I0574445

ST/ESA/STAT/SER.R/45

Department of Economic and Social Affairs
Département des affaires économiques et sociales

2015
Demographic Yearbook
Annuaire démographique

Sixty-sixth issue/Soixante-sixième édition

United Nations
New York, 2016

The Department of Economic and Social Affairs of the United Nations Secretariat is a vital interface between global policies in the economic, social and environmental spheres and national action. The Department works in three main interlinked areas: (i) it compiles, generates and analyses a wide range of economic, social and environmental data and information on which States Members of the United Nations draw to review common problems and to take stock of policy options; (ii) it facilitates the negotiations of Member States in many intergovernmental bodies on joint courses of action to address ongoing or emerging global challenges; and (iii) it advises interested Governments on the ways and means of translating policy frameworks developed in United Nations conferences and summits into programmes at the country level and, through technical assistance, helps build national capacities.

Le Département des affaires économiques et sociales du Secrétariat de l'Organisation des Nations Unies sert de relais entre les orientations arrêtées au niveau international dans les domaines économiques, sociaux et environnementaux et les politiques exécutées à l'échelon national. Il intervient dans trois grands domaines liés les uns aux autres : i) il compile, produit et analyse une vaste gamme de données et d'éléments d'information sur des questions économiques, sociales et environnementales dont les États Membres de l'Organisation se servent pour examiner des problèmes communs et évaluer les options qui s'offrent à eux; ii) il facilite les négociations entre les États Membres dans de nombreux organes intergouvernementaux sur les orientations à suivre de façon collective afin de faire face aux problèmes mondiaux existants ou en voie d'apparition; iii) il conseille les gouvernements intéressés sur la façon de transposer les orientations politiques arrêtées à l'occasion des conférences et sommets des Nations Unies en programmes exécutables au niveau national et aide à renforcer les capacités nationales au moyen de programmes d'assistance technique.

NOTE

Symbols of United Nations documents are composed of capital letters combined with figures. Mention of such a symbol indicates reference to a United Nations document.

The designations employed and the presentation of material in this publication do not imply the expression of any opinion whatsoever on the part of the Secretariat of the United Nations concerning the legal status of any country, territory, city or area, or of its authorities, or concerning the delimitation of its frontiers or boundaries.

Where the designation "country or area" appears in the headings of tables, it covers countries, territories, or areas.

NOTE

Les cotes des documents de l'Organisation des Nations Unies se composent de lettres majuscules et de chiffres. La simple mention d'une cote dans un texte signifie qu'il s'agit d'un document de l'Organisation.

Les appellations employées dans cette publication et la présentation des données qui y figurent n'impliquent de la part du Secrétariat de l'Organisation des Nations Unies aucune prise de position quant au statut juridique des pays, territoires, villes ou zones, ou de leurs autorités, ni quant au tracé de leurs frontières ou limites.

L'appellation "pays ou zone" figurant dans les titres des rubriques des tableaux désigne des pays, des territoires, ou des zones.

ST/ESA/STAT/SER.R/45

UNITED NATIONS PUBLICATION
Sales number: B.17.XIII.1 H

PUBLICATION DES NATIONS UNIES
Numéro de vente: B.17.XIII.1 H

ISBN 978-92-1-051109-4
eISBN 978-92-1-058454-8
Print ISSN: 0082-8041
Online ISSN: 2412-0006

Copyright © United Nations 2016 - Copyright © Nations Unies 2016
All rights reserved - Tous droits réservés

Topics of the Demographic Yearbook series: 1948 - 2015

Sujets des diverses éditions de l'Annuaire démographique : 1948 - 2015

Year Année	Sales No. - Numéro de vente	Issue - Edition	Special topic - Sujet spécial
1948	49.XIII.1	First-Première	General demography-Démographie générale
1949-50	51.XIII.1	Second-Deuxième	Natality statistics-Statistiques de la natalité
1951	52.XIII.1	Third-Trosième	Mortality statistics-Statistiques de la mortalité
1952	53.XIII.1	Fourth-Quatrième	Population distribution-Répartition de la population
1953	54.XIII.1	Fifth-Cinquième	General demography-Démographie générale
1954	55.XIII.1	Sixth-Sixième	Natality statistics -Statistiques de la natalité
1955	56.XIII.1	Seventh-Septième	Population censuses-Recensement de population
1956	57.XIII.1	Eighth-Huitième	Ethnic and economic characteristics of population- Caractéristiques ethniques et économiques de la population
1957	58.XIII.1	Ninth-Neuvième	Mortality statistics- Statistiques de la mortalité
1958	59.XIII.1	Tenth-Dixième	Marriage and divorce statistics- Statistiques de la nuptialitè et de la divortialité
1959	60.XIII.1	Eleventh-Onzième	Natality statistics- Statistiques de la natalité
1960	61.XIII.1	Twelfth-Douzième	Population trends- l' évolution de la population
1961	62.XIII.1	Thirteenth-Treizième	Mortality Statistics- Statistiques de la mortalité
1962	63.XIII.1	Fourteenth-Quatorzième	Population census statistics I- Statistiques des recensements de population I
1963	64.XIII.1	Fifteenth-Quinzième	Population census statistics II- Statistiques des recensements de population II
1964	65.XIII.1	Sixteenth-Seizième	Population census statistics III- Statistiques des recensements de population III
1965	66.XIII.1	Seventeenth-Dix-septième	Natality statistics- Statistiques de la natalité
1966	67.XIII.1	Eighteenth-Dix-huitième	Mortality statistics I- Statistiques de la mortalité I
1967	E/F.68.XIII.1	Nineteenth-Dix-neuvième	Mortality statistics II - Statistiques de la mortalité II
1968	E/F.69.XIII.1	Twentieth-Vingtième	Marriage and divorce statistics-Statistiques de la nuptialité et de la divortialité
1969	E/F.70.XIII.1	Twenty-first-Vingt et unième	Natality statistics-Statistiques de la natalité
1970	E/F.71.XIII.1	Twenty-second-Vingt-deuxième	Population trends-l' évolution de la population
1971	E/F.72.XIII.1	Twenty-third-Vingt-troisième	Population census statistics I- Statistiques de recensements de population I
1972	E/F.73.XIII.1	Twenty-fourth-Vingt-quatrième	Population census statistics II- Statistiques des recensements de population II
1973	E/F.74.XIII.1	Twenty-fifth-Vingt-cinquième	Population census statistics III- Statistiques des recensements de population III
1974	E/F.75.XIII.1	Twenty-sixth-Vingt-sixième	Mortality statistics - Statistiques de la mortalité
1975	E/F.76.XIII.1	Twenty-seventh-Vingt-septième	Natality statistics- Statistiques de la natalité
1976	E/F.77.XIII.1	Twenty-eighth-Vingt-huitième	Marriage and divorce statistics- Statistiques de la nuptialité et de la divortialité
1977	E/F.78.XIII.1	Twenty-ninth-Vingt-neuvième	International Migration Statistics- internationales
1978	E/F.79.XIII.1	Thirtieth-Trentième	General tables- Tableaux de caractère général
1978	E/F.79.XIII.8	Special issue-Edition spéciale	Historical supplement-Supplément rétrospectif
1979	E/F.80.XIII.1	Thirty-first-Trente et unième	Population census statistics- Statistiques des recensements de population
1980	E/F.81.XIII.1	Thirty-second-Trente-deuxième	Mortality statistics- Statistiques de la mortalité
1981	E/F.82.XIII.1	Thirty-third-Trente-troisième	Natality statistics- Statistiques de la natalité
1982	E/F.83.XIII.1	Thirty-fourth-Trente-quatrième	Marriage and divorce statistics- Statistiques de la nuptialité et de la divortialité
1983	E/F.84.XIII.1	Thirty fifth-Trente-cinquième	Population census statistics I- Statistiques des recensements de population I

Year Année	Sales No. - Numéro de vente	Issue - Edition	Special topic - Sujet spécial
1984	E/F.85.XIII.1	Thirty-sixth- Trente-sixième	Population census statistics II- Statistiques des recensements de population II
1985	E/F.86.XIII.1	Thirty-seventh- Trente-septième	Mortality statistics- Statistiques de la mortalité
1986	E/F.87.XIII.1	Thirty-eighth- Trente-huitième	Natality statistics- Statistiques de la natalité
1987	E/F.88.XIII.1	Thirty-ninth- Trente-neuvième	Household composition- Les éléments du ménage
1988	E/F.89.XIII.1	Fortieth- Quarantième	Population census statistics- Statistiques des recensements de population
1989	E/F.90.XIII.1	Forty-first- Quarante-et-unième	International Migration Statistics- Statistiques des migration internationales
1990	E/F.91.XIII.1	Forty-second- Quarante-deuxième	Marriage and divorce statistics- Statistiques de la nuptialité et de la divortialité
1991	E/F.92.XIII.1	Forty-third- Quarante-troisième	General tables- Tableaux de caractère général
1991	E/F.92.XIII.9	Special Issue	Population Ageing and the Situation of Elderly Persons Vieillissement de la population et situation des personnes âgées
1992	E/F.94.XIII.1	Forty-fourth- Quarante-quatrième	Fertility and mortality statistics- Statistiques de la fecondité et de la mortalité
1993	E/F.95.XIII.1	Forty-fifth- Quarante-cinquième	Population census statistics I- Statistiques des recensements de population I
1994	E/F.96.XIII.1	Forty-sixth- Quarante-sixième	Population census statistics II- Statistiques des recensements de population II
1995	E/F.97.XIII.1	Forty-seventh- Quarante-septième	Household composition-Les éléments du ménage
1996	E/F.98.XIII.1	Forty-eighth- Quarante-huitième	Mortality statistics- Statistiques de la mortalité
1997	E/F.99.XIII.1	Forty-ninth- Quarante-neuvième	General tables- Tableaux de caractère général
1997	E/F.99.XIII.12	Special issue- Edition spéciale (CD)	Historical supplement- Supplément rétrospectif
1998	E/F.00.XIII.1	Fiftieth- Cinquantième	General tables- Tableaux de caractère général
1999	E/F.01.XIII.1	Fifty-first- Cinquante-et-unième	General tables- Tableaux de caractère général
1999	E/F.02.XIII.6	Special issue- Edition spéciale (CD)	Natality Statistics- Statistiques de la natalité
2000	E/F.02.XIII.1	Fifty-second- Cinquante-deuxième	General tables- Tableaux de caractère général
2001	E/F.03.XIII.1	Fifty-third- Cinquante- troisième	General tables- Tableaux de caractère général
2002	E/F.05.XIII.1	Fifty-fourth- Cinquante-quatrième	General tables- Tableaux de caractère général
2003	E/F.06.XIII.1	Fifty-fifth- Cinquante-cinquième	General tables- Tableaux de caractère général
2004	E/F.07.XIII.1	Fifty-sixth- Cinquante-sixième	General tables- Tableaux de caractère général
2005	E/F.08.XIII.1	Fifty-seventh- Cinquante-septième	General tables- Tableaux de caractère général
2006	E/F.09.XIII.1	Fifty-eighth- Cinquante-huitième	General tables- Tableaux de caractère général
2007	E/F.10.XIII.1	Fifty-ninth- Cinquante-neuvième	General tables- Tableaux de caractère général
2008	E/F.11.XIII.1	Sixtieth- Soixantième	General tables- Tableaux de caractère général
2009 - 2010	B.12.XIII.1 H	Sixty-first Soixante-et-unième	General tables- Tableaux de caractère général
2011	B.13.XIII.1 H	Sixty-second Soixante- deuxième	General tables- Tableaux de caractère général

Topics of the Demographic Yearbook series: 1948 - 2015

Sujets des diverses éditions de l'Annuaire démographique : 1948 - 2015

Year Année	Sales No. - Numéro de vente	Issue - Edition	Special topic - Sujet spécial
2012	B.14.XIII.1 H	Sixty-third Soixante- troisième	General tables- Tableaux de caractère général
2013	B.15.XIII.1 H	Sixty-fourth Soixante- quatrième	General tables- Tableaux de caractère général
2014	B.16.XIII.1 H	Sixty-fifth Soixante- cinquième	General tables and Whipple's Index, censuses,1985-2014 - Tableaux de caractère général et l'indice de Whipple, recensements, 1985-2014
2015	B.17.XIII.1 H	Sixty-sixth Soixante- sixième	General tables and Whipple's Index, censuses,1985-2015 - Tableaux de caractère général et l'indice de Whipple, recensements, 1985-2015

CONTENTS - TABLE DES MATIERES

FERTILITY

NATALITÉ

FOETAL MORTALITY

MORTALITÉ FŒTALES

INFANT AND MATERNAL MORTALITY

MORTALITÉ INFANTILE ET MORTALITÉ LIÉE À LA MATERNITÉ

GENERAL MORTALITY

MORTALITÉ GÉNÉRALE

NUPTIALITY

DIVORCE

ANNEX

INDEX

NUPTIALITÉ

DIVORTIALITÉ

ANNEX

INDEX

EXPLANATIONS OF SYMBOLS

Category not applicable ....

Data not available... ...

Magnitude zero or less than half of unit employed .... -

Provisional .... *

Data tabulated by year of registration rather than occurrence .... +

Based on less than specified minimum .... ◆

Relatively reliable data .... Roman type

Data of lesser reliability .... *Italics*

EXPLICATION DES SIGNES

Sans objet ....

Données non disponibles ....

Néant ou chiffre inférieur à la moitié de l'unité employée .... -

Données provisoires .... *

Donnée exploitées selon l'année de l'enregistrement et non l'année de l'événement   +

Rapport fondé sur un nombre inférieur à celui spécifié............................ ◆

Données relativement sûres.. Caractères romains

Données dont l'exactitude est moindre .... *Italiques*

INTRODUCTION

The *Demographic Yearbook* is an international compendium of national demographic statistics provided by national statistical authorities to the Statistics Division of the United Nations Department of Economic and Social Affairs. The *Demographic Yearbook* is part of the set of coordinated and interrelated publications issued by the United Nations and its specialized agencies, designed to supply statistical data for such users as demographers, economists, public-health workers and sociologists. Through the co-operation of national statistical services, available official demographic statistics are compiled in the *Demographic Yearbook* for more than 230 countries or areas throughout the world.

The *Demographic Yearbook 2015* is the sixty-sixth issue in a series published by the United Nations since 1948. It contains tables on a wide range of demographic statistics, including a world summary of selected demographic statistics, statistics on the size, distribution and trends in national populations, fertility, foetal mortality, infant and maternal mortality, general mortality, nuptiality and divorce. Data are shown by urban/rural residence, as available. The volume provides Technical Notes, a synoptic table, a historical index and a listing of the issues of the *Demographic Yearbook* published to date. This issue of *Demographic Yearbook* contains data as available including reference year 2015.

This edition of the *Demographic Yearbook* features a special tabulation (table 3a) with Whipple's index by sex and urban/rural residence for the population censuses conducted worldwide since 1985. Whipple's index is an index of age preference in age reporting and can therefore serve to highlight some of the problems related to age distribution.

The Technical Notes on the Statistical Tables are provided to assist the reader in using the tables. Table A, the synoptic table, provides an overview of the completeness of data coverage of the current *Demographic Yearbook*. The cumulative historical index is a guide on content and coverage of all sixty-six issues, and indicates, for each of the topics that have been published, the issues in which they are presented and the years covered. A list of the *Demographic Yearbook* issues, with their corresponding sales numbers and the special topics featured in each issue are shown on pages iii and iv.

Until the 48th issue (1996), each issue consisted of two parts, the general tables and special topic tables, published in the same volume[1]. Beginning with the 49th issue (1997), the special topic tables were being disseminated in digital format as supplements to the regular issues. Two CD-ROMs have been issued: the *Demographic Yearbook Historical Supplement*, which presents a wide panorama of basic demographic statistics for the period 1948 to 1997, and the *Demographic Yearbook: Natality Statistics*, which contains a series of detailed tables dedicated to natality and covering the period from 1980 to 1998. Later on, three volumes of *Demographic Yearbook* Special Census Topics for the 2000 round of censuses, covering the period from 1995 to 2004, were published on-line at http://unstats.un.org/unsd/demographic/products/dyb/dybcens.htm. Current *Demographic Yearbook* population and housing censuses data for the 2000 and 2010 rounds (1995 to the present) are presented at http://unstats.un.org/unsd/demographic/products/dyb/dybcensusdata.htm. These datasets cover basic population characteristics, educational, household, ethnocultural and economic characteristics, and also foreign-born and foreign population. Special tabulations on household and economic characteristics with data based on population censuses since 1995 are available respectively at http://unstats.un.org/unsd/demographic/products/dyb/dyb_Household/dyb_household.htm and http://unstats.un.org/unsd/demographic/products/dyb/dyb_Eco/dyb_eco.htm.

Population statistics are not available for all countries or areas, for a variety of reasons. In an effort to provide estimates of mid-year population and of selected vital statistics for all countries and areas, two annexes are presented. Annex I presents United Nations population estimates for the period 2006-2015 and Annex II presents the medium variant estimates of crude birth and death rates, infant mortality and total fertility rates, as well as life expectancy at birth over the period 2010-2015. These data were produced by the United Nations Population Division and are published in the *2015 Revision of World Population Prospects*[2].

Demographic statistics shown in this issue of the *Demographic Yearbook* are available online at the *Demographic Yearbook* website http://unstats.un.org/unsd/demographic/products/dyb/dyb2015.htm. Information about the Statistics Division's data collection and dissemination programme is also available on the same website. Additional information can be made available by contacting the Statistics Division of the United Nations Department of Economic and Social Affairs at demostat@un.org.

TECHNICAL NOTES ON THE STATISTICAL TABLES

1. GENERAL REMARKS

1.1 Arrangement of Technical Notes

These Technical Notes are designed to provide the reader with relevant information related to the statistical tables. Information pertaining to the *Demographic Yearbook* in general is presented in the sections dealing with geographical aspects, population and vital statistics. In addition, preceding each table are notes describing the variables, remarks on the reliability and limitation of the data, countries and areas covered, and information on the presentation of earlier data. When appropriate, details on computation of rates, ratios or percentages are presented.

1.2 Arrangement of tables

The numbering of tables from one issue of *Demographic Yearbook* to the next is preserved to the extent possible. However, since for some of the tables the numbering may not correspond exactly to those in previous issues, the reader is advised to use the historical index that appears at the end of this book to find the reference to data in earlier issues.

1.3 Source of data

The statistics presented in the *Demographic Yearbook* are national data provided by official statistical authorities unless otherwise indicated. The primary source of data for the *Demographic Yearbook* is a set of questionnaires sent annually by the United Nations Statistics Division to over 230 national statistical services. Data reported on these questionnaires are supplemented, to the extent possible, with data taken from official national publications, official websites and through correspondence with national statistical services. In the interest of comparability, rates, ratios and percentages have been calculated by the Statistics Division of the United Nations, except for the life table functions, the total fertility rate, and also crude birth rate and crude death rate for some countries or areas as appropriately noted. The methods used by the Statistics Division to calculate these rates and ratios are described in the Technical Notes for each table. The population figures used for these computations are those pertaining to the corresponding years published in this or previous issues of the *Demographic Yearbook*.

In cases when data in this issue of the *Demographic Yearbook* differ from those published in earlier issues or related publications, statistics in this issue may be assumed to reflect revisions to the data received by June 2016.

2. GEOGRAPHICAL ASPECTS

2.1 Coverage

Data are shown for all individual countries or areas that provided information. Table 3 is the most comprehensive in geographical coverage, presenting data on population and surface area for all countries or areas with a population of at least 50 persons. Not all of these countries or areas appear in subsequent tables. In many cases the data required for a particular table are not available. In general, the more detailed the data required for a table, the fewer the number of countries or areas that can provide them.

In addition, rates and ratios are presented only for countries or areas reporting at least a minimum number of relevant events. The minimums are stated in the Technical Notes to individual tables.

Except for summary data shown for the world and by major areas and regions in tables 1 and 2 and data shown for capital cities and cities with a population of 100 000 or more in table 8, all data are presented at the national level. The number of countries shown in each table is provided in table A, the synoptic table.

2.2 Territorial composition

To the extent possible, all data, including time series data, relate to the territory within 2015 boundaries. Exceptions are footnoted in individual tables. Relevant clarifications are specified below.

Data relating to **Denmark** exclude Faeroe Islands and Greenland, which are shown separately.

Data relating to **Finland** include Åland Islands, unless otherwise indicated by a footnote.

Data relating to **France** exclude Overseas Departments, namely, French Guiana, Guadeloupe, Martinique and Réunion, which are shown separately, unless otherwise indicated by a footnote.

Data relating to **United Kingdom of Great Britain and Northern Ireland** exclude Guernsey, Isle of Man and Jersey which are shown separately.

Data relating to **Western Sahara** comprise the Northern Region (former Saguia el Hamra) and Southern Region (former Rio de Oro).

2.3 Nomenclature

Because of space limitations, the country or area names listed in the tables are generally the commonly employed short titles currently in use[3] in the United Nations, the full titles being used only when a short form is not available. The latest version of the *Standard Country or Area Codes for Statistics Use* can be accessed at http://unstats.un.org/unsd/methods/m49/m49alpha.htm.

2.3.1 Order of presentation

Countries or areas are listed in English alphabetical order within the following continents: Africa, North America, South America, Asia, Europe and Oceania.

The designations and presentation of the material in this publication were adopted solely for the purpose of providing a convenient geographical basis for the accompanying statistical series. The same qualification applies to all notes and explanations concerning the geographical units for which data are presented.

2.4 Surface area data

Surface area data, shown in tables 1 and 3, represent the total surface area, comprising land area and inland waters (assumed to consist of major rivers and lakes) and excluding only Polar Regions and uninhabited islands. The surface area given is the most recent estimate available. They are presented in square kilometres, a conversion factor of 2.589988 having been applied to surface areas originally reported in square miles.

2.4.1 Comparability over time

Comparability over time in surface area estimates for any given country or area may be affected by changes in the surface area estimation procedures, increases in actual land surface by reclamation, boundary changes, changes in the concept of "land surface area" used or a change in the unit of measurement used. In most cases it was possible to ascertain the reason for a revision; otherwise, the latest figures have generally been accepted as correct and substituted those previously on file.

2.4.2 International comparability

Lack of international comparability between surface area estimates arises primarily from differences in definition. In particular, there is considerable variation in the treatment of coastal bays, inlets and gulfs, rivers and lakes. International comparability is also impaired by the variation in methods employed to estimate surface area. These range from surveys based on modern scientific methods to conjectures based on diverse types of information. Some estimates are recent while others may not be. Since neither the exact method of determining the surface area nor the precise definition of its composition and time reference is known for all countries or areas, the estimates in table 3 should not be considered strictly comparable from one country or area to another.

3. POPULATION

Population statistics, that is, those pertaining to the size, geographical distribution and demographic characteristics of the population, are presented in a number of tables of the *Demographic Yearbook*.

Summary estimates of the mid-year population of the world, major areas and regions for selected years and of its age and sex distribution in 2015 are set forth in tables 1 and 2, respectively.

Data for countries or areas include population census figures, estimates based on results of sample surveys (in the absence of a census), postcensal or intercensal estimates and those derived from continuous population registers. In the present issue of the *Demographic Yearbook*, the latest available census figure of the total population of each country or area and mid-year estimates for 2010 and 2015 are presented in table 3. Mid-year estimates of total population for ten years (2006-2015) are shown in table 5 and mid-year estimates of urban and total population by sex for ten years (2006-2015) are shown in table 6. The latest available data on population by age, sex and urban/rural residence are given in table 7. The latest available figures on the population of capital cities and of cities or urban agglomerations of 100 000 or more inhabitants are presented in table 8.

The statistics on total population, population by age, sex, or urban/rural distribution are used for the calculation of rates in the *Demographic Yearbook*. Vital rates by residence (urban/rural), age or sex were calculated using data presented in tables 6 or 7 in this issue or the corresponding tables of previous issues of the *Demographic Yearbook*.

3.1 Sources of variation of data

The comparability of data is affected by several factors, including (1) the definition of total population; (2) the definition used to classify the population into its urban/rural components; (3) the accuracy of age reporting; (4) the extent of over-enumeration or under-enumeration in the most recent census or other source of benchmark population statistics; and (5) the quality of population estimates. These five factors will be discussed in some detail in sections 3.1.1 to 3.2 below. Other relevant problems are discussed in the technical notes to the individual tables. Readers interested in more detail, relating in particular to the basic concepts of population size, distribution and characteristics as elaborated by the United Nations, should consult the *Principles and Recommendations for Population and Housing Censuses, Revision 3*[4].

3.1.1 Total population

The most important impediment to comparability of total populations is the difference between the concept of a *de facto* and *de jure* population. A *de facto* population includes all persons physically present in the country or area at the reference date. The *de jure* population, by contrast, includes all usual residents of the given country or area, whether or not they were physically present in the area at the reference date. By definition, therefore, a *de facto* total and a *de jure* total are not entirely comparable.

Comparability of even two *de facto* or *de jure* totals is often affected by the fact that strict conformity to either of these concepts is rare. For example, some so-called *de facto* counts do not include foreign military, naval and diplomatic personnel present in the country or area on official duty, and their accompanying family and household members; some do not include foreign visitors in transit through the country or area or transients on ships in harbours. On the other hand, they may include such persons as merchant seamen and fishermen who are temporarily out of the country or area working at their trade.

The *de jure* population figure presents even greater variations in comparability, in part because it depends in the first place on the concept of "usual residence", which varies from one country or area to another and is difficult to apply consistently in a census or survey enumeration. For example, non-national civilians temporarily in a country or area as short-term workers may officially be considered residents after a stay of a specified period of time or they may be considered as non-residents throughout the duration of their stay; at the same time, these individuals may be officially considered as residents or non-residents of the country or area from which they came, depending on the duration and/or purpose of their absence. Furthermore, regardless of the official treatment, individual respondents may apply their own interpretation of residence in responding to the inquiry. In addition, there may be considerable differences in the accuracy with which countries or areas are informed about the number of their residents temporarily out of the country or area.

The population statistics presented in the tables of the *Demographic Yearbook* refer to the *de facto* population or to the *de jure* population. In an effort to overcome, to the extent possible, the effect of the lack of strict conformity to either the *de facto* or the *de jure* concept given above, significant exceptions with respect to inclusions and exclusions of specific population groups, are footnoted when they are known.

A possible source of variation within the statistics of a single country or area may arise from the fact that some countries or areas collect information on both the *de facto* and the *de jure* population in, for example, a census, but prepare detailed tabulations for only the *de jure* population. Hence, even though the total population shown in table 3 is de facto, the figures shown in the tables presenting various characteristics of the population, for example, urban/rural distribution, age and sex distribution, may be on the *de jure* concept.

3.1.2 Urban/rural classification

International comparability of urban/rural distributions is seriously impaired by the wide variation among national definitions of the concept of "urban". The definitions used by individual countries or areas and their implications are shown at the end of technical notes for table 6.

3.1.3 Age distribution

The classification of population by age is a core element of most analyses, estimation and projection of population statistics. Unfortunately, age data are subject to a number of sources of error and non-comparability. Accordingly, the reliability of age data should be of concern to users of these statistics.

3.1.3.1 Collection and compilation of age data

Age is the estimated or calculated interval of time between the date of birth and the date of the census or survey, expressed in completed solar years[5]. There are two methods of collecting information on age. The first is to obtain the date of birth for each member of the population in a census or survey and then to calculate the completed age of the individual by subtracting the date of birth from the date of enumeration[6]. The second method is to record the individual's completed age at the time of the census or survey, that is to say, age at last birthday.

The recommended method is to calculate age at last birthday by subtracting the exact date of birth from the date of the census. Some practices, however, do not use this method but instead calculate the difference between the year of birth and the year of the census. Classifications of this type are footnoted whenever possible. They can be identified to a certain extent by a smaller than expected population under one year of age. However, an irregular number of births from one year to the next or age selective omission of infants may also obscure the expected population under one year of age.

3.1.3.2 Errors in age data

Errors in age data may be due to a variety of causes, including ignorance of the correct age; reporting years of age in terms of a calendar concept other than completed solar years since birth[7]; carelessness in reporting and recording age; a general tendency to state age in figures ending in certain digits (such as zero, two, five and eight); a tendency to exaggerate length of life at advanced ages; a subconscious aversion to certain numbers; and wilful misrepresentations.

These reasons for errors in reported age data are common to most investigations of age and to most countries or areas, and they may significantly impair comparability of the data.

As a result of the above-mentioned difficulties, the age-sex distribution of population in many countries or areas shows irregularities which may be summarized as follows: (1) a deficiency in the number of infants and young children; (2) a concentration at ages ending with zero and five (that is, 5, 10, 15, 20, ...); (3) heaping at even ages (for example, 10, 12, 14, ...) relative to odd ages (for example, 11, 13, 15, ...); (4) unexpectedly large differences between the frequency of males and females at certain ages; and (5) unaccountably large differences between the frequencies in adjacent age groups. Comparing of identical age-sex cohorts from successive censuses, as well as studying the age-sex composition of each census, may reveal these and other inconsistencies, some of which in varying degree are characteristic of even the most modern censuses.

This edition of the *Demographic Yearbook* features a special tabulation (table 3a) with Whipple's index by sex and urban/ rural residence for the past three rounds of population censuses, namely the population censuses conducted worldwide since 1985. Whipple's index is an index of age preference in age reporting and can therefore serve to highlight some of the problems related to age distribution.

4. VITAL STATISTICS

For purposes of the *Demographic Yearbook*, vital statistics of concern are those of live birth, death, foetal death, marriage and divorce.

This volume of the *Demographic Yearbook* presents tables on fertility, nuptiality and divorce as well as tables on mortality referring to foetal mortality, infant and maternal mortality and general mortality.

4.1 Sources of variation of data

Most of the vital statistics data published in this *Demographic Yearbook* come from national civil registration systems. The completeness and the accuracy of the data that these systems produce vary from one country or area to another.

The provision for a national civil registration system is not universal, and in some cases, the registration system covers only certain vital events. For example, in some countries or areas only births and deaths are registered. There are also differences in the effectiveness with which national laws pertaining to civil registration operate in the various countries or areas. The manner in which the law is implemented and the degree to which the public complies with the legislation determine the reliability of vital statistics obtained from the civil registers.

It should be noted that some statistics on marriage and divorce are obtained from sources other than civil registers. For example, in some countries or areas, the only source for data on marriages is church registers. Divorce statistics, on the other hand, are obtained from court records and/or civil registers according to national practice. The actual compilation of these statistics may be the responsibility of the civil registrar, the national statistical office or other government offices.

Other factors affecting international comparability of vital statistics are much the same as those that must be considered in evaluating the variations in other population statistics. Differences in statistical definitions of vital events, differences in geographical and ethnic coverage of the data and diverse tabulation procedures may also influence comparability.

In addition to vital statistics from civil registers, some vital statistics published in the *Demographic Yearbook* are official estimates. These estimates are frequently from population censuses and sample surveys. As such, their comparability may be affected by the national completeness of reporting in population censuses and household surveys, whether a *de facto* or *de jure* based census, non-sampling and sampling errors and other sources of bias.

Readers interested in more detailed information on standards for vital statistics should consult the *Principles and Recommendations for a Vital Statistics System Revision 3*[8]; *Handbook on Civil Registration and Vital Statistics Systems: Preparation of a Legal Framework*[9]; *Handbook on Civil Registration and Vital Statistics Systems: Management, Operation and Maintenance*[10]; *Handbook on Civil Registration and Vital Statistics Systems: Developing Information, Education and Communication*[11]; *Handbook on Civil Registration and Vital Statistics Systems: Policies and Protocols for the Release and Archiving of Individual Records*[12]; and *Handbook on Civil Registration and Vital Statistics Systems: Computerization*[13]. The *Handbook on the Collection of Fertility and Mortality Data*[14] provides information in collection and evaluation of data on fertility and mortality collected in population censuses and household surveys. These publications are also available on the website at http://unstats.un.org/unsd/demographic/standmeth/handbooks/default.htm.

4.1.1 Statistical definition of events

An important source of variation lies in the statistical definition of each vital event. The *Demographic Yearbook* attempts to collect data on vital events, using the standard definitions put forth in Chapter I of *Principles and Recommendations for a Vital Statistics System Revision 3*[8]. These definitions are as follows:

LIVE BIRTH is the complete expulsion or extraction from its mother of a product of conception, irrespective of the duration of pregnancy, which after such separation breathes or shows any other evidence of life such as beating of the heart, pulsation of the umbilical cord, or definite movement of voluntary muscles, whether or not the umbilical cord has been cut or the placenta is attached; each product of such a birth is considered live-born.

DEATH is the permanent disappearance of all evidence of life at any time after the occurrence of live birth, i.e., the postnatal cessation of vital functions without capability of resuscitation. This definition excludes foetal deaths.

FOETAL DEATH is death prior to the complete expulsion or extraction from its mother of a product of conception, irrespective of the duration of the period of gestation. Death is indicated by the fact that after such separation, the foetus does not breathe or show any other evidence of life, such as beating of the heart, pulsation of the umbilical cord, or definite movement of voluntary muscles.

MARRIAGE is an act, ceremony or process by which the legal relationship of spouses is constituted. The legality of the union may be established by civil, religious or other means as recognized by the laws of each country. Countries may wish to expand the definition to cover civil unions if they are registered. In that case, registered partnership usually refers to a legal construct, entailing registration with the public authorities according to the laws of each country, that becomes the basis for legal conjugal obligations between two persons.

DIVORCE is a final legal dissolution of a marriage, that is, the separation of spouses that confers on the parties the right to remarriage under civil, religious and/or other provisions, according to the laws of each country. In the case where a country recognizes registered partnerships, a legal dissolution of a registered partnership constitutes the legal final dissolution of such a partnership, according to national laws, which confers on the parties the right to enter into another partnership or marriage.

In addition to these internationally recommended definitions, the *Demographic Yearbook* collects and presents data on abortions, defined as:

ABORTION is defined, with reference to the woman, as any interruption of pregnancy before 28 weeks of gestation with a dead foetus. There are two major categories of abortion: spontaneous and induced. Induced abortions are those initiated by deliberate action undertaken with the intention of terminating pregnancy; all other abortions are considered spontaneous.

4.1.2 Problems relating to standard definitions

A basic problem affecting international comparability of vital statistics is deviations from the standard definitions of vital events. An example of this can be seen in the cases of live births and foetal deaths. In some countries or areas, an infant must survive for at least 24 hours, to be inscribed in the live-birth register. Infants who die before the expiration of the 24-hour period are classified as late foetal deaths and, barring special tabulation procedures, they would not be counted either as live births or as deaths. Similarly, in several other countries or areas, those infants who are born alive but die before registration of their birth, are also considered late foetal deaths.

Unless special tabulation procedures are adopted in such cases, the live-birth and death statistics will both be deficient by the number of these infants, while the incidence of late foetal deaths will be increased by the same amount. Hence the infant mortality rate is underestimated. Although both components (infant deaths and live births) are deficient by the same absolute amount, the deficiency is proportionately greater in relation to the infant deaths, causing greater errors in the infant mortality rate than in the birth rate.

Moreover, the practice exaggerates the late foetal death ratios. Some countries or areas make provision for correcting this deficiency (at least in the total frequencies) at the tabulation stage. Data for which the correction has not been made are indicated by a footnote whenever possible.

The definitions used for marriage and divorce also present problems for international comparability. Unlike birth and death, which are biological events, marriage and divorce are defined only in terms of law and custom and as such are less amenable to universally applicable statistical definitions. They have therefore been defined for statistical purposes in general terms referring to the laws of individual countries or areas. Laws pertaining to marriage and particularly to divorce, vary from one country or area to another. With respect to marriage, the most widespread requirement relates to the minimum age at which persons may marry but frequently other requirements are specified.

When known the minimum legal age of men and women at which marriage can occur with or without parental consent is presented in table 23-1. Laws and regulations relating to the dissolution of marriage by divorce range from total prohibition, through a wide range of grounds upon which divorces may be granted, to the granting of divorce in response to a simple statement of desire or intention by spouses.

4.1.3 Fragmentary geographical or ethnic coverage

Ideally, vital statistics for any given country or area should cover the entire geographical area and include all ethnic groups. Fragmentary coverage is, however, not uncommon. In some countries or areas, registration is compulsory for only a small part of the population, limited to certain ethnic groups, for example. In other places there is no national provision for compulsory registration, but only municipal or state ordinances that do not cover the entire geographical area. Still others have developed a registration area that comprises only a part of the country or area, the remainder being excluded because of inaccessibility or for economic and cultural considerations that make regular registration practically impossible.

4.1.4 Tabulation procedures

4.1.4.1 By place of occurrence

Vital statistics presented at the national level relate to the de facto, that is, the present-in-area population. Thus, unless otherwise noted, vital statistics for a given country or area cover all the events that occur within its present boundaries and among all segments of the population therein. They may be presumed to include events among nomadic tribes and indigenous peoples, and among nationals and foreigners. When known, deviations from the *de facto* concept are footnoted.

Urban/rural differentials in vital rates for some countries may vary considerably depending on whether the relevant vital events were tabulated on the basis of place of occurrence or place of usual residence. For example, if a substantial number of women residing in rural areas near major urban centres travel to hospitals or maternity homes located in a city to give birth, urban fertility and neo-natal and infant mortality rates will usually be higher (and the corresponding rural rates will usually be lower) if the events are tabulated on the basis of place of occurrence rather than on the basis of place of usual residence. A similar process will affect general mortality differentials if substantial numbers of persons residing in rural areas use urban health facilities when seriously ill.

4.1.4.2 By date of occurrence versus by date of registration

To the extent possible, the vital statistics presented in the *Demographic Yearbook* refer to events that occurred during the specified year, rather than to those that were registered during that period. However, a considerable number of countries or areas tabulate their vital statistics not by date of occurrence, but by date of registration. Because such statistics can be misleading, the countries or areas known to tabulate vital statistics by date of registration are identified in the tables by a plus sign "+". Since information on the method of tabulating vital statistics is not available for all countries and areas, tabulation by date of registration may be more prevalent than the symbols on the vital statistics tables would indicate.

Because quality of data is inextricably related to the timeliness of registration, this must always be considered in conjunction with the quality code description in section 4.2.1 below. If registration of births is complete and timely (code "C"), the ill effects of tabulating by date of registration, are, for all practical purposes, nullified. Similarly, with respect to death statistics, the effect of tabulating events by date of registration may be minimized in many countries or areas in which the sanitary code requires that a death must be registered before a burial permit can be issued, and this regulation tends to make registration prompt. With respect to foetal death, registration is usually done right away or not at all. Therefore, if registration is prompt, the difference between statistics tabulated by date of occurrence and those tabulated by date of registration may be negligible. In many cases, the length of the statutory time period allowed for registering various vital events plays an important part in determining the effects of tabulation by date of registration on comparability of data.

With respect to marriage and divorce, the practice of tabulating data by date of registration does not generally pose serious problems. In many countries or areas marriage is a civil legal contract which, to establish its legality, must be celebrated before a civil officer. It follows that for these countries or areas registration would tend to be almost automatic at the time of, or immediately following, the marriage ceremony. Because the registration of a divorce in many countries or areas is the responsibility solely of the court or the authority which granted it, and since the registration record in such cases is part of the records of the court proceedings, it follows that divorces are likely to be registered soon after the decree is granted.

On the other hand, if registration is not prompt, vital statistics by date of registration will not produce internationally comparable data. Under the best circumstances, statistics by date of registration will include primarily events that occurred in the immediately preceding year; in countries or areas with less developed systems, tabulations will include some events that occurred many years in the past. Examination of available information reveals that delays of many years are not uncommon for birth registration, though the majority is recorded between two to four years after birth.

As long as registration is not prompt, statistics by date of registration will not be internationally comparable either among themselves or with statistics by date of occurrence.

It should also be mentioned that lack of international comparability is not the only limitation introduced by date-of-registration tabulation. Even within the same country or area, comparability over time may be lost by the practice of counting registrations rather than occurrences. If the number of events registered from year to year fluctuates because of *ad hoc* incentives to stimulate registration, or to the sudden need, for example, for proof of (unregistered) birth or death to meet certain requirements, vital statistics tabulated by date of registration are not useful in measuring and analyzing demographic levels and trends. All they can give is an indication of the fluctuations in the need for a birth, death or marriage certificate and the work-load of the registrars. Therefore, statistics tabulated by date of registration may be of very limited use for either national or international studies.

4.2 Methods used to indicate quality of published vital statistics

The quality of vital statistics can be assessed in terms of a number of factors. Most fundamental is the completeness of the civil registration system on which these statistics are based. In some cases, the incompleteness of the data obtained from civil registration systems is revealed when these events are used to compute rates. However, this technique applies only where the data are markedly deficient, where they are tabulated by date of occurrence and where the population base is correctly estimated. Tabulation by date of registration will often produce rates which appear correct, simply because the numerator is artificially inflated by the inclusion of delayed registration and, conversely, rates may be of credible magnitude because the population at risk has been underestimated. Moreover, it should be remembered that knowledge of what is credible in regard to levels of fertility, mortality and nuptiality is extremely scant for many parts of the world, and borderline cases, which are the most difficult to appraise, are frequent.

4.2.1 Quality code for vital statistics from registers.

In the *Demographic Yearbook* annual "Questionnaire on Vital Statistics" national statistical offices are asked to provide their own estimates of the completeness of the births, deaths, late foetal deaths, marriages and divorces recorded in their civil registers.

On the basis of information from the questionnaires, from direct correspondence and from relevant official publications, it has been possible to classify current national statistics from civil registers of birth, death, infant death, late foetal death, marriage and divorce into three broad quality categories, as follows:

C: Data estimated to be virtually complete, that is, representing at least 90 per cent of the events occurring each year.

U: Data estimated to be incomplete, that is representing less than 90 per cent of the events occurring each year.

|: Data not derived from civil registration systems but considered reliable, such as estimates derived from population and housing censuses.

...: Data for which no specific information is available regarding completeness.

These quality codes appear in the first column of the tables which show total frequencies and crude rates (or ratios) over a period of years for all tables on live births, late foetal deaths, infant deaths, deaths, marriages, and divorces. Reliability of maternal mortality statistics is provided by the World Health Organisation.

The classification of countries and areas in terms of these quality codes may not be uniform. Nevertheless, it was felt that national statistical offices were in the best position to judge the quality of their data. It was considered that even the very broad categories that could be established on the basis of the available information would provide useful indicators of the quality of the vital statistics presented in this *Demographic Yearbook*.

Among the countries or areas indicating that the registration of live births was estimated to be 90 per cent or more complete (and hence classified as "C" or "+C" in table 9), the following countries or areas provided information on the method used to evaluate the completeness estimate:

(a) Demographic analysis -- Argentina, Austria, Bulgaria, Chile, China - Hong Kong SAR, Croatia, Egypt, Estonia, Italy, Latvia, Lithuania, Malaysia, Malta, Mauritius, Mexico, New Zealand, Panama, Republic of Korea, Republic of Moldova, Romania, Seychelles, South Africa and Sweden.

(b) Dual record check -- Austria, Bahrain, Cuba, Cyprus, Estonia, Faeroe Islands, Hungary, Israel, Italy, Latvia, Malaysia, Montserrat, New Zealand, Norway, Qatar, Republic of Korea, Saint Vincent and the Grenadines and Uruguay.

(c) Other specified methods -- Aruba, Australia, Curaçao, Denmark, France, Germany, Guatemala, Ireland, Kyrgyzstan, Liechtenstein, Luxembourg, Malaysia, Panama, Poland, Puerto Rico, Singapore, Slovenia, Spain, State of Palestine, Sweden and Uzbekistan.

Among the countries or areas indicating that the registration of late foetal-deaths was estimated to be 90 per cent or more complete (and hence classified as "C" or "+C" in table 12), the following countries or areas provided information on the method used to evaluate the completeness estimate:

(a) Demographic analysis -- Argentina, Austria, Bulgaria, Croatia, Egypt, Estonia, Italy, Latvia, Lithuania, Malta, Mauritius, Mexico, Romania and Sweden.

(b) Dual record check -- Austria, Cuba, Estonia, Hungary, Israel, Italy, Latvia, Lithuania, Montserrat, New Zealand, Norway, Qatar, and Venezuela (Bolivarian Republic of).

(c) Other specified methods – Denmark, Germany, Kyrgyzstan, Luxembourg, Poland, Puerto Rico, Slovenia, Spain, Sweden and Uzbekistan.

Among the countries or areas indicating that the registration of infant deaths was estimated to be 90 per cent or more complete (and hence classified as "C" or "+C" in table 15), the following countries or areas provided information on the method used to evaluate the completeness estimate:

(a) Demographic analysis -- Argentina, Austria, Bulgaria, Chile, China - Hong Kong SAR, Croatia, Egypt, Estonia, Israel, Italy, Latvia, Lithuania, Malta, Mauritius, Mexico, New Zealand, Panama, Republic of Korea, Republic of Moldova, Romania, Seychelles and Sweden.

(b) Dual record check -- Austria, Bahrain, Cuba, Cyprus, Estonia, Faeroe Islands, Hungary, Ireland, Israel, Italy, Latvia, Lithuania, Montserrat, New Zealand, Norway, Qatar, Republic of Korea, and Venezuela (Bolivarian Republic of).

(c) Other specified methods -- Aruba, Australia, Curaçao, Cayman Islands, Denmark, Germany, Kyrgyzstan, Liechtenstein, Luxembourg, Poland, Puerto Rico, Singapore, Slovenia, Spain, Sweden and Uzbekistan.

Among the countries or areas indicating that the registration of deaths was estimated to be 90 per cent or more complete (and hence classified as "C" or "+C" in table 18), the following countries or areas provided information on the method used to evaluate the completeness estimate:

(a) Demographic analysis -- Argentina, Austria, Bulgaria, Chile, China - Hong Kong SAR, Croatia, Egypt, Estonia, Israel, Italy, Latvia, Lithuania, Malaysia, Malta, Mauritius, Mexico, New Zealand, Panama, Republic of Korea, Republic of Moldova, Romania, Seychelles, South Africa, Sweden and Venezuela (Bolivarian Republic of).

(b) Dual record check -- Austria, Bahrain, Cuba, Cyprus, Estonia, Faeroe Islands, Hungary, Israel, Italy, Latvia, Lithuania, Malaysia, Montserrat, New Zealand, Norway, Qatar, Republic of Korea, and Venezuela (Bolivarian Republic of).

(c) Other specified methods -- Aruba, Australia, Brazil, Curaçao, Denmark, France, Germany, Kyrgyzstan, Liechtenstein, Luxembourg, Malaysia, Poland, Puerto Rico, Saint Vincent and the Grenadines, Singapore, Slovenia, Spain, Sweden and Uzbekistan.

Among the countries or areas indicating that the registration of marriages was estimated to be 90 per cent or more complete (and hence classified as "C" or "+C" in table 23), the following countries or areas provided information on the method used to evaluate the completeness estimate:

(a) Demographic analysis -- Argentina, Austria, Bulgaria, Chile, China - Hong Kong SAR, Croatia, Egypt, Estonia, Italy, Latvia, Lithuania, Malta, Mauritius, Mexico, Republic of Korea, Republic of Moldova, Romania, Seychelles and Sweden.

(b) Dual record check – Austria, Cuba, Estonia, Faeroe Islands, Hungary, Israel, Italy, Latvia, New Zealand, Norway, Qatar, Republic of Korea, State of Palestine, and Venezuela (Bolivarian Republic of).

(c) Other specified methods -- Aruba, Australia, Curaçao, Denmark, France, Germany, Kyrgyzstan, Liechtenstein, Luxembourg, Poland, Puerto Rico, Slovenia, Spain, Sweden, Tajikistan and Uzbekistan.

Among the countries or areas indicating that the registration of divorces was estimated to be 90 per cent or more complete (and hence classified as "C" or "+C" in table 24), the following countries or areas provided information on the method used to evaluate the completeness estimate:

(a) Demographic analysis – Austria, Bulgaria, Croatia, Egypt, Estonia, Italy, Latvia, Lithuania, Mexico, Republic of Korea, Republic of Moldova, Romania, Seychelles and Sweden.

(b) Dual record check -- Cuba, Estonia, Faeroe Islands, Hungary, Israel, Italy, Latvia, New Zealand, Norway, Qatar, Republic of Korea, State of Palestine and Venezuela (Bolivarian Republic of).

(c) Other specified methods -- Aruba, Australia, Curaçao, Cyprus, Denmark, Kyrgyzstan, Liechtenstein, Luxembourg, Mauritius, Poland, Puerto Rico, Slovenia, Sweden, Tajikistan and Uzbekistan.

4.2.2 Treatment of vital statistics from registers

On the basis of the quality code described above, the vital statistics shown in all tables of the *Demographic Yearbook* are treated as either reliable or unreliable. Data coded "C" are considered reliable and appear in roman type. Data coded "U" or "..." are considered unreliable and appear in *italics*.

It should be noted that the indications of reliability used for infant mortality rates, maternal mortality ratios and late foetal death ratios (all of which are calculated using the number of live births in the denominator) are determined on the basis of the quality codes for infant deaths, deaths and late foetal deaths respectively. To evaluate these rates and ratios more precisely, one would have to take into account the quality of the live-birth data used in the denominator of these rates and ratios. The quality codes for live births are shown in table 9 and described more fully in the text of the technical notes for that table.

4.2.3 Treatment of time series of vital statistics from registers

The quality of a time series of vital statistics is more difficult to determine than the quality of data for a single year. Since a time series of vital statistics is usually generated only by a system of continuous civil registration, it was assumed that the quality of the entire series was the same as that for the latest year's data obtained from the civil register. The entire series is treated as described in section 4.2.2 above. That is, if the quality code for the latest registered data is "C", the frequencies and rates for earlier years are also considered reliable and appear in roman type. Conversely, if the latest registered data are coded as "U" or "..." then data for earlier years are considered unreliable and appear in *italics*. It is recognized that this method is not entirely satisfactory because it is known that data from earlier years in many of the series were considerably less reliable than the current code implies. Efforts are being made during the past few years to gradually move away from this method, and code the registered data of each year or range of years according to their respective completeness.

4.2.4 Treatment of estimated vital statistics

In addition to data from vital registration systems, estimated frequencies and rates of the events, usually *ad hoc* official estimates that have been derived either from the results of a population census or sample survey or by demographic analyses, also appear in the *Demographic Yearbook*. Estimated frequencies and rates have been included in the tables because it is assumed that they provide information that is more accurate than that from existing civil registration systems. By implication, they are assumed to be reliable and as such they are set in roman type.

In tables showing the quality code, the code applies only to data from civil registers. Estimated data are denoted by the symbol "|".

4.3 Cause of death

World Health Organization (WHO) Member States are bound by the International Nomenclature Regulations to provide the Organization with cause of death data coded in accordance with the current revision of the International Statistical Classification of Diseases and Related Health Problems (ICD). In order to promote international comparability of cause of death statistics, the World Health Organization organizes and conducts an international conference for the revision of the ICD on a regular basis in order to ensure that the Classification is kept current with the most recent clinical and statistical concepts. The data are now usually submitted to WHO at the full four-character level of detail provided by the ICD and are compiled and stored in the WHO Mortality Database at the level of detail as provided by the country. Data from the WHO Mortality Database are available in electronic format at http://www3.who.int/whosis/menu.cfm.

Although revisions provide an up-to-date version of the ICD, such revisions create several problems related to the comparability of cause of death statistics. The first is the lack of comparability over time that inevitably accompanies the use of a new classification. The second problem affects comparability between countries and areas because they may adopt a new classification at different times. The more refined the classification becomes the greater is the need for expert clinical diagnosis of cause of death. In many countries or areas, few of the deaths occur in the presence of an attendant, who is medically trained, i.e., most deaths are certified by a lay attendant. Because the ICD contains many diagnoses that cannot be identified by a non-medical person, the ICD is not always accurately or precisely used, which affects international comparability particularly between countries and areas where the level of medical services differ widely.

The chapters of the tenth revision[15], consist of an alphanumeric coding scheme of one letter followed by three numbers at the four-character level. Chapter one contains infectious and parasitic diseases, chapter two refers to all neoplasms, chapter three to disorders of the immune mechanism including diseases of the blood and blood-forming organs; and chapter four to endocrine, nutritional and metabolic diseases. The remaining chapters group diseases according to the anatomical site affected, except for chapters that refer to mental disorders; complications of pregnancy, childbirth and the puerperium; congenital malformations; and conditions originating in the perinatal period. Finally, an entire chapter is devoted to symptoms, signs, and abnormal findings.

4.3.1 Maternal mortality

According to the tenth revision of the ICD, "Maternal death" is defined as the death of a woman while pregnant or within 42 days of termination of pregnancy, irrespective of the duration and the site of the pregnancy, from any cause related to or aggravated by the pregnancy or its management but not from accidental or incidental causes.

"Maternal deaths" should be subdivided into direct and indirect obstetric deaths. Direct obstetric deaths are those resulting from obstetric complications of the pregnant state (pregnancy, labour and puerperium), from interventions, omissions, incorrect treatment, or from a chain of events resulting from any of the above. Indirect obstetric deaths are those resulting from previous existing disease or disease that developed during pregnancy and which was not due to direct obstetric causes, but which was aggravated by physiologic effects of pregnancy.

While the denominator for the maternal mortality ratio theoretically should be the number of pregnant women, it is impossible to determine the number of pregnant women. A further recommendation by the tenth revision is therefore that maternal mortality ratios be expressed per 100,000 live births or per 100,000 total births (live births and foetal deaths). The maternal mortality ratio calculated here is expressed per 100,000 live births. Although live births do not represent an unbiased estimate of pregnant women, this figure is more reliable than other estimates, in particular, live births are more accurately registered than live births plus foetal deaths.

---

[1] There are two exceptions – the 1978 and 1991 issues, which were disseminated in separate volumes from the respective regular issues.

[2] United Nations, Department of Economic and Social Affairs, Population Division (2015). *2015 Revision of World Population Prospects* (http://esa.un.org/unpd/wpp/).

[3] ST/ESA/STAT/SER.M/49/Rev.4/WWW ; http://unstats.un.org/unsd/methods/m49/m49.htm; see also Standard Country or Area Codes for Statistical Use, Sales No. M.98.XVII.9, United Nations, New York, 1999.

[4] Sales No. E.15.XVII.10, United Nations, New York, 2015.

[5] Ibid, para. 4.151.

[6] Alternatively, if a population register is used, completed ages are calculated by subtracting the date of birth of individuals listed in the register from a reference date to which the age data pertain.

[7] A source of non-comparability may result from differences in the method of reckoning age, for example, the Western versus the Eastern or, as it is usually known, the English versus the Chinese system. By the latter, a child is considered one year old at birth and advances an additional year at each Chinese New Year. The effect of this system is most obvious at the beginning of the age span, where the frequencies in the under-one-year category are markedly understated. The effect on higher age groups is not so apparent. Distributions constructed on this basis are often adjusted before publication, but the possibility of such aberrations should not be excluded when census data by age are compared.

[8]   Sales No. E.13.XVII.10, United Nations, New York, 2014.

[9]   Sales No. E.98.XVII.7, United Nations, New York, 1998.

[10]   Sales No. E.98.XVII.11, United Nations, New York, 1998.

[11]   Sales No. E.98.XVII.4, United Nations, New York, 1998.

[12]   Sales No. E.98.XVII.6, United Nations, New York, 1998.

[13]   Sales No. E.98.XVII.10, United Nations, New York, 1998.

[14]   Sales No. E.03.XVII.11, United Nations, New York, 2004.

[15]   *International Statistical Classification of Diseases and Related Health Problems*, Tenth Revision, Volume 2, World Health Organization, Geneva, 1992.

INTRODUCTION

L'*Annuaire démographique* est un recueil de statistiques démographiques internationales qui est établi par la Division de statistique du Département des affaires économiques et sociales de l'Organisation des Nations Unies. Il fait partie d'un ensemble de publications complémentaires publiées par l'Organisation des Nations Unies et les institutions spécialisées, qui ont pour objet de fournir des statistiques aux démographes, aux économistes, aux spécialistes de la santé publique et aux sociologues. Grâce à la coopération des services nationaux de statistique, il a été possible de faire figurer dans la présente édition de *l'Annuaire démographique* les statistiques officielles disponibles pour plus de 230 pays ou zones du monde entier.

L'*Annuaire démographique 2015* est la soixante-sixième édition d'une série que publie l'ONU depuis 1948. Le présent volume comprend un aperçu mondial des statistiques démographiques de base et des tableaux qui regroupent des statistiques sur la dimension, la répartition et les tendances de la population, la natalité, la mortalité fœtale, la mortalité infantile et la mortalité liée à la maternité, la mortalité générale, la nuptialité et la divortialité. Des données classées selon le lieu de résidence (zone urbaine ou rurale) sont présentées dans un grand nombre de tableaux. L'*Annuaire démographique* contient des notes techniques, un tableau synoptique, un index historique et une liste des éditions de *l'Annuaire démographique* publiées jusqu'à présent. Cette édition de l'*Annuaire démographique* contient les données disponibles couvrant les années de référence jusqu'à 2015.

La présente édition de l'*Annuaire démographique* comprend comme un sujet spécial le tableau 3a avec l'indice de Whipple selon le sexe et la résidence urbaine/rurale pour les recensements de la population effectués dans le monde entier depuis 1985. L'indice de Whipple est un indice de préférence pour certains âges dans la déclaration de l'âge et peut donc servir à mettre en évidence certaines des difficultés liées à la répartition par âge.

Les notes techniques sur les tableaux statistiques sont destinées à aider le lecteur. Le tableau A, qui correspond au tableau synoptique, donne un aperçu de l'"exhaustivité des données publiées dans la présente édition de l'*Annuaire démographique*. Un index cumulatif donne des renseignements sur les matières traitées dans chacune des 66 éditions et sur les années sur lesquelles portent les données. Les numéros de vente des éditions antérieures et une liste des sujets spéciaux traités dans les différentes éditions sont indiqués aux pages iii et iv.

Jusqu'à la 48e édition (1996), chaque édition se composait de deux parties : les tableaux de caractère général et ceux sur des sujets spéciaux, publiés dans le même volume[1]. À partir de 49e édition (1997), les tableaux sur les sujets spéciaux ont été publiés dans un format numérique en tant que suppléments à l'*Annuaire démographique*. Deux CD-ROM ont été produits : l'*Annuaire démographique : Supplément historique*, qui présente un grand nombre de statistiques démographiques pour la période allant de 1948 à 1997, et l'*Annuaire démographique : Statistiques de la natalité*, qui contient des tableaux détaillés sur la natalité pour la période allant de 1980 à 1998. Par la suite, trois volumes concernant l'*Annuaire démographique* consacrés à des thèmes de recensement spéciaux pour le cycle de recensements de 2000 ont été publiés en ligne à l'adresse suivante : http://unstats.un.org/unsd/demographic/products/dyb/dybcens.htm. Les données actuelles sur les thèmes du recensement de l'*Annuaire démographique* pour les années de référence entre 1995 et aujourd'hui, lorsqu'elles sont disponibles, sont présentées sur http://unstats.un.org/unsd/demographic/products/dyb/dybcensusdata.htm. Ils comprennent des données sur la population selon les principales caractéristiques démographiques, scolaires, ethnoculturelles et économiques, les caractéristiques des ménages ainsi que des données sur les étrangers dans le pays ou les personnes nées à l'étranger. Particulièrement, on a présenté sous forme de table aux adresses suivantes, les données des recensements pour les années de référence entre 1995 et aujourd'hui, qui portent sur les thèmes des caractéristiques des ménages et des caractéristiques économiques : http://unstats.un.org/unsd/demographic/products/dyb/dyb_Household/dyb_household.htm et http://unstats.un.org/unsd/demographic/products/dyb/dyb_Eco/dyb_eco.htm

Les statistiques sur la population ne sont pas disponibles pour tous les pays et zones pour plusieurs raisons. Deux annexes sont présentées afin d'offrir des estimations sur la population en milieu d'année et un aperçu des statistiques de l'état civil pour chaque pays ou zone. La première porte sur des estimations concernant la population pour la période 2006-2015. La seconde présente les estimations des variantes moyennes concernant les taux bruts de natalité et de mortalité, la mortalité infantile, les indicateurs synthétiques de fécondité et l'espérance de vie à la naissance pour la période 2010-2015. Ces données ont été établies par la Division de la population de l'ONU et publiées dans les *Perspectives de la population mondiale : La révision de 2015*[2].

Les statistiques démographiques figurant dans la présente édition de l'*Annuaire démographique* sont disponibles en ligne sur les pages Web consacrées à l'*Annuaire démographique* : http://unstats.un.org/unsd/demographic/products/dyb/dyb2015.htm. On trouvera également des renseignements sur le programme de collecte et de diffusion des données de la Division de statistique sur le même site. Il est possible de se procurer d'autres données en contactant la Division de statistique du Département des affaires économiques et sociales de l'Organisation des Nations Unies à l'adresse suivante : demostat@un.org.

NOTES TECHNIQUES SUR LES TABLEAUX STATISTIQUES

1. REMARQUES D'ORDRE GÉNÉRAL

1.1 Notes techniques

Les notes techniques ont pour but de donner au lecteur des informations pertinentes en lien avec les tableaux statistiques. Les renseignements qui concernent l'*Annuaire démographique* en général sont présentés dans des sections portant sur diverses considérations géographiques, sur la population et sur les statistiques de natalité et de mortalité. Les tableaux sont ensuite commentés séparément et l'on trouvera pour chacun une description des variables et des observations sur la fiabilité et les lacunes des données ainsi que sur les pays et zones visés et sur les données publiées antérieurement. Des détails sont également donnés, le cas échéant, sur le mode de calcul des taux, quotients et pourcentages.

1.2 Tableaux

Dans la mesure du possible, la numérotation des tableaux dans les éditions successives de l'*Annuaire démographique* est préservée. Comme la numérotation des tableaux ne correspond pas exactement à celle des éditions précédentes, il est recommandé de se reporter à l'index qui figure à la fin du présent ouvrage pour trouver les données publiées dans les précédentes éditions.

1.3 Origine des données

Sauf indication contraire, les statistiques présentées dans l'*Annuaire démographique* sont des données nationales fournies par les organismes de statistique officiels. Elles sont recueillies essentiellement au moyen de questionnaires qui sont envoyés tous les ans à plus de 230 services nationaux de statistique. Les données communiquées en réponse à ces questionnaires sont complétées, dans toute la mesure possible, par des données tirées de publications nationales officielles et des sites web d'organismes officiels et des renseignements communiqués par les services nationaux de statistique à la demande de l'ONU. Pour que les données soient comparables, les taux, rapports et pourcentages ont été calculés par la Division de statistique de l'ONU, à l'exception des paramètres des tables de mortalité et des indicateurs synthétiques de fécondité ainsi que des taux bruts de natalité et de mortalité pour certains pays et zones, qui ont été dûment signalés en note. Les méthodes suivies par la Division pour le calcul des taux et rapports sont décrites dans les notes techniques relatives à chaque tableau. Les chiffres de population utilisés pour ces calculs sont ceux qui figurent dans la présente édition de l'*Annuaire démographique* ou qui ont paru dans des éditions antérieures.

Chaque fois que l'on constatera des différences entre les données du présent volume et celles des éditions antérieures de l'*Annuaire démographique*, ou de certaines publications apparentées, on pourra en conclure que les statistiques publiées cette année sont des chiffres révisés communiqués à la Division de statistique avant juin 2016.

2. CONSIDÉRATIONS GÉOGRAPHIQUES

2.1 Portée

Des données sont présentées sur tous les pays ou zones qui en ont communiquées. Le tableau 3, le plus complet, contient des données sur la population et la superficie de chaque pays ou zone ayant une population d'au moins 50 habitants. Ces pays ou zones ne figurent pas tous dans les tableaux qui suivent. Dans bien des cas, les données requises pour un tableau particulier n'étaient pas disponibles. En général, les pays ou zones qui peuvent fournir des données sont d'autant moins nombreux que les données demandées sont plus détaillées.
De plus les taux et rapports ne sont présentés que pour les pays ou zones ayant communiqué des chiffres correspondant à un nombre minimal de faits considérés. Les minimums sont indiqués dans les notes techniques relatives à chacun des tableaux.

À l'exception des données récapitulatives présentées dans les tableaux 1 et 2 pour l'ensemble du monde et les grandes zones et régions et des données relatives aux capitales et aux villes de 100 000 habitants ou plus dans le tableau 8, toutes les données se rapportent aux pays. Le nombre de pays sur lequel porte chacun des tableaux est indiqué dans le tableau A.

2.2 Composition territoriale

Autant que possible, toutes les données, y compris les séries chronologiques, se rapportent au territoire de 2015. Les exceptions à cette règle sont signalées en note à la fin des tableaux. Des clarifications importantes sont présentées ci-dessous.

Les données relatives au **Danemark** ne comprennent pas les Iles Féroé et le Groenland, qui font l'objet de rubriques distinctes.

Les données relatives à la **Finlande** comprennent les Îles d'Åland, sauf indication contraire en note de bas de page.

Les données relatives à la **France** ne comprennent pas les départements d'outre-mer, à savoir, la Guyane française, Guadeloupe, la Martinique et La Réunion, qui font l'objet de rubriques distinctes, sauf indication contraire en note de bas de page.

Les données relatives au **Royaume-Uni de Grande-Bretagne et d'Irlande du Nord** ne comprennent pas la Guernesey, l'île de Man et Jersey, qui font l'objet de rubriques distinctes.

Les données relatives au **Sahara Occidental** comprennent la région septentrionale (ancien Saguia-el-Hamra) et la région méridionale (ancien Rio de Oro).

2.3 Nomenclature

En règle générale, pour gagner de la place, on a jugé commode de désigner dans les tableaux les pays ou zones par les noms abrégés couramment utilisés par l'Organisation des Nations Unies[3], les désignations complètes n'étant utilisées que lorsqu'il n'existait pas de forme abrégée. La liste des désignations des pays ou zones est disponible à l'adresse suivante : http://unstats.un.org/unsd/methods/m49/m49alphaf.htm.

2.3.1 Ordre de présentation

Les pays ou zones sont classés dans l'ordre alphabétique anglais et regroupés par continent comme ci-après : Afrique, Amérique du Nord, Amérique du Sud, Asie, Europe et Océanie.

Les appellations employées dans la présente édition et la présentation des données qui y figurent n'ont d'autre objet que de donner un cadre géographique commode aux séries statistiques. La même observation vaut pour toutes les notes et précisions concernant les unités géographiques pour lesquelles des données sont présentées.

2.4 Superficie

Les données relatives à la superficie qui figurent dans les tableaux 1 et 3 représentent la superficie totale, c'est-à-dire qu'elles englobent les terres émergées et les eaux intérieures (qui sont censées comprendre les principaux lacs et cours d'eau), mais excluent les régions polaires et les îles inhabitées. Les données relatives à la superficie correspondent aux chiffres estimatifs les plus récents. Les superficies sont toutes exprimées en kilomètres carrés ; les chiffres qui avaient été communiqués en miles carrés ont été convertis au moyen d'un coefficient de 2,589988.

2.4.1 Comparabilité dans le temps

La révision des estimations antérieures de la superficie, des augmentations effectives de la superficie terrestre due par exemple à des travaux d'assèchement, à des rectifications de frontières, à des changements d'interprétation du concept de « terres émergées » ou à l'utilisation de nouvelles unités de mesure peut avoir des incidences sur la comparabilité dans le temps des estimations relatives à la superficie d'un pays ou d'une zone donnés. Dans la plupart des cas, il a été possible de déterminer la raison de ces révisions; toutefois, même lorsque la raison n'était pas connue, on a remplacé les anciens chiffres par les nouveaux et on a généralement admis que ce sont ces derniers qui sont exacts.

2.4.2 Comparabilité internationale

Le manque de comparabilité internationale entre les données relatives à la superficie est dû principalement à des différences de définition. En particulier, la définition des golfes, baies et criques, lacs et cours d'eau varie sensiblement d'un pays à l'autre. La diversité des méthodes employées pour estimer les superficies nuit elle aussi à la comparabilité internationale. Certaines données proviennent de levés effectués selon des méthodes scientifiques modernes ; d'autres ne représentent que des conjectures reposant sur diverses catégories de renseignements. Certains chiffres sont récents, d'autres pas. Étant donné que ni la méthode de calcul de la superficie ni la composition du territoire et la date à laquelle se rapportent les données ne sont connues avec précision pour tous les pays ou zones, les estimations figurant dans le tableau 3 ne doivent pas être considérées comme rigoureusement comparables d'un pays ou d'une zone à une autre.

3. POPULATION

Les statistiques de la population, c'est-à-dire celles qui se rapportent à la dimension, à la répartition géographique et aux caractéristiques démographiques de la population, sont présentées dans un certain nombre de tableaux de l'*Annuaire démographique*.

Les tableaux 1 et 2 présentent respectivement des estimations récapitulatives de milieu d'année de la population du monde, des grandes zones et régions, pour certaines années présélectionnées, ainsi que de sa répartition selon l'âge et le sexe pour l'année 2015.

Les données concernant les pays ou les zones représentent les résultats de recensements de population, des estimations fondées sur les résultats d'enquêtes par sondage (s'il n'y a pas eu recensement), des estimations postcensitaires ou intercensitaires, ou des estimations établies à partir de données provenant des registres permanents de population. Dans la présente édition, le tableau 3 indique pour chaque pays ou zone le chiffre le plus récent de la population totale issu du dernier recensement et des estimations établies au milieu de l'année 2010 et de l'année 2015. Le tableau 5 contient des estimations de la population totale au milieu de chaque année pendant 10 ans (2006-2015), et le tableau 6 des estimations de la population urbaine et de la population totale, par sexe, au milieu de chaque année pendant 10 ans (2006-2015). Les dernières données disponibles sur la répartition de la population selon l'âge, le sexe et le lieu de résidence (zone urbaine ou rurale) sont présentées dans le tableau 7. Les derniers chiffres disponibles sur la population des capitales et des villes de 100 000 habitants ou plus sont regroupés dans le tableau 8.

On a utilisé pour le calcul des taux les statistiques de la population totale et de la population répartie selon l'âge, le sexe ou le lieu de résidence (zone urbaine ou rurale). Les taux démographiques selon la résidence (urbaine/rurale), l'âge ou le sexe ont été calculés à partir des données présentées dans les tableaux 6 ou 7 de la présente édition ou dans les tableaux correspondants d'éditions précédentes de l'*Annuaire démographique*.

3.1 Sources de variation des données

Plusieurs facteurs influent sur la comparabilité des données : 1) la définition de la population totale ; 2) les définitions utilisées pour faire la distinction entre population urbaine et population rurale ; 3) les difficultés liées aux déclarations d'âge ; 4) l'étendue du surdénombrement ou du sous-dénombrement dans le recensement le plus récent ou dans une autre source de statistiques de référence sur la population ; 5) la qualité des estimations relatives à la population. Ces cinq facteurs sont analysés en détail aux sections 3.1.1 à 3.2 ci-après. D'autres questions seront traitées dans les notes techniques relatives à chaque tableau. Pour plus de précisions concernant, notamment, les notions fondamentales de dimension, de répartition et de caractéristiques de la population qui ont été élaborées par l'Organisation des Nations Unies, le lecteur est invité à se reporter aux *Principes et recommandations concernant les recensements de la population et de l'habitat, Révision 3*[4].

3.1.1 Population totale

Le principal obstacle à la comparabilité des données relatives à la population totale est la différence qui existe entre population de fait et population de droit. La population de fait comprend toutes les personnes présentes dans le pays ou la zone à la date de référence, tandis que la population de droit comprend toutes celles qui résident habituellement dans le pays ou la zone, qu'elles y aient été ou non présentes à la date de référence. Par définition, la population totale de fait et la population totale de droit ne sont donc pas rigoureusement comparables entre elles.

Même lorsque l'on veut comparer deux totaux qui se rapportent à des populations de fait ou deux totaux qui se rapportent à des populations de droit, on risque souvent de faire des erreurs pour cette raison qu'il est rare que l'une et l'autre notions soient appliquées strictement. Pour citer quelques exemples, certains chiffres qui sont censés porter sur la population de fait ne tiennent pas compte du personnel militaire, naval et diplomatique étranger en fonction dans le pays ou la zone, ni des membres de leurs familles et de leurs ménages; d'autres ne comprennent pas les visiteurs étrangers de passage dans le pays ou la zone ni les personnes à bord de navires ancrés dans des ports. En revanche, il arrive que l'on compte des personnes, inscrits maritimes et marins pêcheurs par exemple, qui, en raison de leur activité professionnelle, se trouvent hors du pays ou de la zone de recensement.

Les risques de disparités sont encore plus grands quand il s'agit de comparer des populations de droit, car les comparaisons dépendent au premier chef de la définition que l'on donne à l'expression « lieu de résidence habituel », qui varie d'un pays ou d'une zone à l'autre et qu'il est, de toute façon, difficile d'appliquer uniformément pour le dénombrement lors d'un recensement ou d'une enquête. Par exemple, les civils étrangers qui se trouvent temporairement dans un pays ou une zone comme travailleurs à court terme peuvent officiellement être considérés comme résidents après un séjour d'une durée déterminée, mais ils peuvent aussi être considérés comme non-résidents pendant toute la durée de leur séjour ; ailleurs, ces mêmes personnes peuvent être considérées officiellement comme résidents ou comme non-résidents du pays ou de la zone d'où elles viennent, selon la durée et, éventuellement, la raison de leur absence. Qui plus est, quel que soit son statut officiel, chacun des recensés peut, au moment de l'enquête, interpréter à sa façon la notion de résidence. De plus, les autorités nationales ou les entités responsables des zones ne savent pas toutes avec la même précision combien de leurs résidents se trouvent temporairement à l'étranger.

Les chiffres de population présentés dans les tableaux de l'*Annuaire démographique* représentent la population de fait ou la population de droit. Lorsque l'on savait que les données avaient été recueillies selon une définition de la population de fait ou de la population de droit qui s'écartait sensiblement de celle exposée plus haut, on l'a signalé en note, de manière à compenser dans toute la mesure possible les conséquences des divergences.

Il peut y avoir hétérogénéité dans les statistiques d'un même pays ou d'une même zone dans le cas des pays ou zones qui ne font une exploitation statistique détaillée des données que pour la population de droit alors qu'ils recueillent des données sur la population de droit et sur la population de fait à l'occasion d'un recensement, par exemple. Ainsi, tandis que les chiffres relatifs à la population totale qui figurent au tableau 3 se rapportent à la population de fait, ceux des tableaux qui présentent des données sur diverses caractéristiques de la population, par exemple le lieu de résidence (zone urbaine ou rurale), l'âge et le sexe, peuvent être basés sur le concept de la population de droit.

3.1.2 Lieu de résidence (zone urbaine ou rurale)

L'hétérogénéité des définitions nationales du terme « urbain » nuit considérablement à la comparabilité internationale des données concernant la répartition selon le lieu de résidence. Les définitions utilisées par les différents pays ou zones et leurs implications sont exposées à la fin des notes techniques correspondant au tableau 6.

3.1.3 Répartition par âge

La répartition de la population selon l'âge est un paramètre fondamental de la plupart des analyses, estimations et projections relatives aux statistiques de la population. Malheureusement, ces données sont sujettes à un certain nombre d'erreurs et difficilement comparables. C'est pourquoi pratiquement tous les utilisateurs de ces statistiques doivent considérer ces répartitions avec la plus grande circonspection.

3.1.3.1 Collecte et exploitation des données sur l'âge

L'âge est l'intervalle de temps déterminé par calcul ou par estimation qui sépare la date de naissance de la date du recensement et qui est exprimé en années solaires révolues[5]. Les données sur l'âge peuvent être recueillies selon deux méthodes : la première consiste à obtenir la date de naissance de chaque personne à l'occasion d'un recensement ou d'un sondage, puis à calculer l'âge en années révolues en soustrayant la date de naissance de celle du dénombrement[6]. La seconde consiste à enregistrer l'âge en années révolues au moment du recensement, c'est-à-dire l'âge au dernier anniversaire.

La méthode recommandée consiste à calculer l'âge au dernier anniversaire en soustrayant la date exacte de la naissance de la date du recensement. Toutefois, on n'a pas toujours recours à cette méthode ; certains pays ou zones calculent l'âge en faisant la différence entre l'année du recensement et l'année de la naissance. Lorsque les données sur l'âge ont été établies de cette façon, on l'a signalé chaque fois que possible par une note. On peut d'ailleurs s'en rendre compte dans une certaine mesure, car les chiffres dans la catégorie des moins d'un an sont plus faibles qu'ils ne devraient l'être. Cependant, un nombre irrégulier de naissances d'une année à l'autre ou l'omission de certains âges parmi les moins d'un an peut aussi fausser les chiffres de la population de moins d'un an.

3.1.3.2 Erreurs dans les données sur l'âge

Les causes d'erreurs dans les données sur l'âge sont diverses : on peut citer notamment l'ignorance de l'âge exact, la déclaration d'années d'âge correspondant à un calendrier différent de celui des années solaires révolues depuis la naissance[7], la négligence dans les déclarations et dans la façon dont elles sont consignées, la tendance générale à déclarer des âges se terminant par certains chiffres tels que 0, 2, 5 ou 8, la tendance pour les personnes âgées à exagérer leur âge, une aversion subconsciente pour certains nombres, et les fausses déclarations faites délibérément.

Les causes d'erreurs mentionnées ci-dessus, communes à la plupart des enquêtes sur l'âge et à la plupart des pays ou zones, peuvent nuire sensiblement à la comparabilité.

À cause des difficultés indiquées ci-dessus, les répartitions par âge et par sexe de la population d'un grand nombre de pays ou de zones font apparaître les irrégularités suivantes : 1) sous-estimation des groupes d'âge correspondant aux enfants de moins d'un an et aux jeunes enfants ; 2) polarisation des déclarations sur les âges se terminant par les chiffres 0 ou 5 (c'est-à-dire 5, 10,15, 20...) ; 3) prépondérance des âges pairs (par exemple 10, 12, 14...) au détriment des âges impairs (par exemple 11, 13, 15...) ; 4) écart considérable et surprenant entre le rapport masculin/féminin à certains âges ; 5) différences importantes et difficilement explicables entre les données concernant des groupes d'âge voisins. En comparant les statistiques provenant de recensements successifs pour des cohortes identiques sur le plan de l'âge et de la répartition par sexe et en étudiant la répartition par âge et par sexe de la population à chaque recensement, on peut déceler l'existence de ces incohérences et de quelques autres, un certain nombre d'entre elles se retrouvant à des degrés divers même dans les recensements les plus modernes.

La présente édition de l'*Annuaire démographique* comprend comme un sujet spécial le tableau 3a avec l'indice de Whipple selon le sexe et la résidence urbaine/rurale pour les trois derniers cycles de recensements de la population, à savoir les recensements de la population effectués dans le monde entier depuis 1985. L'indice de Whipple est un indice de préférence pour certains âges dans la déclaration de l'âge et peut donc servir à mettre en évidence certaines des difficultés liées à la répartition par âge.

4. STATISTIQUES DE L'ÉTAT CIVIL

Aux fins de l'*Annuaire démographique*, on entend par statistiques de l'état civil les statistiques des naissances vivantes, des décès, des morts fœtales, des mariages et des divorces.

Dans le présent volume de l'*Annuaire démographique*, on a présenté des tableaux sur la natalité, la mortalité, la nuptialité et la divortialité. Les tableaux consacrés à la mortalité sont groupés sous les rubriques suivantes : mortalité fœtale, mortalité infantile, mortalité liée à la maternité et mortalité générale.

4.1 Sources de variations des données

La plupart des statistiques de l'état civil publiées dans le présent volume de l'*Annuaire démographique* émanent des systèmes nationaux d'enregistrement des faits d'état civil. Le degré d'exhaustivité et d'exactitude de ces données varie d'un pays ou d'une zone à l'autre.

Il n'existe pas partout de système national d'enregistrement des faits d'état civil et, dans quelques cas, seuls certains faits sont enregistrés. Par exemple, dans certains pays ou zones, seuls les naissances et les décès sont enregistrés. Il existe également des différences quant au degré d'efficacité avec lequel les lois relatives à l'enregistrement des faits d'état civil sont appliquées dans les divers pays ou zones. La fiabilité des statistiques provenant des registres d'état civil dépend des modalités d'application de la loi et de la mesure dans laquelle le public s'y soumet.

Il est à signaler que dans certains cas les statistiques de la nuptialité et de la divortialité sont tirées d'autres sources que les registres d'état civil. Dans certains pays ou zones, par exemple, les seules données disponibles sur la nuptialité proviennent des registres des églises. Selon la pratique suivie par chaque pays, les statistiques de la divortialité sont tirées des actes des tribunaux et/ou des registres d'état civil. L'officier de l'état civil, le service national de statistique ou d'autres services administratifs peuvent être chargés d'établir ces statistiques.

Les autres facteurs qui influent sur la comparabilité internationale des statistiques de l'état civil sont à peu près les mêmes que ceux qu'il convient de prendre en considération pour interpréter les variations observées dans les statistiques de la population. La définition des faits d'état civil aux fins de statistique, la portée des données du point de vue géographique et ethnique ainsi que les méthodes d'exploitation des données sont autant d'éléments qui peuvent influer sur la comparabilité.

En plus des statistiques tirées des registres d'état civil, l'*Annuaire démographique* présente des statistiques de l'état civil qui sont des estimations officielles nationales, fondées souvent sur les résultats de sondages ou des recensements de la population. Aussi leur comparabilité varie-t-elle en fonction du degré d'exhaustivité des déclarations recueillies lors des recensements de la population ou d'enquêtes sur les ménages, des erreurs d'échantillonnage ou autres, et des distorsions d'origines diverses.

Pour plus de détails sur les normes d'établissement des statistiques d'état civil, le lecteur pourra se reporter aux : *Principes et recommandations pour un système de statistiques de l'état civil, troisième révision*[8] ; *Manuel des systèmes d'enregistrement des faits d'état civil et de statistiques de l'état civil : Élaboration d'un cadre juridique*[9] ; *Manuel des systèmes d'enregistrement des faits d'état civil et de statistiques de l'état civil : Gestion, fonctionnement et tenue*[10] ; *Manuel des systèmes d'enregistrement des faits d'état civil et de statistiques de l'état civil : Élaboration de programmes d'information, d'éducation et de communication*[11] ; *Manuel des systèmes d'enregistrement des faits d'état civil et de statistiques de l'état civil : Principes et protocoles concernant la communication et l'archivage des documents individuels*[12] ; *Manuel des systèmes d'enregistrement des faits d'état civil et de statistiques de l'état civil : Informatisation*[13]. Le *Manuel de collecte de données sur la fécondité et la mortalité*[14] fournit des informations ayant trait à la collecte et à l'évaluation des données sur la fécondité, sur la mortalité et sur d'autres faits d'état civil, qui ont été recueillies au cours des enquêtes sur les ménages. Ces publications sont également disponibles sur le Web à partir de l'adresse suivante : http://unstats.un.org/unsd/demographic/standmeth/handbooks/default.htm.

4.1.1 Définition des faits d'état civil aux fins de la statistique

Une cause importante d'hétérogénéité dans les données est le manque d'uniformité des définitions des différents faits d'état civil. Aux fins de *l'Annuaire démographique*, il est recommandé de recueillir les données relatives aux faits d'état civil en utilisant les définitions établies au Chapitre I des *Principes et recommandations pour un système de statistiques de l'état civil, troisième révision*[8]. Ces définitions sont les suivantes :

La NAISSANCE VIVANTE est l'expulsion ou l'extraction complète du corps de la mère, indépendamment de la durée de la gestation, d'un produit de la conception qui, après cette séparation, respire ou manifeste tout autre signe de vie, tel que battement de cœur, pulsation du cordon ombilical ou contraction effective d'un muscle soumis à l'action de la volonté, que le cordon ombilical ait été coupé ou non et que le placenta soit ou non demeuré attaché ; tout produit d'une telle naissance est considéré comme « enfant né vivant ».

Le DÉCÈS est la disparition permanente de tout signe de vie à un moment quelconque postérieur à la naissance vivante (cessation des fonctions vitales après la naissance sans possibilité de réanimation). Cette définition ne comprend pas les morts fœtales.

La MORT FŒTALE est le décès d'un produit de la conception lorsque ce décès est survenu avant l'expulsion ou l'extraction complète du corps de la mère, indépendamment de la durée de la gestation. Le décès est indiqué par le fait qu'après cette séparation le fœtus ne respire ni ne manifeste aucun signe de vie, tel que battement de cœur, pulsation du cordon ombilical ou contraction effective d'un muscle soumis à l'action de la volonté.

Le MARIAGE est l'acte, la cérémonie ou la procédure qui établit un rapport légal entre les époux. L'union peut être rendue légale par une procédure civile ou religieuse, ou par toute autre procédure, conformément à la législation du pays.

Le DIVORCE est la dissolution légale et définitive des liens du mariage, c'est-à-dire la séparation des époux qui confère aux parties le droit de se remarier civilement ou religieusement, ou selon toute autre procédure, conformément à la législation du pays.

En plus de ces notions définies internationalement, l'*Annuaire démographique* recueille et met à disposition ces données sur les avortements :

Par référence à la femme, l'AVORTEMENT se définit comme toute interruption de grossesse qui est survenue avant 28 semaines de gestation et dont le produit est un fœtus mort. Il existe deux grandes catégories d'avortement : l'avortement spontané et l'avortement provoqué. L'avortement provoqué a pour origine une action délibérée entreprise en vue d'interrompre une grossesse. Tout autre avortement est considéré comme spontané.

4.1.2 Problèmes posés par les définitions établies

Les variations par rapport aux définitions établies des faits d'état civil sont le principal obstacle à la comparabilité internationale des statistiques de l'état civil. Un exemple en est fourni par le cas des naissances vivantes et celui des morts fœtales. Dans certains pays ou zones, il faut que le nouveau-né ait vécu 24 heures pour pouvoir être inscrit sur le registre des naissances vivantes. Les décès d'enfants qui surviennent avant l'expiration du délai de 24 heures sont classés parmi les morts fœtales tardives et, en l'absence de méthodes spéciales d'exploitation des données, ne sont comptés ni dans les naissances vivantes ni dans les décès. De même, dans plusieurs autres pays ou zones, les décès d'enfants nés vivants et décédés avant l'enregistrement de leur naissance sont également comptés parmi les morts fœtales tardives.

À moins que des méthodes spéciales n'aient été adoptées pour l'exploitation de ces données, les statistiques des naissances vivantes et des décès ne tiendront pas compte de ces cas, qui viendront en revanche accroître d'autant le nombre des morts fœtales tardives. Le taux de mortalité infantile sera donc sous-estimé. Bien que les éléments constitutifs du taux (décès d'enfants de moins d'un an et naissances vivantes) accusent exactement la même insuffisance en valeur absolue, les lacunes sont proportionnellement plus fortes pour les décès de moins d'un an, ce qui cause des erreurs plus importantes dans les taux de mortalité infantile.

De plus, cette pratique augmente les rapports de mortinatalité. Quelques pays ou zones effectuent les ajustements nécessaires pour corriger cette anomalie (du moins dans les fréquences totales) au moment de l'établissement des tableaux. Si aucun ajustement n'a été effectué, cela est indiqué dans les notes chaque fois que possible.

Les définitions du mariage et du divorce posent aussi un problème du point de vue de la comparabilité internationale. Contrairement à la naissance et au décès, qui sont des faits biologiques, le mariage et le divorce sont uniquement déterminés par la législation et la coutume et, de ce fait, il est moins facile d'en donner une définition statistique qui ait une application universelle. À des fins statistiques, ces notions ont donc été définies de manière générale par référence à la législation de chaque pays ou zone. La législation relative au mariage et plus particulièrement au divorce varie d'un pays ou d'une zone à l'autre. En ce qui concerne le mariage, l'âge de nubilité est la condition la plus fréquemment requise, mais il arrive souvent que d'autres conditions soient exigées.

Lorsqu'il est connu, l'âge minimum auquel le mariage peut avoir lieu avec le consentement des parents (et dans certains cas sans le consentement des parents) est indiqué au tableau 23-1. Les lois et règlements relatifs à la dissolution du mariage par le divorce vont de l'interdiction absolue, en passant par diverses conditions requises pour l'obtention du divorce, jusqu'à la simple déclaration, par l'épouse, de son désir ou de son intention de divorcer.

4.1.3 Couverture géographique ou ethnique fragmentaire

En principe, les statistiques de l'état civil devraient s'étendre à l'ensemble du pays ou de la zone auxquels elles se rapportent et englober tous les groupes ethniques. En fait, il n'est pas rare que les données soient fragmentaires. Dans certains pays ou zones, l'enregistrement n'est obligatoire que pour une petite partie de la population, par exemple pour certains groupes ethniques. Dans d'autres, il n'existe pas de disposition qui prescrive l'enregistrement obligatoire sur le plan national, mais seulement des règlements ou décrets des municipalités ou des États, qui ne s'appliquent pas à l'ensemble du territoire. Il en est encore autrement dans d'autres pays ou zones où les autorités ont institué une zone d'enregistrement comprenant seulement une partie du territoire, le reste étant exclu en raison des difficultés d'accès ou parce qu'il est pratiquement impossible, pour des raisons d'ordre économique ou culturel, d'y procéder à un enregistrement régulier.

4.1.4 Méthodes de présentation des données

4.1.4.1 Selon le lieu de l'événement

Les statistiques de l'état civil qui sont présentées pour l'ensemble du territoire national se rapportent à la population de fait ou population présente. En conséquence, sauf indication contraire, les statistiques de l'état civil relatives à une zone ou à un pays donné portent sur tous les faits survenus dans l'ensemble de la population, à l'intérieur des frontières actuelles de la zone ou du pays considéré. On peut donc estimer qu'elles englobent les faits d'état civil survenus dans les tribus nomades et parmi les populations autochtones ainsi que parmi les ressortissants du pays et les étrangers. Des notes signalent les exceptions lorsque celles-ci sont connues.

Pour certains pays, les écarts entre les taux démographiques pour les zones urbaines et pour les zones rurales peuvent varier notablement selon que les faits d'état civil ont été exploités sur la base du lieu de l'événement ou du lieu de résidence habituel. Par exemple, si un nombre appréciable de femmes résidant dans des zones rurales proches de grands centres urbains accouchent dans les hôpitaux ou maternités d'une ville, les taux de fécondité ainsi que les taux de mortalité néo-natale et infantile seront généralement plus élevés dans les zones urbaines (et par conséquent plus faibles dans les zones rurales) si les faits sont exploités en se fondant sur le lieu de l'événement et non sur le lieu de résidence habituel. Le phénomène sera le même dans le cas de la mortalité générale si un bon nombre de personnes résidant dans des zones rurales font appel aux services de santé des villes lorsqu'elles sont gravement malades.

4.1.4.2 Selon la date de l'événement ou la date de l'enregistrement

Autant que possible, les statistiques de l'état civil figurant dans *l'Annuaire démographique* se rapportent aux faits survenus pendant l'année considérée et non aux faits enregistrés au cours de ladite année. Bon nombre de pays ou zones, toutefois, exploitent leurs statistiques de l'état civil selon la date de l'enregistrement et non selon la date de l'événement. Comme ces statistiques risquent d'induire en erreur, les pays ou zones dont on sait qu'ils établissent leurs statistiques d'après la date de l'enregistrement sont signalés dans les tableaux par un signe plus « + ». On ne dispose toutefois pas pour tous les pays ou zones de renseignements complets sur la méthode d'exploitation des statistiques de l'état civil et les données sont peut-être exploitées selon la date de l'enregistrement plus souvent que ne le laisserait supposer l'emploi des signes.

Étant donné que la qualité des données est inextricablement liée aux retards dans l'enregistrement, il faudra toujours considérer en même temps le code de qualité qui est décrit à la section 4.2.1 ci-après. Évidemment, si l'enregistrement des naissances est complet et effectué en temps voulu (code « C »), les effets perturbateurs de la méthode consistant à exploiter les données selon la date de l'enregistrement seront pratiquement annulés. De même, s'agissant des statistiques des décès, les effets pourront bien souvent être réduits au minimum dans les pays ou zones où le code sanitaire subordonne la délivrance du permis d'inhumer à l'enregistrement du décès, ce qui tend à hâter l'enregistrement. Quant aux morts fœtales, elles sont généralement déclarées immédiatement ou ne sont pas déclarées du tout. En conséquence, si l'enregistrement se fait dans un délai très court, la différence entre les statistiques établies selon la date de l'événement et celles qui sont établies selon la date de l'enregistrement peut être négligeable. Dans bien des cas, la durée des délais légaux accordés pour l'enregistrement des faits d'état civil est un facteur dont dépend dans une large mesure l'incidence sur la comparabilité de l'exploitation des données selon la date de l'enregistrement.

En ce qui concerne le mariage et le divorce, la pratique consistant à exploiter les statistiques selon la date de l'enregistrement ne pose généralement pas de graves problèmes. Le mariage étant, dans de nombreux pays ou zones, un contrat juridique civil qui, pour être légal, doit être conclu devant un officier de l'état civil, il s'ensuit que dans ces pays ou zones l'enregistrement a lieu presque systématiquement au moment de la cérémonie ou immédiatement après. De même, dans de nombreux pays ou zones, le tribunal ou l'autorité qui a prononcé le divorce est seul habilité à enregistrer cet acte, et comme l'acte d'enregistrement figure alors sur les registres du tribunal l'enregistrement suit généralement de peu le jugement.

En revanche, si l'enregistrement n'a lieu qu'avec un certain retard, les statistiques de l'état civil établies selon la date de l'enregistrement ne sont pas comparables sur le plan international. Au mieux, les statistiques par date de l'enregistrement prendront surtout en considération des faits survenus au cours de l'année précédente ; dans les pays ou zones où le système d'enregistrement n'est pas très développé, il y entrera des faits datant de plusieurs années. Il ressort des documents dont on dispose que des retards de plusieurs années dans l'enregistrement des naissances ne sont pas rares, encore que, dans la majorité des cas, les retards ne dépassent pas deux à quatre ans.

Tant que l'enregistrement se fera avec retard, les statistiques fondées sur la date d'enregistrement ne seront comparables sur le plan international ni entre elles ni avec les statistiques établies selon la date de fait d'état civil.

Il convient également de noter que l'exploitation des données selon la date de l'enregistrement ne nuit pas seulement à la comparabilité internationale des statistiques. Même à l'intérieur d'un pays ou d'une zone, le procédé qui consiste à compter les enregistrements et non les faits peut compromettre la comparabilité des chiffres sur une longue période. Si le nombre des faits d'état civil enregistrés varie d'une année à l'autre (par suite de l'application de mesures visant tout particulièrement à encourager l'enregistrement ou parce qu'il est subitement devenu nécessaire de produire le certificat d'une naissance ou d'un décès non enregistré pour l'accomplissement de certaines formalités), les statistiques de l'état civil établies d'après la date de l'enregistrement ne permettent pas de quantifier ni d'analyser l'état et l'évolution de la population. Tout au plus peuvent-elles révéler l'évolution des conditions d'exigibilité de l'acte de naissance, de décès ou de mariage et les fluctuations du volume de travail des bureaux d'état civil. Les statistiques établies selon la date de l'enregistrement peuvent donc ne présenter qu'une utilité très réduite pour des études nationales ou internationales.

4.2 Méthodes utilisées pour indiquer la qualité des statistiques de l'état civil qui sont publiées

La qualité des statistiques de l'état civil peut être évaluée en se fondant sur plusieurs facteurs. Le facteur essentiel est la complétude du système d'enregistrement des faits d'état civil d'après lequel ces statistiques sont établies. Dans certains cas, on constate que les données tirées de l'enregistrement ne sont pas complètes lorsque l'on les utilise pour le calcul des taux. Toutefois, cette observation est valable uniquement lorsque les statistiques présentent des lacunes évidentes, qu'elles sont exploitées d'après la date de l'événement et que l'estimation du chiffre de population pris pour base est exacte. L'exploitation des données d'après la date de l'enregistrement donne souvent des taux qui paraissent exacts, tout simplement parce que le numérateur est artificiellement gonflé par suite de l'inclusion d'enregistrements tardifs ; inversement, il arrive que des taux paraissent vraisemblables parce que l'on a sous-évalué la population étudiée. Il ne faut pas non plus oublier que les renseignements dont on dispose sur les taux de fécondité, de mortalité et de nuptialité considérés comme normaux sont extrêmement sommaires dans un grand nombre de régions du monde et que les cas limites, qui sont les plus difficiles à évaluer, sont fréquents.

4.2.1 Codage qualitatif des statistiques provenant des registres de l'état civil

Dans le questionnaire relatif au mouvement de la population qui leur est envoyé chaque année dans le cadre de l'établissement de *l'Annuaire démographique*, les services nationaux de statistique sont invités à donner leur propre évaluation du degré de complétude des données sur les naissances, les décès, les décès d'enfants de moins d'un an, les morts fœtales tardives, les mariages et les divorces figurant dans leurs registres d'état civil.

D'après les renseignements directement communiqués par les gouvernements ou extraits des questionnaires ou de publications officielles pertinentes, il a été possible de classer les statistiques de l'enregistrement des faits d'état civil (naissances, décès, décès d'enfants de moins d'un an, morts fœtales tardives, mariages et divorces) en trois grandes catégories, selon leur qualité :

C : Données jugées pratiquement complètes, c'est-à-dire représentant au moins 90 % des faits d'état civil survenant chaque année.

U : Données jugées incomplètes, c'est-à-dire représentant moins de 90 % des faits survenant chaque année.

| : Données ne provenant pas des systèmes nationaux d'enregistrement des faits d'état civil, mais jugées fiables, telles que les estimations dérivées des recensements de population ou du logement.

... : Données dont le degré de complétude ne fait pas l'objet de renseignements précis.

Ces codes de qualité figurent dans la première colonne des tableaux qui présentent, pour un nombre d'années déterminé les chiffres absolus et les taux (ou rapports) bruts concernant les naissances vivantes, les morts fœtales tardives, les décès d'enfants de moins d'un an, les décès, les mariages et les divorces. Les niveaux de fiabilité des statistiques de mortalité maternelle sont transmis par l'Organisation mondiale de la santé.

La classification des pays ou zones selon ces codes de qualité peut ne pas être uniforme. On a estimé néanmoins que les services nationaux de statistique étaient les mieux placés pour juger de la qualité de leurs données. On a pensé que les catégories que l'on pouvait distinguer sur la base des renseignements disponibles, bien que très larges, permettaient cependant de se faire une idée de la qualité des statistiques de l'état civil publiées dans *l'Annuaire démographique*.

Sur les pays ou zones qui ont estimé à 90 % ou plus le degré d'exhaustivité de leur enregistrement des naissances vivantes (classé « C » ou « +C » dans le tableau 9), les pays ou zones suivants ont communiqué des renseignements concernant les bases sur lesquelles leur estimation reposait :

a) Analyse démographique : Afrique du Sud, Argentine, Autriche, Bulgarie, Chili, Chine - Hong Kong RAS, Croatie, Égypte, Estonie, Italie, Lettonie, Lituanie, Malaisie, Malte, Maurice, Mexique, Nouvelle-Zélande, Panama, République de Corée, République de Moldova, Roumanie, Seychelles et Suède.

b) Double contrôle des registres : Autriche, Bahreïn, Chypre, Cuba, Estonie, Hongrie, Îles Féroé, Israël, Italie, Lettonie, Malaisie, Montserrat, Norvège, Nouvelle-Zélande, Qatar, République de Corée, Roumanie, Saint Vincent et les Grenadines et Uruguay.

c) Autre méthode : Allemagne, Aruba, Australie, Curaçao, Danemark, Espagne, État de Palestine, France, Guatemala, Irlande, Kirghizstan, Liechtenstein, Luxembourg, Malaisie, Mexique, Ouzbékistan, Panama, Pologne, Porto Rico, Singapour, Slovénie et Suède.

Sur les pays ou zones qui ont estimé à 90 % ou plus le degré d'exhaustivité de leur enregistrement des morts fœtales tardives (classé « C » ou « +C » dans le tableau 12), les pays ou zones suivants ont communiqué des renseignements concernant les bases sur lesquelles leur estimation reposait :

a) Analyse démographique : Argentine, Autriche, Bulgarie, Croatie, Égypte, Estonie, Italie, Lettonie, Lituanie, Malte, Maurice, Mexique, Roumanie et Suède.

b) Double contrôle des registres : Autriche, Cuba, Estonie, Hongrie, Israël, Italie, Leetonie, Lituanie, Montserrat, Norvège, Nouvelle-Zélande, Qatar et Venezuela (République bolivarienne du).

c) Autre méthode : Allemagne, Danemark, Espagne, Kirghizstan, Luxembourg, Ouzbékistan, Pologne, Porto Rico, Slovénie et Suède.

Sur les pays ou zones qui ont estimé à 90 % ou plus le degré d'exhaustivité de leur enregistrement des décès à moins d'un an (classé « C » ou « +C » dans le tableau 15), les pays ou zones suivants ont donné des indications touchant la base de cette estimation :

a) Analyse démographique : Argentine, Autriche, Bulgarie, Chili, Chine - Hong Kong RAS, Croatie, Égypte, Estonie, Israël, Italie, Lettonie, Lituanie, Malte, Maurice, Mexique, Nouvelle-Zélande, Panama, République de Corée, République de Moldova, Roumanie, Seychelles et Suède.

b) Double contrôle des registres : Autriche, Bahreïn, Cuba, Chypre, Estonie, Hongrie, Îles Féroé, Irlande, Israël, Italie, Lettonie, Lituanie, Montserrat, Norvège, Nouvelle-Zélande, Qatar, République de Corée et Venezuela (République bolivarienne du).

c) Autre méthode : Allemagne, Aruba, Australie, Curaçao, Danemark, Espagne, Îles Caïmans, Kirghizstan, Liechtenstein, Luxembourg, Ouzbékistan, Pologne, Porto Rico, Singapour, Slovénie et Suède.

Sur les pays ou zones qui ont estimé à 90 % ou plus le degré d'exhaustivité de leur enregistrement des décès (classé « C » ou « +C » dans le tableau 18), les pays ou zones suivants ont donné des indications touchant la base de cette estimation :

a) Analyse démographique : Afrique du Sud, Argentine, Autriche, Bulgarie, Chili, Chine - Hong Kong RAS, Croatie, Égypte, Estonie, Israël, Italie, Lettonie, Lituanie, Malaisie, Malte, Maurice, Mexique, Nouvelle-Zélande, Panama, République de Corée, République de Moldova, Roumanie, Seychelles, Suède et Venezuela (République bolivarienne du).

b) Double contrôle des registres : Autriche, Bahreïn, Cuba, Chypre, Estonie, Hongrie, Îles Féroé, Israël, Italie, Lettonie, Lituanie, Malaisie, Montserrat, Norvège, Nouvelle-Zélande, Qatar, République de Corée et Venezuela (République bolivarienne du).

c) Autre méthode : Allemagne, Aruba, Australie, Brésil, Curaçao, Danemark, Espagne, France, Kirghizstan, Liechtenstein, Luxembourg, Malaisie, Ouzbékistan, Pologne, Porto Rico, Saint Vincent et les Grenadines, Singapour, Slovénie et Suède.

Sur les pays ou zones qui ont estimé à 90 % ou plus le degré d'exhaustivité de leur enregistrement des mariages (classé « C » ou « +C «» dans le tableau 23), les pays ou zones suivants ont communiqué des renseignements concernant les bases sur lesquelles leur estimation reposait :

a) Analyse démographique : Argentine, Autriche, Bulgarie, Chili, Chine - Hong Kong RAS, Croatie, Égypte, Estonie, Italie, Lettonie, Lituanie, Malte, Maurice, Mexique, République de Corée, République de Moldova, Roumanie, Seychelles et Suède.

b) Double contrôle des registres : Autriche, Cuba, Estonie, État de Palestine, Hongrie, Îles Féroé, Israël, Italie, Lettonie, Norvège, Nouvelle-Zélande, Qatar, République de Corée et Venezuela (République bolivarienne du).

c) Autre méthode : Allemagne, Aruba, Australie, Curaçao, Danemark, Espagne, France, Kirghizstan, Liechtenstein, Luxembourg, Ouzbékistan, Pologne, Porto Rico, Slovénie, Suède et Tadjikistan.

Sur les pays ou zones qui ont estimé à 90 % ou plus le degré d'exhaustivité de leur enregistrement des divorces (classé « C » ou « +C » dans le tableau 24), les pays ou zones suivants ont communiqué des renseignements concernant les bases sur lesquelles leur estimation reposait :

a) Analyse démographique : Autriche, Bulgarie, Croatie, Égypte, Estonie, Italie, Lettonie, Lituanie, Mexique, République de Corée, République de Moldova, Roumanie, Seychelles et Suède.

b) Double contrôle des registres : Cuba, Estonie, État de Palestine, Hongrie, Îles Féroé, Israël, Italie, Lettonie, Norvège, Nouvelle-Zélande, Qatar, République de Corée et Venezuela (République bolivarienne du).

c) Autre méthode : Aruba, Australie, Chypre, Curaçao, Danemark, Kirghizstan, Liechtenstein, Luxembourg, Maurice, Ouzbékistan, Pologne, Porto Rico, Slovénie, Suède et Tadjikistan.

4.2.2 Traitement des statistiques tirées des registres d'état civil

Dans tous les tableaux de l'*Annuaire démographique*, on a indiqué le degré de fiabilité des statistiques de l'état civil en se fondant sur le codage qualitatif décrit ci-dessus. Les statistiques codées « C », jugées sûres, sont imprimées en caractères romains. Celles qui sont codées « U » ou « ... », jugées douteuses, sont reproduites en *italique*.

Il convient de noter que, pour les taux de mortalité infantile, les taux de mortalité maternelle et les rapports de morts fœtales tardives (calculées en utilisant au dénominateur le nombre de naissances vivantes), les indications relatives à la fiabilité sont déterminées sur la base des codes de qualité utilisés pour les décès d'enfants de moins d'un an, les décès totaux et les morts fœtales tardives, respectivement. Pour évaluer ces taux et rapports de façon plus précise, il faudrait tenir compte de la qualité des données relatives aux naissances vivantes, utilisées au dénominateur dans leur calcul. Les codes de qualité pour les naissances vivantes figurent au tableau 9 et sont décrits plus en détail dans les notes techniques se rapportant à ce tableau.

4.2.3 Traitement des séries chronologiques de statistiques tirées des registres d'état civil

Il est plus difficile de déterminer la qualité des séries chronologiques de statistiques de l'état civil que celle des données pour une seule année. Étant donné qu'une série chronologique de statistiques de l'état civil ne peut généralement avoir pour source qu'un système permanent d'enregistrement des faits d'état civil, on a arbitrairement supposé que le degré d'exactitude de la série tout entière était le même que celui de la dernière tranche annuelle de données tirées du registre d'état civil. La série tout entière est traitée de la manière décrite à la section 4.2.2 ci-dessus : lorsque le code de qualité relatif aux données d'enregistrement les plus récentes est « C », les fréquences et les taux relatifs aux années antérieures sont eux aussi considérés comme sûrs et figurent en caractères romains. Inversement, si les données d'enregistrement les plus récentes sont codées « U » ou «...», les données des années antérieures sont jugées douteuses et figurent en italique. Cette méthode n'est certes pas entièrement satisfaisante, car les données des premières années de la série sont souvent beaucoup moins sûres que le code actuel ne le laisse supposer. On s'efforce d'abandonner progressivement cette méthode et de coder les données enregistrées pour chaque année séparément.

4.2.4 Traitement des estimations fondées sur les statistiques de l'état civil

En plus des données provenant des systèmes d'enregistrement des faits d'état civil, l'*Annuaire démographique* contient aussi des estimations relatives aux fréquences et aux taux. Il s'agit d'estimations officielles, généralement calculées à partir des résultats d'un recensement de la population ou d'un sondage ou par analyse démographique. Si des estimations concernant les fréquences et les taux figurent dans les tableaux, c'est parce que l'on considère qu'elles fournissent des renseignements plus exacts que les systèmes existants d'enregistrement des faits d'état civil. En conséquence, elles sont également jugées sûres et sont donc imprimées en caractères romains.

Dans les tableaux qui indiquent le code de qualité, ce code ne s'applique qu'aux données tirées des registres d'état civil. Les données estimatives sont dénotées par le «|».

4.3 Causes de décès

Les États membres de l'Organisation mondiale de la santé (OMS) sont tenus de communiquer à celle-ci les données sur les causes de décès codifiées selon la révision en vigueur de la Classification internationale des maladies et des problèmes de santé connexes (CIM). Pour assurer la comparabilité internationale des statistiques des causes de décès, l'OMS organise régulièrement des conférences internationales de révision de la Classification internationale des maladies afin de suivre, au fur et à mesure, les progrès les plus récents de la médecine clinique et de la statistique. Les données sont généralement présentées à l'OMS selon le degré de détail à tous les quatre caractères requis par la CIM et sont compilées et archivées dans la Base de données sur la mortalité de l'OMS au degré de détail présenté par le pays. Les données de la Base de données sur la mortalité de l'OMS sont disponibles sur le site Internet suivant : http://www3.who.int/whosis/menu.cfm.

Les révisions de la CIM permettent certes de disposer d'une version actualisée, mais elles posent plusieurs problèmes de comparabilité des statistiques des causes de décès. Le premier tient au manque de comparabilité dans le temps, qui accompagne inévitablement la mise en œuvre d'une classification nouvelle. Le deuxième est celui de la comparabilité entre pays ou zones, car les différents pays peuvent adopter la nouvelle classification à des époques différentes. Établir la cause des décès exige des compétences de plus en plus poussées à mesure que la classification devient plus précise. Or, dans beaucoup de pays ou zones, il est rare que les décès se produisent en présence d'un témoin possédant une formation médicale et le certificat de décès est le plus souvent établi par quelqu'un qui n'est pas qualifié sur le plan médical. Étant donné que la CIM répertorie de nombreux diagnostics qu'il est impossible d'établir si l'on n'a pas de formation en médecine, la CIM n'est pas toujours exactement ou précisément utilisée ce qui affecte la comparabilité internationale, notamment entre pays ou zones où la qualité des services médicaux est très disparate.

Les chapitres de la dixième révision[15] se fondent sur un système de codification alphanumérique à une lettre suivie de trois chiffres pour les catégories à quatre caractères. Le chapitre 1 concerne les maladies infectieuses et parasitaires et le chapitre 2 l'ensemble des néoplasmes. Le chapitre 3 a trait aux troubles du système immunitaire, aux maladies du sang et aux organes hématopoïétiques. Le chapitre 4 porte sur les maladies du système endocrinien, de la nutrition et du métabolisme. Les autres chapitres groupent les maladies selon leur site anatomique, à l'exception de ceux qui concernent les affections mentales, les complications de la grossesse, de l'accouchement et des suites de couches, les malformations congénitales et les affections de la période périnatale. Enfin, un chapitre entier est consacré aux symptômes, manifestations et résultats anormaux.

4.3.1 Mortalité liée à la maternité

D'après la dixième révision de la CIM, la « mortalité liée à la maternité » est définie comme le décès d'une femme survenu au cours de la grossesse ou dans un délai de 42 jours après sa terminaison, quelle qu'en soit la durée et la localisation, pour une cause quelconque déterminée ou aggravée par la grossesse ou les soins qu'elle a motivés, mais ni accidentelle ni fortuite.

Les « décès liés à la maternité » doivent se répartir en décès par cause obstétricale directe et indirecte. Les décès par cause obstétricale directe sont ceux qui résultent de complications obstétricales de l'état de grossesse (grossesse, travail et suites de couches), d'interventions, d'omissions, d'un traitement incorrect ou d'un enchaînement d'événements de l'un quelconque des facteurs ci-dessus. Les décès par cause obstétricale indirecte sont ceux qui résultent d'une maladie préexistante ou d'une affection apparue au cours de la grossesse, sans qu'elle soit due à des causes obstétricales directes, mais qui a été aggravée par les effets physiologiques de la grossesse.

En théorie, le nombre de femmes enceintes aurait dû être pris comme dénominateur pour le taux de mortalité maternelle, mais il est impossible de déterminer ce nombre. En conséquence, il est en outre recommandé dans la dixième révision d'exprimer les taux de mortalité maternelle sur la base de 100 000 naissances vivantes ou 100 000 naissances totales (naissances vivantes et morts fœtales). Le taux de mortalité maternelle est ici calculé par 100 000 naissances vivantes. Bien que les naissances vivantes ne permettent pas d'évaluer sans distorsion le nombre des femmes enceintes, leur nombre est plus fiable que d'autres estimations car le nombre des naissances vivantes est plus exactement enregistré que celui des naissances vivantes et des morts fœtales.

---

[1] Les éditions de 1978 et de 1991 font exception à la règle, puisque les tableaux sur des sujets spéciaux ont été publiés séparément.

[2] Organisation des Nations Unies, Département des affaires économiques et sociales, Division de la population (2015). *Perspectives de la population mondiale : La révision de 2015* (http://esa.un.org/unpd/wpp/).

[3] ST/ESA/STAT/SER.M/49/Rev.4/WWW ; http://unstats.un.org/unsd/methods/m49/m49frnch.htm; voir également *Code standard des pays et des zones à usage statistique*, numéro de vente : M.98.XVII.9, Nations Unies, New York, 1999.

[4] Numéro de vente : E.15.XVII.10, Nations Unies, New York, 2015.

[5] Ibid., par. 4.151.

[6] Lorsque l'on utilise un registre de la population, on peut également calculer l'âge en années révolues en soustrayant la date de naissance de chaque personne inscrite sur le registre de la date de référence à laquelle se rapportent les données sur l'âge.

[7] L'emploi de méthodes différentes de calcul de l'âge, par exemple la méthode occidentale et la méthode orientale, ou, comme on les désigne plus communément, la méthode anglaise et la méthode chinoise, représente une cause de non-comparabilité. Selon la méthode chinoise, on considère que l'enfant est âgé d'un an à sa naissance et qu'il avance d'un an à chaque nouvelle année chinoise. Les répercussions de cette méthode sont particulièrement apparentes dans les données pour le premier âge : les données concernant les enfants de moins d'un an sont nettement inférieures à la réalité. Les effets sur les chiffres relatifs aux groupes d'âge suivants sont moins visibles. Les séries ainsi établies sont souvent ajustées avant d'être publiées, mais il ne faut pas exclure la possibilité d'aberrations de ce genre lorsque l'on compare des données censitaires sur l'âge.

[8] Numéro de vente : E.13.XVII.10, publication des Nations Unies, New York, 2014.

[9] Numéro de vente : F. 98.XVII.7, publication des Nations Unies, New York, 1998.

[10] Numéro de vente : F.98.XVII.11, publication des Nations Unies, New York, 1998.

[11] Numéro de vente : F.98.XVII.4, publication des Nations Unies, New York, 1998.

[12] Numéro de vente : F.98.XVII.6, publication des Nations Unies, New York, 1998.

[13] Numéro de vente : F.98.XVII.10, publication des Nations Unies, New York, 1998.

[14] Numéro de vente : F.03.XVII.11, United Nations, New York, 2004.

[15] Organisation mondiale de la santé, *Classification statistique internationale des maladies et problèmes de santé connexes,* dixième révision, vol. 2, Genève, 1992.

Table A. Demographic Yearbook 2015 synoptic table: Availability of data by country/area, table and sex, where applicable
Tableau A. Tableau synoptique de l'Annuaire démographique 2015 : Disponibilité des données par pays ou zone, tableau et le sexe, si disponible

General topic and table number - Sujet général et numéro de tableau

Continent and country or area / Continent et pays ou zone	Table totals	Summary - Aperçu 3 Total	3 M/F	4	Population 5	6 Total[1]	6 M/F	7 Total	7 M/F	8 Total	8 M/F	Fertility - Natalité 9	10 Total	10 M/F	11	Foetal mortality - Mortalité foetale 12	13	14
Total number of countries or areas - Total des pays ou zones	..	240	226	188	223	229	229	211	210	206	162	175	151	128	89	89	65	52

AFRICA - AFRIQUE

Continent and country or area / Continent et pays ou zone	Table totals	3 Total	3 M/F	4	5	6 Total[1]	6 M/F	7 Total	7 M/F	8 Total	8 M/F	9	10 Total	10 M/F	11	12	13	14
Algeria - Algérie	17	•	•	•	•	•	•	•	•	•	•	•	...	...	...	•	...	...
Angola	5	•	•	...	•	•	•	•	•	...	...	•	...	...	...	...	...	...
Benin - Bénin	13	•	•	•	•	•	•	•	•	•	•	•	...	...	...	...	...	...
Botswana	20	•	•	•	•	•	•	•	•	•	•	•	•	•	•	...	...	...
Burkina Faso	10	•	•	...	•	•	•	•	•	•	•	•	...	...	...	...	...	...
Burundi	14	•	•	•	•	•	•	•	•	•	•	•	...	...	...	•	•	...
Cabo Verde	13	•	•	...	•	•	•	•	•	•	•	•	...	...	...	...	...	...
Cameroon - Cameroun	8	•	•	•	•	•	•	•	•	...	...	...	...	...	...	...	...	...
Central African Republic - République centrafricaine	2	•	•	...	...	...	...	...	...	...	...	...	...	...	...	...	...	...
Chad - Tchad	4	•	•	...	•	...	...	...	...	...	...	...	...	...	...	...	...	...
Comoros - Comores	2	•	•	...	•	•	•	•	•	...	...	...	...	...	...	...	...	...
Congo	8	•	•	•	•	•	•	•	•	...	...	...	...	...	...	...	...	...
Côte d'Ivoire	10	•	•	•	•	•	•	•	•	•	•	...	...	...	...	...	...	...
Democratic Republic of the Congo - République démocratique du Congo	2	•	•	...	...	...	...	...	...	...	...	...	...	...	...	...	...	...
Djibouti	10	•	•	•	•	•	•	•	•	...	...	•	...	...	...	...	...	...
Egypt - Égypte	27	•	•	•	•	•	•	•	•	•	•	•	•	•	•	•	...	...
Equatorial Guinea - Guinée équatoriale	9	•	•	•	•	•	•	•	•	...	...	...	...	...	...	...	...	...
Eritrea - Érythrée	2	•	•	...	...	...	...	...	...	...	...	...	...	...	...	...	...	...
Ethiopia - Éthiopie	8	•	•	•	•	•	•	•	•	•	...	...	...	...	...	...	...	...
Gabon	6	•	•	...	...	•	•	•	•	...	•	...	...	...	...	...	...	...
Gambia - Gambie	5	•	•	...	•	•	•	...	...	•	•	•	...	...	...	...	...	...
Ghana	17	•	•	•	•	•	•	•	•	•	•	•	•	•	•	...	...	...
Guinea - Guinée	10	•	•	•	•	•	•	•	•	•	...	...	...	...	...	...	...	...
Guinea-Bissau - Guinée-Bissau	10	•	•	•	•	•	•	•	•	•	...	•	•	•	•	...	...	...
Kenya	18	•	•	•	•	•	•	•	•	•	•	•	•	•	•	...	...	...
Lesotho	19	•	•	•	•	•	•	•	•	•	•	•	•	•	•	...	...	...
Liberia - Libéria	12	•	•	•	•	•	•	•	•	•	•	...	•	•	•	...	...	...
Libya - Libye	8	•	•	...	•	•	•	•	...	...	...	...	...	...	...	...	...	...
Madagascar	5	•	•	...	...	...	•	•	•	...	•	•	...	...	...	...	...	...
Malawi	14	•	•	•	•	•	•	•	•	•	•	•	...	•	...	...	...	...
Mali	13	•	•	•	•	•	•	•	•	•	...	•	•	•	•	...	...	...
Mauritania - Mauritanie	11	•	...	•	•	•	•	•	•	•	...	•	•	•	...	...	...	...
Mauritius - Maurice	27	•	•	•	•	•	•	•	•	•	•	•	•	•	•	•	•	...
Mayotte	15	•	•	•	•	•	•	•	•	...	...	•	...	...	...	...	...	...
Morocco - Maroc	13	•	...	•	•	•	•	•	•	•	...	•	...	...	...	...	...	...
Mozambique	12	•	•	•	•	•	•	•	•	•	...	•	...	...	...	...	...	...
Namibia - Namibie	17	•	•	•	•	•	•	•	•	•	•	•	•	...	...	...	...	...
Niger	15	•	•	•	•	•	•	•	•	•	...	•	...	...	...	...	...	...
Nigeria - Nigéria	8	•	•	...	•	•	•	...	...	...	...	•	...	...	...	...	...	...
Republic of South Sudan - République de Soudan du Sud	13	•	•	•	•	•	•	•	•	•	...	...	...	...	...	...	...	...
Reunion - Réunion	26	•	•	•	•	•	•	•	•	•	•	•	•	•	•	•	•	...
Rwanda	13	•	•	•	•	•	•	•	•	•	•	•	•	...	...	...	...	...
Saint Helena ex. dep. - Sainte-Hélène sans dép.	23	•	•	•	•	•	•	•	•	•	•	•	...	...	...	...	...	...
Saint Helena: Ascension - Sainte-Hélène: Ascension	7	•	•	...	•	•	•	•	...	...	...	...	...	...	...	...	...	...
Saint Helena: Tristan da Cunha - Sainte-Hélène: Tristan da Cunha	5	•	•	...	•	•	•	•	•	...	...	...	...	...	...	...	...	...
Sao Tome and Principe - Sao Tomé-et-Principe	15	•	•	•	•	•	•	•	•	•	•	•	...	...	...	...	...	...
Senegal - Sénégal	13	•	•	•	•	•	•	•	•	•	...	•	...	...	...	...	...	...
Seychelles	25	•	•	•	•	•	•	•	•	...	...	•	•	•	•	...	•	...
Sierra Leone	15	•	•	•	•	•	•	•	•	•	•	•	•	...	...	...	...	...
Somalia - Somalie	3	•	•	...	...	...	...	...	...	...	...	...	...	...	...	...	...	...
South Africa - Afrique du Sud	26	•	•	•	•	•	•	•	•	•	•	•	•	•	...	...	...	...
Sudan - Soudan	9	•	•	•	•	•	•	•	•	...	...	...	...	...	...	...	...	...
Swaziland	13	•	•	•	•	•	•	•	•	...	...	•	•	•	•	...	...	...
Togo	8	•	•	...	•	•	•	•	•	...	...	•	...	...	...	...	...	...
Tunisia - Tunisie	19	•	•	•	•	•	•	•	•	•	...	•	•	...	...	...	...	...

Table A. Demographic Yearbook 2015 synoptic table: Availability of data by country/area, table and sex, where applicable
Tableau A. Tableau synoptique de l'Annuaire démographique 2015 : Disponibilité des données par pays ou zone, tableau et le sexe, si disponible

Continent and country or area / Continent et pays ou zone	General topic and table number - Sujet général et numéro de tableau												
	Infant and maternal mortality - Mortalité infantile et mortalité liée à la maternité				General mortality - Mortalité générale						Nuptiality and divorces - Nuptialité et divortialité		
	15	16 Total	16 M/F	17	18	19 Total	19 M/F	20	21	22	23	24	25
Total number of countries or areas - Total des pays ou zones	124	115	112	125	172	150	148	111	72	183	138	110	113
AFRICA - AFRIQUE													
Algeria - Algérie	•	…	…	…	•	•	•	…	…	•	•	…	…
Angola	…	…	…	…	…	…	…	…	…	…	•	…	…
Benin - Bénin	…	…	…	…	•	…	…	…	…	…	•	…	…
Botswana	•	…	…	…	•	•	•	…	…	…	•	•	…
Burkina Faso	…	…	…	…	…	…	…	…	…	•	…	…	…
Burundi	…	…	…	…	…	…	…	…	…	•	…	…	…
Cabo Verde	…	•	…	•	…	…	…	•	…	…	•	…	…
Cameroon - Cameroun	…	…	…	…	…	…	…	…	…	…	…	…	…
Central African Republic - République centrafricaine	…	…	…	…	…	…	…	…	…	…	…	…	…
Chad - Tchad	…	…	…	…	…	…	…	…	…	…	…	…	…
Comoros - Comores	…	…	…	…	…	…	…	…	…	…	…	…	…
Congo	…	…	…	…	…	•	…	…	…	…	…	…	…
Côte d'Ivoire	…	…	…	…	…	…	…	…	…	•	…	…	…
Democratic Republic of the Congo - République démocratique du Congo	…	…	…	…	…	…	…	…	…	…	…	…	…
Djibouti	…	…	…	…	•	…	…	…	…	•	…	…	…
Egypt - Égypte	•	•	•	•	•	•	•	…	…	•	•	•	•
Equatorial Guinea - Guinée équatoriale	…	…	…	…	…	…	…	…	…	•	…	…	…
Eritrea - Érythrée	…	…	…	…	…	…	…	…	…	…	…	…	…
Ethiopia - Éthiopie	…	…	…	…	…	…	…	…	…	…	…	…	…
Gabon	…	…	…	…	…	…	…	…	…	…	…	…	…
Gambia - Gambie	…	…	…	…	…	…	…	…	…	…	…	…	…
Ghana	…	…	…	…	•	•	•	…	…	•	…	…	…
Guinea - Guinée	…	…	…	…	…	…	…	…	…	…	…	…	…
Guinea-Bissau - Guinée-Bissau	…	…	…	…	…	…	…	…	…	…	…	…	…
Kenya	•	…	…	…	•	•	•	…	…	•	…	…	…
Lesotho	…	…	…	…	•	•	•	…	…	•	•	•	•
Liberia - Libéria	…	…	…	…	…	…	…	…	…	…	…	…	…
Libya - Libye	…	…	…	…	…	…	…	…	…	…	…	…	…
Madagascar	…	…	…	…	…	…	…	…	…	…	…	…	…
Malawi	…	…	…	…	•	•	…	…	…	•	…	…	…
Mali	…	…	…	…	•	•	…	…	…	…	…	…	…
Mauritania - Mauritanie	…	…	…	…	…	…	…	…	…	•	…	…	…
Mauritius - Maurice	•	•	•	•	•	•	•	•	…	•	•	•	•
Mayotte	…	…	…	•	•	…	…	•	…	•	•	•	…
Morocco - Maroc	…	…	…	•	•	•	•	•	…	•	…	…	…
Mozambique	…	…	…	…	…	…	…	…	…	•	…	…	…
Namibia - Namibie	…	…	…	…	•	•	•	…	…	•	…	…	…
Niger	…	…	…	…	•	•	•	…	…	…	•	…	…
Nigeria - Nigéria	…	…	…	…	…	…	…	…	…	…	…	…	…
Republic of South Sudan - République de Soudan du Sud	…	…	…	…	•	•	…	•	…	•	…	…	…
Reunion - Réunion	…	•	•	•	•	•	•	•	…	•	•	•	•
Rwanda	…	…	…	…	•	…	…	…	…	•	…	…	…
Saint Helena ex. dep. - Sainte-Hélène sans dép.	•	•	•	…	•	•	…	…	…	•	•	•	•
Saint Helena: Ascension - Sainte-Hélène: Ascension	…	…	…	…	…	…	…	…	…	…	…	…	…
Saint Helena: Tristan da Cunha - Sainte-Hélène: Tristan da Cunha	…	…	…	…	…	…	…	…	…	…	…	…	…
Sao Tome and Principe - Sao Tomé-et-Principe	…	…	…	…	•	•	•	…	…	…	…	…	…
Senegal - Sénégal	…	…	…	…	•	…	…	…	…	•	…	…	…
Seychelles	•	•	•	…	•	•	•	…	…	•	•	•	•
Sierra Leone	•	…	…	…	…	…	…	…	…	…	…	…	…
Somalia - Somalie	…	…	…	…	…	…	…	…	…	…	…	…	…
South Africa - Afrique du Sud	•	…	…	•	•	•	•	…	…	•	•	…	•
Sudan - Soudan	…	…	…	…	…	…	…	…	…	•	•	…	•
Swaziland	…	…	…	…	•	•	…	…	…	•	…	…	…
Togo	…	…	…	…	…	…	…	…	…	…	…	…	…
Tunisia - Tunisie	…	…	…	•	•	…	…	•	…	•	•	•	•

Table A. Demographic Yearbook 2015 synoptic table: Availability of data by country/area, table and sex, where applicable
Tableau A. Tableau synoptique de l'Annuaire démographique 2015 : Disponibilité des données par pays ou zone, tableau et le sexe, si disponible (continued - suite)

General topic and table number - Sujet général et numéro de tableau

Continent and country or area / Continent et pays ou zone	Table totals	Summary - Aperçu 3 Total	3 M/F	4	5	Population 6 Total[1]	6 M/F	7 Total	7 M/F	8 Total	8 M/F	Fertility - Natalité 9	10 Total	10 M/F	11	Foetal mortality - Mortalité foetale 12	13	14
AFRICA - AFRIQUE																		
Uganda - Ouganda	9	•	•	•	•	•	•	•	...	•	...	...	...	...	...	...	...	...
United Republic of Tanzania - République Unie de Tanzanie	10	•	•	•	•	•	•	•	...	•	...	•	...	...	...	...	...	...
Western Sahara - Sahara occidental	3	•	•	...	...	...	•	•	...	•	...	...	...	...	...	...	...	...
Zambia - Zambie	13	•	•	...	•	•	•	•	•	•	...	•	...	...	•	...	...	...
Zimbabwe	11	•	•	...	•	•	•	•	•	•	...	•	...	...	...	...	...	...
AMERICA, NORTH - AMÉRIQUE DU NORD																		
Anguilla	18	•	•	•	•	•	•	...	...	•	•	•	•	•	...	...	...	...
Antigua and Barbuda - Antigua-et-Barbuda	12	•	...	•	•	•	•	•	•	...	...	...	•	•	...	...	...	...
Aruba	25	•	•	•	•	•	•	•	•	•	•	•	•	•	•	...	...	...
Bahamas	26	•	•	•	•	•	•	•	•	•	•	•	•	•	•	...	...	...
Barbados - Barbade	21	•	•	•	•	•	•	•	•	•	•	•	•	•	•	...	...	...
Belize	14	•	•	•	•	•	•	•	•	•	•	•	•	•	...	...	...	...
Bermuda - Bermudes	28	•	•	•	•	•	•	•	•	•	•	•	•	•	•	•	•	•
British Virgin Islands - Îles Vierges britanniques	9	•	•	•	•	•	...	...	•	•	•	•	•	•	...	...	...	...
Canada	26	•	•	•	•	•	•	•	•	•	•	•	•	•	•	•	•	•
Cayman Islands - Îles Caïmanes	20	•	•	•	•	•	•	•	•	•	•	•	•	•	•	...	...	...
Costa Rica	30	•	•	•	•	•	•	•	•	•	•	•	•	•	•	•	•	•
Cuba	29	•	•	•	•	•	•	•	•	...	...	•	•	•	•	•	•	•
Curaçao	22	•	•	•	•	•	•	...	...	•	•	•	•	•	•	...	...	...
Dominica - Dominique	19	•	•	•	•	•	•	•	•	•	•	•	•	•	...	...	...	...
Dominican Republic - République dominicaine	28	•	•	•	•	•	•	•	•	•	•	•	•	•	•	...	...	...
El Salvador	26	•	•	•	•	•	•	•	•	•	•	•	•	•	...	...	...	...
Greenland - Groenland	23	•	•	•	•	•	•	•	•	•	•	•	•	•	...	...	•	•
Grenada - Grenade	12	•	•	•	•	•	•	...	...	•	•	•	•	...	...	...	...	...
Guadeloupe	18	•	•	•	•	•	•	•	•	•	•	•	•	•	...	...	...	...
Guatemala	26	•	•	•	•	•	•	•	•	•	•	•	•	•	•	...	...	...
Haiti - Haïti	9	•	•	...	•	•	•	•	•	•	•	•	...	...	...	...	...	...
Honduras	15	•	•	•	•	•	•	•	•	•	•	•	•	...	...	...	...	...
Jamaica - Jamaïque	24	•	•	•	•	•	•	•	•	•	•	•	•	•	•	...	...	...
Martinique	27	•	•	•	•	•	•	•	•	•	•	•	•	•	•	...	...	...
Mexico - Mexique	30	•	•	•	•	•	•	•	•	•	•	•	•	•	•	•	•	•
Montserrat	22	•	•	•	•	•	•	•	•	•	•	•	•	•	•	...	...	...
Nicaragua	17	•	•	...	•	•	•	•	•	•	•	•	...	...	...	...	...	...
Panama	28	•	•	•	•	•	•	•	•	•	•	•	•	•	•	...	...	...
Puerto Rico - Porto Rico	29	•	•	•	•	•	•	•	•	•	...	•	•	•	•	...	...	...
Saint Kitts and Nevis - Saint-Kitts-et-Nevis	11	•	•	•	•	•	•	...	...	•	•	•	•	...	...	...	...	...
Saint Lucia - Sainte-Lucie	17	•	•	•	•	•	•	•	•	•	•	•	•	...	...	...	...	...
Saint Pierre and Miquelon - Saint Pierre-et-Miquelon	9	•	...	...	•	•	•	•	•	•	•	...	...	...	...	...	...	...
Saint Vincent and the Grenadines - Saint-Vincent-et-les Grenadines	24	•	•	•	•	•	•	•	•	•	•	...	•	•	•	...	...	...
Saint-Barthélemy	1	•	...	...	...	...	...	...	...	...	...	...	...	...	...	...	...	...
Saint-Martin (French part) - Saint-Martin (partie française)	1	•	...	...	...	...	...	...	...	...	...	...	...	...	...	...	...	...
Sint Maarten (Dutch part) - Saint-Martin (partie néerlandaise)	13	•	•	•	•	•	•	...	...	•	•	•	•	•	...	...	...	...
Trinidad and Tobago - Trinité-et-Tobago	23	•	...	•	•	•	•	•	•	•	•	•	•	•	•	...	...	...
Turks and Caicos Islands - Îles Turques et Caïques	11	•	•	...	•	•	•	...	...	•	•	•	...	...	...	...	...	...
United States of America - États-Unis d'Amérique	27	•	•	•	•	•	•	•	•	•	•	...	•	•	•	•	•	...
United States Virgin Islands - Îles Vierges américaines	17	•	•	•	•	•	•	•	•	•	•	...	•	•	...	...	...	...

Table A. Demographic Yearbook 2015 synoptic table: Availability of data by country/area, table and sex, where applicable
Tableau A. Tableau synoptique de l'Annuaire démographique 2015 : Disponibilité des données par pays ou zone, tableau et le sexe, si disponible (continued - suite)

Continent and country or area / Continent et pays ou zone	General topic and table number - Sujet général et numéro de tableau												
	Infant and maternal mortality - Mortalité infantile et mortalité liée à la maternité				General mortality - Mortalité générale						Nuptiality and divorces - Nuptialité et divortialité		
	15	16 Total	16 M/F	17	18	19 Total	19 M/F	20	21	22	23	24	25

AFRICA - AFRIQUE

	15	16 Total	16 M/F	17	18	19 Total	19 M/F	20	21	22	23	24	25
Uganda - Ouganda	...	...	...	...	...	...	...	...	•	...	...	...	...
United Republic of Tanzania - République Unie de Tanzanie	...	...	...	...	•	...	...	...	...	...	...	...	...
Western Sahara - Sahara occidental	...	...	...	...	...	...	...	...	...	...	...	...	...
Zambia - Zambie	...	...	...	...	...	•	•	...	...	...	...	...	...
Zimbabwe	...	...	...	...	...	...	...	•	•	...	...	...	...

AMERICA, NORTH - AMÉRIQUE DU NORD

	15	16 Total	16 M/F	17	18	19 Total	19 M/F	20	21	22	23	24	25
Anguilla	•	...	...	•	•	•	•	•	...	•	•	•	...
Antigua and Barbuda - Antigua-et-Barbuda	...	...	...	•	•	...	•	•	...	•	•	•	...
Aruba	•	...	•	•	•	•	•	•	...	•	•	•	•
Bahamas	•	•	•	•	•	•	•	•	...	•	•	•	•
Barbados - Barbade	•	•	•	•	•	•	•	•	...	•	•	•	•
Belize	...	•	•	•	•	•	•	•	...	•	•	•	•
Bermuda - Bermudes	•	•	•	•	•	•	•	•	...	•	•	•	•
British Virgin Islands - Îles Vierges britanniques	...	...	•	•	•	•	•	•	...	•	•	•	•
Canada	...	•	•	•	•	•	•	•	...	•	•	...	...
Cayman Islands - Îles Caïmanes	•	•	•	•	•	•	•	•	...	•	•	•	•
Costa Rica	•	•	•	•	•	•	•	•	...	•	•	•	•
Cuba	•	•	•	•	•	•	•	•	...	•	•	•	•
Curaçao	•	•	•	...	•	•	•	...	...	•	•	•	•
Dominica - Dominique	•	...	...	•	•	•	•	•	...	•	•	•	...
Dominican Republic - République dominicaine	•	•	•	•	•	•	•	•	...	•	•	•	•
El Salvador	•	•	•	•	•	•	•	•	...	•	•	•	•
Greenland - Groenland	•	•	•	•	•	•	•	...	...	•	...	...	...
Grenada - Grenade	...	...	...	•	•	...	...	•	...	•	...	...	•
Guadeloupe	...	...	...	•	•	...	...	•	...	•	...	...	•
Guatemala	•	•	•	•	•	•	•	•	...	•	•	•	•
Haiti - Haïti	...	...	...	...	...	...	...	...	...	•	...	...	...
Honduras	...	...	...	•	•	•	•	•	...	•	...	...	...
Jamaica - Jamaïque	...	•	•	•	•	•	•	•	...	•	•	•	...
Martinique	...	•	•	•	•	•	•	•	...	•	•	•	•
Mexico - Mexique	•	•	•	•	•	•	•	•	...	•	•	•	•
Montserrat	•	•	•	•	•	•	•	•	...	•	•	•	...
Nicaragua	...	•	•	•	...	•	•	•	...	•	...	...	...
Panama	•	•	•	•	•	•	•	•	...	•	•	•	•
Puerto Rico - Porto Rico	•	•	•	•	•	•	•	•	...	•	•	•	•
Saint Kitts and Nevis - Saint-Kitts-et-Nevis	...	...	...	•	•	•	•	•	...	•	•	•	...
Saint Lucia - Sainte-Lucie	...	...	...	•	•	...	...	•	...	•	•	...	•
Saint Pierre and Miquelon - Saint Pierre-et-Miquelon	...	...	...	•	...	...	...	...	...	...	...	...	...
Saint Vincent and the Grenadines - Saint-Vincent-et-les Grenadines	•	•	•	•	•	•	•	•	...	•	•	•	•
Saint-Barthélemy	...	...	...	•	•	...	...	...	...	•	...	...	...
Saint-Martin (French part) - Saint-Martin (partie française)	...	...	...	...	...	...	...	...	...	...	...	...	...
Sint Maarten (Dutch part) - Saint-Martin (partie néerlandaise)	...	...	...	•	•	...	...	...	...	•	•	...	...
Trinidad and Tobago - Trinité-et-Tobago	•	•	•	•	•	•	•	•	...	•	•	•	...
Turks and Caicos Islands - Îles Turques et Caïques	...	...	...	...	...	...	...	•	...	•	...	•	...
United States of America - États-Unis d'Amérique	•	•	•	•	•	•	•	•	...	•	•	...	•
United States Virgin Islands - Îles Vierges américaines	•	...	...	•	•	•	•	•	...	...	...	...	...

Table A. Demographic Yearbook 2015 synoptic table: Availability of data by country/area, table and sex, where applicable
Tableau A. Tableau synoptique de l'Annuaire démographique 2015 : Disponibilité des données par pays ou zone, tableau et le sexe, si disponible (continued - suite)

General topic and table number - Sujet général et numéro de tableau

Continent and country or area / Continent et pays ou zone	Table totals	Summary - Apercu 3 Total	3 M/F	4	5	Population 6 Total[1]	6 M/F	7 Total	7 M/F	8 Total	8 M/F	Fertility - Natalité 9	10 Total	10 M/F	11	Foetal mortality - Mortalité foetale 12	13	14
AMERICA, SOUTH - AMÉRIQUE DU SUD																		
Argentina - Argentine	24	•	•	•	•	•	•	•	•	•	•	•	•	...	...	•	...	...
Bolivia (Plurinational State of) - Bolivie (État plurinational de)	18	•	•	•	•	•	•	•	•	•	•	•	...	•	•	•	...	...
Brazil - Brésil	26	•	•	•	•	•	•	•	•	•	...	•	•	•	•	•	•	...
Chile - Chili	27	•	•	•	•	•	•	•	•	•	•	•	•	•	•	•	•	...
Colombia - Colombie	26	•	•	•	•	•	•	•	•	•	•	•	•	•	•	•	•	•
Ecuador - Équateur	29	•	•	•	•	•	•	•	•	•	...	•	•	•	•	•	•	•
Falkland Islands (Malvinas) - Îles Falkland (Malvinas)	8	•	•	...	...	•	•	•	•	•	•	•	...	...	...	•	...	...
French Guiana - Guyane française	23	•	•	•	•	•	•	•	•	•	...	•	•	•	•	•	...	...
Guyana	13	•	•	•	•	•	•	•	•	•	...	...	...	...	...	•	...	...
Paraguay	24	•	•	•	•	•	•	•	•	•	•	•	•	•	•	•	...	...
Peru - Pérou	25	•	•	•	•	•	•	•	•	•	•	•	•	•	•	•	...	...
Suriname	23	•	•	•	•	•	•	•	•	•	•	•	•	•	•	•	...	...
Uruguay	24	•	•	•	•	•	•	•	•	•	•	•	•	•	•	•	...	...
Venezuela (Bolivarian Republic of) - Venezuela (République bolivarienne du)	26	•	•	•	•	•	•	•	•	•	...	•	•	•	•	•	...	...
ASIA - ASIE																		
Afghanistan	10	•	•	...	•	•	•	•	•	•	•	...	...	...	...	...	...	...
Armenia - Arménie	29	•	•	•	•	•	•	•	•	•	•	•	•	•	•	•	•	•
Azerbaijan - Azerbaïdjan	29	•	•	•	•	•	•	•	•	•	•	•	•	•	•	•	•	•
Bahrain - Bahreïn	28	•	•	•	•	•	•	•	•	•	•	•	•	•	•	•	•	•
Bangladesh	20	•	•	•	•	•	•	•	•	•	•	•	•	•	...	...	...	...
Bhutan - Bhoutan	10	•	•	...	•	•	•	•	•	•	•	...	...	...	...	•	...	...
Brunei Darussalam - Brunéi Darussalam	25	•	•	•	•	•	•	•	•	•	•	•	•	•	•	•	...	...
Cambodia - Cambodge	9	•	•	...	•	•	•	•	•	•	•	...	...	...	...	...	...	...
China - Chine[2]	17	•	•	•	•	•	•	•	•	•	•	•	•	...	...	•	...	...
China, Hong Kong SAR - Chine, Hong Kong RAS	30	•	•	•	•	•	•	•	•	•	•	•	•	•	•	•	•	•
China, Macao SAR - Chine, Macao RAS	26	•	•	•	•	•	•	•	•	•	•	•	•	•	•	•	•	•
Cyprus - Chypre	25	•	•	•	•	•	•	•	•	•	...	•	•	•	•	•	•	•
Democratic People's Republic of Korea - République populaire démocratique de Corée	13	•	•	...	...	•	•	•	•	•	•	...	•	•	...	•	...	...
Georgia - Géorgie	28	•	•	•	•	•	•	•	•	•	•	•	•	•	•	•	•	•
India - Inde[3]	14	•	•	•	•	•	•	•	•	•	•	•	...	...	•	•	...	...
Indonesia - Indonésie	16	•	•	•	•	•	•	•	•	•	•	•	...	•	•	•	...	...
Iran (Islamic Republic of) - Iran (République islamique d')	21	•	•	•	•	•	•	•	•	•	•	•	•	•	...	•	...	...
Iraq	14	•	•	•	•	•	•	•	•	•	•	•	...	•	•	•	...	...
Israel - Israël[4]	30	•	•	•	•	•	•	•	•	•	•	•	•	•	•	•	•	•
Japan - Japon	30	•	•	•	•	•	•	•	•	•	•	•	•	•	•	•	•	•
Jordan - Jordanie	18	•	•	•	•	•	•	•	•	•	•	•	•	...	...	•	...	...
Kazakhstan	29	•	•	•	•	•	•	•	•	•	•	•	•	•	•	•	•	•
Kuwait - Koweït	25	•	•	•	•	•	•	•	•	•	•	•	•	•	•	•	...	...
Kyrgyzstan - Kirghizstan	30	•	•	•	•	•	•	•	•	•	•	•	•	•	•	•	•	•
Lao People's Democratic Republic - République démocratique populaire lao	11	•	•	•	•	•	•	•	•	•	•	...	...	...	...	...	...	...
Lebanon - Liban	13	•	•	•	...	•	•	•	•	•	•	•	...	...	...	•	...	...
Malaysia - Malaisie	20	•	•	•	•	•	•	•	•	•	...	•	•	•	•	...	...	...
Maldives	24	•	•	•	•	•	•	•	•	•	•	•	•	•	•	•	...	...
Mongolia - Mongolie	26	•	•	•	•	•	•	•	•	•	•	•	•	•	•	•	...	...
Myanmar	21	•	•	•	•	•	•	•	•	•	•	•	•	•	...	•	...	...
Nepal - Népal	14	•	•	•	•	•	•	•	•	•	•	•	•	...	•	•	...	...
Oman	25	•	•	•	•	•	•	•	•	•	•	•	•	•	•	•	...	...
Pakistan[5]	14	•	•	...	•	•	•	•	•	•	•	...	...	•	•	•	...	...
Philippines	24	•	...	•	•	•	•	•	•	•	•	•	•	•	•	•	...	...
Qatar	27	•	•	•	•	•	•	•	•	•	•	•	•	•	•	...	...	...
Republic of Korea - République de Corée	28	•	•	•	•	•	•	•	•	•	•	•	•	•	•	•	•	•
Saudi Arabia - Arabie saoudite	16	•	•	•	•	•	•	•	•	•	•	•	•	...	...	•	...	...
Singapore - Singapour	29	•	•	•	•	•	•	•	•	•	...	•	•	•	•	•	•	•

34

Continent and country or area / Continent et pays ou zone	Infant and maternal mortality - Mortalité infantile et mortalité liée à la maternité				General mortality - Mortalité générale						Nuptiality and divorces - Nuptialité et divortialité		
	15	16 Total	16 M/F	17	18	19 Total	19 M/F	20	21	22	23	24	25

AMERICA, SOUTH - AMÉRIQUE DU SUD

	15	16 T	16 M/F	17	18	19 T	19 M/F	20	21	22	23	24	25
Argentina - Argentine	•	•	•	•	•	•	•	•	•	•	•	...	...
Bolivia (Plurinational State of) - Bolivie (État plurinational de)	...	...	•	...	•	•	•	•	•	•	•	•	•
Brazil - Brésil	•	...	•	...	•	•	•	•	•	•	•	•	•
Chile - Chili	•	•	•	•	•	•	•	•	•	•	•	•	...
Colombia - Colombie	•	•	•	•	•	•	•	...	•	•	...	...	...
Ecuador - Équateur	•	•	•	•	•	•	•	•	•	•	•	...	...
Falkland Islands (Malvinas) - Îles Falkland (Malvinas)	...	...	...	...	...	...	...	...	...	...	•	...	...
French Guiana - Guyane française	...	•	•	•	...	•	•	...	...	...	•	•	...
Guyana	...	...	•	•	...	•	•	...	...	...	•	•	...
Paraguay	•	•	•	•	•	•	•	•	...	•	•	•	...
Peru - Pérou	•	•	•	•	•	•	•	•	...	•	•	...	...
Suriname	•	...	•	•	•	•	•	•	•	•	•	•	•
Uruguay	•	...	•	•	•	•	•	•	•	•	•	...	...
Venezuela (Bolivarian Republic of) - Venezuela (République bolivarienne du)	•	•	•	•	•	•	•	•	...	•	•	•	•

ASIA - ASIE

	15	16 T	16 M/F	17	18	19 T	19 M/F	20	21	22	23	24	25
Afghanistan	...	...	...	...	...	...	...	...	•	...	...	...	...
Armenia - Arménie	•	•	•	•	•	•	•	•	•	•	•	•	•
Azerbaijan - Azerbaïdjan	•	•	•	•	•	•	•	...	•	•	•	•	•
Bahrain - Bahreïn	•	•	•	•	•	•	•	•	•	•	•	•	•
Bangladesh	•	•	•	•	...	•	•	•	•	•	•	...	•
Bhutan - Bhoutan	...	...	...	...	...	...	...	...	•	...	...	...	...
Brunei Darussalam - Brunéi Darussalam	•	...	•	•	•	•	•	•	•	•	•	•	...
Cambodia - Cambodge	...	...	...	...	...	...	...	...	...	...	...	...	...
China - Chine[2]	...	...	...	...	...	...	...	...	•	...	...	...	...
China, Hong Kong SAR - Chine, Hong Kong RAS	•	•	•	•	•	•	•	•	•	•	•	•	•
China, Macao SAR - Chine, Macao RAS	•	•	•	•	•	•	•	•	•	•	•	•	•
Cyprus - Chypre	•	•	•	•	•	•	•	•	•	•	•	•	•
Democratic People's Republic of Korea - République populaire démocratique de Corée	...	...	...	•	...	...	•	...	...	...	...	...	...
Georgia - Géorgie	•	•	•	•	•	•	•	•	•	•	•	•	•
India - Inde[3]	•	...	...	...	...	•	...	...	•	...	...	...	•
Indonesia - Indonésie	...	...	...	...	•	...	...	•	•	...	...	...	•
Iran (Islamic Republic of) - Iran (République islamique d')	•	...	...	•	...	•	...	...	•	...	...	•	•
Iraq	...	...	...	•	...	...	•	...	...	•	...	...	•
Israel - Israël[4]	•	•	•	•	•	•	•	•	•	•	•	•	•
Japan - Japon	•	•	•	•	•	•	•	•	•	•	•	•	•
Jordan - Jordanie	•	•	•	•	...	•	•	•	•	•	•	•	•
Kazakhstan	•	•	•	•	•	•	•	•	•	•	•	•	•
Kuwait - Koweït	•	•	•	•	•	•	•	•	•	...	•	•	•
Kyrgyzstan - Kirghizstan	•	•	•	•	•	•	•	•	•	•	•	•	•
Lao People's Democratic Republic - République démocratique populaire lao	...	...	...	...	...	...	...	...	•	...	...	...	...
Lebanon - Liban	...	...	...	...	...	...	...	...	•	...	...	•	...
Malaysia - Malaisie	•	•	•	•	•	•	•	•	...	•	...	...	•
Maldives	•	•	•	•	•	•	•	•	•	•	•	...	•
Mongolia - Mongolie	•	•	•	•	•	•	•	•	•	•	•	...	•
Myanmar	•	•	•	•	•	•	•	•	•	•	•	...	•
Nepal - Népal	•	•	•	•	•	•	•	•	•	•	•	...	•
Oman	•	•	•	•	•	•	•	•	•	•	•	...	•
Pakistan[5]	...	...	•	•	•	•	•	•	•	•	•	...	•
Philippines	•	•	•	•	•	•	•	•	...	•	•	...	•
Qatar	•	•	•	•	•	•	•	•	•	•	•	•	•
Republic of Korea - République de Corée	•	•	•	•	•	•	•	•	•	•	•	•	•
Saudi Arabia - Arabie saoudite	•	...	...	•	...	...	...	•	...	...	•	•	•
Singapore - Singapour	•	•	•	•	•	•	•	•	•	•	•	•	•

Table A. Demographic Yearbook 2015 synoptic table: Availability of data by country/area, table and sex, where applicable
Tableau A. Tableau synoptique de l'Annuaire démographique 2015 : Disponibilité des données par pays ou zone, tableau et le sexe, si disponible (continued - suite)

General topic and table number - Sujet général et numéro de tableau

Continent and country or area / Continent et pays ou zone	Table totals	Summary - Aperçu 3 Total	3 M/F	4	Population 5	6 Total¹	6 M/F	7 Total	7 M/F	8 Total	8 M/F	Fertility - Natalité 9	10 Total	10 M/F	11	Foetal mortality - Mortalité foetale 12	13	14
ASIA - ASIE																		
Sri Lanka	21	•	•	•	•	•	•	•	•	•	•	•	•	•	...	•	...	...
State of Palestine - État de Palestine	22	•	•	•	•	•	•	•	•	...	•	•	•	•	...	...	...	...
Syrian Arab Republic - République arabe syrienne	10	•	•	...	•	•	•	•	...	...	...	...	...	...	...	...	...	...
Tajikistan - Tadjikistan	24	•	•	•	•	•	•	•	•	•	•	•	•	•	•	•	•	•
Thailand - Thaïlande	22	•	•	•	•	•	•	•	•	•	•	•	•	•	•	...	...	...
Timor-Leste	12	•	•	•	•	•	•	•	•	•	•	...	...	...	...	...	...	...
Turkey - Turquie	27	•	•	•	•	•	•	•	•	•	•	•	•	•	•	...	...	...
Turkmenistan - Turkménistan	6	•	•	...	...	•	•	•	...	...	...	...	...	...	...	...	...	...
United Arab Emirates - Émirats arabes unis	14	•	•	•	•	•	•	•	•	...	•	•	•	•	...	...	...	...
Uzbekistan - Ouzbékistan	29	•	•	•	•	•	•	•	•	•	•	•	•	•	•	•	•	•
Viet Nam	9	•	•	•	•	•	•	•	•	•	...	...	...	...	...	...	...	...
Yemen - Yémen	12	•	•	•	•	•	•	•	•	•	...	•	...	...	...	...	...	...
EUROPE																		
Åland Islands - Îles d'Åland	27	•	•	•	•	•	•	•	•	•	•	•	•	•	•	•	•	•
Albania - Albanie	25	•	•	•	•	•	•	•	•	•	•	•	•	•	•	...	•	...
Andorra - Andorre	20	•	•	•	•	•	•	•	•	•	•	•	•	•	•	...	...	...
Austria - Autriche	28	•	•	•	•	•	•	•	•	•	•	•	•	•	•	•	•	•
Belarus - Bélarus	30	•	•	•	•	•	•	•	•	•	•	•	•	•	•	•	•	•
Belgium - Belgique	29	•	•	•	•	•	•	•	•	•	•	•	•	•	•	...	•	•
Bosnia and Herzegovina - Bosnie-Herzégovine	23	•	...	•	•	•	•	•	...	...	•	•	•	•	•	...	•	...
Bulgaria - Bulgarie	30	•	•	•	•	•	•	•	•	•	•	•	•	•	•	•	•	•
Croatia - Croatie	29	•	•	•	•	•	•	•	•	•	•	•	•	•	•	•	•	•
Czech Republic - République tchèque	30	•	•	•	•	•	•	•	•	•	•	•	•	•	•	•	•	•
Denmark - Danemark	30	•	•	•	•	•	•	•	•	•	•	•	•	•	•	•	•	•
Estonia - Estonie	30	•	•	•	•	•	•	•	•	•	•	•	•	•	•	•	•	•
Faeroe Islands - Îles Féroé	28	•	•	•	•	•	•	•	•	•	•	•	•	•	•	•	•	•
Finland - Finlande	30	•	•	•	•	•	•	•	•	•	•	•	•	•	•	•	•	•
France	29	•	•	•	•	•	•	•	•	•	•	•	•	•	•	...	•	•
Germany - Allemagne	30	•	•	•	•	•	•	•	•	•	•	•	•	•	•	•	•	•
Gibraltar	20	•	•	•	•	•	•	•	•	•	•	•	•	•	•	...	...	...
Greece - Grèce	28	•	•	•	•	•	•	•	•	•	•	•	•	•	•	•	•	•
Guernsey - Guernesey	12	•	•	•	•	•	•	•	•	...	•	•	...	...	...	...	...	...
Holy See - Saint-Siège	6	•	•	...	•	•	•	...	...	...	...	...	...	...	...	...	...	...
Hungary - Hongrie	30	•	•	•	•	•	•	•	•	•	•	•	•	•	•	•	•	•
Iceland - Islande	29	•	•	•	•	•	•	•	•	•	•	•	•	•	•	•	•	•
Ireland - Irlande	27	•	...	•	•	•	•	•	•	•	•	•	•	•	•	...	•	•
Isle of Man - Île de Man	13	•	•	•	•	•	•	•	•	•	•	•	•	•	•	...	•	...
Italy - Italie	30	•	•	•	•	•	•	•	•	•	•	•	•	•	•	•	•	•
Jersey	15	•	•	•	•	•	•	•	•	•	•	•	•	•	•	...	...	...
Latvia - Lettonie	30	•	•	•	•	•	•	•	•	•	•	•	•	•	•	•	•	•
Liechtenstein	22	•	•	•	•	•	•	•	•	•	•	•	•	•	•	...	...	...
Lithuania - Lituanie	30	•	•	•	•	•	•	•	•	•	•	•	•	•	•	•	•	•
Luxembourg	28	•	•	•	•	•	•	•	•	•	•	•	•	•	•	...	...	...
Malta - Malte	28	•	•	•	•	•	•	•	•	•	•	•	•	•	•	•	•	•
Monaco	12	•	•	•	•	•	•	•	•	•	•	...	...	•	•	...	...	...
Montenegro - Monténégro	25	•	•	•	•	•	•	•	•	•	•	•	•	•	•	...	•	...
Netherlands - Pays-Bas	28	•	•	•	•	•	•	•	•	•	•	•	•	•	•	•	•	•
Norway - Norvège	30	•	•	•	•	•	•	•	•	•	•	•	•	•	•	•	•	•
Poland - Pologne	30	•	•	•	•	•	•	•	•	•	•	•	•	•	•	•	•	•
Portugal	30	•	•	•	•	•	•	•	•	•	•	•	•	•	•	•	•	•
Republic of Moldova - République de Moldova	29	•	•	•	•	•	•	•	•	•	•	•	•	•	•	...	•	•
Romania - Roumanie	30	•	•	•	•	•	•	•	•	•	•	•	•	•	•	•	•	•
Russian Federation - Fédération de Russie	30	•	•	•	•	•	•	•	•	•	•	•	•	•	•	•	•	•
San Marino - Saint-Marin	25	•	•	•	•	•	•	•	•	•	•	•	•	•	•	...	...	...
Serbia - Serbie	30	•	•	•	•	•	•	•	•	•	•	•	•	•	•	•	•	•
Slovakia - Slovaquie	30	•	•	•	•	•	•	•	•	•	•	•	•	•	•	•	•	•
Slovenia - Slovénie	29	•	•	•	•	•	•	•	•	•	•	•	•	•	•	•	•	•
Spain - Espagne	30	•	•	•	•	•	•	•	•	•	•	•	•	•	•	•	•	•

Continent and country or area / Continent et pays ou zone	Infant and maternal mortality - Mortalité infantile et mortalité liée à la maternité				General mortality - Mortalité générale						Nuptiality and divorces - Nuptialité et divortialité		
	15	16 Total	16 M/F	17	18	19 Total	19 M/F	20	21	22	23	24	25
ASIA - ASIE													
Sri Lanka	...	...	...	•	•	•	•	...	...	•	•	•	...
State of Palestine - État de Palestine	•	•	•	...	•	•	•	...	...	•	•	•	•
Syrian Arab Republic - République arabe syrienne	...	...	...	•	...	...	...	...	...	•	...	...	•
Tajikistan - Tadjikistan	•	•	•	...	•	•	•	•	•	•	•	•	•
Thailand - Thaïlande	•	•	•	•	•	•	•	•	•	•	...	•	•
Timor-Leste	...	...	...	•	...	...	...	...	...	•	...	...	•
Turkey - Turquie	•	•	•	•	•	•	•	•	•	•	...	•	•
Turkmenistan - Turkménistan	...	...	...	•	...	...	...	...	...	•	...	...	•
United Arab Emirates - Émirats arabes unis	...	...	...	•	•	•	•	...	...	•	•	•	•
Uzbekistan - Ouzbékistan	•	•	•	•	•	•	•	•	•	•	•	•	•
Viet Nam	...	...	...	...	...	...	...	...	...	•	...	...	...
Yemen - Yémen	...	...	...	...	•	...	...	...	...	•	...	...	...
EUROPE													
Åland Islands - Îles d'Åland	•	•	•	...	•	•	•	...	...	•	•	•	•
Albania - Albanie	•	•	•	...	•	•	•	...	•	•	•	•	•
Andorra - Andorre	•	•	•	•	•	•	•	•	•	•	•	•	•
Austria - Autriche	•	•	•	•	•	•	•	•	•	•	•	•	•
Belarus - Bélarus	•	•	•	•	•	•	•	•	•	•	•	•	•
Belgium - Belgique	•	•	•	•	•	•	•	•	•	•	•	•	•
Bosnia and Herzegovina - Bosnie-Herzégovine	•	•	•	•	•	•	•	...	•	•	•	•	•
Bulgaria - Bulgarie	•	•	•	•	•	•	•	•	•	•	•	•	•
Croatia - Croatie	•	•	•	•	•	•	•	...	•	•	•	•	•
Czech Republic - République tchèque	•	•	•	•	•	•	•	•	•	•	•	•	•
Denmark - Danemark	•	•	•	•	•	•	•	•	•	•	•	•	•
Estonia - Estonie	•	•	•	•	•	•	•	•	•	•	•	•	•
Faeroe Islands - Îles Féroé	•	•	•	...	•	•	•	...	•	•	•	•	•
Finland - Finlande	•	•	•	•	•	•	•	•	•	•	•	•	•
France	•	•	•	•	•	•	•	•	•	•	•	•	•
Germany - Allemagne	•	•	•	•	•	•	•	•	•	•	•	•	•
Gibraltar	•	•	•	•	•	•	•	...	•	•	...	•	•
Greece - Grèce	•	•	•	•	•	•	•	•	•	•	•	•	•
Guernsey - Guernesey	...	...	...	•	•	•	•	...	...	•	...	...	...
Holy See - Saint-Siège	...	...	...	...	...	...	...	...	...	...	...	...	...
Hungary - Hongrie	•	•	•	•	•	•	•	•	•	•	•	•	•
Iceland - Islande	•	•	•	•	•	•	•	•	•	•	•	•	•
Ireland - Irlande	•	•	•	•	•	•	•	•	•	•	•	•	•
Isle of Man - Île de Man	...	...	...	•	•	•	•	...	...	•	...	...	•
Italy - Italie	•	•	•	•	•	•	•	•	•	•	•	•	•
Jersey	...	...	...	•	•	•	•	...	...	•	...	...	...
Latvia - Lettonie	•	•	•	•	•	•	•	•	•	•	•	•	•
Liechtenstein	•	•	•	•	•	•	•	•	•	•	•	•	•
Lithuania - Lituanie	•	•	•	•	•	•	•	•	•	•	•	•	•
Luxembourg	•	•	•	•	•	•	•	•	•	•	•	•	•
Malta - Malte	•	•	•	•	•	•	•	•	•	•	•	•	•
Monaco	...	...	...	•	...	...	...	...	...	•	...	...	...
Montenegro - Monténégro	•	•	•	•	•	•	•	•	•	•	•	•	•
Netherlands - Pays-Bas	•	•	•	•	•	•	•	•	•	•	•	•	•
Norway - Norvège	•	•	•	•	•	•	•	•	•	•	•	•	•
Poland - Pologne	•	•	•	•	•	•	•	•	•	•	•	•	•
Portugal	•	•	•	•	•	•	•	•	•	•	•	•	•
Republic of Moldova - République de Moldova	•	•	•	•	•	•	•	•	•	•	•	•	•
Romania - Roumanie	•	•	•	•	•	•	•	•	•	•	•	•	•
Russian Federation - Fédération de Russie	•	•	•	•	•	•	•	•	•	•	•	•	•
San Marino - Saint-Marin	•	•	•	...	•	•	•	...	•	•	•	•	•
Serbia - Serbie	•	•	•	•	•	•	•	•	•	•	•	•	•
Slovakia - Slovaquie	•	•	•	•	•	•	•	•	•	•	•	•	•
Slovenia - Slovénie	•	•	•	•	•	•	•	...	•	•	•	•	•
Spain - Espagne	•	•	•	•	•	•	•	•	•	•	•	•	•

Table A. Demographic Yearbook 2015 synoptic table: Availability of data by country/area, table and sex, where applicable
Tableau A. Tableau synoptique de l'Annuaire démographique 2015 : Disponibilité des données par pays ou zone, tableau et le sexe, si disponible (continued - suite)

General topic and table number - Sujet général et numéro de tableau

Continent and country or area / Continent et pays ou zone	Table totals	Summary - Apercu 3 Total	3 M/F	4	5	Population 6 Total¹	6 M/F	7 Total	7 M/F	8 Total	8 M/F	Fertility - Natalité 9	10 Total	10 M/F	11	Foetal mortality - Mortalité foetale 12	13	14
EUROPE																		
Svalbard and Jan Mayen Islands - Îles Svalbard et Jan Mayen	3	•	•	...	...	...	...	...	...	...	...	...	...	...	...	...	...	...
Sweden - Suède	30	•	•	•	•	•	•	•	•	•	•	•	•	•	•	•	•	•
Switzerland - Suisse	30	•	•	•	•	•	•	•	•	•	•	•	•	•	•	•	•	•
TFYR of Macedonia - L'ex-R. y. de Macédoine	27	•	•	•	•	•	•	•	•	•	•	•	•	•	•	•	...	...
Ukraine	29	•	•	•	•	•	•	•	•	•	•	•	•	•	...	•	•	•
United Kingdom of Great Britain and Northern Ireland - Royaume-Uni de Grande-Bretagne et d'Irlande du Nord	30	•	•	•	•	•	•	•	•	•	•	•	•	•	•	•	•	•
OCEANIA - OCÉANIE																		
American Samoa - Samoas américaines	18	•	•	•	•	•	•	•	•	•	...	•	•	...	...	...	...	...
Australia - Australie	28	•	•	•	•	•	•	•	•	•	•	•	•	•	...	•	•	•
Cook Islands - Îles Cook	17	•	•	•	•	•	•	•	•	•	•	•	•	•	...	...	...	...
Fiji - Fidji	19	•	•	•	•	•	•	•	•	•	•	•	•	•	...	...	...	...
French Polynesia - Polynésie française	17	•	•	•	•	•	•	•	•	•	•	•	•	•	...	...	...	...
Guam	22	•	•	•	•	•	•	•	•	•	•	...	•	•	•	...	...	...
Kiribati	13	•	•	•	•	•	•	•	•	...	...	•	•	...	...	...	...	...
Marshall Islands - Îles Marshall	12	•	•	...	•	•	•	•	•	•	...	...	•	•	...	...	...	...
Micronesia (Federated States of) - Micronésie (États fédérés de)	10	•	•	...	•	•	•	•	•	•	...	...	•	•	...	...	...	...
Nauru	12	•	•	...	...	...	...	...	...	...	•	•	•	...	...	...	...	...
New Caledonia - Nouvelle-Calédonie	20	•	...	•	•	•	•	•	•	•	•	...	•	•	•	...	•	...
New Zealand - Nouvelle-Zélande	29	•	...	•	•	•	•	•	•	•	•	•	•	•	•	•	•	•
Niue - Nioué	17	•	•	•	•	•	•	•	•	•	...	•	•	...	...	...	...	...
Norfolk Island - Île Norfolk	12	•	•	•	•	•	•	•	•	...	•	...	...	...	...	...	...	...
Northern Mariana Islands - Îles Mariannes septentrionales	14	•	•	•	•	•	•	•	•	•	...	•	...	...	...	...	...	...
Palau - Palaos	14	•	•	•	•	•	•	•	•	•	...	•	...	•	...	...	...	...
Papua New Guinea - Papouasie-Nouvelle-Guinée	7	•	•	...	•	•	•	...	...	...	...	...	...	...	...	...	...	...
Pitcairn	12	•	•	•	•	•	•	•	...	•	...	...	...	...	...	...	...	...
Samoa	17	•	•	•	•	•	•	•	•	•	•	•	•	•	•	•	...	...
Solomon Islands - Îles Salomon	9	•	•	•	•	•	•	•	...	•	•	...	...	...	...	...	...	...
Tokelau - Tokélaou	10	•	•	•	•	•	•	...	•	•	...	...	...	...	...	...	...	...
Tonga	12	•	•	...	•	•	•	...	...	...	...	...	...	...	...	...	...	...
Tuvalu	7	•	...	...	•	...	...	•	...	...	...	...	...	...	...	...	...	...
Vanuatu	9	•	•	...	•	•	•	...	...	•	...	...	...	...	...	...	...	...
Wallis and Futuna Islands - Îles Wallis et Futuna	9	•	...	...	...	•	...	...	•	...	...	...	...	...	...	...	...	...

Table A. Demographic Yearbook 2015 synoptic table: Availability of data by country/area, table and sex, where applicable
Tableau A. Tableau synoptique de l'Annuaire démographique 2015 : Disponibilité des données par pays ou zone, tableau et le sexe, si disponible (continued - suite)

Continent and country or area / Continent et pays ou zone	15	16 Total	16 M/F	17	18	19 Total	19 M/F	20	21	22	23	24	25
EUROPE													
Svalbard and Jan Mayen Islands - Îles Svalbard et Jan Mayen	...	...	...	...	...	...	...	...	...	...	...	...	...
Sweden - Suède	•	•	•	•	•	•	•	•	•	•	•	•	•
Switzerland - Suisse	•	•	•	•	•	•	•	•	•	•	•	•	•
TFYR of Macedonia - L'ex-R. y. de Macédoine	•	•	•	•	•	•	•	...	•	•	•	•	•
Ukraine	•	•	•	•	•	•	•	•	•	•	•	•	•
United Kingdom of Great Britain and Northern Ireland - Royaume-Uni de Grande-Bretagne et d'Irlande du Nord	•	•	•	•	•	•	•	•	•	•	•	•	•
OCEANIA - OCÉANIE													
American Samoa - Samoas américaines	•	...	...	...	•	•	•	...	•	•	•	...	•
Australia - Australie	•	•	•	...	•	•	•	•	•	•	•	•	•
Cook Islands - Îles Cook	•	...	...	...	•	•	•	•	...	•	•	•	•
Fiji - Fidji	...	...	...	•	•	•	•	•	...	...	•	•	...
French Polynesia - Polynésie française	•	...	...	...	•	•	•	...	...	•	•	•	•
Guam	•	...	...	...	•	•	•	...	...	•	•	•	•
Kiribati	...	...	...	...	•	•	•	...	...	•	•	...	...
Marshall Islands - Îles Marshall	...	...	...	...	...	•	•	...	...	•	...	...	...
Micronesia (Federated States of) - Micronésie (États fédérés de)	...	...	...	...	...	•	•	...	...	•	...	...	...
Nauru	...	...	...	...	...	•	•	...	...	•	...	...	...
New Caledonia - Nouvelle-Calédonie	•	•	•	...	•	•	•	...	...	•	•	...	•
New Zealand - Nouvelle-Zélande	•	•	•	•	•	•	•	•	•	•	•	•	•
Niue - Nioué	...	...	...	...	•	•	•	...	...	•	...	•	...
Norfolk Island - Île Norfolk	...	...	...	...	•	...	...	...	...	...	•	...	...
Northern Mariana Islands - Îles Mariannes septentrionales	•	...	...	...	•	...	...	...	...	•	...	...	...
Palau - Palaos	•	...	...	...	•	...	...	...	...	•	...	...	...
Papua New Guinea - Papouasie-Nouvelle-Guinée	...	...	...	...	...	...	...	...	...	•	...	...	...
Pitcairn	...	...	...	...	...	•	...	...	...	...	...	...	...
Samoa	...	...	...	...	...	•	...	...	...	•	...	...	...
Solomon Islands - Îles Salomon	...	...	...	...	...	...	...	...	...	•	...	...	...
Tokelau - Tokélaou	...	...	...	...	...	...	...	...	...	•	...	...	...
Tonga	...	...	...	...	...	•	•	...	...	•	...	...	...
Tuvalu	...	...	...	...	...	...	...	...	...	•	...	...	...
Vanuatu	...	...	...	...	...	...	...	...	...	•	...	...	...
Wallis and Futuna Islands - Îles Wallis et Futuna	...	...	...	...	...	•	•	...	...	•	...	•	...

FOOTNOTES - NOTES

• Data presented in the table. - Les données présentées dans le tableau.

... Data not available. - Données non disponibles.

1 Including countries with data on total population by sex but without data on urban population. - Y compris les pays avec des données sur la population totale selon le sexe mais pas sur la population urbaine.

2 For statistical purposes, the data for China do not include those for the Hong Kong Special Administrative Region (Hong Kong SAR), Macao special Administrative Region (Macao SAR) and Taiwan province of China. - Pour la présentation des statistiques, les données pour Chine ne comprennent pas la Région Administrative Spéciale de Hong Kong (Hong Kong RAS), la Région Administrative Spéciale de Macao (Macao RAS) et Taïwan province de Chine.

3 Including data for the Indian-held part of Jammu and Kashmir, the final status of which has not yet been determined. - Y compris les données pour la partie du Jammu et du Cachemire occupée par l'Inde dont le statut définitif n'a pas encore été déterminé.

4 Including data for East Jerusalem and Israeli residents in certain other territories under occupation by Israeli military forces since June 1967. - Y compris les données pour Jérusalem-Est et les résidents israéliens dans certains autres territoires occupés depuis 1967 par les forces armées israéliennes.

5 Excluding data for the Pakistan-held part of Jammu and Kashmir, the final status of which has not yet been determined. - Non compris les données concernant la partie du Jammu et Cachemire occupée par le Pakistan dont le statut définitif n'a pas été déterminé.

Table 1 – *Demographic Yearbook 2015*

Table 1 presents for the world and major areas and regions estimates of the order of magnitude of population size, rates of population increase, crude birth and death rates, surface area as well as population density.

Description of variables: Estimates of world population by major areas and by regions are presented for 1960, 1970, 1980, 1990, 2000, 2010 and 2015. Average annual percentage rates of population growth, crude birth and crude death rates are shown for the period from 2010 to 2015. Surface area in square kilometers and population density estimates relate to 2015.

All population estimates and rates presented in this table were prepared by the Population Division of the United Nations Department of Economic and Social Affairs, and have been published in the *2015 Revision of World Population Prospects*[1].

The scheme of regionalization used for these estimates is described below. Although some continental totals are given, and all can be derived, this table presents six major areas that are so drawn as to obtain greater homogeneity in sizes of population, types of demographic circumstances and accuracy of demographic statistics. Five of the major areas are subdivided into a total of 20 regions, which are arranged within the major areas; these regions together with Northern America, which is not subdivided, make a total of 21 regions.

The major areas of Northern America and Latin America and the Caribbean are distinguished, rather than the conventional continents of North America and South America, because population trends in the middle American mainland and the Caribbean region more closely resemble those of South America than those of America north of Mexico. Data for the traditional continents of North and South America can be obtained by adding Central America and Caribbean region to Northern America and deducting from Latin America. Latin America, as defined here, has somewhat wider limits than it would be if defined only to include the Spanish-speaking, French-speaking and Portuguese-speaking countries.

The average annual percentage rates of population growth are calculated by the Population Division of the United Nations using an exponential rate of increase.

Crude birth and crude death rates are expressed in terms of the average annual number of births and deaths, respectively, per 1 000 mid-year population. These rates are estimated.

Surface area totals are estimated by the Population Division of the United Nations.

Computation: Density, calculated by the Statistics Division of the United Nations, is the number of persons in the total population of 2014 per square kilometer of total surface area.

Reliability of data: With the exception of surface area, all data are set in *italic* type to indicate their conjectural quality.

Limitations: The estimated orders of magnitude of population and surface area are subject to all the basic limitations set forth in connection with table 3, and to the same qualifications set forth for population and surface area statistics in sections 3 and 2.4 of the Technical Notes, respectively.

Likewise, rates of population increase and density index are affected by the limitations of the original figures. However, it may be noted that, in compiling data for regional and major areas totals, errors in the components may tend to compensate each other and the resulting aggregates may be more reliable than the quality of the individual components would imply.

Because of their estimated character, many of the birth and death rates shown should also be considered only as orders of magnitude, and not as measures of the true level of fertility or mortality.

In interpreting the population densities, one should consider that some of the regions include large segments of land that are uninhabitable or barely habitable, and density values calculated as described make no allowance for this, nor for differences in patterns of land settlement.

Composition of major areas and regions

AFRICA

Eastern Africa
Burundi
Comoros
Djibouti
Eritrea
Ethiopia
Kenya
Madagascar
Malawi
Mauritius
Mayotte
Mozambique
Réunion
Rwanda
Seychelles
Somalia
South Sudan
Uganda
United Republic of Tanzania
Zambia
Zimbabwe

Middle Africa
Angola
Cameroon
Central African Republic
Chad
Congo
Democratic Republic of the
  Congo
Equatorial Guinea
Gabon
Sao Tome and Principe

Northern Africa
Algeria
Egypt
Libyan Arab Jamahiriya
Morocco
Sudan
Tunisia
Western Sahara

Southern Africa
Botswana
Lesotho
Namibia
South Africa
Swaziland

Western Africa
Benin
Burkina Faso
Cabo Verde
Côte d'Ivoire
Gambia

Ghana
Guinea
Guinea-Bissau
Liberia
Mali
Mauritania
Niger
Nigeria
Saint Helena
Senegal
Sierra Leone
Togo

ASIA

Eastern Asia
China
China, Hong Kong SAR
China, Macao SAR
Democratic People's
  Republic of Korea
Japan
Mongolia
Republic of Korea

South-Central Asia
Afghanistan
Bangladesh
Bhutan
India
Iran (Islamic Republic of)
Kazakhstan
Kyrgyzstan
Maldives
Nepal
Pakistan
Sri Lanka
Tajikistan
Turkmenistan
Uzbekistan

South-Eastern Asia
Brunei Darussalam
Cambodia
Indonesia
Lao People's Democratic
  Republic
Malaysia
Myanmar
Philippines
Singapore
Thailand
Timor Leste
Viet Nam

Western Asia
Armenia
Azerbaijan

Bahrain
Cyprus
Georgia
Iraq
Israel
Jordan
Kuwait
Lebanon
Oman
Qatar
Saudi Arabia
State of Palestine
Syrian Arab Republic
Turkey
United Arab Emirates
Yemen

EUROPE

Eastern Europe
Belarus
Bulgaria
Czech Republic
Hungary
Poland
Republic of Moldova
Romania
Russian Federation
Slovakia
Ukraine

Northern Europe
Åland Islands
Denmark
Estonia
Faeroe Islands
Finland
Guernsey
Iceland
Ireland
Isle of Man
Jersey
Latvia
Lithuania
Norway
Sweden
United Kingdom of Great Britain
  and Northern Ireland

Southern Europe
Albania
Andorra
Bosnia and Herzegovina
Croatia
Gibraltar
Greece
Holy See

Italy
Malta
Montenegro
Portugal
San Marino
Serbia
Slovenia
Spain
TFYR of Macedonia

Western Europe
Austria
Belgium
France
Germany
Liechtenstein
Luxembourg
Monaco
Netherlands
Switzerland

LATIN AMERICA
 and the CARIBBEAN

Caribbean
Anguilla
Antigua and Barbuda
Aruba
Bahamas
Barbados
Bonaire, Saba and Sint Eustatius
British Virgin Islands
Cayman Islands
Cuba
Curaçao
Dominica
Dominican Republic
Grenada
Guadaloupe
Haiti
Jamaica
Martinique

Montserrat
Puerto Rico
Saint Kitts and Nevis
Saint Lucia
Saint Vincent and the
 Grenadines
Sint Maarten (Dutch part)
Trinidad and Tobago
Turks and Caicos Islands
United States Virgin
 Islands

Central America
Belize
Costa Rica
El Salvador
Guatemala
Honduras
Mexico
Nicaragua
Panama

South America
Argentina
Bolivia (Plurinational State of)
Brazil
Chile
Colombia
Ecuador
Falkland Islands (Malvinas)
French Guiana
Guyana
Paraguay
Peru
Suriname
Uruguay
Venezuela (Bolivarian Republic of)

NORTHERN AMERICA

Bermuda

Canada
Greenland
Saint Pierre and Miquelon
United States of America

OCEANIA

Australia and New Zealand
Australia
New Zealand
Norfolk Island

Melanesia
Fiji
New Caledonia
Papua New Guinea
Solomon Islands
Vanuatu

Micronesia
Guam
Kiribati
Marshall Islands
Micronesia (Federated States of)
Nauru
Northern Mariana Islands
Palau

Polynesia
American Samoa
Cook Islands
French Polynesia
Niue
Pitcairn
Samoa
Tokelau
Tonga
Tuvalu
Wallis and Futuna Islands

---

[1] United Nations, Department of Economic and Social Affairs, Population Division (2015). *2015 Revision of World Population Prospects* (http://esa.un.org/unpd/wpp/).

Tableau 1 – *Annuaire démographique 2015*

Le tableau 1 présente, pour l'ensemble du monde et les grandes zones et régions, des estimations concernant l'ordre de grandeur de la population, les taux d'accroissement démographique, les taux bruts de natalité et de mortalité, la superficie et la densité de peuplement.

Description des variables : des estimations de la population mondiale par grandes zones et régions sont présentées pour 1960, 1970, 1980, 1990, 2000 et 2010 ainsi que pour 2015. Les taux annuels moyens d'accroissement de la population et les taux bruts de natalité et de mortalité portent sur la période allant de 2010 à 2015. Les indications concernant la superficie exprimée en kilomètres carrés et les estimations de la densité de population se rapportent à 2015.

Toutes les estimations de population et les taux de natalité, taux de mortalité et taux annuels d'accroissement de la population qui sont présentés dans le tableau 1 ont été établis par la Division de la population du Département des affaires économiques et sociales de l'Organisation des Nations Unies, et ont été publiés dans les *Perspectives de la population mondiale : La révision de 2015*[1].

Bien que l'on ait donné certains totaux pour les continents (tous les autres pouvant être calculés), on a réparti le monde en six grandes zones qui ont été découpées de manière à obtenir une plus grande homogénéité du point de vue des dimensions de population, des types de situations démographiques et de l'exactitude des statistiques démographiques. Cinq de ces six grandes zones ont été subdivisées en 20 régions. Avec l'Amérique septentrionale, qui n'est pas subdivisée, on arrive à un total de 21 régions.

Au lieu de faire la distinction classique entre l'Amérique du Nord et l'Amérique du Sud, on a choisi d'opérer une comparaison entre l'Amérique septentrionale et l'Amérique latine et Caraïbes, parce que les tendances démographiques dans la partie continentale de l'Amérique centrale et dans la région des Caraïbes se rapprochent davantage de celles de l'Amérique du Sud que de celles de l'Amérique au nord du Mexique. On obtient les données pour les continents traditionnels de l'Amérique du Nord et de l'Amérique du Sud en extrayant les données concernant l'Amérique centrale et les Caraïbes de celles relatives à l'Amérique latine et en les regroupant avec celles relatives à l'Amérique septentrionale. L'Amérique latine ainsi définie a par conséquent des limites plus larges que celles des pays ou zones de langues espagnole, portugaise et française qui constituent l'Amérique latine au sens le plus strict du terme.

Les taux annuels moyens d'accroissement de la population sont calculés par la Division de la population de l'Organisation des Nations Unies en appliquant un taux d'accroissement exponentiel.

Les taux bruts de natalité et de mortalité représentent respectivement le nombre annuel moyen de naissances et de décès par millier d'habitants en milieu d'année. Ces taux sont estimatifs.

La superficie totale a été estimée par la Division de la population de l'Organisation des Nations Unies.

Calculs : la densité, calculée par la Division de statistique de l'Organisation des Nations Unies, est égale au rapport entre l'effectif total de la population en 2014 et la superficie totale exprimée en kilomètres carrés.

Fiabilité des données : á l'exception des données concernant la superficie, toutes les données sont reproduites en *italique* pour en faire ressortir le caractère conjectural.

Insuffisance des données : les estimations concernant l'ordre de grandeur de la population et la superficie reposent en partie sur les données du tableau 3 ; elles appellent donc toutes les réserves fondamentales formulées à propos de ce tableau, et celles qui ont été respectivement formulées aux sections 3 et 2.4 des Notes techniques en ce qui concerne les statistiques relatives à la population et à la superficie.

Les taux d'accroissement et les indices de densité de la population se ressentent eux aussi des insuffisances inhérentes aux données de base. Toutefois, il est à noter que, lorsque l'on additionne des données par territoire pour obtenir des totaux régionaux et par grandes zones, les erreurs qu'elles comportent arrivent parfois à s'équilibrer, de sorte que les agrégats obtenus peuvent être un peu plus exacts que chacun des éléments dont on est parti.

Vu leur caractère estimatif, nombre des taux de natalité et de mortalité du tableau 1 doivent être considérés uniquement comme des ordres de grandeur et ne sont pas censés mesurer exactement le niveau de la natalité ou de la mortalité.

Pour interpréter les valeurs de la densité de population, on se souviendra qu'il existe dans certaines des régions de vastes étendues de terres inhabitables ou à peine habitables et que les chiffres calculés selon la méthode indiquée ne tiennent compte ni de ce fait ni des différences de dispersion de la population selon le mode d'habitat.

Composition des grandes zones et régions

AFRIQUE

Afrique orientale
Burundi
Comores
Djibouti
Érythrée
Éthiopie
Kenya
Madagascar
Malawi
Maurice
Mayotte
Mozambique
Ouganda
République-Unie de Tanzanie
Réunion
Rwanda
Seychelles
Somalie
Soudan du Sud
Zambie
Zimbabwe

Afrique centrale
Angola
Cameroun
Congo
Gabon
Guinée équatoriale
République centrafricaine
République démocratique du Congo
Sao Tomé-et-Principe
Tchad

Afrique septentrionale
Algérie
Égypte
Jamahiriya arabe libyenne
Maroc
Sahara occidental
Soudan
Tunisie

Afrique australe
Afrique du Sud
Botswana
Lesotho
Namibie
Swaziland

Afrique occidentale
Bénin
Burkina Faso
Cabo Verde

Côte d'Ivoire
Gambie
Ghana
Guinée
Guinée-Bissau
Libéria
Mali
Mauritanie
Niger
Nigéria
Sainte-Hélène
Sénégal
Sierra Leone
Togo

AMÉRIQUE LATINE ET CARAÏBES

Caraïbes
Anguilla
Antigua-et-Barbuda
Aruba
Bahamas
Barbade
Bonaire, Saint-Eustache et Saba
Cuba
Curaçao
Dominique
Grenade
Guadeloupe
Haïti
Îles Caïmanes
Îles Turques et Caïques
Îles Vierges américaines
Îles Vierges britanniques
Jamaïque
Martinique
Montserrat
Porto Rico
République dominicaine
Saint-Kitts-et-Nevis
Sainte-Lucie
Saint-Martin
(partie néerlandaise)
Saint-Vincent-et-les
Grenadines
Trinité-et-Tobago

Amérique centrale
Belize
Costa Rica
El Salvador
Guatemala
Honduras

Mexique
Nicaragua
Panama

Amérique du Sud
Argentine
Bolivie (État plurinational de)
Brésil
Chili
Colombie
Équateur
Guyana
Guyane française
Îles Falkland (Malvinas)
Paraguay
Pérou
Suriname
Uruguay
Venezuela (République bolivarienne du)

AMÉRIQUE SEPTENTRIONALE

Bermudes
Canada
États-Unis d'Amérique
Groenland
Saint-Pierre-et-Miquelon

ASIE

Asie orientale
Chine
Chine, Région administrative spéciale de Hong Kong
Chine, Région administrative spéciale de Macao
Japon
Mongolie
République de Corée
République populaire démocratique de Corée

Asie centrale et Asie du Sud
Afghanistan
Bangladesh
Bhoutan
Inde
Iran (République Islamique d')
Kazakhstan
Kirghizistan
Maldives
Népal
Ouzbékistan

Pakistan
Sri Lanka
Tadjikistan
Turkménistan

Asie du Sud-Est
Brunéi Darussalam
Cambodge
Indonésie
Malaisie
Myanmar
Philippines
République démocratique populaire lao
Singapour
Thaïlande
Timor-Leste
Viet Nam

Asie occidentale
Arabie saoudite
Arménie
Azerbaïdjan
Bahreïn
Chypre
Émirats arabes unis
État de Palestine
Géorgie
Iraq
Israël
Jordanie
Koweït
Liban
Oman
Qatar
République arabe syrienne
Turquie
Yémen

EUROPE

Europe orientale
Bélarus
Bulgarie
Fédération de Russie
Hongrie

Pologne
République de Moldova
République tchèque
Roumanie
Slovaquie
Ukraine

Europe septentrionale
Danemark
Estonie
Finlande
Guernesey
Île de Man
Îles d'Åland
Îles Féroé
Îles Svalbard et Jan Mayen
Irlande
Islande
Jersey
Lettonie
Lituanie
Norvège
Royaume-Uni de Grande-Bretagne et d'Irlande du Nord
Suède

Europe méridionale
Albanie
Andorre
Bosnie-Herzégovine
Croatie
Espagne
Gibraltar
Grèce
Italie
L'ex-R. y. de Macédoine
Malte
Monténégro
Portugal
Saint-Marin
Saint-Siège
Serbie
Slovénie

Europe occidentale

Allemagne
Autriche
Belgique
France
Liechtenstein
Luxembourg
Monaco
Pays-Bas
Suisse

OCÉANIE

Australie et Nouvelle-Zélande
Australie
Île Norfolk
Nouvelle-Zélande

Mélanésie
Fidji
Îles Salomon
Nouvelle-Calédonie
Papouasie-Nouvelle-Guinée
Vanuatu

Micronésie
Guam
Îles Mariannes septentrionales
Îles Marshall
Kiribati
Micronésie (États fédérés de)
Nauru
Palaos

Polynésie
Îles Cook
Îles Wallis et Futuna
Nioué
Pitcairn
Polynésie française
Samoa
Samoa américaines
Tokélaou
Tonga
Tuvalu

NOTE

[1] Organisation des Nations Unies, Département des affaires économiques et sociales, Division de la population (2015). *Perspectives de la population mondiale : La révision de 2015* (http://esa.un.org/unpd/wpp/).

1. Population, rate of increase, birth and death rates, surface area and density for the world, major areas and regions: selected years
Population, taux d'accroissement, taux de natalité et taux de mortalité, superficie et densité pour l'ensemble du monde, les régions macro géographiques et les composantes géographiques : diverses années

Major areas and regions / Régions macro géographiques et composantes	Mid-year population estimates - Estimations de population au milieu de l'année (millions)							Annual rate of increase - Taux d'accroissement annuel (%)	Crude birth rate - Taux bruts de natalité	Crude death rate - Taux bruts de mortalité	Surface area (km2) - Superficie (km2) (000s)	Density - Densité[1]
	1960	1970	1980	1990	2000	2010	2015	2010-2015	2010-2015	2010-2015	2015	2015
WORLD TOTAL - ENSEMBLE DU MONDE	3 018.3	3 682.5	4 439.6	5 309.7	6 126.6	6 929.7	7 349.5	1.2	20	8	136 162	54
AFRICA - AFRIQUE	284.9	365.6	478.0	631.6	814.1	1 044.1	1 186.2	2.6	36	10	30 311	39
Eastern Africa - Afrique orientale	84.3	110.4	147.5	198.2	259.4	342.7	394.5	2.8	37	9	7 005	56
Middle Africa - Afrique centrale	32.2	40.8	53.1	70.9	96.1	130.6	152.0	3.0	42	12	6 613	23
Northern Africa - Afrique septentrionale	63.7	82.9	106.9	140.1	171.9	203.7	223.9	1.9	27	6	7 880	28
Southern Africa - Afrique méridionale	19.7	25.5	33.0	42.0	51.5	59.1	62.6	1.2	22	12	2 675	23
Western Africa - Afrique occidentale	84.9	106.0	137.4	180.3	235.2	308.0	353.2	2.7	40	12	6 138	58
LATIN AMERICA AND CARIBBEAN - AMÉRIQUE LATIN ET CARAÏBES	221.2	288.5	365.0	446.9	526.9	599.8	634.4	1.1	18	6	20 546	31
Caribbean - Caraïbes	20.7	25.3	29.7	34.2	38.3	41.6	43.2	0.7	18	8	234	185
Central America - Amérique centrale	51.4	69.7	92.4	114.8	138.8	161.1	172.7	1.4	20	5	2 480	70
South America - Amérique méridionale.................	149.1	193.5	242.9	297.9	349.8	397.1	418.4	1.0	17	6	17 832	23
NORTHERN AMERICA - AMÉRIQUE SEPTENTRIONALE	204.2	231.0	254.2	280.6	313.7	344.1	357.8	0.8	12	8	21 776	16
ASIA - ASIE	1 686.7	2 120.4	2 625.6	3 202.5	3 714.5	4 169.9	4 393.3	1.0	18	7	31 915	138
Eastern Asia - Asie orientale	788.1	978.1	1 173.4	1 368.6	1 496.3	1 575.3	1 612.3	0.5	12	7	11 799	137
South Central Asia - Asie centrale méridionale......	618.6	774.8	980.3	1 239.7	1 507.1	1 765.1	1 890.3	1.4	22	7	10 791	175
South Eastern Asia - Asie méridionale orientale	213.8	281.5	358.1	445.7	526.2	596.7	633.5	1.2	19	7	4 495	141
Western Asia - Asie occidentale...........................	66.2	86.0	113.8	148.6	185.0	232.7	257.2	2.0	23	5	4 831	53
EUROPE	605.6	657.2	693.9	721.1	726.4	735.4	738.4	0.1	11	11	23 049	32
Eastern Europe - Europe orientale........................	253.6	276.4	295.0	310.0	303.8	294.6	292.9	-0.1	12	13	18 814	16
Northern Europe - Europe septentrionale	81.8	87.3	89.8	92.0	94.4	99.7	102.4	0.5	12	9	1 810	57
Southern Europe - Europe méridionale.................	117.9	127.6	138.5	143.4	145.1	153.4	152.3	-0.1	9	10	1 317	116
Western Europe - Europe occidentale...................	152.3	165.9	170.5	175.6	183.2	187.8	190.8	0.3	10	10	1 108	172
OCEANIA - OCÉANIA	15.8	19.7	23.0	27.0	31.1	36.4	39.3	1.5	17	7	8 564	5
Australia and New Zealand - Australie et Nouvelle Zélande	12.7	15.7	17.9	20.5	23.0	26.5	28.5	1.4	14	7	8 012	4
Melanesia - Melanésie	2.6	3.3	4.3	5.5	7.0	8.7	9.6	2.0	28	7	541	18
Micronesia	0.2	0.2	0.3	0.4	0.5	0.5	0.5	0.9	21	6	3	175
Polynesia - Polynésie...	0.3	0.4	0.5	0.5	0.6	0.7	0.7	0.7	21	6	8	86

FOOTNOTES - NOTES

[1] Population per square kilometre of surface area. Figures are estimates of population divided by surface area and are not to be considered as either reflecting density in the urban sense or as indicating the supporting power of a territory's land and resources. - Habitants par kilomètre carré. Il s'agit simplement du quotient calculé en divisant la population par la superficie et n'est par considéré comme indiquant la densité au sens urbain du terme ni l'effectif de population que les terres et les ressources du territoire sont capables de nourrir.

Table 2 - *Demographic Yearbook 2015*

Table 2 presents estimates of population and the percentage distribution by age group and sex as well as the sex ratio for all ages; data are presented for the world, the six major areas and the twenty regions for 2015.

Description of variables: All population estimates presented in this table are prepared by the Population Division of the United Nations Department of Economic and Social Affairs. These estimates are published (using more detailed age groups) in the *2015 Revision of World Population Prospects*[1].

The scheme of regionalization used for these estimates is discussed in detail in the technical notes for table 1. Age groups presented in this table are: 0-14 years, 15-64 years, and 65 years or over. Sex ratio refers to the number of males per 100 females of all ages.

The percentage distributions and the sex ratios that appear in this table were calculated by the Statistics Division of the United Nations Department of Economic and Social Affairs using the estimates prepared by the Population Division of the United Nations Department of Economic and Social Affairs.

Reliability of data: All data are set in *italic* type to indicate their conjectural quality.

Limitations: The data presented in this table are from the same series of estimates, prepared by the Population Division of the United Nations, presented in table 1. The estimated orders of magnitude of population are subject to all the basic limitations set forth for population statistics in section 3 of the Technical Notes. In brief, because they are estimates, these distributions by broad age groups and sex should be considered only as orders of magnitude. However, in compiling data for regional and major areas' totals, errors in the components tend to compensate each other and the resulting aggregates may be somewhat more reliable than the quality of the individual components would imply.

In addition, data in this table are limited by factors affecting data by age. These factors are described in the technical notes for table 7. Because the age groups presented in this table are broad, these problems are minimized.

NOTES

[1] United Nations, Department of Economic and Social Affairs, Population Division (2015). *2015 Revision of World Population Prospects* (http://esa.un.org/unpd/wpp/).

Tableau 2 – *Annuaire démographique 2015*

Le tableau 2 présente, pour l'ensemble du monde, les six grandes zones et les vingt régions, des estimations concernant la population en 2015 ainsi que sa répartition en pourcentage selon des tranches d'âge et le sexe, et le rapport de masculinité pour tous les âges.

Description des variables : toutes les données figurant dans le tableau 2 ont été établies par la Division de la population du Département des affaires économiques et sociales de l'Organisation des Nations Unies, et ont été publiés dans les *Perspectives de la population mondiale : La révision de 2015*[1].

La classification géographique utilisée pour établir ces estimations est exposée en détail dans les notes techniques relatives au tableau 1. Les groupes d'âge présentés dans ce tableau sont définis comme suit : de 0 à 14 ans, de 15 à 64 ans et 65 ans ou plus. Le rapport de masculinité correspond au nombre d'individus de sexe masculin pour 100 individus de sexe féminin sans considération d'âge.

Les pourcentages et les rapports de masculinité qui sont présentés dans le tableau 2 ont été calculés par la Division de statistique du Département des affaires économiques et sociales de l'Organisation des Nations Unies à partir des estimations établies par la Division de la population de l'Organisation des Nations Unies.

Fiabilité des données : toutes les données figurant dans ce tableau sont reproduites en *italique* pour en faire ressortir le caractère conjectural.

Insuffisance des données : les données de ce tableau appartiennent à la même série d'estimations, établie par la Division de la population de l'Organisation des Nations Unies, que celles qui figurent au tableau 1. Les estimations concernant l'ordre de grandeur de la population appellent donc toutes les réserves fondamentales qui ont été formulées à la section 3 des Notes techniques à propos des statistiques relatives à la population. Sans entrer dans le détail, il convient de préciser que les données relatives à la répartition par grand groupe d'âge et par sexe doivent être considérées uniquement comme des ordres de grandeur en raison de leur caractère estimatif. Toutefois, il est à noter que, lorsque l'on additionne des données par territoire pour obtenir des totaux régionaux et par grandes zones, les erreurs qu'elles comportent arrivent parfois à s'équilibrer, de sorte que les agrégats obtenus peuvent être un peu plus exacts que chacun des éléments dont on est parti.

En outre, les donnés figurant dans le tableau 2 comportent certaines imprécisions en raison des facteurs influant sur les données par âge (voir à ce propos les notes techniques relatives au tableau 7). Ces imprécisions sont cependant atténuées du fait de l'étendue des groupes d'âge présentés dans le tableau 2.

NOTE

[1] Organisation des Nations Unies, Département des affaires économiques et sociales, Division de la population (2015). *Perspectives de la population mondiale : La révision de 2015* (http://esa.un.org/unpd/wpp/).

2. Estimates of population and its percentage distribution by age group and sex, and sex ratio, for the world, major areas and regions: 2015

Estimations de la population et pourcentage de répartition selon les tranches d'âge et le sexe, et le rapport de masculinité, pour l'ensemble du monde, les grandes régions et les régions géographiques : 2015

Major areas and regions / Grandes régions et régions	Population (millions)												Sex ratio - Rapport de masculinité[1]
	Both sexes - Les deux sexes				Male - Masculin				Female - Féminin				
	All ages - Tous âges	0-14	15-64	65+	All ages - Tous âges	0-14	15-64	65+	All ages - Tous âges	0-14	15-64	65+	
WORLD TOTAL - ENSEMBLE DU MONDE													
Number - Nombre	7 349	1 916	4 825	608	3 707	990	2 444	273	3 642	925	2 381	336	
Percent - Pourcentage	100.0	26.1	65.7	8.3	100.0	26.7	65.9	7.4	100.0	25.4	65.4	9.2	101.8
AFRICA - AFRIQUE													
Number - Nombre	1 186	486	659	41	593	246	329	19	593	240	330	23	
Percent - Pourcentage	100.0	41.0	55.5	3.5	100.0	41.5	55.4	3.1	100.0	40.4	55.7	3.9	100.1
Eastern Africa - Afrique orientale													
Number - Nombre	394	171	211	12	196	86	104	6	198	85	107	7	
Percent - Pourcentage	100.0	43.4	53.4	3.1	100.0	44.0	53.1	2.8	100.0	42.9	53.7	3.4	98.9
Middle Africa - Afrique centrale													
Number - Nombre	152	69	78	4	76	35	39	2	76	34	39	2	
Percent - Pourcentage	100.0	45.4	51.7	2.9	100.0	45.9	51.5	2.6	100.0	45.0	51.8	3.2	99.5
Northern Africa - Afrique septentrionale													
Number - Nombre	224	72	140	12	112	37	70	5	111	35	70	6	
Percent - Pourcentage	100.0	32.1	62.6	5.2	100.0	32.8	62.5	4.8	100.0	31.5	62.8	5.7	100.8
Southern Africa - Afrique méridionale													
Number - Nombre	63	19	41	3	31	9	20	1	32	9	20	2	
Percent - Pourcentage	100.0	30.0	65.1	4.9	100.0	30.8	65.9	3.3	100.0	29.3	64.4	6.4	96.9
Western Africa - Afrique occidentale													
Number - Nombre	353	155	188	10	178	79	95	5	175	76	94	5	
Percent - Pourcentage	100.0	43.8	53.4	2.8	100.0	44.3	53.1	2.6	100.0	43.4	53.6	3.0	102.0
LATIN AMERICA AND CARIBBEAN - AMÉRIQUE LATIN ET CARAÏBES													
Number - Nombre	634	163	423	48	314	83	209	21	321	80	214	27	
Percent - Pourcentage	100.0	25.7	66.7	7.6	100.0	26.5	66.7	6.7	100.0	24.9	66.6	8.5	97.7
Caribbean - Caraïbes													
Number - Nombre	43	11	28	4	21	6	14	2	22	5	14	2	
Percent - Pourcentage	100.0	25.1	65.6	9.4	100.0	25.8	65.6	8.6	100.0	24.3	65.6	10.1	98.2
Central America - Amérique centrale													
Number - Nombre	173	49	112	11	86	25	55	5	87	24	57	6	
Percent - Pourcentage	100.0	28.6	65.1	6.3	100.0	29.4	64.7	5.9	100.0	27.7	65.5	6.8	98.3
South America - Amérique méridionale													
Number - Nombre	418	103	282	33	206	53	140	14	212	50	143	19	
Percent - Pourcentage	100.0	24.6	67.4	8.0	100.0	25.4	67.7	6.9	100.0	23.8	67.2	9.0	97.4
NORTHERN AMERICA - AMÉRIQUE SEPTENTRIONALE													
Number - Nombre	358	67	238	53	177	34	120	24	180	33	118	30	
Percent - Pourcentage	100.0	18.7	66.4	14.9	100.0	19.2	67.4	13.4	100.0	18.1	65.5	16.4	98.3
ASIA - ASIE													
Number - Nombre	4 393	1 074	2 988	331	2 247	562	1 531	154	2 146	512	1 458	177	
Percent - Pourcentage	100.0	24.5	68.0	7.5	100.0	25.0	68.1	6.9	100.0	23.9	67.9	8.2	104.7
Eastern Asia - Asie orientale													
Number - Nombre	1 612	271	1 164	178	825	145	597	83	788	126	567	95	
Percent - Pourcentage	100.0	16.8	72.2	11.0	100.0	17.5	72.4	10.1	100.0	16.0	72.0	12.0	104.7
South Central Asia - Asie centrale méridionale													
Number - Nombre	1 890	558	1 230	102	972	292	631	49	918	266	599	53	
Percent - Pourcentage	100.0	29.5	65.1	5.4	100.0	30.0	65.0	5.0	100.0	29.0	65.2	5.8	105.8
South Eastern Asia - Asie méridionale orientale													
Number - Nombre	633	168	428	38	316	86	214	16	317	82	214	21	
Percent - Pourcentage	100.0	26.5	67.5	5.9	100.0	27.3	67.6	5.1	100.0	25.8	67.4	6.7	99.6
Western Asia - Asie occidentale													
Number - Nombre	257	77	167	13	134	40	89	6	123	38	78	7	
Percent - Pourcentage	100.0	30.1	64.8	5.1	100.0	29.5	66.1	4.4	100.0	30.6	63.4	6.0	109.0
EUROPE													
Number - Nombre	738	116	492	130	356	60	244	53	382	57	249	77	
Percent - Pourcentage	100.0	15.7	66.7	17.6	100.0	16.7	68.4	14.9	100.0	14.8	65.1	20.1	93.2
Eastern Europe - Europe orientale													
Number - Nombre	293	47	203	43	138	24	99	15	155	23	105	28	
Percent - Pourcentage	100.0	15.9	69.4	14.7	100.0	17.3	71.7	11.0	100.0	14.6	67.4	18.0	88.9
Northern Europe - Europe septentrionale													
Number - Nombre	102	18	66	18	50	9	33	8	52	9	33	10	
Percent - Pourcentage	100.0	17.6	64.4	18.0	100.0	18.3	65.5	16.2	100.0	17.0	63.4	19.6	97.1
Southern Europe - Europe méridionale													
Number - Nombre	152	22	100	31	74	11	50	13	78	11	50	17	
Percent - Pourcentage	100.0	14.5	65.4	20.1	100.0	15.3	67.0	17.7	100.0	13.7	63.8	22.4	95.2

2. Estimates of population and its percentage distribution by age group and sex, and sex ratio, for the world, major areas and regions: 2015

Estimations de la population et pourcentage de répartition selon les tranches d'âge et le sexe, et le rapport de masculinité, pour l'ensemble du monde, les grandes régions et les régions géographiques : 2015 (continued - suite)

Major areas and regions Grandes régions et régions	Population (millions)												Sex ratio - Rapport de masculinité[1]
	Both sexes - Les deux sexes				Male - Masculin				Female - Féminin				
	All ages - Tous âges	0-14	15-64	65+	All ages - Tous âges	0-14	15-64	65+	All ages - Tous âges	0-14	15-64	65+	
Western Europe - Europe occidentale													
Number - Nombre	191	30	123	38	94	15	62	17	97	14	62	21	
Percent - Pourcentage	100.0	15.5	64.7	19.8	100.0	16.2	66.2	17.7	100.0	14.8	63.3	21.9	96.3
OCEANIA - OCÉANIA													
Number - Nombre	39.33	9.23	25.41	4.69	19.71	4.75	12.76	2.19	19.62	4.47	12.64	2.51	
Percent - Pourcentage	100.0	23.5	64.6	11.9	100.0	24.1	64.8	11.1	100.0	22.8	64.4	12.8	100.4
Australia and New Zealand - Australie et Nouvelle Zélande													
Number - Nombre	28.50	5.40	18.82	4.28	14.19	2.77	9.41	2.01	14.31	2.63	9.41	2.27	
Percent - Pourcentage	100.0	18.9	66.0	15.0	100.0	19.5	66.3	14.1	100.0	18.4	65.7	15.9	99.2
Melanesia - Melanésie													
Number - Nombre	9.62	3.47	5.81	0.34	4.90	1.80	2.96	0.15	4.72	1.67	2.86	0.19	
Percent - Pourcentage	100.0	36.1	60.4	3.5	100.0	36.7	60.3	3.0	100.0	35.5	60.5	4.0	103.9
Micronesia													
Number - Nombre	0.53	0.16	0.34	0.03	0.27	0.08	0.17	0.01	0.26	0.08	0.17	0.02	
Percent - Pourcentage	100.0	29.6	64.3	6.1	100.0	30.1	64.4	5.5	100.0	29.1	64.3	6.6	102.2
Polynesia - Polynésie													
Number - Nombre	0.68	0.20	0.44	0.04	0.35	0.11	0.22	0.02	0.34	0.10	0.21	0.02	
Percent - Pourcentage	100.0	29.8	63.7	6.5	100.0	30.2	64.0	5.9	100.0	29.4	63.5	7.1	103.6

FOOTNOTES - NOTES

[1] Males per 100 females of all ages - Hommes pour 100 femmes de tous âges

Table 3 - *Demographic Yearbook 2015*

Table 3 presents for each country or area of the world the total, male and female population enumerated at the latest population census, estimates of the mid-year total population for 2010 and 2015, the average annual exponential rate of population increase (or decrease) for the period 2010 to 2015, the surface area and the population density for 2015.

Description of variables: The total, male and female population is the population enumerated at the most recent census for which data are available. The date of this census is given. Population census data are usually the results of a nation-wide gathering of individual information through full field enumeration. Alternatively other approaches for generating reliable statistics on population and housing can be used by countries, such as the use of population registers. Data that are the result of such an alternative approach are also coded as census and are footnoted accordingly. Also, the results of sample surveys, essentially national in character, may be presented showing the appropriate code.

Mid-year population estimates refer to the population on 1 July. Otherwise, a footnote is appended. Mid-year estimates of the total population are those provided by national statistical offices.

Surface area, expressed in square kilometres, refers to the total surface area, comprising land area and inland waters (assumed to consist of major rivers and lakes) and excluding polar regions as well as uninhabited islands. Exceptions to this are noted. Surface areas, originally reported in square miles by the country or area, have been converted to square kilometres using a conversion factor of 2.589988.

Computation: The annual rate of population increase is the average annual exponential rate of population growth between 2010 and 2015, computed by the Statistics Division of the United Nations Department of Economic and Social Affairs using the unrounded mid-year estimates of 2010 and 2015. This rate is expressed as percentage.

Density is the number of persons in the 2015 total population per square kilometre of total surface area.

Reliability of data: Reliable mid-year population estimates are those that are based on a complete census (or a sample survey) and have been adjusted by a continuous population register or on the basis of the calculated balance of births, deaths and migration. Mid-year estimates of this type are considered reliable and appear in roman type. Mid-year estimates not calculated on this basis are considered less reliable and are shown in italics.

Census data and sample survey results are considered reliable and, therefore, appear in roman type.

Rates of population increase that were calculated using population estimates considered less reliable, as described above, are set in italics rather than roman type.

All surface area data are assumed to be reliable and therefore appear in roman type.

Population density data, however, are considered reliable or less reliable on the basis of the reliability of the 2014 population estimates used as the numerator.

Limitations: Statistics on the total population enumerated at the time of the census, surface area data and estimates of the mid-year total population are subject to the same qualifications as have been set forth for surface area and population data in sections 2.4 and 3 of the Technical Notes, respectively.

Regarding the limitations of census data, it should be noted that although census data are considered reliable, and therefore appear in roman type, the actual quality of census data varies widely from one country or area to another. When known, an estimate of the extent of over-enumeration or under-enumeration is given in footnotes.

Rates of population increase are subject to all the qualifications of the population estimates mentioned above. In some cases, they simply reflect the rate calculated or assumed in constructing the estimates themselves when adequate measures of natural increase and net migration were not available. Despite their shortcomings, these rates provide a useful index for studying population change and can be also useful in evaluating the accuracy of vital and migration statistics.

Population density data as shown in this table give only an indication of actual population density as they do not take account of the dispersion or concentration of population within countries or areas nor the proportion of habitable land. They should not be interpreted as reflecting density in the urban sense or as indicating the supporting power of a territory's land and resources.

Tableau 3 – *Annuaire démographique 2015*

Le tableau 3 indique pour chaque pays ou zone du monde la population totale selon le sexe d'après les derniers recensements effectués, les estimations concernant la population totale au milieu de l'année 2010 et de l'année 2015, le taux moyen d'accroissement annuel exponentiel positif ou négatif de la population pour la période allant de 2010 à 2015, ainsi que la superficie et la densité de population en 2015.

Description des variables : la population masculine et féminine totale est, la population enregistrée lors du recensement le plus récent sur lequel on dispose de données. La date de ce recensement est indiquée. Les données des recensements de la population sont habituellement le résultat d'un collecte à l'échelle nationale des données individuelles obtenues au moyen d'un dénombrement complet. Les pays peuvent recourir à d'autres moyens pour établir des statistiques fiables sur la population et le logement, tels que des registres de la population. Les données obtenues par ce moyen sont présentées comme celles d'un recensement et sont annotées en conséquence. Par ailleurs, les résultats des enquêtes par sondage, réalisées habituellement à l'échelle nationale, peuvent être présentés à l'aide du code correspondant.
Les estimations de la population en milieu d'année sont celles de la population au 1er juillet. Lorsque la date est différente, cela est signalé par une note. Les estimations de la population totale en milieu d'année sont celles qui ont été communiquées par les services nationaux de statistique.

La superficie - exprimée en kilomètres carrés - représente la superficie totale, c'est-à-dire qu'elle englobe les terres émergées et les eaux intérieures (qui sont censées comprendre les principaux lacs et cours d'eau) mais exclut les régions polaires et certaines îles inhabitées. Les exceptions à cette règle sont signalées en note. Les superficies initialement exprimées en miles carrés par les pays ou les zones ont été transformées en kilomètres carrés au moyen d'un coefficient de conversion de 2,589988.

Calculs : le taux d'accroissement annuel est le taux exponentiel annuel moyen de variation (en pourcentage) de la population entre 2010 et 2015, calculé par la Division de statistique du Département des affaires économiques et sociales de l'Organisation des Nations Unies à partir des estimations en milieu d'année non arrondies pour les années 2010 et 2015.

La densité est égale au rapport de l'effectif total de la population en 2015 à la superficie totale, exprimée en kilomètres carrés.

Fiabilité des données : les estimations en milieu d'année qui sont considérées sûres sont fondées sur un recensement complet (ou sur une enquête par sondage) et ont été ajustées en fonction des données provenant d'un registre permanent de population ou en fonction de la balance établie par le calcul des naissances, des décès et des migrations. Les estimations de ce type sont considérées comme sûres et apparaissent en caractères romains. Les estimations en milieu d'année dont le calcul n'a pas été effectué sur cette base sont considérées comme moins sûres et apparaissent en italique.

Les données de recensements ou les résultats d'enquêtes par sondage sont considérés comme sûrs et apparaissent par conséquent en caractères romains.

Les taux d'accroissement de la population, calculés à partir d'estimations jugées moins sûres d'après les normes décrites ci-dessus, sont indiqués en italique plutôt qu'en caractères romains.

Toutes les données de superficie sont présumées sûres et apparaissent par conséquent en caractères romains. En revanche, les données relatives à la densité de la population sont considérées plus ou moins sûres en fonction de la fiabilité des estimations de la population en 2014 ayant servi de numérateur.

Insuffisance des données : les statistiques portant sur la population totale dénombrée lors d'un recensement, les données de superficie et les estimations de la population totale en milieu d'année appellent les mêmes réserves que celles formulées aux sections 2.4 et 3 des Notes techniques à propos des statistiques relatives à la superficie et à la population.

S'agissant de l'insuffisance des données obtenues par recensement, il convient d'indiquer que, bien que ces données soient considérées comme sûres et apparaissent par conséquent en caractères romains, leur qualité réelle varie considérablement d'un pays ou d'une région à l'autre. Lorsque l'on possédait les renseignements voulus, on a donné une estimation du degré de sur-dénombrement ou de sous-dénombrement.
Les taux d'accroissement appellent toutes les réserves formulées plus haut à propos des estimations concernant la population. Dans certains cas, ils représentent seulement le taux calculé ou que l'on a pris

pour base pour établir les estimations elles-mêmes lorsque l'on ne disposait pas de mesures appropriées de l'accroissement naturel et des migrations nettes. Malgré leurs imperfections, ces taux fournissent des indications intéressantes pour l'étude du mouvement de la population et, utilisés avec les précautions nécessaires, ils peuvent également servir à évaluer l'exactitude des statistiques de l'état civil et des migrations.

Les données relatives à la densité de population figurant dans le tableau 3 n'ont qu'une valeur indicative en ce qui concerne la densité de population effective, car elles ne tiennent compte ni de la dispersion ou de la concentration de la population à l'intérieur des pays ou zones, ni de la proportion du territoire qui est habitable. Il ne faut donc y voir d'indication ni de la densité au sens urbain du terme ni du nombre d'habitants qui pourraient vivre sur les terres et avec les ressources naturelles du territoire considéré.

3. Population by sex, annual rate of population increase, surface area and density
Population selon le sexe, taux d'accroissement annuel de la population, superficie et densité

Continent, country or area and census date Continent, pays ou zone et date du recensement	Census type[a]	Population at the latest available census Population d'après le dernier recensement disponible (in units — en unités)			Estimate type[a]	Mid-year estimates Estimations au milieu de l'année (in thousands — en milliers)		Annual rate of increase Taux d' accrois sement annuel 2010-15	Surface area Superficie (km²) 2015	Density Densité 2015[b]
		Both sexes Les deux sexes	Male Masculin	Female Feminin		2010	2015			

AFRICA - AFRIQUE

Algeria - Algérie										
16 IV 2008	DF	34 452 759[1]	17 428 500[1]	17 024 259[1]	DJ	35 978	39 963	2.1	2 381 741	17
Angola										
16 V 2014	DF	25 789 024	12 499 041	13 289 983	DF	17 430	...	...	1 246 700	...
Benin - Bénin										
11 V 2013	DJ	10 008 749	4 887 820	5 120 929	DF	8 779[2]	10 585[3]	3.7	114 763	92
Botswana										
9 VIII 2011	DF	2 024 904	988 957	1 035 947	DJ	1 823	2 195[4]	3.7	582 000	4
Burkina Faso										
9 XII 2006	DF	14 196 259	6 842 560	7 353 699	DJ	15 731[2]	...	...	272 967	...
Burundi										
16 VIII 2008	DF	7 877 728	3 838 045	4 039 683	DF	8 488[5]	9 824[5]	2.9	27 830	353
Cabo Verde										
16 VI 2010	DJ	491 683	243 401	248 282	DF	518	...	...	4 033	...
Cameroon - Cameroun										
11 XI 2005	DF	17 052 134	8 408 495	8 643 639	DJ	19 406[6]	21 918[6]	2.4	475 650	46
Central African Republic - République centrafricaine										
8 XII 2003	DF	3 151 072	1 569 446	1 581 626		...	...	...	622 984	...
Chad - Tchad										
20 V 2009	DJ	11 175 915	5 509 522	5 666 393		...	...	...	1 284 000	...
Comoros - Comores										
1 IX 2003	DF	575 660[7]	285 590[7]	290 070[7]		...	...	...	2 235	...
Congo										
28 IV 2007	DF	3 697 490	1 821 357	1 876 133		...	...	...	342 000	...
Côte d'Ivoire										
15 V 2014	DF	22 224 509	11 441 896	10 782 613		...	...	...	322 463	...
Democratic Republic of the Congo - République démocratique du Congo										
1 VII 1984	DF	29 916 800	14 543 800	15 373 000		...	...	...	2 344 858	...
Djibouti										
29 V 2009	DF	818 159	440 067	378 092	DF	841[8]	...	...	23 200	...
Egypt - Égypte										
21 XI 2006	DF	72 798 031	37 219 056	35 578 975	DF	78 685	88 958	2.5	1 002 000	89
Equatorial Guinea - Guinée équatoriale										
20 VI 2015	DF	1 222 442	651 820	570 622	DF	1 622[9]	...	...	28 051	...
Eritrea - Érythrée										
9 V 1984	DF	2 748 304	1 374 452	1 373 852		...	...	...	117 600	...
Ethiopia - Éthiopie										
29 V 2007	DF	73 750 932	37 217 130	36 533 802	DF	79 634[10]	90 075[10]	2.5	1 104 300	82
Gabon										
22 V 2013	DF	1 811 079	934 072	877 007		...	...	...	267 668	...
Gambia - Gambie										
15 IV 2013	DF	*1 882 450	*930 699	*951 751		...	...	...	11 295	...
Ghana										
26 IX 2010	DF	24 658 823	12 024 845	12 633 978	DF	...	27 670[2]	...	238 537	116
Guinea - Guinée										
1 III 2014	DF	10 523 261	5 084 306	5 438 955	DF	10 537[2]	...	...	245 857	...
Guinea-Bissau - Guinée-Bissau										
15 III 2009	DF	1 520 830	737 634	783 196	DF	1 460[2]	1 531[2]	0.9	36 125	42
Kenya										
24 VIII 2009	DF	38 610 097	19 192 458	19 417 639	DF	40 406	45 509	2.4	591 958	77
Lesotho										
13 IV 2006	DF	1 741 406	818 379	923 027	DF	1 892[2]	...	...	30 355	...
Liberia - Libéria										
21 III 2008	DF	3 476 608	1 739 945	1 736 663	DF	3 627	...	...	111 369	...
Libya - Libye										
15 IV 2006	DF	*5 298 152	*2 687 513	*2 610 639	DF	5 689	6 162	1.6	1 676 198	4
Madagascar										
1 VIII 1993	DF	12 238 914	6 088 116	6 150 798	DF	20 142	...	...	587 295	...

3. Population by sex, annual rate of population increase, surface area and density
Population selon le sexe, taux d'accroissement annuel de la population, superficie et densité (continued - suite)

| Continent, country or area and census date / Continent, pays ou zone et date du recensement | Census type[a] | Population at the latest available census / Population d'après le dernier recensement disponible (in units — en unités) | | | Estimate type[a] | Mid-year estimates Estimations au milieu de l'année (in thousands — en milliers) | | Annual rate of increase Taux d'accrois sement annuel 2010-15 | Surface area Superficie (km²) 2015 | Density Densité 2015[b] |
		Both sexes Les deux sexes	Male Masculin	Female Feminin		2010	2015			
AFRICA - AFRIQUE										
Malawi										
8 VI 2008 .... DF	DF	13 077 160	6 358 933	6 718 227	DF	13 949[11]	...	...	118 484	...
Mali										
1 IV 2009 .... DF	DF	14 528 662	7 204 990	7 323 672	DF	15 370[12]	...	...	1 240 192	...
Mauritania - Mauritanie										
24 III 2013 .... DF	DF	3 460 388[13]	...	...	DF	3 341[2]	...	...	1 030 700	...
Mauritius - Maurice[14]										
4 VII 2011 .... DF	DF	1 237 000	611 053	625 947	DJ	1 281[15]	1 263[16]	-0.3	1 969	641
Mayotte										
21 VIII 2012 .... DJ	DJ	212 645	103 164	109 481	DJ	...	*227[17]	...	...	...
Morocco - Maroc										
1 IX 2014 .... DJ	DJ	33 848 242	...	...	DF	31 894[18]	...	...	446 550	...
Mozambique										
1 VIII 2007 .... DF	DF	20 252 223	9 746 690	10 505 533	DF	22 417[2]	25 728[2]	2.8	799 380	32
Namibia - Namibie										
28 VIII 2011 .... DF	DF	2 113 077	1 021 912	1 091 165	DF	2 143[2]	2 281[19]	1.2	824 116	3
Niger										
10 XII 2012 .... DJ	DJ	17 138 707	8 518 818	8 619 889	DJ	15 204[2]	19 125[20]	4.6	1 267 000	15
Nigeria - Nigéria										
21 III 2006 .... DF	DF	140 431 790	71 345 488	69 086 302	DF	159 619[2]	...	...	923 768	...
Republic of South Sudan - République de Soudan du Sud										
21 IV 2008 .... DF	DF	8 260 490	4 287 300	3 973 190	DF	9 497[21]	...	...	658 841	...
Reunion - Réunion										
1 I 2010 .... DJ	DJ	821 136	398 006	423 130	DJ	...	*844[17]	...	2 513	336
Rwanda										
15 VIII 2012 .... DF	DF	10 393 542	4 981 197	5 412 345	DF	10 413[2]	11 263[22]	1.6	26 338	428
Saint Helena ex. dep. - Sainte-Hélène sans dép.										
7 II 2016 .... DJ	DJ	4 534	2 396	2 138	DF	4	...	...	122	...
Saint Helena: Ascension - Sainte-Hélène: Ascension										
8 III 1998 .... DJ	DJ	712	458	254		...	...	...	88	...
Saint Helena: Tristan da Cunha - Sainte-Hélène: Tristan da Cunha										
31 XII 1988 .... DF	DF	296	139	157		...	...	...	98	...
Sao Tome and Principe - Sao Tomé-et-Principe										
13 V 2012 .... DJ	DJ	178 739	88 867	89 872	DF	164	...	...	964	...
Senegal - Sénégal										
19 XI 2013 .... DF	DF	*12 873 601	*6 428 189	*6 445 412	DJ	12 509[23]	14 357[2]	2.8	196 712[24]	73
Seychelles										
26 VIII 2010 .... DF	DF	90 945	46 912	44 033	DF	90	93	0.8	457	204
Sierra Leone										
4 XII 2015 .... DF	DF	*7 075 641	*3 473 991	*3 601 650	DF	5 747	...	...	72 300	...
Somalia - Somalie										
15 II 1987 .... DF	DF	7 114 431	3 741 664	3 372 767		...	...	...	637 657	...
South Africa - Afrique du Sud										
10 X 2011 .... DF	DF	51 770 560	25 188 791	26 581 769	DF	50 896	...	...	1 221 037	...
Sudan - Soudan										
21 IV 2008 .... DF	DF	30 894 000	15 786 677	15 107 323	DF	32 962	38 454	3.1	...	...
Swaziland										
11 III 2007 .... DF	DF	844 223	405 868	438 355	DF	1 056	1 119[17]	1.2	17 363	64
Togo										
6 XI 2010 .... DJ	DJ	6 191 155	3 009 095	3 182 060	DF	6 191[2]	6 974[2]	2.4	56 785	123
Tunisia - Tunisie										
23 IV 2014 .... DF	DF	10 982 754	5 472 338	5 510 416	DF	10 547	11 154	1.1	163 610	68
Uganda - Ouganda										
27 VIII 2014 .... DF	DF	34 634 650	17 060 832	17 573 818	DF	31 785	...	...	241 550	...

3. Population by sex, annual rate of population increase, surface area and density
Population selon le sexe, taux d'accroissement annuel de la population, superficie et densité (continued - suite)

Continent, country or area and census date / Continent, pays ou zone et date du recensement	Census type[a]	Population at the latest available census / Population d'après le dernier recensement disponible (in units — en unités)			Estimate type[a]	Mid-year estimates / Estimations au milieu de l'année (in thousands — en milliers)		Annual rate of increase / Taux d'accrois sement annuel 2010-15	Surface area / Superficie (km²) 2015	Density / Densité 2015[b]
		Both sexes / Les deux sexes	Male / Masculin	Female / Feminin		2010	2015			
AFRICA - AFRIQUE										
United Republic of Tanzania - République Unie de Tanzanie										
26 VIII 2012 .... DF		44 928 923[25]	21 869 990[25]	23 058 933[25]	DF	*43 188*[26]	*48 776*[22]	2.4	947 303	*51*
Western Sahara - Sahara occidental[27]										
31 XII 1970 .... DF		76 425	43 981	32 444		...	...	...	266 000	...
Zambia - Zambie										
16 X 2010 .... DF		12 526 314	6 117 253	6 409 061	DF	...	*15 474*[2]	...	752 612	*21*
Zimbabwe										
17 VIII 2012 .... DF		13 061 239	6 280 539	6 780 700	DF	...	*13 943*[22]	...	390 757	*36*
AMERICA, NORTH - AMÉRIQUE DU NORD										
Anguilla										
11 V 2011 .... DF		13 572	6 707	6 865	DF	16	15	-2.1	91	162
Antigua and Barbuda - Antigua-et-Barbuda										
27 V 2011 .... DF		88 566	...	...	DF	91	...	...	442	...
Aruba										
29 IX 2010 .... DJ		101 484	48 241	53 243	DJ	102	109	1.4	180	607
Bahamas										
3 V 2010 .... DJ		351 461	170 257	181 204	DF	*335*[2]	...	...	13 940	...
Barbados - Barbade										
1 V 2010 .... DJ		277 821	133 018	144 803	DF	278	275	-0.2	431	637
Belize										
12 V 2010 .... DJ		322 453	161 227	161 226	DF	*324*	*368*	2.6	22 966	*16*
Bermuda - Bermudes										
20 V 2010 .... DJ		64 237[28]	30 858[28]	33 379[28]	DJ	64[29]	62[29]	-0.8	53	1 165
British Virgin Islands - Îles Vierges britanniques										
21 V 2001 .... DF		20 647	10 627	10 020	DF	28	...	...	151	...
Canada										
2 V 2011 .... DJ		33 476 690	16 414 225	17 062 455	DJ	34 005[30]	35 849[31]	1.1	9 984 670	4
Cayman Islands - Îles Caïmanes										
10 X 2010 .... DJ		55 036[32]	27 218[32]	27 818[32]	DJ	56	59	1.2	264	224
Costa Rica										
30 V 2011 .... DJ		4 301 712	2 106 063	2 195 649	DJ	4 538[33]	4 834[34]	1.3	51 100	95
Cuba										
14 IX 2012 .... DF		11 167 325	5 570 825	5 596 500	DJ	11 171	11 239	0.1	109 884	102
Curaçao										
26 III 2011 .... DF		150 563	68 848	81 715	DJ	149[35]	158[36]	1.2	444	356
Dominica - Dominique										
14 V 2011 .... DF		*71 293	*36 411	*34 882	DF	71	...	...	750	...
Dominican Republic - République dominicaine										
1 XII 2010 .... DJ		9 445 281	4 739 038	4 706 243	DF	*9 479*[2]	*9 980*[2]	1.0	48 671	*205*
El Salvador										
12 V 2007 .... DJ		5 744 113	2 719 371	3 024 742	DF	6 183[37]	6 460[37]	0.9	21 041[38]	307
Greenland - Groenland										
1 I 2008 .... DJ		56 462[39]	29 885[39]	26 577[39]	DJ	57[39]	56[39]	-0.1	2 166 086	0
Grenada - Grenade										
25 V 2001 .... DF		102 632	50 481	52 151	DF	105	111	1.0	345	320
Guadeloupe										
1 I 2010 .... DJ		403 355[40]	187 932[40]	215 423[40]	DJ	...	*400*[41]	...	1 705	235
Guatemala										
24 XI 2002 .... DJ		11 237 196	5 496 839	5 740 357	DF	14 362[26]	...	...	108 889	...
Haiti - Haïti										
11 I 2003 .... DJ		8 373 750	4 039 272	4 334 478	DJ	*10 085*[42]	...	...	27 750	...
Honduras										
10 VIII 2013 .... DF		8 303 771	4 052 316	4 251 456	DF	*8 046*[43]	*8 577*[3]	1.3	112 492	*76*

3. Population by sex, annual rate of population increase, surface area and density
Population selon le sexe, taux d'accroissement annuel de la population, superficie et densité (continued - suite)

Continent, country or area and census date — Continent, pays ou zone et date du recensement	Census type[a]	Population at the latest available census — Population d'après le dernier recensement disponible (in units — en unités)			Estimate type[a]	Mid-year estimates — Estimations au milieu de l'année (in thousands — en milliers)		Annual rate of increase — Taux d' accrois sement annuel 2010-15	Surface area Superficie (km²) 2015	Density Densité 2015[b]
		Both sexes Les deux sexes	Male Masculin	Female Feminin		2010	2015			
AMERICA, NORTH - AMÉRIQUE DU NORD										
Jamaica - Jamaïque										
4 IV 2011 .... DJ	DJ	2 697 983[44]	1 334 533[44]	1 363 450[44]	DJ	2 702	*2 726	0.2	10 991	248
Martinique										
1 I 2010 .... DJ	DJ	394 173	182 073	212 100	DJ	...	*378[17]	...	1 128	335
Mexico - Mexique										
12 VI 2010 .... DF	DF	112 336 538[45]	54 855 231[45]	57 481 307[45]	DJ	114 256[2]	121 006[2]	1.1	1 964 375	62
Montserrat										
12 V 2011 .... DJ	DJ	4 922	2 546	2 376	DF	5	5	0.0	103	49
Nicaragua										
4 VI 2005 .... DJ	DJ	5 142 098	2 534 491	2 607 607	DJ	5 816	6 263	1.5	130 373	48
Panama										
16 V 2010 .... DF	DF	3 405 813	1 712 584	1 693 229	DF	3 662[29]	3 975[29]	1.6	75 320	53
Puerto Rico - Porto Rico										
1 IV 2010 .... DJ	DJ	3 725 789[46]	1 785 171[46]	1 940 618[46]	DJ	3 721[47]	3 474[47]	-1.4	8 868	392
Saint Kitts and Nevis - Saint-Kitts-et-Nevis										
15 V 2011 .... DF	DF	*46 398	*22 846	*23 552	DF	*53	...	...	261	...
Saint Lucia - Sainte-Lucie										
10 V 2010 .... DJ	DJ	165 770	83 502	82 268	DF	...	173	...	539[48]	321
Saint Pierre and Miquelon - Saint-Pierre-et-Miquelon										
1 I 2013 .... DJ	DJ	6 286	...	...	...	...	...	...	242	
Saint Vincent and the Grenadines - Saint-Vincent-et-les Grenadines										
12 VI 2012 .... DF	DF	*109 991	*56 419	*53 572	DJ	110	110	0.1	389	283
Saint-Barthélemy										
1 I 2013 .... DJ	DJ	9 417	...	...	...	...	...	...	...	...
Saint-Martin (French part) - Saint-Martin (partie française)										
1 I 2013 .... DJ	DJ	36 457	...	...	...	...	...	...	...	...
Sint Maarten (Dutch part) - Saint-Martin (partie néerlandaise)										
9 IV 2011 .... DF	DF	33 609	15 868	17 741	DJ	36	...	...	34	...
Trinidad and Tobago - Trinité-et-Tobago										
9 I 2011 .... DF	DF	1 332 901	...	...	DF	1 318[15]	1 350[16]	0.5	5 127	263
Turks and Caicos Islands - Îles Turques et Caïques										
25 I 2012 .... DF	DF	31 458	16 037	15 421	DJ	40	...	...	948[49]	...
United States of America - États-Unis d'Amérique										
1 IV 2010 .... DJ	DJ	308 745 538	151 781 326	156 964 212	DJ	309 347[50]	321 419[50]	0.8	9 833 517	33
United States Virgin Islands - Îles Vierges américaines										
1 IV 2010 .... DJ	DJ	106 405[46]	50 854[46]	55 551[46]	DJ	106[51]	...	...	347	...
AMERICA, SOUTH - AMÉRIQUE DU SUD										
Argentina - Argentine										
27 X 2010 .... DF	DF	40 117 096	19 523 766	20 593 330	DF	40 788[52]	43 137[52]	1.1	2 780 400	16
Bolivia (Plurinational State of) - Bolivie (État plurinational de)										
21 XI 2012 .... DF	DF	10 059 856	5 019 447	5 040 409	DF	10 031	10 825	1.5	1 098 581[53]	10
Brazil - Brésil										
31 VII 2010 .... DJ	DJ	190 755 799	93 406 990	97 348 809	DF	195 498[54]	204 451[54]	0.9	8 515 767	24

3. Population by sex, annual rate of population increase, surface area and density
Population selon le sexe, taux d'accroissement annuel de la population, superficie et densité (continued - suite)

Continent, country or area and census date / Continent, pays ou zone et date du recensement	Census type[a]	Population at the latest available census — Population d'après le dernier recensement disponible (in units — en unités)			Estimate type[a]	Mid-year estimates Estimations au milieu de l'année (in thousands — en milliers)		Annual rate of increase Taux d'accrois sement annuel 2010-15	Surface area Superficie (km²) 2015	Density Densité 2015[b]
		Both sexes Les deux sexes	Male Masculin	Female Feminin		2010	2015			
AMERICA, SOUTH - AMÉRIQUE DU SUD										
Chile - Chili										
24 IV 2002	DF	15 116 435	7 447 695	7 668 740	DF	17 094	18 006	1.0	756 102	24
Colombia - Colombie										
22 V 2005	DF	41 468 384	20 336 117	21 132 267	DJ	45 510[55]	48 203[55]	1.2	1 141 748	42
Ecuador - Équateur										
28 XI 2010	DF	14 483 499	7 177 683	7 305 816	DF	15 012[56]	16 279[56]	1.6	257 217	63
Falkland Islands (Malvinas) - Îles Falkland (Malvinas)[57]										
15 IV 2012	DF	2 840[58]	1 491[58]	1 349[58]		...	...	...	12 173	...
French Guiana - Guyane française										
1 I 2013	DJ	244 118	121 653	122 465	DJ	...	*255[17]	...	83 534	3
Guyana										
15 IX 2012	DF	*747 884	*372 547	*375 337	DF	752	742	-0.3	214 969	3
Paraguay										
28 VIII 2002	DF	5 163 198	2 603 242	2 559 956	DF	6 451[26]	...	...	406 752	...
Peru - Pérou										
21 X 2007	DF	27 412 157	13 622 640	13 789 517	DF	29 462[59]	31 152[59]	1.1	1 285 216	24
Suriname										
13 VIII 2012	DJ	541 638	270 629	271 009	DJ	531	...	...	163 820	...
Uruguay										
4 X 2011	DJ	3 286 314	1 577 725[60]	1 708 481[60]	DJ	3 397	3 467[2]	0.4	173 626	20
Venezuela (Bolivarian Republic of) - Venezuela (République bolivarienne du)										
1 IX 2011	DJ	27 227 930	13 549 752	13 678 178	DF	28 524	30 620	1.4	912 050	34
ASIA - ASIE										
Afghanistan										
23 VI 1979	DF	13 051 358[61]	6 712 377[61]	6 338 981[61]	DF	24 486[62]	...	...	652 864	...
Armenia - Arménie										
12 X 2011	DF	2 871 771	1 346 729	1 525 042	DJ	3 256	3 011[17]	-1.6	29 743	101
Azerbaijan - Azerbaïdjan										
13 IV 2009	DJ	8 922 447	4 414 398	4 508 049	DF	9 054	9 593[17]	1.2	86 600	111
Bahrain - Bahreïn										
27 IV 2010	DJ	1 234 571	768 414	466 157	DJ	1 229	...	...	771	...
Bangladesh										
15 III 2011	DF	144 043 697	72 109 796	71 933 901	DF	148 620	...	...	147 570	...
Bhutan - Bhoutan										
30 V 2005	DF	634 982	333 595	301 387	DF	696[63]	757[63]	1.7	38 394	20
Brunei Darussalam - Brunéi Darussalam										
20 VI 2011	DJ	393 372	203 144	190 228	...	387[35]	*417	...	5 765	72
Cambodia - Cambodge										
3 III 2008	DF	13 395 682[64]	6 516 054[64]	6 879 628[64]	DF	14 303[65]	15 405[65]	1.5	181 035	85
China - Chine										
1 XI 2010	DJ	1 339 724 852[66]	686 852 572[66]	652 872 280[66]	DF	1 337 700[67]	1 371 220[67]	0.5	9 600 000	143
China, Hong Kong SAR - Chine, Hong Kong RAS										
30 VI 2011	DJ	7 071 576[68]	3 303 015[68]	3 768 561[68]	DJ	7 024	7 306	0.8	1 106	6 607
China, Macao SAR - Chine, Macao RAS										
12 VIII 2011	DF	625 674	305 398	320 276	DJ	537	643	3.6	30[69]	21 430
Cyprus - Chypre										
1 X 2011	DJ	840 407[70]	408 780[70]	431 627[70]	DJ	829[71]	*847[72]	0.4	9 251	92
Democratic People's Republic of Korea - République populaire démocratique de Corée										
1 X 2008	DJ	24 052 231	11 721 838	12 330 393		...	...	...	120 538	...

3. Population by sex, annual rate of population increase, surface area and density
Population selon le sexe, taux d'accroissement annuel de la population, superficie et densité (continued - suite)

Continent, country or area and census date / Continent, pays ou zone et date du recensement	Census type[a]	Population at the latest available census / Population d'après le dernier recensement disponible (in units — en unités)			Estimate type[a]	Mid-year estimates / Estimations au milieu de l'année (in thousands — en milliers)		Annual rate of increase Taux d' accrois sement annuel 2010-15	Surface area Superficie (km²) 2015	Density Densité 2015[b]
		Both sexes Les deux sexes	Male Masculin	Female Feminin		2010	2015			
ASIA - ASIE										
Georgia - Géorgie										
5 XI 2014 .... DJ	DJ	3 713 804	1 772 864	1 940 940	...	4 453	3 730[17]	...	69 700	54
India - Inde										
9 II 2011 .... DF	DF	1 210 854 977[73]	623 270 258[73]	587 584 719[73]	DF	1 182 105[74]	...	...	3 287 263	...
Indonesia - Indonésie										
1 V 2010 .... DJ	DJ	237 641 326	119 630 913	118 010 413	DJ	238 519	255 462	1.4	1 910 931	134
Iran (Islamic Republic of) - Iran (République islamique d')										
24 X 2011 .... DJ	DJ	75 149 669	37 905 669	37 244 000	DJ	74 340[75]	78 773[75]	1.2	1 628 750[76]	48
Iraq										
16 X 1997 .... DF	DF	19 184 543[77]	9 536 570[77]	9 647 973[77]	DF	32 211	36 659	2.6	435 052	84
Israel - Israël										
27 XII 2008 .... DF	DF	7 412 180[78]	3 663 910[78]	3 748 270[78]	DJ	7 624[79]	...	...	22 072	...
Japan - Japon										
1 X 2015 .... DJ	DJ	*127 110 047	*61 829 237	*65 280 810	DJ	128 070[80]	126 958[80]	-0.2	377 930[81]	336
Jordan - Jordanie										
30 X 2015 .... DF	DF	9 531 712[82]	5 046 822[82]	4 484 890[82]	DF	6 699[83]	9 532[83]	7.1	89 318	107
Kazakhstan										
25 II 2009 .... DF	DF	16 009 597	7 712 224	8 297 373	DF	16 322	...	...	2 724 902	...
Kuwait - Koweït										
21 IV 2011 .... DF	DF	3 065 850	1 738 372	1 327 478	DF	2 933	3 971	6.1	17 818	223
Kyrgyzstan - Kirghizstan										
24 III 2009 .... DJ	DJ	5 362 793	2 645 921	2 716 872	...	5 193[84]	5 957[85]	...	199 949	30
Lao People's Democratic Republic - République démocratique populaire lao										
1 III 2015 .... DJ	DJ	6 492 400	3 254 800	3 237 600	DF	6 230[86]	...	...	236 800	...
Lebanon - Liban										
1 X 2011 .... SDF	SDF	3 779 859[87]	1 840 940[87]	1 938 919[87]		...	...	...	10 452	...
Malaysia - Malaisie										
6 VII 2010 .... DJ	DJ	28 334 135[88]	14 562 638[88]	13 771 497[88]	DJ	28 589[89]	30 996[89]	1.6	330 323	94
Maldives										
20 IX 2014 .... DF	DF	402 071[90]	227 749[90]	174 322[90]	DF	320	348	1.7	300	1 159
Mongolia - Mongolie										
11 XI 2010 .... DF	DF	2 647 199	1 314 246	1 332 953	DF	2 739	3 027	2.0	1 564 116	2
Myanmar										
29 III 2014 .... DF	DF	50 279 900[91]	24 228 714[91]	26 051 186[91]	DF	59 780[92]	...	...	676 577	...
Nepal - Népal										
22 VI 2011 .... DJ	DJ	26 494 504	12 849 041	13 645 463	DJ	28 044	28 038[19]	0.0	147 181	190
Oman										
12 XII 2010 .... DF	DF	2 773 479	1 612 408	1 161 071		...	...	...	309 500	...
Pakistan										
2 III 1998 .... DF	DF	130 579 571[93]	67 840 137[93]	62 739 434[93]	DF	173 510[93]	191 710[93]	2.0	796 095	241
Philippines										
1 VIII 2015 .... DJ	DJ	100 979 303[94]	...	...	DJ	93 135[29]	101 562[29]	1.7	300 000	339
Qatar										
21 IV 2010 .... DF	DF	1 699 435	1 284 739	414 696	DF	1 715	...	...	11 607	...
Republic of Korea - République de Corée										
1 XI 2010 .... DJ	DJ	48 580 293[95]	24 167 098[95]	24 413 195[95]	DJ	49 410	50 617[2]	0.5	100 284	505
Saudi Arabia - Arabie saoudite										
27 IV 2010 .... DF	DF	*27 136 977	*15 306 793	*11 830 184	DF	*27 563[96]	*31 016[96]	2.4	2 206 714	14
Singapore - Singapour										
30 VI 2010 .... DJ	DJ	3 771 721[97]	1 861 133[97]	1 910 588[97]	DJ	5 077[98]	5 535[98]	1.7	719[99]	7 698
Sri Lanka										
27 II 2012 .... DJ	DJ	20 359 439	9 856 634	10 502 805	DF	20 675	20 966	0.3	65 610	320
State of Palestine - État de Palestine										
1 XII 2007 .... DF	DF	3 669 244[100]	1 862 027[100]	1 807 217[100]	DF	4 048	4 682	2.9	6 020	778
Syrian Arab Republic - République arabe syrienne										
22 IX 2004 .... DF	DF	*17 921 000[101]	*9 161 000[101]	*8 760 000[101]	DF	20 619[101]	...	...	185 180	...

3. Population by sex, annual rate of population increase, surface area and density
Population selon le sexe, taux d'accroissement annuel de la population, superficie et densité (continued - suite)

Continent, country or area and census date / Continent, pays ou zone et date du recensement	Census type[a]	Population at the latest available census / Population d'après le dernier recensement disponible (in units — en unités)			Estimate type[a]	Mid-year estimates / Estimations au milieu de l'année (in thousands — en milliers)		Annual rate of increase / Taux d'accroissement annuel 2010-15	Surface area Superficie (km²) 2015	Density Densité 2015[b]
		Both sexes / Les deux sexes	Male / Masculin	Female / Feminin		2010	2015			
ASIA - ASIE										
Tajikistan - Tadjikistan										
21 IX 2010	DF	7 564 502	3 817 004	3 747 498	DF	7 519	*8 440	2.3	142 600	59
Thailand - Thaïlande										
1 IX 2010	DJ	65 981 659	32 355 032	33 626 627	DJ	67 312[2]	...	...	513 120	...
Timor-Leste										
11 VII 2015	DF	*1 167 242	*588 561	*578 681		...	...	...	14 919	...
Turkey - Turquie										
3 X 2011	DJ	74 526 000[102]	37 431 000[102]	37 095 000[102]	...	73 142	77 738[103]	...	783 562	99
Turkmenistan - Turkménistan										
15 XII 2012	DF	4 750 120	2 332 005	2 418 115			...	...	488 100	...
United Arab Emirates - Émirats arabes unis										
5 XII 2005	DF	4 106 427[104]	2 806 141[104]	1 300 286[104]	DF	8 264[104]	...	...	83 600	...
Uzbekistan - Ouzbékistan										
12 I 1989	DJ	19 810 077	9 784 156	10 025 921	DJ	28 562[105]	...	...	448 969	...
Viet Nam										
1 IV 2009	DJ	85 846 997	42 413 143	43 433 854	DF	86 933	91 713	1.1	330 967	277
Yemen - Yémen										
16 XII 2004	DF	19 685 161	10 036 953	9 648 208	DJ	23 154[2]	...	...	527 968	...
EUROPE										
Åland Islands - Îles d'Åland										
31 XII 2000	DJ	25 776[106]	12 700[106]	13 076[106]	DJ	28[39]	29[39]	0.8	1 581	18
Albania - Albanie										
1 X 2011	DJ	2 800 138	1 403 059	1 397 079	DF	2 913	2 889	-0.2	28 748	100
Andorra - Andorre										
31 XII 2000	DJ	65 844[39]	34 268[39]	31 576[39]	DJ	85[39]	...	...	468	...
Austria - Autriche										
31 X 2011	DJ	8 401 940	4 093 938	4 308 002	DJ	8 361	8 576[17]	0.5	83 871	102
Belarus - Bélarus										
14 X 2009	DJ	9 503 807	4 420 039	5 083 768	DJ	9 491	9 481[17]	0.0	207 600	46
Belgium - Belgique										
1 I 2011	DJ	11 000 638	5 401 718	5 598 920	DJ	10 896	11 258[17]	0.7	30 528	369
Bosnia and Herzegovina - Bosnie-Herzégovine										
30 IX 2013	DJ	*3 791 622	...	...	DF	3 843	...	...	51 209	...
Bulgaria - Bulgarie										
1 II 2011	DJ	7 364 570	3 586 571	3 777 999	DJ	7 534	7 202[17]	-0.9	111 002	65
Croatia - Croatie										
1 IV 2011	DJ	4 284 889	2 066 335	2 218 554	DJ	4 295	4 225[17]	-0.3	56 594	75
Czech Republic - République tchèque										
25 III 2011	DJ	10 436 560	5 109 766	5 326 794	DJ	10 474	*10 543	0.1	78 868	134
Denmark - Danemark[107]										
1 I 2011	DJ	5 560 628[39]	2 756 582[39]	2 804 046[39]	DJ	5 545[39]	5 678[39]	0.5	42 921	132
Estonia - Estonie										
31 XII 2011	DJ	1 294 455	600 526	693 929	DJ	1 331	1 313[17]	-0.3	45 227	29
Faeroe Islands - Îles Féroé										
11 XI 2011	DJ	48 346	25 125	23 221	DJ	49	49	0.1	1 393	35
Finland - Finlande										
31 XII 2010	DJ	5 375 276	2 638 416	2 736 860	DJ	5 335[108]	5 472[109]	0.5	336 859[110]	16
France										
1 I 2006	DJ	61 399 541[111]	29 714 539[111]	31 685 002[111]	DJ	62 918[111]	*64 395[111]	0.5	551 500	117
Germany - Allemagne										
9 V 2011	DJ	80 219 695	39 145 941	41 073 754	DJ	81 757	81 198[112]	-0.1	357 376	227
Gibraltar										
12 XI 2012	DJ	32 194[113]	16 061[113]	16 133[113]	DF	31[114]	...	...	6	...
Greece - Grèce										
9 V 2011	DF	10 816 286	5 303 223	5 513 063	DF	11 121	10 858[17]	-0.5	131 957	82
Guernsey - Guernesey										
31 III 2015	DJ	62 612	31 028	31 584	DF	62[115]	...	...	64	...

3. Population by sex, annual rate of population increase, surface area and density
Population selon le sexe, taux d'accroissement annuel de la population, superficie et densité (continued - suite)

Continent, country or area and census date / Continent, pays ou zone et date du recensement	Census type[a]	Population at the latest available census / Population d'après le dernier recensement disponible (in units — en unités)			Estimate type[a]	Mid-year estimates / Estimations au milieu de l'année (in thousands — en milliers)		Annual rate of increase / Taux d' accrois sement annuel 2010-15	Surface area / Superficie (km²) 2015	Density / Densité 2015[b]
		Both sexes / Les deux sexes	Male / Masculin	Female / Féminin		2010	2015			
EUROPE										
Holy See - Saint-Siège[116]										
1 VII 2000 .... DF		798[117]	529[117]	269[117]	DF	0[118]	...	...	0[119]	...
Hungary - Hongrie										
1 X 2011 .... DF		9 937 628	4 718 479	5 219 149	DJ	10 000	*9 843[120]	-0.3	93 024	106
Iceland - Islande										
31 XII 2011 .... DJ		315 556[121]	158 151[121]	157 405[121]	DJ	318[121]	329[122]	0.7	103 000	3
Ireland - Irlande										
24 IV 2016 .... DF		*4 757 976	...	...	...	4 560	4 635[123]	...	69 797	66
Isle of Man - Île de Man										
27 III 2011 .... DJ		84 497	41 971	42 526	DJ	83[124]	87[124]	1.0	572	152
Italy - Italie										
9 X 2011 .... DJ		59 433 744	28 745 507	30 688 237	DJ	59 277	60 796[17]	0.5	302 073	201
Jersey										
27 III 2011 .... DF		97 857	48 296	49 561	DJ	97	103	1.1	116	885
Latvia - Lettonie										
1 III 2011 .... DJ		2 070 371	946 102	1 124 269	DJ	2 098	1 986[17]	-1.1	64 573	31
Liechtenstein										
31 XII 2010 .... DF		36 149	17 886	18 263	DJ	36	37[125]	0.8	160	234
Lithuania - Lituanie										
1 III 2011 .... DJ		3 043 429	1 402 604	1 640 825	DJ	3 097	...	...	65 286	...
Luxembourg										
1 II 2011 .... DJ		512 353	254 967	257 386	DJ	507	563[17]	2.1	2 586	218
Malta - Malte										
20 XI 2011 .... DF		417 432	207 625	209 807	DJ	415[126]	429[127]	0.7	315	1 361
Monaco										
9 VI 2008 .... DJ		31 109	15 076[128]	15 914[128]	DJ	36	...	...	2	...
Montenegro - Monténégro										
1 IV 2011 .... DJ		620 029	306 236	313 793	DJ	617	622[120]	0.2	13 812	45
Netherlands - Pays-Bas										
1 I 2011 .... DJ		16 655 799	8 243 482	8 412 317	DJ	16 615	16 940	0.4	41 542	408
Norway - Norvège										
19 XI 2011 .... DJ		4 979 955[129]	2 495 777[129]	2 484 178[129]	DJ	4 889[120]	5 166[130]	1.1	323 772	16
Poland - Pologne										
31 III 2011 .... DJ		38 044 565[131]	18 420 389[131]	19 624 176[131]	DJ	38 517[120]	38 006[130]	-0.3	312 679	122
Portugal										
21 III 2011 .... DF		10 282 306	4 868 755	5 413 551	DJ	10 573	10 375[17]	-0.4	92 226	112
Republic of Moldova - République de Moldova										
5 X 2004 .... DF		3 386 673[132]	1 629 689[132]	1 756 984[132]	DJ	3 562[132]	3 555[133]	0.0	33 846	105
Romania - Roumanie										
20 X 2011 .... DF		20 039 141	9 736 342	10 302 799	DJ	20 247	19 871[17]	-0.4	238 391	83
Russian Federation - Fédération de Russie										
14 X 2010 .... DF		143 436 145	66 457 074	76 979 071	DJ	142 849	...	...	17 098 246	...
San Marino - Saint-Marin										
7 XI 2010 .... DF		*30 652	*14 791[134]	*15 818[134]	DF	33[39]	34[109]	0.3	61	553
Serbia - Serbie										
1 X 2011 .... DJ		7 186 862[135]	3 499 176[135]	3 687 686[135]	DJ	7 291[135]	7 114[136]	-0.5	88 499[137]	80
Slovakia - Slovaquie										
21 V 2011 .... DJ		5 397 036	2 627 772	2 769 264	DJ	5 391	5 421[17]	0.1	49 035[138]	111
Slovenia - Slovénie										
1 I 2011 .... DF		2 058 051	1 019 826	1 038 225	DJ	2 049	2 063	0.1	20 273	102
Spain - Espagne										
1 XI 2011 .... DJ		46 815 915	23 104 350	23 711 560	DJ	46 562	46 450[122]	0.0	505 944	92
Svalbard and Jan Mayen Islands - Îles Svalbard et Jan Mayen										
1 XI 1960 .... DF		3 431[139]	2 545[139]	886[139]		...	...	...	62 422	...
Sweden - Suède										
31 XII 2011 .... DJ		9 482 855[39]	4 726 834[39]	4 756 021[39]	DJ	9 378[39]	9 747[140]	0.8	438 574	22
Switzerland - Suisse										
31 XII 2011 .... DF		8 035 391	3 973 280	4 062 111	DJ	7 825	8 238[141]	1.0	41 291	200

3. Population by sex, annual rate of population increase, surface area and density
Population selon le sexe, taux d'accroissement annuel de la population, superficie et densité (continued - suite)

Continent, country or area and census date / Continent, pays ou zone et date du recensement	Census type[a]	Population at the latest available census / Population d'après le dernier recensement disponible (in units — en unités)			Estimate type[a]	Mid-year estimates / Estimations au milieu de l'année (in thousands — en milliers)		Annual rate of increase / Taux d' accrois sement annuel 2010-15	Surface area / Superficie (km²) 2015	Density / Densité 2015[b]
		Both sexes / Les deux sexes	Male / Masculin	Female / Feminin		2010	2015			
EUROPE										
TFYR of Macedonia - L'ex-R. y. de Macédoine										
31 X 2002 .... DJ		2 022 547	1 015 377	1 007 170	DF	2 055	2 069[17]	0.1	25 713	80
Ukraine										
5 XII 2001 .... DF		48 240 902	22 316 317	25 924 585	DF	45 871	*42 760[142]	-1.4	603 500	71
United Kingdom of Great Britain and Northern Ireland - Royaume-Uni de Grande-Bretagne et d'Irlande du Nord[143]										
27 III 2011 .... DF		63 379 787	31 126 054	32 253 733	DJ	62 759	64 875[130]	0.7	242 495	268
OCEANIA - OCÉANIE										
American Samoa - Samoas américaines										
1 IV 2010 .... DJ		55 519[46]	28 164[46]	27 355[46]	DJ	67[46]	61[46]	-2.0	199	306
Australia - Australie										
9 VIII 2011 .... DF		21 727 158[144]	10 737 148[144]	10 990 010[144]	DJ	22 032[35]	*23 778[16]	1.5	7 692 024	3
Cook Islands - Îles Cook[145]										
1 XII 2011 .... DF		17 794	8 815	8 979	DF	24	*19	-4.6	236	80
Fiji - Fidji										
16 IX 2007 .... DF		837 271	427 176	410 095	DF	857	867[146]	0.2	18 272	47
French Polynesia - Polynésie française										
22 VIII 2012 .... DJ		268 207	136 996	131 211	DF	265	272	0.5	4 000	68
Guam										
1 IV 2010 .... DJ		159 358	81 552	77 806	DJ	...	162[46]	...	549	295
Kiribati										
10 X 2010 .... DF		103 058	50 796	52 262		...	...	...	726[147]	...
Marshall Islands - Îles Marshall										
3 IV 2011 .... DF		53 158	27 243	25 915	DF	54[148]	...	...	181	...
Micronesia (Federated States of) - Micronésie (États fédérés de)										
1 IV 2010 .... DJ		102 843	52 193	50 650	DJ	108[2]	106[2]	-0.4	702	151
Nauru										
31 X 2011 .... DF		*10 086	*5 105	*4 979		...	...	...	21	...
New Caledonia - Nouvelle-Calédonie										
26 VIII 2014 .... DF		268 767	...	...	DF	250	...	...	18 575	...
New Zealand - Nouvelle-Zélande										
5 III 2013 .... DJ		4 242 048	...	...	DJ	4 351[149]	4 596[149]	1.1	268 107	17
Niue - Nioué										
11 IX 2011 .... DF		1 611	802	809	DJ	1	...	...	260	...
Norfolk Island - Île Norfolk										
9 VIII 2011 .... DF		2 302	1 082	1 220		...	...	...	36	...
Northern Mariana Islands - Îles Mariannes septentrionales										
1 IV 2010 .... DF		53 883	27 746	26 137	DF	48	...	...	457	...
Palau - Palaos										
13 IV 2015 .... DJ		17 661	9 433	8 228	DF	21	...	...	459	...
Papua New Guinea - Papouasie-Nouvelle-Guinée										
10 VII 2011 .... DF		*7 059 653	*3 663 249	*3 396 404		...	...	...	462 840	...
Pitcairn										
31 XII 2013 .... DJ		49	23	26		...	...	...	5	...
Samoa										
7 XI 2011 .... DF		187 820	96 990	90 830	DF	184	...	...	2 842	...

3. Population by sex, annual rate of population increase, surface area and density
Population selon le sexe, taux d'accroissement annuel de la population, superficie et densité (continued - suite)

Continent, country or area and census date / Continent, pays ou zone et date du recensement	Census type[a]	Population at the latest available census / Population d'après le dernier recensement disponible (in units — en unités)			Estimate type[a]	Mid-year estimates / Estimations au milieu de l'année (in thousands — en milliers)		Annual rate of increase / Taux d' accrois sement annuel 2010-15	Surface area / Superficie (km²) 2015	Density / Densité 2015[b]
		Both sexes / Les deux sexes	Male / Masculin	Female / Feminin		2010	2015			
OCEANIA - OCÉANIE										
Solomon Islands - Îles Salomon										
22 XI 2009 .... DF	DF	515 870	264 455	251 415	DF	*531*[2]	...	...	28 896	...
Tokelau - Tokélaou										
18 X 2011 .... DF	DF	1 205	600	605		...	...	...	12	...
Tonga										
30 XI 2011 .... DJ	DJ	103 252	51 979	51 273		...	...	...	747	...
Tuvalu										
4 XI 2012 .... DF	DF	10 782	...	...		...	...	...	26	...
Vanuatu										
16 XI 2009 .... DJ	DJ	234 023	119 091	114 932	DF	*239*	...	...	12 189	...
Wallis and Futuna Islands - Îles Wallis et Futuna										
22 VII 2013 .... DF	DF	12 197	...	...		...	...	...	142	...

FOOTNOTES - NOTES

Italics: estimates which are less reliable. - Italiques : estimations moins sûres.

* Provisional. - Données provisoires.

[a] 'Code' indicates the source of data, as follows:
DF - De facto
DJ - De jure
SDF - Sample survey, de facto
SDJ - Sample survey, de jure

Le 'Code' indique la source des données, comme suit :
DF - Population de fait
DJ - Population de droit
SDF - Enquête par sondage, population de fait
SDJ - Enquête par sondage, Population de droit

[b] Population per square kilometre of surface area. Figures are estimates of population divided by surface area and are not to be considered either as reflecting density in the urban sense or as indicating the supporting power of a territory's land and resources. - Nombre d'habitants au kilomètre carré. Il s'agit simplement d'éstimations de la population divisé par celui de la superficie: il ne faut pas y voir d'indication de la densité au sens urbain du terme ni de l'effectif de population que les terres et les ressources du territoire sont capables de nourrir.

[1] Total resident population including common and collective households of nomadic population, and population counted separately. - Population résidente totale y compris les ménages ordinaires et collectifs de la population nomade, et la population comptée à part.
[2] Data refer to national projections. - Les données se réfèrent aux projections nationales.
[3] Data refer to projections based on the 2013 Population Census. - Les données se réfèrent aux projections basées sur le recensement de la population de 2013.
[4] Data based on the 2011 Census. - Données fondées sur le recensement de 2011.
[5] Data based on the 2008 Population Census. - Données fondées sur le recensement de population de 2008.
[6] Data refer to national projections. Data refer to 1 January. - Les données se réfèrent aux projections nationales. Données se raportent au 1 janvier.
[7] Excluding Mayotte. - Non compris Mayotte.
[8] Data are calculated from the results of the Population and Housing Census of 2009. - Les données sont calculées à partir des résultats du recensement de la population et de l'habitat de 2009.
[9] Data refer to projections based on the 1983 Population Census. - Les données se réfèrent aux projections basées sur le recensement de la population de 1983.

[10] Estimates considering also 2007 Population Census results. - Estimations en prennant en considération les résultats du recensement de la population de 2007.
[11] Revised data. Data refer to national projections. - Données révisées. Les données se réfèrent aux projections nationales.
[12] Projections considering also 2009 Population Census results. - Projections en prennant en considération les résultats du recensement de la population de 2009.
[13] Including nomadic population. - Y compris la population nomade.
[14] Excludes the islands of St. Brandon and Agalega. - Non compris les îles St. Brandon et Agalega.
[15] Based on the results of the 2000 Population Census. - Basé sur les résultats du recencement de la population de 2000.
[16] Based on the results of the 2011 Population Census. - Basé sur les résultats du recensement de la population de 2011.
[17] Data refer to 1 January. - Données se raportent au 1 janvier.
[18] Based on the results of the 2004 Population Census. - D'après des résultats du recensement de la population de 2004.
[19] Data refer to projections based on the 2011 Population Census. - Les données se réfèrent aux projections basées sur le recensement de la population de 2011.
[20] Data are projections based on the 2012 Population and Housing Census. - Projection basée sur le recensement 2012 de la population et des logements.
[21] Data are projections based on the 2008 Population and Housing Census. - Projection basée sur le recensement 2008 de la population et des logements.
[22] Projections based on the 2012 Population Census. - Projections fondées sur le recensement de la population de 2012.
[23] Data refer to 31 December. - Données se raportent au 31 décembre.
[24] Surface area is based on the 2002 population and housing census. - La superficie est fondée sur les données provenant du recensement de la population et du logement de 2002.
[25] Data have not been adjusted for underenumeration, estimated at 7 per cent. - Les données n'ont pas été ajustées pour compenser les lacunes du dénombrement, estimées à 7 p. 100.
[26] Projections based on the 2002 Population Census. - Projections fondées sur le recensement de la population de 2002.
[27] Comprising the Northern Region (former Saguia el Hamra) and Southern Region (former Rio de Oro). - Comprend la région septentrionale (ancien Saguia-el-Hamra) et la région méridionale (ancien Rio de Oro).
[28] Bermuda is 100 per cent urban. - 100 pour cent de la population des Bermudes est urbaine.
[29] Data refer to projections based on the 2010 Population Census. - Les données se réfèrent aux projections basées sur le recensement de la population de 2010.
[30] Final intercensal estimates. - Estimations inter-censitaires definitives.
[31] Updated postcensal estimates. - Estimations post censitaires mises à jour.
[32] Excluding the institutional population. - Non compris la population dans les institutions.

[33] Based on the national household surveys 2010-2014 and the 2011 population census. - D'après les données de l'enquête nationale des ménages 2010-2014 et les résultats du recensement de la population de 2011.

[34] Based on the national household survey of 2015. - Basée sur l' enquête nationale auprès des ménages de 2015.

[35] Intercensal estimates. - Estimations inter-censitaires.

[36] Postcensal estimates. - Estimations post censitaires.

[37] Estimates based on the 2007 Population Census. - Estimations fondées sur le recensement de la population de 2007.

[38] The total surface is 21040.79 square kilometers, without taking into account the last ruling of The Hague. - La superficie totale est égale à 21040.79 km2, sans tenir compte de la dernière décision de la Haye.

[39] Population statistics are compiled from registers. - Les statistiques de la population sont compilées à partir des registres.

[40] Excluding data for Saint Barthélémy and Saint Martin. - Non compris les données pour Saint Barthélémy et Saint Martin.

[41] Excluding data for Saint Barthélémy and Saint Martin. Data refer to 1 January. - Non compris les données pour Saint Barthélémy et Saint Martin. Données se raportent au 1 janvier.

[42] Projections produced by l'Institut Haïtien de Statistique et d'Informatique (IHSI) and the Latin American and Caribbean Demographic Centre (CELADE) - Population Division of ECLAC. - Les données sont projections produits par l'Institut Haïtien de Statistique et d'Informatique (IHSI) et le centre démographique de l'Amérique latine et les Caraïbes - Division de la population de la CEPALC.

[43] Data refer to projections based on the 2001 Population Census. - Les données se réfèrent aux projections basées sur le recensement de la population de 2001.

[44] The figures represent the census counts adjusted for under-coverage. Adjustments are done by applying weights calculated (to 4 decimal places) for each sex and age group to the enumerated population when the tabulations are produced. Minor discrepancies between totals and the sum of the component parts of a table and minor discrepancies between the totals across tables are due to rounding after weights are applied. - Les chiffres représentent le dénombrement résultant du recensement ajusté pour tenir compte du sous-dénombrement. Les ajustements sont effectués en appliquant un coefficient de pondération calculé (à la quatrième décimale) pour chaque sexe et groupe d'âges de la population dénombrée lors de l'établissement des tableaux. Les écarts mineurs entre les totaux et la somme des éléments constitutifs d'un tableau ainsi qu'entre les totaux figurant dans différents tableaux sont dus au fait que les chiffres sont arrondis après la pondération.

[45] Including an estimation of 1 334 585 persons corresponding to 448 195 housing units without information of the occupants. - Y compris une estimation de 1 334 585 personnes correspondant aux 448 195 unités d'habitation sans information sur les occupants.

[46] Including armed forces stationed in the area. - Y compris les militaires en garnison sur le territoire.

[47] Including armed forces stationed in the area. Based on the results of the 2010 Population Census. - Y compris les militaires en garnison sur le territoire. D'après le résultats du recensement de la population de 2010.

[48] Refers to habitable area. Excludes St. Lucia's Forest Reserve. - S'applique à la zone habitable. Exclut la réserve forestière de Sainte-Lucie.

[49] Including low water level for all islands (area to shoreline). - Incluent le niveau de basses eaux pour toutes les îles.

[50] Excluding U.S. Armed Forces overseas and civilian U.S. citizens whose usual place of residence is outside the United States. Postcensal estimates. - Non compris les militaires américains à l'étranger et les civils américains dont le lieu de résidence habituel est en dehors des États-Unis. Estimations post censitaires.

[51] Including armed forces stationed in the area. Source: U.S. National Center for Health Statistics, National Vital Statistics Reports (NVSR). - Y compris les militaires en garnison sur le territoire. Source : US National Center for Health Statistics, National Vital Statistics Reports (NVSR).

[52] Data refer to projections based on the 2010 Population and Housing Census. - Les données se réfèrent aux projections basées sur le recensement 2010 de la population et des logements.

[53] Data updated according to "Superintendencia Agraria". Interior waters correspond to natural or artificial bodies of water or snow. - Données actualisées d'après la « Superintendencia Agraria ». Les eaux intérieures correspondent aux étendues d'eau naturelles ou artificielles et aux étendues neigeuses.

[54] Data include persons in remote areas, military personnel outside the country, merchant seamen at sea, civilian seasonal workers outside the country, and other civilians outside the country, and exclude nomads, foreign military, civilian aliens temporarily in the country, transients on ships and Indian jungle population. Data refer to national projections. - Y compris les personnes vivant dans des régions éloignées, le personel militaire en dehors du pays, les marins marchands, les ouvriers saisonniers en dehors du pays, et autres civils en dehors du pays, et non compris les nomades, les militaires étrangers, les étrangers civils temporairement dans le pays, les transiteurs sur des bateaux et les Indiens de la jungle. Les données se réfèrent aux projections nationales.

[55] Data are revised projections taking into consideration also the results of the 2005 census. - Les données sont des projections révisées tenant compte également des résultats du recensement de 2005.

[56] Data refer to projections based on the 2010 Population Census. Excludes nomadic Indian tribes. - Les données se réfèrent aux projections basées sur le recensement de 2010. Non compris les tribus d'Indiens nomades.

[57] A dispute exists between the governments of Argentina and the United Kingdom of Great Britain and Northern Ireland concerning sovereignty over the Falkland Islands (Malvinas). - La souveraineté sur les îles Falkland (Malvinas) fait l'objet d'un différend entre le Gouvernement argentin et le Gouvernement du Royaume-Uni de Grande-Bretagne et d'Irlande du Nord.

[58] Excluding military personnel and their families, visitors and transients. - Non compris les militaires et leur familles, ni les visiteurs et transients.

[59] Data refer to 30 June. Estimates based on the 2007 Population Census. - Données se raportent au 30 juin. Estimations fondées sur le recensement de la population de 2007.

[60] Figures for male and female population do not add up to the figure for total population, because they exclude 108 homeless people of unknown sex. - Les chiffres relatifs à la population masculine et féminine ne correspondent pas au chiffre de la population totale, parce que l'on en a exclu 108 personnes sans toit dont le sexe n'est pas connu.

[61] Data refer to the settled population based on the 1979 Population Census and the latest household prelisting. The refugees of Afghanistan in Iran, Pakistan, and an estimated 1.5 million nomads, are not included. Excluding nomad population. - Les données se rapportent à la population stationnaire sur la base du recensement de 1979 et du recensement préliminaire des logements le plus récent. Sont exclus les réfugiés d'Afghanistan en Iran et au Pakistan et les nomades estimés à 1,5 million. Non compris les nomades.

[62] Data refer to the settled population based on the 1979 Population Census and the latest household prelisting. The refugees of Afghanistan in Iran, Pakistan, and an estimated 1.5 million nomads, are not included. - Les données se rapportent à la population stationnaire sur la base du recensement de 1979 et du recensement préliminaire des logements le plus récent. Sont exclus les réfugiés d'Afghanistan en Iran et au Pakistan et les nomades estimés à 1,5 million.

[63] Data refer to projected figures based on the Population and Housing Census 2005 (district projection). - Les données se réfèrent aux projections basées sur le recensement de la population et de l'habitat de 2005 (projections locales).

[64] Excluding foreign diplomatic personnel and their dependants. - Non compris le personnel diplomatique étranger et les membres de leur famille les accompagnant.

[65] Excluding foreign diplomatic personnel and their dependants. Data based on the 2008 Population Census. - Non compris le personnel diplomatique étranger et les membres de leur famille les accompagnant. Données fondées sur le recensement de population de 2008.

[66] Data are from Communique of the National Bureau of Statistics of the People's Republic of China on Major Figures of the 2010 Population Census (No.1). For statistical purposes, the data for China do not include those for the Hong Kong Special Administrative Region (Hong Kong SAR), Macao Special Administrative Region (Macao SAR) and Taiwan province of China. - Données issues du communiqué du Bureau national de la statistique de la République populaire de Chine sur les chiffres importants du recensement de 2010 (n° 1). Pour la présentation des statistiques, les données pour la Chine ne comprennent pas la Région Administrative Spéciale de Hong Kong (Hong Kong RAS), la Région Administrative Spéciale de Macao (Macao RAS) et Taïwan province de Chine.

[67] For statistical purposes, the data for China do not include those for the Hong Kong Special Administrative Region (Hong Kong SAR), Macao Special Administrative Region (Macao SAR) and Taiwan province of China. Data have been estimated on the basis of the annual National Sample Survey on Population Changes. - Pour la présentation des statistiques, les données pour la Chine ne comprennent pas la Région Administrative Spéciale de Hong Kong (Hong Kong RAS), la Région Administrative Spéciale de Macao (Macao RAS) et Taïwan province de Chine. Les données ont été estimées sur la base de l'enquête annuelle "National Sample Survey on Population Changes".

[68] Data refer to Hong Kong resident population at the census moment, which covers usual residents and mobile residents. Usual residents refer to two categories of people: (1) Hong Kong permanent residents who had stayed in Hong Kong for at least three months during the six months before or for at least three months during the six months after the census moment, regardless of whether they were in Hong Kong or not at the census moment; and (2) Hong Kong non-permanent residents who were in Hong Kong at the census moment. Mobile Residents, they are Hong Kong permanent residents who had stayed in Hong Kong for at least one month but less than three months during the six

months before or for at least one month but less than three months during the six months after the census moment, regardless of whether they were in Hong Kong or not at the census moment. - Les données se rapportent à la population résidente à Hong Kong au moment du recensement. Cette population est composée des résidants habituels et des résidants mobiles. La population résidente est partagée en deux catégories: (1) les résidents permanents qui ont habité à Hong Kong au moins trois mois pendant les six mois précédents ou les six mois suivants le recensement; (2) les habitants non-permanents de Hong Kong qui étaient à Hong Kong au moment du recensement. La population mobile se rapporte aux résidents permanents de Hong Kong qui ont habité à Hong Kong pendant les six mois après le recensement pour une période comprise entre un mois et trois mois, indépendamment du fait qu'ils étaient à Hong Kong au moment du recensement au pays.

[69] Inland waters include the reservoirs. - Les eaux intérieures comprennent les réservoirs.

[70] Data refer to government controlled areas. - Les données se rapportent aux zones contrôlées par le Gouvernement.

[71] Data refer to government controlled areas. Data refer to annual average population. - Les données se rapportent aux zones contrôlées par le Gouvernement. Les données correspondent à la population annuelle moyenne.

[72] Data refer to government controlled areas. Data refer to 1 January. - Les données se rapportent aux zones contrôlées par le Gouvernement. Données se raportent au 1 janvier.

[73] Includes data for the Indian-held part of Jammu and Kashmir, the final status of which has not yet been determined. - Y compris les données pour la partie du Jammu et du Cachemire occupée par l'Inde dont le statut définitif n'a pas encore été déterminé.

[74] Includes data for the Indian-held part of Jammu and Kashmir, the final status of which has not yet been determined. Data refer to projections based on the 2001 Population Census. - Y compris les données pour la partie du Jammu et du Cachemire occupée par l'Inde dont le statut définitif n'a pas encore été déterminé. Les données se réfèrent aux projections basées sur le recensement de la population de 2001.

[75] Data refer to the Iranian Year which begins on 21 March and ends on 20 March of the following year. - Les données concernent l'année iranienne, qui commence le 21 mars et se termine le 20 mars de l'année suivante.

[76] Land area only. - La superficie des terres seulement.

[77] Excluding the population in three autonomous provinces in the north of the country. - La population des trois provinces autonomes dans le nord du pays est exclue.

[78] Includes data for East Jerusalem and Israeli residents in certain other territories under occupation by Israeli military forces since June 1967. Data are rounded for confidentiality reasons. - Y compris les données pour Jérusalem-Est et les résidents israéliens dans certains autres territoires occupés depuis 1967 par les forces armées israéliennes. Chiffres arrondis pour des raisons de confidentialité.

[79] Includes data for East Jerusalem and Israeli residents in certain other territories under occupation by Israeli military forces since June 1967. - Y compris les données pour Jérusalem-Est et les résidents israéliens dans certains autres territoires occupés depuis 1967 par les forces armées israéliennes.

[80] Excluding diplomatic personnel outside the country and foreign military and civilian personnel and their dependants stationed in the area. Estimates based on the complete counts of the 2010 Population Census. - Non compris le personnel diplomatique hors du pays ni les militaires et agents civils étrangers en poste sur le territoire et les membres de leur famille les accompagnant. Estimations basées sur le dénombrement complet du recensement de la population de 2010.

[81] Data refer to 1 October 2007. - Les données se réfèrent au 1er octobre 2007.

[82] Excluding data for Jordanian territory under occupation since June 1967 by Israeli military forces. - Non compris les données pour le territoire jordanien occupé depuis juin 1967 par les forces armées israéliennes.

[83] Excluding data for Jordanian territory under occupation since June 1967 by Israeli military forces. Data refer to 31 December. - Non compris les données pour le territoire jordanien occupé depuis juin 1967 par les forces armées israéliennes. Données se raportent au 31 décembre.

[84] Data refer to annual average population. Data are calculated from the results of the Population and Housing Census of 2009. - Les données correspondent à la population annuelle moyenne. Les données sont calculées à partir des résultats du recensement de la population et de l'habitat de 2009.

[85] Data refer to annual average population. - Les données correspondent à la population annuelle moyenne.

[86] Data estimated based on the results of 2015 population census. - Estimations fondées sur les résultats du recensement de la population de 2015.

[87] Source: Living conditions of household survey, October 2011 to September 2012. - Source: Enquête sur les conditions de vie des ménages, octobre 2011 à septembre 2012.

[88] Data have been adjusted for underenumeration. - Les données ont été ajustées pour compenser les lacunes du dénombrement.

[89] Estimates based on the adjusted Population and Housing Census of 2010. - Les estimations sont fondée sur les résultats ajustées du recensement de la population et de l'habitat de 2010.

[90] Data refer to resident population that includes Maldivians and foreigners. - Les données concernent la population résidente, qui comprend des Maldiviens et des étrangers.

[91] Data refer to enumerated population. - Les données se rapportent à la population dénombrée.

[92] Data refer to 1 October. - Données se raportent au 1 octobre.

[93] Excluding data for the Pakistan-held part of Jammu and Kashmir, the final status of which has not yet been determined. - Non compris les données concernant la partie du Jammu et Cachemire occupée par le Pakistan dont le statut définitif n'a pas été déterminé.

[94] Excluding 2134 Filipinos in Philippine Embassies, Consulates and Missions Abroad. - Excepté 2134 Philippins travaillant dans les ambassades, les consulats et les missions des Philippines à l'étranger.

[95] Excluding usual residents not in the country at the time of census. - À l'exclusion des résidents habituels qui ne sont pas dans le pays au moment du recensement.

[96] Data based on the preliminary results of the 2010 Population and Housing Census. - D'après les résultats préliminaires du recensement de la population et des logements de 2010.

[97] Data are based on the latest register-based population estimates for 2010. Data refer to resident population which comprises Singapore citizens and permanent residents. Urban and rural breakdown not applicable as Singapore is a city-state. - Données basées sur les estimations démographiques les plus récentes fondées sur les registres de 2010. Les données se rapportent à la population résidente composé des citoyens de Singapour et des résidents permanents. La ventilation entre zones urbaines et zones rurales ne s'applique pas à Singapour, puisqu'il s'agit d'une ville État.

[98] Data refer to total population, which comprises Singapore residents and non-residents. Data refer to 30 June. Data exclude residents who have been away from Singapore for a continuous period of 12 months or longer as at the reference date. - Les données se rapportent à la population totale composé des résidents de Singapour et les non résidents. Données se raportent au 30 juin. Non compris les résidents hors de Singapour pour une période ininterrompue de 12 mois ou plus avant de la date de référence.

[99] The land area of Singapore comprises the mainland and other islands. - La superficie terrestre de Singapour comprend l'île principale et les autres îles.

[100] Data have not been adjusted for underenumeration. - Les données n'ont pas été ajustées pour compenser les lacunes du dénombrement.

[101] Including Palestinian refugees. - Y compris les réfugiés de Palestine.

[102] Because of rounding, totals are not in all cases the sum of the respective components. Based on a sample taken at the time of census. - Les chiffres étant arrondis, les totaux ne correspondent pas toujours rigoureusement à la somme des composants respectifs. D'après un échantillon obtenu au moment du recensement.

[103] Data based on address-based population registration system. - Les données sont basées sur le registre national de la population basé sur l'adresse.

[104] Data include non-national population. - Les données comprennent les non-nationaux.

[105] Data refer to resident population. - Les données concernent la population résidente.

[106] Statistics are compiled from registers. - Les statistiques sont compilées à partir des registres.

[107] Excluding Faeroe Islands and Greenland shown separately, if available. - Non compris les Iles Féroé et le Groenland, qui font l'objet de rubriques distinctes, si disponible.

[108] Population statistics are compiled from registers. Excluding Åland Islands. - Les statistiques de la population sont compilées à partir des registres. Non compris les Îles d'Åland.

[109] Population statistics are compiled from registers. Data refer to 1 January. - Les statistiques de la population sont compilées à partir des registres. Données se raportent au 1 janvier.

[110] Excluding Åland Islands. - Non compris les Îles d'Åland.

[111] Excluding diplomatic personnel outside the country and including members of alien armed forces not living in military camps and foreign diplomatic personnel not living in embassies or consulates. - Non compris le personnel diplomatique hors du pays et y compris les militaires étrangers ne vivant pas dans des camps militaires et le personnel diplomatique étranger ne vivant pas dans les ambassades ou les consulats.

[112] Data refer to 1 January. Data based on the 2011 Census. - Données se raportent au 1 janvier. Données fondées sur le recensement de 2011.

[113] Excluding military personnel, visitors and transients. - Non compris les militaires, ni les visiteurs et transients.

¹¹⁴ Excluding military personnel, visitors and transients. Data refer to 31 December. - Non compris les militaires, ni les visiteurs et transients. Données se raportent au 31 décembre.

¹¹⁵ Data refer to 31 March. - Données se raportent au 31 mars.

¹¹⁶ Data refer to the Vatican City State. - Les données se rapportent à l'Etat de la Cité du Vatican.

¹¹⁷ Population statistics are compiled from registers. Including nationals outside the country. - Les statistiques de la population sont compilées à partir des registres. Y compris les nationaux hors du pays.

¹¹⁸ Data refer to 6 December. The population figure is 466 persons. - Données se raportent au 6 décembre. La population est égale à 466 personnes.

¹¹⁹ Surface area is 0.44 km². - Superficie: 0,44 km².

¹²⁰ Data refer to usually resident population. - Les données concernent la population habituellement résidente.

¹²¹ Data refer to registered resident population. - Les données concernent la population enregistrée résidente.

¹²² Data refer to registered resident population. Data refer to 1 January. - Les données concernent la population enregistrée résidente. Données se raportent au 1 janvier.

¹²³ Data refer to 15 April. Data refer to usually resident population. - Données se raportent au 15 avril. Les données concernent la population habituellement résidente.

¹²⁴ Data refer to 30 April. - Données se raportent au 30 avril.

¹²⁵ Data refer to legal resident population. - Les données concernent la population légalement résidente.

¹²⁶ Including civilian nationals temporarily outside the country. - Y compris les civils nationaux temporairement hors du pays.

¹²⁷ Including civilian nationals temporarily outside the country. Data refer to 1 January. - Y compris les civils nationaux temporairement hors du pays. Données se raportent au 1 janvier.

¹²⁸ Figures for male and female population do not add up to the figure for total population, because they exclude 119 persons of unknown sex. - Les chiffres relatifs à la population masculine et féminine ne correspondent pas au chiffre de la population totale, parce que l'on en a exclu 119 personnes de sexe inconnu.

¹²⁹ Population statistics are compiled from registers. Including residents temporarily outside the country. - Les statistiques de la population sont compilées à partir des registres. Y compris les résidents se trouvant temporairement hors du pays.

¹³⁰ Data refer to 1 January. Data refer to usually resident population. - Données se raportent au 1 janvier. Les données concernent la population habituellement résidente.

¹³¹ Excluding civilian aliens within the country, but including civilian nationals temporarily outside the country. - Non compris les civils étrangers dans le pays, mais y compris les civils nationaux temporairement hors du pays.

¹³² Excluding Transnistria and the municipality of Bender. - Les données ne tiennent pas compte de l'information sur la Transnistria et la municipalité de Bender.

¹³³ Excluding Transnistria and the municipality of Bender. Data refer to 1 January. - Les données ne tiennent pas compte de l'information sur la Transnistria et la municipalité de Bender. Données se raportent au 1 janvier.

¹³⁴ Figures for male and female may not add up to the total, since they do not include the category "Unknown". - La somme des chiffres indiqués pour les sexes masculin et féminin peut n'être pas égale au total parce qu'elle n'inclut pas la catégorie " inconnue ".

¹³⁵ Excludes data for Kosovo and Metohia. - Sans les données pour le Kosovo et Metohie.

¹³⁶ Excludes data for Kosovo and Metohia. Data refer to 1 January. Based on the results of the 2011 Population Census. - Sans les données pour le Kosovo et Metohie. Données se raportent au 1 janvier. Basé sur les résultats du rececement de la population de 2011.

¹³⁷ Changes in total area per year are the result of new measuring and correcting of the administrative borders between former Yugoslavian countries. - Les changements des totaux par année résultent de nouvelles mesures et de corrections des frontières administratives entre pays ex-yougoslaves.

¹³⁸ Excluding inland water. - Exception faite des eaux intérieures.

¹³⁹ Inhabited only during the winter season. The Norwegian population of these islands is included also in the de jure population of Norway. - N'est habitée que pendant la saison d'hiver. La population norvégienne de ces îles est comprise également dans la population de droit de la Norvège.

¹⁴⁰ Data refer to 1 January. Population statistics are compiled from registers. Data refer to registered resident population. - Données se raportent au 1 janvier. Les statistiques de la population sont compilées à partir des registres. Les données concernent la population enregistrée résidente.

¹⁴¹ Data refer to legal resident population. Data refer to 1 January. - Les données concernent la population légalement résidente. Données se raportent au 1 janvier.

¹⁴² Data refer to 1 January. The Government of Ukraine has informed the United Nations that it is not in a position to provide statistical data concerning the Autonomous Republic of Crimea and the city of Sevastopol. - Données se raportent au 1 janvier. Le gouvernement Ukrainien a informé l'ONU qu'il n'est pas en mesure de fournir des données statistiques concernant la République autonome de Crimée et la ville de Sébastopol.

¹⁴³ Excluding Channel Islands (Guernsey and Jersey) and Isle of Man, shown separately, if available. - Non compris les îles Anglo-Normandes (Guerneysey et Jersey) et l'île de Man, qui font l'objet de rubriques distinctes, si disponible.

¹⁴⁴ This data has been randomly rounded to protect confidentiality. Individual figures may not add up to totals, and values for the same data may vary in different tables. Including population in off-shore, migratory and shipping. - Ces données ont été arrondies de façon aléatoire afin d'en préserver la confidentialité. La somme de certains chiffres peut ne pas correspondre aux totaux indiqués et les valeurs des mêmes données peuvent varier d'un tableau à un autre. Y compris les populations extraterritoriales, les populations nomades et les populations maritimes.

¹⁴⁵ Excluding Niue, shown separately, which is part of Cook Islands, but because of remoteness is administered separately. - Non compris Nioué, qui fait l'objet d'une rubrique distincte et qui fait partie des îles Cook, mais qui, en raison de son éloignement, est administrée séparément.

¹⁴⁶ Projections are prepared by the Secretariat of the Pacific Community based on the last population and housing census. - Les projections sont preparées par le Secrétariat de la Communauté du Pacifique à partir des résultats du dernier recensement de la population et de l'habitat.

¹⁴⁷ Land area only. Excluding 84 square km of uninhabited islands. - La superficie des terres seulement. Exclut des îles inhabitées d'une superficie de 84 kilomètres carrés.

¹⁴⁸ Projections are prepared by the Secretariat of the Pacific Community based on 1999 census of population and housing. - Les projections sont preparées par le Secrétariat de la Communauté du Pacifique à partir des résultats du recensement de la population et de l'habitat de 1999.

¹⁴⁹ Because of rounding, totals are not in all cases the sum of the respective components. - Les chiffres étant arrondis, les totaux ne correspondent pas toujours rigoureusement à la somme des composants respectifs.

Table 3a – *Demographic Yearbook 2015*

Table 3a presents the values of the Whipple's index by sex, urban or rural residence, for total area and both sexes combined, according to the availability of the underlying data in the *Demographic Yearbook* database.

The data used to compile these indices are the datasets of population by single years of age, sex, and urban or rural residence, of the population censuses conducted worldwide since 1985. These datasets have been reported by the National Statistical Offices to the United Nations Statistics Division via the *Demographic Yearbook* questionnaires.

The footnotes that appear at the end of this table are notes that refer to the respective dataset of population by single years of age, sex, and urban or rural residence.

Whipple's index is an index of age preference in age reporting. The way it is calculated for this table, it is meant to indicate preference or avoidance of ages ending in digits "0" (zero) or "5" (five) during age reporting for a population census.

The formula used to calculate the values of the Whipple's index for this table is:

$$\frac{P25+P30+P35+P40+P45+P50+P55+P60}{\frac{1}{5}(P23+P24+P25+\cdots+P58+P59+P60+P61+P62)}*100$$

where Px refers to the number of persons of age x in completed years. The sum in brackets in the denominator is the sum of the number of persons of every single age from 23 to 62.

The values of the Whipple's index generally vary between 100, indicating no preference for "0" or "5" (in other words no heaping in ages ending in "0" or "5"), and 500, indicating that age reporting was entirely concentrated in ages ending in digits "0" or "5". The higher than 100 the value of the index, the higher is the heaping of age reporting in ages ending in "0" or "5".

For more information about the measurement of age and digit preference, please refer to *The Methods and Materials of Demography, Second Edition* (2004), Edited by Jacob S. Siegel and David A. Swanson.

Tableau 3a – *Annuaire démographique 2015*

Le tableau 3a présente les valeurs de l'indice de Whipple par sexe, résidence urbaine ou rurale, pour la superficie totale et les sexes combinés, selon la disponibilité des données sous-jacentes dans la base de données de l'*Annuaire démographique.*

Les données utilisées pour établir ces indices sont les séries de données de la population par âge simple, sexe et résidence urbaine ou rurale, pour les recensements de la population effectués dans le monde entier depuis 1985. Ces séries de données sont communiquées par les services nationaux de statistique à la Division de statistique de l'Organisation des Nations Unies par le biais des questionnaires de l'*Annuaire démographique.*

Les notes qui figurent à la fin de ce tableau sont des notes renvoyant aux différentes séries de données de la population par âge simple, sexe et résidence urbaine ou rurale.

L'indice de Whipple est un indice de préférence de certains âges dans les déclarations de l'âge. La manière dont il est calculé pour ce tableau permet d'indiquer l'attraction ou la répulsion pour des âges se terminant par les chiffres « 0 » (zéro) ou « 5 » (cinq) lors de la déclaration de l'âge effectuée dans le cadre d'un recensement de population.

La formule utilisée pour calculer les valeurs de l'indice de Whipple pour ce tableau est la suivante:

$$\frac{P25+P30+P35+P40+P45+P50+P55+P60}{\frac{1}{5}(P23+P24+P25+\cdots+P58+P59+P60+P61+P62)}*100$$

Px étant le nombre de personnes d'âge x en années révolues. La somme entre parenthèses en dénominateur est la somme du nombre de personnes selon l'âge simple de 23 à 62 ans.

Les valeurs de l'indice de Whipple varient généralement entre 100, indication d'absence de préférence pour « 0 » ou « 5 »(en d'autres termes pas de prépondérance des âges se terminant par « 0 » ou « 5 »), et 500, indiquant que les déclarations de l'âge étaient entièrement polarisées sur les âges se terminant par les chiffres « 0 » ou « 5 ». Plus la valeur de l'indice est supérieure à 100, plus les déclarations de l'âge sont polarisées sur les âges se terminant par « 0 » ou « 5 ».

Pour en savoir plus sur la mesure de l'âge et la préférence pour les chiffres, prière de consulter l'ouvrage intitulé *The Methods and Materials of Demography, Second Edition (2004),* publié sous la direction de Jacob S. Siegel et David A. Swanson.

3a. Whipple's Index by sex and urban/rural residence, 1985 - 2015
L'indice de Whipple par le sexe et la résidence urbaine/rurale, 1985 - 2015

Continent, country or area, date and code[a] / Continent, pays ou zone, date et code[a]	Total			Urban - Urbaine			Rural - Rurale		
	Both sexes Les deux sexes	Male Masculin	Female Féminin	Both sexes Les deux sexes	Male Masculin	Female Féminin	Both sexes Les deux sexes	Male Masculin	Female Féminin
AFRICA - AFRIQUE									
Algeria - Algérie[1]									
16 IV 2008 (CDJC)	100.7	100.5	100.9	100.7	100.5	100.9	100.7	100.6	100.8
Benin - Bénin									
15 II 1992 (CDFC)	216.1	205.6	224.6	185.4	171.6	197.9	234.6	228	239.6
11 II 2002 (CDJC)	229.1	218.9	237.8	190.4	180.1	200	257.5	250	263.5
Botswana									
21 VIII 1991 (CDFC)	104.8	106.6	103.3	102.4	103.6	101.4	107.7	110.8	105.3
17 VIII 2001 (CDFC)	100.9	101.8	100.2	...	...	...	...	...	...
9 VIII 2011 (CDFC)	100.8	101.3	100.3	101.7	101.8	101.6	99	100.5	97.5
Burkina Faso									
10 XII 1985 (CDJC)	193	173.8	208.4	153.1	140.9	166.7	198.6	179.4	213.2
10 XII 1996 (CDJC)	162.6[2]	144[2]	177.5[2]	99.5[3]	99.6[3]	99.5[3]	99.6[3]	99.7[3]	99.5[3]
9 XII 2006 (CDJC)	145.1	133.8	154.5	131.1	130.5	131.8	150.2	135.3	161.5
Burundi									
16 VIII 1990 (CDJC)	152.9	141.7	163	...	...	...	...	...	...
16 VIII 2008 (CDJC)	156.8	149.4	164.4	137.2	136.5	138.3	159.4	151.5	167.1
Cabo Verde									
23 VI 1990 (CDFC)	111.9	110.7	112.8	108	107.7	108.3	115.3	113.7	116.4
Cameroon - Cameroun									
11 XI 2005 (CDJC)	173.5	165.1	181.4	...	...	...	...	...	...
Central African Republic - République centrafricaine									
8 XII 1988 (CDFC)	139.4	132	146.1	129.9	125.2	134.3	144.5	135.8	152.3
Congo									
1 I 1985 (CDJC)	107.3	107.5	107.1	...	...	...	...	...	...
28 IV 2007 (CDFC)	103.5	103.1	103.8	...	...	...	...	...	...
Côte d'Ivoire									
1 III 1988 (CDFC)	126.3	117.3	136.2	116.4	112.7	121	132.7	120.5	145
15 V 2014 (CDJC)	116.5	114.3	118.9	112.3	111.8	112.9	121.2	117.1	125.6
Egypt - Égypte									
21 XI 2006 (CDFC)	196.5	175.3	218.2	177.1	162.7	191.9	213.5	186.4	241.4
Ethiopia - Éthiopie									
11 X 1994 (CDFC)	272.3	258.9	285	248.7	232.6	264	276.5	263.7	288.7
29 V 2007 (CDFC)	252.1	241	262.9	232.3	222.5	242.4	256.7	245.4	267.5
Gabon									
31 VII 1993 (CDFC)	116.6	115.9	117.4	...	...	...	...	...	...
Gambia - Gambie									
15 IV 1993 (CDFC)	229.8	215.2	244.5	191.2	183.2	201.2	256.2	241.6	268.9
Ghana									
26 III 2000 (CDFC)	184	175.8	191.6	159.7	154.7	164.5	205.6	195.2	215.3
26 IX 2010 (CDFC)	159.1	155.2	162.5	138.3	136.6	139.8	184.7	178.2	190.6
Guinea - Guinée									
1 III 2014 (CDFC)	200.7	185	214	166.2	160.8	171.9	221.1	202.1	235.4
Guinea-Bissau - Guinée-Bissau									
15 III 2009 (CDJC)	137.8	128.9	145.7	...	...	...	...	...	...
Kenya									
24 VIII 1989 (CDJC)	147.8	142.6	152.8	144.1	140.8	149.4	148.9	143.3	153.5
24 VIII 1999 (CDFC)	148.3	143.2	153.2	...	...	...	...	...	...
24 VIII 2009 (CDFC)	146.4	144.6	148.2	141.1	141.1	141.2	149.8	147.1	152.2
Lesotho									
13 IV 2006 (CDJC)	105.3	105.8	104.9	...	...	...	...	...	...
Liberia - Libéria									
21 III 2008 (CDFC)	142.2	136.3	148.1						
Malawi									
1 IX 1987 (CDFC)	138.5	137.9	139.1	...	...	...	...	...	...
1 IX 1998 (CDFC)	147.7	149.2	146.4	142.6	146.5	137.3	148.7	149.7	147.7
8 VI 2008 (CDFC)	120.6	121	120.2	113	114.7	111	122.2	122.5	121.9
Mali									
1 IV 1987 (CDJC)	184.5	171.4	195.9	163.7	154.1	173	190.4	176.7	202
1 IV 1998 (CDJC)	180.1	166.8	192.3	166.5	158	175.2	185.6	170.7	198.6
1 IV 2009 (CDFC)	156.5	145.7	166.6	142.7	139.1	146.8	161.1	148.2	172.5
Mauritius - Maurice[4]									
1 VII 1990 (CDFC)	103.4	102.4	104.3	...	...	...	...	...	...
2 VII 2000 (CDJC)	102.4	102.1	102.7	102.3	102	102.7	102.5	102.2	102.7
4 VII 2011 (CDJC)	100.6	101	100.3	100.8	101.2	100.3	100.5	100.9	100.2
Mayotte									
31 VII 2007 (CDJC)	124.4	126.9	122.3	...	...	...	...	...	...

3a. Whipple's Index by sex and urban/rural residence, 1985 - 2015
L'indice de Whipple par le sexe et la résidence urbaine/rurale, 1985 - 2015 (continued - suite)

Continent, country or area, date and code[a] / Continent, pays ou zone, date et code[a]	Total			Urban - Urbaine			Rural - Rurale		
	Both sexes Les deux sexes	Male Masculin	Female Féminin	Both sexes Les deux sexes	Male Masculin	Female Féminin	Both sexes Les deux sexes	Male Masculin	Female Féminin
AFRICA - AFRIQUE									
Morocco - Maroc									
1 IX 2004 (CDFC)	113.4	108.4	118	110.1	107.5	112.5	118.2	109.8	126.2
Mozambique									
1 VIII 1997 (CDJC)	118.6	117.9	119.3	111.7	110.9	112.4	121.5	121	121.9
1 VIII 2007 (CDFC)	126	126.2	125.9	...	...	...	...	...	...
Namibie - Namibie									
21 X 1991 (CDFC)	105.8	104.9	106.5	103.5	102.9	104.2	107.1	106.4	107.6
27 VIII 2001 (CDFC)	103.9	103.2	104.5	103.6	102.9	104.4	104.1	103.5	104.6
28 VIII 2011 (CDFC)	103.9	103.8	104	104.3	103.6	105	103.4	104.1	102.9
Niger									
20 V 2001 (CDJC)	270.1	254.7	285.2	...	...	...	...	...	...
10 XII 2012 (CDJC)	105.1	104.7	105.4	...	...	...	...	...	...
Nigeria - Nigéria									
26 XI 1991 (CDFC)	293.5	279.8	307.1	...	...	...	...	...	...
Republic of South Sudan - République de Soudan du Sud									
21 IV 2008 (CDFC)	183.1	178.4	187.9	...	...	...	...	...	...
Reunion - Réunion									
15 III 1990 (CDFC)	99.9	99.8	100.1	...	...	...	...	...	...
8 III 1999 (CDJC)	100	100.3	99.7	...	...	...	...	...	...
Rwanda									
16 VIII 2002 (CDJC)	106.3	106.6	106.1	107.4	108.3	106.2	106	106	106.1
15 VIII 2012 (CDJC)	110.2	110.4	109.9	108.3	109.3	107.1	110.6	110.7	110.5
Saint Helena ex. dep. - Sainte-Hélène sans dép.									
8 III 1998 (CDJC)	101	98.8	103.3	...	...	...	...	...	...
10 II 2008 (CDJC)[5]	98.8	99.9	97.8	...	...	...	...	...	...
Saint Helena: Ascension - Sainte-Hélène: Ascension									
8 III 1998 (CDJC)	117.5	111	130.7	...	...	...	...	...	...
Sao Tome and Principe - Sao Tomé-et-Principe									
4 VIII 1991 (CDFC)	102.7	101.5	103.8	...	...	...	...	...	...
25 VIII 2001 (CDJC)	105.7	106.2	105.3	...	...	...	...	...	...
13 V 2012 (CDJC)	104.1	103.2	105	...	...	...	...	...	...
Seychelles									
17 VIII 1987 (CDFC)	100.9	102.8	99	...	...	...	...	...	...
26 VIII 1994 (CDFC)	100.9	99.9	102	...	...	...	...	...	...
29 VIII 1997 (CDFC)	101.6	100.8	102.5	...	...	...	...	...	...
26 VIII 2002 (CDJC)	100.8	99.2	102.5	...	...	...	...	...	...
26 VIII 2010 (CDFC)	101.3	101.7	101	...	...	...	...	...	...
South Africa - Afrique du Sud									
5 III 1985 (CDFC)	124.3	120.9	127.7	...	...	...	...	...	...
7 III 1991 (CDFC)	113.1	111.5	114.7	...	...	...	...	...	...
10 X 1996 (CDFC)[6]	100.5	100.3	100.7	99.3	99.5	99.1	102.5	101.7	103.1
Swaziland									
25 VIII 1986 (CDFC)	125.9	125.4	126.3	118.3	118.2	118.5	129.3	130.1	128.8
11 V 1997 (CDFC)	120.6	121.5	119.7	116.9	117.9	115.8	122.3	123.7	121.2
11 V 2007 (CDJC)	99.8	101.2	98.6	99	100.7	97.4	100.1	101.5	99.1
Tunisia - Tunisie									
20 IV 1994 (CDFC)	102.4	102.4	102.4	102.4	102.4	102.4	102.4	102.3	102.4
Uganda - Ouganda									
12 I 1991 (CDFC)	168	154.8	180.5	158.6	150.8	167.3	169.4	155.5	182.2
12 IX 2002 (CDFC)	134.2	129.6	138.4	128.2	128.5	128	135.2	129.7	140
United Republic of Tanzania - République Unie de Tanzanie									
28 VIII 1988 (CDFC)	189.2	175.1	201.8	173.7	167.3	180.7	193.3	177.4	206.7
26 VIII 2012 (CDFC)	154.4	152.6	156.1	139.5	141.5	137.7	162.3	158.8	165.5
Zambia - Zambie									
20 VIII 1990 (CDFC)	120.7	121.9	119.6	117.2	119.8	114.2	123.1	123.5	122.7
25 X 2000 (CDFC)	127.6	128.9	126.3	123.9	125.3	122.4	129.9	131.4	128.5
16 X 2010 (CDJC)	123.8	126.8	120.7	122.3	125.2	119.3	124.9	128.2	121.8
Zimbabwe									
18 VIII 1992 (CDFC)	120.6	122.2	119.2	115.9	119.5	111.4	123.7	124.6	123
17 VIII 2002 (CDFC)	115.1	115.2	115	109.7	110.9	108.4	119	119	119.1
17 VIII 2012 (CDFC)	110.8	110.8	110.8	...	...	...	...	...	...

3a. Whipple's Index by sex and urban/rural residence, 1985 - 2015
L'indice de Whipple par le sexe et la résidence urbaine/rurale, 1985 - 2015 (continued - suite)

Continent, country or area, date and code[a] / Continent, pays ou zone, date et code[a]	Total			Urban - Urbaine			Rural - Rurale		
	Both sexes Les deux sexes	Male Masculin	Female Féminin	Both sexes Les deux sexes	Male Masculin	Female Féminin	Both sexes Les deux sexes	Male Masculin	Female Féminin
AMERICA, NORTH - AMÉRIQUE DU NORD									
Anguilla									
13 IV 1992 (CDFC)	104.8	109	100.4	...	...	...	...	...	...
9 V 2001 (CDFC)	104.4	105.8	103.1	...	...	...	...	...	...
Antigua and Barbuda - Antigua-et-Barbuda									
28 V 2001 (CDFC)	104.3	103.1	105.4	...	...	...	...	...	...
Aruba									
6 X 1991 (CDJC)	99.3	99.4	99.3	...	...	...	...	...	...
14 X 2000 (CDJC)	103.9[7]	103.3	104.5	...	...	...	...	...	...
29 IX 2010 (CDJC)[7]	103.4	103.6	103.3	...	...	...	...	...	...
Bahamas									
1 V 1990 (CDFC)	103.4	102.3	104.5	...	...	...	...	...	...
1 V 2000 (CDFC)	101.5	100.4	102.5	...	...	...	...	...	...
3 V 2010 (CDJC)	101.3	101.6	101.1	...	...	...	...	...	...
Barbados - Barbade									
1 V 2000 (CDFC)	103.8	104.4	103.3	...	...	...	...	...	...
Belize									
12 V 1991 (CDFC)	103.5	103.2	103.8	...	...	...	...	...	...
12 V 2010 (CDJC)	104.2	103.9	104.5	...	...	...	...	...	...
Bermuda - Bermudes									
20 V 1991 (CDJC)	99	97.9	100	...	...	...	...	...	...
20 V 2000 (CDJC)[8]	100.2	100	100.3	...	...	...	...	...	...
20 V 2010 (CDJC)[9]	100.9	101.1	100.8	100.9	101.1	100.8	...	...	...
British Virgin Islands - Îles Vierges britanniques									
12 V 1991 (CDJC)	102.6	104.5	100.5	...	...	...	...	...	...
Canada									
4 VI 1991 (CDJC)	99.6	99.6	99.6	99.6	99.6	99.7	99.6	99.6	99.5
14 V 1996 (CDJC)	99.7	99.7	99.7	...	...	...	...	...	...
15 V 2001 (CDJC)	99.7	99.7	99.8	99.8	99.8	99.8	99.6	99.5	99.8
16 V 2006 (CDJC)[7]	99.9	100	99.9	100	100	100	99.6	99.6	99.7
2 V 2011 (CDJC)	100.8	101	100.7	100.9	101.1	100.8	100.4	100.6	100.3
Cayman Islands - Îles Caïmanes									
15 X 1989 (CDFC)	104.1	102.7	105.5	...	...	...	...	...	...
10 X 2010 (CDJC)[8]	102.3	102.8	101.8	102.3	102.8	101.8	...	...	...
Costa Rica									
26 VI 2000 (CDJC)	109.1	109.8	108.4	108.6	108.9	108.3	109.9	111.1	108.6
30 V 2011 (CDJC)	104	104.2	103.9	103.8	103.8	103.9	104.6	105.2	103.9
Cuba									
7 IX 2002 (CDJC)	102.2	102.5	101.9	102.5	102.7	102.2	101.5	102	100.9
14 IX 2012 (CDFC)	101.5	101.6	101.3	...	...	...	...	...	...
Dominican Republic - République dominicaine									
24 IX 1993 (CDJC)	116.5	114.9	118	111.5	109.9	113	123.5	121.4	125.5
18 X 2002 (CDJC)	108	108.9	107.1	105.8	106.3	105.4	112.1	113.5	110.7
1 XII 2010 (CDJC)	111.5	113.8	109.2	109.9	111.9	108.1	116.5	119.3	113.1
El Salvador									
27 IX 1992 (CDFC)	126	127.5	124.6	119.9	119.7	120	133.5	136.6	130.7
12 V 2007 (CDJC)	105.9	107.1	105	105.3	106.3	104.5	107.3	108.7	106.2
Guadeloupe									
8 III 1999 (CDJC)	100.5	100.5	100.4	...	...	...	...	...	...
Honduras									
11 V 1988 (CDFC)	104.1	104.5	103.6	102.4	102.5	102.3	105.3	105.9	104.8
28 VII 2001 (CDJC)	121.8	123.3	120.4	118.5	118.8	118.3	125.1	127.5	122.7
10 VIII 2013 (CDFC)	119.7	121.6	118.1	120	120.9	119.1	119.4	122.4	116.6
Jamaica - Jamaïque									
7 IV 1991 (CDJC)	107.6	108.8	106.5	...	...	...	...	...	...
10 IX 2001 (CDJC)[10]	107.4	108.7	106.1	106.9	107.5	106.4	107.9	110	105.7
4 IV 2011 (CDJC)	103.3	103.4	103.1	103.6	103.6	103.6	102.8	103.2	102.5
Martinique									
15 III 1990 (CDJC)	104.4	104.1	104.6	...	...	...	...	...	...
Mexico - Mexique									
12 III 1990 (CDJC)	125.2	123.5	126.8	...	...	...	...	...	...
14 II 2000 (CDJC)	116.7	116.5	116.9	114.8	114.3	115.3	123.4	124.3	122.7
17 X 2005 (CDJC)	118.8	118.7	118.9	117.5	117	117.9	123.8	124.8	122.8
12 VI 2010 (CDFC)[11]	114	114.1	113.9	113.7	113.6	113.9	115.1	116.2	114.1

3a. Whipple's Index by sex and urban/rural residence, 1985 - 2015
L'indice de Whipple par le sexe et la résidence urbaine/rurale, 1985 - 2015 (continued - suite)

Continent, country or area, date and code[a] Continent, pays ou zone, date et code[a]	Total			Urban - Urbaine			Rural - Rurale		
	Both sexes Les deux sexes	Male Masculin	Female Féminin	Both sexes Les deux sexes	Male Masculin	Female Féminin	Both sexes Les deux sexes	Male Masculin	Female Féminin
AMERICA, NORTH - AMÉRIQUE DU NORD									
Montserrat									
12 V 2011 (CDJC)	101.9	95.9	108.4	...	...	...	...	...	...
Nicaragua									
4 VI 2005 (CDJC)	111.6	112.8	110.5	108.5	109.2	107.8	116.4	117.8	115.1
Panama									
13 V 1990 (CDFC)	109.3	109.2	109.3	104.6	104.5	104.8	115.6	115	116.3
14 V 2000 (CDFC)	103.2	103.3	103.2	...	...	...	...	...	...
Puerto Rico - Porto Rico									
1 IV 1990 (CDJC)	105.6	106.1	105.1	...	...	...	...	...	...
1 IV 2000 (CDJC)	101.7	102	101.6	...	...	...	...	...	...
1 IV 2010 (CDJC)[12]	102	102	102	...	...	...	...	...	...
Saint Lucia - Sainte-Lucie									
12 V 1991 (CDFC)	110.5	110.5	110.4	...	...	...	...	...	...
22 V 2001 (CDFC)	105.5	105.8	105.2	104	100.5	107.3	106.2	108	104.4
Saint Pierre and Miquelon - Saint Pierre-et-Miquelon									
8 III 1999 (CDFC)	100.5	104.6	96.1	...	...	...	...	...	...
Saint Vincent and the Grenadines - Saint-Vincent-et-les Grenadines									
12 V 1991 (CDFC)	106.6	105.2	107.9	...	...	...	...	...	...
Sint Maarten (Dutch part) - Saint-Martin (partie néerlandaise)									
9 IV 2011 (CDFC)	100.7	100.2	101.2	...	...	...	...	...	...
Trinidad and Tobago - Trinité-et-Tobago									
9 I 2011 (CDJC)	106.6	107.2	105.9	...	...	...	...	...	...
Turks and Caicos Islands - Îles Turques et Caïques									
10 IX 2001 (CDFC)	104.2	100.1	108.6	...	...	...	...	...	...
United States of America - États-Unis d'Amérique									
1 IV 1990 (CDJC)	104.5	104.8	104.2	...	...	...	...	...	...
1 IV 2000 (CDJC)[13]	101.8	102.1	101.5	102.1	102.4	101.7	100.8	101	100.5
1 IV 2010 (CDJC)	102.2	102.5	102	102.4	102.7	102.2	101.5	101.7	101.2
AMERICA, SOUTH - AMÉRIQUE DU SUD									
Argentina - Argentine									
15 V 1991 (CDFC)	104.2	103.3	105.2	...	...	...	...	...	...
18 XI 2001 (CDFC)	102.4	101.8	103	...	...	...	...	...	...
27 X 2010 (CDFC)	102.6	102.5	102.7	102.6	102.5	102.7	102.5	102.9	102
Bolivia (Plurinational State of) - Bolivie (État plurinational de)									
3 VI 1992 (CDFC)	125.4	121.1	129.5	111.4	108	114.4	146.1	139.4	152.7
5 IX 2001 (CDFC)	114.6	113.1	116	109.1	108	110.2	124.6	121.9	127.6
21 XI 2012 (CDFC)	110.4	110.5	110.3	108	108.1	108	115.7	115.4	116.1
Brazil - Brésil									
1 IX 1991 (CDJC)	103.3	103.3	103.3	102.3	102.3	102.2	107.2	106.9	107.4
1 VIII 2000 (CDJC)[14]	104.2	104.3	104	103.6	103.7	103.5	107.1	107.3	107
31 VII 2010 (CDJC)	104.8	105.6	104.1	104.7	105.4	104	105.6	106.6	104.4
Chile - Chili									
22 IV 1992 (CDFC)	100.3	98.9	101.7	100.2	98.6	101.7	101	100.2	101.9
24 IV 2002 (CDFC)	99.5	98.5	100.5	99.4	98.2	100.5	100.2	100	100.4
Colombia - Colombie									
15 X 1985 (CDFC)	147.9	146.5	149.2	139.8	136.8	142.4	166.9	166.5	167.3
24 X 1993 (CDFC)	118.9	117.7	120	111.7	108.9	114.1	139.6	139.9	139.4
22 V 2005 (CDFC)	103.5	104.2	102.9	102.1	102.4	101.8	108.6	109.8	107.3
22 V 2005 (CDJC)	103.5	104.2	102.9	102.1	102.4	101.8	108.7	109.9	107.3
Ecuador - Équateur									
25 XI 1990 (CDFC)[15]	132.5	131.2	133.8	122.9	121	124.7	146.6	145.4	147.9
25 XI 2001 (CDFC)[15]	112.1	111.8	112.4	107.9	107	108.7	119.9	120.4	119.4
28 XI 2010 (CDFC)	103.7	104.1	103.3	103	103.4	102.7	104.9	105.4	104.4
French Guiana - Guyane française									
15 III 1990 (CDJC)	106.2	105.7	106.7	...	...	...	...	...	...

Continent, country or area, date and code[a] Continent, pays ou zone, date et code[a]	Total			Urban - Urbaine			Rural - Rurale		
	Both sexes Les deux sexes	Male Masculin	Female Féminin	Both sexes Les deux sexes	Male Masculin	Female Féminin	Both sexes Les deux sexes	Male Masculin	Female Féminin
AMERICA, SOUTH - AMÉRIQUE DU SUD									
8 III 1999 (CDJC)	101.1	100.9	101.3	...	...	...	...	...	...
Paraguay									
26 VIII 1992 (CDFC)........................	108.6	107.9	109.3	105.7	104.3	107	112	111.8	112.3
28 VIII 2002 (CDFC)........................	104.8	104.3	105.2	103.2	102.6	103.7	107.1	106.5	107.8
Peru - Pérou									
21 X 2007 (CDFC)............................	109.4	109.1	109.6	106.9	106.5	107.3	118.8	118.5	119.1
Suriname									
2 VIII 2004 (CDJC)	101.1	100.4	102	102.4[16]	101.4[16]	103.5[16]	98.3[16]	98.2[16]	98.4[16]
13 VIII 2012 (CDJC)	101.7	101.8	101.7	...	...	...	...	...	...
Uruguay									
23 X 1985 (CDFC)............................	106.2	104.9	107.4	106.2	104.7	107.5	106.3	106.1	106.5
22 V 1996 (CDFC)[17]	103.3	102.8	103.8	103.2	102.5	103.8	104	104.5	103.3
1 VI 2004 (CDFC)[18]	106	105.9	106.2	106.1	105.9	106.3	105.4	105.7	105
4 X 2011 (CDJC)	101.8	101.9	101.7	101.8	101.9	101.7	101.8	101.6	102
Venezuela (Bolivarian Republic of) - Venezuela (République bolivarienne du)									
20 X 1990 (CDFC)[19]	106.4	106.5	106.3	105	104.8	105.3	114.9	116.1	113.4
1 IX 2011 (CDJC)	101.3	101.6	101	101.3[20]	101.6[20]	101[20]	101.4[20]	102[20]	100.7[20]
ASIA - ASIE									
Armenia - Arménie									
10 X 2001 (CDJC)	103	102.8	103.3	103.7	103.7	103.8	101.6	101.1	102.1
12 X 2011 (CDJC)	101.8	101.5	102	102.4	102.3	102.6	100.6	100.2	101
Azerbaijan - Azerbaïdjan									
27 I 1999 (CDJC)	100.4	99.8	101	100.3	99.8	100.8	100.5	99.7	101.2
13 IV 2009 (CDJC)	100.4	100.1	100.7	100.8	100.3	101.3	99.9	99.7	100.1
Bahrain - Bahreïn									
16 XI 1991 (CDFC)...........................	96.6	98.3	93.6	...	...	...	...	...	...
7 IV 2001 (CDJC)	100.2	99.9	100.9	...	...	...	...	...	...
27 IV 2010 (CDJC)	100.2	99.3	101.9	...	...	...	...	...	...
Bangladesh[21]									
22 I 2001 (CDFC)............................	299.5	295.8	303.4	283.1	277.9	289.8	305	302.6	307.4
Bhutan - Bhoutan									
30 V 2005 (CDFC)...........................	116.4	117.7	114.9	118.7	119.6	117.4	115.4	116.8	113.9
Brunei Darussalam - Brunéi Darussalam									
7 VIII 1991 (CDFC)...........................	98.8	98.7	98.8	...	...	...	...	...	...
20 VI 2011 (CDJC)	100.9	101.6	100.2	100.6	101.3	99.8	102	102.3	101.6
Cambodia - Cambodge									
3 III 1998 (CDFC)............................	118.1	116.2	119.6	119.8	117.6	121.8	117.6	115.98	119.1
3 III 2008 (CDFC)[22]	109.9	108.2	111.3	109.7	108.5	110.8	109.9	108.1	111.5
China - Chine									
1 VII 1990 (CDFC)...........................	101	101.1	100.9	101.9	102	101.8	100.6	100.7	100.5
1 XI 2000 (CDJC)	101.7	101.7	101.6	101.6	101.8	101.4	101.7	101.7	101.7
1 XI 2010 (CDJC)[23]	98.8	98.9	98.8	98.7	98.9	98.6	98.9	98.9	99
China, Hong Kong SAR - Chine, Hong Kong RAS									
11 III 1986 (CDFC)	101.7	101.4	102.1	101.7	101.3	102.1	102.1	102.5	101.7
15 III 1996 (CDFC)..........................	99.7	99.8	99.7	...	...	...	...	...	...
14 III 2001 (CDJC)[24].......................	100.2	100.3	100.1	...	...	...	...	...	...
14 VII 2006 (CDJC)[25]	98.3	98.4	98.3	...	...	...	...	...	...
30 VI 2011 (CDJC)[24]	99.4	100	98.9	...	...	...	...	...	...
China, Macao SAR - Chine, Macao RAS									
30 VIII 1991 (CDJC)........................	100.8	101.4	100.3	...	...	...	...	...	...
23 VIII 2001 (CDJC)	95.5	94.7	96.2	...	...	...	...	...	...
12 VIII 2011 (CDJC)	98.9	97.6	100	...	...	...	...	...	...
Cyprus - Chypre									
1 X 1992 (CDJC)	98.7	98.3	99	98.8	98.4	99.3	98.4	98.3	98.5
1 X 2001 (CDJC)[26]	100.7	100.7	100.6	100.9	101.4	100.4	100.1	99.1	101.1
1 X 2011 (CDJC)[26]	105.4	106.6	104.4	...	...	...	...	...	...

Continent, country or area, date and code[a] Continent, pays ou zone, date et code[a]	Total			Urban - Urbaine			Rural - Rurale		
	Both sexes Les deux sexes	Male Masculin	Female Féminin	Both sexes Les deux sexes	Male Masculin	Female Féminin	Both sexes Les deux sexes	Male Masculin	Female Féminin
ASIA - ASIE									
Democratic People's Republic of Korea - République populaire démocratique de Corée									
31 XII 1993 (CDJC)	105	105.2	104.7	104.4	104.6	104.2	105.8	106.2	105.5
1 X 2008 (CDJC)	101	100.6	101.3	...	...	...	...	...	...
Georgia - Géorgie									
17 I 2002 (CDJC)	101.4	101.7	101.1	101.6	102	101.3	101.1	101.4	100.8
5 XI 2014 (CDJC)	99.9	99.9	99.8	99.8	99.6	99.9	100	100.4	99.7
India - Inde									
1 III 1991 (CDFC)[27]	290.3	292.6	287.9	258.7	253.8	264.3	302.1	307.7	296.2
1 III 2001 (CDFC)[28]	230	241	218.4	217.2	216.8	217.8	235.5	252	218.7
9 II 2011 (CDFC)[29]	171	174.6	167.4	152.9	151	154.9	180.5	187.1	173.8
Indonesia - Indonésie									
31 X 1990 (CDFC)	163.3	160.2	166.3	139.7	135.8	143.7	174.2	171.7	176.5
30 VI 2000 (CDJC)[30]	152.2	151.3	153.1	136.8	136.4	137.2	164.2	163.1	165.2
1 V 2010 (CDJC)	114.5	114.2	114.9	110.2	110.2	110.2	119	118.4	119.7
Iran (Islamic Republic of) - Iran (République islamique d')									
22 IX 1986 (CDFC)	122.6	121.1	124.1	114.4	113.4	115.5	133.1	131.3	134.8
11 IX 1991 (CDJC)	128.7	127	130.4	122.5	121.3	123.9	138.5	136.4	140.6
11 IX 1994 (CDJC)	107.4	106.8	108.1	107.1	108	106.2	107.8	104.5	111.2
23 X 1996 (CDJC)	108.8	108.6	109	105.7	105.6	105.8	114.1	114	114.3
28 X 2006 (CDJC)[31]	111.6	110.4	112.8	109.3	108.5	110.1	117.2	115.2	119.2
24 X 2011 (CDJC)	103.7	103.8	103.5	103.6	103.8	103.5	103.7[32]	103.8[32]	103.6[32]
Iraq									
16 X 1997 (CDFC)	106.2	105.6	106.8	105.5	104.9	106.1	108	107.6	108.5
Israel - Israël									
4 XI 1995 (CDFC)[33]	101.4	101.8	101	101.3	101.8	100.9	101.9	101.5	102.3
4 XI 1995 (CDJC)	101.1	101.1	101.1	101	101	101	101.5	101.6	101.4
27 XII 2008 (CDFC)[34]	98.9	99	98.9	99	99.1	98.9	98.6	98.3	99
Japan - Japon									
1 X 1985 (CDFC)	98.4	98.4	98.3	98.3	98.4	98.2	98.7	98.5	98.8
1 X 1990 (CDFC)	98.9	98.9	98.9	98.9	99	98.8	98.8	98.6	99
1 X 1995 (CDFC)	99	99	99	99	99.1	99	98.8	98.6	98.9
1 X 2000 (CDJC)	99.1	99.1	99	99.1	99.2	99	99	98.8	99.2
1 X 2005 (CDJC)[35]	99.1	99.2	99.1	99.2	99.2	99.1	99	98.8	99.1
1 X 2010 (CDJC)[35]	100.9	100.9	100.9	100.9	100.9	100.8	101	100.9	101.1
Jordan - Jordanie									
1 X 2004 (CDFC)[36]	100.8	100.4	101.3	...	...	...	...	...	...
30 X 2015 (CDFC)[37]	111.3	112.2	110.3	...	...	...	...	...	...
Kazakhstan									
12 I 1989 (CDFC)	98.9	98.8	99	98.7	98.6	98.8	99.2	99	99.4
26 II 1999 (CDJC)[17]	99.9	99.8	99.9	100.1	100	100.2	99.5	99.5	99.4
Kuwait - Koweït									
20 IV 1985 (CDFC)	139.5	142.6	133.9	...	...	...	...	...	...
21 IV 2011 (CDFC)	102.2	102.6	101.7	102.2	102.6	101.7	...	...	...
Kyrgyzstan - Kirghizstan									
12 I 1989 (CDFC)	99.3	99.1	99.5	98.4	98	98.8	99.9	99.8	100.1
24 III 1999 (CDJC)	99.4	99.2	99.6	99.2	98.9	99.5	99.5	99.3	99.7
24 III 2009 (CDJC)	100.6	100.5	100.8	...	...	...	...	...	...
Lao People's Democratic Republic - République démocratique populaire lao									
1 III 2005 (CDJC)	138.3	136.4	140.2	120.8[38]	120.9[38]	120.6[38]	146[38]	143.3[38]	148.5[38]
1 III 2015 (CDJC)	129.3	128.4	130.2	...	...	...	...	...	...
Malaysia - Malaisie									
14 VIII 1991 (CDFC)	114.2	113.8	114.6	110.3	110.2	110.3	118.8	117.9	119.7
6 VII 2010 (CDJC)	120.4	120.7	120	120.6	120.7	120.5	119.7	120.6	118.7
6 VII 2010 (CDJC)[39]	120.7	121.1	120.3	...	...	...	...	...	...
Maldives									
25 III 1985 (CDFC)	176.7	175.3	178.4	166.3	170.9	159.4	180.7	177.2	184.2
8 III 1990 (CDFC)	156.4	159.9	152.7	149.3	154.5	142.6	159.2	162.4	156.1
25 III 1995 (CDFC)	143.1	144.5	141.7	137.3	137.9	136.7	145.5	147.5	143.5
31 III 2000 (CDFC)	106.9	109.5	104.3	...	...	...	...	...	...
21 III 2006 (CDFC)[40]	103.8	104.9	102.8	104	105.5	102.5	103.7	104.5	102.9
20 IX 2014 (CDFC)[41]	105.4	109.8	99.1	...	...	...	...	...	...

75

Continent, country or area, date and code[a] / Continent, pays ou zone, date et code[a]	Total			Urban - Urbaine			Rural - Rurale		
	Both sexes Les deux sexes	Male Masculin	Female Féminin	Both sexes Les deux sexes	Male Masculin	Female Féminin	Both sexes Les deux sexes	Male Masculin	Female Féminin
ASIA - ASIE									
Mongolia - Mongolie									
5 I 2000 (CDFC)	99.9	99.6	100.2	99.9	99.7	100.1	99.9	99.5	100.2
11 XI 2010 (CDJC)	101.6	101.3	101.9	101.7	101.4	102	101.5	101.3	101.7
Myanmar[42]									
29 III 2014 (CDFC)	123.3	124	122.6	...	...	...	...	...	...
Nepal - Népal									
22 VI 1991 (CDJC)	202.4	195.6	209	186.2	179.2	193.9	204.2	197.6	210.5
22 VI 2001 (CDJC)	206.1	205.7	206.6	...	...	...	...	...	...
22 VI 2011 (CDJC)	188.6	191.3	186.2	169.9	167.8	172	193.1	197.5	189.3
Oman									
7 XII 2003 (CDFC)	158.5	165.6	146.9	154.9	163.1	141.1	170.2	174.1	164.4
Philippines									
1 IX 1995 (CDJC)	115.7	116.5	114.9	...	...	...	...	...	...
1 V 2000 (CDJC)[43]	110.8	111.6	110	...	...	...	...	...	...
1 VIII 2007 (CDJC)	104.8	104.9	104.7	...	...	...	...	...	...
1 V 2010 (CDJC)[44]	108.5	109.1	107.9	...	...	...	...	...	...
Qatar									
16 III 1986 (CDFC)	149.1	151.9	140.2	...	...	...	...	...	...
Republic of Korea - République de Corée									
1 XI 1985 (CDFC)	99.4	98.9	99.8	99.6	99.4	99.8	98.8	97.9	99.6
1 XI 1990 (CDFC)	99.5	99.2	99.8	99.6	99.4	99.8	99.1	98.5	99.7
1 XI 1995 (CDJC)	99.9	99.7	100.1	100	99.8	100.2	99.4	99.2	99.6
1 XI 2000 (CDJC)[45]	100	99.8	100.2	100.2	100	100.4	99.2	98.9	99.4
1 XI 2005 (CDJC)[45]	100.4	100.2	100.6	100.6	100.4	100.8	99.4	99.2	99.7
Singapore - Singapour									
30 VI 2000 (CDJC)	98.2	98.1	98.3	...	...	...	...	...	...
30 VI 2010 (CDJC)[46]	99.7	99.7	99.7	...	...	...	...	...	...
Sri Lanka									
17 VII 2001 (CDFC)[47]	97	97.5	96.4	98.2	98.5	97.8	96.8[48]	97.3[48]	96.2[48]
27 II 2012 (CDJC)	100.2	100.3	100	100.3	100.7	100	100.1	100.2	100.1
State of Palestine - État de Palestine									
9 XII 1997 (CDFC)[49]	109.1	103	115.3	...	...	...	...	...	...
1 XII 2007 (CDFC)[30]	103.8	102.6	104.9	104.4[50]	103.2[50]	105.7[50]	100.8	100	101.6
Syrian Arab Republic - République arabe syrienne[51]									
3 IX 1994 (CDFC)	111.8	109.9	113.8	111.9	110.4	113.5	111.7	109.2	114.1
Tajikistan - Tadjikistan									
12 I 1989 (CDJC)	99	98.9	99.1	97.6	97.1	98	99.9	100	99.9
20 I 2000 (CDFC)	99.3	99.2	99.4	100.1	100	100.1	99	98.9	99.1
21 IX 2010 (CDFC)	103.6	103.9	103.4	105.8	106.6	105	102.8	102.9	102.7
Thailand - Thaïlande									
1 IV 2000 (CDJC)[52]	104.7	104.7	104.8	108.1	108.1	108.1	103	103	103
1 IX 2010 (CDJC)	110.6	111.1	110.1	115.6	116.2	115	106.3	106.8	105.8
Timor-Leste									
11 VII 2010 (CDFC)	130.3	128.9	131.7	126	125.6	126.5	132.3	130.6	134
Turkey - Turquie									
20 X 1985 (CDFC)	149.4	133.8	165.3	...	...	...	...	...	...
21 X 1990 (CDFC)	139.7	128.9	150.8	...	...	...	...	...	...
22 X 2000 (CDFC)	125.7	123.2	128.3	122.7	121.3	124.2	131.7	127.2	136.4
3 X 2011 (CDJC)[53]	101.2	101.7	100.8	101.4	101.7	101.1	100.8	101.5	99.9
Viet Nam									
1 IV 1989 (CDJC)	98.5	98.1	98.8	98.3	97.8	98.8	98.4	98	98.7
1 IV 1999 (CDJC)	99.2	98.8	99.6	99.1	98.6	99.6	99.3	98.8	99.7
1 IV 2009 (CDJC)	100.4	99.8	100.9	100.6	100	101.1	100.3	99.8	100.8
Yemen - Yémen									
16 XII 1994 (CDFC)	293.9	282.6	304.9	245	229.6	265	311.7	305.8	316.8
EUROPE									
Åland Islands - Îles d'Åland[54]									
31 XII 2000 (CDJC)	100.7	101.5	99.8	102.9	101.9	103.8	99	101.2	96.7
Austria - Autriche									
15 V 1991 (CDJC)	97.9	97.9	97.9	97.8	97.9	97.7	98.2	98.1	98.2
15 V 2001 (CDJC)	97.4	97.5	97.3	97.3	97.5	97.2	97.5	97.3	97.6

Continent, country or area, date and code[a] / Continent, pays ou zone, date et code[a]	Total			Urban - Urbaine			Rural - Rurale		
	Both sexes Les deux sexes	Male Masculin	Female Féminin	Both sexes Les deux sexes	Male Masculin	Female Féminin	Both sexes Les deux sexes	Male Masculin	Female Féminin
EUROPE									
31 X 2011 (CDJC)	100	100.1	100	100.2	100.2	100.2	99.7	99.8	99.7
Belarus - Bélarus									
12 I 1989 (CDJC)	99.4	99.3	99.5	98.9	98.8	99.1	100.3	100.3	100.2
16 II 1999 (CDJC)	99.6	99.4	99.8	99.7	99.6	99.9	99.2	98.9	99.5
14 X 2009 (CDJC)	101.5	101.6	101.5	101.7	101.6	101.7	101	101.3	100.7
Belgium - Belgique									
1 X 2001 (CDJC)	99.5	99.4	99.7	99.5	99.4	99.7	99.2	98.9	99.4
1 I 2011 (CDJC)	100	99.9	100.1	100	99.9	100.1	100.3	99.1	101.6
Bosnia and Herzegovina - Bosnie-Herzégovine									
31 III 1991 (CDJC)	100.4	100.5	100.2	...	...	...	...	...	...
Bulgaria - Bulgarie									
1 II 2011 (CDJC)	101.2	101	101.4	101.1	100.9	101.3	101.4	101.4	101.4
Croatia - Croatie									
31 III 1991 (CDFC)	99.1	99.2	99.1	99	99.3	98.8	99.2	99.1	99.4
31 III 2001 (CDJC)	98.2	98.4	98.1	98.3	98.6	98.1	98.1	98.1	98.2
1 IV 2011 (CDJC)	100.3	100.5	100.2	100.3	100.4	100.2	100.4	100.5	100.2
Czech Republic - République tchèque									
3 III 1991 (CDJC)	99	98.8	99.1	...	...	...	...	...	...
1 III 2001 (CDJC)	99.2	99.1	99.3	99	98.9	99.1	99.8	99.8	99.9
25 III 2011 (CDJC)	99.6	99.6	99.7	99.5	99.4	99.6	99.9	100.1	99.8
Denmark - Danemark[55]									
1 I 1991 (CDJC)	100.5	100.6	100.5	...	...	...	...	...	...
Estonia - Estonie									
31 III 2000 (CDJC)	100	99.7	100.3	100.2	100	100.4	99.7	99.1	100.2
31 XII 2011 (CDJC)	100	100	100.1	100.1	100	100.1	100	99.9	100.2
Finland - Finlande									
17 XI 1985 (CDJC)	99.8	99.9	99.6	...	...	...	...	...	...
31 XII 1990 (CDJC)	99.5	99.6	99.5	...	...	...	...	...	...
31 XII 2000 (CDJC)	99.5	99.6	99.4	99.9	100.1	99.7	98.9	98.9	98.8
31 XII 2010 (CDJC)	100.1	100.1	100	100	100.1	99.8	100.3	100	100.5
France									
5 III 1990 (CDJC)	99.2	99	99.3	99.5	99.4	99.6	98.2	98.1	98.4
8 III 1999 (CDJC)[56]	100.5	100.5	100.5	100.5	100.5	100.5	100.8	100.7	100.8
Germany - Allemagne									
9 V 2011 (CDJC)	100	100	100.1	100	100	100.1	100.1	100.1	100.1
Gibraltar									
14 X 1991 (CDFC)	105.7	104.9	106.6	...	...	...	...	...	...
12 XI 2001 (CDFC)[57]	98	98.6	97.5	...	...	...	...	...	...
12 XI 2012 (CDJC)[58]	99.5	100.3	98.7	...	...	...	...	...	...
Greece - Grèce									
17 III 1991 (CDFC)	108.8	107.4	110.1	108.5	107.3	109.7	109.1	107.6	110.7
18 III 2001 (CDJC)[59]	105	104.9	105.1	104.8	104.6	104.9	105.8	105.7	106
9 V 2011 (CDFC)	101.4	101.8	101.1	101.3	101.6	101.1	101.8	102.3	101.2
Guernsey - Guernesey									
23 III 1986 (CDJC)	96.1	96.1	96	...	...	...	...	...	...
13 III 1996 (CDJC)	97.5	98.5	96.6	...	...	...	...	...	...
29 IV 2001 (CDJC)	97.2	97.4	96.9	...	...	...	...	...	...
Hungary - Hongrie									
1 I 1990 (CDFC)	102.1	102.5	101.8	102.4	102.8	102	101.7	101.9	101.5
1 II 2001 (CDFC)	101.6	101.8	101.5	101.9	102.2	101.6	101.2	101.2	101.2
1 X 2011 (CDFC)	100.2	100.2	100.2	100.1	100.2	100.1	100.4	100.3	100.5
Ireland - Irlande									
21 IV 1991 (CDFC)	100.5	100.5	100.4	...	...	...	...	...	...
28 IV 1996 (CDFC)	100.2	100.2	100.1	100.3	100.5	100.2	99.9	99.7	100
28 IV 2002 (CDFC)	99.5	99.8	99.2	99.7	99.9	99.4	99.3	99.5	99
23 IV 2006 (CDFC)	100.9	101	100.8	101	101.2	100.8	100.8	100.7	100.8
10 IV 2011 (CDFC)[60]	100.7	101	100.5	100.9	101.2	100.5	100.5	100.5	100.4
Isle of Man - Île de Man									
6 IV 1986 (CDJC)	99.2	98.6	99.8	...	...	...	...	...	...
14 IV 1991 (CDJC)	97.7	98.1	97.3	...	...	...	...	...	...
14 IV 1996 (CDJC)	97.9	98.9	97	...	...	...	...	...	...
29 IV 2001 (CDJC)	97.8	98	97.5	...	...	...	...	...	...
23 IV 2006 (CDJC)	98.3	98.4	98.3	...	...	...	...	...	...
27 III 2011 (CDJC)	99.3	100.4	98.2	...	...	...	...	...	...

Continent, country or area, date and code[a] Continent, pays ou zone, date et code[a]	Total			Urban - Urbaine			Rural - Rurale		
	Both sexes Les deux sexes	Male Masculin	Female Féminin	Both sexes Les deux sexes	Male Masculin	Female Féminin	Both sexes Les deux sexes	Male Masculin	Female Féminin
EUROPE									
Italy - Italie									
21 X 2001 (CDJC)	101.1	101	101.1	...	...	...	...	...	...
9 X 2011 (CDJC)	99.8	99.8	99.8	...	...	...	...	...	...
Jersey									
23 III 1986 (CDFC)	98	98	98	...	...	...	...	...	...
10 III 1991 (CDJC)	99.2	100.6	97.8	...	...	...	...	...	...
10 III 1996 (CDJC)	99.4	100.7	98.1	...	...	...	...	...	...
11 III 2001 (CDJC)	98.9	99.6	98.3	...	...	...	...	...	...
27 III 2011 (CDFC)	100	100.7	99.3	...	...	...	...	...	...
Latvia - Lettonie									
31 III 2000 (CDJC)[61]	100.5	100.2	100.7	100.4	100.4	100.4	100.6	99.8	101.5
1 III 2011 (CDJC)	99.4	99.6	99.3	99.5	99.7	99.3	99.3	99.3	99.4
Liechtenstein									
31 XII 2010 (CDFC)	100.5	102.1	99	...	...	...	...	...	...
Lithuania - Lituanie									
12 I 1989 (CDJC)	100.6	100.5	100.7	100.7	100.6	100.8	100.3	100.2	100.4
6 IV 2001 (CDJC)	99.8	99.7	99.9	99.4	99	99.7	100.8	101.1	100.5
1 III 2011 (CDJC)	100	100.1	99.9	100	100.2	99.8	100	99.9	100
Luxembourg									
15 II 2001 (CDJC)	99.2	98.9	99.6	...	...	...	...	...	...
1 II 2011 (CDJC)	99.7	99	100.4	...	...	...	...	...	...
Malta - Malte									
26 XI 1995 (CDJC)	101.2	101.2	101.2	101.2	101.2	101.2	125.7	107.6	138.4
27 XI 2005 (CDJC)	101.3	101.9	100.6	101.2	102	100.5	114.3	100	127.3
20 XI 2011 (CDFC)	99.4	100	98.9	99.4	99.9	98.9	100.3	102.3	98.1
Monaco									
21 VI 2000 (CDJC)	100.9	99.9	101.9	...	...	...	...	...	...
Montenegro - Monténégro									
31 X 2003 (CDJC)	100.2	99.9	100.5	100.2	99.6	100.8	100.2	100.3	100
1 IV 2011 (CDJC)	100	99.7	100.3	99.9	99.3	100.5	100.1	100.2	99.9
Netherlands - Pays-Bas									
1 I 2002 (CDJC)	101.2	101.3	101	101.3	101.5	101.1	101	101.1	101
1 I 2011 (CDJC)	100.2	100.2	100.2	...	...	...	...	...	...
Norway - Norvège									
3 XI 1990 (CDJC)	99.9	99.9	99.9	99.9	99.9	100	99.9	100	99.8
3 XI 2001 (CDJC)[62]	100.1	100.1	100.1	100.1	100.1	100.2	99.7	99.9	99.6
19 XI 2011 (CDJC)[62]	99.8	99.8	99.7	99.7[63]	99.6[63]	99.7[63]	100.1[63]	100.4[63]	99.8[63]
Poland - Pologne									
6 XII 1988 (CDFC)	100.5	100.6	100.4	100.5	100.6	100.4	100.5	100.6	100.5
20 V 2002 (CDJC)[64]	100.7	100.7	100.7	100.9	100.8	100.9	100.4	100.5	100.2
31 III 2011 (CDJC)	100.1	100.1	100.1	100.1	100.1	100.1	100.1	100.1	100
Portugal									
15 IV 1991 (CDFC)	101.4	101.7	101.1	101.4	101.7	101.2	101.3	101.6	101.1
21 III 2011 (CDJC)	100.7	100.8	100.5	100.8	101	100.7	100.4	100.4	100.3
Republic of Moldova - République de Moldova									
12 I 1989 (CDJC)	100.5	100.4	100.5	100.2	99.9	100.4	100.7	100.8	100.6
5 X 2004 (CDFC)[65]	103.2	103.3	103.2	102.9	102.9	102.9	103.5	103.5	103.5
Romania - Roumanie									
7 I 1992 (CDJC)	96.2	96.2	96.2	95.6	95.8	95.4	97.1	96.8	97.4
18 III 2002 (CDJC)	95.8	95.9	95.8	95.3	95.5	95.2	96.5	96.3	96.7
20 X 2011 (CDJC)	96.6	96.6	96.6	96.4	96.5	96.3	96.8	96.7	96.9
Russian Federation - Fédération de Russie									
12 I 1989 (CDJC)	97.8	97.7	97.9	97.7	97.6	97.7	98.3	98.2	98.4
14 X 2010 (CDJC)	103	103	103	103.5	103.5	103.5	101.7	101.6	101.7
Serbia - Serbie[66]									
31 III 2002 (CDJC)	99.9	99.9	100	100.4	100.4	100.5	99.2	99.3	99.2
1 X 2011 (CDJC)	99.4	99.2	99.5	99.7	99.3	100	98.9	99.1	98.7
Slovakia - Slovaquie									
3 III 1991 (CDJC)	100	99.8	100.2	...	...	...	...	...	...
25 V 2001 (CDJC)	99.5	99.5	99.6	99.7	99.6	99.8	99.3	99.3	99.3
21 V 2011 (CDJC)	100.2	100.2	100.3	100.3	100.2	100.4	100.2	100.2	100.1
Slovenia - Slovénie									
31 III 1991 (CDJC)	99	99.1	98.9	99.7	99.7	99.6	98.4	98.6	98.1
31 III 2002 (CDJC)	101.9	102.1	101.8	102.2	102.3	102.2	101.6	101.9	101.3
1 I 2011 (CDJC)	100.6	100.1	101.3	100.7	100.1	101.3	100.6	100	101.3

Continent, country or area, date and code[a] Continent, pays ou zone, date et code[a]	Total			Urban - Urbaine			Rural - Rurale		
	Both sexes Les deux sexes	Male Masculin	Female Féminin	Both sexes Les deux sexes	Male Masculin	Female Féminin	Both sexes Les deux sexes	Male Masculin	Female Féminin
EUROPE									
Spain - Espagne									
1 III 1991 (CDJC)	102.4	102.4	102.3	...	...	...	...	...	...
1 XI 2001 (CDFC)[67]	99	99	99	99	99	98.9	99.1	99	99.1
1 XI 2011 (CDJC)	98.3	98.6	98.1	...	...	...	...	...	...
Sweden - Suède									
1 XI 1990 (CDJC)	99.7	99.8	99.6	...	...	...	...	...	...
31 XII 2003 (CDJC)	100	100	100.1	...	...	...	...	...	...
31 XII 2011 (CDJC)	99.7	99.8	99.6	...	...	...	...	...	...
Switzerland - Suisse									
4 XII 1990 (CDJC)	100.6	100.9	100.2	100.7	100.9	100.5	100.2	100.7	99.7
5 XII 2000 (CDFC)	99.7	99.9	99.5	99.7	99.9	99.6	99.5	99.9	99.1
31 XII 2011 (CDJC)	99.9	99.9	99.9	99.9	99.9	99.8	100	99.9	100.1
TFYR of Macedonia - L'ex-R. y. de Macédoine									
20 VI 1994 (CDJC)	100.2	100.2	100.2	100	100.1	99.8	100.6	100.5	100.8
31 X 2002 (CDJC)	100.3	100.3	100.3	...	...	...	...	...	...
Ukraine									
5 XII 2001 (CDFC)...........................	102.7	102.7	102.7	103.1	103.1	103.2	101.7	101.8	101.5
United Kingdom of Great Britain and Northern Ireland - Royaume-Uni de Grande-Bretagne et d'Irlande du Nord[68]									
21 IV 1991 (CDFC)[69].......................	98	98	98	...	...	...	...	...	...
29 IV 2001 (CDFC)[70].......................	98.1	98	98.1	98.2	98.2	98.2	97.6	97.5	97.7
27 III 2011 (CDJC)...........................	100.2	100.3	100.2	100.3	100.3	100.3	99.8	99.8	99.8
OCEANIA - OCÉANIE									
Australia - Australie									
30 VI 1986 (CDFC)..........................	101.6	101.7	101.5	101.6	101.6	101.5	101.8	102	101.6
6 VIII 1991 (CDFC)..........................	101.7	101.4	102.1	...	...	...	...	...	...
9 VIII 1996 (CDFC)..........................	101.6	101.5	101.7	...	...	...	...	...	...
7 VIII 2001 (CDJC)..........................	101.4	101.3	101.5	101.4	101.3	101.5	101.3	101.4	101.3
8 VIII 2006 (CDJC)[71]	100.2[72]	100.3[72]	100.2[72]	100.2	100.2	100.1	100.4	100.5	100.3
9 VIII 2011 (CDJC)[71]	100.8[72]	100.8[72]	100.7[72]	100.7	100.7	100.7	101.3	101.3	101.3
Cook Islands - Îles Cook[73]									
1 XII 1996 (CDJC)	99.1	97.2	101.1	...	...	...	...	...	...
Fiji - Fidji									
31 VIII 1986 (CDFC)........................	105.4	105	105.7	...	...	...	...	...	...
25 VIII 1996 (CDFC)........................	100.2	100.6	99.8	99.8	99.9	99.7	100.6	101.3	99.9
French Polynesia - Polynésie française									
3 IX 1996 (CDFC)...........................	98.6	97.8	99.5	...	...	...	...	...	...
20 VIII 2007 (CDJC)	102.8	103.2	102.4	...	...	...	...	...	...
Guam									
1 IV 1990 (CDJC)...........................	107.1	106.2	108.2	107	105.5	108.7	107.2	106.6	107.8
1 IV 2000 (CDJC)[12]	100.3	100.4	100.3	...	...	...	...	...	...
Kiribati									
10 X 2010 (CDFC)...........................	104.7	103.3	105.9	106	106	106.1	103.3	100.7	105.7
Marshall Islands - Îles Marshall									
13 XI 1988 (CDFC)..........................	101.2	103.3	98.9	...	...	...	...	...	...
1 VI 1999 (CDFC)...........................	104	106.2	101.7	...	...	...	...	...	...
New Caledonia - Nouvelle-Calédonie									
4 IV 1989 (CDFC)...........................	99.5	99.4	99.6	...	...	...	...	...	...
New Zealand - Nouvelle-Zélande									
4 III 1986 (CDJC)	100.7[74]	100.6[74]	100.7[74]	100.7[74]	100.7[74]	100.8[74]	100.2[74]	99.9[74]	100.6[74]
5 III 1991 (CDFC)	100.3	100.4	100.3	100.5	100.6	100.4	99.7	99.3	100
5 III 1996 (CDJC)[75]........................	100	100	100	100.1	100.1	100.1	99.5	99.5	99.5
6 III 2001 (CDJC)[71]	100	99.9	100	100.2	100.1	100.2	99	99	99.1
7 III 2006 (CDFC)[71]	99.7	...	...	...	...	...	...	...	...
7 III 2006 (CDJC)[71]	99.6	99.7	99.6	99.7	99.8	99.7	99.1	99.3	98.9
Niue - Nioué									
29 IX 1986 (CDFC)..........................	105.8	106	105.6	...	...	...	...	...	...
7 IX 2001 (CDFC)...........................	98.5	93.8	103.4	...	...	...	...	...	...

Continent, country or area, date and code[a] Continent, pays ou zone, date et code[a]	Total			Urban - Urbaine			Rural - Rurale		
	Both sexes Les deux sexes	Male Masculin	Female Féminin	Both sexes Les deux sexes	Male Masculin	Female Féminin	Both sexes Les deux sexes	Male Masculin	Female Féminin
OCEANIA - OCÉANIE									
Northern Mariana Islands - Îles Mariannes septentrionales									
1 IV 1990 (CDFC).............	108	108.4	107.4	111.7	111.2	112.1	106.6	107.5	105.3
Palau - Palaos									
15 IV 2000 (CDFC)...........	103.4	105.5	100.5	...	...	...	...	...	...
Papua New Guinea - Papouasie-Nouvelle-Guinée									
11 VII 1990 (CDFC)...........	139	140.1	137.7	...	...	...	...	...	...
9 VII 2000 (CDFC)...........	134	134.2	133.8	131	133.4	128	134.5	134.4	134.7
Pitcairn									
31 XII 1991 (CDFC)...........	96.2	90.9	100	...	...	...	...	...	...
Samoa									
5 XI 2001 (CDFC)...........	96.4	95.9	97	...	...	...	...	...	...
Tokelau - Tokélaou									
18 X 2011 (CDFC)...........	102.7	104.3	101.2	...	...	...	...	...	...
18 X 2011 (CDJC)[76]...........	105.7	109.6	102	...	...	...	...	...	...
Tonga									
28 XI 1986 (CDJC)...........	98.2	99	97.4	...	...	...	...	...	...
30 XI 1996 (CDFC)[77]...........	100.7	101.7	99.6	...	...	...	...	...	...
30 XI 2006 (CDJC)...........	98.6	97.8	99.4	95.2	93.3	97.2	99.7	99.3	100.1
Tuvalu									
1 XI 2002 (CDFC)...........	98.5	100.8	96.4	...	...	...	...	...	...
Vanuatu									
16 V 1989 (CDJC)...........	106.9	104.8	109	102.4	98.1	107.8	108.1	106.8	109.3
16 XI 2009 (CDJC)...........	110.5	111.3	109.7	...	...	...	...	...	...
Wallis and Futuna Islands - Îles Wallis et Futuna									
3 X 1996 (CDFC)...........	96	97.8	94.3	...	...	...	...	...	...

FOOTNOTES - NOTES

Italics: estimates which are less reliable. - Italiques : estimations moins sûres.

* Provisional. - Données provisoires.

[a] 'Code' indicates the source of data, as follows:
CDFC - Census, de facto, complete tabulation
CDFS - Census, de facto, sample tabulation
CDJC - Census, de jure, complete tabulation
CDJS - Census, de jure, sample tabulation
SSDF - Sample survey, de facto
SSDJ - Sample survey, de jure
ESDF - Estimates, de facto
ESDJ - Estimates, de jure

Le 'Code' indique la source des données, comme suit :
CDFC - Recensement, population de fait, tabulation complète
CDFS - Recensement, population de fait, tabulation par sondage
CDJC - Recensement, population de droit, tabulation complète
CDJS - Recensement, population de droit, tabulation par sondage
SSDF - Enquête par sondage, population de fait
SSDJ - Enquête par sondage, population de droit
ESDF - Estimations, population de fait
ESDJ - Estimations, population de droit

[1] Data refer to population in housing units and collective living quarters only. - Correspond aux personnes qui vivent dans des unités d'habitation et dans des logements collectifs seulement.
[2] Data for urban and rural do not add up to the total; reason for discrepancy not ascertained. - La somme des données pour la résidence urbaine et rurale n'est pas égale au total; on ne sait pas comment s'explique la divergence.
[3] Urban and rural data were reported in different years and do not add up to the total. - Les données concernant la population urbaine et la population rurale portent sur des années différentes et leur somme ne correspond pas au total cité.

[4] Excludes the islands of St. Brandon and Agalega. - Non compris les îles St. Brandon et Agalega.
[5] Data refer to Saint Helenian resident population. - Pour la population résidante de Sainte-Hélène.
[6] Data have been adjusted for underenumeration, estimated at 6.8 per cent. - Les données ont été ajustées pour compenser les lacunes du dénombrement estimées à 6,8 p. 100.
[7] Because of rounding, totals are not in all cases the sum of the respective components. - Les chiffres étant arrondis, les totaux ne correspondent pas toujours rigoureusement à la somme des composants respectifs.
[8] Excluding the institutional population. - Non compris la population dans les institutions.
[9] Bermuda is 100 per cent urban. - 100 pour cent de la population des Bermudes est urbaine.
[10] Total represents population in private dwellings, the non-institutional population and persons found on the streets between the hours of 5am and 7am on September 26, 2001; the figures represent the census counts adjusted for under-coverage. - Le total représente la population vivant dans des logements privés et les personnes trouvées dans la rue entre 5 et 7 heures du matin le 26 septembre 2001, mais ne tient pas compte des personnes vivant dans des établissements; les chiffres sont ceux du recensement corrigés pour tenir compte du sous-dénombrement.
[11] Including an estimation of 1 334 585 persons corresponding to 448 195 housing units without information of the occupants. - Y compris une estimation de 1 334 585 personnes correspondant aux 448 195 unités d'habitation sans information sur les occupants.
[12] Including armed forces stationed in the area. - Y compris les militaires en garnison sur le territoire.
[13] Excluding U.S. Armed Forces overseas and civilian U.S. citizens whose usual place of residence is outside the United States. - Non compris les militaires américains à l'étranger et les civils américains dont le lieu de résidence habituel est en dehors des États-Unis.
[14] Data include persons in remote areas, military personnel outside the country, merchant seamen at sea, civilian seasonal workers outside the country, and other civilians outside the country, and exclude nomads, foreign military, civilian aliens temporarily in the country, transients on ships and Indian jungle population. - Y compris les personnes vivant dans des régions éloignées, le personel militaire en

dehors du pays, les marins marchands, les ouvriers saisonniers en dehors du pays, et autres civils en dehors du pays, et non compris les nomades, les militaires étrangers, les étrangers civils temporairement dans le pays, les transiteurs sur des bateaux et les Indiens de la jungle.

[15] Excludes nomadic Indian tribes. - Non compris les tribus d'Indiens nomades.

[16] The districts of Paramaribo and Wanica are considered urban areas, whereas all other districts are considered more or less rural areas. - Les districts de Paramaribo et de Wanica sont considérés comme des zones urbaines, les autres districts étant considérés comme des zones rurales à divers degrés.

[17] Unrevised data. - Les données n'ont pas été révisées.

[18] Unrevised data. Data refer to resident population in Uruguay according to Census Phase 1, carried out between the months of June and July 2004. - Les données n'ont pas été révisées. Les données se rapportent à la population résidente en Uruguay d'après la phase 1 du recensement, qui a eu lieu entre juin et juillet 2004.

[19] Excluding Indian jungle population. - Non compris les Indiens de la jungle.

[20] For operational purposes, population centers with 2,500 and more inhabitants are considered as urban area and less than 2,500 are considered as rural area. - À des fins opérationnelles, les centres de population comptant 2 500 habitants ou plus sont considérés comme zones urbaines, ceux qui en comptent moins de 2 500 comme zones rurales.

[21] Data have not been adjusted for underenumeration, estimated at 4.96 per cent. - Les données n'ont pas été ajustées pour compenser les lacunes du dénombrement, estimées à 4,96 p.100.

[22] Excluding foreign diplomatic personnel and their dependants. - Non compris le personnel diplomatique étranger et les membres de leur famille les accompagnant.

[23] For statistical purposes, the data for China do not include those for the Hong Kong Special Administrative Region (Hong Kong SAR), Macao Special Administrative Region (Macao SAR) and Taiwan province of China. Data exclude 2.3 million servicemen, 4.65 million persons with permanent resident status difficult to define, and 0.12 per cent undercount based on the post enumeration survey. - Pour la présentation des statistiques, les données pour la Chine ne comprennent pas la Région Administrative Spéciale de Hong Kong (Hong Kong RAS), la Région Administrative Spéciale de Macao (Macao RAS) et Taïwan province de Chine. Les données ne comprennent pas 2,3 millions de militaires, 4,65 millions de personnes ayant le statut de résident permanent mais difficiles à définir, et des lacunes estimées à 0,12 pour cent sur la base de l'enquête de vérification du recensement.

[24] Data refer to Hong Kong resident population at the census moment, which covers usual residents and mobile residents. Usual residents refer to two categories of people: (1) Hong Kong permanent residents who had stayed in Hong Kong for at least three months during the six months before or for at least three months during the six months after the census moment, regardless of whether they were in Hong Kong or not at the census moment; and (2) Hong Kong non-permanent residents who were in Hong Kong at the census moment. Mobile Residents, they are Hong Kong permanent residents who had stayed in Hong Kong for at least one month but less than three months during the six months before or for at least one month but less than three months during the six months after the census moment, regardless of whether they were in Hong Kong or not at the census moment. - Les données se rapportent à la population résidente à Hong Kong au moment du recensement. Cette population est composée des résidants habituels et des résidants mobiles. La population résidente est partagée en deux catégories: (1) les résidents permanents qui ont habité à Hong Kong au moins trois mois pendant les six mois précédents ou les six mois suivants le recensement; (2) les habitants non-permanents de Hong Kong qui étaient à Hong Kong au moment du recensement. La population mobile se rapporte aux résidents permanents de Hong Kong qui ont habité à Hong Kong pendant les six mois après le recensement pour une période comprise entre un mois et trois mois, indépendamment du fait qu'ils étaient à Hong Kong au moment du recensement au pays.

[25] Data refer to Hong Kong resident population at the census moment, which covers usual residents and mobile residents. Usual residents refer to two categories of people: (1) Hong Kong permanent residents who had stayed in Hong Kong for at least three months during the six months before or for at least three months during the six months after the census moment, regardless of whether they were in Hong Kong or not at the census moment; and (2) Hong Kong non-permanent residents who were in Hong Kong at the census moment. Mobile Residents, they are Hong Kong permanent residents who had stayed in Hong Kong for at least one month but less than three months during the six months before or for at least one month but less than three months during the six months after the census moment, regardless of whether they were in Hong Kong or not at the census moment. Data are estimates from sample enquiry. - Les données se rapportent à la population résidente à Hong Kong au moment du recensement. Cette population est composée des résidants habituels et des résidants mobiles. La population résidente est partagée en deux catégories: (1) les résidents permanents qui ont habité à Hong Kong au moins trois mois

pendant les six mois précédents ou les six mois suivants le recensement; (2) les habitants non-permanents de Hong Kong qui étaient à Hong Kong au moment du recensement. La population mobile se rapporte aux résidents permanents de Hong Kong qui ont habité à Hong Kong pendant les six mois après le recensement pour une période comprise entre un mois et trois mois, indépendamment du fait qu'ils étaient à Hong Kong au moment du recensement au pays. Les données sont des chiffres estimatifs dérivés d'une enquête par sondage.

[26] Data refer to government controlled areas. - Les données se rapportent aux zones contrôlées par le Gouvernement.

[27] Excluding data for Jammu and Kashmir. - Non compris les données concernant la partie du Jammu et Cachemire.

[28] Includes data for the Indian-held part of Jammu and Kashmir, the final status of which has not yet been determined. Excluding Mao-Maram, Paomata and Purul sub-divisions of Senapati district of Manipur. The population of Manipur including the estimated population of the three sub-divisions of Senapati district is 2,291,125 (Males 1,161,173 and females 1,129,952). - Y compris les données pour la partie du Jammu et du Cachemire occupée par l'Inde dont le statut définitif n'a pas encore été déterminé. Non compris les subdivisions Mao-Maram Paomata et Purul du district de Senapati dans l'État du Manipur. Cet État compte 2 291 125 habitants (1 161 173 hommes et 1 129 952 femmes), y compris la population estimative des trois subdivisions du district de Senapati.

[29] Includes data for the Indian-held part of Jammu and Kashmir, the final status of which has not yet been determined. - Y compris les données pour la partie du Jammu et du Cachemire occupée par l'Inde dont le statut définitif n'a pas encore été déterminé.

[30] Data have not been adjusted for underenumeration. - Les données n'ont pas été ajustées pour compenser les lacunes du dénombrement.

[31] Differences between the total country figures and sum of urban and rural areas are due to the inclusion of unsettled population. - Les différences entre les chiffres pour l'ensemble du pays et la somme des zones urbaines et rurales s'expliquent par l'inclusion de la population non sédentaire.

[32] Including unsettled population. - Y compris la population non sédentaire.

[33] The data is from the census sample. - Données extraites de l'échantillon de recensement.

[34] Because of rounding, totals are not in all cases the sum of the respective components. Includes data for East Jerusalem and Israeli residents in certain other territories under occupation by Israeli military forces since June 1967. Data are rounded for confidentiality reasons. - Les chiffres étant arrondis, les totaux ne correspondent pas toujours rigoureusement à la somme des composants respectifs. Y compris les données pour Jérusalem-Est et les résidents israéliens dans certains autres territoires occupés depuis 1967 par les forces armées israéliennes. Chiffres arrondis pour des raisons de confidentialité.

[35] Excluding diplomatic personnel outside the country and foreign military and civilian personnel and their dependants stationed in the area. - Non compris le personnel diplomatique hors du pays ni les militaires et agents civils étrangers en poste sur le territoire et les membres de leur famille les accompagnant.

[36] Excluding data for Jordanian territory under occupation since June 1967 by Israeli military forces. Including registered Palestinian refugees and Jordanians abroad. - Non compris les données pour le territoire jordanien occupé depuis juin 1967 par les forces armées israéliennes. Y compris les réfugiés palestiniens enregistrés et les Jordaniens à l'étranger.

[37] Excluding data for Jordanian territory under occupation since June 1967 by Israeli military forces. - Non compris les données pour le territoire jordanien occupé depuis juin 1967 par les forces armées israéliennes.

[38] Excluding usual residents not in the country at the time of census. - À l'exclusion des résidents habituels qui ne sont pas dans le pays au moment du recensement.

[39] Data have been adjusted for underenumeration. - Les données ont été ajustées pour compenser les lacunes du dénombrement.

[40] Total population is taken as de facto and de jure together. - Population totale considérée comme de fait et de droit.

[41] Data refer to resident population that includes Maldivians and foreigners. - Les données concernent la population résidente, qui comprend des Maldiviens et des étrangers.

[42] Data refer to enumerated population. - Les données se rapportent à la population dénombrée.

[43] Data refer to projections based on the 1995 Population Census. - Correspond à des projections fondées sur le recensement de population de 1995.

[44] Excluding 2739 Filipinos in Philippine Embassies, Consulates and Missions Abroad. - Excepté 2739 Philippins travaillant dans les ambassades, les consulats et les missions des Philippines à l'étranger.

[45] Excluding foreigners. - Non compris étrangers.

[46] Data are based on the latest register-based population estimates for 2010. Data refer to resident population which comprises Singapore citizens and permanent residents. - Données basées sur les estimations démographiques les

plus récentes fondées sur les registres de 2010. Les données se rapportent à la population résidente composé des citoyens de Singapour et des résidents permanents.

⁴⁷ The Population and Housing Census 2001 did not cover the whole area of the country due to the security problems; data refer to the 18 districts for which the census was completed only (in three districts it was not possible to conduct the census at all and in four districts it was partially conducted). Unrevised data. - Le recensement de la population et du logement de 2001 n'a pas été réalisé sur la superficie totale du pays à cause de problèmes de sécurité; les données ne concernent que les 18 districts entièrement recensés (3 districts n'ont pas été recensés du tout, et 4 ont été recensés en partie). Les données n'ont pas été révisées.

⁴⁸ Data for rural areas include data of estate sectors consist of all plantations which are 20 acres or more in extent and with ten or more resident labourers. - Les données pour les zones rurales comprennent celles pour les domaines, dont l'ensemble des plantations de plus de 10 hectares comptant au moins 10 travailleurs résidents.

⁴⁹ Total population does not include Palestinian population living in those parts of Jerusalem governorate which were annexed by Israel in 1967, amounting to 210 209 persons. Likewise, the results does not include the estimates of not enumerated population based on the findings of the post enumeration study, i.e 83 805 persons. - Les données relatives à la population totale ne comprennent pas la population palestinienne -équivalent à 210 209 personnes - habitant dans les territoires du gouvernorat de Jérusalem qui ont été annexés par Israël en 1967. Egalement, les données ne tiennent pas compte des estimations de la population calculée sur la base des résultats de l'enquête postcensitaire, équivalent à 83 805 personnes.

⁵⁰ Data for urban include population in refugee camps. - Les données pour la population urbaine comprennent la population dans les camps réfugiés.

⁵¹ Including Palestinian refugees. - Y compris les réfugiés de Palestine.

⁵² All persons falling within the scope of the census were enumerated on a de jure basis, except students who were enumerated on a de facto basis. - Toutes les personnes englobées dans le recensement ont été dénombrées comme population de droit, à l'exception des étudiants qui ont été dénombrés comme population de fait.

⁵³ Based on a sample taken at the time of census. Because of rounding, totals are not in all cases the sum of the respective components. The figures were calculated by dividing and rounding to thousand. Therefore, "0" may indicate value of less than 500. - D'après un échantillon obtenu au moment du recensement. Les chiffres étant arrondis, les totaux ne correspondent pas toujours rigoureusement à la somme des composants respectifs. Les chiffres ont été calculés en divisant et en arrondissant au millier. Par conséquent, "0" peut indiquer une valeur inférieure à 500.

⁵⁴ Statistics are compiled from registers. - Les statistiques sont compilées à partir des registres.

⁵⁵ Excluding Faeroe Islands and Greenland shown separately, if available. - Non compris les Iles Féroé et le Groenland, qui font l'objet de rubriques distinctes, si disponible.

⁵⁶ Data include Overseas Departments. - Y compris les données des départements d'outre-mer.

⁵⁷ Excluding families of military personnel, visitors and transients. - Non compris les familles des militaires, ni les visiteurs et transients.

⁵⁸ Excluding military personnel, visitors and transients. - Non compris les militaires, ni les visiteurs et transients.

⁵⁹ Including armed forces stationed outside the country and alien armed forces in the area. - Y compris les militaires nationaux hors du pays et les militaires étrangers en garnison sur le territoire.

⁶⁰ The figures refer to usual residents in private households and persons present in communal establishments during the 2011 census. - Données se rapportant aux résidents habituels membres de ménages privés et aux personnes recensées dans des établissements collectifs au recensement de 2011.

⁶¹ Age classification based on year of birth rather than on completed years of age. - La classification par âge est fondée sur l'année de naissance et non sur l'âge en années révolues.

⁶² Including residents temporarily outside the country. Population statistics are compiled from registers. - Y compris les résidents se trouvant temporairement hors du pays. Les statistiques de la population sont compilées à partir des registres.

⁶³ The total number may include 'Unknown residence', but the categories urban and rural do not. - Le nombre total peut inclure les personnes dont la résidence n'est pas connue, à l'inverse des catégories de population urbaine et rurale.

⁶⁴ Excluding civilian aliens within the country, but including civilian nationals temporarily outside the country. - Non compris les civils étrangers dans le pays, mais y compris les civils nationaux temporairement hors du pays.

⁶⁵ Excluding Transnistria and the municipality of Bender. Excluding non-residents present in country at time of census. - Les données ne tiennent pas compte de l'information sur la Transnistria et la municipalité de Bender. Non compris les non-résidents présents dans le pays au moment du recensement.

⁶⁶ Excludes data for Kosovo and Metohia. - Sans les données pour le Kosovo et Metohie.

⁶⁷ Excluding transients visitors. - Non compris les visiteurs en transit.

⁶⁸ Excluding Channel Islands (Guernsey and Jersey) and Isle of Man, shown separately, if available. - Non compris les îles Anglo-Normandes (Guernesey et Jersey) et l'île de Man, qui font l'objet de rubriques distinctes, si disponible.

⁶⁹ Counts for the 1991 Census are taken from 'Key Statistics for Urban and Rural Areas: Great Britain 1991' published volume basen on the usually resident population. - Les chiffres du recensement de 1991 sont extraits de l'ouvrage « Key Statistics for Urban Areas: Great Britain 1991 » et sont fondés sur la notion de résidence habituelle

⁷⁰ Counts for the 2001 Census are taken from 'Key Statistics table 1 for the Urban/Rural classification: England and Wales' available on CD based on the usually resident population. - Les chiffres du recensement de 2001 proviennent du tableau intitulé « Key Statistics table 1 for the Urban/Rural classification: England and Wales » disponible sur CD-ROM et sont fondés sur la notion de résidence habituelle.

⁷¹ This data has been randomly rounded to protect confidentiality. Individual figures may not add up to totals, and values for the same data may vary in different tables. - Ces données ont été arrondies de façon aléatoire afin d'en préserver la confidentialité. La somme de certains chiffres peut ne pas correspondre aux totaux indiqués et les valeurs des mêmes données peuvent varier d'un tableau à un autre.

⁷² Including population in off-shore, migratory and shipping. - Y compris les populations extraterritoriales, les populations nomades et les populations maritimes.

⁷³ Excluding Niue, shown separately, which is part of Cook Islands, but because of remoteness is administered separately. - Non compris Nioué, qui fait l'objet d'une rubrique distincte et qui fait partie des îles Cook, mais qui, en raison de son éloignement, est administrée séparément.

⁷⁴ Excluding diplomatic personnel and armed forces stationed outside country; also excluding alien armed forces within the country. Data refer to usual residents in country at time of census. - Non compris le personnel diplomatique et les militaires hors du pays; non compris également les militaires étrangers en garnison dans le pays. Pour les personnes qui résident habituellement dans le pays au moment du recensement.

⁷⁵ Summation of frequencies for age groups gives a different total; reason for discrepancy not ascertained. - La somme des fréquences par groupes d'âges donne un total différent; on ne sait pas comment s'explique la divergence.

⁷⁶ Data includes Tokelaun Public Service employees and their immediate families based in Apia but excludes non-residents present at the time of the census. - Les données comprennent les agents de la fonction publique des Tokélaou et leur famille directe basés à Apia mais excluent les non-résidents présents au moment du recensement.

⁷⁷ Data refer to Tongans and part-Tongans only. - Les données ne concernent que la population tongane et partie-Tongans seulement.

Table 4 - Demographic Yearbook 2015

Table 4 presents, for each country or area of the world, basic vital statistics for the period 2011 - 2015: live births, crude birth rate, deaths, crude death rate, rate of natural increase, infant deaths, infant death rate, life expectancy at birth by sex and total fertility rate.

Description of variables: The vital events and rates shown in this table are defined as follows[1]:

Live birth is the complete expulsion or extraction from its mother of a product of conception, irrespective of the duration of pregnancy, which after such separation breathes or shows any other evidence of life such as beating of the heart, pulsation of the umbilical cord, definite movement of voluntary muscles, whether or not the umbilical cord has been cut or the placenta is attached; each product of such a birth is considered live born.

Death is the permanent disappearance of all evidence of life at any time after live birth has taken place (post-natal cessation of vital functions without capability of resuscitation).

Infant deaths are deaths of live born infants under one year of age.

Life expectancy at birth is defined as the average number of years of life for males and females if they continued to be subject to the same mortality experienced in the year(s) to which these life expectancies refer.

The total fertility rate is the average number of children that would be born alive to a hypothetical cohort of women if, throughout their reproductive years, the age-specific fertility rates remained unchanged. The standard method of calculating the total fertility rate is the sum of the age-specific fertility rates.

Crude birth rates and crude death rates presented in this table are calculated using the number of live births and the number of deaths obtained from civil registers. These civil registration data are used only if they are considered reliable (estimated completeness of 90 per cent or more).

Similarly, infant mortality rates presented in this table are calculated using the number of live births and the number of infant deaths obtained from civil registers. If, however, the registration of births or infant deaths for any given country or area is estimated to be less than 90 per cent complete, the rates are not calculated.

For some countries, the data and rates presented in this table are based on vital statistics data sourced from censuses or demographic surveys.

Rate computation: The crude birth and death rates are the annual number of each of these vital events per 1 000 mid-year population. Infant mortality rate is the annual number of deaths of infants under one year of age per 1 000 live births in the same year.

Rates of natural increase are the difference between the crude birth rate and the crude death rate. It should be noted that the rates of natural increase presented here may differ from the population growth rates presented in table 3 as rates of natural increase do not take net international migration into account while the population growth rates do.

Crude birth rates, crude death rates and infant mortality rates that appear in this table have been calculated by the United Nations Statistics Division, unless otherwise noted. Exceptions include official estimated rates for India, which were based on the sample registration system. Rates calculated by the United Nations Statistics Division presented in this table have been limited to those countries or areas having a minimum number of 30 events (for live births, deaths or infant deaths) in a given year.

Reliability of data: Rates calculated on the basis of registered vital statistics which are considered unreliable (estimated to be less than 90 per cent complete) are not calculated. Estimated rates, prepared by individual countries or areas, are presented whenever applicable.

The designation of vital statistics as being either reliable or unreliable is discussed in general in section 4.2 of the Technical Notes. The technical notes for tables 9, 15 and 18 provide specific information on reliability of statistics on live births, infant deaths and deaths, respectively.

The values shown for life expectancy in this table come from official life tables. It is assumed that, if necessary, the basic data (population and deaths classified by age and sex) have been adjusted for deficiencies before their use in constructing the life tables.

Limitations: Statistics on births, deaths and infant deaths are subject to the same qualifications as have been set forth for vital statistics, in general, in section 4 of the Technical Notes and in the technical notes for individual tables presenting detailed data on these events (table 9, live births; table 15, infant deaths; table 18, deaths).

In assessing comparability it is important to take into account the reliability of the data used to calculate the rates, as discussed above.

The problem of obtaining precise correspondence between numerator (births and deaths) and denominator (population for crude birth and death rates) as regards the inclusion or exclusion of armed forces, refugees, displaced persons and other special groups is particularly difficult where vital rates are concerned.

It should also be noted that crude rates are particularly affected by the age-sex structure of the population. Infant mortality rates, and to a much lesser extent crude birth rates and crude death rates, are affected by the variation in the definition of a live birth and tabulation procedures.

NOTES

[1] *Principles and Recommendations for a Vital Statistics System Revision 3,* Sales No. E.13.XVII.10, United Nations, New York, 2014.

Tableau 4 – *Annuaire démographique 2015*

Le tableau 4 présente, pour chaque pays ou zone du monde, des statistiques de base de l'état civil pour les années 2011 – 2015 : les naissances vivantes, le taux brut de natalité, les décès, le taux brut de mortalité et le taux d'accroissement naturel de la population, les décès d'enfants de moins d'un an et le taux de mortalité infantile, l'espérance de vie à la naissance par sexe et l'indice synthétique de fécondité.

Description des variables : les faits d'état civil utilisés aux fins du calcul des taux présentés dans le tableau 4 sont définis comme suit[1] :

La naissance vivante est l'expulsion ou l'extraction complète du corps de la mère, indépendamment de la duré de la gestation, d'un produit de la conception qui après cette séparation, respire ou manifeste tout autre signe de vie, tel que battement de cœur, pulsation du cordon ombilical ou contraction effective d'un muscle soumis à l'action de la volonté, que le cordon ombilical ait été coupé ou non et que le placenta soit ou non demeuré attaché ; tout produit d'une telle naissance est considéré comme « enfant né vivant ».

Le décès est la disparition permanente de tout signe de vie à un moment quelconque postérieur à la naissance vivante (cessation des fonctions vitales après la naissance sans possibilité de réanimation).

Il convient de préciser que les chiffres relatifs aux décès d'enfants de moins d'un an se rapportent aux naissances vivantes.

L'espérance de vie à la naissance est le nombre moyen d'années que vivraient les individus de sexe masculin et de sexe féminin s'ils continuaient d'être soumis aux mêmes conditions de mortalité que celles qui existaient pendant les années auxquelles se rapportent les valeurs indiquées.

L'indice synthétique de fécondité représente le nombre moyen d'enfants que mettrait au monde une cohorte hypothétique de femmes qui seraient soumises, tout au long de leur vie, aux mêmes conditions de fécondité par âge que celles auxquelles sont soumises les femmes, dans chaque groupe d'âge, au cours d'une année ou d'une période donnée. La méthode standard pour calculer l'indice synthétique de fécondité consiste à additionner les taux de fécondité par âge simple.

Les taux bruts de natalité et de mortalité ont été établis sur la base du nombre de naissances vivantes et du nombre de décès inscrits sur les registres de l'état civil. Ces données n'ont été utilisées que lorsqu'elles étaient considérées comme sûres (degré estimatif de complétude égal ou supérieur à 90 p. 100).

De même, les taux de mortalité infantile présentés dans le tableau 4 ont été établis à partir du nombre de naissances vivantes et du nombre de décès d'enfants de moins d'un an inscrits sur les registres de l'état civil. Toutefois, lorsque les données relatives aux naissances ou aux décès d'enfants de moins d'un an pour un pays ou zone quelconque n'étaient pas considérées complètes à 90 p. 100 au moins, les indices n'ont pas été calculés.

Pour quelques pays, les données et les taux présentés dans ce tableau ont été extraites des recensements de la population ou des enquêtes démographiques.

Calcul des taux : les taux bruts de natalité et de mortalité, représentent le nombre annuel de chacun de ces faits d'état civil pour 1 000 habitants au milieu de l'année considérée. Les taux de mortalité infantile correspondent au nombre annuel de décès d'enfants de moins d'un an pour 1 000 naissances vivantes survenues pendant la même année.

Le taux d'accroissement naturel est égal à la différence entre le taux brut de natalité et le taux brut de mortalité. Il y a lieu de noter que les taux d'accroissement naturel indiqués dans le tableau 4 peuvent différer des taux d'accroissement de la population figurant dans le tableau 3, les taux d'accroissement naturel ne tenant pas compte des taux nets de migration internationale, alors que ceux-ci sont inclus dans les taux d'accroissement de la population.

Sauf indication contraire, les taux bruts de natalité et de mortalité, et les taux de mortalité infantile figurant dans le tableau 4, ont été calculés par la Division des statistiques de l'Organisation des Nations Unies. Les exceptions comprennent l'Inde, pour laquelle les taux estimatifs officiels ont été fournis sur la base d'un système d'enregistrement par échantillonnage. Les taux calculés par la Division des statistiques de l'Organisation des Nations Unies qui sont présentés dans le tableau 4 se rapportent aux pays ou zones où l'on a enregistré au moins 30 événements (pour les naissances vivantes, les décès ou pour les décès d'enfants de moins d'un an) au cours d'une année donnée.

Fiabilité des données : les taux n'ont pas été calculés lorsque les statistiques de l'état civil issues de systèmes d'enregistrement d'état civil étaient jugées douteuses (degré estimatif de complétude inférieur à 90 p.100) et des taux estimatifs, calculés par les pays ou zones, ont été présentés lorsqu'ils étaient disponibles.

On trouve à la section 4.2 des Notes techniques des explications générales concernant la façon dont les statistiques de l'état civil ont été classées selon leur degré de fiabilité. Les notes techniques relatives aux tableaux 9, 15 et 18 ont trait respectivement à la fiabilité des statistiques des naissances vivantes, des décès d'enfants de moins d'un an et des décès.

Les valeurs relatives à l'espérance de vie figurant dans le tableau 4 proviennent de tables officielles de mortalité. On présume que les données de base (la population et les décès par sexe et âge) ont été rectifiées d'éventuelles insuffisances avant d'être utilisées pour construire les tables de mortalité.

Insuffisance des données : les statistiques des naissances, décès et décès d'enfants de moins d'un an appellent toutes les réserves qui ont été formulées à propos des statistiques de l'état civil en général à la section 4 des Notes techniques et dans les notes techniques relatives aux différents tableaux présentant des données détaillées sur ces événements [tableau 9 (naissances vivantes), tableau 15 (décès d'enfants de moins d'un an) et tableau 18 (décès)].

Pour évaluer la comparabilité des divers taux, il importe de tenir compte de la fiabilité des données utilisées pour calculer ces taux, comme il a été indiqué précédemment.

Le calcul des taux est particulièrement affecté par la difficulté à obtenir une correspondance parfaite entre le numérateur (naissances et décès) et le dénominateur (population, pour les taux bruts de natalité et de mortalité) en raison de l'inclusion ou non dans la population des forces armées, des réfugiés, des personnes déplacées ou d'autres groupes sociaux.

Il y a lieu de noter que la structure par âge et par sexe de la population influe de façon particulière sur les taux bruts. Le manque d'uniformité dans la définition des naissances vivantes et dans les procédures de mise en tableaux a une incidence sur les taux de mortalité infantile et, à un moindre degré, sur les taux bruts de natalité et les taux bruts de mortalité.

NOTE

[1] *Principles and Recommendations for a Vital Statistics System Revision 3,* Sales No. E.13.XVII.10, United Nations, New York, 2014

4. Vital statistics summary and life expectancy at birth: 2011 - 2015
Aperçu des statistiques de l'état civil et de l'espérance de vie à la naissance : 2011 - 2015

Continent, country or area and year / Continent, pays ou zone et année	Live births / Naissances vivantes			Deaths / Décès			Rate of natural increase Taux d'accrois-sement naturel	Infant deaths / Décès d'enfants de moins d'un an			Life expectancy at birth / Espérance de vie à la naissance		Total fertility rate L'indice synthétique de fécondité
	Code[a]	Number Nombre	Crude birth rate Taux brut de natalité	Code[a]	Number Nombre	Crude death rate Taux brut de mortalité		Code[a]	Number Nombre	Rate (per 1000 births) Taux (par 1000 naiss-ances)	Male[b] Masculin[b]	Female[b] Féminin[b]	
AFRICA - AFRIQUE													
Algeria - Algérie													
2011	C	909 787[1]	24.8	U	161 862[1]	...	...	U	21 055[1]	...	75.6[2]	77.4[2]	2.870
2012	C	978 233[1]	26.1	U	169 815[1]	...	...	U	22 088[1]	...	75.8[2]	77.1[2]	3.020
2013	C	962 722[1]	25.1	U	168 136[1]	...	...	U	21 586[1]	...	76.5[2]	77.6[2]	2.930
2014	C	1 014 248[1]	25.9	U	173 781[1]	...	...	U	22 282[1]	...	76.6[2]	77.8[2]	3.030
2015	C	1 040 285[1]	26.0	U	182 570[1]	...	...	U	23 150[1]	...	76.4[2]	77.8[2]	...
Benin - Bénin[3]													
2011	I	366 889	40.5	I	78 670	8.7	31.8		...	...	...	...	...
2012	I	376 439	40.2	I	79 116	8.4	31.7		...	...	...	...	...
Botswana													
2011	U	39 368[4]	...	+U	13 301[5]	...	...		...	...	...	...	2.689[6]
2012	U	40 856[4]	...	+U	12 270[5]	...	...		...	...	...	...	...
2013	+U	44 794[5]	...	+U	11 967[5]	...	...		...	...	...	...	...
2014	+U	41 741[5]	...	+U	12 177[5]	...	...	+U	1 045[5]	...	...	...	...
Burundi													
2011	+U	216 398[7]	...		...	...	...		...	...	...	...	5.990
2012	+U	221 289[7]	...		...	...	...		...	...	...	...	6.080
2013	+U	248 395[7]	...		...	...	...		...	...	...	...	5.840
2014		...	...		...	...	...		...	...	56.5	60.6	6.140
2015		...	...		...	...	...		...	...	...	...	5.700
Djibouti													
2011	U	10 871	...	U	1 011	...	...		...	...	...	...	...
Egypt - Égypte													
2011	+C	2 442 094	30.3	C	493 086	6.1	24.2	C	35 997	14.7	68.6	71.4	3.000
2012	+C	2 629 769	31.9	C	529 512	6.4	25.4	C	39 942	15.2	...	...	3.000
2013	+C	2 621 902	31.0	C	511 183	6.0	24.9	C	38 753	14.8	...	...	3.000
2014	+C	2 720 495	31.3	C	531 864	6.1	25.2	C	39 679	14.6	...	...	3.500
2015	+C	2 696 231	30.3	C	573 129	6.4	23.9		...	...	...	...	...
Equatorial Guinea - Guinée équatoriale													
2011		...	...		...	...	...		...	...	...	...	5.100
Ghana													
2012	+U	475 731[8]	...	+U	54 551[9]	...	...		...	...	...	...	...
2013	+U	463 409[8]	...	+U	51 466[9]	...	...		...	...	...	...	...
Guinea - Guinée													
2013	+U	205 658	...		...	...	...		...	...	...	...	...
Guinea-Bissau - Guinée-Bissau													
2014		...	...		...	...	...		...	...	51.2	53.6	...
Kenya													
2011	U	771 150	...	U	182 652	...	...	U	23 167	...	...	...	...
2012	U	801 815	...	U	187 811	...	...	U	21 209	...	...	...	...
2013	U	870 599	...	U	194 332	...	...	U	20 888	...	...	...	...
2014	U	954 254	...	U	198 611	...	...	U	18 672	...	...	...	...
Lesotho													
2011	+U	3 931	...	+U	5 314	...	...		...	...	39.4	45.3	3.350
2012	+U	1 718	...	+U	7 751	...	...		...	...	...	...	...
Liberia - Libéria													
2011		...	...		...	...	...		...	...	...	...	4.900
2012		...	...		...	...	...		...	...	...	...	4.800
2013		...	...		...	...	...		...	...	...	...	4.700
2014		...	...		...	...	...		...	...	...	...	4.600
Mauritania - Mauritanie													
2013		...	...		...	...	...		...	...	58.3	61.8	...
Mauritius - Maurice[10]													
2011	+C	14 701	11.7	+C	9 170	7.3	4.4	+C	189	12.9	III69.7	77.0	1.446
2012	+C	14 494	11.5	+C	9 343	7.4	4.1	+C	199	13.7	III70.2	77.1	1.544
2013	+C	13 488	10.7	+C	9 440	7.5	3.2	+C	165	12.2	...	...	1.438
2014	+C	13 283	10.5	+C	9 682	7.7	2.9	+C	194	14.6	III71.0	77.6	1.424
2015	+C	12 640	10.0	+C	9 747	7.7	2.3	+C	173	13.7	III71.1	77.8	...

4. Vital statistics summary and life expectancy at birth: 2011 - 2015
Aperçu des statistiques de l'état civil et de l'espérance de vie à la naissance : 2011 - 2015 (continued - suite)

Continent, country or area and year / Continent, pays ou zone et année	Live births / Naissances vivantes			Deaths / Décès			Rate of natural increase Taux d'accrois-sement naturel	Infant deaths / Décès d'enfants de moins d'un an			Life expectancy at birth / Espérance de vie à la naissance		Total fertility rate L'indice synthétique de fécondité
	Code[a]	Number Nombre	Crude birth rate Taux brut de natalité	Code[a]	Number Nombre	Crude death rate Taux brut de mortalité		Code[a]	Number Nombre	Rate (per 1000 births) Taux (par 1000 naiss-ances)	Male[b] Masculin[b]	Female[b] Féminin[b]	
AFRICA - AFRIQUE													
Mayotte													
2014	C	7 306	33.2	C	590	2.7	30.5		...	...	74.7	77.9	...
Morocco - Maroc													
2013		...	...		...	...	...		...	...	72.4	75.1	...
Mozambique													
2011		...	...		...	...	...		...	...	...	...	5.600
2012	U	624 523[11]	...		...	...	...		...	...	...	...	5.500
2013	U	746 185[11]	...		...	...	...		...	...	...	...	5.400
2014	U	794 718[11]	...		...	...	...		...	...	50.2	55.4	...
Namibia - Namibie													
2011	I	61 523[12]	29.1	I	22 668[12]	10.7	18.4		...	...	53.3	60.5	3.900[13]
Niger													
2011	+U	198 499	...	+U	6 761	...	...		...	...	...	...	...
Reunion - Réunion													
2014	C	14 095[14]	16.8	C	4 355	5.2	11.6		...	...	77.1	83.7	...
Rwanda													
2011	U	406 838	...	U	140 519	...	...		...	...	...	...	5.340
2012	U	404 067	...	U	139 499	...	...		...	...	62.6[15]	66.2[15]	5.300
Saint Helena ex. dep. - Sainte-Hélène sans dép.													
2011	C	34	8.0	C	49	11.5	-3.5	C	-	...	...	...	...
2012	C	32	7.8	C	62	15.0	-7.3	C	1	...	×72.0[16]	79.7[16]	...
2013	C	35	8.3	C	55	13.1	-4.7	C	-	...	...	...	...
2014	C	48	10.9	C	61	13.8	-2.9	C	1	...	...	...	...
Sao Tome and Principe - Sao Tomé-et-Principe													
2011	C	5 232	31.4		...	...	...		...	...	...	...	...
2012	C	5 173	27.6	I	1 287[17]	6.9	20.7		...	...	‖62.1	68.7	...
Senegal - Sénégal													
2011	I	464 464[18]	36.2	I	134 450[18]	10.5	25.7		...	...	56.9[6]	59.8[6]	...
2012	I	471 629[18]	35.7	I	135 468[18]	10.3	25.5		...	...	...	...	...
2013	I	478 898[18]	35.5	I	136 460[18]	10.1	25.3		...	...	...	...	...
Seychelles													
2011	+C	1 625	18.6	+C	691	7.9	10.7	+C	16	...	67.7	78.1	2.380
2012	+C	1 645	18.6	+C	651	7.4	11.3		...	...	...	...	2.420
2013	+C	1 566	17.4	+C	717	8.0	9.4	+C	29	...	69.9	76.5	2.370
2014	+C	1 557	17.0	+C	725	7.9	9.1	+C	17	...	68.4	78.3	2.340
2015	+C	1 592	17.0	+C	703	7.5	9.5	+C	17	...	...	...	...
Sierra Leone													
2011	...	117 207	...	...	13 674	...	...	...	1 289	...	...	...	5.820
2012	...	147 958	...	...	12 767	...	...	...	2 135	...	...	...	5.820
South Africa - Afrique du Sud													
2011	U	1 023 160	...	U	514 938	...	...	U	28 601	...	...	...	...
2012	U	1 020 088	...	U	492 062	...	...	U	27 104	...	...	...	...
2013	U	1 001 195	...	U	473 384	...	...	U	26 630	...	...	...	...
2014	U	988 007	...	U	453 360	...	...	U	25 643	...	...	...	...
Swaziland													
2011		...	...		...	...	...		...	...	...	...	3.700
2012		...	...		...	...	...		...	...	...	...	3.600
2013		...	...		...	...	...		...	...	...	...	3.600
2014		...	...		...	...	...		...	...	...	...	3.600
2015		...	...		...	...	...		...	...	...	...	3.500
Tunisia - Tunisie													
2011	C	201 120	18.8	U	63 258	...	...		...	...	72.9	76.9	2.150
2012	C	214 909	19.9	U	62 224	...	...		...	...	...	...	...
2013	C*	221 147	20.3	U	60 386	...	...		...	...	...	...	...
2014	C*	225 887	20.5	U	62 785	...	...		...	...	...	...	...

4. Vital statistics summary and life expectancy at birth: 2011 - 2015
Aperçu des statistiques de l'état civil et de l'espérance de vie à la naissance : 2011 - 2015 (continued - suite)

Continent, country or area and year / Continent, pays ou zone et année	Live births / Naissances vivantes			Deaths / Décès			Rate of natural increase Taux d'accrois-sement naturel	Infant deaths / Décès d'enfants de moins d'un an			Life expectancy at birth / Espérance de vie à la naissance		Total fertility rate L'indice synthétique de fécondité
	Co-de[a]	Number Nombre	Crude birth rate Taux brut de natalité	Co-de[a]	Number Nombre	Crude death rate Taux brut de mortalité		Co-de[a]	Number Nombre	Rate (per 1000 births) Taux (par 1000 naiss-ances)	Male[b] Masculin[b]	Female[b] Féminin[b]	
AFRICA - AFRIQUE													
Uganda - Ouganda[19]													
2011		...	...		...	...	...		...	...	...	...	6.200
United Republic of Tanzania - République Unie de Tanzanie													
2011	...	1 687 203	...	...	565 099	...	...		...	...	...	...	5.000
2012	...	1 694 943	...	...	555 975	...	...		...	...	...	...	3.685[20]
AMERICA, NORTH - AMÉRIQUE DU NORD													
Anguilla													
2011	+C	185	13.6	+C	55[21]	4.1	9.6	+C	1	...	...	...	...
2012	+C	192	14.0	+C	38[21]	2.8	11.2	+C	-	...	...	...	...
2013	+C	165	11.9	+C	72[21]	5.2	6.7	+C	3	...	...	...	...
2014	+C	151	10.6	+C	59[21]	4.1	6.5		...	...	...	...	...
2015	+C	165	11.2	+C	61[21]	4.1	7.1		...	...	...	...	...
Antigua and Barbuda - Antigua-et-Barbuda													
2011	+C	1 257	14.2	+C	478	5.4	8.8		...	...	...	...	...
2012	+C	1 187	...	+C	510	...	...		...	...	...	...	...
Aruba													
2011	C	1 236	12.0	C	633	6.2	5.9	+C	7	...	II73.9	79.8	1.918
2012	C	1 288	12.3	C	595	5.7	6.6	+C	3	...	...	...	1.973
2013	C	1 346	12.7	C	560	5.3	7.4	+C	5	...	...	...	2.032
2014	C	1 376	12.8	C	643	6.0	6.8	+C	5	...	...	...	2.041
2015	C	1 244	11.4	C	679	6.2	5.2	+C	6	...	...	...	1.821
Bahamas													
2011	+U	4 747	...	+C	2 117	5.9	...	+C	48	...	...	...	1.798
2012	+U	4 469	...	+C	1 995	5.5	...	+C	57	...	...	...	1.740
2013	+U	4 330	...	+C	2 065	5.6	...	+C	51	...	...	...	1.725
2014	+U*	4 196	...		...	...	...		...	...	...	...	1.475*
Barbados - Barbade													
2011	+C	3 283	11.8	+C	2 421	8.7	3.1		...	...	...	...	...
2012	+C	3 185	11.5	+C	2 403	8.7	2.8		...	...	...	...	...
2013	+C	3 020	10.9	+C	2 276	8.2	2.7		...	...	...	...	...
2014	+C	2 902	10.5	+C	2 580	9.3	1.2		...	...	...	...	...
Belize													
2011	U	7 217	...	U	1 554	...	...		...	...	...	...	...
2012		...	...	U	1 535	...	...		...	...	...	...	...
Bermuda - Bermudes													
2011	C	670[22]	10.6	C	429[22]	6.8	3.8	C	-	...	76.6	82.1	1.570
2012	C	648[22]	10.4	C	422[22]	6.8	3.6	C	1	...	77.2	82.4	1.571
2013	C	648[22]	10.5	C	471[22]	7.6	2.9	C	1	...	76.9	84.5	1.594
2014	C	574[22]	9.3	C	480[22]	7.8	1.5	C	2	...	77.1	84.7	1.420
2015	C	583[22]	9.4	C	457[22]	7.4	2.0	C	2	...	77.3	84.9	1.450
British Virgin Islands - Îles Vierges britanniques													
2011	C	333	11.8	C	98	3.5	8.4		...	...	...	...	...
2012	C	286	10.1	C	122	4.3	5.8		...	...	...	...	...
2013	C	277	9.7	C	113	4.0	5.8		...	...	...	...	...
2014	C	280	...	C	111	...	...		...	...	...	...	...
2015	C	266	...	C	136	...	...		...	...	...	...	...
Canada[23]													
2011	C	377 897	11.0	C	243 651	7.1	3.9		...	...	...	...	...
2012	C	382 980	11.0	C	252 309	7.3	3.8		...	...	...	...	...
2013	C	386 044	11.0	C	256 982	7.3	3.7		...	...	...	...	...
2014	C*	388 729	10.9	C*	268 056	7.5	3.4		...	...	...	...	...

89

Continent, country or area and year — Continent, pays ou zone et année	Live births — Naissances vivantes			Deaths — Décès			Rate of natural increase — Taux d'accrois-sement naturel	Infant deaths — Décès d'enfants de moins d'un an			Life expectancy at birth — Espérance de vie à la naissance		Total fertility rate — L'indice synthétique de fécondité
	Code[a]	Number Nombre	Crude birth rate Taux brut de natalité	Code[a]	Number Nombre	Crude death rate Taux brut de mortalité		Code[a]	Number Nombre	Rate (per 1000 births) Taux (par 1000 naiss-ances)	Male[b] Masculin[b]	Female[b] Féminin[b]	
AMERICA, NORTH - AMÉRIQUE DU NORD													
Cayman Islands - Îles Caïmanes													
2011	C	800	14.5	C	176[24]	3.2	11.3		...	...	...	...	...
2012	C	759	13.5	C	184[24]	3.3	10.2		...	...	...	...	...
2013	C	705	12.5	C	182[24]	3.2	9.3		...	...	...	...	...
2014	C	711	12.5	C	163[24]	2.9	9.6		...	...	...	...	...
2015	C	649	11.0	C	170[24]	2.9	8.1		...	...	...	...	...
Costa Rica													
2011	C	73 459	16.0	C	18 801	4.1	11.9	C	666	9.1	...	...	1.870
2012	C	73 326	15.8	C	19 200	4.1	11.6	C	624	8.5	...	...	1.880
2013	C	70 550	15.0	C	19 647	4.2	10.8	C	612	8.7	...	...	1.760
2014	C	71 793	15.0	C	20 553	4.3	10.7	C	575	8.0	77.2	82.3	1.860
2015	C*	71 819	14.9	C*	21 039	4.4	10.5	C*	557	7.8	77.4	82.4	1.750
Cuba													
2011	C	133 067	11.9	C	87 044	7.8	4.1	C	653	4.9	...	...	1.771
2012	C	125 674	11.2	C	89 372	8.0	3.2	C	581	4.6	...	...	1.690
2013	C	125 880	11.2	C	92 273	8.2	3.0	C	525	4.2	[III]76.5	80.4	1.714
2014	C	122 643	10.9	C	96 330	8.6	2.3	C	514	4.2	...	...	1.681
2015	C	125 064	11.1	C*	99 693	8.9	2.3	C*	535	4.3	...	...	...
Curaçao													
2011	C	1 974	13.1	C	1 276	8.5	4.6	C	15	...	...	...	2.076
2012	C	2 039	13.4	C	1 246	8.2	5.2	C	23	...	[II]74.4	80.7	2.168
2013	C	1 962	12.8	C	1 250	8.1	4.6	C	15	...	...	...	2.052
2014	C	1 963	12.6	C	1 370	8.8	3.8	C	24	...	[IV]74.0	81.2	2.009
2015	C	1 874	11.9	C	1 398	8.8	3.0	C	20	...	...	...	1.863
Dominica - Dominique													
2011	+C	944	13.3	+C	592	8.4	5.0		...	...	...	...	...
2012	+C	951	13.4	+C	603	8.5	4.9		...	...	...	...	...
2013	+C	931	13.1	+C	630	8.8	4.2		...	...	...	...	...
2014	+C	858	12.0	+C	590	8.2	3.7		...	...	...	...	...
Dominican Republic - République dominicaine													
2011	U	*158 955*	...	U	*35 490*	...	...	U	*684*	...	...	...	2.440
2012	U	*150 581*	...	U	*35 636*	...	...	U	*472*	...	...	...	2.418
2013	U	*148 719*	...	U	*35 507*	...	...	U	*653*	...	...	...	2.391
2014	U	*138 224*	...	U	*38 997*	...	...	U	*830*	...	...	...	2.364
2015		...	...	U	*35 479*	...	...	U	*436*	...	[VI]70.0	74.8	2.336
El Salvador													
2011	C	109 384[25]	17.6	C	33 211	5.3	12.3	C	826[26]	7.6	...	...	...
2012	C	110 843[25]	17.7	C	32 148	5.1	12.6	C	795[26]	7.2	...	...	2.300
2013		...	...		...	...	...		...	...	...	...	2.200
Greenland - Groenland													
2011	C	821	14.5	C	476	8.4	6.1	C	9	...	[V]68.2	72.9	2.104
2012	C	786	13.8	C	459	8.1	5.8	C	7	...	[V]68.7	73.5	1.987
2013	C	820	14.5	C	444	7.9	6.7	C	7	...	[V]68.5	73.7	2.051
2014	C	805	14.3	C	461	8.2	6.1	C	6	...	[V]69.1	73.7	1.995
2015	C	854	15.2	C	472	8.4	6.8	C	9	...	...	...	...
Grenada - Grenade													
2011	+C	1 812	17.0	+C	803	7.5	9.5		...	...	...	...	...
2012	+C	1 661	15.4	+C	856	8.0	7.5		...	...	...	...	...
2013	+C	1 838	16.9	+C	822	7.6	9.4		...	...	...	...	...
Guadeloupe													
2011	C	5 384[14]	13.3	C	2 835[14]	7.0	6.3		...	...	...	...	...
2012	C	5 233[14]	13.0	C	2 873[14]	7.1	5.9		...	...	...	...	...
2013	C	5 069[14]	12.6	C	2 951[14]	7.3	5.3		...	...	...	...	...
2014	C	5 001[14]	12.5	C	3 290	8.2	4.3		...	...	76.1	83.4	...
Guatemala													
2011	C	373 692	25.4	C	72 354	4.9	20.5	C	7 413	19.8	...	...	...
2012	C	388 613	25.8	C	72 657	4.8	21.0	C	7 121	18.3	...	...	...

4. Vital statistics summary and life expectancy at birth: 2011 - 2015
Aperçu des statistiques de l'état civil et de l'espérance de vie à la naissance : 2011 - 2015 (continued - suite)

Continent, country or area and year / Continent, pays ou zone et année	Live births - Naissances vivantes			Deaths - Décès			Rate of natural increase / Taux d'accroissement naturel	Infant deaths - Décès d'enfants de moins d'un an			Life expectancy at birth - Espérance de vie à la naissance		Total fertility rate / L'indice synthétique de fécondité
	Code[a]	Number Nombre	Crude birth rate Taux brut de natalité	Code[a]	Number Nombre	Crude death rate Taux brut de mortalité		Code[a]	Number Nombre	Rate (per 1000 births) Taux (par 1000 naissances)	Male[b] Masculin[b]	Female[b] Féminin[b]	
AMERICA, NORTH - AMÉRIQUE DU NORD													
Guatemala													
2013	C	387 342	...	C	76 639	...	...	C	7 221	18.6	...	...	...
2014	C	386 195	...	C	77 807	...	...	...	...	...	...	...	...
Honduras													
2011	+U	201 494	...	+U	37 211	...	...	...	...	...	...	...	...
2012	+U	196 119	...		...	...	...	...	...	...	...	...	...
Jamaica - Jamaïque													
2011	C	39 673[27]	14.7	U	16 926[28]	...	...	...	...	...	...	...	...
2012	C	39 348[27]	14.5	U	16 998[28]	...	...	...	...	...	...	...	...
2013	C*	36 745[27]	13.5	U	17 350[28]	...	...	...	...	...	...	...	...
2014	C*	37 892[27]	13.9	U	17 619[28]	...	...	...	...	...	...	...	...
2015	C*	37 556[27]	13.8		...	...	...	...	...	...	...	...	...
Martinique													
2013	C	4 130[14]	10.7		...	...	...		...	...	...	...	1.900
2014	C	4 367[14]	11.4	C	3 319[14]	8.7	2.7		...	...	78.1	83.9	...
Mexico - Mexique													
2011	C	2 262 024[29]	19.6	+C	589 646[30]	5.1	14.5	+U	29 037[30]	...	...	...	...
2012	C	2 190 159[29]	18.7	+C	601 259[30]	5.1	13.6	+U	28 946[30]	...	73.4	78.1	...
2013	C	2 168 933[29]	18.3	+C	622 495[30]	5.3	13.1	+C	27 802[30]	12.8	71.7	77.4	...
2014		...	...	+C	632 587[30]	5.3	...	+C	26 385[30]	...	72.1	77.6	...
Montserrat													
2011	+C	46	9.3	+C	55	11.2	-1.8	+C	-	...	...	...	...
2012	+C	53	10.7	+C	44	8.9	1.8	+C	-	...	...	...	...
2013	+C	41	8.3	+C	45	9.1	-0.8	+C	-	...	...	...	...
2014	+C	50	10.0	+C	32	6.4	3.6	+C	-	...	...	...	...
Panama													
2011	C	73 292	19.7	U	16 367	...	...	U	971	...	...	...	2.500
2012	C	75 486	19.9	U	17 350	...	...	U	1 083	...	74.1[31]	80.4[31]	2.500
2013	C	73 804	19.2	U	17 767	...	...	U	1 106	...	74.4[31]	80.5[31]	2.400
2014	C	75 183	19.2	U	18 171	...	...	U	1 036	...	74.6[31]	80.7[31]	2.400
2015	C*	75 866	19.1	U	18 429	...	...		...	...	...	...	...
Puerto Rico - Porto Rico													
2011	C	41 133	11.2	C	30 147	8.2	3.0	C	364	8.8	...	...	1.604
2012	C	38 974	10.7	C	30 054	8.3	2.4	C	374	9.6	...	...	1.543
2013	C	36 580	10.2	C	29 405	8.2	2.0	C	270	7.4	...	...	1.470
2014	C	34 503	9.7	C	30 330	8.5	1.2	C	242	7.0	...	...	...
2015	C	31 229	9.0	C	28 279	8.1	0.8	C	222	7.1	III76.4	84.0	...
Saint Kitts and Nevis - Saint-Kitts-et-Nevis													
2011	+C	666	14.4	+C	372	8.0	6.3		...	...	...	...	...
2012	+C	636	...	+C	336	...	...		...	...	...	...	...
2013	+C	547	...	+C	348	...	...		...	...	...	...	...
2014	+C	641	...	+C	411	...	...		...	...	...	...	...
Saint Lucia - Sainte-Lucie													
2011	C*	2 009	12.0	C*	983	5.9	6.1		...	...	...	...	...
2012	C*	2 103	12.4	C*	922	5.5	7.0		...	...	75.3	82.5	...
Saint Vincent and the Grenadines - Saint-Vincent-et-les Grenadines													
2011	C	1 725	15.7	C	882	8.0	7.7	C	38	22.0	...	...	1.892
2012	C	1 853	16.8	C	858	7.8	9.0	C	25	...	...	...	2.213
2013	C	1 738	15.8	C	926	8.4	7.4	C	32	18.4	...	...	2.090
2014	C	1 841	16.7	C	1 006	9.1	7.6	C	29	...	68.4	74.6	2.211

4. Vital statistics summary and life expectancy at birth: 2011 - 2015
Aperçu des statistiques de l'état civil et de l'espérance de vie à la naissance : 2011 - 2015 (continued - suite)

Continent, country or area and year / Continent, pays ou zone et année	Live births — Naissances vivantes			Deaths — Décès			Rate of natural increase / Taux d'accrois-sement naturel	Infant deaths — Décès d'enfants de moins d'un an			Life expectancy at birth — Espérance de vie à la naissance		Total fertility rate / L'indice synthétique de fécondité
	Code[a]	Number Nombre	Crude birth rate Taux brut de natalité	Code[a]	Number Nombre	Crude death rate Taux brut de mortalité		Code[a]	Number Nombre	Rate (per 1000 births) Taux (par 1000 naissances)	Male[b] Masculin[b]	Female[b] Féminin[b]	
AMERICA, NORTH - AMÉRIQUE DU NORD													
Sint Maarten (Dutch part) - Saint-Martin (partie néerlandaise)													
2011	+C	432[32]	12.9	+C	173[32]	5.2	7.7		...	...	...	...	...
2012	+C	414[32]	11.9	+C	180[32]	5.2	6.7		...	...	II69.2	77.1	...
2013	+C	511[32]	14.0	+C	171[32]	4.7	9.3		...	...	...	...	...
Trinidad and Tobago - Trinité-et-Tobago													
2011	C*	18 141	13.6	C*	10 007	7.5	6.1	C*	275	15.2	71.4[33]	77.8[33]	1.700[15]
2012	C*	18 729	14.0	C*	10 373	7.8	6.3	C*	239	12.8	...	...	1.700[15]
2013	C*	18 823	14.0	C*	10 661	8.0	6.1		...	...	...	...	...
2014	C*	18 729	13.9	C*	11 461	8.5	5.4		...	...	...	...	...
United States of America - États-Unis d'Amérique													
2011	C	3 953 590	12.7	C	2 515 458	8.1	4.6	C	23 985	6.1	76.3	81.1	1.895
2012	C	3 952 841	12.6	C	2 543 279	8.1	4.5	C	23 629	6.0	76.4	81.2	1.880
2013	C	3 932 181	12.4	C	2 596 993	8.2	4.2	C	23 440	6.0	76.4	81.2	1.857
2014	C	3 988 076	12.5	C	2 626 418	8.2	4.3	C	23 215	5.8	76.4	81.2	1.863
United States Virgin Islands - Îles Vierges américaines[34]													
2011	C	1 491	14.1	C	711	6.7	7.4	C	13	...	...	...	...
2012	C	1 415	13.4	C	723	6.9	6.6	C	13	...	...	...	...
AMERICA, SOUTH - AMÉRIQUE DU SUD													
Argentina - Argentine													
2011	C	758 042	18.4	C	319 059	7.7	10.6	C	8 878	11.7	...	...	2.379
2012	C	738 318	17.7	C	319 539	7.7	10.0	C	8 227	11.1	...	...	...
2013	C	754 603	17.9	C	326 197	7.7	10.2	C	8 174	10.8	...	...	...
2014	C	777 012	18.2	C	325 539	7.6	10.6	C	8 202	10.6	...	...	...
Bolivia (Plurinational State of) - Bolivie (État plurinational de)													
2011	U	160 499	...		...	...	...		...	...	64.6	68.9	3.207
2012	U	128 738	...	I	127 050[35]	12.3	...		...	...	...	...	...
2013	U	149 832	...		...	...	...		...	...	...	...	...
2014	U	153 016	...		...	...	...		...	...	...	...	...
2015	+U	247 754	...		...	...	...		...	...	VI65.0	69.4	...
Brazil - Brésil													
2011	U	2 824 776[36]	...	U	1 148 165[37]	...	...	U	32 184[38]	...	...	...	1.833[39]
2012	U	2 830 458[36]	...	U	1 157 214[37]	...	...	U	31 596[38]	...	70.9[31]	78.2[31]	1.801[39]
2013	U	2 832 590[36]	...	U	1 180 796[37]	...	...	U	31 944[38]	...	71.3[31]	78.5[31]	1.770[39]
2014	U	2 913 121[36]	...	C	1 194 164[37]	5.9	...	U	31 679[38]	...	71.6[31]	78.8[31]	1.742[39]
2015		...	...		...	...	...		...	...	...	...	1.716[39]
Chile - Chili													
2011	C	247 358	14.3	C	94 985	5.5	8.8	C	1 908	7.7	75.7	81.0	1.890
2012	C	243 635	14.0	C	98 711	5.7	8.3	C	1 812	7.4	76.1	81.3	1.840
2013	C	242 005	13.8	C	99 770	5.7	8.1	C	1 692	7.0	76.3	81.4	1.790
2014	C*	252 194	14.2	C*	101 960	5.7	8.4		...	...	...	...	...
Colombia - Colombie													
2011	U	662 783	...	U	192 872	...	...	U	8 082	...	...	...	...
2012	U	675 694	...	U	196 842	...	...	U	8 138	...	...	...	2.350[40]
2013	U	658 835	...	U	203 058	...	...	U	7 551	...	...	...	...
2014	U	669 131	...	U	210 028	...	...	U	7 515	...	...	...	...
2015		...	...		...	...	...		...	...	VI72.1	78.5	...

Continent, country or area and year / Continent, pays ou zone et année	Code[a]	Number Nombre (Live births / Naissances vivantes)	Crude birth rate Taux brut de natalité	Code[a]	Number Nombre (Deaths / Décès)	Crude death rate Taux brut de mortalité	Rate of natural increase Taux d'accroissement naturel	Code[a]	Number Nombre (Infant deaths / Décès d'enfants de moins d'un an)	Rate (per 1000 births) Taux (par 1000 naissances)	Male[b] Masculin[b]	Female[b] Féminin[b]	Total fertility rate L'indice synthétique de fécondité
AMERICA, SOUTH - AMÉRIQUE DU SUD													
Ecuador - Équateur													
2011	+U	229 780	...	U	62 304[41]	...	...	U	3 046[41]	...	...	...	2.737[42]
2012	+U	235 237	...	U	63 511[41]	...	...	U	3 002[41]	...	...	...	2.684[42]
2013	+U	220 896	...	U	63 104[41]	...	...	U	2 928[41]	...	...	...	2.634[42]
2014	+U	229 476	...	U	62 981[41]	...	...	U	2 821[41]	...	73.2[43]	78.6[43]	2.587[42]
2015		...	...		...	...	...		...	...	VI73.2[44]	78.8[44]	2.542[42]
French Guiana - Guyane française													
2014		...	...		...	...	...		...	...	76.7	83.1	...
Guyana													
2011		...	...	+C	4 527	6.0	...						
Paraguay													
2011	+U	111 945	...	+U	22 648	...	...		...		...	...	
2012	+U	118 549	...	+U	22 807	...	...	+U	465		...	...	
2013	+U	114 619	...	+U	24 193	...	...		...		...	...	
2014	+U	116 592	...	+U	22 625	...	...		...		...	...	
Peru - Pérou													
2011	+U	396 839[45]	...	+U	96 852[45]	...	...	+U	4 569[45]	...	...	...	2.445
2012	+U	414 081[45]	...	+U	97 989[45]	...	...	+U	4 523[45]	...	...	...	2.403
2013	+U	475 349[45]	...	+U	98 616[45]	...	...	+U	4 548[45]	...	...	...	2.364
2014	+U	492 008[45]	...	+U	96 460[45]	...	...	+U	4 243[45]	...	...	...	2.328
2015		...	...		...	...	...		...	...	VI71.5[31]	76.8[31]	2.294
Suriname													
2011	C	9 703	18.0	C	3 441	6.4	11.6	C	153	15.8	...	...	2.268
2012	C	10 217	18.9	C	3 687	6.8	12.1	C	162	15.9	...	...	2.406
2013	C	10 012	18.2	C	3 557	6.5	11.7	C	168	16.8	III69.3	75.1	2.323
2014	C	10 407	18.6	C	3 738	6.7	11.9	C	163	15.7	...	...	...
Uruguay													
2011	C	46 712	13.7	C	32 807	9.6	4.1	C	417	8.9	...	...	1.896
2012	C	48 059	14.0	C	33 354	9.7	4.3	C	448	9.3	...	...	1.943
2013	C	48 681	14.2	C	32 795	9.5	4.6		...	...	...	...	1.957
2014	C	48 368	14.0		...	...	...	C	376	7.8	...	...	1.936
Venezuela (Bolivarian Republic of) - Venezuela (République bolivarienne du)													
2011	C	615 132	21.3	C	136 803	4.7	16.5	C	7 121	11.6	...	...	2.466[46]
2012	C	619 530	21.1	C	142 988	4.9	16.2	C	7 331	11.8	...	...	2.446[46]
2013	U	597 902	...	C	147 901	5.0	...	C	7 630	...	...	...	2.427[46]
2014	U	597 773	...	C	159 239	5.3	...	C	8 396	...	...	...	2.410[46]
2015	U	600 860	...	C	163 367	5.3	...	C	9 267	...	...	...	...
ASIA - ASIE													
Armenia - Arménie													
2011	C	43 340	13.3	C	27 963[47]	8.6	4.7	C	507[47]	11.7	...	...	...
2012	C*	42 333	13.4	C*	27 514[47]	8.7	4.7		...	...	...	...	...
2013	C*	41 790	13.8	C*	27 196[47]	9.0	4.8		...	...	...	...	...
2014	C	43 031	...	C	27 714[47]	...	...	C	376[47]	8.7	...	...	...
2015	C	41 763	13.9	C	27 878[47]	9.3	4.6		...	...	...	...	...
Azerbaijan - Azerbaïdjan													
2011	+C	176 072[47]	19.2	+C	53 762[47]	5.9	13.3	+C	1 903[47]	10.8	...	...	...
2012	+C	174 469[47]	18.8	+C	55 017[47]	5.9	12.9	+C	1 884[47]	10.8	71.4	76.3	2.336
2013	+C	172 671[47]	18.3	+C	54 383[47]	5.8	12.6	+C	1 862[47]	10.8	71.4	76.5	...
2014	+C	170 503[47]	17.9	+C	55 648[47]	5.8	12.1	+C	1 655[47]	9.7	72.2	77.3	...
2015	+C	166 210[47]	17.3	+C	54 697[47]	5.7	11.6		...	...	...	...	...

4. Vital statistics summary and life expectancy at birth: 2011 - 2015
Aperçu des statistiques de l'état civil et de l'espérance de vie à la naissance : 2011 - 2015 (continued - suite)

Continent, country or area and year / Continent, pays ou zone et année	Live births / Naissances vivantes			Deaths / Décès			Rate of natural increase / Taux d'accroissement naturel	Infant deaths / Décès d'enfants de moins d'un an			Life expectancy at birth / Espérance de vie à la naissance		Total fertility rate / L'indice synthétique de fécondité
	Code[a]	Number Nombre	Crude birth rate Taux brut de natalité	Code[a]	Number Nombre	Crude death rate Taux brut de mortalité		Code[a]	Number Nombre	Rate (per 1000 births) Taux (par 1000 naiss-ances)	Male[b] Masculin[b]	Female[b] Féminin[b]	
ASIA - ASIE													
Bahrain - Bahreïn													
2011	C	17 573[48]	14.7	C	2 528[48]	2.1	12.6	C	139[49]	7.9	...	...	1.967
2012	C	19 119[48]	15.8	C	2 613[48]	2.2	13.7	C	149[49]	7.8	...	...	2.134
2013	C	19 995[48]	16.0	C	2 588[48]	2.1	13.9	C	141[49]	7.1	...	...	2.157
2014	C	20 931[48]	15.9	C	2 805[48]	2.1	13.8	C	218[49]	10.4	...	...	2.173
2015		...	...		...	...	...		...	...	[VI]75.8	77.4	...
Bangladesh													
2011	U	*2 891 000*	...	U	*828 000*	...	...	U	*100 751*	...	67.9	70.3	2.110
2012	U	*2 933 000*	...	U	*826 000*	...	...	U	*96 254*	...	...	...	2.120
2013		...	...		...	...	...		...	...	68.8	71.4	2.110
Brunei Darussalam - Brunéi Darussalam													
2011	+C	6 724	17.1	+C	1 235	3.1	14.0	+C	56	8.3	...	...	1.900
2012	+C	6 909	17.3	+C	1 216	3.0	14.2	+C	64	9.3	...	...	1.900
2013	+C	6 680	16.4	+C	1 398	3.4	13.0	+C	51	7.6	...	...	1.900
2014	+C	6 891	16.7	+C	1 470	3.6	13.2	+C	51	7.4	75.9	78.8	1.900
2015	+C*	6 699	16.1	+C*	1 547	3.7	12.3		...	...	...	...	...
China - Chine[50]													
2011	I	16 040 000	11.9	I	9 600 000	7.1	4.8		...	...	...	...	...
2012	I	16 350 000	12.1	I	9 660 000	7.2	5.0		...	...	...	...	...
2013	I	16 400 000	12.1	I	9 720 000	7.2	4.9		...	...	...	...	...
2014	I	16 870 000	12.4	I	9 770 000	7.2	5.2		...	...	...	...	...
2015	I	16 550 000	12.1	I	9 750 000	7.1	5.0		...	...	...	...	...
China, Hong Kong SAR - Chine, Hong Kong RAS													
2011	C	95 451	13.5	C	42 346	6.0	7.5	C	127	1.3	80.3	86.7	1.204[51]
2012	C	91 558	12.8	C	43 917	6.1	6.7	C	137	1.5	...	...	1.285[51]
2013	C	57 084	7.9	C	43 397	6.0	1.9	C	100	1.8	81.1	86.7	1.124[51]
2014	C	62 305	8.6	C	45 087	6.2	2.4	C	103	1.7	81.2	86.9	1.234[51]
2015	C*	59 900	8.2	C*	46 100	6.3	1.9		...	...	...	...	...
China, Macao SAR - Chine, Macao RAS													
2011	C	5 852	10.6	C	1 845	3.4	7.3	C	17	...	...	...	1.150
2012	C	7 315	12.9	C	1 841	3.2	9.6	C	18	...	[IV]79.1	85.7	1.357
2013	C	6 571	11.1	C	1 920	3.2	7.9	C	13	...	...	...	1.150
2014	C	7 360	11.8	C	1 939	3.1	8.7	C	15	...	[IV]79.6	86.0	1.224
2015	C	7 055	11.0	C	2 002	3.1	7.9	C	11	...	[IV]79.9	86.3	1.142
Cyprus - Chypre[52]													
2011	C	9 622	11.3	C	5 504	6.5	4.8	C	30	3.1	[II]79.0	82.9	1.349
2012	C	10 161	11.8	C	5 665	6.6	5.2	C	36	3.5	...	...	...
2013	C	9 341	10.8	C	5 141[53]	6.0	4.9	C	15	...	80.0	84.8	...
2014	C	9 258	10.9	C	5 250[53]	6.2	4.7	C	13	...	80.9	84.7	...
2015	C*	9 170	10.8	C*	5 859	6.9	3.9		...	...	...	...	...
Georgia - Géorgie													
2011	C	58 014	12.9	C	49 818[47]	11.1	1.8	C	703[47]	12.1	...	...	1.690
2012	C	57 031	12.7	C	49 348[47]	11.0	1.7	C	715[47]	12.5	...	...	...
2013	C	57 878	...	C	48 553[47]	...	...	C	640[47]	11.1	...	...	...
2014	C	60 635	13.5	C	49 087[47]	10.9	2.6	C	578[47]	9.5	...	...	...
India - Inde[54]													
2011	I	...	21.1 [55]	I	...	7.1 [55]	...	I	...	44.0 [55]	...	...	2.400
2012	I	...	21.6 [55]	I	...	7.0 [55]	...	I	...	42.0 [55]	...	...	2.400
2013	I	...	21.4 [55]	I	...	7.0 [55]	...	I	...	40.0 [55]	...	...	2.300
2014	I	...	21.0 [55]	I	...	6.7 [55]	...	I	...	39.0 [55]	...	...	...

4. Vital statistics summary and life expectancy at birth: 2011 - 2015
Aperçu des statistiques de l'état civil et de l'espérance de vie à la naissance : 2011 - 2015 (continued - suite)

Continent, country or area and year / Continent, pays ou zone et année	Live births / Naissances vivantes			Deaths / Décès			Rate of natural increase / Taux d'accrois-sement naturel	Infant deaths / Décès d'enfants de moins d'un an			Life expectancy at birth / Espérance de vie à la naissance		Total fertility rate / L'indice synthétique de fécondité
	Code[a]	Number / Nombre	Crude birth rate / Taux brut de natalité	Code[a]	Number / Nombre	Crude death rate / Taux brut de mortalité		Code[a]	Number / Nombre	Rate (per 1000 births) / Taux (par 1000 naiss-ances)	Male[b] / Masculin[b]	Female[b] / Féminin[b]	
ASIA - ASIE													
Indonesia - Indonésie													
2012		...	...		...	...	...		...	...	67.7	71.7	2.600[56]
Iran (Islamic Republic of) - Iran (République islamique d')													
2011	+C	1 382 229[57]	18.4	+C	383 504[57]	5.1	13.3	+C	11 021[57]	8.0	71.5	74.0	1.790
2012	+C	1 421 689[57]	18.7	+C	367 539[57]	4.8	13.9	+C	10 401[57]	7.3	...	...	...
2013	+C	1 471 834[57]	19.1	+C	372 279[57]	4.8	14.3	+C	8 015[57]	5.4	...	...	...
2014	+C	1 534 362[57]	19.7	+C	446 333[57]	5.7	14.0	+C	7 430[57]	4.8	...	...	...
Iraq													
2013	U*	1 077 645	...	U*	189 118	...	...						
Israel - Israël[58]													
2011	C	166 296	21.4	C	40 889[59]	5.3	16.1	C	588[59]	3.5	79.9	83.6	3.004
2012	C	170 940	21.6	C	42 100[59]	5.3	16.3	C	611[59]	3.6	79.9	83.6	3.052
2013	C	171 444	21.3	C	41 683[59]	5.2	16.1	C	539[59]	3.1	80.3	83.9	3.030
2014	C	176 427	21.5	C	42 413[59]	5.2	16.3	C	548[59]	3.1	80.3	84.1	3.085
2015	C*	178 723	...	C	44 210[59]	...	...	C	552[59]	3.1	...	...	...
Japan - Japon[60]													
2011	C	1 050 806[61]	8.2	C	1 253 066[61]	9.8	-1.6	C	2 463[61]	2.3	79.4	85.9	1.393[62]
2012	C	1 037 231[61]	8.1	C	1 256 359[61]	9.8	-1.7	C	2 299[61]	2.2	79.9	86.4	1.405[62]
2013	C	1 029 816[61]	8.1	C	1 268 436[61]	10.0	-1.9	C	2 185[61]	2.1	80.2	86.6	1.427[62]
2014	C	1 003 539[61]	7.9	C	1 273 004[61]	10.0	-2.1	C	2 080[61]	2.1	80.5	86.8	1.422[62]
2015	C*	1 005 656	7.9	C*	1 290 428	10.2	-2.2		...	...	...	...	...
Jordan - Jordanie[63]													
2011	C	178 435	25.5	U	21 730	...	...		...	...	71.6	74.4	3.800
2012	C	177 695	23.9	U	22 785	...	...		...	...	72.7	76.7	3.500
2013	C	178 143	22.0	U	23 898	...	...		...	...	...	...	3.500
2014		...	...		...	...	...		...	...	...	...	3.500
2015		...	...		...	...	...		...	...	...	...	3.500
Kazakhstan													
2011	C	372 801[47]	22.5	C	144 944[47]	8.8	13.8	C	5 556[47]	14.9	...	...	2.590
2012	C	381 005[47]	22.7	C	142 880[47]	8.5	14.2	C	5 121[47]	13.4	64.8	74.3	2.620
2013	C	387 227[47]	22.7	C	135 950[47]	8.0	14.8	C	4 367[47]	11.3	...	...	2.640
Kuwait - Koweït													
2011	C	58 198	18.7	C	5 339	1.7	17.0	C	484	8.3	...	...	1.950
2012	C	59 753	18.4	C	5 950	1.8	16.6	C	459	7.7	...	...	1.860
2013	C	59 426	17.3	C	5 909	1.7	15.6	C	453	7.6	...	...	1.720
2014	C	61 313	16.3	C	6 031	1.6	14.7	C	456	7.4	...	...	1.900
Kyrgyzstan - Kirghizstan													
2011	C	149 612	28.4	C	35 941	6.8	21.6	C	3 150	21.1	65.7	73.7	3.085
2012	C	154 918	28.9	C	36 186	6.8	22.2	C	3 091	20.0	66.1	74.1	3.148
2013	C	155 520	27.2	C	34 880	6.1	21.1	C	3 093	19.9	66.3	74.3	3.109
2014	C	161 813	27.7	C	35 564	6.1	21.6	C	3 268	20.2	66.5	74.5	3.186
2015	C*	163 452	27.4	C*	34 808	5.8	21.6	C*	2 945	18.0	...	...	...
Lao People's Democratic Republic - République démocratique populaire lao													
2011		...	...		...	...	...		...	...	...	...	3.700
2012		...	...		...	...	...		...	...	...	...	3.500
2013		...	...		...	...	...		...	...	...	...	3.200
2014		...	...		...	...	...		...	...	...	...	3.060
Lebanon - Liban													
2011	C	98 569	26.1	C	26 070	6.9	19.2		...	...	...	...	...
2012	C	94 842	...	C	23 452	...	...		...	...	...	...	...
2013	C	95 246	...	C	24 013	...	...		...	...	...	...	...
2014	C	104 872	...	C	27 020	...	...		...	...	...	...	...
Malaysia - Malaisie													
2011	C	511 594	17.6	C	135 463	4.7	12.9	C	3 330	6.5	...	...	2.174
2012	C	526 012	17.8	C	138 692	4.7	13.1	C	3 277	6.2	72.2	76.9	2.188

95

4. Vital statistics summary and life expectancy at birth: 2011 - 2015
Aperçu des statistiques de l'état civil et de l'espérance de vie à la naissance : 2011 - 2015 (continued - suite)

Continent, country or area and year / Continent, pays ou zone et année	Live births / Naissances vivantes			Deaths / Décès			Rate of natural increase / Taux d'accrois-sement naturel	Infant deaths / Décès d'enfants de moins d'un an			Life expectancy at birth / Espérance de vie à la naissance		Total fertility rate / L'indice synthétique de fécondité
	Code[a]	Number Nombre	Crude birth rate Taux brut de natalité	Code[a]	Number Nombre	Crude death rate Taux brut de mortalité		Code[a]	Number Nombre	Rate (per 1000 births) Taux (par 1000 naiss-ances)	Male[b] Masculin[b]	Female[b] Féminin[b]	
ASIA - ASIE													
Malaysia - Malaisie													
2013	C	503 914	16.7	C	142 202	4.7	12.0	C	3 199	6.3	...	...	2.022
2014	C*	511 865	16.7	C*	145 648	4.8	12.0	C*	3 156	6.2	...	...	2.018*
Maldives													
2011	C	7 180	22.1	C	1 137	3.5	18.6	C	65	9.1	72.8	74.8	...
2012	C	7 431	22.5	C	1 135	3.4	19.0	C	66	8.9	...	...	...
2013	C	7 153	21.3	C	1 120	3.3	17.9	C	46	6.4	...	...	...
2014	C	7 245	18.0	C	1 143	2.8	15.2	C	59	8.1	73.1	74.8	...
Mongolia - Mongolie													
2011	+C	69 853	25.1	+C	19 155	6.9	18.2	+C	1 152	16.5	...	...	2.600
2012	+C	73 839	26.0	+C	17 761	6.3	19.7	+C	1 143	15.5	...	...	2.700
2013	+C	79 780	27.5	+C	17 247	5.9	21.6	+C	1 166	14.6	65.4	75.0	3.000
2014	+C	82 839	28.0	+C	16 521	5.6	22.4	+C	1 251	15.1	65.9	75.5	3.100
2015	+C	82 130	27.1	+C	17 620	5.8	21.3	+C	1 234	15.0	x65.3	74.8	3.100
Myanmar													
2011	+U	820 293[64]	...	+U	242 584[64]	...	...	+U	10 340[64]	...	...	...	2.286
2012	+U	856 279[64]	...	+U	250 874[64]	...	...	+U	11 406[64]	...	...	...	2.253
2013	+U	835 595[64]	...	+U	257 216[64]	...	...	+U	11 516[64]	...	65.5	69.1	2.222
2014	+U	836 961[64]	...	+U	278 533[64]	...	...	+U	10 668[64]	...	...	...	...
Nepal - Népal													
2011	I	326 725[65]	11.4	I	129 978[65]	4.5	6.9	I	10 132[65]	31.0	65.4	67.9	2.520
Oman													
2011	U	67 922[66]	...	U	7 667[66]	...	...	U	640[66]	...	73.1	77.7	2.900
2012	U	72 867[66]	...	U	7 884[66]	...	...	U	676[66]	...	74.5	78.0	2.800
2013	U	79 417[66]	...	U	7 669[66]	...	...	U	772[66]	...	74.8	78.5	2.900
2014	U	82 981[66]	...	U	7 819[66]	...	...	U	645[66]	...	74.8	78.5	2.900
Philippines													
2011	C	1 746 684	18.4	C	498 486	5.3	13.2	C	22 283	12.8	...	...	...
2012	C	1 790 367	18.6	C	514 745	5.3	13.2	C	22 254	12.4	...	...	...
2013	C	1 761 602	17.9	C	531 280	5.4	12.5	C	21 992	12.5	...	...	...
2014	C	1 748 857	17.5		...	...	...		...	...	...	...	...
Qatar													
2011	C	20 802	12.0	C	1 949	1.1	10.9	C	156	7.5	76.5	81.0	2.118
2012	C	21 423	11.7	C	2 031	1.1	10.6	C	148	6.9	...	...	3.400
2013	C	23 708	11.8	C	2 133	1.1	10.8	C	157	6.6	...	...	...
2014	C*	25 443	11.5	C*	2 366	1.1	10.4		...	...	...	...	...
Republic of Korea - République de Corée													
2011	C	471 265[67]	9.4	C	257 396[68]	5.1	4.3	C	1 435[68]	3.0	77.7	84.5	1.244[68]
2012	C	484 550[67]	9.6	C	267 221[68]	5.3	4.3	C	1 405[68]	2.9	77.9	84.6	1.297[68]
2013	C	436 455[67]	8.6	C	266 257[68]	5.3	3.4	C	1 305[68]	3.0	78.5	85.1	1.187[68]
2014	C	435 435[67]	8.6	C	267 692[68]	5.3	3.3	C	1 305[68]	3.0	79.0	85.5	1.205[68]
Saudi Arabia - Arabie saoudite													
2011	...	...	...	...	102 066[69]	...	...	...	10 023[69]	...	...	...	2.930[70]
2012		...	...	...	104 195[69]	...	...	...	9 843[69]	...	72.8[70]	75.2[70]	2.870[70]
2013	...	607 806	...	...	106 521[69]	...	...		...	...	...	...	2.810[70]
2014		...	...		...	...	...		...	...	...	...	2.750[70]
2015		...	...		...	...	...		...	...	73.1[70]	75.7[70]	2.690[70]
Singapore - Singapour													
2011	C	39 654	10.5	+C	18 027	4.8	5.7	+C	97	2.4	79.5[71]	84.1[71]	1.200[72]
2012	C	42 663	11.2	+C	18 481	4.8	6.3	+C	98	2.3	79.8[71]	84.3[71]	1.290[72]
2013	C	39 720	10.3	+C	18 938	4.9	5.4	+C	94	2.4	80.1[71]	84.5[71]	1.190[72]
2014	C	42 232	10.9	+C	19 393	5.0	5.9	+C	83	2.0	80.3[71]	84.8[71]	1.250[72]
2015	C	42 185	10.8	+C	19 862	5.1	5.7	+C	84	2.0	80.4[73]	84.9[73]	1.240[72]
Sri Lanka													
2011	+C*	363 415	17.4	+C*	123 261	5.9	11.5		...	...	...	...	...
2012	+C*	355 900	17.4	+C*	122 063	6.0	11.4		...	...	...	...	...
2013	+C*	365 792	17.8	+C*	127 124	6.2	11.6		...	...	...	...	...

4. Vital statistics summary and life expectancy at birth: 2011 - 2015
Aperçu des statistiques de l'état civil et de l'espérance de vie à la naissance : 2011 - 2015 (continued - suite)

Continent, country or area and year / Continent, pays ou zone et année	Code[a]	Live births / Naissances vivantes — Number Nombre	Crude birth rate Taux brut de natalité	Code[a]	Deaths / Décès — Number Nombre	Crude death rate Taux brut de mortalité	Rate of natural increase Taux d'accrois-sement naturel	Code[a]	Infant deaths / Décès d'enfants de moins d'un an — Number Nombre	Rate (per 1000 births) Taux (par 1000 naiss-ances)	Life expectancy at birth / Espérance de vie à la naissance — Male[b] Masculin[b]	Female[b] Féminin[b]	Total fertility rate L'indice synthétique de fécondité
ASIA - ASIE													
Sri Lanka													
2014	+C*	349 715	16.8	+C*	127 758	6.2	10.7		...	...	...	...	...
2015	+C*	334 821	16.0	+C*	131 614	6.3	9.7		...	...	...	...	...
State of Palestine - État de Palestine													
2011	U	131 430[74]	...	U	11 333[74]	...	...	U	1 051[74]	...	71.0	73.9	...
2012	U	129 826[74]	...	U	11 676[74]	...	...	U	1 050[74]	...	71.3	74.1	...
2013	U	126 912[74]	...	U	11 013[74]	...	...	U	827[74]	...	71.5	74.4	4.100[75]
2014		...	...		...	...	...		...	...	71.8	74.7	...
2015		...	...		...	...	...		...	...	72.0	75.0	...
Tajikistan - Tadjikistan													
2011	U	224 178[76]	...	U	32 909[47]	...	...	U	3 131[47]	...	70.9	74.1	2.766
2012	U	219 281[76]	...	U	32 828[47]	...	...	U	2 884[47]	...	...	...	2.611
2013	U	209 417[76]	...	U	31 706[47]	...	...	U	3 622[47]	...	...	...	2.616
2014	U	229 460[76]	...	U	32 879[47]	...	...	U	3 273[47]	...	71.6	75.4	2.980
Thailand - Thaïlande													
2011	+U	795 031	...	+U	414 670	...	...	+U	5 275		...	...	...
2012	+U	801 737	...	+U	415 141	...	...		...	...	...	...	...
2013	+U	748 081	...	+U	426 065	...	...		...	...	...	...	...
2014	+U	711 081	...	+U	435 624	...	...		...	...	...	...	...
Timor-Leste													
2015	I	44 854	38.4	I	11 384	9.8	28.7		...	...	...	...	...
Turkey - Turquie													
2011	C	1 247 081	16.8	C	376 162	5.1	11.7	C	14 582	11.7	72.0	77.1	2.020
2012	C	1 290 387	17.2	C	376 338	5.0	12.2	C	14 965	11.6	72.0	77.2	2.080
2013	C	1 291 217	17.0	C	372 686	4.9	12.1	C	13 996	10.8	75.3	80.7	...
2014	C	1 337 504	17.4	C	390 121	5.1	12.3	C	14 821	11.1	75.3	80.7	...
2015	C*	1 325 783	17.1	C	405 218	5.2	11.8		...	...	...	...	...
United Arab Emirates - Émirats arabes unis[77]													
2011	...	83 950	...	...	7 350	...	...		...	...	...	...	...
2012	...	89 578	...	...	7 702	...	...		...	...	...	...	...
Uzbekistan - Ouzbékistan													
2011	+C	622 835	21.2	+C	143 253[47]	4.9	16.3	+C	6 526	10.5	...	...	2.236
2012	+C	625 106	21.0	+C	145 988[47]	4.9	16.1	+C	6 390	10.2	...	...	2.193
2013	+C	679 519	22.5	+C	145 672[47]	4.8	17.7	+C	6 569	9.7	...	...	2.350
2014	+C	718 036	23.3	+C	149 761[47]	4.9	18.5	+C	7 688	10.7	71.1	75.8	2.457
Viet Nam													
2011		...	...		...	...	...		...	...	70.4	75.8	1.990
2012		...	...		...	...	...		...	...	70.4	75.8	2.050
2013		...	...		...	...	...		...	...	70.5	75.8	2.100
2014		...	...		...	...	...		...	...	70.6	76.0	2.090
2015		...	...		...	...	...		...	...	70.7	76.1	2.100
Yemen - Yémen													
2011	U	239 980	...	U	23 662	...	...		...	...	...	...	...
2012	U	279 719	...	U	28 596	...	...		...	...	...	...	...
2013	U	425 165[78]	...	U	35 066[79]	...	...		...	...	...	...	...
EUROPE													
Åland Islands - Îles d'Åland													
2011	C	285	10.1	C	277	9.8	0.3	C	-	...	79.5	84.8	1.801
2012	C	292	10.3	C	323	11.4	-1.1	C	-	...	...	...	1.847
2013	C	287	10.0	C	269	9.4	0.6	C	-	...	79.0	85.9	1.800
2014	C	282	9.8	C	251	8.7	1.1	C	-	...	80.9	84.3	1.780
2015	C*	273	9.4	C*	283	9.8	-0.3		...	...	...	...	...

4. Vital statistics summary and life expectancy at birth: 2011 - 2015
Aperçu des statistiques de l'état civil et de l'espérance de vie à la naissance : 2011 - 2015 (continued - suite)

Continent, country or area and year / Continent, pays ou zone et année	Live births — Naissances vivantes			Deaths — Décès			Rate of natural increase Taux d'accrois-sement naturel	Infant deaths — Décès d'enfants de moins d'un an			Life expectancy at birth — Espérance de vie à la naissance		Total fertility rate L'indice synthétique de fécondité
	Code[a]	Number Nombre	Crude birth rate Taux brut de natalité	Code[a]	Number Nombre	Crude death rate Taux brut de mortalité		Code[a]	Number Nombre	Rate (per 1000 births) Taux (par 1000 naiss-ances)	Male[b] Masculin[b]	Female[b] Féminin[b]	
EUROPE													
Albania - Albanie													
2011	C	34 285	11.8	C	20 012	6.9	4.9	C	299	8.7	...	...	...
2012	C	35 473	12.2	C	20 870	7.2	5.0	C	312	8.8	...	...	...
2013	C	35 750	12.3	C	20 442	7.1	5.3	C	282	7.9	76.0	80.3	...
2014	C	35 760	12.4	C	20 656	7.1	5.2		...	...	...	...	...
2015	C	33 221	11.5	C	22 422	7.8	3.7		...	...	...	...	...
Andorra - Andorre													
2011	C	793	10.0	C	275	3.5	6.5		...	...	...	...	1.260
2012	C	737	9.5	C	303	3.9	5.6	C	4	...	...	...	1.151
Austria - Autriche													
2011	C	78 109	9.3	C	76 479[80]	9.1	0.2	C	281	3.6	78.1	83.4	1.430
2012	C	78 952	9.4	C	79 436[80]	9.4	-0.1	C	252	3.2	78.3	83.3	1.441
2013	C	79 330	9.4	C	79 526[80]	9.4	0.0	C	245	3.1	78.5	83.6	...
2014	C	81 722	9.6	C	78 252[80]	9.2	0.4		...	...	79.1	84.0	...
2015	C	84 381	9.8	C	83 073[80]	9.7	0.2		...	...	...	...	...
Belarus - Bélarus													
2011	C	109 147	11.5	C	135 090	14.3	-2.7	C	420	3.8	64.7	76.7	1.515
2012	C	115 893	12.2	C	126 531	13.4	-1.1	C	386	3.3	66.6	77.6	1.620
2013	C	117 997	12.5	C	125 326	13.2	-0.8	C	407	3.4	67.3	77.9	...
2014	C	118 534	12.5	C	121 542	12.8	-0.3	C	409	3.5	67.8	78.6	...
2015	C	119 028	12.6	C	120 026	12.7	-0.1		...	...	...	...	...
Belgium - Belgique													
2011	C	128 705[81]	11.7	C	104 292[81]	9.4	2.2	C	434[81]	3.4	...	...	1.810
2012	C	128 051[81]	11.5	C	109 076[81]	9.8	1.7	C	483[81]	3.8	...	...	...
2013	C	125 606[81]	11.2	C	109 334[81]	9.8	1.5	C	436[81]	3.5	...	...	...
2014	C	125 014[81]	11.1	C	104 755[81]	9.3	1.8	C	423[81]	3.4	78.8	83.9	...
2015	C*	122 274[81]	10.9	C	110 541[81]	9.8	1.0		...	...	...	...	...
Bosnia and Herzegovina - Bosnie-Herzégovine													
2011	C	31 875	8.3	C	35 522	9.2	-0.9		...	...	...	...	...
2012	C	32 072	8.4	C	35 692	9.3	-0.9	C	161	5.0	...	...	...
2013	C	31 103	8.1	C	35 837	9.3	-1.2	C	161	5.2	...	...	...
2014	C	29 247	7.6	C	34 824	9.1	-1.5	C	140	4.8	...	...	...
Bulgaria - Bulgarie													
2011	C	70 846	9.6	C	108 258	14.7	-5.1	C	601	8.5	[III]70.4	77.4	1.508
2012	C	69 121	9.5	C	109 281	15.0	-5.5	C	536	7.8	[III]70.6	77.5	1.501
2013	C	66 578	9.2	C	104 345	14.4	-5.2	C	489	7.3	...	...	...
2014	C	67 585	9.4	C	108 952	15.1	-5.7	C	517	7.6	71.1	78.0	...
2015	C	65 950	9.2	C	110 117	15.3	-6.1		...	...	...	...	...
Croatia - Croatie													
2011	C	41 197	9.6	C	51 019	11.9	-2.3	C	192	4.7	...	...	1.407
2012	C	41 771	9.8	C	51 710	12.1	-2.3	C	150	3.6	...	...	1.517
2013	C	39 939	9.4	C	50 386	11.8	-2.5	C	162	4.1	...	...	...
2014	C	39 566	9.3	C	50 839	12.0	-2.7	C	199	5.0	74.7	81.0	...
2015	C*	37 503	8.9	C	54 205	12.8	-4.0		...	...	...	...	...
Czech Republic - République tchèque													
2011	C	108 673[82]	10.4	C	106 848	10.2	0.2	C	298	2.7	74.7	80.7	1.426
2012	C	108 576	10.3	C	108 189	10.3	0.0	C	285	2.6	75.0	80.9	1.452
2013	C	106 751	10.2	C	109 160	10.4	-0.2	C	265	2.5	75.2	81.1	...
2014	C	109 860	10.4	C	105 665	10.0	0.4	C	263	2.4	75.8	81.7	...
2015	C*	110 764	10.5	C	111 173	10.5	0.0		...	...	...	...	...
Denmark - Danemark[83]													
2011	C	58 998	10.6	C	52 516	9.4	1.2	C	208	3.5	[II]77.3	81.6	1.756
2012	C	57 916	10.4	C	52 325	9.4	1.0	C	197	3.4	[II]77.9	81.9	1.733
2013	C	55 873	10.0	C	52 471	9.4	0.6	C	195	3.5	[II]78.0	81.9	...
2014	C	56 870	10.1	C	51 340	9.1	1.0	C	229	4.0	78.5	82.7	...
2015	C	58 205	10.3	C	52 555	9.3	1.0		...	...	...	...	...

Continent, country or area and year / Continent, pays ou zone et année	Live births / Naissances vivantes			Deaths / Décès			Rate of natural increase / Taux d'accrois-sement naturel	Infant deaths / Décès d'enfants de moins d'un an			Life expectancy at birth / Espérance de vie à la naissance		Total fertility rate / L'indice synthétique de fécondité
	Code[a]	Number / Nombre	Crude birth rate / Taux brut de natalité	Code[a]	Number / Nombre	Crude death rate / Taux brut de mortalité		Code[a]	Number / Nombre	Rate (per 1000 births) / Taux (par 1000 naissances)	Male[b] / Masculin[b]	Female[b] / Féminin[b]	
EUROPE													
Estonia - Estonie													
2011	C	14 679	11.1	C	15 244	11.5	-0.4	C	36	2.5	71.2	81.3	1.524
2012	C	14 056	10.6	C	15 450	11.7	-1.1	C	50	3.6	71.5	81.5	1.547
2013	C	13 531	10.3	C	15 244	11.6	-1.3	C	28	...	72.7	81.4	...
2014	C	13 551	10.3	C	15 484	11.8	-1.5	C	36	2.7	72.3	81.5	...
2015	C	13 907	10.6	C	15 243	11.6	-1.0		...	...	...	...	...
Faeroe Islands - Îles Féroé													
2011	C	581	12.0	C	385	7.9	4.0	C	3	...	...	...	2.311
2012	C	619	12.8	C	408	8.4	4.4	C	10	...	...	...	2.573
2013	C	626	13.0	C	364	7.5	5.4	C	-	...	...	...	2.537
2014	C	639	13.2	C	394	8.1	5.1	C	4	...	...	...	2.562
2015	C	608	12.4	C	377	7.7	4.7	C	1	...	II78.3	84.5	2.409
Finland - Finlande													
2011	C	59 676[84]	11.1	C	50 308[84]	9.4	1.7	C	143[84]	2.4	...	...	1.827
2012	C	59 201[84]	11.0	C	51 384[84]	9.5	1.5	C	141[84]	2.4	77.5[84]	83.4[84]	1.801
2013	C	57 847[84]	10.7	C	51 203[84]	9.5	1.2	C	102[84]	1.8	...	...	...
2014	C	56 950[84]	10.5	C	51 935[84]	9.6	0.9	C	124[84]	2.2	78.2[84]	83.9[84]	...
2015	C*	55 199[84]	10.1	C	52 209[84]	9.5	0.5		...	...	...	...	...
France													
2011	C	792 996	12.5	C	534 795	8.5	4.1	C	2 604	3.3	III78.1	84.7	1.997
2012	C	790 290	12.4	C	559 227	8.8	3.6	C	2 643	3.3	III78.3[15]	84.8[15]	1.995
2013	C	781 621	12.3	C	558 408	8.8	3.5	C	2 710	3.5	III78.6[15]	85.0[15]	...
2014	C	781 167	12.2	C	547 003	8.5	3.7	C	2 598	3.3	79.3	85.4	...
2015	C*	762 000	11.8	C*	587 000	9.1	2.7		...	...	...	...	...
Germany - Allemagne													
2011	C	662 685	8.3	C	852 328	10.6	-2.4	C	2 408	3.6	III77.7	82.7	1.364
2012	C	673 544	8.4	C	869 582	10.8	-2.4	C	2 202	3.3	III77.7	82.8	...
2013	C	682 069	8.5	C	893 825	11.1	-2.6	C	2 250	3.3	...	...	...
2014	C	714 927	8.8	C	868 356	10.7	-1.9	C	2 284	3.2	78.7	83.6	...
2015	C*	737 575	9.1	C*	925 000	11.4	-2.3		...	...	...	...	...
Gibraltar													
2011	+C	442[85]	13.8	+C	241[86]	7.5	6.3		...	...	...	...	...
2012	+C	461[85]	14.2	+C	264[86]	8.1	6.0		...	...	...	...	...
2013	+C	426[85]	13.0	+C	230[86]	7.0	6.0	+C	-	...	...	...	...
Greece - Grèce													
2011	C	106 428	9.6	C	111 099	10.0	-0.4	C	357	3.4	78.3	83.1	1.390
2012	C	100 371	9.1	C	116 668	10.6	-1.5	C	293	2.9	77.9	83.0	1.340
2013	C	94 134	8.6	C	111 794	10.2	-1.6	C	347	3.7	...	...	...
2014	C	92 149	8.5	C	113 740	10.4	-2.0	C	346	3.8	78.5	83.5	...
2015	C*	91 852	8.5	C*	120 844	11.1	-2.7		...	...	...	...	...
Guernsey - Guernesey													
2011	C	650	10.3	C	535	8.5	1.8		...	...	...	...	...
2012	C	674	10.7	C	547	8.7	2.0		...	...	...	...	...
2013	C	667	10.6	C	556	8.9	1.8		...	...	...	...	...
2014	C	627	10.0	C	526	8.4	1.6		...	...	...	...	...
Hungary - Hongrie													
2011	C	88 049	8.8	C	128 795	12.9	-4.1	C	433	4.9	70.9	78.2	1.238
2012	C	90 269	9.1	C	129 440	13.0	-3.9	C	438	4.9	71.5	78.4	1.337
2013	C	89 524[87]	9.0	C	126 677[88]	12.8	-3.8	C	448[89]	5.0	72.0	78.7	...
2014	C	93 281[90]	9.5	C	126 294[91]	12.8	-3.3	C	418[92]	4.5	72.1	78.9	...
2015	C	92 135[90]	9.4	C	131 575[91]	13.4	-4.0		...	...	...	...	...
Iceland - Islande													
2011	C	4 492[93]	14.1	C	1 986[93]	6.2	7.9	C	4[93]	...	II79.9	82.8	2.017
2012	C	4 533	14.1	C	1 955	6.1	8.0	C	5	...	II80.8	83.9	2.037
2013	C	4 326	13.4	C	2 154	6.7	6.7	C	8	...	II80.8	83.7	...
2014	C	4 375	13.4	C	2 049	6.3	7.1	C	9	...	II80.6	83.6	...
2015	C	4 129	12.5	C	2 178	6.6	5.9		...	...	...	...	...

4. Vital statistics summary and life expectancy at birth: 2011 - 2015
Aperçu des statistiques de l'état civil et de l'espérance de vie à la naissance : 2011 - 2015 (continued - suite)

Continent, country or area and year / Continent, pays ou zone et année	Code[a]	Live births / Naissances vivantes Number Nombre	Crude birth rate Taux brut de natalité	Code[a]	Deaths / Décès Number Nombre	Crude death rate Taux brut de mortalité	Rate of natural increase Taux d'accroissement naturel	Code[a]	Infant deaths / Décès d'enfants de moins d'un an Number Nombre	Rate (per 1000 births) Taux (par 1000 naissances)	Life expectancy at birth / Espérance de vie à la naissance Male[b] Masculin[b]	Female[b] Féminin[b]	Total fertility rate L'indice synthétique de fécondité
EUROPE													
Ireland - Irlande													
2011	C	74 033[94]	16.2[94]	C	28 456[94]	6.2[94]	10.0	+C	262	3.5	...	...	2.020
2012	+C	72 225	15.7	C	29 186[94]	6.4[94]	9.4	+C	250	3.5	...	...	2.010
2013	+C	68 930	15.0	+C	30 018	6.5	8.5	+C	243	3.5	...	...	...
2014	+C	67 285	14.6	+C	29 188	6.3	8.3	+C	224	3.3	79.3[15]	83.5[15]	...
2015	+C*	65 909	14.2	+C*	29 952	6.4	7.7		...	...	...	...	...
Isle of Man - Île de Man													
2011	+C	938	11.1	+C	816	9.7	1.4		...	...	...	...	...
2012	+C	890	10.5	+C	799	9.4	1.1		...	...	...	...	...
2013	+C	859	10.0	+C	792	9.2	0.8		...	...	...	...	...
2014	+C	805	9.3	+C	787	9.1	0.2		...	...	...	...	...
Italy - Italie													
2011	+C	546 585	9.2	C	593 402	10.0	-0.8	C	1 595	2.9	...	...	1.390
2012	+C	534 186	9.0	C	612 883	10.3	-1.3	C	1 532	2.9	...	...	1.390
2013	+C	514 308	8.5	C	600 744	10.0	-1.4	C	1 493	2.9	79.8	84.6	...
2014	C	502 596	8.3	C	598 364	9.8	-1.6	C	1 523	3.0	80.3	85.0	...
2015	C	485 780	8.0	C	647 571	10.7	-2.7		...	...	...	...	...
Jersey													
2011	+C	1 075[29]	11.0	+C	727	7.4	3.5		...	...	...	...	...
2012	+C	1 124[29]	11.4	+C	774	7.8	3.5		...	...	...	...	...
2013	+C	1 029[29]	...	+C	717	...	...		...	...	...	...	...
2014	+C	985[29]	9.8	+C	700	6.9	2.8		...	...	...	...	...
2015	+C	1 021[29]	9.9	+C	756	7.4	2.6		...	...	...	...	...
Latvia - Lettonie													
2011	C	18 828	9.1	C	28 540	13.9	-4.7	C	124	6.6	...	...	...
2012	C	19 897	9.8	C	29 025	14.3	-4.5	C	125	6.3	69.1	78.9	1.444
2013	C	20 596	10.2	C	28 691	14.3	-4.0	C	91	4.4	69.5	79.0	...
2014	C	21 746	10.9	C	28 466	14.3	-3.4	C	83	3.8	69.3	79.5	...
2015	C	21 979	11.1	C	28 478	14.3	-3.3		...	...	...	...	...
Liechtenstein													
2011	C	395	10.9	C	248	6.8	4.1	C	1	...	...	...	1.688
2012	C	357	9.7	C	224	6.1	3.6	C	3	...	...	...	1.507
2013	C	339	9.2	C	246	6.7	2.5	C	2	...	...	...	...
2014	C	372	10.0	C	268	7.2	2.8	C	1	...	...	...	...
2015	C	325	8.7	C	252	6.7	1.9		...	...	...	...	...
Lithuania - Lituanie													
2011	C	30 268	10.0	C	41 037	13.6	-3.6	C	144	4.8	68.1	79.1	1.551
2012	C	30 459	10.2	C	40 938	13.7	-3.5	C	118	3.9	68.4	79.4	1.595
2013	C	29 885	10.1	C	41 511	14.0	-3.9	C	110	3.7	68.5	79.4	...
2014	C	30 369	10.4	C	40 252	13.7	-3.4	C	118	3.9	69.1	79.9	...
2015	C	31 475	...	C	41 776	...	...		...	...	...	...	...
Luxembourg													
2011	C	5 639	10.9	C	3 819	7.4	3.5	C	24	...	...	...	1.513
2012	C	6 026	11.3	C	3 876	7.3	4.0	C	25	...	III79.5	84.3	1.570
2013	C	6 115	11.3	C	3 822	7.0	4.2	C	24	...	III79.9	84.3	...
2014	C	6 070	10.9	C	3 841	6.9	4.0	C	17	...	III80.2	84.8	...
2015	C	6 115	10.9	C	3 983	7.1	3.8		...	...	...	...	...
Malta - Malte													
2011	C	4 165	10.0	C	3 267	7.8	2.2	C	27	...	78.4	82.7	1.448
2012	C	4 130	9.8	C	3 418	8.1	1.7	C	22	...	78.0	82.2	1.435
2013	C	4 032	9.5	C	3 236	7.6	1.9	C	27	...	79.6	84.0	...
2014	C	4 191	9.8	C	3 270	7.7	2.2	C	21	...	79.8	84.3	...
2015	C	4 325	10.1	C	3 442	8.0	2.1		...	...	...	...	...
Monaco[95]													
2011	C	1 028	28.5	C	499	13.8	14.6		...	...	...	...	...
2012	C	979	27.2	C	429	11.9	15.3		...	...	...	...	...
2013	C	992	26.8	C	567[96]	15.3	11.5		...	...	...	...	...
2014	C	974	...	C	524[96]	...	...		...	...	...	...	...

4. Vital statistics summary and life expectancy at birth: 2011 - 2015
Aperçu des statistiques de l'état civil et de l'espérance de vie à la naissance : 2011 - 2015 (continued - suite)

Continent, country or area and year / Continent, pays ou zone et année	Live births Naissances vivantes				Deaths Décès			Rate of natural increase Taux d'accrois-sement naturel	Infant deaths Décès d'enfants de moins d'un an			Life expectancy at birth Espérance de vie à la naissance		Total fertility rate L'indice synthétique de fécondité
	Co-de[a]	Number Nombre	Crude birth rate Taux brut de natalité	Co-de[a]		Number Nombre	Crude death rate Taux brut de mortalité		Co-de[a]	Number Nombre	Rate (per 1000 births) Taux (par 1000 naiss-ances)	Male[b] Masculin[b]	Female[b] Féminin[b]	
EUROPE														
Montenegro - Monténégro														
2011	C	7 215	11.6	C		5 847	9.4	2.2	C	32	4.4	...	...	1.652
2012	C	7 459	12.0	C		5 922	9.5	2.5	C	33	4.4	...	...	1.709
2013	C	7 475	12.0	C		5 917	9.5	2.5	C	33	4.4	...	...	...
2014	C	7 529	12.1	C		6 014	9.7	2.4	C	37	4.9	...	...	...
2015	C	7 386	11.9	C		6 329	10.2	1.7		...	...	...	...	...
Netherlands - Pays-Bas														
2011	C	180 060[97]	10.8	C		135 741[97]	8.1	2.7	C	654[97]	3.6	79.2	82.8	1.760
2012	C	175 959[97]	10.5	C		140 813[97]	8.4	2.1	C	649[97]	3.7	...	...	1.720
2013	C	171 341[97]	10.2	C		141 245[97]	8.4	1.8	C	645[97]	3.8	...	...	...
2014	C	175 181[97]	10.4	C		139 223[97]	8.3	2.1	C	630[97]	3.6	80.0	83.5	...
2015	C*	169 965[97]	10.0	C*		147 010[97]	8.7	1.4		...	...	...	...	...
Norway - Norvège														
2011	C	60 220	12.2	C		41 393[98]	8.4	3.8	C	142[98]	2.4	79.0	83.5	1.880
2012	C	60 255	12.0	C		41 992[98]	8.4	3.6	C	150[98]	2.5	79.4	83.4	1.851
2013	C	58 878	11.6	C		41 131[98]	8.1	3.5	C	140[98]	2.4	...	...	...
2014	C	58 976	11.5	C		40 369[98]	7.9	3.6	C	139[98]	2.4	80.1	84.2	...
2015	C	59 058	11.4	C		40 727[98]	7.9	3.5		...	...	...	...	...
Poland - Pologne														
2011	C	388 416	10.1	C		375 501	9.7	0.3	C	1 836	4.7	72.4	80.9	1.301
2012	C	386 257	10.0	C		384 788	10.0	0.0	C	1 791	4.6	72.7	81.0	1.299
2013	C	369 576	9.7	C		387 312	10.1	-0.5	C	1 684	4.6	...	...	...
2014	C	375 160	9.9	C		376 467	9.9	0.0	C	1 583	4.2	73.7	81.7	...
2015	C	369 308	9.7	C		394 921	10.4	-0.7		...	...	...	...	...
Portugal														
2011	C	96 856[29]	9.2	C		102 848[99]	9.7	-0.6	C	302[99]	3.1	[III]76.4	82.3	1.351
2012	C	89 841[29]	8.5	C		107 612[99]	10.2	-1.7	C	303[99]	3.4	[III]76.7	82.6	1.284
2013	C	82 787[29]	7.9	C		106 543[99]	10.2	-2.3	C	243[99]	2.9	[III]76.9	82.8	...
2014	C	82 367[29]	7.9	C		104 843[99]	10.1	-2.2	C	236[99]	2.9	[III]77.2	83.0	...
2015	C	85 500[29]	8.2	C		108 511[99]	10.5	-2.2		...	...	...	...	...
Republic of Moldova - République de Moldova[100]														
2011	C	39 182	11.0	C		39 249	11.0	0.0	C	431	11.0	...	...	1.266
2012	C	39 435	11.1	C		39 560	11.1	0.0	C	387	9.8	67.2	75.0	1.279
2013	C	37 871	10.6	C		38 060	10.7	-0.1	C	359	9.5	...	...	...
2014	C	38 616	10.9	C		39 494	11.1	-0.2	C	372	9.6	...	...	...
2015	C*	38 612	10.9	C		39 906	11.2	-0.4		...	...	...	...	...
Romania - Roumanie														
2011	C	196 242	9.7	C		251 439	12.5	-2.7	C	1 850	9.4	[III]70.1	77.5	1.251
2012	C	201 104	10.0	C		255 539	12.7	-2.7	C	1 812	9.0	[III]70.7	77.9	1.302
2013	C	182 313	9.1	C		246 967	12.4	-3.2	C	1 677	9.2	[III]71.2	78.3	...
2014	C	193 103	9.7	C		254 237	12.8	-3.1	C	1 628	8.4	[III]72.0	78.9	...
2015	C*	185 006	9.3	C*		260 661	13.1	-3.8		...	...	...	...	...
Russian Federation - Fédération de Russie														
2011	C	1 796 629[47]	12.6	C		1 925 720[47]	13.5	-0.9	C	13 168[47]	7.3	64.0	75.6	...
2012	C	1 902 084[47]	13.3	C		1 906 335[47]	13.3	0.0	C	16 306[47]	8.6	64.6	75.9	...
2013	C*	1 901 182[47]	13.2	C*		1 878 269[47]	13.1	0.2		...	...	...	...	...
San Marino - Saint-Marin														
2011	+C	325	9.7	+C		222	6.6	3.1	+C	1	...	...	...	...
2012	+C	292	8.7	+C		237	7.1	1.6	+C	-	...	81.5	86.1	...
2013	+C	320	9.6	+C		247	7.4	2.2	+C	1	...	81.7	86.4	...
2014	+C	281	8.4	+C		252	7.5	0.9	+C	1	...	...	...	...
2015	+C	269	8.0	+C		235	7.0	1.0		...	...	...	...	...
Serbia - Serbie[101]														
2011	+C	65 598	9.1	+C		102 935	14.2	-5.2	+C	414	6.3	71.6	76.8	1.360
2012	+C	67 257	9.3	+C		102 400	14.2	-4.9	+C	415	6.2	72.2	77.3	1.449
2013	+C	65 554	9.1	+C		100 300	14.0	-4.8	+C	413	6.3	72.5	77.7	...

4. Vital statistics summary and life expectancy at birth: 2011 - 2015
Aperçu des statistiques de l'état civil et de l'espérance de vie à la naissance : 2011 - 2015 (continued - suite)

Continent, country or area and year / Continent, pays ou zone et année	Live births / Naissances vivantes			Deaths / Décès			Rate of natural increase / Taux d'accroissement naturel	Infant deaths / Décès d'enfants de moins d'un an			Life expectancy at birth / Espérance de vie à la naissance		Total fertility rate / L'indice synthétique de fécondité
	Code[a]	Number Nombre	Crude birth rate Taux brut de natalité	Code[a]	Number Nombre	Crude death rate Taux brut de mortalité		Code[a]	Number Nombre	Rate (per 1000 births) Taux (par 1000 naissances)	Male[b] Masculin[b]	Female[b] Féminin[b]	
EUROPE													
Serbia - Serbie[101]													
2014	+C	66 461	9.3	+C	101 247	14.2	-4.9	+C	381	5.7	72.6	77.7	...
2015	+C*	65 657	9.2	+C	103 678	14.6	-5.3		...	...	...	...	...
Slovakia - Slovaquie													
2011	C	60 647	11.2	C	53 594	9.9	1.3	C	300	4.9	72.2	79.4	1.447
2012	C	55 535	10.3	C	52 437	9.7	0.6	C	321	5.8	72.5	79.5	1.339
2013	C	54 823	10.1	C	52 089	9.6	0.5	C	301	5.5	72.9	79.6	...
2014	C	55 033	10.2	C	51 346	9.5	0.7	C	318	5.8	73.2	80.0	...
2015	C	55 602	10.2	C	53 826	9.9	0.3		...	...	...	...	...
Slovenia - Slovénie													
2011	C	21 947	10.7	C	18 699	9.1	1.6	C	64	2.9	76.6	82.9	1.562
2012	C	21 938	10.7	C	19 257	9.4	1.3	C	36	1.6	77.0	82.9	1.581
2013	C	21 111	10.3	C	19 334	9.4	0.9	C	62	2.9	77.0	83.2	...
2014	C	21 165	10.3	C	18 886	9.2	1.1	C	39	1.8	78.0	83.7	...
2015	C	20 641	10.0	C	19 834	9.6	0.4		...	...	...	...	...
Spain - Espagne													
2011	C	470 553	10.1	C	386 017	8.3	1.8	C	1 477	3.1	79.2	85.0	1.342
2012	C	453 348	9.7	C	401 122	8.6	1.1	C	1 389	3.1	79.4	85.1	1.320
2013	C	424 440	9.1	C	388 600	8.3	0.8	C	1 149	2.7	80.0	85.6	...
2014	C	426 076	9.2	C	393 734	8.5	0.7	C	1 202	2.8	80.4	86.2	...
2015	C*	417 265	9.0	C*	420 018	9.0	-0.1		...	...	...	...	...
Sweden - Suède													
2011	C	111 770	11.8	C	89 938	9.5	2.3	C	235	2.1	79.8	83.7	1.900
2012	C	113 177	11.9	C	91 938	9.7	2.2	C	293	2.6	79.9	83.5	1.910
2013	C	113 593	11.8	C	90 402	9.4	2.4	C	306	2.7	...	...	...
2014	C	114 907	11.9	C	88 976	9.2	2.7	C	251	2.2	80.4	84.2	...
2015	C*	114 870	11.8	C	90 907	9.3	2.5		...	...	...	...	...
Switzerland - Suisse													
2011	C	80 808	10.2	C	62 091	7.8	2.4	C	305	3.8	||80.2	84.5	...
2012	C	82 164	10.3	C	64 173	8.0	2.2	C	296	3.6	||80.4	84.6	1.526
2013	C	82 731	10.2	C	64 961	8.0	2.2	C	320	3.9	...	...	...
2014	C	85 287	10.4	C	63 938	7.8	2.6	C	331	3.9	||80.7	84.9	...
2015	C*	84 840	10.3	C*	67 262	8.2	2.1		...	...	...	...	...
TFYR of Macedonia - L'ex-R. y. de Macédoine													
2011	C	22 770	11.1	C	19 465	9.5	1.6	C	172	7.6	73.0	77.0	1.458
2012	C	23 568	11.4	C	20 134	9.8	1.7	C	230	9.8	...	...	1.507
2013	C	23 138	11.2	C	19 208	9.3	1.9	C	237	10.2	...	...	...
2014	C	23 596	11.4	C	19 718	9.5	1.9	C	233	9.9	...	...	...
2015	C	23 075	11.2	C	20 461	9.9	1.3		...	...	...	...	...
Ukraine													
2011	+C	502 595[102]	11.0	+C	664 588[103]	14.5	-3.5	+C	4 511[103]	9.0	66.0	75.9	1.459
2012	+C	520 705[102]	11.4	+C	663 139[103]	14.5	-3.1	+C	4 371[103]	8.4	66.1	76.0	1.531
2013	+C	503 657[102]	11.1	+C	662 368[103]	14.6	-3.5	+C	4 030[103]	8.0	66.3	76.2	...
2014	+C	465 882[104]	10.8	+C	632 296[105]	14.7	-3.9	+C	3 656[105]	7.8	...	...	...
United Kingdom of Great Britain and Northern Ireland - Royaume-Uni de Grande-Bretagne et d'Irlande du Nord[106]													
2011	C	807 776[107]	12.8	+C	552 232	8.7	4.0	+C	3 502	4.3	...	...	1.913
2012	C	812 970[107]	12.8	+C	569 024	8.9	3.8	+C	3 347	4.1	79.0	82.7	1.920
2013	C	778 358[107]	12.1	+C	574 945	9.0	3.2		...	...	...	...	...
2014	C	775 908[107]	12.0	+C	568 840	8.8	3.2	+C	2 990	3.9	...	...	...
2015	C*	777 167[107]	12.0	+C*	602 776	9.3	2.7		...	...	...	...	...

4. Vital statistics summary and life expectancy at birth: 2011 - 2015
Aperçu des statistiques de l'état civil et de l'espérance de vie à la naissance : 2011 - 2015 (continued - suite)

Continent, country or area and year / Continent, pays ou zone et année	Live births / Naissances vivantes			Deaths / Décès			Rate of natural increase / Taux d'accrois-sement naturel	Infant deaths / Décès d'enfants de moins d'un an			Life expectancy at birth / Espérance de vie à la naissance		Total fertility rate / L'indice synthétique de fécondité
	Code[a]	Number / Nombre	Crude birth rate / Taux brut de natalité	Code[a]	Number / Nombre	Crude death rate / Taux brut de mortalité		Code[a]	Number / Nombre	Rate (per 1000 births) / Taux (par 1000 naiss-ances)	Male[b] / Masculin[b]	Female[b] / Féminin[b]	
OCEANIA - OCÉANIE													
American Samoa - Samoas américaines													
2011	C	1 287	20.0	C	283	4.4	15.6	C	9	...	71.1	77.8	...
2012	C	1 175	18.5	C	282	4.4	14.0	C	4	...	...	...	...
2013	C	1 161	18.5	C	270	4.3	14.2	C	5	...	...	...	...
2014	C	1 084	17.5	C	259	4.2	13.3	C	9	...	...	...	...
Australia - Australie													
2011	+C	301 617	13.5	+C	146 932	6.6	6.9	+C	1 140	3.8	[III]79.8	84.2	1.917
2012	+C	309 582	13.6	+C	147 098	6.5	7.1	+C	1 031	3.3	[III]79.9	84.3	1.930
2013	+C	308 065	13.3	+C	147 678	6.4	6.9	+C	1 094	3.6	[III]80.1	84.3	1.883
2014	+C	299 697	12.8	+C	153 580	6.5	6.2	+C	1 012	3.4	[III]80.3	84.4	1.799
Cook Islands - Îles Cook[108]													
2011	+C	262	13.6	+C	72	3.7	9.8	+C	2	...	...	...	...
2012	+C	259	13.3	+C	104	5.3	7.9	+C	1	...	...	...	...
2013	+C	256	13.8	+C	115	6.2	7.6	+C	-	...	...	...	...
2014	+C	204	11.0	+C	113	6.1	4.9	+C	-	...	...	...	...
2015	+C*	205	10.9	+C*	102	5.4	5.5	+C*	-	...	...	...	...
Fiji - Fidji													
2012	+C	20 178	23.5	+C	6 724	7.8	15.7		...	...	...	...	...
2013	+C	20 970	24.4	+C	6 939	8.1	16.3		...	...	...	...	...
French Polynesia - Polynésie française													
2011	C	4 374	16.4	C	1 242	4.7	11.7	C	20	...	...	...	2.060
2012	C	4 296	16.0	C	1 360	5.1	10.9	C	31	7.2	73.3	78.2	2.030
2013	C	4 203	15.6	C	1 441	5.3	10.2	C	37	8.8	72.9	77.4	1.980
2014	C	4 161	15.3	C	1 427	5.3	10.1	C	28	...	73.8	78.0	1.960
2015	C	3 888	14.3	C	1 394	5.1	9.2	C	29	...	...	...	...
Guam													
2011	C	3 298[109]	20.7	C	842[109]	5.3	15.4	C	42[109]	12.7	75.3	81.6	2.480
2012	C	3 604[109]	22.5	C	894[109]	5.6	16.9	C	42[109]	11.7	75.5	81.7	2.450
2013	C	3 329[109]	20.8	C	904[109]	5.6	15.1	C	31[109]	9.3	75.6	81.9	2.410
2014	C	3 396[109]	21.1	C	952[109]	5.9	15.2	C	28[109]	...	75.8	82.1	2.380
2015	C	3 367[109]	20.8	C	1 009[109]	6.2	14.6	C	47[109]	14.0	75.9	82.2	...
Kiribati													
2011		...	...	U	494	...	...		...	...	...	...	...
Nauru													
2011	C	370	36.7	C	75	7.4	29.2		...	...	...	...	...
2012	C	319	...		...	...	...		...	...	...	...	...
2013	C	366	...		...	...	...		...	...	...	...	...
New Caledonia - Nouvelle-Calédonie													
2011	C	4 119	16.2	C	1 320	5.2	11.0	C	20	...	...	...	...
2012	C	4 389	17.0	C	1 322	5.1	11.9	C	17	...	...	...	...
New Zealand - Nouvelle-Zélande													
2011	+C	61 403	14.0	+C	30 082[30]	6.9	7.1	+C	290[30]	4.7	[III]79.1	82.8	2.095
2012	+C	61 178	13.9	+C	30 099[30]	6.8	7.1	+C	256[30]	4.2	[III]79.3	83.0	2.097
2013	+C	58 717	13.2	+C	29 568[30]	6.7	6.6	+C	260[30]	4.4	[III]79.7	83.2	2.007
2014	+C	57 240[110]	12.7	+C	31 062[110]	6.9	5.8	+C	324[110]	5.7	[III]79.6	83.3	1.924
2015	+C	61 038[110]	13.3	+C	31 608[110]	6.9	6.4	+C	252[110]	4.1	...	...	1.994
Niue - Nioué													
2011	C	22[111]	...	C	9[112]	...	...		...	...	...	...	...
Norfolk Island - Île Norfolk[113]													
2011	+C	13	...	+C	18	...	...		...	...	...	...	...
2012	+C	4	...	+C	20	...	...		...	...	...	...	...
2013		...	...	+C	11	...	...		...	...	...	...	...
2014		...	...	+C	13	...	...		...	...	...	...	...

Continent, country or area and year / Continent, pays ou zone et année	Live births Naissances vivantes			Deaths Décès			Rate of natural increase Taux d'accroissement naturel	Infant deaths Décès d'enfants de moins d'un an			Life expectancy at birth Espérance de vie à la naissance		Total fertility rate L'indice synthétique de fécondité
	Code[a]	Number Nombre	Crude birth rate Taux brut de natalité	Code[a]	Number Nombre	Crude death rate Taux brut de mortalité		Code[a]	Number Nombre	Rate (per 1000 births) Taux (par 1000 naissances)	Male[b] Masculin[b]	Female[b] Féminin[b]	
OCEANIA - OCÉANIE													
Northern Mariana Islands - Îles Mariannes septentrionales[34]													
2011	U	*1 033*	...	U	*165*	...	...	U	*2*	...	...	...	...
2012	U	*853*	...	U	*163*	...	...	U	*6*	...	...	...	...
2013	U	*686*	...	U	*185*	...	...	U	*8*	...	...	...	...
2014	U	*517*	...	U	*202*	...	...	U	*7*	...	...	...	...
Palau - Palaos													
2011	C	247	11.8	C	173	8.3	3.5	C	1	...	...	...	...
2012	C	268	12.7	C	164	7.8	4.9	C	2	...	...	...	...
2013	C	229	...	C	192	...	...	C	4	...	...	...	...
Pitcairn													
2011	C	-	...		...	...	...		...	...	...	...	...
2012	C	-	...		...	...	...		...	...	...	...	...
2013	C	-	...		...	...	...		...	...	...	...	...
Samoa													
2011	+U	*2 354*[114]	...	+U	*591*[114]	...	...		...	...	...	...	4.700
Tokelau - Tokélaou[115]													
2011	I	16	...		...	...	...		...	...	...	...	...

FOOTNOTES - NOTES

Italics: data from civil registers which are incomplete or of unknown completeness. - Italiques : données incomplètes ou dont le degré d'exactitude n'est pas connu, provenant des registres de l'état civil.

* Provisional. - Données provisoires.

[a] 'Code' indicates the source of data, as follows:
 C - Civil registration, estimated over 90% complete
 U - Civil registration, estimated less than 90% complete
 | - Other source, estimated reliable
 + - Data tabulated by date of registration rather than occurence
 ... - Information not available

Le 'Code' indique la source des données, comme suit :
 C - Registres de l'état civil considérés complets à 90 p. 100 au moins
 U - Registres de l'état civil qui ne sont pas considérés complets à 90 p. 100 au moins
 | - Autre source, considérée fiable
 + - Données exploitées selon la date de l'enregistrement et non la date de l'événement
 ... - Information non disponible

[b] A Roman number in front of the data for males specifies the range of the reference period of life expectancy for males and females presented on the row. For example, a reference year of 2005 and a range of V years means that the reference period for the life expectancy is 2001 - 2005. The absence of a Roman number means the reference period is one year and the reference period therefore coincides with the reference year. - Un chiffre romain devant la donnée relative aux hommes indique l'étendue de la période de référence concernant l'espérance de vie des hommes et des femmes présentée dans la ligne. Par exemple, une année de référence 2005 et une étendue de V signifie que la période de référence pour l'espérance de vie est 2001-2005. L'absence de chiffre romain signifie que la période de référence est d'un an et donc coïncide avec l'année de référence.

[1] Excluding live-born infants who died before their birth was registered. Data refer to Algerian population only. - Non compris les enfants nés vivants décédés avant l'enregistrement de leur naissance. Les données ne concernent que la population algérienne.
[2] Data refer to Algerian population only. - Les données ne concernent que la population algérienne.
[3] Data are projections presented in Annuaire Statistique 2010. - Les données sont des projections présentées dans l'Annuaire Statistique 2010.
[4] Source: Vital Statistics Report 2012. - Source: Vital Statistics Report 2012.
[5] Source: Vital Statistics Report 2014. - Source: Vital Statistics Report 2014.
[6] Data refer to national projections. - Les données se réfèrent aux projections nationales.
[7] Data refer to the recorded events in Ministry of Health hospitals and health centres only. - Les données se rapportent aux faits d'état civil enregistrés dans les hôpitaux et les dispensaires du Ministère de la santé seulement.
[8] The coverage of registration is estimated at 66 per cent. - Le degré de complétude de l'enregistrement est évalué à 66 pour cent.
[9] The coverage of registration is estimated at 26 per cent. - Le degré de complétude de l'enregistrement est évalué à 26 pour cent.
[10] Excludes the islands of St. Brandon and Agalega. - Non compris les îles St. Brandon et Agalega.
[11] Source: Ministry of Health, National Directorate of Planning and Cooperation. - Source : Ministère de la santé, Direction nationale de la planification et de la coopération.
[12] Data refer to the 12 months preceding the census in August. - Les données se rapportent aux 12 mois précédant le recensement d'août.
[13] Data refer to the 2011 Census. - Les données concernent le recensement de 2011.
[14] Excluding live-born infants who died before their birth was registered. - Non compris les enfants nés vivants décédés avant l'enregistrement de leur naissance.
[15] Provisional data. - Données provisoires.
[16] Data refer to Saint Helenian resident population. - Pour la population résidante de Sainte-Hélène.
[17] Data refer to the 12 months preceding the census in May. - Les données se rapportent aux 12 mois précédant le recensement de mai.
[18] Based on estimates and projections from 'Agence Nationale de la Statistique et de la Démographie'. - Données fondées sur des estimations et des projections provenant de l'Agence Nationale de la Statistique et de la Démographie.

[19] Based on preliminary findings of 2011 Uganda Demographic and Health Survey. - D'après les résultats préliminaires de l'enquête de 2011 sur la démographie et la santé en Ouganda.

[20] Based on the results of the 2012 Population and Housing Census. - D'après les résultats du recensement de la population et des logements de 2012.

[21] Excluding visitors. - Ne comprend pas les visiteurs.

[22] Excluding non-residents and foreign service personnel and their dependants. - À l'exclusion des non-résidents et du personnel diplomatique et de leurs charges de famille.

[23] Including Canadian residents temporarily in the United States, but excluding United States residents temporarily in Canada. Data refer to the twelve months from 1 July of the current year to 30 June of the following year. - Y compris les résidents canadiens se trouvant temporairement aux Etats-Unis, mais ne comprenant pas les résidents des Etats-Unis se trouvant temporairement au Canada. Les données font référence aux douze mois de 1 juillet de l'année actuelle à 30 juin de l'année suivante.

[24] Total includes resident deaths outside of the islands but buried in the islands. - Le total comprend les décès de résidents hors des îles mais inhumés dans les îles.

[25] Excluding children born in the country of non-resident mothers. - Exceptés les enfants nés dans le pays des mères non-résidentes.

[26] Excluding infant deaths to mothers living abroad. - Exception faite des décès d'enfants en bas âge survenus lorsque la mère résidait à l'étranger.

[27] Data have been adjusted for underenumeration. - Les données ont été ajustées pour compenser les lacunes du dénombrement.

[28] Data have been adjusted for undercoverage of infant deaths and sudden and violent deaths. - Ajusté pour la sous-estimation de la mortalité infantile, du nombre de morts soudaines et de morts violentes.

[29] Data refer to births to resident mothers. - Ces données concernent les enfants nés de mères résidentes.

[30] Data refer to resident population only. - Pour la population résidante seulement.

[31] Excluding Indian jungle population. - Non compris les Indiens de la jungle.

[32] Source: Population Registry and STAT/CBS estimates. - Source: Le registre de la population et les estimations du STAT/CBS.

[33] Based on the results of the Population Census. - D'après les résultats du recensement de la population.

[34] Source: U.S. National Center for Health Statistics, National Vital Statistics Reports (NVSR). - Source : US National Center for Health Statistics, National Vital Statistics Reports (NVSR).

[35] Data refer to the 12 months preceding the census in November. - Données se rapportant aux 12 mois précédant le recensement de novembre.

[36] Including births abroad and births of unknown residence of mother. - Y compris les naissances à l'étranger et les naissances pour lesquelles le lieu de résidence de la mère est inconnu.

[37] Including deaths abroad and deaths of unknown place of residence. - Y compris décès à l'étranger et décès dont le lieu de résidence n'est pas connu.

[38] Including deaths abroad and deaths of unknown residence of mother. - Y compris décès à l'étranger et décès de nourrissons nés de mères dont le lieu de résidence n'est pas connu.

[39] Projected value based on the results of 2000 and 2010 censuses, statistics from civil registration and reporting of live births in the ministry of health system. - Projection basée sur les résultats des recensements de 2000 et 2010, des statistiques d'état civil et les registres des naissances vivantes du Ministère de la santé.

[40] Estimate for 2010 – 2015. - Estimation pour la période 2010-2015.

[41] Excludes nomadic Indian tribes. - Non compris les tribus d'Indiens nomades.

[42] Data refer to projections based on the 2010 Population Census. - Les données se réfèrent aux projections basées sur le recensement de la population de 2010.

[43] Excludes nomadic Indian tribes. Data refer to national projections. - Non compris les tribus d'Indiens nomades. Les données se réfèrent aux projections nationales.

[44] Excludes nomadic Indian tribes. Data refer to projections based on the 2010 Population Census. - Non compris les tribus d'Indiens nomades. Les données se réfèrent aux projections basées sur le recensement de la population de 2010.

[45] Source: Reports of the Ministry of Health. - Source : Rapports du Ministère de la Santé.

[46] Indicators based on projected or estimated fertility from the 2001 Population Census. - Les indicateurs sont fondés sur la fécondité projetée ou estimée à partir du recensement de population de 2001.

[47] Excluding infants born alive of less than 28 weeks' gestation, of less than 1 000 grams in weight and 35 centimeters in length, who die within seven days of birth. - Non compris les enfants nés vivants après moins de 28 semaines de gestation, pesant moins de 1 000 grammes, mesurant moins de 35 centimètres et décédés dans les sept jours qui ont suivi leur naissance.

[48] Sources: Births and Deaths National Registration System database, and medical records of government hospitals. - Les sources: Les bases de données des << Births and Deaths National Registration System >> et les dossiers médicaux des hôpitaux du gouvernement.

[49] Deaths include deaths among some visitors. Sources: Births and Deaths National Registration System database, and medical records of government hospitals. - Les décès comprennent des décès parmi certains visiteurs. Les sources: Les bases de données des << Births and Deaths National Registration System >> et les dossiers médicaux des hôpitaux du gouvernement.

[50] For statistical purposes, the data for China do not include those for the Hong Kong Special Administrative Region (Hong Kong SAR), Macao Special Administrative Region (Macao SAR) and Taiwan province of China. Data have been estimated on the basis of the annual National Sample Survey on Population Changes. - Pour la présentation des statistiques, les données pour la Chine ne comprennent pas la Région Administrative Spéciale de Hong Kong (Hong Kong RAS), la Région Administrative Spéciale de Macao (Macao RAS) et Taïwan province de Chine. Les données ont été estimées sur la base de l'enquête annuelle "National Sample Survey on Population Changes".

[51] The fertility rates have been compiled using a population denominator which has excluded female foreign domestic helpers. - Les taux de fécondité ont été compilés pour une population (en dénominateur) ne comprenant pas les domestiques étrangères.

[52] Data refer to government controlled areas. - Les données se rapportent aux zones contrôlées par le Gouvernement.

[53] Data refer to deaths of residents only. - Les données renvoient aux décès de résidents uniquement.

[54] Includes data for the Indian-held part of Jammu and Kashmir, the final status of which has not yet been determined. - Y compris les données pour la partie du Jammu et du Cachemire occupée par l'Inde dont le statut définitif n'a pas encore été déterminé.

[55] Rates were obtained by the Sample Registration System of India, which is a large demographic survey. - Les taux ont été obtenus par le Système de l'enregistrement par échantillon de l'Inde qui est une large enquête démographique.

[56] Data are based on the publication: "Welfare Indicators", table "Health and Nutrition Indicators, Infant Mortality Rates" - Les données sont basées sur la publication : << Welfare Indicators >>, le tableau << Health and Nutrition Indicators, Infant Mortality Rates >>

[57] Data refer to the Iranian Year which begins on 21 March and ends on 20 March of the following year. - Les données concernent l'année iranienne, qui commence le 21 mars et se termine le 20 mars de l'année suivante.

[58] Includes data for East Jerusalem and Israeli residents in certain other territories under occupation by Israeli military forces since June 1967. - Y compris les données pour Jérusalem-Est et les résidents israéliens dans certains autres territoires occupés depuis 1967 par les forces armées israéliennes.

[59] Including deaths abroad of Israeli residents who were out of the country for less than a year. - Y compris les décès à l'étranger de résidents israéliens qui ont quitté le pays depuis moins d'un an.

[60] Data refer to Japanese nationals in Japan only. - Les données se raportent aux nationaux japonais au Japon seulement.

[61] The total number may include 'Unknown residence', but the categories urban and rural do not. - Le nombre total peut inclure les personnes dont la résidence n'est pas connue, à l'inverse des catégories de population urbaine et rurale.

[62] Total fertility rate computed as the sum of the age-specific fertility rates from age 15 to 49 years old. - Le taux de fécondité cumulé est calculé comme somme des taux de fécondité par âge de 15 à 49 ans.

[63] Excluding data for Jordanian territory under occupation since June 1967 by Israeli military forces. Excluding foreigners, including registered Palestinian refugees. - Non compris les données pour le territoire jordanien occupé depuis juin 1967 par les forces armées israéliennes. Non compris les étrangers, mais y compris les réfugiés de Palestine enregistrés.

[64] Data source is "Department of Public Health". - La source des données est << Le Service de la santé publique >>.

[65] Data refer to the 12 months preceding the census in June. - Les données se rapportent aux 12 mois précédant le recensement de juin.

[66] Data from Births and Deaths Notification System (Ministry of Health and all health care providers). - Les données proviennent du système de notification des naissances et des décès (Ministère de la santé et tous prestataires de soins de santé).

[67] Data refer to residence of child. Excluding alien armed forces, civilian aliens employed by armed forces, and foreign diplomatic personnel and their dependants. - Les données correspondent à la résidence de l'enfant. Non compris les militaires étrangers, les civils étrangers employés par les forces armées ni le personnel diplomatique étranger et les membres de leur famille les accompagnant.

68 Excluding alien armed forces, civilian aliens employed by armed forces, and foreign diplomatic personnel and their dependants. - Non compris les militaires étrangers, les civils étrangers employés par les forces armées ni le personnel diplomatique étranger et les membres de leur famille les accompagnant.

69 Projections based on the final results of the 2004 Population and Housing Census. - Projections basées sur les résultats définitifs du recensement de la population et de l'habitat de 2004.

70 Data refer to projections based on the 2010 Population and Housing Census. - Les données se réfèrent aux projections basées sur le recensement 2010 de la population et des logements.

71 Data refer to resident population which comprises Singapore citizens and permanent residents. - Les données se rapportent à la population résidente composé des citoyens de Singapour et des résidents permanents.

72 Data refer to resident total fertility rate. - Les données se rapportent aux indices synthétique de fécondité de la population résidante.

73 Provisional data. Data refer to resident population which comprises Singapore citizens and permanent residents. - Données provisoires. Les données se rapportent à la population résidente composé des citoyens de Singapour et des résidents permanents.

74 Source: Palestinian Central Bureau of Statistics, Population Register, updated version 05/01/2015. - Source: Bureau central de statistique palestinien, registre de la population, version actualisée jusqu'au 05/01/2015.

75 Source: Palestinian Multiple Indicator Cluster Survey 2014. - Source: Enquête palestinienne par grappes à indicateurs multiples, 2014.

76 Data have been adjusted for under-registration. Excluding infants born alive of less than 28 weeks' gestation, of less than 1 000 grams in weight and 35 centimeters in length, who die within seven days of birth. - Y compris un ajustement pour sous-enregistrement. Non compris les enfants nés vivants après moins de 28 semaines de gestations, pesant moins de 1 000 grammes, mesurant moins de 35 centimètres et décédés dans les sept jours qui ont suivi leur naissance.

77 The registration of births and deaths is conducted by the Ministry of Health. An estimate of completeness is not provided. - L'enregistrement des naissances et des décès est mené par le Ministère de la Santé. Le degré estimatif de complétude n'est pas fourni.

78 Including Non-Yemeni births. - Y compris les naissances non-yéménites.

79 Including Non-Yemeni deaths. - Y compris les décès non-yéménites.

80 Including deaths of nationals abroad. - Y compris les décès des nationaux survenus à l'étranger.

81 Including armed forces stationed outside the country, but excluding alien armed forces stationed in the area. - Y compris les militaires nationaux hors du pays, mais non compris les militaires étrangers en garnison sur le territoire.

82 A live-born child is a child fully expelled or removed out of the mother's body, who gives a sign of life and whose birth weight is (a) 500 g or more, or (b) lower than 500 g, if it survives 24 hours after delivery. - Un enfant né vivant est un enfant qui a été entièrement expulsé ou retiré du corps de la mère, qui présente des signes de vie et dont le poids à la naissance est : a) soit égal ou supérieur à 500 grammes; b) soit inférieur à 500 grammes s'il survit plus de 24 heures après l'accouchement.

83 Excluding Faeroe Islands and Greenland shown separately, if available. - Non compris les Îles Féroé et le Groenland, qui font l'objet de rubriques distinctes, si disponible.

84 Excluding Åland Islands. - Non compris les Îles d'Åland.

85 Including live births by military personnel and their dependants. - Y compris les naissances vivantes parmi les membres du personnel militaire et leurs personnes à charge.

86 Excluding armed forces. - Non compris les militaires en garnison.

87 Till 2012 data refer to all live births occurred in Hungary. From 2013 data include the live births of women with Hungarian usual residence regardless of whether the live birth occurred in Hungary or in a foreign country, and do not include the live births of women with foreign country usual residence. - Jusqu'en 2012 les données concernent toutes les naissances vivantes survenues en Hongrie. À partir de 2013, les données concernent les enfants nés vivants de femmes dont la résidence habituelle est en Hongrie, que la naissance vivante ait eu lieu en Hongrie ou dans un pays étranger, et ne comprennent pas les enfants nés vivants de femmes dont la résidence habituelle est dans un pays étranger.

88 Till 2012 data refer to all deaths occurred in Hungary. From 2013 data include the deceased persons with Hungarian usual residence regardless of whether the death occurred in Hungary or in a foreign country, and do not include the deceased persons with foreign country usual residence. - Jusqu'en 2012 les données concernent tous les décès survenus en Hongrie. À partir de 2013, les données comprennent les décès de personnes dont la résidence habituelle était en Hongrie, que le décès ait eu lieu en Hongrie ou dans un pays étranger, et ne comprennent pas les décès de personnes dont la residence habituelle était dans un pays étranger.

89 Till 2012 data refer to all infant deaths occurred in Hungary. From 2013 data include the deceased infants with Hungarian usual residence regardless of whether the death occurred in Hungary or in a foreign country, and do not include the deceased infants with foreign country usual residence. - Jusqu'en 2012 les données concernent tous les décès de nourrissons survenus en Hongrie. À partir de 2013, les données comprennent les nourrissons décédés alors que leur résidence habituelle était en Hongrie, que le décès ait eu lieu en Hongrie ou dans un pays étranger, et ne comprennent pas les nourrissons décédés dont la résidence habituelle était dans un pays étranger.

90 Data include the live births of women with Hungarian usual residence regardless of whether the live birth occurred in Hungary or in a foreign country, and do not include the live births of women with foreign country usual residence. - Les données concernent les enfants nés vivants dont la résidence habituelle est en Hongrie, que la naissance vivante ait eu lieu en Hongrie ou dans un pays étranger, et ne comprennent pas les enfants nés vivants de femmes dont la résidence habituelle est dans un pays étranger.

91 Data include the deceased persons with Hungarian usual residence regardless of whether the death occurred in Hungary or in a foreign country, and do not include the deceased persons with foreign country usual residence. - Les données comprennent tous les décès survenus alors que leur résidence habituelle était en Hongrie, que le décès ait eu lieu en Hongrie ou dans un pays étranger, et ne comprennent pas les décès des personnes dont la residence habituelle était dans un pays étranger.

92 Data include the deceased infants with Hungarian usual residence regardless of whether the death occurred in Hungary or in a foreign country, and do not include the deceased infants with foreign country usual residence. - Les données comprennent les nourrissons décédés alors que leur résidence habituelle était en Hongrie, que le décès ait eu lieu en Hongrie ou dans un pays étranger, et ne comprennent pas les nourrissons décédés dont la residence habituelle était dans un pays étranger.

93 Definition of localities was revised in 2011 causing a break with the previous series. - La rupture par rapport aux séries précédentes s'explique par le fait que la définition des localités a été révisée depuis 2011.

94 Data refer to events registered within one year of occurrence. - Les données portent sur des événements enregistrés dans l'année pendant laquelle ils sont survenus.

95 Including residents outside the country. - Y compris les résidents hors du pays.

96 Including still births. - Les données comprennent les mortinaissances.

97 Including residents outside the country if listed in a Netherlands population register. - Englobe les résidents se trouvant à l'étranger à condition qu'ils soient inscrits sur le registre de population des Pays-Bas.

98 Including residents temporarily outside the country. - Y compris les résidents se trouvant temporairement hors du pays.

99 Data refer to usually resident population. - Les données concernent la population habituellement résidente.

100 Excluding Transnistria and the municipality of Bender. - Les données ne tiennent pas compte de l'information sur la Transnistria et la municipalité de Bender.

101 Excludes data for Kosovo and Metohia. - Sans les données pour le Kosovo et Metohie.

102 Data refer to births with weight 500g and more (if weight is unknown - with length 25 centimeters and more, or with gestation during 22 weeks or more). - Données concernant les nouveau-nés de 500 grammes ou plus (si le poids est inconnu – de 25 centimètres de long ou plus, ou après une grossesse de 22 semaines ou plus).

103 Data includes deaths resulting from births with weight 500g and more (if weight is unknown - with length 25 centimeters and more, or with gestation during 22 weeks or more). - Y compris les décès de nouveau-nés de 500 grammes ou plus (si le poids est inconnu – de 25 centimètres de long ou plus, ou après une grossesse de 22 semaines ou plus).

104 Data refer to births with weight 500g and more (if weight is unknown - with length 25 centimeters and more, or with gestation during 22 weeks or more). The Government of Ukraine has informed the United Nations that it is not in a position to provide statistical data concerning the Autonomous Republic of Crimea and the city of Sevastopol. - Données concernant les nouveau-nés de 500 grammes ou plus (si le poids est inconnu – de 25 centimètres de long ou plus, ou après une grossesse de 22 semaines ou plus). Le gouvernement Ukrainien a informé l'ONU qu'il n'est pas en mesure de fournir des données statistiques concernant la République autonome de Crimée et la ville de Sébastopol.

105 The Government of Ukraine has informed the United Nations that it is not in a position to provide statistical data concerning the Autonomous Republic of Crimea and the city of Sevastopol. Data includes deaths resulting from births with weight 500g and more (if weight is unknown - with length 25 centimeters and more, or with gestation during 22 weeks or more). - Le gouvernement Ukrainien a informé l'ONU qu'il n'est pas en mesure de fournir des données statistiques concernant la République autonome de Crimée et la ville de Sébastopol. Y

compris les décès de nouveau-nés de 500 grammes ou plus (si le poids est inconnu – de 25 centimètres de long ou plus, ou après une grossesse de 22 semaines ou plus).

[106] Excluding Channel Islands (Guernsey and Jersey) and Isle of Man, shown separately, if available. - Non compris les îles Anglo-Normandes (Guernesey et Jersey) et l'île de Man, qui font l'objet de rubriques distinctes, si disponible.

[107] Data tabulated by date of occurrence for England and Wales, and by date of registration for Northern Ireland and Scotland. - Données exploitées selon la date de l'événement pour l'Angleterre et le pays de Galles, et selon la date de l'enregistrement pour l'Irlande du Nord et l'Ecosse.

[108] Excluding Niue, shown separately, which is part of Cook Islands, but because of remoteness is administered separately. - Non compris Nioué, qui fait l'objet d'une rubrique distincte et qui fait partie des îles Cook, mais qui, en raison de son éloignement, est administrée séparément.

[109] Including United States military personnel, their dependants and contract employees. - Y compris les militaires des Etats-Unis, les membres de leur famille les accompagnant et les agents contractuels des Etats-Unis.

[110] Random rounding to base 3 is applied in this table as a confidentiality measure. - Les chiffres sont arrondis à la base 3 de manière aléatoire, pour des raisons de confidentialité.

[111] Includes children born in New Zealand to women resident in Niue who chose to travel to New Zealand to give birth. - Y compris les enfants nés en Nouvelle-Zélande de femmes résidant à Nioué qui ont choisi de se rendre en Nouvelle-Zélande pour accoucher.

[112] Includes deaths occurred in New Zealand but buried in Niue and deaths occurred in Niue but buried elsewhere. - Y compris les personnes décédées en Nouvelle-Zélande qui sont enterrées à Nioué et les personnes décédées à Nioué qui sont enterrées ailleurs.

[113] Data cover the period from 1 July of the previous year to 30 June of the present year. - Pour la période allant du 1er juillet de l'année précédente au 30 juin de l'année en cours.

[114] The coverage of registration is estimated at 70 per cent. - Le degré de complétude de l'enregistrement est évalué à 70 pour cent.

[115] Data refer to usually resident population present on census night. Data refer to the 12 months preceding the census in October. - Les données concernent la population habituellement résidente présente la nuit du recensement. Les données se rapportent aux 12 mois précédant le recensement de octobre.

Table 5 - *Demographic Yearbook 2015*

Table 5 presents national estimates of mid-year population for all available years between 2006 and 2015.

Description of variables: Mid-year estimates of the total population are those provided by national statistical offices. They refer to the *de facto* or *de jure* population on 1 July of the reference year. Exceptions to this are footnoted accordingly. The data are presented in thousands, rounded by the Statistics Division of the United Nations Department of Economic and Social Affairs.

For some countries or areas the figures presented in this table and the figures used to calculate rates in subsequent tables are not the same, as these countries have provided a reference population for vital events that is different than the total population.

Unless otherwise indicated, all estimates relate to the population within present geographical boundaries. Major exceptions to this principle are explained in footnotes.

Reliability of data: Reliable mid-year population estimates are those that are based on a complete census (or on a sample survey) and have been adjusted on a basis of a continuous population register or on the balance of births, deaths and migration. Reliable mid-year estimates appear in roman type. Mid-year estimates that are not calculated on this basis are considered less reliable and are shown in *italics*.

Limitations: Statistics on estimates of the mid-year total population are subject to the same qualifications as have been set forth for population statistics in general in section 3 of the Technical Notes.

International comparability of mid-year population estimates is also affected by the fact that some of these estimates refer to the *de jure*, and not the *de facto*, population. These are indicated in the column titled "Code". The difference between the *de facto* and the *de jure* population is discussed in section 3.1.1 of the Technical Notes.

Earlier data: Estimates of mid-year population have been shown in previous issues of the *Demographic Yearbook*. Information on the years and specific topics covered is presented in the Historical Index.

Tableau 5 – *Annuaire démographique 2015*

Le tableau 5 présente des estimations nationales de la population en milieu d'année pour le plus grand nombre possible d'années entre 2006 et 2015.

Description des variables : les estimations de la population totale en milieu d'année sont celles qui ont été communiquées par les services nationaux de statistique. Elles correspondent à la population de fait ou se réfèrent à la population de droit, au 1er juillet de l'année de référence. Lorsque la date est différente, cela est signalé par une note. Sauf indication contraire, tous les chiffres sont exprimés en milliers. Les données ont été arrondies par la Division de statistique du Département des affaires économiques et sociales de l'Organisation des Nations Unies.

Pour certains pays ou territoires, les données présentées dans ce tableau sont différentes des données utilisées pour calculer les taux dans les tableaux suivants, parce que ces pays ont fourni une population de référence pour les événements démographiques différente de la population totale.

Sauf indication contraire, toutes les estimations se rapportent à la population présente sur le territoire actuel des pays ou zones considérés. Les principales exceptions à cette règle sont expliquées en note.

Fiabilité des données : les estimations de la population en milieu d'année sont considérées sûres quand elles sont fondées sur un recensement complet (ou sur une enquête par sondage) et ont été ajustées en fonction des données provenant d'un registre permanent de population ou en fonction des naissances, décès et mouvements migratoires qui ont eu lieu pendant la période. Les estimations considérées comme sûres apparaissent en caractères romains. Les estimations dont le calcul n'a pas été effectué sur cette base sont considérées comme moins sûres et apparaissent en italique.

Insuffisance des données : les statistiques concernant les estimations de la population totale en milieu d'année appellent toutes les réserves qui ont été formulées à la section 3 des Notes techniques à propos des statistiques de la population en général.

Le fait que certaines des estimations concernant la population en milieu d'année se réfèrent à la population de droit et non à la population de fait influe sur la comparabilité internationale. Ces cas ont été signalés dans la colonne « Code ». La différence entre la population de fait et la population de droit est expliquée à la section 3.1.1 des Notes techniques.

Données publiées antérieurement : des estimations de la population en milieu d'année ont été publiées dans des éditions antérieures de l'*Annuaire démographique*. Pour plus de précisions concernant les années et les sujets pour lesquels des données ont été publiées, se reporter à l'index.

5. Estimates of mid-year population: 2006 - 2015
Estimations de la population au milieu de l'année : 2006 - 2015

Continent and country or area / Continent et pays ou zone	Code[a]	Population estimates (in thousands) - Estimations (en milliers)									
		2006	2007	2008	2009	2010	2011	2012	2013	2014	2015

AFRICA - AFRIQUE

Country	Code	2006	2007	2008	2009	2010	2011	2012	2013	2014	2015
Algeria - Algérie	DJ	33 481	34 096	34 591	35 268	35 978	36 717	37 495	38 297	39 114	39 963
Angola	DF	15 410	15 889	16 368	16 888	17 430	17 991	18 576	19 184	25 789	...
Benin - Bénin	DF	7 700[1]	7 959[1]	8 225[1]	8 498[1]	8 779[1]	9 067[1]	9 365[1]	...	10 293[2]	10 585[2]
Botswana	DJ	1 720	1 736	1 755	1 776	1 823	1 850	2 071[3]	2 115[3]	2 156[3]	2 195[3]
Burkina Faso[1]	DJ	...	14 252	14 731	15 225	15 731	...	...	...	...	...
Burundi[4]	DF	...	...	...	8 263	8 488	8 727	8 981	9 249	9 530	9 824
Cabo Verde		483	491	500	509	518	527	...	...	...	...
Cameroon - Cameroun[5]	DJ	...	...	...	18 928	19 406	19 865	20 387	21 143	21 657	21 918
Congo	DF	3 589[1]	3 616[1]	3 741	3 838	...	...	...	4 278	...	...
Côte d'Ivoire[1]	DF	19 658	20 228	20 807	21 395	...	...	...	...	...	...
Djibouti[6]	DF	754	775	797	...	841	865	...	...	...	...
Egypt - Égypte	DF	72 009	73 644	75 194	76 925	78 685	80 530	82 550	84 629	86 811	88 958
Equatorial Guinea - Guinée équatoriale[7]	DF	1 383	1 446	1 508	1 566	1 622	...	...	...	...	...
Ethiopia - Éthiopie	DF	75 067[8]	77 127[8]	75 719[9]	77 651[9]	79 634[9]	81 668[9]	83 741[9]	85 837[9]	87 952[9]	90 075[9]
Gambia - Gambie	DF	1 510	...	...	...	...	...	...	...	...	...
Ghana[1]	DF	21 876	22 388	22 901	23 417	...	25 235	25 825	26 428	27 043	27 670
Guinea - Guinée[1]	DF	...	...	10 183	10 218	10 537	10 864	...	...	...	...
Guinea-Bissau - Guinée-Bissau[1]	DF	1 357	1 389	...	...	1 460	1 472	1 485	1 499	1 514	1 531
Kenya	DF	36 139	37 184	38 278	...	40 406	41 409	42 436	43 489	44 572	45 509
Lesotho[1]	DF	1 866	1 880	1 884	1 887	1 892	1 897	...	...	...	...
Liberia - Libéria	DF	3 332	3 404	...	3 551	3 627	3 705	3 784	3 865	3 946	...
Libya - Libye	DF	...	5 393	5 490	5 589	5 689	5 791	5 892	5 994	6 096	6 162
Madagascar	DF	18 048	18 556	19 072	19 601	20 142	20 696	...	...	...	...
Malawi[1]	DF	12 758	13 188	13 630	14 085	13 949[10]	14 389[10]	14 845[10]	...	...	...
Mali	DF	12 051[11]	12 378[11]	14 161[12]	14 671[12]	15 370[12]	15 843[12]	16 312[12]	16 808[12]	*17 319[12]	...
Mauritania - Mauritanie[1]	DF	2 990	3 075	3 162	3 251	3 341	3 297	...	...	...	...
Mauritius - Maurice[13]	DJ	1 253[14]	1 260[14]	1 269[14]	1 275[14]	1 281[14]	1 252[15]	1 256[15]	1 259[15]	1 261[15]	1 263[15]
Mayotte[11]	DJ	...	...	...	...	...	...	...	...	*220	*227
Morocco - Maroc[16]	DF	30 509	30 850	31 195	31 543	31 894	32 245	32 597	32 950	33 774	...
Mozambique[1]	DF	19 889	20 632	21 208	21 803	22 417	23 050	23 701	24 366	25 042	25 728
Namibia - Namibie	DF	1 992[1]	2 028[1]	2 065[1]	2 104[1]	2 143[1]	2 116[17]	2 155[17]	2 196[17]	2 238[17]	2 281[17]
Niger	DJ	13 045[1]	13 716[1]	14 198[1]	14 693[1]	15 204[1]	15 731[1]	16 994[18]	17 680[18]	18 389[18]	19 125[18]
Nigeria - Nigéria	DF	*140 004[19]	...	149 652[1]	154 520[1]	159 619[1]	164 729[1]	...	...	...	...
Republic of South Sudan - République de Soudan du Sud[20]	DF	...	...	8 491	8 988	9 497	10 018	10 552	10 809	11 071	...
Reunion - Réunion	DJ	786	794[11]	808[11]	816[11]	...	829[11]	834[11]	835[11]	*839[11]	*844[11]
Rwanda	DF	9 468[1]	9 557[1]	9 832[1]	10 117[1]	10 413[1]	10 718[1]	10 483[21]	10 737[21]	10 997[21]	11 263[21]
Saint Helena ex. dep. - Sainte-Hélène sans dép.	DF	...	4	4	4	4	4	4	4[22]	4	...
Saint Helena: Ascension - Sainte-Hélène: Ascension	DJ	...	...	1	...	...	...	...	...	...	...
Saint Helena: Tristan da Cunha - Sainte-Hélène: Tristan da Cunha[23]	DF	...	0	0	0	...	...	...	...	...	...
Sao Tome and Principe - Sao Tomé-et-Principe	DF	152	155	158	161	164	167	*187	*194	...	...
Senegal - Sénégal	DJ	11 206[22]	11 519[22]	11 841[22]	12 171[22]	12 509[22]	12 842[22]	13 208[1]	13 509[1]	13 926[1]	14 357[1]
Seychelles	DF	85	85	87	87	90	87	88	90	91	93
Sierra Leone	DF	5 217	5 343	5 474	5 608	5 747	5 890	6 038	...	...	...
South Africa - Afrique du Sud	DF	48 270	48 910	49 561	50 223	50 896	51 580	52 275	52 982	54 002	...
Sudan - Soudan	DF	...	...	30 979	31 957	32 962	33 998	35 064	36 163	37 292	38 454
Swaziland	DF	1 146	1 018	1 032	1 044	1 056	1 068	1 080	1 093	1 106	1 119[11]
Togo	DF	5 337	5 465	5 596	5 731	6 191[1]	6 338[1]	6 491[1]	6 648[1]	6 809[1]	6 974[1]
Tunisia - Tunisie	DF	10 128	10 225	10 329	10 440	10 547	10 674	10 778	10 887	11 007	11 154
Uganda - Ouganda	DF	27 629	28 581	29 593	30 661	31 785	32 940	34 131	...	...	...
United Republic of Tanzania - République Unie de Tanzanie	DF	38 251[24]	39 446[24]	40 668[24]	41 916[24]	43 188[24]	44 485[24]	45 798[24]	46 170[21]	47 452[21]	48 776[21]
Zambia - Zambie[1]	DF	11 799	12 161	12 526	12 897	...	13 719	14 145	14 580	15 023	15 474
Zimbabwe	DF	11 930[24]	12 040[24]	12 150[24]	13 668[24]	...	...	...	13 369[21]	13 652[21]	13 943[21]

Continent and country or area / Continent et pays ou zone	Code[a]	Population estimates (in thousands) - Estimations (en milliers)									
		2006	2007	2008	2009	2010	2011	2012	2013	2014	2015
AMERICA, NORTH - AMÉRIQUE DU NORD											
Anguilla	DF	14	15	16	16	16	...	14	14	14	15
Antigua and Barbuda - Antigua-et-Barbuda	DF	84	86	88	89	91	...	...	...	...	...
Aruba	DJ	99	100	101	102	102	103	105	106	108	109
Bahamas[1]	DF	330	334	338	342	335	358	363	368	372	...
Barbados - Barbade	DF	273	274	275	275	278	278	278	277	277	275
Belize	DF	301	311	307	315	324	332	341	350	359	368
Bermuda - Bermudes	DJ	64[25]	64[25]	64[25]	64[25]	64[26]	63[26]	62[26]	62[26]	62[26]	62[26]
British Virgin Islands - Îles Vierges britanniques	DF	26	27	28	28	28	28	28	29	...	...
Canada	DJ	32 571[27]	32 888[27]	33 246[27]	33 629[27]	34 005[27]	34 343[28]	34 751[28]	35 155[29]	35 545[29]	35 849[29]
Cayman Islands - Îles Caïmanes	DJ	53	54	56	57	56	55	56	56	57	59
Costa Rica	DJ	4 354	4 443	4 533[30]	4 620[30]	4 538[31]	4 592[31]	4 651[31]	4 712[31]	4 772[31]	4 834[32]
Cuba	DJ	11 211	11 195	11 181	11 174	11 171	11 172	11 174	11 192	11 224	11 239
Curaçao	DJ	141[33]	144[33]	146[33]	147[33]	149[33]	151[33]	152[34]	154[34]	156[34]	158[34]
Dominica - Dominique	DF	71	71	71	71	71	71	71	71	72	...
Dominican Republic - République dominicaine	DF	9 071	9 174	9 280	9 380	9 479[1]	9 580[1]	9 681[1]	9 785[1]	9 883[1]	9 980[1]
El Salvador[35]	DF	6 074	6 099	6 125	6 153	6 183	6 216	6 251	6 289	6 328	6 460
Greenland - Groenland[36]	DJ	57	57	56	56	57	57	57	56	56	56
Grenada - Grenade	DF	105	105	105	105	105	107	108	109	109	111
Guadeloupe	DJ	458	401[37]	402[37]	402[37]	...	405[37]	403[37]	402[37]	*401[37]	*400[37]
Guatemala[24]	DF	13 019	13 345	13 678	14 017	14 362	14 714	15 073	...	...	...
Haiti - Haïti[38]	DJ	9 445	9 602	9 762	9 923	10 085	10 248	10 413	...	...	...
Honduras	DF	7 367[39]	7 537[39]	7 707[39]	7 877[39]	8 046[39]	8 215[39]	8 385[39]	...	8 432[2]	8 577[2]
Jamaica - Jamaïque	DJ	2 663	2 676	2 687	2 696	2 702	2 700	2 708	2 715	2 721	*2 726
Martinique[11]	DJ	...	398	398	396	...	392	388	386	*382	*378
Mexico - Mexique	DJ	108 409	109 787	111 299	112 853	114 256[1]	115 683[1]	117 054[1]	118 395[1]	119 713[1]	121 006[1]
Montserrat	DF	5	5	5	5	5	5	5	5	5	5
Nicaragua	DJ	5 523	5 596	5 669	5 742	5 816	5 889	6 071	6 134	6 198	6 263
Panama[26]	DF	3 413	3 476	3 538	3 600	3 662	3 724	3 788	3 851	3 913	3 975
Puerto Rico - Porto Rico[40]	DJ	3 805	3 783	3 761	3 740	3 721	3 687	3 642	3 596	3 548	3 474
Saint Kitts and Nevis - Saint-Kitts-et-Nevis	DF	*50	*51	*51	*52	*53	...	...	...	...	...
Saint Lucia - Sainte-Lucie	DF	166	168	170	172	...	167	169	171	173	173
Saint Pierre and Miquelon - Saint Pierre-et-Miquelon[11]	DJ	...	...	...	...	...	6	6	...	...	...
Saint Vincent and the Grenadines - Saint-Vincent-et-les Grenadines	DJ	109	110	110	110	110	110	110	110	110	110
Sint Maarten (Dutch part) - Saint-Martin (partie néerlandaise)	DJ	38	39	40	39	36	33	35	37	37[11]	...
Trinidad and Tobago - Trinité-et-Tobago	DF	1 298[14]	1 303[14]	1 309[14]	1 310[14]	1 318[14]	...	1 335[15]	1 341[15]	1 345[15]	1 350[15]
Turks and Caicos Islands - Îles Turques et Caïques	DJ	33	35	*37	38	40	...	...	...	...	...
United States of America - États-Unis d'Amérique[41]	DJ	298 380[33]	301 231[33]	304 094[33]	306 772[33]	309 347[34]	311 719[34]	314 103[34]	316 427[34]	318 907[34]	321 419[34]
United States Virgin Islands - Îles Vierges américaines[42]	DJ	110	110	110	110[43]	106[43]	106[43]	105[43]	105[43]	104[43]	...
AMERICA, SOUTH - AMÉRIQUE DU SUD											
Argentina - Argentine	DF	38 971	39 356	39 746	40 134	40 788[44]	41 262[44]	41 735[44]	42 206[44]	42 674[44]	43 137[44]
Bolivia (Plurinational State of) - Bolivie (État plurinational de)	DF	9 389	9 550	9 710	9 870	10 031	10 191	10 351	10 508	10 666	10 825
Brazil - Brésil[45]	DF	187 335	189 463	191 532	193 544	195 498	197 397	199 242	201 033	202 769	204 451
Chile - Chili	DF	16 433	16 598	16 763	16 929	17 094	17 248	17 403	17 557	17 819	18 006
Colombia - Colombie[46]	DJ	43 406	43 927	44 451	44 979	45 510	46 045	46 582	47 121	47 662	48 203
Ecuador - Équateur[47]	DF	13 965	14 215	14 473	14 738	15 012	15 266	15 521	15 775	16 027	16 279
French Guiana - Guyane française[11]	DJ	...	213	219	224	...	238	240	...	*249	*255

Continent and country or area / Continent et pays ou zone	Co-de[a]	Population estimates (in thousands) - Estimations (en milliers)									
		2006	2007	2008	2009	2010	2011	2012	2013	2014	2015
AMERICA, SOUTH - AMÉRIQUE DU SUD											
Guyana	DF	768	771	774	753	752	751	749	747	748	742
Paraguay[24]	DF	6 009	6 120	6 230	6 341	6 451	6 562	6 673	6 783	6 894	...
Peru - Pérou[48]	DF	28 151	28 482[35]	28 807[35]	29 132[35]	29 462[35]	29 798[35]	30 136[35]	30 475[35]	30 814[35]	31 152[35]
Suriname	DJ	506	510	517	524	531	540	...	550	559	...
Uruguay	DJ	3 358	3 359	3 363	3 378	3 397	3 413	3 426[1]	3 440[1]	3 454[1]	3 467[1]
Venezuela (Bolivarian Republic of) - Venezuela (République bolivarienne du)	DF	26 858	27 273	27 689	28 106	28 524	28 944	29 366	29 786	30 206	30 620
ASIA - ASIE											
Afghanistan[49]	DF	22 576	23 039	23 511	23 994	24 486	24 988	25 500	26 023	26 557	...
Armenia - Arménie	DJ	3 221	3 227	3 234	3 244	3 256	3 268	3 151	3 022	...	3 011[11]
Azerbaijan - Azerbaïdjan	DF	8 610[33]	8 723[33]	8 839[33]	8 947	9 054	9 173	9 296	9 417	9 529	9 593[11]
Bahrain - Bahreïn	DJ	960	1 039	1 103	1 178	1 229	1 195	1 209	1 253	1 315	...
Bangladesh	DF	140 600	142 600	144 500	146 600	148 620	150 611	152 700	154 790	156 880	...
Bhutan - Bhoutan[50]	DF	647	659	671	683	696	708	721	733	745	757
Brunei Darussalam - Brunéi Darussalam	DF / DJ	365[33]	370[33]	375[33]	380[33]	387[33]	...	400	406	412	*417
Cambodia - Cambodge[51]	DF	14 081[52]	14 364[52]	13 868[4]	14 085[4]	14 303[4]	14 521[4]	14 741[4]	14 963[4]	15 184[4]	15 405[4]
China - Chine[53]	DF	1 314 480[54]	1 317 900[54]	1 324 700[54]	1 331 300[54]	1 337 700[54]	1 344 100[55]	1 350 695[55]	1 357 380[54]	1 364 270[54]	1 371 220[54]
China, Hong Kong SAR - Chine, Hong Kong RAS	DJ	6 857	6 916	6 958	6 973	7 024	7 072	7 155	7 188	7 242	7 306
China, Macao SAR - Chine, Macao RAS	DJ	499	521	541	535	537	550	568	592	622	643
Cyprus - Chypre[56]	DJ	751[57]	767[57]	787[57]	808[57]	829[57]	851[57]	864[57]	862[57]	853[57]	*847[11]
Georgia - Géorgie	DF / DJ	4 398	4 388	4 384	4 411	4 453	4 483	4 491	...	4 490[11]	3 730[11]
India - Inde[58]	DF	1 117 734	1 134 023	1 150 196	1 166 228	1 182 105	1 197 813	1 213 370	...	...	...
Indonesia - Indonésie	DJ	222 747[59]	225 642[59]	228 523[59]	231 370[59]	238 519	241 991	245 425	248 818	252 165	255 462
Iran (Islamic Republic of) - Iran (République islamique d')[60]	DJ	70 603	71 279	72 182	73 202	74 340	...	76 038	76 942	77 856	78 773
Iraq	DF	28 562	29 427	30 315	31 393	32 211	33 052	33 913	34 794	35 736	36 659
Israel - Israël[61]	DJ	7 054	7 180	7 309	7 486	7 624	7 766	7 911	8 059	8 216	...
Japan - Japon[62]	DJ	127 854	128 001	128 063	128 047	128 070	127 817	127 561	127 339	127 132	126 958
Jordan - Jordanie[63]	DF	5 928	6 106	6 293	6 490	6 699	6 993	7 427	8 114	8 804	9 532
Kazakhstan	DF	15 308	15 484	15 674	16 093	16 322	16 557	16 791	17 035	17 161[11]	...
Kuwait - Koweït	DF	2 366	2 495	2 632	2 778	2 933	3 107	3 247	3 428	3 767	3 971
Kyrgyzstan - Kirghizstan[57]	DF / DJ	5 034[6]	5 056[6]	5 078[6]	5 128[6]	5 193[6]	5 260[6]	5 352[6]	5 720	5 836	5 957
Lao People's Democratic Republic - République démocratique populaire lao[64]	DF	5 746	5 869	5 990	6 111	6 230	6 349	6 466	6 581	6 693	...
Malaysia - Malaisie	DJ	26 550[65]	27 058[65]	27 568[65]	28 081[65]	28 589[66]	29 062[66]	29 510[66]	30 214[66]	30 598[66]	30 996[66]
Maldives	DF	...	305	310	315	320	325	331	336	...	348
Mongolia - Mongolie	DF	2 583	2 602	2 643	2 691	2 739	2 786	2 840	2 899	2 963	3 027
Myanmar[67]	DF	56 515	57 504	58 377	59 130	59 780	50 149[68]	50 667[68]	51 184[68]	51 486[68]	...
Nepal - Népal	DJ	25 887	26 427	26 967	27 504	28 044	28 585	26 873[17]	27 257[17]	27 646[17]	28 038[17]
Oman	DF	2 577	2 743	2 867	3 174	...	3 295	3 623	3 855	3 993	...
Pakistan[69]	DF / DJ	147 100	149 860[70]	166 410	169 940	173 510	177 100	...	184 350	188 020	191 710
Philippines	DJ	86 973[25]	88 706[25]	90 457[25]	92 227[25]	93 135[26]	94 824[26]	96 511[26]	98 197[26]	99 880[26]	101 562[26]
Qatar	DF	1 043	1 218	1 448	1 639	1 715	1 733	1 833	2 004	2 216	...
Republic of Korea - République de Corée	DJ	48 372	48 598	48 949	49 182	49 410	49 779[1]	50 004[1]	50 220[1]	50 424[1]	50 617[1]
Saudi Arabia - Arabie saoudite[71]	DF	*24 122	*24 941	*25 787	*26 661	*27 563	*28 376	*29 196	*29 602	*30 301	*31 016
Singapore - Singapour[72]	DJ	4 401	4 589	4 839	4 988	5 077	5 184	5 312	5 399	5 470	5 535
Sri Lanka	DF	19 858	20 039	20 246	20 476	20 675	20 869	20 424	20 579	20 771	20 966
State of Palestine - État de Palestine	DF	3 612	3 719	3 826	3 935	4 048	4 169	4 293	4 421	4 550	4 682
Syrian Arab Republic - République arabe syrienne[73]	DF	18 717	19 172	19 644	20 125	20 619	21 124	...	...	...	...
Tajikistan - Tadjikistan	DF	6 992	7 140	7 295	7 334	7 519	7 714	7 897	8 074	8 257	*8 440
Thailand - Thaïlande[1]	DJ	65 306	66 042	66 480	66 903	67 312	67 599	67 912	...	68 610	...

Continent and country or area Continent et pays ou zone	Code[a]	Population estimates (in thousands) - Estimations (en milliers)									
		2006	2007	2008	2009	2010	2011	2012	2013	2014	2015
ASIA - ASIE											
Timor-Leste[1]	DF	1 015	1 048	1 081	1 115	...	...	...	1 180	1 212	...
Turkey - Turquie	DF	72 971	70 138	71 052	72 039	73 142	74 224	75 176	76 148	...	...
	DJ	...	...	...	...	...	...	...	...	76 903[74]	77 738[74]
United Arab Emirates - Émirats arabes unis[75]	DF	5 012[22]	6 219[22]	8 074[22]	8 200[22]	8 264	...	...	...	...	...
Uzbekistan - Ouzbékistan[76]	DJ	26 488	26 868	27 303	27 767	28 562	29 339	29 774	30 243	30 758	...
Viet Nam	DF	83 313[77]	84 221[77]	85 122[77]	86 025	86 933	87 840	88 773	89 709	90 729	91 713
Yemen - Yémen	DF	20 901[22]	21 539[22]	22 198[22]	...	...	...	...	...	...	...
	DJ	...	...	...	22 492[1]	23 154[1]	23 833[1]	24 527[1]	25 235[1]	25 956[1]	...
EUROPE											
Åland Islands - Îles d'Åland[36]	DJ	27	27	27	28	28	28	28	29	29	29
Albania - Albanie	DF	2 993	2 970	2 947	2 928	2 913	2 905	2 900	2 897	2 894	2 889
Andorra - Andorre[36]	DJ	80	82	84	85	85	79[78]	77	76[11]	...	...
Austria - Autriche	DJ	8 268	8 295	8 322	8 341	8 361	8 389	8 426	8 477	8 542	8 576[11]
Belarus - Bélarus	DJ	9 605	9 561	9 528	9 507	9 491	9 473	9 464	9 466	9 475	9 481[11]
Belgium - Belgique	DJ	10 542	10 623	10 710	10 796	10 896	11 044	11 128	11 183	11 231	11 258[11]
Bosnia and Herzegovina - Bosnie-Herzégovine	DF	3 843	3 843	3 842	3 843	3 843	3 841	*3 837	*3 833	*3 831[11]	...
Bulgaria - Bulgarie	DJ	7 699	7 660	7 623	7 585	7 534	7 348	7 306	7 264	7 224	7 202[11]
Croatia - Croatie	DJ	4 311	4 310	4 310	4 305	4 295	4 281	4 268	4 256	4 238	4 225[11]
Czech Republic - République tchèque	DJ	10 239	10 299	10 385	10 444	10 474	10 496	10 511	10 511	10 525	*10 543
Denmark - Danemark[79]	DJ	5 435	5 457	5 489	5 519	5 545	5 567	5 587	5 609	5 640	5 678
Estonia - Estonie	DJ	1 347	1 341	1 337	1 335	1 331	1 327	1 323	1 318	1 315	1 313[11]
Faeroe Islands - Îles Féroé	DJ	48	48	49	49	49	49	48	48	48	49
Finland - Finlande[36]	DJ	5 239[80]	5 262[80]	5 286[80]	5 311[80]	5 335[80]	5 360[80]	5 386[80]	5 410[80]	5 433[80]	5 472[11]
France[81]	DJ	61 597	61 965	62 300	62 615	62 918	63 223	63 537	63 794	*64 130	*64 395
Germany - Allemagne	DJ	82 366	82 263	82 120	81 875	81 757	80 275[3]	80 426[3]	80 646[3]	80 983[3]	81 198[82]
Gibraltar[83]	DF	30	30	30	31	31	32	33	33	...	...
Greece - Grèce	DF	11 020	11 048	11 078	11 107	11 121	11 105	11 045	10 965	10 892	10 858[11]
Guernsey - Guernesey[84]	DF	61	61	62	62	62	63	63	63	63	...
Holy See - Saint-Siège[85]	DF	...	...	...	0[86]	0[87]	...	0[88]	...	...	...
Hungary - Hongrie	DJ	10 071	10 056	10 038	10 023	10 000	9 972	9 920	9 893	9 866[89]	*9 843[89]
Iceland - Islande[90]	DJ	304	311	319	319	318	319[91]	321	324	327	329[11]
Ireland - Irlande	DF	4 260	4 357	4 426	4 459	4 560	4 577	4 587	4 598[89]	4 606[92]	...
	DJ	...	...	...	...	...	...	...	...	...	4 635[93]
Isle of Man - Île de Man[94]	DJ	...	81	82	82	83	...	85	86	86	87
Italy - Italie	DJ	58 144	58 438	58 827	59 095	59 277	59 379	59 540	60 234	60 789	60 796[11]
Jersey	DJ	92	94	95	96	97	98	99	...	101	103
Latvia - Lettonie	DJ	2 218	2 200	2 177	2 142	2 098	2 060	2 034	2 013	1 994	1 986[11]
Liechtenstein	DJ	35	35	35	36	36	36	37	37	37[95]	37[95]
Lithuania - Lituanie	DJ	3 270	3 231	3 198	3 163	3 097	3 028	2 988	2 958	2 932[89]	...
Luxembourg	DJ	473	480	489	498	507	518	531	543	556	563[11]
Malta - Malte[96]	DJ	405	407	409	413	415	416	420	423	427	429[11]
Monaco	DJ	...	...	...	35	36	36	36	37	...	...
Montenegro - Monténégro	DJ	624	626	629	632	617	621	621	622	622[89]	622[89]
Netherlands - Pays-Bas	DJ	16 346	16 382	16 446	16 530	16 615	16 693	16 755	16 804	16 865	16 940
Norway - Norvège[89]	DJ	4 661	4 709	4 768	4 829	4 889	4 953	5 019	5 080	5 137	5 166[11]
Poland - Pologne[89]	DJ	38 132	38 116	38 116	38 153	38 517	38 526	38 534	38 276	38 012	38 006[11]
Portugal	DJ	10 522	10 543	10 558	10 568	10 573	10 558	10 515	10 457	10 401	10 375[11]
Republic of Moldova - République de Moldova[97]	DJ	3 585	3 577	3 570	3 566	3 562	3 560	3 560	3 559	3 557	3 555[11]
Romania - Roumanie	DJ	21 194	20 883	20 538	20 367	20 247	20 148	20 060	19 986	19 913	19 871[11]
Russian Federation - Fédération de Russie	DJ	143 050	142 805	142 742	142 785	142 849	142 961	143 202	*143 507	...	...
San Marino - Saint-Marin[36]	DF	30	31	32	33	33	33	34	33	34	34[11]
Serbia - Serbie[98]	DJ	7 412	7 382	7 350	7 321	7 291	7 237[15]	7 201[15]	7 167[15]	7 132[15]	7 114[99]
Slovakia - Slovaquie	DJ	5 373	5 375	5 379	5 386	5 391	5 398	5 408	5 413	5 419	5 421[11]
Slovenia - Slovénie	DJ	2 009	2 019	2 023	2 042	2 049	2 052	2 056	2 059	2 062	2 063
Spain - Espagne	DJ	44 361	45 236	45 983	46 368	46 562	46 736	46 766	46 593	46 481[90]	46 450[100]
Svalbard and Jan Mayen Islands - Îles Svalbard et Jan Mayen[101]	DF	...	...	2	...	...	...	...	...	...	...

Continent and country or area / Continent et pays ou zone	Code[a]	Population estimates (in thousands) - Estimations (en milliers)									
		2006	2007	2008	2009	2010	2011	2012	2013	2014	2015
EUROPE											
Sweden - Suède[36]	DJ	9 081	9 148	9 220	9 299	9 378	9 449	9 519	9 600[90]	9 696[90]	9 747[100]
Switzerland - Suisse	DJ	7 484	7 551	7 648	7 744	7 825	7 912	7 997	8 089	8 189[95]	8 238[102]
TFYR of Macedonia - L'ex-R. y. de Macédoine	DF	2 040	2 044	2 047	2 051	2 055	2 059	2 061	2 064	2 067	2 069[11]
Ukraine	DF	46 788	46 509	46 258	46 053	45 871	45 706	45 593	45 553[11]	*42 988[103]	*42 760[104]
United Kingdom of Great Britain and Northern Ireland - Royaume-Uni de Grande-Bretagne et d'Irlande du Nord[105]	DJ	60 827	61 319	61 824	62 260	62 759	63 285	63 705	64 102[89]	64 592[89]	64 875[92]
OCEANIA - OCÉANIE											
American Samoa - Samoas américaines[42]	DJ	67	68	69	70	67	64	64	63	62	61
Australia - Australie	DJ	20 451[33]	20 828[33]	21 249[33]	21 692[33]	22 032[33]	22 340[33]	22 728[15]	23 126[15]	23 491[15]	*23 778[15]
Cook Islands - Îles Cook[106]	DF	24	21	22	23	24	19	20	*19	*19	*19
Fiji - Fidji	DF	830	834	841	843	857	...	858[22]	859[107]	...	867[107]
French Polynesia - Polynésie française	DF	256	259	261	263	265	267	268	270	271	272
Guam[42]	DJ	159	159	159	159	...	160	160	160	161	162
Kiribati[107]	DF	...	...	...	...	...	...	...	109	...	...
Marshall Islands - Îles Marshall	DF	52[108]	53[108]	53[108]	54[108]	54[108]	...	...	54[107]	...	...
Micronesia (Federated States of) - Micronésie (États fédérés de)[1]	DJ	108	108	108	108	108	108	107	107	106	106
New Caledonia - Nouvelle-Calédonie	DF	238	240[11]	242	...	250	254	258	260[11]	...	...
New Zealand - Nouvelle-Zélande[109]	DJ	4 185	4 224	4 260	4 303	4 351	4 384	4 408	4 442	4 510	4 596
Niue - Nioué	DJ	2	2	...	2	1	1	...	...	...	...
Norfolk Island - Île Norfolk	DF	2	...	...	...	...	...	...	...	...	...
Northern Mariana Islands - Îles Marianes septentrionales	DF	61	59	55	51	48	46	51[43]	51[43]	51[43]	...
Palau - Palaos	DF	22	20	20	21	21	21	21	...	...	...
Pitcairn[110]	DF	...	0	0	...	...	...	...	...	...	...
Samoa	DF	185	182	182	183	184	185	189	191	...	...
Solomon Islands - Îles Salomon	DF	483[1]	495[1]	507[1]	518[1]	531[1]	542[1]	554[1]	611[107]	...	...
Tokelau - Tokélaou[111]	DF	...	...	...	...	...	...	...	1	...	...
Tonga[112]	DF	103	103	104	...	...	11	...	11	...	...
Tuvalu	DF	11	11	...	...	...	11	...	11	...	...
Vanuatu	DF	221[1]	...	...	...	239	245	245	265	...	...

FOOTNOTES - NOTES

Italics: estimates which are less reliable. - Italiques : estimations moins sûres.

* Provisional. - Données provisoires.

[a] 'Code' indicates source of data, as follows: - Le 'Code' indique la source des données, comme suit :
DF: Population de facto - Population de fait
DJ : Population de jure - Population de droit

[1] Data refer to national projections. - Les données se réfèrent aux projections nationales.

[2] Data refer to projections based on the 2013 Population Census. - Les données se réfèrent aux projections basées sur le recensement de la population de 2013.

[3] Data based on the 2011 Census. - Données fondées sur le recensement de 2011.

[4] Data based on the 2008 Population Census. - Données fondées sur le recensement de population de 2008.

[5] Data refer to 1 January. Data refer to national projections. - Données se raportent au 1 janvier. Les données se réfèrent aux projections nationales.

[6] Data are calculated from the results of the Population and Housing Census of 2009. - Les données sont calculées à partir des résultats du recensement de la population et de l'habitat de 2009.

[7] Data refer to projections based on the 1983 Population Census. - Les données se réfèrent aux projections basées sur le recensement de la population de 1983.

[8] Projections based on the 1994 Population Census. - Projections fondées sur le recensement de la population de 1994.

[9] Estimates considering also 2007 Population Census results. - Estimations en prennant en considération les résultats du recensement de la population de 2007.

[10] Revised data. - Données révisées.

[11] Data refer to 1 January. - Données se raportent au 1 janvier.

[12] Projections considering also 2009 Population Census results. - Projections en prennant en considération les résultats du recensement de la population de 2009.

[13] Excludes the islands of St. Brandon and Agalega. - Non compris les îles St. Brandon et Agalega.

[14] Based on the results of the 2000 Population Census. - Basé sur les résultats du recensement de la population de 2000.

[15] Based on the results of the 2011 Population Census. - Basé sur les résultats du recensement de la population de 2011.

¹⁶ Based on the results of the 2004 Population Census. - D'après des résultats du recensement de la population de 2004.

¹⁷ Data refer to projections based on the 2011 Population Census. - Les données se réfèrent aux projections basées sur le recensement de la population de 2011.

¹⁸ Data are projections based on the 2012 Population and Housing Census. - Projection basée sur le recensement 2012 de la population et des logements.

¹⁹ Based on the results of the 2006 Population Census. - D'après des résultats du recensement de la population de 2006.

²⁰ Data are projections based on the 2008 Population and Housing Census. - Projection basée sur le recensement 2008 de la population et des logements.

²¹ Projections based on the 2012 Population Census. - Projections fondées sur le recensement de la population de 2012.

²² Data refer to 31 December. - Données se raportent au 31 décembre.

²³ Data refer to 31 December. Based on the results of a population count. The population figures are 264, 263 and 262 persons for 2007, 2008 and 2009 respectively. - Données se raportent au 31 décembre. D'après les rêsultats d'un comptage de la population. La population est respectivement égale à 264, 263 et 262 personnes pour les années 2007, 2008 et 2009.

²⁴ Projections based on the 2002 Population Census. - Projections fondées sur le recensement de la population de 2002.

²⁵ Data refer to projections based on the 2000 Population Census. - Les données se réfèrent aux projections basées sur le recensement de la population de 2000.

²⁶ Data refer to projections based on the 2010 Population Census. - Les données se réfèrent aux projections basées sur le recensement de la population de 2010.

²⁷ Final intercensal estimates. - Estimations inter-censitaires definitives.

²⁸ Final postcensal estimates. - Estimations postcensitaires definitives.

²⁹ Updated postcensal estimates. - Estimations post censitaires mises à jour.

³⁰ The source of data is the national household survey. - La source des données est l'enquête nationale des ménages.

³¹ Based on the national household surveys 2010-2014 and the 2011 population census. - D'après les données de l'enquête nationale des ménages 2010-2014 et les résultats du recensement de la population de 2011.

³² Based on the national household survey of 2015. - Basée sur l' enquête nationale auprès des ménages de 2015.

³³ Intercensal estimates. - Estimations inter-censitaires.

³⁴ Postcensal estimates. - Estimations post censitaires.

³⁵ Estimates based on the 2007 Population Census. - Estimations fondées sur le recensement de la population de 2007.

³⁶ Population statistics are compiled from registers. - Les statistiques de la population sont compilées à partir des registres.

³⁷ Data refer to 1 January. Excluding data for Saint Barthélémy and Saint Martin. - Données se raportent au 1 janvier. Non compris les données pour Saint Barthélémy et Saint Martin.

³⁸ Projections produced by l'Institut Haïtien de Statistique et d'Informatique (IHSI) and the Latin American and Caribbean Demographic Centre (CELADE) - Population Division of ECLAC. - Les données sont projections produits par l'Institut Haïtien de Statistique et d'Informatique (IHSI) et le centre démographique de l'Amérique latine et les Caraïbes - Division de la population de la CEPALC.

³⁹ Data refer to projections based on the 2001 Population Census. - Les données se réfèrent aux projections basées sur le recensement de la population de 2001.

⁴⁰ Including armed forces stationed in the area. Based on the results of the 2010 Population Census. - Y compris les militaires en garnison sur le territoire. D'après le résultats du recensement de la population de 2010.

⁴¹ Excluding U.S. Armed Forces overseas and civilian U.S. citizens whose usual place of residence is outside the United States. - Non compris les militaires américains à l'étranger et les civils américains dont le lieu de résidence habituel est en dehors des États-Unis.

⁴² Including armed forces stationed in the area. - Y compris les militaires en garnison sur le territoire.

⁴³ Source: U.S. National Center for Health Statistics, National Vital Statistics Reports (NVSR). - Source : US National Center for Health Statistics, National Vital Statistics Reports (NVSR).

⁴⁴ Data refer to projections based on the 2010 Population and Housing Census. - Les données se réfèrent aux projections basées sur le recensement 2010 de la population et des logements.

⁴⁵ Data include persons in remote areas, military personnel outside the country, merchant seamen at sea, civilian seasonal workers outside the country, and other civilians outside the country, and exclude nomads, foreign military, civilian aliens temporarily in the country, transients on ships and Indian jungle population. Data refer to national projections. - Y compris les personnes vivant dans des régions éloignées, le personel militaire en dehors du pays, les marins marchands, les ouvriers saisonniers en dehors du pays, et autres civils en dehors du pays, et

non compris les nomades, les militaires étrangers, les étrangers civils temporairement dans le pays, les transiteurs sur des bateaux et les Indiens de la jungle. Les données se réfèrent aux projections nationales.

⁴⁶ Data are revised projections taking into consideration also the results of the 2005 census. - Les données sont des projections révisées tenant compte également des résultats du recensement de 2005.

⁴⁷ Excludes nomadic Indian tribes. Data refer to projections based on the 2010 Population Census. - Non compris les tribus d'Indiens nomades. Les données se réfèrent aux projections basées sur le recensement de la population de 2010.

⁴⁸ Data refer to 30 June. - Données se raportent au 30 juin.

⁴⁹ Data refer to the settled population based on the 1979 Population Census and the latest household prelisting. The refugees of Afghanistan in Iran, Pakistan, and an estimated 1.5 million nomads, are not included. - Les données se rapportent à la population stationnaire sur la base du recensement de 1979 et du recensement préliminaire des logements le plus récent. Sont exclus les réfugiés d'Afghanistan en Iran et au Pakistan et les nomades estimés à 1,5 million.

⁵⁰ Data refer to projected figures based on the Population and Housing Census 2005 (district projection). - Les données se réfèrent aux projections basées sur le recensement de la population et de l'habitat de 2005 (projections locales).

⁵¹ Excluding foreign diplomatic personnel and their dependants. - Non compris le personnel diplomatique étranger et les membres de leur famille les accompagnant.

⁵² Based on the results of 1998 census. - A partir des résultats de recensement de l'année 1998.

⁵³ For statistical purposes, the data for China do not include those for the Hong Kong Special Administrative Region (Hong Kong SAR), Macao Special Administrative Region (Macao SAR) and Taiwan province of China. - Pour la présentation des statistiques, les données pour la Chine ne comprennent pas la Région Administrative Spéciale de Hong Kong (Hong Kong RAS), la Région Administrative Spéciale de Macao (Macao RAS) et Taïwan province de Chine.

⁵⁴ Data have been estimated on the basis of the annual National Sample Survey on Population Changes. - Les données ont été estimées sur la base de l'enquête annuelle "National Sample Survey on Population Changes".

⁵⁵ Data have been adjusted on the basis of the Population Census of 2010. - Les données ont été ajustées à partir des résultats du recensement de la population de 2010.

⁵⁶ Data refer to government controlled areas. - Les données se rapportent aux zones contrôlées par le Gouvernement.

⁵⁷ Data refer to annual average population. - Les données correspondent à la population annuelle moyenne.

⁵⁸ Includes data for the Indian-held part of Jammu and Kashmir, the final status of which has not yet been determined. Data refer to projections based on the 2001 Population Census. - Y compris les données pour la partie du Jammu et du Cachemire occupée par l'Inde dont le statut définitif n'a pas encore été déterminé. Les données se réfèrent aux projections basées sur le recensement de la population de 2001.

⁵⁹ Data are based on the publication: "Indonesia Population Projection 2005-2015" - Les données sont basées sur la publication : << Indonesia Population Projection 2005-2015 >>

⁶⁰ Data refer to the Iranian Year which begins on 21 March and ends on 20 March of the following year. - Les données concernent l'année iranienne, qui commence le 21 mars et se termine le 20 mars de l'année suivante.

⁶¹ Includes data for East Jerusalem and Israeli residents in certain other territories under occupation by Israeli military forces since June 1967. - Y compris les données pour Jérusalem-Est et les résidents israéliens dans certains autres territoires occupés depuis 1967 par les forces armées israéliennes.

⁶² Excluding diplomatic personnel outside the country and foreign military and civilian personnel and their dependants stationed in the area. Estimates based on the complete counts of the 2010 Population Census. - Non compris le personnel diplomatique hors du pays ni les militaires et agents civils étrangers en poste sur le territoire et les membres de leur famille les accompagnant. Estimations basées sur le dénombrement complet du recensement de la population de 2010.

⁶³ Data refer to 31 December. Excluding data for Jordanian territory under occupation since June 1967 by Israeli military forces. - Données se raportent au 31 décembre. Non compris les données pour le territoire jordanien occupé depuis juin 1967 par les forces armées israéliennes.

⁶⁴ Data estimated based on the results of 2015 population census. - Estimations fondées sur les résultats du recensement de la population de 2015.

⁶⁵ Intercensal Mid-Year Population Estimates based on the adjusted Population and Housing Census of 2000 and 2010. - Les estimations inter-censitaires au millieu de l'année sont fondée sur les résultats ajustées des recensements de la population et de l'habitat de 2000 et 2010.

⁶⁶ Estimates based on the adjusted Population and Housing Census of 2010. - Les estimations sont fondée sur les résultats ajustés du recensement de la population et de l'habitat de 2010.

⁶⁷ Data refer to 1 October. - Données se raportent au 1 octobre.

[68] Based on the results of the 2014 Population Census. - D'après les résultats du recensement de la population de 2014.

[69] Excluding data for the Pakistan-held part of Jammu and Kashmir, the final status of which has not yet been determined. - Non compris les données concernant la partie du Jammu et Cachemire occupée par le Pakistan dont le statut définitif n'a pas été déterminé.

[70] Based on the results of the Pakistan Demographic Survey (PDS 2007). - D'après les résultats de l'enquête démographique effectuée par le Pakistan en 2007.

[71] Data based on the preliminary results of the 2010 Population and Housing Census. - D'après les résultats préliminaires du recensement de la population et des logements de 2010.

[72] Data refer to 30 June. Data refer to total population, which comprises Singapore residents and non-residents. Data exclude residents who have been away from Singapore for a continuous period of 12 months or longer as at the reference date. - Données se raportent au 30 juin. Les données se rapportent à la population totale composé des résidents de Singapour et les non résidents. Non compris les résidents hors de Singapour pour une période ininterrompue de 12 mois ou plus avant de la date de référence.

[73] Including Palestinian refugees. - Y compris les réfugiés de Palestine.

[74] Data based on address-based population registration system. - Les données sont basées sur le registre national de la population basé sur l'adresse.

[75] Data include non-national population. - Les données comprennent les non-nationaux.

[76] Data refer to resident population. - Les données concernent la population résidente.

[77] Data are adjusted according to the results of the 1999 and 2009 censuses. - Les données ont été ajustées à partir des résultats des recensements de la population de 1999 et 2009.

[78] Decrease in population due to revision in administrative registers. - Diminution de la population due à la révision des registres administratifs.

[79] Excluding Faeroe Islands and Greenland shown separately, if available. Population statistics are compiled from registers. - Non compris les Iles Féroé et le Groenland, qui font l'objet de rubriques distinctes, si disponible. Les statistiques de la population sont compilées à partir des registres.

[80] Excluding Åland Islands. - Non compris les Îles d'Åland.

[81] Excluding diplomatic personnel outside the country and including members of alien armed forces not living in military camps and foreign diplomatic personnel not living in embassies or consulates. - Non compris le personnel diplomatique hors du pays et y compris les militaires étrangers ne vivant pas dans des camps militaires et le personnel diplomatique étranger ne vivant pas dans les ambassades ou les consulats.

[82] Data refer to 1 January. Data based on the 2011 Census. - Données se raportent au 1 janvier. Données fondées sur le recensement de 2011.

[83] Data refer to 31 December. Excluding military personnel, visitors and transients. - Données se raportent au 31 décembre. Non compris les militaires, ni les visiteurs et transients.

[84] Data refer to 31 March. - Données se raportent au 31 mars.

[85] Data refer to the Vatican City State. - Les données se rapportent à l'Etat de la Cité du Vatican.

[86] The population figure is 466 persons. - La population est égale à 466 personnes.

[87] Data refer to 26 February. The population figure is 460 persons. - Données se raportent au 26 février. La population est égale à 460 personnes.

[88] Data refer to 21 June. The population figure is 451 persons. - Données se raportent au 21 juin. La population est égale à 451 personnes.

[89] Data refer to usually resident population. - Les données concernent la population habituellement résidente.

[90] Data refer to registered resident population. - Les données concernent la population enregistrée résidente.

[91] Definition of localities was revised in 2011 causing a break with the previous series. - La rupture par rapport aux séries précédentes s'explique par le fait que la définition des localités a été révisée depuis 2011.

[92] Data refer to 1 January. Data refer to usually resident population. - Données se raportent au 1 janvier. Les données concernent la population habituellement résidente.

[93] Data refer to 15 April. Data refer to usually resident population. - Données se raportent au 15 avril. Les données concernent la population habituellement résidente.

[94] Data refer to 30 April. - Données se raportent au 30 avril.

[95] Data refer to legal resident population. - Les données concernent la population légalement résidente.

[96] Including civilian nationals temporarily outside the country. - Y compris les civils nationaux temporairement hors du pays.

[97] Excluding Transnistria and the municipality of Bender. - Les données ne tiennent pas compte de l'information sur la Transnistria et la municipalité de Bender.

[98] Excludes data for Kosovo and Metohia. - Sans les données pour le Kosovo et Metohie.

[99] Data refer to 1 January. Based on the results of the 2011 Population Census. - Données se raportent au 1 janvier. Basé sur les résultats du recencement de la population de 2011.

[100] Data refer to 1 January. Data refer to registered resident population. - Données se raportent au 1 janvier. Les données concernent la population enregistrée résidente.

[101] Data refer to 1 January. Data refer to Svalbard only. - Données se raportent au 1 janvier. Données ne concernant que le Svalbard.

[102] Data refer to 1 January. Data refer to legal resident population. - Données se raportent au 1 janvier. Les données concernent la population légalement résidente.

[103] The Government of Ukraine has informed the United Nations that it is not in a position to provide statistical data concerning the Autonomous Republic of Crimea and the city of Sevastopol. - Le gouvernement Ukrainien a informé l'ONU qu'il n'est pas en mesure de fournir des données statistiques concernant la République autonome de Crimée et la ville de Sébastopol.

[104] Data refer to 1 January. The Government of Ukraine has informed the United Nations that it is not in a position to provide statistical data concerning the Autonomous Republic of Crimea and the city of Sevastopol. - Données se raportent au 1 janvier. Le gouvernement Ukrainien a informé l'ONU qu'il n'est pas en mesure de fournir des données statistiques concernant la République autonome de Crimée et la ville de Sébastopol.

[105] Excluding Channel Islands (Guernsey and Jersey) and Isle of Man, shown separately, if available. - Non compris les îles Anglo-Normandes (Guernesey et Jersey) et l'île de Man, qui font l'objet de rubriques distinctes, si disponible.

[106] Excluding Niue, shown separately, which is part of Cook Islands, but because of remoteness is administered separately. - Non compris Nioué, qui fait l'objet d'une rubrique distincte et qui fait partie des îles Cook, mais qui, en raison de son éloignement, est administrée séparément.

[107] Projections are prepared by the Secretariat of the Pacific Community based on the last population and housing census. - Les projections sont préparées par le Secrétariat de la Communauté du Pacifique à partir des résultats du dernier recensement de la population et de l'habitat.

[108] Projections are prepared by the Secretariat of the Pacific Community based on 1999 census of population and housing. - Les projections sont préparées par le Secrétariat de la Communauté du Pacifique à partir des résultats du recensement de la population et de l'habitat de 1999.

[109] Because of rounding, totals are not in all cases the sum of the respective components. - Les chiffres étant arrondis, les totaux ne correspondent pas toujours rigoureusement à la somme des composants respectifs.

[110] Data refer to 31 December. The population figures are 64 and 58 persons for 2007 and 2008 respectively. - Données se raportent au 31 décembre. La population est respectivement égale à 64 et 58 personnes pour les années 2007 et 2008.

[111] Data refer to 1 December. - Données se raportent au 1 décembre.

[112] Data refer to national projections. Based on the results of the 1996 population census. - Les données se réfèrent aux projections nationales. À partir des résultats du recensement de la population de 1996.

Table 6 - *Demographic Yearbook 2015*

Table 6 presents total population by sex for as many years as possible between 2006 and 2015, as well as urban population as available.

Description of variables: Data are from nation-wide population censuses or are estimates, some of which are based on sample surveys of population carried out among all segments of the population. This characteristic of the data is indicated in the column "Code". The codes used are explained at the end of the table.

Urban is defined according to the national census definition. The definition for each country is set forth at the end of the technical notes to this table.

Percentage computation: Urban percentages are the number of persons residing in an area defined as "urban" per 100 total population. They are calculated by the Statistics Division of the United Nations Department of Economic and Social Affairs. In very few cases the data for total population have been revised but the data for the urban and rural population have not been. These data are footnoted accordingly. In these cases, particular caution should be used in interpreting the figures for percentage urban.

Reliability of data: Estimates that are believed to be less reliable are set in *italics* rather than in roman type. Classification in terms of reliability is based on the method of construction of the total population estimate discussed in the technical notes for table 3.

Limitations: Statistics on urban population by sex are subject to the same qualifications as have been set forth for population statistics in general, as discussed in section 3 of the Technical Notes.

The basic limitations imposed by variations in the definition of the total population and in the degree of under-enumeration are perhaps more important in relation to urban/rural than to any other distributions. The classification by urban and rural is affected by variations in defining usual residence for purposes of sub-national tabulations. Likewise, the geographical differentials in the degree of under-enumeration in censuses affect the comparability of these categories throughout the table. The distinction between *de facto* and *de jure* population is also very important with respect to urban/rural distributions. The difference between the *de facto* and the *de jure* population is discussed at length in section 3.1.1 of the Technical Notes.

A most important and specific limitation, however, lies in the national differences in the definition of urban. Because the distinction between urban and rural areas is made in so many different ways, the definitions have been included at the end of this table. The definitions are necessarily brief and, where the classification of urban involves administrative civil divisions, they are often given in the terminology of the particular country or area. As a result of variations in terminology, it may appear that differences between countries or areas are greater than they actually are. On the other hand, similar or identical terms (for example, town, village, district) as used in different countries or areas may have quite different meanings.

It will be seen from an examination of the definitions that they fall roughly into three major types: (1) classification of localities as urban based on size; (2) classification of administrative centres of minor civil divisions as urban and the remainder of the division as rural; and (3) classification of minor civil divisions on a set of criteria, which may include type of local government, number of inhabitants or proportion of population engaged in agriculture.

The designation of areas as urban or rural is so closely bound to historical, political, cultural, and administrative considerations that the process of developing uniform definitions and procedures moves very slowly. Not only do the definitions differ from one country or area to the other, but, they may also no longer reflect the original intention for distinguishing urban from rural. The criteria once established on the basis of administrative subdivisions (as most of these are) become fixed and resistant to change. For this reason, comparisons of time-series data may be severely affected because the definitions used become outdated. Special care must be taken in comparing data from censuses with those from sample surveys because the definitions of urban used may differ.

Despite their shortcomings, however, statistics on urban and rural population are useful in describing the diversity of population distribution within a country or area.

The definition of urban/rural areas is based on both qualitative and quantitative criteria that may include any combination of the following: size of population, population density, distance between built-up areas, predominant type of economic activity, conformity to legal or administrative status and urban characteristics such as specific services and facilities[1].   Although statistics classified by urban/rural areas are widely available, no international standard definition appears to be possible at this time since the meaning differs from one country or area to another. The urban/rural classification of population used here is reported according to the national definition.

Earlier data: Urban and total population by sex have been shown in previous issues of the Demographic Yearbook. For information on specific years covered, readers should consult the Historical Index.

DEFINITION OF "URBAN"

AFRICA

Algeria: The urban/rural delimitation is performed after the census operation based on the classification of built-up areas. Groupings of 100 or more constructions, distant less than 200 metres from one another are considered urban.
Botswana: Agglomeration of 5 000 or more inhabitants where 75 per cent of the economic activity is non-agricultural.
Burundi: Commune of Bujumbura.
Burkina Faso: All administrative centres of provinces (total of 45) plus 4 medium-sized towns are considered as urban areas.
Comoros: Every locality or administrative centre of an island, region or prefecture that has the following facilities: asphalted roads, electricity, a medical centre, telephone services, etc.
Egypt: Governorates of Cairo, Alexandria, Port Said, Ismailia, Suez, frontier governorates and capitals of other governorates, as well as district capitals (Markaz). The definition of urban areas for the 2006 Census is "shiakha", a part of a district.
Equatorial Guinea: District centres and localities with 300 dwellings and/or 1 500 inhabitants or more.
Ethiopia: Localities of 2 000 or more inhabitants.
Kenya: Areas having a population of 2 000 or more inhabitants that have transport systems, build-up areas, industrial/manufacturing structures and other developed structures.
Lesotho: All administrative headquarters and settlements of rapid growth.
Liberia: Localities of 2 000 or more inhabitants.
Malawi: All townships and town planning areas and all district centres.
Mauritius: The five Municipal Council Areas which are subdivided into twenty Municipal Wards defined according to proclaimed boundaries.
Namibia: Proclaimed urban areas for which cadastral data is available and other unplanned squatter areas.
Niger: Capital city, capitals of the departments and districts.
Rwanda: All administrative areas recognized as urban by the law. These are all administrative centres of provinces, and the cities of Kigali, Nyanza, Ruhango and Rwamagana.
Senegal: Agglomerations of 10 000 or more inhabitants.
South Africa: Places with some form of local authority.
Sudan: Localities of administrative and/or commercial importance or with population of 5 000 or more inhabitants.
Swaziland: A geographical area constituting of a city or town, characterized by higher population density and vast human features in comparison to areas surrounding it.
Tunisia: Population living in communes.
Uganda: Gazettes, cities, municipalities and towns.
United Republic of Tanzania: 16 gazetted townships.
Zambia: Localities of 5 000 or more inhabitants, the majority of whom all depend on non-agricultural activities.

AMERICA, NORTH

Canada: Places of 1 000 or more inhabitants, having a population density of 400 or more per square kilometre.
Costa Rica: Administrative centres of cantons.
Cuba: Towns that fulfil a political or administrative function, or that have a population of 2 000 or more and definite urban characteristics.
Dominican Republic: Administrative centres of municipalities and municipal districts, some of which include suburban zones of rural character.
El Salvador: Administrative centres of municipalities.
Greenland: Localities of 200 or more inhabitants.
Guatemala: Municipality of Guatemala Department and officially recognized centres of other departments and municipalities.
Haiti: Administrative centres of communes.
Honduras: Localities of 2 000 or more inhabitants, having essentially urban characteristics.
Jamaica: Localities of 2 000 or more inhabitants, having urban characteristics.
Mexico: Localities of 2 500 or more inhabitants.

Nicaragua: Administrative centres of municipalities and localities of 1 000 or more inhabitants or with more than 150 dwellings, with streets, electric light, water service, school and health centre.

Panama: Localities of 1 500 or more inhabitants having essentially urban characteristics. Beginning 1970, localities of 1 500 or more inhabitants with such urban characteristics as streets, water supply systems, sewerage systems and electric light.

Puerto Rico: Agglomerations of 2 500 or more inhabitants, generally having population densities of 1 000 persons per square mile or more. Two types of urban areas: urbanized areas of 50 000 or more inhabitants and urban clusters of at least 2 500 and less than 50 000 inhabitants.

United States of America: Agglomerations of 2 500 or more inhabitants, generally having population densities of 1 000 persons per square mile or more. Two types of urban areas: urbanized areas of 50 000 or more inhabitants and urban clusters of at least 2 500 and less than 50 000 inhabitants.

United States Virgin Islands: Agglomerations of 2 500 or more inhabitants, generally having population densities of 1 000 persons per square mile or more. Two types of urban areas: urbanized areas of 50 000 or more inhabitants and urban clusters of at least 2 500 and less than 50 000 inhabitants. (As of the 2000 Census, no urbanized areas are identified in the United States Virgin Islands.)

AMERICA, SOUTH

Argentina: Populated centres with 2 000 or more inhabitants.

Bolivia: Localities of 2 000 or more inhabitants.

Brazil: Area inside the urban perimeter of a city or town, defined by municipal law.

Chile: Areas of concentrated housing units with more than 2 000 inhabitants, or between 1 001 and 2 000 inhabitants having 50 per cent or more of its economically active population doing secondary or tertiary activities. As an exception, centres of tourism and recreation with more than 250 housing units that do not satisfy the population requirement are nevertheless considered urban.

Colombia: Areas with a city hall, defined by an urban perimeter established by municipal agreements.

Ecuador: Capitals of provinces and cantons.

Falkland Islands (Malvinas): Town of Stanley.

Paraguay: Cities, towns and administrative centres of departments and districts.

Peru: Populated centres with 100 or more dwellings.

Suriname: The districts of Paramaribo and Wanica.

Uruguay: Cities, villages, towns and other populated areas as defined by the Law of Population Centers.

Venezuela (Bolivarian Republic of): Centres with a population of 2 500 or more inhabitants.

ASIA

Armenia: Cities and urban-type localities, officially designated as such, usually according to the criteria of number of inhabitants and predominance of agricultural, or number of non-agricultural workers and their families.

Azerbaijan: An administrative division which covers more than 15 000 population, engaging mainly in industrial and other economic and social activities and which include administrative and cultural centers.

Bahrain: Communes or villages of 2 500 or more inhabitants.

Cambodia: Areas at the commune level satisfying the following three conditions: (1) Population Density exceeding 200 per square Km, (2) Percentage of male employed in agriculture below 50 per cent, (3) Total population of the commune exceeds 2 000 inhabitants.

China: According to the Regulation on the Classification of Urban/Rural Residence for Statistical Purposes.

Cyprus: As determined by the Department of Town Planning and Housing of the Ministry of Interior.

Georgia: Cities and urban-type localities, officially designated as such, usually according to the criteria of number of inhabitants and predominance of agricultural, or number of non-agricultural workers and their families.

India: Towns (places with municipal corporation, municipal area committee, town committee, notified area committee or cantonment board); also, all places having 5 000 or more inhabitants, a density of not less than 1 000 persons per square mile or 400 per square kilometre, pronounced urban characteristics and at least three fourths of the adult male population employed in pursuits other than agriculture.

Indonesia: Area which satisfies certain criteria in terms of population density, percentage of agricultural households, access to urban facilities, existence of additional facilities, and percentage of built up area not for housing.

Iran (Islamic Republic of): Every district with a municipality.

Israel: Localities with 2 000 or more residents.

Japan: City (shi) having 50 000 or more inhabitants with 60 per cent or more of the houses located in the main built-up areas and 60 per cent or more of the population (including their dependants) engaged in manufacturing, trade or other urban type of business.

Jordan: Localities of 5 000 or more inhabitants.

Kazakhstan: Cities of Republican status (population centres of special national importance or with a population of usually more than one million), Oblast status (population centres that are major economic and cultural centres with developed industrial and social infrastructure and a population of more than 50,000, the country has 40 Oblast status cities), Raion status and settlements located under their administrative jurisdiction.

Kuwait: All localities in Kuwait are urban.

Kyrgyzstan: Cities and urban-type localities, officially designated as such, usually according to the criteria of number of inhabitants and predominance of agricultural, or number of non-agricultural workers and their families.

Lao People's Democratic Republic: Areas or villages that satisfy at least three of the following five conditions: located in metropolitan areas of district or province, there is access to road in dry and rainy seasons, about 70 per cent or 2/3 of the population has access to piped water, about 70 per cent or 2/3 of the population has access to public electricity, there is a market operating every day.

Malaysia: Gazetted areas with their adjoining built-up areas which have a combined population of 10 000 or more. Built-up areas are defined as areas contiguous to a gazetted area and have at least 60 per cent of their population (aged 15 years and over) engaged in non-agricultural activities. The definition of urban areas also takes into account the special development area which is not gazetted and can be indentified and separated from the gazetted area or built-up area of more than 5km and a population of at least 10 000 with 60 per cent of the population (aged 15 years and over) engaged in non-agricultural activities.

Maldives: Malé, the capital.

Mongolia: Capital and district centres.

Nepal: As declared by the government municipalities.

Pakistan: Places with municipal corporation, town committee or cantonment.

Philippines: Cities and municipalities and their central districts with a population density of at least 500 persons per square km. Urban areas are considered other districts regardless of population size that have streets, at least six establishments (commercial, manufacturing, recreational and/or personal services), and at least three public structures such as town hall, church, public park, school, hospital, library, etc.

Republic of Korea: For estimates: Places with 50 000 or more inhabitants. For census: the figures are composed in the basis of the minor administrative divisions such as Dongs (mostly urban areas) and Eups or Myeons (rural areas).

Sri Lanka: All areas administered by municipal and urban councils.

State of Palestine: Any locality where the population amounts to 10 000 persons or more. This applies to all governorates/districts regardless of their size, and to all localities whose populations vary from 4 000 to 9 999 persons provided they have at least four of the following elements: public electricity network, public water network, post office, health center with a full time physician and a school offering a general secondary education certificate.

Syrian Arab Republic: Cities, Mohafaza centres and Mantika centres, and communities with 20 000 or more inhabitants.

Tajikistan: Cities and urban-type localities, officially designated as such, usually according to the criteria of number of inhabitants and predominance of agricultural, or number of non-agricultural workers and their families.

Thailand: Municipal areas.

Turkey: Localities with 20 000 inhabitants or more.

Turkmenistan: Cities and urban-type localities, officially designated as such, usually according to the criteria of number of inhabitants and predominance of agricultural, or number of non-agricultural workers and their families.

Uzbekistan: Cities and urban-type localities, officially designated as such, usually according to the criteria of number of inhabitants and predominance of agricultural, or number of non-agricultural workers and their families.

Viet Nam: Urban areas include inside urban districts of cities, urban quarters and towns. All other local administrative units (communes) belong to rural areas.

EUROPE

Albania: Towns and other industrial centres of more than 400 inhabitants.

Austria: Urban areas are localities with 2 000 or more inhabitants. The delineation of localities goes back to 1991.

Belarus: Urban settlements are settlements authorized under the law as towns, urban-type settlements, workers settlements and health resort areas.

Belgium: All the communes which are not part of the list of rural communes are considered as urban communes. There are 33 communes which are considered rural : Alveringem, Amblève, Bertogne, Bièvre, Bullange, Burg-Reuland, Clavier, Erezée, Fauvillers, Frasnes-lez-Anvaing, Froidchapelle, Gedinne, Gouvy, Havelange, Herstappe, Heuvelland, Houffalize, Houyet, Langemark-Poelkapelle, Léglise, Lierneux, Lo-Reninge, Manhay, Momignies, Ravels, Sainte-Ode, Sint-Laureins, Sivry-Rance, Stoumont, Tenneville, Vaux-sur-Sûre, Vleteren and Vresse-sur-Semois.

Bulgaria: All towns and cities according to the Territorial and Administrative-Territorial Division of the country.

Czech Republic: Localities with 2 000 or more inhabitants.

Estonia: Urban settlements include cities, cities without municipal status and towns.

Finland: Urban communes including those municipalities in which at least 90 per cent of the population lives in urban settlements or in which the population of the largest urban settlement is at least 15 000.

France: Communes containing an agglomeration of more than 2 000 inhabitants living in contiguous houses or with not more than 200 metres between houses, also communes of which the major portion of the population is part of a multi-communal agglomeration of this nature.

Greece: Urban is considered every municipal or communal department of which the largest locality has 2 000 inhabitants and over.

Hungary: Localities recognized by the President of the Republic with the title of town, on the basis of specific (economic, commercial, institutional, cultural etc.) criteria.

Iceland: Localities of 200 or more inhabitants.

Ireland: Cities and towns including suburbs of 1 500 or more inhabitants.

Latvia: Cities and urban-type localities, officially designated as such, usually according to the criteria of number of inhabitants and predominance of agricultural, or number of non-agricultural workers and their families.

Liechtenstein: Communes with 10 000 inhabitants or more.

Lithuania: Urban population refers to persons who live in cities and towns, i.e., the population areas with closely built permanent dwellings and with the resident population of more than 3 000 of which 2/3 of employees work in industry, social infrastructure and business. In a number of towns the population may be less than 3 000 since these areas had already the status of "town" before the law was enforced (July 1994)

Malta: Grid cells of 1 square km with a density of at least 300 inhabitants per square km and a minimum population of 5 000; and densely populated areas (i.e. areas with a density superior to 500 inhabitants per square km).

Montenegro: According to the current law of territorial division of Montenegro. This means that each local community has the obligation to decide which settlements are urban and which are rural.

Netherlands: Urban: Municipalities with a population of 2 000 and more inhabitants. Semi-urban: Municipalities with a population of less than 2 000 but with not more than 20 per cent of their economically active male population engaged in agriculture, and specific residential municipalities of commuters.

Norway: A hub of buildings inhabited by at least 200 people and where the distance between the buildings does not exceed 50 metres. The boundaries are dynamic and may be changed due to developments and population changes.

Poland: All areas which have town rights or the status of a town with provisions of separate laws.

Portugal: Localities with 2 000 or more inhabitants.

Republic of Moldova: Cities and urban-type localities, officially designated as such, usually according to the criteria of number of inhabitants and predominance of agricultural, or number of non-agricultural workers and their families.

Romania: Localities in which the majority of the work resources are employed in non-agricultural activities with a diversified level of endowment, having a constant and significant socio-economic influence on the whole area.

Russian Federation: Cities and urban-type localities, officially designated as such, usually according to the criteria of number of inhabitants and predominance of agricultural, or number of non-agricultural workers and their families.

Serbia: Municipalities, cities and the city of Belgrade.

Slovakia: Municipalities with the status of towns, according to the following criteria: 1) it is an economic, administrative, cultural or tourism centre, 2) provides services for other municipalities, 3) has urban character (at least partly) and 4) has 5 000 inhabitants or more.

Slovenia: Settlements of 3 000 or more inhabitants, settlements that serve as seats of municipalities with at least 1 400 inhabitants, and sub-urban areas that are being gradually integrated with an urban settlement of 5 000 or more inhabitants.

Spain: For the purposes of publishing comparable results at the European level, Eurostat proposes to consider as urban, intermediate and rural, areas formed by municipalities with respectively a population over 10 000 inhabitants, 2 001 to 10 000 inhabitants, and 2 000 or less inhabitants.

Switzerland: Agglomerations and isolated towns (towns not attached to a cluster and with at least 10,000 inhabitants) are the urban space.

Ukraine: Cities and urban-type localities officially designated as such, usually according to the criteria of number of inhabitants and predominance of agricultural, or number of non-agricultural workers and their families.

United Kingdom of Great Britain and Northern Ireland: For England and Wales, the built-up areas of 10 000 or more inhabitants; for Scotland, the settlements of 3 000 or more inhabitants; and for Northern Ireland, the settlements of 5 000 or more inhabitants.

OCEANIA

Australia: Urban are considered all Significant Urban Areas, as defined by the 2011 Australian Statistical Geography Standard. Significant Urban Areas represent concentrations of urban development with population of 10,000 people or more.

American Samoa: Agglomerations of 2 500 or more inhabitants, generally having population densities of 1 000 persons per square mile or more. Two types of urban areas: urbanized areas of 50 000 or more inhabitants and urban clusters of at least 2 500 and less than 50 000 inhabitants. (As of Census 2000, no urbanized areas are identified in American Samoa.)

Cook Islands: Raratonga, the most populous island.

Guam: Agglomerations of 2 500 or more inhabitants, generally having population densities of 1 000 persons per square mile or more, referred to as "urban clusters".

New Caledonia: Nouméa and communes of Païta, Nouvel Dumbéa and Mont-Dore.

New Zealand: All cities, plus boroughs, town districts, townships and country towns with a population of 1 000 or more usual residents.

Northern Mariana Islands: Agglomerations of 2 500 or more inhabitants, generally having population densities of 1 000 persons per square mile or more. Two types of urban areas: urbanized areas of 50 000 or more inhabitants and urban clusters of at least 2 500 and less than 50 000 inhabitants.

Palau: States with 2 500 inhabitants or more (the only state which satisfies this condition is Koror state).

Tokelau: All of Tokelau's population is considered to be rural.

Tonga: Nuku'alofa.

Vanuatu: Luganville centre and Vila urban.

NOTES

[1]   For further information, see *Social and Demographic Statistics: Classifications of Size and Type of Locality and Urban/Rural Areas.* E/CN.3/551, United Nations, New York, 1980.

Tableau 6 – *Annuaire démographique 2015*

Le tableau 6 présente des données sur la population totale selon le sexe pour le plus grand nombre possible d'années entre 2006 et 2015, ainsi que la population urbaine si disponible.

Description des variables : les données proviennent de recensements de la population ou sont des estimations fondées, dans certains cas, sur des enquêtes par sondage portant sur toute la population. Le code qui figure dans la colonne « Code » du tableau indique comment les données ont été obtenues. Les codes utilisés sont expliqués à la fin du tableau.

Le sens donné au terme « urbain » est conforme aux définitions utilisées dans les recensements nationaux. La définition pour chaque pays figure à la fin des présentes notes technique.

Calcul des pourcentages : les pourcentages de la population urbaine sont calculés par la Division de statistique du Département des affaires économiques et sociales de l'Organisation des Nations Unies et représentent le nombre de personnes qui vivent dans des régions considérées comme urbaines pour 100 personnes de la population totale. Dans de très rares cas, les données pour la population totale ont été révisées mais les données pour la population urbaine et la population rurale ne l'ont pas été. Ces données sont indiquées en note. Dans ces cas, les proportions de population urbaine ou rurale sont à interpréter avec précaution.

Fiabilité des données : les estimations considérées comme moins sûres sont indiquées en italique plutôt qu'en caractères romains. Le classement du point de vue de la fiabilité est fondé sur la méthode utilisée pour établir l'estimation de la population totale qui figure au tableau 3 (voir les explications dans les notes techniques relatives à ce même tableau).

Insuffisance des données : les statistiques de la population urbaine selon le sexe appellent toutes les réserves qui ont été formulées à la section 3 des Notes techniques à propos des statistiques de la population en général.

Les limitations fondamentales imposées par les variations de la définition de la population totale et par les lacunes du recensement se font peut-être sentir davantage dans la répartition de la population en population urbaine et population rurale que dans sa répartition suivant toute autre caractéristique. De fait, des différences dans la définition du lieu de résidence habituel utilisée pour l'exploitation des données à l'échelon sous-national influent sur la classification en population urbaine et en population rurale. De même, les différences de degré de sous-dénombrement suivant la zone, à l'occasion des recensements, ont une incidence sur la comparabilité de ces deux catégories dans l'ensemble du tableau. La distinction entre population de fait et population de droit est également très importante du point de vue de la répartition de la population en population urbaine et en population rurale. Cette distinction est expliquée en détail à la section 3.1.1 des Notes techniques.

Toutefois, la difficulté la plus importante tient aux différences de définition du terme « urbain » selon le pays. Les distinctions faites entre « zone urbaine » et « zone rurale » varient tellement que les définitions utilisées ont été reproduites à la fin des notes techniques du tableau 6. Les définitions sont forcément brèves et, lorsque le classement en « zone urbaine » repose sur des divisions administratives, on a souvent désigné celles-ci par le nom qu'elles portent dans la zone ou le pays considéré. Par suite des variations dans la terminologie, les différences entre pays ou zones peuvent sembler plus grandes qu'elles ne le sont réellement. Il se peut aussi que des termes similaires ou identiques, tels que ville, village ou district, aient des significations très différentes selon les pays ou zones.

On constatera, en examinant les définitions adoptées par les différents pays ou zones, qu'elles peuvent être ramenées à trois types principaux : 1) les localités dépassant certaines dimensions sont classées parmi les zones urbaines ; 2) les centres administratifs de petites circonscriptions administratives sont classées parmi les zones urbaines, le reste de la circonscription étant considéré comme zone rurale ; 3) les petites divisions administratives sont classées parmi les zones urbaines selon un critère déterminé, qui peut être soit le type d'administration locale, soit le nombre d'habitants, soit le pourcentage de la population exerçant une activité agricole.

La distinction entre régions urbaines et régions rurales est si étroitement liée à des considérations d'ordre historique, politique, culturel et administratif que l'on ne peut progresser que très lentement vers des définitions et des méthodes uniformes. Non seulement les définitions sont différentes d'une zone ou d'un pays à un autre, mais on n'y retrouve parfois même plus l'intention originale de distinguer les régions rurales des régions urbaines. Lorsque la classification est fondée, en particulier, sur le critère des circonscriptions administratives (comme la plupart le sont), elle a tendance à devenir rigide avec le temps et à décourager toute modification. Pour cette raison, la comparaison des données appartenant à des séries chronologiques risque d'être gravement faussée du fait que les définitions employées sont désormais périmées. Il faut être particulièrement prudent lorsque l'on compare des données issues de recensements avec des données provenant d'enquêtes par sondage, car il se peut que les définitions du terme « urbain » auxquelles ces données se réfèrent respectivement soient différentes.

Malgré leurs insuffisances, les statistiques sur la population urbaine et rurale permettent de mettre en évidence la diversité de la répartition de la population au sein d'un pays ou d'une zone.

La distinction entre « zone urbaine » et « zone rurale » repose sur une série de critères qualitatifs aussi bien que quantitatifs, notamment l'effectif de la population, la densité de peuplement, la distance entre îlots d'habitations, le type prédominant d'activité économique, le statut juridique ou administratif, et les caractéristiques d'une agglomération urbaine, c'est-à-dire l'existence de services publics et d'équipements collectifs[1]. Bien que les statistiques différenciant les zones urbaines des zones rurales soient très répandues, il ne paraît pas possible pour le moment d'adopter une classification internationale type de ces zones, vu la diversité des interprétations nationales. La classification de la population en population urbaine et population rurale retenue ici est celle qui correspond aux définitions nationales.

Données publiées antérieurement : des statistiques concernant la population urbaine et la population totale selon le sexe ont été publiées dans des éditions antérieures de l'*Annuaire démographique*. Pour plus de précisions concernant les années pour lesquelles ces données ont été publiées, se reporter à l'index historique.

DÉFINITIONS DU TERME « URBAIN »

AFRIQUE

Algérie : La délimitation des zones urbaines et rurales se font après l'opération du recensement sur la base de la classification des agglomérations. Regroupement de 100 constructions ou plus distantes l'une à l'autre de moins de 200m ont été considérées comme zones urbaines.
Afrique du Sud : Zones dotées d'une administration locale.
Botswana : Agglomération de 5 000 habitants ou plus dont 75 p. 100 de l'activité économique n'est pas de type agricole.
Burkina Faso : Tous les chefs-lieux de province (45 au total) plus 4 villes moyennes ont été considérées comme zones urbaines.
Burundi : Commune de Bujumbura.
Comores : Toute localité ou chef-lieu d'une île, région/préfecture disposant des infrastructures suivantes : route bitumée, électricité, centre hospitalier, téléphone, etc.
Égypte : Chefs-lieux des gouvernorats du Caire, d'Alexandrie, de Port Saïd, d'Ismaïlia, de Suez ; chefs-lieux des gouvernorats frontaliers, autres chefs-lieux de gouvernorat et chefs-lieux de district (Markaz). La définition des zones urbaines pour le recensement de 2006 est celle de « shiakha », une partie d'un district.
Éthiopie : Localités de 2 000 habitants ou plus.
Guinée équatoriale : Chefs-lieux de district et localités comprenant 300 habitations et/ou 1 500 habitants ou plus.
Kenya : Zone ayant une population de 2 000 habitants ou plus qui dispose de réseaux de transport, comporte des zones bâties, des structures industrielles ou manufacturières et d'autres équipements modernes.
Lesotho : Tous les chefs-lieux administratifs et établissements urbains en forte croissance.
Libéria : Localités de 2 000 habitants ou plus.
Malawi : Toutes les villes et zones urbanisées et tous les chefs-lieux de district.
Maurice : Les cinq circonscriptions municipales, divisées en vingt arrondissements municipaux dont les limites ont été officiellement définies.
Namibie : Zones urbaines déclarées pour lesquelles il existe des données cadastrales et autres zones d'habitat non planifié.
Niger : Ville capital, villes capitales de départements ou de districts.
Ouganda : «Gazettes», villes, municipalités et bourgs.
République-Unie de Tanzanie : 16 townships érigées en communes.

Rwanda : Toutes les zones administratives reconnues comme urbaines par la loi. Il s'agit de tous les chefs - lieux des provinces, de la ville de Kigali ainsi que des villes de Nyanza, Ruhango et Rwamagana.

Sénégal : Agglomérations de 10 000 habitants ou plus.

Soudan : Centres administratifs et/ou commerciaux ou localités ayant une population de 5 000 habitants ou plus.

Swaziland : Zone géographique qui constitue une ville et se caractérise par une densité de population et de constructions humaines plus élevée que dans les zones qui l'entourent.

Tunisie : Population vivant dans les communes.

Zambie : Localités de 5 000 habitants ou plus dont l'activité économique prédominante n'est pas de type agricole.

AMÉRIQUE DU NORD

Canada : Agglomérations de 1 000 habitants ou plus ayant une densité de population d'au moins 400 habitants au kilomètre carré.

Costa Rica : Chefs-lieux de canton.

Cuba : Villes ayant une fonction politique ou administrative, ou une population supérieure à 2 000 habitants et présentant des traits urbains.

El Salvador : Chefs-lieux de municipios.

États-Unis d'Amérique : Agglomérations de 2 500 habitants ou plus ayant généralement une densité de population d'au moins 1 000 habitants au mile carré. Deux types de zones urbaines : zones urbanisées de 50 000 habitants ou plus et groupements urbains comptant au moins 2 500 habitants mais moins de 50 000.

Groenland : Localités d'au moins 200 habitants.

Guatemala : Municipio du département de Guatemala et centres administratifs officiels d'autres départements et municipios.

Haïti : Chefs-lieux de communes.

Honduras : Localités d'au moins 2 000 habitants ayant des caractéristiques essentiellement urbaines.

Îles Vierges américaines : Agglomérations de 2 500 habitants ou plus ayant généralement une densité de population d'au moins 1 000 habitants au mile carré. Deux types de zones urbaines : zones urbanisées de 50 000 habitants ou plus et groupements urbains comptant au moins 2 500 habitants mais moins de 50 000. (D'après les résultats du recensement de 2 000, les Îles Vierges américaines ne comptent aucune zone urbanisée.)

Jamaïque : Localités de 2 000 habitants ou plus présentant des traits urbains.

Mexique : Localités d'au moins 2 500 habitants.

Nicaragua : Centres administratifs des municipalités et localités d'au moins 1 000 habitants ou d'au moins 150 logements, possédant des rues, un éclairage électrique, un réseau de distribution d'eau, une école et un dispensaire.

Panama : Localités d'au moins 1 500 habitants ayant des caractéristiques essentiellement urbaines. À partir de 1970, localités de 1 500 habitants ou plus présentant des caractéristiques urbaines, telles que rues, éclairage électrique, systèmes d'approvisionnement en eau et réseaux d'égouts.

Porto Rico : Agglomérations de 2 500 habitants ou plus ayant généralement une densité de population d'au moins 1 000 habitants au mile carré. Deux types de zones urbaines : zones urbanisées de 50 000 habitants ou plus et groupements urbains comptant au moins 2 500 habitants mais moins de 50 000.

République dominicaine : Chefs-lieux de municipios et districts municipaux, dont certains comprennent des zones suburbaines ayant des caractéristiques rurales.

AMÉRIQUE DU SUD

Argentine : Centres comptant au moins 2 000 habitants.

Bolivie : Localités de 2 000 habitants ou plus.

Brésil : Zone à l'intérieur du périmètre urbain d'une ville, définie par la législation municipale.

Chili : Zones d'habitat concentré comptant 2 000 habitants ou plus, ou comptant entre 1 001 et 2 000 habitants dont 50 pour cent au moins de la population active a une activité secondaire ou tertiaire. Par dérogation, les centres qui ont une fonction touristique ou récréative et plus de 250 unités de logement mais n'atteignent pas le critère de population sont néanmoins considérés comme zones urbaines.

Colombie : Zone avec une mairie, définie par un périmètre urbain qui est établie par des accords municipaux.

Équateur : Capitales des provinces et chefs-lieux de canton.

Îles Falkland (Malvinas) : Ville de Stanley.

Paraguay : Grandes villes, villes et chefs-lieux des départements et des districts.

Pérou : Centres de peuplement comptant plus de 100 logements.

Suriname : Les districts de Paramaribo et de Wanica.

Uruguay : Les villes, villages et autres zones habitées répondant aux définitions de la loi sur les agglomérations.

Venezuela (République bolivarienne du) : Centres de 2 500 habitants ou plus.

ASIE

Arménie : Grandes villes et localités de type urbain, officiellement désignées comme telles, généralement sur la base du nombre d'habitants et de la prédominance des travailleurs agricoles ou non agricoles avec leur famille.

Azerbaïdjan : Division administrative regroupant plus de 15 000 habitants se livrant principalement à des activités industrielles et autres activités économiques et sociales et comprennant des centres administratifs et culturels.

Bahreïn : Communes ou villages comptant au moins 2 500 habitants.

Cambodge : Zones au niveau de la commune répondant aux trois conditions suivantes: 1) Densité démographique supérieure à 200 habitants au km carré, 2) pourcentage d'hommes travaillant dans l'agriculture inférieur à 50 pour cent, 3) population totale de la commune supérieure à 2 000 habitants.

Chine : Suivant la Réglementation sur la classification de la résidence urbaine/rurale à des fins de statistiques.

Chypre : Selon la définition du Département de l'urbanisme et du logement du Ministère de l'intérieur.

État de Palestine : Localités peuplées de plus de 10 000 personnes. L'expression désigne tous les gouvernorats (districts), quelle qu'en soit la taille, ainsi que toutes les villes dont la population est comprise entre 4 000 et 9 999 personnes qui disposent d'au moins quatre des éléments suivants : réseau public de distribution d'électricité, réseau public de distribution d'eau, bureau de poste, centre médical doté d'un médecin à temps plein et école préparant les élèves au certificat général de l'enseignement secondaire.

Géorgie : Grandes villes et localités de type urbain, officiellement désignées comme telles, généralement sur la base du nombre d'habitants et de la prédominance des travailleurs agricoles ou non agricoles avec leur famille.

Inde : Villes [localités dotées d'une charte municipale, d'un comité de zone municipale, d'un comité de zone déclarée urbaine ou d'un comité de zone de regroupement (cantonnement)] ; également toutes les localités qui ont une population de 5 000 habitants au moins, une densité de population d'au moins 1 000 habitants au mile carré ou 400 au kilomètre carré, des caractéristiques urbaines prononcées et où les trois quarts au moins des adultes de sexe masculin ont une occupation non agricole.

Indonésie : Les zones urbaines sont celles qui répondent à certains critères : densité de population, pourcentage de ménages agricoles, accès aux équipements urbains, existence d'équipements supplémentaires, et pourcentage de superficie bâtie à usage autre que l'habitation.

Iran (République islamique d') : Tous les districts comptant une municipalité.

Israël : Tous les lieux comptant au moins 2 000 résidents.

Japon : Villes (shi), comptant au moins 50 000 habitants, où 60 p. 100 au moins des logements sont situés dans les principales zones bâties, et dont 60 p. 100 au moins de population (y compris les personnes à charge) exercent un métier dans l'industrie, le commerce et d'autres branches d'activités essentiellement urbaines.

Jordanie : Localités comptant 5 000 habitants ou plus.

Kazakhstan : Villes ayant statut républicain (centres de population présentant une importance nationale spéciale ou comptant une population généralement de plus d'un million d'habitants), statut régional (Oblast') (centres de population qui sont de grands centres économiques et culturels, dotés d'une infrastructure industrielle et sociale développée et comptant une population de plus 50 000 habitants, le pays compte 40 villes ayant statut régional), statut départemental, et agglomérations relevant de leur juridiction administrative.

Kirghizistan : Grandes villes et localités de type urbain, officiellement désignées comme telles, généralement sur la base du nombre d'habitants et de la prédominance des travailleurs agricoles ou non agricoles avec leur famille.

Koweït : Toutes les localités sont urbaines au Koweït.

Malaisie : Zone ayant le statut de centre urbain et dont la population totale dépasse 10 000 habitants. On nomme périphérie toute zone contiguë à un centre urbain dont au moins 60 % de la population (âgée de 15 ans et plus) a une activité non agricole. La définition des zones urbaines couvre également les zones spéciales de développement qui n'ont pas officiellement le statut de centre urbain, se trouvent à 5 kilomètres ou plus d'un tel centre ou de sa périphérie et comptent au moins 10 000 habitants dont 60 % (parmi les plus de 15 ans) ont une activité non agricole.

Maldives : Malé (capitale).

Mongolie : Capitale et chefs-lieux de district.

Népal : Zones déclarées telles par les municipalités.

Ouzbékistan : Grandes villes et localités de type urbain, officiellement désignées comme telles, généralement sur la base du nombre d'habitants et de la prédominance des travailleurs agricoles ou non agricoles avec leur famille.

Pakistan : Localités dotées d'une charte municipale ou d'un comité municipal et regroupements (cantonments).

Philippines : Villes et municipalités et leurs quartiers centraux dont la densité démographique est d'au moins 500 habitants au km carré. Sont considérés comme zones urbaines les autres quartiers quelle que soit leur population qui sont équipés de routes et possèdent au moins six établissements (commerce, industrie manufacturière, équipements récréatifs ou services aux personnes), et au moins trois équipements publics tels que hôtel de ville, église, parc public, école, hôpital, bibliothèque, etc.

République arabe syrienne : Villes, chefs-lieux de district (Mohafaza) et chefs-lieux de sous district (Mantika), et communes d'au moins 20 000 habitants.

République de Corée : Pour les estimations : localités de 50 000 habitants ou plus. Pour recensements, les données sont établies sont la base des divisions administratives mineures comme les Dongs (principalement en zone urbaines) et des Eups ou Myeons (en zones rurales).

République démocratique populaire lao : Zones ou villages répondant à au moins trois des cinq conditions suivantes: situés dans l'aire métropolitaine du district ou de la province, accessibles par la route en toute saison, quelque 70 pour cent ou deux tiers de la population ayant accès à de l'eau distribuée par canalisation, quelque 70 pour cent ou deux tiers de la population ayant accès au réseau d'électricité et existence d'un marché ouvert tous les jours.

Sri Lanka : Toutes les zones administrées par les conseils municipaux et urbains.

Tadjikistan : Grandes villes et localités de type urbain, officiellement désignées comme telles, généralement sur la base du nombre d'habitants et de la prédominance des travailleurs agricoles ou non agricoles avec leur famille.

Thaïlande : Zones municipales.

Turkménistan : Grandes villes et localités de type urbain, officiellement désignées comme telles, généralement sur la base du nombre d'habitants et de la prédominance des travailleurs agricoles ou non agricoles avec leur famille.

Turquie : Localités comptant 20 000 habitants ou plus.

Viet Nam : Zones urbaines comprises à l'intérieur des districts urbains des villes ainsi que des quartiers urbains et des localités. Toutes les autres unités administratives locales (communes) sont considérées comme zones rurales.

EUROPE

Albanie : Villes et autres centres industriels de plus de 400 habitants.

Autriche :.Les zones urbaines sont les localités comptant 2 000 habitants ou plus. Leur délimitation remonte à 1991.

Bélarus : Les établissements urbains sont des établissements autorisés en vertu de la loi comme les villes, les agglomérations de type urbain, les cités ouvrières et les zones de villégiature de santé.

Belgique : Toutes les communes qui ne sont pas dans la liste des communes rurales sont considérées comme des communes urbaines. Il y a 33 communes qui sont considérées comme rurales: Alveringem, Amblève, Bertogne, Bièvre, Bullange, Burg-Reuland, Clavier, Erezée, Fauvillers, Frasnes-lez-Anvaing, Froidchapelle, Gedinne, Gouvy, Havelange, Herstappe, Heuvelland, Houffalize, Houyet, Langemark-

Poelkapelle, Léglise, Lierneux, Lo-Reninge, Manhay, Momignies, Ravels, Sainte-Ode, Sint-Laureins, Sivry-Rance, Stoumont, Tenneville, Vaux-sur-Sûre, Vleteren et Vresse-sur-Semois.

Bulgarie : Toutes les zones considérées comme villes et bourgs selon la Division territoriale et administrative du pays.

Espagne : Aux fins de la publication de résultats qui soient comparables au niveau européen, Eurostat propose de considérer comme zones urbaines, intermédiaires et rurales les communes comptant respectivement plus de 10 000 habitants, de 2 001 à 10 000 habitants et moins de 2 000 habitants.

Estonie : Les établissements urbains comprennent les villes et les agglomérations n'ayant pas de statut municipal.

Fédération de Russie : Grandes villes et localités de type urbain, officiellement désignées comme telles, généralement sur la base du nombre d'habitants et de la prédominance des travailleurs agricoles ou non agricoles avec leur famille.

Finlande : Communes urbaines (communes où au moins 90 % de la population vit en milieu urbain ou dont le plus grand centre urbain compte au moins 15 000 habitants).

France : Communes comprenant une agglomération de plus de 2 000 habitants vivant dans des habitations contiguës ou qui ne sont pas distantes les unes des autres de plus de 200 mètres et communes où la majeure partie de la population vit dans une agglomération regroupant plusieurs communes de cette nature.

Grèce : Est considérée comme zone urbaine toute municipalité ou commune dont la plus grande localité compte 2 000 habitants ou plus.

Hongrie : Localités dont le statut de ville a été reconnu par le Président de la République compte tenu de critères spécifiques (économiques, commerciaux, institutionnels, culturels, etc.).

Irlande : Localités, y compris leur banlieues, comptant 1 500 habitants ou plus.

Islande : Localités de 200 habitants ou plus.

Lettonie : Grandes villes et localités de type urbain, officiellement désignées comme telles, généralement sur la base du nombre d'habitants et de la prédominance des travailleurs agricoles ou non agricoles avec leur famille.

Liechtenstein : Communes comptant 10 000 habitants ou plus.

Lituanie : Par population urbaine, on entend les personnes qui vivent dans des villes ou des localités, à savoir les zones habitées comportant des logements permanents proches les uns des autres et dont la population est d'au moins 3 000 habitants, les deux tiers desquels étant employés dans le secteur industriel, l'infrastructure sociale ou le commerce. Un certain nombre de villes peuvent compter moins de 3 000 habitants dans la mesure où elles avaient acquis le statut de ville avant l'entrée en vigueur de la nouvelle loi en juillet 1994.

Malte : Zones de 1 kilomètre carré avec une densité minimum de 300 et un minimum de 5 000 habitants au kilomètre carré; et zones à forte densité de population (supérieure à 500 habitants au kilomètre carré).

Monténégro : D'après la législation actuelle relative à l'organisation territoriale du Monténégro, qui oblige chaque collectivité à déterminer quelles sont ses zones urbaines et rurales.

Norvège : Ensemble construit habité par au moins 200 personnes, où les bâtiments ne sont pas éloignés de plus de 50 mètres les uns des autres. Les limites en sont évolutives et peuvent être redéfinies pour tenir compte de l'urbanisation et de l'évolution de la population.

Pays Bas : Zones urbaines : municipalités comptant au moins 2 000 habitants. Zones semi-urbaines : municipalités comptant moins de 2 000 habitants, mais où 20 p. 100 au maximum de la population active de sexe masculin pratiquent l'agriculture, et certaines municipalités de caractère résidentiel dont les habitants travaillent ailleurs.

Pologne : Toutes les zones qui ont les droits d'une ville ou le statut d'une ville avec dispositions de lois distinctes.

Portugal : Localités comptant 2 000 habitants ou davantage.

République de Moldova : Grandes villes et localités de type urbain, officiellement désignées comme telles, généralement sur la base du nombre d'habitants et de la prédominance des travailleurs agricoles ou non agricoles avec leur famille.

République tchèque : Localités d'au moins 2 000 habitants.

Roumanie : Localités où la majorité des ressources en main-d'œuvre est employée dans des activités non agricoles avec un niveau diversifié de ressources, exerçant une influence socioéconomique constante et importante sur l'ensemble de la zone.

Royaume-Uni de Grande-Bretagne et d'Irlande du Nord : Pour l'Angleterre et le Pays de Galles, les zones bâties comptant 10 000 habitants ou plus; pour l'Écosse, les établissements humains comptant 3 000 habitants ou davantage et pour l'Irlande du Nord, les établissements comptant 5 000 habitants.

Serbie : Municipalités, villes et Belgrade.

Slovaquie : Municipalités avec statut de ville, suivant les critères ci-après: 1) est un centre économique, administratif, culturel ou touristique, 2) fournit des services pour d'autres municipalités, 3) a un caractère urbain, au moins en partie, et 4) compte 5 000 habitants ou plus.

Slovénie : Établissements de 3 000 habitants ou plus, chefs-lieux de municipalités comptant au moins 1 400 habitants, et quartiers suburbains qui s'intègrent progressivement dans une ville de 5 000 habitants ou plus.

Suisse : L'espace urbain comprend les agglomérations et les villes isolées (n'appartenant pas à une agglomération et ayant au moins 10 000 habitants à elles seules).

Ukraine : Grandes villes et localités de type urbain, officiellement désignées comme telles, généralement sur la base du nombre d'habitants et de la prédominance des travailleurs agricoles ou non agricoles avec leur famille.

OCÉANIE

Australie : Sont considérées comme urbaines toutes les « zones urbaines importantes » (Significant Urban Areas), telles que définies dans la Norme géographique australienne de statistique de 2011. Il s'agit de concentrations urbanisées comptant 10 000 habitants ou plus.

Guam : Agglomérations de 2 500 habitants ou plus ayant généralement une densité de population d'au moins 1 000 habitants au mile carré et considérées comme étant des groupements urbains.

Îles Cook : Rarotonga, île la plus peuplée.

Îles Mariannes septentrionales : Agglomérations de 2 500 habitants ou plus ayant généralement une densité de population d'au moins 1 000 habitants au mile carré. Deux types de zones urbaines : zones urbanisées de 50 000 habitants ou plus et groupements urbains comptant au moins 2 500 habitants mais moins de 50 000.

Nouvelle-Calédonie : Nouméa et communes de Païta, Dumbéa et Mont-Dore.

Nouvelle-Zélande : Toutes les villes et les quartiers, districts et bourgs ayant 1 000 habitants permanents ou plus.

Palaos : États comptant 2 500 habitants ou plus (le seul État qui remplit cette condition est l'État de Koror).

Samoa américaines : Agglomérations de 2 500 habitants ou plus ayant généralement une densité de population d'au moins 1 000 habitants au mile carré. Deux types de zones urbaines : zones urbanisées de 50 000 habitants ou plus et groupements urbains comptant au moins 2 500 habitants mais moins de 50 000. (D'après les résultats du recensement de 2000, les Samoa américaines ne comptent aucune zone urbanisée.)

Tokélaou : L'ensemble de la population est considéré comme vivant en milieu rural.

Tonga : Nuku'alofa.

Vanuatu : Centre de Luganville et Port-Vila.

NOTES

[1] Pour plus de précisions, voir *Social and Demographic Statistics: Classifications of Size and Type of Locality and Urban/Rural Areas*, E/CN.3/551, publication des Nations Unies, New York, 1980.

6. Total and urban population by sex: 2006 - 2015
Population totale et population urbaine selon le sexe : 2006 - 2015

Continent, country or area, and date / Continent, pays ou zone et date	Code[a]	Both sexes - Les deux sexes			Male - Masculin			Female - Féminin		
		Total	Urban - Urbaine		Total	Urban - Urbaine		Total	Urban - Urbaine	
			Number Nombre	Percent P.100		Number Nombre	Percent P.100		Number Nombre	Percent P.100
AFRICA - AFRIQUE										
Algeria - Algérie										
1 VII 2006 ....ESDJ		33 481 000	...	...	16 915 000	...	...	16 566 000	...	...
1 VII 2007 ....ESDJ		34 096 000	...	...	17 225 000	...	...	16 871 000	...	...
16 IV 2008[1] ....CDFC		34 452 759	...	...	17 428 500	...	...	17 024 259	...	...
1 VII 2008 ....ESDJ		34 591 000	22 808 000	65.9	17 493 000	...	...	17 098 000	...	...
1 VII 2009 ....ESDJ		35 268 000	...	...	17 846 000	...	...	17 422 000	...	...
1 VII 2010 ....ESDJ		35 978 000	...	...	18 205 000	...	...	17 773 000	...	...
1 VII 2011 ....ESDJ		36 717 000	...	...	18 579 000	...	...	18 138 000	...	...
1 VII 2012 ....ESDJ		37 495 000	...	...	18 976 000	...	...	18 519 000	...	...
1 VII 2013 ....ESDJ		38 297 000	...	...	19 383 000	...	...	18 914 000	...	...
1 VII 2014 ....ESDJ		39 114 275	...	...	19 801 163	...	...	19 313 112	...	...
1 VII 2015 ....ESDJ		39 963 249	...	...	20 235 204	...	...	19 728 045	...	...
Angola										
1 VII 2006 ....ESDF		15 410 000	...	...	7 437 000	...	...	7 973 000	...	...
1 VII 2007 ....ESDF		15 889 000	...	...	7 668 000	...	...	8 221 000	...	...
1 VII 2008 ....ESDF		16 368 000	...	...	7 899 000	...	...	8 469 000	...	...
1 VII 2009 ....ESDF		16 888 000	...	...	8 158 000	...	...	8 730 000	...	...
1 VII 2010 ....ESDF		17 430 000	...	...	8 428 000	...	...	9 002 000	...	...
1 VII 2011 ....ESDF		17 991 000	...	...	8 707 000	...	...	9 284 000	...	...
1 VII 2012 ....ESDF		18 576 000	...	...	8 999 000	...	...	9 577 000	...	...
1 VII 2013 ....ESDF		19 184 000	...	...	9 302 000	...	...	9 882 000	...	...
16 V 2014 ....CDFC		25 789 024	...	...	12 499 041	...	...	13 289 983	...	...
1 VII 2014 ....ESDF		25 789 000	16 154 000	62.6	12 499 000	7 861 000	62.9	13 290 000	8 293 000	62.4
Benin - Bénin										
1 VII 2006[2] ....ESDF		7 699 697	3 156 172	41.0	3 755 408	1 544 515	41.1	3 944 289	1 611 657	40.9
1 VII 2007[2] ....ESDF		7 958 813	3 324 220	41.8	3 886 596	1 628 650	41.9	4 072 217	1 695 570	41.6
1 VII 2008[2] ....ESDF		8 224 642	3 499 506	42.5	4 021 094	1 716 411	42.7	4 203 548	1 783 095	42.4
1 VII 2009[2] ....ESDF		8 497 827	3 682 496	43.3	4 159 291	1 808 057	43.5	4 338 536	1 874 439	43.2
1 VII 2010[2] ....ESDF		8 778 648	3 873 462	44.1	4 301 224	1 903 683	44.3	4 477 424	1 969 779	44.0
1 VII 2011[2] ....ESDF		9 067 076	4 072 574	44.9	4 446 877	2 003 366	45.1	4 620 199	2 069 208	44.8
1 VII 2012[2] ....ESDF		9 364 619	4 280 693	45.7	4 597 122	...	...	4 767 497	...	...
11 V 2013 ....CDJC		10 008 749	4 460 503	44.6	4 887 820	...	...	5 120 929	...	...
1 VII 2014[3] ....ESDF		10 293 235	...	...	5 033 372	...	...	5 259 863	...	...
1 VII 2015[3] ....ESDF		10 584 935	...	...	5 182 478	...	...	5 402 457	...	...
Botswana										
1 VII 2006 ....ESDJ		1 719 996	...	...	837 114	...	...	882 882	...	...
1 VIII 2006[4] ....SSDJ		1 773 240	1 000 443	56.4	851 670	473 136	55.6	921 570	527 307	57.2
1 VII 2007 ....ESDJ		1 736 396	...	...	847 539	...	...	888 857	...	...
1 VII 2008 ....ESDJ		1 755 246	...	...	859 167	...	...	896 079	...	...
1 VII 2009 ....ESDJ		1 776 494	...	...	871 964	...	...	904 530	...	...
1 VII 2010 ....ESDJ		1 822 859	...	...	895 007	...	...	927 852	...	...
1 VII 2011 ....ESDJ		1 849 692	...	...	910 404	...	...	939 288	...	...
9 VIII 2011 ....CDFC		2 024 904	1 297 287	64.1	988 957	619 472	62.6	1 035 947	677 815	65.4
1 VII 2012[5] ....ESDJ		2 070 984	1 361 699	65.8	1 010 236	664 243	65.8	1 060 748	697 456	65.8
1 VII 2013[5] ....ESDJ		2 114 890	1 411 436	66.7	1 031 654	688 505	66.7	1 083 236	722 931	66.7
1 VII 2014[5] ....ESDJ		2 156 366	1 460 383	67.7	1 051 886	712 382	67.7	1 104 480	748 001	67.7
1 VII 2015[5] ....ESDJ		2 195 134	1 508 277	68.7	1 070 797	735 745	68.7	1 124 337	772 532	68.7
Burkina Faso										
9 XII 2006 ....CDFC		14 196 259	3 230 504	22.8	6 842 560	1 609 349	23.5	7 353 699	1 621 155	22.0
1 VII 2007[2] ....ESDJ		14 252 012	3 322 360	23.3	6 880 824	1 629 956	23.7	7 371 188	1 692 404	23.0
1 VII 2008[2] ....ESDJ		14 731 167	...	...	7 110 097	...	...	7 621 070	...	...
1 VII 2009[2] ....ESDJ		15 224 780	...	...	7 346 835	...	...	7 877 945	...	...
1 VII 2010[2] ....ESDJ		15 730 977	...	...	7 590 133	...	...	8 140 844	...	...
Burundi										
16 VIII 2008 ....CDFC		7 877 728	799 802	10.2	3 838 045	432 442	11.3	4 039 683	367 360	9.1
1 VII 2009[6] ....ESDF		8 262 912	892 394	10.8	4 065 512	439 075	10.8	4 197 400	453 319	10.8
1 VII 2010[6] ....ESDF		8 487 650	976 080	11.5	4 173 862	479 994	11.5	4 313 788	496 086	11.5
1 VII 2011[6] ....ESDF		8 727 180	1 064 716	12.2	4 289 661	523 339	12.2	4 437 519	541 377	12.2
1 VII 2012[6] ....ESDF		8 981 318	1 158 590	12.9	4 412 830	569 255	12.9	4 568 488	589 335	12.9
1 VII 2013[6] ....ESDF		9 249 336	1 257 910	13.6	4 543 008	617 849	13.6	4 706 328	640 061	13.6
1 VII 2014[6] ....ESDF		9 530 434	1 362 852	14.3	4 679 790	669 210	14.3	4 850 644	693 642	14.3
1 VII 2015[6] ....ESDF		9 823 828	1 473 574	15.0	4 822 838	723 426	15.0	5 000 990	750 148	15.0
Cabo Verde										
1 VII 2006 ....ESDF		483 090	286 687	59.3	233 729	...	...	249 361	...	...
1 VII 2007 ....ESDF		491 419	295 046	60.0	237 842	...	...	253 577	...	...

6. Total and urban population by sex: 2006 - 2015
Population totale et population urbaine selon le sexe : 2006 - 2015 (continued - suite)

Continent, country or area, and date / Continent, pays ou zone et date	Code[a]	Both sexes - Les deux sexes Total	Urban - Urbaine Number Nombre	Urban - Urbaine Percent P.100	Male - Masculin Total	Urban - Urbaine Number Nombre	Urban - Urbaine Percent P.100	Female - Féminin Total	Urban - Urbaine Number Nombre	Urban - Urbaine Percent P.100
AFRICA - AFRIQUE										
Cabo Verde										
1 VII 2008	ESDF	499 796	303 512	60.7	241 914	...	...	257 882	...	...
1 VII 2009	ESDF	508 633	310 958	61.1	246 219	...	...	262 414	...	...
16 VI 2010	CDJC	491 683	303 673	61.8	243 401	151 217	62.1	248 282	152 456	61.4
1 VII 2010	ESDF	517 831	320 111	61.8	250 710	...	...	267 121	...	...
1 VII 2011	ESDF	527 269	328 177	62.2	255 327	...	...	271 942	...	...
Cameroon - Cameroun[2]										
1 I 2010	ESDJ	19 406 100	10 091 172	52.0	9 599 224	5 029 993	52.4	9 806 876	5 061 179	51.6
Chad - Tchad										
20 V 2009	CDJC	11 175 915	...	...	5 509 522	...	...	5 666 393		
Congo										
28 IV 2007	CDFC	3 697 490	2 285 551	61.8	1 821 357	1 132 510	62.2	1 876 133	1 153 041	61.5
1 VII 2008	ESDF	3 740 851	...	...	1 841 589	...	...	1 899 262	...	...
1 VII 2009	ESDF	3 838 238	...	...	1 891 558	...	...	1 946 680	...	...
Côte d'Ivoire										
1 VII 2006[2]	ESDF	19 657 738	...	...	10 023 964	...	...	9 633 774	...	...
1 VII 2007[2]	ESDF	20 227 876	...	...	10 312 061	...	...	9 915 815	...	...
1 VII 2008[2]	ESDF	20 807 216	...	...	10 604 596	...	...	10 202 620	...	...
1 VII 2009[2]	ESDF	21 395 198	...	...	10 901 322	...	...	10 493 876	...	...
15 V 2014	CDFC	22 224 509	10 881 387	49.0	11 441 896	5 495 438	48.0	10 782 613	5 385 949	50.0
Djibouti										
29 V 2009	CDFC	818 159	577 933	70.6	440 067	322 796	73.4	378 092	255 137	67.5
Egypt - Égypte										
1 VII 2006	ESDF	72 008 900	30 699 375	42.6	36 725 501	...	...	35 283 399	...	...
21 XI 2006	CDFC	72 798 031	31 370 925	43.1	37 219 056	16 013 864	43.0	35 578 975	15 357 061	43.2
1 VII 2007	ESDF	73 643 587	31 719 927	43.1	37 643 353	16 186 484	43.0	36 000 234	15 533 443	43.1
1 VII 2008	ESDF	75 193 567	32 248 476	42.9	38 413 404	16 437 464	42.8	36 780 163	15 811 012	43.0
1 VII 2009	ESDF	76 925 139	33 082 770	43.0	39 327 098	16 887 176	42.9	37 598 041	16 195 594	43.1
1 VII 2010	ESDF	78 684 622	33 804 181	43.0	40 228 119	17 255 735	42.9	38 456 503	16 548 446	43.0
1 VII 2011	ESDF	80 529 566	34 495 468	42.8	41 152 525	17 596 284	42.8	39 377 041	16 899 184	42.9
1 VII 2012	ESDF	82 549 976	35 372 982	42.9	42 167 660	18 031 407	42.8	40 382 316	17 341 575	42.9
1 VII 2013	ESDF	84 628 982	36 213 473	42.8	43 217 105	18 470 748	42.7	41 411 877	17 742 725	42.8
1 VII 2014	ESDF	86 811 192	37 098 131	42.7	44 300 565	18 894 134	42.6	42 510 627	18 203 997	42.8
1 VII 2015	ESDF	88 957 833	37 999 018	42.7	45 378 728	19 347 041	42.6	43 579 105	18 651 977	42.8
Equatorial Guinea - Guinée équatoriale										
20 VI 2015	CDFC	1 222 442	863 313	70.6	651 820	...	...	570 622	...	...
Ethiopia - Éthiopie										
1 VII 2006[7]	ESDF	75 067 000	12 172 000	16.2	37 615 000	6 050 000	16.1	37 452 000	6 122 000	16.3
29 V 2007	CDFC	73 750 932	11 862 821	16.1	37 217 130	5 895 916	15.8	36 533 802	5 966 905	16.3
1 VII 2007[7]	ESDF	77 127 000	12 689 000	16.5	38 644 000	6 307 000	16.3	38 483 000	6 382 000	16.6
1 VII 2008[8]	ESDF	75 719 000	12 716 000	16.8	38 215 000	6 353 000	16.6	37 504 000	6 363 000	17.0
1 VII 2009[8]	ESDF	77 651 000	13 318 000	17.2	39 155 000	6 649 000	17.0	38 496 000	6 669 000	17.3
1 VII 2010[8]	ESDF	79 634 000	13 931 000	17.5	40 123 000	6 950 000	17.3	39 511 000	6 981 000	17.7
1 VII 2011[8]	ESDF	81 668 000	14 589 000	17.9	41 119 000	7 274 000	17.7	40 549 000	7 315 000	18.0
1 VII 2012[8]	ESDF	83 741 000	15 246 000	18.2	42 135 000	7 598 000	18.0	41 606 000	7 648 000	18.4
1 VII 2013[8]	ESDF	85 837 000	15 979 000	18.6	43 164 000	7 960 000	18.4	42 673 000	8 019 000	18.8
1 VII 2014[8]	ESDF	87 952 000	16 734 000	19.0	44 204 000	8 332 000	18.8	43 748 000	8 402 000	19.2
1 VII 2015[8]	ESDF	90 075 000	17 521 000	19.5	45 250 000	8 721 000	19.3	44 825 000	8 800 000	19.6
Gabon										
22 V 2013	CDFC	1 811 079	1 577 646	87.1	934 072	813 098	87.0	877 007	764 548	87.2
Gambia - Gambie										
15 IV 2013*	CDFC	1 882 450	...	...	930 699	...	...	951 751	...	...
Ghana										
1 VII 2006[2]	ESDF	21 876 031	...	...	10 833 033	...	...	11 042 998	...	...
1 VII 2007[2]	ESDF	22 387 911	...	...	11 088 060	...	...	11 299 851	...	...
1 VII 2008[2]	ESDF	22 900 927	...	...	11 343 581	...	...	11 557 346	...	...
1 VII 2009[2]	ESDF	23 416 518	10 243 312	43.7	11 600 326	5 006 198	43.2	11 816 192	5 237 114	44.3
26 IX 2010	CDFC	24 658 823	12 545 229	50.9	12 024 845	6 016 059	50.0	12 633 978	6 529 170	51.7
1 VII 2011[2]	ESDF	25 235 268	12 844 745	50.9	12 319 770	6 270 758	50.9	12 915 498	6 573 987	50.9
1 VII 2012[2]	ESDF	25 824 920	13 144 879	50.9	12 621 125	6 424 150	50.9	13 203 795	6 720 729	50.9
1 VII 2013[2]	ESDF	26 427 760	13 451 714	50.9	12 928 916	6 580 808	50.9	13 498 844	6 870 906	50.9
1 VII 2014[2]	ESDF	27 043 093	13 764 931	50.9	13 242 709	6 740 539	50.9	13 800 384	7 024 392	50.9
1 VII 2015[2]	ESDF	27 670 174	13 817 894	49.9	13 562 093	6 903 107	50.9	14 108 081	6 914 787	49.0

6. Total and urban population by sex: 2006 - 2015
Population totale et population urbaine selon le sexe : 2006 - 2015 (continued - suite)

Continent, country or area, and date / Continent, pays ou zone et date	Code[a]	Both sexes - Les deux sexes			Male - Masculin			Female - Féminin		
		Total	Urban - Urbaine		Total	Urban - Urbaine		Total	Urban - Urbaine	
			Number Nombre	Percent P.100		Number Nombre	Percent P.100		Number Nombre	Percent P.100
AFRICA - AFRIQUE										
Guinea - Guinée										
1 VII 2008[2] ....ESDF		10 182 926	2 851 219	28.0	...	...	...	...	...	...
1 VII 2009[2] ....ESDF		10 217 591	...	...	5 038 823	...	...	5 178 768	...	...
1 VII 2010[2] ....ESDF		10 537 234	...	...	5 200 608	...	...	5 336 626	...	...
1 VII 2011[2] ....ESDF		10 863 888	...	...	5 309 110	...	...	5 554 778	...	...
1 III 2014 ....CDFC		10 523 261	3 657 122	34.8	5 084 306	1 821 369	35.8	5 438 955	1 835 753	33.8
Guinea-Bissau - Guinée-Bissau										
15 III 2009 ....CDFC		1 520 830	...	...	737 634	...	...	783 196	...	...
1 VII 2010[2] ....ESDF		1 460 221	584 228	40.0	709 482	283 859	40.0	750 739	300 369	40.0
1 VII 2011[2] ....ESDF		1 472 233	595 358	40.4	716 622	289 796	40.4	755 611	305 562	40.4
1 VII 2012[2] ....ESDF		1 485 189	606 976	40.9	724 208	295 974	40.9	760 981	311 002	40.9
1 VII 2013[2] ....ESDF		1 499 277	619 166	41.3	732 337	302 438	41.3	766 940	316 728	41.3
1 VII 2014[2] ....ESDF		1 514 451	631 938	41.7	740 981	309 191	41.7	773 470	322 747	41.7
1 VII 2015[2] ....ESDF		1 530 673	645 283	42.2	750 119	316 226	42.2	780 554	329 057	42.2
Kenya										
1 VII 2006 ....ESDF		36 138 744	...	...	17 685 163	...	...	18 453 583	...	...
1 VII 2007 ....ESDF		37 183 924	...	...	18 202 701	...	...	18 981 232	...	...
1 VII 2008 ....ESDF		38 277 856	...	...	18 743 686	...	...	19 534 170	...	...
24 VIII 2009 ....CDFC		38 610 097	12 487 375	32.3	19 192 458	6 278 811	32.7	19 417 639	6 208 564	32.0
1 VII 2010 ....ESDF		40 406 412	...	...	19 793 261	...	...	20 613 150	...	...
1 VII 2011 ....ESDF		41 409 344	...	...	20 286 575	...	...	21 122 674	...	...
1 VII 2012 ....ESDF		42 435 596	...	...	20 792 155	...	...	21 643 448	...	...
1 VII 2013 ....ESDF		43 489 032	...	...	21 311 230	...	...	22 177 801	...	...
1 VII 2014 ....ESDF		44 571 640	...	...	21 844 933	...	...	22 726 711	...	...
1 VII 2015 ....ESDF		45 509 212	...	...	22 305 705	...	...	23 203 515	...	...
Lesotho										
13 IV 2006 ....CDFC		1 741 406	403 104	23.1	818 379	181 351	22.2	923 027	221 753	24.0
1 VII 2006[2] ....ESDF		1 866 471	421 655	22.6	...	...	...	...	...	...
Liberia - Libéria										
1 VII 2006 ....ESDF		3 332 320	1 540 608	46.2	1 669 253	760 049	45.5	1 663 067	780 559	46.9
1 VII 2007 ....ESDF		3 403 700	1 586 481	46.6	1 704 232	780 788	45.8	1 699 468	805 693	47.4
21 III 2008 ....CDFC		3 476 608	1 633 719	47.0	1 739 945	802 092	46.1	1 736 663	831 627	47.9
1 VII 2009 ....ESDF		3 551 078	1 682 364	47.4	1 776 406	823 978	46.4	1 774 672	858 386	48.4
1 VII 2010 ....ESDF		3 627 144	1 732 457	47.8	1 813 631	846 461	46.7	1 813 513	885 996	48.9
1 VII 2011 ....ESDF		3 704 838	1 784 042	48.2	1 851 636	869 557	47.0	1 853 202	914 485	49.3
1 VII 2012 ....ESDF		3 784 197	1 837 163	48.5	1 890 438	893 283	47.3	1 893 759	943 880	49.8
1 VII 2013 ....ESDF		3 865 256	1 891 865	48.9	1 930 053	917 657	47.5	1 935 203	974 208	50.3
1 VII 2014 ....ESDF		3 946 311	1 946 567	49.3	1 969 668	942 031	47.8	1 976 643	1 004 536	50.8
Libya - Libye										
15 IV 2006* ....CDFC		5 298 152	4 670 858	88.2	2 687 513	2 372 379	88.3	2 610 639	2 298 479	88.0
1 VII 2007 ....ESDF		5 393 325	4 754 540	88.2	2 735 343	2 414 477	88.3	2 657 982	2 340 064	88.0
1 VII 2008 ....ESDF		5 490 478	4 839 715	88.1	2 784 122	2 457 272	88.3	2 706 356	2 382 443	88.0
1 VII 2009 ....ESDF		5 589 289	4 926 097	88.1	2 833 691	2 500 626	88.2	2 755 598	2 425 471	88.0
1 VII 2010 ....ESDF		5 689 419	5 013 386	88.1	2 883 880	2 544 388	88.2	2 805 538	2 468 998	88.0
1 VII 2011 ....ESDF		5 790 518	5 101 275	88.1	2 934 512	2 588 402	88.2	2 856 006	2 512 874	88.0
1 VII 2012 ....ESDF		5 892 239	5 189 460	88.1	2 985 408	2 632 510	88.2	2 906 831	2 556 950	88.0
1 VII 2013 ....ESDF		5 994 241	5 277 638	88.0	3 036 393	2 676 558	88.1	2 957 849	2 601 081	87.9
1 VII 2014 ....ESDF		6 096 208	5 365 529	88.0	3 087 301	2 720 398	88.1	3 008 907	2 645 131	87.9
1 VII 2015 ....ESDF		6 162 356	5 411 529	87.8	3 129 260	2 707 215	86.5	3 033 156	2 704 314	89.2
Malawi										
1 VII 2006[2] ....ESDF		12 757 883	1 700 379	13.3	6 275 533	875 943	14.0	6 482 350	824 436	12.7
1 VII 2007[2] ....ESDF		13 187 632	1 786 434	13.5	6 490 146	918 991	14.2	6 697 486	867 443	13.0
8 VI 2008 ....CDFC		13 077 160	2 003 309	15.3	6 358 933	1 014 477	16.0	6 718 227	988 832	14.7
1 VII 2008[2] ....ESDF		13 630 164	1 874 199[9]	13.8	6 711 263	962 887[9]	14.3	6 918 901	911 312[9]	13.2
1 VII 2010[10] ....ESDF		13 948 594	...	...	6 804 310	...	...	7 143 284	...	...
1 VII 2011[10] ....ESDF		14 388 551	...	...	7 029 149	...	...	7 359 401	...	...
1 VII 2012[10] ....ESDF		14 844 822	...	...	7 261 499	...	...	7 583 323	...	...
Mali										
1 I 2006 ....ESDF		12 051 021	3 900 404	32.4	5 966 339	1 952 802	32.7	6 084 681	1 947 601	32.0
1 I 2007 ....ESDF		12 377 542	4 102 223	33.1	6 128 544	2 053 767	33.5	6 248 999	2 048 456	32.8
1 IV 2009 ....CDFC		14 528 662	3 274 727	22.5	7 204 990	1 643 671	22.8	7 323 672	1 631 056	22.3
1 VII 2010[11] ....ESDF		15 370 000	...	...	7 679 000	...	...	7 691 000	...	...
1 VII 2011[11] ....ESDF		15 843 000	...	...	7 919 000	...	...	7 924 000	...	...
1 VII 2012[11] ....ESDF		16 312 000	...	...	8 159 000	...	...	8 153 000	...	...

Continent, country or area, and date / Continent, pays ou zone et date	Codea	Both sexes - Les deux sexes			Male - Masculin			Female - Féminin		
		Total	Urban - Urbaine		Total	Urban - Urbaine		Total	Urban - Urbaine	
			Number Nombre	Percent P.100		Number Nombre	Percent P.100		Number Nombre	Percent P.100

AFRICA - AFRIQUE

Mali
| 1 VII 2013[11] .... ESDF | 16 808 000 | ... | ... | 8 411 000 | ... | ... | 8 397 000 | ... | ... |
| 1 VII 2014*[11] .... ESDF | 17 319 000 | ... | ... | 8 671 000 | ... | ... | 8 648 000 | ... | ... |

Mauritania - Mauritanie
1 VII 2008[2] .... ESDF	3 162 338	...	...	1 584 913	...	...	1 577 425	...	...
1 VII 2010[2] .... ESDF	3 340 627	...	...	1 678 324	...	...	1 662 303	...	...
1 VII 2011[2] .... ESDF	3 296 958	...	...	1 644 572	...	...	1 652 386	...	...
24 III 2013 .... CDFC	3 460 388[12]	1 697 792	49.1	...	...	...	...	...	...

Mauritius - Maurice[13]
1 VII 2006[14] .... ESDJ	1 252 698	527 138	42.1	619 243	259 028	41.8	633 455	268 110	42.3
1 VII 2007[14] .... ESDJ	1 260 403	528 961	42.0	622 926	259 800	41.7	637 477	269 161	42.2
1 VII 2008[14] .... ESDJ	1 268 565	531 097	41.9	626 556	260 675	41.6	642 009	270 422	42.1
1 VII 2009[14] .... ESDJ	1 275 032	532 591	41.8	629 157	261 041	41.5	645 875	271 550	42.0
1 VII 2010[14] .... ESDJ	1 280 924	533 771	41.7	631 692	261 489	41.4	649 232	272 282	41.9
1 VII 2011[15] .... ESDJ	1 252 404	509 229	40.7	619 591	249 439	40.3	632 813	259 790	41.1
4 VII 2011 .... CDFC	1 237 000	496 841	40.2	611 053	243 629	39.9	625 947	253 212	40.5
1 VII 2012[15] .... ESDJ	1 255 882	509 177	40.5	621 297	249 422	40.1	634 585	259 755	40.9
1 VII 2013[15] .... ESDJ	1 258 653	519 306	41.3	622 861	254 605	40.9	635 792	264 701	41.6
1 VII 2014[15] .... ESDJ	1 260 934	518 370	41.1	624 002	254 204	40.7	636 932	264 166	41.5
1 VII 2015[15] .... ESDJ	1 262 605	517 482	41.0	624 769	253 796	40.6	637 836	263 686	41.3

Mayotte
31 VII 2007 .... CDJC	186 387	...	...	91 405	...	...	94 982	...	...
21 VIII 2012 .... CDJC	212 645	...	...	103 164	...	...	109 481	...	...
1 I 2014* .... ESDJ	220 300	...	...	106 877	...	...	113 423	...	...
1 I 2015* .... ESDJ	226 915	...	...	110 086	...	...	116 829	...	...

Morocco - Maroc
1 VII 2006[16] .... ESDF	30 509 000	17 082 000	56.0	15 146 000	8 426 000	55.6	15 363 000	8 656 000	56.3
1 VII 2007[16] .... ESDF	30 850 000	17 415 000	56.5	15 314 000	8 579 000	56.0	15 536 000	8 836 000	56.9
1 VII 2008[16] .... ESDF	31 195 000	17 753 000	56.9	15 484 000	8 734 000	56.4	15 711 000	9 019 000	57.4
1 VII 2009[16] .... ESDF	31 543 000	18 097 000	57.4	15 657 000	8 891 000	56.8	15 886 000	9 205 000	57.9
1 VII 2010[16] .... ESDF	31 894 046	18 446 241	57.8	15 831 463	9 051 145	57.2	16 062 583	9 395 096	58.5
1 VII 2011[16] .... ESDF	32 245 120	18 802 208	58.3	16 010 979	9 212 763	57.5	16 234 141	9 589 444	59.1
1 VII 2012[16] .... ESDF	32 596 997	19 157 539	58.8	16 190 815	9 373 546	57.9	16 406 182	9 783 993	59.6
1 VII 2013[16] .... ESDF	32 950 445	19 512 904	59.2	16 371 475	9 533 742	58.2	16 578 971	9 979 162	60.2
1 VII 2014[16] .... ESDF	33 773 630	20 357 619	60.3	...	...	...	...	...	...
1 IX 2014 .... CDJC	33 848 242	20 432 439	60.4	...	...	...	...	...	...

Mozambique
1 VII 2006[2] .... ESDF	19 888 701	...	...	9 603 031	...	...	10 285 670	...	...
1 VII 2007[2] .... ESDF	20 632 434	6 269 621	30.4	9 930 196	3 079 809	31.0	10 702 238	3 189 812	29.8
1 VIII 2007 .... CDFC	20 252 223	6 151 974	30.4	9 746 690	3 021 756	31.0	10 505 533	3 130 218	29.8
1 VII 2008[2] .... ESDF	21 207 929	6 472 214	30.5	10 210 267	3 176 209	31.1	10 997 662	3 296 005	30.0
1 VII 2009[2] .... ESDF	21 802 866	6 685 108	30.7	10 499 954	3 277 805	31.2	11 302 912	3 407 303	30.1
1 VII 2010[2] .... ESDF	22 416 881	6 908 291	30.8	10 799 284	3 384 605	31.3	11 617 597	3 523 686	30.3
1 VII 2011[2] .... ESDF	23 049 621	7 141 715	31.0	11 108 128	3 496 582	31.5	11 941 493	3 645 133	30.5
1 VII 2012[2] .... ESDF	23 700 715	7 385 294	31.2	11 426 321	3 613 684	31.6	12 274 394	3 771 610	30.7
1 VII 2013[2] .... ESDF	24 366 112	7 639 557	31.4	11 751 849	3 736 166	31.8	12 614 263	3 903 391	30.9
1 VII 2014[2] .... ESDF	25 041 922	7 905 004	31.6	12 082 782	3 864 267	32.0	12 959 140	4 040 737	31.2
1 VII 2015[2] .... ESDF	25 727 911	8 181 475	31.8	12 419 014	3 997 895	32.2	13 308 897	4 183 580	31.4

Namibia - Namibie
1 VII 2006[2] .... ESDF	1 991 747	...	...	970 617	...	...	1 021 130	...	...
1 VII 2007[2] .... ESDF	2 027 871	...	...	989 067	...	...	1 038 804	...	...
1 VII 2008[2] .... ESDF	2 065 226	...	...	1 008 115	...	...	1 057 111	...	...
1 VII 2009[2] .... ESDF	2 103 761	...	...	1 027 736	...	...	1 076 025	...	...
1 VII 2010[2] .... ESDF	2 143 410	...	...	1 047 900	...	...	1 095 510	...	...
1 VII 2011[17] .... ESDF	2 116 077	900 163	42.5	1 026 911	439 993	42.8	1 089 166	460 170	42.2
28 VIII 2011 .... CDFC	2 113 077	903 434	42.8	1 021 912	440 334	43.1	1 091 165	463 100	42.4
1 VII 2012[17] .... ESDF	2 155 440	940 825	43.6	1 046 434	459 668	43.9	1 109 006	481 157	43.4
1 VII 2013[17] .... ESDF	2 196 086	982 519	44.7	1 066 541	479 844	45.0	1 129 545	502 675	44.5
1 VII 2014[17] .... ESDF	2 237 894	1 025 147	45.8	1 087 178	500 469	46.0	1 150 716	524 678	45.6
1 VII 2015[17] .... ESDF	2 280 716	1 068 625	46.9	1 108 276	521 496	47.1	1 172 440	547 129	46.7

Niger
1 VII 2006[2] .... ESDJ	13 044 973	2 184 605	16.7	6 506 496	1 092 927	16.8	6 538 477	1 091 678	16.7
1 VII 2007[2] .... ESDJ	13 716 233	2 556 499	18.6	6 851 314	1 280 155	18.7	6 864 919	1 276 344	18.6
1 VII 2008[2] .... ESDJ	14 197 601	2 728 541	19.2	7 088 858	1 366 304	19.3	7 108 743	1 362 237	19.2

Continent, country or area, and date / Continent, pays ou zone et date	Code[a]	Both sexes - Les deux sexes			Male - Masculin			Female - Féminin		
		Total	Urban - Urbaine		Total	Urban - Urbaine		Total	Urban - Urbaine	
			Number Nombre	Percent P.100		Number Nombre	Percent P.100		Number Nombre	Percent P.100
AFRICA - AFRIQUE										
Niger										
1 VII 2009[2]............ESDJ		14 693 112	2 911 006	19.8	7 339 392	1 458 250	19.9	7 353 720	1 452 756	19.8
1 VII 2010[2]............ESDJ		15 203 822	3 104 574	20.4	7 594 565	1 555 187	20.5	7 609 257	1 549 387	20.4
1 VII 2011[2]............ESDJ		15 730 754	...	...	7 857 845	...	...	7 872 909	...	...
1 VII 2012[18]............ESDJ		16 993 563	2 750 279	16.2	8 446 540	1 383 545	16.4	8 547 023	1 366 734	16.0
10 XII 2012............CDJC		17 138 707	2 778 337	16.2	8 518 818	1 397 695	16.4	8 619 889	1 380 642	16.0
1 VII 2013[18]............ESDJ		17 679 760	2 856 533	16.2	8 792 478	1 424 257	16.2	8 887 281	1 432 275	16.1
1 VII 2014[18]............ESDJ		18 389 164	2 965 748	16.1	9 150 266	1 479 064	16.2	9 238 897	1 486 684	16.1
1 VII 2015[18]............ESDJ		19 124 882	3 078 506	16.1	9 521 427	1 535 664	16.1	9 603 456	1 542 842	16.1
Nigeria - Nigéria										
21 III 2006............CDFC		140 431 790	...	...	71 345 488	...	...	69 086 302	...	...
Republic of South Sudan - République de Soudan du Sud										
21 IV 2008............CDFC		8 260 490	1 405 186	17.0	4 287 300	754 086	17.6	3 973 190	651 100	16.4
1 VII 2008[19]............ESDF		8 490 767	1 443 430	17.0	4 406 708	749 140	17.0	4 084 059	694 290	17.0
1 VII 2009[19]............ESDF		8 987 784	1 527 923	17.0	4 323 124	734 931	17.0	4 664 660	792 992	17.0
1 VII 2010[19]............ESDF		9 496 844	1 614 463	17.0	4 567 982	776 557	17.0	4 928 862	837 907	17.0
1 VII 2011[19]............ESDF		10 018 240	1 703 101	17.0	4 818 773	819 191	17.0	5 199 467	883 909	17.0
1 VII 2012[19]............ESDF		10 552 270	1 793 886	17.0	5 075 642	862 859	17.0	5 476 628	931 027	17.0
1 VII 2013[19]............ESDF		10 808 588	1 837 460	17.0	5 198 931	883 818	17.0	5 609 657	953 642	17.0
1 VII 2014[19]............ESDF		11 071 132	1 882 093	17.0	5 325 215	905 286	17.0	5 745 917	976 806	17.0
Reunion - Réunion										
1 I 2006............CDJC		781 962	...	...	379 176	...	...	402 786	...	...
1 VII 2006............ESDJ		786 231	...	...	381 030	...	...	405 202	...	...
1 I 2007............ESDJ		794 107	...	...	385 335	...	...	408 772	...	...
1 I 2008............ESDJ		808 250	...	...	392 041	...	...	416 209	...	...
1 I 2009............ESDJ		816 364	...	...	395 688	...	...	420 676	...	...
1 I 2010............CDJC		821 136	808 540	98.5	398 006	391 623	98.4	423 130	416 917	98.5
1 I 2011............ESDJ		828 581	...	...	401 139	...	...	427 442	...	...
1 I 2012............ESDJ		833 944	...	...	403 504	...	...	430 440	...	...
1 I 2013............ESDJ		835 103	...	...	403 731	...	...	431 372	...	...
1 I 2014*............ESDJ		839 334	...	...	405 618	...	...	433 716	...	...
1 I 2015*............ESDJ		843 529	...	...	407 441	...	...	436 088	...	...
Rwanda										
1 VII 2006[2]............ESDF		9 468 000	1 514 880	16.0	4 487 832	...	...	4 980 168	...	...
1 VII 2007[2]............ESDF		9 556 669	1 726 613	18.1	4 597 277	812 148	17.7	4 959 393	914 465	18.4
1 VII 2008[2]............ESDF		9 831 501	...	...	4 736 104	...	...	5 095 397	...	...
1 VII 2009[2]............ESDF		10 117 029	...	...	4 880 233	...	...	5 236 796	...	...
1 VII 2010[2]............ESDF		10 412 820	1 541 097	14.8	5 029 450	...	...	5 383 371	...	...
1 VII 2011[2]............ESDF		10 718 379	1 564 883	14.6	5 183 505	...	...	5 534 874	...	...
1 VII 2012[20]............ESDF		10 482 641	1 732 175	16.5	5 049 164	889 118	17.6	5 433 477	843 057	15.5
15 VIII 2012............CDFC		10 393 542	1 760 994	16.9	4 981 197	902 501	18.1	5 412 345	858 493	15.9
1 VII 2013[20]............ESDF		10 736 771	1 844 040	17.2	5 178 354	889 382	17.2	5 558 417	954 658	17.2
1 VII 2014[20]............ESDF		10 996 891	1 962 945	17.8	5 310 430	947 912	17.9	5 686 461	1 015 033	17.8
1 VII 2015[20]............ESDF		11 262 564	2 086 390	18.5	5 445 206	1 008 724	18.5	5 817 359	1 077 666	18.5
Saint Helena ex. dep. - Sainte-Hélène sans dép.										
10 II 2008............CDFC		4 257	...	...	2 165	...	...	2 092	...	...
1 VII 2008............ESDF		3 981	...	...	2 022	...	...	1 959	...	...
1 VII 2012............ESDF		4 123	...	...	2 094	...	...	2 029	...	...
31 XII 2013............ESDF		4 211	...	...	2 139	...	...	2 072	...	...
Saint Helena: Ascension - Sainte-Hélène: Ascension										
1 VII 2008............ESDJ		702	...	...	397	...	...	305	...	...
Saint Helena: Tristan da Cunha - Sainte-Hélène: Tristan da Cunha[21]										
31 XII 2009............ESDF		262[22]	...	...	123	...	...	139	...	...
Sao Tome and Principe - Sao Tomé-et-Principe										
1 VII 2006............ESDF		151 912	...	...	74 876	...	...	77 036	...	...
1 VII 2007............ESDF		154 875	...	...	76 256	...	...	78 619	...	...

Continent, country or area, and date / Continent, pays ou zone et date	Code[a]	Both sexes - Les deux sexes			Male - Masculin			Female - Féminin		
		Total	Urban - Urbaine		Total	Urban - Urbaine		Total	Urban - Urbaine	
			Number Nombre	Percent P.100		Number Nombre	Percent P.100		Number Nombre	Percent P.100

AFRICA - AFRIQUE

Sao Tome and Principe - Sao Tomé-et-Principe

1 VII 2008 ....ESDF		157 847	...	...	77 641	...	...	80 206	...	...
1 VII 2009 ....ESDF		160 820	...	...	79 027	...	...	81 794	...	...
1 VII 2010 ....ESDF		163 783	...	...	80 409	...	...	83 375	...	...
1 VII 2011 ....ESDF		166 728	...	...	81 783	...	...	84 945	...	...
13 V 2012 ....CDJC		178 739	119 781	67.0	88 867	58 710	66.1	89 872	61 071	68.0
Senegal - Sénégal										
31 XII 2006 ....ESDJ		11 205 774	4 556 843	40.7	5 515 959	2 259 118	41.0	5 689 815	2 297 725	40.4
31 XII 2007 ....ESDJ		11 519 242	4 684 315	40.7	5 670 261	2 322 314	41.0	5 848 981	2 362 001	40.4
31 XII 2008 ....ESDJ		11 841 137	4 815 214	40.7	5 828 711	2 387 209	41.0	6 012 426	2 428 005	40.4
31 XII 2009 ....ESDJ		12 171 264	4 949 461	40.7	5 991 214	2 453 764	41.0	6 180 050	2 495 697	40.4
31 XII 2010 ....ESDJ		12 509 434	5 086 978	40.7	6 157 675	2 521 940	41.0	6 351 759	2 565 038	40.4
31 XII 2011 ....ESDJ		12 841 702	6 086 966	47.4	6 350 673	3 010 218	47.4	6 491 029	3 076 748	47.4
1 VII 2013[2].................ESDJ		13 508 715	...	...	6 735 420	...	...	6 773 295	...	...
19 XI 2013*.................CDFC		12 873 601	5 824 977	45.2	6 428 189	...	...	6 445 412	...	...
1 VII 2014[2].................ESDJ		13 926 253	...	...	6 941 357	...	...	6 961 847	...	...
1 VII 2015[2].................ESDJ		14 356 575	...	...	7 153 656	...	...	7 202 919	...	...
Seychelles										
1 VII 2006 ....ESDF		84 600	...	...	42 875	...	...	41 725	...	...
1 VII 2007 ....ESDF		85 032	...	...	43 160	...	...	41 872	...	...
1 VII 2008 ....ESDF		86 956	...	...	44 999	...	...	41 957	...	...
1 VII 2009 ....ESDF		87 298	...	...	45 022	...	...	42 276	...	...
1 VII 2010 ....ESDF		89 770	...	...	45 907	...	...	43 863	...	...
26 VIII 2010 ....CDFC		90 945	...	...	46 912	...	...	44 033	...	...
1 VII 2011 ....ESDF		87 441	...	...	43 127	...	...	44 314	...	...
1 VII 2012 ....ESDF		88 303	...	...	43 313	...	...	44 990	...	...
1 VII 2013 ....ESDF		89 949	...	...	44 735	...	...	45 214	...	...
1 VII 2014 ....ESDF		91 359	...	...	45 278	...	...	46 081	...	...
1 VII 2015 ....ESDF		93 419	...	...	46 322	...	...	47 097	...	...
Sierra Leone										
1 VII 2006 ....ESDF		5 216 890	1 999 707	38.3	2 528 430	987 782	39.1	2 688 460	1 011 925	37.6
1 VII 2007 ....ESDF		5 343 200	2 069 160	38.7	2 589 965	1 022 089	39.5	2 753 235	1 047 071	38.0
1 VII 2008 ....ESDF		5 473 530	2 142 918	39.2	2 653 490	1 058 523	39.9	2 820 040	1 084 395	38.5
1 VII 2009 ....ESDF		5 607 930	2 221 331	39.6	2 719 034	1 097 256	40.4	2 888 896	1 124 075	38.9
1 VII 2010 ....ESDF		5 746 800	2 304 955	40.1	2 786 797	1 138 563	40.9	2 960 003	1 166 392	39.4
1 VII 2011 ....ESDF		5 890 080	2 394 041	40.6	2 856 755	1 182 568	41.4	3 033 325	1 211 473	39.9
1 VII 2012 ....ESDF		6 037 660	2 489 123	41.2	2 928 862	1 229 535	42.0	3 108 798	1 259 588	40.5
4 XII 2015*.................CDFC		7 075 641	...	...	3 473 991	...	...	3 601 650	...	...
South Africa - Afrique du Sud										
1 VII 2006 ....ESDF		48 269 753	...	...	23 362 669	...	...	24 907 084	...	...
1 VII 2007 ....ESDF		48 910 248	...	...	23 696 203	...	...	25 214 046	...	...
1 VII 2008 ....ESDF		49 561 256	...	...	24 035 505	...	...	25 525 751	...	...
1 VII 2009 ....ESDF		50 222 996	...	...	24 380 706	...	...	25 842 290	...	...
1 VII 2010 ....ESDF		50 895 698	...	...	24 731 940	...	...	26 163 758	...	...
10 X 2011 ....CDFC		51 770 560	32 559 331	62.9	25 188 791	...	...	26 581 769	...	...
1 VII 2012 ....ESDF		52 274 945	...	...	25 453 074	...	...	26 821 871	...	...
1 VII 2013 ....ESDF		52 981 991	...	...	25 823 270	...	...	27 158 721	...	...
1 VII 2014 ....ESDF		54 001 953	...	...	26 366 008	...	...	27 635 944	...	...
Sudan - Soudan										
21 IV 2008 ....CDFC		30 894 000	...	...	15 786 677	...	...	15 107 323	...	...
1 VII 2008 ....ESDF		30 978 758	10 314 730	33.3	15 790 134	5 350 451	33.9	15 188 624	4 964 279	32.7
1 VII 2009 ....ESDF		31 956 791	10 860 950	34.0	16 275 239	5 531 361	34.0	15 681 552	5 329 589	34.0
1 VII 2010 ....ESDF		32 961 966	11 296 966	34.3	16 774 288	5 749 007	34.3	16 187 678	5 547 959	34.3
1 VII 2011 ....ESDF		33 997 538	11 749 240	34.6	17 289 105	5 974 957	34.6	16 708 434	5 774 283	34.6
1 VII 2012 ....ESDF		35 064 299	12 218 313	34.8	17 820 009	6 209 462	34.8	17 244 290	6 008 851	34.8
1 VII 2013 ....ESDF		36 162 516	12 704 550	35.1	18 367 086	6 452 691	35.1	17 795 430	6 251 858	35.1
1 VII 2014 ....ESDF		37 292 376	13 208 281	35.4	18 930 385	6 704 798	35.4	18 361 991	6 503 483	35.4
1 VII 2015 ....ESDF		38 454 040	13 729 842	35.7	19 509 961	6 965 944	35.7	18 944 080	6 763 898	35.7
Swaziland										
11 III 2007.................CDFC		844 223	186 890	22.1	405 868	93 918	23.1	438 355	92 972	21.2
1 VII 2007 ....ESDF		1 018 449	225 293	22.1	481 428	108 071	22.4	537 021	117 222	21.8
1 VII 2008 ....ESDF		1 031 747	229 516	22.2	488 132	109 937	22.5	543 615	119 579	22.0
1 VII 2009 ....ESDF		1 043 509	233 504	22.4	494 061	111 704	22.6	549 448	121 800	22.2

Continent, country or area, and date / Continent, pays ou zone et date	Code[a]	Both sexes - Les deux sexes			Male - Masculin			Female - Féminin		
		Total	Urban - Urbaine		Total	Urban - Urbaine		Total	Urban - Urbaine	
			Number Nombre	Percent P.100		Number Nombre	Percent P.100		Number Nombre	Percent P.100
AFRICA - AFRIQUE										
Swaziland										
1 VII 2010 ....ESDF		1 055 506	237 641	22.5	500 070	113 554	22.7	555 436	124 087	22.3
1 VII 2011 ....ESDF		1 067 773	241 947	22.7	506 186	115 493	22.8	561 587	126 454	22.5
1 VII 2012 ....ESDF		1 080 337	246 441	22.8	512 432	117 528	22.9	567 905	128 913	22.7
1 VII 2013 ....ESDF		1 093 158	251 122	23.0	518 788	119 658	23.1	574 370	131 464	22.9
1 VII 2014 ....ESDF		1 106 189	255 986	23.1	525 232	121 881	23.2	580 957	134 105	23.1
1 I 2015 ....ESDF		1 119 375	261 028	23.3	531 737	124 195	23.4	587 638	136 833	23.3
Togo										
6 XI 2010 ....CDJC		6 191 155	2 334 495	37.7	3 009 095	1 131 533	37.6	3 182 060	1 202 962	37.8
Tunisia - Tunisie										
1 VII 2006 ....ESDF		10 127 900	...	...	5 062 100	...	...	5 065 800	...	...
1 VII 2007 ....ESDF		10 225 100	...	...	5 105 100	...	...	5 120 000	...	...
1 VII 2008 ....ESDF		10 328 900	...	...	5 156 300	...	...	5 172 600	...	...
1 VII 2009 ....ESDF		10 439 600	...	...	5 207 200	...	...	5 232 400	...	...
1 VII 2010 ....ESDF		10 547 100	...	...	5 261 700	...	...	5 285 400	...	...
1 VII 2011 ....ESDF		10 673 800	...	...	5 316 900	...	...	5 356 800	...	...
23 IV 2014 ....CDFC		10 982 754	7 437 671	67.7	5 472 338	3 713 527	67.9	5 510 416	3 724 144	67.6
Uganda - Ouganda										
1 VII 2006 ....ESDF		27 629 300	4 084 700	14.8	13 386 100	1 953 300	14.6	14 243 200	2 131 400	15.0
1 VII 2007 ....ESDF		28 581 300	4 223 800	14.8	13 866 700	2 022 200	14.6	14 714 600	2 201 600	15.0
1 VII 2008 ....ESDF		29 592 600	4 372 000	14.8	14 383 200	2 095 700	14.6	15 209 400	2 276 300	15.0
1 VII 2009 ....ESDF		30 661 300	4 524 900	14.8	14 933 900	2 171 400	14.5	15 727 400	2 353 500	15.0
1 VII 2010 ....ESDF		31 784 600	...	...	15 516 600	...	...	16 268 000	...	...
1 VII 2011 ....ESDF		32 939 800	...	...	16 118 600	...	...	16 821 200	...	...
1 VII 2012 ....ESDF		34 131 400	...	...	16 741 400	...	...	17 390 000	...	...
27 VIII 2014 ....CDFC		34 634 650	7 425 864	21.4	17 060 832	...	...	17 573 818	...	...
United Republic of Tanzania - République Unie de Tanzanie										
1 VII 2006[23] ....ESDF		38 250 927	9 518 688	24.9	18 748 743	4 691 158	25.0	19 502 184	4 827 530	24.8
1 VII 2007[23] ....ESDF		39 446 061	9 962 731	25.3	19 352 480	4 911 847	25.4	20 093 581	5 050 884	25.1
1 VII 2008[23] ....ESDF		40 667 794	10 419 287	25.6	19 970 944	5 139 187	25.7	20 696 850	5 280 100	25.5
1 VII 2009[23] ....ESDF		41 915 880	10 892 350	26.0	20 604 730	5 375 260	26.1	21 311 150	5 517 090	25.9
1 VII 2010[23] ....ESDF		43 187 823	11 378 015	26.3	21 252 423	5 618 133	26.4	21 935 400	5 759 882	26.3
1 VII 2011[23] ....ESDF		44 484 857	11 875 395	26.7	21 914 229	5 867 287	26.8	22 570 628	6 008 108	26.6
1 VII 2012[23] ....ESDF		45 798 475	12 386 841	27.0	22 585 634	6 123 839	27.1	23 212 841	6 263 002	27.0
26 VIII 2012[24] ....CDFC		44 928 923	13 305 004	29.6	21 869 990	6 407 396	29.3	23 058 933	6 897 608	29.9
1 VII 2013[20] ....ESDF		46 170 154	...	...	22 475 187	...	...	23 694 967	...	...
1 VII 2014[20] ....ESDF		47 451 844	...	...	23 100 125	...	...	24 351 719	...	...
1 VII 2015[20] ....ESDF		48 775 567	...	...	23 745 563	...	...	25 030 004	...	...
Zambia - Zambie										
16 X 2010 ....CDFC		12 526 314	5 021 022	40.1	6 117 253	2 452 904	40.1	6 409 061	2 568 118	40.1
Zimbabwe										
1 VII 2006[23] ....ESDF		11 930 000	4 133 066	34.6	5 778 621	2 039 146	35.3	6 151 379	2 093 919	34.0
1 VII 2007[23] ....ESDF		12 040 000	4 171 175	34.6	5 831 902	2 057 948	35.3	6 208 098	2 113 226	34.0
1 VII 2008[23] ....ESDF		12 150 000	3 495 205	28.8	5 885 184	1 691 434	28.7	6 264 816	1 803 752	28.8
1 VII 2009[23] ....ESDF		13 667 894	...	...	6 642 551	...	...	7 025 344	...	...
17 VIII 2012 ....CDFC		13 061 239	4 284 145	32.8	6 280 539	2 039 224	32.5	6 780 700	2 244 921	33.1
1 VII 2013[20] ....ESDF		13 368 620	...	...	6 428 233	...	...	6 940 389	...	...
1 VII 2014[20] ....ESDF		13 652 297	...	...	6 564 085	...	...	7 088 214	...	...
1 VII 2015[20] ....ESDF		13 943 242	...	...	6 703 559	...	...	7 239 681	...	...
AMERICA, NORTH - AMÉRIQUE DU NORD										
Anguilla										
11 V 2011 ....CDFC		13 572	...	...	6 707	...	...	6 865	...	...
Antigua and Barbuda - Antigua-et-Barbuda										
1 VII 2006 ....ESDF		84 330	...	...	39 603	...	...	44 727	...	...
1 VII 2007 ....ESDF		85 903	...	...	40 342	...	...	45 561	...	...
27 V 2011 ....CDJC		85 567	...	...	40 986	...	...	44 581	...	...

Continent, country or area, and date / Continent, pays ou zone et date	Code[a]	Both sexes - Les deux sexes			Male - Masculin			Female - Féminin		
		Total	Urban - Urbaine		Total	Urban - Urbaine		Total	Urban - Urbaine	
			Number Nombre	Percent P.100		Number Nombre	Percent P.100		Number Nombre	Percent P.100
AMERICA, NORTH - AMÉRIQUE DU NORD										
Aruba										
1 VII 2006	ESDJ	99 405	...	...	47 189	...	...	52 216	...	...
1 VII 2007	ESDJ	100 149	...	...	47 490	...	...	52 660	...	...
1 VII 2008	ESDJ	100 916	...	...	47 890	...	...	53 027	...	...
1 VII 2009	ESDJ	101 604	...	...	48 291	...	...	53 312	...	...
1 VII 2010	ESDJ	101 873	...	...	48 419	...	...	53 454	...	...
29 IX 2010	CDJC	101 484	...	...	48 241	...	...	53 243	...	...
1 VII 2011	ESDJ	102 809	...	...	48 801	...	...	54 008	...	...
1 VII 2012	ESDJ	104 574	...	...	49 558	...	...	55 016	...	...
1 VII 2013	ESDJ	106 390	...	...	50 334	...	...	56 056	...	...
1 VII 2014	ESDJ	107 839	...	...	50 999	...	...	56 840	...	...
1 VII 2015	ESDJ	109 241	...	...	51 691	...	...	57 550	...	...
Bahamas										
1 VII 2006[2]	ESDF	329 500	...	...	160 100	...	...	169 400	...	...
1 VII 2007[2]	ESDF	334 000	...	...	162 300	...	...	171 700	...	...
1 VII 2008[2]	ESDF	338 300	...	...	164 800	...	...	173 500	...	...
1 VII 2009[2]	ESDF	342 400	...	...	166 800	...	...	175 600	...	...
3 V 2010	CDJC	351 461	...	...	170 257	...	...	181 204	...	...
1 VII 2010[2]	ESDF	334 642	...	...	162 730	...	...	171 911	...	...
1 VII 2011[2]	ESDF	357 750	...	...	175 029	...	...	182 721	...	...
1 VII 2012[2]	ESDF	362 590	...	...	177 440	...	...	185 150	...	...
1 VII 2013[2]	ESDF	368 390	...	...	179 850	...	...	188 540	...	...
1 VII 2014[2]	ESDF	372 000	...	...	182 000	...	...	190 000	...	...
Barbados - Barbade										
1 VII 2006	ESDF	273 428	...	...	131 916	...	...	141 512	...	...
1 VII 2007	ESDF	274 162	...	...	132 388	...	...	141 774	...	...
1 VII 2008	ESDF	274 848	...	...	132 786	...	...	142 062	...	...
1 VII 2009	ESDF	275 441	...	...	133 133	...	...	142 308	...	...
1 V 2010	CDJC	277 821	...	...	133 018	...	...	144 803	...	...
1 VII 2010	ESDF	277 758	...	...	133 018	...	...	144 740	...	...
1 VII 2011	ESDF	277 622	...	...	133 119	...	...	144 503	...	...
1 VII 2012	ESDF	277 668	...	...	133 355	...	...	144 313	...	...
1 VII 2013	ESDF	277 492	...	...	133 369	...	...	144 123	...	...
1 VII 2014	ESDF	277 199	...	...	133 343	...	...	143 856	...	...
1 VII 2015	ESDF	274 633	...	...	131 146	...	...	143 487	...	...
Belize										
1 VII 2006	ESDF	301 386	152 583	50.6	149 676	73 495	49.1	151 710	79 089	52.1
1 VII 2008	ESDF	306 809	138 716	45.2	153 570	67 647	44.0	153 239	71 069	46.4
1 VII 2009	ESDF	315 082	142 447	45.2	157 622	69 450	44.1	157 460	72 997	46.4
12 V 2010	CDJC	322 453	145 832	45.2	161 227	71 087	44.1	161 226	74 745	46.4
1 VII 2010	ESDF	323 598	146 322	45.2	161 800	71 328	44.1	161 798	74 995	46.4
1 VII 2011	ESDF	332 084	149 955	45.2	166 043	73 110	44.0	166 041	76 845	46.3
1 VII 2012	ESDF	340 792	153 683	45.1	170 397	74 938	44.0	170 395	78 745	46.2
1 VII 2013	ESDF	349 728	157 508	45.0	174 865	76 815	43.9	174 863	80 693	46.1
1 VII 2014	ESDF	358 899	161 434	45.0	179 451	78 741	43.9	179 448	82 693	46.1
1 VII 2015	ESDF	368 310	165 463	44.9	184 157	80 717	43.8	184 153	84 746	46.0
Bermuda - Bermudes										
1 VII 2006[25]	ESDJ	63 797	...	...	30 504	...	...	33 293	...	...
1 VII 2007[25]	ESDJ	64 009	...	...	30 577	...	...	33 432	...	...
1 VII 2008[25]	ESDJ	64 209	...	...	30 644	...	...	33 565	...	...
1 VII 2009[25]	ESDJ	64 395	...	...	30 704	...	...	33 691	...	...
20 V 2010[26]	CDJC	64 237	64 237	100.0	30 858	30 858	100.0	33 379	33 379	100.0
1 VII 2010[27]	ESDJ	64 129	...	...	30 792	...	...	33 337	...	...
1 VII 2011[27]	ESDJ	63 193	...	...	30 218	...	...	32 975	...	...
1 VII 2012[27]	ESDJ	62 408	...	...	29 819	...	...	32 589	...	...
1 VII 2013[27]	ESDJ	61 954	...	...	29 587	...	...	32 367	...	...
1 VII 2014[27]	ESDJ	61 777	...	...	29 499	...	...	32 278	...	...
1 VII 2015[27]	ESDJ	61 735	...	...	29 480	...	...	32 255	...	...
Canada										
16 V 2006[28]	CDJC	31 612 895	25 350 585	80.2	15 475 970	12 289 025	79.4	16 136 930	13 061 560	80.9
1 VII 2006[29]	ESDJ	32 570 505	...	...	16 144 446	...	...	16 426 059	...	...
1 VII 2007[29]	ESDJ	32 887 928	...	...	16 298 320	...	...	16 589 608	...	...
1 VII 2008[29]	ESDJ	33 245 773	...	...	16 473 545	...	...	16 772 228	...	...
1 VII 2009[29]	ESDJ	33 628 571	...	...	16 663 222	...	...	16 965 349	...	...

Continent, country or area, and date / Continent, pays ou zone et date	Code[a]	Both sexes - Les deux sexes			Male - Masculin			Female - Féminin		
		Total	Urban - Urbaine		Total	Urban - Urbaine		Total	Urban - Urbaine	
			Number Nombre	Percent P.100		Number Nombre	Percent P.100		Number Nombre	Percent P.100
AMERICA, NORTH - AMÉRIQUE DU NORD										
Canada										
1 VII 2010[29] .... ESDJ		34 005 274	...	...	16 847 961	...	...	17 157 313	...	...
2 V 2011 .... CDJC		33 476 690	27 147 190	81.1	16 414 225	13 190 225	80.4	17 062 455	13 956 960	81.8
1 VII 2011[30] .... ESDJ		34 342 780	...	...	17 015 959	...	...	17 326 821	...	...
1 VII 2012[30] .... ESDJ		34 750 545	...	...	17 227 368	...	...	17 523 177	...	...
1 VII 2013[31] .... ESDJ		35 155 451	...	...	17 433 972	...	...	17 721 479	...	...
1 VII 2014[31] .... ESDJ		35 544 564	...	...	17 629 788	...	...	17 914 776	...	...
1 VII 2015[31] .... ESDJ		35 848 610	...	...	17 776 946	...	...	18 071 664	...	...
Cayman Islands - Îles Caïmanes										
31 XII 2006 .... ESDJ		51 992	...	...	26 340	...	...	25 652	...	...
31 XII 2007 .... ESDJ		53 886	...	...	26 773	...	...	27 113	...	...
31 XII 2008 .... ESDJ		57 009	...	...	28 264	...	...	28 745	...	...
31 XII 2009 .... ESDJ		56 005	...	...	27 840	...	...	28 165	...	...
10 X 2010[32] .... CDJC		55 036	55 036	100.0	27 218	27 218	100.0	27 818	27 818	100.0
31 XII 2010 .... ESDJ		55 036	...	...	27 219	...	...	27 817	...	...
31 XII 2011 .... ESDJ		55 517	...	...	27 454	...	...	28 063	...	...
31 XII 2012 .... ESDJ		56 732	...	...	27 753	...	...	28 979	...	...
31 XII 2013 .... ESDJ		55 747	...	...	27 133	...	...	28 614	...	...
31 XII 2014 .... ESDJ		58 238	...	...	28 322	...	...	29 916	...	...
31 XII 2015 .... ESDJ		60 413	...	...	30 264	...	...	30 149	...	...
Costa Rica										
1 VII 2006 .... ESDJ		4 353 843	2 567 797	59.0	2 146 610	1 243 202	57.9	2 207 233	1 324 595	60.0
1 VII 2007 .... ESDJ		4 443 100	2 619 591	59.0	2 195 652	1 273 998	58.0	2 247 448	1 345 593	59.9
1 VII 2008[33] .... ESDJ		4 533 162	2 671 667	58.9	2 246 474	1 299 940	57.9	2 286 688	1 371 727	60.0
1 VII 2009[33] .... ESDJ		4 620 482	2 722 273	58.9	2 291 886	1 325 468	57.8	2 328 596	1 396 805	60.0
1 VII 2010[34] .... ESDJ		4 538 307	3 304 248	72.8	2 206 526	1 579 816	71.6	2 331 781	1 724 432	74.0
30 V 2011 .... CDJC		4 301 712	3 130 871	72.8	2 106 063	1 509 161	71.7	2 195 649	1 621 710	73.9
1 VII 2011[34] .... ESDJ		4 592 346	3 343 241	72.8	2 238 615	1 603 354	71.6	2 353 731	1 739 887	73.9
1 VII 2012[34] .... ESDJ		4 651 166	3 384 925	72.8	2 266 220	1 621 617	71.6	2 384 946	1 763 308	73.9
1 VII 2013[34] .... ESDJ		4 711 986	3 427 548	72.7	2 276 708	1 624 941	71.4	2 435 278	1 802 607	74.0
1 VII 2014[34] .... ESDJ		4 772 098	3 469 802	72.7	2 325 438	1 662 288	71.5	2 446 660	1 807 514	73.9
1 VII 2015[35] .... ESDJ		4 833 752	3 512 683	72.7	2 350 223	1 683 770	71.6	2 483 529	1 828 913	73.6
Cuba										
1 VII 2006 .... ESDJ		11 210 628	8 466 895	75.5	5 613 921	4 165 162	74.2	5 596 706	4 301 733	76.9
1 VII 2007 .... ESDJ		11 195 330	8 446 381	75.4	5 605 756	4 155 581	74.1	5 589 574	4 290 800	76.8
1 VII 2008 .... ESDJ		11 181 012	8 426 393	75.4	5 597 673	4 146 862	74.1	5 583 339	4 279 531	76.6
1 VII 2009 .... ESDJ		11 174 474	8 420 630	75.4	5 594 504	4 145 111	74.1	5 579 971	4 275 519	76.6
1 VII 2010 .... ESDJ		11 171 443	8 416 524	75.3	5 592 729	4 143 388	74.1	5 578 714	4 273 136	76.6
1 VII 2011 .... ESDJ		11 171 679	8 409 543	75.3	5 592 332	4 140 377	74.0	5 579 347	4 269 166	76.5
1 VII 2012 .... ESDJ		11 174 287	8 494 128	76.0	5 583 306	4 159 342	74.5	5 590 981	4 334 786	77.5
14 IX 2012 .... CDFC		11 167 325	8 575 189	76.8	5 570 825	4 177 485	75.0	5 596 500	4 397 704	78.6
1 VII 2013 .... ESDJ		11 191 608	8 596 991	76.8	5 580 810	4 186 436	75.0	5 610 798	4 410 555	78.6
1 VII 2014 .... ESDJ		11 224 190	8 625 144	76.8	5 595 379	4 199 578	75.1	5 628 811	4 425 566	78.6
1 VII 2015 .... ESDJ		11 238 661	8 639 191	76.9	5 600 904	4 205 871	75.1	5 637 757	4 433 320	78.6
Curaçao										
1 VII 2006[36] .... ESDJ		141 249	...	...	64 679	...	...	76 570	...	...
1 VII 2007[36] .... ESDJ		144 061	...	...	65 952	...	...	78 109	...	...
1 VII 2008[36] .... ESDJ		145 882	...	...	66 746	...	...	79 136	...	...
1 VII 2009[36] .... ESDJ		146 833	...	...	67 237	...	...	79 596	...	...
1 VII 2010[36] .... ESDJ		148 703	...	...	68 065	...	...	80 639	...	...
26 III 2011 .... CDFC		150 563	...	...	68 848	...	...	81 715	...	...
1 VII 2011[36] .... ESDJ		150 831	...	...	68 910	...	...	81 921	...	...
1 VII 2012[37] .... ESDJ		152 088	...	...	69 490	...	...	82 598	...	...
1 VII 2013[37] .... ESDJ		153 821	...	...	70 342	...	...	83 479	...	...
1 VII 2014[37] .... ESDJ		155 909	...	...	71 269	...	...	84 640	...	...
1 VII 2015[37] .... ESDJ		157 979	...	...	72 186	...	...	85 793	...	...
Dominica - Dominique										
1 VII 2006 .... ESDF		70 693	...	...	35 585	...	...	35 108	...	...
1 VII 2007 .... ESDF		70 729	...	...	35 603	...	...	35 126	...	...
1 VII 2008 .... ESDF		70 726	...	...	35 602	...	...	35 124	...	...
1 VII 2009 .... ESDF		70 747	...	...	35 811	...	...	34 936	...	...
1 VII 2010 .... ESDF		70 730	...	...	35 604	...	...	35 126	...	...
14 V 2011* .... CDFC		71 293	...	...	36 411	...	...	34 882	...	...

6. Total and urban population by sex: 2006 - 2015
Population totale et population urbaine selon le sexe : 2006 - 2015 (continued - suite)

Continent, country or area, and date / Continent, pays ou zone et date	Code[a]	Both sexes - Les deux sexes Total	Urban - Urbaine Number Nombre	Urban - Urbaine Percent P.100	Male - Masculin Total	Urban - Urbaine Number Nombre	Urban - Urbaine Percent P.100	Female - Féminin Total	Urban - Urbaine Number Nombre	Urban - Urbaine Percent P.100
AMERICA, NORTH - AMÉRIQUE DU NORD										
Dominica - Dominique										
1 VII 2011 .... ESDF		70 755	...	...	35 762	...	...	34 992	...	...
1 VII 2012 .... ESDF		71 042	...	...	36 053	...	...	34 989	...	...
1 VII 2013 .... ESDF		71 221	...	...	36 144	...	...	35 077	...	...
1 VII 2014 .... ESDF		71 575	...	...	36 324	...	...	35 251	...	...
Dominican Republic - République dominicaine										
1 VII 2006 .... ESDF		9 071 458	6 209 005	68.4	4 547 998	3 044 805	66.9	4 523 460	3 164 200	70.0
1 VII 2007 .... ESDF		9 174 058	6 399 362	69.8	4 598 212	3 138 848	68.3	4 575 846	3 260 514	71.3
1 VII 2008 .... ESDF		9 279 602	6 594 497	71.1	4 649 902	3 235 238	69.6	4 629 700	3 359 259	72.6
1 VII 2009 .... ESDF		9 380 152	6 788 782	72.4	4 699 042	3 331 179	70.9	4 681 110	3 457 603	73.9
1 VII 2010[2] .... ESDF		9 478 612	6 992 189	73.8	4 747 103	3 431 480	72.3	4 731 509	3 560 709	75.3
1 XII 2010 .... CDJC		9 445 281	7 013 575	74.3	4 739 038	3 449 122	72.8	4 706 243	3 564 453	75.7
1 VII 2011[2] .... ESDF		9 580 139	7 172 502	74.9	4 796 628	3 520 702	73.4	4 783 511	3 651 800	76.3
1 VII 2012[2] .... ESDF		9 680 963	7 348 975	75.9	4 845 755	3 608 025	74.5	4 835 208	3 740 950	77.4
1 VII 2013[2] .... ESDF		9 784 680	7 524 149	76.9	4 896 319	3 694 713	75.5	4 888 361	3 829 436	78.3
1 VII 2014[2] .... ESDF		9 883 486	7 691 885	77.8	4 944 386	3 777 718	76.4	4 939 100	3 914 167	79.2
1 VII 2015[2] .... ESDF		9 980 243	7 854 203	78.7	4 991 398	3 858 029	77.3	4 988 845	3 996 174	80.1
El Salvador										
1 VII 2006[38] .... ESDF		6 073 859	3 706 525	61.0	2 881 162	1 726 983	59.9	3 192 697	1 979 542	62.0
12 V 2007 .... CDJC		5 744 113	3 598 836	62.7	2 719 371	1 676 313	61.6	3 024 742	1 922 523	63.6
1 VII 2007[38] .... ESDF		6 098 714	3 766 800	61.8	2 887 804	1 752 851	60.7	3 210 910	2 013 949	62.7
1 VII 2008[38] .... ESDF		6 124 705	3 828 004	62.5	2 895 210	1 779 210	61.5	3 229 495	2 048 794	63.4
1 VII 2009[38] .... ESDF		6 152 558	3 890 523	63.2	2 903 737	1 806 310	62.2	3 248 821	2 084 213	64.2
1 VII 2010[38] .... ESDF		6 183 002	3 954 803	64.0	2 913 743	1 834 400	63.0	3 269 259	2 120 404	64.9
1 VII 2011[38] .... ESDF		6 216 143	4 019 742	64.7	2 925 284	1 862 924	63.7	3 290 858	2 156 818	65.5
1 VII 2012[38] .... ESDF		6 251 495	4 086 880	65.4	2 938 123	1 892 642	64.4	3 313 372	2 194 238	66.2
1 VII 2013[38] .... ESDF		6 288 899	4 156 007	66.1	2 952 174	1 923 447	65.2	3 336 726	2 232 560	66.9
1 VII 2014[38] .... ESDF		6 328 196	...	...	2 967 351	...	...	3 360 845	...	...
1 VII 2015[38] .... ESDF		6 460 271	4 502 693	69.7	3 042 036	2 119 867	69.7	3 418 235	2 382 826	69.7
Greenland - Groenland[39]										
1 VII 2006 .... ESDJ		56 775	47 037	82.8	30 094	24 763	82.3	26 681	22 274	83.5
1 VII 2007 .... ESDJ		56 555	47 056	83.2	29 945	24 746	82.6	26 610	22 310	83.8
1 I 2008 .... CDJC		56 462	...	...	29 885	...	...	26 577	...	...
1 VII 2008 .... ESDJ		56 328	47 103	83.6	29 847	24 790	83.1	26 481	22 313	84.3
1 VII 2009 .... ESDJ		56 323	47 230	83.9	29 873	24 865	83.2	26 451	22 366	84.6
1 VII 2010 .... ESDJ		56 534	47 646	84.3	29 939	25 045	83.7	26 595	22 601	85.0
1 VII 2011 .... ESDJ		56 682	48 045	84.8	29 992	25 233	84.1	26 690	22 812	85.5
1 VII 2012 .... ESDJ		56 810	48 224	84.9	30 105	25 331	84.1	26 705	22 893	85.7
1 VII 2013 .... ESDJ		56 483	48 221	85.4	29 867	25 333	84.8	26 616	22 888	86.0
1 VII 2014 .... ESDJ		56 295	48 232	85.7	29 742	25 320	85.1	26 553	22 912	86.3
1 VII 2015 .... ESDJ		56 114	48 284	86.0	29 634	25 329	85.5	26 480	22 955	86.7
Grenada - Grenade										
1 VII 2006 .... ESDF		104 708	...	...	52 310	...	...	52 398	...	...
1 VII 2007 .... ESDF		104 981	...	...	52 472	...	...	52 509	...	...
1 VII 2008 .... ESDF		105 298	...	...	52 655	...	...	52 643	...	...
1 VII 2009 .... ESDF		105 175	...	...	52 720	...	...	52 455	...	...
1 VII 2010 .... ESDF		105 038	...	...	52 788	...	...	52 250	...	...
1 VII 2011 .... ESDF		106 667	...	...	53 898	...	...	52 769	...	...
1 VII 2012 .... ESDF		107 599	...	...	54 435	...	...	53 164	...	...
1 VII 2013 .... ESDF		108 580	...	...	54 926	...	...	53 654	...	...
Guadeloupe[40]										
1 I 2006 .... CDJC		400 736	...	...	188 720	...	...	212 016	...	...
1 I 2007 .... ESDJ		400 584	...	...	188 325	...	...	212 259	...	...
1 I 2008 .... ESDJ		401 784	...	...	188 389	...	...	213 395	...	...
1 I 2009 .... ESDJ		401 554	...	...	187 867	...	...	213 687	...	...
1 I 2010 .... CDJC		403 355	397 070	98.4	187 932	184 752	98.3	215 423	212 318	98.6
1 I 2011 .... ESDJ		404 635	...	...	187 782	...	...	216 853	...	...
1 I 2012 .... ESDJ		403 314	...	...	187 038	...	...	216 276	...	...
1 I 2013 .... ESDJ		402 119	...	...	186 077	...	...	216 042	...	...
1 I 2014* .... ESDJ		401 337	...	...	185 183	...	...	216 154	...	...
1 I 2015* .... ESDJ		400 132	...	...	184 093	...	...	216 039	...	...

Continent, country or area, and date / Continent, pays ou zone et date	Code[a]	Both sexes - Les deux sexes Total	Urban - Urbaine Number Nombre	Urban - Urbaine Percent P.100	Male - Masculin Total	Urban - Urbaine Number Nombre	Urban - Urbaine Percent P.100	Female - Féminin Total	Urban - Urbaine Number Nombre	Urban - Urbaine Percent P.100
AMERICA, NORTH - AMÉRIQUE DU NORD										
Guatemala[23]										
1 VII 2008 ....ESDF	ESDF	13 677 815	...	...	6 673 533	...	...	7 004 282	...	...
1 VII 2009 ....ESDF	ESDF	14 017 057	...	...	6 836 849	...	...	7 180 208	...	...
1 VII 2010 ....ESDF	ESDF	14 361 666	...	...	7 003 337	...	...	7 358 328	...	...
Haiti - Haïti[41]										
1 VII 2006 ....ESDJ	ESDJ	9 445 410	...	...	4 673 089	...	...	4 772 321	...	...
1 VII 2007 ....ESDJ	ESDJ	9 602 304	...	...	4 751 622	...	...	4 850 682	...	...
1 VII 2008 ....ESDJ	ESDJ	9 761 927	...	...	4 831 621	...	...	4 930 306	...	...
1 VII 2009 ....ESDJ	ESDJ	9 923 243	...	...	4 912 515	...	...	5 010 728	...	...
1 VII 2010 ....ESDJ	ESDJ	10 085 214	4 817 666	47.8	4 993 731	2 321 608	46.5	5 091 483	2 496 059	49.0
1 VII 2011 ....ESDJ	ESDJ	10 248 306	...	...	5 075 517	...	...	5 172 789	...	...
1 VII 2012 ....ESDJ	ESDJ	10 413 211	5 154 940	49.5	5 158 254	2 495 108	48.4	5 254 957	2 659 832	50.6
Honduras										
1 VII 2006[42] ....ESDF	ESDF	7 367 021	3 628 228	49.2	3 634 900	1 733 290	47.7	3 732 121	1 894 938	50.8
1 VII 2007[42] ....ESDF	ESDF	7 536 952	3 752 579	49.8	3 717 577	1 793 588	48.2	3 819 375	1 958 991	51.3
1 VII 2008[42] ....ESDF	ESDF	7 706 907	...	...	3 800 300	...	...	3 906 607	...	...
1 VII 2009[42] ....ESDF	ESDF	7 876 662	...	...	3 882 957	...	...	3 993 705	...	...
1 VII 2010[42] ....ESDF	ESDF	8 045 990	...	...	3 965 430	...	...	4 080 560	...	...
10 VIII 2013 ....CDFC	CDFC	8 303 771	4 480 746	54.0	4 052 316	2 116 113	52.2	4 251 456	2 364 633	55.6
1 VII 2014[3] ....ESDF	ESDF	8 432 153	...	...	4 113 061	...	...	4 319 092	...	...
1 VII 2015[3] ....ESDF	ESDF	8 576 532	...	...	4 181 657	...	...	4 394 875	...	...
Jamaica - Jamaïque										
1 VII 2006 ....ESDJ	ESDJ	2 663 106	1 384 145	52.0	1 312 025	660 763	50.4	1 351 081	723 383	53.5
1 VII 2007 ....ESDJ	ESDJ	2 675 831	1 390 754	52.0	1 318 444	663 995	50.4	1 357 387	726 759	53.5
1 VII 2008 ....ESDJ	ESDJ	2 687 241	1 396 470	52.0	1 324 277	666 761	50.3	1 362 964	729 709	53.5
1 VII 2009 ....ESDJ	ESDJ	2 695 583	...	...	1 328 124	...	...	1 367 460	...	...
1 VII 2010 ....ESDJ	ESDJ	2 702 314	...	...	1 324 134	...	...	1 378 180	...	...
4 IV 2011[43] ....CDJC	CDJC	2 697 983	1 454 153	53.9	1 334 533	700 957	52.5	1 363 450	753 196	55.2
1 VII 2011 ....ESDJ	ESDJ	2 699 838	...	...	1 335 466	...	...	1 364 372	...	...
1 VII 2012 ....ESDJ	ESDJ	2 707 805	...	...	1 339 740	...	...	1 368 065	...	...
1 VII 2013 ....ESDJ	ESDJ	2 714 669	...	...	1 343 798	...	...	1 370 871	...	...
1 VII 2014 ....ESDJ	ESDJ	2 720 554	...	...	1 346 711	...	...	1 373 843	...	...
Martinique										
1 I 2006 ....CDJC	CDJC	397 732	355 189	89.3	185 604	165 012	88.9	212 128	190 177	89.7
1 I 2007 ....ESDJ	ESDJ	397 730	...	...	184 970	...	...	212 760	...	...
1 I 2008 ....ESDJ	ESDJ	397 693	...	...	184 437	...	...	213 256	...	...
1 I 2009 ....ESDJ	ESDJ	396 404	...	...	183 655	...	...	212 749	...	...
1 I 2010 ....CDJC	CDJC	394 173	380 973	96.7	182 073	175 573	96.4	212 100	205 400	96.8
1 I 2011 ....ESDJ	ESDJ	392 291	...	...	180 676	...	...	211 615	...	...
1 I 2012 ....ESDJ	ESDJ	388 364	...	...	178 824	...	...	209 540	...	...
1 I 2013 ....ESDJ	ESDJ	385 551	...	...	177 955	...	...	207 596	...	...
1 I 2014* ....ESDJ	ESDJ	381 999	...	...	176 110	...	...	205 889	...	...
1 I 2015* ....ESDJ	ESDJ	378 243	...	...	174 193	...	...	204 050	...	...
Mexico - Mexique										
1 VII 2006 ....ESDJ	ESDJ	108 408 827	...	...	53 011 285	...	...	55 397 542	...	...
1 VII 2007 ....ESDJ	ESDJ	109 787 388	...	...	53 646 464	...	...	56 140 924	...	...
1 VII 2008 ....ESDJ	ESDJ	111 299 015	...	...	54 373 653	...	...	56 925 362	...	...
1 VII 2009 ....ESDJ	ESDJ	112 852 594	...	...	55 144 845	...	...	57 707 749	...	...
12 VI 2010[44] ....CDFC	CDFC	112 336 538	86 287 410	76.8	54 855 231	41 946 540	76.5	57 481 307	44 340 870	77.1
1 VII 2010[2] ....ESDJ	ESDJ	114 255 555	82 629 456	72.3	55 801 919	...	...	58 453 636	...	...
1 VII 2011[2] ....ESDJ	ESDJ	115 682 868	83 726 767	72.4	56 519 798	...	...	59 163 070	...	...
1 VII 2012[2] ....ESDJ	ESDJ	117 053 750	84 776 446	72.4	57 174 268	...	...	59 879 482	...	...
1 VII 2013[2] ....ESDJ	ESDJ	118 395 054	85 792 843	72.5	57 810 955	...	...	60 584 099	...	...
1 VII 2014[2] ....ESDJ	ESDJ	119 713 203	86 782 031	72.5	58 435 900	...	...	61 277 304	...	...
1 VII 2015[2] ....ESDJ	ESDJ	121 005 815	87 743 091	72.5	59 046 837	...	...	61 958 979	...	...
Montserrat										
12 V 2011 ....CDJC	CDJC	4 922	...	...	2 546	...	...	2 376	...	...
Nicaragua										
1 VII 2006 ....ESDJ	ESDJ	5 522 606	3 099 918	56.1	2 741 414	1 488 694	54.3	2 781 192	1 611 224	57.9
1 VII 2007 ....ESDJ	ESDJ	5 595 541	3 152 807	56.3	2 775 638	1 515 432	54.6	2 819 903	1 637 375	58.1
1 VII 2008 ....ESDJ	ESDJ	5 668 866	3 206 205	56.6	2 809 918	1 542 386	54.9	2 858 948	1 663 819	58.2
1 VII 2009 ....ESDJ	ESDJ	5 742 316	3 259 955	56.8	2 844 244	1 569 555	55.2	2 898 072	1 690 400	58.3

Continent, country or area, and date / Continent, pays ou zone et date	Code[a]	Both sexes - Les deux sexes			Male - Masculin			Female - Féminin		
		Total	Urban - Urbaine		Total	Urban - Urbaine		Total	Urban - Urbaine	
			Number Nombre	Percent P.100		Number Nombre	Percent P.100		Number Nombre	Percent P.100
AMERICA, NORTH - AMÉRIQUE DU NORD										
Panama										
1 VII 2006[27] ....ESDF		3 413 399	...	...	1 718 193	...	...	1 695 206	...	...
1 VII 2007[27] ....ESDF		3 475 741	...	...	1 749 211	...	...	1 726 530	...	...
1 VII 2008[27] ....ESDF		3 537 986	...	...	1 780 140	...	...	1 757 846	...	...
1 VII 2009[27] ....ESDF		3 600 000	...	...	1 810 794	...	...	1 789 206	...	...
16 V 2010 ....CDFC		3 405 813	...	...	1 712 584	...	...	1 693 229	...	...
1 VII 2010[27] ....ESDF		3 661 835	2 385 445	65.1	1 841 305	1 171 489	63.6	1 820 530	1 213 956	66.7
1 VII 2011[27] ....ESDF		3 723 821	2 449 917	65.8	1 871 749	1 203 430	64.3	1 852 072	1 246 487	67.3
1 VII 2012[27] ....ESDF		3 787 511	2 514 402	66.4	1 903 085	1 235 377	64.9	1 884 426	1 279 025	67.9
1 VII 2013[27] ....ESDF		3 850 735	2 578 868	67.0	1 934 264	1 267 319	65.5	1 916 471	1 311 549	68.4
1 VII 2014[27] ....ESDF		3 913 275	2 643 353	67.5	1 965 087	1 299 262	66.1	1 948 188	1 344 091	69.0
1 VII 2015[27] ....ESDF		3 975 404	2 707 838	68.1	1 995 695	1 331 207	66.7	1 979 709	1 376 631	69.5
Puerto Rico - Porto Rico[45]										
1 VII 2006[46] ....ESDJ		3 805 214	...	...	1 825 958	...	...	1 979 256	...	...
1 VII 2007[46] ....ESDJ		3 782 995	...	...	1 814 288	...	...	1 968 707	...	...
1 VII 2008[46] ....ESDJ		3 760 866	...	...	1 803 341	...	...	1 957 525	...	...
1 VII 2009[46] ....ESDJ		3 740 410	...	...	1 793 049	...	...	1 947 361	...	...
1 IV 2010 ....CDJC		3 725 789	3 493 256	93.8	1 785 171	...	...	1 940 618	...	...
1 VII 2010[46] ....ESDJ		3 721 208	...	...	1 782 619	...	...	1 938 589	...	...
1 VII 2011[46] ....ESDJ		3 686 771	...	...	1 764 780	...	...	1 921 991	...	...
1 VII 2012[46] ....ESDJ		3 642 281	...	...	1 743 902	...	...	1 898 379	...	...
1 VII 2013[46] ....ESDJ		3 595 839	...	...	1 721 924	...	...	1 873 915	...	...
1 VII 2014[46] ....ESDJ		3 548 397	...	...	1 699 491	...	...	1 848 906	...	...
Saint Kitts and Nevis - Saint-Kitts-et-Nevis										
1 VII 2006* ....ESDF		49 990	...	...	24 445	...	...	25 545	...	...
1 VII 2007* ....ESDF		50 640	...	...	24 765	...	...	25 875	...	...
1 VII 2008* ....ESDF		51 300	...	...	25 085	...	...	26 215	...	...
1 VII 2009* ....ESDF		51 970	...	...	25 415	...	...	26 555	...	...
1 VII 2010* ....ESDF		52 650	...	...	25 750	...	...	26 900	...	...
15 V 2011* ....CDFC		46 398	...	...	22 846	...	...	23 552	...	...
Saint Lucia - Sainte-Lucie										
1 VII 2006 ....ESDF		166 387	...	...	81 558	...	...	84 829	...	...
1 VII 2007 ....ESDF		168 338	...	...	82 426	...	...	85 912	...	...
1 VII 2008 ....ESDF		170 331	...	...	83 478	...	...	86 853	...	...
1 VII 2009 ....ESDF		172 370	...	...	84 465	...	...	87 905	...	...
10 V 2010 ....CDJC		165 770	...	...	83 502	...	...	82 268	...	...
1 VII 2011 ....ESDF		167 366	...	...	82 925	...	...	84 441	...	...
1 VII 2012 ....ESDF		169 170	...	...	83 861	...	...	85 309	...	...
1 VII 2013 ....ESDF		170 925	...	...	84 768	...	...	86 158	...	...
1 VII 2014 ....ESDF		172 623	...	...	85 639	...	...	86 984	...	...
Saint Pierre and Miquelon - Saint Pierre-et-Miquelon										
19 I 2006 ....CDFC		6 125	...	...	3 034	...	...	3 091	...	...
Saint Vincent and the Grenadines - Saint-Vincent-et-les Grenadines										
1 VII 2006 ....ESDJ		109 462	49 790	45.5	55 680	...	...	53 782	...	...
1 VII 2007 ....ESDJ		109 551	49 830	45.5	55 725	...	...	53 826	...	...
1 VII 2008 ....ESDJ		109 639	49 870	45.5	55 770	...	...	53 869	...	...
1 VII 2009 ....ESDJ		109 727	49 911	45.5	55 814	...	...	53 912	...	...
1 VII 2010 ....ESDJ		109 815	49 951	45.5	55 859	...	...	53 956	...	...
1 VII 2011 ....ESDJ		109 903	49 991	45.5	55 904	...	...	53 999	...	...
12 VI 2012* ....CDFC		109 991	...	...	56 419	...	...	53 572	...	...
1 VII 2012 ....ESDJ		109 991	50 926	46.3	56 419	...	...	53 572	...	...
1 VII 2013 ....ESDJ		110 079	50 967	46.3	56 464	...	...	53 615	...	...
1 VII 2014 ....ESDJ		110 167	51 008	46.3	56 509	...	...	53 658	...	...
1 VII 2015 ....ESDJ		110 255	51 048	46.3	56 555	...	...	53 701	...	...

6. Total and urban population by sex: 2006 - 2015
Population totale et population urbaine selon le sexe : 2006 - 2015 (continued - suite)

Continent, country or area, and date / Continent, pays ou zone et date	Code[a]	Both sexes - Les deux sexes			Male - Masculin			Female - Féminin		
		Total	Urban - Urbaine		Total	Urban - Urbaine		Total	Urban - Urbaine	
			Number Nombre	Percent P.100		Number Nombre	Percent P.100		Number Nombre	Percent P.100
AMERICA, NORTH - AMÉRIQUE DU NORD										
Sint Maarten (Dutch part) - Saint-Martin (partie néerlandaise)										
1 VII 2006 .... ESDJ		38 276	...	...	18 510	...	...	19 766	...	...
1 VII 2007 .... ESDJ		39 466	...	...	19 106	...	...	20 361	...	...
1 VII 2008 .... ESDJ		40 461	...	...	19 632	...	...	20 829	...	...
1 VII 2009 .... ESDJ		39 172	...	...	18 918	...	...	20 254	...	...
1 VII 2010 .... ESDJ		35 526	...	...	16 927	...	...	18 600	...	...
9 IV 2011 .... CDFC		33 609	...	...	15 868	...	...	17 741	...	...
1 VII 2011 .... ESDJ		33 436	...	...	15 772	...	...	17 656	...	...
1 VII 2012 .... ESDJ		34 670	...	...	16 656	...	...	18 005	...	...
1 VII 2013 .... ESDJ		36 611	...	...	17 910	...	...	18 701	...	...
1 I 2014 .... ESDJ		37 132	...	...	18 159	...	...	18 973	...	...
Trinidad and Tobago - Trinité-et-Tobago										
1 VII 2006[14] .... ESDF		1 297 944	...	...	650 919	...	...	647 025	...	...
1 VII 2007[14] .... ESDF		1 303 188	...	...	653 549	...	...	649 639	...	...
1 VII 2008[14] .... ESDF		1 308 587	...	...	656 257	...	...	652 330	...	...
1 VII 2009[14] .... ESDF		1 310 106	...	...	657 018	...	...	653 088	...	...
1 VII 2010[14] .... ESDF		1 317 714	...	...	660 822	...	...	656 892	...	...
9 I 2011 .... CDJC		1 328 019	...	...	666 305	...	...	661 714	...	...
1 VII 2012[15] .... ESDF		1 335 194	...	...	669 905	...	...	665 289	...	...
1 VII 2013[15] .... ESDF		1 340 557	...	...	672 596	...	...	667 961	...	...
1 VII 2014[15] .... ESDF		1 345 343	...	...	674 997	...	...	670 346	...	...
1 VII 2015[15] .... ESDF		1 349 667	...	...	677 166	...	...	672 501	...	...
Turks and Caicos Islands - Îles Turques et Caïques										
1 VII 2006 .... ESDJ		*33 202*	...	...	*16 524*	...	...	*16 678*	...	...
1 VII 2007 .... ESDJ		*34 862*	...	...	*18 023*	...	...	*16 839*	...	...
25 I 2012 .... CDFC		31 458	...	...	16 037	...	...	15 421	...	...
United States of America - États-Unis d'Amérique										
1 VII 2006[47] .... ESDJ		298 379 912	...	...	146 647 265	...	...	151 732 647	...	...
1 VII 2007[47] .... ESDJ		301 231 207	...	...	148 064 854	...	...	153 166 353	...	...
1 VII 2008[47] .... ESDJ		304 093 966	...	...	149 489 951	...	...	154 604 015	...	...
1 VII 2009[47] .... ESDJ		306 771 529	...	...	150 807 454	...	...	155 964 075	...	...
1 IV 2010 .... CDJC		308 745 538	249 253 271	80.7	151 781 326	121 698 595	80.2	156 964 212	127 554 676	81.3
1 VII 2010[48] .... ESDJ		309 346 863	...	...	152 088 043	...	...	157 258 820	...	...
1 VII 2011[48] .... ESDJ		311 718 857	...	...	153 291 772	...	...	158 427 085	...	...
1 VII 2012[48] .... ESDJ		314 102 623	...	...	154 521 077	...	...	159 581 546	...	...
1 VII 2013[48] .... ESDJ		316 427 395	...	...	155 706 770	...	...	160 720 625	...	...
1 VII 2014[48] .... ESDJ		318 907 401	...	...	156 955 337	...	...	161 952 064	...	...
1 VII 2015[48] .... ESDJ		321 418 820	...	...	158 229 297	...	...	163 189 523	...	...
United States Virgin Islands - Îles Vierges américaines[45]										
1 VII 2006 .... ESDJ		109 764	...	...	52 113	...	...	57 651	...	...
1 VII 2007 .... ESDJ		109 821	...	...	52 089	...	...	57 732	...	...
1 VII 2008 .... ESDJ		109 840	...	...	52 045	...	...	57 795	...	...
1 IV 2010 .... CDJC		106 405	...	...	50 854	...	...	55 551	...	...
AMERICA, SOUTH - AMÉRIQUE DU SUD										
Argentina - Argentine										
1 VII 2006 .... ESDF		38 970 611	35 304 205	90.6	19 083 828	17 170 659	90.0	19 886 783	18 133 546	91.2
1 VII 2007 .... ESDF		39 356 383	35 719 891	90.8	19 273 494	17 383 239	90.2	20 082 889	18 336 652	91.3
1 VII 2008 .... ESDF		39 745 613	36 137 648	90.9	19 465 305	17 597 280	90.4	20 280 308	18 540 368	91.4
1 VII 2009 .... ESDF		40 134 425	36 553 965	91.1	19 657 086	17 810 843	90.6	20 477 339	18 743 122	91.5
1 VII 2010[49] .... ESDF		40 788 453	37 126 653	91.0	19 940 704	17 996 224	90.2	20 847 749	19 130 429	91.8
27 X 2010 .... CDFC		40 117 096	36 467 245	90.9	19 523 766	17 596 022	90.1	20 593 330	18 871 223	91.6
1 VII 2011[49] .... ESDF		41 262 408	37 603 614	91.1	20 181 263	18 238 292	90.4	21 081 145	19 365 322	91.9

Continent, country or area, and date / Continent, pays ou zone et date	Code[a]	Both sexes - Les deux sexes			Male - Masculin			Female - Féminin		
		Total	Urban - Urbaine		Total	Urban - Urbaine		Total	Urban - Urbaine	
			Number Nombre	Percent P.100		Number Nombre	Percent P.100		Number Nombre	Percent P.100
AMERICA, SOUTH - AMÉRIQUE DU SUD										
Argentina - Argentine										
1 VII 2012[49] .... ESDF		41 735 190	38 079 552	91.2	20 421 377	18 479 951	90.5	21 313 813	19 599 601	92.0
1 VII 2013[49] .... ESDF		42 205 936	38 553 619	91.3	20 660 580	18 720 747	90.6	21 545 356	19 832 872	92.1
1 VII 2014[49] .... ESDF		42 673 657	39 024 881	91.4	20 898 342	18 960 180	90.7	21 775 315	20 064 701	92.1
1 VII 2015[49] .... ESDF		43 137 351	39 492 461	91.6	21 134 115	19 197 773	90.8	22 003 236	20 294 688	92.2
Bolivia (Plurinational State of) - Bolivie (État plurinational de)										
1 VII 2006 .... ESDF		9 389 422	...	...	4 719 637	...	...	4 669 785	...	...
1 VII 2007 .... ESDF		9 549 689	...	...	4 804 855	...	...	4 744 834	...	...
1 VII 2008 .... ESDF		9 709 958	...	...	4 889 348	...	...	4 820 610	...	...
1 VII 2009 .... ESDF		9 870 229	...	...	4 973 094	...	...	4 897 135	...	...
1 VII 2010 .... ESDF		10 030 501	...	...	5 056 056	...	...	4 974 445	...	...
1 VII 2011 .... ESDF		10 190 775	...	...	5 138 206	...	...	5 052 569	...	...
1 VII 2012 .... ESDF		10 351 118	6 965 568	67.3	5 219 006	3 437 451	65.9	5 132 112	3 528 117	68.7
21 XI 2012 .... CDFC		10 059 856	6 788 962	67.5	5 019 447	3 314 824	66.0	5 040 409	3 474 138	68.9
1 VII 2013 .... ESDF		10 507 789	7 110 575	67.7	5 297 727	3 511 796	66.3	5 210 062	3 598 779	69.1
1 VII 2014 .... ESDF		10 665 841	7 256 749	68.0	5 376 880	3 586 449	66.7	5 288 961	3 670 300	69.4
1 VII 2015 .... ESDF		10 825 013	7 403 841	68.4	5 456 332	3 661 290	67.1	5 368 681	3 742 551	69.7
Brazil - Brésil										
1 VII 2006[50] .... ESDF		187 335 137	...	...	92 813 167	...	...	94 521 970	...	...
1 VII 2007[50] .... ESDF		189 462 755	...	...	93 829 262	...	...	95 633 493	...	...
1 VII 2008[50] .... ESDF		191 532 439	...	...	94 816 963	...	...	96 715 476	...	...
1 VII 2009[50] .... ESDF		193 543 969	...	...	95 776 055	...	...	97 767 914	...	...
1 VII 2010[50] .... ESDF		195 497 797	...	...	96 706 703	...	...	98 791 094	...	...
31 VII 2010 .... CDJC		190 755 799	160 925 804	84.4	93 406 990	77 710 179	83.2	97 348 809	83 215 625	85.5
1 VII 2011[50] .... ESDF		197 397 018	...	...	97 610 297	...	...	99 786 721	...	...
1 VII 2012[50] .... ESDF		199 242 462	...	...	98 487 258	...	...	100 755 204	...	...
1 VII 2013[50] .... ESDF		201 032 714	...	...	99 336 858	...	...	101 695 856	...	...
1 VII 2014[50] .... ESDF		202 768 562	...	...	100 159 507	...	...	102 609 055	...	...
1 VII 2015[50] .... ESDF		204 450 649	...	...	100 955 522	...	...	103 495 127	...	...
Chile - Chili										
1 VII 2006 .... ESDF		16 432 674	14 272 454	86.9	8 134 314	6 983 850	85.9	8 298 360	7 288 604	87.8
1 VII 2007 .... ESDF		16 598 074	14 421 386	86.9	8 216 068	7 057 476	85.9	8 382 006	7 363 910	87.9
1 VII 2008 .... ESDF		16 763 470	14 570 311	86.9	8 297 819	7 131 097	85.9	8 465 651	7 439 214	87.9
1 VII 2009 .... ESDF		16 928 873	14 719 246	86.9	8 379 571	7 204 720	86.0	8 549 302	7 514 526	87.9
1 VII 2010 .... ESDF		17 094 275	14 868 172	87.0	8 461 327	7 278 342	86.0	8 632 948	7 589 830	87.9
1 VII 2011 .... ESDF		17 248 450	15 006 226	87.0	8 536 904	7 346 185	86.1	8 711 546	7 660 041	87.9
1 VII 2012 .... ESDF		17 402 630	15 144 277	87.0	8 612 483	7 414 026	86.1	8 790 147	7 730 251	87.9
1 VII 2013 .... ESDF		17 556 815	15 282 334	87.0	8 688 067	7 481 874	86.1	8 868 748	7 800 460	88.0
1 VII 2014 .... ESDF		17 819 054	15 559 039	87.3	8 819 725	7 628 149	86.5	8 999 329	7 930 890	88.1
1 VII 2015 .... ESDF		18 006 407	15 729 803	87.4	8 911 940	7 714 356	86.6	9 094 467	8 015 447	88.1
Colombia - Colombie[51]										
1 VII 2006 .... ESDJ		43 405 956	32 386 530	74.6	21 426 954	15 605 323	72.8	21 979 002	16 781 207	76.4
1 VII 2007 .... ESDJ		43 926 929	32 888 860	74.9	21 683 071	15 850 700	73.1	22 243 858	17 038 160	76.6
1 VII 2008 .... ESDJ		44 451 147	33 396 380	75.1	21 942 355	16 100 320	73.4	22 508 792	17 296 060	76.8
1 VII 2009 .... ESDJ		44 978 832	33 892 634	75.4	22 203 708	16 343 820	73.6	22 775 124	17 548 814	77.1
1 VII 2010 .... ESDJ		45 509 584	34 388 013	75.6	22 466 660	16 587 100	73.8	23 042 924	17 800 913	77.3
1 VII 2011 .... ESDJ		46 044 601	34 883 399	75.8	22 731 299	16 830 795	74.0	23 313 302	18 052 604	77.4
1 VII 2012 .... ESDJ		46 581 823	35 377 138	75.9	22 997 087	17 073 806	74.2	23 584 736	18 303 332	77.6
1 VII 2013 .... ESDJ		47 121 089	35 869 246	76.1	23 264 039	17 315 981	74.4	23 857 050	18 553 265	77.8
1 VII 2014 .... ESDJ		47 661 787	36 359 268	76.3	23 531 670	17 556 826	74.6	24 130 117	18 802 442	77.9
1 VII 2015 .... ESDJ		48 203 405	36 846 935	76.4	23 799 679	17 796 724	74.8	24 403 726	19 050 211	78.1
Ecuador - Équateur										
1 VII 2006[52] .... ESDF		13 964 606	8 733 912	62.5	6 955 272	4 295 578	61.8	7 009 334	4 438 334	63.3
1 VII 2007[52] .... ESDF		14 214 982	8 896 925	62.6	7 071 884	4 371 337	61.8	7 143 098	4 525 588	63.4
1 VII 2008[52] .... ESDF		14 472 881	9 064 267	62.6	7 192 128	4 449 107	61.9	7 280 753	4 615 160	63.4
1 VII 2009[52] .... ESDF		14 738 472	9 236 112	62.7	7 316 020	4 528 987	61.9	7 422 452	4 707 125	63.4
1 VII 2010[52] .... ESDF		15 012 228	9 412 612	62.7	7 443 875	4 611 039	61.9	7 568 353	4 801 573	63.4
28 XI 2010 .... CDFC		14 483 499	9 090 786	62.8	7 177 683	4 451 434	62.0	7 305 816	4 639 352	63.5
1 VII 2011[52] .... ESDF		15 266 431	9 596 628	62.9	7 567 676	4 700 620	62.1	7 698 755	4 896 008	63.6
1 VII 2012[52] .... ESDF		15 520 973	9 780 650	63.0	7 691 912	4 790 437	62.3	7 829 061	4 990 213	63.7
1 VII 2013[52] .... ESDF		15 774 749	9 963 884	63.2	7 815 935	4 880 045	62.4	7 958 814	5 083 839	63.9

Continent, country or area, and date / Continent, pays ou zone et date	Code[a]	Both sexes - Les deux sexes			Male - Masculin			Female - Féminin		
			Urban - Urbaine			Urban - Urbaine			Urban - Urbaine	
		Total	Number Nombre	Percent P.100	Total	Number Nombre	Percent P.100	Total	Number Nombre	Percent P.100
AMERICA, SOUTH - AMÉRIQUE DU SUD										
Ecuador - Équateur										
1 VII 2014[52] .... ESDF		16 027 466	10 145 875	63.3	7 939 552	4 969 197	62.6	8 087 914	5 176 678	64.0
1 VII 2015[52] .... ESDF		16 278 844	10 326 384	63.4	8 062 610	5 057 750	62.7	8 216 234	5 268 634	64.1
Falkland Islands (Malvinas) - Îles Falkland (Malvinas)[53]										
8 X 2006 .... CDFC		2 955	...	...	1 569	...	...	1 386	...	...
15 IV 2012[54] .... CDFC		2 840	...	...	1 491	...	...	1 349	...	...
French Guiana - Guyane française										
1 I 2006 .... CDJC		205 954	167 454	81.3	101 930	81 888	80.3	104 023	85 565	82.3
1 I 2007 .... ESDJ		213 031	...	...	105 546	...	...	107 485	...	...
1 I 2008 .... ESDJ		219 266	...	...	108 673	...	...	110 593	...	...
1 I 2009 .... ESDJ		224 469	...	...	111 201	...	...	113 268	...	...
1 I 2010 .... CDJC		229 040	201 042	87.8	113 599	98 933	87.1	115 441	102 109	88.5
1 I 2011 .... ESDJ		237 549	...	...	117 732	...	...	119 817	...	...
1 I 2012 .... ESDJ		239 648	...	...	119 538	...	...	120 110	...	...
1 I 2013 .... CDJC		244 118	...	...	121 653	...	...	122 465	...	...
1 I 2014* .... ESDJ		249 282	...	...	124 413	...	...	124 869	...	...
1 I 2015* .... ESDJ		254 541	...	...	127 237	...	...	127 304	...	...
Guyana										
1 VII 2006 .... ESDF		768 339	...	...	384 539	...	...	383 800	...	...
1 VII 2007 .... ESDF		770 992	...	...	385 882	...	...	385 110	...	...
1 VII 2008 .... ESDF		774 443	...	...	387 649	...	...	386 794	...	...
1 VII 2009 .... ESDF		753 227	...	...	377 759	...	...	375 468	...	...
1 VII 2010 .... ESDF		752 113	...	...	377 267	...	...	374 846	...	...
1 VII 2011 .... ESDF		750 663	...	...	376 596	...	...	374 067	...	...
1 VII 2012 .... ESDF		748 917	...	...	375 767	...	...	373 150	...	...
15 IX 2012* .... CDFC		747 884	...	...	372 547	...	...	375 337	...	...
1 VII 2013 .... ESDF		746 880	...	...	374 782	...	...	372 098	...	...
Paraguay[23]										
1 VII 2006 .... ESDF		6 009 143	3 430 619	57.1	3 038 590	1 675 752	55.1	2 970 553	1 754 868	59.1
1 VII 2007 .... ESDF		6 119 642	3 513 944	57.4	3 094 044	1 716 874	55.5	3 025 598	1 797 070	59.4
1 VII 2008 .... ESDF		6 230 143	3 597 588	57.7	3 149 475	1 758 138	55.8	3 080 668	1 839 450	59.7
1 VII 2009 .... ESDF		6 340 639	3 681 375	58.1	3 204 871	1 799 444	56.1	3 135 767	1 881 931	60.0
1 VII 2010 .... ESDF		6 451 122	3 765 127	58.4	3 260 223	1 840 694	56.5	3 190 899	1 924 433	60.3
1 VII 2011 .... ESDF		6 561 785	3 848 934	58.7	3 315 636	1 881 940	56.8	3 246 149	1 966 994	60.6
1 VII 2012 .... ESDF		6 672 631	3 932 915	58.9	3 371 117	1 923 249	57.1	3 301 514	2 009 666	60.9
1 VII 2013 .... ESDF		6 783 374	4 016 934	59.2	3 426 508	1 964 541	57.3	3 356 867	2 052 393	61.1
1 VII 2014 .... ESDF		6 893 727	4 100 854	59.5	3 481 648	2 005 735	57.6	3 412 079	2 095 119	61.4
Peru - Pérou										
30 VI 2006 .... ESDF		28 151 443	20 191 318	71.7	14 118 112	9 991 965	70.8	14 033 331	10 199 353	72.7
30 VI 2007[38] .... ESDF		28 481 901	20 594 600	72.3	14 282 346	10 189 918	71.3	14 199 555	10 404 682	73.3
21 X 2007 .... CDFC		27 412 157	20 810 288	75.9	13 622 640	10 226 205	75.1	13 789 517	10 584 083	76.8
30 VI 2008[38] .... ESDF		28 807 034	20 995 699	72.9	14 443 858	10 386 799	71.9	14 363 176	10 608 900	73.9
30 VI 2009[38] .... ESDF		29 132 013	21 398 222	73.5	14 605 206	10 584 348	72.5	14 526 807	10 813 874	74.4
30 VI 2010[38] .... ESDF		29 461 933	21 805 837	74.0	14 768 901	10 784 345	73.0	14 693 032	11 021 492	75.0
30 VI 2011[38] .... ESDF		29 797 694	22 219 201	74.6	14 935 396	10 987 090	73.6	14 862 298	11 232 111	75.6
30 VI 2012[38] .... ESDF		30 135 875	22 635 742	75.1	15 103 003	11 191 332	74.1	15 032 872	11 444 410	76.1
30 VI 2013[38] .... ESDF		30 475 144	23 054 394	75.6	15 271 062	11 396 589	74.6	15 204 082	11 657 805	76.7
30 VI 2014[38] .... ESDF		30 814 175	23 474 069	76.2	15 438 887	11 602 321	75.1	15 375 288	11 871 748	77.2
30 VI 2015[38] .... ESDF		31 151 643	23 893 654	76.7	15 605 814	11 808 006	75.7	15 545 829	12 085 648	77.7
Suriname										
1 VII 2007 .... ESDJ		509 970	...	...	257 181	...	...	252 789	...	...
1 VII 2008 .... ESDJ		517 052	...	...	260 898	...	...	256 154	...	...
13 VIII 2012 .... CDJC		541 638	359 146	66.3	270 629	177 215	65.5	271 009	181 931	67.1
1 VII 2013 .... ESDJ		550 222	...	...	274 859	...	...	275 363	...	...
1 VII 2014 .... ESDJ		558 773	...	...	279 071	...	...	279 702	...	...
Uruguay										
1 VII 2006 .... ESDJ		3 358 005	...	...	1 623 413	...	...	1 734 592	...	...
1 VII 2007 .... ESDJ		3 358 794	...	...	1 623 189	...	...	1 735 604	...	...
1 VII 2008 .... ESDJ		3 363 060	...	...	1 624 932	...	...	1 738 128	...	...
1 VII 2009 .... ESDJ		3 378 083	...	...	1 632 052	...	...	1 746 031	...	...
1 VII 2010 .... ESDJ		3 396 706	...	...	1 640 886	...	...	1 755 820	...	...

Continent, country or area, and date / Continent, pays ou zone et date	Code[a]	Both sexes - Les deux sexes			Male - Masculin			Female - Féminin		
		Total	Urban - Urbaine		Total	Urban - Urbaine		Total	Urban - Urbaine	
			Number Nombre	Percent P.100		Number Nombre	Percent P.100		Number Nombre	Percent P.100
AMERICA, SOUTH - AMÉRIQUE DU SUD										
Uruguay										
1 VII 2011 .... ESDJ		3 412 636	...	...	1 648 466	...	...	1 764 170	...	...
4 X 2011 .... CDJC		3 286 314	3 110 701	94.7	1 577 725[55]	1 478 967[55]	93.7	1 708 481[55]	1 631 626[55]	95.5
1 VII 2012[2] .... ESDJ		3 426 466	...	...	1 655 693	...	...	1 770 774	...	...
1 VII 2013[2] .... ESDJ		3 440 157	...	...	1 662 884	...	...	1 777 273	...	...
1 VII 2014[2] .... ESDJ		3 453 691	...	...	1 670 026	...	...	1 783 665	...	...
1 VII 2015[2] .... ESDJ		3 467 054	...	...	1 677 118	...	...	1 789 936	...	...
Venezuela (Bolivarian Republic of) - Venezuela (République bolivarienne du)										
1 VII 2006 .... ESDF		26 858 165	23 639 927	88.0	13 477 276	11 739 330	87.1	13 380 889	11 900 597	88.9
1 VII 2007 .... ESDF		27 272 712	24 012 062	88.0	13 682 677	11 923 756	87.1	13 590 035	12 088 306	88.9
1 VII 2008 .... ESDF		27 688 638	24 384 883	88.1	13 889 561	12 109 269	87.2	13 799 077	12 275 614	89.0
1 VII 2009 .... ESDF		28 105 913	24 758 144	88.1	14 097 305	12 295 131	87.2	14 008 608	12 463 013	89.0
1 VII 2010 .... ESDF		28 524 411	25 131 837	88.1	14 305 797	12 481 264	87.2	14 218 614	12 650 573	89.0
1 VII 2011 .... ESDF		28 944 070	25 504 003	88.1	14 514 965	12 666 928	87.3	14 429 105	12 837 075	89.0
1 IX 2011 .... CDJC		27 227 930	24 182 998[56]	88.8	13 549 752	11 902 155[56]	87.8	13 678 178	12 280 843[56]	89.8
1 VII 2012 .... ESDF		29 365 589	25 881 720	88.1	14 725 042	12 855 436	87.3	14 640 547	13 026 284	89.0
1 VII 2013 .... ESDF		29 786 263	26 255 358	88.1	14 935 119	13 042 247	87.3	14 851 144	13 213 111	89.0
1 VII 2014 .... ESDF		30 206 307	26 628 251	88.2	15 144 744	13 228 428	87.3	15 061 563	13 399 823	89.0
1 VII 2015 .... ESDF		30 620 404	26 995 334	88.2	15 351 315	13 411 593	87.4	15 269 089	13 583 741	89.0
ASIA - ASIE										
Afghanistan[57]										
1 VII 2006 .... ESDF		22 575 900	4 862 100	21.5	11 545 800	2 503 100	21.7	11 030 100	2 359 000	21.4
1 VII 2007 .... ESDF		23 038 900	5 159 200	22.4	11 783 600	2 656 200	22.5	11 255 300	2 503 000	22.2
1 VII 2008 .... ESDF		23 511 400	5 330 200	22.7	12 025 700	2 744 400	22.8	11 485 700	2 585 800	22.5
1 VII 2009 .... ESDF		23 993 500	5 507 300	23.0	12 272 900	2 835 900	23.1	11 720 600	2 671 400	22.8
1 VII 2010 .... ESDF		24 485 600	5 690 300	23.2	12 524 700	2 929 900	23.4	11 960 900	2 760 400	23.1
1 VII 2011 .... ESDF		24 987 700	5 879 200	23.5	12 782 000	3 027 400	23.7	12 205 700	2 851 800	23.4
1 VII 2012 .... ESDF		25 500 100	6 074 200	23.8	13 044 400	3 127 700	24.0	12 455 700	2 946 500	23.7
1 VII 2013 .... ESDF		26 023 100	6 275 600	24.1	13 312 400	3 231 600	24.3	12 710 700	3 044 000	23.9
1 VII 2014 .... ESDF		26 556 754	6 483 434	24.4	13 585 933	3 338 764	24.6	12 970 821	3 144 670	24.2
Armenia - Arménie										
1 VII 2006 .... ESDJ		3 221 094	2 064 268	64.1	1 555 755	980 272	63.0	1 665 339	1 083 996	65.1
1 VII 2007 .... ESDJ		3 226 520	2 067 650	64.1	1 559 978	982 632	63.0	1 666 542	1 085 018	65.1
1 VII 2008 .... ESDJ		3 234 031	2 071 942	64.1	1 565 411	985 913	63.0	1 668 620	1 086 029	65.1
1 VII 2009 .... ESDJ		3 243 729	2 077 181	64.0	1 572 046	989 609	63.0	1 671 683	1 087 572	65.1
1 VII 2010 .... ESDJ		3 256 066	...	...	1 579 705	...	...	1 676 361	...	...
1 VII 2011 .... ESDJ		3 268 468	...	...	1 586 935	...	...	1 681 533	...	...
12 X 2011 .... CDFC		2 871 771	1 847 124	64.3	1 346 729	851 475	63.2	1 525 042	995 649	65.3
1 I 2012 .... ESDJ		3 274 285	...	...	1 590 285	...	...	1 684 000	...	...
1 I 2015 .... ESDJ		3 010 598	...	...	1 439 148	...	...	1 571 450	...	...
Azerbaijan - Azerbaïdjan										
1 VII 2006[36] .... ESDF		8 609 600	4 533 300	52.7	4 244 200	2 223 100	52.4	4 365 400	2 310 200	52.9
1 VII 2007[36] .... ESDF		8 723 000	4 608 200	52.8	4 305 800	2 262 400	52.5	4 417 200	2 345 800	53.1
1 VII 2008[36] .... ESDF		8 838 500	4 690 000	53.1	4 368 600	2 304 800	52.8	4 469 900	2 385 200	53.4
13 IV 2009 .... CDJC		8 922 447	4 739 123	53.1	4 414 398	2 330 527	52.8	4 508 049	2 408 596	53.4
1 VII 2009 .... ESDF		8 947 300	4 751 400	53.1	4 427 900	2 337 100	52.8	4 519 400	2 414 300	53.4
1 VII 2010 .... ESDF		9 054 300	4 802 200	53.0	4 486 300	2 364 400	52.7	4 568 000	2 437 800	53.4
1 VII 2011 .... ESDF		9 173 100	4 859 100	53.0	4 550 300	2 394 700	52.6	4 622 800	2 464 400	53.3
1 VII 2012 .... ESDF		9 295 784	4 936 922	53.1	4 616 139	2 435 213	52.8	4 679 646	2 501 709	53.5
1 VII 2013 .... ESDF		9 416 800	5 016 000	53.3	4 681 200	2 476 300	52.9	4 735 600	2 539 700	53.6
1 VII 2014 .... ESDF		9 528 900	5 075 700	53.3	4 736 900	2 505 700	52.9	4 792 000	2 570 000	53.6
1 I 2015 .... ESDF		9 593 038	...	...	4 775 857	...	...	4 817 181	...	...
Bahrain - Bahreïn										
1 VII 2006 .... ESDJ		960 425	...	...	580 285	...	...	380 141	...	...
1 VII 2007 .... ESDJ		1 039 297	...	...	632 074	...	...	407 223	...	...
1 VII 2008 .... ESDJ		1 103 496	...	...	676 590	...	...	426 906	...	...
1 VII 2009 .... ESDJ		1 178 415	...	...	731 997	...	...	446 418	...	...
27 IV 2010 .... CDJC		1 234 571	1 234 571	100.0	768 414	768 414	100.0	466 157	466 157	100.0

6. Total and urban population by sex: 2006 - 2015
Population totale et population urbaine selon le sexe : 2006 - 2015 (continued - suite)

Continent, country or area, and date / Continent, pays ou zone et date	Code[a]	Both sexes - Les deux sexes Total	Urban - Urbaine Number Nombre	Urban - Urbaine Percent P.100	Male - Masculin Total	Urban - Urbaine Number Nombre	Urban - Urbaine Percent P.100	Female - Féminin Total	Urban - Urbaine Number Nombre	Urban - Urbaine Percent P.100
ASIA - ASIE										
Bahrain - Bahreïn										
1 VII 2010	ESDJ	1 228 543	...	...	764 357	...	...	464 186	...	...
1 VII 2011	ESDJ	1 195 020	...	...	741 483	...	...	453 537	...	...
1 VII 2012	ESDJ	1 208 964	...	...	760 449	...	...	448 515	...	...
1 VII 2013	ESDJ	1 253 191	...	...	788 381	...	...	464 810	...	...
1 VII 2014	ESDJ	1 314 562	...	...	806 487	...	...	508 075	...	...
Bangladesh										
1 VII 2006	ESDF	140 600 000	34 600 000	24.6	72 000 000	...	...	68 600 000	...	...
1 VII 2007	ESDF	142 600 000	35 700 000	25.0	73 100 000	...	...	69 500 000	...	...
1 VII 2008	ESDF	144 500 000	36 700 000	25.4	74 000 000	...	...	70 500 000	...	...
1 VII 2010	ESDF	148 620 000	38 540 000	25.9	76 120 000	20 427 000	26.8	72 500 000	18 113 000	25.0
15 III 2011[58]	CDFC	149 772 364	...	...	74 980 386	...	...	74 791 978	...	...
1 VII 2011	ESDF	150 611 000	39 000 000	25.9	77 101 062	20 560 587	26.7	73 509 938	18 439 413	25.1
1 VII 2012	ESDF	152 700 000	41 100 000	26.9	78 200 000	...	...	74 500 000	...	...
1 VII 2013	ESDF	154 790 000	42 580 000	27.5	77 510 000	...	...	77 280 000	...	...
1 VII 2014	ESDF	156 880 000	44 110 000	28.1	78 560 000	...	...	78 320 000	...	...
Bhutan - Bhoutan[59]										
1 VII 2006	ESDF	646 851	204 691	31.6	339 403	109 920	32.4	307 448	94 771	30.8
1 VII 2007	ESDF	658 888	213 571	32.4	345 298	114 593	33.2	313 590	98 978	31.6
1 VII 2008	ESDF	671 083	222 753	33.2	351 269	119 342	34.0	319 814	103 411	32.3
1 VII 2009	ESDF	683 407	232 232	34.0	357 305	124 246	34.8	326 102	107 986	33.1
1 VII 2010	ESDF	695 823	242 001	34.8	363 384	129 298	35.6	332 439	112 703	33.9
1 VII 2011	ESDF	708 265	252 038	35.6	369 476	134 484	36.4	338 789	117 554	34.7
1 VII 2012	ESDF	720 679	262 325	36.4	375 554	139 798	37.2	345 125	122 530	35.5
1 VII 2013	ESDF	733 004	272 839	37.2	381 582	145 219	38.1	351 421	127 619	36.3
1 VII 2014	ESDF	745 153	283 543	38.1	387 520	150 737	38.9	357 633	132 806	37.1
1 VII 2015	ESDF	757 042	294 402	38.9	393 324	156 328	39.7	363 718	138 074	38.0
Brunei Darussalam - Brunéi Darussalam										
1 VII 2006[36]	ESDF	364 500	...	...	188 200	...	...	176 300	...	...
1 VII 2007[36]	ESDF	370 000	...	...	191 100	...	...	178 900	...	...
1 VII 2008[36]	ESDF	375 000	...	...	193 700	...	...	181 300	...	...
1 VII 2009[36]	ESDF	380 100	...	...	196 300	...	...	183 800	...	...
1 VII 2010[36]	ESDF	386 800	...	...	199 800	...	...	187 000	...	...
20 VI 2011	CDJC	393 372	296 257	75.3	203 144	151 663	74.7	190 228	144 594	76.0
1 VII 2012	ESDJ	399 800	...	...	206 700	...	...	193 100	...	...
1 VII 2013	ESDJ	406 200	...	...	210 300	...	...	195 900	...	...
1 VII 2014	ESDJ	411 900	...	...	213 500	...	...	198 400	...	...
1 VII 2015*	ESDJ	417 200	...	...	216 600	...	...	200 600	...	...
Cambodia - Cambodge										
1 VII 2006[60]	ESDF	14 080 653	...	...	6 836 759	...	...	7 243 894	...	...
1 VII 2007[60]	ESDF	14 363 519	...	...	6 979 452	...	...	7 384 067	...	...
3 III 2008[61]	CDFC	13 395 682	2 614 027	19.5	6 516 054	1 255 570	19.3	6 879 628	1 358 457	19.7
1 VII 2008[62]	ESDF	13 868 227	2 707 240	19.5	6 745 592	1 299 799	19.3	7 122 635	1 407 441	19.8
1 VII 2009[62]	ESDF	14 085 324	2 814 943	20.0	6 859 756	1 351 939	19.7	7 225 568	1 463 004	20.2
1 VII 2010[62]	ESDF	14 302 779	2 926 810	20.5	6 973 994	1 406 183	20.2	7 328 785	1 520 627	20.7
1 VII 2011[62]	ESDF	14 521 275	3 042 794	21.0	7 088 691	1 462 518	20.6	7 432 584	1 580 276	21.3
1 VII 2012[62]	ESDF	14 741 414	3 165 683	21.5	7 204 166	1 520 722	21.1	7 537 248	1 644 961	21.8
3 III 2013[63]	SSDF	14 676 591	3 146 212	21.4	7 121 508	1 527 479	21.4	7 555 083	1 618 734	21.4
1 VII 2013[62]	ESDF	14 962 591	3 285 951	22.0	7 320 112	1 580 866	21.6	7 642 479	1 705 085	22.3
1 VII 2014[62]	ESDF	15 184 116	3 412 183	22.5	7 436 178	1 642 397	22.1	7 747 938	1 769 786	22.8
1 VII 2015[62]	ESDF	15 405 157	3 540 575	23.0	7 551 944	1 705 018	22.6	7 853 213	1 835 557	23.4
China - Chine[64]										
1 VII 2006[65]	ESDF	1 314 480 000	577 060 000[66]	43.9	677 280 000	...	...	637 200 000	...	...
1 VII 2007[65]	ESDF	1 317 900 000	606 330 000[67]	46.0	680 480 000[28]	...	...	640 810 000[28]	...	...
1 VII 2008[65]	ESDF	1 324 700 000	624 030 000[67]	47.1	683 570 000[28]	...	...	644 450 000[28]	...	...
1 VII 2009[65]	ESDF	1 331 300 000	645 120 000[67]	48.5	686 470 000[28]	...	...	648 030 000[28]	...	...
1 VII 2010[65]	ESDF	1 337 700 000	669 780 000[67]	50.1	687 480 000[28]	...	...	653 430 000[28]	...	...
1 XI 2010[68]	CDJC	1 339 724 852	665 575 306	49.7	686 852 572	...	...	652 872 280	...	...
1 VII 2011[69]	ESDF	1 344 100 000	691 000 000[67]	51.4	691 000 000[28]	...	...	657 000 000[28]	...	...
1 VII 2012[69]	ESDF	1 350 695 000	701 305 000[66]	51.9	692 315 000	...	...	658 380 000	...	...
1 VII 2013[65]	ESDF	1 357 380 000	721 465 000[66]	53.2	695 615 000	...	...	661 765 000	...	...
1 VII 2014[65]	ESDF	1 364 270 000	740 135 000[66]	54.3	699 035 000	...	...	665 235 000	...	...
1 VII 2015[65]	ESDF	1 371 220 000	760 160 000[66]	55.4	702 465 000	...	...	668 755 000	...	...

Continent, country or area, and date / Continent, pays ou zone et date	Code[a]	Both sexes - Les deux sexes Total	Urban - Urbaine Number Nombre	Urban - Urbaine Percent P.100	Male - Masculin Total	Urban - Urbaine Number Nombre	Urban - Urbaine Percent P.100	Female - Féminin Total	Urban - Urbaine Number Nombre	Urban - Urbaine Percent P.100
ASIA - ASIE										
China, Hong Kong SAR - Chine, Hong Kong RAS										
1 VII 2006 .... ESDJ		6 857 100	...	...	3 270 100	...	...	3 587 000	...	...
14 VII 2006[70] .... CDJC		6 864 346	...	...	3 272 956	...	...	3 591 390	...	...
1 VII 2007 .... ESDJ		6 916 300	...	...	3 283 900	...	...	3 632 400	...	...
1 VII 2008 .... ESDJ		6 957 800	...	...	3 290 200	...	...	3 667 600	...	...
1 VII 2009 .... ESDJ		6 972 800	...	...	3 284 800	...	...	3 688 000	...	...
1 VII 2010 .... ESDJ		7 024 200	...	...	3 294 300	...	...	3 729 900	...	...
30 VI 2011[71] .... CDJC		7 071 576	...	...	3 303 015	...	...	3 768 561	...	...
1 VII 2011 .... ESDJ		7 071 600	...	...	3 303 000	...	...	3 768 600	...	...
1 VII 2012 .... ESDJ		7 154 600	...	...	3 327 300	...	...	3 827 300	...	...
1 VII 2013 .... ESDJ		7 187 500	...	...	3 330 700	...	...	3 856 800	...	...
1 VII 2014 .... ESDJ		7 241 700	...	...	3 345 100	...	...	3 896 600	...	...
1 VII 2015 .... ESDJ		7 305 700	...	...	3 367 000	...	...	3 938 700	...	...
China, Macao SAR - Chine, Macao RAS										
1 VII 2006 .... ESDJ		498 852	...	...	243 009	...	...	255 843	...	...
19 VIII 2006 .... CDJC		502 113	...	...	245 167	...	...	256 946	...	...
1 VII 2007 .... ESDJ		520 900	...	...	256 500	...	...	264 400	...	...
1 VII 2008 .... ESDJ		540 700	...	...	264 900	...	...	275 800	...	...
1 VII 2009 .... ESDJ		535 000	...	...	257 900[28]	...	...	277 200[28]	...	...
1 VII 2010 .... ESDJ		537 000	...	...	257 200[28]	...	...	279 700[28]	...	...
1 VII 2011 .... ESDJ		549 600	...	...	263 500	...	...	286 100	...	...
12 VIII 2011 .... CDFC		625 674	...	...	305 398	...	...	320 276	...	...
1 VII 2012 .... ESDJ		567 900	...	...	274 300	...	...	293 600	...	...
1 VII 2013 .... ESDJ		591 900	...	...	285 700	...	...	306 200	...	...
1 VII 2014 .... ESDJ		621 700	...	...	305 500	...	...	316 200	...	...
1 VII 2015 .... ESDJ		642 900	...	...	317 500	...	...	325 400	...	...
Cyprus - Chypre[72]										
1 VII 2006[73] .... ESDJ		750 965	...	...	368 048	...	...	382 917	...	...
1 VII 2007[73] .... ESDJ		767 125	...	...	375 986	...	...	391 139	...	...
1 VII 2008[73] .... ESDJ		786 632	...	...	385 192	...	...	401 440	...	...
1 VII 2009[73] .... ESDJ		808 035	...	...	394 766	...	...	413 270	...	...
1 VII 2010[73] .... ESDJ		829 446	...	...	404 182	...	...	425 264	...	...
1 VII 2011[73] .... ESDJ		850 881	...	...	413 876	...	...	437 006	...	...
1 X 2011 .... CDJC		840 407	566 191	67.4	408 780	273 065	66.8	431 627	293 126	67.9
1 VII 2012[73] .... ESDJ		863 945	...	...	420 015	...	...	443 930	...	...
1 VII 2013[73] .... ESDJ		861 930	...	...	419 183	...	...	442 747	...	...
1 VII 2014[73] .... ESDJ		852 504	...	...	414 682	...	...	437 823	...	...
1 I 2015* .... ESDJ		847 008	...	...	411 825	...	...	435 183	...	...
Democratic People's Republic of Korea - République populaire démocratique de Corée										
1 X 2008 .... CDJC		24 052 231	...	...	11 721 838	...	...	12 330 393	...	...
Georgia - Géorgie										
1 VII 2006 .... ESDF		4 398 000	2 309 700	52.5	2 081 700	...	...	2 316 300	...	...
1 VII 2007 .... ESDF		4 388 400	2 306 400	52.6	2 079 000	...	...	2 309 400	...	...
1 VII 2008 .... ESDF		4 383 800	2 306 500	52.6	2 079 600	...	...	2 304 200	...	...
1 VII 2009 .... ESDF		4 410 900	2 332 700	52.9	2 094 800	...	...	2 316 100	...	...
1 VII 2010 .... ESDF		4 452 800	2 360 900	53.0	2 118 100	...	...	2 334 700	...	...
1 VII 2011 .... ESDF		4 483 400	2 381 500	53.1	2 135 600	...	...	2 347 800	...	...
1 VII 2012 .... ESDF		4 490 700	...	...	2 141 300	...	...	2 349 400	...	...
1 I 2014 .... ESDF		4 490 498	...	...	2 141 372	...	...	2 349 126	...	...
5 XI 2014 .... CDJC		3 713 804	2 122 623	57.2	1 772 864	980 985	55.3	1 940 940	1 141 638	58.8
1 I 2015 .... ESDJ		3 729 500	...	...	1 778 500	...	...	1 951 000	...	...
India - Inde[74]										
1 VII 2006[75] .... ESDF		1 117 733 826	323 827 490	29.0	578 411 677	170 384 885	29.5	539 322 149	153 442 605	28.5
1 VII 2007[75] .... ESDF		1 134 023 232	331 060 644	29.2	586 879 523	174 195 527	29.7	547 143 709	156 865 117	28.7
1 VII 2008[75] .... ESDF		1 150 196 000	338 356 000	29.4	595 291 000	178 041 000	29.9	554 905 000	160 315 000	28.9
9 II 2011 .... CDFC		1 210 854 977	377 106 125	31.1	623 270 258	195 489 200	31.4	587 584 719	181 616 925	30.9
1 VII 2011*[75] .... ESDF		1 192 503 000	...	...	617 315 000	...	...	575 188 000	...	...
Indonesia - Indonésie										
1 VII 2006[76] .... ESDJ		222 746 900	...	...	111 528 600	...	...	111 218 300	...	...
1 VII 2007[76] .... ESDJ		225 642 000	...	...	112 966 900	...	...	112 675 100	...	...

6. Total and urban population by sex: 2006 - 2015
Population totale et population urbaine selon le sexe : 2006 - 2015 (continued - suite)

Continent, country or area, and date — Continent, pays ou zone et date	Code[a]	Both sexes - Les deux sexes Total	Urban - Urbaine Number Nombre	Urban - Urbaine Percent P.100	Male - Masculin Total	Urban - Urbaine Number Nombre	Urban - Urbaine Percent P.100	Female - Féminin Total	Urban - Urbaine Number Nombre	Urban - Urbaine Percent P.100
ASIA - ASIE										
Indonesia - Indonésie										
1 VII 2008[76]	ESDJ	228 523 300	...	...	114 399 200	...	...	114 124 100	...	...
1 VII 2009[76]	ESDJ	231 369 500	...	...	115 817 900	...	...	115 551 600	...	...
1 V 2010	CDJC	237 641 326	118 320 256	49.8	119 630 913	59 559 622	49.8	118 010 413	58 760 634	49.8
1 VII 2010	ESDJ	238 518 787	118 803 981	49.8	119 852 718	59 698 817	49.8	118 666 069	59 105 164	49.8
1 VII 2011	ESDJ	241 990 736	122 164 186	50.5	121 602 475	61 382 741	50.5	120 388 261	60 781 445	50.5
1 VII 2012	ESDJ	245 425 244	125 558 071	51.2	123 331 006	63 081 616	51.1	122 094 238	62 476 455	51.2
1 VII 2013	ESDJ	248 818 090	128 964 283	51.8	125 036 002	64 785 519	51.8	123 782 088	64 178 764	51.8
1 VII 2014	ESDJ	252 164 786	132 387 038	52.5	126 715 188	66 493 813	52.5	125 449 598	65 893 225	52.5
1 VII 2015	ESDJ	255 461 686	135 823 286	53.2	128 366 718	68 214 177	53.1	127 094 968	67 609 109	53.2
Iran (Islamic Republic of) - Iran (République islamique d')										
28 X 2006	CDJC	70 495 782	48 259 964[77]	68.5	35 866 362	24 576 442[77]	68.5	34 629 420	23 683 522[77]	68.4
1 VII 2007[78]	ESDJ	71 278 952	48 874 656	68.6	36 247 296	24 891 876	68.7	35 031 392	23 982 780	68.5
1 VII 2008[78]	ESDJ	72 181 632	49 576 146	68.7	36 691 780	25 253 132	68.8	35 489 488	24 323 014	68.5
1 VII 2009[78]	ESDJ	73 202 096	50 365 184	68.8	37 198 776	25 660 500	69.0	36 003 320	24 704 684	68.6
1 VII 2010[78]	ESDJ	74 339 576	51 242 546	68.9	37 767 220	26 114 342	69.1	36 572 356	25 128 204	68.7
24 X 2011	CDJC	75 149 669	53 646 661	71.4	37 905 669	27 023 638	71.3	37 244 000	26 623 023	71.5
1 VII 2012[78]	ESDJ	76 037 535	54 611 776[79]	71.8	38 336 983	27 547 622[79]	71.9	37 700 552	27 064 154[79]	71.8
1 VII 2013[78]	ESDJ	76 942 276	55 506 192[79]	72.1	38 777 566	27 988 342[79]	72.2	38 164 710	27 517 850[79]	72.1
1 VII 2014[78]	ESDJ	77 856 411	56 412 837	72.5	39 224 036	28 435 933	72.5	38 632 375	27 976 904	72.4
1 VII 2015[78]	ESDJ	78 773 093	57 326 841	72.8	39 672 171	28 887 379	72.8	39 100 922	28 439 462	72.7
Iraq										
1 VII 2006	ESDF	28 562 436	...	...	14 368 462	...	...	14 193 974	...	...
1 VII 2007	ESDF	29 426 942	...	...	14 814 595	...	...	14 612 348	...	...
1 VII 2008	ESDF	30 315 243	...	...	15 261 719	...	...	15 053 524	...	...
1 VII 2009	ESDF	31 392 903	...	...	16 010 232	...	...	15 382 671	...	...
1 VII 2010	ESDF	32 210 813	...	...	16 418 691	...	...	15 792 122	...	...
1 VII 2011	ESDF	33 051 526	...	...	16 839 048	...	...	16 212 479	...	...
1 VII 2012	ESDF	33 913 305	23 475 543	69.2	17 270 036	11 954 703	69.2	16 643 269	11 520 840	69.2
1 VII 2013	ESDF	34 794 194	24 162 634	69.4	17 710 750	12 299 131	69.4	17 083 444	11 863 502	69.4
1 VII 2014	ESDF	35 736 260	24 896 261	69.7	18 182 503	12 667 144	69.7	17 553 757	12 229 117	69.7
1 VII 2015	ESDF	36 658 503	25 631 821	69.9	18 520 532	12 935 587	69.8	18 137 971	12 696 234	70.0
Israel - Israël[80]										
1 VII 2006	ESDJ	7 053 707	6 475 600[81]	91.8	3 485 501	3 189 511[81]	91.5	3 568 206	3 286 089[81]	92.1
1 VII 2007	ESDJ	7 180 115	6 589 632[81]	91.8	3 549 216	3 247 280[81]	91.5	3 630 899	3 342 352[81]	92.1
1 VII 2008	ESDJ	7 308 795	6 701 217[82]	91.7	3 614 125	3 303 732[82]	91.4	3 694 671	3 397 485[82]	92.0
27 XII 2008[83]	CDFC	7 412 180	6 799 340[28]	91.7	3 663 910	3 350 610[28]	91.4	3 748 270	3 448 730[28]	92.0
1 VII 2009	ESDJ	7 485 565	6 864 957[28]	91.7	3 701 159	3 384 295[28]	91.4	3 784 406	3 480 662[28]	92.0
1 VII 2010	ESDJ	7 623 561	6 987 615[28]	91.7	3 771 020	3 446 730[28]	91.4	3 852 541	3 540 885[28]	91.9
1 VII 2011	ESDJ	7 765 832	7 111 015[28]	91.6	3 843 068	3 509 308[28]	91.3	3 922 764	3 601 706[28]	91.8
1 VII 2012	ESDJ	7 910 525	7 235 231[28]	91.5	3 916 125	3 572 531[28]	91.2	3 994 400	3 662 700[28]	91.7
1 VII 2013	ESDJ	8 059 456	7 369 053[28]	91.4	3 991 347	3 640 471[28]	91.2	4 068 109	3 728 581[28]	91.7
1 VII 2014	ESDJ	8 215 668	7 502 325[28]	91.3	4 070 269	3 707 183[28]	91.1	4 145 398	3 795 142[28]	91.6
Japan - Japon										
1 VII 2006[84]	ESDJ	127 854 000	...	...	62 357 000	...	...	65 497 000	...	...
1 VII 2007[84]	ESDJ	128 001 000	...	...	62 401 000[28]	...	...	65 599 000[28]	...	...
1 VII 2008[84]	ESDJ	128 063 000	...	...	62 409 000	...	...	65 654 000	...	...
1 VII 2009[84]	ESDJ	128 047 000	...	...	62 354 000	...	...	65 693 000	...	...
1 VII 2010[84]	ESDJ	128 070 000	...	...	62 330 000	...	...	65 740 000	...	...
1 X 2010[85]	CDJC	128 057 352	116 156 631	90.7	62 327 737	56 569 051	90.8	65 729 615	59 587 580	90.7
1 VII 2011[84]	ESDJ	127 817 000	...	...	62 189 000	...	...	65 628 000	...	...
1 VII 2012[84]	ESDJ	127 561 000	...	...	62 041 000	...	...	65 520 000	...	...
1 VII 2013[84]	ESDJ	127 339 000	...	...	61 918 000[28]	...	...	65 420 000[28]	...	...
1 VII 2014[84]	ESDJ	127 132 000	...	...	61 812 000	...	...	65 320 000	...	...
1 VII 2015[84]	ESDJ	126 958 000	...	...	61 729 000[28]	...	...	65 230 000[28]	...	...
1 X 2015*	CDJC	127 110 047	...	...	61 829 237	...	...	65 280 810	...	...
Jordan - Jordanie[86]										
30 X 2015	CDFC	9 531 712	...	...	5 046 822	...	...	4 484 890	...	...
Kazakhstan										
1 VII 2006	ESDF	15 308 084	8 764 884	57.3	7 367 032	4 094 572	55.6	7 941 052	4 670 312	58.8
1 VII 2007	ESDF	15 484 192	8 195 389	52.9	7 450 418	3 815 422	51.2	8 033 774	4 379 967	54.5
1 VII 2008	ESDF	15 674 000	8 331 030	53.2	7 541 053	3 877 559	51.4	8 132 947	4 453 471	54.8

Continent, country or area, and date Continent, pays ou zone et date	Code[a]	Both sexes - Les deux sexes			Male - Masculin			Female - Féminin		
		Total	Urban - Urbaine		Total	Urban - Urbaine		Total	Urban - Urbaine	
			Number Nombre	Percent P.100		Number Nombre	Percent P.100		Number Nombre	Percent P.100
ASIA - ASIE										
Kazakhstan										
25 II 2009 ....CDFC		16 009 597	8 662 432	54.1	7 712 224	4 055 341	52.6	8 297 373	4 607 091	55.5
1 VII 2009 ....ESDF		16 092 701	8 741 149	54.3	7 753 360	4 092 724	52.8	8 339 341	4 648 425	55.7
1 VII 2010 ....ESDF		16 321 581	8 896 402	54.5	7 866 332	4 165 526	53.0	8 455 249	4 730 876	56.0
1 VII 2011 ....ESDF		16 556 601	9 050 267	54.7	7 983 081	4 237 719	53.1	8 573 520	4 812 548	56.1
1 VII 2012 ....ESDF		16 791 427	9 202 381	54.8	8 100 113	4 309 859	53.2	8 691 314	4 892 522	56.3
1 VII 2013 ....ESDF		17 035 275	9 348 738	54.9	8 221 848	4 380 550	53.3	8 813 427	4 968 188	56.4
1 I 2014 ....ESDF		17 160 774	9 433 482	55.0	8 284 815	4 421 972	53.4	8 875 959	5 011 510	56.5
Kuwait - Koweït										
1 VII 2006 ....ESDF		*2 366 113*	...	...	*1 389 803*	...	...	*976 310*	...	...
1 VII 2007 ....ESDF		*2 495 415*	...	...	*1 455 837*	...	...	*1 039 578*	...	...
1 VII 2008 ....ESDF		*2 631 963*	...	...	*1 525 129*	...	...	*1 106 834*	...	...
1 VII 2009 ....ESDF		*2 777 861*	...	...	*1 597 843*	...	...	*1 180 018*	...	...
1 VII 2010 ....ESDF		*2 933 268*	...	...	*1 674 156*	...	...	*1 259 112*	...	...
21 IV 2011 ....CDFC		3 065 850	3 065 850	100.0	1 738 372	1 738 372	100.0	1 327 478	1 327 478	100.0
1 VII 2011 ....ESDF		*3 106 676*	...	...	*1 767 685*	...	...	*1 338 991*	...	...
1 VII 2012 ....ESDF		*3 246 622*	...	...	*1 856 265*	...	...	*1 390 357*	...	...
1 VII 2013 ....ESDF		*3 427 595*	...	...	*1 968 382*	...	...	*1 459 213*	...	...
1 VII 2014 ....ESDF		*3 767 415*	...	...	*2 161 594*	...	...	*1 605 821*	...	...
Kyrgyzstan - Kirghizstan										
1 VII 2006[87] ....ESDF		5 033 953	1 790 295	35.6	2 460 578	841 414	34.2	2 573 375	948 881	36.9
1 VII 2007[87] ....ESDF		5 055 671	1 791 267	35.4	2 467 458	839 913	34.0	2 588 213	951 354	36.8
1 VII 2008[87] ....ESDF		5 077 722	1 794 620	35.3	2 475 331	839 873	33.9	2 602 391	954 747	36.7
24 III 2009 ....CDJC		5 362 793	1 827 136	34.1	2 645 921	863 002	32.6	2 716 872	964 134	35.5
1 VII 2009[87] ....ESDF		5 128 124	1 809 738	35.3	2 499 977	846 861	33.9	2 628 147	962 877	36.6
1 VII 2010[87] ....ESDF		5 192 806	1 828 955	35.2	2 532 547	856 262	33.8	2 660 259	972 693	36.6
1 VII 2011[87] ....ESDF		5 259 601	1 847 757	35.1	2 566 031	865 260	33.7	2 693 570	982 497	36.5
1 VII 2012[87] ....ESDF		5 352 358	1 856 305	34.7	2 613 586	869 564	33.3	2 738 772	986 741	36.0
1 VII 2013[73] ....ESDJ		5 719 852	1 921 936	33.6	2 827 672	909 216	32.2	2 892 180	1 012 720	35.0
1 VII 2014[73] ....ESDJ		5 835 816	1 965 159	33.7	2 886 758	930 751	32.2	2 949 058	1 034 408	35.1
1 VII 2015[73] ....ESDJ		5 957 271	2 008 148	33.7	2 948 932	952 329	32.3	3 008 339	1 055 819	35.1
Lao People's Democratic Republic - République démocratique populaire lao										
1 VII 2006[88] ....ESDF		*5 746 200*	...	...	*2 863 100*	...	...	*2 883 100*	...	...
1 VII 2007[88] ....ESDF		*5 868 800*	...	...	*2 924 700*	...	...	*2 944 000*	...	...
1 VII 2008[88] ....ESDF		*5 990 100*	...	...	*2 985 800*	...	...	*3 004 300*	...	...
1 VII 2009[88] ....ESDF		*6 110 600*	...	...	*3 046 400*	...	...	*3 064 200*	...	...
1 VII 2010[88] ....ESDF		*6 230 200*	...	...	*3 106 600*	...	...	*3 123 700*	...	...
1 VII 2011[88] ....ESDF		*6 348 800*	...	...	*3 166 300*	...	...	*3 182 500*	...	...
1 VII 2012[88] ....ESDF		*6 465 800*	...	...	*3 225 200*	...	...	*3 240 600*	...	...
1 VII 2013[88] ....ESDF		*6 580 800*	...	...	*3 283 200*	...	...	*3 297 600*	...	...
1 VII 2014[88] ....ESDF		*6 693 300*	...	...	*3 339 800*	...	...	*3 353 400*	...	...
1 III 2015 ....CDJC		6 492 400			3 254 800			3 237 600		
Lebanon - Liban										
3 III 2007[89].................SSDF		3 759 134	...	...	1 857 659	...	...	1 901 475	...	...
1 X 2011[90] ....SSDF		3 779 859	...	...	1 840 940	...	...	1 938 919	...	...
Malaysia - Malaisie										
1 VII 2006[91] ....ESDJ		*26 549 855*	*17 892 686*	*67.4*	*13 627 408*	*9 148 357*	*67.1*	*12 922 447*	*8 744 329*	*67.7*
1 VII 2007[91] ....ESDJ		*27 058 428*	*18 475 499*	*68.3*	*13 903 701*	*9 455 573*	*68.0*	*13 154 727*	*9 019 926*	*68.6*
1 VII 2008[91] ....ESDJ		*27 567 636*	*19 068 738*	*69.2*	*14 179 117*	*9 767 066*	*68.9*	*13 388 519*	*9 301 672*	*69.5*
1 VII 2009[91] ....ESDJ		*28 081 497*	*19 675 873*	*70.1*	*14 456 940*	*10 085 460*	*69.8*	*13 624 557*	*9 590 413*	*70.4*
1 VII 2010[92] ....ESDJ		*28 588 637*	*20 290 864*	*71.0*	*14 730 542*	*10 404 757*	*70.6*	*13 858 095*	*9 886 107*	*71.3*
6 VII 2010[58] ....CDJC		28 334 135	20 124 970	71.0	14 562 638	10 298 698	70.7	13 771 497	9 826 272	71.4
1 VII 2011[92] ....ESDJ		*29 062 036*	*20 606 546*	*70.9*	*14 980 010*	*10 568 602*	*70.6*	*14 082 026*	*10 037 944*	*71.3*
1 VII 2012[92] ....ESDJ		*29 510 022*	*21 355 255*	*72.4*	*15 215 309*	*10 965 006*	*72.1*	*14 294 713*	*10 390 249*	*72.7*
1 VII 2013[92] ....ESDJ		*30 213 664*	*22 041 500*	*73.0*	*15 604 813*	*11 330 984*	*72.6*	*14 608 851*	*10 710 516*	*73.3*
1 VII 2014[92] ....ESDJ		*30 598 041*	*22 509 382*	*73.6*	*15 796 359*	*11 570 594*	*73.2*	*14 801 682*	*10 938 788*	*73.9*
1 VII 2015[92] ....ESDJ		*30 995 706*	*23 015 251*	*74.3*	*15 994 299*	*11 829 562*	*74.0*	*15 001 407*	*11 185 689*	*74.6*
Maldives										
21 III 2006[93]...............CDFC		298 968	103 693	34.7	151 459	51 992	34.3	147 509	51 701	35.0
1 VII 2007 ....ESDF		304 869	...	...	154 391	...	...	150 478	...	...
1 VII 2008 ....ESDF		309 575	...	...	156 714	...	...	152 861	...	...
1 VII 2009 ....ESDF		314 542	...	...	159 159	...	...	155 383	...	...

Continent, country or area, and date / Continent, pays ou zone et date	Code[a]	Both sexes - Les deux sexes			Male - Masculin			Female - Féminin		
		Total	Urban - Urbaine		Total	Urban - Urbaine		Total	Urban - Urbaine	
			Number Nombre	Percent P.100		Number Nombre	Percent P.100		Number Nombre	Percent P.100
ASIA - ASIE										
Maldives										
1 VII 2010 ....ESDF		319 738	...	...	161 708	...	...	158 030	...	...
1 VII 2011 ....ESDF		325 135	...	...	164 349	...	...	160 786	...	...
1 VII 2012 ....ESDF		330 655	...	...	167 058	...	...	163 597	...	...
1 VII 2013 ....ESDF		336 224	...	...	169 800	...	...	166 424	...	...
20 IX 2014[94] ....CDFC		402 071	153 904	38.3	227 749	85 438	37.5	174 322	68 466	39.3
1 VII 2015 ....ESDF		347 552	...	...	175 394	...	...	172 158	...	...
Mongolia - Mongolie										
1 VII 2006 ....ESDF		2 583 254	1 621 686	62.8	1 259 653	780 791	62.0	1 323 601	840 895	63.5
1 VII 2007 ....ESDF		2 601 850	1 638 567	63.0	1 268 447	788 695	62.2	1 333 403	849 872	63.7
1 VII 2008 ....ESDF		2 643 201	1 684 282	63.7	1 289 282	811 224	62.9	1 353 919	873 058	64.5
1 VII 2009 ....ESDF		2 691 115	1 743 008	64.8	1 314 729	840 520	63.9	1 376 386	902 488	65.6
1 VII 2010 ....ESDF		2 738 622	1 799 648	65.7	1 335 111	863 536	64.7	1 403 511	936 112	66.7
11 XI 2010 ....CDFC		2 647 199	1 797 338	67.9	1 314 246	869 827	66.2	1 332 953	927 511	69.6
1 VII 2011 ....ESDF		2 786 322	1 856 224	66.6	1 354 472	886 139	65.4	1 431 850	970 085	67.8
1 VII 2012 ....ESDF		2 839 711	1 911 462	67.3	1 379 091	910 746	66.0	1 460 620	1 000 716	68.5
1 VII 2013 ....ESDF		2 899 011	1 961 169	67.6	1 409 648	936 682	66.4	1 489 363	1 024 487	68.8
1 VII 2014 ....ESDF		2 963 113	1 993 017	67.3	1 446 149	955 833	66.1	1 516 964	1 037 184	68.4
1 VII 2015 ....ESDF		3 026 864	2 043 251	67.5	1 485 034	985 919	66.4	1 541 830	1 057 332	68.6
Myanmar										
1 X 2006 ....ESDF		56 515 349	17 239 318	30.5	28 096 895	8 425 026	30.0	28 418 454	8 814 292	31.0
1 X 2007 ....ESDF		57 504 368	17 567 506	30.5	28 585 910	8 582 809	30.0	28 918 458	8 984 697	31.1
1 X 2008 ....ESDF		58 376 839	17 894 194	30.7	29 025 480	8 798 657	30.3	29 351 359	9 095 537	31.0
1 X 2009 ....ESDF		59 129 900	18 133 654	30.7	29 399 744	8 888 838	30.2	29 730 156	9 244 816	31.1
1 X 2010 ....ESDF		59 780 329	18 342 824	30.7	29 723 184	8 992 226	30.3	30 057 145	9 350 598	31.1
1 X 2011[95] ....ESDF		50 149 496	14 650 579	29.2	24 185 705	7 009 280	29.0	25 963 791	7 641 299	29.4
1 X 2012[95] ....ESDF		50 666 887	14 824 883	29.3	24 435 871	7 092 798	29.0	26 231 016	7 732 085	29.5
1 X 2013[95] ....ESDF		51 184 273	14 999 184	29.3	24 686 034	7 176 313	29.1	26 498 239	7 822 871	29.5
29 III 2014[96] ....CDFC		50 279 900	14 877 943	29.6	24 228 714	7 114 224	29.4	26 051 186	7 763 719	29.8
1 X 2014[95] ....ESDF		51 486 253	...	...	24 824 586	...	...	26 661 667	...	...
Nepal - Népal										
1 VII 2006 ....ESDJ		25 886 736	...	...	12 963 722	...	...	12 923 014	...	...
1 VII 2007 ....ESDJ		26 427 399	...	...	13 240 233	...	...	13 187 166	...	...
1 VII 2008 ....ESDJ		26 966 581	...	...	13 515 938	...	...	13 450 643	...	...
1 VII 2009 ....ESDJ		27 504 280	...	...	13 790 836	...	...	13 713 444	...	...
1 VII 2010 ....ESDJ		28 043 744	...	...	14 066 638	...	...	13 977 106	...	...
22 VI 2011 ....CDJC		26 494 504	4 523 820	17.1	12 849 041	2 306 049	17.9	13 645 463	2 217 771	16.3
1 VII 2011 ....ESDJ		28 584 975	...	...	14 343 343	...	...	14 241 632	...	...
1 VII 2012[17] ....ESDJ		26 873 066	...	...	13 030 795	...	...	13 842 271	...	...
1 VII 2013[17] ....ESDJ		27 257 347	...	...	13 215 791	...	...	14 041 556	...	...
1 VII 2014[17] ....ESDJ		27 646 053	...	...	13 403 432	...	...	14 242 621	...	...
1 VII 2015[17] ....ESDJ		28 037 904	...	...	13 593 069	...	...	14 444 835	...	...
Oman										
1 VII 2006 ....ESDF		2 577 062	1 857 263	72.1	1 498 143	1 093 546	73.0	1 078 919	763 717	70.8
1 VII 2007 ....ESDF		2 743 499	1 984 158	72.3	1 622 119	1 188 537	73.3	1 121 380	795 621	71.0
1 VII 2008 ....ESDF		2 867 428	2 077 862	72.5	1 687 414	1 238 527	73.4	1 180 014	839 335	71.1
1 VII 2009 ....ESDF		3 173 917	2 314 865	72.9	1 971 115	1 457 197	73.9	1 202 802	857 668	71.3
12 XII 2010 ....CDFC		2 773 479	2 079 831	75.0	1 612 408	1 220 557	75.7	1 161 071	859 274	74.0
1 VII 2011 ....ESDF		3 295 298	...	...	2 090 883	...	...	1 204 415	...	...
1 VII 2012 ....ESDF		3 623 001	...	...	2 332 687	...	...	1 290 314	...	...
1 VII 2013 ....ESDF		3 855 206	...	...	2 502 235	...	...	1 352 971	...	...
1 VII 2014 ....ESDF		3 992 893	...	...	2 579 811	...	...	1 413 082	...	...
Pakistan[97]										
1 VII 2006 ....ESDJ		147 099 534	...	...	75 582 494	...	...	71 517 040	...	...
1 VII 2007[98] ....ESDJ		149 860 388	52 807 585	35.2	76 857 737	27 178 203	35.4	73 002 651	25 629 382	35.1
1 VII 2008 ....ESDF		166 410 000	...	...	86 130 000	...	...	80 280 000	...	...
1 VII 2009 ....ESDF		169 940 000	...	...	87 940 000	...	...	82 010 000	...	...
1 VII 2010 ....ESDF		173 510 000	...	...	89 760 000	...	...	83 750 000	...	...
1 VII 2011 ....ESDF		177 100 000	...	...	91 590 000	...	...	85 510 000	...	...
Philippines										
1 VII 2006[25] ....ESDJ		86 972 500	...	...	43 742 100	...	...	43 230 400	...	...
1 VII 2007[25] ....ESDJ		88 706 300	...	...	44 608 300	...	...	44 098 000	...	...
1 VII 2008[25] ....ESDJ		90 457 200	...	...	45 483 100	...	...	44 974 100	...	...
1 VII 2009[25] ....ESDJ		92 226 600	...	...	46 368 900	...	...	45 857 700	...	...
1 V 2010[99] ....CDJC		92 335 113	41 855 571	45.3	46 634 257	20 840 798	44.7	45 700 856	21 014 773	46.0

Continent, country or area, and date / Continent, pays ou zone et date	Code[a]	Both sexes - Les deux sexes			Male - Masculin			Female - Féminin		
		Total	Urban - Urbaine		Total	Urban - Urbaine		Total	Urban - Urbaine	
			Number Nombre	Percent P.100		Number Nombre	Percent P.100		Number Nombre	Percent P.100
ASIA - ASIE										
Philippines										
1 VII 2010[27]	ESDJ	93 135 100	...	...	46 980 200	...	...	46 154 900	...	...
1 VII 2011[27]	ESDJ	94 823 800	...	...	47 832 400	...	...	46 991 400	...	...
1 VII 2012[27]	ESDJ	96 510 900	...	...	48 684 200	...	...	47 826 700	...	...
1 VII 2013[27]	ESDJ	98 196 500	...	...	49 535 100	...	...	48 661 400	...	...
1 VII 2014[27]	ESDJ	99 880 300	...	...	50 385 100	...	...	49 495 200	...	...
1 VII 2015[27]	ESDJ	101 562 300	...	...	51 234 200	...	...	50 328 100	...	...
Qatar										
1 VII 2006	ESDF	1 042 947	...	...	754 298	...	...	288 649	...	...
1 VII 2007	ESDF	1 218 250	...	...	905 747	...	...	312 503	...	...
1 VII 2008	ESDF	1 448 479	...	...	1 111 176	...	...	337 303	...	...
1 VII 2009	ESDF	1 638 626	...	...	1 265 146	...	...	373 480	...	...
21 IV 2010	CDFC	1 699 435	...	...	1 284 739	...	...	414 696	...	...
1 VII 2010	ESDF	1 715 010	...	...	1 296 107	...	...	418 903	...	...
1 VII 2011	ESDF	1 732 717	...	...	1 288 590	...	...	444 127	...	...
1 VII 2012	ESDF	1 832 903	...	...	1 355 199	...	...	477 704	...	...
1 VII 2013	ESDF	2 003 700	...	...	1 477 632	...	...	526 068	...	...
Republic of Korea - République de Corée										
1 VII 2006	ESDJ	48 371 946	...	...	24 302 796	...	...	24 069 150	...	...
1 VII 2007	ESDJ	48 597 652	...	...	24 410 110	...	...	24 187 542	...	...
1 VII 2008	ESDJ	48 948 698	...	...	24 576 155	...	...	24 372 543	...	...
1 VII 2009	ESDJ	49 182 038	...	...	24 664 502	...	...	24 517 536	...	...
1 VII 2010	ESDJ	49 410 366	...	...	24 757 776	...	...	24 652 590	...	...
1 XI 2010[100]	CDJC	48 580 293	39 822 647	82.0	24 167 098	19 798 739	81.9	24 413 195	20 023 908	82.0
1 VII 2011[2]	ESDJ	49 779 440	...	...	24 942 339	...	...	24 837 101	...	...
1 VII 2012[2]	ESDJ	50 004 441	...	...	25 039 557	...	...	24 964 884	...	...
1 VII 2013[2]	ESDJ	50 219 669	...	...	25 132 612	...	...	25 087 057	...	...
1 VII 2014[2]	ESDJ	50 423 955	...	...	25 219 810	...	...	25 204 145	...	...
1 VII 2015[2]	ESDJ	50 617 045	...	...	25 302 520	...	...	25 314 525	...	...
Saudi Arabia - Arabie saoudite										
1 VII 2006*[101]	ESDF	24 121 890	...	...	13 444 010	...	...	10 677 880	...	...
1 VII 2007*[101]	ESDF	24 941 298	...	...	13 947 610	...	...	10 993 688	...	...
1 VII 2008*[101]	ESDF	25 787 025	...	...	14 470 381	...	...	11 316 644	...	...
1 VII 2009*[101]	ESDF	26 660 857	...	...	15 013 600	...	...	11 647 257	...	...
27 IV 2010*	CDFC	27 136 977	...	...	15 306 793	...	...	11 830 184	...	...
1 VII 2010*[101]	ESDF	27 563 432	...	...	15 578 015	...	...	11 985 417	...	...
1 VII 2011*[101]	ESDF	28 376 355	...	...	16 041 361	...	...	12 334 994	...	...
1 VII 2012*[101]	ESDF	29 195 895	...	...	16 543 836	...	...	12 652 059	...	...
1 VII 2013*[101]	ESDF	29 601 529	...	...	16 889 829	...	...	12 711 700	...	...
1 VII 2014*[101]	ESDF	30 300 675	...	...	17 279 880	...	...	13 020 795	...	...
1 VII 2015*[101]	ESDF	31 015 999	...	...	17 652 149	...	...	13 363 850	...	...
Singapore - Singapour[102]										
30 VI 2006[103]	ESDJ	3 525 894	...	...	1 748 242	...	...	1 777 652	...	...
30 VI 2007[103]	ESDJ	3 583 082	...	...	1 775 477	...	...	1 807 605	...	...
30 VI 2008[103]	ESDJ	3 642 659	...	...	1 802 992	...	...	1 839 667	...	...
30 VI 2009[103]	ESDJ	3 733 876	...	...	1 844 732	...	...	1 889 144	...	...
30 VI 2010[104]	CDJC	3 771 721	...	...	1 861 133	...	...	1 910 588	...	...
30 VI 2011[103]	ESDJ	3 789 251	...	...	1 868 170	...	...	1 921 081	...	...
30 VI 2012[103]	ESDJ	3 818 205	...	...	1 880 046	...	...	1 938 159	...	...
30 VI 2013[103]	ESDJ	3 844 751	...	...	1 891 504	...	...	1 953 247	...	...
30 VI 2014[103]	ESDJ	3 870 739	...	...	1 902 410	...	...	1 968 329	...	...
30 VI 2015[103]	ESDJ	3 902 690	...	...	1 916 628	...	...	1 986 062	...	...
Sri Lanka										
1 VII 2006	ESDF	19 858 000	...	...	9 889 000	...	...	9 969 000	...	...
1 VII 2007	ESDF	20 039 000	...	...	9 956 000	...	...	10 083 000	...	...
1 VII 2008	ESDF	20 246 000	...	...	10 060 000	...	...	10 186 000	...	...
1 VII 2009	ESDF	20 476 000	...	...	10 174 000	...	...	10 302 000	...	...
1 VII 2010	ESDF	20 675 000	...	...	10 273 000	...	...	10 402 000	...	...
1 VII 2011	ESDF	20 869 000	...	...	10 357 000	...	...	10 512 000	...	...
27 II 2012	CDJC	20 359 439	3 704 470	18.2	9 856 634	1 800 327	18.3	10 502 805	1 904 143	18.1
1 VII 2012	ESDF	20 424 000	...	...	9 888 000	...	...	10 536 000	...	...
1 VII 2013	ESDF	20 579 000	...	...	9 963 000	...	...	10 616 000	...	...

6. Total and urban population by sex: 2006 - 2015
Population totale et population urbaine selon le sexe : 2006 - 2015 (continued - suite)

Continent, country or area, and date / Continent, pays ou zone et date	Code[a]	Both sexes - Les deux sexes			Male - Masculin			Female - Féminin		
		Total	Urban - Urbaine		Total	Urban - Urbaine		Total	Urban - Urbaine	
			Number Nombre	Percent P.100		Number Nombre	Percent P.100		Number Nombre	Percent P.100
ASIA - ASIE										
Sri Lanka										
1 VII 2014	ESDF	20 771 000	...	...	10 056 000	...	...	10 715 000	...	...
1 VII 2015	ESDF	20 966 000	...	...	10 151 000	...	...	10 815 000	...	...
State of Palestine - État de Palestine										
1 VII 2006	ESDF	3 611 998	2 582 579[105]	71.5	1 833 225	...	...	1 778 773	...	...
1 VII 2007	ESDF	3 719 189	3 086 102[105]	83.0	1 887 628	...	...	1 831 561	...	...
1 XII 2007[106]	CDFC	3 669 244	3 040 039[105]	82.9	1 862 027	1 542 604[105]	82.8	1 807 217	1 497 435[105]	82.9
1 VII 2008	ESDF	3 825 512	3 175 546[105]	83.0	1 941 742	...	...	1 883 770	...	...
1 VII 2009	ESDF	3 935 249	3 267 977[105]	83.0	1 997 625	...	...	1 937 624	...	...
1 VII 2010	ESDF	4 048 403	3 363 385[105]	83.1	2 055 211	...	...	1 993 192	...	...
1 VII 2011	ESDF	4 168 860	3 465 483[105]	83.1	2 116 782	...	...	2 052 078	...	...
1 VII 2012	ESDF	4 293 313	3 571 037[105]	83.2	2 180 386	...	...	2 112 927	...	...
1 VII 2013	ESDF	4 420 549	3 679 034[105]	83.2	2 245 400	...	...	2 175 149	...	...
1 VII 2014	ESDF	4 550 368	3 789 308[105]	83.3	2 311 721	...	...	2 238 647	...	...
1 VII 2015	ESDF	4 682 467	3 901 606[105]	83.3	2 379 184	...	...	2 303 283	...	...
Syrian Arab Republic - République arabe syrienne[107]										
1 VII 2006	ESDF	18 717 000	10 013 000	53.5	9 563 000	5 139 000	53.7	9 154 000	4 874 000	53.2
1 VII 2007	ESDF	19 172 000	10 257 000	53.5	9 798 000	5 265 000	53.7	9 374 000	4 992 000	53.3
1 VII 2008	ESDF	19 644 000	10 511 000	53.5	10 042 000	5 394 000	53.7	9 602 000	5 117 000	53.3
1 VII 2009	ESDF	20 125 000	10 769 000	53.5	10 287 000	5 526 000	53.7	9 838 000	5 243 000	53.3
1 VII 2010	ESDF	20 619 000	11 033 000	53.5	10 539 000	5 661 000	53.7	10 080 000	5 372 000	53.3
1 VII 2011	ESDF	21 124 000	11 297 000	53.5	10 794 000	5 795 000	53.7	10 330 000	5 502 000	53.3
Tajikistan - Tadjikistan										
1 VII 2006	ESDF	6 992 066	1 841 258	26.3	3 508 345	923 963	26.3	3 483 721	917 295	26.3
1 VII 2007	ESDF	7 139 772	1 877 203	26.3	3 581 930	943 032	26.3	3 557 842	934 171	26.3
1 VII 2008	ESDF	7 294 747	1 918 996	26.3	3 659 238	965 220	26.4	3 635 510	953 776	26.2
1 VII 2009	ESDF	7 334 083	1 944 038	26.5	3 699 641	979 510	26.5	3 634 442	964 528	26.5
1 VII 2010	ESDF	7 519 280	1 996 961	26.6	3 794 467	1 007 796	26.6	3 724 813	989 165	26.6
21 IX 2010	CDFC	7 564 502	2 006 605	26.5	3 817 004	1 012 642	26.5	3 747 498	993 963	26.5
1 VII 2011	ESDF	7 714 198	2 042 660	26.5	3 893 798	1 032 106	26.5	3 820 401	1 010 554	26.5
1 VII 2012	ESDF	7 897 313	2 085 698	26.4	3 987 517	1 054 904	26.5	3 909 796	1 030 794	26.4
1 VII 2013	ESDF	8 074 266	2 138 737	26.5	4 078 857	1 083 119	26.6	3 995 409	1 055 618	26.4
1 VII 2014	ESDF	8 256 572	2 193 224	26.6	4 174 269	1 112 352	26.6	4 082 303	1 080 873	26.5
Thailand - Thaïlande										
1 VII 2006[2]	ESDJ	65 305 736	19 792 296	30.3	32 060 034	9 474 510	29.6	33 245 702	10 317 786	31.0
1 VII 2007[2]	ESDJ	66 041 512	20 117 497	30.5	32 467 223	9 733 251	30.0	33 574 289	10 384 246	30.9
1 VII 2008[2]	ESDJ	66 480 004	20 471 816	30.8	32 671 831	9 802 741	30.0	33 808 173	10 669 075	31.6
1 VII 2009[2]	ESDJ	66 903 277	21 133 663	31.6	32 872 931	10 112 852	30.8	34 030 346	11 020 811	32.4
1 VII 2010[2]	ESDJ	67 311 917	23 096 811	34.3	33 067 359	11 070 161	33.5	34 244 558	12 026 650	35.1
1 IX 2010	CDJC	65 981 659	29 133 829	44.2	32 355 032	14 120 842	43.6	33 626 627	15 012 987	44.6
1 VII 2011[2]	ESDJ	67 598 735	23 309 100	34.5	33 190 193	11 167 094	33.6	34 408 542	12 142 006	35.3
1 VII 2012[2]	ESDJ	67 911 720	23 430 180	34.5	33 328 645	11 219 175	33.7	34 583 075	12 211 005	35.3
Timor-Leste										
1 VII 2006[2]	ESDF	1 015 000	...	...	515 000	...	...	500 000	...	...
1 VII 2007[2]	ESDF	1 048 000	...	...	532 000	...	...	516 000	...	...
1 VII 2008[2]	ESDF	1 080 742	...	...	549 000[28]	...	...	532 000[28]	...	...
11 VII 2010	CDFC	1 066 409	316 086	29.6	544 198	166 163	30.5	522 211	149 923	28.7
1 VII 2013[2]	ESDF	1 180 069	...	...	602 526	...	...	577 544	...	...
1 VII 2014[2]	ESDF	1 212 107	...	...	618 789	...	...	593 318	...	...
11 VII 2015*	CDFC	1 167 242	...	...	588 561	...	...	578 681	...	...
Turkey - Turquie										
1 VII 2006	ESDF	72 971 474	...	...	36 796 216	...	...	36 175 258	...	...
1 VII 2007	ESDF	70 137 756	...	...	35 158 437	...	...	34 979 319	...	...
1 VII 2008	ESDF	71 051 678	...	...	35 638 843	...	...	35 412 835	...	...
31 XII 2008[108]	CDJC	71 517 100	...	...	35 901 154	...	...	35 615 946	...	...
1 VII 2009	ESDF	72 039 206	...	...	36 181 812	...	...	35 857 394	...	...
1 VII 2010	ESDF	73 142 150	...	...	36 752 826	...	...	36 389 324	...	...
1 VII 2011	ESDF	74 223 629	...	...	37 288 068	...	...	36 935 561	...	...
3 X 2011[109]	CDJC	74 526 000	53 321 000	71.5	37 431 000	26 777 000	71.5	37 095 000	26 544 000	71.6
1 VII 2012	ESDF	75 175 827	54 168 017	72.1	37 744 561	27 195 122	72.1	37 431 266	26 972 895	72.1

Continent, country or area, and date / Continent, pays ou zone et date	Code[a]	Both sexes - Les deux sexes			Male - Masculin			Female - Féminin		
		Total	Urban - Urbaine		Total	Urban - Urbaine		Total	Urban - Urbaine	
			Number Nombre	Percent P.100		Number Nombre	Percent P.100		Number Nombre	Percent P.100
ASIA - ASIE										
Turkey - Turquie										
31 XII 2013[108] .... ESDJ		76 667 864	66 488 105	86.7	38 473 360	33 344 846	86.7	38 194 504	33 143 259	86.8
31 XII 2014[108] .... ESDJ		77 695 904	67 720 318	87.2	38 984 302	33 954 681	87.1	38 711 602	33 765 637	87.2
Turkmenistan - Turkménistan										
15 XII 2012 .... CDFC		4 750 120	...	...	2 332 005	...	...	2 418 115	...	...
United Arab Emirates - Émirats arabes unis[110]										
31 XII 2006 .... ESDF		5 012 384	...	...	3 533 564	...	...	1 478 820	...	...
31 XII 2007 .... ESDF		6 219 006	...	...	4 533 281	...	...	1 685 725	...	...
31 XII 2008 .... ESDF		8 073 626	...	...	6 039 971	...	...	2 033 655	...	...
31 XII 2009 .... ESDF		8 199 996	...	...	6 120 885	...	...	2 079 111	...	...
1 VII 2010 .... ESDF		8 264 070	...	...	6 161 820	...	...	2 102 250	...	...
Uzbekistan - Ouzbékistan[111]										
1 VII 2006 .... ESDJ		26 488 257	9 539 800[112]	36.0	13 235 336	4 730 700[112]	35.7	13 252 921	4 809 100[112]	36.3
1 VII 2007 .... ESDJ		26 867 998	9 641 400[112]	35.9	13 430 432	4 783 500[112]	35.6	13 437 566	4 857 900[112]	36.2
1 VII 2008 .... ESDJ		27 302 782	14 141 300[112]	51.8	13 653 947	7 037 900[112]	51.5	13 648 835	7 103 400[112]	52.0
1 VII 2009 .... ESDJ		27 767 408	14 330 900[112]	51.6	13 893 825	7 129 600[112]	51.3	13 873 583	7 201 300[112]	51.9
1 VII 2010 .... ESDJ		28 562 405	14 661 700[112]	51.3	14 291 711	7 295 300[112]	51.0	14 270 694	7 366 400[112]	51.6
1 VII 2011 .... ESDJ		29 339 368	15 062 700[112]	51.3	14 680 424	7 496 500[112]	51.1	14 658 944	7 566 200[112]	51.6
1 VII 2012 .... ESDJ		29 774 448	15 285 000[112]	51.3	14 905 603	7 613 400[112]	51.1	14 868 845	7 671 600[112]	51.6
1 VII 2013 .... ESDJ		30 243 172	15 462 637	51.1	15 148 116	7 707 450	50.9	15 095 056	7 755 187	51.4
1 VII 2014 .... ESDJ		30 757 669	15 651 614	50.9	15 414 846	7 809 449	50.7	15 342 823	7 842 165	51.1
Viet Nam										
1 VII 2006[113] .... ESDF		83 312 993	23 046 110	27.7	40 999 887	...	...	42 313 106	...	...
1 VII 2007[113] .... ESDF		84 221 105	23 746 705	28.2	41 448 572	...	...	42 772 533	...	...
1 VII 2008[113] .... ESDF		85 122 271	24 673 681	29.0	41 957 844	...	...	43 164 427	...	...
1 IV 2009 .... CDJC		85 846 997	25 436 896	29.6	42 413 143	12 349 995	29.1	43 433 854	13 086 901	30.1
1 VII 2009 .... ESDF		86 024 979	25 584 740	29.7	42 523 416	...	...	43 501 563	...	...
1 VII 2010 .... ESDF		86 932 527	26 515 940	30.5	42 986 075	...	...	43 946 452	...	...
1 VII 2011 .... ESDF		87 840 038	27 888 152	31.7	43 444 777	...	...	44 395 261	...	...
1 VII 2012 .... ESDF		88 772 884	28 356 363	31.9	43 907 154	...	...	44 865 730	...	...
1 VII 2013 .... ESDF		89 708 892	28 874 850	32.2	44 454 271	...	...	45 254 621	...	...
1 VII 2014 .... ESDF		90 728 941	30 035 405	33.1	44 758 132	...	...	45 970 809	...	...
1 VII 2015 .... ESDF		91 713 345	31 131 496	33.9	45 234 104	...	...	46 479 241	...	...
Yemen - Yémen										
31 XII 2006 .... ESDF		20 900 532	6 070 613	29.0	...	...	...	...	...	...
31 XII 2007 .... ESDF		21 538 995	6 256 462	29.0	...	...	...	...	...	...
1 VII 2008[2] .... ESDJ		21 843 554	6 281 475	28.8	11 127 218	...	...	10 716 336	...	...
1 VII 2009[2] .... ESDJ		22 492 035	6 475 802	28.8	11 454 963	...	...	11 037 072	...	...
1 VII 2010[2] .... ESDJ		23 153 982	6 673 916	28.8	11 789 814	...	...	11 364 168	...	...
1 VII 2011[2] .... ESDJ		23 832 569	6 875 789	28.9	12 133 362	...	...	11 699 207	...	...
1 VII 2012[2] .... ESDJ		24 526 703	7 075 639	28.8	12 485 039	...	...	12 041 664	...	...
1 VII 2013[2] .... ESDJ		25 235 079	7 280 367	28.9	12 844 169	...	...	12 390 910	...	...
EUROPE										
Åland Islands - Îles d'Åland[39]										
1 VII 2006 .... ESDJ		26 845	10 802	40.2	13 299	5 123	38.5	13 546	5 680	41.9
1 VII 2007 .... ESDJ		27 038	10 863	40.2	13 407	5 151	38.4	13 631	5 712	41.9
1 VII 2008 .... ESDJ		27 305	10 954	40.1	13 552	5 189	38.3	13 753	5 765	41.9
1 VII 2009 .... ESDJ		27 595	11 064	40.1	13 724	5 264	38.4	13 871	5 800	41.8
1 VII 2010 .... ESDJ		27 871	11 157	40.0	13 880	5 327	38.4	13 991	5 830	41.7
1 VII 2011 .... ESDJ		28 181	11 227	39.8	14 045	5 364	38.2	14 137	5 863	41.5
1 VII 2012 .... ESDJ		28 429	11 305	39.8	14 172	5 408	38.2	14 257	5 897	41.4
1 VII 2013 .... ESDJ		28 585	11 370	39.8	14 255	5 445	38.2	14 330	5 925	41.3
1 VII 2014 .... ESDJ		28 792	11 437	39.7	14 375	5 490	38.2	14 417	5 947	41.2
1 VII 2015 .... ESDJ		28 950	11 471	39.6	14 466	5 521	38.2	14 484	5 950	41.1
Albania - Albanie										
1 VII 2006 .... ESDF		2 992 547	1 448 706	48.4	1 494 341	717 077	48.0	1 498 206	731 629	48.8
1 VII 2007 .... ESDF		2 970 017	1 472 486	49.6	1 483 616	729 192	49.1	1 486 401	743 294	50.0

Continent, country or area, and date / Continent, pays ou zone et date	Code[a]	Both sexes - Les deux sexes			Male - Masculin			Female - Féminin		
		Total	Urban - Urbaine		Total	Urban - Urbaine		Total	Urban - Urbaine	
			Number Nombre	Percent P.100		Number Nombre	Percent P.100		Number Nombre	Percent P.100
EUROPE										
Albania - Albanie										
1 VII 2008 ....ESDF		2 947 314	1 495 552	50.7	1 472 660	740 747	50.3	1 474 654	754 805	51.2
1 VII 2009 ....ESDF		2 927 519	1 518 397	51.9	1 463 537	752 178	51.4	1 463 982	766 219	52.3
1 VII 2010 ....ESDF		2 913 021	1 541 310	52.9	1 457 661	763 780	52.4	1 455 360	777 530	53.4
1 VII 2011 ....ESDF		2 904 780	1 564 139	53.8	1 455 074	775 313	53.3	1 449 706	788 826	54.4
1 X 2011 ....CDJC		2 800 138	1 498 508	53.5	1 403 059	742 671	52.9	1 397 079	755 837	54.1
1 VII 2012 ....ESDF		2 900 489	1 595 701	55.0	1 455 904	787 167	54.1	1 444 585	808 534	56.0
1 VII 2013 ....ESDF		2 897 364	1 633 617	56.4	1 458 648	798 615	54.8	1 438 716	835 002	58.0
1 I 2014 ....ESDF		2 895 947	...	...	1 459 963	...	...	1 435 984	...	...
Andorra - Andorre[39]										
1 VII 2006 ....ESDJ		80 104	...	...	41 876	...	...	38 228	...	...
1 VII 2007 ....ESDJ		82 392	...	...	43 100	...	...	39 292	...	...
1 VII 2008 ....ESDJ		83 884	...	...	43 911	...	...	39 973	...	...
1 VII 2009 ....ESDJ		85 116	...	...	44 444	...	...	40 672	...	...
1 VII 2010 ....ESDJ		84 549	...	...	43 992	...	...	40 557	...	...
1 VII 2011[114] ....ESDJ		79 280	...	...	40 529	...	...	38 751	...	...
1 VII 2012 ....ESDJ		77 181	...	...	39 351	...	...	37 830	...	...
1 I 2013 ....ESDJ		76 246	...	...	38 838	...	...	37 408	...	...
Austria - Autriche										
1 VII 2006 ....ESDJ		8 267 948	...	...	4 022 516	...	...	4 245 432	...	...
1 VII 2007 ....ESDJ		8 295 189	...	...	4 036 548	...	...	4 258 641	...	...
1 VII 2008 ....ESDJ		8 321 541	...	...	4 050 215	...	...	4 271 326	...	...
1 VII 2009 ....ESDJ		8 341 483	...	...	4 061 195	...	...	4 280 288	...	...
1 VII 2010 ....ESDJ		8 361 069	...	...	4 071 773	...	...	4 289 296	...	...
1 VII 2011 ....ESDJ		8 388 534	...	...	4 087 188	...	...	4 301 346	...	...
31 X 2011 ....CDJC		8 401 940	5 643 239	67.2	4 093 938	2 713 930	66.3	4 308 002	2 929 309	68.0
1 VII 2012 ....ESDJ		8 426 311	...	...	4 109 431	...	...	4 316 880	...	...
1 VII 2013 ....ESDJ		8 477 230	...	...	4 138 693	...	...	4 338 537	...	...
1 VII 2014 ....ESDJ		8 541 575	...	...	4 175 301	...	...	4 366 275	...	...
1 I 2015 ....ESDJ		8 576 261	...	...	4 194 965	...	...	4 381 296	...	...
Belarus - Bélarus										
1 VII 2006 ....ESDJ		9 604 924	6 960 276	72.5	4 475 094	3 235 250	72.3	5 129 830	3 725 026	72.6
1 VII 2007 ....ESDJ		9 560 953	6 976 543	73.0	4 450 877	3 238 281	72.8	5 110 076	3 738 262	73.2
1 VII 2008 ....ESDJ		9 527 985	7 008 135	73.6	4 433 031	3 249 263	73.3	5 094 954	3 758 872	73.8
1 VII 2009 ....ESDJ		9 506 765	7 052 045	74.2	4 421 789	3 266 240	73.9	5 084 976	3 785 805	74.5
14 X 2009 ....CDJC		9 503 807	7 064 529	74.3	4 420 039	3 271 014	74.0	5 083 768	3 793 515	74.6
1 VII 2010 ....ESDJ		9 490 583	7 100 147	74.8	4 413 225	3 285 104	74.4	5 077 358	3 815 043	75.1
1 VII 2011 ....ESDJ		9 473 172	7 148 636	75.5	4 403 227	3 303 932	75.0	5 069 945	3 844 704	75.8
1 VII 2012 ....ESDJ		9 464 495	7 198 575	76.1	4 397 910	3 324 299	75.6	5 066 585	3 874 276	76.5
1 VII 2013 ....ESDJ		9 465 997	7 247 854	76.6	4 399 369	3 345 878	76.1	5 066 628	3 901 976	77.0
1 VII 2014 ....ESDJ		9 474 511	...	...	4 405 204	...	...	5 069 307	...	...
1 I 2015 ....ESDJ		9 480 868	...	...	4 409 197	...	...	5 071 671	...	...
Belgium - Belgique										
1 VII 2006 ....ESDJ		10 541 893	10 389 801	98.6	5 159 947	5 083 829	98.5	5 381 946	5 305 972	98.6
1 VII 2007 ....ESDJ		10 622 604	10 469 341	98.6	5 201 670	5 125 007	98.5	5 420 934	5 344 334	98.6
1 VII 2008 ....ESDJ		10 709 973	10 555 681	98.6	5 246 480	5 169 223	98.5	5 463 493	5 386 458	98.6
1 VII 2009 ....ESDJ		10 796 493	10 641 089	98.6	5 290 436	5 212 557	98.5	5 506 057	5 428 532	98.6
1 VII 2010 ....ESDJ		10 895 638	10 739 291	98.6	5 341 252	5 262 796	98.5	5 554 386	5 476 495	98.6
1 I 2011 ....CDJC		11 000 638	10 842 520	98.6	5 401 718	5 322 172	98.5	5 598 920	5 520 348	98.6
1 VII 2011 ....ESDJ		11 043 788	10 884 939	98.6	5 425 814	5 345 964	98.5	5 617 974	5 538 975	98.6
1 VII 2012 ....ESDJ		11 128 246	...	...	5 469 608	...	...	5 658 638	...	...
1 VII 2013 ....ESDJ		11 182 817	...	...	5 497 753	...	...	5 685 065	...	...
1 VII 2014 ....ESDJ		11 231 213	...	...	5 522 163	...	...	5 709 051	...	...
1 I 2015 ....ESDJ		11 258 434	...	...	5 536 256	...	...	5 722 178	...	...
Bosnia and Herzegovina - Bosnie-Herzégovine										
1 VII 2006 ....ESDF		3 842 762	...	...	1 882 953	...	...	1 959 809	...	...
1 VII 2007 ....ESDF		3 842 562	...	...	1 877 309	...	...	1 965 253	...	...
1 VII 2008 ....ESDF		3 842 265	...	...	1 877 165	...	...	1 965 100	...	...
1 VII 2009 ....ESDF		3 842 566	...	...	1 877 312	...	...	1 965 254	...	...
1 VII 2010 ....ESDF		3 843 126	...	...	1 877 587	...	...	1 965 539	...	...
1 VII 2011 ....ESDF		3 841 224	...	...	1 876 546	...	...	1 964 678	...	...
1 VII 2012* ....ESDF		3 837 455	...	...	1 874 608	...	...	1 962 848	...	...
1 I 2013* ....ESDF		3 835 645	...	...	1 873 605	...	...	1 962 040	...	...

Continent, country or area, and date / Continent, pays ou zone et date	Code[a]	Both sexes - Les deux sexes			Male - Masculin			Female - Féminin		
		Total	Urban - Urbaine		Total	Urban - Urbaine		Total	Urban - Urbaine	
			Number Nombre	Percent P.100		Number Nombre	Percent P.100		Number Nombre	Percent P.100
EUROPE										
Bulgaria - Bulgarie										
1 VII 2006	ESDJ	7 699 020	5 428 388	70.5	3 732 130	2 613 030	70.0	3 966 890	2 815 358	71.0
1 VII 2007	ESDJ	7 659 764	5 414 260	70.7	3 710 315	2 604 175	70.2	3 949 449	2 810 085	71.2
1 VII 2008	ESDJ	7 623 395	5 405 147	70.9	3 690 485	2 597 929	70.4	3 932 910	2 807 218	71.4
1 VII 2009	ESDJ	7 585 131	5 408 330	71.3	3 670 296	2 598 442	70.8	3 914 835	2 809 888	71.8
1 VII 2010	ESDJ	7 534 289	5 388 142	71.5	3 644 560	2 587 844	71.0	3 889 729	2 800 298	72.0
1 II 2011	CDJC	7 364 570	5 338 261	72.5	3 586 571	2 580 734	72.0	3 777 999	2 757 527	73.0
1 VII 2011	ESDJ	7 348 328	5 336 366	72.6	3 577 847	2 579 205	72.1	3 770 481	2 757 161	73.1
1 VII 2012	ESDJ	7 305 888	5 316 384	72.8	3 555 920	2 568 535	72.2	3 749 968	2 747 849	73.3
1 VII 2013	ESDJ	7 263 859	...	...	3 534 276	...	...	3 729 584	...	...
1 VII 2014	ESDJ	7 223 938	...	...	3 513 480	...	...	3 710 458	...	...
1 I 2015	ESDJ	7 202 198	...	...	3 502 015	...	...	3 700 183	...	...
Croatia - Croatie										
1 VII 2006	ESDJ	4 311 159	...	...	2 074 504	...	...	2 236 655	...	...
1 VII 2007	ESDJ	4 310 217	...	...	2 075 547	...	...	2 234 670	...	...
1 VII 2008	ESDJ	4 309 705	...	...	2 076 517	...	...	2 233 188	...	...
1 VII 2009	ESDJ	4 305 181	...	...	2 075 321	...	...	2 229 860	...	...
1 VII 2010	ESDJ	4 295 427	...	...	2 071 195	...	...	2 224 232	...	...
1 IV 2011	CDJC	4 284 889	2 368 506	55.3	2 066 335	1 121 328	54.3	2 218 554	1 247 178	56.2
1 VII 2011	ESDJ	4 280 622	...	...	2 064 314	...	...	2 216 308	...	...
1 VII 2012	ESDJ	4 267 558	...	...	2 058 701	...	...	2 208 857	...	...
1 VII 2013	ESDJ	4 255 689	...	...	2 053 788	...	...	2 201 901	...	...
1 VII 2014	ESDJ	4 238 389	...	...	2 045 801	...	...	2 192 588	...	...
1 I 2015	ESDJ	4 225 316	...	...	2 039 227	...	...	2 186 089	...	...
Czech Republic - République tchèque										
1 VII 2006	ESDJ	10 238 905	...	...	5 000 124	...	...	5 238 781	...	...
1 VII 2007	ESDJ	10 298 828	...	...	5 037 856	...	...	5 260 972	...	...
1 VII 2008	ESDJ	10 384 603	...	...	5 090 898	...	...	5 293 705	...	...
1 VII 2009	ESDJ	10 443 936	...	...	5 126 422	...	...	5 317 514	...	...
1 VII 2010	ESDJ	10 474 410	...	...	5 141 699	...	...	5 332 711	...	...
25 III 2011	CDJC	10 436 560	7 650 450	73.3	5 109 766	3 712 348	72.7	5 326 794	3 938 102	73.9
1 VII 2011	ESDJ	10 496 088	...	...	5 152 721	...	...	5 343 368	...	...
1 VII 2012	ESDJ	10 510 786	...	...	5 161 280	...	...	5 349 506	...	...
1 VII 2013	ESDJ	10 510 719	7 683 793	73.1	5 161 617	3 740 790	72.5	5 349 102	3 943 003	73.7
1 VII 2014	ESDJ	10 524 783	7 693 352	73.1	5 169 146	3 744 873	72.4	5 355 637	3 948 479	73.7
Denmark - Danemark[115]										
1 VII 2006	ESDJ	5 434 567	...	...	2 690 179	...	...	2 744 388	...	...
1 VII 2007	ESDJ	5 457 415	...	...	2 702 894	...	...	2 754 521	...	...
1 VII 2008	ESDJ	5 489 022	...	...	2 720 016	...	...	2 769 006	...	...
1 VII 2009	ESDJ	5 519 441	...	...	2 735 983	...	...	2 783 458	...	...
1 VII 2010	ESDJ	5 545 039	...	...	2 748 439	...	...	2 796 600	...	...
1 I 2011	CDJC	5 560 628	...	...	2 756 582	...	...	2 804 046	...	...
1 VII 2011	ESDJ	5 566 856	...	...	2 760 140	...	...	2 806 716	...	...
1 VII 2012	ESDJ	5 587 085	...	...	2 771 208	...	...	2 815 877	...	...
1 VII 2013	ESDJ	5 608 784	...	...	2 782 661	...	...	2 826 123	...	...
1 VII 2014	ESDJ	5 639 719	...	...	2 799 895	...	...	2 839 824	...	...
1 VII 2015	ESDJ	5 678 348	...	...	2 822 535	...	...	2 855 813	...	...
Estonia - Estonie										
1 VII 2006	ESDJ	1 346 810	922 625	68.5	626 095	416 985	66.6	720 715	505 640	70.2
1 VII 2007	ESDJ	1 340 680	916 015	68.3	623 155	413 710	66.4	717 525	502 305	70.0
1 VII 2008	ESDJ	1 337 090	911 285	68.2	621 685	411 555	66.2	715 405	499 730	69.9
1 VII 2009	ESDJ	1 334 515	907 675	68.0	621 060	410 130	66.0	713 455	497 545	69.7
1 VII 2010	ESDJ	1 331 475	904 365	67.9	620 250	408 720	65.9	711 225	495 645	69.7
1 VII 2011	ESDJ	1 327 439	903 066	68.0	618 919	408 988	66.1	708 520	494 078	69.7
31 XII 2011	CDJC	1 294 455	879 157	67.9	600 526	396 719	66.1	693 929	482 438	69.5
1 VII 2012	ESDJ	1 322 696	902 743	68.3	617 153	409 784	66.4	705 543	492 959	69.9
1 VII 2013	ESDJ	1 317 997	900 071	68.3	615 543	408 564	66.4	702 454	491 507	70.0
1 VII 2014	ESDJ	1 314 545	897 901	68.3	614 654	407 677	66.3	699 891	490 224	70.0
1 I 2015	ESDJ	1 313 271	897 327	68.3	614 389	407 519	66.3	698 882	489 808	70.1
Faeroe Islands - Îles Féroé										
1 VII 2006	ESDJ	48 340	17 624	36.5	25 105	8 877	35.4	23 235	8 747	37.6
1 VII 2007	ESDJ	48 384	17 560	36.3	25 132	8 862	35.3	23 252	8 698	37.4
1 I 2008[39]	CDJC	48 433	...	...	25 174	...	...	23 259	...	...
1 VII 2008	ESDJ	48 555	17 707	36.5	25 218	8 966	35.6	23 337	8 741	37.5

Continent, country or area, and date / Continent, pays ou zone et date	Code[a]	Both sexes - Les deux sexes			Male - Masculin			Female - Féminin		
		Total	Urban - Urbaine Number Nombre	Urban - Urbaine Percent P.100	Total	Urban - Urbaine Number Nombre	Urban - Urbaine Percent P.100	Total	Urban - Urbaine Number Nombre	Urban - Urbaine Percent P.100
EUROPE										
Faeroe Islands - Îles Féroé										
1 VII 2009 ....ESDJ		48 798	18 001	36.9	25 345	9 117	36.0	23 453	8 884	37.9
1 VII 2010 ....ESDJ		48 669	18 131	37.3	25 276	9 195	36.4	23 393	8 936	38.2
1 VII 2011 ....ESDJ		48 563	18 110	37.3	25 179	9 120	36.2	23 384	8 990	38.4
11 XI 2011..................CDJC		48 346	...	...	25 125	...	...	23 221	...	...
1 VII 2012 ....ESDJ		48 319	18 033	37.3	25 074	9 072	36.2	23 245	8 961	38.6
1 VII 2013 ....ESDJ		48 286	18 220	37.7	25 014	9 147	36.6	23 272	9 073	39.0
1 VII 2014 ....ESDJ		48 462	18 373	37.9	25 048	9 207	36.8	23 414	9 166	39.1
1 VII 2015 ....ESDJ		48 958	18 674	38.1	25 330	9 386	37.1	23 628	9 288	39.3
Finland - Finlande										
1 VII 2006[116] ....ESDJ		5 239 423	3 534 480	67.5	2 564 748	1 708 710	66.6	2 674 676	1 825 770	68.3
1 VII 2007[116] ....ESDJ		5 261 682	3 558 585	67.6	2 576 858	1 721 731	66.8	2 684 824	1 836 854	68.4
1 VII 2008[116] ....ESDJ		5 286 095	3 586 744	67.9	2 590 669	1 737 294	67.1	2 695 426	1 849 450	68.6
1 VII 2009[116] ....ESDJ		5 311 276	3 615 933	68.1	2 604 636	1 753 169	67.3	2 706 640	1 862 764	68.8
1 VII 2010[116] ....ESDJ		5 335 481	3 643 170	68.3	2 617 862	1 767 855	67.5	2 717 620	1 875 315	69.0
31 XII 2010 ....CDJC		5 375 276	3 662 915	68.1	2 638 416	1 777 697	67.4	2 736 860	1 885 218	68.9
1 VII 2011[116] ....ESDJ		5 360 091	3 671 777	68.5	2 631 431	1 783 058	67.8	2 728 660	1 888 719	69.2
1 VII 2012[116] ....ESDJ		5 385 543	3 701 923	68.7	2 645 408	1 799 025	68.0	2 740 136	1 902 898	69.4
1 VII 2013[116] ....ESDJ		5 410 389	3 732 928	69.0	2 659 239	1 815 818	68.3	2 751 150	1 917 110	69.7
1 VII 2014[116] ....ESDJ		5 432 721	3 762 906	69.3	2 671 740	1 831 826	68.6	2 760 981	1 931 080	69.9
1 I 2015[39] ....ESDJ		5 471 753	...	...	2 691 863	...	...	2 779 890	...	...
France[117]										
1 I 2006 ....CDJC		61 399 541	...	...	29 714 539	...	...	31 685 002	...	...
1 VII 2006 ....ESDJ		61 597 486	...	...	29 815 995	...	...	31 781 491	...	...
1 VII 2007 ....ESDJ		61 965 052	...	...	30 001 162	...	...	31 963 890	...	...
1 VII 2008 ....ESDJ		62 300 288	...	...	30 166 091	...	...	32 134 197	...	...
1 VII 2009 ....ESDJ		62 615 472	...	...	30 322 692	...	...	32 292 780	...	...
1 I 2010 ....CDJS		62 765 235	48 387 303	77.1	30 393 079	23 208 841	76.4	32 372 156	25 178 462	77.8
1 VII 2010 ....ESDJ		62 917 790	...	...	30 475 789	...	...	32 442 001	...	...
1 VII 2011 ....ESDJ		63 223 158	...	...	30 626 399	...	...	32 596 759	...	...
1 VII 2012 ....ESDJ		63 536 918	...	...	30 782 589	...	...	32 754 329	...	...
1 I 2013 ....ESDJ		63 659 608	...	...	30 852 796	...	...	32 806 812	...	...
1 VII 2014* ....ESDJ		64 129 660	...	...	31 085 556	...	...	33 044 104	...	...
1 VII 2015* ....ESDJ		64 395 242	...	...	31 221 846	...	...	33 173 396	...	...
Germany - Allemagne										
1 VII 2006 ....ESDJ		82 365 810	...	...	40 317 807	...	...	42 048 003	...	...
1 VII 2007 ....ESDJ		82 262 642	...	...	40 287 823	...	...	41 974 819	...	...
1 VII 2008 ....ESDJ		82 119 776	...	...	40 238 595	...	...	41 881 181	...	...
1 VII 2009 ....ESDJ		81 874 770	...	...	40 133 270	...	...	41 741 500	...	...
1 VII 2010 ....ESDJ		81 757 471	...	...	40 099 871	...	...	41 657 600	...	...
9 V 2011 ....CDJC		80 219 695	64 444 232	80.3	39 145 941	31 227 832	79.8	41 073 754	33 216 400	80.9
1 VII 2011[5] ....ESDJ		80 274 983	...	...	39 177 274	...	...	41 097 709	...	...
1 VII 2012[5] ....ESDJ		80 425 823	...	...	39 305 462	...	...	41 120 362	...	...
1 VII 2013[5] ....ESDJ		80 645 605	...	...	39 468 950	...	...	41 176 655	...	...
1 VII 2014[5] ....ESDJ		80 982 500	...	...	39 696 190	...	...	41 286 310	...	...
1 I 2015[5] ....ESDJ		81 197 537	...	...	39 835 457	...	...	41 362 080	...	...
Gibraltar[118]										
31 XII 2006 ....ESDF		29 672	...	...	14 651	...	...	15 021	...	...
31 XII 2007 ....ESDF		30 066	...	...	14 871	...	...	15 195	...	...
31 XII 2008 ....ESDF		30 496	...	...	15 113	...	...	15 383	...	...
31 XII 2009 ....ESDF		30 963	...	...	15 378	...	...	15 585	...	...
31 XII 2010 ....ESDF		31 465	...	...	15 666	...	...	15 799	...	...
31 XII 2011 ....ESDF		32 003	...	...	15 977	...	...	16 026	...	...
12 XI 2012 ....CDJC		32 194	...	...	16 061	...	...	16 133	...	...
31 XII 2012 ....ESDF		32 577	...	...	16 311	...	...	16 266	...	...
31 XII 2013 ....ESDF		32 734	...	...	16 460	...	...	16 274	...	...
Greece - Grèce										
1 VII 2006 ....ESDF		11 020 393	...	...	5 437 830	...	...	5 582 563	...	...
1 VII 2007 ....ESDF		11 048 499	...	...	5 445 100	...	...	5 603 399	...	...
1 VII 2008 ....ESDF		11 077 863	...	...	5 452 027	...	...	5 625 836	...	...
1 VII 2009 ....ESDF		11 107 024	...	...	5 458 449	...	...	5 648 575	...	...
1 VII 2010 ....ESDF		11 121 383	...	...	5 457 186	...	...	5 664 197	...	...
9 V 2011 ....CDFC		10 816 286	8 285 259	76.6	5 303 223	4 022 889	75.9	5 513 063	4 262 370	77.3
1 VII 2011 ....ESDF		11 104 995	...	...	5 438 712	...	...	5 666 283	...	...

Continent, country or area, and date / Continent, pays ou zone et date	Code[a]	Both sexes - Les deux sexes			Male - Masculin			Female - Féminin		
		Total	Urban - Urbaine		Total	Urban - Urbaine		Total	Urban - Urbaine	
			Number Nombre	Percent P.100		Number Nombre	Percent P.100		Number Nombre	Percent P.100
EUROPE										
Greece - Grèce										
1 VII 2012	ESDF	11 045 040	...	...	5 395 104	...	...	5 649 936	...	...
1 VII 2013	ESDF	10 965 241	...	...	5 339 750	...	...	5 625 491	...	...
1 VII 2014	ESDF	10 892 369	...	...	5 290 797	...	...	5 601 572	...	...
1 I 2015	ESDF	10 858 018	...	...	5 268 390	...	...	5 589 628	...	...
Guernsey - Guernesey										
31 III 2006	ESDF	60 993	...	...	30 014	...	...	30 979	...	...
31 III 2007	ESDF	61 139	...	...	30 001	...	...	31 138	...	...
31 III 2008	ESDF	61 688	...	...	30 382	...	...	31 306	...	...
31 III 2009	ESDF	62 236	...	...	30 754	...	...	31 482	...	...
31 III 2010	ESDF	62 390	...	...	30 669	...	...	31 721	...	...
31 III 2011	ESDF	62 878	...	...	31 003	...	...	31 875	...	...
31 III 2012	ESDF	63 033	...	...	31 116	...	...	31 917	...	...
31 III 2013	ESDF	62 675	...	...	31 050	...	...	31 625	...	...
31 III 2014	ESDF	62 576	...	...	30 937	...	...	31 639	...	...
31 III 2015	CDJC	62 612	...	...	31 028	...	...	31 584	...	...
Holy See - Saint-Siège[119]										
1 VII 2009	ESDF	466[120]	...	...	320	...	...	146	...	...
Hungary - Hongrie										
1 VII 2006	ESDJ	10 071 370	6 749 388	67.0	4 781 829	3 163 716	66.2	5 289 541	3 585 673	67.8
1 VII 2007	ESDJ	10 055 780	6 737 792	67.0	4 774 320	3 156 954	66.1	5 281 460	3 580 839	67.8
1 VII 2008	ESDJ	10 038 188	6 810 173	67.8	4 766 306	3 191 030	66.9	5 271 882	3 619 143	68.6
1 VII 2009	ESDJ	10 022 650	6 861 432	68.5	4 759 975	3 215 749	67.6	5 262 675	3 645 683	69.3
1 VII 2010	ESDJ	10 000 023	6 953 071	69.5	4 750 401	3 260 344	68.6	5 249 623	3 692 727	70.3
1 VII 2011	ESDJ	9 971 727	6 945 873	69.7	4 737 813	3 256 796	68.7	5 233 914	3 689 077	70.5
1 X 2011	CDFC	9 937 628	6 903 858	69.5	4 718 479	3 241 911	68.7	5 219 149	3 661 947	70.2
1 VII 2012	ESDJ	9 920 362	6 877 231	69.3	4 720 310	3 234 447	68.5	5 200 052	3 642 785	70.1
1 VII 2013	ESDJ	9 893 082	6 864 757	69.4	4 709 672	3 229 480	68.6	5 183 410	3 635 277	70.1
1 VII 2014[121]	ESDJ	9 866 468	6 950 391	70.4	4 699 585	3 272 050	69.6	5 166 883	3 678 342	71.2
Iceland - Islande[122]										
1 VII 2006	ESDJ	304 334	281 961	92.6	154 287	141 673	91.8	150 047	140 288	93.5
1 VII 2007	ESDJ	311 396	289 119	92.8	158 866	146 168	92.0	152 530	142 951	93.7
1 VII 2008	ESDJ	319 355	298 024	93.3	163 176	151 378	92.8	156 179	146 646	93.9
1 VII 2009	ESDJ	319 246	298 890	93.6	161 548	150 604	93.2	157 698	148 286	94.0
1 VII 2010	ESDJ	318 006	297 432	93.5	159 838	148 901	93.2	158 168	148 531	93.9
1 VII 2011[123]	ESDJ	319 014	314 413	98.6	160 185	157 797	98.5	158 829	156 616	98.6
31 XII 2011	CDJC	315 556	...	...	158 151	...	...	157 405	...	...
1 VII 2012	ESDJ	320 716	300 237	93.6	160 901	150 074	93.3	159 815	150 163	94.0
1 VII 2013	ESDJ	323 764	303 136	93.6	162 378	151 471	93.3	161 386	151 665	94.0
1 VII 2014	ESDJ	327 386	306 633	93.7	164 252	153 265	93.3	163 134	153 368	94.0
1 I 2015	ESDJ	329 100	...	...	165 186	...	...	163 914	...	...
Ireland - Irlande										
23 IV 2006	CDFC	4 239 848	2 574 313	60.7	2 121 171	1 267 960	59.8	2 118 677	1 306 353	61.7
1 VII 2006	ESDF	4 260 341	...	...	2 130 565	...	...	2 129 776	...	...
1 VII 2007	ESDF	4 356 931	...	...	2 177 582	...	...	2 179 349	...	...
1 VII 2008	ESDF	4 425 683	...	...	2 206 165	...	...	2 219 518	...	...
1 VII 2009	ESDF	4 458 942	...	...	2 215 646	...	...	2 243 297	...	...
1 VII 2010	ESDF	4 560 155	...	...	2 265 200	...	...	2 294 955	...	...
10 IV 2011	CDFC	4 588 252	2 846 882	62.0	2 272 699	1 389 160	61.1	2 315 553	1 457 722	63.0
1 VII 2011	ESDF	4 576 794	...	...	2 269 608	...	...	2 307 186	...	...
1 VII 2012	ESDF	4 586 897	...	...	2 271 290	...	...	2 315 607	...	...
1 VII 2013[121]	ESDF	4 598 294	...	...	2 275 508	...	...	2 322 787	...	...
1 I 2014[121]	ESDF	4 605 501	...	...	2 278 225	...	...	2 327 276	...	...
15 IV 2015[121]	ESDJ	4 635 390	...	...	2 289 549	...	...	2 345 841	...	...
Isle of Man - Île de Man										
23 IV 2006	CDJC	80 058	...	...	39 523	...	...	40 535	...	...
30 IV 2007	ESDJ	80 885	...	...	39 995	...	...	40 889	...	...
30 IV 2008	ESDJ	81 722	...	...	40 472	...	...	41 250	...	...
30 IV 2009	ESDJ	82 371	...	...	40 849	...	...	41 522	...	...
30 IV 2010	ESDJ	82 691	...	...	41 053	...	...	41 638	...	...
27 III 2011	CDJC	84 497	...	...	41 971	...	...	42 526	...	...
30 IV 2012	ESDJ	85 047	...	...	42 273	...	...	42 775	...	...
30 IV 2013	ESDJ	85 682	...	...	42 622	...	...	43 060	...	...
30 IV 2014	ESDJ	86 322	...	...	42 971	...	...	43 352	...	...
30 IV 2015	ESDJ	86 963	...	...	43 319	...	...	43 644	...	...

6. Total and urban population by sex: 2006 - 2015
Population totale et population urbaine selon le sexe : 2006 - 2015 (continued - suite)

Continent, country or area, and date / Continent, pays ou zone et date	Code[a]	Both sexes - Les deux sexes			Male - Masculin			Female - Féminin		
		Total	Urban - Urbaine		Total	Urban - Urbaine		Total	Urban - Urbaine	
			Number Nombre	Percent P.100		Number Nombre	Percent P.100		Number Nombre	Percent P.100
EUROPE										
Italy - Italie										
1 VII 2006	ESDJ	58 143 979	...	...	28 175 406	...	...	29 968 574	...	...
1 VII 2007	ESDJ	58 438 310	...	...	28 311 738	...	...	30 126 572	...	...
1 VII 2008	ESDJ	58 826 731	...	...	28 490 625	...	...	30 336 106	...	...
1 VII 2009	ESDJ	59 095 365	...	...	28 609 696	...	...	30 485 669	...	...
1 VII 2010	ESDJ	59 277 417	...	...	28 682 321	...	...	30 595 096	...	...
1 VII 2011	ESDJ	59 379 449	...	...	28 720 928	...	...	30 658 521	...	...
9 X 2011	CDJC	59 433 744	...	...	28 745 507	...	...	30 688 237	...	...
1 VII 2012	ESDJ	59 539 717	...	...	28 808 098	...	...	30 731 619	...	...
1 VII 2013	ESDJ	60 233 948	...	...	29 187 081	...	...	31 046 867	...	...
1 VII 2014	ESDJ	60 789 140	...	...	29 493 077	...	...	31 296 063	...	...
1 I 2015	ESDJ	60 795 612	...	...	29 501 590	...	...	31 294 022	...	...
Jersey										
27 III 2011	CDFC	97 857	...	...	48 296	...	...	49 561	...	...
Latvia - Lettonie										
1 VII 2006	ESDJ	2 218 357	1 505 865	67.9	1 017 925	676 209	66.4	1 200 432	829 656	69.1
1 VII 2007	ESDJ	2 200 325	1 494 615	67.9	1 010 416	671 274	66.4	1 189 909	823 341	69.2
1 VII 2008	ESDJ	2 177 322	1 478 831	67.9	999 845	663 658	66.4	1 177 477	815 173	69.2
1 VII 2009	ESDJ	2 141 669	1 453 570	67.9	981 789	650 486	66.3	1 159 880	803 084	69.2
1 VII 2010	ESDJ	2 097 555	1 422 675	67.8	959 435	634 393	66.1	1 138 120	788 282	69.3
1 III 2011	CDJC	2 070 371	1 404 251	67.8	946 102	625 150	66.1	1 124 269	779 101	69.3
1 VII 2011	ESDJ	2 059 709	1 394 429	67.7	941 375	620 484	65.9	1 118 334	773 945	69.2
1 VII 2012	ESDJ	2 034 319	1 374 215	67.6	930 696	611 604	65.7	1 103 623	762 611	69.1
1 VII 2013	ESDJ	2 012 647	1 362 004	67.7	921 813	606 624	65.8	1 090 834	755 380	69.2
1 VII 2014	ESDJ	1 993 782	1 353 269	67.9	914 126	603 112	66.0	1 079 656	750 157	69.5
1 I 2015	ESDJ	1 986 096	...	...	911 207	...	...	1 074 889	...	...
Liechtenstein										
1 VII 2006	ESDJ	35 010	...	...	17 256	...	...	17 754	...	...
1 VII 2007	ESDJ	35 322	...	...	17 426	...	...	17 896	...	...
1 VII 2008	ESDJ	35 446	...	...	17 508	...	...	17 938	...	...
1 VII 2009	ESDJ	35 789	...	...	17 716	...	...	18 073	...	...
1 VII 2010	ESDJ	36 010	...	...	17 817	...	...	18 193	...	...
31 XII 2010	CDFC	36 149	...	...	17 886	...	...	18 263	...	...
1 VII 2011	ESDJ	36 281	...	...	17 950	...	...	18 331	...	...
1 VII 2012	ESDJ	36 657	...	...	18 145	...	...	18 512	...	...
1 VII 2013	ESDJ	36 984	...	...	18 324	...	...	18 660	...	...
1 VII 2014[124]	ESDJ	37 248	...	...	18 477	...	...	18 771	...	...
1 I 2015[124]	ESDJ	37 366	...	...	18 553	...	...	18 813	...	...
Lithuania - Lituanie										
1 VII 2006	ESDJ	3 269 909	2 179 007	66.6	1 517 629	990 840	65.3	1 752 280	1 188 167	67.8
1 VII 2007	ESDJ	3 231 294	2 155 871	66.7	1 497 107	977 988	65.3	1 734 187	1 177 883	67.9
1 VII 2008	ESDJ	3 198 231	2 134 908	66.8	1 480 386	966 638	65.3	1 717 845	1 168 270	68.0
1 VII 2009	ESDJ	3 162 916	2 112 248	66.8	1 461 776	953 885	65.3	1 701 140	1 158 363	68.1
1 VII 2010	ESDJ	3 097 282	2 068 095	66.8	1 428 711	931 128	65.2	1 668 571	1 136 967	68.1
1 III 2011	CDJC	3 043 429	2 031 211	66.7	1 402 604	912 943	65.1	1 640 825	1 118 268	68.2
1 VII 2011	ESDJ	3 028 115	2 021 365	66.8	1 395 367	907 995	65.1	1 632 748	1 113 370	68.2
1 VII 2012	ESDJ	2 987 773	1 997 436	66.9	1 376 201	896 102	65.1	1 611 572	1 101 334	68.3
1 VII 2013	ESDJ	2 957 689	1 981 924	67.0	1 362 443	888 578	65.2	1 595 246	1 093 346	68.5
1 VII 2014[121]	ESDJ	2 932 367	1 968 596	67.1	1 351 126	881 978	65.3	1 581 241	1 086 618	68.7
Luxembourg										
1 VII 2006	ESDJ	472 637	...	...	233 946	...	...	238 691	...	...
1 VII 2007	ESDJ	479 993	...	...	237 700	...	...	242 294	...	...
1 VII 2008	ESDJ	488 650	...	...	242 221	...	...	246 429	...	...
1 VII 2009	ESDJ	497 782	...	...	247 120	...	...	250 662	...	...
1 VII 2010	ESDJ	506 953	...	...	252 013	...	...	254 941	...	...
1 II 2011	CDJC	512 353	...	...	254 967	...	...	257 386	...	...
1 VII 2011	ESDJ	518 347	...	...	258 220	...	...	260 127	...	...
1 VII 2012	ESDJ	530 946	...	...	265 116	...	...	265 830	...	...
1 VII 2013	ESDJ	543 360	...	...	271 765	...	...	271 595	...	...
1 VII 2014	ESDJ	556 319	...	...	278 544	...	...	277 775	...	...
1 I 2015	ESDJ	562 958	...	...	281 973	...	...	280 985	...	...
Malta - Malte										
1 VII 2006[125]	ESDJ	405 355	...	...	201 201	...	...	204 154	...	...
1 VII 2007[125]	ESDJ	406 778	...	...	202 150	...	...	204 628	...	...
1 VII 2008[125]	ESDJ	409 429	...	...	203 696	...	...	205 733	...	...

158

Continent, country or area, and date / Continent, pays ou zone et date	Code[a]	Both sexes - Les deux sexes			Male - Masculin			Female - Féminin		
		Total	Urban - Urbaine		Total	Urban - Urbaine		Total	Urban - Urbaine	
			Number Nombre	Percent P.100		Number Nombre	Percent P.100		Number Nombre	Percent P.100
EUROPE										
Malta - Malte										
1 VII 2009[125]	ESDJ	412 530	...	...	205 432	...	...	207 098	...	...
1 VII 2010[125]	ESDJ	414 562	...	...	206 333	...	...	208 229	...	...
1 VII 2011[125]	ESDJ	416 318	...	...	207 072	...	...	209 246	...	...
20 XI 2011	CDFC	417 432	400 557	96.0	207 625	199 151	95.9	209 807	201 406	96.0
1 VII 2012[125]	ESDJ	419 507	...	...	208 811	...	...	210 696	...	...
1 VII 2013[125]	ESDJ	423 431	...	...	211 182	...	...	212 249	...	...
1 VII 2014[125]	ESDJ	427 364	...	...	214 735	...	...	212 629	...	...
1 I 2015[125]	ESDJ	429 344	...	...	214 735	...	...	214 609	...	...
Monaco										
9 VI 2008	CDJC	31 109	...	...	15 076[126]	...	...	15 914[126]	...	...
Montenegro - Monténégro										
1 VII 2006	ESDJ	624 241	391 884	62.8	307 271	190 286	61.9	316 970	201 598	63.6
1 VII 2007	ESDJ	626 104	394 653	63.0	308 267	191 692	62.2	317 836	202 961	63.9
1 VII 2008	ESDJ	628 804	397 747	63.3	309 787	193 393	62.4	319 018	204 354	64.1
1 VII 2009	ESDJ	631 536	400 928	63.5	311 258	195 088	62.7	320 278	205 840	64.3
1 VII 2010	ESDJ	617 304	...	...	304 861	...	...	312 443	...	...
1 IV 2011	CDJC	620 029	399 264	64.4	306 236	193 691	63.2	313 793	205 573	65.5
1 VII 2011	ESDJ	620 556	...	...	306 472	...	...	314 084	...	...
1 VII 2012	ESDJ	620 601	...	...	306 580	...	...	314 021	...	...
1 VII 2013	ESDJ	622 149	...	...	307 428	...	...	314 722	...	...
1 VII 2014[121]	ESDJ	621 810	...	...	307 339	...	...	314 472	...	...
1 I 2015[121]	ESDJ	622 099	...	...	307 522	...	...	314 577	...	...
Netherlands - Pays-Bas										
1 VII 2006	ESDJ	16 346 101	10 803 902	66.1	8 082 961	5 311 812	65.7	8 263 141	5 492 090	66.5
1 VII 2007	ESDJ	16 381 696	10 825 307	66.1	8 100 294	5 322 596	65.7	8 281 402	5 502 712	66.4
1 VII 2008	ESDJ	16 445 593	10 877 858	66.1	8 134 235	5 350 572	65.8	8 311 359	5 527 286	66.5
1 VII 2009	ESDJ	16 530 388	10 938 780	66.2	8 179 936	5 383 776	65.8	8 350 452	5 555 004	66.5
1 VII 2010	ESDJ	16 615 394	11 096 288	66.8	8 223 479	5 464 083	66.4	8 391 915	5 632 205	67.1
1 I 2011	CDJC	16 655 799	11 124 721	66.8	8 243 482	5 478 213	66.5	8 412 317	5 646 508	67.1
1 VII 2011	ESDJ	16 693 074		...	8 263 177		...	8 429 897		...
1 VII 2012	ESDJ	16 754 962		...	8 295 105		...	8 459 857		...
1 VII 2013	ESDJ	16 804 432		...	8 320 862		...	8 483 570		...
1 VII 2014	ESDJ	16 865 007		...	8 353 621		...	8 511 386		...
1 I 2015	ESDJ	16 900 726		...	8 372 858		...	8 527 868		...
Norway - Norvège										
1 VII 2006[121]	ESDJ	4 660 677	...	...	2 313 885	...	...	2 346 792	...	...
1 VII 2007[121]	ESDJ	4 709 153	...	...	2 342 739	...	...	2 366 414	...	...
1 VII 2008[121]	ESDJ	4 768 212	...	...	2 377 372	...	...	2 390 840	...	...
1 VII 2009[121]	ESDJ	4 828 726	...	...	2 410 903	...	...	2 417 823	...	...
1 VII 2010[121]	ESDJ	4 889 252	...	...	2 443 801	...	...	2 445 452	...	...
1 VII 2011[121]	ESDJ	4 953 088	...	...	2 479 860	...	...	2 473 228	...	...
19 XI 2011[127]	CDJC	4 979 955	3 951 427[79]	79.3	2 495 777	1 959 424[79]	78.5	2 484 178	1 992 003[79]	80.2
1 VII 2012[121]	ESDJ	5 018 573	...	...	2 517 390	...	...	2 501 183	...	...
1 VII 2013[121]	ESDJ	5 079 623	...	...	2 551 458	...	...	2 528 165	...	...
1 VII 2014[121]	ESDJ	5 137 232	...	...	2 583 105	...	...	2 554 127	...	...
1 I 2015[121]	ESDJ	5 166 493	...	...	2 599 202	...	...	2 567 291	...	...
Poland - Pologne										
1 VII 2006[121]	ESDJ	38 132 177	23 400 565	61.4	18 436 101	11 103 869	60.2	19 696 176	12 296 696	62.4
1 VII 2007[121]	ESDJ	38 115 967	23 350 920	61.3	18 417 074	11 070 886	60.1	19 698 893	12 280 034	62.3
1 VII 2008[121]	ESDJ	38 115 909	23 305 018	61.1	18 408 405	11 041 359	60.0	19 707 504	12 263 659	62.2
1 VII 2009[121]	ESDJ	38 153 389	23 293 906	61.1	18 423 343	11 032 562	59.9	19 730 046	12 261 344	62.1
1 VII 2010[121]	ESDJ	38 516 689	23 448 497	60.9	18 647 604	11 136 164	59.7	19 869 085	12 312 333	62.0
31 III 2011[128]	CDJC	38 044 565	23 116 673	60.8	18 420 389	10 977 424	59.6	19 624 176	12 139 249	61.9
1 VII 2011[121]	ESDJ	38 525 670	23 404 926	60.8	18 650 105	11 111 443	59.6	19 875 565	12 293 483	61.9
1 VII 2012[121]	ESDJ	38 533 789	23 360 022	60.6	18 651 441	11 086 177	59.4	19 882 348	12 273 845	61.7
1 VII 2013[121]	ESDJ	38 275 578	...	...	18 526 649	...	...	19 748 929	...	...
1 VII 2014[121]	ESDJ	38 011 735	...	...	18 400 564	...	...	19 611 172	...	...
1 I 2015[121]	ESDJ	38 005 614	...	...	18 397 163	...	...	19 608 451	...	...
Portugal										
1 VII 2006	ESDJ	10 522 288	...	...	5 061 604	...	...	5 460 684	...	...
1 VII 2007	ESDJ	10 542 964	...	...	5 067 071	...	...	5 475 893	...	...
1 VII 2008	ESDJ	10 558 177	...	...	5 067 993	...	...	5 490 184	...	...
1 VII 2009	ESDJ	10 568 247	...	...	5 064 992	...	...	5 503 255	...	...

Continent, country or area, and date / Continent, pays ou zone et date	Code[a]	Both sexes - Les deux sexes Total	Urban - Urbaine Number Nombre	Urban - Urbaine Percent P.100	Male - Masculin Total	Urban - Urbaine Number Nombre	Urban - Urbaine Percent P.100	Female - Féminin Total	Urban - Urbaine Number Nombre	Urban - Urbaine Percent P.100
EUROPE										
Portugal										
1 VII 2010	ESDJ	10 573 100	...	...	5 058 644	...	...	5 514 456	...	...
21 III 2011	CDFC	10 282 306	6 286 712	61.1	4 868 755	2 949 862	60.6	5 413 551	3 336 850	61.6
1 VII 2011	ESDJ	10 557 560	...	...	5 041 990	...	...	5 515 570	...	...
1 VII 2012	ESDJ	10 514 844	...	...	5 013 067	...	...	5 501 777	...	...
1 VII 2013	ESDJ	10 457 295	...	...	4 976 859	...	...	5 480 437	...	...
1 VII 2014	ESDJ	10 401 062	...	...	4 940 843	...	...	5 460 219	...	...
1 I 2015	ESDJ	10 374 822	...	...	4 923 666	...	...	5 451 156	...	...
Republic of Moldova - République de Moldova[129]										
1 VII 2006	ESDJ	3 585 209	1 481 398	41.3	1 720 139	706 649	41.1	1 865 070	774 749	41.5
1 VII 2007	ESDJ	3 576 910	1 477 062	41.3	1 719 246	694 308	40.4	1 857 664	782 754	42.1
1 VII 2008	ESDJ	3 570 108	1 475 609	41.3	1 716 195	693 550	40.4	1 853 913	782 059	42.2
1 VII 2009	ESDJ	3 565 604	1 476 390	41.4	1 714 209	694 134	40.5	1 851 395	782 257	42.3
1 VII 2010	ESDJ	3 562 045	1 479 196	41.5	1 712 783	695 603	40.6	1 849 262	783 593	42.4
1 VII 2011	ESDJ	3 559 986	1 483 731	41.7	1 711 916	697 492	40.7	1 848 070	786 239	42.5
1 VII 2012	ESDJ	3 559 520	1 488 966	41.8	1 712 036	699 880	40.9	1 847 484	789 086	42.7
1 VII 2014	ESDJ	3 557 328	...	...	1 711 295	...	...	1 846 033	...	...
1 I 2015	ESDJ	3 555 159	...	...	1 710 244	...	...	1 844 915	...	...
Romania - Roumanie										
1 VII 2006	ESDJ	21 193 749	11 748 344	55.4	10 320 907	5 630 452	54.6	10 872 842	6 117 892	56.3
1 VII 2007	ESDJ	20 882 980	11 455 494	54.9	10 169 596	5 489 050	54.0	10 713 384	5 966 444	55.7
1 VII 2008	ESDJ	20 537 848	11 102 802	54.1	10 000 515	5 314 752	53.1	10 537 333	5 788 050	54.9
1 VII 2009	ESDJ	20 367 437	10 976 558	53.9	9 916 107	5 249 975	52.9	10 451 330	5 726 583	54.8
1 VII 2010	ESDJ	20 246 798	10 922 169	53.9	9 856 669	5 223 471	53.0	10 390 129	5 698 698	54.8
1 VII 2011	ESDJ	20 147 657	10 878 099	54.0	9 805 108	5 198 460	53.0	10 342 549	5 679 639	54.9
20 X 2011	CDFC	20 039 141	10 858 790	54.2	9 736 342	5 185 636	53.3	10 302 799	5 673 154	55.1
1 VII 2012	ESDJ	20 060 182	10 823 218	54.0	9 770 353	5 170 875	52.9	10 289 829	5 652 343	54.9
1 VII 2013	ESDJ	19 985 814	10 770 879	53.9	9 754 851	5 152 718	52.8	10 230 963	5 618 161	54.9
1 VII 2014	ESDJ	19 913 193	10 726 149	53.9	9 728 663	5 132 414	52.8	10 184 530	5 593 735	54.9
1 I 2015	ESDJ	19 870 647	...	...	9 707 074	...	...	10 163 573	...	...
Russian Federation - Fédération de Russie										
1 VII 2006	ESDJ	143 049 637	104 775 157	73.2	66 176 725	47 967 026	72.5	76 872 912	56 808 131	73.9
1 VII 2007	ESDJ	142 805 114	104 798 401	73.4	66 013 796	47 923 326	72.6	76 791 318	56 875 075	74.1
1 VII 2008	ESDJ	142 742 366	104 890 297	73.5	65 968 338	47 938 815	72.7	76 774 028	56 951 482	74.2
1 VII 2009	ESDJ	142 785 349	104 988 448	73.5	65 988 356	47 969 474	72.7	76 796 993	57 018 974	74.2
1 VII 2010	ESDJ	142 849 468	105 241 319	73.7	66 033 070	48 081 267	72.8	76 816 398	57 160 052	74.4
14 X 2010	CDFC	143 436 145	...	...	66 457 074	...	...	76 979 071	...	...
1 VII 2011	ESDJ	142 960 908	105 581 615	73.9	66 113 269	48 243 019	73.0	76 847 639	57 338 596	74.6
1 VII 2012	ESDJ	143 201 730	105 930 122	74.0	66 264 910	48 419 208	73.1	76 936 820	57 510 914	74.8
San Marino - Saint-Marin										
1 VII 2006[39]	ESDF	30 184	...	...	14 814	...	...	15 370	...	...
1 VII 2007[39]	ESDF	31 211	...	...	15 664	...	...	15 547	...	...
1 VII 2008[39]	ESDF	31 662	...	...	15 874	...	...	15 788	...	...
1 VII 2009[39]	ESDF	33 066	...	...	16 088	...	...	16 978	...	...
1 VII 2010[39]	ESDF	33 270	...	...	16 171	...	...	17 099	...	...
7 XI 2010*	CDFC	30 652	...	...	14 791[130]	...	...	15 818[130]	...	...
1 VII 2011[39]	ESDF	33 389	...	...	16 221	...	...	17 169	...	...
1 VII 2012[39]	ESDF	33 518	...	...	16 296	...	...	17 222	...	...
1 VII 2013[39]	ESDF	33 469	...	...	16 280	...	...	17 189	...	...
1 VII 2014[39]	ESDF	33 648	...	...	16 396	...	...	17 252	...	...
1 I 2015[39]	ESDF	33 738	...	...	16 425	...	...	17 313	...	...
Serbia - Serbie[131]										
1 VII 2006	ESDJ	7 411 569	4 263 386	57.5	3 603 698	2 034 616	56.5	3 807 871	2 228 770	58.5
1 VII 2007	ESDJ	7 381 579	4 270 400	57.9	3 588 957	2 037 012	56.8	3 792 622	2 233 388	58.9
1 VII 2008	ESDJ	7 350 222	4 275 245	58.2	3 573 814	2 038 642	57.0	3 776 408	2 236 603	59.2
1 VII 2009	ESDJ	7 320 807	4 279 035	58.5	3 560 048	2 039 934	57.3	3 760 759	2 239 101	59.5
1 VII 2010	ESDJ	7 291 436	4 283 985	58.8	3 546 374	2 041 975	57.6	3 745 062	2 242 010	59.9
1 VII 2011[15]	ESDJ	7 236 519	4 275 178	59.1	3 523 911	2 041 228	57.9	3 712 608	2 233 950	60.2
1 X 2011	CDJC	7 186 862	4 271 872	59.4	3 499 176	2 039 105	58.3	3 687 686	2 232 767	60.5
1 VII 2012[15]	ESDJ	7 201 497	4 273 861	59.3	3 506 947	2 039 649	58.2	3 694 550	2 234 212	60.5
1 VII 2013[15]	ESDJ	7 166 552	4 272 061	59.6	3 489 683	2 037 554	58.4	3 676 869	2 234 507	60.8

Continent, country or area, and date / Continent, pays ou zone et date	Code[a]	Both sexes - Les deux sexes			Male - Masculin			Female - Féminin		
		Total	Urban - Urbaine		Total	Urban - Urbaine		Total	Urban - Urbaine	
			Number Nombre	Percent P.100		Number Nombre	Percent P.100		Number Nombre	Percent P.100
EUROPE										
Serbia - Serbie[131]										
1 VII 2014[15] ....ESDJ		7 131 787	4 270 367	59.9	3 472 746	2 035 772	58.6	3 659 041	2 234 595	61.1
1 I 2015[15] ....ESDJ		7 114 393	...	...	3 464 399	...	...	3 649 994	...	...
Slovakia - Slovaquie										
1 VII 2006 ....ESDJ		5 373 054	...	...	2 610 255	...	...	2 762 799	...	...
1 VII 2007 ....ESDJ		5 374 622	...	...	2 612 172	...	...	2 762 451	...	...
1 VII 2008 ....ESDJ		5 379 233	...	...	2 616 013	...	...	2 763 220	...	...
1 VII 2009 ....ESDJ		5 386 406	...	...	2 620 942	...	...	2 765 464	...	...
1 VII 2010 ....ESDJ		5 391 428	...	...	2 624 360	...	...	2 767 069	...	...
21 V 2011 ....CDJC		5 397 036	2 937 735	54.4	2 627 772	1 412 818	53.8	2 769 264	1 524 917	55.1
1 VII 2011 ....ESDJ		5 398 384	2 938 053	54.4	2 628 463	1 412 966	53.8	2 769 922	1 525 087	55.1
1 VII 2012 ....ESDJ		5 407 579	2 935 710	54.3	2 633 866	1 411 738	53.6	2 773 714	1 523 972	54.9
1 VII 2013 ....ESDJ		5 413 393	2 931 444	54.2	2 637 520	1 409 503	53.4	2 775 873	1 521 941	54.8
1 VII 2014 ....ESDJ		5 418 649	2 925 291	54.0	2 640 694	1 406 300	53.3	2 777 955	1 518 991	54.7
1 I 2015 ....ESDJ		5 421 349	...	...	2 642 328	...	...	2 779 021	...	...
Slovenia - Slovénie										
1 VII 2006 ....ESDJ		2 008 516	962 740[132]	47.9	985 876[132]	456 764[132]	46.3	1 022 640[132]	505 976[132]	49.5
1 VII 2007 ....ESDJ		2 019 406	1 006 767	49.9	995 125	490 610	49.3	1 024 281	516 157	50.4
1 VII 2008 ....ESDJ		2 022 629	1 012 477	50.1	996 969	491 605	49.3	1 025 660	520 872	50.8
1 VII 2009 ....ESDJ		2 042 335	1 024 087	50.1	1 011 767	500 253	49.4	1 030 568	523 834	50.8
1 VII 2010 ....ESDJ		2 049 261	1 024 812	50.0	1 014 716	500 063	49.3	1 034 545	524 749	50.7
1 I 2011......................CDFC		2 058 051	1 030 172	50.1	1 019 826	503 083	49.3	1 038 225	527 089	50.8
1 VII 2011 ....ESDJ		2 052 496	1 023 650	49.9	1 015 430	498 490	49.1	1 037 066	525 160	50.6
1 VII 2012 ....ESDJ		2 056 262	1 023 236	49.8	1 017 414	498 297	49.0	1 038 848	524 939	50.5
1 VII 2013 ....ESDJ		2 059 114	1 047 560	50.9	1 019 658	513 084	50.3	1 039 456	534 476	51.4
1 VII 2014 ....ESDJ		2 061 623	1 051 087	51.0	1 021 419	514 828	50.4	1 040 204	536 259	51.6
1 VII 2015 ....ESDJ		2 063 077	1 106 955	53.7	1 022 554	542 847	53.1	1 040 523	564 108	54.2
Spain - Espagne										
1 VII 2006 ....ESDJ		44 360 525	...	...	21 900 707	...	...	22 459 818	...	...
1 VII 2007 ....ESDJ		45 236 002	...	...	22 362 075	...	...	22 873 927	...	...
1 VII 2008 ....ESDJ		45 983 167	...	...	22 756 861	...	...	23 226 306	...	...
1 VII 2009 ....ESDJ		46 367 545	...	...	22 934 497	...	...	23 433 048	...	...
1 VII 2010 ....ESDJ		46 562 486	...	...	23 008 587	...	...	23 553 899	...	...
1 VII 2011 ....ESDJ		46 736 255	...	...	23 073 274	...	...	23 662 981	...	...
1 XI 2011 ....CDJC		46 815 915	...	...	23 104 350	...	...	23 711 560	...	...
1 VII 2012 ....ESDJ		46 766 399	...	...	23 055 715	...	...	23 710 684	...	...
1 VII 2013 ....ESDJ		46 593 236	...	...	22 933 751	...	...	23 659 485	...	...
1 VII 2014[122] ....ESDJ		46 480 882	...	...	22 852 004	...	...	23 628 879	...	...
1 I 2015[122] ....ESDJ		46 449 565	...	...	22 826 546	...	...	23 623 019	...	...
Sweden - Suède[39]										
1 VII 2006 ....ESDJ		9 080 505	...	...	4 505 037	...	...	4 575 468	...	...
1 VII 2007 ....ESDJ		9 148 092	...	...	4 543 722	...	...	4 604 370	...	...
1 VII 2008 ....ESDJ		9 219 637	...	...	4 583 816	...	...	4 635 822	...	...
1 VII 2009 ....ESDJ		9 298 515	...	...	4 626 362	...	...	4 672 153	...	...
1 VII 2010 ....ESDJ		9 378 126	...	...	4 669 629	...	...	4 708 497	...	...
1 VII 2011 ....ESDJ		9 449 213	...	...	4 708 539	...	...	4 740 674	...	...
31 XII 2011 ....CDJC		9 482 855	...	...	4 726 834	...	...	4 756 021	...	...
1 VII 2012 ....ESDJ		9 519 375	...	...	4 746 370	...	...	4 773 005	...	...
1 VII 2013[122] ....ESDJ		9 600 379	...	...	4 790 131	...	...	4 810 248	...	...
1 VII 2014[122] ....ESDJ		9 696 110	...	...	4 843 299	...	...	4 852 811	...	...
1 I 2015[122] ....ESDJ		9 747 355	...	...	4 872 240	...	...	4 875 115	...	...
Switzerland - Suisse										
1 VII 2006 ....ESDJ		7 483 935	5 489 614	73.4	3 665 931	2 671 318	72.9	3 818 004	2 818 296	73.8
1 VII 2007 ....ESDJ		7 551 117	5 543 848	73.4	3 703 187	2 701 296	72.9	3 847 930	2 842 552	73.9
1 VII 2008 ....ESDJ		7 647 675	5 622 042	73.5	3 756 845	2 744 671	73.1	3 890 831	2 877 371	74.0
1 VII 2009 ....ESDJ		7 743 832	5 699 003	73.6	3 808 621	2 786 186	73.2	3 935 211	2 912 817	74.0
1 VII 2010 ....ESDJ		7 824 909	...	...	3 851 028	...	...	3 973 882	...	...
1 VII 2011 ....ESDJ		7 912 398	5 823 816	73.6	3 899 840	2 853 440	73.2	4 012 559	2 970 376	74.0
31 XII 2011 ....CDFC		8 035 391	5 920 706	73.7	3 973 280	2 909 793	73.2	4 062 111	3 010 913	74.1
1 VII 2012 ....ESDJ		7 996 861	5 887 939	73.6	3 945 389	2 887 886	73.2	4 051 473	3 000 053	74.0
1 VII 2013 ....ESDJ		8 089 346	5 958 174	73.7	3 995 308	2 925 500	73.2	4 094 038	3 032 674	74.1
1 VII 2014[124] ....ESDJ		8 188 649	6 033 396	73.7	4 047 986	2 964 948	73.2	4 140 663	3 068 448	74.1
1 I 2015[124] ....ESDJ		8 237 666	6 070 409	73.7	4 073 880	2 984 345	73.3	4 163 786	3 086 064	74.1

6. Total and urban population by sex: 2006 - 2015
Population totale et population urbaine selon le sexe : 2006 - 2015 (continued - suite)

Continent, country or area, and date Continent, pays ou zone et date	Code[a]	Both sexes - Les deux sexes			Male - Masculin			Female - Féminin		
			Urban - Urbaine			Urban - Urbaine			Urban - Urbaine	
		Total	Number Nombre	Percent P.100	Total	Number Nombre	Percent P.100	Total	Number Nombre	Percent P.100
EUROPE										
TFYR of Macedonia - L'ex-R. y. de Macédoine										
1 VII 2006 .... ESDF	ESDF	2 040 228	...	...	1 023 069	...	...	1 017 159	...	...
1 VII 2007 .... ESDF	ESDF	2 043 559	...	...	1 024 489	...	...	1 019 070	...	...
1 VII 2008 .... ESDF	ESDF	2 046 898	...	...	1 026 022	...	...	1 020 876	...	...
1 VII 2009 .... ESDF	ESDF	2 050 671	...	...	1 027 810	...	...	1 022 861	...	...
1 VII 2010 .... ESDF	ESDF	2 055 004	...	...	1 029 848	...	...	1 025 156	...	...
1 VII 2011 .... ESDF	ESDF	2 058 539	...	...	1 031 403	...	...	1 027 136	...	...
1 VII 2012 .... ESDF	ESDF	2 061 044	...	...	1 032 532	...	...	1 028 512	...	...
1 VII 2013 .... ESDF	ESDF	2 064 032	...	...	1 033 990	...	...	1 030 042	...	...
1 VII 2014 .... ESDF	ESDF	2 067 471	...	...	1 035 680	...	...	1 031 791	...	...
1 I 2015 .... ESDF	ESDF	2 069 172	...	...	1 036 518	...	...	1 032 654	...	...
Ukraine										
1 VII 2006 .... ESDF	ESDF	46 787 786	31 827 539	68.0	21 610 648	14 628 495	67.7	25 177 138	17 199 044	68.3
1 VII 2007 .... ESDF	ESDF	46 509 355	31 723 062	68.2	21 472 153	14 567 851	67.8	25 037 202	17 155 212	68.5
1 VII 2008 .... ESDF	ESDF	46 258 189	31 627 980	68.4	21 347 279	14 512 344	68.0	24 910 910	17 115 637	68.7
1 VII 2009 .... ESDF	ESDF	46 053 307	31 556 002	68.5	...	...	...	...	...	...
1 VII 2010 .... ESDF	ESDF	45 870 741	31 483 222	68.6	21 175 816	14 436 554	68.2	24 694 925	17 046 668	69.0
1 VII 2011 .... ESDF	ESDF	45 706 086	31 411 262	68.7	21 110 638	14 401 999	68.2	24 595 448	17 009 263	69.2
1 VII 2012 .... ESDF	ESDF	45 593 342	31 379 757	68.8	21 075 702	14 392 490	68.3	24 517 640	16 987 267	69.3
1 I 2013 .... ESDF	ESDF	45 553 047	31 378 639	68.9	21 068 718	14 397 904	68.3	24 484 329	16 980 735	69.4
1 I 2015*[133] .... ESDF	ESDF	42 759 661	...	...	19 787 826	...	...	22 971 835	...	...
United Kingdom of Great Britain and Northern Ireland - Royaume-Uni de Grande-Bretagne et d'Irlande du Nord[134]										
1 VII 2006 .... ESDJ	ESDJ	60 827 067	...	...	29 761 579	...	...	31 065 488	...	...
1 VII 2007 .... ESDJ	ESDJ	61 319 075	...	...	30 027 882	...	...	31 291 193	...	...
1 VII 2008 .... ESDJ	ESDJ	61 823 772	...	...	30 300 623	...	...	31 523 149	...	...
1 VII 2009 .... ESDJ	ESDJ	62 260 486	...	...	30 532 212	...	...	31 728 274	...	...
1 VII 2010 .... ESDJ	ESDJ	62 759 456	...	...	30 805 493	...	...	31 953 963	...	...
27 III 2011 .... CDFC	CDFC	63 379 787	51 399 714	81.1	31 126 054	25 214 631	81.0	32 253 733	26 185 083	81.2
1 VII 2011 .... ESDJ	ESDJ	63 285 145	...	...	31 097 259	...	...	32 187 886	...	...
1 VII 2012 .... ESDJ	ESDJ	63 705 030	...	...	31 315 072	...	...	32 389 958	...	...
1 VII 2013[121] .... ESDJ	ESDJ	64 102 166	...	...	31 535 963	...	...	32 566 204	...	...
1 VII 2014[121] .... ESDJ	ESDJ	64 591 713	...	...	31 797 813	...	...	32 793 900	...	...
1 I 2015[121] .... ESDJ	ESDJ	64 875 165	...	...	31 947 040	...	...	32 928 125	...	...
OCEANIA - OCÉANIE										
American Samoa - Samoas américaines[45]										
1 IV 2010 .... CDJC	CDJC	55 519	...	...	28 164	...	...	27 355	...	...
Australia - Australie										
1 VII 2006[36] .... ESDJ	ESDJ	20 450 966	17 316 174	84.7	10 159 424	8 555 046	84.2	10 291 542	8 761 128	85.1
8 VIII 2006[135] .... CDFC	CDFC	20 061 646[136]	17 670 009	88.1	9 896 500[136]	8 651 811	87.4	10 165 146[136]	9 018 198	88.7
1 VII 2007[36] .... ESDJ	ESDJ	20 827 622	17 666 467	84.8	10 353 636	8 734 627	84.4	10 473 986	8 931 840	85.3
1 VII 2008[36] .... ESDJ	ESDJ	21 249 199	18 052 915	85.0	10 572 045	8 934 070	84.5	10 677 154	9 118 845	85.4
1 VII 2009[36] .... ESDJ	ESDJ	21 691 653	18 453 978	85.1	10 800 797	9 141 216	84.6	10 890 856	9 312 762	85.5
1 VII 2010[36] .... ESDJ	ESDJ	22 031 750	18 762 982	85.2	10 967 831	9 292 721	84.7	11 063 919	9 470 261	85.6
1 VII 2011[36] .... ESDJ	ESDJ	22 340 024	19 046 939	85.3	11 118 234	9 431 506	84.8	11 221 790	9 615 433	85.7
9 VIII 2011[135] .... CDFC	CDFC	21 727 158[136]	19 312 642	88.9	10 737 148[136]	9 471 918	88.2	10 990 010[136]	9 840 724	89.5
1 VII 2012[15] .... ESDJ	ESDJ	22 728 254	19 402 437	85.4	11 312 823	9 608 375	84.9	11 415 431	9 794 062	85.8
1 VII 2013[15] .... ESDJ	ESDJ	23 125 868	19 770 400	85.5	11 511 548	9 790 875	85.1	11 614 320	9 979 525	85.9
1 VII 2014[15] .... ESDJ	ESDJ	23 490 736	20 109 282	85.6	11 692 500	9 958 617	85.2	11 798 236	10 150 665	86.0
1 VII 2015*[15] .... ESDJ	ESDJ	23 777 777	...	...	11 826 927	...	...	11 950 850	...	...
Cook Islands - Îles Cook[137]										
1 XII 2006 .... CDFC	CDFC	19 342	...	...	9 816	...	...	9 526	...	...
1 XII 2011 .... CDFC	CDFC	17 794	...	...	8 815	...	...	8 979	...	...

Continent, country or area, and date / Continent, pays ou zone et date	Code[a]	Both sexes - Les deux sexes			Male - Masculin			Female - Féminin		
		Total	Urban - Urbaine		Total	Urban - Urbaine		Total	Urban - Urbaine	
			Number Nombre	Percent P.100		Number Nombre	Percent P.100		Number Nombre	Percent P.100
OCEANIA - OCÉANIE										
Fiji - Fidji										
16 IX 2007 ....CDFC		837 271	424 846	50.7	427 176	212 454	49.7	410 095	212 392	51.8
1 VII 2008 ....ESDF		841 351	426 931	50.7	...	...	...	...	...	...
1 VII 2010 ....ESDF		857 000	446 000	52.0	...	...	...	...	...	...
French Polynesia - Polynésie française										
20 VIII 2007 ....CDJC		259 706	...	...	133 109	...	...	126 597	...	...
1 I 2009 ....ESDF		264 000	...	...	135 200	...	...	128 800	...	...
1 I 2011 ....ESDF		269 989	...	...	138 127	...	...	131 862	...	...
22 VIII 2012 ....CDJC		268 207	...	...	136 996	...	...	131 211	...	...
1 I 2015 ....ESDF		271 796	...	...	138 447	...	...	133 349	...	...
Guam										
1 VII 2006[45] ....ESDJ		158 711	...	...	80 851	...	...	77 860	...	...
1 VII 2007[45] ....ESDJ		158 967	...	...	80 930	...	...	78 037	...	...
1 VII 2008[45] ....ESDJ		159 169	...	...	80 982	...	...	78 187	...	...
1 VII 2009[45] ....ESDJ		159 323	...	...	81 010	...	...	78 313	...	...
1 IV 2010 ....CDJC		159 358	149 918	94.1	81 552	...	...	77 806	...	...
1 VII 2011[45] ....ESDJ		159 600	...	...	81 053	...	...	78 547	...	...
1 VII 2012[45] ....ESDJ		159 914	...	...	81 165	...	...	78 749	...	...
1 VII 2013[45] ....ESDJ		160 378	...	...	81 354	...	...	79 024	...	...
1 VII 2014[45] ....ESDJ		161 001	...	...	81 625	...	...	79 376	...	...
1 VII 2015[45] ....ESDJ		161 785	...	...	81 978	...	...	79 807	...	...
Kiribati										
10 X 2010 ....CDFC		103 058	...	...	50 796	...	...	52 262	...	...
Marshall Islands - Îles Marshall										
1 VII 2006[138] ....ESDF		52 163	...	...	26 746	...	...	25 417	...	...
1 VII 2007[138] ....ESDF		52 701	...	...	27 022	...	...	25 679	...	...
1 VII 2008[138] ....ESDF		53 236	...	...	27 297	...	...	25 939	...	...
1 VII 2009[138] ....ESDF		53 763	...	...	27 567	...	...	26 196	...	...
1 VII 2010[138] ....ESDF		54 305	...	...	27 843	...	...	26 462	...	...
3 IV 2011 ....CDFC		53 158	...	...	27 243	...	...	25 915	...	...
Micronesia (Federated States of) - Micronésie (États fédérés de)										
1 VII 2006[2] ....ESDJ		107 965	...	...	54 411	...	...	53 554	...	...
1 VII 2007[2] ....ESDJ		108 031	...	...	54 403	...	...	53 628	...	...
1 VII 2008[2] ....ESDJ		108 026	...	...	54 350	...	...	53 676	...	...
1 VII 2009[2] ....ESDJ		107 973	...	...	54 275	...	...	53 698	...	...
1 IV 2010 ....CDJC		102 843	22 924	22.3	52 193	...	...	50 650	...	...
1 VII 2010[2] ....ESDJ		107 839	...	...	54 158	...	...	53 681	...	...
1 VII 2011[2] ....ESDJ		107 581	...	...	53 975	...	...	53 606	...	...
1 VII 2012[2] ....ESDJ		107 249	...	...	53 749	...	...	53 500	...	...
1 VII 2013[2] ....ESDJ		106 841	...	...	53 488	...	...	53 353	...	...
1 VII 2014[2] ....ESDJ		106 374	...	...	53 200	...	...	53 174	...	...
1 VII 2015[2] ....ESDJ		105 830	...	...	52 883	...	...	52 947	...	...
Nauru										
31 X 2011* ....CDFC		10 086	...	...	5 105	...	...	4 979	...	...
New Caledonia - Nouvelle-Calédonie										
1 I 2006 ....ESDF		236 528	...	...	119 415	...	...	117 113	...	...
1 I 2007 ....ESDF		240 390	150 831	62.7	121 299	...	...	119 091	...	...
1 VII 2008 ....ESDF		242 400	...	...	122 261	...	...	120 139	...	...
27 VII 2009 ....CDFC		245 580	...	...	124 524	...	...	121 056	...	...
1 VII 2010 ....ESDF		250 040	...	...	126 771	...	...	123 269	...	...
1 I 2013 ....ESDF		260 000	...	...	131 481	...	...	128 519	...	...
New Zealand - Nouvelle-Zélande										
7 III 2006[135] ....CDFC		4 143 282	...	...	2 021 277	...	...	2 122 005	...	...
1 VII 2006[28] ....ESDJ		4 184 600	3 606 700[139]	86.2	2 048 300	1 751 400[139]	85.5	2 136 200	1 855 300[139]	86.9
1 VII 2007[28] ....ESDJ		4 223 800	3 640 200[140]	86.2	2 066 400	1 766 900[140]	85.5	2 157 300	1 873 300[140]	86.8
1 VII 2008[28] ....ESDJ		4 259 800	3 669 100[140]	86.1	2 083 400	1 780 600[140]	85.5	2 176 300	1 888 600[140]	86.8
1 VII 2009[28] ....ESDJ		4 302 600	3 703 800[140]	86.1	2 104 700	1 797 800[140]	85.4	2 197 900	1 906 000[140]	86.7
1 VII 2010[28] ....ESDJ		4 350 700	3 743 300[140]	86.0	2 127 700	1 816 700[140]	85.4	2 222 900	1 926 600[140]	86.7
1 VII 2011[28] ....ESDJ		4 384 000	3 765 400[140]	85.9	2 143 600	1 826 900[140]	85.2	2 240 400	1 938 500[140]	86.5

6. Total and urban population by sex: 2006 - 2015
Population totale et population urbaine selon le sexe : 2006 - 2015 (continued - suite)

Continent, country or area, and date / Continent, pays ou zone et date	Code[a]	Both sexes - Les deux sexes Total	Urban - Urbaine Number Nombre	Urban - Urbaine Percent P.100	Male - Masculin Total	Urban - Urbaine Number Nombre	Urban - Urbaine Percent P.100	Female - Féminin Total	Urban - Urbaine Number Nombre	Urban - Urbaine Percent P.100
OCEANIA - OCÉANIE										
New Zealand - Nouvelle-Zélande										
1 VII 2012[28]	ESDJ	4 408 100	3 784 600[140]	85.9	2 155 000	1 836 200[140]	85.2	2 253 100	1 948 500[140]	86.5
1 VII 2013[28]	ESDJ	4 442 100	3 818 300[140]	86.0	2 172 200	1 853 100[140]	85.3	2 269 900	1 965 200[140]	86.6
1 VII 2014[28]	ESDJ	4 509 700	3 884 000[140]	86.1	2 209 600	1 889 100[140]	85.5	2 300 200	1 995 000[140]	86.7
1 VII 2015[28]	ESDJ	4 595 700	3 959 200[140]	86.2	2 257 200	1 931 800[140]	85.6	2 338 500	2 027 400[140]	86.7
Niue - Nioué										
1 VII 2006	ESDJ	1 679	...	...	815	...	...	864	...	...
9 IX 2006	CDFC	1 625	...	...	802	...	...	823	...	...
1 VII 2010	ESDJ	1 496	...	...	754	...	...	740	...	...
11 IX 2011	CDFC	1 611	...	...	802	...	...	809	...	...
Norfolk Island - Île Norfolk										
8 VIII 2006	CDFC	2 523	...	...	1 218	...	...	1 305	...	...
9 VIII 2011	CDFC	2 302	...	...	1 082	...	...	1 220	...	...
Northern Mariana Islands - Îles Mariannes septentrionales										
1 VII 2006	ESDF	60 662	...	...	29 071	...	...	31 591	...	...
1 VII 2007	ESDF	58 629	...	...	28 124	...	...	30 505	...	...
1 VII 2008	ESDF	55 244	...	...	26 524	...	...	28 720	...	...
1 VII 2009	ESDF	51 484	...	...	24 738	...	...	26 746	...	...
1 IV 2010	CDFC	53 883	...	...	27 746	...	...	26 137	...	...
1 VII 2010	ESDF	48 317	...	...	23 231	...	...	25 086	...	...
1 VII 2011	ESDF	46 050	...	...	22 153	...	...	23 897	...	...
Palau - Palaos										
1 XII 2012	CDJC	17 501	14 202	81.1	9 217	7 506	81.4	8 284	6 696	80.8
13 IV 2015	CDJC	17 661	14 209	80.5	9 433	7 620	80.8	8 228	6 589	80.1
Papua New Guinea - Papouasie-Nouvelle-Guinée										
10 VII 2011*	CDFC	7 059 653	...	...	3 663 249	...	...	3 396 404	...	...
Pitcairn										
31 XII 2007	ESDF	64[141]	...	...	37	...	...	27	...	...
31 XII 2008	ESDF	58[141]	...	...	30	...	...	28	...	...
10 VIII 2012	CDJC	48	...	...	22	...	...	26	...	...
31 XII 2013	CDJC	49	...	...	23	...	...	26	...	...
Samoa										
1 VII 2006	ESDF	184 955	40 648	22.0	96 345	20 763	21.6	88 610	19 885	22.4
5 XI 2006	CDFC	180 741	37 708	20.9	93 677	19 120	20.4	87 064	18 588	21.3
1 VII 2007	ESDF	181 588	37 878	20.9	94 101	19 206	20.4	87 458	18 672	21.3
1 VII 2008	ESDF	182 379	38 050	20.9	94 526	19 293	20.4	87 853	18 756	21.3
1 VII 2009	ESDF	183 204	38 222	20.9	94 953	19 381	20.4	88 250	18 841	21.3
1 VII 2010	ESDF	184 032	38 395	20.9	95 383	19 468	20.4	88 649	18 926	21.3
1 VII 2011	ESDF	184 864	38 568	20.9	95 814	19 556	20.4	89 050	19 012	21.3
7 XI 2011	CDFC	187 820	36 735	19.6	96 990	18 485	19.1	90 830	18 250	20.1
1 VII 2012	ESDF	189 236	36 540	19.3	...	...	...	...	...	...
1 VII 2013	ESDF	190 652	36 346	19.1	...	...	...	...	...	...
Solomon Islands - Îles Salomon										
1 VII 2006[2]	ESDF	483 083	...	...	248 944	...	...	234 139	...	...
1 VII 2007[2]	ESDF	495 026	...	...	255 063	...	...	239 963	...	...
1 VII 2008[2]	ESDF	506 992	...	...	261 214	...	...	245 778	...	...
1 VII 2009[2]	ESDF	518 321	...	...	267 704	...	...	250 617	...	...
22 XI 2009	CDFC	515 870	102 030	19.8	264 455	53 596	20.3	251 415	48 434	19.3
1 VII 2013[142]	ESDF	610 800	...	...	311 300	...	...	299 500	...	...
Tokelau - Tokélaou										
19 X 2006	CDFC	1 151	...	...	583	...	...	568	...	...
18 X 2011	CDFC	1 205	...	...	600	...	...	605	...	...
1 XII 2013	ESDF	1 383	...	...	683	...	...	700	...	...
Tonga										
1 VII 2006[143]	ESDF	102 907	...	...	52 561	...	...	50 346	...	...
30 XI 2006	CDJC	101 991	23 658	23.2	51 772	11 860	22.9	50 219	11 798	23.5
1 VII 2007[143]	ESDF	103 289	...	...	52 771	...	...	50 518	...	...

6. Total and urban population by sex: 2006 - 2015
Population totale et population urbaine selon le sexe : 2006 - 2015 (continued - suite)

Continent, country or area, and date / Continent, pays ou zone et date	Code[a]	Both sexes - Les deux sexes Total	Urban - Urbaine Number Nombre	Urban - Urbaine Percent P.100	Male - Masculin Total	Urban - Urbaine Number Nombre	Urban - Urbaine Percent P.100	Female - Féminin Total	Urban - Urbaine Number Nombre	Urban - Urbaine Percent P.100
OCEANIA - OCÉANIE										
Tonga										
1 VII 2008[143] .... ESDF		*103 647*	...	...	*52 972*	...	...	*50 673*	...	...
30 XI 2011 .... CDJC		103 252	24 229	23.5	51 979	12 156	23.4	51 273	12 073	23.5
Tuvalu										
1 VII 2011 .... ESDF		*11 206*	...	...	*5 582*	...	...	*5 625*	...	...
1 VII 2013 .... ESDF		*10 900*	...	...	*5 600*	...	...	*5 400*	...	...
Vanuatu										
1 VII 2006[2] .... ESDF		*221 417*	...	...	*113 034*	...	...	*108 383*	...	...
16 XI 2009 .... CDJC		234 023	57 195	24.4	119 091	29 618	24.9	114 932	27 577	24.0
1 VII 2010 .... ESDF		*239 374*	...	...	*121 726*	...	...	*117 648*	...	...
1 VII 2011 .... ESDF		*244 847*	...	...	*124 420*	...	...	*120 427*	...	...
1 VII 2012 .... ESDF		*244 847*	...	...	*127 173*	...	...	*123 273*	...	...
1 VII 2013 .... ESDF		*264 652*	...	...	*135 170*	...	...	*129 483*	...	...
Wallis and Futuna Islands - Îles Wallis et Futuna										
21 VII 2008 .... CDFC		13 445	...	...	6 669	...	...	6 776	...	...

FOOTNOTES - NOTES

Italics: estimates which are less reliable. - Italiques : estimations moins sûres.

* Provisional. - Données provisoires.

[a] 'Code' indicates the source of data, as follows:
CDFC - Census, de facto, complete tabulation
CDFS - Census, de facto, sample tabulation
CDJC - Census, de jure, complete tabulation
CDJS - Census, de jure, sample tabulation
SSDF - Sample survey, de facto
SSDJ - Sample survey, de jure
ESDF - Estimates, de facto
ESDJ - Estimates, de jure

Le 'Code' indique la source des données, comme suit :
CDFC - Recensement, population de fait, tabulation complète
CDFS - Recensement, population de fait, tabulation par sondage
CDJC - Recensement, population de droit, tabulation complète
CDJS - Recensement, population de droit, tabulation par sondage
SSDF - Enquête par sondage, population de fait
SSDJ - Enquête par sondage, population de droit
ESDF - Estimations, population de fait
ESDJ - Estimations, population de droit

[1] Total resident population including common and collective households of nomadic population, and population counted separately. - Population résidente totale y compris les ménages ordinaires et collectifs de la population nomade, et la population comptée à part.
[2] Data refer to national projections. - Les données se réfèrent aux projections nationales.
[3] Data refer to projections based on the 2013 Population Census. - Les données se réfèrent aux projections basées sur le recensement de la population de 2013.
[4] Based on the results of the 2006 Demographic Survey. - D'après les résultats de l'enquête Démographique par Sondage de 2006.
[5] Data based on the 2011 Census. - Données fondées sur le recensement de 2011.
[6] Data based on the 2008 Population Census. - Données fondées sur le recensement de population de 2008.
[7] Projections based on the 1994 Population Census. - Projections fondées sur le recensement de la population de 1994.
[8] Estimates considering also 2007 Population Census results. - Estimations en prenant en considération les résultats du recensement de la population de 2007.

[9] Reason for discrepancy between these figures and corresponding figures shown elsewhere not ascertained. - On ne sait pas comment s'explique la divergence entre ces chiffres et les chiffres correspondants indiqués ailleurs.
[10] Data refer to national projections. Revised data. - Les données se réfèrent aux projections nationales. Données révisées.
[11] Projections considering also 2009 Population Census results. - Projections en prenant en considération les résultats du recensement de la population de 2009.
[12] Including nomadic population. - Y compris la population nomade.
[13] Excludes the islands of St. Brandon and Agalega. - Non compris les îles St. Brandon et Agalega.
[14] Based on the results of the 2000 Population Census. - Basé sur les résultats du recencement de la population de 2000.
[15] Based on the results of the 2011 Population Census. - Basé sur les résultats du recencement de la population de 2011.
[16] Based on the results of the 2004 Population Census. - D'après des résultats du recencement de la population de 2004.
[17] Data refer to projections based on the 2011 Population Census. - Les données se réfèrent aux projections basées sur le recensement de la population de 2011.
[18] Data are projections based on the 2012 Population and Housing Census. - Projection basée sur le recensement 2012 de la population et des logements.
[19] Data are projections based on the 2008 Population and Housing Census. - Projection basée sur le recensement 2008 de la population et des logements.
[20] Projections based on the 2012 Population Census. - Projections fondées sur le recensement de la population de 2012.
[21] Based on the results of a population count. - D'après les résultats d'un comptage de la population.
[22] The population figures are 264, 263 and 262 persons for 2007, 2008 and 2009 respectively. - La population est respectivement égale à 264, 263 et 262 personnes pour les années 2007, 2008 et 2009.
[23] Projections based on the 2002 Population Census. - Projections fondées sur le recensement de la population de 2002.
[24] Data have not been adjusted for underenumeration, estimated at 7 per cent. - Les données n'ont pas été ajustées pour compenser les lacunes du dénombrement, estimées à 7 p. 100.
[25] Data refer to projections based on the 2000 Population Census. - Les données se réfèrent aux projections basées sur le recensement de la population de 2000.
[26] Bermuda is 100 per cent urban. - 100 pour cent de la population des Bermudes est urbaine.
[27] Data refer to projections based on the 2010 Population Census. - Les données se réfèrent aux projections basées sur le recensement de la population de 2010.

28 Because of rounding, totals are not in all cases the sum of the respective components. - Les chiffres étant arrondis, les totaux ne correspondent pas toujours rigoureusement à la somme des composants respectifs.

29 Final intercensal estimates. - Estimations inter-censitaires definitives.

30 Final postcensal estimates. - Estimations postcensitaires definitives.

31 Updated postcensal estimates. - Estimations post censitaires mises à jour.

32 Excluding the institutional population. - Non compris la population dans les institutions.

33 The source of data is the national household survey. - La source des données est l'enquête nationale des ménages.

34 Based on the national household surveys 2010-2014 and the 2011 population census. - D'après les données de l'enquête nationale des ménages 2010-2014 et les résultats du recensement de la population de 2011.

35 Based on the national household survey of 2015. - Basée sur l' enquête nationale auprès des ménages de 2015.

36 Intercensal estimates. - Estimations inter-censitaires.

37 Postcensal estimates. - Estimations post censitaires.

38 Estimates based on the 2007 Population Census. - Estimations fondées sur le recensement de la population de 2007.

39 Population statistics are compiled from registers. - Les statistiques de la population sont compilées à partir des registres.

40 Excluding data for Saint Barthélémy and Saint Martin. - Non compris les données pour Saint Barthélémy et Saint Martin.

41 Projections produced by l'Institut Haïtien de Statistique et d'Informatique (IHSI) and the Latin American and Caribbean Demographic Centre (CELADE) - Population Division of ECLAC. - Les données sont projections produits par l'Institut Haïtien de Statistique et d'Informatique (IHSI) et le centre démographique de l'Amérique latine et les Caraïbes - Division de la population de la CEPALC.

42 Data refer to projections based on the 2001 Population Census. - Les données se réfèrent aux projections basées sur le recensement de la population de 2001.

43 The figures represent the census counts adjusted for under-coverage. Adjustments are done by applying weights calculated (to 4 decimal places) for each sex and age group to the enumerated population when the tabulations are produced. Minor discrepancies between totals and the sum of the component parts of a table and minor discrepancies between the totals across tables are due to rounding after weights are applied. - Les chiffres représentent le dénombrement résultant du recensement ajusté pour tenir compte du sous-dénombrement. Les ajustements sont effectués en appliquant un coefficient de pondération calculé (à la quatrième décimale) pour chaque sexe et groupe d'âges de la population dénombrée lors de l'établissement des tableaux. Les écarts mineurs entre les totaux et la somme des éléments constitutifs d'un tableau ainsi qu'entre les totaux figurant dans différents tableaux sont dus au fait que les chiffres sont arrondis après la pondération.

44 Including an estimation of 1 334 585 persons corresponding to 448 195 housing units without information of the occupants. - Y compris une estimation de 1 334 585 personnes correspondant aux 448 195 unités d'habitation sans information sur les occupants.

45 Including armed forces stationed in the area. - Y compris les militaires en garnison sur le territoire.

46 Based on the results of the 2010 Population Census. - D'après le résultats du recensement de la population de 2010.

47 Intercensal estimates. Excluding U.S. Armed Forces overseas and civilian U.S. citizens whose usual place of residence is outside the United States. - Estimations inter-censitaires. Non compris les militaires américains à l'étranger et les civils américains dont le lieu de résidence habituel est en dehors des États-Unis.

48 Excluding U.S. Armed Forces overseas and civilian U.S. citizens whose usual place of residence is outside the United States. Postcensal estimates. - Non compris les militaires américains à l'étranger et les civils américains dont le lieu de résidence habituel est en dehors des États-Unis. Estimations post censitaires.

49 Data refer to projections based on the 2010 Population and Housing Census. - Les données se réfèrent aux projections basées sur le recensement 2010 de la population et des logements.

50 Data include persons in remote areas, military personnel outside the country, merchant seamen at sea, civilian seasonal workers outside the country, and other civilians outside the country, and exclude nomads, foreign military, civilian aliens temporarily in the country, transients on ships and Indian jungle population. Data refer to national projections. - Y compris les personnes vivant dans des régions éloignées, le personel militaire en dehors du pays, les marins marchands, les ouvriers saisonniers en dehors du pays, et autres civils en dehors du pays, et non compris les nomades, les militaires étrangers, les étrangers civils temporairement dans le pays, les transiteurs sur des bateaux et les Indiens de la jungle. Les données se réfèrent aux projections nationales.

51 Data are revised projections taking into consideration also the results of the 2005 census. - Les données sont des projections révisées tenant compte également des résultats du recensement de 2005.

52 Data refer to projections based on the 2010 Population Census. Excludes nomadic Indian tribes. - Les données se réfèrent aux projections basées sur le recensement de la population de 2010. Non compris les tribus d'Indiens nomades.

53 A dispute exists between the governments of Argentina and the United Kingdom of Great Britain and Northern Ireland concerning sovereignty over the Falkland Islands (Malvinas). - La souveraineté sur les îles Falkland (Malvinas) fait l'objet d'un différend entre le Gouvernement argentin et le Gouvernement du Royaume-Uni de Grande-Bretagne et d'Irlande du Nord.

54 Excluding military personnel and their families, visitors and transients. - Non compris les militaires et leur familles, ni les visiteurs et transients.

55 Figures for male and female population do not add up to the figure for total population, because they exclude 108 homeless people of unknown sex. - Les chiffres relatifs à la population masculine et féminine ne correspondent pas au chiffre de la population totale, parce que l'on en a exclu 108 personnes sans toit dont le sexe n'est pas connu.

56 For operational purposes, population centers with 2,500 and more inhabitants are considered as urban area and less than 2,500 are considered as rural area. - À des fins opérationnelles, les centres de population comptant 2 500 habitants ou plus sont considérés comme zones urbaines, ceux qui en comptent moins de 2 500 comme zones rurales.

57 Data refer to the settled population based on the 1979 Population Census and the latest household prelisting. The refugees of Afghanistan in Iran, Pakistan, and an estimated 1.5 million nomads, are not included. - Les données se rapportent à la population stationnaire sur la base du recensement de 1979 et du recensement préliminaire des logements le plus récent. Sont exclus les réfugiés d'Afghanistan en Iran et au Pakistan et les nomades estimés à 1,5 million.

58 Data have been adjusted for underenumeration. - Les données ont été ajustées pour compenser les lacunes du dénombrement.

59 Data refer to projected figures based on the Population and Housing Census 2005 (district projection). - Les données se réfèrent aux projections basées sur le recensement de la population et de l'habitat de 2005 (projections locales).

60 Excluding foreign diplomatic personnel and their dependants. Based on the results of 1998 census. - Non compris le personnel diplomatique étranger et les membres de leur famille les accompagnant. A partir des résultats de recensement de l'année 1998.

61 Excluding foreign diplomatic personnel and their dependants. - Non compris le personnel diplomatique étranger et les membres de leur famille les accompagnant.

62 Excluding foreign diplomatic personnel and their dependants. Data based on the 2008 Population Census. - Non compris le personnel diplomatique étranger et les membres de leur famille les accompagnant. Données fondées sur le recensement de population de 2008.

63 Based on the results of the Cambodia Intercensal Population Survey. Data exclude foreign diplomatic personnel and their dependants. - Sur la base de l'enquête intercensitaire de la population de Cambodge. Non compris le personnel diplomatique étranger et les membres de leur famille les accompagnant.

64 For statistical purposes, the data for China do not include those for the Hong Kong Special Administrative Region (Hong Kong SAR), Macao Special Administrative Region (Macao SAR) and Taiwan province of China. - Pour la présentation des statistiques, les données pour la Chine ne comprennent pas la Région Administrative Spéciale de Hong Kong (Hong Kong RAS), la Région Administrative Spéciale de Macao (Macao RAS) et Taïwan province de Chine.

65 Data have been estimated on the basis of the annual National Sample Survey on Population Changes. - Les données ont été estimées sur la base de l'enquête annuelle "National Sample Survey on Population Changes".

66 The military personnel are classified as urban population. - Le personnel militaire est classé dans la population urbaine.

67 The military personnel are classified as urban population. Because of rounding, totals are not in all cases the sum of the respective components. - Le personnel militaire est classé dans la population urbaine. Les chiffres étant arrondis, les totaux ne correspondent pas toujours rigoureusement à la somme des composants respectifs.

68 Data are from Communique of the National Bureau of Statistics of the People's Republic of China on Major Figures of the 2010 Population Census (No.1). - Données issues du communiqué du Bureau national de la statistique de la République populaire de Chine sur les chiffres importants du recensement de 2010 (n° 1).

69 Data have been adjusted on the basis of the Population Census of 2010. - Les données ont été ajustées à partir des résultats du recensement de la population de 2010.

[70] Data are estimates from sample enquiry. Data refer to Hong Kong resident population at the census moment, which covers usual residents and mobile residents. Usual residents refer to two categories of people: (1) Hong Kong permanent residents who had stayed in Hong Kong for at least three months during the six months before or for at least three months during the six months after the census moment, regardless of whether they were in Hong Kong or not at the census moment; and (2) Hong Kong non-permanent residents who were in Hong Kong at the census moment. Mobile Residents, they are Hong Kong permanent residents who had stayed in Hong Kong for at least one month but less than three months during the six months before or for at least one month but less than three months during the six months after the census moment, regardless of whether they were in Hong Kong or not at the census moment. - Les données sont des chiffres estimatifs dérivés d'une enquête par sondage. Les données se rapportent à la population résidente à Hong Kong au moment du recensement. Cette population est composée des résidants habituels et des résidants mobiles. La population résidente est partagée en deux catégories: (1) les résidents permanents qui ont habité à Hong Kong au moins trois mois pendant les six mois précédents ou les six mois suivants le recensement; (2) les habitants non-permanents de Hong Kong qui étaient à Hong Kong au moment du recensement. La population mobile se rapporte aux résidents permanents de Hong Kong qui ont habité à Hong Kong pendant les six mois après le recensement pour une période comprise entre un mois et trois mois, indépendamment du fait qu'ils étaient à Hong Kong au moment du recensement au pays.

[71] Data refer to Hong Kong resident population at the census moment, which covers usual residents and mobile residents. Usual residents refer to two categories of people: (1) Hong Kong permanent residents who had stayed in Hong Kong for at least three months during the six months before or for at least three months during the six months after the census moment, regardless of whether they were in Hong Kong or not at the census moment; and (2) Hong Kong non-permanent residents who were in Hong Kong at the census moment. Mobile Residents, they are Hong Kong permanent residents who had stayed in Hong Kong for at least one month but less than three months during the six months before or for at least one month but less than three months during the six months after the census moment, regardless of whether they were in Hong Kong or not at the census moment. - Les données se rapportent à la population résidente à Hong Kong au moment du recensement. Cette population est composée des résidants habituels et des résidants mobiles. La population résidente est partagée en deux catégories: (1) les résidents permanents qui ont habité à Hong Kong au moins trois mois pendant les six mois précédents ou les six mois suivants le recensement; (2) les habitants non-permanents de Hong Kong qui étaient à Hong Kong au moment du recensement. La population mobile se rapporte aux résidents permanents de Hong Kong qui ont habité à Hong Kong pendant les six mois après le recensement pour une période comprise entre un mois et trois mois, indépendamment du fait qu'ils étaient à Hong Kong au moment du recensement au pays.

[72] Data refer to government controlled areas. - Les données se rapportent aux zones contrôlées par le Gouvernement.

[73] Data refer to annual average population. - Les données correspondent à la population annuelle moyenne.

[74] Includes data for the Indian-held part of Jammu and Kashmir, the final status of which has not yet been determined. - Y compris les données pour la partie du Jammu et du Cachemire occupée par l'Inde dont le statut définitif n'a pas encore été déterminé.

[75] Data refer to projections based on the 2001 Population Census. - Les données se réfèrent aux projections basées sur le recensement de la population de 2001.

[76] Data are based on the publication: "Indonesia Population Projection 2005-2015" - Les données sont basées sur la publication : << Indonesia Population Projection 2005-2015 >>

[77] Differences between the total country figures and sum of urban and rural areas are due to the inclusion of unsettled population. - Les différences entre les chiffres pour l'ensemble du pays et la somme des zones urbaines et rurales s'expliquent par l'inclusion de la population non sédentaire.

[78] Data refer to the Iranian Year which begins on 21 March and ends on 20 March of the following year. - Les données concernent l'année iranienne, qui commence le 21 mars et se termine le 20 mars de l'année suivante.

[79] The total number may include 'Unknown residence', but the categories urban and rural do not. - Le nombre total peut inclure les personnes dont la résidence n'est pas connue, à l'inverse des catégories de population urbaine et rurale.

[80] Includes data for East Jerusalem and Israeli residents in certain other territories under occupation by Israeli military forces since June 1967. - Y compris les données pour Jérusalem-Est et les résidents israéliens dans certains autres territoires occupés depuis 1967 par les forces armées israéliennes.

[81] Because of rounding, totals are not in all cases the sum of the respective components. Excluding residents who had been registered in the Israeli localities (the Jewish localities) in the Gaza Area and northern Samaria, which were evacuated in August 2005, but did not notify the Ministry of Interior of their new address. These residents are included in total. - Les chiffres étant arrondis, les totaux ne correspondent pas toujours rigoureusement à la somme des composants respectifs. Hors résidents enregistrés dans les localités d'Israel (localités juives) de la Bande de Gaza (verfify) et du nord de la Samarie, qui ont été évacués en Août 2005, mais qui n'ont pas notifié leur nouvelle adresse au ministère de l'intérieur. Ces résidents sont inclus dans le total.

[82] Excluding residents who had been registered in the Israeli localities (the Jewish localities) in the Gaza Area and northern Samaria, which were evacuated in August 2005, but did not notify the Ministry of Interior of their new address. These residents are included in total. - Hors résidents enregistrés dans les localités d'Israel (localités juives) de la Bande de Gaza (verfify) et du nord de la Samarie, qui ont été évacués en Août 2005, mais qui n'ont pas notifié leur nouvelle adresse au ministère de l'intérieur. Ces résidents sont inclus dans le total.

[83] Data are rounded for confidentiality reasons. - Chiffres arrondis pour des raisons de confidentialité.

[84] Estimates based on the complete counts of the 2010 Population Census. Excluding diplomatic personnel outside the country and foreign military and civilian personnel and their dependants stationed in the area. - Estimations basées sur le dénombrement complet du recensement de la population de 2010. Non compris le personnel diplomatique hors du pays ni les militaires et agents civils étrangers en poste sur le territoire et les membres de leur famille les accompagnant.

[85] Excluding diplomatic personnel outside the country and foreign military and civilian personnel and their dependants stationed in the area. - Non compris le personnel diplomatique hors du pays ni les militaires et agents civils étrangers en poste sur le territoire et les membres de leur famille les accompagnant.

[86] Excluding data for Jordanian territory under occupation since June 1967 by Israeli military forces. - Non compris les données pour le territoire jordanien occupé depuis juin 1967 par les forces armées israéliennes.

[87] Data refer to annual average population. Data are calculated from the results of the Population and Housing Census of 2009. - Les données correspondent à la population annuelle moyenne. Les données sont calculées à partir des résultats du recensement de la population et de l'habitat de 2009.

[88] Data estimated based on the results of 2015 population census. - Estimations fondées sur les résultats du recensement de la population de 2015.

[89] Based on the results of a household survey. - D'après les résultats d'une enquête des ménages.

[90] Source: Living conditions of household survey, October 2011 to September 2012. - Source: Enquête sur les conditions de vie des ménages, octobre 2011 à septembre 2012.

[91] Intercensal Mid-Year Population Estimates based on the adjusted Population and Housing Census of 2000 and 2010. - Les estimations inter-censitaires au millieu de l'année sont fondée sur les résultats ajustées des recensements de la population et de l'habitat de 2000 et 2010.

[92] Estimates based on the adjusted Population and Housing Census of 2010. - Les estimations sont fondée sur les résultats ajustées du recensement de la population et de l'habitat de 2010.

[93] Total population is taken as de facto and de jure together. - Population totale considérée comme de fait et de droit.

[94] Data refer to resident population that includes Maldivians and foreigners. - Les données concernent la population résidente, qui comprend des Maldiviens et des étrangers.

[95] Based on the results of the 2014 Population Census. - D'après les résultats du recensement de la population de 2014.

[96] Data refer to enumerated population. - Les données se rapportent à la population dénombrée.

[97] Excluding data for the Pakistan-held part of Jammu and Kashmir, the final status of which has not yet been determined. - Non compris les données concernant la partie du Jammu et Cachemire occupée par le Pakistan dont le statut définitif n'a pas été déterminé.

[98] Based on the results of the Pakistan Demographic Survey (PDS 2007). - D'après les résultats de l'enquête démographique effectuée par le Pakistan en 2007.

[99] Excluding 2739 Filipinos in Philippine Embassies, Consulates and Missions Abroad. - Excepté 2739 Philippins travaillant dans les ambassades, les consulats et les missions des Philippines à l'étranger.

[100] Excluding usual residents not in the country at the time of census. - À l'exclusion des résidents habituels qui ne sont pas dans le pays au moment du recensement.

[101] Data based on the preliminary results of the 2010 Population and Housing Census. - D'après les résultats préliminaires du recensement de la population et des logements de 2010.

[102] Data refer to resident population which comprises Singapore citizens and permanent residents. - Les données se rapportent à la population résidente composé des citoyens de Singapour et des résidents permanents.

[103] Data exclude residents who have been away from Singapore for a continuous period of 12 months or longer as at the reference date. - Non compris les résidents hors de Singapour pour une période ininterrompue de 12 mois ou plus avant de la date de référence.

[104] Data are based on the latest register-based population estimates for 2010. Urban and rural breakdown not applicable as Singapore is a city-state. - Données basées sur les estimations démographiques les plus récentes fondées sur les registres de 2010. La ventilation entre zones urbaines et zones rurales ne s'applique pas à Singapour, puisqu'il s'agit d'une ville État.

[105] Data for urban include population in refugee camps. - Les données pour la population urbaine comprennent la population dans les camps réfugiés.

[106] Data have not been adjusted for underenumeration. - Les données n'ont pas été ajustées pour compenser les lacunes du dénombrement.

[107] Including Palestinian refugees. - Y compris les réfugiés de Palestine.

[108] Data based on address-based population registration system. - Les données sont basées sur le registre national de la population basé sur l'adresse.

[109] Because of rounding, totals are not in all cases the sum of the respective components. Based on a sample taken at the time of census. - Les chiffres étant arrondis, les totaux ne correspondent pas toujours rigoureusement à la somme des composants respectifs. D'après un échantillon obtenu au moment du recensement.

[110] Data include non-national population. - Les données comprennent les non-nationaux.

[111] Data refer to resident population. - Les données concernent la population résidente.

[112] Unrevised data. - Les données n'ont pas été révisées.

[113] Data are adjusted according to the results of the 1999 and 2009 censuses. - Les données ont été ajustées à partir des résultats des recensements de la population de 1999 et 2009.

[114] Decrease in population due to revision in administrative registers. - Diminution de la population due à la révision des registres administratifs.

[115] Population statistics are compiled from registers. Excluding Faeroe Islands and Greenland shown separately, if available. - Les statistiques de la population sont compilées à partir des registres. Non compris les Îles Féroé et le Groenland, qui font l'objet de rubriques distinctes, si disponible.

[116] Population statistics are compiled from registers. Excluding Åland Islands. - Les statistiques de la population sont compilées à partir des registres. Non compris les Îles d'Åland.

[117] Excluding diplomatic personnel outside the country and including members of alien armed forces not living in military camps and foreign diplomatic personnel not living in embassies or consulates. - Non compris le personnel diplomatique hors du pays et y compris les militaires étrangers ne vivant pas dans des camps militaires et le personnel diplomatique étranger ne vivant pas dans les ambassades ou les consulats.

[118] Excluding military personnel, visitors and transients. - Non compris les militaires, ni les visiteurs et transients.

[119] Data refer to the Vatican City State. - Les données se rapportent à l'Etat de la Cité du Vatican.

[120] The population figure is 466 persons. - La population est égale à 466 personnes.

[121] Data refer to usually resident population. - Les données concernent la population habituellement résidente.

[122] Data refer to registered resident population. - Les données concernent la population enregistrée résidente.

[123] Definition of localities was revised in 2011 causing a break with the previous series. - La rupture par rapport aux séries précédentes s'explique par le fait que la définition des localités a été révisée depuis 2011.

[124] Data refer to legal resident population. - Les données concernent la population légalement résidente.

[125] Including civilian nationals temporarily outside the country. - Y compris les civils nationaux temporairement hors du pays.

[126] Figures for male and female population do not add up to the figure for total population, because they exclude 119 persons of unknown sex. - Les chiffres relatifs à la population masculine et féminine ne correspondent pas au chiffre de la population totale, parce que l'on en a exclu 119 personnes de sexe inconnu.

[127] Including residents temporarily outside the country. Population statistics are compiled from registers. - Y compris les résidents se trouvant temporairement hors du pays. Les statistiques de la population sont compilées à partir des registres.

[128] Excluding civilian aliens within the country, but including civilian nationals temporarily outside the country. - Non compris les civils étrangers dans le pays, mais y compris les civils nationaux temporairement hors du pays.

[129] Excluding Transnistria and the municipality of Bender. - Les données ne tiennent pas compte de l'information sur la Transnistria et la municipalité de Bender.

[130] Figures for male and female may not add up to the total, since they do not include the category "Unknown". - La somme des chiffres indiqués pour les sexes masculin et féminin peut n'être pas égale au total parce qu'elle n'inclut pas la catégorie " inconnue ".

[131] Excludes data for Kosovo and Metohia. - Sans les données pour le Kosovo et Metohie.

[132] The data for urban and rural exclude the nationals temporarily outside the country. - Les données relatives à la population urbaine et rurale n'englobent pas les nationaux se trouvant provisoirement à l'étranger.

[133] The Government of Ukraine has informed the United Nations that it is not in a position to provide statistical data concerning the Autonomous Republic of Crimea and the city of Sevastopol. - Le gouvernement Ukrainien a informé l'ONU qu'il n'est pas en mesure de fournir des données statistiques concernant la République autonome de Crimée et la ville de Sébastopol.

[134] Excluding Channel Islands (Guernsey and Jersey) and Isle of Man, shown separately, if available. - Non compris les îles Anglo-Normandes (Guernesey et Jersey) et l'île de Man, qui font l'objet de rubriques distinctes, si disponible.

[135] This data has been randomly rounded to protect confidentiality. Individual figures may not add up to totals, and values for the same data may vary in different tables. - Ces données ont été arrondies de façon aléatoire afin d'en préserver la confidentialité. La somme de certains chiffres peut ne pas correspondre aux totaux indiqués et les valeurs des mêmes données peuvent varier d'un tableau à un autre.

[136] Including population in off-shore, migratory and shipping. - Y compris les populations extraterritoriales, les populations nomades et les populations maritimes.

[137] Excluding Niue, shown separately, which is part of Cook Islands, but because of remoteness is administered separately. - Non compris Nioué, qui fait l'objet d'une rubrique distincte et qui fait partie des îles Cook, mais qui, en raison de son éloignement, est administrée séparément.

[138] Projections are prepared by the Secretariat of the Pacific Community based on 1999 census of population and housing. - Les projections sont préparées par le Secrétariat de la Communauté du Pacifique à partir des résultats du recensement de la population et de l'habitat de 1999.

[139] Based on the census, updated for residents missed or counted more than once by the census (net census undercount); residents temporarily overseas on census night, and births, deaths and net migration between the census night and the date of the estimate. Population estimates by urban/rural residence exclude inland waters and oceanic areas. - D'après le recensement, mise à jour pour les résidents omis ou dénombrés plus d'une fois par le recensement (sous-dénombrement net); résidents temporairement à l'étranger la nuit du recensement, et naissances, décès et migration nette entre la nuit du recensement et la date de l'estimation. Les estimations de la population par lieu de résidence urbaine ou rurale excluent les eaux intérieures et les zones océaniques.

[140] Population estimates by urban/rural residence exclude inland waters and oceanic areas. - Les estimations de la population par lieu de résidence urbaine ou rurale excluent les eaux intérieures et les zones océaniques.

[141] The population figures are 64 and 58 persons for 2007 and 2008 respectively. - La population est respectivement égale à 64 et 58 personnes pour les années 2007 et 2008.

[142] Projections are prepared by the Secretariat of the Pacific Community based on the last population and housing census. - Les projections sont préparées par le Secrétariat de la Communauté du Pacifique à partir des résultats du dernier recensement de la population et de l'habitat.

[143] Data refer to national projections. Based on the results of the 1996 population census. - Les données se réfèrent aux projections nationales. À partir des résultats du recensement de la population de 1996.

Table 7 - Demographic Yearbook 2015

Table 7 presents population by age, sex and urban/rural residence for the latest available year between 2006 and 2015.

Description of variables: Data in this table are either population census figures or estimates, some of which are based on sample surveys. The source of data is indicated by the 'code' explained at the end of the table.

The reference date of the census or estimate appears in the left-most column of the table. In general, the estimates refer to mid-year, i.e. 1 July.

Age is defined as age at last birthday, that is, the difference between the date of birth and the reference date of the age distribution expressed in completed solar years. The age classification used in this table is the following: under 1 year, 1-4 years, 5-year groups through 95-99 years, and 100 years or over.

Statistics are presented for one year, the most recent available. However, if more complete disaggregation is available for an earlier year, both are displayed.

The urban/rural classification of population is that provided by each country or area; it is presumed to be based on the national census definitions of urban population that have been set forth at the end of the technical notes to table 6.

Reliability of data: Estimates which are believed to be less reliable are set in *italics* rather than in roman type.

Limitations: Statistics on population by age and sex are subject to the same qualifications as have been set forth for population statistics in general and age distributions in particular, as discussed in sections 3 and 3.1.3, respectively, of the Technical Notes.

Comparability of population data classified by age and sex is limited by variations in the definition of total population, discussed in detail in section 3 of the Technical Notes, and by the accuracy of the original enumeration. Both factors are more important in relation to certain age groups than to others. For example, under-enumeration is known to be more prevalent among infants and young children than among older persons. Similarly, the exclusion from the total population of certain groups that tend to be of selected ages (such as the armed forces) can markedly affect the age structure and its comparability with that for other countries or areas. Consideration should be given to the implications of these basic limitations in using the data.

In addition to these general qualifications are the special problems of comparability that arise in relation to age statistics in particular. Age distributions of population are known to suffer from certain deficiencies that have their origin in irregularities in age reporting. Although some of the irregularities tend to be obscured or eliminated when data are tabulated in five-year age groups rather than by single years, precision still continues to be affected, though the degree of distortion is not always readily seen.

Another factor limiting comparability is the age classification employed by the various countries or areas. Age may be based on the year of birth rather than the age at last birthday, in other words, calculated using the day, month and year of birth. Distributions based only on the year of birth are footnoted when known.

The absence of data in the unknown age group does not necessarily indicate completely accurate reporting and tabulation of the age item. The unknowns may have been eliminated by assigning ages to them before tabulation, or by proportionately distributing the unknown category across the age groups after tabulation.

As noted in connection with table 5, intercensal estimates of total population are usually revised to accord with the results of a census of population if inexplicable discontinuities appear to exist. Postcensal age-sex distributions, however, are less likely to be revised in this way. When it is known that a total population estimate for a given year has been revised and the corresponding age distribution has not been, the age distribution is shown as provisional. Distributions of this type should be used with caution when studying trends over a period of years, though their utility for studying age structure for the specified year is probably unimpaired.

The comparability of data by urban/rural residence is affected by the national definitions of urban and rural used in tabulating these data. When known, the definitions of urban used in national population censuses are presented at the end of the technical notes for table 6. As discussed in detail in the technical notes for table 6, these definitions vary considerably from one country or area to another.

Earlier data: Population by age, sex and urban/rural residence has been shown in previous issues of the *Demographic Yearbook*. For more information on specific topics, and years for which data are reported, readers should consult the Historical Index. In addition, population data by single years of age, sex and urban/rural residence, for censuses conducted since 1995, are shown in the *Demographic Yearbook* webpage http://unstats.un.org/unsd/demographic/products/dyb/dybcensusdata.htm.

Tableau 7 – *Annuaire démographique 2015*

Le tableau 7 présente les données les plus récentes disponibles pour la période 2006-2015 sur la population selon l'âge, le sexe et le lieu de résidence (zone urbaine ou rurale).

Description des variables : les données de ce tableau proviennent de recensements de la population ou correspondent à des estimations, fondées dans certains cas, sur des enquêtes par sondage. Le 'code' indique comment les données ont été obtenues. Les codes utilisés sont expliqués à la fin du tableau.

La date du recensement ou de l'estimation figure dans la colonne de gauche du tableau. En général, les estimations se rapportent au milieu de l'année (1er juillet).

L'âge désigne l'âge au dernier anniversaire, c'est-à-dire la différence entre la date de naissance et la date de référence de la répartition par âge exprimée en années solaires révolues. La classification par âge utilisée dans ce tableau est la suivante : moins d'un an, 1 à 4 ans, groupes quinquennaux jusqu'à 95-99 ans et 100 ans ou plus.

Les statistiques portent sur une année, qui correspond à celle pour laquelle on dispose des statistiques les plus récentes. Toutefois, si l'on dispose de répartitions plus complètes pour des années antérieures, les statistiques sont alors présentées pour les deux années.

La classification par zones urbaines et rurales de la population est celle qui est communiquée par chaque pays ou zone ; on part du principe qu'elle repose sur les définitions de la population urbaine utilisées pour les recensements de la population nationaux telles qu'elles sont reproduites à la fin des notes techniques du tableau 6.

Fiabilité des données : les estimations considérées comme moins sûres sont indiquées en italique plutôt qu'en caractères romains.

Insuffisance des données : les statistiques de la population selon l'âge et le sexe appellent les mêmes réserves que celles qui ont été formulées aux sections 3 et 3.1.3 des Notes technique à propos des statistiques de la population en général et des répartitions par âge en particulier.

La comparabilité des statistiques de la population selon l'âge et le sexe pâtit du manque d'uniformité dans la définition de la population totale (voir la section 3 des Notes techniques) et des lacunes des dénombrements. L'influence de ces deux facteurs varie selon les groupes d'âge. Ainsi, le dénombrement des enfants de moins d'un an et des jeunes enfants comporte souvent plus de lacunes que celui des personnes plus âgées. De même, le fait que certains groupes de personnes appartenant souvent à des groupes d'âge déterminés, par exemple les militaires, ne soient pas pris en compte dans la population totale peut influer sensiblement sur la structure par âge et sur la comparabilité des données avec celles d'autres pays ou zones. Il conviendra de tenir compte de ces facteurs fondamentaux lorsque l'on utilisera les données du tableau.

Outre ces difficultés d'ordre général, la comparabilité pose des problèmes particuliers lorsqu'il s'agit des données par âge. On sait que les répartitions de la population selon l'âge présentent certaines imperfections dues à l'inexactitude des déclarations d'âge. Certaines de ces anomalies ont tendance à s'estomper ou à disparaître lorsque l'on classe les données par groupes d'âge quinquennaux et non par années d'âge, mais une certaine imprécision subsiste, même s'il n'est pas toujours facile de voir à quel point il y a distorsion.

Le degré de comparabilité dépend également de la classification par âge employée dans les divers pays ou zones. L'âge retenu peut être défini par date exacte (jour, mois et année) de naissance ou par celle du dernier anniversaire. Lorsqu'elles étaient connues, les répartitions établies seulement d'après l'année de la naissance ont été signalées en note à la fin du tableau.

Si aucun nombre ne figure dans la rangée réservée aux âges inconnus, cela ne signifie pas nécessairement que les déclarations d'âge et l'exploitation des données par âge aient été tout à fait exactes. C'est souvent une indication que l'on a attribué un âge aux personnes d'âge inconnu avant l'exploitation des données ou qu'elles ont été réparties proportionnellement entre les différents groupes après cette opération.

Comme on l'a indiqué à propos du tableau 5, les estimations intercensitaires de la population totale sont d'ordinaire rectifiées d'après les résultats des recensements de population si l'on constate des discontinuités inexplicables. Les données postcensitaires concernant la répartition de la population par âge et par sexe ont toutefois moins de chance d'être rectifiées de cette manière. Lorsque l'on savait qu'une estimation de la population totale pour une année donnée avait été rectifiée sans qu'il en soit de même pour la répartition par âge correspondante, cette dernière a été indiquée comme ayant un caractère provisoire. Les répartitions de ce type doivent être utilisées avec prudence lorsque l'on étudie les tendances sur un certain nombre d'années, quoique leur utilité pour l'étude de la structure par âge de la population pour l'année visée reste probablement entière.

La comparabilité des données selon le lieu de résidence (zone urbaine ou rurale) peut être limitée par les définitions nationales des termes « urbain » et « rural » utilisées pour la mise en tableaux de ces données. Les définitions du terme « urbain » utilisées pour les recensements nationaux de population ont été présentées à la fin des notes techniques du tableau 6 lorsqu'elles étaient connues. Comme on l'a précisé dans les notes techniques relatives au tableau 6, ces définitions varient considérablement d'un pays ou d'une zone à l'autre.

Données publiées antérieurement : des statistiques concernant la population selon l'âge, le sexe et le lieu de résidence (zone urbaine ou rurale) ont été présentées dans des éditions antérieures de l'*Annuaire démographique*. Pour plus de précisions concernant les années et les sujets pour lesquels des données ont été publiées, se reporter à l'index historique. En plus, des statistiques disponibles concernant la « Population selon chaque année d'âge, le sexe et la résidence urbaine/rurale », pour les recensements depuis 1995, ont été présentées dans la page internet suivante de l'*Annuaire démographique* http://unstats.un.org/unsd/demographic/products/dyb/dybcensusdata.htm.

7. Population by age, sex and urban/rural residence: latest available year, 2006 - 2015
Population selon l'âge, le sexe et la résidence, urbaine/rurale : dernière année disponible, 2006 - 2015

Continent, country or area, date, code[a] and age (in years) / Continent, pays ou zone, date, code[a] et âge (en années)	Total			Urban - Urbaine			Rural - Rurale		
	Both sexes Les deux sexes	Male Masculin	Female Féminin	Both sexes Les deux sexes	Male Masculin	Female Féminin	Both sexes Les deux sexes	Male Masculin	Female Féminin
AFRICA - AFRIQUE									
Algeria - Algérie									
16 IV 2008 (CDJC)[1]									
Total	34 080 030	17 232 753	16 847 277	22 413 189	11 288 724	11 124 466	11 666 841	5 944 029	5 722 812
0 - 4	3 404 918	1 750 097	1 654 821	2 242 705	1 151 239	1 091 466	1 162 213	598 858	563 355
5 - 9	2 888 376	1 475 674	1 412 702	1 888 091	963 262	924 829	1 000 285	512 412	487 873
10 - 14	3 258 773	1 662 262	1 596 511	2 096 819	1 067 727	1 029 092	1 161 954	594 535	567 419
15 - 19	3 635 171	1 847 312	1 787 859	2 309 568	1 169 541	1 140 028	1 325 603	677 772	647 831
20 - 24	3 763 504	1 895 703	1 867 801	2 378 019	1 188 465	1 189 553	1 385 485	707 238	678 247
25 - 29	3 422 377	1 730 411	1 691 966	2 186 560	1 096 016	1 090 545	1 235 816	634 395	601 421
30 - 34	2 740 996	1 379 085	1 361 910	1 802 265	901 021	901 245	938 730	478 064	460 666
35 - 39	2 342 779	1 167 250	1 175 529	1 601 928	793 133	808 795	740 852	374 118	366 734
40 - 44	2 018 327	1 007 683	1 010 644	1 414 371	705 266	709 105	603 956	302 417	301 539
45 - 49	1 629 436	817 005	812 432	1 132 297	570 706	561 591	497 140	246 299	250 841
50 - 54	1 346 695	682 358	664 336	927 655	474 005	453 650	419 040	208 353	210 687
55 - 59	1 062 578	547 180	515 398	720 761	371 528	349 233	341 817	175 652	166 165
60 - 64	711 482	354 694	356 788	479 760	236 949	242 811	231 722	117 745	113 977
65 - 69	631 303	314 958	316 345	420 685	207 760	212 925	210 618	107 198	103 420
70 - 74	504 926	248 672	256 254	336 819	164 109	172 710	168 107	84 563	83 544
75 - 79	363 843	181 478	182 364	240 563	118 362	122 201	123 280	63 116	60 164
80 - 84	187 130	93 472	93 657	121 942	59 267	62 675	65 187	34 205	30 982
85 - 89	89 722	43 307	46 416	58 550	27 171	31 379	31 172	16 136	15 037
90 - 94	29 672	13 575	16 097	19 375	8 488	10 887	10 297	5 087	5 210
95 - 99	10 028	4 178	5 851	6 647	2 638	4 009	3 382	1 540	1 842
100 +	650	252	398	445	170	274	205	82	123
Unknown - Inconnu	37 347	16 146	21 200	27 365	11 901	15 464	9 981	4 245	5 736
1 VII 2015 (ESDJ)									
Total	39 963 249	20 235 204	19 728 045	...	...	...	...	...	...
0	1 001 948	514 553	487 396	...	...	...	...	...	...
1 - 4	3 681 493	1 891 486	1 790 008	...	...	...	...	...	...
5 - 9	3 823 958	1 968 897	1 855 061	...	...	...	...	...	...
10 - 14	3 007 861	1 540 672	1 467 189	...	...	...	...	...	...
15 - 19	3 114 511	1 589 914	1 524 597	...	...	...	...	...	...
20 - 24	3 551 363	1 808 061	1 743 302	...	...	...	...	...	...
25 - 29	3 799 782	1 917 201	1 882 581	...	...	...	...	...	...
30 - 34	3 645 769	1 838 018	1 807 751	...	...	...	...	...	...
35 - 39	3 024 036	1 524 862	1 499 174	...	...	...	...	...	...
40 - 44	2 482 961	1 239 837	1 243 124	...	...	...	...	...	...
45 - 49	2 150 716	1 070 132	1 080 584	...	...	...	...	...	...
50 - 54	1 768 420	882 544	885 876	...	...	...	...	...	...
55 - 59	1 426 468	715 788	710 680	...	...	...	...	...	...
60 - 64	1 145 569	583 152	562 417	...	...	...	...	...	...
65 - 69	782 074	391 709	390 365	...	...	...	...	...	...
70 - 74	581 108	283 923	297 185	...	...	...	...	...	...
75 - 79	463 766	224 389	239 377	...	...	...	...	...	...
80 - 84	306 443	148 198	158 245	...	...	...	...	...	...
85 +	205 001	101 869	103 132	...	...	...	...	...	...
Benin - Bénin									
1 VII 2011 (ESDF)[2]									
Total	9 067 076	4 446 877	4 620 199	4 072 574	2 003 366	2 069 208	4 994 502	2 443 511	2 550 991
0 - 4	1 629 512	828 064	801 448	633 629	321 667	311 962	995 883	506 397	489 486
0	350 292	178 565	171 727	...	...	...	...	...	...
1 - 4	1 279 220	649 499	629 721	...	...	...	...	...	...
5 - 9	1 335 166	675 912	659 254	511 822	251 283	260 539	823 344	424 629	398 715
10 - 14	1 137 068	572 756	564 312	517 373	244 437	272 936	619 695	328 319	291 376
15 - 19	1 081 199	553 241	527 958	550 694	279 420	271 274	530 505	273 821	256 684
20 - 24	767 946	398 920	369 026	406 496	224 092	182 404	361 450	174 828	186 622
25 - 29	609 489	291 598	317 891	303 896	153 731	150 165	305 593	137 867	167 726
30 - 34	537 893	227 400	310 493	264 521	117 596	146 925	273 372	109 804	163 568
35 - 39	494 619	213 385	281 234	236 804	106 800	130 004	257 815	106 585	151 230
40 - 44	378 111	175 956	202 155	178 115	86 225	91 890	199 996	89 731	110 265
45 - 49	308 866	142 056	166 810	145 334	68 351	76 983	163 532	73 705	89 827
50 - 54	232 650	110 074	122 576	101 866	48 831	53 035	130 784	61 243	69 541
55 - 59	171 970	82 190	89 780	77 819	37 319	40 500	94 151	44 871	49 280
60 - 64	135 768	64 968	70 800	52 261	24 642	27 619	83 507	40 326	43 181
65 - 69	75 534	35 915	39 619	31 238	14 546	16 692	44 296	21 369	22 927

Continent, country or area, date, code[a] and age (in years) / Continent, pays ou zone, date, code[a] et âge (en années)	Total			Urban - Urbaine			Rural - Rurale		
	Both sexes Les deux sexes	Male Masculin	Female Féminin	Both sexes Les deux sexes	Male Masculin	Female Féminin	Both sexes Les deux sexes	Male Masculin	Female Féminin
AFRICA - AFRIQUE									
Benin - Bénin									
1 VII 2011 (ESDF)[2]									
70 - 74	82 740	36 511	46 229	30 032	12 558	17 474	52 708	23 953	28 755
75 - 79	36 453	15 591	20 862	14 064	5 573	8 491	22 389	10 018	12 371
80 +	52 092	22 340	29 752	16 610	6 295	10 315	35 482	16 045	19 437
1 VII 2015 (ESDF)[3]									
Total	10 584 935	5 182 478	5 402 457	...	...	...	...	...	...
0 - 4	1 710 027	867 491	842 536	...	...	...	...	...	...
5 - 9	1 695 915	856 846	839 069	...	...	...	...	...	...
10 - 14	1 452 913	744 009	708 904	...	...	...	...	...	...
15 - 19	1 110 397	572 180	538 217	...	...	...	...	...	...
20 - 24	908 355	431 962	476 393	...	...	...	...	...	...
25 - 29	804 474	346 549	457 925	...	...	...	...	...	...
30 - 34	699 479	309 778	389 701	...	...	...	...	...	...
35 - 39	562 066	262 149	299 917	...	...	...	...	...	...
40 - 44	450 071	218 774	231 297	...	...	...	...	...	...
45 - 49	314 668	156 832	157 836	...	...	...	...	...	...
50 - 54	264 881	129 100	135 781	...	...	...	...	...	...
55 - 59	172 060	85 118	86 942	...	...	...	...	...	...
60 - 64	144 394	69 494	74 900	...	...	...	...	...	...
65 - 69	103 178	48 609	54 569	...	...	...	...	...	...
70 - 74	73 117	33 189	39 928	...	...	...	...	...	...
75 - 79	49 124	21 528	27 596	...	...	...	...	...	...
80 +	69 816	28 870	40 946	...	...	...	...	...	...
Botswana									
9 VIII 2011 (CDFC)									
Total	2 024 904	988 957	1 035 947	1 297 287	619 472	677 815	727 617	369 485	358 132
0 - 4	237 314	119 999	117 315	137 134	69 359	67 775	100 180	50 640	49 540
5 - 9	215 162	108 544	106 618	126 224	63 146	63 078	88 938	45 398	43 540
10 - 14	207 294	104 419	102 875	125 427	62 520	62 907	81 867	41 899	39 968
15 - 19	210 746	104 818	105 928	144 299	68 841	75 458	66 447	35 977	30 470
20 - 24	200 350	97 249	103 101	141 377	66 208	75 169	58 973	31 041	27 932
25 - 29	207 852	101 194	106 658	147 689	69 567	78 122	60 163	31 627	28 536
30 - 34	170 542	84 515	86 027	121 956	58 698	63 258	48 586	25 817	22 769
35 - 39	135 219	68 435	66 784	94 329	46 341	47 988	40 890	22 094	18 796
40 - 44	99 297	48 767	50 530	67 345	32 518	34 827	31 952	16 249	15 703
45 - 49	82 261	37 881	44 380	52 842	24 123	28 719	29 419	13 758	15 661
50 - 54	66 362	29 742	36 620	40 264	18 087	22 177	26 098	11 655	14 443
55 - 59	54 049	24 368	29 681	30 470	13 592	16 878	23 579	10 776	12 803
60 - 64	37 584	17 344	20 240	19 235	8 310	10 925	18 349	9 034	9 315
65 - 69	27 747	12 243	15 504	13 597	5 530	8 067	14 150	6 713	7 437
70 - 74	22 261	9 464	12 797	10 696	4 006	6 690	11 565	5 458	6 107
75 - 79	17 892	6 968	10 924	8 578	2 914	5 664	9 314	4 054	5 260
80 - 84	13 219	4 875	8 344	6 112	1 939	4 173	7 107	2 936	4 171
85 - 89	8 247	2 825	5 422	3 946	1 217	2 729	4 301	1 608	2 693
90 - 94	3 921	1 377	2 544	1 842	598	1 244	2 079	779	1 300
95 +	7 585	3 930	3 655	3 925	1 958	1 967	3 660	1 972	1 688
Burkina Faso									
9 XII 2006 (CDJC)									
Total	14 017 262	6 768 739	7 248 523	3 181 967	1 588 895	1 593 072	10 835 295	5 179 844	5 655 451
0	466 516	235 090	231 426	87 021	44 072	42 949	379 495	191 018	188 477
1 - 4	1 970 397	995 520	974 877	333 623	169 737	163 886	1 636 774	825 783	810 991
5 - 9	2 315 710	1 176 473	1 139 237	401 898	200 004	201 894	1 913 812	976 469	937 343
10 - 14	1 746 588	900 103	846 485	369 532	178 639	190 893	1 377 056	721 464	655 592
15 - 19	1 475 285	710 323	764 962	411 383	192 566	218 817	1 063 902	517 757	546 145
20 - 24	1 185 378	530 425	654 953	366 029	178 980	187 049	819 349	351 445	467 904
25 - 29	1 009 285	448 431	560 854	296 420	150 350	146 070	712 865	298 081	414 784
30 - 34	794 820	363 408	431 412	228 658	122 850	105 808	566 162	240 558	325 604
35 - 39	656 824	298 236	358 588	172 705	92 889	79 816	484 119	205 347	278 772
40 - 44	549 287	250 143	299 144	136 961	71 800	65 161	412 326	178 343	233 983
45 - 49	427 739	195 016	232 723	99 671	52 052	47 619	328 068	142 964	185 104
50 - 54	358 810	166 281	192 529	78 866	41 122	37 744	279 944	125 159	154 785
55 - 59	273 563	132 254	141 309	56 234	29 228	27 006	217 329	103 026	114 303
60 - 64	238 962	111 176	127 786	45 740	21 983	23 757	193 222	89 193	104 029
65 - 69	163 609	80 542	83 067	29 765	14 189	15 576	133 844	66 353	67 491

7. Population by age, sex and urban/rural residence: latest available year, 2006 - 2015
Population selon l'âge, le sexe et la résidence, urbaine/rurale : dernière année disponible, 2006 - 2015 (continued - suite)

Continent, country or area, date, codeᵃ and age (in years) / Continent, pays ou zone, date, codeᵃ et âge (en années)	Total			Urban - Urbaine			Rural - Rurale		
	Both sexes Les deux sexes	Male Masculin	Female Féminin	Both sexes Les deux sexes	Male Masculin	Female Féminin	Both sexes Les deux sexes	Male Masculin	Female Féminin
AFRICA - AFRIQUE									
Burkina Faso									
9 XII 2006 (CDJC)									
70 - 74	136 282	63 727	72 555	23 129	10 103	13 026	113 153	53 624	59 529
75 - 79	77 113	37 186	39 927	12 366	5 449	6 917	64 747	31 737	33 010
80 - 84	50 317	21 791	28 526	8 171	2 957	5 214	42 146	18 834	23 312
85 - 89	21 694	9 645	12 049	3 512	1 230	2 282	18 182	8 415	9 767
90 - 94	11 529	4 480	7 049	1 898	619	1 279	9 631	3 861	5 770
95 +	13 067	4 727	8 340	1 956	467	1 489	11 111	4 260	6 851
Unknown - Inconnu	74 487	33 762	40 725	16 429	7 609	8 820	58 058	26 153	31 905
1 VII 2009 (ESDJ)²									
Total	15 224 780	7 346 835	7 877 945	...	...	...	...	...	...
0	652 074	332 861	319 213	...	...	...	...	...	...
1 - 4	2 262 278	1 166 932	1 095 346	...	...	...	...	...	...
5 - 9	2 416 407	1 236 776	1 179 631	...	...	...	...	...	...
10 - 14	1 973 815	988 126	985 689	...	...	...	...	...	...
15 - 19	1 577 324	774 081	803 243	...	...	...	...	...	...
20 - 24	1 309 638	579 080	730 558	...	...	...	...	...	...
25 - 29	1 045 616	455 063	590 553	...	...	...	...	...	...
30 - 34	878 095	389 101	488 994	...	...	...	...	...	...
35 - 39	679 903	308 106	371 797	...	...	...	...	...	...
40 - 44	589 777	263 840	325 937	...	...	...	...	...	...
45 - 49	453 094	206 387	246 707	...	...	...	...	...	...
50 - 54	382 895	172 330	210 565	...	...	...	...	...	...
55 - 59	280 518	133 841	146 677	...	...	...	...	...	...
60 - 64	254 972	118 221	136 751	...	...	...	...	...	...
65 - 69	167 320	81 902	85 418	...	...	...	...	...	...
70 - 74	138 614	64 975	73 639	...	...	...	...	...	...
75 - 79	75 664	37 101	38 563	...	...	...	...	...	...
80 +	86 776	38 112	48 664	...	...	...	...	...	...
Burundi⁴									
1 VII 2015 (ESDF)									
Total	9 823 828	4 822 838	5 000 990	1 473 574	723 426	750 148	8 350 254	4 099 412	4 250 842
0 - 4	1 712 483	856 714	855 769	220 830	99 976	120 854	1 491 653	756 738	734 915
5 - 9	1 379 000	679 740	699 260	172 229	76 843	95 386	1 206 771	602 897	603 874
10 - 14	1 234 086	604 457	629 629	154 449	67 431	87 018	1 079 637	537 026	542 611
15 - 19	1 021 915	496 353	525 562	161 685	74 964	86 721	860 230	421 389	438 841
20 - 24	974 645	467 123	507 522	176 946	89 742	87 204	797 699	377 381	420 318
25 - 29	843 366	397 323	446 043	174 840	90 183	84 657	668 526	307 140	361 386
30 - 34	659 106	321 348	337 758	140 254	76 414	63 840	518 852	244 934	273 918
35 - 39	466 561	236 115	230 446	82 657	46 719	35 938	383 904	189 396	194 508
40 - 44	366 466	182 701	183 765	57 283	33 163	24 120	309 183	149 538	159 645
45 - 49	310 594	153 796	156 798	40 803	22 094	18 709	269 791	131 702	138 089
50 - 54	265 180	134 933	130 247	30 364	16 749	13 615	234 816	118 184	116 632
55 - 59	225 278	113 470	111 808	25 692	13 147	12 545	199 586	100 323	99 263
60 - 64	145 211	74 556	70 655	14 954	7 579	7 375	130 257	66 977	63 280
65 - 69	90 785	44 744	46 041	9 023	4 024	4 999	81 762	40 720	41 042
70 - 74	54 548	25 722	28 826	4 874	2 027	2 847	49 674	23 695	25 979
75 - 79	36 220	16 056	20 164	3 504	1 175	2 329	32 716	14 881	17 835
80 +	38 384	17 687	20 697	3 187	1 196	1 991	35 197	16 491	18 706
Cabo Verde									
1 VII 2011 (ESDF)									
Total	527 269	255 327	271 942	...	...	...	...	...	...
0	13 460	6 778	6 682	...	...	...	...	...	...
1 - 4	50 678	25 438	25 240	...	...	...	...	...	...
5 - 9	57 789	28 923	28 866	...	...	...	...	...	...
10 - 14	57 177	28 773	28 404	...	...	...	...	...	...
15 - 19	60 912	30 486	30 426	...	...	...	...	...	...
20 - 24	61 465	30 479	30 986	...	...	...	...	...	...
25 - 29	48 416	23 782	24 634	...	...	...	...	...	...
30 - 34	35 452	17 379	18 073	...	...	...	...	...	...
35 - 39	27 130	13 085	14 045	...	...	...	...	...	...
40 - 44	26 081	12 350	13 731	...	...	...	...	...	...
45 - 49	24 501	11 490	13 011	...	...	...	...	...	...
50 - 54	19 163	8 591	10 572	...	...	...	...	...	...
55 - 59	13 045	5 240	7 805	...	...	...	...	...	...

7. Population by age, sex and urban/rural residence: latest available year, 2006 - 2015
Population selon l'âge, le sexe et la résidence, urbaine/rurale : dernière année disponible, 2006 - 2015 (continued - suite)

Continent, country or area, date, code[a] and age (in years) / Continent, pays ou zone, date, code[a] et âge (en années)	Total			Urban - Urbaine			Rural - Rurale		
	Both sexes Les deux sexes	Male Masculin	Female Féminin	Both sexes Les deux sexes	Male Masculin	Female Féminin	Both sexes Les deux sexes	Male Masculin	Female Féminin
AFRICA - AFRIQUE									
Cabo Verde									
1 VII 2011 (ESDF)									
60 - 64	6 603	2 691	3 912	...	...	...	...	...	...
65 - 69	5 293	2 140	3 153	...	...	...	...	...	...
70 - 74	7 492	2 838	4 654	...	...	...	...	...	...
75 - 79	6 261	2 425	3 836	...	...	...	...	...	...
80 +	6 351	2 439	3 912	...	...	...	...	...	...
Cameroon - Cameroun[2]									
1 I 2010 (ESDJ)									
Total	19 406 100	9 599 224	9 806 876	...	...	...	...	...	...
0 - 4	3 287 234	1 662 298	1 624 936	...	...	...	...	...	...
5 - 9	2 783 459	1 412 467	1 370 992	...	...	...	...	...	...
10 - 14	2 394 671	1 227 470	1 167 201	...	...	...	...	...	...
15 - 19	2 170 035	1 068 509	1 101 526	...	...	...	...	...	...
20 - 24	1 837 289	855 334	981 955	...	...	...	...	...	...
25 - 29	1 525 816	712 550	813 266	...	...	...	...	...	...
30 - 34	1 209 607	588 210	621 397	...	...	...	...	...	...
35 - 39	942 713	460 394	482 319	...	...	...	...	...	...
40 - 44	793 846	388 539	405 307	...	...	...	...	...	...
45 - 49	640 247	323 507	316 740	...	...	...	...	...	...
50 - 54	521 910	261 626	260 284	...	...	...	...	...	...
55 - 59	337 988	178 876	159 112	...	...	...	...	...	...
60 - 64	315 879	155 208	160 671	...	...	...	...	...	...
65 - 69	227 290	110 645	116 645	...	...	...	...	...	...
70 - 74	189 571	88 969	100 602	...	...	...	...	...	...
75 - 79	98 078	47 173	50 905	...	...	...	...	...	...
80 - 84	71 585	31 609	39 976	...	...	...	...	...	...
85 - 89	26 564	12 109	14 455	...	...	...	...	...	...
90 - 94	15 715	6 942	8 773	...	...	...	...	...	...
95 +	16 603	6 789	9 814	...	...	...	...	...	...
Congo									
1 VII 2009 (ESDF)									
Total	3 838 238	1 891 558	1 946 680	...	...	...	...	...	...
0 - 4	586 578	294 305	292 273	...	...	...	...	...	...
5 - 9	475 864	238 682	237 182	...	...	...	...	...	...
10 - 14	417 074	208 162	208 912	...	...	...	...	...	...
15 - 19	382 673	186 405	196 268	...	...	...	...	...	...
20 - 24	358 745	167 519	191 226	...	...	...	...	...	...
25 - 29	339 133	160 897	178 236	...	...	...	...	...	...
30 - 34	304 009	152 642	151 367	...	...	...	...	...	...
35 - 39	254 997	131 794	123 203	...	...	...	...	...	...
40 - 44	198 594	103 248	95 346	...	...	...	...	...	...
45 - 49	148 798	76 921	71 877	...	...	...	...	...	...
50 - 54	111 812	54 925	56 887	...	...	...	...	...	...
55 - 59	80 842	38 051	42 791	...	...	...	...	...	...
60 - 64	59 601	27 592	32 009	...	...	...	...	...	...
65 - 69	46 706	20 879	25 827	...	...	...	...	...	...
70 - 74	34 961	14 954	20 007	...	...	...	...	...	...
75 - 79	21 868	8 820	13 048	...	...	...	...	...	...
80 +	15 983	5 762	10 221	...	...	...	...	...	...
Côte d'Ivoire									
15 V 2014 (CDJC)									
Total	22 671 331	11 708 244	10 963 087	11 408 513	5 816 059	5 592 354	11 262 818	5 892 185	5 370 733
0 - 4	3 686 747	1 902 052	1 784 695	1 601 086	822 193	778 893	2 085 661	1 079 859	1 005 802
5 - 9	3 165 647	1 635 039	1 530 608	1 391 174	702 830	688 344	1 774 473	932 209	842 264
10 - 14	2 628 957	1 391 732	1 237 225	1 355 885	685 482	670 403	1 273 072	706 250	566 822
15 - 19	2 114 581	1 075 555	1 039 026	1 241 863	617 053	624 810	872 718	458 502	414 216
20 - 24	2 105 594	1 022 190	1 083 404	1 181 634	571 944	609 690	923 960	450 246	473 714
25 - 29	2 050 384	997 460	1 052 924	1 110 948	532 302	578 646	939 436	465 158	474 278
30 - 34	1 770 782	908 792	861 990	947 035	483 237	463 798	823 747	425 555	398 192
35 - 39	1 359 469	744 301	615 168	731 723	403 637	328 086	627 746	340 664	287 082
40 - 44	1 002 585	555 990	446 595	520 065	291 960	228 105	482 520	264 030	218 490
45 - 49	781 041	419 350	361 691	386 878	207 390	179 488	394 163	211 960	182 203
50 - 54	641 975	337 817	304 158	316 518	165 957	150 561	325 457	171 860	153 597
55 - 59	445 441	240 117	205 324	220 963	120 011	100 952	224 478	120 106	104 372

Continent, country or area, date, code[a] and age (in years) / Continent, pays ou zone, date, code[a] et âge (en annèes)	Total			Urban - Urbaine			Rural - Rurale		
	Both sexes Les deux sexes	Male Masculin	Female Féminin	Both sexes Les deux sexes	Male Masculin	Female Féminin	Both sexes Les deux sexes	Male Masculin	Female Féminin
AFRICA - AFRIQUE									
Côte d'Ivoire									
15 V 2014 (CDJC)									
60 - 64	337 681	183 494	154 187	161 143	89 696	71 447	176 538	93 798	82 740
65 - 69	227 209	118 203	109 006	100 675	53 359	47 316	126 534	64 844	61 690
70 - 74	155 547	78 643	76 904	64 012	32 013	31 999	91 535	46 630	44 905
75 - 79	88 561	44 041	44 520	35 235	17 138	18 097	53 326	26 903	26 423
80 - 84	54 684	25 866	28 818	20 377	9 239	11 138	34 307	16 627	17 680
85 - 89	18 767	9 206	9 561	6 866	3 194	3 672	11 901	6 012	5 889
90 - 94	9 370	4 183	5 187	3 218	1 272	1 946	6 152	2 911	3 241
95 - 99	17 555	8 982	8 573	7 323	4 005	3 318	10 232	4 977	5 255
100 +	4 294	1 842	2 452	1 777	737	1 040	2 517	1 105	1 412
Unknown - Inconnu	4 460	3 389	1 071	2 015	1 410	605	2 445	1 979	466
Egypt - Égypte									
1 VII 2014 (ESDF)									
Total	86 813 723	44 304 619	42 509 104	37 094 960	18 904 449	18 190 511	49 718 763	25 400 170	24 318 593
0 - 4	9 829 921	5 101 944	4 727 977	4 200 159	2 176 962	2 023 197	5 629 762	2 924 982	2 704 780
5 - 9	9 126 024	4 728 899	4 397 125	3 899 406	2 017 786	1 881 620	5 226 618	2 711 113	2 515 505
10 - 14	8 183 738	4 224 190	3 959 548	3 496 802	1 802 431	1 694 371	4 686 936	2 421 759	2 265 177
15 - 19	8 388 912	4 311 966	4 076 946	3 584 492	1 839 884	1 744 608	4 804 420	2 472 082	2 332 338
20 - 24	8 929 427	4 564 320	4 365 107	3 815 480	1 947 562	1 867 918	5 113 947	2 616 758	2 497 189
25 - 29	8 398 687	4 279 050	4 119 637	3 588 716	1 825 839	1 762 877	4 809 971	2 453 211	2 356 760
30 - 34	6 731 457	3 412 268	3 319 189	2 876 338	1 455 990	1 420 348	3 855 119	1 956 278	1 898 841
35 - 39	5 281 272	2 677 149	2 604 123	2 256 677	1 142 319	1 114 358	3 024 595	1 534 830	1 489 765
40 - 44	4 739 858	2 391 878	2 347 980	2 025 344	1 020 596	1 004 748	2 714 514	1 371 282	1 343 232
45 - 49	4 350 256	2 194 384	2 155 872	1 858 868	936 327	922 541	2 491 388	1 258 057	1 233 331
50 - 54	3 776 526	1 898 142	1 878 384	1 613 721	809 922	803 799	2 162 805	1 088 220	1 074 585
55 - 59	3 083 900	1 547 040	1 536 860	1 317 764	660 110	657 654	1 766 136	886 930	879 206
60 - 64	2 261 407	1 130 107	1 131 300	966 314	482 208	484 106	1 295 093	647 899	647 194
65 - 69	1 590 425	789 978	800 447	679 605	337 077	342 528	910 820	452 901	457 919
70 - 74	1 049 312	515 680	533 632	448 388	220 036	228 352	600 924	295 644	305 280
75 +	1 092 601	537 624	554 977	466 886	229 400	237 486	625 715	308 224	317 491
1 VII 2015 (ESDF)									
Total	88 957 833	45 378 728	43 579 105	...	...	...	...	...	...
0	1 949 440	1 012 054	937 386	...	...	...	...	...	...
1 - 4	7 699 752	3 996 973	3 702 779	...	...	...	...	...	...
5 - 9	9 457 361	4 907 608	4 549 753	...	...	...	...	...	...
10 - 14	8 301 088	4 295 892	4 005 196	...	...	...	...	...	...
15 - 19	7 936 688	4 088 416	3 848 272	...	...	...	...	...	...
20 - 24	8 392 682	4 301 230	4 091 452	...	...	...	...	...	...
25 - 29	8 611 250	4 391 973	4 219 277	...	...	...	...	...	...
30 - 34	7 565 655	3 838 973	3 726 682	...	...	...	...	...	...
35 - 39	5 865 157	2 965 703	2 899 454	...	...	...	...	...	...
40 - 44	4 805 409	2 427 649	2 377 760	...	...	...	...	...	...
45 - 49	4 412 335	2 222 676	2 189 659	...	...	...	...	...	...
50 - 54	3 949 765	1 983 541	1 966 225	...	...	...	...	...	...
55 - 59	3 309 100	1 651 527	1 657 573	...	...	...	...	...	...
60 - 64	2 543 180	1 259 730	1 283 450	...	...	...	...	...	...
65 - 69	1 768 974	869 000	899 974	...	...	...	...	...	...
70 - 74	1 164 436	566 878	597 558	...	...	...	...	...	...
75 +	1 225 562	598 905	626 656	...	...	...	...	...	...
Ethiopia - Éthiopie									
29 V 2007 (CDFC)									
Total	73 750 932	37 217 130	36 533 802	11 862 821	5 895 916	5 966 905	61 888 111	31 321 214	30 566 897
0 - 4	10 797 022	5 482 792	5 314 230	1 170 955	596 105	574 850	9 626 067	4 886 687	4 739 380
5 - 9	11 981 764	6 106 788	5 874 976	1 287 441	640 097	647 344	10 694 323	5 466 691	5 227 632
10 - 14	10 412 237	5 412 324	4 999 913	1 369 665	658 283	711 382	9 042 572	4 754 041	4 288 531
15 - 19	8 748 048	4 454 710	4 293 338	1 947 281	935 230	1 012 051	6 800 767	3 519 480	3 281 287
20 - 24	6 402 085	3 098 338	3 303 747	1 509 343	750 712	758 631	4 892 742	2 347 626	2 545 116
25 - 29	5 662 188	2 622 759	3 039 429	1 230 544	596 293	634 251	4 431 644	2 026 466	2 405 178
30 - 34	4 220 066	2 088 208	2 131 858	815 179	432 721	382 458	3 404 887	1 655 487	1 749 400
35 - 39	3 776 642	1 827 296	1 949 346	694 895	356 496	338 399	3 081 747	1 470 800	1 610 947
40 - 44	2 872 980	1 464 529	1 408 451	473 929	259 968	213 961	2 399 051	1 204 561	1 194 490
45 - 49	2 247 304	1 150 017	1 097 287	364 212	189 159	175 053	1 883 092	960 858	922 234
50 - 54	1 890 766	928 294	962 472	288 617	138 190	150 427	1 602 149	790 104	812 045
55 - 59	1 171 020	634 053	536 967	178 579	89 368	89 211	992 441	544 685	447 756

7. Population by age, sex and urban/rural residence: latest available year, 2006 - 2015
Population selon l'âge, le sexe et la résidence, urbaine/rurale : dernière année disponible, 2006 - 2015 (continued - suite)

Continent, country or area, date, code[a] and age (in years) Continent, pays ou zone, date, code[a] et âge (en années)	Total			Urban - Urbaine			Rural - Rurale		
	Both sexes Les deux sexes	Male Masculin	Female Féminin	Both sexes Les deux sexes	Male Masculin	Female Féminin	Both sexes Les deux sexes	Male Masculin	Female Féminin
AFRICA - AFRIQUE									
Ethiopia - Éthiopie									
29 V 2007 (CDFC)									
60 - 64	1 235 000	646 359	588 641	178 561	84 582	93 979	1 056 439	561 777	494 662
65 - 69	805 261	446 242	359 019	121 149	59 539	61 610	684 112	386 703	297 409
70 - 74	676 560	359 897	316 663	103 889	47 688	56 201	572 671	312 209	260 462
75 - 79	350 176	203 843	146 333	53 212	26 863	26 349	296 964	176 980	119 984
80 - 84	287 477	159 786	127 691	42 749	18 737	24 012	244 728	141 049	103 679
85 - 89	100 196	62 001	38 195	16 149	8 301	7 848	84 047	53 700	30 347
90 - 94	64 542	38 185	26 357	10 215	4 646	5 569	54 327	33 539	20 788
95 +	49 598	30 709	18 889	6 257	2 938	3 319	43 341	27 771	15 570
Ghana[2]									
1 VII 2015 (ESDF)									
Total	27 670 174	13 562 093	14 108 081	13 817 894	6 903 107	6 914 787	13 852 280	6 658 986	7 193 294
0	841 301	425 611	415 690	403 605	195 150	208 455	437 696	230 461	207 235
1 - 4	3 158 109	1 595 165	1 562 944	1 513 925	731 409	782 516	1 644 184	863 756	780 428
5 - 9	3 312 878	1 688 452	1 624 426	1 579 799	755 911	823 888	1 733 079	932 541	800 538
10 - 14	3 097 352	1 567 043	1 530 309	1 538 503	749 266	789 237	1 558 849	817 777	741 072
15 - 19	2 825 578	1 414 987	1 410 591	1 458 024	735 981	722 043	1 367 554	679 006	688 548
20 - 24	2 537 799	1 251 759	1 286 040	1 377 177	736 425	640 752	1 160 622	515 334	645 288
25 - 29	2 252 493	1 083 877	1 168 616	1 211 633	636 338	575 295	1 040 860	447 539	593 321
30 - 34	1 967 166	935 947	1 031 219	1 014 879	537 402	477 477	952 287	398 545	553 742
35 - 39	1 665 237	785 200	880 037	840 000	437 656	402 344	825 237	347 544	477 693
40 - 44	1 404 309	661 789	742 520	703 098	362 522	340 576	701 211	299 267	401 944
45 - 49	1 145 932	546 030	599 902	560 013	275 131	284 882	585 919	270 899	315 020
50 - 54	933 268	445 531	487 737	477 984	238 760	239 224	455 284	206 771	248 513
55 - 59	728 002	348 118	379 884	337 828	159 376	178 452	390 174	188 742	201 432
60 - 64	570 616	270 642	299 974	271 174	129 651	141 523	299 442	140 991	158 451
65 - 69	419 501	196 219	223 282	178 422	73 727	104 695	241 079	122 492	118 587
70 - 74	313 256	142 378	170 878	149 542	68 333	81 209	163 714	74 045	89 669
75 - 79	223 087	96 514	126 573	90 638	36 406	54 232	132 449	60 108	72 341
80 +	274 290	106 831	167 459	111 650	43 663	67 987	162 640	63 168	99 472
Guinea - Guinée									
1 III 2014 (CDFC)									
Total	10 523 261	5 084 306	5 438 955	3 657 122	1 821 369	1 835 753	6 866 139	3 262 937	3 603 202
0 - 4	1 764 144	890 034	874 110	505 275	254 440	250 835	1 258 869	635 594	623 275
5 - 9	1 699 838	863 214	836 624	488 932	241 360	247 572	1 210 906	621 854	589 052
10 - 14	1 235 102	626 512	608 590	440 827	210 959	229 868	794 275	415 553	378 722
15 - 19	1 108 604	520 540	588 064	468 375	226 124	242 251	640 229	294 416	345 813
20 - 24	906 043	409 385	496 658	435 177	215 462	219 715	470 866	193 923	276 943
25 - 29	782 764	338 166	444 598	321 174	156 550	164 624	461 590	181 616	279 974
30 - 34	630 979	277 205	353 774	241 547	119 817	121 730	389 432	157 388	232 044
35 - 39	512 080	227 303	284 777	182 166	91 481	90 685	329 914	135 822	194 092
40 - 44	437 765	200 650	237 115	150 077	77 979	72 098	287 688	122 671	165 017
45 - 49	328 431	159 533	168 898	107 955	57 478	50 477	220 476	102 055	118 421
50 - 54	298 035	146 067	151 968	92 750	49 856	42 894	205 285	96 211	109 074
55 - 59	211 335	114 646	96 689	67 633	38 018	29 615	143 702	76 628	67 074
60 - 64	204 766	105 390	99 376	59 014	33 468	25 546	145 752	71 922	73 830
65 - 69	127 396	68 065	59 331	33 804	18 584	15 220	93 592	49 481	44 111
70 - 74	116 721	56 862	59 859	28 015	14 135	13 880	88 706	42 727	45 979
75 - 79	63 846	33 920	29 926	14 523	7 371	7 152	49 323	26 549	22 774
80 - 84	50 980	24 678	26 302	10 848	4 760	6 088	40 132	19 918	20 214
85 - 89	20 725	10 788	9 937	4 127	1 795	2 332	16 598	8 993	7 605
90 - 94	11 747	5 631	6 116	2 532	936	1 596	9 215	4 695	4 520
95 +	11 960	5 717	6 243	2 371	796	1 575	9 589	4 921	4 668
Guinea-Bissau - Guinée-Bissau[2]									
1 VII 2015 (ESDF)									
Total	1 530 673	750 119	780 554	645 283	316 226	329 057	885 390	433 893	451 497
0 - 4	269 663	138 069	131 594	93 947	46 630	47 287	175 746	91 439	84 307
5 - 9	208 067	105 099	102 968	75 646	35 838	39 808	132 421	69 261	63 160
10 - 14	188 025	94 466	93 559	79 861	37 176	42 685	108 164	57 290	50 874
15 - 19	160 090	80 758	79 332	76 973	38 006	38 967	83 117	42 752	40 365
20 - 24	150 527	74 501	76 026	77 141	39 679	37 462	73 386	34 822	38 564
25 - 29	129 739	61 895	67 844	62 737	31 830	30 907	67 002	30 065	36 937
30 - 34	114 885	53 113	61 772	55 197	27 116	28 081	59 688	25 997	33 691

7. Population by age, sex and urban/rural residence: latest available year, 2006 - 2015
Population selon l'âge, le sexe et la résidence, urbaine/rurale : dernière année disponible, 2006 - 2015 (continued - suite)

Continent, country or area, date, code[a] and age (in years) / Continent, pays ou zone, date, code[a] et âge (en années)	Total			Urban - Urbaine			Rural - Rurale		
	Both sexes Les deux sexes	Male Masculin	Female Féminin	Both sexes Les deux sexes	Male Masculin	Female Féminin	Both sexes Les deux sexes	Male Masculin	Female Féminin
AFRICA - AFRIQUE									
Guinea-Bissau - Guinée-Bissau[2]									
1 VII 2015 (ESDF)									
35 - 39	78 247	36 440	41 807	34 340	16 937	17 403	43 907	19 503	24 404
40 - 44	63 952	29 420	34 532	28 601	14 055	14 546	35 351	15 365	19 986
45 - 49	45 615	21 089	24 526	19 238	9 453	9 785	26 377	11 636	14 741
50 - 54	39 944	18 465	21 479	16 120	8 089	8 031	23 824	10 376	13 448
55 - 59	28 269	12 731	15 538	10 433	4 847	5 586	17 836	7 884	9 952
60 - 64	19 292	9 287	10 005	6 115	3 016	3 099	13 177	6 271	6 906
65 - 69	14 341	6 640	7 701	4 214	1 877	2 337	10 127	4 763	5 364
70 - 74	9 119	3 989	5 130	2 406	978	1 428	6 713	3 011	3 702
75 - 79	5 226	2 055	3 171	1 223	394	829	4 003	1 661	2 342
80 +	5 672	2 102	3 570	1 121	305	816	4 551	1 797	2 754
Kenya									
24 VIII 2009 (CDFC)									
Total	38 610 097	19 192 458	19 417 639	12 487 375	6 278 811	6 208 564	26 122 722	12 913 647	13 209 075
0	1 221 937	616 843	605 094	388 883	195 861	193 022	833 054	420 982	412 072
1 - 4	4 717 369	2 383 596	2 333 773	1 350 368	679 969	670 399	3 367 001	1 703 627	1 663 374
5 - 9	5 597 716	2 832 669	2 765 047	1 484 285	742 473	741 812	4 113 431	2 090 196	2 023 235
10 - 14	5 034 855	2 565 313	2 469 542	1 312 671	650 438	662 233	3 722 184	1 914 875	1 807 309
15 - 19	4 169 543	2 123 653	2 045 890	1 244 054	587 384	656 670	2 925 489	1 536 269	1 389 220
20 - 24	3 775 103	1 754 105	2 020 998	1 572 026	708 458	863 568	2 203 077	1 045 647	1 157 430
25 - 29	3 201 226	1 529 116	1 672 110	1 442 798	715 957	726 841	1 758 428	813 159	945 269
30 - 34	2 519 506	1 257 035	1 262 471	1 056 483	568 615	487 868	1 463 023	688 420	774 603
35 - 39	2 008 632	1 004 361	1 004 271	785 390	431 054	354 336	1 223 242	573 307	649 935
40 - 44	1 476 169	743 594	732 575	533 174	297 202	235 972	942 995	446 392	496 603
45 - 49	1 272 745	635 276	637 469	422 941	235 467	187 474	849 804	399 809	449 995
50 - 54	956 206	478 346	477 860	286 074	159 814	126 260	670 132	318 532	351 600
55 - 59	711 953	359 466	352 497	187 793	103 563	84 230	524 160	255 903	268 257
60 - 64	593 778	295 197	298 581	139 271	73 800	65 471	454 507	221 397	233 110
65 - 69	390 763	183 151	207 612	83 728	41 299	42 429	307 035	141 852	165 183
70 - 74	339 301	160 301	179 000	68 868	32 691	36 177	270 433	127 610	142 823
75 - 79	218 508	99 833	118 675	42 247	19 276	22 971	176 261	80 557	95 704
80 +	383 701	159 125	224 576	77 003	30 335	46 668	306 698	128 790	177 908
Unknown - Inconnu	21 086	11 478	9 608	9 318	5 155	4 163	11 768	6 323	5 445
1 VII 2014 (ESDF)[5]									
Total	42 961 187	21 289 752	21 671 435	...	...	...	...	...	...
0 - 4	6 739 755	3 385 952	3 353 803	...	...	...	...	...	...
5 - 9	5 842 961	2 941 123	2 901 838	...	...	...	...	...	...
10 - 14	5 248 304	2 661 057	2 587 247	...	...	...	...	...	...
15 - 19	4 618 997	2 345 347	2 273 650	...	...	...	...	...	...
20 - 24	4 109 175	2 031 402	2 077 773	...	...	...	...	...	...
25 - 29	3 668 881	1 713 590	1 955 291	...	...	...	...	...	...
30 - 34	3 051 156	1 437 408	1 613 748	...	...	...	...	...	...
35 - 39	2 378 371	1 189 195	1 189 176	...	...	...	...	...	...
40 - 44	1 871 645	942 826	928 819	...	...	...	...	...	...
45 - 49	1 425 254	709 802	715 452	...	...	...	...	...	...
50 - 54	1 101 693	547 327	554 366	...	...	...	...	...	...
55 - 59	860 917	426 415	434 502	...	...	...	...	...	...
60 - 64	652 824	320 360	332 464	...	...	...	...	...	...
65 - 69	486 113	232 506	253 607	...	...	...	...	...	...
70 - 74	345 646	161 703	183 943	...	...	...	...	...	...
75 - 79	237 838	108 599	129 239	...	...	...	...	...	...
80 +	321 657	135 140	186 517	...	...	...	...	...	...
Lesotho									
13 IV 2006 (CDJC)									
Total	1 862 860	904 392	958 468	421 105	194 097	227 008	1 441 755	710 295	731 460
0 - 4	201 995	101 397	100 598	39 245	19 604	19 641	162 750	81 793	80 957
5 - 9	211 947	106 695	105 252	40 208	20 051	20 157	171 739	86 644	85 095
10 - 14	220 938	110 778	110 160	42 546	20 751	21 795	178 392	90 027	88 365
15 - 19	229 389	114 800	114 589	48 783	21 971	26 812	180 606	92 829	87 777
20 - 24	207 062	101 385	105 677	52 026	21 394	30 632	155 036	79 991	75 045
25 - 29	164 867	82 202	82 665	49 796	21 948	27 848	115 071	60 254	54 817
30 - 34	119 530	60 107	59 423	36 708	17 327	19 381	82 822	42 780	40 042
35 - 39	93 490	45 645	47 845	28 605	13 639	14 966	64 885	32 006	32 879

Continent, country or area, date, code[a] and age (in years) / Continent, pays ou zone, date, code[a] et âge (en années)	Total			Urban - Urbaine			Rural - Rurale		
	Both sexes Les deux sexes	Male Masculin	Female Féminin	Both sexes Les deux sexes	Male Masculin	Female Féminin	Both sexes Les deux sexes	Male Masculin	Female Féminin
AFRICA - AFRIQUE									
Lesotho									
13 IV 2006 (CDJC)									
40 - 44	83 299	39 596	43 703	22 742	10 805	11 937	60 557	28 791	31 766
45 - 49	72 621	34 102	38 519	17 782	8 461	9 321	54 839	25 641	29 198
50 - 54	63 084	28 723	34 361	13 153	6 037	7 116	49 931	22 686	27 245
55 - 59	50 148	23 225	26 923	9 367	4 266	5 101	40 781	18 959	21 822
60 - 64	37 699	16 724	20 975	6 325	2 851	3 474	31 374	13 873	17 501
65 - 69	32 028	13 369	18 659	4 794	1 977	2 817	27 234	11 392	15 842
70 - 74	35 609	13 380	22 229	4 158	1 569	2 589	31 451	11 811	19 640
75 - 79	18 141	6 327	11 814	2 281	742	1 539	15 860	5 585	10 275
80 - 84	10 498	3 251	7 247	1 336	380	956	9 162	2 871	6 291
85 +	10 515	2 686	7 829	1 250	324	926	9 265	2 362	6 903
Liberia - Libéria									
21 III 2008 (CDFC)									
Total	3 476 608	1 739 945	1 736 663	...	...	...	...	...	...
0 - 4	534 475	270 564	263 911	...	...	...	...	...	...
5 - 9	501 931	251 411	250 520	...	...	...	...	...	...
10 - 14	421 666	214 859	206 807	...	...	...	...	...	...
15 - 19	375 695	189 407	186 288	...	...	...	...	...	...
20 - 24	342 930	161 951	180 979	...	...	...	...	...	...
25 - 29	291 858	141 006	150 852	...	...	...	...	...	...
30 - 34	219 632	107 326	112 306	...	...	...	...	...	...
35 - 39	203 536	99 136	104 400	...	...	...	...	...	...
40 - 44	155 737	81 670	74 067	...	...	...	...	...	...
45 - 49	118 807	63 827	54 980	...	...	...	...	...	...
50 - 54	82 940	44 870	38 070	...	...	...	...	...	...
55 - 59	56 460	30 975	25 485	...	...	...	...	...	...
60 - 64	52 830	25 473	27 357	...	...	...	...	...	...
65 - 69	39 807	19 250	20 557	...	...	...	...	...	...
70 - 74	25 746	12 343	13 403	...	...	...	...	...	...
75 - 79	22 913	11 580	11 333	...	...	...	...	...	...
80 - 84	12 007	5 408	6 599	...	...	...	...	...	...
85 +	17 638	8 889	8 749	...	...	...	...	...	...
Libya - Libye									
15 IV 2006* (CDFC)									
Total	5 298 152	2 687 513	2 610 639	4 670 858	2 372 379	2 298 479	627 294	315 134	312 160
0	117 479	60 167	57 312	103 670	53 129	50 541	13 809	7 038	6 771
1 - 4	457 866	234 512	223 354	403 509	206 639	196 870	54 357	27 873	26 484
5 - 9	527 595	269 079	258 516	465 506	237 468	228 038	62 089	31 611	30 478
10 - 14	542 893	277 270	265 623	476 896	243 693	233 203	65 997	33 577	32 420
15 - 19	573 026	290 568	282 458	501 444	254 266	247 178	71 582	36 302	35 280
20 - 24	573 287	289 663	283 624	502 229	253 539	248 690	71 058	36 124	34 934
25 - 29	566 458	287 101	279 357	497 522	252 364	245 158	68 936	34 737	34 199
30 - 34	492 828	248 875	243 953	434 821	220 019	214 802	58 007	28 856	29 151
35 - 39	390 800	195 328	195 472	347 316	174 078	173 238	43 484	21 250	22 234
40 - 44	281 849	140 872	140 977	251 876	126 302	125 574	29 973	14 570	15 403
45 - 49	199 142	100 653	98 489	178 471	90 336	88 135	20 671	10 317	10 354
50 - 54	132 619	64 677	67 942	119 463	58 576	60 887	13 156	6 101	7 055
55 - 59	122 277	61 439	60 838	109 004	55 174	53 830	13 273	6 265	7 008
60 - 64	95 127	51 295	43 832	84 339	45 822	38 517	10 788	5 473	5 315
65 - 69	80 018	42 724	37 294	70 241	37 786	32 455	9 777	4 938	4 839
70 - 74	57 851	30 325	27 526	50 282	26 511	23 771	7 569	3 814	3 755
75 - 79	45 675	23 125	22 550	39 337	19 978	19 359	6 338	3 147	3 191
80 - 84	24 576	12 158	12 418	20 930	10 332	10 598	3 646	1 826	1 820
85 +	16 786	7 682	9 104	14 002	6 367	7 635	2 784	1 315	1 469
1 VII 2015 (ESDF)									
Total	6 162 247	3 129 026	3 033 221	...	...	...	...	...	...
0 - 4	615 556	316 497	299 059	...	...	...	...	...	...
5 - 9	577 905	297 303	280 602	...	...	...	...	...	...
10 - 14	555 149	284 318	270 831	...	...	...	...	...	...
15 - 19	525 115	268 106	257 009	...	...	...	...	...	...
20 - 24	546 408	278 875	267 533	...	...	...	...	...	...
25 - 29	571 230	289 113	282 117	...	...	...	...	...	...
30 - 34	568 834	287 480	281 354	...	...	...	...	...	...
35 - 39	551 606	279 699	271 907	...	...	...	...	...	...

Continent, country or area, date, code[a] and age (in years) / Continent, pays ou zone, date, code[a] et âge (en annèes)	Total			Urban - Urbaine			Rural - Rurale		
	Both sexes Les deux sexes	Male Masculin	Female Féminin	Both sexes Les deux sexes	Male Masculin	Female Féminin	Both sexes Les deux sexes	Male Masculin	Female Féminin
AFRICA - AFRIQUE									
Libya - Libye									
1 VII 2015 (ESDF)									
40 - 44	466 373	235 088	231 285	...	...	...	...	...	...
45 - 49	360 825	180 029	180 796	...	...	...	...	...	...
50 - 54	253 647	126 799	126 848	...	...	...	...	...	...
55 - 59	173 760	87 135	86 625	...	...	...	...	...	...
60 - 64	116 033	56 199	59 834	...	...	...	...	...	...
65 - 69	102 645	51 782	50 863	...	...	...	...	...	...
70 - 74	72 486	38 750	33 736	...	...	...	...	...	...
75 - 79	52 558	26 942	25 616	...	...	...	...	...	...
80 - 84	30 271	15 038	15 233	...	...	...	...	...	...
85 +	21 846	9 873	11 973	...	...	...	...	...	...
Malawi									
8 VI 2008 (CDFC)									
Total	13 077 160	6 358 933	6 718 227	2 003 309	1 014 477	988 832	11 073 851	5 344 456	5 729 395
0	503 385	247 809	255 576	67 264	33 375	33 889	436 121	214 434	221 687
1 - 4	1 866 626	922 138	944 488	248 703	122 976	125 727	1 617 923	799 162	818 761
5 - 9	1 968 299	972 307	995 992	261 838	127 930	133 908	1 706 461	844 377	862 084
10 - 14	1 670 391	826 076	844 315	232 203	110 545	121 658	1 438 188	715 531	722 657
15 - 19	1 276 692	625 664	651 028	218 307	105 746	112 561	1 058 385	519 918	538 467
20 - 24	1 240 329	554 799	685 530	248 790	117 648	131 142	991 539	437 151	554 388
25 - 29	1 102 976	530 103	572 873	236 512	122 761	113 751	866 464	407 342	459 122
30 - 34	827 547	417 599	409 948	162 061	91 637	70 424	665 486	325 962	339 524
35 - 39	623 330	323 643	299 687	105 572	61 564	44 008	517 758	262 079	255 679
40 - 44	441 231	218 546	222 685	67 267	37 061	30 206	373 964	181 485	192 479
45 - 49	343 190	167 285	175 905	47 706	25 811	21 895	295 484	141 474	154 010
50 - 54	269 634	126 778	142 856	33 849	18 400	15 449	235 785	108 378	127 407
55 - 59	258 214	122 616	135 598	26 253	14 525	11 728	231 961	108 091	123 870
60 - 64	184 679	87 008	97 671	16 622	9 256	7 366	168 057	77 752	90 305
65 - 69	153 829	72 038	81 791	11 298	6 217	5 081	142 531	65 821	76 710
70 - 74	106 020	46 481	59 539	6 992	3 573	3 419	99 028	42 908	56 120
75 - 79	106 769	46 003	60 766	5 629	2 769	2 860	101 140	43 234	57 906
80 - 84	55 970	21 945	34 025	2 926	1 262	1 664	53 044	20 683	32 361
85 - 89	40 784	16 680	24 104	1 895	818	1 077	38 889	15 862	23 027
90 - 94	18 739	6 967	11 772	780	323	457	17 959	6 644	11 315
95 +	18 526	6 448	12 078	842	280	562	17 684	6 168	11 516
Mali									
1 IV 2009 (CDFC)									
Total	14 528 662	7 204 990	7 323 672	3 274 727	1 643 671	1 631 056	11 253 935	5 561 319	5 692 616
0 - 4	2 623 385	1 328 871	1 294 514	501 628	253 735	247 893	2 121 757	1 075 136	1 046 621
5 - 9	2 357 823	1 202 875	1 154 948	438 784	220 467	218 317	1 919 039	982 408	936 631
10 - 14	1 784 004	918 866	865 138	382 494	183 203	199 291	1 401 510	735 663	665 847
15 - 19	1 516 146	732 526	783 620	427 554	194 158	233 396	1 088 592	538 368	550 224
20 - 24	1 141 903	529 535	612 368	341 272	171 703	169 569	800 631	357 832	442 799
25 - 29	995 702	449 099	546 603	267 899	132 127	135 772	727 803	316 972	410 831
30 - 34	812 798	385 003	427 795	206 544	109 060	97 484	606 254	275 943	330 311
35 - 39	651 949	325 055	326 894	164 783	89 830	74 953	487 166	235 225	251 941
40 - 44	546 603	271 239	275 364	128 845	70 127	58 718	417 758	201 112	216 646
45 - 49	445 887	228 626	217 261	103 042	56 502	46 540	342 845	172 124	170 721
50 - 54	381 806	189 424	192 382	82 013	44 826	37 187	299 793	144 598	155 195
55 - 59	282 677	148 594	134 083	57 960	31 957	26 003	224 717	116 637	108 080
60 - 64	251 018	127 557	123 461	46 442	23 790	22 652	204 576	103 767	100 809
65 - 69	165 374	88 292	77 082	30 159	15 641	14 518	135 215	72 651	62 564
70 - 74	133 382	67 319	66 063	23 729	11 518	12 211	109 653	55 801	53 852
75 - 79	77 101	40 904	36 197	12 871	6 306	6 565	64 230	34 598	29 632
80 +	85 594	41 992	43 602	14 246	6 009	8 237	71 348	35 983	35 365
Unknown - Inconnu	275 510	129 213	146 297	44 462	22 712	21 750	231 048	106 501	124 547
1 VII 2014* (ESDF)[6]									
Total	17 319 000	8 671 000	8 648 000	...	...	...	...	...	...
0 - 4	3 182 000	1 624 000	1 559 000	...	...	...	...	...	...
5 - 9	2 685 000	1 370 000	1 315 000	...	...	...	...	...	...
10 - 14	2 255 000	1 150 000	1 104 000	...	...	...	...	...	...
15 - 19	1 867 000	952 000	915 000	...	...	...	...	...	...
20 - 24	1 534 000	778 000	756 000	...	...	...	...	...	...
25 - 29	1 298 000	656 000	641 000	...	...	...	...	...	...

181

Population selon l'âge, le sexe et la résidence, urbaine/rurale : dernière année disponible, 2006 - 2015 (continued - suite)

Continent, country or area, date, code[a] and age (in years) / Continent, pays ou zone, date, code[a] et âge (en années)	Total			Urban - Urbaine			Rural - Rurale		
	Both sexes Les deux sexes	Male Masculin	Female Féminin	Both sexes Les deux sexes	Male Masculin	Female Féminin	Both sexes Les deux sexes	Male Masculin	Female Féminin
AFRICA - AFRIQUE									
Mali									
1 VII 2014* (ESDF)[6]									
30 - 34	1 101 000	554 000	547 000	...	...	...	...	...	...
35 - 39	896 000	446 000	451 000	...	...	...	...	...	...
40 - 44	699 000	342 000	358 000	...	...	...	...	...	...
45 - 49	522 000	248 000	275 000	...	...	...	...	...	...
50 - 54	384 000	175 000	209 000	...	...	...	...	...	...
55 - 59	296 000	129 000	167 000	...	...	...	...	...	...
60 - 64	232 000	101 000	131 000	...	...	...	...	...	...
65 - 69	163 000	67 000	96 000	...	...	...	...	...	...
70 - 74	119 000	49 000	70 000	...	...	...	...	...	...
75 - 79	56 000	22 000	34 000	...	...	...	...	...	...
80 +	31 000	12 000	19 000	...	...	...	...	...	...
Mauritania - Mauritanie[7]									
24 III 2013 (CDJC)									
Total	3 537 368	1 743 074	1 794 294	...	...	...	...	...	...
0 - 4	614 692	316 217	298 475	...	...	...	...	...	...
5 - 9	520 102	263 263	256 839	...	...	...	...	...	...
10 - 14	429 505	212 838	216 667	...	...	...	...	...	...
15 - 19	361 404	176 116	185 288	...	...	...	...	...	...
20 - 24	302 440	144 478	157 962	...	...	...	...	...	...
25 - 29	257 353	121 586	135 767	...	...	...	...	...	...
30 - 34	213 525	99 834	113 691	...	...	...	...	...	...
35 - 39	178 957	83 578	95 379	...	...	...	...	...	...
40 - 44	151 336	72 108	79 228	...	...	...	...	...	...
45 - 49	124 813	60 297	64 516	...	...	...	...	...	...
50 - 54	102 490	50 739	51 751	...	...	...	...	...	...
55 - 59	81 720	41 075	40 645	...	...	...	...	...	...
60 - 64	62 119	31 660	30 459	...	...	...	...	...	...
65 - 69	47 175	24 120	23 055	...	...	...	...	...	...
70 - 74	35 296	18 167	17 129	...	...	...	...	...	...
75 - 79	24 901	12 670	12 231	...	...	...	...	...	...
80 - 84	16 664	8 080	8 584	...	...	...	...	...	...
85 +	12 876	6 248	6 628	...	...	...	...	...	...
Mauritius - Maurice[8]									
4 VII 2011 (CDJC)									
Total	1 236 817	610 848	625 969	499 349	244 688	254 661	737 468	366 160	371 308
0 - 4	73 078	36 702	36 376	26 297	13 220	13 077	46 781	23 482	23 299
5 - 9	89 015	44 947	44 068	32 036	16 177	15 859	56 979	28 770	28 209
10 - 14	93 639	47 302	46 337	35 028	17 523	17 505	58 611	29 779	28 832
15 - 19	101 008	50 715	50 293	39 403	19 725	19 678	61 605	30 990	30 615
20 - 24	92 671	46 871	45 800	37 224	18 836	18 388	55 447	28 035	27 412
25 - 29	90 937	45 589	45 348	35 908	17 899	18 009	55 029	27 690	27 339
30 - 34	103 429	52 182	51 247	39 099	19 805	19 294	64 330	32 377	31 953
35 - 39	87 797	44 241	43 556	32 781	16 142	16 639	55 016	28 099	26 917
40 - 44	89 386	45 150	44 236	34 449	17 010	17 439	54 937	28 140	26 797
45 - 49	99 341	49 800	49 541	41 705	20 637	21 068	57 636	29 163	28 473
50 - 54	86 337	42 996	43 341	37 429	18 627	18 802	48 908	24 369	24 539
55 - 59	73 054	35 713	37 341	32 421	15 983	16 438	40 633	19 730	20 903
60 - 64	57 342	27 143	30 199	25 449	12 058	13 391	31 893	15 085	16 808
65 - 69	35 439	15 846	19 593	16 700	7 527	9 173	18 739	8 319	10 420
70 - 74	25 375	10 986	14 389	12 872	5 661	7 211	12 503	5 325	7 178
75 - 79	18 044	7 349	10 695	9 320	3 851	5 469	8 724	3 498	5 226
80 - 84	11 369	4 176	7 193	6 028	2 253	3 775	5 341	1 923	3 418
85 - 89	6 368	2 135	4 233	3 427	1 179	2 248	2 941	956	1 985
90 - 94	1 982	512	1 470	1 046	275	771	936	237	699
95 - 99	491	107	384	297	60	237	194	47	147
100 +	96	13	83	55	7	48	41	6	35
Unknown - Inconnu	619	373	246	375	233	142	244	140	104
1 VII 2015 (ESDJ)[9]									
Total	1 262 605	624 769	637 836	...	...	...	...	...	...
0	13 033	6 638	6 395	...	...	...	...	...	...
1 - 4	56 191	28 540	27 651	...	...	...	...	...	...
5 - 9	82 004	41 593	40 411	...	...	...	...	...	...
10 - 14	96 370	48 897	47 473	...	...	...	...	...	...

7. Population by age, sex and urban/rural residence: latest available year, 2006 - 2015
Population selon l'âge, le sexe et la résidence, urbaine/rurale : dernière année disponible, 2006 - 2015 (continued - suite)

Continent, country or area, date, code[a] and age (in years) / Continent, pays ou zone, date, code[a] et âge (en années)	Total			Urban - Urbaine			Rural - Rurale		
	Both sexes Les deux sexes	Male Masculin	Female Féminin	Both sexes Les deux sexes	Male Masculin	Female Féminin	Both sexes Les deux sexes	Male Masculin	Female Féminin
AFRICA - AFRIQUE									
Mauritius - Maurice[8]									
1 VII 2015 (ESDJ)[9]									
15 - 19	97 507	49 417	48 090	...	...	...	...	...	...
20 - 24	100 168	50 575	49 593	...	...	...	...	...	...
25 - 29	87 880	44 406	43 474	...	...	...	...	...	...
30 - 34	93 116	46 873	46 243	...	...	...	...	...	...
35 - 39	98 535	49 892	48 643	...	...	...	...	...	...
40 - 44	84 424	42 760	41 664	...	...	...	...	...	...
45 - 49	91 152	45 955	45 197	...	...	...	...	...	...
50 - 54	94 090	46 805	47 285	...	...	...	...	...	...
55 - 59	81 724	40 082	41 642	...	...	...	...	...	...
60 - 64	67 776	32 404	35 372	...	...	...	...	...	...
65 - 69	46 477	21 191	25 286	...	...	...	...	...	...
70 - 74	29 503	12 710	16 793	...	...	...	...	...	...
75 - 79	20 309	8 289	12 020	...	...	...	...	...	...
Mayotte									
31 VII 2007 (CDJC)									
Total	186 387	91 405	94 982	...	...	...	...	...	...
0	6 424	3 255	3 169	...	...	...	...	...	...
1 - 4	25 429	12 948	12 481	...	...	...	...	...	...
5 - 9	27 239	13 739	13 500	...	...	...	...	...	...
10 - 14	23 403	11 483	11 920	...	...	...	...	...	...
15 - 19	18 724	9 144	9 580	...	...	...	...	...	...
20 - 24	13 660	5 789	7 871	...	...	...	...	...	...
25 - 29	14 987	6 262	8 725	...	...	...	...	...	...
30 - 34	14 376	6 651	7 725	...	...	...	...	...	...
35 - 39	12 390	6 468	5 922	...	...	...	...	...	...
40 - 44	8 375	4 385	3 990	...	...	...	...	...	...
45 - 49	6 133	3 261	2 872	...	...	...	...	...	...
50 - 54	4 763	2 508	2 255	...	...	...	...	...	...
55 - 59	3 566	1 948	1 618	...	...	...	...	...	...
60 - 64	2 522	1 329	1 193	...	...	...	...	...	...
65 - 69	1 621	833	788	...	...	...	...	...	...
70 - 74	1 266	671	595	...	...	...	...	...	...
75 - 79	689	348	341	...	...	...	...	...	...
80 - 84	459	234	225	...	...	...	...	...	...
85 - 89	199	89	110	...	...	...	...	...	...
90 - 94	101	35	66	...	...	...	...	...	...
95 +	61	25	36	...	...	...	...	...	...
Morocco - Maroc[10]									
1 VII 2013 (ESDF)									
Total	32 950 445	16 371 475	16 578 971	19 512 904	9 533 742	9 979 162	13 437 541	6 837 733	6 599 809
0 - 4	2 903 919	1 482 899	1 421 020	1 538 623	784 659	753 964	1 365 296	698 240	667 056
5 - 9	2 845 161	1 453 315	1 391 847	1 534 498	777 963	756 534	1 310 664	675 351	635 312
10 - 14	2 894 204	1 473 231	1 420 973	1 568 834	789 667	779 167	1 325 370	683 564	641 806
15 - 19	3 043 535	1 547 292	1 496 243	1 648 978	814 055	834 924	1 394 557	733 237	661 319
20 - 24	3 178 851	1 614 483	1 564 368	1 789 076	862 131	926 945	1 389 775	752 352	637 423
25 - 29	2 972 219	1 477 952	1 494 267	1 776 381	851 252	925 128	1 195 838	626 699	569 139
30 - 34	2 747 687	1 338 558	1 409 129	1 722 868	829 862	893 006	1 024 819	508 696	516 123
35 - 39	2 306 566	1 106 764	1 199 802	1 486 948	704 701	782 247	819 618	402 063	417 556
40 - 44	2 045 869	975 428	1 070 441	1 349 956	644 385	705 571	695 913	331 043	364 871
45 - 49	1 809 846	862 688	947 158	1 210 448	575 188	635 260	599 398	287 500	311 898
50 - 54	1 762 347	859 927	902 421	1 147 448	562 942	584 506	614 899	296 985	317 914
55 - 59	1 375 290	704 367	670 923	895 355	464 283	431 072	479 935	240 084	239 851
60 - 64	1 073 646	543 733	529 913	667 089	343 552	323 537	406 556	200 181	206 375
65 - 69	662 674	314 577	348 098	400 434	188 734	211 700	262 241	125 843	136 398
70 - 74	609 636	276 251	333 385	358 211	157 374	200 837	251 425	118 877	132 548
75 +	718 996	340 012	378 983	417 758	182 994	234 764	301 238	157 018	144 220
Mozambique[2]									
1 VII 2015 (ESDF)									
Total	25 727 911	12 419 014	13 308 897	8 181 475	3 997 895	4 183 580	17 546 436	8 421 119	9 125 317
0	933 598	469 724	463 874	...	...	...	...	...	...
1 - 4	3 462 195	1 728 673	1 733 522	879 574	438 652	440 922	2 582 621	1 290 021	1 292 600
5 - 9	3 802 500	1 888 820	1 913 680	1 059 357	526 629	532 728	2 743 143	1 362 191	1 380 952
10 - 14	3 335 853	1 665 556	1 670 297	1 031 991	509 520	522 471	2 303 862	1 156 036	1 147 826

Continent, country or area, date, code[a] and age (in years) / Continent, pays ou zone, date, code[a] et âge (en années)	Total			Urban - Urbaine			Rural - Rurale		
	Both sexes Les deux sexes	Male Masculin	Female Féminin	Both sexes Les deux sexes	Male Masculin	Female Féminin	Both sexes Les deux sexes	Male Masculin	Female Féminin
AFRICA - AFRIQUE									
Mozambique[2]									
1 VII 2015 (ESDF)									
15 - 19	2 772 960	1 378 244	1 394 716	979 579	482 418	497 161	1 793 381	895 826	897 555
20 - 24	2 304 088	1 083 081	1 221 007	887 518	436 533	450 985	1 416 570	646 548	770 022
25 - 29	1 926 947	855 501	1 071 446	740 724	351 770	388 954	1 186 223	503 731	682 492
30 - 34	1 589 845	718 588	871 257	586 039	274 428	311 611	1 003 806	444 160	559 646
35 - 39	1 285 999	603 158	682 841	461 935	220 778	241 157	824 064	382 380	441 684
40 - 44	1 076 563	503 062	573 501	370 753	178 942	191 811	705 810	324 120	381 690
45 - 49	853 052	407 648	445 404	282 760	139 777	142 983	570 292	267 871	302 421
50 - 54	651 875	324 005	327 870	204 028	103 938	100 090	447 847	220 067	227 780
55 - 59	527 245	247 395	279 850	157 435	77 675	79 760	369 810	169 720	200 090
60 - 64	403 635	183 916	219 719	112 496	54 282	58 214	291 139	129 634	161 505
65 - 69	303 784	139 204	164 580	80 270	37 762	42 508	223 514	101 442	122 072
70 - 74	213 490	97 435	116 055	52 137	23 198	28 939	161 353	74 237	87 116
75 - 79	138 702	62 623	76 079	32 820	13 966	18 854	105 882	48 657	57 225
80 +	130 277	56 593	73 684	29 912	11 359	18 553	100 365	45 234	55 131
Namibia - Namibie[11]									
1 VII 2014 (ESDF)									
Total	2 237 894	1 087 178	1 150 716	1 025 147	500 469	524 678	1 212 747	586 709	626 038
0 - 4	313 007	158 229	154 778	135 778	68 604	67 174	177 229	89 625	87 604
5 - 9	263 264	132 713	130 551	90 226	45 189	45 037	173 038	87 524	85 514
10 - 14	239 023	119 477	119 546	83 409	40 489	42 920	155 614	78 988	76 626
15 - 19	243 203	119 995	123 208	90 294	41 602	48 692	152 909	78 393	74 516
20 - 24	228 320	112 074	116 246	112 641	52 586	60 055	115 679	59 488	56 191
25 - 29	196 214	96 205	100 009	125 044	61 032	64 012	71 170	35 173	35 997
30 - 34	159 244	77 560	81 684	101 087	50 183	50 904	58 157	27 377	30 780
35 - 39	133 989	65 263	68 726	79 749	39 953	39 796	54 240	25 310	28 930
40 - 44	108 850	52 124	56 726	61 067	30 481	30 586	47 783	21 643	26 140
45 - 49	86 084	40 171	45 913	45 627	22 976	22 651	40 457	17 195	23 262
50 - 54	69 283	31 124	38 159	34 250	17 242	17 008	35 033	13 882	21 151
55 - 59	51 965	22 549	29 416	23 814	11 704	12 110	28 151	10 845	17 306
60 - 64	41 488	18 291	23 197	15 660	7 548	8 112	25 828	10 743	15 085
65 - 69	33 735	14 572	19 163	9 915	4 380	5 535	23 820	10 192	13 628
70 - 74	24 388	9 982	14 406	6 415	2 680	3 735	17 973	7 302	10 671
75 - 79	17 037	6 934	10 103	4 451	1 790	2 661	12 586	5 144	7 442
80 +	28 800	9 915	18 885	5 720	2 030	3 690	23 080	7 885	15 195
1 VII 2015 (ESDF)									
Total	2 280 716	1 108 276	1 172 440	...	...	...	...	...	...
0	66 240	33 537	32 703	...	...	...	...	...	...
1 - 4	251 263	127 013	124 250	...	...	...	...	...	...
5 - 9	274 401	138 313	136 088	...	...	...	...	...	...
10 - 14	238 160	119 349	118 811	...	...	...	...	...	...
15 - 19	243 482	120 385	123 097	...	...	...	...	...	...
20 - 24	231 466	113 488	117 978	...	...	...	...	...	...
25 - 29	202 828	99 547	103 281	...	...	...	...	...	...
30 - 34	163 689	79 543	84 146	...	...	...	...	...	...
35 - 39	136 985	66 664	70 321	...	...	...	...	...	...
40 - 44	112 821	54 020	58 801	...	...	...	...	...	...
45 - 49	88 195	41 197	46 998	...	...	...	...	...	...
50 - 54	71 893	32 425	39 468	...	...	...	...	...	...
55 - 59	53 922	23 243	30 679	...	...	...	...	...	...
60 - 64	41 878	18 245	23 633	...	...	...	...	...	...
65 - 69	34 576	15 021	19 555	...	...	...	...	...	...
70 - 74	24 718	10 031	14 687	...	...	...	...	...	...
75 - 79	17 148	6 970	10 178	...	...	...	...	...	...
80 +	27 051	9 285	17 766	...	...	...	...	...	...
Niger									
10 XII 2012 (CDJC)									
Total	17 138 707	8 518 818	8 619 889	2 778 337	1 397 695	1 380 642	14 360 370	7 121 123	7 239 247
0 - 4	3 696 791	1 891 826	1 804 965	472 139	240 745	231 394	3 224 652	1 651 081	1 573 571
5 - 9	2 995 004	1 524 504	1 470 500	412 567	206 414	206 153	2 582 437	1 318 090	1 264 347
10 - 14	2 163 813	1 088 679	1 075 134	363 784	176 755	187 029	1 800 029	911 924	888 105
15 - 19	1 727 779	834 345	893 434	314 251	161 949	152 302	1 413 528	672 396	741 132
20 - 24	1 320 316	631 280	689 036	292 612	150 135	142 477	1 027 704	481 145	546 559
25 - 29	1 070 992	521 141	549 851	194 852	96 249	98 603	876 140	424 892	451 248

Continent, country or area, date, code[a] and age (in years) Continent, pays ou zone, date, code[a] et âge (en années)	Total			Urban - Urbaine			Rural - Rurale		
	Both sexes Les deux sexes	Male Masculin	Female Féminin	Both sexes Les deux sexes	Male Masculin	Female Féminin	Both sexes Les deux sexes	Male Masculin	Female Féminin
AFRICA - AFRIQUE									
Niger									
10 XII 2012 (CDJC)									
30 - 34	897 561	430 506	467 055	163 519	81 175	82 344	734 042	349 331	384 711
35 - 39	729 784	349 963	379 821	134 412	66 061	68 351	595 372	283 902	311 470
40 - 44	582 219	285 869	296 350	105 367	55 554	49 813	476 852	230 315	246 537
45 - 49	499 732	243 368	256 364	92 198	46 654	45 544	407 534	196 714	210 820
50 - 54	392 556	195 591	196 965	69 374	35 559	33 815	323 182	160 032	163 150
55 - 59	304 324	151 019	153 305	52 925	26 577	26 348	251 399	124 442	126 957
60 - 64	229 406	114 428	114 978	36 394	18 711	17 683	193 012	95 717	97 295
65 - 69	184 733	90 566	94 167	28 230	13 837	14 393	156 503	76 729	79 774
70 - 74	141 279	69 752	71 527	20 105	9 897	10 208	121 174	59 855	61 319
75 - 79	103 206	50 476	52 730	13 277	6 184	7 093	89 929	44 292	45 637
80 - 84	66 273	31 506	34 767	8 054	3 456	4 598	58 219	28 050	30 169
85 +	32 939	13 999	18 940	4 277	1 783	2 494	28 662	12 216	16 446
1 VII 2013 (ESDJ)[12]									
Total	17 807 117	8 850 137	8 956 980	...	...	...	...	...	...
0 - 4	3 781 472	1 904 227	1 877 245	...	...	...	...	...	...
5 - 9	3 165 490	1 614 326	1 551 164	...	...	...	...	...	...
10 - 14	2 235 375	1 154 040	1 081 334	...	...	...	...	...	...
15 - 19	1 711 861	837 649	874 212	...	...	...	...	...	...
20 - 24	1 370 731	652 981	717 750	...	...	...	...	...	...
25 - 29	1 172 608	536 594	636 014	...	...	...	...	...	...
30 - 34	952 133	444 623	507 510	...	...	...	...	...	...
35 - 39	757 826	359 694	398 132	...	...	...	...	...	...
40 - 44	611 657	293 008	318 649	...	...	...	...	...	...
45 - 49	491 201	241 779	249 422	...	...	...	...	...	...
50 - 54	389 280	200 490	188 790	...	...	...	...	...	...
55 - 59	305 221	162 469	142 751	...	...	...	...	...	...
60 - 64	231 274	121 809	109 465	...	...	...	...	...	...
65 - 69	182 463	99 315	83 148	...	...	...	...	...	...
70 - 74	142 126	74 923	67 203	...	...	...	...	...	...
75 - 79	101 410	53 489	47 920	...	...	...	...	...	...
80 - 84	66 555	31 949	34 606	...	...	...	...	...	...
85 +	76 446	30 686	45 760	...	...	...	...	...	...
Unknown - Inconnu	61 987	36 085	25 902	...	...	...	...	...	...
Nigeria - Nigéria									
21 III 2006 (CDFC)									
Total	140 431 790	71 345 488	69 086 302	...	...	...	...	...	...
0 - 4	22 594 967	11 569 218	11 025 749	...	...	...	...	...	...
5 - 9	20 005 380	10 388 611	9 616 769	...	...	...	...	...	...
10 - 14	16 135 950	8 504 319	7 631 631	...	...	...	...	...	...
15 - 19	14 899 419	7 536 532	7 362 887	...	...	...	...	...	...
20 - 24	13 435 079	6 237 549	7 197 530	...	...	...	...	...	...
25 - 29	12 211 426	5 534 458	6 676 968	...	...	...	...	...	...
30 - 34	9 467 538	4 505 186	4 962 352	...	...	...	...	...	...
35 - 39	7 331 755	3 661 133	3 670 622	...	...	...	...	...	...
40 - 44	6 456 470	3 395 489	3 060 981	...	...	...	...	...	...
45 - 49	4 591 293	2 561 526	2 029 767	...	...	...	...	...	...
50 - 54	4 249 219	2 363 937	1 885 282	...	...	...	...	...	...
55 - 59	2 066 247	1 189 770	876 477	...	...	...	...	...	...
60 - 64	2 450 286	1 363 219	1 087 067	...	...	...	...	...	...
65 - 69	1 151 048	628 436	522 612	...	...	...	...	...	...
70 - 74	1 330 597	765 988	564 609	...	...	...	...	...	...
75 - 79	579 838	327 416	252 422	...	...	...	...	...	...
80 - 84	760 053	408 680	351 373	...	...	...	...	...	...
85 +	715 225	404 021	311 204	...	...	...	...	...	...
Republic of South Sudan - République de Soudan du Sud									
21 IV 2008 (CDFC)									
Total	8 260 490	4 287 300	3 973 190	1 405 186	754 086	651 100	6 855 304	3 533 214	3 322 090
0	231 146	121 882	109 264	43 300	22 617	20 683	187 846	99 265	88 581
1 - 4	1 072 985	567 545	505 440	174 976	91 509	83 467	898 009	476 036	421 973
5 - 9	1 297 816	688 385	609 431	196 136	101 760	94 376	1 101 680	586 625	515 055
10 - 14	1 057 390	569 537	487 853	160 054	84 981	75 073	897 336	484 556	412 780

Continent, country or area, date, code[a] and age (in years) / Continent, pays ou zone, date, code[a] et âge (en années)	Total			Urban - Urbaine			Rural - Rurale		
	Both sexes Les deux sexes	Male Masculin	Female Féminin	Both sexes Les deux sexes	Male Masculin	Female Féminin	Both sexes Les deux sexes	Male Masculin	Female Féminin
AFRICA - AFRIQUE									
Republic of South Sudan - République de Soudan du Sud									
21 IV 2008 (CDFC)									
15 - 19	889 829	462 902	426 927	153 683	81 602	72 081	736 146	381 300	354 846
20 - 24	739 006	360 788	378 218	148 237	78 336	69 901	590 769	282 452	308 317
25 - 29	698 011	335 398	362 613	141 623	76 445	65 178	556 388	258 953	297 435
30 - 34	536 915	258 531	278 384	101 597	56 705	44 892	435 318	201 826	233 492
35 - 39	475 813	238 985	236 828	87 844	49 346	38 498	387 969	189 639	198 330
40 - 44	339 704	173 493	166 211	58 645	33 444	25 201	281 059	140 049	141 010
45 - 49	276 100	149 941	126 159	45 605	26 316	19 289	230 495	123 625	106 870
50 - 54	197 265	104 812	92 453	31 870	17 548	14 322	165 395	87 264	78 131
55 - 59	121 795	67 845	53 950	18 520	10 557	7 963	103 275	57 288	45 987
60 - 64	115 631	64 236	51 395	16 523	8 849	7 674	99 108	55 387	43 721
65 - 69	73 155	41 455	31 700	9 750	5 239	4 511	63 405	36 216	27 189
70 - 74	59 287	34 785	24 502	7 756	4 087	3 669	51 531	30 698	20 833
75 - 79	28 919	17 424	11 495	3 522	1 898	1 624	25 397	15 526	9 871
80 - 84	24 514	14 314	10 200	2 867	1 497	1 370	21 647	12 817	8 830
85 - 89	10 982	6 731	4 251	1 121	550	571	9 861	6 181	3 680
90 - 94	7 361	4 477	2 884	873	472	401	6 488	4 005	2 483
95 +	6 866	3 834	3 032	684	328	356	6 182	3 506	2 676
Reunion - Réunion									
1 I 2013 (ESDJ)									
Total	835 178	404 651	430 527	...	...	...	...	...	...
0 - 4	62 412	31 868	30 544	...	...	...	...	...	...
5 - 9	68 381	35 217	33 164	...	...	...	...	...	...
10 - 14	70 487	36 068	34 419	...	...	...	...	...	...
15 - 19	67 715	34 697	33 018	...	...	...	...	...	...
20 - 24	56 751	27 965	28 785	...	...	...	...	...	...
25 - 29	52 999	24 729	28 270	...	...	...	...	...	...
30 - 34	52 480	23 971	28 509	...	...	...	...	...	...
35 - 39	57 112	26 550	30 562	...	...	...	...	...	...
40 - 44	62 190	29 837	32 352	...	...	...	...	...	...
45 - 49	65 182	31 562	33 620	...	...	...	...	...	...
50 - 54	56 417	27 341	29 077	...	...	...	...	...	...
55 - 59	47 439	23 149	24 290	...	...	...	...	...	...
60 - 64	36 428	17 875	18 554	...	...	...	...	...	...
65 - 69	26 705	12 793	13 912	...	...	...	...	...	...
70 - 74	20 163	9 045	11 118	...	...	...	...	...	...
75 - 79	15 076	6 335	8 741	...	...	...	...	...	...
80 - 84	9 378	3 482	5 896	...	...	...	...	...	...
85 - 89	5 051	1 529	3 522	...	...	...	...	...	...
90 - 94	2 135	503	1 631	...	...	...	...	...	...
95 +	678	133	545	...	...	...	...	...	...
Rwanda[13]									
1 VII 2015 (ESDF)									
Total	11 262 564	5 445 206	5 817 359	2 086 390	1 008 724	1 077 666	9 176 174	4 436 481	4 739 693
0 - 4	1 572 061	789 951	782 110	260 696	123 000	137 696	1 311 365	666 951	644 413
5 - 9	1 526 411	760 099	766 312	227 822	106 543	121 279	1 298 590	653 557	645 033
10 - 14	1 419 149	703 232	715 916	224 132	102 874	121 257	1 195 017	600 358	594 659
15 - 19	1 178 767	579 696	599 071	227 477	99 003	128 474	951 291	480 693	470 597
20 - 24	1 063 880	519 110	544 770	260 180	125 976	134 204	803 700	393 134	410 566
25 - 29	981 733	478 024	503 710	246 792	126 317	120 474	734 941	351 706	383 235
30 - 34	862 303	422 675	439 629	201 132	106 607	94 525	661 172	316 068	345 104
35 - 39	648 536	306 944	341 592	141 113	73 690	67 423	507 423	233 254	274 169
40 - 44	449 731	203 781	245 951	86 335	44 234	42 102	363 396	159 547	203 849
45 - 49	373 831	171 529	202 303	61 861	32 123	29 738	311 970	139 405	172 565
50 - 54	331 208	149 555	181 653	45 583	23 087	22 496	285 625	126 468	159 157
55 - 59	296 157	131 564	164 593	37 156	18 148	19 008	259 001	113 415	145 585
60 - 64	202 409	88 532	113 878	24 260	11 395	12 865	178 150	77 137	101 013
65 - 69	133 645	55 840	77 806	16 118	6 834	9 284	117 527	49 005	68 522
70 - 74	83 992	31 629	52 363	9 532	3 500	6 033	74 459	28 129	46 331
75 - 79	67 224	25 280	41 945	7 889	2 748	5 141	59 335	22 532	36 804
80 +	71 525	27 766	43 758	8 312	2 645	5 667	63 212	25 121	38 091

7. Population by age, sex and urban/rural residence: latest available year, 2006 - 2015
Population selon l'âge, le sexe et la résidence, urbaine/rurale : dernière année disponible, 2006 - 2015 (continued - suite)

Continent, country or area, date, code[a] and age (in years) / Continent, pays ou zone, date, code[a] et âge (en années)	Total			Urban - Urbaine			Rural - Rurale		
	Both sexes Les deux sexes	Male Masculin	Female Féminin	Both sexes Les deux sexes	Male Masculin	Female Féminin	Both sexes Les deux sexes	Male Masculin	Female Féminin
AFRICA - AFRIQUE									
Saint Helena ex. dep. - Sainte-Hélène sans dép.									
31 XII 2013 (ESDF)									
Total..................................	4 211	2 139	2 072	...	...	...	...	...	...
0 - 4	176	89	87	...	...	...	...	...	...
5 - 9	209	115	94	...	...	...	...	...	...
10 - 14	249	131	118	...	...	...	...	...	...
15 - 19	301	157	144	...	...	...	...	...	...
20 - 24	164	84	80	...	...	...	...	...	...
25 - 29	171	77	94	...	...	...	...	...	...
30 - 34	196	88	108	...	...	...	...	...	...
35 - 39	297	138	159	...	...	...	...	...	...
40 - 44	341	178	163	...	...	...	...	...	...
45 - 49	362	179	183	...	...	...	...	...	...
50 - 54	305	166	139	...	...	...	...	...	...
55 - 59	345	182	163	...	...	...	...	...	...
60 - 64	350	208	142	...	...	...	...	...	...
65 - 69	256	138	118	...	...	...	...	...	...
70 - 74	194	111	83	...	...	...	...	...	...
75 - 79	135	57	78	...	...	...	...	...	...
80 - 84	88	28	60	...	...	...	...	...	...
85 - 89	48	10	38	...	...	...	...	...	...
90 - 94	19	2	17	...	...	...	...	...	...
95 - 99	4	-	4	...	...	...	...	...	...
100 + ...	-	-	-	...	...	...	...	...	...
Unknown - Inconnu	1	1	-	...	...	...	...	...	...
Saint Helena: Ascension - Sainte-Hélène: Ascension									
1 VII 2008 (ESDJ)									
Total..................................	702	397	305	...	...	...	...	...	...
0 - 4	32	16	16	...	...	...	...	...	...
5 - 9	19	9	10	...	...	...	...	...	...
10 - 14	41	20	21	...	...	...	...	...	...
15 - 19	30	19	11	...	...	...	...	...	...
20 - 24	63	29	34	...	...	...	...	...	...
25 - 29	73	42	31	...	...	...	...	...	...
30 - 34	76	41	35	...	...	...	...	...	...
35 - 39	92	58	34	...	...	...	...	...	...
40 - 44	85	42	43	...	...	...	...	...	...
45 - 49	65	36	29	...	...	...	...	...	...
50 - 54	51	32	19	...	...	...	...	...	...
55 - 59	43	29	14	...	...	...	...	...	...
60 - 64	21	15	6	...	...	...	...	...	...
65 - 69	10	9	1	...	...	...	...	...	...
70 - 74	-	-	-	...	...	...	...	...	...
75 - 79	-	-	-	...	...	...	...	...	...
80 + ...	1	-	1	...	...	...	...	...	...
Sao Tome and Principe - Sao Tomé-et-Principe									
13 V 2012 (CDJC)									
Total..................................	178 739	88 867	89 872	119 781	58 710	61 071	58 958	30 157	28 801
0 - 4	27 720	13 962	13 758	18 502	9 317	9 185	9 218	4 645	4 573
5 - 9	25 472	12 730	12 742	16 772	8 426	8 346	8 700	4 304	4 396
10 - 14	21 427	10 726	10 701	14 262	7 028	7 234	7 165	3 698	3 467
15 - 19	18 457	9 353	9 104	12 361	6 115	6 246	6 096	3 238	2 858
20 - 24	15 974	7 978	7 996	10 840	5 289	5 551	5 134	2 689	2 445
25 - 29	14 815	7 366	7 449	10 226	4 980	5 246	4 589	2 386	2 203
30 - 34	12 522	6 203	6 319	8 532	4 152	4 380	3 990	2 051	1 939
35 - 39	9 731	4 875	4 856	6 426	3 152	3 274	3 305	1 723	1 582
40 - 44	7 879	3 971	3 908	5 236	2 567	2 669	2 643	1 404	1 239
45 - 49	6 311	3 050	3 261	4 299	2 036	2 263	2 012	1 014	998
50 - 54	5 364	2 606	2 758	3 704	1 769	1 935	1 660	837	823
55 - 59	3 816	1 807	2 009	2 663	1 254	1 409	1 153	553	600
60 - 64	2 661	1 338	1 323	1 786	875	911	875	463	412
65 - 69	1 925	918	1 007	1 253	573	680	672	345	327

Continent, country or area, date, code[a] and age (in years) / Continent, pays ou zone, date, code[a] et âge (en années)	Total			Urban - Urbaine			Rural - Rurale		
	Both sexes Les deux sexes	Male Masculin	Female Féminin	Both sexes Les deux sexes	Male Masculin	Female Féminin	Both sexes Les deux sexes	Male Masculin	Female Féminin
AFRICA - AFRIQUE									
Sao Tome and Principe - Sao Tomé-et-Principe									
13 V 2012 (CDJC)									
70 - 74	1 878	850	1 028	1 156	497	659	722	353	369
75 - 79	1 411	609	802	848	353	495	563	256	307
80 + ...	1 376	525	851	915	327	588	461	198	263
Senegal - Sénégal[2]									
1 VII 2015 (ESDJ)									
Total...............	14 356 575	7 153 656	7 202 919	...	...	...	...	...	...
0 - 4	2 292 171	1 170 409	1 121 762	...	...	...	...	...	...
5 - 9	1 974 285	1 016 146	958 139	...	...	...	...	...	...
10 - 14	1 738 661	895 486	843 175	...	...	...	...	...	...
15 - 19	1 520 692	776 326	744 366	...	...	...	...	...	...
20 - 24	1 322 105	651 680	670 425	...	...	...	...	...	...
25 - 29	1 132 143	542 599	589 544	...	...	...	...	...	...
30 - 34	936 888	450 683	486 205	...	...	...	...	...	...
35 - 39	769 496	371 563	397 933	...	...	...	...	...	...
40 - 44	616 490	292 963	323 527	...	...	...	...	...	...
45 - 49	495 364	232 938	262 426	...	...	...	...	...	...
50 - 54	420 657	201 357	219 300	...	...	...	...	...	...
55 - 59	349 523	170 031	179 492	...	...	...	...	...	...
60 - 64	264 255	129 406	134 849	...	...	...	...	...	...
65 - 69	192 902	94 736	98 166	...	...	...	...	...	...
70 - 74	138 351	67 531	70 820	...	...	...	...	...	...
75 - 79	88 025	41 991	46 034	...	...	...	...	...	...
80 + ...	104 567	47 811	56 756	...	...	...	...	...	...
Seychelles									
1 VII 2015 (ESDF)									
Total...............	93 419	46 322	47 097	...	...	...	...	...	...
0	1 601	832	769	...	...	...	...	...	...
1 - 4	6 310	3 180	3 130	...	...	...	...	...	...
5 - 9	6 193	3 128	3 065	...	...	...	...	...	...
10 - 14	6 099	2 999	3 100	...	...	...	...	...	...
15 - 19	5 497	2 823	2 674	...	...	...	...	...	...
20 - 24	6 509	3 420	3 089	...	...	...	...	...	...
25 - 29	6 750	3 644	3 106	...	...	...	...	...	...
30 - 34	8 188	4 059	4 129	...	...	...	...	...	...
35 - 39	7 325	3 542	3 783	...	...	...	...	...	...
40 - 44	7 536	3 878	3 658	...	...	...	...	...	...
45 - 49	6 722	3 126	3 596	...	...	...	...	...	...
50 - 54	7 385	3 599	3 786	...	...	...	...	...	...
55 - 59	5 457	2 814	2 643	...	...	...	...	...	...
60 - 64	4 062	2 019	2 043	...	...	...	...	...	...
65 - 69	2 705	1 341	1 364	...	...	...	...	...	...
70 - 74	1 953	925	1 028	...	...	...	...	...	...
75 - 79	1 408	528	880	...	...	...	...	...	...
80 - 84	976	294	682	...	...	...	...	...	...
85 - 89	505	126	379	...	...	...	...	...	...
90 + ...	238	45	193	...	...	...	...	...	...
Sierra Leone									
1 VII 2010 (ESDF)									
Total...............	5 746 800	2 786 797	2 960 003	2 304 955	1 138 563	1 166 392	3 441 845	1 648 234	1 793 611
0 - 4	878 231	437 908	440 323	297 865	147 565	150 300	580 366	290 343	290 023
5 - 9	856 605	424 222	432 383	307 007	145 641	161 366	549 598	278 581	271 017
10 - 14	662 651	338 453	324 198	303 094	148 401	154 693	359 557	190 052	169 505
15 - 19	637 914	308 982	328 932	287 597	141 564	146 033	350 317	167 418	182 899
20 - 24	488 054	221 932	266 122	241 599	119 622	121 977	246 455	102 310	144 145
25 - 29	473 952	210 004	263 948	205 137	102 492	102 645	268 815	107 512	161 303
30 - 34	356 727	160 822	195 905	149 414	73 308	76 106	207 313	87 514	119 799
35 - 39	341 470	160 326	181 144	133 461	66 104	67 357	208 009	94 222	113 787
40 - 44	247 978	123 279	124 699	97 102	51 623	45 479	150 876	71 656	79 220
45 - 49	201 708	107 932	93 776	76 536	41 832	34 704	125 172	66 100	59 072
50 - 54	149 167	77 236	71 931	55 139	30 564	24 575	94 028	46 672	47 356
55 - 59	96 801	51 344	45 457	37 477	21 157	16 320	59 324	30 187	29 137
60 - 64	99 394	44 873	54 521	31 058	14 915	16 143	68 336	29 958	38 378

Continent, country or area, date, code[a] and age (in years) / Continent, pays ou zone, date, code[a] et âge (en années)	Total			Urban - Urbaine			Rural - Rurale		
	Both sexes Les deux sexes	Male Masculin	Female Féminin	Both sexes Les deux sexes	Male Masculin	Female Féminin	Both sexes Les deux sexes	Male Masculin	Female Féminin
AFRICA - AFRIQUE									
Sierra Leone									
1 VII 2010 (ESDF)									
65 - 69	71 174	34 054	37 120	24 423	11 420	13 003	46 751	22 634	24 117
70 - 74	61 847	28 198	33 649	18 941	8 268	10 673	42 906	19 930	22 976
75 - 79	41 728	21 586	20 142	12 876	6 356	6 520	28 852	15 230	13 622
80 +	81 399	35 646	45 753	26 229	7 731	18 498	55 170	27 915	27 255
South Africa - Afrique du Sud									
1 VII 2014 (ESDF)									
Total	54 001 953	26 366 008	27 635 944	...	...	...	...	...	...
0 - 4	5 719 329	2 892 219	2 827 110	...	...	...	...	...	...
5 - 9	5 336 710	2 692 433	2 644 277	...	...	...	...	...	...
10 - 14	5 123 726	2 580 229	2 543 497	...	...	...	...	...	...
15 - 19	5 217 561	2 624 166	2 593 395	...	...	...	...	...	...
20 - 24	5 267 117	2 662 829	2 604 288	...	...	...	...	...	...
25 - 29	4 954 532	2 515 096	2 439 436	...	...	...	...	...	...
30 - 34	4 090 283	2 034 229	2 056 054	...	...	...	...	...	...
35 - 39	3 503 217	1 739 688	1 763 529	...	...	...	...	...	...
40 - 44	3 121 822	1 482 086	1 639 736	...	...	...	...	...	...
45 - 49	2 753 470	1 270 867	1 482 603	...	...	...	...	...	...
50 - 54	2 377 730	1 089 941	1 287 789	...	...	...	...	...	...
55 - 59	1 994 390	907 807	1 086 583	...	...	...	...	...	...
60 - 64	1 570 178	703 921	866 257	...	...	...	...	...	...
65 - 69	1 176 466	492 791	683 675	...	...	...	...	...	...
70 - 74	831 263	327 812	503 451	...	...	...	...	...	...
75 - 79	530 877	202 623	328 254	...	...	...	...	...	...
80 +	433 281	147 270	286 011	...	...	...	...	...	...
Sudan - Soudan									
1 VII 2015 (ESDF)									
Total	38 454 040	19 509 961	18 944 080	13 729 842	6 965 944	6 763 898	24 724 198	12 544 017	12 180 181
0	1 458 682	743 535	715 147	...	...	...	...	...	...
1 - 4	5 248 430	2 673 249	2 575 180	2 018 952	993 726	1 025 225	4 688 160	2 423 059	2 265 101
5 - 9	5 171 454	2 648 653	2 522 799	1 645 054	819 246	825 807	3 526 399	1 829 407	1 696 992
10 - 14	4 447 130	2 287 710	2 159 421	1 504 605	758 279	746 326	2 942 526	1 529 431	1 413 095
15 - 19	3 933 704	2 026 071	1 907 632	1 403 261	717 197	686 065	2 530 442	1 308 874	1 221 568
20 - 24	3 452 908	1 769 660	1 683 248	1 320 207	688 113	632 094	2 132 701	1 081 548	1 051 154
25 - 29	2 982 830	1 496 944	1 485 886	1 179 437	609 982	569 454	1 803 392	886 962	916 430
30 - 34	2 555 185	1 259 171	1 296 014	1 030 239	529 658	500 582	1 524 945	729 513	795 432
35 - 39	2 150 504	1 047 861	1 102 642	872 460	444 361	428 099	1 278 045	603 501	674 544
40 - 44	1 783 389	864 689	918 699	713 117	357 319	355 798	1 070 273	507 371	562 901
45 - 49	1 437 590	709 271	728 319	572 778	289 975	282 804	864 812	419 296	445 516
50 - 54	1 135 510	571 770	563 742	453 206	232 202	221 004	682 305	339 568	342 737
55 - 59	859 424	441 102	418 324	340 422	176 339	164 083	519 003	264 763	254 240
60 - 64	634 398	331 713	302 684	246 852	129 178	117 674	387 546	202 535	185 010
65 - 69	459 686	242 742	216 943	174 324	91 048	83 276	285 363	151 696	133 667
70 - 74	317 032	168 301	148 730	115 197	59 363	55 833	201 835	108 937	92 898
75 - 79	205 954	109 504	96 448	69 377	34 565	34 812	136 576	74 939	61 636
80 +	220 231	118 010	102 221	70 356	35 393	34 963	149 876	82 618	67 258
Swaziland									
1 I 2015 (ESDF)									
Total	1 119 375	531 737	587 638	261 028	124 195	136 833	858 347	407 805	450 805
0	32 210	16 325	15 885	5 760	2 925	2 835	26 450	13 400	13 050
1 - 4	117 478	59 909	57 569	20 675	10 525	10 150	96 803	49 384	47 419
5 - 9	130 635	66 666	63 969	22 414	11 435	10 979	108 221	55 231	52 990
10 - 14	130 443	65 576	64 867	20 165	9 730	10 435	110 278	55 846	54 432
15 - 19	127 696	62 743	64 953	21 915	9 674	12 241	105 781	53 069	52 712
20 - 24	119 322	57 695	61 627	28 003	12 185	15 818	91 319	45 510	45 809
25 - 29	102 667	47 802	54 865	33 994	15 617	18 377	68 673	32 185	36 488
30 - 34	85 056	37 362	47 694	32 026	15 460	16 566	53 030	21 902	31 128
35 - 39	67 300	28 364	38 936	23 814	11 663	12 151	43 486	16 701	26 785
40 - 44	51 526	21 704	30 822	17 614	8 592	9 022	33 912	12 670	21 242
45 - 49	40 836	16 996	23 840	12 795	6 253	6 542	28 041	10 743	17 298
50 - 54	31 614	13 545	18 069	8 498	4 239	4 259	23 116	9 306	13 810
55 - 59	24 859	10 830	14 029	5 825	2 831	2 994	19 034	7 999	11 035
60 - 64	19 202	8 570	10 632	3 517	1 596	1 921	15 685	6 974	8 711
65 - 69	14 629	6 715	7 914	1 888	759	1 129	12 741	5 956	6 785

Continent, country or area, date, code[a] and age (in years) / Continent, pays ou zone, date, code[a] et âge (en années)	Total			Urban - Urbaine			Rural - Rurale		
	Both sexes Les deux sexes	Male Masculin	Female Féminin	Both sexes Les deux sexes	Male Masculin	Female Féminin	Both sexes Les deux sexes	Male Masculin	Female Féminin
AFRICA - AFRIQUE									
Swaziland									
1 I 2015 (ESDF)									
70 - 74	10 604	5 036	5 568	1 053	380	673	9 551	4 656	4 895
75 - 79	6 691	3 254	3 437	612	221	391	6 079	3 033	3 046
Togo									
6 XI 2010 (CDJC)									
Total..............................	6 191 155	3 009 095	3 182 060	...	...	...	...	...	...
0	190 136	96 043	94 093	...	...	...	...	...	...
1 - 4	711 135	360 481	350 654	...	...	...	...	...	...
5 - 9	951 700	482 501	469 199	...	...	...	...	...	...
10 - 14	747 726	390 477	357 249	...	...	...	...	...	...
15 - 19	606 401	313 257	293 144	...	...	...	...	...	...
20 - 24	545 245	252 807	292 438	...	...	...	...	...	...
25 - 29	496 822	214 803	282 019	...	...	...	...	...	...
30 - 34	424 380	199 636	224 744	...	...	...	...	...	...
35 - 39	352 008	166 528	185 480	...	...	...	...	...	...
40 - 44	291 584	139 731	151 853	...	...	...	...	...	...
45 - 49	228 446	112 191	116 255	...	...	...	...	...	...
50 - 54	178 233	82 969	95 264	...	...	...	...	...	...
55 - 59	115 950	54 936	61 014	...	...	...	...	...	...
60 - 64	102 694	44 431	58 263	...	...	...	...	...	...
65 - 69	66 324	26 700	39 624	...	...	...	...	...	...
70 - 74	61 756	24 127	37 629	...	...	...	...	...	...
75 - 79	33 574	13 250	20 324	...	...	...	...	...	...
80 + ...	73 591	27 960	45 631	...	...	...	...	...	...
Unknown - Inconnu	13 450	6 267	7 183	...	...	...	...	...	...
Tunisia - Tunisie									
23 IV 2014 (CDFC)									
Total..............................	10 982 753	5 472 333	5 510 420	...	...	...	...	...	...
0 - 4	972 171	505 509	466 662	...	...	...	...	...	...
5 - 9	849 006	440 644	408 362	...	...	...	...	...	...
10 - 14	789 622	407 938	381 684	...	...	...	...	...	...
15 - 19	827 508	421 716	405 792	...	...	...	...	...	...
20 - 24	925 409	459 814	465 595	...	...	...	...	...	...
25 - 29	934 617	449 932	484 685	...	...	...	...	...	...
30 - 34	983 781	477 322	506 459	...	...	...	...	...	...
35 - 39	816 986	397 594	419 392	...	...	...	...	...	...
40 - 44	727 848	357 353	370 495	...	...	...	...	...	...
45 - 49	682 956	331 283	351 673	...	...	...	...	...	...
50 - 54	650 608	324 423	326 185	...	...	...	...	...	...
55 - 59	535 168	268 380	266 788	...	...	...	...	...	...
60 - 64	425 424	212 900	212 524	...	...	...	...	...	...
65 - 69	262 303	127 168	135 135	...	...	...	...	...	...
70 - 74	220 681	107 097	113 584	...	...	...	...	...	...
75 - 79	166 896	81 732	85 164	...	...	...	...	...	...
80 + ...	211 769	101 528	110 241	...	...	...	...	...	...
Uganda - Ouganda									
1 VII 2012 (ESDF)									
Total..............................	34 131 400	...	...	...	...	...	...	...	...
0 - 4	7 220 700	...	...	...	...	...	...	...	...
5 - 9	5 930 300	...	...	...	...	...	...	...	...
10 - 14	4 160 000	...	...	...	...	...	...	...	...
15 - 19	3 661 100	...	...	...	...	...	...	...	...
20 - 24	3 033 800	...	...	...	...	...	...	...	...
25 - 29	2 468 500	...	...	...	...	...	...	...	...
30 - 34	1 969 300	...	...	...	...	...	...	...	...
35 - 39	1 549 200	...	...	...	...	...	...	...	...
40 - 44	1 206 400	...	...	...	...	...	...	...	...
45 - 49	927 600	...	...	...	...	...	...	...	...
50 - 54	695 700	...	...	...	...	...	...	...	...
55 - 59	501 900	...	...	...	...	...	...	...	...
60 - 64	344 400	...	...	...	...	...	...	...	...
65 - 69	221 300	...	...	...	...	...	...	...	...
70 - 74	130 300	...	...	...	...	...	...	...	...

7. Population by age, sex and urban/rural residence: latest available year, 2006 - 2015
Population selon l'âge, le sexe et la résidence, urbaine/rurale : dernière année disponible, 2006 - 2015 (continued - suite)

Continent, country or area, date, code[a] and age (in years) Continent, pays ou zone, date, code[a] et âge (en annèes)	Total			Urban - Urbaine			Rural - Rurale		
	Both sexes Les deux sexes	Male Masculin	Female Féminin	Both sexes Les deux sexes	Male Masculin	Female Féminin	Both sexes Les deux sexes	Male Masculin	Female Féminin
AFRICA - AFRIQUE									
Uganda - Ouganda									
1 VII 2012 (ESDF)									
75 - 79	67 800	...	...	...	...	...	...	...	...
80 + ...	43 100	...	...	...	...	...	...	...	...
United Republic of Tanzania - République Unie de Tanzanie[14]									
1 VII 2013 (ESDF)									
Total.................................	47 132 580	23 267 957	23 864 623	12 909 536	6 386 303	6 523 233	34 223 044	16 881 654	17 341 390
0	1 776 107	895 971	880 136	403 952	203 710	200 242	1 372 155	692 261	679 894
1 - 4	6 536 000	3 295 033	3 240 967	1 521 372	766 466	754 906	5 014 628	2 528 567	2 486 061
5 - 9	7 160 846	3 608 891	3 551 955	1 723 220	857 109	866 111	5 437 626	2 751 782	2 685 844
10 - 14	5 464 181	2 735 494	2 728 687	1 364 854	661 195	703 659	4 099 327	2 074 299	2 025 028
15 - 19	4 985 943	2 494 983	2 490 960	1 427 786	682 734	745 052	3 558 157	1 812 249	1 745 908
20 - 24	4 340 143	2 179 173	2 160 970	1 333 476	672 789	660 687	3 006 667	1 506 384	1 500 283
25 - 29	3 484 607	1 730 600	1 754 007	1 134 814	563 796	571 018	2 349 793	1 166 804	1 182 989
30 - 34	2 852 197	1 289 114	1 563 083	974 580	450 823	523 757	1 877 617	838 291	1 039 326
35 - 39	2 601 610	1 207 182	1 394 428	867 422	418 436	448 986	1 734 188	788 746	945 442
40 - 44	2 121 302	1 032 605	1 088 697	672 984	346 836	326 148	1 448 318	685 769	762 549
45 - 49	1 568 017	770 149	797 868	469 417	248 681	220 736	1 098 600	521 468	577 132
50 - 54	1 234 201	604 621	629 580	339 138	180 385	158 753	895 063	424 236	470 827
55 - 59	881 484	422 141	459 343	223 562	117 172	106 390	657 922	304 969	352 953
60 - 64	734 938	347 604	387 334	172 297	88 004	84 293	562 641	259 600	303 041
65 - 69	466 882	223 365	243 517	100 337	50 363	49 974	366 545	173 002	193 543
70 - 74	387 755	179 960	207 795	78 544	35 541	43 003	309 211	144 419	164 792
75 - 79	245 872	115 076	130 796	46 843	20 380	26 463	199 029	94 696	104 333
80 + ...	290 495	135 995	154 500	54 938	21 883	33 055	235 557	114 112	121 445
Zambia - Zambie									
16 X 2010 (CDJC)									
Total.................................	13 092 666	6 454 647	6 638 019	5 173 450	2 548 011	2 625 439	7 919 216	3 906 636	4 012 580
0 - 4	2 252 748	1 121 468	1 131 280	764 592	380 464	384 128	1 488 156	741 004	747 152
5 - 9	1 916 287	954 332	961 955	656 170	322 268	333 902	1 260 117	632 064	628 053
10 - 14	1 774 134	878 572	895 562	672 089	320 423	351 666	1 102 045	558 149	543 896
15 - 19	1 531 115	748 616	782 499	656 061	311 922	344 139	875 054	436 694	438 360
20 - 24	1 194 642	553 267	641 375	544 640	251 543	293 097	650 002	301 724	348 278
25 - 29	1 057 077	497 774	559 303	492 713	233 826	258 887	564 364	263 948	300 416
30 - 34	840 308	425 227	415 081	393 374	202 930	190 444	446 934	222 297	224 637
35 - 39	682 921	357 097	325 824	307 182	167 113	140 069	375 739	189 984	185 755
40 - 44	473 238	250 415	222 823	200 717	111 062	89 655	272 521	139 353	133 168
45 - 49	376 164	189 047	187 117	151 364	78 278	73 086	224 800	110 769	114 031
50 - 54	284 864	138 764	146 100	111 791	55 850	55 941	173 073	82 914	90 159
55 - 59	194 162	96 718	97 444	75 456	39 790	35 666	118 706	56 928	61 778
60 - 64	168 563	78 301	90 262	55 664	28 866	26 798	112 899	49 435	63 464
65 - 69	122 931	56 814	66 117	35 552	17 637	17 915	87 379	39 177	48 202
70 - 74	93 348	43 945	49 403	24 207	11 599	12 608	69 141	32 346	36 795
75 - 79	63 063	31 929	31 134	15 591	7 323	8 268	47 472	24 606	22 866
80 - 84	33 598	16 569	17 029	8 349	3 788	4 561	25 249	12 781	12 468
85 - 89	19 118	9 651	9 467	4 762	2 118	2 644	14 356	7 533	6 823
90 - 94	6 450	3 245	3 205	1 477	652	825	4 973	2 593	2 380
95 + ...	7 935	2 896	5 039	1 699	559	1 140	6 236	2 337	3 899
Zimbabwe									
17 VIII 2012 (CDFC)									
Total.................................	13 061 239	6 280 539	6 780 700	4 284 145	2 039 224	2 244 921	8 777 094	4 241 315	4 535 779
0 - 4	1 978 474	986 596	991 878	598 256	297 469	300 787	1 380 218	689 127	691 091
5 - 9	1 698 160	845 062	853 098	444 636	216 870	227 766	1 253 524	628 192	625 332
10 - 14	1 695 647	849 473	846 174	436 641	206 681	229 960	1 259 006	642 792	616 214
15 - 19	1 412 033	699 230	712 803	465 606	199 010	266 596	946 427	500 220	446 207
20 - 24	1 195 664	543 466	652 198	491 795	214 391	277 404	703 869	329 075	374 794
25 - 29	1 131 691	519 834	611 857	487 413	224 788	262 625	644 278	295 046	349 232
30 - 34	920 747	443 539	477 208	387 867	192 046	195 821	532 880	251 493	281 387
35 - 39	736 741	362 497	374 244	293 412	152 117	141 295	443 329	210 380	232 949
40 - 44	524 786	268 460	256 326	208 628	113 140	95 488	316 158	155 320	160 838
45 - 49	348 014	161 257	186 757	128 657	64 099	64 558	219 357	97 158	122 199
50 - 54	350 855	139 101	211 754	105 536	49 123	56 413	245 319	89 978	155 341
55 - 59	282 344	120 776	161 568	79 861	39 203	40 658	202 483	81 573	120 910

7. Population by age, sex and urban/rural residence: latest available year, 2006 - 2015
Population selon l'âge, le sexe et la résidence, urbaine/rurale : dernière année disponible, 2006 - 2015 (continued - suite)

Continent, country or area, date, code[a] and age (in years) / Continent, pays ou zone, date, code[a] et âge (en années)	Total			Urban - Urbaine			Rural - Rurale		
	Both sexes Les deux sexes	Male Masculin	Female Féminin	Both sexes Les deux sexes	Male Masculin	Female Féminin	Both sexes Les deux sexes	Male Masculin	Female Féminin
AFRICA - AFRIQUE									
Zimbabwe									
17 VIII 2012 (CDFC)									
60 - 64	226 716	96 779	129 937	52 275	24 852	27 423	174 441	71 927	102 514
65 - 69	167 113	73 055	94 058	34 232	15 508	18 724	132 881	57 547	75 334
70 - 74	137 697	62 230	75 467	24 860	10 889	13 971	112 837	51 341	61 496
75 +	226 894	96 640	130 254	34 907	14 342	20 565	191 987	82 298	109 689
Unknown - Inconnu	27 663	12 544	15 119	9 563	4 696	4 867	18 100	7 848	10 252
AMERICA, NORTH - AMÉRIQUE DU NORD									
Antigua and Barbuda - Antigua-et-Barbuda									
27 V 2011 (CDJC)									
Total	85 567	40 986	44 581	...	...	...	...	...	...
0 - 4	6 623	3 361	3 262	...	...	...	...	...	...
5 - 9	6 460	3 272	3 188	...	...	...	...	...	...
10 - 14	7 329	3 690	3 638	...	...	...	...	...	...
15 - 19	7 073	3 554	3 519	...	...	...	...	...	...
20 - 24	6 624	3 206	3 418	...	...	...	...	...	...
25 - 29	6 647	3 135	3 512	...	...	...	...	...	...
30 - 34	6 617	3 101	3 516	...	...	...	...	...	...
35 - 39	6 748	3 049	3 699	...	...	...	...	...	...
40 - 44	6 712	3 124	3 588	...	...	...	...	...	...
45 - 49	6 241	2 893	3 348	...	...	...	...	...	...
50 - 54	5 110	2 416	2 694	...	...	...	...	...	...
55 - 59	3 721	1 763	1 957	...	...	...	...	...	...
60 - 64	2 968	1 398	1 569	...	...	...	...	...	...
65 - 69	2 238	1 066	1 172	...	...	...	...	...	...
70 - 74	1 500	690	810	...	...	...	...	...	...
75 - 79	1 181	527	654	...	...	...	...	...	...
80 - 84	850	331	520	...	...	...	...	...	...
85 - 89	512	214	298	...	...	...	...	...	...
90 - 94	193	72	122	...	...	...	...	...	...
95 +	84	27	57	...	...	...	...	...	...
Unknown - Inconnu	136	96	40	...	...	...	...	...	...
Aruba									
1 VII 2015 (ESDJ)									
Total	109 241	51 691	57 550	...	...	...	...	...	...
0	1 320	692	628	...	...	...	...	...	...
1 - 4	5 382	2 733	2 648	...	...	...	...	...	...
5 - 9	6 911	3 553	3 357	...	...	...	...	...	...
10 - 14	7 168	3 642	3 526	...	...	...	...	...	...
15 - 19	7 476	3 779	3 696	...	...	...	...	...	...
20 - 24	6 501	3 344	3 156	...	...	...	...	...	...
25 - 29	6 167	3 032	3 135	...	...	...	...	...	...
30 - 34	6 684	3 081	3 603	...	...	...	...	...	...
35 - 39	7 255	3 288	3 967	...	...	...	...	...	...
40 - 44	8 083	3 751	4 331	...	...	...	...	...	...
45 - 49	8 655	3 974	4 681	...	...	...	...	...	...
50 - 54	9 392	4 369	5 022	...	...	...	...	...	...
55 - 59	8 305	3 807	4 498	...	...	...	...	...	...
60 - 64	6 672	3 065	3 608	...	...	...	...	...	...
65 - 69	4 862	2 177	2 685	...	...	...	...	...	...
70 - 74	3 379	1 480	1 898	...	...	...	...	...	...
75 - 79	2 485	1 014	1 471	...	...	...	...	...	...
80 - 84	1 502	570	932	...	...	...	...	...	...
85 - 89	706	243	464	...	...	...	...	...	...
90 - 94	244	72	172	...	...	...	...	...	...
95 +	92	22	70	...	...	...	...	...	...
Bahamas									
1 VII 2014* (ESDF)									
Total	364 000	177 800	186 200	...	...	...	...	...	...
0	6 540	3 300	3 240	...	...	...	...	...	...

Continent, country or area, date, code[a] and age (in years) Continent, pays ou zone, date, code[a] et âge (en années)	Total			Urban - Urbaine			Rural - Rurale		
	Both sexes Les deux sexes	Male Masculin	Female Féminin	Both sexes Les deux sexes	Male Masculin	Female Féminin	Both sexes Les deux sexes	Male Masculin	Female Féminin
AMERICA, NORTH - AMÉRIQUE DU NORD									
Bahamas									
1 VII 2014* (ESDF)									
1 - 4	26 000	13 440	12 570	...	...	...	...	...	...
5 - 9	31 590	16 400	15 090	...	...	...	...	...	...
10 - 14	30 390	15 420	14 950	...	...	...	...	...	...
15 - 19	29 770	14 780	15 010	...	...	...	...	...	...
20 - 24	30 600	15 140	15 470	...	...	...	...	...	...
25 - 29	27 310	13 220	14 080	...	...	...	...	...	...
30 - 34	26 120	12 960	13 150	...	...	...	...	...	...
35 - 39	26 300	12 860	13 440	...	...	...	...	...	...
40 - 44	28 190	13 630	14 560	...	...	...	...	...	...
45 - 49	26 770	12 890	13 940	...	...	...	...	...	...
50 - 54	25 250	12 220	13 030	...	...	...	...	...	...
55 - 59	19 260	9 160	10 120	...	...	...	...	...	...
60 - 64	13 640	6 400	7 240	...	...	...	...	...	...
65 - 69	9 640	4 400	5 230	...	...	...	...	...	...
70 - 74	7 130	3 130	4 000	...	...	...	...	...	...
75 - 79	4 470	1 880	2 600	...	...	...	...	...	...
80 +	3 410	1 030	2 380	...	...	...	...	...	...
Barbados - Barbade									
1 V 2010 (CDJC)									
Total	277 821	133 018	144 803	...	...	...	...	...	...
0 - 4	17 352	8 873	8 479	...	...	...	...	...	...
5 - 9	18 838	9 683	9 155	...	...	...	...	...	...
10 - 14	18 567	9 445	9 122	...	...	...	...	...	...
15 - 19	18 870	9 452	9 418	...	...	...	...	...	...
20 - 24	18 169	9 061	9 108	...	...	...	...	...	...
25 - 29	19 088	9 313	9 775	...	...	...	...	...	...
30 - 34	18 785	9 150	9 635	...	...	...	...	...	...
35 - 39	20 516	9 884	10 632	...	...	...	...	...	...
40 - 44	20 113	9 663	10 450	...	...	...	...	...	...
45 - 49	21 365	10 062	11 303	...	...	...	...	...	...
50 - 54	20 050	9 411	10 639	...	...	...	...	...	...
55 - 59	16 653	7 871	8 782	...	...	...	...	...	...
60 - 64	13 486	6 326	7 160	...	...	...	...	...	...
65 - 69	10 151	4 511	5 640	...	...	...	...	...	...
70 - 74	8 680	3 804	4 876	...	...	...	...	...	...
75 - 79	6 937	2 863	4 074	...	...	...	...	...	...
80 - 84	5 153	1 986	3 167	...	...	...	...	...	...
85 +	5 048	1 660	3 388	...	...	...	...	...	...
Belize									
1 VII 2006 (ESDF)[15]									
Total	301 298	149 598	151 700	151 994	73 576	78 418	149 394	76 101	73 293
0 - 4	36 761	18 145	18 616	17 720	8 446	9 274	19 808	10 070	9 738
5 - 9	40 974	20 850	20 124	19 294	9 792	9 502	21 574	11 011	10 563
10 - 14	40 474	20 611	19 862	19 185	9 790	9 395	21 185	10 775	10 410
15 - 19	33 960	17 192	16 769	16 629	8 785	7 844	17 246	8 369	8 877
20 - 24	24 423	11 939	12 484	12 728	5 973	6 755	11 631	5 939	5 692
25 - 29	20 990	9 733	11 256	11 262	5 018	6 244	9 673	4 693	4 980
30 - 34	20 405	9 522	10 883	11 277	5 183	6 094	9 075	4 318	4 757
35 - 39	18 464	8 747	9 718	9 745	4 294	5 451	8 672	4 433	4 239
40 - 44	15 793	7 735	8 058	8 174	3 931	4 243	7 579	3 787	3 792
45 - 49	12 378	6 295	6 065	6 555	3 305	3 250	5 791	2 976	2 815
50 - 54	9 686	4 983	4 703	5 176	2 385	2 791	4 485	2 586	1 899
55 - 59	6 637	3 363	3 264	3 385	1 636	1 749	3 235	1 720	1 515
60 - 64	5 692	2 913	2 778	2 838	1 376	1 462	2 839	1 531	1 308
65 - 69	4 877	2 547	2 330	2 584	1 201	1 383	2 281	1 341	940
70 - 74	3 867	2 073	1 794	2 203	999	1 204	1 654	1 069	585
75 - 79	2 708	1 374	1 330	1 511	716	795	1 191	656	535
80 - 84	1 578	782	798	794	327	467	784	453	331
85 +	1 629	794	835	934	419	515	691	374	317
1 VII 2015 (ESDF)									
Total	368 310	184 157	184 153	...	...	...	...	...	...
0 - 4	43 208	22 042	21 166	...	...	...	...	...	...

Continent, country or area, date, code[a] and age (in years) / Continent, pays ou zone, date, code[a] et âge (en années)	Total			Urban - Urbaine			Rural - Rurale		
	Both sexes Les deux sexes	Male Masculin	Female Féminin	Both sexes Les deux sexes	Male Masculin	Female Féminin	Both sexes Les deux sexes	Male Masculin	Female Féminin
AMERICA, NORTH - AMÉRIQUE DU NORD									
Belize									
1 VII 2015 (ESDF)									
5 - 9	44 814	22 571	22 243	...	...	...	...	...	...
10 - 14	43 065	21 549	21 516	...	...	...	...	...	...
15 - 19	39 578	19 798	19 780	...	...	...	...	...	...
20 - 24	34 887	17 136	17 751	...	...	...	...	...	...
25 - 29	30 276	14 648	15 628	...	...	...	...	...	...
30 - 34	26 086	12 662	13 424	...	...	...	...	...	...
35 - 39	23 622	11 532	12 090	...	...	...	...	...	...
40 - 44	19 809	9 844	9 965	...	...	...	...	...	...
45 - 49	17 081	8 723	8 358	...	...	...	...	...	...
50 - 54	13 389	6 791	6 598	...	...	...	...	...	...
55 - 59	9 868	5 143	4 725	...	...	...	...	...	...
60 - 64	7 107	3 758	3 349	...	...	...	...	...	...
65 - 69	5 022	2 672	2 350	...	...	...	...	...	...
70 - 74	3 992	2 117	1 875	...	...	...	...	...	...
75 - 79	2 927	1 485	1 442	...	...	...	...	...	...
80 +	3 579	1 686	1 893	...	...	...	...	...	...
Bermuda - Bermudes									
20 V 2010 (CDJC)[16]									
Total	64 237	30 858	33 379	64 237	30 858	33 379	-	-	-
0	709	372	337	709	372	337	-	-	-
1 - 4	2 858	1 479	1 379	2 858	1 479	1 379	-	-	-
5 - 9	3 456	1 759	1 697	3 456	1 759	1 697	-	-	-
10 - 14	3 481	1 706	1 775	3 481	1 706	1 775	-	-	-
15 - 19	3 431	1 682	1 749	3 431	1 682	1 749	-	-	-
20 - 24	3 342	1 608	1 734	3 342	1 608	1 734	-	-	-
25 - 29	4 076	1 947	2 129	4 076	1 947	2 129	-	-	-
30 - 34	4 645	2 259	2 386	4 645	2 259	2 386	-	-	-
35 - 39	5 050	2 572	2 478	5 050	2 572	2 478	-	-	-
40 - 44	5 158	2 588	2 570	5 158	2 588	2 570	-	-	-
45 - 49	5 731	2 811	2 920	5 731	2 811	2 920	-	-	-
50 - 54	5 427	2 531	2 896	5 427	2 531	2 896	-	-	-
55 - 59	4 498	2 146	2 352	4 498	2 146	2 352	-	-	-
60 - 64	3 692	1 733	1 959	3 692	1 733	1 959	-	-	-
65 - 69	2 807	1 290	1 517	2 807	1 290	1 517	-	-	-
70 - 74	2 163	961	1 202	2 163	961	1 202	-	-	-
75 - 79	1 768	747	1 021	1 768	747	1 021	-	-	-
80 - 84	1 120	432	688	1 120	432	688	-	-	-
85 - 89	584	185	399	584	185	399	-	-	-
90 - 94	187	41	146	187	41	146	-	-	-
95 - 99	48	8	40	48	8	40	-	-	-
100 +	6	1	5	6	1	5	-	-	-
1 VII 2015 (ESDJ)[17]									
Total	61 735	29 480	32 255	...	...	...	...	...	...
0	631	317	314	...	...	...	...	...	...
1 - 4	2 552	1 249	1 303	...	...	...	...	...	...
5 - 9	3 205	1 643	1 562	...	...	...	...	...	...
10 - 14	3 027	1 558	1 469	...	...	...	...	...	...
15 - 19	2 937	1 421	1 516	...	...	...	...	...	...
20 - 24	3 027	1 440	1 587	...	...	...	...	...	...
25 - 29	3 435	1 609	1 826	...	...	...	...	...	...
30 - 34	4 184	2 035	2 149	...	...	...	...	...	...
35 - 39	4 293	2 139	2 154	...	...	...	...	...	...
40 - 44	4 585	2 340	2 245	...	...	...	...	...	...
45 - 49	4 809	2 380	2 429	...	...	...	...	...	...
50 - 54	5 494	2 662	2 832	...	...	...	...	...	...
55 - 59	5 131	2 349	2 782	...	...	...	...	...	...
60 - 64	4 184	1 972	2 212	...	...	...	...	...	...
65 - 69	3 379	1 567	1 812	...	...	...	...	...	...
70 - 74	2 566	1 147	1 419	...	...	...	...	...	...
75 - 79	1 857	796	1 061	...	...	...	...	...	...
80 - 84	1 384	542	842	...	...	...	...	...	...
85 +	1 055	314	741	...	...	...	...	...	...

Continent, country or area, date, code[a] and age (in years) Continent, pays ou zone, date, code[a] et âge (en années)	Total			Urban - Urbaine			Rural - Rurale		
	Both sexes Les deux sexes	Male Masculin	Female Féminin	Both sexes Les deux sexes	Male Masculin	Female Féminin	Both sexes Les deux sexes	Male Masculin	Female Féminin
AMERICA, NORTH - AMÉRIQUE DU NORD									
Canada									
2 V 2011 (CDJC)									
Total	33 476 685	16 414 230	17 062 460	27 147 190	13 190 225	13 956 965	6 329 495	3 224 005	3 105 500
0 - 4	1 877 095	961 150	915 945	1 531 620	784 165	747 460	345 480	176 985	168 490
5 - 9	1 809 895	925 960	883 935	1 455 570	743 510	712 060	354 325	182 450	171 875
10 - 14	1 920 355	983 990	936 365	1 526 165	781 760	744 410	394 185	202 230	191 955
15 - 19	2 178 135	1 115 845	1 062 290	1 745 370	890 940	854 430	432 765	224 900	207 860
20 - 24	2 187 450	1 108 780	1 078 670	1 858 035	935 265	922 765	329 415	173 510	155 900
25 - 29	2 169 585	1 077 275	1 092 310	1 879 840	930 835	949 005	289 745	146 445	143 305
30 - 34	2 162 900	1 058 810	1 104 095	1 838 125	897 275	940 855	324 775	161 535	163 235
35 - 39	2 173 930	1 064 195	1 109 735	1 814 025	884 235	929 785	359 910	179 965	179 945
40 - 44	2 324 875	1 141 715	1 183 155	1 908 095	933 115	974 980	416 780	208 605	208 175
45 - 49	2 675 130	1 318 715	1 356 420	2 142 125	1 050 625	1 091 500	533 005	268 085	264 915
50 - 54	2 658 965	1 309 025	1 349 940	2 091 050	1 021 340	1 069 700	567 920	287 680	280 235
55 - 59	2 340 635	1 147 300	1 193 335	1 809 810	876 210	933 600	530 825	271 090	259 735
60 - 64	2 052 670	1 002 685	1 049 980	1 573 340	754 910	818 430	479 330	247 780	231 550
65 - 69	1 521 715	738 010	783 700	1 163 785	549 495	614 290	357 930	188 515	169 415
70 - 74	1 153 065	543 435	609 630	906 035	413 260	492 775	247 025	130 175	116 850
75 - 79	922 695	417 945	504 755	751 575	329 760	421 815	171 125	88 185	82 940
80 - 84	702 070	291 085	410 985	591 015	237 310	353 705	111 055	53 775	57 280
85 - 89	427 015	149 415	277 600	369 925	125 615	244 310	57 090	23 800	33 290
90 - 94	170 285	48 470	121 815	148 965	41 530	107 435	21 315	6 940	14 380
95 - 99	42 390	9 455	32 935	37 515	8 225	29 285	4 875	1 230	3 645
100 +	5 825	955	4 870	5 195	840	4 355	630	115	510
1 VII 2015 (ESDJ)[18]									
Total	35 848 610	17 776 946	18 071 664	...	...	...	...	...	...
0	388 539	199 090	189 449	...	...	...	...	...	...
1 - 4	1 549 462	794 302	755 160	...	...	...	...	...	...
5 - 9	1 951 922	999 609	952 313	...	...	...	...	...	...
10 - 14	1 864 554	957 664	906 890	...	...	...	...	...	...
15 - 19	2 096 626	1 078 131	1 018 495	...	...	...	...	...	...
20 - 24	2 461 124	1 261 033	1 200 091	...	...	...	...	...	...
25 - 29	2 465 126	1 238 745	1 226 381	...	...	...	...	...	...
30 - 34	2 500 293	1 246 691	1 253 602	...	...	...	...	...	...
35 - 39	2 402 168	1 197 432	1 204 736	...	...	...	...	...	...
40 - 44	2 349 450	1 173 338	1 176 112	...	...	...	...	...	...
45 - 49	2 432 472	1 218 794	1 213 678	...	...	...	...	...	...
50 - 54	2 763 325	1 387 142	1 376 183	...	...	...	...	...	...
55 - 59	2 602 374	1 298 602	1 303 772	...	...	...	...	...	...
60 - 64	2 234 268	1 103 792	1 130 476	...	...	...	...	...	...
65 - 69	1 910 821	932 290	978 531	...	...	...	...	...	...
70 - 74	1 372 424	652 916	719 508	...	...	...	...	...	...
75 - 79	1 000 148	457 065	543 083	...	...	...	...	...	...
80 - 84	745 065	320 082	424 983	...	...	...	...	...	...
85 - 89	478 671	180 616	298 055	...	...	...	...	...	...
90 - 94	222 416	68 168	154 248	...	...	...	...	...	...
95 - 99	50 411	10 609	39 802	...	...	...	...	...	...
100 +	6 951	835	6 116	...	...	...	...	...	...
Cayman Islands - Îles Caïmanes									
31 XII 2015 (ESDJ)									
Total	60 413	30 264	30 149	...	...	...	...	...	...
0 - 14	11 044	5 714	5 330	...	...	...	...	...	...
15 - 24	5 564	2 875	2 689	...	...	...	...	...	...
25 - 34	10 005	4 729	5 276	...	...	...	...	...	...
35 - 44	13 145	6 540	6 605	...	...	...	...	...	...
45 - 54	11 134	5 696	5 438	...	...	...	...	...	...
55 - 64	5 481	2 699	2 782	...	...	...	...	...	...
65 +	4 040	2 011	2 029	...	...	...	...	...	...
Costa Rica[19]									
1 VII 2015 (ESDJ)									
Total	4 833 752	2 350 223	2 483 529	3 512 683	1 683 770	1 828 913	1 321 069	666 453	654 616
0 - 4	324 321	163 390	160 931	223 057	115 008	108 049	101 264	48 382	52 882
5 - 9	364 016	186 361	177 655	259 570	130 740	128 830	104 446	55 621	48 825

7. Population by age, sex and urban/rural residence: latest available year, 2006 - 2015
Population selon l'âge, le sexe et la résidence, urbaine/rurale : dernière année disponible, 2006 - 2015 (continued - suite)

Continent, country or area, date, code[a] and age (in years) Continent, pays ou zone, date, code[a] et âge (en annèes)	Total			Urban - Urbaine			Rural - Rurale		
	Both sexes Les deux sexes	Male Masculin	Female Féminin	Both sexes Les deux sexes	Male Masculin	Female Féminin	Both sexes Les deux sexes	Male Masculin	Female Féminin
AMERICA, NORTH - AMÉRIQUE DU NORD									
Costa Rica[19]									
1 VII 2015 (ESDJ)									
10 - 14	373 074	183 371	189 703	254 484	123 538	130 946	118 590	59 833	58 757
15 - 19	423 603	215 969	207 634	297 810	150 260	147 550	125 793	65 709	60 084
20 - 24	434 188	215 559	218 629	319 295	158 359	160 936	114 893	57 200	57 693
25 - 29	412 308	205 655	206 653	308 049	154 959	153 090	104 259	50 696	53 563
30 - 34	365 082	174 288	190 794	270 181	128 717	141 464	94 901	45 571	49 330
35 - 39	334 646	160 352	174 294	247 737	118 323	129 414	86 909	42 029	44 880
40 - 44	299 980	139 163	160 817	219 629	101 015	118 614	80 351	38 148	42 203
45 - 49	310 532	143 259	167 273	224 447	100 559	123 888	86 085	42 700	43 385
50 - 54	304 825	144 506	160 319	223 779	104 881	118 898	81 046	39 625	41 421
55 - 59	250 885	119 940	130 945	185 242	86 672	98 570	65 643	33 268	32 375
60 - 64	192 726	91 721	101 005	146 327	65 282	81 045	46 399	26 439	19 960
65 - 69	151 382	70 286	81 096	114 512	51 929	62 583	36 870	18 357	18 513
70 - 74	101 016	49 371	51 645	72 127	32 181	39 946	28 889	17 190	11 699
75 - 79	81 510	37 772	43 738	61 183	26 562	34 621	20 327	11 210	9 117
80 - 84	53 174	25 035	28 139	41 371	18 190	23 181	11 803	6 845	4 958
85 - 89	32 695	13 786	18 909	24 555	9 102	15 453	8 140	4 684	3 456
90 - 94	13 853	6 172	7 681	11 431	4 294	7 137	2 422	1 878	544
95 - 99	5 079	1 677	3 402	3 500	967	2 533	1 579	710	869
Unknown - Inconnu	4 857	2 590	2 267	4 397	2 232	2 165	460	358	102
Cuba									
1 VII 2015 (ESDJ)									
Total	11 238 661	5 600 904	5 637 757	8 639 191	4 205 871	4 433 320	2 599 470	1 395 033	1 204 438
0	123 351	63 816	59 535	97 894	50 797	47 098	25 457	13 020	12 437
1 - 4	502 615	258 752	243 863	382 299	196 879	185 420	120 317	61 873	58 444
5 - 9	581 823	299 631	282 192	433 021	222 583	210 438	148 802	77 048	71 754
10 - 14	661 201	340 336	320 865	498 706	255 924	242 782	162 495	84 412	78 083
15 - 19	707 405	365 016	342 389	540 645	277 352	263 294	166 760	87 665	79 095
20 - 24	756 614	390 831	365 783	577 420	293 696	283 725	179 194	97 136	82 058
25 - 29	808 353	417 020	391 333	621 300	314 026	307 274	187 053	102 994	84 059
30 - 34	678 572	347 291	331 281	517 518	259 383	258 135	161 054	87 908	73 146
35 - 39	693 953	350 796	343 157	517 923	255 571	262 353	176 030	95 226	80 804
40 - 44	966 103	482 448	483 655	724 548	352 213	372 335	241 556	130 235	111 321
45 - 49	1 012 870	498 919	513 951	772 141	368 959	403 182	240 729	129 960	110 769
50 - 54	942 580	460 703	481 877	743 411	353 722	389 689	199 170	106 981	92 189
55 - 59	644 528	311 553	332 975	503 363	236 030	267 333	141 165	75 523	65 642
60 - 64	588 450	283 955	304 495	465 404	217 118	248 286	123 046	66 837	56 209
65 - 69	508 427	242 702	265 725	403 878	186 622	217 256	104 550	56 081	48 469
70 - 74	408 582	193 733	214 849	324 332	147 855	176 477	84 251	45 879	38 372
75 - 79	292 889	136 171	156 718	231 832	102 346	129 486	61 057	33 826	27 232
80 - 84	185 126	83 588	101 538	145 833	61 599	84 235	39 293	21 989	17 304
85 +	175 225	73 644	101 581	137 727	53 200	84 527	37 498	20 444	17 054
Curaçao[4]									
1 VII 2015 (ESDJ)									
Total	157 979	72 186	85 793	...	...	...	...	...	...
0	1 899	970	929	...	...	...	...	...	...
1 - 4	8 046	4 116	3 931	...	...	...	...	...	...
5 - 9	9 548	4 865	4 683	...	...	...	...	...	...
10 - 14	10 302	5 276	5 027	...	...	...	...	...	...
15 - 19	10 507	5 382	5 125	...	...	...	...	...	...
20 - 24	9 177	4 516	4 661	...	...	...	...	...	...
25 - 29	8 699	3 967	4 732	...	...	...	...	...	...
30 - 34	8 984	3 911	5 073	...	...	...	...	...	...
35 - 39	8 990	3 848	5 142	...	...	...	...	...	...
40 - 44	10 955	4 844	6 111	...	...	...	...	...	...
45 - 49	11 695	5 175	6 520	...	...	...	...	...	...
50 - 54	13 036	5 706	7 330	...	...	...	...	...	...
55 - 59	11 631	5 062	6 569	...	...	...	...	...	...
60 - 64	10 038	4 372	5 666	...	...	...	...	...	...
65 - 69	8 580	3 804	4 776	...	...	...	...	...	...
70 - 74	6 106	2 565	3 541	...	...	...	...	...	...
75 - 79	4 539	1 897	2 642	...	...	...	...	...	...
80 - 84	2 878	1 151	1 728	...	...	...	...	...	...

Continent, country or area, date, code[a] and age (in years) / Continent, pays ou zone, date, code[a] et âge (en annèes)	Total			Urban - Urbaine			Rural - Rurale		
	Both sexes Les deux sexes	Male Masculin	Female Féminin	Both sexes Les deux sexes	Male Masculin	Female Féminin	Both sexes Les deux sexes	Male Masculin	Female Féminin
AMERICA, NORTH - AMÉRIQUE DU NORD									
Curaçao[4]									
1 VII 2015 (ESDJ)									
85 - 89	1 520	532	989	...	...	...	...	...	...
90 - 94	649	191	458	...	...	...	...	...	...
95 - 99	170	29	141	...	...	...	...	...	...
100 +	35	12	23	...	...	...	...	...	...
Dominica - Dominique									
31 XII 2006 (ESDF)									
Total	71 180	36 238	34 942	...	...	...	...	...	...
0 - 4	6 317	3 250	3 067	...	...	...	...	...	...
5 - 9	7 554	3 951	3 603	...	...	...	...	...	...
10 - 14	7 105	3 558	3 547	...	...	...	...	...	...
15 - 19	6 818	3 452	3 366	...	...	...	...	...	...
20 - 24	4 578	2 438	2 140	...	...	...	...	...	...
25 - 29	5 121	2 601	2 520	...	...	...	...	...	...
30 - 34	5 663	2 886	2 777	...	...	...	...	...	...
35 - 39	5 296	2 841	2 455	...	...	...	...	...	...
40 - 44	4 476	2 417	2 059	...	...	...	...	...	...
45 - 49	3 561	1 947	1 614	...	...	...	...	...	...
50 - 54	2 820	1 467	1 353	...	...	...	...	...	...
55 - 59	2 391	1 209	1 182	...	...	...	...	...	...
60 - 64	2 255	1 022	1 233	...	...	...	...	...	...
65 - 69	2 324	1 091	1 233	...	...	...	...	...	...
70 - 74	1 844	871	973	...	...	...	...	...	...
75 - 79	1 332	596	736	...	...	...	...	...	...
80 - 84	901	354	547	...	...	...	...	...	...
85 +	825	288	537	...	...	...	...	...	...
Dominican Republic - République dominicaine[2]									
1 VII 2015 (ESDF)									
Total	9 980 243	4 991 398	4 988 845	7 854 203	3 858 029	3 996 174	2 126 040	1 133 369	992 671
0 - 4	973 795	496 880	476 915	763 008	387 863	375 145	210 787	109 017	101 770
5 - 9	967 269	492 695	474 574	752 046	380 705	371 341	215 223	111 990	103 233
10 - 14	981 483	498 031	483 452	763 114	383 084	380 030	218 369	114 947	103 422
15 - 19	949 228	478 646	470 582	745 262	369 734	375 528	203 966	108 912	95 054
20 - 24	908 335	455 186	453 149	722 178	354 909	367 269	186 157	100 277	85 880
25 - 29	830 004	413 051	416 953	665 299	324 724	340 575	164 705	88 327	76 378
30 - 34	743 334	367 374	375 960	595 753	289 178	306 575	147 581	78 196	69 385
35 - 39	668 488	329 386	339 102	533 971	258 258	275 713	134 517	71 128	63 389
40 - 44	600 405	296 087	304 318	478 192	231 120	247 072	122 213	64 967	57 246
45 - 49	539 125	266 932	272 193	427 994	206 995	220 999	111 131	59 937	51 194
50 - 54	476 771	237 114	239 657	376 979	182 726	194 253	99 792	54 388	45 404
55 - 59	390 663	194 161	196 502	305 626	147 516	158 110	85 037	46 645	38 392
60 - 64	308 197	151 664	156 543	238 347	113 506	124 841	69 850	38 148	31 702
65 - 69	228 216	112 944	115 272	173 855	82 928	90 927	54 361	30 016	24 345
70 - 74	163 853	80 449	83 404	123 906	58 376	65 530	39 947	22 073	17 874
75 - 79	122 605	59 603	63 002	92 123	42 709	49 414	30 482	16 894	13 588
80 +	128 472	61 205	67 267	96 550	43 698	52 852	31 922	17 507	14 415
El Salvador									
12 V 2007 (CDJC)									
Total	5 744 113	2 719 371	3 024 742	3 598 836	1 676 313	1 922 523	2 145 277	1 043 058	1 102 219
0 - 4	555 893	283 272	272 621	324 299	165 397	158 902	231 594	117 875	113 719
5 - 9	684 727	349 150	335 577	390 873	199 184	191 689	293 854	149 966	143 888
10 - 14	706 347	359 523	346 824	404 755	205 222	199 533	301 592	154 301	147 291
15 - 19	600 565	298 384	302 181	355 376	174 488	180 888	245 189	123 896	121 293
20 - 24	486 542	228 001	258 541	309 107	143 779	165 328	177 435	84 222	93 213
25 - 29	457 890	206 963	250 927	306 456	138 320	168 136	151 434	68 643	82 791
30 - 34	402 249	178 400	223 849	274 037	121 278	152 759	128 212	57 122	71 090
35 - 39	353 147	156 514	196 633	242 566	106 882	135 684	110 581	49 632	60 949
40 - 44	303 631	132 218	171 413	209 958	90 559	119 399	93 673	41 659	52 014
45 - 49	252 122	109 957	142 165	170 464	73 027	97 437	81 658	36 930	44 728
50 - 54	215 734	95 275	120 459	143 882	62 014	81 868	71 852	33 261	38 591
55 - 59	183 075	81 718	101 357	119 193	51 574	67 619	63 882	30 144	33 738
60 - 64	151 864	68 207	83 657	97 101	41 821	55 280	54 763	26 386	28 377

7. Population by age, sex and urban/rural residence: latest available year, 2006 - 2015
Population selon l'âge, le sexe et la résidence, urbaine/rurale : dernière année disponible, 2006 - 2015 (continued - suite)

Continent, country or area, date, code[a] and age (in years) / Continent, pays ou zone, date, code[a] et âge (en années)	Total			Urban - Urbaine			Rural - Rurale		
	Both sexes Les deux sexes	Male Masculin	Female Féminin	Both sexes Les deux sexes	Male Masculin	Female Féminin	Both sexes Les deux sexes	Male Masculin	Female Féminin
AMERICA, NORTH - AMÉRIQUE DU NORD									
El Salvador									
12 V 2007 (CDJC)									
65 - 69	125 157	55 781	69 376	79 690	33 492	46 198	45 467	22 289	23 178
70 - 74	97 457	43 449	54 008	62 075	25 726	36 349	35 382	17 723	17 659
75 - 79	75 984	33 658	42 326	48 760	20 096	28 664	27 224	13 562	13 662
80 - 84	46 870	20 401	26 469	30 578	12 261	18 317	16 292	8 140	8 152
85 +	44 859	18 500	26 359	29 666	11 193	18 473	15 193	7 307	7 886
1 VII 2015 (ESDF)[20]									
Total	6 460 271	3 042 036	3 418 235	...	...	...	...	...	...
0	112 144	57 382	54 762	...	...	...	...	...	...
1 - 4	449 672	229 847	219 825	...	...	...	...	...	...
5 - 9	578 687	295 801	282 886	...	...	...	...	...	...
10 - 14	644 362	329 480	314 882	...	...	...	...	...	...
15 - 19	711 346	361 195	350 151	...	...	...	...	...	...
20 - 24	680 843	337 349	343 494	...	...	...	...	...	...
25 - 29	547 691	255 214	292 477	...	...	...	...	...	...
30 - 34	445 367	194 627	250 740	...	...	...	...	...	...
35 - 39	396 379	168 962	227 417	...	...	...	...	...	...
40 - 44	368 590	158 058	210 532	...	...	...	...	...	...
45 - 49	325 570	139 988	185 582	...	...	...	...	...	...
50 - 54	275 901	118 189	157 712	...	...	...	...	...	...
55 - 59	230 362	98 962	131 400	...	...	...	...	...	...
60 - 64	195 220	84 278	110 942	...	...	...	...	...	...
65 - 69	160 195	69 285	90 910	...	...	...	...	...	...
70 - 74	127 212	54 925	72 287	...	...	...	...	...	...
75 - 79	96 576	41 333	55 243	...	...	...	...	...	...
80 - 84	63 234	26 565	36 669	...	...	...	...	...	...
85 +	50 920	20 596	30 324	...	...	...	...	...	...
Greenland - Groenland[21]									
1 VII 2015 (ESDJ)									
Total	56 114	29 634	26 480	48 284	25 329	22 955	7 830	4 305	3 525
0	791	397	394	670	334	336	121	63	58
1 - 4	3 092	1 619	1 473	2 659	1 387	1 272	433	232	201
5 - 9	3 942	2 050	1 892	3 340	1 754	1 586	602	296	306
10 - 14	3 998	2 019	1 979	3 370	1 706	1 664	628	313	315
15 - 19	4 015	2 013	2 002	3 404	1 709	1 695	611	304	307
20 - 24	4 451	2 279	2 172	3 831	1 944	1 887	620	335	285
25 - 29	4 465	2 258	2 207	3 901	1 956	1 945	564	302	262
30 - 34	4 026	2 065	1 961	3 548	1 785	1 763	478	280	198
35 - 39	3 268	1 769	1 499	2 870	1 546	1 324	398	223	175
40 - 44	3 092	1 706	1 386	2 669	1 473	1 196	423	233	190
45 - 49	4 867	2 601	2 266	4 182	2 215	1 967	685	386	299
50 - 54	5 036	2 710	2 326	4 357	2 324	2 033	679	386	293
55 - 59	3 930	2 237	1 693	3 378	1 904	1 474	552	333	219
60 - 64	2 797	1 597	1 200	2 378	1 332	1 046	419	265	154
65 - 69	1 754	1 049	705	1 519	897	622	235	152	83
70 - 74	1 357	721	636	1 157	613	544	200	108	92
75 - 79	690	324	366	579	263	316	111	61	50
80 - 84	370	153	217	317	129	188	53	24	29
85 - 89	144	55	89	128	48	80	16	7	9
90 - 94	26	11	15	24	9	15	2	2	-
95 - 99	3	1	2	3	1	2	-	-	-
Guadeloupe[22]									
1 I 2015* (ESDJ)									
Total	400 132	184 093	216 039	...	...	...	...	...	...
0 - 4	22 486	11 340	11 146	...	...	...	...	...	...
5 - 9	27 314	13 768	13 546	...	...	...	...	...	...
10 - 14	29 880	15 235	14 645	...	...	...	...	...	...
15 - 19	27 984	13 958	14 026	...	...	...	...	...	...
20 - 24	19 810	10 075	9 735	...	...	...	...	...	...
25 - 29	17 916	8 209	9 707	...	...	...	...	...	...
30 - 34	19 782	8 202	11 580	...	...	...	...	...	...
35 - 39	22 009	8 909	13 100	...	...	...	...	...	...
40 - 44	29 714	12 730	16 984	...	...	...	...	...	...

Continent, country or area, date, code[a] and age (in years) Continent, pays ou zone, date, code[a] et âge (en années)	Total			Urban - Urbaine			Rural - Rurale		
	Both sexes Les deux sexes	Male Masculin	Female Féminin	Both sexes Les deux sexes	Male Masculin	Female Féminin	Both sexes Les deux sexes	Male Masculin	Female Féminin
AMERICA, NORTH - AMÉRIQUE DU NORD									
Guadeloupe[22]									
1 I 2015* (ESDJ)									
45 - 49	31 605	14 033	17 572	...	...	...	...	...	...
50 - 54	32 622	15 111	17 511	...	...	...	...	...	...
55 - 59	28 345	13 218	15 127	...	...	...	...	...	...
60 - 64	24 520	11 072	13 448	...	...	...	...	...	...
65 - 69	20 939	9 554	11 385	...	...	...	...	...	...
70 - 74	15 700	7 100	8 600	...	...	...	...	...	...
75 - 79	11 923	5 274	6 649	...	...	...	...	...	...
80 - 84	8 620	3 391	5 229	...	...	...	...	...	...
85 - 89	5 224	1 817	3 407	...	...	...	...	...	...
90 - 94	2 633	803	1 830	...	...	...	...	...	...
95 +	1 106	294	812	...	...	...	...	...	...
Guatemala[14]									
1 VII 2010 (ESDF)									
Total	14 361 666	7 003 337	7 358 328	...	...	...	...	...	...
0 - 4	2 165 745	1 103 521	1 062 224	...	...	...	...	...	...
5 - 9	2 004 670	1 017 180	987 490	...	...	...	...	...	...
10 - 14	1 798 262	906 603	891 659	...	...	...	...	...	...
15 - 19	1 590 147	794 459	795 688	...	...	...	...	...	...
20 - 24	1 322 125	646 911	675 214	...	...	...	...	...	...
25 - 29	1 128 960	538 214	590 746	...	...	...	...	...	...
30 - 34	913 192	418 535	494 657	...	...	...	...	...	...
35 - 39	725 691	323 010	402 681	...	...	...	...	...	...
40 - 44	580 303	258 454	321 849	...	...	...	...	...	...
45 - 49	475 449	215 304	260 145	...	...	...	...	...	...
50 - 54	393 702	182 662	211 040	...	...	...	...	...	...
55 - 59	350 124	165 910	184 214	...	...	...	...	...	...
60 - 64	292 331	139 395	152 936	...	...	...	...	...	...
65 - 69	214 491	103 433	111 058	...	...	...	...	...	...
70 - 74	170 028	81 809	88 219	...	...	...	...	...	...
75 - 79	128 990	60 257	68 733	...	...	...	...	...	...
80 +	107 456	47 678	59 778	...	...	...	...	...	...
Haiti - Haïti[23]									
1 VII 2010 (ESDJ)									
Total	10 085 214	4 993 731	5 091 483	4 817 666	2 321 608	2 496 059	5 267 548	2 672 123	2 595 424
0 - 4	1 263 322	644 550	618 772	532 352	274 597	257 755	730 970	369 953	361 017
5 - 9	1 195 479	608 495	586 984	493 368	249 982	243 386	702 111	358 513	343 598
10 - 14	1 158 478	588 618	569 860	532 573	255 002	277 571	625 905	333 616	292 289
15 - 19	1 092 364	551 467	540 897	583 183	276 258	306 925	509 181	275 209	233 972
20 - 24	1 019 589	509 042	510 547	600 175	296 233	303 943	419 414	212 809	206 604
25 - 29	919 636	454 123	465 513	537 063	267 198	269 865	382 573	186 925	195 648
30 - 34	702 596	340 518	362 078	390 054	189 432	200 622	312 542	151 086	161 456
35 - 39	548 004	261 157	286 847	272 855	128 575	144 280	275 149	132 582	142 567
40 - 44	488 482	235 182	253 300	225 057	106 072	118 985	263 425	129 110	134 315
45 - 49	423 377	204 077	219 300	179 712	81 240	98 472	243 665	122 837	120 828
50 - 54	342 913	166 418	176 495	138 580	61 854	76 726	204 333	104 564	99 769
55 - 59	284 731	136 034	148 697	107 391	46 062	61 329	177 340	89 972	87 368
60 - 64	206 835	95 939	110 896	73 562	29 974	43 588	133 273	65 965	67 308
65 - 69	175 898	81 854	94 044	61 671	24 975	36 696	114 227	56 879	57 348
70 - 74	129 436	58 181	71 255	44 448	17 100	27 347	84 988	41 081	43 908
75 - 79	80 898	35 538	45 360	27 630	10 473	17 158	53 268	25 065	28 202
80 +	53 176	22 538	30 638	17 992	6 581	11 412	35 184	15 957	19 226
1 VII 2011 (ESDJ)									
Total	10 248 306	5 075 517	5 172 789	...	...	...	...	...	...
0 - 4	1 268 897	647 465	621 432	...	...	...	...	...	...
5 - 9	1 201 161	611 472	589 690	...	...	...	...	...	...
10 - 14	1 163 085	591 018	572 066	...	...	...	...	...	...
15 - 19	1 100 883	556 085	544 798	...	...	...	...	...	...
20 - 24	1 029 132	514 235	514 898	...	...	...	...	...	...
25 - 29	940 847	465 396	475 451	...	...	...	...	...	...
30 - 34	737 993	358 927	379 066	...	...	...	...	...	...
35 - 39	566 936	270 574	296 362	...	...	...	...	...	...
40 - 44	495 026	237 754	257 273	...	...	...	...	...	...

Continent, country or area, date, code[a] and age (in years) / Continent, pays ou zone, date, code[a] et âge (en années)	Total			Urban - Urbaine			Rural - Rurale		
	Both sexes Les deux sexes	Male Masculin	Female Féminin	Both sexes Les deux sexes	Male Masculin	Female Féminin	Both sexes Les deux sexes	Male Masculin	Female Féminin
AMERICA, NORTH - AMÉRIQUE DU NORD									
Haiti - Haïti[23]									
1 VII 2011 (ESDJ)									
45 - 49	433 416	208 671	224 746	...	...	...	...	...	...
50 - 54	353 800	171 468	182 332	...	...	...	...	...	...
55 - 59	293 134	140 392	152 742	...	...	...	...	...	...
60 - 64	214 819	99 846	114 973	...	...	...	...	...	...
65 - 69	177 069	82 201	94 868	...	...	...	...	...	...
70 - 74	132 790	59 833	72 957	...	...	...	...	...	...
75 - 79	83 834	36 751	47 083	...	...	...	...	...	...
80 +	55 484	23 431	32 053	...	...	...	...	...	...
Honduras									
10 VIII 2013 (CDFC)									
Total	8 303 771	4 052 316	4 251 456	4 480 746	2 116 113	2 364 633	3 823 025	1 936 203	1 886 823
0 - 4	971 015	494 034	476 980	485 103	247 341	237 762	485 911	246 693	239 218
5 - 9	958 543	489 821	468 723	472 721	240 952	231 769	485 823	248 868	236 954
10 - 14	1 020 406	520 842	499 564	499 521	251 358	248 163	520 885	269 485	251 400
15 - 19	982 164	487 949	494 215	523 989	248 745	275 244	458 175	239 204	218 971
20 - 24	840 800	398 093	442 708	483 289	219 539	263 750	357 511	178 554	178 957
25 - 29	656 443	303 379	353 065	384 221	171 360	212 861	272 222	132 019	140 203
30 - 34	567 367	262 951	304 416	329 661	147 590	182 072	237 705	115 361	122 344
35 - 39	484 740	224 965	259 775	277 833	124 524	153 309	206 907	100 441	106 465
40 - 44	399 555	190 323	209 232	231 557	106 187	125 370	167 998	84 135	83 862
45 - 49	318 026	150 635	167 391	183 503	84 007	99 495	134 524	66 628	67 896
50 - 54	293 256	141 174	152 082	167 798	77 351	90 447	125 458	63 823	61 636
55 - 59	210 708	101 062	109 646	116 409	53 286	63 124	94 299	47 777	46 522
60 - 64	189 636	91 291	98 345	103 821	47 002	56 819	85 815	44 290	41 526
65 - 69	135 709	64 441	71 267	72 921	32 263	40 657	62 788	32 178	30 610
70 - 74	106 566	51 803	54 762	57 407	25 756	31 650	49 159	26 047	23 112
75 - 79	78 407	38 419	39 988	41 388	18 486	22 902	37 019	19 933	17 086
80 - 84	48 965	22 977	25 988	26 407	11 230	15 177	22 558	11 748	10 810
85 - 89	29 532	13 681	15 851	16 153	6 682	9 471	13 380	7 000	6 380
90 - 94	8 241	3 162	5 079	4 867	1 717	3 150	3 374	1 445	1 929
95 +	3 692	1 313	2 379	2 177	738	1 439	1 515	575	940
Jamaica - Jamaïque									
4 IV 2011 (CDJC)									
Total	2 697 983	1 334 533	1 363 450	1 454 151	700 957	753 194	1 243 832	633 576	610 256
0 - 4	209 871	106 107	103 764	109 121	55 157	53 965	100 750	50 950	49 799
5 - 9	226 378	114 792	111 586	114 520	57 817	56 703	111 858	56 975	54 883
10 - 14	266 586	136 183	130 403	138 596	70 428	68 168	127 990	65 755	62 235
15 - 19	274 658	139 777	134 881	143 644	72 173	71 471	131 014	67 604	63 410
20 - 24	250 711	125 243	125 468	140 770	68 692	72 078	109 941	56 551	53 390
25 - 29	226 120	109 919	116 201	129 961	61 980	67 981	96 159	47 939	48 220
30 - 34	185 495	87 810	97 685	106 228	49 452	56 776	79 267	38 358	40 909
35 - 39	183 756	86 647	97 109	103 560	47 408	56 152	80 196	39 239	40 957
40 - 44	173 924	85 656	88 268	97 069	46 377	50 693	76 855	39 279	37 575
45 - 49	155 389	79 201	76 188	88 044	41 385	46 658	67 345	37 816	29 530
50 - 54	137 895	67 297	70 598	74 271	34 341	39 930	63 624	32 956	30 668
55 - 59	100 798	50 717	50 081	54 090	26 020	28 070	46 708	24 697	22 011
60 - 64	88 057	44 407	43 650	46 868	22 549	24 319	41 189	21 858	19 331
65 - 69	65 164	32 543	32 621	33 182	15 691	17 491	31 982	16 852	15 130
70 - 74	51 276	24 627	26 649	25 354	11 785	13 569	25 922	12 842	13 080
75 - 79	42 762	19 847	22 915	20 542	9 085	11 458	22 220	10 762	11 457
80 - 84	30 738	13 258	17 480	14 941	6 132	8 809	15 797	7 126	8 671
85 - 89	18 457	7 267	11 190	8 789	3 151	5 638	9 668	4 116	5 552
90 - 94	6 921	2 303	4 618	3 238	957	2 281	3 683	1 346	2 337
95 - 99	2 503	808	1 695	1 119	326	793	1 384	482	902
100 +	524	124	400	243	53	190	281	71	210
Martinique									
1 I 2013 (ESDJ)									
Total	385 436	178 368	207 068	...	...	...	...	...	...
0 - 4	21 311	10 993	10 318	...	...	...	...	...	...
5 - 9	23 817	11 959	11 858	...	...	...	...	...	...
10 - 14	26 902	13 726	13 175	...	...	...	...	...	...
15 - 19	25 606	13 096	12 510	...	...	...	...	...	...

Continent, country or area, date, code[a] and age (in years) Continent, pays ou zone, date, code[a] et âge (en années)	Total			Urban - Urbaine			Rural - Rurale		
	Both sexes Les deux sexes	Male Masculin	Female Féminin	Both sexes Les deux sexes	Male Masculin	Female Féminin	Both sexes Les deux sexes	Male Masculin	Female Féminin
AMERICA, NORTH - AMÉRIQUE DU NORD									
Martinique									
1 I 2013 (ESDJ)									
20 - 24	20 195	10 409	9 787	...	...	...	...	...	...
25 - 29	18 341	8 122	10 220	...	...	...	...	...	...
30 - 34	17 930	7 568	10 362	...	...	...	...	...	...
35 - 39	22 410	9 300	13 109	...	...	...	...	...	...
40 - 44	28 728	12 630	16 098	...	...	...	...	...	...
45 - 49	32 231	14 324	17 907	...	...	...	...	...	...
50 - 54	31 380	14 450	16 929	...	...	...	...	...	...
55 - 59	27 120	12 675	14 445	...	...	...	...	...	...
60 - 64	23 565	10 737	12 828	...	...	...	...	...	...
65 - 69	18 818	8 920	9 898	...	...	...	...	...	...
70 - 74	15 047	6 749	8 298	...	...	...	...	...	...
75 - 79	13 281	5 691	7 590	...	...	...	...	...	...
80 - 84	9 142	3 792	5 349	...	...	...	...	...	...
85 - 89	5 780	2 102	3 678	...	...	...	...	...	...
90 - 94	2 672	826	1 846	...	...	...	...	...	...
95 +	1 161	299	862	...	...	...	...	...	...
Mexico - Mexique									
12 VI 2010 (CDFC)[24]									
Total	112 336 538	54 855 231	57 481 307	86 287 410	41 946 540	44 340 870	26 049 128	12 908 691	13 140 437
0 - 4	10 528 322	5 346 943	5 181 379	7 766 149	3 945 636	3 820 513	2 762 173	1 401 307	1 360 866
5 - 9	11 047 537	5 604 175	5 443 362	8 124 337	4 124 524	3 999 813	2 923 200	1 479 651	1 443 549
10 - 14	10 939 937	5 547 613	5 392 324	7 974 649	4 041 649	3 933 000	2 965 288	1 505 964	1 459 324
15 - 19	11 026 112	5 520 121	5 505 991	8 191 229	4 097 876	4 093 353	2 834 883	1 422 245	1 412 638
20 - 24	9 892 271	4 813 204	5 079 067	7 725 598	3 775 245	3 950 353	2 166 673	1 037 959	1 128 714
25 - 29	8 788 177	4 205 975	4 582 202	6 985 279	3 354 569	3 630 710	1 802 898	851 406	951 492
30 - 34	8 470 798	4 026 031	4 444 767	6 719 047	3 188 789	3 530 258	1 751 751	837 242	914 509
35 - 39	8 292 987	3 964 738	4 328 249	6 642 253	3 160 713	3 481 540	1 650 734	804 025	846 709
40 - 44	7 009 226	3 350 322	3 658 904	5 633 205	2 676 230	2 956 975	1 376 021	674 092	701 929
45 - 49	5 928 730	2 824 364	3 104 366	4 739 911	2 241 753	2 498 158	1 188 819	582 611	606 208
50 - 54	5 064 291	2 402 451	2 661 840	4 051 487	1 904 317	2 147 170	1 012 804	498 134	514 670
55 - 59	3 895 365	1 869 537	2 025 828	3 043 924	1 443 868	1 600 056	851 441	425 669	425 772
60 - 64	3 116 466	1 476 667	1 639 799	2 403 645	1 119 077	1 284 568	712 821	357 590	355 231
65 - 69	2 317 265	1 095 273	1 221 992	1 719 078	794 137	924 941	598 187	301 136	297 051
70 - 74	1 873 934	873 893	1 000 041	1 338 906	603 945	734 961	535 028	269 948	265 080
75 - 79	1 245 483	579 689	665 794	892 237	399 026	493 211	353 246	180 663	172 583
80 - 84	798 936	355 277	443 659	576 855	244 082	332 773	222 081	111 195	110 886
85 - 89	454 164	197 461	256 703	322 844	132 826	190 018	131 320	64 635	66 685
90 - 94	164 924	68 130	96 794	116 950	45 123	71 827	47 974	23 007	24 967
95 - 99	65 732	25 920	39 812	44 084	16 122	27 962	21 648	9 798	11 850
100 +	18 475	7 228	11 247	10 451	3 753	6 698	8 024	3 475	4 549
Unknown - Inconnu	1 397 406	700 219	697 187	1 265 292	633 280	632 012	132 114	66 939	65 175
1 VII 2015 (ESDJ)[2]									
Total	121 005 815	59 046 837	61 958 979	87 743 091	...	...	33 262 724	...	...
0	2 214 862	1 133 112	1 081 751	...	...	...	...	...	...
1 - 4	8 833 799	4 520 299	4 313 500	...	...	...	...	...	...
5 - 9	11 176 409	5 717 937	5 458 472	...	...	...	...	...	...
10 - 14	11 221 624	5 723 530	5 498 094	...	...	...	...	...	...
15 - 19	11 155 572	5 633 722	5 521 851	...	...	...	...	...	...
20 - 24	10 684 869	5 278 771	5 406 098	...	...	...	...	...	...
25 - 29	9 772 276	4 713 860	5 058 416	...	...	...	...	...	...
30 - 34	9 110 739	4 319 749	4 790 990	...	...	...	...	...	...
35 - 39	8 695 538	4 098 711	4 596 828	...	...	...	...	...	...
40 - 44	8 080 597	3 820 465	4 260 132	...	...	...	...	...	...
45 - 49	7 123 933	3 375 572	3 748 360	...	...	...	...	...	...
50 - 54	5 958 613	2 817 100	3 141 512	...	...	...	...	...	...
55 - 59	4 891 188	2 308 076	2 583 112	...	...	...	...	...	...
60 - 64	3 829 505	1 807 535	2 021 971	...	...	...	...	...	...
65 - 69	2 860 546	1 341 979	1 518 568	...	...	...	...	...	...
70 - 74	2 104 035	974 242	1 129 794	...	...	...	...	...	...
75 - 79	1 473 908	671 906	802 002	...	...	...	...	...	...
80 - 84	958 353	428 041	530 311	...	...	...	...	...	...
85 - 89	530 900	229 071	301 829	...	...	...	...	...	...

Continent, country or area, date, code[a] and age (in years) / Continent, pays ou zone, date, code[a] et âge (en années)	Total			Urban - Urbaine			Rural - Rurale		
	Both sexes Les deux sexes	Male Masculin	Female Féminin	Both sexes Les deux sexes	Male Masculin	Female Féminin	Both sexes Les deux sexes	Male Masculin	Female Féminin
AMERICA, NORTH - AMÉRIQUE DU NORD									
Mexico - Mexique									
1 VII 2015 (ESDJ)[2]									
90 - 94	233 929	96 460	137 469	...	...	...	...	...	...
95 - 99	75 439	29 618	45 821	...	...	...	...	...	...
100 +	19 180	7 082	12 098	...	...	...	...	...	...
Montserrat									
12 V 2011 (CDJC)									
Total	4 922	2 546	2 376	...	...	...	...	...	...
0 - 4	301	157	144	...	...	...	...	...	...
5 - 9	311	146	165	...	...	...	...	...	...
10 - 14	359	187	172	...	...	...	...	...	...
15 - 19	319	179	140	...	...	...	...	...	...
20 - 24	269	152	117	...	...	...	...	...	...
25 - 29	299	154	145	...	...	...	...	...	...
30 - 34	298	138	160	...	...	...	...	...	...
35 - 39	368	172	196	...	...	...	...	...	...
40 - 44	406	189	217	...	...	...	...	...	...
45 - 49	381	196	185	...	...	...	...	...	...
50 - 54	331	183	148	...	...	...	...	...	...
55 - 59	314	181	133	...	...	...	...	...	...
60 - 64	275	165	110	...	...	...	...	...	...
65 - 69	231	130	101	...	...	...	...	...	...
70 - 74	145	75	70	...	...	...	...	...	...
75 - 79	116	61	55	...	...	...	...	...	...
80 - 84	94	44	50	...	...	...	...	...	...
85 +	105	37	68	...	...	...	...	...	...
Nicaragua									
1 VII 2009 (ESDJ)									
Total	5 742 316	2 844 244	2 898 072	3 259 955	1 569 555	1 690 400	2 482 361	1 274 689	1 207 672
0 - 4	680 125	347 205	332 920	335 635	172 875	162 760	344 490	174 330	170 160
5 - 9	660 096	336 817	323 279	332 694	169 358	163 336	327 402	167 459	159 943
10 - 14	677 756	344 831	332 925	359 316	180 457	178 859	318 440	164 374	154 066
15 - 19	660 608	331 536	329 072	363 427	178 690	184 737	297 181	152 846	144 335
20 - 24	576 923	286 484	290 439	332 187	160 315	171 872	244 736	126 169	118 567
25 - 29	511 402	250 672	260 730	306 186	145 137	161 049	205 216	105 535	99 681
30 - 34	412 087	197 120	214 967	251 145	115 523	135 622	160 942	81 597	79 345
35 - 39	337 317	162 472	174 845	208 505	96 540	111 965	128 812	65 932	62 880
40 - 44	279 795	136 223	143 572	177 594	83 709	93 885	102 201	52 514	49 687
45 - 49	239 942	115 914	124 028	154 027	71 955	82 072	85 915	43 959	41 956
50 - 54	206 088	98 355	107 733	130 198	59 417	70 781	75 890	38 938	36 952
55 - 59	154 329	74 173	80 156	95 879	43 653	52 226	58 450	30 520	27 930
60 - 64	93 681	45 221	48 460	57 189	25 734	31 455	36 492	19 487	17 005
65 - 69	89 351	43 121	46 230	54 102	24 079	30 023	35 249	19 042	16 207
70 - 74	67 861	32 418	35 443	41 515	18 145	23 370	26 346	14 273	12 073
75 - 79	48 205	22 249	25 956	30 640	12 935	17 705	17 565	9 314	8 251
80 +	46 750	19 433	27 317	29 716	11 033	18 683	17 034	8 400	8 634
Panama[17]									
1 VII 2015 (ESDF)									
Total	3 975 404	1 995 695	1 979 709	2 707 838	1 331 207	1 376 631	1 267 566	664 488	603 078
0	74 426	38 036	36 390	46 340	23 725	22 615	28 086	14 311	13 775
1 - 4	295 579	150 996	144 583	180 987	92 559	88 428	114 592	58 437	56 155
5 - 9	362 768	185 219	177 549	220 388	112 525	107 863	142 380	72 694	69 686
10 - 14	358 651	183 004	175 647	218 162	110 844	107 318	140 489	72 160	68 329
15 - 19	345 556	176 060	169 496	217 902	109 247	108 655	127 654	66 813	60 841
20 - 24	323 080	163 902	159 178	213 955	107 074	106 881	109 125	56 828	52 297
25 - 29	310 893	157 066	153 827	213 567	105 572	107 995	97 326	51 494	45 832
30 - 34	298 533	150 699	147 834	216 815	107 304	109 511	81 718	43 395	38 323
35 - 39	285 652	143 948	141 704	213 868	106 562	107 306	71 784	37 386	34 398
40 - 44	270 190	135 557	134 633	203 436	100 517	102 919	66 754	35 040	31 714
45 - 49	241 273	120 509	120 764	183 200	89 033	94 167	58 073	31 476	26 597
50 - 54	207 085	102 807	104 278	156 259	75 336	80 923	50 826	27 471	23 355
55 - 59	168 288	82 805	85 483	124 863	59 316	65 547	43 425	23 489	19 936
60 - 64	131 310	63 888	67 422	94 465	43 693	50 772	36 845	20 195	16 650
65 - 69	101 172	48 696	52 476	68 972	31 119	37 853	32 200	17 577	14 623

Continent, country or area, date, code[a] and age (in years) / Continent, pays ou zone, date, code[a] et âge (en annèes)	Total			Urban - Urbaine			Rural - Rurale		
	Both sexes Les deux sexes	Male Masculin	Female Féminin	Both sexes Les deux sexes	Male Masculin	Female Féminin	Both sexes Les deux sexes	Male Masculin	Female Féminin
AMERICA, NORTH - AMÉRIQUE DU NORD									
Panama[17]									
1 VII 2015 (ESDF)									
70 - 74	76 627	36 342	40 285	50 171	22 092	28 079	26 456	14 250	12 206
75 - 79	54 802	25 486	29 316	35 422	15 090	20 332	19 380	10 396	8 984
80 - 84	35 778	16 203	19 575	24 460	9 994	14 466	11 318	6 209	5 109
85 +	...	...	...	24 606	9 605	15 001	9 135	4 867	4 268
85 - 89	20 446	8 956	11 490	...	...	...	...	...	...
90 - 94	9 496	3 994	5 502	...	...	...	...	...	...
95 - 99	3 217	1 296	1 921	...	...	...	...	...	...
100 +	582	226	356	...	...	...	...	...	...
Puerto Rico - Porto Rico[25]									
1 VII 2014 (ESDJ)									
Total	3 548 397	1 699 491	1 848 906	...	...	...	...	...	...
0	35 820	18 475	17 345	...	...	...	...	...	...
1 - 4	151 551	77 752	73 799	...	...	...	...	...	...
5 - 9	208 896	107 432	101 464	...	...	...	...	...	...
10 - 14	228 566	118 403	110 163	...	...	...	...	...	...
15 - 19	250 252	128 795	121 457	...	...	...	...	...	...
20 - 24	259 278	130 927	128 351	...	...	...	...	...	...
25 - 29	225 227	111 135	114 092	...	...	...	...	...	...
30 - 34	222 439	106 660	115 779	...	...	...	...	...	...
35 - 39	225 113	107 716	117 397	...	...	...	...	...	...
40 - 44	226 646	108 762	117 884	...	...	...	...	...	...
45 - 49	229 960	109 133	120 827	...	...	...	...	...	...
50 - 54	233 903	108 663	125 240	...	...	...	...	...	...
55 - 59	224 380	103 047	121 333	...	...	...	...	...	...
60 - 64	209 359	94 927	114 432	...	...	...	...	...	...
65 - 69	199 594	90 649	108 945	...	...	...	...	...	...
70 - 74	154 193	68 940	85 253	...	...	...	...	...	...
75 - 79	113 670	49 728	63 942	...	...	...	...	...	...
80 - 84	75 546	31 027	44 519	...	...	...	...	...	...
85 +	74 004	27 320	46 684	...	...	...	...	...	...
Saint Lucia - Sainte-Lucie									
1 VII 2009 (ESDF)									
Total	172 370	84 465	87 905	...	...	...	...	...	...
0 - 4	15 344	7 808	7 536	...	...	...	...	...	...
5 - 9	13 188	6 514	6 674	...	...	...	...	...	...
10 - 14	16 105	8 047	8 058	...	...	...	...	...	...
15 - 19	17 386	8 735	8 651	...	...	...	...	...	...
20 - 24	17 430	8 553	8 877	...	...	...	...	...	...
25 - 29	15 114	7 422	7 692	...	...	...	...	...	...
30 - 34	13 317	6 469	6 848	...	...	...	...	...	...
35 - 39	12 240	5 895	6 345	...	...	...	...	...	...
40 - 44	11 709	5 644	6 065	...	...	...	...	...	...
45 - 49	10 541	5 107	5 434	...	...	...	...	...	...
50 - 54	7 978	3 988	3 990	...	...	...	...	...	...
55 - 59	5 957	2 977	2 980	...	...	...	...	...	...
60 - 64	4 559	2 142	2 417	...	...	...	...	...	...
65 - 69	3 647	1 662	1 985	...	...	...	...	...	...
70 - 74	3 077	1 410	1 667	...	...	...	...	...	...
75 - 79	2 276	1 034	1 242	...	...	...	...	...	...
80 +	2 502	1 058	1 444	...	...	...	...	...	...
Saint Pierre and Miquelon - Saint Pierre-et-Miquelon									
19 I 2006 (CDFC)									
Total	6 125	3 034	3 091	...	...	...	...	...	...
0 - 4	289	143	146	...	...	...	...	...	...
5 - 9	417	211	206	...	...	...	...	...	...
10 - 14	461	237	224	...	...	...	...	...	...
15 - 19	366	188	178	...	...	...	...	...	...
20 - 24	258	136	122	...	...	...	...	...	...
25 - 29	333	166	167	...	...	...	...	...	...
30 - 34	431	202	229	...	...	...	...	...	...
35 - 39	568	294	274	...	...	...	...	...	...

7. Population by age, sex and urban/rural residence: latest available year, 2006 - 2015
Population selon l'âge, le sexe et la résidence, urbaine/rurale : dernière année disponible, 2006 - 2015 (continued - suite)

Continent, country or area, date, code[a] and age (in years) / Continent, pays ou zone, date, code[a] et âge (en annèes)	Total			Urban - Urbaine			Rural - Rurale		
	Both sexes Les deux sexes	Male Masculin	Female Féminin	Both sexes Les deux sexes	Male Masculin	Female Féminin	Both sexes Les deux sexes	Male Masculin	Female Féminin
AMERICA, NORTH - AMÉRIQUE DU NORD									
Saint Pierre and Miquelon - Saint Pierre-et-Miquelon									
19 I 2006 (CDFC)									
40 - 44	575	293	282	...	...	...	...	...	...
45 - 49	471	246	225	...	...	...	...	...	...
50 - 54	435	238	197	...	...	...	...	...	...
55 - 59	432	231	201	...	...	...	...	...	...
60 - 64	280	143	137	...	...	...	...	...	...
65 - 69	243	115	128	...	...	...	...	...	...
70 - 74	208	83	125	...	...	...	...	...	...
75 - 79	128	42	86	...	...	...	...	...	...
80 - 84	114	35	79	...	...	...	...	...	...
85 - 89	75	19	56	...	...	...	...	...	...
90 - 94	30	12	18	...	...	...	...	...	...
95 +	11	-	11	...	...	...	...	...	...
Saint Vincent and the Grenadines - Saint-Vincent-et-les Grenadines[26]									
1 VII 2008 (ESDF)									
Total	99 086	50 009	49 077	...	...	...	...	...	...
0 - 4	9 302	4 782	4 520	...	...	...	...	...	...
5 - 9	10 684	5 352	5 332	...	...	...	...	...	...
10 - 14	10 391	5 269	5 122	...	...	...	...	...	...
15 - 19	10 531	5 293	5 238	...	...	...	...	...	...
20 - 24	9 060	4 639	4 420	...	...	...	...	...	...
25 - 29	7 941	4 057	3 884	...	...	...	...	...	...
30 - 34	7 155	3 747	3 408	...	...	...	...	...	...
35 - 39	7 525	3 911	3 614	...	...	...	...	...	...
40 - 44	6 243	3 214	3 029	...	...	...	...	...	...
45 - 49	4 410	2 252	2 158	...	...	...	...	...	...
50 - 54	3 481	1 807	1 674	...	...	...	...	...	...
55 - 59	2 595	1 299	1 296	...	...	...	...	...	...
60 - 64	2 550	1 222	1 328	...	...	...	...	...	...
65 - 69	2 379	1 143	1 236	...	...	...	...	...	...
70 - 74	1 819	831	989	...	...	...	...	...	...
75 - 79	1 412	591	821	...	...	...	...	...	...
80 - 84	879	359	520	...	...	...	...	...	...
85 +	729	241	488	...	...	...	...	...	...
Sint Maarten (Dutch part) - Saint-Martin (partie néerlandaise)									
1 I 2013 (ESDJ)									
Total	36 090	17 661	18 429	...	...	...	...	...	...
0 - 4	2 352	1 235	1 117	...	...	...	...	...	...
5 - 9	2 531	1 289	1 242	...	...	...	...	...	...
10 - 14	2 692	1 348	1 344	...	...	...	...	...	...
15 - 19	2 469	1 302	1 167	...	...	...	...	...	...
20 - 24	2 161	1 047	1 114	...	...	...	...	...	...
25 - 29	2 462	1 161	1 300	...	...	...	...	...	...
30 - 34	2 816	1 290	1 526	...	...	...	...	...	...
35 - 39	3 142	1 452	1 689	...	...	...	...	...	...
40 - 44	3 259	1 556	1 703	...	...	...	...	...	...
45 - 49	3 360	1 693	1 667	...	...	...	...	...	...
50 - 54	2 790	1 345	1 445	...	...	...	...	...	...
55 - 59	2 295	1 127	1 167	...	...	...	...	...	...
60 - 64	1 690	835	854	...	...	...	...	...	...
65 - 69	990	490	500	...	...	...	...	...	...
70 - 74	516	258	258	...	...	...	...	...	...
75 - 79	289	143	147	...	...	...	...	...	...
80 - 84	146	51	95	...	...	...	...	...	...
85 +	130	37	93	...	...	...	...	...	...

Continent, country or area, date, code[a] and age (in years) / Continent, pays ou zone, date, code[a] et âge (en années)	Total			Urban - Urbaine			Rural - Rurale		
	Both sexes Les deux sexes	Male Masculin	Female Féminin	Both sexes Les deux sexes	Male Masculin	Female Féminin	Both sexes Les deux sexes	Male Masculin	Female Féminin
AMERICA, NORTH - AMÉRIQUE DU NORD									
Trinidad and Tobago - Trinité-et-Tobago[9]									
1 VII 2015 (ESDF)									
Total	1 349 667	677 166	672 501	...	...	...	...	...	...
0	17 042	8 775	8 268	...	...	...	...	...	...
1 - 4	78 613	39 852	38 761	...	...	...	...	...	...
5 - 9	92 820	47 135	45 685	...	...	...	...	...	...
10 - 14	89 397	45 686	43 711	...	...	...	...	...	...
15 - 19	99 983	50 519	49 463	...	...	...	...	...	...
20 - 24	116 102	58 343	57 759	...	...	...	...	...	...
25 - 29	125 531	63 283	62 248	...	...	...	...	...	...
30 - 34	107 301	54 776	52 525	...	...	...	...	...	...
35 - 39	94 047	47 626	46 422	...	...	...	...	...	...
40 - 44	87 568	44 200	43 368	...	...	...	...	...	...
45 - 49	97 681	49 479	48 202	...	...	...	...	...	...
50 - 54	88 605	44 698	43 907	...	...	...	...	...	...
55 - 59	74 408	37 318	37 091	...	...	...	...	...	...
60 - 64	59 603	30 128	29 475	...	...	...	...	...	...
65 - 69	45 366	21 935	23 431	...	...	...	...	...	...
70 - 74	30 782	14 441	16 341	...	...	...	...	...	...
75 - 79	21 087	9 437	11 650	...	...	...	...	...	...
80 +	23 731	9 537	14 194	...	...	...	...	...	...
United States of America - États-Unis d'Amérique									
1 IV 2010 (CDJC)									
Total	308 745 538	151 781 326	156 964 212	249 253 271	121 698 595	127 554 676	59 492 267	30 082 731	29 409 536
0 - 4	20 201 362	10 319 427	9 881 935	16 838 001	8 597 234	8 240 767	3 363 361	1 722 193	1 641 168
5 - 9	20 348 657	10 389 638	9 959 019	16 597 127	8 464 939	8 132 188	3 751 530	1 924 699	1 826 831
10 - 14	20 677 194	10 579 862	10 097 332	16 576 171	8 466 809	8 109 362	4 101 023	2 113 053	1 987 970
15 - 19	22 040 343	11 303 666	10 736 677	17 946 265	9 149 187	8 797 078	4 094 078	2 154 479	1 939 599
20 - 24	21 585 999	11 014 176	10 571 823	18 653 468	9 450 066	9 203 402	2 932 531	1 564 110	1 368 421
25 - 29	21 101 849	10 635 591	10 466 258	18 163 244	9 110 029	9 053 215	2 938 605	1 525 562	1 413 043
30 - 34	19 962 099	9 996 500	9 965 599	16 857 801	8 409 694	8 448 107	3 104 298	1 586 806	1 517 492
35 - 39	20 179 642	10 042 022	10 137 620	16 629 937	8 249 301	8 380 636	3 549 705	1 792 721	1 756 984
40 - 44	20 890 964	10 393 977	10 496 987	16 837 761	8 347 894	8 489 867	4 053 203	2 046 083	2 007 120
45 - 49	22 708 591	11 209 085	11 499 506	17 847 074	8 760 812	9 086 262	4 861 517	2 448 273	2 413 244
50 - 54	22 298 125	10 933 274	11 364 851	17 279 058	8 401 091	8 877 967	5 019 067	2 532 183	2 486 884
55 - 59	19 664 805	9 523 648	10 141 157	15 060 179	7 204 444	7 855 735	4 604 626	2 319 204	2 285 422
60 - 64	16 817 924	8 077 500	8 740 424	12 750 365	6 020 393	6 729 972	4 067 559	2 057 107	2 010 452
65 - 69	12 435 263	5 852 547	6 582 716	9 299 030	4 275 616	5 023 414	3 136 233	1 576 931	1 559 302
70 - 74	9 278 166	4 243 972	5 034 194	7 011 129	3 115 814	3 895 315	2 267 037	1 128 158	1 138 879
75 - 79	7 317 795	3 182 388	4 135 407	5 693 807	2 409 946	3 283 861	1 623 988	772 442	851 546
80 - 84	5 743 327	2 294 374	3 448 953	4 629 581	1 800 531	2 829 050	1 113 746	493 843	619 903
85 - 89	3 620 459	1 273 867	2 346 592	3 005 285	1 036 583	1 968 702	615 174	237 284	377 890
90 - 94	1 448 366	424 387	1 023 979	1 216 647	351 491	865 156	231 719	72 896	158 823
95 - 99	371 244	82 263	288 981	315 589	69 008	246 581	55 655	13 255	42 400
100 +	53 364	9 162	44 202	45 752	7 713	38 039	7 612	1 449	6 163
1 VII 2015 (ESDJ)[27]									
Total	321 418 820	158 229 297	163 189 523	...	...	...	...	...	...
0	3 978 038	2 035 134	1 942 904	...	...	...	...	...	...
1 - 4	15 929 243	8 142 467	7 786 776	...	...	...	...	...	...
5 - 9	20 487 176	10 459 132	10 028 044	...	...	...	...	...	...
10 - 14	20 622 330	10 520 388	10 101 942	...	...	...	...	...	...
15 - 19	21 108 903	10 797 867	10 311 036	...	...	...	...	...	...
20 - 24	22 739 313	11 667 854	11 071 459	...	...	...	...	...	...
25 - 29	22 461 554	11 409 399	11 052 155	...	...	...	...	...	...
30 - 34	21 675 648	10 889 739	10 785 909	...	...	...	...	...	...
35 - 39	20 374 585	10 173 424	10 201 161	...	...	...	...	...	...
40 - 44	20 215 198	10 030 153	10 185 045	...	...	...	...	...	...
45 - 49	20 853 844	10 334 929	10 518 915	...	...	...	...	...	...
50 - 54	22 334 317	10 963 847	11 370 470	...	...	...	...	...	...
55 - 59	21 807 942	10 597 567	11 210 375	...	...	...	...	...	...
60 - 64	19 069 877	9 117 180	9 952 697	...	...	...	...	...	...
65 - 69	16 067 468	7 596 190	8 471 278	...	...	...	...	...	...

7. Population by age, sex and urban/rural residence: latest available year, 2006 - 2015
Population selon l'âge, le sexe et la résidence, urbaine/rurale : dernière année disponible, 2006 - 2015 (continued - suite)

Continent, country or area, date, code[a] and age (in years) / Continent, pays ou zone, date, code[a] et âge (en années)	Total			Urban - Urbaine			Rural - Rurale		
	Both sexes Les deux sexes	Male Masculin	Female Féminin	Both sexes Les deux sexes	Male Masculin	Female Féminin	Both sexes Les deux sexes	Male Masculin	Female Féminin
AMERICA, NORTH - AMÉRIQUE DU NORD									
United States of America - États-Unis d'Amérique 1 VII 2015 (ESDJ)[27]									
70 - 74	11 483 049	5 296 158	6 186 891	...	...	...	...	...	...
75 - 79	8 123 833	3 610 906	4 512 927	...	...	...	...	...	...
80 - 84	5 799 341	2 412 665	3 386 676	...	...	...	...	...	...
85 - 89	3 864 345	1 442 244	2 422 101	...	...	...	...	...	...
90 - 94	1 850 935	588 978	1 261 957	...	...	...	...	...	...
95 - 99	494 907	127 988	366 919	...	...	...	...	...	...
100 +	76 974	15 088	61 886	...	...	...	...	...	...
United States Virgin Islands - Îles Vierges américaines[28] 1 IV 2010 (CDJC)									
Total	106 405	50 854	55 551	...	...	...	...	...	...
0 - 4	7 500	3 736	3 764	...	...	...	...	...	...
5 - 9	7 150	3 694	3 456	...	...	...	...	...	...
10 - 14	7 484	3 849	3 635	...	...	...	...	...	...
15 - 19	7 560	3 765	3 795	...	...	...	...	...	...
20 - 24	5 894	2 707	3 187	...	...	...	...	...	...
25 - 29	5 969	2 695	3 274	...	...	...	...	...	...
30 - 34	6 137	2 825	3 312	...	...	...	...	...	...
35 - 39	6 675	3 133	3 542	...	...	...	...	...	...
40 - 44	7 450	3 506	3 944	...	...	...	...	...	...
45 - 49	7 743	3 680	4 063	...	...	...	...	...	...
50 - 54	7 900	3 800	4 100	...	...	...	...	...	...
55 - 59	7 192	3 341	3 851	...	...	...	...	...	...
60 - 64	7 367	3 510	3 857	...	...	...	...	...	...
65 - 69	5 853	2 883	2 970	...	...	...	...	...	...
70 - 74	3 717	1 739	1 978	...	...	...	...	...	...
75 - 79	2 328	1 043	1 285	...	...	...	...	...	...
80 - 84	1 332	568	764	...	...	...	...	...	...
85 +	1 154	380	774	...	...	...	...	...	...
AMERICA, SOUTH - AMÉRIQUE DU SUD									
Argentina - Argentine[29] 1 VII 2015 (ESDF)									
Total	43 137 351	21 134 115	22 003 236	39 492 461	19 197 773	20 294 688	3 644 890	1 936 342	1 708 548
0 - 4	3 770 120	1 939 681	1 830 439	3 381 468	1 738 699	1 642 769	388 652	200 982	187 670
5 - 9	3 570 086	1 837 603	1 732 483	3 216 881	1 653 112	1 563 769	353 205	184 491	168 714
10 - 14	3 508 530	1 794 946	1 713 584	3 185 595	1 627 187	1 558 408	322 935	167 759	155 176
15 - 19	3 539 629	1 799 126	1 740 503	3 177 218	1 608 613	1 568 605	362 411	190 513	171 898
20 - 24	3 554 809	1 791 104	1 763 705	3 225 839	1 614 088	1 611 751	328 970	177 016	151 954
25 - 29	3 341 852	1 668 639	1 673 213	3 083 738	1 528 867	1 554 871	258 114	139 772	118 342
30 - 34	3 159 593	1 568 995	1 590 598	2 919 099	1 442 958	1 476 141	240 494	126 037	114 457
35 - 39	3 099 829	1 531 311	1 568 518	2 872 649	1 412 726	1 459 923	227 180	118 585	108 595
40 - 44	2 692 496	1 322 264	1 370 232	2 498 200	1 218 804	1 279 396	194 296	103 460	90 836
45 - 49	2 320 369	1 132 243	1 188 126	2 145 528	1 035 813	1 109 715	174 841	96 430	78 411
50 - 54	2 168 110	1 049 176	1 118 934	2 003 608	957 206	1 046 402	164 502	91 970	72 532
55 - 59	1 995 011	954 332	1 040 679	1 843 250	869 464	973 786	151 761	84 868	66 893
60 - 64	1 782 266	837 633	944 633	1 644 233	760 013	884 220	138 033	77 620	60 413
65 - 69	1 505 505	687 331	818 174	1 390 341	623 393	766 948	115 164	63 938	51 226
70 - 74	1 158 120	504 788	653 332	1 069 750	456 603	613 147	88 370	48 185	40 185
75 - 79	854 994	345 288	509 706	791 062	311 951	479 111	63 932	33 337	30 595
80 - 84	591 451	215 440	376 011	551 052	196 169	354 883	40 399	19 271	21 128
85 - 89	341 807	107 102	234 705	320 269	98 339	221 930	21 538	8 763	12 775
90 - 94	141 747	38 174	103 573	133 788	35 408	98 380	7 959	2 766	5 193
95 - 99	35 100	7 868	27 232	33 327	7 364	25 963	1 773	504	1 269
100 +	5 927	1 071	4 856	5 566	996	4 570	361	75	286

7. Population by age, sex and urban/rural residence: latest available year, 2006 - 2015
Population selon l'âge, le sexe et la résidence, urbaine/rurale : dernière année disponible, 2006 - 2015 (continued - suite)

Continent, country or area, date, code[a] and age (in years) / Continent, pays ou zone, date, code[a] et âge (en années)	Total			Urban - Urbaine			Rural - Rurale		
	Both sexes Les deux sexes	Male Masculin	Female Féminin	Both sexes Les deux sexes	Male Masculin	Female Féminin	Both sexes Les deux sexes	Male Masculin	Female Féminin
AMERICA, SOUTH - AMÉRIQUE DU SUD									
Bolivia (Plurinational State of) - Bolivie (État plurinational de)									
1 VII 2015 (ESDF)									
Total	10 825 013	5 456 332	5 368 681	7 403 841	3 661 290	3 742 551	3 421 172	1 795 042	1 626 130
0	244 188	124 101	120 087	163 454	83 068	80 386	80 734	41 033	39 701
1 - 4	971 455	494 738	476 717	649 545	330 432	319 113	321 910	164 306	157 604
5 - 9	1 202 705	613 613	589 092	793 130	403 199	389 931	409 575	210 414	199 161
10 - 14	1 168 034	595 352	572 682	778 269	392 933	385 336	389 765	202 419	187 346
15 - 19	1 095 489	558 008	537 481	751 938	376 645	375 293	343 551	181 363	162 188
20 - 24	998 835	507 402	491 433	715 211	354 396	360 815	283 624	153 006	130 618
25 - 29	899 584	455 622	443 962	656 320	322 980	333 340	243 264	132 642	110 622
30 - 34	806 815	407 615	399 200	590 274	290 065	300 209	216 541	117 550	98 991
35 - 39	693 830	350 020	343 810	500 301	244 918	255 383	193 529	105 102	88 427
40 - 44	580 557	292 156	288 401	409 541	199 501	210 040	171 016	92 655	78 361
45 - 49	484 347	243 008	241 339	332 762	161 596	171 166	151 585	81 412	70 173
50 - 54	406 544	203 445	203 099	273 496	132 950	140 546	133 048	70 495	62 553
55 - 59	341 122	169 799	171 323	220 977	106 683	114 294	120 145	63 116	57 029
60 - 64	280 440	138 363	142 077	175 850	84 173	91 677	104 590	54 190	50 400
65 - 69	223 061	108 950	114 111	137 429	65 015	72 414	85 632	43 935	41 697
70 - 74	168 757	81 027	87 730	102 526	47 636	54 890	66 231	33 391	32 840
75 - 79	116 432	53 672	62 760	70 022	31 313	38 709	46 410	22 359	24 051
80 - 84	78 554	34 240	44 314	46 259	19 641	26 618	32 295	14 599	17 696
85 - 89	43 747	17 968	25 779	25 099	10 107	14 992	18 648	7 861	10 787
90 - 94	16 506	6 052	10 454	9 243	3 376	5 867	7 263	2 676	4 587
95 +	4 011	1 181	2 830	2 195	663	1 532	1 816	518	1 298
Brazil - Brésil									
31 VII 2010 (CDJC)									
Total	190 755 799	93 406 990	97 348 809	160 925 804	77 710 179	83 215 625	29 829 995	15 696 811	14 133 184
0	2 713 244	1 378 532	1 334 712	2 246 034	1 141 784	1 104 250	467 210	236 748	230 462
1 - 4	11 082 914	5 638 455	5 444 459	9 055 114	4 603 340	4 451 774	2 027 800	1 035 115	992 685
5 - 9	14 969 375	7 624 144	7 345 231	12 135 285	6 169 531	5 965 754	2 834 090	1 454 613	1 379 477
10 - 14	17 166 761	8 725 413	8 441 348	13 956 987	7 062 057	6 894 930	3 209 774	1 663 356	1 546 418
15 - 19	16 990 872	8 558 868	8 432 004	14 039 001	6 998 102	7 040 899	2 951 871	1 560 766	1 391 105
20 - 24	17 245 192	8 630 229	8 614 963	14 706 068	7 276 963	7 429 105	2 539 124	1 353 266	1 185 858
25 - 29	17 104 414	8 460 995	8 643 419	14 772 957	7 225 732	7 547 225	2 331 457	1 235 263	1 096 194
30 - 34	15 744 512	7 717 658	8 026 854	13 611 921	6 586 877	7 025 044	2 132 591	1 130 781	1 001 810
35 - 39	13 888 579	6 766 664	7 121 915	11 975 407	5 750 498	6 224 909	1 913 172	1 016 166	897 006
40 - 44	13 009 364	6 320 568	6 688 796	11 187 429	5 344 982	5 842 447	1 821 935	975 586	846 349
45 - 49	11 833 352	5 692 014	6 141 338	10 181 394	4 806 322	5 375 072	1 651 958	885 692	766 266
50 - 54	10 140 402	4 834 995	5 305 407	8 708 339	4 074 679	4 633 660	1 432 063	760 316	671 747
55 - 59	8 276 221	3 902 344	4 373 877	7 025 474	3 238 531	3 786 943	1 250 747	663 813	586 934
60 - 64	6 509 120	3 041 035	3 468 085	5 474 944	2 479 882	2 995 062	1 034 176	561 153	473 023
65 - 69	4 840 810	2 224 065	2 616 745	4 040 016	1 792 798	2 247 218	800 794	431 267	369 527
70 - 74	3 741 636	1 667 372	2 074 264	3 142 173	1 349 329	1 792 844	599 463	318 043	281 420
75 - 79	2 563 447	1 090 517	1 472 930	2 174 038	889 908	1 284 130	389 409	200 609	188 800
80 - 84	1 666 972	668 623	998 349	1 423 603	546 865	876 738	243 369	121 758	121 611
85 - 89	819 483	310 759	508 724	695 385	251 112	444 273	124 098	59 647	64 451
90 - 94	326 558	114 964	211 594	273 348	90 960	182 388	53 210	24 004	29 206
95 - 99	98 335	31 529	66 806	81 121	24 365	56 756	17 214	7 164	10 050
100 +	24 236	7 247	16 989	19 766	5 562	14 204	4 470	1 685	2 785
1 VII 2015 (ESDF)[30]									
Total	204 450 649	100 955 522	103 495 127	...	...	...	...	...	...
0	2 878 344	1 472 923	1 405 421	...	...	...	...	...	...
1 - 4	11 859 396	6 065 132	5 794 264	...	...	...	...	...	...
5 - 9	15 779 109	8 062 852	7 716 257	...	...	...	...	...	...
10 - 14	16 892 243	8 616 189	8 276 054	...	...	...	...	...	...
15 - 19	17 140 200	8 710 123	8 430 077	...	...	...	...	...	...
20 - 24	17 056 423	8 622 007	8 434 416	...	...	...	...	...	...
25 - 29	17 176 808	8 634 055	8 542 753	...	...	...	...	...	...
30 - 34	17 637 407	8 816 331	8 821 076	...	...	...	...	...	...
35 - 39	15 856 255	7 879 629	7 976 626	...	...	...	...	...	...
40 - 44	13 944 226	6 882 205	7 062 021	...	...	...	...	...	...
45 - 49	12 802 397	6 266 080	6 536 317	...	...	...	...	...	...

Continent, country or area, date, code[a] and age (in years) Continent, pays ou zone, date, code[a] et âge (en années)	Total			Urban - Urbaine			Rural - Rurale		
	Both sexes Les deux sexes	Male Masculin	Female Féminin	Both sexes Les deux sexes	Male Masculin	Female Féminin	Both sexes Les deux sexes	Male Masculin	Female Féminin
AMERICA, SOUTH - AMÉRIQUE DU SUD									
Brazil - Brésil									
1 VII 2015 (ESDF)[30]									
50 - 54	11 687 344	5 659 620	6 027 724	...	...	...	...	...	...
55 - 59	9 799 612	4 678 733	5 120 879	...	...	...	...	...	...
60 - 64	7 797 050	3 655 012	4 142 038	...	...	...	...	...	...
65 - 69	5 844 703	2 672 038	3 172 665	...	...	...	...	...	...
70 - 74	4 076 511	1 793 495	2 283 016	...	...	...	...	...	...
75 - 79	2 913 596	1 222 314	1 691 282	...	...	...	...	...	...
80 - 84	1 796 449	710 926	1 085 523	...	...	...	...	...	...
85 - 89	973 943	361 970	611 973	...	...	...	...	...	...
90 +	538 633	173 888	364 745	...	...	...	...	...	...
Chile - Chili									
1 VII 2015 (ESDF)									
Total	18 006 407	8 911 940	9 094 467	15 729 803	7 714 356	8 015 447	2 276 604	1 197 584	1 079 020
0	248 803	126 633	122 170	218 946	111 541	107 405	29 857	15 092	14 765
1 - 4	987 752	503 250	484 502	884 998	451 199	433 799	102 754	52 051	50 703
5 - 9	1 222 682	623 590	599 092	1 102 437	562 596	539 841	120 245	60 994	59 251
10 - 14	1 207 255	615 595	591 660	1 060 415	540 855	519 560	146 840	74 740	72 100
15 - 19	1 323 480	676 381	647 099	1 146 678	585 672	561 006	176 802	90 709	86 093
20 - 24	1 460 830	743 660	717 170	1 259 054	639 686	619 368	201 776	103 974	97 802
25 - 29	1 498 935	757 921	741 014	1 309 526	658 103	651 423	189 409	99 818	89 591
30 - 34	1 357 954	683 722	674 232	1 202 216	598 678	603 538	155 738	85 044	70 694
35 - 39	1 245 192	623 740	621 452	1 104 983	549 243	555 740	140 209	74 497	65 712
40 - 44	1 243 826	619 735	624 091	1 093 723	540 670	553 053	150 103	79 065	71 038
45 - 49	1 258 457	623 852	634 605	1 093 839	535 807	558 032	164 618	88 045	76 573
50 - 54	1 220 976	601 533	619 443	1 062 036	514 409	547 627	158 940	87 124	71 816
55 - 59	1 050 355	513 547	536 808	914 431	437 819	476 612	135 924	75 728	60 196
60 - 64	822 496	396 985	425 511	715 591	338 151	377 440	106 905	58 834	48 071
65 - 69	642 018	301 766	340 252	552 341	253 224	299 117	89 677	48 542	41 135
70 - 74	487 665	220 125	267 540	414 410	181 573	232 837	73 255	38 552	34 703
75 - 79	342 975	145 320	197 655	284 683	115 600	169 083	58 292	29 720	28 572
80 +	384 756	134 585	250 171	309 496	99 530	209 966	75 260	35 055	40 205
Colombia - Colombie[31]									
1 VII 2015 (ESDJ)									
Total	48 203 405	23 799 679	24 403 726	36 846 935	17 796 724	19 050 211	11 356 470	6 002 955	5 353 515
0 - 4	4 321 637	2 211 071	2 110 566	3 072 805	1 570 283	1 502 522	1 248 832	640 788	608 044
0	873 444	446 997	426 447	...	...	...	...	...	...
1 - 4	3 448 193	1 764 074	1 684 119	...	...	...	...	...	...
5 - 9	4 258 678	2 177 132	2 081 546	3 083 634	1 571 966	1 511 668	1 175 044	605 166	569 878
10 - 14	4 282 708	2 187 619	2 095 089	3 148 129	1 595 191	1 552 938	1 134 579	592 428	542 151
15 - 19	4 345 112	2 218 821	2 126 291	3 252 876	1 632 093	1 620 783	1 092 236	586 728	505 508
20 - 24	4 292 291	2 196 610	2 095 681	3 272 563	1 645 735	1 626 828	1 019 728	550 875	468 853
25 - 29	3 957 939	2 005 736	1 952 203	3 072 100	1 530 193	1 541 907	885 839	475 543	410 296
30 - 34	3 539 724	1 736 122	1 803 602	2 805 801	1 347 546	1 458 255	733 923	388 576	345 347
35 - 39	3 205 979	1 557 606	1 648 373	2 541 515	1 206 475	1 335 040	664 464	351 131	313 333
40 - 44	2 879 410	1 385 333	1 494 077	2 280 163	1 068 444	1 211 719	599 247	316 889	282 358
45 - 49	2 883 795	1 375 401	1 508 394	2 288 488	1 058 669	1 229 819	595 307	316 732	278 575
50 - 54	2 680 490	1 275 603	1 404 887	2 146 454	987 797	1 158 657	534 036	287 806	246 230
55 - 59	2 218 791	1 046 914	1 171 877	1 757 150	797 726	959 424	461 641	249 188	212 453
60 - 64	1 728 396	813 311	915 085	1 354 179	609 904	744 275	374 217	203 407	170 810
65 - 69	1 307 382	608 850	698 532	1 011 194	449 556	561 638	296 188	159 294	136 894
70 - 74	926 841	421 960	504 881	706 958	306 405	400 553	219 883	115 555	104 328
75 - 79	684 618	297 544	387 074	519 919	212 310	307 609	164 699	85 234	79 465
80 +	689 614	284 046	405 568	533 007	206 431	326 576	156 607	77 615	78 992
Ecuador - Équateur[32]									
1 VII 2015 (ESDF)									
Total	16 278 844	8 062 610	8 216 234	10 326 384	5 057 750	5 268 634	5 952 460	3 004 860	2 947 600
0	335 228	171 360	163 868	199 369	102 367	97 002	135 859	68 993	66 866
1 - 4	1 346 286	688 000	658 286	802 238	410 516	391 722	544 048	277 484	266 564
5 - 9	1 685 985	862 323	823 662	1 005 349	514 007	491 342	680 636	348 316	332 320
10 - 14	1 630 352	832 792	797 560	983 919	500 884	483 035	646 433	331 908	314 525
15 - 19	1 534 163	779 282	754 881	959 537	483 475	476 062	574 626	295 807	278 819
20 - 24	1 412 068	710 096	701 972	918 844	457 566	461 278	493 224	252 530	240 694
25 - 29	1 294 477	642 583	651 894	860 972	423 804	437 168	433 505	218 779	214 726

Population selon l'âge, le sexe et la résidence, urbaine/rurale : dernière année disponible, 2006 - 2015 (continued - suite)

Continent, country or area, date, code[a] and age (in years) / Continent, pays ou zone, date, code[a] et âge (en annèes)	Total			Urban - Urbaine			Rural - Rurale		
	Both sexes Les deux sexes	Male Masculin	Female Féminin	Both sexes Les deux sexes	Male Masculin	Female Féminin	Both sexes Les deux sexes	Male Masculin	Female Féminin
AMERICA, SOUTH - AMÉRIQUE DU SUD									
Ecuador - Équateur[32]									
1 VII 2015 (ESDF)									
30 - 34	1 192 678	582 098	610 580	796 606	385 362	411 244	396 072	196 736	199 336
35 - 39	1 081 112	519 334	561 778	721 851	342 493	379 358	359 261	176 841	182 420
40 - 44	958 496	458 294	500 202	643 147	302 528	340 619	315 349	155 766	159 583
45 - 49	845 420	405 129	440 291	569 536	268 266	301 270	275 884	136 863	139 021
50 - 54	737 032	353 969	383 063	492 832	232 909	259 923	244 200	121 060	123 140
55 - 59	619 035	297 828	321 207	404 830	191 345	213 485	214 205	106 483	107 722
60 - 64	497 521	238 963	258 558	313 209	147 101	166 108	184 312	91 862	92 450
65 - 69	386 769	184 248	202 521	232 752	107 592	125 160	154 017	76 656	77 361
70 - 74	289 321	135 790	153 531	168 552	75 955	92 597	120 769	59 835	60 934
75 - 79	202 419	93 762	108 657	116 640	51 497	65 143	85 779	42 265	43 514
80 - 84	126 773	58 627	68 146	73 681	32 476	41 205	53 092	26 151	26 941
85 - 89	66 733	30 993	35 740	39 654	17 561	22 093	27 079	13 432	13 647
90 - 94	27 888	12 911	14 977	17 130	7 523	9 607	10 758	5 388	5 370
95 - 99	8 675	4 023	4 652	5 473	2 398	3 075	3 202	1 625	1 577
100 +	413	205	208	263	125	138	150	80	70
Falkland Islands (Malvinas) - Îles Falkland (Malvinas)[33]									
15 IV 2012 (CDFC)									
Total	2 840	1 491	1 349	...	...	...	...	...	...
0 - 4	152	72	80	...	...	...	...	...	...
5 - 9	161	69	92	...	...	...	...	...	...
10 - 14	152	68	84	...	...	...	...	...	...
15 - 19	143	68	75	...	...	...	...	...	...
20 - 24	165	89	76	...	...	...	...	...	...
25 - 29	203	88	115	...	...	...	...	...	...
30 - 34	217	115	102	...	...	...	...	...	...
35 - 39	256	132	124	...	...	...	...	...	...
40 - 44	266	158	108	...	...	...	...	...	...
45 - 49	225	130	95	...	...	...	...	...	...
50 - 54	235	127	108	...	...	...	...	...	...
55 - 59	189	109	80	...	...	...	...	...	...
60 - 64	145	89	56	...	...	...	...	...	...
65 - 69	109	55	54	...	...	...	...	...	...
70 - 74	72	42	30	...	...	...	...	...	...
75 - 79	62	30	32	...	...	...	...	...	...
80 +	58	29	29	...	...	...	...	...	...
Unknown - Inconnu	30	21	9	...	...	...	...	...	...
French Guiana - Guyane française									
1 I 2013 (CDJC)									
Total	244 118	121 653	122 465	...	...	...	...	...	...
0 - 4	28 241	14 457	13 784	...	...	...	...	...	...
5 - 9	28 592	14 633	13 959	...	...	...	...	...	...
10 - 14	26 503	13 532	12 971	...	...	...	...	...	...
15 - 19	21 485	10 852	10 633	...	...	...	...	...	...
20 - 24	17 401	8 676	8 725	...	...	...	...	...	...
25 - 29	17 354	8 106	9 248	...	...	...	...	...	...
30 - 34	18 477	8 819	9 658	...	...	...	...	...	...
35 - 39	17 087	8 384	8 703	...	...	...	...	...	...
40 - 44	16 538	8 121	8 417	...	...	...	...	...	...
45 - 49	13 792	6 907	6 885	...	...	...	...	...	...
50 - 54	11 611	5 822	5 789	...	...	...	...	...	...
55 - 59	9 176	4 713	4 463	...	...	...	...	...	...
60 - 64	6 781	3 449	3 332	...	...	...	...	...	...
65 - 69	4 437	2 356	2 081	...	...	...	...	...	...
70 - 74	2 576	1 185	1 391	...	...	...	...	...	...
75 - 79	1 800	752	1 048	...	...	...	...	...	...
80 - 84	1 193	544	649	...	...	...	...	...	...
85 - 89	657	211	446	...	...	...	...	...	...
90 - 94	313	93	220	...	...	...	...	...	...
95 +	104	41	63	...	...	...	...	...	...

Continent, country or area, date, code[a] and age (in years) Continent, pays ou zone, date, code[a] et âge (en années)	Total			Urban - Urbaine			Rural - Rurale		
	Both sexes Les deux sexes	Male Masculin	Female Féminin	Both sexes Les deux sexes	Male Masculin	Female Féminin	Both sexes Les deux sexes	Male Masculin	Female Féminin
AMERICA, SOUTH - AMÉRIQUE DU SUD									
Guyana[34]									
1 VII 2010 (ESDF)									
Total	784 894	393 059	391 835	...	...	...	...	...	...
0 - 4	67 701	34 029	33 673	...	...	...	...	...	...
5 - 9	65 201	32 778	32 423	...	...	...	...	...	...
10 - 14	77 921	39 978	37 943	...	...	...	...	...	...
15 - 19	85 004	43 487	41 518	...	...	...	...	...	...
20 - 24	69 423	34 877	34 545	...	...	...	...	...	...
25 - 29	55 510	26 816	28 694	...	...	...	...	...	...
30 - 34	54 824	27 189	27 635	...	...	...	...	...	...
35 - 39	53 454	27 764	25 690	...	...	...	...	...	...
40 - 44	52 434	27 112	25 322	...	...	...	...	...	...
45 - 49	50 689	25 775	24 914	...	...	...	...	...	...
50 - 54	45 438	22 163	23 275	...	...	...	...	...	...
55 - 59	35 160	17 672	17 488	...	...	...	...	...	...
60 - 64	27 873	13 995	13 878	...	...	...	...	...	...
65 - 69	17 455	7 988	9 467	...	...	...	...	...	...
70 - 74	12 451	5 440	7 012	...	...	...	...	...	...
75 - 79	8 114	3 529	4 585	...	...	...	...	...	...
80 +	6 242	2 469	3 773	...	...	...	...	...	...
Paraguay[14]									
1 VII 2014 (ESDF)									
Total	6 893 727	3 481 648	3 412 079	4 100 854	2 005 735	2 095 119	2 792 873	1 475 913	1 316 960
0	149 497	76 292	73 205	82 190	41 921	40 269	67 307	34 371	32 936
1 - 4	592 752	302 081	290 671	329 110	167 318	161 792	263 642	134 763	128 879
5 - 9	732 572	373 032	359 540	414 266	209 925	204 341	318 306	163 107	155 199
10 - 14	718 808	365 801	353 007	409 801	206 133	203 668	309 007	159 668	149 339
15 - 19	695 129	353 337	341 792	396 365	196 907	199 458	298 764	156 430	142 334
20 - 24	660 768	335 017	325 751	374 262	184 053	190 209	286 505	150 963	135 542
25 - 29	609 697	307 963	301 734	350 726	168 983	181 742	258 972	138 979	119 992
30 - 34	531 175	267 895	263 280	335 966	157 173	178 792	195 210	110 722	84 488
35 - 39	420 493	211 739	208 753	290 071	137 473	152 598	130 421	74 266	56 155
40 - 44	351 991	176 306	175 685	237 125	114 658	122 467	114 866	61 649	53 218
45 - 49	324 401	162 786	161 614	209 177	101 643	107 535	115 223	61 144	54 080
50 - 54	285 223	143 859	141 364	178 037	86 922	91 115	107 186	56 937	50 249
55 - 59	243 012	123 235	119 777	148 982	72 588	76 394	94 030	50 647	43 383
60 - 64	196 794	99 963	96 832	119 147	58 279	60 868	77 647	41 684	35 963
65 - 69	141 649	70 841	70 808	84 013	40 163	43 851	57 636	30 679	26 957
70 - 74	101 558	49 351	52 206	60 302	27 893	32 409	41 255	21 458	19 797
75 - 79	71 414	33 466	37 948	41 666	18 111	23 555	29 748	15 356	14 392
80 +	66 795	28 682	38 112	39 648	15 593	24 055	27 146	13 089	14 057
Peru - Pérou[20]									
30 VI 2015 (ESDF)									
Total	31 151 643	15 605 814	15 545 829	23 893 654	11 808 006	12 085 648	7 257 989	3 797 808	3 460 181
0 - 4	2 861 874	1 460 651	1 401 223	1 999 405	1 024 277	975 128	862 469	436 374	426 095
0	569 385	290 929	278 456	...	...	...	...	...	...
1 - 4	2 292 489	1 169 722	1 122 767	...	...	...	...	...	...
5 - 9	2 922 744	1 489 659	1 433 085	2 075 903	1 056 541	1 019 362	846 841	433 118	413 723
10 - 14	2 914 162	1 483 135	1 431 027	2 112 021	1 068 033	1 043 988	802 141	415 102	387 039
15 - 19	2 887 529	1 465 657	1 421 872	2 171 117	1 088 200	1 082 917	716 412	377 457	338 955
20 - 24	2 828 387	1 432 145	1 396 242	2 233 624	1 113 336	1 120 288	594 763	318 809	275 954
25 - 29	2 661 346	1 343 154	1 318 192	2 086 882	1 033 898	1 052 984	574 464	309 256	265 208
30 - 34	2 411 781	1 214 095	1 197 686	1 909 984	940 526	969 458	501 797	273 569	228 228
35 - 39	2 258 372	1 134 864	1 123 508	1 803 662	884 781	918 881	454 710	250 083	204 627
40 - 44	1 977 630	990 241	987 389	1 576 462	770 389	806 073	401 168	219 852	181 316
45 - 49	1 725 353	860 135	865 218	1 392 679	680 417	712 262	332 674	179 718	152 956
50 - 54	1 486 312	736 147	750 165	1 211 513	591 567	619 946	274 799	144 580	130 219
55 - 59	1 205 103	590 957	614 146	972 130	470 219	501 911	232 973	120 738	112 235
60 - 64	967 702	469 267	498 435	762 099	366 031	396 068	205 603	103 236	102 367
65 - 69	736 059	351 637	384 422	570 690	270 856	299 834	165 369	80 781	84 588
70 - 74	545 659	254 420	291 239	419 648	194 190	225 458	126 011	60 230	65 781
75 - 79	394 230	176 971	217 259	303 396	134 156	169 240	90 834	42 815	48 019
80 +	367 400	152 679	214 721	292 439	120 589	171 850	74 961	32 090	42 871

7. Population by age, sex and urban/rural residence: latest available year, 2006 - 2015
Population selon l'âge, le sexe et la résidence, urbaine/rurale : dernière année disponible, 2006 - 2015 (continued - suite)

Continent, country or area, date, code[a] and age (in years) / Continent, pays ou zone, date, code[a] et âge (en années)	Total			Urban - Urbaine			Rural - Rurale		
	Both sexes Les deux sexes	Male Masculin	Female Féminin	Both sexes Les deux sexes	Male Masculin	Female Féminin	Both sexes Les deux sexes	Male Masculin	Female Féminin
AMERICA, SOUTH - AMÉRIQUE DU SUD									
Suriname									
13 VIII 2012 (CDJC)									
Total	541 638	270 629	271 009	359 146	177 215	181 931	182 492	93 414	89 078
0 - 4	50 548	25 968	24 580	30 755	15 787	14 968	19 793	10 181	9 612
5 - 9	47 735	24 549	23 186	28 390	14 549	13 841	19 345	10 000	9 345
10 - 14	50 484	26 166	24 318	31 147	16 037	15 110	19 338	10 130	9 208
15 - 19	45 108	22 772	22 336	30 010	15 040	14 970	15 097	7 731	7 366
20 - 24	43 762	21 656	22 106	31 096	15 201	15 895	12 666	6 455	6 211
25 - 29	43 946	21 761	22 185	30 679	15 107	15 572	13 267	6 654	6 613
30 - 34	39 051	19 355	19 696	26 819	13 234	13 585	12 232	6 121	6 111
35 - 39	36 429	18 316	18 113	24 050	11 860	12 190	12 379	6 456	5 923
40 - 44	37 383	18 763	18 620	24 796	12 167	12 629	12 587	6 596	5 991
45 - 49	36 031	18 083	17 948	24 438	12 032	12 406	11 593	6 051	5 542
50 - 54	30 651	15 313	15 338	21 072	10 258	10 814	9 579	5 055	4 525
55 - 59	22 588	10 929	11 659	15 699	7 417	8 282	6 889	3 512	3 377
60 - 64	16 497	7 734	8 763	11 475	5 304	6 171	5 022	2 430	2 592
65 - 69	13 008	5 951	7 057	9 134	4 166	4 968	3 874	1 785	2 089
70 - 74	10 133	4 619	5 514	6 983	3 211	3 772	3 150	1 408	1 742
75 - 79	7 556	3 393	4 163	5 149	2 296	2 853	2 407	1 097	1 310
80 - 84	4 433	1 934	2 499	3 019	1 308	1 711	1 414	626	788
85 +	2 900	1 081	1 819	2 088	758	1 330	812	323	489
85 - 89	1 978	743	1 235	...	...	...	...	...	...
90 - 94	712	274	438	...	...	...	...	...	...
95 +	210	64	146	...	...	...	...	...	...
Unknown - Inconnu	3 395	2 286	1 109	2 347	1 483	864	1 048	803	245
1 VII 2014 (ESDJ)									
Total	558 773	279 071	279 702	...	...	...	...	...	...
0	10 407	5 229	5 178	...	...	...	...	...	...
1 - 4	40 853	21 087	19 766	...	...	...	...	...	...
5 - 9	49 527	25 499	24 028	...	...	...	...	...	...
10 - 14	48 946	25 071	23 875	...	...	...	...	...	...
15 - 19	47 572	24 215	23 357	...	...	...	...	...	...
20 - 24	45 811	23 095	22 716	...	...	...	...	...	...
25 - 29	43 823	21 946	21 877	...	...	...	...	...	...
30 - 34	41 723	20 854	20 869	...	...	...	...	...	...
35 - 39	39 393	19 667	19 726	...	...	...	...	...	...
40 - 44	37 563	18 789	18 774	...	...	...	...	...	...
45 - 49	34 794	17 388	17 406	...	...	...	...	...	...
50 - 54	30 517	15 117	15 400	...	...	...	...	...	...
55 - 59	25 854	12 659	13 195	...	...	...	...	...	...
60 - 64	20 208	9 683	10 525	...	...	...	...	...	...
65 - 69	15 296	7 147	8 149	...	...	...	...	...	...
70 - 74	11 239	5 120	6 119	...	...	...	...	...	...
75 - 79	7 627	3 368	4 259	...	...	...	...	...	...
80 +	7 620	3 137	4 483	...	...	...	...	...	...
Uruguay									
4 X 2011 (CDJC)									
Total	3 285 877[35]	1 577 416	1 708 461	3 110 264	1 478 658	1 631 606	175 613	98 758	76 855
0 - 4	220 345	112 704	107 641	209 663	107 163	102 500	10 682	5 541	5 141
5 - 9	238 068	121 820	116 248	225 974	115 560	110 414	12 094	6 260	5 834
10 - 14	256 552	131 022	125 530	243 701	124 289	119 412	12 851	6 733	6 118
15 - 19	261 691	133 042	128 649	248 573	125 655	122 918	13 118	7 387	5 731
20 - 24	241 006	119 928	121 078	229 054	112 626	116 428	11 952	7 302	4 650
25 - 29	228 385	112 852	115 533	216 541	105 936	110 605	11 844	6 916	4 928
30 - 34	233 365	113 884	119 481	220 934	106 771	114 163	12 431	7 113	5 318
35 - 39	222 521	108 704	113 817	210 125	101 642	108 483	12 396	7 062	5 334
40 - 44	203 098	98 612	104 486	191 369	92 030	99 339	11 729	6 582	5 147
45 - 49	198 773	95 812	102 961	187 356	89 304	98 052	11 417	6 508	4 909
50 - 54	194 565	93 175	101 390	183 306	86 750	96 556	11 259	6 425	4 834
55 - 59	173 007	81 828	91 179	162 340	75 635	86 705	10 667	6 193	4 474
60 - 64	150 775	69 864	80 911	141 192	64 288	76 904	9 583	5 576	4 007
65 - 69	131 563	58 769	72 794	123 640	54 149	69 491	7 923	4 620	3 303
70 - 74	112 395	47 705	64 690	106 246	44 102	62 144	6 149	3 603	2 546
75 - 79	93 659	36 806	56 853	89 142	34 280	54 862	4 517	2 526	1 991

7. Population by age, sex and urban/rural residence: latest available year, 2006 - 2015
Population selon l'âge, le sexe et la résidence, urbaine/rurale : dernière année disponible, 2006 - 2015 (continued - suite)

Continent, country or area, date, code[a] and age (in years) Continent, pays ou zone, date, code[a] et âge (en années)	Total			Urban - Urbaine			Rural - Rurale		
	Both sexes Les deux sexes	Male Masculin	Female Féminin	Both sexes Les deux sexes	Male Masculin	Female Féminin	Both sexes Les deux sexes	Male Masculin	Female Féminin
AMERICA, SOUTH - AMÉRIQUE DU SUD									
Uruguay									
4 X 2011 (CDJC)									
80 - 84	70 505	24 912	45 593	67 588	23 393	44 195	2 917	1 519	1 398
85 - 89	37 426	11 535	25 891	35 994	10 888	25 106	1 432	647	785
90 - 94	14 113	3 636	10 477	13 599	3 432	10 167	514	204	310
95 - 99	3 546	733	2 813	3 421	694	2 727	125	39	86
100 +	519	73	446	506	71	435	13	2	11
1 VII 2015 (ESDJ)[2]									
Total	3 467 054	1 677 118	1 789 936	...	...	...	...	...	...
0	45 910	23 497	22 413	...	...	...	...	...	...
1 - 4	185 110	94 651	90 458	...	...	...	...	...	...
5 - 9	237 408	121 408	115 999	...	...	...	...	...	...
10 - 14	254 131	129 859	124 272	...	...	...	...	...	...
15 - 19	270 211	137 674	132 537	...	...	...	...	...	...
20 - 24	262 502	132 909	129 593	...	...	...	...	...	...
25 - 29	249 469	125 583	123 886	...	...	...	...	...	...
30 - 34	238 097	118 712	119 384	...	...	...	...	...	...
35 - 39	243 933	120 352	123 580	...	...	...	...	...	...
40 - 44	225 211	110 635	114 575	...	...	...	...	...	...
45 - 49	206 515	100 101	106 413	...	...	...	...	...	...
50 - 54	206 808	99 475	107 333	...	...	...	...	...	...
55 - 59	192 555	91 560	100 995	...	...	...	...	...	...
60 - 64	164 788	76 713	88 075	...	...	...	...	...	...
65 - 69	140 004	63 010	76 994	...	...	...	...	...	...
70 - 74	116 696	50 016	66 680	...	...	...	...	...	...
75 - 79	93 049	36 781	56 268	...	...	...	...	...	...
80 - 84	70 697	25 196	45 501	...	...	...	...	...	...
85 - 89	42 259	13 307	28 952	...	...	...	...	...	...
90 +	21 702	5 675	16 027	...	...	...	...	...	...
Venezuela (Bolivarian Republic of) - Venezuela (République bolivarienne du)									
1 VII 2015 (ESDF)									
Total	30 620 404	15 351 315	15 269 089	26 995 334	13 411 593	13 583 741	3 625 070	1 939 722	1 685 348
0 - 4	2 736 446	1 409 284	1 327 162	2 311 909	1 197 571	1 114 338	424 537	211 713	212 824
0	543 700	280 159	263 541	...	...	...	...	...	...
1 - 4	2 192 746	1 129 125	1 063 621	...	...	...	...	...	...
5 - 9	2 784 674	1 432 711	1 351 963	2 379 987	1 229 715	1 150 272	404 687	202 996	201 691
10 - 14	2 788 676	1 434 198	1 354 478	2 420 389	1 244 903	1 175 486	368 287	189 295	178 992
15 - 19	2 722 694	1 397 705	1 324 989	2 396 209	1 221 073	1 175 136	326 485	176 632	149 853
20 - 24	2 645 112	1 349 072	1 296 040	2 343 806	1 183 417	1 160 389	301 306	165 655	135 651
25 - 29	2 610 871	1 319 472	1 291 399	2 316 010	1 157 755	1 158 255	294 861	161 717	133 144
30 - 34	2 434 990	1 221 222	1 213 768	2 180 398	1 080 585	1 099 813	254 592	140 637	113 955
35 - 39	2 164 315	1 079 530	1 084 785	1 949 978	961 182	988 796	214 337	118 348	95 989
40 - 44	1 965 625	976 470	989 155	1 776 898	872 873	904 025	188 727	103 597	85 130
45 - 49	1 844 227	913 553	930 674	1 665 221	816 387	848 834	179 006	97 166	81 840
50 - 54	1 634 040	805 774	828 266	1 464 340	714 090	750 250	169 700	91 684	78 016
55 - 59	1 312 655	642 492	670 163	1 166 826	561 253	605 573	145 829	81 239	64 590
60 - 64	984 341	477 157	507 184	867 994	410 884	457 110	116 347	66 273	50 074
65 - 69	727 682	345 417	382 265	639 897	294 991	344 906	87 785	50 426	37 359
70 - 74	516 057	240 102	275 955	454 247	205 824	248 423	61 810	34 278	27 532
75 - 79	343 502	154 834	188 668	303 118	132 654	170 464	40 384	22 180	18 204
80 +	404 497	152 322	252 175	358 107	126 436	231 671	46 390	25 886	20 504
80 - 84	208 448	88 114	120 334	...	...	...	...	...	...
85 - 89	114 673	42 302	72 371	...	...	...	...	...	...
90 - 94	54 793	16 170	38 623	...	...	...	...	...	...
95 - 99	21 518	4 722	16 796	...	...	...	...	...	...
100 +	5 065	1 014	4 051	...	...	...	...	...	...

Continent, country or area, date, code[a] and age (in years) / Continent, pays ou zone, date, code[a] et âge (en années)	Total			Urban - Urbaine			Rural - Rurale		
	Both sexes Les deux sexes	Male Masculin	Female Féminin	Both sexes Les deux sexes	Male Masculin	Female Féminin	Both sexes Les deux sexes	Male Masculin	Female Féminin
ASIA - ASIE									
Afghanistan[36]									
1 VII 2014 (ESDF)									
Total	26 556 756	13 585 933	12 970 823	6 483 434	3 338 764	3 144 670	20 073 322	10 247 169	9 826 153
0 - 4	5 183 389	2 522 393	2 660 997	1 220 264	607 176	613 088	3 963 126	1 915 217	2 047 909
5 - 9	3 980 764	2 022 226	1 958 537	991 520	505 319	486 201	2 989 244	1 516 908	1 472 336
10 - 14	3 082 101	1 621 326	1 460 775	804 765	415 948	388 817	2 277 336	1 205 378	1 071 958
15 - 19	2 519 131	1 329 985	1 189 146	664 427	340 034	324 393	1 854 703	989 951	864 752
20 - 24	2 156 300	1 104 060	1 052 240	550 976	274 956	276 020	1 605 324	829 104	776 220
25 - 29	1 779 776	879 132	900 644	442 875	220 003	222 872	1 336 902	659 129	677 773
30 - 34	1 483 076	706 978	776 098	360 667	180 894	179 773	1 122 409	526 084	596 324
35 - 39	1 301 751	622 947	678 803	304 345	155 395	148 950	997 405	467 552	529 853
40 - 44	1 123 853	568 646	555 206	258 490	135 786	122 703	865 363	432 860	432 503
45 - 49	974 149	515 488	458 661	218 672	118 635	100 038	755 477	396 854	358 623
50 - 54	821 885	452 884	369 001	181 411	101 273	80 137	640 475	351 611	288 864
55 - 59	661 715	375 088	286 627	146 085	83 868	62 218	515 630	291 220	224 410
60 - 64	510 789	293 152	217 637	114 518	66 890	47 628	396 271	226 262	170 009
65 - 69	369 018	212 765	156 253	84 257	49 316	34 941	284 761	163 449	121 312
70 - 74	253 765	147 550	106 215	58 422	34 348	24 074	195 343	113 202	82 141
75 - 79	162 203	94 910	67 293	37 253	22 148	15 106	124 950	72 762	52 187
80 - 84	98 003	57 726	40 278	22 558	13 499	9 060	75 445	44 227	31 218
85 +	95 088	58 677	36 411	21 928	13 276	8 651	73 160	45 400	27 760
Armenia - Arménie									
12 X 2011 (CDJC)									
Total	3 018 854	1 448 052	1 570 802	1 911 287	895 372	1 015 915	1 107 567	552 680	554 887
0 - 4	207 572	110 565	97 007	127 653	67 466	60 187	79 919	43 099	36 820
5 - 9	179 929	96 429	83 500	110 826	58 712	52 114	69 103	37 717	31 386
10 - 14	178 637	95 458	83 179	105 685	56 068	49 617	72 952	39 390	33 562
15 - 19	233 075	117 938	115 137	134 853	67 252	67 601	98 222	50 686	47 536
20 - 24	292 234	143 897	148 337	175 999	83 968	92 031	116 235	59 929	56 306
25 - 29	271 929	132 109	139 820	173 093	81 320	91 773	98 836	50 789	48 047
30 - 34	223 005	108 114	114 891	148 671	71 158	77 513	74 334	36 956	37 378
35 - 39	187 421	89 073	98 348	123 792	58 479	65 313	63 629	30 594	33 035
40 - 44	176 964	82 502	94 462	109 718	49 721	59 997	67 246	32 781	34 465
45 - 49	211 060	98 064	112 996	126 779	55 920	70 859	84 281	42 144	42 137
50 - 54	234 532	109 294	125 238	150 258	66 623	83 635	84 274	42 671	41 603
55 - 59	177 758	80 989	96 769	122 931	54 136	68 795	54 827	26 853	27 974
60 - 64	127 599	56 189	71 410	93 673	40 621	53 052	33 926	15 568	18 358
65 - 69	65 373	28 020	37 353	47 797	20 459	27 338	17 576	7 561	10 015
70 - 74	107 678	44 041	63 637	71 461	29 585	41 876	36 217	14 456	21 761
75 - 79	75 377	30 734	44 643	47 483	19 373	28 110	27 894	11 361	16 533
80 - 84	48 906	18 662	30 244	28 738	10 892	17 846	20 168	7 770	12 398
85 +	19 805	5 974	13 831	11 877	3 619	8 258	7 928	2 355	5 573
1 I 2015 (ESDJ)									
Total	3 010 598	1 439 148	1 571 450	...	...	...	...	...	...
0	42 995	22 848	20 147	...	...	...	...	...	...
1 - 4	166 947	88 991	77 956	...	...	...	...	...	...
5 - 9	199 440	106 165	93 275	...	...	...	...	...	...
10 - 14	173 210	92 888	80 322	...	...	...	...	...	...
15 - 19	190 548	99 687	90 861	...	...	...	...	...	...
20 - 24	254 526	124 851	129 675	...	...	...	...	...	...
25 - 29	276 579	133 863	142 716	...	...	...	...	...	...
30 - 34	250 004	120 921	129 083	...	...	...	...	...	...
35 - 39	201 348	95 838	105 510	...	...	...	...	...	...
40 - 44	175 843	82 217	93 626	...	...	...	...	...	...
45 - 49	176 650	80 871	95 779	...	...	...	...	...	...
50 - 54	221 459	101 434	120 025	...	...	...	...	...	...
55 - 59	207 091	93 968	113 123	...	...	...	...	...	...
60 - 64	150 824	66 636	84 188	...	...	...	...	...	...
65 - 69	95 669	39 872	55 797	...	...	...	...	...	...
70 - 74	67 387	27 410	39 977	...	...	...	...	...	...
75 - 79	88 049	34 018	54 031	...	...	...	...	...	...
80 - 84	47 258	18 382	28 876	...	...	...	...	...	...
85 +	24 771	8 288	16 483	...	...	...	...	...	...

7. Population by age, sex and urban/rural residence: latest available year, 2006 - 2015
Population selon l'âge, le sexe et la résidence, urbaine/rurale : dernière année disponible, 2006 - 2015 (continued - suite)

Continent, country or area, date, code[a] and age (in years) Continent, pays ou zone, date, code[a] et âge (en années)	Total			Urban - Urbaine			Rural - Rurale		
	Both sexes Les deux sexes	Male Masculin	Female Féminin	Both sexes Les deux sexes	Male Masculin	Female Féminin	Both sexes Les deux sexes	Male Masculin	Female Féminin
ASIA - ASIE									
Azerbaijan - Azerbaïdjan									
1 VII 2013 (ESDF)									
Total	9 416 801	4 681 171	4 735 630	5 016 014	2 476 345	2 539 669	4 400 787	2 204 826	2 195 961
0	173 570	93 081	80 489	86 660	46 218	40 442	86 910	46 863	40 047
1 - 4	649 116	349 320	299 796	319 660	171 385	148 275	329 456	177 935	151 521
5 - 9	629 478	336 045	293 433	320 693	170 668	150 025	308 785	165 377	143 408
10 - 14	650 650	345 814	304 836	323 728	172 960	150 768	326 922	172 854	154 068
15 - 19	782 374	408 097	374 277	387 662	203 534	184 128	394 712	204 563	190 149
20 - 24	928 770	468 670	460 100	480 394	240 898	239 496	448 376	227 772	220 604
25 - 29	910 905	449 630	461 275	497 908	242 870	255 038	412 997	206 760	206 237
30 - 34	779 354	387 167	392 187	436 312	215 317	220 995	343 042	171 850	171 192
35 - 39	644 717	317 319	327 398	351 258	171 062	180 196	293 459	146 257	147 202
40 - 44	637 984	307 020	330 964	340 244	160 105	180 139	297 740	146 915	150 825
45 - 49	661 348	314 928	346 420	352 678	164 324	188 354	308 670	150 604	158 066
50 - 54	658 917	316 576	342 341	371 405	178 076	193 329	287 512	138 500	149 012
55 - 59	467 876	222 515	245 361	273 059	130 088	142 971	194 817	92 427	102 390
60 - 64	295 787	137 089	158 698	181 006	84 563	96 443	114 781	52 526	62 255
65 - 69	149 923	66 426	83 497	93 078	41 587	51 491	56 845	24 839	32 006
70 - 74	150 419	63 557	86 862	83 410	35 613	47 797	67 009	27 944	39 065
75 - 79	141 182	57 707	83 475	69 273	28 434	40 839	71 909	29 273	42 636
80 - 84	71 159	28 991	42 168	33 005	13 332	19 673	38 154	15 659	22 495
85 - 89	24 448	8 859	15 589	11 179	4 133	7 046	13 269	4 726	8 543
90 - 94	6 756	2 018	4 738	2 879	1 034	1 845	3 877	984	2 893
95 - 99	1 315	313	1 002	381	140	241	934	173	761
100 +	753	29	724	142	4	138	611	25	586
1 I 2015 (ESDF)									
Total	9 593 038	4 775 857	4 817 181	...	...	...	...	...	...
0	170 503	91 410	79 093	...	...	...	...	...	...
1 - 4	680 922	365 532	315 390	...	...	...	...	...	...
5 - 9	666 889	357 141	309 748	...	...	...	...	...	...
10 - 14	634 384	338 185	296 199	...	...	...	...	...	...
15 - 19	724 922	380 500	344 422	...	...	...	...	...	...
20 - 24	902 742	461 306	441 436	...	...	...	...	...	...
25 - 29	936 763	463 564	473 199	...	...	...	...	...	...
30 - 34	816 918	403 718	413 200	...	...	...	...	...	...
35 - 39	680 913	337 743	343 170	...	...	...	...	...	...
40 - 44	620 274	299 237	321 037	...	...	...	...	...	...
45 - 49	656 960	313 177	343 783	...	...	...	...	...	...
50 - 54	666 427	317 938	348 489	...	...	...	...	...	...
55 - 59	536 343	255 352	280 991	...	...	...	...	...	...
60 - 64	327 290	151 938	175 352	...	...	...	...	...	...
65 - 69	190 379	84 637	105 742	...	...	...	...	...	...
70 - 74	118 986	50 004	68 982	...	...	...	...	...	...
75 - 79	149 026	60 641	88 385	...	...	...	...	...	...
80 - 84	74 546	29 993	44 553	...	...	...	...	...	...
85 - 89	27 680	10 762	16 918	...	...	...	...	...	...
90 - 94	8 040	2 581	5 459	...	...	...	...	...	...
95 - 99	1 512	426	1 086	...	...	...	...	...	...
100 +	619	72	547	...	...	...	...	...	...
Bahrain - Bahreïn									
1 VII 2014 (ESDJ)									
Total	1 314 562	806 487	508 075	...	...	...	...	...	...
0	21 379	11 043	10 336	...	...	...	...	...	...
1 - 4	79 217	40 357	38 860	...	...	...	...	...	...
5 - 9	89 812	45 836	43 976	...	...	...	...	...	...
10 - 14	79 179	40 703	38 476	...	...	...	...	...	...
15 - 19	73 589	38 148	35 441	...	...	...	...	...	...
20 - 24	105 972	62 487	43 485	...	...	...	...	...	...
25 - 29	177 999	121 005	56 994	...	...	...	...	...	...
30 - 34	170 791	116 947	53 844	...	...	...	...	...	...
35 - 39	135 098	89 221	45 877	...	...	...	...	...	...
40 - 44	106 200	71 325	34 875	...	...	...	...	...	...
45 - 49	87 287	55 580	31 707	...	...	...	...	...	...
50 - 54	69 440	42 796	26 644	...	...	...	...	...	...
55 - 59	51 854	32 566	19 288	...	...	...	...	...	...

7. Population by age, sex and urban/rural residence: latest available year, 2006 - 2015
Population selon l'âge, le sexe et la résidence, urbaine/rurale : dernière année disponible, 2006 - 2015 (continued - suite)

Continent, country or area, date, code[a] and age (in years) / Continent, pays ou zone, date, code[a] et âge (en années)	Total			Urban - Urbaine			Rural - Rurale		
	Both sexes Les deux sexes	Male Masculin	Female Féminin	Both sexes Les deux sexes	Male Masculin	Female Féminin	Both sexes Les deux sexes	Male Masculin	Female Féminin
ASIA - ASIE									
Bahrain - Bahreïn									
1 VII 2014 (ESDJ)									
60 - 64	29 136	17 917	11 219	...	...	...	...	...	...
65 - 69	14 889	8 583	6 306	...	...	...	...	...	...
70 - 74	9 878	5 285	4 593	...	...	...	...	...	...
75 - 79	6 366	3 303	3 063	...	...	...	...	...	...
80 - 84	3 757	1 969	1 788	...	...	...	...	...	...
85 +	2 719	1 416	1 303	...	...	...	...	...	...
Bangladesh									
15 III 2011 (CDFC)									
Total	144 043 697	72 109 796	71 933 901	33 563 183[37]	17 529 792[37]	16 033 391[37]	110 480 514	54 580 004	55 900 510
0 - 4	15 061 970	7 638 523	7 423 447	3 015 500[37]	1 534 508[37]	1 480 992[37]	12 046 470	6 104 015	5 942 455
5 - 9	18 173 229	9 322 514	8 850 715	3 520 080[37]	1 810 786[37]	1 709 294[37]	14 653 149	7 511 728	7 141 421
10 - 14	16 646 615	8 614 889	8 031 726	3 609 866[37]	1 868 428[37]	1 741 438[37]	13 036 749	6 746 461	6 290 288
15 - 19	12 861 890	6 509 492	6 352 398	3 417 088[37]	1 735 931[37]	1 681 157[37]	9 444 802	4 773 561	4 671 241
20 - 24	13 299 789	5 777 370	7 522 419	3 750 754[37]	1 803 092[37]	1 947 662[37]	9 549 035	3 974 278	5 574 757
25 - 29	13 479 508	6 225 252	7 254 256	3 638 634[37]	1 846 338[37]	1 792 296[37]	9 840 874	4 378 914	5 461 960
30 - 34	10 499 765	5 079 106	5 420 659	2 757 615[37]	1 460 253[37]	1 297 362[37]	7 742 150	3 618 853	4 123 297
35 - 39	9 556 428	4 697 349	4 859 079	2 424 331[37]	1 291 114[37]	1 133 217[37]	7 132 097	3 406 235	3 725 862
40 - 44	8 261 662	4 280 923	3 980 739	2 014 738[37]	1 124 193[37]	890 545[37]	6 246 924	3 156 730	3 090 194
45 - 49	6 380 073	3 363 273	3 016 800	1 504 983[37]	849 659[37]	655 324[37]	4 875 090	2 513 614	2 361 476
50 - 54	5 552 271	2 952 596	2 599 675	1 225 174[37]	703 282[37]	521 892[37]	4 327 097	2 249 314	2 077 783
55 - 59	3 500 997	1 923 534	1 577 463	758 757[37]	448 673[37]	310 084[37]	2 742 240	1 474 861	1 267 379
60 - 64	3 934 014	2 081 306	1 852 708	759 025[37]	425 996[37]	333 029[37]	3 174 989	1 655 310	1 519 679
65 - 69	2 113 490	1 149 569	963 921	386 330[37]	217 634[37]	168 696[37]	1 727 160	931 935	795 225
70 - 74	2 231 712	1 206 398	1 025 314	379 459[37]	207 611[37]	171 848[37]	1 852 253	998 787	853 466
75 - 79	874 727	488 338	386 389	146 831[37]	80 832[37]	65 999[37]	727 896	407 506	320 390
80 - 84	880 079	443 239	436 840	138 128[37]	68 117[37]	70 011[37]	741 951	375 122	366 829
85 - 89	262 611	138 268	124 343	42 824[37]	21 933[37]	20 891[37]	219 787	116 335	103 452
90 - 94	250 189	116 916	133 273	38 679[37]	16 945[37]	21 734[37]	211 510	99 971	111 539
95 +	222 678	100 941	121 737	34 387[37]	14 467[37]	19 920[37]	188 291	86 474	101 817
Bhutan - Bhoutan[38]									
1 VII 2015 (ESDF)									
Total	757 042	393 327	363 718	294 402	156 327	138 077	462 640	237 000	225 641
0 - 4	82 561	41 633	40 928	28 821	14 412	14 409	53 740	27 221	26 519
0	15 650	7 880	7 770	...	...	...	...	...	...
1 - 4	66 911	33 753	33 158	...	...	...	...	...	...
5 - 9	85 171	43 013	42 158	32 984	16 504	16 481	52 187	26 509	25 677
10 - 14	62 054	31 255	30 799	25 968	12 958	13 010	36 086	18 297	17 789
15 - 19	67 765	34 291	33 474	29 789	15 059	14 730	37 976	19 232	18 744
20 - 24	71 524	36 467	35 057	33 496	17 282	16 214	38 028	19 185	18 843
25 - 29	68 976	35 757	33 219	32 499	17 207	15 292	36 477	18 550	17 927
30 - 34	64 212	34 342	29 870	29 576	16 427	13 150	34 636	17 915	16 720
35 - 39	56 625	30 686	25 939	24 647	14 063	10 584	31 978	16 623	15 355
40 - 44	46 399	25 415	20 985	17 557	10 342	7 215	28 842	15 073	13 770
45 - 49	38 480	21 057	17 424	12 883	7 673	5 209	25 597	13 384	12 215
50 - 54	30 568	16 439	14 129	8 636	5 101	3 535	21 932	11 338	10 594
55 - 59	24 636	13 102	11 534	6 070	3 525	2 545	18 566	9 577	8 989
60 - 64	19 415	10 218	9 197	4 154	2 288	1 867	15 261	7 930	7 330
65 - 69	14 838	7 697	7 142	2 875	1 494	1 381	11 963	6 203	5 761
70 - 74	10 696	5 450	5 245	1 918	914	1 004	8 778	4 536	4 241
75 - 79	7 009	3 507	3 503	1 274	539	735	5 735	2 968	2 768
80 +	6 113	2 998	3 115	1 255	539	716	4 858	2 459	2 399
Brunei Darussalam - Brunéi Darussalam									
20 VI 2011 (CDJC)									
Total	393 372	203 144	190 228	296 257	151 663	144 594	97 115	51 481	45 634
0 - 4	30 323	15 690	14 633	23 250	11 966	11 284	7 073	3 724	3 349
5 - 9	33 659	17 271	16 388	25 840	13 253	12 587	7 819	4 018	3 801
10 - 14	35 453	18 424	17 029	26 734	13 946	12 788	8 719	4 478	4 241
15 - 19	34 967	17 954	17 013	25 706	13 158	12 548	9 261	4 796	4 465
20 - 24	38 150	19 916	18 234	28 301	14 585	13 716	9 849	5 331	4 518
25 - 29	39 185	20 756	18 429	29 567	15 337	14 230	9 618	5 419	4 199
30 - 34	36 896	19 324	17 572	28 516	14 629	13 887	8 380	4 695	3 685

215

7. Population by age, sex and urban/rural residence: latest available year, 2006 - 2015
Population selon l'âge, le sexe et la résidence, urbaine/rurale : dernière année disponible, 2006 - 2015 (continued - suite)

Continent, country or area, date, code[a] and age (in years) Continent, pays ou zone, date, code[a] et âge (en années)	Total			Urban - Urbaine			Rural - Rurale		
	Both sexes Les deux sexes	Male Masculin	Female Féminin	Both sexes Les deux sexes	Male Masculin	Female Féminin	Both sexes Les deux sexes	Male Masculin	Female Féminin
ASIA - ASIE									
Brunei Darussalam - Brunéi Darussalam									
20 VI 2011 (CDJC)									
35 - 39	33 796	17 331	16 465	25 962	13 022	12 940	7 834	4 309	3 525
40 - 44	30 122	15 289	14 833	22 900	11 487	11 413	7 222	3 802	3 420
45 - 49	24 610	12 840	11 770	18 737	9 714	9 023	5 873	3 126	2 747
50 - 54	19 781	10 333	9 448	14 978	7 841	7 137	4 803	2 492	2 311
55 - 59	14 044	7 158	6 886	10 214	5 270	4 944	3 830	1 888	1 942
60 - 64	8 518	4 164	4 354	6 112	3 008	3 104	2 406	1 156	1 250
65 - 69	5 088	2 584	2 504	3 522	1 770	1 752	1 566	814	752
70 - 74	3 901	1 827	2 074	2 680	1 208	1 472	1 221	619	602
75 - 79	2 601	1 193	1 408	1 713	764	949	888	429	459
80 - 84	1 405	702	703	943	452	491	462	250	212
85 +	873	388	485	582	253	329	291	135	156
1 VII 2015* (ESDJ)									
Total	417 200	216 600	200 600	...	...	...	...	...	...
0 - 4	32 900	17 100	15 800	...	...	...	...	...	...
5 - 9	31 000	16 100	14 900	...	...	...	...	...	...
10 - 14	34 600	17 800	16 800	...	...	...	...	...	...
15 - 19	35 400	18 300	17 100	...	...	...	...	...	...
20 - 24	35 000	18 200	16 800	...	...	...	...	...	...
25 - 29	39 100	20 700	18 400	...	...	...	...	...	...
30 - 34	39 000	20 900	18 100	...	...	...	...	...	...
35 - 39	36 100	19 000	17 100	...	...	...	...	...	...
40 - 44	33 200	17 000	16 200	...	...	...	...	...	...
45 - 49	28 600	14 800	13 800	...	...	...	...	...	...
50 - 54	23 700	12 500	11 200	...	...	...	...	...	...
55 - 59	18 400	9 500	8 900	...	...	...	...	...	...
60 - 64	12 400	6 300	6 100	...	...	...	...	...	...
65 - 69	7 300	3 500	3 800	...	...	...	...	...	...
70 - 74	4 500	2 200	2 300	...	...	...	...	...	...
75 - 79	3 100	1 400	1 700	...	...	...	...	...	...
80 - 84	1 800	800	1 000	...	...	...	...	...	...
85 - 89	800	400	400	...	...	...	...	...	...
90 - 94	300	100	200	...	...	...	...	...	...
95 - 99	-	-	-	...	...	...	...	...	...
100 +	-	-	-	...	...	...	...	...	...
Unknown - Inconnu	-	-	-	...	...	...	...	...	...
Cambodia - Cambodge[39]									
1 VII 2015 (ESDF)									
Total	15 405 157	7 551 944	7 853 213	3 540 575	1 705 018	1 835 557	11 864 582	5 846 926	6 017 656
0	343 968	175 388	168 580	86 946	44 740	42 206	257 022	130 648	126 374
1 - 4	1 256 559	639 680	616 879	287 909	146 676	141 233	968 650	493 004	475 646
5 - 9	1 478 056	751 537	726 519	266 331	135 468	130 863	1 211 725	616 069	595 656
10 - 14	1 424 533	727 116	697 417	222 335	114 171	108 164	1 202 198	612 945	589 253
15 - 19	1 637 111	838 821	798 290	273 601	136 051	137 550	1 363 510	702 770	660 740
20 - 24	1 698 824	877 158	821 666	407 469	188 296	219 173	1 291 355	688 862	602 493
25 - 29	1 478 710	737 077	741 633	484 549	223 014	261 535	994 161	514 063	480 098
30 - 34	1 333 262	649 670	683 592	427 395	205 047	222 348	905 867	444 623	461 244
35 - 39	879 004	427 791	451 213	237 471	117 764	119 707	641 533	310 027	331 506
40 - 44	761 990	367 586	394 404	177 884	89 396	88 488	584 106	278 190	305 916
45 - 49	793 754	374 975	418 779	175 105	87 482	87 623	618 649	287 493	331 156
50 - 54	677 057	312 718	364 339	144 559	70 342	74 217	532 498	242 376	290 122
55 - 59	533 368	224 272	309 096	119 460	52 954	66 506	413 908	171 318	242 590
60 - 64	398 784	159 105	239 679	89 373	37 736	51 637	309 411	121 369	188 042
65 - 69	282 114	117 449	164 665	58 973	24 909	34 064	223 141	92 540	130 601
70 - 74	191 298	79 144	112 154	36 584	14 784	21 800	154 714	64 360	90 354
75 - 79	126 227	50 567	75 660	23 103	8 844	14 259	103 124	41 723	61 401
80 +	110 538	41 890	68 648	21 528	7 344	14 184	89 010	34 546	54 464
China - Chine[40]									
1 XI 2010 (CDJC)[41]									
Total	1332810869	682 329 104	650 481 765	670 005 546	343 040 783	326 964 763	662 805 323	339 288 321	323 517 002
0 - 4	75 532 610	41 062 566	34 470 044	30 936 470	16 749 729	14 186 741	44 596 140	24 312 837	20 283 303
5 - 9	70 881 549	38 464 665	32 416 884	30 565 659	16 580 910	13 984 749	40 315 890	21 883 755	18 432 135
10 - 14	74 908 462	40 267 277	34 641 185	32 807 526	17 664 790	15 142 736	42 100 936	22 602 487	19 498 449

216

Continent, country or area, date, code[a] and age (in years) / Continent, pays ou zone, date, code[a] et âge (en années)	Total			Urban - Urbaine			Rural - Rurale		
	Both sexes Les deux sexes	Male Masculin	Female Féminin	Both sexes Les deux sexes	Male Masculin	Female Féminin	Both sexes Les deux sexes	Male Masculin	Female Féminin
ASIA - ASIE									
China - Chine[40]									
1 XI 2010 (CDJC)[41]									
15 - 19	99 889 114	51 904 830	47 984 284	53 589 992	27 603 777	25 986 215	46 299 122	24 301 053	21 998 069
20 - 24	127 412 518	64 008 573	63 403 945	71 058 518	36 041 784	35 016 734	56 354 000	27 966 789	28 387 211
25 - 29	101 013 852	50 837 038	50 176 814	57 679 956	28 973 516	28 706 440	43 333 896	21 863 522	21 470 374
30 - 34	97 138 203	49 521 822	47 616 381	56 010 957	28 432 073	27 578 884	41 127 246	21 089 749	20 037 497
35 - 39	118 025 959	60 391 104	57 634 855	65 025 365	33 349 280	31 676 085	53 000 594	27 041 824	25 958 770
40 - 44	124 753 964	63 608 678	61 145 286	63 786 496	32 845 769	30 940 727	60 967 468	30 762 909	30 204 559
45 - 49	105 594 553	53 776 418	51 818 135	53 629 541	27 723 132	25 906 409	51 965 012	26 053 286	25 911 726
50 - 54	78 753 171	40 363 234	38 389 937	39 186 388	20 130 395	19 055 993	39 566 783	20 232 839	19 333 944
55 - 59	81 312 474	41 082 938	40 229 536	37 437 535	18 762 887	18 674 648	43 874 939	22 320 051	21 554 888
60 - 64	58 667 282	29 834 426	28 832 856	26 036 917	13 067 045	12 969 872	32 630 365	16 767 381	15 862 984
65 - 69	41 113 282	20 748 471	20 364 811	17 910 329	8 866 594	9 043 735	23 202 953	11 881 877	11 321 076
70 - 74	32 972 397	16 403 453	16 568 944	14 777 260	7 241 891	7 535 369	18 195 137	9 161 562	9 033 575
75 - 79	23 852 133	11 278 859	12 573 274	10 531 503	5 048 471	5 483 032	13 320 630	6 230 388	7 090 242
80 - 84	13 373 198	5 917 502	7 455 696	5 762 828	2 665 218	3 097 610	7 610 370	3 252 284	4 358 086
85 - 89	5 631 928	2 199 810	3 432 118	2 392 190	982 284	1 409 906	3 239 738	1 217 526	2 022 212
90 - 94	1 578 307	530 872	1 047 435	687 763	246 031	441 732	890 544	284 841	605 703
95 - 99	369 979	117 716	252 263	176 542	60 991	115 551	193 437	56 725	136 712
100 +	35 934	8 852	27 082	15 811	4 216	11 595	20 123	4 636	15 487
31 XII 2011 (ESDF)[42]									
Total	1347304706	690 634 118	656 670 588	...	...	...	...	...	...
0 - 4	76 270 588	41 467 059	34 803 529	...	...	...	...	...	...
5 - 9	72 092 941	39 108 235	32 984 706	...	...	...	...	...	...
10 - 14	73 507 059	39 657 647	33 849 412	...	...	...	...	...	...
15 - 19	94 574 118	49 489 412	45 084 706	...	...	...	...	...	...
20 - 24	127 725 882	64 991 765	62 732 941	...	...	...	...	...	...
25 - 29	105 010 588	52 912 941	52 096 471	...	...	...	...	...	...
30 - 34	96 644 706	49 303 529	47 341 176	...	...	...	...	...	...
35 - 39	113 994 118	58 317 647	55 676 471	...	...	...	...	...	...
40 - 44	126 342 353	64 477 647	61 864 706	...	...	...	...	...	...
45 - 49	118 650 588	60 510 588	58 140 000	...	...	...	...	...	...
50 - 54	73 181 176	37 436 471	35 744 706	...	...	...	...	...	...
55 - 59	84 314 118	42 603 529	41 709 412	...	...	...	...	...	...
60 - 64	62 009 412	31 397 647	30 611 765	...	...	...	...	...	...
65 - 69	42 416 471	21 251 765	21 164 706	...	...	...	...	...	...
70 - 74	33 912 941	16 934 118	16 978 824	...	...	...	...	...	...
75 - 79	24 910 588	11 716 471	13 195 294	...	...	...	...	...	...
80 - 84	14 075 294	6 263 529	7 811 765	...	...	...	...	...	...
85 - 89	5 642 353	2 182 353	3 460 000	...	...	...	...	...	...
90 - 94	1 690 588	524 706	1 165 882	...	...	...	...	...	...
95 +	341 176	85 882	254 118	...	...	...	...	...	...
China, Hong Kong SAR - Chine, Hong Kong RAS									
1 VII 2015 (ESDJ)									
Total	7 305 700	3 367 000	3 938 700	...	...	...	...	...	...
0	55 700	29 100	26 600	...	...	...	...	...	...
1 - 4	227 200	117 700	109 500	...	...	...	...	...	...
5 - 9	279 500	145 100	134 400	...	...	...	...	...	...
10 - 14	265 700	136 100	129 600	...	...	...	...	...	...
15 - 19	360 900	185 900	175 000	...	...	...	...	...	...
20 - 24	447 900	221 900	226 000	...	...	...	...	...	...
25 - 29	514 000	226 100	287 900	...	...	...	...	...	...
30 - 34	582 100	233 900	348 200	...	...	...	...	...	...
35 - 39	562 600	225 400	337 200	...	...	...	...	...	...
40 - 44	579 500	239 100	340 400	...	...	...	...	...	...
45 - 49	572 300	246 300	326 000	...	...	...	...	...	...
50 - 54	655 700	303 700	352 000	...	...	...	...	...	...
55 - 59	610 600	300 900	309 700	...	...	...	...	...	...
60 - 64	474 700	234 500	240 200	...	...	...	...	...	...
65 - 69	363 400	180 300	183 100	...	...	...	...	...	...
70 - 74	214 100	110 500	103 600	...	...	...	...	...	...
75 - 79	209 900	101 600	108 300	...	...	...	...	...	...
80 - 84	166 700	74 000	92 700	...	...	...	...	...	...
85 +	163 200	54 900	108 300	...	...	...	...	...	...

Continent, country or area, date, code[a] and age (in years) / Continent, pays ou zone, date, code[a] et âge (en années)	Total			Urban - Urbaine			Rural - Rurale		
	Both sexes Les deux sexes	Male Masculin	Female Féminin	Both sexes Les deux sexes	Male Masculin	Female Féminin	Both sexes Les deux sexes	Male Masculin	Female Féminin
ASIA - ASIE									
China, Macao SAR - Chine, Macao RAS									
1 VII 2015 (ESDJ)									
Total	642 900	317 500	325 400	...	...	...	...	...	...
0	7 000	3 700	3 300	...	...	...	...	...	...
1 - 4	25 300	13 300	12 000	...	...	...	...	...	...
5 - 9	22 100	11 600	10 500	...	...	...	...	...	...
10 - 14	20 300	10 900	9 400	...	...	...	...	...	...
15 - 19	30 000	15 600	14 400	...	...	...	...	...	...
20 - 24	47 000	23 900	23 100	...	...	...	...	...	...
25 - 29	72 900	36 200	36 700	...	...	...	...	...	...
30 - 34	64 900	32 400	32 500	...	...	...	...	...	...
35 - 39	50 600	25 500	25 100	...	...	...	...	...	...
40 - 44	53 600	25 600	28 000	...	...	...	...	...	...
45 - 49	52 500	23 600	28 900	...	...	...	...	...	...
50 - 54	57 700	27 000	30 700	...	...	...	...	...	...
55 - 59	48 500	24 300	24 200	...	...	...	...	...	...
60 - 64	35 100	17 600	17 500	...	...	...	...	...	...
65 - 69	23 300	12 200	11 100	...	...	...	...	...	...
70 - 74	10 900	5 600	5 300	...	...	...	...	...	...
75 - 79	8 300	3 900	4 400	...	...	...	...	...	...
80 - 84	6 400	2 600	3 800	...	...	...	...	...	...
85 +	6 500	2 000	4 500	...	...	...	...	...	...
Cyprus - Chypre[43]									
1 X 2011 (CDJC)									
Total	840 407	408 780	431 627	566 191	273 065	293 126	274 216	135 715	138 501
0 - 4	45 015	23 061	21 954	29 726	15 202	14 524	15 289	7 859	7 430
5 - 9	42 635	21 921	20 714	28 050	14 386	13 664	14 585	7 535	7 050
10 - 14	47 298	24 179	23 119	30 926	15 730	15 196	16 372	8 449	7 923
15 - 19	55 818	28 683	27 135	36 345	18 593	17 752	19 473	10 090	9 383
20 - 24	66 073	33 891	32 182	44 948	22 847	22 101	21 125	11 044	10 081
25 - 29	74 114	36 992	37 122	51 855	25 842	26 013	22 259	11 150	11 109
30 - 34	69 834	33 149	36 685	48 938	23 133	25 805	20 896	10 016	10 880
35 - 39	61 862	27 754	34 108	43 232	19 204	24 028	18 630	8 550	10 080
40 - 44	59 728	27 031	32 697	41 295	18 416	22 879	18 433	8 615	9 818
45 - 49	57 240	27 059	30 181	39 233	18 225	21 008	18 007	8 834	9 173
50 - 54	56 128	27 517	28 611	38 287	18 499	19 788	17 841	9 018	8 823
55 - 59	47 762	23 771	23 991	31 716	15 541	16 175	16 046	8 230	7 816
60 - 64	45 034	22 057	22 977	29 704	14 438	15 266	15 330	7 619	7 711
65 - 69	36 328	17 656	18 672	23 459	11 295	12 164	12 869	6 361	6 508
70 - 74	29 433	14 044	15 389	18 991	9 048	9 943	10 442	4 996	5 446
75 - 79	21 058	9 647	11 411	13 545	6 239	7 306	7 513	3 408	4 105
80 +	24 948	10 342	14 606	15 853	6 408	9 445	9 095	3 934	5 161
Unknown - Inconnu	99	26	73	88	19	69	11	7	4
1 I 2015* (ESDJ)									
Total	847 008	411 825	435 183	...	...	...	...	...	...
0	9 234	4 844	4 390	...	...	...	...	...	...
1 - 4	38 768	19 776	18 992	...	...	...	...	...	...
5 - 9	46 251	23 750	22 501	...	...	...	...	...	...
10 - 14	44 953	23 063	21 890	...	...	...	...	...	...
15 - 19	52 901	26 900	26 001	...	...	...	...	...	...
20 - 24	66 326	33 701	32 625	...	...	...	...	...	...
25 - 29	71 655	35 953	35 702	...	...	...	...	...	...
30 - 34	68 214	32 182	36 032	...	...	...	...	...	...
35 - 39	60 519	27 638	32 881	...	...	...	...	...	...
40 - 44	57 232	26 307	30 925	...	...	...	...	...	...
45 - 49	54 960	25 983	28 977	...	...	...	...	...	...
50 - 54	55 928	27 234	28 694	...	...	...	...	...	...
55 - 59	50 112	24 823	25 289	...	...	...	...	...	...
60 - 64	46 234	22 737	23 497	...	...	...	...	...	...
65 - 69	41 407	20 007	21 400	...	...	...	...	...	...
70 - 74	30 938	14 691	16 247	...	...	...	...	...	...
75 - 79	23 870	10 943	12 927	...	...	...	...	...	...
80 - 84	15 748	6 680	9 068	...	...	...	...	...	...
85 - 89	8 315	3 321	4 994	...	...	...	...	...	...

7. Population by age, sex and urban/rural residence: latest available year, 2006 - 2015
Population selon l'âge, le sexe et la résidence, urbaine/rurale : dernière année disponible, 2006 - 2015 (continued - suite)

Continent, country or area, date, code[a] and age (in years) / Continent, pays ou zone, date, code[a] et âge (en annèes)	Total			Urban - Urbaine			Rural - Rurale		
	Both sexes Les deux sexes	Male Masculin	Female Féminin	Both sexes Les deux sexes	Male Masculin	Female Féminin	Both sexes Les deux sexes	Male Masculin	Female Féminin
ASIA - ASIE									
Cyprus - Chypre[43]									
1 I 2015* (ESDJ)									
90 - 94	2 739	1 026	1 713	...	...	...	...	...	...
95 - 99	628	223	405	...	...	...	...	...	...
100 +	76	43	33	...	...	...	...	...	...
Democratic People's Republic of Korea - République populaire démocratique de Corée									
1 X 2008 (CDJC)									
Total	24 052 231	11 721 838	12 330 393	...	...	...	...	...	...
0 - 4	1 710 039	872 173	837 866	...	...	...	...	...	...
5 - 9	1 846 785	943 048	903 737	...	...	...	...	...	...
10 - 14	2 021 350	1 035 282	986 068	...	...	...	...	...	...
15 - 19	2 052 342	1 050 113	1 002 229	...	...	...	...	...	...
20 - 24	1 841 400	941 017	900 383	...	...	...	...	...	...
25 - 29	1 737 185	887 573	849 612	...	...	...	...	...	...
30 - 34	1 680 272	853 276	826 996	...	...	...	...	...	...
35 - 39	2 214 929	1 118 391	1 096 538	...	...	...	...	...	...
40 - 44	2 015 514	1 005 140	1 010 374	...	...	...	...	...	...
45 - 49	1 559 527	766 054	793 473	...	...	...	...	...	...
50 - 54	1 315 101	637 737	677 364	...	...	...	...	...	...
55 - 59	902 876	423 625	479 251	...	...	...	...	...	...
60 - 64	1 058 263	476 727	581 536	...	...	...	...	...	...
65 - 69	913 304	379 456	533 848	...	...	...	...	...	...
70 - 74	662 627	228 286	434 341	...	...	...	...	...	...
75 - 79	335 467	79 231	256 236	...	...	...	...	...	...
80 - 84	132 149	18 884	113 265	...	...	...	...	...	...
85 - 89	42 760	4 930	37 830	...	...	...	...	...	...
90 - 94	8 634	809	7 825	...	...	...	...	...	...
95 - 99	1 643	86	1 557	...	...	...	...	...	...
100 +	64	-	64	...	...	...	...	...	...
Georgia - Géorgie									
5 XI 2014 (CDJC)									
Total	3 713 804	1 772 864	1 940 940	2 122 623	980 985	1 141 638	1 591 181	791 879	799 302
0 - 4	255 089	132 700	122 389	152 766	78 799	73 967	102 323	53 901	48 422
5 - 9	230 024	121 245	108 779	139 301	72 526	66 775	90 723	48 719	42 004
10 - 14	206 216	109 481	96 735	119 287	62 645	56 642	86 929	46 836	40 093
15 - 19	226 022	118 877	107 145	130 446	66 924	63 522	95 576	51 953	43 623
20 - 24	266 125	135 305	130 820	162 336	79 100	83 236	103 789	56 205	47 584
25 - 29	278 662	139 945	138 717	168 601	80 608	87 993	110 061	59 337	50 724
30 - 34	262 060	129 921	132 139	160 622	76 264	84 358	101 438	53 657	47 781
35 - 39	248 549	121 943	126 606	150 707	71 177	79 530	97 842	50 766	47 076
40 - 44	243 281	118 318	124 963	143 846	67 326	76 520	99 435	50 992	48 443
45 - 49	239 407	114 036	125 371	133 670	60 443	73 227	105 737	53 593	52 144
50 - 54	271 386	126 710	144 676	150 014	66 843	83 171	121 372	59 867	61 505
55 - 59	245 391	111 641	133 750	133 348	57 828	75 520	112 043	53 813	58 230
60 - 64	211 385	92 412	118 973	114 908	47 738	67 170	96 477	44 674	51 803
65 - 69	155 702	64 889	90 813	84 433	33 489	50 944	71 269	31 400	39 869
70 - 74	123 605	48 483	75 122	61 257	22 399	38 858	62 348	26 084	36 264
75 - 79	135 764	49 895	85 869	64 993	21 828	43 165	70 771	28 067	42 704
80 - 84	71 675	25 100	46 575	32 119	10 106	22 013	39 556	14 994	24 562
85 - 89	34 508	10 166	24 342	15 957	4 154	11 803	18 551	6 012	12 539
90 - 94	7 495	1 620	5 875	3 473	712	2 761	4 022	908	3 114
95 - 99	1 171	163	1 008	456	69	387	715	94	621
100 +	287	14	273	83	7	76	204	7	197
1 I 2015 (ESDJ)									
Total	3 729 500	1 778 500	1 951 000	...	...	...	...	...	...
0	59 800	30 900	28 900	...	...	...	...	...	...
1 - 4	197 000	102 000	95 000	...	...	...	...	...	...
5 - 9	202 600	108 400	94 200	...	...	...	...	...	...
10 - 14	189 700	100 100	89 600	...	...	...	...	...	...
15 - 19	226 100	117 700	108 400	...	...	...	...	...	...
20 - 24	290 100	147 100	143 000	...	...	...	...	...	...
25 - 29	298 100	150 300	147 800	...	...	...	...	...	...

Continent, country or area, date, code[a] and age (in years) Continent, pays ou zone, date, code[a] et âge (en années)	Total			Urban - Urbaine			Rural - Rurale		
	Both sexes Les deux sexes	Male Masculin	Female Féminin	Both sexes Les deux sexes	Male Masculin	Female Féminin	Both sexes Les deux sexes	Male Masculin	Female Féminin
ASIA - ASIE									
Georgia - Géorgie									
1 I 2015 (ESDJ)									
30 - 34	277 200	138 400	138 800	...	...	...	...	...	...
35 - 39	261 300	128 200	133 100	...	...	...	...	...	...
40 - 44	251 100	121 200	129 900	...	...	...	...	...	...
45 - 49	247 500	116 000	131 500	...	...	...	...	...	...
50 - 54	274 900	126 500	148 400	...	...	...	...	...	...
55 - 59	236 200	107 400	128 800	...	...	...	...	...	...
60 - 64	198 800	87 800	111 000	...	...	...	...	...	...
65 - 69	129 900	55 700	74 200	...	...	...	...	...	...
70 - 74	126 700	48 200	78 500	...	...	...	...	...	...
75 - 79	127 100	48 200	78 900	...	...	...	...	...	...
80 - 84	72 300	25 900	46 400	...	...	...	...	...	...
85 +	63 100	18 500	44 600	...	...	...	...	...	...
India - Inde[44]									
9 II 2011 (CDFC)									
Total	1210854977	623 270 258	587 584 719	377 106 125	195 489 200	181 616 925	833 748 852	427 781 058	405 967 794
0 - 4	112 806 778	58 632 074	54 174 704	29 820 118	15 595 697	14 224 421	82 986 660	43 036 377	39 950 283
5 - 9	126 928 126	66 300 466	60 627 660	33 120 514	17 475 207	15 645 307	93 807 612	48 825 259	44 982 353
10 - 14	132 709 212	69 418 835	63 290 377	35 904 718	18 930 677	16 974 041	96 804 494	50 488 158	46 316 336
15 - 19	120 526 449	63 982 396	56 544 053	36 623 977	19 411 839	17 212 138	83 902 472	44 570 557	39 331 915
20 - 24	111 424 222	57 584 693	53 839 529	37 589 176	19 446 031	18 143 145	73 835 046	38 138 662	35 696 384
25 - 29	101 413 965	51 344 208	50 069 757	35 345 695	17 968 219	17 377 476	66 068 270	33 375 989	32 692 281
30 - 34	88 594 951	44 660 674	43 934 277	30 683 172	15 726 482	14 956 690	57 911 779	28 934 192	28 977 587
35 - 39	85 140 684	42 919 381	42 221 303	29 077 977	14 793 820	14 284 157	56 062 707	28 125 561	27 937 146
40 - 44	72 438 112	37 545 386	34 892 726	24 857 104	12 980 151	11 876 953	47 581 008	24 565 235	23 015 773
45 - 49	62 318 327	32 138 114	30 180 213	21 630 099	11 273 844	10 356 255	40 688 228	20 864 270	19 823 958
50 - 54	49 069 254	25 843 266	23 225 988	17 037 466	9 053 719	7 983 747	32 031 788	16 789 547	15 242 241
55 - 59	39 146 055	19 456 012	19 690 043	13 284 541	6 919 483	6 365 058	25 861 514	12 536 529	13 324 985
60 - 64	37 663 707	18 701 749	18 961 958	11 372 462	5 770 157	5 602 305	26 291 245	12 931 592	13 359 653
65 - 69	26 454 983	12 944 326	13 510 657	7 538 713	3 736 015	3 802 698	18 916 270	9 208 311	9 707 959
70 - 74	19 208 842	9 651 499	9 557 343	5 401 242	2 673 320	2 727 922	13 807 600	6 978 179	6 829 421
75 - 79	9 232 503	4 490 603	4 741 900	2 848 786	1 377 179	1 471 607	6 383 717	3 113 424	3 270 293
80 - 84	6 220 229	2 927 040	3 293 189	1 800 347	807 610	992 737	4 419 882	2 119 430	2 300 452
85 - 89	2 383 167	1 120 106	1 263 061	785 179	349 809	435 370	1 597 988	770 297	827 691
90 - 94	1 446 534	652 465	794 069	422 547	180 500	242 047	1 023 987	471 965	552 022
95 - 99	633 297	294 759	338 538	187 628	84 120	103 508	445 669	210 639	235 030
100 +	605 778	289 325	316 453	198 314	95 860	102 454	407 464	193 465	213 999
Unknown - Inconnu	4 489 802	2 372 881	2 116 921	1 576 350	839 461	736 889	2 913 452	1 533 420	1 380 032
Indonesia - Indonésie[45]									
1 VII 2015 (ESDJ)									
Total	*255 182 144*	*128 231 889*	*126 950 255*	*135 613 086*	*68 118 678*	*67 494 408*	*119 569 058*	*60 113 211*	*59 455 847*
0	*4 129 206*	*2 086 586*	*2 042 620*	*2 203 413*	*1 109 637*	*1 093 776*	*1 925 793*	*976 949*	*948 844*
1 - 4	*18 649 805*	*9 556 167*	*9 093 638*	*9 674 406*	*4 940 927*	*4 733 479*	*8 975 399*	*4 615 240*	*4 360 159*
5 - 9	*24 564 098*	*12 588 393*	*11 975 705*	*12 624 775*	*6 489 085*	*6 135 690*	*11 939 323*	*6 099 308*	*5 840 015*
10 - 14	*23 496 807*	*12 029 572*	*11 467 235*	*11 975 376*	*6 101 228*	*5 874 148*	*11 521 431*	*5 928 344*	*5 593 087*
15 - 19	*21 110 721*	*10 788 401*	*10 322 320*	*11 183 002*	*5 651 624*	*5 531 378*	*9 927 719*	*5 136 777*	*4 790 942*
20 - 24	*20 950 475*	*10 634 769*	*10 315 706*	*11 993 749*	*6 046 995*	*5 946 754*	*8 956 726*	*4 587 774*	*4 368 952*
25 - 29	*21 172 507*	*10 585 769*	*10 586 738*	*11 618 534*	*5 839 754*	*5 778 780*	*9 553 973*	*4 746 015*	*4 807 958*
30 - 34	*20 336 001*	*10 150 408*	*10 185 593*	*11 135 834*	*5 589 237*	*5 546 597*	*9 200 167*	*4 561 171*	*4 638 996*
35 - 39	*19 987 441*	*9 936 043*	*10 051 398*	*11 017 643*	*5 476 010*	*5 541 633*	*8 969 798*	*4 460 033*	*4 509 765*
40 - 44	*18 009 072*	*9 063 867*	*8 945 205*	*9 612 758*	*4 880 339*	*4 732 419*	*8 396 314*	*4 183 528*	*4 212 786*
45 - 49	*16 474 327*	*8 247 350*	*8 226 977*	*8 891 443*	*4 423 750*	*4 467 693*	*7 582 884*	*3 823 600*	*3 759 284*
50 - 54	*13 119 231*	*6 638 517*	*6 480 714*	*7 064 986*	*3 515 250*	*3 549 736*	*6 054 245*	*3 123 267*	*2 930 978*
55 - 59	*11 572 736*	*5 729 185*	*5 843 551*	*5 887 496*	*2 988 434*	*2 899 062*	*5 685 240*	*2 740 751*	*2 944 489*
60 - 64	*8 297 601*	*4 206 906*	*4 090 695*	*4 245 745*	*2 143 629*	*2 102 116*	*4 051 856*	*2 063 277*	*1 988 579*
65 - 69	*5 101 072*	*2 427 508*	*2 673 564*	*2 500 758*	*1 203 349*	*1 297 409*	*2 600 314*	*1 224 159*	*1 376 155*
70 - 74	*3 954 635*	*1 772 393*	*2 182 242*	*1 949 235*	*874 108*	*1 075 127*	*2 005 400*	*898 285*	*1 107 115*
75 +	*4 256 409*	*1 790 055*	*2 466 354*	*2 033 933*	*845 322*	*1 188 611*	*2 222 476*	*944 733*	*1 277 743*
Iran (Islamic Republic of) - Iran (République islamique d')[46]									
1 VII 2015 (ESDJ)									
Total	*78 773 093*	*39 672 171*	*39 100 922*	*57 326 841*	*28 887 379*	*28 439 462*	*21 446 252*	*10 784 792*	*10 661 460*
0 - 4	*6 759 788*	*3 454 660*	*3 305 128*	*4 635 262*	*2 370 592*	*2 264 670*	*2 124 526*	*1 084 068*	*1 040 458*

Continent, country or area, date, code[a] and age (in years) / Continent, pays ou zone, date, code[a] et âge (en années)	Total			Urban - Urbaine			Rural - Rurale		
	Both sexes Les deux sexes	Male Masculin	Female Féminin	Both sexes Les deux sexes	Male Masculin	Female Féminin	Both sexes Les deux sexes	Male Masculin	Female Féminin
ASIA - ASIE									
Iran (Islamic Republic of) - Iran (République islamique d')[46]									
1 VII 2015 (ESDJ)									
5 - 9	6 129 170	3 139 243	2 989 927	4 230 649	2 168 386	2 062 263	1 898 521	970 857	927 664
10 - 14	5 596 244	2 864 006	2 732 238	3 933 583	2 011 642	1 921 941	1 662 661	852 364	810 297
15 - 19	5 763 419	2 931 502	2 831 917	4 015 054	2 034 563	1 980 491	1 748 365	896 939	851 426
20 - 24	6 924 685	3 491 776	3 432 909	4 949 401	2 466 005	2 483 396	1 975 284	1 025 771	949 513
25 - 29	8 593 310	4 284 192	4 309 118	6 386 494	3 161 373	3 225 121	2 206 816	1 122 819	1 083 997
30 - 34	8 405 909	4 221 288	4 184 621	6 306 209	3 161 430	3 144 779	2 099 700	1 059 858	1 039 842
35 - 39	6 594 547	3 332 633	3 261 914	4 923 492	2 488 204	2 435 288	1 671 055	844 429	826 626
40 - 44	5 358 394	2 740 397	2 617 997	4 090 368	2 103 562	1 986 806	1 268 026	636 835	631 191
45 - 49	4 689 537	2 369 072	2 320 465	3 628 546	1 847 960	1 780 586	1 060 991	521 112	539 879
50 - 54	3 837 200	1 923 270	1 913 930	2 930 103	1 486 376	1 443 727	907 097	436 894	470 203
55 - 59	3 282 293	1 632 134	1 650 159	2 463 572	1 252 253	1 211 319	818 721	379 881	438 840
60 - 64	2 379 796	1 158 986	1 220 810	1 740 304	869 032	871 272	639 492	289 954	349 538
65 - 69	1 592 739	738 933	853 806	1 143 649	539 414	604 235	449 090	199 519	249 571
70 - 74	1 112 360	526 506	585 854	776 014	365 827	410 187	336 346	160 679	175 667
75 - 79	845 674	418 237	427 437	569 035	276 529	292 506	276 639	141 708	134 931
80 +	908 028	445 336	462 692	605 106	284 231	320 875	302 922	161 105	141 817
Iraq									
1 VII 2015 (ESDF)									
Total	36 658 503	18 520 532	18 137 971	25 631 821	12 935 587	12 696 234	11 026 682	5 584 945	5 441 737
0	1 137 967	584 535	553 432	752 979	386 080	366 899	384 988	198 455	186 533
1 - 4	4 331 718	2 225 935	2 105 783	2 876 835	1 475 521	1 401 314	1 454 883	750 414	704 469
5 - 9	4 910 887	2 527 175	2 383 712	3 286 086	1 687 351	1 598 735	1 624 801	839 824	784 977
10 - 14	4 359 943	2 246 489	2 113 454	2 947 957	1 515 198	1 432 759	1 411 986	731 291	680 695
15 - 19	3 848 199	1 978 743	1 869 456	2 637 780	1 353 470	1 284 310	1 210 419	625 273	585 146
20 - 24	3 328 277	1 703 854	1 624 423	2 331 929	1 192 710	1 139 219	996 348	511 144	485 204
25 - 29	2 895 690	1 471 180	1 424 510	2 057 867	1 045 789	1 012 078	837 823	425 391	412 432
30 - 34	2 486 941	1 245 726	1 241 215	1 791 620	899 685	891 935	695 321	346 041	349 280
35 - 39	2 133 553	1 058 276	1 075 277	1 551 758	772 320	779 438	581 795	285 956	295 839
40 - 44	1 807 120	887 149	919 971	1 322 951	651 530	671 421	484 169	235 619	248 550
45 - 49	1 494 733	727 670	767 063	1 104 497	539 556	564 941	390 236	188 114	202 122
50 - 54	1 171 634	564 478	607 156	880 319	425 836	454 483	291 315	138 642	152 673
55 - 59	915 225	438 062	477 163	694 340	333 828	360 512	220 885	104 234	116 651
60 - 64	675 377	321 617	353 760	515 990	246 884	269 106	159 387	74 733	84 654
65 - 69	480 527	228 559	251 968	369 196	176 457	192 739	111 331	52 102	59 229
70 - 74	304 637	145 516	159 121	235 201	112 862	122 339	69 436	32 654	36 782
75 - 79	147 670	72 473	75 197	113 997	56 096	57 901	33 673	16 377	17 296
80 +	228 407	93 096	135 311	160 521	64 415	96 106	67 886	28 681	39 205
Israel - Israël[47]									
1 VII 2014 (ESDJ)									
Total	8 215 668	4 070 269	4 145 398	7 502 325	3 707 183	3 795 142	713 343	363 086	350 256
0	173 466	89 224	84 242	157 791	81 137	76 654	15 674	8 086	7 588
1 - 4	675 951	346 399	329 551	610 676	312 831	297 845	65 275	33 568	31 706
5 - 9	763 923	391 548	372 376	686 762	351 705	335 057	77 162	39 843	37 319
10 - 14	706 511	361 769	344 742	638 797	326 871	311 926	67 713	34 898	32 816
15 - 19	637 766	326 459	311 307	574 938	293 019	281 920	62 828	33 440	29 388
20 - 24	602 809	307 085	295 724	552 526	280 592	271 934	50 282	26 493	23 789
25 - 29	585 092	294 604	290 488	540 555	271 648	268 907	44 537	22 956	21 581
30 - 34	571 522	285 604	285 918	526 527	263 399	263 127	44 996	22 205	22 791
35 - 39	551 928	274 342	277 586	501 879	250 011	251 868	50 049	24 330	25 719
40 - 44	502 655	248 964	253 691	455 668	225 582	230 086	46 987	23 382	23 604
45 - 49	424 569	209 717	214 852	386 549	190 250	196 298	38 020	19 466	18 554
50 - 54	395 957	192 521	203 436	363 604	175 988	187 616	32 353	16 533	15 820
55 - 59	378 193	181 321	196 872	348 201	165 951	182 250	29 992	15 370	14 622
60 - 64	362 502	172 279	190 223	334 478	157 867	176 611	28 024	14 412	13 612
65 - 69	299 228	140 369	158 859	278 164	129 706	148 459	21 063	10 663	10 401
70 - 74	182 255	83 107	99 148	169 376	76 688	92 688	12 879	6 419	6 460
75 - 79	169 822	73 999	95 824	159 443	69 040	90 403	10 379	4 959	5 420
80 - 84	116 012	47 785	68 227	108 640	44 642	63 998	7 371	3 142	4 229
85 - 89	73 716	27 606	46 110	68 942	25 791	43 151	4 774	1 814	2 959
90 - 94	32 118	11 817	20 301	29 869	10 947	18 921	2 249	869	1 379

Continent, country or area, date, code[a] and age (in years) Continent, pays ou zone, date, code[a] et âge (en années)	Total			Urban - Urbaine			Rural - Rurale		
	Both sexes Les deux sexes	Male Masculin	Female Féminin	Both sexes Les deux sexes	Male Masculin	Female Féminin	Both sexes Les deux sexes	Male Masculin	Female Féminin
ASIA - ASIE									
Israel - Israël[47]									
1 VII 2014 (ESDJ)									
95 - 99	6 775	2 511	4 265	6 254	2 335	3 919	521	176	345
100 +	2 898	1 243	1 655	2 685	1 182	1 503	213	61	152
Japan - Japon[48]									
1 X 2010 (CDJC)									
Total	128 057 352	62 327 737	65 729 615	116 156 631	56 569 051	59 587 580	11 900 721	5 758 686	6 142 035
0 - 4	5 296 748	2 710 581	2 586 167	4 831 346	2 472 475	2 358 871	465 402	238 106	227 296
5 - 9	5 585 661	2 859 805	2 725 856	5 061 966	2 591 629	2 470 337	523 695	268 176	255 519
10 - 14	5 921 035	3 031 943	2 889 092	5 348 569	2 737 977	2 610 592	572 466	293 966	278 500
15 - 19	6 063 357	3 109 229	2 954 128	5 506 483	2 823 085	2 683 398	556 874	286 144	270 730
20 - 24	6 426 433	3 266 240	3 160 193	5 925 984	3 012 027	2 913 957	500 449	254 213	246 236
25 - 29	7 293 701	3 691 723	3 601 978	6 720 343	3 397 748	3 322 595	573 358	293 975	279 383
30 - 34	8 341 497	4 221 011	4 120 486	7 675 385	3 879 081	3 796 304	666 112	341 930	324 182
35 - 39	9 786 349	4 950 122	4 836 227	9 015 173	4 556 572	4 458 601	771 176	393 550	377 626
40 - 44	8 741 865	4 400 375	4 341 490	8 046 407	4 051 948	3 994 459	695 458	348 427	347 031
45 - 49	8 033 116	4 027 969	4 005 147	7 328 789	3 675 150	3 653 639	704 327	352 819	351 508
50 - 54	7 644 499	3 809 576	3 834 923	6 878 402	3 425 836	3 452 566	766 097	383 740	382 357
55 - 59	8 663 734	4 287 489	4 376 245	7 753 645	3 830 707	3 922 938	910 089	456 782	453 307
60 - 64	10 037 249	4 920 468	5 116 781	9 046 242	4 424 879	4 621 363	991 007	495 589	495 418
65 - 69	8 210 173	3 921 774	4 288 399	7 424 237	3 543 535	3 880 702	785 936	378 239	407 697
70 - 74	6 963 302	3 225 503	3 737 799	6 249 910	2 895 658	3 354 252	713 392	329 845	383 547
75 - 79	5 941 013	2 582 940	3 358 073	5 276 323	2 294 753	2 981 570	664 690	288 187	376 503
80 - 84	4 336 264	1 692 584	2 643 680	3 804 707	1 485 631	2 319 076	531 557	206 953	324 604
85 - 89	2 432 588	744 222	1 688 366	2 121 067	649 324	1 471 743	311 521	94 898	216 623
90 - 94	1 021 707	241 799	779 908	889 810	210 257	679 553	131 897	31 542	100 355
95 - 99	296 756	55 739	241 017	258 266	48 545	209 721	38 490	7 194	31 296
100 +	43 882	5 851	38 031	38 068	5 060	33 008	5 814	791	5 023
Unknown - Inconnu	976 423	570 794	405 629	955 509	557 174	398 335	20 914	13 620	7 294
1 VII 2015 (ESDJ)[49]									
Total	126 958 000	61 729 000	65 230 000	...	...	...	...	...	...
0 - 4	5 200 000	2 667 000	2 533 000	...	...	...	...	...	...
5 - 9	5 304 000	2 715 000	2 589 000	...	...	...	...	...	...
10 - 14	5 639 000	2 888 000	2 751 000	...	...	...	...	...	...
15 - 19	5 985 000	3 064 000	2 921 000	...	...	...	...	...	...
20 - 24	6 241 000	3 213 000	3 028 000	...	...	...	...	...	...
25 - 29	6 571 000	3 367 000	3 204 000	...	...	...	...	...	...
30 - 34	7 347 000	3 730 000	3 617 000	...	...	...	...	...	...
35 - 39	8 423 000	4 266 000	4 157 000	...	...	...	...	...	...
40 - 44	9 798 000	4 956 000	4 842 000	...	...	...	...	...	...
45 - 49	8 708 000	4 380 000	4 329 000	...	...	...	...	...	...
50 - 54	7 906 000	3 959 000	3 947 000	...	...	...	...	...	...
55 - 59	7 576 000	3 763 000	3 813 000	...	...	...	...	...	...
60 - 64	8 605 000	4 224 000	4 381 000	...	...	...	...	...	...
65 - 69	9 570 000	4 619 000	4 951 000	...	...	...	...	...	...
70 - 74	7 821 000	3 636 000	4 185 000	...	...	...	...	...	...
75 - 79	6 332 000	2 806 000	3 526 000	...	...	...	...	...	...
80 - 84	4 978 000	1 997 000	2 981 000	...	...	...	...	...	...
85 - 89	3 141 000	1 066 000	2 075 000	...	...	...	...	...	...
90 - 94	1 369 000	337 000	1 032 000	...	...	...	...	...	...
95 - 99	383 000	68 000	315 000	...	...	...	...	...	...
100 +	63 000	8 000	54 000	...	...	...	...	...	...
Jordan - Jordanie[50]									
30 X 2015 (CDFC)									
Total	9 531 712	5 046 822	4 484 890	...	...	...	...	...	...
0	208 775	107 042	101 733	...	...	...	...	...	...
1 - 4	885 868	454 473	431 395	...	...	...	...	...	...
5 - 9	1 170 043	598 252	571 791	...	...	...	...	...	...
10 - 14	1 011 057	520 194	490 863	...	...	...	...	...	...
15 - 19	947 645	498 541	449 104	...	...	...	...	...	...
20 - 24	945 461	518 875	426 586	...	...	...	...	...	...
25 - 29	829 950	459 481	370 469	...	...	...	...	...	...
30 - 34	734 090	395 712	338 378	...	...	...	...	...	...
35 - 39	651 192	352 692	298 500	...	...	...	...	...	...
40 - 44	560 930	304 330	256 600	...	...	...	...	...	...

7. Population by age, sex and urban/rural residence: latest available year, 2006 - 2015
Population selon l'âge, le sexe et la résidence, urbaine/rurale : dernière année disponible, 2006 - 2015 (continued - suite)

Continent, country or area, date, code[a] and age (in years) / Continent, pays ou zone, date, code[a] et âge (en années)	Total			Urban - Urbaine			Rural - Rurale		
	Both sexes Les deux sexes	Male Masculin	Female Féminin	Both sexes Les deux sexes	Male Masculin	Female Féminin	Both sexes Les deux sexes	Male Masculin	Female Féminin
ASIA - ASIE									
Jordan - Jordanie[50]									
30 X 2015 (CDFC)									
45 - 49	473 404	258 560	214 844	...	...	...	...	...	...
50 - 54	349 832	187 185	162 647	...	...	...	...	...	...
55 - 59	244 701	127 361	117 340	...	...	...	...	...	...
60 - 64	167 083	86 259	80 824	...	...	...	...	...	...
65 - 69	135 650	67 493	68 157	...	...	...	...	...	...
70 - 74	99 793	52 669	47 124	...	...	...	...	...	...
75 - 79	64 176	32 423	31 753	...	...	...	...	...	...
80 +	52 062	25 280	26 782	...	...	...	...	...	...
Kazakhstan									
1 I 2014 (ESDF)									
Total	17 160 774	8 284 815	8 875 959	9 433 482	4 421 972	5 011 510	7 727 292	3 862 843	3 864 449
0	383 507	197 722	185 785	206 925	106 746	100 179	176 582	90 976	85 606
1 - 4	1 453 960	747 077	706 883	774 383	398 197	376 186	679 577	348 880	330 697
5 - 9	1 478 444	759 906	718 538	727 159	374 068	353 091	751 285	385 838	365 447
10 - 14	1 142 469	584 661	557 808	541 266	278 151	263 115	601 203	306 510	294 693
15 - 19	1 229 114	627 497	601 617	589 482	299 106	290 376	639 632	328 391	311 241
20 - 24	1 549 891	776 520	773 371	899 705	431 037	468 668	650 186	345 483	304 703
25 - 29	1 593 969	789 257	804 712	941 249	451 323	489 926	652 720	337 934	314 786
30 - 34	1 323 571	655 904	667 667	766 862	370 961	395 901	556 709	284 943	271 766
35 - 39	1 195 873	583 523	612 350	677 270	319 428	357 842	518 603	264 095	254 508
40 - 44	1 112 543	537 147	575 396	628 467	291 881	336 586	484 076	245 266	238 810
45 - 49	1 041 284	495 478	545 806	579 844	264 313	315 531	461 440	231 165	230 275
50 - 54	1 055 814	491 529	564 285	594 574	266 110	328 464	461 240	225 419	235 821
55 - 59	825 252	369 231	456 021	467 435	200 179	267 256	357 817	169 052	188 765
60 - 64	626 713	263 189	363 524	363 041	145 102	217 939	263 672	118 087	145 585
65 - 69	358 005	142 912	215 093	212 061	80 423	131 638	145 944	62 489	83 455
70 - 74	328 827	118 456	210 371	187 797	63 704	124 093	141 030	54 752	86 278
75 - 79	268 284	91 291	176 993	158 629	50 542	108 087	109 655	40 749	68 906
80 - 84	114 520	33 815	80 705	70 087	19 640	50 447	44 433	14 175	30 258
85 - 89	62 266	15 583	46 683	38 006	8 850	29 156	24 260	6 733	17 527
90 - 94	13 270	3 142	10 128	7 688	1 730	5 958	5 582	1 412	4 170
95 - 99	2 224	628	1 596	1 091	305	786	1 133	323	810
100 +	974	347	627	461	176	285	513	171	342
Kuwait - Koweït									
1 VII 2014 (ESDF)									
Total	3 767 415	2 161 594	1 605 821	...	...	...	...	...	...
0	66 474	34 563	31 911	...	...	...	...	...	...
1 - 4	251 311	130 712	120 599	...	...	...	...	...	...
5 - 9	272 062	140 960	131 102	...	...	...	...	...	...
10 - 14	229 368	118 339	111 029	...	...	...	...	...	...
15 - 19	216 068	112 844	103 224	...	...	...	...	...	...
20 - 24	208 012	106 280	101 732	...	...	...	...	...	...
25 - 29	373 992	198 156	175 836	...	...	...	...	...	...
30 - 34	486 880	291 208	195 672	...	...	...	...	...	...
35 - 39	485 789	298 637	187 152	...	...	...	...	...	...
40 - 44	417 976	259 366	158 610	...	...	...	...	...	...
45 - 49	288 750	179 971	108 779	...	...	...	...	...	...
50 - 54	195 478	122 562	72 916	...	...	...	...	...	...
55 - 59	124 637	80 389	44 248	...	...	...	...	...	...
60 - 64	71 182	44 385	26 797	...	...	...	...	...	...
65 - 69	37 103	20 886	16 217	...	...	...	...	...	...
70 - 74	20 497	10 903	9 594	...	...	...	...	...	...
75 - 79	11 929	6 316	5 613	...	...	...	...	...	...
80 +	9 907	5 117	4 790	...	...	...	...	...	...
Kyrgyzstan - Kirghizstan[51]									
1 VII 2015 (ESDJ)									
Total	5 957 271	2 948 932	3 008 339	2 008 148	952 329	1 055 819	3 949 123	1 996 603	1 952 520
0	159 990	82 535	77 455	52 179	27 123	25 056	107 811	55 412	52 399
1 - 4	601 454	308 245	293 209	201 736	103 446	98 290	399 718	204 799	194 919
5 - 9	607 958	310 339	297 619	187 072	95 232	91 840	420 886	215 107	205 779
10 - 14	509 467	259 623	249 844	144 144	72 925	71 219	365 323	186 698	178 625
15 - 19	519 838	264 738	255 100	144 540	73 216	71 324	375 298	191 522	183 776
20 - 24	574 644	292 268	282 376	182 268	89 206	93 062	392 376	203 062	189 314

Continent, country or area, date, code[a] and age (in years) / Continent, pays ou zone, date, code[a] et âge (en années)	Total			Urban - Urbaine			Rural - Rurale		
	Both sexes Les deux sexes	Male Masculin	Female Féminin	Both sexes Les deux sexes	Male Masculin	Female Féminin	Both sexes Les deux sexes	Male Masculin	Female Féminin
ASIA - ASIE									
Kyrgyzstan - Kirghizstan[51]									
1 VII 2015 (ESDJ)									
25 - 29	572 439	286 559	285 880	229 168	106 245	122 923	343 271	180 314	162 957
30 - 34	450 716	226 799	223 917	161 106	76 621	84 485	289 610	150 178	139 432
35 - 39	369 602	184 633	184 969	132 941	62 773	70 168	236 661	121 860	114 801
40 - 44	333 109	162 700	170 409	119 796	53 869	65 927	213 313	108 831	104 482
45 - 49	309 532	149 657	159 875	112 548	51 087	61 461	196 984	98 570	98 414
50 - 54	292 828	138 525	154 303	103 621	46 519	57 102	189 207	92 006	97 201
55 - 59	238 150	110 175	127 975	84 459	36 842	47 617	153 691	73 333	80 358
60 - 64	157 344	69 809	87 535	56 623	23 384	33 239	100 721	46 425	54 296
65 - 69	98 795	41 492	57 303	38 589	14 879	23 710	60 206	26 613	33 593
70 - 74	47 896	19 602	28 294	17 916	6 504	11 412	29 980	13 098	16 882
75 - 79	59 533	22 306	37 227	22 269	7 410	14 859	37 264	14 896	22 368
80 - 84	29 858	10 468	19 390	9 532	2 855	6 677	20 326	7 613	12 713
85 - 89	17 698	6 236	11 462	5 694	1 612	4 082	12 004	4 624	7 380
90 - 94	4 959	1 792	3 167	1 544	476	1 068	3 415	1 316	2 099
95 - 99	1 178	343	835	311	91	220	867	252	615
100 +	283	88	195	92	14	78	191	74	117
Lao People's Democratic Republic - République démocratique populaire lao									
1 III 2015 (CDJC)									
Total	6 492 228	3 254 770	3 237 458	...	...	...	...	...	...
0	118 387	60 356	58 031	...	...	...	...	...	...
1 - 4	563 596	286 106	277 490	...	...	...	...	...	...
5 - 9	679 209	345 380	333 829	...	...	...	...	...	...
10 - 14	718 606	363 026	355 580	...	...	...	...	...	...
15 - 19	699 010	354 360	344 650	...	...	...	...	...	...
20 - 24	654 037	325 601	328 436	...	...	...	...	...	...
25 - 29	615 988	308 988	307 000	...	...	...	...	...	...
30 - 34	496 234	250 383	245 851	...	...	...	...	...	...
35 - 39	420 083	212 523	207 560	...	...	...	...	...	...
40 - 44	343 870	170 808	173 062	...	...	...	...	...	...
45 - 49	295 907	149 656	146 251	...	...	...	...	...	...
50 - 54	267 418	127 272	140 146	...	...	...	...	...	...
55 - 59	197 607	98 615	98 992	...	...	...	...	...	...
60 - 64	147 179	74 106	73 073	...	...	...	...	...	...
65 - 69	98 901	47 563	51 338	...	...	...	...	...	...
70 - 74	71 427	32 930	38 497	...	...	...	...	...	...
75 - 79	47 078	21 871	25 207	...	...	...	...	...	...
80 - 84	30 190	13 519	16 671	...	...	...	...	...	...
85 - 89	15 267	6 744	8 523	...	...	...	...	...	...
90 - 94	7 036	3 041	3 995	...	...	...	...	...	...
95 +	5 198	1 922	3 276	...	...	...	...	...	...
Lebanon - Liban[52]									
3 III 2007 (SSDF)									
Total	3 759 134	1 857 659	1 901 475	...	...	...	...	...	...
0 - 4	261 021	136 514	124 507	...	...	...	...	...	...
5 - 9	312 902	160 577	152 325	...	...	...	...	...	...
10 - 14	354 049	183 613	170 436	...	...	...	...	...	...
15 - 19	363 626	195 984	167 642	...	...	...	...	...	...
20 - 24	367 778	191 471	176 307	...	...	...	...	...	...
25 - 29	305 933	148 321	157 612	...	...	...	...	...	...
30 - 34	276 775	132 105	144 670	...	...	...	...	...	...
35 - 39	249 550	111 833	137 717	...	...	...	...	...	...
40 - 44	233 003	102 405	130 598	...	...	...	...	...	...
45 - 49	208 752	95 595	113 157	...	...	...	...	...	...
50 - 54	179 899	84 091	95 808	...	...	...	...	...	...
55 - 59	143 376	66 993	76 383	...	...	...	...	...	...
60 - 64	140 030	65 701	74 329	...	...	...	...	...	...
65 - 69	122 014	59 900	62 114	...	...	...	...	...	...
70 - 74	105 259	53 267	51 992	...	...	...	...	...	...
75 - 79	71 315	38 353	32 962	...	...	...	...	...	...
80 - 84	45 481	21 083	24 398	...	...	...	...	...	...
85 +	18 371	9 853	8 518	...	...	...	...	...	...

7. Population by age, sex and urban/rural residence: latest available year, 2006 - 2015
Population selon l'âge, le sexe et la résidence, urbaine/rurale : dernière année disponible, 2006 - 2015 (continued - suite)

Continent, country or area, date, code[a] and age (in years) / Continent, pays ou zone, date, code[a] et âge (en années)	Total			Urban - Urbaine			Rural - Rurale		
	Both sexes Les deux sexes	Male Masculin	Female Féminin	Both sexes Les deux sexes	Male Masculin	Female Féminin	Both sexes Les deux sexes	Male Masculin	Female Féminin
ASIA - ASIE									
Malaysia - Malaisie[53]									
1 VII 2015 (ESDJ)									
Total	30 995 706	15 994 299	15 001 407	23 015 251	11 829 562	11 185 689	7 980 455	4 164 737	3 815 718
0	522 295	270 261	252 034	373 782	194 080	179 702	148 513	76 181	72 332
1 - 4	2 070 339	1 072 019	998 320	1 483 477	770 619	712 858	586 862	301 400	285 462
5 - 9	2 510 329	1 290 296	1 220 033	1 828 510	939 278	889 232	681 819	351 018	330 801
10 - 14	2 651 576	1 361 753	1 289 823	1 919 813	984 352	935 461	731 763	377 401	354 362
15 - 19	2 842 381	1 467 520	1 374 861	1 998 349	1 030 789	967 560	844 032	436 731	407 301
20 - 24	3 179 189	1 666 826	1 512 363	2 310 859	1 200 779	1 110 080	868 330	466 047	402 283
25 - 29	3 089 894	1 636 156	1 453 738	2 362 811	1 227 721	1 135 090	727 083	408 435	318 648
30 - 34	2 699 046	1 421 538	1 277 508	2 111 556	1 092 157	1 019 399	587 490	329 381	258 109
35 - 39	2 134 187	1 122 020	1 012 167	1 675 132	868 772	806 360	459 055	253 248	205 807
40 - 44	1 886 582	966 696	919 886	1 457 862	741 545	716 317	428 720	225 151	203 569
45 - 49	1 723 207	866 201	857 006	1 319 719	659 393	660 326	403 488	206 808	196 680
50 - 54	1 556 791	802 194	754 597	1 187 234	617 517	569 717	369 557	184 677	184 880
55 - 59	1 304 323	662 308	642 015	978 245	503 665	474 580	326 078	158 643	167 435
60 - 64	999 498	504 442	495 056	735 436	374 693	360 743	264 062	129 749	134 313
65 - 69	749 828	370 875	378 953	539 009	268 191	270 818	210 819	102 684	108 135
70 - 74	461 636	225 299	236 337	319 972	158 470	161 502	141 664	66 829	74 835
75 - 79	320 631	151 764	168 867	216 773	104 496	112 277	103 858	47 268	56 590
80 - 84	159 155	73 949	85 206	105 920	50 256	55 664	53 235	23 693	29 542
85 - 89	86 339	38 547	47 792	57 653	26 140	31 513	28 686	12 407	16 279
90 - 94	27 742	13 383	14 359	18 094	8 841	9 253	9 648	4 542	5 106
95 +	20 738	10 252	10 486	15 045	7 808	7 237	5 693	2 444	3 249
Maldives									
20 IX 2014 (CDFC)[54]									
Total	402 071	227 749	174 322	153 904	85 438	68 466	248 167	142 311	105 856
0	7 053	3 664	3 389	2 531	1 307	1 224	4 522	2 357	2 165
1 - 4	29 286	15 330	13 956	10 048	5 214	4 834	19 238	10 116	9 122
5 - 9	31 999	16 389	15 610	10 629	5 435	5 194	21 370	10 954	10 416
10 - 14	26 275	13 537	12 738	8 048	4 102	3 946	18 227	9 435	8 792
15 - 19	31 958	16 670	15 288	13 478	6 684	6 794	18 480	9 986	8 494
20 - 24	47 288	28 647	18 641	21 095	12 441	8 654	26 193	16 206	9 987
25 - 29	56 706	35 297	21 409	23 272	14 297	8 975	33 434	21 000	12 434
30 - 34	43 862	26 626	17 236	17 768	10 346	7 422	26 094	16 280	9 814
35 - 39	30 977	18 524	12 453	12 694	7 320	5 374	18 283	11 204	7 079
40 - 44	24 815	14 263	10 552	9 738	5 505	4 233	15 077	8 758	6 319
45 - 49	20 380	11 309	9 071	7 823	4 282	3 541	12 557	7 027	5 530
50 - 54	16 338	8 795	7 543	5 912	3 083	2 829	10 426	5 712	4 714
55 - 59	12 217	6 467	5 750	4 146	2 061	2 085	8 071	4 406	3 665
60 - 64	6 426	3 475	2 951	2 230	1 180	1 050	4 196	2 295	1 901
65 - 69	4 923	2 493	2 430	1 655	786	869	3 268	1 707	1 561
70 - 74	4 856	2 493	2 363	1 315	635	680	3 541	1 858	1 683
75 - 79	3 718	1 972	1 746	873	410	463	2 845	1 562	1 283
80 - 84	1 952	1 161	791	406	212	194	1 546	949	597
85 - 89	727	443	284	169	94	75	558	349	209
90 - 94	231	146	85	54	31	23	177	115	62
95 +	84	48	36	20	13	7	64	35	29
1 VII 2015 (ESDF)									
Total	347 552	175 394	172 158	...	...	...	...	...	...
0	7 083	3 588	3 495	...	...	...	...	...	...
1 - 4	27 364	13 794	13 570	...	...	...	...	...	...
5 - 9	29 250	14 804	14 446	...	...	...	...	...	...
10 - 14	26 729	13 721	13 008	...	...	...	...	...	...
15 - 19	31 841	16 475	15 366	...	...	...	...	...	...
20 - 24	38 819	20 105	18 714	...	...	...	...	...	...
25 - 29	40 228	20 292	19 936	...	...	...	...	...	...
30 - 34	33 430	16 292	17 138	...	...	...	...	...	...
35 - 39	23 576	11 508	12 068	...	...	...	...	...	...
40 - 44	20 332	9 928	10 404	...	...	...	...	...	...
45 - 49	17 795	8 662	9 133	...	...	...	...	...	...
50 - 54	15 381	7 654	7 727	...	...	...	...	...	...
55 - 59	12 282	6 249	6 033	...	...	...	...	...	...
60 - 64	6 764	3 513	3 251	...	...	...	...	...	...
65 - 69	5 095	2 584	2 511	...	...	...	...	...	...

Continent, country or area, date, code[a] and age (in years) / Continent, pays ou zone, date, code[a] et âge (en années)	Total			Urban - Urbaine			Rural - Rurale		
	Both sexes Les deux sexes	Male Masculin	Female Féminin	Both sexes Les deux sexes	Male Masculin	Female Féminin	Both sexes Les deux sexes	Male Masculin	Female Féminin
ASIA - ASIE									
Maldives									
1 VII 2015 (ESDF)									
70 - 74	4 575	2 282	2 293	...	...	...	...	...	...
75 - 79	3 867	2 042	1 825	...	...	...	...	...	...
80 +	3 141	1 901	1 240	...	...	...	...	...	...
Mongolia - Mongolie									
11 XI 2010 (CDJC)									
Total	2 647 545	1 313 968	1 333 577	1 798 147	872 989	925 158	849 398	440 979	408 419
0 - 4	288 497	146 516	141 981	188 882	95 671	93 211	99 615	50 845	48 770
5 - 9	216 214	110 117	106 097	133 740	68 119	65 621	82 474	41 998	40 476
10 - 14	236 865	120 064	116 801	143 846	72 244	71 602	93 019	47 820	45 199
15 - 19	257 645	130 560	127 085	188 334	92 124	96 210	69 311	38 436	30 875
20 - 24	292 183	147 472	144 711	221 784	107 751	114 033	70 399	39 721	30 678
25 - 29	247 983	124 490	123 493	171 685	83 922	87 763	76 298	40 568	35 730
30 - 34	222 522	111 976	110 546	149 461	73 525	75 936	73 061	38 451	34 610
35 - 39	202 383	100 819	101 564	136 034	66 149	69 885	66 349	34 670	31 679
40 - 44	179 267	88 273	90 994	120 105	57 388	62 717	59 162	30 885	28 277
45 - 49	158 756	77 475	81 281	108 736	51 528	57 208	50 020	25 947	24 073
50 - 54	122 082	58 009	64 073	83 084	38 547	44 537	38 998	19 462	19 536
55 - 59	71 989	33 384	38 605	49 342	22 373	26 969	22 647	11 011	11 636
60 - 64	49 453	22 106	27 347	34 724	15 234	19 490	14 729	6 872	7 857
65 - 69	38 232	17 262	20 970	26 004	11 578	14 426	12 228	5 684	6 544
70 - 74	29 332	13 081	16 251	19 556	8 594	10 962	9 776	4 487	5 289
75 - 79	18 617	7 252	11 365	12 384	4 742	7 642	6 233	2 510	3 723
80 - 84	9 166	3 258	5 908	6 234	2 225	4 009	2 932	1 033	1 899
85 - 89	4 415	1 378	3 037	2 948	945	2 003	1 467	433	1 034
90 - 94	1 459	383	1 076	962	274	688	497	109	388
95 - 99	402	80	322	251	47	204	151	33	118
100 +	83	13	70	51	9	42	32	4	28
1 VII 2015 (ESDF)									
Total	3 026 864	1 485 034	1 541 830	...	...	...	...	...	...
0	77 190	39 562	37 628	...	...	...	...	...	...
1 - 4	289 227	147 787	141 440	...	...	...	...	...	...
5 - 9	285 077	144 911	140 167	...	...	...	...	...	...
10 - 14	221 732	112 491	109 242	...	...	...	...	...	...
15 - 19	242 124	122 035	120 089	...	...	...	...	...	...
20 - 24	273 029	136 675	136 354	...	...	...	...	...	...
25 - 29	309 744	153 980	155 764	...	...	...	...	...	...
30 - 34	260 698	128 712	131 987	...	...	...	...	...	...
35 - 39	233 013	114 331	118 682	...	...	...	...	...	...
40 - 44	208 575	101 061	107 515	...	...	...	...	...	...
45 - 49	178 443	84 772	93 671	...	...	...	...	...	...
50 - 54	153 522	71 813	81 709	...	...	...	...	...	...
55 - 59	111 635	50 518	61 117	...	...	...	...	...	...
60 - 64	66 030	28 987	37 043	...	...	...	...	...	...
65 - 69	42 698	17 924	24 775	...	...	...	...	...	...
70 - 74	33 120	14 151	18 969	...	...	...	...	...	...
75 - 79	21 219	8 818	12 401	...	...	...	...	...	...
80 - 84	12 529	4 395	8 134	...	...	...	...	...	...
85 - 89	4 871	1 516	3 355	...	...	...	...	...	...
90 - 94	1 868	497	1 371	...	...	...	...	...	...
95 - 99	429	87	342	...	...	...	...	...	...
100 +	95	15	80	...	...	...	...	...	...
Myanmar[55]									
29 III 2014 (CDFC)									
Total	50 279 900	24 228 714	26 051 186	14 877 943	7 114 224	7 763 719	35 401 957	17 114 490	18 287 467
0	823 378	416 645	406 733	208 571	105 968	102 603	614 807	310 677	304 130
1 - 4	3 648 752	1 846 138	1 802 614	872 557	443 616	428 941	2 776 195	1 402 522	1 373 673
5 - 9	4 819 077	2 438 372	2 380 705	1 146 876	583 310	563 566	3 672 201	1 855 062	1 817 139
10 - 14	5 108 362	2 595 749	2 512 613	1 355 792	703 305	652 487	3 752 570	1 892 444	1 860 126
15 - 19	4 625 989	2 290 998	2 334 991	1 467 120	740 956	726 164	3 158 869	1 550 042	1 608 827
20 - 24	4 331 069	2 091 525	2 239 544	1 460 572	711 405	749 167	2 870 497	1 380 120	1 490 377
25 - 29	4 146 134	1 995 465	2 150 669	1 320 591	638 841	681 750	2 825 543	1 356 624	1 468 919
30 - 34	3 898 861	1 884 549	2 014 312	1 229 010	595 549	633 461	2 669 851	1 289 000	1 380 851
35 - 39	3 563 480	1 705 630	1 857 850	1 092 916	518 880	574 036	2 470 564	1 186 750	1 283 814

226

Continent, country or area, date, code[a] and age (in years) Continent, pays ou zone, date, code[a] et âge (en années)	Total			Urban - Urbaine			Rural - Rurale		
	Both sexes Les deux sexes	Male Masculin	Female Féminin	Both sexes Les deux sexes	Male Masculin	Female Féminin	Both sexes Les deux sexes	Male Masculin	Female Féminin
ASIA - ASIE									
Myanmar[55]									
29 III 2014 (CDFC)									
40 - 44	3 283 073	1 548 942	1 734 131	1 025 669	474 286	551 383	2 257 404	1 074 656	1 182 748
45 - 49	2 946 148	1 375 041	1 571 107	918 610	414 377	504 233	2 027 538	960 664	1 066 874
50 - 54	2 559 232	1 182 341	1 376 891	783 327	346 474	436 853	1 775 905	835 867	940 038
55 - 59	2 051 937	935 979	1 115 958	631 743	275 176	356 567	1 420 194	660 803	759 391
60 - 64	1 576 845	712 040	864 805	477 041	206 172	270 869	1 099 804	505 868	593 936
65 - 69	1 064 493	466 618	597 875	333 747	140 316	193 431	730 746	326 302	404 444
70 - 74	713 170	301 679	411 491	212 747	87 697	125 050	500 423	213 982	286 441
75 - 79	553 298	228 315	324 983	165 732	65 960	99 772	387 566	162 355	225 211
80 - 84	335 576	130 875	204 701	99 573	36 945	62 628	236 003	93 930	142 073
85 - 89	158 069	56 979	101 090	51 127	17 118	34 009	106 942	39 861	67 081
90 - 94	51 382	17 695	33 687	17 705	5 770	11 935	33 677	11 925	21 752
95 +	21 575	7 139	14 436	6 917	2 103	4 814	14 658	5 036	9 622
Nepal - Népal									
22 VI 2011 (CDJC)									
Total	26 494 504	12 849 041	13 645 463	4 523 820	2 306 049	2 217 771	21 970 684	10 542 992	11 427 692
0 - 4	2 567 963	1 314 957	1 253 006	327 100	172 598	154 502	2 240 863	1 142 359	1 098 504
5 - 9	3 204 859	1 635 176	1 569 683	431 121	227 618	203 503	2 773 738	1 407 558	1 366 180
10 - 14	3 475 424	1 764 630	1 710 794	507 618	266 722	240 896	2 967 806	1 497 908	1 469 898
15 - 19	2 931 980	1 443 191	1 488 789	520 714	273 601	247 113	2 411 266	1 169 590	1 241 676
20 - 24	2 358 071	1 043 981	1 314 090	520 546	260 529	260 017	1 837 525	783 452	1 054 073
25 - 29	2 079 354	917 243	1 162 111	452 256	220 230	232 026	1 627 098	697 013	930 085
30 - 34	1 735 305	770 577	964 728	372 219	181 542	190 677	1 363 086	589 035	774 051
35 - 39	1 604 319	740 200	864 119	324 965	161 347	163 618	1 279 354	578 853	700 501
40 - 44	1 386 121	660 290	725 831	263 008	136 600	126 408	1 123 113	523 690	599 423
45 - 49	1 172 959	575 101	597 858	205 833	106 627	99 206	967 126	468 474	498 652
50 - 54	1 005 476	505 864	499 612	165 685	86 471	79 214	839 791	419 393	420 398
55 - 59	818 263	412 892	405 371	123 667	63 841	59 826	694 596	349 051	345 545
60 - 64	756 827	368 451	388 376	105 862	52 258	53 604	650 965	316 193	334 772
65 - 69	554 449	277 782	276 667	76 074	37 256	38 818	478 375	240 526	237 849
70 - 74	395 153	199 610	195 543	55 001	26 400	28 601	340 152	173 210	166 942
75 - 79	235 135	117 358	117 777	35 764	16 538	19 226	199 371	100 820	98 551
80 - 84	128 777	62 787	65 990	21 053	9 435	11 618	107 724	53 352	54 372
85 - 89	52 526	25 810	26 716	9 857	4 350	5 507	42 669	21 460	21 209
90 - 94	20 335	8 940	11 395	3 788	1 474	2 314	16 547	7 466	9 081
95 +	11 208	4 201	7 007	1 689	612	1 077	9 519	3 589	5 930
Oman									
1 VII 2009 (ESDF)									
Total	3 173 917	1 971 115	1 202 802	2 314 865	1 457 197	857 668	859 049	513 917	345 132
0 - 4	272 144	139 614	132 530	184 595	94 803	89 792	87 549	44 811	42 738
5 - 9	245 026	124 776	120 250	162 307	82 954	79 353	82 718	41 821	40 897
10 - 14	254 610	129 964	124 646	168 924	86 326	82 598	85 685	43 638	42 047
15 - 19	284 826	145 215	139 611	194 123	99 854	94 269	90 703	45 361	45 342
20 - 24	387 448	238 483	148 965	285 594	176 341	109 253	101 854	62 142	39 712
25 - 29	475 403	327 686	147 717	362 531	249 782	112 749	112 871	77 904	34 967
30 - 34	367 536	247 107	120 429	288 055	192 969	95 086	79 481	54 138	25 343
35 - 39	272 100	192 483	79 617	212 145	150 865	61 280	59 955	41 618	18 337
40 - 44	207 202	149 090	58 112	161 282	117 670	43 612	45 920	31 420	14 500
45 - 49	145 430	103 908	41 522	111 077	81 065	30 012	34 353	22 843	11 510
50 - 54	113 587	83 057	30 530	84 975	63 752	21 223	28 612	19 305	9 307
55 - 59	59 890	40 488	19 402	42 674	29 489	13 185	17 216	10 999	6 217
60 - 64	39 730	23 538	16 192	26 050	15 494	10 556	13 680	8 044	5 636
65 - 69	20 811	11 811	9 000	13 363	7 537	5 826	7 448	4 274	3 174
70 - 74	14 933	7 721	7 212	9 224	4 703	4 521	5 709	3 018	2 691
75 - 79	6 817	3 303	3 514	4 201	1 981	2 220	2 616	1 322	1 294
80 +	6 424	2 871	3 553	3 745	1 612	2 133	2 679	1 259	1 420
1 VII 2014 (ESDF)[56]									
Total	3 992 893	2 579 811	1 413 082	...	...	...	...	...	...
0	71 009	36 496	34 513	...	...	...	...	...	...
1 - 4	290 786	147 911	142 875	...	...	...	...	...	...
5 - 9	288 291	146 997	141 294	...	...	...	...	...	...
10 - 14	234 597	119 741	114 856	...	...	...	...	...	...
15 - 19	239 220	122 675	116 545	...	...	...	...	...	...
20 - 24	391 869	244 236	147 633	...	...	...	...	...	...

Continent, country or area, date, code[a] and age (in years) Continent, pays ou zone, date, code[a] et âge (en années)	Total			Urban - Urbaine			Rural - Rurale		
	Both sexes Les deux sexes	Male Masculin	Female Féminin	Both sexes Les deux sexes	Male Masculin	Female Féminin	Both sexes Les deux sexes	Male Masculin	Female Féminin
ASIA - ASIE									
Oman									
1 VII 2014 (ESDF)[56]									
25 - 29	691 916	506 642	185 274	...	...	...	...	...	...
30 - 34	552 009	404 263	147 746	...	...	...	...	...	...
35 - 39	386 620	273 648	112 972	...	...	...	...	...	...
40 - 44	269 982	197 869	72 113	...	...	...	...	...	...
45 - 49	186 618	135 911	50 707	...	...	...	...	...	...
50 - 54	136 173	93 478	42 695	...	...	...	...	...	...
55 - 59	98 169	66 267	31 902	...	...	...	...	...	...
60 - 64	54 409	31 028	23 381	...	...	...	...	...	...
65 - 69	33 770	17 657	16 113	...	...	...	...	...	...
70 - 74	28 164	14 059	14 105	...	...	...	...	...	...
75 - 79	17 338	9 572	7 766	...	...	...	...	...	...
80 - 84	11 835	6 125	5 710	...	...	...	...	...	...
85 - 89	5 225	2 714	2 511	...	...	...	...	...	...
90 - 94	3 279	1 651	1 628	...	...	...	...	...	...
95 +	1 614	871	743	...	...	...	...	...	...
Pakistan[57]									
1 VII 2007 (ESDJ)									
Total	149 860 388	76 857 737	73 002 651	52 807 585	27 178 203	25 629 382	97 052 803	49 679 534	47 373 269
0 - 4	19 540 467	9 783 859	9 756 608	5 761 626	2 854 601	2 907 026	13 778 841	6 929 259	6 849 582
5 - 9	22 554 631	11 710 324	10 844 307	6 759 356	3 414 295	3 345 061	15 795 276	8 296 029	7 499 246
10 - 14	20 255 889	10 636 015	9 619 874	6 854 564	3 572 029	3 282 536	13 401 325	7 063 987	6 337 339
15 - 19	17 275 679	9 063 876	8 211 804	6 630 532	3 454 683	3 175 849	10 645 147	5 609 193	5 035 954
20 - 24	13 558 584	6 824 723	6 733 861	5 604 996	2 913 936	2 691 060	7 953 588	3 910 786	4 042 801
25 - 29	10 833 092	5 268 436	5 564 656	4 174 036	2 128 117	2 045 919	6 659 055	3 140 318	3 518 737
30 - 34	8 432 325	3 957 414	4 474 911	3 112 553	1 539 219	1 573 334	5 319 772	2 418 195	2 901 576
35 - 39	8 352 417	4 132 910	4 219 507	3 081 885	1 522 176	1 559 709	5 270 532	2 610 734	2 659 798
40 - 44	6 777 652	3 496 263	3 281 389	2 564 848	1 348 144	1 216 704	4 212 804	2 148 119	2 064 685
45 - 49	6 276 492	3 277 150	2 999 342	2 458 241	1 271 498	1 186 743	3 818 252	2 005 652	1 812 599
50 - 54	4 586 117	2 429 295	2 156 822	1 772 219	967 032	805 188	2 813 897	1 462 263	1 351 634
55 - 59	3 544 175	1 864 568	1 679 608	1 325 845	693 075	632 770	2 218 330	1 171 493	1 046 838
60 - 64	2 933 669	1 637 251	1 296 418	1 003 276	574 578	428 698	1 930 393	1 062 673	867 720
65 - 69	2 038 506	1 106 476	932 030	713 604	371 079	342 526	1 324 901	735 397	589 504
70 - 74	1 464 156	857 310	606 846	499 821	282 013	217 808	964 335	575 297	389 039
75 - 79	654 088	358 255	295 833	244 044	125 467	118 577	410 044	232 788	177 256
80 - 84	428 280	250 734	177 547	129 604	84 073	45 531	298 676	166 661	132 015
85 +	354 168	202 880	151 288	116 534	62 189	54 345	237 634	140 691	96 943
Philippines									
1 V 2010 (CDJC)[58]									
Total	92 335 113	46 634 257	45 700 856	41 855 571	20 840 798	21 014 773	50 479 542	25 793 459	24 686 083
0	1 968 131	1 018 386	949 745	873 792	453 065	420 727	1 094 339	565 321	529 018
1 - 4	8 265 653	4 274 825	3 990 828	3 571 743	1 850 296	1 721 447	4 693 910	2 424 529	2 269 381
5 - 9	10 321 543	5 332 287	4 989 256	4 384 024	2 267 726	2 116 298	5 937 519	3 064 561	2 872 958
10 - 14	10 179 610	5 237 006	4 942 604	4 286 862	2 195 115	2 091 747	5 892 748	3 041 891	2 850 857
15 - 19	9 705 354	4 931 506	4 773 848	4 301 712	2 120 800	2 180 912	5 403 642	2 810 706	2 592 936
20 - 24	8 408 656	4 256 999	4 151 657	4 050 916	1 989 031	2 061 885	4 357 740	2 267 968	2 089 772
25 - 29	7 423 723	3 746 311	3 677 412	3 693 442	1 821 972	1 871 470	3 730 281	1 924 339	1 805 942
30 - 34	6 772 929	3 443 582	3 329 347	3 353 327	1 676 968	1 676 359	3 419 602	1 766 614	1 652 988
35 - 39	6 013 953	3 057 323	2 956 630	2 886 723	1 448 968	1 437 755	3 127 230	1 608 355	1 518 875
40 - 44	5 471 588	2 778 661	2 692 927	2 588 569	1 292 882	1 295 687	2 883 019	1 485 779	1 397 240
45 - 49	4 680 649	2 367 809	2 312 840	2 180 936	1 082 303	1 098 633	2 499 713	1 285 506	1 214 207
50 - 54	3 894 850	1 953 952	1 940 898	1 808 298	890 919	917 379	2 086 552	1 063 033	1 023 519
55 - 59	2 987 148	1 475 861	1 511 287	1 358 685	660 616	698 069	1 628 463	815 245	813 218
60 - 64	2 228 399	1 064 116	1 164 283	979 510	461 508	518 002	1 248 889	602 608	646 281
65 - 69	1 497 557	680 227	817 330	593 219	263 603	329 616	904 338	416 624	487 714
70 - 74	1 142 562	492 152	650 410	437 280	181 972	255 308	705 282	310 180	395 102
75 - 79	707 115	286 079	421 036	265 280	102 308	162 972	441 835	183 771	258 064
80 - 84	394 188	145 937	248 251	145 081	50 979	94 102	249 107	94 958	154 149
85 - 89	188 511	64 125	124 386	67 310	21 250	46 060	121 201	42 875	78 326
90 - 94	60 102	19 598	40 504	21 070	6 202	14 868	39 032	13 396	25 636
95 - 99	18 099	5 684	12 415	6 223	1 753	4 470	11 876	3 931	7 945
100 +	4 793	1 831	2 962	1 569	562	1 007	3 224	1 269	1 955

7. Population by age, sex and urban/rural residence: latest available year, 2006 - 2015
Population selon l'âge, le sexe et la résidence, urbaine/rurale : dernière année disponible, 2006 - 2015 (continued - suite)

Continent, country or area, date, code[a] and age (in years) / Continent, pays ou zone, date, code[a] et âge (en années)	Total			Urban - Urbaine			Rural - Rurale		
	Both sexes Les deux sexes	Male Masculin	Female Féminin	Both sexes Les deux sexes	Male Masculin	Female Féminin	Both sexes Les deux sexes	Male Masculin	Female Féminin
ASIA - ASIE									
Philippines									
1 VII 2015 (ESDJ)[17]									
Total	101 562 300	51 234 200	50 328 100	...	...	...	...	...	...
0 - 4	11 327 300	5 822 000	5 505 300	...	...	...	...	...	...
5 - 9	10 671 000	5 453 300	5 217 700	...	...	...	...	...	...
10 - 14	10 283 900	5 310 500	4 973 400	...	...	...	...	...	...
15 - 19	10 136 900	5 212 100	4 924 800	...	...	...	...	...	...
20 - 24	9 643 400	4 904 000	4 739 400	...	...	...	...	...	...
25 - 29	8 332 500	4 223 300	4 109 200	...	...	...	...	...	...
30 - 34	7 342 000	3 702 300	3 639 700	...	...	...	...	...	...
35 - 39	6 685 300	3 391 300	3 294 000	...	...	...	...	...	...
40 - 44	5 916 400	2 997 000	2 919 400	...	...	...	...	...	...
45 - 49	5 351 200	2 702 900	2 648 300	...	...	...	...	...	...
50 - 54	4 530 000	2 271 400	2 258 600	...	...	...	...	...	...
55 - 59	3 703 100	1 830 900	1 872 200	...	...	...	...	...	...
60 - 64	2 765 500	1 335 800	1 429 700	...	...	...	...	...	...
65 - 69	1 978 400	912 000	1 066 400	...	...	...	...	...	...
70 - 74	1 249 200	538 500	710 700	...	...	...	...	...	...
75 - 79	870 200	349 400	520 800	...	...	...	...	...	...
80 +	776 000	277 500	498 500	...	...	...	...	...	...
Qatar									
1 VII 2013 (ESDF)									
Total	2 003 700	1 477 632	526 068	...	...	...	...	...	...
0	22 441	11 195	11 246	...	...	...	...	...	...
1 - 4	90 700	46 539	44 161	...	...	...	...	...	...
5 - 9	101 189	51 840	49 349	...	...	...	...	...	...
10 - 14	81 233	41 546	39 687	...	...	...	...	...	...
15 - 19	75 897	45 092	30 805	...	...	...	...	...	...
20 - 24	218 475	179 820	38 655	...	...	...	...	...	...
25 - 29	354 242	281 045	73 197	...	...	...	...	...	...
30 - 34	326 348	253 924	72 424	...	...	...	...	...	...
35 - 39	244 013	187 192	56 821	...	...	...	...	...	...
40 - 44	188 078	148 262	39 816	...	...	...	...	...	...
45 - 49	124 089	97 259	26 830	...	...	...	...	...	...
50 - 54	82 169	64 303	17 866	...	...	...	...	...	...
55 - 59	50 050	39 133	10 917	...	...	...	...	...	...
60 - 64	22 108	16 407	5 701	...	...	...	...	...	...
65 - 69	9 925	6 668	3 257	...	...	...	...	...	...
70 - 74	5 375	3 215	2 160	...	...	...	...	...	...
75 - 79	3 574	2 166	1 408	...	...	...	...	...	...
80 +	3 794	2 026	1 768	...	...	...	...	...	...
Republic of Korea - République de Corée									
1 XI 2010 (CDJC)[59]									
Total	47 990 761	23 840 896	24 149 865	39 363 373	19 558 869	19 804 504	8 627 388	4 282 027	4 345 361
0 - 4	2 219 084	1 142 220	1 076 864	1 837 552	945 626	891 926	381 532	196 594	184 938
5 - 9	2 394 663	1 243 294	1 151 369	1 993 280	1 034 401	958 879	401 383	208 893	192 490
10 - 14	3 173 226	1 654 964	1 518 262	2 669 649	1 393 007	1 276 642	503 577	261 957	241 620
15 - 19	3 438 414	1 826 179	1 612 235	2 922 281	1 548 832	1 373 449	516 133	277 347	238 786
20 - 24	3 055 420	1 625 371	1 430 049	2 640 489	1 383 435	1 257 054	414 931	241 936	172 995
25 - 29	3 538 949	1 802 805	1 736 144	3 080 113	1 549 579	1 530 534	458 836	253 226	205 610
30 - 34	3 695 348	1 866 397	1 828 951	3 167 638	1 589 121	1 578 517	527 710	277 276	250 434
35 - 39	4 099 147	2 060 233	2 038 914	3 483 148	1 732 781	1 750 367	615 999	327 452	288 547
40 - 44	4 131 423	2 071 431	2 059 992	3 508 366	1 735 872	1 772 494	623 057	335 559	287 498
45 - 49	4 073 358	2 044 641	2 028 717	3 426 557	1 703 858	1 722 699	646 801	340 783	306 018
50 - 54	3 798 131	1 887 973	1 910 158	3 131 150	1 548 965	1 582 185	666 981	339 008	327 973
55 - 59	2 766 695	1 360 747	1 405 948	2 209 244	1 087 271	1 121 973	557 451	273 476	283 975
60 - 64	2 182 236	1 057 035	1 125 201	1 675 619	813 834	861 785	506 617	243 201	263 416
65 - 69	1 812 168	833 242	978 926	1 307 441	612 023	695 418	504 727	221 219	283 508
70 - 74	1 566 014	672 894	893 120	1 035 369	451 635	583 734	530 645	221 259	309 386
75 - 79	1 084 367	410 726	673 641	676 567	257 200	419 367	407 800	153 526	254 274
80 - 84	595 509	186 008	409 501	370 966	113 906	257 060	224 543	72 102	152 441
85 - 89	271 167	74 118	197 049	168 707	44 883	123 824	102 460	29 235	73 225
90 - 94	78 329	17 770	60 559	48 720	10 873	37 847	29 609	6 897	22 712

Continent, country or area, date, code[a] and age (in years) / Continent, pays ou zone, date, code[a] et âge (en années)	Total			Urban - Urbaine			Rural - Rurale		
	Both sexes Les deux sexes	Male Masculin	Female Féminin	Both sexes Les deux sexes	Male Masculin	Female Féminin	Both sexes Les deux sexes	Male Masculin	Female Féminin
ASIA - ASIE									
Republic of Korea - République de Corée									
1 XI 2010 (CDJC)[59]									
95 - 99	15 278	2 593	12 685	9 424	1 619	7 805	5 854	974	4 880
100 +	1 835	255	1 580	1 093	148	945	742	107	635
1 VII 2015 (ESDJ)[2]									
Total	50 617 045	25 302 520	25 314 525	...	...	...	...	...	...
0	453 515	234 430	219 085	...	...	...	...	...	...
1 - 4	1 843 401	951 472	891 929	...	...	...	...	...	...
5 - 9	2 266 859	1 168 548	1 098 311	...	...	...	...	...	...
10 - 14	2 475 819	1 284 381	1 191 438	...	...	...	...	...	...
15 - 19	3 175 320	1 663 750	1 511 570	...	...	...	...	...	...
20 - 24	3 525 734	1 888 018	1 637 716	...	...	...	...	...	...
25 - 29	3 279 000	1 727 957	1 551 043	...	...	...	...	...	...
30 - 34	3 807 021	1 970 131	1 836 890	...	...	...	...	...	...
35 - 39	3 846 466	1 961 338	1 885 128	...	...	...	...	...	...
40 - 44	4 239 971	2 156 163	2 083 808	...	...	...	...	...	...
45 - 49	4 225 823	2 129 574	2 096 249	...	...	...	...	...	...
50 - 54	4 255 812	2 142 386	2 113 426	...	...	...	...	...	...
55 - 59	3 857 441	1 923 479	1 933 962	...	...	...	...	...	...
60 - 64	2 740 743	1 333 730	1 407 013	...	...	...	...	...	...
65 - 69	2 121 186	1 008 155	1 113 031	...	...	...	...	...	...
70 - 74	1 721 079	763 391	957 688	...	...	...	...	...	...
75 - 79	1 371 183	557 712	813 471	...	...	...	...	...	...
80 - 84	859 318	297 377	561 941	...	...	...	...	...	...
85 - 89	387 911	106 300	281 611	...	...	...	...	...	...
90 - 94	133 620	29 279	104 341	...	...	...	...	...	...
95 - 99	26 498	4 534	21 964	...	...	...	...	...	...
100 +	3 325	415	2 910	...	...	...	...	...	...
Saudi Arabia - Arabie saoudite									
1 VII 2015* (ESDF)									
Total	31 015 999	17 652 149	13 363 850	...	...	...	...	...	...
0 - 4	2 878 783	1 477 380	1 401 403	...	...	...	...	...	...
5 - 9	2 304 881	1 203 723	1 101 158	...	...	...	...	...	...
10 - 14	2 456 229	1 276 618	1 179 611	...	...	...	...	...	...
15 - 19	2 540 329	1 318 768	1 221 561	...	...	...	...	...	...
20 - 24	2 531 574	1 325 306	1 206 268	...	...	...	...	...	...
25 - 29	2 752 658	1 492 216	1 260 442	...	...	...	...	...	...
30 - 34	3 098 467	1 800 682	1 297 785	...	...	...	...	...	...
35 - 39	3 337 479	2 053 885	1 283 594	...	...	...	...	...	...
40 - 44	2 875 337	1 779 112	1 096 225	...	...	...	...	...	...
45 - 49	2 098 909	1 353 202	745 707	...	...	...	...	...	...
50 - 54	1 491 139	972 531	518 608	...	...	...	...	...	...
55 - 59	1 028 355	651 380	376 975	...	...	...	...	...	...
60 - 64	695 355	420 218	275 137	...	...	...	...	...	...
65 - 69	427 888	248 540	179 348	...	...	...	...	...	...
70 - 74	261 148	146 866	114 282	...	...	...	...	...	...
75 - 79	135 130	75 605	59 525	...	...	...	...	...	...
80 +	102 338	56 117	46 221	...	...	...	...	...	...
Singapore - Singapour[60]									
30 VI 2015 (ESDJ)									
Total	3 902 690	1 916 628	1 986 062	...	...	...	...	...	...
0 - 4	183 575	93 852	89 723	...	...	...	...	...	...
5 - 9	204 452	103 861	100 591	...	...	...	...	...	...
10 - 14	214 388	109 401	104 987	...	...	...	...	...	...
15 - 19	242 902	124 287	118 615	...	...	...	...	...	...
20 - 24	264 127	133 493	130 634	...	...	...	...	...	...
25 - 29	271 030	132 504	138 526	...	...	...	...	...	...
30 - 34	290 619	137 847	152 772	...	...	...	...	...	...
35 - 39	301 067	143 795	157 272	...	...	...	...	...	...
40 - 44	316 755	154 460	162 295	...	...	...	...	...	...
45 - 49	303 413	149 607	153 806	...	...	...	...	...	...
50 - 54	315 091	158 465	156 626	...	...	...	...	...	...
55 - 59	295 063	147 860	147 203	...	...	...	...	...	...

7. Population by age, sex and urban/rural residence: latest available year, 2006 - 2015
Population selon l'âge, le sexe et la résidence, urbaine/rurale : dernière année disponible, 2006 - 2015 (continued - suite)

Continent, country or area, date, code[a] and age (in years) / Continent, pays ou zone, date, code[a] et âge (en annèes)	Total			Urban - Urbaine			Rural - Rurale		
	Both sexes Les deux sexes	Male Masculin	Female Féminin	Both sexes Les deux sexes	Male Masculin	Female Féminin	Both sexes Les deux sexes	Male Masculin	Female Féminin
ASIA - ASIE									
Singapore - Singapour[60]									
30 VI 2015 (ESDJ)									
60 - 64	240 493	119 660	120 833	...	...	...	...	...	...
65 - 69	182 425	88 697	93 728	...	...	...	...	...	...
70 - 74	102 631	47 779	54 852	...	...	...	...	...	...
75 - 79	81 211	36 126	45 085	...	...	...	...	...	...
80 - 84	51 785	20 932	30 853	...	...	...	...	...	...
85 - 89	27 494	9 728	17 766	...	...	...	...	...	...
90 - 94	10 011	3 062	6 949	...	...	...	...	...	...
95 - 99	2 982	796	2 186	...	...	...	...	...	...
100 +	1 176	416	760	...	...	...	...	...	...
Sri Lanka									
27 II 2012 (CDJC)									
Total	20 359 439	9 856 634	10 502 805	3 704 470	1 800 327	1 904 143	16 654 969	8 056 307	8 598 662
0 - 4	1 743 862	879 223	864 639	281 707	142 039	139 668	1 462 155	737 184	724 971
5 - 9	1 747 752	882 108	865 644	292 480	147 539	144 941	1 455 272	734 569	720 703
10 - 14	1 640 052	829 069	810 983	286 653	145 640	141 013	1 353 399	683 429	669 970
15 - 19	1 644 249	819 927	824 322	306 654	155 546	151 108	1 337 595	664 381	673 214
20 - 24	1 532 883	742 316	790 567	308 605	151 666	156 939	1 224 278	590 650	633 628
25 - 29	1 552 848	743 510	809 338	290 825	142 387	148 438	1 262 023	601 123	660 900
30 - 34	1 639 415	796 866	842 549	294 944	145 860	149 084	1 344 471	651 006	693 465
35 - 39	1 409 077	686 037	723 040	260 479	127 396	133 083	1 148 598	558 641	589 957
40 - 44	1 359 209	661 623	697 586	253 831	124 363	129 468	1 105 378	537 260	568 118
45 - 49	1 285 830	618 140	667 690	237 646	113 675	123 971	1 048 184	504 465	543 719
50 - 54	1 219 460	581 293	638 167	223 940	106 249	117 691	995 520	475 044	520 476
55 - 59	1 064 229	500 871	563 358	192 715	90 444	102 271	871 514	410 427	461 087
60 - 64	917 910	425 428	492 482	169 167	78 370	90 797	748 743	347 058	401 685
65 - 69	633 289	283 764	349 525	121 751	54 401	67 350	511 538	229 363	282 175
70 - 74	412 414	181 846	230 568	77 909	33 807	44 102	334 505	148 039	186 466
75 - 79	283 186	116 389	166 797	52 087	21 036	31 051	231 099	95 353	135 746
80 - 84	159 379	64 250	95 129	30 707	11 775	18 932	128 672	52 475	76 197
85 - 89	73 441	28 293	45 148	14 121	5 097	9 024	59 320	23 196	36 124
90 - 94	24 258	9 293	14 965	4 932	1 790	3 142	19 326	7 503	11 823
95 +	16 696	6 388	10 308	3 317	1 247	2 070	13 379	5 141	8 238
95 - 99	16 696	6 388	10 308	3 317	1 247	2 070	13 379	5 141	8 238
1 VII 2015 (ESDF)									
Total	20 966 000	10 151 000	10 815 000	...	...	...	...	...	...
0 - 4	1 797 000	906 000	891 000	...	...	...	...	...	...
5 - 9	1 801 000	909 000	892 000	...	...	...	...	...	...
10 - 14	1 690 000	854 000	836 000	...	...	...	...	...	...
15 - 19	1 694 000	845 000	849 000	...	...	...	...	...	...
20 - 24	1 578 000	764 000	814 000	...	...	...	...	...	...
25 - 29	1 599 000	766 000	833 000	...	...	...	...	...	...
30 - 34	1 688 000	820 000	868 000	...	...	...	...	...	...
35 - 39	1 451 000	706 000	745 000	...	...	...	...	...	...
40 - 44	1 399 000	681 000	718 000	...	...	...	...	...	...
45 - 49	1 324 000	637 000	687 000	...	...	...	...	...	...
50 - 54	1 256 000	599 000	657 000	...	...	...	...	...	...
55 - 59	1 096 000	516 000	580 000	...	...	...	...	...	...
60 - 64	945 000	438 000	507 000	...	...	...	...	...	...
65 - 69	652 000	292 000	360 000	...	...	...	...	...	...
70 - 74	424 000	187 000	237 000	...	...	...	...	...	...
75 - 79	291 000	120 000	171 000	...	...	...	...	...	...
80 +	281 000	111 000	170 000	...	...	...	...	...	...
State of Palestine - État de Palestine									
1 XII 2007 (CDFC)[61]									
Total	3 443 828	1 747 284	1 696 544	2 814 623[62]	1 427 861[62]	1 386 762[62]	629 205	319 423	309 782
0	107 187	54 782	52 405	88 830[62]	45 359[62]	43 471[62]	18 357	9 423	8 934
1 - 4	412 748	211 270	201 478	340 784[62]	174 537[62]	166 247[62]	71 964	36 733	35 231
5 - 9	466 880	239 156	227 724	381 348[62]	195 338[62]	186 010[62]	85 532	43 818	41 714
10 - 14	466 273	238 306	227 967	381 583[62]	194 860[62]	186 723[62]	84 690	43 446	41 244
15 - 19	414 439	211 464	202 975	339 534[62]	173 038[62]	166 496[62]	74 905	38 426	36 479
20 - 24	309 935	158 374	151 561	253 464[62]	128 975[62]	124 489[62]	56 471	29 399	27 072
25 - 29	252 227	128 068	124 159	206 038[62]	104 199[62]	101 839[62]	46 189	23 869	22 320

7. Population by age, sex and urban/rural residence: latest available year, 2006 - 2015
Population selon l'âge, le sexe et la résidence, urbaine/rurale : dernière année disponible, 2006 - 2015 (continued - suite)

Continent, country or area, date, code[a] and age (in years) Continent, pays ou zone, date, code[a] et âge (en années)	Total			Urban - Urbaine			Rural - Rurale		
	Both sexes Les deux sexes	Male Masculin	Female Féminin	Both sexes Les deux sexes	Male Masculin	Female Féminin	Both sexes Les deux sexes	Male Masculin	Female Féminin
ASIA - ASIE									
State of Palestine - État de Palestine									
1 XII 2007 (CDFC)[61]									
30 - 34	215 288	108 945	106 343	174 749[62]	88 330[62]	86 419[62]	40 539	20 615	19 924
35 - 39	177 060	90 155	86 905	142 888[62]	72 771[62]	70 117[62]	34 172	17 384	16 788
40 - 44	156 514	81 186	75 328	127 937[62]	66 510[62]	61 427[62]	28 577	14 676	13 901
45 - 49	117 580	60 832	56 748	95 564[62]	49 594[62]	45 970[62]	22 016	11 238	10 778
50 - 54	83 301	41 606	41 695	67 461[62]	33 829[62]	33 632[62]	15 840	7 777	8 063
55 - 59	63 010	32 011	30 999	51 678[62]	26 340[62]	25 338[62]	11 332	5 671	5 661
60 - 64	47 829	22 060	25 769	38 987[62]	18 162[62]	20 825[62]	8 842	3 898	4 944
65 - 69	33 697	13 853	19 844	27 124[62]	11 192[62]	15 932[62]	6 573	2 661	3 912
70 - 74	29 316	12 689	16 627	23 300[62]	10 221[62]	13 079[62]	6 016	2 468	3 548
75 - 79	21 135	8 599	12 536	16 540[62]	6 744[62]	9 796[62]	4 595	1 855	2 740
80 - 84	11 749	4 861	6 888	8 940[62]	3 705[62]	5 235[62]	2 809	1 156	1 653
85 - 89	5 344	2 318	3 026	3 984[62]	1 721[62]	2 263[62]	1 360	597	763
90 - 94	2 004	871	1 133	1 512[62]	646[62]	866[62]	492	225	267
95 +	1 061	464	597	744[62]	331[62]	413[62]	317	133	184
Unknown - Inconnu	49 251	25 414	23 837	41 634[62]	21 459[62]	20 175[62]	7 617	3 955	3 662
1 VII 2015 (ESDF)									
Total	*4 682 467*	*2 379 184*	*2 303 283*	...	...	...	...	...	...
0	*146 668*	*74 998*	*71 670*	...	...	...	...	...	...
1 - 4	*557 304*	*284 918*	*272 386*	...	...	...	...	...	...
5 - 9	*594 449*	*302 977*	*291 472*	...	...	...	...	...	...
10 - 14	*548 201*	*280 082*	*268 119*	...	...	...	...	...	...
15 - 19	*525 706*	*268 313*	*257 393*	...	...	...	...	...	...
20 - 24	*483 189*	*246 357*	*236 832*	...	...	...	...	...	...
25 - 29	*395 360*	*201 718*	*193 642*	...	...	...	...	...	...
30 - 34	*305 702*	*156 257*	*149 445*	...	...	...	...	...	...
35 - 39	*258 088*	*131 317*	*126 771*	...	...	...	...	...	...
40 - 44	*217 334*	*109 908*	*107 426*	...	...	...	...	...	...
45 - 49	*181 971*	*93 122*	*88 849*	...	...	...	...	...	...
50 - 54	*149 473*	*77 605*	*71 868*	...	...	...	...	...	...
55 - 59	*109 672*	*56 276*	*53 396*	...	...	...	...	...	...
60 - 64	*73 512*	*36 623*	*36 889*	...	...	...	...	...	...
65 - 69	*52 751*	*24 649*	*28 102*	...	...	...	...	...	...
70 - 74	*36 325*	*15 391*	*20 934*	...	...	...	...	...	...
75 - 79	*23 839*	*9 622*	*14 217*	...	...	...	...	...	...
80 +	*22 923*	*9 051*	*13 872*	...	...	...	...	...	...
Syrian Arab Republic - République arabe syrienne[63]									
1 VII 2011 (ESDF)									
Total	*21 124 000*	*10 794 000*	*10 330 000*	*11 297 000*	*5 795 000*	*5 502 000*	*9 827 000*	*4 999 000*	*4 828 000*
0 - 4	*2 775 000*	*1 428 000*	*1 347 000*	*1 384 000*	*713 000*	*671 000*	*1 391 000*	*715 000*	*676 000*
5 - 9	*2 654 000*	*1 384 000*	*1 270 000*	*1 357 000*	*719 000*	*638 000*	*1 297 000*	*665 000*	*632 000*
10 - 14	*2 430 000*	*1 232 000*	*1 198 000*	*1 270 000*	*637 000*	*633 000*	*1 160 000*	*595 000*	*565 000*
15 - 19	*2 279 000*	*1 191 000*	*1 088 000*	*1 193 000*	*626 000*	*567 000*	*1 086 000*	*565 000*	*521 000*
20 - 24	*1 979 000*	*1 035 000*	*944 000*	*1 045 000*	*545 000*	*500 000*	*934 000*	*490 000*	*444 000*
25 - 29	*1 737 000*	*864 000*	*873 000*	*937 000*	*475 000*	*462 000*	*800 000*	*389 000*	*411 000*
30 - 34	*1 371 000*	*674 000*	*697 000*	*733 000*	*359 000*	*374 000*	*638 000*	*315 000*	*323 000*
35 - 39	*1 229 000*	*601 000*	*628 000*	*694 000*	*336 000*	*358 000*	*535 000*	*265 000*	*270 000*
40 - 44	*1 096 000*	*545 000*	*551 000*	*644 000*	*325 000*	*319 000*	*452 000*	*220 000*	*232 000*
45 - 49	*870 000*	*437 000*	*433 000*	*536 000*	*272 000*	*264 000*	*334 000*	*165 000*	*169 000*
50 - 54	*792 000*	*387 000*	*405 000*	*458 000*	*232 000*	*226 000*	*334 000*	*155 000*	*179 000*
55 - 59	*573 000*	*293 000*	*280 000*	*322 000*	*168 000*	*154 000*	*251 000*	*125 000*	*126 000*
60 - 64	*481 000*	*254 000*	*227 000*	*260 000*	*139 000*	*121 000*	*221 000*	*115 000*	*106 000*
65 +	*858 000*	*469 000*	*389 000*	*464 000*	*249 000*	*215 000*	*394 000*	*220 000*	*174 000*
Tajikistan - Tadjikistan									
1 VII 2014 (ESDF)									
Total	*8 256 572*	*4 174 269*	*4 082 303*	*2 193 224*	*1 112 352*	*1 080 873*	*6 063 348*	*3 061 917*	*3 001 431*
0	*216 440*	*114 100*	*102 340*	*51 426*	*27 153*	*24 273*	*165 014*	*86 948*	*78 067*
1 - 4	*882 560*	*456 234*	*426 326*	*210 093*	*108 382*	*101 711*	*672 467*	*347 852*	*324 615*
5 - 9	*925 128*	*475 721*	*449 408*	*224 757*	*115 632*	*109 125*	*700 372*	*360 089*	*340 283*
10 - 14	*844 012*	*433 005*	*411 008*	*215 460*	*111 081*	*104 380*	*628 552*	*321 924*	*306 628*
15 - 19	*867 192*	*442 705*	*424 487*	*230 225*	*120 101*	*110 125*	*636 967*	*322 605*	*314 362*

7. Population by age, sex and urban/rural residence: latest available year, 2006 - 2015
Population selon l'âge, le sexe et la résidence, urbaine/rurale : dernière année disponible, 2006 - 2015 (continued - suite)

Continent, country or area, date, code[a] and age (in years) / Continent, pays ou zone, date, code[a] et âge (en années)	Total			Urban - Urbaine			Rural - Rurale		
	Both sexes Les deux sexes	Male Masculin	Female Féminin	Both sexes Les deux sexes	Male Masculin	Female Féminin	Both sexes Les deux sexes	Male Masculin	Female Féminin
ASIA - ASIE									
Tajikistan - Tadjikistan									
1 VII 2014 (ESDF)									
20 - 24	850 400	429 958	420 442	250 113	138 182	111 932	600 287	291 776	308 511
25 - 29	793 282	397 488	395 794	204 805	105 211	99 594	588 478	292 278	296 200
30 - 34	596 625	302 173	294 452	154 035	76 454	77 581	442 590	225 719	216 871
35 - 39	475 028	237 691	237 338	131 898	62 779	69 120	343 130	174 912	168 218
40 - 44	424 616	209 746	214 870	126 370	59 737	66 633	298 247	150 010	148 237
45 - 49	381 217	186 713	194 504	113 273	54 374	58 899	267 944	132 339	135 605
50 - 54	346 740	170 584	176 156	101 114	48 708	52 407	245 626	121 877	123 749
55 - 59	241 422	118 136	123 286	69 084	33 133	35 951	172 338	85 003	87 335
60 - 64	156 423	75 679	80 744	45 239	21 310	23 929	111 185	54 369	56 816
65 - 69	83 359	41 283	42 076	24 008	11 302	12 706	59 351	29 981	29 370
70 - 74	68 103	34 752	33 351	18 103	8 702	9 401	50 001	26 050	23 951
75 - 79	54 116	25 756	28 360	13 026	5 851	7 175	41 090	19 906	21 184
80 - 84	31 351	14 076	17 275	6 609	2 782	3 828	24 742	11 294	13 448
85 - 89	13 688	6 575	7 113	2 637	1 103	1 534	11 051	5 472	5 579
90 - 94	3 962	1 549	2 413	760	281	479	3 202	1 269	1 933
95 - 99	664	256	408	129	62	67	535	195	340
100 +	249	92	157	66	39	28	183	54	129
Thailand - Thaïlande[2]									
1 VII 2012 (ESDJ)									
Total	67 911 720	33 328 645	34 583 075	23 430 180	11 219 175	12 211 005	44 481 540	22 109 470	22 372 070
0 - 4	3 979 864	2 041 071	1 938 793	1 303 276	660 378	642 898	2 676 588	1 380 693	1 295 895
5 - 9	4 624 088	2 353 198	2 270 890	1 653 192	829 716	823 476	2 970 896	1 523 482	1 447 414
10 - 14	4 766 188	2 438 774	2 327 414	1 567 479	790 354	777 125	3 198 709	1 648 420	1 550 289
15 - 19	5 067 031	2 593 629	2 473 402	1 561 571	784 752	776 819	3 505 460	1 808 877	1 696 583
20 - 24	5 237 205	2 673 846	2 563 359	1 615 627	803 045	812 582	3 621 578	1 870 801	1 750 777
25 - 29	5 262 148	2 673 201	2 588 947	1 709 395	839 146	870 249	3 552 753	1 834 055	1 718 698
30 - 34	5 320 960	2 683 015	2 637 945	1 966 999	953 695	1 013 304	3 353 961	1 729 320	1 624 641
35 - 39	5 432 820	2 673 404	2 759 416	2 079 909	992 437	1 087 472	3 352 911	1 680 967	1 671 944
40 - 44	5 543 422	2 672 891	2 870 531	2 045 686	963 854	1 081 832	3 497 736	1 709 037	1 788 699
45 - 49	5 344 099	2 574 423	2 769 676	1 923 474	905 363	1 018 111	3 420 625	1 669 060	1 751 565
50 - 54	4 818 743	2 315 177	2 503 566	1 713 371	804 718	908 653	3 105 372	1 510 459	1 594 913
55 - 59	3 906 749	1 854 719	2 052 030	1 372 422	637 639	734 783	2 534 327	1 217 080	1 317 247
60 - 64	2 881 942	1 347 251	1 534 691	995 295	456 060	539 235	1 886 647	891 191	995 456
65 - 69	2 118 712	963 728	1 154 984	711 804	317 607	394 197	1 406 908	646 121	760 787
70 - 74	1 603 467	695 434	908 033	533 040	226 340	306 700	1 070 427	469 094	601 333
75 - 79	1 111 421	451 737	659 684	375 550	149 055	226 495	735 871	302 682	433 189
80 +	892 861	323 147	569 714	302 090	105 016	197 074	590 771	218 131	372 640
Timor-Leste									
11 VII 2010 (CDFC)									
Total	1 066 409	544 198	522 211	316 086	166 163	149 923	750 323	378 035	372 288
0 - 4	153 334	79 169	74 165	40 622	20 978	19 644	112 712	58 191	54 521
5 - 9	153 108	78 980	74 128	39 668	20 480	19 188	113 440	58 500	54 940
10 - 14	135 464	70 513	64 951	33 309	17 369	15 940	102 155	53 144	49 011
15 - 19	116 535	58 754	57 781	42 791	21 249	21 542	73 744	37 505	36 239
20 - 24	94 427	47 336	47 091	41 612	22 175	19 437	52 815	25 161	27 654
25 - 29	76 836	38 269	38 567	31 190	16 578	14 612	45 646	21 691	23 955
30 - 34	51 911	25 805	26 106	19 454	10 623	8 831	32 457	15 182	17 275
35 - 39	57 508	29 961	27 547	18 377	10 284	8 093	39 131	19 677	19 454
40 - 44	48 372	25 407	22 965	13 599	7 748	5 851	34 773	17 659	17 114
45 - 49	38 917	20 430	18 487	9 971	5 692	4 279	28 946	14 738	14 208
50 - 54	30 084	15 539	14 545	7 205	3 954	3 251	22 879	11 585	11 294
55 - 59	22 346	11 796	10 550	5 007	2 725	2 282	17 339	9 071	8 268
60 - 64	37 333	17 419	19 914	5 419	2 596	2 823	31 914	14 823	17 091
65 - 69	23 106	11 573	11 533	3 407	1 638	1 769	19 699	9 935	9 764
70 - 74	12 705	6 285	6 420	2 079	991	1 088	10 626	5 294	5 332
75 - 79	7 125	3 404	3 721	1 127	508	619	5 998	2 896	3 102
80 - 84	3 755	1 818	1 937	614	275	339	3 141	1 543	1 598
85 +	3 543	1 740	1 803	635	300	335	2 908	1 440	1 468
Turkey - Turquie[64]									
31 XII 2014 (ESDJ)									
Total	77 695 904	38 984 302	38 711 602	67 720 318	33 954 681	33 765 637	9 975 586	5 029 621	4 945 965
0	1 282 180	658 747	623 433	1 142 417	587 147	555 270	139 763	71 600	68 163
1 - 4	5 012 353	2 573 156	2 439 197	4 446 304	2 283 057	2 163 247	566 049	290 099	275 950

7. Population by age, sex and urban/rural residence: latest available year, 2006 - 2015
Population selon l'âge, le sexe et la résidence, urbaine/rurale : dernière année disponible, 2006 - 2015 (continued - suite)

Continent, country or area, date, code[a] and age (in years) / Continent, pays ou zone, date, code[a] et âge (en années)	Total			Urban - Urbaine			Rural - Rurale		
	Both sexes Les deux sexes	Male Masculin	Female Féminin	Both sexes Les deux sexes	Male Masculin	Female Féminin	Both sexes Les deux sexes	Male Masculin	Female Féminin
ASIA - ASIE									
Turkey - Turquie[64]									
31 XII 2014 (ESDJ)									
5 - 9	6 315 628	3 241 355	3 074 273	5 575 619	2 862 121	2 713 498	740 009	379 234	360 775
10 - 14	6 252 269	3 209 897	3 042 372	5 440 368	2 794 324	2 646 044	811 901	415 573	396 328
15 - 19	6 518 921	3 349 081	3 169 840	5 654 637	2 902 546	2 752 091	864 284	446 535	417 749
20 - 24	6 263 460	3 191 641	3 071 819	5 485 430	2 761 133	2 724 297	778 030	430 508	347 522
25 - 29	6 273 202	3 179 412	3 093 790	5 623 162	2 827 169	2 795 993	650 040	352 243	297 797
30 - 34	6 516 294	3 294 389	3 221 905	5 890 223	2 966 599	2 923 624	626 071	327 790	298 281
35 - 39	5 918 336	2 996 001	2 922 335	5 340 040	2 698 675	2 641 365	578 296	297 326	280 970
40 - 44	5 510 337	2 766 305	2 744 032	4 910 254	2 464 415	2 445 839	600 083	301 890	298 193
45 - 49	4 674 262	2 375 494	2 298 768	4 117 379	2 091 375	2 026 004	556 883	284 119	272 764
50 - 54	4 438 422	2 218 311	2 220 111	3 831 563	1 917 619	1 913 944	606 859	300 692	306 167
55 - 59	3 656 563	1 828 486	1 828 077	3 088 573	1 548 340	1 540 233	567 990	280 146	287 844
60 - 64	2 870 715	1 402 604	1 468 111	2 361 729	1 158 685	1 203 044	508 986	243 919	265 067
65 - 69	2 215 704	1 030 716	1 184 988	1 767 075	825 736	941 339	448 629	204 980	243 649
70 - 74	1 557 235	699 604	857 631	1 205 272	542 045	663 227	351 963	157 559	194 404
75 - 79	1 104 178	465 081	639 097	847 001	353 698	493 303	257 177	111 383	145 794
80 - 84	840 410	353 906	486 504	627 866	257 234	370 632	212 544	96 672	115 872
85 - 89	360 158	119 892	240 266	275 152	89 475	185 677	85 006	30 417	54 589
90 +	115 277	30 224	85 053	90 254	23 288	66 966	25 023	6 936	18 087
Uzbekistan - Ouzbékistan[65]									
1 VII 2014 (ESDJ)									
Total	30 757 669	15 414 846	15 342 823	15 651 614	7 809 449	7 842 165	15 106 055	7 605 397	7 500 658
0	671 188	348 592	322 596	305 285	158 537	146 748	365 903	190 055	175 848
1 - 4	2 528 897	1 309 457	1 219 440	1 155 619	599 109	556 510	1 373 278	710 348	662 930
5 - 9	2 901 315	1 491 824	1 409 491	1 338 816	685 725	653 091	1 562 499	806 099	756 400
10 - 14	2 565 282	1 315 653	1 249 629	1 256 711	643 317	613 394	1 308 571	672 336	636 235
15 - 19	2 958 195	1 512 887	1 445 308	1 462 682	747 236	715 446	1 495 513	765 651	729 862
20 - 24	3 234 662	1 645 747	1 588 915	1 586 871	812 868	774 003	1 647 791	832 879	814 912
25 - 29	3 042 651	1 535 745	1 506 906	1 542 327	783 172	759 155	1 500 324	752 573	747 751
30 - 34	2 472 439	1 239 905	1 232 534	1 281 088	643 423	637 665	1 191 351	596 482	594 869
35 - 39	2 095 871	1 046 438	1 049 433	1 109 390	550 518	558 872	986 481	495 920	490 561
40 - 44	1 879 521	933 212	946 309	1 041 911	520 888	521 023	837 610	412 324	425 286
45 - 49	1 637 715	792 645	845 070	893 562	436 942	456 620	744 153	355 703	388 450
50 - 54	1 565 932	757 562	808 370	850 821	408 624	442 197	715 111	348 938	366 173
55 - 59	1 189 451	574 383	615 068	662 923	315 373	347 550	526 528	259 010	267 518
60 - 64	785 066	371 690	413 376	453 846	210 272	243 574	331 220	161 418	169 802
65 - 69	399 272	185 926	213 346	237 680	106 783	130 897	161 592	79 143	82 449
70 - 74	312 849	145 472	167 377	177 960	77 956	100 004	134 889	67 516	67 373
75 - 79	259 841	112 429	147 412	146 657	58 323	88 334	113 184	54 106	59 078
80 - 84	132 526	50 436	82 090	74 115	25 394	48 721	58 411	25 042	33 369
85 +	124 996	44 843	80 153	73 350	24 989	48 361	51 646	19 854	31 792
Viet Nam									
1 IV 2009 (CDJC)									
Total	85 846 997	42 413 143	43 433 854	25 436 896	12 349 995	13 086 901	60 410 101	30 063 148	30 346 953
0 - 4	7 034 144	3 662 889	3 371 255	1 949 105	1 019 547	929 558	5 085 039	2 643 342	2 441 697
5 - 9	6 710 737	3 458 159	3 252 578	1 757 679	910 339	847 340	4 953 058	2 547 820	2 405 238
10 - 14	7 248 378	3 725 369	3 523 009	1 761 650	904 731	856 919	5 486 728	2 820 638	2 666 090
15 - 17	5 236 771	2 681 653	2 555 118	1 311 350	662 369	648 981	3 925 421	2 019 284	1 906 137
18 - 19	3 727 131	1 896 261	1 830 870	1 188 578	562 169	626 409	2 538 553	1 334 092	1 204 461
20 - 24	8 432 867	4 253 618	4 179 249	2 759 456	1 305 436	1 454 020	5 673 411	2 948 182	2 725 229
25 - 29	7 790 003	3 904 730	3 885 273	2 519 920	1 205 518	1 314 402	5 270 083	2 699 212	2 570 871
30 - 34	6 868 158	3 462 905	3 405 253	2 164 824	1 062 838	1 101 986	4 703 334	2 400 067	2 303 267
35 - 39	6 531 607	3 298 266	3 233 341	2 059 356	1 027 075	1 032 281	4 472 251	2 271 191	2 201 060
40 - 44	5 966 856	2 967 934	2 998 922	1 818 188	896 290	921 898	4 148 668	2 071 644	2 077 024
45 - 49	5 450 928	2 642 466	2 808 462	1 728 008	840 047	887 961	3 722 920	1 802 419	1 920 501
50 - 54	4 412 051	2 082 098	2 329 953	1 435 970	683 749	752 221	2 976 081	1 398 349	1 577 732
55 - 59	2 984 619	1 364 319	1 620 300	931 382	421 296	510 086	2 053 237	943 023	1 110 214
60 - 64	1 937 848	861 897	1 076 051	590 161	259 193	330 968	1 347 787	602 704	745 083
65 - 69	1 554 678	653 287	901 391	453 756	195 857	257 899	1 100 922	457 430	643 492
70 - 74	1 412 538	568 312	844 226	378 105	155 224	222 881	1 034 433	413 088	621 345
75 - 79	1 198 893	480 088	718 805	306 226	125 948	180 278	892 667	354 140	538 527
80 - 84	725 985	264 997	460 988	182 550	69 573	112 977	543 435	195 424	348 011
85 +	622 705	183 895	438 810	140 632	42 796	97 836	482 073	141 099	340 974

Continent, country or area, date, code[a] and age (in years) / Continent, pays ou zone, date, code[a] et âge (en années)	Total			Urban - Urbaine			Rural - Rurale		
	Both sexes Les deux sexes	Male Masculin	Female Féminin	Both sexes Les deux sexes	Male Masculin	Female Féminin	Both sexes Les deux sexes	Male Masculin	Female Féminin
ASIA - ASIE									
Viet Nam									
1 VII 2015 (ESDF)									
Total	91 713 345	45 234 104	46 479 241	31 131 496	...	...	60 581 849	...	...
0 - 4	7 556 620	3 978 623	3 577 997	2 360 813	...	...	5 195 807	...	...
5 - 9	7 411 305	3 846 414	3 564 891	2 380 710	...	...	5 030 595	...	...
10 - 14	7 035 913	3 651 887	3 384 026	2 171 908	...	...	4 864 005	...	...
15 - 19	6 546 856	3 364 687	3 182 169	2 028 792	...	...	4 518 064	...	...
20 - 24	7 217 987	3 687 097	3 530 890	2 478 457	...	...	4 739 530	...	...
25 - 29	7 438 733	3 768 467	3 670 266	2 613 869	...	...	4 824 864	...	...
30 - 34	7 437 762	3 655 938	3 781 824	2 714 484	...	...	4 723 278	...	...
35 - 39	6 857 552	3 391 875	3 465 677	2 437 435	...	...	4 420 117	...	...
40 - 44	6 681 780	3 327 657	3 354 123	2 364 978	...	...	4 316 802	...	...
45 - 49	6 095 026	3 054 867	3 040 159	2 151 490	...	...	3 943 536	...	...
50 - 54	6 134 781	2 875 913	3 258 868	2 156 497	...	...	3 978 284	...	...
55 - 59	4 925 911	2 299 228	2 626 683	1 807 166	...	...	3 118 745	...	...
60 - 64	3 420 988	1 571 890	1 849 098	1 211 683	...	...	2 209 305	...	...
65 - 69	2 153 731	944 591	1 209 140	753 671	...	...	1 400 060	...	...
70 - 74	1 546 915	623 234	923 681	530 597	...	...	1 016 318	...	...
75 - 79	1 293 783	507 112	786 671	414 496	...	...	879 287	...	...
80 +	1 957 702	684 624	1 273 078	554 450	...	...	1 403 252	...	...
Yemen - Yémen[2]									
1 VII 2013 (ESDJ)									
Total	25 235 079	12 844 169	12 390 910	...	...	...	...	...	...
0	867 766	442 297	425 470	...	...	...	...	...	...
1 - 4	3 183 851	1 627 558	1 556 293	...	...	...	...	...	...
5 - 9	3 377 146	1 723 755	1 653 391	...	...	...	...	...	...
10 - 14	3 007 245	1 539 447	1 467 798	...	...	...	...	...	...
15 - 19	2 954 657	1 530 854	1 423 803	...	...	...	...	...	...
20 - 24	2 738 574	1 426 490	1 312 083	...	...	...	...	...	...
25 - 29	2 226 915	1 146 775	1 080 140	...	...	...	...	...	...
30 - 34	1 688 248	851 154	837 094	...	...	...	...	...	...
35 - 39	1 276 748	635 492	641 256	...	...	...	...	...	...
40 - 44	916 385	448 186	468 200	...	...	...	...	...	...
45 - 49	758 743	366 733	392 010	...	...	...	...	...	...
50 - 54	644 689	310 025	334 665	...	...	...	...	...	...
55 - 59	488 859	238 877	249 982	...	...	...	...	...	...
60 - 64	352 671	178 041	174 631	...	...	...	...	...	...
65 - 69	266 902	135 090	131 812	...	...	...	...	...	...
70 - 74	195 287	98 257	97 029	...	...	...	...	...	...
75 - 79	133 347	66 656	66 691	...	...	...	...	...	...
80 +	157 047	78 482	78 565	...	...	...	...	...	...
EUROPE									
Åland Islands - Îles d'Åland[21]									
1 VII 2015 (ESDJ)									
Total	28 950	14 466	14 484	11 471	5 521	5 950	17 479	8 945	8 534
0	283	147	136	96	47	49	187	100	87
1 - 4	1 227	611	616	416	212	204	811	399	412
5 - 9	1 623	848	776	547	269	278	1 077	579	498
10 - 14	1 561	819	742	533	269	264	1 028	550	478
15 - 19	1 644	860	784	676	338	338	968	522	446
20 - 24	1 503	809	695	741	400	341	763	409	354
25 - 29	1 660	889	771	806	450	357	854	440	415
30 - 34	1 727	879	849	717	379	338	1 011	500	511
35 - 39	1 772	907	865	684	338	347	1 088	569	519
40 - 44	1 897	965	932	700	341	359	1 197	624	573
45 - 49	2 111	1 043	1 068	805	386	419	1 306	657	649
50 - 54	1 995	990	1 005	751	337	414	1 245	654	591
55 - 59	1 939	921	1 018	728	330	398	1 212	591	621
60 - 64	2 049	979	1 071	825	366	459	1 225	613	612
65 - 69	2 006	1 001	1 006	813	372	442	1 193	629	564
70 - 74	1 452	758	694	589	282	307	864	476	388
75 - 79	1 002	460	542	426	187	239	577	273	304

7. Population by age, sex and urban/rural residence: latest available year, 2006 - 2015
Population selon l'âge, le sexe et la résidence, urbaine/rurale : dernière année disponible, 2006 - 2015 (continued - suite)

Continent, country or area, date, code[a] and age (in years) / Continent, pays ou zone, date, code[a] et âge (en années)	Total			Urban - Urbaine			Rural - Rurale		
	Both sexes Les deux sexes	Male Masculin	Female Féminin	Both sexes Les deux sexes	Male Masculin	Female Féminin	Both sexes Les deux sexes	Male Masculin	Female Féminin
EUROPE									
Åland Islands - Îles d'Åland[21]									
1 VII 2015 (ESDJ)									
80 - 84	738	328	410	309	134	175	429	194	235
85 - 89	494	186	308	196	64	132	299	122	177
90 - 94	214	60	154	94	21	73	120	39	81
95 - 99	52	9	43	22	3	20	30	7	23
100 +	5	1	5	3	-	3	2	1	1
Albania - Albanie									
1 VII 2013 (ESDF)									
Total	2 897 364	1 458 648	1 438 716	1 633 617	798 615	835 002	1 263 747	660 033	603 714
0 - 4	173 349	90 068	83 281	75 341	39 381	35 960	98 008	50 687	47 321
0	35 445	18 414	17 031	...	...	...	...	...	...
1 - 4	137 903	71 653	66 250	...	...	...	...	...	...
5 - 9	171 833	90 701	81 132	100 478	52 421	48 057	71 355	38 280	33 075
10 - 14	220 582	114 164	106 418	117 500	60 576	56 924	103 082	53 587	49 494
15 - 19	261 669	132 810	128 859	134 718	67 303	67 414	126 952	65 507	61 445
20 - 24	235 615	126 936	108 680	153 986	75 706	78 280	81 630	51 230	30 400
25 - 29	209 075	112 236	96 839	136 959	65 999	70 960	72 116	46 237	25 879
30 - 34	187 077	92 149	94 928	95 098	44 074	51 024	91 979	48 075	43 904
35 - 39	173 587	82 445	91 142	89 169	40 432	48 737	84 418	42 013	42 405
40 - 44	189 099	89 772	99 327	106 471	50 381	56 091	82 627	39 391	43 236
45 - 49	197 020	95 657	101 363	113 719	55 342	58 377	83 301	40 315	42 986
50 - 54	209 575	104 084	105 490	121 293	60 655	60 638	88 282	43 430	44 852
55 - 59	184 593	92 037	92 556	105 093	51 906	53 188	79 500	40 131	39 369
60 - 64	141 532	71 276	70 256	83 065	40 768	42 296	58 467	30 508	27 960
65 - 69	106 945	54 278	52 666	60 973	29 333	31 640	45 971	24 945	21 026
70 - 74	102 875	49 827	53 048	55 109	26 020	29 089	47 766	23 807	23 959
75 - 79	71 589	35 241	36 348	41 911	19 956	21 955	29 678	15 285	14 393
80 - 84	38 203	16 977	21 226	25 030	11 374	13 656	13 174	5 603	7 570
85 +	23 147	7 992	15 155	17 705	6 988	10 717	5 443	1 004	4 438
1 I 2014 (ESDF)									
Total	2 895 947	1 459 963	1 435 984	...	...	...	...	...	...
0	35 196	18 328	16 868	...	...	...	...	...	...
1 - 4	137 321	71 092	66 229	...	...	...	...	...	...
5 - 9	166 011	87 690	78 321	...	...	...	...	...	...
10 - 14	216 490	112 159	104 331	...	...	...	...	...	...
15 - 19	256 553	130 580	125 973	...	...	...	...	...	...
20 - 24	229 529	124 337	105 192	...	...	...	...	...	...
25 - 29	210 829	114 197	96 632	...	...	...	...	...	...
30 - 34	191 900	94 950	96 950	...	...	...	...	...	...
35 - 39	176 491	84 004	92 487	...	...	...	...	...	...
40 - 44	186 144	88 592	97 552	...	...	...	...	...	...
45 - 49	197 531	95 598	101 933	...	...	...	...	...	...
50 - 54	210 687	104 617	106 070	...	...	...	...	...	...
55 - 59	189 265	94 245	95 020	...	...	...	...	...	...
60 - 64	143 754	72 519	71 235	...	...	...	...	...	...
65 - 69	108 400	54 945	53 455	...	...	...	...	...	...
70 - 74	104 308	50 427	53 881	...	...	...	...	...	...
75 - 79	73 204	36 096	37 108	...	...	...	...	...	...
80 - 84	39 002	17 349	21 653	...	...	...	...	...	...
85 +	23 332	8 238	15 094	...	...	...	...	...	...
Andorra - Andorre[21]									
1 VII 2012 (ESDJ)									
Total	77 181	39 351	37 830	...	...	...	...	...	...
0	581	288	293	...	...	...	...	...	...
1 - 4	3 126	1 573	1 553	...	...	...	...	...	...
5 - 9	4 016	2 112	1 904	...	...	...	...	...	...
10 - 14	4 246	2 194	2 052	...	...	...	...	...	...
15 - 19	3 794	2 035	1 759	...	...	...	...	...	...
20 - 24	3 834	1 952	1 882	...	...	...	...	...	...
25 - 29	5 039	2 497	2 542	...	...	...	...	...	...
30 - 34	6 768	3 394	3 375	...	...	...	...	...	...
35 - 39	7 536	3 794	3 742	...	...	...	...	...	...
40 - 44	7 281	3 712	3 570	...	...	...	...	...	...
45 - 49	7 002	3 615	3 387	...	...	...	...	...	...

Continent, country or area, date, code[a] and age (in years) / Continent, pays ou zone, date, code[a] et âge (en années)	Total			Urban - Urbaine			Rural - Rurale		
	Both sexes Les deux sexes	Male Masculin	Female Féminin	Both sexes Les deux sexes	Male Masculin	Female Féminin	Both sexes Les deux sexes	Male Masculin	Female Féminin
EUROPE									
Andorra - Andorre[21]									
1 VII 2012 (ESDJ)									
50 - 54	5 884	3 069	2 816	...	...	...	...	...	...
55 - 59	4 646	2 469	2 177	...	...	...	...	...	...
60 - 64	3 699	1 959	1 741	...	...	...	...	...	...
65 - 69	2 912	1 543	1 369	...	...	...	...	...	...
70 - 74	2 009	973	1 036	...	...	...	...	...	...
75 - 79	1 712	838	874	...	...	...	...	...	...
80 - 84	1 477	664	813	...	...	...	...	...	...
85 - 89	929	389	540	...	...	...	...	...	...
90 - 94	448	180	268	...	...	...	...	...	...
95 - 99	174	70	104	...	...	...	...	...	...
100 +	71	36	36	...	...	...	...	...	...
Austria - Autriche									
31 X 2011 (CDJC)									
Total	8 401 940	4 093 938	4 308 002	5 643 239	2 713 930	2 929 309	2 758 701	1 380 008	1 378 693
0 - 4	394 706	202 637	192 069	267 743	137 645	130 098	126 963	64 992	61 971
5 - 9	406 027	207 779	198 248	268 770	137 636	131 134	137 257	70 143	67 114
10 - 14	426 957	218 499	208 458	276 347	141 429	134 918	150 610	77 070	73 540
15 - 19	488 818	251 251	237 567	313 792	160 620	153 172	175 026	90 631	84 395
20 - 24	527 675	267 651	260 024	364 267	181 574	182 693	163 408	86 077	77 331
25 - 29	552 783	277 236	275 547	390 454	193 719	196 735	162 329	83 517	78 812
30 - 34	538 307	270 267	268 040	375 886	187 248	188 638	162 421	83 019	79 402
35 - 39	564 817	280 207	284 610	383 183	187 902	195 281	181 634	92 305	89 329
40 - 44	675 242	338 455	336 787	453 188	224 449	228 739	222 054	114 006	108 048
45 - 49	710 388	358 163	352 225	470 749	234 757	235 992	239 639	123 406	116 233
50 - 54	626 162	312 890	313 272	409 191	200 993	208 198	216 971	111 897	105 074
55 - 59	517 280	253 019	264 261	339 245	161 747	177 498	178 035	91 272	86 763
60 - 64	480 665	231 598	249 067	322 367	151 726	170 641	158 298	79 872	78 426
65 - 69	402 829	189 221	213 608	283 946	130 760	153 186	118 883	58 461	60 422
70 - 74	410 314	187 956	222 358	273 352	123 395	149 957	136 962	64 561	72 401
75 - 79	262 203	110 870	151 333	165 864	68 812	97 052	96 339	42 058	54 281
80 - 84	218 133	83 066	135 067	142 903	52 895	90 008	75 230	30 171	45 059
85 - 89	141 772	40 153	101 619	99 777	27 332	72 445	41 995	12 821	29 174
90 - 94	46 362	10 997	35 365	34 057	7 767	26 290	12 305	3 230	9 075
95 - 99	9 388	1 836	7 552	7 274	1 377	5 897	2 114	459	1 655
100 +	1 112	187	925	884	147	737	228	40	188
1 I 2015 (ESDJ)									
Total	8 576 261	4 194 965	4 381 296	...	...	...	...	...	...
0	80 417	41 521	38 896	...	...	...	...	...	...
1 - 4	325 209	167 558	157 651	...	...	...	...	...	...
5 - 9	403 751	206 557	197 194	...	...	...	...	...	...
10 - 14	415 831	213 313	202 518	...	...	...	...	...	...
15 - 19	459 667	236 135	223 532	...	...	...	...	...	...
20 - 24	547 558	279 416	268 142	...	...	...	...	...	...
25 - 29	568 804	287 783	281 021	...	...	...	...	...	...
30 - 34	584 175	293 775	290 400	...	...	...	...	...	...
35 - 39	544 849	273 611	271 238	...	...	...	...	...	...
40 - 44	609 303	302 250	307 053	...	...	...	...	...	...
45 - 49	706 781	355 676	351 105	...	...	...	...	...	...
50 - 54	691 327	347 043	344 284	...	...	...	...	...	...
55 - 59	580 731	286 228	294 503	...	...	...	...	...	...
60 - 64	473 938	228 627	245 311	...	...	...	...	...	...
65 - 69	424 839	200 525	224 314	...	...	...	...	...	...
70 - 74	426 838	194 885	231 953	...	...	...	...	...	...
75 - 79	302 392	132 205	170 187	...	...	...	...	...	...
80 - 84	214 987	84 387	130 600	...	...	...	...	...	...
85 - 89	141 997	46 715	95 282	...	...	...	...	...	...
90 - 94	62 758	14 813	47 945	...	...	...	...	...	...
95 - 99	8 705	1 700	7 005	...	...	...	...	...	...
100 +	1 404	242	1 162	...	...	...	...	...	...
Belarus - Bélarus									
1 I 2014 (ESDJ)									
Total	9 468 154	4 401 211	5 066 943	7 274 775	3 357 966	3 916 809	2 193 379	1 043 245	1 150 134
0	118 029	60 773	57 256	91 009	46 880	44 129	27 020	13 893	13 127

7. Population by age, sex and urban/rural residence: latest available year, 2006 - 2015
Population selon l'âge, le sexe et la résidence, urbaine/rurale : dernière année disponible, 2006 - 2015 (continued - suite)

Continent, country or area, date, code[a] and age (in years) / Continent, pays ou zone, date, code[a] et âge (en années)	Total			Urban - Urbaine			Rural - Rurale		
	Both sexes Les deux sexes	Male Masculin	Female Féminin	Both sexes Les deux sexes	Male Masculin	Female Féminin	Both sexes Les deux sexes	Male Masculin	Female Féminin
EUROPE									
Belarus - Bélarus									
1 I 2014 (ESDJ)									
1 - 4	444 026	228 597	215 429	346 276	178 225	168 051	97 750	50 372	47 378
5 - 9	479 639	246 370	233 269	373 901	192 245	181 656	105 738	54 125	51 613
10 - 14	447 088	229 555	217 533	336 924	173 072	163 852	110 164	56 483	53 681
15 - 19	482 256	248 418	233 838	387 454	196 404	191 050	94 802	52 014	42 788
20 - 24	671 668	344 808	326 860	582 340	291 203	291 137	89 328	53 605	35 723
25 - 29	781 505	399 208	382 297	649 073	325 264	323 809	132 432	73 944	58 488
30 - 34	727 041	366 062	360 979	603 873	300 562	303 311	123 168	65 500	57 668
35 - 39	667 409	328 482	338 927	533 917	259 919	273 998	133 492	68 563	64 929
40 - 44	649 993	313 157	336 836	496 333	234 179	262 154	153 660	78 978	74 682
45 - 49	659 294	312 426	346 868	491 728	225 158	266 570	167 566	87 268	80 298
50 - 54	763 327	356 227	407 100	574 417	256 895	317 522	188 910	99 332	89 578
55 - 59	696 903	311 780	385 123	528 789	226 859	301 930	168 114	84 921	83 193
60 - 64	562 068	235 845	326 223	428 543	174 181	254 362	133 525	61 664	71 861
65 - 69	359 109	140 810	218 299	264 016	102 942	161 074	95 093	37 868	57 225
70 - 74	317 522	107 773	209 749	208 902	71 856	137 046	108 620	35 917	72 703
75 - 79	309 685	92 407	217 278	187 906	57 157	130 749	121 779	35 250	86 529
80 - 84	197 626	50 828	146 798	107 794	27 573	80 221	89 832	23 255	66 577
85 - 89	104 646	22 549	82 097	61 656	13 854	47 802	42 990	8 695	34 295
90 - 94	25 276	4 504	20 772	16 687	2 999	13 688	8 589	1 505	7 084
95 - 99	3 475	545	2 930	2 726	460	2 266	749	85	664
100 +	569	87	482	511	79	432	58	8	50
1 I 2015 (ESDJ)									
Total	9 480 868	4 409 197	5 071 671	...	...	...	...	...	...
0	118 667	61 299	57 368	...	...	...	...	...	...
1 - 4	454 345	233 850	220 495	...	...	...	...	...	...
5 - 9	502 262	258 189	244 073	...	...	...	...	...	...
10 - 14	443 395	227 672	215 723	...	...	...	...	...	...
15 - 19	465 604	239 685	225 919	...	...	...	...	...	...
20 - 24	631 754	324 467	307 287	...	...	...	...	...	...
25 - 29	775 281	396 607	378 674	...	...	...	...	...	...
30 - 34	744 290	375 255	369 035	...	...	...	...	...	...
35 - 39	673 776	333 121	340 655	...	...	...	...	...	...
40 - 44	653 139	314 962	338 177	...	...	...	...	...	...
45 - 49	642 694	305 209	337 485	...	...	...	...	...	...
50 - 54	743 451	346 439	397 012	...	...	...	...	...	...
55 - 59	715 939	321 461	394 478	...	...	...	...	...	...
60 - 64	567 427	238 277	329 150	...	...	...	...	...	...
65 - 69	408 295	160 953	247 342	...	...	...	...	...	...
70 - 74	286 712	97 779	188 933	...	...	...	...	...	...
75 - 79	322 627	96 048	226 579	...	...	...	...	...	...
80 - 84	190 311	48 424	141 887	...	...	...	...	...	...
85 - 89	108 019	23 794	84 225	...	...	...	...	...	...
90 - 94	28 608	5 006	23 602	...	...	...	...	...	...
95 - 99	3 569	597	2 972	...	...	...	...	...	...
100 +	703	103	600	...	...	...	...	...	...
Belgium - Belgique									
1 I 2011 (CDJC)									
Total	11 000 638	5 401 718	5 598 920	10 842 520	5 322 172	5 520 348	158 118	79 546	78 572
0 - 4	645 512	330 184	315 328	636 217	325 336	310 881	9 295	4 848	4 447
5 - 9	607 325	310 560	296 765	597 723	305 654	292 069	9 602	4 906	4 696
10 - 14	614 460	313 738	300 722	604 574	308 723	295 851	9 886	5 015	4 871
15 - 19	649 018	331 790	317 228	638 725	326 452	312 273	10 293	5 338	4 955
20 - 24	684 093	344 647	339 446	674 173	339 520	334 653	9 920	5 127	4 793
25 - 29	700 373	351 045	349 328	691 593	346 539	345 054	8 780	4 506	4 274
30 - 34	722 936	364 728	358 208	713 667	360 044	353 623	9 269	4 684	4 585
35 - 39	741 204	375 815	365 389	730 809	370 490	360 319	10 395	5 325	5 070
40 - 44	789 895	401 530	388 365	778 159	395 446	382 713	11 736	6 084	5 652
45 - 49	828 167	418 827	409 340	816 018	412 531	403 487	12 149	6 296	5 853
50 - 54	781 240	391 809	389 431	770 016	385 999	384 017	11 224	5 810	5 414
55 - 59	702 331	349 489	352 842	692 496	344 347	348 149	9 835	5 142	4 693
60 - 64	650 904	320 714	330 190	641 771	316 010	325 761	9 133	4 704	4 429
65 - 69	480 199	230 217	249 982	473 668	226 987	246 681	6 531	3 230	3 301
70 - 74	448 374	205 382	242 992	441 884	202 344	239 540	6 490	3 038	3 452

7. Population by age, sex and urban/rural residence: latest available year, 2006 - 2015
Population selon l'âge, le sexe et la résidence, urbaine/rurale : dernière année disponible, 2006 - 2015 (continued - suite)

Continent, country or area, date, code[a] and age (in years) / Continent, pays ou zone, date, code[a] et âge (en années)	Total			Urban - Urbaine			Rural - Rurale		
	Both sexes Les deux sexes	Male Masculin	Female Féminin	Both sexes Les deux sexes	Male Masculin	Female Féminin	Both sexes Les deux sexes	Male Masculin	Female Féminin
EUROPE									
Belgium - Belgique									
1 I 2011 (CDJC)									
75 - 79	401 594	171 538	230 056	395 900	168 962	226 938	5 694	2 576	3 118
80 - 84	304 788	115 591	189 197	300 342	113 821	186 521	4 446	1 770	2 676
85 - 89	180 495	57 963	122 532	177 932	57 048	120 884	2 563	915	1 648
90 - 94	52 708	13 541	39 167	52 007	13 341	38 666	701	200	501
95 - 99	13 392	2 412	10 980	13 233	2 381	10 852	159	31	128
100 +	1 630	198	1 432	1 613	197	1 416	17	1	16
1 I 2015 (ESDJ)									
Total	11 258 434	5 536 256	5 722 178	...	...	...	...	...	...
0	124 903	64 080	60 823	...	...	...	...	...	...
1 - 4	520 762	266 271	254 491	...	...	...	...	...	...
5 - 9	653 169	334 207	318 962	...	...	...	...	...	...
10 - 14	616 452	315 124	301 328	...	...	...	...	...	...
15 - 19	630 120	321 653	308 467	...	...	...	...	...	...
20 - 24	698 786	353 483	345 303	...	...	...	...	...	...
25 - 29	719 235	359 750	359 485	...	...	...	...	...	...
30 - 34	736 721	369 522	367 199	...	...	...	...	...	...
35 - 39	729 580	368 428	361 152	...	...	...	...	...	...
40 - 44	766 628	388 437	378 191	...	...	...	...	...	...
45 - 49	797 598	404 805	392 793	...	...	...	...	...	...
50 - 54	816 666	411 101	405 565	...	...	...	...	...	...
55 - 59	753 248	374 721	378 527	...	...	...	...	...	...
60 - 64	663 444	326 693	336 751	...	...	...	...	...	...
65 - 69	594 542	287 293	307 249	...	...	...	...	...	...
70 - 74	427 902	199 180	228 722	...	...	...	...	...	...
75 - 79	397 290	173 808	223 482	...	...	...	...	...	...
80 - 84	322 965	127 864	195 101	...	...	...	...	...	...
85 - 89	193 283	65 094	128 189	...	...	...	...	...	...
90 - 94	81 104	22 019	59 085	...	...	...	...	...	...
95 - 99	12 035	2 460	9 575	...	...	...	...	...	...
100 +	2 001	263	1 738	...	...	...	...	...	...
Bosnia and Herzegovina - Bosnie-Herzégovine									
1 VII 2010 (ESDF)									
Total	3 843 126	1 877 587	1 965 539	...	...	...	...	...	...
0	33 314	17 123	16 191	...	...	...	...	...	...
1 - 4	133 257	68 494	64 763	...	...	...	...	...	...
5 - 9	229 608	117 330	112 278	...	...	...	...	...	...
10 - 14	274 779	139 862	134 917	...	...	...	...	...	...
15 - 19	279 370	146 390	132 980	...	...	...	...	...	...
20 - 24	284 994	144 777	140 217	...	...	...	...	...	...
25 - 29	268 273	131 991	136 282	...	...	...	...	...	...
30 - 34	240 986	120 975	120 011	...	...	...	...	...	...
35 - 39	246 721	121 633	125 088	...	...	...	...	...	...
40 - 44	283 887	141 943	141 944	...	...	...	...	...	...
45 - 49	306 958	150 410	156 548	...	...	...	...	...	...
50 - 54	266 575	135 687	130 888	...	...	...	...	...	...
55 - 59	231 595	105 145	126 450	...	...	...	...	...	...
60 - 64	182 787	86 092	96 695	...	...	...	...	...	...
65 - 69	202 274	90 012	112 262	...	...	...	...	...	...
70 - 74	184 389	82 422	101 967	...	...	...	...	...	...
75 - 79	120 364	50 553	69 811	...	...	...	...	...	...
80 - 84	47 932	19 605	28 327	...	...	...	...	...	...
85 +	25 063	7 143	17 920	...	...	...	...	...	...
Bulgaria - Bulgarie									
1 VII 2012 (ESDJ)									
Total	7 305 888	3 555 920	3 749 968	5 316 384	2 568 535	2 747 849	1 989 504	987 385	1 002 119
0	66 072	34 082	31 990	49 710	25 724	23 986	16 362	8 358	8 004
1 - 4	280 165	143 865	136 300	208 103	106 901	101 202	72 062	36 964	35 098
5 - 9	324 559	167 057	157 502	235 618	121 101	114 517	88 941	45 956	42 985
10 - 14	314 174	161 486	152 688	226 483	116 269	110 214	87 691	45 217	42 474
15 - 19	346 926	178 574	168 352	250 855	128 646	122 209	96 071	49 928	46 143
20 - 24	466 758	240 138	226 620	360 989	182 904	178 085	105 769	57 234	48 535
25 - 29	489 520	253 779	235 741	380 805	194 743	186 062	108 715	59 036	49 679

239

7. Population by age, sex and urban/rural residence: latest available year, 2006 - 2015
Population selon l'âge, le sexe et la résidence, urbaine/rurale : dernière année disponible, 2006 - 2015 (continued - suite)

Continent, country or area, date, code[a] and age (in years) / Continent, pays ou zone, date, code[a] et âge (en années)	Total			Urban - Urbaine			Rural - Rurale		
	Both sexes Les deux sexes	Male Masculin	Female Féminin	Both sexes Les deux sexes	Male Masculin	Female Féminin	Both sexes Les deux sexes	Male Masculin	Female Féminin
EUROPE									
Bulgaria - Bulgarie									
1 VII 2012 (ESDJ)									
30 - 34	514 109	266 962	247 147	402 004	206 433	195 571	112 105	60 529	51 576
35 - 39	553 955	285 447	268 508	434 249	221 237	213 012	119 706	64 210	55 496
40 - 44	525 895	270 703	255 192	401 223	203 117	198 106	124 672	67 586	57 086
45 - 49	480 082	243 855	236 227	358 986	178 351	180 635	121 096	65 504	55 592
50 - 54	506 689	252 294	254 395	376 212	182 697	193 515	130 477	69 597	60 880
55 - 59	521 824	251 394	270 430	382 836	180 438	202 398	138 988	70 956	68 032
60 - 64	526 885	242 476	284 409	373 390	169 637	203 753	153 495	72 839	80 656
65 - 69	439 615	193 281	246 334	291 001	127 275	163 726	148 614	66 006	82 608
70 - 74	341 305	141 732	199 573	211 176	86 328	124 848	130 129	55 404	74 725
75 - 79	299 387	117 689	181 698	181 312	69 060	112 252	118 075	48 629	69 446
80 - 84	192 907	72 021	120 886	119 850	43 583	76 267	73 057	28 438	44 619
85 - 89	90 647	31 255	59 392	56 432	19 218	37 214	34 215	12 037	22 178
90 - 94	21 736	7 020	14 716	13 463	4 363	9 100	8 273	2 657	5 616
95 - 99	2 366	699	1 667	1 486	437	1 049	880	262	618
100 +	312	111	201	201	73	128	111	38	73
1 I 2015 (ESDJ)									
Total	7 202 198	3 502 015	3 700 183	...	...	...	...	...	...
0	67 216	34 524	32 692	...	...	...	...	...	...
1 - 4	270 440	139 013	131 427	...	...	...	...	...	...
5 - 9	343 330	176 451	166 879	...	...	...	...	...	...
10 - 14	317 210	163 300	153 910	...	...	...	...	...	...
15 - 19	313 313	161 330	151 983	...	...	...	...	...	...
20 - 24	404 960	208 750	196 210	...	...	...	...	...	...
25 - 29	486 621	251 020	235 601	...	...	...	...	...	...
30 - 34	488 268	254 270	233 998	...	...	...	...	...	...
35 - 39	541 664	279 613	262 051	...	...	...	...	...	...
40 - 44	533 378	274 829	258 549	...	...	...	...	...	...
45 - 49	492 411	250 798	241 613	...	...	...	...	...	...
50 - 54	492 977	246 926	246 051	...	...	...	...	...	...
55 - 59	503 714	243 828	259 886	...	...	...	...	...	...
60 - 64	506 367	234 527	271 840	...	...	...	...	...	...
65 - 69	479 107	210 271	268 836	...	...	...	...	...	...
70 - 74	352 291	146 330	205 961	...	...	...	...	...	...
75 - 79	277 738	107 794	169 944	...	...	...	...	...	...
80 - 84	206 460	76 127	130 333	...	...	...	...	...	...
85 - 89	94 392	32 642	61 750	...	...	...	...	...	...
90 - 94	27 213	8 680	18 533	...	...	...	...	...	...
95 - 99	2 770	872	1 898	...	...	...	...	...	...
100 +	358	120	238	...	...	...	...	...	...
Croatia - Croatie									
1 IV 2011 (CDJC)									
Total	4 284 889	2 066 335	2 218 554	2 368 506	1 121 328	1 247 178	1 916 383	945 007	971 376
0 - 4	212 709	109 251	103 458	116 367	59 768	56 599	96 342	49 483	46 859
5 - 9	204 317	104 841	99 476	108 481	55 715	52 766	95 836	49 126	46 710
10 - 14	235 402	120 633	114 769	124 241	63 763	60 478	111 161	56 870	54 291
15 - 19	244 177	124 918	119 259	130 369	66 506	63 863	113 808	58 412	55 396
20 - 24	261 658	133 455	128 203	142 681	72 037	70 644	118 977	61 418	57 559
25 - 29	289 066	147 416	141 650	164 754	82 466	82 288	124 312	64 950	59 362
30 - 34	294 619	149 998	144 621	173 166	86 363	86 803	121 453	63 635	57 818
35 - 39	284 754	143 984	140 770	165 450	81 745	83 705	119 304	62 239	57 065
40 - 44	286 933	143 603	143 330	161 295	78 845	82 450	125 638	64 758	60 880
45 - 49	307 561	152 446	155 115	167 593	80 182	87 411	139 968	72 264	67 704
50 - 54	320 502	157 981	162 521	174 963	81 945	93 018	145 539	76 036	69 503
55 - 59	311 818	153 750	158 068	174 376	81 746	92 630	137 442	72 004	65 438
60 - 64	272 740	127 851	144 889	154 706	69 577	85 129	118 034	58 274	59 760
65 - 69	202 002	89 364	112 638	114 109	49 018	65 091	87 893	40 346	47 547
70 - 74	212 401	88 912	123 489	113 737	47 978	65 759	98 664	40 934	57 730
75 - 79	175 526	66 456	109 070	91 966	35 801	56 165	83 560	30 655	52 905
80 - 84	108 104	35 999	72 105	56 658	19 022	37 636	51 446	16 977	34 469
85 - 89	47 641	12 415	35 226	26 213	7 045	19 168	21 428	5 370	16 058
90 - 94	10 758	2 580	8 178	6 081	1 517	4 564	4 677	1 063	3 614
95 - 99	2 003	446	1 557	1 181	270	911	822	176	646
100 +	198	36	162	119	19	100	79	17	62

Continent, country or area, date, code[a] and age (in years) / Continent, pays ou zone, date, code[a] et âge (en années)	Total			Urban - Urbaine			Rural - Rurale		
	Both sexes Les deux sexes	Male Masculin	Female Féminin	Both sexes Les deux sexes	Male Masculin	Female Féminin	Both sexes Les deux sexes	Male Masculin	Female Féminin
EUROPE									
Croatia - Croatie									
1 I 2015 (ESDJ)									
Total	4 225 316	2 039 227	2 186 089	...	...	...	...	...	...
0	39 425	20 292	19 133	...	...	...	...	...	...
1 - 4	165 736	85 577	80 159	...	...	...	...	...	...
5 - 9	211 122	108 331	102 791	...	...	...	...	...	...
10 - 14	204 767	105 199	99 568	...	...	...	...	...	...
15 - 19	241 956	123 925	118 031	...	...	...	...	...	...
20 - 24	246 590	125 945	120 645	...	...	...	...	...	...
25 - 29	266 817	135 539	131 278	...	...	...	...	...	...
30 - 34	291 402	148 489	142 913	...	...	...	...	...	...
35 - 39	288 558	146 467	142 091	...	...	...	...	...	...
40 - 44	276 652	139 362	137 290	...	...	...	...	...	...
45 - 49	292 380	145 239	147 141	...	...	...	...	...	...
50 - 54	303 185	148 796	154 389	...	...	...	...	...	...
55 - 59	312 206	151 963	160 243	...	...	...	...	...	...
60 - 64	289 373	139 523	149 850	...	...	...	...	...	...
65 - 69	228 050	102 335	125 715	...	...	...	...	...	...
70 - 74	192 999	81 175	111 824	...	...	...	...	...	...
75 - 79	176 934	68 697	108 237	...	...	...	...	...	...
80 - 84	123 084	41 970	81 114	...	...	...	...	...	...
85 - 89	55 375	16 208	39 167	...	...	...	...	...	...
90 - 94	16 640	3 749	12 891	...	...	...	...	...	...
95 - 99	1 751	390	1 361	...	...	...	...	...	...
100 +	314	56	258	...	...	...	...	...	...
Czech Republic - République tchèque									
1 I 2015 (ESDJ)									
Total	10 538 275	5 176 927	5 361 348	7 699 525	3 748 292	3 951 233	2 838 750	1 428 635	1 410 115
0	109 943	56 454	53 489	80 659	41 362	39 297	29 284	15 092	14 192
1 - 4	447 126	229 186	217 940	325 182	166 575	158 607	121 944	62 611	59 333
5 - 9	574 904	294 328	280 576	413 516	211 474	202 042	161 388	82 854	78 534
10 - 14	469 072	241 497	227 575	332 134	170 989	161 145	136 938	70 508	66 430
15 - 19	463 083	237 164	225 919	325 665	166 170	159 495	137 418	70 994	66 424
20 - 24	623 989	319 034	304 955	448 605	227 854	220 751	175 384	91 180	84 204
25 - 29	696 939	357 001	339 938	519 561	265 589	253 972	177 378	91 412	85 966
30 - 34	749 002	385 911	363 091	554 897	285 530	269 367	194 105	100 381	93 724
35 - 39	917 230	470 998	446 232	667 714	341 222	326 492	249 516	129 776	119 740
40 - 44	838 729	431 015	407 714	607 665	308 748	298 917	231 064	122 267	108 797
45 - 49	692 290	354 319	337 971	505 471	254 885	250 586	186 819	99 434	87 385
50 - 54	668 093	338 213	329 880	489 171	244 416	244 755	178 922	93 797	85 125
55 - 59	680 114	335 746	344 368	493 970	239 845	254 125	186 144	95 901	90 243
60 - 64	727 355	348 036	379 319	531 027	250 117	280 910	196 328	97 919	98 409
65 - 69	671 051	308 199	362 852	493 940	222 260	271 680	177 111	85 939	91 172
70 - 74	482 043	209 638	272 405	363 936	156 045	207 891	118 107	53 593	64 514
75 - 79	308 614	122 957	185 657	231 216	91 739	139 477	77 398	31 218	46 180
80 - 84	236 599	84 629	151 970	177 177	63 317	113 860	59 422	21 312	38 110
85 - 89	131 259	40 216	91 043	99 040	30 527	68 513	32 219	9 689	22 530
90 - 94	45 374	11 222	34 152	34 847	8 747	26 100	10 527	2 475	8 052
95 - 99	4 668	991	3 677	3 539	752	2 787	1 129	239	890
100 +	798	173	625	593	129	464	205	44	161
Denmark - Danemark[66]									
1 VII 2015 (ESDJ)									
Total	5 678 348	2 822 535	2 855 813	...	...	...	...	...	...
0	57 214	29 360	27 854	...	...	...	...	...	...
1 - 4	238 074	122 017	116 057	...	...	...	...	...	...
5 - 9	331 703	170 313	161 390	...	...	...	...	...	...
10 - 14	332 601	170 170	162 431	...	...	...	...	...	...
15 - 19	350 604	179 922	170 682	...	...	...	...	...	...
20 - 24	380 329	194 129	186 200	...	...	...	...	...	...
25 - 29	353 741	180 436	173 305	...	...	...	...	...	...
30 - 34	320 428	162 333	158 095	...	...	...	...	...	...
35 - 39	354 977	178 377	176 600	...	...	...	...	...	...
40 - 44	392 173	196 895	195 278	...	...	...	...	...	...
45 - 49	408 841	206 478	202 363	...	...	...	...	...	...

7. Population by age, sex and urban/rural residence: latest available year, 2006 - 2015
Population selon l'âge, le sexe et la résidence, urbaine/rurale : dernière année disponible, 2006 - 2015 (continued - suite)

Continent, country or area, date, code[a] and age (in years) / Continent, pays ou zone, date, code[a] et âge (en années)	Total			Urban - Urbaine			Rural - Rurale		
	Both sexes Les deux sexes	Male Masculin	Female Féminin	Both sexes Les deux sexes	Male Masculin	Female Féminin	Both sexes Les deux sexes	Male Masculin	Female Féminin
EUROPE									
Denmark - Danemark[66]									
1 VII 2015 (ESDJ)									
50 - 54	400 219	201 616	198 603	...	...	...	...	...	...
55 - 59	357 289	178 623	178 666	...	...	...	...	...	...
60 - 64	336 276	166 325	169 951	...	...	...	...	...	...
65 - 69	348 875	171 172	177 703	...	...	...	...	...	...
70 - 74	283 071	135 736	147 335	...	...	...	...	...	...
75 - 79	190 342	87 364	102 978	...	...	...	...	...	...
80 - 84	123 888	52 329	71 559	...	...	...	...	...	...
85 - 89	74 719	27 514	47 205	...	...	...	...	...	...
90 - 94	33 635	9 505	24 130	...	...	...	...	...	...
95 - 99	8 319	1 759	6 560	...	...	...	...	...	...
100 +	1 030	162	868	...	...	...	...	...	...
Estonia - Estonie									
1 I 2015 (ESDJ)									
Total	1 313 271	614 389	698 882	897 327	407 519	489 808	415 944	206 870	209 074
0	13 625	6 957	6 668	9 444	4 773	4 671	4 181	2 184	1 997
1 - 4	58 089	29 871	28 218	38 704	19 894	18 810	19 385	9 977	9 408
5 - 9	74 943	38 578	36 365	49 028	25 105	23 923	25 915	13 473	12 442
10 - 14	62 939	32 280	30 659	40 295	20 606	19 689	22 644	11 674	10 970
15 - 19	59 842	30 759	29 083	37 588	19 127	18 461	22 254	11 632	10 622
20 - 24	78 493	40 480	38 013	53 957	26 713	27 244	24 536	13 767	10 769
25 - 29	98 197	50 866	47 331	73 625	37 154	36 471	24 572	13 712	10 860
30 - 34	92 841	47 635	45 206	66 888	33 964	32 924	25 953	13 671	12 282
35 - 39	89 906	46 068	43 838	61 505	30 997	30 508	28 401	15 071	13 330
40 - 44	91 668	46 282	45 386	61 349	30 087	31 262	30 319	16 195	14 124
45 - 49	84 792	41 717	43 075	55 554	26 438	29 116	29 238	15 279	13 959
50 - 54	90 413	43 457	46 956	60 649	27 863	32 786	29 764	15 594	14 170
55 - 59	89 250	41 007	48 243	61 001	26 597	34 404	28 249	14 410	13 839
60 - 64	81 921	35 436	46 485	56 977	23 346	33 631	24 944	12 090	12 854
65 - 69	69 475	28 117	41 358	47 621	18 222	29 399	21 854	9 895	11 959
70 - 74	57 028	21 058	35 970	38 151	13 293	24 858	18 877	7 765	11 112
75 - 79	54 557	17 613	36 944	38 693	12 057	26 636	15 864	5 556	10 308
80 - 84	36 191	10 140	26 051	25 434	6 902	18 532	10 757	3 238	7 519
85 - 89	21 227	4 760	16 467	15 401	3 464	11 937	5 826	1 296	4 530
90 - 94	6 715	1 150	5 565	4 692	808	3 884	2 023	342	1 681
95 - 99	1 023	143	880	683	97	586	340	46	294
100 +	136	15	121	88	12	76	48	3	45
Faeroe Islands - Îles Féroé									
1 VII 2015 (ESDJ)									
Total	48 958	25 330	23 628	18 674	9 386	9 288	30 284	15 944	14 340
0	633	315	318	256	127	129	377	188	189
1 - 4	2 546	1 305	1 241	995	492	503	1 551	813	738
5 - 9	3 463	1 791	1 672	1 329	661	668	2 134	1 130	1 004
10 - 14	3 621	1 850	1 771	1 403	703	700	2 218	1 147	1 071
15 - 19	3 605	1 884	1 721	1 394	705	689	2 211	1 179	1 032
20 - 24	2 979	1 633	1 346	1 174	634	540	1 805	999	806
25 - 29	2 582	1 429	1 153	950	501	449	1 632	928	704
30 - 34	2 598	1 377	1 221	973	500	473	1 625	877	748
35 - 39	2 956	1 546	1 410	1 156	596	560	1 800	950	850
40 - 44	3 164	1 696	1 468	1 207	638	569	1 957	1 058	899
45 - 49	3 436	1 801	1 635	1 439	715	724	1 997	1 086	911
50 - 54	3 273	1 710	1 563	1 354	702	652	1 919	1 008	911
55 - 59	3 081	1 562	1 519	1 175	580	595	1 906	982	924
60 - 64	2 788	1 451	1 337	1 051	528	523	1 737	923	814
65 - 69	2 580	1 360	1 220	923	470	453	1 657	890	767
70 - 74	2 166	1 134	1 032	733	368	365	1 433	766	667
75 - 79	1 350	657	693	475	214	261	875	443	432
80 - 84	1 101	500	601	321	139	182	780	361	419
85 - 89	655	224	431	232	83	149	423	141	282
90 - 94	301	84	217	103	25	78	198	59	139
95 - 99	70	19	51	24	4	20	46	15	31
100 +	10	2	8	7	1	6	3	1	2

Continent, country or area, date, code[a] and age (in years) / Continent, pays ou zone, date, code[a] et âge (en années)	Total			Urban - Urbaine			Rural - Rurale		
	Both sexes Les deux sexes	Male Masculin	Female Féminin	Both sexes Les deux sexes	Male Masculin	Female Féminin	Both sexes Les deux sexes	Male Masculin	Female Féminin
EUROPE									
Finland - Finlande[21]									
1 VII 2014 (ESDJ)[67]									
Total	5 432 721	2 671 740	2 760 981	3 762 906	1 831 826	1 931 080	1 669 815	839 914	829 901
0	57 754	29 589	28 165	41 315	21 177	20 138	16 438	8 412	8 027
1 - 4	242 311	123 842	118 469	169 277	86 564	82 713	73 035	37 278	35 757
5 - 9	300 906	153 719	147 187	204 426	104 349	100 077	96 480	49 371	47 110
10 - 14	290 168	148 408	141 760	192 183	98 263	93 920	97 985	50 145	47 840
15 - 19	308 376	157 342	151 034	210 594	105 742	104 853	97 782	51 601	46 182
20 - 24	339 941	173 678	166 264	271 179	135 255	135 924	68 763	38 423	30 340
25 - 29	338 165	173 353	164 812	268 405	136 857	131 548	69 761	36 496	33 265
30 - 34	351 343	180 964	170 380	266 702	137 443	129 259	84 641	43 521	41 121
35 - 39	340 499	175 022	165 477	249 437	128 341	121 096	91 062	46 681	44 382
40 - 44	313 382	159 951	153 431	221 687	113 067	108 620	91 695	46 884	44 811
45 - 49	361 628	182 866	178 762	249 996	125 103	124 893	111 632	57 763	53 869
50 - 54	373 305	187 230	186 076	251 032	123 995	127 038	122 273	63 235	59 038
55 - 59	370 624	183 506	187 118	242 422	117 169	125 254	128 202	66 338	61 864
60 - 64	376 156	184 157	191 999	243 028	114 955	128 073	133 129	69 203	63 926
65 - 69	364 434	175 005	189 430	237 850	110 551	127 300	126 584	64 454	62 130
70 - 74	236 042	108 301	127 741	153 077	68 203	84 874	82 965	40 098	42 867
75 - 79	194 015	83 167	110 848	121 812	50 555	71 257	72 203	32 612	39 591
80 - 84	142 891	54 299	88 592	88 669	32 459	56 210	54 223	21 840	32 383
85 - 89	89 057	27 951	61 106	54 234	16 301	37 933	34 823	11 650	23 174
90 - 94	34 336	8 063	26 273	20 874	4 699	16 175	13 463	3 365	10 098
95 - 99	6 672	1 238	5 435	4 268	734	3 534	2 405	504	1 901
100 +	720	94	626	445	49	397	275	46	230
1 I 2015 (ESDJ)									
Total	5 471 753	2 691 863	2 779 890	...	...	...	...	...	...
0	57 670	29 494	28 176	...	...	...	...	...	...
1 - 4	242 466	123 992	118 474	...	...	...	...	...	...
5 - 9	304 173	155 317	148 856	...	...	...	...	...	...
10 - 14	292 299	149 597	142 702	...	...	...	...	...	...
15 - 19	306 582	156 492	150 090	...	...	...	...	...	...
20 - 24	342 086	174 762	167 324	...	...	...	...	...	...
25 - 29	339 565	174 020	165 545	...	...	...	...	...	...
30 - 34	355 387	183 123	172 264	...	...	...	...	...	...
35 - 39	344 429	177 106	167 323	...	...	...	...	...	...
40 - 44	314 679	160 576	154 103	...	...	...	...	...	...
45 - 49	359 317	181 712	177 605	...	...	...	...	...	...
50 - 54	375 585	188 443	187 142	...	...	...	...	...	...
55 - 59	370 897	183 866	187 031	...	...	...	...	...	...
60 - 64	375 230	183 321	191 909	...	...	...	...	...	...
65 - 69	376 614	181 087	195 527	...	...	...	...	...	...
70 - 74	238 873	110 037	128 836	...	...	...	...	...	...
75 - 79	198 424	85 233	113 191	...	...	...	...	...	...
80 - 84	143 437	55 027	88 410	...	...	...	...	...	...
85 - 89	91 054	28 807	62 247	...	...	...	...	...	...
90 - 94	35 527	8 472	27 055	...	...	...	...	...	...
95 - 99	6 718	1 279	5 439	...	...	...	...	...	...
100 +	741	100	641	...	...	...	...	...	...
France[68]									
1 I 2015 (ESDJ)									
Total	64 513 242	31 283 319	33 229 923	...	...	...	...	...	...
0	733 698	375 301	358 397	...	...	...	...	...	...
1 - 4	3 067 012	1 570 037	1 496 975	...	...	...	...	...	...
5 - 9	4 018 545	2 058 056	1 960 489	...	...	...	...	...	...
10 - 14	3 973 212	2 034 130	1 939 082	...	...	...	...	...	...
15 - 19	3 909 265	2 002 292	1 906 973	...	...	...	...	...	...
20 - 24	3 643 281	1 840 860	1 802 421	...	...	...	...	...	...
25 - 29	3 838 291	1 899 373	1 938 918	...	...	...	...	...	...
30 - 34	3 984 808	1 957 783	2 027 025	...	...	...	...	...	...
35 - 39	3 983 773	1 971 651	2 012 122	...	...	...	...	...	...
40 - 44	4 327 249	2 154 683	2 172 566	...	...	...	...	...	...
45 - 49	4 346 984	2 151 053	2 195 931	...	...	...	...	...	...
50 - 54	4 347 157	2 136 471	2 210 686	...	...	...	...	...	...
55 - 59	4 132 132	2 007 511	2 124 621	...	...	...	...	...	...

Continent, country or area, date, code[a] and age (in years) Continent, pays ou zone, date, code[a] et âge (en annèes)	Total			Urban - Urbaine			Rural - Rurale		
	Both sexes Les deux sexes	Male Masculin	Female Féminin	Both sexes Les deux sexes	Male Masculin	Female Féminin	Both sexes Les deux sexes	Male Masculin	Female Féminin
EUROPE									
France[68]									
1 I 2015 (ESDJ)									
60 - 64	3 937 799	1 883 514	2 054 285	...	...	...	...	...	...
65 - 69	3 844 452	1 820 857	2 023 595	...	...	...	...	...	...
70 - 74	2 453 598	1 135 862	1 317 736	...	...	...	...	...	...
75 - 79	2 140 655	934 513	1 206 142	...	...	...	...	...	...
80 - 84	1 845 171	728 178	1 116 993	...	...	...	...	...	...
85 - 89	1 247 557	427 208	820 349	...	...	...	...	...	...
90 - 94	596 356	164 187	432 169	...	...	...	...	...	...
95 +	142 247	29 799	112 448	...	...	...	...	...	...
Germany - Allemagne									
9 V 2011 (CDJC)									
Total	80 219 695	39 145 941	41 073 754	64 444 232	31 227 832	33 216 400	15 775 463	7 918 109	7 857 354
0 - 4	3 338 895	1 714 872	1 624 023	2 712 601	1 393 763	1 318 838	626 294	321 109	305 185
5 - 9	3 525 830	1 809 024	1 716 806	2 798 622	1 435 745	1 362 877	727 208	373 279	353 929
10 - 14	3 940 566	2 021 305	1 919 261	3 074 610	1 575 684	1 498 926	865 956	445 621	420 335
15 - 19	4 013 880	2 057 155	1 956 725	3 144 832	1 606 068	1 538 764	869 048	451 087	417 961
20 - 24	4 835 639	2 463 932	2 371 707	3 993 247	2 003 582	1 989 665	842 392	460 350	382 042
25 - 29	4 872 533	2 455 885	2 416 648	4 113 697	2 057 507	2 056 190	758 836	398 378	360 458
30 - 34	4 751 911	2 385 305	2 366 606	3 942 747	1 977 628	1 965 119	809 164	407 677	401 487
35 - 39	4 742 893	2 378 055	2 364 838	3 833 417	1 920 448	1 912 969	909 476	457 607	451 869
40 - 44	6 351 189	3 209 481	3 141 708	5 029 918	2 540 433	2 489 485	1 321 271	669 048	652 223
45 - 49	6 999 679	3 547 254	3 452 425	5 488 622	2 771 239	2 717 383	1 511 057	776 015	735 042
50 - 54	6 206 294	3 113 463	3 092 831	4 845 747	2 413 038	2 432 709	1 360 547	700 425	660 122
55 - 59	5 419 450	2 668 976	2 750 474	4 252 008	2 066 178	2 185 830	1 167 442	602 798	564 644
60 - 64	4 702 815	2 298 903	2 403 912	3 753 504	1 808 314	1 945 190	949 311	490 589	458 722
65 - 69	4 173 351	1 999 287	2 174 064	3 423 376	1 624 839	1 798 537	749 975	374 448	375 527
70 - 74	4 861 239	2 247 196	2 614 043	3 931 373	1 801 914	2 129 459	929 866	445 282	484 584
75 - 79	3 270 283	1 413 881	1 856 402	2 633 648	1 128 379	1 505 269	636 635	285 502	351 133
80 - 84	2 328 083	878 797	1 449 286	1 890 025	704 565	1 185 460	438 058	174 232	263 826
85 - 89	1 335 076	369 029	966 047	1 108 944	302 059	806 885	226 132	66 970	159 162
90 - 94	430 600	95 074	335 526	368 116	79 884	288 232	62 484	15 190	47 294
95 - 99	106 044	17 388	88 656	93 152	15 094	78 058	12 892	2 294	10 598
100 +	13 445	1 679	11 766	12 026	1 471	10 555	1 419	208	1 211
1 I 2015 (ESDJ)[69]									
Total	81 197 537	39 835 457	41 362 080	...	...	...	...	...	...
0	716 419	367 563	348 856	...	...	...	...	...	...
1 - 4	2 769 992	1 420 377	1 349 615	...	...	...	...	...	...
5 - 9	3 491 478	1 791 964	1 699 514	...	...	...	...	...	...
10 - 14	3 708 834	1 903 744	1 805 090	...	...	...	...	...	...
15 - 19	4 066 788	2 094 653	1 972 135	...	...	...	...	...	...
20 - 24	4 586 328	2 357 904	2 228 424	...	...	...	...	...	...
25 - 29	5 166 826	2 652 021	2 514 805	...	...	...	...	...	...
30 - 34	5 074 081	2 576 055	2 498 026	...	...	...	...	...	...
35 - 39	4 758 616	2 399 445	2 359 171	...	...	...	...	...	...
40 - 44	5 184 279	2 611 144	2 573 135	...	...	...	...	...	...
45 - 49	6 722 424	3 404 196	3 318 228	...	...	...	...	...	...
50 - 54	6 856 652	3 454 804	3 401 848	...	...	...	...	...	...
55 - 59	5 853 132	2 915 733	2 937 399	...	...	...	...	...	...
60 - 64	5 152 977	2 502 129	2 650 848	...	...	...	...	...	...
65 - 69	4 008 894	1 925 969	2 082 925	...	...	...	...	...	...
70 - 74	4 426 214	2 059 860	2 366 354	...	...	...	...	...	...
75 - 79	4 109 305	1 811 505	2 297 800	...	...	...	...	...	...
80 - 84	2 396 702	955 114	1 441 588	...	...	...	...	...	...
85 - 89	1 458 178	479 653	978 525	...	...	...	...	...	...
90 - 94	583 501	133 276	450 225	...	...	...	...	...	...
95 - 99	88 443	15 772	72 671	...	...	...	...	...	...
100 +	17 474	2 576	14 898	...	...	...	...	...	...
Gibraltar[70]									
12 XI 2012 (CDJC)									
Total	32 194	16 061	16 133	...	...	...	...	...	...
0 - 4	1 952	982	970	...	...	...	...	...	...
5 - 9	1 894	967	927	...	...	...	...	...	...
10 - 14	1 987	1 050	937	...	...	...	...	...	...
15 - 19	1 997	1 038	959	...	...	...	...	...	...

7. Population by age, sex and urban/rural residence: latest available year, 2006 - 2015
Population selon l'âge, le sexe et la résidence, urbaine/rurale : dernière année disponible, 2006 - 2015 (continued - suite)

Continent, country or area, date, code[a] and age (in years) / Continent, pays ou zone, date, code[a] et âge (en années)	Total			Urban - Urbaine			Rural - Rurale		
	Both sexes Les deux sexes	Male Masculin	Female Féminin	Both sexes Les deux sexes	Male Masculin	Female Féminin	Both sexes Les deux sexes	Male Masculin	Female Féminin
EUROPE									
Gibraltar[70]									
12 XI 2012 (CDJC)									
20 - 24	2 028	1 042	986	...	...	...	...	...	...
25 - 29	1 985	999	986	...	...	...	...	...	...
30 - 34	2 154	1 107	1 047	...	...	...	...	...	...
35 - 39	2 217	1 080	1 137	...	...	...	...	...	...
40 - 44	2 198	1 076	1 122	...	...	...	...	...	...
45 - 49	2 384	1 203	1 181	...	...	...	...	...	...
50 - 54	2 158	1 072	1 086	...	...	...	...	...	...
55 - 59	2 041	1 054	987	...	...	...	...	...	...
60 - 64	1 954	1 034	920	...	...	...	...	...	...
65 - 69	1 655	853	802	...	...	...	...	...	...
70 - 74	1 176	563	613	...	...	...	...	...	...
75 - 79	1 021	456	565	...	...	...	...	...	...
80 - 84	732	297	435	...	...	...	...	...	...
85 - 89	437	141	296	...	...	...	...	...	...
90 - 94	180	37	143	...	...	...	...	...	...
95 - 99	39	10	29	...	...	...	...	...	...
100 +	5	-	5	...	...	...	...	...	...
Greece - Grèce									
9 V 2011 (CDFC)									
Total	10 816 286	5 303 223	5 513 063	8 285 259	4 022 889	4 262 370	2 531 027	1 280 334	1 250 693
0 - 4	537 243	274 788	262 455	431 611	220 917	210 694	105 632	53 871	51 761
5 - 9	512 596	262 432	250 164	405 436	207 479	197 957	107 160	54 953	52 207
10 - 14	519 429	265 787	253 642	406 962	208 070	198 892	112 467	57 717	54 750
15 - 19	553 276	286 386	266 890	440 869	226 682	214 187	112 407	59 704	52 703
20 - 24	627 097	325 127	301 970	510 067	259 795	250 272	117 030	65 332	51 698
25 - 29	723 771	371 617	352 154	583 506	295 880	287 626	140 265	75 737	64 528
30 - 34	822 475	417 861	404 614	666 145	334 794	331 351	156 330	83 067	73 263
35 - 39	812 829	409 681	403 148	651 826	323 821	328 005	161 003	85 860	75 143
40 - 44	832 666	414 026	418 640	663 331	323 632	339 699	169 335	90 394	78 941
45 - 49	748 429	367 086	381 343	590 034	283 391	306 643	158 395	83 695	74 700
50 - 54	731 486	355 552	375 934	565 986	268 882	297 104	165 500	86 670	78 830
55 - 59	660 368	321 466	338 902	501 507	240 725	260 782	158 861	80 741	78 120
60 - 64	625 769	301 589	324 180	459 249	219 165	240 084	166 520	82 424	84 096
65 - 69	508 276	241 832	266 444	356 701	167 557	189 144	151 575	74 275	77 300
70 - 74	542 165	246 264	295 901	363 133	162 560	200 573	179 032	83 704	95 328
75 - 79	475 077	209 983	265 094	309 622	134 691	174 931	165 455	75 292	90 163
80 - 84	352 373	146 455	205 918	229 214	91 916	137 298	123 159	54 539	68 620
85 - 89	159 841	60 933	98 908	104 058	37 922	66 136	55 783	23 011	32 772
90 - 94	53 445	18 760	34 685	34 608	11 513	23 095	18 837	7 247	11 590
95 - 99	15 187	4 948	10 239	9 822	3 081	6 741	5 365	1 867	3 498
100 +	2 488	650	1 838	1 572	416	1 156	916	234	682
1 I 2015 (ESDF)									
Total	10 858 018	5 268 390	5 589 628	...	...	...	...	...	...
0	91 717	47 150	44 567	...	...	...	...	...	...
1 - 4	407 724	209 608	198 116	...	...	...	...	...	...
5 - 9	548 498	280 498	268 000	...	...	...	...	...	...
10 - 14	529 979	271 270	258 709	...	...	...	...	...	...
15 - 19	537 646	273 727	263 919	...	...	...	...	...	...
20 - 24	575 134	292 470	282 664	...	...	...	...	...	...
25 - 29	611 122	306 636	304 486	...	...	...	...	...	...
30 - 34	751 565	379 459	372 106	...	...	...	...	...	...
35 - 39	814 165	407 210	406 955	...	...	...	...	...	...
40 - 44	819 569	404 599	414 970	...	...	...	...	...	...
45 - 49	817 301	397 226	420 075	...	...	...	...	...	...
50 - 54	739 833	352 642	387 191	...	...	...	...	...	...
55 - 59	707 641	337 250	370 391	...	...	...	...	...	...
60 - 64	637 051	304 751	332 300	...	...	...	...	...	...
65 - 69	608 308	285 907	322 401	...	...	...	...	...	...
70 - 74	486 907	225 349	261 558	...	...	...	...	...	...
75 - 79	492 889	214 733	278 156	...	...	...	...	...	...
80 - 84	377 776	159 496	218 280	...	...	...	...	...	...
85 - 89	211 867	84 042	127 825	...	...	...	...	...	...
90 - 94	67 915	26 038	41 877	...	...	...	...	...	...

Continent, country or area, date, code[a] and age (in years) Continent, pays ou zone, date, code[a] et âge (en années)	Total			Urban - Urbaine			Rural - Rurale		
	Both sexes Les deux sexes	Male Masculin	Female Féminin	Both sexes Les deux sexes	Male Masculin	Female Féminin	Both sexes Les deux sexes	Male Masculin	Female Féminin
EUROPE									
Greece - Grèce									
1 I 2015 (ESDF)									
95 - 99	17 281	6 269	11 012	...	...	...	...	...	...
100 +	6 130	2 060	4 070	...	...	...	...	...	...
Guernsey - Guernesey									
31 III 2015 (ESDF)									
Total	62 612	31 028	31 584	...	...	...	...	...	...
0 - 4	3 267	1 683	1 584	...	...	...	...	...	...
5 - 9	3 205	1 706	1 499	...	...	...	...	...	...
10 - 14	3 056	1 553	1 503	...	...	...	...	...	...
15 - 19	3 475	1 782	1 693	...	...	...	...	...	...
20 - 24	3 970	2 061	1 909	...	...	...	...	...	...
25 - 29	3 914	2 005	1 909	...	...	...	...	...	...
30 - 34	3 964	2 040	1 924	...	...	...	...	...	...
35 - 39	3 708	1 844	1 864	...	...	...	...	...	...
40 - 44	4 414	2 167	2 247	...	...	...	...	...	...
45 - 49	4 958	2 393	2 565	...	...	...	...	...	...
50 - 54	4 904	2 426	2 478	...	...	...	...	...	...
55 - 59	4 341	2 179	2 162	...	...	...	...	...	...
60 - 64	3 758	1 895	1 863	...	...	...	...	...	...
65 - 69	3 771	1 830	1 941	...	...	...	...	...	...
70 - 74	2 476	1 216	1 260	...	...	...	...	...	...
75 - 79	2 235	1 053	1 182	...	...	...	...	...	...
80 - 84	1 589	655	934	...	...	...	...	...	...
85 - 89	1 027	372	655	...	...	...	...	...	...
90 - 94	460	143	317	...	...	...	...	...	...
95 +	120	25	95	...	...	...	...	...	...
Hungary - Hongrie[71]									
1 VII 2014 (ESDJ)									
Total	9 866 468	4 699 585	5 166 883	6 950 391	3 272 050	3 678 342	2 916 077	1 427 536	1 488 542
0	91 100	46 750	44 350	64 182	33 028	31 154	26 917	13 722	13 195
1 - 4	362 584	186 248	176 337	259 683	133 420	126 263	102 902	52 828	50 074
5 - 9	492 815	252 862	239 953	342 135	175 527	166 608	150 680	77 336	73 345
10 - 14	480 003	246 621	233 383	320 240	164 229	156 012	159 763	82 392	77 371
15 - 19	533 406	273 932	259 475	364 978	185 967	179 011	168 429	87 965	80 464
20 - 24	626 533	321 664	304 869	431 605	219 987	211 618	194 928	101 677	93 251
25 - 29	611 714	314 097	297 618	434 466	219 868	214 598	177 249	94 229	83 020
30 - 34	660 475	334 037	326 438	482 116	240 209	241 907	178 359	93 829	84 531
35 - 39	845 728	428 252	417 477	617 458	308 747	308 711	228 271	119 505	108 766
40 - 44	738 024	372 423	365 601	524 017	261 325	262 692	214 007	111 099	102 909
45 - 49	662 749	330 546	332 203	459 728	225 625	234 103	203 021	104 921	98 100
50 - 54	599 455	290 857	308 598	407 177	193 097	214 080	192 279	97 760	94 519
55 - 59	719 769	336 929	382 840	496 850	225 927	270 923	222 920	111 002	111 918
60 - 64	694 094	312 175	381 919	493 480	216 845	276 635	200 614	95 330	105 284
65 - 69	547 904	234 729	313 176	396 620	167 456	229 164	151 285	67 273	84 012
70 - 74	453 664	179 700	273 964	325 199	129 172	196 028	128 465	50 528	77 937
75 - 79	331 241	115 197	216 044	233 306	82 386	150 921	97 935	32 811	65 124
80 - 84	237 633	75 578	162 055	167 898	54 603	113 295	69 735	20 975	48 760
85 - 89	124 935	34 145	90 790	90 239	25 049	65 191	34 696	9 097	25 600
90 - 94	45 441	10 988	34 453	33 536	8 164	25 372	11 906	2 825	9 081
95 - 99	5 822	1 418	4 405	4 423	1 094	3 329	1 399	324	1 076
100 +	1 383	442	942	1 061	330	731	323	112	211
Unknown - Inconnu	-	-	-	-	-	-	-	-	-
Iceland - Islande									
1 VII 2014 (ESDJ)									
Total	327 386	164 252	163 134	306 633	153 265	153 368	20 753	10 987	9 766
0	4 342	2 180	2 162	4 136	2 081	2 055	206	100	107
1 - 4	18 575	9 483	9 092	17 715	9 042	8 673	860	441	419
5 - 9	22 739	11 705	11 035	21 523	11 053	10 470	1 217	652	565
10 - 14	21 251	10 741	10 510	19 991	10 089	9 903	1 260	653	607
15 - 19	22 278	11 409	10 869	20 769	10 643	10 127	1 509	766	743
20 - 24	24 897	12 777	12 120	23 234	11 912	11 323	1 663	865	798
25 - 29	22 993	11 710	11 283	21 744	11 023	10 721	1 249	687	562
30 - 34	23 426	12 001	11 425	22 333	11 427	10 907	1 093	574	519
35 - 39	21 501	10 857	10 644	20 449	10 320	10 129	1 052	538	515

Continent, country or area, date, code[a] and age (in years) / Continent, pays ou zone, date, code[a] et âge (en années)	Total			Urban - Urbaine			Rural - Rurale		
	Both sexes Les deux sexes	Male Masculin	Female Féminin	Both sexes Les deux sexes	Male Masculin	Female Féminin	Both sexes Les deux sexes	Male Masculin	Female Féminin
EUROPE									
Iceland - Islande									
1 VII 2014 (ESDJ)									
40 - 44	21 130	10 675	10 455	19 968	10 073	9 895	1 163	602	561
45 - 49	21 154	10 471	10 683	19 742	9 735	10 007	1 412	736	676
50 - 54	21 602	10 728	10 874	19 960	9 863	10 097	1 642	865	777
55 - 59	20 344	10 198	10 146	18 755	9 325	9 430	1 589	873	716
60 - 64	17 367	8 798	8 570	16 009	8 063	7 946	1 359	735	624
65 - 69	14 179	7 183	6 996	13 010	6 524	6 487	1 169	660	509
70 - 74	10 080	4 849	5 231	9 271	4 407	4 865	809	442	367
75 - 79	7 599	3 585	4 014	6 985	3 247	3 738	614	338	276
80 - 84	6 269	2 796	3 473	5 778	2 535	3 243	491	261	230
85 - 89	3 806	1 521	2 285	3 535	1 379	2 156	271	142	129
90 - 94	1 520	492	1 029	1 420	441	980	100	51	49
95 - 99	307	93	215	277	84	193	30	9	22
100 +	34	6	28	32	5	27	2	1	1
1 I 2015 (ESDJ)[72]									
Total	329 100	165 186	163 914	...	...	...	...	...	...
0	4 358	2 225	2 133	...	...	...	...	...	...
1 - 4	18 321	9 307	9 014	...	...	...	...	...	...
5 - 9	22 998	11 852	11 146	...	...	...	...	...	...
10 - 14	21 325	10 812	10 513	...	...	...	...	...	...
15 - 19	22 110	11 296	10 814	...	...	...	...	...	...
20 - 24	25 039	12 883	12 156	...	...	...	...	...	...
25 - 29	23 234	11 839	11 395	...	...	...	...	...	...
30 - 34	23 369	11 964	11 405	...	...	...	...	...	...
35 - 39	21 781	10 997	10 784	...	...	...	...	...	...
40 - 44	21 222	10 758	10 464	...	...	...	...	...	...
45 - 49	20 978	10 426	10 552	...	...	...	...	...	...
50 - 54	21 605	10 675	10 930	...	...	...	...	...	...
55 - 59	20 626	10 336	10 290	...	...	...	...	...	...
60 - 64	17 593	8 894	8 699	...	...	...	...	...	...
65 - 69	14 487	7 351	7 136	...	...	...	...	...	...
70 - 74	10 378	5 007	5 371	...	...	...	...	...	...
75 - 79	7 624	3 608	4 016	...	...	...	...	...	...
80 - 84	6 275	2 805	3 470	...	...	...	...	...	...
85 - 89	3 889	1 560	2 329	...	...	...	...	...	...
90 - 94	1 542	491	1 051	...	...	...	...	...	...
95 - 99	314	94	220	...	...	...	...	...	...
100 +	32	6	26	...	...	...	...	...	...
Ireland - Irlande									
10 IV 2011 (CDFC)[73]									
Total	4 588 252	2 272 699	2 315 553	2 846 882	1 389 160	1 457 722	1 741 370	883 539	857 831
0 - 4	356 329	182 076	174 253	224 004	114 284	109 720	132 325	67 792	64 533
5 - 9	320 770	164 037	156 733	188 818	96 160	92 658	131 952	67 877	64 075
10 - 14	302 491	155 076	147 415	172 930	88 433	84 497	129 561	66 643	62 918
15 - 19	283 019	144 262	138 757	170 523	86 129	84 394	112 496	58 133	54 363
20 - 24	297 231	146 636	150 595	208 146	100 226	107 920	89 085	46 410	42 675
25 - 29	361 122	173 714	187 408	266 457	126 362	140 095	94 665	47 352	47 313
30 - 34	393 945	194 774	199 171	278 935	137 689	141 246	115 010	57 085	57 925
35 - 39	364 261	182 237	182 024	233 417	116 912	116 505	130 844	65 325	65 519
40 - 44	330 812	166 330	164 482	198 432	99 162	99 270	132 380	67 168	65 212
45 - 49	305 185	151 516	153 669	178 630	87 087	91 543	126 555	64 429	62 126
50 - 54	274 386	136 737	137 649	158 031	77 106	80 925	116 355	59 631	56 724
55 - 59	244 522	122 121	122 401	137 973	66 919	71 054	106 549	55 202	51 347
60 - 64	218 786	109 869	108 917	122 606	59 521	63 085	96 180	50 348	45 832
65 - 69	173 638	86 298	87 340	97 999	46 741	51 258	75 639	39 557	36 082
70 - 74	131 190	63 476	67 714	76 683	35 378	41 305	54 507	28 098	26 409
75 - 79	102 036	46 631	55 405	59 519	25 708	33 811	42 517	20 923	21 594
80 - 84	70 113	28 423	41 690	40 585	15 449	25 136	29 528	12 974	16 554
85 - 89	39 887	13 591	26 296	22 742	7 303	15 439	17 145	6 288	10 857
90 - 94	14 877	4 155	10 722	8 363	2 200	6 163	6 514	1 955	4 559
95 - 99	3 263	682	2 581	1 884	360	1 524	1 379	322	1 057
100 +	389	58	331	205	31	174	184	27	157

Continent, country or area, date, code[a] and age (in years) Continent, pays ou zone, date, code[a] et âge (en années)	Total			Urban - Urbaine			Rural - Rurale		
	Both sexes Les deux sexes	Male Masculin	Female Féminin	Both sexes Les deux sexes	Male Masculin	Female Féminin	Both sexes Les deux sexes	Male Masculin	Female Féminin
EUROPE									
Ireland - Irlande									
15 IV 2015 (ESDJ)[71]									
Total	4 635 390	2 289 549	2 345 841	...	...	...	...	...	...
0	68 078	35 106	32 972	...	...	...	...	...	...
1 - 4	292 793	149 371	143 422	...	...	...	...	...	...
5 - 9	352 356	178 990	173 366	...	...	...	...	...	...
10 - 14	316 079	161 453	154 626	...	...	...	...	...	...
15 - 19	283 200	146 052	137 148	...	...	...	...	...	...
20 - 24	233 501	119 464	114 037	...	...	...	...	...	...
25 - 29	290 419	140 581	149 838	...	...	...	...	...	...
30 - 34	363 852	172 822	191 030	...	...	...	...	...	...
35 - 39	371 537	181 637	189 900	...	...	...	...	...	...
40 - 44	351 826	174 594	177 232	...	...	...	...	...	...
45 - 49	319 450	159 624	159 826	...	...	...	...	...	...
50 - 54	295 774	146 064	149 710	...	...	...	...	...	...
55 - 59	259 858	128 897	130 961	...	...	...	...	...	...
60 - 64	230 656	114 261	116 395	...	...	...	...	...	...
65 - 69	202 639	100 420	102 219	...	...	...	...	...	...
70 - 74	149 367	73 015	76 352	...	...	...	...	...	...
75 - 79	111 109	51 902	59 207	...	...	...	...	...	...
80 - 84	76 922	33 078	43 844	...	...	...	...	...	...
85 - 89	42 422	15 436	26 986	...	...	...	...	...	...
90 - 94	18 034	5 370	12 664	...	...	...	...	...	...
95 +	5 518	1 412	4 106	...	...	...	...	...	...
Isle of Man - Île de Man									
30 IV 2015 (ESDJ)									
Total	86 963	43 319	43 644	...	...	...	...	...	...
0 - 4	4 810	2 450	2 360	...	...	...	...	...	...
5 - 9	4 738	2 495	2 243	...	...	...	...	...	...
10 - 14	4 646	2 443	2 203	...	...	...	...	...	...
15 - 19	5 164	2 655	2 509	...	...	...	...	...	...
20 - 24	5 247	2 711	2 536	...	...	...	...	...	...
25 - 29	4 729	2 408	2 322	...	...	...	...	...	...
30 - 34	4 866	2 372	2 494	...	...	...	...	...	...
35 - 39	5 098	2 502	2 596	...	...	...	...	...	...
40 - 44	6 146	3 028	3 118	...	...	...	...	...	...
45 - 49	6 648	3 358	3 291	...	...	...	...	...	...
50 - 54	6 713	3 381	3 332	...	...	...	...	...	...
55 - 59	5 833	2 922	2 911	...	...	...	...	...	...
60 - 64	5 327	2 681	2 646	...	...	...	...	...	...
65 - 69	5 496	2 762	2 733	...	...	...	...	...	...
70 - 74	4 031	1 971	2 060	...	...	...	...	...	...
75 - 79	3 103	1 477	1 626	...	...	...	...	...	...
80 - 84	2 145	947	1 199	...	...	...	...	...	...
85 - 89	1 366	491	876	...	...	...	...	...	...
90 +	856	268	589	...	...	...	...	...	...
Italy - Italie									
1 I 2014 (ESDJ)									
Total	60 789 140	29 493 077	31 296 063	...	...	...	...	...	...
0	502 840	258 634	244 207	...	...	...	...	...	...
1 - 4	2 185 636	1 123 934	1 061 702	...	...	...	...	...	...
5 - 9	2 868 008	1 476 583	1 391 426	...	...	...	...	...	...
10 - 14	2 859 144	1 471 649	1 387 496	...	...	...	...	...	...
15 - 19	2 863 233	1 478 958	1 384 275	...	...	...	...	...	...
20 - 24	3 098 674	1 588 005	1 510 669	...	...	...	...	...	...
25 - 29	3 292 764	1 662 935	1 629 830	...	...	...	...	...	...
30 - 34	3 647 036	1 831 217	1 815 819	...	...	...	...	...	...
35 - 39	4 343 348	2 173 183	2 170 165	...	...	...	...	...	...
40 - 44	4 848 392	2 414 223	2 434 170	...	...	...	...	...	...
45 - 49	4 982 300	2 468 659	2 513 642	...	...	...	...	...	...
50 - 54	4 568 682	2 240 126	2 328 556	...	...	...	...	...	...
55 - 59	3 981 431	1 931 592	2 049 839	...	...	...	...	...	...
60 - 64	3 630 647	1 749 831	1 880 816	...	...	...	...	...	...
65 - 69	3 504 581	1 671 441	1 833 140	...	...	...	...	...	...
70 - 74	3 003 202	1 385 624	1 617 578	...	...	...	...	...	...

7. Population by age, sex and urban/rural residence: latest available year, 2006 - 2015
Population selon l'âge, le sexe et la résidence, urbaine/rurale : dernière année disponible, 2006 - 2015 (continued - suite)

Continent, country or area, date, code[a] and age (in years) Continent, pays ou zone, date, code[a] et âge (en années)	Total			Urban - Urbaine			Rural - Rurale		
	Both sexes Les deux sexes	Male Masculin	Female Féminin	Both sexes Les deux sexes	Male Masculin	Female Féminin	Both sexes Les deux sexes	Male Masculin	Female Féminin
EUROPE									
Italy - Italie									
1 I 2014 (ESDJ)									
75 - 79	2 681 788	1 174 809	1 506 980	...	...	...	...	...	...
80 - 84	2 030 479	803 891	1 226 589	...	...	...	...	...	...
85 - 89	1 249 960	419 417	830 543	...	...	...	...	...	...
90 - 94	537 199	145 902	391 298	...	...	...	...	...	...
95 - 99	91 310	19 423	71 888	...	...	...	...	...	...
100 +	18 490	3 047	15 443	...	...	...	...	...	...
Jersey									
27 III 2011 (CDFC)									
Total	97 857	48 296	49 561	...	...	...	...	...	...
0 - 4	5 015	2 466	2 549	...	...	...	...	...	...
5 - 9	4 852	2 470	2 382	...	...	...	...	...	...
10 - 14	5 302	2 729	2 573	...	...	...	...	...	...
15 - 19	5 495	2 863	2 632	...	...	...	...	...	...
20 - 24	5 944	3 006	2 938	...	...	...	...	...	...
25 - 29	6 705	3 351	3 354	...	...	...	...	...	...
30 - 34	7 236	3 670	3 566	...	...	...	...	...	...
35 - 39	7 225	3 615	3 610	...	...	...	...	...	...
40 - 44	8 363	4 183	4 180	...	...	...	...	...	...
45 - 49	8 357	4 187	4 170	...	...	...	...	...	...
50 - 54	7 198	3 536	3 662	...	...	...	...	...	...
55 - 59	6 042	2 955	3 087	...	...	...	...	...	...
60 - 64	5 650	2 832	2 818	...	...	...	...	...	...
65 - 69	4 048	1 938	2 110	...	...	...	...	...	...
70 - 74	3 632	1 732	1 900	...	...	...	...	...	...
75 - 79	2 893	1 343	1 550	...	...	...	...	...	...
80 - 84	2 005	822	1 183	...	...	...	...	...	...
85 - 89	1 225	446	779	...	...	...	...	...	...
90 - 94	483	115	368	...	...	...	...	...	...
95 +	187	37	150	...	...	...	...	...	...
Latvia - Lettonie									
1 VII 2014 (ESDJ)									
Total	1 993 782	914 126	1 079 656	1 353 269	603 112	750 157	640 513	311 014	329 499
0	21 043	10 794	10 249	14 623	7 528	7 095	6 420	3 266	3 154
1 - 4	78 698	40 578	38 120	54 272	28 055	26 217	24 426	12 523	11 903
5 - 9	104 485	53 420	51 065	70 392	36 003	34 389	34 093	17 417	16 676
10 - 14	91 826	47 033	44 793	59 507	30 271	29 236	32 319	16 762	15 557
15 - 19	89 815	46 295	43 520	55 694	28 531	27 163	34 121	17 764	16 357
20 - 24	129 363	66 463	62 900	81 581	40 979	40 602	47 782	25 484	22 298
25 - 29	145 913	74 897	71 016	101 342	50 312	51 030	44 571	24 585	19 986
30 - 34	134 981	68 880	66 101	96 226	48 006	48 220	38 755	20 874	17 881
35 - 39	130 565	65 021	65 544	91 248	44 421	46 827	39 317	20 600	18 717
40 - 44	138 007	67 557	70 450	93 782	44 690	49 092	44 225	22 867	21 358
45 - 49	135 123	64 916	70 207	89 687	41 540	48 147	45 436	23 376	22 060
50 - 54	148 307	69 054	79 253	98 902	43 991	54 911	49 405	25 063	24 342
55 - 59	140 716	63 357	77 359	96 004	41 041	54 963	44 712	22 316	22 396
60 - 64	121 595	51 126	70 469	84 881	33 849	51 032	36 714	17 277	19 437
65 - 69	101 375	39 503	61 872	71 108	26 488	44 620	30 267	13 015	17 252
70 - 74	100 856	35 453	65 403	67 723	22 981	44 742	33 133	12 472	20 661
75 - 79	84 927	26 652	58 275	58 933	18 103	40 830	25 994	8 549	17 445
80 - 84	55 230	14 886	40 344	38 098	10 253	27 845	17 132	4 633	12 499
85 - 89	30 592	6 529	24 063	21 967	4 847	17 120	8 625	1 682	6 943
90 - 94	8 979	1 498	7 481	6 340	1 065	5 275	2 639	433	2 206
95 - 99	1 208	194	1 014	846	145	701	362	49	313
100 +	178	20	158	113	13	100	65	7	58
1 I 2015 (ESDJ)									
Total	1 986 096	911 207	1 074 889	...	...	...	...	...	...
0	21 674	11 204	10 470	...	...	...	...	...	...
1 - 4	78 712	40 601	38 111	...	...	...	...	...	...
5 - 9	105 242	53 758	51 484	...	...	...	...	...	...
10 - 14	92 092	47 206	44 886	...	...	...	...	...	...
15 - 19	87 794	45 272	42 522	...	...	...	...	...	...
20 - 24	124 503	63 909	60 594	...	...	...	...	...	...
25 - 29	144 802	74 489	70 313	...	...	...	...	...	...

Continent, country or area, date, code[a] and age (in years) Continent, pays ou zone, date, code[a] et âge (en années)	Total			Urban - Urbaine			Rural - Rurale		
	Both sexes Les deux sexes	Male Masculin	Female Féminin	Both sexes Les deux sexes	Male Masculin	Female Féminin	Both sexes Les deux sexes	Male Masculin	Female Féminin
EUROPE									
Latvia - Lettonie									
1 I 2015 (ESDJ)									
30 - 34	135 861	69 454	66 407	...	...	...	...	...	...
35 - 39	129 127	64 336	64 791	...	...	...	...	...	...
40 - 44	137 503	67 454	70 049	...	...	...	...	...	...
45 - 49	134 134	64 561	69 573	...	...	...	...	...	...
50 - 54	146 613	68 443	78 170	...	...	...	...	...	...
55 - 59	141 822	63 999	77 823	...	...	...	...	...	...
60 - 64	121 141	51 131	70 010	...	...	...	...	...	...
65 - 69	103 499	40 349	63 150	...	...	...	...	...	...
70 - 74	98 023	34 418	63 605	...	...	...	...	...	...
75 - 79	86 939	27 367	59 572	...	...	...	...	...	...
80 - 84	54 752	14 683	40 069	...	...	...	...	...	...
85 - 89	30 999	6 786	24 213	...	...	...	...	...	...
90 - 94	9 439	1 568	7 871	...	...	...	...	...	...
95 - 99	1 231	198	1 033	...	...	...	...	...	...
100 +	194	21	173	...	...	...	...	...	...
Liechtenstein[74]									
1 I 2015 (ESDJ)									
Total	37 366	18 553	18 813	...	...	...	...	...	...
0	373	209	164	...	...	...	...	...	...
1 - 4	1 448	755	693	...	...	...	...	...	...
5 - 9	1 897	1 004	893	...	...	...	...	...	...
10 - 14	1 931	995	936	...	...	...	...	...	...
15 - 19	2 158	1 053	1 105	...	...	...	...	...	...
20 - 24	2 229	1 120	1 109	...	...	...	...	...	...
25 - 29	2 290	1 177	1 113	...	...	...	...	...	...
30 - 34	2 331	1 195	1 136	...	...	...	...	...	...
35 - 39	2 440	1 227	1 213	...	...	...	...	...	...
40 - 44	2 872	1 447	1 425	...	...	...	...	...	...
45 - 49	3 218	1 589	1 629	...	...	...	...	...	...
50 - 54	3 146	1 543	1 603	...	...	...	...	...	...
55 - 59	2 739	1 350	1 389	...	...	...	...	...	...
60 - 64	2 320	1 156	1 164	...	...	...	...	...	...
65 - 69	2 036	1 029	1 007	...	...	...	...	...	...
70 - 74	1 665	801	864	...	...	...	...	...	...
75 - 79	1 004	466	538	...	...	...	...	...	...
80 - 84	665	255	410	...	...	...	...	...	...
85 - 89	405	135	270	...	...	...	...	...	...
90 - 94	168	35	133	...	...	...	...	...	...
95 - 99	26	9	17	...	...	...	...	...	...
100 +	5	3	2	...	...	...	...	...	...
Lithuania - Lituanie[71]									
1 VII 2014 (ESDJ)									
Total	2 932 367	1 351 126	1 581 241	1 968 596	881 978	1 086 618	963 771	469 148	494 623
0	30 110	15 382	14 728	20 621	10 546	10 075	9 489	4 836	4 653
1 - 4	120 680	61 867	58 813	85 667	43 822	41 845	35 013	18 045	16 968
5 - 9	136 834	69 932	66 902	92 715	47 514	45 201	44 119	22 418	21 701
10 - 14	140 151	72 002	68 149	88 203	45 125	43 078	51 948	26 877	25 071
15 - 19	173 797	89 285	84 512	108 476	55 545	52 931	65 321	33 740	31 581
20 - 24	210 113	108 219	101 894	135 895	67 785	68 110	74 218	40 434	33 784
25 - 29	194 891	99 919	94 972	140 488	68 698	71 790	54 403	31 221	23 182
30 - 34	176 592	89 381	87 211	130 071	63 924	66 147	46 521	25 457	21 064
35 - 39	181 554	89 203	92 351	126 720	60 845	65 875	54 834	28 358	26 476
40 - 44	204 087	98 505	105 582	136 013	63 741	72 272	68 074	34 764	33 310
45 - 49	210 752	100 503	110 249	136 528	62 222	74 306	74 224	38 281	35 943
50 - 54	231 860	108 547	123 313	154 181	68 344	85 837	77 679	40 203	37 476
55 - 59	205 451	92 698	112 753	139 507	59 734	79 773	65 944	32 964	32 980
60 - 64	170 568	72 507	98 061	115 945	46 415	69 530	54 623	26 092	28 531
65 - 69	140 442	55 181	85 261	94 796	35 428	59 368	45 646	19 753	25 893
70 - 74	136 285	49 232	87 053	89 466	31 450	58 016	46 819	17 782	29 037
75 - 79	120 485	39 442	81 043	78 501	25 247	53 254	41 984	14 195	27 789
80 - 84	85 715	24 969	60 746	54 370	16 058	38 312	31 345	8 911	22 434
85 - 89	45 903	11 163	34 740	29 800	7 438	22 362	16 103	3 725	12 378
90 - 94	13 907	2 755	11 152	9 090	1 801	7 289	4 817	954	3 863

7. Population by age, sex and urban/rural residence: latest available year, 2006 - 2015
Population selon l'âge, le sexe et la résidence, urbaine/rurale : dernière année disponible, 2006 - 2015 (continued - suite)

Continent, country or area, date, code[a] and age (in years) / Continent, pays ou zone, date, code[a] et âge (en années)	Total			Urban - Urbaine			Rural - Rurale		
	Both sexes Les deux sexes	Male Masculin	Female Féminin	Both sexes Les deux sexes	Male Masculin	Female Féminin	Both sexes Les deux sexes	Male Masculin	Female Féminin
EUROPE									
Lithuania - Lituanie[71]									
1 VII 2014 (ESDJ)									
95 - 99	1 829	357	1 472	1 265	243	1 022	564	114	450
100 +	361	77	284	278	53	225	83	24	59
Luxembourg									
1 VII 2014 (ESDJ)									
Total	556 319	278 544	277 775	...	...	...	...	...	...
0	6 085	3 130	2 955	...	...	...	...	...	...
1 - 4	25 294	12 976	12 318	...	...	...	...	...	...
5 - 9	30 635	15 695	14 940	...	...	...	...	...	...
10 - 14	31 137	16 023	15 114	...	...	...	...	...	...
15 - 19	32 520	16 653	15 867	...	...	...	...	...	...
20 - 24	34 209	17 566	16 643	...	...	...	...	...	...
25 - 29	39 568	20 074	19 494	...	...	...	...	...	...
30 - 34	42 736	21 368	21 368	...	...	...	...	...	...
35 - 39	42 619	21 380	21 239	...	...	...	...	...	...
40 - 44	43 364	22 131	21 233	...	...	...	...	...	...
45 - 49	45 035	23 351	21 684	...	...	...	...	...	...
50 - 54	41 347	21 356	19 991	...	...	...	...	...	...
55 - 59	34 750	17 814	16 936	...	...	...	...	...	...
60 - 64	28 413	14 392	14 021	...	...	...	...	...	...
65 - 69	23 030	11 473	11 557	...	...	...	...	...	...
70 - 74	18 362	8 616	9 746	...	...	...	...	...	...
75 - 79	15 224	6 673	8 551	...	...	...	...	...	...
80 - 84	12 013	4 859	7 154	...	...	...	...	...	...
85 - 89	7 005	2 317	4 688	...	...	...	...	...	...
90 - 94	2 489	601	1 888	...	...	...	...	...	...
95 - 99	420	81	339	...	...	...	...	...	...
100 +	64	15	49	...	...	...	...	...	...
Unknown - Inconnu	-	-	-	...	...	...	...	...	...
Malta - Malte									
20 XI 2011 (CDFC)									
Total	417 432	207 625	209 807	400 557	199 151	201 406	16 875	8 474	8 401
0 - 4	20 061	10 347	9 714	19 247	9 926	9 321	814	421	393
5 - 9	19 419	9 971	9 448	18 602	9 562	9 040	817	409	408
10 - 14	22 248	11 355	10 893	21 218	10 854	10 364	1 030	501	529
15 - 19	26 182	13 509	12 673	25 026	12 907	12 119	1 156	602	554
20 - 24	29 450	15 062	14 388	28 269	14 475	13 794	1 181	587	594
25 - 29	30 320	15 722	14 598	29 154	15 110	14 044	1 166	612	554
30 - 34	30 194	15 641	14 553	29 141	15 074	14 067	1 053	567	486
35 - 39	28 799	14 757	14 042	27 712	14 202	13 510	1 087	555	532
40 - 44	25 236	12 840	12 396	24 151	12 293	11 858	1 085	547	538
45 - 49	26 895	13 574	13 321	25 716	12 972	12 744	1 179	602	577
50 - 54	30 596	15 292	15 304	29 293	14 628	14 665	1 303	664	639
55 - 59	29 246	14 655	14 591	28 127	14 052	14 075	1 119	603	516
60 - 64	30 595	15 130	15 465	29 452	14 551	14 901	1 143	579	564
65 - 69	23 728	11 429	12 299	22 791	10 986	11 805	937	443	494
70 - 74	16 205	7 389	8 816	15 572	7 106	8 466	633	283	350
75 - 79	13 287	5 579	7 708	12 749	5 332	7 417	538	247	291
80 - 84	8 494	3 181	5 313	8 121	3 036	5 085	373	145	228
85 - 89	4 567	1 622	2 945	4 371	1 546	2 825	196	76	120
90 - 94	1 583	480	1 103	1 532	455	1 077	51	25	26
95 - 99	296	82	214	284	77	207	12	5	7
100 +	31	8	23	29	7	22	2	1	1
1 I 2015 (ESDJ)[75]									
Total	429 344	214 735	214 609	...	...	...	...	...	...
0	4 215	2 231	1 984	...	...	...	...	...	...
1 - 4	16 784	8 637	8 147	...	...	...	...	...	...
5 - 9	20 114	10 464	9 650	...	...	...	...	...	...
10 - 14	20 336	10 329	10 007	...	...	...	...	...	...
15 - 19	24 401	12 739	11 662	...	...	...	...	...	...
20 - 24	29 477	15 319	14 158	...	...	...	...	...	...
25 - 29	31 462	16 399	15 063	...	...	...	...	...	...
30 - 34	31 565	16 355	15 210	...	...	...	...	...	...
35 - 39	30 724	15 890	14 834	...	...	...	...	...	...

Continent, country or area, date, code[a] and age (in years) Continent, pays ou zone, date, code[a] et âge (en annèes)	Total			Urban - Urbaine			Rural - Rurale		
	Both sexes Les deux sexes	Male Masculin	Female Féminin	Both sexes Les deux sexes	Male Masculin	Female Féminin	Both sexes Les deux sexes	Male Masculin	Female Féminin
EUROPE									
Malta - Malte									
1 I 2015 (ESDJ)[75]									
40 - 44	27 438	14 055	13 383	...	...	...	...	...	...
45 - 49	25 028	12 699	12 329	...	...	...	...	...	...
50 - 54	29 057	14 663	14 394	...	...	...	...	...	...
55 - 59	30 483	15 257	15 226	...	...	...	...	...	...
60 - 64	28 768	14 289	14 479	...	...	...	...	...	...
65 - 69	29 690	14 411	15 279	...	...	...	...	...	...
70 - 74	17 981	8 389	9 592	...	...	...	...	...	...
75 - 79	14 692	6 437	8 255	...	...	...	...	...	...
80 - 84	9 741	3 695	6 046	...	...	...	...	...	...
85 - 89	5 056	1 806	3 250	...	...	...	...	...	...
90 - 94	1 884	563	1 321	...	...	...	...	...	...
95 - 99	391	94	297	...	...	...	...	...	...
100 +	57	14	43	...	...	...	...	...	...
Monaco									
9 VI 2008 (CDJC)									
Total	31 109[76]	15 076	15 914	...	...	...	...	...	...
0 - 4	1 134	577	557	...	...	...	...	...	...
5 - 9	1 430	706	724	...	...	...	...	...	...
10 - 14	1 401	727	674	...	...	...	...	...	...
15 - 19	1 398	724	674	...	...	...	...	...	...
20 - 24	1 248	647	601	...	...	...	...	...	...
25 - 29	1 305	638	667	...	...	...	...	...	...
30 - 34	1 514	751	766	...	...	...	...	...	...
35 - 39	2 122	1 003	1 119	...	...	...	...	...	...
40 - 44	2 342	1 163	1 179	...	...	...	...	...	...
45 - 64	2 359	1 194	1 165	...	...	...	...	...	...
50 - 54	2 218	1 128	1 090	...	...	...	...	...	...
55 - 59	2 217	1 120	1 097	...	...	...	...	...	...
60 - 64	2 337	1 134	1 203	...	...	...	...	...	...
65 - 69	1 960	945	1 015	...	...	...	...	...	...
70 - 74	1 648	801	847	...	...	...	...	...	...
75 +	3 758	1 530	2 228	...	...	...	...	...	...
Unknown - Inconnu	715[76]	288	308	...	...	...	...	...	...
Montenegro - Monténégro									
1 IV 2011 (CDJC)									
Total	620 029	306 236	313 793	399 264	193 691	205 573	220 765	112 545	108 220
0 - 4	38 950	20 361	18 589	25 277	13 247	12 030	13 673	7 114	6 559
5 - 9	38 430	20 016	18 414	24 781	12 973	11 808	13 649	7 043	6 606
10 - 14	41 371	21 389	19 982	26 526	13 698	12 828	14 845	7 691	7 154
15 - 19	44 093	22 815	21 278	28 376	14 654	13 722	15 717	8 161	7 556
20 - 24	42 816	22 084	20 732	28 218	14 347	13 871	14 598	7 737	6 861
25 - 29	45 793	23 299	22 494	31 083	15 290	15 793	14 710	8 009	6 701
30 - 34	44 495	22 188	22 307	30 133	14 495	15 638	14 362	7 693	6 669
35 - 39	41 879	20 523	21 356	27 869	13 311	14 558	14 010	7 212	6 798
40 - 44	40 496	20 136	20 360	26 265	12 539	13 726	14 231	7 597	6 634
45 - 49	43 089	21 401	21 688	28 332	13 444	14 888	14 757	7 957	6 800
50 - 54	43 613	21 817	21 796	28 705	13 851	14 854	14 908	7 966	6 942
55 - 59	41 223	20 509	20 714	27 021	13 143	13 878	14 202	7 366	6 836
60 - 64	34 196	15 941	18 255	21 738	9 981	11 757	12 458	5 960	6 498
65 - 69	22 121	9 774	12 347	12 692	5 522	7 170	9 429	4 252	5 177
70 - 74	25 141	10 909	14 232	14 441	6 116	8 325	10 700	4 793	5 907
75 - 79	17 184	7 251	9 933	9 665	4 041	5 624	7 519	3 210	4 309
80 - 84	10 021	4 050	5 971	5 375	2 112	3 263	4 646	1 938	2 708
85 - 89	3 739	1 324	2 415	2 038	699	1 339	1 701	625	1 076
90 - 94	885	283	602	453	130	323	432	153	279
95 - 99	202	61	141	103	30	73	99	31	68
100 +	44	13	31	23	7	16	21	6	15
Unknown - Inconnu	248	92	156	150	61	89	98	31	67
1 I 2015 (ESDJ)[71]									
Total	622 099	307 522	314 577	...	...	...	...	...	...
0	7 583	3 969	3 614	...	...	...	...	...	...
1 - 4	29 764	15 431	14 333	...	...	...	...	...	...
5 - 9	37 829	19 875	17 954	...	...	...	...	...	...

7. Population by age, sex and urban/rural residence: latest available year, 2006 - 2015
Population selon l'âge, le sexe et la résidence, urbaine/rurale : dernière année disponible, 2006 - 2015 (continued - suite)

Continent, country or area, date, code[a] and age (in years) / Continent, pays ou zone, date, code[a] et âge (en années)	Total			Urban - Urbaine			Rural - Rurale		
	Both sexes Les deux sexes	Male Masculin	Female Féminin	Both sexes Les deux sexes	Male Masculin	Female Féminin	Both sexes Les deux sexes	Male Masculin	Female Féminin
EUROPE									
Montenegro - Monténégro									
1 I 2015 (ESDJ)[71]									
10 - 14	39 828	20 645	19 183	...	...	...	...	...	...
15 - 19	42 303	21 840	20 463	...	...	...	...	...	...
20 - 24	40 560	21 038	19 522	...	...	...	...	...	...
25 - 29	43 645	22 367	21 278	...	...	...	...	...	...
30 - 34	45 983	23 234	22 749	...	...	...	...	...	...
35 - 39	43 257	21 455	21 802	...	...	...	...	...	...
40 - 44	41 091	20 151	20 940	...	...	...	...	...	...
45 - 49	40 791	20 328	20 463	...	...	...	...	...	...
50 - 54	42 968	21 092	21 876	...	...	...	...	...	...
55 - 59	42 283	21 106	21 177	...	...	...	...	...	...
60 - 64	39 156	18 889	20 267	...	...	...	...	...	...
65 - 69	27 444	12 333	15 111	...	...	...	...	...	...
70 - 74	21 259	9 032	12 227	...	...	...	...	...	...
75 - 79	19 289	8 022	11 267	...	...	...	...	...	...
80 - 84	11 047	4 395	6 652	...	...	...	...	...	...
85 - 89	4 594	1 846	2 748	...	...	...	...	...	...
90 - 94	1 229	423	806	...	...	...	...	...	...
95 - 99	174	44	130	...	...	...	...	...	...
100 +	22	7	15	...	...	...	...	...	...
Netherlands - Pays-Bas									
1 I 2011 (CDJC)									
Total	16 655 799	8 243 482	8 412 317	11 124 721	5 478 213	5 646 508	5 531 078	2 765 269	2 765 809
0 - 4	923 106	472 308	450 798	633 381	323 854	309 527	289 725	148 454	141 271
0	184 007	93 892	90 115	...	...	...	...	...	...
1 - 4	739 099	378 416	360 683	...	...	...	...	...	...
5 - 9	985 229	503 882	481 347	640 541	327 757	312 784	344 688	176 125	168 563
10 - 14	998 740	510 974	487 766	633 115	323 581	309 534	365 625	187 393	178 232
15 - 19	1 006 744	514 830	491 914	658 458	333 676	324 782	348 286	181 154	167 132
20 - 24	1 034 729	522 667	512 062	757 280	373 366	383 914	277 449	149 301	128 148
25 - 29	1 001 538	504 117	497 421	749 880	373 340	376 540	251 658	130 777	120 881
30 - 34	1 004 764	503 323	501 441	736 350	368 630	367 720	268 414	134 693	133 721
35 - 39	1 121 568	560 289	561 279	779 994	391 390	388 604	341 574	168 899	172 675
40 - 44	1 295 925	653 664	642 261	861 292	436 235	425 057	434 633	217 429	217 204
45 - 49	1 298 292	655 302	642 990	850 566	428 796	421 770	447 726	226 506	221 220
50 - 54	1 196 319	601 040	595 279	776 285	388 221	388 064	420 034	212 819	207 215
55 - 59	1 090 247	546 952	543 295	700 036	348 502	351 534	390 211	198 450	191 761
60 - 64	1 103 652	553 446	550 206	700 926	349 188	351 738	402 726	204 258	198 468
65 - 69	790 560	390 725	399 835	488 433	238 792	249 641	302 127	151 933	150 194
70 - 74	637 518	302 542	334 976	401 165	187 850	213 315	236 353	114 692	121 661
75 - 79	499 321	219 108	280 213	316 949	136 949	180 000	182 372	82 159	100 213
80 - 84	360 828	139 348	221 480	234 884	89 412	145 472	125 944	49 936	76 008
85 - 89	212 056	66 949	145 107	141 532	44 184	97 348	70 524	22 765	47 759
90 - 94	76 191	18 812	57 379	51 102	12 438	38 664	25 089	6 374	18 715
95 +	18 472	3 204	15 268	12 552	2 052	10 500	5 920	1 152	4 768
1 I 2015 (ESDJ)									
Total	16 900 726	8 372 858	8 527 868	...	...	...	...	...	...
0	174 681	89 200	85 481	...	...	...	...	...	...
1 - 4	713 641	365 528	348 113	...	...	...	...	...	...
5 - 9	929 655	476 048	453 607	...	...	...	...	...	...
10 - 14	1 009 089	515 675	493 414	...	...	...	...	...	...
15 - 19	1 000 993	512 283	488 710	...	...	...	...	...	...
20 - 24	1 069 032	542 322	526 710	...	...	...	...	...	...
25 - 29	1 050 674	529 400	521 274	...	...	...	...	...	...
30 - 34	1 012 741	508 503	504 238	...	...	...	...	...	...
35 - 39	1 002 000	500 143	501 857	...	...	...	...	...	...
40 - 44	1 176 864	586 818	590 046	...	...	...	...	...	...
45 - 49	1 285 917	647 318	638 599	...	...	...	...	...	...
50 - 54	1 270 184	638 084	632 100	...	...	...	...	...	...
55 - 59	1 151 386	575 631	575 755	...	...	...	...	...	...
60 - 64	1 046 184	522 826	523 358	...	...	...	...	...	...
65 - 69	1 014 432	503 209	511 223	...	...	...	...	...	...
70 - 74	715 743	346 275	369 468	...	...	...	...	...	...
75 - 79	542 534	247 171	295 363	...	...	...	...	...	...

7. Population by age, sex and urban/rural residence: latest available year, 2006 - 2015
Population selon l'âge, le sexe et la résidence, urbaine/rurale : dernière année disponible, 2006 - 2015 (continued - suite)

Continent, country or area, date, code[a] and age (in years) / Continent, pays ou zone, date, code[a] et âge (en années)	Total			Urban - Urbaine			Rural - Rurale		
	Both sexes Les deux sexes	Male Masculin	Female Féminin	Both sexes Les deux sexes	Male Masculin	Female Féminin	Both sexes Les deux sexes	Male Masculin	Female Féminin
EUROPE									
Netherlands - Pays-Bas									
1 I 2015 (ESDJ)									
80 - 84	390 492	158 901	231 591	...	...	...	...	...	...
85 - 89	227 621	77 940	149 681	...	...	...	...	...	...
90 - 94	96 078	25 678	70 400	...	...	...	...	...	...
95 - 99	18 615	3 609	15 006	...	...	...	...	...	...
100 +	2 170	296	1 874	...	...	...	...	...	...
Norway - Norvège									
19 XI 2011 (CDJC)[77]									
Total	4 979 955	2 495 777	2 484 178	3 951 427[78]	1 959 424[78]	1 992 003[78]	1 011 071[78]	524 519[78]	486 552[78]
0 - 4	310 523	159 582	150 941	252 348[78]	129 655[78]	122 693[78]	57 552[78]	29 590[78]	27 962[78]
5 - 9	300 625	153 598	147 027	239 702[78]	122 174[78]	117 528[78]	60 262[78]	31 070[78]	29 192[78]
10 - 14	312 618	160 122	152 496	245 562[78]	125 764[78]	119 798[78]	66 422[78]	34 008[78]	32 414[78]
15 - 19	324 682	167 701	156 981	254 774[78]	131 385[78]	123 389[78]	69 376[78]	36 049[78]	33 327[78]
20 - 24	329 537	167 828	161 709	268 150[78]	135 424[78]	132 726[78]	60 351[78]	31 776[78]	28 575[78]
25 - 29	321 171	163 754	157 417	268 356[78]	135 940[78]	132 416[78]	51 166[78]	26 654[78]	24 512[78]
30 - 34	325 241	166 578	158 663	269 924[78]	137 478[78]	132 446[78]	53 565[78]	27 843[78]	25 722[78]
35 - 39	352 008	180 904	171 104	286 185[78]	146 143[78]	140 042[78]	64 091[78]	33 501[78]	30 590[78]
40 - 44	373 191	191 483	181 708	297 629[78]	151 231[78]	146 398[78]	73 666[78]	38 863[78]	34 803[78]
45 - 49	350 537	180 834	169 703	275 817[78]	140 624[78]	135 193[78]	73 001[78]	38 909[78]	34 092[78]
50 - 54	322 729	165 233	157 496	250 381[78]	126 209[78]	124 172[78]	70 881[78]	37 897[78]	32 984[78]
55 - 59	304 335	154 029	150 306	233 724[78]	116 035[78]	117 689[78]	69 504[78]	37 194[78]	32 310[78]
60 - 64	286 319	144 699	141 620	218 480[78]	108 289[78]	110 191[78]	67 016[78]	35 823[78]	31 193[78]
65 - 69	247 451	122 740	124 711	188 932[78]	91 896[78]	97 036[78]	57 895[78]	30 414[78]	27 481[78]
70 - 74	166 680	78 850	87 830	126 640[78]	58 122[78]	68 518[78]	39 687[78]	20 517[78]	19 170[78]
75 - 79	130 209	58 013	72 196	99 673[78]	42 842[78]	56 831[78]	30 271[78]	15 028[78]	15 243[78]
80 - 84	108 243	44 024	64 219	84 440[78]	32 980[78]	51 460[78]	23 582[78]	10 955[78]	12 627[78]
85 - 89	74 057	25 608	48 449	58 579[78]	19 436[78]	39 143[78]	15 272[78]	6 085[78]	9 187[78]
90 - 94	32 243	8 769	23 474	25 938[78]	6 706[78]	19 232[78]	6 185[78]	2 017[78]	4 168[78]
95 - 99	6 825	1 310	5 515	5 593[78]	1 001[78]	4 592[78]	1 199[78]	300[78]	899[78]
100 +	731	118	613	600[78]	90[78]	510[78]	127[78]	26[78]	101[78]
1 I 2015 (ESDJ)[71]									
Total	5 166 493	2 599 202	2 567 291	...	...	...	...	...	...
0	59 387	30 548	28 839	...	...	...	...	...	...
1 - 4	249 251	127 764	121 487	...	...	...	...	...	...
5 - 9	316 300	162 140	154 160	...	...	...	...	...	...
10 - 14	307 598	157 026	150 572	...	...	...	...	...	...
15 - 19	326 523	168 229	158 294	...	...	...	...	...	...
20 - 24	344 192	176 877	167 315	...	...	...	...	...	...
25 - 29	353 441	179 823	173 618	...	...	...	...	...	...
30 - 34	346 454	178 496	167 958	...	...	...	...	...	...
35 - 39	342 114	176 864	165 250	...	...	...	...	...	...
40 - 44	373 765	192 564	181 201	...	...	...	...	...	...
45 - 49	373 311	192 526	180 785	...	...	...	...	...	...
50 - 54	336 636	172 922	163 714	...	...	...	...	...	...
55 - 59	315 722	160 467	155 255	...	...	...	...	...	...
60 - 64	287 487	144 732	142 755	...	...	...	...	...	...
65 - 69	277 709	138 431	139 278	...	...	...	...	...	...
70 - 74	196 866	95 111	101 755	...	...	...	...	...	...
75 - 79	139 298	63 156	76 142	...	...	...	...	...	...
80 - 84	105 522	43 979	61 543	...	...	...	...	...	...
85 - 89	71 412	25 877	45 535	...	...	...	...	...	...
90 - 94	34 923	9 881	25 042	...	...	...	...	...	...
95 - 99	7 695	1 632	6 063	...	...	...	...	...	...
100 +	887	157	730	...	...	...	...	...	...
Poland - Pologne[71]									
1 VII 2012 (ESDJ)									
Total	38 533 789	18 651 441	19 882 348	23 360 022	11 086 177	12 273 845	15 173 767	7 565 264	7 608 503
0	384 280	197 871	186 409	222 352	114 616	107 736	161 928	83 255	78 673
1 - 4	1 680 663	862 003	818 660	972 484	498 615	473 869	708 179	363 388	344 791
5 - 9	1 843 366	945 643	897 723	1 031 194	528 940	502 254	812 172	416 703	395 469
10 - 14	1 900 015	974 509	925 506	1 012 558	519 440	493 118	887 457	455 069	432 388
15 - 19	2 266 634	1 158 367	1 108 267	1 212 063	617 725	594 338	1 054 571	540 642	513 929
20 - 24	2 736 154	1 394 761	1 341 393	1 573 579	793 273	780 306	1 162 575	601 488	561 087

Continent, country or area, date, code[a] and age (in years) Continent, pays ou zone, date, code[a] et âge (en annèes)	Total			Urban - Urbaine			Rural - Rurale		
	Both sexes Les deux sexes	Male Masculin	Female Féminin	Both sexes Les deux sexes	Male Masculin	Female Féminin	Both sexes Les deux sexes	Male Masculin	Female Féminin
EUROPE									
Poland - Pologne[71]									
1 VII 2012 (ESDJ)									
25 - 29	3 198 618	1 623 072	1 575 546	1 969 888	988 292	981 596	1 228 730	634 780	593 950
30 - 34	3 161 358	1 602 736	1 558 622	1 992 477	998 627	993 850	1 168 881	604 109	564 772
35 - 39	2 903 573	1 470 751	1 432 822	1 782 067	891 666	890 401	1 121 506	579 085	542 421
40 - 44	2 440 834	1 231 083	1 209 751	1 438 923	712 685	726 238	1 001 911	518 398	483 513
45 - 49	2 389 500	1 196 548	1 192 952	1 406 626	681 323	725 303	982 874	515 225	467 649
50 - 54	2 784 254	1 369 258	1 414 996	1 717 873	808 906	908 967	1 066 381	560 352	506 029
55 - 59	2 926 281	1 404 141	1 522 140	1 914 912	880 046	1 034 866	1 011 369	524 095	487 274
60 - 64	2 514 619	1 163 935	1 350 684	1 678 077	751 679	926 398	836 542	412 256	424 286
65 - 69	1 537 157	675 573	861 584	1 022 506	441 278	581 228	514 651	234 295	280 356
70 - 74	1 306 461	529 739	776 722	839 597	334 563	505 034	466 864	195 176	271 688
75 - 79	1 144 656	424 407	720 249	719 337	264 687	454 650	425 319	159 720	265 599
80 - 84	844 554	278 428	566 126	511 821	170 799	341 022	332 733	107 629	225 104
85 - 89	426 601	115 213	311 388	255 282	69 341	185 941	171 319	45 872	125 447
90 - 94	119 788	28 565	91 223	70 696	16 676	54 020	49 092	11 889	37 203
95 - 99	22 879	4 614	18 265	14 423	2 793	11 630	8 456	1 821	6 635
100 +	1 544	224	1 320	1 287	207	1 080	257	17	240
1 I 2015 (ESDJ)									
Total	38 005 614	18 397 163	19 608 451	...	...	...	...	...	...
0	366 768	188 687	178 081	...	...	...	...	...	...
1 - 4	1 559 673	801 828	757 845	...	...	...	...	...	...
5 - 9	1 998 406	1 024 154	974 252	...	...	...	...	...	...
10 - 14	1 789 943	918 424	871 519	...	...	...	...	...	...
15 - 19	2 024 374	1 036 453	987 921	...	...	...	...	...	...
20 - 24	2 507 493	1 278 725	1 228 768	...	...	...	...	...	...
25 - 29	2 875 535	1 466 254	1 409 281	...	...	...	...	...	...
30 - 34	3 153 719	1 604 621	1 549 098	...	...	...	...	...	...
35 - 39	2 985 913	1 514 697	1 471 216	...	...	...	...	...	...
40 - 44	2 589 437	1 308 676	1 280 761	...	...	...	...	...	...
45 - 49	2 284 280	1 145 166	1 139 114	...	...	...	...	...	...
50 - 54	2 460 176	1 214 475	1 245 701	...	...	...	...	...	...
55 - 59	2 890 758	1 392 110	1 498 648	...	...	...	...	...	...
60 - 64	2 659 433	1 235 153	1 424 280	...	...	...	...	...	...
65 - 69	1 963 067	871 331	1 091 736	...	...	...	...	...	...
70 - 74	1 225 948	503 547	722 401	...	...	...	...	...	...
75 - 79	1 144 795	426 621	718 174	...	...	...	...	...	...
80 - 84	862 317	287 704	574 613	...	...	...	...	...	...
85 - 89	475 182	134 520	340 662	...	...	...	...	...	...
90 - 94	160 352	38 185	122 167	...	...	...	...	...	...
95 - 99	22 927	4 777	18 150	...	...	...	...	...	...
100 +	5 118	1 055	4 063	...	...	...	...	...	...
Portugal									
21 III 2011 (CDJC)									
Total	10 562 178	5 046 600	5 515 578	6 438 593	3 047 968	3 390 625	4 123 585	1 998 632	2 124 953
0 - 4	482 647	246 396	236 251	316 068	161 365	154 703	166 579	85 031	81 548
5 - 9	525 087	268 965	256 122	329 692	168 925	160 767	195 395	100 040	95 355
10 - 14	564 595	288 638	275 957	344 809	176 287	168 522	219 786	112 351	107 435
15 - 19	565 250	288 525	276 725	342 328	174 252	168 076	222 922	114 273	108 649
20 - 24	582 065	293 023	289 042	358 412	178 982	179 430	223 653	114 041	109 612
25 - 29	656 076	324 848	331 228	425 629	208 104	217 525	230 447	116 744	113 703
30 - 34	773 567	378 734	394 833	508 225	247 125	261 100	265 342	131 609	133 733
35 - 39	824 683	402 307	422 376	529 287	255 858	273 429	295 396	146 449	148 947
40 - 44	773 098	374 962	398 136	478 840	228 255	250 585	294 258	146 707	147 551
45 - 49	770 294	370 989	399 305	466 564	219 783	246 781	303 730	151 206	152 524
50 - 54	722 360	346 248	376 112	435 982	203 867	232 115	286 378	142 381	143 997
55 - 59	677 651	322 095	355 556	410 020	190 860	219 160	267 631	131 235	136 396
60 - 64	634 741	298 546	336 195	382 547	177 485	205 062	252 194	121 061	131 133
65 - 69	551 701	253 004	298 697	319 398	146 189	173 209	232 303	106 815	125 488
70 - 74	496 438	220 461	275 977	273 513	119 844	153 669	222 925	100 617	122 308
75 - 79	429 706	180 131	249 575	231 208	94 394	136 814	198 498	85 737	112 761
80 - 84	297 888	113 325	184 563	159 578	57 948	101 630	138 310	55 377	82 933
85 - 89	164 356	55 635	108 721	88 444	28 423	60 021	75 912	27 212	48 700
90 - 94	53 847	15 679	38 168	29 038	7 847	21 191	24 809	7 832	16 977

Continent, country or area, date, code[a] and age (in years) / Continent, pays ou zone, date, code[a] et âge (en années)	Total			Urban - Urbaine			Rural - Rurale		
	Both sexes Les deux sexes	Male Masculin	Female Féminin	Both sexes Les deux sexes	Male Masculin	Female Féminin	Both sexes Les deux sexes	Male Masculin	Female Féminin
EUROPE									
Portugal									
21 III 2011 (CDJC)									
95 - 99	14 602	3 816	10 786	8 158	2 029	6 129	6 444	1 787	4 657
100 +	1 526	273	1 253	853	146	707	673	127	546
1 I 2015 (ESDJ)									
Total	10 374 822	4 923 666	5 451 156	...	...	...	...	...	...
0	82 264	42 372	39 892	...	...	...	...	...	...
1 - 4	367 535	187 871	179 664	...	...	...	...	...	...
5 - 9	499 768	255 773	243 995	...	...	...	...	...	...
10 - 14	540 674	277 470	263 204	...	...	...	...	...	...
15 - 19	552 373	282 068	270 305	...	...	...	...	...	...
20 - 24	553 108	279 030	274 078	...	...	...	...	...	...
25 - 29	566 505	282 792	283 713	...	...	...	...	...	...
30 - 34	668 652	325 138	343 514	...	...	...	...	...	...
35 - 39	786 750	378 921	407 829	...	...	...	...	...	...
40 - 44	797 274	382 724	414 550	...	...	...	...	...	...
45 - 49	757 206	362 975	394 231	...	...	...	...	...	...
50 - 54	756 100	360 486	395 614	...	...	...	...	...	...
55 - 59	694 551	328 851	365 700	...	...	...	...	...	...
60 - 64	646 895	303 012	343 883	...	...	...	...	...	...
65 - 69	586 336	267 226	319 110	...	...	...	...	...	...
70 - 74	485 196	213 226	271 970	...	...	...	...	...	...
75 - 79	438 065	182 721	255 344	...	...	...	...	...	...
80 - 84	333 973	128 377	205 596	...	...	...	...	...	...
85 - 89	179 183	59 140	120 043	...	...	...	...	...	...
90 - 94	64 907	18 686	46 221	...	...	...	...	...	...
95 - 99	13 441	3 509	9 932	...	...	...	...	...	...
100 +	4 066	1 298	2 768	...	...	...	...	...	...
Republic of Moldova - République de Moldova[79]									
1 VII 2012 (ESDJ)									
Total	3 559 519	1 712 036	1 847 484	1 488 966	699 880	789 086	2 070 554	1 012 156	1 058 398
0	38 856	20 015	18 842	14 501	7 501	7 000	24 356	12 514	11 842
1 - 4	155 545	80 386	75 159	57 044	29 740	27 305	98 501	50 646	47 855
5 - 9	185 646	95 525	90 121	67 697	35 209	32 489	117 949	60 317	57 632
10 - 14	194 993	100 101	94 893	66 615	34 473	32 142	128 379	65 628	62 751
15 - 19	257 790	131 414	126 376	88 575	45 309	43 267	169 215	86 106	83 110
20 - 24	333 714	169 543	164 171	138 548	69 044	69 505	195 166	100 499	94 667
25 - 29	343 489	174 869	168 620	174 571	84 151	90 420	168 918	90 718	78 200
30 - 34	289 604	146 740	142 864	133 836	65 353	68 483	155 769	81 387	74 382
35 - 39	251 655	124 669	126 986	111 448	54 088	57 360	140 207	70 581	69 627
40 - 44	225 706	109 887	115 819	97 757	46 129	51 629	127 949	63 758	64 191
45 - 49	237 350	112 506	124 844	102 616	46 409	56 207	134 735	66 097	68 638
50 - 54	274 163	127 681	146 482	119 669	52 882	66 787	154 495	74 799	79 696
55 - 59	235 036	106 431	128 605	104 053	44 876	59 177	130 983	61 555	69 428
60 - 64	182 091	79 587	102 504	79 353	34 316	45 038	102 738	45 272	57 467
65 - 69	105 809	44 763	61 046	43 360	18 966	24 394	62 449	25 797	36 652
70 - 74	100 565	38 142	62 423	39 059	15 111	23 948	61 506	23 031	38 475
75 - 79	72 497	25 841	46 656	24 995	8 598	16 397	47 502	17 243	30 259
80 - 84	47 586	15 881	31 706	15 963	5 051	10 912	31 624	10 830	20 794
85 - 89	20 400	5 920	14 480	6 963	1 957	5 006	13 437	3 963	9 474
90 - 94	5 438	1 597	3 841	1 780	526	1 254	3 658	1 071	2 588
95 - 99	1 163	395	768	391	150	241	772	245	527
100 +	429	148	282	177	45	132	253	103	150
1 I 2015 (ESDJ)									
Total	3 555 159	1 710 244	1 844 915	...	...	...	...	...	...
0	38 379	19 813	18 566	...	...	...	...	...	...
1 - 4	153 995	79 115	74 880	...	...	...	...	...	...
5 - 9	190 197	98 168	92 029	...	...	...	...	...	...
10 - 14	185 300	95 476	89 824	...	...	...	...	...	...
15 - 19	219 234	112 110	107 124	...	...	...	...	...	...
20 - 24	296 226	150 859	145 367	...	...	...	...	...	...
25 - 29	355 502	180 817	174 685	...	...	...	...	...	...
30 - 34	311 568	158 799	152 769	...	...	...	...	...	...
35 - 39	266 180	132 992	133 188	...	...	...	...	...	...

Continent, country or area, date, code[a] and age (in years) / Continent, pays ou zone, date, code[a] et âge (en années)	Total			Urban - Urbaine			Rural - Rurale		
	Both sexes Les deux sexes	Male Masculin	Female Féminin	Both sexes Les deux sexes	Male Masculin	Female Féminin	Both sexes Les deux sexes	Male Masculin	Female Féminin
EUROPE									
Republic of Moldova - République de Moldova[79]									
1 I 2015 (ESDJ)									
40 - 44	234 130	114 345	119 785	...	...	...	...	...	...
45 - 49	220 952	105 598	115 354	...	...	...	...	...	...
50 - 54	257 600	119 886	137 714	...	...	...	...	...	...
55 - 59	249 249	112 719	136 530	...	...	...	...	...	...
60 - 64	208 967	91 063	117 904	...	...	...	...	...	...
65 - 69	121 535	51 148	70 387	...	...	...	...	...	...
70 - 74	93 949	36 427	57 522	...	...	...	...	...	...
75 - 79	74 986	26 095	48 891	...	...	...	...	...	...
80 - 84	45 096	14 909	30 187	...	...	...	...	...	...
85 +	32 114	9 905	22 209	...	...	...	...	...	...
Romania - Roumanie									
1 VII 2014 (ESDJ)									
Total	19 913 193	9 728 663	10 184 530	10 726 149	5 132 414	5 593 735	9 187 044	4 596 249	4 590 795
0	186 301	95 812	90 489	101 115	52 120	48 995	85 186	43 692	41 494
1 - 4	774 139	397 693	376 446	407 344	209 824	197 520	366 795	187 869	178 926
5 - 9	1 067 148	548 356	518 792	535 996	275 540	260 456	531 152	272 816	258 336
10 - 14	1 060 881	545 102	515 779	485 520	248 917	236 603	575 361	296 185	279 176
15 - 19	1 084 575	555 367	529 208	503 468	255 191	248 277	581 107	300 176	280 931
20 - 24	1 161 098	602 982	558 116	638 888	320 098	318 790	522 210	282 884	239 326
25 - 29	1 399 152	728 766	670 386	837 288	424 054	413 234	561 864	304 712	257 152
30 - 34	1 367 664	702 313	665 351	814 333	411 340	402 993	553 331	290 973	262 358
35 - 39	1 575 417	803 630	771 787	893 804	445 661	448 143	681 613	357 969	323 644
40 - 44	1 539 532	789 254	750 278	835 098	409 893	425 205	704 434	379 361	325 073
45 - 49	1 468 443	751 219	717 224	846 143	406 311	439 832	622 300	344 908	277 392
50 - 54	1 147 226	574 019	573 207	675 601	317 490	358 111	471 625	256 529	215 096
55 - 59	1 416 026	678 657	737 369	854 767	395 389	459 378	561 259	283 268	277 991
60 - 64	1 328 012	612 214	715 798	755 801	347 570	408 231	572 211	264 644	307 567
65 - 69	986 459	437 580	548 879	496 928	219 386	277 542	489 531	218 194	271 337
70 - 74	801 889	332 965	468 924	370 295	152 290	218 005	431 594	180 675	250 919
75 - 79	745 825	287 422	458 403	327 686	124 156	203 530	418 139	163 266	254 873
80 - 84	488 622	179 296	309 326	208 038	73 256	134 782	280 584	106 040	174 544
85 - 89	234 388	80 885	153 503	101 650	33 488	68 162	132 738	47 397	85 341
90 - 94	70 689	22 232	48 457	31 568	9 136	22 432	39 121	13 096	26 025
95 - 99	8 246	2 466	5 780	4 061	1 095	2 966	4 185	1 371	2 814
100 +	1 461	433	1 028	757	209	548	704	224	480
1 I 2015 (ESDJ)									
Total	19 870 647	9 707 074	10 163 573	...	...	...	...	...	...
0	191 867	98 535	93 332	...	...	...	...	...	...
1 - 4	765 335	393 131	372 204	...	...	...	...	...	...
5 - 9	1 069 067	549 332	519 735	...	...	...	...	...	...
10 - 14	1 054 815	542 064	512 751	...	...	...	...	...	...
15 - 19	1 081 303	553 519	527 784	...	...	...	...	...	...
20 - 24	1 128 713	585 245	543 468	...	...	...	...	...	...
25 - 29	1 405 491	732 741	672 750	...	...	...	...	...	...
30 - 34	1 342 598	690 134	652 464	...	...	...	...	...	...
35 - 39	1 562 558	796 511	766 047	...	...	...	...	...	...
40 - 44	1 524 850	781 476	743 374	...	...	...	...	...	...
45 - 49	1 530 155	783 163	746 992	...	...	...	...	...	...
50 - 54	1 119 092	561 247	557 845	...	...	...	...	...	...
55 - 59	1 393 876	669 221	724 655	...	...	...	...	...	...
60 - 64	1 325 427	611 203	714 224	...	...	...	...	...	...
65 - 69	1 021 358	453 432	567 926	...	...	...	...	...	...
70 - 74	790 417	329 105	461 312	...	...	...	...	...	...
75 - 79	747 826	287 638	460 188	...	...	...	...	...	...
80 - 84	492 717	180 313	312 404	...	...	...	...	...	...
85 - 89	237 902	82 268	155 634	...	...	...	...	...	...
90 - 94	73 968	23 446	50 522	...	...	...	...	...	...
95 - 99	9 754	2 905	6 849	...	...	...	...	...	...
100 +	1 558	445	1 113	...	...	...	...	...	...

7. Population by age, sex and urban/rural residence: latest available year, 2006 - 2015
Population selon l'âge, le sexe et la résidence, urbaine/rurale : dernière année disponible, 2006 - 2015 (continued - suite)

Continent, country or area, date, code[a] and age (in years) / Continent, pays ou zone, date, code[a] et âge (en années)	Total			Urban - Urbaine			Rural - Rurale		
	Both sexes Les deux sexes	Male Masculin	Female Féminin	Both sexes Les deux sexes	Male Masculin	Female Féminin	Both sexes Les deux sexes	Male Masculin	Female Féminin
EUROPE									
Russian Federation - Fédération de Russie									
1 VII 2012 (ESDJ)									
Total	143 201 730	66 264 910	76 936 820	105 930 122	48 419 208	57 510 914	37 271 608	17 845 702	19 425 906
0	1 837 406	944 299	893 107	1 299 253	668 312	630 941	538 153	275 987	262 166
1 - 4	6 695 802	3 433 227	3 262 575	4 714 200	2 419 141	2 295 059	1 981 602	1 014 086	967 516
5 - 9	7 350 838	3 762 806	3 588 032	5 189 787	2 657 166	2 532 621	2 161 051	1 105 640	1 055 411
10 - 14	6 628 125	3 396 364	3 231 761	4 584 611	2 348 219	2 236 392	2 043 514	1 048 145	995 369
15 - 19	7 391 866	3 776 026	3 615 840	5 367 803	2 718 897	2 648 906	2 024 063	1 057 129	966 934
20 - 24	11 223 730	5 708 187	5 515 543	8 636 085	4 330 536	4 305 549	2 587 645	1 377 651	1 209 994
25 - 29	12 442 007	6 262 379	6 179 628	9 541 009	4 744 648	4 796 361	2 900 998	1 517 731	1 383 267
30 - 34	11 231 149	5 583 513	5 647 636	8 675 785	4 272 864	4 402 921	2 555 364	1 310 649	1 244 715
35 - 39	10 419 383	5 087 565	5 331 818	7 966 185	3 854 320	4 111 865	2 453 198	1 233 245	1 219 953
40 - 44	9 451 487	4 589 504	4 861 983	7 068 002	3 394 309	3 673 693	2 383 485	1 195 195	1 188 290
45 - 49	9 784 092	4 632 279	5 151 813	7 108 256	3 298 718	3 809 538	2 675 836	1 333 561	1 342 275
50 - 54	11 498 441	5 279 364	6 219 077	8 339 186	3 721 713	4 617 473	3 159 255	1 557 651	1 601 604
55 - 59	10 298 414	4 480 855	5 817 559	7 573 444	3 197 844	4 375 600	2 724 970	1 283 011	1 441 959
60 - 64	8 534 857	3 523 990	5 010 867	6 428 296	2 585 856	3 842 440	2 106 561	938 134	1 168 427
65 - 69	4 174 510	1 602 839	2 571 671	3 204 644	1 214 486	1 990 158	969 866	388 353	581 513
70 - 74	5 965 072	1 989 724	3 975 348	4 331 090	1 428 165	2 902 925	1 633 982	561 559	1 072 423
75 - 79	3 888 860	1 179 476	2 709 384	2 762 682	822 673	1 940 009	1 126 178	356 803	769 375
80 - 84	2 795 954	722 151	2 073 803	1 965 242	501 515	1 463 727	830 712	220 636	610 076
85 - 89	1 261 655	253 028	1 008 627	927 939	193 530	734 409	333 716	59 498	274 218
90 - 94	266 163	46 736	219 427	200 155	37 401	162 754	66 008	9 335	56 673
95 - 99	52 622	8 634	43 988	39 307	7 154	32 153	13 315	1 480	11 835
100 +	9 297	1 964	7 333	7 161	1 741	5 420	2 136	223	1 913
San Marino - Saint-Marin[21]									
1 I 2015 (ESDF)									
Total	33 738	16 425	17 313	...	...	...	...	...	...
0	300	147	153	...	...	...	...	...	...
1 - 4	1 353	707	646	...	...	...	...	...	...
5 - 9	1 701	897	804	...	...	...	...	...	...
10 - 14	1 695	890	805	...	...	...	...	...	...
15 - 19	1 630	861	769	...	...	...	...	...	...
20 - 24	1 502	763	739	...	...	...	...	...	...
25 - 29	1 568	780	788	...	...	...	...	...	...
30 - 34	1 979	968	1 011	...	...	...	...	...	...
35 - 39	2 600	1 229	1 371	...	...	...	...	...	...
40 - 44	2 972	1 446	1 526	...	...	...	...	...	...
45 - 49	3 157	1 517	1 640	...	...	...	...	...	...
50 - 54	2 869	1 409	1 460	...	...	...	...	...	...
55 - 59	2 286	1 110	1 176	...	...	...	...	...	...
60 - 64	1 912	922	990	...	...	...	...	...	...
65 - 69	1 783	864	919	...	...	...	...	...	...
70 - 74	1 438	686	752	...	...	...	...	...	...
75 - 79	1 169	552	617	...	...	...	...	...	...
80 - 84	930	395	535	...	...	...	...	...	...
85 - 89	551	185	366	...	...	...	...	...	...
90 - 94	277	86	191	...	...	...	...	...	...
95 - 99	59	11	48	...	...	...	...	...	...
100 +	7	-	7	...	...	...	...	...	...
Serbia - Serbie[80]									
1 VII 2014 (ESDJ)									
Total	7 131 787	3 472 746	3 659 041	4 270 367	2 035 772	2 234 595	2 861 420	1 436 974	1 424 446
0	65 616	33 783	31 833	45 430	23 332	22 098	20 186	10 451	9 735
1 - 4	264 361	136 079	128 282	175 693	90 498	85 195	88 668	45 581	43 087
5 - 9	340 205	175 064	165 141	206 473	106 079	100 394	133 732	68 985	64 747
10 - 14	354 243	182 219	172 024	209 085	107 607	101 478	145 158	74 612	70 546
15 - 19	375 525	193 464	182 061	217 888	111 958	105 930	157 637	81 506	76 131
20 - 24	421 250	215 910	205 340	250 504	126 493	124 011	170 746	89 417	81 329
25 - 29	463 847	237 130	226 717	291 484	144 353	147 131	172 363	92 777	79 586
30 - 34	492 218	250 453	241 765	322 367	159 394	162 973	169 851	91 059	78 792
35 - 39	503 508	254 984	248 524	324 050	159 912	164 138	179 458	95 072	84 386
40 - 44	479 646	240 242	239 404	296 738	144 841	151 897	182 908	95 401	87 507
45 - 49	471 585	232 753	238 832	281 161	134 272	146 889	190 424	98 481	91 943

7. Population by age, sex and urban/rural residence: latest available year, 2006 - 2015
Population selon l'âge, le sexe et la résidence, urbaine/rurale : dernière année disponible, 2006 - 2015 (continued - suite)

Continent, country or area, date, code[a] and age (in years) / Continent, pays ou zone, date, code[a] et âge (en années)	Total			Urban - Urbaine			Rural - Rurale		
	Both sexes Les deux sexes	Male Masculin	Female Féminin	Both sexes Les deux sexes	Male Masculin	Female Féminin	Both sexes Les deux sexes	Male Masculin	Female Féminin
EUROPE									
Serbia - Serbie[80]									
1 VII 2014 (ESDJ)									
50 - 54	498 771	243 361	255 410	295 720	138 281	157 439	203 051	105 080	97 971
55 - 59	536 858	259 549	277 309	315 075	145 985	169 090	221 783	113 564	108 219
60 - 64	562 753	266 837	295 916	328 636	149 381	179 255	234 117	117 456	116 661
65 - 69	407 235	185 971	221 264	235 585	103 766	131 819	171 650	82 205	89 445
70 - 74	318 809	138 868	179 941	172 545	73 007	99 538	146 264	65 861	80 403
75 - 79	286 673	117 984	168 689	154 294	62 720	91 574	132 379	55 264	77 115
80 - 84	189 236	73 209	116 027	95 640	36 168	59 472	93 596	37 041	56 555
85 - 89	77 642	27 840	49 802	40 132	13 963	26 169	37 510	13 877	23 633
90 - 94	19 560	6 293	13 267	10 634	3 373	7 261	8 926	2 920	6 006
95 - 99	1 899	637	1 262	1 045	341	704	854	296	558
100 +	347	116	231	188	48	140	159	68	91
1 I 2015 (ESDJ)									
Total	7 114 393	3 464 399	3 649 994	...	...	...	...	...	...
0	66 079	34 101	31 978	...	...	...	...	...	...
1 - 4	263 338	135 433	127 905	...	...	...	...	...	...
5 - 9	338 134	174 043	164 091	...	...	...	...	...	...
10 - 14	355 803	182 959	172 844	...	...	...	...	...	...
15 - 19	369 025	190 179	178 846	...	...	...	...	...	...
20 - 24	418 343	214 606	203 737	...	...	...	...	...	...
25 - 29	457 556	233 956	223 600	...	...	...	...	...	...
30 - 34	491 942	250 291	241 651	...	...	...	...	...	...
35 - 39	503 376	255 089	248 287	...	...	...	...	...	...
40 - 44	481 321	241 289	240 032	...	...	...	...	...	...
45 - 49	471 282	232 782	238 500	...	...	...	...	...	...
50 - 54	493 154	240 592	252 562	...	...	...	...	...	...
55 - 59	524 659	253 507	271 152	...	...	...	...	...	...
60 - 64	566 143	268 489	297 654	...	...	...	...	...	...
65 - 69	423 893	193 777	230 116	...	...	...	...	...	...
70 - 74	312 039	135 867	176 172	...	...	...	...	...	...
75 - 79	283 889	116 861	167 028	...	...	...	...	...	...
80 - 84	191 240	74 167	117 073	...	...	...	...	...	...
85 - 89	79 842	28 854	50 988	...	...	...	...	...	...
90 - 94	20 544	6 635	13 909	...	...	...	...	...	...
95 - 99	2 368	779	1 589	...	...	...	...	...	...
100 +	423	143	280	...	...	...	...	...	...
Slovakia - Slovaquie									
1 VII 2014 (ESDJ)									
Total	5 418 649	2 640 694	2 777 955	2 925 291	1 406 300	1 518 991	2 493 359	1 234 394	1 258 965
0	55 344	28 285	27 060	28 784	14 700	14 083	26 560	13 584	12 976
1 - 4	233 621	119 577	114 045	120 602	61 691	58 912	113 019	57 886	55 133
5 - 9	276 975	142 412	134 564	137 569	70 798	66 771	139 407	71 614	67 793
10 - 14	264 113	135 566	128 547	126 973	65 170	61 803	137 140	70 396	66 744
15 - 19	296 949	152 289	144 661	142 503	73 066	69 437	154 447	79 223	75 224
20 - 24	373 545	190 701	182 845	191 321	97 422	93 899	182 224	93 279	88 946
25 - 29	416 636	212 289	204 347	230 071	116 510	113 561	186 565	95 780	90 786
30 - 34	442 460	227 399	215 061	249 674	127 822	121 852	192 787	99 578	93 209
35 - 39	457 960	235 253	222 707	254 482	129 692	124 790	203 478	105 561	97 917
40 - 44	394 660	200 656	194 004	211 893	105 437	106 457	182 767	95 220	87 548
45 - 49	356 698	178 845	177 853	192 613	92 640	99 974	164 085	86 206	77 879
50 - 54	369 432	183 241	186 192	207 302	98 501	108 801	162 130	84 740	77 391
55 - 59	383 064	185 026	198 038	222 007	103 269	118 739	161 057	81 758	79 299
60 - 64	352 187	164 034	188 153	204 929	93 057	111 872	147 258	70 978	76 281
65 - 69	253 861	110 837	143 024	144 649	62 349	82 300	109 212	48 488	60 724
70 - 74	188 531	75 104	113 427	102 279	40 812	61 467	86 252	34 292	51 960
75 - 79	135 923	48 657	87 266	71 411	26 104	45 307	64 512	22 553	41 959
80 - 84	97 536	31 373	66 163	50 392	16 898	33 494	47 144	14 475	32 669
85 - 89	49 328	13 890	35 439	25 486	7 483	18 003	23 843	6 407	17 436
90 - 94	17 057	4 451	12 606	8 767	2 412	6 355	8 291	2 040	6 251
95 - 99	2 187	615	1 572	1 230	349	882	957	267	691
100 +	586	198	388	358	123	236	228	76	153
1 I 2015 (ESDJ)									
Total	5 421 349	2 642 328	2 779 021	...	...	...	...	...	...
0	55 513	28 334	27 179	...	...	...	...	...	...

Continent, country or area, date, code[a] and age (in years) Continent, pays ou zone, date, code[a] et âge (en annèes)	Total			Urban - Urbaine			Rural - Rurale		
	Both sexes Les deux sexes	Male Masculin	Female Féminin	Both sexes Les deux sexes	Male Masculin	Female Féminin	Both sexes Les deux sexes	Male Masculin	Female Féminin
EUROPE									
Slovakia - Slovaquie									
1 I 2015 (ESDJ)									
1 - 4	231 761	118 504	113 257	...	...	...	...	...	...
5 - 9	279 833	143 930	135 903	...	...	...	...	...	...
10 - 14	263 074	135 149	127 925	...	...	...	...	...	...
15 - 19	291 990	149 772	142 218	...	...	...	...	...	...
20 - 24	367 245	187 508	179 737	...	...	...	...	...	...
25 - 29	412 184	209 940	202 244	...	...	...	...	...	...
30 - 34	438 999	225 648	213 351	...	...	...	...	...	...
35 - 39	459 315	235 935	223 380	...	...	...	...	...	...
40 - 44	403 126	205 226	197 900	...	...	...	...	...	...
45 - 49	354 039	177 702	176 337	...	...	...	...	...	...
50 - 54	370 115	183 578	186 537	...	...	...	...	...	...
55 - 59	380 019	183 831	196 188	...	...	...	...	...	...
60 - 64	357 257	166 676	190 581	...	...	...	...	...	...
65 - 69	259 958	113 985	145 973	...	...	...	...	...	...
70 - 74	191 317	76 440	114 877	...	...	...	...	...	...
75 - 79	137 145	49 099	88 046	...	...	...	...	...	...
80 - 84	97 726	31 484	66 242	...	...	...	...	...	...
85 - 89	50 071	14 132	35 939	...	...	...	...	...	...
90 - 94	17 535	4 549	12 986	...	...	...	...	...	...
95 - 99	2 486	689	1 797	...	...	...	...	...	...
100 +	641	217	424	...	...	...	...	...	...
Slovenia - Slovénie									
1 VII 2014 (ESDJ)									
Total	2 061 623	1 021 419	1 040 204	1 051 087	514 828	536 259	1 010 536	506 591	503 945
0	21 308	10 957	10 351	10 924	5 589	5 335	10 384	5 368	5 016
1 - 4	88 529	45 620	42 909	45 198	23 298	21 900	43 331	22 322	21 009
5 - 9	101 378	52 022	49 356	51 016	26 253	24 763	50 362	25 769	24 593
10 - 14	91 305	47 058	44 247	44 104	22 853	21 251	47 201	24 205	22 996
15 - 19	95 674	49 303	46 371	47 008	24 099	22 909	48 666	25 204	23 462
20 - 24	109 701	56 278	53 423	60 738	30 083	30 655	48 963	26 195	22 768
25 - 29	134 654	70 046	64 608	69 317	35 982	33 335	65 337	34 064	31 273
30 - 34	151 093	79 253	71 840	78 143	40 834	37 309	72 950	38 419	34 531
35 - 39	156 329	81 903	74 426	80 398	41 902	38 496	75 931	40 001	35 930
40 - 44	146 919	76 507	70 412	73 832	38 058	35 774	73 087	38 449	34 638
45 - 49	154 290	78 559	75 731	77 166	38 915	38 251	77 124	39 644	37 480
50 - 54	153 041	77 738	75 303	76 453	38 126	38 327	76 588	39 612	36 976
55 - 59	151 739	76 755	74 984	75 931	37 458	38 473	75 808	39 297	36 511
60 - 64	141 203	70 781	70 422	72 192	35 211	36 981	69 011	35 570	33 441
65 - 69	100 608	47 830	52 778	52 203	24 068	28 135	48 405	23 762	24 643
70 - 74	91 944	40 959	50 985	47 513	20 671	26 842	44 431	20 288	24 143
75 - 79	74 014	30 141	43 873	38 156	15 725	22 431	35 858	14 416	21 442
80 - 84	55 619	19 114	36 505	28 547	9 908	18 639	27 072	9 206	17 866
85 - 89	30 305	8 160	22 145	15 772	4 423	11 349	14 533	3 737	10 796
90 - 94	10 501	2 199	8 302	5 636	1 222	4 414	4 865	977	3 888
95 - 99	1 232	203	1 029	689	126	563	543	77	466
100 +	237	33	204	151	24	127	86	9	77
1 I 2015 (ESDJ)									
Total	2 062 874	1 022 229	1 040 645	...	...	...	...	...	...
0	21 146	10 917	10 229	...	...	...	...	...	...
1 - 4	88 168	45 336	42 832	...	...	...	...	...	...
5 - 9	103 359	53 192	50 167	...	...	...	...	...	...
10 - 14	91 637	47 162	44 475	...	...	...	...	...	...
15 - 19	94 991	48 982	46 009	...	...	...	...	...	...
20 - 24	107 718	55 198	52 520	...	...	...	...	...	...
25 - 29	132 790	69 046	63 744	...	...	...	...	...	...
30 - 34	149 276	78 083	71 193	...	...	...	...	...	...
35 - 39	156 973	82 329	74 644	...	...	...	...	...	...
40 - 44	147 666	76 916	70 750	...	...	...	...	...	...
45 - 49	153 313	78 273	75 040	...	...	...	...	...	...
50 - 54	153 352	77 824	75 528	...	...	...	...	...	...
55 - 59	150 555	76 255	74 300	...	...	...	...	...	...
60 - 64	142 544	71 300	71 244	...	...	...	...	...	...
65 - 69	104 637	49 865	54 772	...	...	...	...	...	...

Continent, country or area, date, code[a] and age (in years) / Continent, pays ou zone, date, code[a] et âge (en années)	Total			Urban - Urbaine			Rural - Rurale		
	Both sexes Les deux sexes	Male Masculin	Female Féminin	Both sexes Les deux sexes	Male Masculin	Female Féminin	Both sexes Les deux sexes	Male Masculin	Female Féminin
EUROPE									
Slovenia - Slovénie									
1 I 2015 (ESDJ)									
70 - 74	90 267	40 357	49 910	...	...	...	...	...	...
75 - 79	74 959	30 816	44 143	...	...	...	...	...	...
80 - 84	56 141	19 388	36 753	...	...	...	...	...	...
85 - 89	30 915	8 467	22 448	...	...	...	...	...	...
90 - 94	10 768	2 225	8 543	...	...	...	...	...	...
95 - 99	1 463	265	1 198	...	...	...	...	...	...
100 +	236	33	203	...	...	...	...	...	...
Spain - Espagne[72]									
1 I 2015 (ESDJ)									
Total	46 449 565	22 826 546	23 623 019	...	...	...	...	...	...
0	426 459	220 124	206 335	...	...	...	...	...	...
1 - 4	1 830 234	943 094	887 140	...	...	...	...	...	...
5 - 9	2 484 377	1 281 689	1 202 688	...	...	...	...	...	...
10 - 14	2 308 009	1 187 484	1 120 525	...	...	...	...	...	...
15 - 19	2 153 295	1 107 970	1 045 325	...	...	...	...	...	...
20 - 24	2 319 300	1 181 542	1 137 758	...	...	...	...	...	...
25 - 29	2 640 340	1 321 886	1 318 454	...	...	...	...	...	...
30 - 34	3 269 864	1 642 804	1 627 060	...	...	...	...	...	...
35 - 39	3 949 789	2 011 296	1 938 493	...	...	...	...	...	...
40 - 44	3 889 668	1 982 453	1 907 215	...	...	...	...	...	...
45 - 49	3 691 008	1 861 330	1 829 678	...	...	...	...	...	...
50 - 54	3 408 998	1 698 889	1 710 109	...	...	...	...	...	...
55 - 59	2 978 374	1 467 133	1 511 241	...	...	...	...	...	...
60 - 64	2 507 836	1 219 620	1 288 216	...	...	...	...	...	...
65 - 69	2 357 514	1 120 627	1 236 887	...	...	...	...	...	...
70 - 74	1 949 029	902 510	1 046 519	...	...	...	...	...	...
75 - 79	1 553 066	673 645	879 421	...	...	...	...	...	...
80 - 84	1 425 564	573 318	852 246	...	...	...	...	...	...
85 - 89	855 423	301 428	553 995	...	...	...	...	...	...
90 - 94	357 162	105 675	251 487	...	...	...	...	...	...
95 - 99	78 777	18 584	60 193	...	...	...	...	...	...
100 +	15 479	3 445	12 034	...	...	...	...	...	...
Sweden - Suède[81]									
1 I 2015 (ESDJ)									
Total	9 747 355	4 872 240	4 875 115	...	...	...	...	...	...
0	115 880	59 584	56 296	...	...	...	...	...	...
1 - 4	468 277	240 600	227 677	...	...	...	...	...	...
5 - 9	571 614	293 755	277 859	...	...	...	...	...	...
10 - 14	526 262	270 418	255 844	...	...	...	...	...	...
15 - 19	527 236	273 055	254 181	...	...	...	...	...	...
20 - 24	671 529	344 583	326 946	...	...	...	...	...	...
25 - 29	655 755	335 238	320 517	...	...	...	...	...	...
30 - 34	609 378	312 360	297 018	...	...	...	...	...	...
35 - 39	604 368	308 109	296 259	...	...	...	...	...	...
40 - 44	650 114	329 565	320 549	...	...	...	...	...	...
45 - 49	670 744	341 083	329 661	...	...	...	...	...	...
50 - 54	622 044	315 278	306 766	...	...	...	...	...	...
55 - 59	579 308	291 556	287 752	...	...	...	...	...	...
60 - 64	561 962	280 372	281 590	...	...	...	...	...	...
65 - 69	599 138	296 189	302 949	...	...	...	...	...	...
70 - 74	479 257	234 581	244 676	...	...	...	...	...	...
75 - 79	335 081	155 541	179 540	...	...	...	...	...	...
80 - 84	242 924	102 596	140 328	...	...	...	...	...	...
85 - 89	161 488	59 867	101 621	...	...	...	...	...	...
90 - 94	76 517	23 648	52 869	...	...	...	...	...	...
95 - 99	16 526	3 941	12 585	...	...	...	...	...	...
100 +	1 953	321	1 632	...	...	...	...	...	...
Switzerland - Suisse[74]									
1 I 2015 (ESDJ)									
Total	8 237 666	4 073 880	4 163 786	6 070 409	2 984 345	3 086 064	2 167 257	1 089 535	1 077 722
0	83 730	43 039	40 691	62 533	32 174	30 359	21 197	10 865	10 332
1 - 4	334 565	171 899	162 666	245 774	126 308	119 466	88 791	45 591	43 200
5 - 9	404 759	208 148	196 611	292 601	150 288	142 313	112 158	57 860	54 298

Continent, country or area, date, code[a] and age (in years) / Continent, pays ou zone, date, code[a] et âge (en années)	Total			Urban - Urbaine			Rural - Rurale		
	Both sexes Les deux sexes	Male Masculin	Female Féminin	Both sexes Les deux sexes	Male Masculin	Female Féminin	Both sexes Les deux sexes	Male Masculin	Female Féminin
EUROPE									
Switzerland - Suisse[74]									
1 I 2015 (ESDJ)									
10 - 14	401 927	206 229	195 698	286 643	147 123	139 520	115 284	59 106	56 178
15 - 19	438 771	224 978	213 793	309 912	158 597	151 315	128 859	66 381	62 478
20 - 24	498 313	253 521	244 792	363 593	183 455	180 138	134 720	70 066	64 654
25 - 29	551 444	278 301	273 143	423 588	212 075	211 513	127 856	66 226	61 630
30 - 34	582 448	294 606	287 842	451 037	227 873	223 164	131 411	66 733	64 678
35 - 39	566 720	285 134	281 586	432 218	217 475	214 743	134 502	67 659	66 843
40 - 44	597 760	301 314	296 446	443 762	223 677	220 085	153 998	77 637	76 361
45 - 49	662 100	334 355	327 745	483 554	243 611	239 943	178 546	90 744	87 802
50 - 54	642 615	325 346	317 269	465 005	234 412	230 593	177 610	90 934	86 676
55 - 59	543 463	274 509	268 954	390 724	195 872	194 852	152 739	78 637	74 102
60 - 64	463 486	228 800	234 686	334 563	162 384	172 179	128 923	66 416	62 507
65 - 69	430 556	208 469	222 087	312 917	148 767	164 150	117 639	59 702	57 937
70 - 74	356 726	167 479	189 247	264 545	122 149	142 396	92 181	45 330	46 851
75 - 79	269 582	119 304	150 278	201 390	88 075	113 315	68 192	31 229	36 963
80 - 84	208 501	84 090	124 411	155 402	62 083	93 319	53 099	22 007	31 092
85 - 89	130 154	45 187	84 967	97 522	33 483	64 039	32 632	11 704	20 928
90 - 94	57 036	16 308	40 728	43 116	12 263	30 853	13 920	4 045	9 875
95 - 99	11 467	2 574	8 893	8 793	1 964	6 829	2 674	610	2 064
100 +	1 543	290	1 253	1 217	237	980	326	53	273
TFYR of Macedonia - L'ex-R. y. de Macédoine									
1 I 2015 (ESDF)									
Total	2 069 172	1 036 518	1 032 654	...	...	...	...	...	...
0	23 373	12 051	11 322	...	...	...	...	...	...
1 - 4	92 819	48 198	44 621	...	...	...	...	...	...
5 - 9	112 693	58 067	54 626	...	...	...	...	...	...
10 - 14	118 759	61 338	57 421	...	...	...	...	...	...
15 - 19	131 455	67 960	63 495	...	...	...	...	...	...
20 - 24	153 943	78 967	74 976	...	...	...	...	...	...
25 - 29	162 874	83 459	79 415	...	...	...	...	...	...
30 - 34	163 444	83 808	79 636	...	...	...	...	...	...
35 - 39	155 124	79 534	75 590	...	...	...	...	...	...
40 - 44	146 605	74 058	72 547	...	...	...	...	...	...
45 - 49	146 740	74 156	72 584	...	...	...	...	...	...
50 - 54	142 332	71 710	70 622	...	...	...	...	...	...
55 - 59	135 722	68 156	67 566	...	...	...	...	...	...
60 - 64	120 847	58 639	62 208	...	...	...	...	...	...
65 - 69	92 561	42 931	49 630	...	...	...	...	...	...
70 - 74	70 302	31 795	38 507	...	...	...	...	...	...
75 - 79	53 146	23 107	30 039	...	...	...	...	...	...
80 - 84	31 919	13 116	18 803	...	...	...	...	...	...
85 - 89	10 832	4 295	6 537	...	...	...	...	...	...
90 - 94	2 546	898	1 648	...	...	...	...	...	...
95 +	828	223	605	...	...	...	...	...	...
Unknown - Inconnu	308	52	256	...	...	...	...	...	...
Ukraine									
1 I 2013 (ESDJ)									
Total	45 372 692	20 962 744	24 409 948	31 123 007	14 259 600	16 863 407	14 249 685	6 703 144	7 546 541
0	517 301	266 820	250 481	339 538	175 547	163 991	177 763	91 273	86 490
1 - 4	2 004 486	1 033 711	970 775	1 327 019	684 897	642 122	677 467	348 814	328 653
5 - 9	2 168 158	1 113 505	1 054 653	1 449 410	745 034	704 376	718 748	368 471	350 277
10 - 14	1 930 653	991 443	939 210	1 203 306	618 657	584 649	727 347	372 786	354 561
15 - 19	2 405 136	1 233 934	1 171 202	1 579 769	804 869	774 900	825 367	429 065	396 302
20 - 24	3 232 157	1 657 101	1 575 056	2 195 942	1 118 307	1 077 635	1 036 215	538 794	497 421
25 - 29	3 868 992	1 969 672	1 899 320	2 801 899	1 408 147	1 393 752	1 067 093	561 525	505 568
30 - 34	3 476 598	1 750 016	1 726 582	2 553 790	1 276 839	1 276 951	922 808	473 177	449 631
35 - 39	3 270 101	1 609 508	1 660 593	2 323 493	1 130 939	1 192 554	946 608	478 569	468 039
40 - 44	3 113 544	1 507 589	1 605 955	2 153 127	1 021 499	1 131 628	960 417	486 090	474 327
45 - 49	3 085 767	1 450 559	1 635 208	2 123 186	966 883	1 156 303	962 581	483 676	478 905
50 - 54	3 500 369	1 594 318	1 906 051	2 461 151	1 084 460	1 376 691	1 039 218	509 858	529 360
55 - 59	3 097 369	1 347 030	1 750 339	2 209 140	931 767	1 277 373	888 229	415 263	472 966
60 - 64	2 796 743	1 157 385	1 639 358	2 006 621	812 407	1 194 214	790 122	344 978	445 144
65 - 69	1 656 868	629 382	1 027 486	1 139 209	432 839	706 370	517 659	196 543	321 116

Continent, country or area, date, code[a] and age (in years) / Continent, pays ou zone, date, code[a] et âge (en années)	Total			Urban - Urbaine			Rural - Rurale		
	Both sexes Les deux sexes	Male Masculin	Female Féminin	Both sexes Les deux sexes	Male Masculin	Female Féminin	Both sexes Les deux sexes	Male Masculin	Female Féminin
EUROPE									
Ukraine									
1 I 2013 (ESDJ)									
70 - 74	2 153 251	742 717	1 410 534	1 391 669	483 905	907 764	761 582	258 812	502 770
75 - 79	1 492 884	489 204	1 003 680	927 376	307 461	619 915	565 508	181 743	383 765
80 - 84	974 774	274 742	700 032	568 852	164 927	403 925	405 922	109 815	296 107
85 - 89	492 650	114 882	377 768	289 117	71 285	217 832	203 533	43 597	159 936
90 - 94	114 583	24 566	90 017	65 707	15 513	50 194	48 876	9 053	39 823
95 - 99	14 543	3 307	11 236	9 446	2 362	7 084	5 097	945	4 152
100 +	5 765	1 353	4 412	4 240	1 056	3 184	1 525	297	1 228
1 I 2015* (ESDF)[82]									
Total	42 759 661	19 787 826	22 971 835	...	...	...	...	...	...
0	463 048	238 366	224 682	...	...	...	...	...	...
1 - 4	1 895 596	976 793	918 803	...	...	...	...	...	...
5 - 9	2 228 912	1 147 223	1 081 689	...	...	...	...	...	...
10 - 14	1 861 615	957 252	904 363	...	...	...	...	...	...
15 - 19	2 073 596	1 063 573	1 010 023	...	...	...	...	...	...
20 - 24	2 740 663	1 408 638	1 332 025	...	...	...	...	...	...
25 - 29	3 487 164	1 777 288	1 709 876	...	...	...	...	...	...
30 - 34	3 496 563	1 765 587	1 730 976	...	...	...	...	...	...
35 - 39	3 142 152	1 554 768	1 587 384	...	...	...	...	...	...
40 - 44	3 026 906	1 470 554	1 556 352	...	...	...	...	...	...
45 - 49	2 791 872	1 323 604	1 468 268	...	...	...	...	...	...
50 - 54	3 178 225	1 453 882	1 724 343	...	...	...	...	...	...
55 - 59	3 042 919	1 332 975	1 709 944	...	...	...	...	...	...
60 - 64	2 654 650	1 098 880	1 555 770	...	...	...	...	...	...
65 - 69	1 938 663	747 937	1 190 726	...	...	...	...	...	...
70 - 74	1 567 950	538 081	1 029 869	...	...	...	...	...	...
75 - 79	1 730 546	548 905	1 181 641	...	...	...	...	...	...
80 - 84	779 304	226 285	553 019	...	...	...	...	...	...
85 - 89	499 082	121 215	377 867	...	...	...	...	...	...
90 - 94	137 501	30 135	107 366	...	...	...	...	...	...
95 - 99	16 363	4 203	12 160	...	...	...	...	...	...
100 +	6 371	1 682	4 689	...	...	...	...	...	...
United Kingdom of Great Britain and Northern Ireland - Royaume-Uni de Grande-Bretagne et d'Irlande du Nord[83]									
27 III 2011 (CDJC)									
Total	63 182 178	31 028 143	32 154 035	51 217 521	25 124 237	26 093 284	11 964 657	5 903 906	6 060 751
0 - 4	3 913 953	2 002 494	1 911 459	3 302 119	1 689 719	1 612 400	611 834	312 775	299 059
5 - 9	3 516 615	1 799 999	1 716 616	2 878 114	1 472 489	1 405 625	638 501	327 510	310 991
10 - 14	3 669 326	1 878 838	1 790 488	2 951 079	1 509 796	1 441 283	718 247	369 042	349 205
15 - 19	3 996 452	2 040 725	1 955 727	3 277 414	1 667 480	1 609 934	719 038	373 245	345 793
20 - 24	4 297 198	2 164 141	2 133 057	3 737 543	1 863 922	1 873 621	559 655	300 219	259 436
25 - 29	4 306 340	2 145 054	2 161 286	3 781 906	1 876 471	1 905 435	524 434	268 583	255 851
30 - 34	4 125 449	2 059 312	2 066 137	3 573 410	1 789 511	1 783 899	552 039	269 801	282 238
35 - 39	4 194 477	2 082 310	2 112 167	3 495 390	1 745 563	1 749 827	699 087	336 747	362 340
40 - 44	4 625 635	2 283 902	2 341 733	3 734 709	1 851 446	1 883 263	890 926	432 456	458 470
45 - 49	4 643 100	2 293 572	2 349 528	3 683 527	1 821 257	1 862 270	959 573	472 315	487 258
50 - 54	4 094 454	2 028 748	2 065 706	3 216 769	1 593 822	1 622 947	877 685	434 926	442 759
55 - 59	3 614 078	1 785 598	1 828 480	2 790 096	1 378 906	1 411 190	823 982	406 692	417 290
60 - 64	3 807 974	1 868 912	1 939 062	2 869 025	1 404 882	1 464 143	938 949	464 030	474 919
65 - 69	3 017 480	1 463 355	1 554 125	2 248 845	1 082 105	1 166 740	768 635	381 250	387 385
70 - 74	2 462 745	1 162 621	1 300 124	1 874 997	873 593	1 001 404	587 748	289 028	298 720
75 - 79	2 006 019	903 433	1 102 586	1 549 014	686 269	862 745	457 005	217 164	239 841
80 - 84	1 498 896	615 163	883 733	1 166 619	470 552	696 067	332 277	144 611	187 666
85 - 89	918 343	324 063	594 280	717 808	249 645	468 163	200 535	74 418	126 117
90 - 94	368 425	104 072	264 353	287 454	80 165	207 289	80 971	23 907	57 064
95 - 99	92 951	19 756	73 195	72 117	15 038	57 079	20 834	4 718	16 116
100 +	12 268	2 075	10 193	9 566	1 606	7 960	2 702	469	2 233
1 I 2015 (ESDJ)[71]									
Total	64 875 165	31 947 040	32 928 125	...	...	...	...	...	...
0	777 052	398 137	378 915	...	...	...	...	...	...
1 - 4	3 246 736	1 663 469	1 583 267	...	...	...	...	...	...

7. Population by age, sex and urban/rural residence: latest available year, 2006 - 2015
Population selon l'âge, le sexe et la résidence, urbaine/rurale : dernière année disponible, 2006 - 2015 (continued - suite)

Continent, country or area, date, code[a] and age (in years) / Continent, pays ou zone, date, code[a] et âge (en annèes)	Total			Urban - Urbaine			Rural - Rurale		
	Both sexes Les deux sexes	Male Masculin	Female Féminin	Both sexes Les deux sexes	Male Masculin	Female Féminin	Both sexes Les deux sexes	Male Masculin	Female Féminin
EUROPE									
United Kingdom of Great Britain and Northern Ireland - Royaume-Uni de Grande-Bretagne et d'Irlande du Nord[83]									
1 I 2015 (ESDJ)[71]									
5 - 9	3 905 542	1 998 962	1 906 580	...	...	...	...	...	...
10 - 14	3 533 925	1 808 830	1 725 095	...	...	...	...	...	...
15 - 19	3 837 607	1 970 554	1 867 053	...	...	...	...	...	...
20 - 24	4 318 636	2 199 715	2 118 921	...	...	...	...	...	...
25 - 29	4 425 006	2 219 275	2 205 731	...	...	...	...	...	...
30 - 34	4 371 113	2 172 031	2 199 082	...	...	...	...	...	...
35 - 39	4 036 354	2 009 739	2 026 615	...	...	...	...	...	...
40 - 44	4 343 853	2 148 614	2 195 239	...	...	...	...	...	...
45 - 49	4 651 253	2 292 328	2 358 925	...	...	...	...	...	...
50 - 54	4 511 640	2 226 857	2 284 783	...	...	...	...	...	...
55 - 59	3 896 812	1 923 965	1 972 847	...	...	...	...	...	...
60 - 64	3 506 186	1 716 505	1 789 681	...	...	...	...	...	...
65 - 69	3 588 600	1 743 239	1 845 361	...	...	...	...	...	...
70 - 74	2 679 833	1 273 348	1 406 485	...	...	...	...	...	...
75 - 79	2 152 004	986 330	1 165 674	...	...	...	...	...	...
80 - 84	1 576 877	672 535	904 342	...	...	...	...	...	...
85 - 89	962 057	361 962	600 095	...	...	...	...	...	...
90 - 94	445 999	136 954	309 045	...	...	...	...	...	...
95 - 99	93 576	21 442	72 134	...	...	...	...	...	...
100 +	14 504	2 249	12 255	...	...	...	...	...	...
OCEANIA - OCÉANIE									
American Samoa - Samoas américaines[28]									
1 IV 2010 (CDJC)									
Total	55 519	28 164	27 355	...	...	...	...	...	...
0 - 4	6 611	3 417	3 194	...	...	...	...	...	...
5 - 9	6 535	3 470	3 065	...	...	...	...	...	...
10 - 14	6 279	3 214	3 065	...	...	...	...	...	...
15 - 19	6 296	3 218	3 078	...	...	...	...	...	...
20 - 24	3 891	1 944	1 947	...	...	...	...	...	...
25 - 29	3 324	1 670	1 654	...	...	...	...	...	...
30 - 34	3 510	1 726	1 784	...	...	...	...	...	...
35 - 39	3 609	1 845	1 764	...	...	...	...	...	...
40 - 44	3 600	1 793	1 807	...	...	...	...	...	...
45 - 49	3 389	1 673	1 716	...	...	...	...	...	...
50 - 54	2 679	1 335	1 344	...	...	...	...	...	...
55 - 59	2 049	1 011	1 038	...	...	...	...	...	...
60 - 64	1 480	755	725	...	...	...	...	...	...
65 - 69	960	500	460	...	...	...	...	...	...
70 - 74	654	321	333	...	...	...	...	...	...
75 - 79	337	155	182	...	...	...	...	...	...
80 - 84	206	76	130	...	...	...	...	...	...
85 +	110	41	69	...	...	...	...	...	...
Australia - Australie[9]									
1 VII 2014 (ESDJ)									
Total	23 490 736	11 692 500	11 798 236	20 109 282	9 958 617	10 150 665	3 381 454	1 733 883	1 647 571
0	300 275	154 115	146 160	262 825	134 828	127 997	37 450	19 287	18 163
1 - 4	1 227 263	630 427	596 836	1 059 189	543 707	515 482	168 074	86 720	81 354
5 - 9	1 488 170	764 441	723 729	1 260 437	647 117	613 320	227 733	117 324	110 409
10 - 14	1 407 178	721 502	685 676	1 182 374	605 955	576 419	224 804	115 547	109 257
15 - 19	1 475 143	758 254	716 889	1 264 863	648 445	616 418	210 280	109 809	100 471
20 - 24	1 652 227	845 407	806 820	1 486 466	756 656	729 810	165 761	88 751	77 010
25 - 29	1 751 348	883 361	867 987	1 577 325	792 934	784 391	174 023	90 427	83 596
30 - 34	1 712 093	859 800	852 293	1 528 090	766 254	761 836	184 003	93 546	90 457
35 - 39	1 560 317	778 307	782 010	1 369 874	682 563	687 311	190 443	95 744	94 699
40 - 44	1 667 775	826 914	840 861	1 437 644	710 868	726 776	230 131	116 046	114 085

264

7. Population by age, sex and urban/rural residence: latest available year, 2006 - 2015
Population selon l'âge, le sexe et la résidence, urbaine/rurale : dernière année disponible, 2006 - 2015 (continued - suite)

Continent, country or area, date, code[a] and age (in years) / Continent, pays ou zone, date, code[a] et âge (en annèes)	Total			Urban - Urbaine			Rural - Rurale		
	Both sexes Les deux sexes	Male Masculin	Female Féminin	Both sexes Les deux sexes	Male Masculin	Female Féminin	Both sexes Les deux sexes	Male Masculin	Female Féminin
OCEANIA - OCÉANIE									
Australia - Australie[9]									
1 VII 2014 (ESDJ)									
45 - 49	1 541 519	763 678	777 841	1 311 213	646 369	664 844	230 306	117 309	112 997
50 - 54	1 561 451	771 725	789 726	1 306 610	641 195	665 415	254 841	130 530	124 311
55 - 59	1 425 771	703 484	722 287	1 176 875	574 684	602 191	248 896	128 800	120 096
60 - 64	1 264 018	623 689	640 329	1 033 201	503 083	530 118	230 817	120 606	110 211
65 - 69	1 120 081	555 407	564 674	910 745	445 218	465 527	209 336	110 189	99 147
70 - 74	819 234	401 418	417 816	667 307	322 085	345 222	151 927	79 333	72 594
75 - 79	612 042	289 632	322 410	506 560	235 395	271 165	105 482	54 237	51 245
80 - 84	448 298	196 036	252 262	377 591	162 531	215 060	70 707	33 505	37 202
85 - 89	295 510	115 261	180 249	252 161	96 924	155 237	43 349	18 337	25 012
90 - 94	129 440	41 784	87 656	111 501	35 287	76 214	17 939	6 497	11 442
95 - 99	27 537	6 975	20 562	23 123	5 776	17 347	4 414	1 199	3 215
100 +	4 046	883	3 163	3 308	743	2 565	738	140	598
Cook Islands - Îles Cook[84]									
1 XII 2011 (CDFC)									
Total	17 794	8 815	8 979	...	...	...	...	...	...
0 - 4	1 584	806	778	...	...	...	...	...	...
5 - 9	1 539	768	771	...	...	...	...	...	...
10 - 14	1 504	794	710	...	...	...	...	...	...
15 - 19	1 495	768	727	...	...	...	...	...	...
20 - 24	1 273	611	662	...	...	...	...	...	...
25 - 29	1 263	590	673	...	...	...	...	...	...
30 - 34	1 122	534	588	...	...	...	...	...	...
35 - 39	1 179	543	636	...	...	...	...	...	...
40 - 44	1 252	605	647	...	...	...	...	...	...
45 - 49	1 282	636	646	...	...	...	...	...	...
50 - 54	1 059	534	525	...	...	...	...	...	...
55 - 59	863	430	433	...	...	...	...	...	...
60 - 64	749	394	355	...	...	...	...	...	...
65 - 69	649	333	316	...	...	...	...	...	...
70 - 74	496	251	245	...	...	...	...	...	...
75 - 79	285	130	155	...	...	...	...	...	...
80 +	200	88	112	...	...	...	...	...	...
Fiji - Fidji									
16 IX 2007 (CDFC)									
Total	837 271	427 176	410 095	424 846	212 454	212 392	412 425	214 722	197 703
0 - 4	82 718	42 835	39 883	39 209	20 264	18 945	43 509	22 571	20 938
5 - 9	78 019	40 441	37 578	35 981	18 528	17 453	42 038	21 913	20 125
10 - 14	82 384	42 369	40 015	38 916	19 790	19 126	43 468	22 579	20 889
15 - 19	79 518	40 818	38 700	42 458	21 051	21 407	37 060	19 767	17 293
20 - 24	80 352	41 325	39 027	45 837	22 896	22 941	34 515	18 429	16 086
25 - 29	73 487	37 390	36 097	40 669	20 260	20 409	32 818	17 130	15 688
30 - 34	63 535	32 825	30 710	33 612	17 017	16 595	29 923	15 808	14 115
35 - 39	56 552	28 778	27 774	29 288	14 674	14 614	27 264	14 104	13 160
40 - 44	56 274	28 598	27 676	28 147	14 058	14 089	28 127	14 540	13 587
45 - 49	50 322	25 835	24 487	25 556	12 780	12 776	24 766	13 055	11 711
50 - 54	40 009	20 215	19 794	20 581	10 118	10 463	19 428	10 097	9 331
55 - 59	31 161	15 735	15 426	15 667	7 715	7 952	15 494	8 020	7 474
60 - 64	24 120	11 956	12 164	11 655	5 647	6 008	12 465	6 309	6 156
65 - 69	16 808	8 098	8 710	7 597	3 509	4 088	9 211	4 589	4 622
70 - 74	10 110	4 716	5 394	4 360	1 887	2 473	5 750	2 829	2 921
75 +	11 902	5 242	6 660	5 313	2 260	3 053	6 589	2 982	3 607
75 - 79	6 138	2 811	3 327	...	...	...	...	...	...
80 - 84	3 236	1 376	1 860	...	...	...	...	...	...
85 - 89	1 638	702	936	...	...	...	...	...	...
90 - 94	572	212	360	...	...	...	...	...	...
95 +	318	141	177	...	...	...	...	...	...
31 XII 2008 (ESDF)									
Total	842 621	430 418	412 203	...	...	...	...	...	...
0	16 852	8 808	8 044	...	...	...	...	...	...
1 - 4	67 137	34 726	32 411	...	...	...	...	...	...
5 - 9	77 959	40 425	37 534	...	...	...	...	...	...
10 - 14	80 218	41 292	38 926	...	...	...	...	...	...
15 - 19	79 267	40 768	38 499	...	...	...	...	...	...

7. Population by age, sex and urban/rural residence: latest available year, 2006 - 2015
Population selon l'âge, le sexe et la résidence, urbaine/rurale : dernière année disponible, 2006 - 2015 (continued - suite)

Continent, country or area, date, code[a] and age (in years) / Continent, pays ou zone, date, code[a] et âge (en années)	Total			Urban - Urbaine			Rural - Rurale		
	Both sexes Les deux sexes	Male Masculin	Female Féminin	Both sexes Les deux sexes	Male Masculin	Female Féminin	Both sexes Les deux sexes	Male Masculin	Female Féminin
OCEANIA - OCÉANIE									
Fiji - Fidji									
31 XII 2008 (ESDF)									
20 - 24	78 985	40 668	38 317	...	...	...	...	...	...
25 - 29	73 799	37 723	36 076	...	...	...	...	...	...
30 - 34	64 585	33 343	31 242	...	...	...	...	...	...
35 - 39	57 517	29 413	28 104	...	...	...	...	...	...
40 - 44	55 676	28 341	27 335	...	...	...	...	...	...
45 - 49	50 813	25 955	24 858	...	...	...	...	...	...
50 - 54	41 579	21 095	20 484	...	...	...	...	...	...
55 - 59	32 329	16 348	15 981	...	...	...	...	...	...
60 - 64	24 662	12 199	12 463	...	...	...	...	...	...
65 - 69	17 754	8 588	9 166	...	...	...	...	...	...
70 - 74	10 865	5 131	5 734	...	...	...	...	...	...
75 +	12 624	5 595	7 029	...	...	...	...	...	...
French Polynesia - Polynésie française									
1 I 2015 (ESDF)									
Total	271 796	138 447	133 349	...	...	...	...	...	...
0 - 4	21 691	10 938	10 753	...	...	...	...	...	...
5 - 9	21 973	11 252	10 721	...	...	...	...	...	...
10 - 14	22 896	11 732	11 164	...	...	...	...	...	...
15 - 19	22 653	11 795	10 858	...	...	...	...	...	...
20 - 24	22 850	11 623	11 227	...	...	...	...	...	...
25 - 29	21 204	10 534	10 670	...	...	...	...	...	...
30 - 34	20 789	10 380	10 409	...	...	...	...	...	...
35 - 39	19 482	9 864	9 618	...	...	...	...	...	...
40 - 44	20 216	10 302	9 914	...	...	...	...	...	...
45 - 49	19 623	10 189	9 434	...	...	...	...	...	...
50 - 54	16 540	8 602	7 938	...	...	...	...	...	...
55 - 59	13 167	6 942	6 225	...	...	...	...	...	...
60 - 64	9 849	5 079	4 770	...	...	...	...	...	...
65 - 69	7 193	3 653	3 540	...	...	...	...	...	...
70 - 74	5 309	2 699	2 610	...	...	...	...	...	...
75 - 79	3 346	1 565	1 781	...	...	...	...	...	...
80 +	3 015	1 298	1 717	...	...	...	...	...	...
Guam[28]									
1 VII 2015 (ESDJ)									
Total	161 785	81 978	79 807	...	...	...	...	...	...
0	2 707	1 393	1 314	...	...	...	...	...	...
1 - 4	10 843	5 576	5 267	...	...	...	...	...	...
5 - 9	13 534	6 959	6 575	...	...	...	...	...	...
10 - 14	14 122	7 261	6 861	...	...	...	...	...	...
15 - 19	14 079	7 376	6 703	...	...	...	...	...	...
20 - 24	13 429	6 891	6 538	...	...	...	...	...	...
25 - 29	11 918	6 004	5 914	...	...	...	...	...	...
30 - 34	10 316	5 190	5 126	...	...	...	...	...	...
35 - 39	9 885	5 013	4 872	...	...	...	...	...	...
40 - 44	10 533	5 323	5 210	...	...	...	...	...	...
45 - 49	10 531	5 455	5 076	...	...	...	...	...	...
50 - 54	10 291	5 330	4 961	...	...	...	...	...	...
55 - 59	8 296	4 211	4 085	...	...	...	...	...	...
60 - 64	6 919	3 444	3 475	...	...	...	...	...	...
65 - 69	5 510	2 694	2 816	...	...	...	...	...	...
70 - 74	3 379	1 619	1 760	...	...	...	...	...	...
75 - 79	2 737	1 189	1 548	...	...	...	...	...	...
80 - 84	1 673	663	1 010	...	...	...	...	...	...
85 - 89	745	288	457	...	...	...	...	...	...
90 - 94	271	85	186	...	...	...	...	...	...
95 - 99	61	13	48	...	...	...	...	...	...
100 +	6	1	5	...	...	...	...	...	...
Kiribati									
10 X 2010 (CDFC)									
Total	103 058	50 796	52 262	50 182	24 233	25 949	52 876	26 563	26 313
0 - 4	13 992	7 126	6 866	6 934	3 563	3 371	7 058	3 563	3 495
5 - 9	11 026	5 739	5 287	4 822	2 504	2 318	6 204	3 235	2 969

Continent, country or area, date, code[a] and age (in years) Continent, pays ou zone, date, code[a] et âge (en années)	Total			Urban - Urbaine			Rural - Rurale		
	Both sexes Les deux sexes	Male Masculin	Female Féminin	Both sexes Les deux sexes	Male Masculin	Female Féminin	Both sexes Les deux sexes	Male Masculin	Female Féminin
OCEANIA - OCÉANIE									
Kiribati									
10 X 2010 (CDFC)									
10 - 14	12 166	6 198	5 968	5 363	2 693	2 670	6 803	3 505	3 298
15 - 19	10 926	5 582	5 344	5 713	2 846	2 867	5 213	2 736	2 477
20 - 24	10 366	5 242	5 124	5 658	2 763	2 895	4 708	2 479	2 229
25 - 29	8 416	4 070	4 346	4 413	2 035	2 378	4 003	2 035	1 968
30 - 34	6 721	3 223	3 498	3 389	1 624	1 765	3 332	1 599	1 733
35 - 39	5 625	2 682	2 943	2 767	1 304	1 463	2 858	1 378	1 480
40 - 44	6 116	2 908	3 208	2 803	1 302	1 501	3 313	1 606	1 707
45 - 49	5 234	2 519	2 715	2 479	1 137	1 342	2 755	1 382	1 373
50 - 54	3 892	1 813	2 079	1 897	855	1 042	1 995	958	1 037
55 - 59	2 927	1 349	1 578	1 437	627	810	1 490	722	768
60 - 64	1 985	919	1 066	922	396	526	1 063	523	540
65 - 69	1 520	642	878	700	278	422	820	364	456
70 - 74	1 108	428	680	438	161	277	670	267	403
75 - 79	637	223	414	264	89	175	373	134	239
80 - 84	272	97	175	119	41	78	153	56	97
85 - 89	89	25	64	48	11	37	41	14	27
90 - 94	29	9	20	15	4	11	14	5	9
95 +	11	2	9	1	-	1	10	2	8
Marshall Islands - Îles Marshall[85]									
1 VII 2010 (ESDF)									
Total	54 305	27 843	26 462	...	...	...	...	...	...
0 - 4	7 899	4 053	3 846	...	...	...	...	...	...
5 - 9	7 131	3 660	3 470	...	...	...	...	...	...
10 - 14	7 207	3 732	3 475	...	...	...	...	...	...
15 - 19	6 120	3 126	2 993	...	...	...	...	...	...
20 - 24	6 347	3 310	3 038	...	...	...	...	...	...
25 - 29	4 808	2 478	2 330	...	...	...	...	...	...
30 - 34	2 761	1 389	1 372	...	...	...	...	...	...
35 - 39	2 128	1 071	1 058	...	...	...	...	...	...
40 - 44	2 039	1 043	996	...	...	...	...	...	...
45 - 49	2 023	1 025	998	...	...	...	...	...	...
50 - 54	1 814	878	936	...	...	...	...	...	...
55 - 59	1 592	854	737	...	...	...	...	...	...
60 - 64	1 089	573	516	...	...	...	...	...	...
65 - 69	572	299	273	...	...	...	...	...	...
70 - 74	361	165	196	...	...	...	...	...	...
75 +	412	184	228	...	...	...	...	...	...
Micronesia (Federated States of) - Micronésie (États fédérés de)[2]									
1 VII 2015 (ESDJ)									
Total	105 830	52 883	52 947	...	...	...	...	...	...
0 - 4	11 865	6 079	5 786	...	...	...	...	...	...
5 - 9	12 365	6 323	6 042	...	...	...	...	...	...
10 - 14	12 243	6 248	5 995	...	...	...	...	...	...
15 - 19	10 782	5 471	5 311	...	...	...	...	...	...
20 - 24	8 344	4 194	4 150	...	...	...	...	...	...
25 - 29	6 945	3 590	3 355	...	...	...	...	...	...
30 - 34	6 753	3 291	3 462	...	...	...	...	...	...
35 - 39	5 731	2 841	2 890	...	...	...	...	...	...
40 - 44	5 911	2 754	3 157	...	...	...	...	...	...
45 - 49	5 485	2 554	2 931	...	...	...	...	...	...
50 - 54	5 242	2 576	2 666	...	...	...	...	...	...
55 - 59	4 823	2 415	2 408	...	...	...	...	...	...
60 - 64	3 887	1 978	1 909	...	...	...	...	...	...
65 - 69	2 492	1 253	1 239	...	...	...	...	...	...
70 - 74	1 285	580	705	...	...	...	...	...	...
75 +	1 677	736	941	...	...	...	...	...	...

Continent, country or area, date, code[a] and age (in years) Continent, pays ou zone, date, code[a] et âge (en annèes)	Total			Urban - Urbaine			Rural - Rurale		
	Both sexes Les deux sexes	Male Masculin	Female Féminin	Both sexes Les deux sexes	Male Masculin	Female Féminin	Both sexes Les deux sexes	Male Masculin	Female Féminin
OCEANIA - OCÉANIE									
New Caledonia - Nouvelle-Calédonie									
1 I 2013 (ESDF)									
Total	260 000	131 481	128 519	...	...	...	...	...	...
0 - 4	20 127	10 368	9 759	...	...	...	...	...	...
5 - 9	20 576	10 626	9 950	...	...	...	...	...	...
10 - 14	22 365	11 403	10 962	...	...	...	...	...	...
15 - 19	21 998	11 335	10 663	...	...	...	...	...	...
20 - 24	18 654	9 516	9 138	...	...	...	...	...	...
25 - 29	19 636	9 907	9 729	...	...	...	...	...	...
30 - 34	19 598	9 756	9 842	...	...	...	...	...	...
35 - 39	19 744	9 830	9 914	...	...	...	...	...	...
40 - 44	20 071	10 103	9 968	...	...	...	...	...	...
45 - 49	17 926	9 111	8 815	...	...	...	...	...	...
50 - 54	14 975	7 562	7 413	...	...	...	...	...	...
55 - 59	12 082	6 147	5 935	...	...	...	...	...	...
60 - 64	10 143	5 267	4 876	...	...	...	...	...	...
65 - 69	8 172	4 197	3 975	...	...	...	...	...	...
70 - 74	5 932	2 834	3 098	...	...	...	...	...	...
75 - 79	3 830	1 812	2 018	...	...	...	...	...	...
80 - 84	2 403	1 028	1 375	...	...	...	...	...	...
85 - 89	1 205	471	734	...	...	...	...	...	...
90 - 94	402	153	249	...	...	...	...	...	...
95 +	161	55	106	...	...	...	...	...	...
New Zealand - Nouvelle-Zélande[86]									
1 VII 2015 (ESDJ)									
Total	4 595 700	2 257 200	2 338 500	3 959 200[87]	1 931 800[87]	2 027 400[87]	635 900[87]	325 000[87]	310 900[87]
0	59 120	30 440	28 670	51 730[87]	26 670[87]	25 060[87]	7 380[87]	3 770[87]	3 610[87]
1 - 4	246 630	126 430	120 200	214 200[87]	109 850[87]	104 350[87]	32 420[87]	16 570[87]	15 850[87]
5 - 9	315 130	161 780	153 350	267 830[87]	137 470[87]	130 360[87]	47 290[87]	24 310[87]	22 980[87]
10 - 14	293 470	150 090	143 390	247 640[87]	126 490[87]	121 150[87]	45 810[87]	23 590[87]	22 230[87]
15 - 19	316 800	163 470	153 330	275 600[87]	141 540[87]	134 060[87]	41 180[87]	21 920[87]	19 260[87]
20 - 24	338 660	175 450	163 200	307 000[87]	157 860[87]	149 140[87]	31 640[87]	17 590[87]	14 050[87]
25 - 29	312 310	155 560	156 760	283 190[87]	140 530[87]	142 660[87]	29 100[87]	15 020[87]	14 090[87]
30 - 34	286 990	138 500	148 490	257 620[87]	124 020[87]	133 600[87]	29 340[87]	14 470[87]	14 870[87]
35 - 39	273 780	130 850	142 930	240 230[87]	114 570[87]	125 670[87]	33 520[87]	16 280[87]	17 240[87]
40 - 44	309 250	146 870	162 380	264 680[87]	125 130[87]	139 550[87]	44 540[87]	21 720[87]	22 820[87]
45 - 49	313 250	150 060	163 190	264 150[87]	125 900[87]	138 250[87]	49 050[87]	24 130[87]	24 920[87]
50 - 54	318 530	153 890	164 650	264 840[87]	127 000[87]	137 840[87]	53 620[87]	26 850[87]	26 780[87]
55 - 59	287 300	139 450	147 850	236 110[87]	113 550[87]	122 560[87]	51 090[87]	25 840[87]	25 250[87]
60 - 64	250 150	121 650	128 500	205 120[87]	98 450[87]	106 670[87]	44 920[87]	23 130[87]	21 790[87]
65 - 69	225 740	110 220	115 510	186 130[87]	89 410[87]	96 720[87]	39 520[87]	20 760[87]	18 760[87]
70 - 74	165 200	79 580	85 620	139 040[87]	65 660[87]	73 370[87]	26 110[87]	13 880[87]	12 230[87]
75 - 79	120 100	56 080	64 010	104 540[87]	47 820[87]	56 720[87]	15 530[87]	8 240[87]	7 290[87]
80 - 84	83 240	37 210	46 030	75 030[87]	32 880[87]	42 150[87]	8 200[87]	4 320[87]	3 880[87]
85 +	80 080	29 610	50 470	74 470[87]	26 980[87]	47 500[87]	5 600[87]	2 620[87]	2 980[87]
85 - 89	52 500	20 990	31 500	...	...	...	...	...	...
90 +	27 580	8 610	18 970	...	...	...	...	...	...
Niue - Nioué									
1 VII 2010 (ESDJ)									
Total	1 496	754[88]	740[88]	...	...	...	...	...	...
0 - 4	135	69[88]	64[88]	...	...	...	...	...	...
5 - 9	134	58	76	...	...	...	...	...	...
10 - 14	116	60	56	...	...	...	...	...	...
15 - 19	124	79	45	...	...	...	...	...	...
20 - 24	100	50	50	...	...	...	...	...	...
25 - 29	90	38	52	...	...	...	...	...	...
30 - 34	71	39	32	...	...	...	...	...	...
35 - 39	85	45	40	...	...	...	...	...	...
40 - 44	101	55	46	...	...	...	...	...	...
45 - 49	92	42	50	...	...	...	...	...	...
50 - 54	107	58	49	...	...	...	...	...	...
55 - 59	89	42	47	...	...	...	...	...	...

7. Population by age, sex and urban/rural residence: latest available year, 2006 - 2015
Population selon l'âge, le sexe et la résidence, urbaine/rurale : dernière année disponible, 2006 - 2015 (continued - suite)

Continent, country or area, date, code[a] and age (in years) / Continent, pays ou zone, date, code[a] et âge (en années)	Total			Urban - Urbaine			Rural - Rurale		
	Both sexes Les deux sexes	Male Masculin	Female Féminin	Both sexes Les deux sexes	Male Masculin	Female Féminin	Both sexes Les deux sexes	Male Masculin	Female Féminin
OCEANIA - OCÉANIE									
Niue - Nioué									
1 VII 2010 (ESDJ)									
60 - 64	70	34	36	...	...	...	...	...	...
65 - 69	75	37	38	...	...	...	...	...	...
70 - 74	53	23	30	...	...	...	...	...	...
75 +	54	25	29	...	...	...	...	...	...
Norfolk Island - Île Norfolk									
9 VIII 2011 (CDFC)									
Total	2 302	1 082	1 220	...	...	...	...	...	...
0 - 4	106	53	53	...	...	...	...	...	...
5 - 9	123	63	60	...	...	...	...	...	...
10 - 14	132	69	63	...	...	...	...	...	...
15 - 19	73	35	38	...	...	...	...	...	...
20 - 24	41	20	21	...	...	...	...	...	...
25 - 29	60	19	41	...	...	...	...	...	...
30 - 34	100	48	52	...	...	...	...	...	...
35 - 39	127	56	71	...	...	...	...	...	...
40 - 44	146	64	82	...	...	...	...	...	...
45 - 49	167	81	86	...	...	...	...	...	...
50 - 54	180	86	94	...	...	...	...	...	...
55 - 59	232	103	129	...	...	...	...	...	...
60 - 64	262	120	142	...	...	...	...	...	...
65 - 69	205	99	106	...	...	...	...	...	...
70 - 74	142	70	72	...	...	...	...	...	...
75 - 79	96	49	47	...	...	...	...	...	...
80 - 84	58	24	34	...	...	...	...	...	...
85 +	52	23	29	...	...	...	...	...	...
Northern Mariana Islands - Îles Mariannes septentrionales									
1 VII 2011 (ESDF)									
Total	46 050	22 153	23 897	...	...	...	...	...	...
0 - 4	4 852	2 495	2 357	...	...	...	...	...	...
5 - 9	3 622	1 883	1 739	...	...	...	...	...	...
10 - 14	3 500	1 971	1 529	...	...	...	...	...	...
15 - 19	3 802	2 121	1 681	...	...	...	...	...	...
20 - 24	3 398	1 607	1 791	...	...	...	...	...	...
25 - 29	3 831	1 050	2 781	...	...	...	...	...	...
30 - 34	3 696	1 008	2 688	...	...	...	...	...	...
35 - 39	3 211	1 550	1 661	...	...	...	...	...	...
40 - 44	3 584	1 858	1 726	...	...	...	...	...	...
45 - 49	3 738	1 967	1 771	...	...	...	...	...	...
50 - 54	3 441	1 824	1 617	...	...	...	...	...	...
55 - 59	2 270	1 260	1 010	...	...	...	...	...	...
60 - 64	1 440	769	671	...	...	...	...	...	...
65 - 69	794	366	428	...	...	...	...	...	...
70 - 74	416	248	168	...	...	...	...	...	...
75 - 79	239	101	138	...	...	...	...	...	...
80 - 84	147	54	93	...	...	...	...	...	...
85 - 89	53	17	36	...	...	...	...	...	...
90 - 94	14	3	11	...	...	...	...	...	...
95 - 99	1	1	-	...	...	...	...	...	...
100 +	1	-	1	...	...	...	...	...	...
Palau - Palaos									
13 IV 2015 (CDJC)									
Total	17 661	9 433	8 228	14 209	7 620	6 589	3 452	1 813	1 639
0 - 4	1 200	653	547	962	528	434	238	125	113
5 - 9	1 219	614	605	932	483	449	287	131	156
10 - 14	1 209	636	573	916	489	427	293	147	146
15 - 19	1 201	624	577	975	495	480	226	129	97
20 - 24	1 195	687	508	1 018	587	431	177	100	77
25 - 29	1 217	694	523	1 041	581	460	176	113	63
30 - 34	1 338	759	579	1 163	661	502	175	98	77
35 - 39	1 420	813	607	1 215	701	514	205	112	93
40 - 44	1 501	861	640	1 235	715	520	266	146	120

7. Population by age, sex and urban/rural residence: latest available year, 2006 - 2015
Population selon l'âge, le sexe et la résidence, urbaine/rurale : dernière année disponible, 2006 - 2015 (continued - suite)

Continent, country or area, date, code[a] and age (in years) / Continent, pays ou zone, date, code[a] et âge (en années)	Total			Urban - Urbaine			Rural - Rurale		
	Both sexes Les deux sexes	Male Masculin	Female Féminin	Both sexes Les deux sexes	Male Masculin	Female Féminin	Both sexes Les deux sexes	Male Masculin	Female Féminin
OCEANIA - OCÉANIE									
Palau - Palaos									
13 IV 2015 (CDJC)									
45 - 49	1 538	820	718	1 248	657	591	290	163	127
50 - 54	1 363	708	655	1 067	549	518	296	159	137
55 - 59	1 126	605	521	856	459	397	270	146	124
60 - 64	851	432	419	641	318	323	210	114	96
65 - 69	554	271	283	414	202	212	140	69	71
70 - 74	314	137	177	233	106	127	81	31	50
75 +	415	119	296	293	89	204	122	30	92
Pitcairn									
31 XII 2013 (CDJC)									
Total	49	23	26	...	...	...	...	...	...
0 - 17	8	3	5	...	...	...	...	...	...
18 - 40	7	4	3	...	...	...	...	...	...
41 - 64	24	13	11	...	...	...	...	...	...
65 +	10	3	7	...	...	...	...	...	...
Samoa									
7 XI 2011 (CDFC)									
Total	187 820	96 990	90 830	...	...	...	...	...	...
0 - 4	26 829	13 953	12 876	...	...	...	...	...	...
5 - 9	23 044	11 899	11 145	...	...	...	...	...	...
10 - 14	22 017	11 497	10 520	...	...	...	...	...	...
15 - 19	19 814	10 391	9 423	...	...	...	...	...	...
20 - 24	14 833	7 700	7 133	...	...	...	...	...	...
25 - 29	12 767	6 601	6 166	...	...	...	...	...	...
30 - 34	11 543	5 945	5 598	...	...	...	...	...	...
35 - 39	10 877	5 735	5 142	...	...	...	...	...	...
40 - 44	10 436	5 602	4 834	...	...	...	...	...	...
45 - 49	8 887	4 574	4 313	...	...	...	...	...	...
50 - 54	7 576	3 966	3 610	...	...	...	...	...	...
55 - 59	5 904	3 007	2 897	...	...	...	...	...	...
60 - 64	3 978	2 002	1 976	...	...	...	...	...	...
65 - 69	3 374	1 605	1 769	...	...	...	...	...	...
70 - 74	2 557	1 187	1 370	...	...	...	...	...	...
75 +	3 354	1 302	2 052	...	...	...	...	...	...
Unknown - Inconnu	30	24	6	...	...	...	...	...	...
Solomon Islands - Îles Salomon									
22 XI 2009 (CDFC)									
Total	515 870	264 455	251 415	102 030	53 596	48 434	413 840	210 859	202 981
0 - 4	76 227	39 728	36 499	12 500	6 573	5 927	63 727	33 155	30 572
5 - 9	71 126	36 974	34 152	11 328	5 853	5 475	59 798	31 121	28 677
10 - 14	61 931	32 562	29 369	10 354	5 382	4 972	51 577	27 180	24 397
15 - 19	51 212	26 189	25 023	10 995	5 525	5 470	40 217	20 664	19 553
20 - 24	45 419	22 399	23 020	12 344	6 360	5 984	33 075	16 039	17 036
25 - 29	42 674	20 794	21 880	11 160	5 696	5 464	31 514	15 098	16 416
30 - 34	37 592	18 807	18 785	8 817	4 568	4 249	28 775	14 239	14 536
35 - 39	33 151	17 010	16 141	7 447	4 000	3 447	25 704	13 010	12 694
40 - 44	23 638	12 070	11 568	5 161	2 808	2 353	18 477	9 262	9 215
45 - 49	19 713	10 189	9 524	4 064	2 265	1 799	15 649	7 924	7 725
50 - 54	14 339	7 498	6 841	2 818	1 650	1 168	11 521	5 848	5 673
55 - 59	11 787	6 111	5 676	2 011	1 198	813	9 776	4 913	4 863
60 - 64	8 916	4 535	4 381	1 272	726	546	7 644	3 809	3 835
65 - 69	7 021	3 693	3 328	822	466	356	6 199	3 227	2 972
70 - 74	4 698	2 402	2 296	478	259	219	4 220	2 143	2 077
75 - 79	3 374	1 784	1 590	279	160	119	3 095	1 624	1 471
80 - 84	1 525	800	725	102	58	44	1 423	742	681
85 - 89	894	512	382	58	34	24	836	478	358
90 - 94	301	170	131	8	4	4	293	166	127
95 - 99	332	228	104	12	11	1	320	217	103
Tokelau - Tokélaou									
1 XII 2013 (ESDF)									
Total	*1 383*	*683*	*700*	...	...	...	...	...	...
0	*25*	*12*	*13*	...	...	...	...	...	...
1 - 4	*115*	*62*	*53*	...	...	...	...	...	...

Continent, country or area, date, code[a] and age (in years) Continent, pays ou zone, date, code[a] et âge (en années)	Total			Urban - Urbaine			Rural - Rurale		
	Both sexes Les deux sexes	Male Masculin	Female Féminin	Both sexes Les deux sexes	Male Masculin	Female Féminin	Both sexes Les deux sexes	Male Masculin	Female Féminin
OCEANIA - OCÉANIE									
Tokelau - Tokélaou									
1 XII 2013 (ESDF)									
5 - 9	139	75	64	...	...	...	...	...	...
10 - 14	134	64	70	...	...	...	...	...	...
15 - 19	142	76	66	...	...	...	...	...	...
20 - 24	130	57	73	...	...	...	...	...	...
25 - 29	93	40	53	...	...	...	...	...	...
30 - 34	78	43	35	...	...	...	...	...	...
35 - 39	59	28	31	...	...	...	...	...	...
40 - 44	75	39	36	...	...	...	...	...	...
45 - 49	84	41	43	...	...	...	...	...	...
50 - 54	66	32	34	...	...	...	...	...	...
55 - 59	63	28	35	...	...	...	...	...	...
60 - 64	62	29	33	...	...	...	...	...	...
65 - 69	34	18	16	...	...	...	...	...	...
70 - 74	32	14	18	...	...	...	...	...	...
75 +	31	13	18	...	...	...	...	...	...
Unknown - Inconnu	21	12	9	...	...	...	...	...	...
Tonga									
30 XI 2006 (CDJC)									
Total	101 991	51 772	50 219	23 658	11 860	11 798	78 333	39 912	38 421
0 - 4	13 782	7 174	6 608	3 015	1 514	1 501	10 767	5 660	5 107
5 - 9	12 804	6 745	6 059	2 721	1 447	1 274	10 083	5 298	4 785
10 - 14	12 320	6 412	5 908	2 631	1 357	1 274	9 689	5 055	4 634
15 - 19	10 280	5 383	4 897	2 362	1 196	1 166	7 918	4 187	3 731
20 - 24	9 191	4 648	4 543	2 503	1 276	1 227	6 688	3 372	3 316
25 - 29	7 304	3 639	3 665	1 872	913	959	5 432	2 726	2 706
30 - 34	6 337	3 146	3 191	1 551	787	764	4 786	2 359	2 427
35 - 39	6 229	3 112	3 117	1 448	711	737	4 781	2 401	2 380
40 - 44	5 014	2 578	2 436	1 240	647	593	3 774	1 931	1 843
45 - 49	3 982	1 923	2 059	982	458	524	3 000	1 465	1 535
50 - 54	3 465	1 634	1 831	844	406	438	2 621	1 228	1 393
55 - 59	2 849	1 359	1 490	639	323	316	2 210	1 036	1 174
60 - 64	2 470	1 169	1 301	556	260	296	1 914	909	1 005
65 - 69	2 174	1 092	1 082	466	211	255	1 708	881	827
70 - 74	1 586	777	809	340	152	188	1 246	625	621
75 - 79	1 099	510	589	253	107	146	846	403	443
80 - 84	625	260	365	144	48	96	481	212	269
85 - 89	246	96	150	45	21	24	201	75	126
90 - 94	86	22	64	15	5	10	71	17	54
95 - 99	20	6	14	5	2	3	15	4	11
100 +	6	-	6	-	-	-	6	-	6
Unknown - Inconnu	122	87	35	26	19	7	96	68	28
1 VII 2008 (ESDF)[89]									
Total	103 647	52 972	50 673	...	...	...	...	...	...
0 - 4	11 970	6 164	5 806	...	...	...	...	...	...
5 - 9	11 419	5 910	5 508	...	...	...	...	...	...
10 - 14	11 968	6 212	5 756	...	...	...	...	...	...
15 - 19	11 383	6 060	5 323	...	...	...	...	...	...
20 - 24	10 612	5 573	5 040	...	...	...	...	...	...
25 - 29	8 609	4 406	4 204	...	...	...	...	...	...
30 - 34	5 874	2 955	2 919	...	...	...	...	...	...
35 - 39	5 397	2 718	2 680	...	...	...	...	...	...
40 - 44	5 250	2 661	2 590	...	...	...	...	...	...
45 - 49	4 471	2 186	2 285	...	...	...	...	...	...
50 - 54	3 914	1 867	2 047	...	...	...	...	...	...
55 - 59	3 294	1 556	1 737	...	...	...	...	...	...
60 - 64	2 844	1 355	1 489	...	...	...	...	...	...
65 - 69	2 482	1 243	1 239	...	...	...	...	...	...
70 - 74	1 896	981	915	...	...	...	...	...	...
75 +	2 263	1 127	1 136	...	...	...	...	...	...
Vanuatu									
16 XI 2009 (CDJC)									
Total	234 023	119 091	114 932	57 195	29 618	27 577	176 828	89 473	87 355
0 - 4	33 367	17 310	16 057	7 224	3 828	3 396	26 143	13 482	12 661

Continent, country or area, date, code[a] and age (in years) / Continent, pays ou zone, date, code[a] et âge (en années)	Total			Urban - Urbaine			Rural - Rurale		
	Both sexes Les deux sexes	Male Masculin	Female Féminin	Both sexes Les deux sexes	Male Masculin	Female Féminin	Both sexes Les deux sexes	Male Masculin	Female Féminin
OCEANIA - OCÉANIE									
Vanuatu									
16 XI 2009 (CDJC)									
5 - 9	29 685	15 455	14 230	5 591	2 850	2 741	24 094	12 605	11 489
10 - 14	27 921	14 762	13 159	5 250	2 755	2 495	22 671	12 007	10 664
15 - 19	23 882	12 027	11 855	6 460	3 122	3 338	17 422	8 905	8 517
20 - 24	21 541	10 415	11 126	7 186	3 606	3 580	14 355	6 809	7 546
25 - 29	18 415	9 124	9 291	5 542	2 937	2 605	12 873	6 187	6 686
30 - 34	15 693	7 790	7 903	4 517	2 300	2 217	11 176	5 490	5 686
35 - 39	14 171	7 076	7 095	3 844	1 965	1 879	10 327	5 111	5 216
40 - 44	11 523	5 814	5 709	3 242	1 710	1 532	8 281	4 104	4 177
45 - 49	10 241	5 066	5 175	2 817	1 474	1 343	7 424	3 592	3 832
50 - 54	7 415	3 789	3 626	1 923	1 036	887	5 492	2 753	2 739
55 - 59	6 363	3 261	3 102	1 495	845	650	4 868	2 416	2 452
60 - 64	4 319	2 192	2 127	826	455	371	3 493	1 737	1 756
65 - 69	3 826	2 054	1 772	590	355	235	3 236	1 699	1 537
70 +	5 661	2 956	2 705	688	380	308	4 973	2 576	2 397

FOOTNOTES - NOTES

Italics: estimates which are less reliable. - Italiques : estimations moins sûres.

* Provisional. - Données provisoires.

[a] 'Code' indicates the source of data, as follows:
CDFC - Census, de facto, complete tabulation
CDFS - Census, de facto, sample tabulation
CDJC - Census, de jure, complete tabulation
CDJS - Census, de jure, sample tabulation
SSDF - Sample survey, de facto
SSDJ - Sample survey, de jure
ESDF - Estimates, de facto
ESDJ - Estimates, de jure

Le 'Code' indique la source des données, comme suit :
CDFC - Recensement, population de fait, tabulation complète
CDFS - Recensement, population de fait, tabulation par sondage
CDJC - Recensement, population de droit, tabulation complète
CDJS - Recensement, population de droit, tabulation par sondage
SSDF - Enquête par sondage, population de fait
SSDJ - Enquête par sondage, population de droit
ESDF - Estimations, population de fait
ESDJ - Estimations, population de droit

[1] Data refer to population in housing units and collective living quarters only. - Correspond aux personnes qui vivent dans des unités d'habitation et dans des logements collectifs seulement.
[2] Data refer to national projections. - Les données se réfèrent aux projections nationales.
[3] Data refer to projections based on the 2013 Population Census. - Les données se réfèrent aux projections basées sur le recensement de la population de 2013.
[4] Postcensal estimates. - Estimations post censitaires.
[5] Post-censal estimates based on the 2009 Population Census. - Les estimations post-censitaire fondées sur le recensement de la population de 2009.
[6] Projections considering also 2009 Population Census results. - Projections en prennant en considération les résultats du recensement de la population de 2009.
[7] Including nomadic population. - Y compris la population nomade.
[8] Excludes the islands of St. Brandon and Agalega. - Non compris les îles St. Brandon et Agalega.
[9] Based on the results of the 2011 Population Census. - Basé sur les résultats du recencement de la population de 2011.

[10] Based on the results of the 2004 Population Census. - D'après des résultats du recensement de la population de 2004.
[11] Data refer to projections based on the 2011 Population Census. - Les données se réfèrent aux projections basées sur le recensement de la population de 2011.
[12] Data refer to national projections. Based on the results of the 2012 Population and Housing Census. - Les données se réfèrent aux projections nationales. D'après les résultats du recensement de la population et des logements de 2012.
[13] Projections based on the 2012 Population Census. - Projections fondées sur le recensement de la population de 2012.
[14] Projections based on the 2002 Population Census. - Projections fondées sur le recensement de la population de 2002.
[15] Data as reported by national statistical authorities. Summation of frequencies gives a different total; reason for discrepancy not ascertained. - Les données comme elles ont été déclarées par l'institut national de la statistique. La somme des fréquences un total différent; on ne sait pas comment s'explique la divergence.
[16] Bermuda is 100 per cent urban. - 100 pour cent de la population des Bermudes est urbaine.
[17] Data refer to projections based on the 2010 Population Census. - Les données se réfèrent aux projections basées sur le recensement de la population de 2010.
[18] Updated postcensal estimates. - Estimations post censitaires mises à jour.
[19] Based on the national household survey of 2015. - Basée sur l' enquête nationale auprès des ménages de 2015.
[20] Estimates based on the 2007 Population Census. - Estimations fondées sur le recensement de la population de 2007.
[21] Population statistics are compiled from registers. - Les statistiques de la population sont compilées à partir des registres.
[22] Excluding data for Saint Barthélemy and Saint Martin. - Non compris les données pour Saint Barthélémy et Saint Martin.
[23] Projections produced by l'Institut Haïtien de Statistique et d'Informatique (IHSI) and the Latin American and Caribbean Demographic Centre (CELADE) - Population Division of ECLAC. - Les données sont projections produits par l'Institut Haïtien de Statistique et d'Informatique (IHSI) et le centre démographique de l'Amérique latine et les Caraïbes - Division de la population de la CEPALC.
[24] Including an estimation of 1 334 585 persons corresponding to 448 195 housing units without information of the occupants. - Y compris une estimation de 1 334 585 personnes correspondant aux 448 195 unités d'habitation sans information sur les occupants.
[25] Including armed forces stationed in the area. Based on the results of the 2010 Population Census. - Y compris les militaires en garnison sur le territoire. D'après le résultat du recensement de la population de 2010.
[26] Because of rounding, totals are not in all cases the sum of the respective components. Unrevised data. - Les chiffres étant arrondis, les totaux ne

correspondent pas toujours rigoureusement à la somme des composants respectifs. Les données n'ont pas été révisées.

27 Excluding U.S. Armed Forces overseas and civilian U.S. citizens whose usual place of residence is outside the United States. Postcensal estimates. - Non compris les militaires américains à l'étranger et les civils américains dont le lieu de résidence habituel est en dehors des États-Unis. Estimations post censitaires.

28 Including armed forces stationed in the area. - Y compris les militaires en garnison sur le territoire.

29 Data refer to projections based on the 2010 Population and Housing Census. - Les données se réfèrent aux projections basées sur le recensement 2010 de la population et des logements.

30 Data include persons in remote areas, military personnel outside the country, merchant seamen at sea, civilian seasonal workers outside the country, and other civilians outside the country, and exclude nomads, foreign military, civilian aliens temporarily in the country, transients on ships and Indian jungle population. Data refer to national projections. - Y compris les personnes vivant dans des régions éloignées, le personel militaire en dehors du pays, les marins marchands, les ouvriers saisonniers en dehors du pays, et autres civils en dehors du pays, et non compris les nomades, les militaires étrangers, les étrangers civils temporairement dans le pays, les transiteurs sur des bateaux et les Indiens de la jungle. Les données se réfèrent aux projections nationales.

31 Data are revised projections taking into consideration also the results of the 2005 census. - Les données sont des projections révisées tenant compte également des résultats du recensement de 2005.

32 Excludes nomadic Indian tribes. Data refer to projections based on the 2010 Population Census. - Non compris les tribus d'Indiens nomades. Les données se réfèrent aux projections basées sur le recensement de la population de 2010.

33 A dispute exists between the governments of Argentina and the United Kingdom of Great Britain and Northern Ireland concerning sovereignty over the Falkland Islands (Malvinas). Excluding military personnel and their families, visitors and transients. - La souveraineté sur les îles Falkland (Malvinas) fait l'objet d'un différend entre le Gouvernement argentin et le Gouvernement du Royaume-Uni de Grande-Bretagne et d'Irlande du Nord. Non compris les militaires et leur familles, ni les visiteurs et transients.

34 Unrevised data. - Les données n'ont pas été révisées.

35 Excluding 437 homeless persons. - On n'a pas pris en compte 437 personnes sans abri.

36 Data refer to the settled population based on the 1979 Population Census and the latest household prelisting. The refugees of Afghanistan in Iran, Pakistan, and an estimated 1.5 million nomads, are not included. - Les données se rapportent à la population stationnaire sur la base du recensement de 1979 et du recensement préliminaire des logements le plus récent. Sont exclus les réfugiés d'Afghanistan en Iran et au Pakistan et les nomades estimés à 1,5 million.

37 Including "Other Urban" (Total of Both Sexes-6094394, Male-3127003, Female-29673941). - Y compris "Autres citadins" (total des deux sexes 6 094 394; hommes : 3 127 003; femmes: 2 967 391).

38 Data refer to projected figures based on the Population and Housing Census 2005 (district projection). - Les données se réfèrent aux projections basées sur le recensement de la population et de l'habitat de 2005 (projections locales).

39 Excluding foreign diplomatic personnel and their dependants. Data based on the 2008 Population Census. - Non compris le personnel diplomatique étranger et les membres de leur famille les accompagnant. Données fondées sur le recensement de population de 2008.

40 For statistical purposes, the data for China do not include those for the Hong Kong Special Administrative Region (Hong Kong SAR), Macao Special Administrative Region (Macao SAR) and Taiwan province of China. - Pour la présentation des statistiques, les données pour la Chine ne comprennent pas les données pour la Région Administrative Spéciale de Hong Kong (Hong Kong RAS), la Région Administrative Spéciale de Macao (Macao RAS) et Taïwan province de Chine.

41 Data exclude 2.3 million servicemen, 4.65 million persons with permanent resident status difficult to define, and 0.12 per cent undercount based on the post enumeration survey. - Les données ne comprennent pas 2,3 millions de militaires, 4,65 millions de personnes ayant le statut de résident permanent mais difficiles à définir, et des lacunes estimées à 0,12 pour cent sur la base de l'enquête de vérification du recensement.

42 Because of rounding, totals are not in all cases the sum of the respective components. Data have been adjusted on the basis of the Population Census of 2010. - Les chiffres étant arrondis, les totaux ne correspondent pas toujours rigoureusement à la somme des composants respectifs. Les données ont été ajustées à partir des résultats du recensement de la population de 2010.

43 Data refer to government controlled areas. - Les données se rapportent aux zones contrôlées par le Gouvernement.

44 Includes data for the Indian-held part of Jammu and Kashmir, the final status of which has not yet been determined. - Y compris les données pour la partie du Jammu et du Cachemire occupée par l'Inde dont le statut définitif n'a pas encore été déterminé.

45 Data refer to the 2015 Intercensal Survey. - Les données concernent l'enquête intercensitaire de 2015.

46 Data refer to the Iranian Year which begins on 21 March and ends on 20 March of the following year. - Les données concernent l'année iranienne, qui commence le 21 mars et se termine le 20 mars de l'année suivante.

47 Because of rounding, totals are not in all cases the sum of the respective components. Includes data for East Jerusalem and Israeli residents in certain other territories under occupation by Israeli military forces since June 1967. - Les chiffres étant arrondis, les totaux ne correspondent pas toujours rigoureusement à la somme des composants respectifs. Y compris les données pour Jérusalem-Est et les résidents israéliens dans certains autres territoires occupés depuis 1967 par les forces armées israéliennes.

48 Excluding diplomatic personnel outside the country and foreign military and civilian personnel and their dependants stationed in the area. - Non compris le personnel diplomatique hors du pays ni les militaires et agents civils étrangers en poste sur le territoire et les membres de leur famille les accompagnant.

49 Because of rounding, totals are not in all cases the sum of the respective components. Estimates based on the complete counts of the 2010 Population Census. - Les chiffres étant arrondis, les totaux ne correspondent pas toujours rigoureusement à la somme des composants respectifs. Estimations basées sur le dénombrement complet du recensement de la population de 2010.

50 Excluding data for Jordanian territory under occupation since June 1967 by Israeli military forces. - Non compris les données pour le territoire jordanien occupé depuis juin 1967 par les forces armées israéliennes.

51 Data refer to annual average population. - Les données correspondent à la population annuelle moyenne.

52 Based on the results of a household survey. - D'après les résultats d'une enquête de ménages.

53 Estimates based on the adjusted Population and Housing Census of 2010. - Les estimations sont fondée sur les résultats ajustées du recensement de la population et de l'habitat de 2010.

54 Data refer to resident population that includes Maldivians and foreigners. - Les données concernent la population résidente, qui comprend des Maldiviens et des étrangers.

55 Data refer to enumerated population. - Les données se rapportent à la population dénombrée.

56 Data refer to registered population data from Royal Oman Police. - Les données portent sur la population enregistrée par la police royale de l'Oman.

57 Excluding data for the Pakistan-held part of Jammu and Kashmir, the final status of which has not yet been determined. Based on the results of the Pakistan Demographic Survey (PDS 2007). - Non compris les données concernant la partie du Jammu et Cachemire occupée par le Pakistan dont le statut définitif n'a pas été déterminé. D'après les résultats de l'enquête démographique effectuée par le Pakistan en 2007.

58 Excluding 2739 Filipinos in Philippine Embassies, Consulates and Missions Abroad. - Excepté 2739 Philippins travaillant dans les ambassades, les consulats et les missions des Philippines à l'étranger.

59 Data refer to Korean population only. - les données ne concernent que la population coréenne.

60 Data refer to resident population which comprises Singapore citizens and permanent residents. - Les données se rapportent à la population résidente composé des citoyens de Singapour et des résidents permanents.

61 Data have not been adjusted for underenumeration. Excluding data from the parts of Jerusalem which were annexed by Israel in 1967. - Les données n'ont pas été ajustées pour compenser les lacunes du dénombrement. Non compris les données provenant des parties de Jérusalem qui ont été annexées par Israël en 1967.

62 Data for urban include population in refugee camps. - Les données pour la population urbaine comprennent la population dans les camps réfugiés.

63 Including Palestinian refugees. - Y compris les réfugiés de Palestine.

64 Data based on address-based population registration system. - Les données sont basées sur le registre national de la population basé sur l'adresse.

65 Data refer to resident population. - Les données concernent la population résidente.

66 Excluding Faeroe Islands and Greenland shown separately, if available. Population statistics are compiled from registers. - Non compris les Iles Féroé et le Groenland, qui font l'objet de rubriques distinctes, si disponible. Les statistiques de la population sont compilées à partir des registres.

67 Excluding Åland Islands. - Non compris les Îles d'Åland.

68 Excluding diplomatic personnel outside the country and including members of alien armed forces not living in military camps and foreign diplomatic personnel not living in embassies or consulates. - Non compris le personnel diplomatique hors du pays et y compris les militaires étrangers ne vivant pas dans des camps militaires et le personnel diplomatique étranger ne vivant pas dans les ambassades ou les consulats.

69 Data based on the 2011 Census. - Données fondées sur le recensement de 2011.

[70] Excluding military personnel, visitors and transients. - Non compris les militaires, ni les visiteurs et transients.

[71] Data refer to usually resident population. - Les données concernent la population habituellement résidente.

[72] Data refer to registered resident population. - Les données concernent la population enregistrée résidente.

[73] The figures refer to usual residents in private households and persons present in communal establishments during the 2011 census. - Données se rapportant aux résidents habituels membres de ménages privés et aux personnes recensées dans des établissements collectifs au recensement de 2011.

[74] Data refer to legal resident population. - Les données concernent la population légalement résidente.

[75] Including civilian nationals temporarily outside the country. - Y compris les civils nationaux temporairement hors du pays.

[76] Figures for male and female population do not add up to the figure for total population, because they exclude 119 persons of unknown sex. - Les chiffres relatifs à la population masculine et féminine ne correspondent pas au chiffre de la population totale, parce que l'on en a exclu 119 personnes de sexe inconnu.

[77] Including residents temporarily outside the country. Population statistics are compiled from registers. - Y compris les résidents se trouvant temporairement hors du pays. Les statistiques de la population sont compilées à partir des registres.

[78] The total number may include 'Unknown residence', but the categories urban and rural do not. - Le nombre total peut inclure les personnes dont la résidence n'est pas connue, à l'inverse des catégories de population urbaine et rurale.

[79] Excluding Transnistria and the municipality of Bender. - Les données ne tiennent pas compte de l'information sur la Transnistria et la municipalité de Bender.

[80] Excludes data for Kosovo and Metohia. Based on the results of the 2011 Population Census. - Sans les données pour le Kosovo et Metohie. Basé sur les résultats du recencement de la population de 2011.

[81] Population statistics are compiled from registers. Data refer to registered resident population. - Les statistiques de la population sont compilées à partir des registres. Les données concernent la population enregistrée résidente.

[82] The Government of Ukraine has informed the United Nations that it is not in a position to provide statistical data concerning the Autonomous Republic of Crimea and the city of Sevastopol. - Le gouvernement Ukrainien a informé l'ONU qu'il n'est pas en mesure de fournir des données statistiques concernant la République autonome de Crimée et la ville de Sébastopol.

[83] Excluding Channel Islands (Guernsey and Jersey) and Isle of Man, shown separately, if available. - Non compris les îles Anglo-Normandes (Guernesey et Jersey) et l'île de Man, qui font l'objet de rubriques distinctes, si disponible.

[84] Excluding Niue, shown separately, which is part of Cook Islands, but because of remoteness is administered separately. - Non compris Nioué, qui fait l'objet d'une rubrique distincte et qui fait partie des îles Cook, mais qui, en raison de son éloignement, est administrée séparément.

[85] Projections are prepared by the Secretariat of the Pacific Community based on 1999 census of population and housing. - Les projections sont preparées par le Secrétariat de la Communauté du Pacifique à partir des résultats du recensement de la population et de l'habitat de 1999.

[86] Because of rounding, totals are not in all cases the sum of the respective components. - Les chiffres étant arrondis, les totaux ne correspondent pas toujours rigoureusement à la somme des composants respectifs.

[87] Population estimates by urban/rural residence exclude inland waters and oceanic areas. - Les estimations de la population par lieu de résidence urbaine ou rurale excluent les eaux intérieures et les zones océaniques.

[88] Figures for male and female may not add up to the total, since they do not include the category "Unknown". - La somme des chiffres indiqués pour les sexes masculin et féminin peut n'être pas égale au total parce qu'elle n'inclut pas la catégorie " inconnue ".

[89] Because of rounding, totals are not in all cases the sum of the respective components. Data refer to national projections. Based on the results of the 1996 population census. - Les chiffres étant arrondis, les totaux ne correspondent pas toujours rigoureusement à la somme des composants respectifs. Les données se réfèrent aux projections nationales. À partir des résultats du recensement de la population de 1996.

Table 8 - *Demographic Yearbook 2015*

Table 8 presents population of capital cities and cities of 100 000 or more inhabitants for the latest available year between 1996 and 2015.

Description of variables: Since the way in which cities are delimited differs from one country or area to another, the table not only presents data for the so-called city proper, but also for the urban agglomeration, if available.

City proper is defined as a locality with legally fixed boundaries and an administratively recognized urban status, usually characterized by some form of local government.

Urban agglomeration has been defined as comprising the city or town proper and also the suburban fringe or densely settled territory lying outside of, but adjacent to, the city boundaries.

For some countries or areas, however, the data relate to entire administrative divisions known, for example, as shi or municipalities (municipios) which are composed of a populated centre and adjoining territory, some of which may contain other, often separate urban localities or may be distinctively rural in character. For this group of countries or areas the type of civil division is given in a footnote.

The surface area of the city or urban agglomeration is presented, when available.

City names are presented in the original language of the country or area in which the cities are located. In cases where the original names are not in the Roman alphabet, they have been romanized. Cities are listed in English alphabetical order.

Capital cities are shown in the table regardless of their population size. The names of the capital cities are printed in capital letters. The designation of any specific city as a capital city is as reported by the country or area.

The table also covers cities whose urban agglomeration's population exceeds 100 000; that is, while the urban agglomeration should have a population of 100 000 or more to be included in the table, the city proper may be of a smaller population size.

The reference date of each population figure appears in the left-most column of the table. Estimates based on results of sample surveys and city censuses or from other sources are explained by the 'code' also appearing in the left-most column of the table. The codes are explained at the end of the table.

Reliability of data: Specific information is generally not available on the reliability of the estimates of the population of cities or urban agglomerations presented in this table.

In the absence of such quality assessment, data from population censuses, sample surveys and city censuses are considered to be reliable and, therefore, set in Roman type. Other estimates are considered to be reliable if they are based on a complete census (or a sample survey), and have been adjusted by a continuous population register or adjusted on the basis of the calculated balance of births, deaths, and migration.

Limitations: Statistics on the population of capital cities and cities of 100 000 or more inhabitants are subject to the same qualifications as have been set forth for population statistics in general as discussed in section 3 of the Technical Notes.

International comparability of data on city population is limited to a great extent by variations in national concepts and definitions. Although an effort is made to reduce the sources of non-comparability somewhat by presenting the data for both city proper and urban agglomeration, many serious problems of comparability remain.

Data presented in the "city proper" column for some countries represent an urban administrative area legally distinguished from surrounding rural territory, while for other countries these data represent a commune or an equally small administrative unit. In still other countries, the administrative units may be relatively extensive and thereby include considerable territories beyond the urban centre itself.

City data are also especially affected by whether the data refer to *de facto* or *de jure* population, as well as variations among countries in how each of these concepts is applied. With reference to the total population, the difference between the *de facto* and *de jure* population is discussed at length in section 3.1.1 of the Technical Notes.

Data on city populations based on intercensal estimates present additional problems: comparability is impaired by the different methods used in making the estimates, and by the loss of precision in applying to selected segments of the population methods best suited for the whole population. For example, it is far more difficult to apply the component method of estimating population growth to cities than it is to the entire country.

Births and deaths occurring in the cities do not all originate in the population present in or resident of that area. Therefore, the use of natural increase to estimate the probable size of the city population is a potential source of error. Internal migration is another component of population change that cannot be measured with accuracy in many areas. Because of these factors, estimates in this table may be less valuable in general and in particular limited for purposes of international comparison.

City data, even when set in Roman type, are often not as reliable as estimates for the total population of the country or area. Furthermore, because the sources of these data include censuses (national or city), surveys and estimates, the years to which they refer vary widely. In addition, because city boundaries may alter over time, comparisons covering different years should be carried out with caution.

Earlier data: Population of capital cities and cities with a population of 100 000 or more have been shown in previous issues of the *Demographic Yearbook*. For more information on specific topics and years for which data are reported, readers should consult the Historical Index.

Tableau 8 – *Annuaire démographique 2015*

Le tableau 8 présente les données les plus récentes disponibles pour la période 1996 – 2015 sur la population des capitales et des villes de 100 000 habitants ou plus.

Description des variables : étant donné que les villes ne sont pas délimitées de la même manière dans tous les pays ou zones, on s'est efforcé de donner, dans ce tableau, des chiffres correspondant non seulement aux villes proprement dites, mais aussi, le cas échéant, aux agglomérations urbaines.

On entend par villes proprement dites les localités qui ont des limites juridiquement définies et sont administrativement considérées comme villes, ce qui se caractérise généralement par l'existence d'une autorité locale.

L'agglomération urbaine comprend, par définition, la ville proprement dite ainsi que la proche banlieue, c'est-à-dire la zone fortement peuplée qui est extérieure, mais contiguë aux limites de la ville.

En outre, dans certains pays ou zones, les données se rapportent à des divisions administratives entières, connues par exemple sous le nom de shi ou de municipios, qui comportent une agglomération et le territoire avoisinant, lequel peut englober d'autres agglomérations urbaines tout à fait distinctes ou être à caractère essentiellement rural. Pour ce groupe de pays ou zones, le type de division administrative est indiqué en note.

On trouvera à la fin du tableau la superficie de la ville ou agglomération urbaine chaque fois que possible.

Les noms des villes sont indiqués dans la langue du pays ou zone où ces villes sont situées. Les noms de villes qui ne sont pas à l'origine libellés en caractères latins ont été romanisés. Les villes sont énumérées dans l'ordre alphabétique anglais.

Les capitales figurent dans le tableau quel que soit le chiffre de leur population et leur nom a été imprimé en lettres majuscules. Ne sont indiquées comme capitales que les villes ainsi désignées par le pays ou zone intéressé.

En ce qui concerne les autres villes, le tableau indique celles dont la population est égale ou supérieure à 100 000 habitants. Ce chiffre limite s'applique à l'agglomération urbaine et non à la ville proprement dite, dont la population peut être moindre.

La date à laquelle se réfère le chiffre correspondant, figure dans la colonne de gauche du tableau. Le 'code' aussi figurant dans la colonne de gauche du tableau, permet de savoir si les estimations sont fondées sur les résultats d'enquêtes par sondage ou de recensements municipaux ou sont tirées d'autres sources. Les codes utilisés sont expliqués à la fin du tableau.

Fiabilité des données : on ne possède généralement pas de renseignements précis sur la fiabilité des estimations de la population des villes ou agglomérations urbaines présentées dans ce tableau.

Les données provenant de recensements de la population, d'enquêtes par sondage ou de recensements municipaux sont jugées sûres et figurent par conséquent en caractères romains. D'autres estimations sont considérées comme sûres si elles sont fondées sur un recensement complet (ou une enquête par sondage) et ont été ajustées en fonction des données provenant d'un registre permanent de population ou en fonction de la balance, établie par le calcul des naissances, des décès et des migrations.

Insuffisance des données : les statistiques portant sur la population des capitales et des villes de 100 000 habitants ou plus appellent toutes les réserves qui ont été formulées à la section 3 des Notes techniques à propos des statistiques de la population en général.

La comparabilité internationale des données portant sur la population des villes est compromise dans une large mesure par la diversité des définitions nationales. Bien que l'on se soit efforcé de réduire les facteurs de non-comparabilité en présentant à la fois dans le tableau les données relatives aux villes proprement dites et celles concernant les agglomérations urbaines, de graves problèmes de comparabilité n'en subsistent pas moins.

Pour certains pays, les données figurant dans la colonne intitulée « Ville proprement dite » correspondent à une zone administrative urbaine juridiquement distincte du territoire rural environnant, tandis que pour d'autres pays ces données correspondent à une commune ou petite unité administrative analogue. Pour d'autres encore, les unités administratives en cause peuvent être relativement étendues et englober par conséquent un vaste territoire au-delà du centre urbain lui-même.

L'emploi de données se rapportant tantôt à la population de fait, tantôt à la population de droit, ainsi que les différences de traitement de ces deux notions d'un pays à l'autre influent particulièrement sur les statistiques urbaines. En ce qui concerne la population totale, la différence entre population de fait et population de droit est expliquée en détail à la section 3.1.1 des Notes techniques.

Les statistiques relatives à la population urbaine qui sont fondées sur des estimations intercensitaires posent encore plus de problèmes que les données issues de recensement. Leur comparabilité est compromise par la diversité des méthodes employées pour établir les estimations, et par l'imprécision qui résulte de l'application de certaines méthodes qui sont conçues pour être appliquées à l'ensemble de la population. La méthode des composantes, par exemple, est beaucoup plus difficile à appliquer en vue de l'estimation de l'accroissement de la population lorsqu'il s'agit de villes que lorsqu'il s'agit d'un pays tout entier.

Les naissances et décès qui surviennent dans les villes ne correspondent pas tous à la population présente ou résidente. En conséquence, des erreurs peuvent se produire si l'on établit pour les villes des estimations fondées sur l'accroissement naturel de la population. Les migrations intérieures constituent un second élément d'estimation que, dans bien des régions, on ne peut pas toujours mesurer avec exactitude. Pour ces raisons, les estimations présentées dans ce tableau risquent dans l'ensemble d'être peu fiables et leur valeur est particulièrement limitée du point de vue des comparaisons internationales.

Même lorsqu'elles figurent en caractères romains, il arrive souvent que les statistiques urbaines ne soient pas aussi fiables que les estimations concernant la population totale de la zone ou du pays considéré. De surcroît, comme ces statistiques proviennent aussi bien de recensements (nationaux ou municipaux) que d'enquêtes ou d'estimations, les années auxquelles elles se rapportent sont extrêmement variables. Enfin, comme les limites urbaines varient parfois d'une époque à une autre, il y a lieu d'être prudent lorsque l'on compare des données se rapportant à des années différentes.

Données publiées antérieurement : des statistiques concernant la population des capitales et des villes de 100 000 habitants ou plus ont été présentées dans des éditions antérieures de l'*Annuaire démographique*. Pour plus de précisions concernant les années et les sujets pour lesquels des données ont été publiées, se reporter à l'index historique.

8. Population of capital cities and cities of 100 000 or more inhabitants: latest available year, 1996 - 2015
Population des capitales et des villes de 100 000 habitants ou plus : dernière année disponible, 1996 - 2015

Continent, country or area, date, code[a] and city / Continent, pays ou zone, date, code[a] et ville	City proper - Ville proprement dite				Urban agglomeration - Agglomération urbaine			
	Population			Surface area - Superficie (km²)	Population			Surface area - Superficie (km²)
	Both sexes - Les deux sexes	Male - Masculin	Female - Féminin		Both sexes - Les deux sexes	Male - Masculin	Female - Féminin	
AFRICA - AFRIQUE								
Algeria - Algérie								
16 IV 2008 (CDJC)								
Adrar	200 834	...	...	...	...	...	...	...
Ain Defla	450 280	...	...	...	...	...	...	...
Ain Temouchent	299 341	...	...	...	...	...	...	...
ALGIERS (EL DJAZAIR)	2 712 944	...	...	...	...	...	...	...
Annaba	442 230	...	...	...	...	...	...	...
Batna	768 444	...	...	...	...	...	...	...
Béchar	236 213	...	...	...	...	...	...	...
Bejaïa	559 981	...	...	...	...	...	...	...
Beskra (Biskra)	563 245	...	...	...	...	...	...	...
Bordj Bou Arreridj	422 986	...	...	...	...	...	...	...
Bouira	372 196	...	...	...	...	...	...	...
Boumerdes	459 250	...	...	...	...	...	...	...
Chlef	521 070	...	...	...	...	...	...	...
El Bayadh	192 958	...	...	...	...	...	...	...
El Boulaïda (Blida)	719 515	...	...	...	...	...	...	...
El Djelfa	825 411	...	...	...	...	...	...	...
El Oued	495 573	...	...	...	...	...	...	...
El Tarf	230 157	...	...	...	...	...	...	...
Ghardaïa	355 701	...	...	...	...	...	...	...
Ghilizane (Relizane)	432 386	...	...	...	...	...	...	...
Guelma	363 716	...	...	...	...	...	...	...
Jijel	391 096	...	...	...	...	...	...	...
Khenchela	288 849	...	...	...	...	...	...	...
Laghouat	371 204	...	...	...	...	...	...	...
Lemdiyya (Médéa)	519 383	...	...	...	...	...	...	...
Mestghanem (Mostaganem)	338 143	...	...	...	...	...	...	...
Mila	440 735	...	...	...	...	...	...	...
Mouaskar (Mascara)	513 432	...	...	...	...	...	...	...
M'Sila	666 848	...	...	...	...	...	...	...
Naama	160 381	...	...	...	...	...	...	...
Oum El Bouaghi	467 997	...	...	...	...	...	...	...
Qacentina (Constantine)	717 646	...	...	...	...	...	...	...
Saïda	248 939	...	...	...	...	...	...	...
Sidi-bel-Abbès	517 836	...	...	...	...	...	...	...
Skikda	543 402	...	...	...	...	...	...	...
Souq Ahras	308 319	...	...	...	...	...	...	...
Stif (Sétif)	856 457	...	...	...	...	...	...	...
Tamanrasset	136 822	...	...	...	...	...	...	...
Tbessa (Tébessa)	515 786	...	...	...	...	...	...	...
Tihert (Tiaret)	637 991	...	...	...	...	...	...	...
Tilimsen (Tlemcen)	672 490	...	...	...	...	...	...	...
Tipaza	343 838	...	...	...	...	...	...	...
Tissemsilt	193 011	...	...	...	...	...	...	...
Tizi Ouzou	585 775	...	...	...	...	...	...	...
Wahran (Oran)	1 165 687	...	...	...	...	...	...	...
Wargla (Ouargla)	473 543	...	...	...	...	...	...	...
Benin - Bénin								
11 V 2013 (CDJC)								
Cotonou	679 012	325 872	353 140	79	...	...	...	...
Parakou	255 478	127 328	128 150	441	...	...	...	...
PORTO-NOVO	264 320	126 016	138 304	50	...	...	...	...
Botswana								
9 VIII 2011 (CDFC)								
GABORONE	231 592	113 580	118 012	169	...	...	...	...
Burkina Faso								
9 XII 2006 (CDFC)								
Banfora	75 917	38 399	37 518	...	109 824	54 581	55 243	...
Bobo Dioulasso	489 967	244 136	245 831	...	554 042	275 703	278 339	...
Dori	21 078	10 431	10 647	...	106 808	52 992	53 816	...
Fada N'gourma	41 785	21 220	20 565	...	124 577	62 193	62 384	...
Gorom-Gorom	8 882	4 509	4 373	...	106 346	53 129	53 217	...
Kaya	54 365	26 989	27 376	...	117 122	56 209	60 913	...
Koudougou	88 184	42 803	45 381	...	138 209	64 362	73 847	...

8. Population of capital cities and cities of 100 000 or more inhabitants: latest available year, 1996 - 2015
Population des capitales et des villes de 100 000 habitants ou plus : dernière année disponible, 1996 - 2015 (continued - suite)

Continent, country or area, date, code[a] and city / Continent, pays ou zone, date, code[a] et ville	City proper - Ville proprement dite				Urban agglomeration - Agglomération urbaine			
	Population			Surface area - Superficie (km²)	Population			Surface area - Superficie (km²)
	Both sexes - Les deux sexes	Male - Masculin	Female - Féminin		Both sexes - Les deux sexes	Male - Masculin	Female - Féminin	
AFRICA - AFRIQUE								
Burkina Faso								
9 XII 2006 (CDFC)								
OUAGADOUGOU	1 475 223	745 289	729 934	...	1 475 223	745 289	729 934	...
Ouahigouya	73 153	36 370	36 783	...	125 030	61 002	64 028	...
Solenzo	16 850	8 557	8 293	...	121 819	59 892	61 927	...
Tenkodogo	44 491	21 476	23 015	...	124 985	58 003	66 982	...
Burundi								
16 VIII 2008 (CDJC)								
BUJUMBURA	497 169	274 979	222 190	...	...	...	...	...
Cabo Verde								
1 VII 2011 (ESDF)								
PRAIA	...	...	...	...	133 863	65 412	68 451	...
Cameroon - Cameroun								
11 XI 2005 (CDJC)								
Bafoussam	239 287	...	...	...	...	...	...	...
Bamenda	269 530	...	...	...	...	...	...	...
Douala	1 907 479	...	...	...	...	...	...	...
Garoua	235 996	...	...	...	...	...	...	...
Kumba	144 268	...	...	...	...	...	...	...
Maroua	201 371	...	...	...	...	...	...	...
Ngaoundéré	152 698	...	...	...	...	...	...	...
Nkongsamba	104 050	...	...	...	...	...	...	...
YAOUNDE	1 817 524	...	...	...	...	...	...	...
Côte d'Ivoire								
15 V 2014 (CDJC)								
Abengourou	100 910	51 153	49 757	...	...	...	...	...
Abidjan	4 395 243	2 180 526	2 214 717	...	...	...	...	...
Anyama	103 297	52 169	51 128	...	...	...	...	...
Bouake	536 719	273 502	263 217	...	...	...	...	...
Daloa	245 360	128 922	116 438	...	...	...	...	...
Divo	105 397	54 614	50 783	...	...	...	...	...
Gagnoa	160 465	82 615	77 850	...	...	...	...	...
Korhogo	243 048	126 493	116 555	...	...	...	...	...
Man	148 945	77 005	71 940	...	...	...	...	...
San Pédro	164 944	85 168	79 776	...	...	...	...	...
Soubre	101 196	53 799	47 397	...	...	...	...	...
YAMOUSSOUKRO	212 670	107 871	104 799	...	...	...	...	...
Djibouti								
29 V 2009 (CDFC)								
DJIBOUTI	475 322	...	...	...	...	...	...	...
Egypt - Égypte								
1 VII 2010* (ESDF)								
6th of October City	802 306	420 009	382 297	...	...	...	...	...
Alexandria	4 358 439	2 225 558	2 132 881	...	...	...	...	...
Assyût	991 929	508 403	483 526	...	...	...	...	...
Aswan	543 396	277 732	265 664	...	...	...	...	...
Behera	985 850	500 999	484 851	...	...	...	...	...
Beni-Suef	582 396	293 887	288 509	...	...	...	...	...
CAIRO	7 248 671	3 682 152	3 566 519	...	...	...	...	...
Dakahlia	1 503 395	758 471	744 924	...	...	...	...	...
Damietta	462 154	236 522	225 632	...	...	...	...	...
Faiyûm	621 268	318 679	302 589	...	...	...	...	...
Gharbia	1 285 492	645 533	639 959	...	...	...	...	...
Giza	3 122 041	1 592 292	1 529 749	...	...	...	...	...
Helwan	1 295 854	660 776	635 078	...	...	...	...	...
Ismailia	472 655	237 174	235 481	...	...	...	...	...
Kafr-Elsheikh	655 002	327 445	327 557	...	...	...	...	...
Kalyoubia	2 053 859	1 051 232	1 002 627	...	...	...	...	...
Luxer	391 460	200 250	191 210	...	...	...	...	...
Matrouh	258 699	136 995	121 704	...	...	...	...	...
Menia	859 719	434 498	425 221	...	...	...	...	...
Menoufia	724 352	368 333	356 019	...	...	...	...	...
North Sinai	229 462	120 302	109 160	...	...	...	...	...
Port Said	610 468	310 881	299 587	...	...	...	...	...
Qena	534 766	270 422	264 344	...	...	...	...	...

8. Population of capital cities and cities of 100 000 or more inhabitants: latest available year, 1996 - 2015
Population des capitales et des villes de 100 000 habitants ou plus : dernière année disponible, 1996 - 2015 (continued - suite)

Continent, country or area, date, code[a] and city / Continent, pays ou zone, date, code[a] et ville	City proper - Ville proprement dite				Urban agglomeration - Agglomération urbaine			
	Population			Surface area - Superficie (km²)	Population			Surface area - Superficie (km²)
	Both sexes - Les deux sexes	Male - Masculin	Female - Féminin		Both sexes - Les deux sexes	Male - Masculin	Female - Féminin	
AFRICA - AFRIQUE								
Egypt - Égypte								
1 VII 2010* (ESDF)								
Red Sea	*295 993*	*180 622*	*115 371*	...	...	...	...	...
Sharkia	*1 340 060*	*682 941*	*657 119*	...	...	...	...	...
Sohag	*870 362*	*443 082*	*427 280*	...	...	...	...	...
Suez	*556 665*	*283 571*	*273 094*	...	...	...	...	...
Equatorial Guinea - Guinée équatoriale								
1 VII 2001 (ESDF)								
MALABO	...	...	...	...	*211 276*	*106 923*	*104 353*	...
Ethiopia - Éthiopie								
29 V 2007 (CDFC)								
ADDIS ABABA	2 739 551	...	...	...	...	...	...	...
Gabon								
22 V 2013 (CDFC)								
Franceville	...	...	...	...	110 568	63 518	47 050	...
LIBREVILLE	...	...	...	...	703 939	360 012	343 927	...
Port-Gentil	...	...	...	...	136 462	69 978	66 484	...
Ghana								
26 IX 2010 (CDFC)								
ACCRA	1 594 419	763 870	830 549	...	...	...	...	...
Ashiaman	190 972	93 727	97 245	...	...	...	...	...
Koforidua	122 300	59 056	63 244	...	...	...	...	...
Kumasi	1 730 249	826 479	903 770	...	...	...	...	...
Madina	111 926	54 271	57 655	...	...	...	...	...
Obuasi	168 641	81 015	87 626	...	...	...	...	...
Tamale	223 252	111 109	112 143	...	...	...	...	...
Tema	292 773	139 958	152 815	...	...	...	...	...
Guinea - Guinée								
1 III 2014 (CDFC)								
Boke	...	...	...	...	450 278	...	...	...
CONAKRY	1 660 973	...	...	...	...	...	...	...
Faranah	...	...	...	...	280 170	...	...	...
Kankan	...	...	...	...	473 359	...	...	...
Kindia	...	...	...	...	439 614	...	...	...
Labé	...	...	...	...	318 938	...	...	...
Mamou	...	...	...	...	318 981	...	...	...
Nzérékoré	...	...	...	...	396 949	...	...	...
Guinea-Bissau - Guinée-Bissau								
15 III 2009 (CDFC)								
BISSAU	387 909	...	...	...	...	...	...	...
Kenya								
24 VIII 2009 (CDFC)								
Eldoret	252 061	127 808	124 253	...	289 380[1]	146 596[1]	142 790[1]	311[1]
Garissa	110 383	56 873	53 490	...	116 317[1]	60 114[1]	56 183[1]	791[1]
Kangundo	13 356	6 544	6 812	...	218 557[1]	107 968[1]	110 589[1]	...
Karuri	99 739	49 692	50 047	...	107 716[1]	53 735[1]	53 981[1]	...
Kericho	42 029	22 199	19 830	...	101 808[1]	52 283[1]	49 525[1]	...
Kikuyu	190 208	93 036	97 172	...	233 231[1]	114 357[1]	118 874[1]	231[1]
Kisumu	259 258	131 062	128 196	...	388 311[1]	193 878[1]	194 433[1]	602[1]
Kitale	75 782	38 081	37 701	...	106 187[1]	54 065[1]	52 122[1]	...
Kitui	20 419	10 338	10 081	...	109 568[1]	53 659[1]	55 909[1]	...
Machakos	41 917	20 448	21 469	...	150 041[1]	74 294[1]	75 747[1]	...
Malindi	84 150	41 911	42 239	...	118 265[1]	59 192[1]	59 073[1]	...
Mavoko/AthiRiver	110 396	59 393	51 003	...	137 211[1]	74 856[1]	62 355[1]	...
Mombasa	915 101	473 433	441 668	...	938 131[1]	486 208[1]	451 923[1]	219[1]
NAIROBI	3 133 518	1 602 104	1 531 414	695	...	...	...	...
Naivasha	91 993	45 253	46 740	...	169 142[1]	84 857[1]	84 285[1]	...
Nakuru	286 411	145 038	141 373	...	307 990[1]	155 881[1]	152 109[1]	412[1]
Ngong	104 073	52 453	51 620	...	107 188[1]	54 040[1]	53 148[1]	...
Nyeri	63 626	31 885	31 741	...	119 353[1]	59 562[1]	59 791[1]	...
Ruiru	236 961	118 143	118 818	...	238 858[1]	119 147[1]	119 711[1]	292[1]
Thika	136 576	68 254	68 322	...	136 917[1]	68 408[1]	68 509[1]	135[1]
Vihiga	36 398	17 608	18 790	...	118 696[1]	56 807[1]	61 889[1]	...

Continent, country or area, date, code[a] and city / Continent, pays ou zone, date, code[a] et ville	City proper - Ville proprement dite				Urban agglomeration - Agglomération urbaine			
	Population			Surface area - Superficie (km²)	Population			Surface area - Superficie (km²)
	Both sexes - Les deux sexes	Male - Masculin	Female - Féminin		Both sexes - Les deux sexes	Male - Masculin	Female - Féminin	
AFRICA - AFRIQUE								
Lesotho								
13 IV 2006 (CDJC)								
MASERU	431 998	205 702	226 296	4 279	...	...	...	...
Liberia - Libéria[2]								
21 III 2008 (CDFC)								
MONROVIA	...	...	...	...	970 824	476 473	494 351	...
Madagascar								
1 VII 2005 (ESDF)								
ANTANANARIVO[3]	1 015 140	495 393	519 747	...	...	...	...	...
Antsirabe	...	...	...	...	180 180	87 691	92 489	...
Fianarantsoa	...	...	...	...	165 220	80 410	84 810	...
Mahajanga	...	...	...	...	152 785	74 359	78 426	...
Toamasina	...	...	...	...	203 469	99 026	104 443	...
Toliara	...	...	...	...	113 993	55 479	58 514	...
Malawi								
1 VII 2012 (ESDF)								
Blantyre City	783 296[4]	396 578[4]	386 718[4]	220	...	...	...	...
LILONGWE	868 800[4]	443 378[4]	425 423[4]	328	...	...	...	...
Mzuzu City	181 690[4]	90 857[4]	90 833[4]	48	...	...	...	...
Zomba City	115 012[4]	57 665[4]	57 347[4]	39	...	...	...	...
Mali								
1 IV 2009 (CDFC)								
BAMAKO[5]	...	...	...	...	1 810 366	907 643	902 723	...
Kayes	...	...	...	...	149 129	76 470	72 659	...
Koutiala	...	...	...	...	141 444	70 905	70 539	...
Mopti	...	...	...	...	120 786	60 080	60 706	...
Ségou	...	...	...	...	133 501	66 819	66 682	...
Sikasso	...	...	...	...	226 618	114 171	112 447	...
Mauritania - Mauritanie[4]								
1 VII 2008 (ESDF)								
NOUAKCHOTT	846 871	471 243	375 628	...	...	...	...	...
Mauritius - Maurice[6]								
1 VII 2015 (ESDJ)								
Beau Bassin - Rose Hill	104 760	51 933	52 827	21	...	...	...	...
PORT LOUIS	149 672	74 677	74 995	61	...	...	...	...
Vacoas - Phoenix	106 413	51 381	55 032	106	...	...	...	...
Morocco - Maroc								
1 VII 2014 (ESDF)								
Agadir	505 765	...	...	...	598 484	...	...	...
Al Hoceima	137 024	...	...	...	399 586	...	...	...
Azilal	100 327	...	...	...	553 121	...	...	...
Béni-Mellal	325 405	...	...	...	549 559	...	...	...
Benslimane	113 341	...	...	...	232 509	...	...	...
Berkane	182 203	...	...	...	288 807	...	...	...
Berrechid	272 356	...	...	...	482 119	...	...	...
Casablanca (Dar-el-Beida)	3 352 399	...	...	...	3 352 399	...	...	...
Chtouka-Ait Baha	111 522	...	...	...	369 706	...	...	...
El Hajeb	121 226	...	...	...	246 461	...	...	...
El Kelâa des Sraghna	152 900	...	...	...	536 191	...	...	...
El-Jadida	311 038	...	...	...	784 432	...	...	...
Errachidia	193 748	...	...	...	418 069	...	...	...
Essaouira	106 319	...	...	...	450 569	...	...	...
Fès	1 126 551	...	...	...	1 146 967	...	...	...
Fquih Ben Salah	204 732	...	...	...	502 021	...	...	...
Guelmim	138 788	...	...	...	187 428	...	...	...
Inezgane ait Melloul	511 209	...	...	...	538 786	...	...	...
Kénitra	604 206	...	...	...	1 058 359	...	...	...
Khemisset	279 890	...	...	...	541 868	...	...	...
Khénifra	228 509	...	...	...	370 952	...	...	...
Khouribga	376 829	...	...	...	541 365	...	...	...
Laayoune	234 870	...	...	...	237 384	...	...	...
Larache	264 802	...	...	...	496 264	...	...	...
Marrakech	978 045	...	...	...	1 325 571	...	...	...
M'Diq-Fnideq	196 586	...	...	...	208 337	...	...	...
Médiouna	119 054	...	...	...	171 684	...	...	...

Continent, country or area, date, code[a] and city Continent, pays ou zone, date, code[a] et ville	City proper - Ville proprement dite				Urban agglomeration - Agglomération urbaine			
	Population			Surface area - Superficie (km²)	Population			Surface area - Superficie (km²)
	Both sexes - Les deux sexes	Male - Masculin	Female - Féminin		Both sexes - Les deux sexes	Male - Masculin	Female - Féminin	
AFRICA - AFRIQUE								
Morocco - Maroc								
1 VII 2014 (ESDF)								
Meknès	685 408	...	...	...	833 456	...	...	...
Midelt	124 684	...	...	...	288 757	...	...	...
Mohammedia	288 131	...	...	...	403 087	...	...	...
Nador	390 913	...	...	...	564 354	...	...	...
Nouaceur	271 052	...	...	...	331 651	...	...	...
Ouarzazate	113 230	...	...	...	297 018	...	...	...
Oued Ed-Dahab	105 193	...	...	...	125 747	...	...	...
Oujda	504 480	...	...	...	550 406	...	...	...
RABAT	578 644	...	...	...	578 644	...	...	...
Rehamna	102 715	...	...	...	314 605	...	...	...
Safi	345 595	...	...	...	691 128	...	...	...
Salé	912 957	...	...	...	979 228	...	...	...
Sefrou	154 973	...	...	...	286 009	...	...	...
Settat	215 665	...	...	...	633 500	...	...	...
Sidi Kacem	168 302	...	...	...	521 694	...	...	...
Sidi Slimane	130 576	...	...	...	319 528	...	...	...
Skhirate-Témara	512 867	...	...	...	570 855	...	...	...
Tanger	998 972	...	...	...	1 059 562	...	...	...
Taourirt	149 604	...	...	...	232 712	...	...	...
Taroudannt	247 428	...	...	...	837 797	...	...	...
Taza	207 719	...	...	...	528 917	...	...	...
Tétouan	396 806	...	...	...	549 062	...	...	...
Youssoufia	100 617	...	...	...	251 692	...	...	...
Mozambique								
1 VII 2015 (ESDF)								
Beira	460 904	231 684	229 220	633	...	...	...	...
Chimoio	314 751	158 700	156 051	174	...	...	...	...
Lichinga	214 614	108 147	106 467	290	...	...	...	...
MAPUTO	1 241 702	597 109	644 593	300	...	...	...	...
Matola	927 123	447 365	479 759	375	...	...	...	...
Maxixe	127 372	57 145	70 227	282	...	...	...	...
Nacala	241 066	118 325	122 741	340	...	...	...	...
Nampula	622 423	313 343	309 080	320	...	...	...	...
Pemba	199 457	99 447	100 010	194	...	...	...	...
Quelimane	241 077	121 599	119 478	117	...	...	...	...
Tete	213 406	107 128	106 278	286	...	...	...	...
Xai-Xai	128 946	59 452	69 494	135	...	...	...	...
Namibia - Namibie								
28 VIII 2011 (CDFC)								
WINDHOEK	325 858	160 730	165 128	...	...	...	...	...
Niger								
10 XII 2012 (CDJC)								
Maradi	267 249	137 051	130 198	...	...	...	...	...
NIAMEY	1 026 848	511 166	515 682	...	...	...	...	...
Tahoua	149 498	74 096	75 402	...	...	...	...	...
Zinder	322 935	162 705	160 230	...	...	...	...	...
Republic of South Sudan - République de Soudan du Sud								
21 IV 2008 (CDFC)								
JUBA	230 195	129 427	100 768	56	...	...	...	...
Malakal	114 528	60 440	54 088	25	...	...	...	...
Wau	118 331	63 777	54 554	75	...	...	...	...
Reunion - Réunion								
1 I 2010 (CDJC)								
SAINT-DENIS	145 022	68 075	76 947	143	174 973	82 815	92 158	230
Saint-Paul	103 346	51 327	52 019	241	172 137	84 793	87 344	376
Rwanda								
15 VIII 2012 (CDJC)								
KIGALI	859 332	451 673	407 659	...	...	...	...	...
Saint Helena ex. dep. - Sainte-Hélène sans dép.								
10 II 2008 (CDFC)								
JAMESTOWN	714	354	360	4	...	...	...	...

8. Population of capital cities and cities of 100 000 or more inhabitants: latest available year, 1996 - 2015
Population des capitales et des villes de 100 000 habitants ou plus : dernière année disponible, 1996 - 2015 (continued - suite)

Continent, country or area, date, code[a] and city / Continent, pays ou zone, date, code[a] et ville	City proper - Ville proprement dite				Urban agglomeration - Agglomération urbaine			
	Population			Surface area - Superficie (km²)	Population			Surface area - Superficie (km²)
	Both sexes - Les deux sexes	Male - Masculin	Female - Féminin		Both sexes - Les deux sexes	Male - Masculin	Female - Féminin	
AFRICA - AFRIQUE								
Sao Tome and Principe - Sao Tomé-et-Principe								
25 VIII 2001 (CDJC)								
SAO TOME	...	...	...	...	49 957	24 003	25 954	...
Senegal - Sénégal								
31 XII 2011 (ESDJ)								
DAKAR	1 056 009[7]	526 299[7]	529 710[7]	500	...	...	...	...
Diourbel[7]	279 667	136 961	142 706	...	...	...	...	...
Guediawaye[7]	317 464	157 992	159 472	...	...	...	...	...
Kaolack[7]	410 577	199 057	211 520	...	...	...	...	...
Mbour[7]	605 346	307 461	297 885	...	...	...	...	...
Pikine[7]	941 245	472 868	468 377	...	...	...	...	...
Rufisque[7]	333 032	167 942	165 090	...	...	...	...	...
Saint Louis[7]	277 245	136 957	140 289	...	...	...	...	...
Thiès[7]	618 436	304 087	314 349	...	...	...	...	...
Ziguinchor[7]	337 295	167 048	170 247	...	...	...	...	...
Seychelles[8]								
26 VIII 2010 (CDFC)								
VICTORIA	...	...	...	...	26 450			
Sierra Leone								
1 VII 2010 (ESDF)								
Bo	231 494	111 731	119 763	...	...	...	...	...
FREETOWN	945 423	479 526	465 897	...	...	...	...	...
Kenema	195 498	95 988	99 510	...	...	...	...	...
Makeni	114 960	55 388	59 572	...	...	...	...	...
Somalia - Somalie								
1 VII 2001 (ESDF)								
MOGADISHU	1 212 000	...	...	...	...	...	...	...
South Africa - Afrique du Sud								
10 X 2011 (CDFC)								
CAPE TOWN[9]	433 688	209 082	224 607	...	...	...	...	...
Durban	595 061	288 871	306 189	...	...	...	...	...
Johannesburg	957 441	484 293	473 148	...	...	...	...	...
PRETORIA[9]	741 651	359 139	382 512	...	...	...	...	...
Togo[4]								
1 VII 2015 (ESDF)								
Kara	104 400	...	...	...	...	...	...	...
LOME	...	...	...	...	1 788 600	...	...	...
Sokode	101 900	...	...	...	...	...	...	...
Tunisia - Tunisie								
1 VII 1998 (ESDF)								
Bizerte	105 520	...	...	...	...	...	...	...
Gabes	104 950	...	...	...	...	...	...	...
Kairouan	110 280	...	...	...	...	...	...	...
Sfax	248 800	...	...	...	...	...	...	...
TUNIS	702 330	...	...	...	...	...	...	...
Uganda - Ouganda								
27 VIII 2014 (CDFC)								
Gulu[10]	...	...	...	...	149 802	...	...	...
Hoima[10]	...	...	...	...	100 126	...	...	...
KAMPALA	1 507 114	...	...	...	...	...	...	...
Kasese[10]	...	...	...	...	101 557	...	...	...
Kira[10]	...	...	...	...	317 428	...	...	...
Lugazi[10]	...	...	...	...	114 163	...	...	...
Makindye Ssabagabo[10]	...	...	...	...	282 664	...	...	...
Masaka[10]	...	...	...	...	103 293	...	...	...
Mbarara[10]	...	...	...	...	195 160	...	...	...
Mukono[10]	...	...	...	...	162 744	...	...	...
Nansana[10]	...	...	...	...	365 857	...	...	...
Western Sahara - Sahara occidental[11]								
1 VII 1999 (ESDF)								
EL AAIUN	169 000	...	...	...	...	...	...	...
Zambia - Zambie								
16 X 2010 (CDJC)								
Chingola	216 626	108 464	108 162	1 678	...	...	...	...
Chipata	455 783	224 934	230 849	...	...	...	...	...

8. Population of capital cities and cities of 100 000 or more inhabitants: latest available year, 1996 - 2015
Population des capitales et des villes de 100 000 habitants ou plus : dernière année disponible, 1996 - 2015 (continued - suite)

Continent, country or area, date, code[a] and city Continent, pays ou zone, date, code[a] et ville	City proper - Ville proprement dite				Urban agglomeration - Agglomération urbaine			
	Population			Surface area - Superficie (km²)	Population			Surface area - Superficie (km²)
	Both sexes - Les deux sexes	Male - Masculin	Female - Féminin		Both sexes - Les deux sexes	Male - Masculin	Female - Féminin	
AFRICA - AFRIQUE								
Zambia - Zambie								
16 X 2010 (CDJC)								
Kabwe	202 360	98 781	103 579	1 572	...	...	...	...
Kasama	231 824	114 208	117 616	...	...	...	...	...
Kitwe	517 543	256 740	260 803	777	...	...	...	...
Livingstone	139 509	68 763	70 746	...	...	...	...	...
Luanshya	156 059	77 368	78 691	811	...	...	...	...
LUSAKA	1 747 152	860 424	886 728	360	...	...	...	...
Mufulira	162 889	81 355	81 534	1 637	...	...	...	...
Ndola	451 246	223 020	228 226	1 103	...	...	...	...
Zimbabwe								
17 VIII 2012 (CDFC)								
Bulawayo	653 337	303 346	349 991	479	...	...	...	...
Chitungwiza	356 840	168 600	188 240	...	...	...	...	...
HARARE	1 485 231	716 595	768 636	872	...	...	...	...
Mutare	262 124	125 850	136 274	...	...	...	...	...
AMERICA, NORTH - AMÉRIQUE DU NORD								
Anguilla								
11 V 2011 (CDFC)								
THE VALLEY	2 812	...	...	...	...	...	...	...
Aruba								
29 IX 2010 (CDJC)								
ORANJESTAD	28 295	13 139	15 156	...	...	...	...	...
Bahamas								
1 VII 2009 (ESDF)								
NASSAU	244 400	119 700	124 700	...	...	...	...	...
Belize								
12 V 2010 (CDJC)								
BELMOPAN	13 939	6 779	7 160	...	...	...	...	...
Bermuda - Bermudes								
1 VII 2010 (ESDJ)								
HAMILTON	3 686	1 986	1 700	1	...	...	...	...
Canada								
1 VII 2014* (ESDJ)								
Abbotsford-Mission	...	...	...	...	178 967[12]	89 970[12]	88 997[12]	605
Barrie	145 544[12]	71 090[12]	74 454[12]	77	200 416[12]	99 194[12]	101 222[12]	898
Brampton	570 290[12]	283 214[12]	287 076[12]	266	...	...	...	...
Brantford	98 874[12]	48 123[12]	50 751[12]	72	143 074[12]	70 204[12]	72 870[12]	1 073
Burlington	193 871[12]	93 946[12]	99 925[12]	186	...	...	...	...
Burnaby	239 059[12]	118 601[12]	120 458[12]	91	...	...	...	...
Calgary	1 265 531[12]	640 832[12]	624 699[12]	825	1 406 721[12]	712 991[12]	693 730[12]	5 108
Cambridge	134 284[12]	66 384[12]	67 900[12]	113	...	...	...	...
Chatham-Kent	105 260[12]	51 470[12]	53 790[12]	2 458	...	...	...	...
Coquitlam	134 962[12]	67 170[12]	67 792[12]	122	...	...	...	...
Edmonton	928 182[12]	470 582[12]	457 600[12]	684	1 328 290[12]	674 022[12]	654 268[12]	9 427
Gatineau	276 338[12]	135 309[12]	141 029[12]	343	328 144[12]	162 186[12]	165 958[12]	...
Greater Sudbury / Grand Sudbury	165 175[12]	81 351[12]	83 824[12]	3 227	165 690[12]	81 555[12]	84 135[12]	3 411
Guelph	129 079[12]	62 950[12]	66 129[12]	87	150 946[12]	74 075[12]	76 871[12]	594
Halifax	414 129[12]	203 584[12]	210 545[12]	5 490	414 398[12]	203 742[12]	210 656[12]	5 496
Hamilton	551 751[12]	271 584[12]	280 167[12]	1 117	765 228[12]	375 015[12]	390 213[12]	1 372
Kelowna	124 951[12]	60 644[12]	64 307[12]	212	191 237[12]	93 711[12]	97 526[12]	2 905
Kingston	129 653[12]	63 289[12]	66 364[12]	451	168 353[12]	82 960[12]	85 393[12]	1 939
Kitchener-Cambridge-Waterloo	...	...	...	...	506 858[12]	251 171[12]	255 687[12]	827
Laval	420 870[12]	206 695[12]	214 175[12]	247	...	...	...	...
Lévis V	142 887[12]	70 546[12]	72 341[12]	449	...	...	...	...
London	388 615[12]	188 802[12]	199 813[12]	421	502 360[12]	245 221[12]	257 139[12]	2 666
Longueuil	241 606[12]	118 475[12]	123 131[12]	116	...	...	...	...
Markham	329 204[12]	161 707[12]	167 497[12]	213	...	...	...	...
Mississauga	781 057[12]	384 469[12]	396 588[12]	292	...	...	...	...
Moncton	72 321[12]	35 488[12]	36 833[12]	141	146 073[12]	72 516[12]	73 557[12]	2 406

285

8. Population of capital cities and cities of 100 000 or more inhabitants: latest available year, 1996 - 2015
Population des capitales et des villes de 100 000 habitants ou plus : dernière année disponible, 1996 - 2015 (continued - suite)

Continent, country or area, date, code[a] and city / Continent, pays ou zone, date, code[a] et ville	City proper - Ville proprement dite				Urban agglomeration - Agglomération urbaine			
	Population			Surface area - Superficie (km²)	Population			Surface area - Superficie (km²)
	Both sexes - Les deux sexes	Male - Masculin	Female - Féminin		Both sexes - Les deux sexes	Male - Masculin	Female - Féminin	

AMERICA, NORTH - AMÉRIQUE DU NORD

Canada
1 VII 2014* (ESDJ)

Montréal	1 741 296[12]	857 007[12]	884 289[12]	365	4 027 121[12]	1 985 787[12]	2 041 334[12]	4 258
Oakville	200 534[12]	97 718[12]	102 816[12]	139	...	...	...	...
Oshawa	162 005[12]	79 344[12]	82 661[12]	146	384 143[12]	189 080[12]	195 063[12]	904
OTTAWA	947 031[12]	462 927[12]	484 104[12]	2 790	989 978[12]	484 176[12]	505 802[12]	...
Ottawa - Gatineau	...	...	...	...	1 318 122[12]	646 362[12]	671 760[12]	6 287
Peterborough	81 779[12]	38 592[12]	43 187[12]	64	123 270[12]	59 259[12]	64 011[12]	1 507
Québec	538 238[12]	263 187[12]	275 051[12]	454	799 632[12]	394 197[12]	405 435[12]	3 349
Regina	216 528[12]	107 981[12]	108 547[12]	145	237 758[12]	119 077[12]	118 681[12]	3 408
Richmond	203 178[12]	98 739[12]	104 439[12]	129	...	...	...	...
Richmond Hill	201 125[12]	98 524[12]	102 601[12]	101	...	...	...	...
Saanich	113 624[12]	55 780[12]	57 844[12]	104	...	...	...	...
Saguenay	146 849[12]	73 196[12]	73 653[12]	1 126	160 138[12]	80 150[12]	79 988[12]	2 564
Saint John	69 734[12]	33 404[12]	36 330[12]	316	127 314[12]	62 090[12]	65 224[12]	3 363
Saskatoon	254 569[12]	127 157[12]	127 412[12]	210	300 634[12]	150 884[12]	149 750[12]	5 215
Sherbrooke	162 638[12]	79 879[12]	82 759[12]	353	212 061[12]	104 592[12]	107 469[12]	1 460
St Catharines-Niagara	...	...	...	...	405 906[12]	197 616[12]	208 290[12]	1 398
St. John's	111 796[12]	54 199[12]	57 597[12]	446	211 724[12]	103 926[12]	107 798[12]	805
Surrey	498 720[12]	249 620[12]	249 100[12]	316	...	...	...	...
Thunder Bay	110 984[12]	54 165[12]	56 819[12]	328	125 112[12]	61 506[12]	63 606[12]	2 556
Toronto	2 808 503[12]	1 360 717[12]	1 447 786[12]	630	6 055 724[12]	2 960 331[12]	3 095 393[12]	5 906
Trois-Rivières	134 846[12]	65 812[12]	69 034[12]	289	155 813[12]	76 557[12]	79 256[12]	1 041
Vancouver	647 540[12]	320 582[12]	326 958[12]	115	2 470 289[12]	1 222 694[12]	1 247 595[12]	2 883
Vaughan	312 176[12]	153 443[12]	158 733[12]	274	...	...	...	...
Victoria	84 289[12]	40 321[12]	43 968[12]	19	358 685[12]	175 242[12]	183 443[12]	696
Whitby	130 341[12]	63 920[12]	66 421[12]	147	...	...	...	...
Windsor	218 270[12]	106 712[12]	111 558[12]	146	333 937[12]	164 367[12]	169 570[12]	1 022
Winnipeg	709 253[12]	348 660[12]	360 593[12]	464	782 640[12]	386 292[12]	396 348[12]	5 303

Cayman Islands - Îles Caïmanes
1 IV 2007 (SSDJ)

GEORGE TOWN	28 836	...	...	...	...	...	...	...

Costa Rica
1 VII 2015 (ESDJ)

Alajuela	293 601	149 041	144 560	388	...	...	...	...
Cartago	157 794	79 287	78 507	288	...	...	...	...
Desamparados	233 360	116 328	117 032	118	...	...	...	...
Goicoechea	132 210	65 130	67 080	32	...	...	...	...
Heredia	135 292	66 495	68 797	283	...	...	...	...
La Unión	106 490	53 479	53 011	45	...	...	...	...
Pérez Zeledón	141 998	70 991	71 007	1 906	...	...	...	...
Pococí	139 975	72 768	67 207	2 403	...	...	...	...
Puntarenas	130 462	66 988	63 474	1 842	...	...	...	...
San Carlos	184 763	95 178	89 585	3 348	...	...	...	...
SAN JOSÉ	333 980	165 070	168 910	45	...	...	...	...

Cuba
31 XII 2015 (ESDJ)

Bayamo	158 905	...	...	27[13]	...	...	...	...
Camagüey	304 738	...	...	82[13]	...	...	...	...
Ciego de Ávila	118 269	...	...	21[13]	...	...	...	...
Cienfuegos	149 145	...	...	46[13]	...	...	...	...
Guantánamo	217 235	...	...	34[13]	...	...	...	...
Holguín	292 581	...	...	58[13]	...	...	...	...
LA HABANA	2 125 320	...	...	721[13]	...	...	...	...
Las Tunas	167 355	...	...	31[13]	...	...	...	...
Matanzas	138 303	...	...	44[13]	...	...	...	...
Pinar del Río	142 689	...	...	32[13]	...	...	...	...
Sancti Spíritus	107 581	...	...	23[13]	...	...	...	...
Santa Clara	215 053	...	...	44[13]	...	...	...	...
Santiago de Cuba	433 527	...	...	70[13]	...	...	...	...

8. Population of capital cities and cities of 100 000 or more inhabitants: latest available year, 1996 - 2015
Population des capitales et des villes de 100 000 habitants ou plus : dernière année disponible, 1996 - 2015 (continued - suite)

Continent, country or area, date, code[a] and city / Continent, pays ou zone, date, code[a] et ville	City proper - Ville proprement dite				Urban agglomeration - Agglomération urbaine			
	Population			Surface area - Superficie (km²)	Population			Surface area - Superficie (km²)
	Both sexes - Les deux sexes	Male - Masculin	Female - Féminin		Both sexes - Les deux sexes	Male - Masculin	Female - Féminin	
AMERICA, NORTH - AMÉRIQUE DU NORD								
Dominican Republic - République dominicaine								
1 VII 2011 (ESDF)								
Azua	102 339[4]	51 620[4]	50 719[4]	155	...	...	...	...
Bajos de Haina	143 807[4]	71 130[4]	72 677[4]	40	...	...	...	...
Baní	177 588[4]	88 818[4]	88 770[4]	740	...	...	...	...
Boca Chica	122 216[4]	61 317[4]	60 899[4]	142	...	...	...	...
Bonao	148 857[4]	73 877[4]	74 980[4]	674	...	...	...	...
Higüey	211 453[4]	106 575[4]	104 878[4]	2 026	...	...	...	...
La Romana	152 454[4]	73 291[4]	79 163[4]	263	...	...	...	...
La Vega	273 547[4]	137 511[4]	136 036[4]	641	...	...	...	...
Los Alcarrizos	249 595[4]	126 001[4]	123 594[4]	46	...	...	...	...
Moca	182 767[4]	91 506[4]	91 261[4]	337	...	...	...	...
Puerto Plata	156 123[4]	76 741[4]	79 382[4]	496	...	...	...	...
San Cristóbal	278 767[4]	138 614[4]	140 153[4]	214	...	...	...	...
San Francisco de Macoris	185 925[4]	92 282[4]	93 643[4]	760	...	...	...	...
San Juan de la Maguana	137 881[4]	70 406[4]	67 475[4]	1 722	...	...	...	...
San Pedro de Macorís	233 255[4]	113 249[4]	120 006[4]	146	...	...	...	...
Santiago de los Caballeros	757 933[4]	372 332[4]	385 601[4]	529	...	...	...	...
SANTO DOMINGO	1 126 306[4]	537 506[4]	588 800[4]	91	1 126 306[4]	537 506[4]	588 800[4]	91
Santo Domingo East - Santo Domingo Este	966 393[4]	468 484[4]	497 909[4]	169	...	...	...	...
Santo Domingo North - Santo Domingo Norte	453 046[4]	228 840[4]	224 206[4]	388	...	...	...	...
Santo Domingo West - Santo Domingo Oeste	349 175[4]	170 849[4]	178 326[4]	54	...	...	...	...
El Salvador[14]								
1 IV 2014 (ESDF)								
Ahuachapán	118 164	55 953	62 212	245	...	...	...	...
Apopa	165 897	74 664	91 232	52	...	...	...	...
Ciudad Delgado	128 635	59 916	68 719	33	...	...	...	...
Ilopango	124 522	55 110	69 413	35	...	...	...	...
Mejicanos	146 915	67 462	79 452	22	...	...	...	...
San Miguel	249 638	114 939	134 700	594	...	...	...	...
SAN SALVADOR	281 870	133 352	148 518	72	...	...	...	...
Santa Ana	265 518	126 100	139 418	400	...	...	...	...
Santa Tecla	135 483	61 289	74 194	112	...	...	...	...
Soyapango	275 868	123 363	152 505	30	...	...	...	...
Greenland - Groenland[15]								
1 VII 2015 (ESDJ)								
NUUK (GODTHAB)	17 036	8 958	8 078	...	...	...	...	...
Guadeloupe								
8 III 1999 (CDJC)								
BASSE-TERRE	12 377	5 687	6 690	...	44 747	21 252	23 495	...
Pointe-à-Pitre	...	...	...	...	171 773	...	...	...
Guatemala								
1 VII 2001 (ESDF)								
CUIDAD DE GUATEMALA	1 022 001	491 891	530 110	228	...	...	...	...
Escuintla	114 626	57 893	56 733	332	...	...	...	...
Mixco	452 134	221 928	230 206	99	...	...	...	...
Quetzaltenango	152 223	76 272	75 951	120	...	...	...	...
Villa Nueva	390 329	192 238	198 091	114	...	...	...	...
Haiti - Haïti								
1 VII 1999 (ESDJ)								
Cap-Haitien	113 555	50 064	63 491	10	...	...	...	...
Carrefour	336 222	146 838	189 384	23	...	...	...	...
Delmas	284 079	124 774	159 305	26	...	...	...	...
PORT-AU-PRINCE	990 558	436 170	554 388	21	...	...	...	...
Honduras								
1 VII 2003 (ESDF)								
La Ceiba	137 815	67 691	70 124	...	...	...	...	...
San Pedro Sula	518 736	251 514	267 222	...	...	...	...	...
TEGUCIGALPA	858 437	411 687	446 749	...	...	...	...	...
Jamaica - Jamaïque								
4 IV 2011 (CDJC)								
KINGSTON[16]	...	...	...	...	592 291	285 509	306 782	149
Montego Bay	...	...	...	...	111 037	53 601	57 436	77

8. Population of capital cities and cities of 100 000 or more inhabitants: latest available year, 1996 - 2015
Population des capitales et des villes de 100 000 habitants ou plus : dernière année disponible, 1996 - 2015 (continued - suite)

Continent, country or area, date, code[a] and city Continent, pays ou zone, date, code[a] et ville	City proper - Ville proprement dite				Urban agglomeration - Agglomération urbaine			
	Population			Surface area - Superficie (km²)	Population			Surface area - Superficie (km²)
	Both sexes - Les deux sexes	Male - Masculin	Female - Féminin		Both sexes - Les deux sexes	Male - Masculin	Female - Féminin	
AMERICA, NORTH - AMÉRIQUE DU NORD								
Jamaica - Jamaïque								
4 IV 2011 (CDJC)								
Portmore	...	...	...	...	182 800	85 380	97 420	182
Spanish Town	...	...	...	...	149 479	72 885	76 594	65
Martinique								
1 I 2006 (CDJC)								
FORT-DE-FRANCE	90 347	40 128	50 219	...	133 281	59 945	73 336	...
Mexico - Mexique[4]								
1 VII 2015 (ESDJ)								
Acapulco	...	...	...	...	919 884	444 439	475 445	...
Acayucan	...	...	...	...	119 367	57 491	61 876	...
Aguascalientes	...	...	...	...	1 016 592	494 702	521 890	...
Apatzingán de la Constitución	...	...	...	...	101 751	...	...	...
Apizaco-Tlaxcala	...	...	...	...	546 348	262 726	283 621	...
Cabo San Lucas	...	...	...	...	160 585	...	...	...
Campeche	...	...	...	...	250 651	...	...	...
Cancún	...	...	...	...	801 924	405 198	396 726	...
Cárdenas	...	...	...	...	102 647	...	...	...
Celaya	...	...	...	...	640 481	306 464	334 017	...
Chetumal	...	...	...	...	180 429	...	...	...
Chihuahua	...	...	...	...	949 606	460 692	488 914	...
Chilpacingo de los Bravo	...	...	...	...	213 849	...	...	...
Ciudad Acuña	...	...	...	...	142 870	...	...	...
Ciudad Del Carmen	...	...	...	...	186 999	...	...	...
Ciudad Guzmán	...	...	...	...	103 019	...	...	...
Ciudad Lázaro Cárdenas	...	...	...	...	143 515	...	...	...
Ciudad Obregón	...	...	...	...	333 988	...	...	...
Ciudad Valles	...	...	...	...	132 766	...	...	...
Ciudad Victoria	...	...	...	...	332 822	...	...	...
Coatzacoalcos	...	...	...	...	370 556	179 830	190 727	...
Colima-Villa de Álvarez	...	...	...	...	370 645	180 420	190 225	...
Comitán de Domínguez	...	...	...	...	109 677	...	...	...
Córdoba	...	...	...	...	333 734	157 916	175 818	...
Cuauhtemoc	...	...	...	...	129 528	...	...	...
Cuautla	...	...	...	...	474 092	228 880	245 212	...
Cuernavaca	...	...	...	...	997 803	479 613	518 190	...
Culiacán Rosales	...	...	...	...	754 092	...	...	...
Delicias	...	...	...	...	130 967	...	...	...
Ensenada	...	...	...	...	306 441	...	...	...
Fresnillo	...	...	...	...	133 147	...	...	...
Guadalajara	...	...	...	...	4 796 050	2 346 539	2 449 511	...
Guanajuato	...	...	...	...	114 285	...	...	...
Guaymas	...	...	...	...	222 839	111 084	111 755	...
Hermosillo	...	...	...	...	788 696	...	...	...
Heroica Nogales	...	...	...	...	235 616	...	...	...
Hidalgo del Parral	...	...	...	...	113 376	...	...	...
Iguala de la Independencia	...	...	...	...	122 873	...	...	...
Irapuato	...	...	...	...	415 060	...	...	...
Juárez	...	...	...	...	1 423 166	703 686	719 480	...
La Laguna	...	...	...	...	1 313 161	643 310	669 851	...
La Paz	...	...	...	...	244 219	...	...	...
La Piedad-Pénjamo	...	...	...	...	261 697	124 215	137 483	...
Lagos de Moreno	...	...	...	...	105 696	...	...	...
León	...	...	...	...	1 714 464	833 412	881 052	...
Los Mochis	...	...	...	...	283 985	...	...	...
Manzanillo	...	...	...	...	157 501	...	...	...
Matamoros	...	...	...	...	524 951	259 553	265 398	...
Mazatlán	...	...	...	...	416 947	...	...	...
Mérida	...	...	...	...	1 064 114	517 721	546 392	...
Mexicali	...	...	...	...	1 025 740	516 172	509 568	...
MEXICO, CIUDAD DE	8 854 560	...	...	...	21 339 781	10 328 238	11 011 543	...
Minatitlán	...	...	...	...	378 003	182 758	195 245	...
Monclova-Frontera	...	...	...	...	338 517	168 015	170 502	...
Monterrey	...	...	...	...	4 477 614	2 224 323	2 253 291	...
Morelia	...	...	...	...	887 593	424 274	463 319	...

8. Population of capital cities and cities of 100 000 or more inhabitants: latest available year, 1996 - 2015
Population des capitales et des villes de 100 000 habitants ou plus : dernière année disponible, 1996 - 2015 (continued - suite)

Continent, country or area, date, code[a] and city / Continent, pays ou zone, date, code[a] et ville	City proper - Ville proprement dite				Urban agglomeration - Agglomération urbaine			
	Population			Surface area - Superficie (km²)	Population			Surface area - Superficie (km²)
	Both sexes - Les deux sexes	Male - Masculin	Female - Féminin		Both sexes - Les deux sexes	Male - Masculin	Female - Féminin	
AMERICA, NORTH - AMÉRIQUE DU NORD								
Mexico - Mexique[4]								
1 VII 2015 (ESDJ)								
Moroleón Uriangato - Moroleón-Uriangato	...	...	...	...	113 862	54 057	59 805	...
Navojoa	...	...	...	...	125 206	...	...	...
Nuevo Laredo	...	...	...	...	414 461	205 074	209 387	...
Oaxaca	...	...	...	...	654 870	308 239	346 631	...
Ocotlán	...	...	...	...	149 565	73 175	76 390	...
Orizaba	...	...	...	...	450 785	214 036	236 750	...
Pachuca	...	...	...	...	570 405	272 554	297 851	...
Piedras Negras	...	...	...	...	191 074	95 768	95 306	...
Playa del Carmen	...	...	...	...	194 103	...	...	...
Poza Rica	...	...	...	...	538 412	259 921	278 492	...
Puebla-Tlaxcala	...	...	...	...	2 954 767	1 417 349	1 537 419	...
Puerto Vallarta	...	...	...	...	443 837	222 865	220 972	...
Querétaro	...	...	...	...	1 213 537	589 653	623 884	...
Reynosa-Río Bravo	...	...	...	...	809 688	402 250	407 438	...
Rioverde-Ciudad Fernández	...	...	...	...	143 575	70 138	73 438	...
Salamanca	...	...	...	...	170 290	...	...	...
Saltillo	...	...	...	...	900 756	446 569	454 187	...
San Cristóbal de las Casas	...	...	...	...	173 550	...	...	...
San Francisco del Rincón	...	...	...	...	195 126	95 226	99 900	...
San José del Cabo	...	...	...	...	116 674	...	...	...
San Juan Bautista Tuxtepec	...	...	...	...	111 792	...	...	...
San Juan del Río	...	...	...	...	151 762	...	...	...
San Luis Potosí-Soledad de Graciano Sánchez	...	...	...	...	1 125 855	542 848	583 007	...
San Luis Rio Colorado	...	...	...	...	174 937	...	...	...
Tampico	...	...	...	...	928 253	450 762	477 491	...
Tapachula de Cordova y Ordoñez	...	...	...	...	232 360	...	...	...
Tecomán	...	...	...	...	156 697	78 604	78 093	...
Tehuacán	...	...	...	...	318 797	150 719	168 079	...
Tehuantepec	...	...	...	...	169 862	82 075	87 787	...
Tepic	...	...	...	...	484 994	235 548	249 446	...
Teziutlán	...	...	...	...	131 122	62 308	68 814	...
Tianguistenco	...	...	...	...	179 517	87 236	92 281	...
Tijuana	...	...	...	...	1 938 597	972 239	966 358	...
Toluca	...	...	...	...	2 189 481	1 068 288	1 121 193	...
Tula	...	...	...	...	220 087	107 195	112 892	...
Tulancingo	...	...	...	...	261 888	124 132	137 756	...
Túxpan de Rodríguez Cano	...	...	...	...	115 653	...	...	...
Tuxtla Gutiérrez	...	...	...	...	762 738	366 003	396 735	...
Uruapan	...	...	...	...	295 852	...	...	...
Veracruz	...	...	...	...	863 709	410 248	453 461	...
Victoria de Durango	...	...	...	...	572 782	...	...	...
Villahermosa	...	...	...	...	824 599	401 925	422 674	...
Xalapa	...	...	...	...	719 476	340 324	379 152	...
Zacatecas-Guadalupe	...	...	...	...	338 167	162 383	175 784	...
Zamora-Jacona	...	...	...	...	262 047	126 293	135 754	...
Nicaragua								
1 VII 2009 (ESDJ)								
Chinandega	...	...	...	...	106 635	...	...	...
León	...	...	...	...	156 049	...	...	...
MANAGUA	...	...	...	...	985 143	...	...	...
Masaya	...	...	...	...	110 491	...	...	...
Tipitapa	...	...	...	...	105 773	...	...	...
Panama								
1 VII 2015 (ESDF)								
CIUDAD DE PANAMÁ	468 843[17]	223 105[17]	245 738[17]	98	1 045 569[17]	511 548[17]	534 020[17]	288
San Miguelito	355 429[17]	173 749[17]	181 680[17]	50	...	...	...	...
Puerto Rico - Porto Rico								
1 VII 2014 (ESDJ)								
Bayamón	193 406[18]	...	...	71	...	...	...	...
Caguas	136 557[18]	...	...	94	...	...	...	...
Carolina	165 269[18]	...	...	73	...	...	...	...
Ponce	152 940[18]	...	...	184	...	...	...	...
SAN JUAN	363 862[18]	...	...	77	...	...	...	...

Continent, country or area, date, code[a] and city / Continent, pays ou zone, date, code[a] et ville	City proper - Ville proprement dite				Urban agglomeration - Agglomération urbaine			
	Population			Surface area - Superficie (km²)	Population			Surface area - Superficie (km²)
	Both sexes - Les deux sexes	Male - Masculin	Female - Féminin		Both sexes - Les deux sexes	Male - Masculin	Female - Féminin	
AMERICA, NORTH - AMÉRIQUE DU NORD								
Saint Lucia - Sainte-Lucie[19]								
10 V 2010* (CDJC)								
CASTRIES	3 661	1 790	1 871	...	...	...	...	...
Saint Pierre and Miquelon - Saint Pierre-et-Miquelon								
8 III 1999 (CDFC)								
SAINT-PIERRE	5 618	2 781	2 837	...	...	...	...	...
Trinidad and Tobago - Trinité-et-Tobago								
9 I 2011 (CDJC)								
PORT-OF-SPAIN	37 074	18 008	19 066	12	...	...	...	...
Turks and Caicos Islands - Îles Turques et Caïques								
1 VII 2006 (ESDJ)								
GRAND TURK	*5 718*	*2 846*	*2 872*	17	...	...	...	...
United States of America - États-Unis d'Amérique[20]								
1 VII 2015 (ESDJ)								
Abilene (TX)	121 721[21]	...	...	276[22]	...	...	...	...
Akron (OH)	197 542[21]	...	...	161[22]	...	...	...	...
Albuquerque (NM)	559 121[21]	...	...	487[22]	...	...	...	...
Alexandria (VA)	153 511[21]	...	...	39[22]	...	...	...	...
Allentown (PA)	120 207[21]	...	...	45[22]	...	...	...	...
Amarillo (TX)	198 645[21]	...	...	259[22]	...	...	...	...
Anaheim (CA)	350 742[21]	...	...	129[22]	...	...	...	...
Anchorage (AK)	298 695[21]	...	...	4 420[22]	...	...	...	...
Ann Arbor (MI)	117 070[21]	...	...	72[22]	...	...	...	...
Antioch (CA)	110 542[21]	...	...	76[22]	...	...	...	...
Arlington (TX)	388 125[21]	...	...	248[22]	...	...	...	...
Arvada (CO)	115 368[21]	...	...	99[22]	...	...	...	...
Athens (GA)	122 604[21]	...	...	301[22]	...	...	...	...
Atlanta (GA)	463 878[21]	...	...	345[22]	...	...	...	...
Augusta (GA)	197 182[21]	...	...	783[22]	...	...	...	...
Aurora (CO)	359 407[21]	...	...	398[22]	...	...	...	...
Aurora (IL)	200 661[21]	...	...	116[22]	...	...	...	...
Austin (TX)	931 830[21]	...	...	810[22]	...	...	...	...
Bakersfield (CA)	373 640[21]	...	...	385[22]	...	...	...	...
Baltimore (MD)	621 849[21]	...	...	210[22]	...	...	...	...
Baton Rouge (LA)	228 590[21]	...	...	223[22]	...	...	...	...
Beaumont (TX)	118 129[21]	...	...	213[22]	...	...	...	...
Bellevue (WA)	139 820[21]	...	...	87[22]	...	...	...	...
Berkeley (CA)	120 972[21]	...	...	27[22]	...	...	...	...
Billings (MT)	110 263[21]	...	...	112[22]	...	...	...	...
Birmingham (AL)	212 461[21]	...	...	378[22]	...	...	...	...
Boise City (ID)	218 281[21]	...	...	208[22]	...	...	...	...
Boston (MA)	667 137[21]	...	...	125[22]	...	...	...	...
Boulder (CO)	107 349[21]	...	...	64[22]	...	...	...	...
Bridgeport (CT)	147 629[21]	...	...	42[22]	...	...	...	...
Broken Arrow (OK)	106 563[21]	...	...	160[22]	...	...	...	...
Brownsville (TX)	183 887[21]	...	...	343[22]	...	...	...	...
Buffalo (NY)	258 071[21]	...	...	105[22]	...	...	...	...
Burbank (CA)	105 319[21]	...	...	45[22]	...	...	...	...
Cambridge (MA)	110 402[21]	...	...	17[22]	...	...	...	...
Cape Coral (FL)	175 229[21]	...	...	274[22]	...	...	...	...
Carlsbad (CA)	113 453[21]	...	...	98[22]	...	...	...	...
Carrollton (TX)	133 168[21]	...	...	94[22]	...	...	...	...
Cary (NC)	159 769[21]	...	...	144[22]	...	...	...	...
Cedar Rapids (IA)	130 405[21]	...	...	183[22]	...	...	...	...
Centennial (CO)	109 741[21]	...	...	76[22]	...	...	...	...
Chandler (AZ)	260 828[21]	...	...	168[22]	...	...	...	...
Charleston (SC)	132 609[21]	...	...	282[22]	...	...	...	...
Charlotte (NC)	827 097[21]	...	...	790[22]	...	...	...	...
Chattanooga (TN)	176 588[21]	...	...	371[22]	...	...	...	...
Chesapeake (VA)	235 429[21]	...	...	883[22]	...	...	...	...
Chicago (IL)	2 720 546[21]	...	...	590[22]	...	...	...	...

8. Population of capital cities and cities of 100 000 or more inhabitants: latest available year, 1996 - 2015
Population des capitales et des villes de 100 000 habitants ou plus : dernière année disponible, 1996 - 2015 (continued - suite)

Continent, country or area, date, code[a] and city Continent, pays ou zone, date, code[a] et ville	City proper - Ville proprement dite				Urban agglomeration - Agglomération urbaine			
	Population			Surface area - Superficie (km²)	Population			Surface area - Superficie (km²)
	Both sexes - Les deux sexes	Male - Masculin	Female - Féminin		Both sexes - Les deux sexes	Male - Masculin	Female - Féminin	

AMERICA, NORTH - AMÉRIQUE DU NORD

United States of America - États-Unis d'Amérique[20]
  1 VII 2015 (ESDJ)

Chula Vista (CA)	265 757[21]	...	...	129[22]	...	...	...	...
Cincinnati (OH)	298 550[21]	...	...	202[22]	...	...	...	...
Clarksville (TN)	149 176[21]	...	...	255[22]	...	...	...	...
Clearwater (FL)	113 003[21]	...	...	67[22]	...	...	...	...
Cleveland (OH)	388 072[21]	...	...	201[22]	...	...	...	...
Clovis (CA)	104 180[21]	...	...	62[22]	...	...	...	...
College Station (TX)	107 889[21]	...	...	131[22]	...	...	...	...
Colorado Springs (CO)	456 568[21]	...	...	506[22]	...	...	...	...
Columbia (MO)	119 108[21]	...	...	167[22]	...	...	...	...
Columbia (SC)	133 803[21]	...	...	346[22]	...	...	...	...
Columbus (GA)	200 579[21]	...	...	561[22]	...	...	...	...
Columbus (OH)	850 106[21]	...	...	565[22]	...	...	...	...
Concord (CA)	128 667[21]	...	...	79[22]	...	...	...	...
Coral Springs (FL)	129 485[21]	...	...	62[22]	...	...	...	...
Corona (CA)	164 226[21]	...	...	101[22]	...	...	...	...
Corpus Christi (TX)	324 074[21]	...	...	452[22]	...	...	...	...
Costa Mesa (CA)	113 204[21]	...	...	41[22]	...	...	...	...
Dallas (TX)	1 300 092[21]	...	...	884[22]	...	...	...	...
Daly City (CA)	106 562[21]	...	...	20[22]	...	...	...	...
Davenport (IA)	102 582[21]	...	...	163[22]	...	...	...	...
Davie (FL)	100 882[21]	...	...	90[22]	...	...	...	...
Dayton (OH)	140 599[21]	...	...	144[22]	...	...	...	...
Denton (TX)	131 044[21]	...	...	241[22]	...	...	...	...
Denver (CO)	682 545[21]	...	...	397[22]	...	...	...	...
Des Moines (IA)	210 330[21]	...	...	230[22]	...	...	...	...
Detroit (MI)	677 116[21]	...	...	359[22]	...	...	...	...
Downey (CA)	114 219[21]	...	...	32[22]	...	...	...	...
Durham (NC)	257 636[21]	...	...	283[22]	...	...	...	...
El Cajon (CA)	103 679[21]	...	...	38[22]	...	...	...	...
El Monte (CA)	116 732[21]	...	...	25[22]	...	...	...	...
El Paso (TX)	681 124[21]	...	...	665[22]	...	...	...	...
Elgin (IL)	112 111[21]	...	...	97[22]	...	...	...	...
Elizabeth (NJ)	129 007[21]	...	...	32[22]	...	...	...	...
Elk Grove (CA)	166 913[21]	...	...	109[22]	...	...	...	...
Escondido (CA)	151 451[21]	...	...	96[22]	...	...	...	...
Eugene (OR)	163 460[21]	...	...	114[22]	...	...	...	...
Evansville (IN)	119 943[21]	...	...	123[22]	...	...	...	...
Everett (WA)	108 010[21]	...	...	86[22]	...	...	...	...
Fairfield (CA)	112 970[21]	...	...	106[22]	...	...	...	...
Fargo (ND)	118 523[21]	...	...	127[22]	...	...	...	...
Fayetteville (NC)	201 963[21]	...	...	383[22]	...	...	...	...
Fontana (CA)	207 460[21]	...	...	112[22]	...	...	...	...
Fort Collins (CO)	161 175[21]	...	...	142[22]	...	...	...	...
Fort Lauderdale (FL)	178 590[21]	...	...	90[22]	...	...	...	...
Fort Wayne (IN)	260 326[21]	...	...	286[22]	...	...	...	...
Fort Worth (TX)	833 319[21]	...	...	882[22]	...	...	...	...
Fremont (CA)	232 206[21]	...	...	201[22]	...	...	...	...
Fresno (CA)	520 052[21]	...	...	294[22]	...	...	...	...
Frisco (TX)	154 407[21]	...	...	175[22]	...	...	...	...
Fullerton (CA)	140 847[21]	...	...	58[22]	...	...	...	...
Gainesville (FL)	130 128[21]	...	...	160[22]	...	...	...	...
Garden Grove (CA)	175 393[21]	...	...	47[22]	...	...	...	...
Garland (TX)	236 897[21]	...	...	148[22]	...	...	...	...
Gilbert (AZ)	247 542[21]	...	...	176[22]	...	...	...	...
Glendale (AZ)	240 126[21]	...	...	153[22]	...	...	...	...
Glendale (CA)	201 020[21]	...	...	79[22]	...	...	...	...
Grand Prairie (TX)	187 809[21]	...	...	187[22]	...	...	...	...
Grand Rapids (MI)	195 097[21]	...	...	115[22]	...	...	...	...
Greeley (CO)	100 883[21]	...	...	124[22]	...	...	...	...

8. Population of capital cities and cities of 100 000 or more inhabitants: latest available year, 1996 - 2015
Population des capitales et des villes de 100 000 habitants ou plus : dernière année disponible, 1996 - 2015 (continued - suite)

Continent, country or area, date, code[a] and city Continent, pays ou zone, date, code[a] et ville	City proper - Ville proprement dite				Urban agglomeration - Agglomération urbaine			
	Population			Surface area - Superficie (km²)	Population			Surface area - Superficie (km²)
	Both sexes - Les deux sexes	Male - Masculin	Female - Féminin		Both sexes - Les deux sexes	Male - Masculin	Female - Féminin	

AMERICA, NORTH - AMÉRIQUE DU NORD

United States of America - États-Unis d'Amérique[20]
1 VII 2015 (ESDJ)

Green Bay (WI)	105 207[21]	...	...	118[22]	...	...	...	...
Greensboro (NC)	285 342[21]	...	...	328[22]	...	...	...	...
Gresham (OR)	110 553[21]	...	...	60[22]	...	...	...	...
Hampton (VA)	136 454[21]	...	...	133[22]	...	...	...	...
Hartford (CT)	124 006[21]	...	...	45[22]	...	...	...	...
Hayward (CA)	158 289[21]	...	...	118[22]	...	...	...	...
Henderson (NV)	285 667[21]	...	...	271[22]	...	...	...	...
Hialeah (FL)	237 069[21]	...	...	56[22]	...	...	...	...
High Point City (NC)	110 268[21]	...	...	143[22]	...	...	...	...
Hillsboro (OR)	102 347[21]	...	...	63[22]	...	...	...	...
Hollywood (FL)	149 728[21]	...	...	71[22]	...	...	...	...
Houston (TX)	2 296 224[21]	...	...	1 631[22]	...	...	...	...
Huntington Beach (CA)	201 899[21]	...	...	70[22]	...	...	...	...
Huntsville (AL)	190 582[21]	...	...	552[22]	...	...	...	...
Independence (MO)	117 255[21]	...	...	202[22]	...	...	...	...
Indianapolis (IN)	853 173[21]	...	...	936[22]	...	...	...	...
Inglewood (CA)	111 666[21]	...	...	23[22]	...	...	...	...
Irvine (CA)	256 927[21]	...	...	170[22]	...	...	...	...
Irving (TX)	236 607[21]	...	...	174[22]	...	...	...	...
Jackson (MS)	170 674[21]	...	...	288[22]	...	...	...	...
Jacksonville (FL)	868 031[21]	...	...	1 936[22]	...	...	...	...
Jersey City (NJ)	264 290[21]	...	...	38[22]	...	...	...	...
Joliet (IL)	147 861[21]	...	...	164[22]	...	...	...	...
Jurupa Valley (CA)	100 314[21]	...	...	111[22]	...	...	...	...
Kansas City (KS)	151 306[21]	...	...	323[22]	...	...	...	...
Kansas City (MO)	475 378[21]	...	...	816[22]	...	...	...	...
Kent (WA)	126 952[21]	...	...	87[22]	...	...	...	...
Killeen (TX)	140 806[21]	...	...	139[22]	...	...	...	...
Knoxville (TN)	185 291[21]	...	...	255[22]	...	...	...	...
Lafayette (LA)	127 657[21]	...	...	139[22]	...	...	...	...
Lakeland (FL)	104 401[21]	...	...	170[22]	...	...	...	...
Lakewood (CO)	152 597[21]	...	...	111[22]	...	...	...	...
Lancaster (CA)	161 103[21]	...	...	244[22]	...	...	...	...
Lansing (MI)	115 056[21]	...	...	101[22]	...	...	...	...
Laredo (TX)	255 473[21]	...	...	253[22]	...	...	...	...
Las Cruces (NM)	101 643[21]	...	...	199[22]	...	...	...	...
Las Vegas (NV)	623 747[21]	...	...	346[22]	...	...	...	...
Lewisville (TX)	104 039[21]	...	...	95[22]	...	...	...	...
Lexington-Fayette (KY)	314 488[21]	...	...	735[22]	...	...	...	...
Lincoln (NE)	277 348[21]	...	...	237[22]	...	...	...	...
Little Rock (AR)	197 992[21]	...	...	307[22]	...	...	...	...
Long Beach (CA)	474 140[21]	...	...	130[22]	...	...	...	...
Los Angeles (CA)	3 971 883[21]	...	...	1 214[22]	...	...	...	...
Louisville (KY)	615 366[21]	...	...	842[22]	...	...	...	...
Lowell (MA)	110 699[21]	...	...	35[22]	...	...	...	...
Lubbock (TX)	249 042[21]	...	...	318[22]	...	...	...	...
Macon-Bibb (GA)	153 515[21]	...	...	646[22]	...	...	...	...
Madison (WI)	248 951[21]	...	...	199[22]	...	...	...	...
Manchester (NH)	110 229[21]	...	...	86[22]	...	...	...	...
McAllen (TX)	140 269[21]	...	...	128[22]	...	...	...	...
McKinney City (TX)	162 898[21]	...	...	161[22]	...	...	...	...
Memphis (TN)	655 770[21]	...	...	822[22]	...	...	...	...
Mesa (AZ)	471 825[21]	...	...	357[22]	...	...	...	...
Mesquite (TX)	144 788[21]	...	...	122[22]	...	...	...	...
Miami (FL)	441 003[21]	...	...	93[22]	...	...	...	...
Miami Gardens (FL)	113 187[21]	...	...	47[22]	...	...	...	...
Midland City (TX)	132 950[21]	...	...	189[22]	...	...	...	...
Milwaukee (WI)	600 155[21]	...	...	249[22]	...	...	...	...
Minneapolis (MN)	410 939[21]	...	...	140[22]	...	...	...	...

8. Population of capital cities and cities of 100 000 or more inhabitants: latest available year, 1996 - 2015
Population des capitales et des villes de 100 000 habitants ou plus : dernière année disponible, 1996 - 2015 (continued - suite)

Continent, country or area, date, code[a] and city / Continent, pays ou zone, date, code[a] et ville	City proper - Ville proprement dite				Urban agglomeration - Agglomération urbaine			
	Population			Surface area - Superficie (km²)	Population			Surface area - Superficie (km²)
	Both sexes - Les deux sexes	Male - Masculin	Female - Féminin		Both sexes - Les deux sexes	Male - Masculin	Female - Féminin	

AMERICA, NORTH - AMÉRIQUE DU NORD

United States of America - États-Unis d'Amérique[20]
  1 VII 2015 (ESDJ)

Miramar (FL)	137 132[21]	...	...	76[22]	...	...	...	...
Mobile (AL)	194 288[21]	...	...	360[22]	...	...	...	...
Modesto (CA)	211 266[21]	...	...	116[22]	...	...	...	...
Montgomery (AL)	200 602[21]	...	...	414[22]	...	...	...	...
Moreno Valley (CA)	204 198[21]	...	...	133[22]	...	...	...	...
Murfreesboro (TN)	126 118[21]	...	...	145[22]	...	...	...	...
Murrieta (CA)	109 830[21]	...	...	87[22]	...	...	...	...
Naperville (IL)	147 100[21]	...	...	100[22]	...	...	...	...
Nashville-Davidson (TN)	654 610[21]	...	...	1 233[22]	...	...	...	...
New Haven (CT)	130 322[21]	...	...	48[22]	...	...	...	...
New Orleans (LA)	389 617[21]	...	...	439[22]	...	...	...	...
New York (NY)	8 550 405[21]	...	...	781[22]	...	...	...	...
Newark (NJ)	281 944[21]	...	...	63[22]	...	...	...	...
Newport News (VA)	182 385[21]	...	...	178[22]	...	...	...	...
Norfolk (VA)	246 393[21]	...	...	140[22]	...	...	...	...
Norman (OK)	120 284[21]	...	...	463[22]	...	...	...	...
North Charleston (SC)	108 304[21]	...	...	191[22]	...	...	...	...
North Las Vegas (NV)	234 807[21]	...	...	254[22]	...	...	...	...
Norwalk (CA)	107 140[21]	...	...	25[22]	...	...	...	...
Oakland (CA)	419 267[21]	...	...	145[22]	...	...	...	...
Oceanside (CA)	175 691[21]	...	...	107[22]	...	...	...	...
Odessa (TX)	118 968[21]	...	...	117[22]	...	...	...	...
Oklahoma City (OK)	631 346[21]	...	...	1 571[22]	...	...	...	...
Olathe (KS)	134 305[21]	...	...	157[22]	...	...	...	...
Omaha (NE)	443 885[21]	...	...	345[22]	...	...	...	...
Ontario (CA)	171 214[21]	...	...	129[22]	...	...	...	...
Orange (CA)	140 992[21]	...	...	66[22]	...	...	...	...
Orlando (FL)	270 934[21]	...	...	266[22]	...	...	...	...
Overland Park (KS)	186 515[21]	...	...	195[22]	...	...	...	...
Oxnard (CA)	207 254[21]	...	...	70[22]	...	...	...	...
Palm Bay City (FL)	107 888[21]	...	...	170[22]	...	...	...	...
Palmdale (CA)	158 351[21]	...	...	274[22]	...	...	...	...
Pasadena (CA)	142 250[21]	...	...	60[22]	...	...	...	...
Pasadena (TX)	153 784[21]	...	...	113[22]	...	...	...	...
Paterson (NJ)	147 754[21]	...	...	22[22]	...	...	...	...
Pearland (TX)	108 821[21]	...	...	120[22]	...	...	...	...
Pembroke Pines (FL)	166 611[21]	...	...	85[22]	...	...	...	...
Peoria (AZ)	171 237[21]	...	...	455[22]	...	...	...	...
Peoria (IL)	115 070[21]	...	...	125[22]	...	...	...	...
Philadelphia (PA)	1 567 442[21]	...	...	348[22]	...	...	...	...
Phoenix (AZ)	1 563 025[21]	...	...	1 341[22]	...	...	...	...
Pittsburgh (PA)	304 391[21]	...	...	143[22]	...	...	...	...
Plano (TX)	283 558[21]	...	...	186[22]	...	...	...	...
Pomona (CA)	153 266[21]	...	...	59[22]	...	...	...	...
Pompano Beach (FL)	107 762[21]	...	...	62[22]	...	...	...	...
Port St. Lucie (FL)	179 413[21]	...	...	307[22]	...	...	...	...
Portland (OR)	632 309[21]	...	...	346[22]	...	...	...	...
Providence (RI)	179 207[21]	...	...	48[22]	...	...	...	...
Provo (UT)	115 264[21]	...	...	108[22]	...	...	...	...
Pueblo (CO)	109 412[21]	...	...	139[22]	...	...	...	...
Raleigh (NC)	451 066[21]	...	...	374[22]	...	...	...	...
Rancho Cucamonga (CA)	175 236[21]	...	...	103[22]	...	...	...	...
Reno (NV)	241 445[21]	...	...	278[22]	...	...	...	...
Renton (WA)	100 242[21]	...	...	61[22]	...	...	...	...
Rialto (CA)	103 132[21]	...	...	58[22]	...	...	...	...
Richardson (TX)	110 815[21]	...	...	74[22]	...	...	...	...
Richmond (CA)	109 708[21]	...	...	78[22]	...	...	...	...
Richmond (VA)	220 289[21]	...	...	155[22]	...	...	...	...
Riverside (CA)	322 424[21]	...	...	210[22]	...	...	...	...

8. Population of capital cities and cities of 100 000 or more inhabitants: latest available year, 1996 - 2015
Population des capitales et des villes de 100 000 habitants ou plus : dernière année disponible, 1996 - 2015 (continued - suite)

Continent, country or area, date, code[a] and city Continent, pays ou zone, date, code[a] et ville	City proper - Ville proprement dite				Urban agglomeration - Agglomération urbaine			
	Population			Surface area - Superficie (km²)	Population			Surface area - Superficie (km²)
	Both sexes - Les deux sexes	Male - Masculin	Female - Féminin		Both sexes - Les deux sexes	Male - Masculin	Female - Féminin	

AMERICA, NORTH - AMÉRIQUE DU NORD

United States of America - États-Unis d'Amérique[20]
1 VII 2015 (ESDJ)

Rochester (MN)	112 225[21]	...	...	141[22]	...	...	...	...
Rochester (NY)	209 802[21]	...	...	93[22]	...	...	...	...
Rockford (IL)	148 278[21]	...	...	164[22]	...	...	...	...
Roseville (CA)	130 269[21]	...	...	109[22]	...	...	...	...
Round Rock (TX)	115 997[21]	...	...	92[22]	...	...	...	...
Sacramento (CA)	490 712[21]	...	...	254[22]	...	...	...	...
Salem (OR)	164 549[21]	...	...	126[22]	...	...	...	...
Salinas (CA)	157 380[21]	...	...	61[22]	...	...	...	...
Salt Lake City (UT)	192 672[21]	...	...	288[22]	...	...	...	...
San Angelo (TX)	100 450[21]	...	...	154[22]	...	...	...	...
San Antonio (TX)	1 469 845[21]	...	...	1 194[22]	...	...	...	...
San Bernardino (CA)	216 108[21]	...	...	159[22]	...	...	...	...
San Buenaventura (CA)	109 708[21]	...	...	57[22]	...	...	...	...
San Diego (CA)	1 394 928[21]	...	...	842[22]	...	...	...	...
San Francisco (CA)	864 816[21]	...	...	121[22]	...	...	...	...
San Jose (CA)	1 026 908[21]	...	...	457[22]	...	...	...	...
San Mateo (CA)	103 536[21]	...	...	31[22]	...	...	...	...
Sandy Springs (GA)	105 330[21]	...	...	98[22]	...	...	...	...
Santa Ana (CA)	335 400[21]	...	...	70[22]	...	...	...	...
Santa Clara (CA)	126 215[21]	...	...	48[22]	...	...	...	...
Santa Clarita (CA)	182 371[21]	...	...	137[22]	...	...	...	...
Santa Maria (CA)	105 093[21]	...	...	59[22]	...	...	...	...
Santa Rosa (CA)	174 972[21]	...	...	107[22]	...	...	...	...
Savannah (GA)	145 674[21]	...	...	268[22]	...	...	...	...
Scottsdale (AZ)	236 839[21]	...	...	476[22]	...	...	...	...
Seattle (WA)	684 451[21]	...	...	217[22]	...	...	...	...
Shreveport (LA)	197 204[21]	...	...	277[22]	...	...	...	...
Simi Valley (CA)	126 788[21]	...	...	107[22]	...	...	...	...
Sioux Falls (SD)	171 544[21]	...	...	194[22]	...	...	...	...
South Bend (IN)	101 516[21]	...	...	107[22]	...	...	...	...
Spokane (WA)	213 272[21]	...	...	178[22]	...	...	...	...
Springfield (IL)	116 565[21]	...	...	155[22]	...	...	...	...
Springfield (MA)	154 341[21]	...	...	83[22]	...	...	...	...
Springfield (MO)	166 810[21]	...	...	213[22]	...	...	...	...
St. Louis (MO)	315 685[21]	...	...	160[22]	...	...	...	...
St. Paul (MN)	300 851[21]	...	...	135[22]	...	...	...	...
St. Petersburg (FL)	257 083[21]	...	...	160[22]	...	...	...	...
Stamford (CT)	128 874[21]	...	...	97[22]	...	...	...	...
Sterling Heights (MI)	132 052[21]	...	...	95[22]	...	...	...	...
Stockton (CA)	305 658[21]	...	...	160[22]	...	...	...	...
Sunnyvale (CA)	151 754[21]	...	...	57[22]	...	...	...	...
Surprise (AZ)	128 422[21]	...	...	279[22]	...	...	...	...
Syracuse (NY)	144 142[21]	...	...	65[22]	...	...	...	...
Tacoma (WA)	207 948[21]	...	...	129[22]	...	...	...	...
Tallahassee (FL)	189 907[21]	...	...	260[22]	...	...	...	...
Tampa (FL)	369 075[21]	...	...	294[22]	...	...	...	...
Temecula (CA)	112 011[21]	...	...	96[22]	...	...	...	...
Tempe (AZ)	175 826[21]	...	...	104[22]	...	...	...	...
Thornton (CO)	133 451[21]	...	...	92[22]	...	...	...	...
Thousand Oaks (CA)	129 339[21]	...	...	143[22]	...	...	...	...
Toledo (OH)	279 789[21]	...	...	209[22]	...	...	...	...
Topeka (KS)	127 265[21]	...	...	158[22]	...	...	...	...
Torrance (CA)	148 475[21]	...	...	53[22]	...	...	...	...
Tucson (AZ)	531 641[21]	...	...	598[22]	...	...	...	...
Tulsa (OK)	403 505[21]	...	...	510[22]	...	...	...	...
Tyler (TX)	103 700[21]	...	...	147[22]	...	...	...	...
Urban Honolulu (HI)	352 769[21]	...	...	157[22]	...	...	...	...
Vallejo (CA)	121 253[21]	...	...	79[22]	...	...	...	...
Vancouver (WA)	172 860[21]	...	...	121[22]	...	...	...	...

8. Population of capital cities and cities of 100 000 or more inhabitants: latest available year, 1996 - 2015
Population des capitales et des villes de 100 000 habitants ou plus : dernière année disponible, 1996 - 2015 (continued - suite)

Continent, country or area, date, code[a] and city / Continent, pays ou zone, date, code[a] et ville	City proper - Ville proprement dite				Urban agglomeration - Agglomération urbaine			
	Population			Surface area - Superficie (km²)	Population			Surface area - Superficie (km²)
	Both sexes - Les deux sexes	Male - Masculin	Female - Féminin		Both sexes - Les deux sexes	Male - Masculin	Female - Féminin	

AMERICA, NORTH - AMÉRIQUE DU NORD

United States of America - États-Unis d'Amérique[20]
  1 VII 2015 (ESDJ)

Victorville City (CA)	122 225[21]	...	...	190[22]	...	...	...	...
Virginia Beach (VA)	452 745[21]	...	...	647[22]	...	...	...	...
Visalia (CA)	130 104[21]	...	...	96[22]	...	...	...	...
Vista (CA)	100 890[21]	...	...	48[22]	...	...	...	...
Waco (TX)	132 356[21]	...	...	231[22]	...	...	...	...
Warren (MI)	135 358[21]	...	...	89[22]	...	...	...	...
WASHINGTON (DC)	672 228[21]	...	...	158[22]	...	...	...	...
Waterbury (CT)	108 802[21]	...	...	74[22]	...	...	...	...
West Covina (CA)	108 484[21]	...	...	42[22]	...	...	...	...
West Jordan (UT)	111 946[21]	...	...	84[22]	...	...	...	...
West Palm Beach (FL)	106 779[21]	...	...	143[22]	...	...	...	...
West Valley City (UT)	136 208[21]	...	...	92[22]	...	...	...	...
Westminster (CO)	113 130[21]	...	...	82[22]	...	...	...	...
Wichita (KS)	389 965[21]	...	...	414[22]	...	...	...	...
Wichita Falls (TX)	104 710[21]	...	...	187[22]	...	...	...	...
Wilmington (NC)	115 933[21]	...	...	134[22]	...	...	...	...
Winston-Salem (NC)	241 218[21]	...	...	343[22]	...	...	...	...
Worcester (MA)	184 815[21]	...	...	97[22]	...	...	...	...
Yonkers (NY)	201 116[21]	...	...	47[22]	...	...	...	...

United States Virgin Islands - Îles Vierges américaines[23]
  1 IV 2010 (CDJC)

CHARLOTTE AMALIE	10 354	...	...	...	...	...	...	...

AMERICA, SOUTH - AMÉRIQUE DU SUD

Argentina - Argentine[24]
  1 VII 2015 (ESDF)

Bahía Blanca-Cerri	...	...	...	...	307 070	147 874	159 196	...
Bariloche	...	...	...	...	154 716	78 079	76 637	...
BUENOS AIRES[25]	...	...	...	...	12 847 328	6 212 253	6 635 075	...
Catamarca	...	...	...	...	210 627	102 333	108 294	...
Comodoro Rivadavia-Rada Tilly	...	...	...	...	213 775	109 020	104 755	...
Concordia	...	...	...	...	160 525	78 302	82 223	...
Córdoba	...	...	...	...	1 517 610	727 682	789 928	...
Corrientes	...	...	...	...	382 208	183 582	198 626	...
Formosa	...	...	...	...	257 004	124 745	132 259	...
La Plata	...	...	...	...	834 530	404 610	429 920	...
La Rioja	...	...	...	...	203 257	100 055	103 202	...
Mar del Plata-Batán	...	...	...	...	635 022	305 237	329 785	...
Mendoza	...	...	...	...	1 079 744	526 105	553 639	...
Neuquén-Plottier	...	...	...	...	308 314	152 432	155 882	...
Paraná	...	...	...	...	274 363	131 274	143 089	...
Posadas	...	...	...	...	353 909	170 406	183 503	...
Rawson-Trelew-Playa Unión	...	...	...	...	138 024	67 421	70 603	...
Resistencia	...	...	...	...	409 056	197 335	211 721	...
Río Cuarto	...	...	...	...	172 267	82 744	89 523	...
Rio Gallegos	...	...	...	...	110 107	55 609	54 498	...
Rosario	...	...	...	...	1 426 517	691 949	734 568	...
Salta	...	...	...	...	623 941	301 577	322 364	...
San Juan	...	...	...	...	514 965	248 959	266 006	...
San Luis - El Chorrillo	...	...	...	...	217 726	106 630	111 096	...
San Nicolás-Villa Constitución	...	...	...	...	188 937	92 359	96 578	...
San Salvador de Jujuy-Palpalá	...	...	...	...	337 748	163 279	174 469	...
Santa Fé	...	...	...	...	529 379	254 311	275 068	...
Santa Rosa-Toay	...	...	...	...	125 513	60 958	64 555	...
Santiago del Estero-La Banda	...	...	...	...	405 054	195 597	209 457	...
Tucumán-Tafí Viejo[26]	...	...	...	...	867 724	417 837	449 887	...
Ushuaia-Río Grande	...	...	...	...	137 371	70 692	66 679	...

8. Population of capital cities and cities of 100 000 or more inhabitants: latest available year, 1996 - 2015
Population des capitales et des villes de 100 000 habitants ou plus : dernière année disponible, 1996 - 2015 (continued - suite)

Continent, country or area, date, code[a] and city Continent, pays ou zone, date, code[a] et ville	City proper - Ville proprement dite				Urban agglomeration - Agglomération urbaine			
	Population			Surface area - Superficie (km²)	Population			Surface area - Superficie (km²)
	Both sexes - Les deux sexes	Male - Masculin	Female - Féminin		Both sexes - Les deux sexes	Male - Masculin	Female - Féminin	

AMERICA, SOUTH - AMÉRIQUE DU SUD

Bolivia (Plurinational State of) - Bolivie (État plurinational de)

1 VII 2010 (ESDF)

Cochabamba	618 376	294 711	323 666	...	...	...	...	...
El Alto	953 253	463 069	490 184	...	...	...	...	...
LA PAZ	835 361	397 608	437 753	...	...	...	...	...
Oruro	216 724	104 294	112 430	...	...	...	...	...
Potosí	154 693	74 591	80 103	...	...	...	...	...
Sacaba	155 668	75 113	80 555	...	...	...	...	...
Santa Cruz	1 616 063	785 941	830 122	...	...	...	...	...
SUCRE	284 032	137 943	146 090	...	...	...	...	...
Tarija	194 313	94 231	100 082	...	...	...	...	...
Yacuiba	112 096	55 346	56 750	...	...	...	...	...

Brazil - Brésil[14]

1 VII 2015 (ESDF)

Abaeteluba	150 431	...	...	...	...	...	...	...
Açailândia	109 685	...	...	...	...	...	...	...
Aguas Lindas de Goiás	187 072	...	...	...	...	...	...	...
Alagoinhas	154 495	...	...	...	...	...	...	...
Almirante Tamandaré	112 870	...	...	...	...	...	...	...
Altamira	108 382	...	...	...	...	...	...	...
Alvorada	206 561	...	...	...	...	...	...	...
Americana	229 322	...	...	...	...	...	...	...
Ananindeua	505 404	...	...	...	...	...	...	...
Anápolis	366 491	...	...	...	...	...	...	...
Angra dos Reis	188 276	...	...	...	...	...	...	...
Aparecida de Goiania	521 910	...	...	...	...	...	...	...
Apucarana	130 430	...	...	...	...	...	...	...
Aracaju	632 744	...	...	...	...	...	...	...
Araçatuba	192 757	...	...	...	...	...	...	...
Araguaina	170 183	...	...	...	...	...	...	...
Araguario	116 267	...	...	...	...	...	...	...
Arapiraca	231 053	...	...	...	...	...	...	...
Arapongas	115 412	...	...	...	...	...	...	...
Araraquara	226 508	...	...	...	...	...	...	...
Araras	128 895	...	...	...	...	...	...	...
Araruama	122 865	...	...	...	...	...	...	...
Araucária	133 428	...	...	...	...	...	...	...
Araxá	102 238	...	...	...	...	...	...	...
Ariquemes	104 401	...	...	...	...	...	...	...
Assis	101 597	...	...	...	...	...	...	...
Atibaia	137 187	...	...	...	...	...	...	...
Bacabal	102 656	...	...	...	...	...	...	...
Bagé	121 749	...	...	...	...	...	...	...
Balneário Camboriú	128 155	...	...	...	...	...	...	...
Barbacena	134 924	...	...	...	...	...	...	...
Barcarena	115 779	...	...	...	...	...	...	...
Barra Mansa	179 915	...	...	...	...	...	...	...
Barreiras	153 918	...	...	...	...	...	...	...
Barretos	119 243	...	...	...	...	...	...	...
Barueri	262 275	...	...	...	...	...	...	...
Bauru	366 992	...	...	...	...	...	...	...
Belém	1 439 561	...	...	...	...	...	...	...
Belford Roxo	481 127	...	...	...	...	...	...	...
Belo Horizonte	2 502 557	...	...	...	...	...	...	...
Bento Gonçalves	113 287	...	...	...	...	...	...	...
Betim	417 307	...	...	...	...	...	...	...
Birigui	118 352	...	...	...	...	...	...	...
Blumenou	338 876	...	...	...	...	...	...	...
Boa Vista	320 714	...	...	...	...	...	...	...
Botucatu	139 483	...	...	...	...	...	...	...
Bragança	121 528	...	...	...	...	...	...	...
Bragança Paulista	160 665	...	...	...	...	...	...	...
BRASILIA	2 914 830	...	...	...	...	...	...	...
Brusque	122 775	...	...	...	...	...	...	...

8. Population of capital cities and cities of 100 000 or more inhabitants: latest available year, 1996 - 2015
Population des capitales et des villes de 100 000 habitants ou plus : dernière année disponible, 1996 - 2015 (continued - suite)

Continent, country or area, date, code[a] and city / Continent, pays ou zone, date, code[a] et ville	City proper - Ville proprement dite				Urban agglomeration - Agglomération urbaine			
	Population			Surface area - Superficie (km²)	Population			Surface area - Superficie (km²)
	Both sexes - Les deux sexes	Male - Masculin	Female - Féminin		Both sexes - Les deux sexes	Male - Masculin	Female - Féminin	

AMERICA, SOUTH - AMÉRIQUE DU SUD

Brazil - Brésil[14]
1 VII 2015 (ESDF)

Cabo de Santo Agostinho	200 546	...	...	...	...	...	...	...
Cabo Frio	208 451	...	...	...	...	...	...	...
Cachoeirinha	125 975	...	...	...	...	...	...	...
Cachoeiro de Itapemirim	208 702	...	...	...	...	...	...	...
Camacari	286 919	...	...	...	...	...	...	...
Camaragibe	154 054	...	...	...	...	...	...	...
Cambé	103 822	...	...	...	...	...	...	...
Cametá	130 868	...	...	...	...	...	...	...
Campina Grande	405 072	...	...	...	...	...	...	...
Campinas	1 164 098	...	...	...	...	...	...	...
Campo Grande	853 622	...	...	...	...	...	...	...
Campo Largo	124 098	...	...	...	...	...	...	...
Campos dos Goytacazes	483 970	...	...	...	...	...	...	...
Canoas	341 343	...	...	...	...	...	...	...
Caraguatatuba	113 317	...	...	...	...	...	...	...
Carapicuíba	392 294	...	...	...	...	...	...	...
Cariacica	381 802	...	...	...	...	...	...	...
Caruaru	347 088	...	...	...	...	...	...	...
Cascavel	312 778	...	...	...	...	...	...	...
Castanhal	189 784	...	...	...	...	...	...	...
Catanduva	119 480	...	...	...	...	...	...	...
Caucaia	353 932	...	...	...	...	...	...	...
Caxias	161 137	...	...	...	...	...	...	...
Caxias do Sul	474 853	...	...	...	...	...	...	...
Chapecó	205 795	...	...	...	...	...	...	...
Codo	120 265	...	...	...	...	...	...	...
Colatina	122 646	...	...	...	...	...	...	...
Colombo	232 432	...	...	...	...	...	...	...
Conselheiro Lafaiete	125 421	...	...	...	...	...	...	...
Contagem	648 766	...	...	...	...	...	...	...
Coronel Fabriciano	109 363	...	...	...	...	...	...	...
Corumbá	108 656	...	...	...	...	...	...	...
Cotia	229 548	...	...	...	...	...	...	...
Crato	128 680	...	...	...	...	...	...	...
Criciúma	206 918	...	...	...	...	...	...	...
Cubatao	127 006	...	...	...	...	...	...	...
Cuiabá	580 489	...	...	...	...	...	...	...
Curitiba	1 879 355	...	...	...	...	...	...	...
Diadema	412 428	...	...	...	...	...	...	...
Divinópolis	230 848	...	...	...	...	...	...	...
Dourados	212 870	...	...	...	...	...	...	...
Duque de Caxias	882 729	...	...	...	...	...	...	...
Embu	261 781	...	...	...	...	...	...	...
Erechim	102 345	...	...	...	...	...	...	...
Eunápolis	113 191	...	...	...	...	...	...	...
Feira de Santana	617 528	...	...	...	...	...	...	...
Ferraz de Vasconcelos	184 700	...	...	...	...	...	...	...
Florianópolis	469 690	...	...	...	...	...	...	...
Formosa	112 236	...	...	...	...	...	...	...
Fortaleza	2 591 188	...	...	...	...	...	...	...
Foz do Iguaçu	263 782	...	...	...	...	...	...	...
Franca	342 112	...	...	...	...	...	...	...
Francisco Morato	168 243	...	...	...	...	...	...	...
Franco da Rocha	145 755	...	...	...	...	...	...	...
Garanhuns	136 949	...	...	...	...	...	...	...
Goiânia	1 430 697	...	...	...	...	...	...	...
Governador Valadares	278 363	...	...	...	...	...	...	...
Gravatai	272 257	...	...	...	...	...	...	...
Guarapari	119 802	...	...	...	...	...	...	...
Guarapuava	178 126	...	...	...	...	...	...	...
Guaratinguetá	119 073	...	...	...	...	...	...	...
Guarujá	311 230	...	...	...	...	...	...	...
Guarulhos	1 324 781	...	...	...	...	...	...	...

8. Population of capital cities and cities of 100 000 or more inhabitants: latest available year, 1996 - 2015
Population des capitales et des villes de 100 000 habitants ou plus : dernière année disponible, 1996 - 2015 (continued - suite)

Continent, country or area, date, code[a] and city / Continent, pays ou zone, date, code[a] et ville	City proper - Ville proprement dite				Urban agglomeration - Agglomération urbaine			
	Population			Surface area - Superficie (km²)	Population			Surface area - Superficie (km²)
	Both sexes - Les deux sexes	Male - Masculin	Female - Féminin		Both sexes - Les deux sexes	Male - Masculin	Female - Féminin	

AMERICA, SOUTH - AMÉRIQUE DU SUD

Brazil - Brésil[14]
1 VII 2015 (ESDF)

	Both sexes	Male	Female	Surface	Both sexes	Male	Female	Surface
Hortolandia	215 819	...	...	...	...	...	...	...
Ibirité	173 873	...	...	...	...	...	...	...
Igarassu	112 463	...	...	...	...	...	...	...
Iguatu	101 386	...	...	...	...	...	...	...
Ilhéus	180 213	...	...	...	...	...	...	...
Imperatriz	253 123	...	...	...	...	...	...	...
Indaiatuba	231 033	...	...	...	...	...	...	...
Ipatinga	257 345	...	...	...	...	...	...	...
Itabiraí	117 634	...	...	...	...	...	...	...
Itaboraí	229 007	...	...	...	...	...	...	...
Itabuna	219 680	...	...	...	...	...	...	...
Itaguaí	119 143	...	...	...	...	...	...	...
Itajaí	205 271	...	...	...	...	...	...	...
Itapecerica da Serra	167 236	...	...	...	...	...	...	...
Itapetininga	157 016	...	...	...	...	...	...	...
Itapevi	223 404	...	...	...	...	...	...	...
Itapipoca	124 950	...	...	...	...	...	...	...
Itaquaquecetuba	352 801	...	...	...	...	...	...	...
Itatiba	113 284	...	...	...	...	...	...	...
Itu	167 095	...	...	...	...	...	...	...
Ituiutaba	103 333	...	...	...	...	...	...	...
Itumbiara	100 548	...	...	...	...	...	...	...
Jaboatao dos Guarapes	686 122	...	...	...	...	...	...	...
Jacareí	226 539	...	...	...	...	...	...	...
Jandira	118 832	...	...	...	...	...	...	...
Jaraguá do Sul	163 735	...	...	...	...	...	...	...
Jaú	143 283	...	...	...	...	...	...	...
Jequié	161 528	...	...	...	...	...	...	...
Ji-Paraná	130 419	...	...	...	...	...	...	...
Joao Pessoa	791 438	...	...	...	...	...	...	...
Joinville	562 151	...	...	...	...	...	...	...
Juazeiro	218 324	...	...	...	...	...	...	...
Juàzeiro do Norte	266 022	...	...	...	...	...	...	...
Juiz de Fora	555 284	...	...	...	...	...	...	...
Jundiaí	401 896	...	...	...	...	...	...	...
Lagarto	102 257	...	...	...	...	...	...	...
Lages	158 732	...	...	...	...	...	...	...
Lauro de Freitas	191 436	...	...	...	...	...	...	...
Lavras	100 243	...	...	...	...	...	...	...
Limeira	296 440	...	...	...	...	...	...	...
Linhares	163 662	...	...	...	...	...	...	...
Londrina	548 249	...	...	...	...	...	...	...
Luziânia	194 039	...	...	...	...	...	...	...
Macae	234 628	...	...	...	...	...	...	...
Macapá	456 171	...	...	...	...	...	...	...
Maceió	1 013 773	...	...	...	...	...	...	...
Magé	234 809	...	...	...	...	...	...	...
Manaus	2 057 711	...	...	...	...	...	...	...
Maraba	262 085	...	...	...	...	...	...	...
Maracanau	221 504	...	...	...	...	...	...	...
Maranguape	123 570	...	...	...	...	...	...	...
Maricá	146 549	...	...	...	...	...	...	...
Marília	232 006	...	...	...	...	...	...	...
Maringá	397 437	...	...	...	...	...	...	...
Marituba	122 916	...	...	...	...	...	...	...
Mauá	453 286	...	...	...	...	...	...	...
Mesquita	170 751	...	...	...	...	...	...	...
Moji das Cruzes	424 633	...	...	...	...	...	...	...
Moji-Guaçu	170 751	...	...	...	...	...	...	...
Montes Claros	394 350	...	...	...	...	...	...	...
Mossoró	288 162	...	...	...	...	...	...	...
Muriaé	107 263	...	...	...	...	...	...	...
Natal	869 954	...	...	...	...	...	...	...

8. Population of capital cities and cities of 100 000 or more inhabitants: latest available year, 1996 - 2015
Population des capitales et des villes de 100 000 habitants ou plus : dernière année disponible, 1996 - 2015 (continued - suite)

Continent, country or area, date, code[a] and city Continent, pays ou zone, date, code[a] et ville	City proper - Ville proprement dite				Urban agglomeration - Agglomération urbaine			
	Population			Surface area - Superficie (km²)	Population			Surface area - Superficie (km²)
	Both sexes - Les deux sexes	Male - Masculin	Female - Féminin		Both sexes - Les deux sexes	Male - Masculin	Female - Féminin	

AMERICA, SOUTH - AMÉRIQUE DU SUD

Brazil - Brésil[14]
  1 VII 2015 (ESDF)

Nilópolis	158 309	...	...	...	...	...	...	...
Niterói	496 696	...	...	...	...	...	...	...
Nossa Senhora do Socorro	177 344	...	...	...	...	...	...	...
Nova Friburgo	184 786	...	...	...	...	...	...	...
Nova Iguaçu	807 492	...	...	...	...	...	...	...
Novo Gama	106 677	...	...	...	...	...	...	...
Nôvo Hamburgo	248 694	...	...	...	...	...	...	...
Olinda	389 494	...	...	...	...	...	...	...
Osasco	694 844	...	...	...	...	...	...	...
Ourinhos	110 282	...	...	...	...	...	...	...
Paço do Lumiar	117 877	...	...	...	...	...	...	...
Palhoça	157 833	...	...	...	...	...	...	...
Palmas	272 726	...	...	...	...	...	...	...
Paragominas	107 010	...	...	...	...	...	...	...
Paranaguá	150 660	...	...	...	...	...	...	...
Parauapebas	189 921	...	...	...	...	...	...	...
Parintins	111 575	...	...	...	...	...	...	...
Parnaíba	149 803	...	...	...	...	...	...	...
Parnamirim	242 384	...	...	...	...	...	...	...
Passo Fundo	196 739	...	...	...	...	...	...	...
Passos	113 122	...	...	...	...	...	...	...
Patos	106 314	...	...	...	...	...	...	...
Patos de Minas	148 762	...	...	...	...	...	...	...
Paulista	322 730	...	...	...	...	...	...	...
Paulo Afonso	119 214	...	...	...	...	...	...	...
Pelotas	342 873	...	...	...	...	...	...	...
Petrolina	331 951	...	...	...	...	...	...	...
Petrópolis	298 142	...	...	...	...	...	...	...
Pindamonhangaba	160 614	...	...	...	...	...	...	...
Pinhais	127 045	...	...	...	...	...	...	...
Piracicaba	391 449	...	...	...	...	...	...	...
Piraquara	104 481	...	...	...	...	...	...	...
Poà	113 793	...	...	...	...	...	...	...
Poços de Caldas	163 677	...	...	...	...	...	...	...
Ponta Grossa	337 865	...	...	...	...	...	...	...
Porto Alegre	1 476 867	...	...	...	...	...	...	...
Porto Seguro	145 431	...	...	...	...	...	...	...
Porto Velho	502 748	...	...	...	...	...	...	...
Pouso Alegre	143 846	...	...	...	...	...	...	...
Praia Grande	299 261	...	...	...	...	...	...	...
Presidente Prudente	222 192	...	...	...	...	...	...	...
Queimados	143 632	...	...	...	...	...	...	...
Recife	1 617 183	...	...	...	...	...	...	...
Resende	125 214	...	...	...	...	...	...	...
Ribeirao das Neves	322 659	...	...	...	...	...	...	...
Ribeirao Pires	120 396	...	...	...	...	...	...	...
Ribeirao Prêto	666 323	...	...	...	...	...	...	...
Rio Branco	370 550	...	...	...	...	...	...	...
Rio Claro	199 961	...	...	...	...	...	...	...
Rio das Ostras	131 976	...	...	...	...	...	...	...
Rio de Janeiro	6 476 631	...	...	...	...	...	...	...
Rio Grande	207 860	...	...	...	...	...	...	...
Rio Verde	207 296	...	...	...	...	...	...	...
Rondonópolis	215 320	...	...	...	...	...	...	...
Sabára	134 382	...	...	...	...	...	...	...
Salto	114 171	...	...	...	...	...	...	...
Salvador	2 921 087	...	...	...	...	...	...	...
Santa Bárbara D'Oeste	190 139	...	...	...	...	...	...	...
Santa Cruz do Capibaribe	101 485	...	...	...	...	...	...	...
Santa Cruz do Sul	126 084	...	...	...	...	...	...	...
Santa Luzia (Minas Gerais)	216 254	...	...	...	...	...	...	...
Santa Maria	276 108	...	...	...	...	...	...	...
Santa Rita	134 940	...	...	...	...	...	...	...

Continent, country or area, date, code[a] and city — Continent, pays ou zone, date, code[a] et ville	City proper - Ville proprement dite				Urban agglomeration - Agglomération urbaine			
	Population			Surface area - Superficie (km²)	Population			Surface area - Superficie (km²)
	Both sexes - Les deux sexes	Male - Masculin	Female - Féminin		Both sexes - Les deux sexes	Male - Masculin	Female - Féminin	
AMERICA, SOUTH - AMÉRIQUE DU SUD								
Brazil - Brésil[14]								
1 VII 2015 (ESDF)								
Santana	112 218	...	...	...	...	...	...	...
Santana de Parnaíba	126 574	...	...	...	...	...	...	...
Santarém	292 520	...	...	...	...	...	...	...
Santo André	710 210	...	...	...	...	...	...	...
Santo Antônio de Jesus	101 548	...	...	...	...	...	...	...
Santos	433 966	...	...	...	...	...	...	...
Sao Bernardo do Campo	816 925	...	...	...	...	...	...	...
Sao Caetano do Sul	158 024	...	...	...	...	...	...	...
Sao Carlo	241 389	...	...	...	...	...	...	...
São Félix do Xingu	116 186	...	...	...	...	...	...	...
Sao Gonçalo	1 038 081	...	...	...	...	...	...	...
Sao Joao de Meriti	460 625	...	...	...	...	...	...	...
Sao José	232 309	...	...	...	...	...	...	...
Sao José de Ribamar	174 267	...	...	...	...	...	...	...
Sao José do Rio Prêto	442 548	...	...	...	...	...	...	...
Sao José dos Campos	688 597	...	...	...	...	...	...	...
Sao José dos Pinhais	297 895	...	...	...	...	...	...	...
Sao Leopoldo	228 370	...	...	...	...	...	...	...
São Lourenço da Mata	110 264	...	...	...	...	...	...	...
Sao Luís	1 073 893	...	...	...	...	...	...	...
São Mateus	124 575	...	...	...	...	...	...	...
Sao Paulo	11 967 825	...	...	...	...	...	...	...
Sao Vicente	355 542	...	...	...	...	...	...	...
Sapucaia do Sul	138 357	...	...	...	...	...	...	...
Senador Canedo	100 367	...	...	...	...	...	...	...
Serra	485 376	...	...	...	...	...	...	...
Sertaozinho	120 152	...	...	...	...	...	...	...
Sete Lagoas	232 107	...	...	...	...	...	...	...
Simoes Filho	133 202	...	...	...	...	...	...	...
Sinop	129 916	...	...	...	...	...	...	...
Sobral	201 756	...	...	...	...	...	...	...
Sorocaba	644 919	...	...	...	...	...	...	...
Sumaré	265 955	...	...	...	...	...	...	...
Susano	285 280	...	...	...	...	...	...	...
Taboao da Serra	272 177	...	...	...	...	...	...	...
Tatuí	116 682	...	...	...	...	...	...	...
Taubaté	302 331	...	...	...	...	...	...	...
Teixeira de Freitas	157 804	...	...	...	...	...	...	...
Teófilo Otoni	141 046	...	...	...	...	...	...	...
Teresina	844 245	...	...	...	...	...	...	...
Teresópolis	173 060	...	...	...	...	...	...	...
Timon	164 869	...	...	...	...	...	...	...
Toledo	132 077	...	...	...	...	...	...	...
Três Lagoas	113 619	...	...	...	...	...	...	...
Trindade	117 454	...	...	...	...	...	...	...
Tubarão	102 883	...	...	...	...	...	...	...
Tucuruí	107 189	...	...	...	...	...	...	...
Ubá	111 012	...	...	...	...	...	...	...
Uberaba	322 126	...	...	...	...	...	...	...
Uberlândia	662 362	...	...	...	...	...	...	...
Umuarama	108 218	...	...	...	...	...	...	...
Uruguaiana	129 652	...	...	...	...	...	...	...
Valinhos	120 258	...	...	...	...	...	...	...
Valparaíso de Goiás	153 255	...	...	...	...	...	...	...
Varginha	132 353	...	...	...	...	...	...	...
Varzea Grande	268 594	...	...	...	...	...	...	...
Varzea Paulista	116 601	...	...	...	...	...	...	...
Vespasiano	118 557	...	...	...	...	...	...	...
Viamao	251 978	...	...	...	...	...	...	...
Vila Velha	472 762	...	...	...	...	...	...	...
Vitória	355 875	...	...	...	...	...	...	...
Vitória da Conquista	343 230	...	...	...	...	...	...	...
Vitória de Santo Antao	135 805	...	...	...	...	...	...	...

8. Population of capital cities and cities of 100 000 or more inhabitants: latest available year, 1996 - 2015
Population des capitales et des villes de 100 000 habitants ou plus : dernière année disponible, 1996 - 2015 (continued - suite)

Continent, country or area, date, code[a] and city / Continent, pays ou zone, date, code[a] et ville	City proper - Ville proprement dite				Urban agglomeration - Agglomération urbaine			
	Population			Surface area - Superficie (km²)	Population			Surface area - Superficie (km²)
	Both sexes - Les deux sexes	Male - Masculin	Female - Féminin		Both sexes - Les deux sexes	Male - Masculin	Female - Féminin	
AMERICA, SOUTH - AMÉRIQUE DU SUD								
Brazil - Brésil[14]								
1 VII 2015 (ESDF)								
Volta Redonda	262 970	...	...	...	...	...	...	...
Votorantim	117 794	...	...	...	...	...	...	...
Chile - Chili								
1 VII 2015 (ESDF)								
Alto Hospicio	112 638	54 412	58 226	17[27]	...	...	...	...
Antofagasta	402 444	209 386	193 058	44[27]	...	...	...	...
Arica	155 399	71 876	83 523	42[27]	...	...	...	...
Calama	149 668	75 851	73 817	18[27]	...	...	...	...
Chiguallante	143 284	66 639	76 645	34[27]	...	...	...	...
Chillán	166 342	79 171	87 171	33[27]	...	...	...	...
Concepción	226 965	109 989	116 976	56[27]	...	...	...	...
Copiapó	171 786	86 151	85 635	48[27]	...	...	...	...
Coquimbo	209 684	103 377	106 307	42[27]	...	...	...	...
Coronel	108 499	52 534	55 965	25[27]	...	...	...	...
Curicó	104 130	51 249	52 881	21[27]	...	...	...	...
Iquique	181 644	86 653	94 991	22[27]	...	...	...	...
La Serena	217 070	105 284	111 786	66[27]	...	...	...	...
Los Ángeles	149 292	73 011	76 281	27[27]	...	...	...	...
Osorno	150 932	74 513	76 419	32[27]	...	...	...	...
Puente Alto	824 579	404 171	420 408	64[27]	...	...	...	...
Puerto Montt	227 698	114 013	113 685	40[27]	...	...	...	...
Punta Arenas	124 474	62 275	62 199	39[27]	...	...	...	...
Quilpué	170 762	83 435	87 327	38[27]	...	...	...	...
Rancagua	249 668	124 976	124 692	50[27]	...	...	...	...
San Bernardo	320 626	157 215	163 411	52[27]	...	...	...	...
San Pedro de la Paz	103 836	49 633	54 203	49[27]	...	...	...	...
SANTIAGO	5 150 010[28]	2 497 665[28]	2 652 345[28]	843[27]	...	...	...	...
Talca	228 044	111 477	116 567	46[27]	...	...	...	...
Talcahuano	123 704	54 631	69 073	51[27]	...	...	...	...
Temuco	275 617	132 789	142 828	46[27]	...	...	...	...
Valdivia	143 305	70 587	72 718	42[27]	...	...	...	...
Valparaíso	248 070	124 189	123 881	47[27]	...	...	...	...
Villa Alemana	143 762	70 500	73 262	31[27]	...	...	...	...
Viña del Mar	287 522	138 051	149 471	87[27]	...	...	...	...
Colombia - Colombie[29]								
1 VII 2015 (ESDJ)								
Apartadó	178 257	90 140	88 117	607[13]	...	...	...	...
Armenia	296 683	143 171	153 512	115[13]	...	...	...	...
Barrancabermeja	191 768	94 605	97 163	1 274[13]	...	...	...	...
Barranquilla	1 218 475	591 098	627 377	166[13]	...	...	...	...
Bello	455 865	220 515	235 350	151[13]	...	...	...	...
BOGOTÁ, D.C.	7 878 783	3 810 013	4 068 770	1 605[13]	...	...	...	...
Bucaramanga	527 913	253 751	274 162	154[13]	...	...	...	...
Buenaventura	399 764	194 424	205 340	6 785[13]	...	...	...	...
Cali	2 369 821	1 132 918	1 236 903	552[13]	...	...	...	...
Cartagena	1 001 755	484 150	517 605	559[13]	...	...	...	...
Cartago	132 249	63 580	68 669	260[13]	...	...	...	...
Caucasia	112 168	54 291	57 877	1 058[13]	...	...	...	...
Chía	126 647	60 886	65 761	76[13]	...	...	...	...
Ciénaga	104 331	52 122	52 209	1 366[13]	...	...	...	...
Cúcuta	650 011	314 402	335 609	1 098[13]	...	...	...	...
Dosquebradas	198 877	96 647	102 230	80[13]	...	...	...	...
Duitama	112 692	52 074	60 618	229[13]	...	...	...	...
Envigado	222 455	107 141	115 314	51[13]	...	...	...	...
Facatativá	132 106	65 914	66 192	160[13]	...	...	...	...
Florencia	172 364	84 708	87 656	2 292[13]	...	...	...	...
Floridablanca	265 407	126 235	139 172	101[13]	...	...	...	...
Fusagasugá	134 523	66 436	68 087	206[13]	...	...	...	...
Girardot	105 085	49 649	55 436	130[13]	...	...	...	...
Girón	180 377	89 891	90 486	681[13]	...	...	...	...

8. Population of capital cities and cities of 100 000 or more inhabitants: latest available year, 1996 - 2015

Population des capitales et des villes de 100 000 habitants ou plus : dernière année disponible, 1996 - 2015 (continued - suite)

Continent, country or area, date, code[a] and city / Continent, pays ou zone, date, code[a] et ville	City proper - Ville proprement dite				Urban agglomeration - Agglomération urbaine			
	Population			Surface area - Superficie (km²)	Population			Surface area - Superficie (km²)
	Both sexes - Les deux sexes	Male - Masculin	Female - Féminin		Both sexes - Les deux sexes	Male - Masculin	Female - Féminin	

AMERICA, SOUTH - AMÉRIQUE DU SUD

Colombia - Colombie[29]
1 VII 2015 (ESDJ)

Gudalajara de Buga	115 234	56 461	58 773	873[13]	...	...	...	...
Ibagué	553 524	268 853	284 671	1 439[13]	...	...	...	...
Ipiales	138 679	68 302	70 377	1 707[13]	...	...	...	...
Itagüí	267 851	130 540	137 311	17[13]	...	...	...	...
Jamundí	119 566	58 143	61 423	603[13]	...	...	...	...
Lorica	118 237	59 177	59 060	890[13]	...	...	...	...
Magangué	123 737	62 585	61 152	1 102[13]	...	...	...	...
Maicao	157 054	77 221	79 833	1 789[13]	...	...	...	...
Malambo	121 281	61 685	59 596	108[13]	...	...	...	...
Manaure	103 961	51 222	52 739	...	...	...	...	...
Manizales	396 075	188 729	207 346	477[13]	...	...	...	...
Medellín	1 756 711	864 549	892 162	387[13]	...	...	...	...
Montería	441 301	214 162	227 139	3 043[13]	...	...	...	...
Neiva	342 117	163 680	178 437	1 468[13]	...	...	...	...
Palmira	304 735	147 242	157 493	1 044[13]	...	...	...	...
Pasto	439 993	212 382	227 611	1 131[13]	...	...	...	...
Pereira	469 612	222 783	246 829	702[13]	...	...	...	...
Piedecuesta	149 248	72 576	76 672	481[13]	...	...	...	...
Pitalito	125 839	62 479	63 360	653[13]	...	...	...	...
Popayán	277 540	134 493	143 047	464[13]	...	...	...	...
Quibdo	115 711	57 873	57 838	3 075[13]	...	...	...	...
Riohacha	259 492	127 672	131 820	3 171[13]	...	...	...	...
Rionegro	120 249	59 751	60 498	198[13]	...	...	...	...
San Andrés de Tumaco	199 659	99 801	99 858	3 778[13]	...	...	...	...
Santa Marta	483 865	236 162	247 703	2 369[13]	...	...	...	...
Sincelejo	275 207	135 152	140 055	292[13]	...	...	...	...
Soacha	511 262	252 292	258 970	187[13]	...	...	...	...
Sogamoso	113 295	53 759	59 536	214[13]	...	...	...	...
Soledad	615 492	304 583	310 909	67[13]	...	...	...	...
Tuluá	211 588	101 693	109 895	818[13]	...	...	...	...
Tunja	188 380	90 106	98 274	118[13]	...	...	...	...
Turbo	159 268	80 604	78 664	3 090[13]	...	...	...	...
Uribia	174 287	85 441	88 846	7 904[13]	...	...	...	...
Valledupar	453 215	220 989	232 226	4 225[13]	...	...	...	...
Villavicencio	484 471	235 037	249 434	1 328[13]	...	...	...	...
Yopal	139 736	69 977	69 759	2 532[13]	...	...	...	...
Yumbo	117 156	58 774	58 382	243[13]	...	...	...	...
Zipaquirá	122 347	60 158	62 189	194[13]	...	...	...	...

Ecuador - Équateur
1 VII 2015 (ESDF)

Ambato	176 197[17]	...	...	31	...	...	...	...
Cuenca	376 584[17]	...	...	56	...	...	...	...
Durán	272 780[17]	...	...	40	...	...	...	...
Esmeraldas	184 115[17]	...	...	8	...	...	...	...
Guayaquil	2 505 200[17]	...	...	369	...	...	...	...
Ibarra	150 877[17]	...	...	36	...	...	...	...
La Libertad[17]	108 565			...	...	...	...	...
Loja	207 752[17]	...	...	25	...	...	...	...
Machala	257 099[17]	...	...	34	...	...	...	...
Manta	241 621[17]	...	...	45	...	...	...	...
Milagro	148 507[17]	...	...	19	...	...	...	...
Portoviejo	229 572[17]	...	...	50	...	...	...	...
Quevedo	171 814[17]	...	...	20	...	...	...	...
QUITO	1 763 111[17]	...	...	181	...	...	...	...
Riobamba	162 481[17]	...	...	29	...	...	...	...
Santo Domingo de los Colorados	314 099[17]	...	...	43	...	...	...	...

Falkland Islands (Malvinas) - Îles Falkland (Malvinas)[30]
15 IV 2012 (CDFC)

STANLEY	2 108	1 055	1 053	...	...	...	...	...

8. Population of capital cities and cities of 100 000 or more inhabitants: latest available year, 1996 - 2015
Population des capitales et des villes de 100 000 habitants ou plus : dernière année disponible, 1996 - 2015 (continued - suite)

Continent, country or area, date, code[a] and city / Continent, pays ou zone, date, code[a] et ville	City proper - Ville proprement dite				Urban agglomeration - Agglomération urbaine			
	Population			Surface area - Superficie (km²)	Population			Surface area - Superficie (km²)
	Both sexes - Les deux sexes	Male - Masculin	Female - Féminin		Both sexes - Les deux sexes	Male - Masculin	Female - Féminin	
AMERICA, SOUTH - AMÉRIQUE DU SUD								
French Guiana - Guyane française								
1 I 2006 (CDJC)								
CAYENNE	58 004	27 412	30 591	24	75 740	36 484	39 256	70
Guyana								
15 IX 2012* (CDFC)								
GEORGETOWN	24 849	...	...	...	118 368	...	...	...
Paraguay								
1 VII 2014 (ESDF)								
ASUNCIÓN[31]	512 919	236 790	276 129	117	2 887 087	1 402 891	1 484 196	2 582
Capiatá	257 116	127 676	129 440	88	...	...	...	...
Ciudad del Este	317 525	159 726	157 799	149	...	...	...	...
Fernando de la Mora	200 112	95 174	104 937	21	...	...	...	...
Lambaré	210 725	101 019	109 706	27	...	...	...	...
Luque	358 265	175 663	182 602	153	...	...	...	...
San Lorenzo	354 283	171 242	183 042	54	...	...	...	...
Peru - Pérou[32]								
30 VI 2015 (ESDF)								
Arequipa	869 351	418 773	450 578	...	...	...	...	...
Ayacucho	180 766	89 393	91 373	...	...	...	...	...
Cajamarca	226 031	111 027	115 004	...	...	...	...	...
Chiclayo	600 440	286 187	314 253	...	...	...	...	...
Chimbote	371 012	186 724	184 288	...	...	...	...	...
Chincha Alta	177 219	88 555	88 664	...	...	...	...	...
Cuzco	427 218	208 228	218 990	...	...	...	...	...
Huancayo	364 725	173 733	190 992	...	...	...	...	...
Huánuco	175 068	83 685	91 383	...	...	...	...	...
Huaraz	127 041	62 464	64 577	...	...	...	...	...
Ica	244 390	120 260	124 130	...	...	...	...	...
Iquitos	437 376	220 352	217 024	...	...	...	...	...
Juliaca	273 882	133 597	140 285	...	...	...	...	...
LIMA[33]	9 886 647	4 808 135	5 078 512	...	...	...	...	...
Pisco	104 656	53 336	51 320	...	...	...	...	...
Piura	436 440	211 687	224 753	...	...	...	...	...
Pucallpa	211 651	108 932	102 719	...	...	...	...	...
Puno	140 839	68 492	72 347	...	...	...	...	...
Sullana	201 302	98 355	102 947	...	...	...	...	...
Tacna	293 116	149 253	143 863	...	...	...	...	...
Tarapoto	144 186	74 883	69 303	...	...	...	...	...
Trujillo	799 550	388 017	411 533	...	...	...	...	...
Tumbes	111 595	60 554	51 041	...	...	...	...	...
Suriname								
13 VIII 2012 (CDJC)								
PARAMARIBO	240 924	119 439	121 485	182	...	...	...	...
Wanica	118 222	57 776	60 446	443	...	...	...	...
Uruguay								
1 VII 2015 (ESDJ)								
Canelones	566 626	277 583	289 043	4 536	...	...	...	...
Colonia	129 127	63 585	65 542	6 106	...	...	...	...
Maldonado	182 504	90 560	91 944	4 793	...	...	...	...
MONTEVIDEO	1 379 560	648 068	731 491	530	...	...	...	...
Paysandú	118 483	58 288	60 194	13 922	...	...	...	...
Rivera	107 782	52 829	54 953	9 370	...	...	...	...
Salto	131 231	64 572	66 659	14 163	...	...	...	...
San José	113 802	56 823	56 979	4 992	...	...	...	...
Venezuela (Bolivarian Republic of) - Venezuela (République bolivarienne du)								
1 VII 2015 (ESDF)								
Anaco(F) (Capital)	140 496	...	...	...	...	...	...	...
Barinas	389 578	...	...	848	...	...	...	...
Barquisimeto	881 127	...	...	2 645	...	...	...	...
Baruta	358 221	...	...	...	...	...	...	...
Cabimas	293 365	...	...	175	...	...	...	...
Cagua	118 290	...	...	...	...	...	...	...
CARACAS	2 082 130	...	...	433	...	...	...	...
Carora	111 963	...	...	...	...	...	...	...

8. Population of capital cities and cities of 100 000 or more inhabitants: latest available year, 1996 - 2015
Population des capitales et des villes de 100 000 habitants ou plus : dernière année disponible, 1996 - 2015 (continued - suite)

| Continent, country or area, date, code[a] and city | City proper - Ville proprement dite | | | | Urban agglomeration - Agglomération urbaine | | | |
| | Population | | | Surface area - Superficie (km²) | Population | | | Surface area - Superficie (km²) |
Continent, pays ou zone, date, code[a] et ville	Both sexes - Les deux sexes	Male - Masculin	Female - Féminin		Both sexes - Les deux sexes	Male - Masculin	Female - Féminin	
AMERICA, SOUTH - AMÉRIQUE DU SUD								
Venezuela (Bolivarian Republic of) - Venezuela (République bolivarienne du)								
1 VII 2015 (ESDF)								
Carúpano	156 380	...	...	203	...	...	...	...
Ciudad Bolívar	407 452	...	...	5 851	...	...	...	...
Ciudad Guayana	877 547	...	...	1 612	...	...	...	...
Ciudad Ojeda	216 489	...	...	...	...	...	...	...
Cua	143 164	...	...	...	...	...	...	...
Cumaná	358 138	...	...	405	...	...	...	...
El Tigre	203 403	...	...	...	...	...	...	...
Guacara	192 536	...	...	...	...	...	...	...
Guanare	160 234	...	...	...	...	...	...	...
Guarenas	247 131	...	...	180	...	...	...	...
Guatire	177 794	...	...	...	...	...	...	...
Los Guayos	173 878	...	...	...	...	...	...	...
Los Teques	216 358	...	...	98	...	...	...	...
Maracaibo	1 653 215	...	...	604	...	...	...	...
Maracay	419 052	...	...	169	...	...	...	...
Maturín	571 276	...	...	...	...	...	...	...
Mérida	248 410	...	...	482	...	...	...	...
Naguanagua	161 658	...	...	...	...	...	...	...
Ocumare Del Tuy	197 952	...	...	...	...	...	...	...
Petare	434 320	...	...	...	...	...	...	...
Pozuelos (F) (Capital)	144 045	...	...	...	...	...	...	...
Puerto Cabello	193 025	...	...	309	...	...	...	...
Punto Fijo	272 239	...	...	31	...	...	...	...
San Cristóbal	282 830	...	...	248	...	...	...	...
San Fernando de Apure	217 590	...	...	...	...	...	...	...
San Francisco	106 763	...	...	...	...	...	...	...
Santa Lucía	133 543	...	...	...	...	...	...	...
Táriba	132 657	...	...	...	...	...	...	...
Tocuyito	186 755	...	...	...	...	...	...	...
Turmero	238 570	...	...	208	...	...	...	...
Valencia	888 109	...	...	1 212	...	...	...	...
Valera	161 771	...	...	55	...	...	...	...
ASIA - ASIE								
Afghanistan								
1 VII 2012 (ESDF)								
Baghalan Center (Puli Khumry)	203 600	104 500	99 100	...	...	...	...	...
Balkh Center (Mazar- Sharif)	368 100	188 800	179 300	...	...	...	...	...
Herat Center	436 300	221 600	214 700	...	...	...	...	...
KABUL CENTER	3 289 000	1 702 300	1 586 700	...	...	...	...	...
Kandhar Center (Kndhar)	491 500	252 900	238 600	...	...	...	...	...
Kunduz Center	304 600	155 500	149 100	...	...	...	...	...
Nngarhar Center (Jlal Abad)	206 500	106 300	100 200	...	...	...	...	...
Armenia - Arménie								
12 X 2011 (CDJC)								
Gyumri (Leninakan)	121 976	57 132	64 844	44	...	...	...	...
YEREVAN	1 060 138	490 362	569 776	223	...	...	...	...
Azerbaijan - Azerbaïdjan								
1 VII 2013 (ESDF)								
BAKU	2 166 355	1 074 374	1 091 981	2 150	...	...	...	...
Ganja	323 860	157 319	166 541	110	...	...	...	...
Sumgayit	327 291	160 791	166 500	80	...	...	...	...
Bahrain - Bahreïn								
1 VII 2006 (ESDF)								
MANAMA	176 909	113 503	63 406	30	...	...	...	...
Bangladesh								
22 I 2001 (CDFC)								
Barisal	...	...	...	...	192 810	103 785	89 025	20
Bogra	...	...	...	...	154 807	82 368	72 439	11
Brahmanbaria	...	...	...	...	129 278	66 890	62 388	18

8. Population of capital cities and cities of 100 000 or more inhabitants: latest available year, 1996 - 2015
Population des capitales et des villes de 100 000 habitants ou plus : dernière année disponible, 1996 - 2015 (continued - suite)

Continent, country or area, date, code[a] and city / Continent, pays ou zone, date, code[a] et ville	City proper - Ville proprement dite				Urban agglomeration - Agglomération urbaine			
	Population			Surface area - Superficie (km²)	Population			Surface area - Superficie (km²)
	Both sexes - Les deux sexes	Male - Masculin	Female - Féminin		Both sexes - Les deux sexes	Male - Masculin	Female - Féminin	
ASIA - ASIE								
Bangladesh								
22 I 2001 (CDFC)								
Chittagong	...	...	...	...	2 023 489	1 127 516	895 973	168
Comilla	...	...	...	...	166 519	88 927	77 592	11
DHAKA	...	...	...	...	5 333 571	3 025 395	2 308 176	154
Dinajpur	...	...	...	...	157 914	82 068	75 846	19
Gazipur	...	...	...	...	122 801	65 522	57 279	49
Jamalpur	...	...	...	...	120 955	62 059	58 896	53
Jessore	...	...	...	...	176 655	94 203	82 452	15
Kadamrasul	...	...	...	...	128 561	66 799	61 762	6
Khulna	...	...	...	...	770 498	412 661	357 837	60
Mymensingh	...	...	...	...	227 204	119 172	108 032	22
Naogaon	...	...	...	...	124 046	65 406	58 640	37
Narayanganj	...	...	...	...	241 393	131 168	110 225	13
Narsingdi	...	...	...	...	124 204	67 575	56 629	9
Nawabganj	...	...	...	...	152 223	75 375	76 848	34
Pabna	...	...	...	...	116 305	60 666	55 639	27
Rajshahi	...	...	...	...	388 811	208 525	180 286	97
Rangpur	...	...	...	...	241 310	124 296	117 014	51
Saidpur	...	...	...	...	112 609	58 289	54 320	34
Sirajganj	...	...	...	...	128 144	66 673	61 471	28
Tangail	...	...	...	...	128 785	66 856	61 929	29
Tongi	...	...	...	...	283 099	156 335	126 764	30
Bhutan - Bhoutan								
30 V 2005 (CDFC)								
THIMPHU	...	...	...	...	79 185	42 465	36 720	...
Brunei Darussalam - Brunéi Darussalam								
21 VIII 2001 (CDFC)								
BANDAR SERI BEGAWAN	27 285	13 639	13 646	100	...	...	...	...
Cambodia - Cambodge								
1 VII 2011 (ESDF)								
Bat Dambang	1 126 345[34]	558 945[34]	567 400[34]	114	...	...	...	...
PHNOM PENH	1 570 791[34]	738 159[34]	832 631[34]	21	...	...	...	...
Seam Reab	999 703[34]	493 184[34]	506 519[34]	292	...	...	...	...
China - Chine								
1 VII 2010 (ESDF)								
BEIJING (PEKING)	19 610 000[36]	10 130 000[36]	9 490 000[36]	16 410	...	...	...	...
China, Hong Kong SAR - Chine, Hong Kong RAS								
1 VII 2015 (ESDJ)								
HONG KONG SAR	7 305 700	3 367 000	3 938 700	1 106	...	...	...	...
China, Macao SAR - Chine, Macao RAS								
1 VII 2015 (ESDJ)								
MACAO	642 900	317 500	325 400	30[35]	...	...	...	...
Cyprus - Chypre								
1 I 2006 (ESDJ)								
LEFKOSIA[37]	...	...	...	...	224 500	...	...	...
Lemesos[38]	...	...	...	...	176 900	...	...	...
Democratic People's Republic of Korea - République populaire démocratique de Corée								
1 X 2008 (CDJC)								
Anju	167 646	79 187	88 459	...	...	...	...	...
Chongjin	614 892	292 741	322 151	...	...	...	...	...
Haeju	241 599	116 594	125 005	...	...	...	...	...
Hamhung	614 198	292 058	322 140	...	...	...	...	...
Huichon	136 093	64 547	71 546	...	...	...	...	...
Hyesan	174 015	82 604	91 411	...	...	...	...	...
Jongju	102 659	48 423	54 236	...	...	...	...	...
Kaechon	262 389	124 222	138 167	...	...	...	...	...
Kaesong	192 578	90 653	101 925	...	...	...	...	...
Kanggye	251 971	120 305	131 666	...	...	...	...	...
Kim Chaek	155 284	73 133	82 151	...	...	...	...	...
Kusong	155 181	73 677	81 504	...	...	...	...	...
Nampho	310 864	150 091	160 773	...	...	...	...	...
Phyongsong	236 583	115 817	120 766	...	...	...	...	...
PYONGYANG	2 581 076	1 233 765	1 347 311	...	...	...	...	...

8. Population of capital cities and cities of 100 000 or more inhabitants: latest available year, 1996 - 2015
Population des capitales et des villes de 100 000 habitants ou plus : dernière année disponible, 1996 - 2015 (continued - suite)

Continent, country or area, date, code[a] and city / Continent, pays ou zone, date, code[a] et ville	City proper - Ville proprement dite				Urban agglomeration - Agglomération urbaine			
	Population			Surface area - Superficie (km²)	Population			Surface area - Superficie (km²)
	Both sexes - Les deux sexes	Male - Masculin	Female - Féminin		Both sexes - Les deux sexes	Male - Masculin	Female - Féminin	
ASIA - ASIE								
Democratic People's Republic of Korea - République populaire démocratique de Corée								
1 X 2008 (CDJC)								
Rason	158 337	74 777	83 560	...	...	...	...	...
Sariwon	271 434	130 181	141 253	...	...	...	...	...
Sinpho	130 951	63 207	67 744	...	...	...	...	...
Sinuiju	334 031	158 139	175 892	...	...	...	...	...
Sunchon	250 738	119 727	131 011	...	...	...	...	...
Tanchon	240 873	113 221	127 652	...	...	...	...	...
Tokchon	210 571	99 655	110 916	...	...	...	...	...
Wonsan	328 467	155 903	172 564	...	...	...	...	...
Georgia - Géorgie								
5 XI 2014 (CDJC)								
Batumi	152 839	72 757	80 082	82	...	...	...	...
Kutaisi	147 635	69 194	78 441	68	...	...	...	...
Rustavi	125 103	59 859	65 244	61	...	...	...	...
TBILISI	1 062 282	480 748	581 534	504	...	...	...	...
India - Inde[39]								
1 III 2001 (CDFC)								
Abohar	124 339	66 445	57 894	23	...	...	...	...
Achalpur	107 316	55 687	51 629	17	...	...	...	...
Adilabad	109 529	55 641	53 888	16	129 403	65 501	63 902	21
Adityapur	119 233	63 837	55 396	50	...	...	...	...
Adoni	157 305	79 639	77 666	30	162 458	82 345	80 113	...
Agartala	189 998	94 742	95 256	16	...	...	...	...
Agra	1 275 134	690 599	584 535	121	1 331 339	720 707	610 632	141
Ahmedabad	3 520 085	1 867 249	1 652 836	191	4 525 013	2 401 422	2 123 591	438
Ahmednagar	307 615	159 564	148 051	18	347 549	184 765	162 784	30
Aizawl	228 280	115 986	112 294	110	...	...	...	...
Ajmer	485 575	254 164	231 411	218	490 520	256 695	233 825	223
Akola	400 520	206 649	193 871	23	...	...	...	...
Alandur	146 287	74 836	71 451	20	...	...	...	...
Alappuzha	177 029	85 725	91 304	70	282 675	137 244	145 431	84
Aligarh	669 087	356 725	312 362	40	...	...	...	...
Alipurduar	...	...	...	...	114 035	58 503	55 532	26
Allahabad	975 393	539 772	435 621	63	1 042 229	576 122	466 107	86
Alwar	260 593	139 585	121 008	...	266 203	143 699	122 504	58
Ambala	139 279	74 016	65 263	17	168 316	92 977	75 339	38
Ambala Sadar	106 568	55 750	50 818	...	...	...	...	...
Ambarnath	203 804	107 325	96 479	36	...	...	...	...
Ambattur	310 967	160 282	150 685	40	...	...	...	...
Amravati	549 510	284 247	265 263	122	...	...	...	...
Amritsar	966 862	518 388	448 474	136	1 003 917	538 744	465 173	...
Amroha	165 129	86 943	78 186	6	...	...	...	...
Anand	130 685	68 074	62 611	21	218 486	115 295	103 191	60
Anantapur	218 808	110 979	107 829	...	243 143	123 713	119 430	...
Anklesvar	...	...	...	...	112 643	60 249	52 394	...
Arcot	...	...	...	...	126 671	62 787	63 884	19
Arrah	203 380	109 867	93 513	31	...	...	...	...
Asansol	475 439	250 886	224 553	128	1 067 369	564 837	502 532	352
Ashoknagar Kalyangarh	111 607	56 490	55 117	...	...	...	...	...
Aurangabad	873 311	459 295	414 016	139	892 483	469 237	423 246	148
Avadi	229 403	117 991	111 412	65	...	...	...	...
Bahadurgarh	119 846	65 859	53 987	21	131 925	72 873	59 052	30
Baharampur	160 143	81 737	78 406	17	170 322	86 969	83 353	19
Bahraich	168 323	89 581	78 742	13	...	...	...	...
Baidyabati	108 229	56 394	51 835	8	...	...	...	...
Baleshwar	106 082	55 691	50 391	...	156 430	82 106	74 324	42
Ballia	101 465	54 496	46 969	16	...	...	...	...
Bally	260 906	149 603	111 303	12	...	...	...	...
Balurghat	135 737	68 871	66 866	10	143 321	72 764	70 557	12
Banda	134 839	72 632	62 207	16	139 436	75 174	64 262	28
Bangalore	4 301 326	2 242 835	2 058 491	...	5 701 446	2 988 561	2 712 885	540
Bangaon	102 163	52 537	49 626	25	...	...	...	...
Bankura	128 781	66 429	62 352	19	...	...	...	...

8. Population of capital cities and cities of 100 000 or more inhabitants: latest available year, 1996 - 2015
Population des capitales et des villes de 100 000 habitants ou plus : dernière année disponible, 1996 - 2015 (continued - suite)

Continent, country or area, date, code[a] and city Continent, pays ou zone, date, code[a] et ville	City proper - Ville proprement dite				Urban agglomeration - Agglomération urbaine			
	Population			Surface area - Superficie (km²)	Population			Surface area - Superficie (km²)
	Both sexes - Les deux sexes	Male - Masculin	Female - Féminin		Both sexes - Les deux sexes	Male - Masculin	Female - Féminin	
ASIA - ASIE								
India - Inde[39]								
1 III 2001 (CDFC)								
Bansberia	104 412	55 389	49 023	9	...	...	...	...
Baranagar	250 768	132 559	118 209	7	...	...	...	...
Barasat	231 521	118 374	113 147	31	...	...	...	...
Barddhaman	285 602	148 562	137 040	23	...	...	...	...
Bareilly	718 395	378 848	339 547	106	748 353	397 304	351 049	125
Baripada	...	...	...	...	100 651	53 606	47 045	38
Barrackpur	144 391	76 299	68 092	11	...	...	...	...
Barshi	104 785	53 848	50 937	36	...	...	...	...
Basirhat	113 159	57 965	55 194	22	...	...	...	...
Basti	107 601	57 053	50 548	19	...	...	...	...
Batala	125 677	66 508	59 169	9	147 872	78 393	69 479	...
Bathinda	217 256	116 946	100 310	110	...	...	...	...
Beawar	123 759	64 417	59 342	18	125 981	65 586	60 395	24
Begusarai	...	...	...	...	107 623	57 541	50 082	12
Belgaum	399 653	204 598	195 055	100	506 480	261 639	244 841	173
Bellary	316 766	162 699	154 067	66	...	...	...	...
Bettiah	116 670	61 753	54 917	8	...	...	...	...
Bhadravati	160 662	81 351	79 311	...	...	...	...	...
Bhadreswar	106 071	58 040	48 031	6	...	...	...	...
Bhagalpur	340 767	182 806	157 961	30	350 133	187 723	162 410	31
Bhalswa Jahangir Pur	152 339	83 802	68 537	7	...	...	...	...
Bharatpur	204 587	110 057	94 530	41	205 235	110 397	94 838	51
Bharuch	148 140	76 506	71 634	18	176 364	91 281	85 083	20
Bhatpara	442 385	243 157	199 228	30	...	...	...	...
Bhavani	...	...	...	...	104 646	52 998	51 648	10
Bhavnagar	511 085	266 838	244 247	90	517 708	270 278	247 430	91
Bheemavaram	137 409	69 473	67 936	26	142 064	71 929	70 135	26
Bhilai Nagar	556 366	291 070	265 296	141	...	...	...	...
Bhilwara	280 128	148 794	131 334	118	...	...	...	...
Bhind	153 752	82 945	70 807	17	...	...	...	...
Bhiwandi	598 741	367 565	231 176	26	621 427	382 184	239 243	28
Bhiwani	169 531	91 697	77 834	28	...	...	...	...
Bhopal	1 437 354	757 408	679 946	285	1 458 416	768 391	690 025	298
Bhubaneswar	648 032	360 739	287 293	135	658 220	366 134	292 086	148
Bhuj	...	...	...	...	136 429	71 056	65 373	...
Bhusawal	172 372	89 208	83 164	13	187 564	97 243	90 321	25
Bid	138 196	71 827	66 369	8	...	...	...	...
Bidar	172 877	89 934	82 943	...	174 257	90 662	83 595	47
Bidhan Nagar	164 221	83 220	81 001	34	...	...	...	...
Bihar	232 071	122 019	110 052	24	...	...	...	...
Bijapur	228 175	117 375	110 800	...	253 891	130 416	123 475	75
Bikaner	529 690	283 067	246 623	166	...	...	...	...
Bilaspur	275 694	143 518	132 176	36	335 293	174 351	160 942	46
Birnagar	...	...	...	...	115 127	59 232	55 895	40
Bokaro Steel City	393 805	213 231	180 574	163	497 780	268 969	228 811	188
Bommanahalli	201 652	108 108	93 544	36	...	...	...	...
Botad	100 194	52 752	47 442	10	...	...	...	...
Brahmapur	307 792	160 354	147 438	80	...	...	...	...
Budaun	148 029	78 141	69 888	4	...	...	...	...
Bulandshahr	176 425	93 531	82 894	12	...	...	...	...
Burhanpur	193 725	99 751	93 974	13	...	...	...	...
Byatarayanapura	181 744	95 508	86 236	45	...	...	...	...
Chakdaha	...	...	...	...	101 320	51 485	49 835	...
Champdani	103 246	57 842	45 404	6	...	...	...	...
Chandan Nagar	162 187	84 181	78 006	22	...	...	...	...
Chandausi	103 749	55 127	48 622	9	...	...	...	...
Chandigarh	808 515	450 122	358 393	79	...	...	...	...
Chandrapur	289 450	151 202	138 248	56	...	...	...	...
Chapra	179 190	95 494	83 696	17	...	...	...	...
Chennai (Madras)	4 343 645	2 219 539	2 124 106	174	6 560 242	3 355 524	3 204 718	702
Cherthala	...	...	...	...	141 558	68 756	72 802	92
Chhatarpur	...	...	...	...	109 078	58 421	50 657	17
Chhindwara	122 247	63 584	58 663	11	153 552	79 889	73 663	22

8. Population of capital cities and cities of 100 000 or more inhabitants: latest available year, 1996 - 2015
Population des capitales et des villes de 100 000 habitants ou plus : dernière année disponible, 1996 - 2015 (continued - suite)

Continent, country or area, date, code[a] and city / Continent, pays ou zone, date, code[a] et ville	City proper - Ville proprement dite				Urban agglomeration - Agglomération urbaine			
	Population			Surface area - Superficie (km²)	Population			Surface area - Superficie (km²)
	Both sexes - Les deux sexes	Male - Masculin	Female - Féminin		Both sexes - Les deux sexes	Male - Masculin	Female - Féminin	
ASIA - ASIE								
India - Inde[39]								
1 III 2001 (CDFC)								
Chikmagalur	101 251	51 694	49 557	33	...	...	...	...
Chirala	...	...	...	...	166 294	82 954	83 340	48
Chirkunda	...	...	...	...	106 227	56 536	49 691	26
Chitradurga	122 702	62 845	59 857	24	125 170	64 112	61 058	26
Chittoor	152 654	76 879	75 775	33	...	...	...	...
Churu	...	...	...	...	101 874	53 079	48 795	30
Coimbatore	930 882	477 937	452 945	106	1 461 139	748 376	712 763	379
Coonoor	...	...	...	...	101 490	51 208	50 282	44
Cuddalore	158 634	80 012	78 622	28	...	...	...	...
Cuddapah	126 505	63 669	62 836	42	262 506	133 224	129 282	78
Cuttack	534 654	285 838	248 816	149	587 182	314 101	273 081	195
Dallo Pura	132 621	71 362	61 259	2	...	...	...	...
Damoh	112 185	58 962	53 223	16	127 967	67 321	60 646	36
Darbhanga	267 348	142 377	124 971	19	...	...	...	...
Darjiling	107 197	55 963	51 234	11	108 830	56 769	52 061	13
Dasarahalli	264 940	143 909	121 031	23	...	...	...	...
Davangere	364 523	187 987	176 536	...	...	...	...	...
Dehradun	426 674	224 546	202 128	52	530 263	283 064	247 199	103
Dehri	119 057	63 540	55 517	21	...	...	...	...
Delhi	9 879 172	5 412 497	4 466 675	554	12 877 470[40]	7 069 371[40]	5 808 099[40]	889[40]
Delhi Cantonment	124 917	75 827	49 090	43	...	...	...	...
Deoghar	...	...	...	...	112 525	61 442	51 083	22
Deoli	119 468	66 594	52 874	10	...	...	...	...
Deoria	104 227	54 681	49 546	16	...	...	...	...
Dewas	231 672	121 075	110 597	100	...	...	...	...
Dhanbad	199 258	108 512	90 746	23	1 065 327	579 150	486 177	223
Dharmavaram	103 357	52 785	50 572	40	...	...	...	...
Dhule	341 755	177 772	163 983	46	...	...	...	...
Dibrugarh	121 893	65 118	56 775	25	137 661	73 307	64 354	26
Dinapur Nizamat	131 176	69 419	61 757	12	...	...	...	...
Dindigul	196 955	99 124	97 831	14	...	...	...	...
Dohad	...	...	...	...	112 026	57 642	54 384	26
Dumdum	101 296	52 890	48 406	9	...	...	...	...
Durg	232 517	119 315	113 202	66	...	...	...	...
Durgapur	493 405	263 721	229 684	154	...	...	...	...
Durg-Bhilai Nagar	...	...	...	...	927 864	482 304	445 560	341
Eluru	190 062	92 790	97 272	15	215 804	105 476	110 328	...
English Bazar	161 456	82 845	78 611	...	224 415	115 356	109 059	19
Erode	150 541	76 462	74 079	8	389 906	198 842	191 064	132
Etah	107 110	56 763	50 347	13	...	...	...	...
Etawah	210 453	111 749	98 704	9	...	...	...	...
Faizabad	144 705	75 935	68 770	33	208 162	114 330	93 832	63
Faridabad	1 055 938	581 069	474 869	199	...	...	...	...
Farrukhabad-cum-Fategarh	228 333	120 829	107 504	17	242 997	129 643	113 354	21
Fatehpur	152 078	80 011	72 067	57	...	...	...	...
Firozabad	279 102	148 263	130 839	9	432 866	230 802	202 064	12
Gadag-Betgeri	154 982	78 713	76 269	35	...	...	...	...
Gajuwaka	259 180	133 469	125 711	128	...	...	...	...
Gandhidham	151 693	79 379	72 314	30	...	...	...	...
Gandhinagar	195 985	103 876	92 109	57	...	...	...	...
Ganganagar	210 713	115 321	95 392	21	222 858	121 865	100 993	...
Gangapur City	...	...	...	...	105 396	56 009	49 387	12
Gangawati	...	...	...	...	101 392	51 211	50 181	16
Gaya	385 432	204 483	180 949	29	394 945	210 410	184 535	32
Ghatlodiya	106 684	56 219	50 465	4	...	...	...	...
Ghaziabad	968 256	521 026	447 230	145	...	...	...	...
Ghazipur	...	...	...	...	103 298	54 371	48 927	20
Giridih	...	...	...	...	105 634	55 490	50 144	11
Godhra	121 879	63 176	58 703	20	131 172	67 969	63 203	23
Gonda	120 301	66 207	54 094	15	...	...	...	...
Gondiya	120 902	61 418	59 484	18	...	...	...	...
Gorakhpur	622 701	329 807	292 894	141	...	...	...	...
Gudivada	113 054	55 867	57 187	13	...	...	...	...

8. Population of capital cities and cities of 100 000 or more inhabitants: latest available year, 1996 - 2015
Population des capitales et des villes de 100 000 habitants ou plus : dernière année disponible, 1996 - 2015 (continued - suite)

Continent, country or area, date, code[a] and city / Continent, pays ou zone, date, code[a] et ville	City proper - Ville proprement dite				Urban agglomeration - Agglomération urbaine			
	Population			Surface area - Superficie (km²)	Population			Surface area - Superficie (km²)
	Both sexes - Les deux sexes	Male - Masculin	Female - Féminin		Both sexes - Les deux sexes	Male - Masculin	Female - Féminin	
ASIA - ASIE								
India - Inde[39]								
1 III 2001 (CDFC)								
Gudiyatham	...	...	...	...	100 115	49 794	50 321	14
Gulbarga	422 569	219 409	203 160	...	430 265	223 594	206 671	43
Guna	137 175	72 538	64 637	46	...	...	...	...
Guntakul	117 103	59 211	57 892	41	...	...	...	...
Guntur	514 461	257 775	256 686	46	...	...	...	...
Gurgaon	172 955	92 934	80 021	15	228 820	123 377	105 443	24
Guruvayur	...	...	...	...	138 681	64 554	74 127	57
Guwahati	809 895	440 288	369 607	217	818 809	446 311	372 498	217
Gwalior	827 026	442 343	384 683	167	865 548	465 057	400 491	180
Habra	127 602	65 141	62 461	18	239 209	121 631	117 578	37
Hajipur	119 412	63 838	55 574	20	...	...	...	...
Haldia	170 673	89 893	80 780	69	...	...	...	...
Haldwani-cum-Kathgodam	129 015	68 755	60 260	11	158 896	84 541	74 355	...
Halisahar	124 510	67 151	57 359	8	...	...	...	...
Hanumangarh	129 556	69 532	60 024	13	...	...	...	...
Haora (Howrah)	1 007 532	547 068	460 464	52	...	...	...	...
Hapur	211 983	113 175	98 808	14	...	...	...	...
Hardoi	112 486	59 876	52 610	6	...	...	...	...
Hardwar	175 340	94 736	80 604	15	220 767	119 234	101 533	42
Hassan	116 574	59 743	56 831	27	133 262	68 242	65 020	30
Hathras	123 244	65 778	57 466	8	126 355	67 436	58 919	8
Hazaribag	127 269	67 900	59 369	26	135 473	72 288	63 185	27
Hindupur	125 074	64 132	60 942	38	...	...	...	...
Hisar	256 689	140 083	116 606	45	263 186	143 795	119 391	49
Hoshiarpur	149 668	79 454	70 214	35	...	...	...	...
Hospet	164 240	83 767	80 473	28	...	...	...	...
Hubli-Dharwad	786 195	403 085	383 110	213	...	...	...	...
Hugli-Chinsurah	170 206	86 788	83 418	17	...	...	...	...
Hyderabad	3 637 483	1 883 064	1 754 419	173	5 742 036	2 973 472	2 768 564	822
Ichalakaranji	257 610	136 063	121 547	30	285 860	150 977	134 883	38
Imphal	221 492	109 815	111 677	33	250 234	123 859	126 375	37
Indore	1 474 968	774 540	700 428	130	1 516 918	796 673	720 245	165
Itarsi	...	...	...	...	107 831	56 347	51 484	24
Jabalpur	932 484	488 479	444 005	119	1 098 000	580 038	517 962	205
Jagadhri	101 290	55 844	45 446	...	...	...	...	...
Jagdalpur	...	...	...	...	103 123	52 909	50 214	26
Jaipur	2 322 575	1 237 765	1 084 810	485	...	...	...	...
Jalandhar	706 043	379 439	326 604	102	714 077	383 624	330 453	...
Jalgaon	368 618	193 496	175 122	62	...	...	...	...
Jalna	235 795	121 922	113 873	82	...	...	...	...
Jalpaiguri	100 348	50 629	49 719	13	...	...	...	...
Jammu	369 959	198 956	171 003	40	612 163	334 452	277 711	202
Jamnagar	443 518	232 845	210 673	26	556 956	292 168	264 788	...
Jamshedpur	573 096	301 433	271 663	60	1 104 713	581 829	522 884	160
Jamuria	129 484	68 695	60 789	73	...	...	...	...
Jaunpur	160 055	84 203	75 852	25	...	...	...	...
Jetpur Navagadh	104 312	54 768	49 544	36	...	...	...	...
Jhansi	383 644	202 745	180 899	58	460 278	244 169	216 109	84
Jhunjhunun	100 485	52 781	47 704	37	...	...	...	...
Jind	135 855	73 407	62 448	15	...	...	...	...
Jodhpur	851 051	454 075	396 976	79	860 818	459 198	401 620	90
Jorhat	...	...	...	...	137 814	73 213	64 601	69
Junagadh	168 515	86 980	81 535	13	252 108	130 461	121 647	...
Kaithal	117 285	63 098	54 187	44	...	...	...	...
Kakinada	296 329	146 476	149 853	39	376 861	187 064	189 797	58
Kalol	100 008	53 110	46 898	17	112 013	59 539	52 474	30
Kalyan	1 193 512	633 508	560 004	105	...	...	...	...
Kamarhati	314 507	168 555	145 952	11	...	...	...	...
Kamptee	...	...	...	...	136 491	71 270	65 221	37
Kancheepuram	153 140	77 069	76 071	12	188 733	95 068	93 665	40
Kanchrapara	126 191	65 264	60 927	9	...	...	...	...
Kanhangad	65 503	31 627	33 876	40	129 367	62 002	67 365	84
Kannur	...	...	...	...	498 207	237 108	261 099	154

8. Population of capital cities and cities of 100 000 or more inhabitants: latest available year, 1996 - 2015
Population des capitales et des villes de 100 000 habitants ou plus : dernière année disponible, 1996 - 2015 (continued - suite)

Continent, country or area, date, code[a] and city / Continent, pays ou zone, date, code[a] et ville	City proper - Ville proprement dite				Urban agglomeration - Agglomération urbaine			
	Population			Surface area - Superficie (km²)	Population			Surface area - Superficie (km²)
	Both sexes - Les deux sexes	Male - Masculin	Female - Féminin		Both sexes - Les deux sexes	Male - Masculin	Female - Féminin	
ASIA - ASIE								
India - Inde[39]								
1 III 2001 (CDFC)								
Kanpur	2 551 337	1 374 121	1 177 216	267	2 715 555	1 465 142	1 250 413	301
Kapra	159 002	82 579	76 423	65	...	...	...	...
Karaikkudi	...	...	...	...	125 717	62 479	63 238	43
Karawal Nagar	148 624	80 495	68 129	5	...	...	...	...
Karimnagar	205 653	105 336	100 317	24	218 302	111 875	106 427	...
Karnal	207 640	110 595	97 045	22	221 236	117 875	103 361	24
Karur	...	...	...	...	153 365	77 207	76 158	33
Katihar	175 199	93 617	81 582	25	190 873	102 161	88 712	...
Khammam	159 544	80 574	78 970	...	198 620	100 930	97 690	26
Khandwa	172 242	88 950	83 292	36	...	...	...	...
Khanna	103 099	55 276	47 823	25	...	...	...	...
Kharagpur	188 761	97 721	91 040	91	272 865	140 730	132 135	125
Khardaha	116 470	61 214	55 256	7	...	...	...	...
Khargone	...	...	...	...	103 448	53 921	49 527	33
Kirari Suleman Nagar	154 633	85 362	69 271	5	...	...	...	...
Kishangarh	116 222	61 075	55 147	25	...	...	...	...
Koch Bihar	...	...	...	...	103 008	52 275	50 733	17
Kochi	595 575	294 756	300 819	95	1 355 972	670 340	685 632	453
Kolar	113 907	58 060	55 847	18	...	...	...	...
Kolhapur	493 167	255 778	237 389	67	505 541	262 258	243 283	67
Kolkata (Calcutta)	4 572 876	2 500 040	2 072 836	185	13 205 697[41]	7 064 138[41]	6 141 559[41]	1 034[41]
Kollam	361 560	177 677	183 883	41	380 091	186 924	193 167	68
Korba	315 690	164 768	150 922	35	...	...	...	...
Kota	694 316	368 451	325 865	221	703 150	373 094	330 056	226
Kothagudem	...	...	...	...	105 266	52 318	52 948	25
Kottayam	...	...	...	...	172 878	84 960	87 918	64
Kozhikode	436 556	211 888	224 668	84	880 247	429 163	451 084	235
Krishnanagar	139 110	70 576	68 534	16	148 709	75 495	73 214	18
Krishnarajapura	186 210	97 412	88 798	25	...	...	...	...
Kukatpalle	292 289	153 331	138 958	72	...	...	...	...
Kulti	289 903	152 821	137 082	100	...	...	...	...
Kumbakonam	139 954	69 785	70 169	13	160 767	80 188	80 579	15
Kurnool	269 122	136 619	132 503	15	342 973	174 190	168 783	46
Lakhimpur	121 486	65 236	56 250	7	...	...	...	...
Lal Bahadur Nagar	268 689	138 667	130 022	85	...	...	...	...
Lalitpur	111 892	58 993	52 899	...	...	...	...	...
Latur	299 985	156 547	143 438	21	...	...	...	...
Loni	120 945	65 278	55 667	7	...	...	...	...
Lucknow	2 185 927	1 156 151	1 029 776	310	2 245 509	1 189 466	1 056 043	338
Ludhiana	1 398 467	793 142	605 325	159	...	...	...	...
Machilipatnam	179 353	89 100	90 253	27	...	...	...	...
Madanapalle	...	...	...	...	107 449	54 497	52 952	13
Madhyamgram	155 451	79 728	75 723	21	...	...	...	...
Madurai	928 869	469 396	459 473	52	1 203 095	608 531	594 564	141
Mahadevapura	135 794	72 882	62 912	53	...	...	...	...
Mahbubnagar	130 986	67 007	63 979	14	139 662	71 516	68 146	14
Mahesana	...	...	...	...	141 453	74 866	66 587	...
Maheshtala	385 266	202 304	182 962	44	...	...	...	...
Mainpuri	...	...	...	...	104 851	55 462	49 389	17
Malappuram	...	...	...	...	170 409	83 709	86 700	111
Malegaon	409 403	208 864	200 539	13	...	...	...	...
Malerkotla	107 009	56 767	50 242	21	...	...	...	...
Malkajgiri	193 863	98 972	94 891	18	...	...	...	...
Mancherial	...	...	...	...	118 195	60 371	57 824	62
Mandsaur	116 505	60 269	56 236	...	117 555	60 859	56 696	...
Mandya	131 179	66 551	64 628	17	...	...	...	...
Mangalore	399 565	200 630	198 935	118	539 387	269 562	269 825	201
Mango	166 125	87 375	78 750	19	...	...	...	...
Mathura	302 770	162 021	140 749	9	323 315	174 335	148 980	22
Maunath Bhanjan	212 657	109 958	102 699	9	...	...	...	...
Medinipur	149 769	76 503	73 266	15	...	...	...	...
Meerut	1 068 772	568 081	500 691	142	1 161 716	621 481	540 235	178
Mira-Bhayandar	520 388	286 391	233 997	79	...	...	...	...

8. Population of capital cities and cities of 100 000 or more inhabitants: latest available year, 1996 - 2015
Population des capitales et des villes de 100 000 habitants ou plus : dernière année disponible, 1996 - 2015 (continued - suite)

Continent, country or area, date, code[a] and city / Continent, pays ou zone, date, code[a] et ville	City proper - Ville proprement dite				Urban agglomeration - Agglomération urbaine			
	Population			Surface area - Superficie (km²)	Population			Surface area - Superficie (km²)
	Both sexes - Les deux sexes	Male - Masculin	Female - Féminin		Both sexes - Les deux sexes	Male - Masculin	Female - Féminin	
ASIA - ASIE								
India - Inde[39]								
1 III 2001 (CDFC)								
Mirzapur-cum-Vindhyachal	205 053	109 647	95 406	39	...	...	...	...
Modinagar	113 218	60 468	52 750	16	139 929	74 788	65 141	23
Moga	125 573	66 888	58 685	16	135 279	72 043	63 236	...
Moradabad	641 583	340 314	301 269	89	...	...	...	...
Morena	150 959	82 305	68 654	12	...	...	...	...
Mormugoa	...	...	...	...	104 758	55 954	48 804	40
Morvi	145 719	75 745	69 974	25	178 055	92 639	85 416	...
Motihari	100 683	54 261	46 422	14	108 428	59 148	49 280	16
Mughalsarai	...	...	...	...	116 308	61 579	54 729	29
Mumbai (Bombay)	11 978 450	6 619 966	5 358 484	603	16 434 386	9 021 789	7 412 597	1 133
Munger	188 050	101 264	86 786	18	...	...	...	...
Murwara (Katni)	187 029	97 843	89 186	107	...	...	...	...
Muzaffarnagar	316 729	167 397	149 332	...	331 668	175 283	156 385	12
Muzaffarpur	305 525	164 000	141 525	26	...	...	...	...
Mysore	755 379	383 480	371 899	89	799 228	406 363	392 865	132
Nabadwip	115 016	58 287	56 729	12	125 341	63 574	61 767	13
Nadiad	192 913	100 322	92 591	28	196 793	102 336	94 457	30
Nagaon	107 667	56 815	50 852	...	123 265	64 895	58 370	16
Nagercoil	208 179	102 907	105 272	24	...	...	...	...
Nagpur	2 052 066	1 059 765	992 301	218	2 129 500	1 102 009	1 027 491	229
Naihati	215 303	113 777	101 526	12	...	...	...	...
Nala Sopara	184 538	98 870	85 668	...	...	...	...	...
Nalgonda	110 286	56 299	53 987	12	111 380	56 848	54 532	51
Nanded	430 733	224 843	205 890	21	...	...	...	...
Nandyal	152 676	77 273	75 403	15	157 120	79 500	77 620	...
Nangloi Jat	150 948	82 687	68 261	7	...	...	...	...
Nashik	1 077 236	575 737	501 499	259	1 152 326	616 088	536 238	322
Navghar-Manikpur	116 723	61 757	54 966	...	...	...	...	...
Navi Mumbai (New Bombay)	704 002	395 705	308 297	133	...	...	...	...
Navsari	134 017	69 794	64 223	...	232 411	122 282	110 129	...
Neemuch	107 663	56 588	51 075	13	112 852	59 320	53 532	13
Nellore	378 428	190 522	187 906	48	404 775	203 823	200 952	...
NEW DELHI[42]	302 363	165 723	136 640	43	...	...	...	...
Neyveli	127 552	65 348	62 204	97	138 035	70 746	67 289	116
Nizamabad	288 722	146 198	142 524	37	...	...	...	...
Noida	305 058	168 958	136 100	90	...	...	...	...
North Barrackpur	123 668	63 796	59 872	9	...	...	...	...
North Dumdum	220 042	113 034	107 008	26	...	...	...	...
Ongole	150 471	76 511	73 960	27	153 829	78 242	75 587	27
Orai	139 318	74 703	64 615	20	...	...	...	...
Ozhukarai	217 707	110 042	107 665	35	...	...	...	...
Palakkad	130 767	64 379	66 388	30	197 369	96 928	100 441	59
Palanpur	110 419	58 055	52 364	20	122 300	64 365	57 935	40
Pali	187 641	99 267	88 374	84	...	...	...	...
Pallavaram	144 623	73 385	71 238	18	...	...	...	...
Palwal	100 722	53 648	47 074	8	...	...	...	...
Panchkula Urban Estate	140 925	75 897	65 028	26	...	...	...	...
Panihati	348 438	180 307	168 131	19	...	...	...	...
Panipat	261 740	143 644	118 096	21	354 148	194 850	159 298	...
Panvel	104 058	54 963	49 095	12	...	...	...	...
Parbhani	259 329	133 959	125 370	58	...	...	...	...
Patan	112 219	59 097	53 122	14	113 749	59 955	53 794	...
Pathankot	157 925	86 520	71 405	22	168 485	92 003	76 482	...
Patiala	303 151	162 573	140 578	65	323 884	173 682	150 202	...
Patna	1 366 444	746 344	620 100	99	1 697 976	922 971	775 005	135
Phagwara	...	...	...	...	102 253	55 335	46 918	...
Phusro	...	...	...	...	174 402	93 700	80 702	84
Pilibhit	124 245	65 853	58 392	10	...	...	...	...
Pimpri Chinchwad	1 012 472	547 050	465 422	171	...	...	...	...
Pollachi	...	...	...	...	128 458	64 657	63 801	29
Pondicherry	220 865	109 389	111 476	20	505 959	253 375	252 584	72
Porbandar	133 051	68 201	64 850	12	197 382	101 824	95 558	...
Proddatur	150 309	75 372	74 937	7	...	...	...	...

8. Population of capital cities and cities of 100 000 or more inhabitants: latest available year, 1996 - 2015
Population des capitales et des villes de 100 000 habitants ou plus : dernière année disponible, 1996 - 2015 (continued - suite)

Continent, country or area, date, code[a] and city / Continent, pays ou zone, date, code[a] et ville	City proper - Ville proprement dite				Urban agglomeration - Agglomération urbaine			
	Population			Surface area - Superficie (km²)	Population			Surface area - Superficie (km²)
	Both sexes - Les deux sexes	Male - Masculin	Female - Féminin		Both sexes - Les deux sexes	Male - Masculin	Female - Féminin	

ASIA - ASIE

India - Inde[39]
1 III 2001 (CDFC)

Pudukkottai	109 217	54 614	54 603	13	...	...	...	...
Pune	2 538 473	1 321 338	1 217 135	430	3 760 636	1 980 621	1 780 015	669
Puri	157 837	82 269	75 568	17	...	...	...	...
Purnia	171 687	92 826	78 861	45	197 211	106 313	90 898	60
Puruliya	113 806	59 092	54 714	14	...	...	...	...
Quthbullapur	231 108	120 690	110 418	47	...	...	...	...
Rae Bareli	169 333	88 911	80 422	50	...	...	...	...
Raichur	207 421	105 763	101 658	...	...	...	...	...
Raiganj	165 212	87 458	77 754	11	175 047	92 703	82 344	15
Raigarh	111 154	57 650	53 504	18	115 908	60 101	55 807	21
Raipur	605 747	314 584	291 163	56	700 113	364 436	335 677	116
Rajahmundry	315 251	158 454	156 797	52	413 616	207 869	205 747	64
Rajapalayam	122 307	61 221	61 086	10	...	...	...	...
Rajarhat Gopalpur	271 811	140 218	131 593	35	...	...	...	...
Rajendranagar	143 240	74 889	68 351	52	...	...	...	...
Rajkot	967 476	506 993	460 483	105	1 003 015	525 898	477 117	163
Rajnandgaon	143 770	72 949	70 821	78	...	...	...	...
Rajpur Sonarpur	336 707	174 140	162 567	55	...	...	...	...
Ramagundam	236 600	120 687	115 913	28	237 686	121 250	116 436	...
Ramgarh	...	...	...	...	110 496	61 591	48 905	50
Rampur	281 494	146 652	134 842	20	...	...	...	...
Ranaghat	...	...	...	...	145 285	73 933	71 352	25
Ranchi	847 093	450 727	396 366	177	863 495	459 462	404 033	182
Raniganj	111 116	59 270	51 846	23	...	...	...	...
Ratlam	222 202	114 370	107 832	39	234 419	120 874	113 545	41
Raurkela	224 987	121 240	103 747	133	484 874	258 731	226 143	157
Raurkela Industrialship	206 693	109 394	97 299	122	...	...	...	...
Rewa	183 274	98 793	84 481	55	...	...	...	...
Rewari	100 684	53 935	46 749	12	...	...	...	...
Rishra	113 305	62 585	50 720	6	...	...	...	...
Robertson Pet	141 424	70 619	70 805	...	157 084	78 578	78 506	...
Rohtak	286 807	154 148	132 659	28	294 577	158 287	136 290	...
Roorkee	...	...	...	...	115 278	64 240	51 038	17
S.A.S. Nagar (Mohali)	123 484	65 642	57 842	24	...	...	...	...
Sagar	232 133	122 385	109 748	36	308 922	162 919	146 003	52
Saharanpur	455 754	241 508	214 246	26	...	...	...	...
Saharasa	125 167	67 718	57 449	21	...	...	...	...
Salem	696 760	353 933	342 827	91	751 438	382 211	369 227	108
Sambalpur	153 643	79 683	73 960	50	226 469	117 745	108 724	90
Sambhal	182 478	97 011	85 467	16	...	...	...	...
Sangli-Miraj-Kupwad	436 781	224 300	212 481	118	447 774	229 958	217 816	121
Santipur	138 235	70 089	68 146	25	...	...	...	...
Sasaram	131 172	69 682	61 490	11	...	...	...	...
Satara	108 048	55 938	52 110	...	...	...	...	...
Satna	225 464	120 277	105 187	...	229 307	122 401	106 906	...
Sawai Madhopur	...	...	...	...	101 997	53 903	48 094	60
Secunderabad	206 102	104 335	101 767	40	...	...	...	...
Serampore	197 857	105 415	92 442	15	...	...	...	...
Serilingampalle	153 364	79 225	74 139	98	...	...	...	...
Shahjahanpur	296 662	160 178	136 484	13	321 885	174 276	147 609	23
Shillong	132 867	66 106	66 761	10	267 662	134 497	133 165	25
Shimla	142 555	81 186	61 369	29	144 975	82 840	62 135	30
Shimoga	274 352	140 224	134 128	...	...	...	...	...
Shivapuri	146 892	78 433	68 459	81	...	...	...	...
Sikar	185 323	96 379	88 944	23	185 925	96 697	89 228	...
Silchar	142 199	72 679	69 520	16	184 105	94 306	89 799	...
Siliguri	472 374	250 645	221 729	42	...	...	...	...
Singrauli	185 190	100 149	85 041	...	...	...	...	...
Sirsa	160 735	85 993	74 742	19	...	...	...	...
Sitapur	151 908	79 767	72 141	26	...	...	...	...
Sivakasi	...	...	...	...	121 358	60 841	60 517	27
Siwan	109 919	58 262	51 657	13	...	...	...	...
Solapur	872 478	444 734	427 744	179	...	...	...	...

Continent, country or area, date, code[a] and city Continent, pays ou zone, date, code[a] et ville	City proper - Ville proprement dite				Urban agglomeration - Agglomération urbaine			
	Population			Surface area - Superficie (km²)	Population			Surface area - Superficie (km²)
	Both sexes - Les deux sexes	Male - Masculin	Female - Féminin		Both sexes - Les deux sexes	Male - Masculin	Female - Féminin	
ASIA - ASIE								
India - Inde[39]								
1 III 2001 (CDFC)								
Sonipat	214 974	117 020	97 954	28	225 074	122 480	102 594	...
South Dum Dum	392 444	200 298	192 146	14	...	...	...	...
Srikakulam	109 905	54 926	54 979	12	117 320	58 753	58 567	14
Srinagar	898 440	484 627	413 813	184	988 210	537 512	450 698	243
Sultan Pur Majra	164 426	88 729	75 697	3	...	...	...	...
Sultanpur	100 065	53 189	46 876	12	...	...	...	...
Surat	2 433 835	1 372 415	1 061 420	112	2 811 614	1 597 156	1 214 458	237
Surendranagar Dudhrej	156 161	81 377	74 784	39	...	...	...	...
Tadepalligudem	102 622	50 925	51 697	21	...	...	...	...
Tambaram	137 933	70 419	67 514	21	...	...	...	...
Tenali	153 756	77 404	76 352	15	...	...	...	...
Tezpur	...	...	...	...	105 377	59 869	45 508	23
Thane	1 262 551	675 147	587 404	128	...	...	...	...
Thanesar	119 687	65 525	54 162	33	122 319	66 978	55 341	36
Thanjavur	215 314	106 625	108 689	15	...	...	...	...
Thiruvananthapuram	744 983	366 235	378 748	142	889 635	437 407	452 228	178
Thoothukkudi (Tuticorin)	216 054	107 758	108 296	13	243 415	121 428	121 987	140
Thrissur	317 526	154 248	163 278	...	330 122	160 443	169 679	88
Tinsukia	...	...	...	...	108 123	59 561	48 562	26
Tiruchirappalli	752 066	376 125	375 941	147	866 354	434 321	432 033	196
Tirunelveli	411 831	203 232	208 599	109	433 352	214 133	219 219	135
Tirupati	228 202	118 187	110 015	16	303 521	155 468	148 053	20
Tiruppur	344 543	179 930	164 613	27	550 826	286 862	263 964	147
Tiruvannamalai	130 567	66 125	64 442	14	...	...	...	...
Tiruvottiyur	212 281	108 720	103 561	21	...	...	...	...
Titagarh	124 213	70 705	53 508	3	...	...	...	...
Tonk	135 689	70 255	65 434	61	...	...	...	...
Tumkur	248 929	129 273	119 656	...	...	...	...	...
Udaipur	389 438	205 335	184 103	64	...	...	...	...
Udupi	113 112	55 893	57 219	64	127 124	62 596	64 528	73
Ujjain	430 427	223 998	206 429	...	431 162	224 475	206 687	92
Ulhasnagar	473 731	251 888	221 843	13	...	...	...	...
Uluberia	202 135	105 843	96 292	34	...	...	...	...
Unnao	144 662	76 254	68 408	21	...	...	...	...
Uppal Kalan	117 217	60 857	56 360	20	...	...	...	...
Uttarpara Kotrung	150 363	78 808	71 555	16	...	...	...	...
Vadakara	...	...	...	...	124 083	59 803	64 280	51
Vadodara	1 306 227	684 013	622 214	108	1 491 045	782 251	708 794	214
Valsad	...	...	...	...	145 592	75 216	70 376	...
Vaniyambadi	...	...	...	...	103 950	51 886	52 064	16
Varanasi	1 091 918	582 096	509 822	92	1 203 961	643 043	560 918	111
Vasai	...	...	...	...	174 396	91 030	83 366	...
Vejalpur	113 445	58 878	54 567	7	...	...	...	...
Vellore	177 230	87 977	89 253	12	386 746	193 176	193 570	62
Veraval	141 357	72 148	69 209	38	158 032	80 889	77 143	41
Vidisha	125 453	66 572	58 881	6	...	...	...	...
Vijayawada	851 282	431 243	420 039	60	1 039 518	527 307	512 211	101
Virar	118 928	63 704	55 224	20	...	...	...	...
Visakhapatnam	982 904	501 406	481 498	112	1 345 938	687 985	657 953	326
Vizianagarm	174 651	86 375	88 276	21	195 801	97 032	98 769	30
Wadhwan	...	...	...	...	219 585	114 175	105 410	59
Warangal	530 636	268 954	261 682	68	579 216	293 709	285 507	97
Wardha	111 118	57 499	53 619	8	...	...	...	...
Yamunanagar	189 696	101 782	87 914	16	306 740	166 137	140 603	42
Yavatmal	120 676	61 780	58 896	10	139 835	71 908	67 927	13
Indonesia - Indonésie								
1 VII 2015 (ESDJ)								
Ambon	411 617	205 684	205 933	359	...	...	...	...
Balikpapan	615 574	317 988	297 586	504	...	...	...	...
Banda Aceh	250 303	128 982	121 321	61	...	...	...	...
Bandar Lampung	979 287	493 411	485 876	296	...	...	...	...
Bandjarmasin	675 440	338 133	337 307	72	...	...	...	...
Bandung	2 481 469	1 253 274	1 228 195	168	...	...	...	...

8. Population of capital cities and cities of 100 000 or more inhabitants: latest available year, 1996 - 2015
Population des capitales et des villes de 100 000 habitants ou plus : dernière année disponible, 1996 - 2015 (continued - suite)

Continent, country or area, date, code[a] and city Continent, pays ou zone, date, code[a] et ville	City proper - Ville proprement dite				Urban agglomeration - Agglomération urbaine			
	Population			Surface area - Superficie (km²)	Population			Surface area - Superficie (km²)
	Both sexes - Les deux sexes	Male - Masculin	Female - Féminin		Both sexes - Les deux sexes	Male - Masculin	Female - Féminin	

ASIA - ASIE								
Indonesia - Indonésie								
1 VII 2015 (ESDJ)								
Batam	1 188 985	607 400	581 585	1 039	...	...	...	...
Bengkulu	351 298	176 535	174 763	145	...	...	...	...
Binjai	264 687	132 197	132 490	90	...	...	...	...
Bitung	205 675	105 094	100 581	330	...	...	...	...
Blitar	137 908	68 401	69 507	33	...	...	...	...
Bogor	1 047 922	532 018	515 904	112	...	...	...	...
Cirebon (Tjirebon)	307 494	154 228	153 266	40	...	...	...	...
Denpasar	880 561	449 666	430 895	128	...	...	...	...
Gorontalo	202 202	99 237	102 965	66	...	...	...	...
JAKARTA	10 154 584	5 103 637	5 050 947	654	...	...	...	...
Jambi	576 067	289 713	286 354	205	...	...	...	...
Jayapura	283 490	151 450	132 040	950	...	...	...	...
Kediri	280 004	139 493	140 511	67	...	...	...	...
Madiun	174 995	84 604	90 391	34	...	...	...	...
Magelang	120 792	59 512	61 280	18	...	...	...	...
Makasar (Ujung Pandang)	1 449 401	717 047	732 354	181	...	...	...	...
Malang	851 298	419 713	431 585	110	...	...	...	...
Manado	425 634	213 613	212 021	167	...	...	...	...
Mataram	450 226	222 596	227 630	61	...	...	...	...
Medan	2 210 624	1 091 937	1 118 687	265	...	...	...	...
Mojokerto	125 706	61 816	63 890	20	...	...	...	...
Padang	902 413	450 598	451 815	695	...	...	...	...
Pakalongan	296 404	148 220	148 184	45	...	...	...	...
Pakanbaru	1 038 118	533 217	504 901	632	...	...	...	...
Palangkaraya	259 865	132 980	126 885	2 400	...	...	...	...
Palembang	1 580 517	791 943	788 574	374	...	...	...	...
Pangkal Pinang	196 202	100 617	95 585	119	...	...	...	...
Pare Pare	138 699	68 094	70 605	89	...	...	...	...
Pasuruan	194 815	96 598	98 217	38	...	...	...	...
Pematang Siantar	247 411	120 597	126 814	80	...	...	...	...
Pontianak	607 618	302 739	304 879	108	...	...	...	...
Probolinggo	229 013	112 689	116 324	56	...	...	...	...
Salatiga	183 815	89 928	93 887	53	...	...	...	...
Samarinda	855 757	442 982	412 775	695	...	...	...	...
Semarang	1 701 114	834 124	866 990	374	...	...	...	...
Sukabumi	318 117	161 188	156 929	49	...	...	...	...
Surabaya	2 848 583	1 406 683	1 441 900	330	...	...	...	...
Surakarta	512 226	249 113	263 113	44	...	...	...	...
Tangerang	2 047 105	1 045 113	1 001 992	154	...	...	...	...
Tanjung Balai	167 012	84 197	82 815	62	...	...	...	...
Tebing Tinggi	156 815	77 509	79 306	38	...	...	...	...
Tegal	246 119	121 884	124 235	34	...	...	...	...
Yogyakarta	412 704	201 082	211 622	33	...	...	...	...
Iran (Islamic Republic of) - Iran (République islamique d')								
24 X 2011 (CDJC)								
Abadan	212 744	106 181	106 563	...	...	...	...	...
Ahwaz	1 112 021	558 346	553 675	...	...	...	...	...
Amol	219 915	110 331	109 584	...	...	...	...	...
Andimeshk	126 811	63 990	62 821	...	...	...	...	...
Arak	484 212	244 614	239 598	...	...	...	...	...
Ardabil	482 632	245 335	237 297	...	...	...	...	...
Babol	219 467	109 407	110 060	...	...	...	...	...
Bam	107 131	53 492	53 639	...	...	...	...	...
Bandar-e-Abbas	435 751	222 798	212 953	...	...	...	...	...
Bandar-e-Anzali	116 664	57 675	58 989	...	...	...	...	...
Bandar-e-Mahshahr	153 778	77 487	76 291	...	...	...	...	...
Behbahan	107 412	54 163	53 249	...	...	...	...	...
Birjand	178 020	90 092	87 928	...	...	...	...	...
Bojnurd	199 791	100 605	99 186	...	...	...	...	...
Borujerd	240 654	118 508	122 146	...	...	...	...	...
Bukand	170 600	85 835	84 765	...	...	...	...	...
Bushehr	195 222	101 362	93 860	...	...	...	...	...

8. Population of capital cities and cities of 100 000 or more inhabitants: latest available year, 1996 - 2015
Population des capitales et des villes de 100 000 habitants ou plus : dernière année disponible, 1996 - 2015 (continued - suite)

Continent, country or area, date, code[a] and city / Continent, pays ou zone, date, code[a] et ville	City proper - Ville proprement dite				Urban agglomeration - Agglomération urbaine			
	Population			Surface area - Superficie (km²)	Population			Surface area - Superficie (km²)
	Both sexes - Les deux sexes	Male - Masculin	Female - Féminin		Both sexes - Les deux sexes	Male - Masculin	Female - Féminin	

ASIA - ASIE

Iran (Islamic Republic of) - Iran (République islamique d')
24 X 2011 (CDJC)

Dezful	248 380	128 430	119 950	...	...	...	...	...
Esfahan	1 756 126	884 018	872 108	...	...	...	...	...
Fasa	104 809	51 907	52 902	...	...	...	...	...
Golestan (Soltanabad)	259 480	133 531	125 949	...	...	...	...	...
Gonbad-e-Kavus	144 546	71 986	72 560	...	...	...	...	...
Gorgan	329 536	165 001	164 535	...	...	...	...	...
Hamadan	525 794	261 577	264 217	...	...	...	...	...
Ilam	172 213	87 221	84 992	...	...	...	...	...
Islam Shahr (Qasemabad)	389 102	198 080	191 022	...	...	...	...	...
Izeh	117 093	58 080	59 013	...	...	...	...	...
Jahrom	114 108	57 865	56 243	...	...	...	...	...
Jiroft	111 034	57 168	53 866	...	...	...	...	...
Kamal Shahr	109 943	56 265	53 678	...	...	...	...	...
Karaj	1 614 626	813 551	801 075	...	...	...	...	...
Kashan	275 325	139 866	135 459	...	...	...	...	...
Kerman	534 441	269 661	264 780	...	...	...	...	...
Kermanshah	851 405	426 129	425 276	...	...	...	...	...
Khomeini shahr	244 696	126 326	118 370	...	...	...	...	...
Khoramabad	348 216	173 264	174 952	...	...	...	...	...
Khoramshahr	129 418	63 804	65 614	...	...	...	...	...
Khoy	200 958	100 593	100 365	...	...	...	...	...
Mahabad	147 268	73 626	73 642	...	...	...	...	...
Malard	290 817	147 954	142 863	...	...	...	...	...
Malayer	159 848	79 477	80 371	...	...	...	...	...
Marand	124 323	62 848	61 475	...	...	...	...	...
Maraqeh	162 275	81 229	81 046	...	...	...	...	...
Marivan	110 464	56 129	54 335	...	...	...	...	...
Marvadsht	138 649	70 221	68 428	...	...	...	...	...
Mashhad	2 766 258	1 384 599	1 381 659	...	...	...	...	...
Masjed Soleyman	103 369	51 852	51 517	...	...	...	...	...
Miandoab	123 081	62 883	60 198	...	...	...	...	...
Mohammad Shahr	100 519	51 359	49 160	...	...	...	...	...
Najafabad	221 814	111 915	109 899	...	...	...	...	...
Nasim Shahr	157 474	80 947	76 527	...	...	...	...	...
Nazar Abad	107 806	54 806	53 000	...	...	...	...	...
Neyshabur	239 185	119 845	119 340	...	...	...	...	...
Orumiyeh	667 499	334 136	333 363	...	...	...	...	...
Pakdasht	206 490	105 814	100 676	...	...	...	...	...
Qaem shahr	196 050	97 358	98 692	...	...	...	...	...
Qarchak	191 588	97 678	93 910	...	...	...	...	...
Qazvin	381 598	192 960	188 638	...	...	...	...	...
Qods	283 517	144 911	138 606	...	...	...	...	...
Qom	1 074 036	545 704	528 332	...	...	...	...	...
Quchan	103 760	52 240	51 520	...	...	...	...	...
Rafsanjan	151 420	75 643	75 777	...	...	...	...	...
Rasht	639 951	316 833	323 118	...	...	...	...	...
Sabzewar	231 557	115 158	116 399	...	...	...	...	...
Sanandaj	373 987	189 047	184 940	...	...	...	...	...
Saqez	139 738	69 856	69 882	...	...	...	...	...
Sari	296 417	147 875	148 542	...	...	...	...	...
Saveh	200 481	102 578	97 903	...	...	...	...	...
Semnan	153 680	77 575	76 105	...	...	...	...	...
Shahinshahr	143 308	71 357	71 951	...	...	...	...	...
Shahr-e-Kord	159 775	79 681	80 094	...	...	...	...	...
Shahreza	123 767	62 314	61 453	...	...	...	...	...
Shahriar	249 473	126 246	123 227	...	...	...	...	...
Shahrud	140 474	70 616	69 858	...	...	...	...	...
Shiraz	1 460 665	732 380	728 285	...	...	...	...	...
Shoosh	106 815	53 747	53 068	...	...	...	...	...
Sirjan	185 623	94 943	90 680	...	...	...	...	...
Tabriz	1 494 998	755 553	739 445	...	...	...	...	...
TEHRAN	8 154 051	4 059 301	4 094 750	...	...	...	...	...

8. Population of capital cities and cities of 100 000 or more inhabitants: latest available year, 1996 - 2015
Population des capitales et des villes de 100 000 habitants ou plus : dernière année disponible, 1996 - 2015 (continued - suite)

Continent, country or area, date, code[a] and city / Continent, pays ou zone, date, code[a] et ville	City proper - Ville proprement dite				Urban agglomeration - Agglomération urbaine			
	Population			Surface area - Superficie (km²)	Population			Surface area - Superficie (km²)
	Both sexes - Les deux sexes	Male - Masculin	Female - Féminin		Both sexes - Les deux sexes	Male - Masculin	Female - Féminin	
ASIA - ASIE								
Iran (Islamic Republic of) - Iran (République islamique d')								
24 X 2011 (CDJC)								
Torbat-e-heydariyeh	131 150	66 310	64 840	...	...	...	...	...
Varamin	218 991	111 074	107 917	...	...	...	...	...
Yasooj	108 505	54 825	53 680	...	...	...	...	...
Yazd	486 152	246 985	239 167	...	...	...	...	...
Zabol	137 722	69 726	67 996	...	...	...	...	...
Zahedan	560 725	283 680	277 045	...	...	...	...	...
Zanjan	386 851	195 382	191 469	...	...	...	...	...
Iraq								
1 VII 2015 (ESDF)								
Abi Gharaq Nahia	108 630	55 009	53 621	191	...	...	...	...
Abna'a Al-Rafidain Nahia	153 712	77 827	75 885	...	...	...	...	...
Abu Al-Khaseeb Qadha Center	215 247	108 228	107 019	1 152	...	...	...	...
Abu-Gharib Qadha Center	149 858	76 274	73 584	431	...	...	...	...
Al-Adhamia Qadha Center	286 036	144 825	141 211	29	...	...	...	...
Al-Amara Qadha Center	541 034	270 426	270 608	2 862	...	...	...	...
Al-Amirya Nahia	101 119	51 899	49 220	2 532	...	...	...	...
Al-Basrah Qadha Center	1 225 793	616 525	609 268	1 085	...	...	...	...
Al-Dair Nahia	101 882	50 969	50 913	825	...	...	...	...
Al-Dijail Qadha Center	105 345	53 240	52 105	1 286	...	...	...	...
Al-Diwaniya Qadha Center	421 571	212 293	209 278	319	...	...	...	...
Al-Fahama Nahia	619 474	313 651	305 823	90	...	...	...	...
Al-Falluja Qadha Center	321 106	165 111	155 995	478	...	...	...	...
Al-Forat Nahia	379 668	192 233	187 435	...	...	...	...	...
Al-Garma Nahia	129 783	66 577	63 206	1 038	...	...	...	...
Al-Gharraf Nahia	118 081	59 318	58 763	623	...	...	...	...
Al-Habbaniya Nahia	133 202	68 366	64 836	714	...	...	...	...
Al-Hamza Qadha Center	128 472	64 739	63 733	600	...	...	...	...
Al-Hartha Nahia	156 391	78 509	77 882	...	...	...	...	...
Al-Hassainya Nahia	147 103	74 383	72 720	334	...	...	...	...
Al-Hawiga Qadha Center	115 910	58 508	57 402	1 903	...	...	...	...
Al-Hilla Qadha Center	559 834	282 142	277 692	161	...	...	...	...
Al-Hindiya Qadha Center	113 021	57 001	56 020	134	...	...	...	...
Al-Hur Nahia	231 635	116 740	114 895	...	...	...	...	...
Al-Iskandaria Nahia	159 516	80 514	79 002	283	...	...	...	...
Al-Jisr Nahia	159 306	81 464	77 842	153	...	...	...	...
Al-Kadimiya Qadha Center	420 968	213 144	207 824	32	...	...	...	...
Al-Kaim Qadha Center	104 989	53 971	51 018	6 460	...	...	...	...
Al-Karkh Qadha Center	113 397	57 415	55 982	...	...	...	...	...
Al-Karrada Al-Sharqia Nahia	318 615	161 321	157 294	49	...	...	...	...
Al-Khalis Qadha Center	139 713	70 624	69 089	1 109	...	...	...	...
Al-Kifl Nahia	140 182	71 029	69 153	526	...	...	...	...
Al-Kufa Qadha Center	232 670	116 667	116 003	129	...	...	...	...
Al-Kut Qadha Center	436 673	220 490	216 183	2 540	...	...	...	...
Al-Madhatiya Nahia	135 941	68 724	67 217	498	...	...	...	...
Al-Mahawil Qadha Center	116 899	59 181	57 718	608	...	...	...	...
Al-Mamoon Nahia	985 798	499 128	486 670	82	...	...	...	...
Al-Mansour Nahia	434 839	220 167	214 672	119	...	...	...	...
Al-Mashroo Nahia	127 344	64 449	62 895	834	...	...	...	...
Al-Mejar Al-Kabir Qadha Center	108 979	54 373	54 606	506	...	...	...	...
Al-Mosal Qadha Center	1 384 260	708 546	675 714	1 783	...	...	...	...
Al-Mounawara Nahia	287 799	145 718	142 081	...	...	...	...	...
Al-Muqdadya Qadha Center	157 593	79 612	77 981	768	...	...	...	...
Al-Najaf Qadha Center	746 180	372 423	373 757	1 133	...	...	...	...
Al-Nasir & Al-Salam Nahia	160 606	82 184	78 422	262	...	...	...	...
Al-Nasiriya Qadha Center	537 544	269 480	268 064	1 277	...	...	...	...
Al-Noamaniya Qadha Center	111 647	56 363	55 284	946	...	...	...	...
Al-Qasim Nahia	159 420	80 545	78 875	528	...	...	...	...
Al-Qayarra Nahia	129 811	66 129	63 682	686	...	...	...	...
Al-Qurna Qadha Center	136 677	68 704	67 973	1 248	...	...	...	...
Al-Ramadi Qadha Center	419 053	215 292	203 761	7 829	...	...	...	...
Al-Rifaai Qadha Center	155 478	78 087	77 391	1 345	...	...	...	...
Al-Rumaitha Qadha Center	118 011	59 581	58 430	106	...	...	...	...

8. Population of capital cities and cities of 100 000 or more inhabitants: latest available year, 1996 - 2015
Population des capitales et des villes de 100 000 habitants ou plus : dernière année disponible, 1996 - 2015 (continued - suite)

Continent, country or area, date, code[a] and city / Continent, pays ou zone, date, code[a] et ville	City proper - Ville proprement dite				Urban agglomeration - Agglomération urbaine			
	Population			Surface area - Superficie (km²)	Population			Surface area - Superficie (km²)
	Both sexes - Les deux sexes	Male - Masculin	Female - Féminin		Both sexes - Les deux sexes	Male - Masculin	Female - Féminin	
ASIA - ASIE								
Iraq								
1 VII 2015 (ESDF)								
Al-Rusafa Qadha Center	118 018	59 755	58 263	...	...	...	...	...
Al-Samawa Qadha Center	288 948	145 984	142 964	941	...	...	...	...
Al-Shamal Nahia	158 475	81 035	77 440	...	...	...	...	...
Al-Shattra Qadha Center	239 680	120 266	119 414	384	...	...	...	...
Al-Shirqat Qadha Center	208 586	105 453	103 133	1 515	...	...	...	...
Al-Sideeq Al-Akbar Nahia	172 057	87 116	84 941	...	...	...	...	...
Al-Suwaira Qadha Center	142 924	72 148	70 776	1 345	...	...	...	...
Al-Taji Nahia	164 894	84 470	80 424	388	...	...	...	...
Al-Wihda Nahia	204 585	104 438	100 147	890	...	...	...	...
Al-Yousifya Nahia	131 507	67 600	63 907	486	...	...	...	...
Al-Zohour Nahia	209 918	106 332	103 586	...	...	...	...	...
Al-Zubair Qadha Center	378 758	190 200	188 558	1 134	...	...	...	...
Arbil Qadha Center	787 997	398 450	389 547	2 790	...	...	...	...
BAGHDAD	1 211 934[43]	613 625[43]	598 309[43]	111	...	...	...	...
Bakrago Nahia	101 892	51 077	50 815	...	...	...	...	...
Baquba Qadha Center	276 029	138 681	137 348	580	...	...	...	...
Bashiqa Nahia	140 258	71 487	68 771	497	...	...	...	...
Beni Saad Nahia	127 268	64 496	62 772	497	...	...	...	...
Beygee Qadha Center	175 395	88 596	86 799	1 188	...	...	...	...
Duhouk Qadha Center	328 113	164 245	163 868	577	...	...	...	...
Kalar Qadha Center	144 235	72 047	72 188	2 201	...	...	...	...
Kerbela Qadha Center	514 356	259 193	255 163	2 397	...	...	...	...
Kirkuk Qadha Center	938 336	471 419	466 917	1 956	...	...	...	...
Mahmudiya Qadha Center	154 741	78 846	75 895	68	...	...	...	...
Qalat Siker Nahia	100 315	50 373	49 942	614	...	...	...	...
Saddat Al-Hindin Nahia	116 247	58 839	57 408	388	...	...	...	...
Sader /1 Qadha Center	130 153	65 899	64 254	...	...	...	...	...
Samarra Qadha Center	203 011	102 444	100 567	4 504	...	...	...	...
Shat Al-Arab Qadha Center	136 043	68 413	67 630	1 516	...	...	...	...
Sulaimania Qadha Center	651 173	325 147	326 026	3 404	...	...	...	...
Suq AL-Shoyolh Qadha Center	126 652	63 493	63 159	285	...	...	...	...
Telafar Qadha Center	206 835	105 780	101 055	3 206	...	...	...	...
That Al Salasil Nahia	277 494	140 647	136 847	147	...	...	...	...
Tikrit Qadha Center	182 464	92 119	90 345	991	...	...	...	...
Tooz-Khormato Qadha Center	117 458	59 233	58 225	1 253	...	...	...	...
Zummar Nahia	128 017	65 210	62 807	1 247	...	...	...	...
Israel - Israël								
1 VII 2014 (ESDJ)								
Ashdod	217 235	106 064	111 171	51	...	...	...	...
Ashqelon	125 149	60 814	64 335	51	...	...	...	...
Bat Yam	128 685	61 233	67 452	8	...	...	...	...
Be'er Sheva	200 210	97 427	102 783	117	...	...	...	...
Bene Beraq	175 386	89 127	86 259	7	...	...	...	...
Haifa	275 130	132 064	143 066	73	...	...	...	...
Holon	186 846	90 218	96 628	19	...	...	...	...
JERUSALEM[44]	839 823	417 702	422 121	125	...	...	...	...
Netanya	199 703	97 400	102 303	35	...	...	...	...
Petah Tiqwa	222 330	108 618	113 712	36	...	...	...	...
Ramat Gan	150 256	71 640	78 615	16	...	...	...	...
Rehovot	126 940	62 126	64 814	24	...	...	...	...
Rishon Leziyyon	239 153	117 047	122 106	59	...	...	...	...
Tel Aviv-Yafo	422 364	208 553	213 811	54	...	...	...	...
Japan - Japon								
1 X 2010 (CDJC)								
Abiko	134 017[45]	65 732[45]	68 285[45]	43[46]	...	...	...	...
Ageo	223 926[45]	111 784[45]	112 142[45]	46[46]	...	...	...	...
Aizuwakamatsu	126 220[45]	59 854[45]	66 366[45]	383[46]	...	...	...	...
Akashi	290 959[45]	141 344[45]	149 615[45]	49[46]	...	...	...	...
Akishima	112 297[45]	56 320[45]	55 977[45]	17[46]	...	...	...	...
Akita	323 600[45]	152 456[45]	171 144[45]	906[46]	...	...	...	...
Amagasaki	453 748[45]	221 216[45]	232 532[45]	50[46]	...	...	...	...
Anjo	178 691[45]	91 424[45]	87 267[45]	86[46]	...	...	...	...
Aomori	299 520[45]	139 084[45]	160 436[45]	825[46]	...	...	...	...

8. Population of capital cities and cities of 100 000 or more inhabitants: latest available year, 1996 - 2015
Population des capitales et des villes de 100 000 habitants ou plus : dernière année disponible, 1996 - 2015 (continued - suite)

Continent, country or area, date, code[a] and city — Continent, pays ou zone, date, code[a] et ville	City proper - Ville proprement dite				Urban agglomeration - Agglomération urbaine			
	Population			Surface area - Superficie (km²)	Population			Surface area - Superficie (km²)
	Both sexes - Les deux sexes	Male - Masculin	Female - Féminin		Both sexes - Les deux sexes	Male - Masculin	Female - Féminin	

ASIA - ASIE

Japan - Japon
1 X 2010 (CDJC)

Asahikawa	347 095[45]	160 094[45]	187 001[45]	748[46]	...	...	...	...
Asaka	129 691[45]	65 503[45]	64 188[45]	18[46]	...	...	...	...
Ashikaga	154 530[45]	75 382[45]	79 148[45]	178[46]	...	...	...	...
Atsugi	224 420[45]	116 927[45]	107 493[45]	94[46]	...	...	...	...
Beppu	125 385[45]	56 868[45]	68 517[45]	125[46]	...	...	...	...
Chiba	961 749[45]	480 194[45]	481 555[45]	272[46]	...	...	...	...
Chigasaki	235 081[45]	115 245[45]	119 836[45]	36[46]	...	...	...	...
Chikusei	108 527[45]	53 680[45]	54 847[45]	205[46]	...	...	...	...
Chikushino	100 172[45]	47 750[45]	52 422[45]	88[46]	...	...	...	...
Chofu	223 593[45]	110 805[45]	112 788[45]	22[46]	...	...	...	...
Daito	127 534[45]	63 810[45]	63 724[45]	18[46]	...	...	...	...
Ebetsu	123 722[45]	59 320[45]	64 402[45]	188[46]	...	...	...	...
Ebina	127 707[45]	64 483[45]	63 224[45]	26[46]	...	...	...	...
Fuchu	255 506[45]	131 558[45]	123 948[45]	29[46]	...	...	...	...
Fuji	254 027[45]	125 240[45]	128 787[45]	245[46]	...	...	...	...
Fujieda	142 151[45]	69 484[45]	72 667[45]	194[46]	...	...	...	...
Fujimi	106 736[45]	53 134[45]	53 602[45]	20[46]	...	...	...	...
Fujimino	105 695[45]	52 640[45]	53 055[45]	15[46]	...	...	...	...
Fujinomiya	132 001[45]	64 909[45]	67 092[45]	389[46]	...	...	...	...
Fujisawa	409 657[45]	203 778[45]	205 879[45]	70[46]	...	...	...	...
Fukaya	144 618[45]	72 146[45]	72 472[45]	138[46]	...	...	...	...
Fukui	266 796[45]	128 692[45]	138 104[45]	536[46]	...	...	...	...
Fukuoka	1 463 743[45]	692 648[45]	771 095[45]	341[46]	...	...	...	...
Fukushima	292 590[45]	140 723[45]	151 867[45]	768[46]	...	...	...	...
Fukuyama	461 357[45]	222 729[45]	238 628[45]	518[46]	...	...	...	...
Funabashi	609 040[45]	306 399[45]	302 641[45]	86[46]	...	...	...	...
Gifu	413 136[45]	196 525[45]	216 611[45]	203[46]	...	...	...	...
Habikino	117 681[45]	55 737[45]	61 944[45]	26[46]	...	...	...	...
Hachinohe	237 615[45]	113 340[45]	124 275[45]	305[46]	...	...	...	...
Hachioji	580 053[45]	293 462[45]	286 591[45]	186[46]	...	...	...	...
Hadano	170 145[45]	87 291[45]	82 854[45]	104[46]	...	...	...	...
Hakodate	279 127[45]	127 046[45]	152 081[45]	678[46]	...	...	...	...
Hakusan	110 459[45]	53 563[45]	56 896[45]	755[46]	...	...	...	...
Hamamatsu	800 866[45]	397 146[45]	403 720[45]	1 558[46]	...	...	...	...
Hanamaki	101 438[45]	48 076[45]	53 362[45]	908[46]	...	...	...	...
Handa	118 828[45]	59 291[45]	59 537[45]	47[46]	...	...	...	...
Hatsukaichi	114 038[45]	54 101[45]	59 937[45]	489[46]	...	...	...	...
Higashihiroshima	190 135[45]	96 952[45]	93 183[45]	635[46]	...	...	...	...
Higashikurume	116 546[45]	57 613[45]	58 933[45]	13[46]	...	...	...	...
Higashimurayama	153 557[45]	75 461[45]	78 096[45]	17[46]	...	...	...	...
Higashiomi	115 479[45]	56 872[45]	58 607[45]	389[46]	...	...	...	...
Higashiosaka	509 533[45]	249 964[45]	259 569[45]	62[46]	...	...	...	...
Hikone	112 156[45]	55 173[45]	56 983[45]	197[46]	...	...	...	...
Himeji	536 270[45]	259 320[45]	276 950[45]	534[46]	...	...	...	...
Hino	180 052[45]	91 236[45]	88 816[45]	28[46]	...	...	...	...
Hirakata	407 978[45]	195 570[45]	212 408[45]	65[46]	...	...	...	...
Hiratsuka	260 780[45]	132 048[45]	128 732[45]	68[46]	...	...	...	...
Hirosaki	183 473[45]	84 064[45]	99 409[45]	524[46]	...	...	...	...
Hiroshima	1 173 843[45]	565 482[45]	608 361[45]	905[46]	...	...	...	...
Hitachi	193 129[45]	96 747[45]	96 382[45]	226[46]	...	...	...	...
Hitachinaka	157 060[45]	79 046[45]	78 014[45]	99[46]	...	...	...	...
Hofu	116 611[45]	56 191[45]	60 420[45]	189[46]	...	...	...	...
Ibaraki	274 822[45]	133 621[45]	141 201[45]	77[46]	...	...	...	...
Ichihara	280 416[45]	143 338[45]	137 078[45]	368[46]	...	...	...	...
Ichikawa	473 919[45]	239 222[45]	234 697[45]	57[46]	...	...	...	...
Ichinomiya	378 566[45]	184 221[45]	194 345[45]	114[46]	...	...	...	...
Ichinoseki	118 578[45]	56 885[45]	61 693[45]	1 133[46]	...	...	...	...
Iida	105 335[45]	50 105[45]	55 230[45]	659[46]	...	...	...	...
Iizuka	131 492[45]	62 166[45]	69 326[45]	214[46]	...	...	...	...

8. Population of capital cities and cities of 100 000 or more inhabitants: latest available year, 1996 - 2015
Population des capitales et des villes de 100 000 habitants ou plus : dernière année disponible, 1996 - 2015 (continued - suite)

Continent, country or area, date, code[a] and city / Continent, pays ou zone, date, code[a] et ville	City proper - Ville proprement dite				Urban agglomeration - Agglomération urbaine			
	Population			Surface area - Superficie (km²)	Population			Surface area - Superficie (km²)
	Both sexes - Les deux sexes	Male - Masculin	Female - Féminin		Both sexes - Les deux sexes	Male - Masculin	Female - Féminin	
ASIA - ASIE								
Japan - Japon								
1 X 2010 (CDJC)								
Ikeda	104 229[45]	50 721[45]	53 508[45]	22[46]	...	...	...	...
Ikoma	118 113[45]	56 311[45]	61 802[45]	53[46]	...	...	...	...
Imabari	166 532[45]	77 893[45]	88 639[45]	420[46]	...	...	...	...
Inazawa	136 442[45]	67 394[45]	69 048[45]	79[46]	...	...	...	...
Iruma	149 872[45]	74 107[45]	75 765[45]	45[46]	...	...	...	...
Isahaya	140 752[45]	66 192[45]	74 560[45]	321[46]	...	...	...	...
Ise	130 271[45]	61 482[45]	68 789[45]	209[46]	...	...	...	...
Isehara	101 039[45]	51 601[45]	49 438[45]	56[46]	...	...	...	...
Isesaki	207 221[45]	103 210[45]	104 011[45]	139[46]	...	...	...	...
Ishinomaki	160 826[45]	77 143[45]	83 683[45]	556[46]	...	...	...	...
Itami	196 127[45]	95 665[45]	100 462[45]	25[46]	...	...	...	...
Iwaki	342 249[45]	165 339[45]	176 910[45]	1 231[46]	...	...	...	...
Iwakuni	143 857[45]	67 597[45]	76 260[45]	874[46]	...	...	...	...
Iwata	168 625[45]	84 716[45]	83 909[45]	164[46]	...	...	...	...
Izumi (Osaka)	184 988[45]	89 613[45]	95 375[45]	85[46]	...	...	...	...
Izumisano	100 801[45]	48 161[45]	52 640[45]	55[46]	...	...	...	...
Izumo	143 796[45]	68 563[45]	75 233[45]	543[46]	...	...	...	...
Joetsu	203 899[45]	99 115[45]	104 784[45]	974[46]	...	...	...	...
Kadoma	130 282[45]	64 423[45]	65 859[45]	12[46]	...	...	...	...
Kagoshima	605 846[45]	281 133[45]	324 713[45]	547[46]	...	...	...	...
Kakamigahara	145 604[45]	71 516[45]	74 088[45]	88[46]	...	...	...	...
Kakegawa	116 363[45]	57 921[45]	58 442[45]	266[46]	...	...	...	...
Kakogawa	266 937[45]	130 931[45]	136 006[45]	139[46]	...	...	...	...
Kamagaya	107 853[45]	53 178[45]	54 675[45]	21[46]	...	...	...	...
Kamakura	174 314[45]	82 235[45]	92 079[45]	40[46]	...	...	...	...
Kanazawa	462 361[45]	224 087[45]	238 274[45]	468[46]	...	...	...	...
Kanoya	105 070[45]	49 808[45]	55 262[45]	448[46]	...	...	...	...
Kanuma	102 348[45]	50 452[45]	51 896[45]	491[46]	...	...	...	...
Karatsu	126 926[45]	59 221[45]	67 705[45]	487[46]	...	...	...	...
Kariya	145 781[45]	76 598[45]	69 183[45]	50[46]	...	...	...	...
Kashihara	125 605[45]	59 879[45]	65 726[45]	40[46]	...	...	...	...
Kashiwa	404 012[45]	201 045[45]	202 967[45]	115[46]	...	...	...	...
Kasuga	106 780[45]	51 445[45]	55 335[45]	14[46]	...	...	...	...
Kasugai	305 569[45]	152 765[45]	152 804[45]	93[46]	...	...	...	...
Kasukabe	237 171[45]	117 798[45]	119 373[45]	66[46]	...	...	...	...
Kawachinagano	112 490[45]	52 964[45]	59 526[45]	110[46]	...	...	...	...
Kawagoe	342 670[45]	171 590[45]	171 080[45]	109[46]	...	...	...	...
Kawaguchi	500 598[45]	255 780[45]	244 818[45]	56[46]	...	...	...	...
Kawanishi	156 423[45]	73 930[45]	82 493[45]	53[46]	...	...	...	...
Kawasaki	1 425 512[45]	728 525[45]	696 987[45]	143[46]	...	...	...	...
Kazo	115 002[45]	57 241[45]	57 761[45]	133[46]	...	...	...	...
Kirishima	127 487[45]	61 135[45]	66 352[45]	604[46]	...	...	...	...
Kiryu	121 704[45]	58 765[45]	62 939[45]	275[46]	...	...	...	...
Kisarazu	129 312[45]	65 242[45]	64 070[45]	139[46]	...	...	...	...
Kishiwada	199 234[45]	95 730[45]	103 504[45]	72[46]	...	...	...	...
Kitakyushu	976 846[45]	459 305[45]	517 541[45]	488[46]	...	...	...	...
Kitami	125 689[45]	60 171[45]	65 518[45]	1 428[46]	...	...	...	...
Kobe	1 544 200[45]	731 114[45]	813 086[45]	553[46]	...	...	...	...
Kochi	343 393[45]	159 644[45]	183 749[45]	309[46]	...	...	...	...
Kodaira	187 035[45]	92 886[45]	94 149[45]	20[46]	...	...	...	...
Kofu	198 992[45]	97 754[45]	101 238[45]	212[46]	...	...	...	...
Koga	142 995[45]	71 450[45]	71 545[45]	124[46]	...	...	...	...
Koganei	118 852[45]	59 515[45]	59 337[45]	11[46]	...	...	...	...
Kokubunji	120 650[45]	59 967[45]	60 683[45]	11[46]	...	...	...	...
Komaki	147 132[45]	74 161[45]	72 971[45]	63[46]	...	...	...	...
Komatsu	108 433[45]	52 465[45]	55 968[45]	371[46]	...	...	...	...
Konosu	119 639[45]	59 152[45]	60 487[45]	67[46]	...	...	...	...
Koriyama	338 712[45]	166 336[45]	172 376[45]	757[46]	...	...	...	...
Koshigaya	326 313[45]	162 374[45]	163 939[45]	60[46]	...	...	...	...

8. Population of capital cities and cities of 100 000 or more inhabitants: latest available year, 1996 - 2015
Population des capitales et des villes de 100 000 habitants ou plus : dernière année disponible, 1996 - 2015 (continued - suite)

Continent, country or area, date, code[a] and city / Continent, pays ou zone, date, code[a] et ville	City proper - Ville proprement dite				Urban agglomeration - Agglomération urbaine			
	Population			Surface area - Superficie (km²)	Population			Surface area - Superficie (km²)
	Both sexes - Les deux sexes	Male - Masculin	Female - Féminin		Both sexes - Les deux sexes	Male - Masculin	Female - Féminin	

ASIA - ASIE

Japan - Japon
1 X 2010 (CDJC)

Kuki	154 310[45]	77 175[45]	77 135[45]	82[46]	...	...	...	...
Kumagaya	203 180[45]	101 430[45]	101 750[45]	160[46]	...	...	...	...
Kumamoto	734 474[45]	344 291[45]	390 183[45]	390[46]	...	...	...	...
Kurashiki	475 513[45]	230 061[45]	245 452[45]	355[46]	...	...	...	...
Kure	239 973[45]	115 432[45]	124 541[45]	354[46]	...	...	...	...
Kurume	302 402[45]	143 885[45]	158 517[45]	230[46]	...	...	...	...
Kusatsu	130 874[45]	67 819[45]	63 055[45]	68[46]	...	...	...	...
Kushiro	181 169[45]	85 474[45]	95 695[45]	1 363[46]	...	...	...	...
Kuwana	140 290[45]	68 914[45]	71 376[45]	137[46]	...	...	...	...
Kyoto	1 474 015[45]	701 088[45]	772 927[45]	828[46]	...	...	...	...
Machida	426 987[45]	209 580[45]	217 407[45]	72[46]	...	...	...	...
Maebashi	340 291[45]	166 043[45]	174 248[45]	312[46]	...	...	...	...
Marugame	110 473[45]	53 633[45]	56 840[45]	112[46]	...	...	...	...
Matsubara	124 594[45]	60 017[45]	64 577[45]	17[46]	...	...	...	...
Matsudo	484 457[45]	240 674[45]	243 783[45]	61[46]	...	...	...	...
Matsue	194 258[45]	93 736[45]	100 522[45]	530[46]	...	...	...	...
Matsumoto	243 037[45]	119 271[45]	123 766[45]	979[46]	...	...	...	...
Matsusaka	168 017[45]	80 960[45]	87 057[45]	624[46]	...	...	...	...
Matsuyama	517 231[45]	241 586[45]	275 645[45]	429[46]	...	...	...	...
Mihara	100 509[45]	47 865[45]	52 644[45]	471[46]	...	...	...	...
Minoh	129 895[45]	62 468[45]	67 427[45]	48[46]	...	...	...	...
Misato	131 415[45]	66 747[45]	64 668[45]	30[46]	...	...	...	...
Mishima	111 838[45]	54 911[45]	56 927[45]	62[46]	...	...	...	...
Mitaka	186 083[45]	91 997[45]	94 086[45]	17[46]	...	...	...	...
Mito	268 750[45]	130 918[45]	137 832[45]	217[46]	...	...	...	...
Miyakonojo	169 602[45]	79 553[45]	90 049[45]	653[46]	...	...	...	...
Miyazaki	400 583[45]	187 619[45]	212 964[45]	645[46]	...	...	...	...
Moriguchi	146 697[45]	71 272[45]	75 425[45]	13[46]	...	...	...	...
Morioka	298 348[45]	141 566[45]	156 782[45]	886[46]	...	...	...	...
Musashino	138 734[45]	66 406[45]	72 328[45]	11[46]	...	...	...	...
Nagahama	124 131[45]	60 973[45]	63 158[45]	681[46]	...	...	...	...
Nagano	381 511[45]	184 128[45]	197 383[45]	835[46]	...	...	...	...
Nagaoka	282 674[45]	137 780[45]	144 894[45]	891[46]	...	...	...	...
Nagareyama	163 984[45]	81 721[45]	82 263[45]	35[46]	...	...	...	...
Nagasaki	443 766[45]	203 574[45]	240 192[45]	406[46]	...	...	...	...
Nagoya	2 263 894[45]	1 116 211[45]	1 147 683[45]	326[46]	...	...	...	...
Naha	315 954[45]	151 848[45]	164 106[45]	39[46]	...	...	...	...
Nara	366 591[45]	171 410[45]	195 181[45]	277[46]	...	...	...	...
Narashino	164 530[45]	83 184[45]	81 346[45]	21[46]	...	...	...	...
Narita	128 933[45]	64 852[45]	64 081[45]	214[46]	...	...	...	...
Nasushiobara	117 812[45]	58 402[45]	59 410[45]	593[46]	...	...	...	...
Neyagawa	238 204[45]	116 132[45]	122 072[45]	25[46]	...	...	...	...
Niigata	811 901[45]	390 406[45]	421 495[45]	726[46]	...	...	...	...
Niihama	121 735[45]	58 219[45]	63 516[45]	234[46]	...	...	...	...
Niiza	158 777[45]	79 416[45]	79 361[45]	23[46]	...	...	...	...
Nishinomiya	482 640[45]	227 660[45]	254 980[45]	99[46]	...	...	...	...
Nishio	106 823[45]	54 066[45]	52 757[45]	76[46]	...	...	...	...
Nishitokyo	196 511[45]	96 437[45]	100 074[45]	16[46]	...	...	...	...
Nobeoka	131 182[45]	61 457[45]	69 725[45]	868[46]	...	...	...	...
Noda	155 491[45]	77 963[45]	77 528[45]	104[46]	...	...	...	...
Numazu	202 304[45]	99 184[45]	103 120[45]	187[46]	...	...	...	...
Obihiro	168 057[45]	80 584[45]	87 473[45]	619[46]	...	...	...	...
Odawara	198 327[45]	96 839[45]	101 488[45]	114[46]	...	...	...	...
Ogaki	161 160[45]	78 282[45]	82 878[45]	207[46]	...	...	...	...
Oita	474 094[45]	227 608[45]	246 486[45]	501[46]	...	...	...	...
Okayama	709 584[45]	341 158[45]	368 426[45]	790[46]	...	...	...	...
Okazaki	372 357[45]	187 649[45]	184 708[45]	387[46]	...	...	...	...
Okinawa	130 249[45]	63 195[45]	67 054[45]	49[46]	...	...	...	...
Ome	139 339[45]	69 742[45]	69 597[45]	103[46]	...	...	...	...

8. Population of capital cities and cities of 100 000 or more inhabitants: latest available year, 1996 - 2015
Population des capitales et des villes de 100 000 habitants ou plus : dernière année disponible, 1996 - 2015 (continued - suite)

Continent, country or area, date, code[a] and city / Continent, pays ou zone, date, code[a] et ville	City proper - Ville proprement dite				Urban agglomeration - Agglomération urbaine			
	Population			Surface area - Superficie (km²)	Population			Surface area - Superficie (km²)
	Both sexes - Les deux sexes	Male - Masculin	Female - Féminin		Both sexes - Les deux sexes	Male - Masculin	Female - Féminin	
ASIA - ASIE								
Japan - Japon								
1 X 2010 (CDJC)								
Omuta	123 638[45]	56 215[45]	67 423[45]	82[46]	...	...	...	...
Onomichi	145 202[45]	69 283[45]	75 919[45]	285[46]	...	...	...	...
Osaka	2 665 314[45]	1 293 798[45]	1 371 516[45]	222[46]	...	...	...	...
Osaki	135 147[45]	65 624[45]	69 523[45]	797[46]	...	...	...	...
Oshu	124 746[45]	59 935[45]	64 811[45]	993[46]	...	...	...	...
Ota	216 465[45]	109 204[45]	107 261[45]	176[46]	...	...	...	...
Otaru	131 928[45]	59 514[45]	72 414[45]	243[46]	...	...	...	...
Otsu	337 634[45]	163 250[45]	174 384[45]	464[46]	...	...	...	...
Oyama	164 454[45]	82 825[45]	81 629[45]	172[46]	...	...	...	...
Saga	237 506[45]	112 173[45]	125 333[45]	431[46]	...	...	...	...
Sagamihara	717 544[45]	361 394[45]	356 150[45]	329[46]	...	...	...	...
Saijo	112 091[45]	53 757[45]	58 334[45]	509[46]	...	...	...	...
Saitama	1 222 434[45]	611 236[45]	611 198[45]	217[46]	...	...	...	...
Sakado	101 700[45]	51 155[45]	50 545[45]	41[46]	...	...	...	...
Sakai	841 966[45]	404 756[45]	437 210[45]	150[46]	...	...	...	...
Sakata	111 151[45]	52 610[45]	58 541[45]	603[46]	...	...	...	...
Saku	100 552[45]	49 090[45]	51 462[45]	424[46]	...	...	...	...
Sakura	172 183[45]	84 246[45]	87 937[45]	104[46]	...	...	...	...
Sanda	114 216[45]	55 175[45]	59 041[45]	210[46]	...	...	...	...
Sanjo	102 292[45]	49 368[45]	52 924[45]	432[46]	...	...	...	...
Sano	121 249[45]	59 499[45]	61 750[45]	356[46]	...	...	...	...
Sapporo	1 913 545[45]	896 850[45]	1 016 695[45]	1 121[46]	...	...	...	...
Sasebo	261 101[45]	122 430[45]	138 671[45]	426[46]	...	...	...	...
Sayama	155 727[45]	78 637[45]	77 090[45]	49[46]	...	...	...	...
Sendai	1 045 986[45]	507 833[45]	538 153[45]	784[46]	...	...	...	...
Seto	132 224[45]	65 123[45]	67 101[45]	112[46]	...	...	...	...
Shibata	101 202[45]	48 606[45]	52 596[45]	533[46]	...	...	...	...
Shimada	100 276[45]	48 876[45]	51 400[45]	316[46]	...	...	...	...
Shimonoseki	280 947[45]	130 105[45]	150 842[45]	716[46]	...	...	...	...
Shizuoka	716 197[45]	348 609[45]	367 588[45]	1 412[46]	...	...	...	...
Shunan	149 487[45]	72 150[45]	77 337[45]	656[46]	...	...	...	...
Soka	243 855[45]	124 553[45]	119 302[45]	27[46]	...	...	...	...
Suita	355 798[45]	171 769[45]	184 029[45]	36[46]	...	...	...	...
Suzuka	199 293[45]	99 925[45]	99 368[45]	195[46]	...	...	...	...
Tachikawa	179 668[45]	89 470[45]	90 198[45]	24[46]	...	...	...	...
Tajimi	112 595[45]	54 342[45]	58 253[45]	91[46]	...	...	...	...
Takamatsu	419 429[45]	203 312[45]	216 117[45]	375[46]	...	...	...	...
Takaoka	176 061[45]	84 292[45]	91 769[45]	209[46]	...	...	...	...
Takarazuka	225 700[45]	105 289[45]	120 411[45]	102[46]	...	...	...	...
Takasaki	371 302[45]	181 667[45]	189 635[45]	459[46]	...	...	...	...
Takatsuki	357 359[45]	171 927[45]	185 432[45]	105[46]	...	...	...	...
Tama	147 648[45]	73 083[45]	74 565[45]	21[46]	...	...	...	...
Tochigi	139 262[45]	67 859[45]	71 403[45]	253[46]	...	...	...	...
Toda	123 079[45]	64 080[45]	58 999[45]	18[46]	...	...	...	...
Tokai	107 690[45]	56 305[45]	51 385[45]	43[46]	...	...	...	...
Tokorozawa	341 924[45]	170 598[45]	171 326[45]	72[46]	...	...	...	...
Tokushima	264 548[45]	125 619[45]	138 929[45]	192[46]	...	...	...	...
TOKYO	8 945 695[47]	4 412 050[47]	4 533 645[47]	622[46]	...	...	...	...
Tomakomai	173 320[45]	84 687[45]	88 633[45]	561[46]	...	...	...	...
Tondabayashi	119 576[45]	56 778[45]	62 798[45]	40[46]	...	...	...	...
Toride	109 651[45]	54 054[45]	55 597[45]	70[46]	...	...	...	...
Tottori	197 449[45]	95 959[45]	101 490[45]	766[46]	...	...	...	...
Toyama	421 953[45]	204 515[45]	217 438[45]	1 242[46]	...	...	...	...
Toyohashi	376 665[45]	188 200[45]	188 465[45]	261[46]	...	...	...	...
Toyokawa	181 928[45]	90 328[45]	91 600[45]	161[46]	...	...	...	...
Toyonaka	389 341[45]	185 103[45]	204 238[45]	36[46]	...	...	...	...
Toyota	421 487[45]	221 198[45]	200 289[45]	918[46]	...	...	...	...
Tsu	285 746[45]	138 643[45]	147 103[45]	711[46]	...	...	...	...
Tsuchiura	143 839[45]	71 600[45]	72 239[45]	123[46]	...	...	...	...

Continent, country or area, date, code[a] and city / Continent, pays ou zone, date, code[a] et ville	City proper - Ville proprement dite				Urban agglomeration - Agglomération urbaine			
	Population			Surface area - Superficie (km²)	Population			Surface area - Superficie (km²)
	Both sexes - Les deux sexes	Male - Masculin	Female - Féminin		Both sexes - Les deux sexes	Male - Masculin	Female - Féminin	
ASIA - ASIE								
Japan - Japon								
1 X 2010 (CDJC)								
Tsukuba	214 590[45]	110 230[45]	104 360[45]	284[46]	...	...	...	...
Tsuruoka	136 623[45]	64 846[45]	71 777[45]	1 312[46]	...	...	...	...
Tsuyama	106 788[45]	50 787[45]	56 001[45]	506[46]	...	...	...	...
Ube	173 772[45]	83 000[45]	90 772[45]	288[46]	...	...	...	...
Ueda	159 597[45]	77 589[45]	82 008[45]	552[46]	...	...	...	...
Uji	189 609[45]	91 971[45]	97 638[45]	68[46]	...	...	...	...
Urasoe	110 351[45]	53 948[45]	56 403[45]	19[46]	...	...	...	...
Urayasu	164 877[45]	82 177[45]	82 700[45]	17[46]	...	...	...	...
Uruma	116 979[45]	58 198[45]	58 781[45]	86[46]	...	...	...	...
Utsunomiya	511 739[45]	254 605[45]	257 134[45]	417[46]	...	...	...	...
Wakayama	370 364[45]	174 104[45]	196 260[45]	209[46]	...	...	...	...
Yachiyo	189 781[45]	93 688[45]	96 093[45]	51[46]	...	...	...	...
Yaizu	143 249[45]	69 901[45]	73 348[45]	71[46]	...	...	...	...
Yamagata	254 244[45]	121 433[45]	132 811[45]	381[46]	...	...	...	...
Yamaguchi	196 628[45]	92 997[45]	103 631[45]	1 023[46]	...	...	...	...
Yamato	228 186[45]	114 700[45]	113 486[45]	27[46]	...	...	...	...
Yao	271 460[45]	131 121[45]	140 339[45]	42[46]	...	...	...	...
Yatsushiro	132 266[45]	61 446[45]	70 820[45]	681[46]	...	...	...	...
Yokkaichi	307 766[45]	152 580[45]	155 186[45]	206[46]	...	...	...	...
Yokohama	3 688 773[45]	1 849 767[45]	1 839 006[45]	437[46]	...	...	...	...
Yokosuka	418 325[45]	208 966[45]	209 359[45]	101[46]	...	...	...	...
Yonago	148 271[45]	70 133[45]	78 138[45]	132[46]	...	...	...	...
Zama	129 436[45]	65 448[45]	63 988[45]	18[46]	...	...	...	...
Jordan - Jordanie								
30 X 2015 (CDFC)								
AMMAN	4 007 526	2 151 569	1 855 957	...	...	...	...	...
Aqaba	188 160	106 435	81 725	...	...	...	...	...
Irbid	1 770 158	914 635	855 523	...	...	...	...	...
Russiefa	481 900	257 888	224 012	...	...	...	...	...
Zarqa	1 364 878	721 601	643 277	...	...	...	...	...
Kazakhstan								
1 I 2013 (ESDF)								
Aktau	181 541	87 636	93 905	29	184 175	89 043	95 132	...
Aktobe	377 752	176 438	201 314	234	428 024	201 192	226 832	...
Almaty	1 507 509	687 027	820 482	319	...	...	...	...
ASTANA	814 435	393 158	421 277	710	...	...	...	...
Atirau	209 699	99 168	110 531	347	280 634	134 498	146 136	...
Ekibastuz	139 778	66 234	73 544	31	149 132	71 017	78 115	...
Karaganda	484 510	221 248	263 262	50	484 768	221 388	263 380	...
Koktshetau	143 267	66 077	77 190	43	154 000	71 225	82 775	...
Kustanai	221 943	99 341	122 602	21	221 943	99 341	122 602	...
Kyzylorda	238 840	116 031	122 809	236	260 524	127 119	133 405	...
Pavlodar	339 153	153 922	185 231	56	352 693	160 532	192 161	...
Petropavlovsk (Severo- Kazakhstanskaya oblast)	207 399	93 015	114 384	22	208 362	93 491	114 871	...
Rudni	127 712	59 700	68 012	19	128 234	59 947	68 287	...
Semipalatinsk	315 750	146 133	169 617	9	337 633	156 958	180 675	...
Shimkent	682 565	323 899	358 666	36	682 565	323 899	358 666	...
Taldykorgan	135 184	62 277	72 907	39	158 984	74 068	84 916	...
Taraz	351 353	164 440	186 913	13	351 353	164 440	186 913	...
Temirtau	182 551	84 577	97 974	30	182 551	84 577	97 974	...
Turkestan	155 552	77 393	78 159	...	248 773	124 719	124 054	...
Uralsk	273 359	125 951	147 408	71	278 086	128 276	149 810	...
Ust-Kamenogorsk	314 069	141 596	172 473	54	325 803	147 288	178 515	...
Zhanaozen	106 220	52 515	53 705	...	130 652	64 533	66 119	...
Kuwait - Koweït								
1 VII 2010 (ESDF)								
Farwanyiah	101 867	68 326	33 541	...	...	...	...	...
Hawalli	127 982	84 506	43 477	...	...	...	...	...
Jaleeb Al-Shuykh	219 629	180 786	38 843	...	...	...	...	...
Salmiya	177 009	103 119	73 890	...	...	...	...	...
South Kheetan	113 426	104 655	8 770	...	...	...	...	...

8. Population of capital cities and cities of 100 000 or more inhabitants: latest available year, 1996 - 2015
Population des capitales et des villes de 100 000 habitants ou plus : dernière année disponible, 1996 - 2015 (continued - suite)

Continent, country or area, date, code[a] and city / Continent, pays ou zone, date, code[a] et ville	City proper - Ville proprement dite				Urban agglomeration - Agglomération urbaine			
	Population			Surface area - Superficie (km²)	Population			Surface area - Superficie (km²)
	Both sexes - Les deux sexes	Male - Masculin	Female - Féminin		Both sexes - Les deux sexes	Male - Masculin	Female - Féminin	
ASIA - ASIE								
Kyrgyzstan - Kirghizstan								
1 VII 2015 (ESDJ)								
BISHKEK	933 753[48]	435 437[48]	498 316[48]	...	947 909[48]	442 437[48]	505 472[48]	127
Osh	245 700[48]	117 616[48]	128 084[48]	...	273 022[48]	131 625[48]	141 397[48]	182
Lao People's Democratic Republic - République démocratique populaire lao[49]								
1 VII 2014 (ESDF)								
VIENTIANE	...	...	...	...	828 494	414 217	414 277	...
Lebanon - Liban[50]								
1 X 2011 (SSDF)								
BEIRUT	...	...	...	...	363 033	179 737	183 296	...
Malaysia - Malaisie[51]								
1 VII 2015 (ESDJ)								
Alor Setar	125 100	...	...	...	...	...	...	...
Bintulu Townland	123 300	...	...	...	...	...	...	...
Georgetown	207 700	...	...	...	...	...	...	...
Klang	262 000	...	...	...	...	...	...	...
Kota Kinabalu	220 200	...	...	...	...	...	...	...
KUALA LUMPUR	1 715 500	...	...	...	...	...	...	...
Kuala Terengganu	212 700	...	...	...	...	...	...	...
Kuantan	404 600	...	...	...	...	...	...	...
Kuching "Bandaraya Kuching Utara dan Selatan"	152 000	...	...	...	...	...	...	...
Majlis Perbandaran Ipoh	469 500	...	...	...	...	...	...	...
MB Johor Bahru (Johor Bahru)	475 800	...	...	...	...	...	...	...
Miri Townland	141 300	...	...	...	...	...	...	...
MP Kota Bharu	307 400	...	...	...	...	...	...	...
Petaling Jaya	199 100	...	...	...	...	...	...	...
Sandakan	173 900	...	...	...	...	...	...	...
Selayang Baru	160 300	...	...	...	...	...	...	...
Seremban	357 300	...	...	...	...	...	...	...
Shah Alam	177 800	...	...	...	...	...	...	...
Sibu "Majlis Perbandaran Sibu"	169 300	...	...	...	...	...	...	...
Subang Jaya	192 800	...	...	...	...	...	...	...
Sungai Petani	192 200	...	...	...	...	...	...	...
Taiping	234 100	...	...	...	...	...	...	...
Tawau	124 400	...	...	...	...	...	...	...
Maldives								
20 IX 2014 (CDFC)								
MALÉ	153 904	85 438	68 466	2	...	...	...	...
Mongolia - Mongolie								
1 VII 2015 (ESDF)								
Darkhan-Uul	100 443	49 098	51 346	...	...	...	...	...
Hovsgol	127 101	63 426	63 676	101	...	...	...	...
Ovorhangay	112 673	56 610	56 063	63	...	...	...	...
Selenge	106 252	54 012	52 240	41	...	...	...	...
ULAANBAATAR	1 379 631	656 002	723 629	5	...	...	...	...
Myanmar								
29 III 2014* (CDFC)								
Bago	491 130	235 612	255 518	...	...	...	...	...
Dawei	125 239	59 941	65 298	...	...	...	...	...
Hpa-an	421 415	203 933	217 482	...	...	...	...	...
Loikaw	128 837	63 404	65 433	...	...	...	...	...
Magway	288 883	134 957	153 926	...	...	...	...	...
Mandalay	1 225 133	597 747	627 386	...	...	...	...	...
Mawlamyine	288 120	138 625	149 495	...	...	...	...	...
Monywa	371 963	172 303	199 660	...	...	...	...	...
Myitkyina	305 347	147 711	157 636	...	...	...	...	...
NAY PYI TAW[52]	...	...	...	...	1 158 367	565 181	593 186	...
Pathein	286 684	137 723	148 961	...	...	...	...	...
Sittway	149 348	71 628	77 720	...	...	...	...	...
Taunggyi	380 665	185 694	194 971	...	...	...	...	...
Yangon	5 209 541	2 468 725	2 740 816	...	...	...	...	...

Continent, country or area, date, code[a] and city / Continent, pays ou zone, date, code[a] et ville	City proper - Ville proprement dite				Urban agglomeration - Agglomération urbaine			
	Population			Surface area - Superficie (km²)	Population			Surface area - Superficie (km²)
	Both sexes - Les deux sexes	Male - Masculin	Female - Féminin		Both sexes - Les deux sexes	Male - Masculin	Female - Féminin	
ASIA - ASIE								
Nepal - Népal								
22 VI 2011 (CDJC)								
Bharatpur	147 777	74 205	73 572	...	...	...	...	...
Bhimdutta	106 666	53 098	53 568	...	...	...	...	...
Biratnagar	204 949	104 935	100 014	58	...	...	...	...
Birgunj	139 068	75 382	63 686	21	...	...	...	...
Butwal	120 982	60 870	60 112	...	...	...	...	...
Dhangadhi	104 047	53 237	50 810	...	...	...	...	...
Dharan	119 915	57 562	62 353	...	...	...	...	...
KATHMANDU	1 003 285	533 127	470 158	49	...	...	...	...
Lalitpur	226 728	117 932	108 796	15	...	...	...	...
Pokhara	264 991	133 318	131 673	55	...	...	...	...
Oman								
7 XII 2003 (CDFC)								
As Seeb	223 449	128 068	95 381	...	...	...	...	...
As Suwayq	101 122	54 997	46 125	...	...	...	...	...
Bawshar	150 420	91 687	58 733	...	...	...	...	...
MUSCAT	24 893	13 695	11 198	...	...	...	...	...
Mutrah	153 526	96 878	56 648	...	...	...	...	...
Salalah	156 530	92 489	64 041	...	...	...	...	...
Sohar	104 312	57 695	46 617	...	...	...	...	...
Pakistan[53]								
2 III 1998 (CDFC)								
Abbotabad	106 101	61 698	44 403	...	...	...	...	...
Bahawalnagar	111 313	57 779	53 534	...	...	...	...	...
Bahawalpur	408 395	222 228	186 167	...	...	...	...	...
Burewala	152 097	78 726	73 371	...	...	...	...	...
Chiniot	172 522	90 474	82 048	...	...	...	...	...
Chishtian	102 287	52 427	49 860	...	...	...	...	...
Dadu	102 550	53 508	49 042	...	...	...	...	...
Daska	102 883	52 359	50 524	...	...	...	...	...
Dera Ghazi Khan	190 542	98 738	91 804	...	...	...	...	...
Faisalabad (Lyallpur)	2 008 861	1 053 085	955 776	...	...	...	...	...
Gojra	117 872	60 598	57 274	...	...	...	...	...
Gujranwala	1 132 509	588 512	543 997	...	...	...	...	...
Gujrat	251 792	128 524	123 268	...	...	...	...	...
Hafizabad	133 678	69 231	64 447	...	...	...	...	...
Hyderabad	1 166 894	612 283	554 611	...	...	...	...	...
ISLAMABAD	529 180	290 717	238 463	...	...	...	...	...
Jacobabad	138 780	71 854	66 926	...	...	...	...	...
Jaranwala	106 785	55 619	51 166	...	...	...	...	...
Jhang	293 366	153 123	140 243	...	...	...	...	...
Jhelum	147 392	79 169	68 223	...	...	...	...	...
Kamoke	152 288	78 848	73 440	...	...	...	...	...
Karachi	9 339 023	5 029 900	4 309 123	...	...	...	...	...
Kasur	245 321	129 553	115 768	...	...	...	...	...
Khairpur	105 637	55 358	50 279	...	...	...	...	...
Khanewal	133 986	69 145	64 841	...	...	...	...	...
Khanpur	120 382	62 371	58 011	...	...	...	...	...
Kohat	126 627	71 505	55 122	...	...	...	...	...
Lahore	5 143 495	2 707 220	2 436 275	...	...	...	...	...
Larkana	270 283	140 622	129 661	...	...	...	...	...
Mangora	173 868	91 742	82 126	...	...	...	...	...
Mardan	245 926	129 247	116 679	...	...	...	...	...
Mirpur Khas	189 671	97 940	91 731	...	...	...	...	...
Multan	1 197 384	637 911	559 473	...	...	...	...	...
Muridke	111 951	58 210	53 741	...	...	...	...	...
Muzaffargharh	123 404	66 556	56 848	...	...	...	...	...
Nawabshah	189 244	98 116	91 128	...	...	...	...	...
Okara	201 815	104 245	97 570	...	...	...	...	...
Pakpattan	109 033	56 676	52 357	...	...	...	...	...
Peshawar	982 816	521 901	460 915	...	...	...	...	...
Quetta	565 137	307 759	257 378	...	...	...	...	...
Rahimyar Khan	233 537	121 446	112 091	...	...	...	...	...
Rawalpindi	1 409 768	750 530	659 238	...	...	...	...	...

8. Population of capital cities and cities of 100 000 or more inhabitants: latest available year, 1996 - 2015
Population des capitales et des villes de 100 000 habitants ou plus : dernière année disponible, 1996 - 2015 (continued - suite)

Continent, country or area, date, code[a] and city / Continent, pays ou zone, date, code[a] et ville	City proper - Ville proprement dite				Urban agglomeration - Agglomération urbaine			
	Population			Surface area - Superficie (km²)	Population			Surface area - Superficie (km²)
	Both sexes - Les deux sexes	Male - Masculin	Female - Féminin		Both sexes - Les deux sexes	Male - Masculin	Female - Féminin	
ASIA - ASIE								
Pakistan[53]								
2 III 1998 (CDFC)								
Sadiqabad	144 391	75 217	69 174	...	...	...	...	...
Sahiwal	208 778	108 992	99 786	...	...	...	...	...
Sargodha	458 440	239 837	218 603	...	...	...	...	...
Shakkarpur	134 883	69 713	65 170	...	...	...	...	...
Sheikhu Pura	280 263	146 739	133 524	...	...	...	...	...
Sialkote	421 502	227 398	194 104	...	...	...	...	...
Sukkur	335 551	175 679	159 872	...	...	...	...	...
Tandoadam	104 907	54 670	50 237	...	...	...	...	...
Wah Cantonment	198 891	104 230	94 661	...	...	...	...	...
Philippines								
1 V 2010 (CDJC)								
Angeles	326 336	161 791	164 545	60	...	...	...	...
Angono	102 407	50 859	51 548	26	...	...	...	...
Antipolo	677 741	338 392	339 349	306	...	...	...	...
Apalit	101 537	51 788	49 749	61	...	...	...	...
Arayat	121 348	61 593	59 755	134	...	...	...	...
Bacolod	511 820	251 910	259 910	163	...	...	...	...
Bacoor City	520 216	255 375	264 841	46	...	...	...	...
Bago	163 045	84 114	78 931	401	...	...	...	...
Baguio	318 676	156 259	162 417	58	...	...	...	...
Baliuag	143 565	71 947	71 618	45	...	...	...	...
Batangas	305 607	152 499	153 108	283	...	...	...	...
Bayambang	111 521	56 423	55 098	144	...	...	...	...
Bayawan (Tulong)	114 074	59 336	54 738	699	...	...	...	...
Baybay	102 841	52 935	49 906	459	...	...	...	...
Biñan	283 396	140 351	143 045	44	...	...	...	...
Binangonan	249 872	125 027	124 845	66	...	...	...	...
Bocaue	106 407	53 248	53 159	32	...	...	...	...
Butuan	309 709	157 204	152 505	817	...	...	...	...
Cabanatuan	272 676	136 432	136 244	283	...	...	...	...
Cabuyao	248 436	123 110	125 326	43	...	...	...	...
Cadiz	151 500	78 049	73 451	525	...	...	...	...
Cagayan de Oro	602 088	300 853	301 235	413	...	...	...	...
Cainta	311 845	152 400	159 445	43	...	...	...	...
Calamba	389 377	191 773	197 604	150	...	...	...	...
Calapan	124 173	62 588	61 585	250	...	...	...	...
Calbayog	172 778	88 540	84 238	881	...	...	...	...
Calumpit	101 068	50 840	50 228	56	...	...	...	...
Candaba	102 399	51 815	50 584	176	...	...	...	...
Candelaria	110 570	55 137	55 433	129	...	...	...	...
Capas	125 852	64 479	61 373	376	...	...	...	...
Carcar	107 323	54 718	52 605	117	...	...	...	...
Cauayan	122 335	62 362	59 973	336	...	...	...	...
Cavite City	101 120	49 710	51 410	11	...	...	...	...
Cebu	866 171	426 738	439 433	315	...	...	...	...
Concepcion	139 832	71 709	68 123	243	...	...	...	...
Consolacion	106 649	53 204	53 445	147	...	...	...	...
Cotabato	271 786	133 457	138 329	176	...	...	...	...
Dagupan	163 676	81 788	81 888	37	...	...	...	...
Danao City	119 252	60 251	59 001	107	...	...	...	...
Daraga (Locsin)	115 804	58 060	57 744	119	...	...	...	...
Dasmariñas	575 817	283 823	291 994	90	...	...	...	...
Davao	1 449 296	724 565	724 731	2 444	...	...	...	...
Digos	149 891	75 664	74 227	287	...	...	...	...
Dipolog	120 460	60 243	60 217	241	...	...	...	...
Dumaguete	120 883	58 711	62 172	34	...	...	...	...
Floridablanca	110 846	56 249	54 597	175	...	...	...	...
Gapan	101 488	51 331	50 157	164	...	...	...	...
Gen. Mariano Alvarez	138 540	69 226	69 314	9	...	...	...	...
General Santos	538 086	272 216	265 870	493	...	...	...	...
General Trias	243 322	118 771	124 551	90	...	...	...	...
Gingoog	117 908	60 628	57 280	568	...	...	...	...
Glan	106 518	54 919	51 599	534	...	...	...	...

8. Population of capital cities and cities of 100 000 or more inhabitants: latest available year, 1996 - 2015
Population des capitales et des villes de 100 000 habitants ou plus : dernière année disponible, 1996 - 2015 (continued - suite)

Continent, country or area, date, code[a] and city / Continent, pays ou zone, date, code[a] et ville	City proper - Ville proprement dite				Urban agglomeration - Agglomération urbaine			
	Population			Surface area - Superficie (km²)	Population			Surface area - Superficie (km²)
	Both sexes - Les deux sexes	Male - Masculin	Female - Féminin		Both sexes - Les deux sexes	Male - Masculin	Female - Féminin	

ASIA - ASIE

Philippines
1 V 2010 (CDJC)

Guagua	111 199	56 191	55 008	49	...	...	...	...
Guimba	104 894	53 633	51 261	245	...	...	...	...
Hagonoy	125 689	63 231	62 458	103	...	...	...	...
Himamaylan	103 006	53 254	49 752	367	...	...	...	...
Ilagan	135 174	69 256	65 918	1 166	...	...	...	...
Iligan	322 821	161 924	160 897	813	...	...	...	...
Iloilo	424 619	207 301	217 318	78	...	...	...	...
Imus City	301 624	145 358	156 266	172	...	...	...	...
Iriga	105 919	53 452	52 467	137	...	...	...	...
Jolo	118 307	58 271	60 036	126	...	...	...	...
Kabankalan	167 666	86 721	80 945	697	...	...	...	...
Kalookan (Caloocan)	1 489 040	742 113	746 927	56	...	...	...	...
Kidapawan	125 447	63 842	61 605	358	...	...	...	...
Koronadal	158 273	79 987	78 286	277	...	...	...	...
La Trinidad	107 188	52 999	54 189	70	...	...	...	...
Laoag	104 904	51 581	53 323	116	...	...	...	...
Lapu-Lapu	350 467	172 839	177 628	58	...	...	...	...
Las Piñas	552 573	268 114	284 459	33	...	...	...	...
Legazpi	182 201	91 174	91 027	154	...	...	...	...
Libmanan	100 002	51 549	48 453	343	...	...	...	...
Liloan	100 500	50 317	50 183	46	...	...	...	...
Lipa	283 468	141 822	141 646	209	...	...	...	...
Los Baños	101 884	50 245	51 639	54	...	...	...	...
Lubao	150 843	76 467	74 376	156	...	...	...	...
Lucena City	246 392	122 774	123 618	80	...	...	...	...
Mabalacat	215 610	107 996	107 614	83	...	...	...	...
Magalang	103 597	52 858	50 739	97	...	...	...	...
Makati	529 039	249 509	279 530	22	...	...	...	...
Malabalay	153 085	79 366	73 719	969	...	...	...	...
Malabon	353 337	176 450	176 887	16	...	...	...	...
Malasiqui	123 566	62 599	60 967	131	...	...	...	...
Malita	109 568	56 155	53 413	883	...	...	...	...
Malolos	234 945	117 260	117 685	67	...	...	...	...
Mandaluyong	328 699	162 235	166 464	9	...	...	...	...
Mandaue	331 320	164 513	166 807	25	...	...	...	...
MANILA	1 652 171	811 788	840 383	25	...	...	...	...
Marawi	187 106	91 003	96 103	88	...	...	...	...
Marikina	424 150	206 821	217 329	22	...	...	...	...
Marilao	185 624	92 323	93 301	34	...	...	...	...
Mariveles	112 707	56 448	56 259	154	...	...	...	...
Mati	126 143	64 742	61 401	589	...	...	...	...
Mexico	146 851	74 426	72 425	117	...	...	...	...
Meycauayan	199 154	99 517	99 637	32	...	...	...	...
Midsayap	134 170	68 475	65 695	290	...	...	...	...
Minglanilla	113 178	57 598	55 580	66	...	...	...	...
Muntinlupa	459 941	233 606	226 335	40	...	...	...	...
Naga (Camarines Sur)	174 931	86 055	88 876	84	...	...	...	...
Naga (Cebu)	101 571	51 551	50 020	102	...	...	...	...
Nasugbu	122 483	61 972	60 511	279	...	...	...	...
Navotas	249 131	125 924	123 207	9	...	...	...	...
Norzagaray	103 095	52 419	50 676	310	...	...	...	...
Olongapo	221 178	109 316	111 862	185	...	...	...	...
Ormoc	191 200	97 722	93 478	614	...	...	...	...
Ozamis	131 527	65 963	65 564	170	...	...	...	...
Pagadian	186 852	93 264	93 588	379	...	...	...	...
Panabo	174 364	88 643	85 721	251	...	...	...	...
Paranaque	588 126	286 371	301 755	47	...	...	...	...
Pasay	392 869	192 097	200 772	14	...	...	...	...
Pasig	669 773	326 875	342 898	48	...	...	...	...
Philippines: Ligao	104 914	53 510	51 404	247	...	...	...	...
Pikit	113 014	56 762	56 252	605	...	...	...	...
Plaridel	101 441	50 554	50 887	32	...	...	...	...
Polomolok	138 273	70 501	67 772	340	...	...	...	...

Continent, country or area, date, code[a] and city Continent, pays ou zone, date, code[a] et ville	City proper - Ville proprement dite				Urban agglomeration - Agglomération urbaine			
	Population			Surface area - Superficie (km²)	Population			Surface area - Superficie (km²)
	Both sexes - Les deux sexes	Male - Masculin	Female - Féminin		Both sexes - Les deux sexes	Male - Masculin	Female - Féminin	
ASIA - ASIE								
Philippines								
1 V 2010 (CDJC)								
Porac	111 441	56 693	54 748	314	...	...	...	...
Puerto Princesa	222 673	114 837	107 836	2 381	...	...	...	...
Quezon City	2 761 720	1 349 016	1 412 704	172	...	...	...	...
Rodriguez (Montalban)	280 904	141 127	139 777	173	...	...	...	...
Rosario	105 561	53 192	52 369	227	...	...	...	...
Roxas	156 197	77 693	78 504	95	...	...	...	...
Sagay City	140 740	72 410	68 330	330	...	...	...	...
San Carlos (Negros Occidental)	129 981	66 600	63 381	452	...	...	...	...
San Carlos (Pangasinan)	175 103	88 715	86 388	169	...	...	...	...
San Fernando (La Union)	114 963	57 002	57 961	103	...	...	...	...
San Fernando (Pampanga)	285 912	143 738	142 174	68	...	...	...	...
San Jose (Occidental Mindoro)	131 188	66 824	64 364	447	...	...	...	...
San Jose City (Nueva Ecija)	129 424	65 867	63 557	186	...	...	...	...
San Jose Del Monte	454 553	227 047	227 506	106	...	...	...	...
San Juan	121 430	54 796	66 634	6	...	...	...	...
San Mateo	205 255	101 991	103 264	55	...	...	...	...
San Miguel	142 854	72 199	70 655	231	...	...	...	...
San Pablo	248 890	123 210	125 680	198	...	...	...	...
San Pedro	294 310	144 967	149 343	24	...	...	...	...
Santa Cruz	110 943	55 794	55 149	39	...	...	...	...
Santa Maria	218 351	109 718	108 633	91	...	...	...	...
Santa Rosa	284 670	137 821	146 849	55	...	...	...	...
Santiago	132 804	67 134	65 670	256	...	...	...	...
Santo Tomas (Davao Del Norte)	109 269	56 703	52 566	222	...	...	...	...
Santo Tomas (Batangas)	124 740	61 500	63 240	95	...	...	...	...
Sariaya	138 894	70 418	68 476	212	...	...	...	...
Silang	213 490	105 117	108 373	209	...	...	...	...
Silay	120 999	61 335	59 664	215	...	...	...	...
Sorsogon	155 144	78 175	76 969	276	...	...	...	...
Surigao	140 540	70 424	70 116	245	...	...	...	...
Tabaco	125 083	63 437	61 646	117	...	...	...	...
Tabuk	103 912	52 894	51 018	700	...	...	...	...
Tacloban	221 174	110 568	110 606	202	...	...	...	...
Taguig	644 473	319 916	324 557	45	...	...	...	...
Tagum	242 801	121 863	120 938	196	...	...	...	...
Talavera	112 515	56 975	55 540	141	...	...	...	...
Talisay	200 772	99 951	100 821	40	...	...	...	...
Tanauan	152 393	75 642	76 751	107	...	...	...	...
Tanza	188 755	93 634	95 121	96	...	...	...	...
Tarlac	318 332	161 365	156 967	275	...	...	...	...
Taytay	288 956	144 538	144 418	39	...	...	...	...
Toledo	157 078	80 619	76 459	216	...	...	...	...
Trece Martires	104 559	52 291	52 268	39	...	...	...	...
Tuguegarao	138 865	68 807	70 058	145	...	...	...	...
Urdaneta	125 451	63 025	62 426	100	...	...	...	...
Valencia	181 556	93 417	88 139	587	...	...	...	...
Valenzuela	575 356	288 659	286 697	47	...	...	...	...
Zamboanga	807 129	405 435	401 694	1 415	...	...	...	...
Qatar								
21 IV 2010 (CDFC)								
Al-Khoor	193 983	181 005	12 978	...	...	...	...	...
Al-Rayyan	455 623	301 842	153 781	...	...	...	...	...
Al-Wakrah	141 222	114 698	26 524	...	...	...	...	...
DOHA	796 947	610 817	186 130	...	...	...	...	...
Republic of Korea - République de Corée								
1 VII 2015 (ESDJ)								
Busan (Pusan)	3 400 069[4]	1 669 381[4]	1 730 688[4]	770	...	...	...	...
Daegu (Taegu)	2 454 733[4]	1 216 581[4]	1 238 152[4]	883	...	...	...	...
Daejeon (Taejon)	1 535 639[4]	770 055[4]	765 584[4]	540	...	...	...	...
Gwangju (Kwangchu)	1 516 527[4]	753 097[4]	763 430[4]	501	...	...	...	...
Incheon	2 886 172[4]	1 452 199[4]	1 433 973[4]	1 041	...	...	...	...
Jeju (Cheju)	587 217[4]	294 781[4]	292 436[4]	1 849	...	...	...	...

8. Population of capital cities and cities of 100 000 or more inhabitants: latest available year, 1996 - 2015
Population des capitales et des villes de 100 000 habitants ou plus : dernière année disponible, 1996 - 2015 (continued - suite)

Continent, country or area, date, code[a] and city Continent, pays ou zone, date, code[a] et ville	City proper - Ville proprement dite				Urban agglomeration - Agglomération urbaine			
	Population			Surface area - Superficie (km²)	Population			Surface area - Superficie (km²)
	Both sexes - Les deux sexes	Male - Masculin	Female - Féminin		Both sexes - Les deux sexes	Male - Masculin	Female - Féminin	
ASIA - ASIE								
Republic of Korea - République de Corée								
1 VII 2015 (ESDJ)								
SEOUL	9 860 372[4]	4 828 103[4]	5 032 269[4]	605	...	...	...	...
Ulsan	1 142 469[4]	594 960[4]	547 509[4]	1 060	...	...	...	...
Saudi Arabia - Arabie saoudite								
27 IV 2010 (CDFC)								
Abha	236 157	136 118	100 039	...	...	...	...	...
Ad-Dammam	903 312	546 924	356 388	...	...	...	...	...
Al-Hawiyah	148 151	78 735	69 416	...	...	...	...	...
Al-Hufuf	660 788	361 672	299 116	...	...	...	...	...
Al-Jubayl	337 778	237 912	99 866	...	...	...	...	...
Al-Khubar	219 679	131 646	88 033	...	...	...	...	...
Al-Madinah	1 100 093	608 720	491 373	...	...	...	...	...
Al-Qatif	118 327	66 504	51 823	...	...	...	...	...
Al-Qurrayyat	116 162	63 412	52 750	...	...	...	...	...
Al-Seeh	234 607	131 391	103 216	...	...	...	...	...
Ar'ar	167 057	90 771	76 286	...	...	...	...	...
Ath-Thuqbah	238 066	149 691	88 375	...	...	...	...	...
At-Ta'if	579 970	306 682	273 288	...	...	...	...	...
Buraydah	467 410	268 604	198 806	...	...	...	...	...
Dhahran	120 521	68 746	51 775	...	...	...	...	...
Hafar al-Batin	271 642	148 396	123 246	...	...	...	...	...
Ha'il	310 897	170 882	140 015	...	...	...	...	...
Jiddah	3 430 697	1 996 716	1 433 981	...	...	...	...	...
Jizan	127 743	76 987	50 756	...	...	...	...	...
Khamis Mushayt	430 828	245 756	185 072	...	...	...	...	...
Makkah	1 534 731	861 737	672 994	...	...	...	...	...
Najran (Aba as-Suud)	298 288	166 143	132 145	...	...	...	...	...
RIYADH	5 188 286	3 059 287	2 128 999	...	...	...	...	...
Sekaka	150 257	84 881	65 376	...	...	...	...	...
Tabuk	512 629	281 672	230 957	...	...	...	...	...
Unayzah	152 895	86 385	66 510	...	...	...	...	...
Yanbu al-Bahr	233 236	140 897	92 339	...	...	...	...	...
Singapore - Singapour								
30 VI 2015 (ESDJ)								
SINGAPORE	5 535 002[54]	...	...	719[55]	...	...	...	...
Sri Lanka[56]								
17 VII 2001 (CDFC)								
COLOMBO	647 100	346 366	300 734	...	...	...	...	...
Dehiwala-Mount Lavinia	210 546	105 522	105 024	...	...	...	...	...
Kandy	109 343	54 288	55 055	...	...	...	...	...
Moratuwa	177 563	87 313	90 250	...	...	...	...	...
Negombo	121 701	60 947	60 754	...	...	...	...	...
Sri Jayawardanapura Kotte	116 366	59 993	56 373	...	...	...	...	...
State of Palestine - État de Palestine								
1 VII 2015 (ESDF)								
EAST JERUSALEM - JÉRUSALEM-EST[57]	246 937	...	...	...	...	...	...	...
Gaza	583 870	...	...	38	...	...	...	...
Hebron	215 452	...	...	49	...	...	...	...
Jabalya	171 642	...	...	...	...	...	...	...
Khan Yunis	185 250	...	...	...	...	...	...	...
Nablus	153 061	...	...	26	...	...	...	...
Rafah	164 000	...	...	...	...	...	...	...
Syrian Arab Republic - République arabe syrienne								
1 VII 2008 (ESDF)								
Aleppo	4 450 000	2 292 000	2 158 000	...	...	...	...	...
Al-Hasakeh	1 392 000	701 000	691 000	...	...	...	...	...
Al-Raqqah	865 000	456 000	409 000	...	...	...	...	...
Al-Sweida	349 000	171 000	178 000	...	...	...	...	...
DAMASCUS	1 680 000	857 000	823 000	...	...	...	...	...
Damasus rural	2 529 000	1 302 000	1 227 000	...	...	...	...	...
Deir El-Zor	1 111 000	563 000	548 000	...	...	...	...	...
Dra'a	930 000	472 000	458 000	...	...	...	...	...
Hama	1 508 000	768 000	740 000	...	...	...	...	...
Homs	1 667 000	852 000	815 000	...	...	...	...	...

8. Population of capital cities and cities of 100 000 or more inhabitants: latest available year, 1996 - 2015
Population des capitales et des villes de 100 000 habitants ou plus : dernière année disponible, 1996 - 2015 (continued - suite)

Continent, country or area, date, code[a] and city / Continent, pays ou zone, date, code[a] et ville	City proper - Ville proprement dite				Urban agglomeration - Agglomération urbaine			
	Population			Surface area - Superficie (km²)	Population			Surface area - Superficie (km²)
	Both sexes - Les deux sexes	Male - Masculin	Female - Féminin		Both sexes - Les deux sexes	Male - Masculin	Female - Féminin	
ASIA - ASIE								
Syrian Arab Republic - République arabe syrienne								
1 VII 2008 (ESDF)								
Idleb	1 376 000	704 000	672 000	...	...	...	...	...
Lattakia	951 000	480 000	471 000	...	...	...	...	...
Tartous	756 000	383 000	373 000	...	...	...	...	...
Tajikistan - Tadjikistan								
1 VII 2014 (ESDF)								
DUSHANBE	782 224	406 802	375 422	...	...	...	...	...
Thailand - Thaïlande								
1 IX 2010 (CDJC)								
Ang Thong	...	...	...	...	109 207	51 540	57 667	...
BANGKOK	...	...	...	...	8 305 218	4 032 586	4 272 632	1 569
Buri Ram	...	...	...	...	375 999	181 546	194 453	...
Chachoengsao	...	...	...	...	206 250	101 475	104 775	...
Chai Nat	...	...	...	...	205 456	97 373	108 083	...
Chaiyaphum	...	...	...	...	205 112	99 280	105 832	...
Chanthaburi	...	...	...	...	243 126	118 221	124 905	...
Chiang Mai	...	...	...	...	967 020	466 145	500 875	...
Chiang Rai	...	...	...	...	455 732	220 391	235 341	...
Chon Buri	...	...	...	...	1 158 989	575 208	583 781	...
Chumphon	...	...	...	...	147 912	75 339	72 573	...
Kalasin	...	...	...	...	428 940	208 863	220 077	...
Kamphaeng Phet	...	...	...	...	211 774	101 456	110 318	...
Kanchanaburi	...	...	...	...	292 521	143 986	148 535	...
Khon Kaen	...	...	...	...	703 123	339 011	364 112	...
Lampang	...	...	...	...	372 463	180 360	192 103	...
Lamphun	...	...	...	...	262 832	126 662	136 170	...
Loei	...	...	...	...	164 180	81 302	82 878	...
Lop Buri	...	...	...	...	235 827	118 964	116 863	...
Maha Sarakham	...	...	...	...	153 740	72 143	81 597	...
Mukdahan	...	...	...	...	180 600	89 190	91 410	...
Nakhon Pathom	...	...	...	...	339 736	166 150	173 586	...
Nakhon Phanom	...	...	...	...	123 720	59 683	64 037	...
Nakhon Ratchasima	...	...	...	...	653 075	316 329	336 746	...
Nakhon Sawan	...	...	...	...	225 903	107 298	118 605	...
Nakhon Si Thammarat	...	...	...	...	265 606	127 460	138 146	...
Narathiwat	...	...	...	...	133 718	64 616	69 102	...
Nong Bua Lam Phu	...	...	...	...	203 142	98 164	104 978	...
Nong Khai	...	...	...	...	232 798	113 989	118 809	...
Nonthaburi	...	...	...	...	797 739	383 826	413 913	...
Pathum Thani	...	...	...	...	757 175	358 679	398 496	...
Pattani	...	...	...	...	104 617	51 305	53 312	...
Phatthalung	...	...	...	...	244 783	117 039	127 744	...
Phayao	...	...	...	...	221 062	106 657	114 405	...
Phetchabun	...	...	...	...	172 275	82 257	90 018	...
Phetchaburi	...	...	...	...	175 675	83 735	91 940	...
Phichit	...	...	...	...	131 283	62 446	68 837	...
Phitsanulok	...	...	...	...	201 466	93 098	108 368	...
Phra Nakhon Si Ayutthaya	...	...	...	...	365 736	173 280	192 456	...
Phrae	...	...	...	...	156 099	75 175	80 924	...
Phuket	...	...	...	...	358 159	175 144	183 015	...
Prachuap Khiri Khan	...	...	...	...	177 011	87 525	89 486	...
Ranong	...	...	...	...	123 596	62 090	61 506	...
Ratchaburi	...	...	...	...	317 886	149 460	168 426	...
Rayong	...	...	...	...	445 939	224 068	221 871	...
Roi Et	...	...	...	...	365 113	176 648	188 465	...
Sa Kaeo	...	...	...	...	135 536	66 447	69 089	...
Sakon Nakhon	...	...	...	...	315 788	153 785	162 003	...
Samut Prakan	...	...	...	...	1 082 993	527 487	555 506	...
Samut Sakhon	...	...	...	...	479 186	237 778	241 408	...
Saraburi	...	...	...	...	239 281	114 885	124 396	...
Si Sa Ket	...	...	...	...	160 508	77 363	83 145	...
Songkhla	...	...	...	...	800 970	382 828	418 142	...
Sukhothai	...	...	...	...	166 782	79 139	87 643	...
Suphan Buri	...	...	...	...	228 496	108 666	119 830	...

8. Population of capital cities and cities of 100 000 or more inhabitants: latest available year, 1996 - 2015
Population des capitales et des villes de 100 000 habitants ou plus : dernière année disponible, 1996 - 2015 (continued - suite)

Continent, country or area, date, code[a] and city / Continent, pays ou zone, date, code[a] et ville	City proper - Ville proprement dite				Urban agglomeration - Agglomération urbaine			
	Population			Surface area - Superficie (km²)	Population			Surface area - Superficie (km²)
	Both sexes - Les deux sexes	Male - Masculin	Female - Féminin		Both sexes - Les deux sexes	Male - Masculin	Female - Féminin	
ASIA - ASIE								
Thailand - Thaïlande								
1 IX 2010 (CDJC)								
Surat Thani	...	...	...	...	410 984	198 909	212 075	...
Surin	...	...	...	...	153 159	73 082	80 077	...
Tak	...	...	...	...	146 769	70 754	76 015	...
Trat	...	...	...	...	110 398	52 309	58 089	...
Ubon Ratchathani	...	...	...	...	411 954	198 655	213 299	...
Udon Thani	...	...	...	...	483 057	232 326	250 731	...
Uttaradit	...	...	...	...	151 047	72 244	78 803	...
Yala	...	...	...	...	119 744	58 041	61 703	...
Yasothon	...	...	...	...	127 173	63 885	63 288	...
Timor-Leste								
11 VII 2010 (CDFC)								
DILI	192 652	102 900	89 752	...	...	...	...	...
Turkey - Turquie[58]								
31 XII 2014 (ESDJ)								
Adana	...	...	...	...	2 165 595	1 082 497	1 083 098	...
Adıyaman	230 630	115 636	114 994	...				...
Afyonkarahisar	209 406	103 896	105 510	...				...
Ağrı	112 339	58 324	54 015	...				...
Aksaray	195 990	97 511	98 479	...				...
ANKARA	...	...	...	...	5 150 072	2 562 805	2 587 267	...
Antalya	...	...	...	...	2 222 562	1 122 997	1 099 565	...
Aydın	...	...	...	...	1 041 979	519 900	522 079	...
Balıkesir	...	...	...	...	1 189 057	593 529	595 528	...
Batman	381 814	191 967	189 847	...				...
Bingöl	103 441	52 592	50 849	...				...
Bolu	144 864	70 959	73 905	...	...	...	...	...
Bursa	...	...	...	...	2 787 539	1 394 715	1 392 824	...
Çanakkale	119 806	60 589	59 217	...	...	...	...	...
Cizre	112 973	57 264	55 709	...				...
Çorum	243 698	120 872	122 826	...	...	...	...	...
Denizli	...	...	...	...	978 700	487 958	490 742	...
Diyarbakır	...	...	...	...	1 635 048	824 133	810 915	...
Düzce	148 061	73 612	74 449	...				...
Edirne	152 628	76 257	76 371	...				...
Elazığ	351 504	173 594	177 910	...				...
Ereğli	112 973	57 264	55 709	...				...
Erzurum	...	...	...	...	763 320	384 356	378 964	...
Eskişehir	...	...	...	...	812 320	405 253	407 067	...
Gaziantep	...	...	...	...	1 889 466	953 760	935 706	...
Giresun	105 748	52 346	53 402	...	...	...	...	...
Hatay	...	...	...	...	1 519 836	763 832	756 004	...
Isparta	207 266	103 595	103 671	...				...
İstanbul	...	...	...	...	14 377 018	7 221 158	7 155 860	...
İzmir	...	...	...	...	4 113 072	2 050 424	2 062 648	...
Kahramanmaraş	...	...	...	...	1 089 038	553 493	535 545	...
Karabük	113 277	57 863	55 414	...				...
Karaman	148 362	73 717	74 645	...	...	...	...	...
Kastamonu	103 724	50 906	52 818	...				...
Kayseri	...	...	...	...	1 322 376	663 249	659 127	...
Kırıkkale	189 044	94 006	95 038	...				...
Kırşehir	120 508	60 035	60 473	...	...	...	...	...
Kocaeli	...	...	...	...	1 722 795	872 403	850 392	...
Konya	...	...	...	...	2 108 808	1 046 182	1 062 626	...
Kütahya	232 123	116 084	116 039	...	...	...	...	...
Lüleburgaz	108 576	55 077	53 499	...				...
Malatya	...	...	...	...	769 544	383 933	385 611	...
Manisa	...	...	...	...	1 367 905	686 379	681 526	...
Mardin	...	...	...	...	788 996	395 968	393 028	...
Mersin	...	...	...	...	1 727 255	860 306	866 949	...
Muğla	...	...	...	...	894 509	454 642	439 867	...
Niğde	127 980	64 508	63 472	...	...	...	...	...
Ordu	...	...	...	...	724 268	361 627	362 641	...
Osmaniye	218 531	109 690	108 841	...	...	...	...	...

330

8. Population of capital cities and cities of 100 000 or more inhabitants: latest available year, 1996 - 2015
Population des capitales et des villes de 100 000 habitants ou plus : dernière année disponible, 1996 - 2015 (continued - suite)

Continent, country or area, date, code[a] and city / Continent, pays ou zone, date, code[a] et ville	City proper - Ville proprement dite				Urban agglomeration - Agglomération urbaine			
	Population			Surface area - Superficie (km²)	Population			Surface area - Superficie (km²)
	Both sexes - Les deux sexes	Male - Masculin	Female - Féminin		Both sexes - Les deux sexes	Male - Masculin	Female - Féminin	
ASIA - ASIE								
Turkey - Turquie[58]								
31 XII 2014 (ESDJ)								
Rize	107 405	52 682	54 723	...	...	...	...	...
Sakarya	...	...	...	...	932 706	467 167	465 539	...
Samsun	...	...	...	...	1 269 989	627 296	642 693	...
Şanlıurfa	...	...	...	...	1 845 667	925 703	919 964	...
Siirt	140 278	72 275	68 003	...	...	...	...	...
Sivas	319 532	157 698	161 834	...	...	...	...	...
Tekirdağ	...	...	...	...	906 732	466 956	439 776	...
Tokat	137 831	69 115	68 716	...	...	...	...	...
Trabzon	...	...	...	...	766 782	378 509	388 273	...
Uşak	196 466	97 695	98 771	...	...	...	...	...
Van	...	...	...	...	1 085 542	554 791	530 751	...
Yalova	107 928	53 025	54 903	...	...	...	...	...
Zonguldak	108 213	53 129	55 084	...	...	...	...	...
United Arab Emirates - Émirats arabes unis								
1 VII 2002 (ESDF)								
ABU DHABI	527 000	359 000	168 000	...	...	...	...	...
Ajman	205 000	122 000	83 000	...	...	...	...	...
Al-Ayn	328 000	215 000	113 000	...	...	...	...	...
Al-Sharjah	488 000	317 000	171 000	...	...	...	...	...
Dubai	1 089 000	759 000	330 000	...	...	...	...	...
Uzbekistan - Ouzbékistan[59]								
1 I 2015 (ESDJ)								
Almalyk	122 588	59 708	62 880	...	...	...	...	...
Andizhan	410 349	205 090	205 259	...	...	...	...	...
Angren	177 714	88 473	89 241	...	...	...	...	...
Bukhara	273 501	134 822	138 679	...	...	...	...	...
Chirchik	150 482	73 783	76 699	...	...	...	...	...
Fergana	268 064	132 594	135 470	...	...	...	...	...
Jizzax	165 036	82 396	82 640	...	...	...	...	...
Karshi	257 738	128 547	129 191	...	...	...	...	...
Kokand	236 838	115 160	121 678	...	...	...	...	...
Margilan	218 838	109 479	109 359	...	...	...	...	...
Namangan	484 921	248 595	236 326	...	...	...	...	...
Navoi	133 540	68 102	65 438	...	...	...	...	...
Nukus	300 658	147 573	153 085	...	...	...	...	...
Samarkand	513 572	247 461	266 111	...	...	...	...	...
Shahrisabz	101 769	51 732	50 037	...	...	...	...	...
TASHKENT	2 371 269	1 154 513	1 216 756	...	...	...	...	...
Termez	137 919	67 717	70 202	...	...	...	...	...
Urgentch	138 016	69 287	68 729	...	...	...	...	...
Yemen - Yémen								
1 VII 2009* (ESDF)								
Adan	684 322	...	...	...	684 322	...	...	...
SANA'A	1 976 286	...	...	...	2 022 867	...	...	...
EUROPE								
Åland Islands - Îles d'Åland								
1 VII 2015 (ESDJ)								
MARIEHAMN	11 471[15]	5 521[15]	5 950[15]	12	...	...	...	...
Albania - Albanie								
1 X 2011 (CDJC)								
Durrës	113 249	56 511	56 738	...	...	...	...	...
TIRANA	418 495	203 239	215 256	31	...	...	...	...
Andorra - Andorre[15]								
1 VII 2011 (ESDJ)								
ANDORRA LA VELLA	...	...	...	...	22 205	11 056	11 149	...
Austria - Autriche								
1 I 2014 (ESDJ)								
Graz	269 997	131 145	138 852	128	...	...	...	...
Innsbruck	124 579	59 726	64 853	105	...	...	...	...
Linz	193 814	92 693	101 121	96	...	...	...	...

8. Population of capital cities and cities of 100 000 or more inhabitants: latest available year, 1996 - 2015
Population des capitales et des villes de 100 000 habitants ou plus : dernière année disponible, 1996 - 2015 (continued - suite)

Continent, country or area, date, code[a] and city / Continent, pays ou zone, date, code[a] et ville	City proper - Ville proprement dite				Urban agglomeration - Agglomération urbaine			
	Population			Surface area - Superficie (km²)	Population			Surface area - Superficie (km²)
	Both sexes - Les deux sexes	Male - Masculin	Female - Féminin		Both sexes - Les deux sexes	Male - Masculin	Female - Féminin	

EUROPE

Austria - Autriche
1 I 2014 (ESDJ)

Salzburg	146 631	69 279	77 352	66	...	...	...	...
WIEN	1 766 746	850 596	916 150	415	...	...	...	...

Belarus - Bélarus
1 VII 2013 (ESDJ)

Baranovichi	173 932	78 644	95 288	85	...	...	...	...
Bobruisk	217 394	101 562	115 832	90	...	...	...	...
Borisov	145 441	68 300	77 141	46	...	...	...	...
Brest	328 681	151 285	177 396	146	...	...	...	...
Gomel	508 839	231 874	276 965	135	...	...	...	...
Grodno	354 521	161 200	193 321	142	...	...	...	...
MINSK	1 911 433	872 393	1 039 040	348	...	...	...	...
Mogilev	368 765	169 579	199 186	119	...	...	...	...
Mozir	111 755	53 086	58 669	44	...	...	...	...
Novopolotsk	101 583	48 342	53 241	48	...	...	...	...
Orsha	116 604	53 942	62 662	39	...	...	...	...
Pinsk	135 858	62 826	73 032	47	...	...	...	...
Soligorsk	105 060	49 326	55 734	15	...	...	...	...
Vitebsk	362 466	160 459	202 007	125	...	...	...	...

Belgium - Belgique
1 I 2011 (CDJC)

Anderlecht	108 940	53 707	55 233	18	...	...	...	...
Antwerpen (Anvers)	498 473	247 192	251 281	205	718 730	354 576	364 154	394
Brugge	117 260	56 952	60 308	138	117 260	56 952	60 308	138
BRUXELLES (BRUSSEL)	174 383	90 317	84 066	33	1 550 299[60]	754 208[60]	796 091[60]	573[60]
Charleroi	204 150	99 221	104 929	102	291 806	141 106	150 700	199
Gent (Gand)	248 358	122 457	125 901	156	280 151	137 980	142 171	207
Liège (Luik)	195 965	96 509	99 456	69	491 767	238 134	253 633	367
Namur	110 175	53 019	57 156	176	110 175	53 019	57 156	176
Schaerbeek	127 525	63 020	64 505	8	...	...	...	...

Bulgaria - Bulgarie
1 VII 2012 (ESDJ)

Burgas	199 284	96 462	102 822	...	...	...	...	...
Pleven	105 045	50 720	54 325	...	...	...	...	...
Plovdiv	338 657	161 523	177 134	...	...	...	...	...
Ruse	148 742	71 960	76 782	...	...	...	...	...
SOFIA	1 210 820	576 142	634 678	...	...	...	...	...
Stara Zagora	137 649	66 670	70 979	...	...	...	...	...
Varna	334 763	162 594	172 169	...	...	...	...	...

Croatia - Croatie
1 IV 2011 (CDJC)

Osijek	108 048	50 357	57 691	174	...	...	...	...
Rijeka	128 624	60 951	67 673	43	...	...	...	...
Split	178 102	84 477	93 625	79	...	...	...	...
ZAGREB	790 017	369 339	420 678	641	...	...	...	...

Czech Republic - République tchèque
1 I 2015 (ESDJ)

Brno	377 440	181 885	195 555	226	...	...	...	...
Liberec	102 562	49 433	53 129	105	...	...	...	...
Ostrava	294 200	142 415	151 785	205	...	...	...	...
Plzen	169 033	82 195	86 838	133	...	...	...	...
PRAHA	1 259 079	610 376	648 703	485	...	...	...	...

Denmark - Danemark[61]
1 VII 2015 (ESDJ)

Ålborg	207 785[15]	104 533[15]	103 252[15]	1 137	...	...	...	...
Århus	326 612[15]	160 492[15]	166 120[15]	468	...	...	...	...
Esbjerg	115 558[15]	57 951[15]	57 607[15]	795	...	...	...	...
Frederiksberg	103 666[15]	48 952[15]	54 714[15]	9	...	...	...	...
KOBENHAVN	583 525[15]	288 448[15]	295 077[15]	86	...	...	...	...
Odense	197 466[15]	97 242[15]	100 224[15]	306	...	...	...	...
Vejle	111 138[15]	55 489[15]	55 649[15]	1 058	...	...	...	...

Estonia - Estonie
1 I 2015 (ESDJ)

TALLINN	413 782	187 050	226 732	158	...	...	...	...

8. Population of capital cities and cities of 100 000 or more inhabitants: latest available year, 1996 - 2015
Population des capitales et des villes de 100 000 habitants ou plus : dernière année disponible, 1996 - 2015 (continued - suite)

Continent, country or area, date, code[a] and city / Continent, pays ou zone, date, code[a] et ville	City proper - Ville proprement dite				Urban agglomeration - Agglomération urbaine			
	Population			Surface area - Superficie (km²)	Population			Surface area - Superficie (km²)
	Both sexes - Les deux sexes	Male - Masculin	Female - Féminin		Both sexes - Les deux sexes	Male - Masculin	Female - Féminin	
EUROPE								
Faeroe Islands - Îles Féroé								
1 VII 2015 (ESDJ)								
TÓRSHAVN	12 713	6 336	6 377	6[62]	18 674[63]	9 386[63]	9 288[63]	15[64]
Finland - Finlande								
1 VII 2014 (ESDJ)								
Espoo	263 148[65]	130 183[65]	132 965[65]	312	...	...	...	...
HELSINKI	616 690[65]	291 035[65]	325 655[65]	214	...	...	...	...
Jyvaskyla	135 219[65]	66 076[65]	69 144[65]	1 171	...	...	...	...
Kuopio	110 701[65]	53 675[65]	57 027[65]	2 776	...	...	...	...
Lahti	103 559[65]	49 253[65]	54 307[65]	135	...	...	...	...
Oulu	195 045[65]	97 028[65]	98 017[65]	3 032	...	...	...	...
Tampere	221 725[65]	107 338[65]	114 388[65]	525	...	...	...	...
Turku	182 948[65]	86 871[65]	96 077[65]	246	...	...	...	...
Vantaa	209 451[65]	103 082[65]	106 369[65]	238	...	...	...	...
France								
1 I 2010 (CDJS)								
Aix-en-Provence	141 438[66]	65 940[66]	75 498[66]	186	...	...	...	...
Amiens	133 448[66]	63 030[66]	70 418[66]	49	162 718	77 241	85 477	137
Angers	147 571[66]	67 521[66]	80 050[66]	43	215 887	100 353	115 534	189
Argenteuil	103 125[66]	50 356[66]	52 769[66]	17	...	...	...	...
Besançon	116 914[66]	54 937[66]	61 977[66]	65	135 050	63 788	71 262	122
Bordeaux	239 157[66]	111 452[66]	127 705[66]	49	843 425	400 423	443 002	1 173
Boulogne-Billancourt	114 205[66]	53 038[66]	61 167[66]	6	...	...	...	...
Brest	141 303[66]	68 083[66]	73 220[66]	50	199 852	96 845	103 007	199
Caen	108 954[66]	50 828[66]	58 126[66]	26	196 743	93 132	103 611	142
Clermont-Ferrand	139 860[66]	65 886[66]	73 974[66]	43	260 681	123 262	137 419	181
Dijon	151 212[66]	71 041[66]	80 171[66]	40	237 117	112 013	125 104	166
Grenoble	155 637[66]	75 558[66]	80 079[66]	18	496 951	241 872	255 079	512
Le Havre	175 497[66]	82 703[66]	92 794[66]	47	241 037	114 634	126 403	195
Le Mans	142 626[66]	66 979[66]	75 647[66]	35	207 658	98 772	108 886	294
Lille	227 560[66]	108 257[66]	119 303[66]	78	1 018 356	486 736	531 620	443
Limoges	139 150[66]	64 643[66]	74 507[66]	48	186 499	87 294	99 205	236
Lyon	484 344[66]	226 203[66]	258 141[66]	53	1 551 108	741 745	809 363	1 178
Marseille	850 726[66]	400 977[66]	449 749[66]	241	1 559 789[67]	741 799[67]	817 990[67]	1 732
Metz	120 738[66]	58 537[66]	62 201[66]	42	288 940	140 573	148 367	307
Montpellier	257 351[66]	119 967[66]	137 384[66]	57	390 962	184 812	206 150	310
Montreuil	102 770[66]	51 166[66]	51 604[66]	9	...	...	...	...
Mulhouse	109 588[66]	52 989[66]	56 599[66]	22	242 353	117 380	124 973	239
Nancy	105 421[66]	49 278[66]	56 143[66]	15	286 215	135 585	150 630	246
Nantes	284 970[66]	134 873[66]	150 097[66]	65	591 461	282 368	309 093	538
Nice	343 304[66]	159 260[66]	184 044[66]	72	941 777	443 854	497 923	744
Nîmes	142 205[66]	66 302[66]	75 903[66]	162	175 503	82 457	93 046	266
Orléans	114 167[66]	54 609[66]	59 558[66]	27	269 724	130 085	139 639	290
PARIS	2 243 833[66]	1 057 233[66]	1 186 600[66]	105	10 460 118[68]	5 037 278[68]	5 422 840[68]	2 845
Perpignan	117 419[66]	54 431[66]	62 988[66]	68	190 668	89 358	101 310	218
Reims	179 992[66]	84 862[66]	95 130[66]	47	208 639	98 645	109 994	94
Rennes	207 178[66]	97 794[66]	109 384[66]	50	310 672	148 841	161 831	284
Rouen	110 933[66]	52 383[66]	58 550[66]	21	463 748	219 416	244 332	453
Saint-Denis	106 785[66]	53 787[66]	52 998[66]	12	...	...	...	...
Saint-Étienne	171 260[66]	80 545[66]	90 715[66]	80	371 281	176 464	194 817	419
Strasbourg	271 782[66]	128 478[66]	143 304[66]	78	449 931	214 580	235 351	240
Toulon	164 532[66]	77 464[66]	87 068[66]	43	557 802	264 944	292 858	764
Toulouse	441 802[66]	213 198[66]	228 604[66]	118	879 683	427 944	451 739	812
Tours	134 817[66]	61 897[66]	72 920[66]	35	346 105	163 682	182 423	664
Villeurbanne	145 150[66]	70 377[66]	74 773[66]	15	...	...	...	...
Germany - Allemagne								
1 I 2015 (ESDJ)								
Aachen	243 336[69]	125 567[69]	117 769[69]	161	...	...	...	...
Augsburg	281 111[69]	137 182[69]	143 929[69]	147	...	...	...	...
Bergisch Gladbach	109 697[69]	52 431[69]	57 266[69]	83	...	...	...	...
BERLIN	3 469 849[69]	1 696 218[69]	1 773 631[69]	892	...	...	...	...
Bielefeld	329 782[69]	159 027[69]	170 755[69]	259	...	...	...	...

8. Population of capital cities and cities of 100 000 or more inhabitants: latest available year, 1996 - 2015
Population des capitales et des villes de 100 000 habitants ou plus : dernière année disponible, 1996 - 2015 (continued - suite)

Continent, country or area, date, code[a] and city / Continent, pays ou zone, date, code[a] et ville	City proper - Ville proprement dite				Urban agglomeration - Agglomération urbaine			
	Population			Surface area - Superficie (km²)	Population			Surface area - Superficie (km²)
	Both sexes - Les deux sexes	Male - Masculin	Female - Féminin		Both sexes - Les deux sexes	Male - Masculin	Female - Féminin	

EUROPE

Germany - Allemagne
1 I 2015 (ESDJ)

Bochum	361 876[69]	174 826[69]	187 050[69]	146	...	...	...	...
Bonn	313 958[69]	148 736[69]	165 222[69]	141	...	...	...	...
Bottrop	116 017[69]	56 128[69]	59 889[69]	101	...	...	...	...
Braunschweig	248 502[69]	122 315[69]	126 187[69]	192	...	...	...	...
Bremen	551 767[69]	270 004[69]	281 763[69]	326	...	...	...	...
Bremerhaven	110 121[69]	54 419[69]	55 702[69]	94	...	...	...	...
Chemnitz	243 521[69]	118 721[69]	124 800[69]	221	...	...	...	...
Darmstadt	151 879[69]	76 716[69]	75 163[69]	122	...	...	...	...
Dortmund	580 511[69]	284 002[69]	296 509[69]	281	...	...	...	...
Dresden	536 308[69]	265 166[69]	271 142[69]	328	...	...	...	...
Duisburg	485 465[69]	237 261[69]	248 204[69]	233	...	...	...	...
Düsseldorf	604 527[69]	291 199[69]	313 328[69]	217	...	...	...	...
Erfurt	206 219[69]	99 624[69]	106 595[69]	270	...	...	...	...
Erlangen	106 423[69]	52 383[69]	54 040[69]	77	...	...	...	...
Essen	573 784[69]	276 462[69]	297 322[69]	210	...	...	...	...
Frankfurt am Main	717 624[69]	353 822[69]	363 802[69]	248	...	...	...	...
Freiburg im Breisgau	222 203[69]	105 265[69]	116 938[69]	153	...	...	...	...
Fürth	121 519[69]	59 090[69]	62 429[69]	63	...	...	...	...
Gelsenkirchen	257 651[69]	127 188[69]	130 463[69]	105	...	...	...	...
Göttingen	117 665[69]	56 922[69]	60 743[69]	117	...	...	...	...
Hagen	186 716[69]	90 536[69]	96 180[69]	160	...	...	...	...
Halle (Saale)	232 470[69]	111 326[69]	121 144[69]	135	...	...	...	...
Hamburg	1 762 791[69]	857 446[69]	905 345[69]	755	...	...	...	...
Hamm	176 580[69]	85 990[69]	90 590[69]	226	...	...	...	...
Hannover	523 642[69]	253 616[69]	270 026[69]	204	...	...	...	...
Heidelberg	154 715[69]	73 988[69]	80 727[69]	109	...	...	...	...
Heilbronn	119 841[69]	59 467[69]	60 374[69]	100	...	...	...	...
Herne	154 608[69]	75 026[69]	79 582[69]	51	...	...	...	...
Ingolstadt	131 002[69]	65 933[69]	65 069[69]	133	...	...	...	...
Jena	108 207[69]	53 520[69]	54 687[69]	115	...	...	...	...
Karlsruhe	300 051[69]	150 881[69]	149 170[69]	173	...	...	...	...
Kassel	194 747[69]	94 406[69]	100 341[69]	107	...	...	...	...
Kiel	243 148[69]	118 032[69]	125 116[69]	119	...	...	...	...
Koblenz	111 434[69]	53 727[69]	57 707[69]	105	...	...	...	...
Köln	1 046 680[69]	508 791[69]	537 889[69]	405	...	...	...	...
Krefeld	222 500[69]	107 548[69]	114 952[69]	138	...	...	...	...
Leipzig	544 479[69]	264 914[69]	279 565[69]	297	...	...	...	...
Leverkusen	161 540[69]	78 267[69]	83 273[69]	79	...	...	...	...
Lübeck	214 420[69]	102 519[69]	111 901[69]	214	...	...	...	...
Ludwigshafen am Rhein	163 832[69]	81 150[69]	82 682[69]	78	...	...	...	...
Magdeburg	232 306[69]	113 573[69]	118 733[69]	201	...	...	...	...
Mainz	206 991[69]	100 006[69]	106 985[69]	98	...	...	...	...
Mannheim	299 844[69]	148 548[69]	151 296[69]	145	...	...	...	...
Moers	102 923[69]	49 756[69]	53 167[69]	68	...	...	...	...
Mönchengladbach	256 853[69]	125 397[69]	131 456[69]	170	...	...	...	...
Mülheim an der Ruhr	167 108[69]	79 848[69]	87 260[69]	91	...	...	...	...
München	1 429 584[69]	694 873[69]	734 711[69]	311	...	...	...	...
Münster (Westf.)	302 178[69]	144 318[69]	157 860[69]	303	...	...	...	...
Neuss	152 644[69]	73 766[69]	78 878[69]	100	...	...	...	...
Nürnberg	501 072[69]	241 878[69]	259 194[69]	186	...	...	...	...
Oberhausen	209 292[69]	102 065[69]	107 227[69]	77	...	...	...	...
Offenbach am Main	120 988[69]	59 848[69]	61 140[69]	45	...	...	...	...
Oldenburg (Oldenburg)	160 907[69]	76 458[69]	84 449[69]	103	...	...	...	...
Osnabrück	156 897[69]	75 449[69]	81 448[69]	120	...	...	...	...
Paderborn	145 176[69]	71 707[69]	73 469[69]	180	...	...	...	...
Pforzheim	119 291[69]	58 089[69]	61 202[69]	98	...	...	...	...
Potsdam	164 042[69]	78 708[69]	85 334[69]	188	...	...	...	...
Recklinghausen	114 147[69]	55 324[69]	58 823[69]	66	...	...	...	...
Regensburg	142 292[69]	68 086[69]	74 206[69]	81	...	...	...	...

8. Population of capital cities and cities of 100 000 or more inhabitants: latest available year, 1996 - 2015
Population des capitales et des villes de 100 000 habitants ou plus : dernière année disponible, 1996 - 2015 (continued - suite)

Continent, country or area, date, code[a] and city / Continent, pays ou zone, date, code[a] et ville	City proper - Ville proprement dite				Urban agglomeration - Agglomération urbaine			
	Population			Surface area - Superficie (km²)	Population			Surface area - Superficie (km²)
	Both sexes - Les deux sexes	Male - Masculin	Female - Féminin		Both sexes - Les deux sexes	Male - Masculin	Female - Féminin	
EUROPE								
Germany - Allemagne								
1 I 2015 (ESDJ)								
Remscheid	109 009[69]	53 266[69]	55 743[69]	75	...	...	...	...
Reutlingen	112 452[69]	55 100[69]	57 352[69]	87	...	...	...	...
Rostock	204 167[69]	99 896[69]	104 271[69]	181	...	...	...	...
Saarbrücken	176 926[69]	86 880[69]	90 046[69]	167	...	...	...	...
Siegen	100 325[69]	48 576[69]	51 749[69]	115	...	...	...	...
Solingen	156 771[69]	75 659[69]	81 112[69]	90	...	...	...	...
Stuttgart	612 441[69]	303 622[69]	308 819[69]	207	...	...	...	...
Trier	108 472[69]	52 766[69]	55 706[69]	117	...	...	...	...
Ulm	120 714[69]	59 144[69]	61 570[69]	119	...	...	...	...
Wiesbaden	275 116[69]	131 324[69]	143 792[69]	204	...	...	...	...
Wolfsburg	123 027[69]	60 791[69]	62 236[69]	204	...	...	...	...
Wuppertal	345 425[69]	167 766[69]	177 659[69]	168	...	...	...	...
Würzburg	124 219[69]	58 587[69]	65 632[69]	88	...	...	...	...
Gibraltar								
31 XII 2013 (ESDF)								
GIBRALTAR	32 734[70]	16 460[70]	16 274[70]	6	...	...	...	...
Greece - Grèce								
9 V 2011 (CDFC)								
ATHINAI	664 046	315 210	348 836	39	...	...	...	...
Calithèa	100 641	46 782	53 859	5	...	...	...	...
Iraclion	140 730	68 024	72 706	52	...	...	...	...
Larissa	144 651	70 797	73 854	88	...	...	...	...
Patrai	167 446	81 114	86 332	57	...	...	...	...
Pésterion	139 981	68 563	71 418	10	...	...	...	...
Pireas	163 688	78 200	85 488	...	...	...	...	...
Thessaloniki	315 196	143 813	171 383	...	...	...	...	...
Guernsey - Guernesey								
29 IV 2001 (CDJC)								
ST. PETER PORT	16 488	...	...	...	...	...	...	...
Holy See - Saint-Siège[71]								
21 VI 2012 (ESDF)								
VATICAN CITY	451	...	...	0[72]	...	...	...	...
Hungary - Hongrie								
1 VII 2014 (ESDJ)								
BUDAPEST	1 751 142	810 552	940 590	525	2 565 035	1 202 943	1 362 093	2 538
Debrecen	203 710	94 932	108 779	462	239 329	112 651	126 678	805
Györ	129 137	60 886	68 251	175	188 477	90 176	98 302	783
Kecskemét	111 954	52 506	59 448	323	144 376	68 573	75 803	840
Miskolc	160 410	74 329	86 081	237	198 583	92 894	105 689	460
Nyiregyhaza	118 145	54 822	63 323	275	134 297	62 739	71 558	405
Pécs	146 283	66 894	79 389	163	171 136	79 179	91 957	430
Szeged	162 257	74 314	87 944	281	200 189	93 057	107 132	713
Iceland - Islande[73]								
1 VII 2014 (ESDJ)								
REYKJAVIK	121 526[74]	60 256[74]	61 271[74]	274	210 017[75]	104 275[75]	105 743[75]	1 044
Ireland - Irlande								
10 IV 2011 (CDFC)								
Cork	119 230	58 812	60 418	40	198 582	97 463	101 119	...
DUBLIN	527 612	257 303	270 309	118	1 110 627	539 742	570 885	...
Isle of Man - Île de Man								
23 IV 2006 (CDJC)								
DOUGLAS	26 218	13 000	13 218	...	...	...	...	...
Italy - Italie								
1 VII 2014 (ESDJ)								
Ancona	101 630	48 302	53 329	125	...	...	...	...
Bari	325 056	155 550	169 506	117	...	...	...	...
Bergamo	118 860	55 504	63 356	40	...	...	...	...
Bologna	385 192	180 840	204 352	141	...	...	...	...
Bolzano	105 912	50 597	55 315	52	...	...	...	...
Brescia	194 829	91 719	103 110	90	...	...	...	...
Cagliari	154 249	71 472	82 777	85	...	...	...	...
Catania	315 589	151 419	164 170	183	...	...	...	...

Continent, country or area, date, code[a] and city / Continent, pays ou zone, date, code[a] et ville	City proper - Ville proprement dite				Urban agglomeration - Agglomération urbaine			
	Population			Surface area - Superficie (km²)	Population			Surface area - Superficie (km²)
	Both sexes - Les deux sexes	Male - Masculin	Female - Féminin		Both sexes - Les deux sexes	Male - Masculin	Female - Féminin	
EUROPE								
Italy - Italie								
1 VII 2014 (ESDJ)								
Ferrara	133 553	62 438	71 115	405	...	...	...	...
Firenze	379 122	177 111	202 012	102	...	...	...	...
Foggia	152 957	73 421	79 536	509	...	...	...	...
Forli	118 307	56 912	61 395	228	...	...	...	...
Genova	594 733	279 182	315 551	240	...	...	...	...
Giugliano in Campania	120 679	59 463	61 216	95	...	...	...	...
Latina	125 436	60 532	64 904	278	...	...	...	...
Livorno	160 027	76 335	83 692	105	...	...	...	...
Messina	241 206	115 426	125 780	214	...	...	...	...
Milano	1 330 662	633 161	697 501	182	...	...	...	...
Modena	184 837	88 173	96 664	183	...	...	...	...
Monza	122 759	58 867	63 893	33	...	...	...	...
Napoli	983 755	468 858	514 897	119	...	...	...	...
Novara	104 594	50 164	54 431	103	...	...	...	...
Padova	210 444	98 652	111 792	93	...	...	...	...
Palermo	678 492	323 975	354 517	161	...	...	...	...
Parma	189 111	89 709	99 402	261	...	...	...	...
Perugia	165 849	78 749	87 100	450	...	...	...	...
Pescara	121 346	56 845	64 501	34	...	...	...	...
Piacenza	102 337	48 622	53 715	118	...	...	...	...
Prato	191 135	92 453	98 683	97	...	...	...	...
Ravenna	158 848	76 821	82 027	654	...	...	...	...
Reggio di Calabria	184 456	88 255	96 201	239	...	...	...	...
Reggio nell'Emilia	172 090	83 569	88 521	231	...	...	...	...
Rimini	147 217	70 376	76 841	136	...	...	...	...
ROMA	2 867 672	1 359 337	1 508 335	1 287	...	...	...	...
Salerno	134 744	62 847	71 897	60	...	...	...	...
Sassari	127 670	61 186	66 485	547	...	...	...	...
Siracusa	122 404	59 986	62 418	208	...	...	...	...
Taranto	202 637	96 588	106 049	250	...	...	...	...
Terni	112 180	52 705	59 476	212	...	...	...	...
Torino	899 455	427 937	471 519	130	...	...	...	...
Trento	117 295	56 084	61 211	158	...	...	...	...
Trieste	205 131	97 035	108 097	85	...	...	...	...
Venezia	264 557	124 717	139 840	416	...	...	...	...
Verona	260 046	122 930	137 116	199	...	...	...	...
Vicenza	113 627	53 770	59 857	81	...	...	...	...
Jersey								
11 III 2001 (CDJC)								
ST. HELIER	28 310	13 669	14 641	9	...	...	...	...
Latvia - Lettonie								
1 VII 2014 (ESDJ)								
RIGA	642 188	283 457	358 731	304	...	...	...	...
Liechtenstein								
1 VII 2013* (ESDJ)								
VADUZ	5 270	2 552	2 718	17	...	...	...	...
Lithuania - Lituanie								
1 VII 2014 (ESDJ)								
Kaunas	302 685	133 046	169 639	157	...	...	...	...
Klaipeda	156 723	70 863	85 860	99	...	...	...	...
Shauliai	105 089	46 446	58 643	81	...	...	...	...
VILNIUS	541 167	242 469	298 698	400	...	...	...	...
Luxembourg								
1 I 2015 (ESDJ)								
LUXEMBOURG-VILLE	111 287	56 743	54 544	51	...	...	...	...
Malta - Malte								
1 VII 2014 (ESDJ)								
VALLETTA	5 689	2 794	2 895	1	...	...	...	...
Monaco								
9 VI 2008 (CDJC)								
MONACO	31 109	15 076[76]	15 914[76]	...	...	...	...	...

Continent, country or area, date, code[a] and city Continent, pays ou zone, date, code[a] et ville	City proper - Ville proprement dite				Urban agglomeration - Agglomération urbaine			
	Population			Surface area - Superficie (km²)	Population			Surface area - Superficie (km²)
	Both sexes - Les deux sexes	Male - Masculin	Female - Féminin		Both sexes - Les deux sexes	Male - Masculin	Female - Féminin	
EUROPE								
Montenegro - Monténégro								
1 IV 2011 (CDJC)								
PODGORICA	185 937	90 614	95 323	1 441	...	...	...	...
Netherlands - Pays-Bas								
1 I 2015 (ESDJ)								
Alkmaar	107 106	52 973	54 133	...	...	...	...	...
Almere	196 932	97 666	99 266	130	...	...	...	...
Alphen aan den	107 396	53 321	54 075	...	...	...	...	...
Amersfoort.............................	152 481	74 967	77 514	63	...	...	...	...
AMSTERDAM	821 752	404 881	416 871	166	...	...	...	...
Apeldoorn	158 099	78 163	79 936	340	...	...	...	...
Arnhem	152 293	75 872	76 421	98	...	...	...	...
Breda	180 937	88 620	92 317	127	...	...	...	...
Delft	101 030	54 035	46 995	...	...	...	...	...
Dordrecht..............................	118 899	58 646	60 253	79	...	...	...	...
Ede	111 575	54 790	56 785	318	...	...	...	...
Eindhoven	223 209	114 034	109 175	88	...	...	...	...
Emmen..................................	107 775	53 399	54 376	337	...	...	...	...
Enschede	158 553	80 411	78 142	141	...	...	...	...
Groningen	200 336	99 657	100 679	78	...	...	...	...
Haarlem	156 645	76 481	80 164	29	...	...	...	...
Haarlemmermeer	144 152	71 642	72 510	179	...	...	...	...
Leeuwarden	107 691	53 264	54 427	...	...	...	...	...
Leiden	121 562	59 084	62 478	22	...	...	...	...
Maastricht..............................	122 397	58 799	63 598	57	...	...	...	...
Nijmegen	170 681	81 934	88 747	54	...	...	...	...
Rotterdam..............................	623 652	307 001	316 651	206	...	...	...	...
s-Gravenhage........................	514 861	254 187	260 674	...	...	...	...	...
s-Hertogenbosch	150 889	74 424	76 465	84	...	...	...	...
Tilburg...................................	211 648	105 179	106 469	117	...	...	...	...
Utrecht..................................	334 176	162 556	171 620	95	...	...	...	...
Venlo	100 536	49 978	50 558	...	...	...	...	...
Westland................................	104 302	51 937	52 365	...	...	...	...	...
Zaanstad	151 418	74 778	76 640	74	...	...	...	...
Zoetermeer	124 025	60 554	63 471	35	...	...	...	...
Zwolle	123 861	60 759	63 102	112	...	...	...	...
Norway - Norvège								
1 I 2014 (ESDJ)								
OSLO	634 293	316 114	318 179	426	...	...	...	...
Poland - Pologne[77]								
1 VII 2012 (ESDJ)								
Bialystok	294 675	138 477	156 198	102[13]	...	...	...	...
Bielsko-Biala..........................	174 291	82 143	92 148	125[13]	...	...	...	...
Bydgoszcz	362 286	170 457	191 829	176[13]	...	...	...	...
Bytom	175 377	84 118	91 259	69[13]	...	...	...	...
Chorzów................................	111 314	53 051	58 263	33[13]	...	...	...	...
Czestochowa..........................	235 156	110 506	124 650	160[13]	...	...	...	...
Dabrowa Górnicza..................	125 063	60 206	64 857	189[13]	...	...	...	...
Elblag	123 977	59 427	64 550	80[13]	...	...	...	...
Gdansk..................................	460 354	218 273	242 081	262[13]	...	...	...	...
Gdynia...................................	248 574	118 140	130 434	135[13]	...	...	...	...
Gliwice	186 347	89 801	96 546	134[13]	...	...	...	...
Gorzów Wielkopolski	124 470	59 306	65 164	86[13]	...	...	...	...
Kalisz....................................	104 867	48 802	56 065	69[13]	...	...	...	...
Katowice	308 269	146 571	161 698	165[13]	...	...	...	...
Kielce....................................	201 363	94 999	106 364	110[13]	...	...	...	...
Koszalin................................	109 183	51 635	57 548	98[13]	...	...	...	...
Kraków	759 131	354 200	404 931	327[13]	...	...	...	...
Legnica	102 708	48 647	54 061	56[13]	...	...	...	...
Lódz......................................	722 022	328 440	393 582	293[13]	...	...	...	...
Lublin....................................	348 120	160 158	187 962	147[13]	...	...	...	...
Olsztyn	175 482	81 778	93 704	88[13]	...	...	...	...
Opole	122 120	57 115	65 005	97[13]	...	...	...	...
Plock.....................................	124 048	58 753	65 295	88[13]	...	...	...	...

8. Population of capital cities and cities of 100 000 or more inhabitants: latest available year, 1996 - 2015
Population des capitales et des villes de 100 000 habitants ou plus : dernière année disponible, 1996 - 2015 (continued - suite)

Continent, country or area, date, code[a] and city / Continent, pays ou zone, date, code[a] et ville	City proper - Ville proprement dite				Urban agglomeration - Agglomération urbaine			
	Population			Surface area - Superficie (km²)	Population			Surface area - Superficie (km²)
	Both sexes - Les deux sexes	Male - Masculin	Female - Féminin		Both sexes - Les deux sexes	Male - Masculin	Female - Féminin	
EUROPE								
Poland - Pologne[77]								
1 VII 2012 (ESDJ)								
Poznan	552 393	257 418	294 975	262[13]	...	...	...	...
Radom	220 062	104 699	115 363	112[13]	...	...	...	...
Ruda Slaska	142 672	69 292	73 380	78[13]	...	...	...	...
Rybnik	140 863	68 798	72 065	148[13]	...	...	...	...
Rzeszów	180 776	85 342	95 434	117[13]	...	...	...	...
Sosnowiec	214 488	101 857	112 631	91[13]	...	...	...	...
Szczecin	409 211	194 601	214 610	301[13]	...	...	...	...
Tarnów	113 188	53 499	59 689	72[13]	...	...	...	...
Torun	204 847	95 219	109 628	116[13]	...	...	...	...
Tychy	129 087	62 377	66 710	82[13]	...	...	...	...
Walbrzych	119 216	56 285	62 931	85[13]	...	...	...	...
WARSZAWA	1 711 324	785 187	926 137	517[13]	...	...	...	...
Wloclawek	115 982	54 738	61 244	84[13]	...	...	...	...
Wroclaw	631 377	294 627	336 750	293[13]	...	...	...	...
Zabrze	179 861	86 939	92 922	80[13]	...	...	...	...
Zielona Góra	119 182	56 032	63 150	58[13]	...	...	...	...
Portugal								
1 VII 2014 (ESDJ)								
Amadora	175 653	82 081	93 573	24[78]	...	...	...	...
LISBOA	513 064	234 521	278 543	100[79]	...	...	...	...
Porto	220 242	99 360	120 882	41[78]	...	...	...	...
Republic of Moldova - République de Moldova								
1 I 2012 (ESDJ)								
Balti (Beltsy)	144 507	66 243	78 264	41	...	...	...	...
CHIŞINĂU (KISHINEV)	669 694	311 575	358 119	123	726 075	339 321	386 755	572
Romania - Roumanie								
1 VII 2014 (ESDJ)								
BUCURESTI	1 859 322	864 006	995 316	238	...	...	...	...
Russian Federation - Fédération de Russie								
1 VII 2012 (ESDJ)								
Abakan	168 655	77 052	91 603	...	...	...	...	...
Achinsk	107 943	48 069	59 874	...	109 229	...	...	...
Almetievsk	148 384	69 433	78 951	...	...	...	...	...
Anapa	...	...	...	...	156 928	...	...	...
Angarsk	231 944	105 405	126 539	...	...	...	...	...
Arkhangelsk	350 258	156 523	193 735	...	357 264	...	...	...
Armavir	190 831	87 524	103 307	...	209 742	...	...	...
Artem (Primorskiy Krai)	102 605	49 147	53 458	...	112 102	...	...	...
Arzamas	105 506	47 208	58 298	...	...	...	...	...
Astrakhan	526 363	241 489	284 874	...	...	...	...	...
Balakovo	196 918	88 075	108 843	...	...	...	...	...
Balashikha	228 567	112 191	116 376	...	238 284	...	...	...
Barnaul	625 679	279 300	346 379	...	686 306	...	...	...
Bataisk	115 016	54 477	60 539	...	...	...	...	...
Belgorod	369 815	167 120	202 695	...	...	...	...	...
Belovo	...	...	...	...	132 144	...	...	...
Berezniki	153 806	68 365	85 441	...	...	...	...	...
Biisk	206 327	91 943	114 384	...	215 780	...	...	...
Blagoveshchensk (Amurskaya oblast)	216 691	97 135	119 556	...	222 065	...	...	...
Bor	...	...	...	...	122 201	...	...	...
Bratsk	242 604	109 596	133 008	...	...	...	...	...
Bryansk	411 798	183 540	228 258	...	430 987	...	...	...
Cheboksary	462 650	206 721	255 948	...	473 189	...	...	...
Chelyabinsk	1 149 829	514 456	635 373	...	...	...	...	...
Cherepovets	315 186	142 977	172 209	...	...	...	...	...
Cherkessk	126 884	55 588	71 296	...	...	...	...	...
Chita	329 391	152 092	177 299	...	329 868	...	...	...
Derbent	119 647	57 527	62 120	...	...	...	...	...
Dimitrovgrad	120 750	55 838	64 912	...	...	...	...	...
Domodedovo	...	...	...	...	142 743	...	...	...
Dzerzhinsk (Nizhegorodskaya oblast)	238 327	105 346	132 981	...	248 649	...	...	...
Ekaterinburg	1 386 909	621 499	765 410	...	1 420 285	...	...	...

8. Population of capital cities and cities of 100 000 or more inhabitants: latest available year, 1996 - 2015
Population des capitales et des villes de 100 000 habitants ou plus : dernière année disponible, 1996 - 2015 (continued - suite)

Continent, country or area, date, code[a] and city / Continent, pays ou zone, date, code[a] et ville	City proper - Ville proprement dite				Urban agglomeration - Agglomération urbaine			
	Population			Surface area - Superficie (km²)	Population			Surface area - Superficie (km²)
	Both sexes - Les deux sexes	Male - Masculin	Female - Féminin		Both sexes - Les deux sexes	Male - Masculin	Female - Féminin	
EUROPE								
Russian Federation - Fédération de Russie								
1 VII 2012 (ESDJ)								
Elektrostal	156 136	71 093	85 043	...	...	...	...	...
Elets	107 347	48 757	58 590	...	...	...	...	...
Elista	104 177	47 317	56 860	...	108 753	...	...	...
Engels	210 190	95 953	114 237	...	211 825	...	...	...
Esentuky	101 851	45 327	56 524	...	...	...	...	...
Groznyi	276 524	136 615	139 909	...	...	...	...	...
Hasaviurt	133 188	63 867	69 321	...	...	...	...	...
Irkutsk	601 993	269 003	332 990	...	...	...	...	...
Ivanovo	408 952	180 083	228 869	...	...	...	...	...
Izhevsk	631 182	281 708	349 474	...	...	...	...	...
Kaliningrad (Kaliningradskaya oblast)	437 456	200 849	236 607	...	...	...	...	...
Kaluga	328 871	146 008	182 863	...	344 766	...	...	...
Kamensk-Uralsky	172 639	77 327	95 312	...	174 493	...	...	...
Kamyshin	117 352	53 822	63 530	...	...	...	...	...
Kaspiysk	102 421	49 393	53 028	...	...	...	...	...
Kazan	1 168 745	520 694	648 051	...	...	...	...	...
Kemerovo	538 188	240 431	297 757	...	...	...	...	...
Khabarovsk	589 596	273 949	315 647	...	...	...	...	...
Khimki	218 275	99 122	119 153	...	...	...	...	...
Kirov	480 594	211 205	269 389	...	505 346	...	...	...
Kiselevsk	...	...	...	...	101 180	...	...	...
Kislovodsk	129 313	58 854	70 459	...	136 142	...	...	...
Kolomna	144 838	66 469	78 369	...	...	...	...	...
Komsomolsk-na-Amure	259 081	120 197	138 884	...	...	...	...	...
Kopeysk	139 161	66 142	73 019	...	141 291	...	...	...
Korolev (Moskovskaya oblast)	186 460	84 232	102 228	...	...	...	...	...
Kostroma	270 366	120 622	149 744	...	...	...	...	...
Kovrov	...	...	...	...	346 922	154 144	192 778	...
Krasnodar	773 970	350 519	423 451	...	861 181	...	...	...
Krasnogorsk	125 198	56 432	68 766	...	125 787	...	...	...
Krasnoyarsk	1 006 856	456 171	550 685	...	1 007 654	...	...	...
Kurgan	326 729	146 140	180 589	...	...	...	...	...
Kursk	425 950	189 025	236 925	...	...	...	...	...
Kyzyl	112 659	52 137	60 522	...	...	...	...	...
Leninsk-Kuznetsky	100 073	45 651	54 422	...	102 285	...	...	...
Lipetsk	508 585	230 178	278 407	...	...	...	...	...
Lyubertsy	178 884	80 564	98 320	...	...	...	...	...
Magadan	95 263	45 084	50 179	...	101 933	...	...	...
Magnitogorsk	410 733	186 534	224 199	...	...	...	...	...
Maikop	144 579	64 512	80 067	...	167 281	...	...	...
Makhachkala	575 243	271 687	303 556	...	701 753	...	...	...
Mezhdurechensk	100 278	46 498	53 780	...	102 465	...	...	...
Miass	150 806	67 824	82 982	...	166 205	...	...	...
MOSKVA	11 918 057	5 495 477	6 422 580	...	...	...	...	...
Murmansk	303 754	139 944	163 810	...	...	...	...	...
Murom	113 330	50 293	63 037	...	122 545	...	...	...
Mytishchi	176 825	80 425	96 400	...	185 204	...	...	...
Naberezhnye Tchelny	517 831	237 620	280 211	...	...	...	...	...
Nakhodka	158 649	75 081	83 568	...	159 633	...	...	...
Naltchik	239 230	106 648	132 582	...	265 051	...	...	...
Nazran	100 574	44 126	56 448	...	...	...	...	...
Neftekamsk	123 202	57 271	65 931	...	135 013	...	...	...
Nefteyugansk	125 528	61 635	63 893	...	...	...	...	...
Nevinnomyssk	117 949	53 611	64 338	...	...	...	...	...
Nizhnekamsk	235 179	111 262	123 917	...	235 279	...	...	...
Nizhnevartovsk	261 011	125 937	135 074	...	...	...	...	...
Nizhny Novgorod	1 257 260	552 285	704 975	...	1 266 231	...	...	...
Nizhny Tagil	358 651	162 731	195 920	...	362 185	...	...	...
Noginsk	101 779	45 741	56 038	...	103 843	...	...	...
Norilsk	177 506	89 198	88 308	...	178 363	...	...	...
Novocheboksarsk	...	...	...	...	124 288	...	...	...
Novocherkassk	171 081	81 921	89 160	...	...	...	...	...
Novokuybishevsk	107 244	48 418	58 826	...	109 521	...	...	...

	City proper - Ville proprement dite				Urban agglomeration - Agglomération urbaine			
	Population				Population			
Continent, country or area, date, code[a] and city Continent, pays ou zone, date, code[a] et ville	Both sexes - Les deux sexes	Male - Masculin	Female - Féminin	Surface area - Superficie (km²)	Both sexes - Les deux sexes	Male - Masculin	Female - Féminin	Surface area - Superficie (km²)

EUROPE

Russian Federation - Fédération de Russie
1 VII 2012 (ESDJ)

Novokuznetsk	549 383	247 386	301 997	...	...	...	...	...
Novomoskovsk (Tulskaya oblast)	129 555	57 961	71 594	...	141 893	...	...	...
Novorossiysk	248 857	117 707	131 150	...	305 421	...	...	...
Novoshakhtinsk	110 243	50 410	59 833	...	...	...	...	...
Novosibirsk	1 511 369	694 959	816 410	...	...	...	...	...
Novotroitsk	...	...	...	...	103 061	...	...	...
Novy Urengoy	114 332	59 841	54 491	...	...	...	...	...
Noyabrsk	108 662	53 237	55 425	...	...	...	...	...
Obninsk	105 722	48 323	57 399	...	...	...	...	...
Odintsovo	137 706	63 405	74 301	...	143 848	...	...	...
Oktyabrsky	111 109	51 956	59 153	...	...	...	...	...
Omsk	1 158 627	526 757	631 870	...	...	...	...	...
Orekhovo-Zuevo	121 341	53 443	67 898	...	...	...	...	...
Orel	318 642	139 662	178 980	...	...	...	...	...
Orenburg	555 420	252 906	302 514	...	571 041	...	...	...
Orsk	237 194	106 127	131 067	...	241 327	...	...	...
Penza	519 948	234 270	285 678	...	...	...	...	...
Perm	1 007 272	444 386	562 886	...	1 007 285	...	...	...
Pervouralsk	125 421	56 144	69 277	...	149 796	...	...	...
Petropavlovsk-Kamchatsky	180 702	88 743	91 959	...	...	...	...	...
Petrozavodsk	267 102	118 638	148 464	...	...	...	...	...
Podolsk	200 059	89 931	110 128	...	...	...	...	...
Prokopyevsk	206 023	91 944	114 079	...	...	...	...	...
Pskov	205 062	92 439	112 623	...	...	...	...	...
Pushkino	104 020	46 649	57 371	...	...	...	...	...
Pyatigorsk	144 603	64 578	80 025	...	212 968	...	...	...
Rostov-na-Donu	1 100 091	501 068	599 023	...	...	...	...	...
Rubtsovsk	146 075	69 084	76 991	...	...	...	...	...
Ryazan	526 919	237 791	289 128	...	...	...	...	...
Rybinsk	197 359	87 921	109 438	...	...	...	...	...
Salavat	155 174	72 449	82 725	...	...	...	...	...
Samara (Samarskaya oblast)	1 170 381	522 660	647 721	...	1 170 485	...	...	...
Saransk	298 103	132 543	165 560	...	326 473	...	...	...
Sarapyul	100 362	44 678	55 684	...	...	...	...	...
Saratov	838 321	373 676	464 645	...	...	...	...	...
Sergiev Posad	109 076	48 786	60 290	...	115 858	...	...	...
Serov	...	...	...	...	107 904	...	...	...
Serpukhov	126 729	57 494	69 235	...	...	...	...	...
Severodvinsk	189 313	87 781	101 532	...	190 513	...	...	...
Seversk	109 630	50 705	58 925	...	116 340	...	...	...
Shakhty	238 031	107 544	130 487	...	...	...	...	...
Shchelkovo	111 406	50 812	60 594	...	113 726	...	...	...
Smolensk	330 451	147 446	183 005	...	...	...	...	...
Sochi	364 171	164 632	199 539	...	441 407	...	...	...
St. Petersburg	4 990 602	2 247 375	2 743 227	...	...	...	...	...
Stary Oskol	220 719	100 902	119 817	...	256 790	...	...	...
Stavropol	408 361	187 593	220 768	...	408 560	...	...	...
Sterlitamak	275 087	125 443	149 644	...	...	...	...	...
Surgut	321 062	153 832	167 230	...	...	...	...	...
Syktivkar	239 341	107 945	131 396	...	255 283	...	...	...
Syzran	177 404	79 804	97 600	...	178 205	...	...	...
Taganrog	255 671	114 508	141 163	...	...	...	...	...
Tambov	281 348	126 427	154 921	...	...	...	...	...
Tobolsk	...	...	...	...	101 955	...	...	...
Tolyatti	719 363	331 248	388 115	...	...	...	...	...
Tomsk	543 596	252 173	291 423	...	565 000	...	...	...
Tula	496 656	220 675	275 981	...	...	...	...	...
Tver	407 896	180 459	227 437	...	...	...	...	...
Tyumen	621 918	288 291	333 627	...	644 799	...	...	...
Ufa	1 075 007	484 893	590 114	...	1 084 420	...	...	...
Uhta	99 680	47 563	52 117	...	121 479	...	...	...
Ulan-Ude	413 850	191 732	222 118	...	...	...	...	...
Ulyanovsk	614 878	278 103	336 775	...	637 637	...	...	...

8. Population of capital cities and cities of 100 000 or more inhabitants: latest available year, 1996 - 2015
Population des capitales et des villes de 100 000 habitants ou plus : dernière année disponible, 1996 - 2015 (continued - suite)

Continent, country or area, date, code[a] and city Continent, pays ou zone, date, code[a] et ville	City proper - Ville proprement dite				Urban agglomeration - Agglomération urbaine			
	Population			Surface area - Superficie (km²)	Population			Surface area - Superficie (km²)
	Both sexes - Les deux sexes	Male - Masculin	Female - Féminin		Both sexes - Les deux sexes	Male - Masculin	Female - Féminin	
EUROPE								
Russian Federation - Fédération de Russie								
1 VII 2012 (ESDJ)								
Ussuriisk	163 465	79 562	83 903	...	189 502	...	...	...
Velikiy Novgorod	219 941	95 446	124 495	...	...	...	...	...
Vladikavkaz (Osetinskaya ASSR)	309 173	139 818	169 355	...	327 448	...	...	...
Vladimir	346 922	154 144	192 778	...	349 525	...	...	...
Vladivostok	598 927	282 260	316 667	...	624 281	...	...	...
Volgodonsk	170 189	78 251	91 938	...	...	...	...	...
Volgograd	1 018 762	460 095	558 667	...	...	...	...	...
Vologda	305 397	135 292	170 105	...	313 679	...	...	...
Volzhsky	320 761	148 339	172 422	...	327 460	...	...	...
Voronezh	997 447	447 484	549 963	...	...	...	...	...
Yakutsk	282 419	132 612	149 807	...	298 926	...	...	...
Yaroslavl	597 161	262 042	335 119	...	...	...	...	...
Yoshkar-Ola	254 987	114 331	140 656	...	265 626	...	...	...
Yuzhno-Sakhalinsk	188 242	89 200	99 042	...	195 104	...	...	...
Zheleznodorozhny	138 814	62 719	76 095	...	...	...	...	...
Zhukovsky	106 555	49 027	57 528	...	...	...	...	...
Zlatoust	172 972	78 071	94 901	...	175 178	...	...	...
San Marino - Saint-Marin								
1 I 2013 (ESDF)								
SAN MARINO	4 438	2 117	2 321	...	...	...	...	...
Serbia - Serbie								
1 VII 2014 (ESDJ)								
BEOGRAD (BELGRADE)	1 363 611[80]	636 105[80]	727 506[80]	236	1 675 043[81]	791 485[81]	883 558[81]	3 158[82]
Čačak	72 754[80]	34 808[80]	37 946[80]	19	113 383[81]	55 082[81]	58 301[81]	633[82]
Kragujevac	150 804[80]	72 828[80]	77 976[80]	34	178 847[81]	86 947[81]	91 900[81]	834[82]
Kraljevo	67 906[80]	32 746[80]	35 160[80]	16	122 782[81]	60 249[81]	62 533[81]	1 525[82]
Kruševac	58 267[80]	27 672[80]	30 595[80]	9	125 853[81]	61 472[81]	64 381[81]	849[82]
Leskovac	64 381[80]	31 214[80]	33 167[80]	2	140 487[81]	69 798[81]	70 689[81]	1 021[82]
Niš	186 568[80]	89 309[80]	97 259[80]	26	258 500[81]	125 530[81]	132 970[81]	594[82]
Novi Sad	284 230[80]	133 120[80]	151 110[80]	50	348 540[81]	165 049[81]	183 491[81]	593[82]
Pancevo	89 927[80]	43 181[80]	46 746[80]	34	122 013[81]	59 355[81]	62 658[81]	736[82]
Šabac	53 529[80]	25 124[80]	28 405[80]	15	113 827[81]	55 651[81]	58 176[81]	788[82]
Smederevo	63 596[80]	30 785[80]	32 811[80]	17	106 470[81]	52 502[81]	53 968[81]	474[82]
Subotica	104 721[80]	49 796[80]	54 925[80]	50	139 612[81]	67 087[81]	72 525[81]	998[82]
Zrenjanin	75 459[80]	35 925[80]	39 534[80]	29	120 709[81]	58 663[81]	62 046[81]	1 286[82]
Slovakia - Slovaquie								
1 VII 2014 (ESDJ)								
BRATISLAVA	418 534	195 681	222 853	368[13]	...	...	...	...
Kosice	239 631	114 891	124 740	244[13]	...	...	...	...
Slovenia - Slovénie								
1 VII 2014 (ESDJ)								
LJUBLJANA	277 905	133 043	144 862	164	279 716	133 952	145 764	171
Maribor	95 338	46 563	48 775	41	109 179	53 437	55 742	99
Spain - Espagne								
1 VII 2013 (ESDJ)								
A Coruña	245 367	113 948	131 419	38	...	...	...	...
Albacete	172 590	84 551	88 039	1 141	...	...	...	...
Alcalá de Henares	202 796	100 688	102 108	88	...	...	...	...
Alcobendas	112 192	54 192	58 000	45	...	...	...	...
Alcorcón	170 055	82 959	87 096	34	...	...	...	...
Algeciras	116 126	57 386	58 740	86	...	...	...	...
Alicante	333 560	162 106	171 454	202	...	...	...	...
Almería	193 024	93 876	99 148	296	...	...	...	...
Badajoz	150 569	73 252	77 317	1 474	...	...	...	...
Badalona	235 633	115 631	120 002	21	...	...	...	...
Baracaldo	100 184	48 558	51 733	25	...	...	...	...
Barcelona	1 607 104	761 009	846 095	103	...	...	...	...
Bilbao	347 965	164 159	183 806	41	...	...	...	...
Burgos	178 437	85 343	93 094	107	...	...	...	...
Cádiz	122 365	57 916	64 449	12	...	...	...	...
Cartagena	217 046	108 889	108 157	558	...	...	...	...
Castellón de la Plana	177 013	86 568	90 445	109	...	...	...	...

8. Population of capital cities and cities of 100 000 or more inhabitants: latest available year, 1996 - 2015
Population des capitales et des villes de 100 000 habitants ou plus : dernière année disponible, 1996 - 2015 (continued - suite)

Continent, country or area, date, codeᵃ and city / Continent, pays ou zone, date, codeᵃ et ville	City proper - Ville proprement dite				Urban agglomeration - Agglomération urbaine			
	Population			Surface area - Superficie (km²)	Population			Surface area - Superficie (km²)
	Both sexes - Les deux sexes	Male - Masculin	Female - Féminin		Both sexes - Les deux sexes	Male - Masculin	Female - Féminin	
EUROPE								
Spain - Espagne								
1 VII 2013 (ESDJ)								
Córdoba	328 373	157 837	170 536	1 263	...	...	...	...
Donostia - San Sebastián	186 313	87 456	98 857	62	...	...	...	...
Dos Hermanas	130 044	64 222	65 822	160	...	...	...	...
Elche	229 436	114 014	115 422	326	...	...	...	...
Fuenlabrada	196 692	98 082	98 610	39	...	...	...	...
Getafe	172 792	84 991	87 801	79	...	...	...	...
Gijón	275 505	130 094	145 411	181	...	...	...	...
Granada	237 679	110 578	127 101	88	...	...	...	...
Hospitalet de Llobregat	236 613	116 287	120 326	13	...	...	...	...
Huelva	147 657	71 077	76 580	152	...	...	...	...
Jaén	116 007	55 979	60 028	424	...	...	...	...
Jérez de la Frontera	211 948	103 825	108 123	1 189	...	...	...	...
Leganés	186 846	91 415	95 431	43	...	...	...	...
León	130 076	59 422	70 654	39	...	...	...	...
Lleida	139 493	69 103	70 390	212	...	...	...	...
Logroño	152 514	73 002	79 512	79	...	...	...	...
MADRID	3 186 241	1 483 791	1 702 450	604	...	...	...	...
Málaga	567 696	273 075	294 621	395	...	...	...	...
Marbella	140 349	68 239	72 110	117	...	...	...	...
Mataró	122 155	61 070	61 085	22	...	...	...	...
Móstoles	206 082	101 337	104 745	45	...	...	...	...
Murcia	438 979	215 065	223 914	886	...	...	...	...
Ourense	107 224	49 168	58 056	85	...	...	...	...
Oviedo	224 427	104 555	119 872	187	...	...	...	...
Palma de Mallorca	398 628	194 281	204 347	...	...	...	...	...
Palmas de Gran Canaria	382 667	186 014	196 653	106	...	...	...	...
Pamplona	196 561	93 706	102 855	25	...	...	...	...
Parla	125 479	63 246	62 233	25	...	...	...	...
Reus	105 876	51 646	54 230	53	...	...	...	...
Sabadell	207 547	101 040	106 507	38	...	...	...	...
Salamanca	148 785	68 236	80 549	40	...	...	...	...
San Cristóbal de La Laguna	152 364	74 229	78 135	107	...	...	...	...
Santa Coloma de Gramanet	166 897	82 879	84 018	7	...	...	...	...
Santa Cruz de Tenerife	205 936	98 529	107 407	156	...	...	...	...
Santander	176 430	81 610	94 820	35	...	...	...	...
Sevilla	698 423	331 916	366 507	141	...	...	...	...
Tarragona	132 872	65 033	67 839	56	...	...	...	...
Telde	102 123	50 607	51 516	104	...	...	...	...
Terrassa	169 808	84 157	85 651	70	...	...	...	...
Torrejón de Ardoz	125 320	62 388	62 932	32	...	...	...	...
Valencia	789 364	376 965	412 399	136	...	...	...	...
Valladolid	308 272	145 691	162 581	197	...	...	...	...
Vigo	295 738	140 843	154 895	105	...	...	...	...
Vitoria-Gasteiz	241 734	118 517	123 217	277	...	...	...	...
Zaragoza	674 031	324 966	349 065	972	...	...	...	...
Sweden - Suède								
1 VII 2007 (ESDJ)								
Göteborg	491 630	242 916	248 714	449	...	...	...	...
Helsingborg	124 188	60 672	63 516	346	...	...	...	...
Jönköping	122 952	60 462	62 490	1 485	...	...	...	...
Linköping	139 474	70 239	69 235	1 431	...	...	...	...
Malmö	278 523	135 997	142 526	154	...	...	...	...
Norrköping	126 072	62 323	63 749	1 491	...	...	...	...
Orebro	129 703	63 123	66 581	1 371	...	...	...	...
STOCKHOLM	789 024	384 243	404 781	187	...	...	...	...
Umeå	111 503	55 549	55 955	2 316	...	...	...	...
Uppsala	186 364	91 149	95 215	2 465	...	...	...	...
Västerås	133 324	66 056	67 269	956	...	...	...	...
Switzerland - Suisse								
1 I 2015 (ESDJ)								
Baden-Brugg	29 774	14 954	14 820	20	123 959	61 872	62 087	124
Bâle	168 620	81 497	87 123	24	513 367	249 886	263 481	481
BERNE	130 015	62 383	67 632	52	365 238	176 835	188 403	479

8. Population of capital cities and cities of 100 000 or more inhabitants: latest available year, 1996 - 2015
Population des capitales et des villes de 100 000 habitants ou plus : dernière année disponible, 1996 - 2015 (continued - suite)

Continent, country or area, date, code[a] and city / Continent, pays ou zone, date, code[a] et ville	City proper - Ville proprement dite				Urban agglomeration - Agglomération urbaine			
	Population			Surface area - Superficie (km²)	Population			Surface area - Superficie (km²)
	Both sexes - Les deux sexes	Male - Masculin	Female - Féminin		Both sexes - Les deux sexes	Male - Masculin	Female - Féminin	
EUROPE								
Switzerland - Suisse								
1 I 2015 (ESDJ)								
Fribourg	38 288	18 938	19 350	9	114 225	56 811	57 414	212
Genève	194 565	93 382	101 183	16	550 866	266 882	283 984	457
Lausanne	133 897	64 337	69 560	41	355 591	173 587	182 004	314
Lugano	63 668	30 612	33 056	76	142 652	68 998	73 654	243
Luzern	81 057	38 813	42 244	29	217 662	106 760	110 902	198
Olten-Zofingen	28 560	14 006	14 554	22	116 186	58 045	58 141	183
St. Gallen	75 310	36 684	38 626	39	154 490	75 991	78 499	175
Winterthur	106 778	52 360	54 418	68	148 619	73 167	75 452	161
Zug	28 603	14 400	14 203	22	115 709	58 451	57 258	180
Zürich	391 359	193 967	197 392	88	1 251 199	622 111	629 088	1 086
TFYR of Macedonia - L'ex-R. y. de Macédoine								
1 VII 2012 (ESDF)								
SKOPJE	536 271	262 676	273 595	...	...	...	...	...
Ukraine								
1 I 2013 (ESDJ)								
Alchevsk	110 878	50 786	60 092	49	...	...	...	...
Berdyansk	116 249	51 540	64 709	83	119 371	53 036	66 335	90
Bila Tserkva	206 990	95 422	111 568	34	...	...	...	...
Cherkasy	283 130	129 279	153 851	67	283 924	129 696	154 228	78
Chernihiv	290 269	133 477	156 792	78	...	...	...	...
Chernivtsi	255 084	117 029	138 055	153	...	...	...	...
Dnepropetrovsk	987 629	448 496	539 133	387	990 025	449 659	540 366	405
Dniprodzerzhynsk	241 330	108 459	132 871	118	248 237	111 564	136 673	138
Donets'k	944 552	418 132	526 420	363	960 646	425 457	535 189	571
Enakievo (Yenakievo)	82 941	36 713	46 228	67	131 250	58 850	72 400	425
Evpatoria	104 289	46 505	57 784	43	120 473	53 898	66 575	66
Gorlivka	254 526	113 970	140 556	186	274 942	123 190	151 752	422
Ivano-Frankivsk	223 165	104 982	118 183	37	240 934	113 229	127 705	84
Kamenets Podolsky	102 039	47 523	54 516	29	...	...	...	...
Kerch	146 559	66 067	80 492	108	...	...	...	...
Kharkiv	1 431 461	659 700	771 761	350	...	...	...	...
Kherson	295 450	132 426	163 024	65	332 767	149 883	182 884	423
Khmelnitsky (Hmilnyk)	262 154	121 083	141 071	86	...	...	...	...
Kirovograd	231 181	104 288	126 893	96	239 253	107 962	131 291	103
Kramatorsk	163 831	72 928	90 903	77	197 392	88 449	108 943	356
Krasny Lutch	82 719	38 155	44 564	58	124 003	57 497	66 506	154
Krementchug	224 912	102 180	122 732	96	...	...	...	...
Krivoy Rog	654 964	294 972	359 992	430	657 760	296 390	361 370	431
KYIV	2 803 716	1 295 137	1 508 579	836	...	...	...	...
Lugansk	422 373	187 593	234 780	257	461 459	206 111	255 348	286
Luts'k	211 644	95 328	116 316	42	...	...	...	...
Lviv	723 605	338 326	385 279	149	751 225	351 409	399 816	171
Lysychansk	104 023	46 935	57 088	76	119 725	54 085	65 640	96
Makijivka	352 227	158 789	193 438	185	390 700	176 633	214 067	426
Mariupol	458 415	208 218	250 197	150	480 263	218 497	261 766	244
Melitopol	156 831	70 894	85 937	43	...	...	...	...
Nikolaev	491 693	222 669	269 024	260	...	...	...	...
Nikopol	120 774	53 710	67 064	50	...	...	...	...
Odessa	997 189	465 200	531 989	162	...	...	...	...
Pavlograd	111 013	50 995	60 018	59	...	...	...	...
Poltava	289 831	132 965	156 866	104	...	...	...	...
Rivne	246 911	113 057	133 854	58	...	...	...	...
Sevastopol	340 735	154 947	185 788	...	381 474	173 812	207 662	864
Sievierodonetsk	109 791	48 887	60 904	32	120 217	53 861	66 356	58
Simferopol	331 936	146 690	185 246	107	356 771	158 116	198 655	107
Slovyansk	115 333	50 262	65 071	61	134 218	58 891	75 327	74
Sumy	268 375	120 965	147 410	111	271 295	122 346	148 949	146
Ternopil	215 636	99 716	115 920	59	...	...	...	...
Uzhhorod	114 789	53 241	61 548	32	...	...	...	...
Vinnitsa	369 860	169 356	200 504	69	...	...	...	...
Yevpatoriya	104 289	46 505	57 784	43	120 473	53 898	66 575	66
Zaporozhye	766 736	346 450	420 286	278	...	...	...	...
Zhytomyr	270 046	124 389	145 657	61	...	...	...	...

8. Population of capital cities and cities of 100 000 or more inhabitants: latest available year, 1996 - 2015
Population des capitales et des villes de 100 000 habitants ou plus : dernière année disponible, 1996 - 2015 (continued - suite)

Continent, country or area, date, code[a] and city / Continent, pays ou zone, date, code[a] et ville	City proper - Ville proprement dite				Urban agglomeration - Agglomération urbaine			
	Population			Surface area - Superficie (km²)	Population			Surface area - Superficie (km²)
	Both sexes - Les deux sexes	Male - Masculin	Female - Féminin		Both sexes - Les deux sexes	Male - Masculin	Female - Féminin	

EUROPE

United Kingdom of Great Britain and Northern Ireland - Royaume-Uni de Grande-Bretagne et d'Irlande du Nord[83]
27 III 2011 (CDJC)

Aberdeen	207 932	102 858	105 078	...	...	...	...	...
Belfast	280 211	134 693	145 518	...	...	...	...	...
Birmingham	1 085 810	534 038	551 772	...	...	...	...	...
Bolton	194 189	95 924	98 265	...	...	...	...	...
Bournemouth	187 503	93 390	94 113	...	...	...	...	...
Bradford	349 561	173 024	176 537	...	...	...	...	...
Brighton and Hove	229 700	115 245	114 455	...	...	...	...	...
Bristol	535 907	265 968	269 939	...	...	...	...	...
Cardiff	335 145	164 427	170 718	...	...	...	...	...
Coventry	325 949	162 069	163 880	...	...	...	...	...
Derby	255 394	126 402	128 992	...	...	...	...	...
Edinburgh	482 005	234 608	247 397	...	...	...	...	...
Glasgow[84]	1 209 143	580 857	628 286	...	...	...	...	...
Kingston-upon-Hull	284 321	141 905	142 416	...	...	...	...	...
Leeds	474 632	233 488	241 144	...	...	...	...	...
Leicester	443 760	218 722	225 038	...	...	...	...	...
Liverpool	552 267	271 342	280 925	...	...	...	...	...
LONDON[85]	8 135 667	4 015 297	4 120 370	...	...	...	...	...
Luton	211 228	105 905	105 323	...	...	...	...	...
Manchester	510 746	256 984	253 762	...	...	...	...	...
Newcastle-upon-Tyne	268 064	134 375	133 689	...	...	...	...	...
Northampton	215 173	105 617	109 556	...	...	...	...	...
Nottingham	289 301	145 855	143 446	...	...	...	...	...
Plymouth	234 982	116 444	118 538	...	...	...	...	...
Portsmouth	238 137	119 369	118 768	...	...	...	...	...
Reading	218 705	109 236	109 469	...	...	...	...	...
Sheffield	518 090	255 755	262 335	...	...	...	...	...
Southampton	253 651	127 630	126 021	...	...	...	...	...
Stoke-on-Trent	270 726	134 642	136 084	...	...	...	...	...
Wolverhampton	210 319	104 047	106 272	...	...	...	...	...

OCEANIA - OCÉANIE

American Samoa - Samoas américaines[23]
1 IV 2010 (CDJC)

PAGO PAGO	3 656	...	...	...	...	...	...	...

Australia - Australie
1 VII 2014 (ESDJ)

Adelaide	1 276 701[86]	627 814[86]	648 887[86]	2 024	...	...	...	...
Brisbane	2 176 799[86]	1 081 185[86]	1 095 614[86]	5 065	...	...	...	...
Cairns	146 778[86]	72 373[86]	74 405[86]	254	...	...	...	...
Canberra-Queanbeyan	422 510[86]	210 337[86]	212 173[86]	482	...	...	...	...
Central Coast	323 079[86]	156 821[86]	166 258[86]	566	...	...	...	...
Darwin	122 571[86]	64 377[86]	58 194[86]	295	...	...	...	...
Geelong	184 182[86]	91 020[86]	93 162[86]	919	...	...	...	...
Gold Coast-Tweed Heads	614 379[86]	300 373[86]	314 006[86]	1 403	...	...	...	...
Greater Adelaide	1 304 631[86]	641 824[86]	662 807[86]	3 258	...	...	...	...
Greater Brisbane	2 274 560[86]	1 130 385[86]	1 144 175[86]	15 826	...	...	...	...
Greater Darwin	140 386[86]	73 725[86]	66 661[86]	3 164	...	...	...	...
Greater Hobart	219 243[86]	108 522[86]	110 721[86]	1 696	...	...	...	...
Greater Melbourne	4 440 328[86]	2 193 542[86]	2 246 786[86]	9 991	...	...	...	...
Greater Perth	2 021 203[86]	1 011 824[86]	1 009 379[86]	6 418	...	...	...	...
Greater Sydney	4 840 628[86]	2 399 534[86]	2 441 094[86]	12 368	...	...	...	...
Hobart	207 663[86]	102 602[86]	105 061[86]	1 213	...	...	...	...
Melbourne	4 269 138[86]	2 108 498[86]	2 160 640[86]	5 679	...	...	...	...
Newcastle-Maitland	430 755[86]	213 962[86]	216 793[86]	1 019	...	...	...	...
Perth	1 945 140[86]	973 244[86]	971 896[86]	3 367	...	...	...	...
Sunshine Coast	297 380[86]	144 191[86]	153 189[86]	1 633	...	...	...	...
Sydney	4 451 841[86]	2 209 478[86]	2 242 363[86]	4 064	...	...	...	...

8. Population of capital cities and cities of 100 000 or more inhabitants: latest available year, 1996 - 2015
Population des capitales et des villes de 100 000 habitants ou plus : dernière année disponible, 1996 - 2015 (continued - suite)

Continent, country or area, date, code[a] and city / Continent, pays ou zone, date, code[a] et ville	City proper - Ville proprement dite				Urban agglomeration - Agglomération urbaine			
	Population			Surface area - Superficie (km²)	Population			Surface area - Superficie (km²)
	Both sexes - Les deux sexes	Male - Masculin	Female - Féminin		Both sexes - Les deux sexes	Male - Masculin	Female - Féminin	
OCEANIA - OCÉANIE								
Australia - Australie								
1 VII 2014 (ESDJ)								
Toowoomba	113 625[86]	55 012[86]	58 613[86]	498	...	...	...	...
Townsville	178 649[86]	89 122[86]	89 527[86]	696	...	...	...	...
Wollongong	289 236[86]	144 030[86]	145 206[86]	572	...	...	...	...
Cook Islands - Îles Cook[87]								
1 XII 2011 (CDFC)								
RAROTONGA	13 095	...	...	...	...	...	...	...
Fiji - Fidji								
16 IX 2007 (CDFC)								
SUVA	74 481	37 032	37 449	...	...	...	...	...
French Polynesia - Polynésie française								
22 VIII 2012 (CDJC)								
PAPEETE	25 763	12 971	12 792	...	...	...	...	...
Guam								
1 VII 2010 (ESDJ)								
AGANA	1 051	...	...	3	...	...	...	...
Kiribati								
7 XII 2005 (CDFC)								
TARAWA	...	...	...	...	40 311	...	...	...
Marshall Islands - Îles Marshall								
3 IV 2011 (CDFC)								
MAJURO	27 797	...	...	...	...	...	...	...
Micronesia (Federated States of) - Micronésie (États fédérés de)								
1 IV 2000 (CDJC)								
PALIKIR	6 227	...	...	...	...	...	...	...
New Caledonia - Nouvelle-Calédonie								
27 VII 2009 (CDFC)								
NOUMEA	97 579	...	...	46	...	...	...	...
New Zealand - Nouvelle-Zélande								
1 VII 2015 (ESDJ)								
Auckland	1 569 900	770 600	799 400	4 938[88]	...	...	...	...
Christchurch	367 800	183 900	183 900	1 415[88]	...	...	...	...
Dunedin	125 800	60 800	65 000	3 287[88]	...	...	...	...
Hamilton	156 800	75 900	81 000	110[88]	...	...	...	...
Lower Hutt	102 000	49 700	52 300	376[88]	...	...	...	...
Napier-Hastings	...	...	...	...	129 700[89]	62 100[89]	67 600[89]	390[88]
Tauranga	124 600	59 400	65 200	134[88]	...	...	...	...
WELLINGTON	203 800	99 600	104 200	290[88]	...	...	...	...
Niue - Nioué								
11 IX 2011 (CDFC)								
ALOFI	639	311	328	...	...	...	...	...
Norfolk Island - Île Norfolk								
1 VII 1997 (ESDF)								
KINGSTON	*800*	...	...	...	...	...	...	...
Northern Mariana Islands - Îles Mariannes septentrionales								
1 IV 2010 (CDFC)								
GARAPAN	3 983	1 953	2 030	...	...	...	...	...
Palau - Palaos								
1 IV 2005 (CDJC)								
KOROR	...	...	...	...	12 676	...	...	...
Papua New Guinea - Papouasie-Nouvelle-Guinée								
9 VII 2000 (CDFC)								
PORT MORESBY	254 158	138 974	115 184	...	...	...	...	...
Pitcairn								
31 XII 2013 (CDJC)								
ADAMSTOWN	49	23	26	...	...	...	...	...
Samoa								
7 XI 2011 (CDFC)								
APIA	36 735	...	...	...	...	...	...	...

8. Population of capital cities and cities of 100 000 or more inhabitants: latest available year, 1996 - 2015
Population des capitales et des villes de 100 000 habitants ou plus : dernière année disponible, 1996 - 2015 (continued - suite)

Continent, country or area, date, code[a] and city Continent, pays ou zone, date, code[a] et ville	City proper - Ville proprement dite				Urban agglomeration - Agglomération urbaine			
	Population			Surface area - Superficie (km²)	Population			Surface area - Superficie (km²)
	Both sexes - Les deux sexes	Male - Masculin	Female - Féminin		Both sexes - Les deux sexes	Male - Masculin	Female - Féminin	
OCEANIA - OCÉANIE								
Solomon Islands - Îles Salomon								
22 XI 2009 (CDFC)								
HONIARA	64 609	...	...	...	80 082	...	...	...
Tonga								
30 XI 2011 (CDJC)								
NUKU'ALOFA	...	...	...	...	36 045	18 100	17 945	...
Tuvalu								
1 XI 2002 (CDFC)								
FUNAFUTI	4 492	2 281	2 211	...	...	...	...	...
Vanuatu								
16 XI 2009 (CDJC)								
PORT VILA	44 039	...	...	...	...	...	...	...
Wallis and Futuna Islands - Îles Wallis et Futuna								
21 VII 2008 (CDFC)								
META-UTU	1 126	...	...	...	...	...	...	...

FOOTNOTES - NOTES

The capital city of each country is shown in capital letters. Figures in italics are estimates of questionnable reliability. For definition of city proper and urban agglomeration, method of evaluation and limitations of data see Technical Notes for this table. - Le nom de la capitale de chaque pays est imprimé en majuscules. Les chiffres en italique sont des estimations dont la fiabilité n'est pas assurée. Pour la définition de la ville proprement dite et de l'agglomération urbaine, et pour les méthodes d'évaluation et les insuffisances de données, voir les notes techniques pour ce tableau.

Italics: estimates which are less reliable. - Italiques : estimations moins sûres.

* Provisional. - Données provisoires.

[a] 'Code' indicates the source of data, as follows:
CDFC - Census, de facto, complete tabulation
CDFS - Census, de facto, sample tabulation
CDJC - Census, de jure, complete tabulation
CDJS - Census, de jure, sample tabulation
SSDF - Sample survey, de facto
SSDJ - Sample survey, de jure
ESDF - Estimates, de facto
ESDJ - Estimates, de jure

Le 'Code' indique la source des données, comme suit :
CDFC - Recensement, population de fait, tabulation complète
CDFS - Recensement, population de fait, tabulation par sondage
CDJC - Recensement, population de droit, tabulation complète
CDJS - Recensement, population de droit, tabulation par sondage
SSDF - Enquête par sondage, population de fait
SSDJ - Enquête par sondage, population de droit
ESDF - Estimations, population de fait
ESDJ - Estimations, population de droit

[1] Data refer to the city proper plus the peri-urban area. - Les données concernent la population de la ville proprement dite et de la zone périurbaine.
[2] Data refer to Greater Monrovia. - Les données concernent la région métropolitaine de Monrovia.
[3] Data refer to the urban commune of Antananarivo. - Pour la commune urbaine de Antananarivo.
[4] Data refer to national projections. - Les données se réfèrent aux projections nationales.
[5] Data refer to District de Bamako. - Les données concernent le district de Bamako.
[6] Excludes the islands of St. Brandon and Agalega. - Non compris les îles St. Brandon et Agalega.

[7] Projections based on the 2002 Population Census. - Projections fondées sur le recensement de la population de 2002.
[8] Data refer to Greater Victoria. - Les données concernent la région métropolitaine de Victoria.
[9] Bloemfontein is the judicial capital, Cape Town is the legislative capital and Pretoria is the administrative capital. - Bloemfontein est la capitale judiciaire, Le Cap est la capitale législative et Pretoria est la capitale administrative.
[10] Data for urban agglomeration refer to Urban Centre (municipalities). - Les données de l'agglomération urbaine se rapportent au centre urbain (commune).
[11] Comprising the Northern Region (former Saguia el Hamra) and Southern Region (former Rio de Oro). - Comprend la région septentrionale (ancien Saguia-el-Hamra) et la région méridionale (ancien Rio de Oro).
[12] Preliminary postcensal estimates. - Estimations post censitaires préliminaires.
[13] Surface area includes interior waters. - La superficie comprend les eaux intérieures.
[14] Data refer to municipalities, which may contain an urban centre as well as rural areas. - Pour municipios qui peuvent comprendre un centre urbain et aussi une zone rurale.
[15] Population statistics are compiled from registers. - Les statistiques de la population sont compilées à partir des registres.
[16] Data refer to Kingston Metropolitan Area. - Données pour la zone métropolitaine de Kingston.
[17] Data refer to projections based on the 2010 Population Census. - Les données se réfèrent aux projections basées sur le recensement de la population de 2010.
[18] Including armed forces stationed in the area. Based on the results of the 2010 Population Census. - Y compris les militaires en garnison sur le territoire. D'après le résultats du recensement de la population de 2010.
[19] Data refer to enumerated household population. - Les données concernent la population des ménages énumérée.
[20] City refers to a type of incorporated place in 49 states and the District of Columbia, that has an elected government and provides a range of government functions and services. Also included among the cities on this list is Urban Honolulu, Hawaii Census Designated Place (CDP), for which the Census Bureau reports data under agreement with the State of Hawaii (instead of the combined city and county of Honolulu). - Par ville, on entend un lieu doté de la personnalité morale dans 49 États et dans le district de Columbia, qui a un gouvernement élu et fournit tout un ensemble de fonctions et de services publics. Sont également inclus Honolulu, lieu chargé du recensement pour Hawaii, pour lequel le Census Bureau établit les données en accord avec l'État de Hawaii (au lieu de la ville et du comté d'Honolulu).
[21] Excluding U.S. Armed Forces overseas and civilian U.S. citizens whose usual place of residence is outside the United States. - Non compris les militaires américains à l'étranger et les civils américains dont le lieu de résidence habituel est en dehors des États-Unis.
[22] Excluding inland water. - Exception faite des eaux intérieures.

²³ Including armed forces stationed in the area. - Y compris les militaires en garnison sur le territoire.

²⁴ Data refer to projections based on the 2010 Population and Housing Census. - Les données se réfèrent aux projections basées sur le recensement 2010 de la population et des logements.

²⁵ The urban agglomeration of Buenos Aires includes the city of Buenos Aires, and the 24 parts of the Buenos Aires province; among them, General San Martín, La Matanza, Lanús, Lomas de Zamora, Morón, Quilmes, San Fernando, San Isidro y Vicente López. - L'agglomération urbaine de Buenos Aires englobe la ville de Buenos Aires et les 24 circonscriptions de la province de Buenos Aires, dont General San Martín, La Matanza, Lanús, Lomas de Zamora, Morón, Quilmes, San Fernando, San Isidro y Vicente López.

²⁶ The urban agglomeration of Tucumán-Tafí Viejo includes San Miguel de Tucumán. - L'agglomération urbaine de Tucumán-Tafí Viejo englobe San Miguel de Tucumán.

²⁷ Excluding interior waters. - Eaux intérieures non comprises.

²⁸ Data exclude the population of the cities of Puente Alto and San Bernardo. - Les données ne comprennent pas la population des villes de Puente Alto et de San Bernardo.

²⁹ Data are revised projections taking into consideration also the results of the 2005 census. - Les données sont des projections révisées tenant compte également des résultats du recensement de 2005.

³⁰ Data excludes "temporary visitors". - Données n'incluant pas les « visiteurs temporaires ».

³¹ The Metropolitan Area of Asunción is made up of Asunción and the 19 Central Department districts. - La zone métropolitaine d'Asunción est composée d'Asunción et de 19 districts du Département central.

³² Estimates based on the 2007 Population Census. - Estimations fondées sur le recensement de la population de 2007.

³³ Data refer to the Province of Lima and the Constitutional Province of Callao. - Les données concernent la province de Lima et la province constitutionnelle de Callao.

³⁴ Excluding foreign diplomatic personnel and their dependants. Data based on the 2008 Population Census. - Non compris le personnel diplomatique étranger et les membres de leur famille les accompagnant. Données fondées sur le recensement de population de 2008.

³⁵ Land area includes inland water (including reservoirs). - La superficie terrestre comprend les eaux intérieures (y compris les réservoirs).

³⁶ Because of rounding, totals are not in all cases the sum of the respective components. - Les chiffres étant arrondis, les totaux ne correspondent pas toujours rigoureusement à la somme des composants respectifs.

³⁷ The urban agglomeration of Lefkosia is composed of Lefkosia municipality, Agios Dometios, Egkomi, Strovolos, Aglangia, Lakatameia, Anthoupoli, Latsia and Geri. - L'agglomération urbaine de Lefkosia est composée de la municipalité de Lefkosia et Agios Dometios, Egkomi, Strovolos, Aglangia, Lakatameia, Anthoupoli, Latsia et Geri.

³⁸ The urban agglomeration of Lemesos is composed of Lemesos municipality, Mesa Geitonia, Agios Athanasios, Germasogeia, Pano Polemidia, Ypsonas, Kato Polemidia, and parts of Mouttagiaka, Agios Tychon, Parekklisia, Monagrouli, Moni, Pyrgos and Tserkezoi. - L'agglomération urbaine de Lemesos est composée de la municipalité de Lemesos et Mesa Geitonia, Agios Athanasios, Germasogeia, Pano Polemidia, Ypsonas, Kato Polemidia, et certaines parties des Mouttagiaka, Agios Tychon, Parekklisia, Monagrouli, Moni, Pyrgos et Tserkezoi.

³⁹ Includes data for the Indian-held part of Jammu and Kashmir, the final status of which has not yet been determined. - Y compris les données pour la partie du Jammu et du Cachemire occupée par l'Inde dont le statut définitif n'a pas encore été déterminé.

⁴⁰ Data for urban agglomeration include New Delhi. - Les données pour l'agglomération urbaine y compris New Delhi.

⁴¹ Data for urban agglomeration include Bally, Baranagar, Barrackpur, Bhatpara, Calcutta Municipal Corporation, Chandan Nagar, Garden Reach, Houghly-Chinsura, Howrah, Jadarpur, Kamarhati, Naihati, Panihati, Serampore, South Dum Dum, South Suburban, and Titagarh. - Les données pour l'agglomération urbaine y compris Bally, Baranagar, Barrackpur, Bhatpara, Calcutta Municipal Corporation, Chandan Nagar, Garden Reach, Houghly Chinsura, Howrah, Jadarpur, Kamarhati, Naihati, Panihati, Serampopre, South Dum Dum, South Suburban et Titagarh.

⁴² Included in urban agglomeration of Delhi. Data refer to the New Delhi Municipal Council. - Comprise dans l'agglomération urbaine de Delhi. Les données se rapportent au New Delhi Municipal Council.

⁴³ Data refer to "Baghdad Al-Jedeeda Nahia" - Les données concernent le district Al-Jadeeda de Bagdad (Baghdad Al-Jedeeda Nahiya).

⁴⁴ Designation and data provided by Israel. The position of the United Nations on the question of Jerusalem is contained in General Assembly resolution 181 (II) and subsequent resolutions of the General Assembly and the Security Council concerning this question. Including East Jerusalem. - Appelation de données fournies par Israel. La position des Nations Unies concernant la question de Jérusalem est décrite dans la resolution 181 (II) de l'Assemblée générale et résolutions ultérieures de l'Assemblée générale et du Conseil de sécurité sur cette question. Y compris Jérusalem-Est.

⁴⁵ Excluding diplomatic personnel outside the country and foreign military and civilian personnel and their dependants stationed in the area. - Non compris le personnel diplomatique hors du pays ni les militaires et agents civils étrangers en poste sur le territoire et les membres de leur famille les accompagnant.

⁴⁶ Land areas are based on the "Municipalities Area Statistics of Japan, 2010" published by the Geospatial Information Authority of Japan, Ministry of Land, Infrastructure, Transport and Tourism. The areas with indefinable boundaries are estimated by the Statistics Bureau, Ministry of Internal Affairs and Communications. - Les zones terrestres sont déterminées selon les statistiques relatives aux municipalités du Japon en 2010, publiées par l'Autorité japonaise d'information géospatiale du Ministère de l'aménagement foncier, des infrastructures, des transports et du tourisme. Les zones sans délimitations définissables font l'objet d'une estimation réalisée par le Bureau de la statistique du Ministère des affaires intérieures et des communications.

⁴⁷ Excluding diplomatic personnel outside the country and foreign military and civilian personnel and their dependants stationed in the area. Data for Tokyo refer to 23 ku (wards) of Tokyo. - Non compris le personnel diplomatique hors du pays ni les militaires et agents civils étrangers en poste sur le territoire et les membres de leur famille les accompagnant. Données relatives à Tokyo concernant 23 ku (arrondissements de la ville).

⁴⁸ Data refer to annual average population. - Les données correspondent à la population annuelle moyenne.

⁴⁹ Based on the results of the 2005 Population and Housing Census. - Données fondées sur les résultats du recensement de la population et de l'habitat de 2005.

⁵⁰ Source: Living conditions of household survey, October 2011 to September 2012. - Source: Enquête sur les conditions de vie des ménages, octobre 2011 à septembre 2012.

⁵¹ Estimates based on the adjusted Population and Housing Census of 2010. - Les estimations sont fondée sur les résultats ajustées du recensement de la population et de l'habitat de 2010.

⁵² Including population from all eight townships. - Y compris la population des huit municipalités.

⁵³ Excluding data for the Pakistan-held part of Jammu and Kashmir, the final status of which has not yet been determined, and for Junagardh, Manavadar, Gilgit and Baltistan. - Non compris les données pour la partie de Jammu-Cachemire occupée par le Pakistan dont le status definitif n'a pas encore été déterminé, et le Junagardh, le Manavadar, le Gilgit et le Baltistan.

⁵⁴ Data exclude residents who have been away from Singapore for a continuous period of 12 months or longer as at the reference date. - Non compris les résidents hors de Singapour pour une période ininterrompue de 12 mois ou plus avant de la date de référence.

⁵⁵ The land area of Singapore comprises the mainland and other islands. - La superficie terrestre de Singapour comprend l'île principale et les autres îles.

⁵⁶ The Population and Housing Census 2001 did not cover the whole area of the country due to the security problems; data refer to the 18 districts for which the census was completed only (in three districts it was not possible to conduct the census at all and in four districts it was partially conducted). - Le recensement de la population et du logement de 2001 n'a pas été réalisé sur la superficie totale du pays à cause de problèmes de sécurité; les données ne concernent que les 18 districts entièrement recensés (3 districts n'ont pas été recensés du tout, et 4 ont été recensés en partie).

⁵⁷ Designation and data provided by the State of Palestine. The position of the United Nations on the question of Jerusalem is contained in General Assembly resolution 181 (II) and subsequent resolutions of the General Assembly and the Security Council concerning this question. - Appellation de données fournies par l'État de Palestine. La position des Nations Unies concernant la question de Jérusalem est décrite dans la résolution 181 (II) de l'Assemblée générale et résolutions ultérieures de l'Assemblée générale et du Conseil de sécurité sur cette question.

⁵⁸ Data based on address-based population registration system. - Les données sont basées sur le registre national de la population basé sur l'adresse.

⁵⁹ Data refer to resident population. - Les données concernent la population résidente.

⁶⁰ Data include Anderlecht and Schaerbeek. - Les données comprennent Anderlecht et Schaerbeek.

⁶¹ Excluding Faeroe Islands and Greenland shown separately, if available. - Non compris les Iles Féroé et le Groenland, qui font l'objet de rubriques distinctes, si disponible.

⁶² Land area refers to built over area. - Partie du territoire désigne une zone bâtie.

⁶³ Urban Agglomeration refers to Tórshavn, Hoyvík, Argir and Hvítanes. - Agglomération urbaine fait référence à Tórshavn, Hoyvík, Argir et Hvitanes.

[64] Urban Agglomeration refers to Tórshavn, Hoyvík, Argir and Hvítanes. Land area refers to built over area. - Agglomération urbaine fait référence à Tórshavn, Hoyvík, Argir et Hvitanes. Partie du territoire désigne une zone bâtie.

[65] Population statistics are compiled from registers. Excluding Åland Islands. - Les statistiques de la population sont compilées à partir des registres. Non compris les Îles d'Åland.

[66] City proper refers to commune or municipality. - La ville proprement dite se rapporte à la commune ou à la municipalité.

[67] The city of Aix-en-Provence is part of the urban agglomeration of Marseille. - La ville d'Aix-en-Provence fait partie de l'agglomération urbaine de Marseille.

[68] The communes of Argenteuil, Boulogne-Billancourt and Montreuil are parts of the urban agglomeration of Paris. - Les communes de Argenteuil, Boulogne-Billancourt et Montreuil font partie de l'agglomération urbaine de Paris.

[69] Data based on the 2011 Census. - Données fondées sur le recensement de 2011.

[70] Excluding military personnel, visitors and transients. - Non compris les militaires, ni les visiteurs et transients.

[71] Data refer to the Vatican City State. - Les données se rapportent à l'Etat de la Cité du Vatican.

[72] Surface area is 0.44 km². - Superficie: 0,44 km².

[73] The boundaries of the city are related to the boundaries of the respective commune. - Les limites de la ville correspondent aux limites de la commune respective.

[74] Data refer to registered resident population. - Les données concernent la population enregistrée résidente.

[75] The urban agglomeration of the capital area includes the following communes: Bessastaðahreppur, Garðabær, Hafnarfjörður, Kjósarhreppur, Kópavogur, Mosfellsbær ,Reykjavík, Seltjarnarnes. Data refer to registered resident population. - L'agglomération urbaine de la capitale comprend les communes suivantes : Bessastaðahreppur, Garðabær, Hafnarfjörður, Kjósarhreppur, Kópavogur, Mosfellsbær ,Reykjavík, Seltjarnarnes. Les données concernent la population enregistrée résidente.

[76] Figures for male and female population do not add up to the figure for total population, because they exclude 119 persons of unknown sex. - Les chiffres relatifs à la population masculine et féminine ne correspondent pas au chiffre de la population totale, parce que l'on en a exclu 119 personnes de sexe inconnu.

[77] City is defined as an administratively separated area entitled to civil (municipal) rights. - Une ville est définie comme une zone administrativement distincte dotée de droits municipaux.

[78] Land area includes inland water. - La zone terrestre comprend les eaux intérieures.

[79] Land area includes inland water. The municipality of Lisboa includes the parish of Parque das Nações as of 30 September 2013. - La zone terrestre comprend les eaux intérieures. La municipalité de Lisbonne comprend la paroisse de Parque das Nações à compter du 30 septembre 2013.

[80] Excludes data for Kosovo and Metohia. - Sans les données pour le Kosovo et Metohie.

[81] Excludes data for Kosovo and Metohia. Data for urban agglomeration refer to communes which are administrative divisions. - Sans les données pour le Kosovo et Metohie. Les données pour l'agglomération urbaine se rapportent aux communes qui sont des divisions administrative.

[82] Data for urban agglomeration refer to communes which are administrative divisions. - Les données pour l'agglomération urbaine se rapportent aux communes qui sont des divisions administrative.

[83] Excluding Channel Islands (Guernsey and Jersey) and Isle of Man, shown separately, if available. - Non compris les îles Anglo-Normandes (Guernesey et Jersey) et l'île de Man, qui font l'objet de rubriques distinctes, si disponible.

[84] Data refer to Greater Glasgow. - Les données concernent la région métropolitaine de Glasgow.

[85] Data refer to Greater London. - Les données concernent la région métropolitaine de London.

[86] Estimates based on the Australian Statistical Geography Standard (ASGS). The populations for Greater Sydney, Melbourne, Brisbane, Perth, Adelaide, Hobart and Darwin are based on the 'Greater Capital City Statistical Area (GCCSA)' statistical area level. All other cities are based on the 'Significant Urban Areas (SUA)' statistical area level. It is not possible to distinguish for all regions between 'city proper' and 'urban agglomeration' areas, therefore data has been included under 'city proper'. - Chiffres estimatifs basés sur la norme géographique australienne de statistique (Australian Statistical Geography Standard - ASGS). Les chiffres de population pour la région métropolitaine de Sydney, Melbourne, Brisbane, Perth, Adelaide, Hobart et Darwin sont basés sur le niveau de division statistique des grandes capitales régionales [Greater Capital City Statistical Area GCCSA)]. Pour toutes les autres villes, les chiffres sont basés sur le niveau de division statistique des grandes zones urbaines [Significant Urban Areas - SUA). Il n'est pas possible de faire la distinction dans toutes les régions entre « ville proprement dite » et « agglomération urbaine », et les données ont donc été incluses dans la catégorie « ville proprement dite ».

[87] Excluding Niue, shown separately, which is part of Cook Islands, but because of remoteness is administered separately. - Non compris Nioué, qui fait l'objet d'une rubrique distincte et qui fait partie des îles Cook, mais qui, en raison de son éloignement, est administrée séparément.

[88] 1. Land area excludes inlet, inland water and oceanic areas. 2. A city is a territorial authority which is a distinct entity, is predominantly urban in character, has a minimum population of 50,000 and is a major centre of activity within its parent region. 3. Urban agglomerations refer to main urban areas that are centres with populations of 30,000 or more. City proper: due to the establishment of new Auckland council in 2011, amalgamating former Auckland cities, including Manukau city, North Shore city, and Waktakere city, separate population estimates for these cities are not available. Napier-Hastings consist of two separate territorial authorities. Napier is a city, while Hastings is a district based on the New Zealand Standard Areas Classification. Urban Agglomeration: all urban agglomerations are presented based on the New Zealand 'Urban Areas' classification, which are statistically defined areas with no administrative or legal basis. The 'Urban area classification' is designed to identify concentrated urban or semi-urban settlements without the distortions of administrative boundaries. Therefore they do not necessarily follow the UN definitions of 'Urban agglomeration'. Some urban areas consist a part of a city (for Auckland, Christchurch, Dunedin), and some are made up from parts over multiple cities/districts (Napier-Hastings, Tauranga, Wellington). For example, Napier-Hastings consist of two separate territorial authorities. Napier is a city, while Hastings is a district. This explains why the data on city proper is greater than the data on urban agglomeration for some areas. - 1. La superficie terrestre ne comprend pas les bras de mer, eaux intérieures et zones océaniques. 2. Une ville est une entité territoriale distincte à caractère essentiellement urbain, comptant au minimum 50 000 habitants et constitue un pôle qui rayonne sur toute la région environnante. 3. Les agglomérations urbaines sont des établissements humains importants comptant 30 000 habitants ou plus. La ville : avec la création de la nouvelle agglomération d'Auckland en 2011, qui regroupe également Manukau, North Shore et Waktakere, il n'y a plus d'estimations démographiques distinctes pour ces différentes villes. Napier-Hastings comprend deux entités territoriales. Napier est une ville, et Hastings est un district selon les critères du classement néozélandais des zones. L'agglomération urbaine : toutes les agglomérations urbaines sont présentées selon le classement néozélandais (zones statistiquement définies hors critères administratifs et juridiques). Le classement des zones urbaines permet de recenser les établissements urbains ou semi-urbains sans les distorsions liées aux frontières administratives. Il ne correspond donc pas forcément à la définition de ce qui constitue une agglomération urbaine pour l'ONU. Certaines zones urbaines sont pour partie des villes (Auckland, Christchurch, Dunedin), et certaines sont des mosaïques de plusieurs villes/districts (Napier-Hastings, Tauranga, Wellington). Ainsi, Napier-Hastings comprend deux entités distinctes, Napier est une ville, et Hastings est un district. C'est la raison pour laquelle il y a parfois plus de données sur la ville elle-même que sur l'agglomération urbaine.

[89] Napier-Hastings consist of two separate territorial authorities. Napier is a city, while Hastings is a district based on the New Zealand Standard Areas Classification. - Napier-Hastings comprend deux entités territoriales. Napier est une ville, et Hastings est un district selon les critères du classement néozélandais des zones.

Table 9 - Demographic Yearbook 2015

Table 9 presents live births and crude birth rates by urban/rural residence for as many years as possible between 2011 and 2015.

Description of variables: Live birth is defined as the complete expulsion or extraction from its mother of a product of conception, irrespective of the duration of pregnancy, which after such separation, breathes or shows any other evidence of life such as beating of the heart, pulsation of the umbilical cord, or definite movements of voluntary muscles, whether or not the umbilical cord has been cut or the placenta is attached; each product of such a birth is considered live-born[1].

Statistics on the number of live births are obtained from civil registers unless otherwise noted. For those countries or areas where civil registration statistics on live births are considered reliable the birth rates shown have been calculated on the basis of registered live births.

For certain countries, there is a discrepancy between the total number of live births shown in this table and those shown in subsequent tables for the same year. Usually this discrepancy arises because the total number of live births occurring in a given year is revised but not the remaining tabulations.

Rate computation: Crude birth rates are the annual number of live births per 1 000 mid-year population.

Rates by urban/rural residence are the annual number of live births, in the appropriate urban or rural category, per 1 000 corresponding mid-year population. Rates are calculated only for data considered complete, that is, coded with a "C" and for estimates and live births statistics for the 12 month period prior to the census date, coded with a "|". These rates are calculated by the Statistics Division of the United Nations based on the appropriate reference population (for example: total population, nationals only, etc.) if known and available. If the reference population is not known or unavailable, the total population is used to calculate the rates. Therefore, if the population that is used to calculate the rates is different from the correct reference population, the rates presented might under- or overstate the true situation in a country or area.

Rates presented in this table are limited to those countries or areas having a minimum number of 30 live births in a given year.

Reliability of data: Each country or area has been asked to indicate the estimated completeness of the live births recorded in its civil register. These national assessments are indicated by the quality codes "C" and "U" that appear in the first column of this table.

"C" indicates that the data are estimated to be virtually complete, that is, representing at least 90 per cent of the live births occurring each year, whereas "U" indicates that data are estimated to be incomplete, that is, representing less than 90 per cent of the live births occurring each year. A third code "..." indicates that no information was provided regarding completeness.

Data from civil registers that are reported as incomplete or of unknown completeness (coded "U" or "...") are considered unreliable. They appear in italics in this table and rates are not calculated for these data.

These quality codes apply only to data from civil registers. If data from other sources are presented, the symbol "|" is shown instead of the quality code. For more information about the quality of vital statistics data in general, and the information available on the basis of the completeness estimates in particular, see section 4.2 of the Technical Notes.

Limitations: Statistics on live births are subject to the same qualifications as have been set forth for vital statistics in general and birth statistics in particular as discussed in section 4 of the Technical Notes.

The reliability of data, an indication of which is described above, is an important factor in considering the limitations. In addition, some live births are tabulated by date of registration and not by date of occurrence; these have been indicated by a plus sign "+". Whenever the lag between the date of occurrence and date of registration is prolonged and, therefore, a large proportion of the live birth registrations are delayed, birth statistics for any given year may be seriously affected.

Another factor that limits international comparability is the practice of some countries or areas not to include in live birth statistics infants who were born alive but died before the registration of the birth or within the first 24 hours of life, thus underestimating the total number of life births. Statistics of this type are footnoted.

In addition, it should be noted that rates are affected also by the quality and limitations of the population estimates that are used in their computation. The problems of under-enumeration or over-enumeration and, to some extent, the differences in definition of total population have been discussed in section 3 of the Technical Notes dealing with population data in general, and specific information pertaining to individual countries or areas is given in the footnotes to table 3.

The rates estimated from the results of sample surveys are subject to possibilities of considerable error as a result of omissions in reporting of births, or as a result of erroneous reporting of births that occurred outside the reference period. However, rates estimated from sample surveys have the advantage of the availability of a built-in and strictly corresponding population base.

It should be emphasized that crude birth rates - like crude death, marriage and divorce rates - may be seriously affected by the age-sex structure of the populations to which they relate. Nevertheless, they do provide a simple measure of the level of and changes in fertility.

The urban/rural classification of birth may refer to the residence of mother or the place of delivery, according to the national practice and it is provided by each country or area. In addition, the comparability of data by urban/rural residence is affected by the national definition of urban and rural used in tabulating these data. It is assumed, in the absence of specific information to the contrary, that the definitions of urban and rural used in connection with the national population census were also used in the compilation of the vital statistics for each country or area. However, it cannot be ruled out that, for a given country or area, different definitions of urban and rural are used for the vital statistics data and the population census data respectively. When known, the definitions of urban used in national population census are presented at the end of the technical notes to table 6. As discussed in detail in the technical notes to table 6, these definitions vary considerably from one area or country to another. Urban/rural differentials in vital rates may also be affected by whether the vital events have been tabulated in terms of place of occurrence or place of usual residence. This problem is discussed in more detail in section 4.1.4.1 of the Technical notes.

Earlier data: Live births have been shown in each issue of the *Demographic Yearbook*. Information on the years and specific topics covered is presented in the Historical Index.

NOTES

[1] *Principles and Recommendations for a Vital Statistics System Revision 3,* Sales No. E.13.XVII.10, United Nations, New York, 2014.

Tableau 9 – *Annuaire démographique 2015*

Le tableau 9 présente des données sur les naissances vivantes et les taux bruts de natalité selon le lieu de résidence (zone urbaine ou rurale) pour le plus grand nombre d'années possible entre 2011 et 2015.

Description des variables : La naissance vivante est l'expulsion ou l'extraction complète du corps de la mère, indépendamment de la durée de gestation, d'un produit de la conception qui, après cette séparation, respire ou manifeste tout autre signe de vie, tel que battement de cœur, pulsation du cordon ombilical ou contraction effective d'un muscle soumis à l'action de la volonté, que le cordon ombilical ait été coupé ou non et que le placenta soit ou non demeuré attaché ; tout produit d'une telle naissance est considéré comme « enfant né vivant »[1].

Sauf indication contraire, les statistiques relatives au nombre de naissances vivantes sont établies sur la base des registres de l'état civil. Pour les pays ou zones où les statistiques obtenues auprès des services de l'état civil sont jugées sûres, les taux de natalité indiqués ont été calculés par la Division de statistique de l'ONU d'après les naissances vivantes enregistrées.

Pour quelques pays il y a une discordance entre le nombre total des décès présenté dans ce tableau et ceux présentés après pour la même année. Habituellement ces différences apparaissent lorsque le nombre total des décès pour une certaine année a été révisé alors que les autres tabulations ne l'ont pas été.

Calcul des taux : Les taux bruts de natalité représentent le nombre annuel de naissances vivantes pour 1 000 habitants au milieu de l'année.

Les taux selon le lieu de résidence (zone urbaine ou rurale) représentent le nombre annuel de naissances vivantes, classées selon la catégorie urbaine ou rurale appropriée pour 1 000 habitants au milieu de l'année. Les taux ont été calculés seulement pour les données considérées complètes, c'est-à-dire celles associées au code « C », ainsi que pour les estimations et les statistiques des naissances vivantes dans la periode des douze mois précédante la date de recensement associées au code « | ». Ces taux sont calculés par la division de statistique des Nations Unies sur la base de la population de référence adéquate (par exemple : population totale, nationaux seulement, etc.) si connue et disponible. Si la population de référence n'est pas connue ou n'est pas disponible, la population totale est utilisée pour calculer les taux. Par conséquent, si la population utilisée pour calculer les taux est différente de la population de référence adéquate, les taux présentés sont susceptibles de sous ou sur estimer la situation réelle d'un pays ou d'un territoire.

Les taux présentés dans ce tableau se rapportent seulement aux pays ou zones où l'on a enregistré un nombre minimal de 30 naissances vivantes au cours d'une année donnée.

Fiabilité des données : Il a été demandé à chaque pays ou zone d'indiquer le degré estimatif de complétude des données sur les naissances vivantes figurant dans ses registres d'état civil. Ces évaluations nationales sont signalées par les codes de qualité "C" et "U" qui apparaissent dans la deuxième colonne du tableau.

La lettre "C" indique que les données sont jugées à peu près complètes, c'est-à-dire qu'elles représentent au moins 90 p. 100 des naissances vivantes survenues chaque année ; la lettre "U" signifie que les données sont jugées incomplètes, c'est-à-dire qu'elles représentent moins de 90 p. 100 des naissances vivantes survenues chaque année. Un troisième code, "...", indique qu'aucun renseignement n'a été communiqué quant à la complétude des données.

Les données provenant des registres de l'état civil qui sont déclarées incomplètes ou dont le degré de complétude n'est pas connu (code "U" ou "...") sont jugées douteuses. Elles apparaissent en italique dans le tableau. Les taux pour ces données ne sont pas calculés.

Les codes de qualité ne s'appliquent qu'aux données provenant des registres de l'état civil. Si l'on présente des données autres que celles de l'état civil, le signe "|" est utilisé à la place du code de qualité. Pour plus de précisions sur la qualité des données reposant sur les statistiques de l'état civil en général et les estimations de complétude en particulier, voir la section 4.2 des Notes techniques.

Insuffisance des données : Les statistiques concernant les naissances vivantes appellent toutes les réserves qui ont été formulées à propos des statistiques de l'état civil en général et des statistiques des naissances en particulier (voir la section 4 des Notes techniques).

La fiabilité des données, au sujet de laquelle des indications ont été fournies plus haut, est un facteur important. Il faut également tenir compte du fait que, dans certains cas, les données relatives aux naissances vivantes sont exploitées selon la date de l'enregistrement et non selon la date de l'événement ; ces cas ont été signalés par le signe '+'. Chaque fois que le décalage entre l'événement et son enregistrement est grand et qu'une forte proportion des naissances vivantes fait l'objet d'un enregistrement tardif, les statistiques des naissances vivantes pour une année donnée peuvent être considérablement faussées.

Un autre facteur qui nuit à la comparabilité internationale est la pratique de certains pays ou zones qui consiste à ne pas inclure dans les statistiques des naissances vivantes les enfants nés vivants mais décédés avant l'enregistrement de leur naissance ou dans les 24 heures qui ont suivi la naissance, pratique qui conduit à sous-estimer le nombre total de naissances vivantes. Lorsque ce facteur a joué, cela a été signalé en note à la fin du tableau.

La qualité et les limitations des estimations concernant la population ont également une incidence sur le calcul des taux. Les problèmes liés au sur-dénombrement ou au sous-dénombrement et, dans une certaine mesure, aux différences dans la définition de la population totale ont été abordés à la section 3 des Notes techniques relative aux données sur la population en général et des précisions sur certains pays ou zones sont données dans les notes se rapportant au tableau 3.

Les taux estimatifs fondés sur les résultats d'enquêtes par sondage comportent des possibilités d'erreurs considérables dues soit à des omissions dans les déclarations, soit au fait que l'on a déclaré à tort des naissances survenues en réalité hors de la période considérée. Toutefois, les taux estimatifs fondés sur les résultats d'enquêtes par sondage présentent un gros avantage : le chiffre de population utilisé comme base est, par définition, rigoureusement correspondant.

Il faut souligner que les taux bruts de natalité, de même que les taux bruts de mortalité, de nuptialité et de divortialité, peuvent varier très sensiblement selon la structure par âge et par sexe de la population à laquelle ils se rapportent. Ils offrent néanmoins un moyen simple de mesurer le niveau et l'évolution de la natalité.

La classification des naissances selon le lieu de résidence (zone urbaine ou rurale) peut se rapporter au lieu de résidence de la mère ou au lieu d'occurrence et correspond à celle indiquée par chaque pays ou zone. En outre, la comparabilité des données selon le lieu de résidence (zone urbaine ou rurale) peut être limitée par les définitions nationales des termes « urbain » et « rural » utilisées pour la mise en tableaux de ces données. En l'absence d'indications contraires, on a supposé que les mêmes définitions avaient servi pour le recensement national de la population et pour l'établissement des statistiques de l'état civil pour chaque pays ou zone. Toutefois, il n'est pas exclu que, pour une zone ou un pays donné, des définitions différentes aient été retenues. Les définitions du terme « urbain » utilisées pour les recensements nationaux de population ont été présentées à la fin des notes techniques du tableau 6 lorsqu'elles étaient connues. Comme on l'a précisé dans les notes techniques relatives au tableau 6, ces définitions varient considérablement d'un pays ou d'une zone à l'autre. La différence entre ces taux pour les zones urbaines et rurales pourra aussi être faussée selon que les faits d'état civil auront été classés d'après le lieu de l'événement ou le lieu de résidence habituel. Ce problème est examiné plus en détail à la section 4.1.4.1 des Notes techniques.

Données publiées antérieurement : Les différentes éditions de l'*Annuaire démographique* contiennent des données sur les naissances vivantes. Pour plus de précisions concernant les années et les sujets pour lesquels des données ont été publiées, se reporter à l'index historique.

NOTES

[1] *Principes et recommandations pour un système de statistique de l'état civil, troisième révision,* numéro de vente : E.13.XVII.10, publication des Nations Unies, New York, 2014.

9. Live births and crude birth rates, by urban/rural residence: 2011 - 2015
Naissances vivantes et taux bruts de natalité selon la résidence, urbaine/rurale : 2011 - 2015

Continent, country or area, and urban/rural residence / Continent, pays ou zone et résidence, urbaine/rurale	Co-de[a]	Number - Nombre					Rate - Taux				
		2011	2012	2013	2014	2015	2011	2012	2013	2014	2015
AFRICA - AFRIQUE											
Algeria - Algérie[1]											
Total	C	909 787	978 233	962 722	1 014 248	1 040 285	24.8	26.1	25.1	25.9	26.0
Benin - Bénin[2]											
Total	I	366 889	376 439	...	...	...	40.5	40.2	...	...	...
Botswana											
Total[3]	U	39 368	40 856	...	...	...	...	...	...	...	...
Total[4]	+U	...	...	44 794	41 741	...	...	...	...	...	...
Burundi[5]											
Total	+U	216 398	221 289	248 395							
Djibouti											
Total	U	10 871	...	...	...	...	...	...	...	...	...
Egypt - Égypte											
Total	+C	2 442 094	2 629 769	2 621 902	2 720 495	2 696 231	30.3	31.9	31.0	31.3	30.3
Urban - Urbaine	+C	942 639	1 009 952	1 186 887	1 228 275	...	27.3	28.6	32.8	33.1	...
Rural - Rurale	+C	1 499 455	1 619 817	1 435 015	1 492 220	...	32.6	34.3	29.6	30.0	...
Ghana[6]											
Total	+U	...	475 731	463 409	...	...	...	...	...	...	...
Guinea - Guinée											
Total	+U	...	...	205 658	...	...	...	...	...	...	...
Kenya											
Total	U	771 150	801 815	870 599	954 254	...	...	...	...	...	...
Lesotho											
Total	+U	3 931	1 718	...	...	...	...	...	...	...	...
Mauritius - Maurice[7]											
Total	+C	14 701	14 494	13 488	13 283	12 640	11.7	11.5	10.7	10.5	10.0
Urban - Urbaine	+C	5 586	5 416	5 059	5 158	5 150	11.0	10.6	9.7	10.0	10.0
Rural - Rurale	+C	9 115	9 078	8 429	8 125	7 490	12.3	12.2	11.4	10.9	10.1
Mayotte											
Total	C	...	...	...	7 306	...	...	...	...	33.2	...
Mozambique[8]											
Total	U	...	624 523	746 185	794 718	...	...	...	...	...	...
Namibia - Namibie[9]											
Total	I	61 523	...	...	...	...	29.1	...	...	...	...
Urban - Urbaine	I	26 836	...	...	...	...	29.8	...	...	...	...
Rural - Rurale	I	34 687	...	...	...	...	28.5	...	...	...	...
Niger											
Total	+U	198 499	...	...	...	...	...	...	...	...	...
Reunion - Réunion[10]											
Total	C	...	...	...	14 095	...	...	...	...	16.8	...
Rwanda											
Total	U	406 838	404 067	...	...	...	...	...	...	...	...
Saint Helena ex. dep. - Sainte-Hélène sans dép.											
Total	C	34	32	35	48	...	8.0	7.8	8.3	10.9	...
Sao Tome and Principe - Sao Tomé-et-Principe											
Total	C	5 232	5 173	...	...	...	31.4	27.6	...	...	...
Senegal - Sénégal[11]											
Total	I	464 464	471 629	478 898	...	...	36.2	35.7	35.5	...	...
Seychelles											
Total	+C	1 625	1 645	1 566	1 557	1 592	18.6	18.6	17.4	17.0	17.0
Sierra Leone											
Total	...	117 207	147 958	...	...	...	...	...	...	...	...
Urban - Urbaine	...	16 270	18 392	...	...	...	...	...	...	...	...
Rural - Rurale	...	100 937	129 566	...	...	...	...	...	...	...	...
South Africa - Afrique du Sud											
Total	U	1 023 160	1 020 088	1 001 195	988 007	...	...	...	...	...	...
Tunisia - Tunisie											
Total	C	201 120	214 909	*221 147	*225 887	...	18.8	19.9	*20.3	*20.5	...
United Republic of Tanzania - République Unie de Tanzanie											
Total	...	1 687 203	1 694 943	...	...	...	...	...	...	...	...

9. Live births and crude birth rates, by urban/rural residence: 2011 - 2015
Naissances vivantes et taux bruts de natalité selon la résidence, urbaine/rurale : 2011 - 2015 (continued - suite)

Continent, country or area, and urban/rural residence / Continent, pays ou zone et résidence, urbaine/rurale	Co-de[a]	Number - Nombre					Rate - Taux				
		2011	2012	2013	2014	2015	2011	2012	2013	2014	2015

AMERICA, NORTH - AMÉRIQUE DU NORD

Anguilla											
Total	+C	185	192	165	151	165	13.6	14.0	11.9	10.6	11.2
Antigua and Barbuda - Antigua-et-Barbuda											
Total	+C	1 257	1 187	...	...	...	14.2	...	...	...	...
Aruba											
Total	C	1 236	1 288	1 346	1 376	1 244	12.0	12.3	12.7	12.8	11.4
Bahamas											
Total	+U	*4 747*	*4 469*	*4 330*	**4 196*	...	...	...	...	...	...
Barbados - Barbade											
Total	+C	3 283	3 185	3 020	2 902	...	11.8	11.5	10.9	10.5	...
Belize											
Total	U	*7 217*	...	...	...	...	...	...	...	...	...
Bermuda - Bermudes[12]											
Total	C	670	648	648	574	583	10.6	10.4	10.5	9.3	9.4
British Virgin Islands - Îles Vierges britanniques											
Total	C	333	286	277	280	266	11.8	10.1	9.7	...	...
Canada[13]											
Total	C	377 897	382 980	386 044	*388 729	...	11.0	11.0	11.0	*10.9	...
Cayman Islands - Îles Caïmanes											
Total	C	800	759	705	711	649	14.5	13.5	12.5	12.5	11.0
Costa Rica											
Total	C	73 459	73 326	70 550	71 793	*71 819	16.0	15.8	15.0	15.0	*14.9
Cuba											
Total	C	133 067	125 674	125 880	122 643	125 064	11.9	11.2	11.2	10.9	11.1
Urban - Urbaine	C	102 342	98 301	98 894	96 930	...	12.2	11.6	11.5	11.2	...
Rural - Rurale	C	30 725	27 373	26 986	25 713	...	11.1	10.2	10.4	9.9	...
Curaçao											
Total	C	1 974	2 039	1 962	1 963	1 874	13.1	13.4	12.8	12.6	11.9
Dominica - Dominique											
Total	+C	944	951	931	858	...	13.3	13.4	13.1	12.0	...
Dominican Republic - République dominicaine											
Total	U	*158 955*	*150 581*	*148 719*	*138 224*	...	...	...	...	...	...
Urban - Urbaine[14]	U	*129 092*	*122 458*	*123 577*	*117 799*	...	...	...	...	...	...
Rural - Rurale[14]	U	*27 996*	*26 347*	*23 946*	*20 072*	...	...	...	...	...	...
El Salvador[15]											
Total	C	109 384	110 843	...	...	...	17.6	17.7	...	...	...
Urban - Urbaine	C	75 495	75 808	...	...	...	18.8	18.5	...	...	...
Rural - Rurale	C	33 889	35 035	...	...	...	15.4	16.2	...	...	...
Greenland - Groenland											
Total	C	821	786	820	805	854	14.5	13.8	14.5	14.3	15.2
Urban - Urbaine	C	705	654	697	703	719	14.7	13.6	14.5	14.6	14.9
Rural - Rurale	C	116	132	123	102	135	13.4	15.4	14.9	12.7	17.2
Grenada - Grenade											
Total	+C	1 812	1 661	1 838	...	...	17.0	15.4	16.9	...	...
Guadeloupe[10]											
Total	C	5 384	5 233	5 069	5 001	...	13.3	13.0	12.6	12.5	...
Guatemala											
Total	C	373 692	388 613	387 342	386 195	...	25.4	25.8	...	...	...
Urban - Urbaine[14]	C	221 638	...	...	...	...	...	...	...	...	...
Rural - Rurale[14]	C	146 505	...	...	...	...	...	...	...	...	...
Honduras											
Total	+U	*201 494*	*196 119*	...	...	...	...	...	...	...	...
Jamaica - Jamaïque[16]											
Total	C	39 673	39 348	*36 745	*37 892	*37 556	14.7	14.5	*13.5	*13.9	*13.8
Martinique[10]											
Total	C	...	...	4 130	4 367	...	...	...	10.7	11.4	...
Mexico - Mexique[17]											
Total	C	2 262 024	2 190 159	2 168 933	...	...	19.6	18.7	18.3	...	...
Urban - Urbaine[14]	C	1 601 091	1 563 853	1 523 223	...	...	19.1	18.4	17.8	...	...
Rural - Rurale[14]	C	541 168	515 520	483 583	...	...	16.9	16.0	14.8	...	...
Montserrat											
Total	+C	46	53	41	50	...	9.3	10.7	8.3	10.0	...

9. Live births and crude birth rates, by urban/rural residence: 2011 - 2015
Naissances vivantes et taux bruts de natalité selon la résidence, urbaine/rurale : 2011 - 2015 (continued - suite)

Continent, country or area, and urban/rural residence / Continent, pays ou zone et résidence, urbaine/rurale	Co-de[a]	Number - Nombre					Rate - Taux				
		2011	2012	2013	2014	2015	2011	2012	2013	2014	2015

AMERICA, NORTH - AMÉRIQUE DU NORD

Panama											
Total	C	73 292	75 486	73 804	75 183	*75 866	19.7	19.9	19.2	19.2	*19.1
Urban - Urbaine	C	46 208	47 801	47 901	49 006	...	18.9	19.0	18.6	18.5	...
Rural - Rurale	C	27 084	27 685	25 903	26 177	...	21.3	21.7	20.4	20.6	...
Puerto Rico - Porto Rico											
Total	C	41 133	38 974	36 580	34 503	31 229	11.2	10.7	10.2	9.7	9.0
Urban - Urbaine	C	23 859	21 481	19 792	19 014[14]	18 986	...	...	...	...	...
Rural - Rurale	C	17 274	17 493	16 788	15 469[14]	12 243	...	...	...	...	...
Saint Kitts and Nevis - Saint-Kitts-et-Nevis											
Total	+C	666	636	547	641	...	14.4	...	...	...	...
Saint Lucia - Sainte-Lucie											
Total	C	*2 009	*2 103	...	...	...	*12.0	*12.4	...	...	...
Saint Vincent and the Grenadines - Saint-Vincent-et-les Grenadines											
Total	C	1 725	1 853	1 738	1 841	...	15.7	16.8	15.8	16.7	...
Sint Maarten (Dutch part) - Saint-Martin (partie néerlandaise)[18]											
Total	+C	432	414	511	...	...	12.9	11.9	14.0	...	...
Trinidad and Tobago - Trinité-et-Tobago											
Total	C	*18 141	*18 729	*18 823	*18 729	...	*13.6	*14.0	*14.0	*13.9	...
United States of America - États-Unis d'Amérique											
Total	C	3 953 590	3 952 841	3 932 181	3 988 076	...	12.7	12.6	12.4	12.5	...
United States Virgin Islands - Îles Vierges américaines[19]											
Total	C	1 491	1 415	...	...	...	14.1	13.4	...	...	...

AMERICA, SOUTH - AMÉRIQUE DU SUD

Argentina - Argentine											
Total	C	758 042	738 318	754 603	777 012	...	18.4	17.7	17.9	18.2	...
Bolivia (Plurinational State of) - Bolivie (État plurinational de)											
Total	U	160 499	128 738	149 832	153 016	...	...	...	...	...	...
Total	+U	...	...	...	...	247 754	...	...	...	...	...
Brazil - Brésil[20]											
Total	U	2 824 776	2 830 458	2 832 590	2 913 121	...	...	...	...	...	...
Chile - Chili											
Total	C	247 358	243 635	242 005	*252 194	...	14.3	14.0	13.8	*14.2	...
Urban - Urbaine	C	223 086	219 348	220 276	...	...	14.9	14.5	14.4	...	...
Rural - Rurale	C	24 272	24 287	21 729	...	...	10.8	10.8	9.6	...	...
Colombia - Colombie											
Total	U	662 783	675 694	658 835	669 131	...	...	...	...	...	...
Urban - Urbaine	U	520 343	529 856	...	...	...	...	...	...	...	...
Rural - Rurale	U	142 440	145 838	...	...	...	...	...	...	...	...
Ecuador - Équateur											
Total	+U	229 780	235 237	220 896	229 476	...	...	...	...	...	...
Urban - Urbaine	+U	190 385	196 473	181 225	185 249	...	...	...	...	...	...
Rural - Rurale	+U	39 395	38 764	39 671	44 227	...	...	...	...	...	...
Paraguay											
Total	+U	111 945	118 549	114 619	116 592	...	...	...	...	...	...
Peru - Pérou[21]											
Total	+U	396 839	414 081	475 349	492 008	...	...	...	...	...	...
Suriname											
Total	C	9 703	10 217	10 012	10 407	...	18.0	18.9	18.2	18.6	...
Urban - Urbaine	C	6 425	6 852	6 792	6 898	...	...	19.1	...	...	...
Rural - Rurale	C	3 278	3 365	3 220	3 509	...	...	18.4	...	...	...
Uruguay											
Total	C	46 712	48 059	48 681	48 368	...	13.7	14.0	14.2	14.0	...

355

9. Live births and crude birth rates, by urban/rural residence: 2011 - 2015
Naissances vivantes et taux bruts de natalité selon la résidence, urbaine/rurale : 2011 - 2015 (continued - suite)

Continent, country or area, and urban/rural residence / Continent, pays ou zone et résidence, urbaine/rurale	Co-de[a]	Number - Nombre					Rate - Taux				
		2011	2012	2013	2014	2015	2011	2012	2013	2014	2015
AMERICA, SOUTH - AMÉRIQUE DU SUD											
Venezuela (Bolivarian Republic of) - Venezuela (République bolivarienne du)											
Total	C	615 132	619 530	...	...	...	21.3	21.1	...	...	...
Total	U	...	...	597 902	597 773	600 860	...	...	...	...	...
ASIA - ASIE											
Armenia - Arménie											
Total	C	43 340	*42 333	*41 790	43 031	41 763	13.3	*13.4	*13.8	...	13.9
Azerbaijan - Azerbaïdjan[22]											
Total	+C	176 072	174 469	172 671	170 503	166 210	19.2	18.8	18.3	17.9	17.3
Urban - Urbaine	+C	85 539	86 364	86 429	...	...	17.6	17.5	17.2	...	...
Rural - Rurale	+C	90 533	88 105	86 242	...	...	21.0	20.2	19.6	...	...
Bahrain - Bahreïn[23]											
Total	C	17 573	19 119	19 995	20 931	...	14.7	15.8	16.0	15.9	...
Bangladesh											
Total	U	2 891 000	2 933 000	...	...	...	...	...	...	...	...
Urban - Urbaine	U	631 000	701 000	...	...	...	...	...	...	...	...
Rural - Rurale	U	2 260 000	2 232 000	...	...	...	...	...	...	...	...
Brunei Darussalam - Brunéi Darussalam											
Total	+C	6 724	6 909	6 680	6 891	*6 699	17.1	17.3	16.4	16.7	*16.1
China - Chine[24]											
Total	I	16 040 000	16 350 000	16 400 000	16 870 000	16 550 000	11.9	12.1	12.1	12.4	12.1
China, Hong Kong SAR - Chine, Hong Kong RAS											
Total	C	95 451	91 558	57 084	62 305	*59 900	13.5	12.8	7.9	8.6	*8.2
China, Macao SAR - Chine, Macao RAS											
Total	C	5 852	7 315	6 571	7 360	7 055	10.6	12.9	11.1	11.8	11.0
Cyprus - Chypre[25]											
Total	C	9 622	10 161	9 341	9 258	*9 170	11.3	11.8	10.8	10.9	*10.8
Urban - Urbaine[14]	C	6 461	...	...	...	...	...	...	...	...	...
Rural - Rurale[14]	C	3 074	...	...	...	...	...	...	...	...	...
Georgia - Géorgie											
Total	C	58 014	57 031	57 878	60 635	...	12.9	12.7	...	13.5	...
Urban - Urbaine	C	33 452	...	...	...	...	14.0	...	...	...	...
Rural - Rurale	C	24 562	...	...	...	...	11.7	...	...	...	...
India - Inde[26]											
Total	I	...	...	...	...	...	21.1	21.6	21.4	21.0	...
Urban - Urbaine	I	...	...	...	...	...	17.6	17.4	17.3	17.4	...
Rural - Rurale	I	...	...	...	...	...	23.3	23.1	22.9	22.7	...
Iran (Islamic Republic of) - Iran (République islamique d')[27]											
Total	+C	1 382 229	1 421 689	1 471 834	1 534 362	...	18.4	18.7	19.1	19.7	...
Urban - Urbaine	+C	1 087 988	1 129 477	1 131 566	1 178 921	...	20.3	20.7	20.4	20.9	...
Rural - Rurale	+C	294 241	292 212	340 268	355 441	...	13.7	13.7	15.9	16.6	...
Iraq											
Total	U	...	...	*1 077 645	...	...	...	...	...	...	...
Israel - Israël[28]											
Total	C	166 296	170 940	171 444	176 427	*178 723	21.4	21.6	21.3	21.5	...
Urban - Urbaine	C	150 895	155 178	155 127	160 223	...	21.2	21.4	21.1	21.4	...
Rural - Rurale	C	15 401	15 762	16 317	16 204	...	23.5	23.3	23.6	22.7	...
Japan - Japon[29]											
Total	C	1 050 806[14]	1 037 231[14]	1 029 816[14]	1 003 539[14]	*1 005 656	8.2	8.1	8.1	7.9	*7.9
Urban - Urbaine[30]	C	963 922	953 933	948 589	926 229	...	...	...	...	...	...
Rural - Rurale[30]	C	86 762	83 231	81 173	77 245	...	...	...	...	...	...
Jordan - Jordanie[31]											
Total	C	178 435	177 695	178 143	...	...	25.5	23.9	22.0	...	...
Kazakhstan[22]											
Total	C	372 801	381 005	387 227	...	...	22.5	22.7	22.7	...	...
Urban - Urbaine	C	197 516	206 198	209 004	...	...	21.8	22.4	22.4	...	...
Rural - Rurale	C	175 285	174 807	178 223	...	...	23.4	23.0	23.2	...	...

9. Live births and crude birth rates, by urban/rural residence: 2011 - 2015
Naissances vivantes et taux bruts de natalité selon la résidence, urbaine/rurale : 2011 - 2015 (continued - suite)

Continent, country or area, and urban/rural residence / Continent, pays ou zone et résidence, urbaine/rurale	Code / Code[a]	Number - Nombre					Rate - Taux				
		2011	2012	2013	2014	2015	2011	2012	2013	2014	2015
ASIA - ASIE											
Kuwait - Koweït											
Total	C	58 198	59 753	59 426	61 313	...	18.7	18.4	17.3	16.3	...
Kyrgyzstan - Kirghizstan											
Total	C	149 612	154 918	155 520	161 813	*163 452	28.4	28.9	27.2	27.7	*27.4
Urban - Urbaine	C	48 906	53 770	53 855	55 463	*52 477	26.5	29.0	28.0	28.2	*26.1
Rural - Rurale	C	100 706	101 148	101 665	106 350	*110 975	29.5	28.9	26.8	27.5	*28.1
Lebanon - Liban											
Total	C	98 569	94 842	95 246	104 872	...	26.1	...	...	...	...
Malaysia - Malaisie											
Total	C	511 594	526 012	503 914	*511 865	...	17.6	17.8	16.7	*16.7	...
Urban - Urbaine	C	341 601	357 877	344 410	...	...	16.6	16.8	15.6	...	...
Rural - Rurale	C	169 993	168 135	159 504	...	...	20.1	20.6	19.5	...	...
Maldives											
Total	C	7 180	7 431	7 153	7 245	...	22.1	22.5	21.3	18.0	...
Urban - Urbaine	C	3 987[32]	4 460[32]	4 698[32]	4 521[14]	...	...	...	...	29.4	...
Rural - Rurale	C	3 155[32]	2 676[32]	2 439[32]	2 378[14]	...	...	...	...	9.6	...
Mongolia - Mongolie											
Total	+C	69 853	73 839	79 780	82 839	82 130	25.1	26.0	27.5	28.0	27.1
Urban - Urbaine	+C	47 193	50 967	57 069	56 148	60 861	25.4	26.7	29.1	28.2	29.8
Rural - Rurale	+C	22 660	22 872	22 711	26 691	21 269	24.4	24.6	24.2	27.5	21.6
Myanmar[33]											
Total	+U	820 293	856 279	835 595	836 961	...	...	...	...	...	...
Urban - Urbaine	+U	...	319 696	333 075	...	...	...	...	...	...	...
Rural - Rurale	+U	...	536 583	502 520	...	...	...	...	...	...	...
Nepal - Népal[34]											
Total	I	326 725	...	...	...	...	11.4	...	...	...	...
Urban - Urbaine	I	41 626	...	...	...	...	...	...	...	...	...
Rural - Rurale	I	285 099	...	...	...	...	...	...	...	...	...
Oman[35]											
Total	U	67 922	72 867	79 417	82 981	...	...	...	...	...	...
Philippines											
Total	C	1 746 684	1 790 367	1 761 602	1 748 857	...	18.4	18.6	17.9	17.5	...
Qatar											
Total	C	20 802	21 423	23 708	*25 443	...	12.0	11.7	11.8	*11.5	...
Republic of Korea - République de Corée[36]											
Total	C	471 265	484 550	436 455	435 435	...	9.4	9.6	8.6	8.6	...
Urban - Urbaine[14]	C	389 640	402 650	365 381	364 615	...	9.6	9.8	8.9	8.8	...
Rural - Rurale[14]	C	81 503	81 843	71 070	70 818	...	8.6	8.7	7.6	7.5	...
Saudi Arabia - Arabie saoudite											
Total	...	...	...	...	607 806	...	...	...	...	...	...
Singapore - Singapour											
Total	C	39 654	42 663	39 720	42 232	42 185	10.5	11.2	10.3	10.9	10.8
Sri Lanka											
Total	+C	*363 415	*355 900	*365 792	*349 715	*334 821	*17.4	*17.4	*17.8	*16.8	*16.0
State of Palestine - État de Palestine[37]											
Total	U	131 430	129 826	126 912	...	...	...	...	...	...	...
Tajikistan - Tadjikistan[38]											
Total	U	224 178	219 281	209 417	229 460	...	...	...	...	...	...
Urban - Urbaine	U	55 081	53 371	50 508	54 878	...	...	...	...	...	...
Rural - Rurale	U	169 097	165 910	158 909	174 582	...	...	...	...	...	...
Thailand - Thaïlande											
Total	+U	795 031	801 737	748 081	711 081	...	...	...	...	...	...
Timor-Leste											
Total	I	...	...	...	...	44 854	...	...	...	...	38.4
Turkey - Turquie											
Total	C	1 247 081	1 290 387	1 291 217	1 337 504	*1 325 783	16.8	17.2	17.0	17.4	*17.1
United Arab Emirates - Émirats arabes unis[39]											
Total	...	83 950	89 578	...	...	...	...	...	...	...	...
Uzbekistan - Ouzbékistan											
Total	+C	622 835	625 106	679 519	718 036	...	21.2	21.0	22.5	23.3	...
Urban - Urbaine	+C	283 090	287 018	310 481	326 231	...	18.8	18.8	20.1	20.8	...
Rural - Rurale	+C	339 745	338 088	369 038	391 805	...	23.8	23.3	25.0	25.9	...

Continent, country or area, and urban/rural residence / Continent, pays ou zone et résidence, urbaine/rurale	Co-de[a]	Number - Nombre					Rate - Taux				
		2011	2012	2013	2014	2015	2011	2012	2013	2014	2015
ASIA - ASIE											
Yemen - Yémen											
Total	U	*239 980*	*279 719*	*425 165[40]*	...	...	...	...	...	...	...
EUROPE											
Åland Islands - Îles d'Åland											
Total	C	285	292	287	282	*273	10.1	10.3	10.0	9.8	*9.4
Urban - Urbaine	C	110	95	104	98	*97	9.8	8.4	9.1	8.6	*8.5
Rural - Rurale	C	175	197	183	184	*176	10.3	11.5	10.6	10.6	*10.1
Albania - Albanie											
Total	C	34 285	35 473	35 750	35 760	33 221	11.8	12.2	12.3	12.4	11.5
Andorra - Andorre											
Total	C	793	737	...	...	...	10.0	9.5	...	...	...
Austria - Autriche											
Total	C	78 109	78 952	79 330	81 722	84 381	9.3	9.4	9.4	9.6	9.8
Belarus - Bélarus											
Total	C	109 147	115 893	117 997	118 534	119 028	11.5	12.2	12.5	12.5	12.6
Urban - Urbaine	C	83 445	89 129	90 436	...	...	11.7	12.4	12.5	...	...
Rural - Rurale	C	25 702	26 764	27 561	...	...	11.1	11.8	12.4	...	...
Belgium - Belgique[41]											
Total	C	128 705	128 051	125 606	125 014	*122 274	11.7	11.5	11.2	11.1	*10.9
Urban - Urbaine	C	126 865	...	...	...	...	11.7	...	...	...	...
Rural - Rurale	C	1 840	...	...	...	...	11.6	...	...	...	...
Bosnia and Herzegovina - Bosnie-Herzégovine											
Total	C	31 875	32 072	31 103	29 247	...	8.3	8.4	8.1	7.6	...
Bulgaria - Bulgarie											
Total	C	70 846	69 121	66 578	67 585	65 950	9.6	9.5	9.2	9.4	9.2
Urban - Urbaine	C	53 396	51 658	...	...	...	10.0	9.7	...	...	...
Rural - Rurale	C	17 450	17 463	...	...	...	8.7	8.8	...	...	...
Croatia - Croatie											
Total	C	41 197	41 771	39 939	39 566	*37 503	9.6	9.8	9.4	9.3	*8.9
Urban - Urbaine	C	23 366	23 839	22 796	22 894	...	...	...	...	...	...
Rural - Rurale	C	17 831	17 932	17 143	16 672	...	...	...	...	...	...
Czech Republic - République tchèque											
Total	C	108 673[42]	108 576	106 751	109 860	*110 764	10.4	10.3	10.2	10.4	*10.5
Urban - Urbaine	C	79 742[42]	79 812	78 469	80 841	...	...	...	10.2	10.5	...
Rural - Rurale	C	28 931[42]	28 764	28 282	29 019	...	...	...	10.0	10.2	...
Denmark - Danemark[43]											
Total	C	58 998	57 916	55 873	56 870	58 205	10.6	10.4	10.0	10.1	10.3
Estonia - Estonie											
Total	C	14 679	14 056	13 531	13 551	13 907	11.1	10.6	10.3	10.3	10.6
Urban - Urbaine	C	10 057	9 653	9 286	9 452	...	11.1	10.7	10.3	10.5	...
Rural - Rurale	C	4 622	4 403	4 245	4 099	...	10.9	10.5	10.2	9.8	...
Faeroe Islands - Îles Féroé											
Total	C	581	619	626	639	608	12.0	12.8	13.0	13.2	12.4
Urban - Urbaine	C	221	250	237	266	229	12.2	13.9	13.0	14.5	12.3
Rural - Rurale	C	360	369	389	373	379	11.8	12.2	12.9	12.4	12.5
Finland - Finlande[44]											
Total	C	59 676	59 201	57 847	56 950	*55 199	11.1	11.0	10.7	10.5	*10.1
Urban - Urbaine	C	42 561	42 329	41 386	41 103	...	11.6	11.4	11.1	10.9	...
Rural - Rurale	C	17 115	16 872	16 461	15 847	...	10.1	10.0	9.8	9.5	...
France											
Total	C	792 996	790 290	781 621	781 167	*762 000	12.5	12.4	12.3	12.2	*11.8
Urban - Urbaine[45]	C	629 283	628 694	623 522	625 957	...	...	...	...	...	...
Rural - Rurale[45]	C	162 102	159 929	156 358	153 342	...	...	...	...	...	...
Germany - Allemagne											
Total	C	662 685	673 544	682 069	714 927	*737 575	8.3	8.4	8.5	8.8	*9.1
Gibraltar[46]											
Total	+C	442	461	426	...	...	13.8	14.2	13.0	...	...
Greece - Grèce											
Total	C	106 428	100 371	94 134	92 149	*91 852	9.6	9.1	8.6	8.5	*8.5
Urban - Urbaine	C	75 224	71 232	64 616	62 785	...	...	...	...	...	...
Rural - Rurale	C	31 204	29 139	29 518	29 364	...	...	...	...	...	...

9. Live births and crude birth rates, by urban/rural residence: 2011 - 2015
Naissances vivantes et taux bruts de natalité selon la résidence, urbaine/rurale : 2011 - 2015 (continued - suite)

Continent, country or area, and urban/rural residence / Continent, pays ou zone et résidence, urbaine/rurale	Co-dea	Number - Nombre					Rate - Taux				
		2011	2012	2013	2014	2015	2011	2012	2013	2014	2015
EUROPE											
Guernsey - Guernesey											
Total	C	650	674	667	627	...	10.3	10.7	10.6	10.0	...
Hungary - Hongrie											
Total	C	88 049	90 269	89 524[48]	93 281[49]	92 135[49]	8.8	9.1	9.0	9.5	9.4
Urban - Urbaine	C	60 698[47]	61 985[47]	61 996[48]	65 095[49]	...	8.7	9.0	9.0	9.4	...
Rural - Rurale	C	26 349[47]	27 278[47]	27 511[48]	28 166[49]	...	8.7	9.0	9.1	9.7	...
Iceland - Islande											
Total	C	4 492[50]	4 533	4 326	4 375	4 129	14.1	14.1	13.4	13.4	12.5
Urban - Urbaine	C	4 441[50]	4 316	4 131	4 164	...	14.1	14.4	13.6	13.6	...
Rural - Rurale	C	51[50]	217	195	211	...	11.1	10.6	9.5	10.2	...
Ireland - Irlande											
Total[51]	C	74 033	...	...	...	...	16.2	...	...	...	...
Total	+C	...	72 225	68 930	67 285	*65 909	...	15.7	15.0	14.6	*14.2
Isle of Man - Île de Man											
Total	+C	938	890	859	805	...	11.1	10.5	10.0	9.3	...
Italy - Italie											
Total	+C	546 585	534 186	514 308	...	...	9.2	9.0	8.5	...	...
Total	C	...	...	...	502 596	485 780	...	...	...	8.3	8.0
Jersey[17]											
Total	+C	1 075	1 124	1 029	985	1 021	11.0	11.4	...	9.8	9.9
Latvia - Lettonie											
Total	C	18 828	19 897	20 596	21 746	21 979	9.1	9.8	10.2	10.9	11.1
Urban - Urbaine	C	12 726	13 582	14 184	15 094	...	9.1	9.9	10.4	11.2	...
Rural - Rurale	C	6 099	6 315	6 412	6 652	...	9.2	9.6	9.9	10.4	...
Liechtenstein											
Total	C	395	357	339	372	325	10.9	9.7	9.2	10.0	8.7
Lithuania - Lituanie											
Total	C	30 268	30 459	29 885	30 369	31 475	10.0	10.2	10.1	10.4	...
Urban - Urbaine	C	20 693	21 393	20 195	20 989	...	10.2	10.7	10.2	10.7	...
Rural - Rurale	C	9 575	9 066	9 690	9 380	...	9.5	9.2	9.9	9.7	...
Luxembourg											
Total	C	5 639	6 026	6 115	6 070	6 115	10.9	11.3	11.3	10.9	10.9
Malta - Malte											
Total	C	4 165	4 130	4 032	4 191	4 325	10.0	9.8	9.5	9.8	10.1
Monaco[52]											
Total	C	1 028	979	992	974	...	28.5	27.2	26.8	...	...
Montenegro - Monténégro											
Total	C	7 215	7 459	7 475	7 529	7 386	11.6	12.0	12.0	12.1	11.9
Netherlands - Pays-Bas[53]											
Total	C	180 060	175 959	171 341	175 181	*169 965	10.8	10.5	10.2	10.4	*10.0
Norway - Norvège											
Total	C	60 220	60 255	58 878	58 976	59 058	12.2	12.0	11.6	11.5	11.4
Poland - Pologne											
Total	C	388 416	386 257	369 576	375 160	369 308	10.1	10.0	9.7	9.9	9.7
Urban - Urbaine	C	225 701	223 815	...	...	...	9.6	9.6	...	...	...
Rural - Rurale	C	162 715	162 442	...	...	...	10.8	10.7	...	...	...
Portugal[17]											
Total	C	96 856	89 841	82 787	82 367	85 500	9.2	8.5	7.9	7.9	8.2
Republic of Moldova - République de Moldova[54]											
Total	C	39 182	39 435	37 871	38 616	*38 612	11.0	11.1	10.6	10.9	*10.9
Urban - Urbaine	C	14 599	14 890	...	...	...	9.8	10.0	...	...	...
Rural - Rurale	C	24 583	24 545	...	...	...	11.8	11.9	...	...	...
Romania - Roumanie											
Total	C	196 242	201 104	182 313	193 103	*185 006	9.7	10.0	9.1	9.7	*9.3
Urban - Urbaine	C	106 667	108 425	98 351	105 389	...	9.8	10.0	9.1	9.8	...
Rural - Rurale	C	89 575	92 679	83 962	87 714	...	9.7	10.0	9.1	9.5	...
Russian Federation - Fédération de Russie[22]											
Total	C	1 796 629	1 902 084	*1 901 182	...	...	12.6	13.3	*13.2	...	...
Urban - Urbaine	C	1 270 047	1 355 674	...	...	...	12.0	12.8	...	...	...
Rural - Rurale	C	526 582	546 410	...	...	...	14.1	14.7	...	...	...
San Marino - Saint-Marin											
Total	+C	325	292	320	281	269	9.7	8.7	9.6	8.4	8.0

9. Live births and crude birth rates, by urban/rural residence: 2011 - 2015
Naissances vivantes et taux bruts de natalité selon la résidence, urbaine/rurale : 2011 - 2015 (continued - suite)

Continent, country or area, and urban/rural residence / Continent, pays ou zone et résidence, urbaine/rurale	Co-de[a]	Number - Nombre					Rate - Taux				
		2011	2012	2013	2014	2015	2011	2012	2013	2014	2015
EUROPE											
Serbia - Serbie[55]											
Total	+C	65 598	67 257	65 554	66 461	*65 657	9.1	9.3	9.1	9.3	*9.2
Urban - Urbaine	+C	45 430	45 869	45 657	46 036	...	10.6	10.7	10.7	10.8	...
Rural - Rurale	+C	20 168	21 388	19 897	20 425	...	6.8	7.3	6.9	7.1	...
Slovakia - Slovaquie											
Total	C	60 647	55 535	54 823	55 033	55 602	11.2	10.3	10.1	10.2	10.2
Urban - Urbaine	C	32 130	29 174	28 692	28 379	...	10.9	9.9	9.8	9.7	...
Rural - Rurale	C	28 517	26 361	26 131	26 654	...	11.6	10.7	10.5	10.7	...
Slovenia - Slovénie											
Total	C	21 947	21 938	21 111	21 165	20 641	10.7	10.7	10.3	10.3	10.0
Urban - Urbaine	C	10 651	10 675	10 698	10 707	...	10.4	10.4	10.2	10.2	...
Rural - Rurale	C	11 296	11 263	10 413	10 458	...	11.0	10.9	10.3	10.3	...
Spain - Espagne											
Total	C	470 553	453 348	424 440	426 076	*417 265	10.1	9.7	9.1	9.2	*9.0
Sweden - Suède											
Total	C	111 770	113 177	113 593	114 907	*114 870	11.8	11.9	11.8	11.9	*11.8
Switzerland - Suisse											
Total	C	80 808	82 164	82 731	85 287	*84 840	10.2	10.3	10.2	10.4	*10.3
Urban - Urbaine	C	60 544	61 490	62 250	64 109	...	10.4	10.4	10.4	10.6	...
Rural - Rurale	C	20 264	20 674	20 481	21 178	...	9.7	9.8	9.6	9.8	...
TFYR of Macedonia - L'ex-R. y. de Macédoine											
Total	C	22 770	23 568	23 138	23 596	23 075	11.1	11.4	11.2	11.4	11.2
Urban - Urbaine	C	13 008	13 379	...	...	...	...	...	...	...	...
Rural - Rurale	C	9 762	10 189	...	...	...	...	...	...	...	...
Ukraine[56]											
Total	+C	502 595	520 705	503 657	465 882[57]	...	11.0	11.4	11.1	10.8	...
Urban - Urbaine	+C	328 934	341 599	330 284	...	...	10.5	10.9	...	...	...
Rural - Rurale	+C	173 661	179 106	173 373	...	...	12.1	12.6	...	...	...
United Kingdom of Great Britain and Northern Ireland - Royaume-Uni de Grande-Bretagne et d'Irlande du Nord[58]											
Total	C	807 776	812 970	778 358	775 908	*777 167	12.8	12.8	12.1	12.0	*12.0
OCEANIA - OCÉANIE											
American Samoa - Samoas américaines											
Total	C	1 287	1 175	1 161	1 084	...	20.0	18.5	18.5	17.5	...
Australia - Australie											
Total	+C	301 617	309 582	308 065	299 697	...	13.5	13.6	13.3	12.8	...
Urban - Urbaine[59]	+C	203 060	210 139	209 397	204 991	...	10.7	10.8	10.6	10.2	...
Rural - Rurale[59]	+C	97 829	98 569	97 514	93 173	...	29.7	29.6	29.1	27.6	...
Cook Islands - Îles Cook[60]											
Total	+C	262	259	256	204	*205	13.6	13.3	13.8	11.0	*10.9
Fiji - Fidji											
Total	+C	...	20 178	20 970	...	...	...	23.5	24.4	...	...
French Polynesia - Polynésie française											
Total	C	4 374	4 296	4 203	4 161	3 888	16.4	16.0	15.6	15.3	14.3
Guam[61]											
Total	C	3 298	3 604	3 329	3 396	3 367	20.7	22.5	20.8	21.1	20.8
Nauru											
Total	C	370	319	366	...	...	36.7	...	...	...	...
New Caledonia - Nouvelle-Calédonie											
Total	C	4 119	4 389	...	...	...	16.2	17.0	...	...	...
New Zealand - Nouvelle-Zélande											
Total	+C	61 403	61 178	58 717	57 240[62]	61 038[62]	14.0	13.9	13.2	12.7	13.3
Urban - Urbaine[14]	+C	53 967	53 917	51 480	50 355[62]	53 202[62]	14.3	14.2	13.5	13.0	13.4
Rural - Rurale[14]	+C	7 419	7 253	7 228	6 873[62]	7 827[62]	12.0	11.6	11.6	11.0	12.3

Continent, country or area, and urban/rural residence — Continent, pays ou zone et résidence, urbaine/rurale	Co-de[a]	Number - Nombre					Rate - Taux				
		2011	2012	2013	2014	2015	2011	2012	2013	2014	2015
OCEANIA - OCÉANIE											
Niue - Nioué[63]											
Total	C	22	...	...	...	...	...	...	...	...	...
Norfolk Island - Île Norfolk[64]											
Total	+C	13	4	...	...	...	...	...	...	...	...
Northern Mariana Islands - Îles Mariannes septentrionales[19]											
Total	U	*1 033*	*853*	*686*	*517*	...	...	...	...	...	...
Palau - Palaos											
Total	C	247	268	229	...	...	11.8	12.7	...	...	...
Pitcairn											
Total	C	-	-	-	...	...	...	...	...	...	...
Samoa[65]											
Total	+U	*2 354*	...	...	...	...	...	...	...	...	...
Tokelau - Tokélaou[66]											
Total		16	...	...	...	...	...	...	...	...	...

FOOTNOTES - NOTES

Italics: data from civil registers which are incomplete or of unknown completeness. - Italiques : données incomplètes ou dont le degré d'exactitude n'est pas connu, provenant des registres de l'état civil.

* Provisional. - Données provisoires.

[a] 'Code' indicates the source of data, as follows:
C - Civil registration, estimated over 90% complete
U - Civil registration, estimated less than 90% complete
| - Other source, estimated reliable
+ - Data tabulated by date of registration rather than occurence
... - Information not available

Le 'Code' indique la source des données, comme suit :
C - Registres de l'état civil considérés complets à 90 p. 100 au moins
U - Registres de l'état civil qui ne sont pas considérés complets à 90 p. 100 au moins
| - Autre source, considérée pas douteuses
+ - Données exploitées selon la date de l'enregistrement et non la date de l'événement
... - Information pas disponible

[1] Excluding live-born infants who died before their birth was registered. Data refer to Algerian population only. - Non compris les enfants nés vivants décédés avant l'enregistrement de leur naissance. Les données ne concernent que la population algérienne.
[2] Data are projections presented in Annuaire Statistique 2010. - Les données sont des projections présentées dans l'Annuaire Statistique 2010.
[3] Source: Vital Statistics Report 2012. - Source: Vital Statistics Report 2012.
[4] Source: Vital Statistics Report 2014. - Source: Vital Statistics Report 2014.
[5] Data refer to the recorded events in Ministry of Health hospitals and health centres only. - Les données se rapportent aux faits d'état civil enregistrés dans les hôpitaux et les dispensaires du Ministère de la santé seulement.
[6] The coverage of registration is estimated at 66 per cent. - Le degré de complétude de l'enregistrement est évalué à 66 pour cent.
[7] Excludes the islands of St. Brandon and Agalega. - Non compris les îles St. Brandon et Agalega.
[8] Source: Ministry of Health, National Directorate of Planning and Cooperation. - Source : Ministère de la santé, Direction nationale de la planification et de la coopération.
[9] Data refer to the 12 months preceding the census in August. - Les données se rapportent aux 12 mois précédant le recensement d'août.
[10] Excluding live-born infants who died before their birth was registered. - Non compris les enfants nés vivants décédés avant l'enregistrement de leur naissance.

[11] Based on estimates and projections from 'Agence Nationale de la Statistique et de la Démographie'. - Données fondées sur des estimations et des projections provenant de l'Agence Nationale de la Statistique et de la Démographie.
[12] Excluding non-residents and foreign service personnel and their dependants. - À l'exclusion des non-résidents et du personnel diplomatique et de leurs charges de famille.
[13] Data refer to the twelve months from 1 July of the current year to 30 June of the following year. Including Canadian residents temporarily in the United States, but excluding United States residents temporarily in Canada. - Les données font référence aux douze mois de 1 juillet de l'année actuelle à 30 juin de l'année suivante. Y compris les résidents canadiens se trouvant temporairement aux Etats-Unis, mais ne comprenant pas les résidents des Etats-Unis se trouvant temporairement au Canada.
[14] The total number may include 'Unknown residence', but the categories urban and rural do not. - Le nombre total peut inclure les personnes dont la résidence n'est pas connue, à l'inverse des catégories de population urbaine et rurale.
[15] Excluding children born in the country of non-resident mothers. - Exceptés les enfants nés dans le pays des mères non-résidentes.
[16] Data have been adjusted for underenumeration. - Les données ont été ajustées pour compenser les lacunes du dénombrement.
[17] Data refer to births to resident mothers. - Ces données concernent les enfants nés de mères résidentes.
[18] Source: Population Registry and STAT/CBS estimates. - Source: Le registre de la population et les estimations du STAT/CBS.
[19] Source: U.S. National Center for Health Statistics, National Vital Statistics Reports (NVSR). - Source : US National Center for Health Statistics, National Vital Statistics Reports (NVSR).
[20] Including births abroad and births of unknown residence of mother. - Y compris les naissances à l'étranger et les naissances pour lesquelles le lieu de résidence de la mère est inconnu.
[21] Source: Reports of the Ministry of Health. - Source : Rapports du Ministère de la Santé.
[22] Excluding infants born alive of less than 28 weeks' gestation, of less than 1 000 grams in weight and 35 centimeters in length, who die within seven days of birth. - Non compris les enfants nés vivants après moins de 28 semaines de gestations, pesant moins de 1 000 grammes, mesurant moins de 35 centimètres et décédés dans les sept jours qui ont suivi leur naissance.
[23] Sources: Births and Deaths National Registration System database, and medical records of government hospitals. - Les sources: Les bases de données des << Births and Deaths National Registration System >> et les dossiers médicaux des hôpitaux du gouvernement.
[24] For statistical purposes, the data for China do not include those for the Hong Kong Special Administrative Region (Hong Kong SAR), Macao Special Administrative Region (Macao SAR) and Taiwan province of China. Data have been estimated on the basis of the annual National Sample Survey on Population Changes. - Pour la présentation des statistiques, les données pour la Chine ne comprennent pas la Région Administrative Spéciale de Hong Kong (Hong Kong RAS), la Région Administrative Spéciale de Macao (Macao RAS) et Taïwan

province de Chine. Les données ont été estimées sur la base de l'enquête annuelle "National Sample Survey on Population Changes".

[25] Data refer to government controlled areas. - Les données se rapportent aux zones contrôlées par le Gouvernement.

[26] Rates were obtained by the Sample Registration System of India, which is a large demographic survey. Includes data for the Indian-held part of Jammu and Kashmir, the final status of which has not yet been determined. - Les taux ont été obtenus par le Système de l'enregistrement par échantillon de l'Inde qui est une large enquête démographique. Y compris les données pour la partie du Jammu et du Cachemire occupée par l'Inde dont le statut définitif n'a pas encore été déterminé.

[27] Data refer to the Iranian Year which begins on 21 March and ends on 20 March of the following year. - Les données concernent l'année iranienne, qui commence le 21 mars et se termine le 20 mars de l'année suivante.

[28] Includes data for East Jerusalem and Israeli residents in certain other territories under occupation by Israeli military forces since June 1967. - Y compris les données pour Jérusalem-Est et les résidents israéliens dans certains autres territoires occupés depuis 1967 par les forces armées israéliennes.

[29] Data refer to Japanese nationals in Japan only. - Les données se raportent aux nationaux japonais au Japon seulement.

[30] The total number may include 'Unknown residence', but the categories urban and rural do not. Urban and rural distribution refers to the residence of the child. - Le nombre total peut inclure les personnes dont la résidence n'est pas connue, à l'inverse des catégories de population urbaine et rurale. La répartition urbain/rural se réfère au domicile de l'enfant.

[31] Excluding data for Jordanian territory under occupation since June 1967 by Israeli military forces. Excluding foreigners, including registered Palestinian refugees. - Non compris les données pour le territoire jordanien occupé depuis juin 1967 par les forces armées israéliennes. Non compris les étrangers, mais y compris les réfugiés de Palestine enregistrés.

[32] Excluding births occurred abroad. - Hormis les naissances intervenues à l'étranger.

[33] Data source is "Department of Public Health". - La source des données est << Le Service de la santé publique >>.

[34] Data refer to the 12 months preceding the census in June. - Les données se rapportent aux 12 mois précédant le recensement de juin.

[35] Data from Births and Deaths Notification System (Ministry of Health and all health care providers). - Les données proviennent du système de notification des naissances et des décès (Ministère de la santé et tous prestataires de soins de santé).

[36] Data refer to residence of child. Excluding alien armed forces, civilian aliens employed by armed forces, and foreign diplomatic personnel and their dependants. - Les données correspondent à la résidence de l'enfant. Non compris les militaires étrangers, les civils étrangers employés par les forces armées ni le personnel diplomatique étranger et les membres de leur famille les accompagnant.

[37] Source: Palestinian Central Bureau of Statistics, Population Register, updated version 05/01/2015. - Source: Bureau central de statistique palestinien, registre de la population, version actualisée jusqu'au 05/01/2015.

[38] Excluding infants born alive of less than 28 weeks' gestation, of less than 1 000 grams in weight and 35 centimeters in length, who die within seven days of birth. Data have been adjusted for under-registration. - Non compris les enfants nés vivants après moins de 28 semaines de gestations, pesant moins de 1 000 grammes, mesurant moins de 35 centimètres et décédés dans les sept jours qui ont suivi leur naissance. Y compris un ajustement pour sous-enregistrement.

[39] The registration of births and deaths is conducted by the Ministry of Health. An estimate of completeness is not provided. - L'enregistrement des naissances et des décès est mené par le Ministère de la Santé. Le degré estimatif de complétude n'est pas fourni.

[40] Including Non-Yemeni births. - Y compris les naissances non-yéménites.

[41] Including armed forces stationed outside the country, but excluding alien armed forces stationed in the area. - Y compris les militaires nationaux hors du pays, mais non compris les militaires étrangers en garnison sur le territoire.

[42] A live-born child is a child fully expelled or removed out of the mother's body, who gives a sign of life and whose birth weight is (a) 500 g or more, or (b) lower than 500 g, if it survives 24 hours after delivery. - Un enfant né vivant est un enfant qui a été entièrement expulsé ou retiré du corps de la mère, qui présente des signes de vie et dont le poids à la naissance est : a) soit égal ou supérieur à 500 grammes; b) soit inférieur à 500 grammes s'il survit plus de 24 heures après l'accouchement.

[43] Excluding Faeroe Islands and Greenland shown separately, if available. - Non compris les Iles Féroé et le Groenland, qui font l'objet de rubriques distinctes, si disponible.

[44] Excluding Åland Islands. - Non compris les Îles d'Åland.

[45] The data for urban and rural exclude the nationals outside the country. - Les données relatives à la population urbaine et rurale n'englobent pas les nationaux se trouvant à l'étranger.

[46] Including live births by military personnel and their dependants. - Y compris les naissances vivantes parmi les membres du personnel militaire et leurs personnes à charge.

[47] The urban and rural categories do not include the data of foreigners, persons of unknown residence and the homeless, whereas the total category includes them. - Les chiffres portant sur la population urbaine et rurale n' incluent pas les données relatives aux étrangers, aux personnes dont la résidence n'est pas connue et aux personnes sans domicile fixe, à l'inverse, le total les inclut.

[48] Till 2012 data refer to all live births occurred in Hungary. From 2013 data include the live births of women with Hungarian usual residence regardless of whether the live birth occurred in Hungary or in a foreign country, and do not include the live births of women with foreign country usual residence. - Jusqu'en 2012 les données concernent toutes les naissances vivantes survenues en Hongrie. À partir de 2013, les données concernent les enfants nés vivants de femmes dont la résidence habituelle est en Hongrie, que la naissance vivante ait eu lieu en Hongrie ou dans un pays étranger, et ne comprennent pas les enfants nés vivants de femmes dont la résidence habituelle est dans un pays étranger.

[49] Data include the live births of women with Hungarian usual residence regardless of whether the live birth occurred in Hungary or in a foreign country, and do not include the live births of women with foreign country usual residence. - Les données concernent les enfants nés vivants de femmes dont la résidence habituelle est en Hongrie, que la naissance vivante ait eu lieu en Hongrie ou dans un pays étranger, et ne comprennent pas les enfants nés vivants de femmes dont la résidence habituelle est dans un pays étranger.

[50] Definition of localities was revised in 2011 causing a break with the previous series. - La rupture par rapport aux séries précédentes s'explique par le fait que la définition des localités a été révisée depuis 2011.

[51] Data refer to events registered within one year of occurrence. - Les données portent sur des événements enregistrés dans l'année pendant laquelle ils sont survenus.

[52] Including residents outside the country. - Y compris les résidents hors du pays.

[53] Including residents outside the country if listed in a Netherlands population register. - Englobe les résidents se trouvant à l'étranger à condition qu'ils soient inscrits sur le registre de population des Pays-Bas.

[54] Excluding Transnistria and the municipality of Bender. - Les données ne tiennent pas compte de l'information sur la Transnistria et la municipalité de Bender.

[55] Excludes data for Kosovo and Metohia. - Sans les données pour le Kosovo et Metohie.

[56] Data refer to births with weight 500g and more (if weight is unknown - with length 25 centimeters and more, or with gestation during 22 weeks or more). - Données concernant les nouveau-nés de 500 grammes ou plus (si le poids est inconnu – de 25 centimètres de long ou plus, ou après une grossesse de 22 semaines ou plus).

[57] The Government of Ukraine has informed the United Nations that it is not in a position to provide statistical data concerning the Autonomous Republic of Crimea and the city of Sevastopol. - Le gouvernement Ukrainien a informé l'ONU qu'il n'est pas en mesure de fournir des données statistiques concernant la République autonome de Crimée et la ville de Sébastopol.

[58] Excluding Channel Islands (Guernsey and Jersey) and Isle of Man, shown separately, if available. Data tabulated by date of occurrence for England and Wales, and by date of registration for Northern Ireland and Scotland. - Non compris les îles Anglo-Normandes (Guernesey et Jersey) et l'île de Man, qui font l'objet de rubriques distinctes, si disponible. Données exploitées selon la date de l'événement pour l'Angleterre et le pays de Galles, et selon la date de l'enregistrement pour l'Irlande du Nord et l'Ecosse.

[59] Urban refers to Greater Capital City Statistical Areas, and rural refers to other areas within the state or territory. Data for urban and rural figures do not add up to the total because they exclude the events occurred in Migratory, Special Purpose and Other Territories. - Urbain renvoie aux zones statistiques de la capitale métropolitaine, et rural aux autres zones de l'État ou territoire. La somme des chiffres des catégories « en zone urbaine » et « en zone rurale » ne correspond pas au total du fait qu'en sont exclus les événements qui ont eu lieu dans les territoires de migration, les territoires à destination spéciale et autres territoires.

[60] Excluding Niue, shown separately, which is part of Cook Islands, but because of remoteness is administered separately. - Non compris Nioué, qui fait l'objet d'une rubrique distincte et qui fait partie des îles Cook, mais qui, en raison de son éloignement, est administrée séparément.

[61] Including United States military personnel, their dependants and contract employees. - Y compris les militaires des Etats-Unis, les membres de leur famille les accompagnant et les agents contractuels des Etats-Unis.

[62] Random rounding to base 3 is applied in this table as a confidentiality measure. - Les chiffres sont arrondis à la base 3 de manière aléatoire, pour des raisons de confidentialité.

[63] Includes children born in New Zealand to women resident in Niue who chose to travel to New Zealand to give birth. - Y compris les enfants nés en Nouvelle-Zélande de femmes résidant à Nioué qui ont choisi de se rendre en Nouvelle-Zélande pour accoucher.

[64] Data cover the period from 1 July of the previous year to 30 June of the present year. - Pour la période allant du 1er juillet de l'année précédente au 30 juin de l'année en cours.

[65] The coverage of registration is estimated at 70 per cent. - Le degré de complétude de l'enregistrement est évalué à 70 pour cent.

[66] Data refer to usually resident population present on census night. Data refer to the 12 months preceding the census in October. - Les données concernent la population habituellement résidente présente la nuit du recensement. Les données se rapportent aux 12 mois précédant le recensement de octobre.

Table 10 - *Demographic Yearbook 2015*

Table 10 presents live births by age of mother and sex of the child, general fertility rate, and age-specific fertility rates for the latest available year between 2006 and 2015.

Description of variables: Age is defined as age at last birthday, that is, the difference between the date of birth and the date of the occurrence of the event, expressed in completed solar years. The age classification used in this table is the following: under 15 years, 5-year age groups through 45-49 years, and 50 years and over. A different classification may appear as provided by the reporting country or area.

Rate computation: Age-specific fertility rates are the annual number of births to women in each age group per 1 000 female population in the same age group. These rates are calculated by the Statistics Division of the United Nations.

Since relatively few births occur to women below 15 or above 50 years of age, age-specific fertility rates for women under 20 years of age and for those 45 years of age or over are computed on the female population aged 15-19 and 45-49, respectively. Similarly, the rate for women of "All ages" is based on all live births irrespective of age of mother, and is computed on the female population aged 15-49 years. This rate for "All ages" is known as the general fertility rate. The age-specific fertility rates for age groups of women below 15 or 50 and above years of age are not calculated.

Births to mothers of unknown age are distributed proportionately across the age groups, by the Statistics Division of the United Nations, in accordance with the distribution of births by age of mother prior to the calculation of the rates.

The population used in computing the rates is the estimated or enumerated distribution of females by age. First priority was given to the estimated population and second priority to the enumerated population, i.e. to census returns of the year to which the births referred.

Rates presented in this table are limited to those for countries or areas having at least a total of 100 live births in a given year.

Reliability of data: Data from civil registers of live births which are reported as incomplete (less than 90 per cent completeness) or of unknown completeness are considered unreliable and are set in *italics* rather than in roman type. Rates are not computed if the data on live births from civil registers are reported as incomplete (less than 90 per cent completeness) or of unknown completeness. Table 9 and the technical notes for that table provide more detailed information on the completeness of live-birth registration. For more information about the quality of vital statistics data in general, see section 4.2 of the Technical Notes.

Limitations: Statistics on live births by age of mother are subject to the same qualifications as have been set forth for vital statistics in general and birth statistics in particular as discussed in section 4 of the Technical Notes. These include differences in the completeness of registration, the method used to determine age of mother and the quality of the reported information relating to age of mother.

The reliability of the data described above, is an important factor in considering the limitations. In addition, some live births are tabulated by date of registration and not by date of occurrence; these are indicated in the table by a plus sign "+". Whenever the lag between the date of occurrence and date of registration is prolonged and, therefore, a large proportion of the live birth registrations are delayed, birth statistics for any given year may be seriously affected. For example, the age of the mother will almost always refer to the date of registration rather than to the date of birth of the child. Hence, in those countries or areas where registration of births is delayed, possibly for years, statistics on births by age of mother should be used with caution.

Another factor which limits international comparability is the practice of some countries or areas of not including in live birth statistics infants who were born alive but died before the registration of the birth or within the first 24 hours of life, thus underestimating the total number of live births. Statistics of this type are footnoted.

Because these statistics are classified according to age, they are subject to the limitations with respect to accuracy of age reporting similar to those already discussed in connection with section 3.1.3 of the Technical Notes. The factors influencing the accuracy of reporting may be somewhat dissimilar in vital statistics (because of the differences in the method of taking a census and registering a birth) but, in general, the same errors can be observed. The absence of frequencies in the unknown age group does not necessarily indicate completely accurate reporting and tabulation of the age item. It is often an indication that the unknowns have been eliminated by assigning ages to them before tabulation, or by proportionate distribution after tabulation.

On the other hand, large frequencies in the unknown age category may indicate that a large proportion of the births are born outside of wedlock, the records for which tend to be incomplete so far as characteristics of the parents are concerned.

Another limitation of age reporting may result from calculating age of mother at birth of child (or at time of registration) from year of birth rather than from day, month and year of birth. Information on this factor is given in footnotes when known.

In few countries, data by age refer to deliveries rather than to live births causing under-enumeration in the event of a multiple birth. This practice leads to lack of strict comparability, both among countries or areas relying on this practice and between data shown in this table and table 9.

Rates shown in this table are subject to the same limitations that affect the corresponding statistics on live births. In cases of rates based on births tabulated by date of registration and not by date of occurrence; the effect of including delayed registration on the distribution of births by age of mother may be noted in the age-specific fertility rates for women at older ages. In some cases, high age-specific rates for women aged 45 years and over may reflect age of mother at registration of birth and not fertility at these older ages.

Earlier data: Live births and live-birth rates by age of mother (i.e. age-specific fertility rates), have been shown for the latest available year in each issue of the Yearbook. Information on the years and specific topics covered is presented in the Historical Index.

Tableau 10 – *Annuaire démographique 2015*

Le tableau 10 présente les données les plus récentes disponibles pour la période 2006 - 2015 sur les naissances vivantes selon l'âge de la mère et le sexe de l'enfant, le taux de fécondité et les taux de fécondité par âge.

Description des variables : l'âge désigne l'âge au dernier anniversaire, c'est-à-dire la différence entre la date de naissance et la date de l'événement exprimée en années solaires révolues. La classification par âge utilisée dans ce tableau comprend les catégories suivantes : moins de 15 ans, groupes quinquennaux jusqu'à 45-49 ans, 50 ans et plus, et âge inconnu. Des groupes d'âge différents sont parfois utilisés lorsque les pays ou territoires ont fourni les données dans une autre classification.

Les taux de fécondité par âge représentent le nombre annuel de naissances vivantes intervenues dans un groupe d'âge donné pour 1 000 femmes du groupe d'âge. Ces taux ont été calculés par la Division de statistique de l'ONU.

Étant donné que le nombre de naissances parmi les femmes de moins de 15 ans ou de plus de 50 ans est relativement peu élevé, les taux de fécondité par âge parmi les femmes âgées de moins de 20 ans et celles de 45 ans et plus ont été calculés sur la base des populations féminines âgées de 15 à 19 ans et de 45 à 49 ans, respectivement. De même, le taux pour les femmes de « tous âges » est fondé sur la totalité des naissances vivantes, indépendamment de l'âge de la mère et ce chiffre est rapporté à l'effectif de la population féminine âgée de 15 à 49 ans. Ce taux « tous âges » est le taux global de fécondité ou simplement taux de fécondité. Les taux de fécondité parmi les femmes âgées de moins de 15 ans ou celles de 50 ans et plus n'ont pas été calculés.

Les naissances pour lesquelles l'âge de la mère était inconnu ont été réparties par la Division de statistique de l'ONU, avant le calcul des taux, suivant les proportions observées pour celles où l'âge de la mère était connu.

Les chiffres de population utilisés pour le calcul des taux proviennent de dénombrements ou de répartitions estimatives de la population féminine selon l'âge. On a utilisé de préférence les estimations de la population; à défaut, on s'est contenté des données censitaires se rapportant à l'année des naissances.

Les taux présentés dans ce tableau ne concernent que les pays ou zones où l'on a enregistré un total d'au moins 100 naissances vivantes dans une année donnée.

Fiabilité des données : les données sur les naissances vivantes provenant des registres de l'état civil qui sont déclarées incomplètes (degré de complétude inférieur à 90 p. 100) ou dont le degré de complétude n'est pas connu, sont jugées douteuses et apparaissent en italique et non en caractères romains. On a choisi de ne pas faire figurer des taux calculés à partir de données sur les naissances vivantes issues de registres de l'état civil qui sont déclarées incomplètes (degré de complétude inférieur à 90 p. 100) ou dont le degré de complétude n'est pas connu. Le tableau 9 et les notes techniques qui s'y rapportent présentent des renseignements plus détaillés sur le degré de complétude de l'enregistrement des naissances vivantes. Pour plus de précisions sur la qualité des statistiques de l'état civil en général, voir la section 4.2 des Notes techniques.

Insuffisance des données : les statistiques relatives aux naissances vivantes selon l'âge de la mère appellent toutes les réserves qui ont été formulées à propos des statistiques de l'état civil en général et des statistiques de naissances en particulier (voir la section 4 des Notes techniques). Ceci inclut les différences de complétude d'enregistrement des faits d'état civil, de méthode pour déterminer l'âge de la mère et de qualité d'information concernant l'âge de la mère.

La fiabilité des données, au sujet de laquelle des indications ont été données plus haut, est un facteur important. Il faut également tenir compte du fait que, dans certains cas, les données relatives aux naissances vivantes sont exploitées selon la date de l'enregistrement et non la date de l'événement ; ces cas ont été signalés dans le tableau par le signe '+'. Chaque fois que le décalage entre l'événement et son enregistrement est grand et qu'une forte proportion des naissances vivantes fait l'objet d'un enregistrement tardif, les statistiques des naissances vivantes pour une année donnée peuvent être considérablement faussées. Par exemple, l'âge de la mère représente presque toujours son âge à la date de l'enregistrement et non à la date de la naissance de l'enfant. Ainsi, dans les pays ou zones où l'enregistrement des naissances est tardif, le retard atteignant parfois plusieurs années, il faut utiliser avec prudence les statistiques concernant les naissances selon l'âge de la mère.

Un autre facteur qui nuit à la comparabilité internationale est la pratique de certains pays ou zones qui consiste à ne pas inclure dans les statistiques des naissances vivantes les enfants nés vivants mais décédés avant l'enregistrement de leur naissance ou dans les 24 heures qui ont suivi la naissance, pratique qui conduit à sous-estimer le nombre total de naissances vivantes. Quand pareil facteur a joué, cela a été signalé en note à la fin du tableau.

Étant donné que les statistiques du tableau 10 sont classées selon l'âge, elles appellent les mêmes réserves concernant l'exactitude des déclarations d'âge que celles formulées à la section 3.1.3 des Notes techniques. Dans le cas des statistiques de l'état civil, les facteurs qui interviennent à cet égard sont parfois différents, étant donné que le recensement de la population et l'enregistrement des naissances se font par des méthodes différentes, mais, d'une manière générale, les erreurs observées seront les mêmes. Si aucun nombre ne figure dans la rangée réservée aux âges inconnus, cela ne signifie pas nécessairement que les déclarations d'âge et l'exploitation des données par âge ont été tout à fait exactes. C'est souvent une indication que l'on a attribué un âge aux personnes d'âge inconnu avant l'exploitation des données ou qu'elles ont été réparties proportionnellement entre les différents groupes après cette opération.

À l'inverse, lorsque le nombre des personnes d'âge inconnu est important, cela peut signifier que la proportion de naissances parmi les mères célibataires est élevée, étant donné qu'en pareil cas l'acte de naissance ne contient pas tous les renseignements concernant les parents.

Les déclarations par âge peuvent comporter des distorsions, du fait que l'âge de la mère au moment de la naissance d'un enfant (ou de la déclaration de naissance) est donné par année de naissance et non par date exacte (jour, mois et année).

Dans quelques pays, la classification par âges se réfère aux accouchements, et non aux naissances vivantes, ce qui conduit à un sous-dénombrement en cas de naissances gémellaires. Cette pratique nuit à la comparabilité des données, à la fois entre pays ou zones qui recourent à cette méthode et entre les données présentées dans le tableau 10 et celles du tableau 9.

Les taux présentés dans ce tableau sont sujets aux mêmes limitations qui affectent les statistiques correspondantes de naissances vivantes. Dans le cas des taux basés sur des naissances par date d'enregistrement et non par date d'occurrence, l'effet peut être visible sur les taux de fécondité par âge des femmes aux âges plus élevés. Dans certains cas, les taux de fécondité des femmes de plus de 45 ans peuvent refléter l'âge de la mère à l'enregistrement plus que la fécondité à ces âges.

Données publiées antérieurement : les différentes éditions de l'*Annuaire démographique* regroupent les dernières statistiques dont on disposait à l'époque sur les naissances vivantes selon l'âge de la mère et les taux des naissances vivantes selon l'âge de la mère (taux de fécondité par âge). Pour plus de précisions concernant les années pour lesquels des données ont été publiées, se reporter à l'index historique.

10. Live births by age of mother and sex of child, general and age-specific fertility rates: latest available year, 2006 - 2015
Naissances vivantes selon l'âge de la mère et le sexe de l'enfant, taux de fécondité et taux de fécondité par âge : dernière année disponible, 2006 - 2015

Continent, country or area, year, code[a] and age of mother (in years) / Continent, pays ou zone, année, code[a] et âge de la mère (en années)	Number - Nombre Total	Male Masculin	Female Féminin	Rate Taux
AFRICA - AFRIQUE				
Botswana[1]				
2014 (+U)				
Total	41 741	21 142	20 599	...
0 - 14	30	13	17	..
15 - 19	3 839	1 949	1 890	...
20 - 24	11 268	5 752	5 516	...
25 - 29	10 767	5 441	5 326	...
30 - 34	9 047	4 575	4 472	...
35 - 39	4 813	2 434	2 379	...
40 - 44	1 475	728	747	...
45 - 49	128	63	65	...
50 +	12	5	7	..
Unknown - Inconnu	362	182	180	..
Egypt - Égypte				
2012 (+C)				
Total	2 629 769	1 343 402	1 286 367	121.1
0 - 19	71 275	36 022	35 253	23.8
20 - 24	1 298 851	665 452	633 399	403.8
25 - 29	399 915	201 967	197 948	127.5
30 - 34	223 307	111 754	111 553	86.0
35 - 39	83 362	41 121	42 241	41.3
40 - 44	21 510	11 229	10 281	12.2
45 +	3 802	2 233	1 569	2.3
Unknown - Inconnu	527 747	273 624	254 123	..
Ghana[2]				
2010 (|)				
Total	623 700	306 159	317 541	98.1
0 - 14	917	381	536	..
15 - 19	40 307	19 067	21 240	31.0
20 - 24	126 417	61 277	65 140	103.4
25 - 29	167 306	82 741	84 565	151.1
30 - 34	130 724	64 600	66 124	147.1
35 - 39	92 751	46 285	46 466	124.6
40 - 44	41 898	20 783	21 115	68.3
45 - 49	14 742	7 071	7 671	30.4
50 +	8 638	3 954	4 684	..
Kenya				
2009 (U)				
Total	691 312	354 154	337 158	...
0 - 14	3 877	2 019	1 858	...
15 - 19	89 664	45 562	44 102	...
20 - 24	221 828	113 572	108 256	...
25 - 29	174 571	89 674	84 897	...
30 - 34	103 940	53 395	50 545	...
35 - 39	49 527	25 424	24 103	...
40 - 44	13 231	6 713	6 518	...
45 - 49	2 165	1 097	1 068	...
50 +	823	423	400	..
Unknown - Inconnu	31 686	16 275	15 411	..
2012 (U)[3]				
Total	754 429	...	...	...
0 - 14	3 047	...	...	...
15 - 19	90 928	...	...	...
20 - 24	234 290	...	...	...
25 - 29	204 221	...	...	...
30 - 34	122 883	...	...	...
35 - 39	64 386	...	...	...
40 - 44	16 674	...	...	...
45 - 49	2 975	...	...	...
50 +	560	...	...	...
Unknown - Inconnu	14 462	...	...	...
Lesotho				
2012 (+U)				
Total	1 718	...	...	..
10 - 14	97	...	...	..
AFRICA - AFRIQUE				
Lesotho				
2012 (+U)				
15 - 19	96	...	...	...
20 - 24	378	...	...	...
25 - 29	506	...	...	...
30 - 34	409	...	...	...
35 - 39	183	...	...	...
40 - 44	42	...	...	...
45 +	7	...	...	...
Liberia - Libéria[4]				
2008 (|)				
Total	63 171	33 511	29 660	73.1
12 - 14	304	157	147	..
15 - 19	6 973	3 668	3 305	37.4
20 - 24	16 181	8 486	7 695	89.4
25 - 29	14 915	8 017	6 898	98.9
30 - 34	10 277	5 433	4 844	91.5
35 - 39	8 336	4 374	3 962	79.8
40 - 44	3 961	2 138	1 823	53.5
45 - 49	2 224	1 238	986	40.5
Libya - Libye[5]				
2009 (+U)				
Total	134 682	...	...	...
0 - 19	733	...	...	...
20 - 24	7 067	...	...	...
25 - 29	17 792	...	...	...
30 - 34	18 491	...	...	...
35 - 39	9 801	...	...	...
40 - 44	3 334	...	...	...
45 +	409	...	...	...
Unknown - Inconnu	77 055	...	...	...
Malawi[6]				
2008 (|)				
Total	516 629	247 753	268 876	160.1
12 - 14	1 621	751	870	..
15 - 19	70 737	34 137	36 600	101.2
20 - 24	169 406	81 379	88 027	284.1
25 - 29	130 331	62 810	67 521	241.6
30 - 34	79 232	37 758	41 474	153.2
35 - 39	43 747	20 776	22 971	116.8
40 - 44	15 956	7 553	8 403	57.8
45 - 49	5 599	2 589	3 010	25.0
Mali[7]				
2009 (|)				
Total	666 216	324 862	341 354	208.9
12 - 14	34 953	17 432	17 521	..
15 - 19	97 788	47 793	49 995	124.8
20 - 24	138 189	67 575	70 614	225.7
25 - 29	140 359	68 914	71 445	256.8
30 - 34	108 467	52 837	55 630	253.5
35 - 39	74 059	35 667	38 392	226.6
40 - 44	45 402	21 748	23 654	164.9
45 +	26 999	12 896	14 103	124.3
Mauritania - Mauritanie[8]				
2013 (|)				
Total	114 420	...	...	137.6
15 - 19	14 258	...	...	77.0
20 - 24	34 153	...	...	216.2
25 - 29	31 533	...	...	232.3
30 - 34	20 082	...	...	176.6
35 - 39	10 479	...	...	109.9
40 - 44	3 421	...	...	43.2
45 - 49	493	...	...	7.6

10. Live births by age of mother and sex of child, general and age-specific fertility rates: latest available year, 2006 - 2015
Naissances vivantes selon l'âge de la mère et le sexe de l'enfant, taux de fécondité et taux de fécondité par âge : dernière année disponible, 2006 - 2015 (continued - suite)

Continent, country or area, year, code[a] and age of mother (in years) / Continent, pays ou zone, année, code[a] et âge de la mère (en années)	Number - Nombre			Rate Taux
	Total	Male Masculin	Female Féminin	
AFRICA - AFRIQUE				
Mauritius - Maurice[9]				
2015 (+C)				
Total	12 640	6 557	6 083	39.1
0 - 14	27	18	9	..
15 - 19	1 107	583	524	23.1
20 - 24	2 899	1 510	1 389	58.8
25 - 29	3 683	1 889	1 794	85.2
30 - 34	3 031	1 572	1 459	65.9
35 - 39	1 498	792	706	31.0
40 - 44	307	156	151	7.4
45 - 49	18	7	11	♦0.4
50 +	2	-	2	..
Unknown - Inconnu	68	30	38	..
Namibia - Namibie[10]				
2011 (|)				
Total	61 523	30 560	30 963	110.8
0 - 14	873	443	430	..
15 - 19	7 593	3 723	3 870	62.5
20 - 24	16 655	8 235	8 420	152.3
25 - 29	14 296	7 109	7 187	157.7
30 - 34	11 017	5 632	5 385	145.3
35 - 39	7 237	3 531	3 706	113.0
40 - 44	2 982	1 451	1 531	58.4
45 +	870	436	434	20.2
Nigeria - Nigéria				
2007 (...)				
Total	1 807 025	...	...	...
0 - 14	2 528	...	...	..
15 - 19	129 716	...	...	..
20 - 24	471 036	...	...	..
25 - 29	588 454	...	...	..
30 - 34	377 593	...	...	..
35 - 39	172 081	...	...	..
40 - 44	49 519	...	...	..
45 - 49	13 411	...	...	..
50 +	2 687	...	...	..
Reunion - Réunion[11]				
2007 (C)				
Total	14 808	7 711	7 097	69.2
0 - 14	23	11	12	..
15 - 19	1 517	769	748	44.1
20 - 24	3 348	1 752	1 596	117.2
25 - 29	3 968	2 075	1 893	144.2
30 - 34	3 429	1 779	1 650	116.2
35 - 39	1 931	1 009	922	58.6
40 - 44	572	307	265	16.8
45 +	20	9	11	♦0.7
Saint Helena ex. dep. - Sainte-Hélène sans dép.				
2014 (C)				
Total	48	25	23	...
0 - 14	-	-	-	..
15 - 19	8	6	2	...
20 - 24	6	2	4	...
25 - 29	8	5	3	...
30 - 34	19	8	11	...
35 - 39	5	3	2	...
40 - 44	2	1	1	...
45 - 49	-	-	-	...
50 +	-	-	-	...
Unknown - Inconnu	-	-	-	..
Seychelles				
2015 (+C)				
Total	1 592	814	778	66.2
0 - 14	5	3	2	..

Continent, country or area, year, code[a] and age of mother (in years) / Continent, pays ou zone, année, code[a] et âge de la mère (en années)	Number - Nombre			Rate Taux
	Total	Male Masculin	Female Féminin	
AFRICA - AFRIQUE				
Seychelles				
2015 (+C)				
15 - 19	187	89	98	69.9
20 - 24	420	211	209	136.0
25 - 29	406	209	197	130.7
30 - 34	325	176	149	78.7
35 - 39	189	99	90	50.0
40 - 44	56	25	31	15.3
45 - 49	4	2	2	♦1.1
50 +	-	-	-	..
South Africa - Afrique du Sud[3]				
2012 (U)				
Total	926 726	467 058	459 668	...
0 - 14	822	415	407	..
15 - 19	112 605	56 816	55 789	...
20 - 24	253 843	128 346	125 497	...
25 - 29	244 006	122 994	121 012	...
30 - 34	178 694	89 924	88 770	...
35 - 39	101 654	51 081	50 573	...
40 - 44	32 046	15 961	16 085	...
45 - 49	2 584	1 289	1 295	...
50 +	237	111	126	...
Unknown - Inconnu	235	121	114	...
Swaziland[12]				
2007 (|)				
Total	33 084	18 905	14 179	152.2
0 - 14	67	33	34	..
15 - 19	3 581	1 775	1 806	71.0
20 - 24	8 303	4 449	3 854	184.4
25 - 29	6 839	3 830	3 009	187.1
30 - 34	5 039	2 969	2 070	188.5
35 - 39	3 839	2 324	1 515	166.8
40 - 44	2 008	1 340	668	104.7
45 - 49	1 246	892	354	75.8
50 +	2 155	1 288	867	..
Unknown - Inconnu	7	5	2	..
Tunisia - Tunisie				
2011 (C)				
Total	201 120	...	...	...
15 - 19	2 550	...	...	...
20 - 24	23 594	...	...	...
25 - 29	52 266	...	...	...
30 - 34	51 003	...	...	...
35 - 39	28 565	...	...	...
40 - 44	7 282	...	...	...
45 - 49	596	...	...	...
Unknown - Inconnu	35 265	...	...	...
Zambia - Zambie[13]				
2010 (|)				
Total	442 998	224 756	218 242	141.4
12 - 14	921	470	451	..
15 - 19	58 999	29 701	29 298	75.4
20 - 24	128 270	65 048	63 222	200.0
25 - 29	114 701	58 366	56 335	205.1
30 - 34	74 066	37 666	36 400	178.4
35 - 39	45 452	23 072	22 380	139.5
40 - 44	16 150	8 181	7 969	72.5
45 - 49	4 439	2 252	2 187	23.7

10. Live births by age of mother and sex of child, general and age-specific fertility rates: latest available year, 2006 - 2015
Naissances vivantes selon l'âge de la mère et le sexe de l'enfant, taux de fécondité et taux de fécondité par âge : dernière année disponible, 2006 - 2015 (continued - suite)

Continent, country or area, year, code[a] and age of mother (in years) / Continent, pays ou zone, année, code[a] et âge de la mère (en années)	Number - Nombre			Rate Taux
	Total	Male Masculin	Female Féminin	
AMERICA, NORTH - AMÉRIQUE DU NORD				
Anguilla				
2006 (+C)				
Total	183	...	...	...
0 - 14	2	...	...	..
15 - 19	26	...	...	...
20 - 24	56	...	...	...
25 - 29	42	...	...	...
30 - 34	26	...	...	...
35 - 39	27	...	...	...
40 +	4	...	...	...
Aruba				
2015 (C)				
Total	1 244	646	598	46.8
0 - 14	1	-	1	..
15 - 19	98	57	41	26.5
20 - 24	306	166	140	96.9
25 - 29	341	175	166	108.8
30 - 34	283	142	141	78.5
35 - 39	164	85	79	41.3
40 - 44	50	20	30	11.5
45 - 49	1	1	-	♦0.2
50 +	-	-	-	..
Bahamas				
2012 (+U)				
Total	4 469	2 279	2 187	...
0 - 14	4	2	2	..
15 - 19	497	261	236	...
20 - 24	1 028	524	504	...
25 - 29	1 123	580	543	...
30 - 34	972	496	476	...
35 - 39	632	318	314	...
40 - 44	193	91	102	...
45 - 49	15	5	10	...
50 +	1	1	-	..
Unknown - Inconnu	1	1	-	..
Barbados - Barbade				
2007 (+C)				
Total	3 537	1 850	1 687	...
0 - 14	10	7	3	..
15 - 19	462	226	236	...
20 - 24	894	487	407	...
25 - 29	805	420	385	...
30 - 34	730	387	343	...
35 - 39	463	235	228	...
40 - 44	164	84	80	...
45 - 49	7	3	4	...
Unknown - Inconnu	2	1	1	..
Bermuda - Bermudes[14]				
2015 (C)				
Total	583	295	288	41.9
0 - 14	-	-	-	..
15 - 19	10	5	5	♦6.6
20 - 24	44	16	28	27.7
25 - 29	112	59	53	61.3
30 - 34	224	119	105	104.2
35 - 39	153	79	74	71.0
40 - 44	37	16	21	16.5
45 - 49	3	1	2	♦1.2
50 +	-	-	-	..
British Virgin Islands - Îles Vierges britanniques				
2015 (C)				
Total	266	...	...	...
13 - 19	22	...	...	...
20 - 24	54	...	...	...

Continent, country or area, year, code[a] and age of mother (in years) / Continent, pays ou zone, année, code[a] et âge de la mère (en années)	Number - Nombre			Rate Taux
	Total	Male Masculin	Female Féminin	
AMERICA, NORTH - AMÉRIQUE DU NORD				
British Virgin Islands - Îles Vierges britanniques				
2015 (C)				
25 - 29	64	...	...	...
30 - 34	64	...	...	...
35 - 39	45	...	...	...
40 +	15	...	...	...
Unknown - Inconnu	2	...	...	..
Canada[15]				
2009 (C)				
Total	380 863	195 445	185 418	46.0
0 - 14	104	52	52	..
15 - 19	15 534	7 997	7 537	14.1
20 - 24	57 778	29 564	28 214	51.2
25 - 29	116 878	60 099	56 779	100.7
30 - 34	120 734	62 132	58 602	107.0
35 - 39	57 733	29 493	28 240	50.6
40 - 44	11 364	5 720	5 644	9.2
45 - 49	605	316	289	0.4
Unknown - Inconnu[16]	133	72	61	..
Cayman Islands - Îles Caïmanes				
2014 (C)				
Total	710	...	...	...
15 - 19	35	...	...	...
20 - 24	129	...	...	...
25 - 29	140	...	...	...
30 - 34	210	...	...	...
35 - 39	142	...	...	...
40 - 44	51	...	...	...
45 - 49	3	...	...	...
Costa Rica				
2015* (C)				
Total	71 819	36 880	34 939	54.2
0 - 14	432	245	187	..
15 - 19	11 177	5 644	5 533	54.1
20 - 24	19 401	9 979	9 422	89.2
25 - 29	18 564	9 497	9 067	90.3
30 - 34	13 810	7 123	6 687	72.7
35 - 39	6 512	3 387	3 125	37.5
40 - 44	1 473	772	701	9.2
45 - 49	91	51	40	0.5
50 +	3	2	1	..
Unknown - Inconnu	356	180	176	..
Cuba				
2014 (C)				
Total	122 643	63 322	59 321	43.6
0 - 14	464	222	242	..
15 - 19	17 179	8 810	8 369	50.4
20 - 24	38 441	19 969	18 472	100.6
25 - 29	35 732	18 394	17 338	93.3
30 - 34	19 157	9 916	9 241	60.1
35 - 39	9 046	4 663	4 383	24.5
40 - 44	2 456	1 254	1 202	4.9
45 - 49	98	55	43	0.2
50 +	43	24	19	..
Unknown - Inconnu	27	15	12	..
Curaçao				
2015 (C)				
Total	1 874	955	919	50.2
0 - 14	3	2	1	..
15 - 19	152	69	83	30.2
20 - 24	415	215	200	90.7
25 - 29	503	246	257	108.3
30 - 34	441	236	205	88.6

10. Live births by age of mother and sex of child, general and age-specific fertility rates: latest available year, 2006 - 2015
Naissances vivantes selon l'âge de la mère et le sexe de l'enfant, taux de fécondité et taux de fécondité par âge : dernière année disponible, 2006 - 2015 (continued - suite)

Continent, country or area, year, code[a] and age of mother (in years) / Continent, pays ou zone, année, code[a] et âge de la mère (en années)	Number - Nombre			Rate Taux
	Total	Male Masculin	Female Féminin	
AMERICA, NORTH - AMÉRIQUE DU NORD				
Curaçao				
2015 (C)				
35 - 39	252	131	121	49.9
40 - 44	67	29	38	11.2
45 - 49	6	3	3	◆0.9
50 +	-	-	-	
Unknown - Inconnu	35	24	11	..
Dominica - Dominique				
2006 (+C)				
Total	1 056	505	551	62.4
0 - 14	3	-	3	..
15 - 19	154	80	74	45.8
20 - 24	250	115	135	116.8
25 - 29	197	91	106	78.2
30 - 34	207	99	108	74.5
35 - 39	179	86	93	72.9
40 - 44	59	29	30	28.7
45 - 49	5	3	2	◆3.1
Dominican Republic - République dominicaine				
2014 (U)				
Total	138 224	71 226	66 998	...
0 - 14	397	216	181	..
15 - 19	21 589	11 204	10 385	...
20 - 24	44 548	22 888	21 660	...
25 - 29	35 347	18 223	17 124	...
30 - 34	22 850	11 778	11 072	...
35 - 39	9 653	4 945	4 708	...
40 - 44	2 058	1 052	1 006	...
45 - 49	157	76	81	...
50 +	129	74	55	..
Unknown - Inconnu	1 496	770	726	..
El Salvador[17]				
2012 (C)				
Total	110 843	57 480	53 363	...
0 - 14	1 033	520	513	..
15 - 19	23 410	12 093	11 317	...
20 - 24	32 655	16 988	15 667	...
25 - 29	24 285	12 567	11 718	...
30 - 34	17 595	9 189	8 406	...
35 - 39	8 687	4 473	4 214	...
40 - 44	2 262	1 193	1 069	...
45 - 49	177	86	91	...
50 +	16	5	11	...
Unknown - Inconnu	739	371	368	...
Greenland - Groenland				
2015 (C)				
Total	854	440	414	63.3
15 - 19	74	37	37	37.0
20 - 24	237	127	110	109.1
25 - 29	274	145	129	124.2
30 - 34	180	87	93	91.8
35 - 39	73	39	34	48.7
40 - 44	15	5	10	◆10.8
45 - 49	1	-	1	◆0.4
Guatemala				
2011 (C)				
Total	373 692	189 724	183 968	...
0 - 14	2 841	1 426	1 415	...
15 - 19	75 175	38 415	36 760	...
20 - 24	108 949	55 558	53 391	...
25 - 29	85 914	43 599	42 315	...
30 - 34	58 050	29 264	28 786	...
35 - 39	30 892	15 540	15 352	...
40 - 44	10 220	5 136	5 084	...

Continent, country or area, year, code[a] and age of mother (in years) / Continent, pays ou zone, année, code[a] et âge de la mère (en années)	Number - Nombre			Rate Taux
	Total	Male Masculin	Female Féminin	
AMERICA, NORTH - AMÉRIQUE DU NORD				
Guatemala				
2011 (C)				
45 - 49	1 176	573	603	...
50 +	290	127	163	..
Unknown - Inconnu	185	86	99	...
Honduras				
2012 (+U)				
Total	196 119	...	...	...
0 - 14	1 571	...	...	..
15 - 19	41 882	...	...	...
20 - 24	56 501	...	...	...
25 - 29	43 429	...	...	...
30 - 34	28 675	...	...	...
35 - 39	14 730	...	...	...
40 - 44	4 791	...	...	...
45 - 49	575	...	...	...
50 +	471	...	...	...
Unknown - Inconnu	3 494	...	...	...
Jamaica - Jamaïque[18]				
2011 (I)				
Total	49 676	23 949[19]	23 339[19]	66.0
15 - 19	6 167	3 034[19]	2 884[19]	50.5
20 - 24	13 977	6 852[19]	6 451[19]	129.9
25 - 29	12 348	5 923[19]	5 900[19]	108.7
30 - 34	8 746	4 182[19]	4 145[19]	73.9
35 - 39	6 001	2 816[19]	2 875[19]	48.9
40 - 44	2 109	1 014[19]	956[19]	21.2
45 - 49	328	128[19]	128[19]	4.8
Martinique[11]				
2007 (C)				
Total	5 317	2 676	2 641	51.0
0 - 14	2	1	1	..
15 - 19	305	165	140	19.8
20 - 24	911	447	464	77.6
25 - 29	1 202	617	585	117.2
30 - 34	1 376	678	698	98.2
35 - 39	1 105	560	545	64.1
40 - 44	393	194	199	20.9
45 +	23	14	9	◆1.4
Mexico - Mexique[20]				
2013 (C)				
Total	2 168 933	1 105 164[19]	1 063 692[19]	...
0 - 14	7 601	3 931[19]	3 670[19]	..
15 - 19	399 650	204 628[19]	195 009[19]	...
20 - 24	658 259	335 726[19]	322 506[19]	...
25 - 29	527 565	268 562[19]	258 993[19]	...
30 - 34	354 986	180 063[19]	174 912[19]	...
35 - 39	171 557	87 088[19]	84 467[19]	...
40 - 44	40 829	20 697[19]	20 131[19]	...
45 - 49	2 672	1 342[19]	1 329[19]	...
50 +	389	199[19]	190[19]	...
Unknown - Inconnu	5 425	2 928[19]	2 485[19]	...
Montserrat				
2014 (+C)				
Total	50	22	28	...
0 - 14	-	-	-	...
15 - 19	9	3	6	...
20 - 24	12	5	7	...
25 - 29	12	6	6	...
30 - 34	7	3	4	...
35 - 39	6	3	3	...
40 - 44	4	2	2	...
45 - 49	-	-	-	...
50 +	-	-	-	...

10. Live births by age of mother and sex of child, general and age-specific fertility rates: latest available year, 2006 - 2015
Naissances vivantes selon l'âge de la mère et le sexe de l'enfant, taux de fécondité et taux de fécondité par âge : dernière année disponible, 2006 - 2015 (continued - suite)

Continent, country or area, year, code[a] and age of mother (in years) / Continent, pays ou zone, année, code[a] et âge de la mère (en années)	Number - Nombre			Rate Taux
	Total	Male Masculin	Female Féminin	

AMERICA, NORTH - AMÉRIQUE DU NORD

	Total	Male Masculin	Female Féminin	Rate Taux
Nicaragua				
2010 (+U)				
Total	132 165	68 726	63 439	...
0 - 14	1 539	793	746	..
15 - 19	33 963	17 752	16 211	...
20 - 24	38 897	20 181	18 716	...
25 - 29	30 273	15 790	14 483	...
30 - 34	17 301	8 942	8 359	...
35 - 39	8 010	4 156	3 854	...
40 - 44	1 943	992	951	...
45 - 49	209	105	104	...
50 +	30	15	15	..
Panama				
2014 (C)				
Total	75 183	38 571	36 612	74.2
0 - 14	669	348	321	
15 - 19	14 354	7 492	6 862	86.0
20 - 24	20 955	10 815	10 140	133.3
25 - 29	18 009	9 164	8 845	118.3
30 - 34	12 868	6 538	6 330	88.2
35 - 39	6 447	3 244	3 203	46.0
40 - 44	1 649	849	800	12.5
45 - 49	117	68	49	1.0
50 +	22	13	9	..
Unknown - Inconnu	93	40	53	
Puerto Rico - Porto Rico				
2015 (C)				
Total	31 229	16 058	15 171	...
0 - 14	43	24	19	...
15 - 19	4 014	2 041	1 973	...
20 - 24	10 536	5 438	5 098	...
25 - 29	8 190	4 204	3 986	...
30 - 34	5 196	2 706	2 490	...
35 - 39	2 683	1 356	1 327	...
40 - 44	540	273	267	...
45 - 49	24	14	10	...
50 +	2	1	1	..
Unknown - Inconnu	1	1	-	..
Saint Vincent and the Grenadines - Saint-Vincent-et-les Grenadines				
2014 (C)				
Total	1 841	912	929	...
0 - 14	10	4	6	..
15 - 19	312	162	150	...
20 - 24	476	240	236	...
25 - 29	426	194	232	...
30 - 34	332	170	162	...
35 - 39	214	113	101	...
40 - 44	67	27	40	...
45 - 49	4	2	2	...
50 +	-	-	-	..
Unknown - Inconnu	-	-	-	..
Trinidad and Tobago - Trinité-et-Tobago				
2009 (C)				
Total	17 949	9 067	8 882	...
0 - 14	24	10	14	..
15 - 19	1 961	961	1 000	...
20 - 24	5 029	2 620	2 409	...
25 - 29	5 258	2 606	2 652	...
30 - 34	3 422	1 715	1 707	...
35 - 39	1 763	910	853	...
40 - 44	432	218	214	...

AMERICA, NORTH - AMÉRIQUE DU NORD

	Total	Male Masculin	Female Féminin	Rate Taux
Trinidad and Tobago - Trinité-et-Tobago				
2009 (C)				
45 - 49	31	13	18	...
50 +	3	1	2	...
Unknown - Inconnu	26	13	13	..
United States of America - États-Unis d'Amérique				
2013 (C)				
Total	3 932 181	2 012 954	1 919 227	...
0 - 14	3 098	1 592	1 506	..
15 - 19	273 105	140 110	132 995	...
20 - 24	896 745	458 528	438 217	...
25 - 29	1 120 777	574 266	546 511	...
30 - 34	1 036 927	530 707	506 220	...
35 - 39	483 873	247 753	236 120	...
40 - 44	109 484	55 858	53 626	...
45 - 49	7 495	3 813	3 682	...
50 - 54	677	327	350	...
2014 (C)				
Total	3 988 076	...	...	...
0 - 14	2 769	...	...	..
15 - 19	249 078	...	...	...
20 - 24	882 567	...	...	...
25 - 29	1 145 392	...	...	...
30 - 34	1 081 058	...	...	...
35 - 39	508 748	...	...	...
40 - 44	110 021	...	...	...
45 - 49	7 700	...	...	...
50 +	743	...	...	...
United States Virgin Islands - Îles Vierges américaines				
2007 (C)				
Total	1 771	...	...	65.9
0 - 14	2	...	...	..
15 - 19	226	...	...	53.1
20 - 24	550	...	...	146.6
25 - 29	424	...	...	146.1
30 - 34	319	...	...	93.9
35 - 39	196	...	...	48.6
40 +	46	...	...	5.5
Unknown - Inconnu	8	...	...	

AMERICA, SOUTH - AMÉRIQUE DU SUD

	Total	Male Masculin	Female Féminin	Rate Taux
Argentina - Argentine				
2014 (C)				
Total	777 012	...	...	72.1
0 - 14	3 007	...	...	
15 - 19	113 945	...	...	65.9
20 - 24	192 415	...	...	111.1
25 - 29	177 190	...	...	108.6
30 - 34	160 012	...	...	101.9
35 - 39	95 509	...	...	62.6
40 - 44	24 305	...	...	18.5
45 +	1 624	...	...	1.4
Unknown - Inconnu	9 005	...	...	...
Brazil - Brésil				
2014 (U)				
Total	2 913 121[21]	1 493 634[19]	1 419 130[19]	...
0 - 14	24 165[21]	12 354[19]	11 809[19]	..
15 - 19	507 928[21]	260 819[19]	247 060[19]	...
20 - 24	725 828[21]	372 663[19]	353 113[19]	...
25 - 29	707 038[21]	362 586[19]	344 400[19]	...

10. Live births by age of mother and sex of child, general and age-specific fertility rates: latest available year, 2006 - 2015
Naissances vivantes selon l'âge de la mère et le sexe de l'enfant, taux de fécondité et taux de fécondité par âge : dernière année disponible, 2006 - 2015 (continued - suite)

Continent, country or area, year, code[a] and age of mother (in years) / Continent, pays ou zone, année, code[a] et âge de la mère (en années)	Number - Nombre			Rate Taux
	Total	Male Masculin	Female Féminin	

AMERICA, SOUTH - AMÉRIQUE DU SUD

	Total	Male Masculin	Female Féminin	Rate Taux
Brazil - Brésil				
2014 (U)				
30 - 34	573 862[21]	293 800[19]	280 031[19]	...
35 - 39	286 000[21]	146 377[19]	139 599[19]	...
40 - 44	67 090[21]	34 284[19]	32 800[19]	...
45 - 49	4 248[21]	2 186[19]	2 062[19]	...
50 +	417[21]	202[19]	215[19]	...
Unknown - Inconnu	16 545[21]	8 363[19]	8 041[19]	..
Chile - Chili				
2013 (C)				
Total	242 005	123 402[19]	118 585[19]	53.0
0 - 14	902	463[19]	439[19]	..
15 - 19	31 506	16 147[19]	15 353[19]	46.0
20 - 24	56 898	29 067[19]	27 827[19]	78.2
25 - 29	58 140	29 576[19]	28 562[19]	83.8
30 - 34	53 625	27 292[19]	26 329[19]	85.9
35 - 39	31 614	16 065[19]	15 547[19]	53.1
40 - 44	8 814	4 547[19]	4 267[19]	14.3
45 - 49	448	206[19]	242[19]	0.7
50 +	12	7[19]	5[19]	..
Unknown - Inconnu	46	25[19]	15[19]	..
Colombia - Colombie				
2014 (U)				
Total	669 131	343 163	325 968	...
0 - 14	6 593	3 463	3 130	..
15 - 19	144 030	73 686	70 344	...
20 - 24	195 473	100 454	95 019	...
25 - 29	150 072	76 926	73 146	...
30 - 34	106 118	54 518	51 600	...
35 - 39	52 432	26 789	25 643	...
40 - 44	12 988	6 602	6 386	...
45 - 49	1 063	533	530	...
50 +	128	51	77	...
Unknown - Inconnu	234	141	93	..
Ecuador - Équateur				
2014 (+U)				
Total	229 476	118 138	111 338	...
0 - 14	1 515	826	689	..
15 - 19	41 451	21 412	20 039	...
20 - 24	62 086	32 115	29 971	...
25 - 29	54 236	27 781	26 455	...
30 - 34	40 735	20 961	19 774	...
35 - 39	22 190	11 374	10 816	...
40 - 44	6 499	3 293	3 206	...
45 - 49	580	289	291	...
50 +	-	-	-	..
Unknown - Inconnu	184	87	97	..
French Guiana - Guyane française[11]				
2007 (C)				
Total	6 386	3 269	3 117	114.5
0 - 14	23	12	11	..
15 - 19	828	428	400	83.3
20 - 24	1 477	726	751	182.2
25 - 29	1 590	821	769	195.5
30 - 34	1 312	707	605	154.0
35 - 39	844	414	430	102.2
40 - 44	289	152	137	40.9
45 - 49	22	8	14	♦3.8
50 +	1	1	-	..
Paraguay				
2008 (+U)				
Total	99 674	51 066	48 608	...
0 - 14	538	269	269	..

AMERICA, SOUTH - AMÉRIQUE DU SUD

	Total	Male Masculin	Female Féminin	Rate Taux
Paraguay				
2008 (+U)				
15 - 19	20 188	10 404	9 784	...
20 - 24	28 246	14 396	13 850	...
25 - 29	23 863	12 261	11 602	...
30 - 34	14 721	7 480	7 241	...
35 - 39	8 899	4 600	4 299	...
40 - 44	2 819	1 440	1 379	...
45 - 49	250	134	116	...
50 +	2	2	-	...
Unknown - Inconnu	148	80	68	...
Peru - Pérou[22]				
2014 (+U)				
Total	492 008	252 135	239 873	...
0 - 14	1 548	791	757	..
15 - 19	65 653	33 755	31 898	...
20 - 24	122 959	63 222	59 737	...
25 - 29	118 198	60 514	57 684	...
30 - 34	97 184	49 726	47 458	...
35 - 39	63 254	32 259	30 995	...
40 - 44	21 583	11 036	10 547	...
45 - 49	1 533	782	751	...
50 +	90	47	43	...
Unknown - Inconnu	6	3	3	..
Suriname				
2014 (C)				
Total	10 407	5 229	5 178	71.9
13 - 14	66	...	...	..
15 - 19	1 390	...	...	59.5
20 - 24	2 643	...	...	116.3
25 - 29	2 866	...	...	131.0
30 - 34	2 134	...	...	102.3
35 - 39	1 006	...	...	51.0
40 - 44	276	...	...	14.7
45 +	26	...	...	♦1.5
Unknown - Inconnu	-	...	...	..
Uruguay				
2014 (C)				
Total	48 368	24 806[19]	23 551[19]	57.1
0 - 14	169	80[19]	89[19]	..
15 - 19	7 779	4 020[19]	3 756[19]	58.2
20 - 24	11 564	5 915[19]	5 648[19]	90.4
25 - 29	10 767	5 563[19]	5 202[19]	87.8
30 - 34	10 304	5 249[19]	5 052[19]	86.0
35 - 39	6 220	3 174[19]	3 044[19]	50.6
40 - 44	1 474	756[19]	718[19]	13.1
45 - 49	67	37[19]	30[19]	0.6
50 +	4	1[19]	3[19]	..
Unknown - Inconnu	20	11[19]	9[19]	..
Venezuela (Bolivarian Republic of) - Venezuela (République bolivarienne du)				
2015 (U)				
Total	600 860	308 901	291 959	...
0 - 14	6 628	3 412	3 216	..
15 - 19	125 739	64 871	60 868	...
20 - 24	174 600	90 042	84 558	...
25 - 29	138 804	71 020	67 784	...
30 - 34	93 722	47 892	45 830	...
35 - 39	44 570	22 993	21 577	...
40 - 44	11 468	5 895	5 573	...
45 - 49	1 038	544	494	...
50 +	310	161	149	...
Unknown - Inconnu	3 981	2 071	1 910	...

10. Live births by age of mother and sex of child, general and age-specific fertility rates: latest available year, 2006 - 2015
Naissances vivantes selon l'âge de la mère et le sexe de l'enfant, taux de fécondité et taux de fécondité par âge : dernière année disponible, 2006 - 2015 (continued - suite)

Continent, country or area, year, code[a] and age of mother (in years) / Continent, pays ou zone, année, code[a] et âge de la mère (en années)	Total	Male Masculin	Female Féminin	Rate Taux	Continent, country or area, year, code[a] and age of mother (in years) / Continent, pays ou zone, année, code[a] et âge de la mère (en années)	Total	Male Masculin	Female Féminin	Rate Taux
ASIA - ASIE					**ASIA - ASIE**				
Armenia - Arménie					China, Hong Kong SAR - Chine, Hong Kong RAS				
2014 (C)					2014 (C)				
Total	43 031	22 869	20 162	...	Total	62 305	32 262	30 043	30.3
0 - 14	-	-	-	..	0 - 14	4	2	2	..
15 - 19	2 192	1 130	1 062	..	15 - 19	555	268	287	3.0
20 - 24	16 387	8 506	7 881	...	20 - 24	4 197	2 206	1 991	18.5
25 - 29	14 630	7 843	6 787	...	25 - 29	14 691	7 598	7 093	50.4
30 - 34	7 173	3 939	3 234	...	30 - 34	24 862	12 817	12 045	71.5
35 - 39	2 260	1 253	1 007	...	35 - 39	14 568	7 568	7 000	43.8
40 - 44	360	181	179	...	40 - 44	3 217	1 688	1 529	9.5
45 - 49	25	13	12	...	45 - 49	161	88	73	0.5
50 +	4	4	-	..	50 +	13	7	6	..
Unknown - Inconnu	-	-	-	..	Unknown - Inconnu	37	20	17	..
Azerbaijan - Azerbaïdjan[23]					China, Macao SAR - Chine, Macao RAS				
2014 (+C)					2015 (C)				
Total	170 503	91 410	79 093	63.4	Total	7 055	3 682	3 373	37.4
0 - 14	-	-	-	..	0 - 24	849	430	419	22.6
15 - 19	19 267	9 931	9 336	52.9	25 - 29	2 826	1 480	1 346	77.0
20 - 24	70 312	37 227	33 085	154.7	30 - 34	2 217	1 135	1 082	68.2
25 - 29	51 021	27 816	23 205	109.2	35 - 39	942	510	432	37.5
30 - 34	21 264	11 707	9 557	53.3	40 +	221	127	94	3.9
35 - 39	7 027	3 904	3 123	21.2	Cyprus - Chypre[25]				
40 - 44	1 443	745	698	4.4	2014 (C)				
45 - 49	138	64	74	0.4	Total	9 258	4 867	4 391	41.0
50 +	31	16	15	..	0 - 14	-	-	-	..
Unknown - Inconnu	-	-	-	..	15 - 19	128	68	60	4.9
Bahrain - Bahreïn[24]					20 - 24	906	487	419	27.6
2014 (C)					25 - 29	2 932	1 522	1 410	81.3
Total	20 931	10 785	10 146	69.3	30 - 34	3 477	1 814	1 663	95.4
0 - 14	-	-	-	..	35 - 39	1 438	776	662	43.5
15 - 19	521	281	240	14.7	40 - 44	316	172	144	10.0
20 - 24	4 370	2 254	2 116	100.5	45 - 49	43	16	27	1.5
25 - 29	6 572	3 340	3 232	115.3	50 +	9	5	4	..
30 - 34	5 497	2 868	2 629	102.1	Unknown - Inconnu	9	7	2	..
35 - 39	3 084	1 586	1 498	67.2	Democratic People's Republic of Korea - République populaire démocratique de Corée[13]				
40 - 44	781	404	377	22.4	2008 (I)				
45 - 49	93	45	48	2.9	Total	345 630	176 399	169 231	53.3
50 +	9	5	4	..	15 - 19	633	330	303	0.6
Unknown - Inconnu	4	2	2	..	20 - 24	52 214	26 657	25 557	58.0
Bangladesh					25 - 29	178 032	90 850	87 182	209.5
2010 (U)					30 - 34	90 973	46 224	44 749	110.0
Total	*2 868 494*	*1 451 664*	*1 416 831*	...	35 - 39	20 275	10 505	9 770	18.5
15 - 19	*404 570*	*209 615*	*194 955*	...	40 - 44	3 202	1 673	1 529	3.2
20 - 24	*1 055 194*	*527 993*	*527 201*	...	45 - 49	301	160	141	0.4
25 - 29	*762 338*	*383 627*	*378 710*	...	Georgia - Géorgie				
30 - 34	*389 547*	*199 767*	*189 780*	...	2014 (C)				
35 - 39	*192 438*	*97 826*	*94 613*	...	Total	60 635	31 325	29 310	53.8
40 - 44	*49 380*	*25 206*	*24 174*	...	0 - 14	21	8	13	..
45 +	*15 027*	*7 630*	*7 397*	...	15 - 19	5 557	2 857	2 700	42.5
Brunei Darussalam - Brunéi Darussalam					20 - 24	19 128	9 918	9 210	110.9
2014 (+C)					25 - 29	18 233	9 376	8 857	102.2
Total	6 891	3 585	3 306	58.9	30 - 34	11 373	5 878	5 495	67.9
0 - 14	5	2	3	..	35 - 39	4 936	2 573	2 363	30.7
15 - 19	195	97	98	11.5	40 - 44	1 148	614	534	7.3
20 - 24	1 078	546	532	62.7	45 - 49	143	59	84	0.9
25 - 29	2 214	1 169	1 045	119.7	50 +	38	18	20	..
30 - 34	2 045	1 065	980	113.0	Unknown - Inconnu	58	24	34	..
35 - 39	1 083	579	504	64.5					
40 - 44	252	119	133	15.8					
45 - 49	16	8	8	♦1.2					
50 +	2	-	2	..					
Unknown - Inconnu	1	-	1	..					

10. Live births by age of mother and sex of child, general and age-specific fertility rates: latest available year, 2006 - 2015
Naissances vivantes selon l'âge de la mère et le sexe de l'enfant, taux de fécondité et taux de fécondité par âge : dernière année disponible, 2006 - 2015 (continued - suite)

Continent, country or area, year, code[a] and age of mother (in years) / Continent, pays ou zone, année, code[a] et âge de la mère (en années)	Number - Nombre			Rate Taux
	Total	Male Masculin	Female Féminin	

ASIA - ASIE

Indonesia - Indonésie[26]
2010 (|)

Total	6 028 921	...	...	92.5
0 - 14	1 054	...	...	..
15 - 19	344 318	...	...	33.5
20 - 24	1 435 265	...	...	143.5
25 - 29	1 787 802	...	...	167.4
30 - 34	1 352 605	...	...	136.9
35 - 39	776 985	...	...	84.8
40 - 44	254 427	...	...	31.0
45 - 49	57 924	...	...	8.3
50 +	18 541	...	...	

Iran (Islamic Republic of) - Iran (République islamique d')[27]
2014 (+C)

Total	1 493 317	768 209	725 108	65.4
0 - 14	1 713	907	806	..
15 - 19	102 549	52 413	50 136	35.6
20 - 24	345 564	177 770	167 794	95.4
25 - 29	474 159	243 543	230 616	108.9
30 - 34	363 457	187 261	176 196	90.8
35 - 39	159 905	82 341	77 564	51.9
40 - 44	34 361	17 747	16 614	13.5
45 - 49	2 541	1 278	1 263	1.1
50 +	264	110	154	..
Unknown - Inconnu	8 804	4 839	3 965	..

Israel - Israël[28]
2014 (C)

Total	176 427	90 780	85 647	91.4
0 - 14	-	-	-	..
15 - 19	3 181	1 656	1 525	10.2
20 - 24	31 589	16 283	15 306	107.0
25 - 29	51 392	26 319	25 073	177.2
30 - 34	51 842	26 690	25 152	181.6
35 - 39	30 041	15 560	14 481	108.4
40 - 44	7 322	3 721	3 601	28.9
45 - 49	656	336	320	3.1
50 +	90	41	49	..
Unknown - Inconnu	314	174	140	..

Japan - Japon[29]
2014 (C)

Total	1 003 539	515 533	488 006	38.1
0 - 14	43	24	19	..
15 - 19	12 968	6 742	6 226	4.4
20 - 24	86 590	44 460	42 130	28.7
25 - 29	267 847	137 557	130 290	81.2
30 - 34	359 323	184 877	174 446	97.2
35 - 39	225 889	115 937	109 952	52.2
40 - 44	49 606	25 299	24 307	10.3
45 - 49	1 214	604	610	0.3
50 +	58	33	25	..
Unknown - Inconnu	1	-	1	..

Kazakhstan[23]
2013 (C)

Total	387 227	199 880	187 347	84.3
0 - 14	20	12	8	..
15 - 19	20 727	10 653	10 074	32.8
20 - 24	124 737	64 434	60 303	155.1
25 - 29	124 145	63 987	60 158	160.1
30 - 34	71 453	36 850	34 603	109.3
35 - 39	37 140	19 237	17 903	61.4
40 - 44	8 560	4 458	4 102	15.1
45 - 49	387	217	170	0.7

Continent, country or area, year, code[a] and age of mother (in years) / Continent, pays ou zone, année, code[a] et âge de la mère (en années)	Number - Nombre			Rate Taux
	Total	Male Masculin	Female Féminin	

ASIA - ASIE

Kazakhstan[23]
2013 (C)

50 +	33	20	13	..
Unknown - Inconnu	25	12	13	..

Kuwait - Koweït
2014 (C)

Total	61 313	31 513	29 800	59.5
15 - 19	772	407	365	8.3
20 - 24	9 140	4 633	4 507	99.4
25 - 29	18 249	9 497	8 752	114.9
30 - 34	16 133	8 247	7 886	91.3
35 - 39	8 460	4 368	4 092	50.0
40 - 44	2 401	1 206	1 195	16.8
45 +	236	121	115	2.4
Unknown - Inconnu	5 922	3 034	2 888	..

Kyrgyzstan - Kirghizstan
2015* (C)

Total	163 452	84 650	78 802	104.6
0 - 14	2	1	1	..
15 - 19	10 789	5 538	5 251	42.3
20 - 24	56 695	29 289	27 406	201.0
25 - 29	49 554	25 855	23 699	173.5
30 - 34	28 822	14 973	13 849	128.8
35 - 39	13 412	6 870	6 542	72.6
40 - 44	3 648	1 834	1 814	21.4
45 - 49	367	197	170	2.3
50 +	12	7	5	..
Unknown - Inconnu	151	86	65	..

Malaysia - Malaisie
2014* (C)

Total	511 865	264 396	247 469	62.5
0 - 14	189	107	82	..
15 - 19	16 966	8 765	8 201	12.4
20 - 24	73 756	38 411	35 345	49.9
25 - 29	172 755	88 950	83 805	123.1
30 - 34	153 583	79 453	74 130	126.8
35 - 39	74 102	38 300	35 802	76.2
40 - 44	18 514	9 385	9 129	20.4
45 - 49	1 458	741	717	1.7
50 +	58	33	25	..
Unknown - Inconnu	484	251	233	..

Maldives
2014 (C)

Total	7 245	3 706	3 539	69.2
0 - 14	-	-	-	..
15 - 19	201	105	96	13.2
20 - 24	1 960	1 029	931	105.2
25 - 29	2 555	1 318	1 237	119.4
30 - 34	1 662	828	834	96.5
35 - 39	654	318	336	52.6
40 - 44	198	102	96	18.8
45 - 49	10	6	4	♦1.1
50 +	-	-	-	..
Unknown - Inconnu	5	-	5	..

Mongolia - Mongolie
2015 (+C)

Total	82 130	42 150	39 980	95.1
0 - 14	22	6	16	..
15 - 19	3 573	1 841	1 732	29.8
20 - 24	21 173	10 860	10 313	155.3
25 - 29	26 276	13 526	12 750	168.7
30 - 34	18 099	9 358	8 741	137.1
35 - 39	10 342	5 200	5 142	87.1
40 - 44	2 524	1 299	1 225	23.5

10. Live births by age of mother and sex of child, general and age-specific fertility rates: latest available year, 2006 - 2015
Naissances vivantes selon l'âge de la mère et le sexe de l'enfant, taux de fécondité et taux de fécondité par âge : dernière année disponible, 2006 - 2015 (continued - suite)

Continent, country or area, year, code[a] and age of mother (in years) / Continent, pays ou zone, année, code[a] et âge de la mère (en années)	Total	Male Masculin	Female Féminin	Rate Taux
ASIA - ASIE				
Mongolia - Mongolie				
2015 (+C)				
45 - 49	112	55	57	1.2
50 +	9	5	4	..
Myanmar				
2013 (+U)				
Total	928 439	483 396	445 043	...
0 - 14	-	-	-	..
15 - 19	49 042	25 646	23 396	...
20 - 24	223 909	116 923	106 986	...
25 - 29	283 164	147 007	136 157	...
30 - 34	208 661	108 722	99 939	...
35 - 39	117 376	60 939	56 437	...
40 - 44	41 724	21 759	19 965	...
45 +	4 563	2 400	2 163	...
Oman[30]				
2014 (U)				
Total	82 981	42 419	40 562	...
0 - 14	12	7	5	..
15 - 19	1 628	825	803	...
20 - 24	15 384	7 826	7 558	...
25 - 29	27 235	14 050	13 185	...
30 - 34	22 000	11 148	10 852	...
35 - 39	12 064	6 190	5 874	...
40 - 44	3 300	1 697	1 603	...
45 - 49	356	190	166	...
50 +	46	28	18	..
Unknown - Inconnu	956	458	498	..
Philippines				
2014 (C)				
Total	1 748 857	912 465	836 392	67.8
0 - 14	1 877	1 015	862	..
15 - 19	207 995	108 401	99 594	42.5
20 - 24	506 451	264 456	241 995	109.8
25 - 29	436 091	227 807	208 284	108.6
30 - 34	331 745	172 908	158 837	92.8
35 - 39	191 321	99 835	91 486	59.4
40 - 44	63 071	32 671	30 400	22.0
45 - 49	6 532	3 323	3 209	2.5
50 +	392	217	175	..
Unknown - Inconnu	3 382	1 832	1 550	..
Qatar				
2013 (C)				
Total	23 708	12 119	11 589	70.0
0 - 19	352	162	190	11.4
20 - 24	3 791	1 955	1 836	98.1
25 - 29	7 687	3 986	3 701	105.0
30 - 34	7 117	3 642	3 475	98.3
35 - 39	3 711	1 865	1 846	65.3
40 - 44	957	459	498	24.0
45 - 49	83	44	39	3.1
50 +	10	6	4	..
Republic of Korea - République de Corée[31]				
2014 (C)				
Total	435 435	223 356	212 079	34.2
0 - 14	22	9	13	..
15 - 19	2 527	1 301	1 226	1.6
20 - 24	21 171	10 779	10 392	13.1
25 - 29	96 192	49 315	46 877	61.6
30 - 34	221 145	113 512	107 633	115.6
35 - 39	82 226	42 294	39 932	43.8
40 - 44	11 523	5 832	5 691	5.4
45 - 49	308	150	158	0.1
ASIA - ASIE				
Republic of Korea - République de Corée[31]				
2014 (C)				
50 +	26	14	12	..
Unknown - Inconnu	295	150	145	..
Singapore - Singapour				
2015 (C)				
Total	42 185	21 755	20 430	41.6
0 - 14	9	4	5	..
15 - 19	332	187	145	2.8
20 - 24	2 557	1 324	1 233	19.6
25 - 29	10 733	5 504	5 229	77.5
30 - 34	17 703	9 196	8 507	115.9
35 - 39	9 102	4 691	4 411	57.9
40 - 44	1 675	815	860	10.3
45 - 49	67	29	38	0.4
50 +	7	5	2	..
Sri Lanka				
2006 (+C)				
Total	373 538	191 263	182 275	67.9
0 - 14	113	57	56	..
15 - 19	20 040	10 335	9 705	21.2
20 - 24	81 003	41 508	39 495	87.5
25 - 29	121 968	62 480	59 488	151.5
30 - 34	90 483	46 346	44 137	118.4
35 - 39	46 534	23 759	22 775	61.6
40 - 44	12 104	6 149	5 955	17.4
45 - 49	1 275	622	653	2.1
50 +	18	7	11	..
State of Palestine - État de Palestine[32]				
2007 (I)				
Total	106 209	54 540	51 671	121.5
0 - 14	2	2	-	..
15 - 19	7 759	4 029	3 731	36.1
20 - 24	31 097	15 970	15 128	189.3
25 - 29	30 535	15 688	14 847	224.1
30 - 34	20 980	10 682	10 298	180.3
35 - 39	11 544	5 974	5 570	118.4
40 - 44	3 821	1 913	1 908	47.5
45 - 49	342	198	144	5.4
50 +	94	66	28	..
Unknown - Inconnu	35	18	17	..
Thailand - Thaïlande				
2011 (+U)				
Total	795 031	409 699	385 332	...
0 - 14	3 415	1 793	1 622	..
15 - 19	129 321	66 645	62 676	...
20 - 24	186 942	96 371	90 571	...
25 - 29	204 684	105 355	99 329	...
30 - 34	167 671	86 515	81 156	...
35 - 39	80 348	41 311	39 037	...
40 - 44	20 089	10 251	9 838	...
45 - 49	1 293	653	640	...
50 +	73	30	43	...
Unknown - Inconnu	1 195	775	420	..
Turkey - Turquie				
2014 (C)				
Total	1 337 504	687 255	650 249	65.2
0 - 14	317	167	150	..
15 - 19	84 359	43 543	40 816	26.8
20 - 24	324 101	166 674	157 427	106.3
25 - 29	413 462	212 713	200 749	134.6
30 - 34	325 138	166 639	158 499	101.6
35 - 39	143 763	73 698	70 065	49.5

10. Live births by age of mother and sex of child, general and age-specific fertility rates: latest available year, 2006 - 2015
Naissances vivantes selon l'âge de la mère et le sexe de l'enfant, taux de fécondité et taux de fécondité par âge : dernière année disponible, 2006 - 2015 (continued - suite)

Continent, country or area, year, code[a] and age of mother (in years) / Continent, pays ou zone, année, code[a] et âge de la mère (en années)	Total	Male Masculin	Female Féminin	Rate Taux
ASIA - ASIE				
Turkey - Turquie				
2014 (C)				
40 - 44	33 892	17 345	16 547	12.4
45 - 49	2 569	1 284	1 285	1.1
50 +	362	213	149	..
Unknown - Inconnu	9 541	4 979	4 562	..
Uzbekistan - Ouzbékistan				
2014 (+C)				
Total	718 036	373 277	344 759	83.4
0 - 14	-	-	-	..
15 - 19	34 922	17 903	17 019	24.2
20 - 24	305 670	158 121	147 549	192.4
25 - 29	244 529	126 995	117 534	162.3
30 - 34	102 728	54 102	48 626	83.3
35 - 39	26 524	14 203	12 321	25.3
40 - 44	3 430	1 825	1 605	3.6
45 - 49	209	111	98	0.2
50 +	24	17	7	..
EUROPE				
Åland Islands - Îles d'Åland				
2014 (C)				
Total	282	148	134	46.9
0 - 14	-	-	-	..
15 - 19	3	-	3	♦3.6
20 - 24	27	13	14	♦38.8
25 - 29	101	58	43	135.8
30 - 34	102	53	49	121.6
35 - 39	41	21	20	47.7
40 - 44	8	3	5	♦8.5
45 - 49	-	-	-	..
50 +	-	-	-	..
Albania - Albanie				
2013 (C)				
Total	35 750	18 661	17 089	49.6
0 - 14	22	16	6	..
15 - 19	2 613	1 337	1 276	20.3
20 - 24	11 737	6 083	5 654	108.2
25 - 29	11 990	6 255	5 735	124.0
30 - 34	6 559	3 482	3 077	69.2
35 - 39	2 298	1 216	1 082	25.3
40 - 44	429	223	206	4.3
45 - 49	33	19	14	0.3
50 +	13	7	6	..
Unknown - Inconnu	56	23	33	..
Andorra - Andorre				
2012 (C)				
Total	737	364	373	36.4
12 - 14	-	-	-	..
15 - 19	5	2	3	♦2.8
20 - 24	43	21	22	22.8
25 - 29	162	86	76	63.7
30 - 34	284	143	141	84.2
35 - 39	197	87	110	52.6
40 - 44	39	19	20	10.9
45 - 49	6	5	1	♦1.8
50 +	1	1	-	..
Austria - Autriche				
2014 (C)				
Total	81 722	42 162	39 560	40.9
0 - 14	15	5	10	..
15 - 19	1 671	865	806	7.4
20 - 24	11 305	5 824	5 481	42.3
EUROPE				
Austria - Autriche				
2014 (C)				
25 - 29	24 498	12 560	11 938	87.8
30 - 34	27 622	14 353	13 269	96.2
35 - 39	13 424	6 927	6 497	49.3
40 - 44	2 996	1 528	1 468	9.6
45 - 49	175	95	80	0.5
50 +	16	5	11	..
Belarus - Bélarus				
2006 (C)				
Total	96 721	49 849	46 872	36.6
0 - 14	10	5	5	..
15 - 19	8 238	4 234	4 004	21.9
20 - 24	36 120	18 613	17 507	88.9
25 - 29	29 846	15 372	14 474	83.0
30 - 34	15 950	8 229	7 721	46.3
35 - 39	5 488	2 846	2 642	16.1
40 - 44	935	488	447	2.4
45 - 49	47	23	24	0.1
50 +	-	-	-	..
Unknown - Inconnu	87	39	48	..
2014 (C)				
Total	118 534	...	...	51.3
0 - 14	14	...	...	..
15 - 19	4 699	...	...	20.4
20 - 24	29 036	...	...	91.6
25 - 29	43 268	...	...	113.7
30 - 34	28 451	...	...	78.0
35 - 39	11 063	...	...	32.6
40 - 44	1 902	...	...	5.6
45 - 49	67	...	...	0.2
50 +	2	...	...	..
Unknown - Inconnu	32	...	...	..
Belgium - Belgique[33]				
2014 (C)				
Total	125 014	64 173	60 841	49.7
0 - 14	11	6	5	..
15 - 19	2 119	1 107	1 012	6.9
20 - 24	15 225	7 787	7 438	44.3
25 - 29	41 977	21 499	20 478	118.4
30 - 34	42 177	21 791	20 386	115.9
35 - 39	18 189	9 255	8 934	51.0
40 - 44	3 908	1 983	1 925	10.4
45 - 49	216	119	97	0.6
50 +	20	11	9	..
Unknown - Inconnu	1 172	615	557	..
Bosnia and Herzegovina - Bosnie-Herzégovine				
2010 (C)				
Total	33 528	17 277	16 251	35.2
12 - 14	8	6	2	..
15 - 19	1 792	950	842	13.5
20 - 24	8 293	4 282	4 011	59.4
25 - 29	11 690	5 949	5 741	86.2
30 - 34	7 985	4 144	3 841	66.8
35 - 39	3 027	1 560	1 467	24.3
40 - 44	557	287	270	3.9
45 - 49	30	14	16	0.2
50 +	1	-	1	..
Unknown - Inconnu	145	85	60	..
Bulgaria - Bulgarie				
2014 (C)				
Total	67 585	34 735	32 850	42.5
0 - 14	324	174	150	..
15 - 19	6 331	3 267	3 064	41.3

10. Live births by age of mother and sex of child, general and age-specific fertility rates: latest available year, 2006 - 2015
Naissances vivantes selon l'âge de la mère et le sexe de l'enfant, taux de fécondité et taux de fécondité par âge : dernière année disponible, 2006 - 2015 (continued - suite)

Continent, country or area, year, code[a] and age of mother (in years) / Continent, pays ou zone, année, code[a] et âge de la mère (en années)	Number - Nombre Total	Male Masculin	Female Féminin	Rate Taux
EUROPE				
Bulgaria - Bulgarie				
2014 (C)				
20 - 24	14 454	7 486	6 968	71.2
25 - 29	20 770	10 571	10 199	88.1
30 - 34	16 204	8 354	7 850	68.5
35 - 39	7 978	4 062	3 916	30.1
40 - 44	1 401	749	652	5.4
45 - 49	105	61	44	0.4
50 +	11	6	5	..
Unknown - Inconnu	7	5	2	...
Croatia - Croatie				
2014 (C)				
Total	39 566	20 374	19 192	41.9
0 - 14	5	3	2	..
15 - 19	1 217	609	608	10.2
20 - 24	5 750	2 981	2 769	47.5
25 - 29	12 376	6 412	5 964	92.6
30 - 34	13 087	6 794	6 293	91.2
35 - 39	5 912	2 975	2 937	41.7
40 - 44	1 161	579	582	8.4
45 - 49	53	18	35	0.4
50 +	-	-	-	..
Unknown - Inconnu	5	3	2	..
Czech Republic - République tchèque				
2014 (C)				
Total	109 860	56 410	53 450	44.9
0 - 14	6	3	3	..
15 - 19	2 728	1 442	1 286	11.7
20 - 24	13 339	6 866	6 473	42.3
25 - 29	32 643	16 663	15 980	95.2
30 - 34	38 620	19 749	18 871	102.5
35 - 39	19 449	10 092	9 357	42.7
40 - 44	2 935	1 530	1 405	7.7
45 - 49	136	63	73	0.4
50 +	4	2	2	..
Denmark - Danemark[34]				
2014 (C)				
Total	56 870	29 254	27 616	45.1
0 - 14	3	1	2	..
15 - 19	629	343	286	3.6
20 - 24	6 254	3 192	3 062	34.5
25 - 29	18 155	9 443	8 712	108.7
30 - 34	19 414	9 925	9 489	122.2
35 - 39	10 192	5 216	4 976	56.3
40 - 44	2 117	1 080	1 037	11.0
45 - 49	103	53	50	0.5
50 +	3	1	2	..
Estonia - Estonie				
2014 (C)				
Total	13 551	6 921	6 630	45.8
0 - 14	1	-	1	..
15 - 19	459	239	220	15.4
20 - 24	2 156	1 104	1 052	52.2
25 - 29	4 510	2 358	2 152	95.6
30 - 34	3 803	1 897	1 906	85.3
35 - 39	2 084	1 049	1 035	47.1
40 - 44	514	266	248	11.3
45 - 49	24	8	16	♦0.6
50 +	-	-	-	..
Faeroe Islands - Îles Féroé				
2015 (C)				
Total	608	292	316	61.1
0 - 14	-	-	-	..
15 - 19	18	10	8	♦10.5

Continent, country or area, year, code[a] and age of mother (in years) / Continent, pays ou zone, année, code[a] et âge de la mère (en années)	Number - Nombre Total	Male Masculin	Female Féminin	Rate Taux
EUROPE				
Faeroe Islands - Îles Féroé				
2015 (C)				
20 - 24	115	60	55	86.1
25 - 29	182	81	101	159.2
30 - 34	176	83	93	145.3
35 - 39	86	42	44	61.5
40 - 44	24	12	12	♦16.5
45 - 49	2	1	1	♦1.2
50 +	-	-	-	..
Unknown - Inconnu	5	3	2	...
Finland - Finlande				
2014 (C)				
Total	57 232	29 272	27 960	49.8
0 - 14	1	1	-	..
15 - 19	1 100	556	544	7.3
20 - 24	8 259	4 364	3 895	49.7
25 - 29	17 158	8 679	8 479	104.1
30 - 34	19 013	9 745	9 268	111.6
35 - 39	9 659	4 907	4 752	58.4
40 - 44	1 897	944	953	12.4
45 - 49	139	73	66	0.8
50 +	6	3	3	..
France[35]				
2012 (C)				
Total	790 290	404 774	385 516	55.6
12 - 14	147	73	74	..
15 - 19	17 512	8 954	8 558	9.4
20 - 24	111 364	57 130	54 234	58.2
25 - 29	253 800	130 005	123 795	131.0
30 - 34	255 606	130 913	124 693	127.2
35 - 39	121 563	62 225	59 338	59.1
40 - 44	28 620	14 598	14 022	12.9
45 - 49	1 557	818	739	0.7
50 +	121	58	63	..
Germany - Allemagne				
2014 (C)				
Total	714 927	366 835	348 092	40.8
0 - 14	135	78	57	..
15 - 19	15 332	7 876	7 456	7.8
20 - 24	80 364	41 530	38 834	35.7
25 - 29	202 696	103 988	98 708	81.4
30 - 34	253 567	129 653	123 914	102.1
35 - 39	133 254	68 365	64 889	57.0
40 - 44	27 484	14 242	13 242	10.4
45 - 49	1 483	775	708	0.4
50 +	91	44	47	..
Unknown - Inconnu	521	284	237	..
Gibraltar[36]				
2013 (+C)				
Total	419	217	202	...
0 - 19	13	3	10	...
20 - 24	66	36	30	...
25 - 29	113	69	44	...
30 - 34	141	66	75	...
35 - 39	71	38	33	...
40 +	15	5	10	...
Greece - Grèce				
2014 (C)				
Total	92 149	47 384	44 765	37.1
0 - 14	124	63	61	..
15 - 19	2 148	1 097	1 051	8.1
20 - 24	7 905	4 081	3 824	27.6
25 - 29	21 682	11 142	10 540	70.1
30 - 34	34 800	17 843	16 957	91.4
35 - 39	20 541	10 598	9 943	50.3

10. Live births by age of mother and sex of child, general and age-specific fertility rates: latest available year, 2006 - 2015
Naissances vivantes selon l'âge de la mère et le sexe de l'enfant, taux de fécondité et taux de fécondité par âge : dernière année disponible, 2006 - 2015 (continued - suite)

Continent, country or area, year, code[a] and age of mother (in years) / Continent, pays ou zone, année, code[a] et âge de la mère (en années)	Number - Nombre			Rate Taux	Continent, country or area, year, code[a] and age of mother (in years) / Continent, pays ou zone, année, code[a] et âge de la mère (en années)	Number - Nombre			Rate Taux
	Total	Male Masculin	Female Féminin			Total	Male Masculin	Female Féminin	
EUROPE					EUROPE				
Greece - Grèce					Jersey[20]				
2014 (C)					2007 (+C)				
40 - 44	4 347	2 261	2 086	10.4	40 - 44	61	27	34	...
45 - 49	536	269	267	1.3	45 - 49	1	-	1	...
50 +	66	30	36	..	50 +	-	-	-	...
Hungary - Hongrie					Latvia - Lettonie				
2013 (C)					2014 (C)				
Total	89 524	45 995	43 529	38.6	Total	21 746	11 230	10 516	48.4
0 - 14	90	58	32	..	0 - 14	3	2	1	..
15 - 19	5 701	2 920	2 781	21.1	15 - 19	863	433	430	19.8
20 - 24	12 736	6 574	6 162	41.7	20 - 24	3 993	2 013	1 980	63.5
25 - 29	22 769	11 742	11 027	76.4	25 - 29	7 357	3 833	3 524	103.6
30 - 34	28 061	14 349	13 712	81.4	30 - 34	5 754	2 962	2 792	87.1
35 - 39	17 091	8 756	8 335	40.7	35 - 39	3 044	1 620	1 424	46.4
40 - 44	2 933	1 521	1 412	8.2	40 - 44	705	353	352	10.0
45 - 49	108	59	49	0.3	45 - 49	23	11	12	♦0.3
50 +	4	2	2	..	50 +	3	2	1	..
Unknown - Inconnu	31	14	17	..	Unknown - Inconnu	1	1	-	..
Iceland - Islande					Liechtenstein				
2014 (C)					2014 (C)				
Total	4 375	2 233	2 142	56.5	Total	372	208	164	42.4
0 - 14	1	1	-	..	0 - 14	-	-	-	..
15 - 19	83	44	39	7.6	15 - 19	5	2	3	♦4.6
20 - 24	784	397	387	64.7	20 - 24	20	12	8	♦18.0
25 - 29	1 380	697	683	122.3	25 - 29	89	51	38	79.2
30 - 34	1 281	641	640	112.1	30 - 34	154	85	69	135.1
35 - 39	692	369	323	65.0	35 - 39	74	46	28	60.8
40 - 44	138	76	62	13.2	40 - 44	30	12	18	♦20.7
45 - 49	16	8	8	♦1.5	45 - 49	-	-	-	-
50 +	-	-	-	..	50 +	-	-	-	..
Unknown - Inconnu	-	-	-	..	Unknown - Inconnu	-	-	-	..
Ireland - Irlande					Lithuania - Lituanie				
2014 (+C)					2012 (C)				
Total	67 285	34 676	32 609	59.4	Total	30 459	15 560	14 899	43.0
0 - 14	4	2	2	..	12 - 14	3	2	1	..
15 - 19	1 222	612	610	9.1	15 - 19	1 380	728	652	14.5
20 - 24	5 954	3 096	2 858	49.0	20 - 24	5 844	2 970	2 874	55.9
25 - 29	13 123	6 741	6 382	80.9	25 - 29	11 104	5 698	5 406	117.0
30 - 34	24 659	12 769	11 890	124.8	30 - 34	7 872	3 985	3 887	88.6
35 - 39	18 188	9 318	8 870	98.1	35 - 39	3 494	1 784	1 710	35.4
40 - 44	3 887	2 019	1 868	22.4	40 - 44	738	384	354	6.7
45 - 49	237	114	123	1.5	45 - 49	19	8	11	♦0.2
50 +	11	5	6	..	50 +	-	-	-	..
Unknown - Inconnu	-	-	-	..	Unknown - Inconnu	5	1	4	..
Italy - Italie					2013 (C)				
2013 (+C)					Total	29 885	...	...	43.2
Total	514 308	264 260	250 048	38.1	0 - 14	6	...	...	..
0 - 14	14	11	3	..	15 - 19	1 262	...	...	14.2
15 - 19	8 071	4 133	3 938	5.9	20 - 24	5 566	...	...	53.6
20 - 24	47 669	24 463	23 206	31.5	25 - 29	10 929	...	...	115.0
25 - 29	114 955	59 117	55 838	70.7	30 - 34	7 825	...	...	89.6
30 - 34	171 151	88 155	82 996	92.8	35 - 39	3 493	...	...	36.7
35 - 39	132 613	68 262	64 351	59.5	40 - 44	766	...	...	7.1
40 - 44	36 852	18 683	18 169	15.2	45 - 49	27	...	...	♦0.2
45 - 49	2 703	1 307	1 396	1.1	50 +	1	...	...	..
50 +	280	129	151	..	Unknown - Inconnu	10	...	...	..
Jersey[20]					Luxembourg				
2007 (+C)					2013 (C)				
Total	1 031	515	516	...	Total	6 115	3 129	2 986	45.8
0 - 14	-	-	-	..	0 - 14	2	2	-	..
15 - 19	29	14	15	...	15 - 19	82	44	38	5.2
20 - 24	114	56	58	...	20 - 24	555	277	278	34.3
25 - 29	228	114	114	...	25 - 29	1 602	833	769	86.7
30 - 34	325	170	155	...	30 - 34	2 245	1 150	1 095	109.0
35 - 39	273	134	139	...	35 - 39	1 311	666	645	64.8

Continent, country or area, year, code[a] and age of mother (in years) / Continent, pays ou zone, année, code[a] et âge de la mère (en années)	Number - Nombre			Rate Taux
	Total	Male Masculin	Female Féminin	
EUROPE				
Luxembourg				
2013 (C)				
40 - 44	297	148	149	14.0
45 - 49	15	5	10	◆0.7
50 +	-	-	-	..
Unknown - Inconnu	6	4	2	..
Malta - Malte				
2014 (C)				
Total	4 191	2 223	1 968	43.4
0 - 14	-	-	-	..
15 - 19	152	89	63	12.9
20 - 24	565	290	275	39.4
25 - 29	1 265	683	582	85.0
30 - 34	1 408	729	679	92.9
35 - 39	689	370	319	46.9
40 - 44	105	60	45	8.0
45 - 49	7	2	5	◆0.6
50 +	-	-	-	..
Unknown - Inconnu	-	-	-	..
Montenegro - Monténégro				
2014 (C)				
Total	7 529	3 947	3 582	51.0
0 - 14	3	-	3	..
15 - 19	223	120	103	11.2
20 - 24	1 366	713	653	72.1
25 - 29	2 409	1 256	1 153	115.5
30 - 34	2 121	1 110	1 011	96.1
35 - 39	951	502	449	45.1
40 - 44	203	108	95	10.0
45 - 49	18	7	11	◆0.9
50 +	2	1	1	..
Unknown - Inconnu	233	130	103	..
Netherlands - Pays-Bas[37]				
2014 (C)				
Total	175 181	89 510	85 671	46.3
0 - 14	-	-	-	..
15 - 19	1 796	941	855	3.7
20 - 24	16 731	8 559	8 172	31.8
25 - 29	54 087	27 580	26 507	104.5
30 - 34	66 460	34 101	32 359	132.1
35 - 39	30 118	15 248	14 870	59.7
40 - 44	5 706	2 947	2 759	9.5
45 - 49	250	118	132	0.4
50 +	33	16	17	..
Unknown - Inconnu	-	-	-	..
Norway - Norvège				
2014 (C)				
Total	58 976	30 323	28 653	49.6
0 - 14	1	-	1	..
15 - 19	793	419	374	5.0
20 - 24	7 485	3 871	3 614	44.8
25 - 29	18 836	9 690	9 146	110.2
30 - 34	20 035	10 257	9 778	120.2
35 - 39	9 671	4 982	4 689	58.3
40 - 44	2 024	1 029	995	11.1
45 - 49	127	73	54	0.7
50 +	4	2	2	..
Poland - Pologne				
2014 (C)				
Total	375 160	193 091	182 069	41.2
0 - 14	51	28	23	..
15 - 19	13 236	6 922	6 314	13.1
20 - 24	60 053	30 807	29 246	48.1
25 - 29	129 245	66 490	62 755	90.2
30 - 34	117 017	60 367	56 650	75.7

Continent, country or area, year, code[a] and age of mother (in years) / Continent, pays ou zone, année, code[a] et âge de la mère (en années)	Number - Nombre			Rate Taux
	Total	Male Masculin	Female Féminin	
EUROPE				
Poland - Pologne				
2014 (C)				
35 - 39	46 891	24 007	22 884	32.1
40 - 44	8 321	4 284	4 037	6.6
45 - 49	339	182	157	0.3
50 +	7	4	3	..
Unknown - Inconnu	-	-	-	..
Portugal[20]				
2014 (C)				
Total	82 367	42 427	39 940	34.3
0 - 14	45	22	23	..
15 - 19	2 446	1 221	1 225	9.1
20 - 24	8 772	4 587	4 185	31.7
25 - 29	19 040	9 787	9 253	65.9
30 - 34	28 645	14 772	13 873	82.0
35 - 39	19 156	9 841	9 315	46.3
40 - 44	4 034	2 080	1 954	9.8
45 - 49	223	114	109	0.6
50 +	6	3	3	..
Republic of Moldova - République de Moldova[38]				
2012 (C)				
Total	39 435	20 380	19 055	40.7
20 - 24	13 022	6 706	6 316	79.3
25 - 29	13 443	6 967	6 476	79.7
30 - 34	6 746	3 411	3 335	47.2
35 - 39	2 591	1 370	1 221	20.4
40 - 44	447	231	216	3.9
45 - 49	8	3	5	◆0.1
50 +	3	3	-	..
Unknown - Inconnu	3	1	2	..
Romania - Roumanie				
2014 (C)				
Total	193 103	99 327	93 776	41.4
0 - 14	704	362	342	..
15 - 19	18 677	9 586	9 091	35.3
20 - 24	39 176	20 117	19 059	70.2
25 - 29	61 486	31 759	29 727	91.7
30 - 34	46 319	23 737	22 582	69.6
35 - 39	22 422	11 571	10 851	29.1
40 - 44	4 092	2 091	2 001	5.5
45 - 49	224	103	121	0.3
50 +	3	1	2	..
Russian Federation - Fédération de Russie[23]				
2011 (C)				
Total	1 796 629	923 804	872 825	48.3
12 - 14	351	174	177	..
15 - 19	103 533	53 162	50 371	25.2
20 - 24	510 184	262 085	248 099	85.1
25 - 29	603 791	311 250	292 541	101.2
30 - 34	379 884	195 518	184 366	68.6
35 - 39	165 364	84 832	80 532	31.8
40 - 44	30 221	15 168	15 053	6.3
45 - 49	1 481	680	801	0.3
50 +	138	65	73	..
Unknown - Inconnu	1 682	870	812	..
San Marino - Saint-Marin				
2014 (+C)				
Total	281	138	143	35.6
0 - 14	-	-	-	..
15 - 19	-	-	-	-
20 - 24	17	9	8	◆23.5
25 - 29	68	37	31	85.2
30 - 34	94	44	50	90.1

10. Live births by age of mother and sex of child, general and age-specific fertility rates: latest available year, 2006 - 2015
Naissances vivantes selon l'âge de la mère et le sexe de l'enfant, taux de fécondité et taux de fécondité par âge : dernière année disponible, 2006 - 2015 (continued - suite)

Continent, country or area, year, code[a] and age of mother (in years) / Continent, pays ou zone, année, code[a] et âge de la mère (en années)	Number - Nombre			Rate Taux
	Total	Male Masculin	Female Féminin	

EUROPE

San Marino - Saint-Marin				
2014 (+C)				
35 - 39	77	33	44	55.8
40 - 44	23	15	8	♦15.1
45 - 49	2	-	2	♦1.2
50 +	-	-	-	..
Serbia - Serbie[39]				
2014 (+C)				
Total	66 461	34 329	32 132	42.0
0 - 14	53	31	22	..
15 - 19	3 243	1 723	1 520	17.9
20 - 24	12 549	6 478	6 071	61.3
25 - 29	20 620	10 546	10 074	91.3
30 - 34	19 317	10 005	9 312	80.2
35 - 39	8 681	4 519	4 162	35.1
40 - 44	1 597	812	785	6.7
45 - 49	137	73	64	0.6
50 +	21	14	7	..
Unknown - Inconnu	243	128	115	..
Slovakia - Slovaquie				
2014 (C)				
Total	55 033	28 100	26 933	41.0
0 - 14	45	24	21	..
15 - 19	3 425	1 761	1 664	23.7
20 - 24	8 938	4 586	4 352	48.9
25 - 29	16 544	8 432	8 112	81.0
30 - 34	16 906	8 589	8 317	78.6
35 - 39	7 891	4 036	3 855	35.4
40 - 44	1 242	646	596	6.4
45 - 49	42	26	16	0.2
50 +	-	-	-	..
Slovenia - Slovénie				
2014 (C)				
Total	21 165	10 928	10 237	46.3
0 - 14	1	-	1	..
15 - 19	232	122	110	5.0
20 - 24	2 256	1 144	1 112	42.2
25 - 29	7 151	3 680	3 471	110.7
30 - 34	7 554	3 868	3 686	105.2
35 - 39	3 413	1 817	1 596	45.9
40 - 44	529	276	253	7.5
45 - 49	29	21	8	♦0.4
50 +	-	-	-	..
Spain - Espagne				
2014 (C)				
Total	426 076	220 034	206 042	39.1
0 - 14	136	75	61	..
15 - 19	8 416	4 389	4 027	8.1
20 - 24	30 752	15 898	14 854	26.7
25 - 29	77 856	40 421	37 435	57.9
30 - 34	153 787	79 649	74 138	92.1
35 - 39	124 271	63 788	60 483	63.6
40 - 44	28 819	14 793	14 026	15.2
45 - 49	1 919	965	954	1.0
50 +	120	56	64	..
Sweden - Suède				
2014 (C)				
Total	114 907	59 098	55 809	53.6
0 - 14	5	3	2	..
15 - 19	1 295	703	592	5.0
20 - 24	14 554	7 431	7 123	44.4
25 - 29	35 425	18 118	17 307	112.6
30 - 34	38 676	19 946	18 730	131.1
35 - 39	20 003	10 340	9 663	67.2
40 - 44	4 663	2 415	2 248	14.6

EUROPE

Sweden - Suède				
2014 (C)				
45 - 49	263	130	133	0.8
50 +	23	12	11	..
Unknown - Inconnu	-	-	-	..
Switzerland - Suisse				
2014 (C)				
Total	85 287	43 850	41 437	44.3
0 - 14	6	2	4	..
15 - 19	627	344	283	2.9
20 - 24	6 963	3 598	3 365	28.4
25 - 29	21 716	11 202	10 514	80.2
30 - 34	32 588	16 737	15 851	114.3
35 - 39	19 058	9 810	9 248	68.1
40 - 44	4 023	2 009	2 014	13.5
45 - 49	276	134	142	0.8
50 +	30	14	16	..
TFYR of Macedonia - L'ex-R. y. de Macédoine				
2014 (C)				
Total	23 596	12 172	11 424	45.4
0 - 14	27	16	11	..
15 - 19	1 165	602	563	17.9
20 - 24	5 001	2 582	2 419	66.4
25 - 29	8 377	4 327	4 050	105.0
30 - 34	6 310	3 245	3 065	79.7
35 - 39	2 293	1 183	1 110	30.4
40 - 44	371	199	172	5.1
45 - 49	33	9	24	0.5
50 +	3	3	-	..
Unknown - Inconnu	16	6	10	..
Ukraine[40]				
2014 (+C)				
Total	465 882	...	...	...
0 - 14	130	...	...	...
15 - 19	27 665	...	...	...
20 - 24	122 988	...	...	...
25 - 29	158 288	...	...	...
30 - 34	103 477	...	...	...
35 - 39	43 718	...	...	...
40 - 44	8 425	...	...	...
45 - 49	466	...	...	...
50 +	64	...	...	...
Unknown - Inconnu	661	...	...	...
United Kingdom of Great Britain and Northern Ireland - Royaume-Uni de Grande-Bretagne et d'Irlande du Nord[41]				
2014 (C)				
Total	775 908	398 145	377 763	51.8
0 - 14	142	72	70	..
15 - 19	29 102	15 142	13 960	15.5
20 - 24	125 377	64 387	60 990	59.0
25 - 29	219 258	112 194	107 064	99.8
30 - 34	241 237	123 918	117 319	110.1
35 - 39	128 610	65 934	62 676	64.0
40 - 44	29 950	15 397	14 553	13.5
45 - 49	1 995	981	1 014	0.8
50 +	177	85	92	..
Unknown - Inconnu	60	35	25	..

10. Live births by age of mother and sex of child, general and age-specific fertility rates: latest available year, 2006 - 2015
Naissances vivantes selon l'âge de la mère et le sexe de l'enfant, taux de fécondité et taux de fécondité par âge : dernière année disponible, 2006 - 2015 (continued - suite)

Continent, country or area, year, code[a] and age of mother (in years) / Continent, pays ou zone, année, code[a] et âge de la mère (en années)	Number - Nombre			Rate Taux
	Total	Male Masculin	Female Féminin	

OCEANIA - OCÉANIE

American Samoa - Samoas américaines				
2014 (C)				
Total	1 084	...	...	...
0 - 14	-	...	...	..
15 - 19	117	...	...	...
20 - 24	291	...	...	...
25 - 29	288	...	...	...
30 - 34	207	...	...	...
35 - 39	135	...	...	...
40 - 44	43	...	...	...
45 - 49	3	...	...	...
50 +	-	...	...	..
Australia - Australie				
2014 (+C)				
Total	299 697	153 592	146 105	53.1
0 - 14	79	38	41	..
15 - 19	9 125	4 716	4 409	12.7
20 - 24	38 558	19 740	18 818	47.8
25 - 29	82 741	42 292	40 449	95.4
30 - 34	102 336	52 405	49 931	120.1
35 - 39	53 839	27 707	26 132	68.9
40 - 44	12 106	6 246	5 860	14.4
45 - 49	707	351	356	0.9
50 +	70	35	35	..
Unknown - Inconnu	136	62	74	..
Cook Islands - Îles Cook[42]				
2015* (+C)				
Total	205	...	...	...
0 - 19	24	...	...	...
20 - 24	63	...	...	...
25 - 29	47	...	...	...
30 - 34	38	...	...	...
35 - 39	21	...	...	...
40 - 44	12	...	...	...
45 +	-	...	...	...
Fiji - Fidji				
2008 (+C)				
Total	17 199	...	...	76.6
0 - 14	3	...	...	..
15 - 19	1 057	...	...	27.5
20 - 24	5 180	...	...	135.3
25 - 29	5 688	...	...	157.8
30 - 34	3 227	...	...	103.4
35 - 39	1 488	...	...	53.0
40 - 44	509	...	...	18.6
45 - 49	34	...	...	1.4
50 +	-	...	...	..
Unknown - Inconnu	13	...	...	..
French Polynesia - Polynésie française				
2014 (C)				
Total	4 161	...	...	...
15 - 19	454	...	...	...
20 - 24	1 079	...	...	...
25 - 29	1 075	...	...	...
30 - 34	888	...	...	...
35 - 39	485	...	...	...
40 - 44	166	...	...	...
45 +	14	...	...	...
Guam[43]				
2015 (C)				
Total	3 367	1 739	1 628	85.4
0 - 14	1	-	1	..
15 - 19	256	131	125	38.2

Continent, country or area, year, code[a] and age of mother (in years) / Continent, pays ou zone, année, code[a] et âge de la mère (en années)	Number - Nombre			Rate Taux
	Total	Male Masculin	Female Féminin	

OCEANIA - OCÉANIE

Guam[43]				
2015 (C)				
20 - 24	904	449	455	138.3
25 - 29	962	506	456	162.7
30 - 34	747	401	346	145.7
35 - 39	398	207	191	81.7
40 - 44	92	42	50	17.7
45 - 49	6	3	3	♦1.2
50 +	1	-	1	..
Unknown - Inconnu	-	-	-	..
Marshall Islands - Îles Marshall[44]				
2006 (+U)				
Total	1 576	...	...	...
0 - 14	2	...	...	...
15 - 19	268	...	...	...
20 - 24	551	...	...	...
25 - 29	431	...	...	...
30 - 34	211	...	...	...
35 - 39	91	...	...	...
40 - 44	19	...	...	...
45 - 49	3	...	...	...
Micronesia (Federated States of) - Micronésie (États fédérés de)				
2006 (+U)				
Total	2 148	...	...	...
10 - 14	8	...	...	...
15 - 17	89	...	...	...
18 - 19	155	...	...	...
20 - 24	619	...	...	...
25 - 29	514	...	...	...
30 - 34	379	...	...	...
35 - 39	259	...	...	...
40 - 44	43	...	...	...
45 +	9	...	...	...
Unknown - Inconnu	73	...	...	...
Nauru				
2011 (C)				
Total	370	190	180	...
15 - 19	40	22	18	...
20 - 24	126	69	57	...
25 - 29	111	57	54	...
30 - 34	55	22	33	...
35 - 39	33	17	16	...
40 - 44	5	3	2	...
45 - 49	-	-	-	...
New Caledonia - Nouvelle-Calédonie				
2012 (C)				
Total	4 389	...	...	...
0 - 19	237	...	...	...
20 - 24	942	...	...	...
25 - 29	1 179	...	...	...
30 - 34	1 169	...	...	...
35 - 39	656	...	...	...
40 - 44	193	...	...	...
45 - 49	11	...	...	...
50 +	2	...	...	...
New Zealand - Nouvelle-Zélande[45]				
2015 (+C)				
Total	61 038	31 356	29 682	56.0
0 - 14	24	12	9	..
15 - 19	2 841	1 473	1 368	18.5

10. Live births by age of mother and sex of child, general and age-specific fertility rates: latest available year, 2006 - 2015
Naissances vivantes selon l'âge de la mère et le sexe de l'enfant, taux de fécondité et taux de fécondité par âge : dernière année disponible, 2006 - 2015 (continued - suite)

Continent, country or area, year, code[a] and age of mother (in years) / Continent, pays ou zone, année, code[a] et âge de la mère (en années)	Number - Nombre			Rate Taux
	Total	Male Masculin	Female Féminin	
OCEANIA - OCÉANIE				
New Zealand - Nouvelle-Zélande[45]				
2015 (+C)				
20 - 24	10 461	5 451	5 007	64.1
25 - 29	16 347	8 385	7 965	104.3
30 - 34	18 597	9 435	9 159	125.3
35 - 39	10 233	5 292	4 938	71.6
40 - 44	2 382	1 221	1 164	14.7
45 +	156	84	72	1.0
Unknown - Inconnu	33	15	18	..
Niue - Nioué[46]				
2009 (C)				
Total	31	...	...	...
0 - 14	-	...	...	..
15 - 19	1	...	...	...
20 - 24	9	...	...	...
25 - 29	12	...	...	...
30 - 34	6	...	...	...
35 - 39	1	...	...	...
40 - 44	1	...	...	...
45 +	1	...	...	...
Samoa[47]				
2011 (|)				
Total	5 703	3 055	2 648	133.8
15 - 19	369	209	160	39.2
20 - 24	1 557	831	726	218.3
25 - 29	1 471	793	678	238.6

Continent, country or area, year, code[a] and age of mother (in years) / Continent, pays ou zone, année, code[a] et âge de la mère (en années)	Number - Nombre			Rate Taux
	Total	Male Masculin	Female Féminin	
OCEANIA - OCÉANIE				
Samoa[47]				
2011 (|)				
30 - 34	1 154	603	551	206.1
35 - 39	741	398	343	144.1
40 - 44	338	180	158	69.9
45 - 49	73	41	32	16.9
Tokelau - Tokélaou[48]				
2011 (|)				
Total	16	...	...	...
0 - 14	-	...	...	...
15 - 19	1	...	...	...
20 - 24	6	...	...	...
25 - 29	4	...	...	...
30 - 34	4	...	...	...
35 - 39	1	...	...	...
Wallis and Futuna Islands - Îles Wallis et Futuna				
2008 (C)				
Total	185	...	...	...
0 - 14	-	...	...	..
15 - 19	9	...	...	...
20 - 24	38	...	...	...
25 - 29	53	...	...	...
30 - 34	51	...	...	...
35 - 39	29	...	...	...
40 - 44	5	...	...	...
45 +	-	...	...	...

FOOTNOTES - NOTES

♦ Rates based on 30 or fewer births. - Taux basés sur 30 naissances ou moins.

* Provisional. - Données provisoires.

[a] 'Code' indicates the source of data, as follows:
C - Civil registration, estimated over 90% complete
U - Civil registration, estimated less than 90% complete
| - Other source, estimated reliable
+ - Data tabulated by date of registration rather than occurrence
... Information not available

Le 'Code' indique la source des données, comme suit :
C - Registres de l'état civil considérés complets à 90 p. 100 au moins
U - Registres de l'état civil qui ne sont pas considérés complets à 90 p. 100 au moins
| - Autre source, considérée fiable
+ - Données exploitées selon la date de l'enregistrement et non la date de l'événement
... Information non disponible

[1] Source: Vital Statistics Report 2014. - Source: Vital Statistics Report 2014.
[2] Data refer to the 12 months preceding the census in September. - Les données se rapportent aux 12 mois précédant le recensement de septembre.
[3] Unrevised data. - Les données n'ont pas été révisées.
[4] Data refer to the 12 months preceding the census in March. - Les données se rapportent aux 12 mois précédant le recensement de mars.
[5] Data refer to Libyan nationals only. - Les données se raportent aux nationaux libyens seulement.
[6] Data refer to the 12 months preceding the census in June. - Les données se raportent aux 12 mois précédant le recensement de juin.
[7] Data refer to the 12 months preceding the census in April. - Les données se rapportent aux douze mois précédant le recensement d'avril.

[8] Data refer to the 12 months preceding the census in March. Including nomadic population. - Les données se rapportent aux 12 mois précédant le recensement de mars. Y compris la population nomade.
[9] Excludes the islands of St. Brandon and Agalega. - Non compris les îles St. Brandon et Agalega.
[10] Data refer to the 12 months preceding the census in August. - Les données se rapportent aux 12 mois précédant le recensement d'août.
[11] Excluding live-born infants who died before their birth was registered. - Non compris les enfants nés vivants décédés avant l'enregistrement de leur naissance.
[12] Data refer to the 12 months preceding the census in May. - Les données se rapportent aux 12 mois précédant le recensement de mai.
[13] Data refer to the 12 months preceding the census in October. - Les données se rapportent aux 12 mois précédant le recensement de octobre.
[14] Excluding non-residents and foreign service personnel and their dependants. - À l'exclusion des non-résidents et du personnel diplomatique et de leurs charges de famille.
[15] Including Canadian residents temporarily in the United States, but excluding United States residents temporarily in Canada. - Y compris les résidents canadiens se trouvant temporairement aux Etats-Unis, mais ne comprenant pas les résidents des Etats-Unis se trouvant temporairement au Canada.
[16] For confidentiality reasons, live births to mothers aged 50 and over and the adopted children with no information on their birth mother are included in 'age of mother Unknown'. - Pour des raisons de confidentialité, on a classé dans la catégorie « âge de la mère Inconnu» les naissances vivantes concernant des femmes âgées de plus de 50 ans et les enfants adoptés nés de mères sur lesquelles on ne dispose pas d'information.
[17] Excluding children born in the country of non-resident mothers. - Exceptés les enfants nés dans le pays des mères non-résidentes.
[18] Data refer to population in private households. Data refer to period from 1 January 2010 to 3 April 2011. - Les données portent sur la population des ménages privés. Les données concernent la période du 1 janvier 2010 au 3 avril 2011.
[19] Figures for male and female may not add up to the total, since they do not include the category "Unknown". - La somme des chiffres indiqués pour les sexes

masculin et féminin peut n'être pas égale au total parce qu'elle n'inclut pas la catégorie " inconnue ".

[20] Data refer to births to resident mothers. - Ces données concernent les enfants nés de mères résidentes.

[21] Including births abroad and births of unknown residence of mother. - Y compris les naissances à l'étranger et les naissances pour lesquelles le lieu de résidence de la mère est inconnu.

[22] Source: Reports of the Ministry of Health. - Source : Rapports du Ministère de la Santé.

[23] Excluding infants born alive of less than 28 weeks' gestation, of less than 1 000 grams in weight and 35 centimeters in length, who die within seven days of birth. - Non compris les enfants nés vivants après moins de 28 semaines de gestations, pesant moins de 1 000 grammes, mesurant moins de 35 centimètres et décédés dans les sept jours qui ont suivi leur naissance.

[24] Sources: Births and Deaths National Registration System database, and medical records of government hospitals. - Les sources: Les bases de données des << Births and Deaths National Registration System >> et les dossiers médicaux des hôpitaux du gouvernement.

[25] Data refer to government controlled areas. - Les données se rapportent aux zones contrôlées par le Gouvernement.

[26] Data are from 1 January 2009 to 1 May 2010. - Les données vont du 1er janvier 2009 au 1er mai 2010.

[27] Data refer to current birth data; excluding delayed birth registrations. Data refer to the Iranian Year which begins on 21 March and ends on 20 March of the following year. - Les données se rapportent aux naissances actuelles; les déclarations tardives des naissances ne sont pas compris. Les données concernent l'année iranienne, qui commence le 21 mars et se termine le 20 mars de l'année suivante.

[28] Includes data for East Jerusalem and Israeli residents in certain other territories under occupation by Israeli military forces since June 1967. - Y compris les données pour Jérusalem-Est et les résidents israéliens dans certains autres territoires occupés depuis 1967 par les forces armées israéliennes.

[29] Data refer to Japanese nationals in Japan only. - Les données se raportent aux nationaux japonais au Japon seulement.

[30] Data from Births and Deaths Notification System (Ministry of Health and all health care providers). - Les données proviennent du système de notification des naissances et des décès (Ministère de la santé et tous prestataires de soins de santé).

[31] Excluding alien armed forces, civilian aliens employed by armed forces, and foreign diplomatic personnel and their dependants. - Non compris les militaires étrangers, les civils étrangers employés par les forces armées ni le personnel diplomatique étranger et les membres de leur famille les accompagnant.

[32] Data have not been adjusted for underenumeration. Data refer to the 12 months preceding the census in December. Excluding data from the parts of Jerusalem which were annexed by Israel in 1967. - Les données n'ont pas été ajustées pour compenser les lacunes du dénombrement. Les données se rapportent aux 12 mois précédant le recensement de décembre. Non compris les données provenant des parties de Jérusalem qui ont été annexées par Israël en 1967.

[33] Including armed forces stationed outside the country, but excluding alien armed forces stationed in the area. - Y compris les militaires nationaux hors du pays, mais non compris les militaires étrangers en garnison sur le territoire.

[34] Excluding Faeroe Islands and Greenland shown separately, if available. - Non compris les Iles Féroé et le Groenland, qui font l'objet de rubriques distinctes, si disponible.

[35] Including armed forces stationed outside the country. - Y compris les militaires nationaux hors du pays.

[36] Total in this table is different from data presented in other tables due to different data source. Including live births by military personnel and their dependants. - Le total figurant dans ce tableau ne correspond pas aux données présentées dans d'autres tableaux parce que les sources de données ne sont pas les mêmes. Y compris les naissances vivantes parmi les membres du personnel militaire et leurs personnes à charge.

[37] Including residents outside the country if listed in a Netherlands population register. - Englobe les résidents se trouvant à l'étranger à condition qu'ils soient inscrits sur le registre de population des Pays-Bas.

[38] Excluding infants born alive of less than 28 weeks' gestation, of less than 1 000 grams in weight and 35 centimeters in length, who die within seven days of birth. Excluding Transnistria and the municipality of Bender. - Non compris les enfants nés vivants après moins de 28 semaines de gestations, pesant moins de 1 000 grammes, mesurant moins de 35 centimètres et décédés dans les sept jours qui ont suivi leur naissance. Les données ne tiennent pas compte de l'information sur la Transnistria et la municipalité de Bender.

[39] Excludes data for Kosovo and Metohia. - Sans les données pour le Kosovo et Metohie.

[40] Data refer to births with weight 500g and more (if weight is unknown - with length 25 centimeters and more, or with gestation during 22 weeks or more). The Government of Ukraine has informed the United Nations that it is not in a position to provide statistical data concerning the Autonomous Republic of Crimea and the city of Sevastopol. - Données concernant les nouveau-nés de 500 grammes ou plus (si le poids est inconnu – de 25 centimètres de long ou plus, ou après une grossesse de 22 semaines ou plus). Le gouvernement Ukrainien a informé l'ONU qu'il n'est pas en mesure de fournir des données statistiques concernant la République autonome de Crimée et la ville de Sébastopol.

[41] Excluding Channel Islands (Guernsey and Jersey) and Isle of Man, shown separately, if available. Data tabulated by date of occurrence for England and Wales, and by date of registration for Northern Ireland and Scotland. - Non compris les îles Anglo-Normandes (Guernesey et Jersey) et l'île de Man, qui font l'objet de rubriques distinctes, si disponible. Données exploitées selon la date de l'événement pour l'Angleterre et le pays de Galles, et selon la date de l'enregistrement pour l'Irlande du Nord et l'Ecosse.

[42] Excluding Niue, shown separately, which is part of Cook Islands, but because of remoteness is administered separately. - Non compris Nioué, qui fait l'objet d'une rubrique distincte et qui fait partie des îles Cook, mais qui, en raison de son éloignement, est administrée séparément.

[43] Including United States military personnel, their dependants and contract employees. - Y compris les militaires des Etats-Unis, les membres de leur famille les accompagnant et les agents contractuels des Etats-Unis.

[44] Excluding United States military personnel, their dependants and contract employees. - Non compris les militaires des Etats-Unis, les membres de leur famille les accompagnant et les agents contractuels des Etats-Unis.

[45] Random rounding to base 3 is applied in this table as a confidentiality measure. - Les chiffres sont arrondis à la base 3 de manière aléatoire, pour des raisons de confidentialité.

[46] Includes children born in New Zealand to women resident in Niue who chose to travel to New Zealand to give birth. - Y compris les enfants nés en Nouvelle-Zélande de femmes résidant à Nioué qui ont choisi de se rendre en Nouvelle-Zélande pour accoucher.

[47] Data refer to the 12 months preceding the census in November. - Données se rapportant aux 12 mois précédant le recensement de novembre.

[48] Data refer to usually resident population present on census night. Data refer to the 12 months preceding the census in October. - Les données concernent la population habituellement résidente présente la nuit du recensement. Les données se rapportent aux 12 mois précédant le recensement de octobre.

Table 11 - *Demographic Yearbook 2015*

Table 11 presents live births by age of father and live birth rates by age of father for the latest available year between 2006 and 2015.

Description of variables: Age is defined as age at last birthday, that is, the difference between the date of birth and the date of the occurrence of the event, expressed in completed solar years. The age classification used in this table is the following: under 20 years, 5-year age groups through 60-64 years, 65 years and over, and age unknown. A different classification may appear as provided by reporting country or area.

Rate computation: Live-birth rates specific to age of father are the annual number of births to a man in each age group per 1 000 male population in the same age group. These rates are calculated by the Statistics Division of the United Nations.

Since relatively few births occur to men below 15 or above 59 years of age, birth rates for men under 20 years of age and for those 55 years of age or over are computed on the male population aged 15-19 and 55-59, respectively. Similarly, the rate for men of "All ages" is based on all live births irrespective of age of father, and is computed on the male population aged 15-59 years.

Births to fathers of unknown age are distributed proportionately across the age groups, by the Statistics Division of the United Nations, in accordance with the distribution of births by age of father prior to the calculation of the rates.

The population used in computing the rates is the estimated or enumerated distribution of males by age. First priority is given to the estimated population and second priority to the enumerated population, i.e. to census returns of the year to which the births refer.

Rates presented in this table are limited to those for countries or areas having at least a total of 100 live births in a given year.

Reliability of data: Data from civil registers of live births which are reported as incomplete (less than 90 per cent completeness) or of unknown completeness are considered unreliable and are set in *italics* rather than in roman type. Rates are not computed if the data on live births from civil registers are reported as incomplete (less than 90 per cent completeness) or of unknown completeness. Table 9 and the technical notes for that table provide more detailed information on the completeness of birth registration. For more information about the quality of vital statistics data in general, see section 4.2 of the Technical Notes.

Limitations: Statistics on live births by age of father are subject to the same qualifications as have been set forth for vital statistics in general and birth statistics in particular as discussed in section 4 of the Technical Notes. These include differences in the completeness of registration, the method used to determine age of father and the quality of the reported information relating to age of father.

The reliability of the data described above, is an important factor in considering the limitations. In addition, some live births are tabulated by date of registration and not by date of occurrence; these are indicated in the table by a plus sign "+". Whenever the lag between the date of occurrence and date of registration is prolonged and, therefore, a large proportion of the live-birth registrations are delayed, birth statistics for any given year may be seriously affected. For example, the age of the father will almost always refer to the date of registration rather than to the date of birth of the child. Hence, in those countries or areas where registration of births is delayed, possibly for years, statistics on births by age of father should be used with caution.

Another factor which limits international comparability is the practice of some countries or areas of not including in live birth statistics infants who were born alive but died before the registration of the birth or within the first 24 hours of life, thus underestimating the total number of live births. Statistics of this type are footnoted.

Because these statistics are classified according to age, they are subject to the limitations with respect to accuracy of age reporting similar to those already discussed in connection with section 3.1.3 of the Technical Notes. The factors influencing the accuracy of reporting may be somewhat dissimilar in vital statistics (because of the differences in the method of taking a census and registering a birth) but, in general, the same errors can be observed. The absence of frequencies in the unknown age group does not necessarily indicate completely accurate reporting and tabulation of the age item. It is often an indication that the unknowns have been eliminated by assigning ages to them before tabulation, or by proportionate distribution after tabulation.

On the other hand, large frequencies in the unknown age category may indicate that a large proportion of the births are born outside of wedlock, the records for which tend to be incomplete so far as characteristics of the parents are concerned.

Another limitation of age reporting may result from calculating age of father at birth of child (or at time of registration) from year of birth rather than from day, month and year of birth. Information on this factor is given in footnotes when known.

In few countries, data by age refer to deliveries rather than to live births causing under-enumeration in the event of a multiple birth. This practice leads to lack of strict comparability, both among countries or areas relying on this practice and between data shown in this table and table 9.

Rates shown in this table are subject to the same limitations that affect the corresponding statistics on live births. In cases of rates based on births tabulated by date of registration and not by date of occurrence; the effect of including delayed registration on the distribution of births by age of father may be noted in the age-specific fertility rates for men at older ages. In some cases, high age-specific rates for men aged 55 years and over may reflect age of father at registration of birth and not fertility at these older ages.

Earlier data: Live births and live birth rates by age of father have been shown in previous issues of the *Demographic Yearbook*. Information on the specific years is presented in the Historical Index.

Tableau 11 – *Annuaire démographique 2015*

Le tableau 11 présente les données les plus récentes disponibles pour la période 2006 - 2015 sur les naissances vivantes selon l'âge du père et les taux des naissances vivantes selon l'âge du père.

Description des variables : l'âge désigne l'âge au dernier anniversaire, c'est-à-dire la différence entre la date de naissance et la date de l'événement exprimée en années solaires révolues. La classification par âge utilisée dans ce tableau comprend les catégories suivantes : moins de 20 ans, groupes quinquennaux jusqu'à 60-64 ans, 65 ans et plus, et âge inconnu. Des groupes d'âge différents sont parfois utilisés lorsque les pays ou territoires ont fourni les données dans une autre classification.

Les taux de natalité selon l'âge du père représentent le nombre annuel de naissances vivantes intervenues dans un groupe d'âge donné pour 1 000 hommes du groupe d'âge. Ces taux ont été calculés par la Division de statistique de l'ONU.

Étant donné que le nombre de naissances parmi les hommes de moins de 15 ans ou de plus de 59 ans est relativement peu élevé, les taux de natalité parmi les hommes âgées de moins de 20 ans et celles de 55 ans et plus ont été calculés sur la base des populations masculines âgées de 15 à 19 ans et de 55 à 59 ans, respectivement. De même, le taux pour les hommes de « tous âges » est fondé sur la totalité des naissances vivantes, indépendamment de l'âge du père et ce chiffre est rapporté à l'effectif de la population masculine âgée de 15 à 59 ans.

Les naissances pour lesquelles l'âge du père était inconnu ont été réparties par la Division de statistique de l'ONU, avant le calcul des taux, suivant les proportions observées pour celles où l'âge du père était connu.

Les chiffres de population utilisés pour le calcul des taux proviennent de dénombrements ou de répartitions estimatives de la population masculine selon l'âge. On a utilisé de préférence les estimations de la population; à défaut, on s'est contenté des données censitaires se rapportant à l'année des naissances.

Les taux présentés dans ce tableau ne concernent que les pays ou zones où l'on a enregistré un total d'au moins 100 naissances vivantes dans une année donnée.

Fiabilité des données : les données sur les naissances vivantes provenant des registres de l'état civil qui sont déclarées incomplètes (degré de complétude inférieur à 90 p. 100) ou dont le degré de complétude n'est pas connu sont jugées douteuses et apparaissent en italique et non en caractères romains. On a choisi de ne pas faire figurer dans le tableau 11 des taux calculés à partir de données sur les naissances vivantes issues de registres de l'état civil qui sont déclarées incomplètes (degré de complétude inférieur à 90 p. 100) ou dont le degré de complétude n'est pas connu. Le tableau 9 et les notes techniques qui s'y rapportent présentent des renseignements plus détaillés sur le degré de complétude de l'enregistrement des naissances vivantes. Pour plus de précisions sur la qualité des statistiques de l'état civil en général, voir la section 4.2 des Notes techniques.

Insuffisance des données : les statistiques relatives aux naissances vivantes selon l'âge du père appellent toutes les réserves qui ont été formulées à propos des statistiques de l'état civil en général et des statistiques de naissances en particulier (voir la section 4 des Notes techniques). Ceci inclut les différences de complétude d'enregistrement des faits d'état civil, de méthode pour déterminer l'âge du père et de qualité d'information concernant l'âge du père.

La fiabilité des données, au sujet de laquelle des indications ont été données plus haut, est un facteur important. Il faut également tenir compte du fait que, dans certains cas, les données relatives aux naissances vivantes sont exploitées selon la date de l'enregistrement et non la date de l'événement ; ces cas ont été signalés dans le tableau par le signe '+'. Chaque fois que le décalage entre l'événement et son enregistrement est grand et qu'une forte proportion des naissances vivantes fait l'objet d'un enregistrement tardif, les statistiques des naissances vivantes pour une année donnée peuvent être considérablement faussées. Par exemple, l'âge du père représente presque toujours son âge à la date de l'enregistrement et non à la date de la naissance de l'enfant. Ainsi, dans les pays ou zones où l'enregistrement des naissances est tardif, le retard atteignant parfois plusieurs années, il faut utiliser avec prudence les statistiques concernant les naissances selon l'âge du père.

Un autre facteur qui nuit à la comparabilité internationale est la pratique de certains pays ou zones qui consiste à ne pas inclure dans les statistiques des naissances vivantes les enfants nés vivants mais décédés avant l'enregistrement de leur naissance ou dans les 24 heures qui ont suivi la naissance, pratique qui conduit à sous-estimer le nombre total de naissances vivantes. Quand pareil facteur a joué, cela a été signalé en note à la fin du tableau.

Étant donné que les statistiques du tableau 11 sont classées selon l'âge, elles appellent les mêmes réserves concernant l'exactitude des déclarations d'âge que celles formulées à la section 3.1.3 des Notes techniques. Dans le cas des statistiques de l'état civil, les facteurs qui interviennent à cet égard sont parfois différents, étant donné que le recensement de la population et l'enregistrement des naissances se font par des méthodes différentes, mais, d'une manière générale, les erreurs observées seront les mêmes. Si aucun nombre ne figure dans la rangée réservée aux âges inconnus, cela ne signifie pas nécessairement que les déclarations d'âge et l'exploitation des données par âge ont été tout à fait exactes. C'est souvent une indication que l'on a attribué un âge aux personnes d'âge inconnu avant l'exploitation des données ou qu'elles ont été réparties proportionnellement entre les différents groupes après cette opération.

À l'inverse, lorsque le nombre des personnes d'âge inconnu est important, cela peut signifier que la proportion de naissances parmi les parents célibataires est élevée, étant donné qu'en pareil cas l'acte de naissance ne contient pas tous les renseignements concernant les parents.

Les déclarations par âge peuvent comporter des distorsions, du fait que l'âge du père au moment de la naissance d'un enfant (ou de la déclaration de naissance) est donné par année de naissance et non par date exacte (jour, mois et année).

Dans quelques pays, la classification par âges se réfère aux accouchements, et non aux naissances vivantes, ce qui conduit à un sous-dénombrement en cas de naissances gémellaires. Cette pratique nuit à la comparabilité des données, à la fois entre pays ou zones qui recourent à cette méthode et entre les données présentées dans le tableau 11 et celles du tableau 9.

Les taux présentés dans ce tableau, sont sujets aux mêmes limitations qui affectent les statistiques correspondantes de naissances vivantes. Dans le cas des taux basés sur des naissances par date d'enregistrement et non par date d'occurrence, l'effet peut être visible sur les taux de fécondité par âge des hommes aux âges plus élevés. Dans certains cas, les taux de fécondité des hommes de plus de 55 ans peuvent refléter l'âge du père à l'enregistrement plus que la fécondité à ces âges.

Données publiées antérieurement : Les données sur les naissances vivantes selon l'âge du père et les taux des naissances vivantes selon l'âge du père ont été publié antérieurement dans l'*Annuaire démographique*. Pour plus de précisions concernant les années pour lesquels des données ont été publiées, se reporter à l'index historique.

11. Live births and live birth rates by age of father: latest available year, 2006 - 2015
Naissances vivantes et taux de natalité selon l'âge du père : dernière année disponible, 2006 - 2015

Continent, country or area, year, code[a] and age of father (in years) / Continent, pays ou zone, année, code[a] et âge du père (en années)	Number - Nombre — Both sexes Les deux sexes	Rate Taux
AFRICA - AFRIQUE		
Egypt - Égypte		
2012 (+C)		
Total	2 629 769	101.6
0 - 19	4 700	1.2
20 - 24	119 826	28.3
25 - 29	1 489 063	364.7
30 - 34	502 329	150.1
35 - 39	288 404	111.4
40 - 44	134 381	59.4
45 - 49	60 206	29.0
50 - 54	19 391	10.6
55 - 59	6 333	4.2
60 +	5 136	..
Mauritius - Maurice[1]		
2015 (+C)		
Total	12 640	30.3
0 - 19	186	4.0
20 - 24	1 391	28.9
25 - 29	2 516	59.6
30 - 34	3 454	77.5
35 - 39	2 767	58.3
40 - 44	1 102	27.1
45 - 49	412	9.4
50 - 54	144	3.2
55 - 59	39	1.0
60 - 64	7	..
65 +	5	..
Unknown - Inconnu	617	..
Reunion - Réunion[2]		
2007 (C)		
Total	14 808	61.9
0 - 19	352	10.0
20 - 24	2 409	88.2
25 - 29	3 283	139.4
30 - 34	3 693	141.6
35 - 39	2 860	96.2
40 - 44	1 488	46.6
45 - 49	491	19.2
50 - 54	151	6.8
55 - 59	53	3.0
60 - 64	28	..
AMERICA, NORTH - AMÉRIQUE DU NORD		
Bahamas		
2014* (+U)		
Total	4 196	...
0 - 19	63	...
20 - 24	576	...
25 - 29	742	...
30 - 34	815	...
35 - 39	659	...
40 - 44	388	...
45 - 49	167	...
50 - 54	60	...
55 - 59	23	...
60 - 64	5	...
65 +	6	..
Unknown - Inconnu	692	..
Barbados - Barbade		
2007 (+C)		
Total	3 537	...
0 - 19	95	...
20 - 24	564	...
25 - 29	745	...
30 - 34	784	...

Continent, country or area, year, code[a] and age of father (in years) / Continent, pays ou zone, année, code[a] et âge du père (en années)	Number - Nombre — Both sexes Les deux sexes	Rate Taux
AMERICA, NORTH - AMÉRIQUE DU NORD		
Barbados - Barbade		
2007 (+C)		
35 - 39	605	...
40 - 44	381	...
45 - 49	163	...
50 - 54	53	...
55 - 59	17	...
60 - 64	8	...
65 +	3	...
Unknown - Inconnu	119	..
Canada[3]		
2009 (C)		
Total	380 863	35.1
0 - 19	4 918	4.5
20 - 24	29 959	26.5
25 - 29	84 206	75.0
30 - 34	117 201	109.5
35 - 39	79 126	72.1
40 - 44	31 813	26.9
45 - 49	9 913	7.5
50 - 54	2 642	2.2
55 - 59	683	0.7
60 - 64	200	..
65 +	77	..
Unknown - Inconnu	20 125	..
Costa Rica		
2015* (C)		
Total	71 819	47.3
0 - 19	1 464	9.8
20 - 24	7 497	50.3
25 - 29	10 937	76.9
30 - 34	10 742	89.1
35 - 39	6 900	62.2
40 - 44	3 216	33.4
45 - 49	1 304	13.2
50 - 54	568	5.7
55 - 59	215	2.6
60 - 64	74	..
65 +	6 757	..
Unknown - Inconnu	22 145	..
Cuba		
2014 (C)		
Total	122 643	33.8
0 - 19	2 788	8.7
20 - 24	20 453	56.5
25 - 29	30 817	85.4
30 - 34	22 140	74.9
35 - 39	14 879	44.9
40 - 44	10 715	24.3
45 - 49	4 668	10.4
50 - 54	1 535	4.0
55 - 59	397	1.5
60 - 64	143	..
65 +	83	..
Unknown - Inconnu	14 025	..
Dominican Republic - République dominicaine[4]		
2014 (U)		
Total	138 224	...
0 - 19	2 990	...
20 - 24	23 128	...
25 - 29	31 302	...
30 - 34	27 841	...
35 - 39	17 735	...
40 - 44	9 136	...
45 - 49	4 521	...
50 - 54	2 164	...
55 - 59	927	...

11. Live births and live birth rates by age of father: latest available year, 2006 - 2015
Naissances vivantes et taux de natalité selon l'âge du père : dernière année disponible, 2006 - 2015 (continued - suite)

Continent, country or area, year, code[a] and age of father (in years) / Continent, pays ou zone, année, code[a] et âge du père (en années)	Number - Nombre Both sexes Les deux sexes	Rate Taux	Continent, country or area, year, code[a] and age of father (in years) / Continent, pays ou zone, année, code[a] et âge du père (en années)	Number - Nombre Both sexes Les deux sexes	Rate Taux
AMERICA, NORTH - AMÉRIQUE DU NORD			**AMERICA, NORTH - AMÉRIQUE DU NORD**		
Dominican Republic - République dominicaine[4]			Martinique[2]		
2014 (U)			2007 (C)		
60 - 64	412	..	Total	5 317	47.3
65 +	264	..	0 - 19	98	6.2
Unknown - Inconnu	17 804	..	20 - 24	710	60.7
El Salvador			25 - 29	1 043	119.9
2011 (C)			30 - 34	1 173	111.7
Total	109 384	65.6	35 - 39	1 293	95.6
0 - 19	6 580	21.5	40 - 44	702	46.1
20 - 24	22 778	94.9	45 - 49	235	16.2
25 - 29	22 364	122.7	50 - 54	42	3.5
30 - 34	19 678	125.6	55 - 59	16	♦1.5
35 - 39	11 744	80.1	60 +	3	..
40 - 44	6 226	47.8	Mexico - Mexique[6]		
45 - 49	3 029	27.3	2013 (C)		
50 - 54	1 396	14.8	Total	2 168 933	...
55 - 59	693	8.5	0 - 19	148 020	...
60 - 64	347	..	20 - 24	496 963	...
65 +	266	..	25 - 29	509 840	...
Unknown - Inconnu	14 283	..	30 - 34	403 658	...
Greenland - Groenland			35 - 39	243 427	...
2008 (C)			40 - 44	109 685	...
Total	834	...	45 - 49	40 290	...
0 - 19	25	...	50 - 54	15 970	...
20 - 24	109	...	55 - 59	6 432	...
25 - 29	169	...	60 - 64	2 533	..
30 - 34	150	...	65 +	1 723	..
35 - 39	112	...	Unknown - Inconnu	190 392	..
40 - 44	91	...	Panama		
45 - 49	35	...	2014 (C)		
50 - 54	9	...	Total	75 183	62.0
55 - 59	1	...	0 - 19	2 946	23.9
60 +	-	..	20 - 24	11 081	96.2
Unknown - Inconnu	133	...	25 - 29	13 046	117.7
Guatemala			30 - 34	11 598	109.4
2011 (C)			35 - 39	7 583	74.8
Total	373 692	...	40 - 44	4 181	44.1
0 - 19	23 425	...	45 - 49	1 810	21.7
20 - 24	82 898	...	50 - 54	736	10.4
25 - 29	83 786	...	55 - 59	278	4.9
30 - 34	64 952	...	60 - 64	133	..
35 - 39	39 412	...	65 +	71	..
40 - 44	20 601	...	Unknown - Inconnu	21 720	..
45 - 49	9 366	...	Puerto Rico - Porto Rico		
50 - 54	3 893	...	2015 (C)		
55 - 59	1 723	...	Total	31 229	...
60 - 64	769	..	0 - 19	1 529	...
65 +	556	..	20 - 24	7 627	...
Unknown - Inconnu	42 311	..	25 - 29	8 165	...
Jamaica - Jamaïque[5]			30 - 34	6 015	...
2006 (C)			35 - 39	3 756	...
Total	42 399	...	40 - 44	1 657	...
0 - 19	496	...	45 - 49	557	...
20 - 24	3 756	...	50 - 54	219	...
25 - 29	5 341	...	55 - 59	77	...
30 - 34	5 069	...	60 - 64	34	...
35 - 39	3 635	...	65 +	25	...
40 - 44	2 166	...	Unknown - Inconnu	1 568	...
45 - 49	986	...	Trinidad and Tobago - Trinité-et-Tobago		
50 - 54	373	...	2009 (C)		
55 - 59	131	...	Total	17 949	...
60 - 64	53	...	0 - 19	389	...
65 +	37	..	20 - 24	3 027	...
Unknown - Inconnu	20 356		25 - 29	4 916	...
			30 - 34	4 149	...
			35 - 39	2 682	...
			40 - 44	1 416	...

Continent, country or area, year, code[a] and age of father (in years) / Continent, pays ou zone, année, code[a] et âge du père (en années)	Number - Nombre — Both sexes Les deux sexes	Rate Taux	Continent, country or area, year, code[a] and age of father (in years) / Continent, pays ou zone, année, code[a] et âge du père (en années)	Number - Nombre — Both sexes Les deux sexes	Rate Taux
AMERICA, NORTH - AMÉRIQUE DU NORD			**AMERICA, SOUTH - AMÉRIQUE DU SUD**		
Trinidad and Tobago - Trinité-et-Tobago			French Guiana - Guyane française[2]		
2009 (C)			2007 (C)		
45 - 49	730	...	Total	6 386	104.6
50 - 54	259	...	0 - 19	323	32.6
55 - 59	73	...	20 - 24	1 263	164.2
60 +	51	..	25 - 29	1 401	203.5
Unknown - Inconnu	257	..	30 - 34	1 334	175.5
United States of America - États-Unis d'Amérique			35 - 39	1 043	138.4
2014 (C)			40 - 44	622	90.0
Total	3 988 076	...	45 - 49	230	38.8
0 - 19	85 002	...	50 - 54	94	19.2
20 - 24	497 940	...	55 - 59	59	16.1
25 - 29	867 330	...	60 - 64	17	..
30 - 34	1 022 910	...	65 +	-	..
35 - 39	629 724	...	Uruguay		
40 - 44	261 320	...	2014 (C)		
45 - 49	87 146	...	Total	48 368	46.9
50 - 54	28 347	...	0 - 19	1 405	15.6
55 +	12 430	...	20 - 24	5 028	59.3
Unknown - Inconnu	495 927	..	25 - 29	6 780	84.2
			30 - 34	7 740	100.9
AMERICA, SOUTH - AMÉRIQUE DU SUD			35 - 39	6 149	79.1
			40 - 44	2 677	38.0
Chile - Chili			45 - 49	967	15.0
2013 (C)			50 - 54	382	5.9
Total	242 005	42.7	55 - 59	145	2.5
0 - 19	13 330	20.9	60 - 64	41	..
20 - 24	40 798	60.5	65 +	9	..
25 - 29	48 693	76.2	Unknown - Inconnu	17 045	..
30 - 34	51 645	90.6	Venezuela (Bolivarian Republic of) - Venezuela (République bolivarienne du)		
35 - 39	35 465	66.0	2015 (U)		
40 - 44	17 462	31.7	Total	600 860	...
45 - 49	6 748	12.3	0 - 19	35 209	...
50 +	3 465	3.7	20 - 24	117 191	...
Unknown - Inconnu	24 399	..	25 - 29	124 572	...
Colombia - Colombie			30 - 34	100 317	...
2014 (U)			35 - 39	61 254	...
Total	669 137	...	40 - 44	31 646	...
0 - 19	43 790	...	45 - 49	14 466	...
20 - 24	156 289	...	50 +	10 213	...
25 - 29	166 282	...	Unknown - Inconnu	105 992	..
30 - 34	137 163	...			
35 - 39	80 662	...	**ASIA - ASIE**		
40 - 44	39 995	...			
45 - 49	16 475	...	Azerbaijan - Azerbaïdjan[7]		
50 - 54	7 150	...	2013 (+C)		
55 - 59	2 355	...	Total	158 195	49.6
60 - 64	898	..	0 - 19	426	1.0
65 +	415	..	20 - 24	25 221	53.8
Unknown - Inconnu	17 663	..	25 - 29	62 750	139.6
Ecuador - Équateur			30 - 34	42 094	108.7
2011 (+U)			35 - 39	18 217	57.4
Total	229 780		40 - 44	6 662	21.7
0 - 19	4 219	...	45 - 49	2 005	6.4
20 - 24	16 514	...	50 - 54	588	1.9
25 - 29	17 040	...	55 +	232	1.0
30 - 34	14 115	...	Bahrain - Bahreïn[8]		
35 - 39	8 339	...	2014 (C)		
40 - 44	4 405	...	Total	20 931	33.2
45 - 49	1 864	...	0 - 19	41	1.1
50 - 54	719	...	20 - 24	1 431	22.9
55 - 59	274	...	25 - 29	4 660	38.5
60 - 64	104	...	30 - 34	5 958	51.0
65 +	94	..	35 - 39	4 656	52.2
Unknown - Inconnu	162 093	..	40 - 44	2 518	35.3

11. Live births and live birth rates by age of father: latest available year, 2006 - 2015
Naissances vivantes et taux de natalité selon l'âge du père : dernière année disponible, 2006 - 2015 (continued - suite)

Continent, country or area, year, code[a] and age of father (in years) Continent, pays ou zone, année, code[a] et âge du père (en années)	Number - Nombre Both sexes Les deux sexes	Rate Taux	Continent, country or area, year, code[a] and age of father (in years) Continent, pays ou zone, année, code[a] et âge du père (en années)	Number - Nombre Both sexes Les deux sexes	Rate Taux
ASIA - ASIE			ASIA - ASIE		
Bahrain - Bahreïn[8]			Israel - Israël[10]		
2014 (C)			2014 (C)		
45 - 49	1 090	19.6	45 - 49	4 309	21.6
50 - 54	383	9.0	50 - 54	1 114	6.1
55 - 59	123	3.8	55 - 59	362	2.1
60 - 64	49	..	60 - 64	132	..
65 +	19	..	65 +	66	..
Unknown - Inconnu	3	..	Unknown - Inconnu	8 878	..
Brunei Darussalam - Brunéi Darussalam			Japan - Japon[11]		
2014 (+C)			2014 (C)		
Total	6 891	46.4	Total	980 688	28.1
0 - 19	23	♦1.4	0 - 19	4 207	1.4
20 - 24	410	23.9	20 - 24	54 377	17.1
25 - 29	1 687	86.7	25 - 29	208 641	60.6
30 - 34	2 016	104.6	30 - 34	326 000	85.7
35 - 39	1 336	78.4	35 - 39	247 634	55.7
40 - 44	635	40.4	40 - 44	106 189	21.6
45 - 49	210	15.7	45 - 49	25 665	6.0
50 - 54	72	6.5	50 - 54	5 730	1.5
55 +	27	♦3.3	55 - 59	1 555	0.4
Unknown - Inconnu	475	..	60 - 64	497	..
China, Hong Kong SAR - Chine, Hong Kong RAS			65 +	190	..
2014 (C)			Unknown - Inconnu	3	..
Total	62 305	28.3	Kazakhstan[12]		
0 - 19	133	0.7	2006 (C)		
20 - 24	1 885	8.6	Total	301 756	61.4
25 - 29	8 860	40.2	0 - 19	2 897	4.2
30 - 34	20 110	87.9	20 - 24	46 772	73.1
35 - 39	17 103	76.8	25 - 29	82 596	152.2
40 - 44	8 213	34.9	30 - 34	66 344	134.3
45 - 49	2 905	11.5	35 - 39	41 180	90.8
50 - 54	1 249	4.1	40 - 44	17 594	38.6
55 - 59	496	1.7	45 - 49	4 336	10.0
60 - 64	160	..	50 - 54	873	2.7
65 +	74	..	55 - 59	296	1.2
Unknown - Inconnu	1 117	..	60 - 64	74	..
China, Macao SAR - Chine, Macao RAS			65 +	74	..
2015 (C)			Unknown - Inconnu	38 720	..
Total	7 055	30.1	Kyrgyzstan - Kirghizstan		
0 - 24	355	9.1	2015* (C)		
25 - 29	2 033	57.0	Total	163 452	90.0
30 - 34	2 202	69.0	0 - 19	535	2.3
35 - 39	1 303	51.9	20 - 24	20 599	78.8
40 - 44	638	25.3	25 - 29	51 510	201.0
45 +	421	5.7	30 - 34	37 445	184.6
Unknown - Inconnu	103	..	35 - 39	21 864	132.4
Cyprus - Chypre[9]			40 - 44	10 124	69.6
2013 (C)			45 - 49	3 019	22.6
Total	9 341	34.7	50 - 54	747	6.0
0 - 19	26	♦0.9	55 - 59	220	2.2
20 - 24	425	12.5	60 - 64	66	..
25 - 29	2 057	57.9	65 +	47	..
30 - 34	3 332	99.3	Unknown - Inconnu	17 276	..
35 - 39	2 094	75.0	Malaysia - Malaisie		
40 - 44	785	29.3	2013 (C)		
45 - 49	292	11.1	Total	503 914	49.6
50 +	143	2.7	0 - 19	3 101	2.2
Unknown - Inconnu	187	..	20 - 24	31 923	20.9
Israel - Israël[10]			25 - 29	129 091	86.1
2014 (C)			30 - 34	149 327	119.0
Total	176 427	76.0	35 - 39	95 306	94.3
0 - 19	344	1.1	40 - 44	47 186	52.6
20 - 24	13 937	47.8	45 - 49	18 516	22.5
25 - 29	38 613	138.0	50 - 54	6 034	8.2
30 - 34	52 514	193.6	55 - 59	1 951	3.3
35 - 39	39 528	151.7	60 - 64	593	..
40 - 44	16 630	70.3			

392

Continent, country or area, year, code[a] and age of father (in years) / Continent, pays ou zone, année, code[a] et âge du père (en années)	Number - Nombre — Both sexes Les deux sexes	Rate Taux
ASIA - ASIE		
Malaysia - Malaisie		
2013 (C)		
65 +	218	..
Unknown - Inconnu	20 668	..
Maldives		
2014 (C)		
Total	7 245	43.5
0 - 19	1	♦0.1
20 - 24	619	22.0
25 - 29	2 249	64.9
30 - 34	1 976	75.6
35 - 39	1 221	67.2
40 - 44	660	47.2
45 - 49	262	23.6
50 - 54	87	10.1
55 - 59	21	♦3.3
60 - 64	10	..
65 +	3	..
Unknown - Inconnu	136	..
Oman[13]		
2014 (U)		
Total	82 981	...
0 - 19	73	...
20 - 24	4 717	...
25 - 29	21 609	...
30 - 34	24 360	...
35 - 39	16 754	...
40 - 44	8 216	...
45 - 49	3 342	...
50 - 54	1 475	...
55 - 59	551	...
60 - 64	288	..
65 +	343	..
Unknown - Inconnu	1 253	..
Philippines		
2014 (C)		
Total	1 748 857	57.1
0 - 19	53 258	11.1
20 - 24	339 142	76.6
25 - 29	422 732	110.4
30 - 34	367 405	108.4
35 - 39	237 948	77.1
40 - 44	123 388	45.0
45 - 49	50 133	20.5
50 - 54	17 548	8.6
55 - 59	6 147	3.8
60 - 64	2 563	..
65 +	1 622	..
Unknown - Inconnu	126 971	..
Qatar		
2010 (C)		
Total	19 504	16.9
0 - 19	17	♦0.5
20 - 24	1 050	6.8
25 - 29	3 770	17.0
30 - 34	5 727	26.3
35 - 39	4 537	23.2
40 - 44	2 584	17.2
45 - 49	1 179	12.2
50 +	637	7.5
Unknown - Inconnu	3	..
Republic of Korea - République de Corée[14]		
2014 (C)		
Total	435 435	24.7
0 - 19	701	0.4
20 - 24	6 360	3.4
25 - 29	46 247	27.1

Continent, country or area, year, code[a] and age of father (in years) / Continent, pays ou zone, année, code[a] et âge du père (en années)	Number - Nombre — Both sexes Les deux sexes	Rate Taux
ASIA - ASIE		
Republic of Korea - République de Corée[14]		
2014 (C)		
30 - 34	193 602	96.3
35 - 39	133 148	69.0
40 - 44	41 732	19.1
45 - 49	7 105	3.4
50 - 54	1 331	0.6
55 - 59	270	0.1
60 - 64	50	..
65 +	10	..
Unknown - Inconnu	4 879	..
Singapore - Singapour		
2015 (C)		
Total	42 185	32.9
0 - 19	85	0.7
20 - 24	967	7.3
25 - 29	6 203	47.3
30 - 34	15 136	111.0
35 - 39	12 111	85.1
40 - 44	5 094	33.3
45 - 49	1 440	9.7
50 - 54	473	3.0
55 - 59	166	1.1
60 - 64	50	..
65 +	18	..
Unknown - Inconnu	442	..
Turkey - Turquie		
2014 (C)		
Total	1 337 504	53.1
0 - 19	8 093	2.4
20 - 24	115 255	36.5
25 - 29	386 906	123.0
30 - 34	425 544	130.5
35 - 39	245 291	82.7
40 - 44	104 601	38.2
45 - 49	27 483	11.7
50 - 54	7 061	3.2
55 - 59	2 011	1.1
60 - 64	805	..
65 +	491	..
Unknown - Inconnu	13 963	..
Uzbekistan - Ouzbékistan		
2014 (+C)		
Total	656 769	65.4
0 - 19	1 393	0.9
20 - 24	105 200	63.9
25 - 29	305 000	198.6
30 - 34	167 914	135.4
35 - 39	58 453	55.9
40 - 44	14 475	15.5
45 - 49	2 930	3.7
50 - 54	824	1.1
55 - 59	332	0.6
60 - 64	157	..
65 +	91	..
EUROPE		
Åland Islands - Îles d'Åland		
2012 (C)		
Total	292	35.4
0 - 19	-	-
20 - 24	20	♦25.1
25 - 29	57	76.1
30 - 34	83	100.3
35 - 39	77	87.8

11. Live births and live birth rates by age of father: latest available year, 2006 - 2015
Naissances vivantes et taux de natalité selon l'âge du père : dernière année disponible, 2006 - 2015 (continued - suite)

Continent, country or area, year, code[a] and age of father (in years) / Continent, pays ou zone, année, code[a] et âge du père (en années)	Number - Nombre — Both sexes Les deux sexes	Rate Taux	Continent, country or area, year, code[a] and age of father (in years) / Continent, pays ou zone, année, code[a] et âge du père (en années)	Number - Nombre — Both sexes Les deux sexes	Rate Taux
EUROPE			EUROPE		
Åland Islands - Îles d'Åland			Bosnia and Herzegovina - Bosnie-Herzégovine		
2012 (C)			2010 (C)		
40 - 44	25	♦27.3	Total	33 528	28.0
45 - 49	10	♦10.2	0 - 19	99	0.7
50 - 54	2	♦2.2	20 - 24	3 174	23.3
55 - 59	1	♦1.1	25 - 29	9 300	75.0
60 - 64	-	..	30 - 34	10 238	90.1
65 +	-	..	35 - 39	5 624	49.2
Unknown - Inconnu	17	..	40 - 44	2 203	16.5
Albania - Albanie			45 - 49	672	4.8
2013 (C)			50 - 54	150	1.2
Total	35 750	38.5	55 - 59	29	0.3
0 - 19	113	0.9	60 - 64	9	..
20 - 24	2 620	21.0	65 +	4	..
25 - 29	10 354	94.0	Unknown - Inconnu	2 026	..
30 - 34	11 683	129.2	Bulgaria - Bulgarie		
35 - 39	6 619	81.8	2012 (C)		
40 - 44	2 667	30.3	Total	69 121	30.8
45 - 49	768	8.2	0 - 19	834	5.7
50 - 54	183	1.8	20 - 24	6 247	31.5
55 - 59	33	0.4	25 - 29	14 643	69.8
60 - 64	15	..	30 - 34	17 865	81.0
65 +	14	..	35 - 39	11 930	50.6
Unknown - Inconnu	681	..	40 - 44	4 065	18.2
Austria - Autriche[15]			45 - 49	1 071	5.3
2013 (C)			50 - 54	325	1.6
Total	46 477	17.7	55 - 59	96	0.5
0 - 19	66	0.3	60 - 64	34	..
20 - 24	2 285	8.3	65 +	12	..
25 - 29	8 964	32.3	Unknown - Inconnu	11 999	..
30 - 34	15 393	55.0	Croatia - Croatie		
35 - 39	11 440	41.9	2014 (C)		
40 - 44	5 568	17.1	Total	39 566	31.0
45 - 49	1 949	5.4	0 - 19	248	2.0
50 - 54	563	1.7	20 - 24	2 544	20.5
55 - 59	161	0.6	25 - 29	8 764	65.0
60 - 64	68	..	30 - 34	13 589	92.7
65 +	20	..	35 - 39	8 803	61.4
Belarus - Bélarus[15]			40 - 44	3 428	25.1
2013 (C)			45 - 49	1 049	7.3
Total	98 991	33.0	50 - 54	240	1.6
0 - 19	876	3.4	55 - 59	84	0.6
20 - 24	15 731	43.0	60 - 64	19	..
25 - 29	36 546	91.5	65 +	-	..
30 - 34	27 117	76.5	Unknown - Inconnu	798	..
35 - 39	12 807	39.4	Czech Republic - République tchèque		
40 - 44	4 312	13.8	2014 (C)		
45 - 49	1 138	3.5	Total	109 860	33.8
50 - 54	346	1.0	0 - 19	439	1.9
55 +	118	0.4	20 - 24	5 329	17.6
Belgium - Belgique			25 - 29	18 939	57.0
2010 (C)			30 - 34	34 567	94.1
Total	130 100	39.7	35 - 39	27 800	63.2
0 - 19	659	2.1	40 - 44	9 721	26.1
20 - 24	7 464	24.1	45 - 49	2 682	8.2
25 - 29	30 127	93.6	50 - 54	899	3.0
30 - 34	41 391	126.4	55 - 59	308	1.0
35 - 39	25 239	71.6	60 - 64	119	..
40 - 44	10 766	28.8	65 +	38	..
45 - 49	3 930	10.2	Unknown - Inconnu	9 019	..
50 - 54	1 222	3.4	Denmark - Danemark[16]		
55 - 59	377	1.2	2014 (C)		
60 - 64	139	..	Total	56 870	34.1
65 +	33	..	0 - 19	101	0.6
Unknown - Inconnu	8 753	..	20 - 24	2 536	15.1
			25 - 29	11 440	74.6
			30 - 34	17 559	122.5

11. Live births and live birth rates by age of father: latest available year, 2006 - 2015
Naissances vivantes et taux de natalité selon l'âge du père : dernière année disponible, 2006 - 2015 (continued - suite)

Continent, country or area, year, code[a] and age of father (in years) / Continent, pays ou zone, année, code[a] et âge du père (en années)	Number - Nombre / Both sexes Les deux sexes	Rate Taux
EUROPE		
Denmark - Danemark[16]		
2014 (C)		
35 - 39	12 145	75.2
40 - 44	4 748	27.4
45 - 49	1 469	7.8
50 - 54	413	2.4
55 - 59	119	0.8
60 - 64	21	..
65 +	23	..
Unknown - Inconnu	6 296	..
Estonia - Estonie		
2014 (C)		
Total	13 551	34.6
0 - 19	97	3.2
20 - 24	1 114	26.4
25 - 29	3 453	72.2
30 - 34	3 869	86.4
35 - 39	2 573	58.8
40 - 44	1 204	27.4
45 - 49	386	9.8
50 - 54	141	3.4
55 - 59	36	0.9
60 - 64	10	..
65 +	4	..
Unknown - Inconnu	664	..
Faeroe Islands - Îles Féroé		
2015 (C)		
Total	608	41.5
0 - 19	4	♦2.3
20 - 24	61	40.2
25 - 29	117	88.1
30 - 34	167	130.5
35 - 39	116	80.7
40 - 44	75	47.6
45 - 49	19	♦11.4
50 - 54	4	♦2.5
55 - 59	2	♦1.4
60 - 64	-	..
65 +	-	..
Unknown - Inconnu	43	..
Finland - Finlande[17]		
2014 (C)		
Total	56 950	36.2
0 - 19	356	2.3
20 - 24	4 620	27.6
25 - 29	12 908	77.2
30 - 34	18 446	105.7
35 - 39	11 979	70.9
40 - 44	4 418	28.6
45 - 49	1 573	8.9
50 - 54	469	2.6
55 - 59	125	0.7
60 - 64	37	..
65 +	12	..
Unknown - Inconnu	2 007	..
France		
2014 (C)		
Total	781 167	43.0
0 - 19	2 801	1.4
20 - 24	43 367	22.7
25 - 29	169 753	89.5
30 - 34	257 676	130.6
35 - 39	177 422	90.4
40 - 44	85 031	38.5
45 - 49	30 269	14.0
50 - 54	10 050	4.8
55 - 59	3 472	1.8
EUROPE		
France		
2014 (C)		
60 - 64	1 191	..
65 +	135	..
Germany - Allemagne		
2014 (C)		
Total	714 927	29.3
0 - 19	2 385	1.2
20 - 24	33 336	15.0
25 - 29	125 929	51.5
30 - 34	216 319	90.8
35 - 39	168 301	75.8
40 - 44	80 513	32.1
45 - 49	29 841	9.3
50 - 54	8 266	2.6
55 - 59	2 155	0.8
60 - 64	646	..
65 +	278	..
Unknown - Inconnu	46 958	..
Greece - Grèce		
2014 (C)		
Total	92 149	29.0
0 - 19	142	0.5
20 - 24	1 637	5.9
25 - 29	10 113	34.4
30 - 34	28 791	78.8
35 - 39	27 675	72.1
40 - 44	12 668	33.2
45 - 49	4 054	11.0
50 - 54	1 012	3.0
55 - 59	263	0.8
60 - 64	76	..
65 +	14	..
Unknown - Inconnu	5 704	..
Hungary - Hongrie[18]		
2014 (C)		
Total	93 281	31.1
0 - 19	1 175	5.0
20 - 24	5 646	20.5
25 - 29	13 258	49.2
30 - 34	24 084	84.1
35 - 39	23 328	63.5
40 - 44	8 878	27.8
45 - 49	2 568	9.1
50 - 54	673	2.7
55 - 59	233	0.8
60 - 64	98	..
65 +	36	..
Unknown - Inconnu	13 304	..
Iceland - Islande		
2014 (C)		
Total	4 375	43.4
0 - 19	21	♦1.9
20 - 24	418	33.3
25 - 29	1 108	96.3
30 - 34	1 370	116.2
35 - 39	869	81.5
40 - 44	364	34.7
45 - 49	91	8.8
50 - 54	38	3.6
55 - 59	11	♦1.1
60 - 64	7	..
65 +	1	..
Unknown - Inconnu	77	..

Continent, country or area, year, code[a] and age of father (in years) Continent, pays ou zone, année, code[a] et âge du père (en années)	Number - Nombre Both sexes Les deux sexes	Rate Taux	Continent, country or area, year, code[a] and age of father (in years) Continent, pays ou zone, année, code[a] et âge du père (en années)	Number - Nombre Both sexes Les deux sexes	Rate Taux
EUROPE			EUROPE		
Ireland - Irlande			Luxembourg		
2006 (+C)			2014 (C)		
Total	64 237	46.6	35 - 39	1 708	82.2
0 - 19	714	5.1	40 - 44	713	33.1
20 - 24	4 382	27.1	45 - 49	257	11.3
25 - 29	10 351	58.3	50 - 54	64	3.1
30 - 34	19 695	118.4	55 - 59	21	♦1.2
35 - 39	16 702	108.8	60 - 64	5	..
40 - 44	6 268	44.1	65 +	3	..
45 - 49	1 585	12.3	Unknown - Inconnu	168	
50 - 54	374	3.2	Malta - Malte		
55 - 59	119	1.1	2014 (C)		
60 - 64	27	..	Total	4 191	31.5
65 +	6	..	0 - 19	37	3.0
Unknown - Inconnu	4 014	..	20 - 24	287	19.5
Italy - Italie			25 - 29	838	53.9
2014 (C)			30 - 34	1 395	90.1
Total	502 596	28.3	35 - 39	943	62.8
0 - 19	1 502	1.1	40 - 44	349	26.6
20 - 24	15 330	10.6	45 - 49	103	8.5
25 - 29	58 384	38.4	50 - 54	23	♦1.6
30 - 34	130 273	77.8	55 - 59	14	♦1.0
35 - 39	142 109	71.5	60 - 64	3	..
40 - 44	77 976	35.3	65 +	1	..
45 - 49	24 823	11.0	Unknown - Inconnu	198	..
50 - 54	6 523	3.2	Montenegro - Monténégro		
55 - 59	1 708	1.0	2009 (C)		
60 - 64	497	..	Total	8 642	43.2
65 +	217	..	0 - 19	32	1.5
Unknown - Inconnu	43 254	..	20 - 24	616	27.3
Latvia - Lettonie			25 - 29	2 011	90.0
2014 (C)			30 - 34	2 268	113.7
Total	21 746	37.1	35 - 39	1 574	85.9
0 - 19	119	2.7	40 - 44	800	43.7
20 - 24	1 898	29.6	45 - 49	287	14.9
25 - 29	5 648	78.3	50 - 54	89	4.6
30 - 34	6 478	97.6	55 - 59	23	♦1.3
35 - 39	3 906	62.4	60 - 64	1	..
40 - 44	1 904	29.3	65 +	6	..
45 - 49	651	10.4	Unknown - Inconnu	935	..
50 - 54	225	3.4	Netherlands - Pays-Bas[19]		
55 - 59	84	1.4	2014 (C)		
60 - 64	30	..	Total	175 181	34.8
65 +	7	..	0 - 19	333	0.7
Unknown - Inconnu	796	..	20 - 24	6 226	12.1
Lithuania - Lituanie			25 - 29	33 346	66.4
2014 (C)			30 - 34	60 729	125.6
Total	30 369	34.7	35 - 39	41 980	87.5
0 - 19	45	0.7	40 - 44	17 247	30.0
20 - 24	1 416	18.4	45 - 49	5 280	8.5
25 - 29	6 462	91.1	50 - 54	1 495	2.5
30 - 34	7 573	119.3	55 - 59	403	0.7
35 - 39	4 115	65.0	60 - 64	97	..
40 - 44	1 415	20.2	65 +	56	..
45 - 49	378	5.3	Unknown - Inconnu	7 989	..
50 - 54	116	1.5	Norway - Norvège		
55 - 59	33	0.5	2012 (C)		
60 - 64	4	..	Total	60 255	38.8
65 +	3	..	0 - 19	271	1.7
Unknown - Inconnu	8 809	..	20 - 24	3 931	23.9
Luxembourg			25 - 29	13 332	83.2
2014 (C)			30 - 34	19 068	116.9
Total	6 070	33.4	35 - 39	13 188	76.5
0 - 19	26	♦1.6	40 - 44	5 590	30.1
20 - 24	263	15.4	45 - 49	1 822	10.3
25 - 29	948	48.6	50 - 54	524	3.3
30 - 34	1 894	91.2	55 - 59	176	1.2

Continent, country or area, year, code[a] and age of father (in years) / Continent, pays ou zone, année, code[a] et âge du père (en années)	Number - Nombre	Rate Taux
	Both sexes Les deux sexes	

EUROPE

Norway - Norvège
2012 (C)

60 - 64	47	..
65 +	9	..
Unknown - Inconnu	2 297	..

Poland - Pologne
2012 (C)

Total	386 257	31.0
0 - 19	2 231	2.0
20 - 24	33 640	25.1
25 - 29	114 291	73.3
30 - 34	126 439	82.1
35 - 39	65 320	46.2
40 - 44	20 696	17.5
45 - 49	6 013	5.2
50 - 54	1 819	1.4
55 - 59	577	0.4
60 +	217	..
Unknown - Inconnu	15 014	..

Portugal[6]
2014 (C)

Total	82 367	27.4
0 - 19	924	3.4
20 - 24	5 259	19.0
25 - 29	14 011	49.7
30 - 34	26 260	80.9
35 - 39	22 278	58.9
40 - 44	8 551	22.8
45 - 49	2 443	6.8
50 - 54	725	2.1
55 - 59	268	0.8
60 - 64	99	..
65 +	32	..
Unknown - Inconnu	1 517	..

Republic of Moldova - République de Moldova[20]
2012 (C)

Total	39 435	32.8
0 - 19	269	2.3
20 - 24	6 290	41.0
25 - 29	13 306	84.1
30 - 34	8 980	67.6
35 - 39	4 561	40.4
40 - 44	1 640	16.5
45 - 49	446	4.4
50 - 54	142	1.2
55 - 59	31	0.3
60 - 64	14	..
65 +	3	..
Unknown - Inconnu	3 753	..

Romania - Roumanie
2014 (C)

Total	193 103	31.2
0 - 19	2 732	5.3
20 - 24	17 870	31.7
25 - 29	48 475	71.2
30 - 34	56 257	85.7
35 - 39	37 322	49.7
40 - 44	12 637	17.1
45 - 49	3 779	5.4
50 - 54	848	1.6
55 - 59	335	0.5
60 - 64	98	..
65 +	34	..
Unknown - Inconnu	12 716	..

EUROPE

Russian Federation - Fédération de Russie[12]
2012 (C)

Total	1 902 084	41.9
0 - 19	12 731	3.9
20 - 24	256 939	51.4
25 - 29	564 777	103.0
30 - 34	431 851	88.4
35 - 39	245 613	55.2
40 - 44	102 880	25.6
45 - 49	33 963	8.4
50 - 54	11 671	2.5
55 - 59	3 196	0.8
60 +	1 203	..
Unknown - Inconnu	237 260	..

San Marino - Saint-Marin
2013 (+C)

Total	320	31.8
0 - 19	-	-
20 - 24	3	♦4.1
25 - 29	26	♦32.4
30 - 34	78	78.8
35 - 39	105	81.1
40 - 44	60	42.2
45 - 49	25	♦16.7
50 - 54	14	♦11.0
55 +	-	-
Unknown - Inconnu	9	..

Serbia - Serbie[21]
2014 (+C)

Total	66 461	31.2
0 - 19	377	2.2
20 - 24	4 351	22.7
25 - 29	14 568	69.1
30 - 34	20 632	92.7
35 - 39	12 769	56.4
40 - 44	4 575	21.4
45 - 49	1 279	6.2
50 - 54	351	1.6
55 - 59	113	0.5
60 - 64	32	..
65 +	11	..
Unknown - Inconnu	7 403	..

Slovakia - Slovaquie
2014 (C)

Total	55 033	31.2
0 - 19	460	3.6
20 - 24	3 473	21.5
25 - 29	10 091	56.1
30 - 34	16 363	84.9
35 - 39	11 283	56.6
40 - 44	3 664	21.5
45 - 49	922	6.1
50 - 54	284	1.8
55 - 59	64	0.4
60 - 64	32	..
65 +	11	..
Unknown - Inconnu	8 386	..

Slovenia - Slovénie
2014 (C)

Total	21 165	32.7
0 - 19	48	1.0
20 - 24	918	16.5
25 - 29	4 864	70.4
30 - 34	7 704	98.6
35 - 39	5 061	62.7
40 - 44	1 642	21.8
45 - 49	453	5.9

Continent, country or area, year, code[a] and age of father (in years) Continent, pays ou zone, année, code[a] et âge du père (en années)	Number - Nombre Both sexes Les deux sexes	Rate Taux	Continent, country or area, year, code[a] and age of father (in years) Continent, pays ou zone, année, code[a] et âge du père (en années)	Number - Nombre Both sexes Les deux sexes	Rate Taux
EUROPE			**EUROPE**		
Slovenia - Slovénie			Ukraine[22]		
2014 (C)			2013 (+C)		
50 - 54	122	1.6	Total	503 657	35.8
55 - 59	29	♦0.4	0 - 19	4 125	3.9
60 - 64	17	..	20 - 24	67 513	48.1
65 +	4	..	25 - 29	149 940	88.2
Unknown - Inconnu	303	..	30 - 34	116 549	75.0
Spain - Espagne			35 - 39	64 684	45.9
2013 (C)			40 - 44	25 378	19.2
Total	424 440	29.3	45 - 49	7 518	6.0
0 - 19	2 376	2.2	50 - 54	2 464	1.8
20 - 24	15 288	12.8	55 +	983	0.8
25 - 29	48 689	35.2	Unknown - Inconnu	64 503	..
30 - 34	132 325	74.8	United Kingdom of Great Britain and Northern Ireland - Royaume-Uni de Grande-Bretagne et d'Irlande du Nord[23]		
35 - 39	139 743	68.7	2012 (C)		
40 - 44	56 906	29.5	Total	812 970	42.9
45 - 49	14 741	8.1	0 - 19	13 166	6.9
50 - 54	3 910	2.4	20 - 24	85 617	41.4
55 - 59	1 056	0.8	25 - 29	168 503	83.1
60 - 64	291	..	30 - 34	226 297	113.8
65 +	106	..	35 - 39	160 698	84.9
Unknown - Inconnu	9 009	..	40 - 44	76 266	35.9
Sweden - Suède			45 - 49	25 537	11.7
2012 (C)			50 - 54	7 396	3.7
Total	113 177	40.2	55 - 59	2 061	1.2
0 - 19	443	1.5	60 - 64	585	..
20 - 24	7 043	21.2	65 +	290	..
25 - 29	23 661	77.8	Unknown - Inconnu	46 554	..
30 - 34	36 139	122.1			
35 - 39	26 932	86.6			
40 - 44	11 433	35.6	**OCEANIA - OCÉANIE**		
45 - 49	4 023	12.0			
50 - 54	1 169	4.0	Australia - Australie		
55 - 59	404	1.4	2014 (+C)		
60 - 64	116	..	Total	299 697	41.7
65 +	52	..	0 - 19	3 481	4.7
Unknown - Inconnu	1 762	..	20 - 24	22 639	27.7
Switzerland - Suisse[15]			25 - 29	59 355	69.5
2014 (C)			30 - 34	96 640	116.2
Total	66 816	26.1	35 - 39	66 500	88.3
0 - 19	10	-	40 - 44	28 784	36.0
20 - 24	1 306	5.2	45 - 49	8 588	11.6
25 - 29	9 528	34.5	50 - 54	2 556	3.4
30 - 34	22 233	76.3	55 - 59	879	1.3
35 - 39	19 805	69.9	60 - 64	285	..
40 - 44	9 403	31.0	65 +	144	..
45 - 49	3 187	9.5	Unknown - Inconnu	9 846	..
50 - 54	948	3.0	New Caledonia - Nouvelle-Calédonie		
55 - 59	266	1.0	2012 (C)		
60 - 64	76	..	Total	4 389	...
65 +	54	..	0 - 19	46	...
Unknown - Inconnu	-	..	20 - 24	447	...
TFYR of Macedonia - L'ex-R. y. de Macédoine			25 - 29	826	...
2012 (C)			30 - 34	1 008	...
Total	23 568	34.3	35 - 39	786	...
0 - 19	197	2.8	40 - 44	394	...
20 - 24	2 321	29.6	45 - 49	158	...
25 - 29	6 789	84.7	50 - 54	39	...
30 - 34	7 672	98.1	55 - 59	19	...
35 - 39	3 842	52.2	60 +	1	...
40 - 44	1 194	17.0	Unknown - Inconnu	665	..
45 - 49	326	4.6	New Zealand - Nouvelle-Zélande[24]		
50 - 54	83	1.2	2015 (+C)		
55 - 59	23	♦0.4	Total	61 038	45.1
60 - 64	6	..	0 - 19	1 410	9.1
65 +	3	..	20 - 24	6 945	41.6
Unknown - Inconnu	1 112	..			

11. Live births and live birth rates by age of father: latest available year, 2006 - 2015
Naissances vivantes et taux de natalité selon l'âge du père : dernière année disponible, 2006 - 2015 (continued - suite)

Continent, country or area, year, code[a] and age of father (in years) / Continent, pays ou zone, année, code[a] et âge du père (en années)	Number - Nombre Both sexes Les deux sexes	Rate Taux	Continent, country or area, year, code[a] and age of father (in years) / Continent, pays ou zone, année, code[a] et âge du père (en années)	Number - Nombre Both sexes Les deux sexes	Rate Taux
OCEANIA - OCÉANIE			**OCEANIA - OCÉANIE**		
New Zealand - Nouvelle-Zélande[24]			New Zealand - Nouvelle-Zélande[24]		
2015 (+C)			2015 (+C)		
25 - 29	12 756	86.3	55 - 59	177	1.3
30 - 34	17 205	130.7	60 - 64	63	..
35 - 39	11 859	95.3	65 +	21	..
40 - 44	5 367	38.4	Unknown - Inconnu	3 018	..
45 - 49	1 710	12.0			
50 - 54	507	3.5			

FOOTNOTES - NOTES

◆ Rates based on 30 or fewer births. - Taux basés sur 30 naissances ou moins.

* Provisional. - Données provisoires.

[a] 'Code' indicates the source of data, as follows:
C - Civil registration, estimated over 90% complete
U - Civil registration, estimated less than 90% complete
| - Other source, estimated reliable
+ - Data tabulated by date of registration rather than occurrence
... Information not available

Le 'Code' indique la source des données, comme suit :
C - Registres de l'état civil considérés complets à 90 p. 100 au moins
U - Registres de l'état civil qui ne sont pas considérés complets à 90 p. 100 au moins
| - Autre source, considérée fiable
+ - Données exploitées selon la date de l'enregistrement et non la date de l'événement
... Information non disponible

[1] Excludes the islands of St. Brandon and Agalega. - Non compris les îles St. Brandon et Agalega.

[2] Excluding live-born infants who died before their birth was registered. - Non compris les enfants nés vivants décédés avant l'enregistrement de leur naissance.

[3] Including Canadian residents temporarily in the United States, but excluding United States residents temporarily in Canada. - Y compris les résidents canadiens se trouvant temporairement aux Etats-Unis, mais ne comprenant pas les résidents des Etats-Unis se trouvant temporairement au Canada.

[4] Data refers to age of father or age of the person reporting. - Les données concernent l'âge du père ou l'âge du répondant.

[5] Data have not been adjusted for underenumeration. - Les données n'ont pas été ajustées pour compenser les lacunes du dénombrement.

[6] Data refer to births to resident mothers. - Ces données concernent les enfants nés de mères résidentes.

[7] Excluding infants born alive of less than 28 weeks' gestation, of less than 1 000 grams in weight and 35 centimeters in length, who die within seven days of birth. Excluding newborns registered by application of mothers. - Non compris les enfants nés vivants après moins de 28 semaines de gestations, pesant moins de 1 000 grammes, mesurant moins de 35 centimètres et décédés dans les sept jours qui ont suivi leur naissance. Exception faite des nouveau-nés qui ont été enregistrés à la demande des mères.

[8] Sources: Births and Deaths National Registration System database, and medical records of government hospitals. - Les sources: Les bases de données des << Births and Deaths National Registration System >> et les dossiers médicaux des hôpitaux du gouvernement.

[9] Data refer to government controlled areas. - Les données se rapportent aux zones contrôlées par le Gouvernement.

[10] Includes data for East Jerusalem and Israeli residents in certain other territories under occupation by Israeli military forces since June 1967. - Y compris les données pour Jérusalem-Est et les résidents israéliens dans certains autres territoires occupés depuis 1967 par les forces armées israéliennes.

[11] Data refer to Japanese nationals in Japan only. Data refer to live births in wedlock only. - Les données se raportent aux nationaux japonais au Japon

seulement. Les données ne concernent que les naissances vivantes de parents mariés.

[12] Excluding infants born alive of less than 28 weeks' gestation, of less than 1 000 grams in weight and 35 centimeters in length, who die within seven days of birth. - Non compris les enfants nés vivants après moins de 28 semaines de gestations, pesant moins de 1 000 grammes, mesurant moins de 35 centimètres et décédés dans les sept jours qui ont suivi leur naissance.

[13] Data from Births and Deaths Notification System (Ministry of Health and all health care providers). - Les données proviennent du système de notification des naissances et des décès (Ministère de la santé et tous prestataires de soins de santé).

[14] Excluding alien armed forces, civilian aliens employed by armed forces, and foreign diplomatic personnel and their dependants. - Non compris les militaires étrangers, les civils étrangers employés par les forces armées ni le personnel diplomatique étranger et les membres de leur famille les accompagnant.

[15] Data refer to live births in wedlock only. - Les données ne concernent que les naissances vivantes de parents mariés.

[16] Excluding Faeroe Islands and Greenland shown separately, if available. - Non compris les îles Féroé et le Groenland, qui font l'objet de rubriques distinctes, si disponible.

[17] Excluding Åland Islands. - Non compris les Îles d'Åland.

[18] Data include the live births of women with Hungarian usual residence regardless of whether the live birth occurred in Hungary or in a foreign country, and do not include the live births of women with foreign country usual residence. - Les données concernent les enfants nés vivants de femmes dont la résidence habituelle est en Hongrie, que la naissance vivante ait eu lieu en Hongrie ou dans un pays étranger, et ne comprennent pas les enfants nés vivants de femmes dont la résidence habituelle est dans un pays étranger.

[19] Including residents outside the country if listed in a Netherlands population register. - Englobe les résidents se trouvant à l'étranger à condition qu'ils soient inscrits sur le registre de population des Pays-Bas.

[20] Excluding Transnistria and the municipality of Bender. - Les données ne tiennent pas compte de l'information sur la Transnistria et la municipalité de Bender.

[21] Excludes data for Kosovo and Metohia. - Sans les données pour le Kosovo et Metohie.

[22] Data refer to births with weight 500g and more (if weight is unknown - with length 25 centimeters and more, or with gestation during 22 weeks or more). - Données concernant les nouveau-nés de 500 grammes ou plus (si le poids est inconnu – de 25 centimètres de long ou plus, ou après une grossesse de 22 semaines ou plus).

[23] Excluding Channel Islands (Guernsey and Jersey) and Isle of Man, shown separately, if available. Data tabulated by date of occurrence for England and Wales, and by date of registration for Northern Ireland and Scotland. - Non compris les îles Anglo-Normandes (Guernesey et Jersey) et l'île de Man, qui font l'objet de rubriques distinctes, si disponible. Données exploitées selon la date de l'événement pour l'Angleterre et le pays de Galles, et selon la date de l'enregistrement pour l'Irlande du Nord et l'Ecosse.

[24] Random rounding to base 3 is applied in this table as a confidentiality measure. - Les chiffres sont arrondis à la base 3 de manière aléatoire, pour des raisons de confidentialité.

Table 12 - *Demographic Yearbook 2015*

Table 12 presents late foetal deaths and late foetal-death ratios by urban/rural residence for as many years as possible between 2011 and 2015.

Description of variables: Late foetal deaths are foetal deaths[1] of 28 or more completed weeks of gestation. Foetal deaths of unknown gestational age are included with those 28 or more weeks.

Statistics on the number of late foetal deaths are obtained from civil registers unless otherwise noted.

The urban/rural classification of late foetal deaths is as provided by each country or area; it is presumed to be based on the national census definitions of urban population that have been set forth at the end of the technical notes for table 6.

Ratio computation: Late foetal-death ratios are the annual number of late foetal deaths per 1 000 live births (as shown in table 9) in the same year. The live-birth base was adopted because it is assumed to be more comparable from one country or area to another than the sum of live births and foetal deaths.

Ratios by urban/rural residence are the annual number of late foetal deaths, in the appropriate urban or rural category, per 1 000 corresponding live births (as shown in table 9). These ratios are calculated by the United Nations Statistics Division.

Ratios presented in this table are limited to those for countries or areas and urban/rural areas having at least a total of 30 late foetal deaths in a given year.

Reliability of data: Each country or area is asked to indicate the estimated completeness of the late foetal deaths recorded in its civil register. These national assessments are indicated by the quality codes "C", "U" and "…" that appear in the first column of this table.

"C" indicates that the data are estimated to be virtually complete, that is, representing at least 90 per cent of the late foetal deaths occurring each year, while "U" indicates that data are estimated to be incomplete, that is, representing less than 90 per cent of the late foetal deaths occurring each year. The code "…" indicates that no information was provided regarding completeness.

Data from civil registers which are reported as incomplete or of unknown completeness (coded "U" or "…") are considered unreliable. They appear in italics in this table. Ratios are not computed for data so coded.

For more information about the quality of vital statistics data in general, see section 4.2 of the Technical Notes.

Limitations: Statistics on late foetal deaths are subject to the same qualifications as have been set forth for vital statistics in general and foetal-death statistics in particular as discussed in section 4 of the Technical Notes.

The reliability of the data is a very important factor. Of all vital statistics, the registration of foetal deaths is probably the most incomplete.

Variation in the definition of foetal deaths, and in particular late foetal deaths, also limits international comparability. The criterion of 28 or more completed weeks of gestation to distinguish late foetal deaths is not universally used; some countries or areas use different durations of gestation or other criteria such as size of the foetus. In addition, the difficulty of accurately determining gestational age further reduces comparability. However, to promote comparability, late foetal deaths shown in this table are restricted to those of at least 28 or more completed weeks of gestation. Wherever this is not possible, a footnote is provided.

Late foetal-death ratios are subject to the limitations of the data on live births with which they have been calculated. These have been set forth in the technical notes for table 9.

It must be pointed out that when late foetal deaths and live births are both under registered, the resulting ratios may be of reasonable magnitude. For the countries or areas where live-birth registration is poorest, the late foetal-death ratios may be the largest, effectively masking the completeness of the base data. For this reason, possible variations in birth-registration completeness as well as the reported completeness of late foetal deaths must always be borne in mind in evaluating late foetal-death ratios.

Finally, it may be noted that the counting of live-born infants as late foetal deaths, because they died before the registration of the birth or within the first 24 hours of life, has the effect of inflating the late foetal-death ratios unduly by decreasing the birth denominator and increasing the foetal-death numerator. This factor should not be overlooked in using data from this table.

The comparability of data by urban/rural residence is affected by the national definitions of urban and rural used in tabulating these data. It is assumed, in the absence of specific information to the contrary, that the definitions of urban and rural used in connection with the national population census were also used in the compilation of the vital statistics for each country or area. However, it cannot be excluded that, for a given country or area, different definitions of urban and rural are used for the vital statistics data and the population census data respectively. When known, the definitions of urban used in national population censuses are presented at the end of the technical notes for table 6. As discussed in detail in the technical notes for table 6, these definitions vary considerably from one country or area to another.

Urban/rural differentials in late foetal death ratios may also be affected by whether the late foetal deaths and live births have been tabulated in terms of place of occurrence or place of usual residence. This problem is discussed in more detail in section 4.1.4.1 of the Introduction.

Earlier data: Late foetal deaths and late foetal-death ratios have been shown in each issue of the Demographic Yearbook beginning with the 1951 issue. A special topic CD on natality published in 2001 presents the data for all available years from 1990 to 1998. For more information on specific topics, and years for which data are reported, readers should consult the Historical Index.

NOTES

[1] For definition, see section 4.1.1 of the Introduction.

Tableau 12 – *Annuaire démographique 2015*

Le tableau 12 présente des données sur les morts fœtales tardives et les rapports de mortinatalité selon le lieu de résidence (zone urbaine ou rurale) pour le plus grand nombre d'années possible entre 2011 et 2015.

Description des variables : Par mort fœtale tardive, on entend le décès d'un fœtus[1] survenu après 28 semaines complètes de gestation au moins. Les morts fœtales pour lesquelles la durée de la période de gestation n'est pas connue sont comprises dans cette catégorie.

Sauf indication contraire, les statistiques du nombre de morts fœtales tardives sont établies sur la base des registres de l'état civil.

La classification des morts fœtales tardives selon le lieu de résidence (zone urbaine ou rurale) est celle qui a été communiquée par chaque pays ou zone ; on part du principe qu'elle repose sur les définitions de la population urbaine utilisées pour les recensements nationaux, telles qu'elles sont reproduites à la fin des notes techniques du tableau 6.

Calcul des rapports : les rapports de mortinatalité représentent le nombre annuel de morts fœtales tardives pour 1 000 naissances vivantes (telles qu'elles sont présentées au tableau 9) survenues pendant la même année. On a pris pour base de calcul les naissances vivantes parce que l'on pense qu'elles sont plus facilement comparables d'un pays ou d'une zone à l'autre que la somme des naissances vivantes et des morts fœtales.

Les rapports selon le lieu de résidence (zone urbaine ou rurale) représentent le nombre annuel de morts fœtales tardives, classées selon la catégorie urbaine ou rurale appropriée pour 1 000 naissances vivantes (telles qu'elles sont présentées au tableau 9) survenues parmi la population correspondante. Ces rapports ont été calculés par la Division des statistiques de l'Organisation des Nations Unies.

Les rapports présentés dans le tableau 12 ne concernent que les pays ou zones où l'on a enregistré un total d'au moins 30 morts fœtales tardives pendant une année donnée.

Fiabilité des données : il a été demandé à chaque pays ou zone d'indiquer le degré estimatif de complétude des données sur les morts fœtales tardives figurant dans ses registres d'état civil. Ces évaluations nationales sont signalées par les codes de qualité "C", "U" et "..." qui apparaissent dans la deuxième colonne du tableau.

La lettre "C" indique que les données sont jugées à peu près complètes, c'est-à-dire qu'elles représentent au moins 90 p. 100 des morts fœtales tardives survenues chaque année ; la lettre "U" signifie que les données sont jugées incomplètes, c'est-à-dire qu'elles représentent moins de 90 p.100 des morts fœtales tardives survenues chaque année. Le code "..." indique qu'aucun renseignement n'a été communiqué quant à la complétude des données.

Les données provenant des registres de l'état civil qui sont déclarées incomplètes ou dont le degré de complétude n'est pas connu (code "U" ou "...") sont jugées douteuses. Elles apparaissent en italique dans le tableau ; les rapports, dans ces cas, n'ont pas été calculés.

Pour plus de précisions sur la qualité des données reposant sur les statistiques de l'état civil en général, voir la section 4.2 des Notes techniques.

Insuffisance des données : les statistiques des morts fœtales tardives appellent toutes les réserves qui ont été formulées à propos des statistiques de l'état civil en général et des statistiques concernant les morts fœtales en particulier (voir la section 4 des Notes techniques).

La fiabilité des données est un facteur très important. Les statistiques concernant les morts fœtales sont probablement les moins complètes de toutes les statistiques de l'état civil.

L'hétérogénéité des définitions de la mort fœtale et, en particulier, de la mort fœtale tardive nuit aussi à la comparabilité internationale des données. Le critère des 28 semaines complètes de gestation au moins n'est pas universellement utilisé ; certains pays ou zones retiennent des critères différents pour la durée de la période de gestation ou d'autres critères tels que la taille du fœtus. De surcroît, la comparabilité est rendue malaisée par le fait qu'il est difficile d'établir avec précision l'âge gestationnel. Pour faciliter les comparaisons, les morts fœtales tardives considérées ici sont exclusivement celles qui sont survenues au terme de 28 semaines de gestation au moins. Les exceptions sont signalées en note.

Les rapports de mortinatalité appellent en outre toutes les réserves qui ont été formulées à propos des statistiques des naissances vivantes qui ont servi à leur calcul (voir à ce sujet les notes techniques relatives au tableau 9).

En ce qui concerne le calcul des rapports, il convient de noter que, si l'enregistrement des morts fœtales tardives et celui des naissances vivantes sont loin d'être exhaustifs, les rapports de mortinatalité peuvent être raisonnables. C'est parfois pour les pays ou zones où l'enregistrement des naissances vivantes laisse le plus à désirer que les rapports de mortinatalité sont les plus élevés, ce qui masque le caractère incomplet des données de base. Aussi, pour porter un jugement sur la qualité des rapports de mortinatalité, il ne faut jamais oublier que la complétude de l'enregistrement des naissances comme celle de l'enregistrement des morts fœtales tardives peuvent varier sensiblement.

Enfin, on notera que l'inclusion parmi les morts fœtales tardives des décès d'enfants nés vivants qui sont décédés avant l'enregistrement de leur naissance ou dans les 24 heures qui ont suivi la naissance conduit à des rapports de mortinatalité exagérés parce que le dénominateur (nombre de naissances) se trouve alors diminué et le numérateur (morts fœtales) augmenté. Il importe de ne pas négliger ce facteur lorsque l'on utilise les données du tableau 12.

La comparabilité des données selon le lieu de résidence (zone urbaine ou rurale) peut être limitée par les définitions nationales des termes « urbain » et « rural » utilisées pour la mise en tableaux de ces données. En l'absence d'indications contraires, on a supposé que les mêmes définitions avaient servi pour le recensement national de la population et pour l'établissement des statistiques de l'état civil pour chaque pays ou zone. Toutefois, il n'est pas exclu que, pour une zone ou un pays donné, des définitions différentes aient été retenues. Les définitions du terme « urbain » utilisées pour les recensements nationaux de population ont été présentées à la fin des notes techniques du tableau 6 lorsqu'elles étaient connues. Comme on l'a précisé dans les notes techniques relatives au tableau 6, ces définitions varient considérablement d'un pays ou d'une zone à l'autre.

La différence entre les rapports de mortinatalité pour les zones urbaines et rurales pourra aussi être faussée selon que les morts fœtales tardives et les naissances vivantes auront été classées d'après le lieu de l'événement ou le lieu de résidence habituel. Ce problème est examiné plus en détail à la section 4.1.4.1 des Notes techniques.

Données publiées antérieurement : les éditions de l'*Annuaire démographique* parues à partir de 1951 contiennent des statistiques concernant les morts fœtales tardives et les rapports de mortinatalité. Un CD-ROM sur la natalité paru en 2001 présente les données pour toutes les années disponibles de 1990 à 1998. Pour plus de précisions concernant les années et les sujets pour lesquels des données ont été publiées, se reporter à l'index.

NOTE

[1] Pour la définition, voir la section 4.1.1 de l'Introduction.

12. Late foetal deaths and late foetal death ratios, by urban/rural residence: 2011 - 2015
Morts foetales tardives et rapports de mortinatalité, selon la résidence, urbaine/rurale : 2011 - 2015

Continent, country or area, and urban/rural residence / Continent, pays ou zone et résidence, urbaine/rurale	Co-de[a]	Number - Nombre					Ratio - Rapport				
		2011	2012	2013	2014	2015	2011	2012	2013	2014	2015
AFRICA - AFRIQUE											
Algeria - Algérie											
Total	+U	15 480	15 795	15 009	15 077	14 620	...	...	...	...	...
Burundi[1]											
Total	+U	3 099	2 448	2 141	...	...	...	...	...	...	...
Egypt - Égypte											
Total	+C	2 465	1 334	...	...	...	1.0	0.5	...	...	...
Urban - Urbaine	+C	1 957	1 093	...	...	...	2.1	1.1	...	...	...
Rural - Rurale	+C	508	241	...	...	...	0.3	0.1	...	...	...
Mauritius - Maurice[2]											
Total	+C	139	140	117	138	125	9.5	9.7	8.7	10.4	9.9
Urban - Urbaine	+C	57	52	46	54	54	10.2	9.6	9.1	10.5	10.5
Rural - Rurale	+C	82	88	71	84	71	9.0	9.7	8.4	10.3	9.5
Sierra Leone											
Total	...	1 663	1 638	...	...	...	...	...	...	...	...
Urban - Urbaine	...	230	572	...	...	...	...	...	...	...	...
Rural - Rurale	...	1 433	1 066	...	...	...	...	...	...	...	...
South Africa - Afrique du Sud											
Total	...	13 852	...	...	...	...	...	...	...	...	...
Tunisia - Tunisie											
Total	U	2 074	...	...	...	...	...	...	...	...	...
AMERICA, NORTH - AMÉRIQUE DU NORD											
Bahamas[3]											
Total	+C	73	59	61	...	...	15.4	13.2	14.1	...	...
Bermuda - Bermudes											
Total	C	2	4	4	1	2	...	...	...	...	...
Canada[4]											
Total	C	*1 115	...	...	...	...	*3.0	...	...	...	...
Costa Rica											
Total	C	471	332	327	319	*326	6.4	4.5	4.6	4.4	*4.5
Urban - Urbaine	C	...	134	108	176	*208	...	5.3	4.3	4.2	*4.2
Rural - Rurale	C	...	198	219	143	*118	...	4.1	4.8	4.7	*5.3
Cuba[5]											
Total	C	1 365	1 262	1 273	1 135	...	10.3	10.0	10.1	9.3	...
Dominican Republic - République dominicaine											
Total	U	1 376	1 131	1 886	1 528	...	...	...	...	...	...
Mexico - Mexique[6]											
Total	+U	11 096	10 442	9 911	9 755	...	...	...	...	...	...
Urban - Urbaine[7]	+U	8 299	7 806	7 249	7 287	...	...	...	...	...	...
Rural - Rurale[7]	+U	2 631	2 469	2 472	2 325	...	...	...	...	...	...
Montserrat											
Total	+C	-	-	-	2	...	...	...	...	...	...
Panama											
Total	U	399	426	370	423	...	...	...	...	...	...
Puerto Rico - Porto Rico[8]											
Total	C	463	382	417	417	358	11.3	9.8	11.4	12.1	11.5
Urban - Urbaine[7]	C	270	236	257	239	205	11.3	11.0	13.0	12.6	10.8
Rural - Rurale[7]	C	190	140	156	151	130	11.0	8.0	9.3	9.8	10.6
Saint Vincent and the Grenadines - Saint-Vincent-et-les Grenadines											
Total	C	29	20	23	...	...	...	...	...	...	...
United States of America - États-Unis d'Amérique											
Total	C	11 857	11 739	11 721	...	...	3.0	3.0	3.0	...	...
AMERICA, SOUTH - AMÉRIQUE DU SUD											
Argentina - Argentine											
Total	C	4 712	3 731	3 809	6 442[8]	...	6.2	5.1	5.0	8.3	...

12. Late foetal deaths and late foetal death ratios, by urban/rural residence: 2011 - 2015
Morts foetales tardives et rapports de mortinatalité, selon la résidence, urbaine/rurale : 2011 - 2015 (continued - suite)

Continent, country or area, and urban/rural residence — Continent, pays ou zone et résidence, urbaine/rurale	Co-de[a]	Number - Nombre					Ratio - Rapport				
		2011	2012	2013	2014	2015	2011	2012	2013	2014	2015
AMERICA, SOUTH - AMÉRIQUE DU SUD											
Brazil - Brésil											
Total	U	24 083	24 823	25 744	25 748	...	...	...	...	...	...
Chile - Chili[9]											
Total	C	1 294	1 276	1 262	...	...	5.2	5.2	5.2	...	...
Urban - Urbaine	C	1 179	996[10]	1 149	...	...	5.3	4.5	5.2	...	...
Rural - Rurale	C	115	125[10]	113	...	...	4.7	5.1	5.2	...	...
Colombia - Colombie											
Total	U	5 276	5 401	5 130	5 178	...	...	...	...	...	...
Urban - Urbaine	U	3 959	3 945	3 780	3 864	...	...	...	...	...	...
Rural - Rurale	U	1 317	1 456	1 350	1 314	...	...	...	...	...	...
Ecuador - Équateur[11]											
Total	...	1 672[8]	1 717[8]	1 040	932	...	...	...	...	...	...
Urban - Urbaine	...	1 432[8]	1 535[8]	875	771	...	...	...	...	...	...
Rural - Rurale	...	240[8]	182[8]	165	161	...	...	...	...	...	...
Suriname											
Total	...	182	...	...	...	...	...	...	...	...	...
Uruguay											
Total	C	...	200	202	229	...	...	4.2	4.1	4.7	...
Venezuela (Bolivarian Republic of) - Venezuela (République bolivarienne du)											
Total	...	1 143	1 006	2 400	2 895	2 457	...	...	...	...	...
ASIA - ASIE											
Armenia - Arménie											
Total	C	...	...	...	746	...	...	...	...	17.3	...
Azerbaijan - Azerbaïdjan											
Total	+C	669	602	643	764	...	3.8	3.5	3.7	4.5	...
Bahrain - Bahreïn[12]											
Total	...	140	125	106	132	...	...	...	...	...	...
Brunei Darussalam - Brunéi Darussalam											
Total	+C	40	43	44	...	...	5.9	6.2	6.6	...	...
China, Hong Kong SAR - Chine, Hong Kong RAS											
Total	...	184	148	119	167	...	...	...	...	...	...
China, Macao SAR - Chine, Macao RAS											
Total	C	12	14	10	12	6	...	...	...	...	...
Georgia - Géorgie											
Total	C	563	...	567	640	...	9.7	...	9.8	10.6	...
Urban - Urbaine	C	323	...	...	...	...	9.7	...	...	...	...
Rural - Rurale	C	240	...	...	...	...	9.8	...	...	...	...
Israel - Israël[13]											
Total	C	530	583	603	...	...	3.2	3.4	3.5	...	...
Urban - Urbaine[7]	C	480	526	535	...	...	3.2	3.4	3.4	...	...
Rural - Rurale[7]	C	47	52	61	...	...	3.1	3.3	3.7	...	...
Japan - Japon[14]											
Total	C	2 137	1 969	1 897	1 790	...	2.0	1.9	1.8	1.8	...
Urban - Urbaine	C	1 946	1 809	1 747	1 657	...	2.0	1.9	1.8	1.8	...
Rural - Rurale	C	191	158	149	131	...	2.2	1.9	1.8	1.7	...
Kazakhstan											
Total	C	3 285	3 453	3 206	...	...	8.8	9.1	8.3	...	...
Urban - Urbaine	C	1 817	1 900	1 673	...	...	9.2	9.2	8.0	...	...
Rural - Rurale	C	1 468	1 553	1 533	...	...	8.4	8.9	8.6	...	...
Kuwait - Koweït											
Total	C	313	355	352	433	...	5.4	5.9	5.9	7.1	...
Kyrgyzstan - Kirghizstan											
Total	C	1 675	1 575	1 549	1 555	*1 484	11.2	10.2	10.0	9.6	*9.1
Urban - Urbaine[15]	C	1 176	1 144	1 142	1 147	*1 080	24.0	21.3	21.2	20.7	*20.6
Rural - Rurale[15]	C	499	431	407	408	*404	5.0	4.3	4.0	3.8	*3.6
Malaysia - Malaisie											
Total	C	2 305	*2 213	...	...	...	4.5	*4.2	...	...	...

Continent, country or area, and urban/rural residence / Continent, pays ou zone et résidence, urbaine/rurale	Code[a]	Number - Nombre					Ratio - Rapport				
		2011	2012	2013	2014	2015	2011	2012	2013	2014	2015
ASIA - ASIE											
Maldives[8]											
Total	...	43	50	51	37	...	...	...	...	...	...
Urban - Urbaine	...	25	29[10]	31	27	...	...	...	...	...	...
Rural - Rurale	...	18	20[10]	20	10	...	...	...	...	...	...
Mongolia - Mongolie											
Total	+C	...	...	...	...	557	...	...	...	...	6.8
Myanmar[16]											
Total	+U	10 986	12 234	11 718	11 926		...	...	...	...	...
Urban - Urbaine	+U	...	5 741	4 898	...		...	...	...	...	...
Rural - Rurale	+U	...	6 493	6 820	...		...	...	...	...	...
Oman[17]											
Total	U	333[18]	...	279	335		...	...	...	...	...
Philippines											
Total	...	4 299	4 219	4 013	...		...	...	...	...	...
Republic of Korea - République de Corée[19]											
Total	C	924	963	931	897	...	2.0	2.0	2.1	2.1	...
Urban - Urbaine[7]	C	697	685	697	611	...	1.8	1.7	1.9	1.7	...
Rural - Rurale[7]	C	153	151	126	135	...	1.9	1.8	1.8	1.9	...
Singapore - Singapour											
Total	+C	106	111	80	86	90	2.7	2.6	2.0	2.0	2.1
Sri Lanka											
Total	+U	998	972	939	708	715	...	...	...	...	...
Tajikistan - Tadjikistan											
Total	U	1 960	1 940	2 234	2 265	...	...	...	...	...	...
Urban - Urbaine	U	775	788	1 301	951	...	...	...	...	...	...
Rural - Rurale	U	1 185	1 152	933	1 314	...	...	...	...	...	...
Uzbekistan - Ouzbékistan											
Total	+C	3 896	3 796	4 122	5 768	...	6.3	6.1	6.1	8.0	...
Urban - Urbaine	+C	2 471	2 425	2 537	3 383	...	8.7	8.4	8.2	10.4	...
Rural - Rurale	+C	1 425	1 371	1 585	2 385	...	4.2	4.1	4.3	6.1	...
EUROPE											
Åland Islands - Îles d'Åland											
Total	C	1	1	-	-	...	...	...	...	...	...
Urban - Urbaine	C	1	-	-	-	...	...	...	...	...	...
Rural - Rurale	C	-	1	-	-	...	...	...	...	...	...
Austria - Autriche											
Total	C	294	260	272	...	...	3.8	3.3	3.4	...	...
Belarus - Bélarus											
Total	C	249	257	260	256	...	2.3	2.2	2.2	2.2	...
Urban - Urbaine	C	174	204	185	...	...	2.1	2.3	2.0	...	...
Rural - Rurale	C	75	53	75	...	...	2.9	2.0	2.7	...	...
Bulgaria - Bulgarie											
Total	C	556	557	483	498	...	7.8	8.1	7.3	7.4	...
Urban - Urbaine	C	401	393	...	...	...	7.5	7.6	...	...	...
Rural - Rurale	C	155	164	...	...	...	8.9	9.4	...	...	...
Croatia - Croatie[20]											
Total	C	145	130	144	150	...	3.5	3.1	3.6	3.8	...
Urban - Urbaine	C	76	78	75	77	...	3.3	3.3	3.3	3.4	...
Rural - Rurale	C	69	52	69	73	...	3.9	2.9	4.0	4.4	...
Czech Republic - République tchèque											
Total	C	303[21]	287[22]	264[22]	296[22]	...	2.8	2.6	2.5	2.7	...
Urban - Urbaine	C	228[21]	211[22]	198[22]	210[22]	...	2.9	2.6	2.5	2.6	...
Rural - Rurale	C	75[21]	76[22]	66[22]	86[22]	...	2.6	2.6	2.3	3.0	...
Denmark - Danemark[23]											
Total	C	262	213	...	234	...	4.4	3.7	...	4.1	...
Estonia - Estonie											
Total	C	42	31	30	38	...	2.9	2.2	2.2	2.8	...
Urban - Urbaine	C	33	17	20	28	...	3.3	...	...	...	...
Rural - Rurale	C	9	14	10	10	...	...	...	...	...	...

Continent, country or area, and urban/rural residence / Continent, pays ou zone et résidence, urbaine/rurale	Co-de[a]	Number - Nombre					Ratio - Rapport				
		2011	2012	2013	2014	2015	2011	2012	2013	2014	2015
EUROPE											
Faeroe Islands - Îles Féroé											
Total	C	...	...	-	-	...	...	...	...	...	...
Urban - Urbaine	C	...	...	-	-	...	...	...	...	...	...
Rural - Rurale	C	...	...	-	-	...	...	...	...	...	...
Finland - Finlande[24]											
Total	C	111	113	106	115	...	1.9	1.9	1.8	2.0	...
Urban - Urbaine	C	76	74	81	83	...	1.8	1.7	2.0	2.0	...
Rural - Rurale	C	35	39	25	32	...	2.0	2.3	...	2.0	...
Germany - Allemagne											
Total	C	2 387	2 400	2 556	2 597	...	3.6	3.6	3.7	3.6	...
Greece - Grèce											
Total	C	431[8]	446[8]	298	353	...	4.0	4.4	3.2	3.8	...
Urban - Urbaine	C	308[8]	332[8]	...	247	...	4.1	4.7	...	3.9	...
Rural - Rurale	C	123[8]	114[8]	...	106	...	3.9	3.9	...	3.6	...
Hungary - Hongrie[25]											
Total	C	392	378	392	421	...	4.5	4.2	4.4	4.5	...
Urban - Urbaine[26]	C	237	234	229	274	...	3.9	3.8	3.7	4.2	...
Rural - Rurale[26]	C	153	140	158	143	...	5.8	5.1	5.7	5.1	...
Iceland - Islande											
Total	C	4[27]	10	4	11	...	...	...	...	...	...
Urban - Urbaine	C	4[27]	10	4	11	...	...	...	...	...	...
Rural - Rurale	C	-[27]	-	-	-	...	...	...	...	...	...
Ireland - Irlande[28]											
Total	C	211	...	...	...	...	2.9	...	...	...	...
Italy - Italie											
Total	C	1 422	1 439	*1 262	1 364	...	2.6	2.7	*2.5	2.7	...
Latvia - Lettonie											
Total	C	87	81	81	83	...	4.6	4.1	3.9	3.8	...
Lithuania - Lituanie[20]											
Total	C	148	117	143	139	...	4.9	3.8	4.8	4.6	...
Urban - Urbaine	C	89	77	87	96	...	4.3	3.6	4.3	4.6	...
Rural - Rurale	C	59	40	56	43	...	6.2	4.4	5.8	4.6	...
Luxembourg											
Total	C	22	28	33	30	...	...	...	5.4	4.9	...
Malta - Malte[20]											
Total	C	18	10	...	...	...	...	...	...	...	...
Netherlands - Pays-Bas[29]											
Total	C	486	438	401	487	...	2.7	2.5	2.3	2.8	...
Norway - Norvège											
Total	C	198	184	171	217	...	3.3	3.1	2.9	3.7	...
Poland - Pologne											
Total	C	1 182	1 174	1 016	928	...	3.0	3.0	2.7	2.5	...
Urban - Urbaine	C	644	638	...	...	...	2.9	2.9	...	...	...
Rural - Rurale	C	538	536	...	...	...	3.3	3.3	...	...	...
Portugal[30]											
Total	C	227	249	180	214	...	2.3	2.8	2.2	2.6	...
Romania - Roumanie											
Total	C	811	779	771	781	...	4.1	3.9	4.2	4.0	...
Urban - Urbaine	C	363	348	325	372	...	3.4	3.2	3.3	3.5	...
Rural - Rurale	C	448	431	446	409	...	5.0	4.7	5.3	4.7	...
Russian Federation - Fédération de Russie											
Total	C	8 109	12 142	...	...	...	4.5	6.4	...	...	...
Urban - Urbaine	C	5 590	8 441	...	...	...	4.4	6.2	...	...	...
Rural - Rurale	C	2 519	3 701	...	...	...	4.8	6.8	...	...	...
Serbia - Serbie[31]											
Total	+C	328	370	307	348	...	5.0	5.5	4.7	5.2	...
Urban - Urbaine	+C	224	252	170	242	...	4.9	5.5	3.7	5.3	...
Rural - Rurale	+C	104	118	137	106	...	5.2	5.5	6.9	5.2	...
Slovakia - Slovaquie[32]											
Total	C	190	180	163	166	...	3.1	3.2	3.0	3.0	...
Urban - Urbaine	C	78	80	72	76	...	2.4	2.7	2.5	2.7	...
Rural - Rurale	C	112	100	91	90	...	3.9	3.8	3.5	3.4	...
Slovenia - Slovénie											
Total	C	59	51	...	...	...	2.7	2.3	...	...	...
Spain - Espagne											
Total	C	1 067	1 050	1 091	1 320	...	2.3	2.3	2.6	3.1	...

12. Late foetal deaths and late foetal death ratios, by urban/rural residence: 2011 - 2015
Morts foetales tardives et rapports de mortinatalité, selon la résidence, urbaine/rurale : 2011 - 2015 (continued - suite)

Continent, country or area, and urban/rural residence / Continent, pays ou zone et résidence, urbaine/rurale	Co-de[a]	Number - Nombre					Ratio - Rapport				
		2011	2012	2013	2014	2015	2011	2012	2013	2014	2015
EUROPE											
Sweden - Suède											
Total	C	429	453	441	456	...	3.8	4.0	3.9	4.0	...
Switzerland - Suisse[8]											
Total	C	349	350	402	368	...	4.3	4.3	4.9	4.3	...
Urban - Urbaine	C	246	282	310	262	...	4.1	4.6	5.0	4.1	...
Rural - Rurale	C	103	68	92	106	...	5.1	3.3	4.5	5.0	...
TFYR of Macedonia - L'ex-R. y. de Macédoine											
Total	C	202	184	196	171	...	8.9	7.8	8.5	7.2	...
Urban - Urbaine	C	120	108	...	...	...	9.2	8.1	...	...	...
Rural - Rurale	C	82	76	...	...	...	8.4	7.5	...	...	...
Ukraine											
Total	+C	3 158	3 230	...	2 820[33]	...	6.3	6.2	...	6.1	...
Urban - Urbaine	+C	2 006	2 120	...	...	...	6.1	6.2	...	...	...
Rural - Rurale	+C	1 152	1 110	...	...	...	6.6	6.2	...	...	...
United Kingdom of Great Britain and Northern Ireland - Royaume-Uni de Grande-Bretagne et d'Irlande du Nord[34]											
Total	C	4 201	3 938	...	...	...	5.2	4.8	...	...	...
OCEANIA - OCÉANIE											
Australia - Australie[35]											
Total	+C	936	1 046	1 295	1 209	...	3.1	3.4	4.2	4.0	...
Guam[8]											
Total	C	...	27	42	36	45	...	...	12.6	10.6	13.4
New Zealand - Nouvelle-Zélande[6]											
Total	+C	184	158	141	144[36]	117[36]	3.0	2.6	2.4	2.5	1.9
Urban - Urbaine	+C	160	141	126	123[37]	108[37]	3.0	2.6	2.4	2.4	2.0
Rural - Rurale	+C	24	17	15	24[37]	12[37]	...	...	...	...	...
Palau - Palaos											
Total	C	1	3	2	...	...	...	...	...	...	...

FOOTNOTES - NOTES

Italics: data from civil registers which are incomplete or of unknown completeness. - Italiques : données incomplètes ou dont le degré d'exactitude n'est pas connu, provenant des registres de l'état civil.

* Provisional. - Données provisoires.

[a] 'Code' indicates the source of data, as follows:
C - Civil registration, estimated over 90% complete
U - Civil registration, estimated less than 90% complete
| - Other source, estimated reliable
+ - Data tabulated by date of registration rather than occurence
... - Information not available

Le 'Code' indique la source des données, comme suit :
C - Registres de l'état civil considérés complets à 90 p. 100 au moins
U - Registres de l'état civil qui ne sont pas considérés complets à 90 p. 100 au moins
| - Autre source, considérée pas douteuses
+ - Données exploitées selon la date de l'enregistrement et non la date de l'événement
... - Information pas disponible

[1] Data refer to the recorded events in Ministry of Health hospitals and health centres only. - Les données se rapportent aux faits d'état civil enregistrés dans les hôpitaux et les dispensaires du Ministère de la santé seulement.
[2] Excludes the islands of St. Brandon and Agalega. - Non compris les îles St. Brandon et Agalega.

[3] Data refer to the death of a foetus at least 22 completed weeks of gestation. - Les données concernent le décès d'un fœtus après 22 semaines de gestation au moins.
[4] Including Canadian residents temporarily in the United States, but excluding United States residents temporarily in Canada. - Y compris les résidents canadiens se trouvant temporairement aux Etats-Unis, mais ne comprenant pas les résidents des Etats-Unis se trouvant temporairement au Canada.
[5] Late foetal death is indicated by the fact that the foetus is at least 500 grams or more in weight. - Les décès foetaux tardifs sont caractérisés par le fait que le foetus pèse au moins 500 grammes.
[6] Data refer to resident population only. - Pour la population résidante seulement.
[7] The total number may include 'Unknown residence', but the categories urban and rural do not. - Le nombre total peut inclure les personnes dont la résidence n'est pas connue, à l'inverse des catégories de population urbaine et rurale.
[8] Data refer to total foetal deaths. - Y compris toutes les morts foetales.
[9] Late foetal death is indicated by the fact that the foetus is at least 22 completed weeks of gestational age. - Les décès intra-utérins tardifs sont définis comme survenant après 22 semaines au moins de gestation.
[10] Excluding deaths of unknown sex. - Non compris les décès dont on ignore le sexe.
[11] Excludes nomadic Indian tribes. - Non compris les tribus d'Indiens nomades.
[12] Sources: Births and Deaths National Registration System database, and medical records of government hospitals. - Les sources: Les bases de données des << Births and Deaths National Registration System >> et les dossiers médicaux des hôpitaux du gouvernement.
[13] Includes data for East Jerusalem and Israeli residents in certain other territories under occupation by Israeli military forces since June 1967. - Y

compris les données pour Jérusalem-Est et les résidents israéliens dans certains autres territoires occupés depuis 1967 par les forces armées israéliennes.

[14] Data refer to Japanese nationals in Japan only. The total number may include 'Unknown residence', but the categories urban and rural do not. Data exclude unknown duration of pregnancy. - Les données se raportent aux nationaux japonais au Japon seulement. Le nombre total peut inclure les personnes dont la résidence n'est pas connue, à l'inverse des catégories de population urbaine et rurale. Exception faite des grossesses dont la durée n'est pas connue.

[15] Urban and rural figures refer to the late foetal deaths collected based on the location of the medical facilities, regardless of the mothers' permanent residence location. - Les chiffres urbains et ruraux concernent les décès tardifs du fœtus recueillis sur la base de l'emplacement des établissements médicaux, indépendamment du lieu de résidence permanente des mères.

[16] Data are from Health Management Information System (HMIS). Including still births. - Les données proviennent de Système d'information de gestion de la santé (HMIS). Les données comprennent les mortinaissances.

[17] Data from Births and Deaths Notification System (Ministry of Health and all health care providers). - Les données proviennent du système de notification des naissances et des décès (Ministère de la santé et tous prestataires de soins de santé).

[18] Data for all population, citizens and foreigners. - Les données portent sur la population entière, les citoyens et les étrangers.

[19] Excluding alien armed forces, civilian aliens employed by armed forces, and foreign diplomatic personnel and their dependants. - Non compris les militaires étrangers, les civils étrangers employés par les forces armées ni le personnel diplomatique étranger et les membres de leur famille les accompagnant.

[20] Late foetal death is defined as an infant born without any signs of life, weighing at least 500 grams, after duration of pregnancy of at least 22 weeks. - On dit qu'il y a mort intra-utérine tardive lorsqu'un enfant pesant au minimum 500 grammes naît sans donner aucun signe de vie au terme d'une grossesse qui a duré au moins 22 semaines.

[21] Late foetal death is defined as an infant born without any signs of life, weighing at least 1000 grams. - La mortalité fœtale en fin de période de gestation s'entend de nourrissons mort-nés et pesant au moins 1 kilo.

[22] Since 1 April 2012, a stillborn child is defined in guidelines for filling in a death certificate as a child fully expelled or removed out of the mother's body, not showing any sign of life and whose birth weight is 500g or more. If the weight is not possible to determine then duration of pregnancy must be 22 weeks or more. If the duration of pregnancy is not possible to determine, the foetus length must be 25cm or more. - Depuis le 1er avril 2012, un enfant mort-né est défini dans les directives relatives à l'établissement du certificat de décès comme un enfant complètement expulsé par la mère ou retiré de son corps, ne montrant aucun signe de vie et ayant atteint un poids de 500 grammes. S'il est impossible d'en déterminer le poids, la durée de gestation doit être au moins de 22 semaines. S'il est impossible de déterminer la durée de gestation, la longueur du fœtus doit être au moins de 25 centimètres.

[23] Excluding Faeroe Islands and Greenland shown separately, if available. - Non compris les Îles Féroé et le Groenland, qui font l'objet de rubriques distinctes, si disponible.

[24] Excluding Åland Islands. - Non compris les Îles d'Åland.

[25] Late foetal death is indicated by the fact that the foetus is at least 24 (it has been 28 weeks until 1996) completed weeks of gestation and does not show any sign of life after the separation from its mother; the foetus has to be 30 cm or more in length or 500 grams or more in weight if its gestational age cannot be determined. - Pour qu'il y ait mort foetale tardive, il faut que le décès d'un foetus survienne après 24 semaines complètes de gestation au moins (28 semaines jusqu'en 1996), que le foetus n'ait pas donné signe de vie après avoir été séparé de la mère, qu'il mesure 30 centimètres au moins ou pèse 500 grammes si la durée de la période de gestation n'est pas connue.

[26] The urban and rural categories do not include the data of foreigners, persons of unknown residence and the homeless, whereas the total category includes them. - Les chiffres portant sur la population urbaine et rurale n' incluent pas les données relatives aux étrangers, aux personnes dont la résidence n'est pas connue et aux personnes sans domicile fixe, à l'inverse, le total les inclut.

[27] Definition of localities was revised in 2011 causing a break with the previous series. - La rupture par rapport aux séries précédentes s'explique par le fait que la définition des localités a été révisée depuis 2011.

[28] Data refer to events registered within one year of occurrence. - Les données portent sur des événements enregistrés dans l'année pendant laquelle ils sont survenus.

[29] Including residents outside the country if listed in a Netherlands population register. - Englobe les résidents se trouvant à l'étranger à condition qu'ils soient inscrits sur le registre de population des Pays-Bas.

[30] Data refer to usually resident population. - Les données concernent la population habituellement résidente.

[31] Data refer to total foetal deaths. Excludes data for Kosovo and Metohia. - Y compris toutes les morts foetales. Sans les données pour le Kosovo et Metohie.

[32] Including foetal deaths of at least 1 000 grams in weight or 28 weeks of gestation. - Y compris les morts de fœtus pesant au moins 1 000 grammes ou après 28 semaines de gestation.

[33] The Government of Ukraine has informed the United Nations that it is not in a position to provide statistical data concerning the Autonomous Republic of Crimea and the city of Sevastopol. - Le gouvernement Ukrainien a informé l'ONU qu'il n'est pas en mesure de fournir des données statistiques concernant la République autonome de Crimée et la ville de Sébastopol.

[34] Excluding Channel Islands (Guernsey and Jersey) and Isle of Man, shown separately, if available. Including unknown sex. - Non compris les îles Anglo-Normandes (Guernesey et Jersey) et l'île de Man, qui font l'objet de rubriques distinctes, si disponible. Y compris le sexe inconnu.

[35] Data include foetal deaths of unknown gestational weeks. - Les données comprennnent les morts foetales où le nombre de semaines de gestation n'est pas connu.

[36] Random rounding to base 3 is applied in this table as a confidentiality measure. - Les chiffres sont arrondis à la base 3 de manière aléatoire, pour des raisons de confidentialité.

[37] Random rounding to base 3 is applied in this table as a confidentiality measure. The total number may include 'Unknown residence', but the categories urban and rural do not. - Les chiffres sont arrondis à la base 3 de manière aléatoire, pour des raisons de confidentialité. Le nombre total peut inclure les personnes dont la résidence n'est pas connue, à l'inverse des catégories de population urbaine et rurale.

Table 13 - *Demographic Yearbook 2015*

Table 13 presents legally induced abortions for as many years as available between 2006 and 2015.

Description of variables: There are two major categories of abortion: spontaneous and induced. Induced abortions are those initiated by deliberate action undertaken with the intention of terminating pregnancy; all other abortions are considered spontaneous.

The induction of abortion is subject to governmental regulation in most, if not all, countries or areas. This regulation varies from complete prohibition in some countries or areas to abortion on request, with services provided by governmental health authorities, in others. More generally, governments have attempted to define the conditions under which a pregnancy may lawfully be terminated and have established procedures for authorizing abortion in individual cases.

Information on abortion policies is collected by the United Nations Population Division and published in the *Abortion Policies and Reproductive Health around the World*[1].

Reliability of data: Unlike data on live births and foetal deaths, which are generally collected through systems of vital registration, data on abortion are collected from a variety of sources. Because of this, the quality specification on the completeness of civil registers, which is presented for other tables, does not appear here.

Limitations: With regard to the collection of information on abortions, a variety of sources are used, but hospital records are the most common source of information. This implies that most cases that have no contact with hospitals are missed. Data from other sources are probably also incomplete. The data in the present table are limited to legally induced abortions, which, by their nature, might be assumed to be more complete than data on all induced abortions.

Earlier data: Legally induced abortions have been shown previously in all issues of the *Demographic Yearbook* since the twenty-third issue. For more information on specific topics and years for which data are reported, readers should consult the Historical Index.

NOTES

[1] United Nations, Department of Economic and Social Affairs, Population Division (2014). *Abortion Policies and Reproductive Health around the World* (United Nations publication, Sales No. E.14.XIII.11).

Tableau 13 – *Annuaire démographique 2015*

Le tableau 13 présente les données disponibles, relatives aux avortements provoqués légalement, entre 2006 et 2015.

Description des variables : l'avortement peut être spontané ou provoqué. L'avortement provoqué est celui qui résulte de manœuvres délibérées, entreprises afin d'interrompre la grossesse ; tous les autres avortements sont considérés comme spontanés.

L'interruption délibérée de la grossesse fait l'objet d'une réglementation officielle dans la plupart des pays ou zones, sinon dans tous. Cette réglementation va de l'interdiction totale à l'autorisation de l'avortement sur demande, pratiqué par des services de santé publique. Le plus souvent, les gouvernements se sont efforcés de définir les circonstances dans lesquelles la grossesse peut être interrompue licitement et de fixer une procédure d'autorisation.

La Division de la population des Nations Unies collecte des informations sur les politiques en matière d'avortement et les publient dans *Abortion Policies and Reproductive Health around the World*[1].

Fiabilité des données : à la différence des données sur les naissances vivantes et les morts fœtales, qui proviennent généralement des registres d'état civil, les données sur l'avortement sont tirées de sources diverses. Aussi ne trouve-t-on pas ici une évaluation de la qualité des données semblable à celle qui indique, pour les autres tableaux, le degré d'exhaustivité des données de l'état civil.

Insuffisance des données : en ce qui concerne les renseignements sur l'avortement, un grand nombre de sources sont utilisées, les relevés hospitaliers restant cependant la source la plus commune. Il s'ensuit que la plupart des cas qui ne passent pas par les hôpitaux sont ignorés. Il faut aussi tenir compte du fait que les données provenant d'autres sources sont probablement incomplètes. Les données du tableau 13 se limitent aux avortements provoqués pour raisons légales dont on peut supposer, en raison de leur nature même, que les statistiques sont plus complètes que les données concernant l'ensemble des avortements provoqués.

Données publiées antérieurement : des statistiques concernant les avortements provoqués pour raisons légales sont publiées dans *l'Annuaire démographique* depuis la vingt-troisième édition. Pour plus de précisions concernant les années et les sujets pour lesquels des données ont été publiées, se reporter à l'index historique.

NOTES

[1] United Nations, Department of Economic and Social Affairs, Population Division (2014). *Abortion Policies and Reproductive Health around the World* (United Nations publication, Sales No. E.14.XIII.11).

13. Legally induced abortions: 2006 - 2015
Avortements provoqués légalement : 2006 - 2015

Continent and country or area Continent et pays ou zone	Number - Nombre									
	2006	**2007**	**2008**	**2009**	**2010**	**2011**	**2012**	**2013**	**2014**	**2015**

AFRICA - AFRIQUE

Burundi[1]	...	...	...	6 329	6 272	3 547	3 630	3 152	...	...
Reunion - Réunion	4 523	4 543	4 564	4 402	4 349	4 508	4 280	...	...	...
Seychelles	443	446	453	471	556	579	533	515	549	478

AMERICA, NORTH - AMÉRIQUE DU NORD

Bermuda - Bermudes	222	90	283	303	284	278	278	275	248	239
Canada[2]	91 310	...	...	...	...	...	...	...	...	...
Costa Rica[3]	8 367[4]	8 504[4]	8 733[4]	7 848	7 697	7 882	7 405	7 283	*7 137	...
Cuba	67 903	66 008	74 905	84 724	71 398	83 943	83 682	84 373	85 782	...
Dominican Republic - République dominicaine	...	29 526	26 318	22 828	22 551	25 284	26 303	26 180	25 999	
Greenland - Groenland	904	887	899	799	858	743	784	875	865	
Martinique	2 392	...	...	...	...	...	...	...	...	
Mexico - Mexique[5]	793	833	764	867	*986	1 041	294	271	...	...
Puerto Rico - Porto Rico[6]	5 538	...	...	...	...	...	...	...	...	...
United States of America - États-Unis d'Amérique[7]	852 385	827 609	825 564	...	...	...	...	...	...	...

AMERICA, SOUTH - AMÉRIQUE DU SUD

Colombia - Colombie	...	...	...	*69*	*81*	*120*	*209*	*628*	*873*	...
Ecuador - Équateur[8]	...	...	...	...	...	...	*41 712*	*40 256*	*35 719*	...
French Guiana - Guyane française	1 661	...	...	...	...	...	...	...	...	...
Paraguay	...	...	...	...	...	...	*4 353*	...	...	...

ASIA - ASIE

Armenia - Arménie	11 132	11 501	12 469	13 797	...	...	...	...	11 892	...
Azerbaijan - Azerbaïdjan	20 864	22 323	25 247	24 554	26 799	27 787	31 037	27 892	27 220	...
Bahrain - Bahreïn[9]	2 297	2 014	2 575	2 394	2 525	2 452	2 463	...	...	...
China, Hong Kong SAR - Chine, Hong Kong RAS	13 510	13 515	13 199	12 028	11 231	11 864	11 298	10 653	10 359	...
Georgia - Géorgie	21 204	20 644	22 062	24 311	25 585	30 590	...	38 018	...	...
Israel - Israël[10]	19 452	19 470	19 638	19 849	19 575	18 974	18 822	18 263	...	...
Japan - Japon	276 352	256 672	242 326	226 878	212 694[11]	202 106	196 639	186 253	181 905	...
Kazakhstan	130 599	125 654	130 599	113 320	106 074	95 288	95 654	84 265	...	...
Kyrgyzstan - Kirghizstan[12]	19 762	21 884	20 800	22 088	21 675	23 728	23 547	21 673	24 456	22 084
Mongolia - Mongolie	12 594	15 817	10 688	12 602	12 492	...	...	...	...	18 168
Singapore - Singapour	12 032	11 933	12 222	12 318	12 082	11 940	10 624	9 282	8 515	7 942
Tajikistan - Tadjikistan	17 489	18 986	18 481	19 470	19 510	17 503	16 618	15 984	17 347	...
Uzbekistan - Ouzbékistan	45 030	42 681	41 758	45 968	40 651	38 809	37 634	38 546	41 352	...

EUROPE

Åland Islands - Îles d'Åland	53	73	67	68	70	73	60	70	66	...
Albania - Albanie	9 552	9 030	8 335	8 139	6 919	7 042	6 755	6 442	...	...
Belarus - Bélarus	58 516	46 285	42 197	35 967	33 262	32 031	28 628	31 206	29 797	...
Belgium - Belgique	17 640	18 033	18 595	18 870	19 095	19 578	...	...	...	...
Bulgaria - Bulgarie	37 272	37 594	36 593	33 733	31 548	31 716	29 992	29 505	28 145	...
Croatia - Croatie	4 733	4 573	4 497	4 450	4 043	4 347	3 571	3 161	3 020	...
Czech Republic - République tchèque	25 352	25 414	25 760	24 636	23 998	24 055	23 032	22 714	21 893	...
Denmark - Danemark[13]	15 202	15 660	16 355	16 736	16 709	15 974	15 608	15 834	15 097	...
Estonia - Estonie[14]	9 378	8 883	8 409	7 542	7 068	6 668	6 056	5 777	6 901	...
Faeroe Islands - Îles Féroé	41	46	37	51	33	33	34	23	30	32
Finland - Finlande[15]	10 636	10 507	10 414	10 437	10 231	10 622	10 177	10 060	9 714	...
France[16]	213 983	212 050	208 003	208 662	211 248	206 888	205 300	...	...	...
Germany - Allemagne	119 710	116 871	114 484	110 694	110 431	108 867	106 815	102 802	99 715	...
Hungary - Hongrie	46 324	43 870	44 089	43 181	40 449	38 443	36 118	34 891	32 663	...
Iceland - Islande	904	905	959	981	977	970	980	963	951	...

Continent and country or area / Continent et pays ou zone	Number - Nombre									
	2006	2007	2008	2009	2010	2011	2012	2013	2014	2015
EUROPE										
Italy - Italie	125 782[17]	125 116[18]	118 891[19]	114 793[20]	112 463[21]	110 041[21]	103 191[22]	100 342	95 400	...
Latvia - Lettonie	11 825	11 814	10 425	8 881	7 443	7 089	6 197	5 557	5 318	...
Lithuania - Lituanie	9 536	9 596	9 031	8 024	6 989	6 205	6 033	5 353	5 231	...
Montenegro - Monténégro	...	...	...	...	...	...	...	...	943	...
Norway - Norvège	14 417	15 165	16 054	15 774	15 735	15 343	...	...	...	...
Poland - Pologne[23]	339	328	506	538	644	669	752	745	970	...
Portugal	1 215	4 325	18 607	19 848	20 137	20 480	19 156	18 281	16 589	...
Republic of Moldova - République de Moldova	15 742	15 843	15 900	14 634	14 785	15 710	14 838	...	...	...
Romania - Roumanie	150 246	137 226	127 907	116 060	101 915	103 386	87 975	86 432	78 371	...
Russian Federation - Fédération de Russie	1 582 398	1 479 010	1 385 600	1 292 389	1 186 108	1 124 880	1 063 982	1 012 399	...	...
Serbia - Serbie[24]	25 665	24 273	22 867	...	...	...	...	...	...	...
Slovakia - Slovaquie	14 243	13 424	13 394	13 240	12 582	11 789	11 214	11 105	10 582	...
Slovenia - Slovénie	5 632	5 176	4 946	4 653	4 328	4 263	4 106	...	...	...
Spain - Espagne	101 592	112 138	115 812	111 482	113 031	118 359	112 390	...	94 796	...
Sweden - Suède	36 045	37 205	38 049	37 524	37 693	37 696	...	...	...	...
Switzerland - Suisse	10 594	10 035[25]	10 310[25]	10 187[25]	10 650[25]	10 715[25]	10 531[25]	10 177[25]	9 990[25]	...
Ukraine	229 618[26]	225 336	217 413	194 845	176 774	169 131	153 147	147 736	116 104[27]	...
United Kingdom of Great Britain and Northern Ireland - Royaume-Uni de Grande-Bretagne et d'Irlande du Nord[28]	214 340	219 376	216 062	208 854	209 048	208 636	203 419[29]	...		...
OCEANIA - OCÉANIE										
Guam[30]	...	...	327	266	269	295	275	213	209	263
New Zealand - Nouvelle-Zélande	17 934	18 382	17 940	17 550	16 630	15 863	14 745	14 073	13 137[31]	...

FOOTNOTES - NOTES

* Provisional. - Données provisoires.

[1] Data refer to the recorded events in Ministry of Health hospitals and health centres only. - Les données se rapportent aux faits d'état civil enregistrés dans les hôpitaux et les dispensaires du Ministère de la santé seulement.

[2] Data refer to resident population only. Significant undercoverage of medically induced abortions in clinics in 2006 due to non response in some provinces. - Pour la population résidante seulement. Sous-dénombrement notable des interruptions volontaires de grossesse pratiquées dans les centres médicaux en 2006 faute de réponse dans certaines provinces.

[3] Excluding abortions performed in private hospitals. - Non comprises les interruptions volontaires de grossesse effectuées dans des hôpitaux privés.

[4] Number of women who report having had a previous abortion when registering a newborn. - Nombre des femmes qui ont signalé d'avoir eu un avortement avant la naissance de l'enfant enregistré.

[5] Data refer to 'Therapeutic Abortions'. According to Mexican law, only induced abortions, prescribed by medical reasons or induced because of pregnancy coming from sexual aggression, are considered as legal; data refer only to the former. Refers to residence of the mother. To calculate the total number of abortions, only foetal deaths of less than 20 weeks of gestation were considered. Excluding abortions in the country by women with usual residence outside of the country. - Les données se rapportent aux « interruptions volontaires de grossesse pour des motifs thérapeutiques ». D'après la loi mexicaine, seuls sont considérés légaux les avortements déclenchés pour des raisons médicales ou parce que la grossesse est le résultat d'une agression sexuelle; les données se réfèrent seulement à la première. Correspond à la résidence de la mère. Seuls les morts fœtales survenues à moins de 20 semaines de gestation ont été prises en compte aux fins du calcul du nombre total d'avortements. Hors avortements dans le pays par des femmes avec résidence habituelle en dehors du pays.

[6] Data refer to the fiscal year from 1 July to 30 June. Excluding abortions performed in a clinic which closed operations without reporting the data. - Les données se réfèrent à l'année budgétaire de 1 juillet au 30 juin. Non comprises les avortements effectuées dans une clinique qui a fermé sans envoyer les données.

[7] Includes areas that reported abortion counts every year during the period of analysis. Excludes states that did not report abortion numbers: Alaska(1998-2002), California (1997-2008), Louisiana (2005), Maryland (2006-2008), New Hampshire (1998-2008), Oklahoma (1998-1999), and West Virginia (2003-2004). - Sont couvertes les régions qui ont indiqué le nombre annuel d'avortements pour la période analysée. Ne sont pas couverts les États qui n'ont pas fourni de chiffres : l'Alaska (1998-2002), la Californie (1997-2008), la Louisiane (2005), le Maryland (2006-2008), le New Hampshire (1998-2008), l'Oklahoma (1998-1999) et la Virginie occidentale (2003-2004).

[8] Data refer to abortions registered in the hospitals due to pregnancy complications. - Les données renvoient aux avortements enregistrés dans les hôpitaux du fait des complications de la grossesse.

[9] Data refer to spontaneous abortions and miscarriages. - Données se rapportant aux avortements spontanés et fausses couches.

[10] Includes data for East Jerusalem and Israeli residents in certain other territories under occupation by Israeli military forces since June 1967. Data refer to applications to commissions for termination of pregnancy and not to authorizations. - Y compris les données pour Jérusalem-Est et les résidents israéliens dans certains autres territoires occupés depuis 1967 par les forces armées israéliennes. Les données relatives aux avortements provoqués légalement se rapportent aux demandes d'autorisation et non aux autorisations elles-mêmes.

[11] Excluding data of cities and towns in the jurisdiction of Sousou Public Health and Welfare Office of Fukushima Prefecture due to the impact of the Great East Japan Earthquake. - Ne sont pas incluses les données relatives aux agglomérations relevant du bureau de la santé publique et des services sociaux de Sousou dans la préfecture de Fukushima, en raison des conséquences du grand séisme dans l'est du Japon.

[12] Based on administrative reporting of the Ministry of Health. - Les données reposent sur les rapports administratifs du Ministère de la santé.

[13] Excluding Faeroe Islands and Greenland shown separately, if available. - Non compris les Îles Féroé et le Groenland, qui font l'objet de rubriques distinctes, si disponible.

[14] Data refer to resident population only. - Pour la population résidante seulement.

[15] Excluding Åland Islands. - Non compris les Îles d'Åland.

¹⁶ Data refer to women between 15 and 49 years of age. - Le total se rapporte uniquement aux femmes dont l'âge est compris entre 15 et 49 ans.

¹⁷ Data are incomplete for Friuli-Venezia Giulia, Campania and Sicilia regions. - Les données sont incomplètes pour les régions Frioul-Vénétie julienne, la Campanie et la Sicile.

¹⁸ Data are incomplete for Campania and Sicilia regions. - Les données sont incomplètes pour les régions de la Campanie et de la Sicile.

¹⁹ Data are incomplete for Campania, Calabria, Sicilia and Sardegna regions. - Les données sont incomplètes pour les régions de Campanie, de Calabrie, de Sicile et de Sardaigne.

²⁰ Data are incomplete for Abruzzo, Campania, Basilicata, Sicilia and Sardegna regions. - Données incomplètes pour les régions des Abruzzes, de Campanie, de Basilicate, de Sicile et de Sardaigne.

²¹ Data are incomplete for Umbria, Campania and Sicilia regions. - Les données sont incomplètes pour l'Ombrie, la Campanie et la Sicile.

²² Data are incomplete for Umbria, Abruzzo, Campania, Puglia and Sicilia regions. - Les données sont incomplètes pour les régions d'Ombrie, des Abruzzes, de Campanie, des Pouilles et de Sicile.

²³ Based on hospital and polyclinic records. - D'après les registres des hôpitaux et des polycliniques.

²⁴ Excludes data for Kosovo and Metohia. Data refer to institutions included in the Health Institutions Network Plan in the Republic of Serbia. - Sans les données pour le Kosovo et Metohie. Les données se rapportent aux institutions membres du "Health Institutions Network Plan" de la République de Serbie.

²⁵ Data refer to termination of pregnancy for women who are Switzerland residents. - Les données portent sur les interruptions de grossesse pratiquées sur des femmes qui résident en Suisse.

²⁶ Data refer to the recorded events in Ministry of Health institutions only. - Données ne concernant que les faits enregistrés dans les institutions du Ministère de la santé.

²⁷ The Government of Ukraine has informed the United Nations that it is not in a position to provide statistical data concerning the Autonomous Republic of Crimea and the city of Sevastopol. - Le gouvernement Ukrainien a informé l'ONU qu'il n'est pas en mesure de fournir des données statistiques concernant la République autonome de Crimée et la ville de Sébastopol.

²⁸ Excluding Northern Ireland. Excluding Channel Islands (Guernsey and Jersey) and Isle of Man, shown separately, if available. - Non compris l'Irlande du Nord. Non compris les îles Anglo-Normandes (Guernesey et Jersey) et l'île de Man, qui font l'objet de rubriques distinctes, si disponible.

²⁹ Including provisional data for Scotland. - Y compris les données provisoires pour l'Écosse.

³⁰ Including United States military personnel, their dependants and contract employees. - Y compris les militaires des Etats-Unis, les membres de leur famille les accompagnant et les agents contractuels des Etats-Unis.

³¹ Random rounding to base 3 is applied in this table as a confidentiality measure. - Les chiffres sont arrondis à la base 3 de manière aléatoire, pour des raisons de confidentialité.

Table 14 - *Demographic Yearbook 2015*

Table 14 presents legally induced abortions by age and number of previous live births of women for the latest available year between 2006 and 2015.

Description of variables: Age is defined as age at last birthday, that is, the difference between the date of birth and the date of the occurrence of the event, expressed in complete solar years. The age classification used in this table is the following: under 15 years, 5-year age groups through 45-49 years and 50 years and over.

Except where otherwise indicated, eight categories are used in classifying the number of previous live births: 0 through 5, 6 or more live births, and, if required, number of live births unknown.

Information on abortion policies is collected by the United Nations Population Division and published in the *Abortion Policies and Reproductive Health around the World*[1].

Reliability of data: Unlike data on live births and foetal deaths, which are generally collected through systems of vital registration, data on abortion are collected from a variety of sources. Because of this, the quality specification on the completeness of civil registers, which is presented for other tables, does not appear here.

Limitations: With regard to the collection of information on abortions, a variety of sources are used, but hospital records are the most common source of information. This implies that most cases that have no contact with hospitals are missed. Data from other sources are probably also incomplete. The data in the present table are limited to legally induced abortions, which, by their nature, might be assumed to be more complete than data on all induced abortions.

In addition, deficiencies in the reporting of age and number of previous live births of the woman, differences in the method used for obtaining the age of the woman, and the proportion of abortions for which age or previous live births of the woman are unknown must all be taken into account in using these data.

Earlier data: Legally induced abortions by age and previous live births of women have been shown previously in most issues of the *Demographic Yearbook* since the twenty-third issue. For more information on specific topics and years for which data are reported, readers should consult the Historical Index.

NOTES

[1] United Nations, Department of Economic and Social Affairs, Population Division (2014). *Abortion Policies and Reproductive Health around the World* (United Nations publication, Sales No. E.14.XIII.11).

415

Tableau 14 – *Annuaire démographique 2015*

Le tableau 14 présente les données les plus récentes disponibles entre 2006 et 2015 sur les avortements provoqués pour des raisons légales, selon l'âge de la mère et le nombre de naissances vivantes précédentes.

Description des variables : L'âge considéré est l'âge au dernier anniversaire, c'est-à-dire la différence entre la date de naissance et la date de l'avortement, exprimée en années solaires révolues. La classification par âge utilisée dans le tableau 14 est la suivante : moins de 15 ans, groupes quinquennaux jusqu'à 45-49 ans, 50 ans et plus, et âge inconnu.

Sauf indication contraire, les naissances vivantes antérieures sont classées dans les huit catégories suivantes: 0 à 5 naissances vivantes, 6 naissances vivantes ou plus et, le cas échéant, nombre de naissances vivantes inconnu.

La Division de la population des Nations Unies collecte des informations sur les politiques en matière d'avortement et les publient dans *Abortion Policies and Reproductive Health around the World*[1].

Fiabilité des données : à la différence des données sur les naissances vivantes et les morts fœtales, qui proviennent généralement des registres d'état civil, les données sur l'avortement sont tirées de sources diverses. Aussi ne trouve-t-on pas ici une évaluation de la qualité des données semblable à celle qui indique, pour les autres tableaux, le degré d'exhaustivité des données de l'état civil.

Insuffisance des données : en ce qui concerne les renseignements sur l'avortement, un grand nombre de sources sont utilisées, les relevés hospitaliers restant cependant la source la plus commune. Il s'ensuit que la plupart des cas qui ne passent pas par les hôpitaux sont ignorés. Il faut aussi tenir compte du fait que les données provenant d'autres sources sont probablement incomplètes. Les données du tableau 14 se limitent aux avortements provoqués pour raisons légales dont on peut supposer, en raison de leur nature même, que les statistiques sont plus complètes que les données concernant l'ensemble des avortements provoqués.

En outre, on doit tenir compte, lorsque l'on utilise ces données, des erreurs de déclaration de l'âge de la mère et du nombre des naissances vivantes précédentes, de l'hétérogénéité des méthodes de calcul de l'âge de la mère et de la proportion d'avortements pour lesquels l'âge de la mère ou le nombre des naissances vivantes ne sont pas connus.

Données publiées antérieurement : Depuis la vingt-troisième édition, la plupart des éditions de l'*Annuaire démographique* contiennent des statistiques concernant les avortements provoqués pour raisons légales, selon l'âge de la mère et le nombre de naissances vivantes antérieures. Pour plus de précisions concernant les années et les sujets pour lesquels des données ont été publiées, se reporter à l'index historique.

NOTES

[1] United Nations, Department of Economic and Social Affairs, Population Division (2014). *Abortion Policies and Reproductive Health around the World* (United Nations publication, Sales No. E.14.XIII.11).

14. Legally induced abortions by age and number of previous live births of women: latest available year, 2006 - 2015
Avortments provoqués légalement selon l'âge de la femme et selon le nombre des naissances vivantes précédentes :
dernière année disponible, 2006 - 2015

Continent, country or area, year and age Continent, pays ou zone, année et âge	Total	Number of previous live births Nombre des naissances vivantes précédentes							Unknown - Inconnu
		0	1	2	3	4	5	6+	

AMERICA, NORTH - AMÉRIQUE DU NORD

Bermuda - Bermudes
2014

Total	248	...	...	...	...	...	...	...	...
0 - 14	-	...	...	...	...	...	...	...	...
15 - 19	17	...	...	...	...	...	...	...	...
20 - 24	54	...	...	...	...	...	...	...	...
25 - 29	78	...	...	...	...	...	...	...	...
30 - 34	57	...	...	...	...	...	...	...	...
35 - 39	33	...	...	...	...	...	...	...	...
40 - 44	9	...	...	...	...	...	...	...	...
45 - 49	-	...	...	...	...	...	...	...	...
50 +	-	...	...	...	...	...	...	...	...
Unknown - Inconnu	-	...	...	...	...	...	...	...	...

Canada[1]
2006

Total	91 310	...	...	...	...	...	...	...	...
0 - 14	267	...	...	...	...	...	...	...	...
15 - 19	15 217	...	...	...	...	...	...	...	...
20 - 24	28 358	...	...	...	...	...	...	...	...
25 - 29	20 315	...	...	...	...	...	...	...	...
30 - 34	13 615	...	...	...	...	...	...	...	...
35 - 39	9 444	...	...	...	...	...	...	...	...
40 +	3 938	...	...	...	...	...	...	...	...
Unknown - Inconnu	156	...	...	...	...	...	...	...	...

Costa Rica[2]
2009

Total	7 848	...	...	...	...	...	...	...	...
10 - 14	68	...	...	...	...	...	...	...	...
15 - 19	1 275	...	...	...	...	...	...	...	...
20 - 44	6 437	...	...	...	...	...	...	...	...
45 +	68	...	...	...	...	...	...	...	...

Cuba
2013

Total	84 373	...	...	...	...	...	...	...	...
12 - 14	1 412	...	...	...	...	...	...	...	...
15 - 19	19 139	...	...	...	...	...	...	...	...
20 - 34	54 077	...	...	...	...	...	...	...	...
35 - 49	9 745	...	...	...	...	...	...	...	...

Mexico - Mexique[3]
2013

Total	271	86	91	45	13	5	2	2	27
0 - 14	2	1	1	-	-	-	-	-	-
15 - 19	31	17	8	-	-	-	-	-	6
20 - 24	72	36	20	7	1	1	-	-	7
25 - 29	69	16	30	10	1	2	-	1	9
30 - 34	49	9	14	15	7	2	-	-	2
35 - 39	31	5	12	11	2	-	-	-	1
40 - 44	10	1	3	1	2	-	1	1	1
45 - 49	1	-	-	1	-	-	-	-	-
50 +	-	-	-	-	-	-	-	-	-
Unknown - Inconnu	6	1	3	-	-	-	1	-	1

Puerto Rico - Porto Rico[4]
2006

Total	5 538	1 991	1 639	1 013	588	229	46	32	-
0 - 14	21	...	...	...	...	...	...	...	...
15 - 19	968	...	...	...	...	...	...	...	...
20 - 24	1 868	...	...	...	...	...	...	...	...
25 - 29	1 413	...	...	...	...	...	...	...	...
30 - 34	767	...	...	...	...	...	...	...	...
35 - 39	351	...	...	...	...	...	...	...	...
40 - 44	129	...	...	...	...	...	...	...	...
45 +	21	...	...	...	...	...	...	...	...

14. Legally induced abortions by age and number of previous live births of women: latest available year, 2006 - 2015
Avortments provoqués légalement selon l'âge de la femme et selon le nombre des naissances vivantes précédentes :
dernière année disponible, 2006 - 2015 (continued - suite)

Continent, country or area, year and age / Continent, pays ou zone, année et âge	Number of previous live births Nombre des naissances vivantes précédentes								
	Total	0	1	2	3	4	5	6+	Unknown - Inconnu

AMERICA, SOUTH - AMÉRIQUE DU SUD

Colombia - Colombie
2014

Total	876	398	243	113	67	31	14	7	3
0 - 14	38	35	1	-	-	-	-	-	2
15 - 19	188	152	30	6	-	-	-	-	-
20 - 24	240	118	88	25	6	2	1	-	-
25 - 29	157	47	51	26	21	6	5	1	-
30 - 34	127	25	42	27	17	10	4	2	-
35 - 39	72	14	23	17	11	4	1	2	-
40 - 44	49	7	6	12	12	8	3	1	-
45 - 49	4	-	2	-	-	1	-	1	-
50 +	-	-	-	-	-	-	-	-	-
Unknown - Inconnu	1	-	-	-	-	-	-	-	1

Ecuador - Équateur[5]
2014

Total	35 719	...	...	...	...	...	...	...	...
0 - 14	447	...	...	...	...	...	...	...	...
15 - 19	5 532	...	...	...	...	...	...	...	...
20 - 24	8 312	...	...	...	...	...	...	...	...
25 - 29	7 804	...	...	...	...	...	...	...	...
30 - 34	6 395	...	...	...	...	...	...	...	...
35 - 39	4 609	...	...	...	...	...	...	...	...
40 - 44	2 188	...	...	...	...	...	...	...	...
45 - 49	432	...	...	...	...	...	...	...	...
50 +	-	...	...	...	...	...	...	...	...
Unknown - Inconnu	-	...	...	...	...	...	...	...	...

ASIA - ASIE

Armenia - Arménie
2014

Total	11 892	...	...	...	...	...	...	...	...
0 - 14	1	...	...	...	...	...	...	...	...
15 - 29	490	...	...	...	...	...	...	...	...
30 - 44	9 251	...	...	...	...	...	...	...	...
45 +	2 150	...	...	...	...	...	...	...	...

Azerbaijan - Azerbaïdjan
2014

Total	27 220	...	...	...	...	...	...	...	...
15 - 19	1 161	...	...	...	...	...	...	...	...
20 - 24	5 738	...	...	...	...	...	...	...	...
25 - 29	8 365	...	...	...	...	...	...	...	...
30 - 34	7 756	...	...	...	...	...	...	...	...
35 +	4 200	...	...	...	...	...	...	...	...
Unknown - Inconnu	-	...	...	...	...	...	...	...	...

China, Hong Kong SAR - Chine, Hong Kong RAS
2014

Total	10 359	5 730	2 013	2 173	358	56	16	13	...
0 - 14	22	22	-	-	-	-	-	-	...
15 - 19	859	820	33	6	-	-	-	-	...
20 - 24	2 035	1 796	169	62	7	1	-	-	...
25 - 29	2 149	1 500	368	249	27	2	2	1	...
30 - 34	2 197	928	568	592	84	19	3	3	...
35 - 39	2 007	487	566	788	137	18	6	5	...
40 - 44	982	165	279	427	90	13	4	4	...
45 - 49	106	11	30	48	13	3	1	-	...
50 +	2	1	-	1	-	-	-	-	...

Georgia - Géorgie
2013

Total	38 018	...	...	...	...	...	...	...	...
0 - 14	34	...	...	...	...	...	...	...	...
15 - 19	1 849	...	...	...	...	...	...	...	...
20 - 29	17 475	...	...	...	...	...	...	...	...
30 - 34	10 007	...	...	...	...	...	...	...	...
35 - 39	6 412	...	...	...	...	...	...	...	...
40 - 44	1 966	...	...	...	...	...	...	...	...

14. Legally induced abortions by age and number of previous live births of women: latest available year, 2006 - 2015
Avortments provoqués légalement selon l'âge de la femme et selon le nombre des naissances vivantes précédentes : dernière année disponible, 2006 - 2015 (continued - suite)

Continent, country or area, year and age Continent, pays ou zone, année et âge	Number of previous live births Nombre des naissances vivantes précédentes								
	Total	0	1	2	3	4	5	6+	Unknown - Inconnu

ASIA - ASIE

Georgia - Géorgie
2013
45 - 49	258	...	...	...	...	...	...	...	...
50 +	17	...	...	...	...	...	...	...	...

Israel - Israël[6]
2013
Total	18 263	7 860	2 509	3 539	2 695	997	387	276	...
0 - 14	46	45	1	-	-	-	-	-	...
15 - 19	1 780	1 706	61	11	2	-	-	-	...
20 - 24	3 600	2 895	414	221	53	17	-	-	...
25 - 29	3 603	1 826	699	618	305	112	28	15	...
30 - 34	3 820	900	735	1 097	696	245	94	53	...
35 - 39	3 506	353	426	1 077	1 006	384	148	112	...
40 - 44	1 719	114	153	468	580	216	105	83	...
45 - 49	176	16	19	45	51	22	11	12	...
50 +	13	5	1	2	2	1	1	1	...

Japan - Japon
2014
Total	181 905	...	...	...	...	...	...	...	...
0 - 14	303	...	...	...	...	...	...	...	...
15 - 19	17 551	...	...	...	...	...	...	...	...
20 - 24	39 851	...	...	...	...	...	...	...	...
25 - 29	36 594	...	...	...	...	...	...	...	...
30 - 34	36 621	...	...	...	...	...	...	...	...
35 - 39	33 111	...	...	...	...	...	...	...	...
40 - 44	16 558	...	...	...	...	...	...	...	...
45 - 49	1 281	...	...	...	...	...	...	...	...
50 +	17	...	...	...	...	...	...	...	...
Unknown - Inconnu	18	...	...	...	...	...	...	...	...

Kyrgyzstan - Kirghizstan[7]
2008
Total	20 800	...	...	...	...	...	...	...	...
0 - 14	1	...	...	...	...	...	...	...	...
15 - 19	1 814	...	...	...	...	...	...	...	...
20 - 24	5 018	...	...	...	...	...	...	...	...
25 - 29	5 462	...	...	...	...	...	...	...	...
30 - 34	4 598	...	...	...	...	...	...	...	...
35 - 39	2 776	...	...	...	...	...	...	...	...
40 - 44	1 019	...	...	...	...	...	...	...	...
45 +	112	...	...	...	...	...	...	...	...

Mongolia - Mongolie
2015
Total	18 168	...	...	...	...	...	...	...	...
0 - 19	935	...	...	...	...	...	...	...	...
20 - 24	3 356	...	...	...	...	...	...	...	...
25 - 29	5 126	...	...	...	...	...	...	...	...
30 - 34	4 219	...	...	...	...	...	...	...	...
35 - 39	3 040	...	...	...	...	...	...	...	...
40 - 44	1 379	...	...	...	...	...	...	...	...
45 - 49	113	...	...	...	...	...	...	...	...
50 +	-	...	...	...	...	...	...	...	...

Singapore - Singapour
2015
Total	7 942	3 433	1 633	2 000	633	^243	...	...	...
0 - 14	5	5	-	-	-	^-	...	...	...
15 - 19	391	362	22	6	1	^-	...	...	...
20 - 24	1 436	1 146	176	82	28	^4	...	...	...
25 - 29	1 985	1 098	447	312	97	^31	...	...	...
30 - 34	1 953	540	495	677	169	^72	...	...	...
35 - 39	1 537	221	368	655	211	^82	...	...	...
40 - 44	593	57	118	247	122	^49	...	...	...
45 +	42	4	7	21	5	^5	...	...	...

Tajikistan - Tadjikistan
2014
Total	17 347	...	...	...	...	...	...	...	...
0 - 14	-	...	...	...	...	...	...	...	...
15 - 17	62	...	...	...	...	...	...	...	...
18 - 19	1 659	...	...	...	...	...	...	...	...

14. Legally induced abortions by age and number of previous live births of women: latest available year, 2006 - 2015
Avortments provoqués légalement selon l'âge de la femme et selon le nombre des naissances vivantes précédentes :
dernière année disponible, 2006 - 2015 (continued - suite)

Continent, country or area, year and age / Continent, pays ou zone, année et âge	Number of previous live births / Nombre des naissances vivantes précédentes								
	Total	0	1	2	3	4	5	6+	Unknown - Inconnu
ASIA - ASIE									
Tajikistan - Tadjikistan									
2014									
20 - 34	11 665	...	...	...	...	...	...	...	...
35 +	3 961	...	...	...	...	...	...	...	...
Uzbekistan - Ouzbékistan									
2014									
Total	41 352	5 920	...	...	...	...	...	...	35 432
0 - 14	-	-	...	...	...	...	...	...	-
15 - 19	1 312	660	...	...	...	...	...	...	652
20 - 34	33 177	4 941	...	...	...	...	...	...	28 236
35 - 49	6 863	319	...	...	...	...	...	...	6 544
50 +	-	-	...	...	...	...	...	...	-
EUROPE									
Åland Islands - Îles d'Åland									
2012									
Total	60	31	12	10	5	-	2	-	...
0 - 14	-	-	-	-	-	-	-	-	...
15 - 19	9	9	-	-	-	-	-	-	...
20 - 24	15	11	3	1	-	-	-	-	...
25 - 29	17	6	4	4	1	-	2	-	...
30 - 34	7	2	1	3	1	-	-	-	...
35 - 39	7	1	3	1	2	-	-	-	...
40 - 44	5	2	1	1	1	-	-	-	...
45 - 49	-	-	-	-	-	-	-	-	...
50 +	-	-	-	-	-	-	-	-	...
2014									
Total	66	...	...	...	...	...	...	...	...
0 - 14	-	...	...	...	...	...	...	...	...
15 - 19	6	...	...	...	...	...	...	...	...
20 - 24	21	...	...	...	...	...	...	...	...
25 - 29	13	...	...	...	...	...	...	...	...
30 - 34	16	...	...	...	...	...	...	...	...
35 - 39	8	...	...	...	...	...	...	...	...
40 - 44	2	...	...	...	...	...	...	...	...
45 - 49	-	...	...	...	...	...	...	...	...
50 +	-	...	...	...	...	...	...	...	...
Belarus - Bélarus									
2014									
Total	29 797	4 426	...	...	...	...	...	...	25 371
0 - 14	14	...	...	...	...	...	...	...	...
15 - 19	1 597	...	...	...	...	...	...	...	...
20 - 24	5 687	...	...	...	...	...	...	...	...
25 - 29	7 909	...	...	...	...	...	...	...	...
30 - 34	7 937	...	...	...	...	...	...	...	...
35 - 39	4 587	...	...	...	...	...	...	...	...
40 - 44	1 885	...	...	...	...	...	...	...	...
45 - 49	181	...	...	...	...	...	...	...	...
Belgium - Belgique									
2011									
Total	19 578	9 145	4 266	3 698	1 636	581	174	78	...
0 - 14	87	86	1	-	-	-	-	-	...
15 - 19	2 575	2 339	207	28	1	-	-	-	...
20 - 24	5 027	3 430	1 070	425	87	12	3	-	...
25 - 29	4 688	1 992	1 249	983	332	104	20	8	...
30 - 34	3 745	863	997	1 131	512	176	46	20	...
35 - 39	2 454	349	538	796	483	184	70	34	...
40 - 44	923	78	188	308	207	99	30	13	...
45 - 49	78	7	16	27	14	6	5	3	...
50 +	1	1	-	-	-	-	-	-	...
Bulgaria - Bulgarie									
2014									
Total	28 145	...	...	...	...	...	...	...	...
0 - 14	130	...	...	...	...	...	...	...	...
15 - 19	2 410	...	...	...	...	...	...	...	...
20 - 24	5 551	...	...	...	...	...	...	...	...

14. Legally induced abortions by age and number of previous live births of women: latest available year, 2006 - 2015
Avortments provoqués légalement selon l'âge de la femme et selon le nombre des naissances vivantes précédentes : dernière année disponible, 2006 - 2015 (continued - suite)

Continent, country or area, year and age / Continent, pays ou zone, année et âge	Number of previous live births / Nombre des naissances vivantes précédentes								
	Total	0	1	2	3	4	5	6+	Unknown - Inconnu
EUROPE									
Bulgaria - Bulgarie									
2014									
25 - 29	7 382	...	...	...	...	...	...	...	...
30 - 34	6 228	...	...	...	...	...	...	...	...
35 - 39	4 885	...	...	...	...	...	...	...	...
40 - 44	1 389	...	...	...	...	...	...	...	...
45 - 49	165	...	...	...	...	...	...	...	...
50 +	5	...	...	...	...	...	...	...	...
Croatia - Croatie									
2014									
Total	3 020	825	549	852	347	86	33	36	292
0 - 14	1	1	-	-	-	-	-	-	-
15 - 19	217	175	11	4	-	-	-	-	27
20 - 24	464	255	86	49	17	3	1	1	52
25 - 29	606	175	147	150	53	11	7	8	55
30 - 34	760	116	159	261	103	34	8	15	64
35 - 39	693	71	112	282	125	24	8	11	60
40 - 44	252	29	31	100	45	13	9	1	24
45 - 49	16	1	1	6	3	1	-	-	4
50 +	2	-	-	-	-	-	-	-	2
Unknown - Inconnu	9	2	2	-	1	-	-	-	4
Czech Republic - République tchèque									
2014									
Total	21 893	6 199	5 633	7 169	2 094	525	170	103	...
0 - 14	34	34	-	-	-	-	-	-	...
15 - 19	1 472	1 274	175	22	1	-	-	-	...
20 - 24	3 852	2 187	1 084	436	112	24	6	3	...
25 - 29	4 424	1 491	1 412	1 104	291	84	29	13	...
30 - 34	4 825	782	1 392	1 948	501	136	35	31	...
35 - 39	4 937	339	1 124	2 456	744	174	61	39	...
40 - 44	2 184	81	420	1 124	411	93	38	17	...
45 - 49	162	10	26	77	34	14	1	-	...
50 +	3	1	-	2	-	-	-	-	...
Denmark - Danemark[8]									
2014									
Total	15 097	...	...	...	...	...	...	...	...
0 - 19	2 051	...	...	...	...	...	...	...	...
20 - 24	4 023	...	...	...	...	...	...	...	...
25 - 29	3 324	...	...	...	...	...	...	...	...
30 - 34	2 609	...	...	...	...	...	...	...	...
35 - 39	2 045	...	...	...	...	...	...	...	...
40 - 44	967	...	...	...	...	...	...	...	...
45 +	78	...	...	...	...	...	...	...	...
Estonia - Estonie[9]									
2014									
Total	6 901	1 903	2 227	1 889	637	157	57	27	4
0 - 14	10	10	-	-	-	-	-	-	-
15 - 19	494	414	71	8	1	-	-	-	-
20 - 24	1 298	676	463	134	23	2	-	-	-
25 - 29	1 591	463	633	391	77	18	8	-	1
30 - 34	1 531	203	526	570	172	39	17	3	1
35 - 39	1 285	94	355	510	230	63	18	14	1
40 - 44	633	41	166	255	121	29	13	7	1
45 - 49	57	2	13	20	12	6	1	3	-
50 +	2	-	-	1	1	-	-	-	-
Faeroe Islands - Îles Féroé									
2013									
Total	23	...	...	...	...	...	...	...	...
0 - 14	-	...	...	...	...	...	...	...	...
15 - 19	1	...	...	...	...	...	...	...	...
20 - 24	5	...	...	...	...	...	...	...	...
25 - 29	4	...	...	...	...	...	...	...	...
30 - 34	7	...	...	...	...	...	...	...	...
35 - 39	5	...	...	...	...	...	...	...	...
40 - 44	1	...	...	...	...	...	...	...	...
45 - 49	-	...	...	...	...	...	...	...	...
50 +	-	...	...	...	...	...	...	...	...

14. Legally induced abortions by age and number of previous live births of women: latest available year, 2006 - 2015
Avortments provoqués légalement selon l'âge de la femme et selon le nombre des naissances vivantes précédentes : dernière année disponible, 2006 - 2015 (continued - suite)

Continent, country or area, year and age Continent, pays ou zone, année et âge	Number of previous live births Nombre des naissances vivantes précédentes								
	Total	0	1	2	3	4	5	6+	Unknown - Inconnu
EUROPE									
Finland - Finlande									
2014									
Total	9 780	4 881	1 818	1 794	778	279	78	46	106
0 - 14	16	16	-	-	-	-	-	-	-
15 - 19	1 379	1 275	74	5	-	-	-	-	25
20 - 24	2 810	2 013	533	186	40	3	-	-	35
25 - 29	2 134	936	501	450	177	37	11	1	21
30 - 34	1 695	407	387	541	225	89	20	12	14
35 - 39	1 210	167	238	419	234	102	26	15	9
40 - 44	493	59	80	179	94	44	19	16	2
45 - 49	43	8	5	14	8	4	2	2	-
50 +	-	-	-	-	-	-	-	-	-
France[10]									
2009									
Total[11]	208 290	...	...	...	...	...	...	...	...
15 - 19	29 004	...	...	...	...	...	...	...	...
20 - 24	52 360	...	...	...	...	...	...	...	...
25 - 29	46 237	...	...	...	...	...	...	...	...
30 - 34	36 351	...	...	...	...	...	...	...	...
35 - 39	30 125	...	...	...	...	...	...	...	...
40 - 44	12 805	...	...	...	...	...	...	...	...
45 - 49	1 408	...	...	...	...	...	...	...	...
Germany - Allemagne									
2014									
Total	99 715	39 261	25 316	23 159	8 310	2 509	740	420	...
0 - 14	369	369	-	-	-	-	-	-	...
15 - 19	8 437	7 662	690	83	2	-	-	-	...
20 - 24	21 761	13 562	5 563	2 072	461	87	10	6	...
25 - 29	24 030	9 385	7 286	5 206	1 582	424	104	43	...
30 - 34	21 706	4 974	6 155	6 976	2 485	765	225	126	...
35 - 39	15 838	2 325	3 914	5 944	2 463	789	258	145	...
40 - 44	6 822	890	1 551	2 574	1 193	400	125	89	...
45 - 49	738	93	154	297	123	43	18	10	...
50 +	14	1	3	7	1	1	-	1	...
Hungary - Hongrie									
2013									
Total	34 891	9 707	8 781	8 536	4 632	1 821	808	606	-
0 - 14	168	165	3	-	-	-	-	-	-
15 - 19	4 423	3 395	869	132	25	2	-	-	-
20 - 24	7 335	3 135	2 182	1 309	542	134	28	5	-
25 - 29	6 935	1 622	1 902	1 692	1 007	450	173	89	-
30 - 34	6 839	837	1 737	2 032	1 229	520	277	207	-
35 - 39	6 624	451	1 528	2 331	1 325	521	240	228	-
40 - 44	2 406	94	526	976	470	184	86	70	-
45 - 49	160	8	34	63	34	10	4	7	-
50 +	1	-	-	1	-	-	-	-	-
Unknown - Inconnu	-	-	-	-	-	-	-	-	-
2014									
Total	32 663	...	...	...	...	...	...	...	...
0 - 14	161	...	...	...	...	...	...	...	...
15 - 19	4 245	...	...	...	...	...	...	...	...
20 - 24	7 109	...	...	...	...	...	...	...	...
25 - 29	6 562	...	...	...	...	...	...	...	...
30 - 34	6 035	...	...	...	...	...	...	...	...
35 - 39	6 066	...	...	...	...	...	...	...	...
40 - 44	2 325	...	...	...	...	...	...	...	...
45 - 49	157	...	...	...	...	...	...	...	...
50 +	3	...	...	...	...	...	...	...	...
Unknown - Inconnu	-	...	...	...	...	...	...	...	...
Iceland - Islande									
2011									
Total	969	415	249	186	83	29	5	2	-
0 - 14	2	2	-	-	-	-	-	-	-
15 - 19	174	155	16	3	-	-	-	-	-
20 - 24	289	182	84	21	2	-	-	-	-
25 - 29	187	46	73	52	10	6	-	-	-
30 - 34	169	25	40	56	36	11	1	-	-
35 - 39	109	5	29	45	20	9	1	-	-
40 - 44	35	-	7	8	12	3	3	2	-

14. Legally induced abortions by age and number of previous live births of women: latest available year, 2006 - 2015
Avortments provoqués légalement selon l'âge de la femme et selon le nombre des naissances vivantes précédentes : dernière année disponible, 2006 - 2015 (continued - suite)

Continent, country or area, year and age / Continent, pays ou zone, année et âge	Total	0	1	2	3	4	5	6+	Unknown - Inconnu
EUROPE									
Iceland - Islande									
2011									
45 - 49	4	-	-	1	3	-	-	-	-
50 +	-	-	-	-	-	-	-	-	-
Unknown - Inconnu	-	-	-	-	-	-	-	-	-
Italy - Italie									
2009[12]									
Total	114 793	45 152	26 909	29 348	8 647	1 918	494	192	2 133
0 - 14	236	222	1	-	-	-	-	-	13
15 - 19	9 603	8 227	753	108	7	2	-	-	506
20 - 24	20 950	13 921	4 461	1 589	242	46	14	6	671
25 - 29	23 302	10 106	6 503	4 865	1 113	206	37	21	451
30 - 34	25 699	6 750	6 895	8 555	2 543	523	109	41	283
35 - 39	22 916	4 038	5 541	9 189	2 994	716	205	74	159
40 - 44	10 228	1 390	2 341	4 405	1 530	369	108	42	43
45 - 49	955	131	192	409	155	40	17	8	3
50 +	25	8	1	13	1	2	-	-	-
Unknown - Inconnu	879	359	221	215	62	14	4		4
2012[13]									
Total	103 191	...	...	...	...	...	...	...	...
0 - 14	262	...	...	...	...	...	...	...	...
15 - 19	8 355	...	...	...	...	...	...	...	...
20 - 24	19 065	...	...	...	...	...	...	...	...
25 - 29	20 955	...	...	...	...	...	...	...	...
30 - 34	22 214	...	...	...	...	...	...	...	...
35 - 39	21 530	...	...	...	...	...	...	...	...
40 - 44	9 808	...	...	...	...	...	...	...	...
45 - 49	889	...	...	...	...	...	...	...	...
50 +	42	...	...	...	...	...	...	...	...
Unknown - Inconnu	71	...	...	...	...	...	...	...	...
Latvia - Lettonie									
2014									
Total	5 318	...	...	...	...	...	...	...	...
0 - 14	3	...	...	...	...	...	...	...	...
15 - 19	291	...	...	...	...	...	...	...	...
20 - 24	1 096	...	...	...	...	...	...	...	...
25 - 29	1 262	...	...	...	...	...	...	...	...
30 - 34	1 197	...	...	...	...	...	...	...	...
35 - 39	929	...	...	...	...	...	...	...	...
40 - 44	494	...	...	...	...	...	...	...	...
45 - 49	46	...	...	...	...	...	...	...	...
50 +	-	...	...	...	...	...	...	...	...
Unknown - Inconnu	-	...	...	...	...	...	...	...	...
Lithuania - Lituanie									
2013									
Total	5 353	...	...	...	...	...	...	...	5 353
0 - 14	2	...	...	...	...	...	...	...	2
15 - 19	401	...	...	...	...	...	...	...	401
20 - 24	1 053	...	...	...	...	...	...	...	1 053
25 - 29	1 205	...	...	...	...	...	...	...	1 205
30 - 34	1 142	...	...	...	...	...	...	...	1 142
35 - 39	985	...	...	...	...	...	...	...	985
40 - 44	501	...	...	...	...	...	...	...	501
45 - 49	64	...	...	...	...	...	...	...	64
2014									
Total	5 231	...	...	...	...	...	...	...	...
0 - 14	5	...	...	...	...	...	...	...	...
15 - 19	362	...	...	...	...	...	...	...	...
20 - 24	1 128	...	...	...	...	...	...	...	...
25 - 29	1 125	...	...	...	...	...	...	...	...
30 - 34	1 070	...	...	...	...	...	...	...	...
35 - 39	1 005	...	...	...	...	...	...	...	...
40 - 44	484	...	...	...	...	...	...	...	...
45 - 49	52	...	...	...	...	...	...	...	...
50 +	-	...	...	...	...	...	...	...	...
Norway - Norvège[10]									
2006									
Total	14 132	...	...	...	...	...	...	...	...
0 - 14	37	...	...	...	...	...	...	...	...

14. Legally induced abortions by age and number of previous live births of women: latest available year, 2006 - 2015
Avortments provoqués légalement selon l'âge de la femme et selon le nombre des naissances vivantes précédentes : dernière année disponible, 2006 - 2015 (continued - suite)

Continent, country or area, year and age / Continent, pays ou zone, année et âge	Number of previous live births / Nombre des naissances vivantes précédentes								
	Total	0	1	2	3	4	5	6+	Unknown - Inconnu
EUROPE									
Norway - Norvège[10]									
2006									
15 - 19	2 307	...	...	...	...	...	...	...	...
20 - 24	3 740	...	...	...	...	...	...	...	...
25 - 29	2 904	...	...	...	...	...	...	...	...
30 - 34	2 495	...	...	...	...	...	...	...	...
35 - 39	1 877	...	...	...	...	...	...	...	...
40 - 44	694	...	...	...	...	...	...	...	...
45 - 49	55	...	...	...	...	...	...	...	...
50 +	-	...	...	...	...	...	...	...	...
Unknown - Inconnu	23	...	...	...	...	...	...	...	...
Poland - Pologne[14]									
2014									
Total	970	...	...	...	...	...	...	...	...
0 - 19	44	...	...	...	...	...	...	...	...
20 - 24	68	...	...	...	...	...	...	...	...
25 - 29	241	...	...	...	...	...	...	...	...
30 - 34	256	...	...	...	...	...	...	...	...
35 +	361	...	...	...	...	...	...	...	...
Portugal									
2014									
Total	16 589	6 855	4 924	3 571	928	215	62	34	...
0 - 14	59	57	1	1	-	-	-	-	...
15 - 19	1 751	1 585	152	13	1	-	-	-	...
20 - 24	3 723	2 426	1 019	254	23	1	-	-	...
25 - 29	3 460	1 445	1 220	629	134	29	3	-	...
30 - 34	3 316	824	1 209	937	264	61	15	6	...
35 - 39	2 889	384	929	1 132	322	81	26	15	...
40 - 44	1 263	118	357	551	170	39	15	13	...
45 - 49	109	9	30	50	13	4	3	-	...
50 +	2	-	-	2	-	-	-	-	...
Unknown - Inconnu	17	7	7	2	1	-	-	-	...
Republic of Moldova - République de Moldova									
2012									
Total	14 838	...	...	...	...	...	...	...	...
0 - 14	9	...	...	...	...	...	...	...	...
15 - 19	1 383	...	...	...	...	...	...	...	...
Unknown - Inconnu	13 446	...	...	...	...	...	...	...	...
Romania - Roumanie									
2012									
Total	87 975	-	-	-	-	-	-	-	87 975
0 - 14	476	-	-	-	-	-	-	-	476
15 - 19	7 547	-	-	-	-	-	-	-	7 547
20 - 24	18 990	-	-	-	-	-	-	-	18 990
25 - 29	20 210	-	-	-	-	-	-	-	20 210
30 - 34	19 635	-	-	-	-	-	-	-	19 635
35 - 39	14 751	-	-	-	-	-	-	-	14 751
40 - 44	5 880	-	-	-	-	-	-	-	5 880
45 - 49	464	-	-	-	-	-	-	-	464
50 +	22	-	-	-	-	-	-	-	22
Unknown - Inconnu	-	-	-	-	-	-	-	-	-
2014									
Total	78 371	...	...	...	...	...	...	...	...
0 - 14	544	...	...	...	...	...	...	...	...
15 - 19	7 287	...	...	...	...	...	...	...	...
20 - 24	15 316	...	...	...	...	...	...	...	...
25 - 29	19 210	...	...	...	...	...	...	...	...
30 - 34	16 656	...	...	...	...	...	...	...	...
35 - 39	13 533	...	...	...	...	...	...	...	...
40 - 44	5 306	...	...	...	...	...	...	...	...
45 - 49	498	...	...	...	...	...	...	...	...
50 +	21	...	...	...	...	...	...	...	...
Russian Federation - Fédération de Russie									
2013									
Total	1 012 399	...	...	...	...	...	...	...	...
0 - 14	474	...	...	...	...	...	...	...	...
15 - 19	47 732	...	...	...	...	...	...	...	...
20 - 24	203 802	...	...	...	...	...	...	...	...

14. Legally induced abortions by age and number of previous live births of women: latest available year, 2006 - 2015
Avortments provoqués légalement selon l'âge de la femme et selon le nombre des naissances vivantes précédentes : dernière année disponible, 2006 - 2015 (continued - suite)

Continent, country or area, year and age / Continent, pays ou zone, année et âge	Number of previous live births / Nombre des naissances vivantes précédentes								
	Total	0	1	2	3	4	5	6+	Unknown - Inconnu

EUROPE

Russian Federation - Fédération de Russie
2013
25 - 29	285 859	...	...	...	...	...	...	...	...
30 - 34	242 437	...	...	...	...	...	...	...	...
35 - 39	165 856	...	...	...	...	...	...	...	...
40 - 44	61 059	...	...	...	...	...	...	...	...
45 - 49	5 029	...	...	...	...	...	...	...	...
50 +	151	...	...	...	...	...	...	...	...

Serbia - Serbie[15]
2008
Total	22 867	6 601	4 346	8 509	2 437	663	198	113	-
0 - 14	9	6	1	2	-	-	-	-	-
15 - 19	975	808	124	35	7	1	-	-	-
20 - 24	3 427	1 823	848	570	122	52	9	3	-
25 - 29	5 117	1 510	1 173	1 757	479	141	47	10	-
30 - 34	5 953	1 240	1 114	2 569	719	212	62	37	-
35 - 39	4 929	806	768	2 354	730	170	59	42	-
40 - 44	2 174	363	279	1 072	347	76	17	20	-
45 - 49	266	40	34	146	31	10	4	1	-
50 +	16	5	4	4	2	1	-	-	-
Unknown - Inconnu	1	-	1	-	-	-	-	-	-

Slovakia - Slovaquie
2014
Total	10 582	3 302	2 934	2 792	942	317	140	155	...
0 - 14	7	7	-	-	-	-	-	-	...
15 - 19	697	590	83	24	-	-	-	-	...
20 - 24	1 681	942	469	198	58	10	4	-	...
25 - 29	2 309	862	719	460	164	71	16	17	...
30 - 34	2 546	556	835	765	220	75	51	44	...
35 - 39	2 240	266	591	888	306	108	36	45	...
40 - 44	1 015	72	221	422	178	49	27	46	...
45 - 49	84	7	15	35	14	4	6	3	...
50 +	3	-	1	-	2	-	-	-	...

Slovenia - Slovénie
2012
Total	4 106	1 365	1 017	1 294	328	73	18	8	3
0 - 14	2	2	-	-	-	-	-	-	-
15 - 19	277	263	11	2	-	-	-	-	1
20 - 24	642	470	124	33	13	2	-	-	-
25 - 29	855	331	264	202	43	12	3	-	-
30 - 34	1 056	183	310	436	98	23	4	1	1
35 - 39	901	89	222	435	119	24	8	4	-
40 - 44	342	24	84	163	53	12	3	3	-
45 - 49	30	3	2	23	2	-	-	-	-
50 +	1	-	-	-	-	-	-	-	1
Unknown - Inconnu	-	-	-	-	-	-	-	-	-

Spain - Espagne
2014
Total	94 796	42 401	25 353	19 229	5 616	^1 541	...	...	656
0 - 14	440	437	3	-	-	^-	...	...	-
15 - 19	9 890	8 911	867	85	21	^4	...	...	2
20 - 24	19 066	12 683	4 676	1 401	260	^36	...	...	10
25 - 29	20 635	9 430	6 345	3 661	932	^192	...	...	75
30 - 34	20 579	6 358	6 402	5 546	1 682	^427	...	...	164
35 - 39	16 909	3 464	5 019	5 836	1 798	^555	...	...	237
40 +	6 727	1 041	1 913	2 471	844	^306	...	...	152
Unknown - Inconnu	550	77	128	229	79	^21	...	...	16

Sweden - Suède[16]
2010
Total	37 693	19 435	6 240	7 203	2 993	814	264	137	607
0 - 14	191	178	4	1	-	-	-	-	8
15 - 19	6 199	5 826	214	14	2	-	-	-	143
20 - 24	10 068	7 708	1 587	480	76	5	2	2	208
25 - 29	7 495	3 558	1 838	1 476	385	79	28	10	121
30 - 34	6 124	1 424	1 336	2 113	884	208	77	18	64
35 - 39	5 073	572	862	2 073	1 053	318	88	62	45
40 - 44	2 248	137	353	948	524	174	58	39	15
45 - 49	238	11	33	85	66	27	10	4	2

14. Legally induced abortions by age and number of previous live births of women: latest available year, 2006 - 2015
Avortments provoqués légalement selon l'âge de la femme et selon le nombre des naissances vivantes précédentes : dernière année disponible, 2006 - 2015 (continued - suite)

Continent, country or area, year and age / Continent, pays ou zone, année et âge	Number of previous live births / Nombre des naissances vivantes précédentes								
	Total	0	1	2	3	4	5	6+	Unknown - Inconnu
EUROPE									
Sweden - Suède[16]									
2010									
50 +	56	20	13	13	3	3	1	2	1
Unknown - Inconnu	1	1	-	-	-	-	-	-	-
Switzerland - Suisse[17]									
2014									
Total	9 990	2 660	1 067	1 046	363	116	...	...	4 738
0 - 14	6	4	-	-	-	-	...	...	2
15 - 19	793	426	17	4	1	-	...	...	345
20 - 24	2 172	949	166	51	1	-	...	...	1 005
25 - 29	2 251	658	284	200	45	11	...	...	1 053
30 - 34	2 175	373	296	324	103	34	...	...	1 045
35 - 39	1 700	167	190	325	136	40	...	...	842
40 - 44	779	70	98	124	67	27	...	...	393
45 - 49	99	8	11	16	10	4	...	...	50
50 +	8	2	2	1	-	-	...	...	3
Unknown - Inconnu	7	3	3	1	-	-	...	...	-
Ukraine[18]									
2014									
Total	116 104	...	...	...	...	...	...	...	...
0 - 14	51	...	...	...	...	...	...	...	...
15 - 19	6 229	...	...	...	...	...	...	...	...
20 - 34	85 575	...	...	...	...	...	...	...	...
35 +	24 249	...	...	...	...	...	...	...	...
United Kingdom of Great Britain and Northern Ireland - Royaume-Uni de Grande-Bretagne et d'Irlande du Nord[19]									
2012									
Total	197 569	...	...	...	...	...	...	...	...
0 - 14	910	...	...	...	...	...	...	...	...
15 - 19	32 967	...	...	...	...	...	...	...	...
20 - 24	58 367	...	...	...	...	...	...	...	...
25 - 29	44 612	...	...	...	...	...	...	...	...
30 - 34	32 139	...	...	...	...	...	...	...	...
35 - 39	19 651	...	...	...	...	...	...	...	...
40 - 44	8 199	...	...	...	...	...	...	...	...
45 - 49	697	...	...	...	...	...	...	...	...
50 +	27	...	...	...	...	...	...	...	...
Unknown - Inconnu	-	...	...	...	...	...	...	...	...
OCEANIA - OCÉANIE									
Guam									
2015									
Total	263	...	...	...	...	...	...	...	...
0 - 14	-	...	...	...	...	...	...	...	...
15 - 19	20	...	...	...	...	...	...	...	...
20 - 24	89	...	...	...	...	...	...	...	...
25 - 29	60	...	...	...	...	...	...	...	...
30 - 34	52	...	...	...	...	...	...	...	...
35 - 39	27	...	...	...	...	...	...	...	...
40 - 44	12	...	...	...	...	...	...	...	...
45 - 49	2	...	...	...	...	...	...	...	...
50 +	-	...	...	...	...	...	...	...	...
Unknown - Inconnu	1	...	...	...	...	...	...	...	...
New Zealand - Nouvelle-Zélande[20]									
2014									
Total	13 137	5 763	2 728	2 681	1 181	485	165	134	...
0 - 14	57	57	...	...	...	...	...	...	...
15 - 19	1 758	1 501	215	37	5	...	...	...	...
20 - 24	4 024	2 319	980	547	136	40	1	1	...
25 - 29	3 075	1 155	693	693	351	128	35	20	...
30 - 34	2 172	479	471	637	331	162	51	41	...
35 - 39	1 384	181	248	521	234	98	50	52	...
40 - 44	611	64	109	225	119	51	25	18	...
45 +	56	7	12	21	5	6	3	2	...

FOOTNOTES - NOTES

* Provisional. - Données provisoires.

^ Indicates an open-ended group, for example 4+. - indique un groupe d'âge ouvert, par exemple 4 ou plus.

[1] Data refer to resident population only. Significant undercoverage of medically induced abortions in clinics in 2006 due to non response in some provinces. - Pour la population résidante seulement. Sous-dénombrement notable des interruptions volontaires de grossesse pratiquées dans les centres médicaux en 2006 faute de réponse dans certaines provinces.

[2] Excluding abortions performed in private hospitals. - Non comprises les interruptions volontaires de grossesse effectuées dans des hôpitaux privés.

[3] Data refer to 'Therapeutic Abortions'. According to Mexican law, only induced abortions, prescribed by medical reasons or induced because of pregnancy coming from sexual aggression, are considered as legal; data refer only to the former. Refers to residence of the mother. To calculate the total number of abortions, only foetal deaths of less than 20 weeks of gestation were considered. Excluding abortions in the country by women with usual residence outside of the country. - Les données se rapportent aux « interruptions volontaires de grossesse pour des motifs thérapeutiques ». D'après la loi mexicaine, seuls sont considérés légaux les avortements déclenchés pour des raisons médicales ou parce que la grossesse est le résultat d'une agression sexuelle; les données se réfèrent seulement à la première. Correspond à la résidence de la mère. Seuls les morts fœtales survenues à moins de 20 semaines de gestation ont été prises en compte aux fins du calcul du nombre total d'avortements. Hors avortements dans le pays par des femmes avec résidence habituelle en dehors du pays.

[4] Data refer to the fiscal year from 1 July to 30 June. Excluding abortions performed in a clinic which closed operations without reporting the data. - Les données se réfèrent à l'année budgétaire de 1 juillet à 30 juin. Non comprises les avortements effectuées dans une clinique qui a fermé sans envoyer les données.

[5] Data refer to abortions registered in the hospitals due to pregnancy complications. - Les données renvoient aux avortements enregistrés dans les hôpitaux du fait des complications de la grossesse.

[6] Includes data for East Jerusalem and Israeli residents in certain other territories under occupation by Israeli military forces since June 1967. Data refer to applications to commissions for termination of pregnancy and not to authorizations. - Y compris les données pour Jérusalem-Est et les résidents israéliens dans certains autres territoires occupés depuis 1967 par les forces armées israéliennes. Les données relatives aux avortements provoqués légalement se rapportent aux demandes d'autorisation et non aux autorisations elles-mêmes.

[7] Based on administrative reporting of the Ministry of Health. - Les données reposent sur les rapports administratifs du Ministère de la santé.

[8] Excluding Faeroe Islands and Greenland shown separately, if available. - Non compris les Iles Féroé et le Groenland, qui font l'objet de rubriques distinctes, si disponible.

[9] Data refer to resident population only. - Pour la population résidante seulement.

[10] Unrevised data. - Les données n'ont pas été révisées.

[11] Data refer to women between 15 and 49 years of age. - Le total se rapporte uniquement aux femmes dont l'âge est compris entre 15 et 49 ans.

[12] Data are incomplete for Abruzzo, Campania, Basilicata, Sicilia and Sardegna regions. - Données incomplètes pour les régions des Abruzzes, de Campanie, de Basilicate, de Sicile et de Sardaigne.

[13] Data are incomplete for Umbria, Abruzzo, Campania, Puglia and Sicilia regions. - Les données sont incomplètes pour les régions d'Ombrie, des Abruzzes, de Campanie, des Pouilles et de Sicile.

[14] Based on hospital and polyclinic records. - D'après les registres des hôpitaux et des polycliniques.

[15] Excludes data for Kosovo and Metohia. Data refer to institutions included in the Health Institutions Network Plan in the Republic of Serbia. - Sans les données pour le Kosovo et Metohie. Les données se rapportent aux institutions membres du "Health Institutions Network Plan" de la République de Serbie.

[16] Data refer to abortions by previous deliveries of mother rather than previous live births of mother. - Avortements selon les accouchements précédents de la mère plutôt que selon les naissances vivantes de la mère.

[17] Data refer to termination of pregnancy for women who are Switzerland residents. - Les données portent sur les interruptions de grossesse pratiquées sur des femmes qui résident en Suisse.

[18] The Government of Ukraine has informed the United Nations that it is not in a position to provide statistical data concerning the Autonomous Republic of Crimea and the city of Sevastopol. - Le gouvernement Ukrainien a informé l'ONU qu'il n'est pas en mesure de fournir des données statistiques concernant la République autonome de Crimée et la ville de Sébastopol.

[19] Excluding Northern Ireland. Excluding Channel Islands (Guernsey and Jersey) and Isle of Man, shown separately, if available. - Non compris l'Irlande du Nord. Non compris les îles Anglo-Normandes (Guernesey et Jersey) et l'île de Man, qui font l'objet de rubriques distinctes, si disponible.

[20] Random rounding to base 3 is applied in this table as a confidentiality measure. - Les chiffres sont arrondis à la base 3 de manière aléatoire, pour des raisons de confidentialité.

Table 15 - *Demographic Yearbook 2015*

Table 15 presents infant deaths and infant mortality rates by urban/rural residence for as many years as possible between 2011 and 2015.

Description of variables: Infant deaths are deaths of live-born infants under one year of age.

Statistics on the number of infant deaths are obtained from civil registers unless otherwise noted. Infant mortality rates are, in most instances, calculated from data on registered infant deaths and registered live births for a country or area where civil registration is considered reliable (that is, with an estimated completeness of 90 per cent or more).

The urban/rural classification of infant deaths is that provided by each reporting country or area; it is presumed to be based on the national census definitions of urban population that have been set forth at the end of the technical notes of table 6.

Rate computation: Infant mortality rates are the annual number of deaths of infants under one year of age per 1 000 live births (as shown in table 9) in the same year.

Rates by urban/rural residence are the annual number of infant deaths, in the appropriate urban or rural category, per 1 000 corresponding live births (as shown in table 9). These rates have been calculated by the United Nations Statistics Division.

Rates presented in this table have been limited to those countries or areas having at least a total of 30 infant deaths in a given year and for which the quality code is represented by a "C" or a symbol "|".

Reliability of data: Each country or area has been asked to indicate the estimated completeness of the infant deaths recorded in its civil register. These national assessments are indicated by the quality codes "C", "U" and "|" that appear in the first column of this table.

"C" indicates that the data are estimated to be virtually complete, that is, representing at least 90 per cent of the infant deaths occurring each year, while "U" indicates that data are estimated to be incomplete that is, representing less than 90 per cent of the infant deaths occurring each year. The code "|" indicates that the source of data is not civil registration, but is still considered reliable. The code "..." indicates that no information was provided regarding completeness.

Data from civil registers that are reported as incomplete or of unknown completeness (coded "U" or "...") are considered unreliable. They appear in italics in this table; rates are not computed for data so coded.

Limitations: Statistics on infant deaths are subject to the same qualifications as have been set forth for vital statistics in general and death statistics in particular as discussed in section 4 of the Technical Notes.

The reliability of the data, an indication of which is described above, is an important factor in considering the limitations. In addition, some infant deaths are tabulated by date of registration and not by date of occurrence; these have been indicated by a plus sign "+". Whenever the lag between the date of occurrence and date of registration is prolonged and, therefore, a large proportion of the infant-death registrations are delayed, infant-death statistics for any given year may be seriously affected.

Another factor that limits international comparability is the practice of some countries or areas not to include in infant-death statistics infants who were born alive but died before the registration of the birth or within the first 24 hours of life, thus underestimating the total number of infant deaths. Statistics of this type are footnoted.

The method of reckoning age at death for infants may also introduce non-comparability. If year alone, rather than completed minutes, hours, days and months elapsed since birth, is used to calculate age at time of death, many of the infants who died during the eleventh month of life and some of those who died at younger ages will be classified as having completed one year of age and thus be excluded. The effect would be to underestimate the number of infant deaths. Information on this factor is given in footnotes when known. Reckoning of infant age is further discussed in the technical notes for table 16.

In addition, infant mortality rates are subject to the limitations of the data on live births that have been used as denominators for these rates. These have been set forth in the technical notes for table 9.

Because the two components of the infant mortality rate, infant deaths in the numerator and live births in the denominator, are both obtained from systems of civil registration, the limitations which affect live birth statistics are very similar to those which have been mentioned above in connection with the infant death statistics. It is important to consider the reliability of the data (the completeness of registration) and the method of tabulation (by date of occurrence or by date of registration) of live birth statistics as well as infant death statistics, both of which are used to calculate infant mortality rates. The quality code and use of italics to indicate unreliable data presented in this table refer only to infant deaths. Similarly, the indication of the basis of tabulation (the use of the symbol "+" to indicate data tabulated by date of registration) presented in this table also refers only to infant deaths. Table 9 provides the corresponding information for live births.

If the registration of infant deaths is more complete than the registration of live births, then infant mortality rates would be biased upwards. If, however, the registration of live births is more complete than registration of infant deaths, infant mortality rates would be biased downwards. If both infant deaths and live births are tabulated by registration, it should be noted that deaths tend to be more promptly reported than births.

Infant mortality rates may be seriously affected by the practice of some countries or areas of not considering infants that were born alive but died before the registration of the birth or within the first 24 hours of life as live birth and subsequently infant death. Although this practice results in both the number of infant deaths in the numerator and the number of live births in the denominator being underestimated, its impact is greater on the numerator of the infant mortality rate. As a result this practice causes infant mortality rates to be biased downwards.

Infant mortality rates will also be underestimated if the method of reckoning age at death results in an underestimation of the number of infant deaths. This point has been discussed above.

Because of all these factors care should be taken in comparing infant mortality rates.

With respect to the method of calculating infant mortality rates used in this table, it should be noted that no adjustment was made to take account of the fact that a proportion of the infant deaths that occur during a given year are deaths of infants that were born during the preceding year and hence are not taken from the universe of births used to compute the rates. However, unless the number of live births or infant deaths is changing rapidly, the error involved is insignificant.

The comparability of data by urban/rural residence is affected by the national definitions of urban and rural used in tabulating these data. It is assumed, in the absence of specific information to the contrary, that the definitions of urban and rural used in connection with the national population census were also used in the compilation of the vital statistics for each country or area. However, it cannot be denied that, for some countries or areas, different definitions of urban and rural may be used for the vital statistics data and the population census data respectively. When known, the definitions of urban used in national population censuses are presented at the end of the technical notes for table 6. As discussed in detail in the technical notes for table 6, these definitions vary considerably from one country or area to another.

Urban/rural differentials in infant mortality rates may also be affected by whether the infant deaths and live births have been tabulated in terms of place of occurrence or place of usual residence. This problem is discussed in more detail in section 4.1.4.1 of the Technical Notes.

Earlier data: Infant deaths and infant mortality rates have been shown in previous issues of the *Demographic Yearbook*. For more information on specific topics and years for which data are reported, readers should consult the Historical Index.

Tableau 15 – *Annuaire démographique 2015*

Le tableau 15 présente des données sur les décès d'enfants de moins d'un an et les taux de mortalité infantile selon le lieu de résidence (zone urbaine ou rurale) pour le plus grand nombre d'années possible entre 2011 et 2015.

Description des variables : les chiffres se rapportent aux décès d'enfants de moins d'un an.

Sauf indication contraire, les statistiques concernant le nombre de décès d'enfants de moins d'un an sont établies à partir des registres de l'état civil. Dans la plupart des cas, les taux de mortalité infantile sont calculés à partir des données relatives aux décès enregistrés d'enfants de moins d'un an et aux naissances vivantes enregistrées dans un pays ou une zone lorsque les registres de l'état civil sont jugés fiables (exhaustivité estimée à 90 p. 100 ou plus).

La classification des décès d'enfants de moins d'un an selon le lieu de résidence (zone urbaine ou rurale) est celle qui a été communiquée par chaque pays ou zone ; on part du principe qu'elle repose sur les définitions de la population urbaine utilisées pour les recensements nationaux, telles qu'elles sont reproduites à la fin des notes techniques du tableau 6.

Calcul des taux : Les taux de mortalité infantile représentent le nombre annuel de décès d'enfants de moins d'un an pour 1 000 naissances vivantes (présentées dans le tableau 9) survenues pendant la même année.

Les taux selon le lieu de résidence (zone urbaine ou rurale) représentent le nombre annuel de décès d'enfants de moins d'un an, classés selon la catégorie urbaine ou rurale appropriée pour 1 000 naissances vivantes survenues parmi la population correspondante (présentées dans le tableau 9). Ces taux ont été calculés par la Division des statistiques de l'Organisation des Nations Unies.

Les taux présentés dans ce tableau se rapportent seulement aux pays ou zones où l'on a enregistré au moins un total de 30 décès d'enfants de moins d'un an au cours d'une année donnée et pour lesquels le code de qualité est soit "C" ou "|".

Fiabilité des données : il a été demandé à chaque pays ou zone d'indiquer le degré estimatif de complétude des données sur les décès d'enfants de moins d'un an figurant dans ses registres d'état civil. Ces évaluations nationales sont signalées par les codes de qualité "C", "U" et "|" qui apparaissent dans la deuxième colonne du tableau.

La lettre "C" indique que les données sont jugées à peu près complètes, c'est-à-dire qu'elles représentent au moins 90 p. 100 des décès d'enfants de moins d'un an survenus chaque année ; la lettre "U" signifie que les données sont jugées incomplètes, c'est-à-dire qu'elles représentent moins de 90 p.100 des décès d'enfants de moins d'un an survenus chaque année. Le symbole 'I' indique que la source des données n'est pas un registre de l'état civil, mais est quand même considérée fiable. Le code "..." dénote qu'aucun renseignement n'a été communiqué quant à la complétude des données.

Les données provenant des registres de l'état civil qui sont déclarées incomplètes ou dont le degré de complétude n'est pas connu (code "U" ou "...") sont jugées douteuses. Elles apparaissent en italique dans le tableau ; les taux, dans ces cas là, n'ont pas été calculés.

Insuffisance des données : les statistiques des décès d'enfants de moins d'un an appellent toutes les réserves qui ont été formulées à propos des statistiques de l'état civil en général et des statistiques concernant les décès en particulier (voir la section 4 des notes techniques).

La fiabilité des données, au sujet de laquelle des indications ont été fournies plus haut, est un facteur important. Il faut également tenir compte du fait que, dans certains cas, les données relatives aux décès d'enfants de moins d'un an sont exploitées selon la date de l'enregistrement et non la date de l'événement ; ces cas ont été signalés par le signe "+". Chaque fois que le décalage entre l'événement et son enregistrement est grand et qu'une forte proportion des décès d'enfants de moins d'un an fait l'objet d'un enregistrement tardif, les statistiques des décès d'enfants de moins d'un an pour une année donnée peuvent être considérablement faussées.

Un autre facteur qui nuit à la comparabilité internationale est la pratique de certains pays ou zones qui consiste à ne pas inclure dans les statistiques des décès d'enfants de moins d'un an les enfants nés vivants mais décédés avant l'enregistrement de leur naissance ou dans les 24 heures qui ont suivi la naissance, pratique qui conduit à sous-estimer le nombre total de décès d'enfants de moins d'un an. Quand pareil facteur a joué, cela a été signalé en note.

Les méthodes appliquées pour calculer l'âge au moment du décès peuvent également nuire à la comparabilité des données. Si l'on utilise à cet effet l'année seulement, et non pas les minutes, heures, jours et mois qui se sont écoulés depuis la naissance, de nombreux enfants décédés au cours du onzième mois qui a suivi leur naissance et certains enfants décédés encore plus jeunes seront classés comme décédés à un an révolu et donc exclus des données. Cette pratique conduit à sous-estimer le nombre de décès d'enfants de moins d'un an. Les renseignements dont on dispose sur ce facteur apparaissent en note à la fin du tableau. La question du calcul de l'âge au moment du décès est examinée plus en détail dans les notes techniques se rapportant au tableau 16.

Les taux de mortalité infantile appellent en outre toutes les réserves qui ont été formulées à propos des statistiques des naissances vivantes qui ont servi à leur calcul (voir à ce sujet les notes techniques relatives au tableau 9).

Les deux composantes du taux de mortalité infantile - décès d'enfants de moins d'un an au numérateur et naissances vivantes au dénominateur - étant obtenues à partir des registres de l'état civil, les statistiques des naissances vivantes appellent des réserves presque identiques à celles qui ont été formulées plus haut à propos des statistiques des décès d'enfants de moins d'un an. Il importe de prendre en considération la fiabilité des données (complétude de l'enregistrement) et le mode d'exploitation (selon la date de l'événement ou selon la date de l'enregistrement) dans le cas des statistiques des naissances vivantes tout comme dans le cas de celles des décès d'enfants de moins d'un an, puisque les unes et les autres servent au calcul des taux de mortalité infantile. Dans le tableau 15, le code de qualité et l'emploi de caractères italiques pour signaler les données moins sûres ne concernent que les décès d'enfants de moins d'un an. L'indication du mode d'exploitation des données (emploi du signe "+" pour signaler les données exploitées selon la date de l'enregistrement) ne porte là aussi que sur les décès d'enfants de moins d'un an. Le tableau 9 contient les renseignements correspondants pour les naissances vivantes.

Si l'enregistrement des décès d'enfants de moins d'un an est plus complet que l'enregistrement des naissances vivantes, les taux de mortalité infantile seront entachés d'une erreur par excès. En revanche, si l'enregistrement des naissances vivantes est plus complet que l'enregistrement des décès d'enfants de moins d'un an, les taux de mortalité infantile seront entachés d'une erreur par défaut. Si les décès d'enfants de moins d'un an et les naissances vivantes sont exploitées selon la date de l'enregistrement, il convient de ne pas perdre de vue que les décès sont, en règle générale, déclarés plus rapidement que les naissances.

Les taux de mortalité infantile peuvent être gravement faussés par la pratique de certains pays ou zones qui consiste à ne pas classer dans les naissances vivantes et ensuite dans les décès d'enfants de moins d'un an les enfants nés vivants mais décédés soit avant l'enregistrement de leur naissance, soit dans les 24 heures qui ont suivi la naissance. Cette pratique conduit à sous-estimer aussi bien le nombre des décès d'enfants de moins d'un an, qui constitue le numérateur, que le nombre des naissances vivantes, qui constitue le dénominateur, mais c'est pour le numérateur du taux de mortalité infantile que la distorsion est la plus marquée. Ce système a pour effet d'introduire une erreur par défaut dans les taux de mortalité infantile.

Les taux de mortalité infantile seront également sous-estimés si la méthode utilisée pour calculer l'âge au moment du décès conduit à sous-estimer le nombre de décès d'enfants de moins d'un an. Cette question a été examinée plus haut.

Tous ces facteurs sont importants et il faut donc en tenir compte lorsque l'on compare les taux de mortalité infantile.

En ce qui concerne la méthode de calcul des taux de mortalité infantile utilisée dans le tableau, il convient de noter qu'il n'a pas été tenu compte du fait qu'une partie des décès survenus pendant une année donnée sont des décès d'enfants nés l'année précédente et ne correspondent donc pas à l'ensemble des naissances utilisé pour le calcul des taux. Toutefois, l'erreur n'est pas grave, à moins que le nombre des naissances vivantes ou des décès d'enfants de moins d'un an ne varie rapidement.

La comparabilité des données selon le lieu de résidence (zone urbaine ou rurale) peut être limitée par les définitions nationales des termes « urbain » et « rural » utilisées pour la mise en tableaux de ces données. En l'absence d'indications contraires, on a supposé que les mêmes définitions avaient servi pour le recensement national de la population et pour l'établissement des statistiques de l'état civil pour chaque pays ou zone. Toutefois, il n'est pas exclu que, pour une zone ou un pays donné, des définitions différentes aient été retenues. Les définitions du terme « urbain » utilisées pour les recensements nationaux de population ont été présentées à la fin des notes techniques du tableau 6 lorsqu'elles étaient connues. Comme on l'a précisé dans les notes techniques relatives au tableau 6, ces définitions varient considérablement d'un pays ou d'une zone à l'autre.

La différence entre les taux de mortalité infantile pour les zones urbaines et rurales pourra aussi être faussée selon que les décès d'enfants de moins d'un an et les naissances vivantes auront été classés d'après le lieu de l'événement ou le lieu de résidence habituel. Ce problème est examiné plus en détail à la section 4.1.4.1 des Notes techniques.

Données publiées antérieurement : des statistiques concernant les décès d'enfants de moins d'un an et les taux de mortalité infantile ont déjà été présentées dans des éditions antérieures de l'*Annuaire démographique*. Pour plus de précisions concernant les années et les sujets pour lesquels des données ont été publiées, se reporter à l'index historique.

15. Infant deaths and infant mortality rates, by urban/rural residence: 2011 - 2015
Décès d'enfants de moins d'un an et taux de mortalité infantile, selon la résidence, urbaine/rurale : 2011 - 2015

Continent, country or area, and urban/rural residence / Continent, pays ou zone et résidence, urbaine/rurale	Co-de[a]	Number - Nombre					Rate - Taux				
		2011	2012	2013	2014	2015	2011	2012	2013	2014	2015
AFRICA - AFRIQUE											
Algeria - Algérie[1]											
Total	U	21 055	22 088	21 586	22 282	23 150	...	...	...	...	...
Botswana[2]											
Total	+U	...	...	...	1 045	...	...	...	...	...	...
Egypt - Égypte											
Total	C	35 997	39 942	38 753	39 679	...	14.7	15.2	14.8	14.6	...
Urban - Urbaine	C	17 601	19 830	22 605	23 952	...	18.7	19.6	19.0	19.5	...
Rural - Rurale	C	18 396	20 112	16 148	15 727	...	12.3	12.4	11.3	10.5	...
Kenya											
Total	U	23 167	21 209	20 888	18 672	...	...	...	...	...	...
Mauritius - Maurice[3]											
Total	+C	189	199	165	194	173	12.9	13.7	12.2	14.6	13.7
Urban - Urbaine	+C	64	65	67	72	81	11.5	12.0	13.2	14.0	15.7
Rural - Rurale	+C	125	134	98	122	92	13.7	14.8	11.6	15.0	12.3
Saint Helena ex. dep. - Sainte-Hélène sans dép.											
Total	C	-	1	-	1	...	...	...	...	...	...
Seychelles											
Total	+C	16	...	29	17	17	...	...	...	...	...
Sierra Leone											
Total	...	1 289	2 135	...	...	...	...	...	...	...	...
Urban - Urbaine	...	547	1 508	...	...	...	...	...	...	...	...
Rural - Rurale	...	742	627	...	...	...	...	...	...	...	...
South Africa - Afrique du Sud											
Total	U	28 601	27 104	26 630	25 643	...	...	...	...	...	...
AMERICA, NORTH - AMÉRIQUE DU NORD											
Anguilla											
Total	+C	1	-	3	...	...	...	...	...	...	...
Aruba											
Total	+C	7	3	5	5	6	...	...	...	...	...
Bahamas											
Total	+C	48	57	51	...	...	10.1	12.8	11.8	...	...
Bermuda - Bermudes											
Total	C	-	1	1	2	2	...	...	...	...	...
Costa Rica											
Total	C	666	624	612	575	*557	9.1	8.5	8.7	8.0	*7.8
Urban - Urbaine	C	303	272	291	362	*404	11.7	10.7	11.7	8.7	*8.1
Rural - Rurale	C	363	352	321	213	*153	7.6	7.4	7.0	7.1	*6.9
Cuba											
Total	C	653	581	525	514	*535	4.9	4.6	4.2	4.2	*4.3
Urban - Urbaine	C	485	462	440	413	...	4.7	4.7	4.4	4.3	...
Rural - Rurale	C	168	119	85	101	...	5.5	4.3	3.1	3.9	...
Curaçao											
Total	C	15	23	15	24	20	...	...	...	...	...
Dominican Republic - République dominicaine											
Total	U	684	472	653	830	436	...	...	...	...	...
Urban - Urbaine[4]	U	515	356	544	703	...	...	...	...	...	...
Rural - Rurale[4]	U	65	40	38	55	...	...	...	...	...	...
El Salvador[5]											
Total	C	826	795	...	...	...	7.6	7.2	...	...	...
Urban - Urbaine	C	563	527	...	...	...	7.5	7.0	...	...	...
Rural - Rurale	C	263	268	...	...	...	7.8	7.6	...	...	...
Greenland - Groenland											
Total	C	9	7	7	6	9	...	...	...	...	...
Urban - Urbaine	C	7	4	7	5	9	...	...	...	...	...
Rural - Rurale	C	2	3	-	1	-	...	...	...	...	...
Guatemala											
Total	C	7 413	7 121	7 221	...	...	19.8	18.3	18.6	...	...

15. Infant deaths and infant mortality rates, by urban/rural residence: 2011 - 2015
Décès d'enfants de moins d'un an et taux de mortalité infantile, selon la résidence, urbaine/rurale : 2011 - 2015 (continued - suite)

Continent, country or area, and urban/rural residence / Continent, pays ou zone et résidence, urbaine/rurale	Co-dea	Number - Nombre					Rate - Taux				
		2011	2012	2013	2014	2015	2011	2012	2013	2014	2015
AMERICA, NORTH - AMÉRIQUE DU NORD											
Mexico - Mexique[6]											
Total	+U	29 037	28 946	...	...	...	...	...	...	...	...
Urban - Urbaine[4]	+U	21 980	22 254	...	...	...	...	...	...	...	...
Rural - Rurale[4]	+U	6 574	6 132	...	...	...	...	...	...	...	...
Total	+C	...	...	27 802	26 385	...	...	...	12.8	...	...
Urban - Urbaine[4]	+C	...	...	21 079	19 987	...	...	...	13.8	...	...
Rural - Rurale[4]	+C	...	...	6 041	5 870	...	...	...	12.5	...	...
Montserrat											
Total	+C	-	-	-	-	...	...	...	...	...	...
Panama											
Total	U	971	1 083	1 106	1 036	...	...	...	...	...	...
Urban - Urbaine	U	509	632	682	585	...	...	...	...	...	...
Rural - Rurale	U	462	451	424	451	...	...	...	...	...	...
Puerto Rico - Porto Rico											
Total	C	364	374	270	242	222	8.8	9.6	7.4	7.0	7.1
Urban - Urbaine	C	261	243	164	141	125[4]	10.9	11.3	8.3	7.4	6.6
Rural - Rurale	C	103	131	106	101	98[4]	6.0	7.5	6.3	6.5	8.0
Saint Vincent and the Grenadines - Saint-Vincent-et-les Grenadines											
Total	C	38	25	32	29	...	22.0	...	18.4	...	...
Trinidad and Tobago - Trinité-et-Tobago											
Total	C	*275	*239	...	...	...	*15.2	*12.8	...	...	...
United States of America - États-Unis d'Amérique											
Total	C	23 985	23 629	23 440	23 215	...	6.1	6.0	6.0	5.8	...
United States Virgin Islands - Îles Vierges américaines[7]											
Total	C	13	13	...	...	...	...	...	...	...	...
AMERICA, SOUTH - AMÉRIQUE DU SUD											
Argentina - Argentine											
Total	C	8 878	8 227	8 174	8 202	...	11.7	11.1	10.8	10.6	...
Brazil - Brésil[8]											
Total	U	32 184	31 596	31 944	31 679	...	...	...	...	...	...
Chile - Chili											
Total	C	1 908	1 812	1 692	...	...	7.7	7.4	7.0	...	...
Urban - Urbaine	C	1 668	1 644	1 540	...	...	7.5	7.5	7.0	...	...
Rural - Rurale	C	240	168	152	...	...	9.9	6.9	7.0	...	...
Colombia - Colombie											
Total	U	8 082	8 138	7 551	7 515	...	...	...	...	...	...
Urban - Urbaine	U	6 116	6 037	5 577	5 642	...	...	...	...	...	...
Rural - Rurale	U	1 966	2 101	1 974	1 873	...	...	...	...	...	...
Ecuador - Équateur[9]											
Total	U	3 046	3 002	2 928	2 821	...	...	...	...	...	...
Urban - Urbaine	U	2 468	2 499	2 455	2 308	...	...	...	...	...	...
Rural - Rurale	U	578	503	473	513	...	...	...	...	...	...
Paraguay											
Total	+U	...	465	...	...	...	...	...	...	...	...
Peru - Pérou[10]											
Total	+U	4 569	4 523	4 548	4 243	...	...	...	...	...	...
Suriname											
Total	C	153	162	168	163	...	15.8	15.9	16.8	15.7	...
Urban - Urbaine	C	101	110	118	117	...	15.7	16.1	17.4	17.0	...
Rural - Rurale	C	52	52	50	46	...	15.9	15.5	15.5	13.1	...
Uruguay											
Total	C	417	448	...	376	...	8.9	9.3	...	7.8	...
Venezuela (Bolivarian Republic of) - Venezuela (République bolivarienne du)											
Total	C	7 121	7 331	7 630	8 396	9 267	11.6	11.8	12.8	14.0	15.4

15. Infant deaths and infant mortality rates, by urban/rural residence: 2011 - 2015
Décès d'enfants de moins d'un an et taux de mortalité infantile, selon la résidence, urbaine/rurale : 2011 - 2015 (continued - suite)

Continent, country or area, and urban/rural residence / Continent, pays ou zone et résidence, urbaine/rurale	Co-de[a]	Number - Nombre					Rate - Taux				
		2011	2012	2013	2014	2015	2011	2012	2013	2014	2015

ASIA - ASIE

Armenia - Arménie[11]											
Total	C	507	...	...	376	...	11.7	...	...	8.7	...
Azerbaijan - Azerbaïdjan[11]											
Total	+C	1 903	1 884	1 862	1 655	...	10.8	10.8	10.8	9.7	...
Urban - Urbaine	+C	1 536	1 524	1 459	...	...	18.0	17.6	16.9	...	...
Rural - Rurale	+C	367	360	403	...	...	4.1	4.1	4.7	...	...
Bahrain - Bahreïn[12]											
Total	C	139	149	141	218	...	7.9	7.8	7.1	10.4	...
Bangladesh											
Total	U	100 751	96 254	...	...	...	...	...	...	...	...
Urban - Urbaine	U	20 484	19 906	...	...	...	...	...	...	...	...
Rural - Rurale	U	80 267	76 348	...	...	...	...	...	...	...	...
Brunei Darussalam - Brunéi Darussalam											
Total	+C	56	64	51	51	...	8.3	9.3	7.6	7.4	...
China, Hong Kong SAR - Chine, Hong Kong RAS											
Total	C	127	137	100	103	...	1.3	1.5	1.8	1.7	...
China, Macao SAR - Chine, Macao RAS											
Total	C	17	18	13	15	11	...	...	...	...	...
Cyprus - Chypre[13]											
Total	C	30	36	15	13	...	3.1	3.5	...	...	...
Georgia - Géorgie[11]											
Total	C	703	715	640	578	...	12.1	12.5	11.1	9.5	...
Urban - Urbaine	C	342	...	...	...	...	10.2	...	...	...	...
Rural - Rurale	C	361	...	...	...	...	14.7	...	...	...	...
India - Inde[14]											
Total	I	...	...	...	...	...	44.0	42.0	40.0	39.0	...
Urban - Urbaine	I	...	...	...	...	...	29.0	28.0	27.0	26.0	...
Rural - Rurale	I	...	...	...	...	...	48.0	46.0	44.0	43.0	...
Iran (Islamic Republic of) - Iran (République islamique d')[15]											
Total	C	11 021	10 401	8 015	7 430	...	8.0	7.3	5.4	4.8	...
Urban - Urbaine	C	7 980[4]	8 173[4]	5 993	5 590	...	7.3	7.2	5.3	4.7	...
Rural - Rurale	C	2 574[4]	2 226[4]	2 022	1 840	...	8.7	7.6	5.9	5.2	...
Israel - Israël[16]											
Total	C	588	611	539	548	552	3.5	3.6	3.1	3.1	3.1
Urban - Urbaine[4]	C	522	545	469	494	488	3.5	3.5	3.0	3.1	...
Rural - Rurale[4]	C	65	65	69	53	62	4.2	4.1	4.2	3.3	...
Japan - Japon[17]											
Total	C	2 463	2 299	2 185	2 080	...	2.3	2.2	2.1	2.1	...
Urban - Urbaine	C	2 244	2 106	2 019	1 891	...	2.3	2.2	2.1	2.0	...
Rural - Rurale	C	214	192	163	187	...	2.5	2.3	2.0	2.4	...
Kazakhstan[11]											
Total	C	5 556	5 121	4 367	...	...	14.9	13.4	11.3	...	...
Urban - Urbaine	C	3 049	2 781	2 383	...	...	15.4	13.5	11.4	...	...
Rural - Rurale	C	2 507	2 340	1 984	...	...	14.3	13.4	11.1	...	...
Kuwait - Koweït											
Total	C	484	459	453	456	...	8.3	7.7	7.6	7.4	...
Kyrgyzstan - Kirghizstan											
Total	C	3 150	3 091	3 093	3 268	*2 945	21.1	20.0	19.9	20.2	*18.0
Urban - Urbaine	C	1 767	1 807	1 886	2 099	*1 853	36.1	33.6	35.0	37.8	*35.3
Rural - Rurale	C	1 383	1 284	1 207	1 169	*1 092	13.7	12.7	11.9	11.0	*9.8
Malaysia - Malaisie											
Total	C	3 330	3 277	3 199	*3 156	...	6.5	6.2	6.3	*6.2	...
Urban - Urbaine	C	2 144	2 087	2 101	...	...	6.3	5.8	6.1	...	...
Rural - Rurale	C	1 186	1 190	1 098	...	...	7.0	7.1	6.9	...	...
Maldives											
Total	C	65	66	46	59	...	9.1	8.9	6.4	8.1	...
Urban - Urbaine	C	41[18]	46[18]	24[18]	15[19]	...	10.3	10.3	...	...	...
Rural - Rurale	C	20[18]	18[18]	19[18]	33[19]	...	...	...	...	13.9	...
Mongolia - Mongolie											
Total	+C	1 152	1 143	1 166	1 251	1 234	16.5	15.5	14.6	15.1	15.0

15. Infant deaths and infant mortality rates, by urban/rural residence: 2011 - 2015
Décès d'enfants de moins d'un an et taux de mortalité infantile, selon la résidence, urbaine/rurale : 2011 - 2015 (continued - suite)

Continent, country or area, and urban/rural residence / Continent, pays ou zone et résidence, urbaine/rurale	Code[a]	Number - Nombre					Rate - Taux				
		2011	2012	2013	2014	2015	2011	2012	2013	2014	2015
ASIA - ASIE											
Myanmar[20]											
Total	+U	10 340	11 406	11 516	10 668	...	...	...	...	...	...
Urban - Urbaine	+U	...	6 170	6 840	...	...	...	...	...	...	...
Rural - Rurale	+U	...	5 236	4 676	...	...	...	...	...	...	...
Nepal - Népal[21]											
Total	|	10 132	...	...	...	...	31.0	...	...	...	...
Urban - Urbaine	|	767	...	...	...	...	18.4	...	...	...	...
Rural - Rurale	|	9 365	...	...	...	...	32.8	...	...	...	...
Oman[22]											
Total	U	640	676	772	645	...	...	...	...	...	...
Philippines											
Total	C	22 283	22 254	21 992	...	...	12.8	12.4	12.5	...	...
Qatar											
Total	C	156	148	157	...	...	7.5	6.9	6.6	...	...
Republic of Korea - République de Corée[23]											
Total	C	1 435	1 405	1 305	1 305	...	3.0	2.9	3.0	3.0	...
Urban - Urbaine	C	1 158[4]	1 135	1 098[4]	1 063[4]	...	3.0	2.8	3.0	2.9	...
Rural - Rurale	C	265[4]	270	203[4]	242[4]	...	3.3	3.3	2.9	3.4	...
Saudi Arabia - Arabie saoudite[24]											
Total	...	10 023	9 843	...	...	...	...	...	...	...	...
Singapore - Singapour											
Total	+C	97	98	94	83	84	2.4	2.3	2.4	2.0	2.0
State of Palestine - État de Palestine[25]											
Total	U	1 051	1 050	827	...	...	...	...	...	...	...
Tajikistan - Tadjikistan[11]											
Total	U	3 131	2 884	3 622	3 273	...	...	...	...	...	...
Urban - Urbaine	U	1 281	1 241	1 817	1 515	...	...	...	...	...	...
Rural - Rurale	U	1 850	1 643	1 805	1 758	...	...	...	...	...	...
Thailand - Thaïlande											
Total	+U	5 275	...	...	...	...	...	...	...	...	...
Turkey - Turquie											
Total	C	14 582	14 965	13 996	14 821	...	11.7	11.6	10.8	11.1	...
Uzbekistan - Ouzbékistan											
Total	+C	6 526	6 390	6 569	7 688	...	10.5	10.2	9.7	10.7	...
Urban - Urbaine	+C	3 664	3 730	3 881	4 312	...	12.9	13.0	12.5	13.2	...
Rural - Rurale	+C	2 862	2 660	2 688	3 376	...	8.4	7.9	7.3	8.6	...
EUROPE											
Åland Islands - Îles d'Åland											
Total	C	-	-	-	-	...	...	...	...	...	...
Urban - Urbaine	C	-	-	-	-	...	...	...	...	...	...
Rural - Rurale	C	-	-	-	-	...	...	...	...	...	...
Albania - Albanie											
Total	C	299	312	282	...	...	8.7	8.8	7.9	...	...
Andorra - Andorre											
Total	C	...	4	...	...	...	...	...	...	...	...
Austria - Autriche											
Total	C	281	252	245	...	...	3.6	3.2	3.1	...	...
Belarus - Bélarus											
Total	C	420	386	407	409	...	3.8	3.3	3.4	3.5	...
Urban - Urbaine	C	286	278	291	...	...	3.4	3.1	3.2	...	...
Rural - Rurale	C	134	108	116	...	...	5.2	4.0	4.2	...	...
Belgium - Belgique[26]											
Total	C	434	483	436	423	...	3.4	3.8	3.5	3.4	...
Urban - Urbaine	C	428	477	...	...	...	3.4	...	...	...	...
Rural - Rurale	C	6	6	...	...	...	...	...	...	...	...
Bosnia and Herzegovina - Bosnie-Herzégovine											
Total	C	...	161	161	140	...	...	5.0	5.2	4.8	...

15. Infant deaths and infant mortality rates, by urban/rural residence: 2011 - 2015
Décès d'enfants de moins d'un an et taux de mortalité infantile, selon la résidence, urbaine/rurale : 2011 - 2015 (continued - suite)

Continent, country or area, and urban/rural residence / Continent, pays ou zone et résidence, urbaine/rurale	Co-de[a]	Number - Nombre					Rate - Taux				
		2011	2012	2013	2014	2015	2011	2012	2013	2014	2015
EUROPE											
Bulgaria - Bulgarie											
Total	C	601	536	489	517	...	8.5	7.8	7.3	7.6	...
Urban - Urbaine	C	412	368	...	...	...	7.7	7.1	...	...	...
Rural - Rurale	C	189	168	...	...	...	10.8	9.6	...	...	...
Croatia - Croatie											
Total	C	192	150	162	199	...	4.7	3.6	4.1	5.0	...
Urban - Urbaine	C	126	95	82	101	...	5.4	4.0	3.6	4.4	...
Rural - Rurale	C	66	55	80	98	...	3.7	3.1	4.7	5.9	...
Czech Republic - République tchèque											
Total	C	298	285	265	263	...	2.7	2.6	2.5	2.4	...
Urban - Urbaine	C	231	208	193	197	...	2.9	2.6	2.5	2.4	...
Rural - Rurale	C	67	77	72	66	...	2.3	2.7	2.5	2.3	...
Denmark - Danemark[27]											
Total	C	208	197	195	229	...	3.5	3.4	3.5	4.0	...
Estonia - Estonie											
Total	C	36	50	28	36	...	2.5	3.6	...	2.7	...
Urban - Urbaine	C	25	36	18	24	...	...	3.7	...	...	...
Rural - Rurale	C	11	14	10	12	...	...	...	...	...	...
Faeroe Islands - Îles Féroé											
Total	C	3	10	-	4	1	...	...	...	...	...
Urban - Urbaine	C	2	6	-	1	-	...	...	...	...	...
Rural - Rurale	C	1	4	-	3	1	...	...	...	...	...
Finland - Finlande[28]											
Total	C	143	141	102	124	...	2.4	2.4	1.8	2.2	...
Urban - Urbaine	C	104	93	65	93	...	2.4	2.2	1.6	2.3	...
Rural - Rurale	C	39	48	37	31	...	2.3	2.8	2.2	2.0	...
France											
Total	C	2 604	2 643	2 710	2 598	...	3.3	3.3	3.5	3.3	...
Urban - Urbaine[29]	C	2 140	2 140	2 233	2 138	...	3.4	3.4	3.6	3.4	...
Rural - Rurale[29]	C	440	485	457	441	...	2.7	3.0	2.9	2.9	...
Germany - Allemagne											
Total	C	2 408	2 202	2 250	2 284	...	3.6	3.3	3.3	3.2	...
Gibraltar											
Total	+C	...	...	-	...	...	...	...	...	...	...
Greece - Grèce											
Total	C	357	293	347	346	...	3.4	2.9	3.7	3.8	...
Urban - Urbaine	C	250	197	...	242	...	3.3	2.8	...	3.9	...
Rural - Rurale	C	107	96	...	104	...	3.4	3.3	...	3.5	...
Hungary - Hongrie											
Total	C	433	438	448[31]	418[32]	...	4.9	4.9	5.0	4.5	...
Urban - Urbaine	C	268[30]	259[30]	273[31]	274[32]	...	4.4	4.2	4.4	4.2	...
Rural - Rurale	C	160[30]	176[30]	175[31]	144[32]	...	6.1	6.5	6.4	5.1	...
Iceland - Islande											
Total	C	4[33]	5	8	9	...	...	...	...	...	...
Urban - Urbaine	C	4[33]	5	8	9	...	...	...	...	...	...
Rural - Rurale	C	-[33]	-	-	-	...	...	...	...	...	...
Ireland - Irlande											
Total	+C	262	250	243	224	...	3.5	3.5	3.5	3.3	...
Italy - Italie											
Total	C	1 595	1 532	1 493	1 523	...	2.9	2.9	2.9	3.0	...
Latvia - Lettonie											
Total	C	124	125	91	83	...	6.6	6.3	4.4	3.8	...
Urban - Urbaine	C	74	87	55	53	...	5.8	6.4	3.9	3.5	...
Rural - Rurale	C	50	38	36	30	...	8.2	6.0	5.6	4.5	...
Liechtenstein											
Total	C	1	3	2	1	...	...	...	...	...	...
Lithuania - Lituanie											
Total	C	144	118	110	118	...	4.8	3.9	3.7	3.9	...
Urban - Urbaine	C	87	77	63	69	...	4.2	3.6	3.1	3.3	...
Rural - Rurale	C	57	41	47	49	...	6.0	4.5	4.9	5.2	...
Luxembourg											
Total	C	24	25	24	17	...	...	...	...	...	...
Malta - Malte											
Total	C	27	22	27	21	...	...	...	...	...	...
Montenegro - Monténégro											
Total	C	32	33	33	37	...	4.4	4.4	4.4	4.9	...

15. Infant deaths and infant mortality rates, by urban/rural residence: 2011 - 2015
Décès d'enfants de moins d'un an et taux de mortalité infantile, selon la résidence, urbaine/rurale : 2011 - 2015 (continued - suite)

Continent, country or area, and urban/rural residence / Continent, pays ou zone et résidence, urbaine/rurale	Co-de[a]	Number - Nombre					Rate - Taux				
		2011	2012	2013	2014	2015	2011	2012	2013	2014	2015
EUROPE											
Netherlands - Pays-Bas[34]											
Total	C	654	649	645	630	...	3.6	3.7	3.8	3.6	...
Norway - Norvège[35]											
Total	C	142	150	140	139	...	2.4	2.5	2.4	2.4	...
Poland - Pologne											
Total	C	1 836	1 791	1 684	1 583	...	4.7	4.6	4.6	4.2	...
Urban - Urbaine	C	1 059	1 006	...	...	...	4.7	4.5	...	...	...
Rural - Rurale	C	777	785	...	...	...	4.8	4.8	...	...	...
Portugal[36]											
Total	C	302	303	243	236	...	3.1	3.4	2.9	2.9	...
Republic of Moldova - République de Moldova[37]											
Total	C	431	387	359	372	...	11.0	9.8	9.5	9.6	...
Urban - Urbaine	C	136	122	...	...	...	9.3	8.2	...	...	...
Rural - Rurale	C	295	265	...	...	...	12.0	10.8	...	...	...
Romania - Roumanie											
Total	C	1 850	1 812	1 677	1 628	...	9.4	9.0	9.2	8.4	...
Urban - Urbaine	C	797	720	738	649	...	7.5	6.6	7.5	6.2	...
Rural - Rurale	C	1 053	1 092	939	979	...	11.8	11.8	11.2	11.2	...
Russian Federation - Fédération de Russie[11]											
Total	C	13 168	16 306	...	...	...	7.3	8.6	...	...	...
Urban - Urbaine	C	8 398	10 843	...	...	...	6.6	8.0	...	...	...
Rural - Rurale	C	4 770	5 463	...	...	...	9.1	10.0	...	...	...
San Marino - Saint-Marin											
Total	+C	1	-	1	1	...	...	...	...	...	...
Serbia - Serbie[38]											
Total	+C	414	415	413	381	...	6.3	6.2	6.3	5.7	...
Urban - Urbaine	+C	283	274	281	268	...	6.2	6.0	6.2	5.8	...
Rural - Rurale	+C	131	141	132	113	...	6.5	6.6	6.6	5.5	...
Slovakia - Slovaquie											
Total	C	300	321	301	318	...	4.9	5.8	5.5	5.8	...
Urban - Urbaine	C	130	151	138	160	...	4.0	5.2	4.8	5.6	...
Rural - Rurale	C	170	170	163	158	...	6.0	6.4	6.2	5.9	...
Slovenia - Slovénie											
Total	C	64	36	62	39	...	2.9	1.6	2.9	1.8	...
Urban - Urbaine	C	28	15	37	19	...	...	...	3.5	...	...
Rural - Rurale	C	36	21	25	20	...	3.2	...	...	...	...
Spain - Espagne											
Total	C	1 477	1 389	1 149	1 202	...	3.1	3.1	2.7	2.8	...
Sweden - Suède											
Total	C	235	293	306	251	...	2.1	2.6	2.7	2.2	...
Switzerland - Suisse											
Total	C	305	296	320	331	...	3.8	3.6	3.9	3.9	...
Urban - Urbaine	C	218	235	258	256	...	3.6	3.8	4.1	4.0	...
Rural - Rurale	C	87	61	62	75	...	4.3	3.0	3.0	3.5	...
TFYR of Macedonia - L'ex-R. y. de Macédoine											
Total	C	172	230	237	233	...	7.6	9.8	10.2	9.9	...
Urban - Urbaine	C	93	123	...	...	...	7.1	9.2	...	...	...
Rural - Rurale	C	79	107	...	...	...	8.1	10.5	...	...	...
Ukraine[39]											
Total	+C	4 511	4 371	4 030	3 656[40]	...	9.0	8.4	8.0	7.8	...
Urban - Urbaine	+C	2 811	2 763	2 536	...	...	8.5	8.1	7.7	...	...
Rural - Rurale	+C	1 700	1 608	1 494	...	...	9.8	9.0	8.6	...	...
United Kingdom of Great Britain and Northern Ireland - Royaume-Uni de Grande-Bretagne et d'Irlande du Nord[41]											
Total	+C	3 502	3 347	...	2 990	...	4.3	4.1	...	3.9	...

438

15. Infant deaths and infant mortality rates, by urban/rural residence: 2011 - 2015
Décès d'enfants de moins d'un an et taux de mortalité infantile, selon la résidence, urbaine/rurale : 2011 - 2015 (continued - suite)

Continent, country or area, and urban/rural residence / Continent, pays ou zone et résidence, urbaine/rurale	Co-de[a]	Number - Nombre					Rate - Taux				
		2011	2012	2013	2014	2015	2011	2012	2013	2014	2015
OCEANIA - OCÉANIE											
American Samoa - Samoas américaines											
Total	C	9	4	5	9	...	...	...	...	...	...
Australia - Australie											
Total	+C	1 140	1 031	1 094	1 012	...	3.8	3.3	3.6	3.4	...
Urban - Urbaine[42]	+C	661	634	658	617	...	3.3	3.0	3.1	3.0	...
Rural - Rurale[42]	+C	443	362	411	380	...	4.5	3.7	4.2	4.1	...
Cook Islands - Îles Cook[43]											
Total	+C	2	1	-	-	*-	...	...	...	...	...
French Polynesia - Polynésie française											
Total	C	20	31	37	28	29	...	7.2	8.8	...	...
Guam[44]											
Total	C	42	42	31	28	47	12.7	11.7	9.3	...	14.0
New Caledonia - Nouvelle-Calédonie											
Total	C	20	17	...	...	...	...	...	...	...	...
New Zealand - Nouvelle-Zélande											
Total	+C	290[6]	256[6]	260[6]	324[45]	252[45]	4.7	4.2	4.4	5.7	4.1
Urban - Urbaine[4]	+C	255[6]	229[6]	222[6]	285[45]	219[45]	4.7	4.2	4.3	5.7	4.1
Rural - Rurale[4]	+C	31[6]	24[6]	33[6]	24[45]	30[45]	4.2	...	4.6	...	3.8
Northern Mariana Islands - Îles Mariannes septentrionales[7]											
Total	U	2	6	8	7	...	...	...	...	...	...
Palau - Palaos											
Total	C	1	2	4	...	...	...	...	...	...	...

FOOTNOTES - NOTES

Italics: data from civil registers which are incomplete or of unknown completeness. - Italiques : données incomplètes ou dont le degré d'exactitude n'est pas connu, provenant des registres de l'état civil.

* Provisional. - Données provisoires.

[a] 'Code' indicates the source of data, as follows:
C - Civil registration, estimated over 90% complete
U - Civil registration, estimated less than 90% complete
| - Other source, estimated reliable
+ - Data tabulated by date of registration rather than occurence
... - Information not available

Le 'Code' indique la source des données, comme suit :
C - Registres de l'état civil considérés complets à 90 p. 100 au moins
U - Registres de l'état civil qui ne sont pas considérés complets à 90 p. 100 au moins
| - Autre source, considérée pas douteuses
+ - Données exploitées selon la date de l'enregistrement et non la date de l'événement
... - Information pas disponible

[1] Excluding live-born infants who died before their birth was registered. Data refer to Algerian population only. - Non compris les enfants nés vivants décédés avant l'enregistrement de leur naissance. Les données ne concernent que la population algérienne.
[2] Source: Vital Statistics Report 2014. - Source: Vital Statistics Report 2014.
[3] Excludes the islands of St. Brandon and Agalega. - Non compris les îles St. Brandon et Agalega.
[4] The total number may include 'Unknown residence', but the categories urban and rural do not. - Le nombre total peut inclure les personnes dont la résidence n'est pas connue, à l'inverse des catégories de population urbaine et rurale.
[5] Excluding infant deaths to mothers living abroad. - Exception faite des décès d'enfants en bas âge survenus lorsque la mère résidait à l'étranger.

[6] Data refer to resident population only. - Pour la population résidante seulement.
[7] Source: U.S. National Center for Health Statistics, National Vital Statistics Reports (NVSR). - Source : US National Center for Health Statistics, National Vital Statistics Reports (NVSR).
[8] Including deaths abroad and deaths of unknown residence of mother. - Y compris décès à l'étranger et décès de nourrissons nés de mères dont le lieu de résidence n'est pas connu.
[9] Excludes nomadic Indian tribes. - Non compris les tribus d'Indiens nomades.
[10] Source: Reports of the Ministry of Health. - Source : Rapports du Ministère de la Santé.
[11] Excluding infants born alive of less than 28 weeks' gestation, of less than 1 000 grams in weight and 35 centimeters in length, who die within seven days of birth. - Non compris les enfants nés vivants après moins de 28 semaines de gestations, pesant moins de 1 000 grammes, mesurant moins de 35 centimètres et décédés dans les sept jours qui ont suivi leur naissance.
[12] Deaths include deaths among some visitors. Sources: Births and Deaths National Registration System database, and medical records of government hospitals. - Les décès comprennent des décès parmi certains visiteurs. Les sources: Les bases de données des << Births and Deaths National Registration System >> et les dossiers médicaux des hôpitaux du gouvernement.
[13] Data refer to government controlled areas. - Les données se rapportent aux zones contrôlées par le Gouvernement.
[14] Rates were obtained by the Sample Registration System of India, which is a large demographic survey. Includes data for the Indian-held part of Jammu and Kashmir, the final status of which has not yet been determined. - Les taux ont été obtenus par le Système de l'enregistrement par échantillon de l'Inde qui est une large enquête démographique. Y compris les données pour la partie du Jammu et du Cachemire occupée par l'Inde dont le statut définitif n'a pas encore été déterminé.
[15] Data refer to the Iranian Year which begins on 21 March and ends on 20 March of the following year. - Les données concernent l'année iranienne, qui commence le 21 mars et se termine le 20 mars de l'année suivante.
[16] Including deaths abroad of Israeli residents who were out of the country for less than a year. Includes data for East Jerusalem and Israeli residents in certain other territories under occupation by Israeli military forces since June 1967. - Y compris les décès à l'étranger de résidents israéliens qui ont quitté le pays depuis

moins d'un an. Y compris les données pour Jérusalem-Est et les résidents israéliens dans certains autres territoires occupés depuis 1967 par les forces armées israéliennes.

[17] The total number may include 'Unknown residence', but the categories urban and rural do not. Data refer to Japanese nationals in Japan only. - Le nombre total peut inclure les personnes dont la résidence n'est pas connue, à l'inverse des catégories de population urbaine et rurale. Les données se raportent aux nationaux japonais au Japon seulement.

[18] Excluding deaths occurred abroad. - Hormis les décès à l'étranger.

[19] Data for urban and rural exclude deaths of unknown residence. - Les données pur la résidence urbaine et rurale non comprent pas les décès dont on ignore la résidence.

[20] Data source is "Department of Public Health". - La source des données est << Le Service de la santé publique >>.

[21] Data refer to the 12 months preceding the census in June. - Les données se rapportent aux 12 mois précédant le recensement de juin.

[22] Data from Births and Deaths Notification System (Ministry of Health and all health care providers). - Les données proviennent du système de notification des naissances et des décès (Ministère de la santé et tous prestataires de soins de santé).

[23] Excluding alien armed forces, civilian aliens employed by armed forces, and foreign diplomatic personnel and their dependants. - Non compris les militaires étrangers, les civils étrangers employés par les forces armées ni le personnel diplomatique étranger et les membres de leur famille les accompagnant.

[24] Projections based on the final results of the 2004 Population and Housing Census. - Projections basées sur les résultats définitifs du recensement de la population et de l'habitat de 2004.

[25] Source: Palestinian Central Bureau of Statistics, Population Register, updated version 05/01/2015. - Source: Bureau central de statistique palestinien, registre de la population, version actualisée jusqu'au 05/01/2015.

[26] Including armed forces stationed outside the country, but excluding alien armed forces stationed in the area. - Y compris les militaires nationaux hors du pays, mais non compris les militaires étrangers en garnison sur le territoire.

[27] Excluding Faeroe Islands and Greenland shown separately, if available. - Non compris les Iles Féroé et le Groenland, qui font l'objet de rubriques distinctes, si disponible.

[28] Excluding Åland Islands. - Non compris les Îles d'Åland.

[29] The data for urban and rural exclude the nationals outside the country. - Les données relatives à la population urbaine et rurale n'englobent pas les nationaux se trouvant à l'étranger.

[30] The urban and rural categories do not include the data of foreigners, persons of unknown residence and the homeless, whereas the total category includes them. - Les chiffres portant sur la population urbaine et rurale n' incluent pas les données relatives aux étrangers, aux personnes dont la résidence n'est pas connue et aux personnes sans domicile fixe, à l'inverse, le total les inclut.

[31] Till 2012 data refer to all infant deaths occurred in Hungary. From 2013 data include the deceased infants with Hungarian usual residence regardless of whether the death occurred in Hungary or in a foreign country, and do not include the deceased infants with foreign country usual residence. - Jusqu'en 2012 les données concernent tous les décès de nourrissons survenus en Hongrie. À partir de 2013, les données comprennent les nourrissons décédés alors que leur résidence habituelle était en Hongrie, que le décès ait eu lieu en Hongrie ou dans un pays étranger, et ne comprennent pas les nourrissons décédés dont la résidence habituelle était dans un pays étranger.

[32] Data include the deceased infants with Hungarian usual residence regardless of whether the death occurred in Hungary or in a foreign country, and do not include the deceased infants with foreign country usual residence. - Les données comprennent les nourrissons décédés alors que leur résidence habituelle était en Hongrie, que le décès ait eu lieu en Hongrie ou dans un pays étranger, et ne comprennent pas les nourrissons décédés dont la residence habituelle était dans un pays étranger.

[33] Definition of localities was revised in 2011 causing a break with the previous series. - La rupture par rapport aux séries précédentes s'explique par le fait que la définition des localités a été révisée depuis 2011.

[34] Including residents outside the country if listed in a Netherlands population register. - Englobe les résidents se trouvant à l'étranger à condition qu'ils soient inscrits sur le registre de population des Pays-Bas.

[35] Including residents temporarily outside the country. - Y compris les résidents se trouvant temporairement hors du pays.

[36] Data refer to usually resident population. - Les données concernent la population habituellement résidente.

[37] Excluding Transnistria and the municipality of Bender. - Les données ne tiennent pas compte de l'information sur la Transnistria et la municipalité de Bender.

[38] Excludes data for Kosovo and Metohia. - Sans les données pour le Kosovo et Metohie.

[39] Data includes deaths resulting from births with weight 500g and more (if weight is unknown - with length 25 centimeters and more, or with gestation during 22 weeks or more). - Y compris les décès de nouveau-nés de 500 grammes ou plus (si le poids est inconnu – de 25 centimètres de long ou plus, ou après une grossesse de 22 semaines ou plus).

[40] The Government of Ukraine has informed the United Nations that it is not in a position to provide statistical data concerning the Autonomous Republic of Crimea and the city of Sevastopol. - Le gouvernement Ukrainien a informé l'ONU qu'il n'est pas en mesure de fournir des données statistiques concernant la République autonome de Crimée et la ville de Sébastopol.

[41] Excluding Channel Islands (Guernsey and Jersey) and Isle of Man, shown separately, if available. - Non compris les îles Anglo-Normandes (Guernesey et Jersey) et l'île de Man, qui font l'objet de rubriques distinctes, si disponible.

[42] Urban refers to Greater Capital City Statistical Areas, and rural refers to other areas within the state or territory. Data for urban and rural figures do not add up to the total because they exclude the events occurred in Migratory, Special Purpose and Other Territories. - Urbain renvoie aux zones statistiques de la capitale métropolitaine, et rural aux autres zones de l'État ou territoire. La somme des chiffres des catégories « en zone urbaine » et « en zone rurale » ne correspond au total du fait qu'en sont exclus les événements qui ont eu lieu dans les territoires de migration, les territoires à destination spéciale et autres territoires.

[43] Excluding Niue, shown separately, which is part of Cook Islands, but because of remoteness is administered separately. - Non compris Nioué, qui fait l'objet d'une rubrique distincte et qui fait partie des îles Cook, mais qui, en raison de son éloignement, est administrée séparément.

[44] Including United States military personnel, their dependants and contract employees. - Y compris les militaires des Etats-Unis, les membres de leur famille les accompagnant et les agents contractuels des Etats-Unis.

[45] Random rounding to base 3 is applied in this table as a confidentiality measure. - Les chiffres sont arrondis à la base 3 de manière aléatoire, pour des raisons de confidentialité.

Table 16 - *Demographic Yearbook 2015*

Table 16 presents infant deaths and infant mortality rates by age and sex for latest available year between 2006 and 2015.

Description of variables: Age is defined as hours, days and months of life completed, based on the difference between the hour, day, month and year of birth and the hour, day, month and year of death. The age classification used in this table is as follows: Main categories are "under 1 day", "1-6 days", "7-27 days" and "28 days – 11 months". Additional subcategories are shown within "7-27 days" and "28 days to 11 months" wherever available.

Rate computation: Infant mortality rates by age and sex are the annual number of infant deaths that occurred in a specific age-sex group per 1 000 live births of the corresponding sex. These rates have been calculated by the Statistics Division of the United Nations Department of Economic and Social Affairs. The denominator for all these rates, regardless of age of infant at death, is the total number of live births by sex.

Infant deaths of unknown age are included only in the rate for under one year of age. Infant deaths of unknown sex are included in the rate for the total and, hence, these rates, should agree with the infant mortality rates shown in table 15. Discrepancies are explained in footnotes.

Rates presented in this table have been limited to those countries or areas having at least a total of 100 deaths in a given year. Moreover, rates specific for individual sub-categories based on 30 or fewer infant deaths are identified by the symbol "♦".

Reliability of data: Data from civil registers of infant deaths which are reported as incomplete (less than 90 percent completeness) or of unknown completeness are considered unreliable and are set in italics rather than in roman type. Rates on these data are not computed. Table 15 and its technical notes provide more detailed information on the completeness of infant death registration. For more information about the quality of vital statistics, and the information available on the basis of the completeness of estimates in particular, see section 4.2 of the Technical Notes.

Limitations: Statistics on infant deaths by age and sex are subject to the same qualifications as have been set forth for vital statistics in general and death statistics in particular as discussed in section 4 of the Technical Notes.

The reliability of the data, an indication of which is described above, is an important factor in considering the limitations. In addition, some infant deaths are tabulated by date of registration and not by date of occurrence; these have been indicated by a plus sign "+". Whenever the lag between the date of occurrence and date of registration is prolonged and, therefore, a large proportion of the infant-death registrations are delayed, infant-death statistics for any given year may be seriously affected.

Another factor that limits international comparability is the practice of some countries or areas of not including in infant-death statistics infants who were born alive but died before the registration of the birth or within the first 24 hours of life, thus underestimating the total number of infant deaths. Statistics of this type are footnoted. In this table in particular, this practice may contribute to the lack of comparability among deaths under one year, under 28 days, under one week and under one day.

Variation in the method of reckoning age at the time of death may also introduce non-comparability. Although it is to some degree a limiting factor throughout the age span, it is an especially important consideration with respect to deaths at ages under one day and under one week (early neonatal deaths) and under 28 days (neonatal deaths). As noted above, the recommended method of reckoning infant age at death is to calculate duration of life in minutes, hours and days, as appropriate. This gives age in completed units of time. In some countries or areas, however, infant age is calculated to the nearest day only, that is, age at death for an infant is the difference between the day, month and year of birth and the day, month and year of death. The result of this procedure is to classify as deaths at age one day, many deaths of infants that occurred before the infants had completed 24 hours of life. The under-one-day class is thus understated while the frequency in the 1-6-day age group is inflated.

A special limitation on comparability of neonatal (under 28 days) deaths is the variation in the classification of infant age used. It is evident from the footnotes that some countries or areas continue to report infant age in calendar, rather than lunar month (4-week or 28-day) periods. This failure to tabulate infant deaths under 4 weeks of age in terms of completed days introduces another source of variation between countries or areas. Deaths classified as occurring under one month usually connote deaths within any one calendar month; these frequencies are not strictly comparable with those referring to deaths within 4 weeks or 27 completed days.

In addition, infant mortality rates by age and sex are subject to the limitations of the data on live births with which they have been calculated. These have been set forth in the technical notes for table 9. These limitations have also been discussed in the technical notes for table 15.

In addition, it should be noted that infant mortality rates by age are affected by the problems related to the practice of excluding infants who were born alive but died before the registration of the birth or within the first 24 hours of life from both infant-death and live-birth statistics and the problems related to the reckoning of infant age at death. These factors, which have been described above, may affect certain age groups more than others. In so far as the numbers of infant deaths for the various age groups are underestimated or overestimated, the corresponding rates for the various age groups will also be underestimated or overestimated. The youngest age groups are more likely to be underestimated than other age groups; the youngest age group (under one day) is likely to be the most seriously affected.

Earlier data: Infant deaths and infant mortality rates by age and sex have been shown in previous issues of the *Demographic Yearbook*. For information on specific years covered, readers should consult the Historical Index.

Tableau 16 – *Annuaire démographique 2015*

Le tableau 16 présente les données les plus récentes disponible, entre 2006 et 2015, sur les décès d'enfants de moins d'un an et les taux de mortalité infantile selon l'âge et le sexe.

Description des variables : l'âge est exprimé en heures, jours et mois révolus et est calculé en retranchant la date de la naissance (heure, jour, mois et année) de celle du décès (heure, jour, mois et année). Les tranches d'âge utilisées dans ce tableau se présentent comme suit : les catégories principales sont « moins d'un jour », « 1-6 jours », « 7-27 jours » et « 28 jours à 11 mois ». Des sous-catégories additionnelles pour « 7-27 jours » et « 28 jours à 11 mois » sont présentées lorsque disponibles.

Calcul des taux : les taux de mortalité infantile selon l'âge et le sexe représentent le nombre annuel de décès d'enfants de moins d'un an intervenu dans un groupe d'âge donné parmi la population de sexe masculin ou féminin pour 1 000 naissances vivantes survenues parmi la population du même sexe. Ces taux ont été calculés par la Division de statistique du Département des affaires économiques et sociales de l'Organisation des Nations Unies. Le dénominateur de tous ces taux, quel que soit l'âge de l'enfant au moment du décès, est le nombre total de naissances vivantes selon le sexe.

Il n'est tenu compte des décès d'enfants d'âge « inconnu » que pour le calcul du taux relatif à l'ensemble des décès de moins d'un an. Étant donné que les décès d'enfants de sexe inconnu sont compris dans le numérateur des taux concernant le total, les chiffres obtenus devraient concorder avec les taux de mortalité infantile du tableau 15. Les divergences sont expliquées en note.

Les taux présentés dans le tableau 16 ne concernent que les pays ou zones où l'on a enregistré un total d'au moins 100 décès au cours d'une année donnée. Les taux relatifs à des sous-catégories qui sont fondées sur un nombre égal ou inférieur à 30 décès d'enfants âgés de moins d'un an sont signalés par le signe "♦".

Fiabilité des données : les données relatives aux décès d'enfants de moins d'un an provenant de registres de l'état civil qui sont déclarées incomplètes (degré de complétude inférieur à 90 p.100) ou dont le degré de complétude n'est pas connu sont jugées douteuses et apparaissent en italique et non en caractères romains. Les taux à partir de ces données n'ont pas été calculés. Le tableau 15 et les notes techniques se rapportant à ce tableau comportent des renseignements plus détaillés sur le degré de complétude de l'enregistrement des décès d'enfants de moins d'un an. Pour plus de précisions sur la qualité des données reposant sur les statistiques de l'état civil en général et les estimations de complétude en particulier, voir la section 4.2 des Notes techniques.

Insuffisance des données : les statistiques des décès d'enfants de moins d'un an selon l'âge et le sexe appellent toutes les réserves qui ont été formulées à propos des statistiques de l'état civil en général et des statistiques concernant les décès en particulier (voir la section 4 des Notes techniques).

La fiabilité des données, au sujet de laquelle des indications ont été fournies plus haut, est un facteur important. Il faut également tenir compte du fait que, dans certains cas, les données relatives aux décès d'enfants de moins d'un an sont exploitées selon la date de l'enregistrement et non la date de l'événement ; ces cas ont été signalés par le signe "+". Chaque fois que le décalage entre l'événement et son enregistrement est grand et qu'une forte proportion des décès d'enfants de moins d'un an fait l'objet d'un enregistrement tardif, les statistiques des décès d'enfants de moins d'un an pour une année donnée peuvent être considérablement faussées.

Un autre facteur qui nuit à la comparabilité internationale est la pratique de certains pays ou zones qui consiste à ne pas inclure dans les statistiques des décès d'enfants de moins d'un an les enfants nés vivants mais décédés soit avant l'enregistrement de leur naissance, soit dans les 24 heures qui ont suivi la naissance, pratique qui conduit à sous-estimer le nombre total de décès d'enfants de moins d'un an. Quand pareil facteur a joué, cela a été signalé en note. Dans le tableau 16 en particulier, ce système peut limiter la comparabilité des données concernant les décès d'enfants de moins d'un an, de moins de 28 jours, de moins d'une semaine et de moins d'un jour.

Le manque d'uniformité des méthodes suivies pour calculer l'âge au moment du décès nuit également à la comparabilité des données. Ce facteur influe dans une certaine mesure sur les données relatives à la mortalité à tous les âges, mais il a des répercussions particulièrement marquées sur les statistiques des décès de moins d'un jour et de moins d'une semaine (mortalité néo-natale précoce) et de moins de 28 jours (mortalité néo-natale). Comme on l'a dit, l'âge d'un enfant de moins d'un an à son décès est calculé, selon la méthode recommandée, en évaluant la durée de vie en minutes, heures et jours, selon le cas. L'âge est ainsi exprimé en unités de temps révolues. Toutefois, dans certains pays ou zones, l'âge de ces enfants est ramené au jour le plus proche en retranchant la date de la naissance (jour, mois et année) de celle du décès (jour, mois et année). Il s'ensuit que de nombreux décès survenus dans les vingt-quatre heures qui suivent la naissance sont classés comme décès d'un jour. Dans ces conditions, les données concernant les décès de moins d'un jour sont entachées d'une erreur par défaut et celles qui se rapportent aux décès de 1 à 6 jours d'une erreur par excès.

La comparabilité des données relatives à la mortalité néo-natale (moins de 28 jours) est influencée par un facteur spécial : l'hétérogénéité de la classification par âge utilisée pour les enfants de moins d'un an. Les notes figurant à la fin des tableaux montrent que, dans un certain nombre de pays ou zones, on continue d'utiliser le mois civil au lieu du mois lunaire (4 semaines ou 28 jours).

Lorsque les données relatives aux décès de moins de 4 semaines ne sont pas exploitées sur la base de l'âge en jours révolus, il existe une nouvelle cause de non-comparabilité internationale. Les décès de moins d'un mois sont généralement ceux qui se produisent au cours d'un mois civil ; les taux calculés sur la base de ces données ne sont pas strictement comparables à ceux qui sont établis à partir des données concernant les décès survenus dans les 4 semaines ou 27 jours révolus qui suivent la naissance.

Les taux de mortalité infantile selon l'âge et le sexe appellent en outre toutes les réserves qui ont été formulées à propos des statistiques des naissances vivantes qui ont servi à leur calcul (voir à ce sujet les notes techniques relatives au tableau 9). Ces insuffisances ont également été examinées dans les notes techniques relatives au tableau 15.

Il convient de signaler aussi que les taux de mortalité infantile selon l'âge peuvent être gravement faussés par la pratique qui consiste à ne pas classer dans les naissances vivantes et ensuite dans les décès d'enfants de moins d'un an les enfants nés vivants mais décédés soit avant l'enregistrement de leur naissance, soit dans les 24 heures qui ont suivi la naissance, et par les problèmes que pose le calcul de l'âge de l'enfant au moment du décès. Ces facteurs, qui ont été décrits plus haut, peuvent fausser les statistiques concernant certains groupes d'âge plus que d'autres. Si le nombre des décès d'enfants de moins d'un an pour chaque groupe d'âge est sous-estimé ou surestimé, les taux correspondants pour chacun de ces groupes d'âge seront eux aussi sous-estimés ou surestimés. Les risques de sous-estimation sont plus grands pour les groupes les plus jeunes ; c'est pour le groupe d'âge le plus jeune de tous (moins d'un jour) que les données risquent de comporter les plus grosses erreurs.

Données publiées antérieurement : des statistiques des décès d'enfants de moins d'un an et des taux de mortalité infantile selon l'âge et le sexe ont déjà été présentées dans des éditions antérieures de l'*Annuaire démographique*. Pour plus de précisions concernant les années pour lesquelles ces données ont été publiées, se reporter à l'index historique.

16. Infant deaths and infant mortality rates by age and sex: latest available year, 2006 - 2015
Décès d'enfants de moins d'un an et taux de mortalité infantile selon l'âge et le sexe : dernière année disponible, 2006 - 2015

Continent, country or area, year, code[a] and age	Number - Nombre			Rate - Taux		
Continent, pays ou zone, année, code[a] et âge	Both sexes Les deux sexes	Male Masculin	Female Féminin	Both sexes Les deux sexes	Male Masculin	Female Féminin

AFRICA - AFRIQUE

Cabo Verde						
2008 (C)						
Total	316	...	...	24.9	...	...
Less than 7 days - Moins de 7 jours	160	...	...	12.6	...	...
7 - 27 days - 7 - 27 jours	52	...	...	4.1	...	...
28 days - 11 months - 28 jours - 11 mois	104	...	...	8.2	...	...
Egypt - Égypte						
2014 (C)						
Total	39 679	21 251	18 428	14.6	15.3	13.9
1 - 6 days - 1 - 6 jours	7 017	4 078	2 939	2.6	2.9	2.2
7 - 27 days - 7 - 27 jours	9 929	5 669	4 260	3.6	4.1	3.2
7 - 13 days - 7 - 13 jours	4 741	2 752	1 989	1.7	2.0	1.5
14 - 20 days - 14 - 20 jours	3 311	1 869	1 442	1.2	1.3	1.1
21 - 27 days - 21 - 27 jours	1 877	1 048	829	0.7	0.8	0.6
28 days - 11 months - 28 jours - 11 mois	22 733	11 504	11 229	8.4	8.3	8.4
28 days - less than 2 months - 28 jours - moins de 2 mois	5 435	2 922	2 513	2.0	2.1	1.9
2 months - 2 mois	3 803	1 897	1 906	1.4	1.4	1.4
3 months - 3 mois	2 827	1 427	1 400	1.0	1.0	1.1
4 months - 4 mois	2 468	1 225	1 243	0.9	0.9	0.9
5 months - 5 mois	1 827	894	933	0.7	0.6	0.7
6 months - 6 mois	1 760	859	901	0.6	0.6	0.7
7 months - 7 mois	1 245	611	634	0.5	0.4	0.5
8 months - 8 mois	1 127	533	594	0.4	0.4	0.4
9 months - 9 mois	974	496	478	0.4	0.4	0.4
10 months - 10 mois	716	372	344	0.3	0.3	0.3
11 months - 11 mois	551	268	283	0.2	0.2	0.2
Mauritius - Maurice[1]						
2015 (+C)						
Total	173	90	83	13.7	13.7	13.6
Less than 1 day - Moins de 1 jour	17	6	11	♦1.3	♦0.9	♦1.8
1 - 6 days - 1 - 6 jours	65	32	33	5.1	4.9	5.4
7 - 27 days - 7 - 27 jours	39	24	15	3.1	♦3.7	♦2.5
7 - 13 days - 7 - 13 jours	16	10	6	♦1.3	♦1.5	♦1.0
14 - 20 days - 14 - 20 jours	16	11	5	♦1.3	♦1.7	♦0.8
21 - 27 days - 21 - 27 jours	7	3	4	♦0.6	♦0.5	♦0.7
28 days - 11 months - 28 jours - 11 mois	52	28	24	4.1	♦4.3	♦3.9
28 days - less than 2 months - 28 jours - moins de 2 mois	23	10	13	♦1.8	♦1.5	♦2.1
2 months - 2 mois	9	8	1	♦0.7	♦1.2	♦0.2
3 months - 3 mois	4	3	1	♦0.3	♦0.5	♦0.2
4 months - 4 mois	2	1	1	♦0.2	♦0.2	♦0.2
5 months - 5 mois	2	2	-	♦0.2	♦0.3	-
6 months - 6 mois	2	-	2	♦0.2	-	♦0.3
7 months - 7 mois	2	1	1	♦0.2	♦0.2	♦0.2
8 months - 8 mois	3	-	3	♦0.2	-	♦0.5
9 months - 9 mois	2	2	-	♦0.2	♦0.3	-
10 months - 10 mois	1	1	-	♦0.1	♦0.2	-
11 months - 11 mois	2	-	2	♦0.2	-	♦0.3
Reunion - Réunion[2]						
2007 (C)						
Total	91	48	43	...	...	...
Less than 1 day - Moins de 1 jour	24	14	10	...	...	...
1 - 6 days - 1 - 6 jours	20	9	11	...	...	...
7 - 27 days - 7 - 27 jours	18	7	11	...	...	...
7 - 13 days - 7 - 13 jours	7	3	4	...	...	...
14 - 20 days - 14 - 20 jours	9	2	7	...	...	...
21 - 27 days - 21 - 27 jours	7	2	5	...	...	...
28 days - 11 months - 28 jours - 11 mois	30	18	12	...	...	...
Saint Helena ex. dep. - Sainte-Hélène sans dép.						
2014 (C)						
Total	1	-	1	...	...	...
Less than 1 day - Moins de 1 jour	-	-	-	...	...	...
1 - 6 days - 1 - 6 jours	1	-	1	...	...	...
7 - 27 days - 7 - 27 jours	-	-	-	...	...	...
7 - 13 days - 7 - 13 jours	-	-	-	...	...	...
14 - 20 days - 14 - 20 jours	-	-	-	...	...	...
21 - 27 days - 21 - 27 jours	-	-	-	...	...	...
28 days - 11 months - 28 jours - 11 mois	-	-	-	...	...	...
28 days - less than 2 months - 28 jours - moins de 2 mois	-	-	-	...	...	...

Continent, country or area, year, code[a] and age Continent, pays ou zone, année, code[a] et âge	Number - Nombre			Rate - Taux		
	Both sexes Les deux sexes	Male Masculin	Female Féminin	Both sexes Les deux sexes	Male Masculin	Female Féminin
AFRICA - AFRIQUE						
Saint Helena ex. dep. - Sainte-Hélène sans dép.						
2014 (C)						
2 months - 2 mois	-	-	-	...	...	...
3 months - 3 mois	-	-	-	...	...	...
4 months - 4 mois	-	-	-	...	...	...
5 months - 5 mois	-	-	-	...	...	...
6 months - 6 mois	-	-	-	...	...	...
7 months - 7 mois	-	-	-	...	...	...
8 months - 8 mois	-	-	-	...	...	...
9 months - 9 mois	-	-	-	...	...	...
10 months - 10 mois	-	-	-	...	...	...
11 months - 11 mois	-	-	-	...	...	...
Seychelles						
2006 (+C)						
Total...	14	5	9	...	...	...
Less than 1 day - Moins de 1 jour	5	1	4	...	...	...
1 - 6 days - 1 - 6 jours	2	1	1	...	...	...
7 - 27 days - 7 - 27 jours	2	-	2	...	...	...
7 - 13 days - 7 - 13 jours	1	-	1	...	...	...
14 - 20 days - 14 - 20 jours	-	-	-	...	...	...
21 - 27 days - 21 - 27 jours	1	-	1	...	...	...
28 days - 11 months - 28 jours - 11 mois............	5	3	2	...	...	...
28 days - less than 2 months - 28 jours - moins de 2 mois	1	1	-	...	...	...
2 months - 2 mois	-	-	-	...	...	...
3 months - 3 mois	-	-	-	...	...	...
4 months - 4 mois	1	-	1	...	...	...
5 months - 5 mois	2	2	-	...	...	...
6 months - 6 mois	1	-	1	...	...	...
7 months - 7 mois	-	-	-	...	...	...
8 months - 8 mois	-	-	-	...	...	...
9 months - 9 mois	-	-	-	...	...	...
10 months - 10 mois	-	-	-	...	...	...
11 months - 11 mois	-	-	-	...	...	...
South Africa - Afrique du Sud[3]						
2006 (...)						
Total...	47 703	25 178[4]	21 810[4]	...	...	...
Less than 1 day - Moins de 1 jour	2 422	1 387[4]	969[4]	...	...	...
1 - 6 days - 1 - 6 jours	7 217	4 146[4]	2 892[4]	...	...	...
7 - 27 days - 7 - 27 jours	3 640	1 991[4]	1 568[4]	...	...	...
7 - 13 days - 7 - 13 jours	1 613	912[4]	667[4]	...	...	...
14 - 20 days - 14 - 20 jours	1 074	589[4]	460[4]	...	...	...
21 - 27 days - 21 - 27 jours	953	490[4]	441[4]	...	...	...
28 days - 11 months - 28 jours - 11 mois............	34 424	17 654[4]	16 381[4]	...	...	...
28 days - less than 2 months - 28 jours - moins de 2 mois	4 770	2 509[4]	2 175[4]	...	...	...
2 months - 2 mois	5 786	2 784[4]	2 934[4]	...	...	...
3 months - 3 mois	5 472	2 783[4]	2 621[4]	...	...	...
4 months - 4 mois	3 711	1 958[4]	1 714[4]	...	...	...
5 months - 5 mois	3 041	1 548[4]	1 465[4]	...	...	...
6 months - 6 mois	2 704	1 393[4]	1 281[4]	...	...	...
7 months - 7 mois	2 258	1 181[4]	1 059[4]	...	...	...
8 months - 8 mois	1 948	1 020[4]	910[4]	...	...	...
9 months - 9 mois	1 811	954[4]	841[4]	...	...	...
10 months - 10 mois	1 544	803[4]	730[4]	...	...	...
11 months - 11 mois	1 379	721[4]	651[4]	...	...	...
AMERICA, NORTH - AMÉRIQUE DU NORD						
Aruba						
2015 (+C)						
Total...	6	5	1	...	...	...
Less than 1 day - Moins de 1 jour	1	1	-	...	...	...
1 - 6 days - 1 - 6 jours	1	1	-	...	...	...
7 - 27 days - 7 - 27 jours	-	-	-	...	...	...
7 - 13 days - 7 - 13 jours	-	-	-	...	...	...
14 - 20 days - 14 - 20 jours	-	-	-	...	...	...

16. Infant deaths and infant mortality rates by age and sex: latest available year, 2006 - 2015
Décès d'enfants de moins d'un an et taux de mortalité infantile selon l'âge et le sexe : dernière année disponible, 2006 - 2015 (continued - suite)

Continent, country or area, year, code[a] and age Continent, pays ou zone, année, code[a] et âge	Number - Nombre			Rate - Taux		
	Both sexes Les deux sexes	Male Masculin	Female Féminin	Both sexes Les deux sexes	Male Masculin	Female Féminin
AMERICA, NORTH - AMÉRIQUE DU NORD						
Aruba						
2015 (+C)						
21 - 27 days - 21 - 27 jours	1	1	-	...	...	...
28 days - 11 months - 28 jours - 11 mois...................................	3	2	1	...	...	...
28 days - less than 2 months - 28 jours - moins de 2 mois	-	-	-	...	...	...
2 months - 2 mois	1	-	1	...	...	...
3 months - 3 mois	-	-	-	...	...	...
4 months - 4 mois	-	-	-	...	...	...
5 months - 5 mois	-	-	-	...	...	...
6 months - 6 mois	-	-	-	...	...	...
7 months - 7 mois	-	-	-	...	...	...
8 months - 8 mois	-	-	-	...	...	...
9 months - 9 mois	1	1	-	...	...	...
10 months - 10 mois	-	-	-	...	...	...
11 months - 11 mois	1	1	-	...	...	...
Bahamas						
2012 (+C)						
Total..	57	26	31	...	...	...
Less than 1 day - Moins de 1 jour	-	-	-	...	...	...
1 - 6 days - 1 - 6 jours	18	10	8	...	...	...
7 - 27 days - 7 - 27 jours	19	8	11	...	...	...
7 - 13 days - 7 - 13 jours	16	6	10	...	...	...
14 - 20 days - 14 - 20 jours	2	1	1	...	...	...
21 - 27 days - 21 - 27 jours	1	1	-	...	...	...
28 days - 11 months - 28 jours - 11 mois..................................	20	8	12	...	...	...
28 days - less than 2 months - 28 jours - moins de 2 mois	9	5	4	...	...	...
2 months - 2 mois	3	1	2	...	...	...
3 months - 3 mois	2	1	1	...	...	...
4 months - 4 mois	3	-	3	...	...	...
5 months - 5 mois	-	-	-	...	...	...
6 months - 6 mois	-	-	-	...	...	...
7 months - 7 mois	1	-	1	...	...	...
8 months - 8 mois	1	1	-	...	...	...
9 months - 9 mois	1	-	1	...	...	...
10 months - 10 mois	-	-	-	...	...	...
11 months - 11 mois	-	-	-	...	...	...
Barbados - Barbade						
2007 (+C)						
Total..	31	18	13	...	...	...
Less than 1 day - Moins de 1 jour	-	1	1	...	...	...
1 - 6 days - 1 - 6 jours	10	8	18	...	...	...
7 - 27 days - 7 - 27 jours	6	4	2	...	...	...
7 - 20 days - 7 - 20 jours	6	4	2	...	...	...
21 - 27 days - 21 - 27 jours	-	-	-	...	...	...
28 days - 11 months - 28 jours - 11 mois..................................	4	2	2	...	...	...
28 days - 2 months - 28 jours - 2 mois	3	2	1	...	...	...
3 - 4 months - 3 - 4 mois	1	-	1	...	...	...
5 - 11 months - 5 - 11 mois	-	-	-	...	...	...
Unknown - Inconnu	2	2	-	...	...	...
Bermuda - Bermudes						
2012 (C)						
Total..	1	1	-	...	...	...
Less than 1 day - Moins de 1 jour	-	-	-	...	...	...
1 - 6 days - 1 - 6 jours	-	-	-	...	...	...
7 - 27 days - 7 - 27 jours	-	-	-	...	...	...
7 - 13 days - 7 - 13 jours	-	-	-	...	...	...
14 - 20 days - 14 - 20 jours	-	-	-	...	...	...
21 - 27 days - 21 - 27 jours	-	-	-	...	...	...
28 days - 11 months - 28 jours - 11 mois..................................	-	-	-	...	...	...
28 days - less than 2 months - 28 jours - moins de 2 mois	-	-	-	...	...	...
2 months - 2 mois	-	-	-	...	...	...
3 months - 3 mois	-	-	-	...	...	...
4 months - 4 mois	-	-	-	...	...	...
5 months - 5 mois	-	-	-	...	...	...
6 months - 6 mois	-	-	-	...	...	...
7 months - 7 mois	-	-	-	...	...	...
8 months - 8 mois	-	-	-	...	...	...
9 months - 9 mois..	-	-	-	...	...	...

16. Infant deaths and infant mortality rates by age and sex: latest available year, 2006 - 2015
Décès d'enfants de moins d'un an et taux de mortalité infantile selon l'âge et le sexe : dernière année disponible, 2006 - 2015 (continued - suite)

Continent, country or area, year, code[a] and age / Continent, pays ou zone, année, code[a] et âge	Number - Nombre			Rate - Taux		
	Both sexes Les deux sexes	Male Masculin	Female Féminin	Both sexes Les deux sexes	Male Masculin	Female Féminin
AMERICA, NORTH - AMÉRIQUE DU NORD						
Bermuda - Bermudes						
2012 (C)						
10 months - 10 mois	-	-	-	...	...	...
11 months - 11 mois	-	-	-	...	...	...
Canada[5]						
2006 (C)						
Total	1 771	983	788	5.0	5.4	4.6
Less than 1 day - Moins de 1 jour	888	481	407	2.5	2.6	2.4
1 - 6 days - 1 - 6 jours	194	110	84	0.5	0.6	0.5
7 - 27 days - 7 - 27 jours	214	123	91	0.6	0.7	0.5
7 - 13 days - 7 - 13 jours	110	62	48	0.3	0.3	0.3
14 - 20 days - 14 - 20 jours	60	34	26	0.2	0.2	♦0.2
21 - 27 days - 21 - 27 jours	44	27	17	0.1	♦0.1	♦0.1
28 days - 11 months - 28 jours - 11 mois	475	269	206	1.3	1.5	1.2
28 days - less than 2 months - 28 jours - moins de 2 mois	141	80	61	0.4	0.4	0.4
2 months - 2 mois	78	42	36	0.2	0.2	0.2
3 months - 3 mois	60	37	23	0.2	0.2	♦0.1
4 months - 4 mois	55	33	22	0.2	0.2	♦0.1
5 months - 5 mois	42	21	21	0.1	♦0.1	♦0.1
6 months - 6 mois	24	16	8	♦0.1	♦0.1	-
7 months - 7 mois	19	9	10	♦0.1	-	♦0.1
8 months - 8 mois	19	14	5	♦0.1	♦0.1	-
9 months - 9 mois	18	8	10	♦0.1	-	♦0.1
10 months - 10 mois	9	4	5	-	-	-
11 months - 11 mois	10	5	5	-	-	-
Cayman Islands - Îles Caïmanes						
2007 (C)						
Total	5	4	1	...	...	...
Less than 1 day - Moins de 1 jour	3	2	1	...	...	...
1 - 6 days - 1 - 6 jours	2	2	-	...	...	...
7 - 27 days - 7 - 27 jours	-	-	-	...	...	...
28 days - 11 months - 28 jours - 11 mois	-	-	-	...	...	...
Costa Rica						
2015* (C)						
Total	557	311	246	7.8	8.4	7.0
Less than 1 day - Moins de 1 jour	156	82	74	2.2	2.2	2.1
1 - 6 days - 1 - 6 jours	167	101	66	2.3	2.7	1.9
7 - 27 days - 7 - 27 jours	100	60	40	1.4	1.6	1.1
7 - 13 days - 7 - 13 jours	56	32	24	0.8	0.9	♦0.7
14 - 20 days - 14 - 20 jours	25	15	10	♦0.3	♦0.4	♦0.3
21 - 27 days - 21 - 27 jours	19	13	6	♦0.3	♦0.4	♦0.2
28 days - 11 months - 28 jours - 11 mois	134	68	66	1.9	1.8	1.9
28 days - less than 2 months - 28 jours - moins de 2 mois	35	18	17	0.5	♦0.5	♦0.5
2 months - 2 mois	30	15	15	0.4	♦0.4	♦0.4
3 months - 3 mois	12	4	8	♦0.2	♦0.1	♦0.2
4 months - 4 mois	10	6	4	♦0.1	♦0.2	♦0.1
5 months - 5 mois	10	6	4	♦0.1	♦0.2	♦0.1
6 months - 6 mois	13	8	5	♦0.2	♦0.2	♦0.1
7 months - 7 mois	6	4	2	♦0.1	♦0.1	♦0.1
8 months - 8 mois	6	3	3	♦0.1	♦0.1	♦0.1
9 months - 9 mois	5	2	3	♦0.1	♦0.1	♦0.1
10 months - 10 mois	5	2	3	♦0.1	♦0.1	♦0.1
11 months - 11 mois	2	-	2	-	-	♦0.1
Cuba						
2014 (C)						
Total	514	309	205	4.2	4.9	3.5
Less than 1 day - Moins de 1 jour	58	41	17	0.5	0.6	♦0.3
1 - 6 days - 1 - 6 jours	125	83	42	1.0	1.3	0.7
7 - 27 days - 7 - 27 jours	103	54	49	0.8	0.9	0.8
7 - 13 days - 7 - 13 jours	41	26	15	0.3	♦0.4	♦0.3
14 - 20 days - 14 - 20 jours	36	19	17	0.3	♦0.3	♦0.3
21 - 27 days - 21 - 27 jours	26	9	17	♦0.2	♦0.1	♦0.3
28 days - 11 months - 28 jours - 11 mois	228	131	97	1.9	2.1	1.6
28 days - less than 2 months - 28 jours - moins de 2 mois	74	41	33	0.6	0.6	0.6
2 months - 2 mois	39	23	16	0.3	♦0.4	♦0.3
3 months - 3 mois	30	18	12	0.2	♦0.3	♦0.2
4 months - 4 mois	21	16	5	♦0.2	♦0.3	♦0.1
5 months - 5 mois	16	9	7	♦0.1	♦0.1	♦0.1

16. Infant deaths and infant mortality rates by age and sex: latest available year, 2006 - 2015

Décès d'enfants de moins d'un an et taux de mortalité infantile selon l'âge et le sexe : dernière année disponible, 2006 - 2015 (continued - suite)

Continent, country or area, year, code[a] and age / Continent, pays ou zone, année, code[a] et âge	Number - Nombre			Rate - Taux		
	Both sexes Les deux sexes	Male Masculin	Female Féminin	Both sexes Les deux sexes	Male Masculin	Female Féminin
AMERICA, NORTH - AMÉRIQUE DU NORD						
Cuba						
2014 (C)						
6 months - 6 mois	12	6	6	♦0.1	♦0.1	♦0.1
7 months - 7 mois	5	3	2	-	-	-
8 months - 8 mois	8	4	4	♦0.1	♦0.1	♦0.1
9 months - 9 mois	13	7	6	♦0.1	♦0.1	♦0.1
10 months - 10 mois	6	4	2	-	♦0.1	-
11 months - 11 mois	4	-	4	-	-	♦0.1
Curaçao						
2011 (C)						
Total	15	6	9	...	...	...
Less than 1 day - Moins de 1 jour	3	2	1	...	...	...
1 - 6 days - 1 - 6 jours	5	1	4	...	...	...
7 - 27 days - 7 - 27 jours	2	2	-	...	...	...
7 - 13 days - 7 - 13 jours	1	1	-	...	...	...
14 - 20 days - 14 - 20 jours	1	1	-	...	...	...
21 - 27 days - 21 - 27 jours	-	-	-	...	...	...
28 days - 11 months - 28 jours - 11 mois	5	1	4	...	...	...
28 days - less than 2 months - 28 jours - moins de 2 mois	2	-	2	...	...	...
2 months - 2 mois	-	-	-	...	...	...
3 months - 3 mois	1	-	1	...	...	...
4 months - 4 mois	2	1	1	...	...	...
5 months - 5 mois	-	-	-	...	...	...
6 months - 6 mois	-	-	-	...	...	...
7 months - 7 mois	-	-	-	...	...	...
8 months - 8 mois	-	-	-	...	...	...
9 months - 9 mois	-	-	-	...	...	...
10 months - 10 mois	-	-	-	...	...	...
11 months - 11 mois	-	-	-	...	...	...
Dominican Republic - République dominicaine						
2014 (U)						
Total	830	494[4]	334[4]	...	...	...
Less than 1 day - Moins de 1 jour	157	87[4]	69[4]	...	...	...
1 - 6 days - 1 - 6 jours	216	143[4]	72[4]	...	...	...
7 - 27 days - 7 - 27 jours	120	70[4]	50[4]	...	...	...
7 - 13 days - 7 - 13 jours	60	35[4]	25[4]	...	...	...
14 - 20 days - 14 - 20 jours	33	17[4]	16[4]	...	...	...
21 - 27 days - 21 - 27 jours	27	18[4]	9[4]	...	...	...
28 days - 11 months - 28 jours - 11 mois	329	186	143	...	...	...
28 days - less than 2 months - 28 jours - moins de 2 mois	75	43[4]	32[4]	...	...	...
2 months - 2 mois	43	28[4]	15[4]	...	...	...
3 months - 3 mois	43	26[4]	17[4]	...	...	...
4 months - 4 mois	42	23[4]	19[4]	...	...	...
5 months - 5 mois	27	12[4]	15[4]	...	...	...
6 months - 6 mois	27	16[4]	11[4]	...	...	...
7 months - 7 mois	16	9[4]	7[4]	...	...	...
8 months - 8 mois	15	8[4]	7[4]	...	...	...
9 months - 9 mois	12	5[4]	7[4]	...	...	...
10 months - 10 mois	12	6[4]	6[4]	...	...	...
11 months - 11 mois	17	10[4]	7[4]	...	...	...
Unknown - Inconnu	8	8[4]	-[4]	...	...	...
El Salvador[6]						
2012 (C)						
Total	795	446	349	7.2	7.8	6.5
Less than 1 day - Moins de 1 jour	102	50	52	0.9	0.9	1.0
1 - 6 days - 1 - 6 jours	144	78	66	1.3	1.4	1.2
7 - 27 days - 7 - 27 jours	129	81	48	1.2	1.4	0.9
7 - 13 days - 7 - 13 jours	56	34	22	0.5	0.6	♦0.4
14 - 20 days - 14 - 20 jours	38	28	10	0.3	♦0.5	♦0.2
21 - 27 days - 21 - 27 jours	35	19	16	0.3	♦0.3	♦0.3
28 days - 11 months - 28 jours - 11 mois	420	237	183	3.8	4.1	3.4
28 days - less than 2 months - 28 jours - moins de 2 mois	95	54	41	0.9	0.9	0.8
2 months - 2 mois	63	35	28	0.6	0.6	♦0.5
3 months - 3 mois	48	25	23	0.4	♦0.4	♦0.4
4 months - 4 mois	57	35	22	0.5	0.6	♦0.4
5 months - 5 mois	30	17	13	0.3	♦0.3	♦0.2
6 months - 6 mois	23	12	11	♦0.2	♦0.2	♦0.2

16. Infant deaths and infant mortality rates by age and sex: latest available year, 2006 - 2015

Décès d'enfants de moins d'un an et taux de mortalité infantile selon l'âge et le sexe : dernière année disponible, 2006 - 2015 (continued - suite)

Continent, country or area, year, code[a] and age Continent, pays ou zone, année, code[a] et âge	Number - Nombre			Rate - Taux		
	Both sexes Les deux sexes	Male Masculin	Female Féminin	Both sexes Les deux sexes	Male Masculin	Female Féminin
AMERICA, NORTH - AMÉRIQUE DU NORD						
El Salvador[6]						
2012 (C)						
7 months - 7 mois	27	15	12	♦0.2	♦0.3	♦0.2
8 months - 8 mois	23	12	11	♦0.2	♦0.2	♦0.2
9 months - 9 mois	12	6	6	♦0.1	♦0.1	♦0.1
10 months - 10 mois	16	11	5	♦0.1	♦0.2	♦0.1
11 months - 11 mois	26	15	11	♦0.2	♦0.3	♦0.2
Greenland - Groenland[3]						
2006 (C)						
Total	13	7	6	...	...	...
Less than 1 day - Moins de 1 jour	8	5	3	...	...	...
1 - 6 days - 1 - 6 jours	-	-	-	...	...	...
7 - 27 days - 7 - 27 jours	-	-	-	...	...	...
28 days - 11 months - 28 jours - 11 mois	5	2	3	...	...	...
28 days - less than 2 months - 28 jours - moins de 2 mois	5	2	3	...	...	...
2 - 11 months - 2 - 11 mois	-	-	-	...	...	...
Guatemala						
2011 (C)						
Total	7 413	4 202	3 211	19.8	22.1	17.5
Less than 1 day - Moins de 1 jour	123	76	47	0.3	0.4	0.3
1 - 6 days - 1 - 6 jours	1 481	860	621	4.0	4.5	3.4
7 - 27 days - 7 - 27 jours	1 684	938	746	4.5	4.9	4.1
7 - 13 days - 7 - 13 jours	813	451	362	2.2	2.4	2.0
14 - 20 days - 14 - 20 jours	521	288	233	1.4	1.5	1.3
21 - 27 days - 21 - 27 jours	350	199	151	0.9	1.0	0.8
28 days - 11 months - 28 jours - 11 mois	4 125	2 328	1 797	11.0	12.3	9.8
28 days - less than 2 months - 28 jours - moins de 2 mois	1 198	694	504	3.2	3.7	2.7
2 months - 2 mois	685	396	289	1.8	2.1	1.6
3 months - 3 mois	475	283	192	1.3	1.5	1.0
4 months - 4 mois	345	196	149	0.9	1.0	0.8
5 months - 5 mois	290	159	131	0.8	0.8	0.7
6 months - 6 mois	265	146	119	0.7	0.8	0.6
7 months - 7 mois	245	129	116	0.7	0.7	0.6
8 months - 8 mois	200	102	98	0.5	0.5	0.5
9 months - 9 mois	207	115	92	0.6	0.6	0.5
10 months - 10 mois	209	107	102	0.6	0.6	0.6
11 months - 11 mois	6	1	5	-	-	-
Martinique[7]						
2007 (C)						
Total	43	26	17	...	...	...
Less than 1 day - Moins de 1 jour	18	10	8	...	...	...
1 - 6 days - 1 - 6 jours	8	7	1	...	...	...
7 - 27 days - 7 - 27 jours	9	3	6	...	...	...
7 - 13 days - 7 - 13 jours	5	1	4	...	...	...
14 - 20 days - 14 - 20 jours	3	2	1	...	...	...
21 - 27 days - 21 - 27 jours	1	-	1	...	...	...
28 days - 11 months - 28 jours - 11 mois	8	6	2	...	...	...
28 days - less than 2 months - 28 jours - moins de 2 mois	-	-	-	...	...	...
2 months - 2 mois	5	3	2	...	...	...
3 months - 3 mois	-	-	-	...	...	...
4 months - 4 mois	1	1	-	...	...	...
5 months - 5 mois	-	-	-	...	...	...
6 months - 6 mois	-	-	-	...	...	...
7 months - 7 mois	1	1	-	...	...	...
8 months - 8 mois	-	-	-	...	...	...
9 - 11 months - 9 - 11 mois	1	1	-	...	...	...
Mexico - Mexique[8]						
2014 (+C)						
Total	26 385	14 872[4]	11 403[4]	...	...	...
Less than 1 day - Moins de 1 jour	5 064	2 846[4]	2 168[4]	...	...	...
1 - 6 days - 1 - 6 jours	6 332	3 645[4]	2 658[4]	...	...	...
7 - 27 days - 7 - 27 jours	5 048	2 811[4]	2 216[4]	...	...	...
7 - 13 days - 7 - 13 jours	2 605	1 463[4]	1 130[4]	...	...	...
14 - 20 days - 14 - 20 jours	1 482	828[4]	649[4]	...	...	...
21 - 27 days - 21 - 27 jours	961	520[4]	437[4]	...	...	...
28 days - 11 months - 28 jours - 11 mois	8 048	4 465	3 577	...	...	...
28 days - less than 2 months - 28 jours - moins de 2 mois	2 822	1 625[4]	1 192[4]	...	...	...

Continent, country or area, year, code[a] and age / Continent, pays ou zone, année, code[a] et âge	Number - Nombre			Rate - Taux		
	Both sexes Les deux sexes	Male Masculin	Female Féminin	Both sexes Les deux sexes	Male Masculin	Female Féminin
AMERICA, NORTH - AMÉRIQUE DU NORD						
Mexico - Mexique[8]						
2014 (+C)						
2 months - 2 mois	1 196	650[4]	545[4]	...	...	...
3 months - 3 mois	935	507[4]	428[4]	...	...	...
4 months - 4 mois	671	373[4]	298[4]	...	...	...
5 months - 5 mois	605	331[4]	274[4]	...	...	...
6 months - 6 mois	466	270[4]	196[4]	...	...	...
7 months - 7 mois	406	220[4]	186[4]	...	...	...
8 months - 8 mois	343	178[4]	165[4]	...	...	...
9 months - 9 mois	300	158[4]	142[4]	...	...	...
10 months - 10 mois	302	152[4]	150[4]	...	...	...
11 months - 11 mois	2	1[4]	1[4]	...	...	...
Montserrat						
2014 (+C)						
Total	-	-	-	...	...	...
Less than 1 day - Moins de 1 jour	-	-	-	...	...	...
1 - 6 days - 1 - 6 jours	-	-	-	...	...	...
7 - 27 days - 7 - 27 jours	-	-	-	...	...	...
7 - 13 days - 7 - 13 jours	-	-	-	...	...	...
14 - 20 days - 14 - 20 jours	-	-	-	...	...	...
21 - 27 days - 21 - 27 jours	-	-	-	...	...	...
28 days - 11 months - 28 jours - 11 mois	-	-	-	...	...	...
28 days - less than 2 months - 28 jours - moins de 2 mois	-	-	-	...	...	...
2 months - 2 mois	-	-	-	...	...	...
3 months - 3 mois	-	-	-	...	...	...
4 months - 4 mois	-	-	-	...	...	...
5 months - 5 mois	-	-	-	...	...	...
6 months - 6 mois	-	-	-	...	...	...
7 months - 7 mois	-	-	-	...	...	...
8 months - 8 mois	-	-	-	...	...	...
9 months - 9 mois	-	-	-	...	...	...
10 months - 10 mois	-	-	-	...	...	...
11 months - 11 mois	-	-	-	...	...	...
Nicaragua						
2008 (+U)						
Total	1 932	1 123	809	...	...	...
Less than 1 day - Moins de 1 jour	386	219	167	...	...	...
1 - 6 days - 1 - 6 jours	664	418	246	...	...	...
7 - 27 days - 7 - 27 jours	277	151	126	...	...	...
7 - 13 days - 7 - 13 jours	156	89	67	...	...	...
14 - 20 days - 14 - 20 jours	74	41	33	...	...	...
21 - 27 days - 21 - 27 jours	47	21	26	...	...	...
28 days - 11 months - 28 jours - 11 mois	591	326	265	...	...	...
28 days - less than 2 months - 28 jours - moins de 2 mois	169	86	83	...	...	...
2 months - 2 mois	116	74	42	...	...	...
3 months - 3 mois	66	38	28	...	...	...
4 months - 4 mois	49	29	20	...	...	...
5 months - 5 mois	45	22	23	...	...	...
6 months - 6 mois	27	13	14	...	...	...
7 months - 7 mois	36	18	18	...	...	...
8 months - 8 mois	27	17	10	...	...	...
9 months - 9 mois	18	8	10	...	...	...
10 months - 10 mois	21	9	12	...	...	...
11 months - 11 mois	17	12	5	...	...	...
Panama						
2014 (U)						
Total	1 036	572	464	...	...	...
Less than 1 day - Moins de 1 jour	137	68	69	...	...	...
1 - 6 days - 1 - 6 jours	307	183	124	...	...	...
7 - 27 days - 7 - 27 jours	153	86	67	...	...	...
7 - 13 days - 7 - 13 jours	78	48	30	...	...	...
14 - 20 days - 14 - 20 jours	40	20	20	...	...	...
21 - 27 days - 21 - 27 jours	35	18	17	...	...	...
28 days - 11 months - 28 jours - 11 mois	439	235	204	...	...	...
28 days - less than 2 months - 28 jours - moins de 2 mois	119	68	51	...	...	...
2 months - 2 mois	69	39	30	...	...	...
3 months - 3 mois	44	25	19	...	...	...

16. Infant deaths and infant mortality rates by age and sex: latest available year, 2006 - 2015
Décès d'enfants de moins d'un an et taux de mortalité infantile selon l'âge et le sexe : dernière année disponible, 2006 - 2015 (continued - suite)

Continent, country or area, year, code[a] and age / Continent, pays ou zone, année, code[a] et âge	Number - Nombre			Rate - Taux		
	Both sexes Les deux sexes	Male Masculin	Female Féminin	Both sexes Les deux sexes	Male Masculin	Female Féminin
AMERICA, NORTH - AMÉRIQUE DU NORD						
Panama						
2014 (U)						
4 months - 4 mois	39	21	18	...	...	...
5 months - 5 mois	32	14	18	...	...	...
6 months - 6 mois	40	20	20	...	...	...
7 months - 7 mois	23	11	12	...	...	...
8 months - 8 mois	18	13	5	...	...	...
9 months - 9 mois	11	6	5	...	...	...
10 months - 10 mois	20	7	13	...	...	...
11 months - 11 mois	24	11	13	...	...	...
Puerto Rico - Porto Rico						
2015 (C)						
Total	222	125	97	7.1	7.8	6.4
Less than 1 day - Moins de 1 jour	35	19	16	1.1	♦1.2	♦1.1
1 - 6 days - 1 - 6 jours	62	38	24	2.0	2.4	♦1.6
7 - 27 days - 7 - 27 jours	50	25	25	1.6	♦1.6	♦1.6
7 - 13 days - 7 - 13 jours	26	8	18	♦0.8	♦0.5	♦1.2
14 - 20 days - 14 - 20 jours	15	11	4	♦0.5	♦0.7	♦0.3
21 - 27 days - 21 - 27 jours	9	6	3	♦0.3	♦0.4	♦0.2
28 days - 11 months - 28 jours - 11 mois	58	31	27	1.9	1.9	♦1.8
28 days - less than 2 months - 28 jours - moins de 2 mois	3	2	1	♦0.1	♦0.1	♦0.1
2 months - 2 mois	18	9	9	♦0.6	♦0.6	♦0.6
3 months - 3 mois	5	1	4	♦0.2	♦0.1	♦0.3
4 months - 4 mois	10	7	3	♦0.3	♦0.4	♦0.2
5 months - 5 mois	2	2	-	♦0.1	♦0.1	-
6 months - 6 mois	5	1	4	♦0.2	♦0.1	♦0.3
7 months - 7 mois	3	2	1	♦0.1	♦0.1	♦0.1
8 months - 8 mois	5	4	1	♦0.2	♦0.2	♦0.1
9 months - 9 mois	4	2	2	♦0.1	♦0.1	♦0.1
10 months - 10 mois	2	-	2	♦0.1	-	♦0.1
11 months - 11 mois	1	1	-	-	♦0.1	-
Unknown - Inconnu	17	12	5	♦0.5	♦0.7	♦0.3
Saint Vincent and the Grenadines - Saint-Vincent-et-les Grenadines						
2014 (C)						
Total	29	19	10	...	...	...
Less than 1 day - Moins de 1 jour	3	3	-	...	...	...
1 - 6 days - 1 - 6 jours	8	6	2	...	...	...
7 - 27 days - 7 - 27 jours	9	4	5	...	...	...
7 - 13 days - 7 - 13 jours	6	4	2	...	...	...
14 - 20 days - 14 - 20 jours	3	-	3	...	...	...
21 - 27 days - 21 - 27 jours	-	-	-	...	...	...
28 days - 11 months - 28 jours - 11 mois	9	6	3	...	...	...
28 days - less than 2 months - 28 jours - moins de 2 mois	4	2	2	...	...	...
2 months - 2 mois	1	-	1	...	...	...
3 months - 3 mois	1	1	-	...	...	...
4 months - 4 mois	2	2	-	...	...	...
5 months - 5 mois	-	-	-	...	...	...
6 months - 6 mois	-	-	-	...	...	...
7 months - 7 mois	1	1	-	...	...	...
8 months - 8 mois	-	-	-	...	...	...
9 months - 9 mois	-	-	-	...	...	...
10 months - 10 mois	-	-	-	...	...	...
11 months - 11 mois	-	-	-	...	...	...
Trinidad and Tobago - Trinité-et-Tobago						
2009 (C)						
Total	275	150	125	15.3	16.5	14.1
Less than 1 day - Moins de 1 jour	65	35	30	3.6	3.9	3.4
1 - 6 days - 1 - 6 jours	81	48	33	4.5	5.3	3.7
7 - 27 days - 7 - 27 jours	51	30	21	2.8	3.3	♦2.4
7 - 13 days - 7 - 13 jours	26	15	11	♦1.4	♦1.7	♦1.2
14 - 20 days - 14 - 20 jours	11	6	5	♦0.6	♦0.7	♦0.6
21 - 27 days - 21 - 27 jours	14	9	5	♦0.8	♦1.0	♦0.6
28 days - 11 months - 28 jours - 11 mois	78	37	41	4.3	4.1	4.6
28 days - less than 2 months - 28 jours - moins de 2 mois	33	17	16	1.8	♦1.9	♦1.8
2 months - 2 mois	11	4	7	♦0.6	♦0.4	♦0.8
3 - 5 months - 3 - 5 mois	12	5	7	♦0.7	♦0.6	♦0.8
6 - 8 months - 6 - 8 mois	12	9	3	♦0.7	♦1.0	♦0.3
9 - 11 months - 9 - 11 mois	10	2	8	♦0.6	♦0.2	♦0.9

16. Infant deaths and infant mortality rates by age and sex: latest available year, 2006 - 2015
Décès d'enfants de moins d'un an et taux de mortalité infantile selon l'âge et le sexe : dernière année disponible, 2006 - 2015 (continued - suite)

Continent, country or area, year, code[a] and age Continent, pays ou zone, année, code[a] et âge	Number - Nombre			Rate - Taux		
	Both sexes Les deux sexes	Male Masculin	Female Féminin	Both sexes Les deux sexes	Male Masculin	Female Féminin
AMERICA, NORTH - AMÉRIQUE DU NORD						
United States of America - États-Unis d'Amérique						
2014 (C)						
Total..	23 215	12 886	10 329	5.8	6.3	5.3
Less than 1 day - Moins de 1 jour	9 814	5 464	4 350	2.5	2.7	2.2
1 - 6 days - 1 - 6 jours	2 942	1 620	1 322	0.7	0.8	0.7
7 - 27 days - 7 - 27 jours	2 964	1 587	1 377	0.7	0.8	0.7
7 - 13 days - 7 - 13 jours	1 387	749	638	0.3	0.4	0.3
14 - 20 days - 14 - 20 jours	886	479	407	0.2	0.2	0.2
21 - 27 days - 21 - 27 jours	691	359	332	0.2	0.2	0.2
28 days - 11 months - 28 jours - 11 mois................	7 495	4 215	3 280	1.9	2.1	1.7
28 days - less than 2 months - 28 jours - moins de 2 mois	1 975	1 094	881	0.5	0.5	0.5
2 months - 2 mois	1 352	751	601	0.3	0.4	0.3
3 months - 3 mois	1 104	633	471	0.3	0.3	0.2
4 months - 4 mois	775	433	342	0.2	0.2	0.2
5 months - 5 mois	652	386	266	0.2	0.2	0.1
6 months - 6 mois	441	258	183	0.1	0.1	0.1
7 months - 7 mois	318	178	140	0.1	0.1	0.1
8 months - 8 mois	295	163	132	0.1	0.1	0.1
9 months - 9 mois	207	109	98	0.1	0.1	0.1
10 months - 10 mois................................	189	104	85	-	0.1	-
11 months - 11 mois	187	106	81	-	0.1	-
AMERICA, SOUTH - AMÉRIQUE DU SUD						
Argentina - Argentine						
2006 (C)						
Total..	8 986	5 063[4]	3 911[4]	12.9	14.1	11.7
Less than 7 days - Moins de 7 jours	4 312	2 465[4]	1 838[4]	6.2	6.8	5.5
7 - 27 days - 7 - 27 jours	1 591	898[4]	691[4]	2.3	2.5	2.1
28 days - 11 months - 28 jours - 11 mois................	3 083	1 700[4]	1 382[4]	4.4	4.7	4.1
Brazil - Brésil						
2014 (U)						
Total..	31 679[9]	17 695	13 899	...	...	...
Less than 1 day - Moins de 1 jour	7 005[9]	3 901	3 049	...	...	...
1 - 6 days - 1 - 6 jours	9 148[9]	5 267	3 861	...	...	...
7 - 27 days - 7 - 27 jours	5 516[9]	3 033	2 476	...	...	...
7 - 13 days - 7 - 13 jours	2 975[9]	1 624	1 347	...	...	...
14 - 20 days - 14 - 20 jours	1 489[9]	839	649	...	...	...
21 - 27 days - 21 - 27 jours	1 052[9]	570	480	...	...	...
28 days - 11 months - 28 jours - 11 mois................	10 010	5 494	4 513	...	...	...
28 days - less than 2 months - 28 jours - moins de 2 mois	3 113[9]	1 718	1 394	...	...	...
2 months - 2 mois	1 700[9]	941	759	...	...	...
3 months - 3 mois	1 170[9]	615	555	...	...	...
4 months - 4 mois	911[9]	504	407	...	...	...
5 months - 5 mois	696[9]	390	306	...	...	...
6 months - 6 mois	579[9]	324	254	...	...	...
7 months - 7 mois	475[9]	267	208	...	...	...
8 months - 8 mois	409[9]	218	191	...	...	...
9 months - 9 mois	381[9]	209	171	...	...	...
10 months - 10 mois................................	302[9]	153	149	...	...	...
11 months - 11 mois	274[9]	155	119	...	...	...
Chile - Chili						
2013 (C)						
Total..	1 692	949[10]	725[10]	7.0	7.7	6.1
Less than 1 day - Moins de 1 jour	700	392[10]	294[10]	2.9	3.2	2.5
1 - 6 days - 1 - 6 jours	314	176[10]	134[10]	1.3	1.4	1.1
7 - 27 days - 7 - 27 jours	239	145	94	1.0	1.2	0.8
7 - 13 days - 7 - 13 jours	120	73	47	0.5	0.6	0.4
14 - 20 days - 14 - 20 jours	63	39	24	0.3	0.3	♦0.2
21 - 27 days - 21 - 27 jours	56	33	23	0.2	0.3	♦0.2
28 days - 11 months - 28 jours - 11 mois................	439	236	203	1.8	1.9	1.7
28 days - less than 2 months - 28 jours - moins de 2 mois	130	74	56	0.5	0.6	0.5
2 months - 2 mois	70	32	38	0.3	0.3	0.3
3 months - 3 mois	48	29	19	0.2	♦0.2	♦0.2
4 months - 4 mois	53	28	25	0.2	♦0.2	♦0.2

16. Infant deaths and infant mortality rates by age and sex: latest available year, 2006 - 2015
Décès d'enfants de moins d'un an et taux de mortalité infantile selon l'âge et le sexe : dernière année disponible, 2006 - 2015 (continued - suite)

Continent, country or area, year, code[a] and age / Continent, pays ou zone, année, code[a] et âge	Number - Nombre			Rate - Taux		
	Both sexes Les deux sexes	Male Masculin	Female Féminin	Both sexes Les deux sexes	Male Masculin	Female Féminin
AMERICA, SOUTH - AMÉRIQUE DU SUD						
Chile - Chili						
2013 (C)						
5 months - 5 mois	31	14	17	0.1	♦0.1	♦0.1
6 months - 6 mois	19	10	9	♦0.1	♦0.1	♦0.1
7 months - 7 mois	23	10	13	♦0.1	♦0.1	♦0.1
8 months - 8 mois	22	14	8	♦0.1	♦0.1	♦0.1
9 months - 9 mois	13	9	4	♦0.1	♦0.1	-
10 months - 10 mois	15	8	7	♦0.1	♦0.1	♦0.1
11 months - 11 mois	15	8	7	♦0.1	♦0.1	♦0.1
Colombia - Colombie[11]						
2014 (U)						
Total	7 589	4 284	3 305	...	...	...
Less than 1 day - Moins de 1 jour	1 565	871	694	...	...	...
1 - 6 days - 1 - 6 jours	1 725	1 023	702	...	...	...
7 - 27 days - 7 - 27 jours	1 510	866	644	...	...	...
7 - 13 days - 7 - 13 jours	805	464	341	...	...	...
14 - 20 days - 14 - 20 jours	408	222	186	...	...	...
21 - 27 days - 21 - 27 jours	297	180	117	...	...	...
28 days - 11 months - 28 jours - 11 mois	2 787	1 523	1 264	...	...	...
28 days - less than 2 months - 28 jours - moins de 2 mois	726	408	318	...	...	...
2 months - 2 mois	487	279	208	...	...	...
3 months - 3 mois	342	189	153	...	...	...
4 months - 4 mois	254	121	133	...	...	...
5 months - 5 mois	218	128	90	...	...	...
6 months - 6 mois	185	98	87	...	...	...
7 months - 7 mois	165	89	76	...	...	...
8 months - 8 mois	127	67	60	...	...	...
9 months - 9 mois	104	55	49	...	...	...
10 months - 10 mois	72	34	38	...	...	...
11 months - 11 mois	107	55	52	...	...	...
Unknown - Inconnu	2	1	1	...	...	...
Ecuador - Équateur[12]						
2014 (U)						
Total	2 821	1 572	1 249	...	...	...
Less than 1 day - Moins de 1 jour	367	203	164	...	...	...
1 - 6 days - 1 - 6 jours	711	398	313	...	...	...
7 - 27 days - 7 - 27 jours	455	265	190	...	...	...
7 - 13 days - 7 - 13 jours	216	128	88	...	...	...
14 - 20 days - 14 - 20 jours	127	77	50	...	...	...
21 - 27 days - 21 - 27 jours	112	60	52	...	...	...
28 days - 11 months - 28 jours - 11 mois	1 288	706	582	...	...	...
28 days - less than 2 months - 28 jours - moins de 2 mois	426	242	184	...	...	...
2 months - 2 mois	177	89	88	...	...	...
3 months - 3 mois	155	79	76	...	...	...
4 months - 4 mois	109	57	52	...	...	...
5 months - 5 mois	88	54	34	...	...	...
6 months - 6 mois	89	50	39	...	...	...
7 months - 7 mois	64	35	29	...	...	...
8 months - 8 mois	50	28	22	...	...	...
9 months - 9 mois	47	25	22	...	...	...
10 months - 10 mois	43	23	20	...	...	...
11 months - 11 mois	40	24	16	...	...	...
French Guiana - Guyane française						
2007 (C)						
Total	73	39	34	...	...	...
Less than 1 day - Moins de 1 jour	18	10	8	...	...	...
1 - 6 days - 1 - 6 jours	15	5	10	...	...	...
7 - 27 days - 7 - 27 jours	17	12	5	...	...	...
7 - 13 days - 7 - 13 jours	9	5	4	...	...	...
14 - 20 days - 14 - 20 jours	3	3	-	...	...	...
21 - 27 days - 21 - 27 jours	5	4	1	...	...	...
28 days - 11 months - 28 jours - 11 mois	23	12	11	...	...	...
28 days - less than 2 months - 28 jours - moins de 2 mois	1	-	1	...	...	...
2 months - 2 mois	7	4	3	...	...	...
3 months - 3 mois	4	1	3	...	...	...
4 months - 4 mois	2	1	1	...	...	...
5 months - 5 mois	2	2	-	...	...	...
6 months - 6 mois	2	1	1	...	...	...

16. Infant deaths and infant mortality rates by age and sex: latest available year, 2006 - 2015
Décès d'enfants de moins d'un an et taux de mortalité infantile selon l'âge et le sexe : dernière année disponible, 2006 - 2015 (continued - suite)

Continent, country or area, year, code[a] and age / Continent, pays ou zone, année, code[a] et âge	Number - Nombre			Rate - Taux		
	Both sexes Les deux sexes	Male Masculin	Female Féminin	Both sexes Les deux sexes	Male Masculin	Female Féminin
AMERICA, SOUTH - AMÉRIQUE DU SUD						
French Guiana - Guyane française						
2007 (C)						
7 months - 7 mois	1	1	-	...	...	...
8 months - 8 mois	1	1	-	...	...	...
9 months - 9 mois	2	1	1	...	...	...
10 months - 10 mois	-	-	-	...	...	...
11 months - 11 mois	1	-	1	...	...	...
Paraguay						
2006 (U)						
Total	549	...	...	...	...	...
Less than 28 days - Moins de 28 jours	270	...	...	...	...	...
28 days - 11 months - 28 jours - 11 mois	279	...	...	...	...	...
Peru - Pérou[13]						
2014 (+U)						
Total	4 243	2 366	1 877	...	...	...
Less than 1 day - Moins de 1 jour	692	390	302	...	...	...
1 - 6 days - 1 - 6 jours	1 038	615	423	...	...	...
7 - 27 days - 7 - 27 jours	633	355	278	...	...	...
7 - 13 days - 7 - 13 jours	309	173	136	...	...	...
14 - 20 days - 14 - 20 jours	163	91	72	...	...	...
21 - 27 days - 21 - 27 jours	161	91	70	...	...	...
28 days - 11 months - 28 jours - 11 mois	1 880	1 006	874	...	...	...
28 days - less than 2 months - 28 jours - moins de 2 mois	483	266	217	...	...	...
2 months - 2 mois	374	200	174	...	...	...
3 months - 3 mois	230	122	108	...	...	...
4 months - 4 mois	164	95	69	...	...	...
5 months - 5 mois	115	61	54	...	...	...
6 months - 6 mois	110	59	51	...	...	...
7 months - 7 mois	102	51	51	...	...	...
8 months - 8 mois	82	44	38	...	...	...
9 months - 9 mois	80	40	40	...	...	...
10 months - 10 mois	69	34	35	...	...	...
11 months - 11 mois	71	34	37	...	...	...
Venezuela (Bolivarian Republic of) - Venezuela (République bolivarienne du)						
2007 (C)						
Total	6 340	3 715	2 625	10.3	11.7	8.8
Less than 28 days - Moins de 28 jours	4 379	2 599	1 780	7.1	8.2	6.0
28 days - 11 months - 28 jours - 11 mois	1 961	1 116	845	3.2	3.5	2.8
28 days - less than 2 months - 28 jours - moins de 2 mois	455	258	197	0.7	0.8	0.7
2 months - 2 mois	325	182	143	0.5	0.6	0.5
3 months - 3 mois	231	136	95	0.4	0.4	0.3
4 months - 4 mois	190	119	71	0.3	0.4	0.2
5 months - 5 mois	157	87	70	0.3	0.3	0.2
6 months - 6 mois	153	89	64	0.2	0.3	0.2
7 months - 7 mois	104	57	47	0.2	0.2	0.2
8 months - 8 mois	122	63	59	0.2	0.2	0.2
9 months - 9 mois	77	39	38	0.1	0.1	0.1
10 months - 10 mois	81	50	31	0.1	0.2	0.1
11 months - 11 mois	66	36	30	0.1	0.1	0.1
ASIA - ASIE						
Armenia - Arménie[14]						
2014 (C)						
Total	376	212	164	8.7	9.3	8.1
Less than 1 day - Moins de 1 jour	67	37	30	1.6	1.6	1.5
1 - 6 days - 1 - 6 jours	140	80	60	3.3	3.5	3.0
7 - 27 days - 7 - 27 jours	80	49	31	1.9	2.1	1.5
28 days - 11 months - 28 jours - 11 mois	89	46	43	2.1	2.0	2.1
Azerbaijan - Azerbaïdjan[14]						
2014 (+C)						
Total	1 655	976	679	9.7	10.7	8.6
Less than 1 day - Moins de 1 jour	242	156	86	1.4	1.7	1.1
1 - 6 days - 1 - 6 jours	735	424	311	4.3	4.6	3.9
7 - 27 days - 7 - 27 jours	55	32	23	0.3	0.4	♦0.3
28 days - 11 months - 28 jours - 11 mois	623	364	259	3.7	4.0	3.3

16. Infant deaths and infant mortality rates by age and sex: latest available year, 2006 - 2015
Décès d'enfants de moins d'un an et taux de mortalité infantile selon l'âge et le sexe : dernière année disponible, 2006 - 2015 (continued - suite)

Continent, country or area, year, code[a] and age Continent, pays ou zone, année, code[a] et âge	Number - Nombre			Rate - Taux		
	Both sexes Les deux sexes	Male Masculin	Female Féminin	Both sexes Les deux sexes	Male Masculin	Female Féminin

ASIA - ASIE

Bahrain - Bahreïn[15]
2014 (C)

Total..	218	113	105	10.4	10.5	10.3
Less than 1 day - Moins de 1 jour	25	12	13	♦1.2	♦1.1	♦1.3
1 - 6 days - 1 - 6 jours	55	34	21	2.6	3.2	♦2.1
7 - 27 days - 7 - 27 jours	23	15	8	♦1.1	♦1.4	♦0.8
7 - 13 days - 7 - 13 jours	8	6	2	♦0.4	♦0.6	♦0.2
14 - 20 days - 14 - 20 jours	7	4	3	♦0.3	♦0.4	♦0.3
21 - 27 days - 21 - 27 jours	8	5	3	♦0.4	♦0.5	♦0.3
28 days - 11 months - 28 jours - 11 mois..................	80	36	44	3.8	3.3	4.3
28 days - less than 2 months - 28 jours - moins de 2 mois	34	11	23	1.6	♦1.0	♦2.3
2 months - 2 mois..	12	5	7	♦0.6	♦0.5	♦0.7
3 months - 3 mois..	6	4	2	♦0.3	♦0.4	♦0.2
4 months - 4 mois..	8	5	3	♦0.4	♦0.5	♦0.3
5 months - 5 mois..	8	5	3	♦0.4	♦0.5	♦0.3
6 months - 6 mois..	5	1	4	♦0.2	♦0.1	♦0.4
7 months - 7 mois..	3	2	1	♦0.1	♦0.2	♦0.1
8 months - 8 mois..	1	1	-	-	♦0.1	-
9 months - 9 mois..	1	1	-	-	♦0.1	-
10 months - 10 mois...	1	-	1	-	-	♦0.1
11 months - 11 mois...	1	1	-	-	♦0.1	-
Unknown - Inconnu	35	16	19	1.7	♦1.5	♦1.9

Bangladesh
2010 (U)

Total..	104 591	55 178	49 413	...	...	...
1 - 6 days - 1 - 6 jours	56 108	30 276	25 832	...	...	...
7 - 27 days - 7 - 27 jours	17 576	9 234	8 342	...	...	...
7 - 13 days - 7 - 13 jours	8 488	4 491	3 997	...	...	...
14 - 20 days - 14 - 20 jours	4 845	2 546	2 299	...	...	...
21 - 27 days - 21 - 27 jours	4 243	2 197	2 046	...	...	...
28 days - 11 months - 28 jours - 11 mois..................	30 907	15 668	15 239	...	...	...
28 days - less than 2 months - 28 jours - moins de 2 mois	7 377	3 906	3 471	...	...	...
2 months - 2 mois..	5 234	2 674	2 560	...	...	...
3 months - 3 mois..	4 381	2 248	2 133	...	...	...
4 months - 4 mois..	2 628	1 333	1 295	...	...	...
5 months - 5 mois..	1 188	606	582	...	...	...
6 months - 6 mois..	2 123	1 050	1 073	...	...	...
7 months - 7 mois..	1 361	669	692	...	...	...
8 months - 8 mois..	1 905	918	987	...	...	...
9 months - 9 mois..	1 420	696	724	...	...	...
10 months - 10 mois...	1 188	566	622	...	...	...
11 months - 11 mois...	2 102	1 002	1 100	...	...	...

China, Hong Kong SAR - Chine, Hong Kong RAS
2014 (C)

Total..	103	44	59	1.7	1.4	2.0
Less than 1 day - Moins de 1 jour	13	8	5	♦0.2	♦0.2	♦0.2
1 - 6 days - 1 - 6 jours	40	15	25	0.6	♦0.5	♦0.8
7 - 27 days - 7 - 27 jours	19	10	9	♦0.3	♦0.3	♦0.3
7 - 13 days - 7 - 13 jours	11	4	7	♦0.2	♦0.1	♦0.2
14 - 20 days - 14 - 20 jours	5	4	1	♦0.1	♦0.1	-
21 - 27 days - 21 - 27 jours	3	2	1	-	♦0.1	-
28 days - 11 months - 28 jours - 11 mois..................	31	11	20	0.5	♦0.3	♦0.7
28 days - less than 2 months - 28 jours - moins de 2 mois	9	2	7	♦0.1	♦0.1	♦0.2
2 months - 2 mois..	3	2	1	-	♦0.1	-
3 months - 3 mois..	3	-	3	-	-	♦0.1
4 months - 4 mois..	4	1	3	♦0.1	-	♦0.1
5 months - 5 mois..	1	1	-	-	-	-
6 months - 6 mois..	3	-	3	-	-	♦0.1
7 months - 7 mois..	1	1	-	-	-	-
8 months - 8 mois..	4	3	1	♦0.1	♦0.1	-
9 months - 9 mois..	3	1	2	-	-	♦0.1
10 months - 10 mois...	-	-	-	-	-	-
11 months - 11 mois...	-	-	-	-	-	-

China, Macao SAR - Chine, Macao RAS
2010 (C)

Total..	15	7	8	...	...	...
Less than 1 day - Moins de 1 jour	7	3	4	...	...	...
1 - 6 days - 1 - 6 jours	4	2	2	...	...	...

16. Infant deaths and infant mortality rates by age and sex: latest available year, 2006 - 2015
Décès d'enfants de moins d'un an et taux de mortalité infantile selon l'âge et le sexe : dernière année disponible, 2006 - 2015 (continued - suite)

Continent, country or area, year, code[a] and age Continent, pays ou zone, année, code[a] et âge	Number - Nombre			Rate - Taux		
	Both sexes Les deux sexes	Male Masculin	Female Féminin	Both sexes Les deux sexes	Male Masculin	Female Féminin
ASIA - ASIE						
China, Macao SAR - Chine, Macao RAS						
2010 (C)						
7 - 27 days - 7 - 27 jours	2	1	1	...	...	...
7 - 13 days - 7 - 13 jours	-	-	-	...	...	...
14 - 20 days - 14 - 20 jours	1	-	1	...	...	...
21 - 27 days - 21 - 27 jours	1	1	-	...	...	...
28 days - 11 months - 28 jours - 11 mois	2	1	1	...	...	...
28 days - less than 2 months - 28 jours - moins de 2 mois	1	-	1	...	...	...
2 months - 2 mois	-	-	-	...	...	...
3 months - 3 mois	-	-	-	...	...	...
4 months - 4 mois	1	1	-	...	...	...
5 months - 5 mois	-	-	-	...	...	...
6 months - 6 mois	-	-	-	...	...	...
7 months - 7 mois	-	-	-	...	...	...
8 months - 8 mois	-	-	-	...	...	...
9 months - 9 mois	-	-	-	...	...	...
10 months - 10 mois	-	-	-	...	...	...
11 months - 11 mois	-	-	-	...	...	...
Cyprus - Chypre[16]						
2011 (C)						
Total	30	18	12	...	...	...
Less than 1 day - Moins de 1 jour	10	6	4	...	...	...
1 - 6 days - 1 - 6 jours	8	4	4	...	...	...
7 - 27 days - 7 - 27 jours	3	2	1	...	...	...
28 days - 11 months - 28 jours - 11 mois	9	6	3	...	...	...
Georgia - Géorgie[14]						
2014 (C)						
Total	578	316	262	9.5	10.1	8.9
Less than 1 day - Moins de 1 jour	89	40	49	1.5	1.3	1.7
1 - 6 days - 1 - 6 jours	161	94	67	2.7	3.0	2.3
7 - 27 days - 7 - 27 jours	143	81	62	2.4	2.6	2.1
28 days - 11 months - 28 jours - 11 mois	185	101	84	3.1	3.2	2.9
Israel - Israël[17]						
2015 (C)						
Total	552	296[4]	252[4]	3.1	...	...
Less than 1 day - Moins de 1 jour	107	58[4]	48[4]	0.6	...	...
1 - 6 days - 1 - 6 jours	145	73[4]	70[4]	0.8	...	...
7 - 27 days - 7 - 27 jours	126	70[4]	56[4]	0.7	...	...
7 - 13 days - 7 - 13 jours	63	35[4]	28[4]	0.4	...	...
14 - 20 days - 14 - 20 jours	40	22[4]	18[4]	0.2	...	...
21 - 27 days - 21 - 27 jours	23	13[4]	10[4]	♦0.1	...	...
28 days - 11 months - 28 jours - 11 mois	174	95	78	1.0	...	...
28 days - less than 2 months - 28 jours - moins de 2 mois	42	21[4]	21[4]	0.2	...	...
2 months - 2 mois	27	15[4]	11[4]	♦0.2	...	...
3 months - 3 mois	34	23[4]	11[4]	0.2	...	...
4 months - 4 mois	16	7[4]	9[4]	♦0.1	...	...
5 months - 5 mois	11	6[4]	5[4]	♦0.1	...	...
6 months - 6 mois	9	5[4]	4[4]	♦0.1	...	...
7 months - 7 mois	7	5[4]	2[4]	-	...	...
8 months - 8 mois	6	3[4]	3[4]	-	...	...
9 months - 9 mois	7	3[4]	4[4]	-	...	...
10 months - 10 mois	10	4[4]	6[4]	♦0.1	...	...
11 months - 11 mois	5	3[4]	2[4]	-	...	...
Japan - Japon[18]						
2014 (C)						
Total	2 080	1 110	970	2.1	2.2	2.0
Less than 1 day - Moins de 1 jour	476	251	225	0.5	0.5	0.5
1 - 6 days - 1 - 6 jours	235	122	113	0.2	0.2	0.2
7 - 27 days - 7 - 27 jours	241	136	105	0.2	0.3	0.2
7 - 13 days - 7 - 13 jours	101	58	43	0.1	0.1	0.1
14 - 20 days - 14 - 20 jours	68	40	28	0.1	0.1	♦0.1
21 - 27 days - 21 - 27 jours	72	38	34	0.1	0.1	0.1
28 days - 11 months - 28 jours - 11 mois	1 128	601	527	1.1	1.2	1.1
28 days - less than 2 months - 28 jours - moins de 2 mois	238	115	123	0.2	0.2	0.3
2 months - 2 mois	158	85	73	0.2	0.2	0.2
3 months - 3 mois	130	73	57	0.1	0.1	0.1
4 months - 4 mois	120	68	52	0.1	0.1	0.1

16. Infant deaths and infant mortality rates by age and sex: latest available year, 2006 - 2015
Décès d'enfants de moins d'un an et taux de mortalité infantile selon l'âge et le sexe : dernière année disponible, 2006 - 2015 (continued - suite)

Continent, country or area, year, code[a] and age	Number - Nombre			Rate - Taux		
Continent, pays ou zone, année, code[a] et âge	Both sexes Les deux sexes	Male Masculin	Female Féminin	Both sexes Les deux sexes	Male Masculin	Female Féminin
ASIA - ASIE						
Japan - Japon[18]						
2014 (C)						
5 months - 5 mois	98	50	48	0.1	0.1	0.1
6 months - 6 mois	85	54	31	0.1	0.1	0.1
7 months - 7 mois	77	45	32	0.1	0.1	0.1
8 months - 8 mois	74	35	39	0.1	0.1	0.1
9 months - 9 mois	57	31	26	0.1	0.1	◆0.1
10 months - 10 mois	44	23	21	-	-	-
11 months - 11 mois	47	22	25	-	-	◆0.1
Kazakhstan[14]						
2013 (C)						
Total	4 367	2 502	1 865	11.3	12.5	10.0
Less than 1 day - Moins de 1 jour	381	209	172	1.0	1.0	0.9
1 - 6 days - 1 - 6 jours	1 439	869	570	3.7	4.3	3.0
7 - 27 days - 7 - 27 jours	927	529	398	2.4	2.6	2.1
7 - 13 days - 7 - 13 jours	534	325	209	1.4	1.6	1.1
14 - 20 days - 14 - 20 jours	233	127	106	0.6	0.6	0.6
21 - 27 days - 21 - 27 jours	160	77	83	0.4	0.4	0.4
28 days - 11 months - 28 jours - 11 mois	1 620	895	725	4.2	4.5	3.9
28 days - less than 2 months - 28 jours - moins de 2 mois	568	330	238	1.5	1.7	1.3
2 months - 2 mois	228	136	92	0.6	0.7	0.5
3 months - 3 mois	161	97	64	0.4	0.5	0.3
4 months - 4 mois	131	63	68	0.3	0.3	0.4
5 months - 5 mois	117	53	64	0.3	0.3	0.3
6 months - 6 mois	118	62	56	0.3	0.3	0.3
7 months - 7 mois	88	47	41	0.2	0.2	0.2
8 months - 8 mois	65	34	31	0.2	0.2	0.2
9 months - 9 mois	61	26	35	0.2	◆0.1	0.2
10 months - 10 mois	42	21	21	0.1	◆0.1	◆0.1
11 months - 11 mois	41	26	15	0.1	◆0.1	◆0.1
Kuwait - Koweït						
2014 (C)						
Total	456	257	199	7.4	8.2	6.7
Less than 1 day - Moins de 1 jour	128	76	52	2.1	2.4	1.7
1 - 6 days - 1 - 6 jours	82	50	32	1.3	1.6	1.1
7 - 27 days - 7 - 27 jours	102	61	41	1.7	1.9	1.4
7 - 13 days - 7 - 13 jours	53	33	20	0.9	1.0	◆0.7
14 - 20 days - 14 - 20 jours	27	16	11	◆0.4	◆0.5	◆0.4
21 - 27 days - 21 - 27 jours	22	12	10	◆0.4	◆0.4	◆0.3
28 days - 11 months - 28 jours - 11 mois	144	70	74	2.3	2.2	2.5
28 days - less than 2 months - 28 jours - moins de 2 mois	56	28	28	0.9	◆0.9	◆0.9
2 months - 2 mois	19	10	9	◆0.3	◆0.3	◆0.3
3 months - 3 mois	21	7	14	◆0.3	◆0.2	◆0.5
4 months - 4 mois	10	8	2	◆0.2	◆0.3	◆0.1
5 months - 5 mois	13	6	7	◆0.2	◆0.2	◆0.2
6 months - 6 mois	4	1	3	◆0.1	-	◆0.1
7 months - 7 mois	4	2	2	◆0.1	◆0.1	◆0.1
8 months - 8 mois	5	2	3	◆0.1	◆0.1	◆0.1
9 months - 9 mois	2	-	2	-	-	◆0.1
10 months - 10 mois	5	2	3	◆0.1	◆0.1	◆0.1
11 months - 11 mois	5	4	1	◆0.1	◆0.1	-
Kyrgyzstan - Kirghizstan						
2015* (C)						
Total	2 945	1 654	1 291	18.0	19.5	16.4
Less than 1 day - Moins de 1 jour	804	457	347	4.9	5.4	4.4
1 - 6 days - 1 - 6 jours	1 184	666	518	7.2	7.9	6.6
7 - 27 days - 7 - 27 jours	300	183	117	1.8	2.2	1.5
7 - 13 days - 7 - 13 jours	168	104	64	1.0	1.2	0.8
14 - 20 days - 14 - 20 jours	77	46	31	0.5	0.5	0.4
21 - 27 days - 21 - 27 jours	55	33	22	0.3	0.4	◆0.3
28 days - 11 months - 28 jours - 11 mois	657	348	309	4.0	4.1	3.9
28 days - less than 2 months - 28 jours - moins de 2 mois	121	65	56	0.7	0.8	0.7
2 months - 2 mois	99	64	35	0.6	0.8	0.4
3 months - 3 mois	87	40	47	0.5	0.5	0.6
4 months - 4 mois	74	45	29	0.5	0.5	◆0.4
5 months - 5 mois	56	29	27	0.3	◆0.3	◆0.3
6 months - 6 mois	49	25	24	0.3	◆0.3	◆0.3
7 months - 7 mois	50	20	30	0.3	◆0.2	0.4

16. Infant deaths and infant mortality rates by age and sex: latest available year, 2006 - 2015
Décès d'enfants de moins d'un an et taux de mortalité infantile selon l'âge et le sexe : dernière année disponible, 2006 - 2015 (continued - suite)

Continent, country or area, year, code[a] and age Continent, pays ou zone, année, code[a] et âge	Number - Nombre			Rate - Taux		
	Both sexes Les deux sexes	Male Masculin	Female Féminin	Both sexes Les deux sexes	Male Masculin	Female Féminin
ASIA - ASIE						
Kyrgyzstan - Kirghizstan						
2015* (C)						
8 months - 8 mois..	45	25	20	0.3	♦0.3	♦0.3
9 months - 9 mois..	22	10	12	♦0.1	♦0.1	♦0.2
10 months - 10 mois..	25	14	11	♦0.2	♦0.2	♦0.1
11 months - 11 mois..	29	11	18	♦0.2	♦0.1	♦0.2
Maldives						
2014 (C)						
Total..	59	32	27	...	...	...
Less than 1 day - Moins de 1 jour	19	11	8	...	...	...
1 - 6 days - 1 - 6 jours	14	10	4	...	...	...
7 - 27 days - 7 - 27 jours	4	1	3	...	...	...
7 - 13 days - 7 - 13 jours	1	-	1	...	...	...
14 - 20 days - 14 - 20 jours	1	1	-	...	...	...
21 - 27 days - 21 - 27 jours	2	-	2	...	...	...
28 days - 11 months - 28 jours - 11 mois...................	22	10	12	...	...	...
28 days - less than 2 months - 28 jours - moins de 2 mois	13	6	7	...	...	...
2 months - 2 mois	1	-	1	...	...	...
3 months - 3 mois	-	-	-	...	...	...
4 months - 4 mois	-	-	-	...	...	...
5 months - 5 mois	3	1	2	...	...	...
6 months - 6 mois	-	-	-	...	...	...
7 months - 7 mois	2	2	-	...	...	...
8 months - 8 mois	3	1	2	...	...	...
9 months - 9 mois	-	-	-	...	...	...
10 months - 10 mois	-	-	-	...	...	...
11 months - 11 mois	-	-	-	...	...	...
Mongolia - Mongolie						
2015 (+C)						
Total..	1 234	723	511	15.0	17.2	12.8
Less than 7 days - Moins de 7 jours..........................	629	374	255	7.7	8.9	6.4
7 - 27 days - 7 - 27 jours	194	107	87	2.4	2.5	2.2
28 days - 11 months - 28 jours - 11 mois....................	411	242	169	5.0	5.7	4.2
Myanmar[19]						
2013 (+U)						
Total..	11 516	6 379	5 137	...	...	...
Less than 1 day - Moins de 1 jour	281	159	122	...	...	...
1 - 6 days - 1 - 6 jours	4 616	2 603	2 013	...	...	...
7 - 27 days - 7 - 27 jours	1 333	753	580	...	...	...
7 - 13 days - 7 - 13 jours	753	435	318	...	...	...
14 - 20 days - 14 - 20 jours	337	202	135	...	...	...
21 - 27 days - 21 - 27 jours	244	117	127	...	...	...
28 days - 11 months - 28 jours - 11 mois...................	5 285	2 864	2 422	...	...	...
28 days - less than 2 months - 28 jours - moins de 2 mois	1 123	638	486	...	...	...
2 months - 2 mois	1 053	615	438	...	...	...
3 months - 3 mois	735	395	341	...	...	...
4 months - 4 mois	456	229	227	...	...	...
5 months - 5 mois	387	198	189	...	...	...
6 months - 6 mois	362	207	155	...	...	...
7 months - 7 mois	304	153	151	...	...	...
8 months - 8 mois	268	134	134	...	...	...
9 months - 9 mois	221	110	111	...	...	...
10 months - 10 mois	194	100	93	...	...	...
11 months - 11 mois	182	85	97	...	...	...
Oman[20]						
2014 (U)						
Total..	645	326	319	...	...	...
Less than 1 day - Moins de 1 jour	161	87	74	...	...	...
1 - 6 days - 1 - 6 jours	176	101	75	...	...	...
7 - 27 days - 7 - 27 jours	91	40	51	...	...	...
7 - 13 days - 7 - 13 jours	43	15	28	...	...	...
14 - 20 days - 14 - 20 jours	33	18	15	...	...	...
21 - 27 days - 21 - 27 jours	15	7	8	...	...	...
28 days - 11 months - 28 jours - 11 mois...................	203	95	108	...	...	...
28 days - less than 2 months - 28 jours - moins de 2 mois	51	24	27	...	...	...
2 months - 2 mois	37	18	19	...	...	...
3 months - 3 mois	16	9	7	...	...	...
4 months - 4 mois	14	7	7	...	...	...

16. Infant deaths and infant mortality rates by age and sex: latest available year, 2006 - 2015
Décès d'enfants de moins d'un an et taux de mortalité infantile selon l'âge et le sexe : dernière année disponible, 2006 - 2015 (continued - suite)

Continent, country or area, year, code[a] and age Continent, pays ou zone, année, code[a] et âge	Number - Nombre			Rate - Taux		
	Both sexes Les deux sexes	Male Masculin	Female Féminin	Both sexes Les deux sexes	Male Masculin	Female Féminin
ASIA - ASIE						
Oman[20]						
2014 (U)						
5 months - 5 mois	18	9	9	...	...	...
6 months - 6 mois	12	8	4	...	...	...
7 months - 7 mois	19	8	11	...	...	...
8 months - 8 mois	12	5	7	...	...	...
9 months - 9 mois	10	4	6	...	...	...
10 months - 10 mois	5	2	3	...	...	...
11 months - 11 mois	9	1	8	...	...	...
Unknown - Inconnu	14	3	11	...	...	...
Pakistan[21]						
2007 (|)						
Total	288 191	167 402	120 789	75.2	83.5	66.2
Less than 1 day - Moins de 1 jour	11 990	8 027	3 963	3.1	4.0	2.2
1 - 6 days - 1 - 6 jours	115 664	74 312	41 352	30.2	37.0	22.7
7 - 27 days - 7 - 27 jours	39 726	23 382	16 344	10.4	11.7	9.0
7 - 13 days - 7 - 13 jours	21 846	13 191	8 655	5.7	6.6	4.7
14 - 20 days - 14 - 20 jours	16 376	9 475	6 901	4.3	4.7	3.8
21 - 27 days - 21 - 27 jours	1 504	716	788	0.4	0.4	0.4
28 days - 11 months - 28 jours - 11 mois	120 811	61 681	59 130	31.5	30.8	32.4
28 days - less than 2 months - 28 jours - moins de 2 mois	23 563	9 553	14 010	6.2	4.8	7.7
2 months - 2 mois	10 666	7 662	3 004	2.8	3.8	1.6
3 months - 3 mois	16 938	9 692	7 246	4.4	4.8	4.0
4 months - 4 mois	10 577	4 135	6 442	2.8	2.1	3.5
5 months - 5 mois	14 148	8 863	5 285	3.7	4.4	2.9
6 months - 6 mois	17 012	6 641	10 371	4.4	3.3	5.7
7 months - 7 mois	8 480	4 209	4 271	2.2	2.1	2.3
8 months - 8 mois	6 221	5 116	1 105	1.6	2.6	0.6
9 months - 9 mois	7 602	3 819	3 783	2.0	1.9	2.1
10 months - 10 mois	3 546	1 291	2 255	0.9	0.6	1.2
11 months - 11 mois	2 058	700	1 358	0.5	0.3	0.7
Philippines						
2013 (C)						
Total	21 992	12 699	9 293	12.5	13.8	11.0
Less than 1 day - Moins de 1 jour	3 112	1 733	1 379	1.8	1.9	1.6
1 - 6 days - 1 - 6 jours	6 136	3 686	2 450	3.5	4.0	2.9
7 - 27 days - 7 - 27 jours	2 836	1 637	1 199	1.6	1.8	1.4
7 - 13 days - 7 - 13 jours	1 416	811	605	0.8	0.9	0.7
14 - 20 days - 14 - 20 jours	776	470	306	0.4	0.5	0.4
21 - 27 days - 21 - 27 jours	644	356	288	0.4	0.4	0.3
28 days - 11 months - 28 jours - 11 mois	9 908	5 643	4 265	5.6	6.2	5.1
28 days - less than 2 months - 28 jours - moins de 2 mois	2 388	1 407	981	1.4	1.5	1.2
2 months - 2 mois	1 308	754	554	0.7	0.8	0.7
3 months - 3 mois	948	528	420	0.5	0.6	0.5
4 months - 4 mois	925	524	401	0.5	0.6	0.5
5 months - 5 mois	814	427	387	0.5	0.5	0.5
6 months - 6 mois	738	412	326	0.4	0.4	0.4
7 months - 7 mois	669	357	312	0.4	0.4	0.4
8 months - 8 mois	640	368	272	0.4	0.4	0.3
9 months - 9 mois	539	319	220	0.3	0.3	0.3
10 months - 10 mois	494	299	195	0.3	0.3	0.2
11 months - 11 mois	445	248	197	0.3	0.3	0.2
Qatar						
2013 (C)						
Total	157	97	60	6.6	8.0	5.2
Less than 1 day - Moins de 1 jour	-	-	-	-	-	-
1 - 6 days - 1 - 6 jours	72	49	23	3.0	4.0	♦2.0
7 - 27 days - 7 - 27 jours	23	16	7	♦1.0	♦1.3	♦0.6
7 - 13 days - 7 - 13 jours	14	9	5	♦0.6	♦0.7	♦0.4
14 - 20 days - 14 - 20 jours	5	3	2	♦0.2	♦0.2	♦0.2
21 - 27 days - 21 - 27 jours	4	4	-	♦0.2	♦0.3	-
28 days - 11 months - 28 jours - 11 mois	62	32	30	2.6	2.6	2.6
28 days - less than 2 months - 28 jours - moins de 2 mois	11	7	4	♦0.5	♦0.6	♦0.3
2 months - 2 mois	16	8	8	♦0.7	♦0.7	♦0.7
3 months - 3 mois	10	5	5	♦0.4	♦0.4	♦0.4
4 months - 4 mois	7	4	3	♦0.3	♦0.3	♦0.3
5 months - 5 mois	4	3	1	♦0.2	♦0.2	♦0.1
6 months - 6 mois	3	1	2	♦0.1	♦0.1	♦0.2

16. Infant deaths and infant mortality rates by age and sex: latest available year, 2006 - 2015
Décès d'enfants de moins d'un an et taux de mortalité infantile selon l'âge et le sexe : dernière année disponible, 2006 - 2015 (continued - suite)

Continent, country or area, year, code[a] and age / Continent, pays ou zone, année, code[a] et âge	Number - Nombre			Rate - Taux		
	Both sexes Les deux sexes	Male Masculin	Female Féminin	Both sexes Les deux sexes	Male Masculin	Female Féminin
ASIA - ASIE						
Qatar						
2013 (C)						
7 months - 7 mois	4	3	1	♦0.2	♦0.2	♦0.1
8 months - 8 mois	1	-	1	-	-	♦0.1
9 months - 9 mois	3	1	2	♦0.1	♦0.1	♦0.2
10 months - 10 mois	1	-	1	-	-	♦0.1
11 months - 11 mois	2	-	2	♦0.1	-	♦0.2
Republic of Korea - République de Corée[22]						
2014 (C)						
Total	1 305	715	590	3.0	3.2	2.8
Less than 1 day - Moins de 1 jour	174	89	85	0.4	0.4	0.4
1 - 6 days - 1 - 6 jours	294	163	131	0.7	0.7	0.6
7 - 27 days - 7 - 27 jours	275	156	119	0.6	0.7	0.6
7 - 13 days - 7 - 13 jours	132	74	58	0.3	0.3	0.3
14 - 20 days - 14 - 20 jours	79	45	34	0.2	0.2	0.2
21 - 27 days - 21 - 27 jours	64	37	27	0.1	0.2	♦0.1
28 days - 11 months - 28 jours - 11 mois	562	307	255	1.3	1.4	1.2
28 days - less than 2 months - 28 jours - moins de 2 mois	162	91	71	0.4	0.4	0.3
2 months - 2 mois	85	41	44	0.2	0.2	0.2
3 months - 3 mois	70	38	32	0.2	0.2	0.2
4 months - 4 mois	58	35	23	0.1	0.2	♦0.1
5 months - 5 mois	47	24	23	0.1	♦0.1	♦0.1
6 months - 6 mois	38	22	16	0.1	♦0.1	♦0.1
7 months - 7 mois	27	18	9	♦0.1	♦0.1	-
8 months - 8 mois	32	18	14	0.1	♦0.1	♦0.1
9 months - 9 mois	15	6	9	-	-	-
10 months - 10 mois	13	6	7	-	-	-
11 months - 11 mois	15	8	7	-	-	-
Singapore - Singapour						
2015 (+C)						
Total	84	56	28	...	...	...
Less than 1 day - Moins de 1 jour	10	5	5	...	...	...
1 - 6 days - 1 - 6 jours	18	12	6	...	...	...
7 - 27 days - 7 - 27 jours	13	8	5	...	...	...
7 - 13 days - 7 - 13 jours	4	2	2	...	...	...
14 - 20 days - 14 - 20 jours	4	2	2	...	...	...
21 - 27 days - 21 - 27 jours	5	4	1	...	...	...
28 days - 11 months - 28 jours - 11 mois	43	31	12	...	...	...
28 days - less than 2 months - 28 jours - moins de 2 mois	13	11	2	...	...	...
2 months - 2 mois	11	7	4	...	...	...
3 months - 3 mois	4	2	2	...	...	...
4 months - 4 mois	5	5	-	...	...	...
5 months - 5 mois	2	1	1	...	...	...
6 months - 6 mois	2	1	1	...	...	...
7 months - 7 mois	3	2	1	...	...	...
8 months - 8 mois	1	1	-	...	...	...
9 months - 9 mois	2	1	1	...	...	...
10 months - 10 mois	-	-	-	...	...	...
11 months - 11 mois	-	-	-	...	...	...
Unknown - Inconnu	-	-	-	...	...	...
State of Palestine - État de Palestine						
2007 (U)						
Total	794	420	374	...	...	...
Less than 1 day - Moins de 1 jour	42	24	18	...	...	...
1 - 6 days - 1 - 6 jours	183	113	70	...	...	...
7 - 27 days - 7 - 27 jours	156	79	77	...	...	...
7 - 13 days - 7 - 13 jours	79	44	35	...	...	...
14 - 20 days - 14 - 20 jours	47	19	28	...	...	...
21 - 27 days - 21 - 27 jours	30	16	14	...	...	...
28 days - 11 months - 28 jours - 11 mois	413	204	209	...	...	...
28 days - less than 2 months - 28 jours - moins de 2 mois	111	64	47	...	...	...
2 months - 2 mois	56	25	31	...	...	...
3 months - 3 mois	50	28	22	...	...	...
4 months - 4 mois	32	14	18	...	...	...
5 months - 5 mois	40	20	20	...	...	...
6 months - 6 mois	28	17	11	...	...	...
7 months - 7 mois	19	8	11	...	...	...
8 months - 8 mois	19	10	9	...	...	...

16. Infant deaths and infant mortality rates by age and sex: latest available year, 2006 - 2015
Décès d'enfants de moins d'un an et taux de mortalité infantile selon l'âge et le sexe : dernière année disponible, 2006 - 2015 (continued - suite)

Continent, country or area, year, code[a] and age Continent, pays ou zone, année, code[a] et âge	Number - Nombre			Rate - Taux		
	Both sexes Les deux sexes	Male Masculin	Female Féminin	Both sexes Les deux sexes	Male Masculin	Female Féminin
ASIA - ASIE						
State of Palestine - État de Palestine						
2007 (U)						
9 months - 9 mois	22	8	14	...	...	...
10 months - 10 mois	21	5	16	...	...	...
11 months - 11 mois	15	5	10	...	...	...
Tajikistan - Tadjikistan[14]						
2008 (U)						
Total	2 480	1 478	1 002	...	...	...
Less than 1 day - Moins de 1 jour	420	255	165	...	...	...
1 - 6 days - 1 - 6 jours	699	443	256	...	...	...
7 - 27 days - 7 - 27 jours	248	140	108	...	...	...
7 - 13 days - 7 - 13 jours	145	87	58	...	...	...
14 - 20 days - 14 - 20 jours	63	33	30	...	...	...
21 - 27 days - 21 - 27 jours	40	20	20	...	...	...
28 days - 11 months - 28 jours - 11 mois	1 113	640	473	...	...	...
28 days - less than 2 months - 28 jours - moins de 2 mois	180	103	77	...	...	...
2 months - 2 mois	155	92	63	...	...	...
3 months - 3 mois	138	77	61	...	...	...
4 months - 4 mois	111	71	40	...	...	...
5 months - 5 mois	106	56	50	...	...	...
6 months - 6 mois	106	62	44	...	...	...
7 months - 7 mois	75	43	32	...	...	...
8 months - 8 mois	79	49	30	...	...	...
9 months - 9 mois	56	23	33	...	...	...
10 months - 10 mois	56	39	17	...	...	...
11 months - 11 mois	51	25	26	...	...	...
Thailand - Thaïlande						
2011 (+U)						
Total	5 275	2 964	2 311	...	...	...
Less than 1 day - Moins de 1 jour	587	326	261	...	...	...
1 - 6 days - 1 - 6 jours	1 612	931	681	...	...	...
7 - 27 days - 7 - 27 jours	987	534	453	...	...	...
7 - 13 days - 7 - 13 jours	527	285	242	...	...	...
14 - 20 days - 14 - 20 jours	276	149	127	...	...	...
21 - 27 days - 21 - 27 jours	184	100	84	...	...	...
28 days - 11 months - 28 jours - 11 mois	2 089	1 173	916	...	...	...
28 days - less than 2 months - 28 jours - moins de 2 mois	556	329	227	...	...	...
2 months - 2 mois	360	203	157	...	...	...
3 months - 3 mois	249	152	97	...	...	...
4 months - 4 mois	193	98	95	...	...	...
5 months - 5 mois	160	91	69	...	...	...
6 months - 6 mois	141	74	67	...	...	...
7 months - 7 mois	103	55	48	...	...	...
8 months - 8 mois	106	51	55	...	...	...
9 months - 9 mois	87	41	46	...	...	...
10 months - 10 mois	77	45	32	...	...	...
11 months - 11 mois	57	34	23	...	...	...
Turkey - Turquie						
2014 (C)						
Total	14 821	8 135	6 686	11.1	11.8	10.3
Less than 1 day - Moins de 1 jour	2 188	1 201	987	1.6	1.7	1.5
1 - 6 days - 1 - 6 jours	4 672	2 646	2 026	3.5	3.9	3.1
7 - 27 days - 7 - 27 jours	2 863	1 608	1 255	2.1	2.3	1.9
7 - 13 days - 7 - 13 jours	1 508	861	647	1.1	1.3	1.0
14 - 20 days - 14 - 20 jours	790	426	364	0.6	0.6	0.6
21 - 27 days - 21 - 27 jours	565	321	244	0.4	0.5	0.4
28 days - 11 months - 28 jours - 11 mois	5 098	2 680	2 418	3.8	3.9	3.7
28 days - less than 2 months - 28 jours - moins de 2 mois	1 546	811	735	1.2	1.2	1.1
2 months - 2 mois	786	401	385	0.6	0.6	0.6
3 months - 3 mois	579	303	276	0.4	0.4	0.4
4 months - 4 mois	458	256	202	0.3	0.4	0.3
5 months - 5 mois	418	236	182	0.3	0.3	0.3
6 months - 6 mois	304	154	150	0.2	0.2	0.2
7 months - 7 mois	252	136	116	0.2	0.2	0.2
8 months - 8 mois	234	103	131	0.2	0.1	0.2
9 months - 9 mois	178	95	83	0.1	0.1	0.1
10 months - 10 mois	153	85	68	0.1	0.1	0.1
11 months - 11 mois	190	100	90	0.1	0.1	0.1

16. Infant deaths and infant mortality rates by age and sex: latest available year, 2006 - 2015
Décès d'enfants de moins d'un an et taux de mortalité infantile selon l'âge et le sexe : dernière année disponible, 2006 - 2015 (continued - suite)

Continent, country or area, year, code[a] and age / Continent, pays ou zone, année, code[a] et âge	Number - Nombre			Rate - Taux		
	Both sexes Les deux sexes	Male Masculin	Female Féminin	Both sexes Les deux sexes	Male Masculin	Female Féminin

ASIA - ASIE

Uzbekistan - Ouzbékistan
2014 (+C)

Total	7 688	4 406	3 282	10.7	11.8	9.5
Less than 1 day - Moins de 1 jour	1 233	679	554	1.7	1.8	1.6
1 - 6 days - 1 - 6 jours	2 679	1 590	1 089	3.7	4.3	3.2
7 - 27 days - 7 - 27 jours	1 169	665	504	1.6	1.8	1.5
7 - 13 days - 7 - 13 jours	720	432	288	1.0	1.2	0.8
14 - 20 days - 14 - 20 jours	253	129	124	0.4	0.3	0.4
21 - 27 days - 21 - 27 jours	196	104	92	0.3	0.3	0.3
28 days - 11 months - 28 jours - 11 mois	2 607	1 472	1 135	3.6	3.9	3.3
28 days - less than 2 months - 28 jours - moins de 2 mois	761	476	285	1.1	1.3	0.8
2 months - 2 mois	359	214	145	0.5	0.6	0.4
3 months - 3 mois	244	132	112	0.3	0.4	0.3
4 months - 4 mois	234	124	110	0.3	0.3	0.3
5 months - 5 mois	197	106	91	0.3	0.3	0.3
6 months - 6 mois	185	99	86	0.3	0.3	0.2
7 months - 7 mois	164	88	76	0.2	0.2	0.2
8 months - 8 mois	141	68	73	0.2	0.2	0.2
9 months - 9 mois	128	49	79	0.2	0.1	0.2
10 months - 10 mois	100	57	43	0.1	0.2	0.1
11 months - 11 mois	94	59	35	0.1	0.2	0.1

EUROPE

Åland Islands - Îles d'Åland
2014 (C)

Total	-	-	-	...	...	...

Albania - Albanie
2013 (C)

Total	282	171	111	7.9	9.2	6.5
Less than 1 day - Moins de 1 jour	100	56	44	2.8	3.0	2.6
1 - 6 days - 1 - 6 jours	59	36	23	1.7	1.9	♦1.3
7 - 27 days - 7 - 27 jours	40	26	14	1.1	♦1.4	♦0.8
7 - 13 days - 7 - 13 jours	25	15	10	♦0.7	♦0.8	♦0.6
14 - 20 days - 14 - 20 jours	11	7	4	♦0.3	♦0.4	♦0.2
21 - 27 days - 21 - 27 jours	4	4	-	♦0.1	♦0.2	-
28 days - 11 months - 28 jours - 11 mois	83	53	30	2.3	2.8	1.8
28 days - less than 2 months - 28 jours - moins de 2 mois	29	22	7	♦0.8	♦1.2	♦0.4
2 months - 2 mois	15	8	7	♦0.4	♦0.4	♦0.4
3 months - 3 mois	8	4	4	♦0.2	♦0.2	♦0.2
4 months - 4 mois	6	1	5	♦0.2	♦0.1	♦0.3
5 months - 5 mois	5	4	1	♦0.1	♦0.2	♦0.1
6 months - 6 mois	5	5	-	♦0.1	♦0.3	-
7 months - 7 mois	2	2	-	♦0.1	♦0.1	-
8 months - 8 mois	5	3	2	♦0.1	♦0.2	♦0.1
9 months - 9 mois	4	1	3	♦0.1	♦0.1	♦0.2
10 months - 10 mois	4	3	1	♦0.1	♦0.2	♦0.1
11 months - 11 mois	-	-	-	-	-	-

Andorra - Andorre
2009 (C)

Total	1	-	1	...	...	...
Less than 1 day - Moins de 1 jour	-	-	-	...	...	...
1 - 6 days - 1 - 6 jours	1	-	1	...	...	...
7 - 27 days - 7 - 27 jours	-	-	-	...	...	...
28 days - 11 months - 28 jours - 11 mois	-	-	-	...	...	...

Austria - Autriche
2013 (C)

Total	245	144	101	3.1	3.5	2.6
Less than 1 day - Moins de 1 jour	111	66	45	1.4	1.6	1.2
1 - 6 days - 1 - 6 jours	43	30	13	0.5	0.7	♦0.3
7 - 27 days - 7 - 27 jours	29	17	12	♦0.4	♦0.4	♦0.3
7 - 13 days - 7 - 13 jours	14	9	5	♦0.2	♦0.2	♦0.1
14 - 20 days - 14 - 20 jours	10	6	4	♦0.1	♦0.1	♦0.1
21 - 27 days - 21 - 27 jours	5	2	3	♦0.1	-	♦0.1
28 days - 11 months - 28 jours - 11 mois	62	31	31	0.8	0.8	0.8
28 days - less than 2 months - 28 jours - moins de 2 mois	24	13	11	♦0.3	♦0.3	♦0.3
2 months - 2 mois	5	3	2	♦0.1	♦0.1	♦0.1

16. Infant deaths and infant mortality rates by age and sex: latest available year, 2006 - 2015
Décès d'enfants de moins d'un an et taux de mortalité infantile selon l'âge et le sexe : dernière année disponible, 2006 - 2015 (continued - suite)

Continent, country or area, year, code[a] and age / Continent, pays ou zone, année, code[a] et âge	Number - Nombre			Rate - Taux		
	Both sexes Les deux sexes	Male Masculin	Female Féminin	Both sexes Les deux sexes	Male Masculin	Female Féminin
EUROPE						
Austria - Autriche						
2013 (C)						
3 months - 3 mois	7	4	3	♦0.1	♦0.1	♦0.1
4 months - 4 mois	6	3	3	♦0.1	♦0.1	♦0.1
5 months - 5 mois	2	2	-	-	-	-
6 months - 6 mois	3	1	2	-	-	♦0.1
7 months - 7 mois	6	-	6	♦0.1	-	♦0.2
8 months - 8 mois	2	1	1	-	-	-
9 months - 9 mois	4	2	2	♦0.1	-	♦0.1
10 months - 10 mois	2	1	1	-	-	-
11 months - 11 mois	1	1	-	-	-	-
Belarus - Bélarus						
2014 (C)						
Total	409	244	165	3.5	4.0	2.9
Less than 1 day - Moins de 1 jour	35	16	19	0.3	♦0.3	♦0.3
1 - 6 days - 1 - 6 jours	87	55	32	0.7	0.9	0.6
7 - 27 days - 7 - 27 jours	79	54	25	0.7	0.9	♦0.4
28 days - 11 months - 28 jours - 11 mois	208	119	89	1.8	1.9	1.6
Belgium - Belgique[23]						
2010 (C)						
Total	465	276	189	3.6	4.1	3.0
Less than 1 day - Moins de 1 jour	123	70	53	0.9	1.1	0.8
1 - 6 days - 1 - 6 jours	101	64	37	0.8	1.0	0.6
7 - 27 days - 7 - 27 jours	68	43	25	0.5	0.6	♦0.4
7 - 13 days - 7 - 13 jours	39	27	12	0.3	♦0.4	♦0.2
14 - 20 days - 14 - 20 jours	16	10	6	♦0.1	♦0.2	♦0.1
21 - 27 days - 21 - 27 jours	13	6	7	♦0.1	♦0.1	♦0.1
28 days - 11 months - 28 jours - 11 mois	173	99	74	1.3	1.5	1.2
28 days - less than 2 months - 28 jours - moins de 2 mois	37	25	12	0.3	♦0.4	♦0.2
2 months - 2 mois	19	13	6	♦0.1	♦0.2	♦0.1
3 months - 3 mois	27	14	13	♦0.2	♦0.2	♦0.2
4 months - 4 mois	13	5	8	♦0.1	♦0.1	♦0.1
5 months - 5 mois	24	16	8	♦0.2	♦0.2	♦0.1
6 months - 6 mois	7	3	4	♦0.1	-	♦0.1
7 months - 7 mois	9	6	3	♦0.1	♦0.1	-
8 months - 8 mois	15	9	6	♦0.1	♦0.1	♦0.1
9 months - 9 mois	7	3	4	♦0.1	-	♦0.1
10 months - 10 mois	13	5	8	♦0.1	♦0.1	♦0.1
11 months - 11 mois	2	-	2	-	-	-
Bosnia and Herzegovina - Bosnie-Herzégovine						
2010 (C)						
Total	216	125	91	6.4	7.2	5.6
Less than 1 day - Moins de 1 jour	74	43	31	2.2	2.5	1.9
1 - 6 days - 1 - 6 jours	89	56	33	2.7	3.2	2.0
7 - 27 days - 7 - 27 jours	19	13	6	♦0.6	♦0.8	♦0.4
7 - 13 days - 7 - 13 jours	10	6	4	♦0.3	♦0.3	♦0.2
14 - 20 days - 14 - 20 jours	6	6	-	♦0.2	♦0.3	-
21 - 27 days - 21 - 27 jours	3	1	2	♦0.1	♦0.1	♦0.1
28 days - 11 months - 28 jours - 11 mois	34	13	21	1.0	♦0.8	♦1.3
28 days - less than 2 months - 28 jours - moins de 2 mois	5	2	3	♦0.1	♦0.1	♦0.2
2 months - 2 mois	10	6	4	♦0.3	♦0.3	♦0.2
3 months - 3 mois	1	-	1	-	-	♦0.1
4 months - 4 mois	5	2	3	♦0.1	♦0.1	♦0.2
5 months - 5 mois	3	1	2	♦0.1	♦0.1	♦0.1
6 months - 6 mois	3	1	2	♦0.1	♦0.1	♦0.1
7 months - 7 mois	-	-	-	-	-	-
8 months - 8 mois	1	-	1	-	-	♦0.1
9 months - 9 mois	4	-	4	♦0.1	-	♦0.2
10 months - 10 mois	1	1	-	-	♦0.1	-
11 months - 11 mois	1	-	1	-	-	♦0.1
Bulgaria - Bulgarie						
2014 (C)						
Total	517	284	233	7.6	8.2	7.1
Less than 1 day - Moins de 1 jour	89	49	40	1.3	1.4	1.2
1 - 6 days - 1 - 6 jours	122	73	49	1.8	2.1	1.5
7 - 27 days - 7 - 27 jours	87	43	44	1.3	1.2	1.3
28 days - 11 months - 28 jours - 11 mois	219	119	100	3.2	3.4	3.0

464

16. Infant deaths and infant mortality rates by age and sex: latest available year, 2006 - 2015
Décès d'enfants de moins d'un an et taux de mortalité infantile selon l'âge et le sexe : dernière année disponible, 2006 - 2015 (continued - suite)

Continent, country or area, year, code[a] and age / Continent, pays ou zone, année, code[a] et âge	Number - Nombre			Rate - Taux		
	Both sexes Les deux sexes	Male Masculin	Female Féminin	Both sexes Les deux sexes	Male Masculin	Female Féminin
EUROPE						
Croatia - Croatie						
2014 (C)						
Total..	199	113	86	5.0	5.5	4.5
Less than 1 day - Moins de 1 jour	71	41	30	1.8	2.0	1.6
1 - 6 days - 1 - 6 jours	51	30	21	1.3	1.5	♦1.1
7 - 27 days - 7 - 27 jours	27	18	9	♦0.7	♦0.9	♦0.5
7 - 13 days - 7 - 13 jours	11	6	5	♦0.3	♦0.3	♦0.3
14 - 20 days - 14 - 20 jours	8	5	3	♦0.2	♦0.2	♦0.2
21 - 27 days - 21 - 27 jours	8	7	1	♦0.2	♦0.3	♦0.1
28 days - 11 months - 28 jours - 11 mois........	50	24	26	1.3	♦1.2	♦1.4
28 days - less than 2 months - 28 jours - moins de 2 mois	19	8	11	♦0.5	♦0.4	♦0.6
2 months - 2 mois	8	7	1	♦0.2	♦0.3	♦0.1
3 months - 3 mois	10	2	8	♦0.3	♦0.1	♦0.4
4 months - 4 mois	2	1	1	♦0.1	-	♦0.1
5 months - 5 mois	1	1	-	-	-	-
6 months - 6 mois	1	1	-	-	-	-
7 months - 7 mois	2	1	1	♦0.1	-	♦0.1
8 months - 8 mois	2	1	1	♦0.1	-	♦0.1
9 months - 9 mois	1	-	1	-	-	♦0.1
10 months - 10 mois	2	1	1	♦0.1	-	♦0.1
11 months - 11 mois	2	1	1	♦0.1	-	♦0.1
Czech Republic - République tchèque						
2014 (C)						
Total..	263	153	110	2.4	2.7	2.1
Less than 1 day - Moins de 1 jour	45	23	22	0.4	♦0.4	♦0.4
1 - 6 days - 1 - 6 jours	70	46	24	0.6	0.8	♦0.4
7 - 27 days - 7 - 27 jours	57	32	25	0.5	0.6	♦0.5
7 - 13 days - 7 - 13 jours	33	17	16	0.3	♦0.3	♦0.3
14 - 20 days - 14 - 20 jours	15	9	6	♦0.1	♦0.2	♦0.1
21 - 27 days - 21 - 27 jours	9	6	3	♦0.1	♦0.1	♦0.1
28 days - 11 months - 28 jours - 11 mois........	91	52	39	0.8	0.9	0.7
28 days - less than 2 months - 28 jours - moins de 2 mois	25	14	11	♦0.2	♦0.2	♦0.2
2 months - 2 mois	14	7	7	♦0.1	♦0.1	♦0.1
3 months - 3 mois	12	9	3	♦0.1	♦0.2	♦0.1
4 months - 4 mois	3	1	2	-	-	-
5 months - 5 mois	11	5	6	♦0.1	♦0.1	♦0.1
6 months - 6 mois	7	6	1	♦0.1	♦0.1	-
7 months - 7 mois	3	2	1	-	-	-
8 months - 8 mois	5	3	2	-	♦0.1	-
9 months - 9 mois	3	1	2	-	-	-
10 months - 10 mois	6	2	4	♦0.1	-	♦0.1
11 months - 11 mois	2	2	-	-	-	-
Denmark - Danemark[24]						
2014 (C)						
Total..	229	134	95	4.0	4.6	3.4
Less than 1 day - Moins de 1 jour	99	56	43	1.7	1.9	1.6
1 - 6 days - 1 - 6 jours	56	38	18	1.0	1.3	♦0.7
7 - 27 days - 7 - 27 jours	20	11	9	♦0.4	♦0.4	♦0.3
7 - 13 days - 7 - 13 jours	10	6	4	♦0.2	♦0.2	♦0.1
14 - 20 days - 14 - 20 jours	4	1	3	♦0.1	-	♦0.1
21 - 27 days - 21 - 27 jours	6	4	2	♦0.1	♦0.1	♦0.1
28 days - 11 months - 28 jours - 11 mois........	54	29	25	0.9	♦1.0	♦0.9
28 days - less than 2 months - 28 jours - moins de 2 mois	20	12	8	♦0.4	♦0.4	♦0.3
2 months - 2 mois	11	6	5	♦0.2	♦0.2	♦0.2
3 months - 3 mois	4	1	3	♦0.1	-	♦0.1
4 months - 4 mois	4	1	3	♦0.1	-	♦0.1
5 months - 5 mois	6	4	2	♦0.1	♦0.1	♦0.1
6 months - 6 mois	3	2	1	♦0.1	♦0.1	-
7 months - 7 mois	2	1	1	-	-	-
8 months - 8 mois	-	-	-	-	-	-
9 months - 9 mois	-	-	-	-	-	-
10 months - 10 mois	2	1	1	-	-	-
11 months - 11 mois	2	1	1	-	-	-
Estonia - Estonie						
2014 (C)						
Total..	36	19	17	...	...	...
Less than 1 day - Moins de 1 jour	7	1	6	...	...	...
1 - 6 days - 1 - 6 jours	8	6	2	...	...	...

465

16. Infant deaths and infant mortality rates by age and sex: latest available year, 2006 - 2015

Décès d'enfants de moins d'un an et taux de mortalité infantile selon l'âge et le sexe : dernière année disponible, 2006 - 2015 (continued - suite)

Continent, country or area, year, code[a] and age Continent, pays ou zone, année, code[a] et âge	Number - Nombre			Rate - Taux		
	Both sexes Les deux sexes	Male Masculin	Female Féminin	Both sexes Les deux sexes	Male Masculin	Female Féminin
EUROPE						
Estonia - Estonie						
2014 (C)						
7 - 27 days - 7 - 27 jours	7	5	2	...	...	...
7 - 13 days - 7 - 13 jours	2	1	1	...	...	...
14 - 20 days - 14 - 20 jours	3	3	-	...	...	...
21 - 27 days - 21 - 27 jours	2	1	1	...	...	...
28 days - 11 months - 28 jours - 11 mois	14	7	7	...	...	...
28 days - less than 2 months - 28 jours - moins de 2 mois	5	3	2	...	...	...
2 months - 2 mois	1	-	1	...	...	...
3 months - 3 mois	1	-	1	...	...	...
4 months - 4 mois	1	-	1	...	...	...
5 months - 5 mois	1	-	1	...	...	...
6 months - 6 mois	1	1	-	...	...	...
7 months - 7 mois	1	1	-	...	...	...
8 months - 8 mois	-	-	-	...	...	...
9 months - 9 mois	-	-	-	...	...	...
10 months - 10 mois	1	-	1	...	...	...
11 months - 11 mois	2	2	-	...	...	...
Faeroe Islands - Îles Féroé						
2014 (C)						
Total	4	4	-	...	...	...
Less than 1 day - Moins de 1 jour	1	1	-	...	...	...
1 - 6 days - 1 - 6 jours	2	2	-	...	...	...
7 - 27 days - 7 - 27 jours	-	-	-	...	...	...
7 - 13 days - 7 - 13 jours	-	-	-	...	...	...
14 - 20 days - 14 - 20 jours	-	-	-	...	...	...
21 - 27 days - 21 - 27 jours	-	-	-	...	...	...
28 days - 11 months - 28 jours - 11 mois	1	1	-	...	...	...
28 days - less than 2 months - 28 jours - moins de 2 mois	-	-	-	...	...	...
2 months - 2 mois	-	-	-	...	...	...
3 months - 3 mois	-	-	-	...	...	...
4 months - 4 mois	-	-	-	...	...	...
5 months - 5 mois	1	1	-	...	...	...
6 months - 6 mois	-	-	-	...	...	...
7 months - 7 mois	-	-	-	...	...	...
8 months - 8 mois	-	-	-	...	...	...
9 months - 9 mois	-	-	-	...	...	...
10 months - 10 mois	-	-	-	...	...	...
11 months - 11 mois	-	-	-	...	...	...
Finland - Finlande[25]						
2014 (C)						
Total	124	68	56	2.2	2.3	2.0
Less than 1 day - Moins de 1 jour	33	18	15	0.6	♦0.6	♦0.5
1 - 6 days - 1 - 6 jours	30	17	13	0.5	♦0.6	♦0.5
7 - 27 days - 7 - 27 jours	20	7	13	♦0.4	♦0.2	♦0.5
7 - 13 days - 7 - 13 jours	7	2	5	♦0.1	♦0.1	♦0.2
14 - 20 days - 14 - 20 jours	8	3	5	♦0.1	♦0.1	♦0.2
21 - 27 days - 21 - 27 jours	5	2	3	♦0.1	♦0.1	♦0.1
28 days - 11 months - 28 jours - 11 mois	41	26	15	0.7	♦0.9	♦0.5
28 days - less than 2 months - 28 jours - moins de 2 mois	15	10	5	♦0.3	♦0.3	♦0.2
2 months - 2 mois	3	2	1	♦0.1	♦0.1	-
3 months - 3 mois	5	3	2	♦0.1	♦0.1	♦0.1
4 months - 4 mois	2	1	1	-	-	-
5 months - 5 mois	3	3	-	♦0.1	♦0.1	-
6 months - 6 mois	5	2	3	♦0.1	♦0.1	♦0.1
7 months - 7 mois	1	1	-	-	-	-
8 months - 8 mois	2	1	1	-	-	-
9 months - 9 mois	2	1	1	-	-	-
10 months - 10 mois	2	1	1	-	-	-
11 months - 11 mois	1	1	-	-	-	-
France						
2014 (C)						
Total	2 598	1 446	1 152	3.3	3.6	3.0
Less than 1 day - Moins de 1 jour	678	361	317	0.9	0.9	0.8
1 - 6 days - 1 - 6 jours	585	339	246	0.7	0.8	0.6
7 - 27 days - 7 - 27 jours	535	320	215	0.7	0.8	0.6
7 - 13 days - 7 - 13 jours	278	163	115	0.4	0.4	0.3
14 - 20 days - 14 - 20 jours	152	94	58	0.2	0.2	0.2

Continent, country or area, year, code[a] and age / Continent, pays ou zone, année, code[a] et âge	Number - Nombre			Rate - Taux		
	Both sexes Les deux sexes	Male Masculin	Female Féminin	Both sexes Les deux sexes	Male Masculin	Female Féminin
EUROPE						
France						
2014 (C)						
21 - 27 days - 21 - 27 jours	105	63	42	0.1	0.2	0.1
28 days - 11 months - 28 jours - 11 mois........................	800	426	374	1.0	1.1	1.0
28 days - less than 2 months - 28 jours - moins de 2 mois	257	147	110	0.3	0.4	0.3
2 months - 2 mois..	112	52	60	0.1	0.1	0.2
3 months - 3 mois..	105	59	46	0.1	0.1	0.1
4 months - 4 mois..	73	43	30	0.1	0.1	0.1
5 months - 5 mois..	59	41	18	0.1	0.1	-
6 months - 6 mois..	55	21	34	0.1	♦0.1	0.1
7 months - 7 mois..	40	17	23	0.1	-	♦0.1
8 months - 8 mois..	35	16	19	-	-	-
9 months - 9 mois..	26	13	13	-	-	-
10 months - 10 mois..	27	11	16	-	-	-
11 months - 11 mois..	11	6	5	-	-	-
Germany - Allemagne						
2014 (C)						
Total...	2 284	1 266	1 018	3.2	3.5	2.9
Less than 1 day - Moins de 1 jour	831	447	384	1.2	1.2	1.1
1 - 6 days - 1 - 6 jours	479	278	201	0.7	0.8	0.6
7 - 27 days - 7 - 27 jours	298	166	132	0.4	0.5	0.4
7 - 13 days - 7 - 13 jours	147	87	60	0.2	0.2	0.2
14 - 20 days - 14 - 20 jours	90	52	38	0.1	0.1	0.1
21 - 27 days - 21 - 27 jours	61	27	34	0.1	♦0.1	0.1
28 days - 11 months - 28 jours - 11 mois........................	676	375	301	0.9	1.0	0.9
28 days - less than 2 months - 28 jours - moins de 2 mois	171	99	72	0.2	0.3	0.2
2 months - 2 mois..	127	70	57	0.2	0.2	0.2
3 months - 3 mois..	103	58	45	0.1	0.2	0.1
4 months - 4 mois..	59	31	28	0.1	0.1	♦0.1
5 months - 5 mois..	53	33	20	0.1	0.1	♦0.1
6 months - 6 mois..	43	23	20	0.1	♦0.1	♦0.1
7 months - 7 mois..	38	22	16	0.1	♦0.1	-
8 months - 8 mois..	27	13	14	-	-	-
9 months - 9 mois..	22	9	13	-	-	-
10 months - 10 mois..	19	10	9	-	-	-
11 months - 11 mois..	14	7	7	-	-	-
Gibraltar						
2006 (+C)						
Total...	1	1	-	...	...	...
Less than 7 days - Moins de 7 jours............................	-	-	-	...	...	...
7 - 27 days - 7 - 27 jours	-	-	-	...	...	...
28 days - 11 months - 28 jours - 11 mois........................	1	1	-	...	...	...
28 days - 2 months - 28 jours - 2 mois...........................	-	-	-	...	...	...
3 months - 3 mois..	1	1	-	...	...	...
4 - 11 months - 4 - 11 mois..	-	-	-	...	...	...
Greece - Grèce						
2014 (C)						
Total...	346	192	154	3.8	4.1	3.4
Less than 1 day - Moins de 1 jour	77	50	27	0.8	1.1	♦0.6
1 - 6 days - 1 - 6 jours	88	54	34	1.0	1.1	0.8
7 - 27 days - 7 - 27 jours	72	42	30	0.8	0.9	0.7
7 - 13 days - 7 - 13 jours	37	19	18	0.4	♦0.4	♦0.4
14 - 20 days - 14 - 20 jours	20	10	10	♦0.2	♦0.2	♦0.2
21 - 27 days - 21 - 27 jours	15	13	2	♦0.2	♦0.3	-
28 days - 11 months - 28 jours - 11 mois........................	108	45	63	1.2	0.9	1.4
28 days - less than 2 months - 28 jours - moins de 2 mois	30	12	18	0.3	♦0.3	♦0.4
2 months - 2 mois..	19	7	12	♦0.2	♦0.1	♦0.3
3 months - 3 mois..	16	8	8	♦0.2	♦0.2	♦0.2
4 months - 4 mois..	7	3	4	♦0.1	♦0.1	♦0.1
5 months - 5 mois..	12	4	8	♦0.1	♦0.1	♦0.2
6 months - 6 mois..	7	4	3	♦0.1	♦0.1	♦0.1
7 months - 7 mois..	3	1	2	-	-	-
8 months - 8 mois..	3	2	1	-	-	-
9 months - 9 mois..	6	2	4	♦0.1	-	♦0.1
10 months - 10 mois..	1	-	1	-	-	-
11 months - 11 mois..	4	2	2	-	-	-

16. Infant deaths and infant mortality rates by age and sex: latest available year, 2006 - 2015
Décès d'enfants de moins d'un an et taux de mortalité infantile selon l'âge et le sexe : dernière année disponible, 2006 - 2015 (continued - suite)

Continent, country or area, year, code[a] and age Continent, pays ou zone, année, code[a] et âge	Number - Nombre			Rate - Taux		
	Both sexes Les deux sexes	Male Masculin	Female Féminin	Both sexes Les deux sexes	Male Masculin	Female Féminin
EUROPE						
Hungary - Hongrie[26]						
2014 (C)						
Total	418	233	185	4.5	4.9	4.1
Less than 1 day - Moins de 1 jour	56	31	25	0.6	0.6	♦0.6
1 - 6 days - 1 - 6 jours	104	57	47	1.1	1.2	1.0
7 - 27 days - 7 - 27 jours	108	64	44	1.2	1.3	1.0
7 - 13 days - 7 - 13 jours	54	35	19	0.6	0.7	♦0.4
14 - 20 days - 14 - 20 jours	35	18	17	0.4	♦0.4	♦0.4
21 - 27 days - 21 - 27 jours	19	11	8	♦0.2	♦0.2	♦0.2
28 days - 11 months - 28 jours - 11 mois	150	81	69	1.6	1.7	1.5
28 days - less than 2 months - 28 jours - moins de 2 mois	42	22	20	0.5	♦0.5	♦0.4
2 months - 2 mois	25	10	15	♦0.3	♦0.2	♦0.3
3 months - 3 mois	16	11	5	♦0.2	♦0.2	♦0.1
4 months - 4 mois	15	7	8	♦0.2	♦0.1	♦0.2
5 months - 5 mois	11	7	4	♦0.1	♦0.1	♦0.1
6 months - 6 mois	11	7	4	♦0.1	♦0.1	♦0.1
7 months - 7 mois	6	3	3	♦0.1	♦0.1	♦0.1
8 months - 8 mois	11	8	3	♦0.1	♦0.2	♦0.1
9 months - 9 mois	3	1	2	-	-	-
10 months - 10 mois	5	3	2	♦0.1	♦0.1	-
11 months - 11 mois	5	2	3	♦0.1	-	♦0.1
Iceland - Islande						
2014 (C)						
Total	9	3	6	...	...	...
Less than 1 day - Moins de 1 jour	3	-	3	...	...	...
1 - 6 days - 1 - 6 jours	1	1	-	...	...	...
7 - 27 days - 7 - 27 jours	3	2	1	...	...	...
7 - 13 days - 7 - 13 jours	-	-	-	...	...	...
14 - 20 days - 14 - 20 jours	1	1	-	...	...	...
21 - 27 days - 21 - 27 jours	2	1	1	...	...	...
28 days - 11 months - 28 jours - 11 mois	2	-	2	...	...	...
28 days - less than 2 months - 28 jours - moins de 2 mois	-	-	-	...	...	...
2 months - 2 mois	2	-	2	...	...	...
3 months - 3 mois	-	-	-	...	...	...
4 months - 4 mois	-	-	-	...	...	...
5 months - 5 mois	-	-	-	...	...	...
6 months - 6 mois	-	-	-	...	...	...
7 months - 7 mois	-	-	-	...	...	...
8 months - 8 mois	-	-	-	...	...	...
9 months - 9 mois	-	-	-	...	...	...
10 months - 10 mois	-	-	-	...	...	...
11 months - 11 mois	-	-	-	...	...	...
Ireland - Irlande						
2011 (+C)						
Total	262	150	112	3.5	4.0	3.1
Less than 1 day - Moins de 1 jour	88	43	45	1.2	1.1	1.2
1 - 6 days - 1 - 6 jours	59	38	21	0.8	1.0	♦0.6
7 - 27 days - 7 - 27 jours	41	30	11	0.6	0.8	♦0.3
7 - 13 days - 7 - 13 jours	18	13	5	♦0.2	♦0.3	♦0.1
14 - 20 days - 14 - 20 jours	17	13	4	♦0.2	♦0.3	♦0.1
21 - 27 days - 21 - 27 jours	6	4	2	♦0.1	♦0.1	♦0.1
28 days - 11 months - 28 jours - 11 mois	74	39	35	1.0	1.0	1.0
28 days - less than 2 months - 28 jours - moins de 2 mois	20	12	8	♦0.3	♦0.3	♦0.2
2 months - 2 mois	17	7	10	♦0.2	♦0.2	♦0.3
3 months - 3 mois	11	4	7	♦0.1	♦0.1	♦0.2
4 months - 4 mois	5	5	-	♦0.1	♦0.1	-
5 months - 5 mois	6	3	3	♦0.1	♦0.1	♦0.1
6 months - 6 mois	3	1	2	-	-	♦0.1
7 months - 7 mois	2	1	1	-	-	-
8 months - 8 mois	1	-	1	-	-	-
9 months - 9 mois	4	3	1	♦0.1	♦0.1	-
10 months - 10 mois	4	2	2	♦0.1	♦0.1	♦0.1
11 months - 11 mois	1	1	-	-	-	-
Italy - Italie						
2013 (C)						
Total	1 493	864	629	2.9	3.3	2.5
Less than 1 day - Moins de 1 jour	268	153	115	0.5	0.6	0.5
1 - 6 days - 1 - 6 jours	447	279	168	0.9	1.1	0.7

16. Infant deaths and infant mortality rates by age and sex: latest available year, 2006 - 2015
Décès d'enfants de moins d'un an et taux de mortalité infantile selon l'âge et le sexe : dernière année disponible, 2006 - 2015 (continued - suite)

Continent, country or area, year, code[a] and age / Continent, pays ou zone, année, code[a] et âge	Number - Nombre			Rate - Taux		
	Both sexes Les deux sexes	Male Masculin	Female Féminin	Both sexes Les deux sexes	Male Masculin	Female Féminin
EUROPE						
Italy - Italie						
2013 (C)						
7 - 27 days - 7 - 27 jours	311	175	136	0.6	0.7	0.5
7 - 13 days - 7 - 13 jours	151	87	64	0.3	0.3	0.3
14 - 20 days - 14 - 20 jours	92	47	45	0.2	0.2	0.2
21 - 27 days - 21 - 27 jours	68	41	27	0.1	0.2	♦0.1
28 days - 11 months - 28 jours - 11 mois	467	257	210	0.9	1.0	0.8
28 days - less than 2 months - 28 jours - moins de 2 mois	149	90	59	0.3	0.3	0.2
2 months - 2 mois	69	31	38	0.1	0.1	0.2
3 months - 3 mois	50	20	30	0.1	♦0.1	0.1
4 months - 4 mois	44	26	18	0.1	♦0.1	♦0.1
5 months - 5 mois	35	21	14	0.1	♦0.1	♦0.1
6 months - 6 mois	33	21	12	0.1	♦0.1	-
7 months - 7 mois	27	10	17	♦0.1	-	♦0.1
8 months - 8 mois	20	16	4	-	♦0.1	-
9 months - 9 mois	18	11	7	-	-	-
10 months - 10 mois	13	6	7	-	-	-
11 months - 11 mois	9	5	4	-	-	-
Latvia - Lettonie						
2014 (C)						
Total	83	45	38	...	...	...
Less than 1 day - Moins de 1 jour	22	11	11	...	...	...
1 - 6 days - 1 - 6 jours	23	15	8	...	...	...
7 - 27 days - 7 - 27 jours	16	10	6	...	...	...
7 - 13 days - 7 - 13 jours	6	4	2	...	...	...
14 - 20 days - 14 - 20 jours	6	3	3	...	...	...
21 - 27 days - 21 - 27 jours	4	3	1	...	...	...
28 days - 11 months - 28 jours - 11 mois	18	7	11	...	...	...
28 days - less than 2 months - 28 jours - moins de 2 mois	6	3	3	...	...	...
2 months - 2 mois	5	1	4	...	...	...
3 months - 3 mois	2	1	1	...	...	...
4 months - 4 mois	2	-	2	...	...	...
5 months - 5 mois	2	1	1	...	...	...
6 months - 6 mois	1	1	-	...	...	...
7 months - 7 mois	-	-	-	...	...	...
8 months - 8 mois	-	-	-	...	...	...
9 months - 9 mois	-	-	-	...	...	...
10 months - 10 mois	-	-	-	...	...	...
11 months - 11 mois	-	-	-	...	...	...
Liechtenstein						
2014 (C)						
Total	1	-	1	...	...	...
Less than 1 day - Moins de 1 jour	-	-	-	...	...	...
1 - 6 days - 1 - 6 jours	-	-	-	...	...	...
7 - 27 days - 7 - 27 jours	-	-	-	...	...	...
28 days - 11 months - 28 jours - 11 mois	1	-	1	...	...	...
Lithuania - Lituanie						
2014 (C)						
Total	118	52	66	3.9	3.3	4.5
Less than 1 day - Moins de 1 jour	29	14	15	♦1.0	♦0.9	♦1.0
1 - 6 days - 1 - 6 jours	21	5	16	♦0.7	♦0.3	♦1.1
7 - 27 days - 7 - 27 jours	25	13	12	♦0.8	♦0.8	♦0.8
7 - 13 days - 7 - 13 jours	14	8	6	♦0.5	♦0.5	♦0.4
14 - 20 days - 14 - 20 jours	5	1	4	♦0.2	♦0.1	♦0.3
21 - 27 days - 21 - 27 jours	6	4	2	♦0.2	♦0.3	♦0.1
28 days - 11 months - 28 jours - 11 mois	43	20	23	1.4	♦1.3	♦1.6
28 days - less than 2 months - 28 jours - moins de 2 mois	16	6	10	♦0.5	♦0.4	♦0.7
2 months - 2 mois	6	3	3	♦0.2	♦0.2	♦0.2
3 months - 3 mois	6	2	4	♦0.2	♦0.1	♦0.3
4 months - 4 mois	7	5	2	♦0.2	♦0.3	♦0.1
5 months - 5 mois	2	1	1	♦0.1	♦0.1	♦0.1
6 months - 6 mois	3	1	2	♦0.1	♦0.1	♦0.1
7 months - 7 mois	2	1	1	♦0.1	♦0.1	♦0.1
8 months - 8 mois	1	1	-	-	♦0.1	-
9 months - 9 mois	-	-	-	-	-	-
10 months - 10 mois	-	-	-	-	-	-
11 months - 11 mois	-	-	-	-	-	-

16. Infant deaths and infant mortality rates by age and sex: latest available year, 2006 - 2015
Décès d'enfants de moins d'un an et taux de mortalité infantile selon l'âge et le sexe : dernière année disponible, 2006 - 2015 (continued - suite)

Continent, country or area, year, code[a] and age / Continent, pays ou zone, année, code[a] et âge	Number - Nombre			Rate - Taux		
	Both sexes Les deux sexes	Male Masculin	Female Féminin	Both sexes Les deux sexes	Male Masculin	Female Féminin
EUROPE						
Luxembourg						
2014 (C)						
Total	17	8	9	...	...	...
Less than 1 day - Moins de 1 jour	6	2	4	...	...	...
1 - 6 days - 1 - 6 jours	4	2	2	...	...	...
7 - 27 days - 7 - 27 jours	1	-	1	...	...	...
7 - 13 days - 7 - 13 jours	1	-	1	...	...	...
14 - 20 days - 14 - 20 jours	-	-	-	...	...	...
21 - 27 days - 21 - 27 jours	-	-	-	...	...	...
28 days - 11 months - 28 jours - 11 mois	6	4	2	...	...	...
28 days - less than 2 months - 28 jours - moins de 2 mois	1	1	-	...	...	...
2 months - 2 mois	1	1	-	...	...	...
3 months - 3 mois	-	-	-	...	...	...
4 months - 4 mois	-	-	-	...	...	...
5 months - 5 mois	2	1	1	...	...	...
6 months - 6 mois	-	-	-	...	...	...
7 months - 7 mois	-	-	-	...	...	...
8 months - 8 mois	-	-	-	...	...	...
9 months - 9 mois	1	-	1	...	...	...
10 months - 10 mois	-	-	-	...	...	...
11 months - 11 mois	1	1	-	...	...	...
Malta - Malte						
2014 (C)						
Total	21	11	10	...	...	...
Less than 1 day - Moins de 1 jour	9	6	3	...	...	...
1 - 6 days - 1 - 6 jours	6	2	4	...	...	...
7 - 27 days - 7 - 27 jours	1	1	-	...	...	...
7 - 13 days - 7 - 13 jours	1	1	-	...	...	...
14 - 20 days - 14 - 20 jours	-	-	-	...	...	...
21 - 27 days - 21 - 27 jours	-	-	-	...	...	...
28 days - 11 months - 28 jours - 11 mois	5	2	3	...	...	...
28 days - less than 2 months - 28 jours - moins de 2 mois	2	2	-	...	...	...
2 months - 2 mois	1	-	1	...	...	...
3 months - 3 mois	-	-	-	...	...	...
4 months - 4 mois	1	-	1	...	...	...
5 months - 5 mois	-	-	-	...	...	...
6 months - 6 mois	1	-	1	...	...	...
7 months - 7 mois	-	-	-	...	...	...
8 months - 8 mois	-	-	-	...	...	...
9 months - 9 mois	-	-	-	...	...	...
10 months - 10 mois	-	-	-	...	...	...
11 months - 11 mois	-	-	-	...	...	...
Montenegro - Monténégro						
2014 (C)						
Total	37	25	12	...	...	...
Less than 1 day - Moins de 1 jour	3	3	-	...	...	...
1 - 6 days - 1 - 6 jours	14	10	4	...	...	...
7 - 27 days - 7 - 27 jours	8	4	4	...	...	...
28 days - 11 months - 28 jours - 11 mois	12	8	4	...	...	...
Netherlands - Pays-Bas[27]						
2014 (C)						
Total	630	354	276	3.6	4.0	3.2
Less than 1 day - Moins de 1 jour	181	97	84	1.0	1.1	1.0
1 - 6 days - 1 - 6 jours	147	89	58	0.8	1.0	0.7
7 - 27 days - 7 - 27 jours	64	31	33	0.4	0.3	0.4
28 days - 11 months - 28 jours - 11 mois	238	137	101	1.4	1.5	1.2
Norway - Norvège[28]						
2014 (C)						
Total	139	77	62	2.4	2.5	2.2
Less than 1 day - Moins de 1 jour	39	22	17	0.7	♦0.7	♦0.6
1 - 6 days - 1 - 6 jours	44	18	26	0.7	♦0.6	♦0.9
7 - 27 days - 7 - 27 jours	22	13	9	♦0.4	♦0.4	♦0.3
28 days - 11 months - 28 jours - 11 mois	34	24	10	0.6	♦0.8	♦0.3
Poland - Pologne						
2014 (C)						
Total	1 583	870	713	4.2	4.5	3.9
Less than 1 day - Moins de 1 jour	473	264	209	1.3	1.4	1.1
1 - 6 days - 1 - 6 jours	308	177	131	0.8	0.9	0.7

16. Infant deaths and infant mortality rates by age and sex: latest available year, 2006 - 2015
Décès d'enfants de moins d'un an et taux de mortalité infantile selon l'âge et le sexe : dernière année disponible, 2006 - 2015 (continued - suite)

Continent, country or area, year, code[a] and age Continent, pays ou zone, année, code[a] et âge	Number - Nombre			Rate - Taux		
	Both sexes Les deux sexes	Male Masculin	Female Féminin	Both sexes Les deux sexes	Male Masculin	Female Féminin
EUROPE						
Poland - Pologne						
2014 (C)						
7 - 27 days - 7 - 27 jours	303	168	135	0.8	0.9	0.7
28 days - 11 months - 28 jours - 11 mois.................................	499	261	238	1.3	1.4	1.3
Portugal[29]						
2014 (C)						
Total...	236	145	91	2.9	3.4	2.3
Less than 1 day - Moins de 1 jour	62	35	27	0.8	0.8	♦0.7
1 - 6 days - 1 - 6 jours	63	42	21	0.8	1.0	♦0.5
7 - 27 days - 7 - 27 jours	49	30	19	0.6	0.7	♦0.5
28 days - 11 months - 28 jours - 11 mois.........................	62	38	24	0.8	0.9	♦0.6
Republic of Moldova - République de Moldova[30]						
2014 (C)						
Total...	372	226	146	9.6	11.3	7.8
Less than 1 day - Moins de 1 jour	75	46	29	1.9	2.3	♦1.6
1 - 6 days - 1 - 6 jours	95	58	37	2.5	2.9	2.0
7 - 27 days - 7 - 27 jours	69	46	23	1.8	2.3	♦1.2
28 days - 11 months - 28 jours - 11 mois.........................	133	76	57	3.4	3.8	3.1
Romania - Roumanie						
2014 (C)						
Total...	1 628	968	660	8.4	9.7	7.0
Less than 1 day - Moins de 1 jour	187	111	76	1.0	1.1	0.8
1 - 6 days - 1 - 6 jours	460	282	178	2.4	2.8	1.9
7 - 27 days - 7 - 27 jours	323	192	131	1.7	1.9	1.4
7 - 13 days - 7 - 13 jours	168	105	63	0.9	1.1	0.7
14 - 20 days - 14 - 20 jours	84	49	35	0.4	0.5	0.4
21 - 27 days - 21 - 27 jours	71	38	33	0.4	0.4	0.4
28 days - 11 months - 28 jours - 11 mois.........................	658	383	275	3.4	3.9	2.9
28 days - less than 2 months - 28 jours - moins de 2 mois	221	130	91	1.1	1.3	1.0
2 months - 2 mois..	97	59	38	0.5	0.6	0.4
3 months - 3 mois..	79	43	36	0.4	0.4	0.4
4 months - 4 mois..	58	35	23	0.3	0.4	♦0.2
5 months - 5 mois..	46	28	18	0.2	♦0.3	♦0.2
6 months - 6 mois..	37	23	14	0.2	♦0.2	♦0.1
7 months - 7 mois..	35	24	11	0.2	♦0.2	♦0.1
8 months - 8 mois..	25	15	10	♦0.1	♦0.2	♦0.1
9 months - 9 mois..	25	10	15	♦0.1	♦0.1	♦0.2
10 months - 10 mois..	13	5	8	♦0.1	♦0.1	♦0.1
11 months - 11 mois..	22	11	11	♦0.1	♦0.1	♦0.1
Russian Federation - Fédération de Russie[14]						
2012 (C)						
Total...	16 306	9 219	7 087	8.6	9.4	7.7
Less than 1 day - Moins de 1 jour	1 897	1 009	888	1.0	1.0	1.0
1 - 6 days - 1 - 6 jours	5 072	2 961	2 111	2.7	3.0	2.3
7 - 27 days - 7 - 27 jours	3 438	1 958	1 480	1.8	2.0	1.6
7 - 13 days - 7 - 13 jours	1 798	1 020	778	0.9	1.0	0.8
14 - 20 days - 14 - 20 jours	952	560	392	0.5	0.6	0.4
21 - 27 days - 21 - 27 jours	688	378	310	0.4	0.4	0.3
28 days - 11 months - 28 jours - 11 mois.........................	5 898	3 290	2 608	3.1	3.4	2.8
28 days - less than 2 months - 28 jours - moins de 2 mois	2 063	1 166	897	1.1	1.2	1.0
2 months - 2 mois..	942	525	417	0.5	0.5	0.5
3 months - 3 mois..	691	372	319	0.4	0.4	0.3
4 months - 4 mois..	562	333	229	0.3	0.3	0.2
5 months - 5 mois..	417	221	196	0.2	0.2	0.2
6 months - 6 mois..	334	184	150	0.2	0.2	0.2
7 months - 7 mois..	252	139	113	0.1	0.1	0.1
8 months - 8 mois..	219	127	92	0.1	0.1	0.1
9 months - 9 mois..	172	86	86	0.1	0.1	0.1
10 months - 10 mois..	134	74	60	0.1	0.1	0.1
11 months - 11 mois..	112	63	49	0.1	0.1	0.1
Unknown - Inconnu	1	1	-	-	-	-
San Marino - Saint-Marin						
2014 (+C)						
Total...	1	1	-	...	...	...
Less than 1 day - Moins de 1 jour	-	-	-	...	...	...
1 - 6 days - 1 - 6 jours	-	-	-	...	...	...
7 - 27 days - 7 - 27 jours	-	-	-	...	...	...
28 days - 11 months - 28 jours - 11 mois.........................	1	1	-	...	...	...

16. Infant deaths and infant mortality rates by age and sex: latest available year, 2006 - 2015

Décès d'enfants de moins d'un an et taux de mortalité infantile selon l'âge et le sexe : dernière année disponible, 2006 - 2015 (continued - suite)

Continent, country or area, year, code[a] and age Continent, pays ou zone, année, code[a] et âge	Number - Nombre			Rate - Taux		
	Both sexes Les deux sexes	Male Masculin	Female Féminin	Both sexes Les deux sexes	Male Masculin	Female Féminin
EUROPE						
Serbia - Serbie[31]						
2014 (+C)						
Total	381	228	153	5.7	6.6	4.8
Less than 1 day - Moins de 1 jour	101	65	36	1.5	1.9	1.1
1 - 6 days - 1 - 6 jours	136	87	49	2.0	2.5	1.5
7 - 27 days - 7 - 27 jours	50	26	24	0.8	♦0.8	♦0.7
7 - 13 days - 7 - 13 jours	26	16	10	♦0.4	♦0.5	♦0.3
14 - 20 days - 14 - 20 jours	14	5	9	♦0.2	♦0.1	♦0.3
21 - 27 days - 21 - 27 jours	10	5	5	♦0.2	♦0.1	♦0.2
28 days - 11 months - 28 jours - 11 mois	94	50	44	1.4	1.5	1.4
28 days - less than 2 months - 28 jours - moins de 2 mois	30	17	13	0.5	♦0.5	♦0.4
2 months - 2 mois	15	7	8	♦0.2	♦0.2	♦0.2
3 months - 3 mois	8	4	4	♦0.1	♦0.1	♦0.1
4 months - 4 mois	9	3	6	♦0.1	♦0.1	♦0.2
5 months - 5 mois	5	5	-	♦0.1	♦0.1	-
6 months - 6 mois	4	2	2	♦0.1	♦0.1	♦0.1
7 months - 7 mois	7	1	6	♦0.1	-	♦0.2
8 months - 8 mois	6	4	2	♦0.1	♦0.1	♦0.1
9 months - 9 mois	1	1	-	-	-	-
10 months - 10 mois	7	6	1	♦0.1	♦0.2	-
11 months - 11 mois	2	-	2	-	-	♦0.1
Slovakia - Slovaquie						
2014 (C)						
Total	318	169	149	5.8	6.0	5.5
Less than 1 day - Moins de 1 jour	65	38	27	1.2	1.4	♦1.0
1 - 6 days - 1 - 6 jours	67	32	35	1.2	1.1	1.3
7 - 27 days - 7 - 27 jours	50	26	24	0.9	♦0.9	♦0.9
7 - 13 days - 7 - 13 jours	21	12	9	♦0.4	♦0.4	♦0.3
14 - 20 days - 14 - 20 jours	22	11	11	♦0.4	♦0.4	♦0.4
21 - 27 days - 21 - 27 jours	7	3	4	♦0.1	♦0.1	♦0.1
28 days - 11 months - 28 jours - 11 mois	136	73	63	2.5	2.6	2.3
28 days - less than 2 months - 28 jours - moins de 2 mois	56	31	25	1.0	1.1	♦0.9
2 months - 2 mois	20	9	11	♦0.4	♦0.3	♦0.4
3 months - 3 mois	16	8	8	♦0.3	♦0.3	♦0.3
4 months - 4 mois	12	8	4	♦0.2	♦0.3	♦0.1
5 months - 5 mois	5	3	2	♦0.1	♦0.1	♦0.1
6 months - 6 mois	4	2	2	♦0.1	♦0.1	♦0.1
7 months - 7 mois	12	6	6	♦0.2	♦0.2	♦0.2
8 months - 8 mois	1	1	-	-	-	-
9 months - 9 mois	5	3	2	♦0.1	♦0.1	♦0.1
10 months - 10 mois	3	1	2	♦0.1	-	♦0.1
11 months - 11 mois	2	1	1	-	-	-
Slovenia - Slovénie						
2014 (C)						
Total	39	19	20	...	...	...
Less than 1 day - Moins de 1 jour	11	6	5	...	...	...
1 - 6 days - 1 - 6 jours	7	4	3	...	...	...
7 - 27 days - 7 - 27 jours	9	3	6	...	...	...
7 - 13 days - 7 - 13 jours	4	2	2	...	...	...
14 - 20 days - 14 - 20 jours	4	1	3	...	...	...
21 - 27 days - 21 - 27 jours	1	-	1	...	...	...
28 days - 11 months - 28 jours - 11 mois	12	6	6	...	...	...
28 days - less than 2 months - 28 jours - moins de 2 mois	4	3	1	...	...	...
2 months - 2 mois	1	1	-	...	...	...
3 months - 3 mois	2	1	1	...	...	...
4 months - 4 mois	1	1	-	...	...	...
5 months - 5 mois	1	-	1	...	...	...
6 months - 6 mois	-	-	-	...	...	...
7 months - 7 mois	-	-	-	...	...	...
8 months - 8 mois	2	-	2	...	...	...
9 months - 9 mois	-	-	-	...	...	...
10 months - 10 mois	-	-	-	...	...	...
11 months - 11 mois	1	-	1	...	...	...
Spain - Espagne						
2014 (C)						
Total	1 202	662	540	2.8	3.0	2.6
Less than 1 day - Moins de 1 jour	314	179	135	0.7	0.8	0.7
1 - 6 days - 1 - 6 jours	279	167	112	0.7	0.8	0.5

16. Infant deaths and infant mortality rates by age and sex: latest available year, 2006 - 2015
Décès d'enfants de moins d'un an et taux de mortalité infantile selon l'âge et le sexe : dernière année disponible, 2006 - 2015 (continued - suite)

Continent, country or area, year, code[a] and age Continent, pays ou zone, année, code[a] et âge	Number - Nombre			Rate - Taux		
	Both sexes Les deux sexes	Male Masculin	Female Féminin	Both sexes Les deux sexes	Male Masculin	Female Féminin
EUROPE						
Spain - Espagne						
2014 (C)						
7 - 27 days - 7 - 27 jours	288	159	129	0.7	0.7	0.6
28 days - 11 months - 28 jours - 11 mois......................................	321	157	164	0.8	0.7	0.8
Sweden - Suède						
2014 (C)						
Total..	251	151	100	2.2	2.6	1.8
Less than 1 day - Moins de 1 jour	64	36	28	0.6	0.6	♦0.5
1 - 6 days - 1 - 6 jours	67	40	27	0.6	0.7	♦0.5
7 - 27 days - 7 - 27 jours	34	20	14	0.3	♦0.3	♦0.3
28 days - 11 months - 28 jours - 11 mois......................................	86	55	31	0.7	0.9	0.6
Switzerland - Suisse						
2014 (C)						
Total..	331	193	138	3.9	4.4	3.3
Less than 1 day - Moins de 1 jour	174	102	72	2.0	2.3	1.7
1 - 6 days - 1 - 6 jours	54	33	21	0.6	0.8	♦0.5
7 - 27 days - 7 - 27 jours	37	21	16	0.4	♦0.5	♦0.4
7 - 13 days - 7 - 13 jours	19	10	9	♦0.2	♦0.2	♦0.2
14 - 20 days - 14 - 20 jours	10	7	3	♦0.1	♦0.2	♦0.1
21 - 27 days - 21 - 27 jours	8	4	4	♦0.1	♦0.1	♦0.1
28 days - 11 months - 28 jours - 11 mois......................................	66	37	29	0.8	0.8	♦0.7
28 days - less than 2 months - 28 jours - moins de 2 mois	13	5	8	♦0.2	♦0.1	♦0.2
2 months - 2 mois......................................	11	7	4	♦0.1	♦0.2	♦0.1
3 months - 3 mois......................................	10	8	2	♦0.1	♦0.2	-
4 months - 4 mois......................................	7	4	3	♦0.1	♦0.1	♦0.1
5 months - 5 mois......................................	6	-	6	♦0.1	-	♦0.1
6 months - 6 mois......................................	2	1	1	-	-	-
7 months - 7 mois......................................	6	6	-	♦0.1	♦0.1	-
8 months - 8 mois......................................	1	1	-	-	-	-
9 months - 9 mois......................................	3	2	1	-	-	-
10 months - 10 mois......................................	6	3	3	♦0.1	♦0.1	♦0.1
11 months - 11 mois......................................	1	-	1	-	-	-
TFYR of Macedonia - L'ex-R. y. de Macédoine						
2014 (C)						
Total..	233	127	106	9.9	10.4	9.3
Less than 1 day - Moins de 1 jour	61	34	27	2.6	2.8	♦2.4
1 - 6 days - 1 - 6 jours	70	34	36	3.0	2.8	3.2
7 - 27 days - 7 - 27 jours	47	26	21	2.0	♦2.1	♦1.8
28 days - 11 months - 28 jours - 11 mois......................................	55	33	22	2.3	2.7	♦1.9
Ukraine[32]						
2014 (+C)						
Total..	3 656	2 124	1 532	7.8	8.8	6.8
Less than 1 day - Moins de 1 jour	544	302	242	1.2	1.3	1.1
1 - 6 days - 1 - 6 jours	977	593	384	2.1	2.5	1.7
7 - 27 days - 7 - 27 jours	748	435	313	1.6	1.8	1.4
28 days - 11 months - 28 jours - 11 mois......................................	1 387	794	593	3.0	3.3	2.6
United Kingdom of Great Britain and Northern Ireland - Royaume-Uni de Grande-Bretagne et d'Irlande du Nord[33]						
2012 (+C)						
Total..	3 347	1 912	1 435	4.1	4.6	3.6
Less than 1 day - Moins de 1 jour	1 083	627	456	1.3	1.5	1.2
1 - 6 days - 1 - 6 jours	693	399	294	0.9	1.0	0.7
7 - 27 days - 7 - 27 jours	542	297	245	0.7	0.7	0.6
7 - 13 days - 7 - 13 jours	274	153	121	0.3	0.4	0.3
14 - 20 days - 14 - 20 jours	154	75	79	0.2	0.2	0.2
21 - 27 days - 21 - 27 jours	114	69	45	0.1	0.2	0.1
28 days - 11 months - 28 jours - 11 mois......................................	1 029	589	440	1.3	1.4	1.1
28 days - less than 2 months - 28 jours - moins de 2 mois	348	202	146	0.4	0.5	0.4
2 months - 2 mois......................................	170	90	80	0.2	0.2	0.2
3 months - 3 mois......................................	115	67	48	0.1	0.2	0.1
4 months - 4 mois......................................	87	58	29	0.1	0.1	♦0.1
5 months - 5 mois......................................	48	34	14	0.1	0.1	-
6 months - 6 mois......................................	68	37	31	0.1	0.1	0.1
7 months - 7 mois......................................	45	22	23	0.1	♦0.1	♦0.1
8 months - 8 mois......................................	45	26	19	0.1	♦0.1	-
9 months - 9 mois......................................	26	10	16	-	-	-
10 months - 10 mois......................................	45	18	27	0.1	-	♦0.1
11 months - 11 mois......................................	32	25	7	-	♦0.1	-

16. Infant deaths and infant mortality rates by age and sex: latest available year, 2006 - 2015
Décès d'enfants de moins d'un an et taux de mortalité infantile selon l'âge et le sexe : dernière année disponible, 2006 - 2015 (continued - suite)

Continent, country or area, year, code[a] and age Continent, pays ou zone, année, code[a] et âge	Number - Nombre			Rate - Taux		
	Both sexes Les deux sexes	Male Masculin	Female Féminin	Both sexes Les deux sexes	Male Masculin	Female Féminin

OCEANIA - OCÉANIE

Australia - Australie[34]
2014 (+C)

Total	1 012	533	479	3.4	3.5	3.3
Less than 1 day - Moins de 1 jour	442	228	214	1.5	1.5	1.5
1 - 6 days - 1 - 6 jours	143	79	64	0.5	0.5	0.4
7 - 27 days - 7 - 27 jours	129	65	64	0.4	0.4	0.4
7 - 13 days - 7 - 13 jours	69	40	29	0.2	0.3	♦0.2
14 - 20 days - 14 - 20 jours	35	12	23	0.1	♦0.1	♦0.2
21 - 27 days - 21 - 27 jours	25	13	12	♦0.1	♦0.1	♦0.1
28 days - 11 months - 28 jours - 11 mois	298	161	135	1.0	1.0	0.9
28 days - less than 2 months - 28 jours - moins de 2 mois	79	38	41	0.3	0.2	0.3
2 months - 2 mois	61	33	28	0.2	0.2	♦0.2
3 months - 3 mois	36	18	18	0.1	♦0.1	♦0.1
4 months - 4 mois	28	18	10	♦0.1	♦0.1	♦0.1
5 months - 5 mois	16	12	2	♦0.1	♦0.1	-
6 months - 6 mois	20	8	12	♦0.1	♦0.1	♦0.1
7 months - 7 mois	17	10	7	♦0.1	♦0.1	-
8 months - 8 mois	12	5	7	-	-	-
9 months - 9 mois	11	8	3	-	♦0.1	-
10 months - 10 mois	7	5	2	-	-	-
11 months - 11 mois	11	6	5	-	-	-

French Polynesia - Polynésie française
2008 (C)

Total	23	...	...	...	...	...
Less than 7 days - Moins de 7 jours	14	...	...	...	...	...
7 - 27 days - 7 - 27 jours	-	...	...	...	...	...
28 days - 11 months - 28 jours - 11 mois	9	...	...	...	...	...

Guam[35]
2015 (C)

Total	47	23	24	...	...	...
Less than 1 day - Moins de 1 jour	10	4	6	...	...	...
1 - 6 days - 1 - 6 jours	16	9	7	...	...	...
7 - 27 days - 7 - 27 jours	7	1	6	...	...	...
7 - 13 days - 7 - 13 jours	2	-	2	...	...	...
14 - 20 days - 14 - 20 jours	4	1	3	...	...	...
21 - 27 days - 21 - 27 jours	1	-	1	...	...	...
28 days - 11 months - 28 jours - 11 mois	14	9	5	...	...	...
28 days - less than 2 months - 28 jours - moins de 2 mois	2	2	-	...	...	...
2 months - 2 mois	3	3	-	...	...	...
3 months - 3 mois	3	-	3	...	...	...
4 months - 4 mois	-	-	-	...	...	...
5 months - 5 mois	-	-	-	...	...	...
6 months - 6 mois	2	1	1	...	...	...
7 months - 7 mois	-	-	-	...	...	...
8 months - 8 mois	2	2	-	...	...	...
9 months - 9 mois	1	1	-	...	...	...
10 months - 10 mois	1	-	1	...	...	...
11 months - 11 mois	-	-	-	...	...	...

New Caledonia - Nouvelle-Calédonie
2007 (C)

Total	25	15	10	...	...	...
Less than 1 day - Moins de 1 jour	-	-	-	...	...	...
1 - 6 days - 1 - 6 jours	11	9	2	...	...	...
7 - 27 days - 7 - 27 jours	6	2	4	...	...	...
7 - 13 days - 7 - 13 jours	6	2	4	...	...	...
14 - 20 days - 14 - 20 jours	-	-	-	...	...	...
21 - 27 days - 21 - 27 jours	-	-	-	...	...	...
28 days - 11 months - 28 jours - 11 mois	8	4	4	...	...	...
28 days - less than 2 months - 28 jours - moins de 2 mois	-	-	-	...	...	...
2 months - 2 mois	-	-	-	...	...	...
3 months - 3 mois	-	2	-	...	...	...
4 months - 4 mois	-	-	-	...	...	...
5 months - 5 mois	-	-	-	...	...	...
6 months - 6 mois	2	2	-	...	...	...
7 months - 7 mois	-	-	-	...	...	...
8 months - 8 mois	-	-	-	...	...	...
9 months - 9 mois	-	-	-	...	...	...

Décès d'enfants de moins d'un an et taux de mortalité infantile selon l'âge et le sexe : dernière année disponible, 2006 - 2015 (continued - suite)

Continent, country or area, year, code[a] and age Continent, pays ou zone, année, code[a] et âge	Number - Nombre			Rate - Taux		
	Both sexes Les deux sexes	Male Masculin	Female Féminin	Both sexes Les deux sexes	Male Masculin	Female Féminin
OCEANIA - OCÉANIE						
New Caledonia - Nouvelle-Calédonie						
2007 (C)						
10 months - 10 mois	-	-	-	...	...	...
11 months - 11 mois	4	-	4	...	...	...
New Zealand - Nouvelle-Zélande[36]						
2015 (+C)						
Total	249	129	120	4.1	4.1	4.0
Less than 1 day - Moins de 1 jour	87	45	42	1.4	1.4	1.4
1 - 6 days - 1 - 6 jours	45	24	24	0.7	♦0.8	♦0.8
7 - 27 days - 7 - 27 jours	30	12	18	0.5	♦0.4	♦0.6
7 - 13 days - 7 - 13 jours	18	9	9	♦0.3	♦0.3	♦0.3
14 - 20 days - 14 - 20 jours	3	3	3	-	♦0.1	♦0.1
21 - 27 days - 21 - 27 jours	6	-	9	♦0.1	-	♦0.3
28 days - 11 months - 28 jours - 11 mois	90	48	42	1.5	1.5	1.4
28 days - less than 2 months - 28 jours - moins de 2 mois	33	18	12	0.5	♦0.6	♦0.4
2 months - 2 mois	18	9	12	♦0.3	♦0.3	♦0.4
3 months - 3 mois	9	3	3	♦0.1	♦0.1	♦0.1
4 months - 4 mois	9	6	3	♦0.1	♦0.2	♦0.1
5 months - 5 mois	6	3	3	♦0.1	♦0.1	♦0.1
6 months - 6 mois	6	3	3	♦0.1	♦0.1	♦0.1
7 months - 7 mois	-	-	3	-	-	♦0.1
8 months - 8 mois	3	3	-	-	♦0.1	-
9 months - 9 mois	3	3	-	-	♦0.1	-
10 months - 10 mois	3	-	3	-	-	♦0.1
11 months - 11 mois	-	-	-			

FOOTNOTES - NOTES

Italics: data from civil registers which are incomplete or of unknown completeness. - Italiques : données incomplètes ou dont le degré d'exactitude n'est pas connu, provenant des registres de l'état civil.

♦ Rates based on 30 or fewer infant deaths. - Taux basés sur 30 décès d'enfants ou moins.

* Provisional. - Données provisoires.

[a] 'Code' indicates the source of data, as follows:
C - Civil registration, estimated over 90% complete
U - Civil registration, estimated less than 90% complete
| - Other source, estimated reliable
+ - Data tabulated by date of registration rather than occurence
... - Information not available

Le 'Code' indique la source des données, comme suit :
C - Registres de l'état civil considérés complèts à 90 p. 100 au moins
U - Registres de l'état civil qui ne sont pas considérés complèts à 90 p. 100 au moins
| - Autre source, considérée pas douteuses
+ - Données exploitées selon la date de l'enregistrement et non la date de l'événement
... - Information pas disponible

[1] Excludes the islands of St. Brandon and Agalega. - Non compris les îles St. Brandon et Agalega.
[2] Excluding live-born infants who died before their birth was registered. - Non compris les enfants nés vivants décédés avant l'enregistrement de leur naissance.
[3] Unrevised data. - Les données n'ont pas été révisées.
[4] Data for male and female categories may exclude infant deaths of unknown sex. - Les données pour les catégories hommes et femmes peuvent exclure décès d'enfant de sexe inconnu.
[5] Including Canadian residents temporarily in the United States, but excluding United States residents temporarily in Canada. - Y compris les résidents canadiens se trouvant temporairement aux Etats-Unis, mais ne comprenant pas les résidents des Etats-Unis se trouvant temporairement au Canada.

[6] Excluding infant deaths to mothers living abroad. - Exception faite des décès d'enfants en bas âge survenus lorsque la mère résidait à l'étranger.
[7] Data refer to urban areas only. - Données ne concernant que les zones urbaines.
[8] Data refer to resident population only. - Pour la population résidante seulement.
[9] Including deaths abroad and deaths of unknown residence of mother. - Y compris décès à l'étranger et décès de nourrissons nés de mères dont le lieu de résidence n'est pas connu.
[10] Figures for male and female may not add up to the total, since they do not include the category "Unknown". - La somme des chiffres indiqués pour les sexes masculin et féminin peut n'être pas égale au total parce qu'elle n'inclut pas la catégorie " inconnue ".
[11] Total in this table is different from data presented in other tables due to different data source. - Le total figurant dans ce tableau ne correspond pas aux données présentées dans d'autres tableaux parce que les sources de données ne sont pas les mêmes.
[12] Excludes nomadic Indian tribes. - Non compris les tribus d'Indiens nomades.
[13] Source: Reports of the Ministry of Health. - Source : Rapports du Ministère de la Santé.
[14] Excluding infants born alive of less than 28 weeks' gestation, of less than 1 000 grams in weight and 35 centimeters in length, who die within seven days of birth. - Non compris les enfants nés vivants après moins de 28 semaines de gestations, pesant moins de 1 000 grammes, mesurant moins de 35 centimètres et décédés dans les sept jours qui ont suivi leur naissance.
[15] Deaths include deaths among some visitors. Sources: Births and Deaths National Registration System database, and medical records of government hospitals. - Les décès comprennent des décès parmi certains visiteurs. Les sources: Les bases de données des << Births and Deaths National Registration System >> et les dossiers médicaux des hôpitaux du gouvernement.
[16] Data refer to government controlled areas. - Les données se rapportent aux zones contrôlées par le Gouvernement.
[17] Includes data for East Jerusalem and Israeli residents in certain other territories under occupation by Israeli military forces since June 1967. Including deaths abroad of Israeli residents who were out of the country for less than a year. - Y compris les données pour Jérusalem-Est et les résidents israéliens dans certains autres territoires occupés depuis 1967 par les forces armées israéliennes. Y compris les décès à l'étranger de résidents israéliens qui ont quitté le pays depuis moins d'un an.
[18] Data refer to Japanese nationals in Japan only. - Les données se raportent aux nationaux japonais au Japon seulement.

[19] Data source is "Department of Public Health". - La source des données est << Le Service de la santé publique >>.

[20] Data from Births and Deaths Notification System (Ministry of Health and all health care providers). - Les données proviennent du système de notification des naissances et des décès (Ministère de la santé et tous prestataires de soins de santé).

[21] Excluding data for the Pakistan-held part of Jammu and Kashmir, the final status of which has not yet been determined. Based on the results of the Pakistan Demographic Survey. - Non compris les données concernant la partie du Jammu et Cachemire occupée par le Pakistan dont le statut définitif n'a pas été déterminé. Données extraites de l'enquête démographique effectuée par le Pakistan.

[22] Excluding alien armed forces, civilian aliens employed by armed forces, and foreign diplomatic personnel and their dependants. - Non compris les militaires étrangers, les civils étrangers employés par les forces armées ni le personnel diplomatique étranger et les membres de leur famille les accompagnant.

[23] Including armed forces stationed outside the country, but excluding alien armed forces stationed in the area. - Y compris les militaires nationaux hors du pays, mais non compris les militaires étrangers en garnison sur le territoire.

[24] Excluding Faeroe Islands and Greenland shown separately, if available. - Non compris les Iles Féroé et le Groenland, qui font l'objet de rubriques distinctes, si disponible.

[25] Excluding Åland Islands. - Non compris les Îles d'Åland.

[26] Data include the deceased infants with Hungarian usual residence regardless of whether the death occurred in Hungary or in a foreign country, and do not include the deceased infants with foreign country usual residence. - Les données comprennent les nourrissons décédés alors que leur résidence habituelle était en Hongrie, que le décès ait eu lieu en Hongrie ou dans un pays étranger, et ne comprennent pas les nourrissons décédés dont la residence habituelle était dans un pays étranger.

[27] Including residents outside the country if listed in a Netherlands population register. - Englobe les résidents se trouvant à l'étranger à condition qu'ils soient inscrits sur le registre de population des Pays-Bas.

[28] Including residents temporarily outside the country. - Y compris les résidents se trouvant temporairement hors du pays.

[29] Data refer to usually resident population. - Les données concernent la population habituellement résidente.

[30] Excluding Transnistria and the municipality of Bender. - Les données ne tiennent pas compte de l'information sur la Transnistria et la municipalité de Bender.

[31] Excludes data for Kosovo and Metohia. - Sans les données pour le Kosovo et Metohie.

[32] Data includes deaths resulting from births with weight 500g and more (if weight is unknown - with length 25 centimeters and more, or with gestation during 22 weeks or more). The Government of Ukraine has informed the United Nations that it is not in a position to provide statistical data concerning the Autonomous Republic of Crimea and the city of Sevastopol. - Y compris les décès de nouveau-nés de 500 grammes ou plus (si le poids est inconnu – de 25 centimètres de long ou plus, ou après une grossesse de 22 semaines ou plus). Le gouvernement Ukrainien a informé l'ONU qu'il n'est pas en mesure de fournir des données statistiques concernant la République autonome de Crimée et la ville de Sébastopol.

[33] Excluding Channel Islands (Guernsey and Jersey) and Isle of Man, shown separately, if available. - Non compris les îles Anglo-Normandes (Guernesey et Jersey) et l'île de Man, qui font l'objet de rubriques distinctes, si disponible.

[34] This data has been randomly rounded to protect confidentiality. Individual figures may not add up to totals, and values for the same data may vary in different tables. - Ces données ont été arrondies de façon aléatoire afin d'en préserver la confidentialité. La somme de certains chiffres peut ne pas correspondre aux totaux indiqués et les valeurs des mêmes données peuvent varier d'un tableau à un autre.

[35] Including United States military personnel, their dependants and contract employees. - Y compris les militaires des Etats-Unis, les membres de leur famille les accompagnant et les agents contractuels des Etats-Unis.

[36] Random rounding to base 3 is applied in this table as a confidentiality measure. - Les chiffres sont arrondis à la base 3 de manière aléatoire, pour des raisons de confidentialité.

Table 17 - *Demographic Yearbook 2015*

Table 17 presents maternal deaths and maternal mortality ratios for as many years available between 2005 and 2014.

Description of variables: Maternal deaths are defined for the purposes of the Demographic Yearbook as those caused by deliveries and complications of pregnancy, childbirth and the puerperium, within 42 days of termination of pregnancy. They are usually defined as deaths coded "38-41" for ICD-9 Basic Tabulation List or as deaths coded "A34", "O00-O95", "O98-O99" for ICD-10, respectively[1]. However, data for ICD-10 shown in this table include deaths due to "O96" and "O97" which refer to deaths from any obstetric cause occurring more than 42 days but less than one year after delivery and death from sequelae of direct obstetric causes occurring one year or more after delivery.

For further information on the definition of maternal mortality from the tenth revisions of the *International Statistical Classification of Diseases and Related Health Problems*[2], see also section 4.3 of the Technical Notes.

Statistics on maternal death presented in this table are provided by the World Health Organisation. They are limited to countries or areas that meet the criterion that cause-of-death statistics are either classified by or convertible to the ninth or tenth revisions mentioned above. Data that are classified by the tenth revision are set in bold in the table.

Ratios computation: Maternal mortality ratios are the annual number of maternal deaths per 100 000 live births (table 9) in the same year. These ratios have been calculated by the Statistics Division of the United Nations Department of Economic and Social Affairs. If maternal mortality data are considered incomplete, or if live birth data for the year are not available, no ratio has been calculated. Ratios based on 30 or fewer maternal deaths are identified by the symbol "♦".

Reliability of data: Countries and areas that have incomplete (less than 90 per cent completeness) or of unknown completeness of cause of deaths data coverage are considered to provide unreliable data, which are set in *italics* rather than in roman type. Ratios on these data are not computed. Information on completeness is normally provided by the World Health Organisation. When this is not the case, information on completeness is set to coincide with that of table 18. The reliability of data for the completeness of cause of death provided by the World Health Organisation[3] may differ from the reliability of data for the total number of reported deaths. Therefore, there are cases when the quality code in table 18 does not correspond with the typeface used in this table.

Territorial composition as set in Section 2.2 of "Technical Notes on the Statistical Tables", including or excluding certain population of a country refers only to the denominator.

Limitations: Statistics on maternal deaths are subject to the same qualifications that have been set forth for vital statistics in general and death statistics in particular as discussed in section 4 of the Technical Notes. The reliability of the data, an indication of which is described above, is an important factor in considering the limitations. In addition, maternal-death statistics are subject to all the qualifications relating to cause-of-death statistics. These have been set forth in section 4 of the Technical Notes.

Maternal mortality ratios are subject to the limitations of the data on live births with which they have been calculated. These have been set forth in the technical notes for table 9. Specific information pertaining to individual countries or areas is given in the footnotes to table 9.

The calculation of the maternal mortality ratios based on the total number of live births approximates the risk of dying from complications of pregnancy, childbirth or puerperium. Ideally this rate should be based on the number of women exposed to the risk of pregnancy, in other words, the number of women conceiving. Since it is impossible to know how many women have conceived, the total number of live births is used in calculating this rate.

Earlier data: Maternal deaths and maternal mortality ratios have been shown in previous issues of the *Demographic Yearbook*. For information on specific years covered, the reader should consult the Index.

It should however be noted that in issues prior to 1975, maternal mortality rates were calculated using the female population rather than live births for the denominators. Therefore, maternal mortality ratios published since 1975 are not comparable to the earlier maternal death rates.

NOTES

[1] Except for Belarus, Russian Federation, Seychelles, Turkmenistan and Ukraine, where A34 and O95 are excluded.

[2] *International Statistical Classification of Diseases and Related Health Problems*, Tenth Revision, Volume 2, World Health Organization, Geneva, 1992. The publication is available online at: http://www.who.int/classifications/icd/en/

[3] For more information on specific method used for countries, see "Mathers CD, Bernard C, Iburg KM, Inoue M, Ma Fat D, Shibuya K et al. *Global burden of disease in 2002: data sources, methods and results*. Geneva, World Health Organization, 2003 (GPE Discussion Paper No. 54).

Tableau 17 – *Annuaire démographique 2015*

Le tableau 17 présente des statistiques et des taux de mortalité liée à la maternité pour les années disponibles entre 2005 et 2014.

Description des variables : aux fins de *l'Annuaire démographique*, les décès liés à la maternité sont ceux entraînés par l'accouchement ou les complications de la grossesse, de l'accouchement et des suites de couches dans un délai de 42 jours après la terminaison de la grossesse. Ils sont généralement associés aux codes 38 à 41 dans le cas de la liste de base pour la mise en tableaux de la CIM-9 et aux codes A34, O00 à O95 et O98 et O99 dans le cas de la CIM-10[1]. Les statistiques associées à des codes correspondant à la CIM-10 englobent des décès de type O96 et O97, qui désignent les décès liés à des causes obstétriques se produisant après 42 jours mais moins d'un an après l'accouchement et les décès entraînés par les séquelles de complications obstétriques directes qui se produisent un an ou plus après l'accouchement.

Pour plus de précisions concernant les définitions de la mortalité liée à la maternité dans la dixième révision de la *Classification statistique internationale des maladies et des problèmes de santé connexes*[2], se reporter également à la section 4.3 des Notes techniques.

Les statistiques de mortalité liée à la maternité présentées dans le tableau 17 émanent de l'Organisation mondiale de la santé. Elles ne se rapportent qu'aux pays ou zones qui répondent aux critères selon lesquels les statistiques relatives à la cause des décès sont conformes à la liste de la neuvième ou de la dixième révision de la CIM ou peuvent être aisément comparées aux catégories de cette liste. Les données conformes à la dixième révision sont indiquées en gras dans le tableau.

Calcul des taux : les taux de mortalité maternelle représentent le nombre annuel de décès dus à la maternité pour 100 000 naissances vivantes (données du tableau 9) de la même année. Ces taux ont été calculés par la Division de statistique du Département des affaires économiques et sociales de l'Organisation des Nations Unies. Si les données des décès dus à la maternité sont incomplètes ou si les naissances vivantes pour l'année ne sont pas disponibles, les taux ne sont pas calculés. Les taux fondés sur 30 décès liés à la maternité ou moins sont signalés par le signe "♦".

Fiabilité des données : les statistiques relatives aux pays et aux zones pour lesquels la couverture des données concernant les causes de décès est incomplète (mois de 90 pour cent) ou dont le degré de complétude n'est pas connue sont jugés douteuses et apparaissent en *italique* et non en caractères romains. Les taux correspondant ne sont pas calculés. L'information sur la complétude est normalement fournie par l'Organisation Mondiale de la Santé. Si ce n'est pas le cas, l'information sur la complétude est reprise de tableau 18. La fiabilité des données relatives aux causes de décès fournie par l'Organisation Mondiale de la Santé[3] peut différer de la fiabilité des données relatives au nombre de décès enregistrés. En conséquence, il peut apparaitre de différences entre les codes de fiabilité du tableau 18 et du présent tableau.

La composition territoriale est définie dans la Section 2.2 des "Notes Techniques sur les tableaux statistiques". L'inclusion ou l'exclusion de certaines populations d'un pays ne concerne que le dénominateur.

Insuffisance des données : les statistiques de la mortalité liée à la maternité appellent toutes les réserves qui ont été formulées à propos des statistiques de l'état civil en général et des statistiques relatives à la mortalité en particulier (voir la section 4 des Notes techniques). La fiabilité des données, au sujet de laquelle des indications ont été fournies plus haut, est un facteur important. En outre, les statistiques de la mortalité liée à la maternité appellent les mêmes réserves que celles exposées à la section 4 des Notes techniques en ce qui concerne les statistiques des causes de décès.

Les taux de mortalité maternelle appellent également toutes les réserves formulées à propos des statistiques des naissances vivantes qui ont servi à leur calcul (voir à ce sujet les notes techniques relatives au tableau 9). Des précisions sur certains pays ou zones sont données dans les notes se rapportant au tableau 9.

En prenant le nombre total des naissances vivantes comme base pour le calcul des taux de mortalité maternelle, on obtient une mesure approximative de la probabilité de décès dus aux complications de la grossesse, de l'accouchement et des suites de couches. Idéalement, ces taux devraient être calculés sur la base du nombre de femmes exposées aux risques liés à la grossesse, c'est-à-dire sur la base du nombre de femmes qui conçoivent. Étant donné qu'il est impossible de connaître le nombre de femmes ayant conçu, c'est le nombre total de naissances vivantes que l'on utilise pour calculer ces taux.

Données publiées antérieurement : des statistiques concernant les décès liés à la maternité (nombre de décès et taux) ont déjà été présentées dans des éditions antérieures de l'*Annuaire démographique*. Pour plus de précisions concernant les années pour lesquelles ces données ont été publiées, se reporter à l'index.

Il faut souligner que, avant 1975, les taux de mortalité maternelle étaient calculés sur la base de la population féminine et non sur celle du nombre de naissances vivantes. Ils ne sont donc pas comparables à ceux qui figurent dans les éditions de l'*Annuaire démographique* parues après 1975.

NOTES

[1] Sauf pour Bélarus, Fédération de Russie, Seychelles, Turkménistan et Ukraine où A34 et O95 sont exclus.
[2] *Classification statistique internationale des maladies et des problèmes de santé connexes*, dixième révision, volume 2. Genève, Organisation mondiale de la santé, 1992.
[3] Pour plus d'information sur les méthodes spécifiques utilisées pour les pays, voir "Mathers CD, Bernard C, Iburg KM, Inoue M, Ma Fat D, Shibuya K et al. *Global burden of disease in 2002: data sources, methods and results*. Geneva, World Health Organization, 2003 (GPE Discussion Paper No. 54).

17. Maternal deaths and maternal mortality ratios: 2005 - 2014
Mortalité liée à la maternité, nombre de décès et taux : 2005 - 2014

Continent and country or area / Continent et pays ou zone	Co-de[a]	2005	2006	2007	2008	2009	2010	2011	2012	2013	2014
AFRICA - AFRIQUE											
Cabo Verde											
Number - Nombre...............	C	...	...	...	...	...	...	5	1	...	...
Egypt - Égypte											
Number - Nombre...............	C	...	604	567	449	579	519	550	531	503	...
Rate - Taux.........................	C	...	32.6	29.1	21.9	26.1	23.0	22.5	20.2	19.2	...
Mauritius - Maurice											
Number - Nombre...............	+C	4	3	6	6	10	4	5	9	9	7
Rate - Taux.........................	+C	♦21.3	♦17.0	♦35.2	♦36.6	♦65.2	♦26.7	♦34.0	♦62.1	♦66.7	♦52.7
Mayotte											
Number - Nombre...............	C	...	...	...	...	...	...	-	1	1	...
Morocco - Maroc											
Number - Nombre...............	U	...	...	...	74	...	65	98	93	...	...
Reunion - Réunion											
Number - Nombre...............	...	4	5	...	2	1	1	5	2	2	...
Seychelles											
Number - Nombre...............	+C	1	-	-	1	1	2	-	-	-	-
Rate - Taux.........................	+C	♦65.1	-	-	♦64.7	♦63.3	♦133.0	-	-	-	-
South Africa - Afrique du Sud											
Number - Nombre...............	...	1 249[1]	1 388[1]	1 762[2]	1 808[2]	1 880[2]	1 658[2]	1 260[2]	1 050[2]	946[2]	1 027[2]
Rate - Taux.........................	...	...	...	163.6	164.3	179.5	162.9	123.1	102.9	94.5	103.9
Tunisia - Tunisie											
Number - Nombre...............	U	...	...	...	...	...	...	...	...	28	...
AMERICA, NORTH - AMÉRIQUE DU NORD											
Anguilla											
Number - Nombre...............	...	-	-	...	1	-	1	-	-	-	-
Antigua and Barbuda - Antigua-et-Barbuda											
Number - Nombre...............	+U	-	-	1	-	-	...	...	1	-	...
Aruba											
Number - Nombre...............	...	...	-	-	-	-	-	2	-	-	...
Bahamas											
Number - Nombre...............	+C	4	...	...	3	7	5	-	3	...	...
Rate - Taux.........................	+C	♦72.1	...	...	♦58.5	♦139.2	♦101.7	-	♦67.1	...	...
Barbados - Barbade											
Number - Nombre...............	C	...	1	...	2	-	-	2	1	...	...
Rate - Taux.........................	C	...	♦29.3	...	♦56.4	-	-	♦60.9	♦31.4	...	...
Belize											
Number - Nombre...............	C	10	3	2	2	4	4	-	2	-	...
Rate - Taux.........................	C	♦119.1	♦41.8	♦28.4	♦28.1	♦53.9	♦55.3	-	...	...	...
Bermuda - Bermudes											
Number - Nombre...............	...	-	1	-	-	-	-	-	-	-	...
British Virgin Islands - Îles Vierges britanniques											
Number - Nombre...............	...	...	...	...	-	-	-	...	...	...	...
Canada											
Number - Nombre...............	C	...	28	24	34	29	24	18	...	...	...
Rate - Taux.........................	C	...	♦7.9	♦6.5	9.0	♦7.6	♦6.4	♦4.8	...	...	...
Cayman Islands - Îles Caïmanes											
Number - Nombre...............	...	...	...	...	-	-	-	...	...	-	...
Costa Rica											
Number - Nombre...............	...	24[3]	24[3]	10[3]	20[3]	10[4]	14[4]	17[4]	22[4]	10[4]	...
Rate - Taux.........................	...	...	...	...	...	♦13.3	♦19.7	♦23.1	♦30.0	♦14.2	...
Cuba											
Number - Nombre...............	C	66	62	42	57	66	61	61	55	56	...
Rate - Taux.........................	C	54.7	55.7	37.3	46.5	50.8	47.8	45.8	43.8	44.5	...
Dominica - Dominique											
Number - Nombre...............	+C	-	-	-	1	-	2	-	-	3	...
Rate - Taux.........................	+C	-	-	-	♦103.7	-	♦214.4	-	-	♦322.2	...
Dominican Republic - République dominicaine											
Number - Nombre...............	U	...	...	...	...	56	37	188	177	...	...
El Salvador											
Number - Nombre...............	+U	23	21	17	18	14	19	16	17	...	...

Continent and country or area / Continent et pays ou zone	Code[a]	2005	2006	2007	2008	2009	2010	2011	2012	2013	2014
AMERICA, NORTH - AMÉRIQUE DU NORD											
Grenada - Grenade											
Number - Nombre	...	-[1]	-[1]	-[1]	-[2]	-[2]	-[2]	-[2]	2[2]	1[2]	...
Rate - Taux	...	...	...	...	-	-	-	-	♦120.4	♦54.4	...
Guadeloupe											
Number - Nombre	...	1	2	...	2	1	1	-	4	1	
Guatemala											
Number - Nombre	...	354[1]	298[1]	310[1]	328[1]	346[1]	355[2]	315[2]	356[2]	318[2]	...
Rate - Taux	...	...	...	...	...	...	98.1	84.3	91.6	82.1	...
Honduras											
Number - Nombre	+U	...	...	...	...	...	28	47	31	37	
Jamaica - Jamaïque											
Number - Nombre	...	...	...	...	...	...	28	28	...	...	
Martinique											
Number - Nombre	...	-	1	...	1	2	-	2	1	3	
Mexico - Mexique											
Number - Nombre	+C	1 269	1 188	1 122	1 135	1 230	1 030	1 027	1 036	969	...
Rate - Taux	+C	59.3	55.2	51.3	50.6	54.6	47.5	45.4	47.3	44.7	...
Montserrat											
Number - Nombre		-	-	-	-	-	-	-	-	-	-
Nicaragua											
Number - Nombre	+U	93	93	...	69	78	80	71	72	71	...
Panama											
Number - Nombre	...	...	36[3]	40[4]	41[4]	29[4]	41[4]	59[4]	49[4]	41[4]	...
Rate - Taux	...	...	...	59.4	59.6	♦42.4	60.3	80.5	64.9	55.6	...
Puerto Rico - Porto Rico											
Number - Nombre	...	5	...	...	6	10	6	5	1	2	
Saint Kitts and Nevis - Saint-Kitts-et-Nevis											
Number - Nombre	+U	-	1	-	1	-	-	1	1	...	
Saint Lucia - Sainte-Lucie											
Number - Nombre	...	...	...	...	1[2]	...	3[1]	1[1]	1[1]	...	
Rate - Taux	...	...	...	...	♦45.2	...	...	...	...	...	
Saint Pierre and Miquelon - Saint Pierre-et-Miquelon											
Number - Nombre	...	...	-	...	-	...	...				
Saint Vincent and the Grenadines - Saint-Vincent-et-les Grenadines											
Number - Nombre	...	...	-	-	2[4]	-[4]	2[4]	1[4]	-[4]	2[4]	...
Rate - Taux	...	...	...	...	♦105.2	-	♦112.1	♦58.0	-	♦115.1	...
Trinidad and Tobago - Trinité-et-Tobago											
Number - Nombre	U	...	12	...	11	...	...	...	...	...	
Turks and Caicos Islands - Îles Turques et Caïques											
Number - Nombre	...	-	...	...	-	1	...	...	...	-	...
United States of America - États-Unis d'Amérique											
Number - Nombre	C	760	756	766	795	962	825	931	990	1 138	...
Rate - Taux	C	18.4	17.7	17.7	18.7	23.3	20.6	23.5	25.0	28.9	...
United States Virgin Islands - Îles Vierges américaines											
Number - Nombre	...	-	...	...	...	-	-	...	...		
AMERICA, SOUTH - AMÉRIQUE DU SUD											
Argentina - Argentine											
Number - Nombre	+C	290	341	332	319	422	331	318	280	274	...
Rate - Taux	+C	40.7	49.0	47.4	42.8	56.6	43.8	42.0	37.9	36.3	...
Brazil - Brésil											
Number - Nombre	...	1 661[1]	1 634[1]	1 613[1]	1 641[2]	1 884[2]	1 728[2]	1 680[2]	1 647[2]	1 788[2]	...
Rate - Taux	...	...	...	...	58.8	68.4	62.6	59.5	58.2	63.1	...
Chile - Chili											
Number - Nombre	C	48	47	42	36	43	46	46	54	52	...
Rate - Taux	C	20.8	20.3	17.5	14.6	17.0	18.4	18.6	22.2	21.5	...

Continent and country or area Continent et pays ou zone	Code[a]	2005	2006	2007	2008	2009	2010	2011	2012	2013	2014
AMERICA, SOUTH - AMÉRIQUE DU SUD											
Colombia - Colombie											
Number - Nombre	...	504[1]	519[2]	503[2]	433[2]	496[2]	474[2]	459[2]	452[2]	...	...
Rate - Taux	...	...	73.8	72.1	61.6	72.3	73.4	69.3	66.9	...	...
Ecuador - Équateur											
Number - Nombre	U	143	135	176	162	208	202	239	202	158	...
French Guiana - Guyane française											
Number - Nombre	...	1	1	...	4	1	3	-	2	1	...
Guyana											
Number - Nombre	U	24	20	...	16	9	20	14	...	...	...
Paraguay											
Number - Nombre	+U	135	123	...	117	128	100	94	91	100	...
Peru - Pérou											
Number - Nombre	+U	...	...	155	192	163	137	148	126	97	...
Suriname											
Number - Nombre	...	4[1]	...	...	9[2]	11[2]	6[2]	7[2]	2[2]	...	...
Rate - Taux	...	...	...	...	♦89.1	♦112.3	♦61.8	♦72.1	♦19.6	...	...
Uruguay											
Number - Nombre	C	...	...	...	6	11	2	...	5	9	...
Rate - Taux	C	...	...	...	♦12.7	♦23.3	♦4.2	...	♦10.4	♦18.5	...
Venezuela (Bolivarian Republic of) - Venezuela (République bolivarienne du)											
Number - Nombre	C	351	356	332	377	434	412	436	416	...	...
Rate - Taux	C	52.7	55.1	54.0	64.8	73.1	69.7	70.9	67.1	...	...
ASIA - ASIE											
Armenia - Arménie											
Number - Nombre	U	...	10	...	16	12	4	6	5	...	8
Azerbaijan - Azerbaïdjan											
Number - Nombre	C	...	...	30	...	...	...	...	...	...	...
Rate - Taux	C	...	...	♦19.7	...	...	...	...	...	...	...
Bahrain - Bahreïn											
Number - Nombre	...	...	-[2]	3[2]	3[2]	3[1]	1[1]	2[1]	2[1]	4[1]	...
Rate - Taux	...	...	...	-	♦18.7	♦17.6	...	...	...	...	...
Brunei Darussalam - Brunéi Darussalam											
Number - Nombre	...	...	...	1[4]	-[4]	1[4]	1[3]	-[3]	3[3]	1[3]	-[3]
Rate - Taux	...	...	...	♦15.8	-	♦15.1	...	...	...	...	...
China, Hong Kong SAR - Chine, Hong Kong RAS											
Number - Nombre	...	2	1	1	2	2	1	1	2	-	...
Cyprus - Chypre											
Number - Nombre	U	2	1	-	1	-	1	-	-	1	...
Georgia - Géorgie											
Number - Nombre	C	...	11	2	...	32	13	21	14	16	18
Rate - Taux	C	...	♦23.0	♦4.1	...	50.5	♦20.8	♦36.2	♦24.5	♦27.6	♦29.7
Iraq											
Number - Nombre	U	...	...	...	62	...	...	...	...	...	...
Israel - Israël											
Number - Nombre	C	4	11	7	8	5	7	2	9	14	...
Rate - Taux	C	♦2.8	♦7.4	♦4.6	♦5.1	♦3.1	♦4.2	♦1.2	♦5.3	♦8.2	...
Japan - Japon											
Number - Nombre	C	66	63	39	41	61	49	43	50	41	...
Rate - Taux	C	6.2	5.8	3.6	3.8	5.7	4.6	4.1	4.8	4.0	...
Jordan - Jordanie											
Number - Nombre	U	...	...	...	25	26	46	34	...	...	...
Kazakhstan											
Number - Nombre	...	81[1]	100[1]	107[1]	86[2]	94[2]	65[2]	48[2]	41[2]	41[2]	37[2]
Rate - Taux	...	...	...	...	24.1	26.4	17.7	12.9	10.8	10.6	...
Kuwait - Koweït											
Number - Nombre	C	...	1	-	5	7	3	6	1	4	7
Rate - Taux	C	...	♦1.9	-	♦9.2	♦12.4	♦5.2	♦10.3	♦1.7	♦6.7	♦11.4
Kyrgyzstan - Kirghizstan											
Number - Nombre	...	66[1]	67[1]	64[1]	70[2]	86[2]	75[2]	81[2]	76[2]	56[2]	...
Rate - Taux	...	...	...	...	55.0	63.5	51.3	54.1	49.1	36.0	...

Continent and country or area Continent et pays ou zone	Co-de[a]	2005	2006	2007	2008	2009	2010	2011	2012	2013	2014
ASIA - ASIE											
Malaysia - Malaisie											
Number - Nombre	U	...	*128*	...	*133*	...	...	...	...	...	...
Maldives											
Number - Nombre	...	*1*[3]	...	*2*[4]	*4*[3]	...	*7*[3]	*4*[3]	...	...	...
Rate - Taux	...	...	...	◆30.4	...	...	...	...	...	...	...
Oman											
Number - Nombre	U	...	...	...	...	*3*	*6*	...	...	...	...
Philippines											
Number - Nombre	U	...	...	...	*1 731*	...	*1 718*	*1 465*	...	...	...
Qatar											
Number - Nombre	...	...	*1*[2]	*5*[2]	*2*[2]	*4*[2]	*2*[1]	*1*[1]	*1*[1]	...	...
Rate - Taux	...	...	◆7.1	◆31.9	◆11.6	◆21.8	...	...	...	...	...
Republic of Korea - République de Corée											
Number - Nombre	C	*53*	*54*	...	*39*	*48*	*75*	*85*	*56*	*51*	...
Rate - Taux	C	*12.2*	*12.0*	...	*8.4*	*10.8*	*16.0*	*18.0*	*11.6*	*11.7*	...
Saudi Arabia - Arabie saoudite											
Number - Nombre	U	...	...	...	...	*54*	...	...	*45*	...	...
Singapore - Singapour											
Number - Nombre	+U	*4*	*3*	...	*2*	-	*1*	*2*	*1*	-	-
Sri Lanka											
Number - Nombre	+U	...	*53*	...	...	...	...	...	...	...	...
Syrian Arab Republic - République arabe syrienne											
Number - Nombre	+C	...	...	...	...	...	*23*	...	...	...	...
Rate - Taux	+C	...	...	...	...	...	◆2.6	...	...	...	...
Tajikistan - Tadjikistan											
Number - Nombre	U	*28*	...	...	...	...	...	...	...	...	...
Thailand - Thaïlande											
Number - Nombre	+U	...	*92*	...	...	...	*78*	*71*	*141*	*166*	*166*
Turkey - Turquie											
Number - Nombre	+U	...	...	...	...	*37*	*46*	*58*	*55*	*302*	...
Turkmenistan - Turkménistan											
Number - Nombre	U	...	...	...	...	...	...	...	*7*	*9*	...
United Arab Emirates - Émirats arabes unis											
Number - Nombre	+U	...	...	...	*1*	*2*	*4*	...	...	...	...
Uzbekistan - Ouzbékistan											
Number - Nombre	U	*145*	...	...	...	...	...	...	...	...	*131*
EUROPE											
Austria - Autriche											
Number - Nombre	C	*3*	*2*	*3*	*2*	*2*	*1*	*2*	*1*	*1*	*7*
Rate - Taux	C	◆3.8	◆2.6	◆3.9	◆2.6	◆2.6	◆1.3	◆2.6	◆1.3	◆1.3	◆8.6
Belarus - Bélarus											
Number - Nombre	C	...	...	*7*	*3*	*1*	*1*	*1*	...	-	*1*
Rate - Taux	C	...	...	◆6.8	◆2.8	◆0.9	◆0.9	◆0.9	...	-	◆0.8
Belgium - Belgique											
Number - Nombre	C	...	*9*	...	*7*	*6*	*8*	*9*	*5*	*3*	...
Rate - Taux	C	...	◆7.3	...	◆5.5	◆4.7	◆6.1	◆7.0	◆3.9	◆2.4	...
Bosnia and Herzegovina - Bosnie-Herzégovine											
Number - Nombre	U	...	...	...	...	...	...	*2*	...	...	-
Bulgaria - Bulgarie											
Number - Nombre	C	*8*	*5*	*8*	*5*	*4*	*6*	*2*	*3*	*8*	...
Rate - Taux	C	◆11.3	◆6.8	◆10.6	◆6.4	◆4.9	◆7.9	◆2.8	◆4.3	◆12.0	...
Croatia - Croatie											
Number - Nombre	C	*3*	*4*	*6*	*3*	*6*	*4*	*4*	*3*	*2*	*1*
Rate - Taux	C	◆7.1	◆9.7	◆14.3	◆6.9	◆13.5	◆9.2	◆9.7	◆7.2	◆5.0	◆2.5
Czech Republic - République tchèque											
Number - Nombre	C	*3*	*9*	*3*	*7*	*3*	*3*	*2*	*6*	*1*	*4*
Rate - Taux	C	◆2.9	◆8.5	◆2.6	◆5.9	◆2.5	◆2.6	◆1.8	◆5.5	◆0.9	◆3.6
Denmark - Danemark											
Number - Nombre	C	-	*5*	...	*4*	*4*	-	*2*	-	...	...
Rate - Taux	C	-	◆7.7	...	◆6.2	◆6.4	-	◆3.4	-	...	...

Continent and country or area / Continent et pays ou zone	Codea	2005	2006	2007	2008	2009	2010	2011	2012	2013	2014
EUROPE											
Estonia - Estonie											
Number - Nombre	C	2	1	-	-	-	1	1	1	1	-
Rate - Taux	C	♦13.9	♦6.7	-	-	-	♦6.3	♦6.8	♦7.1	♦7.4	-
Finland - Finlande											
Number - Nombre	C	3	4	1	5	1	3	-	2	1	3
Rate - Taux	C	♦5.2	♦6.8	♦1.7	♦8.4	♦1.7	♦4.9	-	♦3.4	♦1.7	♦5.3
France											
Number - Nombre	C	41	59	60	52	75	68	45	44	38	...
Rate - Taux	C	5.3	7.4	7.6	6.5	9.5	8.5	5.7	5.6	4.9	...
Germany - Allemagne											
Number - Nombre	C	28	41	28	36	35	37	32	31	29	29
Rate - Taux	C	♦4.1	6.1	♦4.1	5.3	5.3	5.5	4.8	4.6	♦4.3	♦4.1
Greece - Grèce											
Number - Nombre	C	-	3	2	-	4	6	4	...	...	...
Rate - Taux	C	-	♦2.7	♦1.8	-	♦3.4	♦5.2	♦3.8	...	...	...
Hungary - Hongrie											
Number - Nombre	C	5	8	8	17	18	14	9	9	13	6
Rate - Taux	C	♦5.1	♦8.0	♦8.2	♦17.1	♦18.7	♦15.5	♦10.2	♦10.0	♦14.5	♦6.4
Iceland - Islande											
Number - Nombre	C	-	-	-	-	-	...	...	...	...	...
Ireland - Irlande											
Number - Nombre	+C	2	-	1	3	3	3	2	2	3	...
Rate - Taux	+C	♦3.3	-	♦1.4	♦4.0	♦4.0	♦4.0	♦2.7	♦2.8	♦4.4	...
Italy - Italie											
Number - Nombre	C	...	11	13	13	19	16	14	11	...	...
Rate - Taux	C	...	♦2.0	♦2.3	♦2.3	♦3.3	♦2.8	♦2.6	♦2.1	...	...
Latvia - Lettonie											
Number - Nombre	+C	1	2	6	2	7	4	-	4	2	2
Rate - Taux	+C	♦4.6	♦8.7	♦25.0	♦8.2	♦31.8	♦20.2	-	♦20.1	♦9.7	♦9.2
Lithuania - Lituanie											
Number - Nombre	+C	4	-	2	3	-	2	2	3	2	1
Rate - Taux	+C	♦13.6	-	♦6.7	♦9.5	-	♦6.5	♦6.6	♦9.8	♦6.7	♦3.3
Luxembourg											
Number - Nombre	+C	1	-	1	1	-	1	-	1	1	-
Rate - Taux	+C	♦18.6	-	♦18.3	♦17.9	-	♦17.0	-	♦16.6	♦16.4	-
Malta - Malte											
Number - Nombre	+C	-	-	-	1	-	1	-	-	-	-
Rate - Taux	+C	-	-	-	♦24.9	-	♦25.7	-	-	-	-
Montenegro - Monténégro											
Number - Nombre	C	...	-	1	-	-	...	...	...	...	...
Rate - Taux	C	...	-	♦12.8	-	-	...	...	...	...	...
Netherlands - Pays-Bas											
Number - Nombre	+C	16	15	9	8	9	4	3	6	5	...
Rate - Taux	+C	♦8.5	♦8.1	♦5.0	♦4.3	♦4.9	♦2.2	♦1.7	♦3.4	♦2.9	...
Norway - Norvège											
Number - Nombre	+C	2	5	4	3	1	3	3	-	2	2
Rate - Taux	+C	♦3.5	♦8.5	♦6.8	♦5.0	♦1.6	♦4.9	♦5.0	-	♦3.4	♦3.4
Poland - Pologne											
Number - Nombre	C	11	11	11	19	8	9	9	4	7	8
Rate - Taux	C	♦3.0	♦2.9	♦2.8	♦4.6	♦1.9	♦2.2	♦2.3	♦1.0	♦1.9	♦2.1
Portugal											
Number - Nombre	+C	...	...	5	4	7	8	5	4	5	6
Rate - Taux	+C	...	...	♦4.9	♦3.8	♦7.0	♦7.9	♦5.2	♦4.5	♦6.0	♦7.3
Republic of Moldova - République de Moldova											
Number - Nombre	...	8[3]	6[4]	7[4]	17[4]	7[4]	18[4]	6[4]	12[4]	6[4]	7[4]
Rate - Taux	...	...	♦16.0	♦18.4	♦43.6	♦17.2	♦44.5	♦15.3	♦30.4	♦15.8	♦18.1
Romania - Roumanie											
Number - Nombre	+C	37	34	33	30	47	51	50	23	27	24
Rate - Taux	+C	16.7	15.5	15.4	♦13.5	21.1	24.0	25.5	♦11.4	♦14.8	♦12.4
Russian Federation - Fédération de Russie											
Number - Nombre	+C	370	352	356	359	388	298	291	...	...	...
Rate - Taux	+C	25.4	23.8	22.1	20.9	22.0	16.7	16.2	...	...	...
San Marino - Saint-Marin											
Number - Nombre	+U	-	...	...	...	...	...	...	...	...	...
Serbia - Serbie											
Number - Nombre	...	10[3]	9[3]	-[3]	4[3]	6[3]	12[4]	7[4]	10[4]	9[4]	8[4]
Rate - Taux	...	...	...	...	...	...	♦17.6	♦10.7	♦14.9	♦13.7	♦12.0

17. Maternal deaths and maternal mortality ratios: 2005 - 2014
Mortalité liée à la maternité, nombre de décès et taux : 2005 - 2014 (continued - suite)

Continent and country or area / Continent et pays ou zone	Code[a]	2005	2006	2007	2008	2009	2010	2011	2012	2013	2014
EUROPE											
Slovakia - Slovaquie											
Number - Nombre	C	2	3	-	2	6	-	...	3	1	2
Rate - Taux	C	♦3.7	♦5.6	-	♦3.5	♦9.8	-	...	♦5.4	♦1.8	♦3.6
Slovenia - Slovénie											
Number - Nombre	C	1	3	3	2	1	-	...	...	...	...
Rate - Taux	C	♦5.5	♦15.8	♦15.1	♦9.2	♦4.6	-	...	...	...	...
Spain - Espagne											
Number - Nombre	C	18	14	13	24	17	20	14	10	18	9
Rate - Taux	C	♦3.9	♦2.9	♦2.6	♦4.6	♦3.4	♦4.1	♦3.0	♦2.2	♦4.2	♦2.1
Sweden - Suède											
Number - Nombre	C	6	5	2	6	6	3	1	5	7	4
Rate - Taux	C	♦5.9	♦4.7	♦1.9	♦5.5	♦5.4	♦2.6	♦0.9	♦4.4	♦6.2	♦3.5
Switzerland - Suisse											
Number - Nombre	C	4	6	1	8	3	3	3	7	2	...
Rate - Taux	C	♦5.5	♦8.2	♦1.3	♦10.4	♦3.8	♦3.7	♦3.7	♦8.5	♦2.4	...
TFYR of Macedonia - L'ex-R. y. de Macédoine											
Number - Nombre	...	...	...	*1*	-	*-*[2]	*1*[2]	*2*[2]	...	...	...	...
Rate - Taux	...	...	...	...	...	-	♦4.2	♦8.2	...	...	...	...
Ukraine											
Number - Nombre	+C	75	70	...	79	129	116	85	66	...	69
Rate - Taux	+C	17.6	15.2	...	15.5	25.2	23.3	16.9	12.7	...	14.8
United Kingdom of Great Britain and Northern Ireland - Royaume-Uni de Grande-Bretagne et d'Irlande du Nord											
Number - Nombre	+C	51	50	56	49	74	40	53	51	50	...
Rate - Taux	+C	7.1	6.7	7.3	6.2	9.4	5.0	6.6	6.3	6.4	...
OCEANIA - OCÉANIE											
Australia - Australie											
Number - Nombre	C	...	9	...	6	9	12	12	16	6	12
Rate - Taux	C	...	♦3.3	...	♦2.0	♦3.0	♦4.0	♦4.0	♦5.2	♦1.9	♦4.0
Fiji - Fidji											
Number - Nombre	+C	...	...	...	...	5	...	4	8	...	...
Rate - Taux	+C	...	...	...	...	♦27.5	...	...	♦39.6	...	...
New Zealand - Nouvelle-Zélande											
Number - Nombre	+C	6	9	13	7	11	6	7	7	...	...
Rate - Taux	+C	♦10.4	♦15.2	♦20.3	♦10.9	♦17.6	♦9.4	♦11.4	♦11.4	...	...

FOOTNOTES - NOTES

Data in bold refer to maternal deaths based on ICD-10 Classification, otherwise data refer to maternal deaths based on ICD-9 Classification. - Les données en typographie gras se rapportent aux décès maternelles basées sur la classification CIM-10, autrement les données se rapportent aux décès maternelles basées sur la classification CIM-9.

Italics: data from civil registers which are incomplete or of unknown completeness. - Italiques : données incomplètes ou dont le degré d'exactitude n'est pas connu, provenant des registres de l'état civil.

* Provisional. - Données provisoires.

♦ Rates based on 30 or fewer deaths. - Taux basés sur 30 décès ou moins.

[a] 'Code' indicates the source of data, as follows:
  C - Civil registration, estimated over 90% complete
  U - Civil registration, estimated less than 90% complete
  | - Other source, estimated reliable
  + - Data tabulated by date of registration rather than occurence
  ... - Information not available

Le 'Code' indique la source des données, comme suit :

C - Registres de l'état civil considérés complèts à 90 p. 100 au moins
U - Registres de l'état civil qui ne sont pas considérés complèts à 90 p. 100 au moins
| - Autre source, considérée pas douteuses
+ - Données exploitées selon la date de l'enregistrement et non la date de l'événement
... - Information pas disponible

[1] The code is U. - Le code est U.
[2] The code is C. - Le code est C.
[3] The code is +U. - Le code est +U.
[4] The code is +C. - Le code est +C.

Table 18 - *Demographic Yearbook 2015*

Table 18 presents deaths and crude death rates by urban/rural residence for as many years as possible between 2011 and 2015.

Description of variables: Death is defined as the permanent disappearance of all evidence of life at any time after live birth has taken place (post-natal cessation of vital functions without capability of resuscitation).

Statistics on the number of deaths are obtained from civil registers unless otherwise noted. For those countries or areas where civil registration statistics on deaths are considered reliable (estimated completeness of 90 per cent or more), the death rates shown have been calculated on the basis of registered deaths.

The urban/rural classification of deaths is that provided by each country or area; it is presumed to be based on the national census definitions of urban population that have been set forth at the end of the technical notes for table 6.

For certain countries, there is a discrepancy between the total number of deaths shown in this table and those shown in subsequent tables for the same year. Usually this discrepancy arises because the total number of deaths occurring in a given year is revised although the remaining tabulations are not.

Rate computation: Crude death rates are the annual number of deaths per 1 000 mid-year population.

Rates by urban/rural residence are the annual number of deaths, in the appropriate urban or rural category, per 1 000 corresponding mid-year population. These rates are calculated by the Statistics Division of the United Nations based on the appropriate reference population (for example: total population, nationals only etc.) if known and available. If the reference population is not known or unavailable the total population is used to calculate the rates. Therefore, if the population that is used to calculate the rates is different from the correct reference population, the rates presented might under- or overstate the true situation in a country or area.

Rates presented in this table are limited to those countries or areas with a minimum number of 30 deaths in a given year.

Reliability of data: Each country or area has been asked to indicate the estimated completeness of the deaths recorded in its civil register. These national assessments are indicated by the quality codes "C", "U" and "|" that appear in the first column of this table. "C" indicates that the data are estimated to be virtually complete, that is, representing at least 90 per cent of the deaths occurring each year, while "U" indicates that data are estimated to be incomplete that is, representing less than 90 per cent of the deaths occurring each year. The code "|" indicates that the source of data is different than civil registration and is explained by a footnote. The code "..." indicates that no information was provided regarding completeness or no assessment has been done in the country.

Data from civil registers that are reported as incomplete or of unknown completeness (code "U" or "...") are considered unreliable. They appear in italics in this table; rates based on these data are not computed.

Limitations: Statistics on deaths are subject to the same qualifications as have been set forth for vital statistics in general and death statistics in particular as discussed in section 4 of the Introduction.

The reliability of the data, an indication of which is described above, is an important factor in considering the limitations. In addition, some deaths are tabulated by date of registration and not by date of occurrence; these have been indicated with a plus sign "+". Whenever the lag between the date of occurrence and date of registration is prolonged and, therefore, a large proportion of the death registrations are delayed, death statistics for any given year may be seriously affected. However, delays in the registration of deaths are less common and shorter than in the registration of live births.

International comparability in mortality statistics may also be affected by the exclusion of deaths of infants who were born alive but died before the registration of the birth or within the first 24 hours of life. Statistics of this type are footnoted.

In addition, it should be noted that rates are affected also by the quality and limitations of the population estimates that are used in their computation. The problems of under-enumeration or over-enumeration and, to some extent, the differences in definition of total population have been discussed in section 3 of the Introduction dealing with population data in general, and specific information pertaining to individual countries or areas is given in the footnotes to table 3.

It should be emphasized that crude death rates -- like other crude rates, such as of birth, marriage and divorce -- may be seriously affected by the age-sex structure of the populations to which they relate. Nevertheless, they do provide a simple measure of the level and changes in mortality.

The comparability of data by urban/rural residence is affected by the national definitions of urban and rural used in tabulating these data. It is assumed, in the absence of specific information to the contrary, that the definitions of urban and rural used in connection with the national population census were also used in the compilation of the vital statistics for each country or area. However, it cannot be excluded that, for a given country or area, different definitions of urban and rural are used for the vital statistics data and the population census data respectively. When known, the definitions of urban used in national population censuses are presented at the end of the technical notes for table 6. As discussed in detail in the technical notes for table 6, these definitions vary considerably from one country or area to another.

Earlier data: Deaths and crude death rates have been shown in each issue of the Demographic Yearbook. For information on specific years covered, the reader should consult the Index.

Tableau 18 – *Annuaire démographique 2015*

Le tableau 18 présente le nombre des décès et les taux bruts de mortalité selon le lieu de résidence (zone urbaine ou rurale) pour le plus grand nombre d'années possible entre 2011 et 2015.

Description des variables : Le décès est défini comme la disparition permanente de tout signe de vie à un moment quelconque postérieur à la naissance vivante (cessation des fonctions vitales après la naissance sans possibilité de réanimation).

Sauf indication contraire, les statistiques relatives au nombre de décès sont établies sur la base des registres d'état civil. Pour les pays ou zones où les données concernant l'enregistrement des décès par les services de l'état civil sont jugées sûres (complétude estimée à 90 p. 100 ou plus), les taux de mortalité ont été calculés d'après les décès enregistrés.

La répartition des décès entre zones urbaines et zones rurales est celle qui a été communiquée par chaque pays ou zone ; on part du principe qu'elle repose sur les définitions de la population urbaine utilisées pour les recensements nationaux, qui sont reproduites à la fin des notes techniques du tableau 6.

Pour quelques pays il y a une discordance entre le nombre total des décès présenté dans ce tableau et ceux présentés après pour la même année. Habituellement ces différences apparaissent lorsque le nombre total des décès pour une certaine année a été révisé alors que les autres tabulations ne l'ont pas été.

Calcul des taux : Les taux bruts de mortalité représentent le nombre annuel de décès pour 1 000 habitants en milieu d'année.

Les taux selon le lieu de résidence (zone urbaine ou rurale) représentent le nombre annuel de décès, classés selon la catégorie urbaine ou rurale appropriée, pour 1 000 habitants en milieu d'année. Ces taux sont calculés par la division de statistique des Nations Unies sur la base de la population de référence adéquate (par exemple : population totale, nationaux seulement, etc.) si connue et disponible. Si la population de référence n'est pas connue ou n'est pas disponible, la population totale est utilisée pour calculer les taux. Par conséquent, si la population utilisée pour calculer les taux est différente de la population de référence adéquate, les taux présentés sont susceptibles de sous ou sur estimer la situation réelle d'un pays ou d'un territoire.

Les taux présentés dans ce tableau se rapportent seulement aux pays ou zones où l'on a enregistré un nombre minimal de 30 décès au cours d'une année donnée.

Fiabilité des données : Il a été demandé à chaque pays ou zone d'indiquer le degré estimatif de complétude des données sur les décès d'enfants de moins d'un an figurant dans ses registres d'état civil. Ces évaluations nationales sont signalées par les codes de qualité "C", "U" et "|" qui apparaissent dans la deuxième colonne du tableau.

La lettre "C" indique que les données sont jugées à peu près complètes, c'est-à-dire qu'elles représentent au moins 90 p. 100 des décès survenus chaque année ; la lettre "U" signifie que les données sont jugées incomplètes, c'est-à-dire qu'elles représentent moins de 90 p.100 des décès survenus chaque année. Le symbole "|" indique que la source des données n'est pas un registre de l'état civil ; le symbole, dans ce cas, est accompagné par une note explicative. Le code "..." dénote qu'aucun renseignement n'a été communiqué quant à la complétude des données.

Les données provenant des registres de l'état civil qui sont déclarées incomplètes ou dont le degré de complétude n'est pas connu (code "U" ou "...") sont jugées douteuses. Elles apparaissent en italique dans le présent tableau et les taux correspondants n'ont pas été calculés.

Insuffisance des données : Les statistiques relatives à la mortalité appellent les mêmes réserves que celles qui ont été formulées à propos des statistiques de l'état civil en général et des statistiques relatives aux décès en particulier (voir la section 4 des Notes techniques).

La fiabilité des données, au sujet de laquelle des indications ont été fournies plus haut, est un facteur important. Il faut également tenir compte du fait que, dans certains cas, les décès sont classés par date d'enregistrement et non par date d'occurrence ; ces cas ont été signalés par le signe "+". Chaque fois que le décalage entre le décès et son enregistrement est grand et qu'une forte proportion des décès fait l'objet d'un enregistrement tardif, les statistiques relatives aux décès survenus pendant l'année peuvent être considérablement faussées.

En règle générale, toutefois, les décès sont enregistrés beaucoup plus rapidement que les naissances vivantes, et les retards prolongés sont rares.

Un autre facteur qui nuit à la comparabilité internationale est la pratique qui consiste à ne pas inclure dans les statistiques de la mortalité les enfants nés vivants mais décédés avant l'enregistrement de leur naissance ou dans les 24 heures qui ont suivi la naissance. Quand pareil facteur a joué, cela a été signalé en note à la fin du tableau.

Il convient de noter par ailleurs que l'exactitude des taux dépend également de la qualité et des limitations des estimations de la population qui sont utilisées pour leur calcul. Le problème des erreurs par excès ou par défaut commises lors du dénombrement et, dans une certaine mesure, le problème de l'hétérogénéité des définitions de la population totale ont été examinés à la section 3 de l'Introduction, relative à la population en général ; des indications concernant certains pays ou zones sont données en note à la fin du tableau 3.

Il faut souligner que les taux bruts de mortalité, de même que les taux bruts de natalité, de nuptialité et de divortialité, peuvent varier très sensiblement selon la composition par âge et par sexe de la population à laquelle ils se rapportent. Ils offrent néanmoins un moyen simple de mesurer le niveau et l'évolution de la mortalité.

La comparabilité des données selon le lieu de résidence (zone urbaine ou rurale) peut être limitée par les définitions nationales des termes « urbain » et « rural » utilisées pour le classement de ces données. En l'absence d'indications contraires, on a supposé que les mêmes définitions avaient servi pour le recensement national de la population et pour l'établissement des statistiques de l'état civil pour chaque pays ou zone. Toutefois, il n'est pas exclu que, pour une zone ou un pays donné, des définitions différentes aient été retenues. Les définitions du terme « urbain » utilisées pour les recensements nationaux de population ont été présentées à la fin du tableau 6 lorsqu'elles étaient connues. Comme on l'a précisé dans les notes techniques relatives au tableau 6, ces définitions varient considérablement d'un pays ou d'une zone à l'autre.

Données publiées antérieurement : les différentes éditions de l'*Annuaire démographique* contiennent des statistiques des décès et des taux bruts de mortalité. Pour plus de précisions concernant les années pour lesquelles ces données ont été publiées, se reporter à l'index.

18. Deaths and crude death rates, by urban/rural residence: 2011 - 2015
Décès et taux bruts de mortalité, selon la résidence, urbaine/rurale : 2011 - 2015

Continent, country or area, and urban/rural residence / Continent, pays ou zone et résidence, urbaine/rurale	Code[a]	Number - Nombre					Rate - Taux				
		2011	2012	2013	2014	2015	2011	2012	2013	2014	2015
AFRICA - AFRIQUE											
Algeria - Algérie[1]											
Total	U	161 862	169 815	168 136	173 781	182 570	...	...	...	...	...
Benin - Bénin[2]											
Total	I	78 670	79 116	...	...	...	8.7	8.4	...	...	...
Botswana[3]											
Total	+U	13 301	12 270	11 967	12 177	...	...	...	...	...	...
Djibouti											
Total	U	1 011	...	...	...	...	...	...	...	...	...
Egypt - Égypte											
Total	C	493 086	529 512	511 183	531 864	573 129	6.1	6.4	6.0	6.1	6.4
Urban - Urbaine	C	228 368	251 809	285 611	299 490	...	6.6	7.1	7.9	8.1	...
Rural - Rurale	C	264 718	277 703	225 572	232 374	...	5.8	5.9	4.7	4.7	...
Ghana[4]											
Total	+U	...	54 551	51 466	...	...	...	...	...	...	...
Kenya											
Total	U	182 652	187 811	194 332	198 611	...	...	...	...	...	...
Lesotho											
Total	+U	5 314	7 751	...	...	...	...	...	...	...	...
Mauritius - Maurice[5]											
Total	+C	9 170	9 343	9 440	9 682	9 747	7.3	7.4	7.5	7.7	7.7
Urban - Urbaine	+C	4 182	4 117	4 189	4 203	4 454	8.2	8.1	8.1	8.1	8.6
Rural - Rurale	+C	4 988	5 226	5 251	5 479	5 293	6.7	7.0	7.1	7.4	7.1
Mayotte											
Total	C	...	...	...	590	...	...	...	...	2.7	...
Namibia - Namibie[6]											
Total	I	22 668	...	...	...	...	10.7	...	...	...	...
Urban - Urbaine	I	7 858	...	...	...	...	8.7	...	...	...	...
Rural - Rurale	I	14 810	...	...	...	...	12.2	...	...	...	...
Niger											
Total	+U	6 761	...	...	...	...	...	...	...	...	...
Reunion - Réunion											
Total	C	...	...	...	4 355	...	...	...	...	5.2	...
Rwanda											
Total	U	140 519	139 499	...	...	...	...	...	...	...	...
Saint Helena ex. dep. - Sainte-Hélène sans dép.											
Total	C	49	62	55	61	...	11.5	15.0	13.1	13.8	...
Sao Tome and Principe - Sao Tomé-et-Principe[7]											
Total	I	...	1 287	...	...	...	...	6.9	...	...	...
Senegal - Sénégal[8]											
Total	I	134 450	135 468	136 460	...	...	10.5	10.3	10.1	...	...
Seychelles											
Total	+C	691	651	717	725	703	7.9	7.4	8.0	7.9	7.5
Sierra Leone											
Total	...	13 674	12 767	...	...	...	...	...	...	...	...
Urban - Urbaine	...	2 967	4 948	...	...	...	...	...	...	...	...
Rural - Rurale	...	10 707	7 819	...	...	...	...	...	...	...	...
South Africa - Afrique du Sud											
Total	U	514 938	492 062	473 384	453 360	...	...	...	...	...	...
Tunisia - Tunisie											
Total	U	63 258	62 224	60 386	62 785	...	...	...	...	...	...
United Republic of Tanzania - République Unie de Tanzanie											
Total	...	565 099	555 975	...	...	...	...	...	...	...	...
AMERICA, NORTH - AMÉRIQUE DU NORD											
Anguilla[9]											
Total	+C	55	38	72	59	61	4.1	2.8	5.2	4.1	4.1
Antigua and Barbuda - Antigua-et-Barbuda											
Total	+C	478	510	...	...	...	5.4	...	...	...	...

18. Deaths and crude death rates, by urban/rural residence: 2011 - 2015
Décès et taux bruts de mortalité, selon la résidence, urbaine/rurale : 2011 - 2015 (continued - suite)

Continent, country or area, and urban/rural residence / Continent, pays ou zone et résidence, urbaine/rurale	Code[a]	Number - Nombre					Rate - Taux				
		2011	2012	2013	2014	2015	2011	2012	2013	2014	2015

AMERICA, NORTH - AMÉRIQUE DU NORD

Aruba											
Total	C	633	595	560	643	679	6.2	5.7	5.3	6.0	6.2
Bahamas											
Total	+C	2 117	1 995	2 065	...	...	5.9	5.5	5.6	...	...
Barbados - Barbade											
Total	+C	2 421	2 403	2 276	2 580	...	8.7	8.7	8.2	9.3	...
Belize											
Total	U	1 554	1 535	...	...	...	...	...	...	...	...
Bermuda - Bermudes[10]											
Total	C	429	422	471	480	457	6.8	6.8	7.6	7.8	7.4
British Virgin Islands - Îles Vierges britanniques											
Total	C	98	122	113	111	136	3.5	4.3	4.0	...	...
Canada[11]											
Total	C	243 651	252 309	256 982	*268 056	...	7.1	7.3	7.3	*7.5	...
Cayman Islands - Îles Caïmanes[12]											
Total	C	176	184	182	163	170	3.2	3.3	3.2	2.9	2.9
Costa Rica											
Total	C	18 801	19 200	19 647	20 553	*21 039	4.1	4.1	4.2	4.3	*4.4
Urban - Urbaine	C	9 642	9 665	9 891	14 481	*17 103	2.9	2.9	2.9	4.2	*4.9
Rural - Rurale	C	9 159	9 535	9 756	6 072	*3 936	7.3	7.5	7.6	4.7	*3.0
Cuba											
Total	C	87 044	89 372	92 273	96 330	*99 693	7.8	8.0	8.2	8.6	*8.9
Urban - Urbaine	C	...	75 354	78 107	81 866	...	...	8.9	9.1	9.5	...
Rural - Rurale	C	...	14 018	14 166	14 464	...	...	5.2	5.5	5.6	...
Curaçao											
Total	C	1 276	1 246	1 250	1 370	1 398	8.5	8.2	8.1	8.8	8.8
Dominica - Dominique											
Total	+C	592	603	630	590	...	8.4	8.5	8.8	8.2	...
Dominican Republic - République dominicaine											
Total	U	35 490	35 636	35 507	38 997	35 479	...	...	...	...	...
Urban - Urbaine[13]	U	26 913	27 454	27 851	31 532	...	...	...	...	...	...
Rural - Rurale[13]	U	7 811	7 721	7 035	7 077	...	...	...	...	...	...
El Salvador											
Total	C	33 211	32 148	...	...	...	5.3	5.1	...	...	...
Urban - Urbaine	C	23 621	22 153	...	...	...	5.9	5.4	...	...	...
Rural - Rurale	C	9 590	9 995	...	...	...	4.4	4.6	...	...	...
Greenland - Groenland											
Total	C	476	459	444	461	472	8.4	8.1	7.9	8.2	8.4
Urban - Urbaine	C	407	389	379	388	407	8.5	8.1	7.9	8.0	8.4
Rural - Rurale	C	69	70	65	73	65	8.0	8.2	7.9	9.1	8.3
Grenada - Grenade											
Total	+C	803	856	822	...	...	7.5	8.0	7.6	...	...
Guadeloupe											
Total	C	2 835[14]	2 873[14]	2 951[14]	3 290	...	7.0	7.1	7.3	8.2	...
Guatemala											
Total	C	72 354	72 657	76 639	77 807	...	4.9	4.8	...	...	...
Urban - Urbaine[13]	C	37 781	...	...	...	...	...	...	...	...	...
Rural - Rurale[13]	C	33 137	...	...	...	...	...	...	...	...	...
Honduras											
Total	+U	37 211	...	...	...	...	...	...	...	...	...
Jamaica - Jamaïque[15]											
Total	U	16 926	16 998	17 350	17 619	...	...	...	...	...	...
Martinique[14]											
Total	C	...	...	...	3 319	...	...	...	...	8.7	...
Mexico - Mexique[16]											
Total	+C	589 646	601 259	622 495	632 587	...	5.1	5.1	5.3	5.3	...
Urban - Urbaine[13]	+C	444 372	455 905	472 158	482 499	...	5.3	5.4	5.5	5.6	...
Rural - Rurale[13]	+C	133 517	133 577	139 522	140 144	...	4.2	4.1	4.3	4.3	...
Montserrat											
Total	+C	55	44	45	32	...	11.2	8.9	9.1	6.4	...
Panama											
Total	U	16 367	17 350	17 767	18 171	18 429	...	...	...	...	...
Urban - Urbaine	U	11 027	11 712	12 546	12 379	...	...	...	...	...	...
Rural - Rurale	U	5 340	5 638	5 221	5 792	...	...	...	...	...	...

18. Deaths and crude death rates, by urban/rural residence: 2011 - 2015
Décès et taux bruts de mortalité, selon la résidence, urbaine/rurale : 2011 - 2015 (continued - suite)

Continent, country or area, and urban/rural residence / Continent, pays ou zone et résidence, urbaine/rurale	Code[a]	Number - Nombre					Rate - Taux				
		2011	2012	2013	2014	2015	2011	2012	2013	2014	2015
AMERICA, NORTH - AMÉRIQUE DU NORD											
Puerto Rico - Porto Rico											
Total	C	30 147	30 054	29 405	30 330	28 279	8.2	8.3	8.2	8.5	8.1
Urban - Urbaine[13]	C	18 635	16 835	16 424	16 949	14 768	...	...	...	...	...
Rural - Rurale[13]	C	11 460	13 030	12 815	13 153	13 077	...	...	...	...	...
Saint Kitts and Nevis - Saint-Kitts-et-Nevis											
Total	+C	372	336	348	411	...	8.0	...	...	...	...
Saint Lucia - Sainte-Lucie											
Total	C	*983	*922	...	...	...	*5.9	*5.5	...	...	...
Saint Vincent and the Grenadines - Saint-Vincent-et-les Grenadines											
Total	C	882	858	926	1 006	...	8.0	7.8	8.4	9.1	...
Sint Maarten (Dutch part) - Saint-Martin (partie néerlandaise)[17]											
Total	+C	173	180	171	...	...	5.2	5.2	4.7	...	...
Trinidad and Tobago - Trinité-et-Tobago											
Total	C	*10 007	*10 373	*10 661	*11 461	...	*7.5	*7.8	*8.0	*8.5	...
United States of America - États-Unis d'Amérique											
Total	C	2 515 458	2 543 279	2 596 993	2 626 418	...	8.1	8.1	8.2	8.2	...
United States Virgin Islands - Îles Vierges américaines[18]											
Total	C	711	723	...	...	...	6.7	6.9	...	...	...
AMERICA, SOUTH - AMÉRIQUE DU SUD											
Argentina - Argentine											
Total	C	319 059	319 539	326 197	325 539	...	7.7	7.7	7.7	7.6	...
Bolivia (Plurinational State of) - Bolivie (État plurinational de)[19]											
Total	I	...	127 050	...	...	...	...	12.3	...	...	...
Urban - Urbaine	I	...	83 506	...	...	...	...	12.0	...	...	...
Rural - Rurale	I	...	43 544	...	...	...	...	12.9	...	...	...
Brazil - Brésil[20]											
Total	U	1 148 165	1 157 214	1 180 796	...	...	...	...	...	...	...
Total	C	...	...	...	1 194 164	...	...	...	...	5.9	...
Chile - Chili											
Total	C	94 985	98 711	99 770	*101 960	...	5.5	5.7	5.7	*5.7	...
Urban - Urbaine	C	81 552	85 352	86 887	...	...	5.4	5.6	5.7	...	...
Rural - Rurale	C	13 433	13 359	12 883	...	...	6.0	5.9	5.7	...	...
Colombia - Colombie											
Total	U	192 872	196 842	203 058	210 028	...	...	...	...	...	...
Urban - Urbaine	U	156 712	158 795	...	...	...	...	...	...	...	...
Rural - Rurale	U	36 160	38 047	...	...	...	...	...	...	...	...
Ecuador - Équateur[21]											
Total	U	62 304	63 511	63 104	62 981	...	...	...	...	...	...
Urban - Urbaine	U	47 235	50 635	49 912	48 867	...	...	...	...	...	...
Rural - Rurale	U	15 069	12 859	13 192	14 114	...	...	...	...	...	...
Guyana											
Total	+C	4 527	...	...	...	...	6.0	...	...	...	...
Paraguay											
Total	+U	22 648	22 807	24 193	22 625	...	...	...	...	...	...
Urban - Urbaine[22]	+U	...	...	17 354	15 940	...	...	...	...	...	...
Rural - Rurale[22]	+U	...	...	6 742	6 579	...	...	...	...	...	...
Peru - Pérou[23]											
Total	+U	96 852	97 989	98 616	96 460	...	...	...	...	...	...
Suriname											
Total	C	3 441	3 687	3 557	3 738	...	6.4	6.8	6.5	6.7	...
Urban - Urbaine	C	2 401	2 566	2 371	2 519	...	...	7.1	...	...	...
Rural - Rurale	C	1 040	1 121	1 186	1 219	...	...	6.1	...	...	...

18. Deaths and crude death rates, by urban/rural residence: 2011 - 2015
Décès et taux bruts de mortalité, selon la résidence, urbaine/rurale : 2011 - 2015 (continued - suite)

Continent, country or area, and urban/rural residence / Continent, pays ou zone et résidence, urbaine/rurale	Co-de[a]	Number - Nombre					Rate - Taux				
		2011	2012	2013	2014	2015	2011	2012	2013	2014	2015
AMERICA, SOUTH - AMÉRIQUE DU SUD											
Uruguay											
Total	C	32 807	33 354	32 795	...	...	9.6	9.7	9.5	...	...
Venezuela (Bolivarian Republic of) - Venezuela (République bolivarienne du)											
Total	C	136 803	142 988	147 901	159 239	163 367	4.7	4.9	5.0	5.3	5.3
ASIA - ASIE											
Armenia - Arménie[24]											
Total	C	27 963	*27 514	*27 196	27 714	27 878	8.6	*8.7	*9.0	...	9.3
Azerbaijan - Azerbaïdjan[24]											
Total	+C	53 762	55 017	54 383	55 648	54 697	5.9	5.9	5.8	5.8	5.7
Urban - Urbaine	+C	28 567	29 577	28 863	...	...	5.9	6.0	5.8	...	...
Rural - Rurale	+C	25 195	25 440	25 520	...	...	5.8	5.8	5.8	...	...
Bahrain - Bahreïn[25]											
Total	C	2 528	2 613	2 588	2 805		2.1	2.2	2.1	2.1	
Bangladesh											
Total	U	828 000	826 000	...	...	...	...	...	...	...	...
Urban - Urbaine	U	176 000	189 000	...	...	...	...	...	...	...	...
Rural - Rurale	U	652 000	637 000	...	...	...	...	...	...	...	...
Brunei Darussalam - Brunéi Darussalam											
Total	+C	1 235	1 216	1 398	1 470	*1 547	3.1	3.0	3.4	3.6	*3.7
China - Chine[26]											
Total	I	9 600 000	9 660 000	9 720 000	9 770 000	9 750 000	7.1	7.2	7.2	7.2	7.1
China, Hong Kong SAR - Chine, Hong Kong RAS											
Total	C	42 346	43 917	43 397	45 087	*46 100	6.0	6.1	6.0	6.2	*6.3
China, Macao SAR - Chine, Macao RAS											
Total	C	1 845	1 841	1 920	1 939	2 002	3.4	3.2	3.2	3.1	3.1
Cyprus - Chypre[27]											
Total	C	5 504	5 665	5 141[28]	5 250[28]	*5 859	6.5	6.6	6.0	6.2	*6.9
Georgia - Géorgie[24]											
Total	C	49 818	49 348	48 553	49 087	...	11.1	11.0	...	10.9	...
Urban - Urbaine	C	25 771	...	...	...	...	10.8	...	...	...	...
Rural - Rurale	C	24 047	...	...	...	...	11.4	...	...	...	...
India - Inde[29]											
Total	I	...	...	...	...	...	7.1	7.0	7.0	6.7	...
Urban - Urbaine	I	...	...	...	...	...	5.7	5.6	5.6	5.5	...
Rural - Rurale	I	...	...	...	...	...	7.6	7.6	7.5	7.3	...
Iran (Islamic Republic of) - Iran (République islamique d')[30]											
Total	+C	383 504	367 539	372 279	446 333	...	5.1	4.8	4.8	5.7	...
Urban - Urbaine[13]	+C	278 141	281 367	285 117	302 184	...	5.2	5.2	5.1	5.4	...
Rural - Rurale[13]	+C	98 343	86 093	87 063	144 149	...	4.6	4.0	4.1	6.7	...
Iraq											
Total	U	...	...	*189 118	...	...	...	...	...	...	...
Israel - Israël[31]											
Total	C	40 889	42 100	41 683	42 413	44 210	5.3	5.3	5.2	5.2	...
Urban - Urbaine[13]	C	38 435	39 563	39 184	39 871	41 495	5.4	5.5	5.3	5.3	...
Rural - Rurale[13]	C	2 449	2 529	2 494	2 531	2 710	3.7	3.7	3.6	3.5	...
Japan - Japon[32]											
Total	C	1 253 066[13]	1 256 359[13]	1 268 436[13]	1 273 004[13]	*1 290 428	9.8	9.8	10.0	10.0	*10.2
Urban - Urbaine[13]	C	1 103 338	1 112 495	1 124 417	1 130 587	...	...	...	...	...	...
Rural - Rurale[13]	C	147 235	142 359	142 556	141 084	...	...	...	...	...	...
Jordan - Jordanie[33]											
Total	U	21 730	22 785	23 898	...	...	...	...	...	...	...
Kazakhstan[24]											
Total	C	144 944	142 880	135 950	...	...	8.8	8.5	8.0	...	...
Urban - Urbaine	C	83 551	82 943	78 581	...	...	9.2	9.0	8.4	...	...
Rural - Rurale	C	61 393	59 937	57 369	...	...	8.2	7.9	7.5	...	...

18. Deaths and crude death rates, by urban/rural residence: 2011 - 2015
Décès et taux bruts de mortalité, selon la résidence, urbaine/rurale : 2011 - 2015 (continued - suite)

Continent, country or area, and urban/rural residence — Continent, pays ou zone et résidence, urbaine/rurale	Code — Code[a]	Number - Nombre					Rate - Taux				
		2011	2012	2013	2014	2015	2011	2012	2013	2014	2015
ASIA - ASIE											
Kuwait - Koweït											
Total	C	5 339	5 950	5 909	6 031	...	1.7	1.8	1.7	1.6	...
Kyrgyzstan - Kirghizstan											
Total	C	35 941	36 186	34 880	35 564	*34 808	6.8	6.8	6.1	6.1	*5.8
Urban - Urbaine	C	13 098	13 098	12 507	12 802	*12 294	7.1	7.1	6.5	6.5	*6.1
Rural - Rurale	C	22 843	23 088	22 373	22 762	*22 514	6.7	6.6	5.9	5.9	*5.7
Lebanon - Liban											
Total	C	26 070	23 452	24 013	27 020		6.9	...	...	...	...
Malaysia - Malaisie											
Total	C	135 463	138 692	142 202	*145 648	...	4.7	4.7	4.7	*4.8	...
Urban - Urbaine	C	84 382	87 842	90 855	...	...	4.1	4.1	4.1	...	...
Rural - Rurale	C	51 081	50 850	51 347	...	...	6.0	6.2	6.3	...	...
Maldives											
Total	C	1 137	1 135	1 120	1 143	...	3.5	3.4	3.3	2.8	...
Urban - Urbaine[34]	C	468	564	513	546	...	...	...	...	3.5	...
Rural - Rurale[34]	C	615	555	607	492	...	...	...	...	2.0	...
Mongolia - Mongolie											
Total	+C	19 155	17 761	17 247	16 521	17 620	6.9	6.3	5.9	5.6	5.8
Urban - Urbaine	+C	12 462	13 444	11 182	11 406	11 753	6.7	7.0	5.7	5.7	5.8
Rural - Rurale	+C	6 693	4 317	6 065	5 115	5 867	7.2	4.7	6.5	5.3	6.0
Myanmar[35]											
Total	+U	*242 584*	*250 874*	*257 216*	*278 533*	...	...	...	...	...	...
Urban - Urbaine	+U	...	*114 766*	*119 823*	...	...	...	...	...	...	...
Rural - Rurale	+U	...	*136 108*	*137 393*	...	...	...	...	...	...	...
Nepal - Népal[36]											
Total	|	129 978	...	...	...	...	4.5	...	...	...	...
Urban - Urbaine	|	21 844	...	...	...	...	...	...	...	...	...
Rural - Rurale	|	108 134	...	...	...	...	...	...	...	...	...
Oman[37]											
Total	U	*7 667*	*7 884*	*7 669*	*7 819*	...	...	...	...	...	...
Philippines											
Total	C	498 486	514 745	531 280	...	...	5.3	5.3	5.4	...	...
Qatar											
Total	C	1 949	2 031	2 133	*2 366	...	1.1	1.1	1.1	*1.1	...
Republic of Korea - République de Corée[38]											
Total	C	257 396	267 221	266 257	267 692	...	5.1	5.3	5.3	5.3	...
Urban - Urbaine[13]	C	174 974	181 379	182 888	184 631	...	4.3	4.4	4.4	4.5	...
Rural - Rurale[13]	C	82 416	85 840	83 360	83 055	...	8.7	9.1	9.0	8.9	...
Saudi Arabia - Arabie saoudite[39]											
Total	...	*102 066*	*104 195*	*106 521*	...	...	...	...	...	...	...
Singapore - Singapour											
Total	+C	18 027	18 481	18 938	19 393	19 862	4.8	4.8	4.9	5.0	5.1
Sri Lanka											
Total	+C	*123 261	*122 063	*127 124	*127 758	*131 614	*5.9	*6.0	*6.2	*6.2	*6.3
State of Palestine - État de Palestine[40]											
Total	U	*11 333*	*11 676*	*11 013*	...	...	...	...	...	...	...
Tajikistan - Tadjikistan[24]											
Total	U	*32 909*	*32 828*	*31 706*	*32 879*	...	...	...	...	...	...
Urban - Urbaine	U	*9 876*	*9 846*	*10 091*	*9 830*	...	...	...	...	...	...
Rural - Rurale	U	*23 033*	*22 982*	*21 615*	*23 049*	...	...	...	...	...	...
Thailand - Thaïlande											
Total	+U	*414 670*	*415 141*	*426 065*	*435 624*	...	...	...	...	...	...
Timor-Leste											
Total	|	...	...	...	...	11 384	...	...	...	...	9.8
Turkey - Turquie											
Total	C	376 162	376 338	372 686	390 121	405 218	5.1	5.0	4.9	5.1	5.2
United Arab Emirates - Émirats arabes unis[41]											
Total	...	*7 350*	*7 702*	...	...	...	...	...	...	...	...
Uzbekistan - Ouzbékistan[24]											
Total	+C	143 253	145 988	145 672	149 761	...	4.9	4.9	4.8	4.9	...
Urban - Urbaine	+C	76 976	79 675	79 478	81 991	...	5.1	5.2	5.1	5.2	...
Rural - Rurale	+C	66 277	66 313	66 194	67 770	...	4.6	4.6	4.5	4.5	...

18. Deaths and crude death rates, by urban/rural residence: 2011 - 2015
Décès et taux bruts de mortalité, selon la résidence, urbaine/rurale : 2011 - 2015 (continued - suite)

Continent, country or area, and urban/rural residence / Continent, pays ou zone et résidence, urbaine/rurale	Code[a]	Number - Nombre					Rate - Taux				
		2011	2012	2013	2014	2015	2011	2012	2013	2014	2015
ASIA - ASIE											
Yemen - Yémen											
Total	U	23 662	28 596	35 066[42]	...	...	...	...	...	...	...
EUROPE											
Åland Islands - Îles d'Åland											
Total	C	277	323	269	251	*283	9.8	11.4	9.4	8.7	*9.8
Urban - Urbaine	C	120	124	115	104	*113	10.7	11.0	10.1	9.1	*9.9
Rural - Rurale	C	157	199	154	147	*170	9.3	11.6	8.9	8.5	*9.7
Albania - Albanie											
Total	C	20 012	20 870	20 442	20 656	22 422	6.9	7.2	7.1	7.1	7.8
Andorra - Andorre											
Total	C	275	303	...	...	...	3.5	3.9	...	...	...
Austria - Autriche[43]											
Total	C	76 479	79 436	79 526	78 252	83 073	9.1	9.4	9.4	9.2	9.7
Belarus - Bélarus											
Total	C	135 090	126 531	125 326	121 542	120 026	14.3	13.4	13.2	12.8	12.7
Urban - Urbaine	C	78 947	75 234	75 275	...	...	11.0	10.5	10.4	...	...
Rural - Rurale	C	56 143	51 297	50 051	...	...	24.2	22.6	22.6	...	...
Belgium - Belgique[44]											
Total	C	104 292	109 076	109 334	104 755	110 541	9.4	9.8	9.8	9.3	9.8
Urban - Urbaine	C	102 762	107 536	...	...	...	9.4	...	...	...	...
Rural - Rurale	C	1 530	1 540	...	...	...	9.6	...	...	...	...
Bosnia and Herzegovina - Bosnie-Herzégovine											
Total	C	35 522	35 692	35 837	34 824	...	9.2	9.3	9.3	9.1	...
Bulgaria - Bulgarie											
Total	C	108 258	109 281	104 345	108 952	110 117	14.7	15.0	14.4	15.1	15.3
Urban - Urbaine	C	65 182	66 333	...	...	...	12.2	12.5	...	...	...
Rural - Rurale	C	43 076	42 948	...	...	...	21.4	21.6	...	...	...
Croatia - Croatie											
Total	C	51 019	51 710	50 386	50 839	54 205	11.9	12.1	11.8	12.0	12.8
Urban - Urbaine	C	25 774	26 313	25 464	26 230	...	...	...	...	...	...
Rural - Rurale	C	25 245	25 397	24 922	24 609	...	...	...	...	...	...
Czech Republic - République tchèque											
Total	C	106 848	108 189	109 160	105 665	111 173	10.2	10.3	10.4	10.0	10.5
Urban - Urbaine	C	78 209	79 297	79 923	77 826	...	...	...	10.4	10.1	...
Rural - Rurale	C	28 639	28 892	29 237	27 839	...	...	...	10.3	9.8	...
Denmark - Danemark[45]											
Total	C	52 516	52 325	52 471	51 340	52 555	9.4	9.4	9.4	9.1	9.3
Estonia - Estonie											
Total	C	15 244	15 450	15 244	15 484	15 243	11.5	11.7	11.6	11.8	11.6
Urban - Urbaine	C	10 428	10 632	10 044	10 464	...	11.5	11.8	11.2	11.7	...
Rural - Rurale	C	4 816	4 818	5 200	5 020	...	11.3	11.5	12.4	12.0	...
Faeroe Islands - Îles Féroé											
Total	C	385	408	364	394	377	7.9	8.4	7.5	8.1	7.7
Urban - Urbaine	C	144	136	119	131	102	8.0	7.5	6.5	7.1	5.5
Rural - Rurale	C	241	272	245	263	275	7.9	9.0	8.1	8.7	9.1
Finland - Finlande[46]											
Total	C	50 308	51 384	51 203	51 935	52 209	9.4	9.5	9.5	9.6	9.5
Urban - Urbaine	C	31 162	31 838	31 777	32 260	...	8.5	8.6	8.5	8.6	...
Rural - Rurale	C	19 146	19 546	19 426	19 675	...	11.3	11.6	11.6	11.8	...
France											
Total	C	534 795	559 227	558 408	547 003	*587 000	8.5	8.8	8.8	8.5	*9.1
Urban - Urbaine[47]	C	404 706	422 986	422 803	414 410	...	...	...	...	...	...
Rural - Rurale[47]	C	128 444	134 423	133 734	130 755	...	...	...	...	...	...
Germany - Allemagne											
Total	C	852 328	869 582	893 825	868 356	*925 000	10.6	10.8	11.1	10.7	*11.4
Gibraltar[48]											
Total	+C	241	264	230	...	...	7.5	8.1	7.0	...	...
Greece - Grèce											
Total	C	111 099	116 668	111 794	113 740	*120 844	10.0	10.6	10.2	10.4	*11.1
Urban - Urbaine	C	62 095	64 919	...	63 733	...	...	...	...	...	...
Rural - Rurale	C	49 004	51 749	...	50 007	...	...	...	...	...	...

18. Deaths and crude death rates, by urban/rural residence: 2011 - 2015
Décès et taux bruts de mortalité, selon la résidence, urbaine/rurale : 2011 - 2015 (continued - suite)

Continent, country or area, and urban/rural residence / Continent, pays ou zone et résidence, urbaine/rurale	Code[a]	Number - Nombre					Rate - Taux				
		2011	2012	2013	2014	2015	2011	2012	2013	2014	2015
EUROPE											
Guernsey - Guernesey											
Total	C	535	547	556	526	...	8.5	8.7	8.9	8.4	...
Hungary - Hongrie											
Total	C	128 795	129 440	126 677[50]	126 294[51]	131 575[51]	12.9	13.0	12.8	12.8	13.4
Urban - Urbaine	C	85 721[49]	86 137[49]	85 164[50]	85 796[51]	...	12.3	12.5	12.4	12.3	...
Rural - Rurale	C	42 498[49]	42 752[49]	41 383[50]	40 331[51]	...	14.0	14.0	13.7	13.8	...
Iceland - Islande											
Total	C	1 986[52]	1 955	2 154	2 049	2 178	6.2	6.1	6.7	6.3	6.6
Urban - Urbaine	C	1 958[52]	1 815	1 980	1 936	...	6.2	6.0	6.5	6.3	...
Rural - Rurale	C	28[52]	140	174	113	...	...	6.8	8.4	5.4	...
Ireland - Irlande											
Total[53]	C	28 456	29 186	...	...	...	6.2	6.4	...	...	...
Total	+C	...	...	30 018	29 188	*29 952	...	...	6.5	6.3	*6.4
Isle of Man - Île de Man											
Total	+C	816	799	792	787	...	9.7	9.4	9.2	9.1	...
Italy - Italie											
Total	C	593 402	612 883	600 744	598 364	647 571	10.0	10.3	10.0	9.8	10.7
Jersey											
Total	+C	727	774	717	700	756	7.4	7.8	...	6.9	7.4
Latvia - Lettonie											
Total	C	28 540	29 025	28 691	28 466	28 478	13.9	14.3	14.3	14.3	14.3
Urban - Urbaine	C	18 483	18 950	18 764	18 847	...	13.3	13.8	13.8	13.9	...
Rural - Rurale	C	10 057	10 075	9 927	9 619	...	15.1	15.3	15.3	15.0	...
Liechtenstein											
Total	C	248	224	246	268	252	6.8	6.1	6.7	7.2	6.7
Lithuania - Lituanie											
Total	C	41 037	40 938	41 511	40 252	41 776	13.6	13.7	14.0	13.7	...
Urban - Urbaine	C	24 822	25 030	25 403	24 823	...	12.3	12.5	12.8	12.6	...
Rural - Rurale	C	16 215	15 908	16 108	15 429	...	16.1	16.1	16.5	16.0	...
Luxembourg											
Total	C	3 819	3 876	3 822	3 841	3 983	7.4	7.3	7.0	6.9	7.1
Malta - Malte											
Total	C	3 267	3 418	3 236	3 270	3 442	7.8	8.1	7.6	7.7	8.0
Monaco[54]											
Total	C	499	429	567[55]	524[55]	...	13.8	11.9	15.3	...	...
Montenegro - Monténégro											
Total	C	5 847	5 922	5 917	6 014	6 329	9.4	9.5	9.5	9.7	10.2
Netherlands - Pays-Bas[56]											
Total	C	135 741	140 813	141 245	139 223	*147 010	8.1	8.4	8.4	8.3	*8.7
Norway - Norvège[57]											
Total	C	41 393	41 992	41 131	40 369	40 727	8.4	8.4	8.1	7.9	7.9
Poland - Pologne											
Total	C	375 501	384 788	387 312	376 467	394 921	9.7	10.0	10.1	9.9	10.4
Urban - Urbaine	C	225 524	233 015	...	...	...	9.6	10.0	...	...	...
Rural - Rurale	C	149 977	151 773	...	...	...	9.9	10.0	...	...	...
Portugal[58]											
Total	C	102 848	107 612	106 543	104 843	108 511	9.7	10.2	10.2	10.1	10.5
Republic of Moldova - République de Moldova[59]											
Total	C	39 249	39 560	38 060	39 494	39 906	11.0	11.1	10.7	11.1	11.2
Urban - Urbaine	C	12 541	12 792	...	...	...	8.5	8.6	...	...	...
Rural - Rurale	C	26 708	26 768	...	...	...	12.9	12.9	...	...	...
Romania - Roumanie											
Total	C	251 439	255 539	246 967	254 237	*260 661	12.5	12.7	12.4	12.8	*13.1
Urban - Urbaine	C	114 648	117 661	114 091	117 629	...	10.5	10.9	10.6	11.0	...
Rural - Rurale	C	136 791	137 878	132 876	136 608	...	14.8	14.9	14.4	14.9	...
Russian Federation - Fédération de Russie[24]											
Total	C	1 925 720	1 906 335	*1 878 269	...	...	13.5	13.3	*13.1	...	...
Urban - Urbaine	C	1 356 696	1 353 635	...	...	...	12.8	12.8	...	...	...
Rural - Rurale	C	569 024	552 700	...	...	...	15.2	14.8	...	...	...
San Marino - Saint-Marin											
Total	+C	222	237	247	252	235	6.6	7.1	7.4	7.5	7.0
Serbia - Serbie[60]											
Total	+C	102 935	102 400	100 300	101 247	103 678	14.2	14.2	14.0	14.2	14.6
Urban - Urbaine	+C	54 128	53 878	53 169	53 932	...	12.7	12.6	12.4	12.6	...
Rural - Rurale	+C	48 807	48 522	47 131	47 315	...	16.5	16.6	16.3	16.5	...

18. Deaths and crude death rates, by urban/rural residence: 2011 - 2015
Décès et taux bruts de mortalité, selon la résidence, urbaine/rurale : 2011 - 2015 (continued - suite)

Continent, country or area, and urban/rural residence / Continent, pays ou zone et résidence, urbaine/rurale	Code[a]	Number - Nombre					Rate - Taux				
		2011	2012	2013	2014	2015	2011	2012	2013	2014	2015
EUROPE											
Slovakia - Slovaquie											
Total	C	53 594	52 437	52 089	51 346	53 826	9.9	9.7	9.6	9.5	9.9
Urban - Urbaine	C	26 576	26 106	26 482	26 198	...	9.0	8.9	9.0	9.0	...
Rural - Rurale	C	27 018	26 331	25 607	25 148	...	11.0	10.7	10.3	10.1	...
Slovenia - Slovénie											
Total	C	18 699	19 257	19 334	18 886	19 834	9.1	9.4	9.4	9.2	9.6
Urban - Urbaine	C	9 717	10 108	9 268	9 103	...	9.5	9.9	8.8	8.7	...
Rural - Rurale	C	8 982	9 149	10 066	9 783	...	8.7	8.9	10.0	9.7	...
Spain - Espagne											
Total	C	386 017	401 122	388 600	393 734	*420 018	8.3	8.6	8.3	8.5	*9.0
Sweden - Suède											
Total	C	89 938	91 938	90 402	88 976	90 907	9.5	9.7	9.4	9.2	9.3
Switzerland - Suisse											
Total	C	62 091	64 173	64 961	63 938	*67 262	7.8	8.0	8.0	7.8	*8.2
Urban - Urbaine	C	45 451	47 017	47 654	47 089	...	7.8	8.0	8.0	7.8	...
Rural - Rurale	C	16 640	17 156	17 307	16 849	...	8.0	8.1	8.1	7.8	...
TFYR of Macedonia - L'ex-R. y. de Macédoine											
Total	C	19 465	20 134	19 208	19 718	20 461	9.5	9.8	9.3	9.5	9.9
Urban - Urbaine	C	11 478	12 082	...	...	...	...	...	...	...	...
Rural - Rurale	C	7 987	8 052	...	...	...	...	...	...	...	...
Ukraine[61]											
Total	+C	664 588	663 139	662 368	632 296[62]	...	14.5	14.5	14.6	14.7	...
Urban - Urbaine	+C	411 025	411 787	412 553	...	...	13.1	13.1	...	...	...
Rural - Rurale	+C	253 563	251 352	249 815	...	...	17.7	17.7	...	...	...
United Kingdom of Great Britain and Northern Ireland - Royaume-Uni de Grande-Bretagne et d'Irlande du Nord[63]											
Total	+C	552 232	569 024	574 945	568 840	*602 776	8.7	8.9	9.0	8.8	*9.3
OCEANIA - OCÉANIE											
American Samoa - Samoas américaines											
Total	C	283	282	270	259	...	4.4	4.4	4.3	4.2	...
Australia - Australie											
Total	+C	146 932	147 098	147 678	153 580	...	6.6	6.5	6.4	6.5	...
Urban - Urbaine[64]	+C	87 054	87 315	87 835	91 116	...	4.6	4.5	4.4	4.5	...
Rural - Rurale[64]	+C	59 350	59 143	59 265	61 904	...	18.0	17.8	17.7	18.3	...
Cook Islands - Îles Cook[65]											
Total	+C	72	104	115	113	*102	3.7	5.3	6.2	6.1	*5.4
Fiji - Fidji											
Total	+C	...	6 724	6 939	...	...	...	7.8	8.1	...	...
French Polynesia - Polynésie française											
Total	C	1 242	1 360	1 441	1 427	1 394	4.7	5.1	5.3	5.3	5.1
Guam[66]											
Total	C	842	894	904	952	1 009	5.3	5.6	5.6	5.9	6.2
Kiribati											
Total	U	494	...	...	...	...	...	...	...	...	...
Nauru											
Total	C	75	...	...	...	...	7.4	...	...	...	...
New Caledonia - Nouvelle-Calédonie											
Total	C	1 320	1 322	...	...	...	5.2	5.1	...	...	...
New Zealand - Nouvelle-Zélande											
Total	+C	30 082[16]	30 099[16]	29 568[16]	31 062[67]	31 608[67]	6.9	6.8	6.7	6.9	6.9
Urban - Urbaine[13]	+C	27 138[16]	27 050[16]	26 525[16]	27 930[67]	28 458[67]	7.2	7.1	6.9	7.2	7.2
Rural - Rurale[13]	+C	2 920[16]	3 029[16]	3 020[16]	3 102[67]	3 132[67]	4.7	4.9	4.8	5.0	4.9
Niue - Nioué[68]											
Total	C	9	...	...	...	...	...	...	...	...	...

Continent, country or area, and urban/rural residence / Continent, pays ou zone et résidence, urbaine/rurale	Code[a]	Number - Nombre					Rate - Taux				
		2011	2012	2013	2014	2015	2011	2012	2013	2014	2015
OCEANIA - OCÉANIE											
Norfolk Island - Île Norfolk[69]											
Total	+C	18	20	11	13	...	...	...	...	...	...
Northern Mariana Islands - Îles Mariannes septentrionales[18]											
Total	U	*165*	*163*	*185*	*202*	...	...	...	...	...	...
Palau - Palaos											
Total	C	173	164	192	...	...	8.3	7.8	...	...	...
Samoa[70]											
Total	+U	*591*	...	...	...	...	...	...	...	...	...

FOOTNOTES - NOTES

Italics: data from civil registers which are incomplete or of unknown completeness. - Italiques : données incomplètes ou dont le degré d'exactitude n'est pas connu, provenant des registres de l'état civil.

* Provisional. - Données provisoires.

[a] 'Code' indicates the source of data, as follows:
C - Civil registration, estimated over 90% complete
U - Civil registration, estimated less than 90% complete
| - Other source, estimated reliable
+ - Data tabulated by date of registration rather than occurence
... - Information not available

Le 'Code' indique la source des données, comme suit :
C - Registres de l'état civil considérés complets à 90 p. 100 au moins
U - Registres de l'état civil qui ne sont pas considérés complets à 90 p. 100 au moins
| - Autre source, considérée pas douteuses
+ - Données exploitées selon la date de l'enregistrement et non la date de l'événement
... - Information pas disponible

[1] Excluding live-born infants who died before their birth was registered. Data refer to Algerian population only. - Non compris les enfants nés vivants décédés avant l'enregistrement de leur naissance. Les données ne concernent que la population algérienne.
[2] Data are projections presented in Annuaire Statistique 2010. - Les données sont des projections présentées dans l'Annuaire Statistique 2010.
[3] Source: Vital Statistics Report 2014. - Source: Vital Statistics Report 2014.
[4] The coverage of registration is estimated at 26 per cent. - Le degré de complétude de l'enregistrement est évalué à 26 pour cent.
[5] Excludes the islands of St. Brandon and Agalega. - Non compris les îles St. Brandon et Agalega.
[6] Data refer to the 12 months preceding the census in August. - Les données se rapportent aux 12 mois précédant le recensement d'août.
[7] Data refer to the 12 months preceding the census in May. - Les données se rapportent aux 12 mois précédant le recensement de mai.
[8] Based on estimates and projections from 'Agence Nationale de la Statistique et de la Démographie'. - Données fondées sur des estimations et des projections provenant de l'Agence Nationale de la Statistique et de la Démographie.
[9] Excluding visitors. - Ne comprend pas les visiteurs.
[10] Excluding non-residents and foreign service personnel and their dependants. - À l'exclusion des non-résidents et du personnel diplomatique et de leurs charges de famille.
[11] Data refer to the twelve months from 1 July of the current year to 30 June of the following year. Including Canadian residents temporarily in the United States, but excluding United States residents temporarily in Canada. - Les données font référence aux douze mois de 1 juillet de l'année actuelle à 30 juin de l'année suivante. Y compris les résidents canadiens se trouvant temporairement aux Etats-Unis, mais ne comprenant pas les résidents des Etats-Unis se trouvant temporairement au Canada.

[12] Total includes resident deaths outside of the islands but buried in the islands. - Le total comprend les décès de résidents hors des îles mais inhumés dans les îles.
[13] The total number may include 'Unknown residence', but the categories urban and rural do not. - Le nombre total peut inclure les personnes dont la résidence n'est pas connue, à l'inverse des catégories de population urbaine et rurale.
[14] Excluding live-born infants who died before their birth was registered. - Non compris les enfants nés vivants décédés avant l'enregistrement de leur naissance.
[15] Data have been adjusted for undercoverage of infant deaths and sudden and violent deaths. - Ajusté pour la sous-estimation de la mortalité infantile, du nombre de morts soudaines et de morts violentes.
[16] Data refer to resident population only. - Pour la population résidante seulement.
[17] Source: Population Registry and STAT/CBS estimates. - Source: Le registre de la population et les estimations du STAT/CBS.
[18] Source: U.S. National Center for Health Statistics, National Vital Statistics Reports (NVSR). - Source : US National Center for Health Statistics, National Vital Statistics Reports (NVSR).
[19] Data refer to the 12 months preceding the census in November. - Données se rapportant aux 12 mois précédant le recensement de novembre.
[20] Including deaths abroad and deaths of unknown place of residence. - Y compris décès à l'étranger et décès dont le lieu de résidence n'est pas connu.
[21] Excludes nomadic Indian tribes. - Non compris les tribus d'Indiens nomades.
[22] Data for urban and rural exclude deaths of unknown residence. - Les données pur la résidence urbaine et rurale non comprent pas les décès dont on ignore la résidence.
[23] Source: Reports of the Ministry of Health. - Source : Rapports du Ministère de la Santé.
[24] Excluding infants born alive of less than 28 weeks' gestation, of less than 1 000 grams in weight and 35 centimeters in length, who die within seven days of birth. - Non compris les enfants nés vivants après moins de 28 semaines de gestations, pesant moins de 1 000 grammes, mesurant moins de 35 centimètres et décédés dans les sept jours qui ont suivi leur naissance.
[25] Sources: Births and Deaths National Registration System database, and medical records of government hospitals. - Les sources: Les bases de données des << Births and Deaths National Registration System >> et les dossiers médicaux des hôpitaux du gouvernement.
[26] For statistical purposes, the data for China do not include those for the Hong Kong Special Administrative Region (Hong Kong SAR), Macao Special Administrative Region (Macao SAR) and Taiwan province of China. Data have been estimated on the basis of the annual National Sample Survey on Population Changes. - Pour la présentation des statistiques, les données pour la Chine ne comprennent pas la Région Administrative Spéciale de Hong Kong (Hong Kong RAS), la Région Administrative Spéciale de Macao (Macao RAS) et Taïwan province de Chine. Les données ont été estimées sur la base de l'enquête annuelle "National Sample Survey on Population Changes".
[27] Data refer to government controlled areas. - Les données se rapportent aux zones contrôlées par le Gouvernement.
[28] Data refer to deaths of residents only. - Les données renvoient aux décès de résidents uniquement.
[29] Rates were obtained by the Sample Registration System of India, which is a large demographic survey. Includes data for the Indian-held part of Jammu and Kashmir, the final status of which has not yet been determined. - Les taux ont été obtenus par le Système de l'enregistrement par échantillon de l'Inde qui est une

large enquête démographique. Y compris les données pour la partie du Jammu et du Cachemire occupée par l'Inde dont le statut définitif n'a pas encore été déterminé.

[30] Data refer to the Iranian Year which begins on 21 March and ends on 20 March of the following year. - Les données concernent l'année iranienne, qui commence le 21 mars et se termine le 20 mars de l'année suivante.

[31] Includes data for East Jerusalem and Israeli residents in certain other territories under occupation by Israeli military forces since June 1967. Including deaths abroad of Israeli residents who were out of the country for less than a year. - Y compris les données pour Jérusalem-Est et les résidents israéliens dans certains autres territoires occupés depuis 1967 par les forces armées israéliennes. Y compris les décès à l'étranger de résidents israéliens qui ont quitté le pays depuis moins d'un an.

[32] Data refer to Japanese nationals in Japan only. - Les données se raportent aux nationaux japonais au Japon seulement.

[33] Excluding data for Jordanian territory under occupation since June 1967 by Israeli military forces. Excluding foreigners, including registered Palestinian refugees. - Non compris les données pour le territoire jordanien occupé depuis juin 1967 par les forces armées israéliennes. Non compris les étrangers, mais y compris les réfugiés de Palestine enregistrés.

[34] Excluding deaths occurred abroad. Data by the place of occurrence of death, not by the residence of deceased. - Hormis les décès à l'étranger. Données classées selon le lieu du décès, et non selon le lieu de résidence de la personne décédée.

[35] Data source is "Department of Public Health". - La source des données est << Le Service de la santé publique >>.

[36] Data refer to the 12 months preceding the census in June. - Les données se rapportent aux 12 mois précédant le recensement de juin.

[37] Data from Births and Deaths Notification System (Ministry of Health and all health care providers). - Les données proviennent du système de notification des naissances et des décès (Ministère de la santé et tous prestataires de soins de santé).

[38] Excluding alien armed forces, civilian aliens employed by armed forces, and foreign diplomatic personnel and their dependants. - Non compris les militaires étrangers, les civils étrangers employés par les forces armées ni le personnel diplomatique étranger et les membres de leur famille les accompagnant.

[39] Projections based on the final results of the 2004 Population and Housing Census. - Projections basées sur les résultats définitifs du recensement de la population et de l'habitat de 2004.

[40] Source: Palestinian Central Bureau of Statistics, Population Register, updated version 05/01/2015. - Source: Bureau central de statistique palestinien, registre de la population, version actualisée jusqu'au 05/01/2015.

[41] The registration of births and deaths is conducted by the Ministry of Health. An estimate of completeness is not provided. - L'enregistrement des naissances et des décès est mené par le Ministère de la Santé. Le degré estimatif de complétude n'est pas fourni.

[42] Including Non-Yemeni deaths. - Y compris les décès non-yéménites.

[43] Including deaths of nationals abroad. - Y compris les décès des nationaux survenus à l'étranger.

[44] Including armed forces stationed outside the country, but excluding alien armed forces stationed in the area. - Y compris les militaires nationaux hors du pays, mais non compris les militaires étrangers en garnison sur le territoire.

[45] Excluding Faeroe Islands and Greenland shown separately, if available. - Non compris les Iles Féroé et le Groenland, qui font l'objet de rubriques distinctes, si disponible.

[46] Excluding Åland Islands. - Non compris les Îles d'Åland.

[47] The data for urban and rural exclude the nationals outside the country. - Les données relatives à la population urbaine et rurale n'englobent pas les nationaux se trouvant à l'étranger.

[48] Excluding armed forces. - Non compris les militaires en garnison.

[49] The urban and rural categories do not include the data of foreigners, persons of unknown residence and the homeless, whereas the total category includes them. - Les chiffres portant sur la population urbaine et rurale n' incluent pas les données relatives aux étrangers, aux personnes dont la résidence n'est pas connue et aux personnes sans domicile fixe, à l'inverse, le total les inclut.

[50] Till 2012 data refer to all deaths occurred in Hungary. From 2013 data include the deceased persons with Hungarian usual residence regardless of whether the death occurred in Hungary or in a foreign country, and do not include the deceased persons with foreign country usual residence. - Jusqu'en 2012 les données concernent tous les décès survenus en Hongrie. À partir de 2013, les données comprennent les décès de personnes dont la résidence habituelle était en Hongrie, que le décès ait eu lieu en Hongrie ou dans un pays étranger, et ne comprennent pas les décès de personnes dont la residence habituelle était dans un pays étranger.

[51] Data include the deceased persons with Hungarian usual residence regardless of whether the death occurred in Hungary or in a foreign country, and do not include the deceased persons with foreign country usual residence. - Les

données comprennent tous les décès survenus alors que leur résidence habituelle était en Hongrie, que le décès ait eu lieu en Hongrie ou dans un pays étranger, et ne comprennent pas les décès des personnes dont la residence habituelle était dans un pays étranger.

[52] Definition of localities was revised in 2011 causing a break with the previous series. - La rupture par rapport aux séries précédentes s'explique par le fait que la définition des localités a été révisée depuis 2011.

[53] Data refer to events registered within one year of occurrence. - Les données portent sur des événements enregistrés dans l'année pendant laquelle ils sont survenus.

[54] Including residents outside the country. - Y compris les résidents hors du pays.

[55] Including still births. - Les données comprennent les mortinaissances.

[56] Including residents outside the country if listed in a Netherlands population register. - Englobe les résidents se trouvant à l'étranger à condition qu'ils soient inscrits sur le registre de population des Pays-Bas.

[57] Including residents temporarily outside the country. - Y compris les résidents se trouvant temporairement hors du pays.

[58] Data refer to usually resident population. - Les données concernent la population habituellement résidente.

[59] Excluding Transnistria and the municipality of Bender. - Les données ne tiennent pas compte de l'information sur la Transnistria et la municipalité de Bender.

[60] Excludes data for Kosovo and Metohia. - Sans les données pour le Kosovo et Metohie.

[61] Data includes deaths resulting from births with weight 500g and more (if weight is unknown - with length 25 centimeters and more, or with gestation during 22 weeks or more). - Y compris les décès de nouveau-nés de 500 grammes ou plus (si le poids est inconnu – de 25 centimètres de long ou plus, ou après une grossesse de 22 semaines ou plus).

[62] The Government of Ukraine has informed the United Nations that it is not in a position to provide statistical data concerning the Autonomous Republic of Crimea and the city of Sevastopol. - Le gouvernement Ukrainien a informé l'ONU qu'il n'est pas en mesure de fournir des données statistiques concernant la République autonome de Crimée et la ville de Sébastopol.

[63] Excluding Channel Islands (Guernsey and Jersey) and Isle of Man, shown separately, if available. - Non compris les îles Anglo-Normandes (Guernesey et Jersey) et l'île de Man, qui font l'objet de rubriques distinctes, si disponible.

[64] Urban refers to Greater Capital City Statistical Areas, and rural refers to other areas within the state or territory. Data for urban and rural figures do not add up to the total because they exclude the events occurred in Migratory, Special Purpose and Other Territories. - Urbain renvoie aux zones statistiques de la capitale métropolitaine, et rural aux autres zones de l'État ou territoire. La somme des chiffres des catégories « en zone urbaine » et « en zone rurale » ne correspond pas au total du fait qu'en sont exclus les événements qui ont eu lieu dans les territoires de migration, les territoires à destination spéciale et autres territoires.

[65] Excluding Niue, shown separately, which is part of Cook Islands, but because of remoteness is administered separately. - Non compris Nioué, qui fait l'objet d'une rubrique distincte et qui fait partie des îles Cook, mais qui, en raison de son éloignement, est administrée séparément.

[66] Including United States military personnel, their dependants and contract employees. - Y compris les militaires des Etats-Unis, les membres de leur famille les accompagnant et les agents contractuels des Etats-Unis.

[67] Random rounding to base 3 is applied in this table as a confidentiality measure. - Les chiffres sont arrondis à la base 3 de manière aléatoire, pour des raisons de confidentialité.

[68] Includes deaths occurred in New Zealand but buried in Niue and deaths occurred in Niue but buried elsewhere. - Y compris les personnes décédées en Nouvelle-Zélande qui sont enterrées à Nioué et les personnes décédées à Nioué qui sont enterrées ailleurs.

[69] Data cover the period from 1 July of the previous year to 30 June of the present year. - Pour la période allant du 1er juillet de l'année précédente au 30 juin de l'année en cours.

[70] The coverage of registration is estimated at 70 per cent. - Le degré de complétude de l'enregistrement est évalué à 70 pour cent.

Table 19 - *Demographic Yearbook 2015*

Table 19 presents deaths by age and sex and age-specific death rates by sex for the latest available year between 2006 and 2015.

Description of variables: Age is defined as age at last birthday, that is, the difference between the date of birth and the date of the occurrence of the event, expressed in completed solar years. The age classification used in this table is the following: under 1 year, 1-4 years, 5-year age groups through 95-99 years, and 100 years or over.

Rate computation: Age-specific death rates by sex are the annual number of deaths in each age-sex group per 1 000 population in the same age-sex group. These rates are calculated by the Statistics Division of the United Nations.

Deaths at unknown age and the population of unknown age are excluded from age-specific rate calculations but are part of the death rate for all ages combined.

Death rates for infants under one year of age in this table differ from the infant mortality rates shown elsewhere, because the latter are computed per 1 000 live births rather than per 1 000 population.

The population used in computing the rates is the estimated or the enumerated population by age and sex reported to United Nations Statistics Division. First priority is given to an estimate and second priority to census returns of the year to which the deaths refer.

Rates presented in this table have been limited to those countries or areas having at least a total of 100 deaths in a given year. Moreover, rates specific for individual sub-categories that are based on 30 or fewer deaths are identified by the symbol "♦".

Reliability of data: Data from civil registers of deaths that are reported as incomplete (less than 90 per cent completeness) or of unknown completeness are considered unreliable and are set in italics rather than in roman type. Table 18 and the technical notes for that table provide more detailed information on the completeness of death registration. For more information about the quality of vital statistics data in general and the information available on the basis of the completeness estimates in particular, see section 4.2 of the Introduction.

Rates are not computed if data from civil registers of deaths are reported as incomplete (less than 90 per cent completeness) or of unknown completeness, and therefore deemed unreliable.

Limitations: Statistics on deaths by age and sex are subject to the same qualifications as are set forth for vital statistics in general and death statistics in particular as discussed in section 4 of the Introduction.

The reliability of the data is an important factor in considering the limitations. In addition, some deaths are tabulated by date of registration and not by date of occurrence; these have been indicated by a plus sign "+". Whenever the lag between the date of occurrence and date of registration is prolonged and, therefore, a large proportion of the death registrations are delayed, death statistics for any given year may be seriously affected. However, delays in the registration of deaths are less common and shorter than in the registration of live births.

International comparability in mortality statistics may also be affected by the exclusion of deaths of infants who were born alive but died before the registration of the birth or within the first 24 hours of life. Statistics of this type are footnoted.

Because these statistics are classified according to age, they are subject to the limitations with respect to accuracy of age reporting similar to those already discussed in connection with section 3.1.3 of the Introduction. The factors influencing the accuracy of reporting may be somewhat dissimilar in vital statistics (because of the differences in the method of taking a census and registering a death) but, in general, the same errors can be observed.

The absence of data in the unknown age group does not necessarily indicate completely accurate reporting and tabulation of the age item. It is often an indication that the unknowns have been eliminated by assigning ages to them before tabulation, or by proportionate distribution after tabulation.

International comparability of statistics on deaths by age is also affected by the use of different methods to determine age at death. If age is obtained from an item that simply requests age at death in completed years or is derived from information on year of birth and death rather than from information on complete date (day, month and year) of birth and death, the number of deaths classified in the under-one-year age group will tend to be reduced and the number of deaths in the next age group will tend to be somewhat increased. A similar bias may affect other age groups but its impact is usually negligible. Information on this factor is given in the footnotes when known.

Limitations of rates: Rates shown in this table are subject to the same limitations that affect the corresponding data and are set forth in the technical notes for table 18. These include differences in the completeness of registration, the treatment of infants who were born alive but died before the registration of their birth or within the first 24 hours of life, the method used to determine age at death and the quality of the reported information relating to age at death. In addition, some rates are based on deaths tabulated by date of registration and not by date of occurrence; these have been indicated with a plus sign "+".

The problem of obtaining precise correspondence between deaths (numerator) and population (denominator) as regards the inclusion or exclusion of armed forces, refugees, displaced persons and other special groups is particularly difficult where age-specific death rates are concerned. Even when deaths and population do correspond conceptually, comparability of the rates may be affected by abnormal conditions such as absence from the country or area of large numbers of young men in the military forces or working abroad as temporary workers. Death rates may appear high in the younger ages, simply because a large section of the able-bodied members of the age group, whose death rates under normal conditions might be less than the average for persons of their age, is not included. Therefore, care should be exercised in using these rates for comparative purposes.

Also, in a number of cases the rates shown here for all ages combined differ from crude death rates shown elsewhere, because in this table they are computed on the population for which an appropriate age-sex distribution was available, while the crude death rates shown elsewhere may utilize a different total population. The population by age and sex might refer to a census date within the year rather than to the mid-point, or it might be more or less inclusive as regards ethnic groups, armed forces and so forth. In a few instances, the difference is attributable to the fact that the rates in this table were computed on the mean population whereas the corresponding rates in other tables were computed on an estimate for 1 July.

Earlier data: Age-specific deaths and death rates by sex have been shown for the latest available year in each issue of the Yearbook since the 1955 issue. For information on specific years covered, the reader should consult the Historical Index.

Tableau 19 – *Annuaire démographique 2015*

Le tableau 19 présente les données disponibles les plus récentes, entre 2006 et 2015, sur les décès et les taux de mortalité selon l'âge et le sexe.

Description des variables : L'âge considéré est l'âge au dernier anniversaire, c'est-à-dire la différence entre la date de naissance et la date du décès, exprimée en années solaires révolues. La classification par âge est la suivante : moins d'un an, 1 à 4 ans, groupes quinquennaux jusqu'à 95-99 ans et 100 ans et plus.

Calcul des taux : les taux de mortalité selon l'âge et le sexe représentent le nombre annuel de décès survenus pour chaque sexe et chaque groupe d'âge pour 1 000 personnes du même groupe. Ces taux ont été calculés par la Division de statistique de l'ONU.

On n'a pas tenu compte des décès à un âge inconnu ni de la population d'âge inconnu, sauf dans les taux de mortalité pour tous les âges combinés.

Il convient de noter que, dans ce tableau, les taux de mortalité des groupes de moins d'un an sont différents des taux de mortalité infantile qui figurent dans d'autres tableaux, ces derniers ayant été établis pour 1 000 naissances vivantes et non pour 1 000 habitants.

Les chiffres de population utilisés pour le calcul des taux proviennent de dénombrements ou de répartitions estimatives de la population selon l'âge et le sexe. On a utilisé de préférence les estimations de la population; à défaut, on s'est contenté des données censitaires se rapportant à l'année des décès.

Les taux présentés dans ce tableau ne se rapportent qu'aux pays ou zones où l'on a enregistré un total d'au moins 100 décès pendant l'année. Les taux relatifs à des sous-catégories, qui sont fondés sur 30 décès ou moins, sont signalés par le signe "♦".

Fiabilité des données : Les données sur les décès issues des registres d'état civil qui sont déclarées incomplètes (degré d'exhaustivité inférieur à 90 p.100) ou dont le degré d'exhaustivité n'est pas connu sont jugées douteuses et apparaissent en italique et non en caractères romains. Le tableau 18 et les notes techniques s'y rapportant présentent des renseignements plus détaillés sur le degré d'exhaustivité de l'enregistrement des décès. Pour plus de précisions sur la qualité des statistiques de l'état civil en général et le degré de complétude en particulier, voir la section 4.2 de l'Introduction.

On a choisi de ne pas faire figurer dans le tableau 19 des taux calculés à partir de données sur les décès issues de registres d'état civil qui sont déclarées incomplètes (degré d'exhaustivité inférieur à 90 p. 100) ou dont le degré d'exhaustivité n'est pas connu.

Insuffisance des données : Les statistiques des décès selon l'âge et le sexe appellent les mêmes réserves que les statistiques de l'état civil en général et les statistiques relatives à la mortalité en particulier (voir la section 4 de l'Introduction).

La fiabilité des données est un facteur important. Il faut également tenir compte du fait que, dans certains cas, les données relatives aux décès sont classées par date d'enregistrement et non par date d'occurrence ; ces cas ont été signalés par le signe "+". Chaque fois que le décalage entre le décès et son enregistrement est grand et qu'une forte proportion des décès fait l'objet d'un enregistrement tardif, les statistiques des décès de l'année peuvent être considérablement faussées. En règle générale, toutefois, les décès sont enregistrés beaucoup plus rapidement que les naissances vivantes, et les retards prolongés sont rares.

Un autre facteur qui nuit à la comparabilité internationale est la pratique de certains pays ou zones qui consiste à ne pas inclure dans les statistiques des décès les enfants nés vivants mais décédés avant l'enregistrement de leur naissance ou dans les 24 heures qui ont suivi la naissance, pratique qui conduit à sous-évaluer le nombre de décès à moins d'un an. Quand pareil facteur a joué, cela a été signalé en note à la fin du tableau.

Étant donné que les statistiques relatives à la mortalité sont classées selon l'âge, elles appellent les mêmes réserves concernant l'exactitude des déclarations d'âge que celles qui ont été formulées à la section 3.1.3 des Introduction. Dans le cas des données d'état civil, les facteurs qui interviennent à cet égard sont parfois un peu différents, du fait que le recensement et l'enregistrement des décès se font par des méthodes différentes, mais, d'une manière générale, les erreurs observées sont les mêmes.

Si aucun nombre ne figure dans la rangée réservée aux âges inconnus, cela ne signifie pas nécessairement que les déclarations d'âge et le classement par âge sont tout à fait exacts. C'est souvent une indication que l'on a attribué un âge aux personnes d'âge inconnu avant l'exploitation des données ou qu'elles ont été réparties proportionnellement entre les différents groupes après cette opération.

Le manque d'uniformité des méthodes suivies pour obtenir l'âge au moment du décès nuit également à la comparabilité internationale des données. Si l'âge est connu, soit d'après la réponse à une simple question sur l'âge du décès en années révolues, soit d'après l'année de la naissance et l'année du décès, et non d'après des renseignements concernant la date exacte (jour, mois et année) de la naissance et du décès, le nombre de décès classés dans la catégorie « moins d'un an » sera entaché d'une erreur par défaut et le chiffre figurant dans la catégorie suivante d'une erreur par excès.

Les données pour les autres groupes d'âge pourront être entachées d'une distorsion analogue, mais les répercussions seront généralement négligeables. Les imperfections, lorsqu'elles étaient connues, ont été signalées en note à la fin du tableau.

Insuffisance des taux : les taux présentés dans le tableau 19 appellent les mêmes réserves que celles formulées à propos des fréquences correspondantes (voir à ce sujet les notes techniques se rapportant au tableau 18). Leurs imperfections tiennent notamment aux différences d'exhaustivité de l'enregistrement, au classement des enfants nés vivants mais décédés avant l'enregistrement de leur naissance ou dans les 24 heures qui ont suivi la naissance, à la méthode utilisée pour obtenir l'âge au moment du décès, et à la qualité des déclarations concernant l'âge au moment du décès. En outre, dans certains cas, les données relatives aux décès sont classées par date d'enregistrement et non par date de l'événement ; ces cas ont été signalés par le signe "+".

S'agissant des taux de mortalité par âge, il est particulièrement difficile d'établir une correspondance exacte entre les décès (numérateur) et la population (dénominateur) du fait de l'inclusion ou de l'exclusion des militaires, des réfugiés, des personnes déplacées et d'autres groupes spéciaux. Il convient d'ajouter que, même lorsque population et décès correspondent, la comparabilité des taux peut être compromise par des conditions anormales telles que l'absence du pays ou de la zone d'un grand nombre de jeunes gens qui sont sous les drapeaux ou qui travaillent à l'étranger comme travailleurs temporaires. Il arrive ainsi que les taux de mortalité paraissent élevés parmi les groupes les plus jeunes simplement parce que l'on en a exclu un grand nombre d'individus en bonne santé pour lesquels le taux de mortalité pourrait être, dans des conditions normales, inférieur à la moyenne observée pour les personnes du même âge. Par conséquent, il importe d'être prudent quand on les utilise ces taux de mortalité dans des comparaisons.

De même, les taux indiqués pour tous les âges combinés diffèrent dans plusieurs cas des taux bruts de mortalité qui figurent dans d'autres tableaux, parce qu'ils se rapportent à une population pour laquelle on disposait d'une répartition par âge et par sexe appropriée, tandis que les taux bruts de mortalité indiqués ailleurs peuvent avoir été calculés sur la base d'un chiffre de population totale différent. Ainsi, il est possible que les chiffres de population par âge et par sexe proviennent d'un recensement effectué dans le courant de l'année et non au milieu de l'année, et qu'ils se différencient des autres chiffres de population en excluant ou en incluant certains groupes ethniques, les militaires, etc. Quelquefois, la différence tient à ce que les taux du tableau 19 ont été calculés sur la base de la population moyenne, alors que les taux correspondants des autres tableaux reposent sur une estimation au 1er juillet.

Données publiées antérieurement : Les éditions de l'*Annuaire démographique* parues depuis 1955 présentent les statistiques les plus récentes dont on disposait à l'époque sur les décès selon l'âge et le sexe et sur les taux de mortalité selon l'âge et le sexe. Pour plus de précisions concernant les années pour lesquelles ces données ont été publiées, se reporter à l'index historique.

19. Deaths by age and sex and age-specific death rates by sex: latest available year, 2006 - 2015
Décès et taux de mortalité selon l'âge et le sexe : dernière année disponible, 2006 - 2015

Continent, country or area, date, code[a] and age (in years) Continent, pays ou zone, date, code[a] et âge (en années)	Number - Nombre			Rate - Taux		
	Both sexes Les deux sexes	Male Masculin	Female Féminin	Both sexes Les deux sexes	Male Masculin	Female Féminin
AFRICA - AFRIQUE						
Algeria - Algérie[1]						
2015 (U)						
Total	182 570	94 701	87 869	...	...	...
0	23 150	12 600	10 550	...	...	...
1 - 4	3 158	1 607	1 551	...	...	...
5 - 9	1 547	826	721	...	...	...
10 - 14	1 170	703	467	...	...	...
15 - 19	1 857	1 146	711	...	...	...
20 - 24	2 663	1 799	864	...	...	...
25 - 29	3 111	2 005	1 106	...	...	...
30 - 34	3 523	2 094	1 429	...	...	...
35 - 39	3 815	2 092	1 722	...	...	...
40 - 44	4 347	2 251	2 097	...	...	...
45 - 49	5 319	2 753	2 567	...	...	...
50 - 54	6 695	3 696	2 999	...	...	...
55 - 59	7 958	4 552	3 406	...	...	...
60 - 64	10 932	6 302	4 630	...	...	...
65 - 69	11 231	6 274	4 957	...	...	...
70 - 74	13 298	7 075	6 222	...	...	...
75 - 79	18 923	9 653	9 270	...	...	...
80 - 84	22 725	10 857	11 868	...	...	...
85 +	37 149	16 415	20 734	...	...	...
Botswana[2]						
2014 (+U)						
Total	12 177	6 282	5 895	...	...	...
0	1 045	574	471	...	...	...
1 - 4	238	125	113	...	...	...
5 - 9	76	45	31	...	...	...
10 - 14	69	36	33	...	...	...
15 - 19	164	74	90	...	...	...
20 - 24	323	164	159	...	...	...
25 - 29	610	297	313	...	...	...
30 - 34	764	350	414	...	...	...
35 - 39	889	487	402	...	...	...
40 - 44	699	370	329	...	...	...
45 - 49	637	342	295	...	...	...
50 - 54	673	399	274	...	...	...
55 - 59	700	405	295	...	...	...
60 - 64	633	380	253	...	...	...
65 - 69	647	382	265	...	...	...
70 - 74	703	418	285	...	...	...
75 - 79	634	333	301	...	...	...
80 - 84	900	431	469	...	...	...
85 +	1 729	645	1 084	...	...	...
Unknown - Inconnu	44	25	19	..	..	..
Congo[3]						
2009 (+U)						
Total	7 554	...	...	...	...	...
0 - 4	2 150	...	...	...	...	...
5 - 14	2 905	...	...	...	...	...
15 - 59	292	...	...	...	...	...
60 +	2 207	...	...	...	...	...
Egypt - Égypte						
2013 (C)						
Total	511 183	284 212	226 971	6.0	6.6	5.5
0	38 753	20 791	17 962	19.2	19.8	18.5
1 - 4	11 379	6 229	5 150	1.5	1.6	1.4
5 - 9	4 610	2 769	1 841	0.5	0.6	0.4
10 - 14	4 351	2 803	1 548	0.6	0.7	0.4
15 - 19	7 008	5 133	1 875	0.9	1.3	0.5
20 - 24	8 042	5 853	2 189	0.9	1.3	0.5
25 - 29	8 640	5 924	2 716	1.0	1.4	0.7
30 - 34	8 522	5 586	2 936	1.3	1.6	0.9
35 - 39	9 134	5 786	3 348	1.7	2.2	1.3
40 - 44	11 516	7 328	4 188	2.5	3.2	1.8
45 - 49	20 204	13 119	7 085	4.8	6.1	3.4
50 - 54	33 330	21 655	11 675	9.0	11.6	6.3

Continent, country or area, date, code[a] and age (in years) / Continent, pays ou zone, date, code[a] et âge (en années)	Number - Nombre			Rate - Taux		
	Both sexes Les deux sexes	Male Masculin	Female Féminin	Both sexes Les deux sexes	Male Masculin	Female Féminin
AFRICA - AFRIQUE						
Egypt - Égypte						
2013 (C)						
55 - 59	45 099	28 711	16 388	14.7	18.7	10.8
60 - 64	56 319	33 854	22 465	24.7	29.8	19.6
65 - 69	54 246	30 162	24 084	34.0	38.2	29.8
70 - 74	52 817	27 426	25 391	50.5	53.2	47.8
75 - 79	51 372	25 119	26 253	85.5	85.3	85.6
80 +	85 841	35 964	49 877	175.9	148.7	202.7
80 - 84	44 191	19 848	24 343	...	...	...
85 +	41 650	16 116	25 534	...	...	...
Ghana[4]						
2010 (|)						
Total	163 534	84 214	79 320	6.6	7.0	6.3
0	28 068	15 807	12 261	38.4	42.7	34.0
1 - 4	17 868	9 424	8 444	6.7	6.9	6.4
5 - 9	6 275	3 437	2 838	2.0	2.2	1.8
10 - 14	3 641	1 587	2 054	1.2	1.1	1.4
15 - 19	4 399	1 752	2 647	1.7	1.3	2.0
20 - 24	5 467	2 117	3 350	2.4	1.9	2.7
25 - 29	6 325	2 516	3 809	3.1	2.7	3.4
30 - 34	8 218	3 397	4 821	4.9	4.3	5.4
35 - 39	8 215	3 579	4 636	5.8	5.3	6.2
40 - 44	8 855	4 141	4 714	7.5	7.2	7.7
45 - 49	7 573	3 715	3 858	8.1	8.2	8.0
50 - 54	8 577	4 376	4 201	10.3	11.1	9.6
55 - 59	5 656	3 564	2 092	10.8	13.8	7.9
60 - 64	7 159	4 418	2 741	15.0	19.5	11.0
65 - 69	5 670	3 360	2 310	19.3	24.7	14.7
70 - 74	8 443	5 096	3 347	24.0	34.1	16.6
75 - 79	6 197	3 599	2 598	30.1	40.4	22.2
80 - 84	6 543	3 346	3 197	41.1	53.7	33.1
85 - 89	4 436	2 166	2 270	53.4	65.8	45.3
90 - 94	3 650	1 797	1 853	71.5	94.6	57.8
95 +	2 299	1 020	1 279	99.3	116.6	88.9
Kenya[5]						
2011 (U)						
Total	174 487	96 026	78 461	...	...	...
0	23 167	12 119	11 048	...	...	...
1 - 4	12 129	6 530	5 599	...	...	...
5 - 14	9 145	4 949	4 196	...	...	...
15 - 24	11 961	5 931	6 030	...	...	...
25 - 34	21 054	11 329	9 725	...	...	...
35 - 44	21 605	12 382	9 223	...	...	...
45 - 54	18 606	11 124	7 482	...	...	...
55 - 74	29 686	17 525	12 161	...	...	...
75 +	27 134	14 137	12 997	...	...	...
Lesotho						
2010 (+U)						
Total	7 864	4 154	3 710	...	...	...
0 - 4	271	147	124	...	...	...
5 - 9	69	34	35	...	...	...
10 - 14	67	43	24	...	...	...
15 - 19	112	50	62	...	...	...
20 - 24	237	106	131	...	...	...
25 - 29	477	199	278	...	...	...
30 - 34	727	347	380	...	...	...
35 - 39	732	383	349	...	...	...
40 - 44	675	376	299	...	...	...
45 - 49	583	337	246	...	...	...
50 - 54	627	406	221	...	...	...
55 - 59	550	363	187	...	...	...
60 - 64	484	302	182	...	...	...
65 - 69	388	234	154	...	...	...
70 - 74	502	256	246	...	...	...
75 - 79	481	227	254	...	...	...
80 - 84	384	153	231	...	...	...

19. Deaths by age and sex and age-specific death rates by sex: latest available year, 2006 - 2015
Décès et taux de mortalité selon l'âge et le sexe : dernière année disponible, 2006 - 2015 (continued - suite)

Continent, country or area, date, code[a] and age (in years) / Continent, pays ou zone, date, code[a] et âge (en annèes)	Number - Nombre			Rate - Taux		
	Both sexes Les deux sexes	Male Masculin	Female Féminin	Both sexes Les deux sexes	Male Masculin	Female Féminin
AFRICA - AFRIQUE						
Lesotho						
2010 (+U)						
85 +	441	158	283	...	...	...
Unknown - Inconnu	57	33	24	..	..	..
Malawi[6]						
2008 (|)						
Total	135 865	70 991	64 874	10.0	10.6	9.4
0 - 4	56 721	29 832	26 889	20.9	21.9	20.0
0	30 508	16 606	13 902	50.9	54.9	46.9
1 - 4	26 213	13 226	12 987	12.4	12.5	12.4
5 - 9	6 413	3 350	3 063	2.8	2.9	2.7
10 - 14	5 333	3 071	2 262	3.5	4.1	2.9
15 - 19	4 266	1 863	2 403	3.1	2.7	3.4
20 - 24	7 188	3 038	4 150	6.1	5.1	7.0
25 - 29	7 903	3 405	4 498	7.6	6.8	8.3
30 - 34	9 042	4 280	4 762	9.7	10.4	9.2
35 - 39	7 200	3 813	3 387	9.7	10.3	9.0
40 - 44	6 004	3 410	2 594	10.8	12.2	9.4
45 - 49	4 275	2 436	1 839	9.7	11.3	8.2
50 - 54	3 414	2 092	1 322	10.7	13.3	8.2
55 +	18 106	10 401	7 705	34.1	40.9	27.9
55 - 59	2 447	1 523	924	...	...	...
60 - 64	2 978	1 827	1 151	...	...	...
65 - 69	2 314	1 372	942	...	...	...
70 - 74	2 871	1 665	1 206	...	...	...
75 - 79	2 149	1 254	895	...	...	...
80 - 84	2 151	1 138	1 013	...	...	...
85 +	3 196	1 622	1 574	...	...	...
Mali[7]						
2009 (|)						
Total	62 371	34 387	27 984	4.3	4.8	3.8
0 - 4	29 336	16 098	13 238	11.2	12.1	10.2
5 - 9	3 486	1 933	1 553	1.5	1.6	1.3
10 - 14	1 598	914	684	0.9	1.0	0.8
15 - 19	1 638	777	861	1.1	1.1	1.1
20 - 24	1 570	712	858	1.4	1.3	1.4
25 - 29	1 618	752	866	1.6	1.7	1.6
30 - 34	1 729	839	890	2.1	2.2	2.1
35 - 39	1 604	798	806	2.5	2.5	2.5
40 - 44	1 547	858	689	2.8	3.2	2.5
45 - 49	1 462	890	572	3.3	3.9	2.6
50 - 54	1 527	884	643	4.0	4.7	3.3
55 - 59	1 544	954	590	5.5	6.4	4.4
60 - 64	1 960	1 201	759	7.8	9.4	6.1
65 - 69	1 958	1 152	806	11.8	13.0	10.5
70 - 74	2 093	1 198	895	15.7	17.8	13.5
75 - 79	1 891	1 113	778	24.5	27.2	21.5
80 +	3 372	1 836	1 536	39.4	43.7	35.2
Unknown - Inconnu	2 438	1 478	960	..	..	..
Mauritius - Maurice[8]						
2015 (+C)						
Total	9 747	5 444	4 303	7.7	8.7	6.7
0	173	90	83	13.3	13.6	13.0
1 - 4	24	13	11	◆0.4	◆0.5	◆0.4
5 - 9	12	8	4	◆0.1	◆0.2	◆0.1
10 - 14	14	6	8	◆0.1	◆0.1	◆0.2
15 - 19	67	45	22	0.7	0.9	◆0.5
20 - 24	94	63	31	0.9	1.2	0.6
25 - 29	115	83	32	1.3	1.9	0.7
30 - 34	151	105	46	1.6	2.2	1.0
35 - 39	238	179	59	2.4	3.6	1.2
40 - 44	299	208	91	3.5	4.9	2.2
45 - 49	434	289	145	4.8	6.3	3.2
50 - 54	641	439	202	6.8	9.4	4.3
55 - 59	779	502	277	9.5	12.5	6.7
60 - 64	1 056	660	396	15.6	20.4	11.2
65 - 69	1 054	634	420	22.7	29.9	16.6

19. Deaths by age and sex and age-specific death rates by sex: latest available year, 2006 - 2015
Décès et taux de mortalité selon l'âge et le sexe : dernière année disponible, 2006 - 2015 (continued - suite)

Continent, country or area, date, code[a] and age (in years) Continent, pays ou zone, date, code[a] et âge (en années)	Number - Nombre			Rate - Taux		
	Both sexes Les deux sexes	Male Masculin	Female Féminin	Both sexes Les deux sexes	Male Masculin	Female Féminin
AFRICA - AFRIQUE						
Mauritius - Maurice[8]						
2015 (+C)						
70 - 74	991	550	441	33.6	43.3	26.3
75 - 79	1 036	523	513	51.0	63.1	42.7
80 - 84	973	450	523	79.6	99.0	68.2
85 +	1 596	597	999	157.6	186.7	144.2
85 - 89	906	349	557	...	...	...
90 - 94	494	182	312	...	...	...
95 - 99	160	53	107	...	...	...
100 +	36	13	23	...	...	...
Morocco - Maroc						
2007 (U)						
Total	105 222	66 522	38 700	...	...	...
0	5 140	2 823	2 317	...	...	...
1 - 4	2 320	1 266	1 054	...	...	...
5 - 9	1 075	591	484	...	...	...
10 - 14	859	533	326	...	...	...
15 - 19	1 575	1 024	551	...	...	...
20 - 24	2 204	1 442	762	...	...	...
25 - 29	2 503	1 570	933	...	...	...
30 - 34	2 705	1 660	1 045	...	...	...
35 - 39	2 948	1 767	1 181	...	...	...
40 - 44	3 400	2 052	1 348	...	...	...
45 - 49	4 547	2 766	1 781	...	...	...
50 - 54	5 616	3 672	1 944	...	...	...
55 - 59	6 132	4 046	2 086	...	...	...
60 - 64	7 193	4 626	2 567	...	...	...
65 - 69	10 331	6 494	3 837	...	...	...
70 - 74	12 441	7 990	4 451	...	...	...
75 - 79	13 183	8 491	4 692	...	...	...
80 +	20 051	13 159	6 892	...	...	...
Unknown - Inconnu	999	550	449	..	..	..
Namibia - Namibie[9]						
2011 (I)						
Total	22 668	12 491	10 177	10.7	12.2	9.3
0	2 685	1 411	1 274	41.9	44.1	39.6
1 - 4	1 346	719	627	6.1	6.5	5.7
5 - 9	447	255	192	1.9	2.1	1.6
10 - 14	384	212	172	1.6	1.7	1.4
15 - 19	577	298	279	2.4	2.5	2.3
20 - 24	918	537	381	4.3	5.1	3.5
25 - 29	1 233	645	588	7.0	7.4	6.5
30 - 34	1 591	890	701	10.7	12.1	9.2
35 - 39	1 487	873	614	11.9	14.3	9.6
40 - 44	1 323	807	516	13.5	17.2	10.1
45 - 49	1 140	698	442	14.2	18.6	10.3
50 - 54	917	535	382	14.9	19.5	11.2
55 - 59	891	562	329	18.6	26.1	12.5
60 - 64	994	584	410	24.4	31.7	18.3
65 - 69	766	424	342	24.6	32.3	19.0
70 - 74	739	424	315	30.7	41.3	22.8
75 - 79	682	382	300	39.5	54.5	29.3
80 - 84	792	402	390	55.3	76.2	43.1
85 - 89	638	282	356	68.6	90.2	57.6
90 - 94	549	234	315	80.6	98.4	71.1
95 +	1 003	403	600	178.7	228.6	155.8
Unknown - Inconnu	1 566	914	652	..	..	..
Niger						
2011 (+U)						
Total	6 761	...	...	...	...	...
0	236	...	...	...	...	...
1 - 4	329	...	...	...	...	...
5 - 9	120	...	...	...	...	...
10 - 14	81	...	...	...	...	...
15 - 19	147	...	...	...	...	...
20 - 24	242	...	...	...	...	...
25 - 29	319	...	...	...	...	...

19. Deaths by age and sex and age-specific death rates by sex: latest available year, 2006 - 2015
Décès et taux de mortalité selon l'âge et le sexe : dernière année disponible, 2006 - 2015 (continued - suite)

Continent, country or area, date, code[a] and age (in years) Continent, pays ou zone, date, code[a] et âge (en années)	Number - Nombre			Rate - Taux		
	Both sexes Les deux sexes	Male Masculin	Female Féminin	Both sexes Les deux sexes	Male Masculin	Female Féminin

AFRICA - AFRIQUE

Niger
2011 (+U)
30 - 34	378	...	...	...	...	...
35 - 39	414	...	...	...	...	...
40 - 44	470	...	...	...	...	...
45 - 49	485	...	...	...	...	...
50 - 54	495	...	...	...	...	...
55 - 59	443	...	...	...	...	...
60 - 64	541	...	...	...	...	...
65 - 69	443	...	...	...	...	...
70 - 74	517	...	...	...	...	...
75 - 79	347	...	...	...	...	...
80 - 84	298	...	...	...	...	...
85 - 89	112	...	...	...	...	...
90 - 94	90	...	...	...	...	...
95 - 99	26	...	...	...	...	...
100 +	53	...	...	...	...	...
Unknown - Inconnu	175	...	...	..	..	..

Republic of South Sudan - République de Soudan du Sud[10]
2008 (|)
Total	165 898	88 797	77 101	20.1	20.7	19.4
0	29 217	12 384	16 833	126.4	101.6	154.1
1 - 4	55 674	29 144	26 530	51.9	51.4	52.5
5 - 9	22 571	12 351	10 220	17.4	17.9	16.8
10 - 14	12 487	6 785	5 702	11.8	11.9	11.7
15 - 19	11 665	6 297	5 368	13.1	13.6	12.6
20 - 24	9 256	5 556	3 700	12.5	15.4	9.8
25 - 29	6 022	4 063	1 959	8.6	12.1	5.4
30 - 34	4 496	2 634	1 862	8.4	10.2	6.7
35 - 39	3 046	2 237	809	6.4	9.4	3.4
40 - 44	2 627	1 605	1 022	7.7	9.3	6.1
45 - 49	1 656	993	663	6.0	6.6	5.3
50 - 54	1 513	977	536	7.7	9.3	5.8
55 - 59	946	618	328	7.8	9.1	6.1
60 - 64	1 094	668	426	9.5	10.4	8.3
65 - 69	908	528	380	12.4	12.7	12.0
70 - 74	1 036	766	270	17.5	22.0	11.0
75 - 79	487	415	72	16.8	23.8	6.3
80 - 84	493	277	216	20.1	19.4	21.2
85 - 89	355	229	126	32.3	34.0	29.6
90 - 94	177	110	67	24.0	24.6	23.2
95 +	172	160	12	25.1	41.7	♦4.0

Reunion - Réunion
2007 (C)
Total	4 045	2 247	1 798	5.1	5.9	4.4
0 - 4	114	58	56	1.7	1.7	1.7
0	99	49	50	...	...	...
1 - 4	15	9	6	...	...	...
5 - 9	6	6	-	♦0.1	♦0.2	-
10 - 14	10	7	3	♦0.1	♦0.2	♦0.1
15 - 19	32	25	7	0.5	♦0.7	♦0.2
20 - 24	44	35	9	0.8	1.3	♦0.3
25 - 29	39	27	12	0.8	♦1.1	♦0.4
30 - 34	55	37	18	1.0	1.4	♦0.6
35 - 39	97	68	29	1.5	2.3	♦0.9
40 - 44	158	106	52	2.4	3.3	1.5
45 - 49	211	150	61	4.0	5.9	2.3
50 - 54	236	183	53	5.1	8.2	2.2
55 - 59	266	188	78	7.5	10.7	4.4
60 - 64	287	176	111	10.8	14.1	7.9
65 - 69	375	246	129	17.4	24.8	11.1
70 - 74	427	250	177	25.9	34.7	19.1
75 - 79	448	231	217	39.5	50.3	32.2
80 - 84	496	222	274	65.3	78.9	57.3
85 - 89	393	149	244	106.6	140.6	92.9
90 - 94	233	66	167	166.1	182.8	160.3

19. Deaths by age and sex and age-specific death rates by sex: latest available year, 2006 - 2015
Décès et taux de mortalité selon l'âge et le sexe : dernière année disponible, 2006 - 2015 (continued - suite)

Continent, country or area, date, code[a] and age (in years) Continent, pays ou zone, date, code[a] et âge (en annèes)	Number - Nombre			Rate - Taux		
	Both sexes Les deux sexes	Male Masculin	Female Féminin	Both sexes Les deux sexes	Male Masculin	Female Féminin
AFRICA - AFRIQUE						
Reunion - Réunion						
2007 (C)						
95 +	118	17	101	308.9	♦369.6	300.6
95 - 99	96	15	81	...	...	...
100 +	22	2	20	...	...	...
Saint Helena ex. dep. - Sainte-Hélène sans dép.						
2014 (C)						
Total	61	36	25	...	...	...
0	1	-	1	...	...	...
1 - 4	-	-	-	...	...	...
5 - 9	-	-	-	...	...	...
10 - 14	-	-	-	...	...	...
15 - 19	-	-	-	...	...	...
20 - 24	-	-	-	...	...	...
25 - 29	1	1	-	...	...	...
30 - 34	-	-	-	...	...	...
35 - 39	-	-	-	...	...	...
40 - 44	-	-	-	...	...	...
45 - 49	1	1	-	...	...	...
50 - 54	-	-	-	...	...	...
55 - 59	4	2	2	...	...	...
60 - 64	7	5	2	...	...	...
65 - 69	7	5	2	...	...	...
70 - 74	9	6	3	...	...	...
75 - 79	7	6	1	...	...	...
80 - 84	7	4	3	...	...	...
85 - 89	8	4	4	...	...	...
90 - 94	4	1	3	...	...	...
95 - 99	5	1	4	...	...	...
100 +	-	-	-	...	...	...
Sao Tome and Principe - Sao Tomé-et-Principe[11]						
2012 (|)						
Total	1 287	735	552	7.2	8.3	6.1
0	132	82	50	23.1	27.8	18.0
1 - 4	69	41	29	3.1	3.7	♦2.6
5 - 9	18	5	13	♦0.7	♦0.4	♦1.0
10 - 14	29	20	10	♦1.4	♦1.9	♦0.9
15 - 19	29	23	6	♦1.6	♦2.5	♦0.7
20 - 24	54	36	18	3.4	4.5	♦2.3
25 - 29	39	26	13	2.6	♦3.5	♦1.7
30 - 34	41	31	10	3.3	5.0	♦1.6
35 - 39	61	41	20	6.3	8.4	♦4.1
40 - 44	51	34	17	6.5	8.6	♦4.4
45 - 49	49	24	25	7.8	♦7.9	♦7.7
50 - 54	77	44	33	14.4	16.9	12.0
55 - 59	52	21	31	13.6	♦11.6	15.4
60 - 64	86	59	27	32.3	44.1	♦20.4
65 - 69	60	33	27	31.2	35.9	♦26.8
70 - 74	102	60	42	54.3	70.6	40.9
75 - 79	103	51	52	73.0	83.7	64.8
80 +	234	104	130	170.1	198.1	152.8
Seychelles						
2015 (+C)						
Total	703	401	302	7.5	8.7	6.4
0	17	7	10	♦10.6	♦8.4	♦13.0
1 - 4	3	1	2	♦0.5	♦0.3	♦0.6
5 - 9	5	3	2	♦0.8	♦1.0	♦0.7
10 - 14	3	2	1	♦0.5	♦0.7	♦0.3
15 - 19	3	1	2	♦0.5	♦0.4	♦0.7
20 - 24	12	9	3	♦1.8	♦2.6	♦1.0
25 - 29	10	8	2	♦1.5	♦2.2	♦0.6
30 - 34	21	12	9	♦2.6	♦3.0	♦2.2
35 - 39	18	9	9	♦2.5	♦2.5	♦2.4
40 - 44	24	21	3	♦3.2	♦5.4	♦0.8
45 - 49	39	28	11	5.8	♦9.0	♦3.1
50 - 54	45	30	15	6.1	♦8.3	♦4.0
55 - 59	55	38	17	10.1	13.5	♦6.4

19. Deaths by age and sex and age-specific death rates by sex: latest available year, 2006 - 2015
Décès et taux de mortalité selon l'âge et le sexe : dernière année disponible, 2006 - 2015 (continued - suite)

Continent, country or area, date, code[a] and age (in years) Continent, pays ou zone, date, code[a] et âge (en annèes)	Number - Nombre			Rate - Taux		
	Both sexes Les deux sexes	Male Masculin	Female Féminin	Both sexes Les deux sexes	Male Masculin	Female Féminin
AFRICA - AFRIQUE						
Seychelles						
2015 (+C)						
60 - 64	60	43	17	14.8	21.3	♦8.3
65 - 69	59	46	13	21.8	34.3	♦9.5
70 - 74	56	32	24	28.7	34.6	♦23.3
75 - 79	88	46	42	62.5	87.1	47.7
80 - 84	82	35	47	84.0	119.0	68.9
85 - 89	44	12	32	87.1	♦95.2	84.4
90 +	59	18	41	247.9	♦400.0	212.4
90 - 94	41	15	26	...	...	...
95 - 99	12	2	10	...	...	...
100 +	6	1	5	...	...	...
South Africa - Afrique du Sud						
2014 (U)						
Total	453 360	236 613[12]	214 826[12]	...	...	...
0	25 643	13 529[12]	11 618[12]	...	...	...
1 - 4	8 619	4 594[12]	3 964[12]	...	...	...
5 - 9	3 143	1 781[12]	1 353[12]	...	...	...
10 - 14	3 092	1 724[12]	1 361[12]	...	...	...
15 - 19	7 002	3 988[12]	2 995[12]	...	...	...
20 - 24	13 967	7 943[12]	5 948[12]	...	...	...
25 - 29	23 101	12 405[12]	10 530[12]	...	...	...
30 - 34	29 819	16 442[12]	13 213[12]	...	...	...
35 - 39	29 818	17 103[12]	12 569[12]	...	...	...
40 - 44	29 966	17 635[12]	12 225[12]	...	...	...
45 - 49	29 077	16 965[12]	12 039[12]	...	...	...
50 - 54	31 425	18 482[12]	12 873[12]	...	...	...
55 - 59	32 017	18 702[12]	13 256[12]	...	...	...
60 - 64	34 855	20 065[12]	14 754[12]	...	...	...
65 - 69	31 721	17 405[12]	14 294[12]	...	...	...
70 - 74	31 316	15 402[12]	15 897[12]	...	...	...
75 - 79	28 053	12 325[12]	15 710[12]	...	...	...
80 - 84	25 576	9 215[12]	16 344[12]	...	...	...
85 - 89	18 546	6 166[12]	12 370[12]	...	...	...
90 +	15 435	4 115[12]	11 316[12]	...	...	...
Unknown - Inconnu	1 169	627[12]	197[12]	..	..	..
Swaziland[11]						
2007 (|)						
Total	18 367	8 738	9 629	21.8	21.5	22.0
0 - 4	4 843	2 131	2 712	44.1	38.9	49.4
0	3 613	1 555	2 058	...	...	...
1 - 4	1 230	576	654	...	...	...
5 - 9	408	198	210	3.6	3.5	3.8
10 - 14	302	165	137	2.7	3.0	2.4
15 - 19	431	174	257	4.3	3.5	5.1
20 - 24	1 145	353	792	13.0	8.3	17.6
25 - 29	1 773	707	1 066	25.2	20.9	29.2
30 - 34	1 792	839	953	34.3	32.8	35.7
35 - 39	1 586	828	758	36.3	40.0	32.9
40 - 44	1 145	652	493	33.7	44.0	25.7
45 - 49	865	502	363	29.6	39.3	22.1
50 - 54	752	453	299	32.9	43.5	24.0
55 - 59	557	364	193	30.8	43.7	19.8
60 - 64	618	342	276	37.0	51.0	27.6
65 - 69	436	238	198	32.9	43.1	25.6
70 - 74	392	214	178	48.0	66.7	35.9
75 - 79	283	158	125	45.4	68.0	31.9
80 +	612	261	351	95.3	122.1	82.0
Unknown - Inconnu	427	159	268	..	..	..
Zambia - Zambie[13]						
2010 (|)						
Total	164 385	87 693	76 692	12.6	13.6	11.6
0	35 103	18 953	16 150	79.7	86.1	73.2
1 - 4	28 943	15 297	13 646	16.0	17.0	15.0
5 - 9	8 405	4 519	3 886	4.4	4.7	4.0
10 - 14	4 836	2 550	2 286	2.7	2.9	2.6

Continent, country or area, date, code[a] and age (in years) Continent, pays ou zone, date, code[a] et âge (en années)	Number - Nombre			Rate - Taux		
	Both sexes Les deux sexes	Male Masculin	Female Féminin	Both sexes Les deux sexes	Male Masculin	Female Féminin

AFRICA - AFRIQUE

Zambia - Zambie[13]
2010 (|)

15 - 19	5 856	2 821	3 035	3.8	3.8	3.9
20 - 24	7 967	3 746	4 221	6.7	6.8	6.6
25 - 29	10 471	5 112	5 359	9.9	10.3	9.6
30 - 34	11 305	5 986	5 319	13.5	14.1	12.8
35 - 39	9 972	5 698	4 274	14.6	16.0	13.1
40 - 44	7 336	4 334	3 002	15.5	17.3	13.5
45 - 49	6 021	3 603	2 418	16.0	19.1	12.9
50 - 54	4 770	2 687	2 083	16.7	19.4	14.3
55 - 59	3 546	2 056	1 490	18.3	21.3	15.3
60 - 64	3 929	2 146	1 783	23.3	27.4	19.8
65 - 69	3 363	1 732	1 631	27.4	30.5	24.7
70 - 74	4 084	2 138	1 946	43.8	48.7	39.4
75 +	8 478	4 315	4 163	65.1	67.1	63.2

AMERICA, NORTH - AMÉRIQUE DU NORD

Anguilla[14]
2013 (+C)

Total	72	43	29	...	...	...
0	3	2	1	...	...	...
1 - 4	-	-	-	...	...	...
5 - 9	-	-	-	...	...	...
10 - 14	-	-	-	...	...	...
15 - 19	2	2	-	...	...	...
20 - 24	1	1	-	...	...	...
25 - 29	2	2	-	...	...	...
30 - 34	-	-	-	...	...	...
35 - 39	2	1	1	...	...	...
40 - 44	-	-	-	...	...	...
45 - 49	1	1	-	...	...	...
50 - 54	5	3	2	...	...	...
55 - 59	5	3	2	...	...	...
60 - 64	3	3	-	...	...	...
65 - 69	7	3	4	...	...	...
70 - 74	4	3	1	...	...	...
75 - 79	9	5	4	...	...	...
80 - 84	8	5	3	...	...	...
85 +	20	9	11	...	...	...

2015 (+C)

Total	61	...	...	...	...	...
0 - 4	5	...	...	...	...	...
5 - 14	-	...	...	...	...	...
15 - 29	3	...	...	...	...	...
30 - 44	5	...	...	...	...	...
45 - 59	8	...	...	...	...	...
60 - 64	-	...	...	...	...	...
65 - 69	1	...	...	...	...	...
70 - 74	6	...	...	...	...	...
75 - 79	8	...	...	...	...	...
80 - 84	8	...	...	...	...	...
85 +	15	...	...	...	...	...

Aruba
2015 (C)

Total	679	377	302	6.2	7.3	5.2
0	6	5	1	♦4.5	♦7.2	♦1.6
1 - 4	1	1	-	♦0.2	♦0.4	-
5 - 9	-	-	-	-	-	-
10 - 14	2	-	2	♦0.3	-	♦0.6
15 - 19	2	2	-	♦0.3	♦0.5	-
20 - 24	7	5	2	♦1.1	♦1.5	♦0.6
25 - 29	-	-	-	-	-	-
30 - 34	5	4	1	♦0.7	♦1.3	♦0.3
35 - 39	3	2	1	♦0.4	♦0.6	♦0.3
40 - 44	9	6	3	♦1.1	♦1.6	♦0.7

19. Deaths by age and sex and age-specific death rates by sex: latest available year, 2006 - 2015
Décès et taux de mortalité selon l'âge et le sexe : dernière année disponible, 2006 - 2015 (continued - suite)

Continent, country or area, date, codeª and age (in years) Continent, pays ou zone, date, codeª et âge (en annèes)	Number - Nombre			Rate - Taux		
	Both sexes Les deux sexes	Male Masculin	Female Féminin	Both sexes Les deux sexes	Male Masculin	Female Féminin
AMERICA, NORTH - AMÉRIQUE DU NORD						
Aruba						
2015 (C)						
45 - 49	18	9	9	♦2.1	♦2.3	♦1.9
50 - 54	27	16	11	♦2.9	♦3.7	♦2.2
55 - 59	57	37	20	6.9	9.7	♦4.4
60 - 64	54	37	17	8.1	12.1	♦4.7
65 - 69	72	49	23	14.8	22.5	♦8.6
70 - 74	65	40	25	19.2	27.0	♦13.2
75 - 79	89	53	36	35.8	52.2	24.5
80 - 84	104	45	59	69.2	78.9	63.3
85 - 89	87	35	52	123.1	144.3	112.1
90 - 94	44	25	19	180.5	♦346.1	♦110.8
95 +	21	5	16	♦227.4	♦224.1	♦228.5
Bahamas						
2012 (+C)						
Total	1 995	1 094	901	5.5	6.2	4.9
0	57	26	31	8.6	♦7.6	9.7
1 - 4	18	10	8	♦0.7	♦0.8	♦0.7
5 - 9	9	5	4	♦0.3	♦0.3	♦0.3
10 - 14	8	6	2	♦0.3	♦0.4	♦0.1
15 - 19	27	17	10	♦0.9	♦1.1	♦0.6
20 - 24	57	42	15	1.9	2.9	♦1.0
25 - 29	49	42	7	1.8	3.2	♦0.5
30 - 34	72	52	20	2.8	4.1	♦1.5
35 - 39	84	47	37	3.1	3.5	2.6
40 - 44	100	58	42	3.6	4.4	2.9
45 - 49	130	72	58	4.9	5.6	4.2
50 - 54	159	84	75	6.8	7.5	6.2
55 - 59	147	94	53	8.5	11.4	5.9
60 - 64	149	83	66	12.2	14.5	10.2
65 - 69	147	87	60	16.1	21.0	12.1
70 - 74	183	96	87	27.6	32.9	23.5
75 - 79	176	93	83	43.0	54.4	34.9
80 - 84	170	81	89	98.0	154.6	74.0
85 - 89	116	61	55	143.7	279.8	91.5
90 +	137	38	99	259.0	351.9	222.0
90 - 94	90	30	60	...	...	...
95 - 99	36	6	30	...	...	...
100 +	11	2	9	...	...	...
Barbados - Barbade						
2007 (+C)						
Total	2 195	1 143	1 052	...	...	...
0	31	18	13	...	...	...
1 - 4	8	5	3	...	...	...
5 - 9	5	3	2	...	...	...
10 - 14	8	6	2	...	...	...
15 - 19	17	13	4	...	...	...
20 - 24	10	4	6	...	...	...
25 - 29	15	14	1	...	...	...
30 - 34	30	16	14	...	...	...
35 - 39	38	23	15	...	...	...
40 - 44	45	26	19	...	...	...
45 - 49	58	28	30	...	...	...
50 - 54	76	46	30	...	...	...
55 - 59	90	54	36	...	...	...
60 - 64	113	63	50	...	...	...
65 - 69	142	83	59	...	...	...
70 - 74	182	105	77	...	...	...
75 - 79	309	160	149	...	...	...
80 - 84	281	152	129	...	...	...
85 - 89	339	139	200	...	...	...
90 - 94	199	59	140	...	...	...
95 +	97	30	67	...	...	...
Unknown - Inconnu	102	96	6	..	..	..

19. Deaths by age and sex and age-specific death rates by sex: latest available year, 2006 - 2015
Décès et taux de mortalité selon l'âge et le sexe : dernière année disponible, 2006 - 2015 (continued - suite)

Continent, country or area, date, code[a] and age (in years) Continent, pays ou zone, date, code[a] et âge (en années)	Number - Nombre			Rate - Taux		
	Both sexes Les deux sexes	Male Masculin	Female Féminin	Both sexes Les deux sexes	Male Masculin	Female Féminin
AMERICA, NORTH - AMÉRIQUE DU NORD						
Bermuda - Bermudes[15]						
2015 (C)						
Total	457	243	214	7.4	8.2	6.6
0	2	2	-	♦3.2	♦6.3	-
1 - 4	-	-	-	-	-	-
5 - 9	-	-	-	-	-	-
10 - 14	-	-	-	-	-	-
15 - 19	1	1	-	♦0.3	♦0.7	-
20 - 24	3	2	1	♦1.0	♦1.4	♦0.6
25 - 29	1	1	-	♦0.3	♦0.6	-
30 - 34	3	3	-	♦0.7	♦1.5	-
35 - 39	1	-	1	♦0.2	-	♦0.5
40 - 44	3	1	2	♦0.7	♦0.4	♦0.9
45 - 49	6	2	4	♦1.2	♦0.8	♦1.6
50 - 54	14	10	4	♦2.5	♦3.8	♦1.4
55 - 59	29	21	8	♦5.7	♦8.9	♦2.9
60 - 64	28	17	11	♦6.7	♦8.6	♦5.0
65 - 69	39	27	12	11.5	♦17.2	♦6.6
70 - 74	47	30	17	18.3	♦26.2	♦12.0
75 - 79	56	31	25	30.2	38.9	♦23.6
80 - 84	69	34	35	49.9	62.7	41.6
85 +	155	61	94	146.9	194.3	126.9
85 - 89	84	39	45	...	...	...
90 - 94	47	16	31	...	...	...
95 - 99	15	5	10	...	...	...
100 +	9	1	8	...	...	...
Canada[16]						
2008 (C)						
Total	238 617	120 426	118 191	7.2	7.3	7.0
0	1 911	1 057	854	5.3	5.7	4.8
1 - 4	265	153	112	0.2	0.2	0.2
5 - 9	201	117	84	0.1	0.1	0.1
10 - 14	246	160	86	0.1	0.2	0.1
15 - 19	894	607	287	0.4	0.5	0.3
20 - 24	1 264	935	329	0.6	0.8	0.3
25 - 29	1 282	878	404	0.6	0.8	0.4
30 - 34	1 376	911	465	0.6	0.8	0.4
35 - 39	2 064	1 290	774	0.9	1.1	0.7
40 - 44	3 392	2 063	1 329	1.3	1.6	1.0
45 - 49	5 803	3 453	2 350	2.1	2.5	1.7
50 - 54	8 635	5 300	3 335	3.4	4.2	2.6
55 - 59	11 334	6 904	4 430	5.3	6.5	4.1
60 - 64	14 606	8 946	5 660	8.1	10.1	6.2
65 - 69	17 282	10 349	6 933	12.8	15.9	10.0
70 - 74	22 194	13 006	9 188	20.9	26.1	16.3
75 - 79	30 733	17 061	13 672	34.0	42.2	27.4
80 - 84	38 476	19 414	19 062	57.7	72.4	47.8
85 - 89	38 943	16 289	22 654	99.3	120.8	88.0
90 - 94	25 509	8 717	16 792	170.3	207.4	155.8
95 - 99	10 191	2 465	7 726	262.3	284.7	255.9
100 +	2 011	347	1 664	364.8	326.4	373.9
Unknown - Inconnu	5	4	1	..	..	..
Cayman Islands - Îles Caïmanes						
2014 (C)						
Total	153	80	73	2.6	2.8	2.4
0	2	1	1	...	...	...
1 - 4	1	-	1	...	...	...
5 - 9	1	-	1	...	...	...
10 - 14	-	-	-	...	...	...
15 - 19	1	1	-	...	...	...
20 - 24	4	3	1	...	...	...
25 - 29	2	2	-	...	...	...
30 - 34	2	1	1	...	...	...
35 - 39	2	1	1	...	...	...
40 - 44	4	4	-	...	...	...
45 - 49	6	1	5	...	...	...
50 - 54	9	7	2	...	...	...

19. Deaths by age and sex and age-specific death rates by sex: latest available year, 2006 - 2015
Décès et taux de mortalité selon l'âge et le sexe : dernière année disponible, 2006 - 2015 (continued - suite)

Continent, country or area, date, codeª and age (in years) / Continent, pays ou zone, date, codeª et âge (en années)	Number - Nombre			Rate - Taux		
	Both sexes Les deux sexes	Male Masculin	Female Féminin	Both sexes Les deux sexes	Male Masculin	Female Féminin
AMERICA, NORTH - AMÉRIQUE DU NORD						
Cayman Islands - Îles Caïmanes						
2014 (C)						
55 - 59	10	7	3	...	...	...
60 - 64	7	5	2	...	...	...
65 +	102	47	55	26.9	26.6	27.1
Costa Rica						
2015* (C)						
Total	21 039	12 112	8 927	4.4	5.2	3.6
1 - 4	587	314	273	...	...	...
5 - 9	165	91	74	0.5	0.5	0.4
10 - 14	90	54	36	0.2	0.3	0.2
15 - 19	221	158	63	0.5	0.7	0.3
20 - 24	394	324	70	0.9	1.5	0.3
25 - 29	431	334	97	1.0	1.6	0.5
30 - 34	470	350	120	1.3	2.0	0.6
35 - 39	492	315	177	1.5	2.0	1.0
40 - 44	511	347	164	1.7	2.5	1.0
45 - 49	687	442	245	2.2	3.1	1.5
50 - 54	994	653	341	3.3	4.5	2.1
55 - 59	1 302	834	468	5.2	7.0	3.6
60 - 64	1 574	971	603	8.2	10.6	6.0
65 - 69	1 610	988	622	10.6	14.1	7.7
70 - 74	1 878	1 109	769	18.6	22.5	14.9
75 - 79	2 170	1 201	969	26.6	31.8	22.2
80 - 84	2 449	1 316	1 133	46.1	52.6	40.3
85 +	4 848	2 234	2 614	...	...	...
Unknown - Inconnu	166	77	89	..	..	..
Cuba						
2014 (C)						
Total	96 330	51 918	44 412	8.6	9.3	7.9
0	514	309	205	4.2	4.8	3.4
1 - 4	183	100	83	0.4	0.4	0.3
5 - 9	98	48	50	0.2	0.2	0.2
10 - 14	142	89	53	0.2	0.3	0.2
15 - 19	244	153	91	0.3	0.4	0.3
20 - 24	422	293	129	0.5	0.7	0.3
25 - 29	504	337	167	0.6	0.8	0.4
30 - 34	575	392	183	0.9	1.2	0.6
35 - 39	859	552	307	1.2	1.5	0.8
40 - 44	1 738	1 085	653	1.7	2.2	1.3
45 - 49	2 939	1 881	1 058	2.9	3.7	2.0
50 - 54	4 205	2 665	1 540	4.8	6.2	3.4
55 - 59	4 856	2 968	1 888	7.8	9.8	5.9
60 - 64	7 030	4 147	2 883	12.0	14.6	9.6
65 - 69	9 061	5 283	3 778	18.2	22.2	14.5
70 - 74	11 232	6 413	4 819	28.0	33.5	23.0
75 - 79	12 437	6 778	5 659	44.7	52.3	38.1
80 - 84	13 516	6 838	6 678	73.2	82.1	66.0
85 +	25 758	11 572	14 186	151.1	161.6	143.4
85 - 89	12 248	5 932	6 316	...	...	...
90 - 94	8 426	3 618	4 808	...	...	...
95 - 99	3 902	1 549	2 353	...	...	...
100 +	1 182	473	709	...	...	...
Unknown - Inconnu	17	15	2	..	..	..
Curaçao						
2015 (C)						
Total	1 398	731	667	8.8	10.1	7.8
0	20	8	12	♦10.5	♦8.2	♦12.9
1 - 4	2	-	2	♦0.2	-	♦0.5
5 - 9	-	-	-	-	-	-
10 - 14	1	1	-	♦0.1	♦0.2	-
15 - 19	4	4	-	♦0.4	♦0.7	-
20 - 24	10	6	4	♦1.1	♦1.3	♦0.9
25 - 29	4	-	4	♦0.5	-	♦0.8
30 - 34	7	4	3	♦0.8	♦1.0	♦0.6
35 - 39	13	10	3	♦1.4	♦2.6	♦0.6
40 - 44	19	12	7	♦1.7	♦2.5	♦1.1

19. Deaths by age and sex and age-specific death rates by sex: latest available year, 2006 - 2015
Décès et taux de mortalité selon l'âge et le sexe : dernière année disponible, 2006 - 2015 (continued - suite)

Continent, country or area, date, code[a] and age (in years) / Continent, pays ou zone, date, code[a] et âge (en années)	Number - Nombre			Rate - Taux		
	Both sexes Les deux sexes	Male Masculin	Female Féminin	Both sexes Les deux sexes	Male Masculin	Female Féminin
AMERICA, NORTH - AMÉRIQUE DU NORD						
Curaçao						
2015 (C)						
45 - 49	26	19	7	♦2.2	♦3.7	♦1.1
50 - 54	52	37	15	4.0	6.5	♦2.0
55 - 59	73	46	27	6.3	9.1	♦4.1
60 - 64	88	53	35	8.8	12.1	6.2
65 - 69	157	95	62	18.3	25.0	13.0
70 - 74	161	91	70	26.4	35.5	19.8
75 - 79	185	100	85	40.8	52.7	32.2
80 - 84	219	116	103	76.1	100.8	59.6
85 - 89	167	77	90	109.9	144.9	91.0
90 - 94	126	37	89	194.1	193.7	194.3
95 - 99	46	13	33	271.4	♦456.1	234.0
100 +	18	2	16	♦521.7	♦173.9	♦695.7
Dominica - Dominique						
2006 (+C)						
Total	536	285	251	7.5	7.9	7.2
0 - 4	14	12	2	♦2.2	♦3.7	♦0.7
0	13	11	2	...	...	...
1 - 4	1	1	-	...	...	...
5 - 9	1	1	-	♦0.1	♦0.3	-
10 - 14	2	2	-	♦0.3	♦0.6	-
15 - 19	8	7	1	♦1.2	♦2.0	♦0.3
20 - 24	9	6	3	♦2.0	♦2.5	♦1.4
25 - 29	5	3	2	♦1.0	♦1.2	♦0.8
30 - 34	9	5	4	♦1.6	♦1.7	♦1.4
35 - 39	8	6	2	♦1.5	♦2.1	♦0.8
40 - 44	8	5	3	♦1.8	♦2.1	♦1.5
45 - 49	23	7	16	♦6.5	♦3.6	♦9.9
50 - 54	17	9	8	♦6.0	♦6.1	♦5.9
55 - 59	19	11	8	♦7.9	♦9.1	♦6.8
60 - 64	19	13	6	♦8.4	♦12.7	♦4.9
65 - 69	34	16	18	14.6	♦14.7	♦14.6
70 - 74	57	26	31	30.9	♦29.9	31.9
75 - 79	76	39	37	57.1	65.4	50.3
80 - 84	68	38	30	75.5	107.3	♦54.8
85 +	152	73	79	184.2	253.5	147.1
Unknown - Inconnu	7	6	1	..	..	..
Dominican Republic - République dominicaine						
2015 (U)						
Total	35 479	22 540	12 939	...	...	...
0	673	434	239	...	...	...
1 - 4	240	157	83	...	...	...
5 - 9	142	94	48	...	...	...
10 - 14	212	147	65	...	...	...
15 - 19	605	461	144	...	...	...
20 - 24	1 004	776	228	...	...	...
25 - 29	1 016	754	262	...	...	...
30 - 34	1 088	792	296	...	...	...
35 - 39	1 107	772	335	...	...	...
40 - 44	1 280	879	401	...	...	...
45 - 49	1 482	1 022	460	...	...	...
50 - 54	1 854	1 238	616	...	...	...
55 - 59	2 233	1 460	773	...	...	...
60 - 64	2 616	1 689	927	...	...	...
65 - 69	2 688	1 744	944	...	...	...
70 - 74	3 301	2 064	1 237	...	...	...
75 - 79	3 673	2 162	1 511	...	...	...
80 - 84	3 738	2 194	1 544	...	...	...
85 +	5 255	2 871	2 384	...	...	...
Unknown - Inconnu	1 272	830	442	..	..	..
El Salvador						
2012 (C)						
Total	32 148	17 862	14 286	...	...	...
0	795	446	349	...	...	...
1 - 4	214	122	92	...	...	...
5 - 9	114	68	46	...	...	...

Continent, country or area, date, codeᵃ and age (in years) / Continent, pays ou zone, date, codeᵃ et âge (en années)	Number - Nombre			Rate - Taux		
	Both sexes Les deux sexes	Male Masculin	Female Féminin	Both sexes Les deux sexes	Male Masculin	Female Féminin
AMERICA, NORTH - AMÉRIQUE DU NORD						
El Salvador						
2012 (C)						
10 - 14	248	145	103	...	...	...
15 - 19	788	605	183	...	...	...
20 - 24	874	685	189	...	...	...
25 - 29	900	718	182	...	...	...
30 - 34	1 078	858	220	...	...	...
35 - 39	1 107	838	269	...	...	...
40 - 44	1 174	810	364	...	...	...
45 - 49	1 283	811	472	...	...	...
50 - 54	1 529	898	631	...	...	...
55 - 59	1 757	1 012	745	...	...	...
60 - 64	2 116	1 196	920	...	...	...
65 - 69	2 260	1 163	1 097	...	...	...
70 - 74	2 810	1 485	1 325	...	...	...
75 - 79	3 206	1 585	1 621	...	...	...
80 - 84	3 552	1 668	1 884	...	...	...
85 +	6 285	2 703	3 582	...	...	...
Unknown - Inconnu	58	46	12	..	..	..
Greenland - Groenland						
2015 (C)						
Total	472	289	183	8.4	9.8	6.9
0	9	8	1	♦11.4	♦20.2	♦2.5
1 - 4	2	1	1	♦0.6	♦0.6	♦0.7
5 - 9	1	1	-	♦0.3	♦0.5	-
10 - 14	1	1	-	♦0.3	♦0.5	-
15 - 19	11	8	3	♦2.7	♦4.0	♦1.5
20 - 24	17	10	7	♦3.8	♦4.4	♦3.2
25 - 29	5	4	1	♦1.1	♦1.8	♦0.5
30 - 34	5	4	1	♦1.2	♦1.9	♦0.5
35 - 39	6	5	1	♦1.8	♦2.8	♦0.7
40 - 44	6	3	3	♦1.9	♦1.8	♦2.2
45 - 49	16	12	4	♦3.3	♦4.6	♦1.8
50 - 54	29	16	13	♦5.8	♦5.9	♦5.6
55 - 59	39	23	16	9.9	♦10.3	♦9.5
60 - 64	44	34	10	15.7	21.3	♦8.3
65 - 69	62	42	20	35.3	40.0	♦28.4
70 - 74	63	40	23	46.4	55.5	♦36.2
75 - 79	67	41	26	97.1	126.5	♦71.0
80 - 84	53	20	33	143.2	♦130.7	152.1
85 - 89	25	11	14	♦173.6	♦200.0	♦157.3
90 - 94	8	4	4	♦307.7	♦363.6	♦266.7
95 +	3	1	2	...	...	...
Guatemala						
2011 (C)						
Total	72 354	41 295	31 059	...	...	...
0	7 413	4 202	3 211	...	...	...
1 - 4	2 552	1 313	1 239	...	...	...
5 - 9	705	387	318	...	...	...
10 - 14	907	502	405	...	...	...
15 - 19	2 281	1 581	700	...	...	...
20 - 24	2 738	2 111	627	...	...	...
25 - 29	2 864	2 167	697	...	...	...
30 - 34	2 819	2 051	768	...	...	...
35 - 39	2 680	1 855	825	...	...	...
40 - 44	2 659	1 778	881	...	...	...
45 - 49	2 920	1 832	1 088	...	...	...
50 - 54	3 400	1 928	1 472	...	...	...
55 - 59	3 786	1 999	1 787	...	...	...
60 - 64	4 096	2 157	1 939	...	...	...
65 - 69	4 250	2 199	2 051	...	...	...
70 - 74	4 824	2 499	2 325	...	...	...
75 - 79	5 709	2 944	2 765	...	...	...
80 - 84	6 215	3 110	3 105	...	...	...
85 - 89	4 931	2 418	2 513	...	...	...
90 - 94	2 716	1 267	1 449	...	...	...
95 - 99	793	315	478	...	...	...

19. Deaths by age and sex and age-specific death rates by sex: latest available year, 2006 - 2015
Décès et taux de mortalité selon l'âge et le sexe : dernière année disponible, 2006 - 2015 (continued - suite)

Continent, country or area, date, code[a] and age (in years) / Continent, pays ou zone, date, code[a] et âge (en années)	Number - Nombre			Rate - Taux		
	Both sexes Les deux sexes	Male Masculin	Female Féminin	Both sexes Les deux sexes	Male Masculin	Female Féminin
AMERICA, NORTH - AMÉRIQUE DU NORD						
Guatemala						
2011 (C)						
100 +	148	49	99	...	...	...
Unknown - Inconnu	948	631	317	..	..	..
Jamaica - Jamaïque[17]						
2011 (|)						
Total	21 001	10 061[12]	8 618[12]	7.8	7.6	6.3
0 - 4	361	187[12]	163[12]	1.6	1.7	1.5
5 - 9	118	53[12]	61[12]	0.5	0.4	0.5
10 - 14	128	74	54	0.5	0.5	0.4
15 - 19	382	288[12]	90[12]	1.5	2.3	0.7
20 - 24	521	423[12]	92[12]	2.5	4.2	0.9
25 - 29	515	367[12]	136[12]	2.4	3.6	1.2
30 - 34	451	304[12]	134[12]	2.0	2.9	1.1
35 - 39	557	319[12]	224[12]	2.4	3.0	1.8
40 - 44	609	329[12]	268[12]	3.1	3.3	2.7
45 - 49	631	324[12]	299[12]	4.7	4.8	4.4
50 - 54	749	418[12]	320[12]	6.4	6.8	5.7
55 - 59	702	367[12]	319[12]	8.1	8.1	7.8
60 - 64	1 003	501[12]	482[12]	14.6	14.9	13.7
65 - 69	1 031	554[12]	448[12]	15.7	17.5	13.2
70 - 74	1 343	700[12]	610[12]	22.4	24.6	19.3
75 +	9 932	4 853	4 918	94.6	115.9	77.9
75 - 79	1 567	805[12]	722[12]	...	...	...
80 - 84	1 721	876[12]	806[12]	...	...	...
85 - 89	3 057	1 259	1 798	...	...	...
90 +	3 505	1 913	1 592	...	...	...
Unknown - Inconnu	1 968	-	-	..	..	..
Martinique[18]						
2007 (C)						
Total	2 830	1 439	1 391	7.1	7.7	6.5
0 - 4	51	31	20	2.0	2.4	♦1.6
0	47	28	19	...	...	...
1 - 4	4	3	1	...	...	...
5 - 9	4	3	1	♦0.1	♦0.2	♦0.1
10 - 14	7	5	2	♦0.2	♦0.3	♦0.1
15 - 19	16	12	4	♦0.5	♦0.8	♦0.3
20 - 24	26	22	4	♦1.1	♦1.9	♦0.3
25 - 29	19	13	6	♦1.0	♦1.5	♦0.6
30 - 34	35	22	13	1.4	♦2.1	♦0.9
35 - 39	36	22	14	1.2	♦1.6	♦0.8
40 - 44	53	31	22	1.6	2.0	♦1.2
45 - 49	64	46	18	2.0	3.2	♦1.1
50 - 54	107	68	39	4.1	5.6	2.8
55 - 59	97	57	40	4.3	5.5	3.2
60 - 64	146	91	55	7.8	10.3	5.5
65 - 69	226	135	91	14.2	18.7	10.4
70 - 74	305	173	132	21.3	27.2	16.6
75 - 79	382	200	182	35.8	44.2	29.6
80 - 84	443	217	226	59.2	76.6	48.6
85 - 89	388	168	220	92.5	122.1	78.1
90 - 94	269	91	178	137.9	159.6	128.9
95 +	156	32	124	212.8	196.3	217.5
Mexico - Mexique[19]						
2014 (+C)						
Total	632 587	351 288[12]	280 974[12]	5.3	6.0	4.6
0	26 385	14 872[12]	11 403[12]	11.9	13.1	10.5
1 - 4	5 117	2 780[12]	2 332[12]	0.6	0.6	0.5
5 - 9	2 643	1 498[12]	1 145[12]	0.2	0.3	0.2
10 - 14	3 357	1 958[12]	1 399[12]	0.3	0.3	0.3
15 - 19	8 152	5 689[12]	2 463[12]	0.7	1.0	0.4
20 - 24	12 269	9 294[12]	2 974[12]	1.2	1.8	0.6
25 - 29	12 753	9 533[12]	3 216[12]	1.3	2.0	0.6
30 - 34	14 454	10 598[12]	3 853[12]	1.6	2.5	0.8
35 - 39	17 307	12 296[12]	5 007[12]	2.0	3.0	1.1
40 - 44	21 507	14 627[12]	6 878[12]	2.7	3.9	1.6

19. Deaths by age and sex and age-specific death rates by sex: latest available year, 2006 - 2015
Décès et taux de mortalité selon l'âge et le sexe : dernière année disponible, 2006 - 2015 (continued - suite)

Continent, country or area, date, code[a] and age (in years)	Number - Nombre			Rate - Taux		
Continent, pays ou zone, date, code[a] et âge (en années)	Both sexes Les deux sexes	Male Masculin	Female Féminin	Both sexes Les deux sexes	Male Masculin	Female Féminin

AMERICA, NORTH - AMÉRIQUE DU NORD

Mexico - Mexique[19]
2014 (+C)

45 - 49	26 365	16 782[12]	9 581[12]	3.8	5.1	2.6
50 - 54	33 764	20 621[12]	13 139[12]	5.8	7.5	4.3
55 - 59	41 333	24 129[12]	17 203[12]	8.7	10.8	6.9
60 - 64	46 962	26 490[12]	20 469[12]	12.8	15.2	10.6
65 - 69	53 087	29 463[12]	23 624[12]	19.2	22.7	16.2
70 - 74	59 092	31 772[12]	27 320[12]	29.0	33.6	25.0
75 - 79	65 323	34 059[12]	31 263[12]	45.5	51.9	40.1
80 - 84	67 761	33 348[12]	34 413[12]	72.6	79.9	66.7
85 - 89	56 478	25 853[12]	30 625[12]	110.3	116.9	105.3
90 - 94	37 700	16 094[12]	21 604[12]	167.8	173.6	163.8
95 - 99	13 247	5 272[12]	7 975[12]	185.2	187.5	183.6
100 +	4 370	1 661[12]	2 708[12]	233.4	240.4	229.2
Unknown - Inconnu	3 161	2 599[12]	380[12]	..	..	..

Montserrat
2013 (+C)

Total	45	21	24	...	...	...
0	-	-	-	...	...	...
1 - 4	-	-	-	...	...	...
5 - 9	-	-	-	...	...	...
10 - 14	-	-	-	...	...	...
15 - 19	-	-	-	...	...	...
20 - 24	-	-	-	...	...	...
25 - 29	-	-	-	...	...	...
30 - 34	-	-	-	...	...	...
35 - 39	1	-	1	...	...	...
40 - 44	-	-	-	...	...	...
45 - 49	1	-	1	...	...	...
50 - 54	-	-	-	...	...	...
55 - 59	2	1	1	...	...	...
60 - 64	2	2	-	...	...	...
65 - 69	2	1	1	...	...	...
70 - 74	4	2	2	...	...	...
75 - 79	5	3	2	...	...	...
80 - 84	5	2	3	...	...	...
85 - 89	10	3	7	...	...	...
90 - 94	13	7	6	...	...	...
95 - 99	-	-	-	...	...	...
100 +	-	-	-	...	...	...

Nicaragua
2010 (+U)

Total	19 944	11 416	8 528	...	...	...
0	1 891	1 077	814	...	...	...
1 - 4	252	155	97	...	...	...
5 - 9	155	86	69	...	...	...
10 - 14	182	95	87	...	...	...
15 - 19	458	313	145	...	...	...
20 - 24	564	428	136	...	...	...
25 - 29	672	514	158	...	...	...
30 - 34	615	458	157	...	...	...
35 - 39	697	491	206	...	...	...
40 - 44	758	495	263	...	...	...
45 - 49	843	540	303	...	...	...
50 - 54	997	594	403	...	...	...
55 - 59	1 166	693	473	...	...	...
60 - 64	1 258	704	554	...	...	...
65 - 69	1 385	787	598	...	...	...
70 - 74	1 584	863	721	...	...	...
75 - 79	1 740	931	809	...	...	...
80 +	4 727	2 192	2 535	...	...	...

Panama
2014 (U)

Total	18 171	10 442	7 729	...	...	...
0	1 036	572	464	...	...	...
1 - 4	273	141	132	...	...	...
5 - 9	110	66	44	...	...	...

Continent, country or area, date, code[a] and age (in years) Continent, pays ou zone, date, code[a] et âge (en années)	Number - Nombre			Rate - Taux		
	Both sexes Les deux sexes	Male Masculin	Female Féminin	Both sexes Les deux sexes	Male Masculin	Female Féminin

AMERICA, NORTH - AMÉRIQUE DU NORD

Panama
2014 (U)

10 - 14	125	70	55	...	...	...
15 - 19	303	221	82	...	...	...
20 - 24	393	300	93	...	...	...
25 - 29	429	335	94	...	...	...
30 - 34	453	326	127	...	...	...
35 - 39	465	324	141	...	...	...
40 - 44	486	321	165	...	...	...
45 - 49	620	400	220	...	...	...
50 - 54	743	454	289	...	...	...
55 - 59	920	561	359	...	...	...
60 - 64	1 117	653	464	...	...	...
65 - 69	1 329	814	515	...	...	...
70 - 74	1 546	931	615	...	...	...
75 - 79	1 784	1 017	767	...	...	...
80 - 84	1 929	1 045	884	...	...	...
85 - 89	1 792	889	903	...	...	...
90 - 94	1 384	621	763	...	...	...
95 - 99	690	275	415	...	...	...
100 +	203	76	127	...	...	...
Unknown - Inconnu	41	30	11	..	..	...

Puerto Rico - Porto Rico
2015 (C)

Total	28 279	15 287	12 992	...	...	...
0	222	125	97	...	...	...
1 - 4	23	8	15	...	...	...
5 - 9	17	10	7	...	...	...
10 - 14	23	15	8	...	...	...
15 - 19	116	89	27	...	...	...
20 - 24	271	233	38	...	...	...
25 - 29	283	228	55	...	...	...
30 - 34	289	217	72	...	...	...
35 - 39	344	243	101	...	...	...
40 - 44	448	307	141	...	...	...
45 - 49	618	412	206	...	...	...
50 - 54	1 072	706	366	...	...	...
55 - 59	1 446	959	487	...	...	...
60 - 64	1 911	1 204	707	...	...	...
65 - 69	2 561	1 573	988	...	...	...
70 - 74	3 029	1 754	1 275	...	...	...
75 - 79	3 496	1 888	1 608	...	...	...
80 - 84	3 967	1 979	1 988	...	...	...
85 - 89	3 695	1 634	2 061	...	...	...
90 - 94	2 808	1 104	1 704	...	...	...
95 - 99	1 236	453	783	...	...	...
100 +	367	119	248	...	...	...
Unknown - Inconnu	37	27	10	..	..	..

Saint Vincent and the Grenadines -
Saint-Vincent-et-les Grenadines[20]
2013 (C)

Total	928	514	414	...	...	...
0	32	20	12	...	...	...
1 - 4	2	1	1	...	...	...
5 - 9	3	3	-	...	...	...
10 - 14	4	3	1	...	...	...
15 - 19	10	7	3	...	...	...
20 - 24	10	7	3	...	...	...
25 - 29	21	13	8	...	...	...
30 - 34	29	16	13	...	...	...
35 - 39	31	19	12	...	...	...
40 - 44	26	14	12	...	...	...
45 - 49	45	30	15	...	...	...
50 - 54	52	33	19	...	...	...
55 - 59	62	37	25	...	...	...
60 - 64	49	31	18	...	...	...
65 - 69	72	44	28	...	...	...

19. Deaths by age and sex and age-specific death rates by sex: latest available year, 2006 - 2015
Décès et taux de mortalité selon l'âge et le sexe : dernière année disponible, 2006 - 2015 (continued - suite)

Continent, country or area, date, code[a] and age (in years) Continent, pays ou zone, date, code[a] et âge (en années)	Number - Nombre			Rate - Taux		
	Both sexes Les deux sexes	Male Masculin	Female Féminin	Both sexes Les deux sexes	Male Masculin	Female Féminin

AMERICA, NORTH - AMÉRIQUE DU NORD

Saint Vincent and the Grenadines - Saint-Vincent-et-les Grenadines[20]
2013 (C)

70 - 74	87	53	34	...	...	...
75 - 79	114	66	48	...	...	...
80 - 84	101	51	50	...	...	...
85 - 89	90	33	57	...	...	...
90 - 94	53	20	33	...	...	...
95 - 99	23	8	15	...	...	...
100 +	8	1	7	...	...	...
Unknown - Inconnu	4	4	-	..	..	..

Trinidad and Tobago - Trinité-et-Tobago
2009 (C)

Total	9 693	5 548	4 145	7.4	...	...
0	275	150	125	...	...	1.6
1 - 4	41	27	14	...	...	...
5 - 9	20	9	11	...	...	...
10 - 14	37	25	12	...	...	...
15 - 19	128	105	23	0.9	...	...
20 - 24	256	205	51	2.2	...	...
25 - 29	262	201	61	2.6	...	...
30 - 34	264	184	80	2.8	...	...
35 - 39	254	170	84	2.4	...	...
40 - 44	337	207	130	3.6	...	...
45 - 49	514	300	214	6.6	...	...
50 - 54	633	405	228	9.8	...	...
55 - 59	643	384	259	13.3	...	...
60 - 64	830	513	317	21.6	...	...
65 +	5 188	...	...	55.9	...	...
65 - 69	886	514	372	...	...	...
70 - 74	925	519	406	...	...	...
75 - 79	977	543	434	...	...	...
80 - 84	906	424	482	...	...	...
85 +	1 494	654	840	...	...	...
Unknown - Inconnu	11	9	2	..	..	..

United States of America - États-Unis d'Amérique
2014 (C)

Total	2 626 418	1 328 241	1 298 177	...	...	...
0	23 215	12 886	10 329	...	...	...
1 - 4	3 830	2 172	1 658	...	...	...
5 - 9	2 357	1 357	1 000	...	...	...
10 - 14	2 893	1 771	1 122	...	...	...
15 - 19	9 586	6 828	2 758	...	...	...
20 - 24	19 205	14 289	4 916	...	...	...
25 - 29	21 925	15 619	6 306	...	...	...
30 - 34	25 252	17 078	8 174	...	...	...
35 - 39	29 325	18 500	10 825	...	...	...
40 - 44	41 671	25 193	16 478	...	...	...
45 - 49	65 016	39 281	25 735	...	...	...
50 - 54	110 901	67 096	43 805	...	...	...
55 - 59	157 170	95 992	61 178	...	...	...
60 - 64	191 638	116 206	75 432	...	...	...
65 - 69	222 834	129 802	93 032	...	...	...
70 - 74	248 707	138 846	109 861	...	...	...
75 - 79	282 072	149 259	132 813	...	...	...
80 - 84	342 432	167 171	175 261	...	...	...
85 - 89	381 539	164 609	216 930	...	...	...
90 - 94	300 366	107 387	192 979	...	...	...
95 - 99	118 407	32 226	86 181	...	...	...
100 +	25 914	4 563	21 351	...	...	...
Unknown - Inconnu	163	110	53	..	..	..

United States Virgin Islands - Îles Vierges américaines
2007 (C)

Total	727	424	303	6.6	8.1	5.2
0 - 4	14	8	6	♦1.9	♦2.1	♦1.6
0	12	6	6	...	...	...

Continent, country or area, date, code[a] and age (in years) Continent, pays ou zone, date, code[a] et âge (en années)	Number - Nombre			Rate - Taux		
	Both sexes Les deux sexes	Male Masculin	Female Féminin	Both sexes Les deux sexes	Male Masculin	Female Féminin
AMERICA, NORTH - AMÉRIQUE DU NORD						
United States Virgin Islands - Îles Vierges américaines						
2007 (C)						
1 - 4	2	2	-	...	...	...
5 - 9	-	-	-	-	-	-
10 - 14	2	1	1	♦0.2	♦0.2	♦0.2
15 - 19	9	8	1	♦1.1	♦2.0	♦0.2
20 - 24	16	15	1	♦2.3	♦4.7	♦0.3
25 - 29	20	14	6	♦3.7	♦5.7	♦2.1
30 - 34	16	10	6	♦2.6	♦3.7	♦1.8
35 - 39	16	13	3	♦2.2	♦3.9	♦0.7
40 - 44	33	21	12	4.1	♦5.6	♦2.8
45 - 49	26	13	13	♦3.2	♦3.3	♦3.1
50 - 54	50	34	16	6.6	9.6	♦3.9
55 - 59	51	29	22	6.8	♦8.1	♦5.6
60 - 64	79	55	24	10.7	15.3	♦6.3
65 - 69	50	36	14	10.1	14.8	♦5.5
70 - 74	68	43	25	18.8	26.6	♦12.5
75 +	273	120	153	59.0	63.7	55.7
Unknown - Inconnu	4	4	-	..	..	..
AMERICA, SOUTH - AMÉRIQUE DU SUD						
Argentina - Argentine						
2014 (C)						
Total	325 539	168 215[12]	156 987[12]	7.6	8.0	7.2
0	8 202	4 593[12]	3 586[12]	10.9	11.8	9.8
1 - 4	1 278	741[12]	535[12]	0.4	0.5	0.4
5 - 9	710	392[12]	318[12]	0.2	0.2	0.2
10 - 14	900	525[12]	373[12]	0.3	0.3	0.2
15 - 19	2 905	2 129[12]	773[12]	0.8	1.2	0.4
20 - 24	3 714	2 842[12]	864[12]	1.1	1.6	0.5
25 - 29	3 445	2 499[12]	942[12]	1.0	1.5	0.6
30 - 34	3 737	2 488[12]	1 240[12]	1.2	1.6	0.8
35 - 39	4 497	2 853[12]	1 635[12]	1.5	1.9	1.1
40 - 44	5 618	3 387[12]	2 225[12]	2.2	2.6	1.7
45 - 49	7 250	4 475[12]	2 770[12]	3.2	4.0	2.4
50 - 54	11 211	7 005[12]	4 191[12]	5.2	6.7	3.8
55 - 59	16 606	10 543[12]	6 054[12]	8.4	11.2	5.9
60 - 64	22 831	14 348[12]	8 464[12]	13.0	17.4	9.1
65 - 69	28 663	17 684[12]	10 961[12]	19.5	26.4	13.7
70 - 74	33 706	19 869[12]	13 819[12]	30.0	40.6	21.7
75 - 79	38 741	20 912[12]	17 803[12]	46.1	61.7	35.5
80 - 84	46 539	21 893[12]	24 615[12]	79.5	103.1	66.0
85 +	84 385	28 679[12]	55 656[12]	166.1	192.2	155.1
Unknown - Inconnu	601	358[12]	163[12]	..	..	..
Bolivia (Plurinational State of) - Bolivie (État plurinational de)[21]						
2012 (I)						
Total	127 050	59 027	68 023	12.6	11.8	13.5
0	5 363	2 406	2 957	26.6	23.4	29.9
1 - 4	6 695	3 085	3 610	7.5	6.8	8.3
5 - 9	2 531	1 183	1 348	2.5	2.3	2.8
10 - 14	1 961	827	1 134	1.8	1.5	2.1
15 - 19	3 699	1 460	2 239	3.3	2.6	4.1
20 - 24	4 767	1 618	3 149	4.9	3.3	6.5
25 - 29	4 089	1 393	2 696	5.0	3.4	6.6
30 - 34	4 323	1 556	2 767	5.7	4.2	7.3
35 - 39	4 670	1 868	2 802	7.4	6.0	8.7
40 - 44	4 597	1 849	2 748	8.4	6.8	10.0
45 - 49	5 769	2 483	3 286	12.5	10.9	14.0
50 - 54	6 298	2 849	3 449	15.6	14.3	16.9
55 - 59	6 851	2 946	3 905	21.1	18.5	23.7
60 - 64	9 105	4 256	4 849	32.5	31.7	33.3
65 - 69	9 801	4 792	5 009	47.9	48.8	47.1

19. Deaths by age and sex and age-specific death rates by sex: latest available year, 2006 - 2015
Décès et taux de mortalité selon l'âge et le sexe : dernière année disponible, 2006 - 2015 (continued - suite)

Continent, country or area, date, code[a] and age (in years) / Continent, pays ou zone, date, code[a] et âge (en années)	Number - Nombre			Rate - Taux		
	Both sexes Les deux sexes	Male Masculin	Female Féminin	Both sexes Les deux sexes	Male Masculin	Female Féminin
AMERICA, SOUTH - AMÉRIQUE DU SUD						
Bolivia (Plurinational State of) - Bolivie (État plurinational de)[21]						
2012 (I)						
70 - 74	9 701	4 649	5 052	63.6	64.7	62.7
75 - 79	9 798	4 756	5 042	98.7	105.7	92.9
80 - 84	11 190	5 952	5 238	138.0	172.7	112.3
85 - 89	8 493	4 674	3 819	224.0	294.3	173.3
90 - 94	3 927	2 332	1 595	267.8	388.9	184.0
95 +	3 422	2 093	1 329	415.6	633.3	269.6
Brazil - Brésil						
2014 (C)						
Total	1 194 164[22]	675 607[12]	518 044[12]	5.9	6.7	5.0
0	31 679[22]	17 695[12]	13 899[12]	10.9	11.9	9.8
1 - 4	5 809[22]	3 167[12]	2 637[12]	0.5	0.5	0.4
5 - 9	3 443[22]	1 976[12]	1 466[12]	0.2	0.2	0.2
10 - 14	5 025[22]	3 148[12]	1 875[12]	0.3	0.4	0.2
15 - 19	20 910[22]	17 135[12]	3 765[12]	1.2	2.0	0.4
20 - 24	26 868[22]	22 303[12]	4 557[12]	1.6	2.6	0.5
25 - 29	27 137[22]	21 359[12]	5 769[12]	1.6	2.5	0.7
30 - 34	30 163[22]	22 308[12]	7 846[12]	1.7	2.6	0.9
35 - 39	32 760[22]	22 790[12]	9 963[12]	2.1	3.0	1.3
40 - 44	38 376[22]	25 618[12]	12 748[12]	2.8	3.8	1.8
45 - 49	50 457[22]	32 632[12]	17 816[12]	4.0	5.3	2.8
50 - 54	65 480[22]	41 757[12]	23 708[12]	5.7	7.5	4.0
55 - 59	81 151[22]	50 796[12]	30 346[12]	8.6	11.2	6.1
60 - 64	93 430[22]	56 989[12]	36 433[12]	12.5	16.2	9.1
65 - 69	103 272[22]	60 700[12]	42 554[12]	18.5	23.8	14.0
70 - 74	114 695[22]	64 684[12]	49 994[12]	29.2	37.5	22.7
75 - 79	127 565[22]	66 670[12]	60 871[12]	45.3	56.4	37.2
80 - 84	126 627[22]	60 066[12]	66 537[12]	73.1	87.5	63.6
85 - 89	108 823[22]	46 025[12]	62 777[12]	116.8	132.5	107.4
90 +	96 804	35 060	61 708	191.8	215.0	180.7
90 - 94	63 203[22]	23 886[12]	39 307[12]	...	...	...
95 - 99	26 168[22]	8 888[12]	17 256[12]	...	...	...
100 +	7 433[22]	2 286[12]	5 145[12]	...	...	...
Unknown - Inconnu	3 690[22]	2 729[12]	775[12]	..	..	..
Chile - Chili						
2013 (C)						
Total	99 770	52 917[12]	46 835[12]	5.7	6.1	5.3
0	1 692	949[12]	725[12]	6.7	7.4	5.9
1 - 4	285	155	130	0.3	0.3	0.3
5 - 9	169	97	72	0.1	0.2	0.1
10 - 14	233	131	102	0.2	0.2	0.2
15 - 19	625	429	196	0.4	0.6	0.3
20 - 24	924	715	209	0.6	1.0	0.3
25 - 29	982	710	272	0.7	1.0	0.4
30 - 34	1 119	814	305	0.9	1.3	0.5
35 - 39	1 400	983	417	1.2	1.6	0.7
40 - 44	2 079	1 390	689	1.7	2.3	1.1
45 - 49	3 163	2 065	1 098	2.6	3.4	1.8
50 - 54	4 458	2 840	1 618	3.8	4.9	2.7
55 - 59	5 473	3 429	2 044	5.7	7.3	4.1
60 - 64	6 917	4 299	2 618	9.2	12.0	6.7
65 - 69	8 820	5 325	3 495	14.9	19.3	11.0
70 - 74	10 676	6 173	4 503	23.8	30.8	18.2
75 - 79	11 858	6 437	5 421	37.3	48.1	29.5
80 +	38 897	15 976	22 921	108.3	121.7	100.6
80 - 84	14 444	7 137	7 307	...	...	...
85 - 89	12 537	5 278	7 259	...	...	...
90 - 94	7 917	2 627	5 290	...	...	...
95 - 99	3 239	788	2 451	...	...	...
100 +	760	146	614	...	...	...
Colombia - Colombie						
2014 (U)						
Total	210 028	116 380	93 648	...	...	...
0	7 589	4 284	3 305	...	...	...

19. Deaths by age and sex and age-specific death rates by sex: latest available year, 2006 - 2015
Décès et taux de mortalité selon l'âge et le sexe : dernière année disponible, 2006 - 2015 (continued - suite)

Continent, country or area, date, code[a] and age (in years) Continent, pays ou zone, date, code[a] et âge (en années)	Number - Nombre			Rate - Taux		
	Both sexes Les deux sexes	Male Masculin	Female Féminin	Both sexes Les deux sexes	Male Masculin	Female Féminin

AMERICA, SOUTH - AMÉRIQUE DU SUD

Colombia - Colombie
2014 (U)

1 - 4	1 560	876	684	...	...	...
5 - 9	861	494	367	...	...	...
10 - 14	1 222	750	472	...	...	...
15 - 19	4 088	3 162	926	...	...	...
20 - 24	5 600	4 614	986	...	...	...
25 - 29	5 231	4 130	1 101	...	...	...
30 - 34	5 256	3 888	1 368	...	...	...
35 - 39	4 853	3 320	1 533	...	...	...
40 - 44	5 281	3 375	1 906	...	...	...
45 - 49	6 754	3 965	2 789	...	...	...
50 - 54	8 799	5 080	3 719	...	...	...
55 - 59	11 321	6 615	4 706	...	...	...
60 - 64	13 576	7 877	5 699	...	...	...
65 - 69	15 755	8 939	6 816	...	...	...
70 - 74	19 543	10 804	8 739	...	...	...
75 - 79	23 954	12 703	11 251	...	...	...
80 - 84	26 066	12 872	13 194	...	...	...
85 - 89	22 386	10 339	12 047	...	...	...
90 - 94	13 499	5 625	7 874	...	...	...
95 - 99	5 332	2 032	3 300	...	...	...
100 +	1 240	425	815	...	...	...
Unknown - Inconnu	262	211	51	..	..	..

Ecuador - Équateur[23]
2014 (U)

Total	62 981	34 778	28 203	...	...	...
0	2 821	1 572	1 249	...	...	...
1 - 4	845	473	372	...	...	...
5 - 9	443	263	180	...	...	...
10 - 14	557	312	245	...	...	...
15 - 19	1 099	740	359	...	...	...
20 - 24	1 592	1 198	394	...	...	...
25 - 29	1 624	1 243	381	...	...	...
30 - 34	1 610	1 146	464	...	...	...
35 - 39	1 619	1 062	557	...	...	...
40 - 44	1 772	1 121	651	...	...	...
45 - 49	2 112	1 252	860	...	...	...
50 - 54	2 631	1 522	1 109	...	...	...
55 - 59	3 222	1 875	1 347	...	...	...
60 - 64	3 938	2 260	1 678	...	...	...
65 - 69	4 427	2 517	1 910	...	...	...
70 - 74	5 128	2 816	2 312	...	...	...
75 - 79	5 919	3 212	2 707	...	...	...
80 - 84	7 102	3 703	3 399	...	...	...
85 - 89	6 690	3 278	3 412	...	...	...
90 - 94	4 979	2 128	2 851	...	...	...
95 - 99	2 146	825	1 321	...	...	...
100 +	682	247	435	...	...	...
Unknown - Inconnu	23	13	10	..	..	..

French Guiana - Guyane française[18]
2007 (C)

Total	690	405	285	3.2	3.8	2.6
0 - 4	95	50	45	3.5	3.6	3.3
0	77	39	38	...	...	...
1 - 4	18	11	7			
5 - 9	9	4	5	♦0.3	♦0.3	♦0.4
10 - 14	8	5	3	♦0.3	♦0.4	♦0.3
15 - 19	13	10	3	♦0.7	♦1.0	♦0.3
20 - 24	14	12	2	♦0.9	♦1.6	♦0.2
25 - 29	16	11	5	♦1.1	♦1.6	♦0.6
30 - 34	23	15	8	♦1.4	♦2.0	♦0.9
35 - 39	28	21	7	♦1.8	♦2.8	♦0.8
40 - 44	41	24	17	2.9	♦3.5	♦2.4
45 - 49	48	35	13	4.1	5.9	♦2.3
50 - 54	26	16	10	♦2.7	♦3.3	♦2.1
55 - 59	32	24	8	4.6	♦6.5	♦2.4

19. Deaths by age and sex and age-specific death rates by sex: latest available year, 2006 - 2015
Décès et taux de mortalité selon l'âge et le sexe : dernière année disponible, 2006 - 2015 (continued - suite)

Continent, country or area, date, code[a] and age (in years) Continent, pays ou zone, date, code[a] et âge (en années)	Number - Nombre			Rate - Taux		
	Both sexes Les deux sexes	Male Masculin	Female Féminin	Both sexes Les deux sexes	Male Masculin	Female Féminin
AMERICA, SOUTH - AMÉRIQUE DU SUD						
French Guiana - Guyane française[18]						
2007 (C)						
60 - 64	33	25	8	7.4	♦10.5	♦3.8
65 - 69	48	24	24	17.0	♦16.5	♦17.5
70 - 74	46	29	17	21.8	♦28.3	♦15.7
75 - 79	62	32	30	46.6	53.9	♦40.8
80 - 84	57	26	31	60.7	♦66.5	56.6
85 - 89	50	27	23	84.0	♦112.0	♦65.0
90 - 94	28	12	16	♦129.0	♦176.5	♦107.4
95 +	13	3	10	♦123.8	♦111.1	♦128.2
95 - 99	10	3	7	...	...	...
100 +	3	-	3	...	...	...
Paraguay						
2014 (+U)						
Total	22 625	12 645[12]	9 910[12]	...	...	...
0	468	269[12]	198[12]	...	...	...
1 - 4	158	81[12]	77[12]	...	...	...
5 - 9	98	56[12]	42[12]	...	...	...
10 - 14	149	84[12]	65[12]	...	...	...
15 - 19	427	303[12]	123[12]	...	...	...
20 - 24	489	392[12]	97[12]	...	...	...
25 - 29	447	333[12]	111[12]	...	...	...
30 - 34	515	364[12]	146[12]	...	...	...
35 - 39	522	331[12]	190[12]	...	...	...
40 - 44	643	379[12]	260[12]	...	...	...
45 - 49	901	556[12]	342[12]	...	...	...
50 - 54	1 205	732[12]	468[12]	...	...	...
55 - 59	1 474	939[12]	530[12]	...	...	...
60 - 64	1 732	1 055[12]	674[12]	...	...	...
65 - 69	1 905	1 155[12]	741[12]	...	...	...
70 - 74	2 156	1 285[12]	866[12]	...	...	...
75 - 79	2 389	1 302[12]	1 077[12]	...	...	...
80 - 84	2 531	1 234[12]	1 290[12]	...	...	...
85 +	4 416	1 795[12]	2 613[12]	...	...	...
Peru - Pérou[24]						
2014 (+U)						
Total	96 460	51 787	44 673	...	...	...
0	4 243	2 366	1 877	...	...	...
1 - 4	1 262	726	536	...	...	...
5 - 9	658	363	295	...	...	...
10 - 14	620	345	275	...	...	...
15 - 19	1 299	818	481	...	...	...
20 - 24	1 700	1 170	530	...	...	...
25 - 29	1 846	1 285	561	...	...	...
30 - 34	2 034	1 365	669	...	...	...
35 - 39	2 237	1 427	810	...	...	...
40 - 44	2 717	1 652	1 065	...	...	...
45 - 49	3 285	1 886	1 399	...	...	...
50 - 54	4 079	2 282	1 797	...	...	...
55 - 59	4 800	2 610	2 190	...	...	...
60 - 64	5 736	3 093	2 643	...	...	...
65 - 69	7 069	3 868	3 201	...	...	...
70 - 74	8 544	4 684	3 860	...	...	...
75 - 79	10 591	5 724	4 867	...	...	...
80 - 84	12 034	6 191	5 843	...	...	...
85 - 89	11 041	5 432	5 609	...	...	...
90 - 94	7 119	3 168	3 951	...	...	...
95 - 99	2 796	1 099	1 697	...	...	...
100 +	750	233	517	...	...	...
Suriname						
2014 (C)						
Total	3 738	2 111	1 627	6.7	7.6	5.8
0	163	90	73	15.7	17.2	14.1
1 - 4	34	24	10	0.8	♦1.1	♦0.5
5 - 9	15	11	4	♦0.3	♦0.4	♦0.2
10 - 14	24	15	9	♦0.5	♦0.6	♦0.4

19. Deaths by age and sex and age-specific death rates by sex: latest available year, 2006 - 2015
Décès et taux de mortalité selon l'âge et le sexe : dernière année disponible, 2006 - 2015 (continued - suite)

Continent, country or area, date, code[a] and age (in years) / Continent, pays ou zone, date, code[a] et âge (en années)	Number - Nombre			Rate - Taux		
	Both sexes Les deux sexes	Male Masculin	Female Féminin	Both sexes Les deux sexes	Male Masculin	Female Féminin
AMERICA, SOUTH - AMÉRIQUE DU SUD						
Suriname						
2014 (C)						
15 - 19	36	22	14	0.8	♦0.9	♦0.6
20 - 24	40	24	16	0.9	♦1.0	♦0.7
25 - 29	86	51	35	2.0	2.3	1.6
30 - 34	95	58	37	2.3	2.8	1.8
35 - 39	92	50	42	2.3	2.5	2.1
40 - 44	131	80	51	3.5	4.3	2.7
45 - 49	204	120	84	5.9	6.9	4.8
50 - 54	253	176	77	8.3	11.6	5.0
55 - 59	293	182	111	11.3	14.4	8.4
60 - 64	299	183	116	14.8	18.9	11.0
65 - 69	322	190	132	21.1	26.6	16.2
70 - 74	356	189	167	31.7	36.9	27.3
75 - 79	414	229	185	54.3	68.0	43.4
80 +	881	417	464	115.6	132.9	103.5
80 - 84	398	217	181	...	...	...
85 - 89	275	126	149	...	...	...
90 - 94	152	55	97	...	...	...
95 - 99	50	17	33	...	...	...
100 +	6	2	4	...	...	...
Uruguay						
2013 (C)						
Total	32 795	16 631[12]	16 150[12]	...	...	...
0	431	239[12]	192[12]	...	...	...
1 - 4	65	37[12]	28[12]	...	...	...
5 - 9	45	16[12]	29[12]	...	...	...
10 - 14	68	39[12]	29[12]	...	...	...
15 - 19	237	180[12]	57[12]	...	...	...
20 - 24	255	200[12]	55[12]	...	...	...
25 - 29	268	199[12]	69[12]	...	...	...
30 - 34	285	204[12]	81[12]	...	...	...
35 - 39	354	227[12]	127[12]	...	...	...
40 - 44	475	301[12]	174[12]	...	...	...
45 - 49	644	391[12]	253[12]	...	...	...
50 - 54	1 020	683[12]	337[12]	...	...	...
55 - 59	1 533	966[12]	567[12]	...	...	...
60 - 64	2 002	1 288[12]	714[12]	...	...	...
65 - 69	2 596	1 648[12]	948[12]	...	...	...
70 - 74	3 374	2 021[12]	1 352[12]	...	...	...
75 - 79	4 130	2 255[12]	1 875[12]	...	...	...
80 - 84	5 403	2 482[12]	2 919[12]	...	...	...
85 - 89	4 906	1 859[12]	3 041[12]	...	...	...
90 - 94	3 159	974[12]	2 184[12]	...	...	...
95 +	1 341	285[12]	1 056[12]	...	...	...
Unknown - Inconnu	204	137[12]	63[12]	..	..	..
Venezuela (Bolivarian Republic of) - Venezuela (République bolivarienne du)						
2013 (C)						
Total	147 901	90 389	57 512	4.9	6.0	3.8
0 - 4	8 826	5 062	3 764	3.0	3.4	2.6
0	7 630	4 402	3 228	...	...	...
1 - 4	1 196	660	536	...	...	...
5 - 9	705	407	298	0.2	0.3	0.2
10 - 14	888	544	344	0.3	0.4	0.3
15 - 19	4 692	3 976	716	1.7	2.9	0.5
20 - 24	7 173	6 319	854	2.7	4.6	0.6
25 - 29	5 922	4 980	942	2.3	3.9	0.7
30 - 34	5 078	3 966	1 112	2.2	3.4	1.0
35 - 39	4 821	3 467	1 354	2.3	3.4	1.3
40 - 44	4 795	3 218	1 577	2.6	3.5	1.7
45 - 49	5 930	3 775	2 155	3.4	4.4	2.5
50 - 54	7 981	5 139	2 842	5.3	6.9	3.7
55 - 59	9 781	6 151	3 630	7.9	10.2	5.8
60 - 64	11 253	7 096	4 157	11.3	14.6	8.1
65 - 69	11 454	6 958	4 496	15.4	19.5	11.6

19. Deaths by age and sex and age-specific death rates by sex: latest available year, 2006 - 2015
Décès et taux de mortalité selon l'âge et le sexe : dernière année disponible, 2006 - 2015 (continued - suite)

Continent, country or area, date, code[a] and age (in years) / Continent, pays ou zone, date, code[a] et âge (en années)	Number - Nombre			Rate - Taux		
	Both sexes Les deux sexes	Male Masculin	Female Féminin	Both sexes Les deux sexes	Male Masculin	Female Féminin
AMERICA, SOUTH - AMÉRIQUE DU SUD						
Venezuela (Bolivarian Republic of) - Venezuela (République bolivarienne du)						
2013 (C)						
70 - 74	12 139	7 109	5 030	23.7	29.8	18.4
75 - 79	12 988	7 147	5 841	37.2	45.5	30.4
80 +	33 475	15 075	18 400	112.8	117.9	109.0
80 - 84	13 352	6 716	6 636	...	...	...
85 - 89	10 686	4 812	5 874	...	...	...
90 - 94	6 324	2 431	3 893	...	...	...
95 - 99	2 399	882	1 517	...	...	...
100 +	714	234	480	...	...	...
2014 (C)						
Total	159 239	...	...	5.3	...	...
0	8 396	...	...	15.4	...	...
1 - 4	1 326	...	...	0.6	...	...
5 - 9	718	...	...	0.3	...	...
10 - 14	940	...	...	0.3	...	...
15 - 19	4 476	...	...	1.7	...	...
20 - 24	7 061	...	...	2.7	...	...
25 - 29	5 908	...	...	2.3	...	...
30 - 34	5 012	...	...	2.1	...	...
35 - 39	4 749	...	...	2.2	...	...
40 - 44	4 835	...	...	2.5	...	...
45 - 49	6 187	...	...	3.4	...	...
50 - 54	8 174	...	...	5.2	...	...
55 - 59	10 063	...	...	8.0	...	...
60 - 64	12 330	...	...	13.1	...	...
65 - 69	12 594	...	...	18.0	...	...
70 - 74	13 041	...	...	26.3	...	...
75 - 79	14 641	...	...	44.3	...	...
80 - 84	14 822	...	...	73.5	...	...
85 +	23 966	...	...	125.7	...	...
ASIA - ASIE						
Armenia - Arménie[25]						
2014 (C)						
Total	27 714	14 219	13 495	...	...	...
0	376	212	164	...	...	...
1 - 4	69	41	28	...	...	...
5 - 9	32	16	16	...	...	...
10 - 14	25	17	8	...	...	...
15 - 19	84	66	18	...	...	...
20 - 24	138	104	34	...	...	...
25 - 29	184	138	46	...	...	...
30 - 34	195	134	61	...	...	...
35 - 39	283	195	88	...	...	...
40 - 44	430	297	133	...	...	...
45 - 49	720	516	204	...	...	...
50 - 54	1 304	894	410	...	...	...
55 - 59	1 821	1 260	561	...	...	...
60 - 64	2 215	1 421	794	...	...	...
65 - 69	1 892	1 140	752	...	...	...
70 - 74	3 101	1 648	1 453	...	...	...
75 - 79	5 083	2 490	2 593	...	...	...
80 - 84	5 042	2 150	2 892	...	...	...
85 - 89	3 667	1 203	2 464	...	...	...
90 - 94	823	222	601	...	...	...
95 - 99	173	38	135	...	...	...
100 +	57	17	40	...	...	...
Azerbaijan - Azerbaïdjan[25]						
2014 (+C)						
Total	55 648	29 655	25 993	5.9	6.3	5.5
0	1 655	976	679	9.6	10.5	8.5
1 - 4	442	256	186	0.7	0.7	0.6
5 - 9	199	123	76	0.3	0.4	0.3

19. Deaths by age and sex and age-specific death rates by sex: latest available year, 2006 - 2015
Décès et taux de mortalité selon l'âge et le sexe : dernière année disponible, 2006 - 2015 (continued - suite)

Continent, country or area, date, code[a] and age (in years) Continent, pays ou zone, date, code[a] et âge (en années)	Number - Nombre			Rate - Taux		
	Both sexes Les deux sexes	Male Masculin	Female Féminin	Both sexes Les deux sexes	Male Masculin	Female Féminin
ASIA - ASIE						
Azerbaijan - Azerbaïdjan[25]						
2014 (+C)						
10 - 14	200	128	72	0.3	0.4	0.2
15 - 19	376	265	111	0.5	0.7	0.3
20 - 24	612	420	192	0.7	0.9	0.4
25 - 29	644	451	193	0.7	1.0	0.4
30 - 34	750	534	216	0.9	1.4	0.5
35 - 39	878	631	247	1.3	1.9	0.7
40 - 44	1 258	884	374	2.0	2.9	1.1
45 - 49	2 136	1 473	663	3.2	4.7	1.9
50 - 54	3 555	2 338	1 217	5.4	7.3	3.5
55 - 59	4 459	2 950	1 509	9.1	12.6	5.8
60 - 64	4 680	2 926	1 754	15.4	20.7	10.8
65 - 69	3 906	2 336	1 570	23.9	32.3	17.2
70 - 74	5 427	2 843	2 584	39.5	48.9	32.6
75 - 79	9 847	4 487	5 360	67.3	75.4	61.8
80 - 84	8 004	3 456	4 548	112.2	118.5	107.9
85 - 89	4 511	1 722	2 789	173.0	179.4	169.2
90 - 94	1 483	384	1 099	208.5	177.8	221.9
95 - 99	352	47	305	253.4	133.9	293.8
100 +	274	25	249	409.6	♦735.3	392.1
Bahrain - Bahreïn[26]						
2014 (C)						
Total	2 805	1 698	1 107	2.1	2.1	2.2
0	218	113	105	10.2	10.2	10.2
1 - 4	34	9	25	0.4	♦0.2	♦0.6
5 - 9	25	14	11	♦0.3	♦0.3	♦0.3
10 - 14	21	12	9	♦0.3	♦0.3	♦0.2
15 - 19	35	23	12	0.5	♦0.6	♦0.3
20 - 24	64	51	13	0.6	0.8	♦0.3
25 - 29	78	67	11	0.4	0.6	♦0.2
30 - 34	104	78	26	0.6	0.7	♦0.5
35 - 39	111	90	21	0.8	1.0	♦0.5
40 - 44	110	81	29	1.0	1.1	♦0.8
45 - 49	154	112	42	1.8	2.0	1.3
50 - 54	182	126	56	2.6	2.9	2.1
55 - 59	235	156	79	4.5	4.8	4.1
60 - 64	208	127	81	7.1	7.1	7.2
65 - 69	191	109	82	12.8	12.7	13.0
70 - 74	268	153	115	27.1	28.9	25.0
75 - 79	267	126	141	41.9	38.1	46.0
80 - 84	231	107	124	61.5	54.3	69.4
85 +	246	127	119	90.5	89.7	91.3
85 - 89	138	65	73	...	...	...
90 - 94	78	46	32	...	...	...
95 - 99	27	16	11	...	...	...
100 +	3	-	3	...	...	...
Unknown - Inconnu	23	17	6	..	..	..
Brunei Darussalam - Brunéi Darussalam						
2014 (+C)						
Total	1 470	832	638	3.6	3.9	3.2
0	51	30	21	...	...	...
1 - 4	9	6	3	...	...	...
5 - 9	11	5	6	♦0.3	♦0.3	♦0.4
10 - 14	6	5	1	♦0.2	♦0.3	♦0.1
15 - 19	10	6	4	♦0.3	♦0.3	♦0.2
20 - 24	22	17	5	♦0.6	♦0.9	♦0.3
25 - 29	33	24	9	0.8	♦1.1	♦0.5
30 - 34	31	20	11	0.8	♦1.0	♦0.6
35 - 39	47	32	15	1.3	1.7	♦0.9
40 - 44	78	52	26	2.4	3.1	♦1.6
45 - 49	89	60	29	3.2	4.2	♦2.2
50 - 54	90	51	39	4.0	4.3	3.6
55 - 59	103	70	33	6.0	8.0	4.0
60 - 64	116	60	56	10.1	10.3	9.8
65 - 69	122	68	54	18.8	21.3	16.4
70 - 74	145	72	73	31.5	32.7	30.4

19. Deaths by age and sex and age-specific death rates by sex: latest available year, 2006 - 2015
Décès et taux de mortalité selon l'âge et le sexe : dernière année disponible, 2006 - 2015 (continued - suite)

Continent, country or area, date, code[a] and age (in years) Continent, pays ou zone, date, code[a] et âge (en annèes)	Number - Nombre			Rate - Taux		
	Both sexes Les deux sexes	Male Masculin	Female Féminin	Both sexes Les deux sexes	Male Masculin	Female Féminin
ASIA - ASIE						
Brunei Darussalam - Brunéi Darussalam						
2014 (+C)						
75 - 79	160	81	79	57.1	62.3	52.7
80 - 84	158	80	78	87.8	100.0	78.0
85 +	189	93	96	189.0	186.0	192.0
85 - 89	114	59	55	...	...	...
90 - 94	59	28	31	...	...	...
95 - 99	12	4	8	...	...	...
100 +	4	2	2	...	...	...
China - Chine[27]						
2010 (|)						
Total	7 421 990	4 293 783	3 128 207	5.6	6.3	4.8
0	60 217	32 026	28 191	4.4	4.3	4.5
1 - 4	39 591	23 119	16 472	0.6	0.7	0.6
5 - 9	21 183	13 621	7 562	0.3	0.4	0.2
10 - 14	23 088	15 243	7 845	0.3	0.4	0.2
15 - 19	40 469	28 088	12 381	0.4	0.5	0.3
20 - 24	62 552	43 738	18 814	0.5	0.7	0.3
25 - 29	60 661	42 497	18 164	0.6	0.8	0.4
30 - 34	79 960	55 804	24 156	0.8	1.1	0.5
35 - 39	140 531	98 382	42 149	1.2	1.6	0.7
40 - 44	216 353	149 111	67 242	1.7	2.3	1.1
45 - 49	262 531	179 446	83 085	2.5	3.3	1.6
50 - 54	337 397	226 888	110 509	4.3	5.6	2.9
55 - 59	494 339	324 817	169 522	6.1	7.9	4.2
60 - 64	586 160	377 069	209 091	10.0	12.6	7.3
65 - 69	695 662	435 007	260 655	16.9	21.0	12.8
70 - 74	999 653	599 394	400 259	30.3	36.5	24.2
75 - 79	1 162 694	657 140	505 554	48.7	58.3	40.2
80 - 84	1 081 704	553 704	528 000	80.9	93.6	70.8
85 - 89	686 462	306 678	379 784	121.9	139.4	110.7
90 - 94	279 569	104 048	175 521	177.1	196.0	167.6
95 - 99	74 729	23 292	51 437	202.0	197.9	203.9
100 +	16 485	4 671	11 814	458.8	527.7	436.2
China, Hong Kong SAR - Chine, Hong Kong RAS						
2014 (C)						
Total	45 087	24 946[12]	20 140[12]	6.2	7.5	5.2
0	103	44	59	2.1	1.7	2.4
1 - 4	43	21	22	0.2	♦0.2	♦0.2
5 - 9	20	11	9	♦0.1	♦0.1	♦0.1
10 - 14	27	12	15	♦0.1	♦0.1	♦0.1
15 - 19	62	41	21	0.2	0.2	♦0.1
20 - 24	93	62	31	0.2	0.3	0.1
25 - 29	133	85	48	0.3	0.4	0.2
30 - 34	229	127	102	0.4	0.5	0.3
35 - 39	327	207	120	0.6	0.9	0.4
40 - 44	537	330	207	0.9	1.4	0.6
45 - 49	885	527	358	1.5	2.0	1.1
50 - 54	1 533	960	573	2.3	3.1	1.6
55 - 59	2 328	1 524	804	3.9	5.2	2.7
60 - 64	2 794	1 890	904	6.1	8.3	3.9
65 - 69	2 922	1 982	940	8.9	12.2	5.8
70 - 74	3 465	2 451	1 014	16.4	22.3	9.9
75 - 79	5 636	3 575	2 061	26.9	35.7	18.8
80 - 84	7 960	4 596	3 364	48.2	62.5	36.7
85 +	15 973	6 488	9 485	104.4	128.5	92.5
Unknown - Inconnu	17	13[12]	3[12]	..	..	..
China, Macao SAR - Chine, Macao RAS						
2015 (C)						
Total	2 002	1 119	883	3.1	3.5	2.7
0	11	7	4	♦1.6	♦1.9	♦1.2
1 - 14	6	2	4	♦0.1	♦0.1	♦0.1
15 - 39	64	45	19	0.2	0.3	♦0.1
40 - 64	557	379	178	2.3	3.2	1.4
65 - 79	516	336	180	12.1	15.5	8.7
80 +	848	350	498	65.7	76.1	60.0

19. Deaths by age and sex and age-specific death rates by sex: latest available year, 2006 - 2015
Décès et taux de mortalité selon l'âge et le sexe : dernière année disponible, 2006 - 2015 (continued - suite)

Continent, country or area, date, code[a] and age (in years) / Continent, pays ou zone, date, code[a] et âge (en annèes)	Number - Nombre			Rate - Taux		
	Both sexes Les deux sexes	Male Masculin	Female Féminin	Both sexes Les deux sexes	Male Masculin	Female Féminin
ASIA - ASIE						
Cyprus - Chypre[28]						
2014 (C)						
Total	5 250	2 739	2 511	6.2	6.6	5.7
0	13	8	5	♦1.4	♦1.7	♦1.1
1 - 4	2	1	1	♦0.1	-	♦0.1
5 - 9	4	1	3	♦0.1	-	♦0.1
10 - 14	1	1	-	-	-	-
15 - 19	15	12	3	♦0.3	♦0.4	♦0.1
20 - 24	12	7	5	♦0.2	♦0.2	♦0.2
25 - 29	11	7	4	♦0.2	♦0.2	♦0.1
30 - 34	22	12	10	♦0.3	♦0.4	♦0.3
35 - 39	29	22	7	♦0.5	♦0.8	♦0.2
40 - 44	54	33	21	0.9	1.2	♦0.7
45 - 49	68	42	26	1.2	1.6	♦0.9
50 - 54	108	71	37	1.9	2.6	1.3
55 - 59	205	126	79	4.1	5.0	3.1
60 - 64	248	171	77	5.3	7.5	3.3
65 - 69	421	276	145	10.4	14.2	6.9
70 - 74	455	295	160	14.9	20.3	9.9
75 - 79	732	423	309	31.3	39.6	24.3
80 - 84	1 017	455	562	65.7	69.6	62.8
85 - 89	960	428	532	118.3	132.5	108.8
90 - 94	612	250	362	221.1	235.3	212.2
95 - 99	221	87	134	397.5	433.9	376.9
100 +	40	11	29	410.3	♦239.1	♦563.1
Democratic People's Republic of Korea - République populaire démocratique de Corée[13]						
2008 (I)						
Total	216 616	112 827	103 789	9.0	9.6	8.4
0	6 686	3 593	3 093	19.6	20.6	18.5
1 - 4	2 552	1 372	1 180	1.9	2.0	1.8
5 - 9	1 680	960	720	0.9	1.0	0.8
10 - 14	1 614	869	745	0.8	0.8	0.8
15 - 19	2 426	1 348	1 078	1.2	1.3	1.1
20 - 24	3 171	1 922	1 249	1.7	2.0	1.4
25 - 29	3 528	2 160	1 368	2.0	2.4	1.6
30 - 34	3 907	2 424	1 483	2.3	2.8	1.8
35 - 39	5 792	3 655	2 137	2.6	3.3	1.9
40 - 44	6 312	3 907	2 405	3.1	3.9	2.4
45 - 49	6 468	3 915	2 553	4.1	5.1	3.2
50 - 54	7 630	4 715	2 915	5.8	7.4	4.3
55 - 59	11 295	7 113	4 182	12.5	16.8	8.7
60 - 64	26 360	16 815	9 545	24.9	35.3	16.4
65 - 69	34 068	22 281	11 787	37.3	58.7	22.1
70 - 74	34 093	18 886	15 207	51.5	82.7	35.0
75 - 79	28 690	10 991	17 699	85.5	138.7	69.1
80 +	30 344	5 901	24 443	163.8	238.8	152.3
Georgia - Géorgie[25]						
2014 (C)						
Total	49 087	24 851	24 236	10.9	11.6	10.3
0	578	316	262	10.0	10.6	9.4
1 - 4	81	41	40	0.3	0.3	0.3
5 - 9	61	35	26	0.2	0.3	♦0.2
10 - 14	58	41	17	0.3	0.3	♦0.2
15 - 19	140	96	44	0.5	0.7	0.3
20 - 24	214	172	42	0.6	1.0	0.2
25 - 29	290	217	73	0.8	1.2	0.4
30 - 34	400	304	96	1.2	1.8	0.6
35 - 39	535	403	132	1.7	2.6	0.8
40 - 44	808	621	187	2.7	4.2	1.2
45 - 49	1 327	995	332	4.4	7.1	2.1
50 - 54	2 169	1 599	570	6.5	10.5	3.2
55 - 59	2 799	1 966	833	9.8	15.1	5.4
60 - 64	3 524	2 396	1 128	14.7	22.6	8.4
65 - 69	3 584	2 181	1 403	22.8	32.4	15.7
70 - 74	5 342	2 873	2 469	34.9	49.2	26.1
75 - 79	8 909	4 181	4 728	58.1	72.0	49.6

19. Deaths by age and sex and age-specific death rates by sex: latest available year, 2006 - 2015
Décès et taux de mortalité selon l'âge et le sexe : dernière année disponible, 2006 - 2015 (continued - suite)

Continent, country or area, date, code[a] and age (in years) / Continent, pays ou zone, date, code[a] et âge (en annèes)	Number - Nombre			Rate - Taux		
	Both sexes Les deux sexes	Male Masculin	Female Féminin	Both sexes Les deux sexes	Male Masculin	Female Féminin
ASIA - ASIE						
Georgia - Géorgie[25]						
2014 (C)						
80 - 84	8 615	3 481	5 134	98.7	111.3	91.6
85 +	9 446	2 784	6 662	124.1	124.8	123.8
85 - 89	6 744	2 184	4 560	...	...	...
90 - 94	2 130	510	1 620	...	...	...
95 - 99	448	74	374	...	...	...
100 +	124	16	108	...	...	...
Unknown - Inconnu	207	149	58	..	..	..
Indonesia - Indonésie[29]						
2010 (I)						
Total	1 236 154	687 976	548 178	5.2	5.8	4.6
0	106 846	61 546	45 300	24.3	27.2	21.2
1 - 4	37 689	20 958	16 731	2.1	2.2	1.9
5 - 9	19 409	10 807	8 602	0.8	0.9	0.8
10 - 14	15 382	9 029	6 353	0.7	0.8	0.6
15 - 19	23 642	14 948	8 694	1.1	1.4	0.8
20 - 24	27 089	16 020	11 069	1.4	1.6	1.1
25 - 29	31 020	17 855	13 165	1.5	1.7	1.2
30 - 34	31 290	17 168	14 122	1.6	1.7	1.4
35 - 39	38 257	20 382	17 875	2.1	2.2	1.9
40 - 44	49 757	26 901	22 856	3.0	3.2	2.8
45 - 49	65 139	36 351	28 788	4.6	5.2	4.1
50 - 54	89 078	51 820	37 258	7.7	8.8	6.5
55 - 59	86 308	53 355	32 953	10.2	12.1	8.1
60 - 64	105 991	62 663	43 328	17.5	21.4	13.8
65 - 69	107 730	62 508	45 222	23.0	28.1	18.3
70 - 74	138 235	76 159	62 076	40.0	49.7	32.2
75 - 79	92 062	49 343	42 719	46.5	58.6	37.6
80 - 84	86 057	42 547	43 510	75.3	88.4	65.8
85 +	85 173	37 616	47 557	119.4	133.2	110.3
Iran (Islamic Republic of) - Iran (République islamique d')[30]						
2014 (+U)						
Total	338 681	193 394	145 287	...	...	...
0 - 4	11 257	6 137	5 120	...	...	...
0	7 430	4 012	3 418	...	...	...
1 - 4	3 827	2 125	1 702	...	...	...
5 - 9	2 413	1 388	1 025	...	...	...
10 - 14	2 134	1 240	894	...	...	...
15 - 19	4 318	2 981	1 337	...	...	...
20 - 24	6 776	5 006	1 770	...	...	...
25 - 29	8 799	5 784	3 015	...	...	...
30 - 34	8 794	6 018	2 776	...	...	...
35 - 39	8 081	5 523	2 558	...	...	...
40 - 44	8 736	6 014	2 722	...	...	...
45 - 49	10 237	6 827	3 410	...	...	...
50 - 54	14 127	9 401	4 726	...	...	...
55 - 59	18 904	12 142	6 762	...	...	...
60 - 64	21 746	12 765	8 981	...	...	...
65 - 69	23 078	12 953	10 125	...	...	...
70 - 74	27 278	14 836	12 442	...	...	...
75 +	146 095	75 560	70 535	...	...	...
Unknown - Inconnu	15 908	8 819	7 089	..	..	..
Israel - Israël[31]						
2015 (C)						
Total	44 210	22 294	21 912	...	...	...
0	552	296	252	...	...	...
1 - 4	117	68	49	...	...	...
5 - 9	76	51	25	...	...	...
10 - 14	89	51	38	...	...	...
15 - 19	152	111	41	...	...	...
20 - 24	197	152	45	...	...	...
25 - 29	203	146	57	...	...	...
30 - 34	249	174	75	...	...	...
35 - 39	294	181	113	...	...	...
40 - 44	496	314	182	...	...	...

531

19. Deaths by age and sex and age-specific death rates by sex: latest available year, 2006 - 2015
Décès et taux de mortalité selon l'âge et le sexe : dernière année disponible, 2006 - 2015 (continued - suite)

Continent, country or area, date, code[a] and age (in years) / Continent, pays ou zone, date, code[a] et âge (en années)	Number - Nombre			Rate - Taux		
	Both sexes Les deux sexes	Male Masculin	Female Féminin	Both sexes Les deux sexes	Male Masculin	Female Féminin
ASIA - ASIE						
Israel - Israël[31]						
2015 (C)						
45 - 49	653	406	247	...	...	...
50 - 54	1 156	731	425	...	...	...
55 - 59	1 582	996	586	...	...	...
60 - 64	2 384	1 485	899	...	...	...
65 - 69	3 480	2 087	1 393	...	...	...
70 - 74	3 410	1 999	1 411	...	...	...
75 - 79	5 442	2 940	2 502	...	...	...
80 - 84	6 843	3 298	3 545	...	...	...
85 - 89	8 080	3 417	4 663	...	...	...
90 - 94	6 178	2 437	3 741	...	...	...
95 - 99	1 999	746	1 253	...	...	...
100 +	578	208	370	...	...	...
Japan - Japon[32]						
2014 (C)						
Total	1 273 004	660 334	612 670	10.0	10.7	9.4
0 - 4	2 883	1 542	1 341	0.6	0.6	0.5
0	2 080	1 110	970	...	...	...
1 - 4	803	432	371	...	...	...
5 - 9	460	276	184	0.1	0.1	0.1
10 - 14	501	318	183	0.1	0.1	0.1
15 - 19	1 205	840	365	0.2	0.3	0.1
20 - 24	2 320	1 665	655	0.4	0.5	0.2
25 - 29	2 873	1 961	912	0.4	0.6	0.3
30 - 34	3 896	2 574	1 322	0.5	0.7	0.4
35 - 39	5 879	3 715	2 164	0.7	0.8	0.5
40 - 44	10 065	6 449	3 616	1.0	1.3	0.8
45 - 49	13 726	8 750	4 976	1.6	2.0	1.2
50 - 54	19 841	12 954	6 887	2.6	3.3	1.8
55 - 59	30 315	20 277	10 038	3.9	5.3	2.6
60 - 64	57 310	39 570	17 740	6.3	8.8	3.8
65 - 69	85 193	59 068	26 125	9.5	13.6	5.6
70 - 74	114 866	77 300	37 566	14.6	21.1	8.9
75 - 79	156 782	99 061	57 721	25.0	35.9	16.5
80 - 84	221 045	125 619	95 426	45.7	65.1	32.8
85 - 89	249 725	116 956	132 769	82.2	114.8	65.8
90 - 94	186 121	58 659	127 462	144.8	191.7	130.3
95 - 99	84 117	19 021	65 096	236.9	301.9	223.7
100 +	23 411	3 390	20 021	390.2	423.8	385.0
Unknown - Inconnu	470	369	101	..	..	..
Kazakhstan[25]						
2013 (C)						
Total	135 950	74 804	61 146	8.0	9.2	7.0
0	4 367	2 502	1 865	11.6	13.0	10.2
1 - 4	1 071	630	441	0.8	0.9	0.6
5 - 9	433	246	187	0.3	0.3	0.3
10 - 14	376	224	152	0.3	0.4	0.3
15 - 19	921	614	307	0.7	0.9	0.5
20 - 24	1 933	1 421	512	1.2	1.8	0.6
25 - 29	2 751	2 032	719	1.8	2.7	0.9
30 - 34	3 589	2 700	889	2.8	4.2	1.4
35 - 39	4 563	3 386	1 177	3.9	5.9	1.9
40 - 44	5 332	3 887	1 445	4.8	7.3	2.5
45 - 49	6 571	4 686	1 885	6.2	9.3	3.4
50 - 54	9 554	6 743	2 811	9.2	14.0	5.1
55 - 59	10 873	7 312	3 561	13.9	20.9	8.2
60 - 64	12 617	8 045	4 572	20.9	31.8	13.0
65 - 69	9 335	5 601	3 734	30.2	45.1	20.3
70 - 74	15 744	8 170	7 574	41.7	59.9	31.4
75 - 79	17 012	7 901	9 111	72.5	97.9	59.2
80 - 84	13 622	4 908	8 714	108.4	133.5	98.0
85 - 89	10 636	2 823	7 813	187.2	201.9	182.4
90 - 94	3 382	676	2 706	276.8	240.0	287.8
95 - 99	848	141	707	357.1	216.6	410.1
100 +	274	41	233	290.3	139.0	359.0
Unknown - Inconnu	146	115	31	..	..	..

19. Deaths by age and sex and age-specific death rates by sex: latest available year, 2006 - 2015
Décès et taux de mortalité selon l'âge et le sexe : dernière année disponible, 2006 - 2015 (continued - suite)

Continent, country or area, date, code[a] and age (in years) Continent, pays ou zone, date, code[a] et âge (en annèes)	Number - Nombre			Rate - Taux		
	Both sexes Les deux sexes	Male Masculin	Female Féminin	Both sexes Les deux sexes	Male Masculin	Female Féminin
ASIA - ASIE						
Kuwait - Koweït						
2014 (C)						
Total	6 031	3 810	2 221	1.6	1.8	1.4
0	456	257	199	6.9	7.4	6.2
1 - 4	86	55	31	0.3	0.4	0.3
5 - 9	41	31	10	0.2	0.2	♦0.1
10 - 14	50	26	24	0.2	♦0.2	♦0.2
15 - 19	111	77	34	0.5	0.7	0.3
20 - 24	115	81	34	0.6	0.8	0.3
25 - 29	204	166	38	0.5	0.8	0.2
30 - 34	206	147	59	0.4	0.5	0.3
35 - 39	240	186	54	0.5	0.6	0.3
40 - 44	311	244	67	0.7	0.9	0.4
45 - 49	358	273	85	1.2	1.5	0.8
50 - 54	429	322	107	2.2	2.6	1.5
55 - 59	448	316	132	3.6	3.9	3.0
60 - 64	440	284	156	6.2	6.4	5.8
65 - 69	452	253	199	12.2	12.1	12.3
70 - 74	487	241	246	23.8	22.1	25.6
75 - 79	525	259	266	44.0	41.0	47.4
80 +	737	365	372	74.4	71.3	77.7
80 - 84	370	195	175	...	...	...
85 +	367	170	197	...	...	...
Unknown - Inconnu	335	227	108	..	..	..
Kyrgyzstan - Kirghizstan						
2015* (C)						
Total	34 808	19 375	15 433	5.8	6.6	5.1
0	2 945	1 654	1 291	18.4	20.0	16.7
1 - 4	542	296	246	0.9	1.0	0.8
5 - 9	154	92	62	0.3	0.3	0.2
10 - 14	187	121	66	0.4	0.5	0.3
15 - 19	354	232	122	0.7	0.9	0.5
20 - 24	517	362	155	0.9	1.2	0.5
25 - 29	695	513	182	1.2	1.8	0.6
30 - 34	797	540	257	1.8	2.4	1.1
35 - 39	1 121	805	316	3.0	4.4	1.7
40 - 44	1 411	1 019	392	4.2	6.3	2.3
45 - 49	1 711	1 169	542	5.5	7.8	3.4
50 - 54	2 277	1 544	733	7.8	11.1	4.8
55 - 59	2 758	1 785	973	11.6	16.2	7.6
60 - 64	2 846	1 831	1 015	18.1	26.2	11.6
65 - 69	2 523	1 513	1 010	25.5	36.5	17.6
70 - 74	2 192	1 146	1 046	45.8	58.5	37.0
75 - 79	4 172	1 960	2 212	70.1	87.9	59.4
80 - 84	3 504	1 467	2 037	117.4	140.1	105.1
85 - 89	2 772	1 009	1 763	156.6	161.8	153.8
90 - 94	965	258	707	194.6	144.0	223.2
95 - 99	252	38	214	213.9	110.8	256.3
100 +	110	18	92	388.7	♦204.5	471.8
Unknown - Inconnu	3	3	-	..	..	..
Malaysia - Malaisie						
2014* (C)						
Total	145 648	83 862	61 786	4.8	5.4	4.2
0	3 156	1 804	1 352	6.3	6.9	5.6
1 - 4	741	413	328	0.4	0.4	0.3
5 - 9	565	318	247	0.2	0.2	0.2
10 - 14	763	497	266	0.3	0.4	0.2
15 - 19	1 891	1 454	437	0.7	1.0	0.3
20 - 24	2 225	1 688	537	0.7	1.0	0.4
25 - 29	2 237	1 602	635	0.8	1.0	0.5
30 - 34	2 829	2 029	800	1.1	1.5	0.7
35 - 39	3 529	2 432	1 097	1.7	2.3	1.1
40 - 44	4 657	3 232	1 425	2.5	3.4	1.6
45 - 49	6 715	4 460	2 255	4.0	5.2	2.7
50 - 54	9 373	6 025	3 348	6.2	7.7	4.6
55 - 59	12 243	7 928	4 315	9.7	12.4	7.0
60 - 64	14 146	8 822	5 324	14.7	18.2	11.2

533

19. Deaths by age and sex and age-specific death rates by sex: latest available year, 2006 - 2015
Décès et taux de mortalité selon l'âge et le sexe : dernière année disponible, 2006 - 2015 (continued - suite)

Continent, country or area, date, code[a] and age (in years) / Continent, pays ou zone, date, code[a] et âge (en années)	Number - Nombre			Rate - Taux		
	Both sexes Les deux sexes	Male Masculin	Female Féminin	Both sexes Les deux sexes	Male Masculin	Female Féminin
ASIA - ASIE						
Malaysia - Malaisie						
2014* (C)						
65 - 69	15 459	9 511	5 948	21.8	27.1	16.6
70 - 74	16 262	9 347	6 915	37.0	43.4	30.8
75 - 79	18 636	9 742	8 894	60.4	66.6	54.9
80 - 84	14 063	6 334	7 729	94.8	92.9	96.5
85 - 89	9 426	3 931	5 495	111.9	106.1	116.4
90 +	6 732	2 293	4 439	152.0	108.0	192.5
90 - 94	4 857	1 672	3 185	...	...	...
95 +	1 875	621	1 254	...	...	...
Maldives						
2014 (C)						
Total	1 143	663	480	2.8	2.9	2.8
0	59	32	27	8.4	8.7	♦8.0
1 - 4	15	6	9	♦0.5	♦0.4	♦0.6
5 - 9	1	-	1	-	-	♦0.1
10 - 14	7	6	1	♦0.3	♦0.4	♦0.1
15 - 19	18	13	5	♦0.6	♦0.8	♦0.3
20 - 24	17	12	5	♦0.4	♦0.4	♦0.3
25 - 29	26	21	5	♦0.5	♦0.6	♦0.2
30 - 34	13	8	5	♦0.3	♦0.3	♦0.3
35 - 39	7	5	2	♦0.2	♦0.3	♦0.2
40 - 44	21	12	9	♦0.8	♦0.8	♦0.9
45 - 49	29	21	8	♦1.4	♦1.9	♦0.9
50 - 54	53	29	24	3.2	♦3.3	♦3.2
55 - 59	65	43	22	5.3	6.6	♦3.8
60 - 64	64	38	26	10.0	10.9	♦8.8
65 - 69	68	44	24	13.8	17.6	♦9.9
70 - 74	173	96	77	35.6	38.5	32.6
75 - 79	201	110	91	54.1	55.8	52.1
80 - 84	156	74	82	79.9	63.7	103.7
85 - 89	98	59	39	134.8	133.2	137.3
90 - 94	42	29	13	181.8	♦198.6	♦152.9
95 +	10	5	5	♦119.0	♦104.2	♦138.9
95 - 99	8	4	4	...	...	...
100 +	2	1	1	...	...	...
Mongolia - Mongolie						
2014 (+C)						
Total	16 521	9 953	6 568	5.6	6.9	4.3
0	1 251	723	528	17.3	19.5	14.9
1 - 4	304	154	150	1.2	1.2	1.2
5 - 9	115	75	40	0.4	0.6	0.3
10 - 14	120	79	41	0.5	0.7	0.4
15 - 19	200	128	72	0.8	1.0	0.6
20 - 24	311	221	90	1.1	1.5	0.6
25 - 29	440	331	109	1.5	2.2	0.7
30 - 34	511	400	111	2.0	3.2	0.8
35 - 39	734	534	200	3.1	4.7	1.7
40 - 44	960	687	273	4.7	7.0	2.6
45 - 49	1 273	926	347	7.2	11.0	3.7
50 - 54	1 597	1 067	530	10.7	15.2	6.7
55 - 59	1 598	1 064	534	15.6	22.7	9.6
60 - 64	1 408	905	503	22.4	32.5	14.4
65 - 69	1 212	697	515	29.3	39.1	21.9
70 - 74	1 330	703	627	39.0	46.7	32.9
75 - 79	1 174	550	624	58.1	65.6	52.7
80 - 84	972	388	584	78.3	87.2	73.4
85 - 89	579	214	365	125.5	139.5	118.5
90 - 94	301	74	227	159.3	146.5	163.9
95 - 99	99	27	72	256.1	♦325.3	237.2
100 +	32	6	26	329.9	♦387.1	♦319.0
2015 (+C)						
Total	17 620	...	...	5.8	...	...
0	1 234	...	...	16.0	...	...
1 - 4	316	...	...	1.1	...	...
5 - 9	126	...	...	0.4	...	...
10 - 14	108	...	...	0.5	...	...

19. Deaths by age and sex and age-specific death rates by sex: latest available year, 2006 - 2015
Décès et taux de mortalité selon l'âge et le sexe : dernière année disponible, 2006 - 2015 (continued - suite)

Continent, country or area, date, code[a] and age (in years) / Continent, pays ou zone, date, code[a] et âge (en années)	Number - Nombre			Rate - Taux		
	Both sexes Les deux sexes	Male Masculin	Female Féminin	Both sexes Les deux sexes	Male Masculin	Female Féminin
ASIA - ASIE						
Mongolia - Mongolie						
2015 (+C)						
15 - 19	222	...	...	0.9	...	...
20 - 24	322	...	...	1.2	...	...
25 - 29	429	...	...	1.4	...	...
30 - 34	519	...	...	2.0	...	...
35 - 39	717	...	...	3.1	...	...
40 - 44	961	...	...	4.6	...	...
45 - 49	1 258	...	...	7.0	...	...
50 - 54	1 542	...	...	10.0	...	...
55 - 59	1 801	...	...	16.1	...	...
60 - 64	1 454	...	...	22.0	...	...
65 - 69	1 294	...	...	30.3	...	...
70 - 74	1 487	...	...	44.9	...	...
75 - 79	1 433	...	...	67.5	...	...
80 - 84	1 171	...	...	93.5	...	...
85 - 89	675	...	...	138.6	...	...
90 - 94	375	...	...	200.8	...	...
95 - 99	136	...	...	317.0	...	...
100 +	40	...	...	423.3	...	...
Myanmar[33]						
2013 (+U)						
Total	257 216	150 333	106 883	...	...	...
0	11 516	6 731	4 785	...	...	...
1 - 4	1 769	1 034	735	...	...	...
5 - 9	2 551	1 461	1 091	...	...	...
10 - 14	2 381	1 349	1 032	...	...	...
15 - 19	3 682	2 265	1 417	...	...	...
20 - 24	5 165	3 234	1 932	...	...	...
25 - 29	7 598	5 005	2 593	...	...	...
30 - 34	11 104	8 080	3 024	...	...	...
35 - 39	13 265	9 705	3 560	...	...	...
40 - 44	14 970	10 930	4 040	...	...	...
45 - 49	16 302	11 500	4 802	...	...	...
50 - 54	17 336	11 588	5 748	...	...	...
55 - 59	18 524	11 646	6 878	...	...	...
60 - 64	19 656	11 551	8 106	...	...	...
65 - 69	20 421	11 614	8 807	...	...	...
70 - 74	22 822	11 881	10 941	...	...	...
75 - 79	24 684	12 391	12 293	...	...	...
80 - 84	21 216	9 514	11 702	...	...	...
85 +	22 253	8 856	13 397	...	...	...
Oman[34]						
2014 (U)						
Total	7 819	4 948	2 871	...	...	...
0	631	323	308	...	...	...
1 - 4	139	72	67	...	...	...
5 - 9	93	69	24	...	...	...
10 - 14	74	51	23	...	...	...
15 - 19	152	114	38	...	...	...
20 - 24	262	205	57	...	...	...
25 - 29	334	274	60	...	...	...
30 - 34	312	249	63	...	...	...
35 - 39	275	224	51	...	...	...
40 - 44	267	214	53	...	...	...
45 - 49	315	248	67	...	...	...
50 - 54	394	297	97	...	...	...
55 - 59	483	317	166	...	...	...
60 - 64	557	332	225	...	...	...
65 - 69	640	384	256	...	...	...
70 - 74	796	411	385	...	...	...
75 - 79	702	455	247	...	...	...
80 - 84	657	357	300	...	...	...
85 - 89	299	162	137	...	...	...
90 - 94	190	86	104	...	...	...
95 - 99	59	26	33	...	...	...

19. Deaths by age and sex and age-specific death rates by sex: latest available year, 2006 - 2015
Décès et taux de mortalité selon l'âge et le sexe : dernière année disponible, 2006 - 2015 (continued - suite)

Continent, country or area, date, code[a] and age (in years) Continent, pays ou zone, date, code[a] et âge (en années)	Number - Nombre			Rate - Taux		
	Both sexes Les deux sexes	Male Masculin	Female Féminin	Both sexes Les deux sexes	Male Masculin	Female Féminin
ASIA - ASIE						
Oman[34]						
2014 (U)						
100 +	33	12	21	...	...	...
Unknown - Inconnu	155	66	89	..	..	..
Pakistan[35]						
2007 (|)						
Total	1 019 533	598 820	420 713	6.8	7.8	5.8
0 - 4	365 729	205 840	159 889	18.7	21.0	16.4
5 - 9	33 029	16 652	16 376	1.5	1.4	1.5
10 - 14	20 510	6 871	13 640	1.0	0.6	1.4
15 - 19	27 417	16 500	10 917	1.6	1.8	1.3
20 - 24	20 192	11 195	8 997	1.5	1.6	1.3
25 - 29	23 990	13 101	10 888	2.2	2.5	2.0
30 - 34	11 624	8 007	3 617	1.4	2.0	0.8
35 - 39	24 880	11 482	13 398	3.0	2.8	3.2
40 - 44	30 926	18 802	12 124	4.6	5.4	3.7
45 - 49	27 537	17 884	9 652	4.4	5.5	3.2
50 - 54	43 405	30 870	12 535	9.5	12.7	5.8
55 - 59	51 031	35 120	15 911	14.4	18.8	9.5
60 - 64	68 531	41 470	27 061	23.4	25.3	20.9
65 - 69	58 286	35 664	22 621	28.6	32.2	24.3
70 - 74	82 325	49 296	33 029	56.2	57.5	54.4
75 - 79	37 357	24 072	13 285	57.1	67.2	44.9
80 - 84	34 079	21 720	12 359	79.6	86.6	69.6
85 +	58 685	34 274	24 411	165.7	168.9	161.4
Philippines						
2013 (C)						
Total	531 280	304 516	226 764	5.4	6.1	4.7
0 - 4	31 518	17 839	13 679	2.8	3.1	2.5
0	21 992	12 699	9 293	...	...	...
1 - 4	9 526	5 140	4 386	...	...	...
5 - 9	5 391	3 023	2 368	0.5	0.6	0.5
10 - 14	4 708	2 722	1 986	0.5	0.5	0.4
15 - 19	7 885	5 073	2 812	0.8	1.0	0.6
20 - 24	10 955	7 302	3 653	1.2	1.6	0.8
25 - 29	12 013	8 222	3 791	1.5	2.0	1.0
30 - 34	14 354	9 693	4 661	2.0	2.7	1.3
35 - 39	16 758	11 037	5 721	2.6	3.4	1.8
40 - 44	22 311	14 602	7 709	3.9	5.0	2.7
45 - 49	28 005	18 279	9 726	5.5	7.1	3.9
50 - 54	35 598	22 999	12 599	8.3	10.7	5.9
55 - 59	42 388	27 633	14 755	12.4	16.4	8.6
60 - 64	47 952	30 741	17 211	18.8	25.1	13.0
65 - 69	48 561	30 034	18 527	27.3	36.8	19.2
70 - 74	51 801	29 582	22 219	42.9	56.8	32.3
75 - 79	52 375	26 950	25 425	65.2	83.3	52.9
80 +	98 388	38 585	59 803	134.4	147.7	127.1
80 - 84	44 619	19 776	24 843	...	...	...
85 - 89	30 998	11 617	19 381	...	...	...
90 - 94	16 437	5 308	11 129	...	...	...
95 - 99	6 334	1 884	4 450	...	...	...
100 +	-	-	-	...	...	...
Unknown - Inconnu	319	200	119	..	..	..
Qatar						
2013 (C)						
Total	2 133	1 604	529	1.1	1.1	1.0
0	157	97	60	7.0	8.7	5.3
1 - 4	27	18	9	♦0.3	♦0.4	♦0.2
5 - 9	18	12	6	♦0.2	♦0.2	♦0.1
10 - 14	20	15	5	♦0.2	♦0.4	♦0.1
15 - 19	51	45	6	0.7	1.0	♦0.2
20 - 24	115	109	6	0.5	0.6	♦0.2
25 - 29	137	120	17	0.4	0.4	♦0.2
30 - 34	167	146	21	0.5	0.6	♦0.3
35 - 39	139	128	11	0.6	0.7	♦0.2
40 - 44	147	136	11	0.8	0.9	♦0.3
45 - 49	159	134	25	1.3	1.4	♦0.9

19. Deaths by age and sex and age-specific death rates by sex: latest available year, 2006 - 2015
Décès et taux de mortalité selon l'âge et le sexe : dernière année disponible, 2006 - 2015 (continued - suite)

Continent, country or area, date, code[a] and age (in years) Continent, pays ou zone, date, code[a] et âge (en années)	Number - Nombre			Rate - Taux		
	Both sexes Les deux sexes	Male Masculin	Female Féminin	Both sexes Les deux sexes	Male Masculin	Female Féminin
ASIA - ASIE						
Qatar						
2013 (C)						
50 - 54	172	136	36	2.1	2.1	2.0
55 - 59	152	125	27	3.0	3.2	♦2.5
60 - 64	130	88	42	5.9	5.4	7.4
65 - 69	98	52	46	9.9	7.8	14.1
70 - 74	134	66	68	24.9	20.5	31.5
75 - 79	135	70	65	37.8	32.3	46.2
80 +	174	106	68	45.9	52.3	38.5
80 - 84	93	55	38	...	...	...
85 - 89	44	31	13	...	...	...
90 - 94	19	13	6	...	...	...
95 +	18	7	11	...	...	...
Unknown - Inconnu	1	1	-	..	..	..
Republic of Korea - République de Corée[36]						
2014 (C)						
Total	267 692	147 321	120 371	5.3	5.8	4.8
0	1 305	715	590	2.9	3.0	2.7
1 - 4	289	153	136	0.2	0.2	0.2
5 - 9	204	113	91	0.1	0.1	0.1
10 - 14	239	142	97	0.1	0.1	0.1
15 - 19	870	572	298	0.3	0.3	0.2
20 - 24	1 131	777	354	0.3	0.4	0.2
25 - 29	1 449	958	491	0.4	0.6	0.3
30 - 34	2 524	1 613	911	0.6	0.8	0.5
35 - 39	3 416	2 230	1 186	0.9	1.1	0.6
40 - 44	5 854	4 018	1 836	1.3	1.8	0.9
45 - 49	8 757	6 260	2 497	2.1	3.0	1.2
50 - 54	13 628	10 095	3 533	3.2	4.7	1.7
55 - 59	16 167	12 028	4 139	4.4	6.6	2.2
60 - 64	15 888	11 610	4 278	6.2	9.4	3.2
65 - 69	19 521	13 714	5 807	9.6	14.3	5.5
70 - 74	31 261	20 272	10 989	18.1	26.6	11.4
75 - 79	41 399	23 863	17 536	31.5	44.9	22.4
80 - 84	42 575	19 281	23 294	52.8	70.6	43.7
85 - 89	34 239	12 108	22 131	95.3	122.8	84.9
90 - 94	19 944	5 364	14 580	160.8	195.0	151.0
95 - 99	5 827	1 228	4 599	243.9	300.1	232.3
100 +	1 163	186	977	385.4	476.9	371.8
Unknown - Inconnu	42	21	21	..	..	..
Singapore - Singapour						
2015 (+C)						
Total	19 862	10 789	9 073	5.1	5.6	4.6
0	84	56	28	2.4	3.2	♦1.7
1 - 4	32	23	9	0.2	♦0.3	♦0.1
5 - 9	12	10	2	♦0.1	♦0.1	-
10 - 14	31	15	16	0.1	♦0.1	♦0.2
15 - 19	61	37	24	0.3	0.3	♦0.2
20 - 24	120	79	41	0.5	0.6	0.3
25 - 29	146	100	46	0.5	0.8	0.3
30 - 34	173	109	64	0.6	0.8	0.4
35 - 39	219	145	74	0.7	1.0	0.5
40 - 44	349	227	122	1.1	1.5	0.8
45 - 49	522	327	195	1.7	2.2	1.3
50 - 54	845	529	316	2.7	3.3	2.0
55 - 59	1 310	843	467	4.4	5.7	3.2
60 - 64	1 659	1 067	592	6.9	8.9	4.9
65 - 69	2 002	1 302	700	11.0	14.7	7.5
70 - 74	1 993	1 213	780	19.4	25.4	14.2
75 - 79	2 686	1 539	1 147	33.1	42.6	25.4
80 - 84	2 748	1 370	1 378	53.1	65.5	44.7
85 - 89	2 544	1 075	1 469	92.5	110.5	82.7
90 - 94	1 491	497	994	148.9	162.3	143.0
95 - 99	646	185	461	216.6	232.4	210.9
100 +	189	41	148	160.7	98.6	194.7

Continent, country or area, date, code[a] and age (in years)	Number - Nombre			Rate - Taux		
Continent, pays ou zone, date, code[a] et âge (en années)	Both sexes Les deux sexes	Male Masculin	Female Féminin	Both sexes Les deux sexes	Male Masculin	Female Féminin
ASIA - ASIE						
Sri Lanka						
2010 (+C)						
Total	130 337	75 818	54 519	6.3	7.4	5.2
0 - 4	4 451	2 445	2 006	2.5	2.7	2.3
0	3 605	1 964	1 641	...	...	...
1 - 4	846	481	365	...	...	...
5 - 9	796	418	378	0.4	0.5	0.4
10 - 14	844	462	382	0.5	0.5	0.4
15 - 19	1 717	1 016	701	0.9	1.0	0.7
20 - 24	2 874	1 888	986	1.5	1.9	1.0
25 - 29	2 798	1 914	884	1.7	2.4	1.1
30 - 34	2 507	1 717	790	1.6	2.2	1.0
35 - 39	2 739	1 900	839	1.8	2.5	1.1
40 - 44	3 384	2 441	943	2.4	3.5	1.3
45 - 49	5 337	3 844	1 493	4.3	6.3	2.4
50 - 54	6 997	4 887	2 110	6.2	8.8	3.7
55 - 59	8 994	6 211	2 783	11.0	15.9	6.5
60 - 64	11 413	7 373	4 040	18.7	24.8	12.9
65 - 69	12 485	7 728	4 757	25.7	34.3	18.3
70 - 74	14 770	8 443	6 327	39.7	48.5	32.0
75 +	48 160	23 081	25 079	108.5	112.6	104.9
75 - 79	15 063	7 876	7 187	...	...	...
80 - 84	14 961	7 274	7 687	...	...	...
85 - 89	10 828	4 799	6 029	...	...	...
90 - 94	4 939	2 175	2 764	...	...	...
95 - 99	1 877	785	1 092	...	...	...
100 +	492	172	320	...	...	...
Unknown - Inconnu	71	50	21	..	..	..
State of Palestine - État de Palestine[37]						
2013 (U)						
Total	11 013	5 917	5 096	...	...	...
0	827	474	353	...	...	...
1 - 4	310	157	153	...	...	...
5 - 9	129	71	58	...	...	...
10 - 14	114	67	47	...	...	...
15 - 19	192	132	60	...	...	...
20 - 24	204	156	48	...	...	...
25 - 29	157	105	52	...	...	...
30 - 34	171	119	52	...	...	...
35 - 39	192	113	79	...	...	...
40 - 44	229	136	93	...	...	...
45 - 49	376	256	120	...	...	...
50 - 54	510	318	192	...	...	...
55 - 59	694	433	261	...	...	...
60 - 64	825	495	330	...	...	...
65 - 69	1 052	584	468	...	...	...
70 - 74	1 088	525	563	...	...	...
75 - 79	1 286	615	671	...	...	...
80 - 84	1 230	530	700	...	...	...
85 - 89	828	382	446	...	...	...
90 - 94	379	155	224	...	...	...
95 - 99	155	66	89	...	...	...
100 +	65	28	37	...	...	...
Tajikistan - Tadjikistan[25]						
2014 (U)						
Total	32 879	18 540	14 339	...	...	...
0	3 273	1 972	1 301	...	...	...
1 - 4	654	362	292	...	...	...
5 - 9	197	122	75	...	...	...
10 - 14	197	132	65	...	...	...
15 - 19	319	180	139	...	...	...
20 - 24	528	328	200	...	...	...
25 - 29	646	398	248	...	...	...
30 - 34	699	439	260	...	...	...
35 - 39	841	549	292	...	...	...
40 - 44	951	584	367	...	...	...
45 - 49	1 193	706	487	...	...	...

19. Deaths by age and sex and age-specific death rates by sex: latest available year, 2006 - 2015
Décès et taux de mortalité selon l'âge et le sexe : dernière année disponible, 2006 - 2015 (continued - suite)

Continent, country or area, date, code[a] and age (in years) / Continent, pays ou zone, date, code[a] et âge (en années)	Number - Nombre			Rate - Taux		
	Both sexes Les deux sexes	Male Masculin	Female Féminin	Both sexes Les deux sexes	Male Masculin	Female Féminin
ASIA - ASIE						
Tajikistan - Tadjikistan[25]						
2014 (U)						
50 - 54	1 740	1 045	695	...	...	...
55 - 59	2 323	1 389	934	...	...	...
60 - 64	2 565	1 468	1 097	...	...	...
65 - 69	2 266	1 292	974	...	...	...
70 - 74	3 145	1 848	1 297	...	...	...
75 - 79	4 187	2 283	1 904	...	...	...
80 - 84	3 827	1 921	1 906	...	...	...
85 - 89	2 229	1 129	1 100	...	...	...
90 - 94	807	309	498	...	...	...
95 - 99	192	66	126	...	...	...
100 +	100	18	82	...	...	...
Thailand - Thaïlande						
2011 (+U)						
Total	414 670	235 189	179 481	...	...	...
0	5 275	2 964	2 311	...	...	...
1 - 4	7 182	4 102	3 080	...	...	...
5 - 9	1 616	978	638	...	...	...
10 - 14	2 060	1 317	743	...	...	...
15 - 19	5 140	3 896	1 244	...	...	...
20 - 24	5 659	4 383	1 276	...	...	...
25 - 29	7 307	5 531	1 776	...	...	...
30 - 34	10 659	7 862	2 797	...	...	...
35 - 39	13 981	10 135	3 846	...	...	...
40 - 44	18 346	12 894	5 452	...	...	...
45 - 49	23 390	16 016	7 374	...	...	...
50 - 54	27 255	18 201	9 054	...	...	...
55 - 59	29 801	19 075	10 726	...	...	...
60 - 64	33 121	20 047	13 074	...	...	...
65 - 69	34 744	20 202	14 542	...	...	...
70 +	189 134	87 586	101 548	...	...	...
Turkey - Turquie						
2014 (C)						
Total	390 121	213 231	176 890	5.0	5.5	4.6
0	14 821	8 135	6 686	11.6	12.3	10.7
1 - 4	2 938	1 624	1 314	0.6	0.6	0.5
5 - 9	1 509	863	646	0.2	0.3	0.2
10 - 14	1 597	1 026	571	0.3	0.3	0.2
15 - 19	2 992	2 194	798	0.5	0.7	0.3
20 - 24	3 302	2 389	913	0.5	0.7	0.3
25 - 29	3 144	2 285	859	0.5	0.7	0.3
30 - 34	3 860	2 664	1 196	0.6	0.8	0.4
35 - 39	4 677	3 022	1 655	0.8	1.0	0.6
40 - 44	6 836	4 478	2 358	1.2	1.6	0.9
45 - 49	10 128	6 680	3 448	2.2	2.8	1.5
50 - 54	15 897	10 877	5 020	3.6	4.9	2.3
55 - 59	22 172	15 250	6 922	6.1	8.3	3.8
60 - 64	28 719	19 325	9 394	10.0	13.8	6.4
65 - 69	34 537	21 665	12 872	15.6	21.0	10.9
70 - 74	43 327	25 108	18 219	27.8	35.9	21.2
75 - 79	51 121	26 650	24 471	46.3	57.3	38.3
80 - 84	68 133	33 311	34 822	81.1	94.1	71.6
85 - 89	47 491	18 675	28 816	131.9	155.8	119.9
90 +	22 920	7 010	15 910	198.8	231.9	187.1
90 - 94	17 818	5 884	11 934	...	...	...
95 - 99	3 963	930	3 033	...	...	...
100 +	1 139	196	943	...	...	...
Uzbekistan - Ouzbékistan						
2014 (+C)						
Total	149 761	81 465	68 296	4.9	5.3	4.5
0	7 688	4 406	3 282	11.5	12.6	10.2
1 - 4	2 009	1 120	889	0.8	0.9	0.7
5 - 9	930	559	371	0.3	0.4	0.3
10 - 14	889	547	342	0.3	0.4	0.3
15 - 19	1 691	1 001	690	0.6	0.7	0.5
20 - 24	2 403	1 428	975	0.7	0.9	0.6

Continent, country or area, date, codeª and age (in years) / Continent, pays ou zone, date, codeª et âge (en années)	Number - Nombre			Rate - Taux		
	Both sexes Les deux sexes	Male Masculin	Female Féminin	Both sexes Les deux sexes	Male Masculin	Female Féminin
ASIA - ASIE						
Uzbekistan - Ouzbékistan						
2014 (+C)						
25 - 29	2 906	1 852	1 054	1.0	1.2	0.7
30 - 34	3 214	2 016	1 198	1.3	1.6	1.0
35 - 39	3 785	2 449	1 336	1.8	2.3	1.3
40 - 44	4 698	3 001	1 697	2.5	3.2	1.8
45 - 49	6 445	3 994	2 451	3.9	5.0	2.9
50 - 54	9 743	6 176	3 567	6.2	8.2	4.4
55 - 59	12 118	7 546	4 572	10.2	13.1	7.4
60 - 64	14 160	8 460	5 700	18.0	22.8	13.8
65 - 69	11 481	6 407	5 074	28.8	34.5	23.8
70 - 74	14 609	7 924	6 685	46.7	54.5	39.9
75 - 79	19 076	9 432	9 644	73.4	83.9	65.4
80 - 84	16 418	7 382	9 036	123.9	146.4	110.1
85 +	15 498	5 765	9 733	124.0	128.6	121.4
EUROPE						
Åland Islands - Îles d'Åland						
2014 (C)						
Total	251	118	133	8.7	8.2	9.2
0	-	-	-	-	-	-
1 - 4	-	-	-	-	-	-
5 - 9	-	-	-	-	-	-
10 - 14	-	-	-	-	-	-
15 - 19	1	1	-	♦0.6	♦1.2	-
20 - 24	2	1	1	♦1.3	♦1.2	♦1.4
25 - 29	1	1	-	♦0.6	♦1.2	-
30 - 34	-	-	-	-	-	-
35 - 39	-	-	-	-	-	-
40 - 44	4	2	2	♦2.1	♦2.1	♦2.1
45 - 49	2	1	1	♦0.9	♦0.9	♦0.9
50 - 54	7	3	4	♦3.6	♦3.1	♦4.0
55 - 59	8	6	2	♦4.1	♦6.5	♦2.0
60 - 64	10	7	3	♦4.9	♦7.2	♦2.8
65 - 69	26	13	13	♦13.1	♦12.9	♦13.2
70 - 74	13	7	6	♦9.6	♦9.9	♦9.3
75 - 79	23	16	7	♦23.5	♦36.1	♦13.1
80 - 84	36	17	19	50.9	♦54.1	♦48.3
85 - 89	54	22	32	105.3	♦116.1	98.9
90 - 94	47	17	30	224.9	♦285.7	♦200.7
95 - 99	15	4	11	♦315.8	♦444.4	♦285.7
100 +	2	-	2	♦500.0	-	♦666.7
Albania - Albanie						
2013 (C)						
Total	20 442	10 990	9 452	7.1	7.5	6.6
0	282	171	111	8.0	9.3	6.5
1 - 4	70	38	32	0.5	0.5	0.5
5 - 9	42	23	19	0.2	♦0.3	♦0.2
10 - 14	57	32	25	0.3	0.3	♦0.2
15 - 19	156	95	61	0.6	0.7	0.5
20 - 24	164	121	43	0.7	1.0	0.4
25 - 29	143	96	47	0.7	0.9	0.5
30 - 34	165	116	49	0.9	1.3	0.5
35 - 39	185	127	58	1.1	1.5	0.6
40 - 44	290	192	98	1.5	2.1	1.0
45 - 49	450	298	152	2.3	3.1	1.5
50 - 54	705	462	243	3.4	4.4	2.3
55 - 59	954	632	322	5.2	6.9	3.5
60 - 64	1 163	775	388	8.2	10.9	5.5
65 - 69	1 448	962	486	13.5	17.7	9.2
70 - 74	2 622	1 534	1 088	25.5	30.8	20.5
75 - 79	3 426	1 948	1 478	47.9	55.3	40.7
80 - 84	3 582	1 788	1 794	93.8	105.3	84.5
85 +	4 538	1 580	2 958	196.1	197.7	195.2
85 - 89	2 519	943	1 576	...	...	...

19. Deaths by age and sex and age-specific death rates by sex: latest available year, 2006 - 2015
Décès et taux de mortalité selon l'âge et le sexe : dernière année disponible, 2006 - 2015 (continued - suite)

Continent, country or area, date, code[a] and age (in years) / Continent, pays ou zone, date, code[a] et âge (en annèes)	Number - Nombre			Rate - Taux		
	Both sexes Les deux sexes	Male Masculin	Female Féminin	Both sexes Les deux sexes	Male Masculin	Female Féminin
EUROPE						
Albania - Albanie						
2013 (C)						
90 - 94	1 456	510	946	...	...	...
95 - 99	433	102	331	...	...	...
100 +	130	25	105	...	...	...
Andorra - Andorre						
2012 (C)						
Total	303	168	135	3.9	4.3	3.6
0 - 4	4	3	1	♦1.1	♦1.6	♦0.5
0	4	3	1	♦6.9	♦10.4	♦3.4
1 - 4	-	-	-	-	-	-
5 - 9	1	-	1	♦0.2	-	♦0.5
10 - 14	-	-	-	-	-	-
15 - 19	1	-	1	♦0.3	-	♦0.6
20 - 24	1	1	-	♦0.3	♦0.5	-
25 - 29	2	-	2	♦0.4	-	♦0.8
30 - 34	2	2	-	♦0.3	♦0.6	-
35 - 39	3	2	1	♦0.4	♦0.5	♦0.3
40 - 44	6	4	2	♦0.8	♦1.1	♦0.6
45 - 49	10	8	2	♦1.4	♦2.2	♦0.6
50 - 54	7	5	2	♦1.2	♦1.6	♦0.7
55 - 59	14	10	4	♦3.0	♦4.1	♦1.8
60 - 64	20	12	8	♦5.4	♦6.1	♦4.6
65 - 69	26	17	9	♦8.9	♦11.0	♦6.6
70 - 74	31	23	8	15.4	♦23.6	♦7.7
75 - 79	34	24	10	19.9	♦28.6	♦11.4
80 - 84	35	17	18	23.7	♦25.6	♦22.1
85 - 89	51	23	28	54.9	♦59.2	♦51.9
90 - 94	37	12	25	82.6	♦66.7	♦93.3
95 - 99	14	5	9	♦80.7	♦71.9	♦86.5
100 +	4	-	4	♦56.3	-	♦112.7
Austria - Autriche[38]						
2014 (C)						
Total	78 252	37 424	40 828	9.2	9.0	9.4
0	249	130	119	3.1	3.2	3.1
1 - 4	47	27	20	0.1	♦0.2	♦0.1
5 - 9	38	18	20	0.1	♦0.1	♦0.1
10 - 14	42	24	18	0.1	♦0.1	♦0.1
15 - 19	145	104	41	0.3	0.4	0.2
20 - 24	197	144	53	0.4	0.5	0.2
25 - 29	235	159	76	0.4	0.6	0.3
30 - 34	311	199	112	0.5	0.7	0.4
35 - 39	360	227	133	0.7	0.8	0.5
40 - 44	716	459	257	1.2	1.5	0.8
45 - 49	1 316	856	460	1.9	2.4	1.3
50 - 54	2 135	1 395	740	3.1	4.1	2.2
55 - 59	2 949	1 922	1 027	5.2	6.9	3.6
60 - 64	3 997	2 545	1 452	8.5	11.2	5.9
65 - 69	5 571	3 539	2 032	13.2	17.8	9.1
70 - 74	8 316	5 048	3 268	19.1	25.4	13.8
75 - 79	8 333	4 707	3 626	29.3	38.1	22.5
80 - 84	12 456	6 116	6 340	57.6	72.4	48.2
85 - 89	15 471	5 910	9 561	109.4	129.8	99.8
90 - 94	12 046	3 229	8 817	197.5	225.5	188.8
95 - 99	2 633	556	2 077	322.3	349.9	315.6
100 +	689	110	579	496.4	473.1	501.1
Belarus - Bélarus						
2014 (C)						
Total	121 542	61 274	60 268	12.8	13.9	11.9
0	409	244	165	3.5	4.0	2.9
1 - 4	106	65	41	0.2	0.3	0.2
5 - 9	88	49	39	0.2	0.2	0.2
10 - 14	80	47	33	0.2	0.2	0.2
15 - 19	221	166	55	0.5	0.7	0.2
20 - 24	548	442	106	0.8	1.3	0.3
25 - 29	938	748	190	1.2	1.9	0.5
30 - 34	1 453	1 118	335	2.0	3.0	0.9

19. Deaths by age and sex and age-specific death rates by sex: latest available year, 2006 - 2015
Décès et taux de mortalité selon l'âge et le sexe : dernière année disponible, 2006 - 2015 (continued - suite)

Continent, country or area, date, code[a] and age (in years) / Continent, pays ou zone, date, code[a] et âge (en années)	Number - Nombre			Rate - Taux		
	Both sexes Les deux sexes	Male Masculin	Female Féminin	Both sexes Les deux sexes	Male Masculin	Female Féminin
EUROPE						
Belarus - Bélarus						
2014 (C)						
35 - 39	1 924	1 456	468	2.9	4.4	1.4
40 - 44	2 696	1 976	720	4.1	6.3	2.1
45 - 49	3 773	2 828	945	5.8	9.2	2.8
50 - 54	6 511	4 823	1 688	8.6	13.7	4.2
55 - 59	8 831	6 331	2 500	12.5	20.0	6.4
60 - 64	10 727	7 585	3 142	19.0	32.0	9.6
65 - 69	9 996	6 417	3 579	26.1	42.5	15.4
70 - 74	11 711	6 399	5 312	38.8	62.3	26.6
75 - 79	18 372	8 238	10 134	58.1	87.4	45.7
80 - 84	18 922	6 530	12 392	97.6	131.6	85.9
85 - 89	16 400	4 339	12 061	154.2	187.3	145.0
90 - 94	6 351	1 199	5 152	235.7	252.2	232.2
95 - 99	1 184	220	964	336.2	385.3	326.7
100 +	264	29	235	415.1	♦305.3	434.4
Unknown - Inconnu	37	25	12	..	..	..
Belgium - Belgique[39]						
2014 (C)						
Total	104 755	51 579	53 176	9.3	9.3	9.3
0	423	247	176	3.4	3.9	2.9
1 - 4	89	52	37	0.2	0.2	0.1
5 - 9	44	25	19	0.1	♦0.1	♦0.1
10 - 14	65	40	25	0.1	0.1	♦0.1
15 - 19	178	127	51	0.3	0.4	0.2
20 - 24	297	230	67	0.4	0.6	0.2
25 - 29	332	237	95	0.5	0.7	0.3
30 - 34	449	321	128	0.6	0.9	0.3
35 - 39	594	366	228	0.8	1.0	0.6
40 - 44	1 033	624	409	1.3	1.6	1.1
45 - 49	1 658	1 013	645	2.1	2.5	1.6
50 - 54	2 766	1 697	1 069	3.4	4.2	2.6
55 - 59	4 214	2 724	1 490	5.6	7.3	4.0
60 - 64	5 545	3 514	2 031	8.4	10.8	6.1
65 - 69	7 652	4 863	2 789	13.0	17.2	9.2
70 - 74	8 292	5 062	3 230	19.5	25.7	14.2
75 - 79	12 446	7 066	5 380	31.4	40.8	24.1
80 - 84	18 575	9 269	9 306	57.7	73.1	47.7
85 - 89	20 719	8 513	12 206	108.5	133.2	96.1
90 - 94	15 029	4 748	10 281	191.6	224.3	179.5
95 - 99	3 465	729	2 736	303.7	323.2	298.9
100 +	890	112	778	457.5	446.2	459.1
Bosnia and Herzegovina - Bosnie-Herzégovine						
2010 (C)						
Total	35 118	17 900	17 218	9.1	9.5	8.8
0 - 4	252	143	109	1.5	1.7	1.3
0	216	125	91	6.5	7.3	5.6
1 - 4	36	18	18	0.3	♦0.3	♦0.3
5 - 9	28	19	9	♦0.1	♦0.2	♦0.1
10 - 14	27	14	13	♦0.1	♦0.1	♦0.1
15 - 19	84	58	26	0.3	0.4	♦0.2
20 - 24	120	92	28	0.4	0.6	♦0.2
25 - 29	165	130	35	0.6	1.0	0.3
30 - 34	160	109	51	0.7	0.9	0.4
35 - 39	254	180	74	1.0	1.5	0.6
40 - 44	432	265	167	1.5	1.9	1.2
45 - 49	844	553	291	2.7	3.7	1.9
50 - 54	1 465	980	485	5.5	7.2	3.7
55 - 59	2 141	1 429	712	9.2	13.6	5.6
60 - 64	2 610	1 647	963	14.3	19.1	10.0
65 - 69	3 390	2 032	1 358	16.8	22.6	12.1
70 - 74	6 045	3 199	2 846	32.8	38.8	27.9
75 - 79	6 948	3 344	3 604	57.7	66.1	51.6
80 - 84	6 006	2 440	3 566	125.3	124.5	125.9
85 +	4 119	1 254	2 865	164.3	175.6	159.9
85 - 89	3 105	966	2 139	...	...	...
90 - 94	737	210	527	...	...	...

19. Deaths by age and sex and age-specific death rates by sex: latest available year, 2006 - 2015
Décès et taux de mortalité selon l'âge et le sexe : dernière année disponible, 2006 - 2015 (continued - suite)

Continent, country or area, date, code^a and age (in years)	Number - Nombre			Rate - Taux		
Continent, pays ou zone, date, code^a et âge (en années)	Both sexes Les deux sexes	Male Masculin	Female Féminin	Both sexes Les deux sexes	Male Masculin	Female Féminin

EUROPE						
Bosnia and Herzegovina - Bosnie-Herzégovine						
2010 (C)						
95 - 99	245	69	176	...	...	...
100 +	32	9	23	...	...	...
Unknown - Inconnu	28	12	16	..	..	..
Bulgaria - Bulgarie						
2014 (C)						
Total	108 952	56 630	52 322	15.1	16.1	14.1
0	517	284	233	7.8	8.4	7.2
1 - 4	89	46	43	0.3	0.3	0.3
5 - 9	55	30	25	0.2	♦0.2	♦0.2
10 - 14	63	41	22	0.2	0.3	♦0.1
15 - 19	150	108	42	0.5	0.7	0.3
20 - 24	263	186	77	0.6	0.9	0.4
25 - 29	324	222	102	0.7	0.9	0.4
30 - 34	522	366	156	1.1	1.4	0.7
35 - 39	898	648	250	1.6	2.3	0.9
40 - 44	1 365	875	490	2.6	3.2	1.9
45 - 49	2 111	1 500	611	4.3	6.0	2.6
50 - 54	3 798	2 594	1 204	7.7	10.5	4.9
55 - 59	5 711	4 008	1 703	11.3	16.3	6.5
60 - 64	8 515	5 794	2 721	16.6	24.5	9.9
65 - 69	11 090	7 222	3 868	23.6	35.0	14.7
70 - 74	11 995	6 850	5 145	34.3	47.2	25.2
75 - 79	16 347	8 134	8 213	57.8	73.9	47.5
80 - 84	20 514	8 791	11 723	100.9	116.7	91.6
85 - 89	16 213	6 070	10 143	172.3	187.4	164.4
90 - 94	7 283	2 527	4 756	276.4	298.7	265.9
95 - 99	981	288	693	396.0	371.4	407.2
100 +	148	46	102	445.8	420.1	458.4
Croatia - Croatie						
2014 (C)						
Total	50 839	24 965	25 874	12.0	12.2	11.8
0	199	113	86	5.0	5.5	4.5
1 - 4	22	16	6	♦0.1	♦0.2	♦0.1
5 - 9	20	12	8	♦0.1	♦0.1	♦0.1
10 - 14	26	17	9	♦0.1	♦0.2	♦0.1
15 - 19	70	57	13	0.3	0.5	♦0.1
20 - 24	99	72	27	0.4	0.6	♦0.2
25 - 29	124	91	33	0.5	0.7	0.2
30 - 34	169	111	58	0.6	0.7	0.4
35 - 39	267	192	75	0.9	1.3	0.5
40 - 44	373	247	126	1.3	1.8	0.9
45 - 49	810	538	272	2.7	3.7	1.8
50 - 54	1 470	1 045	425	4.8	6.9	2.7
55 - 59	2 518	1 765	753	8.0	11.5	4.7
60 - 64	3 471	2 417	1 054	12.1	17.5	7.1
65 - 69	3 850	2 513	1 337	17.5	25.6	11.0
70 - 74	5 437	3 236	2 201	27.3	38.6	19.1
75 - 79	8 423	4 287	4 136	47.9	62.9	38.3
80 - 84	10 659	4 451	6 208	87.2	107.5	76.7
85 - 89	8 049	2 560	5 489	150.1	164.9	144.1
90 - 94	4 089	1 052	3 037	249.6	279.5	240.7
95 - 99	566	140	426	393.3	440.3	380.0
100 +	128	33	95	421.1	485.3	402.5
Czech Republic - République tchèque						
2014 (C)						
Total	105 665	53 740	51 925	10.1	10.4	9.7
0	263	153	110	2.5	2.8	2.1
1 - 4	65	32	33	0.1	0.1	0.1
5 - 9	53	29	24	0.1	♦0.1	♦0.1
10 - 14	40	27	13	0.1	♦0.1	♦0.1
15 - 19	165	126	39	0.3	0.5	0.2
20 - 24	283	216	67	0.4	0.7	0.2
25 - 29	359	264	95	0.5	0.7	0.3
30 - 34	465	340	125	0.6	0.9	0.3
35 - 39	794	547	247	0.8	1.1	0.5

Continent, country or area, date, code[a] and age (in years) / Continent, pays ou zone, date, code[a] et âge (en années)	Number - Nombre			Rate - Taux		
	Both sexes Les deux sexes	Male Masculin	Female Féminin	Both sexes Les deux sexes	Male Masculin	Female Féminin
EUROPE						
Czech Republic - République tchèque						
2014 (C)						
40 - 44	1 167	818	349	1.5	2.0	0.9
45 - 49	1 772	1 206	566	2.5	3.4	1.7
50 - 54	2 660	1 827	833	4.1	5.6	2.6
55 - 59	4 799	3 279	1 520	6.8	9.4	4.2
60 - 64	8 282	5 609	2 673	11.4	16.1	7.0
65 - 69	11 762	7 653	4 109	17.9	25.4	11.5
70 - 74	12 198	7 291	4 907	26.9	37.2	19.1
75 - 79	13 041	6 879	6 162	43.0	57.2	33.6
80 - 84	17 788	7 879	9 909	75.0	93.3	64.9
85 - 89	17 645	6 252	11 393	137.7	162.8	126.9
90 - 94	10 257	2 927	7 330	244.0	280.2	232.0
95 - 99	1 463	319	1 144	375.7	405.3	368.2
100 +	344	67	277	455.6	385.1	476.8
Denmark - Danemark[40]						
2014 (C)						
Total	51 340	25 694	25 646	9.1	9.2	9.0
0	229	134	95	4.1	4.7	3.5
1 - 4	31	17	14	0.1	◆0.1	◆0.1
5 - 9	14	9	5	-	◆0.1	-
10 - 14	23	13	10	◆0.1	◆0.1	◆0.1
15 - 19	61	41	20	0.2	0.2	◆0.1
20 - 24	111	71	40	0.3	0.4	0.2
25 - 29	118	89	29	0.3	0.5	◆0.2
30 - 34	173	115	58	0.5	0.7	0.4
35 - 39	262	169	93	0.7	0.9	0.5
40 - 44	441	284	157	1.1	1.5	0.8
45 - 49	832	514	318	2.0	2.4	1.5
50 - 54	1 341	832	509	3.4	4.2	2.6
55 - 59	2 035	1 279	756	5.7	7.2	4.3
60 - 64	3 177	1 933	1 244	9.4	11.6	7.3
65 - 69	4 897	2 925	1 972	13.8	16.8	10.9
70 - 74	5 625	3 309	2 316	21.3	26.1	16.8
75 - 79	6 656	3 598	3 058	36.3	43.1	30.6
80 - 84	7 763	3 864	3 899	64.4	76.5	55.7
85 - 89	8 308	3 706	4 602	111.2	137.1	96.5
90 - 94	6 404	2 130	4 274	190.8	227.2	176.7
95 - 99	2 357	584	1 773	303.3	367.5	286.8
100 +	482	78	404	461.7	493.7	456.0
Estonia - Estonie						
2014 (C)						
Total	15 484	7 451	8 033	11.8	12.1	11.5
0	36	19	17	2.7	◆2.7	◆2.6
1 - 4	16	9	7	◆0.3	◆0.3	◆0.2
5 - 9	11	8	3	◆0.2	◆0.2	◆0.1
10 - 14	10	6	4	◆0.2	◆0.2	◆0.1
15 - 19	29	20	9	◆0.5	◆0.6	◆0.3
20 - 24	71	56	15	0.8	1.3	◆0.4
25 - 29	98	77	21	1.0	1.5	◆0.4
30 - 34	145	103	42	1.6	2.2	0.9
35 - 39	154	114	40	1.7	2.5	0.9
40 - 44	188	145	43	2.0	3.1	0.9
45 - 49	326	247	79	3.8	5.9	1.8
50 - 54	518	371	147	5.6	8.4	3.1
55 - 59	807	581	226	9.1	14.3	4.7
60 - 64	1 127	797	330	13.7	22.6	7.0
65 - 69	1 281	830	451	19.8	31.8	11.7
70 - 74	1 650	959	691	27.2	43.1	18.0
75 - 79	2 165	1 045	1 120	41.4	62.3	31.6
80 - 84	2 615	996	1 619	71.2	97.2	61.1
85 - 89	2 504	736	1 768	123.8	164.4	112.2
90 - 94	1 326	267	1 059	219.5	260.0	211.3
95 - 99	332	56	276	327.7	361.3	321.7
100 +	75	9	66	535.7	◆750.0	515.6

19. Deaths by age and sex and age-specific death rates by sex: latest available year, 2006 - 2015
Décès et taux de mortalité selon l'âge et le sexe : dernière année disponible, 2006 - 2015 (continued - suite)

Continent, country or area, date, code[a] and age (in years) Continent, pays ou zone, date, code[a] et âge (en années)	Number - Nombre			Rate - Taux		
	Both sexes Les deux sexes	Male Masculin	Female Féminin	Both sexes Les deux sexes	Male Masculin	Female Féminin
EUROPE						
Faeroe Islands - Îles Féroé						
2015 (C)						
Total	377	192	185	7.7	7.6	7.8
0	-	-	-	-	-	-
1 - 4	2	1	1	♦0.8	♦0.8	♦0.8
5 - 9	-	-	-	-	-	-
10 - 14	1	1	-	♦0.3	♦0.5	-
15 - 19	3	2	1	♦0.8	♦1.1	♦0.6
20 - 24	-	-	-	-	-	-
25 - 29	-	-	-	-	-	-
30 - 34	3	3	-	♦1.2	♦2.2	-
35 - 39	-	-	-	-	-	-
40 - 44	2	1	1	♦0.6	♦0.6	♦0.7
45 - 49	12	6	6	♦3.5	♦3.3	♦3.7
50 - 54	7	5	2	♦2.1	♦2.9	♦1.3
55 - 59	15	11	4	♦4.9	♦7.0	♦2.6
60 - 64	13	12	1	♦4.7	♦8.3	♦0.7
65 - 69	22	12	10	♦8.5	♦8.8	♦8.2
70 - 74	41	29	12	18.9	♦25.6	♦11.6
75 - 79	34	18	16	25.2	♦27.4	♦23.1
80 - 84	68	41	27	61.8	82.0	♦44.9
85 - 89	70	29	41	106.9	♦129.5	95.1
90 - 94	56	15	41	186.0	♦178.6	188.9
95 - 99	25	6	19	♦357.1	♦315.8	♦372.5
100 +	3	-	3	♦300.0	-	♦375.0
Finland - Finlande						
2014 (C)						
Total	52 186	25 748	26 438	9.6	9.6	9.6
0	124	68	56	2.1	2.3	2.0
1 - 4	32	21	11	0.1	♦0.2	♦0.1
5 - 9	28	12	16	♦0.1	♦0.1	♦0.1
10 - 14	26	13	13	♦0.1	♦0.1	♦0.1
15 - 19	88	66	22	0.3	0.4	♦0.1
20 - 24	165	122	43	0.5	0.7	0.3
25 - 29	231	176	55	0.7	1.0	0.3
30 - 34	257	180	77	0.7	1.0	0.5
35 - 39	316	224	92	0.9	1.3	0.6
40 - 44	394	286	108	1.3	1.8	0.7
45 - 49	741	539	202	2.0	2.9	1.1
50 - 54	1 273	849	424	3.4	4.5	2.3
55 - 59	1 971	1 332	639	5.3	7.3	3.4
60 - 64	3 205	2 159	1 046	8.5	11.7	5.4
65 - 69	4 570	2 966	1 604	12.5	16.9	8.5
70 - 74	4 579	2 843	1 736	19.4	26.3	13.6
75 - 79	6 320	3 604	2 716	32.6	43.3	24.5
80 - 84	8 429	4 105	4 324	59.0	75.6	48.8
85 - 89	9 903	3 783	6 120	111.2	135.3	100.2
90 - 94	6 987	1 919	5 068	203.5	238.0	192.9
95 - 99	2 171	436	1 735	325.4	352.2	319.2
100 +	376	45	331	522.2	478.7	528.8
France[41]						
2012 (C)						
Total	559 227	281 468	277 759	8.8	9.1	8.5
0 - 4	3 174	1 788	1 386	0.8	0.9	0.7
0	2 643	1 479	1 164	3.4	3.8	3.1
1 - 4	531	309	222	0.2	0.2	0.1
5 - 9	298	162	136	0.1	0.1	0.1
10 - 14	365	199	166	0.1	0.1	0.1
15 - 19	1 032	729	303	0.3	0.4	0.2
20 - 24	1 751	1 301	450	0.5	0.7	0.2
25 - 29	2 003	1 468	535	0.5	0.8	0.3
30 - 34	2 485	1 753	732	0.6	0.9	0.4
35 - 39	3 724	2 489	1 235	0.9	1.2	0.6
40 - 44	6 509	4 355	2 154	1.5	2.0	1.0
45 - 49	10 827	7 067	3 760	2.5	3.3	1.7
50 - 54	16 881	11 249	5 632	4.0	5.4	2.6
55 - 59	24 454	16 710	7 744	6.0	8.5	3.7

545

19. Deaths by age and sex and age-specific death rates by sex: latest available year, 2006 - 2015
Décès et taux de mortalité selon l'âge et le sexe : dernière année disponible, 2006 - 2015 (continued - suite)

Continent, country or area, date, code[a] and age (in years) Continent, pays ou zone, date, code[a] et âge (en années)	Number - Nombre			Rate - Taux		
	Both sexes Les deux sexes	Male Masculin	Female Féminin	Both sexes Les deux sexes	Male Masculin	Female Féminin
EUROPE						
France[41]						
2012 (C)						
60 - 64	33 129	22 684	10 445	8.2	11.7	5.0
65 - 69	33 793	22 651	11 142	11.2	15.7	7.0
70 - 74	38 076	24 317	13 759	16.4	23.0	10.9
75 - 79	59 955	34 915	25 040	27.2	37.4	19.8
80 - 84	90 672	46 166	44 506	49.7	66.1	39.6
85 - 89	111 079	46 643	64 436	94.4	121.3	81.3
90 - 94	79 942	26 749	53 193	167.7	206.8	153.2
95 - 99	29 993	6 755	23 238	306.8	362.7	293.7
100 +	9 085	1 318	7 767	466.5	474.1	465.3
Germany - Allemagne						
2014 (C)						
Total	868 356	422 225	446 131	10.7	10.6	10.8
0	2 284	1 266	1 018	3.3	3.5	3.0
1 - 4	407	214	193	0.1	0.2	0.1
5 - 9	247	154	93	0.1	0.1	0.1
10 - 14	317	188	129	0.1	0.1	0.1
15 - 19	929	630	299	0.2	0.3	0.2
20 - 24	1 510	1 086	424	0.3	0.5	0.2
25 - 29	1 872	1 350	522	0.4	0.5	0.2
30 - 34	2 546	1 747	799	0.5	0.7	0.3
35 - 39	3 416	2 253	1 163	0.7	0.9	0.5
40 - 44	6 229	4 004	2 225	1.2	1.5	0.8
45 - 49	13 654	8 810	4 844	2.0	2.6	1.4
50 - 54	23 993	15 494	8 499	3.5	4.5	2.5
55 - 59	33 292	21 736	11 556	5.8	7.6	4.0
60 - 64	45 858	29 903	15 955	8.9	12.0	6.1
65 - 69	51 882	32 768	19 114	13.1	17.2	9.3
70 - 74	90 801	56 064	34 737	20.0	26.5	14.3
75 - 79	131 004	74 333	56 671	32.7	42.2	25.3
80 - 84	144 686	71 247	73 439	61.6	76.7	51.8
85 - 89	162 910	62 163	100 747	113.5	134.5	103.5
90 - 94	117 374	30 701	86 673	204.8	236.0	195.7
95 - 99	25 660	5 108	20 552	309.0	351.0	300.1
100 +	7 485	1 006	6 479	443.0	410.3	448.4
Greece - Grèce						
2014 (C)						
Total	113 740	58 132	55 608	10.4	11.0	9.9
0	346	192	154	3.7	4.0	3.4
1 - 4	76	39	37	0.2	0.2	0.2
5 - 9	40	27	13	0.1	♦0.1	-
10 - 14	52	32	20	0.1	0.1	♦0.1
15 - 19	155	121	34	0.3	0.4	0.1
20 - 24	255	186	69	0.4	0.6	0.2
25 - 29	284	205	79	0.5	0.7	0.3
30 - 34	446	328	118	0.6	0.8	0.3
35 - 39	632	429	203	0.8	1.0	0.5
40 - 44	985	654	331	1.2	1.6	0.8
45 - 49	1 719	1 145	574	2.1	2.9	1.4
50 - 54	2 572	1 731	841	3.5	4.9	2.2
55 - 59	3 779	2 628	1 151	5.4	7.8	3.1
60 - 64	5 122	3 490	1 632	8.1	11.5	4.9
65 - 69	7 204	4 906	2 298	12.0	17.3	7.2
70 - 74	8 743	5 531	3 212	17.9	24.5	12.2
75 - 79	15 575	8 714	6 861	31.6	40.5	24.6
80 - 84	23 046	11 188	11 858	61.5	70.6	54.9
85 - 89	24 443	10 265	14 178	118.8	126.7	113.6
90 - 94	13 183	4 748	8 435	200.8	190.1	207.3
95 - 99	4 116	1 318	2 798	249.1	224.6	262.6
100 +	967	255	712	172.0	137.4	189.1
Hungary - Hongrie						
2013 (C)						
Total	126 677	61 820	64 857	12.8	13.1	12.5
0	448	265	183	5.0	5.8	4.2
1 - 4	68	39	29	0.2	0.2	♦0.2
5 - 9	40	22	18	0.1	♦0.1	♦0.1

19. Deaths by age and sex and age-specific death rates by sex: latest available year, 2006 - 2015
Décès et taux de mortalité selon l'âge et le sexe : dernière année disponible, 2006 - 2015 (continued - suite)

Continent, country or area, date, code[a] and age (in years) / Continent, pays ou zone, date, code[a] et âge (en annèes)	Number - Nombre			Rate - Taux		
	Both sexes Les deux sexes	Male Masculin	Female Féminin	Both sexes Les deux sexes	Male Masculin	Female Féminin
EUROPE						
Hungary - Hongrie						
2013 (C)						
10 - 14	61	33	28	0.1	0.1	♦0.1
15 - 19	160	109	51	0.3	0.4	0.2
20 - 24	240	166	74	0.4	0.5	0.2
25 - 29	308	223	85	0.5	0.7	0.3
30 - 34	440	293	147	0.6	0.8	0.4
35 - 39	949	653	296	1.1	1.5	0.7
40 - 44	1 434	968	466	2.0	2.7	1.3
45 - 49	2 716	1 834	882	4.3	5.8	2.7
50 - 54	4 739	3 237	1 502	7.7	10.9	4.7
55 - 59	9 038	6 050	2 988	11.9	17.1	7.4
60 - 64	11 310	7 329	3 981	16.9	24.3	10.8
65 - 69	12 114	7 443	4 671	22.6	32.4	15.2
70 - 74	14 112	7 802	6 310	31.9	45.0	23.5
75 - 79	17 259	8 162	9 097	52.4	71.4	42.4
80 - 84	20 925	8 264	12 661	88.4	110.1	78.4
85 - 89	18 389	5 777	12 612	150.0	173.8	141.2
90 - 94	9 723	2 669	7 054	225.6	254.3	216.3
95 - 99	1 820	405	1 415	346.2	328.6	351.6
100 +	384	77	307	301.5	174.2	369.2
Iceland - Islande						
2014 (C)						
Total	2 049	1 050	999	6.3	6.4	6.1
0	9	3	6	♦2.1	♦1.4	♦2.8
1 - 4	1	-	1	♦0.1	-	♦0.1
5 - 9	2	1	1	♦0.1	♦0.1	♦0.1
10 - 14	-	-	-	-	-	-
15 - 19	7	4	3	♦0.3	♦0.4	♦0.3
20 - 24	10	5	5	♦0.4	♦0.4	♦0.4
25 - 29	8	6	2	♦0.3	♦0.5	♦0.2
30 - 34	14	9	5	♦0.6	♦0.7	♦0.4
35 - 39	15	7	8	♦0.7	♦0.6	♦0.8
40 - 44	19	11	8	♦0.9	♦1.0	♦0.8
45 - 49	22	14	8	♦1.0	♦1.3	♦0.7
50 - 54	57	38	19	2.6	3.5	♦1.7
55 - 59	90	57	33	4.4	5.6	3.3
60 - 64	108	60	48	6.2	6.8	5.6
65 - 69	138	77	61	9.7	10.7	8.7
70 - 74	161	93	68	16.0	19.2	13.0
75 - 79	235	133	102	30.9	37.1	25.4
80 - 84	354	181	173	56.5	64.7	49.8
85 - 89	366	178	188	96.2	117.1	82.3
90 - 94	315	138	177	207.2	280.8	172.1
95 - 99	102	33	69	332.2	356.8	321.7
100 +	16	2	14	♦477.6	♦333.3	♦509.1
Ireland - Irlande						
2014 (+C)						
Total	29 188	14 861	14 327	6.3	6.5	6.2
0	224	131	93	3.2	3.7	2.7
1 - 4	40	23	17	0.1	♦0.2	♦0.1
5 - 9	31	15	16	0.1	♦0.1	♦0.1
10 - 14	25	18	7	♦0.1	♦0.1	-
15 - 19	55	39	16	0.2	0.3	♦0.1
20 - 24	146	120	26	0.6	1.0	♦0.2
25 - 29	164	120	44	0.5	0.8	0.3
30 - 34	222	152	70	0.6	0.8	0.4
35 - 39	255	165	90	0.7	0.9	0.5
40 - 44	378	244	134	1.1	1.4	0.8
45 - 49	525	324	201	1.7	2.1	1.3
50 - 54	822	498	324	2.9	3.5	2.2
55 - 59	1 194	716	478	4.7	5.7	3.7
60 - 64	1 630	991	639	7.2	8.8	5.6
65 - 69	2 363	1 409	954	12.2	14.5	9.8
70 - 74	2 881	1 720	1 161	20.3	24.8	16.0
75 - 79	3 722	2 130	1 592	34.7	42.9	27.6
80 - 84	4 793	2 446	2 347	64.9	77.8	55.3

Continent, country or area, date, code[a] and age (in years) / Continent, pays ou zone, date, code[a] et âge (en annèes)	Number - Nombre			Rate - Taux		
	Both sexes Les deux sexes	Male Masculin	Female Féminin	Both sexes Les deux sexes	Male Masculin	Female Féminin
EUROPE						
Ireland - Irlande						
2014 (+C)						
85 - 89	5 037	2 173	2 864	122.9	148.9	108.5
90 - 94	3 372	1 125	2 247	196.7	224.9	185.0
95 - 99	1 114	272	842	265.8	282.5	260.8
100 +	195	30	165	232.7	♦309.3	222.7
Italy - Italie						
2013 (C)						
Total	600 744	290 354	310 390	10.0	9.9	10.0
0	1 493	864	629	2.9	3.3	2.5
1 - 4	322	191	131	0.1	0.2	0.1
5 - 9	207	132	75	0.1	0.1	0.1
10 - 14	241	144	97	0.1	0.1	0.1
15 - 19	610	433	177	0.2	0.3	0.1
20 - 24	959	695	264	0.3	0.4	0.2
25 - 29	1 149	836	313	0.4	0.5	0.2
30 - 34	1 560	1 058	502	0.4	0.6	0.3
35 - 39	2 659	1 687	972	0.6	0.8	0.4
40 - 44	4 555	2 815	1 740	0.9	1.2	0.7
45 - 49	7 767	4 776	2 991	1.6	2.0	1.2
50 - 54	11 343	6 993	4 350	2.6	3.3	1.9
55 - 59	15 924	9 998	5 926	4.1	5.3	3.0
60 - 64	24 067	15 251	8 816	6.6	8.7	4.7
65 - 69	35 060	22 288	12 772	10.4	13.9	7.3
70 - 74	52 089	31 989	20 100	17.0	22.8	12.2
75 - 79	76 831	43 975	32 856	29.6	38.9	22.4
80 - 84	110 882	55 991	54 891	55.7	71.8	45.3
85 - 89	127 394	52 784	74 610	104.4	130.6	91.4
90 - 94	89 084	29 002	60 082	180.8	217.0	167.4
95 - 99	29 018	7 046	21 972	301.1	342.7	289.8
100 +	7 520	1 406	6 114	438.8	488.9	428.7
Latvia - Lettonie						
2014 (C)						
Total	28 466	13 723	14 743	14.3	15.0	13.7
0	83	45	38	3.9	4.2	3.7
1 - 4	22	11	11	♦0.3	♦0.3	♦0.3
5 - 9	20	13	7	♦0.2	♦0.2	♦0.1
10 - 14	19	10	9	♦0.2	♦0.2	♦0.2
15 - 19	60	46	14	0.7	1.0	♦0.3
20 - 24	111	80	31	0.9	1.2	0.5
25 - 29	174	137	37	1.2	1.8	0.5
30 - 34	244	186	58	1.8	2.7	0.9
35 - 39	380	303	77	2.9	4.7	1.2
40 - 44	541	393	148	3.9	5.8	2.1
45 - 49	680	499	181	5.0	7.7	2.6
50 - 54	1 195	883	312	8.1	12.8	3.9
55 - 59	1 629	1 114	515	11.6	17.6	6.7
60 - 64	2 094	1 429	665	17.2	28.0	9.4
65 - 69	2 423	1 544	879	23.9	39.1	14.2
70 - 74	3 329	1 898	1 431	33.0	53.5	21.9
75 - 79	4 155	1 963	2 192	48.9	73.7	37.6
80 - 84	4 547	1 645	2 902	82.3	110.5	71.9
85 - 89	4 206	1 072	3 134	137.5	164.2	130.2
90 - 94	2 075	373	1 702	231.1	249.0	227.5
95 - 99	397	66	331	328.6	340.2	326.4
100 +	82	13	69	460.7	♦650.0	436.7
Liechtenstein						
2014 (C)						
Total	268	121	147	7.2	6.5	7.8
0	1	-	1	♦2.8	-	♦6.1
1 - 4	-	-	-	-	-	-
5 - 9	-	-	-	-	-	-
10 - 14	-	-	-	-	-	-
15 - 19	-	-	-	-	-	-
20 - 24	1	-	1	♦0.4	-	♦0.9
25 - 29	-	-	-	-	-	-
30 - 34	3	2	1	♦1.3	♦1.7	♦0.9

19. Deaths by age and sex and age-specific death rates by sex: latest available year, 2006 - 2015
Décès et taux de mortalité selon l'âge et le sexe : dernière année disponible, 2006 - 2015 (continued - suite)

Continent, country or area, date, code[a] and age (in years) Continent, pays ou zone, date, code[a] et âge (en annèes)	Number - Nombre			Rate - Taux		
	Both sexes Les deux sexes	Male Masculin	Female Féminin	Both sexes Les deux sexes	Male Masculin	Female Féminin
EUROPE						
Liechtenstein						
2014 (C)						
35 - 39	1	1	-	♦0.4	♦0.8	-
40 - 44	2	2	-	♦0.7	♦1.4	-
45 - 49	5	4	1	♦1.6	♦2.5	♦0.6
50 - 54	6	4	2	♦1.9	♦2.6	♦1.3
55 - 59	15	8	7	♦5.5	♦6.0	♦5.1
60 - 64	12	7	5	♦5.2	♦6.0	♦4.4
65 - 69	22	16	6	♦10.8	♦15.7	♦6.0
70 - 74	27	15	12	♦16.8	♦19.4	♦14.5
75 - 79	31	12	19	31.4	♦26.9	♦35.1
80 - 84	32	16	16	49.3	♦63.7	♦40.2
85 - 89	53	18	35	130.7	♦140.1	126.4
90 - 94	46	12	34	277.1	♦320.0	264.6
95 - 99	9	4	5	♦346.2	♦421.1	♦303.0
100 +	2	-	2	♦400.0	-	♦800.0
Lithuania - Lituanie						
2012 (C)						
Total	40 938	20 691	20 247	13.7	15.0	12.6
0 - 4	141	82	59	0.9	1.1	0.8
0	118	68	50	3.9	4.4	3.4
1 - 4	23	14	9	♦0.2	♦0.2	♦0.2
5 - 9	26	13	13	♦0.2	♦0.2	♦0.2
10 - 14	28	21	7	♦0.2	♦0.3	♦0.1
15 - 19	115	87	28	0.6	0.9	♦0.3
20 - 24	212	180	32	1.0	1.6	0.3
25 - 29	263	220	43	1.4	2.2	0.5
30 - 34	391	326	65	2.2	3.7	0.7
35 - 39	581	433	148	3.0	4.6	1.5
40 - 44	871	648	223	4.1	6.3	2.0
45 - 49	1 330	959	371	6.0	9.1	3.2
50 - 54	2 098	1 521	577	8.8	13.7	4.5
55 - 59	2 349	1 672	677	12.4	19.7	6.5
60 - 64	2 970	2 100	870	17.5	29.3	8.9
65 - 69	3 316	2 153	1 163	23.7	39.4	13.7
70 - 74	4 458	2 567	1 891	31.1	49.3	20.7
75 - 79	5 686	2 775	2 911	47.7	71.4	36.3
80 - 84	6 835	2 613	4 222	80.3	105.1	70.1
85 - 89	5 839	1 544	4 295	139.9	162.2	133.3
90 - 94	2 559	586	1 973	229.1	257.1	221.9
95 - 99	710	143	567	348.9	322.8	356.2
100 +	160	48	112	418.3	484.8	395.1
Luxembourg						
2013 (C)						
Total	3 822	1 864	1 958	7.1	6.9	7.3
0	23	13	10	♦3.8	♦4.2	♦3.4
1 - 4	3	2	1	♦0.1	♦0.2	♦0.1
5 - 9	2	2	-	♦0.1	♦0.1	-
10 - 14	3	2	1	♦0.1	♦0.1	♦0.1
15 - 19	8	4	4	♦0.2	♦0.2	♦0.3
20 - 24	13	11	2	♦0.4	♦0.6	♦0.1
25 - 29	14	7	7	♦0.4	♦0.4	♦0.4
30 - 34	28	13	15	♦0.7	♦0.6	♦0.7
35 - 39	23	13	10	♦0.6	♦0.6	♦0.5
40 - 44	40	24	16	0.9	♦1.1	♦0.8
45 - 49	87	43	44	2.0	1.9	2.1
50 - 54	144	96	48	3.7	4.8	2.5
55 - 59	170	113	57	5.2	6.8	3.5
60 - 64	227	152	75	8.4	11.1	5.6
65 - 69	254	152	102	11.8	14.3	9.4
70 - 74	336	204	132	18.8	24.8	13.6
75 - 79	458	250	208	31.3	38.9	25.3
80 - 84	696	366	330	58.3	76.2	46.2
85 - 89	723	273	450	112.8	140.2	100.9
90 - 94	422	106	316	194.0	193.8	194.1
95 - 99	126	16	110	276.9	♦213.3	289.5
100 +	20	1	19	♦312.5	♦62.5	♦395.8

Continent, country or area, date, code[a] and age (in years) Continent, pays ou zone, date, code[a] et âge (en années)	Number - Nombre			Rate - Taux		
	Both sexes Les deux sexes	Male Masculin	Female Féminin	Both sexes Les deux sexes	Male Masculin	Female Féminin

EUROPE

Malta - Malte
2014 (C)

Total	3 270	1 655	1 615	7.7	7.7	7.6
0	21	11	10	♦5.1	♦5.0	♦5.1
1 - 4	2	1	1	♦0.1	♦0.1	♦0.1
5 - 9	1	1	-	♦0.1	♦0.1	-
10 - 14	4	3	1	♦0.2	♦0.3	♦0.1
15 - 19	6	4	2	♦0.2	♦0.3	♦0.2
20 - 24	7	6	1	♦0.2	♦0.4	♦0.1
25 - 29	8	5	3	♦0.3	♦0.3	♦0.2
30 - 34	21	17	4	♦0.7	♦1.0	♦0.3
35 - 39	18	15	3	♦0.6	♦1.0	♦0.2
40 - 44	34	20	14	1.3	♦1.5	♦1.1
45 - 49	35	21	14	1.4	♦1.6	♦1.1
50 - 54	65	52	13	2.2	3.5	♦0.9
55 - 59	135	83	52	4.4	5.5	3.4
60 - 64	193	112	81	6.7	7.8	5.6
65 - 69	317	195	122	10.7	13.6	8.0
70 - 74	327	200	127	19.3	25.5	14.0
75 - 79	456	268	188	31.6	42.5	23.1
80 - 84	566	256	310	59.2	71.2	52.0
85 - 89	591	226	365	117.8	126.7	112.8
90 - 94	353	133	220	194.8	244.5	173.5
95 - 99	91	22	69	251.4	♦255.8	250.0
100 +	19	4	15	♦327.6	♦235.3	♦365.9

Montenegro - Monténégro
2014 (C)

Total	6 014	3 132	2 882	9.7	10.2	9.2
0	37	25	12	4.8	♦6.3	♦3.3
1 - 4	6	2	4	♦0.2	♦0.1	♦0.3
5 - 9	1	-	1	-	-	♦0.1
10 - 14	7	4	3	♦0.2	♦0.2	♦0.2
15 - 19	12	7	5	♦0.3	♦0.3	♦0.2
20 - 24	20	12	8	♦0.5	♦0.6	♦0.4
25 - 29	31	22	9	0.7	♦1.0	♦0.4
30 - 34	42	29	13	0.9	♦1.3	♦0.6
35 - 39	44	27	17	1.0	♦1.3	♦0.8
40 - 44	68	39	29	1.7	1.9	♦1.4
45 - 49	124	79	45	3.0	3.9	2.2
50 - 54	251	167	84	5.8	7.9	3.8
55 - 59	350	234	116	8.2	11.0	5.5
60 - 64	494	337	157	12.8	18.2	7.8
65 - 69	510	316	194	19.5	26.9	13.4
70 - 74	780	423	357	35.4	45.0	28.3
75 - 79	1 042	525	517	54.8	66.2	46.7
80 - 84	1 059	476	583	98.3	111.0	89.8
85 - 89	754	285	469	165.6	159.8	169.3
90 - 94	326	104	222	266.8	245.6	278.0
95 - 99	41	13	28	275.2	♦366.2	♦246.7
100 +	15	6	9	♦857.1	♦857.1	♦857.1

Netherlands - Pays-Bas[42]
2014 (C)

Total	139 223	67 121	72 102	8.3	8.0	8.5
0	630	354	276	3.6	4.0	3.3
1 - 4	99	52	47	0.1	0.1	0.1
5 - 9	75	43	32	0.1	0.1	0.1
10 - 14	100	51	49	0.1	0.1	0.1
15 - 19	226	142	84	0.2	0.3	0.2
20 - 24	266	165	101	0.2	0.3	0.2
25 - 29	364	234	130	0.3	0.4	0.3
30 - 34	444	285	159	0.4	0.6	0.3
35 - 39	614	377	237	0.6	0.8	0.5
40 - 44	1 232	700	532	1.0	1.2	0.9
45 - 49	2 152	1 215	937	1.7	1.9	1.5
50 - 54	3 647	2 073	1 574	2.9	3.3	2.5
55 - 59	5 335	3 004	2 331	4.7	5.3	4.1
60 - 64	7 880	4 638	3 242	7.5	8.9	6.2

19. Deaths by age and sex and age-specific death rates by sex: latest available year, 2006 - 2015
Décès et taux de mortalité selon l'âge et le sexe : dernière année disponible, 2006 - 2015 (continued - suite)

Continent, country or area, date, code[a] and age (in years) / Continent, pays ou zone, date, code[a] et âge (en années)	Number - Nombre			Rate - Taux		
	Both sexes Les deux sexes	Male Masculin	Female Féminin	Both sexes Les deux sexes	Male Masculin	Female Féminin
EUROPE						
Netherlands - Pays-Bas[42]						
2014 (C)						
65 - 69	11 725	6 951	4 774	11.7	14.0	9.5
70 - 74	13 287	7 853	5 434	18.9	23.2	15.0
75 - 79	17 287	9 833	7 454	32.3	40.5	25.5
80 - 84	23 309	11 783	11 526	60.3	75.4	50.0
85 - 89	24 875	10 254	14 621	110.6	134.5	98.3
90 - 94	18 699	5 715	12 984	199.1	229.3	188.2
95 - 99	5 858	1 237	4 621	...	...	...
100 +	1 119	162	957	...	...	...
Norway - Norvège[43]						
2014 (C)						
Total	40 369	19 693	20 676	7.9	7.6	8.1
0	139	77	62	2.3	2.5	2.1
1 - 4	29	19	10	♦0.1	♦0.1	♦0.1
5 - 9	25	17	8	♦0.1	♦0.1	♦0.1
10 - 14	21	15	6	♦0.1	♦0.1	-
15 - 19	68	44	24	0.2	0.3	♦0.2
20 - 24	135	101	34	0.4	0.6	0.2
25 - 29	163	131	32	0.5	0.7	0.2
30 - 34	190	131	59	0.6	0.7	0.4
35 - 39	249	181	68	0.7	1.0	0.4
40 - 44	343	221	122	0.9	1.1	0.7
45 - 49	576	349	227	1.6	1.8	1.3
50 - 54	906	535	371	2.7	3.1	2.3
55 - 59	1 298	781	517	4.1	4.9	3.3
60 - 64	1 933	1 190	743	6.7	8.2	5.2
65 - 69	3 081	1 859	1 222	11.2	13.5	8.8
70 - 74	3 374	2 059	1 315	17.7	22.5	13.3
75 - 79	4 322	2 442	1 880	31.6	39.5	25.1
80 - 84	6 251	3 212	3 039	59.0	73.0	49.0
85 - 89	7 662	3 321	4 341	106.9	128.8	94.5
90 - 94	6 813	2 357	4 456	197.2	242.5	179.5
95 - 99	2 374	575	1 799	313.7	356.9	302.0
100 +	417	76	341	478.5	482.5	477.6
Poland - Pologne						
2014 (C)						
Total	376 467	195 791	180 676	9.9	10.6	9.2
0	1 583	870	713	4.4	4.7	4.0
1 - 4	277	141	136	0.2	0.2	0.2
5 - 9	192	103	89	0.1	0.1	0.1
10 - 14	228	121	107	0.1	0.1	0.1
15 - 19	834	604	230	0.4	0.6	0.2
20 - 24	1 582	1 268	314	0.6	1.0	0.3
25 - 29	1 957	1 565	392	0.7	1.0	0.3
30 - 34	2 773	2 196	577	0.9	1.4	0.4
35 - 39	3 942	2 989	953	1.3	2.0	0.7
40 - 44	5 542	4 185	1 357	2.2	3.3	1.1
45 - 49	8 086	5 865	2 221	3.5	5.1	1.9
50 - 54	14 851	10 528	4 323	5.9	8.5	3.4
55 - 59	26 479	18 486	7 993	9.1	13.2	5.3
60 - 64	35 675	23 956	11 719	13.5	19.6	8.3
65 - 69	35 785	22 935	12 850	19.1	27.6	12.3
70 - 74	33 909	20 207	13 702	27.4	39.9	18.7
75 - 79	47 917	25 038	22 879	41.9	58.8	31.8
80 - 84	60 595	26 216	34 379	70.5	91.5	59.9
85 - 89	55 682	18 665	37 017	120.2	143.7	111.0
90 - 94	30 726	8 134	22 592	200.4	222.3	193.5
95 - 99	6 377	1 438	4 939	294.5	321.6	287.5
100 +	1 475	281	1 194	307.5	285.0	313.3
Portugal[44]						
2014 (C)						
Total	104 843	53 233	51 610	10.1	10.8	9.5
0	236	145	91	2.9	3.4	2.3
1 - 4	55	28	27	0.1	♦0.1	♦0.1
5 - 9	45	29	16	0.1	♦0.1	♦0.1
10 - 14	50	32	18	0.1	0.1	♦0.1

Continent, country or area, date, code[a] and age (in years) / Continent, pays ou zone, date, code[a] et âge (en années)	Number - Nombre			Rate - Taux		
	Both sexes / Les deux sexes	Male / Masculin	Female / Féminin	Both sexes / Les deux sexes	Male / Masculin	Female / Féminin
EUROPE						
Portugal[44]						
2014 (C)						
15 - 19	135	95	40	0.2	0.3	0.1
20 - 24	182	136	46	0.3	0.5	0.2
25 - 29	257	179	78	0.4	0.6	0.3
30 - 34	382	261	121	0.6	0.8	0.3
35 - 39	701	454	247	0.9	1.2	0.6
40 - 44	1 168	786	382	1.5	2.1	0.9
45 - 49	1 848	1 281	567	2.4	3.5	1.4
50 - 54	2 902	2 056	846	3.9	5.7	2.2
55 - 59	3 881	2 733	1 148	5.6	8.3	3.2
60 - 64	4 827	3 345	1 482	7.5	11.0	4.3
65 - 69	6 567	4 214	2 353	11.3	16.0	7.4
70 - 74	8 717	5 395	3 322	18.1	25.4	12.3
75 - 79	13 925	7 842	6 083	31.9	43.0	23.9
80 - 84	19 614	9 676	9 938	59.6	76.6	49.0
85 - 89	20 873	8 688	12 185	118.1	148.8	103.0
90 - 94	13 534	4 622	8 912	213.4	252.7	197.5
95 - 99	4 024	1 058	2 966	296.1	294.7	296.6
100 +	920	178	742	246.7	155.7	286.9
Republic of Moldova - République de Moldova[45]						
2012 (C)						
Total	39 560	20 774	18 786	11.1	12.1	10.2
0 - 4	484	252	232	2.5	2.5	2.5
0	404	203	201	10.4	10.1	10.7
1 - 4	80	49	31	0.5	0.6	0.4
5 - 9	46	29	17	0.2	♦0.3	♦0.2
10 - 14	64	37	27	0.3	0.4	♦0.3
15 - 19	183	140	43	0.7	1.1	0.3
20 - 24	246	190	56	0.7	1.1	0.3
25 - 29	324	244	80	0.9	1.4	0.5
30 - 34	467	348	119	1.6	2.4	0.8
35 - 39	733	524	209	2.9	4.2	1.6
40 - 44	970	712	258	4.3	6.5	2.2
45 - 49	1 670	1 237	433	7.0	11.0	3.5
50 - 54	2 779	1 939	840	10.1	15.2	5.7
55 - 59	3 521	2 308	1 213	15.0	21.7	9.4
60 - 64	4 194	2 598	1 596	23.0	32.6	15.6
65 - 69	3 249	1 815	1 434	30.7	40.5	23.5
70 - 74	5 351	2 625	2 726	53.2	68.8	43.7
75 - 79	5 726	2 499	3 227	79.0	96.7	69.2
80 - 84	5 308	2 046	3 262	111.5	128.8	102.9
85 - 89	3 038	889	2 149	148.9	150.2	148.4
90 - 94	1 033	306	727	190.0	191.6	189.3
95 - 99	151	31	120	129.8	78.5	156.3
100 +	23	5	18	♦53.6	♦33.8	♦63.8
Romania - Roumanie						
2014 (C)						
Total	254 237	132 742	121 495	12.8	13.6	11.9
0	1 628	968	660	8.7	10.1	7.3
1 - 4	289	155	134	0.4	0.4	0.4
5 - 9	197	113	84	0.2	0.2	0.2
10 - 14	231	154	77	0.2	0.3	0.1
15 - 19	438	307	131	0.4	0.6	0.2
20 - 24	699	519	180	0.6	0.9	0.3
25 - 29	1 048	751	297	0.7	1.0	0.4
30 - 34	1 274	924	350	0.9	1.3	0.5
35 - 39	2 250	1 569	681	1.4	2.0	0.9
40 - 44	3 887	2 818	1 069	2.5	3.6	1.4
45 - 49	6 213	4 472	1 741	4.2	6.0	2.4
50 - 54	8 510	6 058	2 452	7.4	10.6	4.3
55 - 59	16 214	11 383	4 831	11.5	16.8	6.6
60 - 64	20 912	14 167	6 745	15.7	23.1	9.4
65 - 69	21 452	13 616	7 836	21.7	31.1	14.3
70 - 74	27 207	15 471	11 736	33.9	46.5	25.0
75 - 79	41 122	20 300	20 822	55.1	70.6	45.4
80 - 84	45 397	19 273	26 124	92.9	107.5	84.5

19. Deaths by age and sex and age-specific death rates by sex: latest available year, 2006 - 2015
Décès et taux de mortalité selon l'âge et le sexe : dernière année disponible, 2006 - 2015 (continued - suite)

Continent, country or area, date, code[a] and age (in years) / Continent, pays ou zone, date, code[a] et âge (en années)	Number - Nombre			Rate - Taux		
	Both sexes Les deux sexes	Male Masculin	Female Féminin	Both sexes Les deux sexes	Male Masculin	Female Féminin
EUROPE						
Romania - Roumanie						
2014 (C)						
85 - 89	36 073	13 601	22 472	153.9	168.2	146.4
90 - 94	16 262	5 287	10 975	230.0	237.8	226.5
95 - 99	2 409	684	1 725	292.1	277.4	298.4
100 +	525	152	373	359.3	351.0	362.8
Russian Federation - Fédération de Russie[25]						
2011 (C)						
Total	1 925 720	997 494	928 226	13.5	15.1	12.1
0 - 4	16 465	9 472	6 993	2.1	2.3	1.8
0	13 168	7 572	5 596	8.0	9.0	7.0
1 - 4	3 297	1 900	1 397	0.5	0.6	0.5
5 - 9	1 972	1 160	812	0.3	0.3	0.2
10 - 14	2 006	1 249	757	0.3	0.4	0.2
15 - 19	6 656	4 634	2 022	0.8	1.1	0.5
20 - 24	18 666	14 374	4 292	1.5	2.3	0.7
25 - 29	32 160	24 684	7 476	2.7	4.1	1.3
30 - 34	45 451	34 852	10 599	4.1	6.4	1.9
35 - 39	50 630	38 270	12 360	5.0	7.7	2.4
40 - 44	55 007	40 708	14 299	6.0	9.1	3.0
45 - 49	81 813	60 225	21 588	7.7	12.0	3.8
50 - 54	124 961	89 971	34 990	10.9	17.1	5.6
55 - 59	156 587	108 205	48 382	15.6	24.9	8.5
60 - 64	177 990	118 728	59 262	22.7	36.6	12.9
65 - 69	111 156	66 246	44 910	27.8	44.4	17.9
70 - 74	263 633	136 875	126 758	40.8	62.8	29.6
75 - 79	232 616	99 250	133 366	65.5	92.9	53.7
80 - 84	290 314	94 614	195 700	101.1	129.8	91.4
85 - 89	172 178	35 533	136 645	166.8	187.8	162.0
90 - 94	56 714	9 585	47 129	244.6	241.3	245.3
95 - 99	18 647	2 652	15 995	320.7	294.4	325.5
100 +	2 562	320	2 242	352.6	232.1	380.8
Unknown - Inconnu	7 536	5 887	1 649	..	..	..
San Marino - Saint-Marin						
2014 (+C)						
Total	252	128	124	7.5	7.8	7.2
0	1	1	-	♦3.1	♦5.6	-
1 - 4	-	-	-	-	-	-
5 - 9	-	-	-	-	-	-
10 - 14	-	-	-	-	-	-
15 - 19	1	-	1	♦0.6	-	♦1.3
20 - 24	1	1	-	♦0.7	♦1.3	-
25 - 29	-	-	-	-	-	-
30 - 34	-	-	-	-	-	-
35 - 39	-	-	-	-	-	-
40 - 44	1	1	-	♦0.3	♦0.7	-
45 - 49	2	1	1	♦0.6	♦0.7	♦0.6
50 - 54	5	3	2	♦1.8	♦2.2	♦1.4
55 - 59	4	2	2	♦1.8	♦1.9	♦1.8
60 - 64	11	6	5	♦5.7	♦6.4	♦5.1
65 - 69	13	9	4	♦7.7	♦11.0	♦4.5
70 - 74	16	12	4	♦11.2	♦17.5	♦5.4
75 - 79	23	17	6	♦19.6	♦30.8	♦9.6
80 - 84	47	23	24	50.7	♦59.0	♦44.7
85 - 89	60	32	28	112.8	172.0	♦80.9
90 - 94	45	15	30	160.1	♦185.2	♦150.0
95 - 99	15	4	11	♦263.2	♦363.6	♦239.1
100 +	7	1	6	♦777.8	♦1000.0	♦750.0
Serbia - Serbie[46]						
2014 (+C)						
Total	101 247	51 010	50 237	14.2	14.7	13.7
0	381	228	153	5.8	6.7	4.8
1 - 4	60	27	33	0.2	♦0.2	0.3
5 - 9	43	27	16	0.1	♦0.2	♦0.1
10 - 14	47	27	20	0.1	♦0.1	♦0.1
15 - 19	122	88	34	0.3	0.5	0.2
20 - 24	222	159	63	0.5	0.7	0.3

19. Deaths by age and sex and age-specific death rates by sex: latest available year, 2006 - 2015
Décès et taux de mortalité selon l'âge et le sexe : dernière année disponible, 2006 - 2015 (continued - suite)

Continent, country or area, date, code[a] and age (in years) Continent, pays ou zone, date, code[a] et âge (en annèes)	Number - Nombre			Rate - Taux		
	Both sexes Les deux sexes	Male Masculin	Female Féminin	Both sexes Les deux sexes	Male Masculin	Female Féminin
EUROPE						
Serbia - Serbie[46]						
2014 (+C)						
25 - 29	265	189	76	0.6	0.8	0.3
30 - 34	363	249	114	0.7	1.0	0.5
35 - 39	591	394	197	1.2	1.5	0.8
40 - 44	938	589	349	2.0	2.5	1.5
45 - 49	1 683	1 086	597	3.6	4.7	2.5
50 - 54	3 087	2 014	1 073	6.2	8.3	4.2
55 - 59	5 333	3 540	1 793	9.9	13.6	6.5
60 - 64	8 700	5 692	3 008	15.5	21.3	10.2
65 - 69	8 890	5 421	3 469	21.8	29.1	15.7
70 - 74	11 630	6 515	5 115	36.5	46.9	28.4
75 - 79	18 063	8 732	9 331	63.0	74.0	55.3
80 - 84	21 117	8 968	12 149	111.6	122.5	104.7
85 - 89	13 869	5 174	8 695	178.6	185.8	174.6
90 - 94	5 242	1 726	3 516	268.0	274.3	265.0
95 - 99	493	139	354	259.6	218.2	280.5
100 +	108	26	82	311.2	♦224.1	355.0
Slovakia - Slovaquie						
2014 (C)						
Total	51 346	26 499	24 847	9.5	10.0	8.9
0	318	169	149	5.7	6.0	5.5
1 - 4	62	37	25	0.3	0.3	♦0.2
5 - 9	34	23	11	0.1	♦0.2	♦0.1
10 - 14	33	24	9	0.1	♦0.2	♦0.1
15 - 19	111	74	37	0.4	0.5	0.3
20 - 24	182	138	44	0.5	0.7	0.2
25 - 29	224	174	50	0.5	0.8	0.2
30 - 34	345	250	95	0.8	1.1	0.4
35 - 39	561	390	171	1.2	1.7	0.8
40 - 44	738	542	196	1.9	2.7	1.0
45 - 49	1 195	844	351	3.4	4.7	2.0
50 - 54	2 013	1 459	554	5.4	8.0	3.0
55 - 59	3 497	2 473	1 024	9.1	13.4	5.2
60 - 64	4 844	3 302	1 542	13.8	20.1	8.2
65 - 69	4 911	3 181	1 730	19.3	28.7	12.1
70 - 74	5 543	3 165	2 378	29.4	42.1	21.0
75 - 79	6 633	3 226	3 407	48.8	66.3	39.0
80 - 84	8 404	3 362	5 042	86.2	107.2	76.2
85 - 89	7 138	2 383	4 755	144.7	171.6	134.2
90 - 94	3 977	1 117	2 860	233.2	251.0	226.9
95 - 99	468	138	330	214.0	224.4	209.9
100 +	115	28	87	196.2	♦141.4	224.2
Slovenia - Slovénie						
2014 (C)						
Total	18 886	9 208	9 678	9.2	9.0	9.3
0	39	19	20	1.8	♦1.7	♦1.9
1 - 4	6	4	2	♦0.1	♦0.1	-
5 - 9	8	4	4	♦0.1	♦0.1	♦0.1
10 - 14	10	6	4	♦0.1	♦0.1	♦0.1
15 - 19	21	17	4	♦0.2	♦0.3	♦0.1
20 - 24	42	25	17	0.4	♦0.4	♦0.3
25 - 29	47	37	10	0.3	0.5	♦0.2
30 - 34	90	66	24	0.6	0.8	♦0.3
35 - 39	129	94	35	0.8	1.1	0.5
40 - 44	155	108	47	1.1	1.4	0.7
45 - 49	301	198	103	2.0	2.5	1.4
50 - 54	519	363	156	3.4	4.7	2.1
55 - 59	875	611	264	5.8	8.0	3.5
60 - 64	1 333	926	407	9.4	13.1	5.8
65 - 69	1 300	876	424	12.9	18.3	8.0
70 - 74	1 903	1 186	717	20.7	29.0	14.1
75 - 79	2 458	1 346	1 112	33.2	44.7	25.3
80 - 84	3 512	1 579	1 933	63.1	82.6	53.0
85 - 89	3 548	1 167	2 381	117.1	143.0	107.5
90 - 94	2 079	498	1 581	198.0	226.5	190.4

Continent, country or area, date, code[a] and age (in years) Continent, pays ou zone, date, code[a] et âge (en annèes)	Number - Nombre			Rate - Taux		
	Both sexes Les deux sexes	Male Masculin	Female Féminin	Both sexes Les deux sexes	Male Masculin	Female Féminin
EUROPE						
Slovenia - Slovénie						
2014 (C)						
95 - 99	402	63	339	326.3	310.3	329.4
100 +	109	15	94	459.9	♦454.5	460.8
Spain - Espagne						
2014 (C)						
Total	393 734	200 114	193 620	8.5	8.8	8.2
0	1 202	662	540	2.8	3.0	2.6
1 - 4	252	140	112	0.1	0.1	0.1
5 - 9	185	107	78	0.1	0.1	0.1
10 - 14	204	110	94	0.1	0.1	0.1
15 - 19	343	224	119	0.2	0.2	0.1
20 - 24	628	445	183	0.3	0.4	0.2
25 - 29	733	511	222	0.3	0.4	0.2
30 - 34	1 315	891	424	0.4	0.5	0.3
35 - 39	2 070	1 303	767	0.5	0.6	0.4
40 - 44	3 785	2 427	1 358	1.0	1.2	0.7
45 - 49	6 639	4 394	2 245	1.8	2.4	1.2
50 - 54	9 928	6 694	3 234	2.9	4.0	1.9
55 - 59	13 455	9 165	4 290	4.6	6.4	2.9
60 - 64	17 117	11 924	5 193	6.8	9.8	4.0
65 - 69	23 568	16 262	7 306	10.1	14.6	5.9
70 - 74	29 642	19 495	10 147	15.8	22.4	10.0
75 - 79	44 897	26 874	18 023	28.0	38.7	19.9
80 - 84	72 072	37 209	34 863	51.0	65.6	41.2
85 - 89	81 206	34 792	46 414	96.6	118.1	85.0
90 - 94	59 743	20 503	39 240	173.1	201.6	161.2
95 - 99	20 474	5 143	15 331	265.8	285.9	259.7
100 +	4 276	839	3 437	294.0	261.5	303.2
Sweden - Suède						
2014 (C)						
Total	88 976	43 382	45 594	9.2	9.0	9.4
0	251	151	100	2.2	2.6	1.8
1 - 4	51	26	25	0.1	♦0.1	♦0.1
5 - 9	41	17	24	0.1	♦0.1	♦0.1
10 - 14	37	22	15	0.1	♦0.1	♦0.1
15 - 19	130	84	46	0.2	0.3	0.2
20 - 24	301	224	77	0.4	0.7	0.2
25 - 29	313	226	87	0.5	0.7	0.3
30 - 34	374	261	113	0.6	0.8	0.4
35 - 39	340	227	113	0.6	0.7	0.4
40 - 44	595	362	233	0.9	1.1	0.7
45 - 49	1 009	610	399	1.5	1.8	1.2
50 - 54	1 508	895	613	2.5	2.9	2.0
55 - 59	2 320	1 380	940	4.0	4.7	3.3
60 - 64	3 797	2 293	1 504	6.7	8.1	5.3
65 - 69	6 639	3 956	2 683	11.0	13.3	8.8
70 - 74	8 143	4 816	3 327	17.5	21.2	14.0
75 - 79	10 103	5 776	4 327	30.7	38.0	24.5
80 - 84	14 057	7 230	6 827	57.9	70.8	48.5
85 - 89	17 701	7 865	9 836	109.4	131.7	96.4
90 - 94	15 051	5 371	9 680	198.3	229.9	184.3
95 - 99	5 232	1 400	3 832	322.9	366.5	309.4
100 +	983	190	793	513.0	612.9	493.8
Switzerland - Suisse						
2014 (C)						
Total	63 938	30 950	32 988	7.8	7.6	8.0
0	331	193	138	4.0	4.5	3.4
1 - 4	38	17	21	0.1	♦0.1	♦0.1
5 - 9	21	13	8	♦0.1	♦0.1	-
10 - 14	34	15	19	0.1	♦0.1	♦0.1
15 - 19	95	70	25	0.2	0.3	♦0.1
20 - 24	136	93	43	0.3	0.4	0.2
25 - 29	189	132	57	0.3	0.5	0.2
30 - 34	239	156	83	0.4	0.5	0.3
35 - 39	305	199	106	0.5	0.7	0.4
40 - 44	518	330	188	0.9	1.1	0.6

19. Deaths by age and sex and age-specific death rates by sex: latest available year, 2006 - 2015
Décès et taux de mortalité selon l'âge et le sexe : dernière année disponible, 2006 - 2015 (continued - suite)

Continent, country or area, date, code[a] and age (in years) Continent, pays ou zone, date, code[a] et âge (en annèes)	Number - Nombre			Rate - Taux		
	Both sexes Les deux sexes	Male Masculin	Female Féminin	Both sexes Les deux sexes	Male Masculin	Female Féminin
EUROPE						
Switzerland - Suisse						
2014 (C)						
45 - 49	884	555	329	1.3	1.7	1.0
50 - 54	1 488	938	550	2.4	2.9	1.8
55 - 59	2 130	1 353	777	4.0	5.0	2.9
60 - 64	2 793	1 787	1 006	6.1	7.9	4.3
65 - 69	4 306	2 730	1 576	10.0	13.1	7.1
70 - 74	5 341	3 195	2 146	15.3	19.6	11.6
75 - 79	6 967	3 913	3 054	26.0	33.1	20.4
80 - 84	10 428	5 264	5 164	50.5	63.6	41.7
85 - 89	12 918	5 419	7 499	100.3	122.0	88.9
90 - 94	10 427	3 529	6 898	187.5	221.9	173.7
95 - 99	3 576	904	2 672	316.6	357.9	304.7
100 +	774	145	629	509.5	514.2	508.5
TFYR of Macedonia - L'ex-R. y. de Macédoine						
2014 (C)						
Total	19 718	10 210	9 508	9.5	9.9	9.2
0	233	127	106	10.1	10.6	9.5
1 - 4	20	10	10	♦0.2	♦0.2	♦0.2
5 - 9	19	12	7	♦0.2	♦0.2	♦0.1
10 - 14	13	6	7	♦0.1	♦0.1	♦0.1
15 - 19	45	36	9	0.3	0.5	♦0.1
20 - 24	51	33	18	0.3	0.4	♦0.2
25 - 29	70	57	13	0.4	0.7	♦0.2
30 - 34	81	54	27	0.5	0.6	♦0.3
35 - 39	140	85	55	0.9	1.1	0.7
40 - 44	225	137	88	1.5	1.9	1.2
45 - 49	456	303	153	3.1	4.1	2.1
50 - 54	761	511	250	5.4	7.1	3.5
55 - 59	1 143	768	375	8.4	11.3	5.6
60 - 64	1 609	1 049	560	13.5	18.2	9.1
65 - 69	1 926	1 109	817	21.3	26.5	16.9
70 - 74	2 544	1 409	1 135	36.2	44.3	29.6
75 - 79	3 471	1 652	1 819	65.1	71.4	60.2
80 - 84	3 687	1 609	2 078	118.9	126.8	113.5
85 - 89	2 220	886	1 334	208.2	209.4	207.4
90 - 94	858	308	550	339.9	353.0	332.9
95 - 99	121	42	79	...	...	...
100 +	25	7	18	...	...	...
Ukraine[47]						
2014 (+C)						
Total	632 296	310 671	321 625	...	...	...
0	3 656	2 124	1 532	...	...	...
1 - 4	774	421	353	...	...	...
5 - 9	451	280	171	...	...	...
10 - 14	446	276	170	...	...	...
15 - 19	1 359	989	370	...	...	...
20 - 24	3 077	2 437	640	...	...	...
25 - 29	6 334	4 892	1 442	...	...	...
30 - 34	9 510	7 270	2 240	...	...	...
35 - 39	12 525	9 459	3 066	...	...	...
40 - 44	15 098	10 982	4 116	...	...	...
45 - 49	19 036	13 895	5 141	...	...	...
50 - 54	29 714	21 498	8 216	...	...	...
55 - 59	40 342	28 024	12 318	...	...	...
60 - 64	52 238	34 607	17 631	...	...	...
65 - 69	50 416	30 135	20 281	...	...	...
70 - 74	71 113	36 563	34 550	...	...	...
75 - 79	109 901	48 658	61 243	...	...	...
80 - 84	85 913	29 434	56 479	...	...	...
85 - 89	82 792	21 677	61 115	...	...	...
90 - 94	30 848	5 867	24 981	...	...	...
95 - 99	5 602	921	4 681	...	...	...
100 +	1 015	153	862	...	...	...
Unknown - Inconnu	136	109	27	..	..	..

19. Deaths by age and sex and age-specific death rates by sex: latest available year, 2006 - 2015
Décès et taux de mortalité selon l'âge et le sexe : dernière année disponible, 2006 - 2015 (continued - suite)

Continent, country or area, date, code[a] and age (in years) Continent, pays ou zone, date, code[a] et âge (en années)	Number - Nombre			Rate - Taux		
	Both sexes Les deux sexes	Male Masculin	Female Féminin	Both sexes Les deux sexes	Male Masculin	Female Féminin

EUROPE

United Kingdom of Great Britain and Northern Ireland - Royaume-Uni de Grande-Bretagne et d'Irlande du Nord[48]
2014 (+C)

Total	568 840	277 519	291 321	8.8	8.7	8.9
0	2 990	1 631	1 359	3.8	4.0	3.5
1 - 4	501	293	208	0.2	0.2	0.1
5 - 9	317	178	139	0.1	0.1	0.1
10 - 14	333	198	135	0.1	0.1	0.1
15 - 19	939	603	336	0.2	0.3	0.2
20 - 24	1 580	1 103	477	0.4	0.5	0.2
25 - 29	2 002	1 371	631	0.5	0.6	0.3
30 - 34	2 734	1 747	987	0.6	0.8	0.5
35 - 39	3 725	2 364	1 361	0.9	1.2	0.7
40 - 44	6 278	3 823	2 455	1.4	1.8	1.1
45 - 49	9 675	5 873	3 802	2.1	2.6	1.6
50 - 54	13 777	8 143	5 634	3.1	3.7	2.5
55 - 59	18 781	11 174	7 607	4.9	5.9	3.9
60 - 64	27 544	16 382	11 162	7.8	9.5	6.2
65 - 69	42 257	25 065	17 192	11.9	14.5	9.4
70 - 74	52 400	30 192	22 208	19.9	24.2	16.1
75 - 79	71 871	39 413	32 458	33.7	40.4	28.1
80 - 84	94 288	47 244	47 044	60.1	71.0	52.1
85 - 89	102 404	44 788	57 616	107.5	125.8	96.6
90 - 94	81 532	28 242	53 290	185.2	210.8	174.0
95 - 99	26 811	6 749	20 062	288.1	320.4	278.7
100 +	6 101	943	5 158	426.1	434.0	424.7

OCEANIA - OCÉANIE

American Samoa - Samoas américaines
2014 (C)

Total	259	142	117	...	...	...
0	9	4	5	...	...	...
1 - 4	2	-	2	...	...	...
5 - 9	1	-	1	...	...	...
10 - 14	1	1	-	...	...	...
15 - 19	3	1	2	...	...	...
20 - 24	4	2	2	...	...	...
25 - 29	3	2	1	...	...	...
30 - 34	7	6	1	...	...	...
35 - 39	7	6	1	...	...	...
40 - 44	11	5	6	...	...	...
45 - 49	16	5	11	...	...	...
50 - 54	23	11	12	...	...	...
55 - 59	19	11	8	...	...	...
60 - 64	27	14	13	...	...	...
65 - 69	28	19	9	...	...	...
70 - 74	35	23	12	...	...	...
75 - 79	22	14	8	...	...	...
80 - 84	21	14	7	...	...	...
85 +	20	4	16	...	...	...

Australia - Australie
2014 (+C)

Total	153 580	78 341	75 239	6.5	6.7	6.4
0	1 012	533	479	3.4	3.5	3.3
1 - 4	179	103	76	0.1	0.2	0.1
5 - 9	136	69	67	0.1	0.1	0.1
10 - 14	126	66	60	0.1	0.1	0.1
15 - 19	396	256	140	0.3	0.3	0.2
20 - 24	690	498	192	0.4	0.6	0.2
25 - 29	847	572	275	0.5	0.6	0.3
30 - 34	1 100	731	369	0.6	0.9	0.4
35 - 39	1 382	911	471	0.9	1.2	0.6
40 - 44	2 092	1 353	739	1.3	1.6	0.9
45 - 49	2 785	1 692	1 093	1.8	2.2	1.4

Continent, country or area, date, code[a] and age (in years) Continent, pays ou zone, date, code[a] et âge (en années)	Number - Nombre			Rate - Taux		
	Both sexes Les deux sexes	Male Masculin	Female Féminin	Both sexes Les deux sexes	Male Masculin	Female Féminin
OCEANIA - OCÉANIE						
Australia - Australie						
2014 (+C)						
50 - 54	4 302	2 650	1 652	2.8	3.4	2.1
55 - 59	5 831	3 601	2 230	4.1	5.1	3.1
60 - 64	7 955	4 954	3 001	6.3	7.9	4.7
65 - 69	10 825	6 702	4 123	9.7	12.1	7.3
70 - 74	12 991	7 813	5 178	15.9	19.5	12.4
75 - 79	16 988	9 772	7 216	27.8	33.7	22.4
80 - 84	23 209	12 384	10 825	51.8	63.2	42.9
85 - 89	28 629	13 129	15 500	96.9	113.9	86.0
90 - 94	22 381	8 104	14 277	172.9	193.9	162.9
95 - 99	8 024	2 125	5 899	291.4	304.7	286.9
100 +	1 666	305	1 361	411.8	345.4	430.3
Unknown - Inconnu	34	18	16	..	..	..
Cook Islands - Îles Cook[49]						
2009 (+C)						
Total	67	37	30	...	...	...
0	2	1	1	...	...	...
1 - 4	1	1	-	...	...	...
5 - 9	-	-	-	...	...	...
10 - 14	-	-	-	...	...	...
15 - 19	3	2	1	...	...	...
20 - 24	3	3	-	...	...	...
25 - 29	1	1	-	...	...	...
30 - 34	2	1	1	...	...	...
35 - 39	4	3	1	...	...	...
40 - 44	-	-	-	...	...	...
45 - 49	2	1	1	...	...	...
50 - 54	3	1	2	...	...	...
55 - 59	1	1	-	...	...	...
60 - 64	6	3	3	...	...	...
65 - 69	8	4	4	...	...	...
70 - 74	9	1	8	...	...	...
75 - 79	8	5	3	...	...	...
80 +	14	9	5	...	...	...
Fiji - Fidji						
2008 (+C)						
Total	6 471	3 519	2 952	7.7	8.2	7.2
0	319	180	139	18.9	20.4	17.3
1 - 4	128	70	58	1.9	2.0	1.8
5 - 9	45	29	16	0.6	◆0.7	◆0.4
10 - 14	42	25	17	0.5	◆0.6	◆0.4
15 - 19	70	34	36	0.9	0.8	0.9
20 - 24	104	64	40	1.3	1.6	1.0
25 - 29	124	65	59	1.7	1.7	1.6
30 - 34	120	61	59	1.9	1.8	1.9
35 - 39	183	114	69	3.2	3.9	2.5
40 - 44	296	168	128	5.3	5.9	4.7
45 - 49	446	279	167	8.8	10.7	6.7
50 - 54	549	344	205	13.2	16.3	10.0
55 - 59	663	381	282	20.5	23.3	17.6
60 - 64	737	409	328	29.9	33.5	26.3
65 - 69	718	385	333	40.4	44.8	36.3
70 - 74	621	303	318	57.2	59.1	55.5
75 +	1 306	608	698	103.5	108.7	99.3
75 - 79	564	290	274	...	...	...
80 - 84	360	156	204	...	...	...
85 - 89	246	113	133	...	...	...
90 - 94	71	27	44	...	...	...
95 +	65	22	43	...	...	...
Kiribati[50]						
2011 (U)						
Total	481	279	202	...	...	...
0 - 4	132	75	57	...	...	...
5 - 19	14	10	4	...	...	...
20 - 29	34	24	10	...	...	...
30 - 39	28	15	13	...	...	...

19. Deaths by age and sex and age-specific death rates by sex: latest available year, 2006 - 2015
Décès et taux de mortalité selon l'âge et le sexe : dernière année disponible, 2006 - 2015 (continued - suite)

Continent, country or area, date, code[a] and age (in years) Continent, pays ou zone, date, code[a] et âge (en annèes)	Number - Nombre			Rate - Taux		
	Both sexes Les deux sexes	Male Masculin	Female Féminin	Both sexes Les deux sexes	Male Masculin	Female Féminin
OCEANIA - OCÉANIE						
Kiribati[50]						
2011 (U)						
40 - 49	60	37	23	...	...	...
50 - 59	74	42	32	...	...	...
60 - 69	54	34	20	...	...	...
70 +	85	42	43	...	...	...
Marshall Islands - Îles Marshall						
2006 (+U)						
Total	318	171	147	...	...	...
0	27	17	10	...	...	...
1 - 4	13	7	6	...	...	...
5 - 9	4	3	1	...	...	...
10 - 14	1	1	-	...	...	...
15 - 19	11	7	4	...	...	...
20 - 24	8	4	4	...	...	...
25 - 29	6	5	1	...	...	...
30 - 34	10	4	6	...	...	...
35 - 39	15	10	5	...	...	...
40 - 44	20	10	10	...	...	...
45 - 49	16	11	5	...	...	...
50 - 54	26	11	15	...	...	...
55 - 59	38	26	12	...	...	...
60 - 64	21	9	12	...	...	...
65 +	102	46	56	...	...	...
Nauru						
2011 (C)						
Total	75	41	34	...	...	...
0	10	5	5	...	...	...
1 - 4	1	1	-	...	...	...
5 - 9	-	-	-	...	...	...
10 - 14	1	1	-	...	...	...
15 - 19	-	-	-	...	...	...
20 - 24	2	2	-	...	...	...
25 - 29	5	1	4	...	...	...
30 - 34	4	1	3	...	...	...
35 - 39	2	1	1	...	...	...
40 - 44	2	2	-	...	...	...
45 - 49	6	3	3	...	...	...
50 - 54	15	7	8	...	...	...
55 - 59	9	7	2	...	...	...
60 - 64	6	2	4	...	...	...
65 - 69	4	2	2	...	...	...
70 +	8	6	2	...	...	...
New Caledonia - Nouvelle-Calédonie						
2010 (C)						
Total	1 191	701	490	4.8	5.5	4.0
0 - 4	22	10	12	♦1.1	♦1.0	♦1.3
0	19	9	10	...	...	...
1 - 4	3	1	2	...	...	...
5 - 9	9	8	1	♦0.5	♦0.8	♦0.1
10 - 14	1	1	-	-	♦0.1	-
15 - 19	14	11	3	♦0.6	♦1.0	♦0.3
20 - 24	23	17	6	♦1.2	♦1.7	♦0.6
25 - 29	32	23	9	1.7	♦2.5	♦1.0
30 - 34	20	14	6	♦1.1	♦1.5	♦0.6
35 - 39	42	32	10	2.1	3.1	♦1.0
40 - 44	34	25	9	1.8	♦2.6	♦1.0
45 - 49	46	33	13	2.8	3.9	♦1.6
50 - 54	77	46	31	5.6	6.6	4.6
55 - 59	68	49	19	6.0	8.5	♦3.4
60 - 64	114	86	28	11.6	16.6	♦6.0
65 - 69	114	74	40	15.9	20.3	11.4
70 - 74	130	79	51	23.6	29.9	17.8
75 - 79	131	67	64	36.6	39.4	34.1
80 +	314	126	188	80.9	81.4	80.6
80 - 84	132	60	72	...	...	...
85 - 89	97	43	54	...	...	...

19. Deaths by age and sex and age-specific death rates by sex: latest available year, 2006 - 2015
Décès et taux de mortalité selon l'âge et le sexe : dernière année disponible, 2006 - 2015 (continued - suite)

Continent, country or area, date, code[a] and age (in years) / Continent, pays ou zone, date, code[a] et âge (en annèes)	Number - Nombre			Rate - Taux		
	Both sexes Les deux sexes	Male Masculin	Female Féminin	Both sexes Les deux sexes	Male Masculin	Female Féminin
OCEANIA - OCÉANIE						
New Caledonia - Nouvelle-Calédonie						
2010 (C)						
90 - 94	52	17	35	...	...	...
95 +	33	6	27	...	...	...
New Zealand - Nouvelle-Zélande[51]						
2015 (+C)						
Total	31 608	15 801	15 807	6.9	7.0	6.8
0	251	129	122	4.2	4.2	4.3
1 - 4	56	31	25	0.2	0.2	♦0.2
5 - 9	30	18	12	♦0.1	♦0.1	♦0.1
10 - 14	36	22	14	0.1	♦0.1	♦0.1
15 - 19	142	96	46	0.4	0.6	0.3
20 - 24	181	132	49	0.5	0.8	0.3
25 - 29	169	118	51	0.5	0.8	0.3
30 - 34	178	111	67	0.6	0.8	0.5
35 - 39	212	124	88	0.8	0.9	0.6
40 - 44	367	212	155	1.2	1.4	1.0
45 - 49	620	338	282	2.0	2.3	1.7
50 - 54	937	517	420	2.9	3.4	2.6
55 - 59	1 247	723	524	4.3	5.2	3.5
60 - 64	1 658	989	669	6.6	8.1	5.2
65 - 69	2 413	1 400	1 013	10.7	12.7	8.8
70 - 74	3 002	1 761	1 241	18.2	22.1	14.5
75 - 79	3 737	2 050	1 687	31.1	36.6	26.4
80 - 84	4 812	2 452	2 360	57.8	65.9	51.3
85 - 89	5 503	2 562	2 941	104.8	122.1	93.4
90 +	6 057	2 016	4 041	219.6	234.1	213.0
90 - 94	4 251	1 554	2 697	...	...	...
95 - 99	1 520	407	1 113	...	...	...
100 +	286	55	231	...	...	...
Niue - Nioué[52]						
2009 (C)						
Total	12	6	6	...	...	...
0	-	-	-	...	...	...
1 - 4	-	-	-	...	...	...
5 - 9	-	-	-	...	...	...
10 - 14	-	-	-	...	...	...
15 - 19	-	-	-	...	...	...
20 - 24	-	-	-	...	...	...
25 - 29	-	-	-	...	...	...
30 - 34	-	-	-	...	...	...
35 - 39	-	-	-	...	...	...
40 - 44	-	-	-	...	...	...
45 - 49	-	-	-	...	...	...
50 - 54	-	-	-	...	...	...
55 - 59	2	2	-	...	...	...
60 - 64	-	-	-	...	...	...
65 - 69	-	-	-	...	...	...
70 - 74	1	-	1	...	...	...
75 - 79	1	1	-	...	...	...
80 +	8	3	5	...	...	...
Pitcairn						
2007 (C)						
Total	1	...	...	...	...	...
0	-	...	...	...	...	...
1 - 4	-	...	...	...	...	...
5 - 9	-	...	...	...	...	...
10 - 14	-	...	...	...	...	...
15 - 19	-	...	...	...	...	...
20 - 24	-	...	...	...	...	...
25 - 29	-	...	...	...	...	...
30 - 34	-	...	...	...	...	...
35 - 39	-	...	...	...	...	...
40 - 44	-	...	...	...	...	...
45 - 49	-	...	...	...	...	...
50 - 54	-	...	...	...	...	...
55 - 59	-	...	...	...	...	...

19. Deaths by age and sex and age-specific death rates by sex: latest available year, 2006 - 2015
Décès et taux de mortalité selon l'âge et le sexe : dernière année disponible, 2006 - 2015 (continued - suite)

Continent, country or area, date, code[a] and age (in years) Continent, pays ou zone, date, code[a] et âge (en années)	Number - Nombre			Rate - Taux		
	Both sexes Les deux sexes	Male Masculin	Female Féminin	Both sexes Les deux sexes	Male Masculin	Female Féminin
OCEANIA - OCÉANIE						
Pitcairn						
2007 (C)						
60 - 64	-	...	...	...	...	...
65 - 69	-	...	...	...	...	...
70 - 74	-	...	...	...	...	...
75 - 79	1	...	...	...	...	...
80 - 84	-	...	...	...	...	...
85 - 89	-	...	...	...	...	...
90 +	-	...	...	...	...	...
Samoa[21]						
2011 (|)						
Total	812	427	385	4.3	4.4	4.2
0 - 4	92	58	34	3.4	4.2	2.6
0	78	51	27	...	...	...
1 - 4	14	7	7	...	...	...
5 - 9	4	1	3	♦0.2	♦0.1	♦0.3
10 - 14	2	-	2	♦0.1	-	♦0.2
15 - 19	10	7	3	♦0.5	♦0.7	♦0.3
20 - 24	12	5	7	♦0.8	♦0.6	♦1.0
25 - 29	10	8	2	♦0.8	♦1.2	♦0.3
30 - 34	6	4	2	♦0.5	♦0.7	♦0.4
35 - 39	20	8	12	♦1.8	♦1.4	♦2.3
40 - 44	19	12	7	♦1.8	♦2.1	♦1.4
45 - 49	38	20	18	4.3	♦4.4	♦4.2
50 - 54	48	28	20	6.3	♦7.1	♦5.5
55 - 59	49	22	27	8.3	♦7.3	♦9.3
60 - 64	69	37	32	17.3	18.5	16.2
65 - 69	76	36	40	22.5	22.4	22.6
70 - 74	101	59	42	39.5	49.7	30.7
75 +	250	120	130	74.5	92.2	63.4
75 - 79	80	45	35	...	...	...
80 - 84	84	37	47	...	...	...
85 - 89	62	30	32	...	...	...
90 - 94	17	6	11	...	...	...
95 - 99	7	2	5	...	...	...
100 +	-	-	-	...	...	...
Unknown - Inconnu	6	2	4	..	...	..
Tonga[53]						
2006 (|)						
Total	709	402	307	6.9	7.6	6.1
0 - 4	61	38	24	5.1	6.2	♦4.1
0	53	32	21	...	...	...
1 - 4	8	6	3	...	...	...
5 - 9	10	5	4	♦0.9	♦0.8	♦0.7
10 - 14	7	4	4	♦0.6	♦0.6	♦0.7
15 - 19	12	8	3	♦1.1	♦1.3	♦0.6
20 - 24	11	9	2	♦1.0	♦1.6	♦0.4
25 - 29	7	5	2	♦0.9	♦1.2	♦0.5
30 - 34	12	9	4	♦2.1	♦3.2	♦1.4
35 - 39	12	7	5	♦2.1	♦2.4	♦1.8
40 - 44	19	11	8	♦3.8	♦4.4	♦3.2
45 - 49	29	18	11	♦6.8	♦8.8	♦4.9
50 - 54	29	16	13	♦7.7	♦8.9	♦6.5
55 - 59	37	23	15	11.8	♦15.6	♦9.0
60 - 64	53	33	20	18.5	23.9	♦13.5
65 - 69	49	28	21	20.2	♦22.5	♦17.7
70 - 74	70	38	32	37.5	39.7	35.2
75 +	288	149	139	135.1	141.2	129.2
75 - 79	95	54	41	...	...	...
80 +	193	95	98	...	...	...
Wallis and Futuna Islands - Îles Wallis et Futuna						
2008 (C)						
Total	90	51	39	...	...	...
0 - 4	1	1	-	...	...	...
5 - 9	-	-	-	...	...	...
10 - 14	1	1	-	...	...	...
15 - 19	2	1	1	...	...	...

19. Deaths by age and sex and age-specific death rates by sex: latest available year, 2006 - 2015
Décès et taux de mortalité selon l'âge et le sexe : dernière année disponible, 2006 - 2015 (continued - suite)

Continent, country or area, date, code[a] and age (in years) / Continent, pays ou zone, date, code[a] et âge (en années)	Number - Nombre			Rate - Taux		
	Both sexes Les deux sexes	Male Masculin	Female Féminin	Both sexes Les deux sexes	Male Masculin	Female Féminin
OCEANIA - OCÉANIE						
Wallis and Futuna Islands - Îles Wallis et Futuna						
2008 (C)						
20 - 24	4	3	1	...	...	...
25 - 29	4	4	-	...	...	...
30 - 34	3	3	-	...	...	...
35 - 39	2	1	1	...	...	...
40 - 44	-	-	-	...	...	...
45 - 49	2	1	1	...	...	...
50 - 54	2	1	1	...	...	...
55 - 59	4	2	2	...	...	...
60 - 64	5	4	1	...	...	...
65 - 69	12	8	4	...	...	...
70 - 74	15	9	6	...	...	...
75 - 79	13	4	9	...	...	...
80 - 84	11	4	7	...	...	...
85 - 89	5	3	2	...	...	...
90 - 94	4	1	3	...	...	...
95 - 99	-	-	-	...	...	...
100 +	-	-	-	...	...	...

FOOTNOTES - NOTES

✦ Rates based on 30 or fewer deaths. - Taux basés sur 30 décès ou moins.

Italics: estimates which are less reliable. - Italiques : estimations moins sûres.

˙ Provisional. - Données provisoires.

[a] 'Code' indicates the source of data, as follows:
C - Civil registration, estimated over 90% complete
U - Civil registration, estimated less than 90% complete
| - Other source, estimated reliable
+ - Data tabulated by date of registration rather than occurence
... - Information not available

Le 'Code' indique la source des données, comme suit :
C - Registres de l'état civil considérés complets à 90 p. 100 au moins
U - Registres de l'état civil qui ne sont pas considérés complets à 90 p. 100 au moins
| - Autre source, considérée pas douteuses
+ - Données exploitées selon la date de l'enregistrement et non la date de l'événement
... - Information pas disponible

[1] Excluding live-born infants who died before their birth was registered. Data refer to Algerian population only. - Non compris les enfants nés vivants décédés avant l'enregistrement de leur naissance. Les données ne concernent que la population algérienne.
[2] Source: Vital Statistics Report 2014. - Source: Vital Statistics Report 2014.
[3] Data from civil registration centres of Brazzaville, Dolisie, Nkayi, Mossendijo and Ouesso communes. - Données issues des centres d'enregistrement des faits d'état-civil des communes de Brazzaville, Dolisie, Nkayi, Mossendijo et Ouesso.
[4] Data refer to the 12 months preceding the census in September. - Les données se rapportent aux 12 mois précédant le recensement de septembre.
[5] Unrevised data. - Les données n'ont pas été révisées.
[6] Data refer to the 12 months preceding the census in June. - Les données se raportent aux 12 mois précédant le recensement de juin.
[7] Data refer to the 12 months preceding the census in April. - Les données se rapportent aux douze mois précédant le recensement d'avril.
[8] Excludes the islands of St. Brandon and Agalega. - Non compris les îles St. Brandon et Agalega.
[9] Data refer to the 12 months preceding the census in August. - Les données se rapportent aux 12 mois précédant le recensement d'août.
[10] Data refer to the 12 months preceding the census in April. The figures in this table are derived from survey data. They are representative only of private households, internally displaced persons, refugees and nomads, and do not include cattle camps, institutional households, homeless people or overnight travelers. - Les données se rapportent aux douze mois précédant le recensement d'avril. Les chiffres de ce tableau proviennent de données d'enquête. Ils représentent exclusivement les ménages privés et les déplacés, réfugiés et nomades; ils ne comprennent ni les personnes se trouvant dans des camps pastoraux et des établissements collectifs, ni les sans-abri, ni les voyageurs.
[11] Data refer to the 12 months preceding the census in May. - Les données se rapportent aux 12 mois précédant le recensement de mai.
[12] Figures for male and female may not add up to the total, since they do not include the category "Unknown". - La somme des chiffres indiqués pour les sexes masculin et féminin peut n'être pas égale au total parce qu'elle n'inclut pas la catégorie " inconnue ".
[13] Data refer to the 12 months preceding the census in October. - Les données se rapportent aux 12 mois précédant le recensement de octobre.
[14] Excluding visitors. - Ne comprend pas les visiteurs.
[15] Excluding non-residents and foreign service personnel and their dependants. - À l'exclusion des non-résidents et du personnel diplomatique et de leurs charges de famille.
[16] Including Canadian residents temporarily in the United States, but excluding United States residents temporarily in Canada. - Y compris les résidents canadiens se trouvant temporairement aux Etats-Unis, mais ne comprenant pas les résidents des Etats-Unis se trouvant temporairement au Canada.
[17] Data refer to population in private households. Data refer to period from 1 January 2010 to 3 April 2011. - Les données portent sur la population des ménages privés. Les données concernent la période du 1 janvier 2010 au 3 avril 2011.
[18] Excluding live-born infants who died before their birth was registered. - Non compris les enfants nés vivants décédés avant l'enregistrement de leur naissance.
[19] Data refer to resident population only. - Pour la population résidante seulement.
[20] Data refer to resident and non resident deaths that occurred in Saint Vincent and the Grenadines. - Les données concernent les décès de résidents et de non-résidents survenus à St Vincent-et-les-Grenadines.
[21] Data refer to the 12 months preceding the census in November. - Données se rapportant aux 12 mois précédant le recensement de novembre.
[22] Including deaths abroad and deaths of unknown place of residence. - Y compris décès à l'étranger et décès dont le lieu de résidence n'est pas connu.
[23] Excludes nomadic Indian tribes. - Non compris les tribus d'Indiens nomades.
[24] Source: Reports of the Ministry of Health. - Source : Rapports du Ministère de la Santé.
[25] Excluding infants born alive of less than 28 weeks' gestation, of less than 1 000 grams in weight and 35 centimeters in length, who die within seven days of birth. - Non compris les enfants nés vivants après moins de 28 semaines de

gestations, pesant moins de 1 000 grammes, mesurant moins de 35 centimètres et décédés dans les sept jours qui ont suivi leur naissance.

[26] Sources: Births and Deaths National Registration System database, and medical records of government hospitals. - Les sources: Les bases de données des << Births and Deaths National Registration System >> et les dossiers médicaux des hôpitaux du gouvernement.

[27] For statistical purposes, the data for China do not include those for the Hong Kong Special Administrative Region (Hong Kong SAR), Macao Special Administrative Region (Macao SAR) and Taiwan province of China. Data refer to the 12 months preceding the census in November. - Pour la présentation des statistiques, les données pour la Chine ne comprennent pas la Région Administrative Spéciale de Hong Kong (Hong Kong RAS), la Région Administrative Spéciale de Macao (Macao RAS) et Taïwan province de Chine. Données se rapportant aux 12 mois précédant le recensement de novembre.

[28] Data refer to government controlled areas. Data refer to deaths of residents only. - Les données se rapportent aux zones contrôlées par le Gouvernement. Les données renvoient aux décès de résidents uniquement.

[29] Data are from 1 January 2009 to 1 May 2010. - Les données vont du 1er janvier 2009 au 1er mai 2010.

[30] Data refer to the Iranian Year which begins on 21 March and ends on 20 March of the following year. Data refer to current deaths; excluding delayed registrations. - Les données concernent l'année iranienne, qui commence le 21 mars et se termine le 20 mars de l'année suivante. Les données se rapportent aux décès actuels; les déclarations tardives des décès ne sont pas compris.

[31] Includes data for East Jerusalem and Israeli residents in certain other territories under occupation by Israeli military forces since June 1967. Including deaths abroad of Israeli residents who were out of the country for less than a year. - Y compris les données pour Jérusalem-Est et les résidents israéliens dans certains autres territoires occupés depuis 1967 par les forces armées israéliennes. Y compris les décès à l'étranger de résidents israéliens qui ont quitté le pays depuis moins d'un an.

[32] Data refer to Japanese nationals in Japan only. - Les données se raportent aux nationaux japonais au Japon seulement.

[33] Data source is "Department of Public Health". - La source des données est << Le Service de la santé publique >>.

[34] Data from Births and Deaths Notification System (Ministry of Health and all health care providers). - Les données proviennent du système de notification des naissances et des décès (Ministère de la santé et tous prestataires de soins de santé).

[35] Excluding data for the Pakistan-held part of Jammu and Kashmir, the final status of which has not yet been determined. Based on the results of the Pakistan Demographic Survey. - Non compris les données concernant la partie du Jammu et Cachemire occupée par le Pakistan dont le statut définitif n'a pas été déterminé. Données extraites de l'enquête démographique effectuée par le Pakistan.

[36] Excluding alien armed forces, civilian aliens employed by armed forces, and foreign diplomatic personnel and their dependants. - Non compris les militaires étrangers, les civils étrangers employés par les forces armées ni le personnel diplomatique étranger et les membres de leur famille les accompagnant.

[37] Source: Palestinian Central Bureau of Statistics, Population Register, updated version 05/01/2015. - Source: Bureau central de statistique palestinien, registre de la population, version actualisée jusqu'au 05/01/2015.

[38] Including deaths of nationals abroad. - Y compris les décès des nationaux survenus à l'étranger.

[39] Including armed forces stationed outside the country, but excluding alien armed forces stationed in the area. - Y compris les militaires nationaux hors du pays, mais non compris les militaires étrangers en garnison sur le territoire.

[40] Excluding Faeroe Islands and Greenland shown separately, if available. - Non compris les Iles Féroé et le Groenland, qui font l'objet de rubriques distinctes, si disponible.

[41] Including armed forces stationed outside the country. - Y compris les militaires nationaux hors du pays.

[42] Including residents outside the country if listed in a Netherlands population register. - Englobe les résidents se trouvant à l'étranger à condition qu'ils soient inscrits sur le registre de population des Pays-Bas.

[43] Including residents temporarily outside the country. - Y compris les résidents se trouvant temporairement hors du pays.

[44] Data refer to usually resident population. - Les données concernent la population habituellement résidente.

[45] Excluding Transnistria and the municipality of Bender. - Les données ne tiennent pas compte de l'information sur la Transnistria et la municipalité de Bender.

[46] Excludes data for Kosovo and Metohia. - Sans les données pour le Kosovo et Metohie.

[47] Data includes deaths resulting from births with weight 500g and more (if weight is unknown - with length 25 centimeters and more, or with gestation during 22 weeks or more). The Government of Ukraine has informed the United Nations that it is not in a position to provide statistical data concerning the Autonomous Republic of Crimea and the city of Sevastopol. - Y compris les décès de nouveau-nés de 500 grammes ou plus (si le poids est inconnu – de 25 centimètres de long ou plus, ou après une grossesse de 22 semaines ou plus). Le gouvernement Ukrainien a informé l'ONU qu'il n'est pas en mesure de fournir des données statistiques concernant la République autonome de Crimée et la ville de Sébastopol.

[48] Excluding Channel Islands (Guernsey and Jersey) and Isle of Man, shown separately, if available. - Non compris les îles Anglo-Normandes (Guernesey et Jersey) et l'île de Man, qui font l'objet de rubriques distinctes, si disponible.

[49] Excluding Niue, shown separately, which is part of Cook Islands, but because of remoteness is administered separately. Unrevised data. - Non compris Nioué, qui fait l'objet d'une rubrique distincte et qui fait partie des îles Cook, mais qui, en raison de son éloignement, est administrée séparément. Les données n'ont pas été révisées.

[50] Excluding deaths of unknown age or sex. - Les données ne comprennent pas les décès d'âge ou de sexe inconnus.

[51] Random rounding to base 3 is applied in this table as a confidentiality measure. - Les chiffres sont arrondis à la base 3 de manière aléatoire, pour des raisons de confidentialité.

[52] Includes deaths occurred in New Zealand but buried in Niue and deaths occurred in Niue but buried elsewhere. - Y compris les personnes décédées en Nouvelle-Zélande qui sont enterrées à Nioué et les personnes décédées à Nioué qui sont enterrées ailleurs.

[53] Estimate based on results of the Population Census. - Estimation fondeé sur les résultats du recensement de la population.

Table 20 – *Demographic Yearbook 2015*

Table 20 presents deaths and death rates by cause and sex for the two latest available years between 2010 and 2014.

Description of variables: Causes of death are all those diseases, morbid conditions or injuries which either resulted in or contributed to death and the circumstances of the accident or violence which produced any such injuries.[1]

The underlying cause of death, rather than direct or intermediate antecedent cause, is the one recommended as the main cause for tabulation of mortality statistics. It is defined as (a) the disease or injury which initiated the train of events leading directly to death, or (b) the circumstances of the accident or violence which produced the fatal injury.[1]

Statistics on deaths by cause presented in this table are provided by the World Health Organisation. They are limited to countries or areas that meet the criterion that cause-of-death statistics are classified to the ninth or tenth revisions of the International Classification of Diseases (ICD-9 or ICD-10). Data that are classified by the tenth revision are set in bold in the table.

Rate computation: Rates are the annual number of deaths in each cause group by sex reported for the year per 100 000 corresponding mid-year population. For certain causes, the population that more nearly approximates the population at risk is used as denominator, as specified below:
- rates for malignant neoplasm of female breast and malignant neoplasm of cervix uteri are computed per 100 000 female population 15 years and over;
- rates for hyperplasia of prostate are computed per 100 000 male population 50 years and over; and
- rates for direct and indirect obstetric causes, and rates for conditions originating in the perinatal period are computed per 100 000 total live births in the same year.

Rates presented in this table have been limited to those countries or areas having a total of at least 1 000 deaths from all causes in a given year. In certain cases death rates by cause have not been calculated because the population data needed for the denominator are not available (no data on population at risk are available). Moreover, rates based on 30 or fewer deaths shown in this table are identified by the symbol (♦).

Reliability of data: Countries and areas that have incomplete (less than 90 per cent completeness) or of unknown completeness of cause of deaths data coverage are considered unreliable and are set in *italics* rather than in roman type. Rates on these data are not computed. Information on completeness is normally provided by the World Health Organisation, when this is not the case, information on completeness is set to coincide with that of Table 18. Similarly, the reliability of data for the completeness of cause of death is provided by the World Health Organisation and it may differ from the reliability of data for the total number of reported deaths. Therefore, there are cases when the quality code in table 18 does not correspond with the typeface used in this table.

Territorial composition as set in Section 2.2 of "Technical Notes on the Statistical Tables", including or excluding certain population of a country refers only to the denominator.

Limitations: Statistics on deaths by cause are subject to the same qualifications as have been set forth for vital statistics in general and death statistics in particular as discussed in section 4 of the Technical Notes.

In considering cause-of-death statistics it is important to take account of the differences among countries or areas in the quality, availability, and efficiency of medical services, certification procedures, and coding practices. When a death is registered and reported for statistical purposes, the cause of death if available will be stated in the death registration form. This statement of cause may have several sources: (1) If the death has been followed by an autopsy, presumably the "true" cause will have been discovered; (2) If an autopsy is not performed but the decedent was treated prior to death by a medical attendant, the reported cause of death will reflect the opinion of that physician based on observation of the patient while he or she was alive; and (3) If, on the other hand, the decedent has died without medical attendance, the body

---

NOTES

[1] *International Statistical Classification of Diseases and Related Health Problems*, Tenth Revision, Volume 2, World Health Organization, Geneva, 1992

may be examined (without autopsy) by a physician who, aided by the questioning of persons who saw the patient before death, may come to a decision as to the probable cause of death. These three possible sources of information on cause of death constitute in general three degrees of decreasing accuracy in reporting.

Serious difficulties of comparability may stem also from differences in the form of death certificate being used, an increasing tendency to enter more than one cause of death on the certificate and diversity in the principles by which the primary or underlying cause is selected for statistical use when more than one is entered.

Differences in terminology used to identify the same disease also result in lack of comparability in statistics. These differences may arise in the same language in various parts of one country or area, but they are particularly troublesome between different languages.

Coding problems, and problems in interpretation of rules, arise constantly in using the various revisions of the International Statistical Classification of Diseases and Related Health Problems. Lack of uniformity between countries or areas in these interpretations and in adapting rules to national needs, results in a lack of comparability that can be observed in the statistics. It is particularly evident in causes that are coded differently according to the age of the decedent, such as pneumonia, diarrhoeal diseases and others. Changing interpretations and new rules can also introduce disparities into the time series for one country or area. Hence, large increases or decreases in deaths reported from specified diseases should be examined carefully for possible explanations in terms of coding practice, before they are accepted as changes in mortality.

Further limitations of statistics by cause of death result from the periodic revision of the International Classification of Diseases. Data might not be comparable among countries or areas if different revisions of the Classification were used. Similarly, comparison over time for one country or area is not appropriate if different revisions were applied in the country. For a correspondence between ICD-10 and ICD-9, please see table 20-1 below.

In addition to the qualifications explained in footnotes, particular care must be taken in using distributions with relatively large numbers of deaths attributed to ill-defined causes. Large frequencies in this category may indicate that cause of death among whole segments of the population has been undiagnosed, and the distribution of known causes in such cases is likely to be quite unrepresentative of the situation as a whole.

The possibility of error being introduced by the exclusion of deaths of infants who were born alive but died before the registration of the birth or within the first 24 hours of life should not be overlooked. These infant deaths are incorrectly classified as late foetal deaths. In several countries or areas, tabulation procedures have been devised to separate these pseudo-late-foetal deaths from true late foetal deaths and to incorporate them into the total deaths, but even in these cases there is no way of knowing the cause of death.

In addition, it should be noted that rates are affected also by the quality and limitations of the population at risk that are used in their computation. The problems of under-enumeration or over-enumeration and, to some extent, the differences in definition of population and live births have been discussed in section 3 of the Technical Notes dealing with population data in general and section 4 with vital statistics, respectively, Specific information pertaining to individual countries or areas is given in the footnotes to table 3 on total population and to table 9 on live births.

Earlier data: Deaths and death rates by cause have been shown annually since the 1951 issue of the *Demographic Yearbook* and every other year since the 2000 issue. For information on specific years covered, readers should consult the Historical Index.

Table 20-1. Tabulation list for ICD-9 and ICD-10 data for presentation in the Demographic Yearbook

Disease	ICD-10	ICD-9 Basic Tabulation List
All causes	**A00-Y89**	**01-56**
Certain infectious and parasitic diseases	**A00-A33, A35-B99**	**01-07, 184**
Intestinal infectious diseases	A00-A09	01
Tuberculosis	A15-A19	02
Tetanus[1]	A33, A35	037
Diphtheria	A36	033
Whooping cough	A37	034
Meningococcal infection	A39	036
Septicaemia	A40-A41	038
Acute poliomyelitis	A80	040
Measles	B05	042
Viral hepatitis	B15-B19	046
Human immunodeficiency virus [HIV] disease	B20-B24	184
Malaria	B50-B54	052
Neoplasms	**C00-D48**	**08-17**
Malignant neoplasms	**C00-C97**	**08-14**
Malignant neoplasm of lip, oral cavity and pharynx	C00-C14	08
Malignant neoplasm of oesophagus	C15	090
Malignant neoplasm of stomach	C16	091
Malignant neoplasm of colon, rectosigmoid junction, rectum, anus and anal canal	C18-C21	093-094
Malignant neoplasm of liver and intrahepatic bile ducts	C22	095
Malignant neoplasm of pancreas	C25	096
Malignant neoplasm of trachea, bronchus and lung	C33-C34	101
Malignant neoplasm of **female** breast	C50	113
Malignant neoplasm of cervix uteri	C53	120
Malignant neoplasm of prostate	C61	124
Malignant neoplasm of lymphoid, haematopoietic and related tissue	C81-C96	14
Disorders of the blood and blood-forming organs and certain disorders involving the immune mechanism	**D50-D89**	**20**
Anaemias	D50-D64	200
Endocrine, nutritional and metabolic diseases	**E00-E88**	**18-19, minus 184**
Diabetes mellitus	E10-E14	181
Malnutrition	E40-E46	190-192
Mental and behavioural disorders	**F01-F99**	**21**
Diseases of the nervous system	**G00-G98**	**22**
Diseases of the circulatory system	**I00-I99**	**25-30**
Acute rheumatic fever and chronic rheumatic heart diseases	I01-I09	25
Hypertensive diseases	I10-I13	26
Ischaemic heart diseases	I20-I25	27
Cerebrovascular diseases	I60-I69	29
Diseases of arteries, arterioles and capillaries	I70-I79	300-302
Diseases of the respiratory system	**J00-J98**	**31-32**
Influenza	J10-J11	322

Table 20-1. Tabulation list for ICD-9 and ICD-10 data for presentation in the Demographic Yearbook

Disease	ICD-10	ICD-9 Basic Tabulation List
Pneumonia	J12-J18	321
Chronic lower respiratory diseases	J40-J47	323-325
Diseases of the digestive system	**K00-K92**	**33-34**
Gastric and duodenal ulcer	K25-K27	341
Diseases of the liver	K70-K76	347
Diseases of the musculoskeletal system and connective tissue	**M00-M99**	**43**
Diseases of the genitourinary system	**N00-N98**	**35-37**
Disorders of kidney and ureter	N00-N28	350-351
Hyperplasia of prostate	N40	360
Pregnancy, childbirth and the puerperium	**O00-O99, A34**	**38-41**
Pregnancy with abortive outcome	O00-O07	38
Other direct obstetric causes[1]	O10-092, O95, A34	39
Indirect obstetric causes	O98-O99	40
Certain conditions originating in the perinatal period	**P00-P96**	**45**
Congenital malformations, deformations and chromosomal abnormalities	**Q00-Q99**	**44**
Symptoms, signs and abnormal clinical and laboratory findings, not elsewhere classified	**R00-R99**	**46**
All other diseases	**H00-H95, L00-L98**	**23-24, 42**
External causes	**V01-Y89**	**E47-E56**
Accidents	**V01-X59**	**E47-E53**
Transport accidents	V01-V99	E47
Falls	W00-W19	E50
Accidental drowning and submersion	W65-W74	E521
Exposure to smoke, fire and flames	X00-X09	E51
Accidental poisoning by and exposure to noxious substances	X40-X49	E48
Intentional self-harm	**X60-X84**	**E54**
Assault	**X85-Y09**	**E55**
All other external causes	Y10-Y89	E56

---

[1] In ICD-10 obstetrical tetanus is classified to A34 but in this table it is included with "Other direct obstetric causes", except for Belarus, Russian Federation, Seychelles, Turkmenistan and Ukraine, where obstetrical tetanus is included in "Tetanus" and "Other direct obstetric causes" excludes A34 and O95.

Tableau 20 - *Annuaire démographique 2015*

Le tableau 20 présente la statistique des décès par cause et sexe pour les deux dernières années entre 2010 et 2014.

Description des variables : les causes des décès sont toutes les maladies, états morbides ou traumatismes qui ont abouti ou contribué au décès et les circonstances de l'accident ou de la violence qui ont entraîné ces traumatismes[1].

La cause initiale de décès, plutôt que la cause directe du décès, est recommandée pour les statistiques de la mortalité. La cause initiale de décès est définie comme : a) la maladie ou le traumatisme qui a déclenché l'évolution morbide conduisant directement au décès ; b) les circonstances de l'accident ou de la violence qui ont entraîné le traumatisme mortel[1].

Les statistiques sur les décès classés en fonction de la cause qui les a provoqués émanent de l'Organisation mondiale de la santé. Elles ne portent que sur les pays ou les zones dans lesquels les statistiques relatives à la cause des décès sont conformes à la liste de la neuvième ou de la dixième révision de la *Classification statistique internationale des maladies* (CIM-9 ou CIM-10). Les données conformes à la liste de la dixième révision sont indiquées en caractères gras dans le tableau.

Calcul des taux : les taux représentent le nombre annuel de décès signalés dans chaque groupe, pour l'année, dans une population de 100 000 habitants en milieu d'année.

Les taux relatifs à certaines catégories de causes correspondent aux populations les plus semblables à la population exposée comme spécifié ci-dessous :
- les taux correspondant aux catégories « tumeur maligne du sein chez la femme » et « tumeur maligne du col de l'utérus » sont calculés sur une population de 100 000 femmes de 15 ans ou plus.
- les taux correspondant à la catégorie « tumeur maligne de la prostate » sont calculés sur une population de 100 000 personnes de sexe masculin âgées de 50 ans ou plus, et
- les taux pour les catégories « décès maternels directs », « décès maternels indirects » et « affections dont l'origine se situe dans la période périnatale » sont calculés sur 100 000 naissances vivantes dans la même année.

Les taux figurant dans ce tableau ne concernent que les pays ou zones où l'on a relevé au moins 1 000 décès, toutes causes confondues, dans l'année. Dans certains cas, on n'a pas calculé les taux de mortalité selon la cause car l'on ne disposait pas des informations sur la population qui étaient nécessaires pour déterminer le dénominateur (pas d'informations sur la population exposée au risque). De plus, les taux calculés sur la base de 30 décès ou moins, qui sont indiqués dans le tableau, sont signalés par le signe '♦'.

Fiabilité des données : les statistiques relatives aux pays et aux zones pour lesquels la couverture des données concernant les causes de décès est incomplète (mois de 90 pour cent) ou dont le degré de complétude n'est pas connue sont jugés douteuses et apparaissent en *italique* et non en caractères romains. Les taux correspondant ne sont pas calculés. L'information sur la complétude est normalement fournie par l'Organisation Mondiale de la Santé. Si ce n'est pas le cas, l'information sur la complétude est reprise de tableau 18. De même, la fiabilité des données relatives aux causes de décès est fournie par l'Organisation Mondiale de la Santé et peut différer de la fiabilité des données relatives au nombre de décès enregistrés. En conséquence, il peut apparaitre de différences entre les codes de fiabilité du tableau 18 et du présent tableau.

La composition territoriale est définie dans la Section 2.2 des "Notes Techniques sur les tableaux statistiques". L'inclusion ou l'exclusion de certaines populations d'un pays ne concerne que le dénominateur.

Insuffisance des données : les statistiques des décès selon la cause appellent les mêmes réserves que celles qui ont été formulées à propos des statistiques de l'état civil en général et des statistiques relatives aux décès en particulier (voir la section 4 des Notes techniques).

Lorsque l'on étudie les statistiques des causes des décès, il importe de prendre en considération les disparités existant entre pays ou zones du point de vue de la qualité, de la disponibilité et de l'efficacité des services médicaux, ainsi que des méthodes d'établissement des certificats de décès et des procédés de codage. Lorsqu'un décès est enregistré et déclaré aux fins de statistiques, le bulletin établi doit mentionner la cause du décès si elle est connue. Or la déclaration de la cause peut émaner de plusieurs sources : 1) si le décès a été suivi d'une autopsie, il est probable qu'on en aura décelé la cause « véritable » ; 2) s'il n'y a pas eu d'autopsie mais que le défunt a reçu, avant sa mort, les soins d'un médecin, la déclaration de la cause du décès reflétera l'opinion de ce médecin fondée sur l'observation du malade alors qu'il vivait encore ; 3) si, au contraire, le défunt est mort sans avoir reçu de soins médicaux, il se peut qu'un médecin examine le corps (sans qu'il soit fait d'autopsie), auquel cas il pourra, en questionnant les personnes qui ont vu le défunt avant sa mort, se former une opinion sur la cause probable du décès. À ces trois sources de renseignements possibles correspondent généralement trois degrés décroissants d'exactitude des données.

La comparabilité est aussi parfois très difficile à assurer par suite des différences existant dans la forme des certificats de décès utilisés, de la tendance croissante à indiquer plus d'une cause de décès sur le certificat et de la diversité des principes régissant le choix de la cause principale ou initiale à retenir dans les statistiques quand le certificat indique plus d'une cause.

Les différences entre les termes utilisés pour désigner une même maladie compromettent aussi la comparabilité des statistiques. On en rencontre parfois d'une région à l'autre dans un même pays ou une même zone où toute la population parle la même langue, mais elles sont particulièrement gênantes lorsque plusieurs langues interviennent.

En outre, des problèmes de codage et d'interprétation des règles se posent constamment lorsque l'on utilise les diverses révisions de la *Classification statistique internationale des maladies et des problèmes de santé connexes*. Les pays ou zones n'interprètent pas ces règles de manière uniforme et ne les adaptent pas de la même façon à leurs besoins ; la comparabilité s'en ressent comme le montrent les statistiques. Cela est particulièrement vrai pour les causes comme la pneumonie et les maladies diarrhéiques et autres, qui sont codées différemment selon l'âge du défunt. Les changements d'interprétation et l'adoption de nouvelles règles peuvent aussi introduire des divergences dans les séries chronologiques d'un même pays ou d'une même zone. En conséquence, il convient d'examiner attentivement les cas où le nombre de décès attribués à des maladies déterminées s'accroît ou diminue fortement, pour s'assurer, avant de conclure à une évolution de la mortalité, que le changement n'est pas dû à la méthode de codage.

D'autres irrégularités statistiques résultent des révisions périodiques de la *Classification statistique internationale des maladies*. Il est possible que les données ne soient pas comparables d'un pays ou d'une zone à un autre si différentes révisions de la classification ont été utilisées. De même, il n'est pas possible de comparer les données dans le temps pour un même pays ou zone lorsque différentes révisions y ont été utilisées. Pour une correspondance entre CIM-10 et CIM-9, veuillez voir le tableau 20-2 ci-dessous.

Outre les réserves expliquées dans les notes, il faut interpréter avec circonspection les répartitions comportant un nombre relativement élevé de décès attribués à des causes mal définies. Si les chiffres donnés pour cette catégorie sont importants, c'est peut-être parce que les décès survenus parmi des pans entiers de la population n'ont fait l'objet d'aucun diagnostic ; en pareil cas, il est probable que la répartition des causes connues est loin de donner une vue exacte de la situation d'ensemble.

Il ne faut pas négliger non plus le risque d'erreur que peut présenter l'exclusion des enfants nés vivants mais décédés avant l'enregistrement de leur naissance ou dans les 24 heures qui ont suivi la naissance. Ces décès sont classés à tort dans les morts fœtales tardives. Dans plusieurs pays ou zones, les méthodes d'exploitation permettent de différencier ces pseudo-morts fœtales tardives des morts fœtales tardives véritables et de les ajouter au nombre total des décès, mais, là encore, il est impossible de connaître la cause du décès.

De plus, il convient de noter que les taux sont également fonction de la qualité de l'évaluation de la population à risque et des caractéristiques de celle-ci dont il est tenu compte dans leur calcul. Les problèmes du sous-enregistrement et du sur-enregistrement et, à un certain degré, les différences entre les définitions de la population et des naissances vivantes ont été examinés, respectivement, à la section 3 des Notes techniques, qui traite des données démographiques en général, et à la section 4, qui traite des statistiques de l'état civil. Des informations sur certains pays ou certaines zones sont données dans les notes du tableau 3, relatif à la population totale, et dans celles du tableau 9, relatif aux naissances vivantes.

Données antérieures : Le nombre des décès et les taux de mortalité par cause ont été publiés chaque année dans les éditions de l'*Annuaire démographique* 1951 à 2000, et tous les deux ans depuis. Pour obtenir ces informations pour une année donnée, les lecteurs doivent se reporter à l'index historique.

Tableau 20-2. Liste de tabulation pour les données CIM-9 et CIM-10 pour la présentation dans l'annuaire démographique

Maladie	CIM-10	CIM-9 (Liste de base pour la mise en tableaux)
Toutes causes	**A00-Y89**	**01-56**
Certaines maladies infectieuses et parasitaires	**A00-A33, A35-B99**	**01-07, 184**
Maladies infectieuses intestinales	A00-A09	01
Tuberculose	A15-A19	02
Tétanos[2]	A33, A35	037
Diphtérie	A36	033
Coqueluche	A37	034
Infection à méningocoques	A39	036
Septicémie	A40-A41	038
Poliomyélite aiguë	A80	040
Rougeole	B05	042
Hépatite virale	B15-B19	046
Maladies dues au virus de l'immunodéficience humaine (VIH)	B20-B24	184
Malaria	B50-B54	052
Tumeurs	**C00-D48**	**08-17**
Tumeurs malignes	**C00-C97**	**08-14**
Tumeur maligne de la lèvre, de la cavité buccale et du pharynx	C00-C14	08
Tumeur maligne de l'oesophage	C15	090
Tumeur maligne de l'estomac	C16	091
sigmoïdienne, du rectum, de l'anus et du canal anal	C18-C21	093-094
Tumeur maligne du foie et des voies bilaires intrahépatiques	C22	095
Tumeur maligne du pancréas	C25	096
Tumeur maligne de la trachée, des bronches et du poumon	C33-C34	101
Tumeur maligne du sein chez la femme	C50	113
Tumeur maligne du col de l'utérus	C53	120
Tumeur maligne de la prostate	C61	124
Tumeurs malignes primitives ou présumées primitives des tissus lymphoïde, hématopoïétique et apparentés	C81-C96	14
Maladies du sang et des organes hématopoïétiques et certains troubles du système immunitaire	**D50-D89**	**20**
Anémies	D50-D64	200
Maladies endocriniennes, nutritionnelles et métaboliques	**E00-E88**	**18-19, minus 184**
Diabète sucré	E10-E14	181
Malnutrition	E40-E46	190-192
Troubles mentaux et du comportement	**F01-F99**	**21**
Maladies du système nerveux	**G00-G98**	**22**
Maladies de l'appareil circulatoire	**I00-I99**	**25-30**
Rhumatisme articularie aigu et cardiopathies rhumatismales chroniques	I01-I09	25
Maladies hypertensives	I10-I13	26
Cardiopathies ischémiques	I20-I25	27
Maladies cérébrovasculaires	I60-I69	29
Maladies des artères, artérioles et capillaires	I70-I79	300-302
Maladies de l'appareil respiratoire	**J00-J98**	**31-32**

Tableau 20-2. Liste de tabulation pour les données CIM-9 et CIM-10 pour la présentation dans l'annuaire démographique

Maladie	CIM-10	CIM-9 (Liste de base pour la mise en tableaux)
Grippe	J10-J11	322
Pneumopathies	J12-J18	321
Maladies chroniques des voies respiratoires inférieures	J40-J47	323-325
Maladies de l'appareil digestif	**K00-K92**	**33-34**
Ulcère de l'estomac et du duodénum	K25-K27	341
Maladies du foie	K70-K76	347
Maladies du système ostéo-articularie, des muscles et du tissu conjonctif	**M00-M99**	**43**
Maladies de l'appareil génito-urinaire	**N00-N98**	**35-37**
Affections du rein et de l'uretère	N00-N28	350-351
Hyperplasie de la prostate	N40	360
Grossesse, accouchement et puerpéralité	**O00-O99, A34**	**38-41**
Grossesse se terminant par un avortement	O00-O07	38
Autres décès maternels directs[2]	O10-092, O95, A34	39
Décès maternels indirects	O98-O99	40
Certaines affections dont l'origine se situe dans la période périnatale	**P00-P96**	**45**
Malformations congénitales et anomalies chromosomiques	**Q00-Q99**	**44**
Symptômes, signes et résultats anormaux d'examens cliniques et de laboratoire, non classés ailleurs	**R00-R99**	**46**
Toutes autres maladies	**H00-H95, L00-L98**	**23-24, 42**
Causes externes	**V01-Y89**	**E47-E56**
Accidents	**V01-X59**	**E47-E53**
Accidents de transport	V01-V99	E47
Chutes	W00-W19	E50
Noyade et submersion accidentelles	W65-W74	E521
Exposition à la fumée, au feu et aux flammes	X00-X09	E51
Intoxication accidentelle par des substances nocives et exposition à ces substances	X40-X49	E48
Lésions auto-infligées	**X60-X84**	**E54**
Agresssions	**X85-Y09**	**E55**
Toutes autres causes externes	Y10-Y89	E56

NOTES

[1] *Classification statistique internationale des maladies et des problèmes de santé connexes*, dixième révision, volume 2. Genève, Organisation mondiale de la santé, 1992.

[2] Dans la Classification internationale des maladies (CIM-10), le tétanos obstétrique est classé à la rubrique A34 mais, dans ce tableau, il est inclus dans les « Autres causes obstétriques directes », sauf pour Bélarus, Fédération de Russie, Seychelles, Turkménistan et Ukraine où le tétanos obstétrique est inclus dans « Tétanos » et « Autres causes obstétriques directes » exclut A34 et O95.

20. Death and death rates by cause and sex: 2010 - 2014
Décès et taux de mortalité par cause et sexe : 2010 - 2014

Cabo Verde

Cause of death — Cause de décès	2011 (C)				2012 (C)	
	Male — Masculin		Female — Féminin		Male — Masculin	Female — Féminin
	Number Nombre	Rate Taux	Number Nombre	Rate Taux	Number Nombre	Number Nombre
TOTAL	**1 483**	**580.8**	**1 038**	**381.7**	**1 477**	**1 287**
Certain infectious and parasitic diseases — Certaines maladies infectieuses et parasitaires						
Total	121	47.4	69	25.4	102	96
Intestinal infectious diseases — Maladies infectieuses intestinales	19	♦7.4	4	♦1.5	9	16
Tuberculosis — Tuberculose	17	♦6.7	7	♦2.6	11	6
Tetanus — Tétanos	2	♦0.8	-	-	-	-
Diphtheria — Diphtérie....................	-	-	-	-	-	-
Whooping cough — Coqueluche	-	-	-	-	-	-
Meningococcal infection — Infection à méningocoques....................	1	♦0.4	-	-	-	-
Septicaemia — Septicémie	37	14.5	35	12.9	28	43
Acute poliomyelitis — Poliomyélite aiguë	-	-	-	-	-	-
Measles — Rougeole....................	-	-	-	-	-	-
Viral hepatitis — Hépatite virale....................	1	♦0.4	2	♦0.7	3	2
Human immunodeficiency virus [HIV] disease — Maladies dues au virus de l'immunodéficience humaine (VIH)	40	15.7	20	♦7.4	51	28
Malaria — Paludisme....................	4	♦1.6	-	-	-	1
Neoplasms — Tumeurs	**207**	**81.1**	**131**	**48.2**	**202**	**183**
Malignant neoplasms — Tumeurs malignes						
Total	205	80.3	130	47.8	202	180
Malignant neoplasm of lip, oral cavity and pharynx — Tumeur maligne de la lèvre, de la cavité buccale et du pharynx	10	♦3.9	7	♦2.6	8	4
Malignant neoplasm of oesophagus — Tumeur maligne de l'oesophage	27	♦10.6	4	♦1.5	28	7
Malignant neoplasm of stomach — Tumeur maligne de l'estomac	32	12.5	14	♦5.1	32	20
Malignant neoplasm of colon, rectosigmoid junction, rectum, anus and anal canal — Tumeur maligne du côlon, de la jonction recto-sigmoïdienne, du rectum, de l'anus et du canal anal	5	♦2.0	7	♦2.6	8	8
Malignant neoplasm of liver and intrahepatic bile ducts — Tumeur maligne du foie et des voies bilaires intrahépatiques	24	♦9.4	10	♦3.7	14	18
Malignant neoplasm of pancreas — Tumeur maligne du pancréas....................	8	♦3.1	10	♦3.7	6	14
Malignant neoplasm of trachea, bronchus and lung — Tumeur maligne de la trachée, des bronches et du poumon	20	♦7.8	10	♦3.7	19	13
Malignant neoplasm of female breast — Tumeur maligne du sein chez la femme	..	..	18	♦9.8	..	13
Malignant neoplasm of cervix uteri — Tumeur maligne du col de l'utérus....................	..	..	10	♦5.5	..	20
Malignant neoplasm of prostate — Tumeur maligne de la prostate	34	129.0	..	..	46	..
Malignant neoplasm of lymphoid, haematopoietic and related tissue — Tumeurs malignes primitives ou présumées primitives des tissus lymphoïde, hématopoïétique et apparentés	12	♦4.7	3	♦1.1	10	15
Disorders of the blood and blood-forming organs and certain disorders involving the immune mechanism — Maladies du sang et des organes hématopoïétiques et certains troubles du système immunitaire						
Total	5	♦2.0	5	♦1.8	6	8
Anaemias — Anémies	5	♦2.0	5	♦1.8	5	7
Endocrine, nutritional and metabolic diseases — Maladies endocriniennes, nutritionnelles et métaboliques						
Total	19	♦7.4	45	16.5	37	51
Diabetes mellitus — Diabète sucré....................	17	♦6.7	40	14.7	27	46
Malnutrition — Malnutrition	1	♦0.4	2	♦0.7	4	2
Mental and behavioural disorders — Troubles mentaux et du comportement....................	**106**	**41.5**	**9**	**♦3.3**	**72**	**14**
Diseases of the nervous system — Maladies du système nerveux....................	**27**	**♦10.6**	**11**	**♦4.0**	**25**	**14**
Diseases of the circulatory system — Maladies de l'appareil circulatoire						
Total	318	124.5	337	123.9	306	385
Acute rheumatic fever and chronic rheumatic heart diseases — Rhumatisme articularie aigu et cardiopathies rhumatismales chroniques	-	-	1	♦0.4	1	-
Hypertensive diseases — Maladies hypertensives....................	26	♦10.2	15	♦5.5	18	35
Ischaemic heart disease — Cardiopathie ischémique....................	58	22.7	53	19.5	54	70
Cerebrovascular disease — Maladie cérébrovasculaire....................	130	50.9	160	58.8	146	156
Diseases of arteries, arterioles and capillaries — Maladies des artères, artérioles et capillaires	4	♦1.6	10	♦3.7	4	4

20. Death and death rates by cause and sex: 2010 - 2014
Décès et taux de mortalité par cause et sexe : 2010 - 2014

Cabo Verde

Cause of death — Cause de décès	2011 (C)				2012 (C)	
	Male — Masculin		Female — Féminin		Male — Masculin	Female — Féminin
	Number Nombre	Rate Taux	Number Nombre	Rate Taux	Number Nombre	Number Nombre
Diseases of the respiratory system — Maladies de l'appareil respiratoire						
Total	113	44.3	120	44.1	149	111
Influenza — Grippe	-	-	-	-	-	-
Pneumonia — Pneumopathies	71	27.8	55	20.2	96	67
Chronic lower respiratory diseases — Maladies chroniques des voies respiratoires inférieures	8	♦3.1	10	♦3.7	14	11
Diseases of the digestive system — Maladies de l'appareil digestif						
Total	61	23.9	30	♦11.0	52	36
Gastric and duodenal ulcer — Ulcère de l'estomac et du duodénum...............	1	♦0.4	2	♦0.7	1	3
Diseases of the liver — Maladies du foie...............	43	16.8	13	♦4.8	28	18
Diseases of the musculoskeletal system and connective tissue — Maladies du système ostéo-articulaire, des muscles et du tissu conjonctif	1	♦0.4	1	♦0.4	-	3
Diseases of the genitourinary system — Maladies de l'appareil génito-urinaire						
Total	27	♦10.6	13	♦4.8	34	27
Disorders of kidney and ureter — Affections du rein et de l'uretère	25	♦9.8	12	♦4.4	26	24
Hyperplasia of prostate — Hyperplasie de la prostate...............	-	-	..	..	3	..
Pregnancy, childbirth and the puerperium — Grossesse, accouchement et puerpéralité						
Total	..	..	5	...	..	1
Pregnancy with abortive outcome — Grossesse se terminant par un avortement...............	..	..	2	...	..	-
Other direct obstetric causes — Autres décès maternels directs	..	..	3	...	..	1
Indirect obstetric causes — Décès maternels indirects	..	..	-	...	..	-
Certain conditions originating in the perinatal period — Certaines affections dont l'origine se situe dans la période périnatale	93	...	48	...	133	110
Congenital malformations, deformations and chromosomal abnormalities — Malformations congénitales et anomalies chromosomiques	14	...	20	...	25	10
Symptoms, signs and abnormal clinical and laboratory findings, not elsewhere classified — Symptômes, signes et résultats anormaux d'examens cliniques et de laboratoire, non classés ailleurs	121	47.4	146	53.7	123	179
All other diseases — Toutes autres maladies...............	5	♦2.0	4	♦1.5	1	1
External causes — Causes externes						
Total	245	96.0	44	16.2	210	58
Accidents						
Total	44	17.2	7	♦2.6	35	11
Transport accidents — Accidents de transport	1	♦0.4	1	♦0.4	1	1
Falls — Chutes	-	-	-	-	-	-
Accidental drowning and submersion — Noyade et submersion accidentelles...............	33	12.9	3	♦1.1	25	6
Exposure to smoke, fire and flames — Exposition à la fumée, au feu et aux flammes	1	♦0.4	-	-	-	-
Accidental poisoning by and exposure to noxious substances — Intoxication accidentelle par des substances nocives et exposition à ces substances	-	-	-	-	-	-
Intentional self-harm — Lésions auto-infligées...............	37	14.5	5	♦1.8	37	8
Assault — Agresssions...............	44	17.2	7	♦2.6	45	10
All other external causes — Toutes autres causes externes	120	47.0	25	♦9.2	93	29

Egypt - Égypte

Cause of death — Cause de décès	2012 (C)				2013 (C)			
	Male — Masculin		Female — Féminin		Male — Masculin		Female — Féminin	
	Number Nombre	Rate Taux	Number Nombre	Rate Taux	Number Nombre	Rate Taux	Number Nombre	Rate Taux
TOTAL	290 816	698.8	238 417	599.3	284 189	657.6	226 994	548.1
Certain infectious and parasitic diseases — Certaines maladies infectieuses et parasitaires								
Total	10 337	24.8	7 963	20.0	9 631	22.3	7 378	17.8
Intestinal infectious diseases — Maladies infectieuses intestinales	2 187	5.3	2 553	6.4	1 809	4.2	1 921	4.6
Tuberculosis — Tuberculose	340	0.8	126	0.3	140	0.3	76	0.2
Tetanus — Tétanos	65	0.2	12	♦0.0	65	0.2	16	♦0.0
Diphtheria — Diphtérie....................................	-	-	-	-	-	-	-	-
Whooping cough — Coqueluche	2	♦0.0	-	-	-	-	-	-
Meningococcal infection — Infection à méningocoques	12	♦0.0	4	♦0.0	24	♦0.1	16	♦0.0
Septicaemia — Septicémie..............................	1 901	4.6	1 593	4.0	2 232	5.2	1 988	4.8
Acute poliomyelitis — Poliomyélite aiguë	8	♦0.0	6	♦0.0	4	♦0.0	7	♦0.0
Measles — Rougeole	15	♦0.0	7	♦0.0	-	-	3	♦0.0
Viral hepatitis — Hépatite virale	4 968	11.9	3 025	7.6	3 957	9.2	2 348	5.7
Human immunodeficiency virus [HIV] disease — Maladies dues au virus de l'immunodéficience humaine (VIH)........................	11	♦0.0	4	♦0.0	11	♦0.0	1	♦0.0
Malaria — Paludisme......................................	-	-	1	♦0.0	2	♦0.0	1	♦0.0
Neoplasms — Tumeurs	18 246	43.8	14 843	37.3	19 302	44.7	15 631	37.7
Malignant neoplasms — Tumeurs malignes								
Total	16 815	40.4	13 062	32.8	18 119	41.9	14 111	34.1
Malignant neoplasm of lip, oral cavity and pharynx — Tumeur maligne de la lèvre, de la cavité buccale et du pharynx	209	0.5	127	0.3	234	0.5	172	0.4
Malignant neoplasm of oesophagus — Tumeur maligne de l'oesophage	222	0.5	85	0.2	230	0.5	107	0.3
Malignant neoplasm of stomach — Tumeur maligne de l'estomac	818	2.0	697	1.8	936	2.2	811	2.0
Malignant neoplasm of colon, rectosigmoid junction, rectum, anus and anal canal — Tumeur maligne du côlon, de la jonction recto-sigmoïdienne, du rectum, de l'anus et du canal anal..........	748	1.8	695	1.7	816	1.9	697	1.7
Malignant neoplasm of liver and intrahepatic bile ducts — Tumeur maligne du foie et des voies bilaires intrahépatiques	4 073	9.8	1 835	4.6	4 736	11.0	2 221	5.4
Malignant neoplasm of pancreas — Tumeur maligne du pancréas..................	604	1.5	363	0.9	703	1.6	383	0.9
Malignant neoplasm of trachea, bronchus and lung — Tumeur maligne de la trachée, des bronches et du poumon	2 141	5.1	1 094	2.8	2 386	5.5	1 010	2.4
Malignant neoplasm of female breast — Tumeur maligne du sein chez la femme	..	..	2 290	8.2	..	..	2 512	8.7
Malignant neoplasm of cervix uteri — Tumeur maligne du col de l'utérus.........	..	..	135	0.5	..	..	137	0.5
Malignant neoplasm of prostate — Tumeur maligne de la prostate	684	11.0	..	..	738	11.6	..	..
Malignant neoplasm of lymphoid, haematopoietic and related tissue — Tumeurs malignes primitives ou présumées primitives des tissus lymphoïde, hématopoïétique et apparentés..........	1 943	4.7	1 567	3.9	1 876	4.3	1 559	3.8
Disorders of the blood and blood-forming organs and certain disorders involving the immune mechanism — Maladies du sang et des organes hématopoïétiques et certains troubles du système immunitaire								
Total	3 243	7.8	3 122	7.8	2 970	6.9	2 816	6.8
Anaemias — Anémies	379	0.9	440	1.1	379	0.9	489	1.2
Endocrine, nutritional and metabolic diseases — Maladies endocriniennes, nutritionnelles et métaboliques								
Total	6 035	14.5	6 968	17.5	5 382	12.5	6 231	15.0
Diabetes mellitus — Diabète sucré.....................	2 489	6.0	2 811	7.1	2 447	5.7	2 673	6.5
Malnutrition — Malnutrition	151	0.4	121	0.3	102	0.2	107	0.3
Mental and behavioural disorders — Troubles mentaux et du comportement	310	0.7	235	0.6	295	0.7	293	0.7
Diseases of the nervous system — Maladies du système nerveux...............	3 179	7.6	2 986	7.5	3 164	7.3	2 924	7.1
Diseases of the circulatory system — Maladies de l'appareil circulatoire								
Total	130 868	314.5	114 958	289.0	116 327	269.2	102 166	246.7
Acute rheumatic fever and chronic rheumatic heart diseases — Rhumatisme articularie aigu et cardiopathies rhumatismales chroniques	507	1.2	643	1.6	745	1.7	894	2.2
Hypertensive diseases — Maladies hypertensives............................	16 559	39.8	16 850	42.4	18 965	43.9	19 083	46.1
Ischaemic heart disease — Cardiopathie ischémique..................	12 001	28.8	9 712	24.4	10 411	24.1	8 250	19.9
Cerebrovascular disease — Maladie cérébrovasculaire....................	26 105	62.7	21 686	54.5	7 542	17.5	7 555	18.2

Egypt - Égypte

Cause of death — Cause de décès	2012 (C)				2013 (C)			
	Male — Masculin		Female — Féminin		Male — Masculin		Female — Féminin	
	Number Nombre	Rate Taux	Number Nombre	Rate Taux	Number Nombre	Rate Taux	Number Nombre	Rate Taux
Diseases of arteries, arterioles and capillaries — Maladies des artères, artérioles et capillaires	14 415	34.6	13 425	33.7	14 637	33.9	13 265	32.0
Diseases of the respiratory system — Maladies de l'appareil respiratoire								
Total	21 673	52.1	18 961	47.7	21 720	50.3	18 700	45.2
Influenza — Grippe	3	♦0.0	3	♦0.0	5	♦0.0	3	♦0.0
Pneumonia — Pneumopathies	8 651	20.8	7 829	19.7	8 553	19.8	7 646	18.5
Chronic lower respiratory diseases — Maladies chroniques des voies respiratoires inférieures	2 920	7.0	2 329	5.9	2 607	6.0	1 989	4.8
Diseases of the digestive system — Maladies de l'appareil digestif								
Total	36 721	88.2	22 519	56.6	35 027	81.0	21 389	51.6
Gastric and duodenal ulcer — Ulcère de l'estomac et du duodénum	188	0.5	140	0.4	163	0.4	161	0.4
Diseases of the liver — Maladies du foie	34 487	82.9	21 112	53.1	33 560	77.7	20 222	48.8
Diseases of the musculoskeletal system and connective tissue — Maladies du système ostéo-articularie, des muscles et du tissu conjonctif	177	0.4	151	0.4	220	0.5	170	0.4
Diseases of the genitourinary system — Maladies de l'appareil génito-urinaire								
Total	11 228	27.0	8 938	22.5	11 148	25.8	8 624	20.8
Disorders of kidney and ureter — Affections du rein et de l'uretère	11 035	26.5	8 839	22.2	10 992	25.4	8 531	20.6
Hyperplasia of prostate — Hyperplasie de la prostate	102	1.6	..	..	78	1.2	..	..
Pregnancy, childbirth and the puerperium — Grossesse, accouchement et puerpéralité								
Total	..	..	531	20.2	..	..	503	19.2
Pregnancy with abortive outcome — Grossesse se terminant par un avortement	..	..	15	♦0.6	..	..	14	♦0.5
Other direct obstetric causes — Autres décès maternels directs	..	..	493	18.7	..	..	471	18.0
Indirect obstetric causes — Décès maternels indirects	..	..	11	♦0.4	..	..	3	♦0.1
Certain conditions originating in the perinatal period — Certaines affections dont l'origine se situe dans la période périnatale	2 328	173.3	1 625	126.3	2 383	178.0	1 699	132.4
Congenital malformations, deformations and chromosomal abnormalities — Malformations congénitales et anomalies chromosomiques	4 403	327.7	3 746	291.2	4 668	348.7	3 857	300.6
Symptoms, signs and abnormal clinical and laboratory findings, not elsewhere classified — Symptômes, signes et résultats anormaux d'examens cliniques et de laboratoire, non classés ailleurs	27 218	65.4	26 530	66.7	34 445	79.7	30 380	73.4
All other diseases — Toutes autres maladies	168	0.4	288	0.7	172	0.4	231	0.6
External causes — Causes externes								
Total	14 682	35.3	4 053	10.2	17 335	40.1	4 002	9.7
Accidents								
Total	9 774	23.5	2 474	6.2	14 760	34.2	3 207	7.7
Transport accidents — Accidents de transport	5 829	14.0	1 241	3.1	7 571	17.5	1 515	3.7
Falls — Chutes	837	2.0	324	0.8	1 030	2.4	368	0.9
Accidental drowning and submersion — Noyade et submersion accidentelles	1 414	3.4	256	0.6	1 676	3.9	289	0.7
Exposure to smoke, fire and flames — Exposition à la fumée, au feu et aux flammes	259	0.6	181	0.5	416	1.0	380	0.9
Accidental poisoning by and exposure to noxious substances — Intoxication accidentelle par des substances nocives et exposition à ces substances	57	0.1	61	0.2	82	0.2	78	0.2
Intentional self-harm — Lésions auto-infligées	172	0.4	39	0.1	126	0.3	23	♦0.1
Assault — Agresssions	197	0.5	35	0.1	240	0.6	25	♦0.1
All other external causes — Toutes autres causes externes	4 539	10.9	1 505	3.8	2 209	5.1	747	1.8

20. Death and death rates by cause and sex: 2010 - 2014
Décès et taux de mortalité par cause et sexe : 2010 - 2014 (continued - suite)

Mauritius - Maurice

Cause of death — Cause de décès	2013 (+C)				2014 (+C)			
	Male — Masculin		Female — Féminin		Male — Masculin		Female — Féminin	
	Number Nombre	Rate Taux	Number Nombre	Rate Taux	Number Nombre	Rate Taux	Number Nombre	Rate Taux
TOTAL	**5 124**	**822.7**	**4 107**	**646.0**	**5 200**	**833.3**	**4 238**	**665.4**
Certain infectious and parasitic diseases — Certaines maladies infectieuses et parasitaires								
Total	204	32.8	93	14.6	160	25.6	61	9.6
Intestinal infectious diseases — Maladies infectieuses intestinales	13	◆2.1	25	◆3.9	13	◆2.1	5	◆0.8
Tuberculosis — Tuberculose	12	◆1.9	4	◆0.6	13	◆2.1	-	-
Tetanus — Tétanos	-	-	-	-	-	-	-	-
Diphtheria — Diphtérie	-	-	-	-	-	-	-	-
Whooping cough — Coqueluche	-	-	-	-	-	-	-	-
Meningococcal infection — Infection à méningocoques	-	-	-	-	-	-	-	-
Septicaemia — Septicémie	69	11.1	41	6.4	28	◆4.5	33	5.2
Acute poliomyelitis — Poliomyélite aiguë	-	-	-	-	-	-	-	-
Measles — Rougeole	-	-	-	-	-	-	-	-
Viral hepatitis — Hépatite virale	14	◆2.2	4	◆0.6	7	◆1.1	1	◆0.2
Human immunodeficiency virus [HIV] disease — Maladies dues au virus de l'immunodéficience humaine (VIH)	86	13.8	14	◆2.2	92	14.7	20	◆3.1
Malaria — Paludisme	-	-	-	-	-	-	-	-
Neoplasms — Tumeurs	**632**	**101.5**	**602**	**94.7**	**613**	**98.2**	**573**	**90.0**
Malignant neoplasms — Tumeurs malignes								
Total	599	96.2	579	91.1	583	93.4	556	87.3
Malignant neoplasm of lip, oral cavity and pharynx — Tumeur maligne de la lèvre, de la cavité buccale et du pharynx	51	8.2	18	◆2.8	32	5.1	14	◆2.2
Malignant neoplasm of oesophagus — Tumeur maligne de l'oesophage	31	5.0	15	◆2.4	24	◆3.8	5	◆0.8
Malignant neoplasm of stomach — Tumeur maligne de l'estomac	39	6.3	35	5.5	48	7.7	28	◆4.4
Malignant neoplasm of colon, rectosigmoid junction, rectum, anus and anal canal — Tumeur maligne du côlon, de la jonction recto-sigmoïdienne, du rectum, de l'anus et du canal anal	70	11.2	62	9.8	72	11.5	60	9.4
Malignant neoplasm of liver and intrahepatic bile ducts — Tumeur maligne du foie et des voies bilaires intrahépatiques	28	◆4.5	20	◆3.1	18	◆2.9	22	◆3.5
Malignant neoplasm of pancreas — Tumeur maligne du pancréas	29	◆4.7	20	◆3.1	46	7.4	23	◆3.6
Malignant neoplasm of trachea, bronchus and lung — Tumeur maligne de la trachée, des bronches et du poumon	117	18.8	42	6.6	121	19.4	36	5.7
Malignant neoplasm of female breast — Tumeur maligne du sein chez la femme	..	..	164	32.3	..	..	144	28.1
Malignant neoplasm of cervix uteri — Tumeur maligne du col de l'utérus	..	..	35	6.9	..	..	27	◆5.3
Malignant neoplasm of prostate — Tumeur maligne de la prostate	71	44.9	..	..	79	48.2	..	..
Malignant neoplasm of lymphoid, haematopoietic and related tissue — Tumeurs malignes primitives ou présumées primitives des tissus lymphoïde, hématopoïétique et apparentés	45	7.2	25	◆3.9	40	6.4	46	7.2
Disorders of the blood and blood-forming organs and certain disorders involving the immune mechanism — Maladies du sang et des organes hématopoïétiques et certains troubles du système immunitaire								
Total	25	◆4.0	19	◆3.0	23	◆3.7	41	6.4
Anaemias — Anémies	18	◆2.9	16	◆2.5	19	◆3.0	31	4.9
Endocrine, nutritional and metabolic diseases — Maladies endocriniennes, nutritionnelles et métaboliques								
Total	1 181	189.6	1 145	180.1	1 245	199.5	1 201	188.6
Diabetes mellitus — Diabète sucré	1 154	185.3	1 114	175.2	1 206	193.3	1 163	182.6
Malnutrition — Malnutrition	4	◆0.6	12	◆1.9	10	◆1.6	15	◆2.4
Mental and behavioural disorders — Troubles mentaux et du comportement	**76**	**12.2**	**6**	**◆0.9**	**53**	**8.5**	**8**	**◆1.3**
Diseases of the nervous system — Maladies du système nerveux	**78**	**12.5**	**63**	**9.9**	**82**	**13.1**	**59**	**9.3**
Diseases of the circulatory system — Maladies de l'appareil circulatoire								
Total	1 538	246.9	1 320	207.6	1 589	254.6	1 408	221.1
Acute rheumatic fever and chronic rheumatic heart diseases — Rhumatisme articularie aigu et cardiopathies rhumatismales chroniques	1	◆0.2	4	◆0.6	2	◆0.3	3	◆0.5
Hypertensive diseases — Maladies hypertensives	197	31.6	243	38.2	178	28.5	221	34.7
Ischaemic heart disease — Cardiopathie ischémique	653	104.8	459	72.2	705	113.0	534	83.8
Cerebrovascular disease — Maladie cérébrovasculaire	390	62.6	355	55.8	378	60.6	364	57.1

Mauritius - Maurice

Cause of death — Cause de décès	2013 (+C)				2014 (+C)			
	Male — Masculin		Female — Féminin		Male — Masculin		Female — Féminin	
	Number Nombre	Rate Taux	Number Nombre	Rate Taux	Number Nombre	Rate Taux	Number Nombre	Rate Taux
Diseases of arteries, arterioles and capillaries — Maladies des artères, artérioles et capillaires	13	♦2.1	10	♦1.6	14	♦2.2	3	♦0.5
Diseases of the respiratory system — Maladies de l'appareil respiratoire								
Total	466	74.8	329	51.7	529	84.8	378	59.3
Influenza — Grippe	-	-	1	♦0.2	-	-	-	-
Pneumonia — Pneumopathies	111	17.8	95	14.9	132	21.2	118	18.5
Chronic lower respiratory diseases — Maladies chroniques des voies respiratoires inférieures	140	22.5	74	11.6	148	23.7	82	12.9
Diseases of the digestive system — Maladies de l'appareil digestif								
Total	255	40.9	93	14.6	246	39.4	96	15.1
Gastric and duodenal ulcer — Ulcère de l'estomac et du duodénum	4	♦0.6	7	♦1.1	20	♦3.2	5	♦0.8
Diseases of the liver — Maladies du foie	157	25.2	34	5.3	131	21.0	35	5.5
Diseases of the musculoskeletal system and connective tissue — Maladies du système ostéo-articulaire, des muscles et du tissu conjonctif	10	♦1.6	9	♦1.4	10	♦1.6	24	♦3.8
Diseases of the genitourinary system — Maladies de l'appareil génito-urinaire								
Total	117	18.8	89	14.0	76	12.2	65	10.2
Disorders of kidney and ureter — Affections du rein et de l'uretère	100	16.1	79	12.4	58	9.3	48	7.5
Hyperplasia of prostate — Hyperplasie de la prostate	1	♦0.6	..	..	5	♦3.1	..	..
Pregnancy, childbirth and the puerperium — Grossesse, accouchement et puerpéralité								
Total	..	..	9	♦66.7	..	..	7	♦52.7
Pregnancy with abortive outcome — Grossesse se terminant par un avortement	..	..	1	♦7.4	..	..	-	-
Other direct obstetric causes — Autres décès maternels directs	..	..	4	♦29.7	..	..	4	♦30.1
Indirect obstetric causes — Décès maternels indirects	..	..	4	♦29.7	..	..	3	♦22.6
Certain conditions originating in the perinatal period — Certaines affections dont l'origine se situe dans la période périnatale	48	700.3	39	587.9	42	624.8	43	655.4
Congenital malformations, deformations and chromosomal abnormalities — Malformations congénitales et anomalies chromosomiques	28	♦408.5	17	♦256.3	24	♦357.0	31	472.5
Symptoms, signs and abnormal clinical and laboratory findings, not elsewhere classified — Symptômes, signes et résultats anormaux d'examens cliniques et de laboratoire, non classés ailleurs	89	14.3	132	20.8	91	14.6	89	14.0
All other diseases — Toutes autres maladies	14	♦2.2	16	♦2.5	21	♦3.4	27	♦4.2
External causes — Causes externes								
Total	363	58.3	126	19.8	396	63.5	127	19.9
Accidents								
Total	218	35.0	71	11.2	258	41.3	73	11.5
Transport accidents — Accidents de transport	116	18.6	28	♦4.4	128	20.5	30	♦4.7
Falls — Chutes	19	♦3.1	1	♦0.2	44	7.1	8	♦1.3
Accidental drowning and submersion — Noyade et submersion accidentelles	23	♦3.7	6	♦0.9	43	6.9	4	♦0.6
Exposure to smoke, fire and flames — Exposition à la fumée, au feu et aux flammes	9	♦1.4	12	♦1.9	7	♦1.1	13	♦2.0
Accidental poisoning by and exposure to noxious substances — Intoxication accidentelle par des substances nocives et exposition à ces substances	-	-	4	♦0.6	5	♦0.8	1	♦0.2
Intentional self-harm — Lésions auto-infligées	83	13.3	15	♦2.4	96	15.4	24	♦3.8
Assault — Agresssions	28	♦4.5	15	♦2.4	13	♦2.1	10	♦1.6
All other external causes — Toutes autres causes externes	34	5.5	25	♦3.9	29	♦4.6	20	♦3.1

	Mayotte				Morocco - Maroc			
Cause of death — Cause de décès	2012 (C)		2013 (C)		2011 (U)		2012 (U)	
	Male — Masculin	Female — Féminin	Male — Masculin	Female — Féminin	Male — Masculin	Female — Féminin	Male — Masculin	Female — Féminin
	Number Nombre	Number Nombre	Number Nombre	Number Nombre	Number Nombre	Number Nombre	Number Nombre	Number Nombre
TOTAL	232	221	248	166	27 881	19 811	27 431	20 268
Certain infectious and parasitic diseases — Certaines maladies infectieuses et parasitaires								
Total	10	7	7	3	1 059	751	1 066	699
Intestinal infectious diseases — Maladies infectieuses intestinales	1	1	1	-	51	49	74	60
Tuberculosis — Tuberculose	-	-	-	-	308	145	359	134
Tetanus — Tétanos	-	-	-	-	7	2	8	-
Diphtheria — Diphtérie	-	-	-	-	-	-	-	1
Whooping cough — Coqueluche	-	-	-	-	-	2	-	1
Meningococcal infection — Infection à méningocoques	-	-	-	-	1	4	1	-
Septicaemia — Septicémie	1	4	2	2	468	384	413	303
Acute poliomyelitis — Poliomyélite aiguë	-	-	-	-	-	-	-	-
Measles — Rougeole	-	-	-	-	2	-	-	-
Viral hepatitis — Hépatite virale	2	-	1	-	97	111	107	130
Human immunodeficiency virus [HIV] disease — Maladies dues au virus de l'immunodéficience humaine (VIH)	1	1	-	-	46	20	17	14
Malaria — Paludisme	-	-	-	-	-	-	1	3
Neoplasms — Tumeurs	31	42	43	27	2 592	1 873	2 960	2 090
Malignant neoplasms — Tumeurs malignes								
Total	31	41	40	26	2 415	1 702	2 837	2 000
Malignant neoplasm of lip, oral cavity and pharynx — Tumeur maligne de la lèvre, de la cavité buccale et du pharynx	1	-	-	1	65	26	66	37
Malignant neoplasm of oesophagus — Tumeur maligne de l'oesophage	-	-	-	-	30	22	31	15
Malignant neoplasm of stomach — Tumeur maligne de l'estomac	2	1	1	1	195	117	188	98
Malignant neoplasm of colon, rectosigmoid junction, rectum, anus and anal canal — Tumeur maligne du côlon, de la jonction recto-sigmoïdienne, du rectum, de l'anus et du canal anal	2	-	1	1	106	90	150	117
Malignant neoplasm of liver and intrahepatic bile ducts — Tumeur maligne du foie et des voies bilaires intrahépatiques	2	3	6	1	123	88	153	119
Malignant neoplasm of pancreas — Tumeur maligne du pancréas	1	1	5	2	122	53	115	74
Malignant neoplasm of trachea, bronchus and lung — Tumeur maligne de la trachée, des bronches et du poumon	5	2	1	2	549	95	695	134
Malignant neoplasm of female breast — Tumeur maligne du sein chez la femme	..	11	..	5	..	296	..	322
Malignant neoplasm of cervix uteri — Tumeur maligne du col de l'utérus	..	5	..	3	..	88	..	78
Malignant neoplasm of prostate — Tumeur maligne de la prostate	6	..	9	..	243	..	296	..
Malignant neoplasm of lymphoid, haematopoietic and related tissue — Tumeurs malignes primitives ou présumées primitives des tissus lymphoïde, hématopoïétique et apparentés	5	9	8	2	202	143	169	122
Disorders of the blood and blood-forming organs and certain disorders involving the immune mechanism — Maladies du sang et des organes hématopoïétiques et certains troubles du système immunitaire								
Total	1	1	1	-	184	127	164	152
Anaemias — Anémies	-	1	1	-	137	94	121	117
Endocrine, nutritional and metabolic diseases — Maladies endocriniennes, nutritionnelles et métaboliques								
Total	8	18	13	17	1 169	1 070	1 404	1 403
Diabetes mellitus — Diabète sucré	4	14	9	11	1 010	932	1 263	1 295
Malnutrition — Malnutrition	-	1	1	-	16	3	7	7
Mental and behavioural disorders — Troubles mentaux et du comportement	2	4	3	-	75	36	79	34
Diseases of the nervous system — Maladies du système nerveux	6	7	12	6	555	424	596	503
Diseases of the circulatory system — Maladies de l'appareil circulatoire								
Total	49	36	52	34	5 654	4 141	5 156	3 947
Acute rheumatic fever and chronic rheumatic heart diseases — Rhumatisme articularie aigu et cardiopathies rhumatismales chroniques	1	-	2	1	26	28	37	38
Hypertensive diseases — Maladies hypertensives	6	8	9	5	359	459	434	529
Ischaemic heart disease — Cardiopathie ischémique	5	2	7	1	420	188	510	186

20. Death and death rates by cause and sex: 2010 - 2014
Décès et taux de mortalité par cause et sexe : 2010 - 2014 (continued - suite)

	Mayotte				Morocco - Maroc			
	2012 (C)		2013 (C)		2011 (U)		2012 (U)	
Cause of death — Cause de décès	Male — Masculin	Female — Féminin	Male — Masculin	Female — Féminin	Male — Masculin	Female — Féminin	Male — Masculin	Female — Féminin
	Number Nombre	Number Nombre	Number Nombre	Number Nombre	Number Nombre	Number Nombre	Number Nombre	Number Nombre
Cerebrovascular disease — Maladie cérébrovasculaire	18	17	15	13	954	872	984	837
Diseases of arteries, arterioles and capillaries — Maladies des artères, artérioles et capillaires	1	-	3	1	61	19	43	12
Diseases of the respiratory system — Maladies de l'appareil respiratoire								
Total	6	12	9	9	1 577	819	1 514	816
Influenza — Grippe	-	-	-	-	6	6	3	7
Pneumonia — Pneumopathies	1	2	1	1	575	285	571	298
Chronic lower respiratory diseases — Maladies chroniques des voies respiratoires inférieures	2	2	3	7	360	153	325	166
Diseases of the digestive system — Maladies de l'appareil digestif								
Total	3	2	6	-	639	403	731	484
Gastric and duodenal ulcer — Ulcère de l'estomac et du duodénum	-	-	1	-	41	14	31	21
Diseases of the liver — Maladies du foie	2	-	3	-	273	210	286	205
Diseases of the musculoskeletal system and connective tissue — Maladies du système ostéo-articulaire, des muscles et du tissu conjonctif	1	-	-	-	36	43	42	35
Diseases of the genitourinary system — Maladies de l'appareil génito-urinaire								
Total	1	2	4	2	689	464	684	494
Disorders of kidney and ureter — Affections du rein et de l'uretère	1	2	2	1	583	438	581	479
Hyperplasia of prostate — Hyperplasie de la prostate	-	..	1	..	15	..	22	..
Pregnancy, childbirth and the puerperium — Grossesse, accouchement et puerpéralité								
Total	..	1	..	1	..	98	..	93
Pregnancy with abortive outcome — Grossesse se terminant par un avortement	..	1	..	-	..	2	..	1
Other direct obstetric causes — Autres décès maternels directs	..	-	..	1	..	89	..	88
Indirect obstetric causes — Décès maternels indirects	..	-	..	-	..	7	..	4
Certain conditions originating in the perinatal period — Certaines affections dont l'origine se situe dans la période périnatale	12	8	11	12	2 141	1 390	2 272	1 524
Congenital malformations, deformations and chromosomal abnormalities — Malformations congénitales et anomalies chromosomiques	12	9	6	4	259	214	315	236
Symptoms, signs and abnormal clinical and laboratory findings, not elsewhere classified — Symptômes, signes et résultats anormaux d'examens cliniques et de laboratoire, non classés ailleurs	66	55	59	41	8 185	7 168	7 359	6 860
All other diseases — Toutes autres maladies	-	-	3	2	22	31	21	25
External causes — Causes externes								
Total	24	17	19	8	3 045	759	3 068	873
Accidents								
Total	22	17	13	6	808	202	1 134	343
Transport accidents — Accidents de transport	6	3	2	-	482	107	596	185
Falls — Chutes	2	-	-	-	37	8	89	30
Accidental drowning and submersion — Noyade et submersion accidentelles	5	10	4	1	161	32	278	55
Exposure to smoke, fire and flames — Exposition à la fumée, au feu et aux flammes	-	1	1	2	10	5	4	5
Accidental poisoning by and exposure to noxious substances — Intoxication accidentelle par des substances nocives et exposition à ces substances	1	1	1	1	43	30	70	36
Intentional self-harm — Lésions auto-infligées	2	-	3	-	35	12	103	46
Assault — Agresssions	-	-	1	-	65	10	104	16
All other external causes — Toutes autres causes externes	-	-	2	2	2 137	535	1 727	468

Cause of death — Cause de décès	Reunion - Réunion				Seychelles			
	2012 (...)		2013 (...)		2013 (+C)		2014 (+C)	
	Male — Masculin	Female — Féminin	Male — Masculin	Female — Féminin	Male — Masculin	Female — Féminin	Male — Masculin	Female — Féminin
	Number Nombre	Number Nombre	Number Nombre	Number Nombre	Number Nombre	Number Nombre	Number Nombre	Number Nombre
TOTAL	*2 285*	*1 895*	*2 330*	*1 923*	*383*	*334*	*425*	*300*
Certain infectious and parasitic diseases — Certaines maladies infectieuses et parasitaires								
Total	*44*	*48*	*48*	*42*	*28*	*30*	*50*	*32*
Intestinal infectious diseases — Maladies infectieuses intestinales	*8*	*16*	*12*	*10*	*3*	*2*	*1*	*2*
Tuberculosis — Tuberculose	*2*	*1*	*2*	*-*	*1*	*1*	*-*	*-*
Tetanus — Tétanos	*-*	*-*	*-*	*-*	*-*	*-*	*-*	*-*
Diphtheria — Diphtérie	*-*	*-*	*-*	*-*	*-*	*-*	*-*	*-*
Whooping cough — Coqueluche	*-*	*-*	*-*	*-*	*-*	*-*	*-*	*-*
Meningococcal infection — Infection à méningocoques	*-*	*-*	*-*	*-*	*-*	*-*	*-*	*-*
Septicaemia — Septicémie	*20*	*21*	*20*	*23*	*17*	*23*	*26*	*23*
Acute poliomyelitis — Poliomyélite aiguë	*-*	*-*	*-*	*-*	*-*	*-*	*-*	*-*
Measles — Rougeole	*-*	*-*	*-*	*-*	*-*	*-*	*-*	*-*
Viral hepatitis — Hépatite virale	*2*	*1*	*5*	*3*	*-*	*1*	*1*	*-*
Human immunodeficiency virus [HIV] disease — Maladies dues au virus de l'immunodéficience humaine (VIH)	*2*	*-*	*3*	*1*	*-*	*3*	*9*	*6*
Malaria — Paludisme	*1*	*-*	*-*	*-*	*-*	*-*	*-*	*-*
Neoplasms — Tumeurs	*660*	*446*	*609*	*390*	*68*	*51*	*69*	*56*
Malignant neoplasms — Tumeurs malignes								
Total	*630*	*420*	*593*	*374*	*68*	*50*	*69*	*56*
Malignant neoplasm of lip, oral cavity and pharynx — Tumeur maligne de la lèvre, de la cavité buccale et du pharynx	*28*	*6*	*38*	*1*	*6*	*2*	*11*	*1*
Malignant neoplasm of oesophagus — Tumeur maligne de l'oesophage	*32*	*8*	*40*	*1*	*3*	*-*	*2*	*-*
Malignant neoplasm of stomach — Tumeur maligne de l'estomac	*55*	*23*	*39*	*25*	*5*	*1*	*2*	*4*
Malignant neoplasm of colon, rectosigmoid junction, rectum, anus and anal canal — Tumeur maligne du côlon, de la jonction recto-sigmoïdienne, du rectum, de l'anus et du canal anal	*43*	*44*	*58*	*52*	*14*	*4*	*11*	*13*
Malignant neoplasm of liver and intrahepatic bile ducts — Tumeur maligne du foie et des voies bilaires intrahépatiques	*41*	*18*	*41*	*21*	*2*	*1*	*6*	*2*
Malignant neoplasm of pancreas — Tumeur maligne du pancréas	*24*	*38*	*19*	*18*	*1*	*-*	*3*	*1*
Malignant neoplasm of trachea, bronchus and lung — Tumeur maligne de la trachée, des bronches et du poumon	*140*	*31*	*135*	*27*	*7*	*-*	*7*	*3*
Malignant neoplasm of female breast — Tumeur maligne du sein chez la femme	*..*	*52*	*..*	*62*	*..*	*11*	*..*	*10*
Malignant neoplasm of cervix uteri — Tumeur maligne du col de l'utérus	*..*	*17*	*..*	*16*	*..*	*5*	*..*	*7*
Malignant neoplasm of prostate — Tumeur maligne de la prostate	*80*	*..*	*49*	*..*	*15*	*..*	*15*	*..*
Malignant neoplasm of lymphoid, haematopoietic and related tissue — Tumeurs malignes primitives ou présumées primitives des tissus lymphoïde, hématopoïétique et apparentés	*47*	*47*	*43*	*31*	*...*	*...*	*...*	*...*
Disorders of the blood and blood-forming organs and certain disorders involving the immune mechanism — Maladies du sang et des organes hématopoïétiques et certains troubles du système immunitaire								
Total	*4*	*5*	*6*	*9*	*5*	*5*	*6*	*9*
Anaemias — Anémies	*1*	*3*	*4*	*4*	*5*	*5*	*5*	*8*
Endocrine, nutritional and metabolic diseases — Maladies endocriniennes, nutritionnelles et métaboliques								
Total	*112*	*154*	*127*	*152*	*7*	*6*	*9*	*9*
Diabetes mellitus — Diabète sucré	*97*	*122*	*101*	*113*	*3*	*4*	*8*	*9*
Malnutrition — Malnutrition	*2*	*6*	*8*	*11*	*1*	*-*	*-*	*-*
Mental and behavioural disorders — Troubles mentaux et du comportement	*97*	*55*	*82*	*41*	*1*	*1*	*1*	*1*
Diseases of the nervous system — Maladies du système nerveux	*72*	*99*	*72*	*94*	*10*	*1*	*3*	*3*
Diseases of the circulatory system — Maladies de l'appareil circulatoire								
Total	*519*	*560*	*506*	*544*	*96*	*128*	*108*	*94*
Acute rheumatic fever and chronic rheumatic heart diseases — Rhumatisme articularie aigu et cardiopathies rhumatismales chroniques	*6*	*9*	*2*	*12*	*-*	*-*	*2*	*1*
Hypertensive diseases — Maladies hypertensives	*30*	*51*	*38*	*58*	*12*	*32*	*20*	*38*
Ischaemic heart disease — Cardiopathie ischémique	*149*	*137*	*159*	*123*	*16*	*22*	*24*	*12*

	Reunion - Réunion				Seychelles			
	2012 (...)		2013 (...)		2013 (+C)		2014 (+C)	
Cause of death — Cause de décès	Male — Masculin	Female — Féminin	Male — Masculin	Female — Féminin	Male — Masculin	Female — Féminin	Male — Masculin	Female — Féminin
	Number Nombre	Number Nombre	Number Nombre	Number Nombre	Number Nombre	Number Nombre	Number Nombre	Number Nombre
Cerebrovascular disease — Maladie cérébrovasculaire..................................	151	166	145	173	24	28	24	8
Diseases of arteries, arterioles and capillaries — Maladies des artères, artérioles et capillaires	30	17	24	19	...	...	...	...
Diseases of the respiratory system — Maladies de l'appareil respiratoire								
Total	158	121	160	132	62	55	54	41
Influenza — Grippe	4	5	5	6	-	-	-	-
Pneumonia — Pneumopathies	31	34	35	38	43	41	36	29
Chronic lower respiratory diseases — Maladies chroniques des voies respiratoires inférieures	69	35	69	34	14	9	12	4
Diseases of the digestive system — Maladies de l'appareil digestif								
Total	115	67	125	76	31	18	37	17
Gastric and duodenal ulcer — Ulcère de l'estomac et du duodénum...............	6	-	5	2	4	2	4	1
Diseases of the liver — Maladies du foie...	57	27	69	40	10	5	16	8
Diseases of the musculoskeletal system and connective tissue — Maladies du système ostéo-articularie, des muscles et du tissu conjonctif	10	20	8	16	-	-	-	-
Diseases of the genitourinary system — Maladies de l'appareil génito-urinaire								
Total	34	35	31	38	21	20	30	17
Disorders of kidney and ureter — Affections du rein et de l'uretère	25	28	26	31	...	...	...	...
Hyperplasia of prostate — Hyperplasie de la prostate...................................	-	..	-	..	...	...	...	..
Pregnancy, childbirth and the puerperium — Grossesse, accouchement et puerpéralité								
Total	..	2	..	2	..	-	..	-
Pregnancy with abortive outcome — Grossesse se terminant par un avortement	..	-	..	-	..	-	..	-
Other direct obstetric causes — Autres décès maternels directs	..	1	..	1	..	-	..	-
Indirect obstetric causes — Décès maternels indirects	..	1	..	1	..	-	..	-
Certain conditions originating in the perinatal period — Certaines affections dont l'origine se situe dans la période périnatale	37	27	26	19	5	3	8	3
Congenital malformations, deformations and chromosomal abnormalities — Malformations congénitales et anomalies chromosomiques	20	22	7	17	-	2	6	-
Symptoms, signs and abnormal clinical and laboratory findings, not elsewhere classified — Symptômes, signes et résultats anormaux d'examens cliniques et de laboratoire, non classés ailleurs	163	142	281	265	8	7	9	4
All other diseases — Toutes autres maladies..	4	2	2	4	-	1	1	2
External causes — Causes externes								
Total	236	90	240	82	41	6	34	12
Accidents								
Total	153	68	141	59	...	...	...	...
Transport accidents — Accidents de transport	45	5	31	5	9	1	8	4
Falls — Chutes	24	16	25	11	2	-	2	-
Accidental drowning and submersion — Noyade et submersion accidentelles..	6	5	8	3	11	1	8	4
Exposure to smoke, fire and flames — Exposition à la fumée, au feu et aux flammes	3	2	7	3	3	-	3	-
Accidental poisoning by and exposure to noxious substances — Intoxication accidentelle par des substances nocives et exposition à ces substances	30	7	22	8	-	-	-	-
Intentional self-harm — Lésions auto-infligées...	69	15	76	16	9	-	2	2
Assault — Agresssions	11	3	9	3	2	2	6	2
All other external causes — Toutes autres causes externes	3	4	14	4	...	...	...	...

20. Death and death rates by cause and sex: 2010 - 2014
Décès et taux de mortalité par cause et sexe : 2010 - 2014 (continued - suite)

South Africa - Afrique du Sud

Cause of death — Cause de décès	2013 (C)				2014 (C)			
	Male — Masculin		Female — Féminin		Male — Masculin		Female — Féminin	
	Number Nombre	Rate Taux	Number Nombre	Rate Taux	Number Nombre	Rate Taux	Number Nombre	Rate Taux
TOTAL	**239 188**	**926.2**	**217 747**	**801.8**	**236 613**	**897.4**	**214 826**	**777.3**
Certain infectious and parasitic diseases — Certaines maladies infectieuses et parasitaires								
Total	54 469	210.9	48 808	179.7	52 412	198.8	45 980	166.4
Intestinal infectious diseases — Maladies infectieuses intestinales	7 441	28.8	8 259	30.4	6 795	25.8	7 607	27.5
Tuberculosis — Tuberculose	23 791	92.1	16 582	61.1	22 545	85.5	15 174	54.9
Tetanus — Tétanos	8	♦0.0	1	♦0.0	7	♦0.0	4	♦0.0
Diphtheria — Diphtérie	1	♦0.0	1	♦0.0	-	-	-	-
Whooping cough — Coqueluche	1	♦0.0	-	-	2	♦0.0	-	-
Meningococcal infection — Infection à méningocoques	29	♦0.1	22	♦0.1	23	♦0.1	34	0.1
Septicaemia — Septicémie	2 421	9.4	2 895	10.7	2 452	9.3	3 066	11.1
Acute poliomyelitis — Poliomyélite aiguë	-	-	-	-	-	-	-	-
Measles — Rougeole	3	♦0.0	4	♦0.0	1	♦0.0	3	♦0.0
Viral hepatitis — Hépatite virale	188	0.7	128	0.5	166	0.6	113	0.4
Human immunodeficiency virus [HIV] disease — Maladies dues au virus de l'immunodéficience humaine (VIH)	11 643	45.1	11 481	42.3	11 160	42.3	10 685	38.7
Malaria — Paludisme	152	0.6	89	0.3	227	0.9	156	0.6
Neoplasms — Tumeurs	**19 019**	**73.7**	**18 959**	**69.8**	**19 319**	**73.3**	**19 776**	**71.6**
Malignant neoplasms — Tumeurs malignes								
Total	18 373	71.1	18 298	67.4	18 668	70.8	19 098	69.1
Malignant neoplasm of lip, oral cavity and pharynx — Tumeur maligne de la lèvre, de la cavité buccale et du pharynx	778	3.0	336	1.2	737	2.8	297	1.1
Malignant neoplasm of oesophagus — Tumeur maligne de l'oesophage	1 638	6.3	1 021	3.8	1 683	6.4	1 089	3.9
Malignant neoplasm of stomach — Tumeur maligne de l'estomac	706	2.7	455	1.7	631	2.4	471	1.7
Malignant neoplasm of colon, rectosigmoid junction, rectum, anus and anal canal — Tumeur maligne du côlon, de la jonction recto-sigmoïdienne, du rectum, de l'anus et du canal anal	1 206	4.7	1 048	3.9	1 239	4.7	1 142	4.1
Malignant neoplasm of liver and intrahepatic bile ducts — Tumeur maligne du foie et des voies bilaires intrahépatiques	977	3.8	603	2.2	983	3.7	581	2.1
Malignant neoplasm of pancreas — Tumeur maligne du pancréas	656	2.5	616	2.3	671	2.5	659	2.4
Malignant neoplasm of trachea, bronchus and lung — Tumeur maligne de la trachée, des bronches et du poumon	3 443	13.3	1 699	6.3	3 522	13.4	1 720	6.2
Malignant neoplasm of female breast — Tumeur maligne du sein chez la femme	..	..	3 034	15.6	..	..	3 122	15.9
Malignant neoplasm of cervix uteri — Tumeur maligne du col de l'utérus	..	..	3 111	16.0	..	..	3 444	17.6
Malignant neoplasm of prostate — Tumeur maligne de la prostate	2 675	76.1	..	..	2 729	70.5	..	..
Malignant neoplasm of lymphoid, haematopoietic and related tissue — Tumeurs malignes primitives ou présumées primitives des tissus lymphoïde, hématopoïétique et apparentés	1 485	5.8	1 319	4.9	1 532	5.8	1 316	4.8
Disorders of the blood and blood-forming organs and certain disorders involving the immune mechanism — Maladies du sang et des organes hématopoïétiques et certains troubles du système immunitaire								
Total	4 830	18.7	5 483	20.2	4 466	16.9	5 100	18.5
Anaemias — Anémies	905	3.5	1 340	4.9	868	3.3	1 258	4.6
Endocrine, nutritional and metabolic diseases — Maladies endocriniennes, nutritionnelles et métaboliques								
Total	11 859	45.9	17 075	62.9	12 137	46.0	17 465	63.2
Diabetes mellitus — Diabète sucré	8 699	33.7	13 484	49.6	8 914	33.8	13 819	50.0
Malnutrition — Malnutrition	872	3.4	729	2.7	1 006	3.8	858	3.1
Mental and behavioural disorders — Troubles mentaux et du comportement	**835**	**3.2**	**945**	**3.5**	**900**	**3.4**	**1 091**	**3.9**
Diseases of the nervous system — Maladies du système nerveux	**6 046**	**23.4**	**4 926**	**18.1**	**5 722**	**21.7**	**4 520**	**16.4**
Diseases of the circulatory system — Maladies de l'appareil circulatoire								
Total	34 334	133.0	42 009	154.7	35 140	133.3	42 985	155.5
Acute rheumatic fever and chronic rheumatic heart diseases — Rhumatisme articularie aigu et cardiopathies rhumatismales chroniques	120	0.5	245	0.9	122	0.5	203	0.7
Hypertensive diseases — Maladies hypertensives	6 352	24.6	10 388	38.2	6 670	25.3	11 081	40.1
Ischaemic heart disease — Cardiopathie ischémique	6 330	24.5	4 732	17.4	6 200	23.5	4 696	17.0
Cerebrovascular disease — Maladie cérébrovasculaire	9 518	36.9	12 920	47.6	9 908	37.6	13 149	47.6

20. Death and death rates by cause and sex: 2010 - 2014
Décès et taux de mortalité par cause et sexe : 2010 - 2014 (continued - suite)

South Africa - Afrique du Sud

Cause of death — Cause de décès	2013 (C)				2014 (C)			
	Male — Masculin		Female — Féminin		Male — Masculin		Female — Féminin	
	Number Nombre	Rate Taux	Number Nombre	Rate Taux	Number Nombre	Rate Taux	Number Nombre	Rate Taux
Diseases of arteries, arterioles and capillaries — Maladies des artères, artérioles et capillaires	849	3.3	537	2.0	840	3.2	606	2.2
Diseases of the respiratory system — Maladies de l'appareil respiratoire								
Total	25 859	100.1	21 668	79.8	24 576	93.2	20 649	74.7
Influenza — Grippe	216	0.8	278	1.0	192	0.7	280	1.0
Pneumonia — Pneumopathies	11 915	46.1	11 202	41.2	11 011	41.8	10 459	37.8
Chronic lower respiratory diseases — Maladies chroniques des voies respiratoires inférieures	7 262	28.1	4 757	17.5	7 300	27.7	4 785	17.3
Diseases of the digestive system — Maladies de l'appareil digestif								
Total	6 422	24.9	5 458	20.1	6 358	24.1	5 537	20.0
Gastric and duodenal ulcer — Ulcère de l'estomac et du duodénum	725	2.8	764	2.8	766	2.9	720	2.6
Diseases of the liver — Maladies du foie	2 418	9.4	1 698	6.3	2 390	9.1	1 770	6.4
Diseases of the musculoskeletal system and connective tissue — Maladies du système ostéo-articulaire, des muscles et du tissu conjonctif	530	2.1	980	3.6	597	2.3	1 020	3.7
Diseases of the genitourinary system — Maladies de l'appareil génito-urinaire								
Total	4 532	17.6	4 245	15.6	4 534	17.2	4 220	15.3
Disorders of kidney and ureter — Affections du rein et de l'uretère	4 075	15.8	3 799	14.0	4 101	15.6	3 776	13.7
Hyperplasia of prostate — Hyperplasie de la prostate	146	4.2	..	..	156	4.0	..	..
Pregnancy, childbirth and the puerperium — Grossesse, accouchement et puerpéralité								
Total	..	..	946	94.5	..	..	1 027	103.9
Pregnancy with abortive outcome — Grossesse se terminant par un avortement	..	..	107	10.7	..	..	103	10.4
Other direct obstetric causes — Autres décès maternels directs	..	..	547	54.6	..	..	612	61.9
Indirect obstetric causes — Décès maternels indirects	..	..	292	29.2	..	..	312	31.6
Certain conditions originating in the perinatal period — Certaines affections dont l'origine se situe dans la période périnatale	5 085	...	4 119	...	5 041	...	4 035	...
Congenital malformations, deformations and chromosomal abnormalities — Malformations congénitales et anomalies chromosomiques	977	...	947	...	1 127	...	967	...
Symptoms, signs and abnormal clinical and laboratory findings, not elsewhere classified — Symptômes, signes et résultats anormaux d'examens cliniques et de laboratoire, non classés ailleurs	28 299	109.6	29 549	108.8	27 614	104.7	28 937	104.7
All other diseases — Toutes autres maladies	380	1.5	521	1.9	363	1.4	500	1.8
External causes — Causes externes								
Total	35 712	138.3	11 109	40.9	36 307	137.7	11 017	39.9
Accidents								
Total	24 187	93.7	7 874	29.0	23 998	91.0	7 736	28.0
Transport accidents — Accidents de transport	4 190	16.2	1 476	5.4	4 393	16.7	1 504	5.4
Falls — Chutes	129	0.5	52	0.2	129	0.5	54	0.2
Accidental drowning and submersion — Noyade et submersion accidentelles	1 158	4.5	353	1.3	1 225	4.6	343	1.2
Exposure to smoke, fire and flames — Exposition à la fumée, au feu et aux flammes	1 372	5.3	843	3.1	1 416	5.4	854	3.1
Accidental poisoning by and exposure to noxious substances — Intoxication accidentelle par des substances nocives et exposition à ces substances	459	1.8	328	1.2	477	1.8	382	1.4
Intentional self-harm — Lésions auto-infligées	470	1.8	120	0.4	461	1.7	121	0.4
Assault — Agresssions	4 393	17.0	588	2.2	4 670	17.7	601	2.2
All other external causes — Toutes autres causes externes	6 662	25.8	2 527	9.3	7 178	27.2	2 559	9.3

20. Death and death rates by cause and sex: 2010 - 2014
Décès et taux de mortalité par cause et sexe : 2010 - 2014 (continued - suite)

Cause of death — Cause de décès	Tunisia - Tunisie		Anguilla				Antigua and Barbuda - Antigua-et-Barbuda	
	2013 (U)		2013 (...)		2014 (...)		2012 (+U)	
	Male — Masculin	Female — Féminin	Male — Masculin	Female — Féminin	Male — Masculin	Female — Féminin	Male — Masculin	Female — Féminin
	Number Nombre	Number Nombre	Number Nombre	Number Nombre	Number Nombre	Number Nombre	Number Nombre	Number Nombre
TOTAL	12 439	9 446	43	35	39	20	277	216
Certain infectious and parasitic diseases — Certaines maladies infectieuses et parasitaires								
Total	411	273	-	-	-	1	22	13
Intestinal infectious diseases — Maladies infectieuses intestinales	22	18	-	-	-	-	-	1
Tuberculosis — Tuberculose	53	11	-	-	-	-	-	-
Tetanus — Tétanos...	2	-	-	-	-	-	-	-
Diphtheria — Diphtérie...	-	-	-	-	-	-	-	-
Whooping cough — Coqueluche	1	5	-	-	-	-	-	-
Meningococcal infection — Infection à méningocoques............	1	1	-	-	-	-	-	-
Septicaemia — Septicémie...	231	181	-	-	-	1	9	8
Acute poliomyelitis — Poliomyélite aiguë	-	-	-	-	-	-	-	-
Measles — Rougeole...	1	-	-	-	-	-	-	-
Viral hepatitis — Hépatite virale....................................	52	20	-	-	-	-	-	-
Human immunodeficiency virus [HIV] disease — Maladies dues au virus de l'immunodéficience humaine (VIH)................	3	4	-	-	-	-	11	2
Malaria — Paludisme...	-	-	-	-	-	-	-	-
Neoplasms — Tumeurs	2 164	1 294	9	9	8	3	60	43
Malignant neoplasms — Tumeurs malignes								
Total	2 073	1 240	9	9	7	3	56	41
Malignant neoplasm of lip, oral cavity and pharynx — Tumeur maligne de la lèvre, de la cavité buccale et du pharynx	64	29	-	-	-	-	2	1
Malignant neoplasm of oesophagus — Tumeur maligne de l'oesophage	14	6	1	-	-	-	-	-
Malignant neoplasm of stomach — Tumeur maligne de l'estomac	91	59	2	1	1	-	2	1
Malignant neoplasm of colon, rectosigmoid junction, rectum, anus and anal canal — Tumeur maligne du côlon, de la jonction recto-sigmoïdienne, du rectum, de l'anus et du canal anal.................................	147	132	-	1	1	-	5	5
Malignant neoplasm of liver and intrahepatic bile ducts — Tumeur maligne du foie et des voies bilaires intrahépatiques	101	90	1	-	-	-	3	2
Malignant neoplasm of pancreas — Tumeur maligne du pancréas.................	91	55	-	-	-	-	-	-
Malignant neoplasm of trachea, bronchus and lung — Tumeur maligne de la trachée, des bronches et du poumon................................	703	112	-	-	-	-	7	1
Malignant neoplasm of female breast — Tumeur maligne du sein chez la femme	..	255	..	2	..	-	..	11
Malignant neoplasm of cervix uteri — Tumeur maligne du col de l'utérus.........	..	11	..	-	..	2	..	4
Malignant neoplasm of prostate — Tumeur maligne de la prostate	219	..	4	..	3	..	29	..
Malignant neoplasm of lymphoid, haematopoietic and related tissue — Tumeurs malignes primitives ou présumées primitives des tissus lymphoïde, hématopoïétique et apparentés..................................	141	108	-	-	-	1	4	4
Disorders of the blood and blood-forming organs and certain disorders involving the immune mechanism — Maladies du sang et des organes hématopoïétiques et certains troubles du système immunitaire								
Total	52	49	1	1	2	-	5	4
Anaemias — Anémies	31	27	1	1	1	-	4	4
Endocrine, nutritional and metabolic diseases — Maladies endocriniennes, nutritionnelles et métaboliques								
Total	972	1 010	3	2	4	4	24	29
Diabetes mellitus — Diabète sucré	840	865	1	2	3	4	17	20
Malnutrition — Malnutrition	6	8	1	-	-	-	1	-
Mental and behavioural disorders — Troubles mentaux et du comportement	66	38	-	-	-	-	2	1
Diseases of the nervous system — Maladies du système nerveux.................	284	212	3	1	4	1	7	3
Diseases of the circulatory system — Maladies de l'appareil circulatoire								
Total	3 001	2 716	12	16	9	11	86	84
Acute rheumatic fever and chronic rheumatic heart diseases — Rhumatisme articularie aigu et cardiopathies rhumatismales chroniques	9	19	-	-	-	-	-	-
Hypertensive diseases — Maladies hypertensives..............	188	258	2	3	1	1	15	22
Ischaemic heart disease — Cardiopathie ischémique	819	500	4	5	2	-	17	23

Cause of death — Cause de décès	Tunisia - Tunisie 2013 (U) Male — Masculin Number Nombre	Tunisia - Tunisie 2013 (U) Female — Féminin Number Nombre	Anguilla 2013 (...) Male — Masculin Number Nombre	Anguilla 2013 (...) Female — Féminin Number Nombre	Anguilla 2014 (...) Male — Masculin Number Nombre	Anguilla 2014 (...) Female — Féminin Number Nombre	Antigua and Barbuda - Antigua-et-Barbuda 2012 (+U) Male — Masculin Number Nombre	Antigua and Barbuda - Antigua-et-Barbuda 2012 (+U) Female — Féminin Number Nombre
Cerebrovascular disease — Maladie cérébrovasculaire	1 117	1 066	3	4	5	6	17	14
Diseases of arteries, arterioles and capillaries — Maladies des artères, artérioles et capillaires	39	15	-	1	-	-	1	3
Diseases of the respiratory system — Maladies de l'appareil respiratoire								
Total	847	463	3	-	2	-	18	9
Influenza — Grippe	19	16	-	-	-	-	-	-
Pneumonia — Pneumopathies	209	153	-	-	2	-	7	2
Chronic lower respiratory diseases — Maladies chroniques des voies respiratoires inférieures	343	116	1	-	-	-	5	1
Diseases of the digestive system — Maladies de l'appareil digestif								
Total	366	320	3	2	2	-	14	6
Gastric and duodenal ulcer — Ulcère de l'estomac et du duodénum	16	12	1	-	-	-	1	1
Diseases of the liver — Maladies du foie	109	101	2	-	1	-	8	3
Diseases of the musculoskeletal system and connective tissue — Maladies du système ostéo-articularie, des muscles et du tissu conjonctif	20	30	-	-	-	-	2	-
Diseases of the genitourinary system — Maladies de l'appareil génito-urinaire								
Total	245	223	-	-	-	-	10	6
Disorders of kidney and ureter — Affections du rein et de l'uretère	208	214	-	-	-	-	2	2
Hyperplasia of prostate — Hyperplasie de la prostate	13	..	-	..	-	..	3	..
Pregnancy, childbirth and the puerperium — Grossesse, accouchement et puerpéralité								
Total	..	28	..	-	..	-	..	1
Pregnancy with abortive outcome — Grossesse se terminant par un avortement	..	1	..	-	..	-	..	1
Other direct obstetric causes — Autres décès maternels directs	..	27	..	-	..	-	..	-
Indirect obstetric causes — Décès maternels indirects	..	-	..	-	..	-	..	-
Certain conditions originating in the perinatal period — Certaines affections dont l'origine se situe dans la période périnatale	669	502	-	-	2	-	4	-
Congenital malformations, deformations and chromosomal abnormalities — Malformations congénitales et anomalies chromosomiques	310	209	2	2	-	-	-	3
Symptoms, signs and abnormal clinical and laboratory findings, not elsewhere classified — Symptômes, signes et résultats anormaux d'examens cliniques et de laboratoire, non classés ailleurs	2 151	1 673	-	-	-	-	1	3
All other diseases — Toutes autres maladies	36	54	-	-	-	-	3	3
External causes — Causes externes								
Total	845	352	7	2	6	-	19	8
Accidents								
Total	326	75	4	2	6	-	18	6
Transport accidents — Accidents de transport	250	48	2	-	1	-	2	1
Falls — Chutes	8	4	-	-	-	-	-	-
Accidental drowning and submersion — Noyade et submersion accidentelles	31	7	1	1	1	-	4	1
Exposure to smoke, fire and flames — Exposition à la fumée, au feu et aux flammes	3	-	-	-	-	-	-	-
Accidental poisoning by and exposure to noxious substances — Intoxication accidentelle par des substances nocives et exposition à ces substances	7	6	-	-	-	-	-	-
Intentional self-harm — Lésions auto-infligées	9	2	-	-	-	-	-	-
Assault — Agresssions	10	-	1	-	-	-	-	-
All other external causes — Toutes autres causes externes	500	275	2	-	-	-	1	2

20. Death and death rates by cause and sex: 2010 - 2014
Décès et taux de mortalité par cause et sexe : 2010 - 2014 (continued - suite)

Cause of death — Cause de décès	Antigua and Barbuda - Antigua-et-Barbuda				Aruba	
	2013 (+U)		2012 (...)		2013 (...)	
	Male — Masculin	Female — Féminin	Male — Masculin	Female — Féminin	Male — Masculin	Female — Féminin
	Number Nombre	Number Nombre	Number Nombre	Number Nombre	Number Nombre	Number Nombre
TOTAL	**246**	**219**	**309**	**304**	**318**	**255**
Certain infectious and parasitic diseases — Certaines maladies infectieuses et parasitaires						
Total	*13*	*14*	*12*	*10*	*22*	*10*
Intestinal infectious diseases — Maladies infectieuses intestinales	*1*	*1*	-	*1*	-	*1*
Tuberculosis — Tuberculose	-	-	-	-	-	-
Tetanus — Tétanos	-	-	-	-	-	-
Diphtheria — Diphtérie	-	-	-	-	-	-
Whooping cough — Coqueluche	-	-	-	-	-	-
Meningococcal infection — Infection à méningocoques	-	-	-	-	-	-
Septicaemia — Septicémie	*8*	*10*	*10*	*7*	*17*	*5*
Acute poliomyelitis — Poliomyélite aiguë	-	-	-	-	-	-
Measles — Rougeole	-	-	-	-	-	-
Viral hepatitis — Hépatite virale	-	-	-	-	*1*	-
Human immunodeficiency virus [HIV] disease — Maladies dues au virus de l'immunodéficience humaine (VIH)	*3*	*3*	-	-	*2*	*2*
Malaria — Paludisme	-	-	-	-	-	-
Neoplasms — Tumeurs	**53**	**37**	**69**	**80**	**70**	**58**
Malignant neoplasms — Tumeurs malignes						
Total	*52*	*36*	*65*	*80*	*69*	*57*
Malignant neoplasm of lip, oral cavity and pharynx — Tumeur maligne de la lèvre, de la cavité buccale et du pharynx	*3*	-	*1*	*1*	-	-
Malignant neoplasm of oesophagus — Tumeur maligne de l'oesophage	-	-	*2*	*1*	*2*	-
Malignant neoplasm of stomach — Tumeur maligne de l'estomac	*2*	-	*2*	*4*	*4*	*5*
Malignant neoplasm of colon, rectosigmoid junction, rectum, anus and anal canal — Tumeur maligne du côlon, de la jonction recto-sigmoïdienne, du rectum, de l'anus et du canal anal	*2*	*6*	*8*	*5*	*8*	*7*
Malignant neoplasm of liver and intrahepatic bile ducts — Tumeur maligne du foie et des voies bilaires intrahépatiques	*1*	-	*4*	*2*	*3*	*3*
Malignant neoplasm of pancreas — Tumeur maligne du pancréas	*3*	*1*	*2*	*1*	*4*	*3*
Malignant neoplasm of trachea, bronchus and lung — Tumeur maligne de la trachée, des bronches et du poumon	*2*	*1*	*13*	*3*	*8*	*6*
Malignant neoplasm of female breast — Tumeur maligne du sein chez la femme	..	*9*	..	*25*	..	*11*
Malignant neoplasm of cervix uteri — Tumeur maligne du col de l'utérus	..	*2*	..	*5*	..	*1*
Malignant neoplasm of prostate — Tumeur maligne de la prostate	*24*	..	*13*	..	*20*	..
Malignant neoplasm of lymphoid, haematopoietic and related tissue — Tumeurs malignes primitives ou présumées primitives des tissus lymphoïde, hématopoïétique et apparentés	*6*	*4*	*7*	*7*	*3*	*4*
Disorders of the blood and blood-forming organs and certain disorders involving the immune mechanism — Maladies du sang et des organes hématopoïétiques et certains troubles du système immunitaire						
Total	*6*	*1*	*2*	*1*	*1*	*2*
Anaemias — Anémies	*3*	*1*	-	*1*	*1*	*2*
Endocrine, nutritional and metabolic diseases — Maladies endocriniennes, nutritionnelles et métaboliques						
Total	*25*	*34*	*15*	*25*	*13*	*26*
Diabetes mellitus — Diabète sucré	*20*	*30*	*14*	*22*	*9*	*20*
Malnutrition — Malnutrition	*2*	-	-	*1*	*1*	*1*
Mental and behavioural disorders — Troubles mentaux et du comportement	*4*	-	*2*	*4*	*2*	*1*
Diseases of the nervous system — Maladies du système nerveux	*1*	*7*	*7*	*13*	*14*	*21*
Diseases of the circulatory system — Maladies de l'appareil circulatoire						
Total	*87*	*77*	*100*	*91*	*102*	*78*
Acute rheumatic fever and chronic rheumatic heart diseases — Rhumatisme articularie aigu et cardiopathies rhumatismales chroniques	-	-	-	-	-	-
Hypertensive diseases — Maladies hypertensives	*25*	*25*	*5*	*10*	*6*	*5*
Ischaemic heart disease — Cardiopathie ischémique	*24*	*16*	*31*	*16*	*24*	*18*
Cerebrovascular disease — Maladie cérébrovasculaire	*22*	*17*	*25*	*28*	*21*	*23*
Diseases of arteries, arterioles and capillaries — Maladies des artères, artérioles et capillaires	*1*	-	*2*	*1*	*2*	*3*

20. Death and death rates by cause and sex: 2010 - 2014
Décès et taux de mortalité par cause et sexe : 2010 - 2014 (continued - suite)

Cause of death — Cause de décès	Antigua and Barbuda - Antigua-et-Barbuda				Aruba	
	2013 (+U)		2012 (...)		2013 (...)	
	Male — Masculin	Female — Féminin	Male — Masculin	Female — Féminin	Male — Masculin	Female — Féminin
	Number Nombre	Number Nombre	Number Nombre	Number Nombre	Number Nombre	Number Nombre
Diseases of the respiratory system — Maladies de l'appareil respiratoire						
Total	15	21	19	25	15	10
Influenza — Grippe	-	-	-	-	-	-
Pneumonia — Pneumopathies	6	3	10	12	5	7
Chronic lower respiratory diseases — Maladies chroniques des voies respiratoires inférieures	2	3	3	3	4	2
Diseases of the digestive system — Maladies de l'appareil digestif						
Total	5	5	14	16	18	9
Gastric and duodenal ulcer — Ulcère de l'estomac et du duodénum	-	-	1	-	2	1
Diseases of the liver — Maladies du foie	1	1	9	5	8	3
Diseases of the musculoskeletal system and connective tissue — Maladies du système ostéo-articularie, des muscles et du tissu conjonctif	1	5	-	1	1	1
Diseases of the genitourinary system — Maladies de l'appareil génito-urinaire						
Total	4	1	6	8	12	9
Disorders of kidney and ureter — Affections du rein et de l'uretère	2	-	4	4	10	8
Hyperplasia of prostate — Hyperplasie de la prostate	-	..	-	..	-	..
Pregnancy, childbirth and the puerperium — Grossesse, accouchement et puerpéralité						
Total	..	-	..	-	..	-
Pregnancy with abortive outcome — Grossesse se terminant par un avortement	..	-	..	-	..	-
Other direct obstetric causes — Autres décès maternels directs	..	-	..	-	..	-
Indirect obstetric causes — Décès maternels indirects	..	-	..	-	..	-
Certain conditions originating in the perinatal period — Certaines affections dont l'origine se situe dans la période périnatale	3	1	-	-	-	1
Congenital malformations, deformations and chromosomal abnormalities — Malformations congénitales et anomalies chromosomiques	3	-	2	-	-	2
Symptoms, signs and abnormal clinical and laboratory findings, not elsewhere classified — Symptômes, signes et résultats anormaux d'examens cliniques et de laboratoire, non classés ailleurs	4	5	18	17	15	14
All other diseases — Toutes autres maladies	-	-	2	3	1	1
External causes — Causes externes						
Total	22	11	41	10	32	12
Accidents						
Total	22	11	34	5	23	9
Transport accidents — Accidents de transport	-	1	16	3	8	5
Falls — Chutes	-	-	2	-	-	2
Accidental drowning and submersion — Noyade et submersion accidentelles	2	-	6	1	3	1
Exposure to smoke, fire and flames — Exposition à la fumée, au feu et aux flammes	2	2	1	-	-	-
Accidental poisoning by and exposure to noxious substances — Intoxication accidentelle par des substances nocives et exposition à ces substances	-	-	2	1	2	-
Intentional self-harm — Lésions auto-infligées	-	-	1	2	1	1
Assault — Agresssions	-	-	3	1	5	1
All other external causes — Toutes autres causes externes	-	-	3	2	3	1

20. Death and death rates by cause and sex: 2010 - 2014
Décès et taux de mortalité par cause et sexe : 2010 - 2014 (continued - suite)

Bahamas

Cause of death — Cause de décès	2011 (+C)				2012 (+C)			
	Male — Masculin		Female — Féminin		Male — Masculin		Female — Féminin	
	Number Nombre	Rate Taux	Number Nombre	Rate Taux	Number Nombre	Rate Taux	Number Nombre	Rate Taux
TOTAL	1 181	674.7	936	512.3	1 091	614.9	902	487.2
Certain infectious and parasitic diseases — Certaines maladies infectieuses et parasitaires								
Total	93	53.1	84	46.0	83	46.8	81	43.7
Intestinal infectious diseases — Maladies infectieuses intestinales	5	♦2.9	-	-	1	♦0.6	1	♦0.5
Tuberculosis — Tuberculose	2	♦1.1	3	♦1.6	-	-	1	♦0.5
Tetanus — Tétanos	-	-	-	-	-	-	-	-
Diphtheria — Diphtérie.......................................	-	-	-	-	-	-	-	-
Whooping cough — Coqueluche	-	-	-	-	-	-	-	-
Meningococcal infection — Infection à méningocoques	-	-	-	-	-	-	-	-
Septicaemia — Septicémie	14	♦8.0	20	♦10.9	18	♦10.1	30	♦16.2
Acute poliomyelitis — Poliomyélite aiguë	-	-	-	-	-	-	-	-
Measles — Rougeole..	-	-	-	-	-	-	-	-
Viral hepatitis — Hépatite virale	2	♦1.1	1	♦0.5	-	-	-	-
Human immunodeficiency virus [HIV] disease — Maladies dues au virus de l'immunodéficience humaine (VIH)........................	68	38.9	53	29.0	60	33.8	49	26.5
Malaria — Paludisme...	-	-	-	-	-	-	-	-
Neoplasms — Tumeurs	213	121.7	185	101.2	196	110.5	186	100.5
Malignant neoplasms — Tumeurs malignes								
Total	209	119.4	180	98.5	190	107.1	179	96.7
Malignant neoplasm of lip, oral cavity and pharynx — Tumeur maligne de la lèvre, de la cavité buccale et du pharynx	4	♦2.3	1	♦0.5	8	♦4.5	4	♦2.2
Malignant neoplasm of oesophagus — Tumeur maligne de l'oesophage	9	♦5.1	1	♦0.5	7	♦3.9	-	-
Malignant neoplasm of stomach — Tumeur maligne de l'estomac	14	♦8.0	9	♦4.9	5	♦2.8	3	♦1.6
Malignant neoplasm of colon, rectosigmoid junction, rectum, anus and anal canal — Tumeur maligne du côlon, de la jonction recto-sigmoïdienne, du rectum, de l'anus et du canal anal	22	♦12.6	20	♦10.9	20	♦11.3	13	♦7.0
Malignant neoplasm of liver and intrahepatic bile ducts — Tumeur maligne du foie et des voies bilaires intrahépatiques	8	♦4.6	7	♦3.8	11	♦6.2	3	♦1.6
Malignant neoplasm of pancreas — Tumeur maligne du pancréas.................	5	♦2.9	6	♦3.3	4	♦2.3	4	♦2.2
Malignant neoplasm of trachea, bronchus and lung — Tumeur maligne de la trachée, des bronches et du poumon	27	♦15.4	9	♦4.9	16	♦9.0	8	♦4.3
Malignant neoplasm of female breast — Tumeur maligne du sein chez la femme	..	..	60	43.6	..	..	53	37.9
Malignant neoplasm of cervix uteri — Tumeur maligne du col de l'utérus.........	..	..	12	♦8.7	..	..	17	♦12.1
Malignant neoplasm of prostate — Tumeur maligne de la prostate	52	157.3	..	..	62	178.3	..	..
Malignant neoplasm of lymphoid, haematopoietic and related tissue — Tumeurs malignes primitives ou présumées primitives des tissus lymphoïde, hématopoïétique et apparentés	18	♦10.3	9	♦4.9	16	♦9.0	19	♦10.3
Disorders of the blood and blood-forming organs and certain disorders involving the immune mechanism — Maladies du sang et des organes hématopoïétiques et certains troubles du système immunitaire								
Total	20	♦11.4	10	♦5.5	6	♦3.4	9	♦4.9
Anaemias — Anémies	16	♦9.1	8	♦4.4	4	♦2.3	7	♦3.8
Endocrine, nutritional and metabolic diseases — Maladies endocriniennes, nutritionnelles et métaboliques								
Total	49	28.0	62	33.9	78	44.0	80	43.2
Diabetes mellitus — Diabète sucré........................	38	21.7	48	26.3	55	31.0	54	29.2
Malnutrition — Malnutrition	2	♦1.1	1	♦0.5	1	♦0.6	2	♦1.1
Mental and behavioural disorders — Troubles mentaux et du comportement	16	♦9.1	6	♦3.3	14	♦7.9	2	♦1.1
Diseases of the nervous system — Maladies du système nerveux..............	20	♦11.4	36	19.7	18	♦10.1	25	♦13.5
Diseases of the circulatory system — Maladies de l'appareil circulatoire								
Total	354	202.3	353	193.2	313	176.4	302	163.1
Acute rheumatic fever and chronic rheumatic heart diseases — Rhumatisme articularie aigu et cardiopathies rhumatismales chroniques	2	♦1.1	2	♦1.1	-	-	2	♦1.1
Hypertensive diseases — Maladies hypertensives........	99	56.6	116	63.5	65	36.6	88	47.5
Ischaemic heart disease — Cardiopathie ischémique	103	58.8	77	42.1	107	60.3	70	37.8
Cerebrovascular disease — Maladie cérébrovasculaire...........	60	34.3	70	38.3	76	42.8	75	40.5

Bahamas

Cause of death — Cause de décès	2011 (+C)				2012 (+C)			
	Male — Masculin		Female — Féminin		Male — Masculin		Female — Féminin	
	Number Nombre	Rate Taux	Number Nombre	Rate Taux	Number Nombre	Rate Taux	Number Nombre	Rate Taux
Diseases of arteries, arterioles and capillaries — Maladies des artères, artérioles et capillaires	10	♦5.7	9	♦4.9	3	♦1.7	7	♦3.8
Diseases of the respiratory system — Maladies de l'appareil respiratoire								
Total	62	35.4	46	25.2	58	32.7	65	35.1
Influenza — Grippe............	-	-	-	-	-	-	-	-
Pneumonia — Pneumopathies	29	♦16.6	25	♦13.7	26	♦14.7	47	25.4
Chronic lower respiratory diseases — Maladies chroniques des voies respiratoires inférieures	14	♦8.0	6	♦3.3	15	♦8.5	6	♦3.2
Diseases of the digestive system — Maladies de l'appareil digestif								
Total	57	32.6	39	21.3	52	29.3	36	19.4
Gastric and duodenal ulcer — Ulcère de l'estomac et du duodénum............	9	♦5.1	1	♦0.5	6	♦3.4	2	♦1.1
Diseases of the liver — Maladies du foie............	22	♦12.6	9	♦4.9	21	♦11.8	15	♦8.1
Diseases of the musculoskeletal system and connective tissue — Maladies du système ostéo-articularie, des muscles et du tissu conjonctif	3	♦1.7	10	♦5.5	3	♦1.7	10	♦5.4
Diseases of the genitourinary system — Maladies de l'appareil génito-urinaire								
Total	28	♦16.0	20	♦10.9	31	17.5	19	♦10.3
Disorders of kidney and ureter — Affections du rein et de l'uretère	22	♦12.6	12	♦6.6	25	♦14.1	10	♦5.4
Hyperplasia of prostate — Hyperplasie de la prostate............	1	♦3.0	..	..	4	♦11.5	..	..
Pregnancy, childbirth and the puerperium — Grossesse, accouchement et puerpéralité								
Total	..	..	-	-	..	..	3	♦67.1
Pregnancy with abortive outcome — Grossesse se terminant par un avortement	..	..	-	-	..	..	2	♦44.8
Other direct obstetric causes — Autres décès maternels directs	..	..	-	-	..	..	1	♦22.4
Indirect obstetric causes — Décès maternels indirects	..	..	-	-	..	..	-	-
Certain conditions originating in the perinatal period — Certaines affections dont l'origine se situe dans la période périnatale	16	♦676.2	13	♦546.7	15	♦657.9	14	♦639.6
Congenital malformations, deformations and chromosomal abnormalities — Malformations congénitales et anomalies chromosomiques	10	♦422.7	5	♦210.3	7	♦307.0	4	♦182.7
Symptoms, signs and abnormal clinical and laboratory findings, not elsewhere classified — Symptômes, signes et résultats anormaux d'examens cliniques et de laboratoire, non classés ailleurs	12	♦6.9	17	♦9.3	18	♦10.1	12	♦6.5
All other diseases — Toutes autres maladies	11	♦6.3	7	♦3.8	4	♦2.3	14	♦7.6
External causes — Causes externes								
Total	217	124.0	43	23.5	195	109.9	40	21.6
Accidents								
Total	82	46.8	24	♦13.1	67	37.8	24	♦13.0
Transport accidents — Accidents de transport	43	24.6	4	♦2.2	35	19.7	14	♦7.6
Falls — Chutes	1	♦0.6	1	♦0.5	6	♦3.4	1	♦0.5
Accidental drowning and submersion — Noyade et submersion accidentelles............	19	♦10.9	5	♦2.7	16	♦9.0	3	♦1.6
Exposure to smoke, fire and flames — Exposition à la fumée, au feu et aux flammes............	6	♦3.4	9	♦4.9	1	♦0.6	-	-
Accidental poisoning by and exposure to noxious substances — Intoxication accidentelle par des substances nocives et exposition à ces substances	1	♦0.6	1	♦0.5	-	-	-	-
Intentional self-harm — Lésions auto-infligées............	3	♦1.7	1	♦0.5	4	♦2.3	1	♦0.5
Assault — Agresssions	115	65.7	14	♦7.7	116	65.4	13	♦7.0
All other external causes — Toutes autres causes externes	17	♦9.7	4	♦2.2	8	♦4.5	2	♦1.1

20. Death and death rates by cause and sex: 2010 - 2014
Décès et taux de mortalité par cause et sexe : 2010 - 2014 (continued - suite)

Barbados - Barbade

Cause of death — Cause de décès	2011 (C)				2012 (C)			
	Male — Masculin		Female — Féminin		Male — Masculin		Female — Féminin	
	Number Nombre	Rate Taux	Number Nombre	Rate Taux	Number Nombre	Rate Taux	Number Nombre	Rate Taux
TOTAL	1 152	865.4	1 280	885.8	1 159	869.1	1 167	808.7
Certain infectious and parasitic diseases — Certaines maladies infectieuses et parasitaires								
Total	63	47.3	57	39.4	56	42.0	55	38.1
Intestinal infectious diseases — Maladies infectieuses intestinales	2	♦1.5	2	♦1.4	2	♦1.5	4	♦2.8
Tuberculosis — Tuberculose	1	♦0.8	-	-	-	-	-	-
Tetanus — Tétanos..	-	-	-	-	-	-	-	-
Diphtheria — Diphtérie..	-	-	-	-	-	-	-	-
Whooping cough — Coqueluche	-	-	-	-	-	-	-	-
Meningococcal infection — Infection à méningocoques	-	-	-	-	-	-	-	-
Septicaemia — Septicémie..	33	24.8	38	26.3	41	30.7	40	27.7
Acute poliomyelitis — Poliomyélite aiguë	-	-	-	-	-	-	-	-
Measles — Rougeole..	-	-	-	-	-	-	-	-
Viral hepatitis — Hépatite virale	2	♦1.5	-	-	-	-	1	♦0.7
Human immunodeficiency virus [HIV] disease — Maladies dues au virus de l'immunodéficience humaine (VIH)..	9	♦6.8	8	♦5.5	2	♦1.5	1	♦0.7
Malaria — Paludisme..	-	-	-	-	-	-	-	-
Neoplasms — Tumeurs	254	190.8	290	200.7	280	210.0	236	163.5
Malignant neoplasms — Tumeurs malignes								
Total	248	186.3	278	192.4	273	204.7	229	158.7
Malignant neoplasm of lip, oral cavity and pharynx — Tumeur maligne de la lèvre, de la cavité buccale et du pharynx	8	♦6.0	4	♦2.8	12	♦9.0	-	-
Malignant neoplasm of oesophagus — Tumeur maligne de l'oesophage	6	♦4.5	1	♦0.7	6	♦4.5	3	♦2.1
Malignant neoplasm of stomach — Tumeur maligne de l'estomac	9	♦6.8	5	♦3.5	13	♦9.7	5	♦3.5
Malignant neoplasm of colon, rectosigmoid junction, rectum, anus and anal canal — Tumeur maligne du côlon, de la jonction recto-sigmoïdienne, du rectum, de l'anus et du canal anal	36	27.0	43	29.8	36	27.0	22	♦15.2
Malignant neoplasm of liver and intrahepatic bile ducts — Tumeur maligne du foie et des voies bilaires intrahépatiques	6	♦4.5	3	♦2.1	5	♦3.7	4	♦2.8
Malignant neoplasm of pancreas — Tumeur maligne du pancréas...................	6	♦4.5	10	♦6.9	16	♦12.0	11	♦7.6
Malignant neoplasm of trachea, bronchus and lung — Tumeur maligne de la trachée, des bronches et du poumon	14	♦10.5	18	♦12.5	22	♦16.5	10	♦6.9
Malignant neoplasm of female breast — Tumeur maligne du sein chez la femme	..	..	73	...	..	..	63	...
Malignant neoplasm of cervix uteri — Tumeur maligne du col de l'utérus..........	..	..	9	...	..	..	10	...
Malignant neoplasm of prostate — Tumeur maligne de la prostate	94	...	..	..	92	...	..	..
Malignant neoplasm of lymphoid, haematopoietic and related tissue — Tumeurs malignes primitives ou présumées primitives des tissus lymphoïde, hématopoïétique et apparentés.................	16	♦12.0	27	♦18.7	27	♦20.2	27	♦18.7
Disorders of the blood and blood-forming organs and certain disorders involving the immune mechanism — Maladies du sang et des organes hématopoïétiques et certains troubles du système immunitaire								
Total	8	♦6.0	10	♦6.9	14	♦10.5	13	♦9.0
Anaemias — Anémies	4	♦3.0	6	♦4.2	6	♦4.5	8	♦5.5
Endocrine, nutritional and metabolic diseases — Maladies endocriniennes, nutritionnelles et métaboliques								
Total	94	70.6	157	108.6	102	76.5	137	94.9
Diabetes mellitus — Diabète sucré..	77	57.8	129	89.3	73	54.7	112	77.6
Malnutrition — Malnutrition	2	♦1.5	1	♦0.7	-	-	-	-
Mental and behavioural disorders — Troubles mentaux et du comportement	20	♦15.0	32	22.1	21	♦15.7	37	25.6
Diseases of the nervous system — Maladies du système nerveux...............	33	24.8	40	27.7	39	29.2	29	♦20.1
Diseases of the circulatory system — Maladies de l'appareil circulatoire								
Total	324	243.4	384	265.7	310	232.5	369	255.7
Acute rheumatic fever and chronic rheumatic heart diseases — Rhumatisme articularie aigu et cardiopathies rhumatismales chroniques	-	-	-	-	-	-	-	-
Hypertensive diseases — Maladies hypertensives...........................	26	♦19.5	68	47.1	45	33.7	53	36.7
Ischaemic heart disease — Cardiopathie ischémique	87	65.4	75	51.9	79	59.2	89	61.7
Cerebrovascular disease — Maladie cérébrovasculaire...........................	109	81.9	127	87.9	103	77.2	126	87.3

Barbados - Barbade

Cause of death — Cause de décès	2011 (C)				2012 (C)			
	Male — Masculin		Female — Féminin		Male — Masculin		Female — Féminin	
	Number Nombre	Rate Taux	Number Nombre	Rate Taux	Number Nombre	Rate Taux	Number Nombre	Rate Taux
Diseases of arteries, arterioles and capillaries — Maladies des artères, artérioles et capillaires	12	♦9.0	17	♦11.8	9	♦6.7	13	♦9.0
Diseases of the respiratory system — Maladies de l'appareil respiratoire								
Total	96	72.1	120	83.0	108	81.0	112	77.6
Influenza — Grippe..........................	-	-	1	♦0.7	-	-	-	-
Pneumonia — Pneumopathies..........................	33	24.8	51	35.3	44	33.0	46	31.9
Chronic lower respiratory diseases — Maladies chroniques des voies respiratoires inférieures	10	♦7.5	11	♦7.6	12	♦9.0	7	♦4.9
Diseases of the digestive system — Maladies de l'appareil digestif								
Total	50	37.6	35	24.2	48	36.0	35	24.3
Gastric and duodenal ulcer — Ulcère de l'estomac et du duodénum............	7	♦5.3	5	♦3.5	6	♦4.5	3	♦2.1
Diseases of the liver — Maladies du foie..........................	20	♦15.0	3	♦2.1	20	♦15.0	3	♦2.1
Diseases of the musculoskeletal system and connective tissue — Maladies du système ostéo-articularie, des muscles et du tissu conjonctif	5	♦3.8	13	♦9.0	5	♦3.7	12	♦8.3
Diseases of the genitourinary system — Maladies de l'appareil génito-urinaire								
Total	51	38.3	41	28.4	54	40.5	46	31.9
Disorders of kidney and ureter — Affections du rein et de l'uretère	17	♦12.8	21	♦14.5	22	♦16.5	18	♦12.5
Hyperplasia of prostate — Hyperplasie de la prostate..........................	12	...	..		11	...	..	
Pregnancy, childbirth and the puerperium — Grossesse, accouchement et puerpéralité								
Total	..	..	2	♦60.9	..	..	1	♦31.4
Pregnancy with abortive outcome — Grossesse se terminant par un avortement	..	..	1	♦30.5	..	..	1	♦31.4
Other direct obstetric causes — Autres décès maternels directs	..	..	1	♦30.5	..	..	-	-
Indirect obstetric causes — Décès maternels indirects	..	..	-	-	..	..	-	-
Certain conditions originating in the perinatal period — Certaines affections dont l'origine se situe dans la période périnatale	25	...	11	...	13	...	6	...
Congenital malformations, deformations and chromosomal abnormalities — Malformations congénitales et anomalies chromosomiques	10	...	5	...	9	...	7	...
Symptoms, signs and abnormal clinical and laboratory findings, not elsewhere classified — Symptômes, signes et résultats anormaux d'examens cliniques et de laboratoire, non classés ailleurs	17	♦12.8	9	♦6.2	17	♦12.7	10	♦6.9
All other diseases — Toutes autres maladies	17	♦12.8	28	♦19.4	8	♦6.0	22	♦15.2
External causes — Causes externes								
Total	85	63.9	46	31.8	75	56.2	40	27.7
Accidents								
Total	30	♦22.5	12	♦8.3	21	♦15.7	21	♦14.6
Transport accidents — Accidents de transport............	14	♦10.5	7	♦4.8	12	♦9.0	9	♦6.2
Falls — Chutes..........................	2	♦1.5	1	♦0.7	2	♦1.5	1	♦0.7
Accidental drowning and submersion — Noyade et submersion accidentelles..........................	-	-	-	-	-	-	-	-
Exposure to smoke, fire and flames — Exposition à la fumée, au feu et aux flammes..........................	-	-	-	-	-	-	-	-
Accidental poisoning by and exposure to noxious substances — Intoxication accidentelle par des substances nocives et exposition à ces substances	1	♦0.8	1	♦0.7	2	♦1.5	-	-
Intentional self-harm — Lésions auto-infligées..........................	-	-	-	-	-	-	-	-
Assault — Agresssions..........................	10	♦7.5	1	♦0.7	-	-	-	-
All other external causes — Toutes autres causes externes............	45	33.8	33	22.8	54	40.5	19	♦13.2

Belize

Cause of death — Cause de décès	2012 (C)				2013 (C)			
	Male — Masculin		Female — Féminin		Male — Masculin		Female — Féminin	
	Number Nombre	Rate Taux	Number Nombre	Rate Taux	Number Nombre	Rate Taux	Number Nombre	Rate Taux
TOTAL	**906**	**531.7**	**630**	**369.7**	**961**	**549.6**	**650**	**371.7**
Certain infectious and parasitic diseases — Certaines maladies infectieuses et parasitaires								
Total	88	51.6	55	32.3	94	53.8	66	37.7
Intestinal infectious diseases — Maladies infectieuses intestinales	5	♦2.9	2	♦1.2	3	♦1.7	2	♦1.1
Tuberculosis — Tuberculose	5	♦2.9	2	♦1.2	10	♦5.7	5	♦2.9
Tetanus — Tétanos	-	-	-	-	-	-	-	-
Diphtheria — Diphtérie.....................................	-	-	-	-	-	-	-	-
Whooping cough — Coqueluche	-	-	-	-	-	-	-	-
Meningococcal infection — Infection à méningocoques..........	-	-	-	-	-	-	1	♦0.6
Septicaemia — Septicémie	10	♦5.9	10	♦5.9	13	♦7.4	12	♦6.9
Acute poliomyelitis — Poliomyélite aiguë	-	-	-	-	-	-	-	-
Measles — Rougeole	-	-	-	-	-	-	-	-
Viral hepatitis — Hépatite virale	-	-	-	-	-	-	-	-
Human immunodeficiency virus [HIV] disease — Maladies dues au virus de l'immunodéficience humaine (VIH)........	66	38.7	39	22.9	65	37.2	45	25.7
Malaria — Paludisme..	-	-	-	-	-	-	-	-
Neoplasms — Tumeurs	**104**	**61.0**	**98**	**57.5**	**114**	**65.2**	**88**	**50.3**
Malignant neoplasms — Tumeurs malignes								
Total	97	56.9	93	54.6	104	59.5	82	46.9
Malignant neoplasm of lip, oral cavity and pharynx — Tumeur maligne de la lèvre, de la cavité buccale et du pharynx	1	♦0.6	-	-	5	♦2.9	-	-
Malignant neoplasm of oesophagus — Tumeur maligne de l'oesophage	1	♦0.6	-	-	2	♦1.1	1	♦0.6
Malignant neoplasm of stomach — Tumeur maligne de l'estomac	10	♦5.9	7	♦4.1	12	♦6.9	5	♦2.9
Malignant neoplasm of colon, rectosigmoid junction, rectum, anus and anal canal — Tumeur maligne du côlon, de la jonction recto-sigmoïdienne, du rectum, de l'anus et du canal anal..........	8	♦4.7	6	♦3.5	5	♦2.9	9	♦5.1
Malignant neoplasm of liver and intrahepatic bile ducts — Tumeur maligne du foie et des voies bilaires intrahépatiques	10	♦5.9	3	♦1.8	6	♦3.4	6	♦3.4
Malignant neoplasm of pancreas — Tumeur maligne du pancréas..................	1	♦0.6	1	♦0.6	4	♦2.3	3	♦1.7
Malignant neoplasm of trachea, bronchus and lung — Tumeur maligne de la trachée, des bronches et du poumon	11	♦6.5	5	♦2.9	14	♦8.0	4	♦2.3
Malignant neoplasm of female breast — Tumeur maligne du sein chez la femme	..	..	14	♦12.7	..	..	11	♦9.7
Malignant neoplasm of cervix uteri — Tumeur maligne du col de l'utérus..........	..	..	15	♦13.6	..	..	15	♦13.2
Malignant neoplasm of prostate — Tumeur maligne de la prostate	25	♦114.2	..	..	25	♦111.3	..	..
Malignant neoplasm of lymphoid, haematopoietic and related tissue — Tumeurs malignes primitives ou présumées primitives des tissus lymphoïde, hématopoïétique et apparentés..........	9	♦5.3	10	♦5.9	12	♦6.9	5	♦2.9
Disorders of the blood and blood-forming organs and certain disorders involving the immune mechanism — Maladies du sang et des organes hématopoïétiques et certains troubles du système immunitaire								
Total	5	♦2.9	3	♦1.8	10	♦5.7	6	♦3.4
Anaemias — Anémies	3	♦1.8	3	♦1.8	6	♦3.4	5	♦2.9
Endocrine, nutritional and metabolic diseases — Maladies endocriniennes, nutritionnelles et métaboliques								
Total	59	34.6	106	62.2	75	42.9	105	60.0
Diabetes mellitus — Diabète sucré..................	43	25.2	92	54.0	60	34.3	93	53.2
Malnutrition — Malnutrition	5	♦2.9	2	♦1.2	6	♦3.4	1	♦0.6
Mental and behavioural disorders — Troubles mentaux et du comportement	8	♦4.7	2	♦1.2	8	♦4.6	-	-
Diseases of the nervous system — Maladies du système nerveux..................	21	♦12.3	17	♦10.0	19	♦10.9	16	♦9.2
Diseases of the circulatory system — Maladies de l'appareil circulatoire								
Total	194	113.9	153	89.8	174	99.5	161	92.1
Acute rheumatic fever and chronic rheumatic heart diseases — Rhumatisme articularie aigu et cardiopathies rhumatismales chroniques	2	♦1.2	-	-	2	♦1.1	1	♦0.6
Hypertensive diseases — Maladies hypertensives............	35	20.5	35	20.5	24	♦13.7	36	20.6
Ischaemic heart disease — Cardiopathie ischémique	62	36.4	42	24.6	51	29.2	42	24.0
Cerebrovascular disease — Maladie cérébrovasculaire........	54	31.7	42	24.6	53	30.3	43	24.6

Belize

Cause of death — Cause de décès	2012 (C)				2013 (C)			
	Male — Masculin		Female — Féminin		Male — Masculin		Female — Féminin	
	Number Nombre	Rate Taux	Number Nombre	Rate Taux	Number Nombre	Rate Taux	Number Nombre	Rate Taux
Diseases of arteries, arterioles and capillaries — Maladies des artères, artérioles et capillaires	1	♦0.6	1	♦0.6	6	♦3.4	3	♦1.7
Diseases of the respiratory system — Maladies de l'appareil respiratoire								
Total	76	44.6	48	28.2	84	48.0	53	30.3
Influenza — Grippe	-	-	-	-	-	-	-	-
Pneumonia — Pneumopathies	39	22.9	26	♦15.3	44	25.2	36	20.6
Chronic lower respiratory diseases — Maladies chroniques des voies respiratoires inférieures	21	♦12.3	9	♦5.3	24	♦13.7	12	♦6.9
Diseases of the digestive system — Maladies de l'appareil digestif								
Total	34	20.0	34	20.0	60	34.3	43	24.6
Gastric and duodenal ulcer — Ulcère de l'estomac et du duodénum	1	♦0.6	3	♦1.8	3	♦1.7	-	-
Diseases of the liver — Maladies du foie	21	♦12.3	14	♦8.2	38	21.7	26	♦14.9
Diseases of the musculoskeletal system and connective tissue — Maladies du système ostéo-articularie, des muscles et du tissu conjonctif	-	-	8	♦4.7	2	♦1.1	3	♦1.7
Diseases of the genitourinary system — Maladies de l'appareil génito-urinaire								
Total	23	♦13.5	15	♦8.8	23	♦13.2	16	♦9.2
Disorders of kidney and ureter — Affections du rein et de l'uretère	17	♦10.0	11	♦6.5	14	♦8.0	9	♦5.1
Hyperplasia of prostate — Hyperplasie de la prostate	-	-	..	..	4	♦17.8	..	..
Pregnancy, childbirth and the puerperium — Grossesse, accouchement et puerpéralité								
Total	..	..	2	...	..	..	-	...
Pregnancy with abortive outcome — Grossesse se terminant par un avortement	..	..	-	...	..	..	-	...
Other direct obstetric causes — Autres décès maternels directs	..	..	2	...	..	..	-	...
Indirect obstetric causes — Décès maternels indirects	..	..	-	...	..	..	-	...
Certain conditions originating in the perinatal period — Certaines affections dont l'origine se situe dans la période périnatale	41	...	28	...	39	...	30	...
Congenital malformations, deformations and chromosomal abnormalities — Malformations congénitales et anomalies chromosomiques	12	...	13	...	19	...	19	...
Symptoms, signs and abnormal clinical and laboratory findings, not elsewhere classified — Symptômes, signes et résultats anormaux d'examens cliniques et de laboratoire, non classés ailleurs	12	♦7.0	1	♦0.6	5	♦2.9	7	♦4.0
All other diseases — Toutes autres maladies	5	♦2.9	9	♦5.3	5	♦2.9	1	♦0.6
External causes — Causes externes								
Total	224	131.5	38	22.3	230	131.5	36	20.6
Accidents								
Total	81	47.5	20	♦11.7	107	61.2	18	♦10.3
Transport accidents — Accidents de transport	48	28.2	12	♦7.0	62	35.5	7	♦4.0
Falls — Chutes	7	♦4.1	1	♦0.6	8	♦4.6	3	♦1.7
Accidental drowning and submersion — Noyade et submersion accidentelles	17	♦10.0	2	♦1.2	19	♦10.9	3	♦1.7
Exposure to smoke, fire and flames — Exposition à la fumée, au feu et aux flammes	1	♦0.6	1	♦0.6	2	♦1.1	1	♦0.6
Accidental poisoning by and exposure to noxious substances — Intoxication accidentelle par des substances nocives et exposition à ces substances	1	♦0.6	1	♦0.6	5	♦2.9	1	♦0.6
Intentional self-harm — Lésions auto-infligées	16	♦9.4	2	♦1.2	16	♦9.1	1	♦0.6
Assault — Agresssions	119	69.8	9	♦5.3	101	57.8	15	♦8.6
All other external causes — Toutes autres causes externes	8	♦4.7	7	♦4.1	6	♦3.4	2	♦1.1

20. Death and death rates by cause and sex: 2010 - 2014
Décès et taux de mortalité par cause et sexe : 2010 - 2014 (continued - suite)

Cause of death — Cause de décès	Bermuda - Bermudes				British Virgin Islands - Îles Vierges britanniques	
	2012 (...)		2013 (...)		2010 (...)	
	Male — Masculin	Female — Féminin	Male — Masculin	Female — Féminin	Male — Masculin	Female — Féminin
	Number Nombre	Number Nombre	Number Nombre	Number Nombre	Number Nombre	Number Nombre
TOTAL	**244**	**180**	**250**	**222**	**69**	**34**
Certain infectious and parasitic diseases — Certaines maladies infectieuses et parasitaires						
Total	5	3	5	7	3	1
Intestinal infectious diseases — Maladies infectieuses intestinales	3	1	-	-	-	-
Tuberculosis — Tuberculose	-	-	-	-	-	-
Tetanus — Tétanos	-	-	-	-	-	-
Diphtheria — Diphtérie	-	-	-	-	-	-
Whooping cough — Coqueluche	-	-	-	-	-	-
Meningococcal infection — Infection à méningocoques	-	-	-	-	-	-
Septicaemia — Septicémie	1	-	2	5	2	-
Acute poliomyelitis — Poliomyélite aiguë	-	-	-	-	-	-
Measles — Rougeole	-	-	-	-	-	-
Viral hepatitis — Hépatite virale	-	-	-	-	-	-
Human immunodeficiency virus [HIV] disease — Maladies dues au virus de l'immunodéficience humaine (VIH)	1	-	3	2	1	1
Malaria — Paludisme	-	-	-	-	-	-
Neoplasms — Tumeurs	**77**	**50**	**70**	**66**	**11**	**5**
Malignant neoplasms — Tumeurs malignes						
Total	77	50	69	62	11	5
Malignant neoplasm of lip, oral cavity and pharynx — Tumeur maligne de la lèvre, de la cavité buccale et du pharynx	3	-	2	-	-	1
Malignant neoplasm of oesophagus — Tumeur maligne de l'oesophage	2	1	2	-	1	-
Malignant neoplasm of stomach — Tumeur maligne de l'estomac	-	1	2	-	-	-
Malignant neoplasm of colon, rectosigmoid junction, rectum, anus and anal canal — Tumeur maligne du côlon, de la jonction recto-sigmoïdienne, du rectum, de l'anus et du canal anal	8	2	8	9	-	-
Malignant neoplasm of liver and intrahepatic bile ducts — Tumeur maligne du foie et des voies bilaires intrahépatiques	2	2	4	5	-	-
Malignant neoplasm of pancreas — Tumeur maligne du pancréas	4	4	4	5	1	-
Malignant neoplasm of trachea, bronchus and lung — Tumeur maligne de la trachée, des bronches et du poumon	15	10	13	6	2	1
Malignant neoplasm of female breast — Tumeur maligne du sein chez la femme	..	4	..	11	..	2
Malignant neoplasm of cervix uteri — Tumeur maligne du col de l'utérus	..	-	..	3	..	1
Malignant neoplasm of prostate — Tumeur maligne de la prostate	15	..	11	..	-	..
Malignant neoplasm of lymphoid, haematopoietic and related tissue — Tumeurs malignes primitives ou présumées primitives des tissus lymphoïde, hématopoïétique et apparentés	7	3	3	5	3	-
Disorders of the blood and blood-forming organs and certain disorders involving the immune mechanism — Maladies du sang et des organes hématopoïétiques et certains troubles du système immunitaire						
Total	-	1	4	3	1	1
Anaemias — Anémies	-	1	2	2	1	1
Endocrine, nutritional and metabolic diseases — Maladies endocriniennes, nutritionnelles et métaboliques						
Total	18	20	15	19	7	4
Diabetes mellitus — Diabète sucré	16	17	12	11	6	4
Malnutrition — Malnutrition	1	-	-	-	-	-
Mental and behavioural disorders — Troubles mentaux et du comportement	7	1	-	2	-	-
Diseases of the nervous system — Maladies du système nerveux	5	13	16	19	1	1
Diseases of the circulatory system — Maladies de l'appareil circulatoire						
Total	86	66	81	80	18	6
Acute rheumatic fever and chronic rheumatic heart diseases — Rhumatisme articulaire aigu et cardiopathies rhumatismales chroniques	1	-	-	-	-	-
Hypertensive diseases — Maladies hypertensives	6	6	6	8	5	2
Ischaemic heart disease — Cardiopathie ischémique	38	24	44	29	7	2
Cerebrovascular disease — Maladie cérébrovasculaire	17	13	14	17	2	-
Diseases of arteries, arterioles and capillaries — Maladies des artères, artérioles et capillaires	4	7	2	4	-	-

20. Death and death rates by cause and sex: 2010 - 2014
Décès et taux de mortalité par cause et sexe : 2010 - 2014 (continued - suite)

Cause of death — Cause de décès	Bermuda - Bermudes 2012 (...) Male — Masculin Number Nombre	Bermuda - Bermudes 2012 (...) Female — Féminin Number Nombre	Bermuda - Bermudes 2013 (...) Male — Masculin Number Nombre	Bermuda - Bermudes 2013 (...) Female — Féminin Number Nombre	British Virgin Islands - Îles Vierges britanniques 2010 (...) Male — Masculin Number Nombre	British Virgin Islands - Îles Vierges britanniques 2010 (...) Female — Féminin Number Nombre
Diseases of the respiratory system — Maladies de l'appareil respiratoire						
Total	13	14	15	12	4	7
Influenza — Grippe	-	-	-	-	-	-
Pneumonia — Pneumopathies	5	7	5	5	3	3
Chronic lower respiratory diseases — Maladies chroniques des voies respiratoires inférieures	3	1	6	4	-	1
Diseases of the digestive system — Maladies de l'appareil digestif						
Total	6	3	11	5	3	1
Gastric and duodenal ulcer — Ulcère de l'estomac et du duodénum	-	-	1	-	-	-
Diseases of the liver — Maladies du foie	3	-	5	2	2	1
Diseases of the musculoskeletal system and connective tissue — Maladies du système ostéo-articularie, des muscles et du tissu conjonctif	1	2	1	1	-	-
Diseases of the genitourinary system — Maladies de l'appareil génito-urinaire						
Total	4	2	6	4	1	-
Disorders of kidney and ureter — Affections du rein et de l'uretère	3	2	4	4	-	-
Hyperplasia of prostate — Hyperplasie de la prostate	-	..	-	..	-	..
Pregnancy, childbirth and the puerperium — Grossesse, accouchement et puerpéralité						
Total	..	-	..	-	..	-
Pregnancy with abortive outcome — Grossesse se terminant par un avortement	..	-	..	-	..	-
Other direct obstetric causes — Autres décès maternels directs	..	-	..	-	..	-
Indirect obstetric causes — Décès maternels indirects	..	-	..	-	..	-
Certain conditions originating in the perinatal period — Certaines affections dont l'origine se situe dans la période périnatale	1	-	2	-	5	2
Congenital malformations, deformations and chromosomal abnormalities — Malformations congénitales et anomalies chromosomiques	1	-	2	1	1	-
Symptoms, signs and abnormal clinical and laboratory findings, not elsewhere classified — Symptômes, signes et résultats anormaux d'examens cliniques et de laboratoire, non classés ailleurs	1	2	2	2	-	2
All other diseases — Toutes autres maladies	-	2	-	1	-	-
External causes — Causes externes						
Total	19	1	20	-	14	4
Accidents						
Total	14	-	14	-	13	4
Transport accidents — Accidents de transport	9	-	9	-	1	1
Falls — Chutes	-	-	1	-	-	-
Accidental drowning and submersion — Noyade et submersion accidentelles	3	-	2	-	11	3
Exposure to smoke, fire and flames — Exposition à la fumée, au feu et aux flammes	-	-	-	-	-	-
Accidental poisoning by and exposure to noxious substances — Intoxication accidentelle par des substances nocives et exposition à ces substances	-	-	-	-	-	-
Intentional self-harm — Lésions auto-infligées	1	1	-	-	-	-
Assault — Agresssions	3	-	4	-	-	-
All other external causes — Toutes autres causes externes	1	-	2	-	1	-

20. Death and death rates by cause and sex: 2010 - 2014
Décès et taux de mortalité par cause et sexe : 2010 - 2014 (continued - suite)

Canada

Cause of death — Cause de décès	2010 (C)				2011 (C)			
	Male — Masculin		Female — Féminin		Male — Masculin		Female — Féminin	
	Number Nombre	Rate Taux	Number Nombre	Rate Taux	Number Nombre	Rate Taux	Number Nombre	Rate Taux
TOTAL	**120 638**	**716.0**	**119 437**	**696.1**	**121 042**	**711.3**	**121 032**	**698.5**
Certain infectious and parasitic diseases — Certaines maladies infectieuses et parasitaires								
Total	2 648	15.7	2 668	15.6	2 681	15.8	2 893	16.7
Intestinal infectious diseases — Maladies infectieuses intestinales	679	4.0	969	5.6	707	4.2	1 027	5.9
Tuberculosis — Tuberculose	36	0.2	31	0.2	50	0.3	26	♦0.2
Tetanus — Tétanos	-	-	1	♦0.0	-	-	-	-
Diphtheria — Diphtérie.....................	1	♦0.0	-	-	-	-	-	-
Whooping cough — Coqueluche	1	♦0.0	-	-	2	♦0.0	1	♦0.0
Meningococcal infection — Infection à méningocoques	9	♦0.1	5	♦0.0	5	♦0.0	4	♦0.0
Septicaemia — Septicémie.............	1 083	6.4	1 174	6.8	1 124	6.6	1 332	7.7
Acute poliomyelitis — Poliomyélite aiguë	-	-	-	-	-	-	-	-
Measles — Rougeole.....................	-	-	-	-	-	-	1	♦0.0
Viral hepatitis — Hépatite virale	327	1.9	159	0.9	314	1.8	146	0.8
Human immunodeficiency virus [HIV] disease — Maladies dues au virus de l'immunodéficience humaine (VIH)...........	263	1.6	73	0.4	229	1.3	74	0.4
Malaria — Paludisme.....................	3	♦0.0	1	♦0.0	1	♦0.0	-	-
Neoplasms — Tumeurs	**38 234**	**226.9**	**35 005**	**204.0**	**38 645**	**227.1**	**35 267**	**203.5**
Malignant neoplasms — Tumeurs malignes								
Total	37 544	222.8	34 342	200.2	37 917	222.8	34 560	199.5
Malignant neoplasm of lip, oral cavity and pharynx — Tumeur maligne de la lèvre, de la cavité buccale et du pharynx	751	4.5	399	2.3	843	5.0	343	2.0
Malignant neoplasm of oesophagus — Tumeur maligne de l'oesophage	1 368	8.1	429	2.5	1 339	7.9	402	2.3
Malignant neoplasm of stomach — Tumeur maligne de l'estomac	1 141	6.8	742	4.3	1 142	6.7	777	4.5
Malignant neoplasm of colon, rectosigmoid junction, rectum, anus and anal canal — Tumeur maligne du côlon, de la jonction recto-sigmoïdienne, du rectum, de l'anus et du canal anal.....	4 175	24.8	3 647	21.3	4 339	25.5	3 841	22.2
Malignant neoplasm of liver and intrahepatic bile ducts — Tumeur maligne du foie et des voies biliaires intrahépatiques	1 343	8.0	756	4.4	1 465	8.6	808	4.7
Malignant neoplasm of pancreas — Tumeur maligne du pancréas.................	1 923	11.4	1 950	11.4	2 055	12.1	2 027	11.7
Malignant neoplasm of trachea, bronchus and lung — Tumeur maligne de la trachée, des bronches et du poumon	10 531	62.5	8 783	51.2	10 515	61.8	8 707	50.3
Malignant neoplasm of female breast — Tumeur maligne du sein chez la femme	..	..	4 978	34.4	..	..	4 958	34.6
Malignant neoplasm of cervix uteri — Tumeur maligne du col de l'utérus.........	..	..	372	2.6	..	..	397	2.8
Malignant neoplasm of prostate — Tumeur maligne de la prostate	3 833	69.2	..	..	3 693	65.3	..	..
Malignant neoplasm of lymphoid, haematopoietic and related tissue — Tumeurs malignes primitives ou présumées primitives des tissus lymphoïde, hématopoïétique et apparentés.....	3 524	20.9	2 807	16.4	3 714	21.8	2 907	16.8
Disorders of the blood and blood-forming organs and certain disorders involving the immune mechanism — Maladies du sang et des organes hématopoïétiques et certains troubles du système immunitaire								
Total	414	2.5	514	3.0	419	2.5	527	3.0
Anaemias — Anémies	184	1.1	296	1.7	211	1.2	327	1.9
Endocrine, nutritional and metabolic diseases — Maladies endocriniennes, nutritionnelles et métaboliques								
Total	4 890	29.0	4 690	27.3	5 000	29.4	4 808	27.7
Diabetes mellitus — Diabète sucré.....	3 704	22.0	3 238	18.9	3 825	22.5	3 369	19.4
Malnutrition — Malnutrition	83	0.5	119	0.7	87	0.5	131	0.8
Mental and behavioural disorders — Troubles mentaux et du comportement	**4 672**	**27.7**	**8 058**	**47.0**	**5 012**	**29.5**	**8 935**	**51.6**
Diseases of the nervous system — Maladies du système nerveux.............	**5 032**	**29.9**	**7 086**	**41.3**	**5 036**	**29.6**	**7 001**	**40.4**
Diseases of the circulatory system — Maladies de l'appareil circulatoire								
Total	33 744	200.3	33 957	197.9	32 982	193.8	33 196	191.6
Acute rheumatic fever and chronic rheumatic heart diseases — Rhumatisme articularie aigu et cardiopathies rhumatismales chroniques	134	0.8	290	1.7	172	1.0	269	1.6
Hypertensive diseases — Maladies hypertensives..........................	966	5.7	1 541	9.0	1 034	6.1	1 527	8.8
Ischaemic heart disease — Cardiopathie ischémique	19 624	116.5	15 312	89.2	18 823	110.6	14 746	85.1
Cerebrovascular disease — Maladie cérébrovasculaire.................	5 658	33.6	8 048	46.9	5 486	32.2	7 797	45.0

Canada

Cause of death — Cause de décès	2010 (C)				2011 (C)			
	Male — Masculin		Female — Féminin		Male — Masculin		Female — Féminin	
	Number Nombre	Rate Taux	Number Nombre	Rate Taux	Number Nombre	Rate Taux	Number Nombre	Rate Taux
Diseases of arteries, arterioles and capillaries — Maladies des artères, artérioles et capillaires	1 699	10.1	1 570	9.2	1 746	10.3	1 568	9.0
Diseases of the respiratory system — Maladies de l'appareil respiratoire								
Total	10 581	62.8	10 176	59.3	10 946	64.3	11 138	64.3
Influenza — Grippe	29	♦0.2	48	0.3	178	1.0	283	1.6
Pneumonia — Pneumopathies	2 301	13.7	2 722	15.9	2 427	14.3	2 858	16.5
Chronic lower respiratory diseases — Maladies chroniques des voies respiratoires inférieures	5 497	32.6	5 260	30.7	5 551	32.6	5 633	32.5
Diseases of the digestive system — Maladies de l'appareil digestif								
Total	4 796	28.5	4 685	27.3	4 777	28.1	4 882	28.2
Gastric and duodenal ulcer — Ulcère de l'estomac et du duodénum	216	1.3	183	1.1	200	1.2	188	1.1
Diseases of the liver — Maladies du foie............	2 052	12.2	1 133	6.6	2 085	12.3	1 297	7.5
Diseases of the musculoskeletal system and connective tissue — Maladies du système ostéo-articularie, des muscles et du tissu conjonctif	474	2.8	1 004	5.9	530	3.1	1 141	6.6
Diseases of the genitourinary system — Maladies de l'appareil génito-urinaire								
Total	2 544	15.1	3 037	17.7	2 393	14.1	2 618	15.1
Disorders of kidney and ureter — Affections du rein et de l'uretère	1 956	11.6	2 179	12.7	1 801	10.6	1 807	10.4
Hyperplasia of prostate — Hyperplasie de la prostate............	94	1.7	..	..	116	2.1	..	..
Pregnancy, childbirth and the puerperium — Grossesse, accouchement et puerpéralité								
Total	..	..	24	♦6.4	..	..	18	♦4.8
Pregnancy with abortive outcome — Grossesse se terminant par un avortement	..	..	1	♦0.3	..	..	1	♦0.3
Other direct obstetric causes — Autres décès maternels directs	..	..	14	♦3.7	..	..	13	♦3.4
Indirect obstetric causes — Décès maternels indirects	..	..	6	♦1.6	..	..	3	♦0.8
Certain conditions originating in the perinatal period — Certaines affections dont l'origine se situe dans la période périnatale	620	...	510	...	614	...	465	...
Congenital malformations, deformations and chromosomal abnormalities — Malformations congénitales et anomalies chromosomiques	496	...	405	...	474	...	419	...
Symptoms, signs and abnormal clinical and laboratory findings, not elsewhere classified — Symptômes, signes et résultats anormaux d'examens cliniques et de laboratoire, non classés ailleurs	1 060	6.3	1 364	7.9	1 458	8.6	1 559	9.0
All other diseases — Toutes autres maladies............	176	1.0	253	1.5	165	1.0	273	1.6
External causes — Causes externes								
Total	10 257	60.9	6 001	35.0	9 910	58.2	5 892	34.0
Accidents								
Total	6 224	36.9	4 436	25.9	6 123	36.0	4 410	25.5
Transport accidents — Accidents de transport	1 955	11.6	756	4.4	1 720	10.1	631	3.6
Falls — Chutes	1 921	11.4	2 150	12.5	1 966	11.6	2 232	12.9
Accidental drowning and submersion — Noyade et submersion accidentelles............	219	1.3	59	0.3	201	1.2	52	0.3
Exposure to smoke, fire and flames — Exposition à la fumée, au feu et aux flammes............	142	0.8	82	0.5	113	0.7	74	0.4
Accidental poisoning by and exposure to noxious substances — Intoxication accidentelle par des substances nocives et exposition à ces substances	1 053	6.3	520	3.0	1 095	6.4	546	3.2
Intentional self-harm — Lésions auto-infligées............	2 980	17.7	968	5.6	2 780	16.3	946	5.5
Assault — Agresssions............	382	2.3	133	0.8	363	2.1	158	0.9
All other external causes — Toutes autres causes externes	671	4.0	464	2.7	644	3.8	378	2.2

20. Death and death rates by cause and sex: 2010 - 2014
Décès et taux de mortalité par cause et sexe : 2010 - 2014 (continued - suite)

Cause of death — Cause de décès	Cayman Islands - Îles Caïmanes				Costa Rica			
	2010 (...)		2013 (...)		2012 (+C)			
	Male — Masculin	Female — Féminin	Male — Masculin	Female — Féminin	Male — Masculin		Female — Féminin	
	Number Nombre	Number Nombre	Number Nombre	Number Nombre	Number Nombre	Rate Taux	Number Nombre	Rate Taux
TOTAL	85	66	81	89	10 647	469.8	8 266	346.6
Certain infectious and parasitic diseases — Certaines maladies infectieuses et parasitaires								
Total	2	2	2	3	226	10.0	139	5.8
Intestinal infectious diseases — Maladies infectieuses intestinales	-	-	-	-	24	♦1.1	58	2.4
Tuberculosis — Tuberculose	-	-	-	-	30	♦1.3	9	♦0.4
Tetanus — Tétanos	-	-	-	-	-	-	-	-
Diphtheria — Diphtérie	-	-	-	-	-	-	-	-
Whooping cough — Coqueluche	-	-	-	-	1	♦0.0	-	-
Meningococcal infection — Infection à méningocoques	-	-	-	-	-	-	-	-
Septicaemia — Septicémie	2	2	2	1	15	♦0.7	15	♦0.6
Acute poliomyelitis — Poliomyélite aiguë	-	-	-	-	-	-	-	-
Measles — Rougeole	-	-	-	-	-	-	-	-
Viral hepatitis — Hépatite virale	-	-	-	-	6	♦0.3	8	♦0.3
Human immunodeficiency virus [HIV] disease — Maladies dues au virus de l'immunodéficience humaine (VIH)	-	-	-	2	125	5.5	22	♦0.9
Malaria — Paludisme	-	-	-	-	-	-	-	-
Neoplasms — Tumeurs	21	11	28	21	2 411	106.4	2 114	88.6
Malignant neoplasms — Tumeurs malignes								
Total	21	11	28	20	2 259	99.7	1 999	83.8
Malignant neoplasm of lip, oral cavity and pharynx — Tumeur maligne de la lèvre, de la cavité buccale et du pharynx	2	1	1	-	54	2.4	23	♦1.0
Malignant neoplasm of oesophagus — Tumeur maligne de l'oesophage	-	-	1	-	48	2.1	17	♦0.7
Malignant neoplasm of stomach — Tumeur maligne de l'estomac	-	-	-	2	400	17.7	252	10.6
Malignant neoplasm of colon, rectosigmoid junction, rectum, anus and anal canal — Tumeur maligne du côlon, de la jonction recto-sigmoïdienne, du rectum, de l'anus et du canal anal	2	-	3	2	191	8.4	220	9.2
Malignant neoplasm of liver and intrahepatic bile ducts — Tumeur maligne du foie et des voies bilaires intrahépatiques	1	-	2	-	130	5.7	123	5.2
Malignant neoplasm of pancreas — Tumeur maligne du pancréas	-	-	-	3	118	5.2	104	4.4
Malignant neoplasm of trachea, bronchus and lung — Tumeur maligne de la trachée, des bronches et du poumon	6	2	6	1	197	8.7	91	3.8
Malignant neoplasm of female breast — Tumeur maligne du sein chez la femme	..	4	..	3	..	..	283	15.1
Malignant neoplasm of cervix uteri — Tumeur maligne du col de l'utérus	..	-	..	-	..	..	135	7.2
Malignant neoplasm of prostate — Tumeur maligne de la prostate	7	..	5	..	373	72.8	..	..
Malignant neoplasm of lymphoid, haematopoietic and related tissue — Tumeurs malignes primitives ou présumées primitives des tissus lymphoïde, hématopoïétique et apparentés	-	2	3	1	257	11.3	196	8.2
Disorders of the blood and blood-forming organs and certain disorders involving the immune mechanism — Maladies du sang et des organes hématopoïétiques et certains troubles du système immunitaire								
Total	1	-	-	1	27	♦1.2	36	1.5
Anaemias — Anémies	-	-	-	1	15	♦0.7	25	♦1.0
Endocrine, nutritional and metabolic diseases — Maladies endocriniennes, nutritionnelles et métaboliques								
Total	2	7	3	9	345	15.2	451	18.9
Diabetes mellitus — Diabète sucré	2	4	2	6	287	12.7	377	15.8
Malnutrition — Malnutrition	-	-	-	1	17	♦0.8	18	♦0.8
Mental and behavioural disorders — Troubles mentaux et du comportement	-	-	-	1	103	4.5	171	7.2
Diseases of the nervous system — Maladies du système nerveux	5	4	1	3	265	11.7	248	10.4
Diseases of the circulatory system — Maladies de l'appareil circulatoire								
Total	21	22	22	29	3 156	139.3	2 571	107.8
Acute rheumatic fever and chronic rheumatic heart diseases — Rhumatisme articularie aigu et cardiopathies rhumatismales chroniques	-	-	-	-	14	♦0.6	26	♦1.1
Hypertensive diseases — Maladies hypertensives	5	7	7	11	404	17.8	406	17.0
Ischaemic heart disease — Cardiopathie ischémique	7	3	6	5	1 635	72.1	1 029	43.1

20. Death and death rates by cause and sex: 2010 - 2014
Décès et taux de mortalité par cause et sexe : 2010 - 2014 (continued - suite)

Cause of death — Cause de décès	Cayman Islands - Îles Caïmanes				Costa Rica			
	2010 (...)		2013 (...)		2012 (+C)			
	Male — Masculin	Female — Féminin	Male — Masculin	Female — Féminin	Male — Masculin		Female — Féminin	
	Number Nombre	Number Nombre	Number Nombre	Number Nombre	Number Nombre	Rate Taux	Number Nombre	Rate Taux
Cerebrovascular disease — Maladie cérébrovasculaire....................................	4	3	4	3	604	26.7	671	28.1
Diseases of arteries, arterioles and capillaries — Maladies des artères, artérioles et capillaires	2	1	4	2	101	4.5	49	2.1
Diseases of the respiratory system — Maladies de l'appareil respiratoire								
Total	2	8	7	10	883	39.0	725	30.4
Influenza — Grippe	-	-	-	-	1	♦0.0	5	♦0.2
Pneumonia — Pneumopathies	2	4	2	7	267	11.8	194	8.1
Chronic lower respiratory diseases — Maladies chroniques des voies respiratoires inférieures	-	1	3	1	447	19.7	376	15.8
Diseases of the digestive system — Maladies de l'appareil digestif								
Total	2	2	-	1	757	33.4	569	23.9
Gastric and duodenal ulcer — Ulcère de l'estomac et du duodénum...............	-	-	-	-	55	2.4	25	♦1.0
Diseases of the liver — Maladies du foie........................	2	-	-	-	387	17.1	228	9.6
Diseases of the musculoskeletal system and connective tissue — Maladies du système ostéo-articularie, des muscles et du tissu conjonctif	-	-	-	-	52	2.3	119	5.0
Diseases of the genitourinary system — Maladies de l'appareil génito-urinaire								
Total	4	-	1	4	302	13.3	231	9.7
Disorders of kidney and ureter — Affections du rein et de l'uretère	2	-	-	2	249	11.0	155	6.5
Hyperplasia of prostate — Hyperplasie de la prostate........................	-	..	-	..	4	♦0.8	..	..
Pregnancy, childbirth and the puerperium — Grossesse, accouchement et puerpéralité								
Total	..	-	..	-	..	..	22	♦30.0
Pregnancy with abortive outcome — Grossesse se terminant par un avortement	..	-	..	-	..	..	3	♦4.1
Other direct obstetric causes — Autres décès maternels directs	..	-	..	-	..	..	14	♦19.1
Indirect obstetric causes — Décès maternels indirects	..	-	..	-	..	..	5	♦6.8
Certain conditions originating in the perinatal period — Certaines affections dont l'origine se situe dans la période périnatale	1	-	1	1	164	440.8	136	376.5
Congenital malformations, deformations and chromosomal abnormalities — Malformations congénitales et anomalies chromosomiques	-	2	-	-	153	411.2	137	379.3
Symptoms, signs and abnormal clinical and laboratory findings, not elsewhere classified — Symptômes, signes et résultats anormaux d'examens cliniques et de laboratoire, non classés ailleurs	3	3	2	3	142	6.3	70	2.9
All other diseases — Toutes autres maladies........................	1	2	-	1	26	♦1.1	43	1.8
External causes — Causes externes								
Total	20	3	14	2	1 635	72.1	484	20.3
Accidents								
Total	10	3	7	2	971	42.8	352	14.8
Transport accidents — Accidents de transport	5	1	3	1	544	24.0	127	5.3
Falls — Chutes	-	1	-	1	68	3.0	14	♦0.6
Accidental drowning and submersion — Noyade et submersion accidentelles........................	2	-	4	-	106	4.7	10	♦0.4
Exposure to smoke, fire and flames — Exposition à la fumée, au feu et aux flammes........................	-	-	-	-	11	♦0.5	4	♦0.2
Accidental poisoning by and exposure to noxious substances — Intoxication accidentelle par des substances nocives et exposition à ces substances	-	-	-	-	43	1.9	8	♦0.3
Intentional self-harm — Lésions auto-infligées........................	1	-	1	-	260	11.5	42	1.8
Assault — Agresssions........................	9	-	5	-	319	14.1	42	1.8
All other external causes — Toutes autres causes externes	-	-	1	-	85	3.8	48	2.0

20. Death and death rates by cause and sex: 2010 - 2014
Décès et taux de mortalité par cause et sexe : 2010 - 2014 (continued - suite)

	Costa Rica				Cuba			
	2013 (+C)				2012 (C)			
Cause of death — Cause de décès	Male — Masculin		Female — Féminin		Male — Masculin		Female — Féminin	
	Number Nombre	Rate Taux	Number Nombre	Rate Taux	Number Nombre	Rate Taux	Number Nombre	Rate Taux
TOTAL	10 906	479.0	8 459	347.4	48 348	865.9	41 024	733.8
Certain infectious and parasitic diseases — Certaines maladies infectieuses et parasitaires								
Total	248	10.9	132	5.4	630	11.3	358	6.4
Intestinal infectious diseases — Maladies infectieuses intestinales	46	2.0	54	2.2	139	2.5	148	2.6
Tuberculosis — Tuberculose	27	♦1.2	5	♦0.2	24	♦0.4	6	♦0.1
Tetanus — Tétanos..	-	-	-	-	2	♦0.0	-	-
Diphtheria — Diphtérie...	-	-	-	-	-	-	-	-
Whooping cough — Coqueluche	1	♦0.0	-	-	-	-	-	-
Meningococcal infection — Infection à méningocoques	-	-	-	-	1	♦0.0	-	-
Septicaemia — Septicémie	19	♦0.8	16	♦0.7	47	0.8	43	0.8
Acute poliomyelitis — Poliomyélite aiguë	-	-	-	-	-	-	-	-
Measles — Rougeole..	-	-	-	-	-	-	-	-
Viral hepatitis — Hépatite virale	6	♦0.3	-	-	67	1.2	75	1.3
Human immunodeficiency virus [HIV] disease — Maladies dues au virus de l'immunodéficience humaine (VIH)...	106	4.7	27	♦1.1	254	4.5	45	0.8
Malaria — Paludisme	-	-	-	-	1	♦0.0	-	-
Neoplasms — Tumeurs	2 548	111.9	2 119	87.0	13 414	240.3	9 869	176.5
Malignant neoplasms — Tumeurs malignes								
Total	2 389	104.9	2 029	83.3	13 069	234.1	9 586	171.5
Malignant neoplasm of lip, oral cavity and pharynx — Tumeur maligne de la lèvre, de la cavité buccale et du pharynx	58	2.5	18	♦0.7	507	9.1	138	2.5
Malignant neoplasm of oesophagus — Tumeur maligne de l'oesophage	41	1.8	14	♦0.6	612	11.0	129	2.3
Malignant neoplasm of stomach — Tumeur maligne de l'estomac	373	16.4	226	9.3	514	9.2	337	6.0
Malignant neoplasm of colon, rectosigmoid junction, rectum, anus and anal canal — Tumeur maligne du côlon, de la jonction recto-sigmoïdienne, du rectum, de l'anus et du canal anal	228	10.0	231	9.5	1 057	18.9	1 337	23.9
Malignant neoplasm of liver and intrahepatic bile ducts — Tumeur maligne du foie et des voies bilaires intrahépatiques	165	7.2	103	4.2	340	6.1	334	6.0
Malignant neoplasm of pancreas — Tumeur maligne du pancréas...................	94	4.1	127	5.2	449	8.0	382	6.8
Malignant neoplasm of trachea, bronchus and lung — Tumeur maligne de la trachée, des bronches et du poumon	192	8.4	92	3.8	3 287	58.9	1 831	32.7
Malignant neoplasm of female breast — Tumeur maligne du sein chez la femme	..	..	342	...	..	..	1 527	32.7
Malignant neoplasm of cervix uteri — Tumeur maligne du col de l'utérus..........	..	..	131	...	..	..	454	9.7
Malignant neoplasm of prostate — Tumeur maligne de la prostate	401	...	..	..	2 712	164.8	..	..
Malignant neoplasm of lymphoid, haematopoietic and related tissue — Tumeurs malignes primitives ou présumées primitives des tissus lymphoïde, hématopoïétique et apparentés...................................	258	11.3	222	9.1	852	15.3	694	12.4
Disorders of the blood and blood-forming organs and certain disorders involving the immune mechanism — Maladies du sang et des organes hématopoïétiques et certains troubles du système immunitaire								
Total	35	1.5	39	1.6	105	1.9	96	1.7
Anaemias — Anémies	23	♦1.0	28	♦1.1	79	1.4	75	1.3
Endocrine, nutritional and metabolic diseases — Maladies endocriniennes, nutritionnelles et métaboliques								
Total	382	16.8	455	18.7	990	17.7	1 491	26.7
Diabetes mellitus — Diabète sucré...	333	14.6	377	15.5	880	15.8	1 371	24.5
Malnutrition — Malnutrition	13	♦0.6	18	♦0.7	24	♦0.4	23	♦0.4
Mental and behavioural disorders — Troubles mentaux et du comportement	124	5.4	182	7.5	1 801	32.3	2 124	38.0
Diseases of the nervous system — Maladies du système nerveux...................	265	11.6	240	9.9	780	14.0	709	12.7
Diseases of the circulatory system — Maladies de l'appareil circulatoire								
Total	2 941	129.2	2 612	107.3	17 603	315.3	16 586	296.7
Acute rheumatic fever and chronic rheumatic heart diseases — Rhumatisme articularie aigu et cardiopathies rhumatismales chroniques	21	♦0.9	27	♦1.1	65	1.2	83	1.5
Hypertensive diseases — Maladies hypertensives..	291	12.8	314	12.9	1 406	25.2	1 371	24.5
Ischaemic heart disease — Cardiopathie ischémique	1 541	67.7	1 123	46.1	8 144	145.9	7 320	130.9
Cerebrovascular disease — Maladie cérébrovasculaire..................................	608	26.7	669	27.5	4 436	79.5	4 494	80.4

Cause of death — Cause de décès	Costa Rica				Cuba			
	2013 (+C)				2012 (C)			
	Male — Masculin		Female — Féminin		Male — Masculin		Female — Féminin	
	Number Nombre	Rate Taux	Number Nombre	Rate Taux	Number Nombre	Rate Taux	Number Nombre	Rate Taux
Diseases of arteries, arterioles and capillaries — Maladies des artères, artérioles et capillaires	92	4.0	43	1.8	1 297	23.2	1 275	22.8
Diseases of the respiratory system — Maladies de l'appareil respiratoire								
Total	889	39.0	788	32.4	4 763	85.3	4 153	74.3
Influenza — Grippe	3	♦0.1	3	♦0.1	2	♦0.0	3	♦0.1
Pneumonia — Pneumopathies	281	12.3	219	9.0	2 707	48.5	2 495	44.6
Chronic lower respiratory diseases — Maladies chroniques des voies respiratoires inférieures	426	18.7	384	15.8	1 884	33.7	1 520	27.2
Diseases of the digestive system — Maladies de l'appareil digestif								
Total	800	35.1	621	25.5	2 126	38.1	1 405	25.1
Gastric and duodenal ulcer — Ulcère de l'estomac et du duodénum.........	41	1.8	18	♦0.7	248	4.4	148	2.6
Diseases of the liver — Maladies du foie.........	443	19.5	255	10.5	1 022	18.3	367	6.6
Diseases of the musculoskeletal system and connective tissue — Maladies du système ostéo-articularie, des muscles et du tissu conjonctif	52	2.3	131	5.4	226	4.0	404	7.2
Diseases of the genitourinary system — Maladies de l'appareil génito-urinaire								
Total	320	14.1	240	9.9	502	9.0	372	6.7
Disorders of kidney and ureter — Affections du rein et de l'uretère	271	11.9	156	6.4	380	6.8	311	5.6
Hyperplasia of prostate — Hyperplasie de la prostate.........	7	..	..	..	61	3.7	..	..
Pregnancy, childbirth and the puerperium — Grossesse, accouchement et puerpéralité								
Total	..	..	10	♦14.2	..	..	55	43.8
Pregnancy with abortive outcome — Grossesse se terminant par un avortement	..	..	-	-	..	..	9	♦7.2
Other direct obstetric causes — Autres décès maternels directs	..	..	6	♦8.5	..	..	18	♦14.3
Indirect obstetric causes — Décès maternels indirects	..	..	4	♦5.7	..	..	15	♦11.9
Certain conditions originating in the perinatal period — Certaines affections dont l'origine se situe dans la période périnatale	169	467.5	139	404.1	166	255.4	113	186.2
Congenital malformations, deformations and chromosomal abnormalities — Malformations congénitales et anomalies chromosomiques	131	362.4	106	308.1	207	318.5	189	311.5
Symptoms, signs and abnormal clinical and laboratory findings, not elsewhere classified — Symptômes, signes et résultats anormaux d'examens cliniques et de laboratoire, non classés ailleurs	360	15.8	189	7.8	403	7.2	242	4.3
All other diseases — Toutes autres maladies	42	1.8	43	1.8	104	1.9	111	2.0
External causes — Causes externes								
Total	1 600	70.3	413	17.0	4 528	81.1	2 747	49.1
Accidents								
Total	909	39.9	298	12.2	2 381	42.6	1 425	25.5
Transport accidents — Accidents de transport	493	21.7	108	4.4	776	13.9	178	3.2
Falls — Chutes	71	3.1	15	♦0.6	963	17.2	1 104	19.7
Accidental drowning and submersion — Noyade et submersion accidentelles.........	87	3.8	15	♦0.6	191	3.4	18	♦0.3
Exposure to smoke, fire and flames — Exposition à la fumée, au feu et aux flammes.........	9	♦0.4	6	♦0.2	36	0.6	14	♦0.3
Accidental poisoning by and exposure to noxious substances — Intoxication accidentelle par des substances nocives et exposition à ces substances	37	1.6	7	♦0.3	73	1.3	12	♦0.2
Intentional self-harm — Lésions auto-infligées.........	273	12.0	39	1.6	1 199	21.5	294	5.3
Assault — Agressions.........	336	14.8	32	1.3	483	8.7	138	2.5
All other external causes — Toutes autres causes externes.........	82	3.6	44	1.8	465	8.3	890	15.9

20. Death and death rates by cause and sex: 2010 - 2014
Décès et taux de mortalité par cause et sexe : 2010 - 2014 (continued - suite)

Cause of death — Cause de décès	Cuba				Dominica - Dominique			
	2013 (C)				2012 (+C)		2013 (+C)	
	Male — Masculin		Female — Féminin		Male — Masculin	Female — Féminin	Male — Masculin	Female — Féminin
	Number Nombre	Rate Taux	Number Nombre	Rate Taux	Number Nombre	Number Nombre	Number Nombre	Number Nombre
TOTAL	49 706	890.7	42 567	758.7	316	302	331	288
Certain infectious and parasitic diseases — Certaines maladies infectieuses et parasitaires								
Total	715	12.8	413	7.4	11	11	14	12
Intestinal infectious diseases — Maladies infectieuses intestinales	193	3.5	158	2.8	1	1	5	2
Tuberculosis — Tuberculose	29	♦0.5	9	♦0.2	-	-	1	1
Tetanus — Tétanos	-	-	-	-	-	-	-	-
Diphtheria — Diphtérie	-	-	-	-	-	-	-	-
Whooping cough — Coqueluche	-	-	-	-	-	-	-	-
Meningococcal infection — Infection à méningocoques	2	♦0.0	-	-	-	-	-	-
Septicaemia — Septicémie	44	0.8	52	0.9	5	5	4	5
Acute poliomyelitis — Poliomyélite aiguë	-	-	-	-	-	-	-	-
Measles — Rougeole	-	-	-	-	-	-	-	-
Viral hepatitis — Hépatite virale..	64	1.1	81	1.4	-	-	-	-
Human immunodeficiency virus [HIV] disease — Maladies dues au virus de l'immunodéficience humaine (VIH)...	284	5.1	67	1.2	4	2	2	-
Malaria — Paludisme	-	-	-	-	-	-	-	-
Neoplasms — Tumeurs	13 300	238.3	10 221	182.2	64	46	71	50
Malignant neoplasms — Tumeurs malignes								
Total	13 032	233.5	9 950	177.3	60	44	66	48
Malignant neoplasm of lip, oral cavity and pharynx — Tumeur maligne de la lèvre, de la cavité buccale et du pharynx	554	9.9	174	3.1	1	-	2	-
Malignant neoplasm of oesophagus — Tumeur maligne de l'oesophage	617	11.1	144	2.6	-	1	2	-
Malignant neoplasm of stomach — Tumeur maligne de l'estomac	487	8.7	370	6.6	5	3	6	6
Malignant neoplasm of colon, rectosigmoid junction, rectum, anus and anal canal — Tumeur maligne du côlon, de la jonction recto-sigmoïdienne, du rectum, de l'anus et du canal anal	948	17.0	1 381	24.6	-	5	3	2
Malignant neoplasm of liver and intrahepatic bile ducts — Tumeur maligne du foie et des voies bilaires intrahépatiques	407	7.3	360	6.4	1	2	2	1
Malignant neoplasm of pancreas — Tumeur maligne du pancréas...................	393	7.0	430	7.7	4	-	3	2
Malignant neoplasm of trachea, bronchus and lung — Tumeur maligne de la trachée, des bronches et du poumon	3 302	59.2	1 921	34.2	6	1	3	7
Malignant neoplasm of female breast — Tumeur maligne du sein chez la femme	..	..	1 445	30.8	..	12	..	6
Malignant neoplasm of cervix uteri — Tumeur maligne du col de l'utérus.........	..	..	452	9.6	..	4	..	4
Malignant neoplasm of prostate — Tumeur maligne de la prostate	2 800	167.3	..	..	31	..	28	..
Malignant neoplasm of lymphoid, haematopoietic and related tissue — Tumeurs malignes primitives ou présumées primitives des tissus lymphoïde, hématopoïétique et apparentés	828	14.8	701	12.5	7	1	7	4
Disorders of the blood and blood-forming organs and certain disorders involving the immune mechanism — Maladies du sang et des organes hématopoïétiques et certains troubles du système immunitaire								
Total	103	1.8	86	1.5	1	2	2	5
Anaemias — Anémies	65	1.2	57	1.0	1	2	1	4
Endocrine, nutritional and metabolic diseases — Maladies endocriniennes, nutritionnelles et métaboliques								
Total	1 063	19.0	1 523	27.1	23	46	24	27
Diabetes mellitus — Diabète sucré...	934	16.7	1 398	24.9	17	37	22	22
Malnutrition — Malnutrition	33	0.6	16	♦0.3	1	1	-	1
Mental and behavioural disorders — Troubles mentaux et du comportement	2 006	35.9	2 274	40.5	4	3	2	3
Diseases of the nervous system — Maladies du système nerveux.................	830	14.9	674	12.0	5	4	4	6
Diseases of the circulatory system — Maladies de l'appareil circulatoire								
Total	18 223	326.5	16 648	296.7	113	126	105	117
Acute rheumatic fever and chronic rheumatic heart diseases — Rhumatisme articularie aigu et cardiopathies rhumatismales chroniques	44	0.8	81	1.4	-	-	-	1
Hypertensive diseases — Maladies hypertensives.....................................	1 589	28.5	1 445	25.8	12	28	16	17
Ischaemic heart disease — Cardiopathie ischémique	8 478	151.9	7 249	129.2	19	17	11	15

	Cuba				Dominica - Dominique			
Cause of death — Cause de décès	2013 (C)				2012 (+C)		2013 (+C)	
	Male — Masculin		Female — Féminin		Male — Masculin	Female — Féminin	Male — Masculin	Female — Féminin
	Number Nombre	Rate Taux	Number Nombre	Rate Taux	Number Nombre	Number Nombre	Number Nombre	Number Nombre
Cerebrovascular disease — Maladie cérébrovasculaire.....................................	4 502	80.7	4 559	81.3	21	27	23	30
Diseases of arteries, arterioles and capillaries — Maladies des artères, artérioles et capillaires	1 349	24.2	1 272	22.7	3	2	6	4
Diseases of the respiratory system — Maladies de l'appareil respiratoire								
Total	5 085	91.1	4 665	83.1	23	15	25	16
Influenza — Grippe	1	♦0.0	1	♦0.0	-	-	3	-
Pneumonia — Pneumopathies	2 907	52.1	2 702	48.2	4	8	12	9
Chronic lower respiratory diseases — Maladies chroniques des voies respiratoires inférieures	2 023	36.2	1 838	32.8	8	4	7	5
Diseases of the digestive system — Maladies de l'appareil digestif								
Total	2 181	39.1	1 470	26.2	6	6	15	7
Gastric and duodenal ulcer — Ulcère de l'estomac et du duodénum................	231	4.1	133	2.4	-	-	3	-
Diseases of the liver — Maladies du foie..	1 067	19.1	374	6.7	-	2	5	1
Diseases of the musculoskeletal system and connective tissue — Maladies du système ostéo-articulaire, des muscles et du tissu conjonctif	216	3.9	431	7.7	-	3	1	1
Diseases of the genitourinary system — Maladies de l'appareil génito-urinaire								
Total	521	9.3	444	7.9	8	4	6	2
Disorders of kidney and ureter — Affections du rein et de l'uretère	393	7.0	357	6.4	5	4	4	1
Hyperplasia of prostate — Hyperplasie de la prostate....................................	52	3.1	..	..	2	..	1	..
Pregnancy, childbirth and the puerperium — Grossesse, accouchement et puerpéralité								
Total	..	..	56	44.5	..	-	..	3
Pregnancy with abortive outcome — Grossesse se terminant par un avortement	..	..	7	♦5.6	..	-	..	-
Other direct obstetric causes — Autres décès maternels directs	..	..	24	♦19.1	..	-	..	3
Indirect obstetric causes — Décès maternels indirects	..	..	18	♦14.3	..	-	..	-
Certain conditions originating in the perinatal period — Certaines affections dont l'origine se situe dans la période périnatale	168	257.3	125	206.3	14	14	12	16
Congenital malformations, deformations and chromosomal abnormalities — Malformations congénitales et anomalies chromosomiques	205	314.0	176	290.5	1	3	2	4
Symptoms, signs and abnormal clinical and laboratory findings, not elsewhere classified — Symptômes, signes et résultats anormaux d'examens cliniques et de laboratoire, non classés ailleurs	421	7.5	249	4.4	12	11	9	5
All other diseases — Toutes autres maladies..	85	1.5	147	2.6	3	4	3	5
External causes — Causes externes								
Total	4 584	82.1	2 965	52.8	28	4	36	9
Accidents								
Total	2 338	41.9	1 534	27.3	15	3	22	5
Transport accidents — Accidents de transport..	723	13.0	203	3.6	10	1	6	3
Falls — Chutes	949	17.0	1 188	21.2	1	-	1	-
Accidental drowning and submersion — Noyade et submersion accidentelles...	233	4.2	18	♦0.3	2	1	5	-
Exposure to smoke, fire and flames — Exposition à la fumée, au feu et aux flammes...	26	♦0.5	22	♦0.4	-	-	-	1
Accidental poisoning by and exposure to noxious substances — Intoxication accidentelle par des substances nocives et exposition à ces substances	79	1.4	17	♦0.3	-	1	-	-
Intentional self-harm — Lésions auto-infligées...	1 201	21.5	297	5.3	2	-	1	-
Assault — Agresssions...	526	9.4	147	2.6	7	1	12	2
All other external causes — Toutes autres causes externes	519	9.3	987	17.6	4	-	1	2

20. Death and death rates by cause and sex: 2010 - 2014
Décès et taux de mortalité par cause et sexe : 2010 - 2014 (continued - suite)

Cause of death — Cause de décès	Dominican Republic - République dominicaine				El Salvador			
	2011 (U)		2012 (U)		2011 (+U)		2012 (+U)	
	Male — Masculin	Female — Féminin	Male — Masculin	Female — Féminin	Male — Masculin	Female — Féminin	Male — Masculin	Female — Féminin
	Number Nombre	Number Nombre	Number Nombre	Number Nombre	Number Nombre	Number Nombre	Number Nombre	Number Nombre
TOTAL	18 648	13 383	20 805	15 233	18 946	14 216	17 847	14 275
Certain infectious and parasitic diseases — Certaines maladies infectieuses et parasitaires								
Total	903	633	1 080	784	628	477	706	519
Intestinal infectious diseases — Maladies infectieuses intestinales	135	96	85	86	63	58	71	53
Tuberculosis — Tuberculose	191	98	198	100	32	21	44	17
Tetanus — Tétanos	17	2	21	3	1	3	2	-
Diphtheria — Diphtérie	-	1	-	-	-	-	-	-
Whooping cough — Coqueluche	-	-	-	-	-	-	1	1
Meningococcal infection — Infection à méningocoques	2	2	7	2	-	-	1	-
Septicaemia — Septicémie	195	197	284	273	274	278	338	351
Acute poliomyelitis — Poliomyélite aiguë	-	-	-	-	-	-	-	-
Measles — Rougeole	-	-	-	-	-	-	-	-
Viral hepatitis — Hépatite virale	19	18	19	15	4	5	3	4
Human immunodeficiency virus [HIV] disease — Maladies dues au virus de l'immunodéficience humaine (VIH)	273	190	339	221	218	85	207	81
Malaria — Paludisme	3	-	2	2	-	-	1	-
Neoplasms — Tumeurs	2 490	1 983	2 414	2 058	1 599	1 979	1 534	2 049
Malignant neoplasms — Tumeurs malignes								
Total	2 409	1 910	2 331	1 965	1 587	1 972	1 514	2 038
Malignant neoplasm of lip, oral cavity and pharynx — Tumeur maligne de la lèvre, de la cavité buccale et du pharynx	146	62	136	72	35	27	34	28
Malignant neoplasm of oesophagus — Tumeur maligne de l'oesophage	53	26	49	24	27	15	23	14
Malignant neoplasm of stomach — Tumeur maligne de l'estomac	174	111	135	98	255	211	200	193
Malignant neoplasm of colon, rectosigmoid junction, rectum, anus and anal canal — Tumeur maligne du côlon, de la jonction recto-sigmoïdienne, du rectum, de l'anus et du canal anal	168	166	159	158	88	107	75	108
Malignant neoplasm of liver and intrahepatic bile ducts — Tumeur maligne du foie et des voies bilaires intrahépatiques	161	146	159	146	114	137	97	150
Malignant neoplasm of pancreas — Tumeur maligne du pancréas	96	85	108	86	60	72	61	81
Malignant neoplasm of trachea, bronchus and lung — Tumeur maligne de la trachée, des bronches et du poumon	335	215	292	216	122	120	133	124
Malignant neoplasm of female breast — Tumeur maligne du sein chez la femme	..	337	..	360	..	140	..	168
Malignant neoplasm of cervix uteri — Tumeur maligne du col de l'utérus	..	185	..	217	..	185	..	228
Malignant neoplasm of prostate — Tumeur maligne de la prostate	780	..	764	..	216	..	236	..
Malignant neoplasm of lymphoid, haematopoietic and related tissue — Tumeurs malignes primitives ou présumées primitives des tissus lymphoïde, hématopoïétique et apparentés	166	147	182	134	162	137	168	151
Disorders of the blood and blood-forming organs and certain disorders involving the immune mechanism — Maladies du sang et des organes hématopoïétiques et certains troubles du système immunitaire								
Total	84	56	96	108	97	78	78	67
Anaemias — Anémies	61	48	59	69	72	54	67	51
Endocrine, nutritional and metabolic diseases — Maladies endocriniennes, nutritionnelles et métaboliques								
Total	716	725	750	826	735	1 094	834	1 232
Diabetes mellitus — Diabète sucré	637	643	666	743	542	916	663	1 074
Malnutrition — Malnutrition	38	32	37	29	116	93	112	102
Mental and behavioural disorders — Troubles mentaux et du comportement	49	18	47	27	415	22	429	23
Diseases of the nervous system — Maladies du système nerveux	223	164	262	217	350	360	361	326
Diseases of the circulatory system — Maladies de l'appareil circulatoire								
Total	6 094	5 058	6 591	5 547	3 127	3 118	2 752	2 915
Acute rheumatic fever and chronic rheumatic heart diseases — Rhumatisme articularie aigu et cardiopathies rhumatismales chroniques	16	18	8	16	2	4	-	1
Hypertensive diseases — Maladies hypertensives	688	724	754	773	253	229	168	170
Ischaemic heart disease — Cardiopathie ischémique	2 832	2 217	2 921	2 343	1 270	1 162	1 228	1 203

Cause of death — Cause de décès	Dominican Republic - République dominicaine				El Salvador			
	2011 (U)		2012 (U)		2011 (+U)		2012 (+U)	
	Male — Masculin	Female — Féminin	Male — Masculin	Female — Féminin	Male — Masculin	Female — Féminin	Male — Masculin	Female — Féminin
	Number Nombre	Number Nombre	Number Nombre	Number Nombre	Number Nombre	Number Nombre	Number Nombre	Number Nombre
Cerebrovascular disease — Maladie cérébrovasculaire..................................	1 791	1 406	1 947	1 562	452	472	512	605
Diseases of arteries, arterioles and capillaries — Maladies des artères, artérioles et capillaires	68	45	51	46	23	24	20	15
Diseases of the respiratory system — Maladies de l'appareil respiratoire								
Total	1 473	1 263	1 724	1 472	1 219	1 195	1 136	1 181
Influenza — Grippe	1	6	5	5	-	-	-	-
Pneumonia — Pneumopathies	562	481	551	537	667	618	589	593
Chronic lower respiratory diseases — Maladies chroniques des voies respiratoires inférieures	317	249	335	228	229	305	235	305
Diseases of the digestive system — Maladies de l'appareil digestif								
Total	641	450	757	516	966	735	943	717
Gastric and duodenal ulcer — Ulcère de l'estomac et du duodénum...............	75	39	84	56	57	57	54	65
Diseases of the liver — Maladies du foie..	349	232	410	249	597	365	615	352
Diseases of the musculoskeletal system and connective tissue — Maladies du système ostéo-articulaire, des muscles et du tissu conjonctif	13	33	25	49	30	81	34	67
Diseases of the genitourinary system — Maladies de l'appareil génito-urinaire								
Total	205	140	300	194	1 856	884	1 903	954
Disorders of kidney and ureter — Affections du rein et de l'uretère	175	133	272	186	1 759	806	1 801	895
Hyperplasia of prostate — Hyperplasie de la prostate...........................	18	..	16	..	27	..	34	..
Pregnancy, childbirth and the puerperium — Grossesse, accouchement et puerpéralité								
Total	..	188	..	177	..	16	..	17
Pregnancy with abortive outcome — Grossesse se terminant par un avortement	..	17	..	15	..	-	..	3
Other direct obstetric causes — Autres décès maternels directs	..	106	..	122	..	16	..	14
Indirect obstetric causes — Décès maternels indirects	..	65	..	40	..	-	..	-
Certain conditions originating in the perinatal period — Certaines affections dont l'origine se situe dans la période périnatale	1 557	1 224	1 514	1 365	175	132	189	152
Congenital malformations, deformations and chromosomal abnormalities — Malformations congénitales et anomalies chromosomiques	322	219	393	328	125	132	133	119
Symptoms, signs and abnormal clinical and laboratory findings, not elsewhere classified — Symptômes, signes et résultats anormaux d'examens cliniques et de laboratoire, non classés ailleurs	736	591	1 043	806	2 602	2 801	2 934	3 111
All other diseases — Toutes autres maladies...	2	2	4	4	40	74	49	79
External causes — Causes externes								
Total	3 140	636	3 805	755	4 982	1 038	3 832	747
Accidents								
Total	1 471	294	1 663	339	1 475	434	1 338	338
Transport accidents — Accidents de transport	1 180	217	1 400	230	840	228	776	188
Falls — Chutes	20	14	20	9	188	109	170	89
Accidental drowning and submersion — Noyade et submersion accidentelles...	20	4	22	6	208	51	146	30
Exposure to smoke, fire and flames — Exposition à la fumée, au feu et aux flammes..	19	14	11	10	8	5	17	5
Accidental poisoning by and exposure to noxious substances — Intoxication accidentelle par des substances nocives et exposition à ces substances	3	1	4	-	119	9	160	8
Intentional self-harm — Lésions auto-infligées..	187	39	213	43	372	118	398	116
Assault — Agresssions...	851	78	1 130	123	3 122	483	2 055	280
All other external causes — Toutes autres causes externes	631	225	799	250	13	3	41	13

20. Death and death rates by cause and sex: 2010 - 2014
Décès et taux de mortalité par cause et sexe : 2010 - 2014 (continued - suite)

Cause of death — Cause de décès	Grenada - Grenade 2012 (C) Male — Masculin Number Nombre	Grenada - Grenade 2012 (C) Female — Féminin Number Nombre	Grenada - Grenade 2013 (C) Male — Masculin Number Nombre	Grenada - Grenade 2013 (C) Female — Féminin Number Nombre	Guadeloupe 2012 (...) Male — Masculin Number Nombre	Guadeloupe 2012 (...) Female — Féminin Number Nombre	Guadeloupe 2013 (...) Male — Masculin Number Nombre	Guadeloupe 2013 (...) Female — Féminin Number Nombre
TOTAL	448	407	446	374	1 533	1 343	1 618	1 324
Certain infectious and parasitic diseases — Certaines maladies infectieuses et parasitaires								
Total	15	11	16	10	36	37	52	40
Intestinal infectious diseases — Maladies infectieuses intestinales	-	1	-	-	4	2	7	5
Tuberculosis — Tuberculose	-	-	-	-	-	-	-	1
Tetanus — Tétanos	-	-	-	-	-	-	-	-
Diphtheria — Diphtérie	-	-	-	-	-	-	-	-
Whooping cough — Coqueluche	-	-	-	-	-	-	-	-
Meningococcal infection — Infection à méningocoques	-	-	-	-	-	-	-	-
Septicaemia — Septicémie	5	9	8	6	15	19	24	20
Acute poliomyelitis — Poliomyélite aiguë	-	-	-	-	-	-	-	1
Measles — Rougeole	-	-	-	-	-	-	-	-
Viral hepatitis — Hépatite virale	-	-	-	-	1	3	3	3
Human immunodeficiency virus [HIV] disease — Maladies dues au virus de l'immunodéficience humaine (VIH)	7	-	5	-	11	3	6	3
Malaria — Paludisme	-	-	-	-	-	-	-	-
Neoplasms — Tumeurs	107	80	91	65	399	304	400	291
Malignant neoplasms — Tumeurs malignes								
Total	102	75	86	60	379	291	386	281
Malignant neoplasm of lip, oral cavity and pharynx — Tumeur maligne de la lèvre, de la cavité buccale et du pharynx	4	1	3	-	14	4	12	3
Malignant neoplasm of oesophagus — Tumeur maligne de l'oesophage	4	2	1	-	14	1	21	3
Malignant neoplasm of stomach — Tumeur maligne de l'estomac	7	3	2	-	36	30	32	19
Malignant neoplasm of colon, rectosigmoid junction, rectum, anus and anal canal — Tumeur maligne du côlon, de la jonction recto-sigmoïdienne, du rectum, de l'anus et du canal anal	7	8	5	5	41	28	41	28
Malignant neoplasm of liver and intrahepatic bile ducts — Tumeur maligne du foie et des voies bilaires intrahépatiques	1	3	1	1	18	7	12	13
Malignant neoplasm of pancreas — Tumeur maligne du pancréas	1	4	4	6	24	21	31	26
Malignant neoplasm of trachea, bronchus and lung — Tumeur maligne de la trachée, des bronches et du poumon	6	8	7	2	33	17	31	17
Malignant neoplasm of female breast — Tumeur maligne du sein chez la femme	..	18	..	14	..	61	..	53
Malignant neoplasm of cervix uteri — Tumeur maligne du col de l'utérus	..	6	..	8	..	10	..	8
Malignant neoplasm of prostate — Tumeur maligne de la prostate	40	..	36	..	97	..	102	..
Malignant neoplasm of lymphoid, haematopoietic and related tissue — Tumeurs malignes primitives ou présumées primitives des tissus lymphoïde, hématopoïétique et apparentés	14	6	12	7	33	29	37	39
Disorders of the blood and blood-forming organs and certain disorders involving the immune mechanism — Maladies du sang et des organes hématopoïétiques et certains troubles du système immunitaire								
Total	4	4	11	6	6	9	6	14
Anaemias — Anémies	1	3	9	5	5	7	3	11
Endocrine, nutritional and metabolic diseases — Maladies endocriniennes, nutritionnelles et métaboliques								
Total	38	71	41	54	63	101	74	105
Diabetes mellitus — Diabète sucré	34	60	30	49	43	72	48	73
Malnutrition — Malnutrition	1	-	3	-	9	11	12	10
Mental and behavioural disorders — Troubles mentaux et du comportement	4	4	2	5	51	27	54	20
Diseases of the nervous system — Maladies du système nerveux	10	9	6	8	72	84	84	76
Diseases of the circulatory system — Maladies de l'appareil circulatoire								
Total	136	145	144	142	343	356	345	365
Acute rheumatic fever and chronic rheumatic heart diseases — Rhumatisme articularie aigu et cardiopathies rhumatismales chroniques	-	1	4	1	-	4	1	4
Hypertensive diseases — Maladies hypertensives	29	26	27	29	41	69	42	60
Ischaemic heart disease — Cardiopathie ischémique	37	39	51	35	49	31	48	50

	Grenada - Grenade				Guadeloupe			
Cause of death — Cause de décès	2012 (C)		2013 (C)		2012 (...)		2013 (...)	
	Male — Masculin	Female — Féminin	Male — Masculin	Female — Féminin	Male — Masculin	Female — Féminin	Male — Masculin	Female — Féminin
	Number Nombre	Number Nombre	Number Nombre	Number Nombre	Number Nombre	Number Nombre	Number Nombre	Number Nombre
Cerebrovascular disease — Maladie cérébrovasculaire.....................................	46	54	39	53	122	117	121	130
Diseases of arteries, arterioles and capillaries — Maladies des artères, artérioles et capillaires	7	3	4	3	18	15	23	7
Diseases of the respiratory system — Maladies de l'appareil respiratoire								
Total	39	26	42	25	71	70	72	54
Influenza — Grippe	-	-	-	-	1	4	1	4
Pneumonia — Pneumopathies	29	18	22	21	29	34	30	19
Chronic lower respiratory diseases — Maladies chroniques des voies respiratoires inférieures	7	2	8	-	14	13	19	9
Diseases of the digestive system — Maladies de l'appareil digestif								
Total	26	17	26	10	62	48	70	63
Gastric and duodenal ulcer — Ulcère de l'estomac et du duodénum................	-	-	-	-	2	2	4	3
Diseases of the liver — Maladies du foie..	8	4	12	2	27	14	31	13
Diseases of the musculoskeletal system and connective tissue — Maladies du système ostéo-articularie, des muscles et du tissu conjonctif	-	2	1	5	2	10	9	10
Diseases of the genitourinary system — Maladies de l'appareil génito-urinaire								
Total	10	4	7	6	27	22	30	27
Disorders of kidney and ureter — Affections du rein et de l'uretère	2	2	4	3	23	20	21	22
Hyperplasia of prostate — Hyperplasie de la prostate...........................	5	..	2	..	-	..	-	..
Pregnancy, childbirth and the puerperium — Grossesse, accouchement et puerpéralité								
Total	..	2	..	1	..	4	..	1
Pregnancy with abortive outcome — Grossesse se terminant par un avortement	..	-	..	-	..	-	..	-
Other direct obstetric causes — Autres décès maternels directs	..	1	..	1	..	2	..	1
Indirect obstetric causes — Décès maternels indirects	..	1	..	-	..	2	..	-
Certain conditions originating in the perinatal period — Certaines affections dont l'origine se situe dans la période périnatale	5	10	16	13	30	7	16	11
Congenital malformations, deformations and chromosomal abnormalities — Malformations congénitales et anomalies chromosomiques	6	4	1	2	5	5	17	6
Symptoms, signs and abnormal clinical and laboratory findings, not elsewhere classified — Symptômes, signes et résultats anormaux d'examens cliniques et de laboratoire, non classés ailleurs	9	10	4	5	185	170	208	187
All other diseases — Toutes autres maladies..	1	3	3	5	4	8	9	6
External causes — Causes externes								
Total	38	5	35	12	177	81	172	48
Accidents								
Total	32	4	28	9	131	60	108	38
Transport accidents — Accidents de transport	6	-	7	4	55	8	44	4
Falls — Chutes	6	-	4	-	11	10	9	10
Accidental drowning and submersion — Noyade et submersion accidentelles...	3	-	10	-	7	1	13	-
Exposure to smoke, fire and flames — Exposition à la fumée, au feu et aux flammes..	1	-	1	-	1	3	-	1
Accidental poisoning by and exposure to noxious substances — Intoxication accidentelle par des substances nocives et exposition à ces substances	-	-	-	1	4	4	5	4
Intentional self-harm — Lésions auto-infligées..	2	-	-	-	28	12	33	6
Assault — Agresssions..	4	-	5	2	13	2	13	-
All other external causes — Toutes autres causes externes	-	1	2	1	5	7	18	4

	Guatemala						Honduras	
Cause of death — Cause de décès	2012 (C)			2013 (C)			2012 (+U)	
	Male — Masculin	Female — Féminin		Male — Masculin	Female — Féminin		Male — Masculin	Female — Féminin
	Number Nombre	Number Nombre	Rate Taux	Number Nombre	Number Nombre	Rate Taux	Number Nombre	Number Nombre
TOTAL	41 099	31 558	...	42 206	32 660	...	*3 140*	*2 885*
Certain infectious and parasitic diseases — Certaines maladies infectieuses et parasitaires								
Total	2 250	1 861	...	2 396	1 928	...	*266*	*218*
Intestinal infectious diseases — Maladies infectieuses intestinales	1 208	1 085	...	1 212	1 102	...	*41*	*48*
Tuberculosis — Tuberculose	139	96	...	185	116	...	*46*	*36*
Tetanus — Tétanos	5	1	...	9	2	...	*1*	*1*
Diphtheria — Diphtérie	-	-	...	-	-	...	*-*	*-*
Whooping cough — Coqueluche	2	3	...	8	10	...	*6*	*8*
Meningococcal infection — Infection à méningocoques	1	1	...	1	-	...	*-*	*-*
Septicaemia — Septicémie	426	381	...	513	418	...	*37*	*34*
Acute poliomyelitis — Poliomyélite aiguë	-	1	...	2	1	...	*-*	*-*
Measles — Rougeole	-	-	...	1	-	...	*-*	*-*
Viral hepatitis — Hépatite virale	32	24	...	22	25	...	*3*	*1*
Human immunodeficiency virus [HIV] disease — Maladies dues au virus de l'immunodéficience humaine (VIH)	319	168	...	310	135	...	*99*	*66*
Malaria — Paludisme	6	3	...	4	4	...	*-*	*2*
Neoplasms — Tumeurs	3 534	4 378	...	3 529	4 328	...	*212*	*319*
Malignant neoplasms — Tumeurs malignes								
Total	3 396	4 236	...	3 322	4 110	...	*186*	*284*
Malignant neoplasm of lip, oral cavity and pharynx — Tumeur maligne de la lèvre, de la cavité buccale et du pharynx	47	39	...	53	49	...	*2*	*1*
Malignant neoplasm of oesophagus — Tumeur maligne de l'oesophage	83	37	...	77	43	...	*2*	*2*
Malignant neoplasm of stomach — Tumeur maligne de l'estomac	638	762	...	622	724	...	*30*	*25*
Malignant neoplasm of colon, rectosigmoid junction, rectum, anus and anal canal — Tumeur maligne du côlon, de la jonction recto-sigmoïdienne, du rectum, de l'anus et du canal anal	144	156	...	114	165	...	*4*	*13*
Malignant neoplasm of liver and intrahepatic bile ducts — Tumeur maligne du foie et des voies bilaires intrahépatiques	570	666	...	588	693	...	*15*	*16*
Malignant neoplasm of pancreas — Tumeur maligne du pancréas	107	123	...	95	103	...	*4*	*8*
Malignant neoplasm of trachea, bronchus and lung — Tumeur maligne de la trachée, des bronches et du poumon	208	137	...	198	151	...	*19*	*16*
Malignant neoplasm of female breast — Tumeur maligne du sein chez la femme	..	284	...	..	307	...	..	*14*
Malignant neoplasm of cervix uteri — Tumeur maligne du col de l'utérus	..	435	...	..	382	...	..	*47*
Malignant neoplasm of prostate — Tumeur maligne de la prostate	505	..	...	569	..	..	*8*	..
Malignant neoplasm of lymphoid, haematopoietic and related tissue — Tumeurs malignes primitives ou présumées primitives des tissus lymphoïde, hématopoïétique et apparentés	300	316	...	356	292	...	*45*	*61*
Disorders of the blood and blood-forming organs and certain disorders involving the immune mechanism — Maladies du sang et des organes hématopoïétiques et certains troubles du système immunitaire								
Total	310	359	...	297	320	...	*37*	*35*
Anaemias — Anémies	256	310	...	210	242	...	*24*	*26*
Endocrine, nutritional and metabolic diseases — Maladies endocriniennes, nutritionnelles et métaboliques								
Total	3 076	4 079	...	3 221	4 180	...	*222*	*395*
Diabetes mellitus — Diabète sucré	2 070	2 975	...	2 162	3 089	...	*182*	*342*
Malnutrition — Malnutrition	772	878	...	846	890	...	*28*	*32*
Mental and behavioural disorders — Troubles mentaux et du comportement	410	56	...	456	49	...	*25*	*2*
Diseases of the nervous system — Maladies du système nerveux	732	619	...	728	649	...	*54*	*43*
Diseases of the circulatory system — Maladies de l'appareil circulatoire								
Total	5 879	5 833	...	5 965	5 965	...	*515*	*563*
Acute rheumatic fever and chronic rheumatic heart diseases — Rhumatisme articularie aigu et cardiopathies rhumatismales chroniques	3	13	...	10	11	...	*6*	*6*
Hypertensive diseases — Maladies hypertensives	401	464	...	419	561	...	*87*	*86*
Ischaemic heart disease — Cardiopathie ischémique	2 779	2 332	...	2 621	2 256	...	*129*	*134*

20. Death and death rates by cause and sex: 2010 - 2014
Décès et taux de mortalité par cause et sexe : 2010 - 2014 (continued - suite)

Cause of death — Cause de décès	Guatemala						Honduras	
	2012 (C)			2013 (C)			2012 (+U)	
	Male — Masculin	Female — Féminin		Male — Masculin	Female — Féminin		Male — Masculin	Female — Féminin
	Number Nombre	Number Nombre	Rate Taux	Number Nombre	Number Nombre	Rate Taux	Number Nombre	Number Nombre
Cerebrovascular disease — Maladie cérébrovasculaire..................................	1 461	1 697	...	1 523	1 667	...	188	200
Diseases of arteries, arterioles and capillaries — Maladies des artères, artérioles et capillaires	41	52	...	45	55	...	8	15
Diseases of the respiratory system — Maladies de l'appareil respiratoire								
Total	4 659	4 098	...	5 019	4 533	...	263	276
Influenza — Grippe	1	1	...	3	3	...	-	-
Pneumonia — Pneumopathies	3 608	3 207	...	3 889	3 520	...	126	105
Chronic lower respiratory diseases — Maladies chroniques des voies respiratoires inférieures	533	515	...	527	567	...	90	121
Diseases of the digestive system — Maladies de l'appareil digestif								
Total	3 349	2 023	...	3 327	2 077	...	240	179
Gastric and duodenal ulcer — Ulcère de l'estomac et du duodénum..............	336	310	...	309	289	...	6	5
Diseases of the liver — Maladies du foie............................	2 135	927	...	2 127	970	...	169	85
Diseases of the musculoskeletal system and connective tissue — Maladies du système ostéo-articularie, des muscles et du tissu conjonctif	100	146	...	72	162	...	8	23
Diseases of the genitourinary system — Maladies de l'appareil génito-urinaire								
Total	1 547	1 312	...	1 768	1 428	...	74	61
Disorders of kidney and ureter — Affections du rein et de l'uretère	1 410	1 274	...	1 629	1 380	...	53	53
Hyperplasia of prostate — Hyperplasie de la prostate...........................	79	..	..	80	..	..	14	..
Pregnancy, childbirth and the puerperium — Grossesse, accouchement et puerpéralité								
Total	..	356	91.6	..	318	82.1	..	31
Pregnancy with abortive outcome — Grossesse se terminant par un avortement	..	22	♦5.7	..	15	♦3.9	..	2
Other direct obstetric causes — Autres décès maternels directs	..	313	80.5	..	256	66.1	..	26
Indirect obstetric causes — Décès maternels indirects	..	20	♦5.1	..	47	12.1	..	3
Certain conditions originating in the perinatal period — Certaines affections dont l'origine se situe dans la période périnatale	1 536	1 176	...	1 703	1 277	...	559	379
Congenital malformations, deformations and chromosomal abnormalities — Malformations congénitales et anomalies chromosomiques	719	624	...	727	682	...	195	195
Symptoms, signs and abnormal clinical and laboratory findings, not elsewhere classified — Symptômes, signes et résultats anormaux d'examens cliniques et de laboratoire, non classés ailleurs	2 691	2 533	...	2 771	2 583	...	23	22
All other diseases — Toutes autres maladies.................................	47	43	...	22	29	...	19	19
External causes — Causes externes								
Total	10 260	2 062	...	10 205	2 152	...	428	125
Accidents								
Total	6 562	1 501	...	6 208	1 472	...	249	70
Transport accidents — Accidents de transport	810	179	...	952	188	...	63	16
Falls — Chutes	4	2	...	3	-	...	25	15
Accidental drowning and submersion — Noyade et submersion accidentelles..	299	47	...	292	50	...	1	-
Exposure to smoke, fire and flames — Exposition à la fumée, au feu et aux flammes..	85	29	...	69	29	...	3	2
Accidental poisoning by and exposure to noxious substances — Intoxication accidentelle par des substances nocives et exposition à ces substances	964	215	...	945	231	...	38	11
Intentional self-harm — Lésions auto-infligées..	310	110	...	332	124	...	77	34
Assault — Agresssions	3 375	446	...	3 648	544	...	75	7
All other external causes — Toutes autres causes externes	13	5	...	17	12	...	27	14

609

20. Death and death rates by cause and sex: 2010 - 2014
Décès et taux de mortalité par cause et sexe : 2010 - 2014 (continued - suite)

Cause of death — Cause de décès	Honduras		Jamaica - Jamaïque				Martinique	
	2013 (+U)		2010 (...)		2011 (...)		2012 (...)	
	Male — Masculin	Female — Féminin	Male — Masculin	Female — Féminin	Male — Masculin	Female — Féminin	Male — Masculin	Female — Féminin
	Number Nombre	Number Nombre	Number Nombre	Number Nombre	Number Nombre	Number Nombre	Number Nombre	Number Nombre
TOTAL	*3 430*	*3 047*	*8 114*	*7 321*	*9 265*	*7 656*	*1 473*	*1 347*
Certain infectious and parasitic diseases — Certaines maladies infectieuses et parasitaires								
Total	*260*	*217*	*480*	*307*	*421*	*316*	*38*	*22*
Intestinal infectious diseases — Maladies infectieuses intestinales	37	30	1	6	4	2	6	5
Tuberculosis — Tuberculose	52	33	8	2	5	2	1	-
Tetanus — Tétanos	1	3	-	1	-	1	-	-
Diphtheria — Diphtérie...	-	-	-	-	-	-	-	-
Whooping cough — Coqueluche	2	6	-	-	-	-	-	-
Meningococcal infection — Infection à méningocoques	-	-	-	-	-	-	-	-
Septicaemia — Septicémie	45	45	97	71	65	60	16	9
Acute poliomyelitis — Poliomyélite aiguë	-	-	-	-	-	-	-	-
Measles — Rougeole..	-	-	-	-	-	-	-	-
Viral hepatitis — Hépatite virale...	3	4	4	4	7	3	3	1
Human immunodeficiency virus [HIV] disease — Maladies dues au virus de l'immunodéficience humaine (VIH)...........	86	65	300	206	288	235	5	3
Malaria — Paludisme	-	1	-	-	-	-	-	-
Neoplasms — Tumeurs	*240*	*259*	*1 790*	*1 476*	*1 863*	*1 537*	*269*	*205*
Malignant neoplasms — Tumeurs malignes								
Total	*216*	*233*	*1 726*	*1 398*	*1 809*	*1 475*	*255*	*189*
Malignant neoplasm of lip, oral cavity and pharynx — Tumeur maligne de la lèvre, de la cavité buccale et du pharynx	1	4	38	15	31	14	6	-
Malignant neoplasm of oesophagus — Tumeur maligne de l'oesophage	5	-	41	20	39	17	4	-
Malignant neoplasm of stomach — Tumeur maligne de l'estomac	25	19	127	72	112	67	17	13
Malignant neoplasm of colon, rectosigmoid junction, rectum, anus and anal canal — Tumeur maligne du côlon, de la jonction recto-sigmoïdienne, du rectum, de l'anus et du canal anal	11	14	141	132	128	162	34	27
Malignant neoplasm of liver and intrahepatic bile ducts — Tumeur maligne du foie et des voies bilaires intrahépatiques	8	13	47	37	35	36	11	2
Malignant neoplasm of pancreas — Tumeur maligne du pancréas...................	1	6	41	42	44	45	14	12
Malignant neoplasm of trachea, bronchus and lung — Tumeur maligne de la trachée, des bronches et du poumon	26	15	266	79	291	96	33	18
Malignant neoplasm of female breast — Tumeur maligne du sein chez la femme	..	17	..	300	..	294	..	25
Malignant neoplasm of cervix uteri — Tumeur maligne du col de l'utérus.........	..	33	..	158	..	192	..	2
Malignant neoplasm of prostate — Tumeur maligne de la prostate	21	..	590	..	616	..	74	..
Malignant neoplasm of lymphoid, haematopoietic and related tissue — Tumeurs malignes primitives ou présumées primitives des tissus lymphoïde, hématopoïétique et apparentés...........	57	48	155	152	172	148	19	23
Disorders of the blood and blood-forming organs and certain disorders involving the immune mechanism — Maladies du sang et des organes hématopoïétiques et certains troubles du système immunitaire								
Total	*27*	*29*	*94*	*87*	*75*	*67*	*4*	*7*
Anaemias — Anémies	18	24	69	62	58	51	2	4
Endocrine, nutritional and metabolic diseases — Maladies endocriniennes, nutritionnelles et métaboliques								
Total	*224*	*356*	*949*	*1 329*	*985*	*1 482*	*49*	*65*
Diabetes mellitus — Diabète sucré..	176	321	825	1 226	885	1 381	34	47
Malnutrition — Malnutrition	36	23	22	23	32	19	2	6
Mental and behavioural disorders — Troubles mentaux et du comportement	*20*	*4*	*47*	*62*	*16*	*7*	*24*	*23*
Diseases of the nervous system — Maladies du système nerveux.................	*66*	*63*	*191*	*160*	*192*	*189*	*68*	*80*
Diseases of the circulatory system — Maladies de l'appareil circulatoire								
Total	*553*	*590*	*2 431*	*2 598*	*2 483*	*2 615*	*225*	*216*
Acute rheumatic fever and chronic rheumatic heart diseases — Rhumatisme articularie aigu et cardiopathies rhumatismales chroniques	7	12	8	13	15	16	4	1
Hypertensive diseases — Maladies hypertensives....................................	83	104	458	623	553	589	16	20
Ischaemic heart disease — Cardiopathie ischémique	135	151	564	481	557	528	39	26

610

20. Death and death rates by cause and sex: 2010 - 2014
Décès et taux de mortalité par cause et sexe : 2010 - 2014 (continued - suite)

Cause of death — Cause de décès	Honduras		Jamaica - Jamaïque				Martinique	
	2013 (+U)		2010 (...)		2011 (...)		2012 (...)	
	Male — Masculin	Female — Féminin	Male — Masculin	Female — Féminin	Male — Masculin	Female — Féminin	Male — Masculin	Female — Féminin
	Number Nombre	Number Nombre	Number Nombre	Number Nombre	Number Nombre	Number Nombre	Number Nombre	Number Nombre
Cerebrovascular disease — Maladie cérébrovasculaire....................................	194	226	967	1 090	993	1 128	73	75
Diseases of arteries, arterioles and capillaries — Maladies des artères, artérioles et capillaires	16	10	66	61	64	47	12	11
Diseases of the respiratory system — Maladies de l'appareil respiratoire								
Total	305	319	588	334	517	317	44	45
Influenza — Grippe	1	2	1	-	1	3	4	2
Pneumonia — Pneumopathies	141	143	118	131	96	135	13	15
Chronic lower respiratory diseases — Maladies chroniques des voies respiratoires inférieures	115	127	319	87	303	81	6	9
Diseases of the digestive system — Maladies de l'appareil digestif								
Total	267	215	274	171	278	155	41	26
Gastric and duodenal ulcer — Ulcère de l'estomac et du duodénum................	5	6	50	21	47	16	1	2
Diseases of the liver — Maladies du foie..	156	98	79	45	75	35	9	3
Diseases of the musculoskeletal system and connective tissue — Maladies du système ostéo-articulaire, des muscles et du tissu conjonctif	7	26	22	65	15	83	5	9
Diseases of the genitourinary system — Maladies de l'appareil génito-urinaire								
Total	85	65	276	110	257	98	14	13
Disorders of kidney and ureter — Affections du rein et de l'uretère	58	52	129	67	115	66	8	9
Hyperplasia of prostate — Hyperplasie de la prostate...................................	16	..	66	..	76	..	-	..
Pregnancy, childbirth and the puerperium — Grossesse, accouchement et puerpéralité								
Total	..	37	..	28	..	28	..	1
Pregnancy with abortive outcome — Grossesse se terminant par un avortement	..	2	..	4	..	4	..	-
Other direct obstetric causes — Autres décès maternels directs	..	30	..	24	..	23	..	-
Indirect obstetric causes — Décès maternels indirects	..	5	..	-	..	1	..	1
Certain conditions originating in the perinatal period — Certaines affections dont l'origine se situe dans la période périnatale	706	496	242	193	234	212	5	5
Congenital malformations, deformations and chromosomal abnormalities — Malformations congénitales et anomalies chromosomiques	190	205	77	66	80	84	6	6
Symptoms, signs and abnormal clinical and laboratory findings, not elsewhere classified — Symptômes, signes et résultats anormaux d'examens cliniques et de laboratoire, non classés ailleurs	23	34	78	88	61	68	579	576
All other diseases — Toutes autres maladies..	8	10	42	75	54	79	2	14
External causes — Causes externes								
Total	449	122	533	172	1 734	319	100	34
Accidents								
Total	202	61	187	98	369	149	69	26
Transport accidents — Accidents de transport	83	28	77	26	265	80	20	3
Falls — Chutes	24	6	6	3	10	2	5	4
Accidental drowning and submersion — Noyade et submersion accidentelles..	1	-	7	2	17	-	4	-
Exposure to smoke, fire and flames — Exposition à la fumée, au feu et aux flammes..	3	3	4	2	1	6	4	1
Accidental poisoning by and exposure to noxious substances — Intoxication accidentelle par des substances nocives et exposition à ces substances	5	1	2	2	1	1	5	3
Intentional self-harm — Lésions auto-infligées...	63	31	3	-	44	6	16	5
Assault — Agresssions...	127	12	32	11	844	108	4	-
All other external causes — Toutes autres causes externes	57	18	311	63	477	56	11	3

20. Death and death rates by cause and sex: 2010 - 2014
Décès et taux de mortalité par cause et sexe : 2010 - 2014 (continued - suite)

Cause of death — Cause de décès	Martinique 2013 (...)		Mexico - Mexique 2012 (+C)			
	Male — Masculin	Female — Féminin	Male — Masculin		Female — Féminin	
	Number Nombre	Number Nombre	Number Nombre	Rate Taux	Number Nombre	Rate Taux
TOTAL	*1 515*	*1 381*	*329 481*	*576.3*	*257 872*	*430.7*
Certain infectious and parasitic diseases — Certaines maladies infectieuses et parasitaires						
Total	*40*	*36*	10 692	18.7	6 939	11.6
Intestinal infectious diseases — Maladies infectieuses intestinales	*3*	*2*	1 508	2.6	1 760	2.9
Tuberculosis — Tuberculose	-	-	1 540	2.7	636	1.1
Tetanus — Tétanos................	-	-	13	♦0.0	3	♦0.0
Diphtheria — Diphtérie................	-	-	-	-	-	-
Whooping cough — Coqueluche	-	-	26	♦0.0	36	0.1
Meningococcal infection — Infection à méningocoques	-	-	1	♦0.0	1	♦0.0
Septicaemia — Septicémie	*20*	*25*	2 232	3.9	2 206	3.7
Acute poliomyelitis — Poliomyélite aiguë	-	-	-	-	-	-
Measles — Rougeole................	-	-	-	-	-	-
Viral hepatitis — Hépatite virale	*1*	*1*	529	0.9	660	1.1
Human immunodeficiency virus [HIV] disease — Maladies dues au virus de l'immunodéficience humaine (VIH)	*6*	*3*	3 982	7.0	910	1.5
Malaria — Paludisme................	-	-	1	♦0.0	1	♦0.0
Neoplasms — Tumeurs	*472*	*353*	37 927	66.3	38 947	65.0
Malignant neoplasms — Tumeurs malignes						
Total................	*443*	*334*	35 395	61.9	36 445	60.9
Malignant neoplasm of lip, oral cavity and pharynx — Tumeur maligne de la lèvre, de la cavité buccale et du pharynx	*13*	*1*	707	1.2	359	0.6
Malignant neoplasm of oesophagus — Tumeur maligne de l'oesophage	*8*	*5*	754	1.3	222	0.4
Malignant neoplasm of stomach — Tumeur maligne de l'estomac	*38*	*15*	2 912	5.1	2 550	4.3
Malignant neoplasm of colon, rectosigmoid junction, rectum, anus and anal canal — Tumeur maligne du côlon, de la jonction recto-sigmoïdienne, du rectum, de l'anus et du canal anal	*49*	*48*	2 446	4.3	2 195	3.7
Malignant neoplasm of liver and intrahepatic bile ducts — Tumeur maligne du foie et des voies biliaires intrahépatiques	*19*	*10*	2 687	4.7	2 835	4.7
Malignant neoplasm of pancreas — Tumeur maligne du pancréas................	*32*	*31*	1 801	3.2	1 959	3.3
Malignant neoplasm of trachea, bronchus and lung — Tumeur maligne de la trachée, des bronches et du poumon	*41*	*30*	4 069	7.1	2 198	3.7
Malignant neoplasm of female breast — Tumeur maligne du sein chez la femme................	..	*65*	..	..	5 526	...
Malignant neoplasm of cervix uteri — Tumeur maligne du col de l'utérus................	..	*3*	..	..	3 757	...
Malignant neoplasm of prostate — Tumeur maligne de la prostate	*123*	..	5 777	...	..	..
Malignant neoplasm of lymphoid, haematopoietic and related tissue — Tumeurs malignes primitives ou présumées primitives des tissus lymphoïde, hématopoïétique et apparentés	*42*	*27*	4 274	7.5	3 628	6.1
Disorders of the blood and blood-forming organs and certain disorders involving the immune mechanism — Maladies du sang et des organes hématopoïétiques et certains troubles du système immunitaire						
Total	*5*	*7*	2 207	3.9	2 411	4.0
Anaemias — Anémies	*5*	*4*	1 683	2.9	1 883	3.1
Endocrine, nutritional and metabolic diseases — Maladies endocriniennes, nutritionnelles et métaboliques						
Total	*89*	*115*	48 084	84.1	50 654	84.6
Diabetes mellitus — Diabète sucré................	*56*	*79*	40 491	70.8	42 925	71.7
Malnutrition — Malnutrition	*11*	*14*	3 700	6.5	3 776	6.3
Mental and behavioural disorders — Troubles mentaux et du comportement................	*48*	*27*	2 941	5.1	1 023	1.7
Diseases of the nervous system — Maladies du système nerveux................	*100*	*107*	5 420	9.5	4 549	7.6
Diseases of the circulatory system — Maladies de l'appareil circulatoire						
Total	*326*	*373*	72 534	126.9	68 746	114.8
Acute rheumatic fever and chronic rheumatic heart diseases — Rhumatisme articularie aigu et cardiopathies rhumatismales chroniques	*3*	*8*	261	0.5	579	1.0
Hypertensive diseases — Maladies hypertensives................	*39*	*49*	8 227	14.4	10 482	17.5
Ischaemic heart disease — Cardiopathie ischémique	*59*	*35*	40 209	70.3	32 023	53.5
Cerebrovascular disease — Maladie cérébrovasculaire................	*100*	*116*	15 119	26.4	16 005	26.7
Diseases of arteries, arterioles and capillaries — Maladies des artères, artérioles et capillaires	*16*	*20*	1 047	1.8	909	1.5

20. Death and death rates by cause and sex: 2010 - 2014
Décès et taux de mortalité par cause et sexe : 2010 - 2014 (continued - suite)

Cause of death — Cause de décès	Martinique		Mexico - Mexique			
	2013 (...)		2012 (+C)			
	Male — Masculin	Female — Féminin	Male — Masculin		Female — Féminin	
	Number Nombre	Number Nombre	Number Nombre	Rate Taux	Number Nombre	Rate Taux
Diseases of the respiratory system — Maladies de l'appareil respiratoire						
Total	73	64	26 038	45.5	21 351	35.7
Influenza — Grippe...	4	7	72	0.1	65	0.1
Pneumonia — Pneumopathies	27	19	8 264	14.5	6 694	11.2
Chronic lower respiratory diseases — Maladies chroniques des voies respiratoires inférieures	19	10	12 701	22.2	10 531	17.6
Diseases of the digestive system — Maladies de l'appareil digestif						
Total	65	58	35 399	61.9	20 960	35.0
Gastric and duodenal ulcer — Ulcère de l'estomac et du duodénum..............	6	1	1 278	2.2	1 158	1.9
Diseases of the liver — Maladies du foie	18	10	23 655	41.4	8 931	14.9
Diseases of the musculoskeletal system and connective tissue — Maladies du système ostéo-articulaire, des muscles et du tissu conjonctif	11	13	1 679	2.9	3 232	5.4
Diseases of the genitourinary system — Maladies de l'appareil génito-urinaire						
Total	21	22	10 191	17.8	8 819	14.7
Disorders of kidney and ureter — Affections du rein et de l'uretère	12	16	7 901	13.8	6 756	11.3
Hyperplasia of prostate — Hyperplasie de la prostate...........................	1	..	668	...	..	..
Pregnancy, childbirth and the puerperium — Grossesse, accouchement et puerpéralité						
Total	..	3	..	..	1 036	47.3
Pregnancy with abortive outcome — Grossesse se terminant par un avortement..........	..	-	..	..	79	3.6
Other direct obstetric causes — Autres décès maternels directs	..	3	..	..	624	28.5
Indirect obstetric causes — Décès maternels indirects	..	-	..	..	243	11.1
Certain conditions originating in the perinatal period — Certaines affections dont l'origine se situe dans la période périnatale	8	5	8 174	732.4	6 004	559.1
Congenital malformations, deformations and chromosomal abnormalities — Malformations congénitales et anomalies chromosomiques	9	9	4 936	442.3	4 300	400.4
Symptoms, signs and abnormal clinical and laboratory findings, not elsewhere classified — Symptômes, signes et résultats anormaux d'examens cliniques et de laboratoire, non classés ailleurs	126	134	5 064	8.9	4 914	8.2
All other diseases — Toutes autres maladies...........	7	8	733	1.3	991	1.7
External causes — Causes externes						
Total	115	47	57 462	100.5	12 996	21.7
Accidents						
Total	83	34	27 465	48.0	8 257	13.8
Transport accidents — Accidents de transport.........................	23	2	13 583	23.8	3 640	6.1
Falls — Chutes	10	6	1 801	3.2	473	0.8
Accidental drowning and submersion — Noyade et submersion accidentelles........	9	4	1 783	3.1	309	0.5
Exposure to smoke, fire and flames — Exposition à la fumée, au feu et aux flammes	2	2	377	0.7	145	0.2
Accidental poisoning by and exposure to noxious substances — Intoxication accidentelle par des substances nocives et exposition à ces substances	5	5	965	1.7	213	0.4
Intentional self-harm — Lésions auto-infligées.........................	18	9	4 357	7.6	1 052	1.8
Assault — Agresssions..	6	-	21 908	38.3	2 630	4.4
All other external causes — Toutes autres causes externes	8	4	3 732	6.5	1 057	1.8

20. Death and death rates by cause and sex: 2010 - 2014
Décès et taux de mortalité par cause et sexe : 2010 - 2014 (continued - suite)

	Mexico - Mexique				Montserrat			
Cause of death — Cause de décès	2013 (+C)				2013 (...)		2014 (...)	
	Male — Masculin		Female — Féminin		Male — Masculin	Female — Féminin	Male — Masculin	Female — Féminin
	Number Nombre	Rate Taux	Number Nombre	Rate Taux	Number Nombre	Number Nombre	Number Nombre	Number Nombre
TOTAL	*332 706*	*575.5*	*263 053*	*434.2*	*21*	*24*	*23*	*9*
Certain infectious and parasitic diseases — Certaines maladies infectieuses et parasitaires								
Total	11 100	19.2	7 119	11.8	-	-	-	-
Intestinal infectious diseases — Maladies infectieuses intestinales	1 644	2.8	1 787	2.9	-	-	-	-
Tuberculosis — Tuberculose	1 621	2.8	684	1.1	-	-	-	-
Tetanus — Tétanos..........	4	♦0.0	-	-	-	-	-	-
Diphtheria — Diphtérie..........	-	-	-	-	-	-	-	-
Whooping cough — Coqueluche	26	♦0.0	28	♦0.0	-	-	-	-
Meningococcal infection — Infection à méningocoques..........	11	♦0.0	1	♦0.0	-	-	-	-
Septicaemia — Septicémie..........	2 376	4.1	2 422	4.0	-	-	-	-
Acute poliomyelitis — Poliomyélite aiguë	-	-	-	-	-	-	-	-
Measles — Rougeole..........	-	-	-	-	-	-	-	-
Viral hepatitis — Hépatite virale..........	520	0.9	666	1.1	-	-	-	-
Human immunodeficiency virus [HIV] disease — Maladies dues au virus de l'immunodéficience humaine (VIH)..........	4 031	7.0	859	1.4	-	-	-	-
Malaria — Paludisme..........	-	-	1	♦0.0	-	-	-	-
Neoplasms — Tumeurs	37 872	65.5	39 116	64.6	6	3	4	-
Malignant neoplasms — Tumeurs malignes								
Total	35 320	61.1	36 591	60.4	6	3	4	-
Malignant neoplasm of lip, oral cavity and pharynx — Tumeur maligne de la lèvre, de la cavité buccale et du pharynx	697	1.2	360	0.6	-	-	-	-
Malignant neoplasm of oesophagus — Tumeur maligne de l'oesophage	717	1.2	241	0.4	-	-	-	-
Malignant neoplasm of stomach — Tumeur maligne de l'estomac	2 856	4.9	2 510	4.1	-	-	-	-
Malignant neoplasm of colon, rectosigmoid junction, rectum, anus and anal canal — Tumeur maligne du côlon, de la jonction recto-sigmoïdienne, du rectum, de l'anus et du canal anal..........	2 630	4.5	2 355	3.9	-	-	-	-
Malignant neoplasm of liver and intrahepatic bile ducts — Tumeur maligne du foie et des voies bilaires intrahépatiques	2 736	4.7	3 029	5.0	-	2	-	-
Malignant neoplasm of pancreas — Tumeur maligne du pancréas..........	1 701	2.9	2 026	3.3	-	-	-	-
Malignant neoplasm of trachea, bronchus and lung — Tumeur maligne de la trachée, des bronches et du poumon	4 074	7.0	2 360	3.9	2	-	-	-
Malignant neoplasm of female breast — Tumeur maligne du sein chez la femme	..	..	5 338	...	..	-	..	-
Malignant neoplasm of cervix uteri — Tumeur maligne du col de l'utérus..........	..	..	3 694	...	..	-	..	-
Malignant neoplasm of prostate — Tumeur maligne de la prostate	5 770	...	..	..	2	..	3	..
Malignant neoplasm of lymphoid, haematopoietic and related tissue — Tumeurs malignes primitives ou présumées primitives des tissus lymphoïde, hématopoïétique et apparentés..........	4 259	7.4	3 526	5.8	-	-	-	-
Disorders of the blood and blood-forming organs and certain disorders involving the immune mechanism — Maladies du sang et des organes hématopoïétiques et certains troubles du système immunitaire								
Total	2 210	3.8	2 352	3.9	-	-	1	-
Anaemias — Anémies	1 673	2.9	1 869	3.1	-	-	1	-
Endocrine, nutritional and metabolic diseases — Maladies endocriniennes, nutritionnelles et métaboliques								
Total	49 861	86.2	52 689	87.0	6	7	2	2
Diabetes mellitus — Diabète sucré..........	41 357	71.5	43 954	72.6	5	7	2	2
Malnutrition — Malnutrition	3 855	6.7	4 113	6.8	-	-	-	-
Mental and behavioural disorders — Troubles mentaux et du comportement	3 124	5.4	1 089	1.8	-	-	-	-
Diseases of the nervous system — Maladies du système nerveux..........	5 656	9.8	4 654	7.7	-	1	-	1
Diseases of the circulatory system — Maladies de l'appareil circulatoire								
Total	74 801	129.4	70 228	115.9	7	11	7	4
Acute rheumatic fever and chronic rheumatic heart diseases — Rhumatisme articularie aigu et cardiopathies rhumatismales chroniques	238	0.4	505	0.8	-	-	-	-
Hypertensive diseases — Maladies hypertensives..........	8 321	14.4	10 656	17.6	2	2	2	1
Ischaemic heart disease — Cardiopathie ischémique	42 070	72.8	33 054	54.6	2	5	4	1

20. Death and death rates by cause and sex: 2010 - 2014
Décès et taux de mortalité par cause et sexe : 2010 - 2014 (continued - suite)

Cause of death — Cause de décès	Mexico - Mexique 2013 (+C)				Montserrat 2013 (...)		2014 (...)	
	Male — Masculin		Female — Féminin		Male — Masculin	Female — Féminin	Male — Masculin	Female — Féminin
	Number Nombre	Rate Taux	Number Nombre	Rate Taux	Number Nombre	Number Nombre	Number Nombre	Number Nombre
Cerebrovascular disease — Maladie cérébrovasculaire	15 008	26.0	16 221	26.8	2	1	1	2
Diseases of arteries, arterioles and capillaries — Maladies des artères, artérioles et capillaires	1 061	1.8	997	1.6	-	-	-	-
Diseases of the respiratory system — Maladies de l'appareil respiratoire								
Total	27 376	47.4	23 223	38.3	-	1	4	2
Influenza — Grippe	49	0.1	42	0.1	-	-	-	-
Pneumonia — Pneumopathies	9 014	15.6	7 342	12.1	-	-	2	-
Chronic lower respiratory diseases — Maladies chroniques des voies respiratoires inférieures	13 338	23.1	11 526	19.0	-	1	-	-
Diseases of the digestive system — Maladies de l'appareil digestif								
Total	36 417	63.0	21 248	35.1	-	-	2	-
Gastric and duodenal ulcer — Ulcère de l'estomac et du duodénum	1 282	2.2	1 106	1.8	-	-	-	-
Diseases of the liver — Maladies du foie	24 353	42.1	9 054	14.9	-	-	1	-
Diseases of the musculoskeletal system and connective tissue — Maladies du système ostéo-articulaire, des muscles et du tissu conjonctif	1 822	3.2	3 198	5.3	-	-	-	-
Diseases of the genitourinary system — Maladies de l'appareil génito-urinaire								
Total	10 658	18.4	9 053	14.9	-	-	-	-
Disorders of kidney and ureter — Affections du rein et de l'uretère	8 242	14.3	6 725	11.1	-	-	-	-
Hyperplasia of prostate — Hyperplasie de la prostate	724	...	...	..	-	..	-	..
Pregnancy, childbirth and the puerperium — Grossesse, accouchement et puerpéralité								
Total	..	..	969	44.7	..	-	..	-
Pregnancy with abortive outcome — Grossesse se terminant par un avortement	..	..	77	3.6	..	-	..	-
Other direct obstetric causes — Autres décès maternels directs	..	..	541	24.9	..	-	..	-
Indirect obstetric causes — Décès maternels indirects	..	..	229	10.6	..	-	..	-
Certain conditions originating in the perinatal period — Certaines affections dont l'origine se situe dans la période périnatale	7 344	664.5	5 427	510.2	-	-	-	-
Congenital malformations, deformations and chromosomal abnormalities — Malformations congénitales et anomalies chromosomiques	4 900	443.4	4 274	401.8				
Symptoms, signs and abnormal clinical and laboratory findings, not elsewhere classified — Symptômes, signes et résultats anormaux d'examens cliniques et de laboratoire, non classés ailleurs	5 091	8.8	5 082	8.4	-	-	-	-
All other diseases — Toutes autres maladies	627	1.1	948	1.6	-	-	-	-
External causes — Causes externes								
Total	53 847	93.1	12 384	20.4	2	1	3	-
Accidents								
Total	26 349	45.6	7 805	12.9	2	1	2	-
Transport accidents — Accidents de transport	12 833	22.2	3 179	5.2	1	-	-	-
Falls — Chutes	1 981	3.4	521	0.9	1	-	-	-
Accidental drowning and submersion — Noyade et submersion accidentelles	1 725	3.0	273	0.5	-	-	1	-
Exposure to smoke, fire and flames — Exposition à la fumée, au feu et aux flammes	343	0.6	135	0.2	-	-	-	-
Accidental poisoning by and exposure to noxious substances — Intoxication accidentelle par des substances nocives et exposition à ces substances	985	1.7	248	0.4	-	-	-	-
Intentional self-harm — Lésions auto-infligées	4 701	8.1	1 050	1.7	-	-	-	-
Assault — Agresssions	19 134	33.1	2 502	4.1	-	-	-	-
All other external causes — Toutes autres causes externes	3 663	6.3	1 027	1.7	-	-	1	-

20. Death and death rates by cause and sex: 2010 - 2014
Décès et taux de mortalité par cause et sexe : 2010 - 2014 (continued - suite)

Cause of death — Cause de décès	Nicaragua				Panama			
	2012 (+U)		2013 (+U)		2012 (+C)			
	Male — Masculin	Female — Féminin	Male — Masculin	Female — Féminin	Male — Masculin		Female — Féminin	
	Number Nombre	Number Nombre	Number Nombre	Number Nombre	Number Nombre	Rate Taux	Number Nombre	Rate Taux
TOTAL	*11 689*	*8 604*	*12 198*	*9 172*	*10 160*	*533.9*	*7 190*	*381.5*
Certain infectious and parasitic diseases — Certaines maladies infectieuses et parasitaires								
Total	*407*	*231*	*422*	*266*	*741*	*38.9*	*388*	*20.6*
Intestinal infectious diseases — Maladies infectieuses intestinales	55	48	69	53	70	3.7	78	4.1
Tuberculosis — Tuberculose	91	42	70	39	129	6.8	59	3.1
Tetanus — Tétanos	-	-	-	-	1	♦0.1	-	-
Diphtheria — Diphtérie	-	-	-	-	-	-	-	-
Whooping cough — Coqueluche	-	-	-	-	-	-	-	-
Meningococcal infection — Infection à méningocoques	2	-	1	-	-	-	-	-
Septicaemia — Septicémie	67	63	74	93	153	8.0	109	5.8
Acute poliomyelitis — Poliomyélite aiguë	-	-	-	-	-	-	-	-
Measles — Rougeole	-	-	-	-	-	-	-	-
Viral hepatitis — Hépatite virale	14	3	8	5	3	♦0.2	4	♦0.2
Human immunodeficiency virus [HIV] disease — Maladies dues au virus de l'immunodéficience humaine (VIH)	150	58	172	49	358	18.8	120	6.4
Malaria — Paludisme	2	2	-	-	-	-	1	♦0.1
Neoplasms — Tumeurs	*1 284*	*1 368*	*1 334*	*1 489*	*1 647*	*86.5*	*1 376*	*73.0*
Malignant neoplasms — Tumeurs malignes								
Total	*1 247*	*1 320*	*1 282*	*1 438*	*1 598*	*84.0*	*1 330*	*70.6*
Malignant neoplasm of lip, oral cavity and pharynx — Tumeur maligne de la lèvre, de la cavité buccale et du pharynx	29	10	32	13	38	2.0	19	♦1.0
Malignant neoplasm of oesophagus — Tumeur maligne de l'oesophage	26	4	14	8	25	♦1.3	13	♦0.7
Malignant neoplasm of stomach — Tumeur maligne de l'estomac	169	112	199	132	182	9.6	120	6.4
Malignant neoplasm of colon, rectosigmoid junction, rectum, anus and anal canal — Tumeur maligne du côlon, de la jonction recto-sigmoïdienne, du rectum, de l'anus et du canal anal	87	87	88	96	126	6.6	129	6.8
Malignant neoplasm of liver and intrahepatic bile ducts — Tumeur maligne du foie et des voies bilaires intrahépatiques	150	127	149	165	70	3.7	67	3.6
Malignant neoplasm of pancreas — Tumeur maligne du pancréas	28	50	47	52	64	3.4	54	2.9
Malignant neoplasm of trachea, bronchus and lung — Tumeur maligne de la trachée, des bronches et du poumon	119	92	105	87	178	9.4	72	3.8
Malignant neoplasm of female breast — Tumeur maligne du sein chez la femme	..	145	..	170	..	..	204	...
Malignant neoplasm of cervix uteri — Tumeur maligne du col de l'utérus	..	251	..	278	..	..	139	...
Malignant neoplasm of prostate — Tumeur maligne de la prostate	232	..	215	..	356	...	..	..
Malignant neoplasm of lymphoid, haematopoietic and related tissue — Tumeurs malignes primitives ou présumées primitives des tissus lymphoïde, hématopoïétique et apparentés	139	122	146	120	152	8.0	127	6.7
Disorders of the blood and blood-forming organs and certain disorders involving the immune mechanism — Maladies du sang et des organes hématopoïétiques et certains troubles du système immunitaire								
Total	*57*	*50*	*78*	*60*	*58*	*3.0*	*41*	*2.2*
Anaemias — Anémies	*41*	*37*	*58*	*40*	*52*	*2.7*	*33*	*1.8*
Endocrine, nutritional and metabolic diseases — Maladies endocriniennes, nutritionnelles et métaboliques								
Total	*826*	*1 030*	*817*	*1 052*	*561*	*29.5*	*760*	*40.3*
Diabetes mellitus — Diabète sucré	*759*	*954*	*743*	*967*	*458*	*24.1*	*613*	*32.5*
Malnutrition — Malnutrition	*50*	*49*	*57*	*52*	*43*	*2.3*	*67*	*3.6*
Mental and behavioural disorders — Troubles mentaux et du comportement	*277*	*23*	*246*	*16*	*29*	*♦1.5*	*6*	*♦0.3*
Diseases of the nervous system — Maladies du système nerveux	*192*	*158*	*199*	*144*	*261*	*13.7*	*257*	*13.6*
Diseases of the circulatory system — Maladies de l'appareil circulatoire								
Total	*2 706*	*2 630*	*2 913*	*2 831*	*2 625*	*137.9*	*2 042*	*108.4*
Acute rheumatic fever and chronic rheumatic heart diseases — Rhumatisme articularie aigu et cardiopathies rhumatismales chroniques	8	14	12	8	11	♦0.6	8	♦0.4
Hypertensive diseases — Maladies hypertensives	387	389	420	401	197	10.4	189	10.0
Ischaemic heart disease — Cardiopathie ischémique	1 400	1 255	1 471	1 381	999	52.5	673	35.7

	Nicaragua				Panama			
	2012 (+U)		2013 (+U)		2012 (+C)			
Cause of death — Cause de décès	Male — Masculin	Female — Féminin	Male — Masculin	Female — Féminin	Male — Masculin		Female — Féminin	
	Number Nombre	Number Nombre	Number Nombre	Number Nombre	Number Nombre	Rate Taux	Number Nombre	Rate Taux
Cerebrovascular disease — Maladie cérébrovasculaire..................................	594	640	640	719	760	39.9	620	32.9
Diseases of arteries, arterioles and capillaries — Maladies des artères, artérioles et capillaires	36	26	38	20	72	3.8	51	2.7
Diseases of the respiratory system — Maladies de l'appareil respiratoire								
Total	897	735	926	789	908	47.7	864	45.8
Influenza — Grippe	-	-	-	1	3	◆0.2	2	◆0.1
Pneumonia — Pneumopathies	398	327	397	331	337	17.7	289	15.3
Chronic lower respiratory diseases — Maladies chroniques des voies respiratoires inférieures	366	324	415	383	252	13.2	243	12.9
Diseases of the digestive system — Maladies de l'appareil digestif								
Total	1 057	482	1 146	553	471	24.7	309	16.4
Gastric and duodenal ulcer — Ulcère de l'estomac et du duodénum...............	44	20	28	24	12	◆0.6	6	◆0.3
Diseases of the liver — Maladies du foie...	795	257	899	310	236	12.4	119	6.3
Diseases of the musculoskeletal system and connective tissue — Maladies du système ostéo-articulaire, des muscles et du tissu conjonctif	34	89	31	90	26	◆1.4	30	◆1.6
Diseases of the genitourinary system — Maladies de l'appareil génito-urinaire								
Total	990	324	1 128	405	360	18.9	238	12.6
Disorders of kidney and ureter — Affections du rein et de l'uretère	951	311	1 085	393	311	16.3	195	10.3
Hyperplasia of prostate — Hyperplasie de la prostate...............................	23	..	24	..	14	...	..	..
Pregnancy, childbirth and the puerperium — Grossesse, accouchement et puerpéralité								
Total	..	72	..	71	..	..	49	64.9
Pregnancy with abortive outcome — Grossesse se terminant par un avortement	..	2	..	3	..	..	7	◆9.3
Other direct obstetric causes — Autres décès maternels directs	..	58	..	57	..	..	27	◆35.8
Indirect obstetric causes — Décès maternels indirects	..	12	..	11	..	..	15	◆19.9
Certain conditions originating in the perinatal period — Certaines affections dont l'origine se situe dans la période périnatale	699	509	781	533	264	684.9	164	443.9
Congenital malformations, deformations and chromosomal abnormalities — Malformations congénitales et anomalies chromosomiques	232	253	279	286	186	482.6	173	468.3
Symptoms, signs and abnormal clinical and laboratory findings, not elsewhere classified — Symptômes, signes et résultats anormaux d'examens cliniques et de laboratoire, non classés ailleurs	156	164	140	131	307	16.1	188	10.0
All other diseases — Toutes autres maladies..	18	38	33	43	58	3.0	66	3.5
External causes — Causes externes								
Total	1 857	448	1 725	413	1 658	87.1	239	12.7
Accidents								
Total	1 134	292	1 017	270	775	40.7	164	8.7
Transport accidents — Accidents de transport	588	101	519	89	412	21.6	82	4.4
Falls — Chutes	98	80	83	69	105	5.5	28	◆1.5
Accidental drowning and submersion — Noyade et submersion accidentelles..	136	18	114	24	106	5.6	15	◆0.8
Exposure to smoke, fire and flames — Exposition à la fumée, au feu et aux flammes...	6	5	4	4	18	◆0.9	5	◆0.3
Accidental poisoning by and exposure to noxious substances — Intoxication accidentelle par des substances nocives et exposition à ces substances	40	11	47	10	16	◆0.8	5	◆0.3
Intentional self-harm — Lésions auto-infligées..	234	82	276	75	117	6.1	18	◆1.0
Assault — Agresssions	380	40	348	31	671	35.3	41	2.2
All other external causes — Toutes autres causes externes	109	34	84	37	95	5.0	16	◆0.8

20. Death and death rates by cause and sex: 2010 - 2014
Décès et taux de mortalité par cause et sexe : 2010 - 2014 (continued - suite)

Cause of death — Cause de décès	Panama				Puerto Rico - Porto Rico			
	2013 (+C)				2012 (...)		2013 (...)	
	Male — Masculin		Female — Féminin		Male — Masculin	Female — Féminin	Male — Masculin	Female — Féminin
	Number Nombre	Rate Taux	Number Nombre	Rate Taux	Number Nombre	Number Nombre	Number Nombre	Number Nombre
TOTAL	10 248	529.8	7 519	392.3	*16 003*	*13 662*	*15 764*	*13 245*
Certain infectious and parasitic diseases — Certaines maladies infectieuses et parasitaires								
Total	767	39.7	439	22.9	*738*	*574*	*742*	*563*
Intestinal infectious diseases — Maladies infectieuses intestinales	102	5.3	80	4.2	*16*	*26*	*18*	*21*
Tuberculosis — Tuberculose	132	6.8	65	3.4	*13*	-	*10*	*1*
Tetanus — Tétanos	-	-	-	-	*1*	-	-	-
Diphtheria — Diphtérie	-	-	-	-	-	-	-	-
Whooping cough — Coqueluche	1	♦0.1	-	-	-	*2*	*1*	-
Meningococcal infection — Infection à méningocoques	-	-	-	-	-	-	*1*	*1*
Septicaemia — Septicémie	140	7.2	132	6.9	*399*	*399*	*411*	*391*
Acute poliomyelitis — Poliomyélite aiguë	-	-	-	-	-	-	-	-
Measles — Rougeole	-	-	-	-	-	-	-	-
Viral hepatitis — Hépatite virale	2	♦0.1	4	♦0.2	*75*	*34*	*59*	*18*
Human immunodeficiency virus [HIV] disease — Maladies dues au virus de l'immunodéficience humaine (VIH)	371	19.2	144	7.5	*174*	*66*	*171*	*71*
Malaria — Paludisme	-	-	-	-	-	-	-	-
Neoplasms — Tumeurs	1 570	81.2	1 386	72.3	*3 093*	*2 483*	*2 959*	*2 431*
Malignant neoplasms — Tumeurs malignes								
Total	1 495	77.3	1 324	69.1	*3 013*	*2 410*	*2 872*	*2 325*
Malignant neoplasm of lip, oral cavity and pharynx — Tumeur maligne de la lèvre, de la cavité buccale et du pharynx	34	1.8	13	♦0.7	*92*	*33*	*111*	*20*
Malignant neoplasm of oesophagus — Tumeur maligne de l'oesophage	41	2.1	9	♦0.5	*88*	*24*	*100*	*22*
Malignant neoplasm of stomach — Tumeur maligne de l'estomac	187	9.7	100	5.2	*131*	*100*	*126*	*89*
Malignant neoplasm of colon, rectosigmoid junction, rectum, anus and anal canal — Tumeur maligne du côlon, de la jonction recto-sigmoïdienne, du rectum, de l'anus et du canal anal	127	6.6	134	7.0	*392*	*306*	*364*	*305*
Malignant neoplasm of liver and intrahepatic bile ducts — Tumeur maligne du foie et des voies bilaires intrahépatiques	64	3.3	63	3.3	*206*	*101*	*213*	*112*
Malignant neoplasm of pancreas — Tumeur maligne du pancréas	66	3.4	58	3.0	*154*	*163*	*163*	*141*
Malignant neoplasm of trachea, bronchus and lung — Tumeur maligne de la trachée, des bronches et du poumon	177	9.2	107	5.6	*392*	*254*	*385*	*229*
Malignant neoplasm of female breast — Tumeur maligne du sein chez la femme	..	..	217	15.7	..	*435*	..	*415*
Malignant neoplasm of cervix uteri — Tumeur maligne du col de l'utérus	..	..	118	8.5	..	*48*	..	*58*
Malignant neoplasm of prostate — Tumeur maligne de la prostate	326	89.9	..	..	*512*	..	*467*	..
Malignant neoplasm of lymphoid, haematopoietic and related tissue — Tumeurs malignes primitives ou présumées primitives des tissus lymphoïde, hématopoïétique et apparentés	150	7.8	122	6.4	*281*	*201*	*282*	*213*
Disorders of the blood and blood-forming organs and certain disorders involving the immune mechanism — Maladies du sang et des organes hématopoïétiques et certains troubles du système immunitaire								
Total	70	3.6	78	4.1	*160*	*172*	*156*	*160*
Anaemias — Anémies	56	2.9	63	3.3	*91*	*111*	*87*	*99*
Endocrine, nutritional and metabolic diseases — Maladies endocriniennes, nutritionnelles et métaboliques								
Total	656	33.9	754	39.3	*1 881*	*1 857*	*1 906*	*1 854*
Diabetes mellitus — Diabète sucré	488	25.2	614	32.0	*1 564*	*1 527*	*1 609*	*1 518*
Malnutrition — Malnutrition	77	4.0	76	4.0	*21*	*34*	*25*	*26*
Mental and behavioural disorders — Troubles mentaux et du comportement	36	1.9	8	♦0.4	*387*	*376*	*409*	*364*
Diseases of the nervous system — Maladies du système nerveux	262	13.5	256	13.4	*1 029*	*1 575*	*978*	*1 441*
Diseases of the circulatory system — Maladies de l'appareil circulatoire								
Total	2 792	144.3	2 210	115.3	*3 717*	*3 462*	*3 769*	*3 402*
Acute rheumatic fever and chronic rheumatic heart diseases — Rhumatisme articularie aigu et cardiopathies rhumatismales chroniques	4	♦0.2	9	♦0.5	*6*	*9*	*3*	*10*
Hypertensive diseases — Maladies hypertensives	273	14.1	230	12.0	*687*	*680*	*698*	*692*
Ischaemic heart disease — Cardiopathie ischémique	1 059	54.7	743	38.8	*1 640*	*1 361*	*1 687*	*1 300*

20. Death and death rates by cause and sex: 2010 - 2014
Décès et taux de mortalité par cause et sexe : 2010 - 2014 (continued - suite)

Cause of death — Cause de décès	Panama				Puerto Rico - Porto Rico			
	2013 (+C)				2012 (...)		2013 (...)	
	Male — Masculin		Female — Féminin		Male — Masculin	Female — Féminin	Male — Masculin	Female — Féminin
	Number Nombre	Rate Taux	Number Nombre	Rate Taux	Number Nombre	Number Nombre	Number Nombre	Number Nombre
Cerebrovascular disease — Maladie cérébrovasculaire.....................................	792	40.9	654	34.1	661	697	633	709
Diseases of arteries, arterioles and capillaries — Maladies des artères, artérioles et capillaires	76	3.9	60	3.1	78	68	103	65
Diseases of the respiratory system — Maladies de l'appareil respiratoire								
Total	1 033	53.4	885	46.2	1 232	1 179	1 216	1 188
Influenza — Grippe	3	♦0.2	5	♦0.3	5	8	12	13
Pneumonia — Pneumopathies	391	20.2	296	15.4	371	401	356	361
Chronic lower respiratory diseases — Maladies chroniques des voies respiratoires inférieures	273	14.1	221	11.5	540	473	505	493
Diseases of the digestive system — Maladies de l'appareil digestif								
Total	409	21.1	330	17.2	807	450	732	457
Gastric and duodenal ulcer — Ulcère de l'estomac et du duodénum................	13	♦0.7	11	♦0.6	11	9	10	7
Diseases of the liver — Maladies du foie..	213	11.0	116	6.1	518	194	451	214
Diseases of the musculoskeletal system and connective tissue — Maladies du système ostéo-articulaire, des muscles et du tissu conjonctif	25	♦1.3	37	1.9	68	128	65	93
Diseases of the genitourinary system — Maladies de l'appareil génito-urinaire								
Total	347	17.9	250	13.0	690	649	683	568
Disorders of kidney and ureter — Affections du rein et de l'uretère	308	15.9	203	10.6	584	512	587	451
Hyperplasia of prostate — Hyperplasie de la prostate......................................	6	♦1.7	..	..	2	..	-	..
Pregnancy, childbirth and the puerperium — Grossesse, accouchement et puerpéralité								
Total	..	..	41	55.6	..	1	..	2
Pregnancy with abortive outcome — Grossesse se terminant par un avortement	..	..	3	♦4.1	..	-	..	1
Other direct obstetric causes — Autres décès maternels directs	..	..	24	♦32.5	..	1	..	1
Indirect obstetric causes — Décès maternels indirects	..	..	14	♦19.0	..	-	..	-
Certain conditions originating in the perinatal period — Certaines affections dont l'origine se situe dans la période périnatale	264	694.8	205	572.5	113	86	72	54
Congenital malformations, deformations and chromosomal abnormalities — Malformations congénitales et anomalies chromosomiques	162	426.4	156	435.6	67	78	59	47
Symptoms, signs and abnormal clinical and laboratory findings, not elsewhere classified — Symptômes, signes et résultats anormaux d'examens cliniques et de laboratoire, non classés ailleurs	309	16.0	199	10.4	73	79	140	105
All other diseases — Toutes autres maladies..	53	2.7	43	2.2	90	116	86	121
External causes — Causes externes								
Total	1 493	77.2	242	12.6	1 858	397	1 792	395
Accidents								
Total	679	35.1	164	8.6	748	253	746	272
Transport accidents — Accidents de transport...	370	19.1	80	4.2	313	66	302	84
Falls — Chutes	106	5.5	38	2.0	92	47	113	39
Accidental drowning and submersion — Noyade et submersion accidentelles..	98	5.1	20	♦1.0	25	2	23	5
Exposure to smoke, fire and flames — Exposition à la fumée, au feu et aux flammes...	6	♦0.3	3	♦0.2	6	6	5	2
Accidental poisoning by and exposure to noxious substances — Intoxication accidentelle par des substances nocives et exposition à ces substances	12	♦0.6	3	♦0.2	55	8	43	11
Intentional self-harm — Lésions auto-infligées..	117	6.0	13	♦0.7	204	42	204	37
Assault — Agresssions..	627	32.4	49	2.6	870	82	809	53
All other external causes — Toutes autres causes externes	70	3.6	16	♦0.8	36	20	33	33

20. Death and death rates by cause and sex: 2010 - 2014
Décès et taux de mortalité par cause et sexe : 2010 - 2014 (continued - suite)

Cause of death — Cause de décès	Saint Kitts and Nevis - Saint-Kitts-et-Nevis				Saint Lucia - Sainte-Lucie			
	2011 (+U)		2012 (+U)		2011 (U)		2012 (U)	
	Male — Masculin	Female — Féminin	Male — Masculin	Female — Féminin	Male — Masculin	Female — Féminin	Male — Masculin	Female — Féminin
	Number Nombre	Number Nombre	Number Nombre	Number Nombre	Number Nombre	Number Nombre	Number Nombre	Number Nombre
TOTAL	204	169	178	157	538	424	595	555
Certain infectious and parasitic diseases — Certaines maladies infectieuses et parasitaires								
Total	5	5	6	7	21	10	17	22
Intestinal infectious diseases — Maladies infectieuses intestinales ...	-	-	-	1	1	1	-	-
Tuberculosis — Tuberculose	1	-	1	-	-	-	-	1
Tetanus — Tétanos............	-	-	-	-	-	-	-	-
Diphtheria — Diphtérie............	-	-	-	-	-	-	-	-
Whooping cough — Coqueluche	-	-	-	-	-	-	-	-
Meningococcal infection — Infection à méningocoques ...	-	-	-	-	-	-	-	-
Septicaemia — Septicémie............	3	4	-	1	2	4	12	16
Acute poliomyelitis — Poliomyélite aiguë	-	-	-	-	-	-	-	-
Measles — Rougeole............	-	-	-	-	-	-	-	-
Viral hepatitis — Hépatite virale............	-	-	1	-	1	1	1	-
Human immunodeficiency virus [HIV] disease — Maladies dues au virus de l'immunodéficience humaine (VIH)............	-	1	4	4	11	1	-	-
Malaria — Paludisme............	-	-	-	-	-	-	-	-
Neoplasms — Tumeurs	26	35	30	28	79	72	138	124
Malignant neoplasms — Tumeurs malignes								
Total	26	35	30	27	77	70	131	118
Malignant neoplasm of lip, oral cavity and pharynx — Tumeur maligne de la lèvre, de la cavité buccale et du pharynx ...	1	-	1	-	2	1	5	3
Malignant neoplasm of oesophagus — Tumeur maligne de l'oesophage ...	-	-	-	-	3	1	4	1
Malignant neoplasm of stomach — Tumeur maligne de l'estomac ...	-	1	1	-	9	3	12	9
Malignant neoplasm of colon, rectosigmoid junction, rectum, anus and anal canal — Tumeur maligne du côlon, de la jonction recto-sigmoïdienne, du rectum, de l'anus et du canal anal ...	5	3	1	-	3	6	11	14
Malignant neoplasm of liver and intrahepatic bile ducts — Tumeur maligne du foie et des voies bilaires intrahépatiques ...	2	2	3	4	2	1	2	2
Malignant neoplasm of pancreas — Tumeur maligne du pancréas...	2	1	-	1	4	1	5	7
Malignant neoplasm of trachea, bronchus and lung — Tumeur maligne de la trachée, des bronches et du poumon ...	1	-	2	1	7	4	10	4
Malignant neoplasm of female breast — Tumeur maligne du sein chez la femme ...	..	8	..	6	..	17	..	29
Malignant neoplasm of cervix uteri — Tumeur maligne du col de l'utérus...	..	2	..	4	..	3	..	10
Malignant neoplasm of prostate — Tumeur maligne de la prostate ...	11	..	13	..	27	..	41	..
Malignant neoplasm of lymphoid, haematopoietic and related tissue — Tumeurs malignes primitives ou présumées primitives des tissus lymphoïde, hématopoïétique et apparentés...	-	4	3	2	5	10	15	13
Disorders of the blood and blood-forming organs and certain disorders involving the immune mechanism — Maladies du sang et des organes hématopoïétiques et certains troubles du système immunitaire								
Total	3	2	4	2	5	6	4	5
Anaemias — Anémies	2	1	2	-	4	6	3	3
Endocrine, nutritional and metabolic diseases — Maladies endocriniennes, nutritionnelles et métaboliques								
Total	25	25	17	21	67	68	41	64
Diabetes mellitus — Diabète sucré............	19	24	14	19	64	64	36	49
Malnutrition — Malnutrition	1	-	-	-	-	-	-	-
Mental and behavioural disorders — Troubles mentaux et du comportement	3	1	7	4	2	2	-	-
Diseases of the nervous system — Maladies du système nerveux...	3	7	1	4	5	7	10	10
Diseases of the circulatory system — Maladies de l'appareil circulatoire								
Total	64	57	44	66	140	128	170	194
Acute rheumatic fever and chronic rheumatic heart diseases — Rhumatisme articularie aigu et cardiopathies rhumatismales chroniques ...	-	-	-	2	-	1	1	3
Hypertensive diseases — Maladies hypertensives............	8	4	10	9	21	28	36	35
Ischaemic heart disease — Cardiopathie ischémique	17	16	11	19	31	15	30	37

Cause of death — Cause de décès	Saint Kitts and Nevis - Saint-Kitts-et-Nevis				Saint Lucia - Sainte-Lucie			
	2011 (+U)		2012 (+U)		2011 (U)		2012 (U)	
	Male — Masculin	Female — Féminin	Male — Masculin	Female — Féminin	Male — Masculin	Female — Féminin	Male — Masculin	Female — Féminin
	Number Nombre	Number Nombre	Number Nombre	Number Nombre	Number Nombre	Number Nombre	Number Nombre	Number Nombre
Cerebrovascular disease — Maladie cérébrovasculaire	31	24	16	27	40	46	56	83
Diseases of arteries, arterioles and capillaries — Maladies des artères, artérioles et capillaires	1	1	-	1	7	7	11	5
Diseases of the respiratory system — Maladies de l'appareil respiratoire								
Total	5	8	9	2	36	28	44	28
Influenza — Grippe	-	-	-	-	-	-	-	-
Pneumonia — Pneumopathies	3	1	2	-	3	8	12	11
Chronic lower respiratory diseases — Maladies chroniques des voies respiratoires inférieures	-	2	3	-	21	7	19	5
Diseases of the digestive system — Maladies de l'appareil digestif								
Total	20	6	11	3	23	11	29	16
Gastric and duodenal ulcer — Ulcère de l'estomac et du duodénum	1	1	1	-	1	1	6	-
Diseases of the liver — Maladies du foie	7	1	6	-	10	6	13	9
Diseases of the musculoskeletal system and connective tissue — Maladies du système ostéo-articulaire, des muscles et du tissu conjonctif	-	3	-	1	1	3	1	2
Diseases of the genitourinary system — Maladies de l'appareil génito-urinaire								
Total	7	2	11	1	19	14	20	10
Disorders of kidney and ureter — Affections du rein et de l'uretère	5	1	2	-	6	9	9	4
Hyperplasia of prostate — Hyperplasie de la prostate	1	..	2	..	5	..	2	..
Pregnancy, childbirth and the puerperium — Grossesse, accouchement et puerpéralité								
Total	..	1	..	1	..	1	..	1
Pregnancy with abortive outcome — Grossesse se terminant par un avortement	..	-	..	-	..	-	..	-
Other direct obstetric causes — Autres décès maternels directs	..	1	..	1	..	1	..	1
Indirect obstetric causes — Décès maternels indirects	..	-	..	-	..	-	..	-
Certain conditions originating in the perinatal period — Certaines affections dont l'origine se situe dans la période périnatale	1	3	2	-	19	17	14	16
Congenital malformations, deformations and chromosomal abnormalities — Malformations congénitales et anomalies chromosomiques	-	2	1	2	3	2	6	4
Symptoms, signs and abnormal clinical and laboratory findings, not elsewhere classified — Symptômes, signes et résultats anormaux d'examens cliniques et de laboratoire, non classés ailleurs	2	2	3	5	16	29	13	20
All other diseases — Toutes autres maladies	3	4	5	6	4	5	7	17
External causes — Causes externes								
Total	37	6	27	4	98	21	81	22
Accidents								
Total	7	3	6	2	37	11	36	13
Transport accidents — Accidents de transport	2	-	3	1	26	9	11	3
Falls — Chutes	-	-	2	1	4	1	1	1
Accidental drowning and submersion — Noyade et submersion accidentelles	-	-	1	-	3	-	9	1
Exposure to smoke, fire and flames — Exposition à la fumée, au feu et aux flammes	1	-	-	-	3	1	-	-
Accidental poisoning by and exposure to noxious substances — Intoxication accidentelle par des substances nocives et exposition à ces substances	1	-	-	-	-	-	2	-
Intentional self-harm — Lésions auto-infligées	-	1	2	-	8	-	9	1
Assault — Agresssions	25	-	13	1	36	7	31	6
All other external causes — Toutes autres causes externes	5	2	6	1	17	3	5	2

20. Death and death rates by cause and sex: 2010 - 2014
Décès et taux de mortalité par cause et sexe : 2010 - 2014 (continued - suite)

Cause of death — Cause de décès	Saint Pierre and Miquelon - Saint Pierre-et-Miquelon 2010 (...)		Saint Vincent and the Grenadines - Saint-Vincent-et-les Grenadines 2012 (+C)		2013 (+C)		Turks and Caicos Islands - Îles Turques et Caïques 2013 (...)	
	Male — Masculin	Female — Féminin	Male — Masculin	Female — Féminin	Male — Masculin	Female — Féminin	Male — Masculin	Female — Féminin
	Number Nombre	Number Nombre	Number Nombre	Number Nombre	Number Nombre	Number Nombre	Number Nombre	Number Nombre
TOTAL	*19*	*20*	*476*	*383*	*503*	*408*	*53*	*45*
Certain infectious and parasitic diseases — Certaines maladies infectieuses et parasitaires								
Total	-	1	39	38	45	33	2	-
Intestinal infectious diseases — Maladies infectieuses intestinales	-	1	-	-	-	-	1	-
Tuberculosis — Tuberculose	-	-	4	-	1	-	-	-
Tetanus — Tétanos...	-	-	-	-	-	-	-	-
Diphtheria — Diphtérie...	-	-	-	-	-	-	-	-
Whooping cough — Coqueluche	-	-	-	-	-	-	-	-
Meningococcal infection — Infection à méningocoques	-	-	-	-	-	-	-	-
Septicaemia — Septicémie...	-	-	16	28	26	22	-	-
Acute poliomyelitis — Poliomyélite aiguë	-	-	-	-	-	-	-	-
Measles — Rougeole..	-	-	-	-	-	-	-	-
Viral hepatitis — Hépatite virale..	-	-	-	1	-	-	1	-
Human immunodeficiency virus [HIV] disease — Maladies dues au virus de l'immunodéficience humaine (VIH)...	-	-	8	4	13	10	-	-
Malaria — Paludisme	-	-	-	-	-	-	-	-
Neoplasms — Tumeurs	*9*	*8*	*78*	*56*	*94*	*80*	*6*	*10*
Malignant neoplasms — Tumeurs malignes								
Total	8	7	77	55	94	79	6	10
Malignant neoplasm of lip, oral cavity and pharynx — Tumeur maligne de la lèvre, de la cavité buccale et du pharynx	-	-	3	1	4	1	-	-
Malignant neoplasm of oesophagus — Tumeur maligne de l'oesophage	1	-	5	-	1	-	-	1
Malignant neoplasm of stomach — Tumeur maligne de l'estomac	1	-	6	2	5	1	-	-
Malignant neoplasm of colon, rectosigmoid junction, rectum, anus and anal canal — Tumeur maligne du côlon, de la jonction recto-sigmoïdienne, du rectum, de l'anus et du canal anal..	-	1	12	2	3	5	-	2
Malignant neoplasm of liver and intrahepatic bile ducts — Tumeur maligne du foie et des voies bilaires intrahépatiques	2	-	5	2	8	-	1	-
Malignant neoplasm of pancreas — Tumeur maligne du pancréas..................	-	-	6	1	3	-	-	-
Malignant neoplasm of trachea, bronchus and lung — Tumeur maligne de la trachée, des bronches et du poumon	1	-	5	4	9	5	1	1
Malignant neoplasm of female breast — Tumeur maligne du sein chez la femme	..	-	..	14	..	14	..	2
Malignant neoplasm of cervix uteri — Tumeur maligne du col de l'utérus.........	..	1	..	4	..	14	..	1
Malignant neoplasm of prostate — Tumeur maligne de la prostate	2	..	22	..	27	..	2	..
Malignant neoplasm of lymphoid, haematopoietic and related tissue — Tumeurs malignes primitives ou présumées primitives des tissus lymphoïde, hématopoïétique et apparentés..	-	2	5	3	7	4	1	1
Disorders of the blood and blood-forming organs and certain disorders involving the immune mechanism — Maladies du sang et des organes hématopoïétiques et certains troubles du système immunitaire								
Total	-	-	10	5	6	7	-	-
Anaemias — Anémies	-	-	6	5	5	6	-	-
Endocrine, nutritional and metabolic diseases — Maladies endocriniennes, nutritionnelles et métaboliques								
Total	-	-	58	57	57	59	4	5
Diabetes mellitus — Diabète sucré...	-	-	50	54	53	54	3	4
Malnutrition — Malnutrition	-	-	2	-	1	1	-	-
Mental and behavioural disorders — Troubles mentaux et du comportement	-	2	5	1	2	-	1	2
Diseases of the nervous system — Maladies du système nerveux................	-	-	7	8	4	6	-	-
Diseases of the circulatory system — Maladies de l'appareil circulatoire								
Total	4	5	146	155	158	161	*19*	*12*
Acute rheumatic fever and chronic rheumatic heart diseases — Rhumatisme articularie aigu et cardiopathies rhumatismales chroniques	-	-	-	1	-	-	-	-
Hypertensive diseases — Maladies hypertensives...............................	1	-	26	29	26	28	1	1
Ischaemic heart disease — Cardiopathie ischémique	3	1	54	56	57	70	13	6

20. Death and death rates by cause and sex: 2010 - 2014
Décès et taux de mortalité par cause et sexe : 2010 - 2014 (continued - suite)

Cause of death — Cause de décès	Saint Pierre and Miquelon - Saint Pierre-et-Miquelon		Saint Vincent and the Grenadines - Saint-Vincent-et-les Grenadines				Turks and Caicos Islands - Îles Turques et Caïques	
	2010 (...)		2012 (+C)		2013 (+C)		2013 (...)	
	Male — Masculin	Female — Féminin	Male — Masculin	Female — Féminin	Male — Masculin	Female — Féminin	Male — Masculin	Female — Féminin
	Number Nombre	Number Nombre	Number Nombre	Number Nombre	Number Nombre	Number Nombre	Number Nombre	Number Nombre
Cerebrovascular disease — Maladie cérébrovasculaire	-	1	40	47	47	43	2	3
Diseases of arteries, arterioles and capillaries — Maladies des artères, artérioles et capillaires	-	-	4	1	3	1	1	-
Diseases of the respiratory system — Maladies de l'appareil respiratoire								
Total	-	-	31	14	22	11	1	2
Influenza — Grippe	-	-	-	-	-	-	-	-
Pneumonia — Pneumopathies	-	-	10	8	10	7	-	1
Chronic lower respiratory diseases — Maladies chroniques des voies respiratoires inférieures	-	-	13	4	6	-	1	1
Diseases of the digestive system — Maladies de l'appareil digestif								
Total	1	1	16	7	23	15	2	-
Gastric and duodenal ulcer — Ulcère de l'estomac et du duodénum	-	-	2	-	6	1	-	-
Diseases of the liver — Maladies du foie	1	1	7	4	7	3	-	-
Diseases of the musculoskeletal system and connective tissue — Maladies du système ostéo-articularie, des muscles et du tissu conjonctif	-	-	2	3	1	3	-	-
Diseases of the genitourinary system — Maladies de l'appareil génito-urinaire								
Total	-	-	8	9	9	7	-	2
Disorders of kidney and ureter — Affections du rein et de l'uretère	-	-	3	3	5	3	-	1
Hyperplasia of prostate — Hyperplasie de la prostate	-	..	-	..	-	..	-	..
Pregnancy, childbirth and the puerperium — Grossesse, accouchement et puerpéralité								
Total	..	-	..	-	..	2	..	-
Pregnancy with abortive outcome — Grossesse se terminant par un avortement	..	-	..	-	..	1	..	-
Other direct obstetric causes — Autres décès maternels directs	..	-	..	-	..	1	..	-
Indirect obstetric causes — Décès maternels indirects	..	-	..	-	..	-	..	-
Certain conditions originating in the perinatal period — Certaines affections dont l'origine se situe dans la période périnatale	-	-	10	5	11	9	1	1
Congenital malformations, deformations and chromosomal abnormalities — Malformations congénitales et anomalies chromosomiques	-	-	1	1	5	1	1	-
Symptoms, signs and abnormal clinical and laboratory findings, not elsewhere classified — Symptômes, signes et résultats anormaux d'examens cliniques et de laboratoire, non classés ailleurs	4	3	19	13	14	4	-	-
All other diseases — Toutes autres maladies	-	-	-	-	2	1	-	1
External causes — Causes externes								
Total	1	-	46	11	50	9	16	10
Accidents								
Total	-	-	24	3	25	6	13	8
Transport accidents — Accidents de transport	-	-	7	2	5	2	12	6
Falls — Chutes	-	-	7	-	4	-	-	-
Accidental drowning and submersion — Noyade et submersion accidentelles	-	-	4	-	3	1	1	2
Exposure to smoke, fire and flames — Exposition à la fumée, au feu et aux flammes	-	-	2	-	1	-	-	-
Accidental poisoning by and exposure to noxious substances — Intoxication accidentelle par des substances nocives et exposition à ces substances	-	-	1	-	2	-	-	-
Intentional self-harm — Lésions auto-infligées	1	-	7	3	-	-	-	-
Assault — Agresssions	-	-	13	5	21	3	3	1
All other external causes — Toutes autres causes externes	-	-	2	-	4	-	-	1

United States of America - États-Unis d'Amérique

Cause of death — Cause de décès	2012 (C)				2013 (C)			
	Male — Masculin		Female — Féminin		Male — Masculin		Female — Féminin	
	Number Nombre	Rate Taux	Number Nombre	Rate Taux	Number Nombre	Rate Taux	Number Nombre	Rate Taux
TOTAL	1 273 720	824.3	1 269 559	795.6	1 306 031	838.8	1 290 962	803.2
Certain infectious and parasitic diseases — Certaines maladies infectieuses et parasitaires								
Total	35 099	22.7	33 310	20.9	36 235	23.3	34 366	21.4
Intestinal infectious diseases — Maladies infectieuses intestinales	4 130	2.7	6 544	4.1	4 181	2.7	6 457	4.0
Tuberculosis — Tuberculose	314	0.2	196	0.1	357	0.2	198	0.1
Tetanus — Tétanos	1	♦0.0	3	♦0.0	-	-	3	♦0.0
Diphtheria — Diphtérie	-	-	-	-	-	-	-	-
Whooping cough — Coqueluche	9	♦0.0	8	♦0.0	5	♦0.0	7	♦0.0
Meningococcal infection — Infection à méningocoques	42	0.0	32	0.0	34	0.0	25	♦0.0
Septicaemia — Septicémie	16 789	10.9	19 053	11.9	17 994	11.6	20 162	12.5
Acute poliomyelitis — Poliomyélite aiguë	-	-	-	-	-	-	-	-
Measles — Rougeole	1	♦0.0	1	♦0.0	-	-	-	-
Viral hepatitis — Hépatite virale	5 361	3.5	2 701	1.7	5 425	3.5	2 732	1.7
Human immunodeficiency virus [HIV] disease — Maladies dues au virus de l'immunodéficience humaine (VIH)	5 240	3.4	1 976	1.2	5 096	3.3	1 859	1.2
Malaria — Paludisme	3	♦0.0	3	♦0.0	9	♦0.0	1	♦0.0
Neoplasms — Tumeurs	313 574	202.9	284 164	178.1	315 658	202.7	284 505	177.0
Malignant neoplasms — Tumeurs malignes								
Total	305 690	197.8	276 962	173.6	307 568	197.5	277 337	172.6
Malignant neoplasm of lip, oral cavity and pharynx — Tumeur maligne de la lèvre, de la cavité buccale et du pharynx	6 263	4.1	2 661	1.7	6 227	4.0	2 623	1.6
Malignant neoplasm of oesophagus — Tumeur maligne de l'oesophage	11 697	7.6	2 952	1.8	11 732	7.5	2 958	1.8
Malignant neoplasm of stomach — Tumeur maligne de l'estomac	6 611	4.3	4 580	2.9	6 793	4.4	4 468	2.8
Malignant neoplasm of colon, rectosigmoid junction, rectum, anus and anal canal — Tumeur maligne du côlon, de la jonction recto-sigmoïdienne, du rectum, de l'anus et du canal anal	27 038	17.5	24 990	15.7	27 354	17.6	24 898	15.5
Malignant neoplasm of liver and intrahepatic bile ducts — Tumeur maligne du foie et des voies bilaires intrahépatiques	15 563	10.1	7 410	4.6	16 300	10.5	7 732	4.8
Malignant neoplasm of pancreas — Tumeur maligne du pancréas	19 718	12.8	19 079	12.0	19 854	12.8	19 142	11.9
Malignant neoplasm of trachea, bronchus and lung — Tumeur maligne de la trachée, des bronches et du poumon	86 740	56.1	70 759	44.3	85 710	55.0	70 542	43.9
Malignant neoplasm of female breast — Tumeur maligne du sein chez la femme	..	..	41 152	31.8	..	..	40 861	...
Malignant neoplasm of cervix uteri — Tumeur maligne du col de l'utérus	..	..	4 074	3.1	..	..	4 217	...
Malignant neoplasm of prostate — Tumeur maligne de la prostate	27 245	56.2	..	..	27 682	...	..	..
Malignant neoplasm of lymphoid, haematopoietic and related tissue — Tumeurs malignes primitives ou présumées primitives des tissus lymphoïde, hématopoïétique et apparentés	31 936	20.7	25 113	15.7	32 066	20.6	24 894	15.5
Disorders of the blood and blood-forming organs and certain disorders involving the immune mechanism — Maladies du sang et des organes hématopoïétiques et certains troubles du système immunitaire								
Total	4 628	3.0	5 787	3.6	4 600	3.0	5 566	3.5
Anaemias — Anémies	2 172	1.4	3 018	1.9	2 077	1.3	2 817	1.8
Endocrine, nutritional and metabolic diseases — Maladies endocriniennes, nutritionnelles et métaboliques								
Total	53 733	34.8	52 193	32.7	55 773	35.8	53 386	33.2
Diabetes mellitus — Diabète sucré	38 584	25.0	35 348	22.2	39 841	25.6	35 737	22.2
Malnutrition — Malnutrition	1 156	0.7	1 858	1.2	1 284	0.8	1 940	1.2
Mental and behavioural disorders — Troubles mentaux et du comportement	51 605	33.4	96 312	60.4	54 636	35.1	101 779	63.3
Diseases of the nervous system — Maladies du système nerveux	59 496	38.5	86 691	54.3	61 954	39.8	89 830	55.9
Diseases of the circulatory system — Maladies de l'appareil circulatoire								
Total	391 662	253.5	395 769	248.0	402 845	258.7	398 073	247.7
Acute rheumatic fever and chronic rheumatic heart diseases — Rhumatisme articularie aigu et cardiopathies rhumatismales chroniques	1 018	0.7	2 070	1.3	1 141	0.7	2 119	1.3
Hypertensive diseases — Maladies hypertensives	31 113	20.1	36 988	23.2	33 558	21.6	38 373	23.9
Ischaemic heart disease — Cardiopathie ischémique	206 685	133.8	164 784	103.3	208 515	133.9	161 698	100.6
Cerebrovascular disease — Maladie cérébrovasculaire	52 638	34.1	75 908	47.6	53 691	34.5	75 287	46.8

United States of America - États-Unis d'Amérique

Cause of death — Cause de décès	2012 (C)				2013 (C)			
	Male — Masculin		Female — Féminin		Male — Masculin		Female — Féminin	
	Number Nombre	Rate Taux	Number Nombre	Rate Taux	Number Nombre	Rate Taux	Number Nombre	Rate Taux
Diseases of arteries, arterioles and capillaries — Maladies des artères, artérioles et capillaires	12 609	8.2	13 004	8.1	12 685	8.1	12 956	8.1
Diseases of the respiratory system — Maladies de l'appareil respiratoire								
Total	118 820	76.9	127 491	79.9	125 963	80.9	135 108	84.1
Influenza — Grippe	473	0.3	620	0.4	1 611	1.0	1 939	1.2
Pneumonia — Pneumopathies	23 535	15.2	25 995	16.3	25 107	16.1	28 175	17.5
Chronic lower respiratory diseases — Maladies chroniques des voies respiratoires inférieures	67 673	43.8	75 816	47.5	70 317	45.2	78 888	49.1
Diseases of the digestive system — Maladies de l'appareil digestif								
Total	50 452	32.7	44 832	28.1	52 189	33.5	46 194	28.7
Gastric and duodenal ulcer — Ulcère de l'estomac et du duodénum...............	1 460	0.9	1 397	0.9	1 517	1.0	1 433	0.9
Diseases of the liver — Maladies du foie...............	29 402	19.0	17 591	11.0	30 322	19.5	18 290	11.4
Diseases of the musculoskeletal system and connective tissue — Maladies du système ostéo-articularie, des muscles et du tissu conjonctif	4 650	3.0	9 075	5.7	4 629	3.0	8 905	5.5
Diseases of the genitourinary system — Maladies de l'appareil génito-urinaire								
Total	29 172	18.9	32 858	20.6	30 303	19.5	33 782	21.0
Disorders of kidney and ureter — Affections du rein et de l'uretère	24 352	15.8	24 810	15.5	25 362	16.3	25 696	16.0
Hyperplasia of prostate — Hyperplasie de la prostate........................	519	1.1	..	..	558	...		
Pregnancy, childbirth and the puerperium — Grossesse, accouchement et puerpéralité								
Total	..	..	990	25.0	..	..	1 138	28.9
Pregnancy with abortive outcome — Grossesse se terminant par un avortement	..	..	17	♦0.4	..	..	27	♦0.7
Other direct obstetric causes — Autres décès maternels directs	..	..	505	12.8	..	..	575	14.6
Indirect obstetric causes — Décès maternels indirects	..	..	265	6.7	..	..	262	6.7
Certain conditions originating in the perinatal period — Certaines affections dont l'origine se situe dans la période périnatale	6 686	330.8	5 231	270.8	6 723	334.0	5 361	279.3
Congenital malformations, deformations and chromosomal abnormalities — Malformations congénitales et anomalies chromosomiques	5 089	251.8	4 547	235.4	5 052	251.0	4 531	236.1
Symptoms, signs and abnormal clinical and laboratory findings, not elsewhere classified — Symptômes, signes et résultats anormaux d'examens cliniques et de laboratoire, non classés ailleurs	17 592	11.4	24 458	15.3	16 277	10.5	21 478	13.4
All other diseases — Toutes autres maladies........................	1 823	1.2	2 502	1.6	1 946	1.2	2 498	1.6
External causes — Causes externes								
Total	129 639	83.9	63 349	39.7	131 248	84.3	64 462	40.1
Accidents								
Total	78 696	50.9	47 150	29.5	80 659	51.8	48 017	29.9
Transport accidents — Accidents de transport........................	27 191	17.6	11 060	6.9	26 546	17.0	10 638	6.6
Falls — Chutes	14 331	9.3	14 422	9.0	15 205	9.8	15 003	9.3
Accidental drowning and submersion — Noyade et submersion accidentelles........................	2 748	1.8	803	0.5	2 613	1.7	778	0.5
Exposure to smoke, fire and flames — Exposition à la fumée, au feu et aux flammes........................	1 469	1.0	995	0.6	1 653	1.1	1 107	0.7
Accidental poisoning by and exposure to noxious substances — Intoxication accidentelle par des substances nocives et exposition à ces substances	23 266	15.1	13 066	8.2	25 080	16.1	13 771	8.6
Intentional self-harm — Lésions auto-infligées........................	31 727	20.5	8 804	5.5	31 991	20.5	9 069	5.6
Assault — Agresssions........................	13 002	8.4	3 441	2.2	12 516	8.0	3 347	2.1
All other external causes — Toutes autres causes externes	6 214	4.0	3 954	2.5	6 082	3.9	4 029	2.5

Cause of death — Cause de décès	United States Virgin Islands - Îles Vierges américaines				Argentina - Argentine			
	2011 (...)		2012 (...)		2012 (+C)			
	Male — Masculin	Female — Féminin	Male — Masculin	Female — Féminin	Male — Masculin		Female — Féminin	
	Number Nombre	Number Nombre	Number Nombre	Number Nombre	Number Nombre	Rate Taux	Number Nombre	Rate Taux
TOTAL	*410*	*301*	*432*	*291*	165 325	809.6	151 329	710.0
Certain infectious and parasitic diseases — Certaines maladies infectieuses et parasitaires								
Total	*25*	*13*	*18*	*9*	6 935	34.0	6 555	30.8
Intestinal infectious diseases — Maladies infectieuses intestinales	-	*1*	-	-	162	0.8	239	1.1
Tuberculosis — Tuberculose	-	-	-	-	380	1.9	173	0.8
Tetanus — Tétanos	-	-	-	-	1	♦0.0	1	♦0.0
Diphtheria — Diphtérie	-	-	-	-	-	-	-	-
Whooping cough — Coqueluche	-	-	-	-	19	♦0.1	13	♦0.1
Meningococcal infection — Infection à méningocoques	-	-	-	-	14	♦0.1	7	♦0.0
Septicaemia — Septicémie	*12*	*9*	*12*	*4*	4 832	23.7	5 316	24.9
Acute poliomyelitis — Poliomyélite aiguë	-	-	-	-	-	-	-	-
Measles — Rougeole	-	-	-	-	-	-	-	-
Viral hepatitis — Hépatite virale	*5*	*1*	-	-	74	0.4	71	0.3
Human immunodeficiency virus [HIV] disease — Maladies dues au virus de l'immunodéficience humaine (VIH)	*6*	*1*	*5*	*4*	1 004	4.9	422	2.0
Malaria — Paludisme	-	-	-	-	1	♦0.0	-	-
Neoplasms — Tumeurs	*87*	*75*	*91*	*66*	32 361	158.5	29 095	136.5
Malignant neoplasms — Tumeurs malignes								
Total	*87*	*73*	*88*	*66*	31 075	152.2	28 050	131.6
Malignant neoplasm of lip, oral cavity and pharynx — Tumeur maligne de la lèvre, de la cavité buccale et du pharynx	*4*	*2*	*2*	*1*	589	2.9	252	1.2
Malignant neoplasm of oesophagus — Tumeur maligne de l'oesophage	*5*	-	*2*	*3*	1 204	5.9	618	2.9
Malignant neoplasm of stomach — Tumeur maligne de l'estomac	*4*	*2*	*6*	*3*	1 860	9.1	1 067	5.0
Malignant neoplasm of colon, rectosigmoid junction, rectum, anus and anal canal — Tumeur maligne du côlon, de la jonction recto-sigmoïdienne, du rectum, de l'anus et du canal anal	*11*	*9*	*13*	*6*	3 722	18.2	3 194	15.0
Malignant neoplasm of liver and intrahepatic bile ducts — Tumeur maligne du foie et des voies bilaires intrahépatiques	-	*5*	*2*	*3*	1 079	5.3	855	4.0
Malignant neoplasm of pancreas — Tumeur maligne du pancréas	*1*	*2*	*4*	*3*	1 833	9.0	2 072	9.7
Malignant neoplasm of trachea, bronchus and lung — Tumeur maligne de la trachée, des bronches et du poumon	*12*	*9*	*11*	*6*	6 430	31.5	2 741	12.9
Malignant neoplasm of female breast — Tumeur maligne du sein chez la femme	..	*17*	..	*17*	..	..	5 499	34.2
Malignant neoplasm of cervix uteri — Tumeur maligne du col de l'utérus	..	*2*	..	*2*	..	..	1 013	6.3
Malignant neoplasm of prostate — Tumeur maligne de la prostate	*24*	..	*25*	..	3 755	83.4	..	..
Malignant neoplasm of lymphoid, haematopoietic and related tissue — Tumeurs malignes primitives ou présumées primitives des tissus lymphoïde, hématopoïétique et apparentés	*9*	*6*	*4*	*5*	2 039	10.0	1 776	8.3
Disorders of the blood and blood-forming organs and certain disorders involving the immune mechanism — Maladies du sang et des organes hématopoïétiques et certains troubles du système immunitaire								
Total	*4*	*3*	*2*	*1*	566	2.8	672	3.2
Anaemias — Anémies	*2*	*2*	*1*	-	354	1.7	468	2.2
Endocrine, nutritional and metabolic diseases — Maladies endocriniennes, nutritionnelles et métaboliques								
Total	*30*	*33*	*24*	*22*	5 503	26.9	5 663	26.6
Diabetes mellitus — Diabète sucré	*27*	*26*	*23*	*17*	4 114	20.1	3 802	17.8
Malnutrition — Malnutrition	*1*	*1*	-	*1*	421	2.1	514	2.4
Mental and behavioural disorders — Troubles mentaux et du comportement	*13*	*7*	*15*	*9*	1 127	5.5	1 424	6.7
Diseases of the nervous system — Maladies du système nerveux	*12*	*20*	*18*	*18*	2 218	10.9	2 368	11.1
Diseases of the circulatory system — Maladies de l'appareil circulatoire								
Total	*117*	*91*	*108*	*101*	47 132	230.8	47 826	224.4
Acute rheumatic fever and chronic rheumatic heart diseases — Rhumatisme articularie aigu et cardiopathies rhumatismales chroniques	*1*	-	-	*1*	51	0.2	78	0.4
Hypertensive diseases — Maladies hypertensives	*24*	*6*	*19*	*35*	2 747	13.5	3 329	15.6
Ischaemic heart disease — Cardiopathie ischémique	*52*	*36*	*47*	*28*	11 848	58.0	8 204	38.5

Cause of death — Cause de décès	United States Virgin Islands - Îles Vierges américaines				Argentina - Argentine			
	2011 (...)		2012 (...)		2012 (+C)			
	Male — Masculin	Female — Féminin	Male — Masculin	Female — Féminin	Male — Masculin		Female — Féminin	
	Number Nombre	Number Nombre	Number Nombre	Number Nombre	Number Nombre	Rate Taux	Number Nombre	Rate Taux
Cerebrovascular disease — Maladie cérébrovasculaire	17	25	15	16	8 827	43.2	9 434	44.3
Diseases of arteries, arterioles and capillaries — Maladies des artères, artérioles et capillaires	1	3	1	3	1 318	6.5	977	4.6
Diseases of the respiratory system — Maladies de l'appareil respiratoire								
Total	14	8	18	12	24 062	117.8	24 843	116.6
Influenza — Grippe	-	-	-	-	4	♦0.0	7	♦0.0
Pneumonia — Pneumopathies	7	1	4	2	9 536	46.7	10 334	48.5
Chronic lower respiratory diseases — Maladies chroniques des voies respiratoires inférieures	3	6	5	6	3 397	16.6	1 958	9.2
Diseases of the digestive system — Maladies de l'appareil digestif								
Total	17	15	20	8	8 026	39.3	5 409	25.4
Gastric and duodenal ulcer — Ulcère de l'estomac et du duodénum	1	1	1	-	183	0.9	120	0.6
Diseases of the liver — Maladies du foie	9	5	16	3	3 883	19.0	1 387	6.5
Diseases of the musculoskeletal system and connective tissue — Maladies du système ostéo-articulaire, des muscles et du tissu conjonctif	1	2	3	3	279	1.4	697	3.3
Diseases of the genitourinary system — Maladies de l'appareil génito-urinaire								
Total	6	4	8	5	5 223	25.6	5 218	24.5
Disorders of kidney and ureter — Affections du rein et de l'uretère	5	3	6	5	4 108	20.1	3 648	17.1
Hyperplasia of prostate — Hyperplasie de la prostate	-	..	1	..	48	1.1	..	..
Pregnancy, childbirth and the puerperium — Grossesse, accouchement et puerpéralité								
Total	..	-	..	-	..	..	280	37.9
Pregnancy with abortive outcome — Grossesse se terminant par un avortement	..	-	..	-	..	..	32	4.3
Other direct obstetric causes — Autres décès maternels directs	..	-	..	-	..	..	146	19.8
Indirect obstetric causes — Décès maternels indirects	..	-	..	-	..	..	74	10.0
Certain conditions originating in the perinatal period — Certaines affections dont l'origine se situe dans la période périnatale	5	3	3	2	2 261	592.4	1 702	477.4
Congenital malformations, deformations and chromosomal abnormalities — Malformations congénitales et anomalies chromosomiques	3	-	2	-	1 388	363.7	1 213	340.2
Symptoms, signs and abnormal clinical and laboratory findings, not elsewhere classified — Symptômes, signes et résultats anormaux d'examens cliniques et de laboratoire, non classés ailleurs	10	13	16	20	12 562	61.5	12 453	58.4
All other diseases — Toutes autres maladies	2	2	1	-	582	2.8	972	4.6
External causes — Causes externes								
Total	64	12	85	15	15 100	73.9	4 939	23.2
Accidents								
Total	16	6	26	9	8 038	39.4	2 958	13.9
Transport accidents — Accidents de transport	7	1	12	5	4 015	19.7	1 117	5.2
Falls — Chutes	2	-	-	-	183	0.9	104	0.5
Accidental drowning and submersion — Noyade et submersion accidentelles	2	1	7	-	407	2.0	92	0.4
Exposure to smoke, fire and flames — Exposition à la fumée, au feu et aux flammes	-	-	1	2	267	1.3	133	0.6
Accidental poisoning by and exposure to noxious substances — Intoxication accidentelle par des substances nocives et exposition à ces substances	2	-	-	1	219	1.1	97	0.5
Intentional self-harm — Lésions auto-infligées	6	2	6	4	2 632	12.9	631	3.0
Assault — Agresssions	42	3	49	2	1 799	8.8	291	1.4
All other external causes — Toutes autres causes externes	-	1	4	-	2 631	12.9	1 059	5.0

20. Death and death rates by cause and sex: 2010 - 2014
Décès et taux de mortalité par cause et sexe : 2010 - 2014 (continued - suite)

Cause of death — Cause de décès	Argentina - Argentine				Brazil - Brésil			
	2013 (+C)				2012 (C)			
	Male — Masculin		Female — Féminin		Male — Masculin		Female — Féminin	
	Number Nombre	Rate Taux	Number Nombre	Rate Taux	Number Nombre	Rate Taux	Number Nombre	Rate Taux
TOTAL	167 403	810.3	155 533	721.9	670 743	681.0	509 885	506.1
Certain infectious and parasitic diseases — Certaines maladies infectieuses et parasitaires								
Total	7 120	34.5	7 040	32.7	28 389	28.8	21 208	21.0
Intestinal infectious diseases — Maladies infectieuses intestinales	178	0.9	232	1.1	1 918	1.9	2 303	2.3
Tuberculosis — Tuberculose	368	1.8	217	1.0	3 285	3.3	1 132	1.1
Tetanus — Tétanos	4	♦0.0	3	♦0.0	83	0.1	13	♦0.0
Diphtheria — Diphtérie	-	-	-	-	1	♦0.0	-	-
Whooping cough — Coqueluche	2	♦0.0	9	♦0.0	45	0.0	48	0.0
Meningococcal infection — Infection à méningocoques	8	♦0.0	7	♦0.0	234	0.2	180	0.2
Septicaemia — Septicémie	4 950	24.0	5 711	26.5	7 270	7.4	7 617	7.6
Acute poliomyelitis — Poliomyélite aiguë	-	-	-	-	-	-	-	-
Measles — Rougeole	-	-	-	-	-	-	-	-
Viral hepatitis — Hépatite virale	71	0.3	75	0.3	1 801	1.8	1 069	1.1
Human immunodeficiency virus [HIV] disease — Maladies dues au virus de l'immunodéficience humaine (VIH)	1 020	4.9	417	1.9	7 847	8.0	4 225	4.2
Malaria — Paludisme	-	-	-	-	30	♦0.0	30	♦0.0
Neoplasms — Tumeurs	32 552	157.6	29 655	137.6	101 980	103.5	89 607	88.9
Malignant neoplasms — Tumeurs malignes								
Total	31 293	151.5	28 545	132.5	100 022	101.6	87 813	87.2
Malignant neoplasm of lip, oral cavity and pharynx — Tumeur maligne de la lèvre, de la cavité buccale et du pharynx	661	3.2	230	1.1	5 542	5.6	1 528	1.5
Malignant neoplasm of oesophagus — Tumeur maligne de l'oesophage	1 215	5.9	586	2.7	5 988	6.1	1 761	1.7
Malignant neoplasm of stomach — Tumeur maligne de l'estomac	1 810	8.8	1 111	5.2	8 720	8.9	4 991	5.0
Malignant neoplasm of colon, rectosigmoid junction, rectum, anus and anal canal — Tumeur maligne du côlon, de la jonction recto-sigmoïdienne, du rectum, de l'anus et du canal anal	3 810	18.4	3 236	15.0	7 004	7.1	7 608	7.6
Malignant neoplasm of liver and intrahepatic bile ducts — Tumeur maligne du foie et des voies bilaires intrahépatiques	1 067	5.2	784	3.6	5 012	5.1	3 778	3.7
Malignant neoplasm of pancreas — Tumeur maligne du pancréas	1 883	9.1	2 026	9.4	4 017	4.1	4 206	4.2
Malignant neoplasm of trachea, bronchus and lung — Tumeur maligne de la trachée, des bronches et du poumon	6 290	30.4	2 906	13.5	14 275	14.5	9 225	9.2
Malignant neoplasm of female breast — Tumeur maligne du sein chez la femme	..	..	5 635	34.7	..	..	13 591	...
Malignant neoplasm of cervix uteri — Tumeur maligne du col de l'utérus	..	..	1 085	6.7	..	..	5 264	...
Malignant neoplasm of prostate — Tumeur maligne de la prostate	3 740	81.7	..	..	13 354	...	..	..
Malignant neoplasm of lymphoid, haematopoietic and related tissue — Tumeurs malignes primitives ou présumées primitives des tissus lymphoïde, hématopoïétique et apparentés	2 211	10.7	1 769	8.2	7 324	7.4	6 297	6.2
Disorders of the blood and blood-forming organs and certain disorders involving the immune mechanism — Maladies du sang et des organes hématopoïétiques et certains troubles du système immunitaire								
Total	609	2.9	704	3.3	3 214	3.3	3 127	3.1
Anaemias — Anémies	376	1.8	481	2.2	2 226	2.3	2 150	2.1
Endocrine, nutritional and metabolic diseases — Maladies endocriniennes, nutritionnelles et métaboliques								
Total	5 409	26.2	5 722	26.6	32 414	32.9	40 069	39.8
Diabetes mellitus — Diabète sucré	4 155	20.1	3 815	17.7	24 954	25.3	31 800	31.6
Malnutrition — Malnutrition	391	1.9	482	2.2	3 223	3.3	3 185	3.2
Mental and behavioural disorders — Troubles mentaux et du comportement	1 119	5.4	1 538	7.1	8 954	9.1	3 462	3.4
Diseases of the nervous system — Maladies du système nerveux	2 344	11.3	2 629	12.2	13 453	13.7	15 255	15.1
Diseases of the circulatory system — Maladies de l'appareil circulatoire								
Total	46 197	223.6	47 028	218.3	174 428	177.1	158 836	157.6
Acute rheumatic fever and chronic rheumatic heart diseases — Rhumatisme articularie aigu et cardiopathies rhumatismales chroniques	52	0.3	106	0.5	808	0.8	1 366	1.4
Hypertensive diseases — Maladies hypertensives	2 617	12.7	3 360	15.6	21 212	21.5	24 082	23.9
Ischaemic heart disease — Cardiopathie ischémique	11 755	56.9	8 384	38.9	60 735	61.7	43 653	43.3
Cerebrovascular disease — Maladie cérébrovasculaire	9 134	44.2	9 439	43.8	50 530	51.3	49 652	49.3

20. Death and death rates by cause and sex: 2010 - 2014
Décès et taux de mortalité par cause et sexe : 2010 - 2014 (continued - suite)

Cause of death — Cause de décès	Argentina - Argentine 2013 (+C)				Brazil - Brésil 2012 (C)			
	Male — Masculin		Female — Féminin		Male — Masculin		Female — Féminin	
	Number Nombre	Rate Taux	Number Nombre	Rate Taux	Number Nombre	Rate Taux	Number Nombre	Rate Taux
Diseases of arteries, arterioles and capillaries — Maladies des artères, artérioles et capillaires	1 422	6.9	912	4.2	6 603	6.7	5 289	5.2
Diseases of the respiratory system — Maladies de l'appareil respiratoire								
Total	25 281	122.4	26 855	124.6	66 344	67.4	60 838	60.4
Influenza — Grippe	22	◆0.1	18	◆0.1	133	0.1	160	0.2
Pneumonia — Pneumopathies	10 950	53.0	12 169	56.5	30 279	30.7	30 983	30.8
Chronic lower respiratory diseases — Maladies chroniques des voies respiratoires inférieures	3 792	18.4	2 340	10.9	23 492	23.9	17 881	17.7
Diseases of the digestive system — Maladies de l'appareil digestif								
Total	8 292	40.1	5 639	26.2	38 087	38.7	22 408	22.2
Gastric and duodenal ulcer — Ulcère de l'estomac et du duodénum	197	1.0	137	0.6	1 894	1.9	1 203	1.2
Diseases of the liver — Maladies du foie	3 883	18.8	1 404	6.5	20 217	20.5	5 819	5.8
Diseases of the musculoskeletal system and connective tissue — Maladies du système ostéo-articularie, des muscles et du tissu conjonctif	334	1.6	758	3.5	1 635	1.7	2 971	2.9
Diseases of the genitourinary system — Maladies de l'appareil génito-urinaire								
Total	5 461	26.4	5 606	26.0	13 728	13.9	14 245	14.1
Disorders of kidney and ureter — Affections du rein et de l'uretère	4 291	20.8	4 023	18.7	8 333	8.5	7 298	7.2
Hyperplasia of prostate — Hyperplasie de la prostate	46	1.0	..	..	707	...	..	..
Pregnancy, childbirth and the puerperium — Grossesse, accouchement et puerpéralité								
Total	..	..	274	36.3	..	..	1 647	58.2
Pregnancy with abortive outcome — Grossesse se terminant par un avortement	..	..	50	6.6	..	..	120	4.2
Other direct obstetric causes — Autres décès maternels directs	..	..	131	17.4	..	..	1 010	35.7
Indirect obstetric causes — Décès maternels indirects	..	..	62	8.2	..	..	409	14.4
Certain conditions originating in the perinatal period — Certaines affections dont l'origine se situe dans la période périnatale	2 314	595.9	1 762	481.3	12 864	888.2	10 114	731.9
Congenital malformations, deformations and chromosomal abnormalities — Malformations congénitales et anomalies chromosomiques	1 387	357.2	1 235	337.4	5 577	385.1	4 940	357.5
Symptoms, signs and abnormal clinical and laboratory findings, not elsewhere classified — Symptômes, signes et résultats anormaux d'examens cliniques et de laboratoire, non classés ailleurs	12 869	62.3	12 905	59.9	42 519	43.2	32 333	32.1
All other diseases — Toutes autres maladies	573	2.8	1 054	4.9	1 707	1.7	2 191	2.2
External causes — Causes externes								
Total	15 542	75.2	5 129	23.8	125 450	127.4	26 634	26.4
Accidents								
Total	8 231	39.8	3 114	14.5	56 816	57.7	16 341	16.2
Transport accidents — Accidents de transport	4 298	20.8	1 153	5.4	37 680	38.3	8 334	8.3
Falls — Chutes	185	0.9	99	0.5	7 007	7.1	4 640	4.6
Accidental drowning and submersion — Noyade et submersion accidentelles	372	1.8	76	0.4	4 658	4.7	720	0.7
Exposure to smoke, fire and flames — Exposition à la fumée, au feu et aux flammes	237	1.1	155	0.7	696	0.7	323	0.3
Accidental poisoning by and exposure to noxious substances — Intoxication accidentelle par des substances nocives et exposition à ces substances	211	1.0	109	0.5	696	0.7	171	0.2
Intentional self-harm — Lésions auto-infligées	2 407	11.7	590	2.7	8 061	8.2	2 257	2.2
Assault — Agresssions	1 849	8.9	292	1.4	51 544	52.3	4 719	4.7
All other external causes — Toutes autres causes externes	3 055	14.8	1 133	5.3	9 029	9.2	3 317	3.3

20. Death and death rates by cause and sex: 2010 - 2014
Décès et taux de mortalité par cause et sexe : 2010 - 2014 (continued - suite)

	Brazil - Brésil				Chile - Chili			
	2013 (C)				2012 (C)			
Cause of death — Cause de décès	Male — Masculin		Female — Féminin		Male — Masculin		Female — Féminin	
	Number Nombre	Rate Taux	Number Nombre	Rate Taux	Number Nombre	Rate Taux	Number Nombre	Rate Taux
TOTAL	**686 668**	**691.3**	**523 195**	**514.5**	**51 814**	**601.6**	**46 897**	**533.5**
Certain infectious and parasitic diseases — Certaines maladies infectieuses et parasitaires								
Total	29 793	30.0	22 250	21.9	1 257	14.6	910	10.4
Intestinal infectious diseases — Maladies infectieuses intestinales	2 200	2.2	2 614	2.6	112	1.3	165	1.9
Tuberculosis — Tuberculose	3 469	3.5	1 148	1.1	200	2.3	68	0.8
Tetanus — Tétanos...	74	0.1	21	♦0.0	-	-	-	-
Diphtheria — Diphtérie...	-	-	2	♦0.0	-	-	-	-
Whooping cough — Coqueluche	40	0.0	49	0.0	5	♦0.1	9	♦0.1
Meningococcal infection — Infection à méningocoques	182	0.2	166	0.2	17	♦0.2	17	♦0.2
Septicaemia — Septicémie..	7 703	7.8	8 038	7.9	240	2.8	307	3.5
Acute poliomyelitis — Poliomyélite aiguë	-	-	-	-	-	-	-	-
Measles — Rougeole...	-	-	1	♦0.0	-	-	-	-
Viral hepatitis — Hépatite virale	1 759	1.8	1 071	1.1	25	♦0.3	39	0.4
Human immunodeficiency virus [HIV] disease — Maladies dues au virus de l'immunodéficience humaine (VIH)...	8 302	8.4	4 257	4.2	378	4.4	78	0.9
Malaria — Paludisme...	27	♦0.0	13	♦0.0	-	-	-	-
Neoplasms — Tumeurs	**105 220**	**105.9**	**91 734**	**90.2**	**13 140**	**152.6**	**12 281**	**139.7**
Malignant neoplasms — Tumeurs malignes								
Total	103 282	104.0	89 885	88.4	12 627	146.6	11 745	133.6
Malignant neoplasm of lip, oral cavity and pharynx — Tumeur maligne de la lèvre, de la cavité buccale et du pharynx	5 645	5.7	1 499	1.5	179	2.1	90	1.0
Malignant neoplasm of oesophagus — Tumeur maligne de l'oesophage	6 203	6.2	1 727	1.7	396	4.6	237	2.7
Malignant neoplasm of stomach — Tumeur maligne de l'estomac	9 142	9.2	5 040	5.0	2 181	25.3	1 173	13.3
Malignant neoplasm of colon, rectosigmoid junction, rectum, anus and anal canal — Tumeur maligne du côlon, de la jonction recto-sigmoïdienne, du rectum, de l'anus et du canal anal	7 387	7.4	8 024	7.9	1 013	11.8	1 130	12.9
Malignant neoplasm of liver and intrahepatic bile ducts — Tumeur maligne du foie et des voies bilaires intrahépatiques	5 012	5.0	3 759	3.7	637	7.4	529	6.0
Malignant neoplasm of pancreas — Tumeur maligne du pancréas...................	4 373	4.4	4 335	4.3	526	6.1	674	7.7
Malignant neoplasm of trachea, bronchus and lung — Tumeur maligne de la trachée, des bronches et du poumon	14 811	14.9	9 675	9.5	1 680	19.5	1 168	13.3
Malignant neoplasm of female breast — Tumeur maligne du sein chez la femme	..	..	14 206	18.2	..	..	1 367	19.7
Malignant neoplasm of cervix uteri — Tumeur maligne du col de l'utérus..........	..	..	5 430	7.0	..	..	584	8.4
Malignant neoplasm of prostate — Tumeur maligne de la prostate	13 772	70.5	..	..	2 045	98.9	..	..
Malignant neoplasm of lymphoid, haematopoietic and related tissue — Tumeurs malignes primitives ou présumées primitives des tissus lymphoïde, hématopoïétique et apparentés...	7 349	7.4	6 267	6.2	948	11.0	873	9.9
Disorders of the blood and blood-forming organs and certain disorders involving the immune mechanism — Maladies du sang et des organes hématopoïétiques et certains troubles du système immunitaire								
Total	3 118	3.1	3 250	3.2	221	2.6	247	2.8
Anaemias — Anémies	2 119	2.1	2 254	2.2	175	2.0	198	2.3
Endocrine, nutritional and metabolic diseases — Maladies endocriniennes, nutritionnelles et métaboliques								
Total	33 726	34.0	40 996	40.3	2 347	27.3	2 583	29.4
Diabetes mellitus — Diabète sucré..	25 718	25.9	32 296	31.8	1 807	21.0	1 906	21.7
Malnutrition — Malnutrition	3 513	3.5	3 305	3.2	249	2.9	276	3.1
Mental and behavioural disorders — Troubles mentaux et du comportement	**9 325**	**9.4**	**3 585**	**3.5**	**977**	**11.3**	**1 591**	**18.1**
Diseases of the nervous system — Maladies du système nerveux.................	**14 089**	**14.2**	**16 204**	**15.9**	**1 499**	**17.4**	**1 934**	**22.0**
Diseases of the circulatory system — Maladies de l'appareil circulatoire								
Total	178 016	179.2	161 591	158.9	13 798	160.2	13 381	152.2
Acute rheumatic fever and chronic rheumatic heart diseases — Rhumatisme articularie aigu et cardiopathies rhumatismales chroniques	740	0.7	1 263	1.2	38	0.4	93	1.1
Hypertensive diseases — Maladies hypertensives..	22 028	22.2	24 794	24.4	1 698	19.7	2 368	26.9
Ischaemic heart disease — Cardiopathie ischémique	62 235	62.7	44 535	43.8	4 824	56.0	3 109	35.4
Cerebrovascular disease — Maladie cérébrovasculaire................................	50 333	50.7	49 705	48.9	4 350	50.5	4 651	52.9

Cause of death — Cause de décès	Brazil - Brésil 2013 (C)				Chile - Chili 2012 (C)			
	Male — Masculin		Female — Féminin		Male — Masculin		Female — Féminin	
	Number Nombre	Rate Taux	Number Nombre	Rate Taux	Number Nombre	Rate Taux	Number Nombre	Rate Taux
Diseases of arteries, arterioles and capillaries — Maladies des artères, artérioles et capillaires	6 780	6.8	5 642	5.5	523	6.1	434	4.9
Diseases of the respiratory system — Maladies de l'appareil respiratoire								
Total	71 815	72.3	65 993	64.9	4 939	57.3	5 179	58.9
Influenza — Grippe...............	225	0.2	239	0.2	5	♦0.1	2	♦0.0
Pneumonia — Pneumopathies...............	34 055	34.3	34 267	33.7	1 779	20.7	2 069	23.5
Chronic lower respiratory diseases — Maladies chroniques des voies respiratoires inférieures	24 369	24.5	19 121	18.8	1 743	20.2	1 700	19.3
Diseases of the digestive system — Maladies de l'appareil digestif								
Total	38 950	39.2	22 991	22.6	4 282	49.7	2 858	32.5
Gastric and duodenal ulcer — Ulcère de l'estomac et du duodénum...............	1 829	1.8	1 225	1.2	113	1.3	75	0.9
Diseases of the liver — Maladies du foie...............	20 662	20.8	5 913	5.8	2 957	34.3	1 284	14.6
Diseases of the musculoskeletal system and connective tissue — Maladies du système ostéo-articularie, des muscles et du tissu conjonctif	1 768	1.8	3 231	3.2	154	1.8	383	4.4
Diseases of the genitourinary system — Maladies de l'appareil génito-urinaire								
Total	14 609	14.7	15 093	14.8	1 164	13.5	1 438	16.4
Disorders of kidney and ureter — Affections du rein et de l'uretère	8 738	8.8	7 722	7.6	803	9.3	914	10.4
Hyperplasia of prostate — Hyperplasie de la prostate...............	665	3.4	..	..	33	1.6	..	..
Pregnancy, childbirth and the puerperium — Grossesse, accouchement et puerpéralité								
Total	..	..	1 788	63.1	..	..	54	22.2
Pregnancy with abortive outcome — Grossesse se terminant par un avortement	..	..	141	5.0	..	..	4	♦1.6
Other direct obstetric causes — Autres décès maternels directs	..	..	1 097	38.7	..	..	22	♦9.0
Indirect obstetric causes — Décès maternels indirects	..	..	408	14.4	..	..	16	♦6.6
Certain conditions originating in the perinatal period — Certaines affections dont l'origine se situe dans la période périnatale	12 768	879.4	9 898	717.0	468	377.2	341	285.2
Congenital malformations, deformations and chromosomal abnormalities — Malformations congénitales et anomalies chromosomiques	5 575	384.0	5 044	365.4	490	394.9	448	374.7
Symptoms, signs and abnormal clinical and laboratory findings, not elsewhere classified — Symptômes, signes et résultats anormaux d'examens cliniques et de laboratoire, non classés ailleurs	41 239	41.5	30 482	30.0	1 209	14.0	1 377	15.7
All other diseases — Toutes autres maladies...............	1 835	1.8	2 241	2.2	66	0.8	134	1.5
External causes — Causes externes								
Total	124 822	125.7	26 824	26.4	5 803	67.4	1 758	20.0
Accidents								
Total	55 689	56.1	16 608	16.3	3 615	42.0	1 289	14.7
Transport accidents — Accidents de transport...............	35 615	35.9	7 816	7.7	1 673	19.4	456	5.2
Falls — Chutes	7 456	7.5	5 094	5.0	456	5.3	466	5.3
Accidental drowning and submersion — Noyade et submersion accidentelles...............	4 440	4.5	667	0.7	312	3.6	30	♦0.3
Exposure to smoke, fire and flames — Exposition à la fumée, au feu et aux flammes...............	821	0.8	429	0.4	215	2.5	87	1.0
Accidental poisoning by and exposure to noxious substances — Intoxication accidentelle par des substances nocives et exposition à ces substances	778	0.8	202	0.2	212	2.5	58	0.7
Intentional self-harm — Lésions auto-infligées...............	8 309	8.4	2 223	2.2	1 510	17.5	331	3.8
Assault — Agresssions...............	51 937	52.3	4 762	4.7	596	6.9	91	1.0
All other external causes — Toutes autres causes externes	8 887	8.9	3 231	3.2	82	1.0	47	0.5

20. Death and death rates by cause and sex: 2010 - 2014
Décès et taux de mortalité par cause et sexe : 2010 - 2014 (continued - suite)

Cause of death — Cause de décès	Chile - Chili 2013 (C)				Colombia - Colombie 2011 (C)			
	Male — Masculin		Female — Féminin		Male — Masculin		Female — Féminin	
	Number Nombre	Rate Taux	Number Nombre	Rate Taux	Number Nombre	Rate Taux	Number Nombre	Rate Taux
TOTAL	52 916	609.1	46 835	528.1	111 208	489.2	84 590	362.8
Certain infectious and parasitic diseases — Certaines maladies infectieuses et parasitaires								
Total	1 434	16.5	1 060	12.0	3 734	16.4	2 056	8.8
Intestinal infectious diseases — Maladies infectieuses intestinales	150	1.7	201	2.3	281	1.2	293	1.3
Tuberculosis — Tuberculose	188	2.2	87	1.0	594	2.6	259	1.1
Tetanus — Tétanos	2	♦0.0	1	♦0.0	4	♦0.0	2	♦0.0
Diphtheria — Diphtérie..........	-	-	-	-	-	-	-	-
Whooping cough — Coqueluche	3	♦0.0	3	♦0.0	10	♦0.0	6	♦0.0
Meningococcal infection — Infection à méningocoques..........	9	♦0.1	16	♦0.2	8	♦0.0	5	♦0.0
Septicaemia — Septicémie..........	302	3.5	415	4.7	543	2.4	550	2.4
Acute poliomyelitis — Poliomyélite aiguë	-	-	-	-	-	-	-	-
Measles — Rougeole..........	-	-	-	-	-	-	-	-
Viral hepatitis — Hépatite virale..........	40	0.5	40	0.5	52	0.2	45	0.2
Human immunodeficiency virus [HIV] disease — Maladies dues au virus de l'immunodéficience humaine (VIH)..........	456	5.2	67	0.8	1 793	7.9	561	2.4
Malaria — Paludisme..........	-	-	-	-	10	♦0.0	13	♦0.1
Neoplasms — Tumeurs	13 370	153.9	12 318	138.9	17 557	77.2	17 934	76.9
Malignant neoplasms — Tumeurs malignes								
Total	12 803	147.4	11 790	132.9	16 348	71.9	16 706	71.7
Malignant neoplasm of lip, oral cavity and pharynx — Tumeur maligne de la lèvre, de la cavité buccale et du pharynx	196	2.3	79	0.9	327	1.4	237	1.0
Malignant neoplasm of oesophagus — Tumeur maligne de l'oesophage	383	4.4	246	2.8	422	1.9	193	0.8
Malignant neoplasm of stomach — Tumeur maligne de l'estomac	2 132	24.5	1 108	12.5	2 782	12.2	1 727	7.4
Malignant neoplasm of colon, rectosigmoid junction, rectum, anus and anal canal — Tumeur maligne du côlon, de la jonction recto-sigmoïdienne, du rectum, de l'anus et du canal anal..........	1 085	12.5	1 177	13.3	1 288	5.7	1 417	6.1
Malignant neoplasm of liver and intrahepatic bile ducts — Tumeur maligne du foie et des voies bilaires intrahépatiques	587	6.8	525	5.9	754	3.3	846	3.6
Malignant neoplasm of pancreas — Tumeur maligne du pancréas..........	577	6.6	700	7.9	652	2.9	712	3.1
Malignant neoplasm of trachea, bronchus and lung — Tumeur maligne de la trachée, des bronches et du poumon	1 809	20.8	1 225	13.8	2 375	10.4	1 588	6.8
Malignant neoplasm of female breast — Tumeur maligne du sein chez la femme	..	..	1 389	19.8	..	..	2 319	...
Malignant neoplasm of cervix uteri — Tumeur maligne du col de l'utérus..........	..	..	561	8.0	..	..	1 535	...
Malignant neoplasm of prostate — Tumeur maligne de la prostate	2 041	95.2	..	..	2 382	...	..	..
Malignant neoplasm of lymphoid, haematopoietic and related tissue — Tumeurs malignes primitives ou présumées primitives des tissus lymphoïde, hématopoïétique et apparentés	988	11.4	928	10.5	1 758	7.7	1 445	6.2
Disorders of the blood and blood-forming organs and certain disorders involving the immune mechanism — Maladies du sang et des organes hématopoïétiques et certains troubles du système immunitaire								
Total	202	2.3	219	2.5	427	1.9	391	1.7
Anaemias — Anémies	160	1.8	176	2.0	240	1.1	218	0.9
Endocrine, nutritional and metabolic diseases — Maladies endocriniennes, nutritionnelles et métaboliques								
Total	2 301	26.5	2 575	29.0	3 960	17.4	5 030	21.6
Diabetes mellitus — Diabète sucré..........	1 782	20.5	1 961	22.1	2 900	12.8	3 834	16.4
Malnutrition — Malnutrition	245	2.8	271	3.1	787	3.5	800	3.4
Mental and behavioural disorders — Troubles mentaux et du comportement	784	9.0	1 280	14.4	64	0.3	75	0.3
Diseases of the nervous system — Maladies du système nerveux.........	1 656	19.1	2 050	23.1	1 582	7.0	1 330	5.7
Diseases of the circulatory system — Maladies de l'appareil circulatoire								
Total	14 259	164.1	13 400	151.1	30 379	133.6	28 495	122.2
Acute rheumatic fever and chronic rheumatic heart diseases — Rhumatisme articularie aigu et cardiopathies rhumatismales chroniques	54	0.6	58	0.7	90	0.4	121	0.5
Hypertensive diseases — Maladies hypertensives..........	1 909	22.0	2 665	30.0	3 214	14.1	3 444	14.8
Ischaemic heart disease — Cardiopathie ischémique	4 806	55.3	2 935	33.1	16 235	71.4	13 138	56.4
Cerebrovascular disease — Maladie cérébrovasculaire..........	4 450	51.2	4 554	51.3	6 208	27.3	7 203	30.9

	Chile - Chili				Colombia - Colombie			
	2013 (C)				2011 (C)			
Cause of death — Cause de décès	Male — Masculin		Female — Féminin		Male — Masculin		Female — Féminin	
	Number Nombre	Rate Taux	Number Nombre	Rate Taux	Number Nombre	Rate Taux	Number Nombre	Rate Taux
Diseases of arteries, arterioles and capillaries — Maladies des artères, artérioles et capillaires	512	5.9	409	4.6	876	3.9	598	2.6
Diseases of the respiratory system — Maladies de l'appareil respiratoire								
Total	5 109	58.8	5 159	58.2	10 770	47.4	9 768	41.9
Influenza — Grippe	4	♦0.0	5	♦0.1	8	♦0.0	8	♦0.0
Pneumonia — Pneumopathies	2 088	24.0	2 263	25.5	3 019	13.3	2 959	12.7
Chronic lower respiratory diseases — Maladies chroniques des voies respiratoires inférieures	1 627	18.7	1 544	17.4	5 965	26.2	5 108	21.9
Diseases of the digestive system — Maladies de l'appareil digestif								
Total	4 473	51.5	2 877	32.4	5 135	22.6	4 538	19.5
Gastric and duodenal ulcer — Ulcère de l'estomac et du duodénum	97	1.1	77	0.9	359	1.6	248	1.1
Diseases of the liver — Maladies du foie	2 977	34.3	1 244	14.0	1 448	6.4	918	3.9
Diseases of the musculoskeletal system and connective tissue — Maladies du système ostéo-articularie, des muscles et du tissu conjonctif	151	1.7	386	4.4	689	3.0	1 525	6.5
Diseases of the genitourinary system — Maladies de l'appareil génito-urinaire								
Total	1 352	15.6	1 531	17.3	2 769	12.2	2 488	10.7
Disorders of kidney and ureter — Affections du rein et de l'uretère	928	10.7	923	10.4	1 943	8.5	1 538	6.6
Hyperplasia of prostate — Hyperplasie de la prostate	30	♦1.4	..	..	152	...	..	..
Pregnancy, childbirth and the puerperium — Grossesse, accouchement et puerpéralité								
Total	..	..	52	21.5	..	..	459	69.3
Pregnancy with abortive outcome — Grossesse se terminant par un avortement	..	..	2	♦0.8	..	..	43	6.5
Other direct obstetric causes — Autres décès maternels directs	..	..	20	♦8.3	..	..	253	38.2
Indirect obstetric causes — Décès maternels indirects	..	..	16	♦6.6	..	..	153	23.1
Certain conditions originating in the perinatal period — Certaines affections dont l'origine se situe dans la période périnatale	454	367.9	308	259.7	2 384	701.1	1 790	554.6
Congenital malformations, deformations and chromosomal abnormalities — Malformations congénitales et anomalies chromosomiques	468	379.2	459	387.1	1 285	377.9	1 181	365.9
Symptoms, signs and abnormal clinical and laboratory findings, not elsewhere classified — Symptômes, signes et résultats anormaux d'examens cliniques et de laboratoire, non classés ailleurs	1 003	11.5	1 191	13.4	3 102	13.6	2 444	10.5
All other diseases — Toutes autres maladies	99	1.1	155	1.7	495	2.2	654	2.8
External causes — Causes externes								
Total	5 801	66.8	1 815	20.5	26 876	118.2	4 432	19.0
Accidents								
Total	3 699	42.6	1 373	15.5	8 015	35.3	2 080	8.9
Transport accidents — Accidents de transport	1 743	20.1	453	5.1	4 790	21.1	1 127	4.8
Falls — Chutes	436	5.0	505	5.7	871	3.8	263	1.1
Accidental drowning and submersion — Noyade et submersion accidentelles	287	3.3	38	0.4	738	3.2	168	0.7
Exposure to smoke, fire and flames — Exposition à la fumée, au feu et aux flammes	228	2.6	101	1.1	58	0.3	24	♦0.1
Accidental poisoning by and exposure to noxious substances — Intoxication accidentelle par des substances nocives et exposition à ces substances	208	2.4	53	0.6	151	0.7	27	♦0.1
Intentional self-harm — Lésions auto-infligées	1 420	16.3	318	3.6	1 669	7.3	383	1.6
Assault — Agresssions	590	6.8	88	1.0	15 249	67.1	1 423	6.1
All other external causes — Toutes autres causes externes	92	1.1	36	0.4	1 943	8.5	546	2.3

20. Death and death rates by cause and sex: 2010 - 2014
Décès et taux de mortalité par cause et sexe : 2010 - 2014 (continued - suite)

Cause of death — Cause de décès	Colombia - Colombie 2012 (C)				Ecuador - Équateur 2012 (U)		2013 (U)	
	Male — Masculin		Female — Féminin		Male — Masculin	Female — Féminin	Male — Masculin	Female — Féminin
	Number Nombre	Rate Taux	Number Nombre	Rate Taux	Number Nombre	Number Nombre	Number Nombre	Number Nombre
TOTAL	**113 055**	**491.6**	**86 654**	**367.4**	*35 314*	*28 197*	*34 913*	*28 191*
Certain infectious and parasitic diseases — Certaines maladies infectieuses et parasitaires								
Total	3 914	17.0	2 161	9.2	*1 450*	*882*	*1 208*	*733*
Intestinal infectious diseases — Maladies infectieuses intestinales	287	1.2	281	1.2	*126*	*104*	*75*	*88*
Tuberculosis — Tuberculose	618	2.7	279	1.2	*285*	*144*	*255*	*129*
Tetanus — Tétanos..........	24	♦0.1	6	♦0.0	*1*	*1*	*5*	-
Diphtheria — Diphtérie.............	-	-	-	-	-	-	*1*	-
Whooping cough — Coqueluche	28	♦0.1	26	♦0.1	-	*1*	-	-
Meningococcal infection — Infection à méningocoques	13	♦0.1	2	♦0.0	-	*2*	*1*	-
Septicaemia — Septicémie.............	598	2.6	620	2.6	*389*	*380*	*187*	*211*
Acute poliomyelitis — Poliomyélite aiguë	-	-	-	-	*1*	*1*	-	*2*
Measles — Rougeole.............	-	-	-	-	-	-	-	-
Viral hepatitis — Hépatite virale.............	71	0.3	57	0.2	*16*	*9*	*26*	*14*
Human immunodeficiency virus [HIV] disease — Maladies dues au virus de l'immunodéficience humaine (VIH).............	1 739	7.6	538	2.3	*536*	*174*	*559*	*203*
Malaria — Paludisme.............	13	♦0.1	11	♦0.0	-	*1*	*3*	*1*
Neoplasms — Tumeurs	18 319	79.7	19 174	81.3	*5 047*	*5 187*	*4 888*	*5 236*
Malignant neoplasms — Tumeurs malignes								
Total	16 991	73.9	17 778	75.4	*4 888*	*4 987*	*4 625*	*4 984*
Malignant neoplasm of lip, oral cavity and pharynx — Tumeur maligne de la lèvre, de la cavité buccale et du pharynx	332	1.4	197	0.8	*51*	*47*	*54*	*36*
Malignant neoplasm of oesophagus — Tumeur maligne de l'oesophage	410	1.8	202	0.9	*92*	*28*	*76*	*29*
Malignant neoplasm of stomach — Tumeur maligne de l'estomac	2 811	12.2	1 839	7.8	*972*	*747*	*865*	*705*
Malignant neoplasm of colon, rectosigmoid junction, rectum, anus and anal canal — Tumeur maligne du côlon, de la jonction recto-sigmoïdienne, du rectum, de l'anus et du canal anal.............	1 384	6.0	1 467	6.2	*282*	*367*	*270*	*328*
Malignant neoplasm of liver and intrahepatic bile ducts — Tumeur maligne du foie et des voies bilaires intrahépatiques	837	3.6	889	3.8	*328*	*377*	*308*	*329*
Malignant neoplasm of pancreas — Tumeur maligne du pancréas.............	649	2.8	779	3.3	*162*	*203*	*154*	*166*
Malignant neoplasm of trachea, bronchus and lung — Tumeur maligne de la trachée, des bronches et du poumon	2 333	10.1	1 725	7.3	*434*	*321*	*373*	*269*
Malignant neoplasm of female breast — Tumeur maligne du sein chez la femme	..	..	2 489	14.4	..	*513*	..	*518*
Malignant neoplasm of cervix uteri — Tumeur maligne du col de l'utérus..........	..	..	1 521	8.8	..	*329*	..	*357*
Malignant neoplasm of prostate — Tumeur maligne de la prostate	2 499	58.2	..	..	*879*	..	*842*	..
Malignant neoplasm of lymphoid, haematopoietic and related tissue — Tumeurs malignes primitives ou présumées primitives des tissus lymphoïde, hématopoïétique et apparentés.............	1 790	7.8	1 583	6.7	*599*	*432*	*591*	*503*
Disorders of the blood and blood-forming organs and certain disorders involving the immune mechanism — Maladies du sang et des organes hématopoïétiques et certains troubles du système immunitaire								
Total	436	1.9	414	1.8	*210*	*241*	*230*	*249*
Anaemias — Anémies	227	1.0	223	0.9	*171*	*190*	*169*	*200*
Endocrine, nutritional and metabolic diseases — Maladies endocriniennes, nutritionnelles et métaboliques								
Total	4 263	18.5	5 279	22.4	*2 437*	*2 916*	*2 518*	*2 998*
Diabetes mellitus — Diabète sucré.............	3 097	13.5	4 057	17.2	*2 117*	*2 513*	*2 157*	*2 538*
Malnutrition — Malnutrition	832	3.6	816	3.5	*162*	*236*	*191*	*237*
Mental and behavioural disorders — Troubles mentaux et du comportement	76	0.3	93	0.4	*157*	*63*	*132*	*52*
Diseases of the nervous system — Maladies du système nerveux.............	1 523	6.6	1 274	5.4	*632*	*575*	*689*	*633*
Diseases of the circulatory system — Maladies de l'appareil circulatoire								
Total	31 758	138.1	29 275	124.1	*7 501*	*6 886*	*7 625*	*6 846*
Acute rheumatic fever and chronic rheumatic heart diseases — Rhumatisme articularie aigu et cardiopathies rhumatismales chroniques	68	0.3	90	0.4	*26*	*53*	*44*	*65*
Hypertensive diseases — Maladies hypertensives.............	3 394	14.8	3 599	15.3	*2 727*	*2 638*	*2 136*	*2 053*
Ischaemic heart disease — Cardiopathie ischémique	17 516	76.2	13 810	58.6	*1 239*	*829*	*1 783*	*1 159*

Cause of death — Cause de décès	Colombia - Colombie 2012 (C) Male — Masculin Number Nombre	Colombia - Colombie 2012 (C) Male — Masculin Rate Taux	Colombia - Colombie 2012 (C) Female — Féminin Number Nombre	Colombia - Colombie 2012 (C) Female — Féminin Rate Taux	Ecuador - Équateur 2012 (U) Male — Masculin Number Nombre	Ecuador - Équateur 2012 (U) Female — Féminin Number Nombre	Ecuador - Équateur 2013 (U) Male — Masculin Number Nombre	Ecuador - Équateur 2013 (U) Female — Féminin Number Nombre
Cerebrovascular disease — Maladie cérébrovasculaire....................................	6 313	27.5	7 299	30.9	1 657	1 633	1 819	1 748
Diseases of arteries, arterioles and capillaries — Maladies des artères, artérioles et capillaires	890	3.9	604	2.6	156	148	217	177
Diseases of the respiratory system — Maladies de l'appareil respiratoire								
Total	11 037	48.0	10 030	42.5	3 239	2 944	3 387	2 967
Influenza — Grippe	9	♦0.0	3	♦0.0	7	15	36	22
Pneumonia — Pneumopathies	3 294	14.3	3 127	13.3	1 801	1 784	1 905	1 786
Chronic lower respiratory diseases — Maladies chroniques des voies respiratoires inférieures	5 879	25.6	5 230	22.2	775	581	806	619
Diseases of the digestive system — Maladies de l'appareil digestif								
Total	5 197	22.6	4 839	20.5	2 167	1 679	2 149	1 673
Gastric and duodenal ulcer — Ulcère de l'estomac et du duodénum................	407	1.8	281	1.2	124	91	119	102
Diseases of the liver — Maladies du foie...	1 489	6.5	976	4.1	1 286	875	1 161	844
Diseases of the musculoskeletal system and connective tissue — Maladies du système ostéo-articulaire, des muscles et du tissu conjonctif	595	2.6	1 403	5.9	65	167	119	213
Diseases of the genitourinary system — Maladies de l'appareil génito-urinaire								
Total	3 208	13.9	2 603	11.0	1 009	820	1 093	887
Disorders of kidney and ureter — Affections du rein et de l'uretère	2 258	9.8	1 624	6.9	915	776	953	810
Hyperplasia of prostate — Hyperplasie de la prostate...................................	187	4.4	..	..	74	..	81	..
Pregnancy, childbirth and the puerperium — Grossesse, accouchement et puerpéralité								
Total	..	..	452	66.9	..	202	..	158
Pregnancy with abortive outcome — Grossesse se terminant par un avortement	..	..	25	♦3.7	..	13	..	15
Other direct obstetric causes — Autres décès maternels directs	..	..	265	39.2	..	160	..	112
Indirect obstetric causes — Décès maternels indirects	..	..	145	21.5	..	28	..	28
Certain conditions originating in the perinatal period — Certaines affections dont l'origine se situe dans la période périnatale	2 382	687.5	1 782	541.3	862	651	779	611
Congenital malformations, deformations and chromosomal abnormalities — Malformations congénitales et anomalies chromosomiques	1 346	388.5	1 197	363.6	404	366	483	425
Symptoms, signs and abnormal clinical and laboratory findings, not elsewhere classified — Symptômes, signes et résultats anormaux d'examens cliniques et de laboratoire, non classés ailleurs	2 199	9.6	1 700	7.2	2 900	2 726	2 850	2 645
All other diseases — Toutes autres maladies..	423	1.8	611	2.6	11	19	43	52
External causes — Causes externes								
Total	26 379	114.7	4 367	18.5	7 223	1 873	6 720	1 813
Accidents								
Total	8 264	35.9	2 041	8.7	4 510	1 271	4 343	1 197
Transport accidents — Accidents de transport...	5 183	22.5	1 173	5.0	2 529	657	2 497	612
Falls — Chutes	805	3.5	261	1.1	352	116	322	95
Accidental drowning and submersion — Noyade et submersion accidentelles..	714	3.1	139	0.6	396	89	260	69
Exposure to smoke, fire and flames — Exposition à la fumée, au feu et aux flammes..	58	0.3	40	0.2	54	33	65	31
Accidental poisoning by and exposure to noxious substances — Intoxication accidentelle par des substances nocives et exposition à ces substances	170	0.7	47	0.2	117	34	120	35
Intentional self-harm — Lésions auto-infligées..	1 739	7.6	387	1.6	711	265	490	186
Assault — Agresssions	14 417	62.7	1 310	5.6	1 505	201	1 112	159
All other external causes — Toutes autres causes externes	1 959	8.5	629	2.7	497	136	775	271

20. Death and death rates by cause and sex: 2010 - 2014
Décès et taux de mortalité par cause et sexe : 2010 - 2014 (continued - suite)

Cause of death — Cause de décès	French Guiana - Guyane française				Guyana			
	2012 (...)		2013 (...)		2010 (U)		2011 (U)	
	Male — Masculin	Female — Féminin	Male — Masculin	Female — Féminin	Male — Masculin	Female — Féminin	Male — Masculin	Female — Féminin
	Number Nombre	Number Nombre	Number Nombre	Number Nombre	Number Nombre	Number Nombre	Number Nombre	Number Nombre
TOTAL	*479*	*309*	*441*	*321*	*3 033*	*2 400*	*3 085*	*2 306*
Certain infectious and parasitic diseases — Certaines maladies infectieuses et parasitaires								
Total	*24*	*12*	*28*	*21*	*310*	*217*	*329*	*192*
Intestinal infectious diseases — Maladies infectieuses intestinales ...	*2*	*1*	*2*	*2*	*34*	*29*	*28*	*25*
Tuberculosis — Tuberculose	*-*	*-*	*1*	*1*	*92*	*32*	*78*	*23*
Tetanus — Tétanos	*-*	*-*	*-*	*-*	*-*	*-*	*1*	*-*
Diphtheria — Diphtérie	*-*	*-*	*-*	*-*	*-*	*-*	*-*	*-*
Whooping cough — Coqueluche	*-*	*-*	*-*	*-*	*-*	*-*	*-*	*-*
Meningococcal infection — Infection à méningocoques	*-*	*-*	*-*	*-*	*-*	*-*	*-*	*-*
Septicaemia — Septicémie	*6*	*2*	*5*	*4*	*50*	*59*	*48*	*39*
Acute poliomyelitis — Poliomyélite aiguë	*-*	*-*	*-*	*-*	*-*	*-*	*-*	*-*
Measles — Rougeole	*-*	*-*	*-*	*-*	*-*	*-*	*-*	*-*
Viral hepatitis — Hépatite virale	*1*	*-*	*-*	*-*	*-*	*-*	*-*	*2*
Human immunodeficiency virus [HIV] disease — Maladies dues au virus de l'immunodéficience humaine (VIH)	*8*	*6*	*15*	*8*	*109*	*85*	*140*	*90*
Malaria — Paludisme	*2*	*-*	*-*	*-*	*15*	*4*	*27*	*9*
Neoplasms — Tumeurs	*87*	*60*	*76*	*53*	*229*	*227*	*228*	*289*
Malignant neoplasms — Tumeurs malignes								
Total	*84*	*58*	*71*	*50*	*219*	*217*	*215*	*270*
Malignant neoplasm of lip, oral cavity and pharynx — Tumeur maligne de la lèvre, de la cavité buccale et du pharynx	*1*	*-*	*2*	*1*	*7*	*2*	*9*	*1*
Malignant neoplasm of oesophagus — Tumeur maligne de l'oesophage	*1*	*1*	*-*	*-*	*4*	*2*	*3*	*-*
Malignant neoplasm of stomach — Tumeur maligne de l'estomac	*11*	*5*	*4*	*-*	*10*	*5*	*10*	*5*
Malignant neoplasm of colon, rectosigmoid junction, rectum, anus and anal canal — Tumeur maligne du côlon, de la jonction recto-sigmoïdienne, du rectum, de l'anus et du canal anal	*5*	*4*	*7*	*3*	*13*	*16*	*19*	*15*
Malignant neoplasm of liver and intrahepatic bile ducts — Tumeur maligne du foie et des voies bilaires intrahépatiques	*9*	*1*	*5*	*-*	*13*	*5*	*11*	*9*
Malignant neoplasm of pancreas — Tumeur maligne du pancréas	*4*	*4*	*5*	*4*	*9*	*11*	*13*	*6*
Malignant neoplasm of trachea, bronchus and lung — Tumeur maligne de la trachée, des bronches et du poumon	*20*	*6*	*9*	*3*	*19*	*12*	*13*	*8*
Malignant neoplasm of female breast — Tumeur maligne du sein chez la femme	*..*	*13*	*..*	*12*	*..*	*51*	*..*	*39*
Malignant neoplasm of cervix uteri — Tumeur maligne du col de l'utérus	*..*	*3*	*..*	*2*	*..*	*35*	*..*	*45*
Malignant neoplasm of prostate — Tumeur maligne de la prostate	*13*	*..*	*7*	*..*	*76*	*..*	*68*	*..*
Malignant neoplasm of lymphoid, haematopoietic and related tissue — Tumeurs malignes primitives ou présumées primitives des tissus lymphoïde, hématopoïétique et apparentés	*7*	*2*	*8*	*7*	*17*	*14*	*15*	*15*
Disorders of the blood and blood-forming organs and certain disorders involving the immune mechanism — Maladies du sang et des organes hématopoïétiques et certains troubles du système immunitaire								
Total	*2*	*2*	*1*	*3*	*30*	*50*	*43*	*49*
Anaemias — Anémies	*2*	*1*	*-*	*3*	*25*	*47*	*36*	*44*
Endocrine, nutritional and metabolic diseases — Maladies endocriniennes, nutritionnelles et métaboliques								
Total	*20*	*21*	*24*	*18*	*239*	*308*	*250*	*323*
Diabetes mellitus — Diabète sucré	*15*	*15*	*17*	*15*	*166*	*259*	*204*	*277*
Malnutrition — Malnutrition	*-*	*2*	*3*	*1*	*31*	*17*	*17*	*11*
Mental and behavioural disorders — Troubles mentaux et du comportement	*11*	*7*	*11*	*7*	*6*	*3*	*4*	*2*
Diseases of the nervous system — Maladies du système nerveux	*9*	*8*	*14*	*10*	*37*	*40*	*42*	*22*
Diseases of the circulatory system — Maladies de l'appareil circulatoire								
Total	*81*	*61*	*66*	*67*	*1 019*	*966*	*1 016*	*933*
Acute rheumatic fever and chronic rheumatic heart diseases — Rhumatisme articularie aigu et cardiopathies rhumatismales chroniques	*-*	*-*	*1*	*1*	*3*	*6*	*3*	*3*
Hypertensive diseases — Maladies hypertensives	*10*	*11*	*3*	*17*	*184*	*189*	*166*	*198*
Ischaemic heart disease — Cardiopathie ischémique	*13*	*6*	*7*	*7*	*367*	*251*	*350*	*230*

20. Death and death rates by cause and sex: 2010 - 2014
Décès et taux de mortalité par cause et sexe : 2010 - 2014 (continued - suite)

Cause of death — Cause de décès	French Guiana - Guyane française				Guyana			
	2012 (...)		2013 (...)		2010 (U)		2011 (U)	
	Male — Masculin	Female — Féminin	Male — Masculin	Female — Féminin	Male — Masculin	Female — Féminin	Male — Masculin	Female — Féminin
	Number Nombre	Number Nombre	Number Nombre	Number Nombre	Number Nombre	Number Nombre	Number Nombre	Number Nombre
Cerebrovascular disease — Maladie cérébrovasculaire....................................	24	16	31	21	282	322	283	303
Diseases of arteries, arterioles and capillaries — Maladies des artères, artérioles et capillaires	10	7	1	-	2	9	8	8
Diseases of the respiratory system — Maladies de l'appareil respiratoire								
Total	21	18	19	10	181	162	154	120
Influenza — Grippe	1	-	1	-	-	-	-	-
Pneumonia — Pneumopathies	6	10	6	3	103	107	97	85
Chronic lower respiratory diseases — Maladies chroniques des voies respiratoires inférieures	5	1	4	2	49	27	33	14
Diseases of the digestive system — Maladies de l'appareil digestif								
Total	22	5	21	15	245	102	234	80
Gastric and duodenal ulcer — Ulcère de l'estomac et du duodénum...............	-	-	-	-	30	9	17	10
Diseases of the liver — Maladies du foie...	12	1	14	9	148	47	154	32
Diseases of the musculoskeletal system and connective tissue — Maladies du système ostéo-articularie, des muscles et du tissu conjonctif	2	2	4	3	1	5	2	6
Diseases of the genitourinary system — Maladies de l'appareil génito-urinaire								
Total	6	5	11	6	54	50	58	37
Disorders of kidney and ureter — Affections du rein et de l'uretère	4	4	5	6	46	48	47	29
Hyperplasia of prostate — Hyperplasie de la prostate................................	1	..	-	..	3	..	8	..
Pregnancy, childbirth and the puerperium — Grossesse, accouchement et puerpéralité								
Total	..	2	..	1	..	20	..	14
Pregnancy with abortive outcome — Grossesse se terminant par un avortement	..	-	..	-	..	3	..	5
Other direct obstetric causes — Autres décès maternels directs	..	2	..	1	..	17	..	8
Indirect obstetric causes — Décès maternels indirects	..	-	..	-	..	-	..	1
Certain conditions originating in the perinatal period — Certaines affections dont l'origine se situe dans la période périnatale	13	15	10	13	50	45	69	52
Congenital malformations, deformations and chromosomal abnormalities — Malformations congénitales et anomalies chromosomiques	12	11	6	6	17	27	10	19
Symptoms, signs and abnormal clinical and laboratory findings, not elsewhere classified — Symptômes, signes et résultats anormaux d'examens cliniques et de laboratoire, non classés ailleurs	66	52	83	59	27	19	26	17
All other diseases — Toutes autres maladies..	2	2	-	2	-	3	1	4
External causes — Causes externes								
Total	101	26	67	27	588	156	619	147
Accidents								
Total	62	21	42	19	250	57	300	57
Transport accidents — Accidents de transport	31	5	14	4	76	18	125	26
Falls — Chutes	-	-	2	2	3	3	14	-
Accidental drowning and submersion — Noyade et submersion accidentelles..	8	3	8	-	66	9	92	13
Exposure to smoke, fire and flames — Exposition à la fumée, au feu et aux flammes..	2	-	-	2	12	9	11	3
Accidental poisoning by and exposure to noxious substances — Intoxication accidentelle par des substances nocives et exposition à ces substances	5	3	2	-	2	-	2	1
Intentional self-harm — Lésions auto-infligées..	15	4	14	5	157	49	153	39
Assault — Agresssions..	15	1	5	1	88	24	91	33
All other external causes — Toutes autres causes externes	9	-	6	2	93	26	75	18

Cause of death — Cause de décès	Paraguay				Peru - Pérou			
	2012 (+U)		2013 (+U)		2012 (+U)		2013 (+U)	
	Male — Masculin	Female — Féminin	Male — Masculin	Female — Féminin	Male — Masculin	Female — Féminin	Male — Masculin	Female — Féminin
	Number Nombre	Number Nombre	Number Nombre	Number Nombre	Number Nombre	Number Nombre	Number Nombre	Number Nombre
TOTAL	14 401	11 241	15 445	12 242	52 698	45 253	52 822	45 794
Certain infectious and parasitic diseases — Certaines maladies infectieuses et parasitaires								
Total	597	447	800	551	5 159	4 510	5 143	4 620
Intestinal infectious diseases — Maladies infectieuses intestinales	35	46	48	43	231	217	214	195
Tuberculosis — Tuberculose	111	29	123	28	1 005	463	931	405
Tetanus — Tétanos	-	3	1	-	7	-	7	1
Diphtheria — Diphtérie	-	-	-	-	-	-	-	-
Whooping cough — Coqueluche	-	1	2	2	3	3	1	-
Meningococcal infection — Infection à méningocoques	-	-	-	-	4	2	2	1
Septicaemia — Septicémie	189	211	162	157	3 167	3 543	3 352	3 759
Acute poliomyelitis — Poliomyélite aiguë	-	-	-	-	1	-	-	-
Measles — Rougeole	-	-	-	-	-	-	-	-
Viral hepatitis — Hépatite virale	10	1	5	6	44	27	22	15
Human immunodeficiency virus [HIV] disease — Maladies dues au virus de l'immunodéficience humaine (VIH)	132	59	143	70	545	151	540	178
Malaria — Paludisme	-	-	-	-	2	2	1	-
Neoplasms — Tumeurs	1 910	1 796	2 107	1 934	8 722	9 746	8 811	9 712
Malignant neoplasms — Tumeurs malignes								
Total	1 758	1 659	1 938	1 782	8 719	9 746	8 810	9 711
Malignant neoplasm of lip, oral cavity and pharynx — Tumeur maligne de la lèvre, de la cavité buccale et du pharynx	71	13	77	17	119	121	122	105
Malignant neoplasm of oesophagus — Tumeur maligne de l'oesophage	84	24	89	26	123	58	137	58
Malignant neoplasm of stomach — Tumeur maligne de l'estomac	123	67	119	83	1 471	1 260	1 460	1 350
Malignant neoplasm of colon, rectosigmoid junction, rectum, anus and anal canal — Tumeur maligne du côlon, de la jonction recto-sigmoïdienne, du rectum, de l'anus et du canal anal	150	152	147	152	567	711	591	618
Malignant neoplasm of liver and intrahepatic bile ducts — Tumeur maligne du foie et des voies bilaires intrahépatiques	62	40	75	46	639	687	629	713
Malignant neoplasm of pancreas — Tumeur maligne du pancréas	63	84	82	81	338	451	350	413
Malignant neoplasm of trachea, bronchus and lung — Tumeur maligne de la trachée, des bronches et du poumon	346	113	401	103	986	863	907	871
Malignant neoplasm of female breast — Tumeur maligne du sein chez la femme	..	308	..	324	..	904	..	998
Malignant neoplasm of cervix uteri — Tumeur maligne du col de l'utérus	..	255	..	278	..	1 019	..	914
Malignant neoplasm of prostate — Tumeur maligne de la prostate	309	..	301	..	1 510	..	1 503	..
Malignant neoplasm of lymphoid, haematopoietic and related tissue — Tumeurs malignes primitives ou présumées primitives des tissus lymphoïde, hématopoïétique et apparentés	176	133	181	140	910	814	996	895
Disorders of the blood and blood-forming organs and certain disorders involving the immune mechanism — Maladies du sang et des organes hématopoïétiques et certains troubles du système immunitaire								
Total	64	80	84	77	307	377	100	91
Anaemias — Anémies	52	60	63	57	300	374	100	91
Endocrine, nutritional and metabolic diseases — Maladies endocriniennes, nutritionnelles et métaboliques								
Total	1 030	1 374	1 167	1 597	1 877	2 110	1 932	2 095
Diabetes mellitus — Diabète sucré	792	1 103	917	1 301	1 389	1 501	1 597	1 654
Malnutrition — Malnutrition	138	132	142	123	409	489	303	400
Mental and behavioural disorders — Troubles mentaux et du comportement	196	31	200	47	-	-	-	-
Diseases of the nervous system — Maladies du système nerveux	241	187	228	215	504	405	280	245
Diseases of the circulatory system — Maladies de l'appareil circulatoire								
Total	3 723	3 256	3 845	3 506	8 942	8 417	9 148	8 619
Acute rheumatic fever and chronic rheumatic heart diseases — Rhumatisme articularie aigu et cardiopathies rhumatismales chroniques	17	19	12	21	28	47	42	64
Hypertensive diseases — Maladies hypertensives	545	543	565	634	2 138	2 146	1 540	1 552
Ischaemic heart disease — Cardiopathie ischémique	1 416	926	1 519	1 048	2 547	1 867	2 916	2 303

20. Death and death rates by cause and sex: 2010 - 2014
Décès et taux de mortalité par cause et sexe : 2010 - 2014 (continued - suite)

Cause of death — Cause de décès	Paraguay				Peru - Pérou			
	2012 (+U)		2013 (+U)		2012 (+U)		2013 (+U)	
	Male — Masculin	Female — Féminin	Male — Masculin	Female — Féminin	Male — Masculin	Female — Féminin	Male — Masculin	Female — Féminin
	Number Nombre	Number Nombre	Number Nombre	Number Nombre	Number Nombre	Number Nombre	Number Nombre	Number Nombre
Cerebrovascular disease — Maladie cérébrovasculaire.....................................	1 032	1 066	1 053	1 118	1 992	1 981	2 398	2 396
Diseases of arteries, arterioles and capillaries — Maladies des artères, artérioles et capillaires	81	54	74	64	217	153	230	201
Diseases of the respiratory system — Maladies de l'appareil respiratoire								
Total	980	695	987	712	11 307	10 311	11 413	10 681
Influenza — Grippe	22	20	20	27	6	3	22	15
Pneumonia — Pneumopathies	373	352	361	349	6 950	6 525	7 051	6 890
Chronic lower respiratory diseases — Maladies chroniques des voies respiratoires inférieures	352	119	373	163	972	887	1 081	937
Diseases of the digestive system — Maladies de l'appareil digestif								
Total	690	411	693	424	4 082	2 737	3 786	2 728
Gastric and duodenal ulcer — Ulcère de l'estomac et du duodénum...............	27	18	35	19	156	128	159	140
Diseases of the liver — Maladies du foie.........	301	70	296	78	2 434	1 341	2 168	1 302
Diseases of the musculoskeletal system and connective tissue — Maladies du système ostéo-articularie, des muscles et du tissu conjonctif	52	114	65	123	24	59	-	-
Diseases of the genitourinary system — Maladies de l'appareil génito-urinaire								
Total	443	302	451	347	2 253	2 114	2 152	1 975
Disorders of kidney and ureter — Affections du rein et de l'uretère	367	236	361	288	1 974	1 972	1 962	1 949
Hyperplasia of prostate — Hyperplasie de la prostate................	25	..	33	..	106	..	131	..
Pregnancy, childbirth and the puerperium — Grossesse, accouchement et puerpéralité								
Total	..	91	..	100	..	126	..	97
Pregnancy with abortive outcome — Grossesse se terminant par un avortement	..	15	..	20	..	21	..	11
Other direct obstetric causes — Autres décès maternels directs	..	57	..	51	..	103	..	84
Indirect obstetric causes — Décès maternels indirects	..	19	..	29	..	2	..	2
Certain conditions originating in the perinatal period — Certaines affections dont l'origine se situe dans la période périnatale	477	371	482	363	1 140	858	1 083	786
Congenital malformations, deformations and chromosomal abnormalities — Malformations congénitales et anomalies chromosomiques	264	214	267	226	601	503	683	567
Symptoms, signs and abnormal clinical and laboratory findings, not elsewhere classified — Symptômes, signes et résultats anormaux d'examens cliniques et de laboratoire, non classés ailleurs	1 407	1 220	1 628	1 359	212	119	214	103
All other diseases — Toutes autres maladies................	22	40	34	40	27	24	-	-
External causes — Causes externes								
Total	2 305	612	2 407	621	7 541	2 837	8 077	3 475
Accidents								
Total	1 557	428	1 602	456	5 666	2 093	6 988	3 125
Transport accidents — Accidents de transport.........................	985	188	1 012	199	2 110	665	2 043	668
Falls — Chutes	58	14	62	21	136	48	177	63
Accidental drowning and submersion — Noyade et submersion accidentelles...............	134	17	147	28	340	99	310	90
Exposure to smoke, fire and flames — Exposition à la fumée, au feu et aux flammes..........	27	16	24	10	76	34	57	38
Accidental poisoning by and exposure to noxious substances — Intoxication accidentelle par des substances nocives et exposition à ces substances	12	8	17	9	149	61	175	102
Intentional self-harm — Lésions auto-infligées............	190	88	250	74	394	197	246	98
Assault — Agresssions............	464	60	477	60	610	156	484	105
All other external causes — Toutes autres causes externes	94	36	78	31	871	391	359	147

20. Death and death rates by cause and sex: 2010 - 2014
Décès et taux de mortalité par cause et sexe : 2010 - 2014 (continued - suite)

Suriname

Cause of death — Cause de décès	2011 (C)				2012 (C)			
	Male — Masculin		Female — Féminin		Male — Masculin		Female — Féminin	
	Number Nombre	Rate Taux	Number Nombre	Rate Taux	Number Nombre	Rate Taux	Number Nombre	Rate Taux
TOTAL	1 714	...	1 275	...	1 563	577.5	1 252	462.0
Certain infectious and parasitic diseases — Certaines maladies infectieuses et parasitaires								
Total	106	...	94	...	119	44.0	90	33.2
Intestinal infectious diseases — Maladies infectieuses intestinales	4	...	7	...	6	♦2.2	6	♦2.2
Tuberculosis — Tuberculose	8	...	4	...	8	♦3.0	4	♦1.5
Tetanus — Tétanos	-	...	1	...	-	-	-	-
Diphtheria — Diphtérie	-	...	-	...	-	-	-	-
Whooping cough — Coqueluche	-	...	-	...	-	-	-	-
Meningococcal infection — Infection à méningocoques	-	...	-	...	-	-	-	-
Septicaemia — Septicémie	14	...	26	...	34	12.6	28	♦10.3
Acute poliomyelitis — Poliomyélite aiguë	-	...	-	...	-	-	-	-
Measles — Rougeole	-	...	-	...	-	-	-	-
Viral hepatitis — Hépatite virale	5	...	2	...	-	-	2	♦0.7
Human immunodeficiency virus [HIV] disease — Maladies dues au virus de l'immunodéficience humaine (VIH)	63	...	43	...	56	20.7	37	13.7
Malaria — Paludisme	1	...	-	...	-	-	-	-
Neoplasms — Tumeurs	219	...	182	...	192	70.9	169	62.4
Malignant neoplasms — Tumeurs malignes								
Total	219	...	180	...	190	70.2	167	61.6
Malignant neoplasm of lip, oral cavity and pharynx — Tumeur maligne de la lèvre, de la cavité buccale et du pharynx	9	...	7	...	9	♦3.3	4	♦1.5
Malignant neoplasm of oesophagus — Tumeur maligne de l'oesophage	1	...	-	...	-	-	-	-
Malignant neoplasm of stomach — Tumeur maligne de l'estomac	10	...	5	...	11	♦4.1	8	♦3.0
Malignant neoplasm of colon, rectosigmoid junction, rectum, anus and anal canal — Tumeur maligne du côlon, de la jonction recto-sigmoïdienne, du rectum, de l'anus et du canal anal	30	...	14	...	19	♦7.0	15	♦5.5
Malignant neoplasm of liver and intrahepatic bile ducts — Tumeur maligne du foie et des voies bilaires intrahépatiques	15	...	6	...	13	♦4.8	11	♦4.1
Malignant neoplasm of pancreas — Tumeur maligne du pancréas	7	...	6	...	8	♦3.0	6	♦2.2
Malignant neoplasm of trachea, bronchus and lung — Tumeur maligne de la trachée, des bronches et du poumon	25	...	13	...	36	13.3	16	♦5.9
Malignant neoplasm of female breast — Tumeur maligne du sein chez la femme	..	..	33	17.1	..	..	30	♦15.2
Malignant neoplasm of cervix uteri — Tumeur maligne du col de l'utérus	..	..	33	17.1	..	..	33	16.7
Malignant neoplasm of prostate — Tumeur maligne de la prostate	50	101.9	..	..	29	♦56.9	..	..
Malignant neoplasm of lymphoid, haematopoietic and related tissue — Tumeurs malignes primitives ou présumées primitives des tissus lymphoïde, hématopoïétique et apparentés	24	...	11	...	9	♦3.3	10	♦3.7
Disorders of the blood and blood-forming organs and certain disorders involving the immune mechanism — Maladies du sang et des organes hématopoïétiques et certains troubles du système immunitaire								
Total	6	...	5	...	6	♦2.2	7	♦2.6
Anaemias — Anémies	5	...	5	...	6	♦2.2	5	♦1.8
Endocrine, nutritional and metabolic diseases — Maladies endocriniennes, nutritionnelles et métaboliques								
Total	135	...	142	...	101	37.3	128	47.2
Diabetes mellitus — Diabète sucré	121	...	130	...	93	34.4	115	42.4
Malnutrition — Malnutrition	6	...	2	...	2	♦0.7	1	♦0.4
Mental and behavioural disorders — Troubles mentaux et du comportement	4	...	1	...	4	♦1.5	1	♦0.4
Diseases of the nervous system — Maladies du système nerveux	28	...	14	...	26	♦9.6	10	♦3.7
Diseases of the circulatory system — Maladies de l'appareil circulatoire								
Total	438	...	369	...	423	156.3	383	141.3
Acute rheumatic fever and chronic rheumatic heart diseases — Rhumatisme articularie aigu et cardiopathies rhumatismales chroniques	2	...	3	...	2	♦0.7	1	♦0.4
Hypertensive diseases — Maladies hypertensives	58	...	48	...	55	20.3	45	16.6
Ischaemic heart disease — Cardiopathie ischémique	148	...	93	...	159	58.8	94	34.7
Cerebrovascular disease — Maladie cérébrovasculaire	150	...	143	...	140	51.7	148	54.6

20. Death and death rates by cause and sex: 2010 - 2014
Décès et taux de mortalité par cause et sexe : 2010 - 2014 (continued - suite)

Suriname

Cause of death — Cause de décès	2011 (C)				2012 (C)			
	Male — Masculin		Female — Féminin		Male — Masculin		Female — Féminin	
	Number Nombre	Rate Taux	Number Nombre	Rate Taux	Number Nombre	Rate Taux	Number Nombre	Rate Taux
Diseases of arteries, arterioles and capillaries — Maladies des artères, artérioles et capillaires	11	...	8	...	11	♦4.1	12	♦4.4
Diseases of the respiratory system — Maladies de l'appareil respiratoire								
Total	105	...	73	...	97	35.8	74	27.3
Influenza — Grippe	-	...	-	...	2	♦0.7	-	-
Pneumonia — Pneumopathies	68	...	47	...	50	18.5	45	16.6
Chronic lower respiratory diseases — Maladies chroniques des voies respiratoires inférieures	27	...	11	...	35	12.9	17	♦6.3
Diseases of the digestive system — Maladies de l'appareil digestif								
Total	106	...	49	...	91	33.6	47	17.3
Gastric and duodenal ulcer — Ulcère de l'estomac et du duodénum	5	...	3	...	5	♦1.8	2	♦0.7
Diseases of the liver — Maladies du foie	57	...	18	...	41	15.1	15	♦5.5
Diseases of the musculoskeletal system and connective tissue — Maladies du système ostéo-articularie, des muscles et du tissu conjonctif	5	...	7	...	1	♦0.4	5	♦1.8
Diseases of the genitourinary system — Maladies de l'appareil génito-urinaire								
Total	44	...	30	...	54	20.0	31	11.4
Disorders of kidney and ureter — Affections du rein et de l'uretère	27	...	20	...	40	14.8	22	♦8.1
Hyperplasia of prostate — Hyperplasie de la prostate	-	-	..	..	1	♦2.0	..	..
Pregnancy, childbirth and the puerperium — Grossesse, accouchement et puerpéralité								
Total	..	..	7	♦72.1	..	..	2	♦19.6
Pregnancy with abortive outcome — Grossesse se terminant par un avortement	..	..	-	-	..	..	-	-
Other direct obstetric causes — Autres décès maternels directs	..	..	5	♦51.5	..	..	2	♦19.6
Indirect obstetric causes — Décès maternels indirects	..	..	2	♦20.6	..	..	-	-
Certain conditions originating in the perinatal period — Certaines affections dont l'origine se situe dans la période périnatale	56	1 135.4	46	964.2	37	709.8	53	1 059.2
Congenital malformations, deformations and chromosomal abnormalities — Malformations congénitales et anomalies chromosomiques	19	♦385.2	14	♦293.4	14	♦268.6	11	♦219.8
Symptoms, signs and abnormal clinical and laboratory findings, not elsewhere classified — Symptômes, signes et résultats anormaux d'examens cliniques et de laboratoire, non classés ailleurs	137	...	142	...	135	49.9	145	53.5
All other diseases — Toutes autres maladies	12	...	15	...	8	♦3.0	16	♦5.9
External causes — Causes externes								
Total	294	...	85	...	255	94.2	80	29.5
Accidents								
Total	139	...	37	...	117	43.2	30	♦11.1
Transport accidents — Accidents de transport	75	...	19	...	53	19.6	11	♦4.1
Falls — Chutes	6	...	2	...	6	♦2.2	4	♦1.5
Accidental drowning and submersion — Noyade et submersion accidentelles	27	...	5	...	20	♦7.4	5	♦1.8
Exposure to smoke, fire and flames — Exposition à la fumée, au feu et aux flammes	4	...	1	...	1	♦0.4	5	♦1.8
Accidental poisoning by and exposure to noxious substances — Intoxication accidentelle par des substances nocives et exposition à ces substances	2	...	1	...	6	♦2.2	1	♦0.4
Intentional self-harm — Lésions auto-infligées	95	...	32	...	101	37.3	33	12.2
Assault — Agresssions	29	...	6	...	21	♦7.8	9	♦3.3
All other external causes — Toutes autres causes externes	31	...	10	...	16	♦5.9	8	♦3.0

641

Uruguay

Cause of death — Cause de décès	2012 (C)				2013 (C)			
	Male — Masculin		Female — Féminin		Male — Masculin		Female — Féminin	
	Number Nombre	Rate Taux	Number Nombre	Rate Taux	Number Nombre	Rate Taux	Number Nombre	Rate Taux
TOTAL	**16 926**	**1 022.3**	**16 405**	**926.4**	**16 631**	**1 000.1**	**16 150**	**908.7**
Certain infectious and parasitic diseases — Certaines maladies infectieuses et parasitaires								
Total	415	25.1	351	19.8	365	21.9	333	18.7
Intestinal infectious diseases — Maladies infectieuses intestinales	47	2.8	74	4.2	50	3.0	88	5.0
Tuberculosis — Tuberculose	24	♦1.4	9	♦0.5	39	2.3	16	♦0.9
Tetanus — Tétanos...	1	♦0.1	-	-	-	-	1	♦0.1
Diphtheria — Diphtérie..	-	-	-	-	-	-	-	-
Whooping cough — Coqueluche	3	♦0.2	2	♦0.1	2	♦0.1	1	♦0.1
Meningococcal infection — Infection à méningocoques..........................	-	-	1	♦0.1	-	-	1	♦0.1
Septicaemia — Septicémie..	166	10.0	187	10.6	112	6.7	140	7.9
Acute poliomyelitis — Poliomyélite aiguë	-	-	-	-	-	-	-	-
Measles — Rougeole...	-	-	-	-	-	-	-	-
Viral hepatitis — Hépatite virale...	8	♦0.5	6	♦0.3	5	♦0.3	3	♦0.2
Human immunodeficiency virus [HIV] disease — Maladies dues au virus de l'immunodéficience humaine (VIH)...	139	8.4	47	2.7	123	7.4	51	2.9
Malaria — Paludisme...	-	-	-	-	3	♦0.2	-	-
Neoplasms — Tumeurs	**4 348**	**262.6**	**3 391**	**191.5**	**4 383**	**263.6**	**3 510**	**197.5**
Malignant neoplasms — Tumeurs malignes								
Total	4 222	255.0	3 251	183.6	4 229	254.3	3 380	190.2
Malignant neoplasm of lip, oral cavity and pharynx — Tumeur maligne de la lèvre, de la cavité buccale et du pharynx	91	5.5	23	♦1.3	98	5.9	31	1.7
Malignant neoplasm of oesophagus — Tumeur maligne de l'oesophage	181	10.9	75	4.2	137	8.2	75	4.2
Malignant neoplasm of stomach — Tumeur maligne de l'estomac	264	15.9	156	8.8	271	16.3	161	9.1
Malignant neoplasm of colon, rectosigmoid junction, rectum, anus and anal canal — Tumeur maligne du côlon, de la jonction recto-sigmoïdienne, du rectum, de l'anus et du canal anal..	462	27.9	461	26.0	468	28.1	452	25.4
Malignant neoplasm of liver and intrahepatic bile ducts — Tumeur maligne du foie et des voies bilaires intrahépatiques	81	4.9	38	2.1	66	4.0	34	1.9
Malignant neoplasm of pancreas — Tumeur maligne du pancréas..................	224	13.5	270	15.2	261	15.7	267	15.0
Malignant neoplasm of trachea, bronchus and lung — Tumeur maligne de la trachée, des bronches et du poumon	923	55.7	266	15.0	954	57.4	296	16.7
Malignant neoplasm of female breast — Tumeur maligne du sein chez la femme	..	..	582	...	..	..	636	...
Malignant neoplasm of cervix uteri — Tumeur maligne du col de l'utérus.........	..	..	77	...	..	..	92	...
Malignant neoplasm of prostate — Tumeur maligne de la prostate	564	...	..	..	545	...	..	..
Malignant neoplasm of lymphoid, haematopoietic and related tissue — Tumeurs malignes primitives ou présumées primitives des tissus lymphoïde, hématopoïétique et apparentés..	301	18.2	263	14.9	257	15.5	224	12.6
Disorders of the blood and blood-forming organs and certain disorders involving the immune mechanism — Maladies du sang et des organes hématopoïétiques et certains troubles du système immunitaire								
Total	58	3.5	87	4.9	69	4.1	110	6.2
Anaemias — Anémies	39	2.4	64	3.6	50	3.0	81	4.6
Endocrine, nutritional and metabolic diseases — Maladies endocriniennes, nutritionnelles et métaboliques								
Total	504	30.4	608	34.3	512	30.8	646	36.3
Diabetes mellitus — Diabète sucré..	336	20.3	377	21.3	373	22.4	417	23.5
Malnutrition — Malnutrition	34	2.1	36	2.0	36	2.2	30	♦1.7
Mental and behavioural disorders — Troubles mentaux et du comportement	**237**	**14.3**	**448**	**25.3**	**248**	**14.9**	**482**	**27.1**
Diseases of the nervous system — Maladies du système nerveux.................	**481**	**29.1**	**769**	**43.4**	**511**	**30.7**	**726**	**40.8**
Diseases of the circulatory system — Maladies de l'appareil circulatoire								
Total	4 307	260.1	5 062	285.9	4 166	250.5	4 836	272.1
Acute rheumatic fever and chronic rheumatic heart diseases — Rhumatisme articularie aigu et cardiopathies rhumatismales chroniques	13	♦0.8	22	♦1.2	10	♦0.6	21	♦1.2
Hypertensive diseases — Maladies hypertensives..............................	238	14.4	406	22.9	265	15.9	423	23.8
Ischaemic heart disease — Cardiopathie ischémique	1 394	84.2	1 073	60.6	1 333	80.2	984	55.4
Cerebrovascular disease — Maladie cérébrovasculaire.......................	1 007	60.8	1 576	89.0	1 024	61.6	1 558	87.7

Uruguay

Cause of death — Cause de décès	2012 (C)				2013 (C)			
	Male — Masculin		Female — Féminin		Male — Masculin		Female — Féminin	
	Number Nombre	Rate Taux	Number Nombre	Rate Taux	Number Nombre	Rate Taux	Number Nombre	Rate Taux
Diseases of arteries, arterioles and capillaries — Maladies des artères, artérioles et capillaires	266	16.1	211	11.9	268	16.1	209	11.8
Diseases of the respiratory system — Maladies de l'appareil respiratoire								
Total	1 808	109.2	1 718	97.0	1 753	105.4	1 584	89.1
Influenza — Grippe	1	♦0.1	4	♦0.2	2	♦0.1	1	♦0.1
Pneumonia — Pneumopathies	553	33.4	753	42.5	549	33.0	655	36.9
Chronic lower respiratory diseases — Maladies chroniques des voies respiratoires inférieures	764	46.1	335	18.9	756	45.5	359	20.2
Diseases of the digestive system — Maladies de l'appareil digestif								
Total	721	43.5	645	36.4	704	42.3	624	35.1
Gastric and duodenal ulcer — Ulcère de l'estomac et du duodénum	38	2.3	12	♦0.7	28	♦1.7	13	♦0.7
Diseases of the liver — Maladies du foie	253	15.3	81	4.6	233	14.0	69	3.9
Diseases of the musculoskeletal system and connective tissue — Maladies du système ostéo-articularie, des muscles et du tissu conjonctif	57	3.4	132	7.5	83	5.0	198	11.1
Diseases of the genitourinary system — Maladies de l'appareil génito-urinaire								
Total	451	27.2	524	29.6	455	27.4	544	30.6
Disorders of kidney and ureter — Affections du rein et de l'uretère	307	18.5	301	17.0	326	19.6	312	17.6
Hyperplasia of prostate — Hyperplasie de la prostate	10	...	..	..	19	...	..	..
Pregnancy, childbirth and the puerperium — Grossesse, accouchement et puerpéralité								
Total	..	..	5	♦10.4	..	..	9	♦18.5
Pregnancy with abortive outcome — Grossesse se terminant par un avortement	..	..	2	♦4.2	..	..	1	♦2.1
Other direct obstetric causes — Autres décès maternels directs	..	..	2	♦4.2	..	..	5	♦10.3
Indirect obstetric causes — Décès maternels indirects	..	..	1	♦2.1	..	..	3	♦6.2
Certain conditions originating in the perinatal period — Certaines affections dont l'origine se situe dans la période périnatale	117	473.9	71	304.2	111	446.5	66	277.4
Congenital malformations, deformations and chromosomal abnormalities — Malformations congénitales et anomalies chromosomiques	103	417.2	83	355.6	86	345.9	95	399.3
Symptoms, signs and abnormal clinical and laboratory findings, not elsewhere classified — Symptômes, signes et résultats anormaux d'examens cliniques et de laboratoire, non classés ailleurs	1 581	95.5	1 730	97.7	1 452	87.3	1 507	84.8
All other diseases — Toutes autres maladies	61	3.7	122	6.9	55	3.3	137	7.7
External causes — Causes externes								
Total	1 677	101.3	659	37.2	1 678	100.9	743	41.8
Accidents								
Total	958	57.9	467	26.4	1 009	60.7	526	29.6
Transport accidents — Accidents de transport	415	25.1	118	6.7	358	21.5	112	6.3
Falls — Chutes	17	♦1.0	14	♦0.8	35	2.1	14	♦0.8
Accidental drowning and submersion — Noyade et submersion accidentelles	75	4.5	15	♦0.8	55	3.3	15	♦0.8
Exposure to smoke, fire and flames — Exposition à la fumée, au feu et aux flammes	27	♦1.6	17	♦1.0	34	2.0	24	♦1.4
Accidental poisoning by and exposure to noxious substances — Intoxication accidentelle par des substances nocives et exposition à ces substances	29	♦1.8	14	♦0.8	14	♦0.8	10	♦0.6
Intentional self-harm — Lésions auto-infligées	481	29.1	123	6.9	431	25.9	124	7.0
Assault — Agresssions	193	11.7	30	♦1.7	177	10.6	42	2.4
All other external causes — Toutes autres causes externes	45	2.7	39	2.2	61	3.7	51	2.9

Venezuela (Bolivarian Republic of) - Venezuela (République bolivarienne du)

Cause of death — Cause de décès	2011 (C)				2012 (C)			
	Male — Masculin		Female — Féminin		Male — Masculin		Female — Féminin	
	Number Nombre	Rate Taux	Number Nombre	Rate Taux	Number Nombre	Rate Taux	Number Nombre	Rate Taux
TOTAL	86 504	596.0	56 516	391.7	91 034	618.2	57 053	389.7
Certain infectious and parasitic diseases — Certaines maladies infectieuses et parasitaires								
Total	3 778	26.0	2 276	15.8	3 738	25.4	2 180	14.9
Intestinal infectious diseases — Maladies infectieuses intestinales	529	3.6	521	3.6	504	3.4	506	3.5
Tuberculosis — Tuberculose	376	2.6	184	1.3	407	2.8	201	1.4
Tetanus — Tétanos........................	6	♦0.0	2	♦0.0	11	♦0.1	1	♦0.0
Diphtheria — Diphtérie............................	-	-	-	-	-	-	-	-
Whooping cough — Coqueluche	6	♦0.0	11	♦0.1	23	♦0.2	17	♦0.1
Meningococcal infection — Infection à méningocoques	4	♦0.0	6	♦0.0	14	♦0.1	15	♦0.1
Septicaemia — Septicémie..........................	470	3.2	483	3.3	382	2.6	396	2.7
Acute poliomyelitis — Poliomyélite aiguë	-	-	-	-	-	-	-	-
Measles — Rougeole..........................	-	-	-	-	-	-	-	-
Viral hepatitis — Hépatite virale	52	0.4	30	♦0.2	52	0.4	27	♦0.2
Human immunodeficiency virus [HIV] disease — Maladies dues au virus de l'immunodéficience humaine (VIH)................	1 612	11.1	554	3.8	1 603	10.9	558	3.8
Malaria — Paludisme.......................	10	♦0.1	6	♦0.0	7	♦0.0	3	♦0.0
Neoplasms — Tumeurs	12 502	86.1	11 870	82.3	12 749	86.6	12 360	84.4
Malignant neoplasms — Tumeurs malignes								
Total	11 422	78.7	10 905	75.6	11 490	78.0	11 327	77.4
Malignant neoplasm of lip, oral cavity and pharynx — Tumeur maligne de la lèvre, de la cavité buccale et du pharynx	305	2.1	156	1.1	333	2.3	119	0.8
Malignant neoplasm of oesophagus — Tumeur maligne de l'oesophage	236	1.6	84	0.6	253	1.7	68	0.5
Malignant neoplasm of stomach — Tumeur maligne de l'estomac	1 201	8.3	768	5.3	1 113	7.6	822	5.6
Malignant neoplasm of colon, rectosigmoid junction, rectum, anus and anal canal — Tumeur maligne du côlon, de la jonction recto-sigmoïdienne, du rectum, de l'anus et du canal anal...........	822	5.7	812	5.6	756	5.1	801	5.5
Malignant neoplasm of liver and intrahepatic bile ducts — Tumeur maligne du foie et des voies bilaires intrahépatiques	480	3.3	399	2.8	494	3.4	437	3.0
Malignant neoplasm of pancreas — Tumeur maligne du pancréas...................	451	3.1	462	3.2	451	3.1	462	3.2
Malignant neoplasm of trachea, bronchus and lung — Tumeur maligne de la trachée, des bronches et du poumon	1 997	13.8	1 270	8.8	2 039	13.8	1 366	9.3
Malignant neoplasm of female breast — Tumeur maligne du sein chez la femme	..	..	1 942	18.6	..	..	2 067	19.4
Malignant neoplasm of cervix uteri — Tumeur maligne du col de l'utérus..........	..	..	1 331	12.7	..	..	1 321	12.4
Malignant neoplasm of prostate — Tumeur maligne de la prostate	2 431	96.8	..	..	2 419	92.6	..	..
Malignant neoplasm of lymphoid, haematopoietic and related tissue — Tumeurs malignes primitives ou présumées primitives des tissus lymphoïde, hématopoïétique et apparentés.............	1 016	7.0	832	5.8	1 048	7.1	925	6.3
Disorders of the blood and blood-forming organs and certain disorders involving the immune mechanism — Maladies du sang et des organes hématopoïétiques et certains troubles du système immunitaire								
Total	189	1.3	179	1.2	200	1.4	182	1.2
Anaemias — Anémies	130	0.9	128	0.9	138	0.9	106	0.7
Endocrine, nutritional and metabolic diseases — Maladies endocriniennes, nutritionnelles et métaboliques								
Total	5 423	37.4	5 396	37.4	5 686	38.6	5 719	39.1
Diabetes mellitus — Diabète sucré....................	4 955	34.1	4 899	34.0	5 202	35.3	5 328	36.4
Malnutrition — Malnutrition	272	1.9	257	1.8	255	1.7	171	1.2
Mental and behavioural disorders — Troubles mentaux et du comportement	47	0.3	14	♦0.1	81	0.6	20	♦0.1
Diseases of the nervous system — Maladies du système nerveux.................	1 184	8.2	1 036	7.2	1 260	8.6	1 018	7.0
Diseases of the circulatory system — Maladies de l'appareil circulatoire								
Total	24 673	170.0	19 805	137.3	25 115	170.6	19 718	134.7
Acute rheumatic fever and chronic rheumatic heart diseases — Rhumatisme articularie aigu et cardiopathies rhumatismales chroniques	49	0.3	71	0.5	37	0.3	47	0.3
Hypertensive diseases — Maladies hypertensives..........................	2 558	17.6	2 658	18.4	2 628	17.8	2 615	17.9
Ischaemic heart disease — Cardiopathie ischémique	14 189	97.8	9 364	64.9	14 332	97.3	9 262	63.3
Cerebrovascular disease — Maladie cérébrovasculaire...............	5 547	38.2	5 505	38.2	5 759	39.1	5 551	37.9

20. Death and death rates by cause and sex: 2010 - 2014
Décès et taux de mortalité par cause et sexe : 2010 - 2014 (continued - suite)

Venezuela (Bolivarian Republic of) - Venezuela (République bolivarienne du)

Cause of death — Cause de décès	2011 (C)				2012 (C)			
	Male — Masculin		Female — Féminin		Male — Masculin		Female — Féminin	
	Number Nombre	Rate Taux	Number Nombre	Rate Taux	Number Nombre	Rate Taux	Number Nombre	Rate Taux
Diseases of arteries, arterioles and capillaries — Maladies des artères, artérioles et capillaires	366	2.5	314	2.2	416	2.8	341	2.3
Diseases of the respiratory system — Maladies de l'appareil respiratoire								
Total	4 886	33.7	4 766	33.0	5 180	35.2	4 649	31.8
Influenza — Grippe	3	◆0.0	4	◆0.0	4	◆0.0	7	◆0.0
Pneumonia — Pneumopathies	1 959	13.5	1 846	12.8	2 019	13.7	1 750	12.0
Chronic lower respiratory diseases — Maladies chroniques des voies respiratoires inférieures	2 102	14.5	2 002	13.9	2 190	14.9	1 926	13.2
Diseases of the digestive system — Maladies de l'appareil digestif								
Total	3 710	25.6	2 073	14.4	3 837	26.1	2 010	13.7
Gastric and duodenal ulcer — Ulcère de l'estomac et du duodénum	256	1.8	152	1.1	245	1.7	165	1.1
Diseases of the liver — Maladies du foie	2 240	15.4	572	4.0	2 337	15.9	571	3.9
Diseases of the musculoskeletal system and connective tissue — Maladies du système ostéo-articularie, des muscles et du tissu conjonctif	115	0.8	404	2.8	108	0.7	393	2.7
Diseases of the genitourinary system — Maladies de l'appareil génito-urinaire								
Total	1 380	9.5	1 060	7.3	1 438	9.8	1 044	7.1
Disorders of kidney and ureter — Affections du rein et de l'uretère	1 118	7.7	878	6.1	1 128	7.7	840	5.7
Hyperplasia of prostate — Hyperplasie de la prostate	141	5.6	..	..	148	5.7	..	..
Pregnancy, childbirth and the puerperium — Grossesse, accouchement et puerpéralité								
Total	..	..	436	70.9	..	..	416	67.1
Pregnancy with abortive outcome — Grossesse se terminant par un avortement	..	..	37	6.0	..	..	35	5.6
Other direct obstetric causes — Autres décès maternels directs	..	..	251	40.8	..	..	235	37.9
Indirect obstetric causes — Décès maternels indirects	..	..	144	23.4	..	..	143	23.1
Certain conditions originating in the perinatal period — Certaines affections dont l'origine se situe dans la période périnatale	3 184	1 004.8	2 346	786.6	3 189	1 000.4	2 256	750.1
Congenital malformations, deformations and chromosomal abnormalities — Malformations congénitales et anomalies chromosomiques	1 246	393.2	1 055	353.7	1 353	424.4	1 119	372.1
Symptoms, signs and abnormal clinical and laboratory findings, not elsewhere classified — Symptômes, signes et résultats anormaux d'examens cliniques et de laboratoire, non classés ailleurs	310	2.1	369	2.6	413	2.8	335	2.3
All other diseases — Toutes autres maladies	8	◆0.1	8	◆0.1	5	◆0.0	8	◆0.1
External causes — Causes externes								
Total	23 869	164.4	3 423	23.7	26 682	181.2	3 626	24.8
Accidents								
Total	7 037	48.5	1 936	13.4	7 875	53.5	1 990	13.6
Transport accidents — Accidents de transport	4 939	34.0	1 109	7.7	5 796	39.4	1 206	8.2
Falls — Chutes	496	3.4	268	1.9	421	2.9	254	1.7
Accidental drowning and submersion — Noyade et submersion accidentelles	418	2.9	97	0.7	369	2.5	79	0.5
Exposure to smoke, fire and flames — Exposition à la fumée, au feu et aux flammes	90	0.6	33	0.2	110	0.7	31	0.2
Accidental poisoning by and exposure to noxious substances — Intoxication accidentelle par des substances nocives et exposition à ces substances	62	0.4	31	0.2	82	0.6	51	0.3
Intentional self-harm — Lésions auto-infligées	643	4.4	120	0.8	600	4.1	129	0.9
Assault — Agresssions	8 368	57.7	507	3.5	9 362	63.6	583	4.0
All other external causes — Toutes autres causes externes	7 821	53.9	860	6.0	8 845	60.1	924	6.3

	Armenia - Arménie				Bahrain - Bahreïn			
	2012 (U)		2014 (U)		2012 (U)		2013 (U)	
Cause of death — Cause de décès	Male — Masculin	Female — Féminin	Male — Masculin	Female — Féminin	Male — Masculin	Female — Féminin	Male — Masculin	Female — Féminin
	Number Nombre	Number Nombre	Number Nombre	Number Nombre	Number Nombre	Number Nombre	Number Nombre	Number Nombre
TOTAL	*14 268*	*13 332*	*14 219*	*13 495*	*1 549*	*1 063*	*1 549*	*1 020*
Certain infectious and parasitic diseases — Certaines maladies infectieuses et parasitaires								
Total	*230*	*56*	*201*	*79*	*44*	*18*	*23*	*26*
Intestinal infectious diseases — Maladies infectieuses intestinales	*6*	*5*	*6*	*7*	*-*	*2*	*1*	*1*
Tuberculosis — Tuberculose	*111*	*15*	*64*	*11*	*3*	*1*	*3*	*2*
Tetanus — Tétanos	*-*	*-*	*-*	*-*	*-*	*-*	*-*	*-*
Diphtheria — Diphtérie..	*-*	*-*	*-*	*-*	*-*	*-*	*-*	*-*
Whooping cough — Coqueluche	*-*	*-*	*1*	*-*	*-*	*-*	*-*	*-*
Meningococcal infection — Infection à méningocoques	*-*	*-*	*-*	*-*	*-*	*-*	*-*	*-*
Septicaemia — Septicémie	*19*	*11*	*14*	*19*	*20*	*8*	*3*	*11*
Acute poliomyelitis — Poliomyélite aiguë	*-*	*-*	*-*	*-*	*-*	*-*	*-*	*-*
Measles — Rougeole..	*-*	*-*	*-*	*-*	*-*	*-*	*-*	*-*
Viral hepatitis — Hépatite virale	*51*	*8*	*60*	*22*	*17*	*2*	*7*	*6*
Human immunodeficiency virus [HIV] disease — Maladies dues au virus de l'immunodéficience humaine (VIH)...	*19*	*3*	*25*	*5*	*3*	*5*	*5*	*3*
Malaria — Paludisme	*-*	*-*	*-*	*-*	*-*	*-*	*1*	*-*
Neoplasms — Tumeurs	*3 049*	*2 576*	*3 180*	*2 521*	*137*	*119*	*116*	*121*
Malignant neoplasms — Tumeurs malignes								
Total	*3 042*	*2 565*	*3 178*	*2 507*	*135*	*115*	*113*	*115*
Malignant neoplasm of lip, oral cavity and pharynx — Tumeur maligne de la lèvre, de la cavité buccale et du pharynx	*46*	*16*	*61*	*14*	*2*	*2*	*8*	*2*
Malignant neoplasm of oesophagus — Tumeur maligne de l'oesophage	*29*	*13*	*28*	*16*	*4*	*1*	*2*	*1*
Malignant neoplasm of stomach — Tumeur maligne de l'estomac	*270*	*175*	*286*	*181*	*8*	*4*	*5*	*8*
Malignant neoplasm of colon, rectosigmoid junction, rectum, anus and anal canal — Tumeur maligne du côlon, de la jonction recto-sigmoïdienne, du rectum, de l'anus et du canal anal..	*172*	*253*	*215*	*268*	*14*	*9*	*12*	*5*
Malignant neoplasm of liver and intrahepatic bile ducts — Tumeur maligne du foie et des voies bilaires intrahépatiques	*194*	*168*	*193*	*181*	*6*	*3*	*2*	*5*
Malignant neoplasm of pancreas — Tumeur maligne du pancréas..................	*175*	*136*	*200*	*142*	*2*	*5*	*5*	*2*
Malignant neoplasm of trachea, bronchus and lung — Tumeur maligne de la trachée, des bronches et du poumon	*918*	*208*	*967*	*192*	*25*	*6*	*22*	*13*
Malignant neoplasm of female breast — Tumeur maligne du sein chez la femme	*..*	*545*	*..*	*468*	*..*	*46*	*..*	*44*
Malignant neoplasm of cervix uteri — Tumeur maligne du col de l'utérus.........	*..*	*87*	*..*	*51*	*..*	*1*	*..*	*2*
Malignant neoplasm of prostate — Tumeur maligne de la prostate	*260*	*..*	*280*	*..*	*7*	*..*	*9*	*..*
Malignant neoplasm of lymphoid, haematopoietic and related tissue — Tumeurs malignes primitives ou présumées primitives des tissus lymphoïde, hématopoïétique et apparentés...	*147*	*108*	*115*	*104*	*25*	*9*	*21*	*13*
Disorders of the blood and blood-forming organs and certain disorders involving the immune mechanism — Maladies du sang et des organes hématopoïétiques et certains troubles du système immunitaire								
Total	*15*	*7*	*10*	*10*	*26*	*30*	*24*	*16*
Anaemias — Anémies	*9*	*4*	*5*	*6*	*19*	*21*	*19*	*13*
Endocrine, nutritional and metabolic diseases — Maladies endocriniennes, nutritionnelles et métaboliques								
Total	*469*	*860*	*497*	*741*	*166*	*152*	*229*	*220*
Diabetes mellitus — Diabète sucré..	*452*	*843*	*468*	*723*	*136*	*125*	*197*	*188*
Malnutrition — Malnutrition	*-*	*1*	*2*	*-*	*1*	*-*	*-*	*-*
Mental and behavioural disorders — Troubles mentaux et du comportement	*5*	*2*	*1*	*4*	*5*	*4*	*8*	*5*
Diseases of the nervous system — Maladies du système nerveux.................	*65*	*62*	*56*	*58*	*38*	*30*	*31*	*20*
Diseases of the circulatory system — Maladies de l'appareil circulatoire								
Total	*6 494*	*6 836*	*6 422*	*6 845*	*517*	*305*	*550*	*289*
Acute rheumatic fever and chronic rheumatic heart diseases — Rhumatisme articularie aigu et cardiopathies rhumatismales chroniques	*31*	*95*	*33*	*116*	*-*	*-*	*2*	*4*
Hypertensive diseases — Maladies hypertensives..................................	*259*	*497*	*251*	*371*	*128*	*118*	*104*	*94*
Ischaemic heart disease — Cardiopathie ischémique	*4 387*	*4 034*	*4 442*	*4 128*	*78*	*45*	*65*	*36*

Cause of death — Cause de décès	Armenia - Arménie				Bahrain - Bahreïn			
	2012 (U)		2014 (U)		2012 (U)		2013 (U)	
	Male — Masculin	Female — Féminin	Male — Masculin	Female — Féminin	Male — Masculin	Female — Féminin	Male — Masculin	Female — Féminin
	Number Nombre	Number Nombre	Number Nombre	Number Nombre	Number Nombre	Number Nombre	Number Nombre	Number Nombre
Cerebrovascular disease — Maladie cérébrovasculaire....................................	1 204	1 599	1 090	1 547	59	40	52	38
Diseases of arteries, arterioles and capillaries — Maladies des artères, artérioles et capillaires	331	296	364	392	1	3	3	-
Diseases of the respiratory system — Maladies de l'appareil respiratoire								
Total	886	727	981	881	67	61	61	36
Influenza — Grippe	1	-	1	1	3	-	1	1
Pneumonia — Pneumopathies	232	207	252	257	17	15	21	13
Chronic lower respiratory diseases — Maladies chroniques des voies respiratoires inférieures	563	425	581	524	23	19	18	14
Diseases of the digestive system — Maladies de l'appareil digestif								
Total	847	754	863	781	26	26	34	26
Gastric and duodenal ulcer — Ulcère de l'estomac et du duodénum................	123	106	144	124	2	3	2	2
Diseases of the liver — Maladies du foie..	546	410	530	426	14	7	20	10
Diseases of the musculoskeletal system and connective tissue — Maladies du système ostéo-articularie, des muscles et du tissu conjonctif	13	34	15	26	4	11	7	7
Diseases of the genitourinary system — Maladies de l'appareil génito-urinaire								
Total	457	348	446	465	72	48	41	38
Disorders of kidney and ureter — Affections du rein et de l'uretère	386	333	344	460	57	38	35	25
Hyperplasia of prostate — Hyperplasie de la prostate.....................................	60	..	90	..	2	..	2	..
Pregnancy, childbirth and the puerperium — Grossesse, accouchement et puerpéralité								
Total	..	5	..	8	..	2	..	4
Pregnancy with abortive outcome — Grossesse se terminant par un avortement	..	1	..	-	..	-	..	1
Other direct obstetric causes — Autres décès maternels directs	..	4	..	5	..	2	..	1
Indirect obstetric causes — Décès maternels indirects	..	-	..	3	..	-	..	2
Certain conditions originating in the perinatal period — Certaines affections dont l'origine se situe dans la période périnatale	118	82	98	76	33	25	29	20
Congenital malformations, deformations and chromosomal abnormalities — Malformations congénitales et anomalies chromosomiques	236	214	230	226	25	20	22	24
Symptoms, signs and abnormal clinical and laboratory findings, not elsewhere classified — Symptômes, signes et résultats anormaux d'examens cliniques et de laboratoire, non classés ailleurs	357	417	332	396	190	167	186	117
All other diseases — Toutes autres maladies..	8	11	12	14	12	13	7	5
External causes — Causes externes								
Total	1 019	341	875	364	187	32	181	46
Accidents								
Total	329	72	286	69	109	18	125	29
Transport accidents — Accidents de transport...	178	35	153	42	68	13	68	18
Falls — Chutes	12	1	10	3	3	1	9	2
Accidental drowning and submersion — Noyade et submersion accidentelles..	26	-	18	2	9	3	15	3
Exposure to smoke, fire and flames — Exposition à la fumée, au feu et aux flammes	6	3	2	-	5	-	18	2
Accidental poisoning by and exposure to noxious substances — Intoxication accidentelle par des substances nocives et exposition à ces substances	8	4	8	3	11	-	-	-
Intentional self-harm — Lésions auto-infligées...	59	20	43	15	18	1	5	-
Assault — Agresssions...	40	14	20	14	4	-	3	2
All other external causes — Toutes autres causes externes	591	235	526	266	56	13	48	15

20. Death and death rates by cause and sex: 2010 - 2014
Décès et taux de mortalité par cause et sexe : 2010 - 2014 (continued - suite)

Cause of death — Cause de décès	Brunei Darussalam - Brunéi Darussalam				China, Hong Kong SAR - Chine, Hong Kong RAS			
	2013 (+U)		2014 (+U)		2012 (...)		2013 (...)	
	Male — Masculin	Female — Féminin	Male — Masculin	Female — Féminin	Male — Masculin	Female — Féminin	Male — Masculin	Female — Féminin
	Number Nombre	Number Nombre	Number Nombre	Number Nombre	Number Nombre	Number Nombre	Number Nombre	Number Nombre
TOTAL	779	621	833	637	24 346	19 321	24 149	19 244
Certain infectious and parasitic diseases — Certaines maladies infectieuses et parasitaires								
Total	47	28	56	29	702	536	641	575
Intestinal infectious diseases — Maladies infectieuses intestinales	1	-	2	1	25	32	25	37
Tuberculosis — Tuberculose	7	2	7	7	146	49	136	41
Tetanus — Tétanos	-	-	-	-	-	-	-	-
Diphtheria — Diphtérie	-	-	-	-	-	-	-	-
Whooping cough — Coqueluche	-	-	-	-	-	-	-	-
Meningococcal infection — Infection à méningocoques	-	-	-	-	-	1	-	-
Septicaemia — Septicémie	19	16	28	14	430	407	406	446
Acute poliomyelitis — Poliomyélite aiguë	-	-	-	-	-	-	-	-
Measles — Rougeole	-	-	-	-	-	-	-	-
Viral hepatitis — Hépatite virale	4	-	4	1	31	19	18	7
Human immunodeficiency virus [HIV] disease — Maladies dues au virus de l'immunodéficience humaine (VIH)	5	-	1	-	12	1	16	4
Malaria — Paludisme	1	-	-	-	-	-	-	-
Neoplasms — Tumeurs	158	151	147	168	8 087	5 535	8 099	5 793
Malignant neoplasms — Tumeurs malignes								
Total	152	143	138	160	7 933	5 403	7 934	5 655
Malignant neoplasm of lip, oral cavity and pharynx — Tumeur maligne de la lèvre, de la cavité buccale et du pharynx	11	2	6	4	392	129	376	120
Malignant neoplasm of oesophagus — Tumeur maligne de l'oesophage	1	-	2	1	250	63	262	67
Malignant neoplasm of stomach — Tumeur maligne de l'estomac	5	5	11	10	379	278	380	245
Malignant neoplasm of colon, rectosigmoid junction, rectum, anus and anal canal — Tumeur maligne du côlon, de la jonction recto-sigmoïdienne, du rectum, de l'anus et du canal anal	30	17	16	19	1 079	824	1 087	894
Malignant neoplasm of liver and intrahepatic bile ducts — Tumeur maligne du foie et des voies bilaires intrahépatiques	13	8	17	6	1 045	460	1 123	401
Malignant neoplasm of pancreas — Tumeur maligne du pancréas	3	3	4	3	287	251	310	274
Malignant neoplasm of trachea, bronchus and lung — Tumeur maligne de la trachée, des bronches et du poumon	36	28	37	25	2 597	1 296	2 491	1 376
Malignant neoplasm of female breast — Tumeur maligne du sein chez la femme	..	20	..	29	..	601	..	596
Malignant neoplasm of cervix uteri — Tumeur maligne du col de l'utérus	..	11	..	11	..	133	..	142
Malignant neoplasm of prostate — Tumeur maligne de la prostate	10	..	12	..	362	..	372	..
Malignant neoplasm of lymphoid, haematopoietic and related tissue — Tumeurs malignes primitives ou présumées primitives des tissus lymphoïde, hématopoïétique et apparentés	19	10	18	17	471	318	455	330
Disorders of the blood and blood-forming organs and certain disorders involving the immune mechanism — Maladies du sang et des organes hématopoïétiques et certains troubles du système immunitaire								
Total	4	4	4	7	39	44	56	55
Anaemias — Anémies	3	3	2	1	11	20	28	33
Endocrine, nutritional and metabolic diseases — Maladies endocriniennes, nutritionnelles et métaboliques								
Total	83	71	96	70	245	250	231	234
Diabetes mellitus — Diabète sucré	68	63	84	57	198	200	181	179
Malnutrition — Malnutrition	-	-	-	-	1	1	2	3
Mental and behavioural disorders — Troubles mentaux et du comportement	4	8	3	3	341	570	393	613
Diseases of the nervous system — Maladies du système nerveux	28	21	19	14	195	174	204	169
Diseases of the circulatory system — Maladies de l'appareil circulatoire								
Total	205	146	263	145	5 489	4 831	5 253	4 529
Acute rheumatic fever and chronic rheumatic heart diseases — Rhumatisme articularie aigu et cardiopathies rhumatismales chroniques	-	2	-	1	36	65	25	40
Hypertensive diseases — Maladies hypertensives	34	37	32	32	374	423	324	376
Ischaemic heart disease — Cardiopathie ischémique	103	35	134	43	2 524	1 748	2 379	1 628

Cause of death — Cause de décès	Brunei Darussalam - Brunéi Darussalam				China, Hong Kong SAR - Chine, Hong Kong RAS			
	2013 (+U)		2014 (+U)		2012 (...)		2013 (...)	
	Male — Masculin	Female — Féminin	Male — Masculin	Female — Féminin	Male — Masculin	Female — Féminin	Male — Masculin	Female — Féminin
	Number Nombre	Number Nombre	Number Nombre	Number Nombre	Number Nombre	Number Nombre	Number Nombre	Number Nombre
Cerebrovascular disease — Maladie cérébrovasculaire	34	48	51	52	1 680	1 596	1 657	1 595
Diseases of arteries, arterioles and capillaries — Maladies des artères, artérioles et capillaires	4	5	9	-	273	174	262	155
Diseases of the respiratory system — Maladies de l'appareil respiratoire								
Total	86	58	78	69	5 547	4 085	5 385	3 896
Influenza — Grippe	-	1	-	-	37	31	16	9
Pneumonia — Pneumopathies	27	20	33	30	3 683	3 277	3 690	3 140
Chronic lower respiratory diseases — Maladies chroniques des voies respiratoires inférieures	39	27	29	25	1 470	511	1 325	418
Diseases of the digestive system — Maladies de l'appareil digestif								
Total	22	19	23	15	869	664	764	626
Gastric and duodenal ulcer — Ulcère de l'estomac et du duodénum	4	1	2	-	76	48	51	45
Diseases of the liver — Maladies du foie	8	9	7	5	297	168	285	138
Diseases of the musculoskeletal system and connective tissue — Maladies du système ostéo-articularie, des muscles et du tissu conjonctif	6	10	4	9	62	102	83	82
Diseases of the genitourinary system — Maladies de l'appareil génito-urinaire								
Total	12	18	20	20	1 013	1 142	1 000	1 156
Disorders of kidney and ureter — Affections du rein et de l'uretère	9	14	14	13	820	860	779	855
Hyperplasia of prostate — Hyperplasie de la prostate	1	..	3	..	5	..	6	..
Pregnancy, childbirth and the puerperium — Grossesse, accouchement et puerpéralité								
Total	..	1	..	-	..	2	..	-
Pregnancy with abortive outcome — Grossesse se terminant par un avortement	..	-	..	-	..	1	..	-
Other direct obstetric causes — Autres décès maternels directs	..	1	..	-	..	1	..	-
Indirect obstetric causes — Décès maternels indirects	..	-	..	-	..	-	..	-
Certain conditions originating in the perinatal period — Certaines affections dont l'origine se situe dans la période périnatale	16	10	14	10	26	22	20	19
Congenital malformations, deformations and chromosomal abnormalities — Malformations congénitales et anomalies chromosomiques	13	11	13	9	33	40	36	24
Symptoms, signs and abnormal clinical and laboratory findings, not elsewhere classified — Symptômes, signes et résultats anormaux d'examens cliniques et de laboratoire, non classés ailleurs	27	25	29	39	544	651	712	709
All other diseases — Toutes autres maladies	6	7	2	10	85	88	70	106
External causes — Causes externes								
Total	62	33	62	20	1 069	585	1 202	658
Accidents								
Total	50	19	49	12	510	250	521	240
Transport accidents — Accidents de transport	22	8	23	5	89	47	100	40
Falls — Chutes	9	3	8	-	160	74	150	82
Accidental drowning and submersion — Noyade et submersion accidentelles	8	3	6	1	20	9	25	5
Exposure to smoke, fire and flames — Exposition à la fumée, au feu et aux flammes	2	-	2	2	3	-	9	9
Accidental poisoning by and exposure to noxious substances — Intoxication accidentelle par des substances nocives et exposition à ces substances	-	-	2	-	111	33	113	24
Intentional self-harm — Lésions auto-infligées	2	2	3	2	513	309	619	380
Assault — Agresssions	-	-	-	1	10	8	15	12
All other external causes — Toutes autres causes externes	10	12	10	5	36	18	47	26

20. Death and death rates by cause and sex: 2010 - 2014
Décès et taux de mortalité par cause et sexe : 2010 - 2014 (continued - suite)

Cause of death — Cause de décès	Cyprus - Chypre				Georgia - Géorgie			
	2012 (U)		2013 (U)		2013 (C)			
	Male — Masculin	Female — Féminin	Male — Masculin	Female — Féminin	Male — Masculin		Female — Féminin	
	Number Nombre	Number Nombre	Number Nombre	Number Nombre	Number Nombre	Rate Taux	Number Nombre	Rate Taux
TOTAL	*2 868*	*2 632*	*2 888*	*2 384*	24 869	...	23 684	...
Certain infectious and parasitic diseases — Certaines maladies infectieuses et parasitaires								
Total	*43*	*44*	*52*	*38*	395	...	115	...
Intestinal infectious diseases — Maladies infectieuses intestinales	*4*	*13*	*9*	*9*	9	...	5	...
Tuberculosis — Tuberculose	*2*	*1*	*-*	*1*	113	...	20	...
Tetanus — Tétanos..	*-*	*-*	*-*	*-*	*-*	...	1	...
Diphtheria — Diphtérie..	*-*	*-*	*-*	*-*	*-*	...	*-*	...
Whooping cough — Coqueluche	*-*	*-*	*-*	*-*	*-*	...	*-*	...
Meningococcal infection — Infection à méningocoques	*-*	*-*	*-*	*-*	*-*	...	2	...
Septicaemia — Septicémie................................	*26*	*23*	*31*	*22*	26	...	20	...
Acute poliomyelitis — Poliomyélite aiguë	*-*	*-*	*-*	*-*	*-*	...	*-*	...
Measles — Rougeole..	*-*	*-*	*-*	*-*	1	...	*-*	...
Viral hepatitis — Hépatite virale............................	*4*	*-*	*4*	*-*	184	...	32	...
Human immunodeficiency virus [HIV] disease — Maladies dues au virus de l'immunodéficience humaine (VIH)..............	*2*	*-*	*2*	*-*	33	...	6	...
Malaria — Paludisme..	*-*	*-*	*-*	*-*	*-*	...	*-*	...
Neoplasms — Tumeurs	*754*	*509*	*762*	*535*	2 805	...	2 187	...
Malignant neoplasms — Tumeurs malignes								
Total	*730*	*491*	*737*	*513*	2 654	...	2 012	...
Malignant neoplasm of lip, oral cavity and pharynx — Tumeur maligne de la lèvre, de la cavité buccale et du pharynx ...	*11*	*5*	*8*	*4*	111	...	14	...
Malignant neoplasm of oesophagus — Tumeur maligne de l'oesophage	*9*	*3*	*4*	*-*	38	...	15	...
Malignant neoplasm of stomach — Tumeur maligne de l'estomac	*26*	*21*	*35*	*32*	234	...	165	...
Malignant neoplasm of colon, rectosigmoid junction, rectum, anus and anal canal — Tumeur maligne du côlon, de la jonction recto-sigmoïdienne, du rectum, de l'anus et du canal anal.............	*76*	*47*	*67*	*48*	168	...	150	...
Malignant neoplasm of liver and intrahepatic bile ducts — Tumeur maligne du foie et des voies bilaires intrahépatiques	*31*	*15*	*34*	*23*	173	...	101	...
Malignant neoplasm of pancreas — Tumeur maligne du pancréas...................	*40*	*23*	*45*	*23*	94	...	57	...
Malignant neoplasm of trachea, bronchus and lung — Tumeur maligne de la trachée, des bronches et du poumon...........	*200*	*48*	*202*	*32*	720	...	92	...
Malignant neoplasm of female breast — Tumeur maligne du sein chez la femme	*..*	*102*	*..*	*107*	*..*	*..*	453	...
Malignant neoplasm of cervix uteri — Tumeur maligne du col de l'utérus.........	*..*	*7*	*..*	*9*	*..*	*..*	136	...
Malignant neoplasm of prostate — Tumeur maligne de la prostate	*103*	*..*	*99*	*..*	210	...	*..*	*..*
Malignant neoplasm of lymphoid, haematopoietic and related tissue — Tumeurs malignes primitives ou présumées primitives des tissus lymphoïde, hématopoïétique et apparentés...................	*63*	*64*	*78*	*60*	163	...	128	...
Disorders of the blood and blood-forming organs and certain disorders involving the immune mechanism — Maladies du sang et des organes hématopoïétiques et certains troubles du système immunitaire								
Total	*16*	*28*	*16*	*16*	71	...	87	...
Anaemias — Anémies	*13*	*18*	*13*	*9*	56	...	52	...
Endocrine, nutritional and metabolic diseases — Maladies endocriniennes, nutritionnelles et métaboliques								
Total	*215*	*218*	*205*	*239*	497	...	627	...
Diabetes mellitus — Diabète sucré........................	*186*	*178*	*181*	*192*	466	...	586	...
Malnutrition — Malnutrition	*1*	*-*	*3*	*1*	4	...	4	...
Mental and behavioural disorders — Troubles mentaux et du comportement	*34*	*56*	*48*	*46*	27	...	38	...
Diseases of the nervous system — Maladies du système nerveux.................	*83*	*105*	*96*	*79*	306	...	271	...
Diseases of the circulatory system — Maladies de l'appareil circulatoire								
Total	*1 015*	*1 004*	*968*	*855*	8 989	...	9 704	...
Acute rheumatic fever and chronic rheumatic heart diseases — Rhumatisme articulaire aigu et cardiopathies rhumatismales chroniques	*7*	*12*	*4*	*12*	74	...	94	...
Hypertensive diseases — Maladies hypertensives........................	*76*	*136*	*67*	*107*	1 371	...	1 967	...
Ischaemic heart disease — Cardiopathie ischémique	*427*	*214*	*438*	*205*	2 505	...	2 338	...

Cause of death — Cause de décès	Cyprus - Chypre				Georgia - Géorgie			
	2012 (U)		2013 (U)		2013 (C)			
	Male — Masculin	Female — Féminin	Male — Masculin	Female — Féminin	Male — Masculin		Female — Féminin	
	Number Nombre	Number Nombre	Number Nombre	Number Nombre	Number Nombre	Rate Taux	Number Nombre	Rate Taux
Cerebrovascular disease — Maladie cérébrovasculaire	174	226	165	201	2 231	...	2 639	...
Diseases of arteries, arterioles and capillaries — Maladies des artères, artérioles et capillaires	38	34	39	21	161	...	99	...
Diseases of the respiratory system — Maladies de l'appareil respiratoire								
Total	220	204	235	189	701	...	441	...
Influenza — Grippe	-	2	-	-	13	...	11	...
Pneumonia — Pneumopathies	35	37	23	38	218	...	150	...
Chronic lower respiratory diseases — Maladies chroniques des voies respiratoires inférieures	85	34	108	45	196	...	111	...
Diseases of the digestive system — Maladies de l'appareil digestif								
Total	78	78	124	80	861	...	434	...
Gastric and duodenal ulcer — Ulcère de l'estomac et du duodénum	3	6	7	5	66	...	39	...
Diseases of the liver — Maladies du foie	31	14	48	16	448	...	134	...
Diseases of the musculoskeletal system and connective tissue — Maladies du système ostéo-articularie, des muscles et du tissu conjonctif	13	17	7	20	13	...	46	...
Diseases of the genitourinary system — Maladies de l'appareil génito-urinaire								
Total	92	106	93	87	268	...	199	...
Disorders of kidney and ureter — Affections du rein et de l'uretère	68	70	63	44	225	...	192	...
Hyperplasia of prostate — Hyperplasie de la prostate	6	..	4	..	18	...	..	..
Pregnancy, childbirth and the puerperium — Grossesse, accouchement et puerpéralité								
Total	..	-	..	1	..	..	16	♦27.6
Pregnancy with abortive outcome — Grossesse se terminant par un avortement	..	-	..	-	..	..	1	♦1.7
Other direct obstetric causes — Autres décès maternels directs	..	-	..	1	..	..	11	♦19.0
Indirect obstetric causes — Décès maternels indirects	..	-	..	-	..	..	4	♦6.9
Certain conditions originating in the perinatal period — Certaines affections dont l'origine se situe dans la période périnatale	19	10	5	2	262	872.5	171	614.0
Congenital malformations, deformations and chromosomal abnormalities — Malformations congénitales et anomalies chromosomiques	10	9	4	5	75	249.8	65	233.4
Symptoms, signs and abnormal clinical and laboratory findings, not elsewhere classified — Symptômes, signes et résultats anormaux d'examens cliniques et de laboratoire, non classés ailleurs	88	131	57	92	8 406	...	8 917	...
All other diseases — Toutes autres maladies	11	20	11	15	9	...	11	...
External causes — Causes externes								
Total	177	93	205	85	1 184	...	355	...
Accidents								
Total	120	82	148	74	926	...	301	...
Transport accidents — Accidents de transport	52	15	44	10	220	...	59	...
Falls — Chutes	17	9	23	9	71	...	21	...
Accidental drowning and submersion — Noyade et submersion accidentelles	4	2	10	5	46	...	16	...
Exposure to smoke, fire and flames — Exposition à la fumée, au feu et aux flammes	1	2	2	-	40	...	27	...
Accidental poisoning by and exposure to noxious substances — Intoxication accidentelle par des substances nocives et exposition à ces substances	7	1	7	1	16	...	7	...
Intentional self-harm — Lésions auto-infligées	34	2	40	5	131	...	22	...
Assault — Agresssions	15	4	9	3	33	...	12	...
All other external causes — Toutes autres causes externes	8	5	8	3	94	...	20	...

20. Death and death rates by cause and sex: 2010 - 2014
Décès et taux de mortalité par cause et sexe : 2010 - 2014 (continued - suite)

Cause of death — Cause de décès	Georgia - Géorgie 2014 (C)				Israel - Israël 2012 (C)			
	Male — Masculin		Female — Féminin		Male — Masculin		Female — Féminin	
	Number Nombre	Rate Taux	Number Nombre	Rate Taux	Number Nombre	Rate Taux	Number Nombre	Rate Taux
TOTAL	24 851	1 160.5	24 236	1 031.7	20 688	528.3	21 189	530.5
Certain infectious and parasitic diseases — Certaines maladies infectieuses et parasitaires								
Total	419	19.6	135	5.7	1 051	26.8	1 171	29.3
Intestinal infectious diseases — Maladies infectieuses intestinales	9	♦0.4	5	♦0.2	93	2.4	132	3.3
Tuberculosis — Tuberculose	88	4.1	23	♦1.0	6	♦0.2	7	♦0.2
Tetanus — Tétanos	-	-	-	-	-	-	-	-
Diphtheria — Diphtérie	-	-	-	-	-	-	-	-
Whooping cough — Coqueluche	-	-	-	-	1	♦0.0	-	-
Meningococcal infection — Infection à méningocoques	3	♦0.1	1	♦0.0	-	-	-	-
Septicaemia — Septicémie	33	1.5	22	♦0.9	796	20.3	930	23.3
Acute poliomyelitis — Poliomyélite aiguë	-	-	-	-	-	-	-	-
Measles — Rougeole	-	-	-	-	-	-	-	-
Viral hepatitis — Hépatite virale	205	9.6	48	2.0	53	1.4	40	1.0
Human immunodeficiency virus [HIV] disease — Maladies dues au virus de l'immunodéficience humaine (VIH)	37	1.7	8	♦0.3	24	♦0.6	9	♦0.2
Malaria — Paludisme	-	-	-	-	-	-	-	-
Neoplasms — Tumeurs	3 132	146.3	2 493	106.1	5 520	141.0	5 380	134.7
Malignant neoplasms — Tumeurs malignes								
Total	2 992	139.7	2 381	101.4	5 398	137.8	5 242	131.2
Malignant neoplasm of lip, oral cavity and pharynx — Tumeur maligne de la lèvre, de la cavité buccale et du pharynx	104	4.9	25	♦1.1	62	1.6	43	1.1
Malignant neoplasm of oesophagus — Tumeur maligne de l'oesophage	47	2.2	19	♦0.8	81	2.1	61	1.5
Malignant neoplasm of stomach — Tumeur maligne de l'estomac	289	13.5	190	8.1	294	7.5	199	5.0
Malignant neoplasm of colon, rectosigmoid junction, rectum, anus and anal canal — Tumeur maligne du côlon, de la jonction recto-sigmoïdienne, du rectum, de l'anus et du canal anal	175	8.2	165	7.0	684	17.5	677	16.9
Malignant neoplasm of liver and intrahepatic bile ducts — Tumeur maligne du foie et des voies bilaires intrahépatiques	188	8.8	137	5.8	189	4.8	139	3.5
Malignant neoplasm of pancreas — Tumeur maligne du pancréas	114	5.3	105	4.5	471	12.0	401	10.0
Malignant neoplasm of trachea, bronchus and lung — Tumeur maligne de la trachée, des bronches et du poumon	780	36.4	136	5.8	1 178	30.1	583	14.6
Malignant neoplasm of female breast — Tumeur maligne du sein chez la femme	..	..	515	...	..	..	994	34.2
Malignant neoplasm of cervix uteri — Tumeur maligne du col de l'utérus	..	..	158	...	..	..	76	2.6
Malignant neoplasm of prostate — Tumeur maligne de la prostate	235	...	..	..	417	46.9	..	..
Malignant neoplasm of lymphoid, haematopoietic and related tissue — Tumeurs malignes primitives ou présumées primitives des tissus lymphoïde, hématopoïétique et apparentés	181	8.5	172	7.3	740	18.9	626	15.7
Disorders of the blood and blood-forming organs and certain disorders involving the immune mechanism — Maladies du sang et des organes hématopoïétiques et certains troubles du système immunitaire								
Total	112	5.2	130	5.5	117	3.0	169	4.2
Anaemias — Anémies	76	3.5	94	4.0	73	1.9	115	2.9
Endocrine, nutritional and metabolic diseases — Maladies endocriniennes, nutritionnelles et métaboliques								
Total	495	23.1	632	26.9	1 326	33.9	1 713	42.9
Diabetes mellitus — Diabète sucré	461	21.5	576	24.5	1 029	26.3	1 258	31.5
Malnutrition — Malnutrition	3	♦0.1	2	♦0.1	14	♦0.4	20	♦0.5
Mental and behavioural disorders — Troubles mentaux et du comportement	47	2.2	49	2.1	473	12.1	804	20.1
Diseases of the nervous system — Maladies du système nerveux	310	14.5	289	12.3	667	17.0	761	19.1
Diseases of the circulatory system — Maladies de l'appareil circulatoire								
Total	9 680	452.0	10 939	465.7	4 889	124.8	5 268	131.9
Acute rheumatic fever and chronic rheumatic heart diseases — Rhumatisme articularie aigu et cardiopathies rhumatismales chroniques	55	2.6	75	3.2	53	1.4	91	2.3
Hypertensive diseases — Maladies hypertensives	1 296	60.5	1 875	79.8	318	8.1	533	13.3
Ischaemic heart disease — Cardiopathie ischémique	2 943	137.4	3 043	129.5	2 196	56.1	1 848	46.3
Cerebrovascular disease — Maladie cérébrovasculaire	2 592	121.0	3 153	134.2	1 143	29.2	1 350	33.8

20. Death and death rates by cause and sex: 2010 - 2014
Décès et taux de mortalité par cause et sexe : 2010 - 2014 (continued - suite)

Cause of death — Cause de décès	Georgia - Géorgie 2014 (C)				Israel - Israël 2012 (C)			
	Male — Masculin		Female — Féminin		Male — Masculin		Female — Féminin	
	Number Nombre	Rate Taux	Number Nombre	Rate Taux	Number Nombre	Rate Taux	Number Nombre	Rate Taux
Diseases of arteries, arterioles and capillaries — Maladies des artères, artérioles et capillaires	159	7.4	114	4.9	208	5.3	163	4.1
Diseases of the respiratory system — Maladies de l'appareil respiratoire								
Total	767	35.8	574	24.4	1 687	43.1	1 662	41.6
Influenza — Grippe	5	♦0.2	4	♦0.2	4	♦0.1	3	♦0.1
Pneumonia — Pneumopathies	256	12.0	225	9.6	490	12.5	480	12.0
Chronic lower respiratory diseases — Maladies chroniques des voies respiratoires inférieures	198	9.2	101	4.3	676	17.3	564	14.1
Diseases of the digestive system — Maladies de l'appareil digestif								
Total	875	40.9	470	20.0	674	17.2	800	20.0
Gastric and duodenal ulcer — Ulcère de l'estomac et du duodénum	75	3.5	45	1.9	15	♦0.4	22	♦0.6
Diseases of the liver — Maladies du foie	476	22.2	127	5.4	226	5.8	167	4.2
Diseases of the musculoskeletal system and connective tissue — Maladies du système ostéo-articularie, des muscles et du tissu conjonctif	21	♦1.0	45	1.9	143	3.7	174	4.4
Diseases of the genitourinary system — Maladies de l'appareil génito-urinaire								
Total	284	13.3	243	10.3	1 170	29.9	1 045	26.2
Disorders of kidney and ureter — Affections du rein et de l'uretère	247	11.5	224	9.5	950	24.3	787	19.7
Hyperplasia of prostate — Hyperplasie de la prostate	15	...	..	..	10	♦1.1	..	..
Pregnancy, childbirth and the puerperium — Grossesse, accouchement et puerpéralité								
Total	..	..	18	♦29.7	..	..	9	♦5.3
Pregnancy with abortive outcome — Grossesse se terminant par un avortement	..	..	2	♦3.3	..	..	-	-
Other direct obstetric causes — Autres décès maternels directs	..	..	13	♦21.4	..	..	6	♦3.5
Indirect obstetric causes — Décès maternels indirects	..	..	3	♦4.9	..	..	3	♦1.8
Certain conditions originating in the perinatal period — Certaines affections dont l'origine se situe dans la période périnatale	217	692.7	171	583.4	146	166.9	108	129.4
Congenital malformations, deformations and chromosomal abnormalities — Malformations congénitales et anomalies chromosomiques	79	252.2	74	252.5	154	176.1	140	167.7
Symptoms, signs and abnormal clinical and laboratory findings, not elsewhere classified — Symptômes, signes et résultats anormaux d'examens cliniques et de laboratoire, non classés ailleurs	6 998	326.8	7 424	316.0	1 291	33.0	1 082	27.1
All other diseases — Toutes autres maladies	15	♦0.7	16	♦0.7	202	5.2	280	7.0
External causes — Causes externes								
Total	1 400	65.4	534	22.7	1 178	30.1	623	15.6
Accidents								
Total	1 051	49.1	432	18.4	606	15.5	453	11.3
Transport accidents — Accidents de transport	473	22.1	153	6.5	226	5.8	98	2.5
Falls — Chutes	92	4.3	91	3.9	58	1.5	61	1.5
Accidental drowning and submersion — Noyade et submersion accidentelles	38	1.8	11	♦0.5	35	0.9	9	♦0.2
Exposure to smoke, fire and flames — Exposition à la fumée, au feu et aux flammes	62	2.9	19	♦0.8	18	♦0.5	9	♦0.2
Accidental poisoning by and exposure to noxious substances — Intoxication accidentelle par des substances nocives et exposition à ces substances	23	♦1.1	14	♦0.6	1	♦0.0	-	-
Intentional self-harm — Lésions auto-infligées	153	7.1	36	1.5	346	8.8	81	2.0
Assault — Agresssions	59	2.8	26	♦1.1	111	2.8	25	♦0.6
All other external causes — Toutes autres causes externes	137	6.4	40	1.7	115	2.9	64	1.6

Cause of death — Cause de décès	Israel - Israël				Japan - Japon			
	2013 (C)				2012 (C)			
	Male — Masculin		Female — Féminin		Male — Masculin		Female — Féminin	
	Number Nombre	Rate Taux	Number Nombre	Rate Taux	Number Nombre	Rate Taux	Number Nombre	Rate Taux
TOTAL	**20 479**	**513.1**	**21 000**	**516.2**	**655 526**	**1 056.6**	**600 833**	**917.0**
Certain infectious and parasitic diseases — Certaines maladies infectieuses et parasitaires								
Total	1 020	25.6	1 130	27.8	12 975	20.9	13 764	21.0
Intestinal infectious diseases — Maladies infectieuses intestinales	101	2.5	139	3.4	1 147	1.8	1 567	2.4
Tuberculosis — Tuberculose	5	♦0.1	4	♦0.1	1 279	2.1	831	1.3
Tetanus — Tétanos	-	-	-	-	6	♦0.0	2	♦0.0
Diphtheria — Diphtérie........................	-	-	-	-	-	-	-	-
Whooping cough — Coqueluche	-	-	-	-	2	♦0.0	1	♦0.0
Meningococcal infection — Infection à méningocoques........................	5	♦0.1	-	-	1	♦0.0	1	♦0.0
Septicaemia — Septicémie........................	764	19.1	861	21.2	5 556	9.0	5 930	9.1
Acute poliomyelitis — Poliomyélite aiguë	-	-	-	-	-	-	-	-
Measles — Rougeole........................	-	-	-	-	-	-	-	-
Viral hepatitis — Hépatite virale........................	43	1.1	37	0.9	2 336	3.8	2 904	4.4
Human immunodeficiency virus [HIV] disease — Maladies dues au virus de l'immunodéficience humaine (VIH)........................	23	♦0.6	10	♦0.2	48	0.1	2	♦0.0
Malaria — Paludisme........................	-	-	-	-	-	-	-	-
Neoplasms — Tumeurs	**5 455**	**136.7**	**5 507**	**135.4**	**220 764**	**355.8**	**151 175**	**230.7**
Malignant neoplasms — Tumeurs malignes								
Total	5 322	133.3	5 376	132.1	215 113	346.7	145 854	222.6
Malignant neoplasm of lip, oral cavity and pharynx — Tumeur maligne de la lèvre, de la cavité buccale et du pharynx	77	1.9	49	1.2	5 166	8.3	2 001	3.1
Malignant neoplasm of oesophagus — Tumeur maligne de l'oesophage	80	2.0	55	1.4	9 724	15.7	1 868	2.9
Malignant neoplasm of stomach — Tumeur maligne de l'estomac	287	7.2	187	4.6	32 206	51.9	16 923	25.8
Malignant neoplasm of colon, rectosigmoid junction, rectum, anus and anal canal — Tumeur maligne du côlon, de la jonction recto-sigmoïdienne, du rectum, de l'anus et du canal anal	676	16.9	698	17.2	25 718	41.5	21 961	33.5
Malignant neoplasm of liver and intrahepatic bile ducts — Tumeur maligne du foie et des voies bilaires intrahépatiques	174	4.4	128	3.1	20 060	32.3	10 630	16.2
Malignant neoplasm of pancreas — Tumeur maligne du pancréas........................	429	10.7	456	11.2	15 517	25.0	14 399	22.0
Malignant neoplasm of trachea, bronchus and lung — Tumeur maligne de la trachée, des bronches et du poumon	1 242	31.1	604	14.8	51 372	82.8	20 146	30.7
Malignant neoplasm of female breast — Tumeur maligne du sein chez la femme	..	..	1 052	35.5	..	..	12 529	21.8
Malignant neoplasm of cervix uteri — Tumeur maligne du col de l'utérus.........	..	..	82	2.8	..	..	2 712	4.7
Malignant neoplasm of prostate — Tumeur maligne de la prostate	372	40.8	..	..	11 143	43.0	..	..
Malignant neoplasm of lymphoid, haematopoietic and related tissue — Tumeurs malignes primitives ou présumées primitives des tissus lymphoïde, hématopoïétique et apparentés	651	16.3	554	13.6	12 970	20.9	9 886	15.1
Disorders of the blood and blood-forming organs and certain disorders involving the immune mechanism — Maladies du sang et des organes hématopoïétiques et certains troubles du système immunitaire								
Total	129	3.2	168	4.1	1 926	3.1	2 503	3.8
Anaemias — Anémies	74	1.9	107	2.6	756	1.2	1 168	1.8
Endocrine, nutritional and metabolic diseases — Maladies endocriniennes, nutritionnelles et métaboliques								
Total	1 365	34.2	1 695	41.7	10 980	17.7	11 188	17.1
Diabetes mellitus — Diabète sucré........................	1 065	26.7	1 249	30.7	7 639	12.3	6 847	10.5
Malnutrition — Malnutrition	12	♦0.3	10	♦0.2	875	1.4	872	1.3
Mental and behavioural disorders — Troubles mentaux et du comportement	**477**	**12.0**	**789**	**19.4**	**3 310**	**5.3**	**7 458**	**11.4**
Diseases of the nervous system — Maladies du système nerveux.................	**658**	**16.5**	**828**	**20.4**	**11 547**	**18.6**	**12 814**	**19.6**
Diseases of the circulatory system — Maladies de l'appareil circulatoire								
Total	4 819	120.7	5 217	128.2	166 023	267.6	184 889	282.2
Acute rheumatic fever and chronic rheumatic heart diseases — Rhumatisme articularie aigu et cardiopathies rhumatismales chroniques	54	1.4	93	2.3	773	1.2	1 738	2.7
Hypertensive diseases — Maladies hypertensives........................	301	7.5	497	12.2	2 738	4.4	4 523	6.9
Ischaemic heart disease — Cardiopathie ischémique	2 179	54.6	1 786	43.9	43 501	70.1	34 078	52.0
Cerebrovascular disease — Maladie cérébrovasculaire........................	1 064	26.7	1 265	31.1	58 625	94.5	62 977	96.1

	Israel - Israël				Japan - Japon			
Cause of death — Cause de décès	2013 (C)				2012 (C)			
	Male — Masculin		Female — Féminin		Male — Masculin		Female — Féminin	
	Number Nombre	Rate Taux	Number Nombre	Rate Taux	Number Nombre	Rate Taux	Number Nombre	Rate Taux
Diseases of arteries, arterioles and capillaries — Maladies des artères, artérioles et capillaires	233	5.8	173	4.3	9 980	16.1	9 458	14.4
Diseases of the respiratory system — Maladies de l'appareil respiratoire								
Total	1 607	40.3	1 565	38.5	113 518	183.0	88 280	134.7
Influenza — Grippe	7	♦0.2	9	♦0.2	582	0.9	693	1.1
Pneumonia — Pneumopathies	458	11.5	446	11.0	66 386	107.0	57 539	87.8
Chronic lower respiratory diseases — Maladies chroniques des voies respiratoires inférieures	621	15.6	589	14.5	14 081	22.7	5 566	8.5
Diseases of the digestive system — Maladies de l'appareil digestif								
Total	760	19.0	690	17.0	24 908	40.1	22 347	34.1
Gastric and duodenal ulcer — Ulcère de l'estomac et du duodénum...............	22	♦0.6	20	♦0.5	1 697	2.7	1 435	2.2
Diseases of the liver — Maladies du foie...............	236	5.9	154	3.8	10 441	16.8	5 539	8.5
Diseases of the musculoskeletal system and connective tissue — Maladies du système ostéo-articularie, des muscles et du tissu conjonctif	127	3.2	174	4.3	2 166	3.5	3 602	5.5
Diseases of the genitourinary system — Maladies de l'appareil génito-urinaire								
Total	1 011	25.3	1 027	25.2	15 714	25.3	20 068	30.6
Disorders of kidney and ureter — Affections du rein et de l'uretère	809	20.3	742	18.2	13 808	22.3	16 591	25.3
Hyperplasia of prostate — Hyperplasie de la prostate...............	9	♦1.0	..	..	105	0.4	..	..
Pregnancy, childbirth and the puerperium — Grossesse, accouchement et puerpéralité								
Total	..	..	14	♦8.2	..	..	50	4.8
Pregnancy with abortive outcome — Grossesse se terminant par un avortement	..	..	-	-	..	..	1	♦0.1
Other direct obstetric causes — Autres décès maternels directs	..	..	6	♦3.5	..	..	34	3.3
Indirect obstetric causes — Décès maternels indirects	..	..	2	♦1.2	..	..	7	♦0.7
Certain conditions originating in the perinatal period — Certaines affections dont l'origine se situe dans la période périnatale	135	153.1	96	115.3	316	59.4	285	56.4
Congenital malformations, deformations and chromosomal abnormalities — Malformations congénitales et anomalies chromosomiques	152	172.3	130	156.2	946	177.9	1 095	216.6
Symptoms, signs and abnormal clinical and laboratory findings, not elsewhere classified — Symptômes, signes et résultats anormaux d'examens cliniques et de laboratoire, non classés ailleurs	1 374	34.4	1 090	26.8	24 298	39.2	52 453	80.1
All other diseases — Toutes autres maladies...............	226	5.7	291	7.2	555	0.9	973	1.5
External causes — Causes externes								
Total	1 164	29.2	589	14.5	45 580	73.5	27 889	42.6
Accidents								
Total	693	17.4	388	9.5	23 714	38.2	17 317	26.4
Transport accidents — Accidents de transport...............	273	6.8	81	2.0	4 294	6.9	2 120	3.2
Falls — Chutes	75	1.9	51	1.3	4 471	7.2	3 290	5.0
Accidental drowning and submersion — Noyade et submersion accidentelles...............	46	1.2	9	♦0.2	4 129	6.7	3 834	5.9
Exposure to smoke, fire and flames — Exposition à la fumée, au feu et aux flammes...............	18	♦0.5	8	♦0.2	836	1.3	511	0.8
Accidental poisoning by and exposure to noxious substances — Intoxication accidentelle par des substances nocives et exposition à ces substances	1	♦0.0	-	-	501	0.8	288	0.4
Intentional self-harm — Lésions auto-infligées...............	291	7.3	80	2.0	18 485	29.8	7 948	12.1
Assault — Agresssions...............	95	2.4	36	0.9	183	0.3	200	0.3
All other external causes — Toutes autres causes externes	85	2.1	85	2.1	3 198	5.2	2 424	3.7

20. Death and death rates by cause and sex: 2010 - 2014
Décès et taux de mortalité par cause et sexe : 2010 - 2014 (continued - suite)

	Japan - Japon				Jordan - Jordanie			
Cause of death — Cause de décès	2013 (C)				2010 (U)		2011 (U)	
	Male — Masculin		Female — Féminin		Male — Masculin	Female — Féminin	Male — Masculin	Female — Féminin
	Number Nombre	Rate Taux	Number Nombre	Rate Taux	Number Nombre	Number Nombre	Number Nombre	Number Nombre
TOTAL	**658 684**	**1 063.8**	**609 752**	**932.1**	*8 960*	*6 771*	*9 694*	*7 198*
Certain infectious and parasitic diseases — Certaines maladies infectieuses et parasitaires								
Total	12 503	20.2	13 230	20.2	*167*	*133*	*196*	*150*
Intestinal infectious diseases — Maladies infectieuses intestinales	1 102	1.8	1 484	2.3	*7*	*18*	*11*	*10*
Tuberculosis — Tuberculose	1 246	2.0	841	1.3	*12*	*8*	*13*	*7*
Tetanus — Tétanos.......................................	2	✦0.0	3	✦0.0	-	-	-	-
Diphtheria — Diphtérie.................................	-	-	-	-	-	-	-	-
Whooping cough — Coqueluche	1	✦0.0	-	-	-	-	-	-
Meningococcal infection — Infection à méningocoques...	1	✦0.0	1	✦0.0	-	-	-	-
Septicaemia — Septicémie............................	5 342	8.6	5 816	8.9	*108*	*78*	*115*	*103*
Acute poliomyelitis — Poliomyélite aiguë	-	-	-	-	-	-	-	-
Measles — Rougeole....................................	1	✦0.0	1	✦0.0	-	-	-	-
Viral hepatitis — Hépatite virale...................	2 227	3.6	2 655	4.1	*33*	*18*	*47*	*28*
Human immunodeficiency virus [HIV] disease — Maladies dues au virus de l'immunodéficience humaine (VIH)................	42	0.1	3	✦0.0	-	-	*1*	*1*
Malaria — Paludisme....................................	-	-	-	-	*1*	-	-	-
Neoplasms — Tumeurs	**222 617**	**359.5**	**153 287**	**234.3**	*1 376*	*1 085*	*1 474*	*1 160*
Malignant neoplasms — Tumeurs malignes								
Total	216 977	350.4	147 900	226.1	*1 311*	*1 032*	*1 400*	*1 085*
Malignant neoplasm of lip, oral cavity and pharynx — Tumeur maligne de la lèvre, de la cavité buccale et du pharynx	5 128	8.3	2 051	3.1	*39*	*7*	*42*	*14*
Malignant neoplasm of oesophagus — Tumeur maligne de l'oesophage	9 667	15.6	1 876	2.9	*13*	*8*	*16*	*7*
Malignant neoplasm of stomach — Tumeur maligne de l'estomac	31 978	51.6	16 654	25.5	*66*	*49*	*61*	*58*
Malignant neoplasm of colon, rectosigmoid junction, rectum, anus and anal canal — Tumeur maligne du côlon, de la jonction recto-sigmoïdienne, du rectum, de l'anus et du canal anal................	25 976	42.0	22 026	33.7	*142*	*109*	*150*	*109*
Malignant neoplasm of liver and intrahepatic bile ducts — Tumeur maligne du foie et des voies bilaires intrahépatiques	19 816	32.0	10 359	15.8	*41*	*35*	*47*	*34*
Malignant neoplasm of pancreas — Tumeur maligne du pancréas...................	15 873	25.6	14 799	22.6	*78*	*50*	*64*	*46*
Malignant neoplasm of trachea, bronchus and lung — Tumeur maligne de la trachée, des bronches et du poumon...........	52 054	84.1	20 680	31.6	*303*	*74*	*342*	*79*
Malignant neoplasm of female breast — Tumeur maligne du sein chez la femme	..	..	13 148	22.9	*..*	*235*	*..*	*279*
Malignant neoplasm of cervix uteri — Tumeur maligne du col de l'utérus.........	..	..	2 656	4.6	*..*	*16*	*..*	*10*
Malignant neoplasm of prostate — Tumeur maligne de la prostate	11 560	44.3	..	..	*97*	*..*	*100*	*..*
Malignant neoplasm of lymphoid, haematopoietic and related tissue — Tumeurs malignes primitives ou présumées primitives des tissus lymphoïde, hématopoïétique et apparentés................	13 209	21.3	10 390	15.9	*180*	*153*	*221*	*168*
Disorders of the blood and blood-forming organs and certain disorders involving the immune mechanism — Maladies du sang et des organes hématopoïétiques et certains troubles du système immunitaire								
Total	1 985	3.2	2 492	3.8	*49*	*42*	*40*	*36*
Anaemias — Anémies	740	1.2	1 270	1.9	*24*	*26*	*20*	*14*
Endocrine, nutritional and metabolic diseases — Maladies endocriniennes, nutritionnelles et métaboliques								
Total	10 638	17.2	10 846	16.6	*674*	*630*	*725*	*705*
Diabetes mellitus — Diabète sucré................	7 294	11.8	6 518	10.0	*624*	*580*	*677*	*662*
Malnutrition — Malnutrition	805	1.3	888	1.4	*1*	*2*	*1*	*1*
Mental and behavioural disorders — Troubles mentaux et du comportement	**3 588**	**5.8**	**8 346**	**12.8**	*5*	-	*4*	*3*
Diseases of the nervous system — Maladies du système nerveux................	**12 478**	**20.2**	**14 407**	**22.0**	*171*	*151*	*202*	*168*
Diseases of the circulatory system — Maladies de l'appareil circulatoire								
Total	162 508	262.5	183 142	279.9	*3 160*	*2 510*	*3 635*	*2 725*
Acute rheumatic fever and chronic rheumatic heart diseases — Rhumatisme articularie aigu et cardiopathies rhumatismales chroniques	709	1.1	1 640	2.5	*9*	*12*	*8*	*8*
Hypertensive diseases — Maladies hypertensives...	2 657	4.3	4 508	6.9	*698*	*826*	*842*	*918*
Ischaemic heart disease — Cardiopathie ischémique	42 084	68.0	32 725	50.0	*1 331*	*636*	*1 495*	*693*

Cause of death — Cause de décès	Japan - Japon 2013 (C)				Jordan - Jordanie 2010 (U)		2011 (U)	
	Male — Masculin		Female — Féminin		Male — Masculin	Female — Féminin	Male — Masculin	Female — Féminin
	Number Nombre	Rate Taux	Number Nombre	Rate Taux	Number Nombre	Number Nombre	Number Nombre	Number Nombre
Cerebrovascular disease — Maladie cérébrovasculaire	56 718	91.6	61 629	94.2	721	691	805	700
Diseases of arteries, arterioles and capillaries — Maladies des artères, artérioles et capillaires	9 991	16.1	9 673	14.8	37	16	47	22
Diseases of the respiratory system — Maladies de l'appareil respiratoire								
Total	115 149	186.0	88 524	135.3	488	342	574	367
Influenza — Grippe	732	1.2	782	1.2	-	2	-	-
Pneumonia — Pneumopathies	66 362	107.2	56 607	86.5	243	187	263	195
Chronic lower respiratory diseases — Maladies chroniques des voies respiratoires inférieures	14 214	23.0	5 314	8.1	172	84	214	67
Diseases of the digestive system — Maladies de l'appareil digestif								
Total	25 076	40.5	22 535	34.4	233	197	269	218
Gastric and duodenal ulcer — Ulcère de l'estomac et du duodénum	1 588	2.6	1 240	1.9	16	8	14	7
Diseases of the liver — Maladies du foie	10 360	16.7	5 570	8.5	84	74	99	74
Diseases of the musculoskeletal system and connective tissue — Maladies du système ostéo-articulaire, des muscles et du tissu conjonctif	2 248	3.6	3 601	5.5	18	34	16	29
Diseases of the genitourinary system — Maladies de l'appareil génito-urinaire								
Total	16 126	26.0	20 261	31.0	230	173	233	184
Disorders of kidney and ureter — Affections du rein et de l'uretère	14 067	22.7	16 515	25.2	212	162	209	165
Hyperplasia of prostate — Hyperplasie de la prostate	108	0.4	..	..	7	..	4	..
Pregnancy, childbirth and the puerperium — Grossesse, accouchement et puerpéralité								
Total	..	..	41	4.0	..	46	..	34
Pregnancy with abortive outcome — Grossesse se terminant par un avortement	..	..	1	♦0.1	..	-	..	1
Other direct obstetric causes — Autres décès maternels directs	..	..	27	♦2.6	..	43	..	32
Indirect obstetric causes — Décès maternels indirects	..	..	8	♦0.8	..	3	..	1
Certain conditions originating in the perinatal period — Certaines affections dont l'origine se situe dans la période périnatale	316	59.9	245	48.8	585	469	588	425
Congenital malformations, deformations and chromosomal abnormalities — Malformations congénitales et anomalies chromosomiques	1 002	189.9	1 077	214.5	401	337	392	353
Symptoms, signs and abnormal clinical and laboratory findings, not elsewhere classified — Symptômes, signes et résultats anormaux d'examens cliniques et de laboratoire, non classés ailleurs	27 211	43.9	59 702	91.3	256	211	262	224
All other diseases — Toutes autres maladies	571	0.9	917	1.4	6	12	20	19
External causes — Causes externes								
Total	44 668	72.1	27 099	41.4	1 141	399	1 064	398
Accidents								
Total	23 043	37.2	16 531	25.3	731	254	644	217
Transport accidents — Accidents de transport	4 119	6.7	1 941	3.0	507	163	452	121
Falls — Chutes	4 501	7.3	3 265	5.0	50	8	44	10
Accidental drowning and submersion — Noyade et submersion accidentelles	3 961	6.4	3 562	5.4	48	16	33	9
Exposure to smoke, fire and flames — Exposition à la fumée, au feu et aux flammes	818	1.3	486	0.7	41	25	40	32
Accidental poisoning by and exposure to noxious substances — Intoxication accidentelle par des substances nocives et exposition à ces substances	424	0.7	270	0.4	19	21	21	16
Intentional self-harm — Lésions auto-infligées	18 158	29.3	7 905	12.1	16	3	16	3
Assault — Agresssions	178	0.3	164	0.3	111	26	122	24
All other external causes — Toutes autres causes externes	3 289	5.3	2 499	3.8	283	116	282	154

657

20. Death and death rates by cause and sex: 2010 - 2014
Décès et taux de mortalité par cause et sexe : 2010 - 2014 (continued - suite)

Kazakhstan

Cause of death — Cause de décès	2013 (C)				2014 (C)			
	Male — Masculin		Female — Féminin		Male — Masculin		Female — Féminin	
	Number Nombre	Rate Taux	Number Nombre	Rate Taux	Number Nombre	Rate Taux	Number Nombre	Rate Taux
TOTAL	75 038	912.7	61 223	694.7	71 929	868.2	59 966	675.6
Certain infectious and parasitic diseases — Certaines maladies infectieuses et parasitaires								
Total	1 205	14.7	586	6.6	1 056	12.7	551	6.2
Intestinal infectious diseases — Maladies infectieuses intestinales	28	♦0.3	19	♦0.2	19	♦0.2	16	♦0.2
Tuberculosis — Tuberculose	731	8.9	241	2.7	621	7.5	231	2.6
Tetanus — Tétanos	-	-	-	-	-	-	-	-
Diphtheria — Diphtérie....................	-	-	1	♦0.0	-	-	-	-
Whooping cough — Coqueluche	-	-	-	-	-	-	-	-
Meningococcal infection — Infection à méningocoques........	13	♦0.2	10	♦0.1	16	♦0.2	13	♦0.1
Septicaemia — Septicémie....................	187	2.3	152	1.7	150	1.8	142	1.6
Acute poliomyelitis — Poliomyélite aiguë	-	-	-	-	-	-	1	♦0.0
Measles — Rougeole....................	-	-	-	-	-	-	-	-
Viral hepatitis — Hépatite virale........	16	♦0.2	23	♦0.3	29	♦0.4	22	♦0.2
Human immunodeficiency virus [HIV] disease — Maladies dues au virus de l'immunodéficience humaine (VIH)........	134	1.6	50	0.6	140	1.7	41	0.5
Malaria — Paludisme....................	-	-	-	-	-	-	-	-
Neoplasms — Tumeurs	9 354	113.8	7 962	90.3	8 828	106.6	7 567	85.3
Malignant neoplasms — Tumeurs malignes								
Total	9 208	112.0	7 830	88.8	8 680	104.8	7 429	83.7
Malignant neoplasm of lip, oral cavity and pharynx — Tumeur maligne de la lèvre, de la cavité buccale et du pharynx	319	3.9	173	2.0	338	4.1	157	1.8
Malignant neoplasm of oesophagus — Tumeur maligne de l'oesophage	571	6.9	409	4.6	533	6.4	378	4.3
Malignant neoplasm of stomach — Tumeur maligne de l'estomac	1 373	16.7	737	8.4	1 303	15.7	702	7.9
Malignant neoplasm of colon, rectosigmoid junction, rectum, anus and anal canal — Tumeur maligne du côlon, de la jonction recto-sigmoïdienne, du rectum, de l'anus et du canal anal	788	9.6	838	9.5	767	9.3	806	9.1
Malignant neoplasm of liver and intrahepatic bile ducts — Tumeur maligne du foie et des voies bilaires intrahépatiques	464	5.6	316	3.6	477	5.8	254	2.9
Malignant neoplasm of pancreas — Tumeur maligne du pancréas....................	438	5.3	413	4.7	473	5.7	392	4.4
Malignant neoplasm of trachea, bronchus and lung — Tumeur maligne de la trachée, des bronches et du poumon	2 494	30.3	524	5.9	2 234	27.0	530	6.0
Malignant neoplasm of female breast — Tumeur maligne du sein chez la femme	..	..	1 383	20.8	..	..	1 252	18.7
Malignant neoplasm of cervix uteri — Tumeur maligne du col de l'utérus.........	..	..	607	9.1	..	..	630	9.4
Malignant neoplasm of prostate — Tumeur maligne de la prostate	402	27.2	..	..	347	22.7	..	..
Malignant neoplasm of lymphoid, haematopoietic and related tissue — Tumeurs malignes primitives ou présumées primitives des tissus lymphoïde, hématopoïétique et apparentés	443	5.4	382	4.3	441	5.3	368	4.1
Disorders of the blood and blood-forming organs and certain disorders involving the immune mechanism — Maladies du sang et des organes hématopoïétiques et certains troubles du système immunitaire								
Total	51	0.6	85	1.0	71	0.9	98	1.1
Anaemias — Anémies	29	♦0.4	48	0.5	35	0.4	50	0.6
Endocrine, nutritional and metabolic diseases — Maladies endocriniennes, nutritionnelles et métaboliques								
Total	802	9.8	1 476	16.7	963	11.6	1 763	19.9
Diabetes mellitus — Diabète sucré....................	690	8.4	1 319	15.0	873	10.5	1 584	17.8
Malnutrition — Malnutrition	38	0.5	37	0.4	24	♦0.3	45	0.5
Mental and behavioural disorders — Troubles mentaux et du comportement	286	3.5	490	5.6	404	4.9	724	8.2
Diseases of the nervous system — Maladies du système nerveux....................	3 680	44.8	4 675	53.0	4 897	59.1	6 268	70.6
Diseases of the circulatory system — Maladies de l'appareil circulatoire								
Total	21 978	267.3	19 707	223.6	19 042	229.8	16 801	189.3
Acute rheumatic fever and chronic rheumatic heart diseases — Rhumatisme articularie aigu et cardiopathies rhumatismales chroniques	144	1.8	232	2.6	109	1.3	189	2.1
Hypertensive diseases — Maladies hypertensives....................	727	8.8	866	9.8	574	6.9	615	6.9
Ischaemic heart disease — Cardiopathie ischémique....................	8 110	98.6	6 500	73.8	7 269	87.7	5 759	64.9
Cerebrovascular disease — Maladie cérébrovasculaire....................	6 924	84.2	8 093	91.8	6 076	73.3	6 882	77.5

Kazakhstan

Cause of death — Cause de décès	2013 (C)				2014 (C)			
	Male — Masculin		Female — Féminin		Male — Masculin		Female — Féminin	
	Number Nombre	Rate Taux	Number Nombre	Rate Taux	Number Nombre	Rate Taux	Number Nombre	Rate Taux
Diseases of arteries, arterioles and capillaries — Maladies des artères, artérioles et capillaires	1 134	13.8	1 175	13.3	886	10.7	988	11.1
Diseases of the respiratory system — Maladies de l'appareil respiratoire								
Total	8 948	108.8	7 153	81.2	9 112	110.0	7 462	84.1
Influenza — Grippe	5	♦0.1	7	♦0.1	10	♦0.1	4	♦0.0
Pneumonia — Pneumopathies	1 947	23.7	1 092	12.4	1 974	23.8	1 256	14.2
Chronic lower respiratory diseases — Maladies chroniques des voies respiratoires inférieures	6 376	77.5	5 624	63.8	6 549	79.0	5 765	65.0
Diseases of the digestive system — Maladies de l'appareil digestif								
Total	7 600	92.4	5 972	67.8	7 519	90.8	5 980	67.4
Gastric and duodenal ulcer — Ulcère de l'estomac et du duodénum	380	4.6	224	2.5	462	5.6	241	2.7
Diseases of the liver — Maladies du foie	5 945	72.3	4 731	53.7	5 859	70.7	4 697	52.9
Diseases of the musculoskeletal system and connective tissue — Maladies du système ostéo-articularie, des muscles et du tissu conjonctif	282	3.4	709	8.0	201	2.4	637	7.2
Diseases of the genitourinary system — Maladies de l'appareil génito-urinaire								
Total	1 910	23.2	2 049	23.2	1 928	23.3	2 153	24.3
Disorders of kidney and ureter — Affections du rein et de l'uretère	1 441	17.5	2 010	22.8	1 513	18.3	2 127	24.0
Hyperplasia of prostate — Hyperplasie de la prostate	416	28.1	..	..	378	24.7	..	..
Pregnancy, childbirth and the puerperium — Grossesse, accouchement et puerpéralité								
Total	..	..	41	10.6	..	..	37	...
Pregnancy with abortive outcome — Grossesse se terminant par un avortement	..	..	2	♦0.5	..	..	2	...
Other direct obstetric causes — Autres décès maternels directs	..	..	26	♦6.7	..	..	24	...
Indirect obstetric causes — Décès maternels indirects	..	..	13	♦3.4	..	..	11	...
Certain conditions originating in the perinatal period — Certaines affections dont l'origine se situe dans la période périnatale	1 468	734.4	1 024	546.6	1 252	...	910	...
Congenital malformations, deformations and chromosomal abnormalities — Malformations congénitales et anomalies chromosomiques	596	298.2	533	284.5	621	...	536	...
Symptoms, signs and abnormal clinical and laboratory findings, not elsewhere classified — Symptômes, signes et résultats anormaux d'examens cliniques et de laboratoire, non classés ailleurs	4 037	49.1	4 968	56.4	4 151	50.1	5 099	57.4
All other diseases — Toutes autres maladies	54	0.7	69	0.8	61	0.7	67	0.8
External causes — Causes externes								
Total	12 787	155.5	3 724	42.3	11 823	142.7	3 313	37.3
Accidents								
Total	7 194	87.5	2 278	25.8	6 827	82.4	2 131	24.0
Transport accidents — Accidents de transport	2 367	28.8	882	10.0	2 109	25.5	702	7.9
Falls — Chutes	473	5.8	168	1.9	530	6.4	181	2.0
Accidental drowning and submersion — Noyade et submersion accidentelles	608	7.4	142	1.6	652	7.9	157	1.8
Exposure to smoke, fire and flames — Exposition à la fumée, au feu et aux flammes	247	3.0	97	1.1	273	3.3	94	1.1
Accidental poisoning by and exposure to noxious substances — Intoxication accidentelle par des substances nocives et exposition à ces substances	1 498	18.2	469	5.3	1 442	17.4	453	5.1
Intentional self-harm — Lésions auto-infligées	2 839	34.5	675	7.7	2 560	30.9	563	6.3
Assault — Agresssions	829	10.1	251	2.8	796	9.6	226	2.5
All other external causes — Toutes autres causes externes	1 925	23.4	520	5.9	1 640	19.8	393	4.4

20. Death and death rates by cause and sex: 2010 - 2014
Décès et taux de mortalité par cause et sexe : 2010 - 2014 (continued - suite)

Kuwait - Koweït

Cause of death — Cause de décès	2013 (C)				2014 (C)			
	Male — Masculin		Female — Féminin		Male — Masculin		Female — Féminin	
	Number Nombre	Rate Taux	Number Nombre	Rate Taux	Number Nombre	Rate Taux	Number Nombre	Rate Taux
TOTAL	3 753	190.7	2 156	147.8	3 810	176.3	2 221	138.3
Certain infectious and parasitic diseases — Certaines maladies infectieuses et parasitaires								
Total	122	6.2	128	8.8	187	8.7	188	11.7
Intestinal infectious diseases — Maladies infectieuses intestinales	3	♦0.2	3	♦0.2	2	♦0.1	1	♦0.1
Tuberculosis — Tuberculose	5	♦0.3	2	♦0.1	4	♦0.2	4	♦0.2
Tetanus — Tétanos....................	-	-	-	-	1	♦0.0	-	-
Diphtheria — Diphtérie....................	-	-	-	-	-	-	-	-
Whooping cough — Coqueluche	-	-	-	-	-	-	-	-
Meningococcal infection — Infection à méningocoques	1	♦0.1	-	-	-	-	-	-
Septicaemia — Septicémie	105	5.3	115	7.9	165	7.6	179	11.1
Acute poliomyelitis — Poliomyélite aiguë	-	-	-	-	-	-	-	-
Measles — Rougeole....................	-	-	-	-	-	-	-	-
Viral hepatitis — Hépatite virale	6	♦0.3	5	♦0.3	12	♦0.6	2	♦0.1
Human immunodeficiency virus [HIV] disease — Maladies dues au virus de l'immunodéficience humaine (VIH)....................	-	-	-	-	1	♦0.0	1	♦0.1
Malaria — Paludisme....................	-	-	-	-	-	-	-	-
Neoplasms — Tumeurs	425	21.6	367	25.2	436	20.2	412	25.7
Malignant neoplasms — Tumeurs malignes								
Total	417	21.2	363	24.9	412	19.1	386	24.0
Malignant neoplasm of lip, oral cavity and pharynx — Tumeur maligne de la lèvre, de la cavité buccale et du pharynx	7	♦0.4	4	♦0.3	10	♦0.5	4	♦0.2
Malignant neoplasm of oesophagus — Tumeur maligne de l'oesophage	7	♦0.4	3	♦0.2	7	♦0.3	2	♦0.1
Malignant neoplasm of stomach — Tumeur maligne de l'estomac	15	♦0.8	8	♦0.5	18	♦0.8	13	♦0.8
Malignant neoplasm of colon, rectosigmoid junction, rectum, anus and anal canal — Tumeur maligne du côlon, de la jonction recto-sigmoïdienne, du rectum, de l'anus et du canal anal....................	59	3.0	32	2.2	45	2.1	33	2.1
Malignant neoplasm of liver and intrahepatic bile ducts — Tumeur maligne du foie et des voies bilaires intrahépatiques	37	1.9	17	♦1.2	24	♦1.1	12	♦0.7
Malignant neoplasm of pancreas — Tumeur maligne du pancréas....................	24	♦1.2	25	♦1.7	29	♦1.3	17	♦1.1
Malignant neoplasm of trachea, bronchus and lung — Tumeur maligne de la trachée, des bronches et du poumon	71	3.6	24	♦1.6	85	3.9	25	♦1.6
Malignant neoplasm of female breast — Tumeur maligne du sein chez la femme	..	..	87	7.6	..	..	121	10.0
Malignant neoplasm of cervix uteri — Tumeur maligne du col de l'utérus.........	..	..	4	♦0.3	..	..	7	♦0.6
Malignant neoplasm of prostate — Tumeur maligne de la prostate	24	♦11.6	..	..	32	11.0	..	..
Malignant neoplasm of lymphoid, haematopoietic and related tissue — Tumeurs malignes primitives ou présumées primitives des tissus lymphoïde, hématopoïétique et apparentés....................	49	2.5	35	2.4	62	2.9	32	2.0
Disorders of the blood and blood-forming organs and certain disorders involving the immune mechanism — Maladies du sang et des organes hématopoïétiques et certains troubles du système immunitaire								
Total	4	♦0.2	14	♦1.0	12	♦0.6	13	♦0.8
Anaemias — Anémies	2	♦0.1	8	♦0.5	6	♦0.3	9	♦0.6
Endocrine, nutritional and metabolic diseases — Maladies endocriniennes, nutritionnelles et métaboliques								
Total	71	3.6	98	6.7	83	3.8	76	4.7
Diabetes mellitus — Diabète sucré....................	57	2.9	81	5.6	68	3.1	59	3.7
Malnutrition — Malnutrition	-	-	-	-	-	-	-	-
Mental and behavioural disorders — Troubles mentaux et du comportement	1	♦0.1	1	♦0.1	3	♦0.1	3	♦0.2
Diseases of the nervous system — Maladies du système nerveux..................	30	♦1.5	22	♦1.5	33	1.5	35	2.2
Diseases of the circulatory system — Maladies de l'appareil circulatoire								
Total	1 737	88.2	754	51.7	1 579	73.0	694	43.2
Acute rheumatic fever and chronic rheumatic heart diseases — Rhumatisme articularie aigu et cardiopathies rhumatismales chroniques	1	♦0.1	1	♦0.1	3	♦0.1	-	-
Hypertensive diseases — Maladies hypertensives....................	64	3.3	67	4.6	64	3.0	77	4.8
Ischaemic heart disease — Cardiopathie ischémique	865	43.9	216	14.8	1 085	50.2	228	14.2
Cerebrovascular disease — Maladie cérébrovasculaire....................	250	12.7	156	10.7	248	11.5	164	10.2

Kuwait - Koweït

Cause of death — Cause de décès	2013 (C)				2014 (C)			
	Male — Masculin		Female — Féminin		Male — Masculin		Female — Féminin	
	Number Nombre	Rate Taux	Number Nombre	Rate Taux	Number Nombre	Rate Taux	Number Nombre	Rate Taux
Diseases of arteries, arterioles and capillaries — Maladies des artères, artérioles et capillaires	13	♦0.7	2	♦0.1	11	♦0.5	3	♦0.2
Diseases of the respiratory system — Maladies de l'appareil respiratoire								
Total	288	14.6	259	17.7	280	13.0	297	18.5
Influenza — Grippe	1	♦0.1	3	♦0.2	5	♦0.2	1	♦0.1
Pneumonia — Pneumopathies	238	12.1	226	15.5	236	10.9	251	15.6
Chronic lower respiratory diseases — Maladies chroniques des voies respiratoires inférieures	21	♦1.1	10	♦0.7	15	♦0.7	15	♦0.9
Diseases of the digestive system — Maladies de l'appareil digestif								
Total	85	4.3	68	4.7	64	3.0	62	3.9
Gastric and duodenal ulcer — Ulcère de l'estomac et du duodénum	6	♦0.3	1	♦0.1	5	♦0.2	-	-
Diseases of the liver — Maladies du foie	39	2.0	27	♦1.9	23	♦1.1	16	♦1.0
Diseases of the musculoskeletal system and connective tissue — Maladies du système ostéo-articularie, des muscles et du tissu conjonctif	2	♦0.1	11	♦0.8	1	♦0.0	10	♦0.6
Diseases of the genitourinary system — Maladies de l'appareil génito-urinaire								
Total	42	2.1	67	4.6	48	2.2	48	3.0
Disorders of kidney and ureter — Affections du rein et de l'uretère	23	♦1.2	44	3.0	24	♦1.1	23	♦1.4
Hyperplasia of prostate — Hyperplasie de la prostate	-	-	..	..	-	-	..	..
Pregnancy, childbirth and the puerperium — Grossesse, accouchement et puerpéralité								
Total	..	..	4	♦6.7	..	..	7	♦11.4
Pregnancy with abortive outcome — Grossesse se terminant par un avortement	..	..	1	♦1.7	..	..	1	♦1.6
Other direct obstetric causes — Autres décès maternels directs	..	..	3	♦5.0	..	..	6	♦9.8
Indirect obstetric causes — Décès maternels indirects	..	..	-	-	..	..	-	-
Certain conditions originating in the perinatal period — Certaines affections dont l'origine se situe dans la période périnatale	121	396.0	88	304.8	139	441.1	96	322.1
Congenital malformations, deformations and chromosomal abnormalities — Malformations congénitales et anomalies chromosomiques	101	330.6	102	353.3	119	377.6	102	342.3
Symptoms, signs and abnormal clinical and laboratory findings, not elsewhere classified — Symptômes, signes et résultats anormaux d'examens cliniques et de laboratoire, non classés ailleurs	38	1.9	35	2.4	55	2.5	32	2.0
All other diseases — Toutes autres maladies	-	-	2	♦0.1	3	♦0.1	-	-
External causes — Causes externes								
Total	686	34.9	136	9.3	768	35.5	146	9.1
Accidents								
Total	557	28.3	101	6.9	620	28.7	104	6.5
Transport accidents — Accidents de transport	404	20.5	60	4.1	434	20.1	69	4.3
Falls — Chutes	52	2.6	8	♦0.5	73	3.4	11	♦0.7
Accidental drowning and submersion — Noyade et submersion accidentelles	24	♦1.2	2	♦0.1	13	♦0.6	3	♦0.2
Exposure to smoke, fire and flames — Exposition à la fumée, au feu et aux flammes	11	♦0.6	14	♦1.0	26	♦1.2	7	♦0.4
Accidental poisoning by and exposure to noxious substances — Intoxication accidentelle par des substances nocives et exposition à ces substances	9	♦0.5	3	♦0.2	19	♦0.9	3	♦0.2
Intentional self-harm — Lésions auto-infligées	29	♦1.5	15	♦1.0	52	2.4	19	♦1.2
Assault — Agresssions	18	♦0.9	-	-	20	♦0.9	11	♦0.7
All other external causes — Toutes autres causes externes	82	4.2	20	♦1.4	76	3.5	12	♦0.7

20. Death and death rates by cause and sex: 2010 - 2014
Décès et taux de mortalité par cause et sexe : 2010 - 2014 (continued - suite)

Kyrgyzstan - Kirghizstan

Cause of death — Cause de décès	2012 (C)				2013 (C)			
	Male — Masculin		Female — Féminin		Male — Masculin		Female — Féminin	
	Number Nombre	Rate Taux	Number Nombre	Rate Taux	Number Nombre	Rate Taux	Number Nombre	Rate Taux
TOTAL	20 270	775.6	15 916	581.1	19 714	697.2	15 166	524.4
Certain infectious and parasitic diseases — Certaines maladies infectieuses et parasitaires								
Total	685	26.2	293	10.7	685	24.2	317	11.0
Intestinal infectious diseases — Maladies infectieuses intestinales	83	3.2	69	2.5	56	2.0	46	1.6
Tuberculosis — Tuberculose	456	17.4	150	5.5	436	15.4	175	6.1
Tetanus — Tétanos................	-	-	-	-	-	-	-	-
Diphtheria — Diphtérie..............	-	-	1	♦0.0	-	-	1	♦0.0
Whooping cough — Coqueluche	-	-	-	-	1	♦0.0	-	-
Meningococcal infection — Infection à méningocoques	3	♦0.1	7	♦0.3	3	♦0.1	5	♦0.2
Septicaemia — Septicémie............	19	♦0.7	6	♦0.2	32	1.1	17	♦0.6
Acute poliomyelitis — Poliomyélite aiguë	-	-	-	-	-	-	1	♦0.0
Measles — Rougeole..............	-	-	-	-	-	-	-	-
Viral hepatitis — Hépatite virale	21	♦0.8	21	♦0.8	30	♦1.1	20	♦0.7
Human immunodeficiency virus [HIV] disease — Maladies dues au virus de l'immunodéficience humaine (VIH)...............	72	2.8	14	♦0.5	90	3.2	32	1.1
Malaria — Paludisme................	-	-	-	-	-	-	-	-
Neoplasms — Tumeurs	1 752	67.0	1 578	57.6	1 809	64.0	1 678	58.0
Malignant neoplasms — Tumeurs malignes								
Total	1 725	66.0	1 553	56.7	1 789	63.3	1 648	57.0
Malignant neoplasm of lip, oral cavity and pharynx — Tumeur maligne de la lèvre, de la cavité buccale et du pharynx	70	2.7	25	♦0.9	67	2.4	44	1.5
Malignant neoplasm of oesophagus — Tumeur maligne de l'oesophage	107	4.1	53	1.9	91	3.2	55	1.9
Malignant neoplasm of stomach — Tumeur maligne de l'estomac	381	14.6	185	6.8	401	14.2	198	6.8
Malignant neoplasm of colon, rectosigmoid junction, rectum, anus and anal canal — Tumeur maligne du côlon, de la jonction recto-sigmoïdienne, du rectum, de l'anus et du canal anal...............	104	4.0	94	3.4	115	4.1	109	3.8
Malignant neoplasm of liver and intrahepatic bile ducts — Tumeur maligne du foie et des voies bilaires intrahépatiques	151	5.8	109	4.0	163	5.8	128	4.4
Malignant neoplasm of pancreas — Tumeur maligne du pancréas...............	83	3.2	67	2.4	75	2.7	79	2.7
Malignant neoplasm of trachea, bronchus and lung — Tumeur maligne de la trachée, des bronches et du poumon	322	12.3	86	3.1	361	12.8	116	4.0
Malignant neoplasm of female breast — Tumeur maligne du sein chez la femme	..	..	227	11.4	..	..	217	...
Malignant neoplasm of cervix uteri — Tumeur maligne du col de l'utérus..........	..	..	206	10.3	..	..	215	...
Malignant neoplasm of prostate — Tumeur maligne de la prostate	48	12.8	..	..	71	...	..	..
Malignant neoplasm of lymphoid, haematopoietic and related tissue — Tumeurs malignes primitives ou présumées primitives des tissus lymphoïde, hématopoïétique et apparentés	91	3.5	63	2.3	93	3.3	80	2.8
Disorders of the blood and blood-forming organs and certain disorders involving the immune mechanism — Maladies du sang et des organes hématopoïétiques et certains troubles du système immunitaire								
Total	25	♦1.0	27	♦1.0	29	♦1.0	21	♦0.7
Anaemias — Anémies	16	♦0.6	14	♦0.5	17	♦0.6	15	♦0.5
Endocrine, nutritional and metabolic diseases — Maladies endocriniennes, nutritionnelles et métaboliques								
Total	158	6.0	172	6.3	172	6.1	247	8.5
Diabetes mellitus — Diabète sucré...............	140	5.4	159	5.8	160	5.7	234	8.1
Malnutrition — Malnutrition	11	♦0.4	2	♦0.1	3	♦0.1	3	♦0.1
Mental and behavioural disorders — Troubles mentaux et du comportement	34	1.3	27	♦1.0	33	1.2	19	♦0.7
Diseases of the nervous system — Maladies du système nerveux...............	305	11.7	170	6.2	323	11.4	188	6.5
Diseases of the circulatory system — Maladies de l'appareil circulatoire								
Total	9 302	355.9	9 268	338.4	9 019	319.0	8 610	297.7
Acute rheumatic fever and chronic rheumatic heart diseases — Rhumatisme articularie aigu et cardiopathies rhumatismales chroniques	74	2.8	114	4.2	80	2.8	94	3.3
Hypertensive diseases — Maladies hypertensives...............	300	11.5	290	10.6	290	10.3	242	8.4
Ischaemic heart disease — Cardiopathie ischémique...............	5 775	221.0	6 026	220.0	5 575	197.2	5 574	192.7
Cerebrovascular disease — Maladie cérébrovasculaire...............	2 488	95.2	2 464	90.0	2 417	85.5	2 361	81.6

Kyrgyzstan - Kirghizstan

Cause of death — Cause de décès	2012 (C)				2013 (C)			
	Male — Masculin		Female — Féminin		Male — Masculin		Female — Féminin	
	Number Nombre	Rate Taux	Number Nombre	Rate Taux	Number Nombre	Rate Taux	Number Nombre	Rate Taux
Diseases of arteries, arterioles and capillaries — Maladies des artères, artérioles et capillaires	114	4.4	97	3.5	111	3.9	99	3.4
Diseases of the respiratory system — Maladies de l'appareil respiratoire								
Total	1 486	56.9	1 050	38.3	1 280	45.3	889	30.7
Influenza — Grippe	41	1.6	31	1.1	27	♦1.0	18	♦0.6
Pneumonia — Pneumopathies	427	16.3	283	10.3	395	14.0	254	8.8
Chronic lower respiratory diseases — Maladies chroniques des voies respiratoires inférieures	893	34.2	648	23.7	741	26.2	540	18.7
Diseases of the digestive system — Maladies de l'appareil digestif								
Total	1 621	62.0	827	30.2	1 641	58.0	827	28.6
Gastric and duodenal ulcer — Ulcère de l'estomac et du duodénum	64	2.4	26	♦0.9	59	2.1	29	♦1.0
Diseases of the liver — Maladies du foie	1 399	53.5	704	25.7	1 442	51.0	701	24.2
Diseases of the musculoskeletal system and connective tissue — Maladies du système ostéo-articularie, des muscles et du tissu conjonctif	50	1.9	83	3.0	32	1.1	77	2.7
Diseases of the genitourinary system — Maladies de l'appareil génito-urinaire								
Total	314	12.0	237	8.7	306	10.8	205	7.1
Disorders of kidney and ureter — Affections du rein et de l'uretère	307	11.7	235	8.6	301	10.6	203	7.0
Hyperplasia of prostate — Hyperplasie de la prostate	4	♦1.1	..	..	2	...	..	..
Pregnancy, childbirth and the puerperium — Grossesse, accouchement et puerpéralité								
Total	..	..	76	49.1	..	..	56	36.0
Pregnancy with abortive outcome — Grossesse se terminant par un avortement	..	..	2	♦1.3	..	..	2	♦1.3
Other direct obstetric causes — Autres décès maternels directs	..	..	61	39.4	..	..	41	26.4
Indirect obstetric causes — Décès maternels indirects	..	..	10	♦6.5	..	..	13	♦8.4
Certain conditions originating in the perinatal period — Certaines affections dont l'origine se situe dans la période périnatale	1 113	1 398.7	846	1 122.8	1 144	1 431.4	832	1 100.6
Congenital malformations, deformations and chromosomal abnormalities — Malformations congénitales et anomalies chromosomiques	274	344.3	249	330.5	296	370.4	277	366.4
Symptoms, signs and abnormal clinical and laboratory findings, not elsewhere classified — Symptômes, signes et résultats anormaux d'examens cliniques et de laboratoire, non classés ailleurs	475	18.2	195	7.1	494	17.5	195	6.7
All other diseases — Toutes autres maladies	12	♦0.5	7	♦0.3	14	♦0.5	9	♦0.3
External causes — Causes externes								
Total	2 664	101.9	811	29.6	2 437	86.2	719	24.9
Accidents								
Total	1 762	67.4	549	20.0	1 665	58.9	518	17.9
Transport accidents — Accidents de transport	704	26.9	222	8.1	760	26.9	264	9.1
Falls — Chutes	67	2.6	15	♦0.5	61	2.2	16	♦0.6
Accidental drowning and submersion — Noyade et submersion accidentelles	218	8.3	66	2.4	147	5.2	67	2.3
Exposure to smoke, fire and flames — Exposition à la fumée, au feu et aux flammes	42	1.6	18	♦0.7	31	1.1	11	♦0.4
Accidental poisoning by and exposure to noxious substances — Intoxication accidentelle par des substances nocives et exposition à ces substances	354	13.5	92	3.4	308	10.9	64	2.2
Intentional self-harm — Lésions auto-infligées	402	15.4	122	4.5	349	12.3	97	3.4
Assault — Agresssions	189	7.2	59	2.2	167	5.9	50	1.7
All other external causes — Toutes autres causes externes	311	11.9	81	3.0	256	9.1	54	1.9

20. Death and death rates by cause and sex: 2010 - 2014
Décès et taux de mortalité par cause et sexe : 2010 - 2014 (continued - suite)

Cause of death — Cause de décès	Maldives				Oman		Philippines	
	2010 (+U)		2011 (+U)		2010 (U)		2010 (U)	
	Male — Masculin	Female — Féminin	Male — Masculin	Female — Féminin	Male — Masculin	Female — Féminin	Male — Masculin	Female — Féminin
	Number Nombre	Number Nombre	Number Nombre	Number Nombre	Number Nombre	Number Nombre	Number Nombre	Number Nombre
TOTAL	**679**	**462**	**686**	**458**	**4 460**	**2 534**	**282 371**	**205 884**
Certain infectious and parasitic diseases — Certaines maladies infectieuses et parasitaires								
Total	22	7	20	15	241	152	27 167	16 130
Intestinal infectious diseases — Maladies infectieuses intestinales	1	-	2	1	6	8	2 604	2 013
Tuberculosis — Tuberculose	6	-	3	2	7	5	17 099	7 610
Tetanus — Tétanos	-	-	-	-	-	-	439	151
Diphtheria — Diphtérie	-	-	-	-	-	-	10	13
Whooping cough — Coqueluche	-	-	-	-	-	-	3	-
Meningococcal infection — Infection à méningocoques	-	-	-	-	17	7	32	33
Septicaemia — Septicémie	12	6	4	8	162	118	4 660	4 765
Acute poliomyelitis — Poliomyélite aiguë	-	-	-	-	-	1	13	9
Measles — Rougeole	-	-	-	-	-	-	27	24
Viral hepatitis — Hépatite virale	1	-	-	1	14	6	505	230
Human immunodeficiency virus [HIV] disease — Maladies dues au virus de l'immunodéficience humaine (VIH)	-	-	-	-	12	2	28	6
Malaria — Paludisme	-	-	-	-	1	-	33	21
Neoplasms — Tumeurs	**57**	**36**	**62**	**44**	**200**	**150**	**26 822**	**25 678**
Malignant neoplasms — Tumeurs malignes								
Total	55	34	59	43	184	140	25 389	24 433
Malignant neoplasm of lip, oral cavity and pharynx — Tumeur maligne de la lèvre, de la cavité buccale et du pharynx	2	6	2	2	11	3	1 379	834
Malignant neoplasm of oesophagus — Tumeur maligne de l'oesophage	2	1	1	2	5	2	348	140
Malignant neoplasm of stomach — Tumeur maligne de l'estomac	1	-	2	1	18	10	820	588
Malignant neoplasm of colon, rectosigmoid junction, rectum, anus and anal canal — Tumeur maligne du côlon, de la jonction recto-sigmoïdienne, du rectum, de l'anus et du canal anal	1	-	1	1	11	8	2 828	2 330
Malignant neoplasm of liver and intrahepatic bile ducts — Tumeur maligne du foie et des voies bilaires intrahépatiques	8	1	7	2	15	6	4 140	1 793
Malignant neoplasm of pancreas — Tumeur maligne du pancréas	3	-	1	2	6	4	673	658
Malignant neoplasm of trachea, bronchus and lung — Tumeur maligne de la trachée, des bronches et du poumon	7	1	14	2	25	7	5 899	2 344
Malignant neoplasm of female breast — Tumeur maligne du sein chez la femme	..	5	..	6	..	19	..	5 972
Malignant neoplasm of cervix uteri — Tumeur maligne du col de l'utérus	..	2	..	5	..	2	..	1 660
Malignant neoplasm of prostate — Tumeur maligne de la prostate	-	..	4	..	17	..	2 448	..
Malignant neoplasm of lymphoid, haematopoietic and related tissue — Tumeurs malignes primitives ou présumées primitives des tissus lymphoïde, hématopoïétique et apparentés	8	-	3	4	16	13	2 198	1 982
Disorders of the blood and blood-forming organs and certain disorders involving the immune mechanism — Maladies du sang et des organes hématopoïétiques et certains troubles du système immunitaire								
Total	8	5	8	6	33	21	1 522	1 680
Anaemias — Anémies	6	3	6	4	15	11	1 164	1 283
Endocrine, nutritional and metabolic diseases — Maladies endocriniennes, nutritionnelles et métaboliques								
Total	24	26	29	21	137	115	13 249	14 968
Diabetes mellitus — Diabète sucré	14	15	18	18	109	87	10 483	11 030
Malnutrition — Malnutrition	-	2	1	-	-	1	878	1 174
Mental and behavioural disorders — Troubles mentaux et du comportement	-	4	1	2	10	9	179	166
Diseases of the nervous system — Maladies du système nerveux	16	10	14	9	39	39	3 691	2 805
Diseases of the circulatory system — Maladies de l'appareil circulatoire								
Total	296	187	277	175	860	540	95 740	75 749
Acute rheumatic fever and chronic rheumatic heart diseases — Rhumatisme articularie aigu et cardiopathies rhumatismales chroniques	1	1	-	2	17	17	796	1 145
Hypertensive diseases — Maladies hypertensives	127	82	36	43	174	124	8 997	7 844
Ischaemic heart disease — Cardiopathie ischémique	67	21	82	31	201	113	36 648	25 038

Cause of death — Cause de décès	Maldives				Oman		Philippines	
	2010 (+U)		2011 (+U)		2010 (U)		2010 (U)	
	Male — Masculin	Female — Féminin	Male — Masculin	Female — Féminin	Male — Masculin	Female — Féminin	Male — Masculin	Female — Féminin
	Number Nombre	Number Nombre	Number Nombre	Number Nombre	Number Nombre	Number Nombre	Number Nombre	Number Nombre
Cerebrovascular disease — Maladie cérébrovasculaire	31	25	72	36	135	87	33 338	26 213
Diseases of arteries, arterioles and capillaries — Maladies des artères, artérioles et capillaires	-	-	2	2	13	4	1 334	1 438
Diseases of the respiratory system — Maladies de l'appareil respiratoire								
Total	46	57	66	62	224	170	41 022	32 079
Influenza — Grippe	-	-	-	-	1	2	39	47
Pneumonia — Pneumopathies	6	2	2	3	85	68	22 647	22 944
Chronic lower respiratory diseases — Maladies chroniques des voies respiratoires inférieures	18	33	39	41	25	18	15 805	7 072
Diseases of the digestive system — Maladies de l'appareil digestif								
Total	17	11	15	9	102	59	14 865	5 729
Gastric and duodenal ulcer — Ulcère de l'estomac et du duodénum	-	2	2	-	9	4	3 842	1 899
Diseases of the liver — Maladies du foie	12	5	6	3	54	29	6 467	2 009
Diseases of the musculoskeletal system and connective tissue — Maladies du système ostéo-articulaire, des muscles et du tissu conjonctif	-	2	1	-	13	8	571	911
Diseases of the genitourinary system — Maladies de l'appareil génito-urinaire								
Total	25	18	19	16	100	52	10 752	7 486
Disorders of kidney and ureter — Affections du rein et de l'uretère	22	16	17	14	77	40	9 734	6 708
Hyperplasia of prostate — Hyperplasie de la prostate	1	..	2	..	2	..	419	..
Pregnancy, childbirth and the puerperium — Grossesse, accouchement et puerpéralité								
Total	..	7	..	4	..	6	..	1 718
Pregnancy with abortive outcome — Grossesse se terminant par un avortement	..	-	..	-	..	1	..	155
Other direct obstetric causes — Autres décès maternels directs	..	5	..	3	..	5	..	1 468
Indirect obstetric causes — Décès maternels indirects	..	2	..	1	..	-	..	95
Certain conditions originating in the perinatal period — Certaines affections dont l'origine se situe dans la période périnatale	33	23	22	20	110	96	7 242	4 845
Congenital malformations, deformations and chromosomal abnormalities — Malformations congénitales et anomalies chromosomiques	14	10	8	7	75	78	2 853	2 336
Symptoms, signs and abnormal clinical and laboratory findings, not elsewhere classified — Symptômes, signes et résultats anormaux d'examens cliniques et de laboratoire, non classés ailleurs	78	45	110	53	1 737	897	6 076	6 056
All other diseases — Toutes autres maladies	2	2	3	2	19	18	662	860
External causes — Causes externes								
Total	41	12	31	13	560	124	29 958	6 688
Accidents								
Total	27	8	27	13	342	71	13 135	3 927
Transport accidents — Accidents de transport	4	2	3	-	298	57	6 738	1 685
Falls — Chutes	5	2	5	-	13	3	1 389	631
Accidental drowning and submersion — Noyade et submersion accidentelles	12	1	9	5	20	9	2 268	776
Exposure to smoke, fire and flames — Exposition à la fumée, au feu et aux flammes	1	-	1	2	2	-	278	200
Accidental poisoning by and exposure to noxious substances — Intoxication accidentelle par des substances nocives et exposition à ces substances	-	-	1	-	-	-	435	74
Intentional self-harm — Lésions auto-infligées	1	-	2	-	16	-	1 630	488
Assault — Agresssions	2	-	1	-	2	1	11 302	1 016
All other external causes — Toutes autres causes externes	11	4	1	-	200	52	3 891	1 257

Cause of death — Cause de décès	Philippines		Qatar			
	2011 (U)		2011 (U)		2012 (U)	
	Male — Masculin	Female — Féminin	Male — Masculin	Female — Féminin	Male — Masculin	Female — Féminin
	Number Nombre	Number Nombre	Number Nombre	Number Nombre	Number Nombre	Number Nombre
TOTAL	*288 702*	*209 739*	*1 402*	*547*	*1 470*	*561*
Certain infectious and parasitic diseases — Certaines maladies infectieuses et parasitaires						
Total	*27 480*	*15 814*	*12*	*11*	*14*	*10*
Intestinal infectious diseases — Maladies infectieuses intestinales	*2 864*	*2 089*	*1*	*-*	*-*	*-*
Tuberculosis — Tuberculose	*16 810*	*7 552*	*1*	*1*	*2*	*-*
Tetanus — Tétanos	*449*	*149*	*-*	*-*	*-*	*-*
Diphtheria — Diphtérie	*6*	*12*	*-*	*-*	*-*	*-*
Whooping cough — Coqueluche	*1*	*1*	*-*	*-*	*-*	*-*
Meningococcal infection — Infection à méningocoques	*31*	*23*	*-*	*-*	*-*	*1*
Septicaemia — Septicémie	*5 027*	*4 757*	*1*	*1*	*2*	*4*
Acute poliomyelitis — Poliomyélite aiguë	*5*	*2*	*-*	*-*	*-*	*-*
Measles — Rougeole	*27*	*11*	*-*	*-*	*-*	*-*
Viral hepatitis — Hépatite virale	*527*	*203*	*4*	*5*	*4*	*2*
Human immunodeficiency virus [HIV] disease — Maladies dues au virus de l'immunodéficience humaine (VIH)	*73*	*7*	*-*	*-*	*-*	*-*
Malaria — Paludisme	*16*	*12*	*1*	*-*	*1*	*-*
Neoplasms — Tumeurs	*27 044*	*26 407*	*109*	*87*	*114*	*104*
Malignant neoplasms — Tumeurs malignes						
Total	*25 588*	*25 176*	*102*	*84*	*113*	*104*
Malignant neoplasm of lip, oral cavity and pharynx — Tumeur maligne de la lèvre, de la cavité buccale et du pharynx	*1 462*	*835*	*-*	*2*	*3*	*2*
Malignant neoplasm of oesophagus — Tumeur maligne de l'oesophage	*343*	*96*	*7*	*-*	*3*	*1*
Malignant neoplasm of stomach — Tumeur maligne de l'estomac	*786*	*604*	*5*	*5*	*11*	*5*
Malignant neoplasm of colon, rectosigmoid junction, rectum, anus and anal canal — Tumeur maligne du côlon, de la jonction recto-sigmoïdienne, du rectum, de l'anus et du canal anal	*2 962*	*2 423*	*11*	*13*	*7*	*12*
Malignant neoplasm of liver and intrahepatic bile ducts — Tumeur maligne du foie et des voies bilaires intrahépatiques	*4 040*	*1 691*	*15*	*8*	*12*	*9*
Malignant neoplasm of pancreas — Tumeur maligne du pancréas	*684*	*693*	*8*	*2*	*10*	*5*
Malignant neoplasm of trachea, bronchus and lung — Tumeur maligne de la trachée, des bronches et du poumon	*5 969*	*2 389*	*18*	*6*	*20*	*3*
Malignant neoplasm of female breast — Tumeur maligne du sein chez la femme	*..*	*6 162*	*..*	*24*	*..*	*36*
Malignant neoplasm of cervix uteri — Tumeur maligne du col de l'utérus	*..*	*1 788*	*..*	*2*	*..*	*-*
Malignant neoplasm of prostate — Tumeur maligne de la prostate	*2 467*	*..*	*5*	*..*	*8*	*..*
Malignant neoplasm of lymphoid, haematopoietic and related tissue — Tumeurs malignes primitives ou présumées primitives des tissus lymphoïde, hématopoïétique et apparentés	*2 232*	*2 040*	*19*	*4*	*16*	*7*
Disorders of the blood and blood-forming organs and certain disorders involving the immune mechanism — Maladies du sang et des organes hématopoïétiques et certains troubles du système immunitaire						
Total	*1 575*	*1 611*	*5*	*3*	*6*	*3*
Anaemias — Anémies	*1 221*	*1 254*	*-*	*-*	*-*	*-*
Endocrine, nutritional and metabolic diseases — Maladies endocriniennes, nutritionnelles et métaboliques						
Total	*13 650*	*15 160*	*78*	*81*	*72*	*62*
Diabetes mellitus — Diabète sucré	*10 718*	*11 175*	*71*	*74*	*62*	*50*
Malnutrition — Malnutrition	*845*	*961*	*-*	*1*	*-*	*-*
Mental and behavioural disorders — Troubles mentaux et du comportement	*208*	*233*	*-*	*-*	*-*	*-*
Diseases of the nervous system — Maladies du système nerveux	*3 405*	*2 645*	*15*	*8*	*26*	*10*
Diseases of the circulatory system — Maladies de l'appareil circulatoire						
Total	*99 538*	*77 820*	*168*	*71*	*182*	*66*
Acute rheumatic fever and chronic rheumatic heart diseases — Rhumatisme articularie aigu et cardiopathies rhumatismales chroniques	*790*	*1 103*	*3*	*1*	*-*	*-*
Hypertensive diseases — Maladies hypertensives	*8 995*	*7 728*	*23*	*14*	*16*	*13*
Ischaemic heart disease — Cardiopathie ischémique	*38 743*	*25 986*	*85*	*19*	*97*	*22*
Cerebrovascular disease — Maladie cérébrovasculaire	*33 885*	*26 672*	*34*	*21*	*33*	*9*
Diseases of arteries, arterioles and capillaries — Maladies des artères, artérioles et capillaires	*1 359*	*1 460*	*4*	*2*	*4*	*1*

Cause of death — Cause de décès	Philippines		Qatar			
	2011 (U)		2011 (U)		2012 (U)	
	Male — Masculin	Female — Féminin	Male — Masculin	Female — Féminin	Male — Masculin	Female — Féminin
	Number Nombre	Number Nombre	Number Nombre	Number Nombre	Number Nombre	Number Nombre
Diseases of the respiratory system — Maladies de l'appareil respiratoire						
Total	43 004	33 564	45	24	34	40
Influenza — Grippe	20	18	-	-	-	-
Pneumonia — Pneumopathies	24 279	24 151	11	8	6	10
Chronic lower respiratory diseases — Maladies chroniques des voies respiratoires inférieures	16 042	7 216	5	4	7	2
Diseases of the digestive system — Maladies de l'appareil digestif						
Total	14 935	5 862	36	17	29	17
Gastric and duodenal ulcer — Ulcère de l'estomac et du duodénum......................	3 964	1 854	-	-	-	-
Diseases of the liver — Maladies du foie............................	6 216	2 070	15	6	18	13
Diseases of the musculoskeletal system and connective tissue — Maladies du système ostéo-articulaire, des muscles et du tissu conjonctif	534	821	-	-	-	2
Diseases of the genitourinary system — Maladies de l'appareil génito-urinaire						
Total	10 946	7 387	24	21	20	29
Disorders of kidney and ureter — Affections du rein et de l'uretère	9 987	6 602	24	19	18	27
Hyperplasia of prostate — Hyperplasie de la prostate...................	349	..	-	..	-	..
Pregnancy, childbirth and the puerperium — Grossesse, accouchement et puerpéralité						
Total	..	1 465	..	1	..	1
Pregnancy with abortive outcome — Grossesse se terminant par un avortement...................	..	121	..	-	..	-
Other direct obstetric causes — Autres décès maternels directs	..	1 253	..	-	..	1
Indirect obstetric causes — Décès maternels indirects	..	91	..	-	..	-
Certain conditions originating in the perinatal period — Certaines affections dont l'origine se situe dans la période périnatale	7 110	4 871	48	27	34	28
Congenital malformations, deformations and chromosomal abnormalities — Malformations congénitales et anomalies chromosomiques	2 686	2 117	25	34	39	23
Symptoms, signs and abnormal clinical and laboratory findings, not elsewhere classified — Symptômes, signes et résultats anormaux d'examens cliniques et de laboratoire, non classés ailleurs	6 548	6 094	495	117	555	126
All other diseases — Toutes autres maladies......................	636	834	2	4	1	1
External causes — Causes externes						
Total	29 403	7 034	340	41	344	39
Accidents						
Total	13 145	4 301	291	36	300	33
Transport accidents — Accidents de transport	6 496	1 527	205	20	208	23
Falls — Chutes	1 352	676	19	6	24	2
Accidental drowning and submersion — Noyade et submersion accidentelles...................	2 677	978	20	2	18	3
Exposure to smoke, fire and flames — Exposition à la fumée, au feu et aux flammes	213	133	5	7	14	3
Accidental poisoning by and exposure to noxious substances — Intoxication accidentelle par des substances nocives et exposition à ces substances	293	56	2	-	3	1
Intentional self-harm — Lésions auto-infligées.........................	1 879	570	45	5	38	5
Assault — Agresssions..	10 903	1 081	4	-	6	1
All other external causes — Toutes autres causes externes	3 476	1 082	-	-	-	-

20. Death and death rates by cause and sex: 2010 - 2014
Décès et taux de mortalité par cause et sexe : 2010 - 2014 (continued - suite)

Republic of Korea - République de Corée

Cause of death — Cause de décès	2012 (C)				2013 (C)			
	Male — Masculin		Female — Féminin		Male — Masculin		Female — Féminin	
	Number Nombre	Rate Taux	Number Nombre	Rate Taux	Number Nombre	Rate Taux	Number Nombre	Rate Taux
TOTAL	147 372	585.1	119 849	476.4	146 599	579.8	119 658	473.4
Certain infectious and parasitic diseases — Certaines maladies infectieuses et parasitaires								
Total	3 878	15.4	3 228	12.8	3 563	14.1	3 120	12.3
Intestinal infectious diseases — Maladies infectieuses intestinales	301	1.2	496	2.0	257	1.0	473	1.9
Tuberculosis — Tuberculose	1 588	6.3	878	3.5	1 455	5.8	775	3.1
Tetanus — Tétanos.............	1	⬧0.0	3	⬧0.0	2	⬧0.0	5	⬧0.0
Diphtheria — Diphtérie.............	-	-	-	-	-	-	-	-
Whooping cough — Coqueluche	-	-	-	-	-	-	-	-
Meningococcal infection — Infection à méningocoques	1	⬧0.0	-	-	-	-	-	-
Septicaemia — Septicémie.............	912	3.6	1 228	4.9	910	3.6	1 286	5.1
Acute poliomyelitis — Poliomyélite aiguë	-	-	-	-	-	-	-	-
Measles — Rougeole.............	-	-	-	-	-	-	-	-
Viral hepatitis — Hépatite virale	539	2.1	351	1.4	445	1.8	318	1.3
Human immunodeficiency virus [HIV] disease — Maladies dues au virus de l'immunodéficience humaine (VIH).............	115	0.5	9	⬧0.0	111	0.4	8	⬧0.0
Malaria — Paludisme.............	2	⬧0.0	2	⬧0.0	3	⬧0.0	-	-
Neoplasms — Tumeurs	47 104	187.0	27 886	110.8	47 768	188.9	28 853	114.2
Malignant neoplasms — Tumeurs malignes								
Total	46 462	184.5	27 297	108.5	47 079	186.2	28 255	111.8
Malignant neoplasm of lip, oral cavity and pharynx — Tumeur maligne de la lèvre, de la cavité buccale et du pharynx	809	3.2	227	0.9	821	3.2	257	1.0
Malignant neoplasm of oesophagus — Tumeur maligne de l'oesophage	1 278	5.1	120	0.5	1 320	5.2	128	0.5
Malignant neoplasm of stomach — Tumeur maligne de l'estomac	6 090	24.2	3 252	12.9	5 995	23.7	3 185	12.6
Malignant neoplasm of colon, rectosigmoid junction, rectum, anus and anal canal — Tumeur maligne du côlon, de la jonction recto-sigmoïdienne, du rectum, de l'anus et du canal anal.............	4 692	18.6	3 506	13.9	4 687	18.5	3 583	14.2
Malignant neoplasm of liver and intrahepatic bile ducts — Tumeur maligne du foie et des voies bilaires intrahépatiques	8 494	33.7	2 841	11.3	8 421	33.3	2 984	11.8
Malignant neoplasm of pancreas — Tumeur maligne du pancréas.............	2 616	10.4	2 162	8.6	2 615	10.3	2 216	8.8
Malignant neoplasm of trachea, bronchus and lung — Tumeur maligne de la trachée, des bronches et du poumon	12 175	48.3	4 479	17.8	12 519	49.5	4 658	18.4
Malignant neoplasm of female breast — Tumeur maligne du sein chez la femme	..	..	1 993	9.3	..	..	2 231	10.4
Malignant neoplasm of cervix uteri — Tumeur maligne du col de l'utérus.........	..	..	889	4.2	..	..	892	4.1
Malignant neoplasm of prostate — Tumeur maligne de la prostate	1 460	20.1	..	..	1 629	21.5	..	..
Malignant neoplasm of lymphoid, haematopoietic and related tissue — Tumeurs malignes primitives ou présumées primitives des tissus lymphoïde, hématopoïétique et apparentés.............	2 411	9.6	1 745	6.9	2 411	9.5	1 719	6.8
Disorders of the blood and blood-forming organs and certain disorders involving the immune mechanism — Maladies du sang et des organes hématopoïétiques et certains troubles du système immunitaire								
Total	279	1.1	347	1.4	307	1.2	383	1.5
Anaemias — Anémies	165	0.7	242	1.0	184	0.7	247	1.0
Endocrine, nutritional and metabolic diseases — Maladies endocriniennes, nutritionnelles et métaboliques								
Total	6 340	25.2	6 203	24.7	5 872	23.2	5 972	23.6
Diabetes mellitus — Diabète sucré.............	5 849	23.2	5 708	22.7	5 382	21.3	5 506	21.8
Malnutrition — Malnutrition	24	⬧0.1	32	0.1	27	⬧0.1	34	0.1
Mental and behavioural disorders — Troubles mentaux et du comportement	2 214	8.8	3 360	13.4	2 138	8.5	3 052	12.1
Diseases of the nervous system — Maladies du système nerveux.............	3 382	13.4	4 756	18.9	4 115	16.3	5 699	22.5
Diseases of the circulatory system — Maladies de l'appareil circulatoire								
Total	27 818	110.4	31 142	123.8	27 097	107.2	30 084	119.0
Acute rheumatic fever and chronic rheumatic heart diseases — Rhumatisme articularie aigu et cardiopathies rhumatismales chroniques	57	0.2	171	0.7	55	0.2	121	0.5
Hypertensive diseases — Maladies hypertensives.............	1 620	6.4	3 619	14.4	1 497	5.9	3 235	12.8
Ischaemic heart disease — Cardiopathie ischémique	7 698	30.6	6 872	27.3	7 155	28.3	6 419	25.4
Cerebrovascular disease — Maladie cérébrovasculaire.............	12 380	49.2	13 364	53.1	12 096	47.8	13 351	52.8

Republic of Korea - République de Corée

Cause of death — Cause de décès	2012 (C)				2013 (C)			
	Male — Masculin		Female — Féminin		Male — Masculin		Female — Féminin	
	Number Nombre	Rate Taux	Number Nombre	Rate Taux	Number Nombre	Rate Taux	Number Nombre	Rate Taux
Diseases of arteries, arterioles and capillaries — Maladies des artères, artérioles et capillaires	653	2.6	533	2.1	763	3.0	552	2.2
Diseases of the respiratory system — Maladies de l'appareil respiratoire								
Total	12 685	50.4	10 085	40.1	12 485	49.4	10 005	39.6
Influenza — Grippe	37	0.1	40	0.2	16	♦0.1	15	♦0.1
Pneumonia — Pneumopathies	5 203	20.7	5 111	20.3	5 411	21.4	5 398	21.4
Chronic lower respiratory diseases — Maladies chroniques des voies respiratoires inférieures	4 844	19.2	2 987	11.9	4 400	17.4	2 674	10.6
Diseases of the digestive system — Maladies de l'appareil digestif								
Total	7 407	29.4	3 869	15.4	7 279	28.8	3 892	15.4
Gastric and duodenal ulcer — Ulcère de l'estomac et du duodénum	246	1.0	255	1.0	231	0.9	233	0.9
Diseases of the liver — Maladies du foie	5 364	21.3	1 429	5.7	5 186	20.5	1 479	5.9
Diseases of the musculoskeletal system and connective tissue — Maladies du système ostéo-articularie, des muscles et du tissu conjonctif	615	2.4	1 152	4.6	606	2.4	1 054	4.2
Diseases of the genitourinary system — Maladies de l'appareil génito-urinaire								
Total	2 575	10.2	2 863	11.4	2 609	10.3	3 043	12.0
Disorders of kidney and ureter — Affections du rein et de l'uretère	2 311	9.2	2 314	9.2	2 343	9.3	2 537	10.0
Hyperplasia of prostate — Hyperplasie de la prostate	61	0.8	..	..	72	0.9	..	..
Pregnancy, childbirth and the puerperium — Grossesse, accouchement et puerpéralité								
Total	..	..	56	11.6	..	..	51	11.7
Pregnancy with abortive outcome — Grossesse se terminant par un avortement	..	..	3	♦0.6	..	..	2	♦0.5
Other direct obstetric causes — Autres décès maternels directs	..	..	28	♦5.8	..	..	36	8.2
Indirect obstetric causes — Décès maternels indirects	..	..	17	♦3.5	..	..	12	♦2.7
Certain conditions originating in the perinatal period — Certaines affections dont l'origine se situe dans la période périnatale	429	172.3	335	142.2	378	168.8	311	146.3
Congenital malformations, deformations and chromosomal abnormalities — Malformations congénitales et anomalies chromosomiques	257	103.2	242	102.7	249	111.2	260	122.3
Symptoms, signs and abnormal clinical and laboratory findings, not elsewhere classified — Symptômes, signes et résultats anormaux d'examens cliniques et de laboratoire, non classés ailleurs	11 137	44.2	13 978	55.6	10 863	43.0	13 703	54.2
All other diseases — Toutes autres maladies	144	0.6	302	1.2	126	0.5	305	1.2
External causes — Causes externes								
Total	21 108	83.8	10 045	39.9	21 144	83.6	9 871	39.1
Accidents								
Total	9 248	36.7	4 194	16.7	8 906	35.2	4 176	16.5
Transport accidents — Accidents de transport	4 785	19.0	1 717	6.8	4 398	17.4	1 630	6.4
Falls — Chutes	1 577	6.3	527	2.1	1 761	7.0	572	2.3
Accidental drowning and submersion — Noyade et submersion accidentelles	571	2.3	141	0.6	491	1.9	131	0.5
Exposure to smoke, fire and flames — Exposition à la fumée, au feu et aux flammes	217	0.9	94	0.4	203	0.8	96	0.4
Accidental poisoning by and exposure to noxious substances — Intoxication accidentelle par des substances nocives et exposition à ces substances	213	0.8	69	0.3	175	0.7	77	0.3
Intentional self-harm — Lésions auto-infligées	9 622	38.2	4 538	18.0	10 060	39.8	4 367	17.3
Assault — Agresssions	297	1.2	245	1.0	300	1.2	264	1.0
All other external causes — Toutes autres causes externes	1 941	7.7	1 068	4.2	1 878	7.4	1 064	4.2

Cause of death — Cause de décès	Saudi Arabia - Arabie saoudite		Singapore - Singapour			
	2012 (U)		2013 (+U)		2014 (+U)	
	Male — Masculin	Female — Féminin	Male — Masculin	Female — Féminin	Male — Masculin	Female — Féminin
	Number Nombre	Number Nombre	Number Nombre	Number Nombre	Number Nombre	Number Nombre
TOTAL	29 994	15 642	9 624	8 186	9 802	8 434
Certain infectious and parasitic diseases — Certaines maladies infectieuses et parasitaires						
Total	808	614	129	64	130	65
Intestinal infectious diseases — Maladies infectieuses intestinales	66	54	8	20	13	20
Tuberculosis — Tuberculose	135	127	35	11	41	14
Tetanus — Tétanos	5	1	-	-	-	-
Diphtheria — Diphtérie	-	-	-	-	-	-
Whooping cough — Coqueluche	-	1	-	-	-	-
Meningococcal infection — Infection à méningocoques	-	-	1	-	-	-
Septicaemia — Septicémie	449	348	24	21	16	19
Acute poliomyelitis — Poliomyélite aiguë	-	-	-	-	-	-
Measles — Rougeole	1	-	-	-	-	-
Viral hepatitis — Hépatite virale	45	23	4	4	1	-
Human immunodeficiency virus [HIV] disease — Maladies dues au virus de l'immunodéficience humaine (VIH)	84	50	41	3	46	1
Malaria — Paludisme	9	1	-	-	-	-
Neoplasms — Tumeurs	1 094	936	3 069	2 492	3 038	2 470
Malignant neoplasms — Tumeurs malignes						
Total	1 091	935	3 026	2 467	2 997	2 431
Malignant neoplasm of lip, oral cavity and pharynx — Tumeur maligne de la lèvre, de la cavité buccale et du pharynx	26	23	185	51	180	68
Malignant neoplasm of oesophagus — Tumeur maligne de l'oesophage	16	17	83	20	70	21
Malignant neoplasm of stomach — Tumeur maligne de l'estomac	48	43	184	138	164	130
Malignant neoplasm of colon, rectosigmoid junction, rectum, anus and anal canal — Tumeur maligne du côlon, de la jonction recto-sigmoïdienne, du rectum, de l'anus et du canal anal	107	67	409	391	405	377
Malignant neoplasm of liver and intrahepatic bile ducts — Tumeur maligne du foie et des voies bilaires intrahépatiques	175	88	359	162	393	165
Malignant neoplasm of pancreas — Tumeur maligne du pancréas	46	31	156	136	164	127
Malignant neoplasm of trachea, bronchus and lung — Tumeur maligne de la trachée, des bronches et du poumon	113	51	805	404	828	398
Malignant neoplasm of female breast — Tumeur maligne du sein chez la femme	..	149	..	451	..	411
Malignant neoplasm of cervix uteri — Tumeur maligne du col de l'utérus	..	10	..	69	..	77
Malignant neoplasm of prostate — Tumeur maligne de la prostate	51	..	180	..	173	..
Malignant neoplasm of lymphoid, haematopoietic and related tissue — Tumeurs malignes primitives ou présumées primitives des tissus lymphoïde, hématopoïétique et apparentés	121	95	212	142	192	144
Disorders of the blood and blood-forming organs and certain disorders involving the immune mechanism — Maladies du sang et des organes hématopoïétiques et certains troubles du système immunitaire						
Total	135	133	4	8	10	8
Anaemias — Anémies	83	79	1	3	5	2
Endocrine, nutritional and metabolic diseases — Maladies endocriniennes, nutritionnelles et métaboliques						
Total	668	531	97	147	124	161
Diabetes mellitus — Diabète sucré	546	404	96	144	114	154
Malnutrition — Malnutrition	16	8	-	-	-	-
Mental and behavioural disorders — Troubles mentaux et du comportement	2	1	-	3	-	1
Diseases of the nervous system — Maladies du système nerveux	287	228	70	60	72	64
Diseases of the circulatory system — Maladies de l'appareil circulatoire						
Total	4 854	3 362	2 997	2 395	3 064	2 540
Acute rheumatic fever and chronic rheumatic heart diseases — Rhumatisme articularie aigu et cardiopathies rhumatismales chroniques	9	9	11	11	9	19
Hypertensive diseases — Maladies hypertensives	726	638	318	246	351	312
Ischaemic heart disease — Cardiopathie ischémique	1 385	693	1 712	1 044	1 741	1 151
Cerebrovascular disease — Maladie cérébrovasculaire	1 350	1 055	723	857	714	823
Diseases of arteries, arterioles and capillaries — Maladies des artères, artérioles et capillaires	18	7	83	68	102	80

Cause of death — Cause de décès	Saudi Arabia - Arabie saoudite		Singapore - Singapour			
	2012 (U)		2013 (+U)		2014 (+U)	
	Male — Masculin	Female — Féminin	Male — Masculin	Female — Féminin	Male — Masculin	Female — Féminin
	Number Nombre	Number Nombre	Number Nombre	Number Nombre	Number Nombre	Number Nombre
Diseases of the respiratory system — Maladies de l'appareil respiratoire						
Total	1 093	833	2 043	1 875	2 133	1 944
Influenza — Grippe	1	-	-	-	-	-
Pneumonia — Pneumopathies	625	444	1 689	1 707	1 754	1 803
Chronic lower respiratory diseases — Maladies chroniques des voies respiratoires inférieures	204	160	301	117	325	105
Diseases of the digestive system — Maladies de l'appareil digestif						
Total	542	300	204	185	241	210
Gastric and duodenal ulcer — Ulcère de l'estomac et du duodénum	17	12	24	17	24	10
Diseases of the liver — Maladies du foie	406	204	92	64	105	68
Diseases of the musculoskeletal system and connective tissue — Maladies du système ostéo-articularie, des muscles et du tissu conjonctif	2	22	32	27	39	38
Diseases of the genitourinary system — Maladies de l'appareil génito-urinaire						
Total	928	630	339	608	333	596
Disorders of kidney and ureter — Affections du rein et de l'uretère	882	594	193	269	183	236
Hyperplasia of prostate — Hyperplasie de la prostate	-	..	-	..	-	..
Pregnancy, childbirth and the puerperium — Grossesse, accouchement et puerpéralité						
Total	..	45	..	-	..	-
Pregnancy with abortive outcome — Grossesse se terminant par un avortement	..	1	..	-	..	-
Other direct obstetric causes — Autres décès maternels directs	..	42	..	-	..	-
Indirect obstetric causes — Décès maternels indirects	..	1	..	-	..	-
Certain conditions originating in the perinatal period — Certaines affections dont l'origine se situe dans la période périnatale	2 055	1 567	13	18	18	20
Congenital malformations, deformations and chromosomal abnormalities — Malformations congénitales et anomalies chromosomiques	667	577	18	20	25	18
Symptoms, signs and abnormal clinical and laboratory findings, not elsewhere classified — Symptômes, signes et résultats anormaux d'examens cliniques et de laboratoire, non classés ailleurs	9 127	4 554	27	27	26	22
All other diseases — Toutes autres maladies	108	73	38	74	45	73
External causes — Causes externes						
Total	7 624	1 236	544	183	504	204
Accidents						
Total	2 788	386	252	57	213	83
Transport accidents — Accidents de transport	2 426	318	104	13	102	26
Falls — Chutes	165	24	95	34	71	40
Accidental drowning and submersion — Noyade et submersion accidentelles	10	3	6	1	5	-
Exposure to smoke, fire and flames — Exposition à la fumée, au feu et aux flammes	-	-	3	-	2	1
Accidental poisoning by and exposure to noxious substances — Intoxication accidentelle par des substances nocives et exposition à ces substances	-	-	11	3	7	2
Intentional self-harm — Lésions auto-infligées	59	17	245	112	250	105
Assault — Agresssions	-	-	5	3	4	5
All other external causes — Toutes autres causes externes	4 777	833	42	11	37	11

20. Death and death rates by cause and sex: 2010 - 2014
Décès et taux de mortalité par cause et sexe : 2010 - 2014 (continued - suite)

Cause of death — Cause de décès	Syrian Arab Republic - République arabe syrienne 2010 (+C)				Thailand - Thaïlande 2013 (+U)		2014 (+U)	
	Male — Masculin		Female — Féminin		Male — Masculin	Female — Féminin	Male — Masculin	Female — Féminin
	Number Nombre	Rate Taux	Number Nombre	Rate Taux	Number Nombre	Number Nombre	Number Nombre	Number Nombre
TOTAL	38 220	362.7	28 804	285.8	241 819	184 246	245 902	189 722
Certain infectious and parasitic diseases — Certaines maladies infectieuses et parasitaires								
Total	853	8.1	714	7.1	23 849	18 612	23 385	18 095
Intestinal infectious diseases — Maladies infectieuses intestinales	39	0.4	42	0.4	771	739	868	886
Tuberculosis — Tuberculose	17	◆0.2	6	◆0.1	3 921	1 575	4 202	1 734
Tetanus — Tétanos..............................	5	◆0.0	2	◆0.0	24	12	24	11
Diphtheria — Diphtérie..............................	-	-	-	-	6	4	1	2
Whooping cough — Coqueluche	-	-	2	◆0.0	-	-	-	-
Meningococcal infection — Infection à méningocoques	-	-	-	-	3	1	4	2
Septicaemia — Septicémie..............................	662	6.3	569	5.6	13 556	12 967	13 001	12 382
Acute poliomyelitis — Poliomyélite aiguë	2	◆0.0	1	◆0.0	-	-	-	-
Measles — Rougeole..............................	-	-	-	-	-	1	-	-
Viral hepatitis — Hépatite virale..............................	68	0.6	44	0.4	433	192	430	214
Human immunodeficiency virus [HIV] disease — Maladies dues au virus de l'immunodéficience humaine (VIH)..............................	-	-	-	-	3 649	2 034	3 641	2 064
Malaria — Paludisme..............................	-	-	-	-	31	11	29	9
Neoplasms — Tumeurs	2 394	22.7	1 774	17.6	38 965	28 726	40 161	29 914
Malignant neoplasms — Tumeurs malignes								
Total	2 368	22.5	1 668	16.5	38 689	28 492	39 935	29 738
Malignant neoplasm of lip, oral cavity and pharynx — Tumeur maligne de la lèvre, de la cavité buccale et du pharynx	17	◆0.2	11	◆0.1	1 693	782	1 769	826
Malignant neoplasm of oesophagus — Tumeur maligne de l'oesophage	16	◆0.2	11	◆0.1	1 208	205	1 319	229
Malignant neoplasm of stomach — Tumeur maligne de l'estomac	164	1.6	118	1.2	772	729	907	753
Malignant neoplasm of colon, rectosigmoid junction, rectum, anus and anal canal — Tumeur maligne du côlon, de la jonction recto-sigmoïdienne, du rectum, de l'anus et du canal anal	102	1.0	123	1.2	1 866	1 541	1 843	1 573
Malignant neoplasm of liver and intrahepatic bile ducts — Tumeur maligne du foie et des voies bilaires intrahépatiques	129	1.2	105	1.0	10 874	4 541	10 800	4 505
Malignant neoplasm of pancreas — Tumeur maligne du pancréas..............................	96	0.9	54	0.5	568	510	632	551
Malignant neoplasm of trachea, bronchus and lung — Tumeur maligne de la trachée, des bronches et du poumon	517	4.9	174	1.7	7 756	3 913	7 934	4 151
Malignant neoplasm of female breast — Tumeur maligne du sein chez la femme	..	..	201	3.2	..	3 246	..	3 455
Malignant neoplasm of cervix uteri — Tumeur maligne du col de l'utérus.........	..	..	16	◆0.3	..	2 031	..	2 062
Malignant neoplasm of prostate — Tumeur maligne de la prostate	154	11.2	..	..	1 069	..	1 156	..
Malignant neoplasm of lymphoid, haematopoietic and related tissue — Tumeurs malignes primitives ou présumées primitives des tissus lymphoïde, hématopoïétique et apparentés..............................	288	2.7	180	1.8	1 601	1 373	1 525	1 249
Disorders of the blood and blood-forming organs and certain disorders involving the immune mechanism — Maladies du sang et des organes hématopoïétiques et certains troubles du système immunitaire								
Total	79	0.7	81	0.8	361	419	324	400
Anaemias — Anémies	70	0.7	77	0.8	201	239	180	238
Endocrine, nutritional and metabolic diseases — Maladies endocriniennes, nutritionnelles et métaboliques								
Total	571	5.4	600	6.0	4 805	6 724	5 563	7 740
Diabetes mellitus — Diabète sucré..............................	355	3.4	396	3.9	3 888	5 815	4 613	6 776
Malnutrition — Malnutrition	13	◆0.1	5	◆0.0	126	131	117	156
Mental and behavioural disorders — Troubles mentaux et du comportement	36	0.3	35	0.3	806	111	928	115
Diseases of the nervous system — Maladies du système nerveux..................	349	3.3	295	2.9	3 631	3 723	3 960	4 545
Diseases of the circulatory system — Maladies de l'appareil circulatoire								
Total	18 488	175.4	15 292	151.7	30 777	23 593	32 817	25 859
Acute rheumatic fever and chronic rheumatic heart diseases — Rhumatisme articulaire aigu et cardiopathies rhumatismales chroniques	29	◆0.3	38	0.4	48	67	43	79
Hypertensive diseases — Maladies hypertensives..............................	274	2.6	322	3.2	2 578	2 608	3 357	3 758
Ischaemic heart disease — Cardiopathie ischémique	5 934	56.3	3 976	39.4	10 266	7 128	10 761	7 318

672

Cause of death — Cause de décès	Syrian Arab Republic - République arabe syrienne				Thailand - Thaïlande			
	2010 (+C)				2013 (+U)		2014 (+U)	
	Male — Masculin		Female — Féminin		Male — Masculin	Female — Féminin	Male — Masculin	Female — Féminin
	Number Nombre	Rate Taux	Number Nombre	Rate Taux	Number Nombre	Number Nombre	Number Nombre	Number Nombre
Cerebrovascular disease — Maladie cérébrovasculaire	1 983	18.8	1 546	15.3	13 336	9 886	14 216	10 894
Diseases of arteries, arterioles and capillaries — Maladies des artères, artérioles et capillaires	62	0.6	40	0.4	658	446	745	429
Diseases of the respiratory system — Maladies de l'appareil respiratoire								
Total	7 558	71.7	4 635	46.0	20 831	13 002	24 203	15 434
Influenza — Grippe	1	◆0.0	8	◆0.1	6	6	31	26
Pneumonia — Pneumopathies	5 337	50.6	3 028	30.0	11 613	8 480	14 128	10 174
Chronic lower respiratory diseases — Maladies chroniques des voies respiratoires inférieures	185	1.8	141	1.4	5 366	1 927	5 668	2 218
Diseases of the digestive system — Maladies de l'appareil digestif								
Total	1 006	9.5	805	8.0	11 500	5 156	12 001	5 457
Gastric and duodenal ulcer — Ulcère de l'estomac et du duodénum	18	◆0.2	5	◆0.0	194	128	236	137
Diseases of the liver — Maladies du foie	798	7.6	658	6.5	6 885	2 673	7 098	2 734
Diseases of the musculoskeletal system and connective tissue — Maladies du système ostéo-articularie, des muscles et du tissu conjonctif	1	◆0.0	5	◆0.0	798	1 067	864	1 104
Diseases of the genitourinary system — Maladies de l'appareil génito-urinaire								
Total	491	4.7	491	4.9	8 116	8 662	9 364	10 306
Disorders of kidney and ureter — Affections du rein et de l'uretère	484	4.6	482	4.8	7 466	7 696	8 419	8 752
Hyperplasia of prostate — Hyperplasie de la prostate	-	-	..	..	111	..	120	..
Pregnancy, childbirth and the puerperium — Grossesse, accouchement et puerpéralité								
Total	..	..	23	◆2.6	..	166	..	166
Pregnancy with abortive outcome — Grossesse se terminant par un avortement	..	..	-	-	..	30	..	19
Other direct obstetric causes — Autres décès maternels directs	..	..	14	◆1.6	..	101	..	112
Indirect obstetric causes — Décès maternels indirects	..	..	-	-	..	35	..	35
Certain conditions originating in the perinatal period — Certaines affections dont l'origine se situe dans la période périnatale	1 515	354.3	1 045	236.1	1 470	1 089	1 283	1 005
Congenital malformations, deformations and chromosomal abnormalities — Malformations congénitales et anomalies chromosomiques	1 095	256.1	852	192.5	714	674	785	667
Symptoms, signs and abnormal clinical and laboratory findings, not elsewhere classified — Symptômes, signes et résultats anormaux d'examens cliniques et de laboratoire, non classés ailleurs	1 433	13.6	1 395	13.8	63 253	63 166	59 071	59 446
All other diseases — Toutes autres maladies	5	◆0.0	6	◆0.1	914	974	1 050	1 161
External causes — Causes externes								
Total	2 346	22.3	756	7.5	31 029	8 382	30 143	8 308
Accidents								
Total	1 562	14.8	460	4.6	18 896	5 352	18 603	5 351
Transport accidents — Accidents de transport	1 162	11.0	315	3.1	11 595	3 206	11 783	3 286
Falls — Chutes	138	1.3	63	0.6	1 332	440	1 497	510
Accidental drowning and submersion — Noyade et submersion accidentelles	108	1.0	24	◆0.2	2 958	754	2 838	730
Exposure to smoke, fire and flames — Exposition à la fumée, au feu et aux flammes	-	-	-	-	172	78	186	87
Accidental poisoning by and exposure to noxious substances — Intoxication accidentelle par des substances nocives et exposition à ces substances	17	◆0.2	12	◆0.1	48	28	43	37
Intentional self-harm — Lésions auto-infligées	26	◆0.2	6	◆0.1	3 105	856	3 074	878
Assault — Agresssions	170	1.6	43	0.4	2 628	395	2 248	404
All other external causes — Toutes autres causes externes	588	5.6	247	2.5	6 400	1 779	6 218	1 675

20. Death and death rates by cause and sex: 2010 - 2014
Décès et taux de mortalité par cause et sexe : 2010 - 2014 (continued - suite)

Cause of death — Cause de décès	Turkey - Turquie				Turkmenistan - Turkménistan			
	2012 (+U)		2013 (+U)		2012 (U)		2013 (U)	
	Male — Masculin	Female — Féminin	Male — Masculin	Female — Féminin	Male — Masculin	Female — Féminin	Male — Masculin	Female — Féminin
	Number Nombre	Number Nombre	Number Nombre	Number Nombre	Number Nombre	Number Nombre	Number Nombre	Number Nombre
TOTAL	175 980	144 987	196 709	160 824	16 092	13 116	17 197	13 313
Certain infectious and parasitic diseases — Certaines maladies infectieuses et parasitaires								
Total	2 957	2 647	3 428	2 908	501	239	505	237
Intestinal infectious diseases — Maladies infectieuses intestinales	146	154	248	306	32	20	43	28
Tuberculosis — Tuberculose	303	149	255	129	319	112	289	103
Tetanus — Tétanos...	2	7	5	3	-	-	-	-
Diphtheria — Diphtérie..	-	1	-	-	-	-	-	-
Whooping cough — Coqueluche	-	-	-	-	-	-	-	-
Meningococcal infection — Infection à méningocoques	11	4	13	9	1	-	7	3
Septicaemia — Septicémie	1 623	1 722	1 822	1 698	70	77	84	53
Acute poliomyelitis — Poliomyélite aiguë	-	-	-	-	-	-	-	-
Measles — Rougeole...	-	-	2	5	-	-	-	-
Viral hepatitis — Hépatite virale...	445	314	540	390	56	14	39	19
Human immunodeficiency virus [HIV] disease — Maladies dues au virus de l'immunodéficience humaine (VIH)..	53	8	54	16	-	-	-	-
Malaria — Paludisme	1	1	4	-	-	-	-	-
Neoplasms — Tumeurs	44 924	24 345	49 700	26 523	1 242	1 296	1 195	1 306
Malignant neoplasms — Tumeurs malignes								
Total	44 105	23 672	48 797	25 802	1 235	1 292	1 181	1 290
Malignant neoplasm of lip, oral cavity and pharynx — Tumeur maligne de la lèvre, de la cavité buccale et du pharynx	458	232	542	292	92	62	75	39
Malignant neoplasm of oesophagus — Tumeur maligne de l'oesophage	403	263	491	325	118	121	107	111
Malignant neoplasm of stomach — Tumeur maligne de l'estomac	3 672	2 022	4 317	2 294	172	87	172	96
Malignant neoplasm of colon, rectosigmoid junction, rectum, anus and anal canal — Tumeur maligne du côlon, de la jonction recto-sigmoïdienne, du rectum, de l'anus et du canal anal	3 261	2 449	3 720	2 702	81	64	56	48
Malignant neoplasm of liver and intrahepatic bile ducts — Tumeur maligne du foie et des voies bilaires intrahépatiques	1 624	848	1 817	1 018	96	66	81	63
Malignant neoplasm of pancreas — Tumeur maligne du pancréas...................	2 108	1 508	2 543	1 830	46	27	31	17
Malignant neoplasm of trachea, bronchus and lung — Tumeur maligne de la trachée, des bronches et du poumon	17 236	3 063	19 017	3 169	148	52	149	49
Malignant neoplasm of female breast — Tumeur maligne du sein chez la femme	..	2 852	..	3 541	..	236	..	252
Malignant neoplasm of cervix uteri — Tumeur maligne du col de l'utérus.........	..	405	..	515	..	169	..	159
Malignant neoplasm of prostate — Tumeur maligne de la prostate	2 900	..	3 526	..	30	..	32	..
Malignant neoplasm of lymphoid, haematopoietic and related tissue — Tumeurs malignes primitives ou présumées primitives des tissus lymphoïde, hématopoïétique et apparentés...	3 152	2 294	3 523	2 606	...	...	...	...
Disorders of the blood and blood-forming organs and certain disorders involving the immune mechanism — Maladies du sang et des organes hématopoïétiques et certains troubles du système immunitaire								
Total	640	737	684	800	40	19	32	27
Anaemias — Anémies	276	344	286	374	21	16	18	17
Endocrine, nutritional and metabolic diseases — Maladies endocriniennes, nutritionnelles et métaboliques								
Total	8 174	11 084	8 529	11 501	242	272	231	293
Diabetes mellitus — Diabète sucré..	6 876	9 423	6 908	9 435	237	262	221	278
Malnutrition — Malnutrition	130	165	194	319	-	2	3	1
Mental and behavioural disorders — Troubles mentaux et du comportement	355	271	285	275	13	5	15	5
Diseases of the nervous system — Maladies du système nerveux.................	6 330	7 427	6 756	7 896	166	132	187	153
Diseases of the circulatory system — Maladies de l'appareil circulatoire								
Total	60 548	61 200	70 477	71 750	7 324	6 862	7 701	6 606
Acute rheumatic fever and chronic rheumatic heart diseases — Rhumatisme articularie aigu et cardiopathies rhumatismales chroniques	70	130	95	214	33	51	36	33
Hypertensive diseases — Maladies hypertensives...	5 465	8 828	7 009	11 129	1 332	1 370	1 584	1 407
Ischaemic heart disease — Cardiopathie ischémique	22 980	15 009	32 257	22 987	3 545	3 121	3 493	2 968

20. Death and death rates by cause and sex: 2010 - 2014
Décès et taux de mortalité par cause et sexe : 2010 - 2014 (continued - suite)

Cause of death — Cause de décès	Turkey - Turquie				Turkmenistan - Turkménistan			
	2012 (+U)		2013 (+U)		2012 (U)		2013 (U)	
	Male — Masculin	Female — Féminin	Male — Masculin	Female — Féminin	Male — Masculin	Female — Féminin	Male — Masculin	Female — Féminin
	Number Nombre	Number Nombre	Number Nombre	Number Nombre	Number Nombre	Number Nombre	Number Nombre	Number Nombre
Cerebrovascular disease — Maladie cérébrovasculaire..................................	14 045	17 262	16 167	19 704	1 978	1 927	2 003	1 745
Diseases of arteries, arterioles and capillaries — Maladies des artères, artérioles et capillaires	1 391	830	1 534	841	...	...	...	...
Diseases of the respiratory system — Maladies de l'appareil respiratoire								
Total	18 784	12 240	21 077	14 073	821	627	993	726
Influenza — Grippe	15	26	52	49	3	2	17	7
Pneumonia — Pneumopathies	2 265	2 089	3 505	3 126	381	293	430	324
Chronic lower respiratory diseases — Maladies chroniques des voies respiratoires inférieures	13 292	7 417	15 007	8 762	89	62	105	67
Diseases of the digestive system — Maladies de l'appareil digestif								
Total	4 440	3 921	5 038	4 415	1 187	763	1 275	802
Gastric and duodenal ulcer — Ulcère de l'estomac et du duodénum...............	185	148	322	198	82	17	82	37
Diseases of the liver — Maladies du foie..	1 856	1 281	2 015	1 409	1 038	674	1 115	698
Diseases of the musculoskeletal system and connective tissue — Maladies du système ostéo-articulaire, des muscles et du tissu conjonctif	510	849	393	738	14	21	16	25
Diseases of the genitourinary system — Maladies de l'appareil génito-urinaire								
Total	5 450	5 099	5 518	5 233	235	232	243	179
Disorders of kidney and ureter — Affections du rein et de l'uretère	4 790	4 643	4 770	4 718	...	...	...	...
Hyperplasia of prostate — Hyperplasie de la prostate............................	247	..	276	..	...	..	...	..
Pregnancy, childbirth and the puerperium — Grossesse, accouchement et puerpéralité								
Total	..	55	..	302	..	7	..	9
Pregnancy with abortive outcome — Grossesse se terminant par un avortement	..	-	..	2	..	-	..	1
Other direct obstetric causes — Autres décès maternels directs	..	49	..	155	..	6	..	8
Indirect obstetric causes — Décès maternels indirects	..	6	..	141	..	-	..	-
Certain conditions originating in the perinatal period — Certaines affections dont l'origine se situe dans la période périnatale	3 075	2 496	3 863	2 928	701	519	780	505
Congenital malformations, deformations and chromosomal abnormalities — Malformations congénitales et anomalies chromosomiques	2 036	1 887	2 505	2 299	501	394	450	370
Symptoms, signs and abnormal clinical and laboratory findings, not elsewhere classified — Symptômes, signes et résultats anormaux d'examens cliniques et de laboratoire, non classés ailleurs	8 295	6 787	4 054	3 707	2 169	1 393	2 520	1 557
All other diseases — Toutes autres maladies..	99	132	110	160	3	-	3	3
External causes — Causes externes								
Total	9 363	3 810	14 292	5 316	933	335	1 051	510
Accidents								
Total	7 427	3 202	10 627	4 300	...	...	...	...
Transport accidents — Accidents de transport	3 193	920	5 146	1 531	142	39	116	28
Falls — Chutes	1 343	1 364	1 861	1 747	18	5	22	5
Accidental drowning and submersion — Noyade et submersion accidentelles..	154	46	527	119	66	16	52	14
Exposure to smoke, fire and flames — Exposition à la fumée, au feu et aux flammes	115	60	224	125	25	25	28	30
Accidental poisoning by and exposure to noxious substances — Intoxication accidentelle par des substances nocives et exposition à ces substances	161	134	378	152	38	29	31	15
Intentional self-harm — Lésions auto-infligées....................................	1 072	378	1 348	462	105	33	73	28
Assault — Agresssions..	791	153	1 074	227	50	29	57	27
All other external causes — Toutes autres causes externes	73	77	1 243	327	...	...	...	...

20. Death and death rates by cause and sex: 2010 - 2014
Décès et taux de mortalité par cause et sexe : 2010 - 2014 (continued - suite)

Cause of death — Cause de décès	United Arab Emirates - Émirats arabes unis 2010 (+U)		Uzbekistan - Ouzbékistan 2014 (U)		Austria - Autriche 2013 (C)			
	Male — Masculin	Female — Féminin	Male — Masculin	Female — Féminin	Male — Masculin		Female — Féminin	
	Number Nombre	Number Nombre	Number Nombre	Number Nombre	Number Nombre	Rate Taux	Number Nombre	Rate Taux
TOTAL	5 281	2 132	*81 465*	*68 296*	37 958	920.5	41 568	960.4
Certain infectious and parasitic diseases — Certaines maladies infectieuses et parasitaires								
Total	24	8	*1 987*	*1 066*	366	8.9	370	8.5
Intestinal infectious diseases — Maladies infectieuses intestinales	1	2	58	43	35	0.8	58	1.3
Tuberculosis — Tuberculose	23	6	*1 253*	569	36	0.9	18	♦0.4
Tetanus — Tétanos	-	-	-	-	-	-	1	♦0.0
Diphtheria — Diphtérie	...	...	-	-	-	-	-	-
Whooping cough — Coqueluche	-	-	-	-	-	-	1	♦0.0
Meningococcal infection — Infection à méningocoques	1	-	16	14	6	♦0.1	2	♦0.0
Septicaemia — Septicémie	138	112	278	216	44	1.1	63	1.5
Acute poliomyelitis — Poliomyélite aiguë	...	...	-	-	-	-	-	-
Measles — Rougeole	-	-	1	1	1	♦0.0	-	-
Viral hepatitis — Hépatite virale	...	...	139	103	126	3.1	123	2.8
Human immunodeficiency virus [HIV] disease — Maladies dues au virus de l'immunodéficience humaine (VIH)	...	...	212	97	40	1.0	11	♦0.3
Malaria — Paludisme	2	1	-	-	-	-	-	-
Neoplasms — Tumeurs	...	...	*6 005*	*6 309*	11 115	269.5	9 661	223.2
Malignant neoplasms — Tumeurs malignes								
Total	...	...	*5 970*	*6 253*	10 818	262.3	9 279	214.4
Malignant neoplasm of lip, oral cavity and pharynx — Tumeur maligne de la lèvre, de la cavité buccale et du pharynx			327	196	338	8.2	119	2.7
Malignant neoplasm of oesophagus — Tumeur maligne de l'oesophage	...	...	336	282	287	7.0	71	1.6
Malignant neoplasm of stomach — Tumeur maligne de l'estomac	23	19	978	671	496	12.0	379	8.8
Malignant neoplasm of colon, rectosigmoid junction, rectum, anus and anal canal — Tumeur maligne du côlon, de la jonction recto-sigmoïdienne, du rectum, de l'anus et du canal anal	22	18	374	304	1 184	28.7	994	23.0
Malignant neoplasm of liver and intrahepatic bile ducts — Tumeur maligne du foie et des voies bilaires intrahépatiques	...	...	503	394	613	14.9	284	6.6
Malignant neoplasm of pancreas — Tumeur maligne du pancréas	...	...	183	167	717	17.4	771	17.8
Malignant neoplasm of trachea, bronchus and lung — Tumeur maligne de la trachée, des bronches et du poumon	72	23	916	353	2 411	58.5	1 301	30.1
Malignant neoplasm of female breast — Tumeur maligne du sein chez la femme	..	73	..	*1 226*	..	..	1 568	42.0
Malignant neoplasm of cervix uteri — Tumeur maligne du col de l'utérus	..	14	..	626	..	..	146	3.9
Malignant neoplasm of prostate — Tumeur maligne de la prostate	...	..	167	..	1 144	78.2	..	..
Malignant neoplasm of lymphoid, haematopoietic and related tissue — Tumeurs malignes primitives ou présumées primitives des tissus lymphoïde, hématopoïétique et apparentés	...	...	496	387	931	22.6	808	18.7
Disorders of the blood and blood-forming organs and certain disorders involving the immune mechanism — Maladies du sang et des organes hématopoïétiques et certains troubles du système immunitaire								
Total	...	...	167	163	87	2.1	111	2.6
Anaemias — Anémies	23	18	125	134	29	♦0.7	53	1.2
Endocrine, nutritional and metabolic diseases — Maladies endocriniennes, nutritionnelles et métaboliques								
Total	...	...	*2 387*	*2 466*	1 701	41.3	2 139	49.4
Diabetes mellitus — Diabète sucré	181	126	*2 356*	*2 419*	1 233	29.9	1 639	37.9
Malnutrition — Malnutrition	5	8	4	4	-	-	-	-
Mental and behavioural disorders — Troubles mentaux et du comportement	3	1	26	12	817	19.8	799	18.5
Diseases of the nervous system — Maladies du système nerveux	350	219	*1 581*	*1 051*	1 215	29.5	1 690	39.0
Diseases of the circulatory system — Maladies de l'appareil circulatoire								
Total	507	254	*47 415*	*43 442*	14 257	345.7	19 844	458.5
Acute rheumatic fever and chronic rheumatic heart diseases — Rhumatisme articulaire aigu et cardiopathies rhumatismales chroniques	...	...	231	336	69	1.7	149	3.4
Hypertensive diseases — Maladies hypertensives	149	101	*10 292*	*9 827*	1 325	32.1	3 227	74.6
Ischaemic heart disease — Cardiopathie ischémique	134	45	*22 300*	*19 592*	7 266	176.2	7 571	174.9

Cause of death — Cause de décès	United Arab Emirates - Émirats arabes unis 2010 (+U)		Uzbekistan - Ouzbékistan 2014 (U)		Austria - Autriche 2013 (C)			
	Male — Masculin	Female — Féminin	Male — Masculin	Female — Féminin	Male — Masculin		Female — Féminin	
	Number Nombre	Number Nombre	Number Nombre	Number Nombre	Number Nombre	Rate Taux	Number Nombre	Rate Taux
Cerebrovascular disease — Maladie cérébrovasculaire	224	108	7 588	6 673	1 990	48.3	3 160	73.0
Diseases of arteries, arterioles and capillaries — Maladies des artères, artérioles et capillaires	143	47	1 783	2 350	600	14.6	716	16.5
Diseases of the respiratory system — Maladies de l'appareil respiratoire								
Total	355	68	4 166	3 287	2 132	51.7	1 818	42.0
Influenza — Grippe	1	-	101	110	19	♦0.5	16	♦0.4
Pneumonia — Pneumopathies	117	77	1 905	1 461	313	7.6	426	9.8
Chronic lower respiratory diseases — Maladies chroniques des voies respiratoires inférieures	20	12	902	725	1 589	38.5	1 199	27.7
Diseases of the digestive system — Maladies de l'appareil digestif								
Total	...	...	5 032	3 679	1 635	39.6	1 361	31.4
Gastric and duodenal ulcer — Ulcère de l'estomac et du duodénum	7	7	354	183	78	1.9	104	2.4
Diseases of the liver — Maladies du foie	87	34	4 192	3 115	1 103	26.7	437	10.1
Diseases of the musculoskeletal system and connective tissue — Maladies du système ostéo-articularie, des muscles et du tissu conjonctif	...	...	60	105	86	2.1	169	3.9
Diseases of the genitourinary system — Maladies de l'appareil génito-urinaire								
Total	...	...	1 500	1 177	558	13.5	857	19.8
Disorders of kidney and ureter — Affections du rein et de l'uretère	82	53	1 430	1 158	481	11.7	701	16.2
Hyperplasia of prostate — Hyperplasie de la prostate	-	..	36	..	10	♦0.7	..	..
Pregnancy, childbirth and the puerperium — Grossesse, accouchement et puerpéralité								
Total	..	4	..	131	..	..	1	♦1.3
Pregnancy with abortive outcome — Grossesse se terminant par un avortement	..	1	..	4	..	..	-	-
Other direct obstetric causes — Autres décès maternels directs	..	3	..	109	..	..	1	♦1.3
Indirect obstetric causes — Décès maternels indirects	..	...	..	17	..	..	-	-
Certain conditions originating in the perinatal period — Certaines affections dont l'origine se situe dans la période périnatale	113	87	2 439	1 764	78	190.5	47	122.5
Congenital malformations, deformations and chromosomal abnormalities — Malformations congénitales et anomalies chromosomiques	139	114	475	371	141	344.3	120	312.7
Symptoms, signs and abnormal clinical and laboratory findings, not elsewhere classified — Symptômes, signes et résultats anormaux d'examens cliniques et de laboratoire, non classés ailleurs	1 065	274	1 261	994	1 042	25.3	946	21.9
All other diseases — Toutes autres maladies	...	...	16	19	20	♦0.5	40	0.9
External causes — Causes externes								
Total	927	148	6 948	2 260	2 708	65.7	1 595	36.9
Accidents								
Total	816	120	4 720	1 315	1 436	34.8	1 067	24.7
Transport accidents — Accidents de transport	630	92	2 048	494	352	8.5	107	2.5
Falls — Chutes	133	16	234	45	467	11.3	386	8.9
Accidental drowning and submersion — Noyade et submersion accidentelles	...	...	624	205	38	0.9	15	♦0.3
Exposure to smoke, fire and flames — Exposition à la fumée, au feu et aux flammes	34	7	200	122	11	♦0.3	9	♦0.2
Accidental poisoning by and exposure to noxious substances — Intoxication accidentelle par des substances nocives et exposition à ces substances	16	5	276	102	11	♦0.3	8	♦0.2
Intentional self-harm — Lésions auto-infligées	89	23	1 408	690	967	23.5	324	7.5
Assault — Agresssions	22	5	309	107	15	♦0.4	21	♦0.5
All other external causes — Toutes autres causes externes	...	...	511	148	290	7.0	183	4.2

20. Death and death rates by cause and sex: 2010 - 2014
Décès et taux de mortalité par cause et sexe : 2010 - 2014 (continued - suite)

	Austria - Autriche				Belarus - Bélarus			
Cause of death — Cause de décès	2014 (C)				2013 (C)			
	Male — Masculin		Female — Féminin		Male — Masculin		Female — Féminin	
	Number Nombre	Rate Taux	Number Nombre	Rate Taux	Number Nombre	Rate Taux	Number Nombre	Rate Taux
TOTAL	37 424	900.6	40 828	938.0	63 012	1 432.3	62 314	1 229.9
Certain infectious and parasitic diseases — Certaines maladies infectieuses et parasitaires								
Total	364	8.8	348	8.0	720	16.4	245	4.8
Intestinal infectious diseases — Maladies infectieuses intestinales	28	♦0.7	54	1.2	3	♦0.1	3	♦0.1
Tuberculosis — Tuberculose	32	0.8	16	♦0.4	460	10.5	87	1.7
Tetanus — Tétanos	-	-	-	-	-	-	-	-
Diphtheria — Diphtérie..	-	-	-	-	-	-	-	-
Whooping cough — Coqueluche	1	♦0.0	-	-	-	-	-	-
Meningococcal infection — Infection à méningocoques...............................	1	♦0.0	-	-	9	♦0.2	4	♦0.1
Septicaemia — Septicémie	55	1.3	61	1.4	36	0.8	26	♦0.5
Acute poliomyelitis — Poliomyélite aiguë	-	-	-	-	-	-	-	-
Measles — Rougeole..	-	-	-	-	-	-	-	-
Viral hepatitis — Hépatite virale	133	3.2	132	3.0	13	♦0.3	5	♦0.1
Human immunodeficiency virus [HIV] disease — Maladies dues au virus de l'immunodéficience humaine (VIH)..	35	0.8	7	♦0.2	161	3.7	79	1.6
Malaria — Paludisme..	-	-	1	♦0.0	-	-	-	-
Neoplasms — Tumeurs	11 157	268.5	10 003	229.8	9 976	226.8	7 344	144.9
Malignant neoplasms — Tumeurs malignes								
Total	10 884	261.9	9 618	221.0	9 851	223.9	7 212	142.3
Malignant neoplasm of lip, oral cavity and pharynx — Tumeur maligne de la lèvre, de la cavité buccale et du pharynx	387	9.3	123	2.8	661	15.0	69	1.4
Malignant neoplasm of oesophagus — Tumeur maligne de l'oesophage	282	6.8	79	1.8	358	8.1	47	0.9
Malignant neoplasm of stomach — Tumeur maligne de l'estomac	493	11.9	360	8.3	1 171	26.6	768	15.2
Malignant neoplasm of colon, rectosigmoid junction, rectum, anus and anal canal — Tumeur maligne du côlon, de la jonction recto-sigmoïdienne, du rectum, de l'anus et du canal anal...	1 175	28.3	989	22.7	1 094	24.9	1 186	23.4
Malignant neoplasm of liver and intrahepatic bile ducts — Tumeur maligne du foie et des voies bilaires intrahépatiques	602	14.5	297	6.8	224	5.1	107	2.1
Malignant neoplasm of pancreas — Tumeur maligne du pancréas...................	786	18.9	833	19.1	443	10.1	401	7.9
Malignant neoplasm of trachea, bronchus and lung — Tumeur maligne de la trachée, des bronches et du poumon	2 450	59.0	1 458	33.5	2 477	56.3	339	6.7
Malignant neoplasm of female breast — Tumeur maligne du sein chez la femme	..	..	1 535	40.8	..	..	1 169	...
Malignant neoplasm of cervix uteri — Tumeur maligne du col de l'utérus..........	..	..	157	4.2	..	..	321	...
Malignant neoplasm of prostate — Tumeur maligne de la prostate	1 115	74.4	..	..	745	...	..	..
Malignant neoplasm of lymphoid, haematopoietic and related tissue — Tumeurs malignes primitives ou présumées primitives des tissus lymphoïde, hématopoïétique et apparentés...	903	21.7	861	19.8	...	...	...	...
Disorders of the blood and blood-forming organs and certain disorders involving the immune mechanism — Maladies du sang et des organes hématopoïétiques et certains troubles du système immunitaire								
Total	67	1.6	119	2.7	29	♦0.7	32	0.6
Anaemias — Anémies	23	♦0.6	69	1.6	11	♦0.3	11	♦0.2
Endocrine, nutritional and metabolic diseases — Maladies endocriniennes, nutritionnelles et métaboliques								
Total	1 824	43.9	2 139	49.1	132	3.0	165	3.3
Diabetes mellitus — Diabète sucré...	1 403	33.8	1 718	39.5	82	1.9	114	2.3
Malnutrition — Malnutrition	1	♦0.0	-	-	3	♦0.1	3	♦0.1
Mental and behavioural disorders — Troubles mentaux et du comportement	757	18.2	769	17.7	828	18.8	670	13.2
Diseases of the nervous system — Maladies du système nerveux..................	1 128	27.1	1 518	34.9	895	20.3	964	19.0
Diseases of the circulatory system — Maladies de l'appareil circulatoire								
Total	13 964	336.0	19 172	440.5	32 437	737.3	33 771	666.5
Acute rheumatic fever and chronic rheumatic heart diseases — Rhumatisme articularie aigu et cardiopathies rhumatismales chroniques	81	1.9	186	4.3	117	2.7	173	3.4
Hypertensive diseases — Maladies hypertensives.......................................	1 486	35.8	3 145	72.3	101	2.3	84	1.7
Ischaemic heart disease — Cardiopathie ischémique	7 041	169.4	7 244	166.4	23 586	536.1	24 032	474.3
Cerebrovascular disease — Maladie cérébrovasculaire................................	1 904	45.8	3 040	69.8	6 064	137.8	7 913	156.2

20. Death and death rates by cause and sex: 2010 - 2014
Décès et taux de mortalité par cause et sexe : 2010 - 2014 (continued - suite)

	Austria - Autriche				Belarus - Bélarus			
Cause of death — Cause de décès	2014 (C)				2013 (C)			
	Male — Masculin		Female — Féminin		Male — Masculin		Female — Féminin	
	Number Nombre	Rate Taux	Number Nombre	Rate Taux	Number Nombre	Rate Taux	Number Nombre	Rate Taux
Diseases of arteries, arterioles and capillaries — Maladies des artères, artérioles et capillaires	547	13.2	665	15.3	...	...	...	...
Diseases of the respiratory system — Maladies de l'appareil respiratoire								
Total	2 054	49.4	1 680	38.6	1 707	38.8	431	8.5
Influenza — Grippe..................................	5	♦0.1	8	♦0.2	3	♦0.1	-	-
Pneumonia — Pneumopathies	324	7.8	380	8.7	551	12.5	110	2.2
Chronic lower respiratory diseases — Maladies chroniques des voies respiratoires inférieures	1 491	35.9	1 131	26.0	978	22.2	265	5.2
Diseases of the digestive system — Maladies de l'appareil digestif								
Total	1 573	37.9	1 168	26.8	2 432	55.3	1 744	34.4
Gastric and duodenal ulcer — Ulcère de l'estomac et du duodénum.................	77	1.9	75	1.7	136	3.1	73	1.4
Diseases of the liver — Maladies du foie..........................	1 056	25.4	411	9.4	1 431	32.5	906	17.9
Diseases of the musculoskeletal system and connective tissue — Maladies du système ostéo-articularie, des muscles et du tissu conjonctif	82	2.0	164	3.8	39	0.9	112	2.2
Diseases of the genitourinary system — Maladies de l'appareil génito-urinaire								
Total	537	12.9	911	20.9	395	9.0	329	6.5
Disorders of kidney and ureter — Affections du rein et de l'uretère	465	11.2	775	17.8	...	...	...	...
Hyperplasia of prostate — Hyperplasie de la prostate.............................	9	♦0.6	..	..	...	...	...	...
Pregnancy, childbirth and the puerperium — Grossesse, accouchement et puerpéralité								
Total	..	..	7	♦8.6	..	..	-	-
Pregnancy with abortive outcome — Grossesse se terminant par un avortement	..	..	-	-	..	..	-	-
Other direct obstetric causes — Autres décès maternels directs	..	..	5	♦6.1	..	..	-	-
Indirect obstetric causes — Décès maternels indirects	..	..	2	♦2.4	..	..	-	-
Certain conditions originating in the perinatal period — Certaines affections dont l'origine se situe dans la période périnatale	69	163.7	65	164.3	107	176.1	76	132.8
Congenital malformations, deformations and chromosomal abnormalities — Malformations congénitales et anomalies chromosomiques	138	327.3	135	341.3	136	223.8	110	192.2
Symptoms, signs and abnormal clinical and laboratory findings, not elsewhere classified — Symptômes, signes et résultats anormaux d'examens cliniques et de laboratoire, non classés ailleurs	1 053	25.3	967	22.2	4 931	112.1	14 037	277.0
All other diseases — Toutes autres maladies................................	13	♦0.3	43	1.0	42	1.0	34	0.7
External causes — Causes externes								
Total	2 644	63.6	1 620	37.2	8 206	186.5	2 250	44.4
Accidents								
Total	1 332	32.1	1 085	24.9	...	...	...	...
Transport accidents — Accidents de transport..........................	334	8.0	115	2.6	832	18.9	286	5.6
Falls — Chutes	476	11.5	419	9.6	616	14.0	224	4.4
Accidental drowning and submersion — Noyade et submersion accidentelles..........................	22	♦0.5	8	♦0.2	493	11.2	83	1.6
Exposure to smoke, fire and flames — Exposition à la fumée, au feu et aux flammes..........................	9	♦0.2	16	♦0.4	521	11.8	183	3.6
Accidental poisoning by and exposure to noxious substances — Intoxication accidentelle par des substances nocives et exposition à ces substances	15	♦0.4	10	♦0.2	1 584	36.0	421	8.3
Intentional self-harm — Lésions auto-infligées.............................	989	23.8	324	7.4	1 569	35.7	334	6.6
Assault — Agresssions.............................	21	♦0.5	17	♦0.4	290	6.6	106	2.1
All other external causes — Toutes autres causes externes	302	7.3	194	4.5	...	...	...	...

20. Death and death rates by cause and sex: 2010 - 2014
Décès et taux de mortalité par cause et sexe : 2010 - 2014 (continued - suite)

Cause of death — Cause de décès	Belarus - Bélarus				Belgium - Belgique			
	2014 (C)				2012 (C)			
	Male — Masculin		Female — Féminin		Male — Masculin		Female — Féminin	
	Number Nombre	Rate Taux	Number Nombre	Rate Taux	Number Nombre	Rate Taux	Number Nombre	Rate Taux
TOTAL	61 274	1 390.9	60 268	1 188.9	53 830	984.2	55 246	976.3
Certain infectious and parasitic diseases — Certaines maladies infectieuses et parasitaires								
Total	661	15.0	232	4.6	1 260	23.0	1 327	23.5
Intestinal infectious diseases — Maladies infectieuses intestinales	2	♦0.0	5	♦0.1	78	1.4	139	2.5
Tuberculosis — Tuberculose	383	8.7	62	1.2	24	♦0.4	8	♦0.1
Tetanus — Tétanos	-	-	-	-	-	-	-	-
Diphtheria — Diphtérie	-	-	-	-	-	-	-	-
Whooping cough — Coqueluche	-	-	-	-	-	-	1	♦0.0
Meningococcal infection — Infection à méningocoques	3	♦0.1	6	♦0.1	5	♦0.1	4	♦0.1
Septicaemia — Septicémie	31	0.7	23	♦0.5	746	13.6	701	12.4
Acute poliomyelitis — Poliomyélite aiguë	-	-	-	-	-	-	-	-
Measles — Rougeole	-	-	-	-	-	-	-	-
Viral hepatitis — Hépatite virale	23	♦0.5	8	♦0.2	46	0.8	42	0.7
Human immunodeficiency virus [HIV] disease — Maladies dues au virus de l'immunodéficience humaine (VIH)	179	4.1	96	1.9	28	♦0.5	11	♦0.2
Malaria — Paludisme	-	-	-	-	-	-	-	-
Neoplasms — Tumeurs	10 156	230.5	7 171	141.5	15 920	291.1	12 497	220.8
Malignant neoplasms — Tumeurs malignes								
Total	10 050	228.1	7 018	138.4	15 214	278.2	11 819	208.9
Malignant neoplasm of lip, oral cavity and pharynx — Tumeur maligne de la lèvre, de la cavité buccale et du pharynx	706	16.0	88	1.7	443	8.1	138	2.4
Malignant neoplasm of oesophagus — Tumeur maligne de l'oesophage	351	8.0	40	0.8	514	9.4	201	3.6
Malignant neoplasm of stomach — Tumeur maligne de l'estomac	1 124	25.5	719	14.2	495	9.1	311	5.5
Malignant neoplasm of colon, rectosigmoid junction, rectum, anus and anal canal — Tumeur maligne du côlon, de la jonction recto-sigmoïdienne, du rectum, de l'anus et du canal anal	1 089	24.7	1 107	21.8	1 590	29.1	1 416	25.0
Malignant neoplasm of liver and intrahepatic bile ducts — Tumeur maligne du foie et des voies bilaires intrahépatiques	213	4.8	114	2.2	525	9.6	320	5.7
Malignant neoplasm of pancreas — Tumeur maligne du pancréas	510	11.6	409	8.1	788	14.4	799	14.1
Malignant neoplasm of trachea, bronchus and lung — Tumeur maligne de la trachée, des bronches et du poumon	2 550	57.9	339	6.7	4 578	83.7	1 730	30.6
Malignant neoplasm of female breast — Tumeur maligne du sein chez la femme	..	..	1 106	25.5	..	..	2 312	48.8
Malignant neoplasm of cervix uteri — Tumeur maligne du col de l'utérus	..	..	318	7.3	..	..	179	3.8
Malignant neoplasm of prostate — Tumeur maligne de la prostate	799	60.0	..	..	1 394	73.1	..	..
Malignant neoplasm of lymphoid, haematopoietic and related tissue — Tumeurs malignes primitives ou présumées primitives des tissus lymphoïde, hématopoïétique et apparentés	...	...	...	...	1 231	22.5	978	17.3
Disorders of the blood and blood-forming organs and certain disorders involving the immune mechanism — Maladies du sang et des organes hématopoïétiques et certains troubles du système immunitaire								
Total	34	0.8	34	0.7	186	3.4	240	4.2
Anaemias — Anémies	7	♦0.2	19	♦0.4	83	1.5	136	2.4
Endocrine, nutritional and metabolic diseases — Maladies endocriniennes, nutritionnelles et métaboliques								
Total	131	3.0	154	3.0	1 206	22.0	1 746	30.9
Diabetes mellitus — Diabète sucré	84	1.9	110	2.2	728	13.3	980	17.3
Malnutrition — Malnutrition	2	♦0.0	2	♦0.0	69	1.3	142	2.5
Mental and behavioural disorders — Troubles mentaux et du comportement	831	18.9	883	17.4	1 736	31.7	2 881	50.9
Diseases of the nervous system — Maladies du système nerveux	1 094	24.8	1 299	25.6	2 282	41.7	3 161	55.9
Diseases of the circulatory system — Maladies de l'appareil circulatoire								
Total	32 671	741.6	34 802	686.5	14 299	261.4	17 157	303.2
Acute rheumatic fever and chronic rheumatic heart diseases — Rhumatisme articularie aigu et cardiopathies rhumatismales chroniques	107	2.4	158	3.1	69	1.3	218	3.9
Hypertensive diseases — Maladies hypertensives	92	2.1	59	1.2	326	6.0	613	10.8
Ischaemic heart disease — Cardiopathie ischémique	24 096	547.0	24 881	490.8	4 934	90.2	3 564	63.0
Cerebrovascular disease — Maladie cérébrovasculaire	5 810	131.9	7 904	155.9	2 832	51.8	4 177	73.8

	Belarus - Bélarus				Belgium - Belgique			
Cause of death — Cause de décès	2014 (C)				2012 (C)			
	Male — Masculin		Female — Féminin		Male — Masculin		Female — Féminin	
	Number Nombre	Rate Taux	Number Nombre	Rate Taux	Number Nombre	Rate Taux	Number Nombre	Rate Taux
Diseases of arteries, arterioles and capillaries — Maladies des artères, artérioles et capillaires	...	...	...	...	797	14.6	551	9.7
Diseases of the respiratory system — Maladies de l'appareil respiratoire								
Total	1 508	34.2	357	7.0	5 935	108.5	5 392	95.3
Influenza — Grippe	-	-	4	◆0.1	35	0.6	72	1.3
Pneumonia — Pneumopathies	468	10.6	81	1.6	1 687	30.8	1 931	34.1
Chronic lower respiratory diseases — Maladies chroniques des voies respiratoires inférieures	868	19.7	222	4.4	2 793	51.1	1 991	35.2
Diseases of the digestive system — Maladies de l'appareil digestif								
Total	2 235	50.7	1 646	32.5	2 412	44.1	2 521	44.6
Gastric and duodenal ulcer — Ulcère de l'estomac et du duodénum	132	3.0	65	1.3	91	1.7	111	2.0
Diseases of the liver — Maladies du foie	1 302	29.6	815	16.1	977	17.9	555	9.8
Diseases of the musculoskeletal system and connective tissue — Maladies du système ostéo-articularie, des muscles et du tissu conjonctif	51	1.2	88	1.7	234	4.3	348	6.1
Diseases of the genitourinary system — Maladies de l'appareil génito-urinaire								
Total	340	7.7	324	6.4	1 085	19.8	1 421	25.1
Disorders of kidney and ureter — Affections du rein et de l'uretère	...	...	...	...	869	15.9	1 100	19.4
Hyperplasia of prostate — Hyperplasie de la prostate	...	...	..	..	13	◆0.7	..	..
Pregnancy, childbirth and the puerperium — Grossesse, accouchement et puerpéralité								
Total	..	..	1	◆0.8	..	..	5	◆3.9
Pregnancy with abortive outcome — Grossesse se terminant par un avortement	..	..	-	-	..	..	-	-
Other direct obstetric causes — Autres décès maternels directs	..	..	-	-	..	..	5	◆3.9
Indirect obstetric causes — Décès maternels indirects	..	..	-	-	..	..	-	-
Certain conditions originating in the perinatal period — Certaines affections dont l'origine se situe dans la période périnatale	107	174.6	72	125.7	128	195.9	82	130.8
Congenital malformations, deformations and chromosomal abnormalities — Malformations congénitales et anomalies chromosomiques	140	228.5	113	197.4	157	240.3	138	220.1
Symptoms, signs and abnormal clinical and laboratory findings, not elsewhere classified — Symptômes, signes et résultats anormaux d'examens cliniques et de laboratoire, non classés ailleurs	3 693	83.8	10 949	216.0	2 712	49.6	3 298	58.3
All other diseases — Toutes autres maladies	34	0.8	47	0.9	68	1.2	195	3.4
External causes — Causes externes								
Total	7 588	172.3	2 096	41.3	4 210	77.0	2 837	50.1
Accidents								
Total	...	...	...	...	2 309	42.2	2 032	35.9
Transport accidents — Accidents de transport	747	17.0	255	5.0	584	10.7	186	3.3
Falls — Chutes	531	12.1	173	3.4	706	12.9	776	13.7
Accidental drowning and submersion — Noyade et submersion accidentelles	535	12.1	94	1.9	35	0.6	18	◆0.3
Exposure to smoke, fire and flames — Exposition à la fumée, au feu et aux flammes	569	12.9	211	4.2	42	0.8	44	0.8
Accidental poisoning by and exposure to noxious substances — Intoxication accidentelle par des substances nocives et exposition à ces substances	1 388	31.5	367	7.2	136	2.5	66	1.2
Intentional self-harm — Lésions auto-infligées	1 466	33.3	276	5.4	1 484	27.1	539	9.5
Assault — Agresssions	238	5.4	118	2.3	81	1.5	49	0.9
All other external causes — Toutes autres causes externes	...	...	...	...	336	6.1	217	3.8

20. Death and death rates by cause and sex: 2010 - 2014
Décès et taux de mortalité par cause et sexe : 2010 - 2014 (continued - suite)

Cause of death — Cause de décès	Belgium - Belgique				Bosnia and Herzegovina - Bosnie-Herzégovine			
	2013 (C)				2011 (U)		2014 (U)	
	Male — Masculin		Female — Féminin		Male — Masculin	Female — Féminin	Male — Masculin	Female — Féminin
	Number Nombre	Rate Taux	Number Nombre	Rate Taux	Number Nombre	Number Nombre	Number Nombre	Number Nombre
TOTAL	53 908	980.5	55 426	974.9	*17 965*	*17 063*	*18 360*	*17 620*
Certain infectious and parasitic diseases — Certaines maladies infectieuses et parasitaires								
Total	1 328	24.2	1 547	27.2	*193*	*106*	*168*	*126*
Intestinal infectious diseases — Maladies infectieuses intestinales ...	133	2.4	254	4.5	*2*	*1*	*5*	*8*
Tuberculosis — Tuberculose	18	♦0.3	10	♦0.2	*117*	*43*	*74*	*35*
Tetanus — Tétanos	1	♦0.0	1	♦0.0	-	-	-	-
Diphtheria — Diphtérie..................	-	-	-	-	-	-	-	-
Whooping cough — Coqueluche	-	-	1	♦0.0	-	-	-	-
Meningococcal infection — Infection à méningocoques	5	♦0.1	6	♦0.1	-	-	-	*2*
Septicaemia — Septicémie	734	13.4	732	12.9	*44*	*52*	*48*	*58*
Acute poliomyelitis — Poliomyélite aiguë	-	-	-	-	-	-	-	-
Measles — Rougeole..................	-	-	-	-	-	-	-	-
Viral hepatitis — Hépatite virale..................	39	0.7	45	0.8	*19*	*8*	*23*	*15*
Human immunodeficiency virus [HIV] disease — Maladies dues au virus de l'immunodéficience humaine (VIH)..................	37	0.7	16	♦0.3	-	-	*1*	*1*
Malaria — Paludisme..................	-	-	1	♦0.0	-	-	-	-
Neoplasms — Tumeurs	16 009	291.2	12 721	223.8	*4 316*	*2 898*	*4 569*	*3 252*
Malignant neoplasms — Tumeurs malignes								
Total	15 227	277.0	12 066	212.2	*4 285*	*2 876*	*4 531*	*3 231*
Malignant neoplasm of lip, oral cavity and pharynx — Tumeur maligne de la lèvre, de la cavité buccale et du pharynx	449	8.2	146	2.6	*105*	*26*	*106*	*26*
Malignant neoplasm of oesophagus — Tumeur maligne de l'oesophage	589	10.7	179	3.1	*70*	*21*	*77*	*16*
Malignant neoplasm of stomach — Tumeur maligne de l'estomac	458	8.3	284	5.0	*285*	*176*	*315*	*196*
Malignant neoplasm of colon, rectosigmoid junction, rectum, anus and anal canal — Tumeur maligne du côlon, de la jonction recto-sigmoïdienne, du rectum, de l'anus et du canal anal	1 507	27.4	1 391	24.5	*505*	*307*	*527*	*382*
Malignant neoplasm of liver and intrahepatic bile ducts — Tumeur maligne du foie et des voies bilaires intrahépatiques	549	10.0	346	6.1	*230*	*205*	*212*	*181*
Malignant neoplasm of pancreas — Tumeur maligne du pancréas..................	823	15.0	839	14.8	*199*	*163*	*234*	*203*
Malignant neoplasm of trachea, bronchus and lung — Tumeur maligne de la trachée, des bronches et du poumon	4 597	83.6	1 886	33.2	*1 438*	*349*	*1 468*	*390*
Malignant neoplasm of female breast — Tumeur maligne du sein chez la femme	..	..	2 290	48.2	..	*429*	..	*520*
Malignant neoplasm of cervix uteri — Tumeur maligne du col de l'utérus.........	..	..	176	3.7	..	*100*	..	*107*
Malignant neoplasm of prostate — Tumeur maligne de la prostate	1 455	75.0	..	..	*308*	..	*383*	..
Malignant neoplasm of lymphoid, haematopoietic and related tissue — Tumeurs malignes primitives ou présumées primitives des tissus lymphoïde, hématopoïétique et apparentés..................	1 281	23.3	1 032	18.2	*186*	*149*	*189*	*161*
Disorders of the blood and blood-forming organs and certain disorders involving the immune mechanism — Maladies du sang et des organes hématopoïétiques et certains troubles du système immunitaire								
Total	156	2.8	228	4.0	*20*	*38*	*14*	*26*
Anaemias — Anémies	71	1.3	132	2.3	*10*	*21*	*8*	*20*
Endocrine, nutritional and metabolic diseases — Maladies endocriniennes, nutritionnelles et métaboliques								
Total	1 175	21.4	1 709	30.1	*761*	*1 179*	*925*	*1 342*
Diabetes mellitus — Diabète sucré..................	711	12.9	903	15.9	*746*	*1 159*	*907*	*1 324*
Malnutrition — Malnutrition	71	1.3	146	2.6	*4*	*1*	*1*	-
Mental and behavioural disorders — Troubles mentaux et du comportement	1 843	33.5	3 055	53.7	*88*	*63*	*130*	*65*
Diseases of the nervous system — Maladies du système nerveux..................	2 354	42.8	3 139	55.2	*210*	*201*	*198*	*185*
Diseases of the circulatory system — Maladies de l'appareil circulatoire								
Total	14 424	262.4	16 890	297.1	*8 504*	*9 892*	*8 320*	*9 586*
Acute rheumatic fever and chronic rheumatic heart diseases — Rhumatisme articularie aigu et cardiopathies rhumatismales chroniques	81	1.5	202	3.6	*9*	*13*	*11*	*5*
Hypertensive diseases — Maladies hypertensives..................	329	6.0	682	12.0	*456*	*677*	*529*	*801*
Ischaemic heart disease — Cardiopathie ischémique	4 783	87.0	3 444	60.6	*1 769*	*1 428*	*2 082*	*1 800*

Cause of death — Cause de décès	Belgium - Belgique				Bosnia and Herzegovina - Bosnie-Herzégovine			
	2013 (C)				2011 (U)		2014 (U)	
	Male — Masculin		Female — Féminin		Male — Masculin	Female — Féminin	Male — Masculin	Female — Féminin
	Number Nombre	Rate Taux	Number Nombre	Rate Taux	Number Nombre	Number Nombre	Number Nombre	Number Nombre
Cerebrovascular disease — Maladie cérébrovasculaire....................................	2 841	51.7	4 144	72.9	2 050	2 601	1 893	2 293
Diseases of arteries, arterioles and capillaries — Maladies des artères, artérioles et capillaires	812	14.8	584	10.3	352	476	317	379
Diseases of the respiratory system — Maladies de l'appareil respiratoire								
Total	6 032	109.7	5 330	93.8	711	539	822	549
Influenza — Grippe	61	1.1	82	1.4	6	6	1	2
Pneumonia — Pneumopathies	1 824	33.2	1 963	34.5	90	85	77	82
Chronic lower respiratory diseases — Maladies chroniques des voies respiratoires inférieures	2 855	51.9	1 892	33.3	439	273	532	291
Diseases of the digestive system — Maladies de l'appareil digestif								
Total	2 282	41.5	2 334	41.1	537	330	544	403
Gastric and duodenal ulcer — Ulcère de l'estomac et du duodénum...............	98	1.8	107	1.9	45	33	36	42
Diseases of the liver — Maladies du foie..	889	16.2	561	9.9	269	110	305	101
Diseases of the musculoskeletal system and connective tissue — Maladies du système ostéo-articularie, des muscles et du tissu conjonctif	197	3.6	348	6.1	12	32	16	44
Diseases of the genitourinary system — Maladies de l'appareil génito-urinaire								
Total	1 143	20.8	1 490	26.2	301	249	259	273
Disorders of kidney and ureter — Affections du rein et de l'uretère	924	16.8	1 102	19.4	283	246	243	269
Hyperplasia of prostate — Hyperplasie de la prostate..............................	16	♦0.8	..	..	17	..	7	..
Pregnancy, childbirth and the puerperium — Grossesse, accouchement et puerpéralité								
Total	..	..	3	♦2.4	..	2	..	-
Pregnancy with abortive outcome — Grossesse se terminant par un avortement	..	..	-	-	..	..	..	-
Other direct obstetric causes — Autres décès maternels directs	..	..	3	♦2.4	..	2	..	-
Indirect obstetric causes — Décès maternels indirects	..	..	-	-	..	-	..	-
Certain conditions originating in the perinatal period — Certaines affections dont l'origine se situe dans la période périnatale	116	180.2	95	155.1	67	51	42	44
Congenital malformations, deformations and chromosomal abnormalities — Malformations congénitales et anomalies chromosomiques	147	228.4	119	194.3	30	28	20	28
Symptoms, signs and abnormal clinical and laboratory findings, not elsewhere classified — Symptômes, signes et résultats anormaux d'examens cliniques et de laboratoire, non classés ailleurs	2 638	48.0	3 368	59.2	1 270	1 212	1 512	1 432
All other diseases — Toutes autres maladies..	90	1.6	193	3.4	2	10	16	21
External causes — Causes externes								
Total	3 974	72.3	2 857	50.3	943	233	805	244
Accidents								
Total	2 196	39.9	2 007	35.3	8	1	448	138
Transport accidents — Accidents de transport	566	10.3	192	3.4	3	1	196	48
Falls — Chutes	714	13.0	772	13.6	-	-	26	6
Accidental drowning and submersion — Noyade et submersion accidentelles...	47	0.9	20	♦0.4	3	-	45	17
Exposure to smoke, fire and flames — Exposition à la fumée, au feu et aux flammes..	38	0.7	34	0.6	1	-	16	8
Accidental poisoning by and exposure to noxious substances — Intoxication accidentelle par des substances nocives et exposition à ces substances	115	2.1	80	1.4	-	-	7	5
Intentional self-harm — Lésions auto-infligées...	1 363	24.8	532	9.4	5	-	243	70
Assault — Agresssions	57	1.0	53	0.9	-	-	34	12
All other external causes — Toutes autres causes externes	358	6.5	265	4.7	930	232	80	24

20. Death and death rates by cause and sex: 2010 - 2014
Décès et taux de mortalité par cause et sexe : 2010 - 2014 (continued - suite)

Bulgaria - Bulgarie

Cause of death — Cause de décès	2012 (C)				2013 (C)			
	Male — Masculin		Female — Féminin		Male — Masculin		Female — Féminin	
	Number Nombre	Rate Taux	Number Nombre	Rate Taux	Number Nombre	Rate Taux	Number Nombre	Rate Taux
TOTAL	56 702	1 594.6	52 579	1 402.1	54 827	1 551.3	49 518	1 327.7
Certain infectious and parasitic diseases — Certaines maladies infectieuses et parasitaires								
Total	399	11.2	227	6.1	320	9.1	198	5.3
Intestinal infectious diseases — Maladies infectieuses intestinales	12	♦0.3	8	♦0.2	11	♦0.3	14	♦0.4
Tuberculosis — Tuberculose	131	3.7	33	0.9	117	3.3	32	0.9
Tetanus — Tétanos......	-	-	-	-	1	♦0.0	-	-
Diphtheria — Diphtérie......	-	-	-	-	-	-	-	-
Whooping cough — Coqueluche	-	-	-	-	-	-	-	-
Meningococcal infection — Infection à méningocoques	6	♦0.2	1	♦0.0	2	♦0.1	2	♦0.1
Septicaemia — Septicémie......	189	5.3	148	3.9	138	3.9	114	3.1
Acute poliomyelitis — Poliomyélite aiguë	-	-	-	-	-	-	-	-
Measles — Rougeole......	-	-	-	-	-	-	-	-
Viral hepatitis — Hépatite virale......	12	♦0.3	6	♦0.2	9	♦0.3	7	♦0.2
Human immunodeficiency virus [HIV] disease — Maladies dues au virus de l'immunodéficience humaine (VIH)......	12	♦0.3	-	-	5	♦0.1	3	♦0.1
Malaria — Paludisme......	-	-	-	-	1	♦0.0	-	-
Neoplasms — Tumeurs	10 701	300.9	7 598	202.6	10 934	309.4	7 340	196.8
Malignant neoplasms — Tumeurs malignes								
Total	10 614	298.5	7 543	201.1	10 842	306.8	7 273	195.0
Malignant neoplasm of lip, oral cavity and pharynx — Tumeur maligne de la lèvre, de la cavité buccale et du pharynx	333	9.4	78	2.1	375	10.6	87	2.3
Malignant neoplasm of oesophagus — Tumeur maligne de l'oesophage	159	4.5	38	1.0	159	4.5	40	1.1
Malignant neoplasm of stomach — Tumeur maligne de l'estomac	794	22.3	494	13.2	780	22.1	478	12.8
Malignant neoplasm of colon, rectosigmoid junction, rectum, anus and anal canal — Tumeur maligne du côlon, de la jonction recto-sigmoïdienne, du rectum, de l'anus et du canal anal	1 478	41.6	1 075	28.7	1 549	43.8	1 041	27.9
Malignant neoplasm of liver and intrahepatic bile ducts — Tumeur maligne du foie et des voies bilaires intrahépatiques	443	12.5	235	6.3	427	12.1	234	6.3
Malignant neoplasm of pancreas — Tumeur maligne du pancréas......	596	16.8	464	12.4	654	18.5	437	11.7
Malignant neoplasm of trachea, bronchus and lung — Tumeur maligne de la trachée, des bronches et du poumon	2 889	81.2	705	18.8	2 959	83.7	665	17.8
Malignant neoplasm of female breast — Tumeur maligne du sein chez la femme	..	..	1 364	41.7	..	..	1 274	...
Malignant neoplasm of cervix uteri — Tumeur maligne du col de l'utérus......	..	..	382	11.7	..	..	352	...
Malignant neoplasm of prostate — Tumeur maligne de la prostate	936	71.5	..	..	994	...	..	..
Malignant neoplasm of lymphoid, haematopoietic and related tissue — Tumeurs malignes primitives ou présumées primitives des tissus lymphoïde, hématopoïétique et apparentés......	524	14.7	396	10.6	528	14.9	432	11.6
Disorders of the blood and blood-forming organs and certain disorders involving the immune mechanism — Maladies du sang et des organes hématopoïétiques et certains troubles du système immunitaire								
Total	73	2.1	62	1.7	74	2.1	69	1.9
Anaemias — Anémies	47	1.3	48	1.3	46	1.3	43	1.2
Endocrine, nutritional and metabolic diseases — Maladies endocriniennes, nutritionnelles et métaboliques								
Total	759	21.3	964	25.7	632	17.9	814	21.8
Diabetes mellitus — Diabète sucré......	745	21.0	938	25.0	609	17.2	784	21.0
Malnutrition — Malnutrition	3	♦0.1	2	♦0.1	1	♦0.0	1	♦0.0
Mental and behavioural disorders — Troubles mentaux et du comportement	47	1.3	40	1.1	41	1.2	41	1.1
Diseases of the nervous system — Maladies du système nerveux......	573	16.1	551	14.7	491	13.9	468	12.5
Diseases of the circulatory system — Maladies de l'appareil circulatoire								
Total	34 456	969.0	37 188	991.7	33 094	936.4	34 816	933.5
Acute rheumatic fever and chronic rheumatic heart diseases — Rhumatisme articularie aigu et cardiopathies rhumatismales chroniques	12	♦0.3	42	1.1	30	♦0.8	40	1.1
Hypertensive diseases — Maladies hypertensives......	3 670	103.2	4 509	120.2	3 396	96.1	4 007	107.4
Ischaemic heart disease — Cardiopathie ischémique	7 405	208.2	6 447	171.9	6 944	196.5	5 734	153.7
Cerebrovascular disease — Maladie cérébrovasculaire......	9 964	280.2	11 819	315.2	9 316	263.6	11 147	298.9

Bulgaria - Bulgarie

Cause of death — Cause de décès	2012 (C)				2013 (C)			
	Male — Masculin		Female — Féminin		Male — Masculin		Female — Féminin	
	Number Nombre	Rate Taux	Number Nombre	Rate Taux	Number Nombre	Rate Taux	Number Nombre	Rate Taux
Diseases of arteries, arterioles and capillaries — Maladies des artères, artérioles et capillaires	1 698	47.8	2 029	54.1	1 290	36.5	1 556	41.7
Diseases of the respiratory system — Maladies de l'appareil respiratoire								
Total	2 459	69.2	1 515	40.4	2 158	61.1	1 354	36.3
Influenza — Grippe	4	♦0.1	4	♦0.1	5	♦0.1	5	♦0.1
Pneumonia — Pneumopathies	893	25.1	594	15.8	727	20.6	559	15.0
Chronic lower respiratory diseases — Maladies chroniques des voies respiratoires inférieures	967	27.2	475	12.7	910	25.7	449	12.0
Diseases of the digestive system — Maladies de l'appareil digestif								
Total	2 349	66.1	1 204	32.1	2 367	67.0	1 262	33.8
Gastric and duodenal ulcer — Ulcère de l'estomac et du duodénum	188	5.3	112	3.0	176	5.0	104	2.8
Diseases of the liver — Maladies du foie	1 430	40.2	448	11.9	1 364	38.6	414	11.1
Diseases of the musculoskeletal system and connective tissue — Maladies du système ostéo-articularie, des muscles et du tissu conjonctif	13	♦0.4	35	0.9	18	♦0.5	22	♦0.6
Diseases of the genitourinary system — Maladies de l'appareil génito-urinaire								
Total	769	21.6	581	15.5	734	20.8	555	14.9
Disorders of kidney and ureter — Affections du rein et de l'uretère	748	21.0	574	15.3	719	20.3	551	14.8
Hyperplasia of prostate — Hyperplasie de la prostate	14	♦1.1	..	..	7	...	..	..
Pregnancy, childbirth and the puerperium — Grossesse, accouchement et puerpéralité								
Total	..	..	3	♦4.3	..	..	8	♦12.0
Pregnancy with abortive outcome — Grossesse se terminant par un avortement	..	..	1	♦1.4	..	..	-	-
Other direct obstetric causes — Autres décès maternels directs	..	..	2	♦2.9	..	..	8	♦12.0
Indirect obstetric causes — Décès maternels indirects	..	..	-	-	..	..	-	-
Certain conditions originating in the perinatal period — Certaines affections dont l'origine se situe dans la période périnatale	145	406.6	92	275.0	136	399.5	102	313.5
Congenital malformations, deformations and chromosomal abnormalities — Malformations congénitales et anomalies chromosomiques	86	241.2	57	170.4	102	299.6	54	166.0
Symptoms, signs and abnormal clinical and laboratory findings, not elsewhere classified — Symptômes, signes et résultats anormaux d'examens cliniques et de laboratoire, non classés ailleurs	1 524	42.9	1 714	45.7	1 556	44.0	1 775	47.6
All other diseases — Toutes autres maladies	21	♦0.6	18	♦0.5	17	♦0.5	28	♦0.8
External causes — Causes externes								
Total	2 328	65.5	730	19.5	2 153	60.9	612	16.4
Accidents								
Total	1 348	37.9	434	11.6	1 328	37.6	390	10.5
Transport accidents — Accidents de transport	421	11.8	121	3.2	458	13.0	125	3.4
Falls — Chutes	193	5.4	74	2.0	269	7.6	100	2.7
Accidental drowning and submersion — Noyade et submersion accidentelles	104	2.9	31	0.8	97	2.7	18	♦0.5
Exposure to smoke, fire and flames — Exposition à la fumée, au feu et aux flammes	73	2.1	36	1.0	54	1.5	37	1.0
Accidental poisoning by and exposure to noxious substances — Intoxication accidentelle par des substances nocives et exposition à ces substances	60	1.7	23	♦0.6	72	2.0	27	♦0.7
Intentional self-harm — Lésions auto-infligées	673	18.9	199	5.3	572	16.2	148	4.0
Assault — Agresssions	83	2.3	27	♦0.7	59	1.7	31	0.8
All other external causes — Toutes autres causes externes	224	6.3	70	1.9	194	5.5	43	1.2

20. Death and death rates by cause and sex: 2010 - 2014
Décès et taux de mortalité par cause et sexe : 2010 - 2014 (continued - suite)

Croatia - Croatie

Cause of death — Cause de décès	2013 (C)				2014 (C)			
	Male — Masculin		Female — Féminin		Male — Masculin		Female — Féminin	
	Number Nombre	Rate Taux	Number Nombre	Rate Taux	Number Nombre	Rate Taux	Number Nombre	Rate Taux
TOTAL	24 988	1 215.1	25 398	1 151.5	24 965	1 218.0	25 874	1 177.7
Certain infectious and parasitic diseases — Certaines maladies infectieuses et parasitaires								
Total	156	7.6	155	7.0	182	8.9	165	7.5
Intestinal infectious diseases — Maladies infectieuses intestinales	10	◆0.5	11	◆0.5	14	◆0.7	29	◆1.3
Tuberculosis — Tuberculose	34	1.7	19	◆0.9	28	◆1.4	12	◆0.5
Tetanus — Tétanos	-	-	-	-	-	-	-	-
Diphtheria — Diphtérie................	-	-	-	-	-	-	-	-
Whooping cough — Coqueluche	-	-	-	-	-	-	-	-
Meningococcal infection — Infection à méningocoques	1	◆0.0	1	◆0.0	-	-	-	-
Septicaemia — Septicémie.........	69	3.4	104	4.7	90	4.4	103	4.7
Acute poliomyelitis — Poliomyélite aiguë	-	-	-	-	-	-	-	-
Measles — Rougeole.........	-	-	-	-	-	-	-	-
Viral hepatitis — Hépatite virale	30	◆1.5	10	◆0.5	37	1.8	15	◆0.7
Human immunodeficiency virus [HIV] disease — Maladies dues au virus de l'immunodéficience humaine (VIH)................	4	◆0.2	3	◆0.1	4	◆0.2	-	-
Malaria — Paludisme.........	-	-	-	-	-	-	-	-
Neoplasms — Tumeurs	8 012	389.6	6 000	272.0	8 063	393.4	6 143	279.6
Malignant neoplasms — Tumeurs malignes								
Total	7 888	383.6	5 900	267.5	7 911	385.9	6 028	274.4
Malignant neoplasm of lip, oral cavity and pharynx — Tumeur maligne de la lèvre, de la cavité buccale et du pharynx	271	13.2	40	1.8	307	15.0	68	3.1
Malignant neoplasm of oesophagus — Tumeur maligne de l'oesophage	138	6.7	34	1.5	170	8.3	24	◆1.1
Malignant neoplasm of stomach — Tumeur maligne de l'estomac	492	23.9	357	16.2	464	22.6	307	14.0
Malignant neoplasm of colon, rectosigmoid junction, rectum, anus and anal canal — Tumeur maligne du côlon, de la jonction recto-sigmoïdienne, du rectum, de l'anus et du canal anal.........	1 182	57.5	855	38.8	1 237	60.3	857	39.0
Malignant neoplasm of liver and intrahepatic bile ducts — Tumeur maligne du foie et des voies bilaires intrahépatiques	347	16.9	190	8.6	294	14.3	197	9.0
Malignant neoplasm of pancreas — Tumeur maligne du pancréas................	370	18.0	339	15.4	325	15.9	353	16.1
Malignant neoplasm of trachea, bronchus and lung — Tumeur maligne de la trachée, des bronches et du poumon	2 090	101.6	712	32.3	2 074	101.2	753	34.3
Malignant neoplasm of female breast — Tumeur maligne du sein chez la femme	..	..	994	...	..	..	1 071	56.6
Malignant neoplasm of cervix uteri — Tumeur maligne du col de l'utérus.........	..	..	127	...	..	..	130	6.9
Malignant neoplasm of prostate — Tumeur maligne de la prostate	739	...	..	..	750	99.9	..	..
Malignant neoplasm of lymphoid, haematopoietic and related tissue — Tumeurs malignes primitives ou présumées primitives des tissus lymphoïde, hématopoïétique et apparentés.........	478	23.2	425	19.3	491	24.0	411	18.7
Disorders of the blood and blood-forming organs and certain disorders involving the immune mechanism — Maladies du sang et des organes hématopoïétiques et certains troubles du système immunitaire								
Total	12	◆0.6	11	◆0.5	9	◆0.4	11	◆0.5
Anaemias — Anémies	5	◆0.2	6	◆0.3	4	◆0.2	4	◆0.2
Endocrine, nutritional and metabolic diseases — Maladies endocriniennes, nutritionnelles et métaboliques								
Total	567	27.6	708	32.1	557	27.2	813	37.0
Diabetes mellitus — Diabète sucré................	550	26.7	693	31.4	536	26.1	797	36.3
Malnutrition — Malnutrition	-	-	-	-	-	-	-	-
Mental and behavioural disorders — Troubles mentaux et du comportement	509	24.8	644	29.2	484	23.6	704	32.0
Diseases of the nervous system — Maladies du système nerveux................	424	20.6	426	19.3	416	20.3	440	20.0
Diseases of the circulatory system — Maladies de l'appareil circulatoire								
Total	10 445	507.9	13 787	625.1	10 312	503.1	13 800	628.1
Acute rheumatic fever and chronic rheumatic heart diseases — Rhumatisme articularie aigu et cardiopathies rhumatismales chroniques	44	2.1	78	3.5	53	2.6	96	4.4
Hypertensive diseases — Maladies hypertensives.........	647	31.5	1 300	58.9	507	24.7	1 082	49.2
Ischaemic heart disease — Cardiopathie ischémique	4 945	240.5	5 827	264.2	4 912	239.6	5 919	269.4
Cerebrovascular disease — Maladie cérébrovasculaire................	3 026	147.1	4 217	191.2	3 016	147.1	4 284	195.0

Croatia - Croatie

Cause of death — Cause de décès	2013 (C)				2014 (C)			
	Male — Masculin		Female — Féminin		Male — Masculin		Female — Féminin	
	Number Nombre	Rate Taux	Number Nombre	Rate Taux	Number Nombre	Rate Taux	Number Nombre	Rate Taux
Diseases of arteries, arterioles and capillaries — Maladies des artères, artérioles et capillaires	572	27.8	739	33.5	479	23.4	641	29.2
Diseases of the respiratory system — Maladies de l'appareil respiratoire								
Total	1 251	60.8	893	40.5	1 344	65.6	883	40.2
Influenza — Grippe	13	♦0.6	19	♦0.9	3	♦0.1	4	♦0.2
Pneumonia — Pneumopathies	148	7.2	151	6.8	220	10.7	169	7.7
Chronic lower respiratory diseases — Maladies chroniques des voies respiratoires inférieures	1 025	49.8	679	30.8	1 051	51.3	670	30.5
Diseases of the digestive system — Maladies de l'appareil digestif								
Total	1 325	64.4	827	37.5	1 300	63.4	849	38.6
Gastric and duodenal ulcer — Ulcère de l'estomac et du duodénum	137	6.7	95	4.3	90	4.4	94	4.3
Diseases of the liver — Maladies du foie...........................	811	39.4	228	10.3	806	39.3	258	11.7
Diseases of the musculoskeletal system and connective tissue — Maladies du système ostéo-articularie, des muscles et du tissu conjonctif	17	♦0.8	90	4.1	29	♦1.4	127	5.8
Diseases of the genitourinary system — Maladies de l'appareil génito-urinaire								
Total	284	13.8	392	17.8	362	17.7	462	21.0
Disorders of kidney and ureter — Affections du rein et de l'uretère	168	8.2	234	10.6	245	12.0	282	12.8
Hyperplasia of prostate — Hyperplasie de la prostate.........	32	...	..	..	33	4.4	..	..
Pregnancy, childbirth and the puerperium — Grossesse, accouchement et puerpéralité								
Total	..	..	2	♦5.0	..	..	1	♦2.5
Pregnancy with abortive outcome — Grossesse se terminant par un avortement	..	..	-	-	..	..	-	-
Other direct obstetric causes — Autres décès maternels directs	..	..	1	♦2.5	..	..	-	-
Indirect obstetric causes — Décès maternels indirects	..	..	1	♦2.5	..	..	1	♦2.5
Certain conditions originating in the perinatal period — Certaines affections dont l'origine se situe dans la période périnatale	56	270.1	45	234.3	71	348.5	50	260.5
Congenital malformations, deformations and chromosomal abnormalities — Malformations congénitales et anomalies chromosomiques	61	294.2	44	229.1	59	289.6	50	260.5
Symptoms, signs and abnormal clinical and laboratory findings, not elsewhere classified — Symptômes, signes et résultats anormaux d'examens cliniques et de laboratoire, non classés ailleurs	201	9.8	272	12.3	159	7.8	235	10.7
All other diseases — Toutes autres maladies..	4	♦0.2	8	♦0.4	2	♦0.1	7	♦0.3
External causes — Causes externes								
Total	1 664	80.9	1 094	49.6	1 616	78.8	1 134	51.6
Accidents								
Total	1 056	51.3	849	38.5	1 029	50.2	866	39.4
Transport accidents — Accidents de transport	324	15.8	104	4.7	293	14.3	77	3.5
Falls — Chutes	412	20.0	627	28.4	450	22.0	664	30.2
Accidental drowning and submersion — Noyade et submersion accidentelles...	83	4.0	17	♦0.8	63	3.1	16	♦0.7
Exposure to smoke, fire and flames — Exposition à la fumée, au feu et aux flammes..	16	♦0.8	12	♦0.5	17	♦0.8	13	♦0.6
Accidental poisoning by and exposure to noxious substances — Intoxication accidentelle par des substances nocives et exposition à ces substances	77	3.7	20	♦0.9	81	4.0	21	♦1.0
Intentional self-harm — Lésions auto-infligées..	546	26.6	145	6.6	536	26.1	186	8.5
Assault — Agresssions..	25	♦1.2	22	♦1.0	17	♦0.8	21	♦1.0
All other external causes — Toutes autres causes externes	37	1.8	78	3.5	34	1.7	61	2.8

20. Death and death rates by cause and sex: 2010 - 2014
Décès et taux de mortalité par cause et sexe : 2010 - 2014 (continued - suite)

Czech Republic - République tchèque

Cause of death — Cause de décès	2013 (C)				2014 (C)			
	Male — Masculin		Female — Féminin		Male — Masculin		Female — Féminin	
	Number Nombre	Rate Taux	Number Nombre	Rate Taux	Number Nombre	Rate Taux	Number Nombre	Rate Taux
TOTAL	55 098	1 066.9	54 062	1 010.2	53 740	1 041.0	51 925	970.6
Certain infectious and parasitic diseases — Certaines maladies infectieuses et parasitaires								
Total	696	13.5	843	15.8	844	16.3	893	16.7
Intestinal infectious diseases — Maladies infectieuses intestinales	82	1.6	165	3.1	119	2.3	144	2.7
Tuberculosis — Tuberculose	40	0.8	20	♦0.4	25	♦0.5	9	♦0.2
Tetanus — Tétanos	-	-	-	-	-	-	-	-
Diphtheria — Diphtérie	-	-	-	-	-	-	-	-
Whooping cough — Coqueluche	-	-	-	-	-	-	-	-
Meningococcal infection — Infection à méningocoques	4	♦0.1	1	♦0.0	2	♦0.0	-	-
Septicaemia — Septicémie	468	9.1	549	10.3	585	11.3	603	11.3
Acute poliomyelitis — Poliomyélite aiguë	-	-	-	-	1	♦0.0	-	-
Measles — Rougeole	-	-	-	-	-	-	-	-
Viral hepatitis — Hépatite virale	14	♦0.3	14	♦0.3	16	♦0.3	27	♦0.5
Human immunodeficiency virus [HIV] disease — Maladies dues au virus de l'immunodéficience humaine (VIH)	7	♦0.1	-	-	12	♦0.2	5	♦0.1
Malaria — Paludisme	-	-	-	-	-	-	-	-
Neoplasms — Tumeurs	15 208	294.5	12 241	228.7	15 252	295.4	12 351	230.9
Malignant neoplasms — Tumeurs malignes								
Total	15 039	291.2	12 045	225.1	14 976	290.1	12 074	225.7
Malignant neoplasm of lip, oral cavity and pharynx — Tumeur maligne de la lèvre, de la cavité buccale et du pharynx	563	10.9	155	2.9	569	11.0	159	3.0
Malignant neoplasm of oesophagus — Tumeur maligne de l'oesophage	439	8.5	94	1.8	416	8.1	107	2.0
Malignant neoplasm of stomach — Tumeur maligne de l'estomac	670	13.0	430	8.0	631	12.2	468	8.7
Malignant neoplasm of colon, rectosigmoid junction, rectum, anus and anal canal — Tumeur maligne du côlon, de la jonction recto-sigmoïdienne, du rectum, de l'anus et du canal anal	2 101	40.7	1 471	27.5	2 041	39.5	1 499	28.0
Malignant neoplasm of liver and intrahepatic bile ducts — Tumeur maligne du foie et des voies bilaires intrahépatiques	521	10.1	309	5.8	554	10.7	272	5.1
Malignant neoplasm of pancreas — Tumeur maligne du pancréas	1 014	19.6	980	18.3	1 012	19.6	986	18.4
Malignant neoplasm of trachea, bronchus and lung — Tumeur maligne de la trachée, des bronches et du poumon	3 741	72.4	1 685	31.5	3 588	69.5	1 671	31.2
Malignant neoplasm of female breast — Tumeur maligne du sein chez la femme	..	..	1 692	36.8	..	..	1 581	34.5
Malignant neoplasm of cervix uteri — Tumeur maligne du col de l'utérus	..	..	369	8.0	..	..	310	6.8
Malignant neoplasm of prostate — Tumeur maligne de la prostate	1 422	81.1	..	..	1 509	85.1	..	..
Malignant neoplasm of lymphoid, haematopoietic and related tissue — Tumeurs malignes primitives ou présumées primitives des tissus lymphoïde, hématopoïétique et apparentés	1 007	19.5	855	16.0	1 021	19.8	853	15.9
Disorders of the blood and blood-forming organs and certain disorders involving the immune mechanism — Maladies du sang et des organes hématopoïétiques et certains troubles du système immunitaire								
Total	94	1.8	110	2.1	83	1.6	122	2.3
Anaemias — Anémies	29	♦0.6	47	0.9	28	♦0.5	41	0.8
Endocrine, nutritional and metabolic diseases — Maladies endocriniennes, nutritionnelles et métaboliques								
Total	1 914	37.1	2 372	44.3	1 830	35.4	2 260	42.2
Diabetes mellitus — Diabète sucré	1 687	32.7	2 061	38.5	1 598	31.0	1 902	35.6
Malnutrition — Malnutrition	72	1.4	64	1.2	54	1.0	85	1.6
Mental and behavioural disorders — Troubles mentaux et du comportement	478	9.3	708	13.2	512	9.9	698	13.0
Diseases of the nervous system — Maladies du système nerveux	1 163	22.5	1 438	26.9	1 213	23.5	1 451	27.1
Diseases of the circulatory system — Maladies de l'appareil circulatoire								
Total	23 701	458.9	28 030	523.8	22 489	435.6	26 138	488.6
Acute rheumatic fever and chronic rheumatic heart diseases — Rhumatisme articularie aigu et cardiopathies rhumatismales chroniques	118	2.3	189	3.5	124	2.4	203	3.8
Hypertensive diseases — Maladies hypertensives	1 089	21.1	1 762	32.9	1 126	21.8	1 572	29.4
Ischaemic heart disease — Cardiopathie ischémique	13 412	259.7	14 524	271.4	12 603	244.1	13 436	251.1
Cerebrovascular disease — Maladie cérébrovasculaire	4 249	82.3	6 067	113.4	3 885	75.3	5 525	103.3

20. Death and death rates by cause and sex: 2010 - 2014
Décès et taux de mortalité par cause et sexe : 2010 - 2014 (continued - suite)

Czech Republic - République tchèque

Cause of death — Cause de décès	2013 (C)				2014 (C)			
	Male — Masculin		Female — Féminin		Male — Masculin		Female — Féminin	
	Number Nombre	Rate Taux	Number Nombre	Rate Taux	Number Nombre	Rate Taux	Number Nombre	Rate Taux
Diseases of arteries, arterioles and capillaries — Maladies des artères, artérioles et capillaires	1 264	24.5	1 389	26.0	1 090	21.1	1 260	23.6
Diseases of the respiratory system — Maladies de l'appareil respiratoire								
Total	3 853	74.6	2 980	55.7	3 520	68.2	2 690	50.3
Influenza — Grippe	101	2.0	82	1.5	13	♦0.3	26	♦0.5
Pneumonia — Pneumopathies	1 164	22.5	1 077	20.1	1 167	22.6	1 091	20.4
Chronic lower respiratory diseases — Maladies chroniques des voies respiratoires inférieures	2 140	41.4	1 444	27.0	1 896	36.7	1 232	23.0
Diseases of the digestive system — Maladies de l'appareil digestif								
Total	2 609	50.5	1 998	37.3	2 537	49.1	1 937	36.2
Gastric and duodenal ulcer — Ulcère de l'estomac et du duodénum	219	4.2	213	4.0	196	3.8	190	3.6
Diseases of the liver — Maladies du foie....	1 474	28.5	700	13.1	1 429	27.7	701	13.1
Diseases of the musculoskeletal system and connective tissue — Maladies du système ostéo-articularie, des muscles et du tissu conjonctif	66	1.3	107	2.0	79	1.5	120	2.2
Diseases of the genitourinary system — Maladies de l'appareil génito-urinaire								
Total	516	10.0	649	12.1	554	10.7	666	12.4
Disorders of kidney and ureter — Affections du rein et de l'uretère	399	7.7	531	9.9	393	7.6	487	9.1
Hyperplasia of prostate — Hyperplasie de la prostate....................................	27	♦1.5	..	..	29	♦1.6	..	..
Pregnancy, childbirth and the puerperium — Grossesse, accouchement et puerpéralité								
Total	..	..	1	♦0.9	..	..	4	♦3.6
Pregnancy with abortive outcome — Grossesse se terminant par un avortement	..	..	-	-	..	..	-	-
Other direct obstetric causes — Autres décès maternels directs	..	..	1	♦0.9	..	..	4	♦3.6
Indirect obstetric causes — Décès maternels indirects	..	..	-	-	..	..	-	-
Certain conditions originating in the perinatal period — Certaines affections dont l'origine se situe dans la période périnatale	83	151.7	55	105.7	82	145.4	61	114.1
Congenital malformations, deformations and chromosomal abnormalities — Malformations congénitales et anomalies chromosomiques	96	175.5	87	167.2	91	161.3	75	140.3
Symptoms, signs and abnormal clinical and laboratory findings, not elsewhere classified — Symptômes, signes et résultats anormaux d'examens cliniques et de laboratoire, non classés ailleurs	711	13.8	615	11.5	724	14.0	498	9.3
All other diseases — Toutes autres maladies...	62	1.2	78	1.5	70	1.4	107	2.0
External causes — Causes externes								
Total	3 848	74.5	1 750	32.7	3 860	74.8	1 854	34.7
Accidents								
Total	2 270	44.0	1 276	23.8	2 343	45.4	1 369	25.6
Transport accidents — Accidents de transport	590	11.4	170	3.2	598	11.6	188	3.5
Falls — Chutes	408	7.9	249	4.7	374	7.2	198	3.7
Accidental drowning and submersion — Noyade et submersion accidentelles....	135	2.6	42	0.8	112	2.2	29	♦0.5
Exposure to smoke, fire and flames — Exposition à la fumée, au feu et aux flammes...	31	0.6	12	♦0.2	34	0.7	14	♦0.3
Accidental poisoning by and exposure to noxious substances — Intoxication accidentelle par des substances nocives et exposition à ces substances	300	5.8	119	2.2	274	5.3	121	2.3
Intentional self-harm — Lésions auto-infligées...................................	1 291	25.0	282	5.3	1 195	23.1	293	5.5
Assault — Agresssions	46	0.9	46	0.9	48	0.9	31	0.6
All other external causes — Toutes autres causes externes	241	4.7	146	2.7	274	5.3	161	3.0

20. Death and death rates by cause and sex: 2010 - 2014
Décès et taux de mortalité par cause et sexe : 2010 - 2014 (continued - suite)

Denmark - Danemark

Cause of death — Cause de décès	2011 (C)				2012 (C)			
	Male — Masculin		Female — Féminin		Male — Masculin		Female — Féminin	
	Number Nombre	Rate Taux	Number Nombre	Rate Taux	Number Nombre	Rate Taux	Number Nombre	Rate Taux
TOTAL	25 718	931.8	26 487	943.7	25 695	928.7	26 316	935.3
Certain infectious and parasitic diseases — Certaines maladies infectieuses et parasitaires								
Total	374	13.6	406	14.5	415	15.0	461	16.4
Intestinal infectious diseases — Maladies infectieuses intestinales	99	3.6	144	5.1	89	3.2	135	4.8
Tuberculosis — Tuberculose	10	♦0.4	5	♦0.2	15	♦0.5	6	♦0.2
Tetanus — Tétanos..	-	-	-	-	-	-	-	-
Diphtheria — Diphtérie...	-	-	-	-	-	-	-	-
Whooping cough — Coqueluche	-	-	-	-	-	-	-	-
Meningococcal infection — Infection à méningocoques	2	♦0.1	6	♦0.2	2	♦0.1	-	-
Septicaemia — Septicémie	138	5.0	125	4.5	162	5.9	183	6.5
Acute poliomyelitis — Poliomyélite aiguë	3	♦0.1	-	-	2	♦0.1	1	♦0.0
Measles — Rougeole...	1	♦0.0	-	-	1	♦0.0	-	-
Viral hepatitis — Hépatite virale	11	♦0.4	9	♦0.3	12	♦0.4	8	♦0.3
Human immunodeficiency virus [HIV] disease — Maladies dues au virus de l'immunodéficience humaine (VIH)..	16	♦0.6	2	♦0.1	23	♦0.8	3	♦0.1
Malaria — Paludisme	-	-	1	♦0.0	-	-	-	-
Neoplasms — Tumeurs	8 121	294.2	7 382	263.0	8 226	297.3	7 613	270.6
Malignant neoplasms — Tumeurs malignes								
Total	7 990	289.5	7 247	258.2	8 062	291.4	7 444	264.6
Malignant neoplasm of lip, oral cavity and pharynx — Tumeur maligne de la lèvre, de la cavité buccale et du pharynx	233	8.4	91	3.2	206	7.4	107	3.8
Malignant neoplasm of oesophagus — Tumeur maligne de l'oesophage	307	11.1	101	3.6	323	11.7	125	4.4
Malignant neoplasm of stomach — Tumeur maligne de l'estomac	260	9.4	127	4.5	259	9.4	155	5.5
Malignant neoplasm of colon, rectosigmoid junction, rectum, anus and anal canal — Tumeur maligne du côlon, de la jonction recto-sigmoïdienne, du rectum, de l'anus et du canal anal	984	35.7	958	34.1	981	35.5	917	32.6
Malignant neoplasm of liver and intrahepatic bile ducts — Tumeur maligne du foie et des voies bilaires intrahépatiques	246	8.9	125	4.5	255	9.2	143	5.1
Malignant neoplasm of pancreas — Tumeur maligne du pancréas..................	452	16.4	425	15.1	514	18.6	467	16.6
Malignant neoplasm of trachea, bronchus and lung — Tumeur maligne de la trachée, des bronches et du poumon	1 825	66.1	1 742	62.1	1 960	70.8	1 785	63.4
Malignant neoplasm of female breast — Tumeur maligne du sein chez la femme	..	..	1 200	...	..	..	1 123	...
Malignant neoplasm of cervix uteri — Tumeur maligne du col de l'utérus.........	..	..	75	...	..	..	95	...
Malignant neoplasm of prostate — Tumeur maligne de la prostate	1 228	...	..	..	1 153	...	..	..
Malignant neoplasm of lymphoid, haematopoietic and related tissue — Tumeurs malignes primitives ou présumées primitives des tissus lymphoïde, hématopoïétique et apparentés	628	22.8	465	16.6	603	21.8	449	16.0
Disorders of the blood and blood-forming organs and certain disorders involving the immune mechanism — Maladies du sang et des organes hématopoïétiques et certains troubles du système immunitaire								
Total	126	4.6	139	5.0	126	4.6	150	5.3
Anaemias — Anémies	87	3.2	103	3.7	81	2.9	119	4.2
Endocrine, nutritional and metabolic diseases — Maladies endocriniennes, nutritionnelles et métaboliques								
Total	891	32.3	774	27.6	875	31.6	784	27.9
Diabetes mellitus — Diabète sucré..	772	28.0	583	20.8	744	26.9	570	20.3
Malnutrition — Malnutrition	4	♦0.1	11	♦0.4	2	♦0.1	3	♦0.1
Mental and behavioural disorders — Troubles mentaux et du comportement	1 306	47.3	1 700	60.6	1 353	48.9	1 749	62.2
Diseases of the nervous system — Maladies du système nerveux................	778	28.2	1 034	36.8	831	30.0	1 046	37.2
Diseases of the circulatory system — Maladies de l'appareil circulatoire								
Total	6 373	230.9	6 720	239.4	6 442	232.8	6 654	236.5
Acute rheumatic fever and chronic rheumatic heart diseases — Rhumatisme articularie aigu et cardiopathies rhumatismales chroniques	20	♦0.7	31	1.1	28	♦1.0	43	1.5
Hypertensive diseases — Maladies hypertensives..	362	13.1	523	18.6	364	13.2	488	17.3
Ischaemic heart disease — Cardiopathie ischémique	2 456	89.0	2 004	71.4	2 426	87.7	1 944	69.1
Cerebrovascular disease — Maladie cérébrovasculaire................................	1 447	52.4	1 953	69.6	1 499	54.2	1 847	65.6

690

20. Death and death rates by cause and sex: 2010 - 2014
Décès et taux de mortalité par cause et sexe : 2010 - 2014 (continued - suite)

Denmark - Danemark

Cause of death — Cause de décès	2011 (C)				2012 (C)			
	Male — Masculin		Female — Féminin		Male — Masculin		Female — Féminin	
	Number Nombre	Rate Taux	Number Nombre	Rate Taux	Number Nombre	Rate Taux	Number Nombre	Rate Taux
Diseases of arteries, arterioles and capillaries — Maladies des artères, artérioles et capillaires	526	19.1	422	15.0	520	18.8	468	16.6
Diseases of the respiratory system — Maladies de l'appareil respiratoire								
Total	2 668	96.7	3 055	108.8	2 637	95.3	3 069	109.1
Influenza — Grippe	5	♦0.2	7	♦0.2	4	♦0.1	9	♦0.3
Pneumonia — Pneumopathies	813	29.5	1 017	36.2	829	30.0	949	33.7
Chronic lower respiratory diseases — Maladies chroniques des voies respiratoires inférieures	1 569	56.8	1 804	64.3	1 530	55.3	1 893	67.3
Diseases of the digestive system — Maladies de l'appareil digestif								
Total	1 257	45.5	1 187	42.3	1 157	41.8	1 086	38.6
Gastric and duodenal ulcer — Ulcère de l'estomac et du duodénum	138	5.0	194	6.9	114	4.1	158	5.6
Diseases of the liver — Maladies du foie	563	20.4	320	11.4	544	19.7	305	10.8
Diseases of the musculoskeletal system and connective tissue — Maladies du système ostéo-articularie, des muscles et du tissu conjonctif	118	4.3	210	7.5	111	4.0	272	9.7
Diseases of the genitourinary system — Maladies de l'appareil génito-urinaire								
Total	377	13.7	389	13.9	395	14.3	355	12.6
Disorders of kidney and ureter — Affections du rein et de l'uretère	222	8.0	218	7.8	281	10.2	217	7.7
Hyperplasia of prostate — Hyperplasie de la prostate	32	...	..	..	29	...	..	..
Pregnancy, childbirth and the puerperium — Grossesse, accouchement et puerpéralité								
Total	..	..	2	♦3.4	..	..	-	-
Pregnancy with abortive outcome — Grossesse se terminant par un avortement	..	..	1	♦1.7	..	..	-	-
Other direct obstetric causes — Autres décès maternels directs	..	..	1	♦1.7	..	..	-	-
Indirect obstetric causes — Décès maternels indirects	..	..	-	-	..	..	-	-
Certain conditions originating in the perinatal period — Certaines affections dont l'origine se situe dans la période périnatale	58	193.2	53	182.9	57	191.4	49	174.2
Congenital malformations, deformations and chromosomal abnormalities — Malformations congénitales et anomalies chromosomiques	62	206.6	62	213.9	72	241.7	74	263.1
Symptoms, signs and abnormal clinical and laboratory findings, not elsewhere classified — Symptômes, signes et résultats anormaux d'examens cliniques et de laboratoire, non classés ailleurs	1 844	66.8	2 512	89.5	1 687	61.0	2 108	74.9
All other diseases — Toutes autres maladies	25	♦0.9	42	1.5	25	♦0.9	40	1.4
External causes — Causes externes								
Total	1 340	48.5	820	29.2	1 286	46.5	806	28.6
Accidents								
Total	789	28.6	619	22.1	727	26.3	597	21.2
Transport accidents — Accidents de transport	173	6.3	56	2.0	141	5.1	49	1.7
Falls — Chutes	240	8.7	279	9.9	222	8.0	289	10.3
Accidental drowning and submersion — Noyade et submersion accidentelles	22	♦0.8	7	♦0.2	28	♦1.0	6	♦0.2
Exposure to smoke, fire and flames — Exposition à la fumée, au feu et aux flammes	31	1.1	28	♦1.0	38	1.4	18	♦0.6
Accidental poisoning by and exposure to noxious substances — Intoxication accidentelle par des substances nocives et exposition à ces substances	166	6.0	57	2.0	131	4.7	44	1.6
Intentional self-harm — Lésions auto-infligées	437	15.8	152	5.4	494	17.9	167	5.9
Assault — Agresssions	31	1.1	12	♦0.4	11	♦0.4	7	♦0.2
All other external causes — Toutes autres causes externes	83	3.0	37	1.3	54	2.0	35	1.2

20. Death and death rates by cause and sex: 2010 - 2014
Décès et taux de mortalité par cause et sexe : 2010 - 2014 (continued - suite)

Estonia - Estonie

Cause of death — Cause de décès	2013 (C)				2014 (C)			
	Male — Masculin		Female — Féminin		Male — Masculin		Female — Féminin	
	Number Nombre	Rate Taux	Number Nombre	Rate Taux	Number Nombre	Rate Taux	Number Nombre	Rate Taux
TOTAL	7 337	1 190.7	8 037	1 141.6	7 465	1 214.0	8 005	1 142.1
Certain infectious and parasitic diseases — Certaines maladies infectieuses et parasitaires								
Total	80	13.0	35	5.0	68	11.1	59	8.4
Intestinal infectious diseases — Maladies infectieuses intestinales	1	♦0.2	-	-	-	-	-	-
Tuberculosis — Tuberculose	16	♦2.6	4	♦0.6	13	♦2.1	9	♦1.3
Tetanus — Tétanos	-	-	-	-	-	-	-	-
Diphtheria — Diphtérie...	-	-	-	-	-	-	-	-
Whooping cough — Coqueluche	-	-	-	-	-	-	-	-
Meningococcal infection — Infection à méningocoques.........................	1	♦0.2	-	-	-	-	-	-
Septicaemia — Septicémie	5	♦0.8	3	♦0.4	5	♦0.8	15	♦2.1
Acute poliomyelitis — Poliomyélite aiguë	-	-	-	-	-	-	-	-
Measles — Rougeole...	-	-	-	-	-	-	-	-
Viral hepatitis — Hépatite virale	8	♦1.3	2	♦0.3	3	♦0.5	8	♦1.1
Human immunodeficiency virus [HIV] disease — Maladies dues au virus de l'immunodéficience humaine (VIH)........................	39	6.3	13	♦1.8	36	5.9	11	♦1.6
Malaria — Paludisme...	-	-	-	-	-	-	-	-
Neoplasms — Tumeurs	1 999	324.4	1 747	248.2	2 060	335.0	1 827	260.7
Malignant neoplasms — Tumeurs malignes								
Total	1 978	321.0	1 698	241.2	2 021	328.7	1 790	255.4
Malignant neoplasm of lip, oral cavity and pharynx — Tumeur maligne de la lèvre, de la cavité buccale et du pharynx	77	12.5	22	♦3.1	78	12.7	15	♦2.1
Malignant neoplasm of oesophagus — Tumeur maligne de l'oesophage	34	5.5	15	♦2.1	56	9.1	17	♦2.4
Malignant neoplasm of stomach — Tumeur maligne de l'estomac	169	27.4	122	17.3	170	27.6	139	19.8
Malignant neoplasm of colon, rectosigmoid junction, rectum, anus and anal canal — Tumeur maligne du côlon, de la jonction recto-sigmoïdienne, du rectum, de l'anus et du canal anal................................	210	34.1	251	35.7	215	35.0	240	34.2
Malignant neoplasm of liver and intrahepatic bile ducts — Tumeur maligne du foie et des voies bilaires intrahépatiques	56	9.1	39	5.5	42	6.8	41	5.8
Malignant neoplasm of pancreas — Tumeur maligne du pancréas...................	131	21.3	129	18.3	107	17.4	144	20.5
Malignant neoplasm of trachea, bronchus and lung — Tumeur maligne de la trachée, des bronches et du poumon	484	78.6	174	24.7	533	86.7	182	26.0
Malignant neoplasm of female breast — Tumeur maligne du sein chez la femme	..	..	209	...	..	..	251	41.8
Malignant neoplasm of cervix uteri — Tumeur maligne du col de l'utérus..........	..	..	63	...	..	..	66	11.0
Malignant neoplasm of prostate — Tumeur maligne de la prostate	259	...	..	..	271	134.9	..	..
Malignant neoplasm of lymphoid, haematopoietic and related tissue — Tumeurs malignes primitives ou présumées primitives des tissus lymphoïde, hématopoïétique et apparentés	147	23.9	172	24.4	135	22.0	156	22.3
Disorders of the blood and blood-forming organs and certain disorders involving the immune mechanism — Maladies du sang et des organes hématopoïétiques et certains troubles du système immunitaire								
Total	3	♦0.5	17	♦2.4	8	♦1.3	10	♦1.4
Anaemias — Anémies	2	♦0.3	12	♦1.7	5	♦0.8	7	♦1.0
Endocrine, nutritional and metabolic diseases — Maladies endocriniennes, nutritionnelles et métaboliques								
Total	69	11.2	104	14.8	59	9.6	108	15.4
Diabetes mellitus — Diabète sucré	61	9.9	85	12.1	53	8.6	97	13.8
Malnutrition — Malnutrition	-	-	1	♦0.1	-	-	-	-
Mental and behavioural disorders — Troubles mentaux et du comportement	71	11.5	37	5.3	71	11.5	36	5.1
Diseases of the nervous system — Maladies du système nerveux..................	142	23.0	149	21.2	147	23.9	136	19.4
Diseases of the circulatory system — Maladies de l'appareil circulatoire								
Total	3 287	533.5	5 006	711.1	3 342	543.5	4 908	700.2
Acute rheumatic fever and chronic rheumatic heart diseases — Rhumatisme articularie aigu et cardiopathies rhumatismales chroniques	7	♦1.1	24	♦3.4	5	♦0.8	13	♦1.9
Hypertensive diseases — Maladies hypertensives................................	765	124.2	1 522	216.2	877	142.6	1 727	246.4
Ischaemic heart disease — Cardiopathie ischémique	1 506	244.4	2 039	289.6	1 495	243.1	1 909	272.4
Cerebrovascular disease — Maladie cérébrovasculaire.........................	451	73.2	758	107.7	363	59.0	581	82.9

20. Death and death rates by cause and sex: 2010 - 2014
Décès et taux de mortalité par cause et sexe : 2010 - 2014 (continued - suite)

Estonia - Estonie

Cause of death — Cause de décès	2013 (C)				2014 (C)			
	Male — Masculin		Female — Féminin		Male — Masculin		Female — Féminin	
	Number Nombre	Rate Taux	Number Nombre	Rate Taux	Number Nombre	Rate Taux	Number Nombre	Rate Taux
Diseases of arteries, arterioles and capillaries — Maladies des artères, artérioles et capillaires	104	16.9	148	21.0	117	19.0	138	19.7
Diseases of the respiratory system — Maladies de l'appareil respiratoire								
Total	344	55.8	173	24.6	372	60.5	178	25.4
Influenza — Grippe	7	♦1.1	2	♦0.3	11	♦1.8	4	♦0.6
Pneumonia — Pneumopathies	153	24.8	79	11.2	158	25.7	94	13.4
Chronic lower respiratory diseases — Maladies chroniques des voies respiratoires inférieures	158	25.6	79	11.2	174	28.3	62	8.8
Diseases of the digestive system — Maladies de l'appareil digestif								
Total	323	52.4	247	35.1	339	55.1	245	35.0
Gastric and duodenal ulcer — Ulcère de l'estomac et du duodénum	37	6.0	28	♦4.0	32	5.2	28	♦4.0
Diseases of the liver — Maladies du foie	179	29.1	83	11.8	198	32.2	78	11.1
Diseases of the musculoskeletal system and connective tissue — Maladies du système ostéo-articularie, des muscles et du tissu conjonctif	12	♦1.9	33	4.7	13	♦2.1	26	♦3.7
Diseases of the genitourinary system — Maladies de l'appareil génito-urinaire								
Total	59	9.6	67	9.5	52	8.5	68	9.7
Disorders of kidney and ureter — Affections du rein et de l'uretère	40	6.5	55	7.8	35	5.7	54	7.7
Hyperplasia of prostate — Hyperplasie de la prostate	10	...	..	..	5	♦2.5	..	..
Pregnancy, childbirth and the puerperium — Grossesse, accouchement et puerpéralité								
Total	..	..	1	♦7.4	..	..	-	-
Pregnancy with abortive outcome — Grossesse se terminant par un avortement	..	..	-	-	..	..	-	-
Other direct obstetric causes — Autres décès maternels directs	..	..	1	♦7.4	..	..	-	-
Indirect obstetric causes — Décès maternels indirects	..	..	-	-	..	..	-	-
Certain conditions originating in the perinatal period — Certaines affections dont l'origine se situe dans la période périnatale	6	♦86.9	6	♦90.5	7	♦101.1	6	♦90.5
Congenital malformations, deformations and chromosomal abnormalities — Malformations congénitales et anomalies chromosomiques	11	♦159.4	12	♦181.0	17	♦245.6	12	♦181.0
Symptoms, signs and abnormal clinical and laboratory findings, not elsewhere classified — Symptômes, signes et résultats anormaux d'examens cliniques et de laboratoire, non classés ailleurs	162	26.3	153	21.7	152	24.7	158	22.5
All other diseases — Toutes autres maladies	5	♦0.8	11	♦1.6	4	♦0.7	7	♦1.0
External causes — Causes externes								
Total	764	124.0	239	33.9	754	122.6	221	31.5
Accidents								
Total	506	82.1	156	22.2	492	80.0	152	21.7
Transport accidents — Accidents de transport	65	10.5	29	♦4.1	64	10.4	28	♦4.0
Falls — Chutes	84	13.6	25	♦3.6	71	11.5	30	♦4.3
Accidental drowning and submersion — Noyade et submersion accidentelles	28	♦4.5	12	♦1.7	54	8.8	11	♦1.6
Exposure to smoke, fire and flames — Exposition à la fumée, au feu et aux flammes	30	♦4.9	14	♦2.0	33	5.4	11	♦1.6
Accidental poisoning by and exposure to noxious substances — Intoxication accidentelle par des substances nocives et exposition à ces substances	189	30.7	48	6.8	188	30.6	49	7.0
Intentional self-harm — Lésions auto-infligées	171	27.8	47	6.7	193	31.4	48	6.8
Assault — Agresssions	34	5.5	18	♦2.6	33	5.4	9	♦1.3
All other external causes — Toutes autres causes externes	53	8.6	18	♦2.6	36	5.9	12	♦1.7

20. Death and death rates by cause and sex: 2010 - 2014
Décès et taux de mortalité par cause et sexe : 2010 - 2014 (continued - suite)

Finland - Finlande

Cause of death — Cause de décès	2013 (C)				2014 (C)			
	Male — Masculin		Female — Féminin		Male — Masculin		Female — Féminin	
	Number Nombre	Rate Taux	Number Nombre	Rate Taux	Number Nombre	Rate Taux	Number Nombre	Rate Taux
TOTAL	25 627	961.0	25 851	936.6	25 864	964.9	26 545	958.0
Certain infectious and parasitic diseases — Certaines maladies infectieuses et parasitaires								
Total	155	5.8	157	5.7	139	5.2	171	6.2
Intestinal infectious diseases — Maladies infectieuses intestinales	16	♦0.6	19	♦0.7	6	♦0.2	11	♦0.4
Tuberculosis — Tuberculose	9	♦0.3	3	♦0.1	12	♦0.4	8	♦0.3
Tetanus — Tétanos..	-	-	-	-	-	-	-	-
Diphtheria — Diphtérie..	-	-	-	-	-	-	-	-
Whooping cough — Coqueluche	-	-	-	-	1	♦0.0	-	-
Meningococcal infection — Infection à méningocoques	3	♦0.1	2	♦0.1	1	♦0.0	1	♦0.0
Septicaemia — Septicémie	67	2.5	78	2.8	63	2.4	83	3.0
Acute poliomyelitis — Poliomyélite aiguë	-	-	-	-	-	-	-	-
Measles — Rougeole	-	-	-	-	-	-	-	-
Viral hepatitis — Hépatite virale.......................................	5	♦0.2	3	♦0.1	4	♦0.1	5	♦0.2
Human immunodeficiency virus [HIV] disease — Maladies dues au virus de l'immunodéficience humaine (VIH)................................	3	♦0.1	1	♦0.0	-	-	3	♦0.1
Malaria — Paludisme..	-	-	-	-	-	-	-	-
Neoplasms — Tumeurs	6 410	240.4	5 816	210.7	6 476	241.6	5 794	209.1
Malignant neoplasms — Tumeurs malignes								
Total	6 284	235.7	5 614	203.4	6 318	235.7	5 602	202.2
Malignant neoplasm of lip, oral cavity and pharynx — Tumeur maligne de la lèvre, de la cavité buccale et du pharynx	134	5.0	70	2.5	143	5.3	74	2.7
Malignant neoplasm of oesophagus — Tumeur maligne de l'oesophage	187	7.0	66	2.4	185	6.9	89	3.2
Malignant neoplasm of stomach — Tumeur maligne de l'estomac	262	9.8	217	7.9	244	9.1	169	6.1
Malignant neoplasm of colon, rectosigmoid junction, rectum, anus and anal canal — Tumeur maligne du côlon, de la jonction recto-sigmoïdienne, du rectum, de l'anus et du canal anal	617	23.1	583	21.1	646	24.1	583	21.0
Malignant neoplasm of liver and intrahepatic bile ducts — Tumeur maligne du foie et des voies bilaires intrahépatiques	266	10.0	187	6.8	303	11.3	186	6.7
Malignant neoplasm of pancreas — Tumeur maligne du pancréas...................	499	18.7	526	19.1	535	20.0	545	19.7
Malignant neoplasm of trachea, bronchus and lung — Tumeur maligne de la trachée, des bronches et du poumon	1 503	56.4	722	26.2	1 381	51.5	771	27.8
Malignant neoplasm of female breast — Tumeur maligne du sein chez la femme	..	..	866	...	..	..	813	34.8
Malignant neoplasm of cervix uteri — Tumeur maligne du col de l'utérus..........	..	..	54	...	..	..	53	2.3
Malignant neoplasm of prostate — Tumeur maligne de la prostate	853	...	..	..	859	84.9	..	..
Malignant neoplasm of lymphoid, haematopoietic and related tissue — Tumeurs malignes primitives ou présumées primitives des tissus lymphoïde, hématopoïétique et apparentés	577	21.6	568	20.6	604	22.5	578	20.9
Disorders of the blood and blood-forming organs and certain disorders involving the immune mechanism — Maladies du sang et des organes hématopoïétiques et certains troubles du système immunitaire								
Total	29	♦1.1	41	1.5	35	1.3	29	♦1.0
Anaemias — Anémies	9	♦0.3	17	♦0.6	13	♦0.5	12	♦0.4
Endocrine, nutritional and metabolic diseases — Maladies endocriniennes, nutritionnelles et métaboliques								
Total	325	12.2	307	11.1	352	13.1	327	11.8
Diabetes mellitus — Diabète sucré....................................	264	9.9	224	8.1	270	10.1	228	8.2
Malnutrition — Malnutrition	2	♦0.1	2	♦0.1	1	♦0.0	-	-
Mental and behavioural disorders — Troubles mentaux et du comportement	859	32.2	1 431	51.8	853	31.8	1 472	53.1
Diseases of the nervous system — Maladies du système nerveux.................	2 507	94.0	4 543	164.6	2 805	104.6	5 111	184.5
Diseases of the circulatory system — Maladies de l'appareil circulatoire								
Total	9 575	359.1	10 079	365.2	9 496	354.3	10 147	366.2
Acute rheumatic fever and chronic rheumatic heart diseases — Rhumatisme articularie aigu et cardiopathies rhumatismales chroniques	14	♦0.5	22	♦0.8	8	♦0.3	17	♦0.6
Hypertensive diseases — Maladies hypertensives............................	450	16.9	865	31.3	518	19.3	1 061	38.3
Ischaemic heart disease — Cardiopathie ischémique	5 558	208.4	4 994	180.9	5 532	206.4	4 805	173.4
Cerebrovascular disease — Maladie cérébrovasculaire.................	1 843	69.1	2 576	93.3	1 786	66.6	2 642	95.3

Finland - Finlande

Cause of death — Cause de décès	2013 (C)				2014 (C)			
	Male — Masculin		Female — Féminin		Male — Masculin		Female — Féminin	
	Number Nombre	Rate Taux	Number Nombre	Rate Taux	Number Nombre	Rate Taux	Number Nombre	Rate Taux
Diseases of arteries, arterioles and capillaries — Maladies des artères, artérioles et capillaires	559	21.0	516	18.7	550	20.5	472	17.0
Diseases of the respiratory system — Maladies de l'appareil respiratoire								
Total	1 186	44.5	707	25.6	1 149	42.9	688	24.8
Influenza — Grippe..........	11	♦0.4	17	♦0.6	9	♦0.3	17	♦0.6
Pneumonia — Pneumopathies..........	125	4.7	133	4.8	99	3.7	81	2.9
Chronic lower respiratory diseases — Maladies chroniques des voies respiratoires inférieures	821	30.8	413	15.0	813	30.3	443	16.0
Diseases of the digestive system — Maladies de l'appareil digestif								
Total	1 476	55.4	978	35.4	1 478	55.1	951	34.3
Gastric and duodenal ulcer — Ulcère de l'estomac et du duodénum..........	84	3.2	60	2.2	94	3.5	51	1.8
Diseases of the liver — Maladies du foie..........	925	34.7	352	12.8	904	33.7	335	12.1
Diseases of the musculoskeletal system and connective tissue — Maladies du système ostéo-articularie, des muscles et du tissu conjonctif	74	2.8	132	4.8	72	2.7	133	4.8
Diseases of the genitourinary system — Maladies de l'appareil génito-urinaire								
Total	163	6.1	210	7.6	141	5.3	174	6.3
Disorders of kidney and ureter — Affections du rein et de l'uretère	131	4.9	183	6.6	124	4.6	149	5.4
Hyperplasia of prostate — Hyperplasie de la prostate..........	16	...	..	..	9	♦0.9	..	..
Pregnancy, childbirth and the puerperium — Grossesse, accouchement et puerpéralité								
Total	..	..	1	♦1.7	..	..	3	♦5.3
Pregnancy with abortive outcome — Grossesse se terminant par un avortement	..	..	-	-	..	..	-	-
Other direct obstetric causes — Autres décès maternels directs	..	..	1	♦1.7	..	..	2	♦3.5
Indirect obstetric causes — Décès maternels indirects	..	..	-	-	..	..	1	♦1.8
Certain conditions originating in the perinatal period — Certaines affections dont l'origine se situe dans la période périnatale	24	♦80.8	18	♦64.0	20	♦68.7	26	♦93.4
Congenital malformations, deformations and chromosomal abnormalities — Malformations congénitales et anomalies chromosomiques	69	232.3	98	348.3	87	298.7	90	323.4
Symptoms, signs and abnormal clinical and laboratory findings, not elsewhere classified — Symptômes, signes et résultats anormaux d'examens cliniques et de laboratoire, non classés ailleurs	317	11.9	164	5.9	426	15.9	259	9.3
All other diseases — Toutes autres maladies	10	♦0.4	12	♦0.4	17	♦0.6	11	♦0.4
External causes — Causes externes								
Total	2 448	91.8	1 157	41.9	2 318	86.5	1 159	41.8
Accidents								
Total	1 614	60.5	872	31.6	1 525	56.9	874	31.5
Transport accidents — Accidents de transport..........	240	9.0	78	2.8	232	8.7	69	2.5
Falls — Chutes..........	596	22.4	517	18.7	587	21.9	554	20.0
Accidental drowning and submersion — Noyade et submersion accidentelles..........	101	3.8	30	♦1.1	87	3.2	28	♦1.0
Exposure to smoke, fire and flames — Exposition à la fumée, au feu et aux flammes..........	34	1.3	13	♦0.5	50	1.9	20	♦0.7
Accidental poisoning by and exposure to noxious substances — Intoxication accidentelle par des substances nocives et exposition à ces substances	440	16.5	157	5.7	383	14.3	110	4.0
Intentional self-harm — Lésions auto-infligées..........	666	25.0	221	8.0	595	22.2	188	6.8
Assault — Agresssions..........	58	2.2	19	♦0.7	48	1.8	27	♦1.0
All other external causes — Toutes autres causes externes	110	4.1	45	1.6	150	5.6	70	2.5

20. Death and death rates by cause and sex: 2010 - 2014
Décès et taux de mortalité par cause et sexe : 2010 - 2014 (continued - suite)

France

Cause of death — Cause de décès	2012 (C)				2013 (C)			
	Male — Masculin		Female — Féminin		Male — Masculin		Female — Féminin	
	Number Nombre	Rate Taux	Number Nombre	Rate Taux	Number Nombre	Rate Taux	Number Nombre	Rate Taux
TOTAL	**280 821**	**912.3**	**277 631**	**847.6**	**279 954**	**907.4**	**276 077**	**841.5**
Certain infectious and parasitic diseases — Certaines maladies infectieuses et parasitaires								
Total	5 544	18.0	6 011	18.4	5 086	16.5	5 574	17.0
Intestinal infectious diseases — Maladies infectieuses intestinales	948	3.1	1 564	4.8	766	2.5	1 195	3.6
Tuberculosis — Tuberculose	135	0.4	131	0.4	124	0.4	75	0.2
Tetanus — Tétanos	1	♦0.0	1	♦0.0	-	-	1	♦0.0
Diphtheria — Diphtérie	-	-	-	-	1	♦0.0	-	-
Whooping cough — Coqueluche	3	♦0.0	7	♦0.0	2	♦0.0	8	♦0.0
Meningococcal infection — Infection à méningocoques	8	♦0.0	5	♦0.0	9	♦0.0	14	♦0.0
Septicaemia — Septicémie	2 729	8.9	2 603	7.9	2 551	8.3	2 647	8.1
Acute poliomyelitis — Poliomyélite aiguë	-	-	-	-	-	-	-	-
Measles — Rougeole	-	-	1	♦0.0	-	-	-	-
Viral hepatitis — Hépatite virale	371	1.2	289	0.9	337	1.1	274	0.8
Human immunodeficiency virus [HIV] disease — Maladies dues au virus de l'immunodéficience humaine (VIH)	304	1.0	108	0.3	320	1.0	129	0.4
Malaria — Paludisme	8	♦0.0	4	♦0.0	10	♦0.0	2	♦0.0
Neoplasms — Tumeurs	**92 665**	**301.0**	**68 141**	**208.0**	**92 045**	**298.3**	**67 673**	**206.3**
Malignant neoplasms — Tumeurs malignes								
Total	89 121	289.5	64 857	198.0	88 516	286.9	64 255	195.9
Malignant neoplasm of lip, oral cavity and pharynx — Tumeur maligne de la lèvre, de la cavité buccale et du pharynx	3 000	9.7	784	2.4	3 021	9.8	819	2.5
Malignant neoplasm of oesophagus — Tumeur maligne de l'oesophage	3 038	9.9	758	2.3	2 877	9.3	775	2.4
Malignant neoplasm of stomach — Tumeur maligne de l'estomac	2 938	9.5	1 654	5.0	2 985	9.7	1 680	5.1
Malignant neoplasm of colon, rectosigmoid junction, rectum, anus and anal canal — Tumeur maligne du côlon, de la jonction recto-sigmoïdienne, du rectum, de l'anus et du canal anal	9 058	29.4	8 096	24.7	9 044	29.3	7 882	24.0
Malignant neoplasm of liver and intrahepatic bile ducts — Tumeur maligne du foie et des voies bilaires intrahépatiques	5 856	19.0	2 180	6.7	5 911	19.2	2 209	6.7
Malignant neoplasm of pancreas — Tumeur maligne du pancréas	4 839	15.7	4 772	14.6	5 143	16.7	4 974	15.2
Malignant neoplasm of trachea, bronchus and lung — Tumeur maligne de la trachée, des bronches et du poumon	22 311	72.5	8 246	25.2	22 190	71.9	8 021	24.4
Malignant neoplasm of female breast — Tumeur maligne du sein chez la femme	..	..	11 691	...	..	..	11 678	...
Malignant neoplasm of cervix uteri — Tumeur maligne du col de l'utérus	..	..	786	...	..	..	749	...
Malignant neoplasm of prostate — Tumeur maligne de la prostate	8 574	...	..	..	8 590	...	..	..
Malignant neoplasm of lymphoid, haematopoietic and related tissue — Tumeurs malignes primitives ou présumées primitives des tissus lymphoïde, hématopoïétique et apparentés	7 302	23.7	6 247	19.1	7 379	23.9	6 207	18.9
Disorders of the blood and blood-forming organs and certain disorders involving the immune mechanism — Maladies du sang et des organes hématopoïétiques et certains troubles du système immunitaire								
Total	894	2.9	1 152	3.5	900	2.9	1 134	3.5
Anaemias — Anémies	461	1.5	734	2.2	466	1.5	708	2.2
Endocrine, nutritional and metabolic diseases — Maladies endocriniennes, nutritionnelles et métaboliques								
Total	8 712	28.3	10 822	33.0	8 608	27.9	10 869	33.1
Diabetes mellitus — Diabète sucré	5 493	17.8	5 730	17.5	5 450	17.7	5 720	17.4
Malnutrition — Malnutrition	1 013	3.3	1 980	6.0	1 017	3.3	1 975	6.0
Mental and behavioural disorders — Troubles mentaux et du comportement	**8 879**	**28.8**	**12 752**	**38.9**	**9 038**	**29.3**	**13 140**	**40.1**
Diseases of the nervous system — Maladies du système nerveux	**13 724**	**44.6**	**22 059**	**67.3**	**13 455**	**43.6**	**21 522**	**65.6**
Diseases of the circulatory system — Maladies de l'appareil circulatoire								
Total	65 412	212.5	75 925	231.8	64 213	208.1	74 681	227.6
Acute rheumatic fever and chronic rheumatic heart diseases — Rhumatisme articularie aigu et cardiopathies rhumatismales chroniques	558	1.8	1 065	3.3	614	2.0	1 034	3.2
Hypertensive diseases — Maladies hypertensives	3 211	10.4	6 091	18.6	3 424	11.1	6 415	19.6
Ischaemic heart disease — Cardiopathie ischémique	20 064	65.2	14 665	44.8	19 439	63.0	13 990	42.6
Cerebrovascular disease — Maladie cérébrovasculaire	13 333	43.3	18 978	57.9	13 074	42.4	18 525	56.5

20. Death and death rates by cause and sex: 2010 - 2014
Décès et taux de mortalité par cause et sexe : 2010 - 2014 (continued - suite)

France

Cause of death — Cause de décès	2012 (C)				2013 (C)			
	Male — Masculin		Female — Féminin		Male — Masculin		Female — Féminin	
	Number Nombre	Rate Taux	Number Nombre	Rate Taux	Number Nombre	Rate Taux	Number Nombre	Rate Taux
Diseases of arteries, arterioles and capillaries — Maladies des artères, artérioles et capillaires	4 392	14.3	3 313	10.1	4 206	13.6	3 393	10.3
Diseases of the respiratory system — Maladies de l'appareil respiratoire								
Total	19 251	62.5	18 848	57.5	18 994	61.6	17 836	54.4
Influenza — Grippe	229	0.7	421	1.3	240	0.8	357	1.1
Pneumonia — Pneumopathies	5 518	17.9	6 604	20.2	5 589	18.1	6 218	19.0
Chronic lower respiratory diseases — Maladies chroniques des voies respiratoires inférieures	5 938	19.3	4 122	12.6	6 183	20.0	4 136	12.6
Diseases of the digestive system — Maladies de l'appareil digestif								
Total	12 252	39.8	10 440	31.9	12 062	39.1	10 383	31.6
Gastric and duodenal ulcer — Ulcère de l'estomac et du duodénum	450	1.5	406	1.2	398	1.3	422	1.3
Diseases of the liver — Maladies du foie	5 571	18.1	2 465	7.5	5 347	17.3	2 420	7.4
Diseases of the musculoskeletal system and connective tissue — Maladies du système ostéo-articularie, des muscles et du tissu conjonctif	1 509	4.9	2 439	7.4	1 551	5.0	2 479	7.6
Diseases of the genitourinary system — Maladies de l'appareil génito-urinaire								
Total	4 204	13.7	4 493	13.7	4 322	14.0	4 412	13.4
Disorders of kidney and ureter — Affections du rein et de l'uretère	3 235	10.5	3 551	10.8	3 278	10.6	3 484	10.6
Hyperplasia of prostate — Hyperplasie de la prostate	59	...	..	..	71	...	..	..
Pregnancy, childbirth and the puerperium — Grossesse, accouchement et puerpéralité								
Total	..	..	44	5.6	..	..	38	4.9
Pregnancy with abortive outcome — Grossesse se terminant par un avortement	..	..	3	◆0.4	..	..	2	◆0.3
Other direct obstetric causes — Autres décès maternels directs	..	..	30	◆3.8	..	..	30	◆3.8
Indirect obstetric causes — Décès maternels indirects	..	..	9	◆1.1	..	..	6	◆0.8
Certain conditions originating in the perinatal period — Certaines affections dont l'origine se situe dans la période périnatale	784	193.7	580	150.4	778	194.4	627	164.4
Congenital malformations, deformations and chromosomal abnormalities — Malformations congénitales et anomalies chromosomiques	754	186.3	686	177.9	791	197.7	709	185.9
Symptoms, signs and abnormal clinical and laboratory findings, not elsewhere classified — Symptômes, signes et résultats anormaux d'examens cliniques et de laboratoire, non classés ailleurs	23 747	77.1	27 551	84.1	26 323	85.3	29 560	90.1
All other diseases — Toutes autres maladies	459	1.5	819	2.5	467	1.5	852	2.6
External causes — Causes externes								
Total	22 031	71.6	14 869	45.4	21 321	69.1	14 588	44.5
Accidents								
Total	13 387	43.5	11 615	35.5	12 864	41.7	11 382	34.7
Transport accidents — Accidents de transport	2 587	8.4	854	2.6	2 317	7.5	701	2.1
Falls — Chutes	2 838	9.2	3 247	9.9	3 146	10.2	3 400	10.4
Accidental drowning and submersion — Noyade et submersion accidentelles	630	2.0	316	1.0	644	2.1	310	0.9
Exposure to smoke, fire and flames — Exposition à la fumée, au feu et aux flammes	251	0.8	164	0.5	234	0.8	164	0.5
Accidental poisoning by and exposure to noxious substances — Intoxication accidentelle par des substances nocives et exposition à ces substances	1 109	3.6	925	2.8	1 104	3.6	885	2.7
Intentional self-harm — Lésions auto-infligées	7 312	23.8	2 410	7.4	7 217	23.4	2 372	7.2
Assault — Agresssions	237	0.8	158	0.5	245	0.8	150	0.5
All other external causes — Toutes autres causes externes	1 095	3.6	686	2.1	995	3.2	684	2.1

20. Death and death rates by cause and sex: 2010 - 2014
Décès et taux de mortalité par cause et sexe : 2010 - 2014 (continued - suite)

Germany - Allemagne

Cause of death — Cause de décès	2013 (C)				2014 (C)			
	Male — Masculin		Female — Féminin		Male — Masculin		Female — Féminin	
	Number Nombre	Rate Taux	Number Nombre	Rate Taux	Number Nombre	Rate Taux	Number Nombre	Rate Taux
TOTAL	429 645	1 088.6	464 180	1 127.3	422 223	1 067.4	446 133	1 082.6
Certain infectious and parasitic diseases — Certaines maladies infectieuses et parasitaires								
Total	8 357	21.2	10 123	24.6	8 350	21.1	9 637	23.4
Intestinal infectious diseases — Maladies infectieuses intestinales	2 136	5.4	3 624	8.8	1 904	4.8	3 277	8.0
Tuberculosis — Tuberculose	189	0.5	122	0.3	146	0.4	115	0.3
Tetanus — Tétanos.........	1	♦0.0	-	-	1	♦0.0	1	♦0.0
Diphtheria — Diphtérie.........	-	-	-	-	-	-	-	-
Whooping cough — Coqueluche	1	♦0.0	1	♦0.0	-	-	1	♦0.0
Meningococcal infection — Infection à méningocoques	15	♦0.0	18	♦0.0	11	♦0.0	19	♦0.0
Septicaemia — Septicémie.........	3 894	9.9	4 103	10.0	4 325	10.9	4 194	10.2
Acute poliomyelitis — Poliomyélite aiguë	-	-	-	-	-	-	1	♦0.0
Measles — Rougeole.........	1	♦0.0	1	♦0.0	1	♦0.0	-	-
Viral hepatitis — Hépatite virale	529	1.3	462	1.1	448	1.1	406	1.0
Human immunodeficiency virus [HIV] disease — Maladies dues au virus de l'immunodéficience humaine (VIH).........	335	0.8	66	0.2	305	0.8	83	0.2
Malaria — Paludisme.........	5	♦0.0	-	-	4	♦0.0	1	♦0.0
Neoplasms — Tumeurs	125 054	316.8	105 786	256.9	125 120	316.3	105 651	256.4
Malignant neoplasms — Tumeurs malignes								
Total	121 748	308.5	102 094	247.9	121 766	307.8	101 992	247.5
Malignant neoplasm of lip, oral cavity and pharynx — Tumeur maligne de la lèvre, de la cavité buccale et du pharynx	4 084	10.3	1 389	3.4	4 095	10.4	1 353	3.3
Malignant neoplasm of oesophagus — Tumeur maligne de l'oesophage	4 244	10.8	1 192	2.9	4 107	10.4	1 236	3.0
Malignant neoplasm of stomach — Tumeur maligne de l'estomac	5 591	14.2	4 031	9.8	5 545	14.0	4 065	9.9
Malignant neoplasm of colon, rectosigmoid junction, rectum, anus and anal canal — Tumeur maligne du côlon, de la jonction recto-sigmoïdienne, du rectum, de l'anus et du canal anal	13 608	34.5	12 085	29.3	13 580	34.3	11 932	29.0
Malignant neoplasm of liver and intrahepatic bile ducts — Tumeur maligne du foie et des voies bilaires intrahépatiques	5 000	12.7	2 467	6.0	5 246	13.3	2 440	5.9
Malignant neoplasm of pancreas — Tumeur maligne du pancréas.........	8 273	21.0	8 328	20.2	8 231	20.8	8 384	20.3
Malignant neoplasm of trachea, bronchus and lung — Tumeur maligne de la trachée, des bronches et du poumon	29 708	75.3	15 140	36.8	29 560	74.7	15 524	37.7
Malignant neoplasm of female breast — Tumeur maligne du sein chez la femme	..	..	17 853	49.0	..	..	17 670	49.0
Malignant neoplasm of cervix uteri — Tumeur maligne du col de l'utérus.........	..	..	1 550	4.3	..	..	1 506	4.2
Malignant neoplasm of prostate — Tumeur maligne de la prostate	13 408	83.9	..	..	13 704	86.1	..	..
Malignant neoplasm of lymphoid, haematopoietic and related tissue — Tumeurs malignes primitives ou présumées primitives des tissus lymphoïde, hématopoïétique et apparentés	10 255	26.0	8 576	20.8	10 009	25.3	8 600	20.9
Disorders of the blood and blood-forming organs and certain disorders involving the immune mechanism — Maladies du sang et des organes hématopoïétiques et certains troubles du système immunitaire								
Total	1 205	3.1	1 711	4.2	1 198	3.0	1 733	4.2
Anaemias — Anémies	489	1.2	921	2.2	480	1.2	895	2.2
Endocrine, nutritional and metabolic diseases — Maladies endocriniennes, nutritionnelles et métaboliques								
Total	13 347	33.8	17 850	43.3	12 646	32.0	16 624	40.3
Diabetes mellitus — Diabète sucré.........	10 484	26.6	13 773	33.4	9 941	25.1	12 702	30.8
Malnutrition — Malnutrition	69	0.2	194	0.5	91	0.2	178	0.4
Mental and behavioural disorders — Troubles mentaux et du comportement	14 241	36.1	21 876	53.1	13 974	35.3	21 961	53.3
Diseases of the nervous system — Maladies du système nerveux.........	12 470	31.6	13 284	32.3	12 636	31.9	13 222	32.1
Diseases of the circulatory system — Maladies de l'appareil circulatoire								
Total	153 309	388.4	201 184	488.6	148 538	375.5	189 518	459.9
Acute rheumatic fever and chronic rheumatic heart diseases — Rhumatisme articularie aigu et cardiopathies rhumatismales chroniques	978	2.5	1 913	4.6	1 022	2.6	2 089	5.1
Hypertensive diseases — Maladies hypertensives.........	11 896	30.1	27 740	67.4	11 311	28.6	25 865	62.8
Ischaemic heart disease — Cardiopathie ischémique	67 175	170.2	61 633	149.7	64 467	163.0	56 699	137.6
Cerebrovascular disease — Maladie cérébrovasculaire.........	23 167	58.7	35 389	85.9	22 012	55.6	33 220	80.6

Germany - Allemagne

Cause of death — Cause de décès	2013 (C)				2014 (C)			
	Male — Masculin		Female — Féminin		Male — Masculin		Female — Féminin	
	Number Nombre	Rate Taux	Number Nombre	Rate Taux	Number Nombre	Rate Taux	Number Nombre	Rate Taux
Diseases of arteries, arterioles and capillaries — Maladies des artères, artérioles et capillaires	8 391	21.3	10 113	24.6	8 256	20.9	9 621	23.3
Diseases of the respiratory system — Maladies de l'appareil respiratoire								
Total	34 431	87.2	30 487	74.0	31 744	80.2	26 860	65.2
Influenza — Grippe	130	0.3	171	0.4	33	0.1	34	0.1
Pneumonia — Pneumopathies	9 824	24.9	10 094	24.5	8 474	21.4	8 237	20.0
Chronic lower respiratory diseases — Maladies chroniques des voies respiratoires inférieures	18 046	45.7	14 704	35.7	17 086	43.2	13 402	32.5
Diseases of the digestive system — Maladies de l'appareil digestif								
Total	20 564	52.1	19 548	47.5	19 993	50.5	18 544	45.0
Gastric and duodenal ulcer — Ulcère de l'estomac et du duodénum	1 149	2.9	1 418	3.4	1 025	2.6	1 194	2.9
Diseases of the liver — Maladies du foie	9 950	25.2	5 305	12.9	9 590	24.2	5 154	12.5
Diseases of the musculoskeletal system and connective tissue — Maladies du système ostéo-articularie, des muscles et du tissu conjonctif	1 270	3.2	2 254	5.5	1 175	3.0	2 142	5.2
Diseases of the genitourinary system — Maladies de l'appareil génito-urinaire								
Total	9 463	24.0	12 425	30.2	9 779	24.7	12 468	30.3
Disorders of kidney and ureter — Affections du rein et de l'uretère	7 280	18.4	9 469	23.0	7 441	18.8	9 366	22.7
Hyperplasia of prostate — Hyperplasie de la prostate	162	1.0	..	..	145	0.9	..	..
Pregnancy, childbirth and the puerperium — Grossesse, accouchement et puerpéralité								
Total	..	..	29	◆4.3	..	..	29	◆4.1
Pregnancy with abortive outcome — Grossesse se terminant par un avortement	..	..	1	◆0.1	..	..	2	◆0.3
Other direct obstetric causes — Autres décès maternels directs	..	..	22	◆3.2	..	..	23	◆3.2
Indirect obstetric causes — Décès maternels indirects	..	..	5	◆0.7	..	..	4	◆0.6
Certain conditions originating in the perinatal period — Certaines affections dont l'origine se situe dans la période périnatale	635	181.5	482	145.1	704	191.9	533	153.1
Congenital malformations, deformations and chromosomal abnormalities — Malformations congénitales et anomalies chromosomiques	887	253.6	819	246.5	866	236.1	799	229.5
Symptoms, signs and abnormal clinical and laboratory findings, not elsewhere classified — Symptômes, signes et résultats anormaux d'examens cliniques et de laboratoire, non classés ailleurs	13 518	34.2	11 671	28.3	14 130	35.7	11 669	28.3
All other diseases — Toutes autres maladies	471	1.2	941	2.3	525	1.3	921	2.2
External causes — Causes externes								
Total	20 423	51.7	13 710	33.3	20 845	52.7	13 822	33.5
Accidents								
Total	10 975	27.8	9 343	22.7	11 294	28.6	9 634	23.4
Transport accidents — Accidents de transport	2 789	7.1	982	2.4	2 796	7.1	927	2.2
Falls — Chutes	4 972	12.6	5 870	14.3	5 363	13.6	6 219	15.1
Accidental drowning and submersion — Noyade et submersion accidentelles	335	0.8	130	0.3	287	0.7	102	0.2
Exposure to smoke, fire and flames — Exposition à la fumée, au feu et aux flammes	241	0.6	174	0.4	214	0.5	133	0.3
Accidental poisoning by and exposure to noxious substances — Intoxication accidentelle par des substances nocives et exposition à ces substances	478	1.2	172	0.4	476	1.2	176	0.4
Intentional self-harm — Lésions auto-infligées	7 449	18.9	2 627	6.4	7 624	19.3	2 585	6.3
Assault — Agresssions	180	0.5	214	0.5	174	0.4	194	0.5
All other external causes — Toutes autres causes externes	1 819	4.6	1 526	3.7	1 753	4.4	1 409	3.4

20. Death and death rates by cause and sex: 2010 - 2014
Décès et taux de mortalité par cause et sexe : 2010 - 2014 (continued - suite)

Greece - Grèce

Cause of death — Cause de décès	2010 (C)				2011 (C)			
	Male — Masculin		Female — Féminin		Male — Masculin		Female — Féminin	
	Number Nombre	Rate Taux	Number Nombre	Rate Taux	Number Nombre	Rate Taux	Number Nombre	Rate Taux
TOTAL	56 480	1 029.0	52 604	923.7	57 999	1 063.5	53 100	936.5
Certain infectious and parasitic diseases — Certaines maladies infectieuses et parasitaires								
Total	515	9.4	561	9.9	469	8.6	501	8.8
Intestinal infectious diseases — Maladies infectieuses intestinales	-	-	-	-	-	-	1	♦0.0
Tuberculosis — Tuberculose	50	0.9	21	♦0.4	41	0.8	26	♦0.5
Tetanus — Tétanos..................	3	♦0.1	-	-	3	♦0.1	1	♦0.0
Diphtheria — Diphtérie..................	-	-	-	-	-	-	-	-
Whooping cough — Coqueluche	-	-	-	-	-	-	-	-
Meningococcal infection — Infection à méningocoques..................	1	♦0.0	2	♦0.0	-	-	-	-
Septicaemia — Septicémie..................	369	6.7	502	8.8	335	6.1	418	7.4
Acute poliomyelitis — Poliomyélite aiguë	1	♦0.0	-	-	-	-	-	-
Measles — Rougeole..................	-	-	-	-	-	-	-	-
Viral hepatitis — Hépatite virale..................	52	0.9	23	♦0.4	48	0.9	29	♦0.5
Human immunodeficiency virus [HIV] disease — Maladies dues au virus de l'immunodéficience humaine (VIH)..................	16	♦0.3	2	♦0.0	13	♦0.2	5	♦0.1
Malaria — Paludisme..................	1	♦0.0	-	-	1	♦0.0	-	-
Neoplasms — Tumeurs	16 418	299.1	10 759	188.9	16 726	306.7	10 631	187.5
Malignant neoplasms — Tumeurs malignes								
Total	16 407	298.9	10 752	188.8	16 716	306.5	10 625	187.4
Malignant neoplasm of lip, oral cavity and pharynx — Tumeur maligne de la lèvre, de la cavité buccale et du pharynx	173	3.2	86	1.5	192	3.5	86	1.5
Malignant neoplasm of oesophagus — Tumeur maligne de l'oesophage	168	3.1	48	0.8	139	2.5	50	0.9
Malignant neoplasm of stomach — Tumeur maligne de l'estomac	767	14.0	492	8.6	767	14.1	522	9.2
Malignant neoplasm of colon, rectosigmoid junction, rectum, anus and anal canal — Tumeur maligne du côlon, de la jonction recto-sigmoïdienne, du rectum, de l'anus et du canal anal..................	1 314	23.9	1 064	18.7	1 336	24.5	1 102	19.4
Malignant neoplasm of liver and intrahepatic bile ducts — Tumeur maligne du foie et des voies bilaires intrahépatiques	210	3.8	88	1.5	193	3.5	58	1.0
Malignant neoplasm of pancreas — Tumeur maligne du pancréas..................	729	13.3	730	12.8	841	15.4	720	12.7
Malignant neoplasm of trachea, bronchus and lung — Tumeur maligne de la trachée, des bronches et du poumon	5 263	95.9	1 144	20.1	5 367	98.4	1 214	21.4
Malignant neoplasm of female breast — Tumeur maligne du sein chez la femme	..	..	2 028	41.4	..	..	1 842	37.8
Malignant neoplasm of cervix uteri — Tumeur maligne du col de l'utérus.........	..	..	174	3.6	..	..	168	3.4
Malignant neoplasm of prostate — Tumeur maligne de la prostate	1 558	80.9	..	..	1 533	78.9	..	..
Malignant neoplasm of lymphoid, haematopoietic and related tissue — Tumeurs malignes primitives ou présumées primitives des tissus lymphoïde, hématopoïétique et apparentés	1 124	20.5	822	14.4	1 122	20.6	857	15.1
Disorders of the blood and blood-forming organs and certain disorders involving the immune mechanism — Maladies du sang et des organes hématopoïétiques et certains troubles du système immunitaire								
Total	188	3.4	159	2.8	197	3.6	174	3.1
Anaemias — Anémies	29	♦0.5	30	♦0.5	26	♦0.5	22	♦0.4
Endocrine, nutritional and metabolic diseases — Maladies endocriniennes, nutritionnelles et métaboliques								
Total	663	12.1	679	11.9	791	14.5	704	12.4
Diabetes mellitus — Diabète sucré..................	529	9.6	546	9.6	629	11.5	523	9.2
Malnutrition — Malnutrition	-	-	-	-	-	-	-	-
Mental and behavioural disorders — Troubles mentaux et du comportement	57	1.0	41	0.7	58	1.1	68	1.2
Diseases of the nervous system — Maladies du système nerveux..................	754	13.7	775	13.6	749	13.7	768	13.5
Diseases of the circulatory system — Maladies de l'appareil circulatoire								
Total	22 413	408.3	25 293	444.1	22 744	417.1	24 997	440.9
Acute rheumatic fever and chronic rheumatic heart diseases — Rhumatisme articularie aigu et cardiopathies rhumatismales chroniques	2	♦0.0	2	♦0.0	-	-	3	♦0.1
Hypertensive diseases — Maladies hypertensives..................	723	13.2	842	14.8	769	14.1	817	14.4
Ischaemic heart disease — Cardiopathie ischémique	7 066	128.7	4 266	74.9	7 226	132.5	4 274	75.4
Cerebrovascular disease — Maladie cérébrovasculaire..................	6 238	113.6	8 672	152.3	6 334	116.1	8 707	153.6

Greece - Grèce

Cause of death — Cause de décès	2010 (C)				2011 (C)			
	Male — Masculin		Female — Féminin		Male — Masculin		Female — Féminin	
	Number Nombre	Rate Taux	Number Nombre	Rate Taux	Number Nombre	Rate Taux	Number Nombre	Rate Taux
Diseases of arteries, arterioles and capillaries — Maladies des artères, artérioles et capillaires	559	10.2	202	3.5	606	11.1	269	4.7
Diseases of the respiratory system — Maladies de l'appareil respiratoire								
Total	5 318	96.9	5 023	88.2	5 320	97.6	5 015	88.4
Influenza — Grippe	30	♦0.5	25	♦0.4	64	1.2	48	0.8
Pneumonia — Pneumopathies	497	9.1	455	8.0	521	9.6	441	7.8
Chronic lower respiratory diseases — Maladies chroniques des voies respiratoires inférieures	1 411	25.7	1 002	17.6	1 362	25.0	908	16.0
Diseases of the digestive system — Maladies de l'appareil digestif								
Total	1 460	26.6	1 116	19.6	1 596	29.3	1 176	20.7
Gastric and duodenal ulcer — Ulcère de l'estomac et du duodénum	200	3.6	174	3.1	237	4.3	203	3.6
Diseases of the liver — Maladies du foie	581	10.6	185	3.2	602	11.0	207	3.7
Diseases of the musculoskeletal system and connective tissue — Maladies du système ostéo-articularie, des muscles et du tissu conjonctif	249	4.5	299	5.3	243	4.5	333	5.9
Diseases of the genitourinary system — Maladies de l'appareil génito-urinaire								
Total	928	16.9	970	17.0	909	16.7	873	15.4
Disorders of kidney and ureter — Affections du rein et de l'uretère	864	15.7	852	15.0	848	15.5	777	13.7
Hyperplasia of prostate — Hyperplasie de la prostate	-	-	..	..	-	-	..	..
Pregnancy, childbirth and the puerperium — Grossesse, accouchement et puerpéralité								
Total	..	..	6	♦5.2	..	..	4	♦3.8
Pregnancy with abortive outcome — Grossesse se terminant par un avortement	..	..	1	♦0.9	..	..	1	♦0.9
Other direct obstetric causes — Autres décès maternels directs	..	..	5	♦4.4	..	..	3	♦2.8
Indirect obstetric causes — Décès maternels indirects	..	..	-	-	..	..	-	-
Certain conditions originating in the perinatal period — Certaines affections dont l'origine se situe dans la période périnatale	98	165.7	87	156.4	90	164.0	56	108.6
Congenital malformations, deformations and chromosomal abnormalities — Malformations congénitales et anomalies chromosomiques	134	226.6	122	219.3	131	238.8	108	209.4
Symptoms, signs and abnormal clinical and laboratory findings, not elsewhere classified — Symptômes, signes et résultats anormaux d'examens cliniques et de laboratoire, non classés ailleurs	4 486	81.7	5 928	104.1	5 313	97.4	6 874	121.2
All other diseases — Toutes autres maladies	8	♦0.1	23	♦0.4	7	♦0.1	14	♦0.2
External causes — Causes externes								
Total	2 791	50.8	763	13.4	2 656	48.7	804	14.2
Accidents								
Total	2 296	41.8	687	12.1	2 106	38.6	684	12.1
Transport accidents — Accidents de transport	1 143	20.8	287	5.0	1 060	19.4	279	4.9
Falls — Chutes	301	5.5	137	2.4	245	4.5	139	2.5
Accidental drowning and submersion — Noyade et submersion accidentelles	302	5.5	108	1.9	277	5.1	110	1.9
Exposure to smoke, fire and flames — Exposition à la fumée, au feu et aux flammes	53	1.0	36	0.6	64	1.2	36	0.6
Accidental poisoning by and exposure to noxious substances — Intoxication accidentelle par des substances nocives et exposition à ces substances	254	4.6	34	0.6	216	4.0	38	0.7
Intentional self-harm — Lésions auto-infligées	336	6.1	41	0.7	393	7.2	84	1.5
Assault — Agresssions	132	2.4	33	0.6	152	2.8	34	0.6
All other external causes — Toutes autres causes externes	27	♦0.5	2	♦0.0	5	♦0.1	2	♦0.0

20. Death and death rates by cause and sex: 2010 - 2014
Décès et taux de mortalité par cause et sexe : 2010 - 2014 (continued - suite)

Hungary - Hongrie

Cause of death — Cause de décès	2013 (C)				2014 (C)			
	Male — Masculin		Female — Féminin		Male — Masculin		Female — Féminin	
	Number Nombre	Rate Taux	Number Nombre	Rate Taux	Number Nombre	Rate Taux	Number Nombre	Rate Taux
TOTAL	61 894	1 314.2	64 884	1 251.8	61 992	1 319.1	64 316	1 244.8
Certain infectious and parasitic diseases — Certaines maladies infectieuses et parasitaires								
Total	396	8.4	508	9.8	366	7.8	444	8.6
Intestinal infectious diseases — Maladies infectieuses intestinales	144	3.1	288	5.6	129	2.7	217	4.2
Tuberculosis — Tuberculose	54	1.1	22	♦0.4	40	0.9	14	♦0.3
Tetanus — Tétanos	-	-	1	♦0.0	-	-	1	♦0.0
Diphtheria — Diphtérie	-	-	-	-	-	-	-	-
Whooping cough — Coqueluche	-	-	-	-	-	-	-	-
Meningococcal infection — Infection à méningocoques	6	♦0.1	5	♦0.1	1	♦0.0	2	♦0.0
Septicaemia — Septicémie	24	♦0.5	33	0.6	19	♦0.4	37	0.7
Acute poliomyelitis — Poliomyélite aiguë	1	♦0.0	-	-	-	-	-	-
Measles — Rougeole	-	-	-	-	-	-	-	-
Viral hepatitis — Hépatite virale	97	2.1	107	2.1	93	2.0	107	2.1
Human immunodeficiency virus [HIV] disease — Maladies dues au virus de l'immunodéficience humaine (VIH)	7	♦0.1	-	-	14	♦0.3	1	♦0.0
Malaria — Paludisme	-	-	-	-	-	-	-	-
Neoplasms — Tumeurs	18 060	383.5	15 214	293.5	17 997	382.9	15 295	296.0
Malignant neoplasms — Tumeurs malignes								
Total	17 815	378.3	14 933	288.1	17 763	378.0	14 985	290.0
Malignant neoplasm of lip, oral cavity and pharynx — Tumeur maligne de la lèvre, de la cavité buccale et du pharynx	1 146	24.3	285	5.5	1 157	24.6	303	5.9
Malignant neoplasm of oesophagus — Tumeur maligne de l'oesophage	522	11.1	105	2.0	432	9.2	112	2.2
Malignant neoplasm of stomach — Tumeur maligne de l'estomac	942	20.0	677	13.1	904	19.2	698	13.5
Malignant neoplasm of colon, rectosigmoid junction, rectum, anus and anal canal — Tumeur maligne du côlon, de la jonction recto-sigmoïdienne, du rectum, de l'anus et du canal anal	2 865	60.8	2 242	43.3	2 848	60.6	2 202	42.6
Malignant neoplasm of liver and intrahepatic bile ducts — Tumeur maligne du foie et des voies bilaires intrahépatiques	553	11.7	279	5.4	625	13.3	279	5.4
Malignant neoplasm of pancreas — Tumeur maligne du pancréas	943	20.0	1 033	19.9	958	20.4	1 041	20.1
Malignant neoplasm of trachea, bronchus and lung — Tumeur maligne de la trachée, des bronches et du poumon	5 418	115.0	3 173	61.2	5 456	116.1	3 277	63.4
Malignant neoplasm of female breast — Tumeur maligne du sein chez la femme	..	..	2 167	...	..	..	2 107	47.1
Malignant neoplasm of cervix uteri — Tumeur maligne du col de l'utérus	..	..	405	...	..	..	420	9.4
Malignant neoplasm of prostate — Tumeur maligne de la prostate	1 211	...	..	..	1 280	80.4	..	..
Malignant neoplasm of lymphoid, haematopoietic and related tissue — Tumeurs malignes primitives ou présumées primitives des tissus lymphoïde, hématopoïétique et apparentés	916	19.4	883	17.0	897	19.1	846	16.4
Disorders of the blood and blood-forming organs and certain disorders involving the immune mechanism — Maladies du sang et des organes hématopoïétiques et certains troubles du système immunitaire								
Total	81	1.7	126	2.4	97	2.1	138	2.7
Anaemias — Anémies	39	0.8	69	1.3	47	1.0	76	1.5
Endocrine, nutritional and metabolic diseases — Maladies endocriniennes, nutritionnelles et métaboliques								
Total	1 244	26.4	1 672	32.3	1 256	26.7	1 646	31.9
Diabetes mellitus — Diabète sucré	1 121	23.8	1 463	28.2	1 128	24.0	1 455	28.2
Malnutrition — Malnutrition	6	♦0.1	10	♦0.2	7	♦0.1	9	♦0.2
Mental and behavioural disorders — Troubles mentaux et du comportement	1 179	25.0	1 927	37.2	1 231	26.2	1 928	37.3
Diseases of the nervous system — Maladies du système nerveux	807	17.1	923	17.8	838	17.8	909	17.6
Diseases of the circulatory system — Maladies de l'appareil circulatoire								
Total	27 600	586.0	35 379	682.5	27 642	588.2	35 144	680.2
Acute rheumatic fever and chronic rheumatic heart diseases — Rhumatisme articularie aigu et cardiopathies rhumatismales chroniques	107	2.3	211	4.1	103	2.2	206	4.0
Hypertensive diseases — Maladies hypertensives	2 721	57.8	4 903	94.6	2 712	57.7	4 937	95.6
Ischaemic heart disease — Cardiopathie ischémique	14 635	310.7	17 469	337.0	14 589	310.4	17 550	339.7
Cerebrovascular disease — Maladie cérébrovasculaire	5 427	115.2	7 401	142.8	5 269	112.1	7 121	137.8

20. Death and death rates by cause and sex: 2010 - 2014
Décès et taux de mortalité par cause et sexe : 2010 - 2014 (continued - suite)

Hungary - Hongrie

Cause of death — Cause de décès	2013 (C)				2014 (C)			
	Male — Masculin		Female — Féminin		Male — Masculin		Female — Féminin	
	Number Nombre	Rate Taux	Number Nombre	Rate Taux	Number Nombre	Rate Taux	Number Nombre	Rate Taux
Diseases of arteries, arterioles and capillaries — Maladies des artères, artérioles et capillaires	1 413	30.0	1 722	33.2	1 411	30.0	1 665	32.2
Diseases of the respiratory system — Maladies de l'appareil respiratoire								
Total	3 822	81.2	3 187	61.5	3 794	80.7	3 114	60.3
Influenza — Grippe	5	♦0.1	2	♦0.0	2	♦0.0	1	♦0.0
Pneumonia — Pneumopathies	428	9.1	367	7.1	408	8.7	409	7.9
Chronic lower respiratory diseases — Maladies chroniques des voies respiratoires inférieures	2 996	63.6	2 494	48.1	3 006	64.0	2 379	46.0
Diseases of the digestive system — Maladies de l'appareil digestif								
Total	3 741	79.4	2 649	51.1	3 863	82.2	2 527	48.9
Gastric and duodenal ulcer — Ulcère de l'estomac et du duodénum	359	7.6	351	6.8	354	7.5	334	6.5
Diseases of the liver — Maladies du foie	2 391	50.8	933	18.0	2 468	52.5	972	18.8
Diseases of the musculoskeletal system and connective tissue — Maladies du système ostéo-articularie, des muscles et du tissu conjonctif	115	2.4	292	5.6	128	2.7	287	5.6
Diseases of the genitourinary system — Maladies de l'appareil génito-urinaire								
Total	419	8.9	489	9.4	416	8.9	497	9.6
Disorders of kidney and ureter — Affections du rein et de l'uretère	255	5.4	388	7.5	235	5.0	372	7.2
Hyperplasia of prostate — Hyperplasie de la prostate	92	...	..	..	89	5.6	..	..
Pregnancy, childbirth and the puerperium — Grossesse, accouchement et puerpéralité								
Total	..	..	13	♦14.5	..	..	6	♦6.4
Pregnancy with abortive outcome — Grossesse se terminant par un avortement	..	..	2	♦2.2	..	..	-	-
Other direct obstetric causes — Autres décès maternels directs	..	..	6	♦6.7	..	..	2	♦2.1
Indirect obstetric causes — Décès maternels indirects	..	..	5	♦5.6	..	..	4	♦4.3
Certain conditions originating in the perinatal period — Certaines affections dont l'origine se situe dans la période périnatale	170	369.6	109	250.4	131	273.9	107	235.4
Congenital malformations, deformations and chromosomal abnormalities — Malformations congénitales et anomalies chromosomiques	158	343.5	118	271.1	173	361.7	147	323.5
Symptoms, signs and abnormal clinical and laboratory findings, not elsewhere classified — Symptômes, signes et résultats anormaux d'examens cliniques et de laboratoire, non classés ailleurs	77	1.6	74	1.4	74	1.6	107	2.1
All other diseases — Toutes autres maladies	44	0.9	61	1.2	50	1.1	68	1.3
External causes — Causes externes								
Total	3 981	84.5	2 143	41.3	3 936	83.8	1 952	37.8
Accidents								
Total	2 128	45.2	1 482	28.6	2 222	47.3	1 354	26.2
Transport accidents — Accidents de transport	571	12.1	212	4.1	595	12.7	215	4.2
Falls — Chutes	826	17.5	950	18.3	974	20.7	841	16.3
Accidental drowning and submersion — Noyade et submersion accidentelles	99	2.1	24	♦0.5	103	2.2	23	♦0.4
Exposure to smoke, fire and flames — Exposition à la fumée, au feu et aux flammes	71	1.5	41	0.8	56	1.2	42	0.8
Accidental poisoning by and exposure to noxious substances — Intoxication accidentelle par des substances nocives et exposition à ces substances	69	1.5	34	0.7	83	1.8	18	♦0.3
Intentional self-harm — Lésions auto-infligées	1 588	33.7	505	9.7	1 480	31.5	447	8.7
Assault — Agresssions	73	1.6	52	1.0	49	1.0	42	0.8
All other external causes — Toutes autres causes externes	192	4.1	104	2.0	185	3.9	109	2.1

20. Death and death rates by cause and sex: 2010 - 2014
Décès et taux de mortalité par cause et sexe : 2010 - 2014 (continued - suite)

Ireland - Irlande

Cause of death — Cause de décès	2012 (+C)				2013 (+C)			
	Male — Masculin		Female — Féminin		Male — Masculin		Female — Féminin	
	Number Nombre	Rate Taux	Number Nombre	Rate Taux	Number Nombre	Rate Taux	Number Nombre	Rate Taux
TOTAL	14 945	658.4	14 241	615.7	14 958	658.1	14 546	627.4
Certain infectious and parasitic diseases — Certaines maladies infectieuses et parasitaires								
Total	116	5.1	107	4.6	119	5.2	126	5.4
Intestinal infectious diseases — Maladies infectieuses intestinales ...	11	◆0.5	18	◆0.8	14	◆0.6	30	◆1.3
Tuberculosis — Tuberculose	12	◆0.5	9	◆0.4	12	◆0.5	5	◆0.2
Tetanus — Tétanos...............	-	-	-	-	-	-	-	-
Diphtheria — Diphtérie...............	-	-	-	-	-	-	-	-
Whooping cough — Coqueluche	1	◆0.0	-	-	-	-	-	-
Meningococcal infection — Infection à méningocoques ...	-	-	1	◆0.0	2	◆0.1	1	◆0.0
Septicaemia — Septicémie...............	39	1.7	43	1.9	42	1.8	49	2.1
Acute poliomyelitis — Poliomyélite aiguë	-	-	-	-	-	-	1	◆0.0
Measles — Rougeole...............	-	-	-	-	-	-	-	-
Viral hepatitis — Hépatite virale...............	13	◆0.6	10	◆0.4	20	◆0.9	7	◆0.3
Human immunodeficiency virus [HIV] disease — Maladies dues au virus de l'immunodéficience humaine (VIH)...............	11	◆0.5	1	◆0.0	7	◆0.3	3	◆0.1
Malaria — Paludisme...............	-	-	-	-	-	-	-	-
Neoplasms — Tumeurs	4 677	206.1	4 105	177.5	4 742	208.6	4 219	182.0
Malignant neoplasms — Tumeurs malignes								
Total	4 569	201.3	4 002	173.0	4 606	202.7	4 119	177.7
Malignant neoplasm of lip, oral cavity and pharynx — Tumeur maligne de la lèvre, de la cavité buccale et du pharynx	117	5.2	52	2.2	117	5.1	46	2.0
Malignant neoplasm of oesophagus — Tumeur maligne de l'oesophage	230	10.1	146	6.3	258	11.4	114	4.9
Malignant neoplasm of stomach — Tumeur maligne de l'estomac	192	8.5	121	5.2	179	7.9	119	5.1
Malignant neoplasm of colon, rectosigmoid junction, rectum, anus and anal canal — Tumeur maligne du côlon, de la jonction recto-sigmoïdienne, du rectum, de l'anus et du canal anal........	581	25.6	401	17.3	592	26.0	440	19.0
Malignant neoplasm of liver and intrahepatic bile ducts — Tumeur maligne du foie et des voies bilaires intrahépatiques	144	6.3	92	4.0	184	8.1	122	5.3
Malignant neoplasm of pancreas — Tumeur maligne du pancréas...............	246	10.8	230	9.9	237	10.4	258	11.1
Malignant neoplasm of trachea, bronchus and lung — Tumeur maligne de la trachée, des bronches et du poumon	1 073	47.3	728	31.5	1 074	47.3	757	32.7
Malignant neoplasm of female breast — Tumeur maligne du sein chez la femme	..	..	689	...	..	..	704	...
Malignant neoplasm of cervix uteri — Tumeur maligne du col de l'utérus.........	..	..	93	...	..	..	76	...
Malignant neoplasm of prostate — Tumeur maligne de la prostate	519	...	..	..	499	...	..	..
Malignant neoplasm of lymphoid, haematopoietic and related tissue — Tumeurs malignes primitives ou présumées primitives des tissus lymphoïde, hématopoïétique et apparentés...............	436	19.2	331	14.3	382	16.8	340	14.7
Disorders of the blood and blood-forming organs and certain disorders involving the immune mechanism — Maladies du sang et des organes hématopoïétiques et certains troubles du système immunitaire								
Total	35	1.5	59	2.6	36	1.6	66	2.8
Anaemias — Anémies	16	◆0.7	30	◆1.3	17	◆0.7	39	1.7
Endocrine, nutritional and metabolic diseases — Maladies endocriniennes, nutritionnelles et métaboliques								
Total	374	16.5	339	14.7	385	16.9	369	15.9
Diabetes mellitus — Diabète sucré...............	288	12.7	248	10.7	320	14.1	253	10.9
Malnutrition — Malnutrition	-	-	1	◆0.0	-	-	2	◆0.1
Mental and behavioural disorders — Troubles mentaux et du comportement	354	15.6	619	26.8	387	17.0	820	35.4
Diseases of the nervous system — Maladies du système nerveux...............	622	27.4	734	31.7	602	26.5	776	33.5
Diseases of the circulatory system — Maladies de l'appareil circulatoire								
Total	4 779	210.5	4 701	203.2	4 791	210.8	4 682	202.0
Acute rheumatic fever and chronic rheumatic heart diseases — Rhumatisme articularie aigu et cardiopathies rhumatismales chroniques	20	◆0.9	42	1.8	18	◆0.8	33	1.4
Hypertensive diseases — Maladies hypertensives...............	123	5.4	226	9.8	117	5.1	191	8.2
Ischaemic heart disease — Cardiopathie ischémique	2 753	121.3	2 005	86.7	2 707	119.1	1 935	83.5
Cerebrovascular disease — Maladie cérébrovasculaire...............	773	34.1	1 162	50.2	803	35.3	1 156	49.9

Ireland - Irlande

Cause of death — Cause de décès	2012 (+C)				2013 (+C)			
	Male — Masculin		Female — Féminin		Male — Masculin		Female — Féminin	
	Number Nombre	Rate Taux	Number Nombre	Rate Taux	Number Nombre	Rate Taux	Number Nombre	Rate Taux
Diseases of arteries, arterioles and capillaries — Maladies des artères, artérioles et capillaires	254	11.2	238	10.3	268	11.8	227	9.8
Diseases of the respiratory system — Maladies de l'appareil respiratoire								
Total	1 683	74.1	1 814	78.4	1 685	74.1	1 819	78.5
Influenza — Grippe..	5	♦0.2	2	♦0.1	6	♦0.3	10	♦0.4
Pneumonia — Pneumopathies	446	19.6	640	27.7	410	18.0	573	24.7
Chronic lower respiratory diseases — Maladies chroniques des voies respiratoires inférieures	809	35.6	778	33.6	808	35.6	849	36.6
Diseases of the digestive system — Maladies de l'appareil digestif								
Total	581	25.6	577	24.9	533	23.5	536	23.1
Gastric and duodenal ulcer — Ulcère de l'estomac et du duodénum................	38	1.7	40	1.7	31	1.4	33	1.4
Diseases of the liver — Maladies du foie.............	254	11.2	171	7.4	239	10.5	127	5.5
Diseases of the musculoskeletal system and connective tissue — Maladies du système ostéo-articularie, des muscles et du tissu conjonctif	80	3.5	154	6.7	60	2.6	160	6.9
Diseases of the genitourinary system — Maladies de l'appareil génito-urinaire								
Total	293	12.9	377	16.3	309	13.6	324	14.0
Disorders of kidney and ureter — Affections du rein et de l'uretère	222	9.8	247	10.7	264	11.6	210	9.1
Hyperplasia of prostate — Hyperplasie de la prostate............................	8	...	..	..	7	...	..	..
Pregnancy, childbirth and the puerperium — Grossesse, accouchement et puerpéralité								
Total	..	..	2	♦2.8	..	..	3	♦4.4
Pregnancy with abortive outcome — Grossesse se terminant par un avortement	..	..	-	-	..	..	-	-
Other direct obstetric causes — Autres décès maternels directs	..	..	2	♦2.8	..	..	2	♦2.9
Indirect obstetric causes — Décès maternels indirects	..	..	-	-	..	..	1	♦1.5
Certain conditions originating in the perinatal period — Certaines affections dont l'origine se situe dans la période périnatale	52	139.7	59	168.5	64	181.4	43	127.8
Congenital malformations, deformations and chromosomal abnormalities — Malformations congénitales et anomalies chromosomiques	101	271.4	85	242.8	114	323.2	82	243.6
Symptoms, signs and abnormal clinical and laboratory findings, not elsewhere classified — Symptômes, signes et résultats anormaux d'examens cliniques et de laboratoire, non classés ailleurs	40	1.8	50	2.2	46	2.0	61	2.6
All other diseases — Toutes autres maladies...	16	♦0.7	24	♦1.0	21	♦0.9	33	1.4
External causes — Causes externes								
Total	1 142	50.3	435	18.8	1 064	46.8	427	18.4
Accidents								
Total	618	27.2	298	12.9	596	26.2	302	13.0
Transport accidents — Accidents de transport..........	115	5.1	47	2.0	128	5.6	39	1.7
Falls — Chutes	139	6.1	107	4.6	103	4.5	94	4.1
Accidental drowning and submersion — Noyade et submersion accidentelles...	49	2.2	10	♦0.4	44	1.9	7	♦0.3
Exposure to smoke, fire and flames — Exposition à la fumée, au feu et aux flammes...	25	♦1.1	11	♦0.5	13	♦0.6	12	♦0.5
Accidental poisoning by and exposure to noxious substances — Intoxication accidentelle par des substances nocives et exposition à ces substances	198	8.7	63	2.7	203	8.9	79	3.4
Intentional self-harm — Lésions auto-infligées...............................	445	19.6	96	4.2	391	17.2	96	4.1
Assault — Agresssions	30	♦1.3	8	♦0.3	22	♦1.0	4	♦0.2
All other external causes — Toutes autres causes externes	49	2.2	33	1.4	55	2.4	25	♦1.1

20. Death and death rates by cause and sex: 2010 - 2014
Décès et taux de mortalité par cause et sexe : 2010 - 2014 (continued - suite)

Italy - Italie

Cause of death — Cause de décès	2011 (C)				2012 (C)			
	Male — Masculin		Female — Féminin		Male — Masculin		Female — Féminin	
	Number Nombre	Rate Taux	Number Nombre	Rate Taux	Number Nombre	Rate Taux	Number Nombre	Rate Taux
TOTAL	288 522	1 004.8	305 631	997.2	295 831	1 029.8	317 689	1 035.9
Certain infectious and parasitic diseases — Certaines maladies infectieuses et parasitaires								
Total	5 355	18.6	5 720	18.7	6 158	21.4	6 388	20.8
Intestinal infectious diseases — Maladies infectieuses intestinales	211	0.7	315	1.0	237	0.8	426	1.4
Tuberculosis — Tuberculose	192	0.7	126	0.4	162	0.6	118	0.4
Tetanus — Tétanos	6	♦0.0	16	♦0.1	9	♦0.0	14	♦0.0
Diphtheria — Diphtérie	-	-	-	-	-	-	-	-
Whooping cough — Coqueluche	-	-	-	-	-	-	-	-
Meningococcal infection — Infection à méningocoques	7	♦0.0	10	♦0.0	14	♦0.0	14	♦0.0
Septicaemia — Septicémie	2 451	8.5	3 020	9.9	3 095	10.8	3 588	11.7
Acute poliomyelitis — Poliomyélite aiguë	-	-	-	-	-	-	-	-
Measles — Rougeole	-	-	-	-	1	♦0.0	2	♦0.0
Viral hepatitis — Hépatite virale	1 390	4.8	1 622	5.3	1 501	5.2	1 591	5.2
Human immunodeficiency virus [HIV] disease — Maladies dues au virus de l'immunodéficience humaine (VIH)	641	2.2	190	0.6	678	2.4	203	0.7
Malaria — Paludisme	2	♦0.0	1	♦0.0	3	♦0.0	-	-
Neoplasms — Tumeurs	99 055	345.0	76 917	251.0	99 794	347.4	77 559	252.9
Malignant neoplasms — Tumeurs malignes								
Total	94 706	329.8	73 177	238.8	95 464	332.3	73 716	240.4
Malignant neoplasm of lip, oral cavity and pharynx — Tumeur maligne de la lèvre, de la cavité buccale et du pharynx	1 971	6.9	888	2.9	2 002	7.0	841	2.7
Malignant neoplasm of oesophagus — Tumeur maligne de l'oesophage	1 368	4.8	441	1.4	1 366	4.8	449	1.5
Malignant neoplasm of stomach — Tumeur maligne de l'estomac	5 772	20.1	4 213	13.7	5 811	20.2	4 189	13.7
Malignant neoplasm of colon, rectosigmoid junction, rectum, anus and anal canal — Tumeur maligne du côlon, de la jonction recto-sigmoïdienne, du rectum, de l'anus et du canal anal	10 272	35.8	8 848	28.9	10 406	36.2	8 796	28.7
Malignant neoplasm of liver and intrahepatic bile ducts — Tumeur maligne du foie et des voies bilaires intrahépatiques	6 523	22.7	3 531	11.5	6 638	23.1	3 478	11.3
Malignant neoplasm of pancreas — Tumeur maligne du pancréas	5 264	18.3	5 545	18.1	5 154	17.9	5 568	18.2
Malignant neoplasm of trachea, bronchus and lung — Tumeur maligne de la trachée, des bronches et du poumon	25 239	87.9	8 580	28.0	24 885	86.6	8 653	28.2
Malignant neoplasm of female breast — Tumeur maligne du sein chez la femme	..	..	12 001	45.1	..	..	12 004	45.1
Malignant neoplasm of cervix uteri — Tumeur maligne du col de l'utérus	..	..	441	1.7	..	..	422	1.6
Malignant neoplasm of prostate — Tumeur maligne de la prostate	7 536	70.0	..	..	7 282	67.0	..	..
Malignant neoplasm of lymphoid, haematopoietic and related tissue — Tumeurs malignes primitives ou présumées primitives des tissus lymphoïde, hématopoïétique et apparentés	7 578	26.4	6 739	22.0	7 992	27.8	6 873	22.4
Disorders of the blood and blood-forming organs and certain disorders involving the immune mechanism — Maladies du sang et des organes hématopoïétiques et certains troubles du système immunitaire								
Total	1 142	4.0	1 783	5.8	1 244	4.3	1 868	6.1
Anaemias — Anémies	762	2.7	1 271	4.1	802	2.8	1 367	4.5
Endocrine, nutritional and metabolic diseases — Maladies endocriniennes, nutritionnelles et métaboliques								
Total	11 272	39.3	15 529	50.7	11 734	40.8	15 899	51.8
Diabetes mellitus — Diabète sucré	9 056	31.5	12 103	39.5	9 272	32.3	12 264	40.0
Malnutrition — Malnutrition	163	0.6	290	0.9	194	0.7	322	1.0
Mental and behavioural disorders — Troubles mentaux et du comportement	5 299	18.5	10 671	34.8	5 593	19.5	11 763	38.4
Diseases of the nervous system — Maladies du système nerveux	9 710	33.8	13 493	44.0	10 379	36.1	14 576	47.5
Diseases of the circulatory system — Maladies de l'appareil circulatoire								
Total	97 168	338.4	125 942	410.9	99 661	346.9	130 499	425.5
Acute rheumatic fever and chronic rheumatic heart diseases — Rhumatisme articularie aigu et cardiopathies rhumatismales chroniques	678	2.4	1 517	4.9	703	2.4	1 626	5.3
Hypertensive diseases — Maladies hypertensives	9 891	34.4	18 863	61.5	10 880	37.9	20 365	66.4
Ischaemic heart disease — Cardiopathie ischémique	37 673	131.2	37 039	120.8	37 958	132.1	37 140	121.1
Cerebrovascular disease — Maladie cérébrovasculaire	23 915	83.3	36 609	119.4	23 951	83.4	37 304	121.6

20. Death and death rates by cause and sex: 2010 - 2014
Décès et taux de mortalité par cause et sexe : 2010 - 2014 (continued - suite)

Italy - Italie

Cause of death — Cause de décès	2011 (C)				2012 (C)			
	Male — Masculin		Female — Féminin		Male — Masculin		Female — Féminin	
	Number Nombre	Rate Taux	Number Nombre	Rate Taux	Number Nombre	Rate Taux	Number Nombre	Rate Taux
Diseases of arteries, arterioles and capillaries — Maladies des artères, artérioles et capillaires	4 272	14.9	3 448	11.2	4 256	14.8	3 567	11.6
Diseases of the respiratory system — Maladies de l'appareil respiratoire								
Total	22 489	78.3	18 070	59.0	23 603	82.2	19 841	64.7
Influenza — Grippe	168	0.6	232	0.8	154	0.5	300	1.0
Pneumonia — Pneumopathies	4 024	14.0	4 359	14.2	4 351	15.1	4 925	16.1
Chronic lower respiratory diseases — Maladies chroniques des voies respiratoires inférieures	12 718	44.3	8 194	26.7	13 109	45.6	8 732	28.5
Diseases of the digestive system — Maladies de l'appareil digestif								
Total	11 313	39.4	11 608	37.9	11 504	40.0	11 912	38.8
Gastric and duodenal ulcer — Ulcère de l'estomac et du duodénum	382	1.3	342	1.1	390	1.4	321	1.0
Diseases of the liver — Maladies du foie	4 952	17.2	3 285	10.7	4 864	16.9	3 207	10.5
Diseases of the musculoskeletal system and connective tissue — Maladies du système ostéo-articularie, des muscles et du tissu conjonctif	895	3.1	2 248	7.3	947	3.3	2 205	7.2
Diseases of the genitourinary system — Maladies de l'appareil génito-urinaire								
Total	5 271	18.4	5 832	19.0	5 604	19.5	6 364	20.8
Disorders of kidney and ureter — Affections du rein et de l'uretère	4 497	15.7	5 002	16.3	4 686	16.3	5 426	17.7
Hyperplasia of prostate — Hyperplasie de la prostate	171	1.6	..	..	196	1.8	..	..
Pregnancy, childbirth and the puerperium — Grossesse, accouchement et puerpéralité								
Total	..	..	14	♦2.6	..	..	11	♦2.1
Pregnancy with abortive outcome — Grossesse se terminant par un avortement	..	..	2	♦0.4	..	..	1	♦0.2
Other direct obstetric causes — Autres décès maternels directs	..	..	12	♦2.2	..	..	9	♦1.7
Indirect obstetric causes — Décès maternels indirects	..	..	-	-	..	..	-	-
Certain conditions originating in the perinatal period — Certaines affections dont l'origine se situe dans la période périnatale	575	204.6	445	167.6	548	199.6	472	181.8
Congenital malformations, deformations and chromosomal abnormalities — Malformations congénitales et anomalies chromosomiques	762	271.1	664	250.1	701	255.3	624	240.4
Symptoms, signs and abnormal clinical and laboratory findings, not elsewhere classified — Symptômes, signes et résultats anormaux d'examens cliniques et de laboratoire, non classés ailleurs	3 917	13.6	6 254	20.4	4 238	14.8	6 984	22.8
All other diseases — Toutes autres maladies	348	1.2	699	2.3	340	1.2	732	2.4
External causes — Causes externes								
Total	13 951	48.6	9 742	31.8	13 783	48.0	9 992	32.6
Accidents								
Total	9 743	33.9	7 666	25.0	9 551	33.2	7 851	25.6
Transport accidents — Accidents de transport	3 473	12.1	1 012	3.3	3 273	11.4	881	2.9
Falls — Chutes	2 148	7.5	1 772	5.8	2 172	7.6	2 006	6.5
Accidental drowning and submersion — Noyade et submersion accidentelles	326	1.1	73	0.2	298	1.0	65	0.2
Exposure to smoke, fire and flames — Exposition à la fumée, au feu et aux flammes	132	0.5	99	0.3	151	0.5	101	0.3
Accidental poisoning by and exposure to noxious substances — Intoxication accidentelle par des substances nocives et exposition à ces substances	277	1.0	115	0.4	337	1.2	167	0.5
Intentional self-harm — Lésions auto-infligées	3 289	11.5	863	2.8	3 323	11.6	933	3.0
Assault — Agresssions	328	1.1	123	0.4	333	1.2	131	0.4
All other external causes — Toutes autres causes externes	591	2.1	1 090	3.6	576	2.0	1 077	3.5

20. Death and death rates by cause and sex: 2010 - 2014
Décès et taux de mortalité par cause et sexe : 2010 - 2014 (continued - suite)

Latvia - Lettonie

Cause of death — Cause de décès	2013 (+C)				2014 (+C)			
	Male — Masculin		Female — Féminin		Male — Masculin		Female — Féminin	
	Number Nombre	Rate Taux	Number Nombre	Rate Taux	Number Nombre	Rate Taux	Number Nombre	Rate Taux
TOTAL	13 511	1 458.2	15 176	1 383.1	13 557	1 483.1	14 644	1 356.4
Certain infectious and parasitic diseases — Certaines maladies infectieuses et parasitaires								
Total	210	22.7	144	13.1	184	20.1	105	9.7
Intestinal infectious diseases — Maladies infectieuses intestinales	2	♦0.2	2	♦0.2	1	♦0.1	3	♦0.3
Tuberculosis — Tuberculose	61	6.6	22	♦2.0	37	4.0	10	♦0.9
Tetanus — Tétanos	-	-	-	-	-	-	-	-
Diphtheria — Diphtérie..	-	-	1	♦0.1	-	-	1	♦0.1
Whooping cough — Coqueluche	-	-	1	♦0.1	-	-	-	-
Meningococcal infection — Infection à méningocoques	1	♦0.1	1	♦0.1	-	-	-	-
Septicaemia — Septicémie	9	♦1.0	13	♦1.2	15	♦1.6	18	♦1.7
Acute poliomyelitis — Poliomyélite aiguë	-	-	-	-	-	-	-	-
Measles — Rougeole...	-	-	-	-	-	-	-	-
Viral hepatitis — Hépatite virale..................................	29	♦3.1	23	♦2.1	28	♦3.1	18	♦1.7
Human immunodeficiency virus [HIV] disease — Maladies dues au virus de l'immunodéficience humaine (VIH)............................	65	7.0	45	4.1	70	7.7	32	3.0
Malaria — Paludisme..	-	-	-	-	-	-	-	-
Neoplasms — Tumeurs	3 215	347.0	2 831	258.0	3 273	358.0	2 807	260.0
Malignant neoplasms — Tumeurs malignes								
Total	3 183	343.5	2 773	252.7	3 233	353.7	2 739	253.7
Malignant neoplasm of lip, oral cavity and pharynx — Tumeur maligne de la lèvre, de la cavité buccale et du pharynx	168	18.1	32	2.9	154	16.8	37	3.4
Malignant neoplasm of oesophagus — Tumeur maligne de l'oesophage	101	10.9	15	♦1.4	113	12.4	20	♦1.9
Malignant neoplasm of stomach — Tumeur maligne de l'estomac	279	30.1	206	18.8	252	27.6	202	18.7
Malignant neoplasm of colon, rectosigmoid junction, rectum, anus and anal canal — Tumeur maligne du côlon, de la jonction recto-sigmoïdienne, du rectum, de l'anus et du canal anal..........	304	32.8	376	34.3	336	36.8	353	32.7
Malignant neoplasm of liver and intrahepatic bile ducts — Tumeur maligne du foie et des voies bilaires intrahépatiques	87	9.4	58	5.3	85	9.3	65	6.0
Malignant neoplasm of pancreas — Tumeur maligne du pancréas...................	166	17.9	190	17.3	173	18.9	202	18.7
Malignant neoplasm of trachea, bronchus and lung — Tumeur maligne de la trachée, des bronches et du poumon	780	84.2	215	19.6	760	83.1	186	17.2
Malignant neoplasm of female breast — Tumeur maligne du sein chez la femme	..	..	434	...	..	..	439	46.9
Malignant neoplasm of cervix uteri — Tumeur maligne du col de l'utérus..........	..	..	132	...	..	..	111	11.9
Malignant neoplasm of prostate — Tumeur maligne de la prostate	368	...	..	..	409	132.7	..	..
Malignant neoplasm of lymphoid, haematopoietic and related tissue — Tumeurs malignes primitives ou présumées primitives des tissus lymphoïde, hématopoïétique et apparentés..........	183	19.8	226	20.6	195	21.3	238	22.0
Disorders of the blood and blood-forming organs and certain disorders involving the immune mechanism — Maladies du sang et des organes hématopoïétiques et certains troubles du système immunitaire								
Total	6	♦0.6	18	♦1.6	16	♦1.8	24	♦2.2
Anaemias — Anémies	3	♦0.3	15	♦1.4	10	♦1.1	15	♦1.4
Endocrine, nutritional and metabolic diseases — Maladies endocriniennes, nutritionnelles et métaboliques								
Total	169	18.2	336	30.6	187	20.5	342	31.7
Diabetes mellitus — Diabète sucré............................	151	16.3	307	28.0	178	19.5	326	30.2
Malnutrition — Malnutrition	1	♦0.1	-	-	1	♦0.1	1	♦0.1
Mental and behavioural disorders — Troubles mentaux et du comportement	170	18.3	171	15.6	145	15.9	161	14.9
Diseases of the nervous system — Maladies du système nerveux..............	145	15.6	164	14.9	150	16.4	156	14.4
Diseases of the circulatory system — Maladies de l'appareil circulatoire								
Total	6 714	724.6	9 644	878.9	6 699	732.8	9 372	868.1
Acute rheumatic fever and chronic rheumatic heart diseases — Rhumatisme articularie aigu et cardiopathies rhumatismales chroniques	13	♦1.4	42	3.8	9	♦1.0	40	3.7
Hypertensive diseases — Maladies hypertensives............................	397	42.8	714	65.1	374	40.9	703	65.1
Ischaemic heart disease — Cardiopathie ischémique	3 606	389.2	4 686	427.1	3 551	388.5	4 536	420.1
Cerebrovascular disease — Maladie cérébrovasculaire....................	1 639	176.9	3 248	296.0	1 717	187.8	3 157	292.4

Latvia - Lettonie

Cause of death — Cause de décès	2013 (+C)				2014 (+C)			
	Male — Masculin		Female — Féminin		Male — Masculin		Female — Féminin	
	Number Nombre	Rate Taux	Number Nombre	Rate Taux	Number Nombre	Rate Taux	Number Nombre	Rate Taux
Diseases of arteries, arterioles and capillaries — Maladies des artères, artérioles et capillaires	209	22.6	239	21.8	202	22.1	228	21.1
Diseases of the respiratory system — Maladies de l'appareil respiratoire								
Total	534	57.6	297	27.1	476	52.1	220	20.4
Influenza — Grippe	29	♦3.1	32	2.9	-	-	2	♦0.2
Pneumonia — Pneumopathies	234	25.3	155	14.1	220	24.1	126	11.7
Chronic lower respiratory diseases — Maladies chroniques des voies respiratoires inférieures	227	24.5	85	7.7	218	23.8	64	5.9
Diseases of the digestive system — Maladies de l'appareil digestif								
Total	550	59.4	504	45.9	529	57.9	460	42.6
Gastric and duodenal ulcer — Ulcère de l'estomac et du duodénum	69	7.4	81	7.4	66	7.2	75	6.9
Diseases of the liver — Maladies du foie.............................	250	27.0	162	14.8	249	27.2	164	15.2
Diseases of the musculoskeletal system and connective tissue — Maladies du système ostéo-articularie, des muscles et du tissu conjonctif	35	3.8	60	5.5	25	♦2.7	46	4.3
Diseases of the genitourinary system — Maladies de l'appareil génito-urinaire								
Total	182	19.6	206	18.8	186	20.3	188	17.4
Disorders of kidney and ureter — Affections du rein et de l'uretère	109	11.8	179	16.3	113	12.4	152	14.1
Hyperplasia of prostate — Hyperplasie de la prostate....................................	51	...	..	..	46	14.9	..	..
Pregnancy, childbirth and the puerperium — Grossesse, accouchement et puerpéralité								
Total	..	..	2	♦9.7	..	..	2	♦9.2
Pregnancy with abortive outcome — Grossesse se terminant par un avortement	..	..	-	-	..	..	-	-
Other direct obstetric causes — Autres décès maternels directs	..	..	2	♦9.7	..	..	1	♦4.6
Indirect obstetric causes — Décès maternels indirects	..	..	-	-	..	..	1	♦4.6
Certain conditions originating in the perinatal period — Certaines affections dont l'origine se situe dans la période périnatale	25	♦239.1	25	♦246.6	26	♦231.5	16	♦152.1
Congenital malformations, deformations and chromosomal abnormalities — Malformations congénitales et anomalies chromosomiques	25	♦239.1	19	♦187.4	27	♦240.4	20	♦190.2
Symptoms, signs and abnormal clinical and laboratory findings, not elsewhere classified — Symptômes, signes et résultats anormaux d'examens cliniques et de laboratoire, non classés ailleurs	194	20.9	247	22.5	191	20.9	215	19.9
All other diseases — Toutes autres maladies..	13	♦1.4	29	♦2.6	24	♦2.6	59	5.5
External causes — Causes externes								
Total	1 324	142.9	479	43.7	1 419	155.2	451	41.8
Accidents								
Total	779	84.1	321	29.3	863	94.4	283	26.2
Transport accidents — Accidents de transport	146	15.8	48	4.4	182	19.9	58	5.4
Falls — Chutes	125	13.5	55	5.0	115	12.6	62	5.7
Accidental drowning and submersion — Noyade et submersion accidentelles	109	11.8	22	♦2.0	152	16.6	30	♦2.8
Exposure to smoke, fire and flames — Exposition à la fumée, au feu et aux flammes	75	8.1	40	3.6	73	8.0	37	3.4
Accidental poisoning by and exposure to noxious substances — Intoxication accidentelle par des substances nocives et exposition à ces substances	101	10.9	42	3.8	121	13.2	29	♦2.7
Intentional self-harm — Lésions auto-infligées...	321	34.6	61	5.6	311	34.0	71	6.6
Assault — Agresssions...	86	9.3	34	3.1	97	10.6	40	3.7
All other external causes — Toutes autres causes externes	138	14.9	63	5.7	148	16.2	57	5.3

20. Death and death rates by cause and sex: 2010 - 2014
Décès et taux de mortalité par cause et sexe : 2010 - 2014 (continued - suite)

Lithuania - Lituanie

Cause of death — Cause de décès	2013 (+C)				2014 (+C)			
	Male — Masculin		Female — Féminin		Male — Masculin		Female — Féminin	
	Number Nombre	Rate Taux	Number Nombre	Rate Taux	Number Nombre	Rate Taux	Number Nombre	Rate Taux
TOTAL	20 789	1 518.7	20 722	1 292.7	20 110	1 483.0	20 142	1 268.8
Certain infectious and parasitic diseases — Certaines maladies infectieuses et parasitaires								
Total	403	29.4	232	14.5	406	29.9	271	17.1
Intestinal infectious diseases — Maladies infectieuses intestinales	3	♦0.2	2	♦0.1	1	♦0.1	6	♦0.4
Tuberculosis — Tuberculose	168	12.3	42	2.6	171	12.6	51	3.2
Tetanus — Tétanos...	1	♦0.1	1	♦0.1	-	-	1	♦0.1
Diphtheria — Diphtérie...	-	-	-	-	-	-	-	-
Whooping cough — Coqueluche	-	-	-	-	-	-	-	-
Meningococcal infection — Infection à méningocoques	7	♦0.5	5	♦0.3	3	♦0.2	3	♦0.2
Septicaemia — Septicémie	153	11.2	157	9.8	166	12.2	174	11.0
Acute poliomyelitis — Poliomyélite aiguë	-	-	-	-	-	-	-	-
Measles — Rougeole...	-	-	-	-	-	-	-	-
Viral hepatitis — Hépatite virale	23	♦1.7	9	♦0.6	19	♦1.4	13	♦0.8
Human immunodeficiency virus [HIV] disease — Maladies dues au virus de l'immunodéficience humaine (VIH)...	23	♦1.7	3	♦0.2	17	♦1.3	5	♦0.3
Malaria — Paludisme	-	-	-	-	-	-	-	-
Neoplasms — Tumeurs	4 409	322.1	3 618	225.7	4 597	339.0	3 584	225.8
Malignant neoplasms — Tumeurs malignes								
Total	4 337	316.8	3 541	220.9	4 525	333.7	3 503	220.7
Malignant neoplasm of lip, oral cavity and pharynx — Tumeur maligne de la lèvre, de la cavité buccale et du pharynx	215	15.7	39	2.4	218	16.1	30	♦1.9
Malignant neoplasm of oesophagus — Tumeur maligne de l'oesophage	155	11.3	20	♦1.2	173	12.8	29	♦1.8
Malignant neoplasm of stomach — Tumeur maligne de l'estomac	396	28.9	247	15.4	413	30.5	285	18.0
Malignant neoplasm of colon, rectosigmoid junction, rectum, anus and anal canal — Tumeur maligne du côlon, de la jonction recto-sigmoïdienne, du rectum, de l'anus et du canal anal...	476	34.8	456	28.4	496	36.6	436	27.5
Malignant neoplasm of liver and intrahepatic bile ducts — Tumeur maligne du foie et des voies bilaires intrahépatiques	99	7.2	57	3.6	113	8.3	79	5.0
Malignant neoplasm of pancreas — Tumeur maligne du pancréas...................	228	16.7	213	13.3	235	17.3	240	15.1
Malignant neoplasm of trachea, bronchus and lung — Tumeur maligne de la trachée, des bronches et du poumon	1 059	77.4	250	15.6	1 076	79.4	262	16.5
Malignant neoplasm of female breast — Tumeur maligne du sein chez la femme	..	..	564	...	..	..	512	...
Malignant neoplasm of cervix uteri — Tumeur maligne du col de l'utérus..........	..	..	180	...	..	..	181	...
Malignant neoplasm of prostate — Tumeur maligne de la prostate	529	...	..	..	521	...	..	..
Malignant neoplasm of lymphoid, haematopoietic and related tissue — Tumeurs malignes primitives ou présumées primitives des tissus lymphoïde, hématopoïétique et apparentés...	242	17.7	272	17.0	245	18.1	267	16.8
Disorders of the blood and blood-forming organs and certain disorders involving the immune mechanism — Maladies du sang et des organes hématopoïétiques et certains troubles du système immunitaire								
Total	12	♦0.9	26	♦1.6	18	♦1.3	22	♦1.4
Anaemias — Anémies	9	♦0.7	15	♦0.9	8	♦0.6	11	♦0.7
Endocrine, nutritional and metabolic diseases — Maladies endocriniennes, nutritionnelles et métaboliques								
Total	150	11.0	187	11.7	125	9.2	181	11.4
Diabetes mellitus — Diabète sucré..	135	9.9	172	10.7	113	8.3	167	10.5
Malnutrition — Malnutrition	4	♦0.3	3	♦0.2	2	♦0.1	-	-
Mental and behavioural disorders — Troubles mentaux et du comportement	36	2.6	68	4.2	49	3.6	65	4.1
Diseases of the nervous system — Maladies du système nerveux.................	295	21.6	302	18.8	282	20.8	320	20.2
Diseases of the circulatory system — Maladies de l'appareil circulatoire								
Total	9 899	723.1	13 462	839.8	9 451	697.0	13 072	823.4
Acute rheumatic fever and chronic rheumatic heart diseases — Rhumatisme articularie aigu et cardiopathies rhumatismales chroniques	35	2.6	70	4.4	28	♦2.1	60	3.8
Hypertensive diseases — Maladies hypertensives..	239	17.5	333	20.8	265	19.5	366	23.1
Ischaemic heart disease — Cardiopathie ischémique	6 393	467.0	8 729	544.5	6 248	460.8	8 481	534.2
Cerebrovascular disease — Maladie cérébrovasculaire..	2 215	161.8	3 682	229.7	1 973	145.5	3 537	222.8

Lithuania - Lituanie

Cause of death — Cause de décès	2013 (+C)				2014 (+C)			
	Male — Masculin		Female — Féminin		Male — Masculin		Female — Féminin	
	Number Nombre	Rate Taux	Number Nombre	Rate Taux	Number Nombre	Rate Taux	Number Nombre	Rate Taux
Diseases of arteries, arterioles and capillaries — Maladies des artères, artérioles et capillaires	231	16.9	153	9.5	207	15.3	161	10.1
Diseases of the respiratory system — Maladies de l'appareil respiratoire								
Total	981	71.7	489	30.5	820	60.5	359	22.6
Influenza — Grippe	4	♦0.3	5	♦0.3	-	-	2	♦0.1
Pneumonia — Pneumopathies	383	28.0	207	12.9	305	22.5	167	10.5
Chronic lower respiratory diseases — Maladies chroniques des voies respiratoires inférieures	532	38.9	248	15.5	468	34.5	167	10.5
Diseases of the digestive system — Maladies de l'appareil digestif								
Total	1 209	88.3	1 025	63.9	1 131	83.4	960	60.5
Gastric and duodenal ulcer — Ulcère de l'estomac et du duodénum	135	9.9	147	9.2	136	10.0	138	8.7
Diseases of the liver — Maladies du foie	662	48.4	380	23.7	574	42.3	326	20.5
Diseases of the musculoskeletal system and connective tissue — Maladies du système ostéo-articularie, des muscles et du tissu conjonctif	29	♦2.1	63	3.9	32	2.4	57	3.6
Diseases of the genitourinary system — Maladies de l'appareil génito-urinaire								
Total	141	10.3	176	11.0	161	11.9	178	11.2
Disorders of kidney and ureter — Affections du rein et de l'uretère	114	8.3	161	10.0	128	9.4	154	9.7
Hyperplasia of prostate — Hyperplasie de la prostate	15	...	..	..	13	...	..	..
Pregnancy, childbirth and the puerperium — Grossesse, accouchement et puerpéralité								
Total	..	..	2	♦6.7	..	..	1	♦3.3
Pregnancy with abortive outcome — Grossesse se terminant par un avortement	..	..	-	-	..	..	-	-
Other direct obstetric causes — Autres décès maternels directs	..	..	2	♦6.7	..	..	1	♦3.3
Indirect obstetric causes — Décès maternels indirects	..	..	-	-	..	..	-	-
Certain conditions originating in the perinatal period — Certaines affections dont l'origine se situe dans la période périnatale	27	♦177.4	14	♦95.5	18	♦115.6	23	♦155.4
Congenital malformations, deformations and chromosomal abnormalities — Malformations congénitales et anomalies chromosomiques	42	275.9	37	252.3	45	289.1	49	331.0
Symptoms, signs and abnormal clinical and laboratory findings, not elsewhere classified — Symptômes, signes et résultats anormaux d'examens cliniques et de laboratoire, non classés ailleurs	344	25.1	173	10.8	379	27.9	194	12.2
All other diseases — Toutes autres maladies	23	♦1.7	22	♦1.4	25	♦1.8	39	2.5
External causes — Causes externes								
Total	2 789	203.7	826	51.5	2 571	189.6	767	48.3
Accidents								
Total	1 507	110.1	494	30.8	1 429	105.4	480	30.2
Transport accidents — Accidents de transport	240	17.5	76	4.7	241	17.8	84	5.3
Falls — Chutes	250	18.3	128	8.0	230	17.0	122	7.7
Accidental drowning and submersion — Noyade et submersion accidentelles	162	11.8	36	2.2	189	13.9	40	2.5
Exposure to smoke, fire and flames — Exposition à la fumée, au feu et aux flammes	66	4.8	14	♦0.9	38	2.8	21	♦1.3
Accidental poisoning by and exposure to noxious substances — Intoxication accidentelle par des substances nocives et exposition à ces substances	355	25.9	82	5.1	346	25.5	83	5.2
Intentional self-harm — Lésions auto-infligées	887	64.8	198	12.4	769	56.7	161	10.1
Assault — Agresssions	103	7.5	41	2.6	82	6.0	30	♦1.9
All other external causes — Toutes autres causes externes	292	21.3	93	5.8	291	21.5	96	6.0

20. Death and death rates by cause and sex: 2010 - 2014
Décès et taux de mortalité par cause et sexe : 2010 - 2014 (continued - suite)

Luxembourg

Cause of death — Cause de décès	2013 (+C)				2014 (+C)			
	Male — Masculin		Female — Féminin		Male — Masculin		Female — Féminin	
	Number Nombre	Rate Taux	Number Nombre	Rate Taux	Number Nombre	Rate Taux	Number Nombre	Rate Taux
TOTAL	1 765	657.6	1 906	709.5	1 919	697.5	1 786	650.5
Certain infectious and parasitic diseases — Certaines maladies infectieuses et parasitaires								
Total	43	16.0	41	15.3	25	♦9.1	28	♦10.2
Intestinal infectious diseases — Maladies infectieuses intestinales	3	♦1.1	8	♦3.0	-	-	-	-
Tuberculosis — Tuberculose	-	-	-	-	1	♦0.4	-	-
Tetanus — Tétanos	-	-	-	-	-	-	-	-
Diphtheria — Diphtérie	-	-	-	-	-	-	-	-
Whooping cough — Coqueluche	-	-	-	-	-	-	-	-
Meningococcal infection — Infection à méningocoques	-	-	-	-	-	-	1	♦0.4
Septicaemia — Septicémie	27	♦10.1	24	♦8.9	13	♦4.7	19	♦6.9
Acute poliomyelitis — Poliomyélite aiguë	-	-	-	-	-	-	-	-
Measles — Rougeole	-	-	-	-	-	-	-	-
Viral hepatitis — Hépatite virale	4	♦1.5	3	♦1.1	4	♦1.5	2	♦0.7
Human immunodeficiency virus [HIV] disease — Maladies dues au virus de l'immunodéficience humaine (VIH)	3	♦1.1	2	♦0.7	3	♦1.1		
Malaria — Paludisme	-	-	-	-	-	-	-	-
Neoplasms — Tumeurs	566	210.9	480	178.7	651	236.6	480	174.8
Malignant neoplasms — Tumeurs malignes								
Total	544	202.7	465	173.1	635	230.8	460	167.5
Malignant neoplasm of lip, oral cavity and pharynx — Tumeur maligne de la lèvre, de la cavité buccale et du pharynx	5	♦1.9	1	♦0.4	17	♦6.2	4	♦1.5
Malignant neoplasm of oesophagus — Tumeur maligne de l'oesophage	25	♦9.3	1	♦0.4	22	♦8.0	4	♦1.5
Malignant neoplasm of stomach — Tumeur maligne de l'estomac	22	♦8.2	12	♦4.5	31	11.3	19	♦6.9
Malignant neoplasm of colon, rectosigmoid junction, rectum, anus and anal canal — Tumeur maligne du côlon, de la jonction recto-sigmoïdienne, du rectum, de l'anus et du canal anal	65	24.2	67	24.9	66	24.0	40	14.6
Malignant neoplasm of liver and intrahepatic bile ducts — Tumeur maligne du foie et des voies bilaires intrahépatiques	33	12.3	25	♦9.3	32	11.6	12	♦4.4
Malignant neoplasm of pancreas — Tumeur maligne du pancréas	33	12.3	38	14.1	49	17.8	45	16.4
Malignant neoplasm of trachea, bronchus and lung — Tumeur maligne de la trachée, des bronches et du poumon	137	51.0	59	22.0	171	62.2	82	29.9
Malignant neoplasm of female breast — Tumeur maligne du sein chez la femme	..	..	92	41.0	..	..	85	37.0
Malignant neoplasm of cervix uteri — Tumeur maligne du col de l'utérus	..	..	9	♦4.0	..	..	8	♦3.5
Malignant neoplasm of prostate — Tumeur maligne de la prostate	42	50.6	..	..	48	55.5	..	..
Malignant neoplasm of lymphoid, haematopoietic and related tissue — Tumeurs malignes primitives ou présumées primitives des tissus lymphoïde, hématopoïétique et apparentés	51	19.0	45	16.8	46	16.7	40	14.6
Disorders of the blood and blood-forming organs and certain disorders involving the immune mechanism — Maladies du sang et des organes hématopoïétiques et certains troubles du système immunitaire								
Total	10	♦3.7	9	♦3.4	6	♦2.2	10	♦3.6
Anaemias — Anémies	3	♦1.1	2	♦0.7	4	♦1.5	5	♦1.8
Endocrine, nutritional and metabolic diseases — Maladies endocriniennes, nutritionnelles et métaboliques								
Total	44	16.4	68	25.3	61	22.2	64	23.3
Diabetes mellitus — Diabète sucré	32	11.9	45	16.8	51	18.5	43	15.7
Malnutrition — Malnutrition	2	♦0.7	9	♦3.4	-	-	9	♦3.3
Mental and behavioural disorders — Troubles mentaux et du comportement	68	25.3	120	44.7	79	28.7	106	38.6
Diseases of the nervous system — Maladies du système nerveux	83	30.9	91	33.9	72	26.2	80	29.1
Diseases of the circulatory system — Maladies de l'appareil circulatoire								
Total	523	194.8	650	242.0	543	197.4	620	225.8
Acute rheumatic fever and chronic rheumatic heart diseases — Rhumatisme articularie aigu et cardiopathies rhumatismales chroniques	3	♦1.1	14	♦5.2	6	♦2.2	10	♦3.6
Hypertensive diseases — Maladies hypertensives	19	♦7.1	41	15.3	13	♦4.7	38	13.8
Ischaemic heart disease — Cardiopathie ischémique	189	70.4	159	59.2	205	74.5	119	43.3
Cerebrovascular disease — Maladie cérébrovasculaire	108	40.2	137	51.0	85	30.9	139	50.6

20. Death and death rates by cause and sex: 2010 - 2014
Décès et taux de mortalité par cause et sexe : 2010 - 2014 (continued - suite)

Luxembourg

Cause of death — Cause de décès	2013 (+C)				2014 (+C)			
	Male — Masculin		Female — Féminin		Male — Masculin		Female — Féminin	
	Number Nombre	Rate Taux	Number Nombre	Rate Taux	Number Nombre	Rate Taux	Number Nombre	Rate Taux
Diseases of arteries, arterioles and capillaries — Maladies des artères, artérioles et capillaires	30	♦11.2	28	♦10.4	29	♦10.5	25	♦9.1
Diseases of the respiratory system — Maladies de l'appareil respiratoire								
Total	136	50.7	140	52.1	132	48.0	125	45.5
Influenza — Grippe	1	♦0.4	4	♦1.5	-	-	2	♦0.7
Pneumonia — Pneumopathies	28	♦10.4	41	15.3	33	12.0	33	12.0
Chronic lower respiratory diseases — Maladies chroniques des voies respiratoires inférieures	80	29.8	68	25.3	65	23.6	63	22.9
Diseases of the digestive system — Maladies de l'appareil digestif								
Total	82	30.6	67	24.9	98	35.6	73	26.6
Gastric and duodenal ulcer — Ulcère de l'estomac et du duodénum	1	♦0.4	2	♦0.7	1	♦0.4	4	♦1.5
Diseases of the liver — Maladies du foie...........................	44	16.4	20	♦7.4	52	18.9	19	♦6.9
Diseases of the musculoskeletal system and connective tissue — Maladies du système ostéo-articulaire, des muscles et du tissu conjonctif	6	♦2.2	8	♦3.0	6	♦2.2	12	♦4.4
Diseases of the genitourinary system — Maladies de l'appareil génito-urinaire								
Total	24	♦8.9	33	12.3	42	15.3	37	13.5
Disorders of kidney and ureter — Affections du rein et de l'uretère	22	♦8.2	30	♦11.2	31	11.3	33	12.0
Hyperplasia of prostate — Hyperplasie de la prostate...........................	-	-	..	..	1	♦1.2	..	..
Pregnancy, childbirth and the puerperium — Grossesse, accouchement et puerpéralité								
Total	..	..	1	♦16.4	..	..	-	-
Pregnancy with abortive outcome — Grossesse se terminant par un avortement	..	..	-	-	..	..	-	-
Other direct obstetric causes — Autres décès maternels directs	..	..	-	-	..	..	-	-
Indirect obstetric causes — Décès maternels indirects	..	..	-	-	..	..	-	-
Certain conditions originating in the perinatal period — Certaines affections dont l'origine se situe dans la période périnatale	6	♦191.8	2	♦67.0	4	♦127.4	6	♦204.7
Congenital malformations, deformations and chromosomal abnormalities — Malformations congénitales et anomalies chromosomiques	4	♦127.8	7	♦234.4	5	♦159.3	2	♦68.2
Symptoms, signs and abnormal clinical and laboratory findings, not elsewhere classified — Symptômes, signes et résultats anormaux d'examens cliniques et de laboratoire, non classés ailleurs	31	11.5	68	25.3	47	17.1	47	17.1
All other diseases — Toutes autres maladies..............................	-	-	2	♦0.7	2	♦0.7	2	♦0.7
External causes — Causes externes								
Total	139	51.8	119	44.3	146	53.1	94	34.2
Accidents								
Total	89	33.2	76	28.3	77	28.0	62	22.6
Transport accidents — Accidents de transport.............................	23	♦8.6	9	♦3.4	23	♦8.4	6	♦2.2
Falls — Chutes	28	♦10.4	23	♦8.6	24	♦8.7	28	♦10.2
Accidental drowning and submersion — Noyade et submersion accidentelles...............................	1	♦0.4	-	-	-	-	1	♦0.4
Exposure to smoke, fire and flames — Exposition à la fumée, au feu et aux flammes........................	-	-	-	-	1	♦0.4	2	♦0.7
Accidental poisoning by and exposure to noxious substances — Intoxication accidentelle par des substances nocives et exposition à ces substances	5	♦1.9	2	♦0.7	6	♦2.2	2	♦0.7
Intentional self-harm — Lésions auto-infligées.............................	24	♦8.9	16	♦6.0	52	18.9	15	♦5.5
Assault — Agresssions...	-	-	1	♦0.4	2	♦0.7	2	♦0.7
All other external causes — Toutes autres causes externes	26	♦9.7	26	♦9.7	15	♦5.5	15	♦5.5

20. Death and death rates by cause and sex: 2010 - 2014
Décès et taux de mortalité par cause et sexe : 2010 - 2014 (continued - suite)

Malta - Malte

Cause of death — Cause de décès	2013 (+C)				2014 (+C)			
	Male — Masculin		Female — Féminin		Male — Masculin		Female — Féminin	
	Number Nombre	Rate Taux	Number Nombre	Rate Taux	Number Nombre	Rate Taux	Number Nombre	Rate Taux
TOTAL	1 636	774.7	1 600	753.8	1 655	770.7	1 615	759.5
Certain infectious and parasitic diseases — Certaines maladies infectieuses et parasitaires								
Total	13	◆6.2	11	◆5.2	13	◆6.1	12	◆5.6
Intestinal infectious diseases — Maladies infectieuses intestinales	2	◆0.9	2	◆0.9	-	-	-	-
Tuberculosis — Tuberculose	-	-	1	◆0.5	1	◆0.5	-	-
Tetanus — Tétanos	-	-	-	-	-	-	-	-
Diphtheria — Diphtérie	-	-	-	-	-	-	-	-
Whooping cough — Coqueluche	-	-	-	-	-	-	-	-
Meningococcal infection — Infection à méningocoques	-	-	-	-	-	-	-	-
Septicaemia — Septicémie	2	◆0.9	6	◆2.8	9	◆4.2	8	◆3.8
Acute poliomyelitis — Poliomyélite aiguë	-	-	-	-	-	-	-	-
Measles — Rougeole	-	-	-	-	-	-	-	-
Viral hepatitis — Hépatite virale	2	◆0.9	-	-	1	◆0.5	2	◆0.9
Human immunodeficiency virus [HIV] disease — Maladies dues au virus de l'immunodéficience humaine (VIH)	1	◆0.5	-	-	2	◆0.9	1	◆0.5
Malaria — Paludisme	-	-	-	-	-	-	-	-
Neoplasms — Tumeurs	467	221.1	404	190.3	532	247.7	401	188.6
Malignant neoplasms — Tumeurs malignes								
Total	461	218.3	388	182.8	523	243.6	389	182.9
Malignant neoplasm of lip, oral cavity and pharynx — Tumeur maligne de la lèvre, de la cavité buccale et du pharynx	9	◆4.3	8	◆3.8	17	◆7.9	10	◆4.7
Malignant neoplasm of oesophagus — Tumeur maligne de l'oesophage	9	◆4.3	3	◆1.4	20	◆9.3	5	◆2.4
Malignant neoplasm of stomach — Tumeur maligne de l'estomac	31	14.7	15	◆7.1	27	◆12.6	14	◆6.6
Malignant neoplasm of colon, rectosigmoid junction, rectum, anus and anal canal — Tumeur maligne du côlon, de la jonction recto-sigmoïdienne, du rectum, de l'anus et du canal anal	61	28.9	48	22.6	60	27.9	46	21.6
Malignant neoplasm of liver and intrahepatic bile ducts — Tumeur maligne du foie et des voies bilaires intrahépatiques	13	◆6.2	8	◆3.8	16	◆7.5	10	◆4.7
Malignant neoplasm of pancreas — Tumeur maligne du pancréas	34	16.1	38	17.9	47	21.9	41	19.3
Malignant neoplasm of trachea, bronchus and lung — Tumeur maligne de la trachée, des bronches et du poumon	117	55.4	37	17.4	142	66.1	28	◆13.2
Malignant neoplasm of female breast — Tumeur maligne du sein chez la femme	..	..	83	45.5	..	..	75	40.8
Malignant neoplasm of cervix uteri — Tumeur maligne du col de l'utérus	..	..	4	◆2.2	..	..	4	◆2.2
Malignant neoplasm of prostate — Tumeur maligne de la prostate	37	47.9	..	..	43	54.5	..	..
Malignant neoplasm of lymphoid, haematopoietic and related tissue — Tumeurs malignes primitives ou présumées primitives des tissus lymphoïde, hématopoïétique et apparentés	34	16.1	30	◆14.1	35	16.3	32	15.0
Disorders of the blood and blood-forming organs and certain disorders involving the immune mechanism — Maladies du sang et des organes hématopoïétiques et certains troubles du système immunitaire								
Total	1	◆0.5	3	◆1.4	2	◆0.9	6	◆2.8
Anaemias — Anémies	1	◆0.5	3	◆1.4	2	◆0.9	3	◆1.4
Endocrine, nutritional and metabolic diseases — Maladies endocriniennes, nutritionnelles et métaboliques								
Total	58	27.5	55	25.9	85	39.6	87	40.9
Diabetes mellitus — Diabète sucré	54	25.6	51	24.0	80	37.3	77	36.2
Malnutrition — Malnutrition	-	-	-	-	-	-	1	◆0.5
Mental and behavioural disorders — Troubles mentaux et du comportement	38	18.0	83	39.1	46	21.4	93	43.7
Diseases of the nervous system — Maladies du système nerveux	44	20.8	40	18.8	34	15.8	42	19.8
Diseases of the circulatory system — Maladies de l'appareil circulatoire								
Total	633	299.7	665	313.3	577	268.7	654	307.6
Acute rheumatic fever and chronic rheumatic heart diseases — Rhumatisme articularie aigu et cardiopathies rhumatismales chroniques	-	-	-	-	-	-	4	◆1.9
Hypertensive diseases — Maladies hypertensives	13	◆6.2	15	◆7.1	13	◆6.1	19	◆8.9
Ischaemic heart disease — Cardiopathie ischémique	387	183.3	318	149.8	352	163.9	337	158.5
Cerebrovascular disease — Maladie cérébrovasculaire	113	53.5	161	75.9	116	54.0	160	75.2

Malta - Malte

Cause of death — Cause de décès	2013 (+C)				2014 (+C)			
	Male — Masculin		Female — Féminin		Male — Masculin		Female — Féminin	
	Number Nombre	Rate Taux	Number Nombre	Rate Taux	Number Nombre	Rate Taux	Number Nombre	Rate Taux
Diseases of arteries, arterioles and capillaries — Maladies des artères, artérioles et capillaires	18	♦8.5	31	14.6	22	♦10.2	13	♦6.1
Diseases of the respiratory system — Maladies de l'appareil respiratoire								
Total	187	88.5	157	74.0	171	79.6	140	65.8
Influenza — Grippe	-	-	-	-	-	-	-	-
Pneumonia — Pneumopathies	61	28.9	74	34.9	51	23.8	57	26.8
Chronic lower respiratory diseases — Maladies chroniques des voies respiratoires inférieures	66	31.3	12	♦5.7	74	34.5	24	♦11.3
Diseases of the digestive system — Maladies de l'appareil digestif								
Total	50	23.7	51	24.0	53	24.7	61	28.7
Gastric and duodenal ulcer — Ulcère de l'estomac et du duodénum	4	♦1.9	6	♦2.8	3	♦1.4	4	♦1.9
Diseases of the liver — Maladies du foie	22	♦10.4	5	♦2.4	23	♦10.7	4	♦1.9
Diseases of the musculoskeletal system and connective tissue — Maladies du système ostéo-articularie, des muscles et du tissu conjonctif	4	♦1.9	8	♦3.8	8	♦3.7	12	♦5.6
Diseases of the genitourinary system — Maladies de l'appareil génito-urinaire								
Total	38	18.0	58	27.3	28	♦13.0	35	16.5
Disorders of kidney and ureter — Affections du rein et de l'uretère	19	♦9.0	32	15.1	14	♦6.5	16	♦7.5
Hyperplasia of prostate — Hyperplasie de la prostate	2	♦2.6	..	..	3	♦3.8	..	..
Pregnancy, childbirth and the puerperium — Grossesse, accouchement et puerpéralité								
Total	..	..	-	-	..	..	-	-
Pregnancy with abortive outcome — Grossesse se terminant par un avortement	..	..	-	-	..	..	-	-
Other direct obstetric causes — Autres décès maternels directs	..	..	-	-	..	..	-	-
Indirect obstetric causes — Décès maternels indirects	..	..	-	-	..	..	-	-
Certain conditions originating in the perinatal period — Certaines affections dont l'origine se situe dans la période périnatale	6	♦284.5	6	♦312.0	6	♦269.9	7	♦355.7
Congenital malformations, deformations and chromosomal abnormalities — Malformations congénitales et anomalies chromosomiques	5	♦237.1	5	♦260.0	10	♦449.8	4	♦203.3
Symptoms, signs and abnormal clinical and laboratory findings, not elsewhere classified — Symptômes, signes et résultats anormaux d'examens cliniques et de laboratoire, non classés ailleurs	10	♦4.7	12	♦5.7	9	♦4.2	11	♦5.2
All other diseases — Toutes autres maladies	4	♦1.9	14	♦6.6	6	♦2.8	18	♦8.5
External causes — Causes externes								
Total	78	36.9	28	♦13.2	75	34.9	32	15.0
Accidents								
Total	51	24.1	26	♦12.2	42	19.6	25	♦11.8
Transport accidents — Accidents de transport	18	♦8.5	6	♦2.8	7	♦3.3	4	♦1.9
Falls — Chutes	28	♦13.3	18	♦8.5	23	♦10.7	18	♦8.5
Accidental drowning and submersion — Noyade et submersion accidentelles	-	-	1	♦0.5	2	♦0.9	-	-
Exposure to smoke, fire and flames — Exposition à la fumée, au feu et aux flammes	-	-	-	-	-	-	-	-
Accidental poisoning by and exposure to noxious substances — Intoxication accidentelle par des substances nocives et exposition à ces substances	-	-	-	-	4	♦1.9	-	-
Intentional self-harm — Lésions auto-infligées	21	♦9.9	1	♦0.5	27	♦12.6	5	♦2.4
Assault — Agresssions	6	♦2.8	-	-	4	♦1.9	-	-
All other external causes — Toutes autres causes externes	-	-	1	♦0.5	2	♦0.9	2	♦0.9

Netherlands - Pays-Bas

Cause of death — Cause de décès	2012 (+C)				2013 (+C)			
	Male — Masculin		Female — Féminin		Male — Masculin		Female — Féminin	
	Number Nombre	Rate Taux	Number Nombre	Rate Taux	Number Nombre	Rate Taux	Number Nombre	Rate Taux
TOTAL	67 907	819.8	72 906	863.1	68 360	822.9	72 885	860.3
Certain infectious and parasitic diseases — Certaines maladies infectieuses et parasitaires								
Total	1 092	13.2	1 139	13.5	1 528	18.4	1 655	19.5
Intestinal infectious diseases — Maladies infectieuses intestinales	76	0.9	118	1.4	177	2.1	366	4.3
Tuberculosis — Tuberculose	9	٠0.1	6	٠0.1	13	٠0.2	10	٠0.1
Tetanus — Tétanos	-	-	-	-	-	-	-	-
Diphtheria — Diphtérie............	-	-	-	-	-	-	-	-
Whooping cough — Coqueluche	1	٠0.0	1	٠0.0	-	-	-	-
Meningococcal infection — Infection à méningocoques............	1	٠0.0	-	-	1	٠0.0	2	٠0.0
Septicaemia — Septicémie............	596	7.2	567	6.7	897	10.8	785	9.3
Acute poliomyelitis — Poliomyélite aiguë	-	-	-	-	1	٠0.0	-	-
Measles — Rougeole............	-	-	-	-	-	-	-	-
Viral hepatitis — Hépatite virale............	38	0.5	20	٠0.2	39	0.5	16	٠0.2
Human immunodeficiency virus [HIV] disease — Maladies dues au virus de l'immunodéficience humaine (VIH)............	38	0.5	6	٠0.1	30	٠0.4	4	٠0.0
Malaria — Paludisme............	-	-	-	-	-	-	1	٠0.0
Neoplasms — Tumeurs	24 161	291.7	20 508	242.8	23 766	286.1	20 390	240.7
Malignant neoplasms — Tumeurs malignes								
Total............	23 545	284.3	19 836	234.8	22 887	275.5	19 456	229.6
Malignant neoplasm of lip, oral cavity and pharynx — Tumeur maligne de la lèvre, de la cavité buccale et du pharynx	408	4.9	221	2.6	408	4.9	238	2.8
Malignant neoplasm of oesophagus — Tumeur maligne de l'oesophage	1 289	15.6	448	5.3	1 238	14.9	429	5.1
Malignant neoplasm of stomach — Tumeur maligne de l'estomac	827	10.0	534	6.3	811	9.8	529	6.2
Malignant neoplasm of colon, rectosigmoid junction, rectum, anus and anal canal — Tumeur maligne du côlon, de la jonction recto-sigmoïdienne, du rectum, de l'anus et du canal anal............	2 805	33.9	2 569	30.4	2 625	31.6	2 351	27.7
Malignant neoplasm of liver and intrahepatic bile ducts — Tumeur maligne du foie et des voies bilaires intrahépatiques	522	6.3	317	3.8	487	5.9	272	3.2
Malignant neoplasm of pancreas — Tumeur maligne du pancréas............	1 308	15.8	1 260	14.9	1 221	14.7	1 233	14.6
Malignant neoplasm of trachea, bronchus and lung — Tumeur maligne de la trachée, des bronches et du poumon	6 324	76.4	3 998	47.3	6 215	74.8	4 062	47.9
Malignant neoplasm of female breast — Tumeur maligne du sein chez la femme	..	..	3 197	...	..	..	3 161	...
Malignant neoplasm of cervix uteri — Tumeur maligne du col de l'utérus.........	..	..	215	...	..	..	222	...
Malignant neoplasm of prostate — Tumeur maligne de la prostate	2 566	...	..	..	2 535	...	..	..
Malignant neoplasm of lymphoid, haematopoietic and related tissue — Tumeurs malignes primitives ou présumées primitives des tissus lymphoïde, hématopoïétique et apparentés............	1 810	21.9	1 386	16.4	1 827	22.0	1 447	17.1
Disorders of the blood and blood-forming organs and certain disorders involving the immune mechanism — Maladies du sang et des organes hématopoïétiques et certains troubles du système immunitaire								
Total............	189	2.3	284	3.4	222	2.7	282	3.3
Anaemias — Anémies	117	1.4	207	2.5	140	1.7	205	2.4
Endocrine, nutritional and metabolic diseases — Maladies endocriniennes, nutritionnelles et métaboliques								
Total............	1 592	19.2	2 010	23.8	1 680	20.2	2 097	24.8
Diabetes mellitus — Diabète sucré............	1 329	16.0	1 482	17.5	1 313	15.8	1 586	18.7
Malnutrition — Malnutrition	21	٠0.3	58	0.7	26	٠0.3	31	0.4
Mental and behavioural disorders — Troubles mentaux et du comportement	2 527	30.5	6 054	71.7	3 447	41.5	7 012	82.8
Diseases of the nervous system — Maladies du système nerveux............	2 360	28.5	3 200	37.9	2 900	34.9	3 801	44.9
Diseases of the circulatory system — Maladies de l'appareil circulatoire								
Total............	18 027	217.6	20 344	240.8	18 026	217.0	20 437	241.2
Acute rheumatic fever and chronic rheumatic heart diseases — Rhumatisme articulaire aigu et cardiopathies rhumatismales chroniques	-	-	7	٠0.1	61	0.7	162	1.9
Hypertensive diseases — Maladies hypertensives............	441	5.3	692	8.2	564	6.8	929	11.0
Ischaemic heart disease — Cardiopathie ischémique............	5 691	68.7	4 029	47.7	5 354	64.4	3 912	46.2
Cerebrovascular disease — Maladie cérébrovasculaire............	3 286	39.7	5 186	61.4	3 747	45.1	5 653	66.7

20. Death and death rates by cause and sex: 2010 - 2014
Décès et taux de mortalité par cause et sexe : 2010 - 2014 (continued - suite)

Netherlands - Pays-Bas

Cause of death — Cause de décès	2012 (+C)				2013 (+C)			
	Male — Masculin		Female — Féminin		Male — Masculin		Female — Féminin	
	Number Nombre	Rate Taux	Number Nombre	Rate Taux	Number Nombre	Rate Taux	Number Nombre	Rate Taux
Diseases of arteries, arterioles and capillaries — Maladies des artères, artérioles et capillaires	1 757	21.2	1 367	16.2	1 500	18.1	1 115	13.2
Diseases of the respiratory system — Maladies de l'appareil respiratoire								
Total	7 380	89.1	7 097	84.0	6 312	76.0	5 957	70.3
Influenza — Grippe	51	0.6	90	1.1	95	1.1	167	2.0
Pneumonia — Pneumopathies	2 570	31.0	2 846	33.7	1 594	19.2	1 869	22.1
Chronic lower respiratory diseases — Maladies chroniques des voies respiratoires inférieures	3 748	45.3	3 226	38.2	3 661	44.1	3 050	36.0
Diseases of the digestive system — Maladies de l'appareil digestif								
Total	2 331	28.1	2 929	34.7	2 084	25.1	2 402	28.4
Gastric and duodenal ulcer — Ulcère de l'estomac et du duodénum..............	94	1.1	98	1.2	81	1.0	86	1.0
Diseases of the liver — Maladies du foie..............	595	7.2	391	4.6	575	6.9	391	4.6
Diseases of the musculoskeletal system and connective tissue — Maladies du système ostéo-articularie, des muscles et du tissu conjonctif	297	3.6	627	7.4	347	4.2	731	8.6
Diseases of the genitourinary system — Maladies de l'appareil génito-urinaire								
Total	1 537	18.6	2 137	25.3	1 316	15.8	1 691	20.0
Disorders of kidney and ureter — Affections du rein et de l'uretère	860	10.4	1 124	13.3	864	10.4	1 024	12.1
Hyperplasia of prostate — Hyperplasie de la prostate..............	44	...	..		34	...		
Pregnancy, childbirth and the puerperium — Grossesse, accouchement et puerpéralité								
Total	..	..	6	♦3.4	..	..	5	♦2.9
Pregnancy with abortive outcome — Grossesse se terminant par un avortement	..	..	1	♦0.6	..	..	-	-
Other direct obstetric causes — Autres décès maternels directs	..	..	5	♦2.8	..	..	5	♦2.9
Indirect obstetric causes — Décès maternels indirects	..	..	-	-	..	..	-	-
Certain conditions originating in the perinatal period — Certaines affections dont l'origine se situe dans la période périnatale	209	231.8	152	177.2	204	231.9	135	161.9
Congenital malformations, deformations and chromosomal abnormalities — Malformations congénitales et anomalies chromosomiques	226	250.6	205	239.0	214	243.3	221	265.0
Symptoms, signs and abnormal clinical and laboratory findings, not elsewhere classified — Symptômes, signes et résultats anormaux d'examens cliniques et de laboratoire, non classés ailleurs	2 465	29.8	2 988	35.4	2 662	32.0	2 960	34.9
All other diseases — Toutes autres maladies..............	121	1.5	282	3.3	97	1.2	221	2.6
External causes — Causes externes								
Total	3 393	41.0	2 944	34.9	3 555	42.8	2 888	34.1
Accidents								
Total	1 904	23.0	2 007	23.8	1 940	23.4	1 963	23.2
Transport accidents — Accidents de transport	498	6.0	186	2.2	434	5.2	154	1.8
Falls — Chutes	837	10.1	1 202	14.2	944	11.4	1 230	14.5
Accidental drowning and submersion — Noyade et submersion accidentelles..............	64	0.8	17	♦0.2	59	0.7	25	♦0.3
Exposure to smoke, fire and flames — Exposition à la fumée, au feu et aux flammes..............	14	♦0.2	14	♦0.2	27	♦0.3	12	♦0.1
Accidental poisoning by and exposure to noxious substances — Intoxication accidentelle par des substances nocives et exposition à ces substances	106	1.3	36	0.4	88	1.1	47	0.6
Intentional self-harm — Lésions auto-infligées	1 186	14.3	567	6.7	1 305	15.7	549	6.5
Assault — Agresssions	95	1.1	50	0.6	69	0.8	56	0.7
All other external causes — Toutes autres causes externes	208	2.5	320	3.8	241	2.9	320	3.8

Norway - Norvège

Cause of death — Cause de décès	2013 (+C)				2014 (+C)			
	Male — Masculin		Female — Féminin		Male — Masculin		Female — Féminin	
	Number Nombre	Rate Taux	Number Nombre	Rate Taux	Number Nombre	Rate Taux	Number Nombre	Rate Taux
TOTAL	19 924	785.7	21 254	845.0	19 685	766.8	20 659	813.0
Certain infectious and parasitic diseases — Certaines maladies infectieuses et parasitaires								
Total	430	17.0	548	21.8	411	16.0	503	19.8
Intestinal infectious diseases — Maladies infectieuses intestinales	54	2.1	97	3.9	44	1.7	67	2.6
Tuberculosis — Tuberculose	5	♦0.2	2	♦0.1	4	♦0.2	1	♦0.0
Tetanus — Tétanos	-	-	-	-	1	♦0.0	-	-
Diphtheria — Diphtérie...........................	-	-	-	-	-	-	-	-
Whooping cough — Coqueluche	-	-	-	-	1	♦0.0	-	-
Meningococcal infection — Infection à méningocoques...........................	1	♦0.0	-	-	-	-	-	-
Septicaemia — Septicémie...........................	203	8.0	206	8.2	168	6.5	173	6.8
Acute poliomyelitis — Poliomyélite aiguë	-	-	-	-	-	-	-	-
Measles — Rougeole...........................	-	-	-	-	-	-	-	-
Viral hepatitis — Hépatite virale...........................	7	♦0.3	4	♦0.2	13	♦0.5	5	♦0.2
Human immunodeficiency virus [HIV] disease — Maladies dues au virus de l'immunodéficience humaine (VIH)...........................	4	♦0.2	-	-	8	♦0.3	3	♦0.1
Malaria — Paludisme...........................	2	♦0.1	-	-	-	-	-	-
Neoplasms — Tumeurs	5 788	228.2	5 037	200.2	5 889	229.4	5 199	204.6
Malignant neoplasms — Tumeurs malignes								
Total	5 650	222.8	4 900	194.8	5 766	224.6	5 075	199.7
Malignant neoplasm of lip, oral cavity and pharynx — Tumeur maligne de la lèvre, de la cavité buccale et du pharynx	94	3.7	56	2.2	69	2.7	41	1.6
Malignant neoplasm of oesophagus — Tumeur maligne de l'oesophage	161	6.3	48	1.9	170	6.6	56	2.2
Malignant neoplasm of stomach — Tumeur maligne de l'estomac	181	7.1	139	5.5	179	7.0	122	4.8
Malignant neoplasm of colon, rectosigmoid junction, rectum, anus and anal canal — Tumeur maligne du côlon, de la jonction recto-sigmoïdienne, du rectum, de l'anus et du canal anal	760	30.0	780	31.0	784	30.5	780	30.7
Malignant neoplasm of liver and intrahepatic bile ducts — Tumeur maligne du foie et des voies bilaires intrahépatiques	145	5.7	87	3.5	120	4.7	84	3.3
Malignant neoplasm of pancreas — Tumeur maligne du pancréas...........	350	13.8	350	13.9	349	13.6	364	14.3
Malignant neoplasm of trachea, bronchus and lung — Tumeur maligne de la trachée, des bronches et du poumon	1 209	47.7	954	37.9	1 198	46.7	960	37.8
Malignant neoplasm of female breast — Tumeur maligne du sein chez la femme	..	..	631	...	..	..	663	...
Malignant neoplasm of cervix uteri — Tumeur maligne du col de l'utérus.........	..	..	75	...	..	..	63	...
Malignant neoplasm of prostate — Tumeur maligne de la prostate	988	...	..	..	1 093	...	..	..
Malignant neoplasm of lymphoid, haematopoietic and related tissue — Tumeurs malignes primitives ou présumées primitives des tissus lymphoïde, hématopoïétique et apparentés...........	494	19.5	396	15.7	457	17.8	414	16.3
Disorders of the blood and blood-forming organs and certain disorders involving the immune mechanism — Maladies du sang et des organes hématopoïétiques et certains troubles du système immunitaire								
Total	63	2.5	76	3.0	72	2.8	82	3.2
Anaemias — Anémies	34	1.3	50	2.0	36	1.4	54	2.1
Endocrine, nutritional and metabolic diseases — Maladies endocriniennes, nutritionnelles et métaboliques								
Total	453	17.9	529	21.0	425	16.6	520	20.5
Diabetes mellitus — Diabète sucré...........................	327	12.9	329	13.1	307	12.0	307	12.1
Malnutrition — Malnutrition	22	♦0.9	68	2.7	29	♦1.1	66	2.6
Mental and behavioural disorders — Troubles mentaux et du comportement	738	29.1	1 466	58.3	847	33.0	1 570	61.8
Diseases of the nervous system — Maladies du système nerveux...............	759	29.9	970	38.6	841	32.8	1 094	43.1
Diseases of the circulatory system — Maladies de l'appareil circulatoire								
Total	5 630	222.0	6 455	256.6	5 477	213.4	6 239	245.5
Acute rheumatic fever and chronic rheumatic heart diseases — Rhumatisme articularie aigu et cardiopathies rhumatismales chroniques	16	♦0.6	36	1.4	18	♦0.7	37	1.5
Hypertensive diseases — Maladies hypertensives...........................	182	7.2	307	12.2	180	7.0	301	11.8
Ischaemic heart disease — Cardiopathie ischémique...........................	2 384	94.0	2 005	79.7	2 220	86.5	1 872	73.7
Cerebrovascular disease — Maladie cérébrovasculaire...........................	1 133	44.7	1 621	64.4	1 114	43.4	1 591	62.6

20. Death and death rates by cause and sex: 2010 - 2014
Décès et taux de mortalité par cause et sexe : 2010 - 2014 (continued - suite)

Norway - Norvège

Cause of death — Cause de décès	2013 (+C)				2014 (+C)			
	Male — Masculin		Female — Féminin		Male — Masculin		Female — Féminin	
	Number Nombre	Rate Taux	Number Nombre	Rate Taux	Number Nombre	Rate Taux	Number Nombre	Rate Taux
Diseases of arteries, arterioles and capillaries — Maladies des artères, artérioles et capillaires	392	15.5	282	11.2	350	13.6	279	11.0
Diseases of the respiratory system — Maladies de l'appareil respiratoire								
Total	1 918	75.6	2 106	83.7	1 865	72.7	1 885	74.2
Influenza — Grippe	33	1.3	44	1.7	19	♦0.7	21	♦0.8
Pneumonia — Pneumopathies	636	25.1	801	31.8	575	22.4	691	27.2
Chronic lower respiratory diseases — Maladies chroniques des voies respiratoires inférieures	1 045	41.2	1 067	42.4	1 028	40.0	1 013	39.9
Diseases of the digestive system — Maladies de l'appareil digestif								
Total	531	20.9	674	26.8	581	22.6	629	24.8
Gastric and duodenal ulcer — Ulcère de l'estomac et du duodénum	57	2.2	90	3.6	64	2.5	75	3.0
Diseases of the liver — Maladies du foie	160	6.3	113	4.5	141	5.5	83	3.3
Diseases of the musculoskeletal system and connective tissue — Maladies du système ostéo-articularie, des muscles et du tissu conjonctif	89	3.5	162	6.4	104	4.1	162	6.4
Diseases of the genitourinary system — Maladies de l'appareil génito-urinaire								
Total	383	15.1	404	16.1	399	15.5	409	16.1
Disorders of kidney and ureter — Affections du rein et de l'uretère	243	9.6	235	9.3	239	9.3	224	8.8
Hyperplasia of prostate — Hyperplasie de la prostate	19	...	..	..	36	...	..	..
Pregnancy, childbirth and the puerperium — Grossesse, accouchement et puerpéralité								
Total	..	..	2	♦3.4	..	..	2	♦3.4
Pregnancy with abortive outcome — Grossesse se terminant par un avortement	..	..	-	-	..	..	-	-
Other direct obstetric causes — Autres décès maternels directs	..	..	2	♦3.4	..	..	2	♦3.4
Indirect obstetric causes — Décès maternels indirects	..	..	-	-	..	..	-	-
Certain conditions originating in the perinatal period — Certaines affections dont l'origine se situe dans la période périnatale	44	146.3	35	121.6	39	128.6	40	139.6
Congenital malformations, deformations and chromosomal abnormalities — Malformations congénitales et anomalies chromosomiques	67	222.7	71	246.6	65	214.4	53	185.0
Symptoms, signs and abnormal clinical and laboratory findings, not elsewhere classified — Symptômes, signes et résultats anormaux d'examens cliniques et de laboratoire, non classés ailleurs	1 509	59.5	1 576	62.7	1 087	42.3	1 162	45.7
All other diseases — Toutes autres maladies	46	1.8	59	2.3	36	1.4	82	3.2
External causes — Causes externes								
Total	1 476	58.2	1 084	43.1	1 547	60.3	1 028	40.5
Accidents								
Total	1 050	41.4	870	34.6	1 101	42.9	854	33.6
Transport accidents — Accidents de transport	179	7.1	53	2.1	148	5.8	38	1.5
Falls — Chutes	239	9.4	259	10.3	275	10.7	250	9.8
Accidental drowning and submersion — Noyade et submersion accidentelles	40	1.6	12	♦0.5	62	2.4	12	♦0.5
Exposure to smoke, fire and flames — Exposition à la fumée, au feu et aux flammes	35	1.4	22	♦0.9	27	♦1.1	21	♦0.8
Accidental poisoning by and exposure to noxious substances — Intoxication accidentelle par des substances nocives et exposition à ces substances	233	9.2	83	3.3	244	9.5	92	3.6
Intentional self-harm — Lésions auto-infligées	377	14.9	176	7.0	401	15.6	147	5.8
Assault — Agresssions	32	1.3	18	♦0.7	22	♦0.9	9	♦0.4
All other external causes — Toutes autres causes externes	17	♦0.7	20	♦0.8	23	♦0.9	18	♦0.7

20. Death and death rates by cause and sex: 2010 - 2014
Décès et taux de mortalité par cause et sexe : 2010 - 2014 (continued - suite)

Poland - Pologne

Cause of death — Cause de décès	2013 (C)				2014 (C)			
	Male — Masculin		Female — Féminin		Male — Masculin		Female — Féminin	
	Number Nombre	Rate Taux	Number Nombre	Rate Taux	Number Nombre	Rate Taux	Number Nombre	Rate Taux
TOTAL	201 696	1 081.5	185 616	933.5	195 791	1 063.9	180 676	921.2
Certain infectious and parasitic diseases — Certaines maladies infectieuses et parasitaires								
Total	1 150	6.2	813	4.1	1 102	6.0	821	4.2
Intestinal infectious diseases — Maladies infectieuses intestinales	122	0.7	197	1.0	164	0.9	258	1.3
Tuberculosis — Tuberculose	416	2.2	116	0.6	413	2.2	113	0.6
Tetanus — Tétanos	2	♦0.0	2	♦0.0	-	-	2	♦0.0
Diphtheria — Diphtérie	-	-	-	-	-	-	-	-
Whooping cough — Coqueluche	-	-	-	-	-	-	-	-
Meningococcal infection — Infection à méningocoques	10	♦0.1	5	♦0.0	1	♦0.0	4	♦0.0
Septicaemia — Septicémie	255	1.4	261	1.3	139	0.8	170	0.9
Acute poliomyelitis — Poliomyélite aiguë	-	-	-	-	-	-	-	-
Measles — Rougeole	-	-	-	-	-	-	-	-
Viral hepatitis — Hépatite virale	141	0.8	92	0.5	183	1.0	138	0.7
Human immunodeficiency virus [HIV] disease — Maladies dues au virus de l'immunodéficience humaine (VIH)	92	0.5	31	0.2	93	0.5	32	0.2
Malaria — Paludisme	-	-	-	-	1	♦0.0	-	-
Neoplasms — Tumeurs	54 728	293.5	44 209	222.3	55 255	300.2	45 074	229.8
Malignant neoplasms — Tumeurs malignes								
Total	52 197	279.9	41 919	210.8	52 688	286.3	42 873	218.6
Malignant neoplasm of lip, oral cavity and pharynx — Tumeur maligne de la lèvre, de la cavité buccale et du pharynx	1 884	10.1	581	2.9	2 004	10.9	671	3.4
Malignant neoplasm of oesophagus — Tumeur maligne de l'oesophage	1 153	6.2	318	1.6	1 171	6.4	344	1.8
Malignant neoplasm of stomach — Tumeur maligne de l'estomac	3 361	18.0	1 871	9.4	3 379	18.4	1 874	9.6
Malignant neoplasm of colon, rectosigmoid junction, rectum, anus and anal canal — Tumeur maligne du côlon, de la jonction recto-sigmoïdienne, du rectum, de l'anus et du canal anal	6 222	33.4	5 074	25.5	6 423	34.9	4 988	25.4
Malignant neoplasm of liver and intrahepatic bile ducts — Tumeur maligne du foie et des voies bilaires intrahépatiques	1 089	5.8	891	4.5	1 084	5.9	840	4.3
Malignant neoplasm of pancreas — Tumeur maligne du pancréas	2 375	12.7	2 355	11.8	2 464	13.4	2 519	12.8
Malignant neoplasm of trachea, bronchus and lung — Tumeur maligne de la trachée, des bronches et du poumon	16 002	85.8	6 653	33.5	15 847	86.1	7 363	37.5
Malignant neoplasm of female breast — Tumeur maligne du sein chez la femme	..	..	5 816	...	..	..	5 975	...
Malignant neoplasm of cervix uteri — Tumeur maligne du col de l'utérus	..	..	1 669	...	..	..	1 628	...
Malignant neoplasm of prostate — Tumeur maligne de la prostate	4 281	...	..	..	4 440	...	..	..
Malignant neoplasm of lymphoid, haematopoietic and related tissue — Tumeurs malignes primitives ou présumées primitives des tissus lymphoïde, hématopoïétique et apparentés	3 150	16.9	2 733	13.7	3 269	17.8	2 805	14.3
Disorders of the blood and blood-forming organs and certain disorders involving the immune mechanism — Maladies du sang et des organes hématopoïétiques et certains troubles du système immunitaire								
Total	125	0.7	175	0.9	101	0.5	111	0.6
Anaemias — Anémies	55	0.3	88	0.4	40	0.2	47	0.2
Endocrine, nutritional and metabolic diseases — Maladies endocriniennes, nutritionnelles et métaboliques								
Total	3 389	18.2	4 440	22.3	3 150	17.1	4 056	20.7
Diabetes mellitus — Diabète sucré	3 217	17.2	4 224	21.2	2 965	16.1	3 821	19.5
Malnutrition — Malnutrition	72	0.4	89	0.4	80	0.4	87	0.4
Mental and behavioural disorders — Troubles mentaux et du comportement	1 205	6.5	326	1.6	1 176	6.4	314	1.6
Diseases of the nervous system — Maladies du système nerveux	2 591	13.9	3 188	16.0	2 339	12.7	2 851	14.5
Diseases of the circulatory system — Maladies de l'appareil circulatoire								
Total	82 518	442.5	94 910	477.3	78 817	428.3	90 917	463.5
Acute rheumatic fever and chronic rheumatic heart diseases — Rhumatisme articularie aigu et cardiopathies rhumatismales chroniques	299	1.6	557	2.8	286	1.6	454	2.3
Hypertensive diseases — Maladies hypertensives	1 838	9.9	2 435	12.2	1 669	9.1	2 269	11.6
Ischaemic heart disease — Cardiopathie ischémique	22 299	119.6	18 570	93.4	21 044	114.3	17 494	89.2
Cerebrovascular disease — Maladie cérébrovasculaire	14 073	75.5	18 689	94.0	13 365	72.6	17 644	90.0

Poland - Pologne

Cause of death — Cause de décès	2013 (C)				2014 (C)			
	Male — Masculin		Female — Féminin		Male — Masculin		Female — Féminin	
	Number Nombre	Rate Taux	Number Nombre	Rate Taux	Number Nombre	Rate Taux	Number Nombre	Rate Taux
Diseases of arteries, arterioles and capillaries — Maladies des artères, artérioles et capillaires	14 468	77.6	24 139	121.4	14 050	76.3	23 881	121.8
Diseases of the respiratory system — Maladies de l'appareil respiratoire								
Total	13 106	70.3	9 841	49.5	11 611	63.1	8 760	44.7
Influenza — Grippe	56	0.3	59	0.3	7	♦0.0	4	♦0.0
Pneumonia — Pneumopathies	7 022	37.7	6 340	31.9	6 491	35.3	5 759	29.4
Chronic lower respiratory diseases — Maladies chroniques des voies respiratoires inférieures	5 037	27.0	2 685	13.5	4 174	22.7	2 264	11.5
Diseases of the digestive system — Maladies de l'appareil digestif								
Total	9 280	49.8	7 268	36.6	8 729	47.4	6 669	34.0
Gastric and duodenal ulcer — Ulcère de l'estomac et du duodénum.................	1 177	6.3	1 031	5.2	1 246	6.8	1 021	5.2
Diseases of the liver — Maladies du foie........................	4 676	25.1	2 181	11.0	4 504	24.5	2 077	10.6
Diseases of the musculoskeletal system and connective tissue — Maladies du système ostéo-articularie, des muscles et du tissu conjonctif	158	0.8	454	2.3	157	0.9	431	2.2
Diseases of the genitourinary system — Maladies de l'appareil génito-urinaire								
Total	2 018	10.8	2 278	11.5	1 329	7.2	1 516	7.7
Disorders of kidney and ureter — Affections du rein et de l'uretère	1 769	9.5	1 965	9.9	991	5.4	1 073	5.5
Hyperplasia of prostate — Hyperplasie de la prostate....................	6	...	..	..	25	...	..	..
Pregnancy, childbirth and the puerperium — Grossesse, accouchement et puerpéralité								
Total	..	..	7	♦1.9	..	..	8	♦2.1
Pregnancy with abortive outcome — Grossesse se terminant par un avortement	..	..	-	-	..	..	1	♦0.3
Other direct obstetric causes — Autres décès maternels directs	..	..	7	♦1.9	..	..	7	♦1.9
Indirect obstetric causes — Décès maternels indirects	..	..	-	-	..	..	-	-
Certain conditions originating in the perinatal period — Certaines affections dont l'origine se situe dans la période périnatale	456	240.1	378	210.4	457	236.7	348	191.1
Congenital malformations, deformations and chromosomal abnormalities — Malformations congénitales et anomalies chromosomiques	494	260.1	424	236.0	446	231.0	432	237.3
Symptoms, signs and abnormal clinical and laboratory findings, not elsewhere classified — Symptômes, signes et résultats anormaux d'examens cliniques et de laboratoire, non classés ailleurs	13 391	71.8	11 367	57.2	14 829	80.6	13 049	66.5
All other diseases — Toutes autres maladies...............................	70	0.4	102	0.5	94	0.5	118	0.6
External causes — Causes externes								
Total	17 017	91.2	5 436	27.3	16 199	88.0	5 201	26.5
Accidents								
Total	9 442	50.6	3 892	19.6	9 073	49.3	3 740	19.1
Transport accidents — Accidents de transport.............................	3 124	16.8	886	4.5	2 965	16.1	872	4.4
Falls — Chutes	2 589	13.9	2 073	10.4	2 655	14.4	2 063	10.5
Accidental drowning and submersion — Noyade et submersion accidentelles..	722	3.9	162	0.8	648	3.5	108	0.6
Exposure to smoke, fire and flames — Exposition à la fumée, au feu et aux flammes...	413	2.2	146	0.7	372	2.0	115	0.6
Accidental poisoning by and exposure to noxious substances — Intoxication accidentelle par des substances nocives et exposition à ces substances	1 121	6.0	216	1.1	1 028	5.6	192	1.0
Intentional self-harm — Lésions auto-infligées.............................	5 375	28.8	840	4.2	5 122	27.8	811	4.1
Assault — Agresssions...	304	1.6	119	0.6	247	1.3	89	0.5
All other external causes — Toutes autres causes externes	1 896	10.2	585	2.9	1 757	9.5	561	2.9

Portugal

Cause of death — Cause de décès	2013 (+C)				2014 (+C)			
	Male — Masculin		Female — Féminin		Male — Masculin		Female — Féminin	
	Number Nombre	Rate Taux	Number Nombre	Rate Taux	Number Nombre	Rate Taux	Number Nombre	Rate Taux
TOTAL	54 406	1 093.2	52 469	957.4	53 498	1 082.8	51 721	947.2
Certain infectious and parasitic diseases — Certaines maladies infectieuses et parasitaires								
Total	1 307	26.3	1 131	20.6	1 206	24.4	1 014	18.6
Intestinal infectious diseases — Maladies infectieuses intestinales	72	1.4	157	2.9	79	1.6	135	2.5
Tuberculosis — Tuberculose	91	1.8	27	⬧0.5	87	1.8	26	⬧0.5
Tetanus — Tétanos...................	-	-	-	-	-	-	1	⬧0.0
Diphtheria — Diphtérie...................	-	-	-	-	-	-	-	-
Whooping cough — Coqueluche	1	⬧0.0	1	⬧0.0	-	-	-	-
Meningococcal infection — Infection à méningocoques	1	⬧0.0	4	⬧0.1	2	⬧0.0	1	⬧0.0
Septicaemia — Septicémie...................	527	10.6	679	12.4	431	8.7	570	10.4
Acute poliomyelitis — Poliomyélite aiguë	-	-	-	-	-	-	-	-
Measles — Rougeole...................	-	-	-	-	-	-	-	-
Viral hepatitis — Hépatite virale...................	97	1.9	43	0.8	105	2.1	53	1.0
Human immunodeficiency virus [HIV] disease — Maladies dues au virus de l'immunodéficience humaine (VIH)...................	359	7.2	99	1.8	317	6.4	102	1.9
Malaria — Paludisme...................	4	⬧0.1	-	-	5	⬧0.1	1	⬧0.0
Neoplasms — Tumeurs	15 746	316.4	10 661	194.5	15 934	322.5	10 808	197.9
Malignant neoplasms — Tumeurs malignes								
Total	15 463	310.7	10 457	190.8	15 649	316.7	10 571	193.6
Malignant neoplasm of lip, oral cavity and pharynx — Tumeur maligne de la lèvre, de la cavité buccale et du pharynx	568	11.4	128	2.3	584	11.8	110	2.0
Malignant neoplasm of oesophagus — Tumeur maligne de l'oesophage	485	9.7	59	1.1	482	9.8	83	1.5
Malignant neoplasm of stomach — Tumeur maligne de l'estomac	1 350	27.1	916	16.7	1 382	28.0	911	16.7
Malignant neoplasm of colon, rectosigmoid junction, rectum, anus and anal canal — Tumeur maligne du côlon, de la jonction recto-sigmoïdienne, du rectum, de l'anus et du canal anal	2 237	44.9	1 611	29.4	2 200	44.5	1 608	29.4
Malignant neoplasm of liver and intrahepatic bile ducts — Tumeur maligne du foie et des voies bilaires intrahépatiques	726	14.6	311	5.7	777	15.7	313	5.7
Malignant neoplasm of pancreas — Tumeur maligne du pancréas...................	732	14.7	644	11.8	742	15.0	620	11.4
Malignant neoplasm of trachea, bronchus and lung — Tumeur maligne de la trachée, des bronches et du poumon	3 153	63.4	857	15.6	3 084	62.4	853	15.6
Malignant neoplasm of female breast — Tumeur maligne du sein chez la femme	..	..	1 646	34.8	..	..	1 664	35.2
Malignant neoplasm of cervix uteri — Tumeur maligne du col de l'utérus.........	..	..	205	4.3	..	..	210	4.4
Malignant neoplasm of prostate — Tumeur maligne de la prostate	1 717	93.5	..	..	1 791	96.5	..	..
Malignant neoplasm of lymphoid, haematopoietic and related tissue — Tumeurs malignes primitives ou présumées primitives des tissus lymphoïde, hématopoïétique et apparentés...................	1 202	24.2	1 001	18.3	1 190	24.1	1 029	18.8
Disorders of the blood and blood-forming organs and certain disorders involving the immune mechanism — Maladies du sang et des organes hématopoïétiques et certains troubles du système immunitaire								
Total	212	4.3	244	4.5	217	4.4	250	4.6
Anaemias — Anémies	125	2.5	170	3.1	137	2.8	176	3.2
Endocrine, nutritional and metabolic diseases — Maladies endocriniennes, nutritionnelles et métaboliques								
Total	2 393	48.1	3 382	61.7	2 331	47.2	3 166	58.0
Diabetes mellitus — Diabète sucré...................	1 910	38.4	2 638	48.1	1 853	37.5	2 422	44.4
Malnutrition — Malnutrition	28	⬧0.6	42	0.8	28	⬧0.6	31	0.6
Mental and behavioural disorders — Troubles mentaux et du comportement	887	17.8	1 336	24.4	1 082	21.9	1 557	28.5
Diseases of the nervous system — Maladies du système nerveux...................	1 596	32.1	1 931	35.2	1 618	32.7	1 932	35.4
Diseases of the circulatory system — Maladies de l'appareil circulatoire								
Total	13 981	280.9	17 547	320.2	14 574	295.0	17 712	324.4
Acute rheumatic fever and chronic rheumatic heart diseases — Rhumatisme articularie aigu et cardiopathies rhumatismales chroniques	61	1.2	126	2.3	70	1.4	131	2.4
Hypertensive diseases — Maladies hypertensives...................	836	16.8	1 458	26.6	846	17.1	1 539	28.2
Ischaemic heart disease — Cardiopathie ischémique	3 711	74.6	3 225	58.8	4 178	84.6	3 278	60.0
Cerebrovascular disease — Maladie cérébrovasculaire...................	5 362	107.7	6 911	126.1	5 117	103.6	6 691	122.5

Portugal

Cause of death — Cause de décès	2013 (+C)				2014 (+C)			
	Male — Masculin		Female — Féminin		Male — Masculin		Female — Féminin	
	Number Nombre	Rate Taux	Number Nombre	Rate Taux	Number Nombre	Rate Taux	Number Nombre	Rate Taux
Diseases of arteries, arterioles and capillaries — Maladies des artères, artérioles et capillaires	739	14.8	889	16.2	767	15.5	834	15.3
Diseases of the respiratory system — Maladies de l'appareil respiratoire								
Total	6 565	131.9	6 062	110.6	6 308	127.7	5 856	107.2
Influenza — Grippe............................	10	♦0.2	15	♦0.3	11	♦0.2	13	♦0.2
Pneumonia — Pneumopathies.............	2 988	60.0	2 947	53.8	2 813	56.9	2 816	51.6
Chronic lower respiratory diseases — Maladies chroniques des voies respiratoires inférieures	1 715	34.5	1 005	18.3	1 726	34.9	1 030	18.9
Diseases of the digestive system — Maladies de l'appareil digestif								
Total	2 578	51.8	2 005	36.6	2 619	53.0	1 985	36.4
Gastric and duodenal ulcer — Ulcère de l'estomac et du duodénum................	141	2.8	108	2.0	112	2.3	99	1.8
Diseases of the liver — Maladies du foie............	1 208	24.3	407	7.4	1 194	24.2	346	6.3
Diseases of the musculoskeletal system and connective tissue — Maladies du système ostéo-articularie, des muscles et du tissu conjonctif	155	3.1	236	4.3	161	3.3	246	4.5
Diseases of the genitourinary system — Maladies de l'appareil génito-urinaire								
Total	1 301	26.1	1 629	29.7	1 216	24.6	1 666	30.5
Disorders of kidney and ureter — Affections du rein et de l'uretère	787	15.8	862	15.7	710	14.4	829	15.2
Hyperplasia of prostate — Hyperplasie de la prostate....................	41	2.2	..	..	43	2.3	..	..
Pregnancy, childbirth and the puerperium — Grossesse, accouchement et puerpéralité								
Total	..	..	5	♦6.0	..	..	6	♦7.3
Pregnancy with abortive outcome — Grossesse se terminant par un avortement	..	..	-	-	..	..	-	-
Other direct obstetric causes — Autres décès maternels directs	..	..	4	♦4.8	..	..	3	♦3.6
Indirect obstetric causes — Décès maternels indirects	..	..	1	♦1.2	..	..	3	♦3.6
Certain conditions originating in the perinatal period — Certaines affections dont l'origine se situe dans la période périnatale	88	208.4	52	128.2	83	195.6	61	152.7
Congenital malformations, deformations and chromosomal abnormalities — Malformations congénitales et anomalies chromosomiques	85	201.3	75	184.9	97	228.6	68	170.3
Symptoms, signs and abnormal clinical and laboratory findings, not elsewhere classified — Symptômes, signes et résultats anormaux d'examens cliniques et de laboratoire, non classés ailleurs	4 655	93.5	4 703	85.8	2 836	57.4	3 640	66.7
All other diseases — Toutes autres maladies............	35	0.7	65	1.2	65	1.3	87	1.6
External causes — Causes externes								
Total	2 822	56.7	1 405	25.6	3 151	63.8	1 667	30.5
Accidents								
Total	1 366	27.4	661	12.1	1 545	31.3	811	14.9
Transport accidents — Accidents de transport	599	12.0	168	3.1	653	13.2	162	3.0
Falls — Chutes	322	6.5	211	3.9	371	7.5	247	4.5
Accidental drowning and submersion — Noyade et submersion accidentelles....................................	58	1.2	23	♦0.4	58	1.2	20	♦0.4
Exposure to smoke, fire and flames — Exposition à la fumée, au feu et aux flammes.......................................	38	0.8	19	♦0.3	25	♦0.5	23	♦0.4
Accidental poisoning by and exposure to noxious substances — Intoxication accidentelle par des substances nocives et exposition à ces substances	30	♦0.6	20	♦0.4	53	1.1	21	♦0.4
Intentional self-harm — Lésions auto-infligées...	812	16.3	241	4.4	925	18.7	298	5.5
Assault — Agresssions.......................	62	1.2	35	0.6	52	1.1	57	1.0
All other external causes — Toutes autres causes externes	582	11.7	468	8.5	629	12.7	501	9.2

20. Death and death rates by cause and sex: 2010 - 2014
Décès et taux de mortalité par cause et sexe : 2010 - 2014 (continued - suite)

Republic of Moldova - République de Moldova

Cause of death — Cause de décès	2013 (+C)				2014 (+C)			
	Male — Masculin		Female — Féminin		Male — Masculin		Female — Féminin	
	Number Nombre	Rate Taux	Number Nombre	Rate Taux	Number Nombre	Rate Taux	Number Nombre	Rate Taux
TOTAL	19 876	...	18 184	...	20 606	1 204.1	18 888	1 023.2
Certain infectious and parasitic diseases — Certaines maladies infectieuses et parasitaires								
Total	343	...	94	...	361	21.1	110	6.0
Intestinal infectious diseases — Maladies infectieuses intestinales	3	...	2	...	3	◆0.2	2	◆0.1
Tuberculosis — Tuberculose	276	...	41	...	258	15.1	55	3.0
Tetanus — Tétanos	-	...	-	...	-	-	-	-
Diphtheria — Diphtérie	-	...	-	...	-	-	-	-
Whooping cough — Coqueluche	-	...	-	...	-	-	-	-
Meningococcal infection — Infection à méningocoques	1	...	2	...	3	◆0.2	4	◆0.2
Septicaemia — Septicémie	4	...	6	...	8	◆0.5	7	◆0.4
Acute poliomyelitis — Poliomyélite aiguë	-	...	-	...	-	-	-	-
Measles — Rougeole	-	...	-	...	-	-	-	-
Viral hepatitis — Hépatite virale	-	...	2	...	2	◆0.1	2	◆0.1
Human immunodeficiency virus [HIV] disease — Maladies dues au virus de l'immunodéficience humaine (VIH)	45	...	28	...	69	4.0	28	◆1.5
Malaria — Paludisme	-	...	-	...	-	-	-	-
Neoplasms — Tumeurs	3 412	...	2 471	...	3 438	200.9	2 534	137.3
Malignant neoplasms — Tumeurs malignes								
Total	3 389	...	2 440	...	3 424	200.1	2 519	136.5
Malignant neoplasm of lip, oral cavity and pharynx — Tumeur maligne de la lèvre, de la cavité buccale et du pharynx	228	...	37	...	270	15.8	36	2.0
Malignant neoplasm of oesophagus — Tumeur maligne de l'oesophage	45	...	11	...	72	4.2	11	◆0.6
Malignant neoplasm of stomach — Tumeur maligne de l'estomac	297	...	186	...	284	16.6	196	10.6
Malignant neoplasm of colon, rectosigmoid junction, rectum, anus and anal canal — Tumeur maligne du côlon, de la jonction recto-sigmoïdienne, du rectum, de l'anus et du canal anal	440	...	375	...	452	26.4	381	20.6
Malignant neoplasm of liver and intrahepatic bile ducts — Tumeur maligne du foie et des voies bilaires intrahépatiques	329	...	178	...	291	17.0	176	9.5
Malignant neoplasm of pancreas — Tumeur maligne du pancréas	213	...	125	...	222	13.0	145	7.9
Malignant neoplasm of trachea, bronchus and lung — Tumeur maligne de la trachée, des bronches et du poumon	752	...	192	...	750	43.8	200	10.8
Malignant neoplasm of female breast — Tumeur maligne du sein chez la femme	..	...	477	...	..	..	482	...
Malignant neoplasm of cervix uteri — Tumeur maligne du col de l'utérus	..	...	161	...	..	..	169	...
Malignant neoplasm of prostate — Tumeur maligne de la prostate	195	...	..	..	207	...	..	..
Malignant neoplasm of lymphoid, haematopoietic and related tissue — Tumeurs malignes primitives ou présumées primitives des tissus lymphoïde, hématopoïétique et apparentés	176	...	137	...	162	9.5	135	7.3
Disorders of the blood and blood-forming organs and certain disorders involving the immune mechanism — Maladies du sang et des organes hématopoïétiques et certains troubles du système immunitaire								
Total	7	...	5	...	6	◆0.4	11	◆0.6
Anaemias — Anémies	4	...	3	...	4	◆0.2	5	◆0.3
Endocrine, nutritional and metabolic diseases — Maladies endocriniennes, nutritionnelles et métaboliques								
Total	149	...	226	...	165	9.6	227	12.3
Diabetes mellitus — Diabète sucré	140	...	220	...	155	9.1	221	12.0
Malnutrition — Malnutrition	1	...	-	...	-	-	-	-
Mental and behavioural disorders — Troubles mentaux et du comportement	40	...	14	...	141	8.2	27	◆1.5
Diseases of the nervous system — Maladies du système nerveux	238	...	98	...	246	14.4	113	6.1
Diseases of the circulatory system — Maladies de l'appareil circulatoire								
Total	9 994	...	12 136	...	10 267	600.0	12 583	681.6
Acute rheumatic fever and chronic rheumatic heart diseases — Rhumatisme articularie aigu et cardiopathies rhumatismales chroniques	37	...	45	...	32	1.9	40	2.2
Hypertensive diseases — Maladies hypertensives	428	...	700	...	532	31.1	899	48.7
Ischaemic heart disease — Cardiopathie ischémique	6 565	...	7 866	...	6 533	381.8	8 090	438.2
Cerebrovascular disease — Maladie cérébrovasculaire	2 589	...	3 342	...	2 701	157.8	3 293	178.4

Republic of Moldova - République de Moldova

Cause of death — Cause de décès	2013 (+C)				2014 (+C)			
	Male — Masculin		Female — Féminin		Male — Masculin		Female — Féminin	
	Number Nombre	Rate Taux	Number Nombre	Rate Taux	Number Nombre	Rate Taux	Number Nombre	Rate Taux
Diseases of arteries, arterioles and capillaries — Maladies des artères, artérioles et capillaires	127	...	55	...	117	6.8	67	3.6
Diseases of the respiratory system — Maladies de l'appareil respiratoire								
Total	1 190	...	521	...	1 185	69.2	522	28.3
Influenza — Grippe	6	...	8	...	1	♦0.1	1	♦0.1
Pneumonia — Pneumopathies	542	...	170	...	636	37.2	233	12.6
Chronic lower respiratory diseases — Maladies chroniques des voies respiratoires inférieures	592	...	334	...	511	29.9	270	14.6
Diseases of the digestive system — Maladies de l'appareil digestif								
Total	1 775	...	1 589	...	1 866	109.0	1 753	95.0
Gastric and duodenal ulcer — Ulcère de l'estomac et du duodénum	141	...	51	...	144	8.4	71	3.8
Diseases of the liver — Maladies du foie	1 341	...	1 304	...	1 428	83.4	1 412	76.5
Diseases of the musculoskeletal system and connective tissue — Maladies du système ostéo-articularie, des muscles et du tissu conjonctif	8	...	19	...	14	♦0.8	17	♦0.9
Diseases of the genitourinary system — Maladies de l'appareil génito-urinaire								
Total	148	...	143	...	145	8.5	138	7.5
Disorders of kidney and ureter — Affections du rein et de l'uretère	125	...	133	...	126	7.4	132	7.2
Hyperplasia of prostate — Hyperplasie de la prostate.................	14	...	..	..	13	...	..	..
Pregnancy, childbirth and the puerperium — Grossesse, accouchement et puerpéralité								
Total	..	..	6	♦15.8	..	..	7	♦18.1
Pregnancy with abortive outcome — Grossesse se terminant par un avortement	..	..	-	-	..	..	1	♦2.6
Other direct obstetric causes — Autres décès maternels directs	..	..	3	♦7.9	..	..	6	♦15.5
Indirect obstetric causes — Décès maternels indirects	..	..	3	♦7.9	..	..	-	-
Certain conditions originating in the perinatal period — Certaines affections dont l'origine se situe dans la période périnatale	76	391.3	77	417.4	87	436.4	60	321.2
Congenital malformations, deformations and chromosomal abnormalities — Malformations congénitales et anomalies chromosomiques	83	427.4	61	330.6	92	461.5	63	337.3
Symptoms, signs and abnormal clinical and laboratory findings, not elsewhere classified — Symptômes, signes et résultats anormaux d'examens cliniques et de laboratoire, non classés ailleurs	192	...	73	...	185	10.8	62	3.4
All other diseases — Toutes autres maladies	18	...	15	...	16	♦0.9	18	♦1.0
External causes — Causes externes								
Total	2 203	...	636	...	2 392	139.8	643	34.8
Accidents								
Total	1 406	...	441	...	1 585	92.6	462	25.0
Transport accidents — Accidents de transport	328	...	69	...	315	18.4	71	3.8
Falls — Chutes	133	...	50	...	141	8.2	33	1.8
Accidental drowning and submersion — Noyade et submersion accidentelles	119	...	40	...	138	8.1	45	2.4
Exposure to smoke, fire and flames — Exposition à la fumée, au feu et aux flammes	126	...	53	...	79	4.6	34	1.8
Accidental poisoning by and exposure to noxious substances — Intoxication accidentelle par des substances nocives et exposition à ces substances	228	...	84	...	300	17.5	114	6.2
Intentional self-harm — Lésions auto-infligées	487	...	89	...	498	29.1	83	4.5
Assault — Agresssions	175	...	61	...	131	7.7	53	2.9
All other external causes — Toutes autres causes externes	135	...	45	...	178	10.4	45	2.4

20. Death and death rates by cause and sex: 2010 - 2014
Décès et taux de mortalité par cause et sexe : 2010 - 2014 (continued - suite)

Romania - Roumanie

Cause of death — Cause de décès	2013 (+C)				2014 (+C)			
	Male — Masculin		Female — Féminin		Male — Masculin		Female — Féminin	
	Number Nombre	Rate Taux	Number Nombre	Rate Taux	Number Nombre	Rate Taux	Number Nombre	Rate Taux
TOTAL	**130 579**	**1 338.6**	**119 325**	**1 166.3**	**133 056**	**1 365.2**	**121 735**	**1 193.3**
Certain infectious and parasitic diseases — Certaines maladies infectieuses et parasitaires								
Total	1 553	15.9	808	7.9	1 676	17.2	996	9.8
Intestinal infectious diseases — Maladies infectieuses intestinales	43	0.4	49	0.5	44	0.5	74	0.7
Tuberculosis — Tuberculose	903	9.3	233	2.3	876	9.0	249	2.4
Tetanus — Tétanos................................	2	♦0.0	2	♦0.0	-	-	-	-
Diphtheria — Diphtérie................................	-	-	-	-	-	-	-	-
Whooping cough — Coqueluche	-	-	-	-	-	-	-	-
Meningococcal infection — Infection à méningocoques	6	♦0.1	2	♦0.0	5	♦0.1	3	♦0.0
Septicaemia — Septicémie	417	4.3	391	3.8	512	5.3	514	5.0
Acute poliomyelitis — Poliomyélite aiguë	-	-	-	-	-	-	-	-
Measles — Rougeole	-	-	-	-	-	-	-	-
Viral hepatitis — Hépatite virale	21	♦0.2	25	♦0.2	34	0.3	41	0.4
Human immunodeficiency virus [HIV] disease — Maladies dues au virus de l'immunodéficience humaine (VIH)................	112	1.1	60	0.6	138	1.4	65	0.6
Malaria — Paludisme	1	♦0.0	-	-	-	-	-	-
Neoplasms — Tumeurs	**29 392**	**301.3**	**20 341**	**198.8**	**30 112**	**309.0**	**20 472**	**200.7**
Malignant neoplasms — Tumeurs malignes								
Total	29 235	299.7	20 210	197.5	29 958	307.4	20 355	199.5
Malignant neoplasm of lip, oral cavity and pharynx — Tumeur maligne de la lèvre, de la cavité buccale et du pharynx	1 864	19.1	280	2.7	1 890	19.4	268	2.6
Malignant neoplasm of oesophagus — Tumeur maligne de l'oesophage	576	5.9	103	1.0	606	6.2	104	1.0
Malignant neoplasm of stomach — Tumeur maligne de l'estomac	2 232	22.9	1 189	11.6	2 285	23.4	1 163	11.4
Malignant neoplasm of colon, rectosigmoid junction, rectum, anus and anal canal — Tumeur maligne du côlon, de la jonction recto-sigmoïdienne, du rectum, de l'anus et du canal anal	3 317	34.0	2 498	24.4	3 345	34.3	2 518	24.7
Malignant neoplasm of liver and intrahepatic bile ducts — Tumeur maligne du foie et des voies bilaires intrahépatiques	1 800	18.5	1 022	10.0	1 916	19.7	1 043	10.2
Malignant neoplasm of pancreas — Tumeur maligne du pancréas................	1 569	16.1	1 261	12.3	1 633	16.8	1 268	12.4
Malignant neoplasm of trachea, bronchus and lung — Tumeur maligne de la trachée, des bronches et du poumon	7 795	79.9	2 195	21.5	8 000	82.1	2 188	21.4
Malignant neoplasm of female breast — Tumeur maligne du sein chez la femme	..	..	3 241	...	..	..	3 343	...
Malignant neoplasm of cervix uteri — Tumeur maligne du col de l'utérus.........	..	..	1 688	...	..	..	1 713	...
Malignant neoplasm of prostate — Tumeur maligne de la prostate	2 174	...	..	..	2 243	...	..	..
Malignant neoplasm of lymphoid, haematopoietic and related tissue — Tumeurs malignes primitives ou présumées primitives des tissus lymphoïde, hématopoïétique et apparentés	1 271	13.0	1 143	11.2	1 405	14.4	1 143	11.2
Disorders of the blood and blood-forming organs and certain disorders involving the immune mechanism — Maladies du sang et des organes hématopoïétiques et certains troubles du système immunitaire								
Total	62	0.6	70	0.7	53	0.5	72	0.7
Anaemias — Anémies	40	0.4	46	0.4	34	0.3	49	0.5
Endocrine, nutritional and metabolic diseases — Maladies endocriniennes, nutritionnelles et métaboliques								
Total	1 144	11.7	1 211	11.8	1 126	11.6	1 280	12.5
Diabetes mellitus — Diabète sucré................................	1 070	11.0	1 149	11.2	1 043	10.7	1 198	11.7
Malnutrition — Malnutrition	48	0.5	39	0.4	55	0.6	37	0.4
Mental and behavioural disorders — Troubles mentaux et du comportement	155	1.6	55	0.5	155	1.6	67	0.7
Diseases of the nervous system — Maladies du système nerveux................	1 395	14.3	1 727	16.9	1 532	15.7	1 921	18.8
Diseases of the circulatory system — Maladies de l'appareil circulatoire								
Total	68 607	703.3	78 911	771.3	68 905	707.0	80 155	785.7
Acute rheumatic fever and chronic rheumatic heart diseases — Rhumatisme articularie aigu et cardiopathies rhumatismales chroniques	139	1.4	203	2.0	144	1.5	243	2.4
Hypertensive diseases — Maladies hypertensives................	11 342	116.3	15 980	156.2	11 834	121.4	16 897	165.6
Ischaemic heart disease — Cardiopathie ischémique	24 834	254.6	24 879	243.2	25 174	258.3	25 496	249.9
Cerebrovascular disease — Maladie cérébrovasculaire................	20 558	210.7	25 634	250.6	19 867	203.8	24 815	243.3

726

Romania - Roumanie

Cause of death — Cause de décès	2013 (+C)				2014 (+C)			
	Male — Masculin		Female — Féminin		Male — Masculin		Female — Féminin	
	Number Nombre	Rate Taux	Number Nombre	Rate Taux	Number Nombre	Rate Taux	Number Nombre	Rate Taux
Diseases of arteries, arterioles and capillaries — Maladies des artères, artérioles et capillaires	4 709	48.3	6 435	62.9	4 710	48.3	6 518	63.9
Diseases of the respiratory system — Maladies de l'appareil respiratoire								
Total	7 859	80.6	4 831	47.2	8 323	85.4	5 065	49.7
Influenza — Grippe	9	♦0.1	5	♦0.0	9	♦0.1	7	♦0.1
Pneumonia — Pneumopathies	3 256	33.4	2 212	21.6	3 385	34.7	2 296	22.5
Chronic lower respiratory diseases — Maladies chroniques des voies respiratoires inférieures	3 623	37.1	1 856	18.1	3 968	40.7	2 017	19.8
Diseases of the digestive system — Maladies de l'appareil digestif								
Total	8 415	86.3	5 632	55.0	8 688	89.1	5 859	57.4
Gastric and duodenal ulcer — Ulcère de l'estomac et du duodénum	272	2.8	186	1.8	310	3.2	176	1.7
Diseases of the liver — Maladies du foie	6 025	61.8	3 564	34.8	6 213	63.7	3 806	37.3
Diseases of the musculoskeletal system and connective tissue — Maladies du système ostéo-articularie, des muscles et du tissu conjonctif	20	♦0.2	25	♦0.2	12	♦0.1	29	♦0.3
Diseases of the genitourinary system — Maladies de l'appareil génito-urinaire								
Total	1 647	16.9	1 510	14.8	1 699	17.4	1 569	15.4
Disorders of kidney and ureter — Affections du rein et de l'uretère	1 518	15.6	1 476	14.4	1 563	16.0	1 532	15.0
Hyperplasia of prostate — Hyperplasie de la prostate	113	...	..	..	112	...	..	..
Pregnancy, childbirth and the puerperium — Grossesse, accouchement et puerpéralité								
Total	..	..	27	♦14.8	..	..	24	♦12.4
Pregnancy with abortive outcome — Grossesse se terminant par un avortement	..	..	6	♦3.3	..	..	6	♦3.1
Other direct obstetric causes — Autres décès maternels directs	..	..	14	♦7.7	..	..	11	♦5.7
Indirect obstetric causes — Décès maternels indirects	..	..	7	♦3.8	..	..	7	♦3.6
Certain conditions originating in the perinatal period — Certaines affections dont l'origine se situe dans la période périnatale	372	395.8	291	329.5	404	406.7	238	253.8
Congenital malformations, deformations and chromosomal abnormalities — Malformations congénitales et anomalies chromosomiques	277	294.7	223	252.5	240	241.6	198	211.1
Symptoms, signs and abnormal clinical and laboratory findings, not elsewhere classified — Symptômes, signes et résultats anormaux d'examens cliniques et de laboratoire, non classés ailleurs	1 730	17.7	1 303	12.7	2 235	22.9	1 506	14.8
All other diseases — Toutes autres maladies	34	0.3	53	0.5	35	0.4	62	0.6
External causes — Causes externes								
Total	7 917	81.2	2 307	22.5	7 861	80.7	2 222	21.8
Accidents								
Total	5 402	55.4	1 733	16.9	5 490	56.3	1 678	16.4
Transport accidents — Accidents de transport	1 775	18.2	596	5.8	1 778	18.2	556	5.5
Falls — Chutes	979	10.0	265	2.6	1 020	10.5	284	2.8
Accidental drowning and submersion — Noyade et submersion accidentelles	510	5.2	124	1.2	583	6.0	142	1.4
Exposure to smoke, fire and flames — Exposition à la fumée, au feu et aux flammes	205	2.1	145	1.4	206	2.1	138	1.4
Accidental poisoning by and exposure to noxious substances — Intoxication accidentelle par des substances nocives et exposition à ces substances	549	5.6	240	2.3	528	5.4	228	2.2
Intentional self-harm — Lésions auto-infligées	2 054	21.1	366	3.6	1 886	19.4	322	3.2
Assault — Agresssions	244	2.5	124	1.2	241	2.5	119	1.2
All other external causes — Toutes autres causes externes	217	2.2	84	0.8	244	2.5	103	1.0

Russian Federation - Fédération de Russie

Cause of death — Cause de décès	2010 (+C)				2011 (+C)			
	Male — Masculin		Female — Féminin		Male — Masculin		Female — Féminin	
	Number Nombre	Rate Taux	Number Nombre	Rate Taux	Number Nombre	Rate Taux	Number Nombre	Rate Taux
TOTAL	1 050 676	1 591.1	977 840	1 273.0	997 494	1 510.3	928 226	1 208.5
Certain infectious and parasitic diseases — Certaines maladies infectieuses et parasitaires								
Total	25 239	38.2	8 370	10.9	25 089	38.0	8 583	11.2
Intestinal infectious diseases — Maladies infectieuses intestinales	213	0.3	179	0.2	213	0.3	195	0.3
Tuberculosis — Tuberculose	17 463	26.4	4 366	5.7	16 228	24.6	4 015	5.2
Tetanus — Tétanos	2	◆0.0	-	-	2	◆0.0	4	◆0.0
Diphtheria — Diphtérie...	-	-	1	◆0.0	-	-	1	◆0.0
Whooping cough — Coqueluche	3	◆0.0	2	◆0.0	-	-	1	◆0.0
Meningococcal infection — Infection à méningocoques	186	0.3	111	0.1	154	0.2	168	0.2
Septicaemia — Septicémie	1 084	1.6	692	0.9	1 162	1.8	791	1.0
Acute poliomyelitis — Poliomyélite aiguë	-	-	-	-	-	-	-	-
Measles — Rougeole...	-	-	-	-	1	◆0.0	1	◆0.0
Viral hepatitis — Hépatite virale....................................	775	1.2	488	0.6	754	1.1	507	0.7
Human immunodeficiency virus [HIV] disease — Maladies dues au virus de l'immunodéficience humaine (VIH)................	4 879	7.4	1 905	2.5	5 940	9.0	2 307	3.0
Malaria — Paludisme...	2	◆0.0	-	-	1	◆0.0	2	◆0.0
Neoplasms — Tumeurs	156 301	236.7	136 870	178.2	156 144	236.4	136 301	177.5
Malignant neoplasms — Tumeurs malignes								
Total	155 006	234.7	135 130	175.9	154 882	234.5	134 653	175.3
Malignant neoplasm of lip, oral cavity and pharynx — Tumeur maligne de la lèvre, de la cavité buccale et du pharynx	7 310	11.1	1 709	2.2	7 428	11.2	1 748	2.3
Malignant neoplasm of oesophagus — Tumeur maligne de l'oesophage	5 093	7.7	1 389	1.8	5 300	8.0	1 498	2.0
Malignant neoplasm of stomach — Tumeur maligne de l'estomac	19 553	29.6	14 885	19.4	19 031	28.8	14 182	18.5
Malignant neoplasm of colon, rectosigmoid junction, rectum, anus and anal canal — Tumeur maligne du côlon, de la jonction recto-sigmoïdienne, du rectum, de l'anus et du canal anal..........................	17 032	25.8	21 158	27.5	17 082	25.9	20 871	27.2
Malignant neoplasm of liver and intrahepatic bile ducts — Tumeur maligne du foie et des voies bilaires intrahépatiques	4 682	7.1	3 700	4.8	4 753	7.2	3 799	4.9
Malignant neoplasm of pancreas — Tumeur maligne du pancréas...................	7 783	11.8	7 823	10.2	7 930	12.0	7 764	10.1
Malignant neoplasm of trachea, bronchus and lung — Tumeur maligne de la trachée, des bronches et du poumon	42 583	64.5	8 739	11.4	41 767	63.2	8 673	11.3
Malignant neoplasm of female breast — Tumeur maligne du sein chez la femme	..	..	23 282	35.4	..	..	23 320	...
Malignant neoplasm of cervix uteri — Tumeur maligne du col de l'utérus.........	..	..	6 193	9.4	..	..	6 376	...
Malignant neoplasm of prostate — Tumeur maligne de la prostate	10 251	57.2	..	..	10 555	...	..	..
Malignant neoplasm of lymphoid, haematopoietic and related tissue — Tumeurs malignes primitives ou présumées primitives des tissus lymphoïde, hématopoïétique et apparentés.........	...	...	...	...	...	...	...	...
Disorders of the blood and blood-forming organs and certain disorders involving the immune mechanism — Maladies du sang et des organes hématopoïétiques et certains troubles du système immunitaire								
Total	503	0.8	681	0.9	562	0.9	724	0.9
Anaemias — Anémies	275	0.4	426	0.6	329	0.5	457	0.6
Endocrine, nutritional and metabolic diseases — Maladies endocriniennes, nutritionnelles et métaboliques								
Total	3 246	4.9	7 013	9.1	3 160	4.8	6 777	8.8
Diabetes mellitus — Diabète sucré..................................	2 723	4.1	6 393	8.3	2 684	4.1	6 193	8.1
Malnutrition — Malnutrition	112	0.2	108	0.1	83	0.1	70	0.1
Mental and behavioural disorders — Troubles mentaux et du comportement	4 366	6.6	2 251	2.9	3 394	5.1	1 618	2.1
Diseases of the nervous system — Maladies du système nerveux...............	10 433	15.8	7 872	10.2	10 475	15.9	8 494	11.1
Diseases of the circulatory system — Maladies de l'appareil circulatoire								
Total	518 284	784.9	633 633	824.9	486 018	735.9	590 440	768.7
Acute rheumatic fever and chronic rheumatic heart diseases — Rhumatisme articularie aigu et cardiopathies rhumatismales chroniques	1 383	2.1	2 557	3.3	1 150	1.7	2 149	2.8
Hypertensive diseases — Maladies hypertensives...........................	11 507	17.4	17 600	22.9	10 251	15.5	15 765	20.5
Ischaemic heart disease — Cardiopathie ischémique	283 058	428.7	314 863	409.9	268 484	406.5	299 698	390.2
Cerebrovascular disease — Maladie cérébrovasculaire................	142 587	215.9	229 662	299.0	128 650	194.8	204 154	265.8

20. Death and death rates by cause and sex: 2010 - 2014
Décès et taux de mortalité par cause et sexe : 2010 - 2014 (continued - suite)

Russian Federation - Fédération de Russie

Cause of death — Cause de décès	2010 (+C)				2011 (+C)			
	Male — Masculin		Female — Féminin		Male — Masculin		Female — Féminin	
	Number Nombre	Rate Taux	Number Nombre	Rate Taux	Number Nombre	Rate Taux	Number Nombre	Rate Taux
Diseases of arteries, arterioles and capillaries — Maladies des artères, artérioles et capillaires	...	...	...	...	...	...	...	...
Diseases of the respiratory system — Maladies de l'appareil respiratoire								
Total	52 944	80.2	21 864	28.5	52 144	79.0	22 075	28.7
Influenza — Grippe	111	0.2	121	0.2	275	0.4	255	0.3
Pneumonia — Pneumopathies	27 080	41.0	10 693	13.9	27 151	41.1	10 942	14.2
Chronic lower respiratory diseases — Maladies chroniques des voies respiratoires inférieures	22 292	33.8	9 513	12.4	21 065	31.9	9 091	11.8
Diseases of the digestive system — Maladies de l'appareil digestif								
Total	52 500	79.5	39 495	51.4	50 387	76.3	38 523	50.2
Gastric and duodenal ulcer — Ulcère de l'estomac et du duodénum	5 426	8.2	3 058	4.0	5 258	8.0	3 241	4.2
Diseases of the liver — Maladies du foie	30 082	45.6	20 621	26.8	28 653	43.4	19 668	25.6
Diseases of the musculoskeletal system and connective tissue — Maladies du système ostéo-articularie, des muscles et du tissu conjonctif	626	0.9	1 219	1.6	592	0.9	1 196	1.6
Diseases of the genitourinary system — Maladies de l'appareil génito-urinaire								
Total	5 617	8.5	6 134	8.0	5 331	8.1	5 804	7.6
Disorders of kidney and ureter — Affections du rein et de l'uretère	...	...	...	...	...	...	...	...
Hyperplasia of prostate — Hyperplasie de la prostate	...	...	...	...	...	...	..	...
Pregnancy, childbirth and the puerperium — Grossesse, accouchement et puerpéralité								
Total	..	..	298	16.7	..	..	291	16.2
Pregnancy with abortive outcome — Grossesse se terminant par un avortement	..	..	42	2.3	..	..	32	1.8
Other direct obstetric causes — Autres décès maternels directs	..	..	175	9.8	..	..	182	10.1
Indirect obstetric causes — Décès maternels indirects	..	..	77	4.3	..	..	77	4.3
Certain conditions originating in the perinatal period — Certaines affections dont l'origine se situe dans la période périnatale	3 611	392.7	2 541	292.3	3 712	401.8	2 534	290.3
Congenital malformations, deformations and chromosomal abnormalities — Malformations congénitales et anomalies chromosomiques	2 770	301.2	2 435	280.1	2 836	307.0	2 322	266.0
Symptoms, signs and abnormal clinical and laboratory findings, not elsewhere classified — Symptômes, signes et résultats anormaux d'examens cliniques et de laboratoire, non classés ailleurs	46 187	69.9	56 175	73.1	43 054	65.2	55 695	72.5
All other diseases — Toutes autres maladies	989	1.5	1 182	1.5	1 052	1.6	1 035	1.3
External causes — Causes externes								
Total	167 060	253.0	49 807	64.8	153 544	232.5	45 814	59.6
Accidents								
Total	...	...	...	...	...	...	...	...
Transport accidents — Accidents de transport	20 982	31.8	7 576	9.9	21 643	32.8	7 699	10.0
Falls — Chutes	6 987	10.6	2 729	3.6	6 408	9.7	2 557	3.3
Accidental drowning and submersion — Noyade et submersion accidentelles	10 156	15.4	1 825	2.4	7 190	10.9	1 340	1.7
Exposure to smoke, fire and flames — Exposition à la fumée, au feu et aux flammes	6 296	9.5	2 717	3.5	5 548	8.4	2 351	3.1
Accidental poisoning by and exposure to noxious substances — Intoxication accidentelle par des substances nocives et exposition à ces substances	26 560	40.2	7 958	10.4	22 664	34.3	6 743	8.8
Intentional self-harm — Lésions auto-infligées	27 675	41.9	5 805	7.6	25 564	38.7	5 580	7.3
Assault — Agerssions	14 190	21.5	4 761	6.2	12 758	19.3	4 037	5.3
All other external causes — Toutes autres causes externes	...	...	...	...	...	...	...	...

20. Death and death rates by cause and sex: 2010 - 2014
Décès et taux de mortalité par cause et sexe : 2010 - 2014 (continued - suite)

Serbia - Serbie

Cause of death — Cause de décès	2013 (+C)				2014 (+C)			
	Male — Masculin		Female — Féminin		Male — Masculin		Female — Féminin	
	Number Nombre	Rate Taux	Number Nombre	Rate Taux	Number Nombre	Rate Taux	Number Nombre	Rate Taux
TOTAL	50 910	1 455.8	49 390	1 340.5	51 010	1 465.9	50 237	1 370.0
Certain infectious and parasitic diseases — Certaines maladies infectieuses et parasitaires								
Total	330	9.4	253	6.9	305	8.8	250	6.8
Intestinal infectious diseases — Maladies infectieuses intestinales	41	1.2	73	2.0	52	1.5	84	2.3
Tuberculosis — Tuberculose	74	2.1	36	1.0	54	1.6	33	0.9
Tetanus — Tétanos	-	-	1	♦0.0	-	-	-	-
Diphtheria — Diphtérie...	-	-	-	-	-	-	-	-
Whooping cough — Coqueluche	-	-	-	-	-	-	-	-
Meningococcal infection — Infection à méningocoques.............	-	-	-	-	-	-	1	♦0.0
Septicaemia — Septicémie..	94	2.7	102	2.8	120	3.4	83	2.3
Acute poliomyelitis — Poliomyélite aiguë	-	-	-	-	-	-	-	-
Measles — Rougeole...	-	-	-	-	-	-	-	-
Viral hepatitis — Hépatite virale	28	♦0.8	16	♦0.4	28	♦0.8	13	♦0.4
Human immunodeficiency virus [HIV] disease — Maladies dues au virus de l'immunodéficience humaine (VIH)................	27	♦0.8	1	♦0.0	11	♦0.3	1	♦0.0
Malaria — Paludisme...	1	♦0.0	-	-	-	-	-	-
Neoplasms — Tumeurs	12 391	354.3	9 255	251.2	12 374	355.6	9 432	257.2
Malignant neoplasms — Tumeurs malignes								
Total	12 101	346.0	8 990	244.0	12 117	348.2	9 205	251.0
Malignant neoplasm of lip, oral cavity and pharynx — Tumeur maligne de la lèvre, de la cavité buccale et du pharynx	365	10.4	103	2.8	401	11.5	110	3.0
Malignant neoplasm of oesophagus — Tumeur maligne de l'oesophage	226	6.5	48	1.3	203	5.8	50	1.4
Malignant neoplasm of stomach — Tumeur maligne de l'estomac	610	17.4	372	10.1	618	17.8	339	9.2
Malignant neoplasm of colon, rectosigmoid junction, rectum, anus and anal canal — Tumeur maligne du côlon, de la jonction recto-sigmoïdienne, du rectum, de l'anus et du canal anal	1 642	47.0	1 014	27.5	1 545	44.4	1 050	28.6
Malignant neoplasm of liver and intrahepatic bile ducts — Tumeur maligne du foie et des voies bilaires intrahépatiques	429	12.3	336	9.1	455	13.1	279	7.6
Malignant neoplasm of pancreas — Tumeur maligne du pancréas...............	586	16.8	485	13.2	573	16.5	483	13.2
Malignant neoplasm of trachea, bronchus and lung — Tumeur maligne de la trachée, des bronches et du poumon	3 807	108.9	1 422	38.6	3 798	109.1	1 427	38.9
Malignant neoplasm of female breast — Tumeur maligne du sein chez la femme	..	..	1 647	...	..	..	1 648	...
Malignant neoplasm of cervix uteri — Tumeur maligne du col de l'utérus.........	..	..	468	...	..	..	415	...
Malignant neoplasm of prostate — Tumeur maligne de la prostate	942	...	..	..	977	...	..	..
Malignant neoplasm of lymphoid, haematopoietic and related tissue — Tumeurs malignes primitives ou présumées primitives des tissus lymphoïde, hématopoïétique et apparentés............	654	18.7	485	13.2	667	19.2	534	14.6
Disorders of the blood and blood-forming organs and certain disorders involving the immune mechanism — Maladies du sang et des organes hématopoïétiques et certains troubles du système immunitaire								
Total	87	2.5	130	3.5	93	2.7	158	4.3
Anaemias — Anémies	48	1.4	77	2.1	53	1.5	101	2.8
Endocrine, nutritional and metabolic diseases — Maladies endocriniennes, nutritionnelles et métaboliques								
Total	1 323	37.8	1 586	43.0	1 138	32.7	1 505	41.0
Diabetes mellitus — Diabète sucré...............................	1 277	36.5	1 526	41.4	1 096	31.5	1 417	38.6
Malnutrition — Malnutrition	4	♦0.1	2	♦0.1	7	♦0.2	5	♦0.1
Mental and behavioural disorders — Troubles mentaux et du comportement	594	17.0	625	17.0	606	17.4	697	19.0
Diseases of the nervous system — Maladies du système nerveux..............	845	24.2	930	25.2	812	23.3	960	26.2
Diseases of the circulatory system — Maladies de l'appareil circulatoire								
Total	24 505	700.7	28 862	783.3	24 691	709.5	29 302	799.1
Acute rheumatic fever and chronic rheumatic heart diseases — Rhumatisme articularie aigu et cardiopathies rhumatismales chroniques	32	0.9	42	1.1	34	1.0	47	1.3
Hypertensive diseases — Maladies hypertensives...............	1 939	55.4	2 881	78.2	2 292	65.9	3 431	93.6
Ischaemic heart disease — Cardiopathie ischémique............	5 427	155.2	4 434	120.3	5 382	154.7	4 589	125.1
Cerebrovascular disease — Maladie cérébrovasculaire............	5 845	167.1	7 319	198.6	5 477	157.4	6 842	186.6

Serbia - Serbie

Cause of death — Cause de décès	2013 (+C)				2014 (+C)			
	Male — Masculin		Female — Féminin		Male — Masculin		Female — Féminin	
	Number Nombre	Rate Taux	Number Nombre	Rate Taux	Number Nombre	Rate Taux	Number Nombre	Rate Taux
Diseases of arteries, arterioles and capillaries — Maladies des artères, artérioles et capillaires	1 078	30.8	1 347	36.6	1 159	33.3	1 461	39.8
Diseases of the respiratory system — Maladies de l'appareil respiratoire								
Total	2 819	80.6	2 014	54.7	2 877	82.7	2 192	59.8
Influenza — Grippe	12	♦0.3	3	♦0.1	3	♦0.1	3	♦0.1
Pneumonia — Pneumopathies	583	16.7	470	12.8	553	15.9	449	12.2
Chronic lower respiratory diseases — Maladies chroniques des voies respiratoires inférieures	1 580	45.2	997	27.1	1 517	43.6	982	26.8
Diseases of the digestive system — Maladies de l'appareil digestif								
Total	1 940	55.5	1 497	40.6	1 922	55.2	1 429	39.0
Gastric and duodenal ulcer — Ulcère de l'estomac et du duodénum	281	8.0	262	7.1	282	8.1	232	6.3
Diseases of the liver — Maladies du foie	656	18.8	183	5.0	674	19.4	188	5.1
Diseases of the musculoskeletal system and connective tissue — Maladies du système ostéo-articularie, des muscles et du tissu conjonctif	47	1.3	121	3.3	32	0.9	109	3.0
Diseases of the genitourinary system — Maladies de l'appareil génito-urinaire								
Total	1 097	31.4	961	26.1	1 153	33.1	901	24.6
Disorders of kidney and ureter — Affections du rein et de l'uretère	1 013	29.0	936	25.4	1 081	31.1	881	24.0
Hyperplasia of prostate — Hyperplasie de la prostate..................................	44	...	..	..	30	...	..	..
Pregnancy, childbirth and the puerperium — Grossesse, accouchement et puerpéralité								
Total	..	..	9	♦13.7	..	..	8	♦12.0
Pregnancy with abortive outcome — Grossesse se terminant par un avortement	..	..	-	-	..	..	-	-
Other direct obstetric causes — Autres décès maternels directs	..	..	7	♦10.7	..	..	5	♦7.5
Indirect obstetric causes — Décès maternels indirects	..	..	2	♦3.1	..	..	3	♦4.5
Certain conditions originating in the perinatal period — Certaines affections dont l'origine se situe dans la période périnatale	174	516.2	118	370.6	158	460.3	94	292.5
Congenital malformations, deformations and chromosomal abnormalities — Malformations congénitales et anomalies chromosomiques	68	201.7	45	141.3	61	177.7	59	183.6
Symptoms, signs and abnormal clinical and laboratory findings, not elsewhere classified — Symptômes, signes et résultats anormaux d'examens cliniques et de laboratoire, non classés ailleurs	2 318	66.3	2 118	57.5	2 494	71.7	2 255	61.5
All other diseases — Toutes autres maladies..	36	1.0	30	♦0.8	47	1.4	58	1.6
External causes — Causes externes								
Total	2 336	66.8	836	22.7	2 247	64.6	828	22.6
Accidents								
Total	1 069	30.6	367	10.0	1 052	30.2	400	10.9
Transport accidents — Accidents de transport	465	13.3	133	3.6	418	12.0	111	3.0
Falls — Chutes	234	6.7	107	2.9	241	6.9	134	3.7
Accidental drowning and submersion — Noyade et submersion accidentelles....................................	55	1.6	17	♦0.5	56	1.6	17	♦0.5
Exposure to smoke, fire and flames — Exposition à la fumée, au feu et aux flammes...	28	♦0.8	15	♦0.4	37	1.1	19	♦0.5
Accidental poisoning by and exposure to noxious substances — Intoxication accidentelle par des substances nocives et exposition à ces substances	39	1.1	6	♦0.2	31	0.9	15	♦0.4
Intentional self-harm — Lésions auto-infligées..	902	25.8	296	8.0	857	24.6	277	7.6
Assault — Agresssions..	95	2.7	57	1.5	82	2.4	32	0.9
All other external causes — Toutes autres causes externes	270	7.7	116	3.1	256	7.4	119	3.2

Slovakia - Slovaquie

Cause of death — Cause de décès	2013 (C)				2014 (C)			
	Male — Masculin		Female — Féminin		Male — Masculin		Female — Féminin	
	Number Nombre	Rate Taux	Number Nombre	Rate Taux	Number Nombre	Rate Taux	Number Nombre	Rate Taux
TOTAL	**26 863**	**1 019.1**	**25 221**	**908.9**	**26 498**	**1 004.1**	**24 847**	**894.8**
Certain infectious and parasitic diseases — Certaines maladies infectieuses et parasitaires								
Total	166	6.3	167	6.0	168	6.4	200	7.2
Intestinal infectious diseases — Maladies infectieuses intestinales	12	♦0.5	12	♦0.4	21	♦0.8	28	♦1.0
Tuberculosis — Tuberculose	14	♦0.5	5	♦0.2	21	♦0.8	11	♦0.4
Tetanus — Tétanos...	-	-	-	-	-	-	-	-
Diphtheria — Diphtérie...	-	-	-	-	-	-	-	-
Whooping cough — Coqueluche	-	-	-	-	1	♦0.0	-	-
Meningococcal infection — Infection à méningocoques	3	♦0.1	-	-	4	♦0.2	4	♦0.1
Septicaemia — Septicémie	107	4.1	121	4.4	92	3.5	121	4.4
Acute poliomyelitis — Poliomyélite aiguë	-	-	-	-	-	-	-	-
Measles — Rougeole...	-	-	-	-	-	-	-	-
Viral hepatitis — Hépatite virale	9	♦0.3	7	♦0.3	11	♦0.4	10	♦0.4
Human immunodeficiency virus [HIV] disease — Maladies dues au virus de l'immunodéficience humaine (VIH)...	2	♦0.1	-	-	1	♦0.0	-	-
Malaria — Paludisme...	1	♦0.0	1	♦0.0	-	-	-	-
Neoplasms — Tumeurs	**7 755**	**294.2**	**5 708**	**205.7**	**7 650**	**289.9**	**5 978**	**215.3**
Malignant neoplasms — Tumeurs malignes								
Total	7 725	293.1	5 652	203.7	7 616	288.6	5 927	213.4
Malignant neoplasm of lip, oral cavity and pharynx — Tumeur maligne de la lèvre, de la cavité buccale et du pharynx	598	22.7	92	3.3	554	21.0	89	3.2
Malignant neoplasm of oesophagus — Tumeur maligne de l'oesophage	245	9.3	32	1.2	251	9.5	37	1.3
Malignant neoplasm of stomach — Tumeur maligne de l'estomac	426	16.2	268	9.7	371	14.1	285	10.3
Malignant neoplasm of colon, rectosigmoid junction, rectum, anus and anal canal — Tumeur maligne du côlon, de la jonction recto-sigmoïdienne, du rectum, de l'anus et du canal anal..	1 255	47.6	836	30.1	1 133	42.9	856	30.8
Malignant neoplasm of liver and intrahepatic bile ducts — Tumeur maligne du foie et des voies bilaires intrahépatiques	272	10.3	140	5.0	278	10.5	149	5.4
Malignant neoplasm of pancreas — Tumeur maligne du pancréas....................	381	14.5	335	12.1	428	16.2	394	14.2
Malignant neoplasm of trachea, bronchus and lung — Tumeur maligne de la trachée, des bronches et du poumon	1 684	63.9	547	19.7	1 607	60.9	567	20.4
Malignant neoplasm of female breast — Tumeur maligne du sein chez la femme	..	..	973	...	..	..	898	...
Malignant neoplasm of cervix uteri — Tumeur maligne du col de l'utérus..........	..	..	240	...	..	..	228	...
Malignant neoplasm of prostate — Tumeur maligne de la prostate	626	...	..	..	738	...	..	..
Malignant neoplasm of lymphoid, haematopoietic and related tissue — Tumeurs malignes primitives ou présumées primitives des tissus lymphoïde, hématopoïétique et apparentés...	535	20.3	457	16.5	507	19.2	513	18.5
Disorders of the blood and blood-forming organs and certain disorders involving the immune mechanism — Maladies du sang et des organes hématopoïétiques et certains troubles du système immunitaire								
Total	25	♦0.9	35	1.3	24	♦0.9	30	♦1.1
Anaemias — Anémies	9	♦0.3	10	♦0.4	7	♦0.3	12	♦0.4
Endocrine, nutritional and metabolic diseases — Maladies endocriniennes, nutritionnelles et métaboliques								
Total	422	16.0	546	19.7	451	17.1	583	21.0
Diabetes mellitus — Diabète sucré..	350	13.3	442	15.9	392	14.9	503	18.1
Malnutrition — Malnutrition	16	♦0.6	12	♦0.4	14	♦0.5	18	♦0.6
Mental and behavioural disorders — Troubles mentaux et du comportement	289	11.0	436	15.7	405	15.3	542	19.5
Diseases of the nervous system — Maladies du système nerveux.................	440	16.7	486	17.5	527	20.0	620	22.3
Diseases of the circulatory system — Maladies de l'appareil circulatoire								
Total	10 989	416.9	13 139	473.5	10 540	399.4	12 349	444.7
Acute rheumatic fever and chronic rheumatic heart diseases — Rhumatisme articularie aigu et cardiopathies rhumatismales chroniques	31	1.2	69	2.5	30	♦1.1	54	1.9
Hypertensive diseases — Maladies hypertensives....................................	608	23.1	737	26.6	534	20.2	778	28.0
Ischaemic heart disease — Cardiopathie ischémique	6 466	245.3	7 904	284.8	6 138	232.6	7 200	259.3
Cerebrovascular disease — Maladie cérébrovasculaire................................	2 236	84.8	2 803	101.0	2 358	89.3	2 829	101.9

20. Death and death rates by cause and sex: 2010 - 2014
Décès et taux de mortalité par cause et sexe : 2010 - 2014 (continued - suite)

Slovakia - Slovaquie

Cause of death — Cause de décès	2013 (C)				2014 (C)			
	Male — Masculin		Female — Féminin		Male — Masculin		Female — Féminin	
	Number Nombre	Rate Taux	Number Nombre	Rate Taux	Number Nombre	Rate Taux	Number Nombre	Rate Taux
Diseases of arteries, arterioles and capillaries — Maladies des artères, artérioles et capillaires	270	10.2	200	7.2	246	9.3	239	8.6
Diseases of the respiratory system — Maladies de l'appareil respiratoire								
Total	1 712	64.9	1 320	47.6	1 578	59.8	1 150	41.4
Influenza — Grippe	8	♦0.3	6	♦0.2	1	♦0.0	-	-
Pneumonia — Pneumopathies	984	37.3	864	31.1	860	32.6	717	25.8
Chronic lower respiratory diseases — Maladies chroniques des voies respiratoires inférieures	554	21.0	309	11.1	574	21.8	310	11.2
Diseases of the digestive system — Maladies de l'appareil digestif								
Total	1 705	64.7	1 138	41.0	1 734	65.7	1 158	41.7
Gastric and duodenal ulcer — Ulcère de l'estomac et du duodénum	139	5.3	99	3.6	124	4.7	108	3.9
Diseases of the liver — Maladies du foie	1 064	40.4	424	15.3	1 113	42.2	409	14.7
Diseases of the musculoskeletal system and connective tissue — Maladies du système ostéo-articularie, des muscles et du tissu conjonctif	22	♦0.8	54	1.9	29	♦1.1	51	1.8
Diseases of the genitourinary system — Maladies de l'appareil génito-urinaire								
Total	328	12.4	427	15.4	367	13.9	441	15.9
Disorders of kidney and ureter — Affections du rein et de l'uretère	268	10.2	350	12.6	300	11.4	351	12.6
Hyperplasia of prostate — Hyperplasie de la prostate...............	7	...	..	..	7	...	..	..
Pregnancy, childbirth and the puerperium — Grossesse, accouchement et puerpéralité								
Total	..	..	1	♦1.8	..	..	2	♦3.6
Pregnancy with abortive outcome — Grossesse se terminant par un avortement	..	..	1	♦1.8	..	..	1	♦1.8
Other direct obstetric causes — Autres décès maternels directs	..	..	-	-	..	..	1	♦1.8
Indirect obstetric causes — Décès maternels indirects	..	..	-	-	..	..	-	-
Certain conditions originating in the perinatal period — Certaines affections dont l'origine se situe dans la période périnatale	80	285.0	47	175.7	78	277.6	63	233.9
Congenital malformations, deformations and chromosomal abnormalities — Malformations congénitales et anomalies chromosomiques	78	277.9	100	373.8	101	359.4	69	256.2
Symptoms, signs and abnormal clinical and laboratory findings, not elsewhere classified — Symptômes, signes et résultats anormaux d'examens cliniques et de laboratoire, non classés ailleurs	545	20.7	630	22.7	553	21.0	571	20.6
All other diseases — Toutes autres maladies	53	2.0	102	3.7	71	2.7	96	3.5
External causes — Causes externes								
Total	2 254	85.5	885	31.9	2 222	84.2	944	34.0
Accidents								
Total	1 508	57.2	723	26.1	1 228	46.5	543	19.6
Transport accidents — Accidents de transport	279	10.6	88	3.2	316	12.0	112	4.0
Falls — Chutes	689	26.1	500	18.0	426	16.1	305	11.0
Accidental drowning and submersion — Noyade et submersion accidentelles...............	113	4.3	31	1.1	103	3.9	26	♦0.9
Exposure to smoke, fire and flames — Exposition à la fumée, au feu et aux flammes...............	25	♦0.9	6	♦0.2	14	♦0.5	6	♦0.2
Accidental poisoning by and exposure to noxious substances — Intoxication accidentelle par des substances nocives et exposition à ces substances	111	4.2	36	1.3	118	4.5	31	1.1
Intentional self-harm — Lésions auto-infligées...............	533	20.2	83	3.0	471	17.8	82	3.0
Assault — Agresssions...............	37	1.4	30	♦1.1	29	♦1.1	18	♦0.6
All other external causes — Toutes autres causes externes	176	6.7	49	1.8	494	18.7	301	10.8

733

20. Death and death rates by cause and sex: 2010 - 2014
Décès et taux de mortalité par cause et sexe : 2010 - 2014 (continued - suite)

Cause of death — Cause de décès	Slovenia - Slovénie 2010 (C)				Spain - Espagne 2013 (C)			
	Male — Masculin		Female — Féminin		Male — Masculin		Female — Féminin	
	Number Nombre	Rate Taux	Number Nombre	Rate Taux	Number Nombre	Rate Taux	Number Nombre	Rate Taux
TOTAL	9 292	915.7	9 317	900.6	199 834	871.4	190 585	805.5
Certain infectious and parasitic diseases — Certaines maladies infectieuses et parasitaires								
Total	42	4.1	42	4.1	3 166	13.8	3 042	12.9
Intestinal infectious diseases — Maladies infectieuses intestinales	-	-	3	♦0.3	300	1.3	501	2.1
Tuberculosis — Tuberculose	11	♦1.1	8	♦0.8	164	0.7	74	0.3
Tetanus — Tétanos	-	-	-	-	2	♦0.0	2	♦0.0
Diphtheria — Diphtérie	-	-	1	♦0.1	-	-	-	-
Whooping cough — Coqueluche	-	-	-	-	2	♦0.0	2	♦0.0
Meningococcal infection — Infection à méningocoques	1	♦0.1	-	-	13	♦0.1	8	♦0.0
Septicaemia — Septicémie	9	♦0.9	16	♦1.5	1 345	5.9	1 572	6.6
Acute poliomyelitis — Poliomyélite aiguë	-	-	-	-	-	-	-	-
Measles — Rougeole	-	-	-	-	-	-	-	-
Viral hepatitis — Hépatite virale	6	♦0.6	2	♦0.2	402	1.8	439	1.9
Human immunodeficiency virus [HIV] disease — Maladies dues au virus de l'immunodéficience humaine (VIH)	-	-	-	-	603	2.6	146	0.6
Malaria — Paludisme	-	-	-	-	-	-	-	-
Neoplasms — Tumeurs	3 245	319.8	2 640	255.2	67 711	295.2	43 310	183.1
Malignant neoplasms — Tumeurs malignes								
Total	3 227	318.0	2 616	252.9	65 642	286.2	41 494	175.4
Malignant neoplasm of lip, oral cavity and pharynx — Tumeur maligne de la lèvre, de la cavité buccale et du pharynx	138	13.6	31	3.0	1 861	8.1	598	2.5
Malignant neoplasm of oesophagus — Tumeur maligne de l'oesophage	63	6.2	12	♦1.2	1 509	6.6	289	1.2
Malignant neoplasm of stomach — Tumeur maligne de l'estomac	241	23.8	153	14.8	3 443	15.0	2 183	9.2
Malignant neoplasm of colon, rectosigmoid junction, rectum, anus and anal canal — Tumeur maligne du côlon, de la jonction recto-sigmoïdienne, du rectum, de l'anus et du canal anal	443	43.7	343	33.2	9 236	40.3	6 364	26.9
Malignant neoplasm of liver and intrahepatic bile ducts — Tumeur maligne du foie et des voies bilaires intrahépatiques	129	12.7	62	6.0	3 373	14.7	1 709	7.2
Malignant neoplasm of pancreas — Tumeur maligne du pancréas	165	16.3	198	19.1	3 169	13.8	2 870	12.1
Malignant neoplasm of trachea, bronchus and lung — Tumeur maligne de la trachée, des bronches et du poumon	805	79.3	316	30.5	17 577	76.6	4 112	17.4
Malignant neoplasm of female breast — Tumeur maligne du sein chez la femme	..	..	416	46.5	..	..	6 477	32.0
Malignant neoplasm of cervix uteri — Tumeur maligne du col de l'utérus	..	..	43	4.8	..	..	640	3.2
Malignant neoplasm of prostate — Tumeur maligne de la prostate	358	103.0	..	..	5 787	73.8	..	..
Malignant neoplasm of lymphoid, haematopoietic and related tissue — Tumeurs malignes primitives ou présumées primitives des tissus lymphoïde, hématopoïétique et apparentés	220	21.7	209	20.2	4 503	19.6	3 798	16.1
Disorders of the blood and blood-forming organs and certain disorders involving the immune mechanism — Maladies du sang et des organes hématopoïétiques et certains troubles du système immunitaire								
Total	11	♦1.1	25	♦2.4	688	3.0	951	4.0
Anaemias — Anémies	-	-	12	♦1.2	383	1.7	689	2.9
Endocrine, nutritional and metabolic diseases — Maladies endocriniennes, nutritionnelles et métaboliques								
Total	134	13.2	161	15.6	5 063	22.1	7 143	30.2
Diabetes mellitus — Diabète sucré	117	11.5	138	13.3	3 985	17.4	5 406	22.8
Malnutrition — Malnutrition	-	-	-	-	61	0.3	75	0.3
Mental and behavioural disorders — Troubles mentaux et du comportement	114	11.2	28	♦2.7	5 772	25.2	11 205	47.4
Diseases of the nervous system — Maladies du système nerveux	147	14.5	156	15.1	8 352	36.4	13 116	55.4
Diseases of the circulatory system — Maladies de l'appareil circulatoire								
Total	3 071	302.6	4 260	411.8	53 487	233.2	63 997	270.5
Acute rheumatic fever and chronic rheumatic heart diseases — Rhumatisme articularie aigu et cardiopathies rhumatismales chroniques	30	♦3.0	50	4.8	411	1.8	1 041	4.4
Hypertensive diseases — Maladies hypertensives	173	17.0	357	34.5	3 648	15.9	7 595	32.1
Ischaemic heart disease — Cardiopathie ischémique	1 108	109.2	943	91.2	19 402	84.6	14 011	59.2
Cerebrovascular disease — Maladie cérébrovasculaire	829	81.7	1 144	110.6	11 593	50.5	16 257	68.7

Cause of death — Cause de décès	Slovenia - Slovénie 2010 (C)				Spain - Espagne 2013 (C)			
	Male — Masculin		Female — Féminin		Male — Masculin		Female — Féminin	
	Number Nombre	Rate Taux	Number Nombre	Rate Taux	Number Nombre	Rate Taux	Number Nombre	Rate Taux
Diseases of arteries, arterioles and capillaries — Maladies des artères, artérioles et capillaires	178	17.5	247	23.9	2 966	12.9	2 204	9.3
Diseases of the respiratory system — Maladies de l'appareil respiratoire								
Total	561	55.3	558	53.9	24 305	106.0	18 260	77.2
Influenza — Grippe	1	♦0.1	2	♦0.2	44	0.2	44	0.2
Pneumonia — Pneumopathies	209	20.6	303	29.3	4 317	18.8	4 016	17.0
Chronic lower respiratory diseases — Maladies chroniques des voies respiratoires inférieures	270	26.6	151	14.6	11 377	49.6	4 010	16.9
Diseases of the digestive system — Maladies de l'appareil digestif								
Total	651	64.2	501	48.4	10 245	44.7	9 133	38.6
Gastric and duodenal ulcer — Ulcère de l'estomac et du duodénum	27	♦2.7	41	4.0	256	1.1	186	0.8
Diseases of the liver — Maladies du foie	443	43.7	181	17.5	4 033	17.6	1 677	7.1
Diseases of the musculoskeletal system and connective tissue — Maladies du système ostéo-articularie, des muscles et du tissu conjonctif	22	♦2.2	59	5.7	1 121	4.9	2 240	9.5
Diseases of the genitourinary system — Maladies de l'appareil génito-urinaire								
Total	93	9.2	181	17.5	5 236	22.8	6 453	27.3
Disorders of kidney and ureter — Affections du rein et de l'uretère	71	7.0	126	12.2	3 496	15.2	3 970	16.8
Hyperplasia of prostate — Hyperplasie de la prostate	-	-	..	..	141	1.8	..	..
Pregnancy, childbirth and the puerperium — Grossesse, accouchement et puerpéralité								
Total	..	..	-	-	..	..	18	♦4.2
Pregnancy with abortive outcome — Grossesse se terminant par un avortement	..	..	-	-	..	..	2	♦0.5
Other direct obstetric causes — Autres décès maternels directs	..	..	-	-	..	..	16	♦3.8
Indirect obstetric causes — Décès maternels indirects	..	..	-	-	..	..	-	-
Certain conditions originating in the perinatal period — Certaines affections dont l'origine se situe dans la période périnatale	20	♦173.9	22	♦203.0	403	184.5	310	150.4
Congenital malformations, deformations and chromosomal abnormalities — Malformations congénitales et anomalies chromosomiques	13	♦113.0	18	♦166.1	387	177.2	371	180.0
Symptoms, signs and abnormal clinical and laboratory findings, not elsewhere classified — Symptômes, signes et résultats anormaux d'examens cliniques et de laboratoire, non classés ailleurs	172	17.0	103	10.0	4 209	18.4	4 739	20.0
All other diseases — Toutes autres maladies	7	♦0.7	37	3.6	424	1.8	884	3.7
External causes — Causes externes								
Total	989	97.5	526	50.8	9 265	40.4	5 413	22.9
Accidents								
Total	548	54.0	356	34.4	5 852	25.5	4 087	17.3
Transport accidents — Accidents de transport	130	12.8	34	3.3	1 625	7.1	500	2.1
Falls — Chutes	255	25.1	270	26.1	1 339	5.8	1 333	5.6
Accidental drowning and submersion — Noyade et submersion accidentelles	22	♦2.2	6	♦0.6	344	1.5	78	0.3
Exposure to smoke, fire and flames — Exposition à la fumée, au feu et aux flammes	6	♦0.6	3	♦0.3	82	0.4	58	0.2
Accidental poisoning by and exposure to noxious substances — Intoxication accidentelle par des substances nocives et exposition à ces substances	51	5.0	15	♦1.4	620	2.7	252	1.1
Intentional self-harm — Lésions auto-infligées	336	33.1	78	7.5	2 911	12.7	959	4.1
Assault — Agresssions	5	♦0.5	5	♦0.5	206	0.9	109	0.5
All other external causes — Toutes autres causes externes	100	9.9	87	8.4	296	1.3	258	1.1

20. Death and death rates by cause and sex: 2010 - 2014
Décès et taux de mortalité par cause et sexe : 2010 - 2014 (continued - suite)

	Spain - Espagne				Sweden - Suède			
	2014 (C)				2013 (C)			
Cause of death — Cause de décès	Male — Masculin		Female — Féminin		Male — Masculin		Female — Féminin	
	Number Nombre	Rate Taux	Number Nombre	Rate Taux	Number Nombre	Rate Taux	Number Nombre	Rate Taux
TOTAL	**201 571**	**882.1**	**194 259**	**822.1**	**43 728**	**912.9**	**46 777**	**972.4**
Certain infectious and parasitic diseases — Certaines maladies infectieuses et parasitaires								
Total	3 263	14.3	3 245	13.7	1 063	22.2	1 217	25.3
Intestinal infectious diseases — Maladies infectieuses intestinales	278	1.2	475	2.0	114	2.4	227	4.7
Tuberculosis — Tuberculose	150	0.7	66	0.3	14	♦0.3	10	♦0.2
Tetanus — Tétanos....................	-	-	1	♦0.0	-	-	-	-
Diphtheria — Diphtérie....................	-	-	-	-	-	-	-	-
Whooping cough — Coqueluche	3	♦0.0	2	♦0.0	-	-	-	-
Meningococcal infection — Infection à méningocoques	4	♦0.0	4	♦0.0	-	-	3	♦0.1
Septicaemia — Septicémie....................	1 482	6.5	1 775	7.5	523	10.9	519	10.8
Acute poliomyelitis — Poliomyélite aiguë	-	-	-	-	-	-	-	-
Measles — Rougeole....................	-	-	-	-	-	-	-	-
Viral hepatitis — Hépatite virale	488	2.1	431	1.8	65	1.4	16	♦0.3
Human immunodeficiency virus [HIV] disease — Maladies dues au virus de l'immunodéficience humaine (VIH)....................	531	2.3	169	0.7	11	♦0.2	4	♦0.1
Malaria — Paludisme....................	3	♦0.0	-	-	1	♦0.0	-	-
Neoplasms — Tumeurs	**67 278**	**294.4**	**43 000**	**182.0**	**11 907**	**248.6**	**11 226**	**233.4**
Malignant neoplasms — Tumeurs malignes								
Total	65 163	285.2	41 106	174.0	11 462	239.3	10 720	222.9
Malignant neoplasm of lip, oral cavity and pharynx — Tumeur maligne de la lèvre, de la cavité buccale et du pharynx	1 769	7.7	571	2.4	206	4.3	113	2.3
Malignant neoplasm of oesophagus — Tumeur maligne de l'oesophage	1 545	6.8	289	1.2	326	6.8	109	2.3
Malignant neoplasm of stomach — Tumeur maligne de l'estomac	3 334	14.6	2 200	9.3	384	8.0	262	5.4
Malignant neoplasm of colon, rectosigmoid junction, rectum, anus and anal canal — Tumeur maligne du côlon, de la jonction recto-sigmoïdienne, du rectum, de l'anus et du canal anal	9 260	40.5	6 216	26.3	1 415	29.5	1 344	27.9
Malignant neoplasm of liver and intrahepatic bile ducts — Tumeur maligne du foie et des voies bilaires intrahépatiques	3 401	14.9	1 654	7.0	410	8.6	276	5.7
Malignant neoplasm of pancreas — Tumeur maligne du pancréas....................	3 199	14.0	3 088	13.1	798	16.7	877	18.2
Malignant neoplasm of trachea, bronchus and lung — Tumeur maligne de la trachée, des bronches et du poumon	17 212	75.3	4 058	17.2	1 840	38.4	1 791	37.2
Malignant neoplasm of female breast — Tumeur maligne du sein chez la femme	..	..	6 231	...	..	..	1 473	...
Malignant neoplasm of cervix uteri — Tumeur maligne du col de l'utérus.........	..	..	590	...	..	..	166	...
Malignant neoplasm of prostate — Tumeur maligne de la prostate	5 863	...	..	..	2 343	...	..	..
Malignant neoplasm of lymphoid, haematopoietic and related tissue — Tumeurs malignes primitives ou présumées primitives des tissus lymphoïde, hématopoïétique et apparentés....................	4 536	19.8	3 781	16.0	1 060	22.1	917	19.1
Disorders of the blood and blood-forming organs and certain disorders involving the immune mechanism — Maladies du sang et des organes hématopoïétiques et certains troubles du système immunitaire								
Total	781	3.4	1 003	4.2	132	2.8	168	3.5
Anaemias — Anémies	445	1.9	698	3.0	76	1.6	110	2.3
Endocrine, nutritional and metabolic diseases — Maladies endocriniennes, nutritionnelles et métaboliques								
Total	5 431	23.8	7 582	32.1	1 270	26.5	1 162	24.2
Diabetes mellitus — Diabète sucré....................	4 100	17.9	5 525	23.4	1 087	22.7	884	18.4
Malnutrition — Malnutrition	90	0.4	97	0.4	16	♦0.3	52	1.1
Mental and behavioural disorders — Troubles mentaux et du comportement	**6 343**	**27.8**	**12 363**	**52.3**	**2 019**	**42.1**	**3 920**	**81.5**
Diseases of the nervous system — Maladies du système nerveux.................	**8 907**	**39.0**	**14 466**	**61.2**	**1 689**	**35.3**	**2 299**	**47.8**
Diseases of the circulatory system — Maladies de l'appareil circulatoire								
Total	53 581	234.5	63 812	270.1	15 972	333.4	17 597	365.8
Acute rheumatic fever and chronic rheumatic heart diseases — Rhumatisme articularie aigu et cardiopathies rhumatismales chroniques	482	2.1	1 186	5.0	50	1.0	90	1.9
Hypertensive diseases — Maladies hypertensives....................	3 699	16.2	7 874	33.3	765	16.0	1 531	31.8
Ischaemic heart disease — Cardiopathie ischémique	19 101	83.6	13 463	57.0	7 265	151.7	5 925	123.2
Cerebrovascular disease — Maladie cérébrovasculaire....................	11 573	50.6	16 006	67.7	2 873	60.0	4 046	84.1

20. Death and death rates by cause and sex: 2010 - 2014
Décès et taux de mortalité par cause et sexe : 2010 - 2014 (continued - suite)

Cause of death — Cause de décès	Spain - Espagne 2014 (C)				Sweden - Suède 2013 (C)			
	Male — Masculin		Female — Féminin		Male — Masculin		Female — Féminin	
	Number Nombre	Rate Taux	Number Nombre	Rate Taux	Number Nombre	Rate Taux	Number Nombre	Rate Taux
Diseases of arteries, arterioles and capillaries — Maladies des artères, artérioles et capillaires	2 908	12.7	2 123	9.0	971	20.3	903	18.8
Diseases of the respiratory system — Maladies de l'appareil respiratoire								
Total	24 906	109.0	18 935	80.1	2 989	62.4	3 096	64.4
Influenza — Grippe...........	199	0.9	181	0.8	62	1.3	84	1.7
Pneumonia — Pneumopathies	4 357	19.1	4 088	17.3	1 086	22.7	987	20.5
Chronic lower respiratory diseases — Maladies chroniques des voies respiratoires inférieures	11 434	50.0	4 112	17.4	1 312	27.4	1 611	33.5
Diseases of the digestive system — Maladies de l'appareil digestif								
Total	10 071	44.1	9 314	39.4	1 377	28.7	1 352	28.1
Gastric and duodenal ulcer — Ulcère de l'estomac et du duodénum........	211	0.9	200	0.8	155	3.2	147	3.1
Diseases of the liver — Maladies du foie........	3 823	16.7	1 630	6.9	458	9.6	268	5.6
Diseases of the musculoskeletal system and connective tissue — Maladies du système ostéo-articularie, des muscles et du tissu conjonctif	1 268	5.5	2 411	10.2	142	3.0	297	6.2
Diseases of the genitourinary system — Maladies de l'appareil génito-urinaire								
Total	5 050	22.1	6 480	27.4	579	12.1	539	11.2
Disorders of kidney and ureter — Affections du rein et de l'uretère	3 283	14.4	3 794	16.1	388	8.1	374	7.8
Hyperplasia of prostate — Hyperplasie de la prostate........	183	...	..	..	44	...	..	..
Pregnancy, childbirth and the puerperium — Grossesse, accouchement et puerpéralité								
Total	..	..	9	♦2.1	..	..	7	♦6.2
Pregnancy with abortive outcome — Grossesse se terminant par un avortement	..	..	1	♦0.2	..	..	1	♦0.9
Other direct obstetric causes — Autres décès maternels directs	..	..	8	♦1.9	..	..	4	♦3.5
Indirect obstetric causes — Décès maternels indirects	..	..	-	-	..	..	1	♦0.9
Certain conditions originating in the perinatal period — Certaines affections dont l'origine se situe dans la période périnatale	446	202.7	332	161.1	93	159.1	51	92.5
Congenital malformations, deformations and chromosomal abnormalities — Malformations congénitales et anomalies chromosomiques	430	195.4	398	193.2	126	215.5	124	225.0
Symptoms, signs and abnormal clinical and laboratory findings, not elsewhere classified — Symptômes, signes et résultats anormaux d'examens cliniques et de laboratoire, non classés ailleurs	3 981	17.4	4 502	19.1	1 239	25.9	1 854	38.5
All other diseases — Toutes autres maladies........	447	2.0	892	3.8	87	1.8	96	2.0
External causes — Causes externes								
Total	9 388	41.1	5 515	23.3	3 044	63.5	1 772	36.8
Accidents								
Total	6 028	26.4	4 258	18.0	1 794	37.5	1 174	24.4
Transport accidents — Accidents de transport......	1 608	7.0	465	2.0	235	4.9	67	1.4
Falls — Chutes	1 433	6.3	1 316	5.6	533	11.1	434	9.0
Accidental drowning and submersion — Noyade et submersion accidentelles......	335	1.5	99	0.4	68	1.4	15	♦0.3
Exposure to smoke, fire and flames — Exposition à la fumée, au feu et aux flammes........	112	0.5	61	0.3	39	0.8	25	♦0.5
Accidental poisoning by and exposure to noxious substances — Intoxication accidentelle par des substances nocives et exposition à ces substances	625	2.7	296	1.3	343	7.2	94	2.0
Intentional self-harm — Lésions auto-infligées........	2 938	12.9	972	4.1	861	18.0	366	7.6
Assault — Agresssions........	201	0.9	116	0.5	54	1.1	24	♦0.5
All other external causes — Toutes autres causes externes	221	1.0	169	0.7	335	7.0	208	4.3

20. Death and death rates by cause and sex: 2010 - 2014
Décès et taux de mortalité par cause et sexe : 2010 - 2014 (continued - suite)

	Sweden - Suède				Switzerland - Suisse			
Cause of death — Cause de décès	2014 (C)				2012 (C)			
	Male — Masculin		Female — Féminin		Male — Masculin		Female — Féminin	
	Number Nombre	Rate Taux	Number Nombre	Rate Taux	Number Nombre	Rate Taux	Number Nombre	Rate Taux
TOTAL	**43 440**	**896.9**	**45 622**	**940.1**	**30 697**	**782.6**	**33 476**	**830.2**
Certain infectious and parasitic diseases — Certaines maladies infectieuses et parasitaires								
Total	1 046	21.6	1 068	22.0	335	8.5	417	10.3
Intestinal infectious diseases — Maladies infectieuses intestinales	107	2.2	152	3.1	40	1.0	91	2.3
Tuberculosis — Tuberculose	4	♦0.1	7	♦0.1	5	♦0.1	6	♦0.1
Tetanus — Tétanos...	-	-	-	-	-	-	-	-
Diphtheria — Diphtérie..	-	-	-	-	-	-	-	-
Whooping cough — Coqueluche	-	-	2	♦0.0	-	-	1	♦0.0
Meningococcal infection — Infection à méningocoques	-	-	1	♦0.0	1	♦0.0	-	-
Septicaemia — Septicémie...	558	11.5	499	10.3	86	2.2	91	2.3
Acute poliomyelitis — Poliomyélite aiguë	-	-	-	-	-	-	-	-
Measles — Rougeole	-	-	-	-	-	-	-	-
Viral hepatitis — Hépatite virale...	41	0.8	19	♦0.4	10	♦0.3	2	♦0.0
Human immunodeficiency virus [HIV] disease — Maladies dues au virus de l'immunodéficience humaine (VIH).................................	6	♦0.1	3	♦0.1	30	♦0.8	15	♦0.4
Malaria — Paludisme	-	-	-	-	-	-	-	-
Neoplasms — Tumeurs	**12 194**	**251.8**	**11 143**	**229.6**	**9 290**	**236.9**	**7 769**	**192.7**
Malignant neoplasms — Tumeurs malignes								
Total	11 692	241.4	10 635	219.2	9 024	230.1	7 466	185.1
Malignant neoplasm of lip, oral cavity and pharynx — Tumeur maligne de la lèvre, de la cavité buccale et du pharynx	193	4.0	109	2.2	306	7.8	138	3.4
Malignant neoplasm of oesophagus — Tumeur maligne de l'oesophage	357	7.4	95	2.0	333	8.5	97	2.4
Malignant neoplasm of stomach — Tumeur maligne de l'estomac	355	7.3	257	5.3	332	8.5	191	4.7
Malignant neoplasm of colon, rectosigmoid junction, rectum, anus and anal canal — Tumeur maligne du côlon, de la jonction recto-sigmoïdienne, du rectum, de l'anus et du canal anal...	1 417	29.3	1 354	27.9	919	23.4	821	20.4
Malignant neoplasm of liver and intrahepatic bile ducts — Tumeur maligne du foie et des voies bilaires intrahépatiques	435	9.0	263	5.4	484	12.3	201	5.0
Malignant neoplasm of pancreas — Tumeur maligne du pancréas...................	863	17.8	929	19.1	563	14.4	606	15.0
Malignant neoplasm of trachea, bronchus and lung — Tumeur maligne de la trachée, des bronches et du poumon	1 805	37.3	1 845	38.0	1 949	49.7	1 143	28.3
Malignant neoplasm of female breast — Tumeur maligne du sein chez la femme	..	..	1 398	...	..	..	1 371	...
Malignant neoplasm of cervix uteri — Tumeur maligne du col de l'utérus.........	..	..	132	...	..	..	90	...
Malignant neoplasm of prostate — Tumeur maligne de la prostate	2 398	...	..	..	1 278	...	..	..
Malignant neoplasm of lymphoid, haematopoietic and related tissue — Tumeurs malignes primitives ou présumées primitives des tissus lymphoïde, hématopoïétique et apparentés...	1 141	23.6	887	18.3	803	20.5	679	16.8
Disorders of the blood and blood-forming organs and certain disorders involving the immune mechanism — Maladies du sang et des organes hématopoïétiques et certains troubles du système immunitaire								
Total	104	2.1	152	3.1	69	1.8	107	2.7
Anaemias — Anémies	56	1.2	96	2.0	46	1.2	73	1.8
Endocrine, nutritional and metabolic diseases — Maladies endocriniennes, nutritionnelles et métaboliques								
Total	1 263	26.1	1 135	23.4	761	19.4	843	20.9
Diabetes mellitus — Diabète sucré...	1 029	21.2	851	17.5	592	15.1	650	16.1
Malnutrition — Malnutrition	35	0.7	49	1.0	17	♦0.4	35	0.9
Mental and behavioural disorders — Troubles mentaux et du comportement	**2 049**	**42.3**	**3 937**	**81.1**	**1 572**	**40.1**	**3 132**	**77.7**
Diseases of the nervous system — Maladies du système nerveux..................	**1 679**	**34.7**	**2 404**	**49.5**	**1 401**	**35.7**	**2 049**	**50.8**
Diseases of the circulatory system — Maladies de l'appareil circulatoire								
Total	15 652	323.2	16 896	348.2	9 745	248.5	11 929	295.8
Acute rheumatic fever and chronic rheumatic heart diseases — Rhumatisme articularie aigu et cardiopathies rhumatismales chroniques	51	1.1	70	1.4	26	♦0.7	41	1.0
Hypertensive diseases — Maladies hypertensives.................................	882	18.2	1 476	30.4	1 000	25.5	1 993	49.4
Ischaemic heart disease — Cardiopathie ischémique..............................	6 947	143.4	5 626	115.9	4 227	107.8	3 764	93.3
Cerebrovascular disease — Maladie cérébrovasculaire............................	2 857	59.0	3 731	76.9	1 454	37.1	2 162	53.6

20. Death and death rates by cause and sex: 2010 - 2014
Décès et taux de mortalité par cause et sexe : 2010 - 2014 (continued - suite)

	Sweden - Suède				Switzerland - Suisse			
Cause of death — Cause de décès	2014 (C)				2012 (C)			
	Male — Masculin		Female — Féminin		Male — Masculin		Female — Féminin	
	Number Nombre	Rate Taux	Number Nombre	Rate Taux	Number Nombre	Rate Taux	Number Nombre	Rate Taux
Diseases of arteries, arterioles and capillaries — Maladies des artères, artérioles et capillaires	816	16.8	844	17.4	524	13.4	509	12.6
Diseases of the respiratory system — Maladies de l'appareil respiratoire								
Total	2 775	57.3	2 777	57.2	2 057	52.4	1 849	45.9
Influenza — Grippe	17	♦0.4	12	♦0.2	10	♦0.3	22	♦0.5
Pneumonia — Pneumopathies	922	19.0	843	17.4	599	15.3	684	17.0
Chronic lower respiratory diseases — Maladies chroniques des voies respiratoires inférieures	1 281	26.4	1 583	32.6	1 089	27.8	858	21.3
Diseases of the digestive system — Maladies de l'appareil digestif								
Total	1 481	30.6	1 344	27.7	1 227	31.3	1 333	33.1
Gastric and duodenal ulcer — Ulcère de l'estomac et du duodénum	137	2.8	133	2.7	60	1.5	70	1.7
Diseases of the liver — Maladies du foie........	544	11.2	268	5.5	491	12.5	260	6.4
Diseases of the musculoskeletal system and connective tissue — Maladies du système ostéo-articularie, des muscles et du tissu conjonctif	148	3.1	334	6.9	177	4.5	389	9.6
Diseases of the genitourinary system — Maladies de l'appareil génito-urinaire								
Total	543	11.2	581	12.0	468	11.9	529	13.1
Disorders of kidney and ureter — Affections du rein et de l'uretère	358	7.4	394	8.1	308	7.9	354	8.8
Hyperplasia of prostate — Hyperplasie de la prostate....................	30	...	..	..	40	...	..	..
Pregnancy, childbirth and the puerperium — Grossesse, accouchement et puerpéralité								
Total	..	..	4	♦3.5	..	..	7	♦8.5
Pregnancy with abortive outcome — Grossesse se terminant par un avortement	..	..	-	-	..	..	1	♦1.2
Other direct obstetric causes — Autres décès maternels directs	..	..	4	♦3.5	..	..	4	♦4.9
Indirect obstetric causes — Décès maternels indirects	..	..	-	-	..	..	1	♦1.2
Certain conditions originating in the perinatal period — Certaines affections dont l'origine se situe dans la période périnatale	71	120.1	48	86.0	81	190.9	77	193.8
Congenital malformations, deformations and chromosomal abnormalities — Malformations congénitales et anomalies chromosomiques	131	221.7	126	225.8	138	325.2	116	292.0
Symptoms, signs and abnormal clinical and laboratory findings, not elsewhere classified — Symptômes, signes et résultats anormaux d'examens cliniques et de laboratoire, non classés ailleurs	1 203	24.8	1 754	36.1	1 195	30.5	1 353	33.6
All other diseases — Toutes autres maladies...	73	1.5	106	2.2	30	♦0.8	78	1.9
External causes — Causes externes								
Total	3 028	62.5	1 813	37.4	2 151	54.8	1 499	37.2
Accidents								
Total	1 825	37.7	1 236	25.5	1 311	33.4	1 152	28.6
Transport accidents — Accidents de transport...	234	4.8	86	1.8	257	6.6	84	2.1
Falls — Chutes	551	11.4	449	9.3	703	17.9	892	22.1
Accidental drowning and submersion — Noyade et submersion accidentelles..	91	1.9	19	♦0.4	36	0.9	16	♦0.4
Exposure to smoke, fire and flames — Exposition à la fumée, au feu et aux flammes..	37	0.8	25	♦0.5	11	♦0.3	19	♦0.5
Accidental poisoning by and exposure to noxious substances — Intoxication accidentelle par des substances nocives et exposition à ces substances	388	8.0	117	2.4	95	2.4	33	0.8
Intentional self-harm — Lésions auto-infligées...	785	16.2	363	7.5	752	19.2	285	7.1
Assault — Agresssions..................................	52	1.1	26	♦0.5	23	♦0.6	18	♦0.4
All other external causes — Toutes autres causes externes	366	7.6	188	3.9	65	1.7	44	1.1

20. Death and death rates by cause and sex: 2010 - 2014
Décès et taux de mortalité par cause et sexe : 2010 - 2014 (continued - suite)

Cause of death — Cause de décès	Switzerland - Suisse 2013 (C)				TFYR of Macedonia - L'ex-R. y. de Macédoine 2010 (C)			
	Male — Masculin		Female — Féminin		Male — Masculin		Female — Féminin	
	Number Nombre	Rate Taux	Number Nombre	Rate Taux	Number Nombre	Rate Taux	Number Nombre	Rate Taux
TOTAL	31 257	787.6	33 704	828.0	10 168	987.3	8 945	872.6
Certain infectious and parasitic diseases — Certaines maladies infectieuses et parasitaires								
Total	352	8.9	415	10.2	43	4.2	19	✦1.9
Intestinal infectious diseases — Maladies infectieuses intestinales	47	1.2	76	1.9	1	✦0.1	-	-
Tuberculosis — Tuberculose	7	✦0.2	5	✦0.1	24	✦2.3	8	✦0.8
Tetanus — Tétanos	-	-	1	✦0.0	-	-	-	-
Diphtheria — Diphtérie	-	-	-	-	-	-	-	-
Whooping cough — Coqueluche	-	-	-	-	-	-	-	-
Meningococcal infection — Infection à méningocoques	1	✦0.0	1	✦0.0	2	✦0.2	-	-
Septicaemia — Septicémie	96	2.4	105	2.6	14	✦1.4	6	✦0.6
Acute poliomyelitis — Poliomyélite aiguë	-	-	-	-	-	-	-	-
Measles — Rougeole	-	-	1	✦0.0	-	-	-	-
Viral hepatitis — Hépatite virale	9	✦0.2	3	✦0.1	-	-	1	✦0.1
Human immunodeficiency virus [HIV] disease — Maladies dues au virus de l'immunodéficience humaine (VIH)	24	✦0.6	12	✦0.3	-	-	-	-
Malaria — Paludisme	-	-	1	✦0.0	-	-	-	-
Neoplasms — Tumeurs	9 446	238.0	7 803	191.7	2 218	215.4	1 487	145.1
Malignant neoplasms — Tumeurs malignes								
Total	9 199	231.8	7 476	183.7	2 211	214.7	1 474	143.8
Malignant neoplasm of lip, oral cavity and pharynx — Tumeur maligne de la lèvre, de la cavité buccale et du pharynx	302	7.6	145	3.6	31	3.0	17	✦1.7
Malignant neoplasm of oesophagus — Tumeur maligne de l'oesophage	361	9.1	116	2.8	18	✦1.7	4	✦0.4
Malignant neoplasm of stomach — Tumeur maligne de l'estomac	344	8.7	225	5.5	252	24.5	126	12.3
Malignant neoplasm of colon, rectosigmoid junction, rectum, anus and anal canal — Tumeur maligne du côlon, de la jonction recto-sigmoïdienne, du rectum, de l'anus et du canal anal	894	22.5	766	18.8	219	21.3	163	15.9
Malignant neoplasm of liver and intrahepatic bile ducts — Tumeur maligne du foie et des voies bilaires intrahépatiques	494	12.4	221	5.4	127	12.3	78	7.6
Malignant neoplasm of pancreas — Tumeur maligne du pancréas	576	14.5	638	15.7	118	11.5	71	6.9
Malignant neoplasm of trachea, bronchus and lung — Tumeur maligne de la trachée, des bronches et du poumon	1 960	49.4	1 209	29.7	667	64.8	135	13.2
Malignant neoplasm of female breast — Tumeur maligne du sein chez la femme	..	..	1 329	...	..	..	308	36.2
Malignant neoplasm of cervix uteri — Tumeur maligne du col de l'utérus	..	..	70	...	..	..	31	3.6
Malignant neoplasm of prostate — Tumeur maligne de la prostate	1 356	...	..	..	165	56.5	..	..
Malignant neoplasm of lymphoid, haematopoietic and related tissue — Tumeurs malignes primitives ou présumées primitives des tissus lymphoïde, hématopoïétique et apparentés	851	21.4	667	16.4	109	10.6	54	5.3
Disorders of the blood and blood-forming organs and certain disorders involving the immune mechanism — Maladies du sang et des organes hématopoïétiques et certains troubles du système immunitaire								
Total	73	1.8	87	2.1	8	✦0.8	7	✦0.7
Anaemias — Anémies	38	1.0	58	1.4	6	✦0.6	5	✦0.5
Endocrine, nutritional and metabolic diseases — Maladies endocriniennes, nutritionnelles et métaboliques								
Total	787	19.8	942	23.1	310	30.1	431	42.0
Diabetes mellitus — Diabète sucré	615	15.5	700	17.2	308	29.9	429	41.8
Malnutrition — Malnutrition	20	✦0.5	45	1.1	1	✦0.1	-	-
Mental and behavioural disorders — Troubles mentaux et du comportement	1 671	42.1	3 382	83.1	18	✦1.7	1	✦0.1
Diseases of the nervous system — Maladies du système nerveux	1 430	36.0	1 908	46.9	99	9.6	58	5.7
Diseases of the circulatory system — Maladies de l'appareil circulatoire								
Total	9 719	244.9	11 793	289.7	5 500	534.1	5 567	543.0
Acute rheumatic fever and chronic rheumatic heart diseases — Rhumatisme articularie aigu et cardiopathies rhumatismales chroniques	24	✦0.6	43	1.1	9	✦0.9	5	✦0.5
Hypertensive diseases — Maladies hypertensives	1 020	25.7	2 017	49.6	283	27.5	398	38.8
Ischaemic heart disease — Cardiopathie ischémique	4 097	103.2	3 628	89.1	1 086	105.5	666	65.0
Cerebrovascular disease — Maladie cérébrovasculaire	1 465	36.9	2 238	55.0	1 801	174.9	2 017	196.8

Cause of death — Cause de décès	Switzerland - Suisse				TFYR of Macedonia - L'ex-R. y. de Macédoine			
	2013 (C)				2010 (C)			
	Male — Masculin		Female — Féminin		Male — Masculin		Female — Féminin	
	Number Nombre	Rate Taux	Number Nombre	Rate Taux	Number Nombre	Rate Taux	Number Nombre	Rate Taux
Diseases of arteries, arterioles and capillaries — Maladies des artères, artérioles et capillaires	548	13.8	472	11.6	155	15.1	225	21.9
Diseases of the respiratory system — Maladies de l'appareil respiratoire								
Total	2 167	54.6	1 949	47.9	401	38.9	310	30.2
Influenza — Grippe	20	◆0.5	39	1.0	5	◆0.5	3	◆0.3
Pneumonia — Pneumopathies	554	14.0	709	17.4	50	4.9	43	4.2
Chronic lower respiratory diseases — Maladies chroniques des voies respiratoires inférieures	1 186	29.9	891	21.9	235	22.8	152	14.8
Diseases of the digestive system — Maladies de l'appareil digestif								
Total	1 243	31.3	1 269	31.2	240	23.3	130	12.7
Gastric and duodenal ulcer — Ulcère de l'estomac et du duodénum	51	1.3	74	1.8	26	◆2.5	14	◆1.4
Diseases of the liver — Maladies du foie	469	11.8	217	5.3	136	13.2	46	4.5
Diseases of the musculoskeletal system and connective tissue — Maladies du système ostéo-articularie, des muscles et du tissu conjonctif	188	4.7	426	10.5	1	◆0.1	5	◆0.5
Diseases of the genitourinary system — Maladies de l'appareil génito-urinaire								
Total	451	11.4	518	12.7	148	14.4	114	11.1
Disorders of kidney and ureter — Affections du rein et de l'uretère	274	6.9	341	8.4	146	14.2	114	11.1
Hyperplasia of prostate — Hyperplasie de la prostate	33	...	..	..	2	◆0.7	..	..
Pregnancy, childbirth and the puerperium — Grossesse, accouchement et puerpéralité								
Total	..	..	2	◆2.4	..	..	2	◆8.2
Pregnancy with abortive outcome — Grossesse se terminant par un avortement	..	..	-	-	..	..	-	-
Other direct obstetric causes — Autres décès maternels directs	..	..	1	◆1.2	..	..	2	◆8.2
Indirect obstetric causes — Décès maternels indirects	..	..	1	◆1.2	..	..	-	-
Certain conditions originating in the perinatal period — Certaines affections dont l'origine se situe dans la période périnatale	95	223.0	69	171.9	70	554.2	55	471.5
Congenital malformations, deformations and chromosomal abnormalities — Malformations congénitales et anomalies chromosomiques	163	382.7	132	328.9	17	◆134.6	15	◆128.6
Symptoms, signs and abnormal clinical and laboratory findings, not elsewhere classified — Symptômes, signes et résultats anormaux d'examens cliniques et de laboratoire, non classés ailleurs	1 265	31.9	1 283	31.5	672	65.3	578	56.4
All other diseases — Toutes autres maladies	30	◆0.8	84	2.1	1	◆0.1	-	-
External causes — Causes externes								
Total	2 177	54.9	1 642	40.3	422	41.0	166	16.2
Accidents								
Total	1 312	33.1	1 285	31.6	302	29.3	117	11.4
Transport accidents — Accidents de transport	231	5.8	89	2.2	105	10.2	31	3.0
Falls — Chutes	746	18.8	1 020	25.1	34	3.3	35	3.4
Accidental drowning and submersion — Noyade et submersion accidentelles	42	1.1	14	◆0.3	17	◆1.7	7	◆0.7
Exposure to smoke, fire and flames — Exposition à la fumée, au feu et aux flammes	14	◆0.4	12	◆0.3	5	◆0.5	4	◆0.4
Accidental poisoning by and exposure to noxious substances — Intoxication accidentelle par des substances nocives et exposition à ces substances	98	2.5	41	1.0	15	◆1.5	6	◆0.6
Intentional self-harm — Lésions auto-infligées	786	19.8	284	7.0	87	8.4	35	3.4
Assault — Agresssions	18	◆0.5	27	◆0.7	31	3.0	13	◆1.3
All other external causes — Toutes autres causes externes	61	1.5	46	1.1	2	◆0.2	1	◆0.1

Ukraine

Cause of death — Cause de décès	2012 (+C)				2014 (+C)			
	Male — Masculin		Female — Féminin		Male — Masculin		Female — Féminin	
	Number Nombre	Rate Taux	Number Nombre	Rate Taux	Number Nombre	Rate Taux	Number Nombre	Rate Taux
TOTAL	325 584	1 544.3	337 555	1 374.9	310 671	...	321 625	...
Certain infectious and parasitic diseases — Certaines maladies infectieuses et parasitaires								
Total	10 226	48.5	3 696	15.1	8 005	...	2 969	...
Intestinal infectious diseases — Maladies infectieuses intestinales	22	♦0.1	20	♦0.1	12	...	18	...
Tuberculosis — Tuberculose	5 584	26.5	1 278	5.2	4 326	...	914	...
Tetanus — Tétanos	3	♦0.0	4	♦0.0	3	...	2	...
Diphtheria — Diphtérie	-	-	-	-	1	...	1	...
Whooping cough — Coqueluche	3	♦0.0	-	-	1	...	-	...
Meningococcal infection — Infection à méningocoques	31	0.1	27	♦0.1	28	...	32	...
Septicaemia — Septicémie	275	1.3	210	0.9	207	...	179	...
Acute poliomyelitis — Poliomyélite aiguë	-	-	-	-	-	...	-	...
Measles — Rougeole	2	♦0.0	1	♦0.0	-	...	-	...
Viral hepatitis — Hépatite virale	101	0.5	75	0.3	149	...	103	...
Human immunodeficiency virus [HIV] disease — Maladies dues au virus de l'immunodéficience humaine (VIH)	3 835	18.2	1 851	7.5	2 880	...	1 519	...
Malaria — Paludisme	2	♦0.0	-	-	3	...	-	...
Neoplasms — Tumeurs	51 241	243.0	41 655	169.7	46 545	...	37 349	...
Malignant neoplasms — Tumeurs malignes								
Total	50 796	240.9	41 168	167.7	46 194	...	36 887	...
Malignant neoplasm of lip, oral cavity and pharynx — Tumeur maligne de la lèvre, de la cavité buccale et du pharynx	3 267	15.5	479	2.0	3 179	...	456	...
Malignant neoplasm of oesophagus — Tumeur maligne de l'oesophage	1 479	7.0	184	0.7	1 381	...	165	...
Malignant neoplasm of stomach — Tumeur maligne de l'estomac	5 520	26.2	3 632	14.8	4 860	...	3 051	...
Malignant neoplasm of colon, rectosigmoid junction, rectum, anus and anal canal — Tumeur maligne du côlon, de la jonction recto-sigmoïdienne, du rectum, de l'anus et du canal anal	6 296	29.9	6 324	25.8	5 771	...	5 733	...
Malignant neoplasm of liver and intrahepatic bile ducts — Tumeur maligne du foie et des voies bilaires intrahépatiques	1 221	5.8	913	3.7	992	...	706	...
Malignant neoplasm of pancreas — Tumeur maligne du pancréas	2 640	12.5	2 163	8.8	2 486	...	2 072	...
Malignant neoplasm of trachea, bronchus and lung — Tumeur maligne de la trachée, des bronches et du poumon	12 508	59.3	2 541	10.3	10 959	...	2 284	...
Malignant neoplasm of female breast — Tumeur maligne du sein chez la femme	..	..	8 076	37.9	..	..	7 275	...
Malignant neoplasm of cervix uteri — Tumeur maligne du col de l'utérus	..	..	2 187	10.3	..	..	2 102	...
Malignant neoplasm of prostate — Tumeur maligne de la prostate	3 787	59.8	..	..	3 715	...	..	..
Malignant neoplasm of lymphoid, haematopoietic and related tissue — Tumeurs malignes primitives ou présumées primitives des tissus lymphoïde, hématopoïétique et apparentés	...	...	...	...	...	...	...	...
Disorders of the blood and blood-forming organs and certain disorders involving the immune mechanism — Maladies du sang et des organes hématopoïétiques et certains troubles du système immunitaire								
Total	138	0.7	158	0.6	117	...	124	...
Anaemias — Anémies	52	0.2	79	0.3	47	...	59	...
Endocrine, nutritional and metabolic diseases — Maladies endocriniennes, nutritionnelles et métaboliques								
Total	1 045	5.0	1 484	6.0	923	...	1 299	...
Diabetes mellitus — Diabète sucré	893	4.2	1 312	5.3	780	...	1 168	...
Malnutrition — Malnutrition	19	♦0.1	11	♦0.0	22	...	15	...
Mental and behavioural disorders — Troubles mentaux et du comportement	1 092	5.2	473	1.9	1 082	...	527	...
Diseases of the nervous system — Maladies du système nerveux	3 624	17.2	2 223	9.1	3 528	...	2 354	...
Diseases of the circulatory system — Maladies de l'appareil circulatoire								
Total	186 869	886.4	249 576	1 016.6	183 219	...	242 388	...
Acute rheumatic fever and chronic rheumatic heart diseases — Rhumatisme articularie aigu et cardiopathies rhumatismales chroniques	464	2.2	692	2.8	345	...	494	...
Hypertensive diseases — Maladies hypertensives	442	2.1	283	1.2	356	...	222	...
Ischaemic heart disease — Cardiopathie ischémique	128 376	608.9	169 056	688.6	126 762	...	164 683	...
Cerebrovascular disease — Maladie cérébrovasculaire	37 211	176.5	55 721	227.0	35 465	...	52 425	...

Ukraine

Cause of death — Cause de décès	2012 (+C)				2014 (+C)			
	Male — Masculin		Female — Féminin		Male — Masculin		Female — Féminin	
	Number Nombre	Rate Taux	Number Nombre	Rate Taux	Number Nombre	Rate Taux	Number Nombre	Rate Taux
Diseases of arteries, arterioles and capillaries — Maladies des artères, artérioles et capillaires	...	...	...	...	...	...	...	...
Diseases of the respiratory system — Maladies de l'appareil respiratoire								
Total	12 197	57.9	4 912	20.0	10 619	...	4 191	...
Influenza — Grippe	2	♦0.0	-	-	7	...	7	...
Pneumonia — Pneumopathies	3 999	19.0	1 381	5.6	3 713	...	1 270	...
Chronic lower respiratory diseases — Maladies chroniques des voies respiratoires inférieures	6 813	32.3	3 098	12.6	5 816	...	2 532	...
Diseases of the digestive system — Maladies de l'appareil digestif								
Total	17 117	81.2	10 602	43.2	15 759	...	9 466	...
Gastric and duodenal ulcer — Ulcère de l'estomac et du duodénum	1 312	6.2	825	3.4	1 086	...	616	...
Diseases of the liver — Maladies du foie	11 754	55.8	6 352	25.9	11 021	...	5 766	...
Diseases of the musculoskeletal system and connective tissue — Maladies du système ostéo-articularie, des muscles et du tissu conjonctif	230	1.1	355	1.4	201	...	318	...
Diseases of the genitourinary system — Maladies de l'appareil génito-urinaire								
Total	1 598	7.6	1 569	6.4	1 414	...	1 281	...
Disorders of kidney and ureter — Affections du rein et de l'uretère	...	...	...	...	...	...	...	...
Hyperplasia of prostate — Hyperplasie de la prostate	...	...	...	...	...	...	...	..
Pregnancy, childbirth and the puerperium — Grossesse, accouchement et puerpéralité								
Total	..	..	66	12.7	..	..	69	14.8
Pregnancy with abortive outcome — Grossesse se terminant par un avortement	..	..	3	♦0.6	..	..	3	♦0.6
Other direct obstetric causes — Autres décès maternels directs	..	..	30	♦5.8	..	..	41	8.8
Indirect obstetric causes — Décès maternels indirects	..	..	30	♦5.8	..	..	24	♦5.2
Certain conditions originating in the perinatal period — Certaines affections dont l'origine se situe dans la période périnatale	1 320	491.2	991	393.3	1 159	482.8	799	353.8
Congenital malformations, deformations and chromosomal abnormalities — Malformations congénitales et anomalies chromosomiques	980	364.7	863	342.5	800	333.3	713	315.7
Symptoms, signs and abnormal clinical and laboratory findings, not elsewhere classified — Symptômes, signes et résultats anormaux d'examens cliniques et de laboratoire, non classés ailleurs	5 148	24.4	9 343	38.1	5 236	...	9 163	...
All other diseases — Toutes autres maladies	320	1.5	315	1.3	253	...	291	...
External causes — Causes externes								
Total	32 439	153.9	9 274	37.8	31 811	...	8 324	...
Accidents								
Total	...	...	...	...	...	...	...	...
Transport accidents — Accidents de transport	4 456	21.1	1 449	5.9	3 947	...	1 217	...
Falls — Chutes	1 864	8.8	642	2.6	1 646	...	505	...
Accidental drowning and submersion — Noyade et submersion accidentelles	2 303	10.9	410	1.7	1 921	...	322	...
Exposure to smoke, fire and flames — Exposition à la fumée, au feu et aux flammes	1 132	5.4	549	2.2	1 004	...	429	...
Accidental poisoning by and exposure to noxious substances — Intoxication accidentelle par des substances nocives et exposition à ces substances	5 283	25.1	1 407	5.7	4 173	...	1 070	...
Intentional self-harm — Lésions auto-infligées	7 363	34.9	1 697	6.9	6 414	...	1 556	...
Assault — Agresssions	1 641	7.8	695	2.8	2 124	...	721	...
All other external causes — Toutes autres causes externes	...	...	...	...	...	...	...	...

20. Death and death rates by cause and sex: 2010 - 2014
Décès et taux de mortalité par cause et sexe : 2010 - 2014 (continued - suite)

United Kingdom of Great Britain and Northern Ireland - Royaume-Uni de Grande-Bretagne et d'Irlande du Nord

Cause of death — Cause de décès	2012 (+C)				2013 (+C)			
	Male — Masculin		Female — Féminin		Male — Masculin		Female — Féminin	
	Number Nombre	Rate Taux	Number Nombre	Rate Taux	Number Nombre	Rate Taux	Number Nombre	Rate Taux
TOTAL	273 347	875.9	295 677	915.7	279 171	888.4	297 287	915.5
Certain infectious and parasitic diseases — Certaines maladies infectieuses et parasitaires								
Total	2 636	8.4	3 329	10.3	2 825	9.0	3 440	10.6
Intestinal infectious diseases — Maladies infectieuses intestinales	631	2.0	1 183	3.7	670	2.1	1 118	3.4
Tuberculosis — Tuberculose	183	0.6	100	0.3	183	0.6	121	0.4
Tetanus — Tétanos	-	-	1	♦0.0	-	-	-	-
Diphtheria — Diphtérie	-	-	-	-	-	-	-	-
Whooping cough — Coqueluche	2	♦0.0	5	♦0.0	2	♦0.0	1	♦0.0
Meningococcal infection — Infection à méningocoques	23	♦0.1	18	♦0.1	25	♦0.1	28	♦0.1
Septicaemia — Septicémie	1 009	3.2	1 449	4.5	1 111	3.5	1 566	4.8
Acute poliomyelitis — Poliomyélite aiguë	-	-	-	-	-	-	-	-
Measles — Rougeole	-	-	1	♦0.0	1	♦0.0	1	♦0.0
Viral hepatitis — Hépatite virale	161	0.5	100	0.3	175	0.6	90	0.3
Human immunodeficiency virus [HIV] disease — Maladies dues au virus de l'immunodéficience humaine (VIH)	167	0.5	60	0.2	171	0.5	53	0.2
Malaria — Paludisme	2	♦0.0	-	-	5	♦0.0	2	♦0.0
Neoplasms — Tumeurs	87 056	279.0	78 753	243.9	87 511	278.5	78 331	241.2
Malignant neoplasms — Tumeurs malignes								
Total	85 209	273.1	76 881	238.1	85 563	272.3	76 423	235.3
Malignant neoplasm of lip, oral cavity and pharynx — Tumeur maligne de la lèvre, de la cavité buccale et du pharynx	1 662	5.3	793	2.5	1 762	5.6	885	2.7
Malignant neoplasm of oesophagus — Tumeur maligne de l'oesophage	5 245	16.8	2 464	7.6	5 277	16.8	2 475	7.6
Malignant neoplasm of stomach — Tumeur maligne de l'estomac	3 022	9.7	1 740	5.4	2 950	9.4	1 754	5.4
Malignant neoplasm of colon, rectosigmoid junction, rectum, anus and anal canal — Tumeur maligne du côlon, de la jonction recto-sigmoïdienne, du rectum, de l'anus et du canal anal	8 916	28.6	7 593	23.5	8 781	27.9	7 501	23.1
Malignant neoplasm of liver and intrahepatic bile ducts — Tumeur maligne du foie et des voies bilaires intrahépatiques	2 690	8.6	1 847	5.7	2 933	9.3	1 912	5.9
Malignant neoplasm of pancreas — Tumeur maligne du pancréas	4 279	13.7	4 389	13.6	4 232	13.5	4 290	13.2
Malignant neoplasm of trachea, bronchus and lung — Tumeur maligne de la trachée, des bronches et du poumon	19 327	61.9	16 076	49.8	19 511	62.1	16 011	49.3
Malignant neoplasm of female breast — Tumeur maligne du sein chez la femme	..	..	11 662	...	..	..	11 476	...
Malignant neoplasm of cervix uteri — Tumeur maligne du col de l'utérus	..	..	920	...	..	..	886	...
Malignant neoplasm of prostate — Tumeur maligne de la prostate	10 845	...	..	..	10 873	...	..	..
Malignant neoplasm of lymphoid, haematopoietic and related tissue — Tumeurs malignes primitives ou présumées primitives des tissus lymphoïde, hématopoïétique et apparentés	7 038	22.6	5 696	17.6	7 061	22.5	5 557	17.1
Disorders of the blood and blood-forming organs and certain disorders involving the immune mechanism — Maladies du sang et des organes hématopoïétiques et certains troubles du système immunitaire								
Total	483	1.5	613	1.9	512	1.6	590	1.8
Anaemias — Anémies	158	0.5	298	0.9	173	0.6	248	0.8
Endocrine, nutritional and metabolic diseases — Maladies endocriniennes, nutritionnelles et métaboliques								
Total	3 779	12.1	4 174	12.9	3 767	12.0	4 207	13.0
Diabetes mellitus — Diabète sucré	2 836	9.1	3 022	9.4	2 793	8.9	3 064	9.4
Malnutrition — Malnutrition	35	0.1	53	0.2	34	0.1	52	0.2
Mental and behavioural disorders — Troubles mentaux et du comportement	13 358	42.8	27 347	84.7	14 335	45.6	28 872	88.9
Diseases of the nervous system — Maladies du système nerveux	10 754	34.5	13 591	42.1	11 510	36.6	14 266	43.9
Diseases of the circulatory system — Maladies de l'appareil circulatoire								
Total	79 049	253.3	82 215	254.6	79 935	254.4	79 860	245.9
Acute rheumatic fever and chronic rheumatic heart diseases — Rhumatisme articularie aigu et cardiopathies rhumatismales chroniques	382	1.2	855	2.6	320	1.0	728	2.2
Hypertensive diseases — Maladies hypertensives	2 275	7.3	3 268	10.1	2 368	7.5	3 239	10.0
Ischaemic heart disease — Cardiopathie ischémique	42 818	137.2	30 865	95.6	43 056	137.0	29 968	92.3
Cerebrovascular disease — Maladie cérébrovasculaire	16 197	51.9	25 204	78.1	16 260	51.7	24 027	74.0

20. Death and death rates by cause and sex: 2010 - 2014
Décès et taux de mortalité par cause et sexe : 2010 - 2014 (continued - suite)

United Kingdom of Great Britain and Northern Ireland - Royaume-Uni de Grande-Bretagne et d'Irlande du Nord

Cause of death — Cause de décès	2012 (+C)				2013 (+C)			
	Male — Masculin		Female — Féminin		Male — Masculin		Female — Féminin	
	Number Nombre	Rate Taux	Number Nombre	Rate Taux	Number Nombre	Rate Taux	Number Nombre	Rate Taux
Diseases of arteries, arterioles and capillaries — Maladies des artères, artérioles et capillaires	5 363	17.2	4 788	14.8	5 217	16.6	4 491	13.8
Diseases of the respiratory system — Maladies de l'appareil respiratoire								
Total	37 686	120.8	42 232	130.8	39 372	125.3	44 014	135.5
Influenza — Grippe	42	0.1	54	0.2	86	0.3	119	0.4
Pneumonia — Pneumopathies	12 253	39.3	16 721	51.8	12 501	39.8	16 847	51.9
Chronic lower respiratory diseases — Maladies chroniques des voies respiratoires inférieures	16 260	52.1	16 324	50.6	16 953	54.0	17 097	52.7
Diseases of the digestive system — Maladies de l'appareil digestif								
Total	13 481	43.2	14 592	45.2	13 406	42.7	14 501	44.7
Gastric and duodenal ulcer — Ulcère de l'estomac et du duodénum	1 200	3.8	1 105	3.4	1 119	3.6	1 046	3.2
Diseases of the liver — Maladies du foie..........	5 336	17.1	3 326	10.3	5 427	17.3	3 343	10.3
Diseases of the musculoskeletal system and connective tissue — Maladies du système ostéo-articularie, des muscles et du tissu conjonctif	1 539	4.9	3 220	10.0	1 522	4.8	3 168	9.8
Diseases of the genitourinary system — Maladies de l'appareil génito-urinaire								
Total	4 649	14.9	6 609	20.5	4 690	14.9	6 374	19.6
Disorders of kidney and ureter — Affections du rein et de l'uretère	2 303	7.4	2 904	9.0	2 364	7.5	2 941	9.1
Hyperplasia of prostate — Hyperplasie de la prostate..........	202	...	..	..	159	...	..	..
Pregnancy, childbirth and the puerperium — Grossesse, accouchement et puerpéralité								
Total	..	..	51	6.3	..	..	50	6.4
Pregnancy with abortive outcome — Grossesse se terminant par un avortement	..	..	-	-	..	..	3	♦0.4
Other direct obstetric causes — Autres décès maternels directs	..	..	35	4.3	..	..	30	♦3.9
Indirect obstetric causes — Décès maternels indirects	..	..	15	♦1.8	..	..	17	♦2.2
Certain conditions originating in the perinatal period — Certaines affections dont l'origine se situe dans la période périnatale	1 014	243.1	760	192.0	950	237.9	693	182.8
Congenital malformations, deformations and chromosomal abnormalities — Malformations congénitales et anomalies chromosomiques	1 027	246.2	929	234.6	970	242.9	854	225.3
Symptoms, signs and abnormal clinical and laboratory findings, not elsewhere classified — Symptômes, signes et résultats anormaux d'examens cliniques et de laboratoire, non classés ailleurs	3 028	9.7	8 397	26.0	3 089	9.8	8 629	26.6
All other diseases — Toutes autres maladies..........	652	2.1	1 237	3.8	699	2.2	1 252	3.9
External causes — Causes externes								
Total	13 156	42.2	7 628	23.6	14 078	44.8	8 186	25.2
Accidents								
Total	8 013	25.7	5 835	18.1	8 498	27.0	6 267	19.3
Transport accidents — Accidents de transport	1 417	4.5	448	1.4	1 341	4.3	451	1.4
Falls — Chutes	2 332	7.5	2 343	7.3	2 551	8.1	2 596	8.0
Accidental drowning and submersion — Noyade et submersion accidentelles..........	196	0.6	46	0.1	199	0.6	63	0.2
Exposure to smoke, fire and flames — Exposition à la fumée, au feu et aux flammes..........	117	0.4	120	0.4	159	0.5	137	0.4
Accidental poisoning by and exposure to noxious substances — Intoxication accidentelle par des substances nocives et exposition à ces substances	1 815	5.8	734	2.3	2 061	6.6	817	2.5
Intentional self-harm — Lésions auto-infligées..........	3 511	11.3	932	2.9	3 828	12.2	992	3.1
Assault — Agresssions..........	99	0.3	48	0.1	111	0.4	34	0.1
All other external causes — Toutes autres causes externes	1 533	4.9	813	2.5	1 641	5.2	893	2.7

20. Death and death rates by cause and sex: 2010 - 2014
Décès et taux de mortalité par cause et sexe : 2010 - 2014 (continued - suite)

Australia - Australie

Cause of death — Cause de décès	2013 (C)				2014 (C)			
	Male — Masculin		Female — Féminin		Male — Masculin		Female — Féminin	
	Number Nombre	Rate Taux	Number Nombre	Rate Taux	Number Nombre	Rate Taux	Number Nombre	Rate Taux
TOTAL	75 782	658.3	71 896	619.0	78 341	670.0	75 239	637.7
Certain infectious and parasitic diseases — Certaines maladies infectieuses et parasitaires								
Total	1 322	11.5	1 359	11.7	1 411	12.1	1 319	11.2
Intestinal infectious diseases — Maladies infectieuses intestinales	97	0.8	180	1.5	116	1.0	158	1.3
Tuberculosis — Tuberculose	33	0.3	17	♦0.1	29	♦0.2	14	♦0.1
Tetanus — Tétanos..	-	-	1	♦0.0	-	-	-	-
Diphtheria — Diphtérie...	1	♦0.0	-	-	-	-	-	-
Whooping cough — Coqueluche	-	-	2	♦0.0	2	♦0.0	2	♦0.0
Meningococcal infection — Infection à méningocoques	1	♦0.0	4	♦0.0	2	♦0.0	5	♦0.0
Septicaemia — Septicémie	744	6.5	842	7.2	785	6.7	867	7.3
Acute poliomyelitis — Poliomyélite aiguë	-	-	-	-	-	-	-	-
Measles — Rougeole..	1	♦0.0	-	-	-	-	-	-
Viral hepatitis — Hépatite virale	190	1.7	92	0.8	202	1.7	86	0.7
Human immunodeficiency virus [HIV] disease — Maladies dues au virus de l'immunodéficience humaine (VIH).................	55	0.5	7	♦0.1	54	0.5	2	♦0.0
Malaria — Paludisme	-	-	-	-	-	-	-	-
Neoplasms — Tumeurs	25 236	219.2	19 437	167.4	24 994	213.8	19 740	167.3
Malignant neoplasms — Tumeurs malignes								
Total	24 611	213.8	18 888	162.6	24 356	208.3	19 193	162.7
Malignant neoplasm of lip, oral cavity and pharynx — Tumeur maligne de la lèvre, de la cavité buccale et du pharynx	581	5.0	237	2.0	552	4.7	229	1.9
Malignant neoplasm of oesophagus — Tumeur maligne de l'oesophage	882	7.7	363	3.1	869	7.4	329	2.8
Malignant neoplasm of stomach — Tumeur maligne de l'estomac	796	6.9	430	3.7	705	6.0	432	3.7
Malignant neoplasm of colon, rectosigmoid junction, rectum, anus and anal canal — Tumeur maligne du côlon, de la jonction recto-sigmoïdienne, du rectum, de l'anus et du canal anal	2 332	20.3	1 902	16.4	2 279	19.5	1 890	16.0
Malignant neoplasm of liver and intrahepatic bile ducts — Tumeur maligne du foie et des voies bilaires intrahépatiques	1 040	9.0	534	4.6	1 131	9.7	601	5.1
Malignant neoplasm of pancreas — Tumeur maligne du pancréas...................	1 335	11.6	1 223	10.5	1 292	11.0	1 255	10.6
Malignant neoplasm of trachea, bronchus and lung — Tumeur maligne de la trachée, des bronches et du poumon	4 994	43.4	3 221	27.7	4 947	42.3	3 304	28.0
Malignant neoplasm of female breast — Tumeur maligne du sein chez la femme	..	..	2 862	30.2	..	..	2 814	29.2
Malignant neoplasm of cervix uteri — Tumeur maligne du col de l'utérus.........	..	..	224	2.4	..	..	223	2.3
Malignant neoplasm of prostate — Tumeur maligne de la prostate	3 112	86.1	..	..	3 102	83.7	..	..
Malignant neoplasm of lymphoid, haematopoietic and related tissue — Tumeurs malignes primitives ou présumées primitives des tissus lymphoïde, hématopoïétique et apparentés...	2 355	20.5	1 738	15.0	2 413	20.6	1 862	15.8
Disorders of the blood and blood-forming organs and certain disorders involving the immune mechanism — Maladies du sang et des organes hématopoïétiques et certains troubles du système immunitaire								
Total	219	1.9	282	2.4	249	2.1	286	2.4
Anaemias — Anémies	101	0.9	166	1.4	105	0.9	149	1.3
Endocrine, nutritional and metabolic diseases — Maladies endocriniennes, nutritionnelles et métaboliques								
Total	3 094	26.9	3 011	25.9	3 108	26.6	3 096	26.2
Diabetes mellitus — Diabète sucré...	2 301	20.0	2 031	17.5	2 213	18.9	2 135	18.1
Malnutrition — Malnutrition	23	♦0.2	47	0.4	52	0.4	44	0.4
Mental and behavioural disorders — Troubles mentaux et du comportement	2 954	25.7	5 244	45.2	3 269	28.0	5 734	48.6
Diseases of the nervous system — Maladies du système nerveux.................	3 374	29.3	4 146	35.7	3 789	32.4	4 321	36.6
Diseases of the circulatory system — Maladies de l'appareil circulatoire								
Total	21 113	183.4	22 494	193.7	21 633	185.0	23 420	198.5
Acute rheumatic fever and chronic rheumatic heart diseases — Rhumatisme articularie aigu et cardiopathies rhumatismales chroniques	128	1.1	251	2.2	119	1.0	257	2.2
Hypertensive diseases — Maladies hypertensives.................................	764	6.6	1 387	11.9	797	6.8	1 428	12.1
Ischaemic heart disease — Cardiopathie ischémique	11 018	95.7	8 751	75.3	11 082	94.8	9 091	77.1
Cerebrovascular disease — Maladie cérébrovasculaire...........................	4 178	36.3	6 372	54.9	4 279	36.6	6 486	55.0

20. Death and death rates by cause and sex: 2010 - 2014
Décès et taux de mortalité par cause et sexe : 2010 - 2014 (continued - suite)

Australia - Australie

Cause of death — Cause de décès	2013 (C)				2014 (C)			
	Male — Masculin		Female — Féminin		Male — Masculin		Female — Féminin	
	Number Nombre	Rate Taux	Number Nombre	Rate Taux	Number Nombre	Rate Taux	Number Nombre	Rate Taux
Diseases of arteries, arterioles and capillaries — Maladies des artères, artérioles et capillaires	976	8.5	846	7.3	973	8.3	866	7.3
Diseases of the respiratory system — Maladies de l'appareil respiratoire								
Total	6 556	57.0	5 914	50.9	7 173	61.3	6 605	56.0
Influenza — Grippe...............................	35	0.3	36	0.3	116	1.0	126	1.1
Pneumonia — Pneumopathies	1 094	9.5	1 323	11.4	1 178	10.1	1 436	12.2
Chronic lower respiratory diseases — Maladies chroniques des voies respiratoires inférieures	3 801	33.0	3 348	28.8	4 164	35.6	3 646	30.9
Diseases of the digestive system — Maladies de l'appareil digestif								
Total	2 765	24.0	2 653	22.8	2 812	24.0	2 667	22.6
Gastric and duodenal ulcer — Ulcère de l'estomac et du duodénum.................	140	1.2	111	1.0	130	1.1	132	1.1
Diseases of the liver — Maladies du foie........	1 182	10.3	590	5.1	1 229	10.5	525	4.4
Diseases of the musculoskeletal system and connective tissue — Maladies du système ostéo-articularie, des muscles et du tissu conjonctif	377	3.3	806	6.9	420	3.6	815	6.9
Diseases of the genitourinary system — Maladies de l'appareil génito-urinaire								
Total	1 404	12.2	1 704	14.7	1 427	12.2	1 815	15.4
Disorders of kidney and ureter — Affections du rein et de l'uretère	1 074	9.3	1 191	10.3	1 062	9.1	1 256	10.6
Hyperplasia of prostate — Hyperplasie de la prostate......................................	61	1.7	..	..	58	1.6	..	..
Pregnancy, childbirth and the puerperium — Grossesse, accouchement et puerpéralité								
Total	..	..	6	♦1.9	..	..	12	♦4.0
Pregnancy with abortive outcome — Grossesse se terminant par un avortement	..	..	-	-	..	..	1	♦0.3
Other direct obstetric causes — Autres décès maternels directs	..	..	6	♦1.9	..	..	10	♦3.3
Indirect obstetric causes — Décès maternels indirects	..	..	-	-	..	..	1	♦0.3
Certain conditions originating in the perinatal period — Certaines affections dont l'origine se situe dans la période périnatale	295	185.9	264	176.8	286	186.2	257	175.9
Congenital malformations, deformations and chromosomal abnormalities — Malformations congénitales et anomalies chromosomiques	320	201.6	301	201.5	313	203.8	301	206.0
Symptoms, signs and abnormal clinical and laboratory findings, not elsewhere classified — Symptômes, signes et résultats anormaux d'examens cliniques et de laboratoire, non classés ailleurs	699	6.1	718	6.2	850	7.3	892	7.6
All other diseases — Toutes autres maladies..............	197	1.7	251	2.2	217	1.9	287	2.4
External causes — Causes externes								
Total	5 857	50.9	3 306	28.5	6 390	54.7	3 672	31.1
Accidents								
Total	3 414	29.7	2 368	20.4	3 688	31.5	2 644	22.4
Transport accidents — Accidents de transport..	1 064	9.2	377	3.2	1 007	8.6	373	3.2
Falls — Chutes	913	7.9	1 008	8.7	1 087	9.3	1 214	10.3
Accidental drowning and submersion — Noyade et submersion accidentelles......................................	160	1.4	52	0.4	148	1.3	38	0.3
Exposure to smoke, fire and flames — Exposition à la fumée, au feu et aux flammes..	32	0.3	24	♦0.2	37	0.3	22	♦0.2
Accidental poisoning by and exposure to noxious substances — Intoxication accidentelle par des substances nocives et exposition à ces substances	715	6.2	347	3.0	813	7.0	411	3.5
Intentional self-harm — Lésions auto-infligées........	1 919	16.7	649	5.6	2 157	18.4	704	6.0
Assault — Agresssions	145	1.3	82	0.7	147	1.3	88	0.7
All other external causes — Toutes autres causes externes	379	3.3	207	1.8	398	3.4	236	2.0

20. Death and death rates by cause and sex: 2010 - 2014
Décès et taux de mortalité par cause et sexe : 2010 - 2014 (continued - suite)

Cause of death — Cause de décès	Fiji - Fidji					New Zealand - Nouvelle-Zélande
	2011 (+C)		2012 (+C)			2011 (+C)
	Male — Masculin	Female — Féminin	Male — Masculin	Female — Féminin		Male — Masculin
	Number Nombre	Number Nombre	Number Nombre	Number Nombre	Rate Taux	Number Nombre
TOTAL	3 663	3 000	3 757	3 009	...	14 942
Certain infectious and parasitic diseases — Certaines maladies infectieuses et parasitaires						
Total	192	163	213	150	...	135
Intestinal infectious diseases — Maladies infectieuses intestinales	60	46	73	43	...	29
Tuberculosis — Tuberculose	20	11	22	13	...	5
Tetanus — Tétanos	-	-	-	-	...	-
Diphtheria — Diphtérie	-	-	-	-	...	-
Whooping cough — Coqueluche	-	-	-	-	...	-
Meningococcal infection — Infection à méningocoques	1	-	-	-	...	7
Septicaemia — Septicémie	70	76	65	63	...	30
Acute poliomyelitis — Poliomyélite aiguë	-	-	-	-	...	-
Measles — Rougeole	-	-	-	-	...	-
Viral hepatitis — Hépatite virale	8	4	4	4	...	26
Human immunodeficiency virus [HIV] disease — Maladies dues au virus de l'immunodéficience humaine (VIH)	-	-	2	3	...	7
Malaria — Paludisme	-	-	-	-	...	-
Neoplasms — Tumeurs	300	427	275	425	...	4 678
Malignant neoplasms — Tumeurs malignes						
Total	272	402	247	399	...	4 597
Malignant neoplasm of lip, oral cavity and pharynx — Tumeur maligne de la lèvre, de la cavité buccale et du pharynx	10	3	7	5	...	81
Malignant neoplasm of oesophagus — Tumeur maligne de l'oesophage	11	7	6	3	...	174
Malignant neoplasm of stomach — Tumeur maligne de l'estomac	13	8	11	4	...	193
Malignant neoplasm of colon, rectosigmoid junction, rectum, anus and anal canal — Tumeur maligne du côlon, de la jonction recto-sigmoïdienne, du rectum, de l'anus et du canal anal	19	17	19	24	...	602
Malignant neoplasm of liver and intrahepatic bile ducts — Tumeur maligne du foie et des voies bilaires intrahépatiques	46	14	35	20	...	164
Malignant neoplasm of pancreas — Tumeur maligne du pancréas	9	8	8	2	...	219
Malignant neoplasm of trachea, bronchus and lung — Tumeur maligne de la trachée, des bronches et du poumon	30	19	21	12	...	909
Malignant neoplasm of female breast — Tumeur maligne du sein chez la femme	..	112	..	114	...	..
Malignant neoplasm of cervix uteri — Tumeur maligne du col de l'utérus	..	89	..	76	...	
Malignant neoplasm of prostate — Tumeur maligne de la prostate	34	..	41	..	..	585
Malignant neoplasm of lymphoid, haematopoietic and related tissue — Tumeurs malignes primitives ou présumées primitives des tissus lymphoïde, hématopoïétique et apparentés	30	16	42	28	...	479
Disorders of the blood and blood-forming organs and certain disorders involving the immune mechanism — Maladies du sang et des organes hématopoïétiques et certains troubles du système immunitaire						
Total	26	27	34	38	...	20
Anaemias — Anémies	19	16	22	26	...	5
Endocrine, nutritional and metabolic diseases — Maladies endocriniennes, nutritionnelles et métaboliques						
Total	786	801	778	785	...	548
Diabetes mellitus — Diabète sucré	707	756	712	740	...	438
Malnutrition — Malnutrition	10	5	5	6	...	6
Mental and behavioural disorders — Troubles mentaux et du comportement	1	-	1	2	...	376
Diseases of the nervous system — Maladies du système nerveux	53	27	60	39	...	611
Diseases of the circulatory system — Maladies de l'appareil circulatoire						
Total	1 377	949	1 405	859	...	4 988
Acute rheumatic fever and chronic rheumatic heart diseases — Rhumatisme articularie aigu et cardiopathies rhumatismales chroniques	21	22	25	24	...	32
Hypertensive diseases — Maladies hypertensives	456	435	480	408	...	154
Ischaemic heart disease — Cardiopathie ischémique	517	158	585	169	...	2 934
Cerebrovascular disease — Maladie cérébrovasculaire	81	68	76	76	...	1 011
Diseases of arteries, arterioles and capillaries — Maladies des artères, artérioles et capillaires	10	6	18	10	...	238

20. Death and death rates by cause and sex: 2010 - 2014
Décès et taux de mortalité par cause et sexe : 2010 - 2014 (continued - suite)

Cause of death — Cause de décès	Fiji - Fidji					New Zealand - Nouvelle-Zélande
	2011 (+C)		2012 (+C)			2011 (+C)
	Male — Masculin	Female — Féminin	Male — Masculin	Female — Féminin		Male — Masculin
	Number Nombre	Number Nombre	Number Nombre	Number Nombre	Rate Taux	Number Nombre
Diseases of the respiratory system — Maladies de l'appareil respiratoire						
Total	233	142	223	171	...	1 317
Influenza — Grippe	-	-	-	-	...	8
Pneumonia — Pneumopathies	81	58	56	50	...	228
Chronic lower respiratory diseases — Maladies chroniques des voies respiratoires inférieures	119	60	140	88	...	893
Diseases of the digestive system — Maladies de l'appareil digestif						
Total	95	51	105	52	...	427
Gastric and duodenal ulcer — Ulcère de l'estomac et du duodénum....................	11	2	16	5	...	44
Diseases of the liver — Maladies du foie....................	40	14	27	15	...	116
Diseases of the musculoskeletal system and connective tissue — Maladies du système ostéo-articularie, des muscles et du tissu conjonctif	17	29	26	40		84
Diseases of the genitourinary system — Maladies de l'appareil génito-urinaire						
Total	136	80	124	72	...	191
Disorders of kidney and ureter — Affections du rein et de l'uretère	107	72	103	58	...	143
Hyperplasia of prostate — Hyperplasie de la prostate........	17	..	13	..	..	15
Pregnancy, childbirth and the puerperium — Grossesse, accouchement et puerpéralité						
Total	..	4	..	8	♦39.6	..
Pregnancy with abortive outcome — Grossesse se terminant par un avortement....................	..	1	..	1	♦5.0	..
Other direct obstetric causes — Autres décès maternels directs	..	3	..	7	♦34.7	..
Indirect obstetric causes — Décès maternels indirects	..	-	..	-	-	..
Certain conditions originating in the perinatal period — Certaines affections dont l'origine se situe dans la période périnatale	78	51	61	66	...	84
Congenital malformations, deformations and chromosomal abnormalities — Malformations congénitales et anomalies chromosomiques	46	45	65	42	...	94
Symptoms, signs and abnormal clinical and laboratory findings, not elsewhere classified — Symptômes, signes et résultats anormaux d'examens cliniques et de laboratoire, non classés ailleurs	75	102	116	131	...	61
All other diseases — Toutes autres maladies........	23	14	27	18	...	47
External causes — Causes externes						
Total	225	88	244	111	...	1 281
Accidents						
Total	140	58	150	74	...	807
Transport accidents — Accidents de transport........	41	15	34	12	...	265
Falls — Chutes	12	2	8	2	...	231
Accidental drowning and submersion — Noyade et submersion accidentelles........	43	11	51	16	...	58
Exposure to smoke, fire and flames — Exposition à la fumée, au feu et aux flammes	12	14	15	14	...	7
Accidental poisoning by and exposure to noxious substances — Intoxication accidentelle par des substances nocives et exposition à ces substances	-	-	1	-	...	71
Intentional self-harm — Lésions auto-infligées........	30	8	24	10	...	377
Assault — Agresssions	6	2	10	2	...	35
All other external causes — Toutes autres causes externes	49	20	60	25	...	62

20. Death and death rates by cause and sex: 2010 - 2014
Décès et taux de mortalité par cause et sexe : 2010 - 2014 (continued - suite)

New Zealand - Nouvelle-Zélande

Cause of death — Cause de décès	2011 (+C)				2012 (+C)			
	Male — Masculin	Female — Féminin		Male — Masculin		Female — Féminin		
	Rate Taux	Number Nombre	Rate Taux	Number Nombre	Rate Taux	Number Nombre	Rate Taux	
TOTAL	697.1	15 348	685.1	15 148	702.9	15 129	671.5	
Certain infectious and parasitic diseases — Certaines maladies infectieuses et parasitaires								
Total	6.3	161	7.2	145	6.7	169	7.5	
Intestinal infectious diseases — Maladies infectieuses intestinales	1.4	53	2.4	37	1.7	59	2.6	
Tuberculosis — Tuberculose	0.2	1	◆0.0	4	◆0.2	-	-	
Tetanus — Tétanos..................................	-	-	-	-	-	-	-	
Diphtheria — Diphtérie..............................	-	-	-	-	-	-	-	
Whooping cough — Coqueluche.....................	-	-	-	-	-	2	◆0.1	
Meningococcal infection — Infection à méningocoques	0.3	6	◆0.3	-	-	4	◆0.2	
Septicaemia — Septicémie...........................	1.4	57	2.5	43	2.0	67	3.0	
Acute poliomyelitis — Poliomyélite aiguë	-	-	-	-	-	-	-	
Measles — Rougeole..................................	-	-	-	-	-	-	-	
Viral hepatitis — Hépatite virale.....................	1.2	11	◆0.5	31	1.4	8	◆0.4	
Human immunodeficiency virus [HIV] disease — Maladies dues au virus de l'immunodéficience humaine (VIH)............................	0.3	1	◆0.0	8	◆0.4	3	◆0.1	
Malaria — Paludisme..................................	-	-	-	-	-	-	-	
Neoplasms — Tumeurs	218.2	4 281	191.1	4 767	221.2	4 216	187.1	
Malignant neoplasms — Tumeurs malignes								
Total	214.5	4 189	187.0	4 671	216.8	4 120	182.9	
Malignant neoplasm of lip, oral cavity and pharynx — Tumeur maligne de la lèvre, de la cavité buccale et du pharynx	3.8	46	2.1	74	3.4	41	1.8	
Malignant neoplasm of oesophagus — Tumeur maligne de l'oesophage	8.1	88	3.9	161	7.5	66	2.9	
Malignant neoplasm of stomach — Tumeur maligne de l'estomac	9.0	103	4.6	178	8.3	123	5.5	
Malignant neoplasm of colon, rectosigmoid junction, rectum, anus and anal canal — Tumeur maligne du côlon, de la jonction recto-sigmoïdienne, du rectum, de l'anus et du canal anal	28.1	589	26.3	664	30.8	619	27.5	
Malignant neoplasm of liver and intrahepatic bile ducts — Tumeur maligne du foie et des voies bilaires intrahépatiques	7.7	76	3.4	154	7.1	82	3.6	
Malignant neoplasm of pancreas — Tumeur maligne du pancréas............................	10.2	210	9.4	229	10.6	234	10.4	
Malignant neoplasm of trachea, bronchus and lung — Tumeur maligne de la trachée, des bronches et du poumon	42.4	773	34.5	891	41.3	737	32.7	
Malignant neoplasm of female breast — Tumeur maligne du sein chez la femme	..	636	35.2	..	..	617	34.0	
Malignant neoplasm of cervix uteri — Tumeur maligne du col de l'utérus.........................	..	53	2.9	..	..	56	3.1	
Malignant neoplasm of prostate — Tumeur maligne de la prostate	89.1	..	..	607	90.2	..	..	
Malignant neoplasm of lymphoid, haematopoietic and related tissue — Tumeurs malignes primitives ou présumées primitives des tissus lymphoïde, hématopoïétique et apparentés	22.3	346	15.4	463	21.5	348	15.4	
Disorders of the blood and blood-forming organs and certain disorders involving the immune mechanism — Maladies du sang et des organes hématopoïétiques et certains troubles du système immunitaire								
Total	0.9	38	1.7	31	1.4	30	◆1.3	
Anaemias — Anémies	0.2	20	◆0.9	15	◆0.7	17	◆0.8	
Endocrine, nutritional and metabolic diseases — Maladies endocriniennes, nutritionnelles et métaboliques								
Total	25.6	515	23.0	551	25.6	512	22.7	
Diabetes mellitus — Diabète sucré..................	20.4	397	17.7	430	20.0	377	16.7	
Malnutrition — Malnutrition	0.3	5	◆0.2	5	◆0.2	5	◆0.2	
Mental and behavioural disorders — Troubles mentaux et du comportement................	17.5	774	34.5	447	20.7	859	38.1	
Diseases of the nervous system — Maladies du système nerveux................	28.5	682	30.4	617	28.6	699	31.0	
Diseases of the circulatory system — Maladies de l'appareil circulatoire								
Total	232.7	5 553	247.9	5 023	233.1	5 336	236.8	
Acute rheumatic fever and chronic rheumatic heart diseases — Rhumatisme articularie aigu et cardiopathies rhumatismales chroniques	1.5	64	2.9	46	2.1	69	3.1	
Hypertensive diseases — Maladies hypertensives.........................	7.2	221	9.9	144	6.7	200	8.9	
Ischaemic heart disease — Cardiopathie ischémique	136.9	2 599	116.0	2 953	137.0	2 387	105.9	
Cerebrovascular disease — Maladie cérébrovasculaire........................	47.2	1 653	73.8	968	44.9	1 643	72.9	

750

20. Death and death rates by cause and sex: 2010 - 2014
Décès et taux de mortalité par cause et sexe : 2010 - 2014 (continued - suite)

New Zealand - Nouvelle-Zélande

Cause of death — Cause de décès	2011 (+C)			2012 (+C)			
	Male — Masculin	Female — Féminin		Male — Masculin		Female — Féminin	
	Rate Taux	Number Nombre	Rate Taux	Number Nombre	Rate Taux	Number Nombre	Rate Taux
Diseases of arteries, arterioles and capillaries — Maladies des artères, artérioles et capillaires	11.1	230	10.3	230	10.7	220	9.8
Diseases of the respiratory system — Maladies de l'appareil respiratoire							
Total	61.4	1 406	62.8	1 369	63.5	1 452	64.4
Influenza — Grippe	0.4	8	♦0.4	16	♦0.7	23	♦1.0
Pneumonia — Pneumopathies	10.6	376	16.8	284	13.2	394	17.5
Chronic lower respiratory diseases — Maladies chroniques des voies respiratoires inférieures	41.7	875	39.1	851	39.5	865	38.4
Diseases of the digestive system — Maladies de l'appareil digestif							
Total	19.9	513	22.9	430	20.0	481	21.3
Gastric and duodenal ulcer — Ulcère de l'estomac et du duodénum	2.1	41	1.8	38	1.8	29	♦1.3
Diseases of the liver — Maladies du foie	5.4	58	2.6	104	4.8	68	3.0
Diseases of the musculoskeletal system and connective tissue — Maladies du système ostéo-articularie, des muscles et du tissu conjonctif	3.9	167	7.5	80	3.7	160	7.1
Diseases of the genitourinary system — Maladies de l'appareil génito-urinaire							
Total	8.9	244	10.9	215	10.0	217	9.6
Disorders of kidney and ureter — Affections du rein et de l'uretère	6.7	148	6.6	140	6.5	128	5.7
Hyperplasia of prostate — Hyperplasie de la prostate	2.3	..	..	25	♦3.7	..	..
Pregnancy, childbirth and the puerperium — Grossesse, accouchement et puerpéralité							
Total	..	7	♦11.4	..	..	7	♦11.4
Pregnancy with abortive outcome — Grossesse se terminant par un avortement	..	-	-	..	..	-	-
Other direct obstetric causes — Autres décès maternels directs	..	2	♦3.3	..	..	2	♦3.3
Indirect obstetric causes — Décès maternels indirects	..	5	♦8.1	..	..	5	♦8.2
Certain conditions originating in the perinatal period — Certaines affections dont l'origine se situe dans la période périnatale	266.9	67	223.9	78	249.7	70	233.8
Congenital malformations, deformations and chromosomal abnormalities — Malformations congénitales et anomalies chromosomiques	298.6	88	294.0	96	307.3	64	213.8
Symptoms, signs and abnormal clinical and laboratory findings, not elsewhere classified — Symptômes, signes et résultats anormaux d'examens cliniques et de laboratoire, non classés ailleurs	2.8	58	2.6	47	2.2	89	4.0
All other diseases — Toutes autres maladies	2.2	49	2.2	37	1.7	68	3.0
External causes — Causes externes							
Total	59.8	745	33.3	1 215	56.4	700	31.1
Accidents							
Total	37.6	577	25.8	723	33.5	492	21.8
Transport accidents — Accidents de transport	12.4	88	3.9	305	14.2	100	4.4
Falls — Chutes	10.8	264	11.8	226	10.5	290	12.9
Accidental drowning and submersion — Noyade et submersion accidentelles	2.7	13	♦0.6	38	1.8	9	♦0.4
Exposure to smoke, fire and flames — Exposition à la fumée, au feu et aux flammes	0.3	5	♦0.2	10	♦0.5	5	♦0.2
Accidental poisoning by and exposure to noxious substances — Intoxication accidentelle par des substances nocives et exposition à ces substances	3.3	44	2.0	62	2.9	41	1.8
Intentional self-harm — Lésions auto-infligées	17.6	116	5.2	404	18.7	145	6.4
Assault — Agresssions	1.6	18	♦0.8	31	1.4	25	♦1.1
All other external causes — Toutes autres causes externes	2.9	34	1.5	57	2.6	38	1.7

FOOTNOTES — NOTES

Data in bold refer to deaths based on ICD-10 Classification, otherwise data refer to deaths based on ICD-9 Classification. - Les données en typographie gras se rapportent aux décès basées sur la classification CIM-10, autrement les données se rapportent aux décès basées sur la classification CIM-9.

Italics: data from civil registers that are incomplete or of unknown completeness. — Italiques : données incomplètes ou dont le degré d'exactitude n'est pas connu provenant des registres de l'état civil.

* Provisional. - Données provisoires.

♦ Rates based on 30 or fewer deaths. - Taux basés sur 30 décès ou moins.

'Code' indicates the source of data, as follows:

C - Civil registration, estimated over 90% complete
U - Civil registration, estimated less than 90% complete
| - Other source, estimated reliable
+ - Data tabulated by date of registration rather than occurence
... - Information not available

Le 'Code' indique la source des données, comme suit :
C - Registres de l'état civil considérés complèts à 90 p. 100 au moins
U - Registres de l'état civil qui ne sont pas considérés complèts à 90 p. 100 au moins
| - Autre source, considérée pas douteuses
+ - Données exploitées selon la date de l'enregistrement et non la date de l'événement
... - Information pas disponible

Table 21 - *Demographic Yearbook 2015*

Table 21 presents the life tables' probabilities of dying in the five year interval following specified ages ($_5q_x$), for each sex, for the latest available year between 2001 and 2015. The probabilities are multiplied by a thousand, that is, the values presented in the table are $1000*_5q_x$.

Male and female probabilities of dying are shown separately for selected ages beginning at birth and proceeding at every fifth age thereafter up to age 100.

The values presented in the table are derived by the United Nations Statistics Division from the official complete life tables reported by the countries or areas.

Data are shown with one decimal regardless of the number of digits provided in the original computation.

The life table is a statistical device for summarizing the mortality experience of a population, from which the probability of dying, survivorship and expectation of life can be calculated. It is based on the assumption that the theoretical cohort is subject, throughout its existence, to the age-specific mortality rates observed at a particular time. Thus, levels of mortality prevailing at the time a life table is constructed are assumed to remain unchanged into the future until all members of the cohort have died.

Reliability of data: The values shown in this table are derived from official complete life tables. It is assumed that, if necessary, the basic data (population and deaths classified by age and sex) have been adjusted for deficiencies before their use in constructing the complete life tables.

Limitations: The life tables' probabilities of dying are subject to the same qualifications as have been set forth for population statistics in general and death statistics in particular, as discussed in sections 3 and 4, respectively, of the Technical Notes. They must be interpreted strictly using the underlying assumption that surviving cohorts are subjected to the same age-specific mortality rates of the period to which the life table refers.

Earlier data: The life tables' probabilities of dying at specified ages, for each sex, have been shown in previous issues of the *Demographic Yearbook*. For information on specific years covered, the reader should consult the Historical Index.

Tableau 21 – *Annuaire démographique 2015*

Le tableau 21 donne les probabilités de décès dans l'intervalle de cinq ans que suit l'âge spécifié ($_5q_x$), pour chaque sexe, pour la dernière année disponible entre 2001 et 2015. Les probabilités sont multipliées par mille, c'est-à-dire que les valeurs indiquées dans le tableau sont égales à $1000*_5q_x$.

Les probabilités de décès sont indiquées séparément pour les hommes et les femmes pour différents âges, depuis la naissance puis tous les cinq ans jusqu'à 100 ans.

Les chiffres indiqués dans ce tableau ont été calculés par la Division de statistique de l'Organisation des Nations Unies à partir des tables de mortalité complètes communiquées par les pays ou zones.

Les données sont arrondies à la première décimale, indépendamment du nombre de décimales qui figurent dans le calcul initial.

La table de mortalité est un moyen statistique que s'utilise pour donner un aperçu complet de la mortalité d'une population incluant les probabilités de décès et l'espérance de vie à chaque âge. Les tables de mortalité reposent sur l'hypothèse que chaque cohorte théoriquement distinguée connaît, pendant toute son existence, les taux de mortalité par âge observé à un moment donné. Les taux de mortalité correspondant à l'époque à laquelle sont calculées les tables de mortalité sont ainsi censés demeurer inchangées dans l'avenir jusqu'au décès de tous les membres de la cohorte.

Fiabilité des donnés : Les chiffres indiqués dans ce tableau ont été calculés à partir des tables officielles de mortalité complètes. En ce qui concerne les chiffres extraits de tables officielles de mortalité, on part du principe que les données de base (effectif de la population et nombre de décès selon l'âge et le sexe) ont été ajustées, en tant que de besoin, avant de servir à l'établissement de la table de mortalité.

Insuffisance des données : Les probabilités de décès appellent les mêmes réserves que celles qui ont été formulées à propos des statistiques de la population en général et des statistiques de mortalité en particulier (voir les sections 3 et 4 des Notes techniques). Lorsque l'on interprète les données, il ne faut jamais perdre de vue que, par hypothèse, les cohortes de survivants sont soumises, pour chaque âge, aux conditions de mortalité de la période visée par la table de mortalité.

Données publiées antérieurement : Les probabilités de décès pour chaque sexe figuraient déjà dans des éditions antérieures de l'*Annuaire démographique*. Pour plus de précisions concernant les années pour lesquelles ces données ont été publiées, se reporter à l'index historique.

21. Probability of dying in the five year interval following specified age (5qx), by sex, latest available year: 2001 - 2015
Probabilité de décès dans l'intervalle de cinq ans qui suit un âge donné (5qx), par sexe, dernière année disponible : 2001 - 2015

Continent, country or area and date / Continent, pays ou zone et date	0	5	10	15	20	25	30	35	40	45	50	55	60	65	70	75	80	85	90	95	100
AFRICA - AFRIQUE																					
Republic of South Sudan - République de Soudan du Sud 2010																					
Male - Hommes	130.6	14.1	10.8	18.5	25.6	27.0	28.8	33.1	40.1	51.8	70.0	98.7	143.7	213.2	316.6	457.7	624.2	785.1	907.0	...	...
Female - Femmes	111.9	13.7	10.7	18.4	25.9	27.8	30.2	35.2	43.3	56.8	78.0	111.6	164.6	245.8	362.8	513.5	678.3	826.7	931.7	...	...
Zimbabwe 2001 - 2002																					
Male - Hommes	116.9	18.0	12.8	12.2	30.6	70.9	129.9	193.2	193.5	186.2	175.7	177.3	167.1	186.5	197.2	270.7	297.7	432.4	545.1	...	...
Female - Femmes	100.5	15.2	10.8	15.2	46.7	97.4	141.4	159.8	125.9	122.9	101.0	99.6	100.9	122.5	128.8	161.1	223.5	304.5	438.0	...	...
AMERICA, NORTH - AMÉRIQUE DU NORD																					
Canada 2000 - 2002																					
Male - Hommes	6.9	0.5	1.3	3.6	4.2	4.2	4.9	6.0	9.8	14.2	23.1	35.7	58.9	93.6	147.5	232.0	356.1	522.1	699.2	832.4	...
Female - Femmes	5.5	0.4	0.7	1.5	1.7	1.7	2.3	3.6	5.5	8.8	13.9	22.4	35.1	55.7	88.8	145.8	244.8	402.2	576.2	750.4	...
Costa Rica 2015																					
Male - Hommes	9.4	0.9	1.2	3.5	6.0	7.0	7.9	9.2	11.8	16.3	23.6	34.7	52.8	82.6	126.5	197.9	294.3	422.1	585.0	757.8	*1000
Female - Femmes	7.7	0.5	0.9	1.5	1.9	2.0	2.7	3.6	5.2	8.4	12.5	20.6	32.6	53.0	84.4	139.5	233.3	366.5	533.8	720.1	*1000
Cuba 2011 - 2013																					
Male - Hommes	6.0	1.0	1.3	2.4	3.5	4.5	5.7	7.3	10.5	17.5	29.3	44.9	67.2	100.5	148.8	223.2	334.7	477.3	602.9	645.4	*1000
Female - Femmes	5.6	0.9	0.9	1.4	1.9	2.4	3.0	4.1	6.5	11.0	18.7	29.3	44.6	67.0	104.8	168.7	270.2	421.1	577.7	655.4	*1000
Curaçao 2011 - 2014																					
Male - Hommes	8.3	1.2	1.7	2.6	6.7	9.2	9.0	11.4	16.4	24.0	35.3	52.0	76.3	111.6	162.1	232.6	327.7	449.3	593.0	743.1	*1000
Female - Femmes	13.0	0.4	0.5	0.7	1.0	1.5	2.3	3.5	5.5	8.6	13.6	21.8	35.2	57.0	92.6	149.5	238.3	369.4	544.9	742.7	*1000
Greenland - Groenland 2009 - 2013																					
Male - Hommes	15.4	0.5	2.8	15.7	22.9	16.2	14.3	13.6	18.4	25.9	35.9	72.3	87.1	167.8	303.9	470.3	648.6	758.8	...	...	...
Female - Femmes	7.0	0.5	2.7	10.3	8.0	2.5	6.9	10.8	9.1	20.1	26.0	50.6	83.8	147.4	209.0	326.2	565.3	731.9	970.6	...	...
Guadeloupe 2002																					
Male - Hommes	8.7	1.1	2.1	4.6	9.3	11.1	10.0	12.7	14.6	24.3	31.1	45.3	68.9	95.0	141.6	219.3	290.6	421.7	994.4	*1000	...
Female - Femmes	6.0	0.3	0.3	1.2	2.9	1.4	4.3	5.8	8.0	8.1	10.9	22.1	39.9	55.5	87.1	112.0	212.4	331.5	984.3	*1000	...
Jamaica - Jamaïque 2006																					
Male - Hommes	31.7	2.8	2.5	4.5	6.5	6.5	7.0	9.4	14.5	23.2	37.5	60.5	96.9	153.2	236.8	353.8	502.7	667.6	817.2	921.8	*1000
Female - Femmes	18.0	1.3	1.1	1.7	2.6	3.4	4.3	5.9	8.7	13.9	22.8	38.0	63.2	104.5	169.8	268.2	405.3	574.1	747.0	883.6	*1000
Martinique 2007																					
Male - Hommes	11.6	1.0	1.1	4.2	8.8	7.5	8.8	8.5	10.4	13.5	26.7	28.9	42.2	87.6	122.7	202.9	325.3	532.7	663.7	834.4	*1000
Female - Femmes	7.8	0.4	0.7	0.6	2.1	2.9	4.6	4.1	4.8	5.3	11.3	14.8	28.6	45.6	76.8	135.3	216.7	362.2	508.4	810.4	*1000
Mexico - Mexique 2005																					
Male - Hommes	21.6	1.7	2.2	4.3	7.4	9.9	12.0	15.1	20.3	28.7	41.3	59.9	86.6	124.3	176.5	246.8	337.7	448.7	574.2	702.2	*1000
Female - Femmes	17.4	1.3	1.2	1.8	2.4	3.1	4.3	6.4	9.9	15.4	23.9	37.2	57.5	88.4	134.4	201.1	293.6	414.1	557.1	705.8	*1000
Panama[1] 2014																					
Male - Hommes	22.0	2.0	2.5	7.2	12.9	14.5	13.4	12.9	14.7	19.5	27.9	41.1	60.8	89.9	132.0	191.2	272.0	376.8	503.2	641.1	*1000
Female - Femmes	16.7	1.3	1.5	2.4	3.4	4.4	5.4	6.7	8.5	11.6	16.5	24.6	37.8	58.9	92.1	143.3	219.6	327.0	466.3	625.7	*1000
Puerto Rico - Porto Rico 2013 - 2015																					
Male - Hommes	8.4	0.5	0.6	4.1	10.7	11.4	11.4	12.5	14.7	21.0	31.7	46.6	63.1	86.4	121.4	179.3	281.7	*1000	...	...	...
Female - Femmes	6.7	0.5	0.4	1.1	1.8	2.4	3.2	4.7	6.5	10.1	15.3	21.4	31.5	46.0	73.6	121.6	208.2	*1000	...	...	...

21. Probability of dying in the five year interval following specified age (5qx), by sex, latest available year: 2001 - 2015
Probabilité de décès dans l'intervalle de cinq ans qui suit un âge donné (5qx), par sexe, dernière année disponible : 2001 - 2015 (continued - suite)

Continent, country or area and date / Continent, pays ou zone et date	Age (in years) - Age (en années)																				
	0	5	10	15	20	25	30	35	40	45	50	55	60	65	70	75	80	85	90	95	100

AMERICA, NORTH - AMÉRIQUE DU NORD

United States of America - États-Unis d'Amérique
2014

	0	5	10	15	20	25	30	35	40	45	50	55	60	65	70	75	80	85	90	95	100
Male - Hommes	7.4	0.6	0.8	3.1	6.1	7.0	7.9	9.3	12.2	18.8	29.8	45.1	63.7	86.6	130.0	198.4	311.2	481.1	670.9	828.2	*1000
Female - Femmes	6.2	0.5	0.6	1.3	2.2	2.9	3.8	5.4	7.9	12.1	18.9	27.3	38.4	56.6	89.8	145.1	239.4	390.6	588.0	774.4	*1000

AMERICA, SOUTH - AMÉRIQUE DU SUD

Argentina - Argentine
2008 - 2010

	0	5	10	15	20	25	30	35	40	45	50	55	60	65	70	75	80	85	90	95	100
Male - Hommes	15.8	1.3	1.8	5.3	7.5	7.9	8.1	10.0	14.5	22.1	37.3	59.5	89.5	133.8	194.0	289.6	431.2	568.1	692.6	804.3	*1000
Female - Femmes	13.0	1.0	1.2	2.2	2.6	3.1	4.0	5.7	8.4	13.2	20.4	31.0	45.5	68.2	105.9	175.1	309.8	460.7	614.6	762.3	*1000

Bolivia (Plurinational State of) - Bolivie (État plurinational de)[2]
2015 - 2016

	0	5	10	15	20	25	30	35	40	45	50	55	60	65	70	75	80	85	90	95	100
Male - Hommes	46.7	5.6	4.4	9.2	14.1	14.8	16.7	19.7	25.1	31.7	42.6	58.4	84.5	118.9	169.6	235.3	332.5	419.1	612.9	*1000	...
Female - Femmes	37.3	3.9	2.6	5.1	5.7	6.3	8.0	10.5	15.2	20.8	28.9	40.6	59.4	86.7	122.7	168.7	239.6	320.2	492.7	*1000	...

Brazil - Brésil[1]
2014

	0	5	10	15	20	25	30	35	40	45	50	55	60	65	70	75	80	85	90	95	100
Male - Hommes	18.1	1.5	1.9	8.4	12.8	12.9	13.9	16.1	20.7	28.8	41.1	57.9	80.4	116.1	171.3	250.0	*1000	...	...	...	...
Female - Femmes	15.2	1.1	1.3	2.3	2.8	3.6	4.8	6.6	9.8	15.1	22.1	32.2	47.6	73.2	114.3	176.7	*1000	...	...	...	...

Chile - Chili
2013

	0	5	10	15	20	25	30	35	40	45	50	55	60	65	70	75	80	85	90	95	100
Male - Hommes	9.1	0.7	1.0	3.0	4.2	5.0	6.3	8.0	10.7	15.8	23.8	36.4	54.1	93.8	143.7	227.6	383.1	543.0	*1000	...	...
Female - Femmes	7.8	0.7	0.6	1.4	1.5	1.6	2.6	3.3	5.5	8.0	12.7	21.3	33.9	55.2	89.2	144.2	261.0	416.0	*1000	...	...

Ecuador - Équateur[3]
2010 - 2016

	0	5	10	15	20	25	30	35	40	45	50	55	60	65	70	75	80	85	90	95	100
Male - Hommes	22.7	0.9	1.1	3.1	4.7	6.9	10.5	11.4	13.3	19.4	29.0	43.2	67.8	104.2	164.4	252.2	381.3	551.5	723.7	854.4	*1000
Female - Femmes	19.4	0.9	0.8	1.9	2.3	2.3	2.8	4.0	6.2	9.3	14.1	21.4	33.7	56.6	99.8	182.4	314.3	496.5	680.7	833.1	*1000

French Guiana - Guyane française
2007

	0	5	10	15	20	25	30	35	40	45	50	55	60	65	70	75	80	85	90	95	100
Male - Hommes	16.3	1.5	2.1	4.9	7.7	8.1	10.0	14.0	17.2	29.4	16.0	32.3	52.4	79.5	135.5	261.3	306.7	474.0	733.7	...	...
Female - Femmes	15.1	1.9	1.3	1.4	1.2	3.0	4.6	4.2	11.9	11.0	10.4	11.6	26.7	85.4	77.4	203.8	253.1	321.1	434.3	...	...

Uruguay
2004

	0	5	10	15	20	25	30	35	40	45	50	55	60	65	70	75	80	85	90	95	100
Male - Hommes	20.0	1.3	1.3	3.5	5.8	6.8	7.2	9.0	12.8	21.2	36.4	62.2	95.4	145.2	204.6	305.7	430.5	610.5	776.7	862.5	*1000
Female - Femmes	15.5	1.0	1.1	1.6	1.9	2.7	3.8	5.2	7.9	12.5	19.4	30.5	41.2	63.4	97.2	177.7	292.9	472.0	654.3	820.5	*1000

ASIA - ASIE

Armenia - Arménie
2006 - 2007

	0	5	10	15	20	25	30	35	40	45	50	55	60	65	70	75	80	85	90	95	100
Male - Hommes	15.3	1.1	1.1	2.9	3.9	4.9	7.3	11.4	20.4	28.6	45.0	68.2	112.2	173.3	246.9	350.8	495.4	691.9	870.7	975.9	...
Female - Femmes	11.9	1.0	0.9	0.9	1.6	1.8	2.7	4.4	7.8	11.3	18.4	29.4	52.7	95.7	158.1	254.3	413.9	670.0	851.3	957.0	...

Azerbaijan - Azerbaïdjan
2013

	0	5	10	15	20	25	30	35	40	45	50	55	60	65	70	75	80	85	90	95	100
Male - Hommes	13.5	1.8	1.6	2.9	4.6	5.3	6.7	10.1	15.7	24.9	39.2	62.3	98.4	134.0	223.2	325.1	533.1	630.5	532.8	706.7	...
Female - Femmes	12.4	1.2	1.3	1.8	2.1	2.1	2.7	4.0	6.0	10.1	17.1	28.5	51.8	84.3	154.6	268.6	439.6	616.2	686.1	823.8	...

China, Hong Kong SAR - Chine, Hong Kong RAS
2014

	0	5	10	15	20	25	30	35	40	45	50	55	60	65	70	75	80	85	90	95	100
Male - Hommes	2.0	0.4	0.5	0.9	1.4	1.9	2.8	4.5	6.8	10.0	15.5	25.9	39.8	61.5	103.9	168.3	274.4	420.5	597.5	775.7	*1000
Female - Femmes	2.9	0.4	0.5	0.6	0.7	0.9	1.4	1.8	3.1	5.3	8.4	13.2	19.2	28.9	48.3	91.7	171.4	288.3	450.1	642.9	*1000

21. Probability of dying in the five year interval following specified age (5qx), by sex, latest available year: 2001 - 2015
Probabilité de décès dans l'intervalle de cinq ans qui suit un âge donné (5qx), par sexe, dernière année disponible : 2001 - 2015 (continued - suite)

Continent, country or area and date / Continent, pays ou zone et date	0	5	10	15	20	25	30	35	40	45	50	55	60	65	70	75	80	85	90	95	100
ASIA - ASIE																					
China, Macao SAR - Chine, Macao RAS 2002 - 2005																					
Male - Hommes	7.2	0.6	0.4	1.7	3.9	5.4	6.2	7.6	9.0	13.6	17.8	25.8	43.1	72.1	128.9	239.9	369.5	574.4	841.2	991.4	*1000
Female - Femmes	5.2	0.4	0.2	0.9	1.5	1.9	2.3	3.8	4.7	5.9	7.4	10.9	19.3	33.3	70.4	186.2	317.0	485.2	717.3	923.7	*1000
Israel - Israël[4] 2010 - 2014																					
Male - Hommes	4.5	0.5	0.7	1.7	2.7	3.0	3.2	4.1	6.2	10.0	16.6	27.6	45.5	74.2	119.4	188.0	287.9	423.9	591.2	760.9	*1000
Female - Femmes	4.0	0.4	0.4	0.6	0.9	1.2	1.7	2.4	3.6	5.7	9.3	15.5	26.4	45.6	78.9	135.9	229.3	372.2	565.4	769.2	*1000
Japan - Japon 2010																					
Male - Hommes	3.4	0.5	0.6	1.3	3.0	3.3	3.7	5.0	7.6	12.0	19.1	30.4	47.3	70.0	108.1	183.7	306.5	473.8	658.4	820.7	...
Female - Femmes	2.9	0.4	0.4	0.8	1.3	1.5	2.0	2.8	4.2	6.4	9.6	13.6	19.9	29.1	48.0	86.8	161.1	302.6	506.4	721.5	...
Kazakhstan 2012																					
Male - Hommes	18.1	2.1	2.1	4.9	9.5	15.0	22.5	30.6	37.5	49.5	72.7	107.0	157.3	204.8	286.8	397.7	531.1	638.2	732.6	812.3	...
Female - Femmes	14.5	1.6	1.2	2.4	3.3	4.9	7.4	10.3	13.8	18.6	28.5	43.8	68.1	99.5	161.7	268.0	427.7	602.1	790.3	887.7	...
Kyrgyzstan - Kirghizstan 2014																					
Male - Hommes	24.4	1.8	2.1	3.9	6.1	9.0	14.3	22.5	30.5	40.4	60.0	84.5	138.0	173.8	285.4	403.1	592.4	736.3	860.1	917.3	*1000
Female - Femmes	20.9	1.3	1.5	2.2	2.9	4.2	5.9	8.5	11.7	15.9	22.5	38.8	64.2	92.3	175.3	252.7	435.9	629.8	765.5	875.4	*1000
Qatar 2006																					
Male - Hommes	10.2	0.8	1.8	9.4	8.9	6.5	5.6	6.6	7.1	9.0	16.1	22.1	42.2	88.0	167.5	248.6	376.7	*1000	...	...	...
Female - Femmes	9.0	1.3	0.9	2.2	1.4	2.4	1.2	1.8	3.8	6.7	9.8	22.1	76.0	120.2	253.6	354.1	348.3	*1000	...	...	...
Republic of Korea - République de Corée 2014																					
Male - Hommes	3.8	0.5	0.5	1.6	2.2	2.9	4.0	5.6	8.7	14.1	22.3	31.7	45.5	68.6	117.7	200.5	328.6	492.2	656.2	791.4	*1000
Female - Femmes	3.4	0.4	0.4	0.9	1.1	1.6	2.3	3.1	4.1	5.8	8.1	11.1	16.4	27.0	52.4	103.6	206.1	360.3	544.1	712.0	*1000
Singapore - Singapour[5] 2015																					
Male - Hommes	2.8	0.3	0.4	1.2	1.7	1.9	2.5	3.7	6.0	9.3	15.7	27.6	42.7	69.6	117.3	189.8	291.6	439.1	616.4	790.8	*1000
Female - Femmes	1.9	0.1	0.4	0.7	0.7	0.8	1.4	1.8	3.3	6.0	9.8	15.6	22.9	37.6	67.8	122.4	208.4	347.9	529.5	720.7	*1000
Turkey - Turquie 2014																					
Male - Hommes	14.7	1.4	1.7	3.2	3.7	3.6	4.0	5.2	8.3	14.5	25.2	42.6	68.1	106.5	168.8	256.5	385.3	548.1	692.6	787.7	*1000
Female - Femmes	12.9	1.2	1.0	1.3	1.4	1.5	2.0	2.9	4.5	7.4	11.7	19.1	32.0	56.4	103.7	179.4	299.4	457.7	602.2	694.5	*1000
EUROPE																					
Austria - Autriche 2013																					
Male - Hommes	4.3	0.4	0.7	1.8	2.9	3.1	3.2	4.8	6.5	12.9	21.7	35.6	56.8	86.6	117.9	191.9	324.0	506.5	722.3	882.0	...
Female - Femmes	3.2	0.5	0.4	0.8	1.1	1.0	1.6	2.3	3.9	6.8	11.0	17.5	29.5	44.9	66.6	117.0	224.6	416.8	647.8	850.0	...
Belarus - Bélarus 2013																					
Male - Hommes	5.2	1.0	1.0	3.0	6.9	10.1	16.1	24.5	33.7	45.7	67.1	104.2	150.7	198.0	271.8	375.2	497.3	630.3	760.6	870.5	...
Female - Femmes	4.0	0.8	0.7	1.3	2.2	2.8	4.8	7.2	10.2	14.4	21.5	33.9	50.5	77.8	127.7	224.5	364.5	545.3	741.0	899.6	...
Belgium - Belgique 2006																					
Male - Hommes	4.4	0.6	0.7	2.6	4.6	4.4	5.6	7.1	10.7	17.3	27.2	42.4	65.1	93.3	149.7	248.7	387.2	570.9	751.3	886.0	...
Female - Femmes	3.9	0.5	0.6	1.3	1.1	1.8	2.4	3.8	5.8	10.2	16.3	22.5	33.8	48.2	79.3	149.1	270.8	466.0	663.7	835.2	...
Bulgaria - Bulgarie 2010 - 2012																					
Male - Hommes	11.9	1.0	1.6	3.1	4.8	5.6	7.1	9.7	17.2	30.5	51.7	80.4	116.1	155.2	225.0	325.9	472.1	632.4	764.1	886.4	...
Female - Femmes	9.1	1.0	1.0	1.8	1.8	2.1	3.1	5.5	8.7	13.7	21.2	31.4	47.2	72.7	127.0	231.4	395.0	597.0	738.0	891.0	...
Czech Republic - République tchèque 2014																					
Male - Hommes	3.2	0.5	0.6	2.5	3.4	3.7	4.3	5.8	9.8	16.9	27.1	46.6	77.6	119.7	165.7	251.1	376.5	542.6	730.0	890.0	...
Female - Femmes	2.7	0.4	0.3	0.8	1.1	1.4	1.7	2.7	4.6	8.3	12.8	21.3	34.6	56.2	89.1	155.5	279.8	474.1	720.7	922.2	...

21. Probability of dying in the five year interval following specified age (5qx), by sex, latest available year: 2001 - 2015
Probabilité de décès dans l'intervalle de cinq ans qui suit un âge donné (5qx), par sexe, dernière année disponible : 2001 - 2015 (continued - suite)

Continent, country or area and date / Continent, pays ou zone et date	0	5	10	15	20	25	30	35	40	45	50	55	60	65	70	75	80	85	90	95	100
EUROPE																					
Denmark - Danemark[6]																					
2014																					
Male - Hommes	4.1	0.2	0.4	1.5	1.8	2.5	3.3	4.9	7.3	12.1	21.6	36.0	57.1	79.2	126.5	199.6	332.6	509.2	686.7	878.3	...
Female - Femmes	3.9	0.3	0.3	0.5	1.1	0.9	1.6	2.3	4.4	7.4	13.4	21.1	34.5	52.0	81.8	142.6	250.6	394.1	600.2	771.2	
Estonia - Estonie																					
2014																					
Male - Hommes	3.8	1.0	0.9	3.1	6.6	7.6	10.8	12.3	15.6	29.3	41.5	69.0	107.1	144.8	196.7	264.4	388.8	564.8	735.8	897.8	*1000
Female - Femmes	3.1	0.4	0.7	1.5	1.9	2.2	4.7	4.5	4.7	9.1	15.3	23.1	34.8	55.8	87.6	145.9	268.6	436.2	664.3	803.6	*1000
Faeroe Islands - Îles Féroé																					
2014 - 2015																					
Male - Hommes	18.5	0.0	2.9	5.8	3.1	0.0	3.7	0.0	3.2	23.4	17.7	38.4	33.0	43.1	117.4	162.5	361.1	481.0	826.0	916.7	...
Female - Femmes	3.2	0.0	0.0	0.0	0.0	0.0	0.0	0.0	6.6	15.2	3.3	13.4	14.7	54.3	51.2	130.8	184.5	378.9	742.7	807.5	
Finland - Finlande[7]																					
2014																					
Male - Hommes	3.0	0.4	0.4	2.0	3.5	5.0	5.0	6.4	8.8	14.6	22.4	35.4	56.7	81.9	124.0	197.1	318.1	504.8	716.8	848.1	...
Female - Femmes	2.4	0.5	0.4	0.7	1.3	1.7	2.3	2.8	3.4	5.6	11.2	16.9	26.8	41.6	66.0	116.8	217.1	404.2	642.9	817.4	...
France[8]																					
2011 - 2013																					
Male - Hommes	4.4	0.4	0.5	1.9	3.4	3.9	4.5	6.3	9.9	16.1	26.8	41.1	56.2	76.2	108.5	170.7	284.6	462.6	671.0	841.6	...
Female - Femmes	3.7	0.4	0.4	0.8	1.1	1.3	1.9	3.0	5.0	8.3	12.9	18.3	24.8	34.7	53.3	92.4	178.5	338.1	561.7	773.5	...
Germany - Allemagne																					
2010 - 2012																					
Male - Hommes	4.5	0.5	0.5	1.7	2.8	3.0	3.6	4.9	7.9	14.0	24.8	39.8	59.6	86.8	129.2	213.2	345.1	526.5	726.6	867.2	...
Female - Femmes	3.8	0.4	0.4	0.8	1.1	1.2	1.7	2.6	4.4	7.9	13.5	20.5	31.0	45.6	70.7	131.7	247.0	435.7	657.0	828.1	...
Greece - Grèce																					
2014																					
Male - Hommes	4.8	0.5	0.7	2.0	3.1	3.4	4.1	5.3	8.3	14.6	24.4	38.9	56.0	83.0	117.0	189.6	315.2	466.3	613.5	769.1	...
Female - Femmes	4.0	0.4	0.4	0.7	1.1	1.3	1.6	2.5	4.2	7.1	10.9	16.2	24.3	37.4	65.2	131.3	265.4	427.6	581.6	745.6	...
Hungary - Hongrie																					
2014																					
Male - Hommes	6.1	0.6	0.8	1.9	2.8	3.4	4.6	7.2	13.3	26.4	51.4	82.6	115.1	152.7	203.7	298.3	421.5	625.7	863.9	987.1	...
Female - Femmes	4.7	0.4	0.4	0.7	0.9	1.4	2.2	3.5	6.7	12.8	22.7	35.6	52.6	74.7	110.1	191.9	318.1	548.7	839.0	987.7	...
Iceland - Islande																					
2013 - 2014																					
Male - Hommes	2.6	0.4	0.5	1.3	2.5	2.6	5.4	3.5	5.3	8.0	15.7	25.4	32.2	60.3	97.0	172.9	302.0	499.7	724.2	842.8	...
Female - Femmes	5.9	0.4	0.0	1.2	1.6	0.9	1.5	3.1	3.8	5.1	9.4	14.5	28.9	44.2	72.8	126.0	224.1	389.6	574.4	823.5	...
Ireland - Irlande																					
2005 - 2007																					
Male - Hommes	4.9	0.6	0.8	3.6	5.4	4.7	5.1	5.7	8.6	13.3	21.1	33.3	54.5	88.7	148.8	247.0	395.4	567.3	730.3	919.0	...
Female - Femmes	4.5	0.4	0.7	1.6	1.5	1.6	2.0	3.0	5.2	9.2	13.6	21.3	33.8	53.6	90.1	153.4	284.4	460.3	643.4	800.7	...
Italy - Italie																					
2014																					
Male - Hommes	3.9	0.4	0.5	1.5	2.3	2.5	2.9	4.0	5.9	9.7	15.8	25.6	42.3	66.3	107.7	172.9	299.4	481.1	670.0	841.3	...
Female - Femmes	3.3	0.3	0.4	0.7	0.8	1.0	1.3	2.2	3.5	5.9	9.2	14.4	22.6	35.4	58.7	102.8	200.9	367.6	573.6	785.0	...
Latvia - Lettonie																					
2006																					
Male - Hommes	10.5	1.4	1.6	3.0	6.2	11.3	18.6	28.3	40.6	56.3	76.6	104.3	143.2	199.8	282.1	397.7	547.0	712.6	...	...	...
Female - Femmes	12.7	1.3	1.2	1.5	2.2	3.2	4.8	7.3	11.2	17.3	26.7	41.0	63.0	96.1	145.1	215.5	312.2	436.5	...	...	...
Lithuania - Lituanie																					
2014																					
Male - Hommes	4.9	1.2	1.2	4.5	8.4	9.8	15.4	23.2	31.1	41.7	59.4	86.1	126.0	169.1	217.9	291.4	413.0	565.0	772.4	885.0	*1000
Female - Femmes	5.2	0.6	1.0	1.3	1.6	2.4	4.6	5.0	8.9	13.7	19.8	29.6	43.4	64.1	95.7	157.3	291.8	486.5	692.4	830.5	*1000
Luxembourg																					
2012 - 2014																					
Male - Hommes	2.2	0.6	0.6	1.9	2.0	2.4	3.4	4.5	6.2	10.1	21.3	33.6	49.9	77.2	118.4	183.7	310.5	529.7	671.1	*1000	...
Female - Femmes	2.1	0.1	0.2	1.2	0.7	1.5	1.8	2.3	3.2	7.0	11.4	17.7	26.3	45.8	66.7	117.2	214.0	397.4	628.4	*1000	...
Malta - Malte																					
2012																					
Male - Hommes	5.6	0.5	0.4	0.4	2.3	2.2	5.4	4.8	6.1	12.6	14.8	26.8	46.3	77.4	112.0	220.3	378.6	640.6	887.5	975.9	*1000
Female - Femmes	6.0	0.6	0.9	0.8	0.0	2.0	2.7	1.8	5.6	4.5	11.8	13.5	27.6	41.3	67.7	130.5	273.1	474.9	737.6	853.6	*1000
Netherlands - Pays-Bas																					
2009																					
Male - Hommes	4.8	0.5	0.6	1.4	2.3	2.4	3.0	4.1	6.6	10.7	18.7	30.3	49.9	79.1	132.1	225.2	363.5	539.8	738.0	...	...
Female - Femmes	4.1	0.4	0.5	0.8	1.0	1.3	1.7	2.9	5.0	8.9	15.0	21.5	32.5	47.8	76.4	136.1	249.6	428.5	644.7		

21. Probability of dying in the five year interval following specified age (5qx), by sex, latest available year: 2001 - 2015
Probabilité de décès dans l'intervalle de cinq ans qui suit un âge donné (5qx), par sexe, dernière année disponible : 2001 - 2015 (continued - suite)

Continent, country or area and date / Continent, pays ou zone et date	0	5	10	15	20	25	30	35	40	45	50	55	60	65	70	75	80	85	90	95	100
EUROPE																					
Norway - Norvège 2012																					
Male - Hommes	3.3	0.4	0.6	1.5	3.2	3.3	4.2	4.9	6.0	9.5	17.2	26.3	45.2	70.3	111.2	192.3	335.0	513.3	727.7	859.1	...
Female - Femmes	2.7	0.4	0.6	0.8	1.0	1.2	1.4	2.4	3.9	6.7	10.6	17.1	28.2	46.4	75.5	127.0	232.7	402.3	640.0	837.9	...
Poland - Pologne 2012																					
Male - Hommes	5.9	0.6	0.7	3.1	5.0	5.6	6.9	10.8	17.5	28.8	46.4	70.1	100.4	137.3	189.2	271.9	388.8	529.1	679.2	814.9	...
Female - Femmes	4.8	0.4	0.6	1.1	1.1	1.3	2.0	3.3	5.8	10.5	17.9	28.2	42.6	61.6	93.6	160.8	278.6	436.3	614.7	781.5	...
Portugal 2012 - 2014																					
Male - Hommes	4.2	0.5	0.6	1.6	2.8	3.1	4.3	6.3	11.1	18.3	29.1	40.7	55.5	80.9	123.6	200.7	359.4	636.3	857.8	969.1	...
Female - Femmes	3.4	0.5	0.4	0.7	1.0	1.3	1.6	2.9	4.8	7.7	11.2	15.3	23.0	36.6	62.2	117.4	253.9	518.3	783.9	946.4	...
Republic of Moldova - République de Moldova 2012																					
Male - Hommes	12.2	1.4	2.0	4.4	5.6	7.1	11.3	19.8	30.9	50.0	71.2	102.2	157.9	176.7	292.1	388.4	503.1	558.6	*1000	...	...
Female - Femmes	12.1	1.1	1.2	1.6	1.8	2.4	3.6	8.1	10.6	16.1	26.8	44.1	78.0	103.1	191.4	289.0	418.9	550.8	*1000	...	...
Romania - Roumanie 2012 - 2014																					
Male - Hommes	10.5	1.0	1.4	2.8	4.1	4.2	5.4	8.6	14.9	27.7	47.4	74.7	105.4	145.2	206.3	296.0	420.2	571.5	716.9	838.4	...
Female - Femmes	8.8	0.8	0.8	1.3	1.6	1.7	2.3	3.7	6.3	11.1	19.0	29.3	45.2	70.9	116.2	206.1	347.8	518.7	686.1	825.3	...
Russian Federation - Fédération de Russie 2012																					
Male - Hommes	11.6	1.7	1.8	5.4	11.6	19.0	30.3	36.8	42.1	56.4	77.9	110.6	155.6	193.8	273.2	361.6	481.9	577.2	694.9	771.0	*1000
Female - Femmes	9.5	1.1	1.2	2.5	3.4	5.6	9.0	11.6	14.3	18.9	26.2	39.5	57.7	84.1	137.1	230.5	372.9	543.1	716.4	825.0	*1000
San Marino - Saint-Marin 2013																					
Male - Hommes	2.4	0.6	1.2	2.7	2.7	2.3	0.9	2.6	5.2	3.0	10.8	28.9	31.0	53.1	81.0	167.4	300.6	458.9	674.0	923.3	...
Female - Femmes	1.3	0.0	0.7	1.5	0.7	0.0	0.8	0.7	4.4	4.9	8.3	11.7	16.6	30.5	56.9	81.0	171.2	350.3	539.6	820.0	...
Serbia - Serbie[9] 2010 - 2012																					
Male - Hommes	8.1	0.5	0.9	2.4	3.7	4.7	6.4	8.2	13.3	25.5	44.0	69.0	101.6	145.8	216.4	334.2	492.1	676.0	856.4	973.0	...
Female - Femmes	6.5	0.6	0.9	1.1	1.5	2.0	2.6	4.3	7.4	12.8	21.1	33.3	50.4	82.2	147.2	265.6	432.9	632.3	840.3	975.2	...
Slovakia - Slovaquie 2014																					
Male - Hommes	7.2	0.7	0.9	2.5	3.6	4.1	5.3	8.4	13.6	23.6	38.7	64.9	96.2	135.9	191.7	286.7	422.0	597.0	782.9	924.8	...
Female - Femmes	6.3	0.4	0.4	1.3	1.2	1.3	2.1	3.6	5.3	9.9	14.8	25.3	40.1	60.4	99.3	179.3	324.9	553.2	813.3	970.5	...
Slovenia - Slovénie 2014																					
Male - Hommes	2.1	0.4	0.6	1.7	2.2	2.6	4.1	5.7	7.1	12.5	23.1	39.1	63.9	88.4	136.8	202.6	347.9	521.5	697.2	787.1	...
Female - Femmes	2.1	0.4	0.5	0.4	1.6	0.8	1.7	2.4	3.3	6.7	10.3	17.5	28.7	40.3	69.2	119.7	235.8	430.7	643.5	826.4	...
Spain - Espagne 2013																					
Male - Hommes	3.4	0.4	0.4	1.1	1.7	2.0	2.6	3.5	6.3	12.1	20.5	32.2	49.0	71.3	108.6	177.3	291.9	464.9	641.1	770.1	*1000
Female - Femmes	3.0	0.4	0.4	0.6	0.7	0.9	1.2	2.2	3.5	6.3	10.1	14.4	20.0	29.9	50.0	94.8	190.0	357.1	569.6	739.3	*1000
Sweden - Suède 2012																					
Male - Hommes	3.5	0.4	0.5	1.4	3.2	3.6	3.2	3.8	5.4	9.2	15.2	25.0	40.8	65.6	109.3	186.3	322.6	519.0	727.6	886.1	...
Female - Femmes	2.7	0.3	0.5	0.9	1.1	1.1	1.6	2.8	3.4	6.4	11.0	16.2	26.3	45.6	71.4	126.8	229.8	416.2	644.1	827.2	...
Switzerland - Suisse 2014																					
Male - Hommes	4.8	0.2	0.4	1.2	2.2	2.1	2.6	3.6	5.2	8.5	14.5	24.5	39.9	61.6	95.4	157.6	274.3	468.4	696.5	852.3	...
Female - Femmes	3.7	0.3	0.4	0.6	0.7	1.1	1.4	1.9	3.0	5.2	8.8	14.2	22.1	34.4	56.1	99.6	189.8	363.6	605.9	805.4	...
TFYR of Macedonia - L'ex-R. y. de Macédoine 2011																					
Male - Hommes	9.9	0.8	1.0	2.0	2.5	2.9	3.6	6.5	10.3	20.4	35.3	57.5	89.0	138.0	209.4	334.4	526.7	713.5	830.7	...	...
Female - Femmes	8.8	0.4	0.6	1.1	0.8	1.4	2.1	3.5	6.3	11.1	18.4	30.6	48.4	84.5	155.5	275.7	468.1	674.9	751.2	...	...
Ukraine 2013																					
Male - Hommes	10.5	1.1	1.4	4.0	7.2	12.0	20.3	29.3	36.5	50.9	72.3	101.9	151.5	197.4	267.0	363.8	483.5	578.1	671.9	756.8	...
Female - Femmes	8.2	0.7	1.0	1.7	2.5	4.0	6.6	10.0	13.1	17.6	24.1	37.0	57.7	87.7	143.3	244.9	390.8	557.8	731.5	877.1	...

21. Probability of dying in the five year interval following specified age (5qx), by sex, latest available year: 2001 - 2015
Probabilité de décès dans l'intervalle de cinq ans qui suit un âge donné (5qx), par sexe, dernière année disponible : 2001 - 2015 (continued - suite)

Continent, country or area and date / Continent, pays ou zone et date	Age (in years) - Age (en années)																				
	0	5	10	15	20	25	30	35	40	45	50	55	60	65	70	75	80	85	90	95	100
EUROPE																					
United Kingdom of Great Britain and Northern Ireland - Royaume-Uni de Grande-Bretagne et d'Irlande du Nord[10] 2012																					
Male - Hommes	5.3	0.5	0.6	1.6	2.5	3.1	4.1	5.8	8.7	12.5	18.6	29.9	46.9	73.2	120.2	192.2	316.4	492.9	672.1	843.0	...
Female - Femmes	4.2	0.4	0.4	0.8	1.1	1.5	2.2	3.2	5.2	8.2	13.0	20.6	31.2	48.8	81.1	137.4	243.5	406.5	604.7	791.1	...
OCEANIA - OCÉANIE																					
Australia - Australie 2012 - 2014																					
Male - Hommes	4.6	0.5	0.5	1.9	3.1	3.4	4.2	5.7	7.9	11.4	17.2	26.0	39.4	62.0	98.6	164.9	281.2	458.7	661.2	813.2	...
Female - Femmes	4.0	0.4	0.5	1.1	1.3	1.5	2.1	3.0	4.5	7.0	10.7	15.7	24.2	37.5	62.2	108.3	199.9	365.3	586.5	776.9	...
New Zealand - Nouvelle-Zélande 2012 - 2014																					
Male - Hommes	5.9	0.7	0.9	3.2	4.1	4.0	4.2	5.6	7.6	11.6	17.6	26.2	40.3	65.4	108.3	176.2	298.2	485.4	667.7	822.5	*1000
Female - Femmes	4.9	0.5	0.7	1.5	1.6	1.5	2.3	3.2	5.1	8.0	12.5	17.9	28.2	43.2	71.4	126.3	219.4	391.0	615.3	807.3	*1000

FOOTNOTES - NOTES

* Open-ended group (e.g. 80 years or over). - Groupe d'âge ouvert (par exemple, 80 ans ou plus).

[1] Excluding Indian jungle population. - Non compris les Indiens de la jungle.

[2] Data refer to the 12 months from 30 June 2015 to 30 June 2016. - Les données font référence aux douze mois de 30 juin 2015 à 30 juin 2016.

[3] Data refer to projections based on the 2010 Population Census. Excludes nomadic Indian tribes. - Les données se réfèrent aux projections basées sur le recensement de la population de 2010. Non compris les tribus d'Indiens nomades.

[4] Includes data for East Jerusalem and Israeli residents in certain other territories under occupation by Israeli military forces since June 1967. - Y compris les données pour Jérusalem-Est et les résidents israéliens dans certains autres territoires occupés depuis 1967 par les forces armées israéliennes.

[5] Provisional data. Data refer to resident population which comprises Singapore citizens and permanent residents. - Données provisoires. Les données se rapportent à la population résidente composé des citoyens de Singapour et des résidents permanents.

[6] Excluding Faeroe Islands and Greenland shown separately, if available. - Non compris les Iles Féroé et le Groenland, qui font l'objet de rubriques distinctes, si disponible.

[7] Excluding Åland Islands. - Non compris les Îles d'Åland.

[8] Provisional data. - Données provisoires.

[9] Excludes data for Kosovo and Metohia. - Sans les données pour le Kosovo et Metohie.

[10] Excluding Channel Islands (Guernsey and Jersey) and Isle of Man, shown separately, if available. - Non compris les îles Anglo-Normandes (Guernesey et Jersey) et l'île de Man, qui font l'objet de rubriques distinctes, si disponible.

Table 22 - *Demographic Yearbook 2015*

Table 22 presents life expectancy at specified ages for each sex, for the latest available year between 1996 and 2015.

Description of variables: Life expectancy at age x, e_x, is defined as the average number of years of life remaining to persons who have reached age *x* if they continue to be subject to the mortality conditions of the period indicated in the life table.

Male and female life expectancy values are shown separately at selected ages beginning at birth and proceeding at every fifth age thereafter up to age 100.

The table shows life expectancy derived from a complete or abridged life table as reported by the country or area.

Data are shown with one decimal regardless of the number of digits provided in the original computation.

The life table is a statistical device for summarizing the mortality experience of a population, from which the probability of dying, survivorship and life expectancy can be calculated. It is based on the assumption that the theoretical cohort is subject, throughout its existence, to the age-specific mortality rates observed at a particular time period. Thus, levels of mortality prevailing at the time a life table is constructed are assumed to remain unchanged into the future until all members of the cohort have died.

Reliability of data: The values shown in this table come from official life tables. It is assumed that, if necessary, the basic data (population and deaths classified by age and sex) have been adjusted for deficiencies before their use in constructing the life tables.

Limitations: Life expectancy values are subject to the same qualifications as have been set forth for population statistics in general and death statistics in particular, as discussed in sections 3 and 4, respectively, of the Technical Notes. They must be interpreted strictly using the underlying assumption that surviving cohorts are subjected to the same age-specific mortality rates of the period to which the life table refers.

Earlier data: Life expectancy values at specified ages for each sex have been shown in previous issues of the *Demographic Yearbook*. For information on specific years covered, the reader should consult the Historical Index.

Tableau 22 – *Annuaire démographique 2015*

Le tableau 22 présente les espérances de vie à des âges déterminés, pour chaque sexe, pour la dernière année disponible entre 1996 et 2015.

Description des variables : L'espérance de vie à l'âge x, e_x, se définit comme le nombre moyen d'années restant à vivre aux hommes et aux femmes qui ont atteint l'âge x, à supposer qu'ils continuent de connaître les mêmes conditions de mortalité observées pendant la période sur laquelle porte la table de mortalité.

Les chiffres sont présentés séparément pour chaque sexe à partir de la naissance et puis tous les cinq ans jusqu'à 100 ans.

Dans le tableau figurent les espérances de vie calculées selon les tables de mortalité complètes ou abrégées communiquées par les pays et les zones.

Les données sont arrondies à la première décimale, indépendamment du nombre de décimales qui figurent dans le calcul initial.

La table de mortalité est un moyen statistique que s'utilise pour donner un aperçu complet de la mortalité d'une population incluant les probabilités de décès et l'espérance de vie à chaque âge. Les tables de mortalité reposent sur l'hypothèse que chaque cohorte théoriquement distinguée connaît, pendant toute son existence, les taux de mortalité par âge observé à un moment donné. Les taux de mortalité correspondant à l'époque à laquelle sont calculées les tables de mortalité sont ainsi censés demeurer inchangées dans l'avenir jusqu'au décès de tous les membres de la cohorte.

Fiabilité des donnés : Les chiffres figurant dans ce tableau proviennent de tables officielles de mortalité. En ce qui concerne les chiffres extraits de tables officielles de mortalité, on part du principe que les données de base (effectif de la population et nombre de décès selon l'âge et le sexe) ont été ajustées, en tant que de besoin, avant de servir à l'établissement de la table de mortalité.

Insuffisance des données : les espérances de vie appellent les mêmes réserves que celles qui ont été formulées à propos des statistiques de la population en général et des statistiques de mortalité en particulier (voir les sections 3 et 4 des Notes techniques). Lorsque l'on interprète les données, il ne faut jamais perdre de vue que, par hypothèse, les cohortes de survivants sont soumises, pour chaque âge, aux conditions de mortalité de la période visée par la table de mortalité.

Données publiées antérieurement : les espérances de vie à des âges déterminés pour chaque sexe figuraient déjà dans des éditions antérieures de *l'Annuaire démographique*. Pour plus de précisions concernant les années pour lesquelles ces données ont été publiées, se reporter à l'index historique.

22. Life expectancy at specified ages for each sex: latest available year, 1996 - 2015
Espérance de vie à un âge donné pour chaque sexe : dernière année disponible, 1996 - 2015

Continent, country or area and date / Continent, pays ou zone et date	Age (in years) - Age (en années)																				
	0	5	10	15	20	25	30	35	40	45	50	55	60	65	70	75	80	85	90	95	100

AFRICA - AFRIQUE

Algeria - Algérie[1]
2015
| Male - Hommes | 76.4 | 73.5 | 68.7 | 63.8 | 59.1 | 54.3 | 49.6 | 44.9 | 40.2 | 35.5 | 30.9 | 26.5 | 22.3 | 18.4 | 14.7 | 11.4 | 8.5 | 6.2 | ... | ... | ... |
| Female - Femmes | 77.8 | 74.7 | 69.8 | 64.9 | 60.1 | 55.2 | 50.4 | 45.5 | 40.8 | 36.1 | 31.5 | 27.0 | 22.6 | 18.5 | 14.5 | 10.8 | 7.6 | 5.0 | ... | ... | ... |

Benin - Bénin[2]
2002
| Male - Hommes | 57.2 | 63.4 | 59.1 | 54.7 | 50.2 | 45.9 | 41.8 | 37.8 | 33.8 | 30.0 | 26.2 | 22.7 | 19.4 | 16.2 | 13.2 | 10.6 | 8.1 | 5.5 | 3.8 | ... | ... |
| Female - Femmes | 61.3 | 65.4 | 61.2 | 56.7 | 52.3 | 48.1 | 43.9 | 39.9 | 36.0 | 32.1 | 28.3 | 24.6 | 21.2 | 18.0 | 14.2 | 10.8 | 7.7 | 4.8 | 2.9 | ... | ... |

Botswana[3]
2006
| Male - Hommes | 54.0 | 57.6 | 54.0 | 49.7 | 45.6 | 41.8 | 37.9 | 34.0 | 30.0 | 26.2 | 22.4 | 19.9 | 15.4 | 12.3 | 9.4 | 7.0 | 4.8 | ... | ... | ... | ... |
| Female - Femmes | 66.0 | 65.7 | 61.4 | 56.8 | 52.3 | 47.8 | 43.4 | 39.1 | 34.7 | 30.4 | 26.2 | 22.1 | 18.2 | 14.5 | 11.2 | 8.3 | 5.8 | ... | ... | ... | ... |

Burkina Faso[4]
2006
| Male - Hommes | 55.8 | 60.0 | 55.9 | 51.3 | 46.9 | 42.8 | 38.6 | 34.5 | 30.5 | 26.6 | 22.8 | 19.3 | 16.0 | 12.9 | 10.3 | 8.1 | 6.2 | 4.8 | ... | ... | ... |
| Female - Femmes | 57.5 | 61.6 | 57.6 | 53.1 | 48.6 | 44.4 | 40.2 | 36.1 | 32.0 | 28.0 | 24.1 | 20.3 | 16.8 | 13.5 | 10.7 | 8.4 | 6.4 | 4.9 | ... | ... | ... |

Burundi
2008
| Male - Hommes | 46.0 | 49.7 | 46.5 | 42.5 | 39.0 | 35.8 | 32.4 | 28.9 | 25.4 | 21.9 | 18.6 | 15.3 | 12.3 | 9.5 | 7.2 | 5.2 | 3.8 | ... | ... | ... | ... |
| Female - Femmes | 51.8 | 55.4 | 52.1 | 47.9 | 44.0 | 40.3 | 36.7 | 33.0 | 29.2 | 25.4 | 21.5 | 17.8 | 14.2 | 11.0 | 8.3 | 6.0 | 4.4 | ... | ... | ... | ... |
2014
| Male - Hommes | 56.5 | ... | ... | ... | ... | ... | ... | ... | ... | ... | ... | ... | ... | ... | ... | ... | ... | ... | ... | ... | ... |
| Female - Femmes | 60.6 | ... | ... | ... | ... | ... | ... | ... | ... | ... | ... | ... | ... | ... | ... | ... | ... | ... | ... | ... | ... |

Côte d'Ivoire
2006
| Male - Hommes | 49.6 | ... | ... | ... | ... | ... | ... | ... | ... | ... | ... | ... | ... | ... | ... | ... | ... | ... | ... | ... | ... |
| Female - Femmes | 53.0 | ... | ... | ... | ... | ... | ... | ... | ... | ... | ... | ... | ... | ... | ... | ... | ... | ... | ... | ... | ... |

Djibouti
1998
| Male - Hommes | 49.0 | ... | ... | ... | ... | ... | ... | ... | ... | ... | ... | ... | ... | ... | ... | ... | ... | ... | ... | ... | ... |
| Female - Femmes | 52.0 | ... | ... | ... | ... | ... | ... | ... | ... | ... | ... | ... | ... | ... | ... | ... | ... | ... | ... | ... | ... |

Egypt - Égypte
2011
| Male - Hommes | 68.6 | 65.5 | 60.6 | 55.7 | 50.9 | 46.1 | 41.4 | 36.6 | 31.9 | 27.3 | 23.1 | 19.2 | 15.7 | 12.2 | 9.1 | 6.4 | 3.4 | ... | ... | ... | ... |
| Female - Femmes | 71.4 | 68.1 | 63.2 | 58.2 | 53.3 | 48.4 | 43.5 | 38.7 | 33.9 | 29.1 | 24.5 | 20.1 | 16.1 | 12.3 | 8.8 | 5.7 | 2.4 | ... | ... | ... | ... |

Equatorial Guinea - Guinée équatoriale
2001
| Male - Hommes | ... | ... | ... | ... | ... | ... | ... | ... | ... | ... | ... | ... | ... | ... | ... | ... | ... | ... | ... | ... | ... |
| Female - Femmes | 59.3 | ... | ... | ... | ... | ... | ... | ... | ... | ... | ... | ... | ... | ... | ... | ... | ... | ... | ... | ... | ... |

Ghana
2005
| Male - Hommes | 58.3 | ... | ... | ... | ... | ... | ... | ... | ... | ... | ... | ... | ... | ... | ... | ... | ... | ... | ... | ... | ... |
| Female - Femmes | 62.0 | ... | ... | ... | ... | ... | ... | ... | ... | ... | ... | ... | ... | ... | ... | ... | ... | ... | ... | ... | ... |

Guinea-Bissau - Guinée-Bissau
2008 - 2009
| Male - Hommes | 49.2 | 49.8 | 45.3 | 41.0 | 36.8 | 32.8 | 29.3 | 26.2 | 23.3 | 20.7 | 18.0 | 15.5 | 13.1 | 11.2 | 9.4 | 8.0 | 6.8 | ... | ... | ... | ... |
| Female - Femmes | 51.2 | 50.1 | 45.7 | 41.5 | 37.8 | 34.4 | 31.3 | 28.4 | 25.6 | 22.9 | 20.0 | 17.4 | 14.9 | 12.8 | 10.6 | 8.8 | 7.1 | ... | ... | ... | ... |
2014
| Male - Hommes | 51.2 | ... | ... | ... | ... | ... | ... | ... | ... | ... | ... | ... | ... | ... | ... | ... | ... | ... | ... | ... | ... |
| Female - Femmes | 53.6 | ... | ... | ... | ... | ... | ... | ... | ... | ... | ... | ... | ... | ... | ... | ... | ... | ... | ... | ... | ... |

Kenya
1989 - 1999
| Male - Hommes | 52.9 | 54.8 | 51.1 | 46.6 | 42.3 | 38.3 | 34.5 | 31.0 | 27.7 | 24.4 | 21.0 | 17.7 | 14.5 | 11.6 | 8.9 | 6.7 | 5.0 | 3.8 | 3.1 | 2.5 | ... |
| Female - Femmes | 60.4 | 63.0 | 59.0 | 54.3 | 49.9 | 45.9 | 42.2 | 38.6 | 34.8 | 30.9 | 27.0 | 23.1 | 19.3 | 15.6 | 12.2 | 9.2 | 6.7 | 4.8 | 3.6 | 2.5 | ... |
2009
| Male - Hommes | 58.0 | ... | ... | ... | ... | ... | ... | ... | ... | ... | ... | ... | ... | ... | ... | ... | ... | ... | ... | ... | ... |
| Female - Femmes | 61.0 | ... | ... | ... | ... | ... | ... | ... | ... | ... | ... | ... | ... | ... | ... | ... | ... | ... | ... | ... | ... |

Lesotho
2006[5]
| Male - Hommes | 39.8 | 40.4 | 36.0 | 31.5 | 27.2 | 23.6 | 20.9 | 19.2 | 18.2 | 17.3 | 16.4 | 14.9 | 13.2 | 11.3 | 9.4 | 7.4 | 5.3 | 2.9 | ... | ... | ... |
| Female - Femmes | 42.9 | 42.7 | 38.4 | 33.8 | 29.6 | 26.3 | 24.2 | 23.2 | 22.8 | 22.3 | 21.5 | 20.2 | 18.6 | 16.7 | 14.5 | 12.1 | 9.6 | 7.4 | ... | ... | ... |
2011
| Male - Hommes | 39.4 | ... | ... | ... | ... | ... | ... | ... | ... | ... | ... | ... | ... | ... | ... | ... | ... | ... | ... | ... | ... |
| Female - Femmes | 45.3 | ... | ... | ... | ... | ... | ... | ... | ... | ... | ... | ... | ... | ... | ... | ... | ... | ... | ... | ... | ... |

Continent, country or area and date / Continent, pays ou zone et date	Age (in years) - Age (en années)																				
	0	5	10	15	20	25	30	35	40	45	50	55	60	65	70	75	80	85	90	95	100

AFRICA - AFRIQUE

Malawi
1992 - 1997
| Male - Hommes | 43.5 | 52.1 | 49.5 | 45.7 | 41.9 | 38.4 | 34.8 | 31.2 | 27.6 | 24.0 | 20.6 | 17.3 | 14.1 | 11.2 | 8.6 | 6.3 | 4.4 | ... | ... | ... | ... |
| Female - Femmes | 46.8 | 54.5 | 52.0 | 48.2 | 44.4 | 40.6 | 36.9 | 33.2 | 29.6 | 25.9 | 22.2 | 18.6 | 15.1 | 11.9 | 9.2 | 6.8 | 4.6 | ... | ... | ... | ... |
2008
| Male - Hommes | 47.4 | ... | ... | ... | ... | ... | ... | ... | ... | ... | ... | ... | ... | ... | ... | ... | ... | ... | ... | ... | ... |
| Female - Femmes | 50.6 | ... | ... | ... | ... | ... | ... | ... | ... | ... | ... | ... | ... | ... | ... | ... | ... | ... | ... | ... | ... |

Mauritania - Mauritanie
2013
| Male - Hommes | 58.3 | 61.5 | 57.5 | 53.0 | 48.7 | 44.6 | 40.5 | 36.4 | 32.2 | 28.2 | 24.2 | 20.4 | 16.8 | 13.5 | 10.5 | 8.0 | 6.0 | ... | ... | ... | ... |
| Female - Femmes | 61.8 | 63.8 | 59.8 | 55.3 | 50.9 | 46.6 | 42.4 | 38.1 | 33.9 | 29.8 | 25.6 | 21.7 | 17.8 | 14.3 | 11.2 | 8.5 | 6.4 | ... | ... | ... | ... |

Mauritius - Maurice[6]
2013 - 2015
| Male - Hommes | 71.1 | 67.1 | 62.2 | 57.3 | 52.5 | 47.8 | 43.2 | 38.6 | 34.2 | 30.0 | 25.9 | 22.0 | 18.3 | 15.0 | 12.0 | 9.4 | 7.2 | 5.5 | ... | ... | ... |
| Female - Femmes | 77.8 | 73.8 | 68.9 | 64.0 | 59.1 | 54.2 | 49.4 | 44.6 | 39.9 | 35.3 | 30.8 | 26.4 | 22.3 | 18.4 | 14.8 | 11.6 | 8.9 | 6.6 | ... | ... | ... |

Mayotte
2014
| Male - Hommes | 74.7 | ... | ... | ... | 56.2 | ... | ... | ... | 37.4 | ... | ... | ... | 19.4 | ... | ... | ... | ... | | | | |
| Female - Femmes | 77.9 | ... | ... | ... | 59.0 | ... | ... | ... | 39.7 | ... | ... | ... | 21.4 | ... | ... | ... | ... | | | | |

Morocco - Maroc
2013
| Male - Hommes | 72.4 | ... | ... | ... | ... | ... | ... | ... | ... | ... | ... | ... | ... | ... | ... | ... | ... | ... | ... | ... | ... |
| Female - Femmes | 75.1 | ... | ... | ... | ... | ... | ... | ... | ... | ... | ... | ... | ... | ... | ... | ... | ... | ... | ... | ... | ... |

Mozambique
2014
| Male - Hommes | 50.2 | 54.0 | 50.0 | 45.6 | 41.6 | 37.7 | 33.9 | 30.1 | 26.5 | 22.9 | 19.6 | 16.4 | 13.5 | 10.9 | 8.7 | 6.8 | 5.0 | ... | ... | ... | ... |
| Female - Femmes | 55.4 | 59.0 | 54.8 | 50.3 | 46.1 | 42.1 | 38.1 | 34.1 | 30.2 | 26.3 | 22.5 | 19.0 | 15.7 | 12.7 | 10.0 | 7.7 | 5.8 | ... | ... | ... | ... |

Namibia - Namibie
2011
| Male - Hommes | 53.3 | 52.4 | 48.0 | 43.4 | 39.0 | 35.1 | 31.5 | 28.6 | 25.8 | 23.2 | 20.6 | 17.7 | 15.1 | 12.6 | 9.8 | 7.4 | 5.6 | ... | ... | ... | ... |
| Female - Femmes | 60.5 | 59.6 | 55.1 | 50.5 | 46.1 | 42.0 | 38.4 | 35.2 | 32.0 | 28.7 | 25.2 | 21.6 | 17.9 | 14.5 | 11.3 | 8.6 | 6.5 | ... | ... | ... | ... |

Republic of South Sudan - République de Soudan du Sud
2010
| Male - Hommes | 54.4 | 57.4 | 53.2 | 48.8 | 44.6 | 40.7 | 36.8 | 32.8 | 28.9 | 25.0 | 21.2 | 17.6 | 14.2 | 11.2 | 8.5 | 6.3 | 4.5 | 3.2 | 2.2 | 1.5 | ... |
| Female - Femmes | 54.5 | 56.2 | 51.9 | 47.5 | 43.3 | 39.4 | 35.4 | 31.5 | 27.5 | 23.7 | 19.9 | 16.4 | 13.1 | 10.2 | 7.7 | 5.6 | 4.1 | 2.9 | 2.0 | 1.4 | ... |

Reunion - Réunion
2014
| Male - Hommes | 77.1 | ... | ... | ... | 57.8 | ... | ... | ... | 38.9 | ... | ... | ... | 21.7 | ... | ... | ... | ... | | | | |
| Female - Femmes | 83.7 | ... | ... | ... | 64.6 | ... | ... | ... | 45.0 | ... | ... | ... | 26.3 | ... | ... | ... | ... | | | | |

Rwanda
2002
| Male - Hommes | 48.4 | 58.4 | 54.4 | 49.9 | 45.6 | 41.6 | 37.5 | 33.5 | 29.4 | 25.4 | 21.6 | 17.9 | 14.5 | 11.4 | 8.6 | 6.3 | 4.6 | ... | ... | ... | ... |
| Female - Femmes | 53.8 | 63.1 | 58.8 | 54.3 | 49.9 | 45.7 | 41.4 | 37.2 | 32.9 | 28.7 | 24.5 | 20.4 | 16.5 | 12.9 | 9.8 | 7.1 | 5.1 | ... | ... | ... | ... |
2012[7]
| Male - Hommes | 62.6 | ... | ... | ... | ... | ... | ... | ... | ... | ... | ... | ... | ... | ... | ... | ... | ... | ... | ... | ... | ... |
| Female - Femmes | 66.2 | ... | ... | ... | ... | ... | ... | ... | ... | ... | ... | ... | ... | ... | ... | ... | ... | ... | ... | ... | ... |

Saint Helena ex. dep. - Sainte-Hélène sans dép.[8]
2003 - 2012
| Male - Hommes | 72.0 | 68.1 | 63.4 | ... | 53.9 | ... | 44.2 | ... | 35.5 | ... | 27.1 | ... | 19.3 | ... | 12.5 | ... | 7.2 | ... | ... | ... | ... |
| Female - Femmes | 79.7 | 75.3 | 70.3 | ... | 60.3 | ... | 51.0 | ... | 41.8 | ... | 32.0 | ... | 23.0 | ... | 15.5 | ... | 8.6 | ... | ... | ... | ... |

Sao Tome and Principe - Sao Tomé-et-Principe
2011 - 2012
| Male - Hommes | 62.1 | 59.5 | 54.6 | 50.1 | 45.8 | 41.6 | 37.5 | 33.4 | 29.6 | 25.8 | 22.1 | 18.4 | 15.2 | 12.0 | 9.8 | 7.4 | 5.0 | ... | ... | ... | ... |
| Female - Femmes | 68.7 | 65.9 | 61.2 | 56.5 | 51.8 | 47.1 | 42.5 | 38.0 | 33.5 | 29.3 | 25.3 | 21.7 | 18.2 | 14.9 | 11.8 | 9.0 | 6.6 | ... | ... | ... | ... |

Senegal - Sénégal[9]
2011
| Male - Hommes | 56.9 | ... | ... | ... | ... | ... | ... | ... | ... | ... | ... | ... | ... | ... | ... | ... | ... | ... | ... | ... | ... |
| Female - Femmes | 59.8 | ... | ... | ... | ... | ... | ... | ... | ... | ... | ... | ... | ... | ... | ... | ... | ... | ... | ... | ... | ... |

22. Life expectancy at specified ages for each sex: latest available year, 1996 - 2015
Espérance de vie à un âge donné pour chaque sexe : dernière année disponible, 1996 - 2015 (continued - suite)

Continent, country or area and date / Continent, pays ou zone et date	Age (in years) - Age (en années)																				
	0	5	10	15	20	25	30	35	40	45	50	55	60	65	70	75	80	85	90	95	100

AFRICA - AFRIQUE

Seychelles
2007
Male - Hommes	68.9	65.0	60.2	55.3	50.5	45.9	41.6	37.0	32.7	28.7	24.4	20.9	17.1	14.1	11.0	9.0	7.4	...	...	...	...
Female - Femmes	77.7	73.3	68.5	63.5	58.5	53.7	48.9	44.3	39.5	35.3	31.0	26.4	22.2	18.5	15.1	12.1	9.2	...	...	...	...

2014
Male - Hommes	68.4	...	...	...	...	...	...	...	...	...	...	...	...	...	...	...	...	...	...	...	...
Female - Femmes	78.3	...	...	...	...	...	...	...	...	...	...	...	...	...	...	...	...	...	...	...	...

Sierra Leone
2004
Male - Hommes	47.5	...	...	...	...	...	...	...	...	...	...	...	...	...	...	...	...	...	...	...	...
Female - Femmes	49.4	...	...	...	...	...	...	...	...	...	...	...	...	...	...	...	...	...	...	...	...

South Africa - Afrique du Sud
2009
Male - Hommes	53.5	...	...	...	...	...	...	...	...	...	...	...	...	...	...	...	...	...	...	...	...
Female - Femmes	57.2	...	...	...	...	...	...	...	...	...	...	...	...	...	...	...	...	...	...	...	...

Swaziland
2007
Male - Hommes	42.2	44.9	40.5	36.0	31.5	27.5	24.9	23.3	22.1	20.9	19.1	17.4	15.4	13.6	10.9	8.9	...	...	...	...	...
Female - Femmes	43.1	48.2	43.9	39.3	35.0	32.3	30.9	30.3	29.5	27.6	25.1	22.7	19.5	16.8	13.5	10.5	...	...	...	...	...

Tunisia - Tunisie
2011
Male - Hommes	72.9	...	...	...	...	...	...	...	...	...	...	...	...	...	...	...	...	...	...	...	...
Female - Femmes	76.9	...	...	...	...	...	...	...	...	...	...	...	...	...	...	...	...	...	...	...	...

Uganda - Ouganda[10]
2002
Male - Hommes	48.8	53.0	49.2	44.8	40.5	36.6	33.6	31.0	28.4	25.8	23.2	20.4	17.2	14.4	11.6	9.2	6.7	4.1	...	...	...
Female - Femmes	52.0	56.0	52.1	47.6	43.3	39.6	36.7	34.2	31.5	28.6	25.6	22.3	18.9	15.7	12.6	9.9	7.0	4.2	...	...	...

Zimbabwe
2001 - 2002
Male - Hommes	45.8	44.2	40.0	35.4	30.9	26.8	23.8	22.1	21.8	21.3	20.4	19.2	17.7	15.7	13.7	11.4	9.5	7.5	6.2	5.2	...
Female - Femmes	50.3	48.6	44.2	39.7	35.3	32.1	30.4	30.1	30.2	29.0	27.6	25.3	22.9	20.2	17.6	14.8	12.2	9.9	8.1	7.3	...

AMERICA, NORTH - AMÉRIQUE DU NORD

Anguilla
2000 - 2002
Male - Hommes	76.5	72.1	67.1	62.1	57.3	53.1	48.4	43.7	39.4	34.7	30.2	25.4	21.1	16.5	12.7	10.0	8.0	6.9	...	...	...
Female - Femmes	81.1	76.4	71.4	66.4	61.4	57.1	52.7	47.7	42.7	38.3	33.5	28.7	24.0	19.4	15.3	10.8	8.3	7.6	...	...	...

Antigua and Barbuda - Antigua-et-Barbuda
2010
Male - Hommes	74.0	...	...	...	...	...	...	...	...	...	...	...	...	...	...	...	...	...	...	...	...
Female - Femmes	79.7	...	...	...	...	...	...	...	...	...	...	...	...	...	...	...	...	...	...	...	...

Aruba
2010 - 2011
Male - Hommes	73.9	69.4	64.4	59.5	54.6	50.0	45.4	40.8	36.3	31.7	27.3	23.1	19.1	15.3	12.3	9.4	7.3	5.0	3.5	2.7	...
Female - Femmes	79.8	76.2	71.2	66.2	61.3	56.4	51.5	46.6	42.0	37.3	32.6	27.9	23.8	19.7	16.0	12.5	9.5	6.8	5.0	3.8	...

Bahamas
1999 - 2001
Male - Hommes	69.9	...	...	...	...	...	...	...	...	...	...	...	...	...	...	...	...	...	...	...	...
Female - Femmes	76.4	...	...	...	...	...	...	...	...	...	...	...	...	...	...	...	...	...	...	...	...

Bermuda - Bermudes
2015
Male - Hommes	77.3	72.6	67.6	62.7	57.9	53.4	48.8	44.2	39.6	35.1	30.5	26.1	21.8	17.8	14.1	10.7	7.7	5.0	...	...	...
Female - Femmes	84.9	80.1	75.1	70.1	65.1	60.2	55.2	50.3	45.4	40.6	35.8	31.1	26.6	22.2	18.0	13.9	10.6	7.6	...	...	...

British Virgin Islands - Îles Vierges britanniques
2004
Male - Hommes	69.9	...	...	...	...	...	...	...	...	...	...	...	...	...	...	...	...	...	...	...	...
Female - Femmes	78.5	...	...	...	...	...	...	...	...	...	...	...	...	...	...	...	...	...	...	...	...

22. Life expectancy at specified ages for each sex: latest available year, 1996 - 2015
Espérance de vie à un âge donné pour chaque sexe : dernière année disponible, 1996 - 2015 (continued - suite)

Continent, country or area and date / Continent, pays ou zone et date	Age (in years) - Age (en années)																				
	0	5	10	15	20	25	30	35	40	45	50	55	60	65	70	75	80	85	90	95	100
AMERICA, NORTH - AMÉRIQUE DU NORD																					
Canada																					
2006 - 2008																					
Male - Hommes	78.5	74.0	69.1	64.1	59.3	54.5	49.7	44.9	40.2	35.5	30.9	26.5	22.3	18.3	14.7	11.4	8.5	6.2	4.5	...	...
Female - Femmes	83.2	78.6	73.6	68.7	63.8	58.9	53.9	49.1	44.2	39.4	34.7	30.2	25.7	21.5	17.4	13.7	10.4	7.5	5.4	...	...
Cayman Islands - Îles Caïmanes[11]																					
2006																					
Male - Hommes	76.3	72.1	67.1	62.1	57.7	53.3	48.9	44.0	39.3	34.5	29.8	25.3	20.8	17.1	13.6	10.2	8.2	6.4	3.3	5.3	2.5
Female - Femmes	83.8	79.8	74.8	69.8	65.1	60.1	55.2	50.2	45.3	40.4	35.7	30.9	26.1	21.9	17.5	13.9	10.4	6.9	7.0	3.1	2.5
Costa Rica																					
2015																					
Male - Hommes	77.4	73.1	68.2	63.2	58.5	53.8	49.2	44.5	39.9	35.3	30.9	26.6	22.4	18.5	15.0	11.8	9.0	6.7	4.8	3.3	2.1
Female - Femmes	82.4	78.1	73.1	68.2	63.3	58.4	53.5	48.6	43.8	39.0	34.3	29.7	25.3	21.1	17.1	13.4	10.2	7.4	5.3	3.6	2.3
Cuba																					
2011 - 2013																					
Male - Hommes	76.5	72.0	67.0	62.1	57.3	52.5	47.7	42.9	38.2	33.6	29.2	25.0	21.0	17.3	14.0	11.0	8.4	6.3	4.9	3.8	2.0
Female - Femmes	80.4	75.9	71.0	66.0	61.1	56.2	51.4	46.5	41.7	36.9	32.3	27.9	23.6	19.6	15.8	12.4	9.4	6.9	5.1	3.8	2.1
Curaçao																					
2011 - 2014																					
Male - Hommes	74.0	70.1	65.2	60.3	55.4	50.8	46.3	41.6	37.1	32.7	28.4	24.4	20.5	17.0	13.8	11.0	8.6	6.5	4.9	3.6	2.9
Female - Femmes	81.2	77.8	72.8	67.8	62.9	57.9	53.0	48.1	43.3	38.5	33.8	29.3	24.9	20.7	16.8	13.2	10.1	7.4	5.2	3.6	2.7
Dominica - Dominique																					
2008																					
Male - Hommes	73.8	...	...	...	...	...	...	...	...	...	...	...	...	...	...	...	...	...	...	...	...
Female - Femmes	78.2	...	...	...	...	...	...	...	...	...	...	...	...	...	...	...	...	...	...	...	...
Dominican Republic - République dominicaine																					
2010 - 2015																					
Male - Hommes	70.0	67.5	62.6	57.7	53.0	48.7	44.3	40.0	35.6	31.3	27.2	23.3	19.6	16.2	13.2	10.5	...	...	...	...	...
Female - Femmes	74.8	71.8	66.9	62.0	57.1	52.4	47.7	43.1	38.5	34.1	29.7	25.5	21.6	17.9	14.6	11.7	...	...	...	...	...
El Salvador[12]																					
2000 - 2005																					
Male - Hommes	65.4	62.6	57.8	52.9	48.7	45.0	41.5	37.8	34.1	30.4	26.8	23.3	20.0	16.7	13.8	11.1	9.0	...	...	...	...
Female - Femmes	74.9	72.0	67.1	62.3	57.5	52.9	48.2	43.6	39.0	34.6	30.3	26.1	22.1	18.4	15.0	12.0	9.6	...	...	...	...
Greenland - Groenland																					
2010 - 2014																					
Male - Hommes	69.1	65.4	60.4	55.5	51.1	47.3	42.9	38.5	34.0	29.6	25.3	21.0	17.1	13.4	10.2	7.8	6.0	4.7	3.2	4.0	...
Female - Femmes	73.7	69.3	64.4	59.5	54.9	50.5	45.7	40.9	36.4	31.7	27.2	22.7	18.5	14.8	11.7	8.8	6.3	4.5	3.3	3.1	...
Guadeloupe																					
2014																					
Male - Hommes	76.1	...	...	...	57.2	...	...	...	39.2	...	...	...	22.1	...	...	...	...	...	...	...	...
Female - Femmes	83.4	...	...	...	64.2	...	...	...	45.1	...	...	...	26.8	...	...	...	...	...	...	...	...
Guatemala																					
1995 - 2000																					
Male - Hommes	61.4	60.6	56.0	51.2	46.8	42.7	38.8	34.9	31.2	27.4	23.7	20.1	16.8	13.6	10.7	8.2	6.1	...	...	...	...
Female - Femmes	67.2	66.2	62.6	56.9	52.3	47.7	43.3	38.9	34.6	30.4	26.3	22.3	18.6	15.2	12.0	9.2	6.9	...	...	...	...
Jamaica - Jamaïque																					
2006																					
Male - Hommes	69.7	67.0	62.2	57.3	52.6	47.9	43.2	38.5	33.8	29.3	24.9	20.8	16.9	13.5	10.4	7.8	5.8	4.1	2.9	2.1	1.5
Female - Femmes	75.2	71.6	66.7	61.7	56.8	52.0	47.1	42.3	37.6	32.9	28.3	23.9	19.7	15.9	12.4	9.4	6.9	5.0	3.5	2.4	1.7
Martinique																					
2014																					
Male - Hommes	78.1	...	...	...	59.0	...	...	...	40.9	...	...	...	23.1	...	...	...	...	...	...	...	...
Female - Femmes	83.9	...	...	...	64.6	...	...	...	45.3	...	...	...	26.7	...	...	...	...	...	...	...	...
Mexico - Mexique																					
2008																					
Male - Hommes	72.8	69.2	64.3	59.4	54.7	50.0	45.5	40.9	36.5	32.1	27.9	23.9	20.2	16.8	13.7	11.0	8.7	6.6	4.9	3.5	2.6
Female - Femmes	77.5	73.8	68.9	63.9	59.0	54.2	49.3	44.5	39.7	35.1	30.6	26.2	22.1	18.3	14.8	11.7	9.0	6.8	4.9	3.5	2.6
2014																					
Male - Hommes	72.1	...	...	...	...	...	...	...	...	...	...	...	...	...	...	...	...	...	...	...	...
Female - Femmes	77.6	...	...	...	...	...	...	...	...	...	...	...	...	...	...	...	...	...	...	...	...

22. Life expectancy at specified ages for each sex: latest available year, 1996 - 2015
Espérance de vie à un âge donné pour chaque sexe : dernière année disponible, 1996 - 2015 (continued - suite)

Continent, country or area and date / Continent, pays ou zone et date	0	5	10	15	20	25	30	35	40	45	50	55	60	65	70	75	80	85	90	95	100
AMERICA, NORTH - AMÉRIQUE DU NORD																					
Nicaragua																					
2005 - 2010																					
Male - Hommes	63.4	61.1	56.5	51.8	47.9	44.2	40.5	36.5	32.5	28.6	24.9	21.3	17.7	14.6	11.6	9.0	6.5	...	...	...	...
Female - Femmes	68.9	66.2	61.4	56.7	52.1	47.6	43.0	38.5	34.1	29.8	25.7	21.9	18.1	14.9	11.8	9.3	6.9	...	...	...	...
Panama[13]																					
2014																					
Male - Hommes	74.6	71.3	66.4	61.6	57.0	52.7	48.5	44.1	39.6	35.2	30.8	26.6	22.6	18.9	15.6	12.5	9.9	7.6	5.7	4.1	2.5
Female - Femmes	80.7	77.1	72.2	67.3	62.4	57.6	52.9	48.2	43.5	38.8	34.2	29.8	25.4	21.3	17.5	14.0	10.9	8.3	6.1	4.2	2.5
Puerto Rico - Porto Rico																					
2013 - 2015																					
Male - Hommes	76.4	72.0	67.1	62.1	57.4	52.9	48.5	44.1	39.6	35.1	30.8	26.8	22.9	19.3	15.9	12.7	9.9	7.8	...	...	...
Female - Femmes	84.0	79.6	74.6	69.6	64.7	59.8	55.0	50.1	45.4	40.6	36.0	31.5	27.2	23.0	18.9	15.2	12.0	9.4	...	...	...
Saint Kitts and Nevis - Saint-Kitts-et-Nevis																					
1998																					
Male - Hommes	68.2	65.0	60.1	55.3	50.5	45.8	41.1	36.5	32.7	28.5	24.3	20.6	16.6	13.3	11.0	9.1	6.6	4.7	3.4	2.2	0.4
Female - Femmes	70.7	67.5	62.5	57.6	52.7	48.0	43.4	38.8	34.4	29.8	25.4	21.3	17.6	14.3	11.3	8.9	6.3	4.6	3.3	2.2	0.4
Saint Lucia - Sainte-Lucie																					
2005																					
Male - Hommes	69.9	66.4	61.5	56.6	52.0	47.4	43.1	38.6	34.3	30.1	25.9	21.7	17.9	14.7	11.8	9.0	7.2	5.2	...	...	...
Female - Femmes	75.7	72.2	67.3	62.4	57.5	52.6	47.8	43.2	38.4	33.8	29.2	25.0	20.8	17.2	13.8	10.4	7.7	4.8	...	...	...
2012																					
Male - Hommes	75.3	...	...	...	...	...	...	...	...	...	...	...	...	...	...	...	...	...	...	...	...
Female - Femmes	82.5	...	...	...	...	...	...	...	...	...	...	...	...	...	...	...	...	...	...	...	...
Saint Vincent and the Grenadines - Saint-Vincent-et-les Grenadines																					
2001																					
Male - Hommes	66.9	63.9	59.2	54.3	49.6	45.1	40.7	36.5	32.3	28.2	24.1	19.9	16.2	12.8	9.7	7.3	4.3	4.1	...	...	...
Female - Femmes	72.9	69.3	64.5	59.5	54.7	49.8	45.2	40.7	36.1	31.7	27.3	23.0	19.0	14.6	10.8	7.3	4.1	3.6	...	...	...
2014																					
Male - Hommes	68.4	...	...	...	...	...	...	...	...	...	...	...	...	...	...	...	...	...	...	...	...
Female - Femmes	74.6	...	...	...	...	...	...	...	...	...	...	...	...	...	...	...	...	...	...	...	...
Sint Maarten (Dutch part) - Saint-Martin (partie néerlandaise)																					
2011 - 2012																					
Male - Hommes	69.2	65.5	60.6	55.7	51.0	46.9	42.5	38.2	33.9	29.5	25.3	21.2	17.6	13.8	10.4	7.4	5.2	4.0	...	...	...
Female - Femmes	77.1	72.3	67.4	62.6	57.8	52.8	48.0	43.1	38.2	33.5	28.6	24.0	19.4	14.9	11.5	8.1	5.0	1.8	...	...	...
Trinidad and Tobago - Trinité-et-Tobago[2]																					
2011																					
Male - Hommes	71.4	67.6	62.7	57.8	53.2	49.0	44.7	40.4	36.0	31.7	27.5	23.5	19.6	16.2	12.9	10.2	7.9	6.0	...	...	...
Female - Femmes	77.8	74.1	69.2	64.2	59.4	54.6	49.9	45.3	40.6	36.2	31.7	27.5	23.3	19.4	15.9	12.6	9.7	7.6	...	...	...
Turks and Caicos Islands - Îles Turques et Caïques																					
2001																					
Male - Hommes	79.0	75.3	70.3	65.3	60.3	55.8	50.8	46.0	41.2	37.1	33.0	28.4	24.3	20.8	17.5	12.5	7.5	4.1	...	...	...
Female - Femmes	77.4	72.5	67.5	62.5	57.5	52.9	48.2	43.4	38.6	33.8	29.6	25.0	20.0	17.0	13.2	11.7	10.3	8.8	...	...	...
United States of America - États-Unis d'Amérique																					
2014																					
Male - Hommes	76.4	72.0	67.0	62.1	57.3	52.6	48.0	43.3	38.7	34.2	29.8	25.6	21.7	18.0	14.4	11.2	8.3	5.9	4.1	2.9	2.1
Female - Femmes	81.2	76.7	71.7	66.8	61.9	57.0	52.1	47.3	42.6	37.9	33.3	28.9	24.7	20.5	16.6	13.0	9.7	7.0	4.8	3.3	2.3

Continent, country or area and date / Continent, pays ou zone et date	Age (in years) - Age (en années)																				
	0	5	10	15	20	25	30	35	40	45	50	55	60	65	70	75	80	85	90	95	100
AMERICA, SOUTH - AMÉRIQUE DU SUD																					
Argentina - Argentine 2008 - 2010																					
Male - Hommes	72.1	68.2	63.3	58.4	53.7	49.1	44.5	39.8	35.2	30.7	26.3	22.2	18.5	15.0	11.9	9.2	6.9	5.2	4.0	3.1	2.6
Female - Femmes	78.8	74.8	69.9	65.0	60.1	55.3	50.5	45.6	40.9	36.2	31.7	27.3	23.1	19.0	15.2	11.7	8.6	6.3	4.7	3.5	2.9
Bolivia (Plurinational State of) - Bolivie (État plurinational de)[14] 2015 - 2016																					
Male - Hommes	68.6	66.9	62.3	57.6	53.1	48.8	44.5	40.2	36.0	31.8	27.8	23.9	20.2	16.8	13.8	11.0	8.7	6.7	4.8	3.7	...
Female - Femmes	75.3	73.2	68.5	63.6	58.9	54.3	49.6	45.0	40.4	36.0	31.7	27.6	23.6	20.0	16.6	13.6	10.8	8.4	6.2	4.7	...
Brazil - Brésil[13] 2014																					
Male - Hommes	71.6	67.9	63.0	58.2	53.6	49.3	44.9	40.5	36.1	31.8	27.7	23.8	20.1	16.6	13.4	10.6	8.3	...	...	...	...
Female - Femmes	78.8	75.0	70.1	65.2	60.4	55.5	50.7	46.0	41.2	36.6	32.1	27.8	23.6	19.7	16.0	12.8	9.9	...			
Chile - Chili 2013																					
Male - Hommes	76.2	71.9	67.0	62.1	57.2	52.5	47.7	43.0	38.3	33.7	29.2	24.9	20.7	16.7	13.2	10.0	7.1	5.0	3.1	...	...
Female - Femmes	81.4	77.1	72.1	67.2	62.3	57.3	52.4	47.6	42.7	37.9	33.2	28.6	24.2	19.9	15.9	12.2	8.9	6.1	3.5	...	...
Colombia - Colombie 2010 - 2015																					
Male - Hommes	72.1	68.9	64.0	59.1	54.5	50.1	45.7	41.3	36.8	32.3	27.9	23.7	19.7	16.0	12.7	9.8	7.4	...	...	...	...
Female - Femmes	78.5	74.9	70.0	65.1	60.2	55.4	50.6	45.8	41.0	36.3	31.7	27.2	22.9	18.8	15.0	11.6	8.7	...	...	...	...
Ecuador - Équateur[15] 2010 - 2016																					
Male - Hommes	73.7	70.4	65.4	60.5	55.7	50.9	46.3	41.7	37.2	32.6	28.2	24.0	20.0	16.2	12.8	9.8	7.3	5.2	3.6	2.4	0.5
Female - Femmes	79.3	75.9	70.9	66.0	61.1	56.2	51.4	46.5	41.7	36.9	32.2	27.7	23.2	18.9	14.9	11.3	8.2	5.7	3.9	2.6	0.5
French Guiana - Guyane française 2014																					
Male - Hommes	76.7	...	...	...	58.0	...	...	...	39.7	...	...	...	22.0	...	...	...	...	...	...	...	...
Female - Femmes	83.1	...	...	...	64.2	...	...	...	44.8	...	...	...	26.6	...	...	...	...	...	...	...	...
Paraguay 2005 - 2010																					
Male - Hommes	69.7	...	...	...	...	...	...	...	...	...	...	...	...	...	...	...	...	...	...	...	...
Female - Femmes	73.9	...	...	...	...	...	...	...	...	...	...	...	...	...	...	...	...	...	...	...	...
Peru - Pérou[13] 2010 - 2015																					
Male - Hommes	71.5	69.0	64.3	59.4	54.7	50.0	45.5	40.9	36.4	32.0	27.7	23.6	19.8	16.2	13.0	10.1	7.7	...	...	...	...
Female - Femmes	76.8	73.8	69.0	64.1	59.3	54.5	49.7	45.0	40.3	35.7	31.2	26.9	22.7	18.7	15.0	11.7	8.8	...	...	...	...
Suriname 2011 - 2013																					
Male - Hommes	69.3	65.7	60.8	55.9	51.3	46.8	42.3	37.9	33.7	29.5	25.5	21.7	18.1	14.8	11.8	9.1	6.5	4.7	...	...	...
Female - Femmes	75.1	71.6	66.6	61.8	57.0	52.3	47.7	43.1	38.4	33.9	29.5	25.2	21.1	17.0	13.3	9.9	6.9	4.7	...	...	...
Uruguay 2010																					
Male - Hommes	72.8	68.5	63.6	58.7	54.0	49.4	44.8	40.2	35.6	31.0	26.6	22.4	18.6	15.1	12.0	9.3	7.0	5.2	4.0	...	...
Female - Femmes	80.0	75.6	70.7	65.8	60.9	56.1	51.2	46.4	41.6	36.9	32.3	27.9	23.6	19.5	15.6	12.0	8.9	6.4	4.5	...	...
Venezuela (Bolivarian Republic of) - Venezuela (République bolivarienne du) 1995 - 2000																					
Male - Hommes	68.6	66.6	61.8	56.9	52.3	47.8	43.3	38.8	34.3	29.9	25.6	21.6	17.9	14.5	11.4	8.6	5.9	...	...	...	...
Female - Femmes	74.5	72.1	67.2	62.3	57.5	52.6	47.8	43.1	38.4	33.7	29.2	24.9	20.8	16.9	13.3	9.9	6.9	...	...	...	...
2007																					
Male - Hommes	70.7	...	...	...	...	...	...	...	...	...	...	...	...	...	...	...	...	...	...	...	...
Female - Femmes	76.6	...	...	...	...	...	...	...	...	...	...	...	...	...	...	...	...	...	...	...	...
ASIA - ASIE																					
Afghanistan 2004																					
Male - Hommes	45.0	...	...	...	...	...	...	...	...	...	...	...	...	...	...	...	...	...	...	...	...
Female - Femmes	44.0	...	...	...	...	...	...	...	...	...	...	...	...	...	...	...	...	...	...	...	...

22. Life expectancy at specified ages for each sex: latest available year, 1996 - 2015
Espérance de vie à un âge donné pour chaque sexe : dernière année disponible, 1996 - 2015 (continued - suite)

Continent, country or area and date / Continent, pays ou zone et date	Age (in years) - Age (en années)																				
	0	5	10	15	20	25	30	35	40	45	50	55	60	65	70	75	80	85	90	95	100
ASIA - ASIE																					
Armenia - Arménie																					
2006 - 2007																					
Male - Hommes	70.2	66.3	61.4	56.4	51.6	46.8	42.0	37.3	32.7	28.3	24.1	20.1	16.4	13.1	10.3	7.8	5.7	3.9	2.6	1.6	0.7
Female - Femmes	76.6	72.5	67.6	62.7	57.7	52.8	47.9	43.0	38.2	33.5	28.8	24.3	20.0	15.9	12.4	9.2	6.4	4.1	2.7	1.8	0.7
Azerbaijan - Azerbaïdjan																					
2013																					
Male - Hommes	71.6	67.6	62.7	57.8	53.0	48.2	43.4	38.7	34.1	29.6	25.3	21.2	17.4	14.1	10.8	8.2	5.9	5.0	5.1	3.3	0.5
Female - Femmes	76.8	72.8	67.9	63.0	58.1	53.2	48.3	43.4	38.6	33.8	29.1	24.6	20.2	16.2	12.4	9.2	6.6	4.8	3.7	2.6	0.8
2014																					
Male - Hommes	72.2	...	...	...	...	...	...	...	...	...	...	...	...	...	...	...	...	...	...	...	...
Female - Femmes	77.3	...	...	...	...	...	...	...	...	...	...	...	...	...	...	...	...	...	...	...	...
Bahrain - Bahreïn																					
2001																					
Male - Hommes	73.2	69.3	64.4	59.5	54.7	49.9	45.2	40.4	35.6	30.9	26.4	22.0	17.8	14.1	11.3	9.5	...	...	...	...	...
Female - Femmes	76.2	72.0	67.1	62.1	57.2	52.3	47.4	42.5	37.7	32.9	28.2	23.7	19.6	15.9	12.9	10.9	...	...	...	...	...
2010 - 2015																					
Male - Hommes	75.8	...	...	...	...	...	...	...	...	...	...	...	...	...	...	...	...	...	...	...	...
Female - Femmes	77.4	...	...	...	...	...	...	...	...	...	...	...	...	...	...	...	...	...	...	...	...
Bangladesh																					
2011																					
Male - Hommes	67.9	65.5	60.8	56.1	51.3	46.5	41.8	37.1	32.6	28.2	24.1	20.2	16.6	13.2	10.0	6.7	4.4	...	...	...	...
Female - Femmes	70.3	67.8	63.1	58.3	53.6	48.8	44.0	39.3	34.7	30.1	25.6	21.4	17.4	13.8	10.3	6.7	5.6	...	...	...	...
2013																					
Male - Hommes	68.8	...	...	...	...	...	...	...	...	...	...	...	...	...	...	...	...	...	...	...	...
Female - Femmes	71.4	...	...	...	...	...	...	...	...	...	...	...	...	...	...	...	...	...	...	...	...
Bhutan - Bhoutan																					
2005																					
Male - Hommes	65.7	...	...	...	...	...	...	...	...	...	...	...	...	...	...	...	...	...	...	...	...
Female - Femmes	66.9	...	...	...	...	...	...	...	...	...	...	...	...	...	...	...	...	...	...	...	...
Brunei Darussalam - Brunéi Darussalam																					
2014																					
Male - Hommes	75.9	...	...	...	...	...	...	...	...	...	...	...	...	...	...	...	...	...	...	...	...
Female - Femmes	78.8	...	...	...	...	...	...	...	...	...	...	...	...	...	...	...	...	...	...	...	...
China - Chine[16]																					
2010																					
Male - Hommes	66.8	...	...	...	...	...	...	...	...	...	...	...	...	...	...	...	...	...	...	...	...
Female - Femmes	70.5	...	...	...	...	...	...	...	...	...	...	...	...	...	...	...	...	...	...	...	...
China, Hong Kong SAR - Chine, Hong Kong RAS																					
2014																					
Male - Hommes	81.2	76.3	71.4	66.4	61.5	56.5	51.6	46.8	42.0	37.3	32.6	28.1	23.7	19.6	15.7	12.2	9.2	6.7	4.7	3.3	2.2
Female - Femmes	86.9	82.1	77.2	72.2	67.2	62.3	57.3	52.4	47.5	42.6	37.8	33.1	28.6	24.1	19.7	15.6	11.9	8.7	6.2	4.3	2.9
China, Macao SAR - Chine, Macao RAS																					
2012 - 2015																					
Male - Hommes	79.9	75.2	70.3	65.3	60.4	55.6	50.7	45.9	41.2	36.6	32.0	27.6	23.4	19.3	15.5	12.1	9.2	7.3	...	...	...
Female - Femmes	86.3	81.5	76.5	71.6	66.6	61.8	56.8	51.9	47.1	42.2	37.5	32.9	28.3	23.8	19.4	15.5	12.2	9.6	...	...	...
Cyprus - Chypre[17]																					
2013																					
Male - Hommes	80.0	75.1	70.2	65.3	60.4	55.5	50.7	45.8	41.0	36.3	31.6	27.0	22.6	18.5	14.7	11.2	8.2	5.9	...	...	...
Female - Femmes	84.8	79.8	74.9	69.9	64.9	60.0	55.0	50.1	45.2	40.3	35.4	30.6	25.9	21.4	17.2	13.1	9.5	6.6	...	...	...
2014																					
Male - Hommes	80.9	...	...	...	...	...	...	...	...	...	...	...	...	...	...	...	...	...	...	...	...
Female - Femmes	84.7	...	...	...	...	...	...	...	...	...	...	...	...	...	...	...	...	...	...	...	...
Democratic People's Republic of Korea - République populaire démocratique de Corée																					
2008																					
Male - Hommes	65.6	...	...	...	...	...	...	...	...	...	...	...	...	...	...	...	...	...	...	...	...
Female - Femmes	72.7	...	...	...	...	...	...	...	...	...	...	...	...	...	...	...	...	...	...	...	...

22. Life expectancy at specified ages for each sex: latest available year, 1996 - 2015
Espérance de vie à un âge donné pour chaque sexe : dernière année disponible, 1996 - 2015 (continued - suite)

Continent, country or area and date / Continent, pays ou zone et date	0	5	10	15	20	25	30	35	40	45	50	55	60	65	70	75	80	85	90	95	100
ASIA - ASIE																					
Georgia - Géorgie 2010																					
Male - Hommes	70.2	66.3	61.3	56.4	51.6	46.9	42.2	37.6	33.0	28.7	24.7	20.9	17.4	14.2	11.5	9.2	7.5	6.5	...	...	...
Female - Femmes	78.6	74.5	69.6	64.6	59.7	54.8	49.9	45.0	40.2	35.5	30.8	26.3	22.0	18.0	14.3	11.1	8.8	7.5	...	...	...
India - Inde[18] 2002 - 2006																					
Male - Hommes	62.6	63.8	59.3	54.6	49.9	45.4	40.9	36.5	32.2	28.0	24.0	20.2	16.7	13.6	10.9	...	...	...	...		
Female - Femmes	64.2	67.4	62.9	58.2	53.7	49.2	44.8	40.2	35.7	31.3	26.9	22.7	18.9	15.4	12.4	...	...	...	...		
Indonesia - Indonésie 2012																					
Male - Hommes	67.7	...	...	...	...	...	...	...	...	...	...	...	...	...	...	...	...	...	...	...	...
Female - Femmes	71.7	...	...	...	...	...	...	...	...	...	...	...	...	...	...	...	...	...	...	...	...
Iran (Islamic Republic of) - Iran (République islamique d') 1996																					
Male - Hommes	66.1	64.6	59.9	55.1	50.5	46.0	41.4	36.8	32.3	27.9	23.7	19.8	16.2	12.9	10.1	7.7	5.7	4.2	3.1	...	...
Female - Femmes	68.4	66.8	62.1	57.3	52.7	48.0	43.5	39.0	34.5	30.1	25.8	21.7	17.8	14.3	11.1	8.4	6.2	4.5	3.2	...	...
2011																					
Male - Hommes	71.5	...	...	...	...	...	...	...	...	...	...	...	...	...	...	...	...	...	...	...	...
Female - Femmes	74.0	...	...	...	...	...	...	...	...	...	...	...	...	...	...	...	...	...	...	...	...
Iraq 1997																					
Male - Hommes	58.0	...	...	...	...	...	...	...	...	...	...	...	...	...	...	...	...	...	...	...	...
Female - Femmes	59.0	...	...	...	...	...	...	...	...	...	...	...	...	...	...	...	...	...	...	...	...
Israel - Israël[19] 2010 - 2014																					
Male - Hommes	80.0	75.3	70.4	65.4	60.5	55.7	50.8	46.0	41.2	36.4	31.8	27.2	22.9	18.9	15.2	11.9	9.1	6.7	4.8	3.4	2.4
Female - Femmes	83.7	79.1	74.1	69.1	64.2	59.2	54.3	49.4	44.5	39.6	34.9	30.2	25.6	21.2	17.1	13.3	10.0	7.2	5.0	3.3	2.2
Japan - Japon[20] 2014																					
Male - Hommes	80.5	75.7	70.8	65.8	60.9	56.1	51.2	46.4	41.6	36.8	32.2	27.7	23.4	19.3	15.5	11.9	8.8	6.2	4.4	3.0	2.1
Female - Femmes	86.8	82.1	77.1	72.1	67.2	62.2	57.3	52.4	47.6	42.7	38.0	33.3	28.7	24.2	19.8	15.6	11.7	8.4	5.7	3.8	2.4
Jordan - Jordanie[21] 2012																					
Male - Hommes	72.7	69.1	64.2	59.3	54.4	49.6	44.8	40.0	35.2	30.5	26.0	21.7	17.8	14.2	10.9	8.2	6.0	...	...	...	...
Female - Femmes	76.7	73.1	68.1	63.2	58.2	53.3	48.4	43.6	38.7	33.9	29.3	24.7	20.3	16.2	12.4	9.2	6.8	...	...	...	...
Kazakhstan 2012																					
Male - Hommes	64.8	61.0	56.1	51.3	46.5	41.9	37.5	33.3	29.3	25.3	21.5	18.0	14.8	12.1	9.6	7.4	5.7	4.5	3.7	2.9	2.0
Female - Femmes	74.3	70.4	65.5	60.6	55.7	50.9	46.2	41.5	36.9	32.4	27.9	23.7	19.6	15.9	12.3	9.2	6.6	4.7	3.2	2.4	1.8
Kyrgyzstan - Kirghizstan 2014																					
Male - Hommes	66.5	63.2	58.3	53.4	48.6	43.9	39.3	34.8	30.5	26.4	22.4	18.7	15.2	12.2	9.2	6.9	4.9	3.6	2.6	2.1	1.7
Female - Femmes	74.5	71.1	66.2	61.3	56.4	51.6	46.8	42.0	37.4	32.8	28.3	23.8	19.7	15.9	12.2	9.2	6.5	4.5	3.4	2.5	1.8
Lao People's Democratic Republic - République démocratique populaire lao[22] 2005																					
Male - Hommes	59.0	...	...	...	...	...	...	...	...	...	...	...	...	...	...	...	...	...	...	...	...
Female - Femmes	63.0	...	...	...	...	...	...	...	...	...	...	...	...	...	...	...	...	...	...	...	...
Malaysia - Malaisie 2012																					
Male - Hommes	72.2	67.8	62.9	58.0	53.3	48.6	43.9	39.2	34.6	30.2	25.9	21.8	18.0	14.5	11.3	8.5	6.0	...	...	...	...
Female - Femmes	76.9	72.5	67.5	62.6	57.7	52.8	47.9	43.1	38.3	33.6	29.0	24.6	20.4	16.4	12.7	9.5	6.8	...	...	...	...
Maldives 2009																					
Male - Hommes	72.5	68.7	63.8	59.0	54.1	49.2	44.4	39.5	34.7	29.9	25.2	20.6	16.3	12.3	8.8	6.1	...	...	...	...	...
Female - Femmes	74.2	70.2	65.3	60.4	55.5	50.6	45.6	40.8	35.8	31.0	26.3	21.6	17.1	12.9	9.1	6.0	...	...	...	...	...
2014																					
Male - Hommes	73.1	...	...	...	...	...	...	...	...	...	...	...	...	...	...	...	...	...	...	...	...
Female - Femmes	74.8	...	...	...	...	...	...	...	...	...	...	...	...	...	...	...	...	...	...	...	...

22. Life expectancy at specified ages for each sex: latest available year, 1996 - 2015
Espérance de vie à un âge donné pour chaque sexe : dernière année disponible, 1996 - 2015 (continued - suite)

Continent, country or area and date / Continent, pays ou zone et date	0	5	10	15	20	25	30	35	40	45	50	55	60	65	70	75	80	85	90	95	100
ASIA - ASIE																					
Mongolia - Mongolie 2006 - 2015																					
Male - Hommes	65.3	62.1	57.3	52.4	47.7	43.2	38.7	34.4	30.3	26.5	23.0	19.8	17.0	14.5	12.3	...	...	...	...	...	...
Female - Femmes	74.8	71.4	66.5	61.6	56.8	52.0	47.2	42.5	37.9	33.4	29.2	25.2	21.4	18.0	15.1	...	...	...	...	...	...
Myanmar 2013																					
Male - Hommes	65.5	63.1	58.3	53.5	48.8	44.3	39.9	35.9	32.1	28.4	24.8	21.2	17.9	14.6	11.9	9.6	7.7	6.3	...	...	...
Female - Femmes	69.1	69.7	64.9	60.1	55.3	50.6	46.0	41.5	37.0	32.6	28.3	24.1	20.1	16.4	13.1	10.4	8.2	6.8	...	...	...
Nepal - Népal 2011																					
Male - Hommes	65.4	...	...	...	...	...	...	...	...	...	...	...	...	...	...	...	...	...	...	...	...
Female - Femmes	67.9	...	...	...	...	...	...	...	...	...	...	...	...	...	...	...	...	...	...	...	...
Oman 2013																					
Male - Hommes	74.8	70.9	66.0	61.1	56.4	51.8	47.1	42.4	37.6	33.0	28.5	24.3	20.4	16.9	13.6	10.4	...	...	...	...	...
Female - Femmes	78.5	74.3	69.4	64.4	59.5	54.6	49.7	44.8	39.9	35.1	30.5	25.9	21.6	17.5	13.8	10.2	...	...	...	...	...
2014																					
Male - Hommes	74.8	...	...	...	...	...	...	...	...	...	...	...	...	...	...	...	...	...	...	...	...
Female - Femmes	78.5	...	...	...	...	...	...	...	...	...	...	...	...	...	...	...	...	...	...	...	...
Pakistan[23] 2007																					
Male - Hommes	63.6	65.3	60.7	55.9	51.3	46.7	42.2	37.7	33.3	29.0	25.0	21.3	18.1	15.2	12.7	10.8	9.2	7.3	...	...	...
Female - Femmes	67.6	68.6	64.1	59.5	54.9	50.3	45.7	41.1	36.5	32.1	27.7	23.5	19.6	16.2	13.4	10.9	8.6	6.1	...	...	...
Qatar 2008																					
Male - Hommes	77.9	73.7	68.8	63.9	59.1	54.3	49.4	44.6	39.8	35.0	30.3	25.6	21.2	17.0	13.3	9.9	7.1	...	...	...	...
Female - Femmes	78.1	73.9	68.9	64.0	59.1	54.1	49.2	44.3	39.3	34.5	29.6	24.9	20.5	16.6	13.2	10.0	7.8	...	...	...	...
2011																					
Male - Hommes	76.5	...	...	...	...	...	...	...	...	...	...	...	...	...	...	...	...	...	...	...	...
Female - Femmes	81.0	...	...	...	...	...	...	...	...	...	...	...	...	...	...	...	...	...	...	...	...
Republic of Korea - République de Corée 2014																					
Male - Hommes	79.0	74.3	69.3	64.4	59.5	54.6	49.7	44.9	40.2	35.5	31.0	26.6	22.4	18.3	14.5	11.1	8.2	5.9	4.3	3.2	2.4
Female - Femmes	85.5	80.8	75.8	70.8	65.9	61.0	56.1	51.2	46.3	41.5	36.7	32.0	27.4	22.8	18.3	14.2	10.5	7.5	5.3	3.8	2.9
Saudi Arabia - Arabie saoudite[24] 2015																					
Male - Hommes	73.1	...	...	...	...	...	...	...	...	...	...	...	...	...	...	...	...	...	...	...	...
Female - Femmes	75.7	...	...	...	...	...	...	...	...	...	...	...	...	...	...	...	...	...	...	...	...
Singapore - Singapour[25] 2015																					
Male - Hommes	80.4	75.6	70.7	65.7	60.8	55.9	51.0	46.1	41.2	36.5	31.8	27.3	23.0	18.9	15.1	11.7	8.9	6.4	4.6	3.1	2.1
Female - Femmes	84.9	80.1	75.1	70.1	65.2	60.2	55.3	50.3	45.4	40.6	35.8	31.1	26.6	22.1	17.9	14.0	10.6	7.7	5.4	3.7	2.5
Sri Lanka 2000 - 2002																					
Male - Hommes	68.8	...	...	...	...	...	...	...	...	...	...	...	...	...	...	...	...	...	...	...	...
Female - Femmes	77.2	...	...	...	...	...	...	...	...	...	...	...	...	...	...	...	...	...	...	...	...
State of Palestine - État de Palestine 2001																					
Male - Hommes	70.5	67.5	62.7	57.8	53.1	48.4	43.6	38.9	34.2	29.6	25.2	21.1	17.2	13.8	10.7	8.1	6.1	...	...	...	...
Female - Femmes	73.6	70.3	65.5	60.5	55.7	50.9	46.1	41.3	36.6	32.0	27.5	23.2	19.0	15.2	11.7	8.8	6.4	...	...	...	...
2015																					
Male - Hommes	72.0	...	...	...	...	...	...	...	...	...	...	...	...	...	...	...	...	...	...	...	...
Female - Femmes	75.0	...	...	...	...	...	...	...	...	...	...	...	...	...	...	...	...	...	...	...	...
Tajikistan - Tadjikistan 2008																					
Male - Hommes	69.7	67.9	63.0	58.1	53.3	48.5	43.7	39.1	34.6	30.1	25.7	21.6	17.9	14.7	12.2	10.4	9.2	...	...	...	...
Female - Femmes	74.8	72.5	67.6	62.7	57.8	52.9	48.1	43.4	38.6	33.9	29.4	25.0	21.0	17.5	14.7	12.5	11.1	...	...	...	...
2014																					
Male - Hommes	71.6	...	...	...	...	...	...	...	...	...	...	...	...	...	...	...	...	...	...	...	...
Female - Femmes	75.4	...	...	...	...	...	...	...	...	...	...	...	...	...	...	...	...	...	...	...	...

22. Life expectancy at specified ages for each sex: latest available year, 1996 - 2015
Espérance de vie à un âge donné pour chaque sexe : dernière année disponible, 1996 - 2015 (continued - suite)

Continent, country or area and date / Continent, pays ou zone et date	Age (in years) - Age (en années)																				
	0	5	10	15	20	25	30	35	40	45	50	55	60	65	70	75	80	85	90	95	100
ASIA - ASIE																					
Thailand - Thaïlande 2005 - 2006																					
Male - Hommes	69.9	...	...	...	...	...	...	...	...	...	...	...	...	...	...	...	...	...	...	...	...
Female - Femmes	77.6	...	...	...	...	...	...	...	...	...	...	...	...	...	...	...	...	...	...	...	...
Turkey - Turquie 2014																					
Male - Hommes	75.3	71.4	66.5	61.6	56.8	52.0	47.2	42.4	37.6	32.9	28.3	24.0	19.9	16.2	12.8	9.9	7.4	5.4	4.1	3.4	3.8
Female - Femmes	80.7	76.8	71.9	66.9	62.0	57.1	52.2	47.3	42.4	37.6	32.9	28.2	23.7	19.4	15.4	11.9	8.9	6.6	5.1	4.4	4.5
United Arab Emirates - Émirats arabes unis 2006																					
Male - Hommes	76.7	72.5	67.6	62.7	57.9	53.1	48.3	43.5	38.7	33.9	29.3	24.8	20.7	16.9	13.8	11.3	10.2	...	...	...	...
Female - Femmes	78.8	74.5	69.5	64.6	59.7	54.8	49.8	44.9	40.0	35.2	30.4	25.8	21.6	18.0	15.4	14.0	14.5	...	...	...	...
Uzbekistan - Ouzbékistan 2014																					
Male - Hommes	71.1	67.2	62.3	57.4	52.6	47.8	43.1	38.4	33.8	29.3	25.0	21.0	17.2	14.0	11.2	8.9	7.3	...	...	...	...
Female - Femmes	75.8	71.8	66.9	62.0	57.1	52.3	47.5	42.7	37.9	33.3	28.7	24.3	20.1	16.4	13.1	10.5	8.6	...	...	...	...
Viet Nam 2015																					
Male - Hommes	70.7	67.8	62.9	58.1	53.4	48.6	43.9	39.2	34.6	30.1	25.8	21.9	18.2	15.0	12.3	10.0	8.3	...	...	...	...
Female - Femmes	76.1	72.2	67.3	62.3	57.4	52.6	47.7	42.9	38.1	33.5	29.0	24.7	20.6	16.9	13.6	11.0	8.9	...	...	...	...
Yemen - Yémen 2004																					
Male - Hommes	60.2	...	...	...	...	...	...	...	...	...	...	...	...	...	...	...	...	...	...	...	...
Female - Femmes	62.0	...	...	...	...	...	...	...	...	...	...	...	...	...	...	...	...	...	...	...	...
EUROPE																					
Åland Islands - Îles d'Åland 2014																					
Male - Hommes	80.9	75.9	70.9	65.9	61.3	56.7	52.0	47.0	42.0	37.4	32.6	28.1	24.0	19.8	15.9	11.6	8.5	5.5	3.1	1.6	1.0
Female - Femmes	84.3	79.3	74.3	69.3	64.3	59.8	54.8	49.8	44.8	40.2	35.4	31.0	26.3	21.7	18.0	13.7	9.5	6.4	4.1	2.7	1.5
Albania - Albanie 2013																					
Male - Hommes	76.0	71.9	66.9	62.0	57.3	52.5	47.7	43.0	38.3	33.7	29.2	24.8	20.6	16.6	12.9	9.6	6.9	5.0	...	...	...
Female - Femmes	80.3	75.9	71.0	66.1	61.3	56.4	51.5	46.6	41.8	37.0	32.2	27.6	23.0	18.6	14.3	10.6	7.4	5.1	...	...	...
Austria - Autriche 2013																					
Male - Hommes	78.5	73.8	68.8	63.9	59.0	54.1	49.3	44.4	39.7	34.9	30.3	25.9	21.8	17.9	14.4	11.0	7.9	5.5	3.7	2.4	...
Female - Femmes	83.6	78.8	73.9	68.9	63.9	59.0	54.1	49.2	44.3	39.4	34.7	30.0	25.5	21.2	17.1	13.1	9.5	6.5	4.2	2.8	...
2014																					
Male - Hommes	79.1	...	...	...	...	...	...	...	...	...	...	...	...	...	...	...	...	...	...	...	...
Female - Femmes	84.0	...	...	...	...	...	...	...	...	...	...	...	...	...	...	...	...	...	...	...	...
Belarus - Bélarus 2013																					
Male - Hommes	67.3	62.6	57.7	52.7	47.9	43.2	38.6	34.2	30.0	25.9	22.0	18.4	15.3	12.5	10.0	7.8	6.0	4.5	3.4	2.5	1.8
Female - Femmes	77.9	73.2	68.2	63.3	58.3	53.5	48.6	43.8	39.1	34.5	30.0	25.6	21.4	17.4	13.6	10.2	7.4	5.2	3.5	2.3	1.4
2014																					
Male - Hommes	67.8	...	...	...	...	...	...	...	...	...	...	...	...	...	...	...	...	...	...	...	...
Female - Femmes	78.6	...	...	...	...	...	...	...	...	...	...	...	...	...	...	...	...	...	...	...	...
Belgium - Belgique 2006																					
Male - Hommes	77.0	71.4	66.5	61.5	56.7	51.9	47.1	42.4	37.7	33.1	28.6	24.3	20.3	16.5	12.9	9.7	7.1	5.0	3.4	2.5	...
Female - Femmes	82.7	77.0	72.1	67.1	62.2	57.3	52.4	47.5	42.6	37.9	33.2	28.7	24.3	20.1	16.0	12.1	8.8	6.1	4.1	2.8	...
2014																					
Male - Hommes	78.8	...	...	...	...	...	...	...	...	...	...	...	...	...	...	...	...	...	...	...	...
Female - Femmes	83.9	...	...	...	...	...	...	...	...	...	...	...	...	...	...	...	...	...	...	...	...
Bosnia and Herzegovina - Bosnie-Herzégovine 2003																					
Male - Hommes	71.3	...	...	...	...	...	...	...	...	...	...	...	...	...	...	...	...	...	...	...	...
Female - Femmes	76.7	...	...	...	...	...	...	...	...	...	...	...	...	...	...	...	...	...	...	...	...

Continent, country or area and date / Continent, pays ou zone et date	Age (in years) - Age (en années)																				
	0	5	10	15	20	25	30	35	40	45	50	55	60	65	70	75	80	85	90	95	100
EUROPE																					
Bulgaria - Bulgarie																					
2010 - 2012																					
Male - Hommes	70.6	66.5	61.5	56.6	51.8	47.0	42.3	37.6	32.9	28.4	24.2	20.4	17.0	13.9	10.9	8.4	6.2	4.5	3.3	2.5	0.5
Female - Femmes	77.5	73.2	68.3	63.4	58.5	53.6	48.7	43.8	39.1	34.4	29.8	25.4	21.2	17.1	13.2	9.7	6.9	4.7	3.2	2.2	0.5
2014																					
Male - Hommes	71.1	...	...	...	...	...	...	...	...	...	...	...	...	...	...	...	...	...	...	...	...
Female - Femmes	78.0	...	...	...	...	...	...	...	...	...	...	...	...	...	...	...	...	...	...	...	...
Croatia - Croatie																					
2014																					
Male - Hommes	74.7	...	...	...	...	...	...	...	...	...	...	...	...	...	...	...	...	...	...	...	...
Female - Femmes	81.0	...	...	...	...	...	...	...	...	...	...	...	...	...	...	...	...	...	...	...	...
Czech Republic - République tchèque																					
2014																					
Male - Hommes	75.8	71.0	66.1	61.1	56.2	51.4	46.6	41.8	37.0	32.4	27.9	23.6	19.6	16.0	12.8	9.9	7.3	5.2	3.6	2.4	1.6
Female - Femmes	81.7	76.9	71.9	67.0	62.0	57.1	52.2	47.2	42.4	37.5	32.8	28.2	23.8	19.5	15.5	11.8	8.5	5.7	3.6	2.2	1.3
Denmark - Danemark[26]																					
2014																					
Male - Hommes	78.5	73.9	68.9	63.9	59.0	54.1	49.2	44.4	39.6	34.9	30.3	25.9	21.7	17.9	14.2	10.9	7.9	5.6	3.9	2.5	...
Female - Femmes	82.7	78.0	73.1	68.1	63.1	58.2	53.2	48.3	43.4	38.6	33.9	29.3	24.9	20.7	16.6	12.9	9.6	6.9	4.7	3.3	...
Estonia - Estonie																					
2014																					
Male - Hommes	72.3	67.6	62.7	57.7	52.9	48.2	43.6	39.0	34.5	30.0	25.8	21.8	18.2	15.1	12.2	9.5	7.1	5.1	3.6	2.5	1.5
Female - Femmes	81.5	76.8	71.8	66.9	62.0	57.1	52.2	47.4	42.6	37.8	33.1	28.6	24.2	20.0	16.0	12.3	9.0	6.3	4.2	2.9	1.9
Faeroe Islands - Îles Féroé																					
2014 - 2015																					
Male - Hommes	78.3	74.8	69.8	65.0	60.3	55.5	50.5	45.7	40.7	35.8	31.6	27.1	23.1	18.8	14.5	11.0	7.6	5.4	3.4	2.8	2.0
Female - Femmes	84.5	79.8	74.8	69.8	64.8	59.8	54.8	49.8	44.8	40.1	35.6	30.7	26.1	21.5	17.6	13.4	10.0	6.5	3.8	2.8	2.0
Finland - Finlande[27]																					
2014																					
Male - Hommes	78.2	73.4	68.4	63.4	58.6	53.8	49.0	44.3	39.5	34.8	30.3	26.0	21.8	18.0	14.3	11.0	8.0	5.6	3.8	2.7	1.9
Female - Femmes	83.9	79.1	74.1	69.1	64.2	59.3	54.4	49.5	44.6	39.8	35.0	30.3	25.8	21.4	17.3	13.3	9.7	6.6	4.4	2.9	1.8
France																					
2014																					
Male - Hommes	79.3	...	...	...	59.8	...	...	...	40.6	...	...	...	23.1	...	...	...	...	...	...	...	...
Female - Femmes	85.4	...	...	...	65.8	...	...	...	46.2	...	...	...	27.7	...	...	...	...	...	...	...	...
Germany - Allemagne																					
2010 - 2012																					
Male - Hommes	77.7	73.1	68.1	63.1	58.2	53.4	48.5	43.7	38.9	34.2	29.7	25.3	21.3	17.5	13.9	10.5	7.7	5.4	3.7	2.6	1.9
Female - Femmes	82.8	78.1	73.1	68.2	63.2	58.3	53.4	48.4	43.6	38.7	34.0	29.5	25.0	20.7	16.6	12.7	9.2	6.3	4.2	2.9	2.1
2014																					
Male - Hommes	78.7	...	...	...	...	...	...	...	...	...	...	...	...	...	...	...	...	...	...	...	...
Female - Femmes	83.6	...	...	...	...	...	...	...	...	...	...	...	...	...	...	...	...	...	...	...	...
Gibraltar																					
2001																					
Male - Hommes	78.5	73.5	68.5	63.5	58.5	53.5	...	43.5	...	33.9	...	25.8	...	17.9	...	11.3	...	...	...	...	...
Female - Femmes	83.3	79.5	75.0	70.0	65.0	60.0	...	50.3	...	40.3	...	30.3	...	20.6	...	13.7	...	...	...	...	...
Greece - Grèce																					
2014																					
Male - Hommes	78.5	73.8	68.9	63.9	59.0	54.2	49.4	44.6	39.8	35.1	30.6	26.3	22.2	18.4	14.8	11.5	8.5	6.3	4.6	3.3	2.3
Female - Femmes	83.5	78.8	73.9	68.9	63.9	59.0	54.1	49.2	44.3	39.5	34.7	30.1	25.5	21.1	16.8	12.8	9.3	6.7	4.9	3.5	2.4
Hungary - Hongrie																					
2014																					
Male - Hommes	72.1	67.6	62.6	57.7	52.8	47.9	43.1	38.2	33.5	28.9	24.6	20.8	17.4	14.4	11.5	8.8	6.5	4.4	2.6	1.5	0.6
Female - Femmes	78.9	74.3	69.3	64.3	59.4	54.4	49.5	44.6	39.8	35.0	30.4	26.1	21.9	18.0	14.2	10.7	7.6	4.9	2.8	1.5	0.6
Iceland - Islande																					
2013 - 2014																					
Male - Hommes	80.6	75.8	70.9	65.9	61.0	56.1	51.3	46.5	41.7	36.9	32.2	27.7	23.3	19.0	15.0	11.4	8.2	5.6	3.6	2.6	1.5
Female - Femmes	83.6	79.1	74.1	69.1	64.2	59.3	54.3	49.4	44.5	39.7	34.9	30.2	25.6	21.3	17.1	13.3	9.8	6.9	4.6	2.7	1.5
Ireland - Irlande																					
2005 - 2007																					
Male - Hommes	76.8	72.2	67.2	62.3	57.5	52.8	48.0	43.3	38.5	33.8	29.2	24.8	20.6	16.6	13.0	9.8	7.1	5.1	3.6	2.6	1.9
Female - Femmes	81.6	76.9	72.0	67.0	62.1	57.2	52.3	47.4	42.5	37.7	33.1	28.5	24.0	19.8	15.8	12.1	8.8	6.2	4.3	3.1	2.1

22. Life expectancy at specified ages for each sex: latest available year, 1996 - 2015
Espérance de vie à un âge donné pour chaque sexe : dernière année disponible, 1996 - 2015 (continued - suite)

Continent, country or area and date / Continent, pays ou zone et date	Age (in years) - Age (en années)																				
	0	5	10	15	20	25	30	35	40	45	50	55	60	65	70	75	80	85	90	95	100
EUROPE																					
2014[7]																					
Male - Hommes	79.3	...	...	...	...	...	...	...	...	...	...	...	...	...	...	...	...	...	...	...	...
Female - Femmes	83.5	...	...	...	...	...	...	...	...	...	...	...	...	...	...	...	...	...	...	...	...
Isle of Man - Île de Man																					
1996																					
Male - Hommes	73.6	68.6	63.6	58.6	53.6	49.1	44.6	40.2	35.8	31.2	26.7	22.4	18.4	15.1	12.0	9.3	7.5	5.2	4.7	3.2	0.5
Female - Femmes	79.9	75.1	70.1	65.1	60.1	55.1	50.1	45.1	40.2	35.4	30.7	26.2	22.0	18.3	14.5	11.3	8.6	5.9	3.7	2.0	1.5
Italy - Italie																					
2014																					
Male - Hommes	80.3	75.6	70.6	65.7	60.8	55.9	51.0	46.2	41.3	36.6	31.9	27.4	23.0	18.9	15.1	11.6	8.4	5.9	4.1	2.8	1.8
Female - Femmes	85.0	80.3	75.3	70.3	65.4	60.4	55.5	50.5	45.6	40.8	36.0	31.3	26.8	22.3	18.0	14.0	10.3	7.2	4.8	3.2	2.1
Latvia - Lettonie																					
2014																					
Male - Hommes	69.3	64.7	59.7	54.8	50.0	45.3	40.7	36.2	31.9	27.8	23.7	20.1	16.6	13.7	11.1	8.7	6.6	4.7	3.3	2.3	1.9
Female - Femmes	79.5	74.8	69.9	65.0	60.1	55.2	50.3	45.5	40.8	36.1	31.6	27.2	22.9	18.9	15.1	11.4	8.2	5.6	3.6	2.5	1.9
Lithuania - Lituanie																					
2014																					
Male - Hommes	69.1	64.5	59.5	54.6	49.8	45.2	40.7	36.3	32.1	28.0	24.1	20.5	17.1	14.2	11.6	9.2	6.9	5.0	3.4	2.5	1.8
Female - Femmes	79.9	75.3	70.3	65.4	60.5	55.6	50.7	45.9	41.1	36.5	32.0	27.6	23.3	19.2	15.4	11.7	8.4	5.8	4.0	2.8	2.1
Luxembourg																					
2012 - 2014																					
Male - Hommes	80.2	75.4	70.4	65.5	60.6	55.7	50.8	46.0	41.2	36.4	31.8	27.4	23.2	19.2	15.5	12.1	9.0	6.5	5.0	3.4	...
Female - Femmes	84.8	80.0	75.0	70.0	65.1	60.1	55.2	50.3	45.4	40.6	35.8	31.2	26.7	22.3	18.2	14.2	10.7	7.6	5.2	3.3	...
Malta - Malte																					
2014																					
Male - Hommes	79.8	75.3	70.3	65.4	60.5	55.6	50.7	45.9	41.1	36.4	31.7	27.1	22.8	18.5	14.6	11.3	8.4	6.0	...	...	...
Female - Femmes	84.3	79.7	74.7	69.7	64.8	59.8	54.9	50.0	45.0	40.2	35.5	30.6	26.0	21.7	17.4	13.5	9.8	6.9	...	...	...
Netherlands - Pays-Bas																					
2009																					
Male - Hommes	78.5	73.8	68.8	63.9	59.0	54.1	49.2	44.4	39.5	34.8	30.1	25.6	21.4	17.3	13.6	10.3	7.5	5.3	3.6	2.6	...
Female - Femmes	82.7	77.8	72.8	67.9	62.9	58.0	53.1	48.2	43.3	38.5	33.8	29.3	24.9	20.6	16.5	12.7	9.2	6.4	4.3	2.9	...
2014																					
Male - Hommes	80.0	...	...	...	...	...	...	...	...	...	...	...	...	...	...	...	...	...	...	...	...
Female - Femmes	83.5	...	...	...	...	...	...	...	...	...	...	...	...	...	...	...	...	...	...	...	...
Norway - Norvège																					
2012																					
Male - Hommes	79.4	74.7	69.7	64.8	59.8	55.0	50.2	45.4	40.6	35.8	31.2	26.7	22.3	18.2	14.4	10.9	7.8	5.5	3.7	2.6	2.3
Female - Femmes	83.4	78.6	73.7	68.7	63.8	58.8	53.9	49.0	44.1	39.2	34.5	29.8	25.3	21.0	16.9	13.0	9.5	6.6	4.3	2.8	1.9
2014																					
Male - Hommes	80.1	...	...	...	...	...	...	...	...	...	...	...	...	...	...	...	...	...	...	...	...
Female - Femmes	84.2	...	...	...	...	...	...	...	...	...	...	...	...	...	...	...	...	...	...	...	...
Poland - Pologne																					
2012																					
Male - Hommes	72.7	68.1	63.2	58.2	53.4	48.7	43.9	39.2	34.6	30.2	26.0	22.1	18.6	15.4	12.4	9.7	7.4	5.5	4.1	3.0	2.2
Female - Femmes	81.0	76.4	71.4	66.5	61.5	56.6	51.7	46.8	41.9	37.1	32.5	28.0	23.8	19.7	15.8	12.2	9.0	6.5	4.6	3.2	2.3
2014																					
Male - Hommes	73.7	...	...	...	...	...	...	...	...	...	...	...	...	...	...	...	...	...	...	...	...
Female - Femmes	81.7	...	...	...	...	...	...	...	...	...	...	...	...	...	...	...	...	...	...	...	...
Portugal																					
2012 - 2014																					
Male - Hommes	77.2	72.5	67.5	62.6	57.6	52.8	48.0	43.2	38.4	33.8	29.4	25.2	21.2	17.2	13.5	10.1	6.9	4.3	2.7	1.7	1.1
Female - Femmes	83.0	78.3	73.3	68.4	63.4	58.5	53.5	48.6	43.8	39.0	34.2	29.6	25.0	20.6	16.2	12.1	8.4	5.3	3.2	1.9	1.2
Republic of Moldova - République de Moldova[28]																					
2012																					
Male - Hommes	67.2	63.1	58.1	53.3	48.5	43.7	39.0	34.5	30.1	26.0	22.2	18.7	15.5	13.0	10.2	8.4	7.1	6.9	7.8	...	...
Female - Femmes	75.0	70.9	66.0	61.0	56.1	51.2	46.4	41.5	36.8	32.2	27.7	23.4	19.3	15.7	12.2	9.5	7.4	5.9	5.3	...	...
Romania - Roumanie																					
2012 - 2014																					
Male - Hommes	72.0	67.8	62.8	57.9	53.1	48.3	43.5	38.7	34.0	29.5	25.2	21.4	17.9	14.7	11.7	9.1	6.9	5.1	3.8	2.8	2.1
Female - Femmes	78.9	74.6	69.7	64.7	59.8	54.9	50.0	45.1	40.2	35.5	30.8	26.4	22.1	18.0	14.2	10.7	7.8	5.6	4.0	2.9	2.1

Continent, country or area and date / Continent, pays ou zone et date	Age (in years) - Age (en années)																				
	0	5	10	15	20	25	30	35	40	45	50	55	60	65	70	75	80	85	90	95	100
EUROPE																					
Russian Federation - Fédération de Russie																					
2012																					
Male - Hommes	64.6	60.3	55.4	50.5	45.8	41.3	37.0	33.1	29.3	25.4	21.8	18.4	15.4	12.8	10.2	8.1	6.4	5.1	4.0	3.0	1.4
Female - Femmes	75.9	71.6	66.7	61.7	56.9	52.1	47.3	42.8	38.2	33.7	29.3	25.1	21.0	17.1	13.4	10.2	7.4	5.3	3.8	2.8	1.8
San Marino - Saint-Marin																					
2013																					
Male - Hommes	81.7	76.9	72.0	67.0	62.2	57.4	52.5	47.6	42.7	37.9	33.0	28.3	24.1	19.7	15.7	11.8	8.6	6.1	4.1	2.3	...
Female - Femmes	86.4	81.5	76.5	71.5	66.6	61.6	56.6	51.7	46.7	41.9	37.1	32.4	27.7	23.2	18.8	14.8	10.8	7.4	5.0	2.7	...
Serbia - Serbie[29]																					
2014																					
Male - Hommes	72.6	68.2	63.2	58.2	53.4	48.6	43.7	39.0	34.2	29.6	25.3	21.2	17.6	14.3	11.1	8.4	6.1	4.3	...	...	...
Female - Femmes	77.7	73.1	68.2	63.2	58.3	53.4	48.4	43.6	38.7	34.0	29.4	24.9	20.7	16.6	12.8	9.4	6.6	4.5	...	...	...
Slovakia - Slovaquie																					
2014																					
Male - Hommes	73.2	68.7	63.8	58.8	54.0	49.1	44.3	39.6	34.9	30.3	26.0	21.9	18.3	14.9	11.9	9.0	6.7	4.7	3.2	2.1	0.8
Female - Femmes	80.0	75.5	70.5	65.6	60.6	55.7	50.8	45.9	41.0	36.2	31.6	27.0	22.6	18.5	14.5	10.8	7.6	4.9	3.0	1.7	0.7
Slovenia - Slovénie																					
2014																					
Male - Hommes	78.0	73.1	68.2	63.2	58.3	53.4	48.6	43.8	39.0	34.2	29.6	25.3	21.2	17.5	13.9	10.7	7.8	5.5	3.9	3.1	2.0
Female - Femmes	83.7	78.9	73.9	68.9	63.9	59.0	54.1	49.2	44.3	39.4	34.7	30.0	25.5	21.2	16.9	13.0	9.4	6.5	4.4	3.0	2.1
Spain - Espagne																					
2013																					
Male - Hommes	80.0	75.2	70.3	65.3	60.4	55.5	50.6	45.7	40.8	36.1	31.5	27.1	22.9	19.0	15.2	11.7	8.7	6.2	4.5	3.5	3.4
Female - Femmes	85.6	80.9	75.9	70.9	66.0	61.0	56.0	51.1	46.2	41.4	36.6	32.0	27.4	22.9	18.5	14.4	10.6	7.4	5.1	3.7	3.1
2014																					
Male - Hommes	80.4	...	...	...	...	...	...	...	...	...	...	...	...	...	...	...	...	...	...	...	...
Female - Femmes	86.2	...	...	...	...	...	...	...	...	...	...	...	...	...	...	...	...	...	...	...	...
Sweden - Suède																					
2012																					
Male - Hommes	79.9	75.1	70.2	65.2	60.3	55.5	50.7	45.8	41.0	36.2	31.5	27.0	22.6	18.4	14.5	11.0	7.9	5.4	3.6	2.4	1.6
Female - Femmes	83.5	78.8	73.8	68.8	63.9	59.0	54.0	49.1	44.2	39.4	34.6	30.0	25.4	21.0	16.9	13.0	9.5	6.5	4.3	2.9	1.9
2014																					
Male - Hommes	80.4	...	...	...	...	...	...	...	...	...	...	...	...	...	...	...	...	...	...	...	...
Female - Femmes	84.2	...	...	...	...	...	...	...	...	...	...	...	...	...	...	...	...	...	...	...	...
Switzerland - Suisse																					
2014																					
Male - Hommes	81.0	76.4	71.4	66.4	61.5	56.6	51.7	46.9	42.0	37.2	32.5	28.0	23.6	19.5	15.6	11.9	8.7	5.9	3.9	2.7	2.1
Female - Femmes	85.2	80.5	75.5	70.5	65.6	60.6	55.7	50.8	45.8	41.0	36.2	31.5	26.9	22.4	18.1	14.1	10.3	7.1	4.6	3.0	2.1
TFYR of Macedonia - L'ex-R. y. de Macédoine																					
2011																					
Male - Hommes	73.0	68.7	63.8	58.8	53.9	49.1	44.2	39.3	34.6	29.9	25.5	21.3	17.4	13.9	10.7	7.8	5.5	3.8	2.8	2.4	...
Female - Femmes	77.0	72.7	67.8	62.8	57.9	52.9	48.0	43.1	38.2	33.4	28.8	24.3	20.0	15.8	12.1	8.8	6.1	4.3	3.4	2.9	...
Ukraine																					
2013																					
Male - Hommes	66.3	62.0	57.1	52.2	47.4	42.7	38.2	33.9	29.9	25.9	22.2	18.7	15.5	12.8	10.3	8.2	6.4	5.2	4.2	3.3	2.2
Female - Femmes	76.2	71.8	66.9	62.0	57.1	52.2	47.4	42.7	38.1	33.6	29.1	24.8	20.6	16.7	13.1	9.8	7.2	5.1	3.6	2.5	1.6
United Kingdom of Great Britain and Northern Ireland - Royaume-Uni de Grande-Bretagne et d'Irlande du Nord[30]																					
2012																					
Male - Hommes	79.0	74.4	69.4	64.5	59.6	54.7	49.9	45.1	40.3	35.6	31.1	26.6	22.3	18.3	14.5	11.2	8.2	5.8	4.0	2.8	2.2
Female - Femmes	82.7	78.0	73.1	68.1	63.1	58.2	53.3	48.4	43.5	38.7	34.0	29.5	25.0	20.7	16.7	12.9	9.5	6.7	4.6	3.2	2.3

22. Life expectancy at specified ages for each sex: latest available year, 1996 - 2015
Espérance de vie à un âge donné pour chaque sexe : dernière année disponible, 1996 - 2015 (continued - suite)

Continent, country or area and date / Continent, pays ou zone et date	Age (in years) - Age (en années)																				
	0	5	10	15	20	25	30	35	40	45	50	55	60	65	70	75	80	85	90	95	100

OCEANIA - OCÉANIE

American Samoa - Samoas américaines
2011
| Male - Hommes | 71.1 | 66.8 | 61.9 | 57.0 | 52.2 | 47.4 | 42.6 | 38.0 | 33.5 | 29.1 | 25.3 | 21.4 | 18.0 | 14.6 | 11.7 | 9.6 | ... | ... | ... | ... | ... |
| Female - Femmes | 77.8 | 73.3 | 68.3 | 63.4 | 58.5 | 53.6 | 48.9 | 44.4 | 39.6 | 35.0 | 30.6 | 26.5 | 22.8 | 19.2 | 16.1 | 13.8 | ... | ... | ... | ... | ... |

Australia - Australie
2012 - 2014
| Male - Hommes | 80.3 | 75.6 | 70.7 | 65.7 | 60.8 | 56.0 | 51.2 | 46.4 | 41.7 | 37.0 | 32.4 | 27.9 | 23.5 | 19.4 | 15.5 | 11.9 | 8.7 | 6.1 | 4.2 | 3.0 | 2.3 |
| Female - Femmes | 84.4 | 79.7 | 74.8 | 69.8 | 64.9 | 60.0 | 55.0 | 50.2 | 45.3 | 40.5 | 35.8 | 31.1 | 26.6 | 22.2 | 17.9 | 13.9 | 10.3 | 7.2 | 4.8 | 3.3 | 2.4 |

Cook Islands - Îles Cook[31]
2006
| Male - Hommes | 69.5 | 66.0 | 61.3 | 56.5 | 52.0 | 47.4 | 42.8 | 38.1 | 33.6 | 29.1 | 24.8 | 20.9 | 17.5 | 14.3 | 11.4 | 9.0 | 7.3 | ... | ... | ... | ... |
| Female - Femmes | 76.2 | 72.4 | 67.4 | 62.4 | 57.4 | 52.7 | 48.0 | 43.2 | 38.4 | 33.6 | 29.1 | 24.7 | 20.4 | 16.4 | 12.6 | 9.5 | 6.9 | ... | ... | ... | ... |

Fiji - Fidji
1996
| Male - Hommes | 64.5 | ... | ... | ... | ... | 42.4 | ... | ... | ... | ... | ... | ... | ... | 10.7 | ... | ... | ... | ... | ... | ... | ... |
| Female - Femmes | 68.7 | ... | ... | ... | ... | 46.4 | ... | ... | ... | ... | ... | ... | ... | 13.0 | ... | ... | ... | ... | ... | ... | ... |
2007
| Male - Hommes | 65.3 | ... | ... | ... | ... | ... | ... | ... | ... | ... | ... | ... | ... | ... | ... | ... | ... | ... | ... | ... | ... |
| Female - Femmes | 69.6 | ... | ... | ... | ... | ... | ... | ... | ... | ... | ... | ... | ... | ... | ... | ... | ... | ... | ... | ... | ... |

French Polynesia - Polynésie française
2012
| Male - Hommes | 73.3 | 69.6 | 64.6 | 59.8 | 55.0 | 50.3 | 45.7 | 41.0 | 36.2 | 31.6 | 27.1 | 22.7 | 18.3 | 14.8 | 11.4 | 8.5 | 6.5 | 4.7 | ... | ... | ... |
| Female - Femmes | 78.2 | 73.8 | 68.8 | 63.9 | 59.1 | 54.1 | 49.3 | 44.5 | 39.7 | 35.0 | 30.4 | 26.1 | 22.0 | 17.9 | 14.2 | 10.6 | 7.6 | 5.0 | ... | ... | ... |
2014
| Male - Hommes | 73.8 | ... | ... | ... | ... | ... | ... | ... | ... | ... | ... | ... | ... | ... | ... | ... | ... | ... | ... | ... | ... |
| Female - Femmes | 78.0 | ... | ... | ... | ... | ... | ... | ... | ... | ... | ... | ... | ... | ... | ... | ... | ... | ... | ... | ... | ... |

Guam
2015
| Male - Hommes | 75.9 | ... | ... | ... | ... | ... | ... | ... | ... | ... | ... | ... | ... | ... | ... | ... | ... | ... | ... | ... | ... |
| Female - Femmes | 82.2 | ... | ... | ... | ... | ... | ... | ... | ... | ... | ... | ... | ... | ... | ... | ... | ... | ... | ... | ... | ... |

Kiribati
2005
| Male - Hommes | 58.9 | 58.2 | 53.6 | 48.9 | 44.4 | 40.0 | 35.6 | 31.3 | 27.1 | 23.1 | 19.4 | 16.0 | 13.0 | 10.4 | 8.3 | 6.6 | 5.3 | 4.2 | ... | ... | ... |
| Female - Femmes | 63.1 | 62.6 | 57.9 | 53.1 | 48.6 | 44.1 | 39.7 | 35.4 | 31.2 | 27.1 | 23.2 | 19.5 | 16.1 | 13.1 | 10.4 | 8.1 | 6.2 | 4.7 | ... | ... | ... |

Marshall Islands - Îles Marshall
2004
| Male - Hommes | 67.0 | ... | ... | ... | ... | ... | ... | ... | ... | ... | ... | ... | ... | ... | ... | ... | ... | ... | ... | ... | ... |
| Female - Femmes | 70.6 | ... | ... | ... | ... | ... | ... | ... | ... | ... | ... | ... | ... | ... | ... | ... | ... | ... | ... | ... | ... |

Micronesia (Federated States of) - Micronésie (États fédérés de)
2000
| Male - Hommes | 66.5 | ... | ... | ... | ... | ... | ... | ... | ... | ... | ... | ... | ... | ... | ... | ... | ... | ... | ... | ... | ... |
| Female - Femmes | 67.5 | ... | ... | ... | ... | ... | ... | ... | ... | ... | ... | ... | ... | ... | ... | ... | ... | ... | ... | ... | ... |

Nauru
2006
| Male - Hommes | 55.2 | ... | ... | ... | ... | ... | ... | ... | ... | ... | ... | ... | ... | ... | ... | ... | ... | ... | ... | ... | ... |
| Female - Femmes | 57.1 | ... | ... | ... | ... | ... | ... | ... | ... | ... | ... | ... | ... | ... | ... | ... | ... | ... | ... | ... | ... |

New Caledonia - Nouvelle-Calédonie
2010
| Male - Hommes | 74.4 | 69.8 | 65.0 | 60.0 | 55.3 | 50.8 | 46.3 | 41.7 | 37.3 | 32.8 | 28.4 | 24.3 | 20.3 | 17.0 | 13.9 | 11.0 | 8.3 | 6.1 | 4.7 | 5.0 | ... |
| Female - Femmes | 80.7 | 76.2 | 71.2 | 66.2 | 61.3 | 56.5 | 51.8 | 46.9 | 42.1 | 37.3 | 32.6 | 28.4 | 23.9 | 19.6 | 15.6 | 12.0 | 9.0 | 6.6 | 4.7 | 3.1 | ... |

New Zealand - Nouvelle-Zélande
2012 - 2014
| Male - Hommes | 79.5 | 74.9 | 70.0 | 65.1 | 60.3 | 55.5 | 50.7 | 45.9 | 41.2 | 36.4 | 31.8 | 27.4 | 23.0 | 18.9 | 15.0 | 11.5 | 8.4 | 5.9 | 4.1 | 2.9 | 2.2 |
| Female - Femmes | 83.2 | 78.6 | 73.6 | 68.7 | 63.8 | 58.9 | 54.0 | 49.1 | 44.2 | 39.5 | 34.8 | 30.2 | 25.7 | 21.3 | 17.2 | 13.3 | 9.8 | 6.8 | 4.6 | 3.1 | 2.5 |

Niue - Nioué
2006
| Male - Hommes | 67.0 | ... | ... | ... | ... | ... | ... | ... | ... | ... | ... | ... | ... | ... | ... | ... | ... | ... | ... | ... | ... |
| Female - Femmes | 76.0 | ... | ... | ... | ... | ... | ... | ... | ... | ... | ... | ... | ... | ... | ... | ... | ... | ... | ... | ... | ... |

22. Life expectancy at specified ages for each sex: latest available year, 1996 - 2015
Espérance de vie à un âge donné pour chaque sexe : dernière année disponible, 1996 - 2015 (continued - suite)

Continent, country or area and date / Continent, pays ou zone et date	Age (in years) - Age (en années)																				
	0	5	10	15	20	25	30	35	40	45	50	55	60	65	70	75	80	85	90	95	100
OCEANIA - OCÉANIE																					
Northern Mariana Islands - Îles Mariannes septentrionales																					
2009																					
Male - Hommes	74.5	...	...	...	...	...	...	...	...	...	...	...	...	...	...	...	...	...	...	...	...
Female - Femmes	79.9	...	...	...	...	...	...	...	...	...	...	...	...	...	...	...	...	...	...	...	...
Palau - Palaos																					
2005																					
Male - Hommes	66.3	...	...	...	...	...	...	...	...	...	...	...	...	...	...	...	...	...	...	...	...
Female - Femmes	72.1	...	...	...	...	...	...	...	...	...	...	...	...	...	...	...	...	...	...	...	...
Papua New Guinea - Papouasie-Nouvelle-Guinée																					
2000																					
Male - Hommes	53.7	54.1	50.2	45.7	41.6	37.7	33.7	29.8	25.9	22.1	18.5	15.0	11.9	9.2	6.9	5.0	3.6	2.6	1.7	0.6	...
Female - Femmes	54.8	54.7	50.8	46.3	42.1	38.1	34.1	30.1	26.2	22.3	18.6	15.2	12.0	9.2	6.8	5.0	3.6	2.5	1.6	0.6	...
Samoa																					
2006																					
Male - Hommes	71.5	...	...	...	...	...	...	...	...	...	...	...	...	...	...	...	...	...	...	...	...
Female - Femmes	74.2	...	...	...	...	...	...	...	...	...	...	...	...	...	...	...	...	...	...	...	...
Solomon Islands - Îles Salomon																					
1999																					
Male - Hommes	60.6	...	...	...	...	...	...	...	...	...	...	...	...	...	...	...	...	...	...	...	...
Female - Femmes	61.6	...	...	...	...	...	...	...	...	...	...	...	...	...	...	...	...	...	...	...	...
Tonga																					
2006																					
Male - Hommes	67.3	64.1	59.3	54.5	49.9	45.4	40.7	36.2	31.6	27.2	23.4	19.4	15.9	13.0	9.4	6.3	4.0	...	...	...	...
Female - Femmes	73.0	69.3	64.6	59.8	55.0	50.1	45.2	40.4	35.7	31.3	27.1	23.0	19.0	15.3	11.6	8.6	6.1	...	...	...	...
Tuvalu																					
1997 - 2002																					
Male - Hommes	61.7	59.5	54.8	50.0	45.2	40.6	35.9	32.1	28.0	24.1	20.0	17.1	13.7	10.8	9.0	6.9	5.4	...	...	...	...
Female - Femmes	65.1	62.6	57.7	53.7	50.0	45.3	40.9	36.6	32.2	28.1	23.8	20.3	16.9	13.2	10.6	7.9	6.4	...	...	...	...
Vanuatu																					
1999																					
Male - Hommes	65.6	...	...	...	...	...	...	...	...	...	...	...	...	...	...	...	...	...	...	...	...
Female - Femmes	69.0	...	...	...	...	...	...	...	...	...	...	...	...	...	...	...	...	...	...	...	...
Wallis and Futuna Islands - Îles Wallis et Futuna																					
2003																					
Male - Hommes	73.1	...	...	...	...	...	...	...	...	...	...	...	...	...	...	...	...	...	...	...	...
Female - Femmes	75.5	...	...	...	...	...	...	...	...	...	...	...	...	...	...	...	...	...	...	...	...

FOOTNOTES - NOTES

[1] Data refer to Algerian population only. - Les données ne concernent que la population algérienne.

[2] Based on the results of the Population Census. - D'après les résultats du recensement de la population.

[3] Based on the results of the Botswana Demographic Survey. - Données extraites de l'enquête démographique effectuée par le Botswana.

[4] Based on the results of the 2006 Population and Housing Census. - Données fondées sur les résultats du recensement de la population et de l'habitat de 2006.

[5] Data refer to the 12 months preceding the census in April. - Les données se rapportent aux douze mois précédant le recensement d'avril.

[6] Excludes the islands of St. Brandon and Agalega. - Non compris les îles St. Brandon et Agalega.

[7] Provisional data. - Données provisoires.

[8] Data refer to Saint Helenian resident population. - Pour la population résidante de Sainte-Hélène.

[9] Data refer to national projections. - Les données se réfèrent aux projections nationales.

[10] Based on underlying data of the 2002 Population Census. - Données fondées sur le recensement de la population de 2002.

[11] Data are based on a small number of deaths. - Les données sont basées sur un nombre limité de décès.

[12] Data refer to projections based on the 1992 Population Census. - Les données se réfèrent aux projections basées sur le recensement de la population de 1992.

[13] Excluding Indian jungle population. - Non compris les Indiens de la jungle.

[14] Data refer to the 12 months from 30 June 2015 to 30 June 2016. - Les données font référence aux douze mois de 30 juin 2015 à 30 juin 2016.

[15] Data refer to projections based on the 2010 Population Census. Excludes nomadic Indian tribes. - Les données se réfèrent aux projections basées sur le recensement de la population de 2010. Non compris les tribus d'Indiens nomades.

[16] For statistical purposes, the data for China do not include those for the Hong Kong Special Administrative Region (Hong Kong SAR), Macao Special Administrative Region (Macao SAR) and Taiwan province of China. - Pour la présentation des statistiques, les données pour la Chine ne comprennent pas la Région Administrative Spéciale de Hong Kong (Hong Kong RAS), la Région Administrative Spéciale de Macao (Macao RAS) et Taïwan province de Chine.

¹⁷ Data refer to government controlled areas. - Les données se rapportent aux zones contrôlées par le Gouvernement.

¹⁸ Includes data for the Indian-held part of Jammu and Kashmir, the final status of which has not yet been determined. - Y compris les données pour la partie du Jammu et du Cachemire occupée par l'Inde dont le statut définitif n'a pas encore été déterminé.

¹⁹ Includes data for East Jerusalem and Israeli residents in certain other territories under occupation by Israeli military forces since June 1967. - Y compris les données pour Jérusalem-Est et les résidents israéliens dans certains autres territoires occupés depuis 1967 par les forces armées israéliennes.

²⁰ Data refer to Japanese nationals in Japan only. - Les données se raportent aux nationaux japonais au Japon seulement.

²¹ Excluding data for Jordanian territory under occupation since June 1967 by Israeli military forces. Excluding foreigners, including registered Palestinian refugees. - Non compris les données pour le territoire jordanien occupé depuis juin 1967 par les forces armées israéliennes. Non compris les étrangers, mais y compris les réfugiés de Palestine enregistrés.

²² Based on the results of the 2005 Population and Housing Census. - Données fondées sur les résultats du recensement de la population et de l'habitat de 2005.

²³ Based on the results of the Pakistan Demographic Survey. Excluding data for the Pakistan-held part of Jammu and Kashmir, the final status of which has not yet been determined. - Données extraites de l'enquête démographique effectuée par le Pakistan. Non compris les données concernant la partie du Jammu et Cachemire occupée par le Pakistan dont le statut définitif n'a pas été déterminé.

²⁴ Data refer to projections based on the 2010 Population and Housing Census. - Les données se réfèrent aux projections basées sur le recensement 2010 de la population et des logements.

²⁵ Data refer to resident population which comprises Singapore citizens and permanent residents. Provisional data. - Les données se rapportent à la population résidente composé des citoyens de Singapour et des résidents permanents. Données provisoires.

²⁶ Excluding Faeroe Islands and Greenland shown separately, if available. - Non compris les Iles Féroé et le Groenland, qui font l'objet de rubriques distinctes, si disponible.

²⁷ Excluding Åland Islands. - Non compris les Îles d'Åland.

²⁸ Excluding Transnistria and the municipality of Bender. - Les données ne tiennent pas compte de l'information sur la Transnistria et la municipalité de Bender.

²⁹ Excludes data for Kosovo and Metohia. - Sans les données pour le Kosovo et Metohie.

³⁰ Excluding Channel Islands (Guernsey and Jersey) and Isle of Man, shown separately, if available. - Non compris les îles Anglo-Normandes (Guernesey et Jersey) et l'île de Man, qui font l'objet de rubriques distinctes, si disponible.

³¹ Excluding Niue, shown separately, which is part of Cook Islands, but because of remoteness is administered separately. - Non compris Nioué, qui fait l'objet d'une rubrique distincte et qui fait partie des îles Cook, mais qui, en raison de son éloignement, est administrée séparément.

Table 23 - *Demographic Yearbook 2015*

Table 23 presents the number of marriages and crude marriage rates by urban/rural residence for every year with available data between 2011 and 2015.

Description of variables: Marriage is defined as the act, ceremony or process by which the legal relationship of spouses is constituted. The legality of the union may be established by civil, religious or other means as recognized by the laws of each country[1].

Marriage statistics in this table, therefore, include both first marriages and remarriages after divorce, widowhood or annulment. They do not, unless otherwise noted, include resumption of marriage ties after legal separation. These statistics refer to the number of marriages performed, and not to the number of persons marrying.

Statistics shown are obtained from civil registers of marriage. Exceptions, such as data from church registers, are identified in footnotes.

The urban/rural classification of marriages is that provided by each country or area; it is presumed to be based on the national census definitions of urban population which have been set forth at the end of the notes for table 6.

For certain countries, there is a discrepancy between the total number of marriages shown in this table and those shown in subsequent tables for the same year. Usually this discrepancy arises because the total number of marriages occurring in a given year is revised although the remaining tabulations are not.

Rate computation: Crude marriage rates are the annual number of marriages per 1 000 mid-year population. Rates by urban/rural residence are the annual number of marriages, in the appropriate urban or rural category, per 1 000 corresponding mid-year population. Rates presented in this table have been limited to those for countries or areas having at least a total of 30 marriages in a given year. These rates are calculated by the Statistics Division of the United Nations based on the appropriate reference population (for example: total population, nationals only, etc.) if known and available. If the reference population is not known or unavailable the total population is used to calculate the rates. Therefore, if the population that is used to calculate the rates is different from the correct reference population, the rates presented might under- or overstate the true situation in a country or area.

Reliability of data: Each country or area has been asked to indicate the estimated completeness of the number of marriages recorded in its civil register. These national assessments are indicated by the quality codes "C" and "U" that appear in the first column of this table.

"C" indicates that the data are estimated to be virtually complete, that is, representing at least 90 per cent of the marriages occurring each year, while "U" indicates that data are estimated to be incomplete, that is representing less than 90 per cent of the marriages occurring each year. The code "..." indicates that no information was provided regarding completeness.

Data from civil registers which are reported as incomplete or of unknown completeness (coded "U" or "...") are considered unreliable. They appear in italics in this table; rates are not computed for these data.

These quality codes apply only to data from civil registers. For more information about the quality of vital statistics data in general, see section 4.2 of the Technical Notes.

Limitations: Statistics on marriages are subject to the same qualifications that have been set forth for vital statistics in general and marriage statistics in particular as discussed in section 4 of the Technical Notes.

The fact that marriage is a legal event, unlike birth and death that are biological events, has implications for international comparability of data. Marriage has been defined, for statistical purposes, in terms of the laws of individual countries or areas. These laws vary throughout the world. In addition, comparability is further limited because some countries or areas compile statistics only for civil marriages although religious marriages may also be legally recognized; in other countries or areas, the only available records are church registers and, therefore, the statistics may not reflect marriages that are civil marriages only.

Because in many countries or areas marriage is a civil legal contract which, to establish its legality, must be celebrated before a civil officer, it follows that for these countries or areas registration would tend to be almost automatic at the time of, or immediately following, the marriage ceremony. This factor should be kept in mind when considering the reliability of data, described above. For this reason the practice of tabulating data by date of registration does not generally pose serious problems of comparability as it does in the case of birth and death statistics.

As indicators of family formation, the statistics on the number of marriages presented in this table are bound to be deficient to the extent that they do not include either customary unions, which are not registered even though they are considered legal and binding under customary law, or consensual unions (also known as extra-legal or de facto unions). In general, lower marriage rates over a period of years are an indication of higher incidence of customary or consensual unions.

In addition, rates are affected also by the quality and limitations of the population estimates that are used in their computation. The problems of under-enumeration or over-enumeration and, to some extent, the differences in definition of total population have been discussed in section 3 of the Technical Notes dealing with population data in general, and specific information pertaining to individual countries or areas is given in the footnotes to table 3.

Strict correspondence between the numerator of the rate and the denominator is not always obtained; for example, marriages among civilian and military segments of the population may be related to civilian population. The effect of this may be to increase the rates, but, in most cases, this effect is negligible.

It should be emphasized that crude marriage rates like crude birth, death and divorce rates, may be seriously affected by the age-sex-marital structure of the population to which they relate. Crude marriage rates do, however, provide a simple measure of the level and changes in marriage.

The comparability of data by urban/rural residence is affected by the national definitions of urban and rural used in tabulating these data. It is assumed, in the absence of specific information to the contrary, that the definitions of urban and rural used in connection with the national population census were also used in the compilation of the vital statistics for each country or area. However, it cannot be excluded that, for a given country or area, different definitions of urban and rural are used for the vital statistics data and the population census data respectively. When known, the definitions of urban in national population censuses are presented at the end of the technical notes for table 6. As discussed in detail in the notes, these definitions vary considerably from one country or area to another.

In addition to problems of comparability, marriage rates classified by urban/rural residence are also subject to certain special types of bias. If, when calculating marriage rates, different definitions of urban are used in connection with the vital events and the population data, and if this results in a net difference between the numerator and denominator of the rate in the population at risk, then the marriage rates would be biased. Urban/rural differentials in marriage rates may also be affected by whether the vital events have been tabulated in terms of place of occurrence or place of usual residence. This problem is discussed in more detail in section 4.1.4.1 of the Technical Notes.

Earlier data: Marriages and crude marriage rates have been shown in each issue of the *Demographic Yearbook*. For more information on specific topics, and years for which data are reported, readers should consult the Historical Index.

NOTES

[1] *Principles and Recommendations for a Vital Statistics System Revision 3,* Sales No. E.13.XVII.10, United Nations, New York, 2014.

Tableau 23 – *Annuaire démographique 2015*

Le tableau 23 présente des données sur les mariages et les taux bruts de nuptialité selon le lieu de résidence (zone urbaine ou rurale) pour les années où l'information est disponible entre 2011 et 2015.

Description des variables : le mariage désigne l'acte, la cérémonie ou la procédure qui établit un rapport légal entre les époux. L'union peut être rendue légale par une procédure civile ou religieuse, ou par toute autre procédure, conformément à la législation du pays[1].

Les statistiques de la nuptialité présentées dans ce tableau comprennent donc les premiers mariages et les remariages faisant suite à un divorce, un veuvage ou une annulation. Toutefois, sauf indication contraire, elles ne comprennent pas les unions reconstituées après une séparation légale. Ces statistiques se rapportent au nombre de mariages célébrés, non au nombre de personnes qui se marient.

Les statistiques présentées reposent sur l'enregistrement des mariages par les services de l'état civil. Les exceptions (données provenant des registres des églises, par exemple) font l'objet d'une note à la fin du tableau.

La classification des mariages selon le lieu de résidence (zone urbaine ou rurale) est celle qui a été communiquée par chaque pays ou zone ; on part du principe qu'elle repose sur les définitions de la population urbaine utilisées pour les recensements nationaux telles qu'elles sont reproduites à la fin des notes se rapportant au tableau 6.

Pour quelques pays il y a une discordance entre le nombre total de mariages présenté dans ce tableau et ceux présentés après pour la même année. Habituellement ces différences apparaissent lorsque le nombre total des mariages pour une certaine année a été révisé alors que les autres tabulations ne l'ont pas été.

Calcul des taux : les taux bruts de nuptialité représentent le nombre annuel de mariages pour 1 000 habitants au milieu de l'année. Les taux selon le lieu de résidence (zone urbaine ou rurale) représentent le nombre annuel de mariages, classés selon la catégorie urbaine ou rurale appropriée, pour 1 000 habitants au milieu de l'année. Les taux de ce tableau ne se rapportent qu'aux pays ou zones où l'on a enregistré un total d'au moins 30 mariages pendant une année donnée. Ces taux sont calculés par la division de statistique des Nations Unies sur la base de la population de référence adéquate (par exemple : population totale, nationaux seulement, etc.) si connue et disponible. Si la population de référence n'est pas connue ou n'est pas disponible, la population totale est utilisée pour calculer les taux. Par conséquent, si la population utilisée pour calculer les taux est différente de la population de référence adéquate, les taux présentés sont susceptibles de sous ou sur estimer la situation réelle d'un pays ou d'un territoire.

Fiabilité des données : il a été demandé à chaque pays ou zone d'indiquer le degré estimatif de complétude des données sur les mariages figurant dans ses registres d'état civil. Ces évaluations nationales sont signalées par les codes de qualité "C" et "U" qui apparaissent dans la deuxième colonne du tableau.

La lettre "C" indique que les données sont jugées à peu près complètes, c'est-à-dire qu'elles représentent au moins 90 p. 100 des mariages survenus chaque année ; la lettre "U" signale que les données sont jugées incomplètes, c'est-à-dire qu'elles représentent moins de 90 p. 100 des mariages survenus chaque année. Le code "..." indique qu'aucun renseignement n'a été communiqué quant à la complétude des données.

Les données issues des registres de l'état civil qui sont déclarées incomplètes ou dont le degré de complétude n'est pas connu (code "U" ou "...") sont jugées douteuses. Elles apparaissent en italique dans le tableau et les taux correspondants n'ont pas été calculés.

Les codes de qualité ne s'appliquent qu'aux données provenant des registres de l'état civil. Pour plus de précisions sur la qualité des données reposant sur les statistiques de l'état civil en général, voir la section 4.2 des Notes techniques.

Insuffisance des données : les statistiques relatives aux mariages appellent les mêmes réserves que celles qui ont été formulées à propos des statistiques de l'état civil en général et des statistiques concernant la nuptialité en particulier (voir la section 4 des Notes techniques).

Le fait que le mariage soit un acte juridique, à la différence de la naissance et du décès, qui sont des faits biologiques, a des répercussions sur la comparabilité internationale des données. Aux fins de la statistique, le mariage est défini par la législation de chaque pays ou zone. Cette législation varie d'un pays à l'autre. La comparabilité est limitée en outre du fait que certains pays ou zones ne réunissent des statistiques que pour les mariages civils, bien que les mariages religieux y soient également reconnus par la loi ; dans d'autres, les seuls relevés disponibles sont les registres des églises et, en conséquence, les statistiques peuvent ne pas rendre compte des mariages exclusivement civils.

Étant donné que, dans de nombreux pays ou zones, le mariage est un contrat juridique civil qui, pour être légal, doit être conclu devant un officier d'état civil, il s'ensuit que dans ces pays ou zones l'enregistrement se fait à peu près systématiquement au moment de la cérémonie ou immédiatement après. Il faut tenir compte de cet élément lorsque l'on évalue la fiabilité des données, dont il est question plus haut. C'est pourquoi la pratique consistant à exploiter les données selon la date de l'enregistrement ne pose généralement pas les graves problèmes de comparabilité auxquels on se heurte dans le cas des statistiques concernant les naissances et les décès.

Les statistiques relatives au nombre des mariages présentées dans ce tableau donnent une idée forcément trompeuse de la formation des familles, dans la mesure où elles ne tiennent compte ni des mariages coutumiers, qui ne sont pas enregistrés bien qu'ils soient considérés comme légaux et créateurs d'obligations en vertu du droit coutumier, ni des unions consensuelles (appelées également unions non légalisées ou unions de fait). En général, une diminution du taux de nuptialité pendant un certain nombre d'années indique une augmentation des mariages coutumiers ou des unions consensuelles.

L'exactitude des taux dépend également de la qualité et des insuffisances des estimations de population qui sont utilisées pour leur calcul. Le problème des erreurs par excès ou par défaut commises lors du dénombrement et, dans une certaine mesure, le problème de l'hétérogénéité des définitions de la population totale ont été examinés à la section 3 des Notes techniques relative à la population en général ; des indications concernant les différents pays ou zones sont données en note à la fin du tableau 3.

Il n'a pas toujours été possible d'obtenir une correspondance rigoureuse entre le numérateur et le dénominateur pour le calcul des taux. Par exemple, les mariages parmi la population civile et les militaires sont parfois rapportés à la population civile. Cela peut avoir pour effet d'accroître les taux, mais, dans la plupart des cas, il est probable que la différence sera négligeable.

Il faut souligner que les taux bruts de nuptialité, de même que les taux bruts de natalité, de mortalité et de divortialité, peuvent varier sensiblement selon la structure par âge et par sexe de la population à laquelle ils se rapportent. Les taux bruts de nuptialité offrent néanmoins un moyen simple de mesurer la fréquence et l'évolution des mariages.

La comparabilité des données selon le lieu de résidence (zone urbaine ou rurale) peut être limitée par les définitions nationales des termes « urbain » et « rural » utilisées pour le classement de ces données. En l'absence d'indications contraires, on a supposé que les mêmes définitions avaient servi pour le recensement national de la population et pour l'établissement des statistiques de l'état civil pour chaque pays ou zone. Toutefois, il n'est pas exclu que, pour une zone ou un pays donné, des définitions différentes aient été retenues. Les définitions du terme « urbain » utilisées pour les recensements nationaux de population ont été présentées à la fin des notes techniques du tableau 6 lorsqu'elles étaient connues. Comme on l'a précisé dans les notes techniques relatives au tableau 6, ces définitions varient considérablement d'un pays ou d'une zone à l'autre.

Outre les problèmes de comparabilité, les taux de nuptialité classés selon le lieu de résidence (zone urbaine ou rurale) sont également sujets à des distorsions particulières. Si l'on utilise des définitions différentes du terme « urbain » pour classer les faits d'état civil et les données relatives à la population lors du calcul des taux et qu'il en résulte une différence nette entre le numérateur et le dénominateur pour le taux de la population exposée au risque, les taux de nuptialité s'en trouveront faussés. La différence entre ces taux pour les zones urbaines et rurales pourra aussi être faussée selon que les faits d'état civil auront été classés d'après le lieu où ils se sont produits ou d'après le lieu de résidence habituel. Ce problème est examiné plus en détail à la section 4.1.4.1 des Notes techniques.

Données publiées antérieurement : les différentes éditions de l'*Annuaire démographique* regroupent des données sur le nombre des mariages. Pour plus de précisions concernant les années et les sujets pour lesquels des données ont été publiées, se reporter à l'index historique.

NOTE

[1] *Principes et recommandations pour un système de statistique de l'état civil, troisième révision,* numéro de vente : E.13.XVII.10, publication des Nations Unies, New York, 2014.

23. Marriages and crude marriage rates, by urban/rural residence: 2011 - 2015
Mariages et taux bruts de nuptialité, selon la résidence, urbaine/rurale : 2011 - 2015

Continent, country or area, and urban/rural residence / Continent, pays ou zone et résidence, urbaine/rurale	Co-de[a]	Number - Nombre					Rate - Taux				
		2011	2012	2013	2014	2015	2011	2012	2013	2014	2015
AFRICA - AFRIQUE											
Algeria - Algérie[1]											
Total	...	369 031	371 280	387 947	386 422	369 074	...	...	...	...	...
Botswana											
Total	+U	4 601	5 214	5 333[2]	5 591[2]	...	...	...	...	...	...
Cabo Verde											
Total	+C	1 158	...	...	...	...	2.2	...	...	...	...
Egypt - Égypte[3]											
Total	+C	897 969	922 425	909 350	953 137	...	11.2	11.2	10.7	11.0	...
Urban - Urbaine	+C	353 048	416 060	371 995	384 799	...	10.2	11.8	10.3	10.4	...
Rural - Rurale	+C	544 921	506 365	537 355	568 338	...	11.8	10.7	11.1	11.4	...
Lesotho											
Total	+U	3 188	...	...	...	...	...	...	...	...	...
Mauritius - Maurice[4]											
Total	+C	10 499	10 382	9 575	9 959	9 709	8.4	8.3	7.6	7.9	7.7
Urban - Urbaine	+C	3 195	3 096	2 902	3 216	3 194	6.3	6.1	5.6	6.2	6.2
Rural - Rurale	+C	7 304	7 286	6 673	6 743	6 515	9.8	9.8	9.0	9.1	8.7
Mayotte											
Total	C	...	...	...	467		...	...	...	2.1	...
Niger											
Total	+U	6 750	...	...	...		...	...	...	...	...
Reunion - Réunion											
Total	C	...	...	...	2 771		...	...	...	3.3	...
Saint Helena ex. dep. - Sainte-Hélène sans dép.											
Total	C	15	12	8	7		...	...	...	...	...
Seychelles[5]											
Total	+C	1 525	1 748	1 708	1 655	1 845	17.4	19.8	19.0	18.1	19.7
South Africa - Afrique du Sud											
Total	...	167 264	161 112	158 642	150 852		...	...	...	...	...
Sudan - Soudan											
Total	U	...	...	...	...	158 051	...	...	...	...	...
Tunisia - Tunisie											
Total	...	91 590	...	...	...		...	...	...	...	...
AMERICA, NORTH - AMÉRIQUE DU NORD											
Anguilla[6]											
Total	C	47	56	42	64	39	3.5	4.1	3.0	4.5	2.6
Aruba											
Total	C	550	574	523	617	705	5.3	5.5	4.9	5.7	6.5
Bahamas											
Total	+C	1 916	1 941	2 122	...	...	5.4	5.4	5.8	...	...
Barbados - Barbade											
Total	+C	2 200	2 135	1 829	1 855	...	7.9	7.7	6.6	6.7	...
Bermuda - Bermudes											
Total	C	555	601	471	477	509	8.8	9.6	7.6	7.7	8.2
Cayman Islands - Îles Caïmanes[7]											
Total	+C	533	473	527	452	468	9.6	8.4	9.4	7.9	7.9
Costa Rica[8]											
Total	C	25 013	26 112	25 725	25 909	*26 512	5.4	5.6	5.5	5.4	*5.5
Urban - Urbaine	C	13 127	13 567	12 229	17 905	*21 258	3.9	4.0	3.6	5.2	*6.1
Rural - Rurale	C	11 886	12 545	13 496	8 004	*5 254	9.5	9.9	10.5	6.1	*4.0
Cuba[9]											
Total	C	59 676	55 759	61 449	63 954	61 902	5.3	5.0	5.5	5.7	5.5
Urban - Urbaine	C	54 847	49 837	56 462	58 137	...	6.5	5.9	6.6	6.7	...
Rural - Rurale	C	4 829	5 922	4 987	5 817	...	1.7	2.2	1.9	2.2	...
Curaçao											
Total	C	859	741	665	696	703	5.7	4.9	4.3	4.5	4.4
Dominica - Dominique											
Total	+C	240	...	...	...	...	3.4	...	...	...	...
Dominican Republic - République dominicaine											
Total	+C	44 253	43 307	45 163	47 235	...	4.6	4.5	4.6	4.8	...

23. Marriages and crude marriage rates, by urban/rural residence: 2011 - 2015
Mariages et taux bruts de nuptialité, selon la résidence, urbaine/rurale : 2011 - 2015 (continued - suite)

Continent, country or area, and urban/rural residence / Continent, pays ou zone et résidence, urbaine/rurale	Co-de[a]	Number - Nombre					Rate - Taux				
		2011	2012	2013	2014	2015	2011	2012	2013	2014	2015

AMERICA, NORTH - AMÉRIQUE DU NORD

El Salvador[10]											
Total	...	31 220	29 267	...	...	...	...	...	...	...	...
Urban - Urbaine	...	11 702	7 757	...	...	...	...	...	...	...	...
Rural - Rurale	...	19 518	21 510	...	...	...	...	...	...	...	...
Grenada - Grenade											
Total	+C	589	610	...	...	...	5.5	5.7	...	...	...
Guadeloupe											
Total	C	1 259	1 291	1 136	1 198	...	3.1	3.2	2.8	3.0	...
Guatemala											
Total	C	78 285	84 253	80 750	79 496	...	5.3	5.6	...	...	...
Jamaica - Jamaïque											
Total	+C	20 685	20 175	18 835	18 480	...	7.7	7.5	6.9	6.8	...
Martinique											
Total	C	...	...	...	968	...	...	...	...	2.5	...
Mexico - Mexique[11]											
Total	+C	570 954	585 434	583 264	577 713	...	4.9	5.0	4.9	4.8	...
Urban - Urbaine[12]	+C	417 583	430 852	418 686	420 856	...	5.0	5.1	4.9	4.8	...
Rural - Rurale[12]	+C	121 839	120 188	114 574	119 600	...	3.8	3.7	3.5	3.6	...
Montserrat											
Total	+...	19	16	18	14	...	...	...	...	...	...
Panama[8]											
Total	C	15 135[13]	14 201	13 213	12 869	...	4.1	3.7	3.4	3.3	...
Urban - Urbaine	C	11 625[13]	10 995	10 535	10 443	...	4.7	4.4	4.1	4.0	...
Rural - Rurale	C	3 510[13]	3 206	2 678	2 426	...	2.8	2.5	2.1	1.9	...
Puerto Rico - Porto Rico											
Total	C	18 001	17 948	17 010	16 668	16 987	4.9	4.9	4.7	4.7	4.9
Saint Lucia - Sainte-Lucie											
Total	C	*492	*305	...	...	...	*2.9	*1.8	...	...	...
Saint Vincent and the Grenadines - Saint-Vincent-et-les Grenadines											
Total	C	507	514	511	526	574	4.6	4.7	4.6	4.8	5.2
Sint Maarten (Dutch part) - Saint-Martin (partie néerlandaise)											
Total	+C	187	166	230	...	...	5.6	4.8	6.3	...	...
Trinidad and Tobago - Trinité-et-Tobago											
Total	C	*7 877	...	...	...	...	*5.9	...	...	...	...
United States of America - États-Unis d'Amérique											
Total	C	2 118 000	...	...	...	...	6.8	...	...	...	...

AMERICA, SOUTH - AMÉRIQUE DU SUD

Argentina - Argentine											
Total	C	128 797	131 922	123 810	119 266	...	3.1	3.2	2.9	2.8	...
Bolivia (Plurinational State of) - Bolivie (État plurinational de)											
Total	U	25 531	34 542	...	...	...	...	...	...	...	...
Total	+U	...	...	40 871	57 267	34 123	...	...	...	...	...
Brazil - Brésil											
Total	+U	1 026 736	1 041 440	1 052 477[11]	1 106 440[11]	...	...	...	...	...	...
Chile - Chili											
Total	+C	64 768	63 736	61 446	...	...	3.8	3.7	3.5	...	...
Urban - Urbaine[14]	+C	59 619	58 606	56 758	...	...	4.0	3.9	3.7	...	...
Rural - Rurale[14]	+C	5 149	5 130	4 688	...	...	2.3	2.3	2.1	...	...
Ecuador - Équateur[15]											
Total	U	73 579	57 753	53 986	60 328	...	...	...	...	...	...
Urban - Urbaine	U	...	...	44 721	50 434	...	...	...	...	...	...
Rural - Rurale	U	...	...	9 265	9 894	...	...	...	...	...	...
Guyana[16]											
Total	C	4 846	5 128	4 667	4 679	...	6.5	6.8	6.2	6.3	...

23. Marriages and crude marriage rates, by urban/rural residence: 2011 - 2015
Mariages et taux bruts de nuptialité, selon la résidence, urbaine/rurale : 2011 - 2015 (continued - suite)

Continent, country or area, and urban/rural residence / Continent, pays ou zone et résidence, urbaine/rurale	Co-de[a]	Number - Nombre					Rate - Taux				
		2011	2012	2013	2014	2015	2011	2012	2013	2014	2015
AMERICA, SOUTH - AMÉRIQUE DU SUD											
Paraguay											
Total	U	*19 491*	*20 967*	*19 076*	*19 527*	...	...	...	...	...	...
Peru - Pérou[17]											
Total	+C	97 693	107 380	89 763	95 770	...	3.3	3.6	2.9	3.1	...
Suriname											
Total	C	2 337	2 204	2 190	2 143	...	4.3	4.1	4.0	3.8	...
Uruguay											
Total	C	9 604	9 631	10 034	10 226	...	2.8	2.8	2.9	3.0	...
Venezuela (Bolivarian Republic of) - Venezuela (République bolivarienne du)											
Total	C	103 004	102 077	99 065	94 519	90 812	3.6	3.5	3.3	3.1	3.0
ASIA - ASIE											
Armenia - Arménie											
Total	+C	19 706	...	...	18 912	...	6.0	...	...	...	...
Azerbaijan - Azerbaïdjan											
Total	+C	88 145	79 065	86 852	84 912	...	9.6	8.5	9.2	8.9	...
Urban - Urbaine	+C	45 494	42 293	46 324	...	...	9.4	8.6	9.2	...	...
Rural - Rurale	+C	42 651	36 772	40 528	...	...	9.9	8.4	9.2	...	...
Bahrain - Bahreïn											
Total	...	*6 769*	*7 559*	*7 463*	*7 673*	*6 953*	...	...	...	...	...
Bangladesh											
Total	...	*2 066 820*	*2 027 350*	...	...	...	...	...	...	...	...
Urban - Urbaine	...	*443 040*	*446 516*	...	...	...	...	...	...	...	...
Rural - Rurale	...	*1 623 780*	*1 580 834*	...	...	...	...	...	...	...	...
Brunei Darussalam - Brunéi Darussalam											
Total	...	*2 726*	*2 671*	*2 741*	*2 992*	...	...	...	...	...	...
China - Chine[18]											
Total	+C	12 471 000	12 971 000	...	...	...	9.3	9.6	...	...	...
China, Hong Kong SAR - Chine, Hong Kong RAS											
Total	C	58 369	60 459	55 274	56 454	...	8.3	8.5	7.7	7.8	...
China, Macao SAR - Chine, Macao RAS											
Total	+C	3 545	3 783	4 153	4 085	3 719	6.5	6.7	7.0	6.6	5.8
Cyprus - Chypre[19]											
Total	C	6 210	5 806	5 493	...	...	7.3	6.7	6.4	...	...
Georgia - Géorgie											
Total	C	30 863	30 412	34 693	31 526	...	6.9	6.8	...	7.0	...
Urban - Urbaine[14]	C	17 625	...	...	...	...	7.4	...	...	...	...
Rural - Rurale[14]	C	13 238	...	...	...	...	6.3	...	...	...	...
Indonesia - Indonésie											
Total	U	*2 319 821*	...	...	...	...	...	...	...	...	...
Iran (Islamic Republic of) - Iran (République islamique d')[20]											
Total	+C	874 792	829 968	774 513	724 324	...	11.6	10.9	10.1	9.3	...
Israel - Israël[21]											
Total	C	51 271	50 474	52 705	...	...	6.6	6.4	6.5	...	...
Urban - Urbaine[22]	C	46 034	45 371	47 506	...	...	6.5	6.3	6.4	...	...
Rural - Rurale[22]	C	4 034	3 900	3 951	...	...	6.2	5.8	5.7	...	...
Japan - Japon[23]											
Total	+C	661 895	668 869	660 613	643 749	...	5.2	5.2	5.2	5.1	...
Urban - Urbaine[14]	+C	613 035	620 373	613 648	598 792	...	...	...	...	...	...
Rural - Rurale[14]	+C	48 860	48 496	46 965	44 957	...	...	...	...	...	...
Jordan - Jordanie[24]											
Total	+C	64 665	70 621	70 965	81 209	...	9.2	9.5	8.7	9.2	...
Kazakhstan											
Total	C	160 494	164 681	168 447	...	...	9.7	9.8	9.9	...	...
Urban - Urbaine	C	97 321	102 889	107 494	...	...	10.8	11.2	11.5	...	...
Rural - Rurale	C	63 173	61 792	60 953	...	...	8.4	8.1	7.9	...	...

23. Marriages and crude marriage rates, by urban/rural residence: 2011 - 2015
Mariages et taux bruts de nuptialité, selon la résidence, urbaine/rurale : 2011 - 2015 (continued - suite)

Continent, country or area, and urban/rural residence / Continent, pays ou zone et résidence, urbaine/rurale	Code[a]	Number - Nombre					Rate - Taux				
		2011	2012	2013	2014	2015	2011	2012	2013	2014	2015
ASIA - ASIE											
Kuwait - Koweït											
Total	C	19 860	14 320	15 118	15 086	...	6.4	4.4	4.4	4.0	...
Kyrgyzstan - Kirghizstan											
Total	C	56 509	55 176	53 578	54 942	*52 043	10.7	10.3	9.4	9.4	*8.7
Urban - Urbaine	C	15 930	16 622	17 329	17 150	*15 875	8.6	9.0	9.0	8.7	*7.9
Rural - Rurale	C	40 579	38 554	36 249	37 792	*36 168	11.9	11.0	9.5	9.8	*9.2
Lebanon - Liban											
Total	C	42 500	38 691	38 737	41 049	...	11.2	...	...	...	...
Mongolia - Mongolie											
Total	+C	11 869	12 822	15 785	17 332	17 586	4.3	4.5	5.4	5.8	5.8
Urban - Urbaine	+C	8 245	8 718	10 613	12 075	12 506	4.4	4.6	5.4	6.1	6.1
Rural - Rurale	+C	3 624	4 104	5 172	5 257	5 080	3.9	4.4	5.5	5.4	5.2
Oman[25]											
Total	+U	26 540	29 840	...	...	...	...	...	...	...	...
Philippines											
Total	U	476 408	482 399	442 603	429 732	...	...	...	...	...	...
Qatar											
Total	C	3 293	3 532	3 619	...	...	1.9	1.9	1.8	...	...
Republic of Korea - République de Corée[26]											
Total	+C	329 087	327 073	322 807	305 507	302 828	6.6	6.5	6.4	6.0	5.9
Urban - Urbaine[22]	+C	266 713	266 463	263 992	248 965	247 486	6.6	6.5	6.4	6.0	6.0
Rural - Rurale[22]	+C	54 441	52 829	50 906	48 818	48 638	5.8	5.6	5.5	5.2	5.1
Singapore - Singapour[27]											
Total	+C	27 258	27 936	26 254	28 407	28 322	7.2	7.3	6.8	7.3	7.3
Sri Lanka											
Total	+U	*200 314	*198 710	*180 760	*175 728	*175 939	...	...	...	...	...
State of Palestine - État de Palestine											
Total	C	36 284	40 292	42 698	43 732	...	8.7	9.4	9.7	9.6	...
Tajikistan - Tadjikistan											
Total	+C	94 730	97 653	96 989	95 537	...	12.3	12.4	12.0	11.6	...
Urban - Urbaine	+C	25 068	25 115	25 306	25 757	...	12.3	12.0	11.8	11.7	...
Rural - Rurale	+C	69 662	72 538	71 683	69 780	...	12.3	12.5	12.1	11.5	...
Turkey - Turquie[28]											
Total	C	592 775	603 751	600 138	599 704	...	8.0	8.0	7.9	7.8	...
United Arab Emirates - Émirats arabes unis											
Total	...	15 105	14 934	16 441	16 917	...	...	...	...	...	...
Uzbekistan - Ouzbékistan											
Total	+C	287 793	299 048	304 859	296 055	...	9.8	10.0	10.1	9.6	...
Urban - Urbaine	+C	143 250	144 174	140 958	136 707	...	9.5	9.4	9.1	8.7	...
Rural - Rurale	+C	144 543	154 874	163 901	159 348	...	10.1	10.7	11.1	10.5	...
EUROPE											
Åland Islands - Îles d'Åland											
Total	C	113	141	118	115	*118	4.0	5.0	4.1	4.0	*4.1
Urban - Urbaine	C	44	59	46	53	*50	3.9	5.2	4.0	4.6	*4.4
Rural - Rurale	C	69	82	72	62	*68	4.1	4.8	4.2	3.6	*3.9
Albania - Albanie											
Total	C	25 556	22 891	23 820	...	...	8.8	7.9	8.2	...	...
Andorra - Andorre											
Total	C	283	288	...	...	...	3.6	3.7	...	...	...
Austria - Autriche[29]											
Total	C	36 426	38 592	36 140	...	...	4.3	4.6	4.3	...	...
Belarus - Bélarus											
Total	C	86 785	76 245	87 127	83 942	...	9.2	8.1	9.2	8.9	...
Urban - Urbaine	C	71 795	62 828	71 702	...	...	10.0	8.7	9.9	...	...
Rural - Rurale	C	14 990	13 417	15 425	...	...	6.4	5.9	7.0	...	...
Belgium - Belgique[30]											
Total	C	41 001	*40 500	...	...	...	3.7	*3.6	...	...	...
Urban - Urbaine	C	40 455	...	...	...	...	3.7	...	...	...	...
Rural - Rurale	C	546	...	...	...	...	3.4	...	...	...	...

23. Marriages and crude marriage rates, by urban/rural residence: 2011 - 2015
Mariages et taux bruts de nuptialité, selon la résidence, urbaine/rurale : 2011 - 2015 (continued - suite)

Continent, country or area, and urban/rural residence — Continent, pays ou zone et résidence, urbaine/rurale	Code[a]	Number - Nombre					Rate - Taux				
		2011	2012	2013	2014	2015	2011	2012	2013	2014	2015
EUROPE											
Bosnia and Herzegovina - Bosnie-Herzégovine											
Total	C	19 156	18 980	18 387	18 409	...	5.0	4.9	4.8	4.8	...
Bulgaria - Bulgarie[31]											
Total	C	21 448	21 167	21 943	24 596	...	2.9	2.9	3.0	3.4	...
Urban - Urbaine	C	16 704	16 357	...	...	...	3.1	3.1	...	...	...
Rural - Rurale	C	4 744	4 810	...	...	...	2.4	2.4	...	...	...
Croatia - Croatie											
Total	C	20 211	20 323	19 169	19 501	...	4.7	4.8	4.5	4.6	...
Urban - Urbaine	C	11 333	11 386	10 691	10 924	...	...	...	...	...	...
Rural - Rurale	C	8 878	8 937	8 478	8 577	...	...	...	...	...	...
Czech Republic - République tchèque											
Total	C	45 137	45 206	43 499	45 575	...	4.3	4.3	4.1	4.3	...
Urban - Urbaine	C	33 601	33 403	31 976	33 356	...	...	...	4.2	4.3	...
Rural - Rurale	C	11 536	11 803	11 523	12 219	...	...	...	4.1	4.3	...
Denmark - Danemark[32]											
Total	C	27 198	28 503	27 503	28 331	...	4.9	5.1	4.9	5.0	...
Estonia - Estonie											
Total	C	5 499	5 888	5 630	6 220	...	4.1	4.5	4.3	4.7	...
Urban - Urbaine[33]	C	3 837	4 000	3 963	4 232	...	4.2	4.4	4.4	4.7	...
Rural - Rurale[33]	C	1 396	1 594	1 368	1 496	...	3.3	3.8	3.3	3.6	...
Faeroe Islands - Îles Féroé											
Total	C	206	237	259	236	217	4.2	4.9	5.4	4.9	4.4
Finland - Finlande[34]											
Total	C	28 295	28 737	25 001	24 347	...	5.3	5.3	4.6	4.5	...
Urban - Urbaine	C	21 343	21 485	18 856	18 485	...	5.8	5.8	5.1	4.9	...
Rural - Rurale	C	6 952	7 252	6 145	5 862	...	4.1	4.3	3.7	3.5	...
France											
Total	C	231 100	239 840	233 108	235 315	...	3.7	3.8	3.7	3.7	...
Urban - Urbaine[35]	C	178 548	186 141	181 513	182 905	...	...	...	...	...	...
Rural - Rurale[35]	C	50 308	51 425	49 361	49 824	...	...	...	...	...	...
Germany - Allemagne											
Total	C	377 816	387 423	373 655	385 952	...	4.7	4.8	4.6	4.8	...
Gibraltar[7]											
Total	+C	176	204	195	...	...	5.5	6.3	6.0	...	...
Greece - Grèce											
Total	C	55 099	49 705	51 256	53 105	...	5.0	4.5	4.7	4.9	...
Urban - Urbaine	C	39 624	35 464	...	37 743	...	...	...	...	...	...
Rural - Rurale	C	15 475	14 241	...	15 362	...	...	...	...	...	...
Guernsey - Guernesey											
Total	C	340	325	...	...	...	5.4	5.2	...	...	...
Hungary - Hongrie[9]											
Total	C	35 812	36 161	36 986	38 780	...	3.6	3.6	3.7	3.9	...
Urban - Urbaine[36]	C	26 793	26 678	27 189	28 854	...	3.9	3.9	4.0	4.2	...
Rural - Rurale[36]	C	8 607	9 117	9 424	9 538	...	2.8	3.0	3.1	3.3	...
Iceland - Islande[37]											
Total	C	1 456	...	...	...	...	4.6	...	...	...	...
Urban - Urbaine	C	1 432	...	...	...	...	4.6	...	...	...	...
Rural - Rurale	C	24	...	...	...	...	...	...	...	...	...
Ireland - Irlande											
Total	+C	19 855	20 713	20 680	22 045	...	4.3	4.5	4.5	4.8	...
Italy - Italie											
Total	C	204 830	207 138	194 057	189 765	...	3.4	3.5	3.2	3.1	...
Jersey											
Total	+C	515	557	...	...	...	5.2	5.6	...	...	...
Latvia - Lettonie[8]											
Total	C	10 760	11 244	11 436	12 515	...	5.2	5.5	5.7	6.3	...
Liechtenstein[8]											
Total	C	163	185	...	...	...	4.5	5.0	...	...	...
Lithuania - Lituanie											
Total	C	19 221	20 660	20 469	22 142	...	6.3	6.9	6.9	7.6	...
Urban - Urbaine	C	13 546	14 432	14 166	15 250	...	6.7	7.2	7.1	7.7	...
Rural - Rurale	C	5 675	6 228	6 303	6 892	...	5.6	6.3	6.5	7.2	...
Luxembourg[7]											
Total	C	1 714	1 782	1 722	1 657	...	3.3	3.4	3.2	3.0	...

23. Marriages and crude marriage rates, by urban/rural residence: 2011 - 2015
Mariages et taux bruts de nuptialité, selon la résidence, urbaine/rurale : 2011 - 2015 (continued - suite)

Continent, country or area, and urban/rural residence Continent, pays ou zone et résidence, urbaine/rurale	Co-de[a]	Number - Nombre					Rate - Taux				
		2011	2012	2013	2014	2015	2011	2012	2013	2014	2015
EUROPE											
Malta - Malte											
Total	C	2 562	2 823	2 578	2 871	...	6.2	6.7	6.1	6.7	...
Montenegro - Monténégro											
Total	C	3 528	3 305	3 847	3 527	...	5.7	5.3	6.2	5.7	...
Netherlands - Pays-Bas[38]											
Total	C	71 572	70 315	64 549	65 333	...	4.3	4.2	3.8	3.9	...
Norway - Norvège[11]											
Total	C	23 135	24 346	23 916	23 462	...	4.7	4.9	4.7	4.6	...
Poland - Pologne											
Total	C	206 471	203 850	180 396	188 488	...	5.4	5.3	4.7	5.0	...
Urban - Urbaine	C	122 737	119 401	...	...	...	5.2	5.1	...	...	...
Rural - Rurale	C	83 734	84 449	...	...	...	5.5	5.6	...	...	...
Portugal[39]											
Total	C	36 035	34 423	31 998	31 478	...	3.4	3.3	3.1	3.0	...
Republic of Moldova - République de Moldova											
Total	C	25 900	24 262	24 449	25 624	...	7.3	6.8	6.9	7.2	...
Urban - Urbaine	C	13 191	12 287	...	...	...	8.9	8.3	...	...	...
Rural - Rurale	C	12 709	11 975	...	...	...	6.1	5.8	...	...	...
Romania - Roumanie											
Total	C	105 599	107 760	107 507	118 075	...	5.2	5.4	5.4	5.9	...
Urban - Urbaine	C	67 962	68 821	68 985	76 833	...	6.2	6.4	6.4	7.2	...
Rural - Rurale	C	37 637	38 939	38 522	41 242	...	4.1	4.2	4.2	4.5	...
Russian Federation - Fédération de Russie[40]											
Total	C	1 316 011	1 213 598	1 225 501	...	...	9.2	8.5	8.5	...	...
Urban - Urbaine	C	978 039	911 015	...	...	...	9.3	8.6	...	...	...
Rural - Rurale	C	337 972	302 583	...	...	...	9.0	8.1	...	...	...
San Marino - Saint-Marin[41]											
Total	C	205	203	221	187	...	6.1	6.1	6.6	5.6	...
Serbia - Serbie[42]											
Total	+C	35 808	34 639	36 209	36 429	...	4.9	4.8	5.1	5.1	...
Urban - Urbaine	+C	23 564	22 622	23 573	23 718	...	5.5	5.3	5.5	5.6	...
Rural - Rurale	+C	12 244	12 017	12 636	12 711	...	4.1	4.1	4.4	4.4	...
Slovakia - Slovaquie[8]											
Total	C	25 621	26 006	25 491	26 737	...	4.7	4.8	4.7	4.9	...
Urban - Urbaine	C	14 608	14 950	14 491	15 280	...	5.0	5.1	4.9	5.2	...
Rural - Rurale	C	11 013	11 056	11 000	11 457	...	4.5	4.5	4.4	4.6	...
Slovenia - Slovénie[43]											
Total	C	6 671	7 057	6 254	6 571	...	3.3	3.4	3.0	3.2	...
Urban - Urbaine	C	3 430	3 622	3 295	3 365	...	3.4	3.5	3.1	3.2	...
Rural - Rurale	C	3 241	3 435	2 959	3 206	...	3.2	3.3	2.9	3.2	...
Spain - Espagne											
Total	C	158 220	163 173	151 433	160 256	...	3.4	3.5	3.3	3.4	...
Sweden - Suède[11]											
Total	C	47 564	50 616	51 554	53 051	...	5.0	5.3	5.4	5.5	...
Switzerland - Suisse[44]											
Total	C	42 083	42 654	39 794	41 891	...	5.3	5.3	4.9	5.1	...
Urban - Urbaine	C	32 279	32 589	30 455	32 019	...	5.5	5.5	5.1	5.3	...
Rural - Rurale	C	9 804	10 065	9 339	9 872	...	4.7	4.8	4.4	4.6	...
TFYR of Macedonia - L'ex-R. y. de Macédoine											
Total	C	*14 797	13 991	13 982	13 813	...	*7.2	6.8	6.8	6.7	...
Ukraine											
Total	+C	355 880	278 276	304 232	294 962[45]	...	7.8	6.1	6.7	6.9	...
Urban - Urbaine	+C	270 245	211 819	235 108	...	...	8.6	6.8	...	...	...
Rural - Rurale	+C	85 635	66 457	69 124	...	...	6.0	4.7	...	...	...
United Kingdom of Great Britain and Northern Ireland - Royaume-Uni de Grande-Bretagne et d'Irlande du Nord[46]											
Total	C	285 391	...	...	...	...	4.5	...	...	...	...

789

Continent, country or area, and urban/rural residence Continent, pays ou zone et résidence, urbaine/rurale	Co-de[a]	Number - Nombre					Rate - Taux				
		2011	2012	2013	2014	2015	2011	2012	2013	2014	2015
OCEANIA - OCÉANIE											
American Samoa - Samoas américaines											
Total	C	204	155	186	217	...	3.2	2.4	3.0	3.5	...
Australia - Australie											
Total	+C	121 752	123 244	118 962	121 197	...	5.4	5.4	5.1	5.2	...
Cook Islands - Îles Cook[47]											
Total	+C	918	894	843	746	*720	47.6	45.8	45.3	40.1	*38.3
French Polynesia - Polynésie française											
Total	C	1 431	1 699	1 474	1 480	1 456	5.4	6.3	5.5	5.5	5.3
Guam[48]											
Total	C	1 579	1 658	1 462	1 463	1 348[11]	9.9	10.4	9.1	9.1	8.3
New Caledonia - Nouvelle-Calédonie											
Total	C	880	994	...	...	...	3.5	3.9	...	...	...
New Zealand - Nouvelle-Zélande											
Total	+C	20 231[8]	20 521[8]	19 237[49]	20 125[50]	...	4.6	4.7	4.3	4.5	...
Norfolk Island - Île Norfolk[51]											
Total	+C	34	31	19	15	24	14.8	...	...	...	...
Samoa											
Total	U	*953*	...	...	...	*865*	...	...	...	...	...

FOOTNOTES - NOTES

Italics: data from civil registers which are incomplete or of unknown completeness. - Italiques : données incomplètes ou dont le degré d'exactitude n'est pas connu, provenant des registres de l'état civil.

* Provisional. - Données provisoires.

[a] 'Code' indicates the source of data, as follows:
C - Civil registration, estimated over 90% complete
U - Civil registration, estimated less than 90% complete
| - Other source, estimated reliable
+ - Data tabulated by date of registration rather than occurence
... - Information not available

Le 'Code' indique la source des données, comme suit :
C - Registres de l'état civil considérés complèts à 90 p. 100 au moins
U - Registres de l'état civil qui ne sont pas considérés complèts à 90 p. 100 au moins
| - Autre source, considérée pas douteuses
+ - Données exploitées selon la date de l'enregistrement et non la date de l'événement
... - Information pas disponible

[1] Data refer to Algerian population only. - Les données ne concernent que la population algérienne.
[2] Source: Vital Statistics Report 2014. - Source: Vital Statistics Report 2014.
[3] Including marriages resumed after 'revocable divorce' (among Moslem population), which approximates legal separation. - Y compris les unions reconstituées après un 'divorce révocable' (parmi la population musulmane), qui est à peu près l'équivalent d'une séparation légale.
[4] Excludes the islands of St. Brandon and Agalega. - Non compris les îles St. Brandon et Agalega.
[5] Including visitors. - Y compris les visiteurs.
[6] Excluding visitors. - Ne comprend pas les visiteurs.
[7] Data refer to marriages where one or both partners are residents. - Les données portent sur les mariages pour lesquels l'un des deux partenaires ou les deux sont résidents.
[8] Data refer to marriages by residence of the groom. - Les données concernent les mariages selon la résidence du marié.
[9] Marriages registered by residence of bride. - Les mariages sont enregistrés selon le lieu de résidence de la mariée.

[10] Including marriages where bride/groom are non-residents. - Y compris les mariages pour lesquels le marié et la mariée sont des non-résidents.
[11] Including same sex marriages. - Y compris les mariages entre personnes du même sexe.
[12] The total number may include 'Unknown residence', but the categories urban and rural do not. - Le nombre total peut inclure les personnes dont la résidence n'est pas connue, à l'inverse des catégories de population urbaine et rurale.
[13] The increase in marriages is due to the project "Legally united families", coordinated by the Ministry of the Presidency. - L'augmentation des mariages est une conséquence du projet <<Familles légalement unies >> organisé par le ministère de la présidence.
[14] Urban and rural residence refers to the place of usual residence of groom. - Le lieu de résidence (zone urbaine ou zone rurale) correspond au lieu de résidence habituel du marié.
[15] Excludes nomadic Indian tribes. - Non compris les tribus d'Indiens nomades.
[16] Excluding Amerindians. - Non compris les Amérindiens.
[17] Data are compiled from the National Registers of Identification and Civil Status (RENIEC). - Les données sont rédigées à partir des Registres Nationaux d'Identification et d'État Civil (RENIEC).
[18] For statistical purposes, the data for China do not include those for the Hong Kong Special Administrative Region (Hong Kong SAR), Macao Special Administrative Region (Macao SAR) and Taiwan province of China. - Pour la présentation des statistiques, les données pour la Chine ne comprennent pas la Région Administrative Spéciale de Hong Kong (Hong Kong RAS), la Région Administrative Spéciale de Macao (Macao RAS) et Taïwan province de Chine.
[19] Data refer to government controlled areas. Data refer to marriages of residents only. - Les données se rapportent aux zones contrôlées par le Gouvernement. Les données ne portent que sur les mariages de résidents.
[20] Data refer to the Iranian Year which begins on 21 March and ends on 20 March of the following year. - Les données concernent l'année iranienne, qui commence le 21 mars et se termine le 20 mars de l'année suivante.
[21] Includes data for East Jerusalem and Israeli residents in certain other territories under occupation by Israeli military forces since June 1967. - Y compris les données pour Jérusalem-Est et les résidents israéliens dans certains autres territoires occupés depuis 1967 par les forces armées israéliennes.
[22] The total number may include 'Unknown residence', but the categories urban and rural do not. Urban and rural residence refers to the place of usual residence of groom. - Le nombre total peut inclure les personnes dont la résidence n'est pas connue, à l'inverse des catégories de population urbaine et rurale. Le lieu de résidence (zone urbaine ou zone rurale) correspond au lieu de résidence habituel du marié.
[23] Data refer to Japanese nationals in Japan only. - Les données se raportent aux nationaux japonais au Japon seulement.

24 Excluding data for Jordanian territory under occupation since June 1967 by Israeli military forces. Excluding foreigners, including registered Palestinian refugees. - Non compris les données pour le territoire jordanien occupé depuis juin 1967 par les forces armées israéliennes. Non compris les étrangers, mais y compris les réfugiés de Palestine enregistrés.

25 Data refer to registered events only. - Les données ne concernent que les événements enregistrés.

26 Excluding alien armed forces, civilian aliens employed by armed forces, and foreign diplomatic personnel and their dependants. - Non compris les militaires étrangers, les civils étrangers employés par les forces armées ni le personnel diplomatique étranger et les membres de leur famille les accompagnant.

27 Excluding marriages previously officiated outside Singapore or under religious and customary rites. Data comprise civil marriages registered under the Women's Charter and Muslim marriages registered under the Administration of Muslim Law Act. - Ne comprend pas les mariages prononcés ailleurs qu'à Singapour ni les mariages religieux ou coutumiers.

28 Data from MERNIS (Central Population Administrative System). - Données de MERNIS (Système central de données démographiques).

29 Excluding aliens temporarily in the area. - Non compris les étrangers se trouvant temporairement dans le territoire.

30 Including armed forces stationed outside the country and alien armed forces in the area, if the marriage is performed by local authority. - Y compris les militaires nationaux hors du pays et les militaires étrangers en garnison sur le territoire, si le mariage a été célébré par l'autorité locale.

31 Including nationals outside the country, but excluding foreigners in the country. - Y compris les nationaux à l'étranger, mais non compris les étrangers sur le territoire.

32 Excluding Faeroe Islands and Greenland shown separately, if available. - Non compris les Iles Féroé et le Groenland, qui font l'objet de rubriques distinctes, si disponible.

33 The difference between 'Total' and the sum of urban and rural is due to the unknown place of residence of grooms and to grooms living outside the country. Urban and rural residence refers to the place of usual residence of groom. - La différence entre le « Total » et la somme des chiffres urbains et ruraux s'explique par le fait que la résidence du marié n'est pas toujours connue ou est située à l'étranger. Le lieu de résidence (zone urbaine ou zone rurale) correspond au lieu de résidence habituel du marié.

34 Excluding Åland Islands. - Non compris les Îles d'Åland.

35 The data for urban and rural exclude the nationals outside the country. - Les données relatives à la population urbaine et rurale n'englobent pas les nationaux se trouvant à l'étranger.

36 The urban and rural categories do not include the data of foreigners, persons of unknown residence and the homeless, whereas the total category includes them. - Les chiffres portant sur la population urbaine et rurale n' incluent pas les données relatives aux étrangers, aux personnes dont la résidence n'est pas connue et aux personnes sans domicile fixe, à l'inverse, le total les inclut.

37 Definition of localities was revised in 2011 causing a break with the previous series. Data for residence abroad are excluded. Data refer to common residence after marriage. - La rupture par rapport aux séries précédentes s'explique par le fait que la définition des localités a été révisée depuis 2011. Les données relatives aux résidents à l'étranger sont exclues. Données se rapportant à la résidence commune après le mariage.

38 Data exclude registered partnerships. Marriages of couples of which at least one partner is recorded in a Dutch municipal register, irrespective of the country where the marriage was performed. Including same sex marriages. Including residents outside the country if listed in a Netherlands population register. - Les données ne comprennent pas les partenariats d'un pacte civil enregistrés. Correspond aux mariages pour lesquels au moins l'un des partenaires est inscrit sur un registre municipal néerlandais, quel que soit le pays dans lequel le mariage est célébré. Y compris les mariages entre personnes du même sexe. Englobe les résidents se trouvant à l'étranger à condition qu'ils soient inscrits sur le registre de population des Pays-Bas.

39 Marriages registered by place of occurrence of marriage. - Mariages enregistrés en fonction du lieu de l'événement.

40 Data refer to population 15 years of age or more. - Les données concernent la population âgée de 15 ans ou plus.

41 Includes civil and religious marriages as well as not specified. - Englobe les mariages civils et religieux et ceux pour lesquels rien n'a été indiqué.

42 Excludes data for Kosovo and Metohia. - Sans les données pour le Kosovo et Metohie.

43 Data refer to residence of groom or bride before marriage. - Données relatives au lieu de résidence du marié ou de la mariée avant le mariage.

44 Data based on the residence of groom if he has permanent address in the country, otherwise, based on the residence of bride. If neither partner is a permanent resident, the marriage is not included in the official statistics. - Les données sont fondées sur la résidence du marié si celui-ci a une adresse permanente dans le pays, sinon elles sont fondées sur la résidence de la mariée.

Si aucun des deux partenaires n'est un résident permanent, le mariage n'apparaît pas dans les statistiques officielles.

45 The Government of Ukraine has informed the United Nations that it is not in a position to provide statistical data concerning the Autonomous Republic of Crimea and the city of Sevastopol. - Le gouvernement Ukrainien a informé l'ONU qu'il n'est pas en mesure de fournir des données statistiques concernant la République autonome de Crimée et la ville de Sébastopol.

46 Excluding Channel Islands (Guernsey and Jersey) and Isle of Man, shown separately, if available. - Non compris les îles Anglo-Normandes (Guernesey et Jersey) et l'île de Man, qui font l'objet de rubriques distinctes, si disponible.

47 Excluding Niue, shown separately, which is part of Cook Islands, but because of remoteness is administered separately. - Non compris Nioué, qui fait l'objet d'une rubrique distincte et qui fait partie des îles Cook, mais qui, en raison de son éloignement, est administrée séparément.

48 Including United States military personnel, their dependants and contract employees. - Y compris les militaires des Etats-Unis, les membres de leur famille les accompagnant et les agents contractuels des Etats-Unis.

49 Including same sex marriages. Data refer to marriages by residence of the groom. - Y compris les mariages entre personnes du même sexe. Les données concernent les mariages selon la résidence du marié.

50 Data refer to marriages and civil unions by residence of 'partner 2'. Random rounding to base 3 is applied in this table as a confidentiality measure. Including same sex marriages. - Les données concernent les mariages et les unions civiles selon la résidence du « partenaire 2 ». Les chiffres sont arrondis à la base 3 de manière aléatoire, pour des raisons de confidentialité. Y compris les mariages entre personnes du même sexe.

51 Data cover the period from 1 July of the previous year to 30 June of the present year. - Pour la période allant du 1er juillet de l'année précédente au 30 juin de l'année en cours.

Table 24 - *Demographic Yearbook 2015*

Table 24 presents the marriages cross-classified by age of groom and age of bride for the latest available year between 2006 and 2015.

Description of variables: Marriage is defined as the act, ceremony or process by which the legal relationship of spouses is constituted. The legality of the union may be established by civil, religious or other means as recognized by the laws of each country[1].

Marriage statistics in this table, therefore, include both first marriages and remarriages after divorce, widowhood or annulment. They do not, unless otherwise noted, include resumption of marriage ties after legal separation. These statistics refer to the number of marriages performed, and not to the number of persons marrying.

Age is defined as age at last birthday, that is, the difference between the date of birth and the date of the occurrence of the event, expressed in completed solar years. The age classification used for brides in this table is the following: under 15 years, 5-year age groups through 90-94, and 95 years and over, depending on the availability of data. Age classification for grooms is restricted to: under 15 years, 5-year age groups from 15 to 59, and 60 years and over.

In an effort to provide interpretation of these statistics, countries or areas providing data on marriages by age of groom and bride have been requested to specify "the minimum legal age at which marriage can take place with and without parental consent". This information is presented in the table 24-1 below.

Reliability of data: Data from civil registers of marriages that are reported as incomplete (less than 90 per cent completeness) or of unknown completeness are considered unreliable and are set in *italics* rather than in roman type. Table 23 and the technical notes for that table provide more detailed information on the completeness of marriage registration. For more information about the quality of vital statistics data in general, see Section 4.2 of the Technical Notes.

Limitations: Statistics on marriages by age of groom and age of bride are subject to the same qualifications as have been set forth for vital statistics in general and marriage statistics in particular as discussed in Section 4 of the Technical Notes.

The fact that marriage is a legal event, unlike birth and death that are biological events, has implications for international comparability of data. Marriage has been defined, for statistical purposes, in terms of the laws of individual countries or areas. These laws vary throughout the world. In addition, comparability is further limited because some countries or areas compile statistics only for civil marriages although religious marriages may also be legally recognized; in other countries or areas, the only available records are church registers and, therefore, the statistics may not reflect marriages that are civil marriages only.

Because in many countries or areas marriage is a civil legal contract which, to establish its legality, must be celebrated before a civil officer, it follows that for these countries or areas registration would tend to be almost automatic at the time of, or immediately following, the marriage ceremony. This factor should be kept in mind when considering the reliability of data, described above.

Because these statistics are classified according to age, they are subject to the limitations with respect to accuracy of age reporting similar to those already discussed in connection with Section 3.1.3 of the Technical Notes.   It is probable that biases are less pronounced in marriage statistics, because information is obtained from the persons concerned and since marriage is a legal act, the participants are likely to give correct information. However, in some countries or areas, there appears to be a concentration of marriages at the legal minimum age for marriage and at the age at which valid marriage may be contracted without parental consent, indicating perhaps an overstatement in some cases to comply with the law.

Aside from the possibility of age misreporting, it should be noted that marriage patterns at younger ages, that is, for ages up to 24 years, are influenced to a large extent by laws regarding the minimum age for marriage.

Factors that may influence age reporting, particularly at older ages include an inclination to understate the age of the bride in order that it may be equal to or less than that of the groom.

The absence of data in the unknown age group does not necessarily indicate completely accurate reporting and tabulation of the age item. It is sometimes an indication that the unknowns have been eliminated by assigning ages to them before tabulation, or by proportionate distribution after tabulation.

Another age-reporting factor that must be kept in mind in using these data is the variation that may result from calculating age at marriage from year of birth rather than from day, month and year of birth. Information on this factor is given in footnotes when known.

Earlier data: Marriages by age of groom and age of bride have been shown for the latest available year in most issues of the *Demographic Yearbook*. Data cross-classified by age of groom and bride have been presented in previous issues featuring marriage and divorce statistics. For information on the specific topics and the years covered, readers should consult the Historical Index.

24-1 Minimum legal age at which marriage can take place

Country or area	With parental consent		Without parental consent	
	Groom	*Bride*	*Groom*	*Bride*
Africa				
Botswana	18	18	21	21
Burkina Faso[2]	18	15	20	17
Burundi[4]			21	18
Egypt	18	18		
Ghana			18	18
Liberia	16	16	21	18
Libya[3]	18	18		
Malawi[4]			18	18
Mauritius	16	16	18	18
Morocco[4]			18	18
Namibia	18	18	21	21
Saint Helena ex. Dep.	16	16	21	21
Senegal	Under 18	Under 18	18	18
Seychelles	16	16	18	18
Sierra Leone[4]			18	18
South Africa[5]	Under 18	Under 18	18	18
Swaziland	18	18	21	21
Uganda[4, 6]			18	18
Zimbabwe	16	16	18	18
America, North				
Anguilla	16	16	18	18
Aruba[7]	16	16	18	18
Bermuda	16	16	18	18
Canada[8]	16	16	18	18
Cayman Islands	16	16	18	18
Costa Rica	15	15	18	18
Cuba	16	14	18	16
Curaçao	16	16	18	18
Dominican Republic	16	15	18	18

Country or area	With parental consent		Without parental consent	
	Groom	Bride	Groom	Bride
El Salvador	15	14	18	18
Greenland[4]			18	18
Jamaica	16	16	18	18
Mexico[9]	Under 18	Under 18	18	18
Montserrat[10]	16	16	18	18
Panama	16	14	18	18
Puerto Rico	17	17	21	21
Saint Vincent and the Grenadines			18	18
Trinidad and Tobago[11]	Under 18	Under 18	18	18
America, South				
Brazil	16	16	18	18
Chile	16	16	18	18
Colombia	14	14	18	18
Ecuador	14	12	18	18
Suriname	17	15	21	21
Uruguay	16	16	18	18
Venezuela (Bolivarian Republic of)	14	12	18	18
Asia				
Armenia			18	17
Azerbaijan	18	17		
Bahrain			15	
Cambodia			18	18
China, Hong Kong SAR	16	16	21	21
China, Macao SAR	16	16	18	18
Cyprus	16	16	18	18
Georgia	16	16	18	18
Indonesia			19	16
Iran	18	15		
Israel[4]			17	17
Japan	18	16	20	20
Kazakhstan	16	16	18	17
Kyrgyzstan			18	18
Malaysia[12]	18	16 and 18	18 and 21	18 and 21
Nepal	18	18	20	20
Oman[4]			18	18
Philippines	18	18	21	21
Republic of Korea	18	18	20	20
Singapore[13]	Under 21	Under 21	21	21

Country or area	With parental consent		Without parental consent	
	Groom	*Bride*	*Groom*	*Bride*
State of Palestine[14]		14.5	15.5	
Tajikistan	17	17	18	18
Turkey	16	16	18	18
Uzbekistan			17	17
Europe				
Åland Islands[18]			18	18
Albania			18	18
Austria[15]	16	16	18	18
Belarus[16]			18	18
Belgium			18	18
Bosnia and Herzegovina			18	18
Bulgaria	16	16	18	18
Croatia	16	16	18	18
Czech Republic[17]	16	16	18	18
Denmark	15	15	18	18
Estonia	15	15	18	18
Faeroe Islands[4]			18	18
Finland[18]			18	18
France[4]			18	18
Germany[19]	16	16	18	18
Gibraltar	16	16	18	18
Greece[20]			18	18
Hungary	16	16	18	18
Iceland	No limit	No limit	18	18
Ireland[4, 21]			18	18
Isle of Man	16	16	18	18
Italy	16	16	18	18
Jersey	16	16	18	18
Latvia	16	16	18	18
Liechtenstein[15]			18	18
Lithuania[22]	15	15	18	18
Luxembourg			18	18
Malta			16	16
Montenegro	16	16	18	18
Netherlands	16	16	18	18
Norway	16	16	18	18
Poland[23]			18	18
Portugal	16	16	18	18
Republic of Moldova			18	16

Country or area	With parental consent		Without parental consent	
	Groom	Bride	Groom	Bride
Romania	16	16	18	18
Russian Federation	16	16	18	18
Serbia[24]	16	16	18	18
Slovakia			16	16
Slovenia	15	15	18	18
Spain	14	14	18	18
Sweden[25]			18	18
Switzerland			18	18
TFYR of Macedonia	16	16	18	18
Ukraine[15]	16	16	18	18
United Kingdom of Great Britain and Northern Ireland	16	16	18	18
Oceania				
Australia	16	16	18	18
Cook Islands	16	16	21	21
Guam[26]	17	17	18	18
New Caledonia			18	18
New Zealand	16	16	18	18

NOTES

[1] *Principles and Recommendations for a Vital Statistics System Revision 3,* Sales No. E.13.XVII.10, United Nations, New York, 2014.

[2] In addition, an age waiver may be granted by a civil court for a serious reason from 15 years for women and 18 years for men.

[3] According to the Islamic law, marriage requires parental consent. Consent of the bride herself, as well as the guardian's consent are fundamental in the marriage contract. Young men usually choose the consent of the parents. Minimum age at marriage is usually 18 years. According to the law, marriage is not restricted to individuals over the age of 18 years.

[4] The minimum legal age at which marriage can take place is the same with or without parental consent.

[5] Marriages under the age of 18 can be performed with parental consent or with judicial permission if parental consent has been unreasonably refused. Additionally, boys under the age of 18 and girls under the age of 16 may also be required to seek the consent of the Minister of Home Affairs.

[6] As reported by Uganda Bureau of Statistics, marriages with or without parental consent may occur much earlier than 18 years of age.

[7] The legal minimum marriage age is 18, with two exceptions: if the persons concerned are older than 16 and the woman is pregnant or has given birth or the Minister of Security and Justice grants a dispensation based on their request.

[8] Marriage is under provincial and territory legislations. Without parental consent, the minimum legal age at which marriage can take place is 18 years of age in all provinces and territories in Canada except in British Columbia, Newfoundland and Labrador, Nova Scotia, Nunavut, and Yukon where the minimum legal age is 19 years. With parental consent, the minimum legal age is 16 years in all provinces except in Northwest Territories, Nunavut, and Yukon. With parental consent, in Northwest Territories, and Yukon the minimum legal age is 15 years whereas in Nunavut, the minimum legal age is 18 years.

[9] Each of the 31 Federal States and the Federal District has its own civil code for marriage. Marriages under 18 require parental consent. Additionally, in the Federal District and in the states of Guanajuato, Morelos, Puebla and San Luis Potosí the minimum age with parental consent is 16 for both bride and groom and in the states of Michoacán, Nayarit, Sinaloa and Sonora the minimum age with parental consent is 14 for the bride and 16 for the groom..

[10] Consent can be given by a guardian or a person who has custody of the child wishing to marry. Also the Governor has discretion to permit persons as young as 15 years and 1 day old to marry, if he thinks that getting married is in the best interest of the persons who are intending to marry and the persons in this instance must have also received the necessary consent.

[11] With parental consent, age for marriage is 14 years for males and 12 years for females in a civil marriage; 16 years for males and 12 years for females in a Muslim marriage; 18 years for males and 14 years for females in a Hindu marriage; and 18 years for males and 16 for females in Orisa marriage.

[12] For marriage with parental consent, it is 18 years of age for males whereas it is 18 years of age for non-Muslim females and 16 years of age for Muslim females. Without parental consent, it is 21 years of age for non-Muslims and 18 years of age for Muslims.

[13] Specified minimum legal marriage age refers to marriages contracted under the Women's Charter. For Muslim marriages under the Administration of Muslim Law Act, no marriage shall be solemnised when either party is below the age of 18 years. Notwithstanding that, Muslim women below the age of 18 years who have attained the age of puberty may be married under the Administration of the Muslim Law Act.

[14] The legal marriage age for females is 14 years, 6 months and 22 days. There must be parental consent (father or brother if the father is dead). The legal marriage age for males is 15 years, 6 months and 21 days. Parental consent is not required.

[15] Persons less than 18 years old need a decision of the court.

[16] In compliance with the Marriage and Family Code of the Republic of Belarus, in the exclusive cases related to pregnancy, childbirth, and in case of acquiring by a juvenile of a full legal capacity under lawful age, the civil registration offices are in a position to reduce the marriage age of espousing persons, but not more than by 3 years. The marriage age is to be reduced by an application of espousing persons; the parental consent is not required.

[17] If it is in accordance with the social purpose of marriage, only the court may, for important reasons, allow the marriage of a minor over 16 years.

[18] Persons less than 18 years old need the permission of the Ministry of Justice.

[19] Marriage at 16-17 years of age requires that the other spouse be an adult already betrothed (18 years) and an exemption from the requirement of majority by a competent family court.

[20] Under some conditions (e.g. pregnancy) the marriage can take place without age restrictions.

[21] An exemption on the minimum age can be granted by court order if granting of such an exemption is in the best interests of the parties to the intended marriage and good reasons for the application can be demonstrated.

[22] In addition to parental consent, persons less than 18 years old need judicial approval. In case of pregnancy, marriage can be allowed below 15 years of age.

[23] Females can marry at the age of 16 or 17 years with parental and court consent.

[24] Marriage is not allowed for persons below the age of 18; only the court may, for good cause, permit marriage to a minor who has attained the age of 16 years of age, and attained physical and mental maturity to exercise the rights and responsibilities of marriage. Parental consent is not required.

[25] With parental consent, no limit but authorities must approve; without parental consent, 18 years of age for Swedish citizens.

[26] Under 18, both a court order and parent or legal guardian consent are needed.

Tableau 24 – *Annuaire démographique 2015*

Le tableau 24 présente des statistiques concernant les mariages classés selon l'âge de l'époux et selon l'âge de l'épouse pour les années où les données sont disponibles entre 2006 et 2015.

Description des variables : le mariage désigne l'acte, la cérémonie ou la procédure qui établit un rapport légal entre les époux. L'union peut être rendue légale par une procédure civile ou religieuse, ou par toute autre procédure, conformément à la législation du pays[1].

Les statistiques de la nuptialité présentées dans ce tableau comprennent donc les premiers mariages et les remariages faisant suite à un divorce, un veuvage ou une annulation. Toutefois, sauf indication contraire, elles ne comprennent pas les unions reconstituées après une séparation légale. Ces statistiques se rapportent au nombre de mariages célébrés, non au nombre de personnes qui se marient.

L'âge désigne l'âge au dernier anniversaire, c'est-à-dire la différence entre la date de naissance et la date de l'événement, exprimée en années solaires révolues. Le classement par âge pour l'épouse utilisé dans ce tableau comprend les groupes suivants : moins de 15 ans, groupes quinquennaux jusqu'à 90-94 ans, et 95 ans et plus, selon la disponibilité des données. Le classement par âge pour l'époux est : moins de 15 ans, groupes quinquennal de 15 jusqu' à 59 ans et 60 ans et plus.

Dans un effort de fournir l'interprétation de ces statistiques, les pays ou les zones fournissant des données sur les mariages par l'âge de l'épouse et de par l'âge de l'époux ont été demandés d'indiquer "l'âge légal minimum avec auquel le mariage peut avoir lieu avec et sans consentement parental". Cette information est présentée dans le tableau 24-1 ci-dessous.

Fiabilité des données : les données sur les mariages issues des registres de l'état civil qui sont déclarées incomplètes (degré de complétude inférieur à 90 p. 100) ou dont le degré de complétude n'est pas connu sont jugées douteuses et apparaissent en italique et non en caractères romains. Le tableau 23 et les notes techniques s'y rapportant présentent des renseignements plus détaillés sur le degré de complétude de l'enregistrement des mariages. Pour plus de précisions sur la qualité des données reposant sur les statistiques de l'état civil en général, voir la section 4.2 des notes techniques.

Insuffisance des données : les statistiques des mariages selon l'âge de l'époux et selon l'âge de l'épouse appellent les mêmes réserves que celles formulées à propos des statistiques de l'état civil en général et des statistiques de la nuptialité en particulier (voir la section 4 des Notes techniques).

Le fait que le mariage soit un acte juridique, à la différence de la naissance et du décès, qui sont des faits biologiques, a des répercussions sur la comparabilité internationale des données. Aux fins de la statistique, le mariage est défini par la législation de chaque pays ou zone. Cette législation varie d'un pays à l'autre. La comparabilité est limitée en outre du fait que certains pays et zones ne réunissent des statistiques que pour les mariages civils, bien que les mariages religieux y soient également reconnus par la loi ; dans d'autres, les seuls relevés disponibles sont les registres des églises et, en conséquence, les statistiques peuvent ne pas rendre compte des mariages exclusivement civils.

Le mariage étant, dans de nombreux pays ou zones, un contrat juridique civil qui, pour être légal, doit être conclu devant un officier d'état civil, il s'ensuit que, dans ces pays ou zones, l'enregistrement se fait à peu près systématiquement au moment de la cérémonie ou immédiatement après. Il faut tenir compte de cet élément lorsque l'on évalue la fiabilité des données, dont il est question plus haut.

Étant donné que ces statistiques sont classées selon l'âge, elles appellent les mêmes réserves concernant l'exactitude des déclarations d'âge que celles dont il a déjà été question à la section 3.1.3 des Notes techniques. Il est probable que les statistiques de la nuptialité sont moins faussées par ce genre d'erreur, car les renseignements sont donnés par les intéressés eux-mêmes, et, comme le mariage est un acte juridique, il y a toutes chances que leurs déclarations soient exactes. Toutefois, dans certains pays ou zones, il semble y avoir une concentration de mariages à l'âge minimal légal de nubilité ainsi qu'à l'âge auquel le mariage peut être valablement contracté sans le consentement des parents, ce qui peut indiquer que certains déclarants se vieillissent pour se conformer à la loi.

Outre la possibilité d'erreurs dans les déclarations d'âge, il convient de noter que la législation fixant l'âge minimal de nubilité influe notablement sur les caractéristiques de la nuptialité pour les premiers âges, c'est-à-dire jusqu'à 24 ans.

Parmi les facteurs pouvant exercer une influence sur les déclarations d'âge, en particulier celles qui sont faites par des personnes plus âgées, il faut citer la tendance à diminuer l'âge de l'épouse de façon qu'il soit égal ou inférieur à celui de l'époux.

Si aucun nombre ne figure dans la rangée réservée aux âges inconnus, cela ne signifie pas nécessairement que les déclarations d'âge et l'exploitation des données par âge aient été tout à fait exactes. C'est parfois une indication que l'on a attribué un âge aux personnes d'âge inconnu avant l'exploitation des données ou qu'elles ont été réparties proportionnellement entre les différents groupes après cette opération.

Il importe de ne pas oublier non plus, lorsque l'on utilisera ces données, que l'on calcule parfois l'âge des conjoints au moment du mariage sur la base de l'année de naissance seulement et non d'après la date exacte (jour, mois et année) de naissance. Des renseignements à ce sujet sont donnés en note chaque fois que possible.

Donnés publiées antérieurement : on trouve dans la plupart des éditions de l'*Annuaire démographique* des statistiques concernant les mariages selon l'âge de l'époux et selon l'âge de l'épouse qui ont été établies à partir des données les plus récentes dont on disposait à l'époque. Des données croisant l'âge des époux ont été présentées dans des éditions antérieurs, plus particulièrement consacrées aux statistiques de la nuptialité et de la divortialité. Pour plus de précisions concernant les années et les sujets pour lesquels des données ont été publiées, se reporter à l'index historique.

24-1 L'âge légal minimum avec auquel le mariage peut avoir lieu

Pays ou zone	Avec consentement parental		Sans consentement parental	
	Epoux	Epouse	Epoux	Epouse
Afrique				
Afrique du Sud[2]	moins de 18	moins de 18	18	18
Botswana	18	18	21	21
Burkina Faso[3]	18	15	20	17
Burundi[5]			21	18
Egypte	18	18		
Ghana			18	18
Libéria	16	16	21	18
Libye[4]	18	18		
Malawi[5]			18	18
Maurice	16	16	18	18
Maroc[5]			18	18
Namibie	18	18	21	21
Ouganda[5, 6]			18	18
Sainte-Hélène sans dép.	16	16	21	21
Sénégal	moins de 18	moins de 18	18	18
Seychelles	16	16	18	18
Sierra Leone[5]			18	18
Swaziland	18	18	21	21
Zimbabwe	16	16	18	18
Amérique du Nord				
Anguilla	16	16	18	18
Aruba[7]	16	16	18	18
Bermudes	16	16	18	18

Pays ou zone	Avec consentement parental		Sans consentement parental	
	Epoux	Epouse	Epoux	Epouse
Canada[8]	16	16	18	18
Costa Rica	15	15	18	18
Cuba	16	14	18	16
Curaçao	16	16	18	18
El Salvador	15	14	18	18
Groenland[5]			18	18
Îles Caïmanes	16	16	18	18
Jamaïque	16	16	18	18
Mexique[9]	moins de 18	moins de 18	18	18
Montserrat[10]	16	16	18	18
Panama	16	14	18	18
Porto Rico	17	17	21	21
République dominicaine	16	15	18	18
Saint-Vincent-et-les Grenadines			18	18
Trinité-et-Tobago[11]	moins de 18	moins de 18	18	18
Amérique du Sud				
Brésil	16	16	18	18
Chili	16	16	18	18
Colombie	14	14	18	18
Equateur	14	12	18	18
Suriname	17	15	21	21
Uruguay	16	16	18	18
Venezuela (République bolivarienne du)	14	12	18	18
Asie				
Arménie			18	17
Azerbaïdjan	18	17		
Bahreïn			15	
Cambodge			18	18
Chine, Hong Kong RAS	16	16	21	21
Chine, Macao RAS	16	16	18	18
Chypre	16	16	18	18
État de Palestine[12]		14.5	15.5	
Géorgie	16	16	18	18
Indonésie			19	16
Iran (République islamique d')	18	15		
Israël[5]			17	17

Pays ou zone	Avec consentement parental		Sans consentement parental	
	Epoux	*Epouse*	*Epoux*	*Epouse*
Japon	18	16	20	20
Kazakhstan	16	16	18	17
Kirghizistan			18	18
Malaisie[13]	18	16 et 18	18 et 21	18 et 21
Népal	18	18	20	20
Oman[5]			18	18
Ouzbékistan			17	17
Philippines	18	18	21	21
République de Corée	18	18	20	20
Singapour[14]	moins de 21	moins de 21	21	21
Tadjikistan	17	17	18	18
Turquie	16	16	18	18
Europe				
Albanie			18	18
Allemagne[15]	16	16	18	18
Autriche[16]	16	16	18	18
Bélarus[17]			18	18
Belgique			18	18
Bosnie-Herzégovine			18	18
Bulgarie	16	16	18	18
Croatie	16	16	18	18
Danemark	15	15	18	18
Espagne	14	14	18	18
Estonie	15	15	18	18
Fédération de Russie	16	16	18	18
Finlande[18]			18	18
France[5]			18	18
Gibraltar	16	16	18	18
Grèce[19]			18	18
Hongrie	16	16	18	18
Île de Man	16	16	18	18
Îles d'Åland[18]			18	18
Îles Féroé[5]			18	18
Irlande[5, 20]			18	18
Islande	Pas de limites	Pas de limites	18	18
Italie	16	16	18	18
Jersey	16	16	18	18
L'ex-R. y. de Macédoine	16	16	18	18

Pays ou zone	Avec consentement parental		Sans consentement parental	
	Epoux	Epouse	Epoux	Epouse
Lettonie	16	16	18	18
Liechtenstein[16]			18	18
Lituanie[21]	15	15	18	18
Luxembourg			18	18
Malte			16	16
Monténégro	16	16	18	18
Norvège	16	16	18	18
Pays-Bas	16	16	18	18
Pologne[22]			18	18
Portugal	16	16	18	18
République de Moldova			18	16
République tchèque	16	16	18	18
Roumanie	16	16	18	18
Royaume-Uni de Grande-Bretagne et d'Irlande du Nord	16	16	18	18
Serbie[23]	16	16	18	18
Slovaque			16	16
Slovénie	15	15	18	18
Suede[24]			18	18
Suisse	16	16	18	18
Ukraine[16]	16	16	18	18
Océanie				
Australie	16	16	18	18
Guam	17	17	18	18
Îles Cook	16	16	21	21
Nouvelle-Calédonie			18	18
Nouvelle-Zélande	16	16	18	18

NOTES

[1] *Principes et recommandations pour un système de statistique de l'état civil, troisième révision,* numéro de vente : E.13.XVII.10, publication des Nations Unies, New York, 2014.

[2] Il est possible de se marier avant 18 ans avec consentement parental, ou autorisation judiciaire si le consentement parental a été refusé sans motif raisonnable. De plus, les garçons âgés de moins de 18 ans et les filles âgées de moins de 16 ans peuvent être également tenus de demander le consentement du Ministère de l'intérieur.

[3] De plus, une dispense d'âge peut être accordée par un tribunal civil pour motif grave à partir de 15 ans pour les femmes et de 18 ans pour les hommes.

[4] Conformément à la loi islamique, le mariage requiert le consentement parental. Le consentement de la mariée, elle-même ainsi que le consentement du tuteur sont fondamentaux dans le contrat de mariage. Les jeunes hommes choisissent habituellement le consentement des parents. L'âge minimum du mariage est généralement 18 ans. Conformément à la loi, le mariage n'est pas limité aux individus âgés de plus de 18 ans.

[5] L'âge minimum légal du mariage est le même avec ou sans le consentement parental.

[6] Tel que le signale l' "Uganda Bureau of Statistics", les mariages avec ou sans le consentement parental peuvent se produire beaucoup plus tôt que 18 ans.

[7] L'âge minimum légal du mariage est 18 ans, avec deux exceptions : si les personnes en cause ont plus de 16 ans et la femme est enceinte ou a accouché, ou si le Ministre de la sécurité et de la justice leur a accordé une dispense sur leur demande.

[8] Le mariage est en vertu des législations provinciales et territoriales. Sans le consentement des parents, l'âge minimum légal du mariage est de 18 ans dans toutes les provinces et territoires du Canada sauf en Colombie-Britannique, Terre-Neuve-et-Labrador, la Nouvelle-Écosse, du Nunavut et du Yukon, où l'âge minimum légal est de 19 ans. Avec le consentement des parents, l'âge minimum légal est de 16 ans dans toutes les provinces sauf dans les Territoires du Nord-Ouest, Nunavut et Yukon. Avec le consentement des parents, dans les Territoires du Nord-Ouest et le Yukon l'âge minimum légal est de 15 ans alors que dans le Nunavut, l'âge minimum légal est de 18 ans.

[9] Chacun des 31 Etats fédéraux et du District fédéral a son propre code civil pour le mariage. Avant 18 ans, il faut le consentement parental pour pouvoir se marier. De plus, dans le District fédéral et les États de Guanajuato, Morelos, Puebla et San Luis Potosí l'âge minimum, avec consentement parental, est de 16 ans pour le fiancé et la fiancée, et dans les États de Michoacán, Nayarit, Sinaloa et Sonora, l'âge minimum avec consentement parental est de 14 ans pour la fiancée et 16 ans pour le fiancé.

[10] Le consentement peut être donné par un tuteur ou une personne qui a la garde de l'enfant qui souhaitent se marier. En outre, le gouverneur a la faculté de permettre aux personnes âgés d'au moins 15 ans et 1 jour de se marier, s'il pense que le mariage est dans le meilleur intérêt des personnes qui ont l'intention de s'unir et que les personnes concernées aient également reçu le consentement nécessaire.

[11] Avec l'âge du le consentement parental, l'âge minimum du mariage pour se marier est de 14 ans pour les hommes et de 12 ans pour les femmes pour un mariage civil ; de 16 ans pour les hommes et de 12 ans pour les femmes pour un mariage musulman ; de 18 ans pour les hommes et de 14 ans pour les femmes pour un mariage hindou, et de18 ans pour les hommes et de 16 pour les femmes pour un mariage orisa.

[12] L'âge légal du mariage pour les femmes est de 14 ans, 6 mois et 22 jours. Le consentement parental (du père ou du frère si le père est mort) est requis. L'âge légal du mariage pour les hommes est de 15 ans, 6 mois et 21 jours. Le consentement parental n'est pas nécessaire.

[13] Pour le mariage avec le consentement parental, il est de 18 ans pour les hommes alors qu'il est de 18 ans pour les femmes non-musulmanes et il est de 16 ans pour les femmes musulmanes. Sans le consentement parental, il est de 21 ans pour les non-musulmans et de 18 ans pour les musulmans.

[14] L'âge minimum légal du mariage spécifié correspond à des mariages contractés en vertu de la Charte des femmes. Pour les mariages musulmans sous l'administration de la « Loi sur le Droit Musulman », aucun mariage ne doit être célébré lorsque l'une des parties est en dessous de l'âge de 18 ans. Néanmoins, les femmes musulmanes en dessous de l'âge de 18 ans qui ont atteint l'âge de la puberté peuvent être mariées dans le cadre de l'administration de la « Loi sur le Droit Musulman ».

[15] Le mariage à 16-17 ans exige que l'autre conjoint soit un adulte déjà fiancée (18 ans) ainsi qu'une exemption de l'obligation de la majorité par un juge aux affaires familiales.

[16] Les personnes âgées de moins de 18 ans doivent obtenir l'autorisation de la justice.

[17] En conformité avec le Code du mariage et la famille de la République du Bélarus, dans les cas exclusifs liés à la maternité, l'accouchement et en cas d'acquisition par un mineur d'une pleine capacité juridique en vertu de l'âge légal, les bureaux d'état civil sont en mesure de de réduire l'âge du mariage des personnes souhaitant se marier, de 3 ans au plus. L'âge du mariage est abaissé suite à une demande des personnes se mariant, le consentement parental n'est pas nécessaire.

[18] Les personnes âgées de moins de 18 ans doivent obtenir l'autorisation du ministère de la justice.

[19] Dans certaines conditions (par exemple la grossesse), le mariage peut avoir lieu sans restriction d'âge.

[20] Une exemption sur l'âge minimum peut être accordée par ordonnance du tribunal si l'octroi d'une telle exemption est dans le meilleur intérêt des parties ayant l'intention de se marier et si la demande est appuyée par de bonnes raisons.

[21] En plus du consentement parental, les personnes de moins de 18 ans doivent obtenir l'autorisation du tribunal l'approbation judiciaire. En cas de grossesse, le mariage peut être autorisé en dessous de 15 ans.

[22] Les femmes peuvent se marier à l'âge de 16 ou 17 ans avec l'autorisation des parents et du tribunal de la cour.

[23] Il n'est pas permis de se marier avant 18 ans ; seul le tribunal peut, pour un motif valable, y autoriser une personne mineure ayant atteint l'âge de 16 ans et parvenue à la maturité physique et mentale voulue pour exercer les droits et les responsabilités du mariage. Le consentement parental n'est pas requis.

[24] Avec le consentement des parents, aucune limite mais les autorités doivent approuver. Sans le consentement parental, l'âge minimum légal du mariage est de 18 ans pour les citoyens suédois.

24. Marriages by age of groom and by age of bride: latest available year, 2006 - 2015
Mariages selon l'âge de l'époux et selon l'âge de l'épouse : dernière année disponible, 2006 - 2015

Continent, country or area, year, code[a] and age of bride / Continent, pays ou zone, date, code[a] et âge de l'épouse	Total	0-14	15-19	20-24	25-29	30-34	35-39	40-44	45-49	50-54	55-59	60+	Unknown Inconnu
AFRICA - AFRIQUE													
Botswana[1]													
2014 (+U)													
Total	5 591	-	-	59	572	1 389	1 275	847	540	329	235	345	...
0 - 14	-	-	-	-	-	-	-	-	-	-	-	-	...
15 - 19	9	-	-	2	6	-	1	-	-	-	-	-	...
20 - 24	401	-	-	39	166	119	53	13	8	3	-	-	...
25 - 29	1 407	-	-	14	325	626	303	84	37	9	6	3	...
30 - 34	1 631	-	-	3	63	552	565	264	111	35	24	14	...
35 - 39	965	-	-	1	10	71	274	322	179	72	23	13	...
40 - 44	499	-	-	-	2	13	63	133	136	89	40	23	...
45 - 49	266	-	-	-	-	3	10	26	55	79	50	43	...
50 - 54	206	-	-	-	-	4	4	5	12	38	70	73	...
55 - 59	91	-	-	-	-	-	2	-	2	3	18	66	...
60 - 64	56	-	-	-	-	1	-	-	-	1	4	50	...
65 +	60	-	-	-	-	-	-	-	-	-	-	60	...
Egypt - Égypte[2]													
2014 (+C)													
Total	953 137	...	12 499[j]	190 513	412 452	183 640	60 404	29 161	19 505	15 614	10 471	15 443	3 435
18 - 19	247 837	...	7 329[j]	84 124	119 632	30 984	4 213	744	284	236	103	151	37
20 - 24	375 611	...	4 081[j]	92 422	194 695	66 307	12 074	2 980	1 384	771	379	473	45
25 - 29	184 412	...	698[j]	11 011	83 947	57 490	18 024	6 210	3 230	1 799	1 024	957	22
30 - 34	69 705	...	198[j]	1 850	10 308	23 072	16 047	7 767	4 314	2 817	1 593	1 714	25
35 - 39	33 731	...	65[j]	463	2 144	4 080	7 579	7 073	4 688	3 345	2 008	2 280	6
40 - 44	17 262	...	44[j]	161	587	912	1 643	3 218	3 359	2 992	1 860	2 482	4
45 - 49	10 689	...	35[j]	174	555	415	537	830	1 669	2 263	1 652	2 558	1
50 - 54	5 708	...	22[j]	80	223	178	185	248	449	1 070	1 245	2 008	-
55 - 59	2 378	...	6[j]	47	57	34	38	52	80	226	444	1 394	-
60 - 64	1 100	...	6[j]	32	44	35	14	16	27	47	117	762	-
65 - 69	498	...	2[j]	14	16	12	7	4	7	21	27	388	-
70 - 74	189	...	-[j]	5	12	5	5	-	3	4	10	145	-
75 +	201	...	-[j]	16	33	17	5	7	1	5	2	115	-
Unknown - Inconnu	3 816	...	13[j]	114	199	99	33	12	10	18	7	16	3 295
Lesotho													
2011 (+U)													
Total	3 162	-	10	265	980	764	458	268	183	109	66	59	-
0 - 14	-	-	-	-	-	-	-	-	-	-	-	-	-
15 - 19	144	-	8	69	55	10	1	-	-	1	-	-	-
20 - 24	924	-	2	178	524	159	48	5	4	1	2	1	-
25 - 29	979	-	-	16	360	397	122	44	18	14	4	4	-
30 - 34	574	-	-	1	37	184	196	77	45	21	7	6	-
35 - 39	299	-	-	-	3	12	85	109	56	19	10	5	-
40 - 44	122	-	-	1	-	2	4	32	44	22	11	6	-
45 - 49	60	-	-	-	-	-	2	1	16	19	14	8	-
50 - 54	32	-	-	-	-	-	-	-	-	11	13	8	-
55 - 59	16	-	-	-	1	-	-	-	-	1	5	9	-
60 - 64	8	-	-	-	-	-	-	-	-	-	-	8	-
65 - 69	2	-	-	-	-	-	-	-	-	-	-	2	-
70 - 74	2	-	-	-	-	-	-	-	-	-	-	2	-
75 +	-	-	-	-	-	-	-	-	-	-	-	-	-
Unknown - Inconnu	-	-	-	-	-	-	-	-	-	-	-	-	-
Mauritius - Maurice[3]													
2015 (+C)													
Total	9 709	-	106	1 155	2 817	2 415	1 293	710	463	359	202	188	1
0 - 14	-	-	-	-	-	-	-	-	-	-	-	-	-
15 - 19	698	-	68	331	187	77	27	5	2	1	-	-	-
20 - 24	2 506	-	29	642	1 138	505	146	30	9	6	1	-	-
25 - 29	2 929	-	8	143	1 242	1 025	358	95	34	17	6	1	-
30 - 34	1 557	-	1	26	194	641	419	174	70	21	5	6	-
35 - 39	806	-	-	10	42	123	245	216	109	40	13	8	-
40 - 44	480	-	-	1	10	34	71	127	112	84	32	9	-
45 - 49	314	-	-	1	3	8	21	43	81	98	33	26	-
50 - 54	231	-	-	-	1	2	4	18	35	68	63	40	-
55 - 59	113	-	-	1	-	-	1	2	8	19	38	44	-
60 +	74	-	-	-	-	-	1	-	3	5	11	54	-
Unknown - Inconnu	1	-	-	-	-	-	-	-	-	-	-	-	1

24. Marriages by age of groom and by age of bride: latest available year, 2006 - 2015
Mariages selon l'âge de l'époux et selon l'âge de l'épouse : dernière année disponible, 2006 - 2015 (continued - suite)

Continent, country or area, year, code[a] and age of bride / Continent, pays ou zone, date, code[a] et âge de l'épouse	Total	0-14	15-19	20-24	25-29	30-34	35-39	40-44	45-49	50-54	55-59	60+	Unknown Inconnu
AFRICA - AFRIQUE													
Reunion - Réunion													
2008 (C)													
Total	3 149	-	15	338	787	681	514	306	185	150	62	111	-
0 - 14	1	-	1	-	-	-	-	-	-	-	-	-	-
15 - 19	91	-	8	45	26	7	2	2	1	-	-	-	-
20 - 24	679	-	4	235	296	99	28	13	3	-	1	-	-
25 - 29	858	-	2	42	391	264	117	30	7	4	1	-	-
30 - 34	584	-	-	12	52	232	185	56	29	10	4	4	-
35 - 39	384	-	-	3	16	55	134	106	38	25	4	3	-
40 - 44	234	-	-	-	4	16	34	77	49	28	13	13	-
45 - 49	144	-	-	1	1	7	11	18	34	40	18	14	-
50 - 54	94	-	-	-	1	1	3	4	19	30	12	24	-
55 - 59	39	-	-	-	-	-	-	-	3	10	7	19	-
60 - 64	16	-	-	-	-	-	-	-	2	2	1	11	-
65 - 69	16	-	-	-	-	-	-	-	-	1	1	14	-
70 - 74	7	-	-	-	-	-	-	-	-	-	-	7	-
75 +	2	-	-	-	-	-	-	-	-	-	-	2	-
Saint Helena ex. dep. - Sainte-Hélène sans dép.													
2012 (C)													
Total	12	-	-	-	1	3	-	2	5	-	-	1	...
0 - 14	-	-	-	-	-	-	-	-	-	-	-	-	...
15 - 19	-	-	-	-	-	-	-	-	-	-	-	-	...
20 - 24	-	-	-	-	-	-	-	-	-	-	-	-	...
25 - 29	2	-	-	-	1	1	-	-	-	-	-	-	...
30 - 34	2	-	-	-	-	1	-	1	-	-	-	-	...
35 - 39	3	-	-	-	-	1	-	-	2	-	-	-	...
40 - 44	2	-	-	-	-	-	-	1	1	-	-	-	...
45 - 49	1	-	-	-	-	-	-	-	1	-	-	-	...
50 - 54	1	-	-	-	-	-	-	-	1	-	-	-	...
55 - 59	1	-	-	-	-	-	-	-	-	-	-	1	...
60 - 64	-	-	-	-	-	-	-	-	-	-	-	-	...
65 - 69	-	-	-	-	-	-	-	-	-	-	-	-	...
70 - 74	-	-	-	-	-	-	-	-	-	-	-	-	...
75 +	-	-	-	-	-	-	-	-	-	-	-	-	...
Seychelles[4]													
2015 (+C)													
Total	1 845	-	3	73	318	452	346	237	183	118	60	55	...
0 - 14	-	-	-	-	-	-	-	-	-	-	-	-	...
15 - 19	15	-	2	7	4	1	1	-	-	-	1	2	...
20 - 24	127	-	-	38	48	25	4	5	4	-	1	2	...
25 - 29	481	-	-	18	176	168	67	24	15	3	7	3	...
30 - 34	519	-	-	8	64	202	147	56	26	11	5	-	...
35 - 39	295	-	-	1	17	41	94	79	33	21	8	1	...
40 - 44	182	-	-	1	7	13	27	54	42	25	7	6	...
45 - 49	111	-	-	-	1	-	3	12	45	27	14	9	...
50 - 54	58	-	-	-	1	-	2	4	13	23	10	5	...
55 - 59	44	-	1	-	-	2	1	3	4	8	6	19	...
60 - 64	9	-	-	-	-	-	-	-	1	-	2	6	...
65 - 69	3	-	-	-	-	-	-	-	-	-	-	3	...
70 - 74	1	-	-	-	-	-	-	-	-	-	-	1	...
75 +	-	-	-	-	-	-	-	-	-	-	-	-	...
South Africa - Afrique du Sud													
2011 (...)													
Total	167 264	2	189	8 719	36 903	38 827	30 474	19 424	13 105	7 955	5 028	6 638	...
0 - 14	4	-	-	2	-	2	-	-	-	-	-	-	...
15 - 19	2 199	-	96	1 002	703	256	90	33	8	4	4	3	...
20 - 24	25 542	-	72	5 690	12 489	4 977	1 589	431	172	67	36	19	...
25 - 29	50 977	-	13	1 598	19 588	18 847	7 485	2 245	786	246	105	64	...
30 - 34	35 124	-	2	308	3 266	11 855	12 206	4 737	1 764	620	210	156	...
35 - 39	22 456	-	4	84	637	2 266	7 236	6 955	3 296	1 209	479	290	...
40 - 44	13 030	-	1	26	167	456	1 449	3 799	3 943	1 859	783	547	...
45 - 49	8 221	-	-	6	44	129	310	940	2 365	2 270	1 203	954	...
50 - 54	4 674	-	-	3	7	25	88	228	586	1 294	1 293	1 150	...
55 - 59	2 480	-	-	-	2	9	16	44	140	285	692	1 292	...
60 - 64	1 340	1	-	-	-	3	4	8	31	81	177	1 035	...

24. Marriages by age of groom and by age of bride: latest available year, 2006 - 2015
Mariages selon l'âge de l'époux et selon l'âge de l'épouse : dernière année disponible, 2006 - 2015 (continued - suite)

Continent, country or area, year, code[a] and age of bride / Continent, pays ou zone, date, code[a] et âge de l'épouse	Total	0-14	15-19	20-24	25-29	30-34	35-39	40-44	45-49	50-54	55-59	60+	Unknown Inconnu
AFRICA - AFRIQUE													
South Africa - Afrique du Sud													
2011													
65 - 69	653	-	1	-	-	1	-	3	13	12	36	587	...
70 - 74	322	-	-	-	-	-	-	1	1	6	8	306	...
75 +	242	1	-	-	-	1	1	-	-	2	2	235	...
Tunisia - Tunisie													
2011 (...)													
Total	91 590	...	228[f]	5 724	24 725	30 919	15 770	5 904	2 881	4 652[s]	...	...	787
0 - 19	6 504	...	...	...	...	...	...	...	...	...	...	...	...
20 - 24	24 862	...	...	...	...	...	...	...	...	...	...	...	...
25 - 29	31 959	...	...	...	...	...	...	...	...	...	...	...	...
30 - 34	15 109	...	...	...	...	...	...	...	...	...	...	...	...
35 - 39	6 123	...	...	...	...	...	...	...	...	...	...	...	...
40 - 44	3 104	...	...	...	...	...	...	...	...	...	...	...	...
45 - 49	1 744	...	...	...	...	...	...	...	...	...	...	...	...
50 +	1 267	...	...	...	...	...	...	...	...	...	...	...	...
Unknown - Inconnu	918	...	...	...	...	...	...	...	...	...	...	...	...
AMERICA, NORTH - AMÉRIQUE DU NORD													
Anguilla[5]													
2013 (C)													
Total	42	4	9	9	4	4	4	1	-	1	...	...	6
0 - 14	5	2	2	-	-	-	1	-	-	-	...	...	-
15 - 19	12	1	5	3	3	-	-	-	-	-	...	...	-
20 - 24	9	-	1	5	1	1	1	-	-	-	...	...	-
25 - 29	5	1	1	1	-	2	-	-	-	-	...	...	-
30 - 34	3	-	-	-	-	-	2	1	-	-	...	...	-
35 - 39	2	-	-	-	-	1	-	-	-	1	...	...	-
40 - 44	-	-	-	-	-	-	-	-	-	-	...	...	-
45 - 49	-	-	-	-	-	-	-	-	-	-	...	...	-
50 - 54	-	-	-	-	-	-	-	-	-	-	...	...	-
Unknown - Inconnu	6	-	-	-	-	-	-	-	-	-	...	...	6
Aruba													
2014 (C)													
Total	617	-	5	45	121	111	77	78	55	47	46	32	-
0 - 14	-	-	-	-	-	-	-	-	-	-	-	-	-
15 - 19	11	-	2	5	1	2	-	1	-	-	-	-	-
20 - 24	85	-	2	22	35	17	5	2	2	-	-	-	-
25 - 29	159	-	1	16	54	45	19	18	6	-	-	-	-
30 - 34	88	-	-	2	16	24	19	13	8	2	1	3	-
35 - 39	74	-	-	-	7	16	19	13	9	5	4	1	-
40 - 44	68	-	-	-	2	5	8	19	11	14	6	3	-
45 - 49	57	-	-	-	1	2	3	5	11	12	15	8	-
50 - 54	41	-	-	-	1	-	2	5	5	10	11	7	-
55 - 59	18	-	-	-	1	-	-	1	2	1	7	6	-
60 - 64	7	-	-	-	-	-	2	1	-	1	2	1	-
65 - 69	4	-	-	-	-	-	-	-	1	1	-	2	-
70 - 74	-	-	-	-	-	-	-	-	-	-	-	-	-
75 +	2	-	-	-	-	-	-	-	-	1	-	1	-
Unknown - Inconnu	3	-	-	-	3	-	-	-	-	-	-	-	-
Bahamas													
2013 (+C)													
Total	2 122	...	...	...	104	472	498	325	223	163	106	226	5
25 - 29	171	...	...	...	24	64	39	16	3	5	-	20	-
30 - 34	543	...	...	...	27	202	161	62	42	13	12	24	-
35 - 39	391	...	...	...	9	61	131	87	48	24	12	18	1
40 - 44	249	...	...	...	5	21	53	70	50	28	9	13	-
45 - 49	219	...	...	...	5	24	33	28	38	44	23	24	-
50 - 54	192	...	...	...	6	21	28	26	22	38	21	30	-
55 - 59	133	...	...	...	6	17	20	17	9	6	18	39	1
60 +	216	...	...	...	22	62	33	17	10	4	11	56	1
Unknown - Inconnu	8	...	...	...	-	-	-	2	1	1	-	2	2

24. Marriages by age of groom and by age of bride: latest available year, 2006 - 2015
Mariages selon l'âge de l'époux et selon l'âge de l'épouse : dernière année disponible, 2006 - 2015 (continued - suite)

Continent, country or area, year, code[a] and age of bride / Continent, pays ou zone, date, code[a] et âge de l'épouse	Total	0-14	15-19	20-24	25-29	30-34	35-39	40-44	45-49	50-54	55-59	60+	Unknown Inconnu
AMERICA, NORTH - AMÉRIQUE DU NORD													
Bermuda - Bermudes													
2015 (C)													
Total	509	-	1	16	89	113	66	52	46	46	42	38	-
0 - 14	-	-	-	-	-	-	-	-	-	-	-	-	-
15 - 19	2	-	1	1	-	-	-	-	-	-	-	-	-
20 - 24	38	-	-	12	17	5	1	1	2	-	-	-	-
25 - 29	116	-	-	2	51	40	12	10	1	-	-	-	-
30 - 34	115	-	-	1	16	54	25	10	4	3	-	2	-
35 - 39	56	-	-	-	1	12	20	11	8	3	1	-	-
40 - 44	49	-	-	-	4	-	6	13	12	7	4	3	-
45 - 49	40	-	-	-	-	2	1	4	12	13	8	-	-
50 - 54	44	-	-	-	-	-	-	2	6	13	16	7	-
55 - 59	26	-	-	-	-	-	1	1	-	5	11	8	-
60 - 64	16	-	-	-	-	-	-	-	1	2	1	12	-
65 - 69	2	-	-	-	-	-	-	-	-	-	-	2	-
70 - 74	3	-	-	-	-	-	-	-	-	-	1	2	-
75 +	2	-	-	-	-	-	-	-	-	-	-	2	-
Unknown - Inconnu	-	-	-	-	-	-	-	-	-	-	-	-	-
Costa Rica[6]													
2015* (C)													
Total	26 512	-	314	3 491	6 705	5 739	3 517	2 175	1 453	1 061	774	1 227	56
0 - 14	-	-	-	-	-	-	-	-	-	-	-	-	-
15 - 19	1 480	-	185	764	346	116	31	18	8	5	3	1	3
20 - 24	5 391	-	93	1 794	2 161	823	275	114	64	34	13	16	4
25 - 29	7 264	-	26	631	3 018	2 227	832	271	125	59	40	27	8
30 - 34	4 941	-	5	194	852	1 812	1 145	511	214	97	59	43	9
35 - 39	2 846	-	4	81	222	525	832	557	303	158	91	70	3
40 - 44	1 631	-	-	19	66	155	247	416	326	178	122	102	-
45 - 49	1 166	-	-	6	21	54	93	189	253	247	139	163	1
50 - 54	762	-	-	1	10	13	35	71	97	198	149	188	-
55 - 59	454	-	-	-	1	3	12	13	43	57	95	229	1
60 - 64	243	-	-	-	3	-	8	8	8	17	44	154	1
65 - 69	130	-	-	-	1	-	1	4	7	2	12	103	-
70 - 74	85	-	-	-	1	-	-	-	-	2	5	77	-
75 +	55	-	-	-	-	-	-	-	-	1	5	-	49	-
Unknown - Inconnu	64	-	1	1	3	11	6	3	4	2	2	5	26
Cuba[7]													
2014 (C)													
Total	63 954	-	874	7 184	11 740	9 040	7 420	7 804	6 730	4 764	2 668	5 729	1
0 - 14	54	-	7	26	15	5	1	-	-	-	-	-	-
15 - 19	3 874	-	496	1 780	1 022	317	121	67	27	19	6	19	-
20 - 24	11 169	-	265	3 324	4 038	1 715	747	522	270	128	55	105	-
25 - 29	12 433	-	68	1 244	4 120	3 126	1 724	1 071	579	262	95	144	-
30 - 34	8 098	-	17	435	1 320	2 020	1 787	1 331	649	277	118	143	1
35 - 39	6 431	-	4	150	582	916	1 419	1 515	1 077	452	152	164	-
40 - 44	6 781	-	6	102	326	514	919	1 749	1 638	890	319	318	-
45 - 49	5 786	-	3	67	160	246	434	958	1 489	1 217	539	673	-
50 - 54	4 267	-	7	35	88	95	169	421	704	1 039	724	985	-
55 - 59	2 097	-	-	4	28	37	54	103	184	306	432	949	-
60 - 64	1 476	-	1	12	23	28	24	43	61	122	146	1 016	-
65 - 69	837	-	-	2	6	8	9	15	32	34	58	673	-
70 - 74	408	-	-	3	6	6	6	8	14	10	15	340	-
75 +	241	-	-	-	6	7	6	1	6	8	9	198	-
Unknown - Inconnu	2	-	-	-	-	-	-	-	-	-	-	2	-
Curaçao													
2015 (C)													
Total	703	-	2	44	112	124	87	79	74	70	57	45	9
0 - 14	-	-	-	-	-	-	-	-	-	-	-	-	-
15 - 19	3	-	-	3	-	-	-	-	-	-	-	-	-
20 - 24	81	-	1	30	30	12	8	-	-	-	-	-	-
25 - 29	143	-	1	10	54	44	23	6	2	2	1	-	-
30 - 34	131	-	-	1	23	44	26	20	12	3	-	2	-
35 - 39	93	-	-	-	2	14	23	27	8	10	6	3	-
40 - 44	71	-	-	-	1	10	4	17	23	9	4	3	-
45 - 49	70	-	-	-	2	-	3	5	21	18	13	8	-
50 - 54	50	-	-	-	-	-	-	4	7	17	17	5	-

807

24. Marriages by age of groom and by age of bride: latest available year, 2006 - 2015
Mariages selon l'âge de l'époux et selon l'âge de l'épouse : dernière année disponible, 2006 - 2015 (continued - suite)

Continent, country or area, year, code[a] and age of bride / Continent, pays ou zone, date, code[a] et âge de l'épouse	Total	0-14	15-19	20-24	25-29	30-34	35-39	40-44	45-49	50-54	55-59	60+	Unknown Inconnu
AMERICA, NORTH - AMÉRIQUE DU NORD													
Curaçao													
2015													
55 - 59	31	-	-	-	-	-	-	-	1	7	10	13	-
60 - 64	11	-	-	-	-	-	-	-	-	2	4	5	-
65 - 69	9	-	-	-	-	-	-	-	-	2	2	5	-
70 - 74	1	-	-	-	-	-	-	-	-	-	-	1	-
75 +	-	-	-	-	-	-	-	-	-	-	-	-	-
Unknown - Inconnu	9	-	-	-	-	-	-	-	-	-	-	-	9
Dominican Republic - République dominicaine													
2014 (+C)													
Total	47 235	-	406	5 915	9 494	8 050	6 003	4 919	4 054	2 994	1 953	2 969	478
0 - 14	-	-	-	-	-	-	-	-	-	-	-	-	-
15 - 19	2 285	-	165	1 101	559	214	93	60	46	24	11	11	1
20 - 24	10 127	-	133	3 166	3 581	1 636	711	347	230	143	72	105	3
25 - 29	10 041	-	52	985	3 376	2 723	1 253	704	445	231	127	137	8
30 - 34	7 494	-	15	366	1 091	2 099	1 693	922	581	349	183	189	6
35 - 39	5 416	-	13	144	464	732	1 259	1 229	718	409	229	215	4
40 - 44	4 057	-	9	66	219	305	540	934	860	522	254	345	3
45 - 49	3 151	-	7	39	101	177	272	425	719	666	357	386	2
50 - 54	1 980	-	4	15	43	80	118	188	298	436	356	438	4
55 - 59	1 115	-	3	10	16	40	25	69	99	134	245	472	2
60 - 64	564	-	-	3	6	14	15	23	31	47	79	344	2
65 - 69	281	-	1	1	6	1	3	6	10	19	24	209	1
70 - 74	87	-	-	1	3	1	-	2	3	5	8	64	-
75 +	56	-	-	1	2	3	-	2	3	2	2	41	-
Unknown - Inconnu	581	-	4	17	27	25	21	8	11	7	6	13	442
El Salvador[8]													
2012 (...)													
Total	29 267	-	1 098	6 586	6 762	5 101	3 026	2 078	1 528	989	671	1 294	134
0 - 14	37	-	10	16	6	3	2	-	-	-	-	-	-
15 - 19	3 670	-	544	1 856	787	250	113	53	25	12	5	9	16
20 - 24	8 329	-	414	3 407	2 652	1 113	374	176	90	37	12	19	35
25 - 29	6 227	-	80	933	2 304	1 713	647	264	153	70	27	23	13
30 - 34	4 049	-	16	230	704	1 360	902	414	223	82	47	53	18
35 - 39	2 433	-	14	69	179	436	654	509	272	134	74	84	8
40 - 44	1 604	-	4	25	58	118	208	410	348	175	107	149	2
45 - 49	1 144	-	2	6	18	54	80	174	290	234	125	157	4
50 - 54	633	-	-	3	6	15	16	43	84	162	140	164	-
55 - 59	403	-	1	1	1	6	5	10	23	61	89	206	-
60 - 64	242	-	1	-	1	2	2	10	10	12	26	177	1
65 +	279	-	2	1	-	2	3	3	3	7	13	245	-
Unknown - Inconnu	217	-	10	39	46	29	20	12	7	3	6	8	37
Guatemala													
2011 (C)													
Total	78 286	17	9 779	27 197	18 081	9 430	4 619	2 550	1 635	1 375	1 126	2 362	115
0 - 14	1 122	4	513	458	109	31	5	1	1	-	-	-	-
15 - 19	22 191	12	6 733	11 231	3 124	788	191	52	27	9	6	6	12
20 - 24	25 037	1	2 199	12 176	7 600	2 137	592	162	69	39	16	25	21
25 - 29	13 633	-	267	2 705	5 632	3 393	1 009	338	135	61	39	42	12
30 - 34	6 599	-	46	494	1 284	2 336	1 504	497	192	115	64	63	4
35 - 39	3 263	-	11	83	240	588	933	780	283	165	77	96	7
40 - 44	1 869	-	2	19	49	112	266	504	401	255	116	144	1
45 - 49	1 436	-	1	8	17	31	78	156	373	379	184	205	4
50 - 54	1 094	-	-	1	6	8	26	41	107	260	335	306	4
55 - 59	760	-	-	-	1	-	8	13	32	70	225	410	1
60 - 64	511	-	-	2	-	-	1	2	8	15	44	438	1
65 - 69	332	-	1	-	1	1	-	2	2	3	14	308	-
70 - 74	183	-	-	-	-	-	-	-	-	2	2	178	1
75 +	139	-	-	-	-	-	-	-	-	1	1	137	-
Unknown - Inconnu	117	-	6	20	18	5	6	2	5	1	3	4	47
Jamaica - Jamaïque													
2006 (+C)													
Total	23 181	-	70	2 153	5 477	4 987	3 749	2 672	1 676	1 032	568	797	-
0 - 14	-	-	-	-	-	-	-	-	-	-	-	-	-
15 - 19	368	-	31	168	89	35	23	11	6	1	1	3	-

24. Marriages by age of groom and by age of bride: latest available year, 2006 - 2015
Mariages selon l'âge de l'époux et selon l'âge de l'épouse : dernière année disponible, 2006 - 2015 (continued - suite)

Continent, country or area, year, code[a] and age of bride / Continent, pays ou zone, date, code[a] et âge de l'épouse	Total	Age of groom - - âge de l'époux											
		0-14	15-19	20-24	25-29	30-34	35-39	40-44	45-49	50-54	55-59	60+	Unknown Inconnu
AMERICA, NORTH - AMÉRIQUE DU NORD													
Jamaica - Jamaïque													
2006													
20 - 24	3 726	-	22	1 251	1 579	531	195	86	31	19	4	8	-
25 - 29	6 263	-	11	501	2 670	1 870	742	277	108	43	15	26	-
30 - 34	4 635	-	4	136	715	1 660	1 242	525	199	86	41	27	-
35 - 39	3 194	-	1	62	266	571	940	765	360	123	55	51	-
40 - 44	2 190	-	1	18	105	221	402	635	440	202	102	64	-
45 - 49	1 452	-	-	15	35	75	147	273	364	292	133	118	-
50 - 54	708	-	-	1	15	18	39	63	122	200	105	145	-
55 - 59	327	-	-	1	-	5	17	24	28	45	71	136	-
60 - 64	179	-	-	-	2	1	1	10	15	15	27	108	-
65 - 69	84	-	-	-	1	-	-	2	1	4	10	66	-
70 - 74	35	-	-	-	-	-	-	1	2	1	3	28	-
75 +	20	-	-	-	-	-	1	-	-	1	1	17	-
Martinique													
2007 (C)													
Total	1 341	-	19	128	297	284	185	155	117	63	32	61	-
0 - 14	-	-	-	-	-	-	-	-	-	-	-	-	-
15 - 19	55	-	11	35	8	1	-	-	-	-	-	-	-
20 - 24	217	-	4	63	108	25	13	4	-	-	-	-	-
25 - 29	273	-	3	20	123	99	16	7	1	4	-	-	-
30 - 34	243	-	1	4	38	97	65	24	11	2	1	-	-
35 - 39	173	-	-	4	12	42	54	49	9	3	-	-	-
40 - 44	146	-	-	1	3	11	26	47	45	10	3	-	-
45 - 49	84	-	-	1	3	6	6	19	29	14	5	1	-
50 - 54	53	-	-	-	2	3	3	3	15	11	10	6	-
55 - 59	31	-	-	-	-	-	1	-	7	12	3	8	-
60 - 64	24	-	-	-	-	-	-	1	-	4	8	11	-
65 - 69	12	-	-	-	-	-	1	-	-	2	-	9	-
70 - 74	16	-	-	-	-	-	-	1	-	1	2	12	-
75 +	14	-	-	-	-	-	-	-	-	-	-	14	-
Mexico - Mexique[9]													
2014 (+C)													
Total	577 713	31	39 504	157 190	150 530	92 273	48 320	28 482	17 305	12 368	9 420	19 579	2 711
0 - 14	791	7	399	276	57	36	10	-	1	-	1	2	2
15 - 19	96 388	12	28 422	49 707	13 068	3 322	1 046	314	132	45	25	38	257
20 - 24	173 463	5	9 347	84 683	55 593	16 187	4 536	1 518	556	216	110	120	592
25 - 29	136 320	4	1 018	18 204	64 725	35 528	10 651	3 529	1 252	473	241	229	466
30 - 34	71 071	1	198	3 141	13 380	28 422	15 511	5 909	2 268	1 005	481	490	265
35 - 39	36 469	-	54	749	2 696	6 538	11 797	7 753	3 365	1 676	811	901	129
40 - 44	22 158	1	21	192	669	1 550	3 405	6 700	4 380	2 420	1 265	1 495	60
45 - 49	14 534	-	11	69	152	428	944	1 934	3 725	3 080	1 885	2 272	34
50 - 54	10 261	-	6	28	56	124	239	573	1 143	2 493	2 344	3 231	24
55 - 59	6 763	-	2	22	21	34	71	145	311	654	1 626	3 860	17
60 - 64	4 049	-	3	5	6	13	28	39	94	198	427	3 223	13
65 - 69	2 214	1	1	7	6	8	18	18	33	63	135	1 918	6
70 - 74	1 160	-	-	3	3	6	2	4	8	20	46	1 066	2
75 +	753	-	-	3	2	5	1	3	6	10	10	711	2
Unknown - Inconnu	1 319	-	22	101	96	72	61	43	31	15	13	23	842
Montserrat													
2013 (+...)													
Total	18	-	-	1	3	1	5	2	5	1	-	-	...
0 - 14	-	-	-	-	-	-	-	-	-	-	-	-	...
15 - 19	-	-	-	-	-	-	-	-	-	-	-	-	...
20 - 24	3	-	-	1	1	1	-	-	-	-	-	-	...
25 - 29	3	-	-	-	1	-	2	-	-	-	-	-	...
30 - 34	2	-	-	-	-	-	-	-	-	2	-	-	...
35 - 39	3	-	-	-	1	-	1	-	1	-	-	-	...
40 - 44	5	-	-	-	-	-	2	1	1	1	-	-	...
45 - 49	1	-	-	-	-	-	-	1	-	-	-	-	...
50 - 54	1	-	-	-	-	-	-	-	1	-	-	-	...
55 - 59	-	-	-	-	-	-	-	-	-	-	-	-	...
60 - 64	-	-	-	-	-	-	-	-	-	-	-	-	...
65 - 69	-	-	-	-	-	-	-	-	-	-	-	-	...
70 - 74	-	-	-	-	-	-	-	-	-	-	-	-	...
75 +	-	-	-	-	-	-	-	-	-	-	-	-	...

24. Marriages by age of groom and by age of bride: latest available year, 2006 - 2015
Mariages selon l'âge de l'époux et selon l'âge de l'épouse : dernière année disponible, 2006 - 2015 (continued - suite)

Continent, pays ou zone, date, code[a] et âge de l'épouse	Total	0-14	15-19	20-24	25-29	30-34	35-39	40-44	45-49	50-54	55-59	60+	Unknown Inconnu

Age of groom - - âge de l'époux

AMERICA, NORTH - AMÉRIQUE DU NORD

Panama[6]
2014 (C)

Total	12 869	-	132	1 562	2 867	2 535	1 648	1 913[n]	...	920[o]	...	835	457
0 - 14	2	-	1	1	-	-	-	-[n]	...	-[o]	...	-	-
15 - 19	589	-	71	282	140	46	19	11[n]	...	-[o]	...	-	20
20 - 24	2 433	-	44	851	907	367	117	58[n]	...	10[o]	...	7	72
25 - 29	3 104	-	6	269	1 254	904	348	204[n]	...	23[o]	...	11	85
30 - 34	2 171	-	1	77	339	782	511	331[n]	...	66[o]	...	22	42
35 - 39	1 324	-	1	23	84	236	379	421[n]	...	100[o]	...	40	40
40 - 49	1 602	-	1	4	52	86	192	680[n]	...	368[o]	...	168	51
50 - 59	749	-	-	-	2	8	18	109[n]	...	281[o]	...	317	14
60 - 69	240	-	-	1	-	-	-	11[n]	...	34[o]	...	191	3
70 +	67	-	-	-	-	-	-	-[n]	...	4[o]	...	62	1
Unknown - Inconnu	588	-	7	54	89	106	64	88[n]	...	34[o]	...	17	129

Puerto Rico - Porto Rico
2015 (C)

Total	16 987	-	310	2 464	3 444	2 690	2 073	1 619	1 247	1 015	769	1 350	6
0 - 14	4	-	3	1	-	-	-	-	-	-	-	-	-
15 - 19	680	-	204	351	96	18	5	2	4	-	-	-	-
20 - 24	2 953	-	87	1 505	959	252	99	32	9	7	1	2	-
25 - 29	3 714	-	12	438	1 745	943	352	151	43	23	5	2	-
30 - 34	2 626	-	3	111	446	953	640	293	109	44	8	19	-
35 - 39	1 931	-	-	39	147	363	573	424	219	102	38	26	-
40 - 44	1 472	-	1	11	38	112	255	437	308	169	83	58	-
45 - 49	1 206	-	-	5	12	35	105	183	330	253	159	124	-
50 - 54	923	-	-	1	1	13	26	62	147	254	218	201	-
55 - 59	580	-	-	1	-	-	13	26	50	93	150	247	-
60 - 64	456	-	-	-	-	1	5	7	16	45	70	312	-
65 - 69	253	-	-	-	-	-	-	1	7	16	26	203	-
70 - 74	102	-	-	1	-	-	-	1	1	5	7	87	-
75 +	81	-	-	-	-	-	-	-	4	4	4	69	-
Unknown - Inconnu	6	-	-	-	-	-	-	-	-	-	-	-	6

Saint Vincent and the Grenadines - Saint-Vincent-et-les Grenadines
2015 (C)

Total	572	-	-	26	83	113	84	76	48	60	32	50	...
0 - 14	-	-	-	-	-	-	-	-	-	-	-	-	...
15 - 19	5	-	-	1	1	1	1	-	-	-	-	1	...
20 - 24	60	-	-	14	27	11	5	2	1	-	-	-	...
25 - 29	130	-	-	10	39	42	27	8	2	1	-	1	...
30 - 34	98	-	-	-	6	37	23	17	6	7	1	1	...
35 - 39	91	-	-	1	7	10	21	26	10	10	5	1	...
40 - 44	68	-	-	-	2	8	3	15	15	15	6	4	...
45 - 49	51	-	-	-	-	3	3	3	12	15	3	12	...
50 - 54	31	-	-	-	1	1	1	3	1	8	10	6	...
55 - 59	17	-	-	-	-	-	-	-	-	3	4	10	...
60 - 64	15	-	-	-	-	-	-	2	1	1	2	9	...
65 - 69	3	-	-	-	-	-	-	-	-	-	-	3	...
70 - 74	3	-	-	-	-	-	-	-	-	-	1	2	...
75 +	-	-	-	-	-	-	-	-	-	-	-	-	...

Trinidad and Tobago - Trinité-et-Tobago
2009 (C)

Total	8 638	-	77	1 276	2 494	1 653	1 028	691	521	376	203	319	-
0 - 14	15	-	4	9	-	-	1	-	-	1	-	-	-
15 - 19	531	-	41	277	157	45	8	2	1	-	-	-	-
20 - 24	2 180	-	23	700	944	336	114	40	13	5	5	-	-
25 - 29	2 410	-	4	209	1 052	677	268	120	54	19	4	3	-
30 - 34	1 311	-	5	51	235	399	313	161	75	47	12	13	-
35 - 39	781	-	-	16	82	139	191	174	102	44	18	15	-
40 - 44	530	-	-	7	16	37	86	134	120	70	38	22	-
45 - 49	387	-	-	4	5	15	35	37	105	99	42	45	-
50 - 54	249	-	-	2	1	2	10	17	35	71	47	64	-

24. Marriages by age of groom and by age of bride: latest available year, 2006 - 2015
Mariages selon l'âge de l'époux et selon l'âge de l'épouse : dernière année disponible, 2006 - 2015 (continued - suite)

Continent, country or area, year, code[a] and age of bride / Continent, pays ou zone, date, code[a] et âge de l'épouse	Total	0-14	15-19	20-24	25-29	30-34	35-39	40-44	45-49	50-54	55-59	60+	Unknown Inconnu
AMERICA, NORTH - AMÉRIQUE DU NORD													
Trinidad and Tobago - Trinité-et-Tobago													
2009													
55 - 59	124	-	-	1	2	3	2	3	9	15	26	63	-
60 - 64	70	-	-	-	-	-	-	2	5	4	10	49	-
65 +	49	-	-	-	-	-	-	1	1	1	1	45	-
Unknown - Inconnu	1	-	-	-	-	-	-	-	1	-	-	-	-
Turks and Caicos Islands - Îles Turques et Caïques													
2008 (C)													
Total	486	...	-	20	110	114	94	63	51	17	10	7	-
15 - 19	2	...	...	...	...	...	...	...	...	...	...	...	...
20 - 24	47	...	...	...	...	...	...	...	...	...	...	...	...
25 - 29	134	...	...	...	...	...	...	...	...	...	...	...	...
30 - 34	127	...	...	...	...	...	...	...	...	...	...	...	...
35 - 39	94	...	...	...	...	...	...	...	...	...	...	...	...
40 - 44	37	...	...	...	...	...	...	...	...	...	...	...	...
45 - 49	26	...	...	...	...	...	...	...	...	...	...	...	...
50 - 54	12	...	...	...	...	...	...	...	...	...	...	...	...
55 - 59	6	...	...	...	...	...	...	...	...	...	...	...	...
60 - 64	-	...	...	...	...	...	...	...	...	...	...	...	...
65 +	1	...	...	...	...	...	...	...	...	...	...	...	...
Unknown - Inconnu	-	...	...	...	...	...	...	...	...	...	...	...	...
AMERICA, SOUTH - AMÉRIQUE DU SUD													
Bolivia (Plurinational State of) - Bolivie (État plurinational de)													
2012 (U)													
Total	34 542	...	...	...	...	...	...	...	...	...	1 864[t]	...	11
15 - 24	11 851	...	...	...	...	...	...	...	...	...	...	...	...
25 - 34	16 113	...	...	...	...	...	...	...	...	...	...	...	...
35 - 44	3 944	...	...	...	...	...	...	...	...	...	...	...	...
45 - 54	1 335	...	...	...	...	...	...	...	...	...	...	...	...
55 +	1 247	...	...	...	...	...	...	...	...	...	...	...	...
Unknown - Inconnu	52	...	...	...	...	...	...	...	...	...	...	...	...
Brazil - Brésil													
2014 (+U)													
Total	1101586	37	32 811	204 427	282 339	221 094	128 800	78 322	53 494	36 837	24 354	38 723	348
0 - 14	345	13	133	132	46	15	3	2	-	-	-	1	-
15 - 19	127 843	12	21 463	67 184	27 197	8 220	2 445	792	262	132	62	60	14
20 - 24	252 927	6	8 443	94 252	97 462	35 741	10 917	3 631	1 402	597	255	203	18
25 - 29	263 904	5	1 901	30 207	108 159	80 118	27 402	9 270	3 844	1 689	700	593	16
30 - 34	186 229	-	556	8 740	35 817	66 774	42 916	17 612	7 637	3 439	1 518	1 207	13
35 - 39	105 478	-	194	2 654	9 691	21 143	28 738	21 486	11 070	5 491	2 577	2 429	5
40 - 44	63 886	-	64	839	2 775	6 199	10 624	15 390	12 976	7 456	3 774	3 783	6
45 - 49	43 627	-	32	265	804	2 005	3 958	6 697	10 124	8 825	5 229	5 686	2
50 - 54	27 363	-	10	80	238	606	1 262	2 408	4 193	6 028	5 408	7 129	1
55 - 59	14 615	-	6	23	68	175	345	713	1 354	2 043	3 109	6 778	1
60 - 64	8 080	-	1	12	21	56	101	196	425	768	1 218	5 281	1
65 - 69	3 849	-	-	6	12	11	35	69	127	256	343	2 990	-
70 - 74	1 871	-	1	5	7	5	19	26	48	79	97	1 584	-
75 +	1 169	1	2	4	15	11	11	16	22	29	64	994	-
Unknown - Inconnu	400	-	5	24	27	15	24	14	10	5	-	5	271
Chile - Chili													
2013 (+C)													
Total	61 446	-	601	7 339	15 418	13 921	7 886	4 758	3 436	2 611	1 842	3 634	...
0 - 14	-	-	-	-	-	-	-	-	-	-	-	-	...
15 - 19	1 912	-	334	1 030	390	110	35	8	4	-	-	1	...
20 - 24	10 998	-	209	4 435	4 345	1 424	385	121	52	12	8	7	...
25 - 29	17 115	-	42	1 448	8 033	5 413	1 441	480	170	68	12	8	...
30 - 34	12 242	-	10	334	2 094	5 263	2 908	1 014	385	125	63	46	...
35 - 39	6 399	-	6	62	400	1 275	2 108	1 398	663	306	101	80	...
40 - 44	4 047	-	-	22	111	331	693	1 073	891	488	231	207	...

24. Marriages by age of groom and by age of bride: latest available year, 2006 - 2015
Mariages selon l'âge de l'époux et selon l'âge de l'épouse : dernière année disponible, 2006 - 2015 (continued - suite)

Continent, country or area, year, code[a] and age of bride / Continent, pays ou zone, date, code[a] et âge de l'épouse	Total	Age of groom - - âge de l'époux											Unknown Inconnu
		0-14	15-19	20-24	25-29	30-34	35-39	40-44	45-49	50-54	55-59	60+	
AMERICA, SOUTH - AMÉRIQUE DU SUD													
Chile - Chili													
2013													
45 - 49	3 061	-	-	5	34	82	231	445	756	694	392	422	...
50 - 54	2 358	-	-	3	9	17	68	158	362	551	509	681	...
55 - 59	1 557	-	-	-	1	4	14	43	116	244	353	782	...
60 - 64	879	-	-	-	-	2	1	14	25	91	116	630	...
65 - 69	476	-	-	-	1	-	-	4	9	25	42	395	...
70 - 74	245	-	-	-	-	-	2	-	2	5	10	226	...
75 +	157	-	-	-	-	-	-	-	1	2	5	149	...
Ecuador - Équateur[10]													
2014 (U)													
Total	60 328	13	3 559	15 111	16 653	10 309	5 330	3 010	2 067	1 401	970	1 902	3
0 - 14	362	1	156	141	42	12	8	2	-	-	-	-	-
15 - 19	9 121	5	2 446	4 671	1 457	385	100	36	13	3	4	1	-
20 - 24	17 820	5	810	8 095	6 279	1 875	518	142	56	16	14	10	-
25 - 29	14 849	2	113	1 791	6 970	4 133	1 235	355	157	48	21	23	1
30 - 34	7 670	-	21	307	1 503	2 903	1 774	698	275	109	42	37	1
35 - 39	3 974	-	7	60	305	767	1 193	858	434	198	78	74	-
40 - 44	2 396	-	1	21	55	171	367	640	586	273	148	134	-
45 - 49	1 512	-	-	9	19	43	97	197	375	372	204	196	-
50 - 54	1 047	-	2	2	10	14	27	67	127	279	235	284	-
55 - 59	661	-	1	1	2	2	6	11	35	74	157	372	-
60 - 64	399	-	1	2	-	-	1	2	6	23	50	314	-
65 - 69	218	-	-	2	3	1	-	1	2	5	9	195	-
70 - 74	139	-	-	2	1	-	1	-	-	1	4	130	-
75 +	149	-	1	3	4	2	2	-	1	-	4	132	-
Unknown - Inconnu	11	-	-	4	3	1	1	1	-	-	-	-	1
French Guiana - Guyane française													
2007 (C)													
Total	667	...	5	48	123	150	108	79	47	48	26	33	-
15 - 19	30	...	-	10	13	4	-	1	1	-	1	-	-
20 - 24	93	...	3	22	33	15	8	7	-	1	2	2	-
25 - 29	151	...	1	5	51	57	17	7	5	2	6	-	-
30 - 34	135	...	1	8	16	41	35	18	7	7	2	-	-
35 - 39	98	...	-	3	6	20	27	20	11	2	6	3	-
40 - 44	62	...	-	-	4	7	10	15	10	9	2	5	-
45 - 49	55	...	-	-	-	3	5	9	10	16	4	8	-
50 - 54	23	...	-	-	-	2	4	2	3	6	2	4	-
55 - 59	13	...	-	-	-	1	2	-	-	3	1	6	-
60 - 64	2	...	-	-	-	-	-	-	-	1	-	1	-
65 - 69	4	...	-	-	-	-	-	-	-	1	-	3	-
70 - 74	1	...	-	-	-	-	-	-	-	-	-	1	-
75 - 79	-	...	-	-	-	-	-	-	-	-	-	-	-
80 - 84	-	...	-	-	-	-	-	-	-	-	-	-	-
85 +	-	...	-	-	-	-	-	-	-	-	-	-	-
Paraguay													
2014 (U)													
Total	19 527	-	522	4 026	5 754	4 204	1 953	1 143	687	472	279	481	6
0 - 14	6	-	2	1	3	-	-	-	-	-	-	-	-
15 - 19	2 725	-	373	1 359	659	224	68	24	7	7	2	2	-
20 - 24	5 192	-	119	1 962	2 002	788	192	74	27	15	3	9	1
25 - 29	5 035	-	21	527	2 250	1 541	441	147	57	23	12	16	-
30 - 34	3 249	-	4	120	687	1 227	669	310	112	64	24	31	1
35 - 39	1 355	-	3	35	102	284	396	285	142	66	17	25	-
40 - 44	725	-	-	13	32	78	123	187	158	69	22	43	-
45 - 49	496	-	-	3	15	40	43	65	116	115	60	39	-
50 - 54	322	-	-	3	2	14	14	32	46	68	72	71	-
55 - 59	181	-	-	1	1	5	2	11	15	32	37	77	-
60 - 64	110	-	-	-	-	1	2	4	3	6	19	75	-
65 - 69	66	-	-	-	-	2	1	2	3	4	10	44	-
70 - 74	30	-	-	1	-	-	-	1	1	1	1	25	-
75 +	27	-	-	-	-	-	1	-	-	-	2	-	24	-
Unknown - Inconnu	8	-	-	1	1	-	1	1	-	-	-	-	4

24. Marriages by age of groom and by age of bride: latest available year, 2006 - 2015
Mariages selon l'âge de l'époux et selon l'âge de l'épouse : dernière année disponible, 2006 - 2015 (continued - suite)

Continent, country or area, year, code[a] and age of bride / Continent, pays ou zone, date, code[a] et âge de l'épouse	Total	0-14	15-19	20-24	25-29	30-34	35-39	40-44	45-49	50-54	55-59	60+	Unknown Inconnu
AMERICA, SOUTH - AMÉRIQUE DU SUD													
Peru - Pérou[11,12]													
2014 (+C)													
Total	33 679	-	293	3 312	7 894	8 431	5 683	3 182	1 802	1 153	688	1 241	...
0 - 14	-	-	-	-	-	-	-	-	-	-	-	-	...
15 - 19	954	-	176	473	197	69	21	9	7	-	2	-	...
20 - 24	5 564	-	102	2 010	2 278	794	289	59	28	4	-	-	...
25 - 29	9 429	-	10	660	4 014	3 067	1 094	434	85	29	17	19	...
30 - 34	7 882	-	5	144	1 148	3 446	2 067	680	228	72	32	60	...
35 - 39	4 492	-	-	24	187	901	1 710	976	393	160	69	72	...
40 - 44	2 293	-	-	1	49	136	387	766	507	265	85	97	...
45 - 49	1 332	-	-	-	21	-	73	193	426	298	177	144	...
50 - 54	749	-	-	-	-	8	20	38	96	231	155	201	...
55 - 59	434	-	-	-	-	2	-	12	19	47	128	226	...
60 +	550	-	-	-	-	8	22	15	13	47	23	422	...
Venezuela (Bolivarian Republic of) - Venezuela (République bolivarienne du)													
2014 (C)													
Total	94 519	216	8 759	23 551	25 178	15 417	8 565	5 362	3 351	2 072	990	1 058	...
0 - 14	20	3	8	6	1	-	-	-	-	1	-	1	...
15 - 19	2 550	58	1 595	658	136	45	25	10	7	7	2	7	...
20 - 24	17 462	93	4 458	9 340	2 641	635	180	61	22	13	3	16	...
25 - 29	26 166	41	1 849	9 035	11 250	2 884	749	232	70	24	11	21	...
30 - 34	18 537	13	537	2 989	7 086	5 613	1 587	495	150	41	9	17	...
35 - 39	11 206	4	177	942	2 499	3 550	2 588	940	352	102	24	28	...
40 - 44	6 898	3	66	337	937	1 510	1 816	1 453	527	171	43	35	...
45 - 49	4 568	1	36	137	359	673	898	1 124	889	333	77	41	...
50 - 54	2 906	-	12	55	157	294	405	574	667	526	146	70	...
55 - 59	1 717	-	9	22	56	110	180	263	351	371	231	124	...
60 +	2 489	-	12	30	56	103	137	210	316	483	444	698	...
ASIA - ASIE													
Armenia - Arménie													
2009 (+C)													
Total	18 773	...	153	4 608	7 796	3 482	1 313	560	325	208	132	196	-
15 - 19	2 010	...	122	928	825	124	11	-	-	-	-	-	-
20 - 24	9 521	...	28	3 366	4 655	1 278	170	19	2	3	-	-	-
25 - 29	4 516	...	2	282	2 151	1 474	478	95	27	7	-	-	-
30 - 34	1 467	...	-	26	130	539	455	215	76	17	9	-	-
35 - 39	528	...	-	4	20	47	165	154	92	32	10	4	-
40 - 44	238	...	-	2	8	13	22	52	72	42	16	11	-
45 - 49	161	...	1	-	2	4	6	14	39	53	20	22	-
50 - 54	153	...	-	-	4	3	4	8	8	45	47	34	-
55 - 59	101	...	-	-	-	-	1	2	4	5	25	64	-
60 +	78	...	-	-	1	-	1	1	5	4	5	61	-
Azerbaijan - Azerbaïdjan													
2013 (+C)													
Total	86 852	...	712	26 208	34 344	13 402	5 464	2 920	1 522	967	550	763	...
15 - 19	20 791	...	437	9 759	8 643	1 763	162	17	6	1	-	3	...
20 - 24	38 318	...	242	14 391	17 418	5 100	943	185	28	9	-	2	...
25 - 29	15 285	...	26	1 769	7 099	4 153	1 588	490	115	34	9	2	...
30 - 34	6 147	...	3	226	988	1 902	1 673	914	312	96	27	6	...
35 - 39	2 914	...	2	40	139	384	830	766	445	200	63	45	...
40 - 44	1 562	...	1	11	36	72	216	414	359	249	124	80	...
45 - 49	916	...	-	4	6	19	41	106	200	236	144	160	...
50 - 54	523	...	-	1	2	7	8	23	45	122	122	193	...
55 - 59	225	...	1	1	5	-	2	5	10	17	52	132	...
60 +	171	...	-	6	8	2	1	-	2	3	9	140	...
Bahrain - Bahreïn													
2015 (...)													
Total	6 953	-	190	2 266	2 449	899	417	242	150	272[s]	...	...	68
0 - 14	10	-	-	9	1	-	-	-	-	-[s]	...	...	-
15 - 19	1 270	-	137	763	310	41	14	1	1	1[s]	...	...	2
20 - 24	2 639	-	31	1 149	1 155	213	40	15	9	5[s]	...	...	22

24. Marriages by age of groom and by age of bride: latest available year, 2006 - 2015
Mariages selon l'âge de l'époux et selon l'âge de l'épouse : dernière année disponible, 2006 - 2015 (continued - suite)

Continent, country or area, year, code[a] and age of bride / Continent, pays ou zone, date, code[a] et âge de l'épouse	Total	\multicolumn{11}{c}{Age of groom - - âge de l'époux}	Unknown Inconnu
		0-14	15-19	20-24	25-29	30-34	35-39	40-44	45-49	50-54	55-59	60+	

Continent, country or area, year, code and age of bride	Total	0-14	15-19	20-24	25-29	30-34	35-39	40-44	45-49	50-54	55-59	60+	Unknown Inconnu
ASIA - ASIE													
Bahrain - Bahreïn													
2015													
25 - 29	1 207	-	2	102	568	324	105	46	21	21[s]	...	...	18
30 - 34	457	-	-	12	80	149	115	55	13	28[s]	...	...	5
35 - 39	252	-	-	6	15	26	57	54	39	50[s]	...	...	5
40 - 44	143	-	-	1	10	12	19	26	28	46[s]	...	...	1
45 - 49	58	-	-	2	2	3	6	4	12	29[s]	...	...	-
50 +	49	-	-	-	1	1	3	3	5	36[s]	...	...	-
Unknown - Inconnu	868	-	20	222	307	130	58	38	22	56[s]	...	...	15
Brunei Darussalam - Brunéi Darussalam													
2014 (...)													
Total	2 992	-	66	560	1 227	591	256	123	71	40	23	35	-
0 - 14	5	...	...	...	...	...	...	...	...	...	...	...	...
15 - 19	197	...	...	...	...	...	...	...	...	...	...	...	...
20 - 24	792	...	...	...	...	...	...	...	...	...	...	...	...
25 - 29	1 160	...	...	...	...	...	...	...	...	...	...	...	...
30 - 34	448	...	...	...	...	...	...	...	...	...	...	...	...
35 - 39	162	...	...	...	...	...	...	...	...	...	...	...	...
40 - 44	107	...	...	...	...	...	...	...	...	...	...	...	...
45 - 49	63	...	...	...	...	...	...	...	...	...	...	...	...
50 - 54	31	...	...	...	...	...	...	...	...	...	...	...	...
55 - 59	19	...	...	...	...	...	...	...	...	...	...	...	...
60 - 64	6	...	...	...	...	...	...	...	...	...	...	...	...
65 - 69	-	...	...	...	...	...	...	...	...	...	...	...	...
70 - 74	2	...	...	...	...	...	...	...	...	...	...	...	...
75 +	-	...	...	...	...	...	...	...	...	...	...	...	...
Unknown - Inconnu	-	...	...	...	...	...	...	...	...	...	...	...	...
China, Hong Kong SAR - Chine, Hong Kong RAS													
2014 (C)													
Total	56 454	-	182	3 555	13 528	15 354	8 230	5 122	3 375	2 737	1 976	2 395	...
0 - 14	-	-	-	-	-	-	-	-	-	-	-	-	...
15 - 19	562	-	87	274	137	40	16	5	3	-	-	-	...
20 - 24	6 883	-	78	2 325	2 654	1 097	348	175	101	58	35	12	...
25 - 29	19 114	-	13	751	8 655	6 138	1 989	784	394	220	110	60	...
30 - 34	14 692	-	2	142	1 703	6 796	3 276	1 321	642	409	235	166	...
35 - 39	6 634	-	2	32	261	979	1 977	1 423	797	519	351	293	...
40 - 44	4 146	-	-	22	81	224	458	1 049	769	629	435	479	...
45 - 49	2 270	-	-	6	28	60	126	272	476	502	341	459	...
50 - 54	1 207	-	-	1	5	15	28	81	158	300	255	364	...
55 - 59	555	-	-	-	4	3	5	9	34	79	160	261	...
60 - 64	220	-	-	1	-	-	5	2	1	17	41	153	...
65 - 69	92	-	-	1	-	1	1	1	-	2	10	76	...
70 - 74	34	-	-	-	-	-	-	-	-	2	3	29	...
75 +	45	-	-	-	-	1	1	-	-	-	-	43	...
China, Macao SAR - Chine, Macao RAS													
2009 (+C)													
Total	3 035	-	18	608	1 023	697	286	157	98	68	39	41	-
0 - 14	-	-	-	-	-	-	-	-	-	-	-	-	-
15 - 19	66	-	5	40	17	3	1	-	-	-	-	-	-
20 - 24	993	-	12	445	353	125	36	14	5	3	-	-	-
25 - 29	1 166	-	1	109	575	313	94	42	13	11	7	1	-
30 - 34	444	-	-	10	62	212	83	33	25	12	5	2	-
35 - 39	195	-	-	4	9	30	62	41	26	8	8	7	-
40 - 44	72	-	-	-	5	8	9	17	12	9	6	6	-
45 - 49	58	-	-	-	1	4	1	7	16	14	8	7	-
50 - 54	20	-	-	-	1	2	-	3	1	9	2	2	-
55 - 59	11	-	-	-	-	-	-	-	-	1	2	8	-
60 - 64	4	-	-	-	-	-	-	-	-	1	1	2	-
65 - 69	1	-	-	-	-	-	-	-	-	-	-	1	-
70 +	5	-	-	-	-	-	-	-	-	-	-	5	-
2015 (+C)													
Total	3 719	...	...	418[g]	...	...	...	...	392[r]	...	...	...	...
0 - 24	861	...	...	...	...	...	...	...	...	...	...	...	...

24. Marriages by age of groom and by age of bride: latest available year, 2006 - 2015
Mariages selon l'âge de l'époux et selon l'âge de l'épouse : dernière année disponible, 2006 - 2015 (continued - suite)

Continent, country or area, year, code[a] and age of bride / Continent, pays ou zone, date, code[a] et âge de l'épouse	Age of groom - - âge de l'époux												
	Total	0-14	15-19	20-24	25-29	30-34	35-39	40-44	45-49	50-54	55-59	60+	Unknown Inconnu
ASIA - ASIE													
China, Macao SAR - Chine, Macao RAS													
2015													
25 - 34	2 317	...	...	...	...	...	...	...	...	...	...	...	...
35 - 44	348	...	...	...	...	...	...	...	...	...	...	...	...
45 +	193	...	...	...	...	...	...	...	...	...	...	...	...
Cyprus - Chypre[13,14]													
2013 (C)													
Total	5 493	-	22	437	1 854	1 711	597	322	187	127	69	132	35
0 - 14	-	-	-	-	-	-	-	-	-	-	-	-	-
15 - 19	80	-	7	41	18	10	2	-	2	-	-	-	-
20 - 24	805	-	8	237	395	130	22	9	4	-	-	-	-
25 - 29	2 298	-	5	111	1 161	785	147	44	26	12	3	4	-
30 - 34	1 290	-	2	23	215	639	241	102	31	23	5	8	1
35 - 39	521	-	-	19	48	117	134	102	57	23	11	10	-
40 - 44	214	-	-	6	10	23	38	44	29	31	15	18	-
45 - 49	129	-	-	-	5	6	8	16	30	22	13	29	-
50 - 54	64	-	-	-	2	-	3	4	6	13	14	22	-
55 - 59	30	-	-	-	-	-	1	1	2	2	6	18	-
60 +	27	-	-	-	-	-	1	-	-	1	2	23	-
Unknown - Inconnu	35	-	-	-	-	1	-	-	-	-	-	-	34
Georgia - Géorgie													
2011 (C)													
Total	30 863	...	1 013[h]	7 972	8 522	5 705	3 513	1 915	1 047	534	285	353	4
16 - 19	4 554	...	...	...	...	...	...	...	...	...	...	...	...
20 - 24	10 875	...	...	...	...	...	...	...	...	...	...	...	...
25 - 29	7 155	...	...	...	...	...	...	...	...	...	...	...	...
30 - 34	4 052	...	...	...	...	...	...	...	...	...	...	...	...
35 - 39	2 053	...	...	...	...	...	...	...	...	...	...	...	...
40 - 44	1 040	...	...	...	...	...	...	...	...	...	...	...	...
45 - 49	567	...	...	...	...	...	...	...	...	...	...	...	...
50 - 54	280	...	...	...	...	...	...	...	...	...	...	...	...
55 - 59	145	...	...	...	...	...	...	...	...	...	...	...	...
60 +	142	...	...	...	...	...	...	...	...	...	...	...	...
Unknown - Inconnu	-	...	...	...	...	...	...	...	...	...	...	...	...
Iran (Islamic Republic of) - Iran (République islamique d')[15]													
2014 (+C)													
Total	724 324	321	32 266	241 850	267 410	107 062	32 689	14 644	7 943	5 450	4 403	10 286	-
0 - 14	40 404	126	6 505	23 898	8 837	807	141	54	16	7	11	2	-
15 - 19	214 086	139	20 054	114 460	68 612	9 415	973	230	99	46	21	37	-
20 - 24	225 921	41	4 658	83 717	104 710	27 538	3 934	784	267	132	72	68	-
25 - 29	142 239	11	837	16 507	69 737	41 344	9 521	2 561	924	353	184	260	-
30 - 34	59 201	3	167	2 628	13 049	22 661	11 639	4 985	1 948	956	483	682	-
35 - 39	22 086	1	39	524	2 069	4 417	5 103	4 014	2 383	1 427	886	1 223	-
40 - 44	9 861	-	4	84	306	720	1 154	1 627	1 594	1 348	1 073	1 951	-
45 - 49	4 853	-	2	25	64	127	177	318	589	801	860	1 890	-
50 - 54	2 638	-	-	4	21	21	35	58	91	300	538	1 570	-
55 - 59	1 462	-	-	2	4	6	9	9	24	67	200	1 141	-
60 - 64	802	-	-	-	-	2	1	4	5	10	51	729	-
65 - 69	444	-	-	-	1	1	1	-	3	2	20	416	-
70 - 74	184	-	-	-	-	1	-	-	-	-	4	179	-
75 +	143	-	-	1	-	2	1	-	-	1	-	138	-
Unknown - Inconnu	-	-	-	-	-	-	-	-	-	-	-	-	-
Israel - Israël[16]													
2013 (C)													
Total	52 705	...	1 744	12 625	19 204	10 735	3 592	1 518	709	456	344	555	1 223
15 - 19	6 910	...	1 260	3 609	1 455	249	27	3	1	1	-	-	305
20 - 24	18 315	...	432	8 203	7 120	1 776	257	48	12	4	-	1	462
25 - 29	16 841	...	4	525	9 521	5 277	1 012	213	57	16	3	1	212
30 - 34	5 777	...	-	29	793	2 917	1 372	400	107	33	12	6	108
35 - 39	2 019	...	-	7	79	326	725	511	188	70	28	20	65
40 - 44	800	...	1	1	7	37	93	232	199	104	47	38	41
45 - 49	430	...	-	1	1	2	19	43	93	121	76	61	13
50 - 54	285	...	-	-	-	-	2	9	18	68	93	86	9

815

Continent, country or area, year, code[a] and age of bride / Continent, pays ou zone, date, code[a] et âge de l'épouse	Total	Age of groom - - âge de l'époux											Unknown Inconnu
		0-14	15-19	20-24	25-29	30-34	35-39	40-44	45-49	50-54	55-59	60+	
ASIA - ASIE													
Israel - Israël[16]													
2013													
55 - 59	185	...	-	-	-	1	-	-	5	13	48	116	2
60 - 64	113	...	-	-	-	-	-	-	-	1	13	96	3
65 - 69	56	...	-	-	-	1	-	-	-	-	2	50	3
70 - 74	24	...	-	-	-	-	-	-	-	-	-	24	-
75 +	10	...	-	-	-	-	-	-	-	-	-	10	-
Unknown - Inconnu	940	...	47	250	228	149	85	59	29	25	22	46	-
Japan - Japon[17]													
2014 (+C)													
Total	525 361	-	5 360	53 635	167 357	129 251	79 546	44 106	20 055	10 248	6 137	9 666	-
0 - 14	-	-	-	-	-	-	-	-	-	-	-	-	-
15 - 19	10 150	-	4 039	4 051	1 109	531	211	102	46	33	15	13	-
20 - 24	79 921	-	1 172	36 448	26 512	9 818	3 788	1 310	433	200	119	121	-
25 - 29	194 919	-	105	10 517	113 367	48 194	15 618	4 838	1 464	434	202	180	-
30 - 34	122 406	-	29	2 023	21 646	55 990	28 474	9 890	2 848	874	346	286	-
35 - 39	65 018	-	12	499	3 981	12 317	25 407	15 124	5 038	1 611	580	449	-
40 - 44	27 782	-	3	74	628	2 034	5 019	10 455	5 651	2 278	933	707	-
45 - 49	11 194	-	-	17	96	319	858	1 911	3 572	2 345	1 188	888	-
50 - 54	6 039	-	-	3	11	38	148	390	802	1 972	1 359	1 316	-
55 - 59	3 228	-	-	2	5	8	19	72	161	386	1 097	1 478	-
60 - 64	2 141	-	-	-	1	-	4	12	30	82	222	1 790	-
65 - 69	1 373	-	-	1	-	-	-	2	8	25	58	1 279	-
70 - 74	733	-	-	-	-	1	-	-	2	5	16	709	-
75 +	457	-	-	-	1	1	-	-	-	3	2	450	-
Unknown - Inconnu	-	-	-	-	-	-	-	-	-	-	-	-	-
Jordan - Jordanie													
2010[18] (+C)													
Total	62 107	...	16 151	25 559	12 760	4 002	1 795	1 151	437	252[s]	...	...	-
18 - 19	1 262	...	1 017	191	40	11	1	2	-	-[s]	...	...	-
20 - 24	14 272	...	6 768	6 453	835	139	42	20	7	8[s]	...	...	-
25 - 29	25 434	...	6 276	12 608	5 720	633	120	45	16	16[s]	...	...	-
30 - 34	11 523	...	1 603	4 782	3 679	1 153	197	70	25	14[s]	...	...	-
35 - 39	4 064	...	299	1 043	1 434	819	350	92	19	8[s]	...	...	-
40 - 44	2 365	...	99	321	681	647	358	217	35	7[s]	...	...	-
45 - 49	1 139	...	35	81	220	283	249	196	57	18[s]	...	...	-
50 - 54	639	...	14	37	73	152	169	121	53	20[s]	...	...	-
55 - 59	425	...	12	18	35	80	95	107	56	22[s]	...	...	-
60 - 64	318	...	11	7	21	40	66	97	39	37[s]	...	...	-
65 +	666	...	17	18	22	45	148	184	130	102[s]	...	...	-
Kazakhstan													
2013 (C)													
Total	168 447	101[d]	3 612[j]	57 563	60 803	22 537	10 618	5 553	3 077	2 126	1 229	1 228	...
0 - 17	1 392	38[d]	367[j]	789	174	19	3	1	-	1	-	-	...
18 - 19	19 707	49[d]	2 280[j]	12 409	4 319	555	73	17	3	1	1	-	...
20 - 24	79 862	11[d]	889[j]	39 230	33 107	5 486	899	178	36	14	9	3	...
25 - 29	37 703	2[d]	63[j]	4 541	19 985	9 429	2 705	668	220	64	21	5	...
30 - 34	14 237	-[d]	12[j]	481	2 642	5 502	3 632	1 345	408	145	48	22	...
35 - 39	7 447	-[d]	1[j]	85	460	1 273	2 563	1 834	776	308	98	49	...
40 - 44	3 675	1[d]	-[j]	21	85	225	598	1 178	826	471	177	93	...
45 - 49	1 932	-[d]	-[j]	3	24	42	114	256	594	523	234	142	...
50 - 54	1 249	-[d]	-[j]	2	4	4	26	60	173	448	303	229	...
55 - 59	674	-[d]	-[j]	-	2	1	5	14	30	119	266	237	...
60 +	568	-[d]	-[j]	1	1	1	-	2	11	32	72	448	...
Unknown - Inconnu	1	-[d]	-[j]	1	-	-	-	-	-	-	-	-	...
Kuwait - Koweït													
2014 (C)													
Total	15 086	-	305	4 175	5 172	2 541	1 151	668	1 074[r]	...	...	...	...
0 - 14	1	-	1	-	-	-	-	-	-[r]	...	...	...	...
15 - 19	2 517	-	229	1 529	637	98	15	3	6[r]	...	...	...	...
20 - 24	5 574	-	62	2 328	2 451	579	105	19	30[r]	...	...	...	...
25 - 29	3 663	-	9	271	1 739	1 079	349	116	100[r]	...	...	...	...
30 - 34	1 642	-	3	32	256	551	377	220	203[r]	...	...	...	...
35 - 39	847	-	1	12	51	174	204	173	232[r]	...	...	...	...

Continent, country or area, year, code[a] and age of bride / Continent, pays ou zone, date, code[a] et âge de l'épouse	Total	0-14	15-19	20-24	25-29	30-34	35-39	40-44	45-49	50-54	55-59	60+	Unknown Inconnu
ASIA - ASIE													
Kuwait - Koweït													
2014													
40 - 44	431	-	-	1	23	35	65	100	207[r]	...	...	...	...
45 +	411	-	-	2	15	25	36	37	296[r]	...	...	...	...
Kyrgyzstan - Kirghizstan													
2015* (C)													
Total	52 043	-	715	17 260	20 300	6 879	2 994	1 661	932	585	373	344	-
0 - 14	-	-	-	-	-	-	-	-	-	-	-	-	-
15 - 19	10 629	-	559	6 536	3 217	289	21	5	-	1	-	1	-
20 - 24	24 442	-	150	10 081	11 880	2 014	265	36	10	3	2	1	-
25 - 29	9 531	-	6	588	4 738	3 001	903	214	55	15	9	2	-
30 - 34	3 594	-	-	49	408	1 377	1 098	450	140	52	15	5	-
35 - 39	1 841	-	-	6	50	160	572	613	274	99	44	23	-
40 - 44	970	-	-	-	5	31	112	296	265	140	89	32	-
45 - 49	515	-	-	-	1	6	20	38	154	165	78	53	-
50 - 54	269	-	-	-	1	1	2	7	28	90	72	68	-
55 - 59	123	-	-	-	-	-	-	1	4	16	49	53	-
60 - 64	78	-	-	-	-	-	1	-	-	4	13	60	-
65 - 69	39	-	-	-	-	-	-	1	2	-	2	34	-
70 - 74	4	-	-	-	-	-	-	-	-	-	-	4	-
75 +	8	-	-	-	-	-	-	-	-	-	-	8	-
Unknown - Inconnu	-	-	-	-	-	-	-	-	-	-	-	-	-
Mongolia - Mongolie													
2015 (+C)													
Total	17 586	...	217[j]	5 157	6 874	2 546	1 299	767	409	317[s]	...	...	...
18 - 19	553	...	...	...	...	...	...	...	...	...	...	...	...
20 - 24	6 630	...	...	...	...	...	...	...	...	...	...	...	...
25 - 29	6 065	...	...	...	...	...	...	...	...	...	...	...	...
30 - 34	2 049	...	...	...	...	...	...	...	...	...	...	...	...
35 - 39	1 126	...	...	...	...	...	...	...	...	...	...	...	...
40 - 44	646	...	...	...	...	...	...	...	...	...	...	...	...
45 - 49	325	...	...	...	...	...	...	...	...	...	...	...	...
50 +	192	...	...	...	...	...	...	...	...	...	...	...	...
Philippines[19]													
2014 (U)													
Total	428 936	-	9 235	106 752	150 545	88 068	35 783	15 519	8 354	5 456	3 689	5 495	40
0 - 14	10	-	2	8	-	-	-	-	-	-	-	-	-
15 - 19	41 837	-	5 437	24 038	8 997	2 168	686	241	121	69	36	41	3
20 - 24	149 752	-	3 408	65 912	56 886	16 189	4 230	1 486	638	420	261	315	7
25 - 29	134 637	-	319	14 179	68 940	36 363	9 458	2 749	1 171	603	388	463	4
30 - 34	60 118	-	45	2 028	12 969	26 888	11 640	3 588	1 343	729	406	479	3
35 - 39	21 727	-	13	408	2 096	4 994	7 271	3 743	1 551	765	396	489	1
40 - 44	9 472	-	7	115	445	1 040	1 821	2 572	1 676	850	454	491	1
45 - 49	5 133	-	1	36	128	304	519	815	1 300	916	527	587	-
50 - 54	2 921	-	1	10	33	75	104	223	390	811	577	696	1
55 - 59	1 653	-	-	4	15	22	31	62	113	205	461	740	-
60 - 64	935	-	1	-	6	5	11	27	35	68	132	650	-
65 - 69	414	-	-	2	5	5	6	7	11	13	37	328	-
70 - 74	157	-	-	-	-	2	2	5	2	4	10	132	-
75 +	114	-	-	5	13	5	2	1	1	1	3	83	-
Unknown - Inconnu	56	-	1	7	12	8	2	-	2	2	1	1	20
Qatar													
2012 (C)													
Total	3 532	...	71	963	1 214	678	256	145	104	55	21	25	...
0 - 19	687	...	57	390	199	33	8	-	-	-	-	-	...
20 - 24	1 359	...	12	506	597	192	32	8	9	2	1	-	...
25 - 29	798	...	1	51	336	275	81	29	11	8	5	1	...
30 - 34	371	...	1	11	58	129	73	53	33	9	3	1	...
35 - 39	181	...	-	3	19	31	44	29	32	13	5	5	...
40 - 44	72	...	-	1	4	12	9	16	11	11	4	4	...
45 - 49	40	...	-	1	1	3	6	8	5	7	3	6	...
50 - 54	19	...	-	-	-	-	3	2	3	5	-	6	...
55 - 59	3	...	-	-	-	2	-	-	-	-	-	1	...
60 +	2	...	-	-	-	1	-	-	-	-	-	1	...

24. Marriages by age of groom and by age of bride: latest available year, 2006 - 2015
Mariages selon l'âge de l'époux et selon l'âge de l'épouse : dernière année disponible, 2006 - 2015 (continued - suite)

Continent, country or area, year, code[a] and age of bride / Continent, pays ou zone, date, code[a] et âge de l'épouse	Total	0-14	15-19	20-24	25-29	30-34	35-39	40-44	45-49	50-54	55-59	60+	Unknown Inconnu
ASIA - ASIE													
2013 (C)													
Total	3 619	...	70[f]	983	1 325	593	270	152	120	62	20	24	...
0 - 19	582	...	...	...	...	...	...	...	...	...	...	...	...
20 - 24	1 412	...	...	...	...	...	...	...	...	...	...	...	...
25 - 29	877	...	...	...	...	...	...	...	...	...	...	...	...
30 - 34	369	...	...	...	...	...	...	...	...	...	...	...	...
35 - 39	206	...	...	...	...	...	...	...	...	...	...	...	...
40 - 44	112	...	...	...	...	...	...	...	...	...	...	...	...
45 - 49	41	...	...	...	...	...	...	...	...	...	...	...	...
50 - 54	17	...	...	...	...	...	...	...	...	...	...	...	...
55 - 59	3	...	...	...	...	...	...	...	...	...	...	...	...
60 +	-	...	...	...	...	...	...	...	...	...	...	...	...
Republic of Korea - République de Corée[20]													
2015 (+C)													
Total	302 828	-	929	9 595	67 107	121 185	49 507	22 290	11 946	8 645	5 919	5 705	...
0 - 14	6	-	3	-	2	-	1	-	-	-	-	-	...
15 - 19	3 465	-	667	866	452	353	548	463	101	12	3	-	...
20 - 24	25 499	-	222	6 527	9 862	5 352	1 773	1 207	458	71	19	8	...
25 - 29	109 287	-	31	1 822	46 529	51 339	7 235	1 497	575	201	42	16	...
30 - 34	96 085	-	6	305	9 460	58 260	23 107	3 780	811	243	86	27	...
35 - 39	29 953	-	-	65	696	5 226	14 371	7 427	1 565	404	145	54	...
40 - 44	14 112	-	-	8	81	574	2 043	6 113	3 505	1 275	372	141	...
45 - 49	9 747	-	-	2	20	77	372	1 448	3 672	2 784	1 036	336	...
50 - 54	7 343	-	-	-	4	4	52	299	1 019	2 818	2 244	903	...
55 - 59	4 424	-	-	-	1	-	5	52	216	735	1 661	1 754	...
60 - 64	1 754	-	-	-	-	-	-	3	23	90	289	1 349	...
65 - 69	665	-	-	-	-	-	-	1	1	11	20	632	...
70 - 74	334	-	-	-	-	-	-	-	-	-	1	333	...
75 +	154	-	-	-	-	-	-	-	-	1	1	152	...
Singapore - Singapour[21,22]													
2015 (+C)													
Total	28 322	-	72	1 534	9 698	8 524	3 689	2 024	1 106	747	486	442	...
0 - 14	-	-	-	-	-	-	-	-	-	-	-	-	...
15 - 19	278	-	47	126	45	28	17	9	3	1	1	1	...
20 - 24	3 772	-	21	942	1 806	582	229	105	57	17	7	6	...
25 - 29	12 763	-	2	394	6 792	4 110	881	333	131	73	31	16	...
30 - 34	6 713	-	2	49	871	3 247	1 526	607	220	91	66	34	...
35 - 39	2 501	-	-	14	125	445	828	569	267	143	72	38	...
40 - 44	1 183	-	-	8	39	86	165	302	237	173	104	69	...
45 - 49	582	-	-	1	14	16	35	80	137	140	83	76	...
50 - 54	310	-	-	-	4	8	7	13	41	92	81	64	...
55 - 59	121	-	-	-	2	2	1	6	11	14	32	53	...
60 +	99	-	-	-	-	-	-	-	2	3	9	85	...
Sri Lanka													
2007 (+U)													
Total	*196 236*	-	*4 874*	*50 475*	*77 223*	*37 758*	*13 636*	*5 693*	*3 065*	*1 585*	*988*	*939*	-
0 - 14	*20*	-	*7*	*7*	*5*	*1*	-	-	-	-	-	-	-
15 - 19	*35 127*	-	*3 814*	*19 794*	*10 010*	*1 301*	*168*	*27*	*6*	*3*	*1*	*3*	-
20 - 24	*73 649*	-	*899*	*26 759*	*35 730*	*8 980*	*1 043*	*174*	*44*	*12*	*4*	*4*	-
25 - 29	*55 088*	-	*135*	*3 335*	*29 096*	*18 013*	*3 732*	*560*	*160*	*29*	*16*	*12*	-
30 - 34	*17 764*	-	*15*	*432*	*1 881*	*8 373*	*5 319*	*1 316*	*310*	*74*	*29*	*15*	-
35 - 39	*7 468*	-	*3*	*123*	*400*	*864*	*2 930*	*2 070*	*815*	*185*	*47*	*31*	-
40 - 44	*3 529*	-	-	*10*	*74*	*184*	*350*	*1 307*	*1 008*	*389*	*157*	*50*	-
45 - 49	*1 852*	-	-	*8*	*14*	*31*	*74*	*194*	*600*	*536*	*278*	*117*	-
50 - 54	*958*	-	*1*	*5*	*8*	*8*	*18*	*39*	*98*	*299*	*294*	*188*	-
55 - 59	*471*	-	-	*1*	*5*	*2*	*2*	*6*	*17*	*43*	*138*	*257*	-
60 - 64	*193*	-	-	*1*	-	*1*	-	-	*6*	*13*	*21*	*151*	-
65 - 69	*71*	-	-	-	-	-	-	-	*1*	*1*	*1*	*68*	-
70 - 74	*31*	-	-	-	-	-	-	-	-	*1*	*2*	*28*	-
75 +	*15*	-	-	-	-	-	-	-	-	-	-	*15*	-
State of Palestine - État de Palestine													
2014 (C)													
Total	43 732	...	2 670	17 903	14 762	4 370	1 498	801	508	397	279	544	...
12 - 14	670	...	180	386	90	14	-	-	-	-	-	-	...

24. Marriages by age of groom and by age of bride: latest available year, 2006 - 2015
Mariages selon l'âge de l'époux et selon l'âge de l'épouse : dernière année disponible, 2006 - 2015 (continued - suite)

Continent, country or area, year, code[a] and age of bride / Continent, pays ou zone, date, code[a] et âge de l'épouse	Total	0-14	15-19	20-24	25-29	30-34	35-39	40-44	45-49	50-54	55-59	60+	Unknown Inconnu
ASIA - ASIE													
State of Palestine - État de Palestine													
2014													
15 - 19	17 999	...	2 183	10 028	4 962	704	86	15	9	7	2	3	...
20 - 24	17 953	...	284	7 052	7 719	2 203	477	133	51	16	12	6	...
25 - 29	4 326	...	21	383	1 779	1 086	524	267	123	74	47	22	...
30 - 34	1 412	...	1	40	162	303	284	224	160	105	58	75	...
35 - 39	733	...	1	10	28	43	99	112	96	110	78	156	...
40 - 44	371	...	-	4	13	12	20	36	51	50	48	137	...
45 - 49	160	...	-	-	5	4	7	12	16	21	26	69	...
50 - 54	74	...	-	-	4	1	1	2	2	13	6	45	...
55 - 59	21	...	-	-	-	-	-	-	-	1	2	18	...
60 - 64	7	...	-	-	-	-	-	-	-	-	-	7	...
65 +	6	...	-	-	-	-	-	-	-	-	-	6	...
Tajikistan - Tadjikistan													
2014 (+C)													
Total	95 537	-	3 916	49 719	26 233	7 001	3 804	2 303	1 050	541	331	419	220
0 - 14	-	-	-	-	-	-	-	-	-	-	-	-	-
15 - 19	42 931	-	3 445	29 805	9 138	514	-	-	-	-	-	-	29
20 - 24	33 873	-	471	19 218	12 317	1 572	222	36	12	-	-	-	25
25 - 29	10 093	-	-	696	4 502	3 337	1 131	274	85	32	19	3	14
30 - 34	4 523	-	-	-	275	1 489	1 646	662	236	87	63	57	8
35 - 39	2 374	-	-	-	1	87	749	916	298	148	72	98	5
40 - 44	1 072	-	-	-	-	2	55	401	315	137	72	89	1
45 - 49	323	-	-	-	-	-	1	14	96	97	39	76	-
50 - 54	151	-	-	-	-	-	-	-	8	37	49	57	-
55 - 59	49	-	-	-	-	-	-	-	-	3	16	30	-
60 - 64	5	-	-	-	-	-	-	-	-	-	1	4	-
65 - 69	5	-	-	-	-	-	-	-	-	-	-	5	-
70 - 74	-	-	-	-	-	-	-	-	-	-	-	-	-
75 +	-	-	-	-	-	-	-	-	-	-	-	-	-
Unknown - Inconnu	138	-	-	-	-	-	-	-	-	-	-	-	138
Turkey - Turquie[23]													
2014 (C)													
Total	599 704	...	12 619[f]	152 863	239 621	105 095	37 504	17 958	10 576	7 068	4 881	8 112	3 407
0 - 19	116 275	...	9 218[f]	56 677	41 288	7 528	950	136	35	9	2	4	428
20 - 24	213 112	...	2 860[f]	78 084	100 229	26 138	3 992	705	181	63	15	16	829
25 - 29	147 355	...	304[f]	14 012	80 645	39 439	9 031	2 181	574	192	83	45	849
30 - 34	54 787	...	74[f]	1 660	10 964	22 590	11 875	4 492	1 551	598	212	165	606
35 - 39	23 916	...	17[f]	328	1 679	4 660	7 328	5 143	2 536	1 064	481	357	323
40 - 44	12 851	...	4[f]	77	370	935	1 810	3 224	2 855	1 734	857	773	212
45 - 49	6 710	...	-[f]	5	60	159	295	623	1 601	1 651	1 065	1 166	85
50 - 54	4 048	...	-[f]	6	14	17	55	127	340	930	1 043	1 472	44
55 - 59	2 307	...	-[f]	-	2	5	9	16	62	200	553	1 440	20
60 - 64	1 174	...	-[f]	-	-	-	1	4	4	34	120	1 006	5
65 - 69	580	...	-[f]	-	1	3	-	1	3	8	25	535	4
70 - 74	243	...	-[f]	-	-	-	-	1	-	1	3	238	-
75 +	167	...	-[f]	1	-	1	-	1	1	1	4	156	2
Unknown - Inconnu	16 179	...	142[f]	2 013	4 369	3 620	2 158	1 304	833	583	418	739	-
Uzbekistan - Ouzbékistan													
2014 (+C)													
Total	296 055	-	4 030	125 032	128 477	20 698	7 867	4 329	2 233	1 480	910	999	...
0 - 14	-	-	-	-	-	-	-	-	-	-	-	-	...
15 - 19	68 624	-	3 211	42 167	22 427	734	56	26	1	1	-	1	...
20 - 24	169 600	-	794	80 319	81 740	6 017	555	122	39	8	4	2	...
25 - 29	38 281	-	23	2 415	23 230	9 344	2 312	621	234	63	27	12	...
30 - 34	11 156	-	2	110	982	4 252	3 439	1 392	538	280	91	70	...
35 - 39	4 366	-	-	18	77	300	1 334	1 437	595	330	175	100	...
40 - 44	1 998	-	-	2	17	41	133	652	515	321	176	141	...
45 - 49	936	-	-	-	3	9	31	70	254	239	174	156	...
50 - 54	616	-	-	1	1	1	3	4	48	194	146	218	...
55 - 59	280	-	-	-	-	-	3	3	9	35	93	137	...
60 - 64	118	-	-	-	-	-	1	2	-	7	20	88	...
65 - 69	46	-	-	-	-	-	-	-	-	2	3	41	...

24. Marriages by age of groom and by age of bride: latest available year, 2006 - 2015
Mariages selon l'âge de l'époux et selon l'âge de l'épouse : dernière année disponible, 2006 - 2015 (continued - suite)

Continent, country or area, year, code[a] and age of bride / Continent, pays ou zone, date, code[a] et âge de l'épouse	Total	0-14	15-19	20-24	25-29	30-34	35-39	40-44	45-49	50-54	55-59	60+	Unknown Inconnu
ASIA - ASIE													
Uzbekistan - Ouzbékistan													
2014													
70 - 74	21	-	-	-	-	-	-	-	-	-	1	20	...
75 +	13	-	-	-	-	-	-	-	-	-	-	13	...
EUROPE													
Åland Islands - Îles d'Åland													
2014 (C)													
Total	115	-	-	7	17	22	19	12	12	12	10	4	...
0 - 14	-	-	-	-	-	-	-	-	-	-	-	-	...
15 - 19	-	-	-	-	-	-	-	-	-	-	-	-	...
20 - 24	11	-	-	2	5	3	1	-	-	-	-	-	...
25 - 29	24	-	-	3	10	9	1	1	-	-	-	-	...
30 - 34	22	-	-	2	2	7	8	-	1	2	-	-	...
35 - 39	19	-	-	-	-	3	6	5	4	-	1	-	...
40 - 44	11	-	-	-	-	-	2	4	2	2	1	-	...
45 - 49	14	-	-	-	-	-	1	-	4	6	2	1	...
50 - 54	6	-	-	-	-	-	-	2	1	1	2	-	...
55 - 59	5	-	-	-	-	-	-	-	1	2	2	...
60 - 64	3	-	-	-	-	-	-	-	-	-	2	1	...
65 - 69	-	-	-	-	-	-	-	-	-	-	-	-	...
70 - 74	-	-	-	-	-	-	-	-	-	-	-	-	...
75 +	-	-	-	-	-	-	-	-	-	-	-	-	...
Albania - Albanie													
2013 (C)													
Total	23 820	...	154[f]	4 209	10 364	5 730	1 906	749	315	193	99	101	...
0 - 19	5 635	...	107[f]	1 842	2 922	693	65	5	1	-	-	-	...
20 - 24	10 054	...	42[f]	2 123	5 023	2 395	416	48	4	3	-	-	...
25 - 29	5 277	...	3[f]	205	2 191	1 955	733	148	33	8	1	-	...
30 - 34	1 710	...	2[f]	27	192	607	491	277	84	23	3	4	...
35 - 39	644	...	-[f]	9	30	65	168	199	101	40	26	6	...
40 - 44	251	...	-[f]	2	4	11	26	58	64	54	22	10	...
45 - 49	126	...	-[f]	-	2	3	7	11	22	43	18	20	...
50 - 54	63	...	-[f]	-	-	1	-	2	5	18	17	20	...
55 - 59	38	...	-[f]	-	-	-	-	1	1	4	9	23	...
60 - 64	12	...	-[f]	1	-	-	-	-	-	-	3	8	...
65 - 69	6	...	-[f]	-	-	-	-	-	-	-	-	6	...
70 - 74	4	...	-[f]	-	-	-	-	-	-	-	-	4	...
75 +	-	...	-[f]	-	-	-	-	-	-	-	-	-	...
Austria - Autriche[24]													
2013 (C)													
Total	36 140	-	166	2 648	7 180	8 897	5 657	3 801	2 815	2 049	1 355	1 572	...
0 - 14	-	-	-	-	-	-	-	-	-	-	-	-	...
15 - 19	680	-	93	408	139	31	7	2	-	-	-	-	...
20 - 24	4 764	-	60	1 694	2 026	679	186	60	35	14	3	7	...
25 - 29	9 572	-	12	417	3 919	3 680	1 033	313	129	43	18	8	...
30 - 34	8 223	-	-	92	882	3 640	2 333	813	301	100	37	25	...
35 - 39	4 459	-	-	24	146	667	1 551	1 235	515	208	63	50	...
40 - 44	3 004	-	1	9	43	151	413	917	788	406	171	105	...
45 - 49	2 330	-	-	3	15	35	101	332	714	595	316	219	...
50 - 54	1 666	-	-	1	6	7	27	111	270	497	432	315	...
55 - 59	824	-	-	-	3	5	3	15	45	149	230	374	...
60 - 64	357	-	-	-	1	-	2	2	11	26	60	255	...
65 - 69	179	-	-	-	-	1	1	1	5	8	20	143	...
70 - 74	62	-	-	-	-	-	-	-	2	2	2	56	...
75 +	20	-	-	-	-	1	-	-	-	1	3	15	...
Belarus - Bélarus													
2013 (C)													
Total	87 127	89[d]	1 659[j]	24 508	28 498	12 840	6 927	4 253	2 979	2 434	1 507	1 433	...
0 - 17	961	45[d]	283[j]	495	118	13	5	2	-	-	-	-	...
18 - 19	5 554	31[d]	692[j]	3 446	1 177	155	37	10	2	3	1	-	...
20 - 24	33 436	11[d]	565[j]	16 490	13 191	2 487	516	115	38	17	6	-	...
25 - 29	22 354	2[d]	102[j]	3 418	11 072	5 353	1 627	531	157	57	26	9	...

Continent, country or area, year, code[a] and age of bride / Continent, pays ou zone, date, code[a] et âge de l'épouse	Total	0-14	15-19	20-24	25-29	30-34	35-39	40-44	45-49	50-54	55-59	60+	Unknown Inconnu
EUROPE													
Belarus - Bélarus													
2013													
30 - 34	10 147	-d	13j	534	2 336	3 417	2 304	960	390	146	33	14	...
35 - 39	5 405	-d	3j	106	490	1 068	1 644	1 175	576	239	68	36	...
40 - 44	3 346	-d	1j	12	95	264	587	1 003	803	369	155	57	...
45 - 49	2 146	-d	-j	5	13	63	151	315	650	618	224	107	...
50 - 54	1 825	-d	-j	2	5	18	47	116	278	696	469	194	...
55 - 59	1 057	-d	-j	-	1	1	8	20	72	238	385	332	...
60 +	896	-d	-j	-	-	1	1	6	13	51	140	684	...
Belgium - Belgique[25,26]													
2010 (C)													
Total	42 159	-	100	3 343	11 662	8 743	5 567	4 016	3 093	2 416	1 527	1 692	...
0 - 14	-	-	-	-	-	-	-	-	-	-	-	-	...
15 - 19	672	-	46	363	197	43	11	6	3	2	-	1	...
20 - 24	6 935	-	43	2 186	3 442	886	206	107	34	16	11	4	...
25 - 29	13 021	-	8	632	6 768	3 925	1 089	343	170	55	21	10	...
30 - 34	7 218	-	1	109	966	2 934	1 971	738	311	117	41	30	...
35 - 39	4 622	-	1	28	182	684	1 531	1 229	580	243	85	59	...
40 - 44	3 335	-	1	15	68	175	511	1 056	799	456	145	109	...
45 - 49	2 707	-	-	5	29	68	185	387	779	679	336	239	...
50 - 54	1 895	-	-	2	6	15	45	122	307	620	462	316	...
55 - 59	1 006	-	-	2	3	13	12	18	80	182	320	376	...
60 - 64	428	-	-	-	-	-	3	9	25	33	82	276	...
65 - 69	174	-	-	1	-	-	1	1	3	10	17	141	...
70 - 74	83	-	-	-	-	-	-	-	2	3	4	74	...
75 +	63	-	-	-	1	-	2	-	-	-	3	57	...
Bosnia and Herzegovina - Bosnie-Herzégovine													
2012 (C)													
Total	18 235	-	147	3 617	6 959	3 922	1 571	739	438	259	185	398	-
0 - 14	-	-	-	-	-	-	-	-	-	-	-	-	-
15 - 19	1 885	-	91	1 028	606	122	27	6	2	1	-	2	-
20 - 24	6 191	-	48	2 130	2 958	844	160	36	7	5	2	1	-
25 - 29	5 764	-	8	403	2 936	1 833	431	113	26	10	2	2	-
30 - 34	2 228	-	-	42	405	941	581	172	66	14	2	5	-
35 - 39	871	-	-	10	35	150	292	240	92	34	14	4	-
40 - 44	437	-	-	1	9	20	56	117	122	60	19	33	-
45 - 49	349	-	-	2	6	6	13	41	85	76	52	68	-
50 - 54	237	-	-	-	2	4	6	10	30	39	52	94	-
55 - 59	136	-	-	-	-	-	2	3	6	17	34	74	-
60 - 64	78	-	-	-	-	2	1	1	-	1	7	66	-
65 - 69	27	-	-	-	-	-	-	-	1	2	1	23	-
70 - 74	18	-	-	-	-	-	-	-	1	-	-	17	-
75 +	9	-	-	-	-	-	-	-	-	-	-	9	-
Unknown - Inconnu	5	-	-	1	2	-	2	-	-	-	-	-	-
Bulgaria - Bulgarie[27]													
2012 (C)													
Total	21 167	-	202	2 957	7 343	5 173	2 571	1 169	559	419	281	493	...
0 - 14	-	-	-	-	-	-	-	-	-	-	-	-	...
15 - 19	1 357	-	157	788	316	78	12	1	3	2	-	-	...
20 - 24	6 045	-	37	1 751	2 953	1 034	220	29	10	6	2	3	...
25 - 29	7 196	-	7	355	3 546	2 357	724	140	38	17	6	6	...
30 - 34	3 199	-	1	45	440	1 362	913	294	84	37	14	9	...
35 - 39	1 582	-	-	13	72	286	548	420	147	64	18	14	...
40 - 44	702	-	-	4	8	38	115	218	166	87	43	23	...
45 - 49	390	-	-	1	3	15	31	57	83	91	65	44	...
50 - 54	270	-	-	-	4	2	6	9	23	83	75	68	...
55 - 59	177	-	-	-	1	1	2	1	3	28	43	98	...
60 - 64	130	-	-	-	-	-	-	-	2	4	13	111	...
65 - 69	73	-	-	-	-	-	-	-	-	-	2	71	...
70 - 74	31	-	-	-	-	-	-	-	-	-	-	31	...
75 +	15	-	-	-	-	-	-	-	-	-	-	15	...
Croatia - Croatie													
2014 (C)													
Total	19 501	-	118	2 086	6 731	5 660	2 267	1 045	555	364	224	450	1
0 - 14	-	-	-	-	-	-	-	-	-	-	-	-	-

24. Marriages by age of groom and by age of bride: latest available year, 2006 - 2015
Mariages selon l'âge de l'époux et selon l'âge de l'épouse : dernière année disponible, 2006 - 2015 (continued - suite)

Continent, country or area, year, code[a] and age of bride / Continent, pays ou zone, date, code[a] et âge de l'épouse	Total	0-14	15-19	20-24	25-29	30-34	35-39	40-44	45-49	50-54	55-59	60+	Unknown Inconnu
EUROPE													
Croatia - Croatie													
2014													
15 - 19	742	-	80	385	198	54	16	7	1	1	-	-	-
20 - 24	4 299	-	32	1 213	2 092	756	154	35	11	2	2	2	-
25 - 29	7 423	-	6	402	3 619	2 565	607	156	48	12	6	2	-
30 - 34	4 034	-	-	70	715	1 914	896	284	99	36	11	8	1
35 - 39	1 393	-	-	16	90	315	454	315	120	59	17	7	-
40 - 44	607	-	-	-	10	41	112	174	138	63	34	35	-
45 - 49	370	-	-	-	3	6	21	61	97	94	44	44	-
50 - 54	245	-	-	-	-	3	7	9	31	64	53	78	-
55 - 59	175	-	-	-	1	-	-	3	7	29	40	95	-
60 - 64	105	-	-	-	-	1	-	1	1	2	12	88	-
65 - 69	56	-	-	-	-	-	-	-	-	2	4	50	-
70 - 74	24	-	-	-	-	-	-	-	-	-	1	23	-
75 +	19	-	-	-	-	-	-	-	1	-	-	18	-
Unknown - Inconnu	9	-	-	-	3	5	-	-	1	-	-	-	-
Czech Republic - République tchèque													
2014 (C)													
Total	45 575	-	73	2 568	11 803	13 019	7 925	3 738	2 113	1 631	1 079	1 626	...
0 - 14	-	-	-	-	-	-	-	-	-	-	-	-	...
15 - 19	385	-	29	200	99	34	12	6	2	3	-	-	...
20 - 24	6 090	-	32	1 504	2 801	1 182	389	107	39	22	8	6	...
25 - 29	16 381	-	7	630	7 090	5 985	1 965	503	125	47	13	16	...
30 - 34	10 604	-	-	164	1 435	4 546	3 016	946	312	114	46	25	...
35 - 39	5 284	-	3	53	309	1 025	1 913	1 136	452	238	105	50	...
40 - 44	2 539	-	1	10	46	188	465	731	538	325	139	96	...
45 - 49	1 616	-	1	5	15	45	124	217	443	398	215	153	...
50 - 54	1 141	-	-	-	7	12	32	73	148	349	247	273	...
55 - 59	756	-	-	1	1	2	8	15	44	101	229	355	...
60 - 64	434	-	-	1	-	-	-	2	9	27	58	337	...
65 - 69	234	-	-	-	-	-	-	2	1	6	17	208	...
70 - 74	77	-	-	-	-	-	1	-	-	-	2	74	...
75 +	34	-	-	-	-	-	-	-	-	1	-	33	...
Denmark - Danemark[28]													
2014 (C)													
Total	28 331	-	29	1 339	5 679	6 294	4 279	2 938	2 305	1 841	1 218	1 751	658
0 - 14	-	-	-	-	-	-	-	-	-	-	-	-	-
15 - 19	188	-	20	93	35	10	4	3	-	-	-	-	23
20 - 24	2 755	-	8	894	1 185	371	92	39	34	6	2	3	121
25 - 29	7 358	-	-	223	3 479	2 449	657	204	78	33	12	9	214
30 - 34	5 665	-	-	37	651	2 605	1 562	479	145	67	19	17	83
35 - 39	3 377	-	-	9	101	475	1 330	888	349	98	40	20	67
40 - 44	2 250	-	-	4	18	90	305	828	556	274	71	43	61
45 - 49	1 872	-	-	2	4	19	69	234	675	535	197	101	36
50 - 54	1 434	-	-	-	2	3	14	66	227	513	363	223	23
55 - 59	899	-	-	1	-	-	4	16	33	141	311	373	20
60 - 64	550	-	-	-	-	-	-	3	8	38	93	403	5
65 - 69	299	-	-	-	-	-	-	-	1	6	22	267	3
70 - 74	131	-	-	-	-	-	-	-	2	1	2	124	2
75 +	87	-	-	-	-	-	-	-	-	-	3	84	-
Unknown - Inconnu	1 466	-	1	76	204	272	242	178	197	129	83	84	-
Estonia - Estonie													
2014 (C)													
Total	6 220	-	34	569	1 649	1 397	921	586	368	247	162	179	108
0 - 14	-	-	-	-	-	-	-	-	-	-	-	-	-
15 - 19	133	-	20	62	30	10	5	-	1	1	-	-	4
20 - 24	1 029	-	9	342	468	129	32	16	5	2	1	1	24
25 - 29	1 965	-	4	135	907	592	212	64	14	5	-	1	31
30 - 34	1 200	-	1	14	163	495	322	117	49	17	4	3	15
35 - 39	713	-	-	5	54	110	247	173	72	32	9	2	9
40 - 44	481	-	-	3	11	39	72	157	112	52	18	5	12
45 - 49	252	-	-	1	5	7	18	46	71	56	26	15	7
50 - 54	185	-	-	1	-	3	8	5	33	56	51	25	3
55 - 59	107	-	-	-	-	-	-	-	5	17	38	46	1
60 - 64	63	-	-	-	-	-	-	-	-	6	14	41	2

Continent, country or area, year, code[a] and age of bride / Continent, pays ou zone, date, code[a] et âge de l'épouse	Total	0-14	15-19	20-24	25-29	30-34	35-39	40-44	45-49	50-54	55-59	60+	Unknown Inconnu
EUROPE													
Estonia - Estonie													
2014													
65 - 69	20	-	-	-	-	-	-	1	1	-	1	17	-
70 - 74	15	-	-	-	-	-	-	-	-	-	-	15	-
75 +	9	-	-	-	-	-	-	-	-	-	1	-	8	-
Unknown - Inconnu	48	-	-	6	11	12	5	7	5	2	-	-	-
Faeroe Islands - Îles Féroé													
2015 (C)													
Total	217	-	1	16	37	38	48	25	19	21	4	8	...
0 - 14	-	-	-	-	-	-	-	-	-	-	-	-	...
15 - 19	1	-	-	1	-	-	-	-	-	-	-	-	...
20 - 24	32	-	1	9	14	5	1	-	2	-	-	-	...
25 - 29	49	-	-	6	17	16	10	-	-	-	-	-	...
30 - 34	53	-	-	-	3	15	20	10	4	1	-	-	...
35 - 39	32	-	-	-	2	1	15	9	3	2	-	-	...
40 - 44	16	-	-	-	1	1	1	4	5	3	1	-	...
45 - 49	17	-	-	-	-	-	1	2	4	10	-	-	...
50 - 54	7	-	-	-	-	-	-	-	1	5	1	-	...
55 - 59	1	-	-	-	-	-	-	-	-	-	1	-	...
60 - 64	6	-	-	-	-	-	-	-	-	-	1	5	...
65 - 69	1	-	-	-	-	-	-	-	-	-	-	1	...
70 - 74	1	-	-	-	-	-	-	-	-	-	-	1	...
75 +	1	-	-	-	-	-	-	-	-	-	-	1	...
Finland - Finlande[29]													
2014 (C)													
Total	24 347	-	183	2 204	5 916	5 749	3 302	2 005	2 057	1 139	828	964	...
0 - 14	-	-	-	-	-	-	-	-	-	-	-	-	...
15 - 19	506	-	114	281	83	19	6	3	-	-	-	-	...
20 - 24	3 442	-	62	1 473	1 378	367	113	23	14	10	-	2	...
25 - 29	6 854	-	4	356	3 479	2 269	547	135	40	14	7	3	...
30 - 34	5 162	-	2	51	754	2 464	1 308	380	143	40	13	7	...
35 - 39	2 718	-	-	26	151	485	961	674	297	78	32	14	...
40 - 44	1 619	-	1	5	39	98	241	489	503	147	70	26	...
45 - 49	1 925	-	-	9	14	27	92	235	855	418	187	88	...
50 - 54	931	-	-	2	10	12	29	54	151	310	231	132	...
55 - 59	592	-	-	1	7	5	4	10	42	100	211	212	...
60 - 64	315	-	-	-	-	2	1	1	9	16	65	221	...
65 - 69	185	-	-	-	1	1	-	-	2	4	10	167	...
70 - 74	55	-	-	-	-	-	-	1	-	-	2	52	...
75 +	43	-	-	-	-	-	-	-	1	2	-	40	...
France[30]													
2014 (C)													
Total	224 878	-	196	10 434	51 634	54 208	32 481	23 557	16 157	13 474	9 963	12 774	-
0 - 14	10	-	2	5	2	1	-	-	-	-	-	-	-
15 - 19	1 556	-	81	744	500	175	40	9	3	1	2	1	-
20 - 24	22 352	-	89	6 930	11 077	3 131	724	218	103	46	14	20	-
25 - 29	62 682	-	13	2 231	32 869	20 541	4 710	1 489	476	206	84	63	-
30 - 34	49 542	-	5	338	5 614	24 486	12 548	4 258	1 405	534	206	148	-
35 - 39	27 741	-	2	107	953	4 241	10 571	7 328	2 693	1 097	447	302	-
40 - 44	20 382	-	2	43	366	1 071	2 850	7 365	4 846	2 319	918	602	-
45 - 49	14 438	-	1	22	158	366	709	2 089	4 365	3 783	1 748	1 197	-
50 - 54	11 801	-	1	8	58	138	228	614	1 719	3 872	3 034	2 129	-
55 - 59	7 318	-	-	4	22	44	68	139	410	1 205	2 469	2 957	-
60 - 64	3 995	-	-	2	10	10	20	31	104	318	793	2 707	-
65 - 69	1 850	-	-	-	1	1	9	11	26	69	195	1 538	-
70 - 74	710	-	-	-	2	-	2	3	6	17	39	641	-
75 +	501	-	-	-	2	3	2	3	1	7	14	469	-
Unknown - Inconnu	-	-	-	-	-	-	-	-	-	-	-	-	-
Germany - Allemagne													
2014 (C)													
Total	385 952	-	613	21 101	84 787	96 326	55 168	34 802	31 543	26 005	16 490	19 117	...
0 - 14	-	-	-	-	-	-	-	-	-	-	-	-	...
15 - 19	3 467	-	321	1 985	868	186	58	17	16	11	3	2	...
20 - 24	43 831	-	222	13 771	21 243	6 240	1 467	472	265	92	37	22	...
25 - 29	111 427	-	40	4 349	50 407	41 002	10 779	3 101	1 150	385	137	77	...
30 - 34	88 702	-	16	711	10 278	40 842	24 192	8 148	3 010	1 017	308	180	...

823

24. Marriages by age of groom and by age of bride: latest available year, 2006 - 2015
Mariages selon l'âge de l'époux et selon l'âge de l'épouse : dernière année disponible, 2006 - 2015 (continued - suite)

Continent, country or area, year, code[a] and age of bride / Continent, pays ou zone, date, code[a] et âge de l'épouse	Total	0-14	15-19	20-24	25-29	30-34	35-39	40-44	45-49	50-54	55-59	60+	Unknown Inconnu
EUROPE													
Germany - Allemagne													
2014													
35 - 39	41 984	-	8	177	1 506	6 579	14 681	10 900	5 377	1 785	631	340	...
40 - 44	25 776	-	6	71	300	1 035	2 912	7 844	7 748	3 801	1 308	751	...
45 - 49	26 755	-	-	26	115	296	775	3 048	9 150	8 165	3 360	1 820	...
50 - 54	22 272	-	-	5	49	102	228	994	3 797	7 906	5 553	3 638	...
55 - 59	11 850	-	-	4	14	33	56	226	808	2 237	3 819	4 653	...
60 - 64	5 684	-	-	2	6	7	16	40	186	487	1 055	3 885	...
65 - 69	2 292	-	-	-	-	-	2	6	32	90	215	1 947	...
70 - 74	1 241	-	-	-	-	2	2	4	4	18	47	1 164	...
75 +	671	-	-	-	1	2	-	2	-	11	17	638	...
Greece - Grèce													
2014 (C)													
Total	53 105	-	199	1 916	10 631	18 764	11 221	4 900	2 347	1 250	761	1 116	...
0 - 14	18	-	13	4	1	-	-	-	-	-	-	-	...
15 - 19	894	-	158	377	222	102	24	6	5	-	-	-	...
20 - 24	5 397	-	21	1 014	2 432	1 358	441	87	34	6	2	2	...
25 - 29	16 904	-	5	397	5 891	7 202	2 597	610	143	40	12	7	...
30 - 34	17 391	-	2	83	1 775	8 461	4 860	1 577	460	122	30	21	...
35 - 39	7 053	-	-	30	241	1 405	2 695	1 634	673	238	81	56	...
40 - 44	2 647	-	-	6	53	201	497	761	575	306	136	112	...
45 - 49	1 280	-	-	3	11	28	85	163	317	277	199	197	...
50 - 54	804	-	-	1	4	4	15	49	109	182	180	260	...
55 - 59	428	-	-	1	1	1	6	13	29	59	99	219	...
60 - 64	182	-	-	-	-	1	1	-	2	14	17	147	...
65 - 69	75	-	-	-	-	1	-	-	-	4	5	65	...
70 - 74	22	-	-	-	-	-	-	-	-	1	-	21	...
75 +	10	-	-	-	-	-	-	-	-	1	-	9	...
Hungary - Hongrie[7]													
2014 (C)													
Total	38 780	-	211	2 026	8 790	10 760	7 375	3 548	2 076	1 208	1 063	1 723	-
0 - 14	-	-	-	-	-	-	-	-	-	-	-	-	-
15 - 19	757	-	158	358	149	49	19	15	5	1	2	1	-
20 - 24	4 721	-	38	1 102	2 115	982	348	93	29	5	6	3	-
25 - 29	12 514	-	8	421	5 043	4 690	1 733	432	125	39	12	11	-
30 - 34	8 784	-	5	93	1 130	3 788	2 595	759	271	82	34	27	-
35 - 39	5 346	-	1	34	282	1 009	2 021	1 202	504	145	77	71	-
40 - 44	2 474	-	1	16	60	191	504	737	537	238	116	74	-
45 - 49	1 518	-	-	1	7	37	137	234	420	322	201	159	-
50 - 54	987	-	-	1	3	12	12	55	134	248	273	249	-
55 - 59	757	-	-	-	1	2	6	14	33	91	233	377	-
60 - 64	529	-	-	-	-	-	-	6	14	25	86	398	-
65 - 69	250	-	-	-	-	-	-	1	3	10	17	219	-
70 - 74	106	-	-	-	-	-	-	-	-	2	6	98	-
75 +	37	-	-	-	-	-	-	-	1	-	-	36	-
Unknown - Inconnu	-	-	-	-	-	-	-	-	-	-	-	-	-
Iceland - Islande[31,32]													
2011 (C)													
Total	1 458	-	3	77	302	334	272	161	111	74	64	55	5
0 - 14	-	-	-	-	-	-	-	-	-	-	-	-	-
15 - 19	6	-	-	2	4	-	-	-	-	-	-	-	-
20 - 24	152	-	3	52	69	21	1	3	1	1	-	-	1
25 - 29	371	-	-	19	173	115	44	9	5	3	1	1	1
30 - 34	350	-	-	3	43	157	104	25	9	3	4	1	1
35 - 39	243	-	-	1	7	33	101	62	22	9	6	1	1
40 - 44	113	-	-	-	3	6	14	44	28	11	3	4	-
45 - 49	94	-	-	-	1	-	6	15	36	24	7	4	1
50 - 54	68	-	-	-	-	1	1	2	9	18	25	12	-
55 - 59	30	-	-	-	-	-	1	-	1	4	15	9	-
60 - 64	18	-	-	-	-	-	-	1	-	1	2	14	-
65 - 69	7	-	-	-	-	-	-	-	-	-	1	6	-
70 - 74	2	-	-	-	-	-	-	-	-	-	-	2	-
75 +	1	-	-	-	-	-	-	-	-	-	-	1	-
Unknown - Inconnu	3	-	-	-	2	1	-	-	-	-	-	-	-

Continent, country or area, year, code[a] and age of bride / Continent, pays ou zone, date, code[a] et âge de l'épouse	Total	0-14	15-19	20-24	25-29	30-34	35-39	40-44	45-49	50-54	55-59	60+	Unknown Inconnu
EUROPE													
Ireland - Irlande													
2012 (+C)													
Total	20 713	...	102	516	4 523	8 245	3 896	1 585	766	452	258	370	...
15 - 19	237	...	80	91	43	17	5	-	-	-	1	-	...
20 - 24	968	...	22	258	457	168	40	13	7	3	-	-	...
25 - 29	6 485	...	-	136	2 944	2 670	578	110	33	10	-	4	...
30 - 34	8 016	...	-	25	930	4 640	1 858	419	102	28	11	3	...
35 - 39	2 827	...	-	5	120	673	1 149	588	200	67	15	10	...
40 - 44	995	...	-	1	20	54	228	331	198	99	40	24	...
45 - 49	542	...	-	-	8	18	29	97	157	120	71	42	...
50 - 54	340	...	-	-	-	3	6	21	53	97	81	79	...
55 - 59	168	...	-	-	1	2	2	4	12	25	33	89	...
60 - 64	89	...	-	-	-	-	1	2	2	3	6	75	...
65 - 69	26	...	-	-	-	-	-	-	1	-	-	25	...
70 - 74	17	...	-	-	-	-	-	-	1	-	-	16	...
75 +	3	...	-	-	-	-	-	-	-	-	-	3	...
Italy - Italie													
2014 (C)													
Total	189 765	-	292	6 715	36 375	57 566	37 478	20 513	11 310	7 241	4 666	7 609	-
0 - 14	-	-	-	-	-	-	-	-	-	-	-	-	-
15 - 19	1 677	-	142	867	469	145	30	17	5	1	-	1	-
20 - 24	17 619	-	128	4 068	8 577	3 514	916	259	91	37	16	13	-
25 - 29	55 814	-	17	1 372	21 275	23 678	6 916	1 785	483	173	59	56	-
30 - 34	53 040	-	2	268	4 997	24 822	15 966	4 891	1 308	477	160	149	-
35 - 39	27 151	-	2	76	774	4 403	10 541	6 955	2 670	1 014	404	312	-
40 - 44	14 765	-	-	35	175	769	2 510	4 909	3 391	1 695	695	586	-
45 - 49	8 553	-	1	15	66	177	459	1 340	2 399	1 900	1 111	1 085	-
50 - 54	5 451	-	-	5	29	41	106	297	757	1 418	1 232	1 566	-
55 - 59	3 048	-	-	4	6	13	20	54	163	402	703	1 683	-
60 - 64	1 480	-	-	2	7	3	9	4	30	89	228	1 108	-
65 - 69	699	-	-	2	-	-	4	1	10	30	43	609	-
70 - 74	275	-	-	-	-	1	1	1	2	4	12	254	-
75 +	193	-	-	1	-	-	-	-	1	1	3	187	-
Unknown - Inconnu	-	-	-	-	-	-	-	-	-	-	-	-	-
Latvia - Lettonie[6]													
2014 (C)													
Total	12 515	-	45	1 073	3 764	2 777	1 536	1 086	734	515	369	616	-
0 - 14	-	-	-	-	-	-	-	-	-	-	-	-	-
15 - 19	203	-	25	113	40	17	4	4	-	-	-	-	-
20 - 24	2 145	-	19	657	1 080	282	72	29	3	2	1	-	-
25 - 29	4 099	-	-	254	2 144	1 186	347	124	35	6	2	1	-
30 - 34	2 280	-	1	34	376	963	524	237	91	33	13	8	-
35 - 39	1 230	-	-	13	94	254	376	294	121	51	18	9	-
40 - 44	854	-	-	1	25	55	159	263	203	83	41	24	-
45 - 49	591	-	-	1	4	17	42	99	184	133	66	45	-
50 - 54	443	-	-	-	1	3	9	26	75	141	91	97	-
55 - 59	284	-	-	-	-	-	3	9	18	51	99	104	-
60 - 64	165	-	-	-	-	-	-	1	2	12	26	124	-
65 - 69	104	-	-	-	-	-	-	-	2	2	8	92	-
70 - 74	68	-	-	-	-	-	-	-	-	1	3	64	-
75 +	49	-	-	-	-	-	-	-	-	-	1	48	-
Unknown - Inconnu	-	-	-	-	-	-	-	-	-	-	-	-	-
Liechtenstein[6]													
2012 (C)													
Total	185	-	-	8	30	59	33	19	20	10	2	4	...
Lithuania - Lituanie													
2014 (C)													
Total	22 142	-	114	2 953	8 076	4 802	2 286	1 422	894	683	396	516	-
0 - 14	3	-	2	-	1	-	-	-	-	-	-	-	-
15 - 19	598	-	71	340	145	33	7	-	2	-	-	-	-
20 - 24	5 615	-	33	1 976	2 810	616	119	45	7	7	-	2	-
25 - 29	8 123	-	5	554	4 389	2 341	581	178	46	20	7	2	-
30 - 34	3 361	-	2	60	599	1 405	785	332	112	50	11	5	-
35 - 39	1 668	-	1	19	103	316	553	400	179	69	19	9	-
40 - 44	1 019	-	-	3	19	71	175	313	233	134	41	30	-
45 - 49	713	-	-	1	10	17	52	112	223	188	71	39	-

825

24. Marriages by age of groom and by age of bride: latest available year, 2006 - 2015
Mariages selon l'âge de l'époux et selon l'âge de l'épouse : dernière année disponible, 2006 - 2015 (continued - suite)

Continent, country or area, year, code[a] and age of bride / Continent, pays ou zone, date, code[a] et âge de l'épouse	Total	0-14	15-19	20-24	25-29	30-34	35-39	40-44	45-49	50-54	55-59	60+	Unknown Inconnu
EUROPE													
Lithuania - Lituanie													
2014													
50 - 54	495	-	-	-	-	2	12	36	74	161	113	97	-
55 - 59	269	-	-	-	-	1	2	5	13	50	99	99	-
60 - 64	124	-	-	-	-	-	-	1	2	3	22	96	-
65 - 69	84	-	-	-	-	-	-	-	2	1	11	70	-
70 - 74	43	-	-	-	-	-	-	-	1	-	2	40	-
75 +	27	-	-	-	-	-	-	-	-	-	-	27	-
Unknown - Inconnu	-	-	-	-	-	-	-	-	-	-	-	-	-
Luxembourg[33]													
2014 (C)													
Total	1 657	-	1	90	366	420	269	167	125	101	56	62	-
0 - 14	-	-	-	-	-	-	-	-	-	-	-	-	-
15 - 19	13	-	1	10	2	-	-	-	-	-	-	-	-
20 - 24	168	-	-	50	77	30	7	2	2	-	-	-	-
25 - 29	465	-	-	20	198	169	52	13	10	1	-	2	-
30 - 34	420	-	-	4	74	172	105	39	13	8	3	2	-
35 - 39	217	-	-	3	9	36	74	45	31	14	3	2	-
40 - 44	154	-	-	2	4	5	22	48	29	27	11	6	-
45 - 49	103	-	-	-	2	6	6	16	26	24	9	14	-
50 - 54	60	-	-	1	-	1	2	2	8	20	17	9	-
55 - 59	40	-	-	-	-	1	-	1	5	7	12	14	-
60 - 64	12	-	-	-	-	-	1	1	1	-	1	8	-
65 - 69	3	-	-	-	-	-	-	-	-	-	-	3	-
70 - 74	2	-	-	-	-	-	-	-	-	-	-	2	-
75 +	-	-	-	-	-	-	-	-	-	-	-	-	-
Unknown - Inconnu	-	-	-	-	-	-	...	-	-	-	-	-	-
Malta - Malte													
2014 (C)													
Total	2 871	-	1	144	931	876	335	207	132	87	66	84	8
0 - 14	-	-	-	-	-	-	-	-	-	-	-	-	-
15 - 19	22	-	1	5	12	3	1	-	-	-	-	-	-
20 - 24	376	-	-	87	207	68	7	4	2	-	1	-	-
25 - 29	1 152	-	-	41	570	415	85	35	5	1	-	-	-
30 - 34	692	-	-	7	118	319	145	57	26	11	4	5	-
35 - 39	233	-	-	-	17	57	71	55	18	10	5	-	-
40 - 44	124	-	-	1	4	7	20	38	24	12	12	6	-
45 - 49	126	-	-	2	2	4	5	16	42	27	19	9	-
50 - 54	69	-	-	1	1	1	1	1	10	21	13	20	-
55 - 59	37	-	-	-	-	2	-	1	3	4	6	21	-
60 - 64	21	-	-	-	-	-	-	-	2	1	5	13	-
65 - 69	7	-	-	-	-	-	-	-	-	-	1	6	-
70 - 74	4	-	-	-	-	-	-	-	-	-	-	4	-
75 +	-	-	-	-	-	-	-	-	-	-	-	-	-
Unknown - Inconnu	8	-	-	-	-	-	-	-	-	-	-	-	8
Montenegro - Monténégro													
2009 (C)													
Total	3 829	...	26	619	1 371	876	425	232	131	66	31	52	-
0 - 14	-	...	-	-	-	-	-	-	-	-	-	-	...
15 - 19	376	...	15	172	131	41	11	4	1	-	-	1	-
20 - 24	1 268	...	9	358	600	217	53	22	6	2	1	-	-
25 - 29	1 243	...	1	75	549	406	151	47	12	1	1	-	-
30 - 34	517	...	-	8	81	176	135	79	33	5	-	-	-
35 - 39	203	...	-	3	8	32	60	47	33	16	2	2	-
40 - 44	96	...	-	2	1	2	15	25	31	10	7	3	-
45 - 49	55	...	1	1	-	1	-	7	12	15	7	11	-
50 - 54	34	...	-	-	1	1	-	1	1	15	6	9	-
55 - 59	22	...	-	-	-	-	-	-	2	1	5	14	-
60 - 64	8	...	-	-	-	-	-	-	-	1	2	5	-
65 - 69	7	...	-	-	-	-	-	-	-	-	-	7	-
70 - 74	-	...	-	-	-	-	-	-	-	-	-	-	-
75 +	-	...	-	-	-	-	-	-	-	-	-	-	-
Netherlands - Pays-Bas[9,34,35]													
2014 (C)													
Total	75 696	...	93	5 415	18 406	18 053	10 388	7 078	5 065	4 156	2 989	4 053	...
15 - 19	707	...	53	359	202	57	17	12	4	2	1	-	...

24. Marriages by age of groom and by age of bride: latest available year, 2006 - 2015
Mariages selon l'âge de l'époux et selon l'âge de l'épouse : dernière année disponible, 2006 - 2015 (continued - suite)

Continent, country or area, year, code[a] and age of bride / Continent, pays ou zone, date, code[a] et âge de l'épouse	Total	0-14	15-19	20-24	25-29	30-34	35-39	40-44	45-49	50-54	55-59	60+	Unknown Inconnu
EUROPE													
Netherlands - Pays-Bas[9,34,35]													
2014													
20 - 24	11 835	...	30	4 051	5 752	1 433	345	130	62	21	3	8	...
25 - 29	22 426	...	7	856	10 426	8 207	1 966	609	201	95	36	23	...
30 - 34	15 494	...	3	105	1 726	7 034	4 306	1 512	478	202	73	55	...
35 - 39	7 942	...	-	24	214	1 050	2 925	2 245	929	329	136	90	...
40 - 44	5 397	...	-	9	53	205	641	1 840	1 499	730	259	161	...
45 - 49	4 147	...	-	8	26	54	137	529	1 325	1 229	503	336	...
50 - 54	3 524	...	-	3	7	8	42	162	427	1 163	1 036	676	...
55 - 59	2 113	...	-	-	-	3	8	31	107	302	702	960	...
60 - 64	1 153	...	-	-	-	2	1	5	27	60	189	869	...
65 - 69	569	...	-	-	-	-	-	2	4	18	44	501	...
70 - 74	251	...	-	-	-	-	-	1	1	4	5	240	...
75 +	138	...	-	-	-	-	-	-	1	1	2	134	...
Norway - Norvège													
2012 (C)													
Total	24 077	-	38	1 503	5 000	5 362	3 852	2 786	1 989	1 440	1 018	1 089	...
0 - 14	-	-	-	-	-	-	-	-	-	-	-	-	...
15 - 19	352	-	19	164	105	35	14	10	3	1	-	1	...
20 - 24	3 246	-	15	1 069	1 372	457	164	79	51	21	7	11	...
25 - 29	6 632	-	3	226	2 933	2 215	721	289	140	61	25	19	...
30 - 34	5 312	-	-	29	486	2 197	1 503	614	245	129	64	45	...
35 - 39	3 099	-	1	13	82	386	1 128	840	352	154	79	64	...
40 - 44	2 083	-	-	1	19	55	259	718	553	270	128	80	...
45 - 49	1 463	-	-	1	2	10	51	180	477	416	201	125	...
50 - 54	981	-	-	-	1	4	9	48	137	301	291	190	...
55 - 59	505	-	-	-	-	1	2	6	24	74	177	221	...
60 - 64	231	-	-	-	-	1	1	2	5	13	37	172	...
65 - 69	129	-	-	-	-	-	-	-	2	-	8	119	...
70 - 74	28	-	-	-	-	-	-	-	-	-	1	27	...
75 +	15	-	-	-	-	-	-	-	-	-	-	15	...
Unknown - Inconnu	1	-	-	-	-	1	-	-	-	-	-	-	...
Poland - Pologne													
2012 (C)													
Total	203 850	-	911	35 828	89 905	41 502	15 386	6 593	3 804	3 013	2 515	4 393	-
0 - 14	-	-	-	-	-	-	-	-	-	-	-	-	-
15 - 19	6 351	-	560	4 117	1 382	232	50	5	3	1	1	-	-
20 - 24	66 827	-	321	25 910	33 537	5 899	884	188	58	22	5	3	-
25 - 29	79 944	-	22	5 237	48 694	20 706	4 055	868	230	63	51	18	-
30 - 34	26 609	-	6	457	5 500	12 168	5 912	1 621	551	260	84	50	-
35 - 39	9 907	-	1	91	655	2 098	3 539	2 081	844	353	172	73	-
40 - 44	4 354	-	1	13	112	316	722	1 299	944	560	245	142	-
45 - 49	2 837	-	-	2	14	69	163	350	773	708	437	321	-
50 - 54	2 586	-	-	1	9	11	45	135	274	695	697	719	-
55 - 59	2 024	-	-	-	1	3	9	37	86	253	607	1 028	-
60 - 64	1 246	-	-	-	-	-	5	4	28	71	166	972	-
65 - 69	650	-	-	-	1	-	-	4	7	19	30	589	-
70 - 74	324	-	-	-	-	-	-	-	2	6	13	303	-
75 +	191	-	-	-	-	-	2	1	4	2	7	175	-
Unknown - Inconnu	-	-	-	-	-	-	-	-	-	-	-	-	-
Portugal[36]													
2014 (C)													
Total	31 478	-	110	2 231	8 141	8 644	4 838	2 581	1 523	1 082	874	1 454	...
0 - 14	-	-	-	-	-	-	-	-	-	-	-	-	...
15 - 19	427	-	60	229	97	25	11	3	2	-	-	-	...
20 - 24	3 937	-	37	1 365	1 750	562	147	54	14	7	1	-	...
25 - 29	9 770	-	8	513	4 827	3 275	827	210	67	25	11	7	...
30 - 34	7 722	-	5	87	1 204	3 730	1 866	536	186	61	25	22	...
35 - 39	3 856	-	-	31	197	831	1 416	814	321	139	66	41	...
40 - 44	2 111	-	-	3	55	168	413	641	435	190	120	86	...
45 - 49	1 357	-	-	3	7	41	118	231	328	289	165	175	...
50 - 54	992	-	-	-	1	5	27	68	130	258	249	254	...
55 - 59	629	-	-	-	2	6	8	16	34	75	172	316	...
60 - 64	374	-	-	-	1	1	2	5	4	28	52	281	...
65 - 69	177	-	-	-	-	-	1	1	1	9	6	159	...

24. Marriages by age of groom and by age of bride: latest available year, 2006 - 2015
Mariages selon l'âge de l'époux et selon l'âge de l'épouse : dernière année disponible, 2006 - 2015 (continued - suite)

Continent, pays ou zone, date, code[a] et âge de l'épouse	Total	0-14	15-19	20-24	25-29	30-34	35-39	40-44	45-49	50-54	55-59	60+	Unknown Inconnu
EUROPE													
Portugal[36]													
2014													
70 - 74	72	-	-	-	-	-	1	2	1	1	6	61	...
75 +	54	-	-	-	-	-	1	-	-	-	1	52	...
Republic of Moldova - République de Moldova[37]													
2012 (C)													
Total	18 565	-	308	7 229	7 959	2 219	583	143	61	37	12	13	1
0 - 14	-	-	-	-	-	-	-	-	-	-	-	-	-
15 - 19	2 706	-	189	1 743	675	83	11	3	1	1	-	-	-
20 - 24	10 091	-	108	4 720	4 452	710	92	5	2	-	2	-	-
25 - 29	4 470	-	9	714	2 535	975	188	39	7	2	-	1	-
30 - 34	938	-	1	41	274	384	191	33	9	4	1	-	-
35 - 39	241	-	-	8	19	64	79	44	17	9	-	1	-
40 - 44	66	-	-	3	4	1	20	17	15	5	1	-	-
45 - 49	25	-	1	-	-	1	1	1	9	10	1	1	-
50 - 54	11	-	-	-	-	-	1	1	1	2	3	3	-
55 - 59	10	-	-	-	-	-	-	-	-	3	3	4	-
60 - 64	5	-	-	-	-	1	-	-	-	1	1	2	-
65 - 69	-	-	-	-	-	-	-	-	-	-	-	-	-
70 - 74	1	-	-	-	-	-	-	-	-	-	-	1	-
75 +	-	-	-	-	-	-	-	-	-	-	-	-	-
Unknown - Inconnu	1	-	-	-	-	-	-	-	-	-	-	-	1
Romania - Roumanie													
2014 (C)													
Total	118 075	-	475	14 468	44 913	27 942	13 903	6 451	4 100	2 019	1 727	2 077	...
0 - 14	1	-	-	-	1	-	-	-	-	-	-	-	...
15 - 19	6 716	-	309	3 200	2 466	578	138	22	1	-	1	1	...
20 - 24	33 116	-	137	8 668	17 543	5 258	1 178	240	64	18	7	3	...
25 - 29	41 115	-	22	2 260	21 274	12 695	3 764	765	221	63	31	20	...
30 - 34	17 184	-	4	263	2 962	7 231	4 542	1 424	520	133	59	46	...
35 - 39	8 982	-	1	59	539	1 757	3 205	2 073	902	237	126	83	...
40 - 44	4 431	-	1	11	101	336	793	1 331	1 159	356	208	135	...
45 - 49	3 059	-	-	5	24	80	245	500	971	621	364	249	...
50 - 54	1 506	-	-	1	1	4	33	77	204	419	456	311	...
55 - 59	1 038	-	-	-	2	3	4	16	44	132	362	475	...
60 - 64	572	-	-	1	-	-	1	1	9	33	91	436	...
65 - 69	209	-	1	-	-	-	-	1	3	4	19	181	...
70 - 74	95	-	-	-	-	-	-	1	2	2	1	89	...
75 +	51	-	-	-	-	-	-	-	-	1	2	48	...
Russian Federation - Fédération de Russie													
2012[38] (C)													
Total	1213598	...	15 848	312 104	402 995	191 131	105 357	63 778	43 196	34 745	21 315	23 078	51
15 - 19	81 342	...	9 599	50 495	18 055	2 523	468	130	38	20	7	6	1
20 - 24	425 562	...	5 186	200 558	173 664	35 196	7 918	2 062	620	221	80	54	3
25 - 29	337 474	...	802	50 809	166 737	80 206	26 188	8 444	2 758	1 022	326	182	-
30 - 34	154 765	...	189	8 034	34 743	52 674	34 829	15 241	5 645	2 339	749	318	4
35 - 39	83 803	...	50	1 683	7 769	15 610	25 204	18 450	9 030	4 074	1 366	564	3
40 - 44	45 822	...	17	377	1 571	3 745	7 817	13 055	10 391	5 807	2 044	996	2
45 - 49	31 345	...	1	94	327	880	2 159	4 456	9 684	8 528	3 435	1 778	3
50 - 54	25 096	...	1	37	89	230	606	1 487	3 793	9 098	6 198	3 553	4
55 - 59	14 880	...	1	7	22	46	121	360	985	2 837	5 299	5 202	-
60 +	13 481	...	2	8	16	20	47	91	252	798	1 811	10 424	12
Unknown - Inconnu	28	...	-	2	2	1	-	2	-	1	-	1	19
San Marino - Saint-Marin[39]													
2011 (C)													
Total	205	-	-	8	40	55	28	18	13	6	5	10	22
0 - 14	-	-	-	-	-	-	-	-	-	-	-	-	-
15 - 19	1	-	-	-	-	-	-	-	-	-	-	-	1
20 - 24	6	-	-	-	5	1	-	-	-	-	-	-	-
25 - 29	49	-	-	2	20	14	1	2	2	-	-	-	8
30 - 34	42	-	-	-	5	16	9	1	2	2	-	-	7
35 - 39	22	-	-	-	-	2	9	5	1	-	1	1	3
40 - 44	12	-	-	-	-	1	1	4	3	1	-	-	2
45 - 49	8	-	-	-	-	-	1	-	1	1	3	2	-

24. Marriages by age of groom and by age of bride: latest available year, 2006 - 2015
Mariages selon l'âge de l'époux et selon l'âge de l'épouse : dernière année disponible, 2006 - 2015 (continued - suite)

Continent, country or area, year, code[a] and age of bride / Continent, pays ou zone, date, code[a] et âge de l'épouse	Total	Age of groom - - âge de l'époux											
		0-14	15-19	20-24	25-29	30-34	35-39	40-44	45-49	50-54	55-59	60+	Unknown Inconnu
EUROPE													
San Marino - Saint-Marin[39]													
2011													
50 - 54	5	-	-	-	-	-	-	1	-	2	-	1	1
55 - 59	1	-	-	-	-	-	-	-	-	-	-	1	-
60 - 64	1	-	-	-	-	-	-	-	-	-	-	1	-
65 - 69	-	-	-	-	-	-	-	-	-	-	-	-	-
70 - 74	1	-	-	-	-	-	-	-	-	-	-	1	-
75 +	-	-	-	-	-	-	-	-	-	-	-	-	-
Unknown - Inconnu	57	-	-	6	10	21	7	5	4	-	1	3	-
Serbia - Serbie[40]													
2014 (+C)													
Total	36 429	-	277	3 970	11 397	10 215	4 554	2 117	1 202	809	593	1 203	92
0 - 14	-	-	-	-	-	-	-	-	-	-	-	-	-
15 - 19	1 819	-	181	923	528	140	26	9	2	2	2	3	3
20 - 24	8 173	-	86	2 298	3 918	1 432	310	82	21	8	1	6	11
25 - 29	12 356	-	7	603	5 685	4 483	1 190	251	74	23	10	12	18
30 - 34	7 111	-	1	80	1 047	3 458	1 717	523	180	53	21	15	16
35 - 39	2 910	-	-	26	142	536	1 029	698	288	109	44	33	5
40 - 44	1 393	-	-	7	28	95	185	398	337	191	72	76	4
45 - 49	902	-	-	6	11	27	50	105	197	233	123	148	2
50 - 54	673	-	1	1	2	2	12	30	63	138	183	241	-
55 - 59	424	-	1	1	3	4	7	4	26	32	88	258	-
60 - 64	266	-	-	1	1	2	-	5	7	9	33	206	2
65 - 69	143	-	-	1	-	-	2	2	3	3	8	124	-
70 - 74	66	-	-	2	1	1	-	1	2	1	1	56	1
75 +	25	-	-	-	-	2	-	-	-	-	2	21	-
Unknown - Inconnu	168	-	-	21	31	33	26	9	2	7	5	4	30
Slovakia - Slovaquie[6]													
2014 (C)													
Total	26 737	-	458	2 260	8 218	7 864	3 890	1 654	794	580	400	619	...
0 - 14	-	-	-	-	-	-	-	-	-	-	-	-	...
15 - 19	1 040	-	358	495	139	31	13	4	-	-	-	-	...
20 - 24	4 699	-	91	1 274	2 247	809	213	37	14	8	1	5	...
25 - 29	10 290	-	7	389	4 814	3 756	1 019	219	55	22	8	1	...
30 - 34	5 842	-	1	77	845	2 676	1 493	509	134	68	21	18	...
35 - 39	2 361	-	1	18	139	490	887	485	188	84	42	27	...
40 - 44	983	-	-	5	27	67	208	300	200	107	35	34	...
45 - 49	570	-	-	1	5	25	42	75	144	146	63	69	...
50 - 54	409	-	-	-	2	7	10	22	48	104	109	107	...
55 - 59	269	-	-	-	-	3	4	2	9	31	89	131	...
60 - 64	151	-	-	-	-	-	1	1	1	6	21	121	...
65 - 69	70	-	-	-	-	-	-	-	1	3	9	57	...
70 - 74	41	-	-	1	-	-	-	-	-	-	2	38	...
75 +	12	-	-	-	-	-	-	-	-	1	-	11	...
Slovenia - Slovénie[41]													
2014 (C)													
Total	6 571	...	99	900	2 351	1 601	773	363	190	142	81	71	...
15 - 19	23	...	11	6	4	1	1	-	-	-	-	-	...
20 - 24	417	...	44	258	90	13	8	2	1	-	1	-	...
25 - 29	1 898	...	31	448	1 141	236	28	9	2	3	-	-	...
30 - 34	1 866	...	5	140	827	720	139	29	3	2	-	1	...
35 - 39	1 090	...	6	33	212	460	312	55	11	1	-	-	...
40 - 44	549	...	-	5	60	120	178	138	33	15	-	-	...
45 - 49	256	...	1	6	11	34	58	74	49	17	6	-	...
50 - 54	187	...	-	3	4	12	26	33	47	43	13	6	...
55 - 59	124	...	1	-	-	3	15	14	29	30	23	9	...
60 - 64	78	...	-	1	2	2	6	7	9	16	17	18	...
65 - 69	34	...	-	-	-	-	-	1	4	6	12	11	...
70 - 74	23	...	-	-	-	-	1	-	1	4	3	14	...
75 +	26	...	-	-	-	-	1	1	1	5	6	12	...
Spain - Espagne													
2013 (C)													
Total	151 433	-	191	3 603	25 108	48 666	33 715	16 470	8 845	5 526	3 753	5 556	-
0 - 14	1	-	-	1	-	-	-	-	-	-	-	-	-
15 - 19	861	-	69	388	245	112	32	9	3	1	1	1	-
20 - 24	8 194	-	72	1 834	3 712	1 721	553	150	87	33	13	19	-

829

Continent, country or area, year, code[a] and age of bride / Continent, pays ou zone, date, code[a] et âge de l'épouse	Total	0-14	15-19	20-24	25-29	30-34	35-39	40-44	45-49	50-54	55-59	60+	Unknown Inconnu
EUROPE													
Spain - Espagne													
2013													
25 - 29	37 970	-	28	947	15 421	15 994	4 023	1 009	325	123	50	50	-
30 - 34	47 991	-	15	319	4 619	24 677	13 577	3 240	915	330	169	130	-
35 - 39	27 302	-	5	72	794	5 059	12 127	6 026	1 954	724	320	221	-
40 - 44	13 081	-	2	26	190	802	2 694	4 508	2 639	1 200	544	476	-
45 - 49	7 317	-	-	12	75	194	547	1 187	2 093	1 563	821	825	-
50 - 54	4 463	-	-	4	36	73	123	276	658	1 166	1 018	1 109	-
55 - 59	2 341	-	-	-	11	19	27	47	136	309	607	1 185	-
60 - 64	1 158	-	-	-	4	13	9	11	31	60	184	846	-
65 - 69	452	-	-	-	1	2	3	5	3	11	20	407	-
70 - 74	175	-	-	-	-	-	-	-	-	5	3	167	-
75 +	127	-	-	-	-	-	-	2	1	1	3	120	-
Unknown - Inconnu	-	-	-	-	-	-	-	-	-	-	-	-	-
Sweden - Suède													
2012 (C)													
Total	50 044	-	69	1 803	7 703	10 419	8 284	5 587	4 328	2 880	2 142	2 688	4 141
0 - 14	-	-	-	-	-	-	-	-	-	-	-	-	-
15 - 19	668	-	33	130	81	26	7	1	1	-	-	1	388
20 - 24	4 680	-	27	1 194	1 729	551	164	63	30	7	4	2	909
25 - 29	11 233	-	5	378	4 640	3 898	1 046	288	123	41	15	12	787
30 - 34	10 932	-	2	71	1 004	4 783	3 106	858	319	104	37	30	618
35 - 39	7 543	-	1	12	183	930	3 005	1 924	666	218	81	54	469
40 - 44	5 154	-	1	10	43	175	732	1 768	1 317	434	192	87	395
45 - 49	3 922	-	-	5	19	42	178	525	1 383	905	407	180	278
50 - 54	2 665	-	-	2	2	7	36	127	395	863	690	383	160
55 - 59	1 595	-	-	1	2	6	5	28	75	242	526	647	63
60 - 64	934	-	-	-	-	1	5	4	16	58	150	657	43
65 - 69	468	-	-	-	-	-	-	1	2	8	36	396	25
70 - 74	160	-	-	-	-	-	-	-	-	-	4	153	3
75 +	90	-	-	-	-	-	-	-	1	-	-	86	3
Switzerland - Suisse[42]													
2014 (C)													
Total	41 891	-	62	2 658	8 917	11 646	7 126	4 007	2 613	1 922	1 294	1 646	-
0 - 14	-	-	-	-	-	-	-	-	-	-	-	-	-
15 - 19	466	-	30	259	129	30	10	3	1	2	1	1	-
20 - 24	5 162	-	25	1 736	2 316	715	194	97	41	22	6	10	-
25 - 29	11 645	-	5	511	4 757	4 328	1 299	408	174	94	35	34	-
30 - 34	11 520	-	1	103	1 298	5 265	3 074	1 059	415	187	64	54	-
35 - 39	5 589	-	1	25	263	1 015	1 987	1 309	581	215	107	86	-
40 - 44	2 761	-	-	10	81	183	395	775	649	375	168	125	-
45 - 49	1 855	-	-	6	38	61	100	249	490	464	253	194	-
50 - 54	1 454	-	-	3	25	25	39	79	203	402	363	315	-
55 - 59	810	-	-	4	7	14	19	18	40	124	231	353	-
60 - 64	342	-	-	1	1	4	6	6	13	22	46	243	-
65 - 69	153	-	-	-	1	5	2	2	5	10	11	117	-
70 - 74	91	-	-	-	-	1	1	2	1	4	5	77	-
75 +	43	-	-	-	1	-	-	-	-	1	4	37	-
Unknown - Inconnu	-	-	-	-	-	-	-	-	-	-	-	-	-
TFYR of Macedonia - L'ex-R. y. de Macédoine													
2012 (C)													
Total	13 991	-	268	3 264	5 246	3 025	1 039	479	287	158	87	138	...
0 - 14	-	-	-	-	-	-	-	-	-	-	-	-	...
15 - 19	1 727	-	208	1 024	405	74	11	3	-	2	-	-	...
20 - 24	4 972	-	58	1 953	2 238	605	94	15	4	2	2	1	...
25 - 29	4 413	-	2	261	2 313	1 467	284	64	18	3	-	1	...
30 - 34	1 618	-	-	18	257	770	377	132	36	18	4	6	...
35 - 39	578	-	-	3	27	87	219	143	73	14	6	6	...
40 - 44	309	-	-	1	4	17	46	96	82	33	14	16	...
45 - 49	178	-	-	1	-	1	7	20	54	47	19	29	...
50 - 54	112	-	-	1	-	3	1	4	16	31	21	35	...
55 - 59	42	-	-	-	-	-	-	1	1	4	19	17	...
60 - 64	24	-	-	-	-	-	-	-	3	3	1	17	...
65 - 69	6	-	-	-	1	-	-	-	-	-	-	5	...

24. Marriages by age of groom and by age of bride: latest available year, 2006 - 2015
Mariages selon l'âge de l'époux et selon l'âge de l'épouse : dernière année disponible, 2006 - 2015 (continued - suite)

Continent, country or area, year, code[a] and age of bride / Continent, pays ou zone, date, code[a] et âge de l'épouse	Total	0-14	15-19	20-24	25-29	30-34	35-39	40-44	45-49	50-54	55-59	60+	Unknown Inconnu
EUROPE													
TFYR of Macedonia - L'ex-R. y. de Macédoine													
2012													
70 - 74	5	-	-	-	-	-	-	1	-	1	-	3	...
75 +	7	-	-	2	1	1	-	-	-	-	1	2	...
Ukraine													
2013 (+C)													
Total	304 232	-	5 638	82 689	101 854	47 671	24 031	14 047	9 174	7 491	4 907	6 730	-
0 - 14	-	-	-	-	-	-	-	-	-	-	-	-	-
15 - 19	29 768	-	3 569	17 949	6 954	1 094	151	33	14	2	1	1	-
20 - 24	115 048	-	1 792	52 456	47 373	10 539	2 148	479	149	69	20	23	-
25 - 29	78 596	-	207	10 455	38 179	20 214	6 593	1 969	627	238	79	35	-
30 - 34	33 936	-	52	1 452	7 460	11 676	7 831	3 448	1 237	520	176	84	-
35 - 39	17 460	-	9	280	1 534	3 220	5 127	3 905	1 977	929	314	165	-
40 - 44	10 066	-	6	55	267	729	1 602	2 875	2 283	1 398	556	295	-
45 - 49	6 781	-	3	33	67	140	441	989	1 864	1 902	834	508	-
50 - 54	5 469	-	-	4	13	44	107	273	784	1 810	1 422	1 012	-
55 - 59	3 332	-	-	2	3	13	26	60	198	481	1 119	1 430	-
60 +	3 776	-	-	3	4	2	5	16	41	142	386	3 177	-
Unknown - Inconnu	-	-	-	-	-	-	-	-	-	-	-	-	-
United Kingdom of Great Britain and Northern Ireland - Royaume-Uni de Grande-Bretagne et d'Irlande du Nord[43]													
2010 (C)													
Total	280 444	-	953	21 358	71 229	66 208	41 473	27 517	19 583	12 562	8 140	11 421	-
0 - 14	-	-	-	-	-	-	-	-	-	-	-	-	-
15 - 19	3 052	-	582	1 556	612	176	70	35	9	5	5	2	-
20 - 24	38 975	-	292	13 649	17 116	5 325	1 667	566	239	66	26	29	-
25 - 29	85 307	-	57	4 743	41 761	26 417	8 245	2 632	933	311	119	89	-
30 - 34	59 525	-	13	952	9 172	26 368	14 655	5 457	1 967	604	204	133	-
35 - 39	33 497	-	5	314	1 907	5 998	11 699	8 013	3 658	1 250	376	277	-
40 - 44	21 842	-	4	97	454	1 405	3 719	7 062	5 289	2 421	871	520	-
45 - 49	16 193	-	-	31	147	405	1 112	2 792	5 151	3 647	1 693	1 215	-
50 - 54	10 119	-	-	10	48	83	247	772	1 767	3 015	2 327	1 850	-
55 - 59	5 562	-	-	5	7	23	43	138	447	918	1 734	2 247	-
60 - 64	3 484	-	-	1	4	7	12	38	99	262	623	2 438	-
65 - 69	1 641	-	-	-	1	1	3	10	19	52	130	1 425	-
70 - 74	746	-	-	-	-	-	-	2	3	7	27	707	-
75 +	501	-	-	-	-	-	1	-	2	4	5	489	-
Unknown - Inconnu	-	-	-	-	-	-	-	-	-	-	-	-	-
OCEANIA - OCÉANIE													
Australia - Australie[44]													
2014 (+C)													
Total	121 197	-	458	12 077	36 564	30 300	14 350	9 068	5 810	4 747	3 369	4 449	-
0 - 14	-	-	-	-	-	-	-	-	-	-	-	-	-
15 - 19	1 621	-	226	859	389	95	25	13	4	3	3	-	-
20 - 24	20 182	-	204	8 363	8 502	2 135	549	205	106	60	29	36	-
25 - 29	42 429	-	20	2 367	22 522	13 020	2 911	914	356	161	94	64	-
30 - 34	26 183	-	8	369	4 297	12 317	5 788	2 085	681	341	146	148	-
35 - 39	11 078	-	-	77	629	2 160	3 769	2 554	1 049	472	222	149	-
40 - 44	7 040	-	-	31	151	440	1 007	2 320	1 597	854	374	266	-
45 - 49	4 834	-	-	7	44	81	223	725	1 408	1 283	634	420	-
50 - 54	3 593	-	-	5	17	26	62	185	492	1 157	939	700	-
55 - 59	2 063	-	-	-	3	11	14	56	94	341	692	844	-
60 - 64	1 128	-	-	-	-	8	3	10	25	68	190	835	-
65 - 69	602	-	-	-	-	-	-	3	-	13	43	538	-
70 - 74	274	-	-	-	-	-	-	-	-	-	7	264	-
75 +	185	-	-	-	-	-	-	-	-	-	-	177	-
Unknown - Inconnu	-	-	-	-	-	-	-	-	-	-	-	-	-

24. Marriages by age of groom and by age of bride: latest available year, 2006 - 2015
Mariages selon l'âge de l'époux et selon l'âge de l'épouse : dernière année disponible, 2006 - 2015 (continued - suite)

Continent, pays ou zone, date, code[a] et âge de l'épouse	Total	0-14	15-19	20-24	25-29	30-34	35-39	40-44	45-49	50-54	55-59	60+	Unknown Inconnu
OCEANIA - OCÉANIE													
Fiji - Fidji													
2008 (+C)													
Total	8 180	...	99	1 960	2 932	1 346	741	454	296	158	95	99	-
15 - 19	1 050	...	...	...	...	...	...	...	...	...	...	...	...
20 - 24	3 049	...	...	...	...	...	...	...	...	...	...	...	...
25 - 29	2 024	...	...	...	...	...	...	...	...	...	...	...	...
30 - 34	903	...	...	...	...	...	...	...	...	...	...	...	...
35 - 39	493	...	...	...	...	...	...	...	...	...	...	...	...
40 - 44	310	...	...	...	...	...	...	...	...	...	...	...	...
45 - 49	200	...	...	...	...	...	...	...	...	...	...	...	...
50 - 54	83	...	...	...	...	...	...	...	...	...	...	...	...
55 - 59	44	...	...	...	...	...	...	...	...	...	...	...	...
60 - 64	14	...	...	...	...	...	...	...	...	...	...	...	...
65 +	10	...	...	...	...	...	...	...	...	...	...	...	...
Unknown - Inconnu	-	...	...	...	...	...	...	...	...	...	...	...	...
New Caledonia - Nouvelle-Calédonie													
2010 (C)													
Total	908	...	2[f]	62	149	200	171	169[n]	...	90[o]	...	65	-
0 - 19	13	...	1[f]	6	2	2	1	1[n]	...	-[o]	...	-	-
20 - 24	118	...	-[f]	36	51	18	10	2[n]	...	1[o]	...	-	-
25 - 29	194	...	1[f]	16	77	63	20	13[n]	...	3[o]	...	1	-
30 - 34	205	...	-[f]	4	14	94	62	27[n]	...	4[o]	...	-	-
35 - 39	139	...	-[f]	-	3	19	55	52[n]	...	7[o]	...	3	-
40 - 49	150	...	-[f]	-	2	4	22	65[n]	...	41[o]	...	16	-
50 - 59	59	...	-[f]	-	-	-	1	9[n]	...	30[o]	...	19	-
60 +	30	...	-[f]	-	-	-	-	-[n]	...	4[o]	...	26	-
New Zealand - Nouvelle-Zélande[9,45,46,47]													
2014 (+C)													
Total	20 125	-	68	1 699	5 002	4 537	2 554	1 783	1 371	1 133	793	1 185	...
0 - 14	-	-	-	-	-	-	-	-	-	-	-	-	...
15 - 19	409	-	68	247	71	13	5	2	1	2	-	-	...
20 - 24	3 737	-	-	1 452	1 752	394	86	26	19	4	3	1	...
25 - 29	6 288	-	-	-	3 179	2 353	496	160	56	29	9	6	...
30 - 34	3 689	-	-	-	-	1 777	1 251	439	134	58	15	15	...
35 - 39	1 865	-	-	-	-	-	716	714	279	87	45	24	...
40 - 44	1 375	-	-	-	-	-	-	442	564	248	81	40	...
45 - 49	1 066	-	-	-	-	-	-	-	318	450	177	121	...
50 - 54	804	-	-	-	-	-	-	-	-	255	324	225	...
55 - 59	409	-	-	-	-	-	-	-	-	-	139	270	...
60 - 64	237	-	-	-	-	-	-	-	-	-	-	237	...
65 - 69	146	-	-	-	-	-	-	-	-	-	-	146	...
70 - 74	66	-	-	-	-	-	-	-	-	-	-	66	...
75 +	34	-	-	-	-	-	-	-	-	-	-	34	...
Niue - Nioué													
2009 (C)													
Total	12	...	-	2	3	4	-	1	1	-	1	-	-
15 - 19	-	...	...	...	...	...	...	...	...	...	...	...	...
20 - 24	-	...	...	...	...	...	...	...	...	...	...	...	...
25 - 29	3	...	...	...	...	...	...	...	...	...	...	...	...
30 - 34	4	...	...	...	...	...	...	...	...	...	...	...	...
35 - 39	3	...	...	...	...	...	...	...	...	...	...	...	...
40 - 44	-	...	...	...	...	...	...	...	...	...	...	...	...
45 - 49	1	...	...	...	...	...	...	...	...	...	...	...	...
50 - 54	1	...	...	...	...	...	...	...	...	...	...	...	...
55 - 59	-	...	...	...	...	...	...	...	...	...	...	...	...
60 - 64	-	...	...	...	...	...	...	...	...	...	...	...	...
65 +	-	...	...	...	...	...	...	...	...	...	...	...	...
Wallis and Futuna Islands - Îles Wallis et Futuna													
2008 (C)													
Total	53	-	1	14	23	8	3	2	-	2	-	-	-
0 - 14	-	...	...	...	...	...	...	...	...	...	...	...	...
15 - 19	9	...	...	...	...	...	...	...	...	...	...	...	...
20 - 24	18	...	...	...	...	...	...	...	...	...	...	...	...

Continent, country or area, year, code[a] and age of bride / Continent, pays ou zone, date, code[a] et âge de l'épouse	Age of groom - - âge de l'époux												
	Total	0-14	15-19	20-24	25-29	30-34	35-39	40-44	45-49	50-54	55-59	60+	Unknown Inconnu

OCEANIA - OCÉANIE

Wallis and Futuna Islands - Îles Wallis et Futuna
2008

	Total	0-14	15-19	20-24	25-29	30-34	35-39	40-44	45-49	50-54	55-59	60+	Unknown
25 - 29	12	...	...	...	...	...	...	...	...	...	...	...	...
30 - 34	7	...	...	...	...	...	...	...	...	...	...	...	...
35 - 39	5	...	...	...	...	...	...	...	...	...	...	...	...
40 - 44	-	...	...	...	...	...	...	...	...	...	...	...	...
45 - 49	1	...	...	...	...	...	...	...	...	...	...	...	...
50 - 54	-	...	...	...	...	...	...	...	...	...	...	...	...
55 - 59	-	...	...	...	...	...	...	...	...	...	...	...	...
60 - 64	1	...	...	...	...	...	...	...	...	...	...	...	...
65 - 69	-	...	...	...	...	...	...	...	...	...	...	...	...
70 - 74	-	...	...	...	...	...	...	...	...	...	...	...	...
75 +	-	...	...	...	...	...	...	...	...	...	...	...	...

FOOTNOTES - NOTES

Italics: data from civil registers which are incomplete or of unknown completeness. - Italiques : données incomplètes ou dont le degré d'exactitude n'est pas connu, provenant des registres de l'état civil.

* Provisional. - Données provisoires.

[a] 'Code' indicates the source of data, as follows:
C - Civil registration, estimated over 90% complete
U - Civil registration, estimated less than 90% complete
| - Other source, estimated reliable
+ - Data tabulated by date of registration rather than occurence
... - Information not available

Le 'Code' indique la source des données, comme suit :
C - Registres de l'état civil considérés complets à 90 p. 100 au moins
U - Registres de l'état civil qui ne sont pas considérés complets à 90 p. 100 au moins
| - Autre source, considérée pas douteuses
+ - Données exploitées selon la date de l'enregistrement et non la date de l'événement
... - Information pas disponible

[b] Refers to 0-15 years of age. - Données se raportent au groupe d'âges 0-15.
[c] Refers to 0-16 years of age. - Données se raportent au groupe d'âges 0-16.
[d] Refers to 0-17 years of age. - Données se raportent au groupe d'âges 0-17.
[e] Refers to 0-18 years of age. - Données se raportent au groupe d'âges 0-18.
[f] Refers to 0-19 years of age. - Données se raportent au groupe d'âges 0-19.
[g] Refers to 0-24 years of age. - Données se raportent au groupe d'âges 0-24.
[h] Refers to 16-19 years of age. - Données se raportent au groupe d'âges 16-19.
[i] Refers to 17-19 years of age. - Données se raportent au groupe d'âges 17-19.
[j] Refers to 18-19 years of age. - Données se raportent au groupe d'âges 18-19.
[k] Refers to 19-24 years of age. - Données se raportent au groupe d'âges 19-24.
[l] Refers to 20-29 years of age. - Données se raportent au groupe d'âges 20-29.
[m] Refers to 30-39 years of age. - Données se raportent au groupe d'âges 30-39.
[n] Refers to 40-49 years of age. - Données se raportent au groupe d'âges 40-49.
[o] Refers to 50-59 years of age. - Données se raportent au groupe d'âges 50-59.
[p] Refers to 35+ years of age. - Données se raportent au groupe d'âges 35+.
[q] Refers to 40+ years of age. - Données se raportent au groupe d'âges 40+.
[r] Refers to 45+ years of age. - Données se raportent au groupe d'âges 45+.
[s] Refers to 50+ years of age. - Données se raportent au groupe d'âges 50+.
[t] Refers to 55+ years of age. - Données se raportent au groupe d'âges 55+.

[1] Source: Vital Statistics Report 2014. - Source: Vital Statistics Report 2014.
[2] Including marriages resumed after 'revocable divorce' (among Moslem population), which approximates legal separation. - Y compris les unions reconstituées après un 'divorce révocable' (parmi la population musulmane), qui est à peu près l'équivalent d'une séparation légale.

[3] Excludes the islands of St. Brandon and Agalega. - Non compris les îles St. Brandon et Agalega.
[4] Including visitors. - Y compris les visiteurs.
[5] Excluding visitors. - Ne comprend pas les visiteurs.
[6] Data refer to marriages by residence of the groom. - Les données concernent les mariages selon la résidence du marié.
[7] Marriages registered by residence of bride. - Les mariages sont enregistrés selon le lieu de résidence de la mariée.
[8] Including marriages where bride/groom are non-residents. - Y compris les mariages pour lesquels le marié et la mariée sont des non-résidents.
[9] Including same sex marriages. - Y compris les mariages entre personnes du même sexe.
[10] Excludes nomadic Indian tribes. - Non compris les tribus d'Indiens nomades.
[11] Data are compiled from the National Registers of Identification and Civil Status (RENIEC). - Les données sont rédigées à partir des Registres Nationaux d'Identification et d'État Civil (RENIEC).
[12] Data refers to metropolitan Lima and Callao. - Les données font référence à la région métropolitaine de Lima et Callao.
[13] Data refer to marriages of residents only. - Les données ne portent que sur les mariages de résidents.
[14] Data refer to government controlled areas. - Les données se rapportent aux zones contrôlées par le Gouvernement.
[15] Data refer to the Iranian Year which begins on 21 March and ends on 20 March of the following year. - Les données concernent l'année iranienne, qui commence le 21 mars et se termine le 20 mars de l'année suivante.
[16] Includes data for East Jerusalem and Israeli residents in certain other territories under occupation by Israeli military forces since June 1967. - Y compris les données pour Jérusalem-Est et les résidents israéliens dans certains autres territoires occupés depuis 1967 par les forces armées israéliennes.
[17] Data refer to Japanese nationals in Japan only; and to grooms and brides married for the first time whose marriages occurred and were registered in the same year. - Les données se raportent aux nationaux japonais au Japon seulement; et aux époux et épouses mariés pour la première fois, dont le mariage a été célébré et enregistré la même année.
[18] Excluding data for Jordanian territory under occupation since June 1967 by Israeli military forces. Excluding foreigners, including registered Palestinian refugees. - Non compris les données pour le territoire jordanien occupé depuis juin 1967 par les forces armées israéliennes. Non compris les étrangers, mais y compris les réfugiés de Palestine enregistrés.
[19] Excluding marriages by groom and bride that are under "Married" status. - Sauf mariages entre personnes qui ont le statut de « marié(e) ».
[20] Excluding alien armed forces, civilian aliens employed by armed forces, and foreign diplomatic personnel and their dependants. - Non compris les militaires étrangers, les civils étrangers employés par les forces armées ni le personnel diplomatique étranger et les membres de leur famille les accompagnant.
[21] Data comprise civil marriages registered under the Women's Charter and Muslim marriages registered under the Administration of Muslim Law Act. -
[22] Excluding marriages previously officiated outside Singapore or under religious and customary rites. - Ne comprend pas les mariages prononcés ailleurs qu'à Singapour ni les mariages religieux ou coutumiers.

²³ Data from MERNIS (Central Population Administrative System). - Données de MERNIS (Système central de données démographiques).

²⁴ Excluding aliens temporarily in the area. - Non compris les étrangers se trouvant temporairement dans le territoire.

²⁵ Since 2003, marriage between persons of the same sex is authorized in Belgium, but the sex of spouses is not revealed. In this table, husband is used for first spouse, whereas wife is used for second spouse. - Depuis 2003, le mariage entre personnes de même sexe est autorisé en Belgique, mais le sexe des conjoints n'est pas indiqué. Dans ce tableau, la mention "époux" est utilisée pour le premier conjoint et la mention "épouse" pour le second conjoint.

²⁶ Including armed forces stationed outside the country and alien armed forces in the area, if the marriage is performed by local authority. - Y compris les militaires nationaux hors du pays et les militaires étrangers en garnison sur le territoire, si le mariage a été célébré par l'autorité locale.

²⁷ Including nationals outside the country, but excluding foreigners in the country. - Y compris les nationaux à l'étranger, mais non compris les étrangers sur le territoire.

²⁸ Excluding Faeroe Islands and Greenland shown separately, if available. - Non compris les Iles Féroé et le Groenland, qui font l'objet de rubriques distinctes, si disponible.

²⁹ Excluding Åland Islands. - Non compris les Îles d'Åland.

³⁰ Data refer to marriages between persons of different sex. - Les données se rapportent aux mariages entre personnes de sexe différent.

³¹ Data for residence abroad are excluded. - Les données relatives aux résidents à l'étranger sont exclues.

³² Data refer to common residence after marriage. - Données se rapportant à la résidence commune après le mariage.

³³ Data refer to marriages where one or both partners are residents. - Les données portent sur les mariages pour lesquels l'un des deux partenaires ou les deux sont résidents.

³⁴ Marriages of couples of which at least one partner is recorded in a Dutch municipal register, irrespective of the country where the marriage was performed. - Correspond aux mariages pour lesquels au moins l'un des partenaires est inscrit sur un registre municipal néerlandais, quel que soit le pays dans lequel le mariage est célébré.

³⁵ Including residents outside the country if listed in a Netherlands population register. - Englobe les résidents se trouvant à l'étranger à condition qu'ils soient inscrits sur le registre de population des Pays-Bas.

³⁶ Groom refers to the man for opposite sex marriages, and to spouse 1 as specified in the Civil Register for same sex marriages. Bride refers to the woman for opposite sex marriages, and to spouse 2 as specified in the Civil Register for same sex marriages. - Marié se réfère à l'homme en cas de mariage entre personnes de sexe différent et à l'époux 1 inscrit sur le Registre d'état civil en cas de mariage entre personnes du même sexe. Mariée se réfère à la femme en cas de mariage entre personnes de sexe différent et à l'époux 2 inscrit sur le Registre d'état civil en cas de mariage entre personnes du même sexe.

³⁷ Data refer to first marriages only. - Données se rapportent aux premiers mariages seulement.

³⁸ Data refer to population 15 years of age or more. - Les données concernent la population âgée de 15 ans ou plus.

³⁹ Includes civil and religious marriages as well as not specified. - Englobe les mariages civils et religieux et ceux pour lesquels rien n'a été indiqué.

⁴⁰ Excludes data for Kosovo and Metohia. - Sans les données pour le Kosovo et Metohie.

⁴¹ Data refer to residence of groom or bride before marriage. - Données relatives au lieu de résidence du marié ou de la mariée avant le mariage.

⁴² Data based on the residence of groom if he has permanent address in the country, otherwise, based on the residence of bride. If neither partner is a permanent resident, the marriage is not included in the official statistics. - Les données sont fondées sur la résidence du marié si celui-ci a une adresse permanente dans le pays, sinon elles sont fondées sur la résidence de la mariée. Si aucun des deux partenaires n'est un résident permanent, le mariage n'apparaît pas dans les statistiques officielles.

⁴³ Excluding Channel Islands (Guernsey and Jersey) and Isle of Man, shown separately, if available. - Non compris les îles Anglo-Normandes (Guernesey et Jersey) et l'île de Man, qui font l'objet de rubriques distinctes, si disponible.

⁴⁴ This data has been randomly rounded to protect confidentiality. Individual figures may not add up to totals, and values for the same data may vary in different tables. - Ces données ont été arrondies de façon aléatoire afin d'en préserver la confidentialité. La somme de certains chiffres peut ne pas correspondre aux totaux indiqués et les valeurs des mêmes données peuvent varier d'un tableau à un autre.

⁴⁵ Data refer to marriages and civil unions by residence of 'partner 2'. - Les données concernent les mariages et les unions civiles selon la résidence du « partenaire 2 ».

⁴⁶ The first row of the table title is 'age of the oldest partner' and the first column title is 'age of youngest partner'. - L'intitulé de la première rangée est « âge du partenaire le plus âgé », et celui de la première colonne est « âge du partenaire le plus jeune ».

⁴⁷ Random rounding to base 3 is applied in this table as a confidentiality measure. - Les chiffres sont arrondis à la base 3 de manière aléatoire, pour des raisons de confidentialité.

Table 25 - *Demographic Yearbook 2015*

Table 25 presents the number of divorces and crude divorce rates for as many years as possible between 2011 and 2015.

Description of variables: Divorce is defined as a final legal dissolution of a marriage, that is, the separation of husband and wife which confers on the parties the right to remarriage under civil, religious and/or other provisions, according to the laws of each country[1].

Unless otherwise noted, divorce statistics exclude legal separations that do not allow remarriage. These statistics refer to the number of divorces granted, and not to the number of persons divorcing.

Divorce statistics are obtained from court records and/or civil registers according to national practice. The actual compilation of these statistics may be the responsibility of the civil registrar, the national statistical office or other government offices.

The urban/rural classification of divorces is that provided by each country or area; it is presumed to be based on the national census definitions of urban population, which have been set forth at the end of the technical notes for table 6.

Rate computation: Crude divorce rates by urban/rural residence are the annual number of divorces per 1 000 mid-year population. Rates presented in this table have been limited to those countries or areas having at least a total of 30 divorces in a given year. These rates are calculated by the Statistics Division of the United Nations based on the appropriate reference population (for example: total population, nationals only etc.) if known and available. If the reference population is not known or unavailable the total population is used to calculate the rates. Therefore, if the population that is used to calculate the rates is different from the correct reference population, the rates presented might under- or overstate the true situation in a country or area.

Reliability of data: Each country or area has been asked to indicate the estimated completeness of the divorces recorded in its civil register. These national assessments are indicated by the quality codes "C" and "U" that appear in the first column of this table.

"C" indicates that the data are estimated to be virtually complete, that is, representing at least 90 per cent of the divorces that occur each year, while "U" indicates that data are estimated to be incomplete, that is, representing less than 90 per cent of the divorces occurring each year. The code "..." indicates that no information was provided regarding completeness.

Data from civil registers that are reported as incomplete or of unknown completeness (coded "U" or "...") are considered unreliable. They appear in *italics* in this table and the rates were not computed on data so coded. These quality codes apply only to data from civil registers. For more information about the quality of vital statistics data in general, see section 4.2 of the Technical Notes.

Limitations: Statistics on divorces are subject to the same qualifications as have been set forth for vital statistics in general and divorce statistics in particular as discussed in section 4 of the Technical Notes.

Divorce, like marriage, is a legal event, and this has implications for international comparability of data. Divorce has been defined, for statistical purposes, in terms of the laws of individual countries or areas. The laws pertaining to divorce vary considerably from one country or area to another. This variation in the legal provision for divorce also affects the incidence of divorce, which is relatively low in countries or areas where divorce decrees are difficult to obtain.

Since divorces are granted by courts and statistics on divorce refer to the actual divorce decree, effective as of the date of the decree, marked year-to-year fluctuations may reflect court delays and clearances rather than trends in the incidence of divorce. The comparability of divorce statistics may also be affected by tabulation procedures. In some countries or areas annulments and/or legal separations may be included. This practice is more common for countries or areas in which the number of divorces is small. Information on this practice is given in the footnotes when known.

The registration of a divorce in many countries or areas is the responsibility solely of the court or the authority which granted it. Since the registration recording such cases is part of the records of the court proceedings, divorces are likely to be registered soon after the decree is granted.   For this reason the practice of tabulating data by date of registration does not generally pose serious problems of comparability as it does in the case of birth and death statistics.

As noted briefly above, the incidence of divorce is affected by the relative ease or difficulty of obtaining a divorce according to the laws of individual countries or areas. The incidence of divorce is also affected by the ability of individuals to meet financial and other costs of the court procedures. Connected with this aspect is the influence of certain religious faiths on the incidence of divorce. For all these reasons, divorce statistics are not strictly comparable as measures of family dissolution by legal means. Furthermore, family dissolution by other than legal means, such as separation, is not measured in statistics for divorce.

For certain countries or areas there is or was no legal provision for divorce in the sense used here, and therefore no data for these countries or areas appear in this table.

In addition, it should be noted that rates are affected also by the quality and limitations of the population estimates that are used in their computation. The problems of under-enumeration or over-enumeration, and to some extent, the differences in definition of total population, have been discussed in section 3 of the Technical Notes dealing with population data in general, and specific information pertaining to individual countries or areas is given in the footnotes to table 3.

As will be seen from the footnotes, strict correspondence between the numerator of the rate and the denominator is not always obtained; for example, divorces among civilian plus military segments of the population may be related to civilian population only. The effect of this may be to increase the rates but, in most cases, the effect is negligible.

As mentioned above, data for some countries or areas may include annulments and/or legal separations. This practice affects the comparability of the crude divorce rates. For example, inclusion of annulments in the numerator of the rates produces a negligible effect on the rates, but inclusion of legal separations may have a measurable effect on the level.

It should be emphasized that crude divorce rates like crude birth, death and marriage rates may be seriously affected by age-sex structure of the populations to which they relate. Like crude marriage rates, they are also affected by the existing distribution of the population by marital status. Nevertheless, crude divorce rates provide a simple measure of the level and changes in divorces.

The comparability of data by urban/rural residence is affected by the national definitions of urban and rural used in tabulating these data. It is assumed, in the absence of specific information to the contrary, that the definitions of urban and rural used in connection with the national population census were also used in the compilation of the vital statistics for each country or area. However, it cannot be excluded that, for a given country or area, different definitions of urban and rural are used for the vital statistics data and the population census data respectively. When known, the definitions of urban in national population censuses are presented at the end of the technical notes for table 6. As discussed in detail in the notes, these definitions vary considerably from one country or area to another.

In addition to problems of comparability, divorce rates classified by urban/rural residence are also subject to certain special types of bias. If, when calculating divorce rates, different definitions of urban are used in connection with the vital events and the population data, and if this results in a net difference between the numerator and denominator of the rate in the population at risk, then the divorce rates would be biased. Urban/rural differentials in divorce rates may also be affected by whether the vital events have been tabulated in terms of place of occurrence or place of usual residence. This problem is discussed in more detail in section 4.1.4.1 of the Technical Notes.

Earlier data: Divorces have been shown in previous issues of the Demographic Yearbook. The earliest data, which were for 1935, appeared in the 1951 issue. For more information on specific topics and years for which data are reported, readers should consult the Historical Index.

NOTES

[1] For definition, please see section 4.1.1 of the Technical Notes.

Tableau 25 – *Annuaire démographique 2015*

Le tableau 25 présente des statistiques concernant les divorces et les taux bruts de divortialité, pour le plus grand nombre d'années possible entre 2011 et 2015.

Description des variables : le divorce est la dissolution légale et définitive des liens du mariage, c'est-à-dire la séparation de l'époux et de l'épouse qui confère aux parties le droit de se remarier civilement ou religieusement, ou selon toute autre procédure, conformément à la législation du pays[1].

Sauf indication contraire, les statistiques de la divortialité n'englobent pas les séparations légales qui excluent un remariage. Ces statistiques se rapportent aux jugements de divorce prononcés, non aux personnes divorcées.

Les statistiques de la divortialité proviennent, selon la pratique suivie par chaque pays, des actes des tribunaux et/ou des registres de l'état civil. L'officier d'état civil, les services nationaux de statistique ou d'autres services gouvernementaux peuvent être chargés d'établir ces statistiques.

La classification des divorces selon le lieu de résidence (zone urbaine ou rurale) est celle qui a été communiquée par chaque pays ou zone ; on part du principe qu'elle repose sur les définitions de la population urbaine utilisées pour les recensements nationaux, qui sont reproduites à la fin des notes techniques du tableau 6.

Calcul des taux : les taux bruts de divortialité selon le lieu de résidence (zone urbaine ou rurale) représentent le nombre annuel de divorces enregistrés pour 1 000 habitants au milieu de l'année. Les taux de ce tableau ne se rapportent qu'aux pays ou zones où l'on a enregistré un total d'au moins 30 divorces pendant une année donnée. Ces taux sont calculés par la division de statistique des Nations Unies sur la base de la population de référence adéquate (par exemple : population totale, nationaux seulement, etc.) si connue et disponible. Si la population de référence n'est pas connue ou n'est pas disponible, la population totale est utilisée pour calculer les taux. Par conséquent, si la population utilisée pour calculer les taux est différente de la population de référence adéquate, les taux présentés sont susceptibles de sous ou sur estimer la situation réelle d'un pays ou d'un territoire.

Fiabilité des données : il a été demandé à chaque pays ou zone d'indiquer le degré estimatif de complétude des données sur les divorces figurant dans ses registres d'état civil. Ces évaluations nationales sont désignées par les codes de qualité "C" et "U" qui apparaissent dans la deuxième colonne du tableau.

La lettre "C" indique que les données sont jugées à peu près complètes, c'est-à-dire qu'elles représentent au moins 90 p. 100 des divorces survenus chaque année ; la lettre "U" signale que les données sont jugées incomplètes, c'est-à-dire qu'elles représentent moins de 90 p. 100 des divorces survenus chaque année. Le code "..." indique qu'aucun renseignement n'a été communiqué quant à la complétude des données.

Les données issues des registres de l'état civil qui sont déclarées incomplètes ou dont le degré de complétude n'est pas connu (code "U" ou "...") sont jugées douteuses. Elles apparaissent en italique dans le tableau et les taux correspondants n'ont pas été calculés. Les codes de qualité ne s'appliquent qu'aux données extraites des registres de l'état civil. Pour plus de précisions sur la qualité des données reposant sur les statistiques de l'état civil en général, voir la section 4.2 des notes techniques.

Insuffisance des données : les statistiques des divorces appellent les mêmes réserves que celles formulées à propos des statistiques de l'état civil en général et des statistiques de divortialité en particulier (voir la section 4 des notes techniques).

Le divorce est, comme le mariage, un acte juridique, et ce fait influe sur la comparabilité internationale des données. Aux fins de la statistique, le divorce est défini par la législation de chaque pays ou zone. La législation sur le divorce varie considérablement d'un pays ou d'une zone à l'autre, ce qui influe aussi sur la fréquence des divorces, laquelle est relativement faible dans les pays ou zones où le jugement de divorce est difficile à obtenir.

Du fait que les divorces sont prononcés par les tribunaux et que les statistiques de la divortialité se rapportent aux jugements de divorce proprement dits, qui prennent effet à la date où ces jugements sont rendus, il se peut que des fluctuations annuelles accusées traduisent le rythme plus ou moins rapide auquel les affaires sont jugées plutôt que l'évolution de la fréquence des divorces. Les méthodes d'exploitation des données peuvent aussi influer sur la comparabilité des statistiques de la divortialité. Dans certains pays ou zones, ces statistiques peuvent comprendre les annulations et/ou les séparations légales. C'est notamment le cas dans les pays ou zones où les divorces sont peu nombreux. Lorsqu'ils sont connus, des renseignements à ce propos sont donnés en note à la fin du tableau.

Étant donné que dans de nombreux pays ou zones, le tribunal ou l'autorité qui a prononcé le divorce est seul habilité à enregistrer cet acte, et, comme l'acte d'enregistrement figure alors sur les registres du tribunal, l'enregistrement suit généralement de peu le jugement. C'est pourquoi la pratique consistant à exploiter les données selon la date de l'enregistrement ne pose généralement pas les graves problèmes de comparabilité auxquels on se heurte dans le cas des statistiques des naissances et des décès.

Comme on l'a brièvement mentionné ci-dessus, la fréquence des divorces est fonction notamment de la facilité relative avec laquelle la législation de chaque pays ou zone permet d'obtenir le divorce. Elle dépend également de la capacité des intéressés à supporter les frais de procédure. Il faut aussi citer l'influence de certaines religions sur la fréquence des divorces. Pour toutes ces raisons, les statistiques de divortialité ne sont pas rigoureusement comparables et ne permettent pas de mesurer exactement la fréquence des dissolutions légales des mariages. De plus, elles ne rendent pas compte des cas de dissolution extrajudiciaire du mariage, comme la séparation.

Dans certains pays ou zones, il n'existe ou il n'existait pas de législation sur le divorce selon l'acception retenue aux fins de ce tableau, si bien que l'on ne dispose pas de données les concernant.

De surcroît, il convient de noter que l'exactitude des taux dépend également de la qualité et des insuffisances des estimations de population qui sont utilisées pour leur calcul. Le problème des erreurs par excès ou par défaut commises lors du dénombrement et, dans une certaine mesure, le problème de l'hétérogénéité des définitions de la population totale ont été examinés à la section 3 des notes techniques, relative à la population en général ; des explications concernant les différents pays ou zones sont données en note à la fin du tableau 3.

Comme on le verra dans les notes, il n'a pas toujours été possible d'obtenir une correspondance rigoureuse entre le numérateur et le dénominateur pour le calcul des taux. Par exemple, les divorces parmi la population civile et les militaires sont parfois rapportés à la population civile seulement. Cela peut avoir pour effet d'accroître les taux, mais, dans la plupart des cas, il est probable que la différence sera négligeable.

Comme indiqué plus haut, les données concernant certains pays ou zones peuvent comprendre les annulations et/ou les séparations légales. Cette pratique influe sur la comparabilité des taux bruts de divortialité. Par exemple, l'inclusion des annulations dans le numérateur a une influence négligeable, mais l'inclusion des séparations légales peut avoir un effet appréciable.

Il faut souligner que les taux bruts de divortialité, de même que les taux bruts de natalité, de mortalité et de nuptialité, peuvent varier sensiblement selon la structure par âge et par sexe. Comme les taux bruts de nuptialité, ils peuvent également varier en raison de la répartition de la population selon l'état matrimonial. Les taux bruts de divortialité offrent néanmoins un moyen simple de mesurer la fréquence et l'évolution des divorces.

La comparabilité des données selon le lieu de résidence (zone urbaine ou rurale) peut être limitée par les définitions nationales des termes « urbain » et « rural » utilisées pour la mise en tableaux de ces données. En l'absence d'indications contraires, on a supposé que les mêmes définitions avaient servi pour le recensement national de la population et pour l'établissement des statistiques de l'état civil pour chaque pays ou zone. Toutefois, il n'est pas exclu que, pour une zone ou un pays donné, des définitions différentes aient été retenues. Les définitions du terme « urbain » utilisées pour les recensements nationaux de population ont été présentées à la fin des notes techniques du tableau 6 lorsqu'elles étaient connues. Comme on l'a précisé dans les notes techniques relatives au tableau 6, ces définitions varient considérablement d'un pays ou d'une zone à l'autre.

Outre les problèmes de comparabilité, les taux de divortialité classés selon le lieu de résidence (zone urbaine ou rurale) sont également sujets à des distorsions particulières. Si l'on utilise des définitions différentes du terme « urbain » pour classer les faits d'état civil et les données relatives à la population lors du calcul des taux et qu'il en résulte une différence nette entre le numérateur et le dénominateur pour le taux de la population exposée au risque, les taux de divortialité s'en trouveront faussés. La différence entre ces taux pour les zones urbaines et rurales pourra aussi être faussée selon que les faits d'état civil auront été classés d'après le lieu de l'événement ou d'après le lieu de résidence habituel. Ce problème est examiné plus en détail à la section 4.1.4.1 des notes techniques.

Données publiées antérieurement : des statistiques concernant les divorces ont déjà été présentées dans des éditions antérieures de l'*Annuaire démographique*. Les plus anciennes, qui portaient sur 1935, ont été publiées dans l'édition de 1951. Pour plus de précisions concernant les années et les sujets pour lesquels des données ont été publiées, se reporter à l'index historique.

NOTE

[1] Pour la définition, voir la section 4.1.1 des Notes techniques.

25. Divorces and crude divorce rates by urban/rural residence: 2011 - 2015
Divorces et taux bruts de divortialité selon la résidence, urbaine/rurale : 2011 - 2015

Continent, country or area, and urban/rural residence / Continent, pays ou zone et résidence, urbaine/rurale	Co-de[a]	Number - Nombre					Rate - Taux				
		2011	2012	2013	2014	2015	2011	2012	2013	2014	2015
AFRICA - AFRIQUE											
Egypt - Égypte[1]											
Total	+C	151 933	155 261	162 583	180 344	...	1.9	1.9	1.9	2.1	...
Urban - Urbaine	+C	87 091	91 789	91 040	97 953	...	2.5	2.6	2.5	2.6	...
Rural - Rurale	+C	64 842	63 472	71 543	82 391	...	1.4	1.3	1.5	1.7	...
Lesotho											
Total	+U	143	142	...	...	...	...	...	...	...	...
Mauritius - Maurice[2]											
Total	+C	1 788	2 003	1 584	2 262	2 161	1.4	1.6	1.3	1.8	1.7
Mayotte											
Total	C	...	...	...	155	...	...	...	...	0.7	...
Reunion - Réunion											
Total	C	...	...	...	1 420	...	...	...	...	1.7	...
Saint Helena ex. dep. - Sainte-Hélène sans dép.											
Total	C	1	5	7	4	...	...	...	...	...	...
Seychelles											
Total	+C	165	158	193	158	149	1.9	1.8	2.1	1.7	1.6
South Africa - Afrique du Sud											
Total	...	20 980	21 998	23 885	24 689	...	...	...	...	...	...
Sudan - Soudan											
Total	U	...	...	...	...	43 926	...	...	...	...	...
Tunisia - Tunisie											
Total	...	12 651	...	...	...	...	...	...	...	...	...
AMERICA, NORTH - AMÉRIQUE DU NORD											
Aruba											
Total	C	470	464	477	468	366	4.6	4.4	4.5	4.3	3.4
Barbados - Barbade											
Total	+C	452	472	459	443	...	1.6	1.7	1.7	1.6	...
Bermuda - Bermudes											
Total	C	177	145	165	104	116	2.8	2.3	2.7	1.7	1.9
Costa Rica											
Total	C	...	11 593	13 349	10 864	*10 111	...	2.5	2.8	2.3	*2.1
Cuba											
Total	C	29 712	32 005	32 848	32 934	33 174	2.7	2.9	2.9	2.9	3.0
Urban - Urbaine	C	27 654	30 028	30 819	30 906	...	3.3	3.5	3.6	3.6	...
Rural - Rurale	C	2 058	1 977	2 029	2 028	...	0.7	0.7	0.8	0.8	...
Curaçao											
Total	C	396	386	366	344	375	2.6	2.5	2.4	2.2	2.4
Dominica - Dominique											
Total	+C	78	82	81	80	...	1.1	1.2	1.1	1.1	...
Dominican Republic - République dominicaine											
Total	+C	17 927	17 820	18 882	19 244	...	1.9	1.8	1.9	1.9	...
El Salvador											
Total	...	6 053	6 674[4]	...	...	...	...	...	...	...	...
Urban - Urbaine	...	3 022[3]	6 463[4]	...	...	...	...	...	...	...	...
Rural - Rurale	...	3 031[3]	211[4]	...	...	...	...	...	...	...	...
Grenada - Grenade											
Total	+C	150	174	...	...	...	1.4	1.6	...	...	...
Guadeloupe											
Total	C	860	902	806	729	...	2.1	2.2	2.0	1.8	...
Guatemala											
Total	C	4 344	5 157	5 542	5 575	...	0.3	0.3	...	...	...
Jamaica - Jamaïque											
Total	+C	1 960	2 409	2 410	1 744	...	0.7	0.9	0.9	0.6	...
Martinique											
Total	C	...	...	...	414	...	...	...	...	1.1	...
Mexico - Mexique											
Total	+C	91 285	99 509	108 727	*113 481[7]	...	0.8	0.9	0.9	*0.9	...
Urban - Urbaine[5]	+C	82 623[6]	89 927[6]	97 087[6]	*101 095[7]	...	1.0	1.1	1.1	*1.2	...
Rural - Rurale[5]	+C	4 122[6]	4 723[6]	5 305[6]	*5 786[7]	...	0.1	0.1	0.2	*0.2	...

25. Divorces and crude divorce rates by urban/rural residence: 2011 - 2015
Divorces et taux bruts de divortialité selon la résidence, urbaine/rurale : 2011 - 2015 (continued - suite)

Continent, country or area, and urban/rural residence — Continent, pays ou zone et résidence, urbaine/rurale	Co-de[a]	Number - Nombre					Rate - Taux				
		2011	2012	2013	2014	2015	2011	2012	2013	2014	2015
AMERICA, NORTH - AMÉRIQUE DU NORD											
Panama											
Total	C	3 848	4 132	4 083	4 336	...	1.0	1.1	1.1	1.1	...
Urban - Urbaine	C	3 300	3 514	3 453	3 781	...	1.3	1.4	1.3	1.4	...
Rural - Rurale	C	548	618	630	555	...	0.4	0.5	0.5	0.4	...
Puerto Rico - Porto Rico											
Total	C	13 349	14 325	12 908	11 776	11 877	3.6	3.9	3.6	3.3	3.4
Saint Lucia - Sainte-Lucie											
Total	C	*31	*117	...	...	...	*0.2	*0.7	...	...	...
Saint Vincent and the Grenadines - Saint-Vincent-et-les Grenadines											
Total	C	26	34	29	39	...	...	0.3	...	0.4	...
Sint Maarten (Dutch part) - Saint-Martin (partie néerlandaise)											
Total	+C	95	...	99	...	...	2.8	...	2.7	...	...
United States of America - États-Unis d'Amérique[8]											
Total	C	877 000	...	...	...	...	2.8	...	...	...	...
AMERICA, SOUTH - AMÉRIQUE DU SUD											
Brazil - Brésil											
Total	...	347 583	341 600	324 921	341 181	...	...	...	...	...	...
Ecuador - Équateur[9]											
Total	U	21 466	20 299	21 122	24 771	...	...	...	...	...	...
Urban - Urbaine	U	...	...	19 458	22 854	...	...	...	...	...	...
Rural - Rurale	U	...	...	1 664	1 917	...	...	...	...	...	...
Peru - Pérou[10]											
Total	+C	5 625	13 126	14 103	13 598	...	0.2	0.4	0.5	0.4	...
Suriname[11]											
Total	C	488	528	602	778	...	0.9	1.0	1.1	1.4	...
Venezuela (Bolivarian Republic of) - Venezuela (République bolivarienne du)											
Total	...	28 653	30 660	31 355	26 127	24 089	...	...	...	...	...
ASIA - ASIE											
Armenia - Arménie											
Total	+C	3 188	...	...	4 496	...	1.0	...	...	...	...
Azerbaijan - Azerbaïdjan											
Total	+C	10 747	11 087	11 730	12 088	...	1.2	1.2	1.2	1.3	...
Urban - Urbaine	+C	7 931	8 212	8 451	...	...	1.6	1.7	1.7	...	...
Rural - Rurale	+C	2 816	2 875	3 279	...	...	0.7	0.7	0.7	...	...
Bahrain - Bahreïn											
Total	...	1 408	1 649	1 824	1 795	1 745	...	...	...	...	...
Bangladesh											
Total	...	124 110	125 787	...	...	...	...	...	...	...	...
Urban - Urbaine	...	29 250	31 483	...	...	...	...	...	...	...	...
Rural - Rurale	...	94 860	94 304	...	...	...	...	...	...	...	...
Brunei Darussalam - Brunéi Darussalam											
Total	...	475	570	502	522	...	...	...	...	...	...
China - Chine[12]											
Total	+C	2 111 000	2 388 000	...	...	...	1.6	1.8	...	...	...
China, Hong Kong SAR - Chine, Hong Kong RAS											
Total	...	19 597	21 125	22 271	20 019	20 075	...	...	...	...	...
China, Macao SAR - Chine, Macao RAS											
Total	+C	998	1 147	1 172	1 308	1 168	1.8	2.0	2.0	2.1	1.8

25. Divorces and crude divorce rates by urban/rural residence: 2011 - 2015
Divorces et taux bruts de divortialité selon la résidence, urbaine/rurale : 2011 - 2015 (continued - suite)

Continent, country or area, and urban/rural residence / Continent, pays ou zone et résidence, urbaine/rurale	Co-de[a]	Number - Nombre					Rate - Taux				
		2011	2012	2013	2014	2015	2011	2012	2013	2014	2015
ASIA - ASIE											
Cyprus - Chypre[13]											
Total	C	1 934	2 036	1 857	...	...	2.3	2.4	2.2	...	...
Urban - Urbaine[14]	C	1 518	1 597	1 444	...	...	...	...	...	...	...
Rural - Rurale[14]	C	354	363	333	...	...	...	...	...	...	...
Georgia - Géorgie											
Total	C	5 850	7 136	8 089	9 119	...	1.3	1.6	...	2.0	...
Urban - Urbaine	C	4 384	...	...	...	...	1.8	...	...	...	...
Rural - Rurale	C	1 466	...	...	...	...	0.7	...	...	...	...
Indonesia - Indonésie											
Total	U	276 791	...	...	...	...	...	...	...	...	...
Iran (Islamic Republic of) - Iran (République islamique d')[15]											
Total	+C	142 841	150 324	155 369	163 569	...	1.9	2.0	2.0	2.1	...
Israel - Israël[16]											
Total	C	13 460	13 685	14 735	...	...	1.7	1.7	1.8	...	...
Urban - Urbaine[14]	C	12 244	12 451	13 392	...	...	1.7	1.7	1.8	...	...
Rural - Rurale[14]	C	932	955	1 021	...	...	1.4	1.4	1.5	...	...
Japan - Japon[17]											
Total	+C	235 719	235 406	231 383	222 107	...	1.8	1.8	1.8	1.7	...
Urban - Urbaine	+C	216 337	216 322	212 844	204 352	...	...	...	...	...	...
Rural - Rurale	+C	19 382	19 084	18 539	17 755	...	...	...	...	...	...
Jordan - Jordanie[18]											
Total	+C	16 086	17 696	18 976	20 911	...	2.3	2.4	2.3	2.4	...
Kazakhstan											
Total	C	44 862	48 513	51 482	...	...	2.7	2.9	3.0	...	...
Urban - Urbaine	C	33 792	36 232	38 365	...	...	3.7	3.9	4.1	...	...
Rural - Rurale	C	11 070	12 281	13 117	...	...	1.5	1.6	1.7	...	...
Kuwait - Koweït											
Total	C	6 254	6 672	6 904	7 327	...	2.0	2.1	2.0	1.9	...
Kyrgyzstan - Kirghizstan											
Total	C	8 705	8 698	9 052	9 235	*8 588	1.7	1.6	1.6	1.6	*1.4
Urban - Urbaine	C	4 497	4 609	5 255	5 324	*4 797	2.4	2.5	2.7	2.7	*2.4
Rural - Rurale	C	4 208	4 089	3 797	3 911	*3 791	1.2	1.2	1.0	1.0	*1.0
Lebanon - Liban											
Total	+C	6 879	6 498	6 644	7 206	...	1.8	...	...	...	...
Mongolia - Mongolie											
Total	+C	3 222	2 467	3 522	3 750	3 873	1.2	0.9	1.2	1.3	1.3
Urban - Urbaine	+C	2 760	2 096	2 978	3 333	3 455	1.5	1.1	1.5	1.7	1.7
Rural - Rurale	+C	462	371	544	417	418	0.5	0.4	0.6	0.4	0.4
Oman[19]											
Total	+U	3 805	3 570	...	...	...	...	...	...	...	...
Qatar											
Total	C	1 108	1 420	1 325	...	...	0.6	0.8	0.7	...	...
Republic of Korea - République de Corée[20]											
Total	+C	114 284	114 316	115 292	115 510	109 153	2.3	2.3	2.3	2.3	2.1
Urban - Urbaine[14]	+C	88 273	88 785	89 793	89 689	84 958	2.2	2.2	2.2	2.2	2.0
Rural - Rurale[14]	+C	22 398	22 213	22 218	22 596	21 384	2.4	2.4	2.4	2.4	2.3
Singapore - Singapour											
Total	+C	7 234	6 893	7 133	6 861	7 117	1.9	1.8	1.9	1.8	1.8
State of Palestine - État de Palestine											
Total	C	6 155	6 574	7 114	7 603	...	1.5	1.5	1.6	1.7	...
Tajikistan - Tadjikistan											
Total	+C	6 762	7 417	7 920	9 037	...	0.9	0.9	1.0	1.1	...
Urban - Urbaine	+C	2 811	2 973	3 264	3 279	...	1.4	1.4	1.5	1.5	...
Rural - Rurale	+C	3 951	4 444	4 656	5 758	...	0.7	0.8	0.8	0.9	...
Turkey - Turquie[21]											
Total	C	120 117	123 325	125 305	130 913	...	1.6	1.6	1.6	1.7	...
United Arab Emirates - Émirats arabes unis											
Total	...	4 145	3 901	4 233	4 809	...	...	...	...	...	...
Uzbekistan - Ouzbékistan											
Total	+C	18 603	17 879	24 025	28 811	...	0.6	0.6	0.8	0.9	...
Urban - Urbaine	+C	12 799	12 413	16 524	19 634	...	0.8	0.8	1.1	1.3	...
Rural - Rurale	+C	5 804	5 466	7 501	9 177	...	0.4	0.4	0.5	0.6	...

Continent, country or area, and urban/rural residence / Continent, pays ou zone et résidence, urbaine/rurale	Co-de[a]	Number - Nombre					Rate - Taux				
		2011	2012	2013	2014	2015	2011	2012	2013	2014	2015
EUROPE											
Åland Islands - Îles d'Åland											
Total	C	53	63	54	50	*77	1.9	2.2	1.9	1.7	*2.7
Urban - Urbaine	C	26	34	29	20	*45	...	3.0	...	...	*3.9
Rural - Rurale	C	27	29	25	30	*32	...	...	...	1.7	*1.8
Albania - Albanie											
Total	C	3 642	3 561	3 747	...	...	1.3	1.2	1.3	...	...
Austria - Autriche[22]											
Total	C	17 295	17 006	15 958	...	...	2.1	2.0	1.9	...	...
Belarus - Bélarus											
Total	C	38 584	39 034	36 105	34 864	...	4.1	4.1	3.8	3.7	...
Urban - Urbaine	C	33 105	33 197	31 239	...	...	4.6	4.6	4.3	...	...
Rural - Rurale	C	5 479	5 837	4 866	...	...	2.4	2.6	2.2	...	...
Belgium - Belgique[23]											
Total	C	27 522	*27 400	...	...	...	2.5	*2.5	...	...	...
Urban - Urbaine	C	27 216	...	...	...	...	2.5	...	...	...	...
Rural - Rurale	C	306	...	...	...	...	1.9	...	...	...	...
Bosnia and Herzegovina - Bosnie-Herzégovine											
Total	C	2 309	2 294	1 608	1 655	...	0.6	0.6	0.4	0.4	...
Bulgaria - Bulgarie[24]											
Total	C	10 581	11 947	10 908	10 584	...	1.4	1.6	1.5	1.5	...
Urban - Urbaine	C	8 849	9 861	...	...	...	1.7	1.9	...	...	...
Rural - Rurale	C	1 732	2 086	...	...	...	0.9	1.0	...	...	...
Croatia - Croatie											
Total	C	5 662	5 659	5 992	6 570	...	1.3	1.3	1.4	1.6	...
Urban - Urbaine	C	3 955	3 894	4 105	4 585	...	...	...	...	...	...
Rural - Rurale	C	1 707	1 765	1 887	1 985	...	...	...	...	...	...
Czech Republic - République tchèque											
Total	C	28 113	26 402	27 895	26 764	...	2.7	2.5	2.7	2.5	...
Urban - Urbaine	C	22 170	20 753	21 882	20 676	...	...	...	2.8	2.7	...
Rural - Rurale	C	5 943	5 649	6 013	6 088	...	...	...	2.1	2.2	...
Denmark - Danemark[25]											
Total	C	14 484	15 709	18 875	19 435	...	2.6	2.8	3.4	3.4	...
Estonia - Estonie											
Total	C	3 099	3 142	3 343	3 218	...	2.3	2.4	2.5	2.4	...
Urban - Urbaine[26]	C	2 169	2 168	2 275	2 197	...	2.4	2.4	2.5	2.4	...
Rural - Rurale[26]	C	848	892	888	836	...	2.0	2.1	2.1	2.0	...
Faeroe Islands - Îles Féroé											
Total	C	87	78	78	84	79	1.8	1.6	1.6	1.7	1.6
Finland - Finlande[27]											
Total	C	13 416	12 977	13 712	13 632	...	2.5	2.4	2.5	2.5	...
Urban - Urbaine	C	10 019	9 637	10 257	10 229	...	2.7	2.6	2.7	2.7	...
Rural - Rurale	C	3 397	3 340	3 455	3 403	...	2.0	2.0	2.1	2.0	...
France											
Total	C	129 802	125 217	121 849	...	...	2.1	2.0	1.9	...	...
Germany - Allemagne											
Total	C	187 640	179 147	169 833	166 199	...	2.3	2.2	2.1	2.1	...
Gibraltar											
Total	+C	93	91	84	...	...	2.9	2.8	2.6	...	...
Greece - Grèce											
Total	C	12 705	14 880	16 717	...	...	1.1	1.3	1.5	...	...
Hungary - Hongrie[11]											
Total	C	23 335	21 830	20 209	19 576	...	2.3	2.2	2.0	2.0	...
Urban - Urbaine[28]	C	17 132	16 164	15 044	14 801	...	2.5	2.4	2.2	2.1	...
Rural - Rurale[28]	C	5 998	5 457	4 928	4 536	...	2.0	1.8	1.6	1.6	...
Iceland - Islande[29]											
Total	C	516	...	...	...	...	1.6	...	...	...	...
Urban - Urbaine[30]	C	504	...	...	...	...	1.6	...	...	...	...
Rural - Rurale[30]	C	4	...	...	...	...	...	...	...	...	...
Ireland - Irlande											
Total	+C	2 819	2 892	...	2 629	...	0.6	0.6	...	0.6	...
Italy - Italie											
Total	C	53 806	51 319	52 943	52 355	...	0.9	0.9	0.9	0.9	...
Latvia - Lettonie											
Total	C	8 302	7 311	7 031	6 271	...	4.0	3.6	3.5	3.1	...

Continent, country or area, and urban/rural residence / Continent, pays ou zone et résidence, urbaine/rurale	Co-de[a]	Number - Nombre					Rate - Taux				
		2011	2012	2013	2014	2015	2011	2012	2013	2014	2015
EUROPE											
Liechtenstein[31]											
Total	C	91	*87	...	...	...	2.5	*2.4	...	...	...
Lithuania - Lituanie											
Total	C	10 341	10 399	9 974	9 806	...	3.4	3.5	3.4	3.3	...
Urban - Urbaine	C	7 128	7 359	6 924	6 831	...	3.5	3.7	3.5	3.5	...
Rural - Rurale	C	3 213	3 040	3 050	2 975	...	3.2	3.1	3.1	3.1	...
Luxembourg											
Total	C	1 218	1 074	1 163	1 453	...	2.3	2.0	2.1	2.6	...
Malta - Malte											
Total	C	42	441	338	323	...	0.1	1.1	0.8	0.8	...
Montenegro - Monténégro											
Total	C	471	515	499	584	...	0.8	0.8	0.8	0.9	...
Netherlands - Pays-Bas[32]											
Total	C	32 510	33 273	33 636	35 409	...	1.9	2.0	2.0	2.1	...
Norway - Norvège[7]											
Total	C	10 207	9 929	10 212	9 918	...	2.1	2.0	2.0	1.9	...
Poland - Pologne											
Total	C	64 594	64 432	66 132	65 761	...	1.7	1.7	1.7	1.7	...
Urban - Urbaine[33]	C	49 186	48 552	...	...	...	2.1	2.1	...	...	...
Rural - Rurale[33]	C	14 855	15 336	...	...	...	1.0	1.0	...	...	...
Portugal[34]											
Total	C	26 751	25 380	22 525	...	...	2.5	2.4	2.2	...	...
Republic of Moldova - République de Moldova											
Total	C	11 120	10 637	...	...	...	3.1	3.0	...	...	...
Urban - Urbaine	C	8 647	7 765	...	...	...	5.8	5.2	...	...	...
Rural - Rurale	C	2 473	2 872	...	...	...	1.2	1.4	...	...	...
Romania - Roumanie											
Total	C	35 780	31 324	28 507	27 188	...	1.8	1.6	1.4	1.4	...
Urban - Urbaine	C	25 152	21 790	19 594	18 692	...	2.3	2.0	1.8	1.7	...
Rural - Rurale	C	10 628	9 534	8 913	8 496	...	1.1	1.0	1.0	0.9	...
Russian Federation - Fédération de Russie											
Total	C	669 376	644 101	...	...	...	4.7	4.5	...	...	...
Urban - Urbaine	C	523 697	502 494	...	...	...	5.0	4.7	...	...	...
Rural - Rurale	C	145 679	141 607	...	...	...	3.9	3.8	...	...	...
San Marino - Saint-Marin											
Total	+C	82	49	54	51		2.5	1.5	1.6	1.5	
Serbia - Serbie[35]											
Total	+C	8 251	7 372	8 170	7 614	...	1.1	1.0	1.1	1.1	...
Urban - Urbaine	+C	6 192	5 410	5 761	5 322	...	1.4	1.3	1.3	1.2	...
Rural - Rurale	+C	2 059	1 962	2 409	2 292	...	0.7	0.7	0.8	0.8	...
Slovakia - Slovaquie											
Total	C	11 102	10 948	10 946	10 514	...	2.1	2.0	2.0	1.9	...
Urban - Urbaine	C	7 053	6 804	6 840	6 490	...	2.4	2.3	2.3	2.2	...
Rural - Rurale	C	4 049	4 144	4 106	4 024	...	1.6	1.7	1.7	1.6	...
Slovenia - Slovénie											
Total	C	2 298	2 509	2 351	2 469	...	1.1	1.2	1.1	1.2	...
Urban - Urbaine	C	1 308	1 422	1 307	1 399	...	1.3	1.4	1.2	1.3	...
Rural - Rurale	C	990	1 087	1 044	1 070	...	1.0	1.1	1.0	1.1	...
Spain - Espagne											
Total	C	103 290	104 262	95 427	100 746	...	2.2	2.2	2.0	2.2	...
Sweden - Suède[7]											
Total	C	23 389	23 422	26 933	26 143	...	2.5	2.5	2.8	2.7	...
Switzerland - Suisse											
Total	U	17 566[36]	17 550	17 119	16 756	...	...	...	...	...	...
Urban - Urbaine	U	13 603[36]	13 457	13 123	...	...	...	...	...	...	...
Rural - Rurale	U	3 963[36]	4 093	3 996	...	...	...	...	...	...	...
TFYR of Macedonia - L'ex-R. y. de Macédoine											
Total	C	1 753	1 926	2 045	2 210	...	0.9	0.9	1.0	1.1	...
Ukraine											
Total	+C	182 490	168 508	164 939	130 673[37]	...	4.0	3.7	3.6	3.0	...

Continent, country or area, and urban/rural residence / Continent, pays ou zone et résidence, urbaine/rurale	Code[a]	Number - Nombre					Rate - Taux				
		2011	2012	2013	2014	2015	2011	2012	2013	2014	2015
EUROPE											
United Kingdom of Great Britain and Northern Ireland - Royaume-Uni de Grande-Bretagne et d'Irlande du Nord[38]											
Total	C	129 764	130 469	...	...	...	2.1	2.0	...	...	...
OCEANIA - OCÉANIE											
American Samoa - Samoas américaines											
Total	C	70	52	61	63	...	1.1	0.8	1.0	1.0	...
Australia - Australie											
Total	C	48 935	49 917	47 638	46 498	...	2.2	2.2	2.1	2.0	...
Guam[39]											
Total	C	878	869	742	749	581	5.5	5.4	4.6	4.7	3.6
New Zealand - Nouvelle-Zélande											
Total	+C	8 551	8 785	8 279	8 171[40]	...	2.0	2.0	1.9	1.8	...

FOOTNOTES - NOTES

Italics: data from civil registers which are incomplete or of unknown completeness. - Italiques : données incomplètes ou dont le degré d'exactitude n'est pas connu, provenant des registres de l'état civil.

* Provisional. - Données provisoires.

a 'Code' indicates the source of data, as follows:
C - Civil registration, estimated over 90% complete
U - Civil registration, estimated less than 90% complete
| - Other source, estimated reliable
+ - Data tabulated by date of registration rather than occurence
... - Information not available

Le 'Code' indique la source des données, comme suit :
C - Registres de l'état civil considérés complets à 90 p. 100 au moins
U - Registres de l'état civil qui ne sont pas considérés complets à 90 p. 100 au moins
| - Autre source, considérée pas douteuses
+ - Données exploitées selon la date de l'enregistrement et non la date de l'événement
... - Information pas disponible

1 Including 'revocable divorces' (among Muslim population), which approximate legal separations. - Y compris les 'divorces révocables' (parmi la population musulmane), qui sont plus au moins l'équivalent des séparations légales.
2 Excludes the islands of St. Brandon and Agalega. - Non compris les îles St. Brandon et Agalega.
3 Urban and rural distribution refers to the usual residence of the wife. Unrevised data. - La répartition entre résidence urbaine et résidence rurale fait référence au lieu de résidence habituel de la femme. Les données n'ont pas été révisées.
4 Data refer to the usual residence of the wife and excludes divorces granted in the country of wives living abroad. - Données relatives à la résidence habituelle de l'épouse, sauf cas de divorces prononcés dans les pays d'épouses vivant à l'étranger.
5 The total number may include 'Unknown residence', but the categories urban and rural do not. - Le nombre total peut inclure les personnes dont la résidence n'est pas connue, à l'inverse des catégories de population urbaine et rurale.
6 Urban and rural distribution refers to the usual residence of the wife. - La répartition entre résidence urbaine et résidence rurale fait référence au lieu de résidence habituel de la femme.
7 Including same sex divorces. - Y compris les divorces entre conjoints du même sexe.

8 Excluding data for California, Georgia, Hawaii, Indiana, Louisiana, and Minnesota. - Non compris les données pour la Californie, la Géorgie, Hawaii, l'Indiana, la Louisiane et le Minnesota.
9 Excludes nomadic Indian tribes. - Non compris les tribus d'Indiens nomades.
10 Data are compiled from the National Registers of Identification and Civil Status (RENIEC). - Les données sont rédigées à partir des Registres Nationaux d'Identification et d'État Civil (RENIEC).
11 Including annulments. - Y compris les annulations.
12 Including annulments. For statistical purposes, the data for China do not include those for the Hong Kong Special Administrative Region (Hong Kong SAR), Macao Special Administrative Region (Macao SAR) and Taiwan province of China. - Y compris les annulations. Pour la présentation des statistiques, les données pour la Chine ne comprennent pas la Région Administrative Spéciale de Hong Kong (Hong Kong RAS), la Région Administrative Spéciale de Macao (Macao RAS) et Taïwan province de Chine.
13 Data refer to government controlled areas. - Les données se rapportent aux zones contrôlées par le Gouvernement.
14 The total number may include 'Unknown residence', but the categories urban and rural do not. Urban and rural residence refers to the place of usual residence of husband. - Le nombre total peut inclure les personnes dont la résidence n'est pas connue, à l'inverse des catégories de population urbaine et rurale. Le lieu de résidence (zone urbaine ou zone rurale) correspond au lieu de résidence habituel du mari.
15 Data refer to the Iranian Year which begins on 21 March and ends on 20 March of the following year. - Les données concernent l'année iranienne, qui commence le 21 mars et se termine le 20 mars de l'année suivante.
16 Includes data for East Jerusalem and Israeli residents in certain other territories under occupation by Israeli military forces since June 1967. - Y compris les données pour Jérusalem-Est et les résidents israéliens dans certains autres territoires occupés depuis 1967 par les forces armées israéliennes.
17 Data refer to Japanese nationals in Japan only. - Les données se raportent aux nationaux japonais au Japon seulement.
18 Excluding data for Jordanian territory under occupation since June 1967 by Israeli military forces. Excluding foreigners, including registered Palestinian refugees. - Non compris les données pour le territoire jordanien occupé depuis juin 1967 par les forces armées israéliennes. Non compris les étrangers, mais y compris les réfugiés de Palestine enregistrés.
19 Data refer to registered events only. - Les données ne concernent que les événements enregistrés.
20 Excluding alien armed forces, civilian aliens employed by armed forces, and foreign diplomatic personnel and their dependants. - Non compris les militaires étrangers, les civils étrangers employés par les forces armées ni le personnel diplomatique étranger et les membres de leur famille les accompagnant.
21 Data from MERNIS (Central Population Administrative System). - Données de MERNIS (Système central de données démographiques).

²² Excluding aliens temporarily in the area. - Non compris les étrangers se trouvant temporairement dans le territoire.

²³ Including divorces among armed forces stationed outside the country and alien armed forces in the area. - Y compris les divorces de militaires nationaux hors du pays et les militaires étrangers en garnison sur le territoire.

²⁴ Including nationals outside the country, but excluding foreigners in the country. Including annulments. - Y compris les nationaux à l'étranger, mais non compris les étrangers sur le territoire. Y compris les annulations.

²⁵ Excluding Faeroe Islands and Greenland shown separately, if available. - Non compris les Iles Féroé et le Groenland, qui font l'objet de rubriques distinctes, si disponible.

²⁶ Urban and rural residence refers to the place of usual residence of husband. The difference between 'Total' and the sum of urban and rural is due to the unknown place of residence of husbands and to husbands living outside the country. - Le lieu de résidence (zone urbaine ou zone rurale) correspond au lieu de résidence habituel du mari. La différence entre le « Total » et la somme des chiffres urbains et ruraux s'explique par le fait que la résidence du mari n'est pas toujours connue ou est située à l'étranger.

²⁷ Excluding Åland Islands. - Non compris les Îles d'Åland.

²⁸ The urban and rural categories do not include the data of foreigners, persons of unknown residence and the homeless, whereas the total category includes them. - Les chiffres portant sur la population urbaine et rurale n' incluent pas les données relatives aux étrangers, aux personnes dont la résidence n'est pas connue et aux personnes sans domicile fixe, à l'inverse, le total les inclut.

²⁹ Data refer to common residence before divorce. - Données se rapportant à la résidence commune avant le divorce.

³⁰ Total includes residence abroad, but the categories urban and rural do not. - Le total compris résidence à l'étranger, à l'inverse des catégories de population urbaine et rurale.

³¹ Data refer to divorces by residence of the husband. - Les données concernent les divorces selon la résidence du mari.

³² Including same sex divorces. Based on the general office for civil registration. - Y compris les divorces entre conjoints du même sexe. Données provenant des services généraux d'état civil.

³³ Data for urban and rural exclude divorces if both persons live abroad. - Les données pour les zones urbaines et rurales excluent le divorce si les deux personnes vivent à l'étranger.

³⁴ Data refer to resident spouses only. - Les données concernent uniquement les conjoints résidents.

³⁵ Excludes data for Kosovo and Metohia. - Sans les données pour le Kosovo et Metohie.

³⁶ Since 2011, there is a break in series. The information on divorces of spouses that are both of foreign nationality are not entirely available for statistics. - A partir de 2011, il y a une rupture de série dans la statistique des divorces. Les informations sur les divorces concernant deux époux de nationalité étrangère ne sont plus toutes disponibles pour la statistique.

³⁷ The Government of Ukraine has informed the United Nations that it is not in a position to provide statistical data concerning the Autonomous Republic of Crimea and the city of Sevastopol. - Le gouvernement Ukrainien a informé l'ONU qu'il n'est pas en mesure de fournir des données statistiques concernant la République autonome de Crimée et la ville de Sébastopol.

³⁸ Excluding Channel Islands (Guernsey and Jersey) and Isle of Man, shown separately, if available. - Non compris les îles Anglo-Normandes (Guernesey et Jersey) et l'île de Man, qui font l'objet de rubriques distinctes, si disponible.

³⁹ Including United States military personnel, their dependants and contract employees. - Y compris les militaires des Etats-Unis, les membres de leur famille les accompagnant et les agents contractuels des Etats-Unis.

⁴⁰ Random rounding to base 3 is applied in this table as a confidentiality measure. - Les chiffres sont arrondis à la base 3 de manière aléatoire, pour des raisons de confidentialité.

Continent and country or area Continent et pays ou zone	Population estimates (in thousands) - Estimations de population (en milliers)									
	2006	**2007**	**2008**	**2009**	**2010**	**2011**	**2012**	**2013**	**2014**	**2015**

AFRICA - AFRIQUE

	2006	2007	2008	2009	2010	2011	2012	2013	2014	2015
Algeria - Algérie	33 749	34 262	34 811	35 402	36 036	36 717	37 439	38 186	38 934	39 667
Angola	18 541	19 184	19 842	20 520	21 220	21 942	22 686	23 448	24 228	25 022
Benin - Bénin	8 444	8 708	8 974	9 241	9 510	9 779	10 050	10 322	10 598	10 880
Botswana	1 896	1 930	1 968	2 007	2 048	2 090	2 133	2 177	2 220	2 262
Burkina Faso	13 834	14 264	14 709	15 166	15 632	16 107	16 591	17 085	17 589	18 106
Burundi	8 218	8 515	8 822	9 138	9 461	9 790	10 125	10 466	10 817	11 179
Cabo Verde	478	481	484	487	490	495	501	507	514	521
Cameroon - Cameroun	18 597	19 078	19 570	20 075	20 591	21 119	21 659	22 211	22 773	23 344
Central African Republic - République centrafricaine	4 127	4 202	4 280	4 361	4 445	4 531	4 620	4 711	4 804	4 900
Chad - Tchad	10 424	10 780	11 140	11 511	11 896	12 299	12 715	13 146	13 587	14 037
Comoros - Comores	634	649	665	682	699	716	734	752	770	788
Congo	3 605	3 716	3 833	3 951	4 066	4 177	4 286	4 394	4 505	4 620
Côte d'Ivoire	18 486	18 862	19 262	19 685	20 132	20 604	21 103	21 622	22 157	22 702
Democratic Republic of the Congo - République démocratique du Congo	57 927	59 835	61 809	63 845	65 939	68 087	70 291	72 553	74 877	77 267
Djibouti	789	799	810	820	831	842	853	865	876	888
Egypt - Égypte	76 274	77 605	78 976	80 442	82 041	83 788	85 661	87 614	89 580	91 508
Equatorial Guinea - Guinée équatoriale	646	666	686	707	729	751	774	797	821	845
Eritrea - Érythrée	4 304	4 406	4 501	4 594	4 690	4 790	4 892	4 999	5 110	5 228
Ethiopia - Éthiopie	78 736	80 892	83 080	85 302	87 562	89 859	92 191	94 558	96 959	99 391
Gabon	1 409	1 441	1 474	1 507	1 542	1 577	1 613	1 650	1 688	1 725
Gambia - Gambie	1 488	1 536	1 587	1 639	1 693	1 749	1 807	1 867	1 928	1 991
Ghana	21 952	22 528	23 116	23 713	24 318	24 929	25 545	26 164	26 787	27 410
Guinea - Guinée	9 898	10 153	10 427	10 716	11 012	11 316	11 629	11 949	12 276	12 609
Guinea-Bissau - Guinée-Bissau	1 495	1 527	1 561	1 597	1 634	1 674	1 715	1 757	1 801	1 844
Kenya	36 286	37 251	38 244	39 270	40 328	41 420	42 543	43 693	44 864	46 050
Lesotho	1 940	1 956	1 972	1 990	2 011	2 033	2 057	2 083	2 109	2 135
Liberia - Libéria	3 385	3 522	3 673	3 821	3 958	4 080	4 190	4 294	4 397	4 503
Libya - Libye	5 907	6 018	6 123	6 209	6 266	6 289	6 283	6 266	6 259	6 278
Madagascar	18 826	19 371	19 927	20 496	21 080	21 679	22 294	22 925	23 572	24 235
Malawi	13 112	13 498	13 905	14 329	14 770	15 227	15 700	16 190	16 695	17 215
Mali	13 310	13 759	14 223	14 695	15 167	15 639	16 112	16 592	17 086	17 600
Mauritania - Mauritanie	3 242	3 328	3 415	3 502	3 591	3 683	3 777	3 873	3 970	4 068
Mauritius - Maurice[1]	1 228	1 233	1 238	1 243	1 248	1 253	1 258	1 264	1 269	1 273
Mayotte	184	190	196	203	209	215	221	227	234	240
Morocco - Maroc	30 691	31 011	31 351	31 715	32 108	32 532	32 984	33 453	33 921	34 378
Mozambique	21 738	22 360	22 995	23 648	24 321	25 017	25 733	26 467	27 216	27 978
Namibia - Namibie	2 054	2 083	2 116	2 152	2 194	2 240	2 292	2 347	2 403	2 459
Niger	13 996	14 528	15 085	15 672	16 292	16 946	17 636	18 359	19 114	19 899
Nigeria - Nigéria	143 318	147 153	151 116	155 207	159 425	163 771	168 240	172 817	177 476	182 202
Republic of South Sudan - République de Soudan du Sud	8 446	8 815	9 209	9 623	10 056	10 510	10 981	11 454	11 911	12 340
Reunion - Réunion	801	809	817	824	831	837	843	849	855	861
Rwanda	9 231	9 481	9 750	10 025	10 294	10 556	10 817	11 078	11 342	11 610
Sao Tome and Principe - Sao Tomé-et-Principe	157	160	164	167	171	175	178	182	186	190
Senegal - Sénégal	11 578	11 897	12 230	12 582	12 957	13 357	13 780	14 221	14 673	15 129
Seychelles	90	91	92	92	93	94	95	95	96	96
Sierra Leone	5 243	5 391	5 522	5 647	5 776	5 909	6 043	6 179	6 316	6 453
Somalia - Somalie	8 687	8 909	9 133	9 357	9 582	9 807	10 034	10 268	10 518	10 787
South Africa - Afrique du Sud	49 028	49 694	50 349	50 992	51 622	52 237	52 837	53 417	53 969	54 490
Sudan - Soudan	32 809	33 638	34 470	35 297	36 115	36 918	37 712	38 515	39 350	40 235
Swaziland	1 118	1 135	1 154	1 174	1 193	1 212	1 232	1 251	1 269	1 287
Togo	5 732	5 890	6 053	6 220	6 391	6 566	6 746	6 929	7 115	7 305
Tunisia - Tunisie	10 196	10 299	10 408	10 522	10 639	10 759	10 881	11 006	11 130	11 254
Uganda - Ouganda	29 001	29 992	31 014	32 067	33 149	34 260	35 401	36 573	37 783	39 032
United Republic of Tanzania - République Unie de Tanzanie	40 261	41 522	42 845	44 222	45 649	47 123	48 646	50 213	51 823	53 470
Western Sahara - Sahara occidental	449	467	483	498	512	525	538	550	561	573
Zambia - Zambie	12 382	12 739	13 115	13 508	13 917	14 344	14 787	15 246	15 721	16 212
Zimbabwe	13 128	13 298	13 495	13 721	13 974	14 256	14 565	14 898	15 246	15 603

AMERICA, NORTH - AMÉRIQUE DU NORD

	2006	2007	2008	2009	2010	2011	2012	2013	2014	2015
Anguilla	13	13	13	14	14	14	14	14	14	15
Antigua and Barbuda - Antigua-et-Barbuda	83	84	85	86	87	88	89	90	91	92
Aruba	101	101	101	101	102	102	102	103	103	104
Bahamas	336	342	349	355	361	367	372	378	383	388
Barbados - Barbade	275	276	277	278	280	281	282	283	283	284

Continent and country or area Continent et pays ou zone	Population estimates (in thousands) - Estimations de population (en milliers)									
	2006	2007	2008	2009	2010	2011	2012	2013	2014	2015

AMERICA, NORTH - AMÉRIQUE DU NORD

Belize...........	291	298	306	314	322	329	337	344	352	359
Bermuda - Bermudes	65	65	65	64	64	64	63	63	62	62
Bonaire, Saba and Sint Eustatius - Bonaire, Saba et Saint-Eustache	15	17	18	20	21	22	23	24	24	25
British Virgin Islands - Îles Vierges britanniques	24	25	26	26	27	28	29	29	30	30
Canada	32 611	32 982	33 363	33 747	34 126	34 500	34 868	35 231	35 588	35 940
Cayman Islands - Îles Caïmanes	50	51	53	54	56	57	58	58	59	60
Costa Rica	4 309	4 369	4 430	4 488	4 545	4 600	4 654	4 706	4 758	4 808
Cuba	11 275	11 284	11 290	11 297	11 308	11 324	11 343	11 363	11 379	11 390
Curaçao	132	136	140	144	148	150	153	154	156	157
Dominica - Dominique	71	71	71	71	71	71	72	72	72	73
Dominican Republic - République dominicaine...............	9 371	9 504	9 636	9 768	9 898	10 027	10 155	10 281	10 406	10 528
El Salvador	5 968	5 986	6 004	6 021	6 038	6 055	6 072	6 090	6 108	6 127
Greenland - Groenland	57	57	57	57	57	56	56	56	56	56
Grenada - Grenade	103	104	104	104	105	105	105	106	106	107
Guadeloupe[2]	453	454	455	456	457	459	461	464	466	468
Guatemala	13 490	13 798	14 107	14 418	14 732	15 049	15 369	15 691	16 015	16 343
Haiti - Haïti	9 409	9 557	9 705	9 853	10 000	10 145	10 289	10 431	10 572	10 711
Honduras	7 007	7 134	7 259	7 383	7 504	7 621	7 736	7 849	7 962	8 075
Jamaica - Jamaïque	2 691	2 705	2 717	2 730	2 741	2 752	2 763	2 773	2 783	2 793
Martinique	397	397	396	395	395	395	395	396	396	396
Mexico - Mexique	111 383	113 139	114 973	116 816	118 618	120 365	122 071	123 740	125 386	127 017
Montserrat	5	5	5	5	5	5	5	5	5	5
Nicaragua	5 450	5 522	5 595	5 667	5 738	5 808	5 877	5 946	6 014	6 082
Panama	3 379	3 438	3 499	3 559	3 621	3 682	3 744	3 806	3 868	3 929
Puerto Rico - Porto Rico...............	3 750	3 739	3 728	3 718	3 710	3 702	3 696	3 691	3 687	3 683
Saint Kitts and Nevis - Saint-Kitts-et-Nevis	50	50	51	52	52	53	54	54	55	56
Saint Lucia - Sainte-Lucie	168	170	173	175	177	179	181	182	184	185
Saint Pierre and Miquelon - Saint Pierre-et-Miquelon..........	6	6	6	6	6	6	6	6	6	6
Saint Vincent and the Grenadines - Saint-Vincent-et-les Grenadines	109	109	109	109	109	109	109	109	109	109
Sint Maarten (Dutch part) - Saint-Martin (partie néerlandaise)...............	33	32	32	33	33	34	35	36	38	39
Trinidad and Tobago - Trinité-et-Tobago	1 303	1 309	1 315	1 322	1 328	1 335	1 342	1 348	1 354	1 360
Turks and Caicos Islands - Îles Turques et Caïques...........	28	29	29	30	31	32	32	33	34	34
United States of America - États-Unis d'Amérique...............	298 861	301 656	304 473	307 232	309 876	312 390	314 799	317 136	319 449	321 774
United States Virgin Islands - Îles Vierges américaines.......	107	107	107	107	106	106	106	106	106	106

AMERICA, SOUTH - AMÉRIQUE DU SUD

Argentina - Argentine	39 559	39 970	40 382	40 799	41 223	41 656	42 095	42 538	42 980	43 417
Bolivia (Plurinational State of) - Bolivie (État plurinational de)	9 283	9 441	9 600	9 759	9 918	10 078	10 239	10 400	10 562	10 725
Brazil - Brésil	190 698	192 785	194 770	196 701	198 614	200 518	202 402	204 259	206 078	207 848
Chile - Chili	16 280	16 463	16 646	16 830	17 015	17 201	17 388	17 576	17 763	17 948
Colombia - Colombie	43 836	44 375	44 902	45 416	45 918	46 406	46 881	47 342	47 791	48 229
Ecuador - Équateur	13 967	14 205	14 448	14 691	14 935	15 177	15 419	15 661	15 903	16 144
Falkland Islands (Malvinas) - Îles Falkland (Malvinas)........	3	3	3	3	3	3	3	3	3	3
French Guiana - Guyane française	210	216	222	228	234	240	247	254	261	269
Guyana...............	744	746	748	751	753	756	758	761	764	767
Paraguay	5 883	5 966	6 047	6 128	6 210	6 294	6 379	6 466	6 553	6 639
Peru - Pérou	27 950	28 293	28 642	29 002	29 374	29 760	30 159	30 565	30 973	31 377
Suriname	496	501	507	513	518	523	529	533	538	543
Uruguay...............	3 331	3 340	3 351	3 363	3 374	3 386	3 397	3 408	3 420	3 432
Venezuela (Bolivarian Republic of) - Venezuela (République bolivarienne du)	27 221	27 671	28 117	28 559	28 996	29 428	29 854	30 276	30 694	31 108

ASIA - ASIE

Afghanistan	25 184	25 878	26 529	27 207	27 962	28 809	29 727	30 683	31 628	32 527
Armenia - Arménie	3 002	2 988	2 975	2 966	2 963	2 968	2 978	2 992	3 006	3 018
Azerbaijan - Azerbaïdjan[3]	8 662	8 763	8 869	8 980	9 100	9 228	9 361	9 497	9 630	9 754
Bahrain - Bahreïn	941	1 027	1 116	1 197	1 261	1 306	1 334	1 349	1 362	1 377
Bangladesh	144 839	146 593	148 252	149 906	151 617	153 406	155 257	157 157	159 078	160 996
Bhutan - Bhoutan	667	681	695	708	720	732	744	755	765	775
Brunei Darussalam - Brunéi Darussalam	368	374	381	387	393	399	406	411	417	423

Continent and country or area Continent et pays ou zone	Population estimates (in thousands) - Estimations de population (en milliers)									
	2006	2007	2008	2009	2010	2011	2012	2013	2014	2015

ASIA - ASIE

	2006	2007	2008	2009	2010	2011	2012	2013	2014	2015
Cambodia - Cambodge	13 525	13 729	13 934	14 144	14 364	14 593	14 832	15 079	15 328	15 578
China - Chine[4]	1 312 601	1 319 625	1 326 691	1 333 807	1 340 969	1 348 174	1 355 387	1 362 514	1 369 436	1 376 049
China, Hong Kong SAR - Chine, Hong Kong RAS	6 856	6 879	6 910	6 949	6 994	7 044	7 102	7 164	7 227	7 288
China, Macao SAR - Chine, Macao RAS	480	493	507	521	535	547	558	568	578	588
Cyprus - Chypre[5]	1 048	1 063	1 077	1 090	1 104	1 117	1 129	1 142	1 154	1 165
Democratic People's Republic of Korea - République populaire démocratique de Corée	23 970	24 112	24 244	24 372	24 501	24 631	24 763	24 896	25 027	25 155
Georgia - Géorgie[6]	4 429	4 386	4 343	4 299	4 250	4 196	4 139	4 083	4 035	4 000
India - Inde	1 162 088	1 179 686	1 197 070	1 214 182	1 230 985	1 247 446	1 263 590	1 279 499	1 295 292	1 311 051
Indonesia - Indonésie	229 264	232 297	235 361	238 465	241 613	244 808	248 038	251 268	254 455	257 564
Iran (Islamic Republic of) - Iran (République islamique d')	70 923	71 721	72 531	73 371	74 253	75 184	76 157	77 152	78 144	79 109
Iraq	27 717	28 424	29 163	29 971	30 868	31 868	32 958	34 107	35 273	36 423
Israel - Israël	6 755	6 921	7 094	7 263	7 420	7 563	7 695	7 818	7 939	8 064
Japan - Japon	127 137	127 250	127 318	127 341	127 320	127 253	127 140	126 985	126 795	126 573
Jordan - Jordanie	5 530	5 759	6 010	6 267	6 518	6 760	6 994	7 215	7 416	7 595
Kazakhstan	15 603	15 755	15 916	16 098	16 311	16 554	16 821	17 100	17 372	17 625
Kuwait - Koweït	2 389	2 539	2 705	2 881	3 059	3 239	3 420	3 594	3 753	3 892
Kyrgyzstan - Kirghizstan	5 167	5 229	5 301	5 380	5 465	5 554	5 648	5 746	5 844	5 940
Lao People's Democratic Republic - République démocratique populaire lao	5 839	5 940	6 045	6 153	6 261	6 367	6 473	6 580	6 689	6 802
Lebanon - Liban	4 057	4 085	4 109	4 182	4 337	4 592	4 924	5 287	5 612	5 851
Malaysia - Malaisie[7]	26 263	26 731	27 197	27 661	28 120	28 573	29 022	29 465	29 902	30 331
Maldives	310	316	321	327	333	339	345	351	357	364
Mongolia - Mongolie	2 558	2 593	2 630	2 670	2 713	2 759	2 808	2 859	2 910	2 959
Myanmar	50 356	50 699	51 030	51 370	51 733	52 125	52 544	52 984	53 437	53 897
Nepal - Népal	25 794	26 064	26 325	26 593	26 876	27 179	27 501	27 835	28 175	28 514
Oman	2 553	2 594	2 652	2 762	2 944	3 210	3 545	3 907	4 236	4 491
Pakistan	156 524	159 768	163 097	166 521	170 044	173 670	177 392	181 193	185 044	188 925
Philippines	87 593	88 966	90 297	91 642	93 039	94 501	96 017	97 572	99 139	100 699
Qatar	988	1 179	1 389	1 591	1 766	1 905	2 016	2 101	2 172	2 235
Republic of Korea - République de Corée	47 902	48 205	48 510	48 807	49 090	49 357	49 608	49 847	50 074	50 293
Saudi Arabia - Arabie saoudite	25 420	26 084	26 743	27 409	28 091	28 788	29 496	30 201	30 887	31 540
Singapore - Singapour	4 615	4 733	4 850	4 965	5 079	5 191	5 300	5 405	5 507	5 604
Sri Lanka	19 672	19 814	19 950	20 079	20 201	20 316	20 422	20 522	20 619	20 715
State of Palestine - État de Palestine	3 663	3 755	3 855	3 960	4 069	4 181	4 298	4 418	4 542	4 668
Syrian Arab Republic - République arabe syrienne	18 728	19 426	20 097	20 567	20 721	20 501	19 979	19 323	18 772	18 502
Tajikistan - Tadjikistan	6 950	7 099	7 254	7 415	7 582	7 754	7 931	8 112	8 296	8 482
Thailand - Thaïlande	66 174	66 354	66 453	66 548	66 692	66 903	67 164	67 451	67 726	67 959
Timor-Leste	1 008	1 021	1 031	1 042	1 057	1 078	1 102	1 129	1 157	1 185
Turkey - Turquie	68 705	69 515	70 344	71 261	72 310	73 517	74 849	76 224	77 524	78 666
Turkmenistan - Turkménistan	4 802	4 858	4 918	4 979	5 042	5 107	5 173	5 240	5 307	5 374
United Arab Emirates - Émirats arabes unis	5 171	6 010	6 900	7 705	8 329	8 735	8 953	9 040	9 086	9 157
Uzbekistan - Ouzbékistan	26 243	26 587	26 953	27 338	27 740	28 158	28 592	29 033	29 470	29 893
Viet Nam	84 980	85 771	86 589	87 449	88 358	89 322	90 336	91 379	92 423	93 448
Yemen - Yémen	21 094	21 701	22 323	22 954	23 592	24 235	24 883	25 533	26 184	26 832

EUROPE

	2006	2007	2008	2009	2010	2011	2012	2013	2014	2015
Albania - Albanie	3 051	3 011	2 968	2 930	2 902	2 886	2 881	2 883	2 890	2 897
Andorra - Andorre	83	85	86	85	84	82	79	76	73	70
Austria - Autriche	8 269	8 301	8 331	8 361	8 392	8 424	8 455	8 487	8 517	8 545
Belarus - Bélarus	9 594	9 556	9 526	9 505	9 492	9 488	9 491	9 497	9 500	9 496
Belgium - Belgique	10 632	10 705	10 779	10 854	10 930	11 005	11 080	11 153	11 226	11 299
Bosnia and Herzegovina - Bosnie-Herzégovine	3 839	3 840	3 840	3 838	3 835	3 832	3 828	3 824	3 818	3 810
Bulgaria - Bulgarie	7 625	7 568	7 514	7 460	7 407	7 355	7 304	7 253	7 201	7 150
Croatia - Croatie	4 369	4 357	4 344	4 330	4 316	4 302	4 287	4 271	4 256	4 240
Czech Republic - République tchèque	10 271	10 330	10 398	10 460	10 507	10 534	10 545	10 545	10 543	10 543
Denmark - Danemark	5 441	5 467	5 495	5 524	5 551	5 577	5 601	5 624	5 647	5 669
Estonia - Estonie	1 349	1 344	1 340	1 336	1 332	1 328	1 324	1 320	1 316	1 313
Faeroe Islands - Îles Féroé	49	49	49	49	49	48	48	48	48	48
Finland - Finlande[8]	5 267	5 289	5 314	5 340	5 368	5 396	5 425	5 453	5 480	5 503
France	61 610	61 966	62 310	62 641	62 961	63 268	63 562	63 845	64 121	64 395
Germany - Allemagne	81 056	80 855	80 666	80 520	80 435	80 425	80 478	80 566	80 646	80 689
Gibraltar	29	30	30	30	31	31	31	32	32	32
Greece - Grèce	11 098	11 131	11 162	11 179	11 178	11 153	11 110	11 055	11 001	10 955
Holy See - Saint-Siège	1	1	1	1	1	1	1	1	1	1
Hungary - Hongrie	10 078	10 064	10 051	10 035	10 015	9 989	9 958	9 925	9 890	9 855

Annex I: Mid-year population, United Nations estimates: 2006 - 2015
Annexe I : Population au milieu de l'année, estimations des Nations Unies : 2006 - 2015 (continued - suite)

Continent and country or area Continent et pays ou zone	Population estimates (in thousands) - Estimations de population (en milliers)									
	2006	2007	2008	2009	2010	2011	2012	2013	2014	2015

EUROPE

	2006	2007	2008	2009	2010	2011	2012	2013	2014	2015
Iceland - Islande	301	305	310	314	318	321	323	325	327	329
Ireland - Irlande	4 294	4 389	4 480	4 559	4 617	4 653	4 668	4 671	4 675	4 688
Isle of Man - Île de Man	81	82	83	84	84	85	86	86	87	88
Italy - Italie	58 918	59 139	59 319	59 467	59 588	59 679	59 738	59 771	59 789	59 798
Latvia - Lettonie	2 199	2 171	2 144	2 117	2 091	2 064	2 037	2 012	1 989	1 971
Liechtenstein	35	35	36	36	36	37	37	37	37	38
Lithuania - Lituanie	3 306	3 264	3 220	3 172	3 123	3 071	3 016	2 964	2 917	2 878
Luxembourg	466	475	485	496	508	520	532	545	557	567
Malta - Malte	400	403	406	409	412	414	416	417	418	419
Monaco	34	35	36	36	37	37	37	38	38	38
Montenegro - Monténégro	617	619	620	621	622	623	624	625	625	626
Netherlands - Pays-Bas	16 401	16 463	16 520	16 575	16 632	16 690	16 749	16 809	16 868	16 925
Norway - Norvège[9]	4 667	4 717	4 772	4 830	4 891	4 954	5 018	5 083	5 148	5 211
Poland - Pologne	38 479	38 500	38 526	38 551	38 575	38 594	38 609	38 619	38 620	38 612
Portugal	10 517	10 551	10 577	10 590	10 585	10 559	10 515	10 460	10 402	10 350
Republic of Moldova - République de Moldova[10]	4 145	4 128	4 111	4 096	4 084	4 078	4 075	4 074	4 072	4 069
Romania - Roumanie	21 206	20 980	20 742	20 510	20 299	20 112	19 945	19 794	19 652	19 511
Russian Federation - Fédération de Russie	143 338	143 180	143 123	143 127	143 158	143 211	143 288	143 367	143 429	143 457
San Marino - Saint-Marin	30	30	30	30	31	31	31	31	32	32
Serbia - Serbie[11]	9 155	9 130	9 110	9 087	9 059	9 024	8 983	8 938	8 893	8 851
Slovakia - Slovaquie	5 388	5 392	5 397	5 402	5 407	5 411	5 415	5 419	5 423	5 426
Slovenia - Slovénie	2 006	2 017	2 031	2 043	2 052	2 059	2 063	2 065	2 066	2 068
Spain - Espagne[12]	44 538	45 210	45 817	46 295	46 601	46 708	46 637	46 455	46 260	46 122
Sweden - Suède	9 087	9 153	9 226	9 303	9 382	9 462	9 543	9 624	9 703	9 779
Switzerland - Suisse	7 480	7 560	7 647	7 737	7 831	7 926	8 023	8 119	8 211	8 299
TFYR of Macedonia - L'ex-R. y. de Macédoine	2 047	2 051	2 055	2 059	2 062	2 066	2 069	2 073	2 076	2 078
Ukraine[13]	46 503	46 249	46 028	45 831	45 647	45 478	45 320	45 165	45 002	44 824
United Kingdom of Great Britain and Northern Ireland - Royaume-Uni de Grande-Bretagne et d'Irlande du Nord	60 649	61 152	61 690	62 221	62 717	63 165	63 574	63 956	64 331	64 716

OCEANIA - OCÉANIE

	2006	2007	2008	2009	2010	2011	2012	2013	2014	2015
American Samoa - Samoas américaines	59	58	57	56	56	55	55	55	55	56
Australia - Australie[14]	20 606	20 976	21 370	21 771	22 163	22 542	22 911	23 270	23 622	23 969
Cook Islands - Îles Cook	20	20	20	20	20	20	21	21	21	21
Fiji - Fidji	827	835	843	852	860	867	874	880	886	892
French Polynesia - Polynésie française	258	260	263	265	268	271	274	277	280	283
Guam	158	158	158	159	159	161	163	165	168	170
Kiribati	94	96	98	101	103	105	107	109	110	112
Marshall Islands - Îles Marshall	52	52	52	52	52	53	53	53	53	53
Micronesia (Federated States of) - Micronésie (États fédérés de)	106	105	104	104	104	103	104	104	104	104
Nauru	10	10	10	10	10	10	10	10	10	10
New Caledonia - Nouvelle-Calédonie	232	236	239	243	246	250	253	256	260	263
New Zealand - Nouvelle-Zélande	4 188	4 238	4 285	4 329	4 369	4 404	4 436	4 465	4 495	4 529
Niue - Nioué	2	2	2	2	2	2	2	2	2	2
Northern Mariana Islands - Îles Mariannes septentrionales	62	60	57	55	54	53	53	54	55	55
Palau - Palaos	20	20	20	20	20	21	21	21	21	21
Papua New Guinea - Papouasie-Nouvelle-Guinée	6 236	6 387	6 540	6 694	6 848	7 001	7 155	7 309	7 464	7 619
Samoa	181	182	183	185	186	187	189	190	192	193
Solomon Islands - Îles Salomon	481	492	503	515	526	538	549	561	572	584
Tokelau - Tokélaou	1	1	1	1	1	1	1	1	1	1
Tonga	102	102	103	103	104	104	105	105	106	106
Tuvalu	10	10	10	10	10	10	10	10	10	10
Vanuatu	215	220	225	231	236	242	247	253	259	265
Wallis and Futuna Islands - Îles Wallis et Futuna	14	14	14	14	14	13	13	13	13	13

SOURCE

United Nations, Department of Economic and Social Affairs, Population Division (2015). 2015 Revision of World Population Prospects - Organisation des Nations Unies, Département des affaires économiques et sociales, Division de la population (2015). Perspectives de la population mondiale : La révision de 2015

FOOTNOTES - NOTES

[1] Including Agalega, Rodrigues and Saint Brandon. - Y compris Agalega, Rodrigues et Saint Brandon.

[2] Including Saint-Barthélemy and Saint-Martin (French part). - Y compris Saint-Barthélemy et Saint-Martin (partie française).

[3] Including Nagorno-Karabakh. - Y compris le Haut-Karabakh.

[4] For statistical purposes, the data for China do not include Hong Kong and Macao Special Administrative Regions (SAR) of China. - A des fins statistiques, les données pour la Chine ne comprennent pas les Régions Administratives Spéciales (SAR) de Hong Kong et Macao.

[5] Refers to the whole country. - Les données se rapportent au pays en entier.

[6] Including Abkhazia and South Ossetia. - Y compris l'Abkhazie et l'Ossétie du Sud.

[7] Including Sabah and Sarawak. - Y compris le Sabah et le Sarawak.

[8] Including Åland Islands. - Y compris les îles Åland.

[9] Including Svalbard and Jan Mayen Islands. - Y compris Svalbard et l'île Jan Mayen.

[10] Including Transnistria. - Y compris la Transnistrie.

[11] Including Kosovo. - Y compris le Kosovo.

[12] Including Canary Islands, Ceuta and Melilla. - Y compris les îles Canaries, Ceuta et Melilla.

[13] Including Crimea. - Y compris la Crimée.

[14] Including Christmas Island, Cocos (Keeling) Islands and Norfolk Island. - Y compris les îles Christmas, Cocos (Keeling) et Norfolk.

Annex II: Vital statistics summary, United Nations estimates: 2010-2015
Annexe II: Aperçu des statistiques de l'état civil, estimations des Nations Unies : 2010-2015

Continent and country or area Continent et pays ou zone	Crude birth rate - Taux bruts de natalité	Crude death rate - Taux bruts de mortalité	Infant mortality rate - Décès d'enfants de moins d'un an	Life expectancy at birth - Espérance de vie à la naissance		Total fertility rate - Indice synthétique de fécondité	Natural increase - Accroissement naturel
				Male - Masculin	Female - Féminin		
AFRICA - AFRIQUE							
Algeria - Algérie..	25.1	5.1	30.3	72.1	76.8	2.93	19.9
Angola..	46.2	14.2	96.2	50.2	53.2	6.20	32.0
Benin - Bénin...	36.6	9.6	68.7	57.8	60.6	4.89	27.1
Botswana...	25.6	7.5	32.5	61.8	66.5	2.90	18.1
Burkina Faso..	40.8	10.0	66.5	56.7	59.3	5.65	30.8
Burundi..	44.2	11.7	77.9	54.2	58.0	6.08	32.5
Cabo Verde..	21.8	5.5	20.1	71.1	74.7	2.37	16.3
Cameroon - Cameroun...	37.5	11.9	73.5	53.7	56.0	4.82	25.6
Central African Republic - République centrafricaine............	34.3	15.2	93.5	47.8	51.3	4.41	19.1
Chad - Tchad...	45.9	14.5	95.8	50.1	52.2	6.31	31.5
Comoros - Comores...	34.6	7.7	58.1	61.2	64.5	4.60	26.8
Congo..	37.3	9.0	50.6	60.0	62.9	4.95	28.3
Côte d'Ivoire..	37.4	13.9	73.4	50.2	51.9	5.10	23.5
Democratic Republic of the Congo - République démocratique du Congo	42.6	10.7	73.2	56.7	59.5	6.15	31.9
Djibouti..	25.7	8.7	55.3	60.0	63.2	3.30	17.0
Egypt - Égypte...	28.5	6.2	18.9	68.7	73.1	3.38	22.3
Equatorial Guinea - Guinée équatoriale..............................	35.5	11.0	70.1	55.9	58.6	4.97	24.5
Eritrea - Érythrée...	35.0	6.9	46.5	60.9	65.2	4.40	28.2
Ethiopia - Éthiopie...	33.2	7.8	50.0	61.3	65.0	4.59	25.4
Gabon..	30.8	9.0	43.2	63.2	64.1	4.00	21.8
Gambia - Gambie...	42.8	9.0	47.1	58.5	61.2	5.78	33.8
Ghana..	33.5	9.2	51.1	60.1	62.0	4.25	24.3
Guinea - Guinée..	37.6	10.4	59.2	57.6	58.5	5.14	27.2
Guinea-Bissau - Guinée-Bissau...	37.7	12.4	91.9	53.0	56.5	4.95	25.3
Kenya..	35.4	8.7	52.5	59.1	62.2	4.44	26.7
Lesotho..	28.9	14.9	60.1	49.2	49.6	3.26	13.9
Liberia - Libéria...	35.7	9.0	61.2	59.3	61.2	4.83	26.7
Libya - Libye..	21.7	5.3	24.3	68.8	74.4	2.53	16.4
Madagascar...	34.8	6.9	36.8	63.0	66.0	4.50	27.9
Malawi...	39.6	8.6	60.1	59.9	62.0	5.25	31.0
Mali..	44.4	11.0	84.0	57.4	57.0	6.35	33.4
Mauritania - Mauritanie...	34.0	8.1	67.3	61.3	64.3	4.69	25.9
Mauritius - Maurice[1]...	11.4	7.3	12.0	70.7	77.7	1.50	4.0
Mayotte..	31.7	2.5	4.2	76.0	82.9	4.10	29.2
Morocco - Maroc...	21.3	5.7	26.3	72.6	74.6	2.56	15.5
Mozambique...	40.0	11.8	64.4	52.9	56.2	5.45	28.2
Namibia - Namibie...	30.2	7.3	33.5	61.6	67.0	3.60	22.9
Niger..	49.8	9.6	59.8	59.9	61.6	7.63	40.2
Nigeria - Nigéria..	40.3	13.3	76.3	52.0	52.6	5.74	27.0
Republic of South Sudan - République de Soudan du Sud ...	37.3	12.0	77.7	54.1	56.0	5.15	25.3
Reunion - Réunion...	15.7	5.5	4.2	76.0	82.9	2.24	10.2
Rwanda..	32.9	7.5	49.2	59.7	66.3	4.05	25.4
Sao Tome and Principe - Sao Tomé-et-Principe	34.9	7.1	43.5	64.2	68.2	4.67	27.8
Senegal - Sénégal...	38.9	6.6	44.3	63.9	67.6	5.18	32.4
Seychelles...	18.0	7.6	10.2	68.7	77.9	2.33	10.4
Sierra Leone..	36.9	14.1	94.4	49.7	50.7	4.79	22.8
Somalia - Somalie	43.9	12.4	79.5	53.3	56.5	6.61	31.5
South Africa - Afrique du Sud...	21.0	12.5	38.3	54.9	59.1	2.40	8.6
Sudan - Soudan	33.7	7.9	53.3	61.6	64.6	4.46	25.8
Swaziland	30.2	14.1	64.6	49.7	48.5	3.36	16.1
Togo...	36.3	9.3	50.2	58.3	59.7	4.69	27.0
Tunisia - Tunisie..	18.4	6.6	18.7	72.3	77.0	2.16	11.8
Uganda - Ouganda..	43.7	10.2	61.2	55.7	58.8	5.91	33.4
United Republic of Tanzania - République Unie de Tanzanie	39.7	7.3	37.0	62.6	65.6	5.24	32.4
Western Sahara - Sahara occidental	19.1	5.6	37.2	65.9	69.8	2.20	13.5
Zambia - Zambie	40.6	9.7	55.4	57.2	60.3	5.45	30.9
Zimbabwe...	36.1	11.1	48.4	53.6	56.0	4.02	25.0
AMERICA, NORTH - AMÉRIQUE DU NORD							
Antigua and Barbuda - Antigua-et-Barbuda	16.5	6.2	9.1	73.3	78.2	2.10	10.4
Aruba...	10.3	8.3	14.8	72.9	77.8	1.68	2.0
Bahamas..	15.4	6.0	9.1	72.0	78.1	1.89	9.4
Barbados - Barbade	12.2	10.5	9.6	72.9	77.7	1.79	1.8
Belize...	23.3	5.6	14.3	67.2	72.7	2.64	17.7

Continent and country or area Continent et pays ou zone	Crude birth rate - Taux bruts de natalité	Crude death rate - Taux bruts de mortalité	Infant mortality rate - Décès d'enfants de moins d'un an	Life expectancy at birth - Espérance de vie à la naissance		Total fertility rate - Indice synthétique de fécondité	Natural increase - Accroissement naturel
				Male - Masculin	Female - Féminin		
AMERICA, NORTH - AMÉRIQUE DU NORD							
Canada..	10.9	7.3	4.7	79.7	83.8	1.61	3.6
Costa Rica...	15.1	4.7	9.3	76.7	81.7	1.85	10.4
Cuba...	10.5	7.7	5.5	77.1	81.3	1.63	2.8
Curaçao...	13.3	8.2	10.3	74.5	80.7	2.10	5.1
Dominican Republic - République dominicaine...................	21.4	6.0	25.1	70.2	76.5	2.53	15.3
El Salvador..	17.5	6.7	17.0	67.9	77.1	1.97	10.8
Grenada - Grenade...	19.4	7.2	9.6	70.8	75.6	2.18	12.1
Guadeloupe[2]..	13.7	7.1	5.8	76.8	84.0	2.17	6.6
Guatemala..	27.7	5.4	22.6	67.9	75.0	3.30	22.3
Haiti - Haïti..	25.5	8.9	47.0	60.2	64.4	3.13	16.6
Honduras...	21.7	5.0	27.8	70.4	75.4	2.47	16.7
Jamaica - Jamaïque...	17.6	6.8	15.0	73.1	77.9	2.08	10.8
Martinique..	11.7	8.0	6.4	77.8	84.4	1.95	3.8
Mexico - Mexique..	19.3	4.8	18.8	74.0	78.9	2.29	14.5
Nicaragua..	21.0	4.8	20.0	71.4	77.5	2.32	16.2
Panama...	19.8	5.0	15.2	74.3	80.5	2.48	14.9
Puerto Rico - Porto Rico...	12.1	7.9	6.3	75.2	83.2	1.64	4.2
Saint Lucia - Sainte-Lucie.......................................	15.5	7.2	10.9	72.2	77.6	1.92	8.3
Saint Vincent and the Grenadines - Saint-Vincent-et-les Grenadines..	16.4	7.0	16.5	70.7	74.9	2.01	9.4
Trinidad and Tobago - Trinité-et-Tobago......................	14.7	9.2	24.8	66.9	73.8	1.80	5.5
United States of America - États-Unis d'Amérique..........	12.6	8.2	6.0	76.5	81.3	1.89	4.4
United States Virgin Islands - Îles Vierges américaines.........	14.1	7.4	9.4	77.2	82.9	2.30	6.6
AMERICA, SOUTH - AMÉRIQUE DU SUD							
Argentina - Argentine...	17.8	7.6	13.7	72.2	79.8	2.35	10.2
Bolivia (Plurinational State of) - Bolivie (État plurinational de)...	24.4	7.6	42.9	65.3	70.2	3.04	16.8
Brazil - Brésil...	15.1	6.1	20.3	70.3	77.9	1.82	9.1
Chile - Chili..	13.5	5.1	7.2	78.1	84.1	1.78	8.4
Colombia - Colombie..	16.2	5.8	17.9	70.2	77.4	1.93	10.4
Ecuador - Équateur...	21.2	5.2	21.1	72.8	78.4	2.59	16.1
French Guiana - Guyane française.............................	26.1	3.2	9.5	75.8	82.6	3.48	22.9
Guyana...	18.8	8.0	33.2	64.0	68.6	2.60	10.8
Paraguay...	21.7	5.6	28.8	70.7	74.9	2.60	16.1
Peru - Pérou..	20.4	5.6	18.6	71.5	76.8	2.50	14.8
Suriname...	18.6	7.3	17.4	67.8	74.2	2.40	11.2
Uruguay..	14.4	9.3	12.7	73.3	80.4	2.04	5.1
Venezuela (Bolivarian Republic of) - Venezuela (République bolivarienne du)...	20.0	5.5	13.8	69.9	78.2	2.41	14.5
ASIA - ASIE							
Afghanistan..	35.6	8.6	71.1	58.7	61.1	5.14	27.1
Armenia - Arménie...	13.3	9.0	13.2	70.7	78.4	1.55	4.3
Azerbaijan - Azerbaïdjan[3].....................................	21.2	7.0	39.6	67.5	73.8	2.30	14.2
Bahrain - Bahreïn..	15.4	2.3	6.9	75.6	77.4	2.10	13.0
Bangladesh..	20.4	5.5	33.1	69.9	72.3	2.23	14.8
Bhutan - Bhoutan..	18.2	6.3	30.5	68.6	69.1	2.10	11.9
Brunei Darussalam - Brunéi Darussalam.....................	16.6	3.0	4.2	76.6	80.4	1.90	13.6
Cambodia - Cambodge...	24.5	6.3	29.9	65.5	69.6	2.70	18.2
China - Chine[4]..	12.4	7.0	11.6	74.0	77.0	1.55	5.4
China, Hong Kong SAR - Chine, Hong Kong RAS............	10.1	6.0	1.8	80.9	86.6	1.20	4.0
China, Macao SAR - Chine, Macao RAS.......................	11.2	4.8	4.1	78.1	82.5	1.19	6.4
Cyprus - Chypre[5]..	11.5	6.8	4.2	77.7	82.2	1.46	4.7
Democratic People's Republic of Korea - République populaire démocratique de Corée..........................	14.4	9.2	22.0	66.3	73.3	2.00	5.3
Georgia - Géorgie[6]..	13.7	11.5	13.7	70.9	78.1	1.81	2.2
India - Inde..	20.4	7.4	41.4	66.1	68.9	2.48	13.0
Indonesia - Indonésie...	20.5	7.2	25.0	66.6	70.7	2.50	13.3
Iran (Islamic Republic of) - Iran (République islamique d').....	18.1	4.7	14.8	74.0	76.2	1.75	13.4
Iraq..	35.1	5.3	32.1	67.0	71.4	4.64	29.8
Israel - Israël...	21.5	5.3	3.5	80.2	83.8	3.05	16.1
Japan - Japon..	8.3	10.0	2.2	80.0	86.5	1.40	-1.7

853

Continent and country or area / Continent et pays ou zone	Crude birth rate - Taux bruts de natalité	Crude death rate - Taux bruts de mortalité	Infant mortality rate - Décès d'enfants de moins d'un an	Life expectancy at birth - Espérance de vie à la naissance		Total fertility rate - Indice synthétique de fécondité	Natural increase - Accroissement naturel
				Male - Masculin	Female - Féminin		
ASIA - ASIE							
Jordan - Jordanie	27.9	3.9	17.1	72.2	75.5	3.51	24.0
Kazakhstan..	22.5	8.9	14.1	64.3	73.9	2.64	13.6
Kuwait - Koweït	20.7	2.5	8.6	73.3	75.6	2.15	18.1
Kyrgyzstan - Kirghizstan....................................	27.1	6.4	19.6	66.4	74.3	3.12	20.7
Lao People's Democratic Republic - République démocratique populaire lao	27.2	7.0	46.8	64.1	66.8	3.10	20.2
Lebanon - Liban	15.0	4.6	9.3	77.1	80.9	1.72	10.3
Malaysia - Malaisie[7]	16.9	4.8	6.8	72.2	76.9	1.97	12.1
Maldives	21.7	3.8	9.0	75.4	77.4	2.18	17.9
Mongolia - Mongolie	24.6	6.2	25.8	64.8	73.3	2.68	18.4
Myanmar	18.2	8.3	46.5	63.6	67.7	2.25	10.0
Nepal - Népal	21.0	6.5	32.4	67.6	70.5	2.32	14.5
Oman...	20.8	2.7	7.3	74.7	78.9	2.88	18.1
Pakistan..	29.8	7.5	69.8	65.0	66.8	3.72	22.2
Philippines	24.0	6.7	23.2	64.7	71.6	3.04	17.3
Qatar	12.1	1.5	6.5	77.1	79.7	2.08	10.6
Republic of Korea - République de Corée...........	9.2	5.5	2.9	78.0	84.6	1.26	3.6
Saudi Arabia - Arabie saoudite..........................	20.8	3.4	15.3	72.8	75.5	2.85	17.4
Singapore - Singapour	9.3	4.5	1.8	79.6	85.6	1.23	4.8
Sri Lanka	16.4	6.7	8.2	71.2	78.0	2.11	9.8
State of Palestine - État de Palestine.................	33.1	3.6	20.6	70.7	74.7	4.28	29.5
Syrian Arab Republic - République arabe syrienne	24.1	5.6	17.9	64.0	76.3	3.03	18.5
Tajikistan - Tadjikistan.......................................	31.0	5.7	39.9	65.9	72.8	3.55	25.3
Thailand - Thaïlande	11.2	7.7	11.2	70.8	77.6	1.54	3.5
Timor-Leste	38.7	7.0	43.9	66.1	69.5	5.91	31.7
Turkey - Turquie	17.3	5.7	12.6	71.5	78.1	2.10	11.5
Turkmenistan - Turkménistan.............................	21.5	7.8	46.7	61.3	69.7	2.34	13.7
United Arab Emirates - Émirats arabes unis	11.2	1.5	6.2	76.0	78.2	1.82	9.7
Uzbekistan - Ouzbékistan	23.3	7.0	44.0	64.9	71.6	2.48	16.3
Viet Nam	17.4	5.8	19.3	70.7	80.3	1.96	11.6
Yemen - Yémen	33.2	7.1	53.6	62.2	64.9	4.35	26.1
EUROPE							
Albania - Albanie	13.1	7.2	14.4	75.0	80.2	1.78	6.0
Austria - Autriche..	9.5	9.4	3.1	78.5	83.6	1.47	0.1
Belarus - Bélarus..	11.7	14.2	4.0	65.3	77.0	1.58	-2.5
Belgium - Belgique	11.6	9.8	3.3	78.0	83.0	1.82	1.8
Bosnia and Herzegovina - Bosnie-Herzégovine...	9.1	10.3	7.6	73.7	78.8	1.28	-1.2
Bulgaria - Bulgarie	9.4	15.1	9.0	70.6	77.6	1.52	-5.7
Croatia - Croatie	9.8	12.4	3.9	73.6	80.4	1.52	-2.6
Czech Republic - République tchèque	10.2	10.1	2.5	75.4	81.3	1.45	0.1
Denmark - Danemark...	10.4	9.7	3.5	78.0	81.9	1.73	0.8
Estonia - Estonie	10.7	11.9	3.2	71.6	81.1	1.59	-1.2
Finland - Finlande[8]	10.7	9.6	2.3	77.6	83.4	1.75	1.0
France	12.4	8.9	3.3	78.8	84.9	2.00	3.5
Germany - Allemagne	8.3	10.8	3.1	78.2	83.1	1.39	-2.5
Greece - Grèce...	8.9	10.5	2.8	77.6	83.6	1.34	-1.6
Hungary - Hongrie...	9.3	13.2	4.6	71.2	78.5	1.34	-3.8
Iceland - Islande	13.6	6.3	2.0	80.7	83.8	1.96	7.3
Ireland - Irlande	15.4	6.4	2.9	78.4	82.7	2.01	9.1
Italy - Italie	8.6	9.7	2.3	80.3	85.2	1.43	-1.1
Latvia - Lettonie..	10.0	14.5	6.5	68.9	78.7	1.48	-4.6
Lithuania - Lituanie...	10.2	15.2	3.8	67.4	78.8	1.57	-5.0
Luxembourg	11.3	7.4	1.6	78.9	83.7	1.57	3.9
Malta - Malte	8.9	8.8	4.8	78.6	82.0	1.44	0.2
Montenegro - Monténégro	11.9	9.9	4.4	73.8	78.2	1.71	2.0
Netherlands - Pays-Bas	10.6	8.4	3.5	79.4	83.1	1.75	2.2
Norway - Norvège[9]	11.7	8.4	2.5	79.2	83.4	1.80	3.3
Poland - Pologne	10.4	9.8	4.6	73.1	81.1	1.37	0.6
Portugal..	8.5	10.3	3.3	77.4	83.5	1.28	-1.8
Republic of Moldova - République de Moldova[10]	10.9	11.2	10.9	67.2	75.4	1.27	-0.3
Romania - Roumanie	9.4	12.9	9.6	70.9	78.1	1.48	-3.5
Russian Federation - Fédération de Russie........	12.7	13.9	8.2	64.2	75.6	1.66	-1.1
Serbia - Serbie[11]	10.2	12.7	9.8	71.8	77.5	1.56	-2.4
Slovakia - Slovaquie	10.5	9.8	4.9	72.2	79.7	1.37	0.7

Continent and country or area Continent et pays ou zone	Crude birth rate - Taux bruts de natalité	Crude death rate - Taux bruts de mortalité	Infant mortality rate - Décès d'enfants de moins d'un an	Life expectancy at birth - Espérance de vie à la naissance		Total fertility rate - Indice synthétique de fécondité	Natural increase - Accroissement naturel
				Male - Masculin	Female - Féminin		
EUROPE							
Slovenia - Slovénie...............................	10.5	9.4	2.9	76.9	83.1	1.58	1.0
Spain - Espagne[12]...............................	9.3	8.8	3.0	79.4	85.1	1.32	0.5
Sweden - Suède..................................	12.0	9.4	2.8	80.1	83.7	1.92	2.6
Switzerland - Suisse............................	10.2	8.1	3.7	80.4	84.7	1.52	2.1
TFYR of Macedonia - L'ex-R. y. de Macédoine.............	11.3	9.2	10.1	72.9	77.5	1.51	2.0
Ukraine[13]	10.8	15.3	9.2	65.7	75.7	1.49	-4.5
United Kingdom of Great Britain and Northern Ireland - Royaume-Uni de Grande-Bretagne et d'Irlande du Nord	12.6	9.2	4.2	78.5	82.4	1.92	3.5
OCEANIA - OCÉANIE							
Australia - Australie[14]	13.5	6.7	4.0	79.9	84.3	1.92	6.8
Fiji - Fidji..	20.7	6.8	16.0	66.9	72.9	2.61	13.9
French Polynesia - Polynésie française	16.5	5.5	6.9	74.0	78.6	2.07	11.0
Guam..	17.5	4.8	9.7	76.1	81.5	2.42	12.7
Kiribati...	29.2	7.1	46.7	62.6	68.9	3.79	22.1
Micronesia (Federated States of) - Micronésie (États fédérés de)	23.6	6.2	32.7	68.0	69.9	3.33	17.4
New Caledonia - Nouvelle-Calédonie	15.7	6.9	13.1	73.6	79.3	2.13	8.7
New Zealand - Nouvelle-Zélande.................	13.7	6.8	4.3	79.7	83.4	2.05	6.8
Papua New Guinea - Papouasie-Nouvelle-Guinée	29.1	7.7	47.6	60.3	64.5	3.84	21.3
Samoa..	26.4	5.4	19.7	70.0	76.4	4.16	21.0
Solomon Islands - Îles Salomon.................	30.9	5.9	38.0	66.2	69.0	4.06	25.0
Tonga..	25.7	6.1	20.4	69.7	75.6	3.79	19.6
Vanuatu	26.9	4.8	23.9	69.6	73.6	3.41	22.2

SOURCE

United Nations, Department of Economic and Social Affairs, Population Division (2015). 2015 Revision of World Population Prospects - Organisation des Nations Unies, Département des affaires économiques et sociales, Division de la population (2015). Perspectives de la population mondiale : La révision de 2015

FOOTNOTES - NOTES

[1] Including Agalega, Rodrigues and Saint Brandon. - Y compris Agalega, Rodrigues et Saint Brandon.

[2] Including Saint-Barthélemy and Saint-Martin (French part). - Y compris Saint-Barthélemy et Saint-Martin (partie française).

[3] Including Nagorno-Karabakh. - Y compris le Haut-Karabakh.

[4] For statistical purposes, the data for China do not include Hong Kong and Macao Special Administrative Regions (SAR) of China. - A des fins statistiques, les données pour la Chine ne comprennent pas les Régions Administratives Spéciales (SAR) de Hong Kong et Macao.

[5] Refers to the whole country. - Les données se rapportent au pays en entier.

[6] Including Abkhazia and South Ossetia. - Y compris l'Abkhazie et l'Ossétie du Sud.

[7] Including Sabah and Sarawak. - Y compris le Sabah et le Sarawak.

[8] Including Åland Islands. - Y compris les îles Åland.

[9] Including Svalbard and Jan Mayen Islands. - Y compris Svalbard et l'île Jan Mayen.

[10] Including Transnistria. - Y compris la Transnistrie.

[11] Including Kosovo. - Y compris le Kosovo.

[12] Including Canary Islands, Ceuta and Melilla. - Y compris les îles Canaries, Ceuta et Melilla.

[13] Including Crimea. - Y compris la Crimée.

[14] Including Christmas Island, Cocos (Keeling) Islands and Norfolk Island. - Y compris les îles Christmas, Cocos (Keeling) et Norfolk.

Index
Historical index
(See notes at end of index)

Subject-matter	Year of issue	Time coverage
	1984	1980-84
	1985	1981-85
	1986	1967-86
	1987	1983-87
	1988	1984-88
	1989	1985-89
	1990	1986-90
	1991	1987-91
	1992	1983-92
	1993	1989-93
	1994	1990-94
	1995	1991-95
	1996	1992-96
	1997	1993-97
	1997HS[iii]	1948-97
	1998	1994-98
	1999	1995-99
	1999CD[iv]	1980-99
	2000	1996-00
	2001	1997-01
	2002	1998-02
	2003	1999-03
	2004	2000-04
	2005	2001-05
	2006	2002-06
	2007	2003-07
	2008	2004-08
	2009-2010	2006-10
	2011	2007-11
	2012	2008-12
	2013	2009-13
	2014	2010-14
	2015	2011-15
- by age of father	1949/50	1942-49
	1954	1936-53
	1959	1949-58
	1965	1955-64
	1969	1963-68
	1975	1966-74
	1981	1972-80
	1999CD[iv]	1990-98
	2007-2015	Latest
- by age of mother	1948	1936-47
	1949/50	1936-49
	1954	1936-53
	1955-1956	Latest
	1958	Latest
	1959	1949-58

Subject-matter	Year of issue	Time coverage
	1960-1964	Latest
	1965	1955-64
	1966-1968	Latest
	1969	1963-68
	1970-1974	Latest
	1975	1966-74
	1976-1978	Latest
	1978HS[ii]	1948-77
	1979-1980	Latest
	1981	1972-80
	1982-1985	Latest
	1986	1977-85
	1987-1991	Latest
	1992	1983-92
	1993-1997	Latest
	1997HS[iii] [3]	1948-96
	1998-99	Latest
	1999CD[iv]	1990-98
	2000-2015	Latest
- by age of mother and birth order	1949/50	1936-47
	1954	Latest
	1959	1949-58
	1965	1955-64
	1969	1963-68
	1975	1966-74
	1981	1972-80
	1986	1977-85
	1999CD[iv]	1990-98
- by age of mother and sex of child	1965-1968	Latest
	1969	1963-68
	1970-1974	Latest
	1975	1966-74
	1976-1978	Latest
	1978HS[ii]	1948-77
	1979-1980	Latest
	1981	1972-80
	1982-1985	Latest
	1986	1977-85
	1987-1991	Latest
	1992	1983-92
	1993-1997	Latest
	1997HS[iii]	1948-96
	1998-99	Latest

Subject-matter	Year of issue	Time coverage
	1999CD[iv]	1990-98
	2000-2015	Latest
- by age of mother and urban/rural residence (see: by urban/rural residence, below)		
- by birth order	1948	1936-47
	1949/50	1936-49
	1954	1936-53
	1955	Latest
	1959	1949-58
	1965	1955-64
	1969	1963-68
	1975	1966-74
	1981	1972-80
	1986	1977-85
	1999CD[iv]	1990-98
- by birth weight	1975	Latest
	1981	1972-80
	1986	1977-85
	1999CD[iv]	1990-98
- by gestational age	1975	Latest
	1981	1972-80
	1986	1977-85
	1999CD[iv]	1990-98
- by legitimacy status	1959	1949-58
	1965	1955-64
	1969	1963-68
	1975	1966-74
	1981	1972-80
	1986	1977-85
	1999CD[iv]	1990-98
- by month	2002	1980-02
- by occupation of father	1965	Latest
	1969	Latest
- by sex	1959	1949-58

Subject-matter	Year of issue	Time coverage
	1965	1955-64
	1967-1968	Latest
	1969	1963-68
	1970-1974	Latest
	1975	1956-75
	1976-1980	Latest
	1981	1962-81
	1982-1985	Latest
	1986	1967-86
	1987-1991	Latest
	1992	1983-92
	1993-1999	Latest
	1999CD[iv]	1990-98
	2000-2015	Latest
- by plurality	1965	Latest
	1969	Latest
	1975	Latest
	1981	1972-80
	1986	1977-85
	1999CD[iv]	1990-98
- by urban/rural residence	1965	Latest
	1967	Latest
	1968	1964-68
	1969	1964-68
	1970	1966-70
	1971	1967-71
	1972	1968-72
	1973	1969-73
	1974	1970-74
	1975	1956-75
	1976	1972-76
	1977	1973-77
	1978	1974-78
	1979	1975-79
	1980	1976-80
	1981	1962-81
	1982	1978-82
	1983	1979-83
	1984	1980-84
	1985	1981-85
	1986	1967-86
	1987	1983-87
	1988	1984-88
	1989	1985-89
	1990	1986-90
	1991	1987-91

Subject-matter	Year of issue	Time coverage	Subject-matter	Year of issue	Time coverage
	1992	1983-92	- legitimate	1948	1936-47
	1993	1989-93		1949/50	1936-49
	1994	1990-94		1954	1936-53
	1995	1991-95		1959	1949-58
	1996	1992-96		1965	1955-64
	1997	1993-97		1969	1963-68
	1998	1994-98		1975	1966-74
	1999	1995-99		1981	1972-80
	1999CD[iv]	1980-99		1986	1977-85
	2000	1996-00		1999CD[iv]	1990-98
	2001	1997-01			
	2002	1998-02	- legitimate, by age of father	1959	1949-58
	2003	1999-03		1965	1955-64
	2004	2000-04		1969	1963-68
	2005	2001-05		1975	1966-74
	2006	2002-06		1981	1972-80
	2007	2003-07		1986	1977-85
	2008	2004-08	- legitimate, by age of mother	1954	1936-53
	2009-2010	2006-10		1959	1949-58
	2011	2007-11		1965	1955-64
	2012	2008-12		1969	1963-68
	2013	2009-13		1975	1966-74
	2014	2010-14		1981	1972-80
	2015	2011-15		1986	1977-85
- by urban/rural residence and age of mother	1965	Latest	- legitimate, by duration of marriage	1948	1936-47
	1969-1974	Latest		1949/50	1936-49
	1975	1966-74		1954	1936-53
	1976-1980	Latest		1959	1949-58
	1981	1972-80		1965	1955-64
	1982-1985	Latest		1969	1963-68
	1986	1977-85		1975	1966-74
	1987-1991	Latest		1981	1972-80
	1992	1983-92		1986	1977-85
	1993-1997	Latest		1999CD[iv]	1990-98
	1997HS[iii]	1948-96			
	1998-1999	Latest	Birth rates	1948	1932-47
	1999CD[iv]	1990-98		1949/50	1932-49
	2000-2006	Latest		1951	1905-30[v]
					1930-50
- illegitimate	1959	1949-58		1952	1920-34[v]
	1965	1955-64			1934-51
	1969	1963-68		1953	1920-39[v]
	1975	1966-74			1940-52
	1981	1972-80		1954	1920-39[v]
	1986	1977-85			
	1999CD[iv]	1990-98			

Subject-matter	Year of issue	Time coverage	Subject-matter	Year of issue	Time coverage
		1939-53		1998	1994-98
	1955	1920-34[v]		1999	1995-99
		1946-54		1999CD[iv]	1985-99
	1956	1947-55		2000	1996-00
	1957	1948-56		2001	1997-01
	1958	1948-57		2002	1998-02
	1959	1920-54[v]		2003	1999-03
		1953-58		2004	2000-04
	1960	1950-59		2005	2001-05
	1961	1945-59[v]		2006	2002-06
		1952-61		2007	2003-07
	1962	1945-54[v]		2008	2004-08
		1952-62		2009-2010	2006-10
	1963	1945-59[v]		2011	2007-11
		1954-63		2012	2008-12
	1964	1960-64		2013	2009-13
	1965	1920-64[v]		2014	2010-14
		1950-65		2015	2011-15
	1966	1950-64[v]	- by age of father	1949/50	1942-49
		1957-66		1954	1936-53
	1967	1963-67		1959	1949-58
	1968	1964-68		1965	1955-64
	1969	1925-69[v]		1969	1963-68
		1954-69		1975	1966-74
	1970	1966-70		1981	1972-80
	1971	1967-71		1986	1977-85
	1972	1968-72		1999CD[iv]	1990-98
	1973	1969-73		2007-2015	Latest
	1974	1970-74			
	1975	1956-75	- by age of mother	1948	1936-47
	1976	1972-76		1949/50	1936-49
	1977	1973-77		1951	1936-50
	1978	1974-78		1952	1936-50
	1978HS[ii]	1948-78		1953	1936-52
	1979	1975-79		1954	1936-53
	1980	1976-80		1955-1956	Latest
	1981	1962-81		1959	1949-58
	1982	1978-82		1965	1955-64
	1983	1979-83		1969	1963-68
	1984	1980-84		1975	1966-74
	1985	1981-85		1976-1978	Latest
	1986	1967-86		1978HS[ii]	1948-77
	1987	1983-87		1979-1980	Latest
	1988	1984-88		1981	1972-80
	1989	1985-89		1982-1985	Latest
	1990	1986-90		1986	1977-85
	1991	1987-91		1987-1991	Latest
	1992	1983-92		1992	1983-92
	1993	1989-93		1993-1997	Latest
	1994	1990-94			
	1995	1991-95			
	1996	1992-96			
	1997	1993-97			
	1997HS[iii]	1948-97			

Subject-matter	Year of issue	Time coverage	Subject-matter	Year of issue	Time coverage
	1997HS[iii]	1948-96		1980	1976-80
	1998-1999	Latest		1981	1962-81
	1999CD[iv]	1990-98		1982	1978-82
	2000-2015	Latest		1983	1979-83
				1984	1980-84
- by age of mother and birth order	1954	1948 and 1951		1985	1981-85
				1986	1967-86
	1959	1949-58		1987	1983-87
	1965	1955-64		1988	1984-88
	1969	1963-68		1989	1985-89
	1975	1966-74		1990	1986-90
	1981	1972-80		1991	1987-91
	1986	1977-85		1992	1983-92
	1999CD[iv]	1990-98		1993	1989-93
				1994	1990-94
- by age of mother and urban/rural residence (see: by urban/rural residence, below)				1995	1991-95
				1996	1992-96
				1997	1993-97
				1998	1994-98
				1999	1995-99
- by birth order	1951	1936-49		1999CD[iv]	1985-99
	1952	1936-50		2000	1996-00
	1953	1936-52		2001	1997-01
	1954	1936-53		2002	1998-02
	1955	Latest		2003	1999-03
	1959	1949-58		2004	2000-04
	1965	1955-64		2005	2001-05
	1969	1963-68		2006	2002-06
	1975	1966-74		2007	2003-07
	1981	1972-80		2008	2004-08
	1986	1977-85		2009-2010	2006-10
	1999CD[iv]	1990-98		2011	2007-11
				2012	2008-12
- by urban/rural residence	1965	Latest		2013	2009-13
	1967	Latest		2014	2010-14
	1968	1964-68		2015	2011-15
	1969	1964-68	- by urban/rural residence and age of mother		
	1970	1966-70		1965	Latest
	1971	1967-71		1969	Latest
	1972	1968-72		1975	1966-74
	1973	1969-73		1976-1980	Latest
	1974	1970-74		1981	1972-80
	1975	1956-75		1982-1985	Latest
	1976	1972-76		1986	1977-85
	1977	1973-77		1987-1991	Latest
	1978	1974-78		1992	1983-92
	1979	1975-79		1993-1997	Latest
				1997HS[iii]	1948-96
				1998-1999	Latest
				1999CD[iv]	1990-98

Subject-matter	Year of issue	Time coverage	Subject-matter	Year of issue	Time coverage
	2000-2006	Latest	- illegitimate	1959	1949-58
- estimated:			- legitimate	1954	1936-53
for continents	1949/50	1947		1959	1949-58
	1956-1977	Latest		1965	Latest
	1978-1979	1970-75		1969	Latest
	1980-1983	1975-80		1975	Latest
	1984-1986	1980-85		1981	Latest
	1987-1992	1985-90		1986	Latest
	1993-1997	1990-95	- legitimate by age of father	1959	1949-58
	1998-2000	1995-00		1965	Latest
	2001-2005	2000-05		1969	Latest
	2006-2010	2005-10		1975	Latest
	2011-2015	2010-15		1981	Latest
				1986	Latest
for macro regions	1964-1977	Latest	- legitimate by age of mother	1954	1936-53
	1978-1979	1970-75		1959	1949-58
	1980-1983	1975-80		1965	Latest
	1984-1986	1980-85		1969	Latest
	1987-1992	1985-90		1975	Latest
	1993-1997	1990-95		1981	Latest
	1998-2000	1995-00		1986	Latest
	2001-2005	2000-05	- legitimate by duration of marriage	1959	1950-57
	2006-2010	2005-10		1965	Latest
	2011-2015	2010-15		1969	Latest
for regions	1949/1950	1947		1975	Latest
	1956-1977	Latest	**Birth Ratios**		
	1978-1979	1970-75	- fertility	1949/1950	Latest
	1980-1983	1975-80		1954	Latest
	1984-1986	1980-85		1959	1949-58
	1987-1992	1985-90		1965	1955-65
	1993-1997	1990-95		1969	1963-68
	1998-2000	1995-00		1975	1965-74
	2001-2005	2000-05		1978HS[ii]	1948-77
	2006-2010	2005-10		1981	1972-80
	2011-2015	2010-15		1986	1977-85
for the world	1949/50	1947		1997HS[iii]	1948-96
	1956-1977	Latest		1999CD[iv]	1980-99
	1978-1979	1970-75	- illegitimate	1959	1949-58
	1980-1983	1975-80		1965	1955-64
	1984-1986	1980-85		1969	1963-68
	1987-1992	1985-90		1975	1965-74
	1993-1997	1990-95		1981	1972-80
	1998-2000	1995-00		1986	1977-85
	2001-2005	2000-05			
	2006-2010	2005-10			
	2011-2015	2010-15			

Subject-matter	Year of issue	Time coverage	Subject-matter	Year of issue	Time coverage
	1978HS[ii]	1948-78		1992	1983-92
	1979	1975-79		1993-1995	Latest
	1980	1971-80		1996	1987-95
	1981	1977-81		1997	Latest
	1982	1978-82		1997HS[iii]	1948-96
	1983	1979-83		1998-2015	Latest
	1984	1980-84			
	1985	1976-85	- by age and sex and urban/rural residence		
	1986	1982-86		1967-1973	Latest
	1987	1983-87		1974	1965-73
	1988	1984-88		1975-1979	Latest
	1989	1985-89		1980	1971-79
	1990	1986-90		1981-1984	Latest
	1991	1987-91		1985	1976-84
	1992	1983-92		1986-1991	Latest
	1993	1989-93		1992	1983-92
	1994	1990-94		1993-1995	Latest
	1995	1991-95		1996	1987-95
	1996	1987-96		1997	Latest
	1997	1993-97		1997HS[iii]	1948-96
	1997HS[iii]	1948-97		1998-2006	Latest
	1998	1994-98			
	1999	1995-99	- by cause	1951	1947-50
	2000	1996-00		1952	1947-51[vi]
	2001	1997-01		1953	Latest
	2002	1998-02		1954	1945-53
	2003	1999-03		1955-1956	Latest
	2004	2000-04		1957	1952-56
	2005	2001-05		1958-1960	Latest
	2006	2002-06		1961	1955-60
	2007	2003-07		1962-1965	Latest
	2008	2004-08		1966	1960-65
	2009-2010	2006-10		1967-1973	Latest
	2011	2007-11		1974	1965-73
	2012	2008-12		1975-1979	Latest
	2013	2009-13		1980	1971-79
	2014	2010-14		1981-1984	Latest
	2015	2011-15		1985	1976-84
- by age and sex	1948	1936-47		1986-1991	Latest
	1951	1936-50		1991PA[vii]	1960-90
	1955-1956	Latest		1992-1995	Latest
	1957	1948-56		1996	1987-95
	1958-1960	Latest		1997-2000	Latest
	1961	1955-60		2002	1995-02
	1962-1965	Latest		2004	1995-04
	1966	1961-65		2006	2002-06
	1967-1973	Latest		2008	2004-08
	1974	1965-73		2011	2006-10
	1975-1979	Latest		2013	2008-12
	1978HS[ii]	1948-77		2015	2010-14
	1980	1971-79			
	1981-1984	Latest	- by cause, age and sex	1951	Latest
	1985	1976-84		1952	Latest
	1986-1991	Latest			

Subject-matter	Year of issue	Time coverage	Subject-matter	Year of issue	Time coverage
	1957	Latest		1961	1955-60
	1961	Latest		1966	1960-65
	1967	Latest		1974	1965-73
	1974	Latest		1980	1971-79
	1980	Latest		1985	1976-84
	1985	Latest	- by urban/rural residence		
	1991PA[vii]	1960-90		1967	Latest
	1996	Latest		1968	1964-68
- by cause, age and sex and urban/rural residence				1969	1965-69
				1970	1966-70
				1971	1967-71
	1967	Latest		1972	1968-72
				1973	1969-73
- by cause and sex	1967	Latest		1974	1965-74
	1974	Latest		1975	1971-75
	1980	Latest		1976	1972-76
	1985	Latest		1977	1973-77
	1996	Latest		1978	1974-78
	2006	2002-06		1979	1975-79
	2008	2004-08		1980	1971-80
	2011	2006-10		1981	1977-81
	2013	2008-12		1982	1978-82
	2015	2010-14		1983	1979-83
				1984	1980-84
- by marital status, age and sex	1958	Latest		1985	1976-85
	1961	Latest		1986	1982-86
	1967	Latest		1987	1983-87
	1974	Latest		1988	1984-88
	1980	Latest		1989	1985-89
	1985	Latest		1990	1986-90
	1991PA[vii]	1950-90		1991	1987-91
	1996	Latest		1992	1983-92
	2003	Latest		1993	1989-93
				1994	1990-94
- by month	1951	1946-50		1995	1991-95
	1967	1962-66		1996	1987-96
	1974	1965-73		1997	1993-97
	1980	1971-79		1998	1994-98
	1985	1976-84		1999	1995-99
	2001	1985-00		2000	1996-00
	2005	2001-05		2001	1997-01
				2002	1998-02
				2003	1999-03
- by occupation and age, males	1957	Latest		2004	2000-04
	1961	1957-60		2006	2002-06
	1967	1962-66		2007	2003-07
				2008	2004-08
- by type of certification and cause:				2009-2010	2006-10
				2011	2007-11
				2012	2008-12
numbers	1957	Latest		2013	2009-13
	1974	1965-73		2014	2010-14
	1980	1971-79		2015	2011-15
	1985	1976-84			
percent	1957	Latest	- of infants (see		

Subject-matter	Year of issue	Time coverage	Subject-matter	Year of issue	Time coverage
infant deaths)				1991	1987-91
				1992	1983-92
Death rates	1948	1932-47		1993	1989-93
	1949/50	1932-49		1994	1990-94
	1951	1905-30[v]		1995	1991-95
		1930-50		1996	1987-96
	1952	1920-34[v]		1997	1993-97
		1934-51		1997HS[iii]	1948-97
	1953	1920-39[v]		1998	1994-98
		1940-52		1999	1995-99
	1954	1920-39[v]		2000	1996-00
		1946-53		2001	1997-01
	1955	1920-34[v]		2002	1998-02
		1946-54		2003	1999-03
	1956	1947-55		2004	2000-04
	1957	1930-56		2005	2001-05
	1958	1948-57		2006	2002-06
	1959	1949-58		2007	2003-07
	1960	1950-59		2008	2004-08
	1961	1945-59[v]		2009-2010	2006-10
		1952-61		2011	2007-11
	1962	1945-54[v]		2012	2008-12
		1952-62		2013	2009-13
	1963	1945-59[v]		2014	2010-14
		1954-63		2015	2011-15
	1964	1960-64			
	1965	1961-65	- by age and sex	1948	1935-47
	1966	1920-64[v]		1949/50	1936-49
		1951-66		1951	1936-50
	1967	1963-67		1952	1936-51
	1968	1964-68		1953	1940-52
	1969	1965-69		1954	1946-53
	1970	1966-70		1955-1956	Latest
	1971	1967-71		1957	1948-56
	1972	1968-72		1961	1952-60
	1973	1969-73		1966	1950-65
	1974	1965-74		1972	Latest
	1975	1971-75		1974	1965-73
	1976	1972-76		1975-1979	Latest
	1977	1973-77		1978HS[ii]	1948-77
	1978	1974-78		1980	1971-79
	1978HS[ii]	1948-78		1981-1984	Latest
	1979	1975-79		1985	1976-84
	1980	1971-80		1986-1991	Latest
	1981	1977-81		1991PA[vii]	1950-1990
	1982	1978-82		1992	1983-1992
	1983	1979-83		1993-1995	Latest
	1984	1980-84		1996	1987-95
	1985	1976-85		1997	Latest
	1986	1982-86		1997HS[iii]	1948-96
	1987	1983-87		1998-2015	Latest
	1988	1984-88			
	1989	1985-89	- by age and sex and urban/rural residence	1967	Latest
	1990	1986-90			

Subject-matter	Year of issue	Time coverage	Subject-matter	Year of issue	Time coverage
	1972	Latest		2008	2004-08
	1974	1965-73		2011	2006-10
	1975-1979	Latest		2013	2008-12
	1980	1971-79		2015	2010-14
	1981-1984	Latest	- by marital status, age and sex	1961	Latest
	1985	1976-84		1967	Latest
	1986-1991	Latest		1974	Latest
	1991PA[vii]	1950-1990		1980	Latest
	1992	1983-1992		1985	Latest
	1993-1995	Latest		1996	Latest
	1996	1987-95		2003	Latest
	1997	Latest	- by occupation, age and sex	1957	Latest
	1997HS[iii]	1948-96			
	1998-2006	Latest	- by occupation and age, males	1961	Latest
- by cause	1951	1947-49		1967	Latest
	1952	1947-51[vi]	- by urban/rural residence	1967	Latest
	1953	1947-52		1968	1964-68
	1954	1945-53		1969	1965-69
	1955-1956	Latest		1970	1966-70
	1957	1952-56		1971	1967-71
	1958-1960	Latest		1972	1968-72
	1961	1955-60		1973	1969-73
	1962-1965	Latest		1974	1965-74
	1966	1960-65		1975	1971-75
	1967-1973	Latest		1976	1972-76
	1974	1965-73		1977	1973-77
	1975-1979	Latest		1978	1974-78
	1980	1971-79		1979	1975-79
	1981-1984	Latest		1980	1971-80
	1985	1976-84		1981	1977-81
	1986-1991	Latest		1982	1978-82
	1991PA[vii]	1960-90		1983	1979-83
	1992-1995	Latest		1984	1980-84
	1996	1987-95		1985	1976-85
	1997-2000	Latest		1986	1982-86
	2002	1995-02		1987	1983-87
	2004	1995-04		1988	1984-88
	2006	2002-06		1989	1985-89
	2008	2004-08		1990	1986-90
	2011	2006-10		1991	1987-91
	2013	2008-12		1992	1983-92
	2015	2010-14		1993	1989-93
- by cause, age and sex	1957	Latest		1994	1990-94
	1961	Latest		1995	1991-95
	1991PA[vii]	1960-90		1996	1987-96
				1997	1993-97
- by cause and sex	1967	Latest		1998	1994-98
	1974	Latest		1999	1995-99
	1980	Latest		1987	1983-87
	1985	Latest		1988	1984-88
	1996	Latest			
	2006	2002-06			

Subject-matter	Year of issue	Time coverage	Subject-matter	Year of issue	Time coverage
	1989	1985-89		1978-1979	1970-75
	1990	1986-90		1980-1983	1975-80
	1991	1987-91		1984-1986	1980-85
	1992	1983-92		1987-1992	1985-90
	1993	1989-93		1993-1997	1990-95
	1994	1990-94		1998-2000	1995-00
	1995	1991-95		2001-2005	2000-05
	1996	1987-96		2006-2010	2005-10
	1997	1993-97		2011-2015	2010-15
	1998	1994-98			
	1999	1995-99	for the world	1949/50	1947
	2000	1996-00		1956-1977	Latest
	2001	1997-01		1978-1979	1970-75
	2002	1998-02		1980-1983	1975-80
	2003	1999-03		1984-1986	1980-85
	2004	2000-04		1987-1992	1985-90
	2005	2001-05		1993-1997	1990-95
	2006	2002-06		1998-2000	1995-00
	2007	2003-07		2001-2005	2000-05
	2008	2004-08		2006-2010	2005-10
	2009-2010	2006-10		2011-2015	2010-15
	2011	2007-11			
	2012	2008-12	- of infants (see: Infant deaths)		
	2013	2009-13			
	2014	2010-14	**Density of population**:		
	2015	2011-15	- of continents	1949/50	1920-49
- estimated				1951-1999	Latest
for continents	1949/50	1947		2000	2000
	1956-1977	Latest		2001	2001
	1978-1979	1970-75		2002	2002
	1980-1983	1975-80		2003	2003
	1984-1986	1980-85		2004	2004
	1984-1986	1980-85		2005	2005
	1987-1992	1985-90		2006	2006
	1993-1997	1990-95		2007	2007
	1998-2000	1995-00		2008	2008
	2001-2005	2000-05		2009-2010	2010
	2006-2010	2005-10		2011	2011
	2011-2015	2010-15		2012	2012
for macro regions				2013	2013
	1964-1977	Latest		2014	2014
	1978-1979	1970-75		2015	2015
	1980-1983	1975-80			
	1984-1986	1980-85	- of countries	1948-1999	Latest
	1987-1992	1985-90		2000	2000
	1993-1997	1990-95		2001	2001
	1998-2000	1995-00		2002	2002
	2001-2005	2000-05		2003	2003
	2006-2010	2005-10		2004	2004
	2011-2015	2010-15		2005	2005
				2006	2006
for regions	1949/50	1947		2007	2007
	1956-1977	Latest		2008	2008
				2009-2010	2010

Subject-matter	Year of issue	Time coverage
	1978	1974-78
	1979	1975-79
	1980	1976-80
	1969	1965-69
	1970	1966-70
	1971	1967-71
	1972	1968-72
	1973	1969-73
	1974	1970-74
	1975	1971-75
	1976	1957-76
	1977	1973-77
	1978	1974-78
	1979	1975-79
	1980	1976-80
	1969	1965-69
	1970	1966-70
	1971	1967-71
	1972	1968-72
	1973	1969-73
	1974	1970-74
	1975	1971-75
	1976	1957-76
	1977	1973-77
	1978	1974-78
	1979	1975-79
	1980	1976-80
	1981	1977-81
	1982	1963-82
	1983	1979-83
	1984	1980-84
	1985	1981-85
	1986	1982-86
	1987	1983-87
	1988	1984-88
	1989	1985-89
	1990	1971-90
	1991	1987-91
	1992	1988-92
	1993	1989-93
	1994	1990-94
	1995	1991-95
	1996	1992-96
	1997	1993-97
	1998	1994-98
	1999	1995-99
	2000	1996-00
	2001	1997-01
	2002	1998-02
	2003	1999-03
	2004	2000-04
	2005	2001-05
	2006	2002-06
	2007	2003-07

Subject-matter	Year of issue	Time coverage
	2008	2004-08
	2009-2010	2006-10
	2011	2007-11
	2012	2008-12
	2013	2009-13
	2014	2010-14
	2015	2011-15
- by age of husband	1968	Latest
	1976	Latest
	1982	Latest
	1987	1975-86
	1990	Latest
- by age of wife	1968	Latest
	1976	Latest
	1982	Latest
	1987	1975-86
	1990	Latest
- for married couples	1953	1935-52
	1954	1935-53
	1958	1935-56
	1968	1935-67
	1976	1966-75
	1978HS[ii]	1948-77
	1982	1972-81
	1990	1980-89
- by urban/rural residence	2002	1998-02
	2003	1999-03
	2004	2000-04
	2005	2001-05
	2006	2002-06
	2007	2003-07
	2008	2004-08
	2009-2010	2006-10
	2011	2007-11
	2012	2008-12
	2013	2009-13
	2014	2010-14
	2015	2011-15

E

Economically active population (see: Population)

Economically inactive population (see: Population)

Emigrants (see: Migration)

Subject-matter	Year of issue	Time coverage	Subject-matter	Year of issue	Time coverage
	1965	1955-64		2015	2011-15
	1966	1947-65			
	1967	1962-66	- by age of mother	1954	1936-53
	1968	1963-67		1959	1949-58
	1969	1959-68		1965	1955-64
	1970	1965-69		1969	1963-68
	1971	1966-70		1975	1966-74
	1972	1967-71		1981	1972-80
	1973	1968-72		1986	1977-85
	1974	1965-73	- by age of mother		
	1975	1966-74	and birth order	1954	Latest
	1976	1971-75		1959	1949-58
	1977	1972-76		1965	3-Latest
	1978	1973-77		1969	1963-68
	1979	1974-78		1975	1966-74
	1980	1971-79		1981	1972-80
	1981	1972-80		1986	1977-85
	1982	1977-81	- by period of		
	1983	1978-82	gestation	1957	1950-56
	1984	1979-83		1959	1949-58
	1985	1975-84		1961	1952-60
	1986	1977-85		1965	5-Latest
	1987	1982-86		1966	1956-65
	1988	1983-87		1967-1968	Latest
	1989	1984-88		1969	1963-68
	1990	1985-89		1974	1965-73
	1991	1986-90		1975	1966-74
	1992	1987-91		1980	1971-79
	1993	1988-92		1981	1972-80
	1994	1989-93		1985	1976-84
	1995	1990-94		1986	1977-85
	1996	1987-95		1996	1987-95
	1997	1992-96			
	1998	1993-97	- by sex	1961	1952-60
	1999	1994-98		1965	5 Latest
	1999CD[iv]	1990-98		1969	1963-68
	2000	1995-99		1975	1966-74
	2001	1997-01		1981	1972-80
	2002	1998-02		1986	1977-85
	2003	1999-03			
	2004	2000-04	- by urban/rural		
	2005	2001-05	residence	1971	1966-70
	2006	2002-06		1972	1967-71
	2007	2003-07		1973	1968-72
	2008	2004-08		1974	1965-73
	2009-2010	2006-10		1975	1966-74
	2011	2007-11		1976	1971-75
	2012	2008-12		1977	1972-76
	2013	2009-13		1978	1973-77
	2014	2010-14		1979	1974-78
				1980	1971-79
				1981	1972-80
				1982	1977-81
				1983	1978-82
				1984	1979-83

Subject-matter	Year of issue	Time coverage	Subject-matter	Year of issue	Time coverage
	1985	1975-84		1981	1972-80
	1986	1977-85		1986	1977-85
	1987	1982-86	- legitimate by age of mother		
	1988	1983-87		1959	1949-58
	1989	1984-88		1965	1955-64
	1990	1985-89		1969	1963-68
	1991	1986-90		1975	1966-74
	1992	1987-91		1981	1972-80
	1993	1988-92		1986	1977-85
	1994	1989-93		1996	1987-95
	1995	1990-94			
	1996	1987-95	**Foetal Death Ratios**		
	1997	1992-96	- by period of gestation	1957	1950-56
	1998	1993-97		1959	1949-58
	1999	1994-98		1961	1952-60
	1999CD[iv]	1990-98		1965	5-Latest
	2000	1995-99		1966	1956-65
	2001	1997-01		1967-1968	Latest
	2002	1998-02		1969	1963-68
	2003	1999-03		1974	1965-73
	2004	2000-04		1975	1966-74
	2005	2001-05		1980	1971-79
	2006	2002-06		1981	1972-80
	2007	2003-07		1985	1976-84
	2008	2004-08		1986	1977-85
	2009-2010	2006-10		1996	1987-95
	2011	2007-11		1999CD[iv]	1990-98
	2012	2008-12			
	2013	2009-13	Foetal death ratios, late..........	1951	1935-50
	2014	2010-14		1952	1935-51
	2015	2011-15		1953	1936-52
- illegitimate	1961	1952-60		1954	1938-53
	1965	5-Latest		1955	1946-54
	1969	1963-68		1956	1947-55
	1975	1966-74		1957	1948-56
	1981	1972-80		1958	1948-57
	1986	1977-85		1959	1920-54[v]
					1953-58
- illegitimate, percent	1961	1952-60		1960	1950-59
	1965	5-Latest		1961	1945-49[v]
	1969	1963-68			1952-60
	1975	1966-74		1962	1945-54[v]
	1981	1972-80			1952-61
	1986	1977-85		1963	1945-59[v]
					1953-62
- legitimate	1959	1949-58		1964	1959-63
	1965	1955-64		1965	1950-64[v]
	1969	1963-68			1955-64
	1975	1966-74		1966	1950-64[v]
					1956-65

Subject-matter	Year of issue	Time coverage	Subject-matter	Year of issue	Time coverage
	1967	1962-66		2015	2011-15
	1968	1963-67			
	1969	1950-64[v]	- by age of mother	1954	1936-53
		1959-68		1959	1949-58
	1970	1965-69		1965	1955-64
	1971	1966-70		1969	1963-68
	1972	1967-71		1975	1966-74
	1973	1968-72		1981	1972-80
	1974	1965-73		1986	1977-85
	1975	1966-74		1996	1987-95
	1976	1971-75		1999CD[iv]	1990-98
	1977	1972-76			
	1978	1973-77	- by age of mother and birth order	1954	Latest
	1979	1974-78		1959	1949-58
	1980	1971-79		1965	3-Latest
	1981	1972-80		1969	1963-68
	1982	1977-81		1975	1966-74
	1983	1978-82		1981	1972-80
	1984	1979-83		1986	1977-85
	1985	1975-84		1999CD[iv]	1990-98
	1986	1977-85			
	1987	1982-86	- by period of gestation	1957	1950-56
	1988	1983-87		1959	1949-58
	1989	1984-88		1961	1952-60
	1990	1985-89		1965	5-Latest
	1991	1986-90		1966	1956-65
	1992	1987-91		1967-1968	Latest
	1993	1988-92		1969	1963-68
	1994	1989-93		1974	1965-73
	1995	1990-94		1975	1966-74
	1996	1987-95		1980	1971-79
	1997	1992-96		1981	1972-80
	1998	1993-97		1985	1976-84
	1999	1994-98		1986	1977-85
	1999CD[iv]	1990-98	- by urban/rural residence	1971	1966-70
	2000	1995-99		1972	1967-71
	2001	1997-01		1973	1968-72
	2002	1998-02		1974	1965-73
	2003	1999-03		1975	1966-74
	2004	2000-04		1976	1971-75
	2005	2001-05		1977	1972-76
	2006	2002-06		1978	1973-77
	2007	2003-07		1979	1974-78
	2008	2004-08		1980	1971-79
	2009-2010	2006-10		1981	1972-80
	2011	2007-11		1982	1977-81
	2012	2008-12		1983	1978-82
	2013	2009-13			
	2014	2010-14			

Subject-matter	Year of issue	Time coverage	Subject-matter	Year of issue	Time coverage
	1984	1979-83	**G**		
	1985	1975-84			
	1986	1977-85	**Gestational age of foetal deaths (see: Foetal deaths)**		
	1987	1982-86			
	1988	1983-87	**Gross reproduction rates (see: Reproduction rates)**		
	1989	1984-88			
	1990	1985-89	**H**		
	1991	1986-90			
	1992	1987-91	**Homeless (see: Population)**		
	1993	1988-92			
	1994	1989-93	**Households**		
	1995	1990-94	- average size of	1962	1955-62
	1996	1987-95		1963	1955-63[vi]
	1997	1992-96		1968	Latest
	1998	1993-97		1971	1962-71
	1999	1994-98		1973	1965-73[vi]
	1999CD[iv]	1990-98		1976	Latest
	2000	1995-99		1982	Latest
	2001	1997-01		1987	1975-86
	2002	1998-02		1990	1980-89
	2003	1999-03	- by age, sex of householder, size and urban/rural residence	1987	1975-86
	2004	2000-04	- by family type and urban/rural residence	1987	1975-86
	2005	2001-05	- by marital status of householder and urban/rural residence	1987	1975-86
	2006	2002-06		1995	1985-95
	2007	2003-07	- by relationship to householder and urban/rural residence	1987	1975-86
	2008	2004-08		1995	1985-95
	2009-2010	2006-10	- by size	1955	1945-54
	2011	2007-11		1962	1955-62
	2012	2008-12		1963	1955-63[vi]
	2013	2009-13		1971	1962-71
	2014	2010-14		1973	1965-73[vi]
	2015	2011-15		1976	Latest
- illegitimate	1961	1952-60		1982	Latest
	1965	5-Latest		1987	1975-86
- legitimate	1959	1949-58		1990	1980-89
	1965	1955-64		1995	1985-95
	1969	1963-68	- and number of persons 60+	1991PA[vii]	Latest
	1975	1966-74	- by urban/rural residence	1968	Latest
	1981	1972-80		1971	1962-71
	1986	1977-85			
- legitimate by age of mother	1959	1949-58			
	1965	1955-64			
	1969	1963-68			
	1975	1966-74			
	1981	1972-80			
	1986	1977-85			

Index
Historical index
(See notes at end of index)

Subject-matter	Year of issue	Time coverage	Subject-matter	Year of issue	Time coverage
Migration)				1999	1995-99
				2000	1996-00
Infant deaths...........................	1948	1932-47		2001	1997-01
	1949/50	1934-49		2002	1998-02
	1951	1935-50		2003	1999-03
	1952	1936-51		2004	2000-04
	1953	1950-52		2005	2001-05
	1954	1946-53		2006	2002-06
	1955	1946-54		2007	2003-07
	1956	1947-55		2008	2004-08
	1957	1948-56		2009-2010	2006-10
	1958	1948-57		2011	2007-11
	1959	1949-58		2012	2008-12
	1960	1950-59		2013	2009-13
	1961	1952-61		2014	2010-14
	1962	1953-62		2015	2011-15
	1963	1954-63	- by age and sex	1948	1936-47
	1964	1960-64		1951	1936-49
	1965	1961-65		1957	1948-56
	1966	1947-66		1961	1952-60
	1967	1963-67		1962-1965	Latest
	1968	1964-68		1966	1956-65
	1969	1965-69		1967-1973	Latest
	1970	1966-70		1974	1965-73
	1971	1967-71		1975-1979	Latest
	1972	1968-72		1980	1971-79
	1973	1969-73		1981-1984	Latest
	1974	1965-74		1985	1976-84
	1975	1971-75		1986-1991	Latest
	1976	1972-76		1992	1983-92
	1977	1973-77		1993-1995	Latest
	1978	1974-78		1996	1987-95
	1978HS[ii]	1948-78		1997-2004	Latest
	1979	1975-79		2005	1996-05
	1980	1971-80		2006-2015	Latest
	1981	1977-81			
	1982	1978-82			
	1983	1979-83	- by age and sex and urban/rural residence	1967-1973	Latest
	1984	1980-84		1974	1965-73
	1985	1976-85		1975-1979	Latest
	1986	1982-86		1980	1971-79
	1987	1983-87		1981-1984	Latest
	1988	1984-88		1985	1976-84
	1989	1985-89		1986-1991	Latest
	1990	1986-90		1992	1983-92
	1991	1987-91		1993-1995	Latest
	1992	1983-92		1996	1987-95
	1993	1989-93		1997-1999	Latest
	1994	1990-94			
	1995	1991-95			
	1996	1987-96	- by month	1967	1962-66
	1997	1993-97		1974	1965-73
	1997HS[iii]	1948-97		1980	1971-79
	1998	1994-98		1985	1976-84

Index
Historical index
(See notes at end of index)

Subject-matter	Year of issue	Time coverage	Subject-matter	Year of issue	Time coverage
	1998	1994-98		1971	1967-71
	1999	1995-99		1972	1968-72
	2000	1996-00		1973	1969-73
	2001	1997-01		1974	1965-74
	2002	1998-02		1975	1971-75
	2003	1999-03		1976	1972-76
	2004	2000-04		1977	1973-77
	2005	2001-05		1978	1974-78
	2006	2002-06		1979	1975-79
	2007	2003-07		1980	1971-80
	2008	2004-08		1981	1977-81
	2009-2010	2006-10		1982	1978-82
	2011	2007-11		1983	1979-83
	2012	2008-12		1984	1980-84
	2013	2009-13		1985	1976-85
	2014	2010-14		1986	1982-86
	2015	2011-15		1987	1983-87
- by age and sex	1948	1936-47		1988	1984-88
	1951	1936-49		1989	1985-89
	1957	1948-56		1990	1986-90
	1961	1952-60		1991	1987-91
	1966	1956-65		1992	1983-92
	1967	1962-66		1993	1989-93
	1971-1973	Latest		1994	1990-94
	1974	1965-73		1995	1991-95
	1975-1979	Latest		1996	1987-96
	1980	1971-79		1997	1993-97
	1981-1984	Latest		1998	1994-98
	1985	1976-84		1999	1995-99
	1986-1991	Latest		2000	1996-00
	1992	1983-92		2001	1997-01
	1993-1995	Latest		2002	1998-02
	1996	1987-95		2003	1999-03
	1997-2015	Latest		2004	2000-04
				2005	2001-05
- by age and sex and urban/rural residence	1971-1973	Latest		2006	2002-06
	1974	1965-73		2007	2003-07
	1975-1979	Latest		2008	2004-08
	1980	1971-79		2009-2010	2006-10
	1981-1984	Latest		2011	2007-11
	1985	1976-84		2012	2008-12
	1986-1991	Latest		2013	2009-13
	1992	1983-92		2014	2010-14
	1993-1995	Latest		2015	2011-15
	1996	1987-95	**Intercensal rates of population increase**	1948	1900-48
	1997-1999	Latest		1949/50	1900-50
				1951	1900-51
- by urban/rural residence	1967	Latest		1952	1850-1952
	1968	1964-68		1953	1850-1953
	1969	1965-69		1955	1850-1954
	1970	1966-70		1960	1900-61
				1962	1900-62
				1964	1955-64
				1970	1900-70

Index
Historical index
(See notes at end of index)

Index
Historical index
(See notes at end of index)

Subject-matter	Year of issue	Time coverage
	1990	Latest
	2006-2015	Latest
- by age of bride and previous marital status	1958	1948-57
	1968	Latest
	1976	Latest
	1982	Latest
	1990	Latest
- by age of groom	1948	1936-47
	1949/50	1936-49
	1958	1948-57
	1959-1967	Latest
	1968	1958-67
	1969-1975	Latest
	1976	1966-75
	1977-1981	Latest
	1982	1972-81
	1983-1986	Latest
	1987	1975-86
	1988-1989	Latest
	1990	1980-1989
	1990-1997	Latest
	1998	1993-97
	1999	1994-98
	2000	1995-99
	2001	1997-01
	2002	1998-02
	2003	1999-03
	2004	2000-04
	2005	2001-05
	2006-2015	Latest
- by age of groom classified by age of bride	1958	1948-57
	1968	Latest
	1976	Latest
	1982	Latest
	1990	Latest
	2006-2015	Latest
- by age of groom and previous marital status	1958	1948-57
	1968	Latest
	1976	Latest
	1982	Latest
	1990	Latest
- by month	1968	1963-67
- by previous marital status of		

Subject-matter	Year of issue	Time coverage
bride:		
and age	1958	1946-57
	1968	Latest
	1976	Latest
	1982	Latest
	1990	Latest
and previous marital status of groom	1949/50	Latest
	1958	1948-57
	1968	1958-67
	1976	1966-75
	1982	1972-81
	1990	1980-89
- by previous marital status of groom: and age	1958	1946-57
	1968	Latest
	1976	Latest
	1982	Latest
	1990	Latest
and previous marital status of bride	1949/50	Latest
	1958	1948-57
	1968	1958-67
	1976	1966-75
	1982	1972-81
	1990	1980-89
-by urban/rural residence	1968	Latest
	1969	1965-69
	1970	1966-70
	1971	1967-71
	1972	1968-72
	1973	1969-73
	1974	1970-74
	1975	1971-75
	1976	1957-76
	1977	1973-77
	1978	1974-78
	1979	1975-79
	1980	1976-80
	1981	1977-81
	1982	1963-82
	1983	1979-83
	1984	1980-84
	1985	1981-85
	1986	1982-86
	1987	1983-87
	1988	1984-88
	1989	1985-89
	1990	1971-90
	1991	1987-91
	1992	1988-92

Subject-matter	Year of issue	Time coverage	Subject-matter	Year of issue	Time coverage
	1982	1972-81		2013	2009-13
	1987	1975-86		2014	2010-14
	1990	1980-89		2015	2011-15
- by sex among marriageable population	1958	1935-56	**Marriage rates, first** -by detailed age of groom and bride	1982	1972-81
	1968	1935-67		1990	1980-89
	1976	1966-75			
	1982	1972-81			
	1990	1980-89	**Married population by age and sex (see: Population by marital status)**		
- by urban/rural residence	1968	Latest			
	1969	1965-69			
	1970	1966-70	**Maternal death**	1951	1947-50
	1971	1967-71		1952	1947-51
	1972	1968-72		1953	Latest
	1973	1969-73		1954	1945-53
	1974	1970-74		1955-1956	Latest
	1975	1971-75		1957	1952-56
	1976	1957-76		1958-1960	Latest
	1977	1973-77		1961	1955-60
	1978	1974-78		1962-1965	Latest
	1979	1975-79		1966	1960-65
	1980	1976-80		1967-1973	Latest
	1981	1977-81		1974	1965-73
	1982	1963-82		1975-1979	Latest
	1983	1979-83		1980	1971-79
	1984	1980-84		1981	1972-80
	1985	1981-85		1982	1972-81
	1986	1982-86		1983	1973-82
	1987	1983-87		1984	1974-83
	1988	1984-88		1985	1975-84
	1989	1985-89		1986	1976-85
	1990	1971-90		1987	1977-86
	1991	1987-91		1988	1978-87
	1992	1988-92		1989	1979-88
	1993	1989-93		1990	1980-89
	1994	1990-94		1991	1981-90
	1995	1991-95		1992	1982-91
	1996	1992-96		1993	1983-92
	1997	1993-97		1994	1984-93
	1998	1994-98		1995	1985-94
	1999	1995-99		1996	1986-95
	2000	1996-00		1997	1987-96
	2001	1997-01		1998	1988-97
	2002	1998-02		1999	1989-98
	2003	1999-03		2000	1991-00
	2004	2000-04		2001	1991-00
	2005	2001-05		2002	1995-02
	2006	2002-06		2003	1995-02
	2007	2003-07		2004	1995-04
	2008	2004-08		2005	1995-04
	2009-2010	2006-10		2006	1997-06
	2011	2007-11		2007	1997-06
	2012	2008-12		2008	1999-08

Subject-matter	Year of issue	Time coverage
	1977	1967-76
	1985	1975-84
	1989	1979-88
	1996	1986-95
- emigrants, long term:		
by age and sex	1948	1945-47
	1949/50	1946-48
	1951	1948-50
	1952	1949-51
	1954	1950-53
	1957	1953-56
	1959	1955-58
	1962	1958-61
	1966	1960-65
	1970	1962-69
	1977	1967-76
	1989	1975-88
by country or area of intended residence	1948	1945-47
	1949/50	1945-48
	1951	1948-50
	1952	1949-51
	1954	1950-53
	1957	1953-56
	1959	1956-58
	1977	1958-76
	1989	1975-88
- immigrants, long term		
by age and sex	1948	1945-47
	1949/50	1946-48
	1951	1948-50
	1952	1949-51
	1954	1950-53
	1957	1953-56
	1959	1955-58
	1962	1958-61
	1966	1960-65
	1970	1962-69
	1977	1967-76
	1989	1975-88
by country or area of last residence	1948	1945-47
	1949/50	1945-48
	1951	1948-50
	1952	1949-51
	1954	1950-53
	1957	1953-56

Subject-matter	Year of issue	Time coverage
	1959	1956-58
	1977	1958-76
	1989	1975-88
	1948	1945-47
	1949/50	1945-48
- refugees, by country or area of destination:		
repatriated by the International Refugee Organization	1952	1947-51
resettled by the International Refugee Organization	1952	1947-51

Mortality [see: Death(s), Death rates, infant deaths, infant mortality rates, Foetal death(s), Foetal death ratios, Life tables, Maternal deaths, Maternal mortality rates, Neonatal deaths, Neo-natal mortality rates, Perinatal mortality, Post-neo-natal deaths, Post-neo-natal mortality rates]

N

Natality (see: Births and Birth rates)

Subject-matter	Year of issue	Time coverage
Natural increase rate	1958-1978	Latest
	1978HS[ii]	1948-78
	1979-1997	Latest
	1998	1995-98
	1999	1996-99
	2000	1995-00
	2001	1997-01
	2002	1998-02
	2003	1999-03

Subject-matter	Year of issue	Time coverage	Subject-matter	Year of issue	Time coverage
	2004	2000-04		1986-1991	Latest
	2005	2001-05		1992	1983-92
	2006	2002-06		1993-1995	Latest
	2007	2003-07		1996	1987-95
	2008	2004-08		1997	Latest
	2009-2010	2006-10		1997HS[iii]	1948-96
	2011	2007-11		1998-1999	Latest
	2012	2008-12			
	2013	2009-13	**Net reproduction rates**		
	2014	2010-14	(see: Reproduction rates)		
	2015	2011-15			
			Nuptiality (see: Marriages)		

P

Subject-matter	Year of issue	Time coverage	Subject-matter	Year of issue	Time coverage
Neo-natal mortality			**Perinatal deaths**......................	1961	1952-60
- by sex	1948	1936-47		1966	1956-65
	1951	1936-50		1971	1966-70
	1957	1948-56		1974	1965-73
	1961	1952-60		1980	1971-79
	1963-1965	Latest		1985	1976-84
	1966	1961-65		1996	1987-95
	1967	1962-66	- by urban/rural		
	2000-2015	Latest	residence	1971	1966-70
- by sex and				1974	1965-73
urban/rural				1980	1971-79
residence	1968-1973	Latest		1985	1976-84
	1974	1965-73		1996	1987-95
	1975-1979	Latest			
	1980	1971-79	**Perinatal death ratios**	1961	1952-60
	1981-1984	Latest		1966	1956-65
	1985	1976-84		1971	1966-70
	1986-1991	Latest		1974	1965-73
	1992	1983-92		1980	1971-79
	1993-1995	Latest		1985	1976-84
	1996	1987-95		1996	1987-95
	1997	Latest	- by urban/rural		
	1997HS[iii]	1948-96	residence	1971	1966-70
	1998-1999	Latest		1974	1965-73
Neo-natal mortality rates				1980	1971-79
- by sex	1948	1936-47		1985	1976-84
	1951	1936-50		1996	1987-95
	1957	1948-56			
	1961	1952-60	**Population**		
	1966	1956-65	- Ageing		
	1967	1962-66	selected indicators	1991PA[vii]	1950-90
	2000-2015	Latest			
- by sex and			- by age groups		
urban/rural			and sex:		
residence	1971-1973	Latest	enumerated	1948-1952	Latest
	1974	1965-73		1953	1950-52
	1975-1979	Latest		1954-1959	Latest[vi]
	1980	1971-79		1960	1940-60
	1981-1984	Latest		1961	Latest
	1985	1976-84			

Index
Historical index
(See notes at end of index)

Subject-matter	Year of issue	Time coverage	Subject-matter	Year of issue	Time coverage
	1962	1955-62	sex		
	1963	1955-63		1963	1955-63
	1964	1955-64[vi]		1964	1955-64[vi]
	1965-1969	Latest		1971	1962-71
	1970	1950-70		1973	1965-73[vi]
	1971	1962-71		1979	1970-79[vi]
	1972	Latest		1983	1974-83
	1973	1965-73		1988	1980-88[vi]
	1974-1978	Latest		1993	1985-93
	1978HS[ii]	1948-77	- by households, number and size (see also: Households)		
	1979-1991	Latest		1955	1945-54
	1991PA[vii]	1950-90		1962	1955-62
	1992-1997	Latest		1963	1955-63[vi]
	1997HS[iii]	1948-97		1968	Latest
	1998-2015	Latest		1971	1962-71
estimated	1948-1949/50	1945 and Latest[vi]		1973	1965-73[vi]
	1951-1959	Latest		1976	Latest
	1960	1940-60		1982	Latest
	1961-1969	Latest		1987	1975-86
	1970	1950-70		1990	1980-89
	1971-1997	Latest		1995	1985-95
	1997HS[iii]	1948-97	- by language and sex		
	1998-2015	Latest		1956	1945-55
percentage distribution	1948-1949/50	1945 and Latest[vi]		1963	1955-63
	1951-1952	Latest		1964	1955-64[vi]
- by country or area of birth and sex (see also: foreign-born, below)				1971	1962-71
	1956	1945-55		1973	1965-73[vi]
	1963	1955-63		1979	1970-79[vi]
	1964	1955-64[vi]		1983	1974-83
	1971	1962-71		1988	1980-88[vi]
	1973	1965-73[vi]		1993	1985-93
- by country or area of birth and sex and age (see also: foreign-born, below)			- by level of education, age and sex		
	1977	Latest		1956	1945-55
	1983	1974-83		1963	1955-63
	1989	1980-88[vi]		1964	1955-64[vi]
- by citizenship	1956	1945-55		1971	1962-71
	1963	1955-63		1973	1965-73[vi]
	1964	1955-64[vi]		1979	1970-79[vi]
	1971	1962-71		1983	1974-83
	1973	1965-73[vi]		1988	1980-88[vi]
- by citizenship, sex and age	1977	Latest		1993	1985-93
	1983	1974-83	- by literacy, age and sex (see also: illiteracy, below)	1948	Latest
	1989	Latest		1955	1945-54
- by ethnic composition and	1956	1945-55		1963	1955-63
				1964	1955-64[vi]
				1971	1962-71
			- by literacy, age and sex and urban/rural residence	1973	1965-73[vi]
				1979	1970-79[vi]
				1983	1974-83

Subject-matter	Year of issue	Time coverage
	1971	1962-71
	1972	Latest
	1973	1965-73
	1974-1978	Latest
	1978HS[ii]	1948-78
	1979-1982	Latest
	1983	1974-83
	1984-1997	Latest
	1997HS[iii]	1948-97
	1998-2015	Latest
estimated	1948-1949/50	1945and latest
	1951-1954	Latest
	1955-1959	Latest
	1960	1940-60
	1961-1969	Latest
	1970	1950-70
	1971	1962-71
	1972	Latest
	1973	1965-73
	1974-1997	Latest
	1997HS[iii]	1948-97
	1998-1999	Latest
	2000	1991-00
	2001	1992-01
	2002	1993-02
	2003	1994-03
	2004	1995-04
	2005	1996-05
	2006	1997-06
	2007	1998-07
	2008	1999-08
	2009-2010	2001-10
	2011	2002-11
	2012	2003-12
	2013	2004-13
	2014	2005-14
	2015	2006-15
- by single years of age and sex	1955	1945-54
	1962	1955-62
	1963	1955-63[vi]
	1971	1962-71
	1973	1965-73[vi]
	1979	1970-79[vi]
	1983	1974-83
	1988	1980-88[vi]
	1993	1985-93
- cities (see: of cities, below)		
- civil division (see: by major civil divisions, above)		

Subject-matter	Year of issue	Time coverage
- density (see: Density)		
- Disabled	1991PA[vii]	Latest
- economically active:		
by age and sex	1945	1945-54
	1956	1945-55
	1964	1955-64
	1972	1962-72
by age and sex and urban/rural residence	1973	1965-73[vi]
	1979	1970-79[vi]
	1984	1974-84
	1988	1980-88[vi]
	1994	1985-94
by age and sex, per cent	1949/50	1930-48
	1954	Latest
	1955	1945-54
	1956	1945-55
	1964	1955-64
	1972	1962-72
by age and sex, per cent and urban/rural residence	1973	1965-73[vi]
	1979	1970-79[vi]
	1984	1974-84
	1988	1980-88[vi]
	1994	1985-94
by industry, age and sex	1956	1945-55
	1964	1955-64
	1972	1962-72
by industry, age, sex and urban/rural residence	1973	1965-74[vi]
	1979	1970-79[vi]
	1984	1974-84
	1988	1980-88[vi]
	1994	1985-94
by industry, status and sex	1948	Latest
	1949/50	Latest
	1955	1945-54
	1964	1955-64
	1972	1962-72

Index
Historical index
(See notes at end of index)

Subject-matter	Year of issue	Time coverage	Subject-matter	Year of issue	Time coverage
	1969	1963-69		1960	1950-59
	1970	1963-70		1961	1950-60
	1971	1963-71		1962	1950-61
	1972	1963-72		1963	1958-62
	1973	1970-73			1960-62
	1974	1970-74		1964	1958-63
	1975	1970-75			1960-63
	1976	1970-76		1965	1958-64
	1977	1970-77			1960-64
	1978	1975-78		1966	1958-66
	1979	1975-79			1960-66
	1980	1975-80		1967	1960-67
	1981	1975-81			1963-67
	1982	1975-82		1968	1960-68
	1983	1980-83			1963-68
	1984	1980-84		1969	1960-69
	1985	1980-85			1963-69
	1986	1980-86		1970	1963-70
	1987	1980-87			1965-70
	1988	1985-88		1971	1963-71
	1989	1985-89			1965-71
	1990	1985-90		1972	1963-72
	1991	1985-91			1965-72
	1992	1985-92		1973	1965-73
	1993	1990-93			1970-73
	1994	1990-94		1974	1965-74
	1995	1990-95			1970-74
	1996	1990-96		1975	1965-75
	1997	1990-97			1970-75
	1998	1993-98		1976	1965-76
	1999	1995-99			1970-76
	2000	1995-00		1977	1965-77
	2001	1995-01			1970-77
	2002	1995-02		1978-1979	1970-75
	2003	2000-03		1980-1983	1975-80
	2004	2000-04		1984-1986	1980-85
	2005	2000-05		1987-1992	1985-90
	2006	2000-06		1993-1997	1990-95
	2007	2005-07		1998-2000	1995-00
	2008	2005-08		2001-2005	2000-05
	2009-2010	2005-10		2006-2010	2005-10
	2011	2005-11		2011-2015	2010-15
	2012	2005-12			
	2013	2010-13	- Homeless by age and sex		
	2014	2010-14		1991PA[vii]	Latest
	2015	2010-15	- illiteracy rates by sex		
average annual for the world, macro-regions (continents) and regions				1948	Latest
				1955	1945-54
				1960	1920-60
				1963	1955-63[vi]
				1964	1955-64[vi]
				1970	1950-70
	1957	1950-56			
	1958	1950-57			
	1959	1950-58			

Subject-matter	Year of issue	Time coverage	Subject-matter	Year of issue	Time coverage
- of cities:				1954	1920-54
capital city	1952	Latest		1955	1920-55
	1955	1945-54		1956	1920-56
	1957	Latest		1957	1940-57
	1960	1939-61		1958	1939-58
	1962	1955-62		1959	1940-59
	1963	1955-63		1960	1920-60
	1964-1969	Latest		1961	1941-61
	1970	1950-70		1962	1942-62
	1971	1962-71		1963	1943-63
	1972	Latest		1964	1955-64
	1973	1965-73		1965	1946-65
	1974-2015	Latest		1966	1947-66
				1967	1958-67
of 100000+				1968	1959-68
inhabitants	1952	Latest		1969	1960-69
	1955	1945-54		1970	1950-70
	1957	Latest		1971	1962-71
	1960	1939-61		1972	1963-72
	1962	1955-62		1973	1964-73
	1963	1955-63		1974	1965-74
	1964-1969	Latest		1975	1966-75
	1970	1950-70		1976	1967-76
	1971	1962-71		1977	1968-77
	1972	Latest		1978	1969-78
	1973	1965-73		1978HS[ii]	1948-78
	1974-2015	Latest		1979	1970-79
				1980	1971-80
- of continents				1981	1972-81
(see: of macro				1982	1973-82
regions, below)				1983	1974-83
- of countries or				1984	1975-84
areas (totals):				1985	1976-85
enumerated	1948	1900-48		1986	1977-86
	1949/50	1900-50		1987	1978-87
	1951	1900-51		1988	1979-88
	1952	1850-1952		1989	1980-89
	1953	1850-1953		1990	1981-90
	1954	Latest		1991	1982-91
	1955	1850-1954		1992	1983-92
	1956-1961	Latest		1993	1984-93
	1962	1900-62		1994	1985-94
	1963	Latest		1995	1986-95
	1964	1955-64		1996	1987-96
	1965-1978	Latest		1997	1988-97
	1978HS[ii]	1948-78		1997HS[iii]	1948-97
	1979-1997	Latest		1998	1989-98
	1997HS[iii]	1948-97		1999	1990-99
	1998-2015	Latest		2000	1991-00
estimated	1948	1932-47		2001	1992-01
	1949/50	1932-49		2002	1993-02
	1951	1930-50		2003	1994-03
	1952	1920-51		2004	1995-04
	1953	1920-53		2005	1996-05

Index
Historical index
(See notes at end of index)

Subject-matter	Year of issue	Time coverage	Subject-matter	Year of issue	Time coverage
	2006	1997-06		1994	1950-94
	2007	1998-07		1995	1950-95
	2008	1999-08		1996	1950-96
	2009-2010	2001-10		1997	1950-97
	2011	2002-11		1998-1999	1950-00
	2012	2003-12		2000	1950-00
	2013	2004-13		2001	1950-01
	2014	2005-14		2002	1950-02
	2015	2006-15		2003	1950-03
				2004	1950-04
- of major regions	1949/50	1920-49		2005	1950-05
	1951	1950		2006	1950-06
	1952	1920-51		2007	1950-07
	1953	1920-52		2008	1950-08
	1954	1920-53		2009-2010	1950-10
	1955	1920-54		2011	1960-11
	1956	1920-55		2012	1960-12
	1957	1920-56		2013	1960-13
	1958	1920-57		2014	1960-14
	1959	1920-58		2015	1960-15
	1960	1920-59			
	1961	1920-60	- of regions	1949/50	1920-49
	1962	1920-61		1952	1920-51
	1963	1930-62		1953	1920-52
	1964	1930-63		1954	1920-53
	1965	1930-65		1955	1920-54
	1966	1930-66		1956	1920-55
	1967	1930-67		1957	1920-56
	1968	1930-68		1958	1920-57
	1969	1930-69		1959	1920-58
	1970	1950-70		1960	1920-59
	1971	1950-71		1961	1920-60
	1972	1950-72		1962	1920-61
	1973	1950-73		1963	1930-62
	1974	1950-74		1964	1930-63
	1975	1950-75		1965	1930-65
	1976	1950-76		1966	1930-66
	1977	1950-77		1967	1930-67
	1978	1950-78		1968	1930-68
	1979	1950-79		1969	1930-69
	1980	1950-80		1970	1950-70
	1981	1950-81		1971	1950-71
	1982	1950-82		1972	1950-72
	1983	1950-83		1973	1950-73
	1984	1950-84		1974	1950-74
	1985	1950-85		1975	1950-75
	1986	1950-86		1976	1950-76
	1987	1950-87		1977	1950-77
	1988	1950-88		1978	1950-78
	1989	1950-89		1979	1950-79
	1990	1950-90		1980	1950-80
	1991	1950-91		1981	1950-81
	1992	1950-92		1982	1950-82
	1993	1950-93		1983	1950-83

Subject-matter	Year of issue	Time coverage	Subject-matter	Year of issue	Time coverage
	1984	1950-84		1973	1950-73
	1985	1950-85		1974	1950-74
	1986	1950-86		1975	1950-75
	1987	1950-87		1976	1950-76
	1988	1950-88		1977	1950-77
	1989	1950-89		1978	1950-78
	1990	1950-90		1979	1950-79
	1991	1950-91		1980	1950-80
	1992	1950-92		1981	1950-81
	1993	1950-93		1982	1950-82
	1994	1950-94		1983	1950-83
	1995	1950-95		1984	1950-84
	1996	1950-96		1985	1950-85
	1997	1950-97		1986	1950-86
	1998-1999	1950-00		1987	1950-87
	2000	1950-00		1988	1950-88
	2001	1950-01		1989	1950-89
	2002	1950-02		1990	1950-90
	2003	1950-03		1991	1950-91
	2004	1950-04		1992	1950-92
	2005	1950-05		1993	1950-93
	2006	1950-06		1994	1950-94
	2007	1950-07		1995	1950-95
	2008	1950-08		1996	1950-96
	2009-2010	1950-10		1997	1950-97
	2011	1960-11		1998-1999	1950-00
	2012	1960-12		2000	1950-00
	2013	1960-13		2001	1950-01
	2014	1960-14		2002	1950-02
	2015	1960-15		2003	1950-03
				2004	1950-04
- of the world	1949/50	1920-49		2005	1950-05
	1951	1950		2006	1950-06
	1952	1920-51		2007	1950-07
	1953	1920-52		2008	1950-08
	1954	1920-53		2009-2010	1950-10
	1955	1920-54		2011	1960-11
	1956	1920-55		2012	1960-12
	1957	1920-56		2013	1960-13
	1958	1920-57		2014	1960-14
	1959	1920-58		2015	1960-15
	1960	1920-59			
	1961	1920-60	- rural residence (see: urban/rural residence, below)		
	1962	1920-61			
	1963	1930-62			
	1964	1930-63	- single, by age and sex (see also: by marital status, above):		
	1965	1930-65			
	1966	1930-66			
	1967	1930-67			
	1968	1930-68	numbers	1960	1920-60
	1969	1930-69		1970	1950-70
	1970	1950-70	percent	1949/50	1926-48
	1971	1950-71		1960	1920-60
	1972	1950-72		1970	1950-70

Subject-matter	Year of issue	Time coverage
- urban/rural residence		
	1968	1964-68
	1969	1965-69
	1970	1950-70
	1971	1962-71
	1972	1968-72
	1973	1965-73
	1974	1966-74
	1975	1967-75
	1976	1967-76
	1977	1968-77
	1978	1969-78
	1979	1970-79
	1980	1971-80
	1981	1972-81
	1982	1973-82
	1983	1974-83
	1984	1975-84
	1985	1976-85
	1986	1977-86
	1987	1978-87
	1988	1979-88
	1989	1980-89
	1990	1981-90
	1991	1982-91
	1992	1983-92
	1993	1984-93
	1994	1985-94
	1995	1986-95
	1996	1987-96
	1997	1988-97
	1998	1989-98
	1999	1990-99
	2000	1991-00
	2001	1992-01
	2002	1993-02
	2003	1994-03
	2004	1995-04
	2005	1996-05
	2006	1997-06
	2007	1998-07
	2008	1999-08
	2009-2010	2001-10
	2011	2002-11
	2012	2003-12
	2013	2004-13
	2014	2005-14
	2015	2006-15
by age and sex:		
enumerated	1963	1955-63
	1964	1955-64[vi]
	1967	Latest
	1970	1950-70

Subject-matter	Year of issue	Time coverage
	1971	1962-71
	1972	Latest
	1973	1965-73
	1974-1978	Latest
	1978HS[ii]	1948-77
	1979-1996	Latest
	1979-1997	Latest
	1997HS[iii]	1948-96
	1998-2015	Latest
estimated	1963	Latest
	1967	Latest
	1970	1950-70
	1971-1997	Latest
	1997HS[iii]	1948-96
	1998-2015	Latest
by country or area of birth and sex	1971	1962-71
	1973	1965-73[vi]
by country or area of birth and sex and age	1977	Latest
by citizenship and sex	1971	1962-71
	1973	1965-73[vi]
by citizenship and sex and age	1977	Latest
	1983	1974-83
	1989	1980-88
by ethnic composition and sex	1971	Latest
	1973	1965-73[vi]
	1979	1970-79[vi]
	1983	1974-83
	1988	1980-88[vi]
	1993	1985-93
by households, number and size (see also: Households)	1968	Latest
	1971	1962-71
	1973	1965-73[vi]
	1976	Latest
	1982	Latest
	1987	1975-86
	1990	1980-89
	1995	1985-95
by language and sex	1971	1962-71
	1973	1965-73[vi]
	1979	1970-79[vi]

Subject-matter	Year of issue	Time coverage
	1977	1968-77
	1978	1969-78
	1979	1970-79
	1980	1971-80
	1981	1972-81
	1982	1973-82
	1983	1974-83
	1984	1975-84
	1985	1976-85
	1986	1977-86
	1987	1978-87
	1988	1979-88
	1989	1980-89
	1990	1981-90
	1991	1982-91
	1992	1983-92
	1993	1984-93
	1994	1985-94
	1995	1986-95
	1996	1987-96
	1997	1988-97
	1998	1989-98
	1999	1990-99
	2000	1991-00
	2001	1992-01
	2002	1993-02
	2003	1994-03
	2004	1995-04
	2005	1996-05
	2006	1997-06
	2007	1998-07
	2008	1999-08
	2009-2010	2001-10
	2011	2002-11
	2012	2003-12
	2013	2004-13
	2014	2005-14
	2015	2006-15
by single years of age and sex	1971	1962-71
	1973	1965-73[vi]
	1979	1970-79[vi]
	1983	1974-83
	1993	1985-93
female: by number of children born alive and age	1971	1962-71
	1973	1965-73[vi]
	1975	1965-74
	1978HS[ii]	1948-77
	1981	1972-80

Subject-matter	Year of issue	Time coverage
	1986	1977-85
	1997HS[iii]	1948-96
female: by number of children living and age	1971	1962-71
	1973	1965-73[vi]
	1975	1965-74
	1978HS[ii]	1948-77
	1981	1972-80
	1986	1977-85
	1997HS[iii]	1948-96
Post-neo-natal deaths:		
- by sex	1948	1936-47
	1951	1936-50
	1957	1948-56
	1961	1952-60
	1963-1965	Latest
	1966	1961-65
	1967	1962-66
	1968-1973	Latest
	1974	1965-73
	1975-1979	Latest
	1980	1971-79
	1981-1984	Latest
	1985	1976-84
	1986-1991	Latest
	1992	1983-92
	1993-1995	Latest
	1996	1987-95
	1997	Latest
	1997HS[ii]	1948-96
	1998-2015	Latest
- by urban/rural residence	1971-1973	Latest
	1974	1965-73
	1975-1979	Latest
	1980	1971-79
	1981-1984	Latest
	1985	1976-84
	1986-1991	Latest
	1992	1983-92
	1993-1995	Latest
	1996	1987-95
	1997	Latest
	1997 HS[ii]	1948-96
	1998-1999	Latest
Post-neo-natal mortality rates:		
- by sex	1948	1936-47
	1951	1936-50
	1957	1948-56

Subject-matter	Year of issue	Time coverage
	1961	1952-60
	1966	1956-65
	1967	1962-66
	1968-1973	Latest
	1974	1965-73
	1975-1979	Latest
	1980	1971-79
	1981-1984	Latest
	1985	1976-84
	1986-1991	Latest
	1992	1983-92
	1993-1995	Latest
	1996	1987-95
	1997	Latest
	1997HS [ii]	1948-96
	1998-2015	Latest
- by urban/rural residence	1971-1973	Latest
	1974	1965-73
	1975-1979	Latest
	1980	1971-79
	1981-1984	Latest
	1985	1976-84
	1986-1991	Latest
	1992	1983-92
	1993-1995	Latest
	1996	1987-95
	1997	Latest
	1997HS [ii]	1948-96
	1998-1999	Latest

R

Rates (see under following subject-matter headings: Annulments, Births, Deaths, Divorces, Fertility, Illiteracy, Infant Mortality, Intercensal, Life Tables, Literacy Marriages, Maternal mortality, Natural increase, Neo-natal mortality, Population growth, Post-neo-natal mortality, Reproduction)

Ratios (see under following subject matter headings: Births, Child-woman, Fertility, Foetal deaths, Perinatal mortality)

Refugees, by country or area of destination:

Subject-matter	Year of issue	Time coverage
- repatriated by the International Refugee Organization	1952	1947-51
- resettled by the International Refugee Organization	1952	1947-51

Religion and sex (see: Population)

Subject-matter	Year of issue	Time coverage
Reproduction rates, gross and net	1948	1920-47
	1949/50	1900-48
	1954	1920-53
	1965	1930-64
	1969	1963-68
	1975	1966-74
	1978HS [ii]	1948-77
	1981	1962-80
	1986	1967-85
	1997HS [iii]	1948-96
	1999CD [iv]	1980-99

Rural/urban births [see: Birth(s)]

Rural/urban population (see: Population: urban/rural residence)

S

Sex (see appropriate subject entry, e.g., Births, Death rates, Migration, Population, etc.)

Subject-matter	Year of issue	Time coverage
Size of (living) family: - female population by age (see also: Children)	1949/50	Latest
	1954	1930-53
	1955	1945-54
	1959	1949-58
	1963	1955-63
	1965	1955-65
	1968	1955-67
	1969	Latest
	1971	1962-71
	1973	1965-73 [vi]
	1975	1965-74
	1978HS [ii]	1948-77
	1981	1972-80
	1986	1977-85
	1997HS [iii]	1948-96

Special text (see separate listing in Appendix to this Index)

Subject-matter	Year of issue	Time coverage	Subject-matter	Year of issue	Time coverage
	1957	1930-56		1973	1965-73[vi]
	1961	1945-61		1979	1970-79[vi]
	1966	1920-66		1983	1974-83
	1967	1900-67		1988	1980-88[vi]
	1974	1965-74		1993	1985-93
	1980	1971-80	Fertility characteristics		
	1985	1976-85		1940/50	1900-50
	1992	1983-92		1954	1900-53
	1996	1987-96		1955	1945-54
				1959	1935-59
- Natality	1949/50	1932-49		1963	1955-63
	1954	1920-53		1965	1955-65
	1959	1920-58		1969	Latest
	1965	1920-65		1971	1962-71
	1969	1925-69		1973	1965-73[vi]
	1975	1956-75		1975	1965-75
	1981	1962-81		1981	1972-81
	1986	1967-86		1986	1977-86
	1992	1983-92		1992	1983-92
	1999CD[iv]	1980-99	Geographic characteristics		
- Nuptiality (see: Marriage and Divorce, above)				1952	1900-51
				1955	1945-54
				1962	1955-62
				1964	1955-64[vi]
- Population Ageing and the Situation of Elderly Persons	1991PA[vii]	1950-90		1971	1962-71
				1973	1965-73[vi]
				1979	1970-79[vi]
- Population Census:				1983	1974-83
Economic characteristics				1988	1980-88[vi]
	1956	1945-55		1993	1985-93
	1964	1955-64	Household characteristics		
	1972	1962-72		1955	1945-54
	1973	1965-73[vi]		1962	1955-62
	1979	1970-79[vi]		1963	1955-63[vi]
	1984	1974-84		1971	1962-71
	1988	1980-88[vi]		1973	1965-73[vi]
	1994	1985-94		1976	1966-75
	2014	1995-2014		1983	1974-83
Educational characteristics				1987	1975-86
	1955	1945-54		1995	1985-95
	1956	1945-55		2013	1995-2013
	1963	1955-63	Personal characteristics		
	1964	1955-64[vi]		1955	1945-54
	1971	1962-71		1962	1955-62
	1973	1965-73[vi]		1971	1962-71
	1979	1970-79[vi]		1973	1965-73[vi]
	1983	1974-83		1979	1970-79[vi]
	1988	1980-88[vi]		1983	1974-83
	1993	1985-93		1988	1980-88[vi]
Ethnic characteristics				1993	1985-93
	1956	1945-55	-Population trends	1960	1920-60
	1963	1955-63		1970	1950-70
	1964	1955-64[vi]			
	1971	1962-71			

Subject-matter	Year of issue	Time coverage	Subject-matter	Year of issue	Time coverage
U			(see: Infant deaths)		
Urban/rural births (see: Births)			**Urban/rural population** (see: Population: urban/rural residence)		
Urban/rural deaths (see: Deaths)			**Urban/rural population** **by average size of** **households** (see: Households)		
Urban/rural infant deaths					

APPENDIX

Special text of each Demographic Yearbook:

Divorce:

'Uses of Marriage and Divorce Statistics', 1958.

Marriage:

'Uses of Marriage and Divorce Statistics', 1958.

Households:

'Concepts and definitions of households, householder and institutional population', 1987.

Migration:

'Statistics of International Migration', 1977.

Mortality:

'Recent Mortality Trends', 1951.
'Development of Statistics of Causes of Death', 1951.
'Factors in Declining Mortality', 1957.
'Notes on Methods of Evaluating the Reliability of Conventional Mortality Statistics', 1961.
'Recent Trends of Mortality', 1966.
'Mortality Trends among Elderly Persons', 1991PA[vii].

Natality:

'Graphic Presentation of Trends in Fertility', 1959.
'Recent Trends in Birth Rates', 1965.
'Recent Changes in World Fertility', 1969.

Population

'World Population Trends, 1920-1949', 1949/50.
'Urban Trends and Characteristics', 1952.
'Background to the1950 Censuses of Population', 1955.
'The World Demographic Situation', 1956.
'How Well Do We Know the Present Size and Trend of the World's Population?', 1960.
'Notes on Availability of National Population Census Data and Methods of Estimating their Reliability', 1962.
'Availability and Adequacy of Selected Data Obtained from Population Censuses Taken 1955-1963', 1963.
'Availability of Selected Population Census Statistics: 1955-1964', 1964.
'Statistical Concepts and Definitions of Urban and Rural Population', 1967.
'Statistical Concepts and Definitions of Household', 1968.
'How Well Do We Know the Present Size and Trend of the World's Population?', 1970.
'United Nations Recommendations on Topics to be Investigated in a Population Census
Compared with Country Practice in National Censuses taken 1965-1971', 1971.
'Statistical Definitions of Urban Population and their Use in Applied Demography', 1972.
'Dates of National Population and Housing Census carried out during the decade1965-1974', 1974.
'Dates of National Population and/or Housing Censuses taken or anticipated during the decade 1975-1984', 1979.
'Dates of National Population and/or Housing Censuses taken during the decade1965-1974 and taken or anticipated during the decade 1975-1984', 1983.
'Dates of National Population and/or Housing Censuses taken during the decade1975-1984 and taken or anticipated during the decade 1985-1994', 1988 and 1993.
'Statistics Concerning the Economically Active Population: An Overview', 1984.

'Disability', 1991PA[vii].
'Population Ageing', 1991PA[vii].
'Special Needs for the Study of Population Ageing and Elderly Persons', 1991PA[vii].

General Notes

This cumulative index covers the contents of each of the 66 issues of the Demographic Yearbook. 'Year of issue' stands for the particular issue in which the indicated subject-matter appears. Unless otherwise specified, 'Time coverage' designates the years for which annual statistics are shown in the Demographic Yearbook referred to in 'Year of issue' column. 'Latest' or '2-Latest' indicates that data are for latest available year(s) only.

[i] Only titles not available for preceding bibliography.

[ii] Historical Supplement to the 30th DYB published in a separate volume in year 1979.

[iii] Historical Supplement to the 49th DYB published in a separate volume (CD-ROM) in year 2000.

[iv] Supplement to the 51st DYB focusing on natality published in a separate volume (CD-ROM) in year 2002.

[v] Five-year average rates.

[vi] Only data not available for preceding issue.

[vii] Population ageing published in separate volume.

Index
Index historique (suite)
(Voir notes à la fin de l'index)

Index
Index historique (suite)
(Voir notes à la fin de l'index)

Index
Index historique (suite)
(Voir notes à la fin de l'index)

Index
Index historique (suite)
(Voir notes à la fin de l'index)

Index
Index historique (suite)
(Voir notes à la fin de l'index)

Index
Index historique (suite)
(Voir notes à la fin de l'index)

Sujet	Année de l'édition	Période considérée
	2015	2010-14
-selon l'état matrimonial, l'âge et le sexe	1961	Dernière
	1967	Dernière
	1974	Dernière
	1980	Dernière
	1985	Dernière
	1996	Dernière
	2003	Dernière
-selon la profession, l'âge et le sexe	1957	Dernière
-selon la profession et l'âge (sexe masculin)	1961	Dernière
	1967	Dernière
-selon la résidence (urbaine/rurale)	1967	Dernière
	1968	1964-68
	1969	1965-69
	1970	1966-70
	1971	1967-71
	1972	1968-72
	1973	1969-73
	1974	1965-74
	1975	1971-75
	1976	1972-76
	1977	1973-77
	1978	1974-78
	1979	1975-79
	1980	1971-80
	1981	1977-81
	1982	1978-82
	1983	1979-83
	1984	1980-84
	1985	1976-85
	1986	1982-86
	1987	1983-87
	1988	1984-88
	1989	1985-89
	1990	1986-90
	1991	1987-91
	1992	1983-92
	1993	1989-93
	1994	1990-94
	1995	1991-95
	1996	1987-96
	1997	1993-97
	1998	1994-98
	1999	1995-99
	2000	1996-00
	2001	1997-01
	2002	1998-02
	2003	1999-03
	2004	2000-04
	2005	2001-05
	2006	2002-06
	2007	2003-07
	2008	2004-08
	2009-2010	2006-10
	2011	2007-11
	2012	2008-12

Sujet	Année de l'édition	Période considérée
	2013	2009-13
	2014	2010-14
	2015	2011-15
Densité de population:		
-des continents	1949/50	1920-49
	1951-1999	Dernière
	2001	2001
	2002	2002
	2003	2003
	2004	2004
	2005	2005
	2006	2006
	2007	2007
	2008	2008
	2009-2010	2010
	2011	2011
	2012	2012
	2013	2013
	2014	2014
	2015	2015
-des grandes régions (continentales)	1964-1999	Dernière
	2000	2000
	2001	2001
	2002	2002
	2003	2003
	2004	2004
	2005	2005
	2006	2006
	2007	2007
	2008	2008
	2009-2010	2010
	2011	2011
	2012	2012
	2013	2013
	2014	2014
	2015	2015
-des pays ou zones	1948-1999	Dernière
	2000	2000
	2001	2001
	2002	2002
	2003	2003
	2004	2004
	2005	2005
	2006	2006
	2007	2007
	2008	2008
	2009-2010	2010
	2011	2011
	2012	2012
	2013	2013
	2014	2014
	2015	2015
-des régions	1949/50	1920-49
	1952-1999	Dernière
	2000	2000
	2001	2001
	2002	2002

Index
Index historique (suite)
(Voir notes à la fin de l'index)

Sujet	Année de l'édition	Période considérée	Sujet	Année de l'édition	Période considérée
	2003	2003		1963	1954-63
	2004	2004		1964	1960-64
	2005	2005		1965	1961-65
	2006	2006		1966	1962-66
	2007	2007		1967	1963-67
	2008	2008		1968	1949-68
	2009-2010	2010		1969	1965-69
	2011	2011		1970	1966-70
	2012	2012		1971	1967-71
	2013	2013		1972	1968-72
	2014	2014		1973	1969-73
	2015	2015		1974	1970-74
				1975	1971-75
-du monde	1949/50	1920-49		1976	1957-76
	1952-1999	Dernière		1977	1973-77
	2000	2000		1962	1953-62
	2001	2001		1963	1954-63
	2002	2002		1964	1960-64
	2003	2003		1965	1961-65
	2004	2004		1966	1962-66
	2005	2005		1967	1963-67
	2006	2006		1968	1949-68
	2007	2007		1969	1965-69
	2008	2008		1970	1966-70
	2009-2010	2010		1971	1967-71
	2011	2011		1972	1968-72
	2012	2012		1973	1969-73
	2013	2013		1974	1970-74
	2014	2014		1975	1971-75
	2015	2015		1976	1957-76
				1977	1973-77
Dimension de la famille vivante:				1978	1974-78
-selon l'âge des femmes (voir également: Enfants)	1949-1950	Dernière		1979	1975-79
	1954	1930-53		1980	1976-80
	1955	1945-54		1981	1977-81
	1959	1949-58		1982	1963-82
	1963	1955-63		1983	1979-83
	1965	1955-65		1984	1980-84
	1968	1955-67		1985	1981-85
	1969	Dernière		1986	1982-86
	1971	1962-71		1987	1983-87
	1973	1965-73 [iii]		1988	1984-88
	1975	1965-74		1989	1985-89
	1978SR [i]	1948-77		1990	1971-90
	1981	1972-80		1991	1987-91
	1986	1977-85		1992	1988-92
	1997SR [ii]	1948-96		1993	1989-93
				1994	1990-94
Divorces	1951	1935-50		1995	1991-95
	1952	1936-51		1996	1992-96
	1953	1950-52		1997	1993-97
	1954	1946-53		1998	1994-98
	1955	1946-54		1999	1995-99
	1956	1947-55		2000	1996-00
	1957	1948-56		2001	1997-01
	1958	1940-57		2002	1998-02
	1959	1949-58		2003	1999-03
	1960	1950-59		2004	2000-04
	1961	1952-61		2005	2001-05
	1962	1953-62		2006	2002-06
				2007	2003-07
				2008	2004-08

Index
Index historique (suite)
(Voir notes à la fin de l'index)

Index
Index historique (suite)
(Voir notes à la fin de l'index)

Sujet	Année de l'édition	Période considérée
	1986	1982-86
	1987	1983-87
	1988	1984-88
	1989	1985-89
	1990	1971-90
	1991	1987-91
	1992	1988-92
	1993	1989-93
	1994	1990-94
	1995	1991-95
	1996	1992-96
	1997	1993-97
	1998	1994-98
	1999	1995-99
	2000	1996-00
	2001	1997-01
	2002	1998-02
	2003	1999-03
	2004	2000-04
	2005	2001-05
	2006	2002-06
	2007	2003-07
	2008	2004-08
	2009-2010	2006-10
	2011	2007-11
	2012	2008-12
	2013	2009-13
	2014	2010-14
	2015	2011-15
-pour la population mariée	1953	1935-52
	1954	1935-53
	1958	1935-56
	1968	1935-67
	1976	1966-75
	1978SR [i]	1948-77
	1982	1972-81
	1990	1980-89
-selon l'âge de l'épouse	1968	Dernière
	1976	Dernière
	1982	Dernière
	1987	1975-86
	1990	Dernière
-selon l'âge de l'époux	1968	Dernière
	1976	Dernière
	1982	Dernière
	1987	1975-86
	1990	Dernière
-selon la résidence (urbaine/rurale)	2002	1998-02
	2003	1999-03
	2004	2000-04
	2005	2001-05
	2006	2002-06
	2007	2003-07
	2008	2004-08
	2009-2010	2006-10
	2011	2007-11
	2012	2008-12

Sujet	Année de l'édition	Période considérée
	2013	2009-13
	2014	2010-14
	2015	2011-15
Durée du mariage (voir: Divorces)		

E

Emigrants (voir: Migration internationale)

Enfants, nombre:

Sujet	Année de l'édition	Période considérée
-dont il est tenu compte dans les divorces	1958	1948-57
	1968	1958-67
	1976	1966-75
	1982	1972-81
	1990	1980-89
-mis au monde, selon l'âge de la mère	1949/50	Dernière
	1954	1930-53
	1955	1945-54
	1959	1949-58
	1963	1955-63
	1965	1955-65
	1969	Dernière
	1971	1962-71
	1973	1965-73 [iii]
	1975	1965-74
	1978SR [i]	1948-77
	1981	1972-80
	1986	1977-85
	1997SR [ii]	1948-96
-vivants, selon l'âge de la mère	1940/50	Dernière
	1954	1930-53
	1955	1945-54
	1959	1949-58
	1963	1955-63
	1965	1955-65
	1968	1955-67
	1969	Dernière
	1971	1962-71
	1973	1965-73 [iii]
	1975	1965-74
	1978SR [i]	1948-77
	1981	1972-80
	1986	1977-85
	1997SR [ii]	1948-96

Espérance de vie (voir: Mortalité, tables de)

Etat matrimonial (voir la rubrique appropriée par sujet, p.ex., Décès, Population, etc.)

F

Sujet	Année de l'édition	Période considérée
Fécondité, indice synthétique	1987-1997	Dernière

Index
Index historique (suite)
(Voir notes à la fin de l'index)

I

Index
Index historique (suite)
(Voir notes à la fin de l'index)

Sujet	Année de l'édition	Période considérée	Sujet	Année de l'édition	Période considérée
	1963	1954-63		1982	1972-81
	1964	1960-64		1983-1986	Dernière
	1965	1956-65		1987	1975-86
	1966	1962-66		1988-1989	Dernière
	1967	1963-67		1990	1980-89
	1968	1949-68		1991-1997	Dernière
	1969	1965-69		1998	1993-97
	1970	1966-70		1999	1994-98
	1971	1967-71		2000	1995-99
	1972	1968-72		2001	1997-01
	1973	1969-73		2002	1998-02
	1974	1970-74		2003	1999-03
	1975	1971-75		2004	2000-04
	1976	1957-76		2005	2001-05
	1977	1973-77		2006-2015	Dernière
	1978	1974-78			
	1979	1975-79	-selon l'âge de l'épouse et l'âge de l'époux	1958	1948-57
	1980	1976-80		1968	Dernière
	1981	1977-81		1976	Dernière
	1982	1963-82		1982	Dernière
	1983	1979-83		1990	Dernière
	1984	1980-84		2006-2015	Dernière
	1985	1981-85			
	1986	1982-86	-selon l'âge de l'épouse et l'état matrimonial antérieur	1958	1948-57
	1987	1983-87		1968	Dernière
	1988	1984-88		1976	Dernière
	1989	1985-89		1982	Dernière
	1990	1971-90		1990	Dernière
	1991	1987-91			
	1992	1988-92	-selon l'âge de l'époux	1948	1936-47
	1993	1989-93		1949/50	1936-49
	1994	1990-94		1958	1948-57
	1995	1991-95		1959-1967	Dernière
	1996	1992-96		1968	1958-67
	1997	1993-97		1969-1975	Dernière
	1998	1994-98		1976	1966-75
	1999	1995-99		1977-1981	Dernière
	2000	1996-00		1982	1972-81
	2001	1997-01		1983-1986	Dernière
	2002	1998-02		1987	1975-86
	2003	1999-03		1988-1989	Dernière
	2004	2000-04		1990	1980-89
	2005	2001-05		1991-1997	Dernière
	2006	2002-06		1998	1993-97
	2007	2003-07		1999	1994-98
	2008	2004-08		2000	1995-99
	2009-2010	2006-10		2001	1997-01
	2011	2007-11		2002	1998-02
	2012	2008-12		2003	1999-03
	2013	2009-13		2004	2000-04
	2014	2010-14		2005	2001-05
	2015	2011-15		2006-2015	Dernière
-selon l'âge de l'épouse			-selon l'âge de l'époux et l'âge de l'épouse	1958	1948-57
	1948	1936-47		1968	Dernière
	1949/50	1936-49		1976	Dernière
	1958	1948-57		1982	Dernière
	1959-1967	Dernière		1990	Dernière
	1968	1958-67		2006-2015	Dernière
	1969-1975	Dernière			
	1976	1966-75			
	1977-1981	Dernière			

Index
Index historique (suite)
(Voir notes à la fin de l'index)

Index
Index historique (suite)
(Voir notes à la fin de l'index)

Index
Index historique (suite)
(Voir notes à la fin de l'index)

Index
Index historique (suite)
(Voir notes à la fin de l'index)

Index
Index historique (suite)
(Voir notes à la fin de l'index)

Sujet	Année de l'édition	Période considérée	Sujet	Année de l'édition	Période considérée
	1999	1994-98		1992	1983-92
	1999CD [vii]	1990-98		1993	1989-93
	2000	1995-99		1994	1990-94
	2001	1997-01		1995	1991-95
	2002	1998-02		1996	1987-96
	2003	1999-03		1997	1993-97
	2004	2000-04		1997SR [ii]	1948-97
	2005	2001-05		1998	1994-98
	2006	2002-06		1999	1995-99
	2007	2003-07		2000	1996-00
	2008	2004-08		2001	1997-01
	2009-2010	2006-10		2002	1998-02
	2011	2007-11		2003	1999-03
	2012	2008-12		2004	2000-04
	2013	2009-13		2005	2001-05
	2014	2010-14		2006	2002-06
	2015	2011-15		2007	2003-07
				2008	2004-08
Mortalité infantile (nombres).....	1948	1932-47		2009-2010	2006-10
	1949/50	1934-49		2011	2007-11
	1951	1935-50		2012	2008-12
	1952	1936-51		2013	2009-13
	1953	1950-52		2014	2010-14
	1954	1946-53		2015	2011-15
	1955	1946-54			
	1956	1947-55	-selon l'âge et le sexe	1948	1936-47
	1957	1948-56		1951	1936-49
	1958	1948-57		1957	1948-56
	1959	1949-58		1961	1952-60
	1960	1950-59		1962-1965	Dernière
	1961	1952-61		1966	1956-65
	1962	1953-62		1967-1973	Dernière
	1963	1954-63		1974	1965-73
	1964	1960-64		1975-1979	Dernière
	1965	1961-65		1980	1971-79
	1966	1947-66		1981-1984	Dernière
	1967	1963-67		1985	1976-84
	1968	1964-68		1986-1991	Dernière
	1969	1965-69		1992	1983-92
	1970	1966-70		1993-1995	Dernière
	1971	1967-71		1996	1987-95
	1972	1968-72		1997-2004	Dernière
	1973	1969-73		2005	1996-05
	1974	1965-74		2006-2015	Dernière
	1975	1971-75			
	1976	1972-76	-selon l'âge et le sexe et la résidence (urbaine/rurale)	1968-1973	Dernière
	1977	1973-77		1974	1965-73
	1978	1974-78		1975-1979	Dernière
	1978SR [i]	1948-78		1980	1971-79
	1979	1975-79		1981-1984	Dernière
	1980	1971-80		1985	1976-84
	1981	1977-81		1986-1991	Dernière
	1982	1978-82		1992	1983-92
	1983	1979-83		1993-1995	Dernière
	1984	1980-84		1996	1987-95
	1985	1976-85		1997-1999	Dernière
	1986	1982-86			
	1987	1983-87	-selon la résidence (urbaine/rurale)	1967	Dernière
	1988	1984-88		1968	1964-68
	1989	1985-89		1969	1965-69
	1990	1986-90		1970	1966-70
	1991	1987-91			

Index
Index historique (suite)
(Voir notes à la fin de l'index)

Index
Index historique (suite)
(Voir notes à la fin de l'index)

Index
Index historique (suite)
(Voir notes à la fin de l'index)

Index
Index historique (suite)
(Voir notes à la fin de l'index)

Index
Index historique (suite)
(Voir notes à la fin de l'index)

Index
Index historique (suite)
(Voir notes à la fin de l'index)

Sujet	Année de l'édition	Période considérée	Sujet	Année de l'édition	Période considérée
	1988	1983-87		1981	1972-80
	1989	1984-88		1986	1977-85
	1990	1985-89		1999CD [vii]	1990-98
	1991	1986-90	-selon l'âge de la mère et le rang de naissance	1954	Dernière
	1992	1987-91		1959	1949-58
	1993	1988-92		1965	3-Dernières
	1994	1989-93		1969	1963-68
	1995	1990-94		1975	1966-74
	1996	1987-95		1981	1972-80
	1997	1992-96		1986	1977-85
	1998	1993-97		1999CD [vii]	1990-98
	1999	1994-98			
	1999CD [vii]	1990-98	-selon la période de gestation	1957	1950-56
	2000	1995-99		1959	1949-58
	2001	1997-01		1961	1952-60
	2002	1998-02		1965	5-Dernières
	2003	1999-03		1966	1956-65
	2004	2000-04		1967-1968	Dernière
	2005	2001-05		1969	1963-68
	2006	2002-06		1974	1965-73
	2007	2003-07		1975	1966-74
	2008	2004-08		1980	1971-79
	2009-2010	2006-10		1981	1972-80
	2011	2007-11		1985	1976-84
	2012	2008-12		1986	1977-85
	2013	2009-13		1996	1987-95
	2014	2010-14			
	2015	2011-15	-selon la résidence (urbaine/rurale)	1971	1966-70
-illégitimes	1961	1952-60		1972	1967-71
	1965	5-Dernières		1973	1968-72
	1969	1963-68		1974	1965-73
	1975	1966-74		1975	1966-74
	1981	1972-80		1976	1971-75
	1986	1977-85		1977	1972-76
-illégitimes, en pourcentage	1961	1952-60		1978	1973-77
	1965	5-Dernières		1979	1974-78
	1969	1963-68		1980	1971-79
	1975	1966-74		1981	1972-80
	1981	1972-80		1982	1977-81
	1986	1977-85		1983	1978-82
-légitimes	1959	1949-58		1984	1979-83
	1965	1955-64		1985	1975-84
	1969	1963-68		1986	1977-85
	1975	1966-74		1987	1982-86
	1981	1972-80		1988	1983-87
	1986	1977-85		1989	1984-88
-légitimes selon l'âge de la mère	1959	1949-58		1990	1985-89
	1965	1955-64		1991	1986-90
	1969	1963-68		1992	1987-91
	1975	1966-74		1993	1988-92
	1981	1972-80		1994	1989-93
	1986	1977-85		1995	1990-94
-selon l'âge de la mère	1954	1936-53		1996	1987-95
	1959	1949-58		1997	1992-96
	1965	1955-64		1998	1993-97
	1969	1963-68		1999	1994-98
	1975	1966-74		1999CD [vii]	1990-98
				2000	1995-99
				2001	1997-01

Index
Index historique (suite)
(Voir notes à la fin de l'index)

Index
Index historique (suite)
(Voir notes à la fin de l'index)

Index
Index historique (suite)
(Voir notes à la fin de l'index)

Index
Index historique (suite)
(Voir notes à la fin de l'index)

Index
Index historique (suite)
(Voir notes à la fin de l'index)

Index
Index historique (suite)
(Voir notes à la fin de l'index)

Index
Index historique (suite)
(Voir notes à la fin de l'index)

Sujet	Année de l'édition	Période considérée	Sujet	Année de l'édition	Période considérée
	1978	1975-78		1970	1963-70
	1979	1975-79			1965-70
	1980	1975-80		1971	1963-71
	1981	1975-81			1965-71
	1982	1975-82		1972	1963-72
	1983	1980-83			1965-72
	1984	1980-84		1973	1965-73
	1985	1980-85			1970-73
	1986	1980-86		1974	1965-74
	1987	1980-87			1970-74
	1988	1985-88		1975	1965-75
	1989	1985-89			1970-75
	1990	1985-90		1976	1965-76
	1991	1985-91			1970-76
	1992	1985-92		1977	1965-77
	1993	1990-93			1970-77
	1994	1990-94		1978-1979	1970-75
	1995	1990-95		1980-1983	1975-80
	1996	1990-96		1984-1986	1980-85
	1997	1990-97		1987-1992	1985-90
	1998	1993-98		1993-1997	1990-95
	1999	1995-99		1998-2000	1995-00
	2000	1995-00		2001-2005	2000-05
	2001	1995-01		2006-2010	2005-10
	2002	1995-02		2011-2015	2010-15
	2003	2000-03			
	2004	2000-04	-active:		
	2005	2000-05	féminin, selon l'état		
	2006	2000-06	matrimonial et l'âge	1956	1945-55
	2007	2005-07		1967	1955-64
	2008	2005-08		1968	Dernière
	2009-2010	2005-10		1972	1962-77
	2011	2005-11	féminin, selon l'état		
	2012	2005-12	matrimonial et l'âge et la		
	2013	2010-13	résidence (urbaine/rurale)	1973	1965-73
	2014	2010-14		1979	1970-79
	2015	2010-15		1984	1974-84
				1988	1980-88 [iii]
annuels moyens pour le			née â l'étranger selon la		
monde, les grandes			profession, l'âge et le		
régions (continentes) et			sexe	1984	1974-84
les régions				1989	1980-88
géographiques	1957	1950-56	née â l'étranger selon la		
	1958	1950-57	profession, l'âge et le		
	1959	1950-58	sexe	1977	Dernière
	1960	1950-59			
	1961	1950-60	selon l'âge et le sexe	1955	1945-54
	1962	1950-61		1956	1945-55
	1963	1958-62		1964	1955-64
		1960-62		1972	1962-72
	1964	1958-63			
		1960-63	selon l'âge et le sexe	1973	1965-73 [iii]
	1965	1958-64	et la résidence	1979	1970-79 [iii]
		1960-64	(urbaine/rurale)	1984	1974-84
	1966	1958-66		1988	1980-88 [iii]
		1960-66		1994	1985-94
	1967	1960-67	selon l'âge et le sexe en		
		1963-67	pourcentage	1948	Dernière
	1968	1960-68		1949/50	1930-48
		1963-68		1955	1945-54
	1969	1960-69		1956	1945-55
		1963-69		1964	1955-64

Index
Index historique (suite)
(Voir notes à la fin de l'index)

Index
Index historique (suite)
(Voir notes à la fin de l'index)

Index
Index historique (suite)
(Voir notes à la fin de l'index)

Sujet	Année de l'édition	Période considérée
	1962	1920-61
	1963	1930-62
	1964	1930-63
	1965	1930-65
	1966	1930-66
	1967	1930-67
	1968	1930-68
	1969	1930-69
	1970	1950-70
	1971	1950-71
	1972	1950-72
	1973	1950-73
	1974	1950-74
	1975	1950-75
	1976	1950-76
	1977	1950-77
	1978	1950-78
	1979	1950-79
	1980	1950-80
	1981	1950-81
	1982	1950-82
	1983	1950-83
	1984	1950-84
	1985	1950-85
	1986	1950-86
	1987	1950-87
	1988	1950-88
	1989	1950-89
	1990	1950-90
	1991	1950-91
	1992	1950-92
	1993	1950-93
	1994	1950-94
	1995	1950-95
	1996	1950-96
	1997	1950-97
	1998-2000	1950-00
	2001	1950-01
	2002	1950-02
	2003	1950-03
	2004	1950-04
	2005	1950-05
	2006	1950-06
	2007	1950-07
	2008	1950-08
	2009-2010	1950-10
	2011	1960-11
	2012	1960-12
	2013	1960-13
	2014	1960-14
	2015	1960-15
-des pays ou zones (total): dénombrée		
	1948	1900-48
	1949/50	1900-50
	1951	1900-51
	1952	1850-1952
	1953	1850-1953
	1954	Dernière
	1955	1850-1954
	1956-1961	Dernière
	1962	1900-62

Sujet	Année de l'édition	Période considérée
	1963	Dernière
	1964	1955-64
	1965-1978	Dernière
	1978SR [i]	1948-78
	1979-1997	Dernière
	1979SR [ii]	1948-78
	1998-2015	Dernière
estimée	1948	1932-47
	1949/50	1932-49
	1951	1930-50
	1952	1920-51
	1953	1920-53
	1954	1920-54
	1955	1920-55
	1956	1920-56
	1957	1940-57
	1958	1939-58
	1959	1940-59
	1960	1920-60
	1961	1941-61
	1962	1942-62
	1963	1943-63
	1964	1955-64
	1965	1946-65
	1966	1947-66
	1967	1958-67
	1968	1959-68
	1969	1960-69
	1970	1950-70
	1971	1962-71
	1972	1963-72
	1973	1964-73
	1974	1965-74
	1975	1966-75
	1976	1967-76
	1977	1968-77
	1978	1969-78
	1978SR [i]	1948-78
	1979	1970-79
	1980	1971-80
	1981	1972-81
	1982	1973-82
	1983	1974-83
	1984	1975-84
	1985	1976-85
	1986	1977-86
	1987	1978-87
	1988	1979-88
	1989	1980-89
	1990	1981-90
	1991	1982-91
	1992	1983-92
	1993	1984-93
	1994	1985-94
	1995	1986-95
	1996	1987-96
	1997	1988-97
	1997SR [ii]	1948-97
	1998	1989-98
	1999	1990-99
	2000	1991-00

Index
Index historique (suite)
(Voir notes à la fin de l'index)

Index
Index historique (suite)
(Voir notes à la fin de l'index)

Index
Index historique (suite)
(Voir notes à la fin de l'index)

Index
Index historique (suite)
(Voir notes à la fin de l'index)

Index
Index historique (suite)
(Voir notes à la fin de l'index)

Index
Index historique (suite)
(Voir notes à la fin de l'index)

Index
Index historique (suite)
(Voir notes à la fin de l'index)

Sujet	Année de l'édition	Période considérée
	1981	1972-81
	1982	1973-82
	1983	1974-83
	1984	1975-84
	1985	1976-85
	1986	1977-86
	1987	1978-87
	1988	1979-88
	1989	1980-89
	1990	1981-90
	1991	1982-91
	1992	1983-92
	1993	1984-93
	1994	1985-94
	1995	1986-95
	1996	1987-96
	1997	1988-97
	1998	1989-98
	1999	1990-99
	2000	1991-00
	2001	1992-01
	2002	1993-02
	2003	1994-03
	2004	1995-04
	2005	1996-05
	2006	1997-06
	2007	1998-07
	2008	1999-08
	2009-2010	2001-10
	2011	2002-11
	2012	2003-12
	2013	2004-13
	2014	2005-14
	2015	2006-15
-Vieillissement indicateurs divers	1991 VP [v]	1950-90
-Villes (voir: des villes, ci-dessus)		

R

Rapports (voir: Fécondité proportionnelle; Mortalité fœtale (tardive), rapports de; Mortalité périnatale, rapports de; Natalité proportionnelle; Rapports enfants-femmes)

Sujet	Année de l'édition	Période considérée
Rapports enfants-femmes	1949/50	1900-50
	1954	1900-52
	1955	1945-54
	1959	1935-59
	1963	1955-63
	1965	1945-65
	1969	Dernière
	1975	1966-74
	1978SR [i]	1948-77
	1981	1962-80
	1986	1967-85
	1997SR [ii]	1948-96

Sujet	Année de l'édition	Période considérée
	1999CD [vii]	1980-1999
-dans les zones (urbaines/rurales)	1965	Dernière
	1969	Dernière

Réfugiés selon le pays ou zone de destination:

Sujet	Année de l'édition	Période considérée
-rapatriés par l'Organisation Internationale pour les réfugiés	1952	1947-51
-réinstallés par l'Organisation Internationale pour les réfugiés	1952	1947-51

Religion (voir: Population)

Sujet	Année de l'édition	Période considérée
Reproduction, taux bruts et nets de	1948	1920-47
	1949/50	1900-48
	1954	1920-53
	1965	1930-64
	1969	1963-68
	1975	1966-74
	1978SR [i]	1948-77
	1981	1962-80
	1986	1967-85
	1997SR [ii]	1948-96
	1999CD [vii]	1980-99

S

Sans abri (voir : Population)

Sexe (voir: la rubrique appropriée par sujet, p. ex., Immigrants; Mortalité, taux de; Naissance; Population, etc.)

Situation dans la profession (voir: Population active)

Sujet spécial des divers Annuaires démographiques:

Sujet	Année de l'édition	Période considérée
-Démographie générale	1948	1900-48
	1953	1850-1953
-Divorce (voir: Mariage et divorce, ci-dessous)		
-Mariage et Divorce	1958	1930-57
	1968	1920-68
	1976	1957-76
	1982	1963-82
	1990	1971-90
-Migration (Internationale)	1977	1958-76
	1989	1975-88
-Mortalité	1951	1905-50
	1957	1930-56
	1961	1945-61
	1966	1920-66
-Mortalité (suite):	1967	1900-67
	1974	1965-74
	1980	1971-80

Index
Index historique (suite)
(Voir notes à la fin de l'index)

Index
Index historique (suite)
(Voir notes à la fin de l'index)

Index
Index historique (suite)
(Voir notes à la fin de l'index)

APPENDICE

Texte spécial de chaque Annuaire démographique

Divorce:

"Application des statistiques de la nuptialité et de la divortialité", 1958.

Mariage:

"Application des statistiques de la nuptialité et de la divortialité", 1958.

Ménages:

"Concepts et définitions des ménages, du chef de ménage et de la population des collectivités", 1987.

Migration:

"'Statistiques des migrations internationales",1977.

Mortalité:

"Tendances récentes de la mortalité", 1951.
"Développement des statistiques des causes de décès",1951.
"Les facteurs du fléchissement de la mortalité",1957.
"Notes sur les méthodes d'évaluation de la fiabilité des statistiques classiques de la mortalité",1961.
"Mortalité: Tendances récentes",1966.
"Tendances de la mortalité chez les personnes âgées",1991VP [v].

Natalité:

"Présentation graphiques des tendances de la fécondité",1959.

"Taux de natalité: Tendances récentes",1965.

Population: ..

"Tendances démo-graphiques mondiales,1920-1949",1949/50.
"Mouvements d'urbanisation et ses caractéristiques",1952.
"Les recensements de population de 1950",1955.
"Situation démographique mondiale",1956.
"Ce que nous savons de l'état et de l'évolution de la population mondiale",1960.
"Notes sur les statistiques disponibles des recensements nationaux de population et méthodes d'évaluation de leur exactitude",1962.
"Disponibilité et qualité de certaines données statistiques fondées sur les recensements de population effectués entre 1955 et 1963",1963.
"Disponibilité de certaines statistiques fondées sur les recensements de population: 1955-1964",1964.

"Définitions et concepts statistiques de la population urbaine et de la population rurale",1967.
"Application des statistiques de la nuptialité et de la divortialité",1958.
"Ce que nous savons de l'état et de l'évolution de la population mondiale",1970.
"Recommandations de l'Organisation des Nations Unies quant aux sujets sur lesquels doit porter un recensement de population, en regard de la pratique adoptée par les différents pays dans les recensements nationaux effectués de 1965 à 1971",1971.
"Les définitions statistiques de la population urbaine et leurs usages en démographie appliquée",1972.

"Evolution récente de la fécondité dans le monde",1969.
"Dates des recensements nationaux de la population et de l'habitation effectués au cours de la décennie

Index
Index historique (suite)
(Voir notes à la fin de l'index)

1965-1974", 1974.

"Dates des recensements nationaux de la population et de l'habitation effectués ou prévus, au cours de la décennie 1975-1984",1979.

"Dates des recensements nationaux de la population et/ou de l'habitation effectués au cours de la décennie 1965-1974 et effectués ou prévus au cours de la décennie1975-1984",1983.

"Définitions et concepts statistiques du ménage",1968.

"Dates des recensements nationaux de la population et/ou de l'habitation effectués au cours de la décennie 1975-1984 et effectués ou prévus au cours de la décennie1985-1994", 1988, 1993.

"Statistiques concernant la population active: un aperçu",1984.

"'Etude du vieillissement et de la situation des personnes âgées: Besoins particuliers",1991VP [v].

"Les incapacités", 1991VP [v].

"Le vieillissement", 1991VP [v].

Notes générales

Cet index alphabétique donne la liste des sujets traités dans chacune de 66 éditions de l'Annuaire démographique. La colonne "Année de l'édition" indique l'édition spécifique dans laquelle le sujet a été traité. Sauf indication contraire, la colonne "Période considérée" désigne les années pour lesquelles les statistiques annuelles apparaissant dans l'Annuaire démographique sont indiquées sous la colonne "Année de l'édition". La rubrique "Dernière" ou " 2-Dernières" indique que les données représentent la ou les dernières années disponibles seulement.

[i] Le Supplément rétrospectif du 30ème Annuaire Démographique fait l'objet d'un tirage spécial publié en 1979.

[ii] Le Supplément rétrospectif du 49ème Annuaire Démographique fait l'objet d'un tirage spécial (CD-ROM) publié en 2000

[iii] Données non disponibles dans l'édition précédente seulement.

[iv] Titres non disponibles dans la bibliographie précédente seulement.

[v] Taux moyens pour 5 ans.

[vi] Vieillissement de la population.

[vii] Le Supplément du 51 Annuaire Démographique, ayant comme suject la natalité, fait l'objet d'un tirage spécial (CD-ROM) publié en 2002.